WORLD CARS®
1979

Published annually by
THE AUTOMOBILE CLUB OF ITALY

Edited by
L'EDITRICE DELL'AUTOMOBILE LEA

Management
ARNOLDO MONDADORI EDITORE
OFFICINE GRAFICHE

HERALD BOOKS, PELHAM, NEW YORK

Cover pictures

Bertone Sibilo (front)
BMW M1 engine, Dome-O,
Mercedes C 111, Fiat X1/9 five speed (back)

Cover and layout

Ovidio Ricci, Francesco Ricciardi

Editor

Annamaria Lösch

Contributors and correspondents

Alberto Bellucci

Carlo Acri
Mario Bilancioni
Gianni Costa (China, India)
John Crawford (Australia)
Filippo Crispolti
Antonio di Fazio
Flora Di Giovanni
Bob Irvin (USA)
Alan Langley (Great Britain)
Antonio Lioy
Roberto Nobilio
Hilmar Schmitt (Germany)
L.J.K. Setright
Jack K. Yamaguchi (Japan)

Language consultant

Jean Gribble

Editorial offices

L'Editrice dell'Automobile LEA
Viale Regina Margherita 279
00198 Rome, Italy

Composition and printing

Arnoldo Mondadori Editore
Stabilimento Grafico di Roma, Italy

Illustrations

Riproduzioni-Lith - Rome, Italy

ISBN 0-910714-11-8
LC 74-643381

Published in the English language
edition throughout the world in 1979
by Herald Books, Pelham, New York

WORLD CARS and WORLD CAR CATALOGUE
are trademarks registered by
Herald Books in the United States of America

© World Copyright
L'Editrice dell'Automobile LEA - 1979
Printed in Italy

The publishers assume no responsibility
for any errors or omissions

SUMMARY

Editor's note

The aim of *World Cars* is to present accurate information that is as complete as possible and to present it in a concise form. It is not always easy to reconcile the search for accuracy and completeness, for clarity and uniformity, and one or two preliminary remarks may help readers consulting this reference book.

The technical data is based on questionnaires completed by motor manufacturers throughout the world, and only when this information was incomplete or not made available has it been supplemented from other reliable sources.

Different cultures have always used different formulae to express maximum power and torque. DIN and SAE standards are familiar to most readers, while Japan alone uses the Japanese Industrial Standard (JIS). Expressed in DIN, power or torque is 20% lower than when expressed in SAE, while JIS ratings roughly correspond to SAE gross ratings. Horsepower in Anglo-Saxon countries expresses slightly higher power than the horsepower used by other countries (1.0139:1).

The innovation that marks recent editions of *World Cars* stems from the new units of measurement established by the Système Internationale d'Unites (SI). These are the kilowatt (kW), which replaces horsepower (hp), and the Newton metre (Nm), which replaces lb/ft. The conversation ratios are:

1 hp = 0.736 kW or 1 kW = 1.360 hp	
1 kg m = 7 lb ft = 9.807 Nm or 1 Nm = 0.714 lb ft = 0.012 kg m	

Fuel consumption, indicated by figures that are inevitably only a rough calculation, is based on a medium load and a cruising speed of about 60% of the car's maximum speed on a varied run. By dry weight is meant the fully-equipped car ready for the road plus water, oil and petrol.

Since two valves per cylinder are now the norm and dual braking circuits are prevalent, only exceptions to the two have been indicated. Again, when in V8 engines the cylinders are slanted at 90°, this indication has been omitted. The turning circle should be taken as between walls unless otherwise specified.

Quite often a model is available with engines differing both in size and power. For the production of the United States, Canada, South Africa, and Australia, and some German, British and Japanese makes, each of these engines is described separately. In this case, whenever they are not given, the measurements and weight are the same as in the standard version. When the power-weight ratio is given, this usually refers to the 4-door sedan version. For other countries, the various engines have been listed under "Variations" at the foot of the basic description and — except when otherwise specifically indicated — should be taken as being available for all the models that refer back to the basic description. The "Optional Accessories" also apply to all the models that refer back to the basic description, except when otherwise specified. Some accessories may become "standard" or not be available, and others may be added, but this is always specified.

Editorial problems have prevented us from making certain corrections to the prices in the main body of the volume after the end of 1978 and so the reader is advised to refer to the price index for more recent prices of models, many of which may be raised in the course of the year. When prices are shown in the currency of the country of origin, these should be taken as ex-factory and therefore subject to revision if the car is imported into another country. Prices with a single asterisk include VAT (value added tax) or its equivalent in other European countries, and in Great Britain also SCT (special car tax). Prices with two asterisks are ex-showroom. The prices for American cars refer to models equipped with a standard engine of the lowest power listed (generally a four- or six-cylinder engine). Any surcharge for higher power standard engines is indicated at the foot of the list of models and prices. For cars imported into the United States, asterisked figures denote prices ex-showroom. In view of the requirements of Federal legislation, cars imported into the United States differ from the ones on sale in the respective countries of origin. Every attempt is made to quote accurate prices but both variations in what the companies include in the price quoted and frequent price modifications make our task a difficult one.

Technical and photographic coverage is given to over 1,500 models at present in production. It has sometimes been necessary to exclude models produced in very small numbers or visually almost identical to others illustrated, and also models that, even if built or assembled under another name outside the country of origin, are to all purposes a repetition of the model presented as part of the maker's standard range.

MONOCOQUES IN SKIRTS

by Filippo Crispolti

Every now and then, a voice is raised complaining there is nothing more to invent for the automobile, that we are at the end of an historical cycle and Formula 1 races are no longer the maximum expression of motor racing because there is nothing new to be discovered in them any more: the same old mixture served up over and over again, with just a slight change in the minor ingredients, if there is that.

The 1978 World Drivers' Championship provided an eloquent retort to these complaints. Won by the Italo-American Mario Andretti, it was a walkover for the Lotus which has successfully developed a totally new technical principle. A deciding factor in ensuring overwhelming supremacy, it is a point of reference for all the new designs for monocoques that will see the light of day in the coming years, heaven knows for how long! This technical principle is called "ground effect", but it might more justly be renamed "Lotus effect" and no objections would be raised. For there is no doubt that Colin Chapman was the first to believe in the beneficial effects, for roadholding purposes, of a marked vacuum, created by natural means under the belly of the monocoque. The principle which — paradoxically — gave the Lotus 78 and 79 wings by gluing them to the ground and thus allowing their drivers to get round corners at much higher speeds, is very different from the one applied by the genial American Jim Hall on his Chaparral, built to dominate the lucrative Can-Am series but shelved by the sporting organs whose power was clearly greater in 1969-70 than it would seem to be today.

It could be said that, until yesterday, in order to adhere to the ground, monocoques could count — aerodynamically speaking — on front and rear wings and spoilers, as well as on the shape of the so-called body, generally wedge-shaped to a greater or lesser degree.

The wings, or more correctly speaking, their angle of incidence, are however always a compromise between downforce and speed. Roughly speaking, the greater the angle of the wings, the better the vehicle's roadholding and thus the faster it will be on the more twisting parts of the circuit that require greater "holding" qualities. The price paid is however that any increase in the angle of the wing enlarges the front section of the car, increasing

resistance. The obvious consequence is a lower top speed on the straight where the need to flatten the car to the ground is practically nil. The adjustment of the wings also has marked effects on the already excessively delicate functioning of the tyres which, with the increase in the "holding", heat up more.

A new system therefore had to be found that would allow the car to hug the ground without worsening its aerodynamic penetration characteristics. It seemed a little like wanting to have your cake and eat it, a contradiction in terms. But the ideal solution did exist, and at the Lotus works, after a couple of experimental but rather disappointing chassis, but above all after months spent

Mario Andretti, 38 years old, born in Montona, Italy, but living in Nazareth, Pennsylvania, took the World Championship ten years after his debut in Formula 1 racing.

checking new profiles in the wind gallery, they managed to find it. Exploiting the venturi effect, Colin Chapman and his collaborators managed to create under the monocoque a marked vacuum that — instead of sticking the machine to the ground by means of pressure coming from above, as wings do — held it down in accordance with the vacuum principle of the suction pad. In order to understand at a glance what it is that so greatly improves the road-holding of the present Lotuses, think of the Hovercraft, but turning the working principle upside down. Air cushion vehicles create (artificially, by means of a motor) a pressure that keeps them raised above the ground. The Lotus does exactly the contrary, exploiting a vacuum obtained by making air flow through the side pods, over them and under them, but with the latter movement counting most. The air encouraged under the car is kept there by mobile teflon and ceramics flaps or skirts. The acceleration of the rearward flow of air increases the effect, enhancing straight-line speed. Thanks to the narrow crankcase of the 90° V8 Cosworth engine there is a lot of venturi area and these channels formed by the underside of the side sections, the skirts and the track make brilliant use of the underflow of air. Another innovation on the Lotus 79 is that the engine exhaust pipes have been moved higher up and the rear suspension has also been designed with springs and dampers close to the gearbox so as to eliminate as far as possible any obstacle that would hinder the free flow of the air coming from the channels and reduce the downforce.

In passing, it should be mentioned that these skirts, since they are mobile aerodynamic elements, have been held by some — the International Sporting Commission (CSI) included for some time — to be contrary to the regulations. The CSI at first accepted the telling argument that the skirts, by favouring the ground effect, markedly increased the speed of the machines on the bends, a factor that would demand the immediate upgrading of the already inadequate protective systems of the circuits. This led to their prohibition and robbed the "Lotus effect" of much of its efficacy. Then, as has too often happened in Formula 1 racing, the CSI ate its words, allowing the free-for-all that is already being seen, with skirts sprouting on all the marques. Even during the course of the 1978 season no less than seven other monocoques (Wolf, Arrows, Shadow, Ferrari, Brabham-Alfa, Copersucar and ATS) felt bound to imitate the

Lotus 78/79 in some way or other. There is no doubt that this aerodynamic innovation is a milestone in the history of Formula 1 racing.

Leaving aside the undoubted qualities of Mario Andretti, an extremely combative driver, full of courage and character, as truly professional as any of his colleagues, he clearly had the best machine of the moment at his disposal. This was eloquently demonstrated in the final of the North-American season, when the Frenchman Jean-Pierre Jarier inherited the second Lotus from the unlucky Ronnie Peterson. He had succumbed to the consequences of the absurd accident at Monza at the end of a year that had finally done justice once more to his great class and even more to the admirable way he respected the promise given to Colin Chapman to remain loyal to his role of "second" driver. Jarier, though rather short of practice and knowing little or nothing about the car and the tracks, was able to go very fast at once and even come close to victory.

There is an old proverb that states 'needs must when the devil drives'. There is no doubt that from 1974 on it was clear to the British teams that something had to be done to stem the advance of the twelve-cylinder cars. It was however equally clear that Britain's role as supermarket of speed, thanks to the industries that supply all the separate parts to assemble a Formula 1 monocoque, would allow every possible innovation to be studied. Only the Cosworth engine had to remain more or less the same, since by now practically no further substantial developments remained unexplored as far as maximum power was concerned.

This reasoning was just the opposite of the line being followed in the Ferrari stable, where the apparently inexhaustible potential of the engine was partly responsible for a relatively stagnant situation in the progress of the chassis. It was, it is true, being continuously altered and improved but without a marked enhancement of its qualities. And the policy adopted by Goodyear seemed for some time to be the real villain in the Ferraris' reduced increase in competitiveness from one season to another. Tyres have in the last few years been a variable factor whose importance has been very difficult to calculate precisely and impartially, even for the men looking after them.

I have no illusions of having, with these technical premises, explained all the factors that led to the changing of the guard between Ferrari and Lotus, or — if you will — between Niki Lauda, the outgoing champion, and Mario Andretti who took over the number one slot.

If we glance at the two teams' balance sheets, we see that Lotus marked up eight wins in 1978, as compared with Ferrari's five. Andretti took the chequered flag six times while Reutemann had this honour four times. Lauda, on the contrary, carried off only two victories, both — it must be admitted — rather questionable. In Sweden Niki beat Andretti thanks to the notorious ventilator, a gadget that created, by means of a large suction fan connected directly to the gear shaft, a dynamic vacuum under the car even stronger than the one characteristic of the Lotus school, obtained by aerodynamic systems. Gordon Murray had carefully followed in the wake of the Chaparral's

The start of the Monte Carlo GP. Reutemann's and Lauda's cars have just touched and for the Argentinian it is the end of the race. The chicanes often cause trouble.

experience in his attempt to make the Brabham-Alfa Romeo BT 46 competitive, since on the same car the special aerodynamic surfaces (originated for use in aeronautics) had not worked as a replacement for the more conventional (but bulky and heavy) radiators. The return to radiators on the nose strongly conditioned the BT 46, especially the front which Murray had intended to make much slenderer to limit the chronic understeering phenomena typical of the earlier BT 45. It also prevented Lauda and Watson from playing leading roles and so the ventilator solution was thought up, blocked however at once by the CSI before everyone inevitably followed suit. At Monza, in a Grand Prix already tarnished by a muddled start that led to tragedy, Lauda won on paper thanks to the penalty inflicted on Andretti and Villeneuve who crossed the chequered flag first and second but were penalized for anticipating the start. To the shortcomings of the BT 46 was added the high mortality rate of the twelve-cylinder Alfa Romeo engine which several times brought Lauda in particular to a halt on the way, if not to victory, at least to a good placing. It is a fairly widespread opinion that — as was only to be expected — the Lauda-Ferrari divorce left both sides dissatisfied. For the Ferrari team the outcome was less negative, though there was never any hope of keeping the title. For, even if the Lotus often seemed vulnerable when there was someone able to test its drivers to the utmost, forcing them to drive their engines at full revs, Andretti was almost always able to win by keeping his engine about 400 to 500 revs below its ceiling. It must however be admitted that these are empty thoughts, for the history of motor racing is full of ifs.

It would seem a good idea, at this point, to run quickly through the sixteen chapters of the '78 book of Formula 1 racing. Not all of them were interesting, indeed monotony often reared its ugly head but less frequently than might have been feared.

It all began as usual in Argentina, in January. There it is summer and suffocatingly hot — especially difficult conditions for the Ferrari making its debut with the new Michelin radial tyres. The French tyres pick up the dirt from the track and their efficiency is rapidly lowered, forcing Reutemann, who in practice had earned his place beside Andretti in the front row of the grid, to drop back. Andretti wins handsomely and Lauda is second. A promising placing for the Austrian in his first Grand Prix with the Brabham-Alfa, but...

The cockpit where it all happened. Mario Andretti, often hard-pressed by his team-mate, Ronnie Peterson, had to curb his natural impetuousness.

Two weeks later on the new Rio de Janeiro circuit in the Brazilian Grand Prix, Andretti and Reutemann are once again side by side on the starting line, but in the second row. In front of them are Peterson and Hunt. However, this does not stop Reutemann from tearing away at the starting signal and this time there is no catching him thanks to a correct choice of tyres. Andretti has gearbox problems, but his tyres too bother him, while Peterson has a snarl-up with Villeneuve's car. Emerson Fittipaldi is unexpectedly second with his Copersucar and Lauda third.

More than a month later it is the turn of the South African Grand Prix. In the front row at Kyalami are Lauda and Andretti but the victory goes to Ronnie Peterson because the future world champion runs first into tyre trouble here and then fuel feed problems. The Italian Riccardo Patrese with the Arrows breaks his engine after leading for much of the race. The race is a débâcle for the Ferraris, lagging in practice and in the race, while Lauda inaugurates a series of vulnerable engines.

Another month's pause, valuable for taking advantage of the experience of these first races of the season, and it is the turn of Long Beach in California for the Western America Grand Prix. Here it is once more the Ferrari driven by Reutemann that carries off the honours after young Villeneuve — the leader for much of the race — lets himself down with a risky overtaking manoeuvre involving Regazzoni. The Ferraris had monopolized, thanks to their fine practice time, the first row of the grid. Andretti is second while Niki Lauda has ignition trouble.

In 1978 the first European Grand Prix

was at Monte Carlo, early in May. Depailler's is one of the few outstanding wins of the season with his conventional Tyrrell 008. Reutemann, the hot favourite, makes a mess of the start and is bumped by Lauda who goes on to drive a magnificent pursuit race, finishing second. Reutemann had started out in the first row of the grid with Watson. Mario Andretti is slowed down by a fuel leak.

In Belgium at Zolder, Reutemann makes up for his failure to get away from the start at Monte Carlo, by touching off a collision behind him (he had started out in the first row of the grid alongside Andretti) that eliminated Hunt, Lauda and Fittipaldi right from the start. And this was the first of Andretti and Peterson's Lotus doubles.

The double is promptly repeated at the next Grand Prix in Spain where, in practice too, the Lotuses sweep all before them. During the race Reutemann runs off the strack due to a snapped semiaxle and Lauda's engine as usual lets him down. Decidedly, the Austrian is out of luck. However, Murray, the team mechanic in the next race in Sweden, unveils the absolute novelty of the shortlived ventilators. The device works so well that Lauda wins and Andretti, to keep up with the impossible pace of the Brabham-Alfa fitted with its fan, breaks his engine. The people responsible for the Anglo-Italian team claim however that the ventilator is to improve the engine cooling! In Sweden the first row of the grid was formed by Andretti and Watson. Patrese took second place.

The French Grand Prix at Castellet witnesses another Lotus double, yet another engine breakdown for Lauda and

Left, Scheckter follows the future World Champion round the toboggan at Monte Carlo. Above, a thoughtful Forghieri kneeling beside the the young Villeneuve: maybe the tyres are causing a headache in spite of the new anti-roll bars. Right, Laffite's Renault Turbo was often in the pits with teething troubles. But it looks as though the "turbo" solution may well catch on if not blocked by the regulations.

(photos by Filippo Crispolti)

Above, Depailler at the wheel of the winning Tyrrell at Monte Carlo. Right, the controversial fan of the Brabham-Alfa which won in Sweden. Below, the start of the Austrian Grand Prix.

In 1978 Carlos Reutemann, winner of four Grands Prix, confirmed the quality of the Ferrari, always a car to beat even when it seemed to have hit a moment of crisis.

tyre trouble for the two Ferrari men. In the first row at the start were Watson and Mario Andretti.

The British Grand Prix is one of the finest of the year. The Lotuses, looking for a home win, have to give over due to mechanical trouble and at the height of the duel between Lauda and Reutemann there is an unforgettable overtaking manoeuvre by Carlos Reutemann who wins as a result. Peterson and Andretti had, however, started out in the first row of the grid.

From the German Grand Prix on, there is a series of fast circuits in theory favourable to the twelve-cylinder cars. But forecasts are proved wrong. In practice, the best times are put up by Andretti and Peterson and in the race the victory goes to the Italo-American, while some of the difficulties of the Ferrari and Alfa Romeo engines must be put down to the torrid conditions. Second place is taken by Jody Scheckter who announces he is moving over to the Ferrari team this year.

The Austrian Grand Prix is marred by the rain which leads to a second start after a cloudburst has made the interruption of the race inevitable. Mario Andretti had, however, already thrown his chance away through over-eagerness, running off the track, even though here again the two Lotuses had monopolized the best positions at the start. The race is won by Ronnie Peterson who demonstrates remarkable class and versatility. In fact, all the drivers near the top of the table sooner or later make mistakes or run off the track: Lauda, Reutemann, Scheckter and — as has already been mentioned — Andretti. Second place goes to an improving De-pailler.

But in Holland, it is the same story all over again: two Lotuses in the first row at the start and first and second across the finishing line, with Mario Andretti taking first place as usual because Ronnie Peterson scrupulously respects his instructions not to challenge his team mate.

And so we come to the tragic Italian Grand Prix. A badly communicated start (the monocoques in the back rows start away in a rush), a bottleneck that had always been a recognized hazard, risky even if not blameworthy manoeuvres by some drivers — all these led to a collision that was a holocaust because it took place at such a speed. Ronnie Peterson was to die from the injuries he received while Vittorio Brambilla managed to come through thanks to exceptional toughness. Andretti and Villeneuve, penalized for anticipating the second start, present first and second points to Lauda and Watson.

The conviction that the Ferraris are coming to a peak in this final stage of the season is amply confirmed by the last two races in North America. At Watkins Glen the winner is Reutemann who has managed to get back into the front row at the start alongside Andretti who however breaks his engine. The new Canadian circuit in Montreal sees instead Villeneuve's first success, for Andretti — already confirmed world champion — is dogged by mechanical trouble and has to see the first row in the grid filled by Jarier (Lotus) and Scheckter (Wolf). Who knows, perhaps this is a sign that Formula 1 racing is looking for new protagonists while waiting for the more coherent legislative structures it needs in order to avoid undisciplined and chaotic starts and all

the other countless chicaneries and uncorrect behaviour that over the last few years have increased the potential dangers in the speed circus.

The season closed with a worthy world champion, and can list some interesting technical content but also a tragedy that could perhaps have been avoided. But motor racing, by its very nature, is not only exalting but dangerous, as for that matter are many other sports.

There is no doubt that, if Formula 1 had its unchallenged master last season the same is true of Formula 2. The Italian Bruno Giacomelli, even though his March-BMW could not boast of a superiority to match that of the Lotus was capable of taking eight races out of a total of twelve, and almost always took the pole position. Although the new European champion of Formula 2 racing beat every earlier record for the number of successes, he nevertheless failed to find a place in a Formula 1 team at any rate for the start of the 1979 season.

There was more of a battle for the Formula 3 title which was still at stake in the sixteenth and last race at Vallelunga near Rome. Here the champion's crown was taken by the Dutchman Jan Lammers at the wheel of a Ralt-Toyota who had won only four times this year the same number of victories as the Swede Olafsson who was his most dangerous and determined rival.

In the rallies, Fiat for the second time running took the world title thanks to the Finn Markku Alen and the Fiat Abarth 131, beating Vatanen and the Ford who at the end of the 1000 Lakes rally were the only ones still in the running for the title. The Fiats used to go faster on the dry and the Fords on the dirt. But then the racing section of the Italian make improved their cars and wiped out the handicap and the Fords had to be content with second place even on the surfaces most congenial to them. There are even rumours that they will shortly abandon this kind of racing, at any rate as far as official entries are concerned. The trumps of the Fiat 131 were perfect organization incredible reliability and excellent professional drivers.

Public interest in rallies is constantly increasing and the main obstacle now lies in the difficulty in obtaining information. If the media — television and press — devote more space to the sport, as would only be fair, rallying could shortly become a rival to Formula 1 racing. And that would not be a bad thing.

Special bodies

Illustrations and technical information

ARCADIPANE — Taipan — **AUSTRALIA**

The second prototype of the Australian coachbuilders, again based on the Holden Torana hatchback, is the Taipan.
Economy, simplicity and ease of maintenance are once again the criteria followed
by Arcadipane who provide Australian manufacturers with concept studies.

BAUR — BMW Hardtop Cabriolet — **GERMANY (FR)**

Using the mechanics of the entire range of the BMW Series 3, the Stuttgart coachbuilder has designed this
streamlined cabriolet, fitted with an ample rollbar to give the entire shell rigidity. For the front
part of the roof there is a hardtop (which can be stowed in the boot) and a folding hood for the rear.

he lure of the XJS's 12 cylinders led Bertone to design this refined and harmonious 3-door sports car.
Great ingenuity marks the solution for the air filter which has its own housing, separate
rom the rest of the bonnet, making it look lower although it is 20 cm shorter than the original.

he 'hiss' is based on the Lancia Stratos running gear and chassis but is 4 in (10 cm) longer. Taking his dream-car
ne step further, Bertone tries to integrate the glass area into the body. An original steering wheel fits
e natural grip of the hand and also houses warning lights, switches and a loudspeaker.

*A wedge-shaped convertible spider with lively performance from
a 1500 cc 85 hp (DIN) engine centrally mounted is Bertone's version of the Fiat X1/9,
distinguished by a 5-speed gearbox and modified front end and bumpers.*

 BERTONE   Fiat Abarth 131 Rally   **ITALY**

*Four hundred blue and yellow 131s are being built at Rivalta for homologation in
Group 4 - GT Special - to be raced in 1979, replacing the 124 Spider. The 132 twinshaft engine
and fuel injection are used. The cars will race in the blue and yellow colours of Fiat oils.*

Derived from the Volvo 264 GL saloon, this elegant limousine is destined for diplomats and the like. The hull has been reinforced and lengthened by the insertion of new doors, windows, roof and various other elements. The sumptuous equipment includes a radio telephone and refrigerator. Overall length 220.47 in (560 cm), height 56.69 in (144 cm).

Bertone is building the 262 C to Volvo specifications aimed at providing maximum comfort and low noise levels in a 4-seater coupé for an exclusive clientèle. The spare tire is stowed flat in the boot, to be blown up with a compressed air cylinder when needed.

Simple, pleasing lines characterize this 2+2 coupé with Turbo-Hydramatic 3-speed automatic gearbox.
Its dimensions are: 190.94 in (485 cm) long, 72.44 in (184 cm) wide, weight 4,443 lb (2,015 kg).
The 8-cylinder 5,354 cc engine develops 230 bhp (DIN) at 4,700 rpm, with a maximum speed in the region of 137 mph (220 km/h).

Like the god, Coggiola's study for a new coupé is two-faced. It is an exercise in style which demonstrates
how a car can be given a different character simply by modifying its form. The dimensions
of the two sides are identical and a mirror allows the unequal natures to be appreciated from all angles.

n extra 10 in (25 cm) of rear compartment leg room is built into the Minster derived from the 2.8 litre
ord Granada. The designers cut the body in body in half and weld in additional bodywork, fitting larger rear
oors and a distinctive front end. Air-conditioning and electric windows and partition are among the extras.

istributed worldwide by Bristol Street Motors, the new 'T' Bar Convertible is a handsome car
r the young at heart. An exclusive seat style provides
irtually the same leg and head room for front and rear passengers as in the normal saloon model.

This sophisticated town car also offers open air four-seater luxury.
The car's high standard of refinement plus outstanding roominess for passengers
and luggage makes it a most luxurious four-seater convertible.

 **DOME**   **Dome-O**   **JAPAN**

"Child's dream" is a literal translation of Dome. Designed by a group of young enthusiasts,
the Dome-O is a brand new mid-engined aerodynamic road car of steel monocoque construction. The first prototype
is powered by Nissan's L28 fuel injection inline six conforming to Japan's stringent emission standards.

On the chassis of the Series 5, Frua has created this snappy coupé with wheelbase shortened to 94.49 in (240 cm).
BMW 520 I mechanics with a 1,990 cc injection engine and 5-speed gearbox are used. The belt line is low to increase lateral
vision and a tailgate gives access to the luggage area. Overall length 167.32 in (425 cm) and width 69.68 in (177 cm).

Derived from the Lamborghini Espada, Frua's low four-door 12-cylinder saloon offers roomy accommodation for four
and excellent visibility, thanks to the multiple rear window treatment. The wheelbase is 111 in (283 cm),
width 75 in (190 cm) and height 49 in (125 cm). The Lamborghini 12-cylinder engine allows a top speed of 155 mph (250 km/h).

This 2+2 coupé is called Kyalami, after the famous South African Grand Prix track near Johannesburg.
The mechanical parts are by Maserati, with the V8 4,136 cc 265 bhp engine developing a
maximum speed in the region of 150 mph (240 km/h).

GHIA

Action

ITALY

Both the Action and the Microsport form part of a study on aerodynamics and energy conservation.
The mid-engined Action mounts the Ford Cosworth 8-cylinder F1 engine. The front spoiler is extended laterally
to give increased down force. Each panel of the body in designed to contribute to overall aerodynamic efficiency.

This 5-seater prototype mounted on a Ford Taunus 2000 chassis is the adaptation of the Megastar concept to the theme of a sports coupé for the family. The spare wheel is now housed in the engine compartment, the nose is longer and more "chiseled", and there is a tailgate. It was invited to the USA by Ford to celebrate the Foundation's 75th anniversary.

ITALY   Microsport   GHIA

Ghia Operations has given the Fiesta a superlight 2-seater 2-door body. The wheelbase has been cut by 254 mm and the front end extended to reduce the front section, greatly improving the drag coefficient. The Fiesta 957 cc engine is retained. This prototype is 143 lb (65 kg) lighter than the standard Fiesta thanks to aluminium doors, hood and rear deck.

Presented at the 1978 Geneva Show, this off-road vehicle derived from the Ford Fiesta was designed in collaboration with the Ford Design Center of Dearborn. The modified suspension increases the ground clearance. A robust roll bar and special off-road tyres complete the transformation.

 GRANDEUR MOTOR CAR   **Opera Coupé**   **USA**

The rear seat portion of a Cadillac Seville has been removed and the nose extended in this pretentious coupé with two false side-mount spare tyres. Thirty a month are being built in Florida. A four-door Formal Sedan is also on the production line.

*This special Range Rover has 6 wheels, an extended chassis, 4 doors, hydraulically raised
hunting seats, a sunroof eight feet long, leather-trimmed interior, long-range fuel and water tanks,
camel bars, automatic transmission, a special V8 power unit and air conditioning. Eighty are being made.*

*For the intermediate model of the Audi range, Giugiaro has designed a sober,
pleasing body with excellent all-round visibility thanks to three side windows. Every attention has been given to passenger comfort,
particularly for driving in the colder areas of the world. The overall length is 169 in (430 cm) and the weight 1,874 lb (850 kg).*

Starting from the Mitsubishi mechanics of the Korean Hyundai Pony Coupé, Giugiaro has freely developed a sports version of the saloon. A generous roll bar makes excellent side visibility possible with very high rear end. Even with the lower bonnet, the headlamps remain fixed. Wheelbase 92 in (234 cm).

ITAL DESIGN   Maserati Quattroporte   ITALY

In close collaboration with Maserati, Ital Design has created a thoroughbred high-performance 4-seater beautifully finished throughout. The side lines are upswept with respect to the belt line and the rear quarter lights set well forward to give the rear seat passengers privacy. Overall length 192.13 in (488 cm), width 66.54 in (169 cm) and height 52.76 in (134 cm).

For once Ital Design has concentrated on comfort, safety and rationality.
The height of the Lancia Gamma has been increased for extra passenger comfort and luggage space, while the fuel tank and spare tyre fit under the doorstep-level humpfree floor. Overall length is only 169 in (429.5 cm). The aesthetic result is new and surprising.

A numbered series of 50 will be built of the 4-seater luxury touring car reminiscent of the '30s.
Based on a modified Ford van chassis with Ford running gear and 400 cc V8 engine, it rides and handles well. There is a choice of automatic or manual transmission. The wheelbase is 144 in (366 cm).

An immensely strong T-bar for maximum rigidity, and the original upper safety belt
mounting points give this 4-seater convertible based on the Cavalier Coupé exceptional safety
qualities. It is powered by a 1,979 cc engine and has received British National Type approval.

MICHELOTTI   Every 4R   ITALY

Derived from the Fiat 127, the "Every" is a rational and economical interpretation of our favourite plaything.
A simple, robust structure with fiberglass panels, doors, roof and bonnet — the latter a nostalgic
two-piece unit. It is available both in an open and a closed version. Production is expected to begin in the summer.

Dual-chambered air-cushion restraints at the front and force limiters combined with 3-point harnesses at the rear afford excellent protection for the occupants of this safety car in a frontal collision. Resilient plastic covers the energy-absorbent, foam-filled steel structure.

USA   LRSV   MINICARS MINICARS, INC.

This Large Research Safety Vehicle based on a 1977 Chevrolet Impala has an improved power-weight ration, lower emissions and can do 27.5 mpg. It provides occupant crash protection in 40 mph (64 km/h) frontal crashes. It seats six and mounts a Volvo Lambda-Sond engine.

Moretti has moved into the market — a neglected one in Italy — for large estate cars with the Folk based on the Alfa Romeo Giulietta chassis. A fifth door has been set into the rear end, hinging up from bumper level. Electrically winding down windows are fitted behind the rear air vents, and there is a rear wiper. The dimensions are unchanged.

Based on Fiat Campagnola frame and running gear, this 8-seater squarerigger with 6 seats folding away to create ample cargo space offers more comfort than most off-road vehicles. Wheelbase 91 in (230 cm), weight 4,230 lb (1,920 kg) dry.

The Leyland Princess, the first car to use the Triplex advanced safety windscreen, has been restyled as a one-off estate car to demonstrate the latest skills in automotive glass. It has a curved, all-glass rear door, Hyviz windscreen for demisting, de-icing and radio reception, flexing glass sunroof and glassed rear extension. There is an all-round protective buffer.

USA   **Di Napoli Coupé**   **PACIFIC COACHBUILDERS** (PC)

One hundred units are being built of this nostalgic de luxe coupé which has however its full compliment of safety equipment. A 3.8 turbocharged Buick V6 engine and Turbo-Hydramaitc automatic transmission are standard. It also features automatic air conditioning, electric windows and a power sunshine roof. Wheelbase 150 in (381 cm).

Phaeton have based this Executive Limousine, and also the Presidential and Town Car limousines, on a Toyota chassis, using a 6-cylinder single overhead camshaft engine with varying wheelbases. Every passenger comfort is catered for.

In this version, destined for the United States only, the famous spider has been slightly modified, above all externally. American-type bumpers are fitted and light alloy wheels. The engine is the well-established 2-litre injection with twin overhead camshaft.

Pininfarina used his wind gallery to ensure more markedly aerodynamic lines for
the 308 GTB. It features large spoilers and a wing set behind the passenger area.
The choice and distribution of the colours emphasize its sporting personality.

Derived from the Ferrari 308 GTB berlinetta, this comfortable spider with modern lines
and marked sporting characteristics does not fail to respect the contemporary demand
for safety features and reliability. It is produced by Ferrari and the Carrozzeria Scaglietti.

31

PININFARINA   **Ferrari 400 Automatic**   **ITALY**

This Ferrari, which is the evolution of the 365 GT4, whose lines it retains unchanged, is notable for the innovations in the mechanics and the interior. It is in fact the first Ferrari with automatic transmission but this has meant no loss in its traditional high performance characteristics. Space has been found in the interior for four comfortable seats.

PININFARINA   **Ferrari 512 B.B.**   **ITALY**

The fascination of this car, typical of all the others of the marque of the rampant horse does not lie merely in its high performance figures. The great attraction is the smooth, clean lines, studied specially to allow the powerful 12-cylinder engine developing 360 bhp (DIN) to top 300 km/h (186 mph).

To date over 150 thousand of these cars, which are at present sold only in the United States, have been built. At present the 124 Spider has a 2-litre twin overhead camshaft engine. The body has been updated both internally and externally.

This aerodynamic prototype spider, based on the XJS coupé, harks back to the glorious models D and E, re-evoking their rounded lines and the oval front air intake. A soft back and soft nose have replaced the traditional bumpers. The interior, surprisingly simple, is dictated by safety principles. Luggage space is unusually ample.

PININFARINA   **Lancia Beta Monte-Carlo**   **ITALY**

Low, wide and aggressive at the same time, this car has orignial lines and several stylistic innovations.
The central-rear engine geometry, typical of modern sports cars, makes comfortable and safe seating possible.
The arrangement of the various instruments is rational and they are in easy reach.

PININFARINA   **Lancia Gamma Coupé**   **ITALY**

More compact than the saloon version, this coupé, besides being easier to handle, has the advantage of a lower drag
coefficient with higher performance at the same power. The high level of the finishings and the great comfort can be further
enhanced by the adoption of the optional accessories offered, including hide upholstery and air-conditioning.

logical outcome of the coupé's success, the prototype Pininfarina spider looks even more
ashing and elegant. The rollbar already used in the coupé is fully exploited in the T-roof
olution which guarantees maximum safety. The transparent vinyl rear window zips open.

SA   Turbo Phantom   THE PHANTOM

esigned to be built on a custom basis only, this 3-wheeled luxury sports car has a tilt canopy door and is powered by a special
rbocharged version of the Honda Gold Wing engine. Power is delivered through a 5-speed transmission to the shaft driven rear wheel.
igid urethane foam surrounds the passenger compartment for structural safety. Length 168 in (427 cm), top speed 130 mph (209 km/h).

The 2-seater Vector W2, a blend of aerospace and sports racing technology, aims to be America's challenge to Maserati and Lamborghini. Urethane foam sandwich allows its front and rear panels to double as bumpers. The engine is a twin turbocharged V8 with Bosch fuel injection designed to produce 600 bhp at 5,000 rpm. The sun-roof is removable.

Modification of the front end has entailed the replacement of round headlamps by rectangular ones. The paintwork is extremely original with a shaded band running along the waistline and the edges of the roof. The effect on the look of the car is to make it slimmer and more streamlined. The passenger accommodation is neat and pleasing with a combination of felt and vinyl.

For his Lancia Beta Spider destined for the American market, Zagato has replaced the canvas section around the rear window by a fibreglass hardtop which will stand up to the rigours of harsh winters or to razor blades and sharp knives.

ITALY   Z 80   ZAGATO

This is Zagato's proposal for a spacious 4-seater sports car of the future the 'eighties, as the name suggests. To reduce consumption to the minimum, great attention has been paid to the aerodynamics, above all wind resistance. Overall length 166.14 in (422 cm).

Electric vehicles

Illustrations and technical information

AM GENERAL   Electruck DJ-5E

Like the Jeep it is derived from, the Electruck has sliding doors, but it has only one bucket driver's seat and rear wheel drive only. The 54 V 30 bhp dc motor has SCR chopper regulation. Top speed is 40 mph (64 km/h) and town autonomy with frequent stops 30 miles (50 km). The chassis and body are all of steel construction. Dimensions: wheelbase 81 in (206 cm), front track 51.50 in (131 cm), rear track 50 in (127 cm), overall length 136 in (345 cm), width 59.88 in (152 cm), height 69.49 in (176 cm), dry weight 3,618 lb (1641 kg), maximum weight 4,304 lb (1,952 kg), weight of batteries 1,301 lb (590 kg). Many are in use for US postal deliveries in urban areas with pollution problems.

B & Z   Electra King PFS 125

Already in production for mixed transport purposes, the Minivan is built in plastic on a steel frame to Battronic's own design. The dc series wound motor has SCR control and develops 31.5 kW at 2,300 rpm. 2 packs of 56-cell lead-acid batteries are placed on each side of the van. On- and off-board recharging is possible and takes 8 hours. Maximum speed is 60 mph (96 km/h) and range at cruising speed 40 miles (64 km). Dimensions: wheelbase 94.49 in (240 cm), front track 61.02 in (155 cm), rear track 63.39 in (161 cm), overall length 145 in (368 cm), width 74 in (188 cm), height 92 in (234 cm), maximum weight with batteries 5,700 lb (2,585 kg). It features sliding doors and two seats.

BATTRONIC   Minivan

This two-seater coupé designed by B & Z staff has a fiberglass-reinforced body with sliding glass windows. A series motor developing 6 kW at 1400 rpm and 2 kW at 2,800 rpm is regulated by the electromechanical switching of the series resistance. Six 6 V lead-acid batteries in a single pack under the seat give 190 Ah. Top speed, which is also cruising speed, is 20 mph (30 km/h) and the range is 22 miles (35 km). A larger motor and larger batteries, available as optionals, give increased speed and range. The length is 101 in (256 cm), width 45 in (114 cm) and height 60 in (152 cm), while the wheelbase is 65 in (165 cm). Curb weight with batteries is 1,100 lb (500 kg). Price $ 3,965.

C.E.D.R.E.   Midinette 1000

Already in production, this 3-wheeler is based on a 1974 prototype. The iron square tube and fiberglass body is described as having one and a half seats, with sliding doors. There is a permanent luggage rack on the roof and a rear movable compartment. The series motor with electromagnetic variable voltage develops 5 kW at 4,000 rpm and 1 kW at 5,000 rpm. The 6 V batteries are mounted 2 in front and 4 at the rear. The on-board, self-regulated high energy rate recharging system is original, without electronic charging system. Top speed is 28 mph (45 km/h) and range 75 miles (120 km). Length is 73 in (185 cm), width 35 in (88 cm) and height 61 in (155 cm). Curb weight is 662 lb (300 kg). Price 14,500 francs.

COMMUTER   111-DW Comuta-Car

Commuter's little 2-door two-seater is, as its name suggests, built for short trips in town. Access is by two side doors and a rear hatchback door. Rally stripes, aerodynamic styling and high impact energy absorbing bumpers are featured. The series-wound dc motor develops 5.76 kW at 4,100 revs and has high current contacters for battery switching. 8 6 V 106 Ah lead-acid batteries in 3 packs are mounted front and rear. There is a built-in charger for overnight charging from a wall socket. At the top speed of 50 mph (80 km/h), range is 30 miles (48 km), but 40 miles (64 km) at cruising speed. Overall length is 120 in (285 cm), wheelbase 65 in (166 cm) and curb weight 1,400 lb (635 kg). Price $ 4,000.

COMMUTER   121-CV Comuta-Van

The 121-CV Van is basically a variation of the Comuta-Car, but a little longer and heavier. Like the Car, it is already in production, as is a taxi version. The chief dimensions are: wheelbase 76 in (193 cm), length 140 in (336 cm), width 55 in (139 cm) and height 60 in (151 cm). Weight with batteries — at 500 lb (662 kg) — is 1,460 lb (662 kg). Both Car and Van fit hydraulic dual master nonservo drum brakes all round and electric braking is available at extra cost. The Van only can be supplied with solar panels: photovoltaic cells convert the sunlight directly into electricity, allowing a 10% increase in range after 8 hours' charging. Price $ 4,500. For other details, see Comuta Car.

COPPER   Runabout

The mass of the Runabout, CDA's latest prototype, is about two-thirds the Town Car's. Designed by them, but using many Renault R5 components, it has 3 doors and seats four, 2 facing rearwards. The height ensures good visibility and a tinted glass sunroof improves ventilation. The 28 kW separately excited Reliance motor is powered by 126 V 160 Ah Globe Union batteries mounted centrally under the car and sliding out lengthwise on teflon rails. They have common venting and a single-point water fill system. Top speed is 59 mph (95 km/h) and range 72 miles (116 km). The suspension has a large amount of front and rear antilift to minimize pitch altitude changes. Weight with batteries is only 3,036 lb (1,377 kg).

COPPER   Town Car

This 2-seater hatchback prototype is built by the Copper Development Association using existing components and innovative technology. The streamlined car's range is 103 miles (165 km) at 40 mph (64 km/h) with a top speed of 59 mph (95 km/h). The 18 6 V batteries are housed in the central tunnel, sliding out from the rear. They power a separately excited 42 kW motor with a proprietary control system. The unusual doors swing outward until they clear the car's body and then travel rearward parallel to the body. The wheelbase is 80 in (203 cm), length 145 in (368 cm), width 60 in (152 cm), and height 54.5 in (138 cm). Weight with the batteries — which weigh 1,206 lb (547 kg) — is 3,036 lb (1,377 kg).

DAIHATSU   Masters Seven GBC

The smallest vehicle in Daihatsu's electric range is this open 3-wheeled golf buggy, already in production in Japan. The single central seat has no backrest. The dc electric motor has two-step regulation and develops 25 W x 2 kW. There are three 12 V 100 Ah lead acid batteries mounted under the seat and they are recharged by means of a 100 V or 200 V ac converter. Transmission is direct and the Masters Seven is fitted with 15-6.0-8-S P tyres. Speed is obviously not an important factor in a golf buggy. The Masters Seven can do 4 mph (7 km/h). The chief dimensions are: overall length 76 in (194 cm), width 36 in (92 cm), and height 39 in (99 cm). Curb weight with batteries is 430 lb (195 kg).

DAIHATSU   Masters 4

Daihatsu's neat and sturdy four-wheeled open golf buggy seats two comfortably with grab rails offering side support. No windscreen is fitted in view of the fact that the top speed of the Masters 4 is only 11 mph (18 km/h). The dc electric motor with three-step regulation develops 2.3 kW. Three 12 V lead-acid batteries are housed under the seat and recharging is by means of a 200 V ac converter. Simplicity is the key word. The transmission is direct and braking mechanical. 19-8.00 tyres are fitted. The weight with batteries is 1,003 lb (455 kg). Overall length is 102 in (260 cm), width 46 in (116 cm) and height 48 in (123 cm). Golf bags are conveniently stowed at the rear.

DAIHATSU   S60-TSD

The S60 TSD pickup is also produced in two other versions, the TSD03-1 and TSD04. Like the S603-DOV van it is based on the 550 cc Hijet and uses the same motor, regulation and batteries as the DOV. The DO3s are connected in series and the DO4 in parallel. A 200 V power source is used for charging. Top speed is 43 mph (70 km/h) in the DO3 and DO3-1 and 22 mph (35 km/h) in the DO4. The range varies: 34 miles (55 km) in the DO3-1, 56 miles (90 km) in the DO3-1, and 62 miles (100 km) in the DO4. The dimensions are the same in all three: length 126 in (319.5 cm), width 55 in (139 cm) and height 66 in (166.5 cm). The DO3 and DO4 weigh 2,172 lb (985 kg) and the DO3-1 1,951 lb (885 kg).

DAIHATSU   S60V-W03

Daihatsu's new mini pickup is already in production and is also available in DO3-1 and DO4 versions. Based on the 550 cc Hijet vehicles, it has a 14 kW 90 V dc shunt motor with a maximum torque of 5 kgm and a 3-step regulator TR chopper. 8 12 V lead batteries are mounted in all three versions, developing 120 Ah in the DO3 and DO4 and 100 Ah in the DO3-1. The connection is in series in the former and in parallel in the latter. Dimensions are identical in all three: length 126 in (319.5 cm), width 55 in (139.5 cm) and height 62 in (157.5 cm). The DO3-1 is lighter than the others at 2,106 lb (955 kg). Top speed is 43 mph (70 km/h) in the DOZ and DO3-1 but only 22 mph (35 km/h) in the DO4.

DAIHATSU   Mini-Elec Bus Z045-7

Daihatsu's latest electric vehicle is a 7-passenger open bus commissioned for resort use. Only eight will in fact be built. The ML dc electric motor develops a maximum power of 7.2 kW. It is powered by eight 12 V lead-acid batteries giving 100 Ah/5 hr. They are mounted under the floor. Recharging takes 8 hours using an ac 200 V input. The mechanical gearbox has two forward speeds and reverse. The maximum speed, in view of the use for which the bus is designed, is only 9 mph (15 km/h) and the range between charges 31 miles (50 km). Overall length is 138 in (350 cm), width 59 in (150 cm) and height 73 in (185 cm). The wheelbase is 70 in (178 mm) and the weight with batteries 2,095 lb (950 kg).

DIE MESH   Spider

The infinite speed traction transmission invented by Die Mesh's president, Domenic Borello, is being evaluated by the Federal Energy Research and Development Administration. The University of Michigan, too, is interested in a transmission that has no gears and does not work by friction, but combines parallel cone-shaped components with a power transfer wheel. Mounted on a Fiat 850 sport spider body, 16 6 V lead acid batteries in two packs power a 10 hp motor. Top speed is 50 mph (80 km/h) and range 35 miles (55 km). The weight (batteries included) is slightly greater than the original model at 2,600 lb (1,179 kg) but the overall length and height are unchanged. The wheelbase is 77.80 in (203 cm). Price $ 8,200.

E.A.C.   Electric Limousine

EAC's engineering team is backed by the long experience in this field of Electric Fuel Propulsion (EFP). Limited quantities of this super luxury 6-seater derived from a GM Cadillac will be built in 1979. The 180 V series motor has SCR chopper control and develops 80 kW at 4,500 rpm. 2 EFP TPX battery packs are mounted, one forward and one rear. On--board charging takes 8 hours but 45 minutes are enough for an external fast charge. A new small on-board gasoline-fueled auxiliary power unit supplies the air conditioning, heating, power brakes and steering, and extends the range from 70-100 miles (112-161 km). Top speed is 70 mph (112 km/h). Overall length 221 in (561 cm) width 78 in (198 cm), height 57 in (145 cm).

E.A.C.   1979 Silver Volt

Based on a GM Buick Century, this 5-seater wagon has aerodynamic bodywork and crash designed front and rear bumpers. Limited production is foreseen in 1979. It has a separately excited motor with a 50 kW peak and 20 kW continuous rating, transistor field control, automatic transmission with a continuously variable torque convertor and regenerative braking down to 15 mph (24 km/h). 2 packs of EFP TPX batteries giving 144 V and 240 amp at a 2 hr rate are mounted, one forward and one rear. Top speed is 70 mph (112 km/h) and range at 50 mph (80 km/h) 60 miles (96 km). A gasoline-powered auxiliary power unit extends the range and provides air conditioning, heating, and power steering and brakes.

ELECTRICAR   Lectric Leopard

C.H. Waterman, who gave his initials to the CHW electric cars, presides over the US Electricar Corp. Their 3-door 4-seater hatchback sedan, already in production, is designed for short haul driving and claims to be virtually maintenance free. The compound wound Prestolite 48 V dc motor is regulated by voltage switching control. 16 6 V lead-acid batteries developing 440 Ah are mounted in 2 packs at the front and rear. Maximum speed is 50 mph (80 km/h) and the range is from 60-80 miles (96-128 km), depending on the driving conditions. The overall length is 142 in (361 cm), width 60 in (152 cm), height 55 in (140 cm) and wheelbase 95 in (241 cm). Weight with batteries is 2,580 lb (1,170 kg). Price $ 6,995.

EPC   Hummingbird Hydrid Mk II

A Ford Pinto station wagon is the basis of the longer-range Mk II Hummingbird. The 17.6 hp Onan Model X-100 shunt wound motor with constantly variable rate transmission is powered by 8 Globe Union EV 27-15 batteries placed at the rear. Recharging is by means of an onboard Lester automatic recharger. The heat engine hybrid is designed to replace energy drained from the batteries during operation. At the Hummingbird's top speed of 58 mph (93 km/h) its range is 40 miles (64 km) rising to 50 miles (80 km) at cruising speed. The chief dimensions are: overall length 169.3 in (430 cm), width 69 in (175 cm), height 51 in (129 cm) and wheelbase 94 in (239 cm). Regenerative braking is used. Price $ 10,500.

EVA   Change of Pace

Based, like a previous EVA model, on the AMC Pacer, this station wagon seats 4 and has a fold-down rear seat for additional cargo space. It is supplied complete with every detail including a gas heater. The series motor develops 26 kW at 3,000 revs with SCR speed control and is powered by 20 6 V lead-acid batteries housed front and rear in 2 packs. An on-board charger fits standard wall outlets. Transmission is automatic and there are disc brakes at the front and drum at the rear. Top speed is 55 mph (88 km/h) and range 40-50 miles (64-80 km) at cruising speed or 30 miles (48 km) at maximum speed. Overall length is 216 in (549 cm), width 77 in (196 cm) and height 57 in (145 cm). Price $ 12,360.

EXXON   Experimental Electric Vehicle

The striking gull-wing door body of this prototype is based on the Bradley GT II design but incorporates graphite fiber reinforced plastics. A proprietary direct current shunt motor is powered by twelve 6 V batteries weighing 750 lb (340 kg), 9 mounted amidships and 3 in the nose. The propulsion unit allows a top speed of 55 mph (88 km/h) to be reached, while a cruising speed of 45 mph (72 km/h) is recommended. Range between charges varies according to how the car is driven but is roughly 30 miles (48 km). Regenerative electric braking is used. The Exxon is not a small car: overall length 177 in (450 cm), width 69 in (175 cm), height 43.50 in (110 cm), wheelbase 95 in (241 cm) and curb weight 2,350 lb (1,066 kg).

FIAT   X 1/23

The Fiat X 1/23 is a little two-seater experimental car for town use. It was presented some years ago at the Turin Motor Show minus power unit and in 1976 it was fitted with a 14 kW electric motor with separate exciting field and lead-acid bateries. The traditional brakes are supplemented by a regenerating brake. Cooling is by a fan driven by an auxiliary electric motor. An electronic impulse traction regulator adjusts the speed of the vehicle continuously from zero to top speed, ensures that it functions in a regular manner at all speeds and provides for energy-recovery braking. The X 1/23 has front wheel drive while the batteries are housed at the rar. Top speed is 45 mph (75 km/h) and the range about 50 miles (80 km).

FIAT   900 T Elettrico

Fiat's experimental electric van is derived from their standard '900 T commercial vehicle and is powered by a Fiat electric motor weighing 121 lb (55 kg) and developing a nominal power of 14 kW at 3,200 rpm. The 12 V batteries are connected .in series and housed in a single central tray. An electronic traction regulator adjusts the speed and provides electric braking with recovery of kinetic energy. The van has a top speed of 37 mph (60 km/h) and a range between charges of 30 miles (50 km). The chief dimensions are: overall length 146.85 in (373 cm), overall width 58.66 in (149 cm), and overall height 65.35 in (166 cm). The curb weight is 4,095 lb (1,857 kg).

FIAT   242 Electric Van Prototype

The Fiat Research Centre has derived this electric van from the 242, retaining the same geometry of the traction organs. The dc series excited motor with 24 kW nominal power and the electronic controller with energy-recovery braking are front-mounted under the bonnet, while the batteries are housed in two compartments along the sides of the van, leaving ample cargo space. They are accessible from the exterior for easy removal by means of a fork-lift truck. In an alternative version, the batteries are stowed under the floor. The maximum speed is 50 mph (80 km/h) and the range in normal town conditions 40-50 miles (65-81 km). The curb weight is 7,720 lb (3,500 kg) and the payload capacity 1,918 lb (870 kg).

FLINDERS   Investigator Mk II

The Flinders University team has spent five years developing its twin-module motor electric version of a Fiat 127. A practical and viable propulsion system is linked to advanced battery developments to give exceptional acceleration and hill-climbing and a range of up to 50 miles (80 km) at 37-47 mph (60-75 km/h). The novelty is a printed circuit motor and a method of matching impedance with a series-pass transistor. The motor and control system is designed as a modular assembly and the Flinders linear current control system (FLCC) allows infinitely variable power control of both output and regenerative power. There are plans to add a third motor module to the two 5 kW motors.

FSM   Polski-Fiat 126

The FSM (Fabryka Samochodów Malolitrazo- wych), which builds cars derived from Italian Fiat models in Poland, has also prepared an experimental electric version of the 126. The body is unchanged but the petrol engine has been replaced by an ac electric motor with a power of 5 kW (about 7 bhp). A current invertor is used to transform the dc current of the lead batteries into alternating current. The car has a top speed of roughly 43 mph (70 km/h) and an autonomy of 25 miles (40 km). But forth- coming improvements should more than double the autonomy, making it adequate for city use. An air-zinc battery is also being studied giving an energy-weight ratio that is five times better than the lead batteries and would greatly im- prove the autonomy.

GARRETT   Doe Electric

This all plastic prototype is due to be delivered to the Department of Energy this year. Two 21 kW dc motors with field control are powered by 18 6 V lead-acid batteries mounted in the central tunnel. There is an on-board charger for a 110 V receptical. An experimental elec- tromechanical fully automatic gearbox is con- trolled by a computer-micro processor. This 4-seater compact has a passing speed of 68 mph (109 km/h) and a range of 120 miles (193 km) at a cruising speed of 40 mph (64 km/h). A composite wound flywheel housed in a low- pressure aluminum chamber stores energy to provide high transient power capability for acceleration and recovery of kinetic energy dur- ing braking.

GE   Centennial Electric

Designed to provide hard data on the present state of the technology of electric cars and to celebrate GE's 100th birthday, this hatchback prototype was built to GE specifications by Triad Services of Dearborn. It carries 4, with the 2 at the back facing rearwards. The 24 hp dc series traction motor driving the front wheels is centrally mounted and has solid state controller and power conditioner, plus a blower for cooling the motor and electric components. 18 6 V lead-acid batteries are slung centrally and longitudinally on a movable trolley beneath the vehicle. Top speed is 60 mph (96 km/h) with a range of 75 miles (120 km) at a con- stant 40 mph (64 km/h). Length is 92 in (234 in), width 66 in (168 cm) and height 54 in (137 cm). Curb weight is 3,350 lb (1,519 kg).

GLOBE UNION   Endura

This lightweight fiberglass prototype is design- ed as a test vehicle for Globe Union's techno- logy in batteries. Using a four individual seat configuration, it has the flexibility of a combin- ed sport sedan and station wagon thanks to the easy interchange of a rear quarter panel. The 20 Globe Union high energy density advanc- ed lead-acid 12 V batteries are mounted on an aluminium frame and roller subassembly tray. A Monopanel electronic control board controls ignition, lights, wipers and other accessories. The 20 hp series wound motor allows a top speed of over 60 mph (96 km/h) and a range at cruising speed of 100 miles (161 km). Over- all length is 184 in (467 cm), width 72 in (183 cm) and wheelbase 108 in (277 cm).

GM   Electrovette

Confident that electric vehicles have a definite place in the future of transportation, GM are developing a new series of test cars. The first prototype is a 2-seater coupé with a removable sun roof based on the Chevrolet Chevette. In the space once occupied by the engine are mounted an on-board computer that is a control signal processor and "brain" of the system; a chopper which is a motor-power controller; a "choke" or motor current smoothing reactor; a dc motor/generator; a 110/220 V ac transformerless charger, a gear box and an auxiliary battery. 20 12 V lead-acid batteries are mounted in two packs in the rear seat area. Top speed is 53 mph (85 km/h) and range 50 miles (80 km) at cruising speed.

GMC   Vandura G31003

GMC's 2-seater prototype commercial van is based on a conventional van body with the batteries housed under the vehicle to allow unobstructed load space. A dc series motor with chain gear reduction is combined with solid state continuous electronic speed control. Max power is 37 1/2 kW at 3,250 rpm. The 36 6 V lead-acid batteries are in a single pack and recharging is automatic. It has vacuum assist hydraulic brakes with electric regeneration. Top speed is 50 mph (80 km/h) and range 40 miles (64 km) on S.A.E. schedule "C". Length is 178.2 in (452 cm), width 79.5 in (202 cm) and height 81.2 in (206 cm). Several will be used in service in Southern California in 1979 as part of a U.S. Department of Energy demonstration project.

GOULD   Electric Van

This prototype with aerodynamic fiberglass nose — derived from the Ford E-250 Econoline — has utility or minibus configurations and seats up to 12. A Gould motor with direct chain drive and dual SCR power chopper regulation develops 105 kW at 1,000 rpm. There is regenerative braking from 20-50 mph (32-80 km/h). 32 3 V advanced lead-acid batteries are mounted under the floor and give 440 Ah at a 20 hour rate. Recharging can be carried out overnight by an automatic ferroresonant system. Top speed is 55 mph (88 km/h) and range at cruising speed about 40 miles (64 km). Overall length is 207 in (525 cm), width 92 in (234 cm) and height 83 in (210 cm). The batteries weigh 2,200 lb (1,000 kg).

GURGEL   Itaipu Mod. 1

Gurgel's little four-wheeled Itaipu Mod. 1 is a prototype mounting a 3 kW motor powered by ten 12 V batteries giving 68 Ah. The batteries are placed behind the seats. The wedge-nosed Mod. 12 has a maximum speed of 31 mph (50 km/h) and an autonomy of 37 miles (60 km) at that speed. It is designed to seat two persons and can carry a load of 66 lb (30 kg). The chief dimensions are: overall length 102 in (260 cm), overall width 61 in (155 cm), overall height 57 in (145 cm) and ground clearance 6 in (16 cm). It weighs 1,103 lb (500 kg) without the batteries which account for 706 lb (320 kg) of the total weight.

GURGEL — Itaipu Mod. 2

The Brazilian firm's unusual Itaipu Mod. 2 is an open-bodied test vehicle being developed by Gurgel to carry four passengers besides the driver or to seat two with ample cargo space for a 551 lb (250 kg) load. The 8 kW motor is powered by six 12 V batteries developing 225 Ah which are housed on the floor behind the front seats. The Mod. 2 has a top speed of 53 mph (85 km/h) and a range of 62 miles (100 km) at a cruising speed of 19 mph (30 km/h). The chief dimensions are: overall length 142 in (360 cm) and overall width 71 in (180 cm). The prototype weighs 1,544 lb (700 kg) without the batteries which weigh 948 lb (430 kg).

H-M-VEHICLES — Free-Way

Limited production in 1979 is foreseen for this 3-wheel commuter hatchback with tandem seating for two presented at the EV Expo II. The original design with small frontal profile and low air drag features a steel frame and fiberglass body. Regulation of the permanent magnet motor is by mechanical variation of variable speed belt drive with on/off contactor. 4 12 V deep cycle batteries in the rear motor compartment provide 8.5 kW at 2,600 rpm. Mounted in a fiberglass case, they slide out from the side. Regenerative braking is controlled through the accelerator pedal. Top speed is 55 mph (88 km/h) and range at cruising speed 75 miles (121 km). Length is 115 in (292 cm) and height 51 in (130 cm). Price $ 2,495.

HYBRICON — Centaur

Based on a restyled Honda 600 sedan, the 2-door 4-seater body is styled by George Barris. Two double shuntfield electric motors drive the rear wheels through electric clutches and helical gears, while the Honda 600 2-cylinder engine driving the front wheels through a 4-speed transaxle can charge the batteries 80% in an hour at 50 mph (80 km/). There is a common regenerative and hydraulic brake. 7 lead-acid 6 V batteries are placed under the rear seat. Regulation is by a power transister chopper on the armatures. Top speed is 35 mph (56 km/h) or 70 mph (112 km/h) with the I.C. engine. The electric motor provides one hour's range but the hybrid system offers obvious range and economy advantages.

JET INDUSTRIES — Electra Van 600

Based on a Fuji Heavy Industries model, this 5-door steel-bodied van is tailored for use on fixed routes such as postal services. It has energy absorbing bumpers. A 20 hp Prestolite motor with General Electric EV-1 control is powered by 17 6 V lead-acid batteries housed in a single pack at the centre of the vehicle. There is an onboard charger for 115/220 V at 30 Ah and a 4-speed manual gearbox. At its maximum speed of 54 mph (87 km/h) the range is 40 miles (64 km) but cruising speed gives a range of 60 miles (96 km). The hydraulic system has drum brakes. Length is 126 in (320 cm), wheelbase 72 in (183 cm), width 55 in (140 cm) and height 64 in (162 cm). Weight with batteries is 2,690 lb (1,220 kg). Price $ 7,995.

JET INDUSTRIES   Electra Van 1000 P

The Model 1000 P is a heavy duty pick-up designed for use in industry or municipalities. Available as a long or short bed pick-up, it is geared for heavy loads and steep inclines. The central watering system minimizes maintenance requirements and stabilizes the level of battery efficiency. Unlike the other models, it has a bench front seat for three. Motor and regulation are identical to the 1000 as are the type and number of batteries, but in the 1000 P these are stowed in two packs only at the front and back. Speeds, too, are the same as in the 1000 and 1400. The wheelbase is either 115 or 131 in (292 or 333 cm) with overall length 190 or 210 in (483 or 533 cm). The batteries in all three models weigh 1,652 lb (749 kg). Price $ 11,605.30.

JET INDUSTRIES   Electra Van 1000

Jet Industries' three larger vans are all derived from Chrysler Corporation models. The 1000 is a multi-purpose utility vehicle with maximum cargo area. There are 2 separate front seats. The 1000 van, like the 1000 P and the 1400, mounts a General Electric motor developing 32 hp at 3,900 rpm, with GE EV-1 control. 24 6 V batteries are mounted in 3 packs at the front, middle and rear. The weight with batteries is 4,760 lb (2,159 kg) and it has the same alternative lengths and wheelbases as the 1400. Overall width, as in the 1000 P and 1400, is 80 in (203 cm) and the height is 77 in (196 cm). Maintenance is simplified by easy access to all components through the front compartment. Price $ 12.508.

JET INDUSTRIES   Electra Van 1400

The Electra Van Model 1400 is a plus 8-passenger window van designed for use as a personnel carrier and for transporting guests beween convention facilities, hotels and airports. The General Electric motor with GE EV-1 control develops 32 hp at 3,900 rpm. 24 6 V lead acid batteries are mounted in three packs, front, middle and rear. Disc brakes are used at the front and drum at the rear. The van fits 15 x 6.70 tyres like the 1000 and 1000 P. The top speed is 60 mph (96 km/h) and range at cruising speed 40 miles (64 km). Overall length is either 176 in (447 cm) with a wheelbase of 109 in (277 cm) or 194 in (493 cm) with a wheelbase of 127 in (323 cm). Weight with batteries is 5,420 lb (2,458 kg). Price $ 14,080.94.

LUCAS   CF Electric Van

In 1979 Lucas is concentrating on perfecting an electric drive system in a short wheelbase Bedford CE. It can be a van, truck or personnel carrier, the latter seating up to 12. The aim is to increase in-service experience and optimise vehicle efficiency and operating cost for on-line production in the early 1980s. A Lucas CAV 40 kW motor with thyristor chopper control is mounted transversely behind the rear axle. 36 6 V lead-acid batteries giving a nominal 180 Ah are housed in a strong rectangular tray suspended beween the axles. Direct drive to the rear wheels is through a double reduction unit. Top speed is over 50 mph (80 km/h) and range 140 miles at 30 mph or 225 kilometers at 50 km/h.

MARATHON   C-360

This 6-wheel 3-axle all metal step-van accommodates driver and one passenger with 2 additional seats optional. It has two sliding side doors and two hinged rear cargo doors. The front-mounted 8 hp dc traction motor is powered by 12 6 V 225 Ah batteries carried on the independently sprung third axle, giving greatly increased drive train efficiency. Top speed is 42 mph (62 km/h); range at cruising speed is 60 miles (96 km) and at top speed 50 miles (80 km). The chief dimensions are: length 151 in (383 cm), width 62 in (157 cm) and height 70 in (178 cm). Weight with batteries is 2,600 lb (1,179 kg), the batteries accounting for 1,050 lb (476 kg). A payload of 1,000 lb (453 kg) can be carried. Price $ 10,500.

McKEE   Sundancer

McKee's two-seater commuter car has an upward opening top for easy access. The 12 6 V lead-acid batteries plus an auxiliary battery fit into a battery tray which can be rolled out and replaced in 5 minutes. The tray is housed in the backbone frame pioneered by McKee, because this battery location ensures a low centre of gravity and isolation from the car's occupants. The 8 hp motor allows a top speed of 60 mph (96 km/h) and a range of 120 miles (193 km) at 30 mph (48 km/h), or 75-85 miles (120-136 km) of city driving. Curb weight, complete with batteries, is 1,600 lb (725 kg), and the car has a wheelbase of 72 in (183 cm). It is only 40 in (102 cm) high.

MERCEDES-BENZ   307 E Van

Daimler-Benz AG's new experimental electric van is very closely based on the successful Bremen range. The fully electronic drive control and quick-service horizontal battery changing technique employed on the preceding model have been discontinued for cost reasons. It has a hydraulic converter and features a simplified electronic system with start control regulating the drive motor's shunt field in a relatively simple manner. The energy storage unit is located under the floor in two units of 90 V each, with a lifting device integrated into the battery supporting bracket. Payload is 1.5 tons. 58 vehicles have been built and tested in cooperation with the Association for Electric Road Transport GES.

P.G.E.   6 P

This snub-nosed little open runabout, built of light alloy flat panels riveted and framed with square section steel, can carry six passengers in addition to the driver. The motor, which weighs 99 lb (45 kg), develops a continuous power of 5 kW. The nominal tension of the batteries, which are housed in a central tray, is 72 V. The instruments provided include an ammeter for the armature current, a voltmeter for the tension of the batteries, a tachometer and an instrument indicating the state of charge of the batteries. The maximum speed that can be reached by the 6 P is about 37 mph (60 km/h) and it has a range between charges of about 62 miles (100 km) when driven in normal town conditions.

P.G.E.   Scuolabus

P.G.E.'s school bus can carry ten children and driver. The 5 kW electric motor has a peak power of 10 kW and is fed by twelve 6 V batteries each with a capacity of 185 Ah. The main dimensions are: overall length 135 in (342 cm), overall width 58 in (147 cm), overall height 55 in (140 cm), and the curb weight is 2,646 lb (1,200 kg). It has a top speed of 31 mph (50 km/h), while the range in town driving is about 47 miles (75 km) and 65 miles (105 km) at a constant cruising speed. The instruments fitted include an ammeter for the armature current, a voltmeter for the battery tension, a speedometer and an indicator of the battery level.

P.G.E.   Ambulanza

P.G.E.'s ambulance can carry three passengers. The same 5 kW electric motor and the same body are used as for the Scuolabus but clearly with interior finishings suited for the work it is destined to carry out. As in the school bus, there are twelve 6 V batteries but the top speed is only 28 mph (45 km/h), with a range at that speed of 65 miles (105 km). The ambulance can tackle a maximum gradient of 18% at 12 mph (20 km/h) or a continuous gradient of 6% at 15 mph (25 km/h). The vehicle is fitted with disc brakes at the front and drum brakes at the rear and has front-wheel drive.

P.G.E.   Furgone M3

This angular little van has a cargo load of 662 lb (300 kg) besides the driver. It can be powered either by a 5 kW electric motor or an internal combustion engine. The main dimensions are: overall length 118 in (300 cm), overall width 63 in (160 cm), overall height 60 in (153 cm). The curb weight is 2,139 lb (970 kg). The braking system is mixed, with disc brakes at the front and drum at the rear. The van can reach a top speed of 37 mph (60 km/h) and has a range of 62 miles (100 km). The performance in the version fitted with an internal combustion engine is about the same as the Fiat 500, since this is the type of engine mounted.

P.G.E.   Van 8

First presented at the 1978 Philadelphia Show, this unusual van with revolutionary lines can be transformed into minibus and pick-up versions. There are 3 front seats with cargo space for a payload of 1,764 lb (800 kg) at the rear. The electric motor driving the front wheels has a maximum continuous power of 15 kW and a peak power of 30 kW, allowing the van to reach a top speed of 37 mph (60 km/h). The batteries are mounted under the platform in two packs and have a nominal tension of 144 V. Regulation is by a thyristor partializer complete with static circuit for regenerative braking. Range is 37 miles (60 km) in town. The maximum gradient is 18% and acceleration from 0-30 km/h takes 6 seconds.

PIAGGIO   Ape Elettrocar

Piaggio's electric van, derived from the 3-wheel-ed Ape running on petroil mixture fits a Bosch rear-mounted electric motor developing 8 kW at 2,400 rpm. Transmission is by reduction gears with a built-in differential. The twelve batteries are connected in series with 6 V tension and are divided into three groups. A Bosch electronic group looks after speed adjustment. Top speed is a respectable 28 mph (45 km/h) and the van has a range between charges of 30 miles (50 km). The chief dimensions are: overall length 128.74 in (327 cm), overall width 57.09 in (145 cm) and overall height 68.11 in (173 cm). The total weight is 2,796 lb (1,268 kg).

PILCAR   4-seater

A three-year guarantee or unlimited mileage goes with this handy little 4-seater with three doors. The body is reinforced polyester with independent suspension all round. The 22 hp (DIN) 8/16 kW motor has an output of 84 V and is powered by improved batteries with a 40 W/kg capacity that can be completely recharged in 8 hours. There is an onboard charger. Automatic transmission and hydraulic brakes on all four wheels with electric braking on the rear wheels are features of the Pilcar. Top speed is 56 mph (90 km/h), cruising speed 37 mph (60 km/h) and the range as much as 75 miles (120 km). The overall length is 120 in (306 cm), overall width 57 in (145 cm) and weight 2,646 lb (1,700 kg). Price 16,000 francs.

PININFARINA   Ecos

Pininfarina is collaborating with Fiat on the development of electric cars on an experimental basis. Ease of entry, good visibility and comfort plus ample battery housing are ensured in the 4-seater Ecos by a forward motor, front-wheel drive and battery pouffs under the seats. Fiat, mostly Ritmo, components are used. An electronic regulator provides energy recovery during braking. 16 6 V high energy and high power density batteries are recharged on board by an automatic current rectifier. The rear seats fold independently for easy access to the batteries and to increase luggage space. Top speed is 50 mph (80 km/h) and range in town 37 miles (60 km). Length is 154 in (390 cm) and height 59 in (149 cm).

QUINCEY-LYNN   Urba Car

In an aim to avoid unnecessary energy loss, generally caused above all by the speed control system, Quincey-Lynn have patented a continuously variable transmission (CVT). It starts the compound wound Jack & Heinz motor at full voltage, putting the current directly to the 25 hp motor, which runs at constant voltage and speed. Vehicle speed is controlled through the transmission. The CVT shifts in response to a signal from a foot pedal, controlling the speed from 10 to 60 mph (16 to 96 km/h). Transmission efficiency is about 90%. Top speed is 55 mph (88 km/h) or 60 plus with field weakening circuit and range up to 65 miles (104 km). Length is 126 in (320 cm). Cost of this build-it-yourself project is about $ 2,500.

SAAB   Prototype

Saab-Scania is cooperating with AGA Innovation and the Swedish Post Office on the development of an electric van based on Saab components. Field trials are now in progress and two vans are being used in mail deliveries in one of Stockholm's satellite towns. The van is powered by modified AGA/Tudor lead batteries with an output of 144 V. A Bosch motor provides feedback current when braking and it is estimated that this system offers a feedback of 10-15% of the energy. With the current capacity of the batteries, the van's range is roughly 25 miles (40 km) with 300 stops and starts or, in normal urban traffic 43-50 miles (70-80 km). Front-wheel drive · and excellent weight distribution make for good handling.

SEARS   XDR-1

Created to mark the 10th anniversary of the famous Die Hard Battery used in USAC races, Sears' 3-door hatchback prototype based on the Fiat 128 3P has front-wheel drive and 2 bucket seats. A compound-wound 40 hp motor with regulation by solid state field weakening is mounted transversely. 20 6 V batteries are mounted in 2 packs, 5 under the hood and 15 in the former rear-seat area. Top speed is a lively 75 mph (120 km/h) with a range of 90 miles (145 km) at a cruising speed of 47 mph (75 km/h). Sears steel belted radial tyres are fitted and the car's weight, with batteries, is 3,110 lb (1,410 kg). Overall length is 151 in (386 cm), width 61 in (155 cm), height 52 in (132 cm) and the wheelbase 88 in (223 cm).

TEILHOL   Messagette

The successful Messagette is now available in various versions — the 2-seater Series B, Series D with canvas hood, 4-seater beach buggy, golf buggy with no lighting and space for clubs, and Series P for industrial use. All have stratified polyester bodies and welded steel tubing frames and are powered by a 2 kW motor driving the rear wheel through a two-stage helicoidal pinion reduction gear. There is a built-in charger for the 8 143 Ah batteries which weigh 441 lb (200 kg) and allow a maximum speed in the Series B of 15 mph (25 km/h) and autonomy of about 55 miles (90 km). The overall length is 90.55 in (230 cm), width 54.33 in (138 cm), height 61.02 in (155 cm), dry weight minus batteries 882 lb (400 kg). No driving licence is needed in France.

TEILHOL   Handicar

This 4-wheeler is primarily intended for the disabled or invalids using a wheel-chair. By pressing a button the floor descends to ground level allowing simple access in a wheel-chair by the rear door. The floor is then raised again. The rear door can be opened from the driving seat by pressing a button. The 2-seater stratified polyester body is mounted on a steel frame and has lateral boxes for the eight 12 V Ah batteries. The Handicar has a 4 kW motor, independent wheels and hydraulic drum brakes on all 4 wheels. Dimensions: overall length 95.28 in (242 cm), width 53.15 in (135 cm), height 61.02 in (155 cm), dry weight with batteries 1,389 lb (630 kg). Top speed is 30 mph (50 km/h) and range 25-38 miles (40-60 km).

TEILHOL   Citacome K 5 and K 10

Teilhol's economical Citacome van comes in two versions, the K 10 being the more powerful. For both, the body is reinforced polyester and the chassis steel tubes. They are powered by a 96 V 4 kW motor connected in series and have an onboard charger. The 8 12 V batteries weighing 452 lb (205 kg) of the model K 5 develop 105 Ah and allow a range of 30 miles (50 km), while the 16 10 V batteries weighing 970 lb (440 kg) of the K 10 develop 105 Ah with a range of 62 miles (100 km). For both versions, the top speed is 30 mph (50 km/h). They are identical in overall length, width and height at 112.99 in (287 cm), 54.33 in (138 cm), and 66.93 in (170 cm) respectively. The K 5 weighs 1,411 lb (640 kg) and the K 10 1,962 lb (890 kg).

TP LABORATORIES   Kesling Yare

This bright yellow egg-shaped prototype is the brainchild of a 77 year-old dentist. The low-slung fiberglass body seats three adults and two children. Centre wheels front and back take care of the steering while the two drive wheels are at the sides, slightly rear of centre. The tricycle arrangement (two side and rear wheels) carrying the 12 6 V lead-acid batteries is easily detached for service. The single gull-wing door affords easy access and exit from the kerb side only. Regulation of the 2-speed dc gearless motor is by Borisoff Engineering controls. Top speed is over 55 mph (88 km/h) and range 35-40 miles (56-64 km). Dimensions are: overall length 168 in (427 cm), height 52 in (132 cm) and wheelbase 144 in (366 cm).

VOLKSWAGEN   Elektrotransporter

The trend in Germany seems to be towards large-scale electric vehicles, not runabouts. The explanation is simple: in a heavy vehicle, the weight of the batteries and the complexity of the electrical equipment pose fewer problems. The VW truck presented at the 1977 Frankfurt Motor Show mounts a 44 hp separately excited motor connected in parallel with thyristor control. The electric current is automatically reduced should the motor overheat or the minimum value of the battery voltage fall. Maximum speed is 43 mph (70 km/h) and the range between charges is 30-50 miles (50-80 km). The lead-acid batteries weigh 1,896 lb (860 kg) and a load of 1,763 lb (800 kg) can be carried. The curb weight with driver is 5,016 lb (2,275 kg).

VOLVO   Prototype

To gain know-how about electric cars while waiting for developments in batteries, Volvo has built two prototypes which are narrower and higher than the smallest Volvo production model but weigh 2,205 lb (1,000 kg). Rear-wheel drive, button selection of forward or reverse and an electronically actuated transmission make for easy driving. Thyristors aid starting and slow running, making them jerk-free. The 4-seater passenger car has a 8 kW 11 hp motor and the 2-seater van with sliding door mounts a 9.5 kW 13 hp motor. The 12 traction batteries of the 4-seater provide 72 V and the 10 of the van 60 V. The battery containers allows swift replacement. Top speed is 43 mph (70 km/h) cruising speed 31 mph (50 km/h) and range 31 miles (50 km).

WITKOFF — Henney Kilowatt

This Renault Dauphine based 4-door sedan is already in production. The compact unitized, laminated steel body has 2 front seats with cargo space or optional jump seats at the rear. 14 heavy-duty 6 V lead-acid batteries power a traction GE 7.1 HF series wound motor with GE EVI SCR regulation. The transmission is automatic with forward and reverse control operated by a switch on the dashboard. The motor is connected directly to a single unitized gear housing. Top speed is 50 mph (80 km/h) with a range of 60-80 miles (96-128 km) at cruising speed. The weight is 2,545 lb (1,154 kg), with the batteries accounting for 1,129 lb (512 kg). The overall length is 89 in (226 cm). Price $ 5,995.

ZAGATO — Zele Golf

Zagato's latest electric vehicle reflects the growing interest in golf in Italy where golf buggies have not previously been manufactured. The Zele Golf is a variation on the well-established Zele. It carries 2 plus 4 golf bags. The body is completely open to allow easy access but there is an overhead roll-bar allowing a winding back sun-awning to be fitted. The unbreakable windscreen ensures excellent visibility. A 2.5 hp motor is powered by six 6 V batteries and braking is hydraulic all round. A warning light shows when the batteries need recharging. The Zele Golf was awarded a prize in its category in the French Interministerial Competition for Electric Cars held in 1978.

ZAGATO — Zele 1000 and 2000

Various versions of the Zele are produced, the 1000 and the 2000, and the Van and Golf, carrying two plus luggage, with bodywork in reinforced polyester. They are driven by accumulator traction in four 12 V groups of 160 Ah batteries. Suspension is independent at the front and drum brakes are used all round. Dimensions: overall length 76.77 in (195 cm), width 53.15 in (135 cm), height 63.39 in (161 cm), curb weight 1,091 lb (495 kg), wheelbase 51.18 in (130 cm), front track 43.31 in (110 cm), rear track 42.52 in (108 cm), turning circle about 11.5 ft (3.5 m). For the 1000 version top speed is 25 mph (40 km/h) and range about 43 miles (70 km), and for the 2000 34 mph (55 km/h) and 31 miles (50 km).

ZAGATO — Zele Van

In view of the success of the Zeles, Zagato presented a new electric Van at the Chicago International Electric Vehicle Show. The range, top speed and battery recharging and replacement have been improved. Eight 6 V 215 Ah batteries power a 48 V dc motor which allows a top speed of over 30 mph (50 km/h) and a range of about 37 miles (60 km). It is expected that a more powerful motor and improved batteries will shortly be adopted. The batteries are housed under the car's floor in an independent sliding tray. The chief dimensions are: overall length 81.89 in (208 cm), overall width 55.12 in (140 cm), height 60.63 in (154 cm) and wheelbase 53.15 in (135 cm). The compact reinforced glass fibre body is designed by the Zagato styling centre.

Europe

THE EMANCIPATION OF THE COMMON CAR

by L.J.K. Setright

If we cannot now end our differences, at least we can help make the world safe for diversity. As in so much of what he said, there is a terrible irony in this quotation from the late President of the USA, John Kennedy. Apply it to the motor industry rather than to the political world at large, and the irony bites even deeper, for he said it in 1963 when motoring was riding towards the crest of a popularity wave in which the diversity of cars from which to choose, and the diversity of motoring experiences that we were free to explore, were more kaleidoscopic than ever before or since. By the beginning of 1978, ending our differences meant something else in the motor industry, something more desperate, more overlaid with tones of the sinister and the cynical. While the convergence of technology and of legislation was making cars more and more alike, the call was yet for less diversity.

Most members of the European motor industry were keenly aware of the dangers of competition from elsewhere, and only by uniting could they stand. The head of Rolls-Royce Motors, Mr David Plastow, might have been thought immune from such worries, but at the time he also held office as president of Britain's Society of Motor Manufacturers and Traders; and on the eve of the 1978 Brussels Show, he declared that only by coöperation and collective development among themselves could the European manufacturers survive competition from the Americans and the Japanese.

All the countries of Europe combined could produce more than twice the number of cars built by Japan alone, so there was clearly something in what Mr Plastow said. Heading the list with an annual output of 3.8 million cars was West Germany, the home of only three major carmaking groups (of which one was American-controlled). Almost at the other extreme was Britain, that home of diversity where small firms proliferated: her output was not 1.4 million, less than that of Italy, not much more than that of Belgium — and who has heard of a Belgian brand since the days of Minerva? Yet Austins, Fords, Opels, Vauxhalls and the Lord knows what else are made there, to the tune of more than a million a year. As a scene for the Plastow pronouncement, Brussels was curiously appropriate.

The neighbouring French had already begun to set their house in order, by the amalgamation of Citroën with Peugeot. Some remarkable offspring were expected of this gifted couple, but effective coupling was somewhat delayed by one of the parties being already in labour: late in 1977 Peugeot was safely delivered of a 305, which demonstrated itself healthy by promptly taking a sizable bite out of the medium-sized family saloon market previously exploited by Peugeot. In 1290 and 1472 cm³ versions, its overhead-camshaft light-alloy engine displayed familiar Peugeot characteristics in a front-wheel-drive vehicle that likewise had all the suavity associated with the make; but the discovery that the 305 combined these attributes with an impressive degree of roadholding and handling, not to mention a quite captivating sweetness in all the controls, made us realise that the car was something more than just another Peugeot. It was above all a demonstration of the emancipation of the common car: the ordinary everyday run-of-the-mill middling-small saloon had until this year been a deplor-

able aggregation of compromises held uncertainly together by an implausible congregation of promises. Now it has matured into something so practical and pleasurable, so sensibly sufficient and sufficiently sensible, that the industry no longer has any real need of flagships: it can be proud of its ordinary line. A look at the specification of the 305 might suggest that none of the year's cars could have been more ordinary; that suggestion merely emphasizes how extraordinary the standards of the category have become.

Their association with Peugeot has not robbed Citroën of all their flair for producing cars that are extraordinary in themselves, cars so individual and uncategorizable that they defy all ordinary standards. In due course the Visa was issued in two forms, one substantially alloyed with Peugeot parts and another more purely Citroën, to point the differences between the firms and to show how well the ending of other differences had served them both. Intended to occupy that niche in the Citroën range once the lodging of the quaint Ami, the Visa spreads its appeal more widely by exploiting Peugeot components to carry it up to a level with the GS range. The smaller Visa has a flat-twin air-cooled engine of characteristic Citroën design — albeit brand new and better detailed than ever before — which endows the car with more liveliness than might be expected of 650 cm^3; the larger borrows the transverse water-cooled four of the Peugeot 104 and is not unnaturally a little faster and smoother. However, whereas the Peu-

geot-Visa is just a car, the Citroën-Visa is rather exceptional: its suspension and steering geometry could be (and were) modified to improve the handling and roadholding, which are every bit as stupefying as in other small Citroëns. The new flat-twin engine boasts in addition a simple but very efficient electronic ignition system.

Electronics were also a feature of another small French car, though not as small as the Visa: the new SX version of the Chrysler-Simca Horizon carries a miniature computer on its facia, with which the driver can occupy himself playing with calculations of average speed, fuel consumption, journey time, and all the other things that can be produced by combining a clock with a speedometer and a flowmeter. How long he will play with this toy before tiring of it is difficult to forecast, but he will go on boasting about it to his friends a

lot longer. More practically important in the SX was the speed-hold device, something popular enough already in big luxury cars but not hitherto seen in Europe outside the Rolls-Royce and Bristol bracket. More important still was the new small automatic transmission now being built by Chrysler and likely to figure in many forthcoming small cars: perhaps not as smooth as the eternally impressive Chrysler Torqueflite for big cars, it is still quite a good little box. The same, indeed, may be said of the Horizon itself; at any rate, enough of my colleagues on the jury panel thought it merited selection as the international Car of the Year, practically all of us (myself included) giving it some of our votes.

Had there been an award for the Deal of the Year, these three French firms aforesaid would have figured in that too. The Chrysler Corporation had

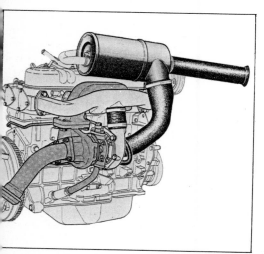

Above, the Peugeot 604's 2,300 cc diesel engine with turbocompressor and left, how Pininfarina has designed the large French saloon. Top, the new Jaguar XJ12 5.3 Series III with aesthetic and mechanical innovations. Bottom right, the sports version of the Chrysler-Sunbeam prepared by Lotus with a 16-valve 2,127 cc engine.

The experimental Mercedes C 111 with 230 bhp turbo diesel engine derived from the series 5-cylinder 3,000 cc. This car has cracked the speed record for its category, reaching 325 km/h.

been making a loss on its European operation, and sold out to the Peugeot-Citroën group for 1.8 million shares and 230 million dollars. As a result, the French not only took control of the Simca continental factories but also gained a foothold in Britain through the Chrysler plants that had once belonged to the Rootes Group — Hillman, Humber, Sunbeam and such.

Renault, enjoying the strength of a nationalised company, carried the war into the enemy's camp in their own way: the boss of the Régie whizzed across the Atlantic in a Concorde, flourished his pen, and whizzed back to be at work in his office again that same evening back in the summer of '78, leaving the dignitaries of the American Motors Corporation gazing fondly at his signature. AMC were on short commons, and will happily provide a dealer network for the RS. A modern equivalent of the veteran R12, the new R18 will not replace any existing model but will prove once again that Renault are inveterate gap-fillers: using engines, gearboxes and sundry bits from other models, they have produced four versions of the new car. Two rely on the elderly iron-blocked engine long familiar in the R12, the other on the beautiful lightweight engine of the R16. The rest is fairly conventional front-drive stuff, but the transmission options include a five-speed synchromesh gearbox and Renault's own and good electronically controlled automatic. That same automatic, built in a specially tailored version to fit beneath a notably small bonnet, featured in a new variant of the R5 theme, to rank promptly as the nicest small automatic on the market. Yet another variant — the Alpine or Gordini, with fat tyres and 93 bhp — offered to the public some hint of the fireworks that must have culminated in the two factory-entered specials which very nearly won the Monte Carlo Rally at the beginning of the year.

The car that ought to have been the nicest small automatic, the erstwhile Daf 66, was in trouble because Volvo — who had taken over and turned it into a 343 — were themselves in trouble. After wooing the Saab-Scania group unsuccessfully, they sought Norwegian government cash to help them out of their dire financial straits, but their Swedish shareholders vetoed the deal. Saab for their part were quite happy with the way things were going, revamping their 99 saloons during the year to create a new 900 series — new from the scuttle forward, at least, and with the wheelbase extended by two inches to make room for four feet behind the front wheel arches. Saab were among several manufacturers who took up the latest in tyres during the year: the five-door Turbo was fitted out with Michelin TRX tyres and wheels, the three-door version (which they reckoned would be driven more enterprisingly) was graced with the Pirelli P6.

In Pirelli's home country, where the annual output of cars is about 1.5 million, there was yet another manufacturer in financial difficulties — a nationalised manufacturer, at that. Alfa Romeo, it was revealed, had lost £400 million in the past six years. Still they persevered with their new big six-cylinder car, nearing the end of its development, while the Giulietta that had taken its bow at the end of 1977 was being well received. Rumours of trials of the P6 on the Giulietta mentioned cornering rates of 1.2 *g*; people who tried the new Fiat 131 Racing, announced in the autumn of '78 and wearing the same rubberware, would not have been at all surprised. Other versions of the 131 had been brought out by Fiat at the beginning of the year, but they had involved changes of a mainly styling nature, most successfully in the 1756 cm³ Supermirafiori. The little Bertone-styled X1/9 two-seater was more mechanically uprated with a 1.5 litre engine supplanting the old 1.3 litre derivative of the 128 power plant and with a five-speed gearbox to accompany it. More important to the future prosperity of Fiat was the Ritmo saloon, a superbly engineered Golf-sized front-drive saloon that did not feel as Fiats were wont to feel but was a good car nevertheless, and had some styling features of such originality as to make JFK's comments about making the world safe for diversity have some meaning.

The new off-road Mercedes-Steyr, built in 40 different versions. There is an ample choice of engines: two diesels, a 2,400 cc 4-cylinder and a 3,000 cc 5-cylinder, and two petrol engines, a 2,300 cc and a 2,800 cc.

The Panorama 1,600 cc version of the Fiat 131 Mirafiori. There is an exceptionally wide range of optionals.

even after fifteen years. Fiat had gone to enormous trouble over this car, not only in its design but also in the provisions for its production, which had been automated to an extent never before seen.

If their compatriots Lamborghini could have survived their crises half as well, they would by now be making the BMW M1 coupé. They could not, and in the end they did not: BMW had to take the work away and farm it out in Germany, losing some more time in the process so that production was delayed beyond the end of the year. The only other detrimental effect of this change is likely to be that the M1 will cost even more than it was going to; but it promises to be a car of such prodigious potential that there will doubtless be no shortage of customers. Meanwhile, a simpler 12-valved lower-powered version of their 3.5 litre six-cylinder engine was inserted into their biggest and costliest production coupé (front-engined,

The new Alfa 6 powered by a 160 bhp 2,492 cc cylinder Vee engine. Top speed is 195 km/h.

of course, unlike the M1) to make the 635, a car as fast and as well-behaved as the 633 ought to have been. Better still, BMW brought out a new high-performance version of the 3-series saloons, the 323i with a fuel-injected 2.3 litre engine, some lovely Getrag gearbox options, stronger anti-roll bars, disc brakes at all four wheels (those at the front ventilated, as in the larger BMW coupés), and with the front suspension more thoroughly damped as in the 7-series saloons. It had all it needed to make it a sports car and not just another 3-series runabout; and although it does not look very different from the others of the series, it really is a sports car. The mere facts of its performance (the top speed is at least 119 mph, even with the four-speed gearbox) are enough to make any car offering more, and costing more, begin to smell of superfluity; but even more to the point is that the whole character of the car is so crisp and responsive.

In terms of dynamic delight, the 323i is the best BMW yet.

The biggest and most expensive cars of the BMW range have their own claims to a distinction more vital than JFK's diversity. Working closely with Bosch, BMW developed an anti-lock braking system that can be relied on to work safely and positively at all times. Daimler-Benz, who had been sharing the development work, stole a march on them by breaking an alleged agreement for simultaneous announcement of their accomplishment; but whereas the Mercedes-Benz ABS system has three lock sensors, the odd one being centrally mounted at the differential between the driving wheels at the rear of the 450, the BMW arrangement is at once purer and simpler, with a separate sensor for each wheel. They made up for the publicity they lost to Daimler-Benz by showing the world's press some of their long-term future developments in technology, and although some of it was the usual sort of electronic toys looking for a serious and worthwhile job of work to do (and in due course somebody will surely find one), some of the other work was fascinating and very impressive. The range of engine ideas welling up at Munich is broader and much more diverse than one might have imagined bigger and richer companies undertaking, but there are many other notions being explored too. A new split- or stepped-reflector headlamp is one of the most immediately promising of these, and its imminent adoption for production will do much for drivers and other road users, as well as for Lucas whose collaboration was crucial.

Elsewhere in Germany, Porsche were making their 924 into a genuinely fast car by the overpopularized expedient of

59

The new "little" Lancia with two-volume body designed by Giugiaro. There is a choice of two engines, either a 1,300 cc 75 bhp or a 1,500 cc 85 bhp, the latter with a 5-speed box.

turbocharging its engine. Good may yet come of it, for the necessarily uprated suspension and brakes and running gear are likely to be exploited by a 924 of intermediate performance, its engine tuned but still normally aspirated. Recollection of the humble origins of the 924 (most of the parts came off the Audi shelves) makes the latest Audi itself something of a disappointment: the new Audi 80 makes considerable use of floor and other pressings from the old one, while yet contriving to look like an ugly miniature version of the 100 Avant and to feel less alive than either.

Despite the loss of the demonstrably very competent Charles 'Chuck' Chapman to the General Motors establishment in Australia (where he is making the Holden V8 version of the Monza the best of them all), Opel contrived to do very well in the spring of 1978 when they gave us their new Senator and Monza at the Geneva Show. The two cars are closely related mechanically, combining a well-sorted six-cylinder engine with even better-sorted all-independent suspension to result in far better roadholding and handling than might be expected of cars in that class. The Senator is a saloon that is sensible, sensual and sumptuous all at the same time; the Monza is a coupé that is more, and when it is delivered with the optional P6 Pirellis at each corner it assumes a degree of roadworthiness and balance that is probably without equal in cars of comparable size. These Opels are handsome too, but not the last word; that was left to Vauxhall, the British corner of the GM empire, where slightly restyled Rekords will be built and sold

as Vauxhall Carltons, and similarly sleekened Senators and Monzas will assume the guises of Vauxhall Royales, whether saloons or coupés.

What a pity British Leyland could not enjoy similar luck: the Princess ought to be handsome but somehow turns out to be rather gross when you see it on the road — which is not nearly as often as it should be. Its chances were not greatly improved by the introduction of a second series featuring the new 'O' series engine, a rather unenterprising replacement for the hoary old B-series inherited from a prehistoric incarnation of Austin. After 'BMC' and 'British Leyland' and 'Leyland' simpliciter, they have now decided to go back to the good old names that everybody knew and at least occasionally loved. What with that and a new model policy, and some harsh things to do to the new Mini presently in gestation (it is being bloated into a Super Mini so as to rival the likes of the Fiesta and R5), Leyland's new management hardly have time to manage the really urgent campaigns they must wage against the undermining influence of the unions. Their new boss, Mr Michael Edwardes, seems gradually to be gathering people on his side but the workforce is still a long way from unanimity, let alone competence and conscientiousness. Alas, the parties not only cannot now end their differences, they cannot even provide for diversity to be harmless. The lesson is available to those who will learn; Mr Seisi Kato, president of Toyota, should have been heard by the right ears when he attributed his company's high productivity to 'the excellent coöperation between our management and workers.

Our unions remember that we almos went bankrupt in 1951'.

It seems a dreadful business, th motor industry, so fraught with financia disaster, so readily thrown into chao by external politics. Perhaps it is n different from other industries; perhap on the other hand, not all the motor i dustry is like that. It is not easy t know how smoothly the car manufact ries of the Eastern Bloc countries fun tion, but the output seems to issu smoothly enough — in more senses tha one, if the unexpectedly modern stylin of the new front-wheel-drive Polone saloon from the Polski-Fiat factory b any guide. That there can be interru tions in the plans of even the best (o shall we say, the most rigorously?) r gulated organizations was shown at th end of 1978, when it was announce that the mighty VAZ factory would n after all exploit its expanded capaci to increase substantially the output cars, but would use it for trucks. Pro pects of a world flooded wth Lada Zhiguli 'Fiats' thereupon faded, thoug with the introduction of a new and be ter version of the eternal 124/125 sy thesis in the form of a Lada 1600, th prospect would not have been quite daunting. Maybe there was more si nificance in Lada's other newcomer, sort of poor man's Range Rover wi permanent four-wheel drive, rang change gearboxes, and an off-highwa competence that would do credit to tank. Real efforts to make it smart a safe as well as functional have m success, and the result is a car th can truly go anywhere. Is the intentio one wonders, that it should eventual go everywhere?

Japan

THE YEAR OF UNCERTAINTY?

by Jack K. Yamaguchi

"Uncertainty" has suddenly become a favorite Japanese description of the state of affairs, be it political, social, economic or industrial, thanks to John Kenneth Galbraith's best seller, *The Age of Uncertainty*. It is certainly a convenient synonym for the age's inherent difficulties and problems, fears and worries, or mere queasiness.

Japan emerged relatively unscathed from the bout of the heavy weather that was 1978. She attained a real economic growth rate of 6% with an enviably low inflation rate. The domestic growth rate was actually 7.7%, but lower export growth, partly deliberate and partly caused by the continuing dollar-yen disparity, brought it down to an aggregate 6%, which fell short of the projected 7%. President Carter obviously considered Japan's performance lukewarm, and conveyed his disappointment to the Prime Minister. The summit prodding was followed by another at government level, whereupon the Japanese got sullen. By world standards, they might still be an economic paragon, but by their own yardstick, the domestic economy was cool and sluggish, and that was the very best they could achieve. In fact several key industries, including the once mighty shipbuilding industry, were declared structurally depressed, and ominous talk of redundancies was heard in many quarters, although the year's unemployment rate was held at a controlled 2.3%, or 1.3 million workers.

The motor industry once again proved to be immune from the national depression, and turned out 9.26 million vehicles, which was the absolute record in its history, bettering the previous season's performance by 8.8%.

Datsun has transformed its Z sports car into a fully-equipped and comfortable GT.

More remarkable, and gratifying for the industry members, was the return of the home market buyers, who consumed 4.68 million vehicles. Even the stagnant light vehicle class (engine capacity under 550 cc) showed an increase of 7.3%, and for the first time since 1974 recovered to the 700,000 unit-per-annum level.

The home market thaw was long overdue. It should have happened in 1977, which turned out to be a sour and dismal year domestically. When it finally arrived in 1978, however, it came with welcome dispatch, in fact, several months sooner than the most optimistic anticipated. In spring, there were already signs that the cautious buyer was returning to the market place. Buyer Yamada, the Japanese "man-in-the-street", who had quickly adjusted his life style to the bleak economic climate of the post energy crisis era, was at last shaking off his qualms and started buying things and spending on leisure. A new car had not been high on his priority list. Earlier, spiralling car prices were beyond his means and comprehension. The Japanese government was determined to cleanse automotive exhausts and tightened the governing emission standards in four quick instalments, starting out in 1973. Unlike the American legislators, whose original Clean Air Act of 1970 served as a model for Japan, the Japanese did not compromise or relent halfway, despite hell and Arab sheikhs. Good citizen that he was, Mr. Yamada shared the environmental conscience, but the

Toyota has brought back a 5-door sedan in the revamped Corona range.

solid middle class in him also had an inbred mistrust for anything interim, which the 1975 and 1976 emission standard models were, especially when the ultimate rule of 1978 was in sight. Horror stories on earlier "clean" models which displayed an atrocious thirst for expensive fuel and most peculiar quirks in drive ability, exaggerated though they were, did nothing to encourage Mr. Yamada to part with his hard-earned yen.

Now all these outside factors were things of the past. Prices seemed to have stabilized, and he had accustomed himself to the inflated value of yen. Most of the glittering new models offered by the industry met the 1978 exhaust emission standards with improved fuel consumption and driveability. And Mr. Yamada's car was showing signs of old age.

The Japanese motor industry was ready for the spring thaw with the typical foresight and alertness which has marked its short history. It conceived 1978 as "the year of the Grand Public Car", a vague classification that would apply to small cars in the Honda Civic-Toyota Corolla size and price category with engine capacities ranging from 1 to 1.6 liters, and had several interesting new models ready for launching in quick succession. Actually many had thought that 1 liter cars were long dead due to stringent emission control standards which would steal a lot of horsepower from small displacement engines and make them hopelessly underpowered. Pleasantly they were proven wrong by Daihatsu, whose unique 3-cylinder frontwheel drive Charade became an overnight success when announced in late 1977, and promptly won the coveted Japanese Car of the Year award. Dai-

hatsu's parent company, mighty Toyota, did not wait very long before it released the revamped Starlet, curiously now sans Publica (public-car) name. The Starlet followed the two-box hatchback sedan trend, with either 2 or 4 doors for passenger ingress/egress, but did not go FWD, yet. It had a fully detoxined 1300 cc engine at the front, driving the rear wheels which were mounted on a rigid axle now properly located by four links and sprung by coil springs. The Starlet was a peppy and relaxed runabout, thanks to a relatively "big" engine and tall gearing, and was easy on fuel. With this sound package, Toyota combined generous equipment and specifications, including 5-speed gearbox and 2-speed automatic, all offered at very attractive

prices. Starlet production, by the way is undertaken by Daihatsu at its Ikeda factory where Charades are also manufactured. It is a fascinating sight to behold these two models wtih entirely different mechanical configuration and no major interchangeable components rolling out from the same assembly line, at a rate no slower than that of a typical European or American volume producer (knowing no work stoppage by the labor force, Daihatsu's overall performance should be considerably better). And as Daihatsu is a smaller member of the industry, the factory isn't that much automated. For example, parts bins are not aligned and delivered by a central computor as in major factories, but merely color coded and placed on sub-belts or manually pushed to the assembly line. A Daihatsu worker nonchalantly and conscientiously works on a front-wheel driven Charade, which is followed by a front-engined, rear-wheel drive Starlet. And occasionally he sees Charmants which are really rebodied Corollas. Japanese automotive ingenuity and diligence at their very best.

Mitsubishi Motor Corporation joined the two-box econocar battle with its handsome Mirage hatchback, first with a 2-door body followed by a 4-door version. The Mirage follows the contemporary transverse engine, FWD school of design, with 1200, 1400 and 1600 cc engine options. The Mirage's publicity gathering feature is undoubtedly its two side-by-side gear levers that transform Mitsubishi's 4-speed corporate gearbox into an eight-speed unit. Called "Super Shift" in Japan, and "Twin

The Mitsubishi Mirage, a "two-box" front wheel drive car. It is a stylish and peppy runabout with a unique "Super Shift (or Twin Stick for the U.S.)" two-range gearbox.

Above, Honda's Prelude to sporting motoring. A front wheel drive coupé with outstanding dynamic qualities. Below, Nissan-Datsun has added a diesel version to the Laurel series.

Later in the year, Honda followed suit, and built up a second dealer network comprised of 91 independent dealers under the banner of "Verno (Latin for young) shops", to market the new Prelude, a sporting 2+2 coupe.

In May Nissan-Datsun announced the Pulsar 4-door sedan, eventually to replace the Cherry front-wheel drive range. The old Cherry had never been a hot seller in Japan, and its U.S. launching was abortive, hardly making a dent in the Rabbit-Civic sector. Like recent European upgrades, the Pulsar is essentially a widened Cherry with crisper clothing and important detail improvement. The Pulsar is a roomy, roadable and economical runabout, and must rank as the most improved car of the year, successfully inheriting the title from last year's Sunny/210 range. It deserves rechristening. Originally announced with 1.2 and 1.4 liter carbureted engines, it was supplemented by a more powerful E version with the ubiquitous Bosch L-jetronic fuel injection. And in autumn, the sedan was joined by a hatchback 2-door sedan, a coupé and a wagon/van. This is Nissan's re-entry vehicle to the U.S. FWD market as the Datsun 310. Nissan obviously considers that sophisticated engineering is the road to follow, now that the REAP (Reliability, Equipment, Availability and Petrol economy) of the Japanese car is taken for granted. In a recent press conference, President Ishihara of Nissan stressed consorted efforts and heavier spending on R&D, and at the same time hinted that future Datsun cars smaller than the Cedric/Gloria 260C might go FWD.

Stick" by Chrysler's copywriters in the U.S., the idea has been a feature of every Jeep Mitsubishi produces under license, but of course the Mirage does not have 4WD. This neat dual-range transmission with an alternative pair of transfer gears was a product of logical development work. The design criteria specified the use of the company's Orion SOHC inline 4-cylinder engine. Placed in the Mirage prototype shell, it had a forward-facing carburettor and quickly ran into icing problems. Turn around the engine, then you would have to change the direction of revolution. Chief engineer Kisuna and his designers and engineers came up with a clever solution. Insert a transfer gear train, give it two alternative ratios, and they could kill two birds with a single stone. And the cost consideration was about the same as if they had developed a brand new 5-speed gearbox. Everybody else had a 5-speed box, but not a twin lever, 8-speed one.

Mitsubishi had ambitious marketing plans for the Mirage as well as the popular Galant range. As proved by the Big Two, the most effective way to increase sales is to increase dealer networks. It enlisted the services and resources of local entrepreneurs, many new to the car retail business, established a second network, and gave them the Mirage as well as rectangular-headlamped Eterna versions of the Sigma sedan and its coupé sister, the Lambda. The ploy had a slow start, but is gathering momentum, contributing handsomely to the overall growth of the Mitsubishi group. The corporation was thus able to secure the third position in the 1978 domestic car sales chart wth 224,014 units, and for the first time since its independence from the giant Mitsubishi Heavy Industries, paid dividends to its two stockholders, Mitsubishi HI and Chrysler Corp.

If anyone built bland cars, they would have a hard time beating Toyota, who have turned out myriads of bland solidmobiles from time immemorial. This was changing rapidly, and such technical sophistications as four-wheel independent suspension, four-disc brakes and rack-and-pinion steering were appearing in the latest Toyota cars. The Number One factory is ahead of others in several important fields, like the smooth new 2.2 liter diesel engine that powers certain Crown models and an automatic transmission with overdrive 4th ratio offered in the Crown, Mark II/Chaser (Cressida for export) and now new Corona ranges. And now Toyota has finally got on the FWD bandwagon with the Corsa/Tercel twins. Unlike most of the recent crop of FWD minis, the Corsa/Tercel has its engine mounted longitudinally and "upstairs" over gearbox and final drive. Thanks to this layout, Toyota claims, the power unit occupies no more room lengthwise

TOTAL MOTOR VEHICLE PRODUCTION

1973	7,082,757
1974	6,551,840
1975	6,941,591
1976	7,841,447
1977	8,514,522
1978 estimate	9,260,000

1978 Jan-Nov		
Passenger car	5,483,516	(+10.6%) *
Truck	2,961,104	(+ 7.3%) *
Bus	51,106	(+14.0%) *

* Change from previous year.

HOME MARKET REGISTRATIONS

	1977	1978 (estimate)	1979 (forecast)
Passenger car, normal	2,335,066	2,672,000	2,812,000
Passenger car, light	165,067	171,000	164,000
Truck, normal	135,364	148,000	166,000
Truck, small	1,028,498	1,093,000	1,118,000
Truck, light	507,375	545,000	533,000
Bus	22,904	24,000	24,000
Grand Total	4,194,274	4,653,000*	4,817,000

Note: 1) Based on Nissan Motor estimate and forecast.
     2) * Actual production aggregate 4,681,864.

EXPORT

	1977	1978 (estimate)	1979 (forecast)
Passenger car, normal	2,948,972	3,030,000	3,000,000
Passenger car, light	9,907	8,000	8,000
Truck, normal	265,179	314,000	315,000
Truck, small	1,023,102	1,146,000	987,000
Truck, light	81,636	62,000	60,000
Bus	24,021	30,000	30,000
Grand Total	4,352,817	4,590,000	4,400,000

DOMESTIC NEW CAR REGISTRATIONS BY MAKES, 1978

	Number	Comparison with 1977	Market share
Toyota	1,081,919	121.2%	40.3%
Nissan-Datsun	834,502	110.5%	31.1%
Toyo Kogyo	171,665	97.4%	6.4%
Mitsubishi	224,014	121.4%	8.3%
Honda	171,274	103.3%	6.4%
Daihatsu	65,383	200.5%	2.4%
Fuji Heavy Ind.	37,617	77.3%	1.4%
Isuzu	48,613	127.6%	1.8%
Import	50,374	120.5%	1.9%
Total	2,685,361	115.0%	100.0%
Light car, estimated (Daihatsu, Mitsubishi, Fuji and Suzuki)	171,000	103.6%	
Grand Total	2,856,361		

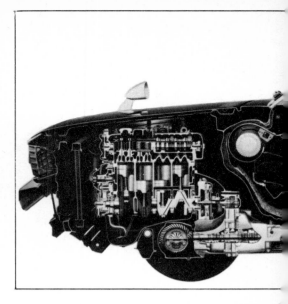

than a typical transverse one. This is a rare all-new car. Its engine is a Type 1A-U, a single overhead camshaft inline four with almost square cylinder dimensions (77.5 x 77 mm) for a total cubic capacity of 1,452 cc. It incorporates Toyota's TTC-L leanburn cylinder head with a tiny dead-end auxiliary combustion chamber in each cylinder that generates powerful turbulence in the incoming charge. Transmission options are 4- and 5-speed manual gearboxes which are THE sweetest and most direct shifting box in any FWD car, thanks to the gearbox's proximity to the driver's hand. The suspension is all-independent by front McPherson struts and rear semi-trailing arms. A rack-and-pinion steering and a front-disc, rear-drum brake combination complete the mechanical package. Curiously in this age of wider cars, Toyota chose a relatively narrow proportion, overall width of only 155 cm. And for its 396 cm length, the wheelbase is unusually long, at 250 cm. The package provides four occupants with ample space. Those in the back are particularly well catered for. Toyota's intentions are very honorable indeed but the C-T, the company's latest offering, feels underdeveloped. On-the-road-performance does not confirm its engine's claimed output of 80 hp, even after adding a generous pinch of salt to the lenient Japanese Industrial Standard rating. A year's digestion on home soil should help iron out its few shortcomings.

The older hands in the econobox gage met new challengers with bigger engines in the existing shells. Honda injected 97 cc of combustion volume into the basic Civic which is now the Civic 1300. They also enlarged the 1600 cc CVCC in the Accord, which became "1800", or 1,770 cc to be exact. The 1800 is shared with the new Prelude coupé. Once a champion of the clean air race, Honda's CVCC stratified charge engine has of late been subjected to some critical comments, certainly not on its exhaust cleasing ability, but on performance and fuel efficiency. There are speculations that this pioneering company may soon join the catalyst school, at least with certain performance-oriented models. Toyo Kogyo, maker of Mazda cars, also added a 1400 cc engine to the Familia/GLC/323 range

...ange which was also joined by a station wagon/van variant. Mazda is seriously looking at a FWD alternative, and, according to R&D chief Kenichi Yamamoto of rotary engine fame, when it appears in a few years' time, it will have both a new high performance gasoline engine and a small capacity diesel. Later a single rotor Wankel with improved low-and medium-speed torque characteristics may be added! The Hiroshima-based company has also signed a contract with Ford Motor Company for the former to supply transaxles for the latter's new FWD car, code name Erica, which will debut as a 1981 model.

The millionth Mazda rotary-engined car rolled off the assembly line on November 10th. Few fanfares accompanied this memorable occasion, which was indicative of Toyo Kogyo's newly-adopted balanced engineering policy.

the three pillars of power unit wisdom. The rotary will not be sent to the battle field as a shocktrooper, but will be an important integral part of the Mazda Force, together with reciprocal piston engine and high speed diesel.

It must have taken considerable courage for the Toyo Kogyo management to approve Project X605, conceived in the darkest days of the company's history, in 1974. It was to be a rotary-powered sports car designed to fill a large gap in the lucrative market sector, which was a "study of frustration and compromise", reflects Yoshiki Yamasaki, who took over the presidency of the Hiroshima-based company, after Kohei Matsuda was elevated to a more or less honorary chairmanship by his bankers. The world was in need of a new sports car, and the success formula was only too obvious: a good

measure of performance, excellent road manners, combined with comfort and convenience features, all wrapped up in modern and obvious sports car clothing. Thus the birth of a new legend, the RX7. In the first eight months after its introduction on the domestic market, 30,923 RX7s were delivered to eager customers, and another 15,990 exported to the U.S. and Canada. Kenichi Yamamoto, former chief of rotary development, now in charge of the entire Mazda R&D, is proud of his "victory car", which was also a come-back car for troubled Mazda in the U.S. Pride, yes, but intoxication, no, asserts Yamamoto. He will nurture the RX7 and the rotary. He hints at a possibility of a Super RX7, incorporating such sophisticated fea-

Mazda's Pan-European looking Capella/626 sedan. A thoroughly conventional car powered by the company's sturdy single overhead camshaft inline four.

tures as independent rear suspension, four-wheel discs and a more powerful engine. To broaden rotary application, the engine must overcome its inherent shortcoming of lean low and mid-range torque. His engine men are now working on a semi-supercharging system utilizing a more efficient airpump (if you can develop a workable rotary engine, improving airpump sealing presents no major problem). He foresees 15 to 19% improvement in low-speed torque characteristics.

Rather than resurrecting its original 1970 ideal, Nissan made a refined GT out of the new Fairlady Z/280ZX, which is bigger and heavier, and obviously better equipped than ever before, with an inflated price tag. The new Z did not break any new technical ground or send Pininfarina scurrying to his drawing-board. It is unmistakably the Z with more refinement. It has given up the strut-type independent rear suspension for a semi-trailing system which is similar to that of the middle class Bluebird (810) sedan. The official reason given by Chief Engineer Sakagami of Nissan is to reduce the intrusion of final drive noise into the cabin. Comfort features and opulence are abundant, including a four-speaker stereo system, fully automatic air-conditioning, cruise-control, genuine leather upholstery, et al. And Nissan was able to bring back big displacement Zs in the domestic market, the first time since the demise of the 240Z in the aftermath of the Oil Crisis. The spring thaw must

have affected the most die-hard bureaucrats who had been known for their dislike of sports cars and like. Mazda's RX7 got their blessings with pop-up headlamps and all. And the Z got the 280Z version back. But don't think our government agency has been completely liberated. They still have some strange notions about cars. They pretend they have never seen a crop of the latest ultra low-profile radials, thus no " 60 " or " 55 " Bridgestones or Yokohamas are sold in Japan (Porsche manages to import certain registered Pirelli P7s for exclusive use on the Turbo and 928). A few enterprising designers are said to have approached the ministry responsible to probe the possibility of getting detachable glass tops approved for their new cars. Whereupon a technocrat inquired, " Suppose a truck driver drops a lighted cigarette butt on to it "? To which, our designer-engineer replied that he could come up with a fire-resistant plastic. The official retorted, " Could it take a great ball of fire falling from the sky "? They must really believe in UFOs!

Honda's new front-wheel-drive sports coupé, the Prelude, will have a solid metal sliding roof for the home market, while the U.S. version will feature a glass top which should give the occupants a wee bit more head space. At a glance, the Prelude may look like a shortened and rebodied Accord with intentional detail resemblance to the Mercedes 450SLC, but it is actually a brand new chassis with superior hand-

ling and roadholding combination. The work of Honda R&D's " Le CAP (Civic, Accord, Prelude) " — Hiroshi Kizawa and his young and brilliant engineers — it is the company's prelude to a sporting symphony.

The year saw activities in the middle class sector. Toyo Kogyo announced the new Capella 626, a conventional front-engined, rear-wheel drive car with 4-door sedan and 2-door hardtop body styles, powered by Mazda's low emission inline 4-cylinder engine. It is a very Pan European looking car which should not feel uncomfortable in the company of the new Opels, Peugeots and Renaults. Toyota updated the solid Corona range, and resurrected a 5-door sedan model. The Corona is available with a fuel-injected 2 litre twin cam four which is shared with the Celica GT and Carna GT models. Another twin cam engine in the immortal Giugiaro designed Isuzu 117 has been brought up to full 2 liter size which gives more sting to this sleek GT. Across the board, it was the year of rectangular headlamps, thanks to Detroit who had set the trend. Among converts were Nissan's Bluebird (810/180B) and Laurel (200L). The latter now has a 2-liter diesel version which is the third model after Toyota's Crown and Isuzu's Florian.

The light car class, now with engine capacity under 550 cc, has been stagnant, selling only 171,000 cars in 1978 which was quite a sharp drop from the peak 1970 record of 717,000 units. Most active was the Hamamatsu-based motorcycle manufacturer Suzuki, who added a Fronte Coupé CX-L version, L standing for Ladies. It is a retrimmed brighter Fronte catering for our fair sex. Suzuki has also terminated its contract with Toyota whereby it bought Daihatsu developed 550 cc 4-stroke engines for Fronte cars, now that Suzuki's own 2-stroke 3-cylinder engine fully meets the Japanese emission standards by a clever two-stage catalyst.

The prospect for 1979 is no prospect at all. It will be a year of no growth. The industry hopes the domestic buyer will continue buying, assuming his autonomous buying cycle, as described by President Kato of Toyota Motor Sales, has been fully restored. The darker side of the coin is in exports. In November, exports fell to 325,984 vehicles which was 17.9% less than in November 1977. The slide is expected to continue throughout 1979. The Big Two's production forecast for 1979 is modest. Toyota expects no growth, while Nissan should increase by a mere 2.2%. The Third Power members have more ambitious plans.

Sportscar of the '80's, Mazda's exciting RX7 powered by the latest twin rotor Wankel.

SURVIVAL OF THE FITTEST

by Bob Irvin

The state of the American auto industry in 1979 can be summed up simply: the strong are getting stronger and the weak are getting weaker. And this has a direct bearing on the kinds of cars Americans are able to buy this year and what will be on the market in the 1980s.

It is a matter of General Motors and Ford seeming to benefit at the expense of Chrysler and American Motors. To be sure, all four American companies have new cars to market this year. But only GM and Ford can claim to have cars which are actually new from the ground up. Chrysler's and AMC's " new " nameplates for 1979 are actually redesigns, or new body styles, based on existing cars.

All this is the result of the energy crisis and the U.S. laws it prompted which require the firms to build small economy cars replacing the traditionally big, heavy American cars. Five years ago American cars on the average got 12 miles per gallon. In 1974 the government in Washington persuaded the firms to agree to a voluntary program to increase mileage by 50%, to 18 mpg by 1980.

But then the U.S. Congress decided that if a voluntary program was good, a mandatory one with tougher requirements would be better. So Congress passed a law setting Corporate Average Fuel Economy (CAFE) standards. This raised the goal another 50%, to 27.5 mpg by 1985. Moreover, the companies had to begin meeting the 18 mpg standard in 1978.

The requirement for 1979 is 19 mpg and 20 for 1980. Meeting it has been no easy task for an industry where the average car weighed two tons only a

few years ago. The law is the reason for the frantic rush at the U.S. auto engineering centers to design cars which are smaller, weigh less and have more economical engines. It has stretched the resources of all car manufacturers. The cost so far is about what the U.S. spent to get to the moon. And by 1985, the American firms will have spent another $80 billion, more than three times the $26 billion outlay for the Apollo lunar landings.

Over half the money is being spent by GM alone to protect its nearly 60% share of the domestic car market. By the spring of this year it completed the first phase of the program. The all-new compact-sized cars with front-wheel drive being introduced this spring as early 1980 models are the latest in GM's downsizing evolutionary chain starting with redesigned standard cars in 1977, intermediate cars in 1978 and new small 1979 model luxury cars.

The Giugiaro-designed rear-engined DeLorean DMC-12 is aimed mainly at the American market but will be built in Northern Ireland. It has a steel body mounted on a plastic frame with major mechanical components mounted on sub-frames. Elastic Reservoir Moulding is used with unstressed outer panels of brushed stainless steel.

The other firms have been hard put to keep up. Indeed, gone forever are the old days when the major companies were in lock-step on styling changes — each introducing a new full size car line one year, new specialty cars another years. Even the appearance of the cars seemed pretty much the same. Now the American auto industry is changing like a kaleidoscope. Each company is going its own way. They have in recent years stopped trying to match each other model for model. AMC has been forced out of the intermediate size car market. Chrysler has retrenched in the standard and intermediate markets.

Mistakes have been made under pressure of conforming with the new mileage law with the money available. Chrysler, in financial difficulty, has dropped out of the standard car market entirely with its Plymouth, once considered part of the American "low priced three" — the others being Ford and Chevrolet.

Chrysler does have a new nameplate for 1979, the Dodge St. Regis, competing in the standard car market. But it replaces an intermediate car, the Dodge Monaco, and in fact is built from the same underbody components as its predecessor. Thus it cannot be consi-

dered an all-new car, just a new nameplate. The Chrysler New Yorker, formerly a large-bodied car, shares the new intermediate size underbody with the Dodge St. Regis.

Chrysler has introduced two sporty models as well for 1979, carrying names obviously inspired by the movie *Star Wars*. One is the Dodge Omni 024, the other the Plymouth Horizon TC3. The numbers and letters have no special meaning. Originally, the intention was to give the cars new names. They are actually two-door versions of the four-door Omni and Horizon, but could be sold as distinct cars because they look sporty with a slope-nose front and fastback rear while the four-doors have a family car look about them. However, Chrysler decided it didn't have the money necessary to introduce the two-doors as all-new cars. So it chose the less expensive route of calling them models of existing cars.

These decisions to retrench in the big car market and do a cheap introduction of the sporty models were questioned by the new Chrysler president, Lee A. Iacocca, who joined Chrysler some four months after being fired in July, 1978 as president of Ford — the most dramatic event of the year in the American auto industry. Iacocca, regarded

This is the Dodge version of the two-door Omni. The transverse front-drive powerplant is the same as the four-door's while the chassis has been shortened to a 96.7 in wheelbase. A smooth appearance is gained through the use of a soft facia covering aluminum bumpers at both front and rear. This new car has no common body panels with the sedan.

as the father of the Ford Mustang and an auto marketing genius, admitted there was little he could do for two years to change Chrysler's products, such is the lead time in car building.

Meanwhile, Ford was introducing the 1979 cars developed under Iacocca's direction — new downsized Ford and Mercury standard size models carrying the LTD and Marquis names. These are all-new, like GM's cars, but they are two years behind GM which redesigned its standard cars for the 1977 model year. And Ford is more than two years behind in the standard luxury car market. The Lincoln-Continental is not scheduled to be changed until the 1980 model year, three years after GM downsized its Cadillac sedans. Cadillac downsized its "personal luxury car" the Eldorado, in 1979 but again Ford is not due until 1980. "We just don't have their money", explained Henry Ford II, chairman of the Ford Motor Co.

Ford also introduced 1979 replacements for its sporty models, the Mustang and the Capri. The Capri heretofore had been built in Europe only, the one sold in America coming from Germany. But the rising value of the German mark sent Capri prices up and that hurt sales in America. So the decision was made to build a 1979 version for America off the same new body being used for the Mustang.

The Mustang/Capri cars do share some mechanical components with the Ford Fairmont and Mercury Zephyr which were all-new as 1978 models. The Mustang/Capri platform on which the car

This 'phantom' view of the new Mercury Marquis reveals the full perimeter frame for strength. The traditional smooth ride is attained by using four-link coil spring rear suspension, new 'A' arm coil spring design for the front and a forward-mounted reduced ratio steering system.

A fourth model for the Camaro series is the top-of-the-line Berlinetta. Unlike the basic coupé or sporty Rally and Z28 versions it has special paint stripes, custom interior trim, body-color styled wheels and a unique two-tier grille as standard features. The basic engine is the 4.1 litre L6 with 5.0 and 5.7-litre as options.

body is built is a shortened version of the Fairmont/Zephyr platform.

American Motors, which has had a struggle to survive for most of its 25 years existence, had to be content for 1979 to redesign as cheaply as possible its subcompact car, the Gremlin, and call it by a new name, Spirit. Along the way AMC had to shelve plans for an all-new subcompact size car, lacking the money. It has had to buy engines from Volkswagen (it will use Pontiac engines in some cars next year). Chrysler, too, bought engines from VW for its Omni/Horizon cars because it wanted to conserve its precious funds.

AMC and Chrysler have also had to seek alliances with foreign auto firms.

After protracted negotiations for over nine months, AMC announced early this year that they had concluded an agreement with Renault of France to sell their model R5 (Le Car) through AMC's 2,300 dealers in the United States and Canada. Later, AMC plans to import the R18 although the French firm had originally wanted to have their larger model built at AMC's Wisconsin plants. Reciprocally, Renault will sell the AMC Jeeps through their dealer network in Europe and South America.

Chrysler, for its part, has allied itself with another French auto maker, Peugeot. It sold its European automotive operation to Peugeot for more than $500 million in cash and stock. In a later move to raise additional capital Chrysler sold its European financial subsidiaries to PSA Peugeot-Citroën for an estimated $80 million.

What seemed clear was that only GM and Ford could remain fully independent auto firms. In fact, a government-funded study in late 1978 predicted AMC would have to phase out its car business entirely by the mid-1980s and Chrysler's share of the market would dwindle to under 10% because of the fuel-economy pressures.

AMC has a thriving business selling Jeep vehicles, based on the World War II utility vehicle, but has consistently said it will not abandon the regular passenger car business. Chrysler maintains it will continue to be represented in all major phases of the car business. But denials notwithstanding, auto observers believe there is little hope that Chrysler or AMC can continue to offer a wide range of cars. That is, they could not as things now stand. They could if they were given federal help or had closer ties with major overseas auto firms.

In the meantime, American auto firms are facing new competition at home from foreign companies. In 1978, Volkswagen began production of its Rabbit at a plant in Pennsylvania and three Japanese firms (Toyota, Nissan and Honda) all investigated American assembly plants but took no action to begin U.S. car production, although Honda is going to build motorcycles at an Ohio plant.

GM's new X-line front-wheel drive cars the Chevrolet Citation, Pontiac Phoenix, Buick Skylark and Oldsmobile Omega — are clearly the most important new cars to be introduced during the 1979 model run period, even though they carry an early 1980 model designation. They are the first post-oil-embargo cars with new engineering, all done in America.

These replacements for GM's compacts have cost $2.5 billion to bring to market, and GM expects to build one million a year, double the production of the old ones. They are 16 inches shorter than the old compacts and 850 pounds lighter. Two feet longer than the VW Rabbit, they come in five body styles: 1- and 4-door hatchbacks, 2- and 4-door notchbacks and a sporty 2-door slant-back for Chevrolet. Front-drive transverse engines — a 2.5 liter in-line four built by Pontiac and a 2.8 liter V-6 built by Chevrolet are used with either a four-speed manual or three-speed automatic transmission. The V-6 is rated at 24 mpg with the automatic and 26 mpg with the manual while the four is

rated at 27 mpg with the automatic and 29 mpg with the manual. The four will accelerate from 0-60 miles an hour in 15 seconds and the V-6 in 13 seconds.

The new X-lines weigh 2,400 pounds, have a 13.2 gallon fuel tank, are 54.8 inches high, have an overall length of 176.7 inches and a wheelbase of 104.5 inches. The transaxle is a new GM design. There is also a unique ladder and cable structure to support the drive train. The cars have McPherson strut front suspension, four coil springs all round, rack and pinion steering, 13-inch tires and a long list of optional equipment.

Most of the features found on a Cadillac are available as options: power steering, brakes, and door locks; air conditioning; cruise control; reclining seat backs; tilt steering wheel; a removable sunroof and a power trunk-lid release. The AM radio is standard with a wide variety of optional radios and tape systems offered. The auto firms traditionally make money on options and this is why GM is offering such a long list.

Inside, the X-body models have the room of the GM intermediates introduced in 1978. What GM has done is to take European engineering features and put them inside cars designed to American tastes and equipped with options Americans have come to expect in a family car.

The most important cars GM introduced at the start of the model run were its three downsized front-drive luxury models, the Cadillac Eldorado, Oldsmobile Toronado and Buick Riviera. They feature independent rear suspension and automatic load leveling. The Toronado/Eldorado models were the sole survivors of the old standard GM car

Newest flagship of the Chrysler fleet is the high-style New Yorker Fifth Avenue Edition. This four-door pillared hardtop features opera windows on the rear doors and a heavily padded vinyl landau roof. Like other luxury cars it comes with all-leather upholstery.

body, abandoned on other GM regular cars in 1977. The Riviera did undergo one downsizing in 1977. The new versions are as much as 1,000 pounds lighter and a foot shorter but have more interior room. They are also loaded with standard equipment including air conditioning; AM/FM radio, power windows seats and doorlocks, and radio antenna. GM's digital trip computer, offered initially on the Seville in early 1978, is available in another version on the Riviera. The Eldorado has four-wheel disc brakes. The others have front discs, rear drums.

The three downsized luxury models are basically the new GM intermediates but stretched to provide more rear seat room. Essentially the same car underneath, each has some unique feature. Buick offers its turbo V-6 as standard equipment on the Riviera "S" model. Eldorado models come standard with the fuel-injected 350 cubic inch V-8 pioneered on the Seville. Olds offers its diesel engine as optional equipment on the Toronado.

The elite Corvette entered its 26th year with refinements in performance, handling and interior comfort. These include high performance L82-type dual snorkel intakes for the air cleaner to improve engine breathing, horsepower and torque; larger diameter "Y" pipe behind the emission converter; open-flow mufflers to reduce exhaust gas back pressure; and high-backed bucket seats as standard. The Camaro Berlinetta, similarly with strong appeal to the sporty driver, is going as fast as it can be built. The demand currently is about three buyers for every one off the production line.

At Ford, the LTD and Marquis are viewed as improvements on the GM downsized regular cars, such as the Chevrolet Impala, introduced two years

The Pontiac Phoenix hatchback sedan, one of the new X-bodies which represent stage 3 (compact series cars) in General Motors resizing programme. They feature front-wheel-drive and weigh about 2,500 lb. Power comes either from a V6 mounted transversely or the 2.5 litre L4 crossflow shown above. The crossflow cylinder head features separation of the intake manifold to the right side of the head and exhaust to the left. The improved gas flow and ease of engine breathing are now similar to that of a V8. Weight has been reduced by 35 lb and horsepower increased to 90 hp.

arlier. "We were last out but we are
est dressed", said William O. Bourke,
ord executive vice president. The new
TD and Marquis are about eight inches
horter and 700 pounds lighter than the
ld ones. Still, the dimensions and
eight are very close to the 1977 Chev-
olet Impala. They are available in
wo-door coupé, four-door sedan and
our-door station wagon versions. The
rs show a family resemblance to the
ery popular Fairmont/Zephyr, with
rge windows and what Ford calls
command position seating".

The new LTD is only the third com-
etely new regular Ford since World
War II and only the ninth in the firm's
5-year history. Ford expects to sell
00,000 of the new models, about half
gain as many as 1978 when deliveries
taled 330,000. The most popular model
the four-door, accounting for 46% of
les. About 30% are two-door models,
4% wagons.

The LTD has room for six passengers
ut maneuvers like a small car and
oesn't nosedive in heavy braking. It
a far cry from 1978 models which
eemed to maneuver like an ocean liner.
owever, the Ford ride is still softer
an the new GM regular cars, which
em to have a more European firm
de.

The new Mustang/Capri models aver-
ge about four inches longer than last
ear but are still about 300 pounds light-
r. The extra length is to provide more
ear seat room. The cars use the Fair-
ont/Zephyr suspension and steering
ystem. A 2.3 liter turbocharged engine
optional. The Mustang is available
two-door notchback and three-door
atchback models while the Capri only
omes as a three-door hatchback.

The Continental Mark V, unchanged
is the Lincoln Continental for 1979,
as a new electronic AM/FM stereo
earch radio with digital frequency read-
ut. Ford also offers Citizen Band radios
at automatically scan the frequencies,
opping at the first conversation moni-
red.

Over at American Motors, Dick
eague, styling vice president, says his
ew Spirit GT models "are geared to
e youth market with a luxurious sports
terior and full instrumentation". In
ddition to the GT, the Spirit is available
a basic model (the DL) and the more
aborate LTD. While basically a rede-
gned Gremlin, Teague maintains "it
a lot different from the Gremlin.
uch more attention has been paid to
oise, vibration and harshness. It now
ts into the luxury compact group rather
an the economy group as did the
remlin".

The other "domestic" car is the
VW Rabbit, somewhat different from the
one made in Germany. Square headlamps and a more American style color-
coordinated interior are the most no-
ticeable changes. But the major differ-
ence is that it is American made. And
the American Rabbit is actually better
made than the German one, according
to U.S. competitors of VW. John Mc-
Dougall, a Ford executive vicepresident,
said the firm bought some of the American Rabbits and checked them minu-
tely before concluding they were better
than the German Rabbits in terms of
"fit and finish" — perceived quality on
the showroom floor. American VW is
the first to offer a diesel engine in a
small economy car, and in its 5-speed
version has the best fuel rating of any
U.S. car — 41 mpg.

With cars getting smaller, the American firms have been able to discon-
tinue some big engines. They include
the Pontiac 400-inch V-8, the Chrysler
400 and 440-inch V-8s and the Ford
460-inch V-8. New GM engines include
an Olds 260-inch V-8 diesel and a 267-
inch Chevrolet V-8. The Buick turbo
was added to the intermediate Century
line and the turbo four is optional on
the Mustang/Capri.

GM says recent studies show diesel
engines present no significant health
hazard. This year it is tripling diesel
engine production for light trucks and

cars to 190,000 and is adding the smaller V-8 diesel for medium-size cars.
Olds expects to sell 125,000 of the
diesels which provide a 25% improvement in fuel economy over comparable
gasoline engines but cost $800 more.
GM engineers have found a way substantially to reduce start-up time for
diesels in cold weather. A few seconds
instead of a minute is all that's needed
now.

Detroit is well into plans for its
downsized cars in the 1980s. Besides
the Lincolns and Continental Mark cars
for 1980 (which will be 10 inches shorter and 1,000 pounds lighter), Ford is
going to downsize the Thunderbird and
XR-7 models. Now built off an intermediate body shell used for the LTD II
and Cougar (which are being discontinued after 1979), the new T-Bird and
XR-7 models will be built off the Fair-
mont/Zephyr bodies. The dimensions
of the two sets of cars will thus be
close in 1980.

Chrysler in 1980 will downsize its
Magnum and Cordoba two-door specialty
cars. They will have a 112.7-inch wheelbase, down from 114 inches now. The
Le Baron and Diplomat coupés also drop
from 112 to 108 inches in wheelbase.
Midway in the 1980 model run, Chrysler
will introduce a new luxury two-door on
a 112.7-inch wheelbase, probably to be
called the Imperial. It will compete with

*To show how profoundly they believe in diesel engines Oldsmobile is offering a new 4.3-litre
V8 version as an option in their Cutlass coupés, sedans and wagons. Fuel economy
figures show that mileage should be 24 mpg with the automatic and 25 mpg
with the five-speed manual transmission.*

the new Continental Mark and the Eldorado cars.

GM, meanwhile, will introduce as a 1980 model a redesigned Seville. It will be the most controversial car of the year, featuring a luggage-box trunk, similar to that found on classic cars of a generation or two ago. "Suddenly it's 1930", was the comment of one observer who saw a prototype. The car, a four-door model, uses the front-drive powertrain developed for the Eldorado. In fact, most GM cars by the late 1980s will be front-drive, according to sources.

Early in the 1979 model year, the U.S. Secretary of Transportation, Brock Adams, called on Detroit to "re-invent the automobile". He challenged Detroit auto executives to begin another program after they reach 27.5 mpg in 1985 — to build a 50 mpg car or find a power source other than oil. Adams got a cool reception from U.S. auto executives. "You just can't order inventions", said Henry Ford II.

In 1978 Americans bought cars and trucks in a combined record total of 15.4 million units. Truck sales alone topped four million. Small cars increased their share of the market to 44%. Imports still remained strong despite price increases caused by the weakened dollar. Foreign car sales of two million were almost equal to the record set in 1977 but their market share fell from 18.5% to 17.7%.

Of the new cars introduced as 1978 models, the runaway success clearly was the Fairmont Zephyr line from Ford and Mercury, with combined sales of over half a million — up 135% over the Maverick/Comet line it replaced. Fairmont, incidentally, became the most popular car ever introduced. Its 1978 sales

just broke the 418,000 first-year record of the 1965 Ford Mustang.

The Chevette, with the help of a four-door model, reached the quarter million sales mark, up 32%. For a while, General Motors did not fare as well with its other new mid-size cars for 1978. The so-called personal cars — Chevrolet Monte Carlo and Pontiac Grand Prix — got off to a slow start because many prospective buyers objected to the downsized 1978 versions and kept their earlier cars or went elsewhere for their new cars. In addition, Oldsmobile and Buick ran into opposition from would-be buyers who didn't like the fastback versions of the new intermediate Cutlass and Century four-door sedans. As a result, GM is going to offer traditional notchback sedan versions in the 1980 model year. GM wound up the 1978 model year with all-time record sales of passenger cars.

Chrysler got off to a strong start with its Omni/Horizon front-drive subcompacts, although they were late on the market. But then sales fell off midway through the model year when Consumer Reports magazine rated them unacceptable, charging a handling problem. U.S. safety officials ruled there was nothing wrong but sales suffered nonetheless. To make matters worse, the Omni/Horizon subcompact line apparently took sales from Chrysler's

compact Volare/Aspen line which wa off by one-third. All three makes – Chrysler, Dodge and Plymouth — wer down in 1978.

Likewise, American Motors, despit a 51% increase in sales of its new Cor cord line over the predecessor Horne line, suffered losses in other AMC line which more than offset the gains.

In short, 1978 was a good year fo GM and Ford because of their wid range of cars but Chrysler and America Motors continued to lose — both i market share and overall sales.

Clearly, GM was finding in the ene gy crisis and the mileage law an op portunity to strengthen its position a the No. 1 automaker. Chairman Thoma A. Murphy recalled what it was lik in 1974, during the recession and energ crisis. "A lot of people in the industr thought that General Motors was i trouble because we were making al those big, not very fuel-efficient cars Well, it was a risk but we changed al of them as fast as we could". And GM is now reaping the benefits of tha unprecedented change while plannin to change as much again in the 1980s

One independent Detroit auto ana lyst who advises banks and institutions Arvid Jouppi, noted that the "weigh of the average American car has dropp ed from 3,950 pounds in 1975 to 3,30 in 1979 — 650 pounds in four years. Bu there is still a long way to go. It wi have to drop to 2,700 pounds by 198 to meet the 27.5 mpg figure". But h adds that while the American car wi continue to get smaller the America public will still cling to personal trans portation. "Autos will remain th mainstay of U.S. transportation", h said.

Europe

Models now in production

Illustrations and technical information

CUSTOCA   AUSTRIA

Hurrycane

PRICE EX WORKS: 125,000 schillings

ENGINE Volkswagen, rear, 4 stroke; 4 cylinders, horizontally opposed; 96.7 cu in, 1,584 cc (3.37 x 2.72 in, 85.5 x 69 mm); max power (DIN): 50 hp (36.8 kW) at 4,000 rpm; max torque (DIN): 78 lb ft, 10.8 kg m (105.9 Nm) at 2,800 rpm; 31.6 hp/l (23.2 kW/l).

PERFORMANCE max speeds: (I) 22 mph, 35 km/h; (II) 47 mph, 75 km/h; (III) 68 mph, 110 km/h; (IV) 96 mph, 155 km/h; power-weight ratio: 30.9 lb/hp (41.9 lb/kW), 14 kg/hp (19 kg/kW); acceleration: standing ¼ mile 12.5 sec; consumption: 23.5 m/imp gal, 19.6 m/US gal, 12 l x 100 km.

STEERING turns lock to lock: 2.50.

ELECTRICAL EQUIPMENT 12 V; 4 headlamps.

DIMENSIONS AND WEIGHT wheel base: 94.49 in, 240 cm; tracks: 55.12 in, 140 cm front, 55.91 in, 142 cm rear; length: 171.26 in, 435 cm; width: 67.72 in, 172 cm; height: 44.09 in, 112 cm; ground clearance: 6.30 in, 16 cm; weight: 1,544 lb, 700 kg; weight distribution: 46% front, 54% rear; turning circle: 41 ft, 12.5 m; fuel tank: 9.2 imp gal, 11.1 US gal, 42 l.

BODY coupé in plastic material; 2 doors; 2 + 2 seats.

PRACTICAL INSTRUCTIONS tyre pressure: front 19 psi, 1.2 atm, rear 22 psi, 1.5 atm.

For further data, see Volkswagen.

Strato ES

See Hurrycane, except for:

PRICE EX WORKS: 130,000 schillings

PERFORMANCE power-weight ratio: 30 lb/hp (40.7 lb/kW), 13.6 kg/hp (18.5 kg/kW).

DIMENSIONS AND WEIGHT length: 164.57 in, 418 cm; width: 62.99 in, 160 cm; weight: 1,499 lb, 680 kg.

ŠKODA   CZECHOSLOVAKIA

105 S

PRICE IN GB: £ 1,698*

ENGINE rear, 4 stroke; 4 cylinders slanted 30° to right, in line; 63.8 cu in, 1,046 cc (2.68 x 2.83 in, 68 x 72 mm); compression ratio: 8.5:1; max power (DIN): 46 hp (33.9 kW) at 4,800 rpm; max torque (DIN): 55 lb ft, 7.6 kg m (74.5 Nm) at 3,000 rpm; max engine rpm: 5,200; 43.2 hp/l (31.8 kW/l); light alloy block, cast iron head, wet liners; 3 crankshaft bearings; valves: overhead, in line, push-rods and rockers; camshafts: 1, side; lubrication: gear pump, cartridge on by-pass, 7 imp pt, 8.5 US pt, 4 l; 1 Jikov EDS R downdraught carburettor; fuel feed: mechanical pump; water-cooled, front radiator, 22 imp pt, 26.4 US pt, 12.5 l.

TRANSMISSION driving wheels: rear; clutch: single dry plate, hydraulically-controlled; gearbox: mechanical; gears: 4, fully synchronized; ratios: I 3.800, II 2.120, III 1.410, IV 0.960, rev 3.270; lever: central; final drive: spiral bevel; axle ratio: 4.444; width of rims: 4.5''; tyres: 165 SR x 13.

PERFORMANCE max speeds: (I) 20 mph, 32 km/h; (II) 34 mph, 55 km/h; (III) 53 mph, 85 km/h; (IV) 81 mph, 130 km/h; power-weight ratio: 41 lb/hp (55.6 lb/kW), 18.6 kg/hp (25.2 kg/kW); carrying capacity: 882 lb, 400 kg; speed in top at 1,000 rpm: 15.5 mph, 25 km/h; consumption: 40.4 m/imp gal, 33.6 m/US gal, 7 l x 100 km.

CHASSIS integral; front suspension: independent, wishbones, coil springs, anti-roll bar, telescopic dampers; rear: independent, swinging semi-axles, swinging longitudinal leading arms, coil springs, telescopic dampers.

STEERING screw and nut; turns lock to lock: 2.50.

BRAKES servo, front disc (diameter 9.92 in, 25.2 cm), rear drum; lining area: front 11.8 sq in, 76 sq cm, rear 59.7 sq in, 385 sq cm, total 71.5 sq in, 461 sq cm.

CUSTOCA Strato ES

ELECTRICAL EQUIPMENT 12 V; 35 Ah battery; 490 W alternator; Pal distributor; 2 headlamps.

DIMENSIONS AND WEIGHT wheel base: 94.49 in, 240 cm; tracks: 50.39 in, 128 cm front, 49.21 in, 125 cm rear; length: 163.78 in, 416 cm; width: 62.60 in, 159 cm; height: 55.12 in, 140 cm; ground clearance: 6.69 in, 17 cm; weight: 1,885 lb, 855 kg; turning circle: 36.1 ft, 11 m; fuel tank: 8.4 imp gal, 10 US gal, 38 l.

BODY saloon/sedan; 4 doors; 5 seats, separate front seats.

PRACTICAL INSTRUCTIONS fuel: 90 oct petrol; oil: engine 7 imp pt, 8.5 US pt, 4 l, SAE 20W (winter) 40W (summer), change every 3,100 miles, 5,000 km - gearbox and final drive 4.4 imp pt, 5.3 US pt, 2.5 l, SAE 90, change every 12,400 miles, 20,000 km; greasing: every 6,200 miles, 10,000 km, 4 points; tyre pressure: front 21 psi, 1.4 atm, rear 23 psi, 1.6 atm.

VARIATIONS

(only for export).
ENGINE max power (DIN) 45 hp (33.1 kW) at 4,800 rpm, 43 hp/l (31.6 kW/l).
PERFORMANCE power-weight ratio 41.9 lb/hp (56.9 lb/kW), 19 kg/hp (25.8 kg/kW).

OPTIONALS 4.666 axle ratio: 5.5'' light alloy wheels.

105 L

See 105 S, except for:

PRICE IN GB: £ 1,825*

PERFORMANCE power-weight ratio: 41.9 lb/hp (56.9 lb/kW), 19 kg/hp (25.8 kg/kW).

DIMENSIONS AND WEIGHT weight: 1,929 lb, 875 kg.

120 L

See 105 S, except for:

PRICE IN GB: £ 1,898*

ENGINE 71.6 cu in, 1,174 cc (2.83 x 2.83 in, 72 x 72 mm); max power (DIN): 52 hp (38.3 kW) at 5,000 rpm; max torque (DIN): 63 lb ft, 8.7 kg m (85.2 Nm) at 3,000 rpm; max engine rpm: 5,400; 44.3 hp/l (32.6 kW/l).

PERFORMANCE max speed: 87 mph, 140 km/h; power-weight ratio: 37.1 lb/hp (50.4 lb/kW), 16.8 kg/hp (22 kg/kW); consumption: 35.8 m/imp gal, 29.8 m/US gal, 8 l x 100 km.

ŠKODA 105 S

DIMENSIONS AND WEIGHT weight: 1,929 lb, 875 kg.

VARIATIONS

one.

120 LS

ee 120 L, except for:

ICE IN GB: £ 2,098*

NGINE compression ratio: 9.5:1; max power (DIN): 58 hp
2.7 kW) at 5,200 rpm; max torque (DIN): 67 lb ft, 9.2 kg
(90.2 Nm) at 3,250 rpm; max engine rpm: 5,500; 49.4
/l (36.2 kW/l); lubrication: oil cooler, 8.1 imp pt, 9.7
pt, 4.6 l.

RANSMISSION width of rims: 5.5''.

ERFORMANCE max speed: 93 mph, 150 km/h; power-
eight ratio: 33.7 lb/hp (45.6 lb/kW), 15.3 kg/hp (20.7
/kW); consumption: 32.8 m/imp gal, 27.3 m/US gal, 8.6
100 km.

ECTRICAL EQUIPMENT 4 headlamps.

IMENSIONS AND WEIGHT weight: 1,951 lb, 885 kg.

RACTICAL INSTRUCTIONS fuel: 95 oct petrol; oil: engine
1 imp pt, 9.7 US pt, 4.6 l.

S 110 R Coupé

ICE IN GB: £ 1,749*

NGINE rear, 4 stroke; 4 cylinders slanted 30° to right, in
ne; 67.5 cu in, 1,107 cc (2.83 x 2.68 in, 72 x 68 mm);
mpression ratio: 9.5:1; max power (DIN): 52 hp (38.3 kW)
4,650 rpm; max torque (DIN): 59 lb ft, 8.1 kg m (79.4
m) at 3,500 rpm; max engine rpm: 5,800; 47 hp/l (34.6
V/l); light alloy block, cast iron head, wet liners; 3
ankshaft bearings; valves: overhead, in line, push-rods
d rockers; camshafts: 1, side; lubrication: gear pump,
rtridge on by-pass, oil cooler, 8.1 imp pt, 9.7 US pt,
6 l; 1 jikov 32 DDS R downdraught twin barrel carbu-
ttor; fuel feed: mechanical pump; water-cooled, front
diator, 13 imp pt, 15.6 US pt, 7.4 l.

RANSMISSION driving wheels: rear; clutch: single dry
ate, hydraulically-controlled; gearbox: mechanical; gears:
fully synchronized; ratios: I 3.800, II 2.120, III 1.410, IV
960, rev 3.270; lever: central; final drive: spiral bevel;
le ratio: 4.444; width of rims: 4.5''; tyres: 155 SR x 14.

ERFORMANCE max speeds: (I) 20 mph, 32 km/h; (II) 35
ph, 56 km/h; (III) 54 mph, 87 km/h; (IV) 90 mph, 145
n/h; power-weight ratio: 35.4 lb/hp (48.1 lb/kW), 16 kg/hp
1.8 kg/kW); carrying capacity: 805 lb, 365 kg; speed in
p at 1,000 rpm: 15.5 mph, 25 km/h; consumption: 33.2
/imp gal, 27.7 m/US gal, 8.5 l x 100 km.

HASSIS integral; front suspension: independent, wish-

bones, coil springs, anti-roll bar, telescopic dampers; rear:
independent, swinging semi-axles, swinging longitudinal
leading arms, coil springs, telescopic dampers.

STEERING screw and nut; turns lock to lock: 2.50.

BRAKES servo, front disc (diameter 9.92 in, 25.2 cm),
rear drum; lining area: front 11.8 sq in, 76 sq cm, rear,
59.7 sq in, 385 sq cm, total 71.5 sq in, 461 sq cm.

ELECTRICAL EQUIPMENT 12 V; 35 Ah battery; 35 A alternator; Pal distributor; 4 headlamps (2 halogen).

DIMENSIONS AND WEIGHT wheel base: 94.49 in, 240 cm;
tracks: 50.39 in, 128 cm front, 49.21 in, 125 cm rear; length:
163.39 in, 415 cm; width: 63.78 in, 162 cm; height: 52.76
in, 134 cm; ground clearance: 6.89 in, 17.5 cm; weight:
1,841 lb, 835 kg; turning circle: 33.5 ft, 10.2 m; fuel tank:
8.4 imp gal, 10 US gal, 38 l.

BODY coupé; 2-dr; 2 + 2 seats, built-in headrests.

PRACTICAL INSTRUCTIONS fuel: 95 oct petrol; oil: engine
8.1 imp pt, 9.7 US pt, 4.6 l, SAE 20W (winter) 40W
(summer), change every 3,100 miles, 5,000 km - gearbox
and final drive 4.4 imp pt, 5.3 US pt, 2.5 l, SAE 90, change
every 12,400 miles, 20,000 km; greasing: every 6,200 miles,
10,000 km, 4 points; valve timing: 18° 49° 53° 14°; tyre
pressure: front 21 psi, 1.4 atm, rear 23 psi, 1.6 atm.

OPTIONALS 4.666 axle ratio.

TATRA CZECHOSLOVAKIA

T 613

ENGINE rear, 4 stroke; 8 cylinders, Vee-slanted at 90°;
213.3 cu in, 3,495 cc (3.35 x 3.03 in, 85 x 77 mm); compression ratio: 9.2:1; max power (DIN): 165 hp (121.4 kW)
at 5,200 rpm; max torque (DIN): 196 lb ft, 27 kg m (264.8
Nm) at 2,500 rpm; max engine rpm: 5,600; 47.2 hp/l (34.7
kW/l); cast iron block, light alloy head; 5 crankshaft bearings; valves: overhead, Vee-slanted, rockers; camshafts: 2 per
block, overhead; lubrication: gear pump, full flow filter
(cartridge), oil cooler, 16.7 imp pt, 20.1 US pt, 9.5 l; 2 Jikov
EDSR 32/34 downdraught twin barrel carburettors; fuel feed:
mechanical pump; air-cooled.

TRANSMISSION driving wheels: rear; clutch: single dry
plate, hydraulically controlled; gearbox: mechanical; gears:
4, fully synchronized; ratios: I 3.394, II 1.889, III 1.165, IV
0.862, rev 3.243; lever: central; final drive: hypoid bevel;
axle ratio: 3.909; width of rims: 6''; tyres: 215/70 HR x 14.

PERFORMANCE max speeds: (I) 29 mph, 47 km/h; (II) 53
mph, 85 km/h; (III) 86 mph, 138 km/h; (IV) 116 mph, 186
km/h; power-weight ratio: 21.4 lb/hp (29.1 lb/kW), 9.7
kg/hp (13.2 kg/kW); carrying capacity: 1,036 lb, 470 kg;
speed in top at 1,000 rpm: 22.2 mph, 35.8 km/h; consumption: 15.7 m/imp gal, 13.1 m/US gal, 18 l x 100 km.

ŠKODA 110 R Coupé

CHASSIS integral; front suspension: independent (by Mc-
Pherson), wishbones, coil springs, anti-roll bar, telescopic
dampers; rear: independent, swinging semi-axles, swinging
longitudinal trailing arms, coil springs, telescopic dampers.

STEERING rack-and-pinion, damper; turns lock to lock: 4.25.

BRAKES disc, servo; lining area: front 30.7 sq in, 198 sq
cm, rear 21.1 sq in, 136 sq cm, total 51.8 sq in, 334 sq cm.

ELECTRICAL EQUIPMENT 12 V; 75 Ah 2 x 6 V batteries; 55
A alternator; PAL Magneton distributor; electronic ignition;
4 headlamps, 2 iodine fog lamps.

DIMENSIONS AND WEIGHT wheel base: 117.32 in, 298 cm;
tracks: 60 in, 152 cm front, 60 in, 152 cm rear; length:
198 in, 503 cm; width: 71 in, 180 cm; height: 59.25 in,
151 cm; ground clearance: 6.30 in, 16 cm; weight: 3,528
lb, 1,600 kg; weight distribution: 43% front, 57% rear;
turning circle: 41 ft, 12.5 m; fuel tank: 15.8 imp gal, 19
US gal, 72 l.

BODY saloon/sedan; 4 doors; 5 seats, separate front seats,
reclining backrests, built-in headrests.

PRACTICAL INSTRUCTIONS fuel: 96 oct petrol; oil: engine
16.7 imp pt, 20.1 US pt, 9.5 l, SAE 20W-50, change every
6,200 miles, 10,000 km - gearbox 3.5 imp pt, 4.2 US pt,
2 l, SAE 90, change every 18,600 miles, 30,000 km - final
drive 1.8 imp pt, 2.1 US pt, 1 l, SAE 90, change every
6,200 miles, 10,000 km; greasing: none; sparking plug: 200°;
tappet clearances: inlet 0.004 in, 0.10 mm, exhaust 0.004 in,
0.10 mm; valve timing: 0° 30° 30° 0°; tyre pressure (max
load): front 24 psi, 1.7 atm, rear 33 psi, 2.3 atm.

TATRA T 613

ALPINE   FRANCE

A 310 V6

PRICE EX WORKS: 81,700** francs

ENGINE Renault, rear, 4 stroke; 6 cylinders, Vee-slanted at 90°; 162.6 cu in, 2,664 cc (3.46 x 2.87 in, 88 x 73 mm); compression ratio: 10.1:1; max power (DIN): 150 hp (108 kW) at 6,000 rpm; max torque (DIN): 151 lb ft, 20.8 kg m (204 Nm) at 3,500 rpm; max engine rpm: 6,400; 56.3 hp/l 40.5 kW/l); light alloy block and head, wet liners, hemispherical combustion chambers; 4 crankshaft bearings; valves: overhead, Vee-slanted, rockers; camshafts: 2 1 per bank, overhead; lubrication: gear pump, full flow filter, 10.6 imp pt, 12.7 US pt, 6 l; 1 Solex 34 TBIA downdraught single barrel carburettor and 1 Solex 35 CEEI downdraught twin barrel carburettor; fuel feed: mechanical pump; sealed circuit cooling, expansion tank, 21.1 imp pt, 25.4 US pt, 12 l, viscous coupling thermostatic fan.

TRANSMISSION driving wheels: rear; clutch: single dry plate (diaphragm), hydraulically controlled; gearbox: mechanical; gears: 4, fully synchronized; ratios: I 3.364, II 2.059, III 1.318, IV 0.931, rev 3.182; lever: central; final drive: hypoid bevel; axle ratio: 3.444; width of rims: 7''; tyres: 185/70 VR x 13 front, 205/70 VR x 13 rear.

ALPINE A 310 V6

PERFORMANCE max speeds: (I) 39 mph, 62 km/h; (II) 63 mph, 102 km/h; (III) 99 mph, 159 km/h; (IV) 137 mph, 220 km/h; power-weight ratio: 14.4 lb/hp (20 lb/kW), 6.5 kg/hp (9.1 kg/kW); carrying capacity: 794 lb, 360 kg; acceleration: standing ¼ mile 15.4 sec; speed in top at 1,000 rpm: 22 mph, 35.4 km/h; consumption: 30.7 m/imp gal, 25.6 m/US gal, 9.2 l x 100 km at 75 mph, 120 km/h.

CHASSIS integral, central steel backbone; front suspension: independent, wishbones, rubber elements, coil springs, anti-roll bar, telescopic dampers; rear: independent, wishbones, coil springs, anti-roll bar, telescopic dampers.

STEERING rack-and-pinion; turns lock to lock: 3.60.

BRAKES disc, front internal radial fins, dual circuit, servo; lining area: total 22.5 sq in, 145 sq cm.

ELECTRICAL EQUIPMENT 12 V; 50 Ah battery; 50 A alternator; Ducellier distributor; 4 headlamps.

DIMENSIONS AND WEIGHT wheel base: 89.37 in, 227 cm; tracks: 55.28 in, 140 cm front, 56.30 in, 143 cm rear; length: 164.57 in, 418 cm; width: 64.57 in, 164 cm; height: 45.28 in, 115 cm; ground clearance: 6.30 in, 16 cm; weight: 2,161 lb, 990 kg; turning circle: 34.8 ft, 10.6 m; fuel tank: 13.6 imp gal, 16.4 US gal, 62 l.

BODY coupé in plastic material; 2 doors; 2+2 seats; separate front seats, reclining backrests; electric windows; heated rear window.

PRACTICAL INSTRUCTIONS fuel: 98-100 oct petrol; oil: engine 10.6 imp pt, 12.7 US pt, 6 l, SAE 10W-30, change every 4,650 miles, 7,500 km - gearbox and final drive 6.5 imp pt, 7.8 US pt, 3.7 l, SAE 80, change every 9,300 miles, 15,000 km; tappet clearances: inlet 0.004-0.006 in, 0.10-0.15 mm, exhaust 0.010-0.012 in, 0.25-0.30 mm; valve timing: 9° 45° 45° 9° (left), 7° 43° 43° 7° (right); tyre pressure: front 23 psi, 1.6 atm, rear 38 psi, 2.7 atm.

OPTIONALS tinted glass; leather upholstery; metallic spray.

CHRYSLER FRANCE   FRANCE

Simca 1100 Series

PRICES IN GB AND EX WORKS:	£	francs
1 1100 LE 2-dr Berline	2,326*	20,400**
2 1100 LE 4-dr Berline	2,396*	22,100**
3 1100 LE Break	—	24,700**
4 1100 GLS 4-dr Berline	2,569*	25,200**
5 1100 GLS Break	2,803*	26,900**

Power team:	Standard for:	Optional for:
50 hp	1,2	3
58 hp	3 to 5	—

50 hp power team

ENGINE front, transverse, slanted 41° to rear, 4 stroke; 4 cylinders, in line; 68.2 cu in, 1,118 cc (2.91 x 2.56 in, 74 x 65 mm); compression ratio: 8.8:1; max power (DIN): 50 hp (36.8 kW) at 5,800 rpm; max torque (DIN): 57 ft, 7.8 kg m (76.5 Nm) at 3,000 rpm; max engine rpm: 6,000; 44.7 hp/l (32.9 kW/l); cast iron block, light alloy head; 5 crankshaft bearings; valves: overhead, in line, push-rods and rockers; camshafts: 1, side; lubrication: gear pump, full flow filter, 5.3 imp pt, 6.3 US pt, 3 l; 1 Bressel Weber 32 IBSA downdraught single barrel carburettor; fuel feed: mechanical pump; sealed circuit cooling, liquid expansion tank, 10.6 imp pt, 12.7 US pt, 6 l, electric thermostatic fan.

TRANSMISSION driving wheels: front; clutch: single dry plate (diaphragm), hydraulically controlled; gearbox: mechanical, in unit with final drive; gears: 4, fully synchronized; ratios: I 3.900, II 2.312, III 1.524, IV 1.080, rev 3.769; lever: central; final drive: cylindrical gears; axle ratio: 3.937; width of rims: 5''; tyres: 145 SR x 13 or 155 SR x 13.

PERFORMANCE max speeds: (I) 25 mph, 40 km/h; (II) 42 mph, 68 km/h; (III) 64 mph, 103 km/h; (IV) 87 mph, 140 km/h; power-weight ratio: 4-dr 41 lb/hp (55.7 lb/kW), 18.6 kg/hp (25.3 kg/kW) - 2-dr 40.1 lb/hp (54.5 lb/kW), 18.2 kg/hp (24.7 kg/kW); carrying capacity: 882 lb, 400 kg; speed in top at 1,000 rpm: 15 mph, 24 km/h; consumption: 30 m/imp gal, 25 m/US gal, 9.4 l x 100 km.

CHASSIS integral; front suspension: independent, wishbones, longitudinal torsion bars, anti-roll bar, telescopic dampers; rear: independent, longitudinal trailing arms, transverse torsion bars, anti-roll bar, telescopic dampers.

STEERING rack-and-pinion; turns lock to lock: 3.25.

BRAKES front disc (diameter 9.21 in, 23.4 cm), rear drum, rear compensator, servo; swept area: front 146.2 sq in, 943 sq cm, rear 73.8 sq in, 476 sq cm, total 220 sq in, 1,419 sq cm.

ELECTRICAL EQUIPMENT 12 V; 36 Ah battery; 40 A alternator; Chrysler transistorized ignition; 2 headlamps.

DIMENSIONS AND WEIGHT wheel base: 99.21 in, 252 cm; front track: 53.94 in, 137 cm - 2-dr 54.33 in, 138 cm; rear track: 51.57 in, 131 cm - 2-dr 52.36 in, 133 cm; length: 155.11 in, 394 cm; width: 62.60 in, 159 cm; height: 57.48 in, 146 cm; ground clearance: 5.12 in, 13 cm; weight: 2,051 lb, 930 kg - 2-dr 2,007 lb, 910 kg; turning circle: 34.1 ft, 10.4 m; fuel tank: 9.2 imp gal, 11.1 US gal, 42 l.

BODY 5 seats, separate front seats; folding rear seat, heated rear window.

PRACTICAL INSTRUCTIONS fuel: 85 oct petrol; oil: engine 5.3 imp pt, 6.3 US pt, 3 l, SAE 20W-40, change every 4,650 miles, 7,500 km - gearbox and final drive 1,9 imp pt, 2 US pt, 1.1 l, SAE 90 EP, change every 9,300 miles, 15,000 km; greasing: none; tyre pressure: front 25 psi, 1.7 atm, rear 26 psi, 1.8 atm.

OPTIONALS sunshine roof; light alloy wheels; tinted glass; metallic spray.

CHRYSLER FRANCE Simca 1100 GLS 4-dr Berline

CHRYSLER FRANCE Simca Horizon SX

BODY saloon/sedan; 4 + 1 doors; 5 seats, separate front seats, reclining backrests; heated rear window; folding rear seat.

PRACTICAL INSTRUCTIONS fuel: 98-100 oct petrol; oil: engine 5.3 imp pt, 6.3 US pt, 3 l, SAE 20W-40, change every 4,650 miles, 7,500 km - gearbox and final drive 1.9 imp pt, 2.3 US pt, 1.1 l, SAE 90 EP, change every 9,300 miles, 15,000 km; greasing: none.

OPTIONALS metallic spray; iodine headlamps; rear window wiper-washer; tinted glass; adjustable headrests on front seats; vinyl roof.

68 hp power team

See 59 hp power team, except for:

ENGINE 79 cu in, 1,294 cc (3.02 x 2.76 in, 76.7 x 70 mm); compression ratio: 9.5:1; max power (DIN): 68 hp (50 kW) at 5,600 rpm; max torque (DIN): 76 lb ft, 10.5 kg m (103 Nm) at 2,800 rpm; 52.6 hp/l (38.7 kW/l).

TRANSMISSION axle ratio: 3.588.

PERFORMANCE max speed: 96 mph, 155 km/h; power-weight ratio: 31.1 lb/hp (42.3 lb/kW), 14.1 kg/hp (19.2 kg/kW); carrying capacity: 948 lb, 430 kg; acceleration: standing ¼ mile 19.5 sec; consumption: 30.1 m/imp gal, 25 m/US gal, 9.4 l x 100 km.

DIMENSIONS AND WEIGHT weight: 2,117 lb, 960 kg.

69 hp power team

See 59 hp power team, except for:

ENGINE 88 cu in, 1,442 cc (3.02 x 3.07 in, 76.7 x 78 mm); compression ratio: 9.5:1; max power (DIN): 69 hp (50.8 kW) at 5,200 rpm; max torque (DIN): 85 lb ft, 11.7 kg m (114.7 Nm) at 3,000 rpm; 47.9 hp/l (35.2 kW/l); 1 Solex 32 BISA 7 or Weber 32 IBSA single barrel carburettor.

TRANSMISSION gearbox ratios: I 3.900, II 2.312, III 1.524, IV 1.040, rev 3.769; axle ratio: 3 471.

PERFORMANCE max speed: 96 mph, 155 km/h; power-weight ratio: 32.6 lb/hp (42.3 lb/kW), 14.1 kg/hp (19.2 kg/kW); carrying capacity: 915 lb, 415 kg; acceleration: standing ¼ mile 19.5 sec; consumption: 31.7 m/imp gal, 26.4 m/US gal, 8.9 l x 100 km.

ELECTRICAL EQUIPMENT iodine headlamps (standard).

DIMENSIONS AND WEIGHT weight: 2,150 lb, 975 kg.

BODY (standard) adjustable backrests on front seats, rear window wiper-washer.

OPTIONALS light alloy wheels; headlamps with wiper-washers.

83 hp power team

See 59 hp power team, except for:

ENGINE 88 cu in, 1,442 cc (3.02 x 3.07 in, 76.7 x 78 mm); compression ratio: 9.5:1; max power (DIN): 83 hp (61.1 kW) at 5,600 rpm; max torque (DIN): 89 lb ft, 12.3 kg m (120.6 Nm) at 3,000 rpm; 57.6 hp/l (42.4 kW/l); 1 Weber 36 DCA 2 downdraught twin barrel carburettor; liquid-cooled, 11.3 imp pt, 13.5 US pt, 6.4 l.

TRANSMISSION gearbox: Chrysler 415 automatic transmission, hydraulic torque converter and planetary gears with 3 ratios, max ratio of converter at stall 1.224, possible manual selection; ratios: I 2.475, II 1.475, III 1, rev 2.103; axle ratio: 3,000; width of rims: 5''; tyres: 155 SR x 13.

PERFORMANCE max speed: 100 mph, 161 km/h; power-weight ratio: 27.2 lb/hp (37 lb/kW), 12.3 kg/hp (16.8 kg/kW); carrying capacity: 882 lb, 400 kg; consumption: 29.4 m/imp gal, 24.5 m/US gal, 9.6 l x 100 km.

ELECTRICAL EQUIPMENT 50 A alternator; iodine headlamps (standard).

DIMENSIONS AND WEIGHT rear track: 54.33 in, 138 cm; weight: 2,260 lb, 1,025 kg.

BODY (standard) adjustable backrests on front seats, rear window wiper-washer, automatic speed control, trip computer.

PRACTICAL INSTRUCTIONS oil: automatic transmission 11.3 imp pt, 13.5 US pt, 6.4 l.

OPTIONALS light alloy wheels; headlamps with wiper-washers.

58 hp power team

50 hp power team, except for:

ENGINE compression ratio: 9.6:1; max power (DIN): 58 hp (..7 kW) at 6,000 rpm; max torque (DIN): 64 lb ft, 8.8 ..m (86.3 Nm) at 3,000 rpm; 51.9 hp/l (38.2 kW/l); 1 ..ex 32 BISA or Weber or Bressel 32 IBSA downdraught ..gle barrel carburettor.

..RFORMANCE max speed: 91 mph, 146 km/h - breaks 87 ..h, 140 km/h; power-weight ratio: 35.4 lb/hp (48 lb/kW), ..kg/hp (21.8 kg/kW); carrying capacity: Breaks 992 lb, ..kg; consumption: 29.1 m/imp gal, 24.2 m/US gal, 9.7 ..100 km.

..MENSIONS AND WEIGHT length: Breaks 154.72 in, 393 ..; height: Breaks 58.27 in, 148 cm; ground clearance: ..aks 5.51 in, 14 cm; weight: 2,051 lb, 930 kg.

..DY built-in headrests on front seats (except for Breaks).

..ACTICAL INSTRUCTIONS fuel: 98-100 oct petrol.

..TIONALS Ferodo 3-speed semi-automatic transmission, ..raulic torque converter (I 2.469, II 1.650, III 1.080, rev ..74), max ratio of converter at stall 2, possible manual ..ection, max speeds (I) 40 mph, 64 km/h, (II) 59 mph, ..km/h, (III) 91 mph, 146 km/h (Breaks 87 mph, 140 ../h), consumption 29.4 m/imp gal, 24.5 m/US gal, 9.6 ..100 km.

Simca Horizon Series

..CES EX WORKS:

..orizon LS	26,770**	francs
..orizon GL	27,970**	francs
..orizon GLS	30,190**	francs
..orizon SX	33,800**	francs

..er team:	Standard for:	Optional for:
..hp	1	—
..hp	2	—
..hp	3	—
..hp	4	—

59 hp power team

..GINE front, transverse, slanted 41° to rear, 4 stroke; ..ylinders, in line; 68.2 cu in, 1,118 cc (2.91 x 2.56 in, ..x 65 mm); compression ratio: 9.6:1; max power (DIN): ..hp (43.4 kW) at 5,600 rpm; max torque (DIN): 66 lb ft, ..kg m (89.2 Nm) at 3,000 rpm; max engine rpm: 6,300; ..hp/l (38.8 kW/l); cast iron block, light alloy head; 5 ..nkshaft bearings; valves: overhead, push-rods and rockers, ..ble tappets; camshafts: 1, side; lubrication: gear pump, ..flow filter, 5.3 imp pt, 6.3 US pt, 3 l; 1 Solex 32 BISA ..r Weber 32 IBSA single barrel carburettor; fuel feed: ..chanical pump; sealed circuit cooling, expansion tank, ..id, 10.6 imp pt, 12.7 US pt, 6 l, electric thermostatic fan.

..ANSMISSION driving wheels: front; clutch: single dry ..te (diaphragm), hydraulically controlled; gearbox: mecha-..; gears: 4, fully synchronized; ratios: I 3.900, II 2.312, ..1.524, IV 1.080, rev 3.769; lever: central; final drive:

cylindrical gears; axle ratio: 3.705; width of rims: 4.5''; tyres: 145 SR x 13.

PERFORMANCE max speed: 92 mph, 148 km/h; power-weight ratio: 35.3 lb/hp (48 lb/kW), 16 kg/hp (21.8 kg/kW); carrying capacity: 981 lb, 445 kg; acceleration: standing ¼ mile 20.7 sec; consumption: 29.4 m/imp gal, 24.5 m/US gal, 9.6 l x 100 km.

CHASSIS integral; front suspension: independent, longitudinal torsion bars, wishbones, anti-roll bar, telescopic dampers; rear: independent, swinging longitudinal trailing arms, coil springs, anti-roll bar, telescopic dampers.

STEERING rack-and-pinion; turns lock to lock: 4.35.

BRAKES front disc (diameter 9.37 in, 23.8 cm), rear drum, rear compensator, servo; swept area: front 155 sq in, 1,000 sq cm, rear 89 sq in, 574 sq cm, total 244 sq in, 1,574 sq cm.

ELECTRICAL EQUIPMENT 12 V; 40 Ah battery; 40 A alternator; Chrysler transistorized ignition; 2 headlamps.

DIMENSIONS AND WEIGHT wheel base: 99.21 in, 252 cm; tracks: 55.91 in, 142 cm front, 53.94 in, 137 cm rear; length: 155.91 in, 396 cm; width: 66.14 in, 168 cm; height: 55.51 in, 141 cm; ground clearance: 7.09 in, 18 cm; weight: 2,084 lb, 945 kg; weight distribution: 59.4% front, 40.6% rear; turning circle: 33.5 ft, 10.2 m; fuel tank: 10.3 imp gal, 12.4 US gal, 47 l.

CHRYSLER FRANCE Simca Horizon SX

CHRYSLER FRANCE Simca 1309 SX

Simca 1307 GLS

PRICE EX WORKS: 29,600** francs

ENGINE front, transverse, slanted 41° to rear, 4 stroke; 4 cylinders, in line; 79 cu in, 1,294 cc (3.02 x 2.76 in, 76.7 x 70 mm); compression ratio: 9.5:1; max power (DIN): 68 hp (50 kW) at 5,600 rpm; max torque (DIN): 78 lb ft, 10.7 kg m (104.9 Nm) at 2,800 rpm; max engine rpm: 6,300; 52.6 hp/l (38.6 kW/l); cast iron block, light alloy head; 5 crankshaft bearings; valves: overhead, in line, push-rods and rockers; camshafts: 1, side; lubrication: gear pump, full flow filter, 5.3 imp pt, 6.3 US pt, 3 l; 1 Solex 32 BISA 5 A or Weber 32 IBSA 9 downdraught single barrel carburettor; fuel feed: mechanical pump; sealed circuit cooling, expansion tank, liquid, 10.7 imp pt, 12.9 US pt, 6.1 l, electric thermostatic fan.

TRANSMISSION driving wheels: front; clutch: single dry plate (diaphragm), hydraulically controlled; gearbox: mechanical; gears: 4, fully synchronized; ratios: I 3.900, II 2.312, III 1.524, IV 1.080, rev 3.769; lever: central; final drive: cylindrical gears; axle ratio: 3.706; width of rims: 5''; tyres: 155 SR x 13.

PERFORMANCE max speed: 94 mph, 152 km/h; power-weight ratio: 34 lb/hp (46.3 lb/kW), 15.4 kg/hp (21 kg/kW); carrying capacity: 882 lb, 400 kg; acceleration: standing ¼ mile 19.8 sec, 0-50 mph (0-80 km/h) 10.7 sec; speed in top at 1,000 rpm: 16.4 mph, 26.4 km/h; consumption: 33.6 m/imp gal, 28 m/US gal, 8.4 l x 100 km.

CHASSIS integral; front suspension: independent, wishbones, longitudinal torsion bars, anti-roll bar, telescopic dampers; rear: independent, swinging longitudinal trailing arms, coil springs, anti-roll bar, telescopic dampers.

STEERING rack-and-pinion; turns lock to lock: 4.15.

BRAKES front disc (diameter 9.45 in, 24 cm), rear drum, rear compensator, servo; swept area: front 169.3 sq in, 1,092 sq cm, rear 90.2 sq in, 582 sq cm, total 259.5 sq in, 1,674 sq cm.

ELECTRICAL EQUIPMENT 12 V; 40 Ah battery; 40 A alternator; Chrysler transistorized ignition; 2 headlamps.

DIMENSIONS AND WEIGHT wheel base: 102.36 in, 260 cm; tracks: 55.51 in, 141 cm front, 54.72 in, 139 cm rear; length: 166.93 in, 424 cm; width: 66.14 in, 168 cm; height: 54.72 in, 139 cm; ground clearance: 5.12 in, 13 cm; weight: 2,315 lb, 1,050 kg; turning circle: 36.1 ft, 11 m; fuel tank: 12.8 imp gal, 15.3 US gal, 58 l.

BODY saloon/sedan; 4 doors; 5 seats, separate front seats, reclining backrests; heated rear window; folding rear seat.

PRACTICAL INSTRUCTIONS fuel: 98-100 oct petrol; oil: engine 5.3 imp pt, 6.3 US pt, 3 l, SAE 20W-40, change every 4,650 miles, 7,500 km - gearbox and final drive 1.9 imp pt, 2.3 US pt, 1.1 l, SAE 90 EP, change every 9,300 miles, 15,000 km; greasing: none.

OPTIONALS metallic spray; iodine headlamps; adjustable headrests on front seats; tinted glass; vinyl roof; sunshine roof; rear window wiper-washer.

Simca 1307 S

See Simca 1307 GLS, except for:

PRICE EX WORKS: 32,900** francs

ENGINE 88 cu in, 1,442 cc (3.02 x 3.07 in, 76.7 x 78 mm); max power (DIN): 85 hp (62.6 kW) at 5,600 rpm; max torque (DIN): 92 lb ft, 12.7 kg m (124.5 Nm) at 3,000 rpm; 58.9 hp/l (43.4 kW/l); 1 Weber 36 DCNV A downdraught twin barrel carburettor.

TRANSMISSION axle ratio: 3.588.

PERFORMANCE max speed: 102 mph, 164 km/h; power-weight ratio: 27.9 lb/hp (37.9 lb/kW), 12.6 kg/hp (17.2 kg/kW); carrying capacity: 1,103 lb, 500 kg; acceleration: standing ¼ mile 19 sec, 0-50 mph (0-80 km/h) 8.9 sec; speed in top at 1,000 rpm: 17.6 mph, 28.3 km/h; consumption: 28.5 m/imp gal, 23.8 m/US gal, 9.9 l x 100 km.

ELECTRICAL EQUIPMENT iodine headlamps (standard).

DIMENSIONS AND WEIGHT weight: 2,370 lb, 1,075 kg.

BODY adjustable headrests on front seats (standard).

OPTIONALS light alloy wheels; headlamps with wiper-washers; power steering; electric windows.

Simca 1308 GT

See Simca 1307 GLS, except for:

PRICE EX WORKS: 35,200** francs

ENGINE 88 cu in, 1,442 cc (3.02 x 3.07 in, 76.7 x 78 mm); max power (DIN): 85 hp (62.6 kW) at 5,600 rpm; max torque (DIN): 92 lb ft, 12.7 kg m (124.5 Nm) at 3,000 rpm; 58.9 hp/l (43.4 kW/l); 1 Weber 36 DCVN A downdraught twin barrel carburettor.

TRANSMISSION axle ratio: 3.588.

PERFORMANCE max speed: 102 mph, 164 km/h; power-weight ratio: 27.9 lb/hp (37.9 lb/kW), 12.6 kg/hp (17 kg/kW); carrying capacity: 1,103 lb, 500 kg; acceleration: standing ¼ mile 19 sec, 0-50 mph (0-80 km/h) 8.9 sec; speed in top at 1,000 rpm: 17.6 mph, 28.3 km/h; consumption: 28.5 m/imp gal, 23.8 m/US gal, 9.9 l x 100 km.

ELECTRICAL EQUIPMENT iodine headlamps with wiper-washers (standard).

DIMENSIONS AND WEIGHT weight: 2,370 lb, 1,075 kg.

BODY (standard) adjustable backrests on front seats; electric windows.

OPTIONALS light alloy wheels; power steering.

Simca 1309 SX

See Simca 1307 GLS, except for:

PRICE EX WORKS: 41,650** francs

ENGINE 97.1 cu in, 1,592 cc (3.17 x 3.07 in, 80.6 x 78 mm); compression ratio: 9.35:1; max power (DIN): 88 hp (64 kW) at 5,400 rpm; max torque (DIN): 99 lb ft, 13.7 kg m (134.4 Nm) at 3,000 rpm; 55.3 hp/l (40.7 kW/l); 1 Weber 36 DCA 100 downdraught twin barrel carburettor; liquid cooled, 11.1 imp pt, 13.3 US pt, 6.3 l.

TRANSMISSION gearbox: Chrysler 415 automatic transmission, hydraulic torque converter and planetary gears with 3 ratios, max ratio of converter at stall 1.224, possible manual selection; ratios: I 2.475, II 1.475, III 1, rev 2.103; axle ratio: 3.000.

PERFORMANCE max speed: 106 mph, 170 km/h; power-weight ratio: 27.4 lb/hp (37.3 lb/kW), 12.4 kg/hp (16 kg/kW); carrying capacity: 882 lb, 400 kg; speed in direct drive at 1,000 rpm: 17.8 mph, 28.7 km/h; consumption: 26.9 m/imp gal, 22.4 m/US gal, 10.5 l x 100 km.

STEERING servo; turns lock to lock: 2.80.

BRAKES front disc (diameter 9.45 in, 24 cm), rear drum, rear compensator, servo; swept area: front 169.3 sq in, 1,092 sq cm, rear 89 sq in, 574 sq cm, total 258.3 sq in, 1,666 sq cm.

ELECTRICAL EQUIPMENT 50 A alternator; iodine headlamps with wiper-washers (standard).

DIMENSIONS AND WEIGHT weight: 2,414 lb, 1,095 kg; turning circle: 34.1 ft, 10.4 m.

BODY (standard) adjustable backrests on front seats, rear window wiper-washer, automatic speed control.

CHRYSLER FRANCE Simca 1309 SX

PRACTICAL INSTRUCTIONS oil: automatic transmission 11.3 imp pt, 13.5 US pt, 6.4 l.

OPTIONALS light alloy wheels; leather upholstery.

Simca 1610

PRICE EX WORKS: 33.620** francs

ENGINE front, slanted 15º to right, 4 stroke: 4 cylinders, in line; 120.9 cu in, 1,981 cc (3.61 x 2.95 in, 91.7 x 75 mm); compression ratio: 9.45:1; max power (DIN): 110 hp (81 kW) at 5,800 rpm; max torque (DIN): 117 lb ft, 16.2 kg m (158.9 Nm) at 3,400 rpm; max engine rpm: 5,800; 55.5 hp/l (40.9 kW/l); cast iron block, light alloy head; 5 crankshaft bearings; valves: overhead, rockers; camshafts: 1, overhead; lubrication: gear pump, full flow filter, 7 imp pt, 8.5 US pt, 4 l; 1 Weber 34 ADS-D downdraught twin barrel carburettor; fuel feed: mechanical pump; water-cooled, 17.6 imp pt, 21.1 US pt, 10 l, electric thermostatic fan.

TRANSMISSION driving wheels: rear; clutch: single dry plate (diaphragm), hydraulically controlled; gearbox: mechanical; gears: 4, fully synchronized; ratios: I 3.546, II 2.175, III 1.418, IV 1, rev 3.226; lever: central; final drive: hypoid bevel; axle ratio: 3.727; width of rims: 5.5''; tyres: 175 SR x 14 or 175 HR x 14.

PERFORMANCE max speed: 109 mph, 175 km/h; power-weight ratio: 22.6 lb/hp (30.6 lb/kW), 10.2 kg/hp (13.9 kg/kW); carrying capacity: 882 lb, 400 kg; speed in direct drive at 1,000 rpm: 18.8 mph, 30.2 km/h; consumption: 25.9 m/imp gal, 21.6 m/US gal, 10.9 l x 100 km.

CHASSIS integral; front suspension: independent, by McPherson, coil springs/telescopic damper struts, lower wishbones, anti-roll bar; rear: rigid axle, lower longitudinal trailing arms, upper torque arms, transverse linkage bar, coil springs, telescopic dampers.

STEERING rack-and-pinion; turns lock to lock: 4.

BRAKES disc (front diameter 9.92 in, 25.2 cm, rear 9.02 in, 22.9 cm), rear compensator, servo; swept area: front 186 sq in, 1,200 sq cm, rear 140.8 sq in, 908 sq cm, total 326.8 sq in, 2,108 sq cm.

ELECTRICAL EQUIPMENT 12 V; 36 Ah battery; 35 A alternator; Chrysler transistorized ignition; 2 headlamps, iodine long-distance lights.

DIMENSIONS AND WEIGHT wheel base: 105.12 in, 267 cm; tracks: 55.12 in, 140 cm front, 55.12 in, 140 cm rear; length: 178.35 in, 453 cm; width: 68.11 in, 173 cm; height: 56.69 in, 144 cm; ground clearance: 5.71 in, 14.5 cm; weight: 2,481 lb, 1,125 kg; turning circle: 33.8 ft, 10.3 m; fuel tank: 14.3 imp gal, 17.2 US gal, 65 l.

BODY saloon/sedan; 4 doors; 5 seats, separate front seats; built-in headrests; heated rear window; tinted glass.

PRACTICAL INSTRUCTIONS fuel: 98-100 oct petrol; oil: engine 7 imp pt, 8.5 US pt, 4 l, SAE 10 W-50, change every 4,650 miles, 7,500 km - gearbox 2.6 imp pt, 3.2 US pt, 1.5 l, SAE 90 EP, change every 12,400 miles, 20,000 km - final

CHRYSLER FRANCE Simca 1610

drive 2.3 imp pt, 2.7 US pt, 1.3 l, SAE 90 EP, change every 12,400 miles, 20,000 km; greasing: none; sparking plug: 225º; tappet clearances: inlet 0.010 in, 0.25 mm, exhaust 0.014 in, 0.35 mm; tyre pressure: front 24 psi, 1.7 atm, rear 27 psi, 1.9 atm.

OPTIONALS light alloy wheels; vinyl roof; metallic spray.

Simca 2 L Automatic

See Simca 1610, except for:

PRICE EX WORKS: 36,350** francs

TRANSMISSION gearbox: Chrysler A904 automatic transmission, hydraulic torque converter and planetary gears with 3 ratios + reverse, max ratio of converter at stall. 2.2, possible manual selection; ratios: I 2.450, II 1.450, III 1, rev 2.200.

PERFORMANCE max speed: 106 mph, 170 km/h; acceleration: standing ¼ mile 18.7 sec; speed in direct drive at 1,000 rpm: 18.3 mph, 29.5 km/h; consumption: 23.7 m/imp gal, 19.8 m/US gal, 11.9 l x 100 km.

STEERING turns lock to lock: 4.50.

PRACTICAL INSTRUCTIONS oil: automatic transmission 14.1 imp pt,, 16.9 US pt, 8 l.

CITROËN   FRANCE

2 CV Spécial

PRICE EX WORKS: 14,750** francs

ENGINE front, 4 stroke; 2 cylinders, horizontally opposed; 26.5 cu in, 435 cc (2.70 x 2.32 in, 68.5 x 59 mm); compression ratio: 8.5:1; max power (DIN): 24 hp (17.7 kW) at 6,750 rpm; max torque (DIN): 21 lb ft, 2.9 kg m (28.4 Nm) at 3,750 rpm; max engine rpm: 6,750; 55.2 hp/l (40.7 kW/l); cast iron block, light alloy head, dry liners, light alloy sump, hemispherical combustion chambers; 2 crankshaft bearings; valves: overhead, Vee-slanted at 70º, pushrods and rockers; camshafts: 1, central, lower; lubrication: rotary pump, filter in sump, oil cooler, 3.9 imp pt, 4.7 US pt, 2.2 l; 1 Solex 34 PICS downdraught carburettor; fuel feed: mechanical pump; air-cooled.

TRANSMISSION driving wheels: front (double homokinetic joints); clutch: single dry plate; gearbox: mechanical; gears: 4, II, III and IV synchronized; ratios: I 6.961, II 3.554, III 2.133, IV 1.474, rev 6.961; lever: on facia; final drive: spiral bevel; axle ratio: 4.125; width of rims: 4''; tyres: 125 x 15.

PERFORMANCE max speeds: (I) 16 mph, 25 km/h; (II) 30 mph, 49 km/h; (III) 52 mph, 83 km/h; (IV) 63 mph, 102 km/h; power-weight ratio: 51.4 lb/hp (69.8 lb/kW), 23.3 kg/hp (31.6 kg/kW); carrying capacity: 739 lb, 335 kg; acceleration: standing ¼ mile 24.3 sec; speed in top at 1,000 rpm: 11 mph, 17.7 km/h; consumption: 53.3 m/imp gal, 44.4 m/US gal, 5.3 l x 100 km at 56 mph, 90 km/h.

CHASSIS platform; front suspension: independent, swinging leading arms, 2 friction dampers, 2 inertia-type patter dampers; rear: independent, swinging longitudinal trailing arms linked to front suspension by longitudinal coil springs, 2 inertia-type patter dampers, 2 telescopic dampers.

STEERING rack-and-pinion; turns lock to lock: 3.25.

BRAKES drum, single circuit; lining area: front 30.4 sq in, 196 sq cm, rear 34.7 sq in, 224 sq cm, total 65.1 sq in, 420 sq cm.

ELECTRICAL EQUIPMENT 12 V; 25 Ah battery; 390 W alternator; 2 headlamps, height adjustable from driving seat.

DIMENSIONS AND WEIGHT wheel base: 94.49 in, 240 cm; tracks: 49.61 in, 126 cm front, 49.61 in, 126 cm rear; length: 150.79 in, 383 cm; width: 58.27 in, 148 cm; height: 62.99 in, 160 cm; ground clearance: 5.91 in, 15 cm; weight: 1,235 lb, 560 kg; weight distribution: 58% front, 42% rear; turning circle: 36.7 ft, 11.2 m; fuel tank: 4.4 imp gal, 5.3 US gal, 20 l.

BODY saloon/sedan; 4 doors; 4 seats, bench front seats; folding rear seat; fully opening canvas sunshine roof.

PRACTICAL INSTRUCTIONS fuel: 80-85 oct petrol; oil: engine 3.5 imp pt, 4.2 US pt, 2 l, SAE 20W-50, change every 4,600 miles, 7,500 km - gearbox 1.6 imp pt, 1.9 US pt, 0.9 l, SAE 80, change every 14,000 miles, 22,500 km - final drive 0.9 imp pt, 1.1 US pt, 0.5 l; greasing: every 1,900 miles, 3,000 km, 4 points; sparking plug: 225º; tappet clearances: inlet 0.008 in, 0.20 mm, exhaust 0.008

CITROËN 2 CV Spécial

in, 0.20 mm; valve timing: 2°5' 41°30' 35°55' 3°30'; tyre pressure: front 20 psi, 1.4 atm, rear 26 psi, 1.8 atm.

OPTIONALS centrifugal clutch; separate front seats.

2 CV 6

See 2 CV Spécial, except for:

PRICE IN GB: £ 1,767*
PRICE EX WORKS: 17,100** francs

ENGINE 36.7 cu in, 602 cc (2.91 x 2.76 in, 74 x 70 mm); max power (DIN): 29 hp (21.3 kW) at 5,750 rpm; max torque (DIN): 29 lb ft, 4 kg m (39.2 Nm) at 3,500 rpm; max engine rpm: 5,900; 48.2 hp/l (35.4 kW/l); lubricating system: 4 imp pt, 4.9 US pt, 2.3 l; 1 Solex 26/35 CSIC downdraught twin barrel carburettor.

TRANSMISSION gearbox ratios: I 5.203, II 2.656, III 1.786, IV 1.316, rev 5.203.

PERFORMANCE max speeds: (I) 19 mph, 30 km/h; (II) 37 mph, 59 km/h; (III) 55 mph, 88 km/h; (IV) 68 mph, 110 km/h; power-weight ratio: 42.6 lb/hp (58 lb/kW), 19.3 kg/hp (26.3 kg/kW); acceleration: standing ¼ mile 22.7 sec; speed in top at 1,000 rpm: 12.7 mph, 20.4 km/h; consumption: 47.1 m/imp gal, 39.2 m/US gal, 6 l x 100 km at 56 mph, 90 km/h.

PRACTICAL INSTRUCTIONS valve timing: 0°5' 49°15' 35°55' 3°30'.

Mehari

PRICE EX WORKS: 18,228** francs

ENGINE front, 4 stroke; 2 cylinders, horizontally opposed; 36.7 cu in, 602 cc (2.91 x 2.76 in, 74 x 70 mm); compression ratio: 8.5:1; max power (DIN): 29 hp (21.3 kW) at 5,750 rpm; max torque (DIN): 29 lb ft, 4 kg m (39.2 Nm) at 3,500 rpm; max engine rpm: 5,900; 48.2 hp/l (35.4 kW/l); cast iron block, light alloy head, dry liners, light alloy sump, hemispherical combustion chambers; 2 crankshaft bearings; valves: overhead, Vee-slanted at 70°, push-rods and rockers; camshafts: 1, central, lower; lubrication: rotary pump, filter in sump, oil cooler, 4 imp pt, 4.9 US pt, 2.3 l; 1 Solex 26/35 CSIC downdraught twin barrel carburettor; fuel feed: mechanical pump; air-cooled.

TRANSMISSION driving wheels: front (double homokinetic joints); clutch: single dry plate; gearbox: mechanical; gears: 4, II, III and IV synchronized; ratios: I 6.051, II 3.089, III 1.293, IV 1.421, rev 6.051; lever: on facia; final drive: spiral bevel; axle ratio: 3.875; width of rims: 4''; tyres: 135 x 15.

PERFORMANCE max speeds: (I) 15 mph, 24 km/h; (II) 29 mph, 46 km/h; (III) 47 mph, 75 km/h; (IV) 62 mph, 100 km/h; power-weight ratio: 42.2 lb/hp (57.5 lb/kW), 19.1 kg/hp (26.1 kg/kW); carrying capacity: 838 lb, 380 kg; acceleration: standing ¼ mile 23.6 sec; speed in top at 1,000 rpm: 12.7 mph, 20.4 km/h; consumption: 37.2 m/imp gal, 30.9 m/US gal, 7.6 l x 100 km at 56 mph, 90 km/h.

CHASSIS platform; front suspension: independent, swinging leading arms, 2 friction dampers, 2 inertia-type patter dampers; rear: independent, swinging longitudinal trailing arms linked to front suspension by longitudinal coil springs, 2 inertia-type patter dampers, 2 telescopic dampers.

STEERING rack-and-pinion; turns lock to lock: 3.25.

BRAKES front disc (diameter 9.61 in, 24.4 cm), rear drum, single circuit; lining area: front 13 sq in, 84 sq cm, rear 34.7 sq in, 224 sq cm, total 47.7 sq in, 308 sq cm.

ELECTRICAL EQUIPMENT 12 V; 25 Ah battery; 390 W alternator; 2 headlamps, height adjustable from driving seat.

DIMENSIONS AND WEIGHT wheel base: 93.31 in, 237 cm; tracks: 49.61 in, 126 cm front, 49.61 in, 126 cm rear; length: 138.58 in, 352 cm; width: 60.24 in, 153 cm; height: 64.37 in, 163 cm; ground clearance: 7.09 in, 18 cm; weight: 1,224 lb, 555 kg; weight distribution: 60% front, 40% rear; turning circle: 37.5 ft, 11.4 m; fuel tank: 5.5 imp gal, 6.6 US gal, 25 l.

BODY open in plastic material; 2 doors; 2 seats.

PRACTICAL INSTRUCTIONS fuel: 98 oct petrol; oil: engine 4 imp pt, 4.9 US pt, 2.3 l, SAE 20W-50, change every 4,600 miles, 7,500 km - gearbox 1.6 imp pt, 1.9 US pt, 0.9 l, SAE 80, change every 14,000 miles, 22,500 km - final drive 0.9 imp pt, 1.1 US pt, 0.5 l; greasing: every 1,900 miles, 3,000 km, 4 point; sparking plug: 225°; tappet clearances: inlet 0.008 in, 0.20 mm, exhaust 0.008 in, 0.20 mm; valve timing: 2°5' 41°30' 35°55' 3°30'; tyre pressure: front 20 psi, 1.4 atm, rear 26 psi, 1.8 atm.

OPTIONALS centrifugal clutch; tonneau cover.

Mehari 2+2

See Mehari except for:

PRICE EX WORKS: 20,200** francs

DIMENSIONS AND WEIGHT weight distribution: 63% front, 37% rear; turning circle: 36.1 ft, 11 m.

BODY 2 + 1 doors; 4 seats, separate front seats.

Dyane 6

PRICE IN GB: £ 1,950*
PRICE EX WORKS: 18,160** francs

ENGINE front, 4 stroke; 2 cylinders, horizontally opposed; 36.7 cu in, 602 cc (2.91 x 2.76 in, 74 x 70 mm); compression ratio: 9:1; max power (DIN): 32 hp (23.6 kW) at 5,750 rpm; max torque (DIN): 30 lb ft, 4.2 kg m (41.2 Nm) at 4,000 rpm; max engine rpm: 5,900; 53.3 hp/l (39.2 kW/l); cast iron block, light alloy head, dry liners, light alloy sump, hemispherical combustion chambers; 2 crankshaft bearings; valves: overhead, Vee-slanted at 70°, push-rods and rockers; camshafts: 1, central, lower; lubrication: rotary pump, filter in sump, oil cooler, 4 imp pt, 4.9 US pt, 2.3 l; 1 Solex 26/35 CSIC downdraught twin barrel carburettor; fuel feed: mechanical pump; air-cooled.

TRANSMISSION driving wheels: front (double homokinetic joints); clutch: single dry plate; gearbox: mechanical; gears: 4, fully synchronized; ratios: I 5.749, II 2.935, III 1.923, IV 1.350, rev 5.749; lever: on facia; final drive: spiral bevel; axle ratio: 3.875; width of rims: 4''; tyres: 125 x 15.

PERFORMANCE max speeds: (I) 17 mph, 28 km/h; (II) 35 mph, 56 km/h; (III) 53 mph, 85 km/h; (IV) 75 mph, 120 km/h; power-weight ratio: 41.3 lb/hp (56.1 lb/kW), 18.7 kg/hp (25.4 kg/kW); carrying capacity: 728 lb, 330 kg; acceleration: standing ¼ mile 22 sec; speed in top at 1,000 rpm: 12.8 mph, 20.6 km/h; consumption: 49.6 m/imp gal, 41.3 m/US gal, 5.7 l x 100 km at 56 mph, 90 km/h.

CHASSIS platform; front suspension: independent, swinging leading arms, 2 friction dampers, 2 inertia-type patter dampers; rear: independent, swinging longitudinal trailing arms linked to front suspension by longitudinal coil springs, 2 inertia-type patter dampers, 2 telescopic dampers.

STEERING rack-and-pinion; turns lock to lock: 3.25.

BRAKES front disc (diameter 9.61 in, 24.4 cm), rear drum, single circuit; lining area: front 13 sq in, 84 sq cm, rear 34.7 sq in, 224 sq cm, total 47.7 sq in, 308 sq cm.

ELECTRICAL EQUIPMENT 12 V; 25 Ah battery; 390 W alternator; 2 headlamps, height adjustable from driving seat.

DIMENSIONS AND WEIGHT wheel base: 94.49 in, 240 cm; front and rear tracks: 49.16 in, 126 cm; length: 152.36 in, 387 cm; width: 59.06 in, 150 cm; height: 60.63 in, 154 cm; ground clearance: 5.91 in, 15 cm; weight: 1,323 lb, 600 kg; weight distribution: 61% front, 39% rear; turning circle: 36.4 ft, 11.1 m; fuel tank: 5.5 imp gal, 6.6 US gal, 25 l.

CITROËN Mehari

CITROËN Dyane 6

BODY saloon/sedan: 4+1 doors; 4 seats, bench front seats; fully opening canvas·sunshine roof.

PRACTICAL INSTRUCTIONS fuel: 80-85 oct petrol; oil: engine 4 imp pt, 4.9 US pt, 2.3 l, SAE 20W-50, change every 4,600 miles, 7,500 km - gearbox 1.6 imp pt, 1.9 US pt, 0.9 l, SAE 80, change every 14,000 miles, 22,500 km - final drive 0.9 imp pt, 1.1 US pt, 0.5 l; greasing: every 1,900 miles, 3,000 km, 4 points; sparking plug: 225°; tappet clearances: inlet 0.008 in, 0.20 mm, exhaust 0.008 in, 0.20 mm; valve timing: 0°5' 49°15' 35°55' 3°30'; tyre pressure: front 20 psi, 1.4 atm, rear 26 psi, 1.8 atm.

OPTIONALS centrifugal clutch; separate front seats; folding rear seat.

LN

PRICE EX WORKS: 20.700** francs

ENGINE front, 4 stroke; 2 cylinders, horizontally opposed; 36.7 cu in, 602 cc (2.91 x 2.76 in, 74 x 70 mm); compression ratio: 9:1; max power (DIN): 32 hp (23.6 kW) at 5,750 rpm; max torque (DIN): 30 lb ft, 4.2 kg m (41.2 Nm) at 3,500 rpm; max engine rpm: 6,150; 53.3 hp/l (39.2 kW/l); cast iron block, light alloy head, dry liners, light alloy sump, hemispherical combustion chambers; 2 crankshaft bearings; valves: overhead, Vee-slanted at 70°, push-rods and rockers; camshafts: 1, central, lower; lubrication: rotary pump, filter in sump, oil cooler, 4.8 imp pt, 5.7 US pt, 2.7 l; 1 Solex 26/35 CSIC downdraught twin barrel carburettor; fuel feed: mechanical pump; air-cooled.

TRANSMISSION driving wheels: front (double homokinetic joints); clutch: single dry plate (diaphragm); gearbox: mechanical; gears: 4, II, III and IV synchronized; ratios: I 4.545, II 2.500, III 1.643, IV 1.147, rev 4.184; lever: central; final drive: spiral bevel; axle ratio: 4.375; width of rims: 4''; tyres: 135 SR x 13.

PERFORMANCE max speeds: (I) 19 mph, 30 km/h; (II) 34 mph, 55 km/h; (III) 52 mph, 84 km/h; (IV) 75 mph, 120 km/h; power-weight ratio: 48.6 lb/hp (70 lb/kW), 22.1 kg/hp (29.9 kg/kW); carrying capacity: 728 lb, 320 kg; acceleration: standing 1/4 mile 23.2 sec; speed in top at 1,000 rpm: 12 mph, 20 km/h; consumption: 47.9 m/imp gal, 39.9 m/US gal, 5.9 l x 100 km at 56 mph, 90 km/h.

CHASSIS platform; front suspension: independent, swinging leading arms, 2 friction dampers, 2 inertia-type patter dampers; rear: independent, swinging longitudinal trailing arms linked to front suspension by longitudinal coil springs, 2 inertia-type patter dampers, 2 telescopic dampers.

STEERING rack-and-pinion; turns lock to lock: 3.33.

BRAKES front disc (diameter 9.49 in, 24.1 cm), rear drum, rear compensator; lining area: front 19.8 sq in, 128 sq cm, rear 24.5 sq in, 158 sq cm, total 44.3 sq in, 286 sq cm.

ELECTRICAL EQUIPMENT 12 V; 28 Ah battery; 420 W alternator; 2 headlamps, height adjustable from driving seat.

DIMENSIONS AND WEIGHT wheel base: 87.80 in, 223 cm; tracks: 50.79 in, 129 cm front, 48.82 in, 124 cm rear; length: 133.07 in, 338 cm; width: 59.84 in, 152 cm; height: 53.94 in, 137 cm; ground clearance: 4.72 in, 12 cm; weight: 1,557 lb, 706 kg; turning circle: 30.8 ft, 9.4 m; fuel tank: 8.8 imp gal, 10.6 US gal, 40 l.

BODY coupé; 2 + 1 doors; 4 seats, separate front and rear seats, reclining driver's seat, folding rear seats.

PRACTICAL INSTRUCTIONS fuel: 80-85 oct petrol; oil: engine 4 imp pt, 4.9 US pt, 2.3 l, SAE 20W-50, change every 4,600 miles, 7,500 km - gearbox 2.5 imp pt, 3 US pt, 1.4 l, SAE 80, change every 14,000 miles, 22,500 km - final drive 0.9 imp pt, 1.1 US pt, 0.5 l; greasing: every 4,600 miles, 7,500 km, 1 point; sparking plug: 225°; tappet clearances: inlet 0.008 in, 0.20 mm, exhaust 0.008 in, 0.20 mm; valve timing: 0°5' 49°15' 35°55' 3°30'; tyre pressure: front 20 psi, 1.4 atm, rear 26 psi, 1.8 atm.

OPTIONALS centrifugal clutch; rear window wiper-washer; heated rear window; metallic spray; reclining backrests.

LNA

See LN, except for:

PRICE EX WORKS: 21,900** francs

ENGINE 39.8 cu in, 652 cc (3.03 x 2.76 in, 77 x 70 mm); max power (DIN): 36 hp (26.5 kW) at 5,500 rpm; max torque (DIN): 38 lb ft, 5.3 kg m (52 Nm) at 3,500 rpm; max engine rpm: 5,850; 55.2 hp/l (40.6 kW/l); light alloy block and head; 3 crankshaft bearings; valves: overhead, Vee-slanted at 33°, push-rods and rockers; lubrication: rotary pump, filter in sump, oil cooler, 5.8 imp pt, 7 US pt, 3.3 l.

TRANSMISSION gears: 4, fully synchronized; axle ratio: 4.125.

CITROËN LN

PERFORMANCE max speeds: (I) 19 mph, 31 km/h; (II) 35 mph, 57 km/h; (III) 53 mph, 86 km/h; (IV) 77 mph, 125 km/h; power-weight ratio: 43.5 lb/hp (59.1 lb/kW), 19.7 kg/hp (26.8 kg/kW); acceleration: standing 1/4 mile 21.5 sec; speed in top at 1,000 rpm: 13.2 mph, 21.2 km/h; consumption: 54.3 m/imp gal, 45.2 m/US gal, 5.2 l x 100 km at 56 mph, 90 km/h.

ELECTRICAL EQUIPMENT 36 Ah battery; 460 W alternator; Thomson fully electronic ignition.

DIMENSIONS AND WEIGHT weight: 1,566 lb, 710 kg.

BODY luxury equipment.

PRACTICAL INSTRUCTIONS fuel: 98 oct petrol; oil: engine 5.3 imp pt, 6.3 US pt, 3 l, SAE 15W-40 (summer) 10W-30 (winter); valve timing: 7° 42° 35° 6°.

OPTIONALS centrifugal clutch not available.

Visa Spécial

PRICE EX WORKS: 22,660** francs

ENGINE front, longitudinal, slanted 7°13' to rear, 4 stroke; 2 cylinders, horizontally opposed; 39.8 cu in, 652 cc (3.03 x 2.76 in, 77 x 70 mm); compression ratio: 9:1; max power (DIN): 36 hp (26.5 kW) at 5,500 rpm; max torque (DIN): 38 lb ft, 5.3 kg m (52 Nm) at 3,500 rpm; max engine rpm: 5,850; 55.2 hp/l (40.6 kW/l); light alloy block and head; 3 crankshaft bearings; valves: overhead, Vee-slanted at 33°, push-rods and rockers; camshafts: 1, central; lubrication: rotary pump, filter in sump, oil cooler, 5.8 imp pt, 7 US pt, 3.3 l; 1 Solex 26/35 CSIC downdraught twin barrel carburettor; fuel feed: mechanical pump; air-cooled.

TRANSMISSION driving wheels: front (double homokinetic joints); clutch: single dry plate; gearbox: mechanical; gears: 4, fully synchronized; ratios: I 4.545, II 2.500, III 1.643, IV 1.147, rev 4.184; lever: central; final drive: spiral bevel; axle ratio: 4.125; width of rims: 4''; tyres: 135 SR x 13.

PERFORMANCE max speeds: (I) 19 mph, 31 km/h; (II) 35 mph, 57 km/h; (III) 53 mph, 86 km/h; (IV) 77 mph, 124 km/h; power-weight ratio: 45 lb/hp (61.2 lb/kW), 20.4 kg/h (27.7 kg/kW); carrying capacity: 728 lb, 330 kg; acceleration, standing 1/4 mile 21.9 sec; speed in top at 1,000 rpm: 13.2 mph, 21.2 km/h consumption: 49.6 m/imp gal, 41.3 m/US gal, 5.7 l x 100 km at 56 mph, 90 km/h.

CHASSIS integral; front suspension: independent, by McPherson, coil springs/telescopic damper struts, lower wishbones (trailing links), anti-roll bar; rear: independent, swinging longitudinal trailing arms, coil springs, telescopic dampers.

STEERING rack-and-pinion; turns lock to lock: 3.33.

BRAKES front disc (diameter 9.49 in, 24.1 cm), rear drum; lining area: front 23.9 sq in, 154 sq cm, rear 24.5 sq in, 158 sq cm, total 48.4 sq in, 312 sq cm.

CITROËN Visa Club

VISA SPÉCIAL

ELECTRICAL EQUIPMENT 12 V; 35 Ah battery; 460 W alternator; Thomson fully electronic ignition; 2 headlamps, height adjustable from driving seat.

DIMENSIONS AND WEIGHT wheel base: 95.67 in, 243 cm; tracks: 50.79 in, 129 cm front, 48.82 in, 124 cm rear; length: 145.28 in, 369 cm; width: 59.45 in, 151 cm; height: 55.51 in, 141 cm; ground clearance: 5.16 in, 13.1 cm; weight: 1,621 lb, 735 kg; weight distribution: 59% front, 41% rear; turning circle: 32.1 ft, 9.8 m; fuel tank: 8.8 imp gal, 10.6 US gal, 40 l.

BODY saloon/sedan; 4 + 1 doors; 4 seats, separate front seats.

PRACTICAL INSTRUCTIONS fuel: 98 oct petrol; oil: engine 5.3 imp pt, 6.3 US pt, 3 l, SAE 15W-40 (summer) 10W-30 (winter), change every 4,600 miles, 7,500 km - gearbox 5.3 imp pt, 6.3 US pt, 3 l, SAE 80 EP, change every 14,000 miles, 22,500 km - final drive 0.4 imp pt, 0.4 US pt, 0.2 l; greasing: none; tappet clearances: inlet 0.008 in, 0.20 mm; exhaust 0.008 in, 0.20 mm; valve timing: 7° 42° 35° 6°; tyre pressure: front 24 psi, 1.7 atm, rear 28 psi, 2 atm.

OPTIONALS heated rear window; rear window wiper-washer; metallic spray; reclining backrests.

Visa Club

See Visa Spécial, except for:

PRICE EX WORKS 23,300** francs

BODY luxury equipment; reclining backrests (standard).

OPTIONALS headrests on front seats; tinted glass.

Visa Super

See Visa Spécial, except for:

PRICE EX WORKS 25,800** francs

ENGINE Peugeot, transverse, slanted 72° to rear; 4 cylinders, in line; 68.6 cu in, 1,124 cc (2.83 x 2.72 in, 72 x 69 mm); compression ratio: 9.2:1; max power (DIN) 57 hp (42 kW) at 6,250 rpm; max torque (DIN) 59 lb ft, 8.2 kg m (80.4 Nm) at 3,000 rpm; max engine rpm: 6,500; 50.7 hp/l (37.4 kW/l); light alloy block and head, wet liners, bi-spherical combustion chambers; 5 crankshaft bearings; valves: overhead, Vee-slanted, rockers; camshafts: 1, overhead; lubrication: gear pump, full flow filter, 7.9 imp pt, 9.5 US pt, 4.5 l; Solex 32 PBISA 7 horizontal single barrel carburettor; sealed circuit cooling, liquid, expansion tank, 13.2 imp pt, 15.9 US pt, 7.5 l, electric thermostatic fan.

TRANSMISSION gearbox ratios: I 3.882, II 2.297, III 1.500, IV 1.042, rev 3.569; axle ratio: 3.562; width of rims: 4.5''; tyres: 145 SR x 13.

PERFORMANCE max speeds: (I) 24 mph, 39 km/h; (II) 40 mph, 65 km/h; (III) 62 mph, 100 km/h; (IV) 89 mph, 144 km/h; power-weight ratio: 30.9 lb/hp (42 lb/kW), 14 kg/hp (19 kg/kW); carrying capacity: 904 lb, 410 kg; acceleration: standing ¼ mile 19.9 sec; speed in top at 1,000 rpm: 17.3 mph, 27.8 km/h; consumption: 45.6 m/imp gal, 37.9 m/US gal, 6.2 l x 100 km at 56 mph, 90 km/h - 33.6 m/imp gal, 28 m/US gal, 8.4 l x 100 km at 75 mph, 120 km/h.

CHASSIS rear suspension: anti-roll bar.

ELECTRICAL EQUIPMENT Ducellier or Paris-Rhône distributor.

DIMENSIONS AND WEIGHT wheel base: 95.28 in, 242 cm; width: 60.39 in, 153 cm; height: 55.71 in, 141 cm; ground clearance: 5.91 in, 15 cm; weight: 1,764 lb, 800 kg; weight distribution: 62% front, 38% rear; turning circle: 32.5 ft, 9.9 m.

BODY folding rear seat.

PRACTICAL INSTRUCTIONS oil: engine 7.9 imp pt, 9.5 US pt, 4.5 l - gearbox 7.9 imp pt, 9.5 US pt, 4.5 l; tappet clearances: inlet 0.006 in, 0.15 mm, exhaust 0.010 in, 0.25 mm; valve timing: 5°20' 36°50' 36°50' 5°20'; tyre pressure: front 24 psi, 1.7 atm, rear 27 psi, 1.9 atm.

OPTIONALS headrests on front seats; tinted glass.

G Spécial Berline

PRICE IN GB: £ 2,797*
PRICE EX WORKS: 25,800** francs

ENGINE front, 4 stroke; 4 cylinders, horizontally opposed; 68.9 cu in, 1,129 cc (2.91 x 2.58 in, 74 x 65.6 mm); compression ratio: 9:1; max power (DIN): 56 hp (41.2 kW) at 5,750 rpm; max torque (DIN): 59 lb ft, 8.1 kg m (79.4 Nm) at 3,500 rpm; max engine rpm: 6,000; 49.6 hp/l (36.5 kW/l); light alloy block, head with cast iron liners, light alloy fins, hemispherical combustion chambers; 3 crankshaft bearings; valves: overhead, Vee-slanted; camshafts: 1, per block, overhead, cogged belt; lubrication: gear pump, full flow filter, oil cooler, 7 imp pt, 8.5 US pt, 4 l; 1 Solex 28 CIC 2 or Weber 30 DGS 14/250 downdraught twin barrel carburettor; fuel feed: mechanical pump; air-cooled.

TRANSMISSION driving wheels: front; clutch: single dry plate (diaphragm); gearbox: mechanical; gears: 4, fully synchronized; ratios: I 3.818, II 2.295, III 1.500, IV 1.031, rev 4.182; lever: central; final drive: spiral bevel; axle ratio: 4.125; width of rims: 4.5''; tyres: 145 SR x 15.

PERFORMANCE max speeds: (I) 28 mph, 45 km/h; (II) 45 mph, 73 km/h; (III) 71 mph, 114 km/h; (IV) 93 mph, 149 km/h; power-weight ratio: 36.4 lb/hp (49.5 lb/kW), 16.5 kg/hp (22.4 kg/kW); carrying capacity: 904 lb, 410 kg; acceleration: standing ¼ mile 20.7 sec; speed in top at 1,000 rpm: 16.4 mph, 26.4 km/h; consumption: 44.1 m/imp gal, 36.8 m/US gal, 6.4 l x 100 km at 56 mph, 90 km/h - 33.6 m/imp gal, 28 m/US gal, 8.4 l x 100 km at 75 mph, 120 km/h.

CHASSIS integral; front suspension: independent, wishbones, hydropneumatic suspension, anti-roll bar, automatic levelling control; rear: independent, swinging trailing arms, hydropneumatic suspension, anti-roll bar, automatic levelling control.

STEERING rack-and-pinion; turns lock to lock: 3.80.

BRAKES disc (front diameter 10.63 in, 27 cm, rear diameter 7.01 in, 17.8 cm), servo; lining area: front 22.6 sq in, 146 sq cm, rear 11.2 sq in, 72 sq cm, total 33.8 sq in, 218 sq cm.

ELECTRICAL EQUIPMENT 12 V; 40 Ah battery; 490 W alternator; Sev distributor; 2 headlamps.

DIMENSIONS AND WEIGHT wheel base: 100.39 in, 255 cm; tracks: 54.33 in, 138 cm front, 52.36 in, 133 cm rear; length: 162.20 in, 412 cm; width: 63.39 in, 161 cm; constant height 53.15 in, 135 cm; ground clearance (variable): 6.06 in, 15.4 cm; weight: 2,040 lb, 925 kg; weight distribution: 63% front, 37% rear turning circle: 34.1 ft, 10.4 m; fuel tank: 9.5 imp gal, 11.4 US gal, 43 l.

BODY saloon/sedan; 4 doors; 5 seats, separate front seat reclining backrests.

PRACTICAL INSTRUCTIONS fuel: 98 oct peetrol; oil: engine 7 imp pt, 8.5 US pt, 4 l, SAE 20W-50, change ever 4,600 miles, 7,500 km - gearbox and final drive 2.5 imp pt, 3 US pt, 1.4 l, SAE 90, change every 14,000 miles, 22,500 km - hydropneumatic suspension 7.4 imp pt, 8.9 US pt, 4.2 l; greasing: none; sparking plug: 200°; tappet clearances: inlet 0.008 in, 0.20 mm, exhaust 0.008 in, 0.20 mm; valve timing: 4°10' 31°50' 36°10' 0°20'; tyre pressure: front 26 psi, 1.8 atm, rear 27 psi, 1.9 atm.

OPTIONALS folding rear seat; heated rear window; tinted glass; sunshine roof; metallic spray.

GS X

See G Spécial Berline, except for:

PRICE EX WORKS: 26,850** francs

TRANSMISSION axle ratio: 4.375.

PERFORMANCE power-weight ratio: 36.8 lb/hp (50 lb/kW), 16.7 kg/hp (22.7 kg/kW); carrying capacity: 882 lb, 400 kg; acceleration: standing ¼ mile 20.3 sec; speed in top at 1,000 rpm: 15.5 mph, 24.9 km/h; consumption: 43.5 m/imp gal, 36.2 m/US gal, 6.5 l x 100 km at 56 mph, 90 km/h - 32.5 m/imp gal, 27 m/US gal, 8.7 l x 100 km at 75 mph 120 km/h.

ELECTRICAL EQUIPMENT 45 Ah battery.

DIMENSIONS AND WEIGHT weight: 2,062 lb, 935 kg.

BODY built-in headrests on front seats; luxury equipment

G Spécial Break

See G Spécial Berline, except for:

PRICE IN GB: £ 3,046*
PRICE EX WORKS: 27,250** francs

PERFORMANCE max speed: 91 mph, 146 km/h; power weight ratio: 36.8 lb/hp (50 lb/kW), 16.7 kg/hp (22.7 kg/kW); carrying capacity: 893 lb, 405 kg; acceleration: standing ¼ mile 20.9 sec; consumption: 43.5 m/imp gal, 36.2 m/US gal, 6.5 l x 100 km at 56 mph, 90 km/h - 32. m/imp gal, 27 m/US gal, 8.7 l x 100 km at 75 mph 120 km/h.

DIMENSIONS AND WEIGHT ground clearance (variable) 5.91 in, 15 cm; weight: 2,062 lb, 935 kg.

BODY estate car/st. wagon; 4 + 1 doors; rear window wiper-washer; folding rear seat (standard).

OPTIONALS sunshine roof not available.

GS Club Berline

See G Spécial Berline, except for:

PRICE IN GB: £ 3,099*
PRICE EX WORKS: 28,250** francs

ENGINE 74.6 cu in, 1,222 cc (3.03 x 2.58 in, 77 x 65.6 mm) compression ratio: 8.2:1; max power (DIN) 59 hp (43.4 kW) at 5,750 rpm; max torque (DIN) 64 lb ft, 8.9 kg m (87.3 Nm) at 3,250 rpm; max engine rpm: 6,500; 48.3 hp/l (35.5 kW/l); 1 Solex 28 CIC or Weber 30 DGS 11/250 downdraugh twin barrel carburettor.

TRANSMISSION gearbox ratios: I 3.818, II 2.294, III 1.500 IV 1.097, rev 4.182.

PERFORMANCE max speeds: (I) 29 mph, 46 km/h; (II) 4 mph, 77 km/h; (III) 72 mph, 116 km/h; (IV) 94 mph, 15 km/h; power-weight ratio: 34.8 lb/hp (47.3 lb/kW), 15. kg/hp (21.4 kg/kW); acceleration: standing ¼ mile 19.7 sec speed in top at 1,000 rpm: 15.4 mph, 24.8 km/h; consump tion: 41.5 m/imp gal, 34.6 m/US gal, 6.8 l x 100 km a

CITROËN GS Club Berline

56 mph, 90 km/h - 29.4 m/imp gal, 24.5 m/US gal, 9.6 l x 100 km at 75 mph, 120 km/h.

DIMENSIONS AND WEIGHT weight: 2,051 lb, 930 kg.

PRACTICAL INSTRUCTIONS valve timing: 5°30' 34°30' 32° 4°30'.

GS Club Berline C Matic

See GS Club Berline, except for:

PRICE IN GB: £ 3,304*
PRICE EX WORKS: 29,750 francs**

TRANSMISSION gearbox: semi-automatic transmission, hydraulic torque converter and planetary gears with 3 ratios, max ratio of converter at stall 2, possible manual selection; ratios: I 2.786, II 1.700, III 1.120, rev 2.500.

PERFORMANCE max speeds: (I) 42 mph, 68 km/h; (II) 63 mph, 101 km/h; (III) 92 mph, 148 km/h; power-weight ratio: 35.2 lb/hp (47.9 lb/kW), 16 kg/hp (21.7 kg/kW); carrying capacity: 889 lb, 403 kg; acceleration: standing ¼ mile 20.9 sec; speed in top at 1,000 rpm: 15.4 mph, 24.8 km/h; consumption: 38.2 m/imp gal, 31.8 m/US gal, 7.4 l x 100 km at 56 mph, 90 km/h - 27.4 m/imp gal, 22.8 m/US gal, 10.3 l x 100 km at 75 mph, 120 km/h.

DIMENSIONS AND WEIGHT weight: 2,077 lb, 942 kg; weight distribution: 65% front, 35% rear.

CITROËN G Spécial Break

CITROËN GS X3

GS Club Break

See GS Club Berline, except for:

PRICE IN GB: £ 3,318*
PRICE EX WORKS: 29,700 francs**

PERFORMANCE max speed: 93 mph, 149 km/h; power-weight ratio: 35.1 lb/hp (47.8 lb/kW), 15.9 kg/hp (21.6 kg/kW); carrying capacity: 882 lb, 400 kg; consumption: 41.5 m/imp gal, 34.6 m/US gal, 6.8 l x 100 km at 56 mph, 90 km/h - 28.8 m/imp gal, 24 m/US gal, 9.8 l x 100 km at 75 mph, 120 km/h.

DIMENSIONS AND WEIGHT weight: 2,073 lb, 940 kg.

BODY estate car/st. wagon; 4 + 1 doors; rear window wiper-washer.

OPTIONALS Targa equipment; sunshine roof not available.

GS X3

See G Spécial Berline, except for:

PRICE EX WORKS: 29,800 francs**

ENGINE 79.3 cu in, 1,299 cc (3.13 x 2.58 in, 79.4 x 65.6 mm); compression ratio: 8.7:1; max power (DIN): 65 hp (47.8 kW) at 5,500 rpm; max torque (DIN): 72 lb ft, 10 kg m (98.1 Nm) at 3,500 rpm; max engine rpm: 6,500; 50 hp/l (36.8 kW/l); 1 Weber 30 DGS 13/250 downdraught twin barrel carburettor.

CITROËN GS X3

TRANSMISSION gearbox ratios: I 3.818, II 2.294, III 1.500, IV 1.097, rev 4.182.

PERFORMANCE max speeds: (I) 29 mph, 46 km/h; (II) 42 mph, 67 km/h; (III) 73 mph, 118 km/h; (IV) 98 mph, 158 km/h; power-weight ratio: 31.9 lb/hp (43.4 lb/kW), 14.5 kg/hp (19.7 kg/kW); carrying capacity: 882 lb, 400 kg; acceleration: standing ¼ mile 19.1 sec; speed in top at 1,000 rpm: 15.4 mph, 24.8 km/h; consumption: 41.5 m/imp gal, 34.6 m/US gal, 6.8 l x 100 km at 56 mph, 90 km/h - 29.1 m/imp gal, 24.2 m/US gal, 9.7 l x 100 km at 75 mph, 120 km/h.

ELECTRICAL EQUIPMENT 45 Ah battery.

DIMENSIONS AND WEIGHT weight: 2,073 lb, 940 kg.

BODY heated rear window (standard).

PRACTICAL INSTRUCTIONS valve timing: 5°30' 34°30' 32° 4°30'.

GS Pallas

See GS Club Berline, except for:

PRICE IN GB: £ 3,421*
PRICE EX WORKS: 30,350 francs**

PERFORMANCE power-weight ratio: 35.3 lb/hp (48 lb/kW), 16 kg/hp (21.8 kg/kW).

DIMENSIONS AND WEIGHT weight: 2,084 lb, 945 kg.

BODY (standard) luxury equipment, heated rear window, metallic spray.

GS Pallas C Matic

See GS Pallas, except for:

PRICE IN GB: £ 3,626*
PRICE EX WORKS: 31,850 francs**

TRANSMISSION gearbox: semi-automatic transmission, hydraulic torque converter and planetary gears with 3 ratios, max ratio of converter at stall 2, possible manual selection; ratios: I 2.786, II 1.700, III 1.120, rev 2.500.

PERFORMANCE max speeds: (I) 39 mph, 62 km/h; (II) 63 mph, 101 km/h; (III) 92 mph, 148 km/h; power-weight ratio: 35.8 lb/hp (48.6 lb/kW), 16.2 kg/hp (22 kg/kW); carrying capacity: 856 lb, 388 kg; acceleration: standing ¼ mile 20.9 sec; speed in top at 1,000 rpm: 15.1 mph, 24.3 km/h; consumption: 38.2 m/imp gal, 31.8 m/US gal, 7.4 l x 100 km at 56 mph, 90 km/h - 27.4 m/imp gal, 22.8 m/US gal, 10.3 l x 100 km at 75 mph, 120 km/h.

DIMENSIONS AND WEIGHT weight: 2,110 lb, 957 kg; weight distribution: 63.5% front, 36.5% rear.

CX 2000 Confort

PRICE IN GB: £ 4,967* (with power steering)
PRICE EX WORKS: 38,960 francs**

ENGINE front, transverse, slanted 30° to front, 4 stroke; 4 cylinders, in line; 121.1 cu in, 1,985 cc (3.39 x 3.37 in, 86 x 85.5 mm); compression ratio: 9:1; max power (DIN): 102 hp (75.1 kW) at 5,500 rpm; max torque (DIN): 112 lb ft, 15.5 kg m (152 Nm) at 3,000 rpm; max engine rpm: 5,600; 51.4 hp/l (37.8 kW/l); cast iron block, light alloy head; 5 crankshaft bearings; valves: overhead, Vee-slanted at 60°, push-rods and rockers; camshafts: 1, side; lubrication: rotary pump, full flow filter, 9.3 imp pt, 11.2 US pt, 5.3 l; 1 Weber 34 DMTR 25/250 downdraught twin barrel carburettor; fuel feed: mechanical pump; water-cooled, 18.7 imp pt, 22.4 US pt, 10.6 l, electric thermostatic fan.

TRANSMISSION driving wheels: front; clutch: single dry plate (diaphragm); gearbox: mechanical; gears: 4, fully synchronized; ratios: I 3.166, II 1.833, III 1.133, IV 0.800, rev 3.153; lever: central; final drive: spiral bevel; axle ratio: 4.769; width of rims: 5.5''; tyres: 185 SR x 14 front, 175 SR x 14 rear.

PERFORMANCE max speeds: (I) 29 mph, 47 km/h; (II) 50 mph, 81 km/h; (III) 81 mph, 131 km/h; (IV) 108 mph, 174 km/h; power-weight ratio: 27.3 lb/hp (37.1 lb/kW), 12.4 kg/hp (16.8 kg/kW); carrying capacity: 1,091 lb, 495 kg; acceleration: standing ¼ mile 18.3 sec; speed in top at 1,000 rpm: 19.3 mph, 31 km/h; consumption: 34.4 m/imp gal, 28.7 m/US gal, 8.2 l x 100 km at 56 mph, 90 km/h - 27.7 m/imp gal, 23.1 m/US gal, 10.2 l x 100 km at 75 mph, 120 km/h.

CHASSIS integral with front and rear subframes; front suspension: independent, wishbones, hydropneumatic suspension, anti-roll bar, automatic levelling control; rear: independent, swinging trailing arms, hydropneumatic suspension, anti-roll bar, automatic levelling control.

CX 2000 CONFORT

STEERING rack-and-pinion; turns lock to lock: 4.50.

BRAKES disc (front diameter 10.24 in, 26 cm, rear diameter 8.82 in, 22.4 cm), internal radial fins, rear compensator, servo; lining area: front 40.3 sq in, 260 sq cm, rear 34.7 sq in, 224 sq cm, total 75 sq in, 484 sq cm.

ELECTRICAL EQUIPMENT 12 V; 45 Ah battery; 1,008 W alternator; Ducellier distributor; 2 halogen headlamps.

DIMENSIONS AND WEIGHT wheel base: 111.81 in, 284 cm; tracks: 57.87 in, 147 cm front, 53.54 in, 136 cm rear; length: 183.46 in, 466 cm; width: 68.11 in, 173 cm; height: 53.54 in, 136 cm; ground clearance: 6.10 in, 15.5 cm; weight: 2,789 lb, 1,265 kg; weight distribution: 67% front, 33% rear; turning circle: 38.7 ft, 11.8 m; fuel tank: 15 imp gal, 18 US gal, 68 l.

BODY saloon/sedan; 4 doors; 5 seats, separate front seats, reclining backrests, built-in headrests, heated rear window.

PRACTICAL INSTRUCTIONS fuel: 95 oct petrol; oil: engine 8.1 imp pt, 9.7 US pt, 4.6 l, SAE 20W-50, change every 4,600 miles, 7,500 km - gearbox and final drive 2.8 imp pt, 3.4 US pt, 1.6 l, SAE 80, change every 14,000 miles, 22,500 km - hydraulic suspension 7.4 imp pt, 8.9 US pt, 4.2 l; greasing: none; sparking plug: 225°; tappet clearances: inlet 0.006 in, 0.15 mm, exhaust 0.008 in, 0.20 mm;

PRACTICAL INSTRUCTIONS tyre pressure: front 31 psi, 2.2 atm, rear 31 psi, 2.2 atm.

OPTIONALS metallic spray.

CX 2000 Super

See CX 2000 Confort, except for:

PRICE IN GB: £ 5,199* (with power steering)
PRICE EX WORKS: 41,900** francs

PERFORMANCE power-weight ratio: 29.1 lb/hp (39.5 lb/kW), 13.2 kg/hp (17.9 kg/kW); carrying capacity: 915 lb, 415 kg.

DIMENSIONS AND WEIGHT weight: 2,966 lb, 1,345 kg.

BODY luxury equipment; electric front windows.

OPTIONALS metallic spray.

CX 2000 Pallas

See CX 2000 Confort, except for:

PRICE EX WORKS: 44,700** francs

PERFORMANCE power-weight ratio: 29.1 lb/hp (39.5 lb/kW), 13.2 kg/hp (17.9 kg/kW); carrying capacity: 915 lb, 415 kg.

DIMENSIONS AND WEIGHT weight: 2,966 lb, 1,345 kg.

BODY luxury equipment; metallic spray.

CX 2400 Super

See CX 2000 Confort, except for:

PRICE IN GB: £ 5,814* (with power steering)
PRICE EX WORKS: 44,300** francs

ENGINE 143.2 cu in, 2,347 cc (3.68 x 3.37 in, 93.5 x 85.5 mm); compression ratio: 8.75:1; max power (DIN): 115 hp (84.6 kW) at 5,500 rpm; max torque (DIN): 133 lb ft, 18.3 kg m (179.5 Nm) at 2,750 rpm; max engine rpm: 5,750; 49 hp/l (36 kW/l); 1 Weber 34 DMTR 35/250 or Solex 34 CICF downdraught twin barrel carburettor.

TRANSMISSION tyres: 185 HR x 14 front, 175 HR x 14 rear.

PERFORMANCE max speeds: (I) 29 mph, 46 km/h; (II) 49 mph, 79 km/h; (III) 80 mph, 128 km/h; (IV) 112 mph, 181 km/h; power-weight ratio: 24.9 lb/hp (33.9 lb/kW), 11.3 kg/hp (15.4 kg/kW); carrying capacity: 1,080 lb, 490 kg; acceleration: standing ¼ mile 17.5 sec; consumption: 34 m/imp gal, 28.3 m/US gal, 8.3 l x 100 km at 56 mph, 90 km/h - 26.9 m/imp gal, 22.4 m/US gal, 10.5 l x 100 km at 75 mph, 120 km/h.

ELECTRICAL EQUIPMENT 55 Ah battery.

DIMENSIONS AND WEIGHT weight: 2,867 lb, 1,300 kg.

PRACTICAL INSTRUCTIONS sparking plug: 175°; valve timing: 0°30' 42°30' 38°30' 4°30'.

OPTIONALS « C Matic » semi-automatic transmission, hydraulic torque converter and planetary gears with 3 ratios (I 1.944, II 1.133, III 0.800, rev 2.389), max speeds (I) 45 mph, 72 km/h, (II) 77 mph, 124 km/h, (III) 110 mph, 177 km/h, acceleration: standing ¼ mile 19.3 sec, consumption: 24.6 m/imp gal, 20.5 m/US gal, 11.5 l x 100 km at 75 mph, 120 km/h; 5-speed fully synchronized mechanical gearbox (I 3.166, II 1.833, III 1.250, IV 0.939, V 0.733, rev 3.153), 4.357 axle ratio, max speed 112 mph, 180 km/h, acceleration: standing ¼ mile 17.9 sec, speed in top at 1,000 rpm: 23 mph, 37 km/h, consumption: 30.1 m/imp gal, 25 m/US gal, 9.4 l x 100 km at 75 mph, 120 km/h.

CX 2400 Break Super

See CX 2400 Super, except for:

PRICE IN GB: £ 5,972* (with power steering)
PRICE EX WORKS: 49,600** francs

TRANSMISSION tyres: 185 SR x 14 front and rear.

PERFORMANCE max speed: 108 mph, 174 km/h; power-weight ratio: 26.9 lb/hp (36.6 lb/kW), 12.2 kg/hp (16.6 kg/kW); carrying capacity: 1,521 lb, 690 kg; acceleration: standing ¼ mile 18 sec; consumption: 30.7 m/imp gal, 25.6 m/US gal, 9.2 l x 100 km at 56 mph, 90 km/h - 24.6 m/imp gal, 20.5 m/US gal, 11.5 l x 100 km at 75 mph, 120 km/h.

CITROËN CX 2000/2400 Pallas

valve timing: 0°30' 42°30' 38°30' 0°30'; tyre pressure: front 27 psi, 2 atm, rear 30 psi, 2.1 atm.

OPTIONALS power steering; tinted glass; electric sunshine roof; air-conditioning.

CX 2000 Break Confort

See CX 2000 Confort, except for:

PRICE EX WORKS: 44,260** francs

TRANSMISSION tyres: 185 SR x 14 front and rear.

PERFORMANCE max speed: 106 mph, 171 km/h; power-weight ratio: 29.9 lb/hp (40.7 lb/kW), 13.6 kg/hp (18.4 kg/kW); carrying capacity: 1,510 lb, 685 kg; acceleration: standing ¼ mile 19.3 sec; consumption: 33.6 m/imp gal, 28 m/US gal, 8.4 l x 100 km at 56 mph, 90 km/h - 26.2 m/imp gal, 21.8 m/US gal, 10.8 l x 100 km at 75 mph, 120 km/h.

CHASSIS reinforced suspension.

BRAKES lining area: front 34.1 sq in, 220 sq cm, rear 22.5 sq in, 145 sq cm, total 56.6 sq in, 365 sq cm.

DIMENSIONS AND WEIGHT wheel base: 121.65 in, 309 cm; length: 194.96 in, 495 cm; height: 57.48 in, 146 cm; weight: 3,054 lb, 1,385 kg; weight distribution: 63.5% front, 36.5% rear; turning circle: 41.7 ft, 12.7 m.

BODY estate car/st. wagon; 4 + 1 doors; folding rear seat; heated rear window with wiper-washers.

CITROËN CX 2400 Break Super

CITROËN CX Prestige

CHASSIS reinforced suspension.

BRAKES lining area: front 34.1 sq in, 220 sq cm, rear 22.5 sq in, 145 sq cm, total 56.6 sq in, 365 sq cm.

DIMENSIONS AND WEIGHT wheel base: 121.65 in, 309 cm; length: 194.96 in, 495 cm; height: 57.48 in, 146 cm; weight: 3,098 lb, 1,405 kg; weight distribution: 64% front, 36% rear; turning circle: 41.7 ft, 12.7 m.

BODY estate car/st. wagon; 4 + 1 doors; folding rear seat; heated rear window with wiper-washer.

PRACTICAL INSTRUCTIONS tyre pressure: front 30 psi, 2.1 atm, rear 31 psi, 2.2 atm.

OPTIONALS metallic spray; « C Matic » semi-automatic transmission and 5-speed fully synchronized mechanical gearbox not available.

CX 2400 Familiale Super

See CX 2400 Break Super, except for:

PRICE IN GB: £ 6,082* (with power steering)
PRICE EX WORKS: 51,100** francs

PERFORMANCE power-weight ratio: 27.1 lb/hp (36.9 lb/kW), 12.3 kg/hp (16.7 kg/kW); carrying capacity: 1,488 lb, 675 kg.

DIMENSIONS AND WEIGHT weight: 3,120 lb, 1,415 kg.

BODY 8 seats.

CX 2400 Pallas

See CX 2400 Super, except for:

PRICE IN GB: £ 6,399* (with power steering)
PRICE EX WORKS: 47,100** francs

PERFORMANCE power-weight ratio: 25.2 lb/hp (34.3 lb/kW), 11.4 kg/hp (15.5 kg/kW); carrying capacity: 1,047 lb, 475 kg.

DIMENSIONS AND WEIGHT weight: 2,900 lb, 1,315 kg.

BODY luxury equipment; metallic spray.

CX 2400 GTI

See CX 2400 Super, except for:

PRICE IN GB: £ 6,979*
PRICE EX WORKS: 55,400** francs

ENGINE max power (DIN): 128 hp ,94.2 kW) at 4,800 rpm; max torque (DIN): 146 lb ft, 20.1 kg m (197.1 Nm) at 3,600 rpm; max engine rpm: 5,500; 54.5 hp/l (40.1 kW/l); Bosch L-Jetronic fuel injection system; fuel feed: electric pump; cooling system: 21.6 imp pt, 26 US pt, 12.3 l.

TRANSMISSION gears: 5, fully synchronized; ratios: I 3.166, II 1.833, III 1.250, IV 0.939, rev 3.153; axle ratio: 4.769; width of rims: 6''; tyres: 185 HR x 14.

PERFORMANCE max speeds: (I) 27 mph, 44 km/h; (II) 47 mph, 76 km/h; (III) 69 mph, 111 km/h; (IV) 92 mph,

148 km/h; (V) 117 mph, 189 km/h; power-weight ratio: 23.7 lb/hp (32.2 lb/kW), 10.7 kg/hp (14.6 kg/kW); acceleration: standing ¼ mile 17.1 sec; speed in top at 1,000 rpm: 21 mph, 33.8 km/h; consumption: 34.9 m/imp gal, 29 m/US gal, 8.1 l x 100 km at 56 mph, 90 km/h - 28 m/imp gal, 23.3 m/US gal, 10.1 l x 100 km at 75 mph, 120 km/h.

STEERING servo, variable ratio (standard); turns lock to lock: 2.50.

ELECTRICAL EQUIPMENT 60 Ah battery; 1,120 W alternator.

DIMENSIONS AND WEIGHT weight: 3,032 lb, 1,375 kg; weight distribution: 68% front, 32% rear.

BODY metallic spray.

PRACTICAL INSTRUCTIONS tyre pressure: front 30 psi, 2.1 atm, rear 31 psi, 2.2 atm.

OPTIONALS leather upholstery; « C Matic » semi-automatic transmission not available.

CX 2400 Pallas Injection C Matic

See CX 2400 GTI, except for:

PRICE IN GB: £ 6,998*
PRICE EX WORKS: 56,100** francs

TRANSMISSION gearbox: « C Matic » semi-automatic transmission, hydraulic torque converter and planetary gears with 3 ratios, possible manual selection; ratios: I 2.176, II 1.133, III 0.750, rev 2.389; width of rims: 5.5''.

PERFORMANCE max speeds: (I) 39 mph, 62 km/h; (II) 73 mph, 118 km/h; (III) 112 mph, 180 km/h; power-weight ratio: 23.9 lb/hp (32.5 lb/kW), 10.8 kg/hp (14.7 kg/kW); carrying capacity: 1,021 lb, 463 kg; acceleration: standing ¼ mile 18.6 sec; speed in top at 1,000 rpm: 20.5 mph, 33 km/h; consumption: 31.4 m/imp gal, 26.1 m/US gal, 9 l x 100 km at 56 mph, 90 km/h - 24.1 m/imp gal, 20.1 m/US gal, 11.7 l x 100 km at 75 mph, 120 km/h.

DIMENSIONS AND WEIGHT weight: 3,058 lb, 1,387 kg; weight distribution: 68.9% front, 31.1% rear.

PRACTICAL INSTRUCTIONS oil: semi-automatic transmission 7.9 imp pt, 9.5 US pt, 4.5 l.

CX Prestige

See CX 2400 GTI, except for:

PRICE IN GB: £ 9,255*
PRICE EX WORKS: 70,400** francs

TRANSMISSION axle ratio: 4.357; width of rims: 5.5''.

PERFORMANCE max speeds: (I) 27 mph, 43 km/h; (II) 47 mph, 75 km/h; (III) 52 mph, 84 km/h; (IV) 91 mph, 147 km/h; (V) 118 mph, 190 km/h; power-weight ratio: 25.4 lb/hp (34.5 lb/kW), 11.5 kg/hp (15.7 kg/kW); carrying capacity: 992 lb, 450 kg; acceleration: standing ¼ mile 17.6 sec; speed in top at 1,000 rpm: 23 mph, 37 km/h; consumption: 37.2 m/imp gal, 30.9 m/US gal, 7.6 l x 100 km at 56 mph, 90 km/h - 29.1 m/imp gal, 24.2 m/US gal, 9.7 l x 100 km at 75 mph, 120 km/h.

ELECTRICAL EQUIPMENT 70 Ah battery.

DIMENSIONS AND WEIGHT wheel base: 121.65 in, 309 cm; length: 193.70 in, 492 cm; height: in, 137 cm; weight: 3,252 lb, 1,475 kg; weight distribution: 67.5% front, 32.5% rear.

BODY luxury equipment; metallic spray; air-conditioning.

PRACTICAL INSTRUCTIONS tyre pressure: front 31 psi, 2.2 atm, rear 31 psi, 2.2 atm.

OPTIONALS « C Matic » semi-automatic transmission with 3 ratios (I 2.176, II 1.133, III 0.750, rev 2.389), 4.769 axle ratio, max speed 112 mph, 180 km/h, acceleration standing ¼ mile 19.1 sec, speed in top at 1,000 rpm 20.5 mph, 33 km/h, consumption 31.4 m/imp gal, 26.1 m/US gal, 9 l x 100 km at 56 mph, 90 km/h - 24.1 m/imp gal, 20.1 m/US gal, 11.7 l x 100 km at 75 mph, 120 km/h; leather upholstery; tinted glass; vinyl roof.

CX 2500 Diesel Confort

See CX 2000 Confort, except for:

PRICE IN GB: £ 6,041* (with power steering)
PRICE EX WORKS: 45,760** francs

ENGINE Diesel, 4 stroke; 152.6 cu in, 2,500 cc (3.66 x 3.62 in, 93 x 92 mm); compression ratio: 22.25: 1; max power (DIN): 75 hp (55.2 kW) at 4,250 rpm; max torque (DIN): 111 lb ft, 15.3 kg m (150 Nm) at 2,000 rpm; max engine rpm: 4,525; 30 hp/l (22.1 kW/l); lubricating system: 8.3 imp pt, 9.9 US pt, 4.7 l; Roto-Diesel fuel injection; cooling system: 21.6 imp pt, 26 US pt, 12.3 l.

TRANSMISSION axle ratio: 4.538.

PERFORMANCE max speeds: (I) 23 mph, 37 km/h; (II) 40 mph, 64 km/h; (III) 65 mph, 104 km/h; (IV) 91 mph, 147 km/h; power-weight ratio: 39.1 lb/hp, 17.7 kg/hp (24.1 kg/kW); carrying capacity: 1,036 lb, 470 kg; acceleration: standing ¼ mile 20.7 sec; speed in top at 1,000 rpm: 20.3 mph, 32.6 km/h; consumption: 43.5 m/imp gal, 36.2 m/US gal, 6.5 l x 100 km at 56 mph, 90 km/h - 32.5 m/imp gal, 27 m/US gal, 8.7 l x 100 km at 75 mph, 120 km/h.

ELECTRICAL EQUIPMENT 88 Ah battery.

DIMENSIONS AND WEIGHT weight: 2,933 lb, 1,330 kg; weight distribution: 68.4% front, 31.6% rear.

PRACTICAL INSTRUCTIONS fuel: Diesel oil; oil: engine 8.1 imp pt, 9.7 US pt, 4.6 l, SAE 30, change every 3,100 miles, 5,000 km; tappet clearances: inlet 0.006 in, 0.15 mm, exhaust 0.008 in, 0.20 mm; valve timing: 2°52' 33°08' 37°48' 4°12'; tyre pressure: front 30 psi, 2.1 atm, rear 30 psi, 2.1 atm.

OPTIONALS 5-speed fully synchronized mechanical gearbox (I 3.166, II 1.833, III 1.250, IV 0.939, V 0.733, rev 3.153), max speed 97 mph, 156 km/h, acceleration standing ¼ mile 20.4 sec, speed in top at 1,000 rpm 22.1 mph, 35.5 km/h, consumption 46.3 m/imp gal, 38.6 m/US gal, 6.1 l x 100 km at 56 mph, 90 km/h - 34.9 m/imp gal, 29 m/US gal, 8.1 l x 100 km at 75 mph, 120 km/h.

CX 2500 Diesel Break Confort

See CX 2500 Diesel Confort, except for:

PRICE IN GB: £ 6,316* (with power steering)
PRICE EX WORKS: 51,060** francs

PERFORMANCE power-weight ratio: 42.6 lb/hp (57.9 lb/kW), 19.3 kg/hp (26.3 kg/kW); carrying capacity: 1,455 lb, 660 kg; acceleration: standing ¼ mile 21.6 sec.

DIMENSIONS AND WEIGHT wheel base: 121.65 in, 309 cm; length: 194.96 in, 495 cm; height: 57.48 in, 146 cm; weight: 3,197 lb, 1,450 kg; weight distribution: 64.8% front, 35.2% rear; turning circle: 41.7 ft, 12.7 m.

BODY estate car/st. wagon; 4 + 1 doors; folding rear seat; heated rear window with wiper-washer.

PRACTICAL INSTRUCTIONS tyre pressure: front 27 psi, 2 atm, rear 31 psi, 2.2 atm.

OPTIONALS metallic spray.

CX 2500 Diesel Super

See CX 2500 Diesel Confort, except for:

PRICE EX WORKS: 48,700** francs

PERFORMANCE power-weight ratio: 39.5 lb/hp (53.7 lb/kW), 17.9 kg/hp (24.4 kg/kW); carrying capacity: 1,003 lb, 455 kg.

DIMENSIONS AND WEIGHT weight 2,966 lb, 1,345 kg.

CX 2500 Diesel Break Super

See CX 2500 Diesel Confort, except for:

PRICE EX WORKS: 54,000** francs

PERFORMANCE power-weight ratio: 43.1 lb/hp (58.5 lb/kW), 19.5 kg/hp (26.5 kg/kW); carrying capacity: 1,422 lb, 645 kg; acceleration: standing ¼ mile 21.6 sec.

DIMENSIONS AND WEIGHT wheel base: 121.65 in, 309 cm; length: 194.96 in, 495 cm; height: 57.48 in, 146 cm; weight: 3,230 lb, 1,465 kg; weight distribution: 64.8% front, 35.2% rear; turning circle: 41.7 ft, 12.7 m.

BODY estate car/st. wagon; 4 + 1 doors; folding rear seat; heated rear window with wiper-washer.

PRACTICAL INSTRUCTIONS tyre pressure: front 27 psi, 2 atm, rear 31 psi, 2.2 atm.

OPTIONALS metallic spray.

CX 2500 Diesel Familiale Super

See CX 2500 Diesel Break Super, except for:

PRICE IN GB: £ 6,422* (with power steering)
PRICE EX WORKS: 55,500** francs

PERFORMANCE power-weight ratio: 43.2 lb/hp (58.7 lb/kW), 19.6 kg/hp (26.6 kg/kW); carrying capacity: 1,411 lb, 640 kg.

DIMENSIONS AND WEIGHT weight: 3,241 lb, 1,470 kg.

BODY 8 seats.

CX 2500 Diesel Pallas

See CX 2500 Diesel Confort, except for:

PRICE EX WORKS: 59,500** francs

PERFORMANCE power-weight ratio: 39.5 lb/hp (53.7 lb/kW), 17.9 kg/hp (24.4 kg/kW); carrying capacity: 1,003 lb, 455 kg.

DIMENSIONS AND WEIGHT weight: 2,966 lb, 1,345 kg.

BODY luxury equipment; metallic spray.

OPTIONALS leather upholstery.

MATRA-SIMCA   FRANCE

Rancho

PRICE IN GB: £ 5,650*
PRICE EX WORKS: 39,950** francs

ENGINE Simca, front, transverse, slanted 41° to rear, 4 stroke; 4 cylinders, in line; 88 cu in, 1,442 cc (3.02 x 3.07 in, 76.7 x 78 mm); compression ratio: 9.5:1; max power (DIN): 80 hp (58.9 kW) at 5,600 rpm; max torque (DIN): 87 lb ft, 12 kg m (117.7 Nm) at 3,000 rpm; max engine rpm: 6,000; 55.5 hp/l (40.8 kW/l); cast iron block, light alloy head; 5 crankshaft bearings; valves: overhead, in line, push-rods and rockers; camshafts: 1, side; lubrication: gear pump, full flow filter, 5.3 imp pt, 6.3 US pt, 3 l; 1 Weber 36 DCNVA downdraught twin barrel carburettor; fuel feed: mechanical pump; sealed circuit cooling, expansion tank, liquid, 10.6 imp pt, 12.7 US pt, 6 l, electric thermostatic fan.

TRANSMISSION driving wheels: front; clutch: single dry plate (diaphragm), hydraulically controlled; gearbox: mechanical; gears: 4, fully synchronized; ratios: I 3.900, II 2.312, III 1.524, IV 1.080, rev 3.769; lever: central; final drive: cylindrical gears; axle ratio: 3.706; width of rims: 5.5''; tyres: 185/70 SR x 14.

PERFORMANCE max speed: 90 mph, 145 km/h; power-weight ratio: 31.1 lb/hp (42.3 lb/kW), 14.1 kg/hp (19.2 kg/kW); carrying capacity: 1,147 lb, 520 kg; speed in top at 1,000 rpm: 17.6 mph, 28.4 km/h; consumption: 24.6 m/imp gal, 20.5 m/US gal, 11.5 l x 100 km at 75 mph, 120 km/h.

CHASSIS integral, box-type reinforced platform; front suspension: independent, wishbones, longitudinal torsion bars, anti-roll bar, telescopic dampers; rear: independent, swinging longitudinal trailing arms, transverse torsion bars, anti-roll bar, telescopic dampers.

STEERING rack-and-pinion; turns lock to lock: 3.75.

BRAKES front disc (diameter 9.37 in, 23.8 cm), rear drum, rear compensator, servo; swept area: front 158.8 sq in,

MATRA-SIMCA Rancho

1,024 sq cm, rear 90.2 sq in, 582 sq cm, total 249 sq in, 1,606 sq cm.

ELECTRICAL EQUIPMENT 12 V; 40 Ah battery; 40 A alternator; Chrysler transistorized ignition; 4 iodine headlamps.

DIMENSIONS AND WEIGHT wheel base: 99.21 in, 252 cm; tracks: 55.51 in, 141 cm front, 53.15 in, 135 cm rear; length: 169.68 in, 431 cm; width: 65.35 in, 166 cm; height: 68.11 in, 173 cm; ground clearance: 6.57 in, 16.7 cm front, 6.69 in, 17 cm rear; weight: 2,492 lb, 1,130 kg; turning circle: 36.1 ft, 11 m; fuel tank: 13.2 imp gal, 15.8 US gal, 60 l.

BODY estate car/st. wagon in plastic material; 2 doors; 5 seats, separate front seats, reclining backrests with built-in headrests; folding rear seat; heated rear window with wiper-washer.

PRACTICAL INSTRUCTIONS fuel: 98-100 oct petrol; oil: engine 5.3 imp pt, 6.3 US pt, 3 l, SAE 20W-40, change every 3,100 miles, 5,000 km - gearbox and final drive 1.9 imp pt, 2.3 US pt, 1.1 l, SAE 90 EP, change every 6,200 miles, 10,000 km; greasing: none.

VARIATIONS

ENGINE Simca, 8.8:1 compression ratio, max power (DIN) 78 hp (57.4 kW) at 5,600 rpm, max torque (DIN) 86 lb ft, 11.8 kg m (115.7 Nm) at 3,000 rpm, 54.1 hp/l (39.8 kW/l).
TRANSMISSION 3.937 axle ratio.
PERFORMANCE power-weight ratio 31.9 lb/hp (43.4 lb/kW), 14.5 kg/hp (19.7 kg/kW), consumption 23.5 m/imp gal, 19. m/US gal, 12 l x 100 km at 75 mph, 120 km/h.
PRACTICAL INSTRUCTIONS 85 oct petrol.

OPTIONALS light alloy wheels; metallic spray; tinted glass electric winch.

Bagheera

PRICE EX WORKS: 42,500** francs

ENGINE Simca, central, transverse, slanted 41° to rear, stroke; 4 cylinders, in line; 88 cu in, 1,442 cc (3.02 x 3.0 in, 76.7 x 78 mm); compression ratio: 9.5:1; max power (DIN): 84 hp (61.8 kW) at 5,600 rpm; max torque (DIN) 91 lb ft, 12.6 kg m (123.6 Nm) at 3,200 rpm; max engin rpm: 6,300; 58.3 hp/l (42.9 kW/l); cast iron block, light a loy head; 5 crankshaft bearings; valves: overhead, push rods and rockers; camshafts: 1, side; lubrication: gear pump full flow filter, 5.3 imp pt, 6.3 US pt, 3 l; 1 Weber 3 DCNF downdraught twin barrel carburettor; fuel feed: me chanical pump; sealed circuit cooling, expansion tank, ra diator on front, electric thermostatic fan, 17.6 imp pt, 21. US pt, 10 l.

TRANSMISSION driving wheels: rear; clutch: single dr plate (diaphragm), hydraulically controlled; gearbox: me chanical; gears: 4, fully synchronized; ratios: I 3.900, I 2.312, III 1.524, IV 1.080, rev 3.769; lever: central; fina

MATRA-SIMCA Bagheera

ive: cylindrical gears; axle ratio: 3.470; width of rims: 5.5''
res: 155 HR x 13 front, 185 HR x 13 rear.

PERFORMANCE max speed: 115 mph, 185 km/h; power-
eight ratio: 25.7 lb/hp (35 lb/kW), 11.7 kg/hp (15.9 kg/kW);
onsumption: 28.5 m/imp gal, 23.8 m/US gal, 9.9 l x 100 km.

HASSIS integral, box-type reinforced platform; front sus-
nsion: independent, wishbones, longitudinal torsion bars,
ti-roll bar, telescopic dampers; rear: independent, swing-
g longitudinal trailing arms, transverse torsion bars, anti-
ll bar, telescopic dampers.

TEERING rack-and-pinion; turns lock to lock: 3.25.

RAKES disc (front diameter 9.37 in, 23.8 cm, rear 9.21 in,
.4 cm), rear compensator, servo; swept area: front 158.8
q in, 1,024 sq cm, rear 161.6 sq in, 1,042 sq cm, total
20.4 sq in, 2,066 sq cm.

LECTRICAL EQUIPMENT 12 V; 40 Ah battery; 40 A alterna-
r; Ducellier distributor; 4 headlamps, 2 retractable iodine
ng-distance lights.

IMENSIONS AND WEIGHT wheel base: 93.31 in, 237 cm;
acks: 55.12 in, 140 cm front, 57.48 in, 146 cm rear; length:
7.87 in, 401 cm; width: 68.39 in, 174 cm; height: 48.03
, 122 cm; ground clearance: 6.73 in, 17.1 cm front, 7.48
, 19 cm rear; weight: 2,161 lb, 980 kg; weight distribution:
% front, 59% rear; turning circle: 32.8 ft, 10 m; fuel tank:
.3 imp gal, 14.8 US gal, 56 l.

ODY coupé in plastic material; 2 doors; 3 front seats in
row, separate driving seat, built-in headrests; heated
ar window.

RACTICAL INSTRUCTIONS fuel: 98-100 oct petrol; oil:
gine 5.3 imp pt, 6.3 US pt, 3 l, SAE 20W-40, change
ery 3,100 miles, 5,000 km - gearbox and final drive 1.9
p pt, 2.3 US pt, 1.1 l, SAE 90 EP, change every 6,200
les, 10,000 km; greasing: none; tyre pressure: front 20
i, 1.4 atm, rear 28 psi, 2 atm.

PTIONALS light alloy wheels; metallic spray; sunshine
of; tinted glass; electric windows.

Bagheera S

e Bagheera, except for:

RICE IN GB: £ 5,370*
RICE EX WORKS: 47,150** francs

NGINE max power (DIN): 90 hp (66.2 kW) at 5,800 rpm;
ax torque (DIN): 88 lb ft, 12.2 kg m (119.6 Nm) at 3,200
m; 62.4 hp/l (45.9 kW/l); 2 Weber 36 DCNF downdraught
in barrel carburettors.

ERFORMANCE max speed: 118 mph, 190 km/h; power-
eight ratio: 24.9 lb/hp (33.8 lb/kW), 11.3 kg/hp (15.3
/kW); consumpiton: 28 m/imp gal, 23.3 m/US gal, 10.1
x 100 km.

ECTRICAL EQUIPMENT 48 Ah battery; 50 A alternator.

MENSIONS AND WEIGHT weight: 2,238 lb, 1,015 kg.

ODY electric tinted glass (standard).

PEUGEOT 104 S Berline

PEUGEOT 104 S Berline

Bagheera X

See Bagheera S, except for:

PRICE EX WORKS: 51,350** francs

TRANSMISSION light alloy wheels.

BODY luxury equipment; heated rear window with wiper-
washer.

PEUGEOT   FRANCE

104 GL Berline

PRICE IN GB: £ 2,539*
PRICE EX WORKS: 23,250** francs

ENGINE front, transverse, slanted 72° to rear, 4 stroke; 4
cylinders, in line: 58.2 cu in, 954 cc (2.76 x 2.44 in, 70 x 62
mm); compression ratio: 8.8:1; max power (DIN): 44.5 hp
(32 kW) at 6,000 rpm; max torque (DIN): 45 lb ft, 6.2
kg m (61.3 Nm) at 3,000 rpm; max engine rpm: 6,250;
46.1 hp/l (34 kW/l); light alloy block and head, wet
liners, bi-hemispherical combustion chambers; 5 crankshaft bearings; valves: overhead, Vee-slanted, rockers;
camshafts: 1, overhead; lubrication: gear pump, full flow
filter, 7.9 imp pt, 9.5 US pt, 4.5 l; 1 Solex 32 HSA2 horizontal single barrel carburettor; fuel feed: mechanical
pump; water-cooled, 9.9 imp pt, 11.8 US pt, 5.6 l, electric thermostatic fan.

TRANSMISSION driving wheels: front; clutch: single dry
plate (diaphragm); gearbox: mechanical, in unit with engine
and final drive; gears: 4, fully synchronized; ratios: I 3.882,
II 2.296, III 1.501, IV 1.042, rev 3.568; lever: central; final
drive: spiral bevel; axle ratio: 4.067; width of rims: 4'';
tyres: 135 SR x 13.

PERFORMANCE max speeds: (I) 28 mph, 45 km/h; (II) 47
mph, 76 km/h; (III) 72 mph, 116 km/h; (IV) 84 mph, 135
km/h; power-weight ratio: 38.7 lb/hp (53.7 lb/kW), 17.5
kg/hp (24.4 kg/kW); carrying capacity: 882 lb, 400 kg;
acceleration: standing ¼ mile 20.5 sec; speed in top at
1,000 rpm: 14.7 mph, 23.6 km/h; consumption: 32.5 m/imp
gal, 27 m/US gal, 8.7 l x 100 km.

CHASSIS integral; front suspension: independent, by Mc-
Pherson, coil springs/telescopic damper struts, lower wishbones (trailing links), anti-roll bar; rear: independent,
swinging longitudinal trailing arms, coil springs, telescopic
dampers.

STEERING rack-and-pinion; turns lock to lock: 3.33.

BRAKES front disc (diameter 9.49 in, 24.1 cm), rear drum,
dual circuit, rear compensator; swept area: front 176.1 sq
in, 1,136 sq cm, rear 68.4 sq in, 441 sq cm, total 244.5 sq
in, 1,577 sq cm.

ELECTRICAL EQUIPMENT 12 V; 28 Ah battery; 350 W alternator; Ducellier or Paris-Rhone distributor; 2 headlamps.

DIMENSIONS AND WEIGHT wheel base: 95.28 in, 242 cm;

tracks: 50.79 in, 129 cm front, 48.82 in, 124 cm rear;
length: 140.94 in, 358 cm; width: 59.84 in, 152 cm; height:
55.12 in, 140 cm; ground clearance: 5.04 in, 12.8 cm; weight:
1,720 lb, 780 kg; turning circle: 33.1 ft, 10.1 m; fuel tank:
8.8 imp gal, 10.6 US gal, 40 l.

BODY saloon/sedan: 4 + 1 doors; 4 seats, separate front
seats; back seat folding down to luggage table.

PRACTICAL INSTRUCTIONS fuel: 88 oct petrol; oil: engine,
gearbox and final drive 7 imp pt, 8.5 US pt, 4 l, SAE
10W-50, change every 3,100 miles, 5,000 km; greasing: every
3,100 miles, 5,000 km, 1 point; valve timing: -2° 32° 33°30'
-2°; tyre pressure: front 26 psi, 1.8 atm, rear 28 psi, 2 atm.

OPTIONALS heated rear window with 500 W alternator;
sunshine roof; tinted glass; headrests.

104 GL6 Berline

See 104 GL Berline, except for:

PRICE EX WORKS: 24,370** francs

ENGINE 68.6 cu in, 1,124 cc (2.83 x 2.72 in, 72 x 69 mm);
compression ratio: 9.2:1; max power (DIN): 57 hp (41 kW)
at 6,000 rpm; max torque (DIN): 59 lb ft, 8.2 kg m (80.4
Nm) at 3,000 rpm; max engine rpm: 6.500; 50.7 hp/l (36.5
kW/l); lubricating system: 8.8 imp pt, 10.6 US pt, 5 l;
1 Solex 32 PBISA7 downdraught twin barrel carburettor.

TRANSMISSION axle ratio: 3.867.

PERFORMANCE max speed: 90 mph, 145 km/h; power-weight
ratio: 30.6 lb/hp (42.5 lb/kW), 13.9 kg/hp (19.3 kg/kW);
acceleration: standing ¼ mile 20 sec; speed in top at
1,000 rpm: 15.5 mph, 24.9 km/h.

DIMENSIONS AND WEIGHT length: 142.36 in, 362 cm;
height: 55.35 in, 141 cm; ground clearance: 4.80 in, 12.2
cm; weight: 1,742 lb, 790 kg.

PRACTICAL INSTRUCTIONS fuel: 95 oct petrol; oil: engine,
gearbox and final drive 7.9 imp pt, 9.5 US pt, 4.5 l; valve
timing: 5°20' 36°50' 36°50' 5°20'.

104 SL Berline

See 104 GL6 Berline, except for:

PRICE IN GB: £ 2,856*
PRICE EX WORKS: 25,870** francs

TRANSMISSION axle ratio: 4.067; width of rims: 4.5'';
tyres: 145 SR x 13.

PERFORMANCE power-weight ratio: 30.9 lb/hp (43 lb/kW),
14 kg/hp (19.5 kg/kW); speed in top at 1,000 rpm: 14.5
mph, 24.3 km/h.

ELECTRICAL EQUIPMENT 500 W alternator.

DIMENSIONS AND WEIGHT weight: 1,764 lb, 800 kg.

BODY heated rear window (standard).

OPTIONALS metallic spray; light alloy wheels; rear window
wiper-washer.

104 S Berline

See 104 GL6 Berline, except for:

PRICE EX WORKS: 28,170** francs

ENGINE max power (DIN): 66 hp (47.5 kW) at 6,200 rpm; max torque (DIN): 62 lb ft, 8.5 kg m (83.4 Nm) at 4,000 rpm; 58.5 hp/l (42.3 kW/l); 1 Solex 32 TMMIA downdraught twin barrel carburettor.

TRANSMISSION width of rims: 4.5''; tyres: 145 SR x 13.

PERFORMANCE max speed: 96 mph, 155 km/h; power-weight ratio: 26.7 lb/hp (37.1 lb/kW), 12.1 kg/hp (16.8 kg/kW); acceleration: standing ¼ mile 19 sec; speed in top at 1,000 rpm: 15.9 mph, 25.6 km/h; consumption: 30.7 m/imp gal, 25.6 m/US gal, 9.2 l x 100 km.

CHASSIS rear suspension: anti-roll bar.

BRAKES servo.

ELECTRICAL EQUIPMENT 500 W alternator.

DIMENSIONS AND WEIGHT weight: 1.764 lb, 800 kg.

BODY heated rear window (standard).

104 ZL Coupé

See 104 GL Berline, except for:

PRICE IN GB: £ 2,583*
PRICE EX WORKS: 23,550** francs

PERFORMANCE max speed: over 84 mph, 135 km/h; power-weight ratio: 36.7 lb/hp (51 lb/kW), 16.6 kg/hp (23.1 kg/kW); carrying capacity: 706 lb, 320 kg; consumption: 34 m/imp gal, 28.3 m/US gal, 8.3 l x 100 km.

DIMENSIONS AND WEIGHT wheel base: 87.80 in, 223 cm; length: 128.92 in, 330 cm; height: 52.76 in, 134 cm; ground clearance: 4.72 in, 12 cm; weight: 1,632 lb, 740 kg; turning circle: 30.8 ft, 9.4 m.

BODY coupé; 2 + 1 doors.

OPTIONALS tinted glass with rear window wiper-washer.

104 ZS Coupé

See 104 ZL Coupé, except for:

PRICE IN GB: £ 2,984*
PRICE EX WORKS: 26,870** francs

ENGINE 68.6 cu in, 1,124 cc (2.83 x 2.72 in, 72 x 69 mm); compression ratio: 9.2:1; max power (DIN): 66 hp (47.5 kW) at 6,200 rpm; max torque (DIN): 62 lb ft, 8.5 kg m (83.4 Nm) at 4,000 rpm; max engine rpm: 6,500; 58.5 hp/l (42.3 kW/l); lubricating system: 8.8 imp pt, 10.6 US pt, 5 l; 1 Solex 32 TMMIA downdraught twin barrel carburettor.

TRANSMISSION axle ratio: 3.867; width of rims: 4.5''; tyres: 145 SR x 13.

PERFORMANCE max speed: over 96 mph, 155 km/h; power-weight ratio: 26.1 lb/hp (36.2 lb/kW), 11.8 kg/hp (16.4 kg/kW); acceleration: standing ¼ mile 19 sec; speed in top at 1,000 rpm: 15.9 mph, 25.6 km/h; consumption: 33.2 m/imp gal, 27.7 m/US gal, 8.5 l x 100 km.

CHASSIS rear suspension: anti-roll bar.

BRAKES servo.

ELECTRICAL EQUIPMENT 500 W alternator; halogen head-lamps.

DIMENSIONS AND WEIGHT weight: 1,720 lb, 780 kg.

BODY (standard) reclining backrests with built-in headrests, heated rear window, rev counter.

PRACTICAL INSTRUCTIONS fuel: 95 oct petrol; oil: engine, gearbox and final drive 7.9 imp pt, 9.5 US pt, 4.5 l; valve timing: 5°20' 36°50' 36°50' 5°20'.

OPTIONALS metallic spray; tinted glass; light alloy wheels; rear window wiper-washer.

304 GL Berline

PRICE IN GB: £ 2,895*
PRICE EX WORKS: 26,090** francs

ENGINE front, transverse, slanted 20° to front, 4 stroke; 4 cylinders, in line; 78.7 cu in, 1,290 cc (3.07 x 2.66 in, 78 x 67.5 mm); compression ratio: 8.8:1; max power (DIN): 65 hp (47 kW) at 6,000 rpm; max torque (DIN): 70 lb ft, 9.6 kg m (9.41 Nm) at 3,750 rpm; max engine rpm: 6,100; 50.4 hp/l (36.4 kW/l); light alloy block and head,

PEUGEOT 304 GL Berline

PEUGEOT 304 SL Break

wet liners, bi-hemispherical combustion chambers; 5 crank-shaft bearings; valves: overhead, Vee-slanted, rockers; camshafts: 1 overhead; lubrication: rotary pump, cartridge on by-pass, 7 imp pt, 8.5 US pt, 4 l; Solex 34 PBISA-5 downdraught single barrel carburettor; fuel feed: mechanical pump; water-cooled, 10.2 imp pt, 12.3 US pt, 5.8 l, electromagnetically-operated fan.

TRANSMISSION driving wheels: front; clutch: single dry plate (diaphragm), hydraulically controlled; gearbox: mechanical; gears: 4, fully synchronized; ratios: I 3.647, II 2.213, III 1.451, IV 0.985, rev 3.942; lever: steering column; final drive: helical spur gears; axle ratio: 4.067; width of rims: 4.5''; tyres: 145 SR x 14.

PERFORMANCE max speeds: (I) 27 mph, 44 km/h; (II) 45 mph, 73 km/h; (III) 69 mph, 111 km/h; (IV) 93 mph, 150 km/h; power-weight ratio: 30.5 lb/hp (42.2 lb/kW), 13.8 kg/hp (19.1 kg/kW); carrying capacity: 882 lb, 400 kg; acceleration: standing ¼ mile 20.1 sec; speed in top at 1,000 rpm: 16.7 mph, 26.9 km/h; consumption: 29.7 m/imp gal, 24.8 m/US gal, 9.5 l x 100 km.

CHASSIS integral; front suspension: independent, by Mc-Pherson, coil springs/telescopic dampers, lower wishbones, anti-roll bar; rear: independent, swinging longitudinal trailing arms, anti-roll bar, coil springs/telescopic dampers.

STEERING rack-and-pinion; turns lock to lock: 3.60.

BRAKES front disc (diameter 10.08 in, 25.6 cm), rear drum, dual circuit, rear compensator, servo; swept area: front 192.2 sq in, 1,240 sq cm, rear 89.1 sq in, 575 sq cm, total 281.3 sq in, 1,815 sq cm.

ELECTRICAL EQUIPMENT 12 V; 36 Ah battery; 500 alternator; Ducellier distributor; 2 headlamps.

DIMENSIONS AND WEIGHT wheel base: 101.97 in, 259 c tracks: 53.94 in, 1.37 cm front, 50.79 in, 129 cm rear; leng 162.99 in, 414 cm; width: 61.81 in, 157 cm; height: 55.51 141 cm; ground clearance: 4.72 in, 12 cm; weight: 1,9 lb, 900 kg; turning circle: 34.8 ft, 10.6 m; fuel tank: imp gal, 11.1 US gal, 42 l.

BODY saloon/sedan; 4 doors; 5 seats, separate front sea reclining backrests; heated rear window.

PRACTICAL INSTRUCTIONS fuel: 95 oct petrol; oil: engi gearbox and final drive 7 imp pt, 8.5 US pt, 4 l, S 20W-40, change every 3,100 miles, 5,000 km; greasing: eve 3,100 miles, 5,000 km, 5 points; tyre pressure: front 23 p 1.6 atm, rear 27 psi, 1.9 atm.

OPTIONALS sunshine roof; metallic spray.

304 GL Break

See 304 GL Berline, except for:

PRICE IN GB: £ 3,056*
PRICE EX WORKS: 26,150** francs

PERFORMANCE power-weight ratio: 31.7 lb/hp (43.9 lb/kW 14.4 kg/hp (19.9 kg/kW); carrying capacity: 1,014 lb, 4 kg.

DIMENSIONS AND WEIGHT length: 157.87 in, 401 c height: 56 in, 142 cm; weight: 2,062 lb, 935 kg.

...DY estate car/station wagon; 4 + 1 doors; back seat ...ding down to luggage table.

304 SL Break

...e 304 GL Break, except for:

...ICE IN GB: £ 3,299*
...ICE EX WORKS: 29,090** francs

...ANSMISSION lever: central.

...RFORMANCE power-weight ratio: 32.2 lb/hp (44.6 lb/kW), ...6 kg/hp (20.2 kg/kW).

...ECTRICAL EQUIPMENT halogen headlamps.

...MENSIONS AND WEIGHT weight: 2,095 lb, 950 kg.

...DY built-in headrests; metallic spray and sunshine roof ...andard).

...TIONALS tinted glass; rear window wiper-washer.

304 GLD Berline

...e 304 GL Berline, except for:

...ICE EX WORKS: 30,850** francs

...GINE Diesel; 82.8 cu in, 1,357 cc (3.07 x 2.80 in, 78 x 71 ...n); compression ratio: 23.3:1; max power (DIN): 45 hp ... kW) at 5,000 rpm; max torque (DIN): 57 lb ft, 7.8 ...m (76.5 Nm) at 2,500 rpm; max engine rpm: 5,450 rpm; ...2 hp/l (24.4 kW/l); lubricating system: 8.8 imp pt, ...6 US pt, 5 l; heating plugs on head; Bosch injection ...mp; cooling system: 11.4 imp pt, 13.7 US pt, 6.5 l.

...ANSMISSION gearbox ratios: I 3.733, II 2.264, III 1.485, ...1.008, rev 4.034.

...RFORMANCE max speed: 81 mph, 130 km/h; power-...ight ratio: 45.8 lb/hp (66.5 lb/kW), 20.8 kg/hp (30.2 ...kW); acceleration: standing ¼ mile 22.5 sec; consump-...n: 45.6 m/imp gal, 37.9 m/US gal, 6.2 l x 100 km.

...ECTRICAL EQUIPMENT 60 Ah battery.

...MENSIONS AND WEIGHT weight: 2,062 lb, 935 kg.

...ACTICAL INSTRUCTIONS fuel: Diesel oil; oil: engine, ...arbox and final drive 8.8 imp pt, 10.6 US pt, 5 l, change ...ery 1,600 miles, 2,500 rpm; tyre pressure: front 24 psi, ...atm.

304 GLD Break

...e 304 GLD Berline, except for:

...ICE EX WORKS: 30,900* francs

...RFORMANCE power-weight ratio: 47.5 lb/hp (69 lb/kW), ...6 kg/hp (31.3 kg/kW); carrying capacity: 1,014 lb, 460 kg.

PEUGEOT 305 SR

DIMENSIONS AND WEIGHT length: 157.87 in, 401 cm; height: 56.30 in, 143 cm; weight: 2,139 lb, 970 kg.

BODY estate car/station wagon; 4 + 1 doors; back seat folding down to luggage table.

305 GL/305 GR

PRICES IN GB: 305 GL £ 3,235*
              305 GR £ 3,515*
PRICES EX WORKS: 305 GL 29,290** francs
                   305 GR 30,990** francs

ENGINE front, transverse, slanted 20° to front, 4 stroke; 4 cylinders, in line; 78.7 cu in, 1,290 cc (3.07 x 2.66 in, 78 x 67.5 mm); compression ratio: 8.8:1; max power (DIN): 65 hp (47 kW) at 6,000 rpm; max torque (DIN): 70 lb ft, 9.6 kg m (94.1 Nm) at 3,750 rpm; max engine rpm: 6,500; 50.4 hp/l (36.4 kW/l); light alloy block and head, wet liners, bi-hemispherical combustion chambers; 5 crank-shaft bearings; valves: overhead, Vee-slanted, rockers; camshafts: 1, overhead; lubrication: rotary pump, cartridge on by-pass, 7 imp pt, 8.5 US pt, 4 l; 1 Solex 34 PBISA5 downdraught single barrel carburettor; fuel feed: mechanical pump; water-cooled, 10.2 imp pt, 12.3 US pt, 5.8 l, electro-magnetically-operated fan.

TRANSMISSION driving wheels: front; clutch: single dry plate (diaphragm); gearbox: mechanical; gears: 4, fully synchronized; ratios: I 3.647, II 2.213, III 1.451, IV 0.985, rev

3.942; lever: central; final drive: helical spur gears; axle ratio: 4.065; width of rims: 4.5''; tyres: 165 SR x 13.

PERFORMANCE max speed: 91 mph, 147 km/h; power-weight ratio: 31.3 lb/hp (43.4 lb/kW), 14.2 kg/hp (19.7 kg/kW); carrying capacity: 915 lb, 415 kg; acceleration: standing ¼ mile 19.9 sec; speed in top at 1,000 rpm: 16.7 mph, 26.9 km/h; consumption: 29.7 m/imp gal, 24.8 m/US gal, 9.5 l x 100 km.

CHASSIS integral; front suspension: independent, by Mc-Pherson, coil springs/telescopic dampers, lower wishbones, anti-roll bar; rear: independent, coil springs, anti-roll bar, telescopic dampers.

STEERING rack-and-pinion; turns lock to lock: 3.60.

BRAKES front disc (diameter 10.35 in, 26.3 cm), rear drum, dual circuit, rear compensator, servo; swept area: total 275.2 sq in, 1,775 sq cm.

ELECTRICAL EQUIPMENT 12 V; 45 Ah battery; 500 W alternator; Ducellier distributor; 2 headlamps.

DIMENSIONS AND WEIGHT wheel base: 103.15 in, 262 cm; tracks: 53.94 in, 137 cm front, 51.97 in, 132 cm rear; length: 166.93 in, 424 cm; width: 64.17 in, 163 cm; height: 55.12 in, 140 cm; ground clearance: 4.96 in, 12.6 cm; weight: 2,040 lb, 925 kg; turning circle: 35.4 ft, 10.8 m; fuel tank: 9.5 imp gal, 11.4 US gal, 43 l.

BODY saloon/sedan; 4 doors; 5 seats, separate front seats, reclining backrests, heated rear window.

PRACTICAL INSTRUCTIONS fuel: 97 oct petrol; oil: engine, gearbox and final drive 7 imp pt, 8.5 US pt, 4 l, SAE 10W-40, change every 4,750 miles, 7,500 km; valve timing: 6° 38° 45° 1°; tyre pressure: front 26 psi, 1.8 atm, rear 30 psi, 2.1 atm.

OPTIONALS sunshine roof.

305 SR

See 305 GL/305 GR, except for:

PRICE IN GB: £ 3,815*
PRICE EX WORKS: 33,160* francs

ENGINE 89.8 cu in, 1,472 cc (3.07 x 3.03 in, 78 x 77 mm); compression ratio: 9.2:1; max power (DIN): 74 hp (53 kW) at 6,000 rpm; max torque (DIN): 86 lb ft, 11.8 kg m (115.7 Nm) at 3,000 rpm; 50.3 hp/l (36 kW/l); 1 Solex 35 PBISA9 downdraught single barrel carburettor.

TRANSMISSION gearbox ratios: I 3.334, II 1.929, III 1.312, IV 0.929, rev 3.436.

PERFORMANCE max speed: 95 mph, 153 km/h; power-weight ratio: 28 lb/hp (39.1 lb/kW), 12.7 kg/hp (17.7 kg/kW); acceleration: standing ¼ mile 18.5 sec; speed in top at 1,000 rpm: 17.8 mph, 28.6 km/h; consumption: 31.7 m/imp gal, 26.4 m/US gal, 8.9 l x 100 km.

DIMENSIONS AND WEIGHT ground clearance: 4.72 in, 12 cm; weight: 2,073 lb, 940 kg.

PRACTICAL INSTRUCTIONS valve timing: 3° 41° 42° 2°.

504 Berline

PRICE IN GB: £ 3,985*
PRICE EX WORKS: 32,900* francs

ENGINE front, slanted 45° to right, 4 stroke; 4 cylinders, in line; 109.6 cu in, 1,796 cc (3.31 x 3.19 in, 84 x 81 mm); compression ratio: 7.5:1; max power (DIN): 79 hp (57 kW) at 5,100 rpm; max torque (DIN): 105 lb ft, 14.5 kg m (142.2 Nm) at 2,500 rpm; max engine rpm: 5,500; 44 hp/l (31.7 kW/l); cast iron block, wet liners, light alloy head, hemispherical combustion chambers; 5 crankshaft bearings; valves: overhead, Vee-slanted, push-rods and rockers; camshafts: 1, side; lubrication: gear pump, metal gauze filter, 7 imp pt, 8.5 US pt, 4 l; 1 Solex 34 BICSA 3 downdraught single barrel carburettor; fuel feed: mechanical pump; water-cooled, 13.7 imp pt, 16.5 US pt, 7.8 l, electromagnetic thermostatic fan.

TRANSMISSION driving wheels: rear; clutch: single dry plate (diaphragm), hydraulically controlled; gearbox: mechanical; gears: 4, fully synchronized; ratios: I 3.704, II 2.170, III 1.409, IV 1, rev 3.747; lever: steering column; final drive: hypoid bevel; axle ratio: 3.889; width of rims: 5''; tyres: 165 SR x 14.

PERFORMANCE max speeds: (I) 25 mph, 40 km/h; (II) 43 mph, 70 km/h; (III) 65 mph, 105 km/h; (IV) 96 mph, 154 km/h; power-weight ratio: 32.4 lb/hp (44.9 lb/kW), 14.7 kg/hp (20.3 kg/kW); carrying capacity: 1,169 lb, 530 kg; acceleration: standing ¼ mile 19.6 sec, 0-50 mph (0-80 km/h) 10.6 sec; speed in direct drive at 1,000 rpm: 18.1 mph, 29.1 km/h; consumption: 26.9 m/imp gal, 22.4 m/US gal, 10.5 l x 100 km.

PEUGEOT 305 SR

504 BERLINE

CHASSIS integral; front suspension: independent, by Mc-Pherson, coil springs/telescopic damper struts, lower wishbones, anti-roll bar; rear: rigid axle, trailing lower radius arms, upper oblique torque arms, coil springs, anti-roll bar, telescopic dampers.

STEERING rack-and-pinion; turns lock to lock: 4.50.

BRAKES front disc (diameter 10.75 in, 27.3 cm), rear drum, dual circuit, rear compensator, servo; swept area: total 400.5 sq in, 2,583 sq cm.

ELECTRICAL EQUIPMENT 12 V; 44 Ah battery; 500 W alternator; Ducellier distributor; 2 headlamps.

DIMENSIONS AND WEIGHT wheel base: 107.87 in, 274 cm; tracks: 55.91 in, 142 cm front, 53.54 in, 136 cm rear; length: 176.77 in, 449 cm; width: 66.54 in, 169 cm; height: 57.48 in, 146 cm; ground clearance: 6.30 in, 16 cm; weight: 2,558 lb, 1,160 kg; turning circle (between walls): 35.8 ft, 10.9 m; fuel tank: 12.3 imp gal, 14.8 US gal, 56 l.

BODY saloon/sedan; 4 doors; 5 seats, separate front seats, reclining backrests; heated rear window.

PRACTICAL INSTRUCTIONS fuel: 85 oct petrol; oil: engine 7 imp pt, 8.5 US pt, 4 l, SAE 20W-40, change every 3,100 miles, 5,000 km - gearbox 1.9 imp pt, 2.3 US pt, 1.1 l, SAE 20W-40, change every 6,200 miles, 10,000 km - final drive 2.1 imp pt, 1.5 US pt, 1.2 l, GP 90, change every 6,200 miles, 10,000 km; greasing: every 3,100 miles, 5,000 km, 6 points; tappet clearances: inlet 0.004 in, 0.10 mm, exhaust 0.010 in, 0.25 mm; tyre pressure: front 21 psi, 1.5 atm, rear 26 psi, 1.8 atm.

VARIATIONS

ENGINE Diesel, 128.9 cu in, 2,112 cc (3.54 x 3.27 in, 90 x 83 mm), 22.2:1 compression ratio, max power (DIN) 65 hp (45.5 kW) at 4,500 rpm, max torque (DIN) 88 lb ft, 12.1 kg m (118.7 Nm) at 2,500 rpm, max engine rpm 4,750, 30.8 hp/l (21.5 kW/l), Bosch injection pump.
TRANSMISSION 3.778 axle ratio.
PERFORMANCE max speed 84 mph, 135 km/h, power-weight ratio 41 lb/hp (58.6 lb/kW), 18.6 kg/hp (26.6 kg/kW), acceleration standing ¼ mile 21.8 sec, speed in direct drive at 1,000 rpm 18.6 mph, 30 km/h, consumption 33.6 m/imp gal, 28 m/US gal, 8.4 l x 100 km.
ELECTRICAL EQUIPMENT 60 Ah battery.
DIMENSIONS AND WEIGHT weight 2,668, 1,210 kg.

OPTIONALS metallic spray.

504 Break

See 504 Berline, except for:

PRICE IN GB: £ 4,368*
PRICE EX WORKS: 34,500** francs

ENGINE (max power (DIN) 73 hp (52.5 kW) at 5,000 rpm; max torque (DIN): 101 lb ft, 14 kg m (137.7 Nm) at 2,500 rpm; 40.6 hp/l (29.2 kW/l).

PEUGEOT 504 GL Berline

TRANSMISSION axle ratio: 4.222; tyres: 185 SR x 14.

PERFORMANCE max speed: 91 mph, 146 km/h; power-weight ratio: 38.5 lb/hp (53.5 lb/kW), 17.5 kg/hp (24.3 kg/kW); carrying capacity: 1,477 lb, 670 kg; speed in direct drive at 1,000 rpm: 17.4 mph, 28 km/h; consumption: 20.6 m/imp gal, 17.2 m/US gal, 13.7 l x 100 km.

CHASSIS rear suspension: rigid axle, 4 coil springs.

DIMENSIONS AND WEIGHT wheel base: 114.17 in, 290 cm; length: 118.98 in, 480 cm; height: 61.02 in, 155 cm; ground clearance: 6.50 in, 16.5 cm; weight: 2,811 lb, 1,275 kg; turning circle: 37.4 ft, 11.4 m; fuel tank: 13.2 imp gal, 15.8 US gal, 60 l.

BODY estate car/station wagon; 4 + 1 doors; back seat folding down to luggage table.

VARIATIONS

ENGINE Diesel, 2,112 cc (3.54 x 3.27 in, 90 x 83 mm), 22.2:1 compression ratio, max power (DIN) 65 hp (45.5 kW) at 4,500 rpm, max torque (DIN): 88 lb ft, 12.1 kg m (118.7 Nm) at 2,500 rpm, max engine rpm 4,750, 30.8 hp/l (21.5 kW/l), Bosch injection pump.
PERFORMANCE max speed 78 mph, 126 km/h, power-weight ratio 45.8 lb/hp (65.4 lb/kW), 20.8 kg/hp (29.7 kg/kW), acceleration standing ¼ mile 23.1 sec, consumption 31.7 m/imp gal, 26.4 m/US gal, 8.9 l x 100 km.
ELECTRICAL EQUIPMENT 60 Ah battery.
DIMENSIONS AND WEIGHT weight, 2,977 lb, 1,350 kg.

504 GL Berline

See 504 Berline, except for:

PRICE IN GB: £ 4,486*
PRICE IN USA: $ 9,432*

ENGINE 120.3 cu in, 1,971 cc (3.46 x 3.19 in, 88 x 81 mm) compression ratio: 8.8:1; max power (DIN): 96 hp (69 k at 5,200 rpm; max torque (DIN): 119 lb ft, 16.4 kg m (16 Nm) at 3,000 rpm; 48.7 hp/l (35 kW/l); 1 Zenith 35-40 IN or Solex 32-35 TMIMA downdraught twin barrel carburett

TRANSMISSION gearbox ratios: I 3.592, II 2.104, III 1.3 IV 1, rev 3.634; lever: central; tyres: 175 SR x 14.

PERFORMANCE max speed: 102 mph, 164 km/h; pow weight ratio: 28.2 lb/hp (39.3 lb/kW), 12.8 kg/hp (1 kg/kW); carrying capacity: 1,058 lb, 480 kg; accelerati standing ¼ mile 18.4 sec; consumption: 23.7 m/imp g 19.8 m/US gal, 11.9 l x 100 km.

CHASSIS rear suspension: independent, oblique semi-tra ing arms, coil springs/telescopic dampers, anti-roll bar

BRAKES disc (diameter 10.75 in, 27.3 cm), dual circuit, re compensator, servo; swept area: front 236.9 sq in, 1,5 sq cm, rear 201.6 sq in, 1,300 sq cm, total 438.5 sq 2,828 sq cm.

ELECTRICAL EQUIPMENT halogen headlamps.

DIMENSIONS AND WEIGHT weight: 2,712 lb, 1,230 kg.

BODY built-in adjustable headrests.

PRACTICAL INSTRUCTIONS fuel: 95 oct petrol.

VARIATIONS

ENGINE Diesel, slanted 20°, 140.6 cu in, 2,304 cc (3.7 3.27 in, 94 x 83 mm), 22.2:1 compression ratio, max pow (DIN) 70 hp (50.5 kW) at 4,500 rpm, max torque (DI 97 lb ft, 13.4 kg m (131.4 Nm) at 2,200 rpm, 30.4 hp/l (2 kW/l), Bosch injection pump.
PERFORMANCE max speed 88 mph, 141 km/h, power-wei ratio 40.9 lb/hp (56.7 lb/kW), 18.6 kg/hp (25.7 kg/kV consumption 34 m/imp gal, 28.3 m/US gal, 8.3 l x 100 k
ELECTRICAL EQUIPMENT 60 Ah battery.
DIMENSIONS AND WEIGHT weight 2,866 lb, 1,300 kg.

OPTIONALS ZF automatic transmission, hydraulic torc converter and planetary gears with 3 ratios (I 2.564, II 1.5 III 1, rev 2), max ratio of converter at stall 2.3, max spe 91 mph, 146 km/h; leather upholstery; sunshine roof; tint glass; metallic spray.

504 GL Break

See 504 GL Berline, except for:

PRICE IN GB: £ 4,870*
PRICE IN USA: $ 10,032*

TRANSMISSION lever: steering column; axle ratio: 4.2 tyres: 185 SR x 14.

PEUGEOT 504 GL Break

PERFORMANCE max speed: 101 mph, 162 km/h; power-weight ratio: 30.6 lb/hp (42.5 lb/kW), 13.9 kg/hp (19.3 g/kW); carrying capacity: 1,411 lb, 640 kg; speed in direct drive at 1,000 rpm: 17 mph, 28 km/h; consumption: 1.6 m/imp gal, 18 m/US gal, 13.1 l x 100 km.

CHASSIS rear suspension: rigid axle, 4 coil springs.

BRAKES rear drum; swept area: total 400.5 sq in, 2,583 sq cm.

DIMENSIONS AND WEIGHT wheel base: 114.17 in, 290 cm; length: 188.98 in, 480 cm; height: 61.02 in, 155 cm; ground clearance: 6.50 in, 16.5 cm; weight: 2,933 lb, 1,330 kg; turning circle: 37.4 ft, 11.4 m; fuel tank: 13.2 imp gal, 15.8 US gal, 60 l.

BODY estate car/station wagon; 4+1 doors; back seat folding down to luggage table.

OPTIONALS ZF automatic transmission, 4.110 axle ratio, max speed 96 mph, 154 km/h; tinted glass; metallic spray; rear window wiper-washer.

504 Break Familial

See 504 GL Berline, except for:

PRICE IN GB: £ 4,902*
PRICE EX WORKS: 39,320** francs

TRANSMISSION lever: steering column; axle ratio: 4.222; tyres: 185 SR x 14.

PERFORMANCE max speed: 101 mph, 162 km/h; power-weight ratio: 30.6 lb/hp (42.5 lb/kW), 13.9 kg/hp (19.3 kg/kW); carrying capacity: 1,411 lb, 640 kg; speed in direct drive at 1,000 rpm: 17 mph, 28 km/h; consumption: 21.6 m/imp gal, 18 m/US gal, 13.1 l x 100 km.

CHASSIS rear suspension: rigid axle, 4 coil springs.

BRAKES rear drum; swept area: total 400.5 sq in, 2,583 cm.

DIMENSIONS AND WEIGHT wheel base: 114.17 in, 290 cm; length: 188.98 in, 480 cm; height: 61.02 in, 155 cm; ground clearance: 6.50 in, 16.5 cm; weight: 2,933 lb, 1,330 kg; turning circle: 37.4 ft, 11.4 m; fuel tank: 13.2 imp gal, 15.8 gal, 60 l.

BODY estate car/station wagon; 4 + 1 doors; 7 seats; back seat folding down to luggage table.

VARIATIONS

with Diesel engine).
PERFORMANCE max speed 81 mph, 130 km/h, power-weight ratio 44.4 lb/hp (61.6 lb/kW), 20.1 kg/hp (27.9 kg/kW), consumption 30.1 m/imp gal, 25 m/US gal, 9.4 l x 100 km.
DIMENSIONS AND WEIGHT weight 3,109 lb, 1,410 kg.

OPTIONALS tinted glass; metallic spray; wiper and washer rear window; ZF automatic transmission not available.

504 TI Berline

See 504 Berline, except for:

PRICE IN GB: £ 4,927*
PRICE EX WORKS: 41,20** francs

ENGINE 120.3 cu in, 1.971 cc (3.46 x 3.19 in, 88 x 81 mm); compression ratio: 8.8:1; max power (DIN): 106 hp (76.5 kW) at 5,200 rpm; max torque (DIN): 125 lb ft, 17.2 kg m (168.7 Nm) at 3,000 rpm; 53.8 hp/l (38.8 kW/l); 4-cylinder injection pump in inlet pipes (Kugelfischer system); fuel feed: electric pump.

TRANSMISSION gearbox ratio: I 3.592, II 2.104, III 1.366, IV 1, rev 3.634; lever: central; axle ratio: 3.778; tyres: 175 HR x 14.

PERFORMANCE max speeds: (I) 29 mph, 46 km/h; (II) 48 mph, 78 km/h; (III) 75 mph, 121 km/h; (IV) 107 mph, 173 km/h; power-weight ratio: 25.8 lb/hp (35.7 lb/kW), 11.7 kg/hp (16.2 kg/kW); carrying capacity: 1,058 lb, 480 kg; acceleration: standing ¼ mile 17.7 sec. speed in direct drive at 1,000 rpm: 19 mph, 30.6 km/h; consumption: 23.2 m/imp gal, 19.3 m/US gal, 12.2 l x 100 km.

CHASSIS rear suspension: independent, oblique semi-trailing arms, coil springs/telescopic dampers, anti-roll bar.

BRAKES disc (diameter 10.75 in, 27.3 cm), dual circuit, rear compensator, servo; swept area: front 236.9 sq in, 1,528 sq cm, rear 201.6 sq in, 1,300 sq cm, total 438.5 sq in, 2,828 sq cm.

ELECTRICAL EQUIPMENT halogen headlamps.

DIMENSIONS AND WEIGHT weight: 2,734 lb, 1,240 kg.

BODY sunshine roof; built-in adjustable headrests; electrically-controlled front windows.

PRACTICAL INSTRUCTIONS fuel: 95 oct petrol.

VARIATIONS

None.

OPTIONALS ZF automatic transmission, hydraulic torque converter and planetary gears with 3 ratios (I 2.564, II 1.520, III 1, rev 2), max ratio of converter at stall 2.3, max speed 104 mph, 167 km/h; leather upholstery; tinted glass; metallic spray.

504 Cabriolet

PRICE EX WORKS: 55,920** francs

ENGINE front, slanted 45º to right, 4 stroke; 4 cylinders, in line; 120.3 cu in, 1,971 cc (3.46 x 3.19 in, 88 x 81 mm); compression ratio: 8.8:1; max power (DIN): 106 hp (76.5 kW) at 5,200 rpm; max torque (DIN): 125 lb ft, 17.2 kg m (168.7 Nm) at 3,000 rpm; max engine rpm: 5,500; 53.8 hp/l (38.8 kW/l); cast iron block, wet liners, light alloy head, hemispherical combustion chambers; 5 crankshaft bearings; valves: overhead, Vee-slanted, push-rods and rockers; camshafts: 1, side; lubrication: gear pump, metal gauze filter, 7 imp pt, 8.5 US pt, 4 l; 4 cylinder injection pump

in inlet pipes (Kugelfischer system); fuel feed: electric pump; water-cooled, 13.7 imp pt, 16.5 US pt, 7.8 l, electromagnetic thermostatic fan.

TRANSMISSION driving wheels: rear; clutch: single dry plate (diaphragm), hydraulically controlled; gearbox: mechanical; gears: 4, fully synchronized; ratios: I 3.592, II 2.104, III 1.366, IV 1, rev 3.634; lever: central; final drive: hypoid bevel; axle ratio: 3.700; width of rims: 5.5''; tyres: 175 HR x 14.

PERFORMANCE max speed: 111 mph, 179 km/h; power-weight ratio: 22.7 lb/hp (35.6 lb/kW), 11.6 kg/hp (16.1 kg/kW); carrying capacity: 706 lb(320 kg; speed in direct drive at 1,000 rpm: 19.4 mph, 31.3 km/h; consumption: 21.9 m/imp gal, 18.2 m/US gal, 12.9 l x 100 km.

CHASSIS integral; front suspension: independent, by McPherson, coil springs/telescopic damper struts, lower wishbones, anti-roll bar; rear: independent, oblique semi-trailing arms, coil springs/telescopic damper struts, anti-roll bar.

STEERING rack-and-pinion, servo; turns lock to lock: 3.50.

BRAKES disc (diameter 10.75 in, 27.3 cm), front internal radial fins, dual circuit, rear compensator, servo; lining area: front 22.9 sq in, 148 sq cm, rear 16.7 sq in, 108 sq cm, total 39.6 sq in, 256 sq cm.

ELECTRICAL EQUIPMENT 12 V; 45 Ah battery; 750 W alternator; Ducellier distributor; 4 halogen headlamps.

DIMENSIONS AND WEIGHT wheel base: 100.39 in, 255 cm; tracks: 58.66 in, 149 cm front, 56.30 in, 143 cm rear; length: 171.65 in, 436 cm; width: 66.93 in, 170 cm; height: 53.34 in, 136 cm; ground clearance: 4.72 in, 12 cm; weight: 2,723 lb, 1,235 kg; turning circle: 34.8 ft, 10.6 m; fuel tank: 12.3 imp gal, 14.8 US gal, 56 l.

BODY convertible; 2 doors; 2 + 2 seats, separate front seats, reclining backrests with built-in-headrests; electrically-controlled windows; tinted glass.

PRACTICAL INSTRUCTIONS fuel: 95 oct petrol; oil: engine 7 imp pt, 8.5 US pt, 4 l, SAE 20W-40, change every 3,100 miles, 5,000 km - gearbox 2.3 imp pt, 2.7 US pt, 1.3 l, SAE 20W-40, change every 6,200 miles, 10,000 km - final drive 2.6 imp pt, 3.2 US pt, 1.5 l, SAE 80, change every 6,200 miles, 10,000 km; greasing every 3,100 miles, 5,000 km, 6 points.

OPTIONALS metallic spray.

504 Coupé

See 504 Cabriolet, except for:

PERFORMANCE power-weight ratio: 26 lb/hp (36 lb/kW), 11.8 kg/hp (16.3 kg/kW).

DIMENSIONS AND WEIGHT height: 53.15 in, 135 cm; weight: 2,756 lb, 1,250 kg.

BODY coupé; 4 seats; heated rear window.

OPTIONALS ZF automatic transmission.

504 V6 Coupé

See 504 Coupé, except for:

PRICE EX WORKS: 68,100** francs

ENGINE 6 cylinders, Vee-slanted at 90º; 162.6 cu in, 2,664 cc (3.46 x 2.87 in, 88 x 73 mm); compression ratio: 8.65:1; max power (DIN): 144 hp (104 kW) at 5,500 rpm; max torque (DIN): 160 lb ft, 22.1 kg m (216.7 Nm) at 3,000 rpm; max engine rpm: 6,000; 54 hp/l (39 kW/l); light alloy block and head, wet liners, bi-hemispherical combustion chambers; 4 crankshaft bearings; valves: overhead, Vee-slanted, rockers; camshafts: 2, 1 per bank, overhead; lubrication: gear pump, full flow filter, 10.6 imp pt, 12.7 US pt, 6 l; Bosch K-Jetronic fuel injection system; fuel feed: mechanical pump; water-cooled, expansion tank, 18.1 imp pt, 21.8 US pt, 10.3 l, viscous coupling thermostatic fan.

TRANSMISSION gears: 5, fully synchronized; gearbox ratios: I 3.862, II 2.183, III 1.445, IV 1, V 0.844, rev 3.587; tyres: 190/65 HR x 390.

PERFORMANCE max speed: 117 mph, 189 km/h; power-weight ratio: 19.8 lb/hp (27.4 lb/kW), 9 kg/hp (12.4 kg/kW); speed in direct drive at 1,000 rpm: 23 mph, 37.1 km/h; consumption: 17.5 m/imp gal, 14.6 m/US gal, 16.1 l x 100 km.

ELECTRICAL EQUIPMENT electronic ignition.

DIMENSIONS AND WEIGHT height: 52.76 in, 134 cm; weight: 2,855 lb, 1,295 kg; fuel tank: 13.2 imp gal, 15.8 US gal, 60 l.

PRACTICAL INSTRUCTIONS oil: engine 10.6 imp pt, 12.7 US pt, 6 l, SAE 10W-50; tappet clearances: inlet 0.006 in, 0.15 mm, exhaust 0.012 in, 0.30 mm; xalxe timing: 32º 72º 20º 32º.

PEUGEOT 504 V6 Coupé

PEUGEOT 604 TI

604 SL

PRICE IN GB: £ 6,715*
PRICE IN USA: $ 11,969*

ENGINE front, 4 stroke; 6 cylinders, Vee-slanted at 90°; 162.6 cu in, 2,664 cc (3.46 x 2.87 in, 88 x 73 mm); compression ratio: 8.65:1; max power (DIN): 136 hp (98 kW) at 5,750 rpm; max torque (DIN): 153 lb ft, 21.1 kg m (207 Nm) at 3,500 rpm; max engine rpm: 6,000; 51 hp/l (36.8 kW/l); light alloy block and head, wet liners, bi-hemispherical combustion chambers; 4 crankshaft bearings; valves: overhead, Vee-slanted, rockers; camshafts: 2, 1 per bank, overhead; lubrication: gear pump, full flow filter, 10.6 imp pt, 12.7 US pt, 6 l; 1 Solex 34 TBIA downdraught single barrel carburettor and 1 Solex 35 CEEI downdraught twin barrel carburettor; fuel feed: mechanical pump; water-cooled, expansion tank, 18.1 imp pt, 21.8 US pt, 10.3 l, viscous coupling thermostatic fan.

TRANSMISSION driving wheels: rear; clutch: single dry plate (diaphragm), hydraulically controlled; gearbox: mechanical; gears: 4, fully synchronized; ratios: I 3.862, II 2.183, III 1.445, IV 1, rev 3.587: lever: central; final drive: hypoid bevel; axle ratio. 3.580; width of rims: 5.5''; tyres: 175 HR x 14.

PERFORMANCE max speeds: (I) 32 mph, 52 km/h; (II) 55 mph, 88 km/h; (III) 80 mph, 129 km/h; (IV) 113 mph, 182 km/h; power-weight ratio: 22.5 lb/hp (30.6 lb/kW), 10.2 kg/hp (13.9 kg/kW); carrying capacity: 1,257 lb, 570 kg; acceleration: standing ¼ mile 17.2 sec; speed in direct drive at 1,000 rpm: 20 mph, 32.3 km/h; consumption: 17.7 m/imp gal, 14.7 m/US gal, 16 l x 100 km.

CHASSIS integral; front suspension: independent, by McPherson, coil springs/telescopic damper struts, lower wishbones, anti-roll bar; rear: independent, oblique semi-trailing arms, coil springs, anti-roll bar, telescopic dampers.

STEERING rack-and-pinion, servo; turns lock to lock: 3.50.

BRAKES disc (diameter 10.75 in, 27.3 cm), front internal radial fins, dual circuit, rear compensator, servo; swept area: front 223 sq in, 1,438 sq cm, rear 192 sq in, 1,239 sq cm, total 415 sq in, 2,677 sq cm.

ELECTRICAL EQUIPMENT 12 V; 45 Ah battery; 750 W alternator; Ducellier distributor; 4 halogen headlamps.

DIMENSIONS AND WEIGHT wheel base: 110.24 in, 280 cm; tracks: 58.66 in, 149 cm front, 56.30 in, 143 cm rear; length: 185.83 in, 472 cm; width: 69.68 in, 177 cm; height: 56.30 in, 143 cm; ground clearance: 5.91 in, 15 cm; weight: 3,065 lb, 1,390 kg; turning circle: 37.7 ft, 11.5 m; fuel tank: 15.4 imp gal, 18.5 US gal, 70 l.

BODY saloon/sedan; 4 doors, 5 seats, separate front seats, reclining backrests with built-in headrests; electric windows; heated rear window.

PRACTICAL INSTRUCTIONS fuel: 95 oct petrol; oil: engine 10.6 imp pt, 12.7 US pt, 6 l, SAE 10W-50, change every 3,100 miles, 5,000 km - gearbox 2.3 imp pt, 2.7 US pt, 1.3 l, SAE 20W-40, change every 6,200 miles, 10,000 km - final drive 2.6 imp pt, 3.2 US pt, 1.5 l, SAE 80, change every 6,200 miles, 10,000 km; greasing: every 3,100 miles, 5,000 km; tappet clearances: inlet 0.006 in, 0.15 mm, exhaust 0.012 in, 0.30 mm; valve timing: 32° 72° 20° 32°.

OPTIONALS automatic transmission with 3 ratios (I 2.400,

II 1.480, III 1, rev 1.920), max ratio of converter at stall 2.3, possible manual selection, max speed 111 mph, 178 km/h, acceleration standing ¼ mile 18.3 sec, consumption 21.7 m/imp gal, 18.1 m/US gal, 13 l x 100 km; electrically-controlled sunshine roof; leather upholstery; metallic spray.

604 TI

See 604 SL, except for:

PRICE IN GB: £ 7,961*
PRICE EX WORKS: 58,700** francs

ENGINE max power (DIN): 144 hp (104 kW) at 5,500 rpm; max torque (DIN): 160 lb ft, 22.1 kg m (216.7 Nm) at 3,000 rpm; 54 hp/l (39 kW/l); Bosch K-Jetronic fuel injection system; fuel feed: electric pump.

TRANSMISSION gears: 5, fully synchronized; gearbox ratios: I 3.862, II 2.183, III 1.445, IV 1, V 0.844, rev 3.587; axle ratio: 3.700.

PERFORMANCE max speed: 115 mph, 185 km/h; power-weight ratio: 21.6 lb/hp (29.9 lb/kW), 9.8 kg/hp (13.6 kg/kW); consumption: 16.8 m/imp gal, 14 m/US gal, 16.8 l x 100 km.

ELECTRICAL EQUIPMENT electronic ignition.

DIMENSIONS AND WEIGHT weight: 3,109 lb, 1,410 kg.

OPTIONALS air-conditioning.

4

(For France only).

PRICE EX WORKS: 17,100** francs

ENGINE front, 4 stroke; 4 cylinders, vertical, in line; 47.7 cu in, 782 cc (2.20 x 3.15 in, 55.8 x 80 mm); compression ratio 8.5:1; max power (DIN): 27 hp (19.5 kW) at 5,000 rpm; max torque (DIN): 38 lb ft, 5.2 kg m (51 Nm) at 2,500 rpm; max engine rpm: 5,000; 34.5 hp/l (24.9 kW/l); cast iron block wet liners, light alloy head; 3 crankshaft bearings; valves overhead, in line, push-rods and rockers; camshafts: 1, side lubrication: gear pump, filter in sump, 8.4 imp pt, 10.1 US pt, 4.8 l; 1 Zenith 28 IF downdraught single barrel carburettor; fuel feed: mechanical pump; sealed circuit cooling liquid, expansion tank, 10.4 imp pt, 18.1 US pt, 5.9 l.

TRANSMISSION driving wheels: front; clutch: single dry plate (diaphragm); gearbox: mechanical; gears: 4, fully synchronized; ratios: I 3.833, II 2.235, III 1.458, IV 1.026, rev 3.545; lever: on facia; final drive: spiral bevel; axle ratio: 4.125; width of rims: 4''; tyres: 135 SR x 13.

PERFORMANCE max speeds: (I) 21 mph, 33 km/h; (II) 34 mph 54 km/h; (III) 52 mph, 83 km/h; (IV) 68 mph, 110 km/h; power-weight ratio: 56.7 lb/hp (78.6 lb/kW), 25.7 kg/hp (35.6 kg/kW); carrying capacity: 728 lb, 330 kg; acceleration: standing ¼ mile 23.8 sec, 0-50 mph (0-80 km/h) 34 sec; speed in top at 1,000 rpm: 14.7 mph, 23.7 km/h; consumption: 34 m/imp gal, 28.3 m/US gal, 8.3 l x 100 km.

CHASSIS platform; front suspension: independent, wishbones, longitudinal torsion bars, anti-roll bar, telescopic dampers; rear: independent, swinging longitudinal trailing arms, transverse torsion bars, telescopic dampers.

STEERING rack-and-pinion; turns lock to lock: 3.

BRAKES drum (front diameter 7.87 in, 20 cm, rear 6.30 in 16 cm), dual circuit, rear compensator; lining area: front 36.4 sq in, 235 sq cm, rear 17.4 sq in, 112 sq cm, total 53.8 sq in, 347 sq cm.

ELECTRICAL EQUIPMENT 12 V; 28 Ah battery; 35 A alternator; 2 headlamps.

DIMENSIONS AND WEIGHT wheel base: 96.46 in, 245 cm (right), 94.49 in, 240 cm (left); tracks: 50.39 in, 128 cm front, 48.82 in, 124 cm rear; length: 144.49 in, 367 cm width: 58.27 in, 148 cm; height: 61.02 in, 155 cm; ground clearance: 6.89 in, 17.5 cm; weight: 1,532 lb, 695 kg; weight distribution: 56.1% front, 43.9% rear; turning circle: 33 ft, 10.1 m; fuel tank: 7.5 imp gal, 9 US gal, 34 l.

BODY estate car/station wagon; 4 + 1 doors; 4 seats, bench front seats; folding rear seat heated rear window.

PRACTICAL INSTRUCTIONS fuel: 85 oct petrol; oil: engine 8.4 imp pt, 10.1 US pt, 4.8 l, SAE 10W-40, change every 4,650 miles, 7,500 km - gearbox and final drive 3.2 imp pt 3.8 US pt, 1.8 l, SAE 80 EP, change every 9,300 miles, 15,000

RENAULT 4 GTL

m; greasing: none; tappet clearances: inlet 0.006-0.007 in, .15-0.18 mm, exhaust 0.007-0.009 in, 0.18-0.22 mm; valve iming: 10° 34° 49° 11°; tyre pressure: front 20 psi, 1.4 atm, rear 24 psi, 1.7 atm.

OPTIONALS luxury interior.

4 TL

(For France only).

See 4, except for:

PRICE EX WORKS: 19,500** francs

BODY separate front seats.

OPTIONALS sunshine roof; metallic spray; reclining back-rests.

VARIATIONS

(for export only)
ENGINE 51.6 cu in, 845 cc (2.28 x 3.15 in, 58 x 80 mm); compression ratio: 8:1; max power (DIN): 34 hp (25 kW) at 5,000 rpm; max torque (DIN): 43 lb ft, 5.9 kg m (57.9 Nm) at 2,500 rpm; 40.2 hp/l (29.6 kW/l); water-cooled, 9.7 imp pt, 11.6 US pt, 5.5 l.
PERFORMANCE max speed: 78 mph, 125 km/h; power-weight ratio: 45 lb/hp (61.3 lb/kW), 20.4 kg/hp (27.8 kg/kW).

RENAULT 4 TL

RENAULT 4 Rodeo

4 GTL

See 4, except for:

PRICE EX WORKS: 20,300** francs

ENGINE 67.6 cu in, 1,108 cc (2.76 x 2.83 in, 70 x 72 mm); compression ratio: 9.5:1; max power (DIN): 34 hp (25 kW) at 4,000 rpm; max torque (DIN): 54.3 lb/ft, 7.5 kg m (73.6 Nm) at 2,500 rpm; 42.4 hp/l (22.6 kW/l); lubrication 4.3 imp pt, 6.3 US pt, 3 l.

TRANSMISSION axle ratio: 3.100.

PERFORMANCE max speed: 75 mph, 120 km/h; power-weight ratio: 46.7 lb/hp, (63.5 lb/kW), 21.2 kg/hp (28.8 kg/kW); acceleration: standing ¼ mile 22.9 sec; speed in direct drive/top at 1,000 rpm: 19.6 mph, 31.5 km/h; consumption: 40.4 m/imp gal, 33.6 m/US gal, 7 l x 100 km.

STEERING turns lock to lock: 3.75.

BRAKES drum (front diameter 8.9 in, 23 cm, rear 7.1 in, 18 cm); lining area: front 49.3 sq in, 318 sq cm, rear 24.8 sq in, 160 sq cm, total 74.1 sq in, 478 sq cm.

DIMENSIONS AND WEIGHT weight: 1,588 lb, 720 kg.

BODY separate front seats.

PRACTICAL INSTRUCTIONS fuel: 98-100 oct petrol; oil: engine 5.3 imp pt, 6.3 US pt, 3 l; tappet clearances: inlet 0.012 in, 0.30 mm, exhaust 0.012 in, 0.30 mm; valve timing: 12° 48° 52° 8°; tyre pressure: rear 21.3 psi, 1.5 atm.

OPTIONALS sunshine roof; metallic spray; reclining back-rests.

4 Rodeo

See 4, except for:

PRICE EX WORKS: 23,600** francs

ENGINE 51.6 cu in, 845 cc (2.28 x 3.15 in, 58 x 80 mm); compression ratio: 8:1; max power (DIN): 34 hp (25 kW) at 5,000 rpm; max torque (DIN): 43 lb ft, 6 kg m (57.9 Nm) at 2,500 rpm; 40.2 hp/l (29.6 kW/l); water-cooled, 9.7 imp pt, 11.6 US pt, 5.5 l.

TRANSMISSION tyres: 145 SR x 13.

PERFORMANCE max speeds: (I) 21 mph, 34 km/h; (II) 35 mph, 56 km/h; (III) 53 mph, 86 km/h; (IV) 68 mph, 110 km/h; power-weight ratio: 43.4 lb/hp (59.1 lb/kW), 19.7 kg/hp (26.8 kg/kW); speed in top at 1,000 rpm: 15.2 mph, 24.4 km/h.

CHASSIS reinforced platform; rear suspension: anti-roll bar.

STEERING turns lock to lock: 3.33.

BRAKES drum (front diameter 8.98 in, 22.8 cm, rear 6.30 in, 16 cm), rear compensator; lining area: front 44.8 sq in, 289 sq cm, rear 17.4 sq in, 112 sq cm, total 62.2 sq in, 401 sq cm.

ELECTRICAL EQUIPMENT 30/40 A alternator.

DIMENSIONS AND WEIGHT length: 146.85 in, 373 cm; width: 60.79 in, 154 cm; height: 62.99 in, 160 cm; ground clear-ance: 5.51 in, 14 cm; weight: 1,477 lb, 670 kg.

BODY open, in plastic material; 2 doors; 2 or 4 seats.

PRACTICAL INSTRUCTIONS valve timing: 16° 52° 52° 16°; tyre pressure: front 18 psi, 1.3 atm, rear 24 psi, 1.7 atm.

OPTIONALS 4-wheel drive; « Evasion » version; « Chantier » version; « Coursière » version; « Quatre saisons » version; « Artisane » version.

6 Rodeo

See 4 Rodeo, except for:

PRICE EX WORKS: 25,725** francs

ENGINE 67.6 cu in, 1,108 cc (2.76 x 2.83 in, 70 x 72 mm); compression ratio: 9.5:1; max power (DIN): 48 hp (34.5 kW) at 5,300 rpm; max torque (DIN): 57 lb ft, 7.9 kg m (77.5 Nm) at 3,000 rpm; max engine rpm: 5,400; 43.3 hp/l (31.1 kW/l); lubricating system: 5.3 imp pt, 6.3 US pt, 3 l; 1 Zenith 32 IF 8 downdraught single barrel carburettor; water-cooled, 11.1 imp pt, 13.3 US pt, 6.3 l.

PERFORMANCE max speeds: (I) 23 mph, 37 km/h; (II) 37 mph, 60 km/h; (III) 58 mph, 93 km/h; (IV) 81 mph, 130 km/h; power-weight ratio: 34.2 lb/hp (47.6 lb/kW), 15.5 kg/hp (21.6 kg/kW).

STEERING turns lock to lock: 3.25.

BRAKES front disc (diameter 8.98 in, 22.8 cm), rear drum, rear compensator; lining area: front 19.8 sq in, 128 sq cm, rear 22.2 sq in, 143 sq cm, total 42 sq in, 271 sq cm.

DIMENSIONS AND WEIGHT tracks: 50.63 in, 129 cm front, 49.13 in, 125 cm rear; length: 148.62 in, 377 cm; height: 61.18 in, 155 cm; ground clearance: 5.71 in, 14.5 cm; weight: 1,643 lb, 745 kg; turning circle: 35.4 ft, 10.8 m; fuel tank: 8.8 imp gal, 10.6 US gal, 40 l.

BODY 2 seats.

PRACTICAL INSTRUCTIONS oil: engine 5.3 imp pt, 6.3 US pt, 3 l; tappet clearances: inlet 0.006 in, 0.15 mm, exhaust 0.008 in, 0.20 mm; valve timing: 18° 54° 53° 23°; tyre pres-sure: front 20 psi, 1.4 atm, rear 24 psi, 1.7 atm.

5

PRICE IN GB: £ 2,232*
PRICE EX WORKS: 20,400** francs

ENGINE front, 4 stroke; 4 cylinders, vertical, in line: 51.6 cu in, 845 cc (2.28 x 3.15 in, 58 x 80 mm); compression ratio: 8:1; max power (DIN): 36 hp (26.5 kW) at 5,500 rpm; max torque (DIN): 42 lb ft, 5.8 kg m (56.9 Nm) at 2,500 rpm; max engine rpm: 6,000; 42.6 hp/l (31.4 kW/l); cast iron block, wet liners, light alloy head; 3 crankshaft bearings; valves: overhead, in line, push-rods and rockers; camshafts: 1, side; lubrication: gear pump, filter in sump (cartridge), 4.4 imp pt, 5.3 US pt, 2.5 l; 1 Solex 32 DIS downdraught single barrel carburettor; fuel feed: mechanical pump; seal-ed circuit cooling, liquid, expansion tank, 10.2 imp pt, 12.3 US pt, 5.8 l.

TRANSMISSION driving wheels: front; clutch: single dry plate (diaphragm); gearbox: mechanical; gears: 4, fully synchronized; ratios: I 3.833, II 2.235, III 1.458, IV 1.026, rev 3.545; lever: central; final drive: spiral bevel; axle ratio: 4.125; width of rims: 4''; tyres; 135 SR x 13.

PERFORMANCE max. speeds: (I) 24 mph, 38 km/h; (II) 39 mph, 63 km/h; (III) 60 mph, 97 km/h; (IV) 76 mph, 123 km/h; power-weight ratio: 44.7 lb/hp (60.7 lb/kW), 20.3 kg/hp (27.5 kg/kW); carrying capacity: 728 lb, 330 kg; speed in top at 1,000 rpm: 14.7 mph, 23.7 km/h; consump-tion: 34.9 m/imp gal, 29 m/US gal, 8.1 l x 100 km.

CHASSIS integral; front suspension: independent, wishbones, longitudinal torsion bar, anti-roll bar, telescopic dampers; rear: independent, swinging longitudinal trailing arms, trans-verse torsion bars, telescopic dampers.

STEERING rack-and-pinion; turns lock to lock: 3.75.

BRAKES drum (diameter 7.87 in, 20 cm front, 6.30 in, 16 cm rear), dual circuit, rear compensator; lining area: front 68.2 sq in, 440 sq cm, rear 38.9 sq in, 251 sq cm, total 107.1 sq in, 691 sq cm.

ELECTRICAL EQUIPMENT 12 V; 28 Ah battery; 35 A alter-nator; R 220 distributor; 2 headlamps.

DIMENSIONS AND WEIGHT wheel base: 94.49 in, 240 cm (right), 95.67 in, 243 cm (left); tracks: 50.39 in, 128 cm front, 48.82 in, 124 cm rear; length: 138.19 in, 351 cm;

5

width: 59.84 in, 152 cm; height: 55.12 in, 140 cm; ground clearance: 7.87 in, 20 cm; weight: 1,610 lb, 730 kg; weight distribution: 58.2% front, 41.8% rear; turning circle: 33.1 ft, 10.1 m; fuel tank: 8.4 imp gal, 10 US gal, 38 l.

BODY saloon/sedan; 2 + 1 doors; 4 seats, separate front seats; heated rear window; folding rear seat.

PRACTICAL INSTRUCTIONS fuel: 98-100 oct petrol; oil: engine 4.4 imp pt, 5.3 US pt, 2.5 l, SAE 20W-40, change every 4,650 miles, 7,500 km - gearbox and final drive 3.2 imp pt, 3.8 US pt, 1.8 l, SAE 80 EP, change every 9,300 miles, 15,000 km; greasing: none; tappet clearances: inlet 0.006-0.007 in, 0.15-0.18 mm, exhaust 0.007-0.009 in, 0.18-0.22 mm; valve timing: 20° 56° 53° 23°; tyre pressure: front 24 psi, 1.7 atm, rear 28 psi, 1.9 atm.

OPTIONALS luxury interior; metallic spray.

5 TL

See 5, except for:

PRICE IN GB: £ 2,524*
PRICE EX WORKS: 22,700** francs

RENAULT 5 L

ENGINE 58.3 cu in, 956 cc (2.56 x 2.83 in, 65 x 72 mm); compression ratio: 9.25:1; max power (DIN): 44 hp (31.7 kW) at 5,500 rpm; max torque (DIN): 48 lb ft, 6.5 kg m (63.8 Nm) at 3,500 rpm; 46 hp/l (33.2 kW/l); 5 crankshaft bearings; lubricating system: 5.3 imp pt, 6.3 US pt, 3 l; sealed circuit cooling, liquid, electric thermostatic fan, 11.1 imp pt, 13.3 US pt, 6.3 l.

PERFORMANCE max speeds: (I) 24 mph, 39 km/h; (II) 40 mph, 64 km/h; (III) 62 mph, 100 km/h; (IV) 85 mph, 136 km/h; power-weight ratio: 38.8 lb/hp (53.9 lb/kW), 17.6 kg/hp (24.4 kg/kW); carrying capacity: 882 lb, 400 kg; consumption: 31.4 m/imp gal, 26.1 m/US gal, 9 l x 100 km.

BRAKES front disc (diameter 8.98 iin, 22.8 cm), rear drum, dual circuit, rear compensator; swept area: front 157.2 sq in, 1,014 sq cm, rear 52.6 sq in, 339 sq cm, total 209.8 sq in, 1,353 sq cm.

ELECTRICAL EQUIPMENT 30/40 A alternator; R 248 C 33 distributor.

DIMENSIONS AND WEIGHT front track: 50.71 in, 129 cm; weight: 1,709 lb, 775 kg; weight distribution: 60% front, 40% rear.

BODY 5 seats, reclining backrests.

PRACTICAL INSTRUCTIONS oil: engine 5.3 imp pt, 6.3 US pt, 3 l; tappet clearances: inlet 0.006 in, 0.15 mm, exhaust 0.008 in, 0.20 mm; valve timing: 18° 54° 53° 23°.

OPTIONALS tinted glass; sunshine roof; rear window wiper-washer.

5 GTL

See 5 TL, except for:

PRICE IN GB: £ 2,724*
PRICE IN USA: $ 3,895*

ENGINE 78.7 cu in, 1,289 cc (2.87 x 3.03 in, 73 x 77 mm); compression ratio: 9.5:1; max power (DIN): 42 hp (30.2 kW) at 5,000 rpm; max torque (DIN): 61 lb ft, 8.4 kg m (82.4 Nm) at 2,500 rpm; max engine rpm: 5,000; 32.6 hp/l (23.4 kW/l); 1 Solex 32 SEIA downdraught carburettor.

TRANSMISSION axle ratio: 3.100.

PERFORMANCE max speeds: (I) 26 mph, 42 km/h; (II) 45 mph, 72 km/h; (III) 68 mph, 110 km/h; (IV) 85 mph, 136 km/h; power-weight ratio: 41.2 lb/hp (57.3 lb/kW), 18.7 kg/hp (26 kg/kW); speed in top at 1,000 rpm: 19.6 mph, 31.5 km/h; consumption: 32.5 m/imp gal, 27 m/US gal, 8.7 l x 100 km.

BRAKES servo.

DIMENSIONS AND WEIGHT width: 61.02 in, 155 cm; weight: 1,731 lb, 785 kg.

PRACTICAL INSTRUCTIONS valve timing: 22° 62° 65° 25°.

RENAULT 5 Alpine

5 Automatic

See 5 TL, except for:

PRICE IN GB: £ 3,050*
PRICE EX WORKS: 27,800** francs

ENGINE 78.7 cu in, 1,289 cc (2.87 x 3.03 in, 73 x 77 mm); compression ratio: 9.5:1; max power (DIN): 55 hp (40 kW) at 5,750 rpm; max torque (DIN): 70 lb ft, 9.6 kg m (94. Nm) at 2,500 rpm; max engine rpm: 5,750; 42.7 hp/l (3 kW/l); 1 Solex 32 SEIA downdraught.

TRANSMISSION gearbox: automatic transmission, hydrauli torque converter and planetary gears with 3 ratios, ma torque of converter at stall 2, possible manual selectio ratios: I 2.666, II 1.403, III 0.971, rev 1.942; axle rati 3.555.

PERFORMANCE max speeds: (I) 32 mph, 52 km/h; (II) 6 mph, 100 km/h; (III) 89 mph, 144 km/h; power-weigh ratio: 32.5 lb/hp (44.6 lb/kW), 14.7 kg/hp (20.2 kg/kW) speed in top at 1,000 rpm: 17.8 mph, 28.7 km/h; consump tion: 34 m/imp gal, 28.3 m/US gal, 8.3 l x 100 km.

BRAKES servo.

DIMENSIONS AND WEIGHT weight: 1,786 lb, 810 kg.

PRACTICAL INSTRUCTIONS valve timing: 22° 62° 65° 25°

5 TS

See 5 TL, except for:

PRICE IN GB: £ 3,050*
PRICE EX WORKS: 27,400** francs

ENGINE 78.7 cu in, 1,289 cc (2.87 x3.03 in, 73 x 77 mm) compression ratio: 9.5:1; max power (DIN): 64 hp (46. kW) at 6,000 rpm; max torque (DIN): 70 lb ft, 9.6 kg (94.1 Nm) at 3,500 rpm; 49.6 hp/l (36 kW/l); 1 Webe 32 DIR 62 downdraught twin barrel carburettor.

TRANSMISSION ratios: I 3.833, II 2.375, III 1.522, IV 1.02 rev 3.545; axle ratio: 3.625; width of rims: 4.5''; tyres: 14 SR x 13.

PERFORMANCE max speeds: (I) 29 mph, 47 km/h; (II 45 mph, 73 km/h; (III) 70 mph, 113 km/h; (IV) 94 mp 151 km/h; power-weight ratio: 27.6 lb/hp (38 lb/kW), 12. kg/hp (17.2 kg/kW); speed in top at 1,000 rpm: 17.2 mp 27.7 km/h; consumption: 31.7 m/imp gal, 26.4 m/US ga 8.9 l x 100 km.

CHASSIS rear suspension: anti-roll bar.

BRAKES servo.

ELECTRICAL EQUIPMENT 36 Ah battery; 50 A alternato iodine headlamps.

DIMENSIONS AND WEIGHT weight: 1,764 lb, 800 kg.

BODY rear window wiper-washer (standard).

PRACTICAL INSTRUCTIONS valve timing: 22° 62° 65° 25° tyre pressure: front 23 psi, 1.6 atm, rear 27 psi, 1.9 atm

5 Alpine

See 5 TL, except for:

PRICE EX WORKS: 37,700** francs

ENGINE 85.2 cu in, 1,397 cc (2.99 x 3.03 in, 76 x 77 mm) compression ratio: 10:1; max power (DIN): 93 hp (67 kW at 6,400 rpm; max torque (DIN): 86 lb ft, 11.8 kg m (115. Nm) at 4,000 rpm; max engine rpm: 6,500; 66.6 hp/l (4 kW/l); 1 Weber 32 DIR 58 downdraught twin barrel ca burettor.

TRANSMISSION gears: 5 fully synchronized; ratios: I 3.818 II 2.235, III 1.478, IV 1.036, V 0.861, rev 3.083; axle ratio 3.875; width of rims: 4.5''; tyres: 155/70 HR x 13.

PERFORMANCE max speeds: (I) 27 mph, 44 km/h; (II) 4 mph, 74 km/h; (III) 70 mph, 113 km/h; (IV) 100 mph, 16 km/h; (V) 109 mph, 175 km/h; power-weight ratio: 20. lb/hp (28 lb/kW), 9.1 kg/hp (12.7 kg/kW); carrying ca pacity: 992 lb, 450 kg; speed in top at 1,000 rpm: 18. mph, 30.2 km/h; consumption: 26.4 m/imp gal, 22 m/U gal, 10.7 l x 100 km.

CHASSIS rear suspension: anti-roll bar.

STEERING turns lock to lock: 3.66.

BRAKES servo.

ELECTRICAL EQUIPMENT 36 Ah battery; 50 A alternator; i dine headlamps.

RENAULT 5 Alpine

IMENSIONS AND WEIGHT wheel base: 94.96 in, 241 cm (ight), 96.14 in, 244 cm (left); tracks: 50.94 in, 129 cm ont, 50 in, 127 cm rear; length: 139.49 in, 354 cm; height: .17 in, 138 cm; ground clearance: 4.72 in, 12 cm; weight 374 lb, 850 kg.

DY tinted glass, rear window wiper-washer (standard).

RACTICAL INSTRUCTIONS gearbox and final drive oil: 3 1p pt, 3.6 US pt, 1.7 l; tappet clearances: inlet 0.008- 009 in, 0.20-0.22 mm, exhaust 0.010-0.011 in, 0.25-0.27 mm; lve timing: 30° 72° 72° 30°; tyre pressure: front 23 psi, 1.6 m, rear 28 psi, 2 atm.

PTIONALS luxury equipment; metallic spray.

6

ICE EX WORKS: 21,700 francs

IGINE front, 4 stroke; 4 cylinders, vertical, in line; 51.6 in, 845 cc (2.28 x 3.15 in, 58 x 80 mm); compression tio: 8:1; max power (DIN): 34 hp (25 kW) at 5,000 rpm; ax torque (DIN): 42 lb ft, 5.8 kg m (56.9 Nm) at 3,000 m; max engine rpm: 5,200; 40.2 hp/l (29.6 kW/l); cast n block, wet liners, light alloy head; 3 crankshaft bear- gs; valves: overhead, in line, push-rods and rockers; mshafts: 1, side; lubrication: gear pump, filter in sump, 4 imp pt. 5.3 US pt, 2.5 l; 1 Solex 32 DIS downdraught rburettor; fuel feed: mechanical pump; sealed circuit oling, liquid, expansion tank, 9.7 imp pt, 11.6 US pt, 5.5 l.

ANSMISSION driving wheels: front; clutch: single dry ate (diaphragm); gearbox: mechanical; gears: 4, fully nchronized; ratios: I 3.833, II 2.235, III 1.458, IV 1.026, v 3.545; lever: on facia; final drive: spiral bevel; axle tio: 4.125; width of rims: 4''; tyres: 135 SR x 13.

RFORMANCE max speeds: (I) 24 mph, 39 km/h; (II) 39 ph, 63 km/h; (III) 60 mph, 97 km/h; (IV) 73 mph, 8 km/h; power-weight ratio: 50.9 lb/hp (69.2 lb/kW), 23.1 /hp (31.4 kg/kW); carrying capacity: 816 lb, 370 kg; eed in top at 1,000 rpm: 14.7 mph, 23.7 km/h; consump- n: 32.1 m/imp gal, 26.7 m/US gal, 8.8 l x 100 km.

ASSIS platform; front suspension: independent, wish- nes, longitudinal torsion bars, anti-roll bar, telescopic mpers; rear: independent, swinging longitudinal trailing ns, transverse torsion bars, telescopic dampers.

EERING rack-and-pinion; turns lock to lock: 3.75.

AKES drum (diameter 8.98 in, 22.8 cm front, 6.30 in, 16 rear), dual circuit, rear compensator; lining area: front .8 sq in, 289 sq cm, rear 17.4 sq in, 112 sq cm, total .2 sq in, 401 sq cm.

ECTRICAL EQUIPMENT 12 V; 28 Ah battery; 35 A alter- tor; Lucas distributor; 2 headlamps.

MENSIONS AND WEIGHT wheel base: 96.46 in, 245 cm ght), 94.49 in, 240 cm (left); tracks: 50.39 in, 128 cm nt, 48.82 in, 124 cm rear; length: 151.97 in, 386 cm; dth: 59.06 in, 150 cm; height: 57.87 in, 147 cm; ground earance: 4.92 in, 12.5 cm; weight: 1,731 lb, 785 kg; weight stribution: 56.5% front, 43.5% rear; turning circle: 34.1 , 10.4 m; fuel tank: 8.6 imp gal, 10.3 US gal, 39 l.

BODY saloon/sedan; 4 + 1 doors; 4 seats, separate front seats; folding rear seat; heated rear window.

PRACTICAL INSTRUCTIONS fuel: 90 oct petrol; oil: engine 4.4 imp pt, 5.3 US pt, 2.5 l, SAE 10 or 20W-40, change every 4,650 miles, 7,500 km - gearbox and final drive 3.2 imp pt, 3.8 US pt, 1.8 l, SAE 80 EP, change every 9,300 miles, 15,000 km; greasing: none; tappet clearances: inlet 0.006-0.007 in, 0.15-0.18 mm, exhaust 0.007-0.009 in, 0.18-0.22 mm; valve timing: 16° 52° 52° 22°; tyre pressure: front 21 psi, 1.5 atm, rear 24 psi, 1.7 atm.

OPTIONALS reclining backrests; luxury interior.

6 TL

See 6, except for:

PRICE IN GB: £ 2,794*
PRICE EX WORKS: 23,200 francs**

ENGINE 67.6 cu in, 1,108 cc (2.76 x 2.83 in, 70 x 72 mm); compression ratio: 9.5:1; max power (DIN): 48 hp (34.5 kW) at 5,300 rpm; max torque (DIN): 57 lb ft, 7.9 kg m (77.5 Nm) at 3,000 rpm; max engine rpm: 5,700; 43.3 hp/l (31.2 kW/l); 5 crankshaft bearings; valves: slanted; lubrication: full flow filter, 5.3 imp pt, 6.3 US pt, 3 l; 1 Zenith 32 IF 8 or Solex 32 SEIA downdraught carburettor; cooling system: 11.1 imp pt, 13.3 US pt, 6.3 l, electric thermostatic fan.

RENAULT 6 TL

TRANSMISSION tyres: 145 SR x 13.

PERFORMANCE max speeds: (I) 22 mph, 35 km/h; (II) 39 mph, 63 km/h; (III) 60 mph, 97 km/h; (IV) 84 mph, 135 km/h; power-weight ratio: 37.7 lb/hp (52.2 lb/kW), 17.1 kg/hp (23.7 kg/kW); carrying capacity: 882 lb, 400 kg; speed in top at 1,000 rpm: 15.2 mph, 24.4 km/h; consump- tion: 30.7 m/imp gal, 25.6 m/US gal, 9.2 l x 100 km.

CHASSIS rear suspension: anti-roll bar.

BRAKES front disc (diameter 8.98 in, 22.8 cm), rear drum, dual circuit, rear compensator; lining area: front 19.8 sq in, 128 sq cm, rear 52.6 sq in, 339 sq cm, total 72.4 sq in, 467 sq cm.

ELECTRICAL EQUIPMENT 30/40 A alternator.

DIMENSIONS AND WEIGHT tracks: 50.79 in, 129 cm front, 49.21 in, 125 cm rear; weight: 1,808 lb, 820 kg; weight distribution: 56.1% front, 43.9% rear.

BODY 5 seats; reclining backrests (standard).

PRACTICAL INSTRUCTIONS oil: engine 5.3 imp pt, 6.3 US pt, 3 l; tappet clearances: inlet 0.006 in, 0.15 mm, ex- haust 0.009 in, 0.22 mm; valve timing: 18° 54° 53° 23°; tyre pressure: front 20 psi, 1.4 atm.

OPTIONALS tinted glass; metallic spray.

12 Berline

PRICE IN GB: £ 2,682*
PRICE EX WORKS: 25,500 francs**

ENGINE front, 4 stroke; 4 cylinders, vertical, in line; 78.7 cu in, 1,289 cc (2.87 x 3.03 in, 73 x 77 mm); compression ratio: 8.5:1; max power (DIN): 50 hp (36 kW) at 5,000 rpm; max torque (DIN): 64.5 lb ft, 8.9 kg m (87.3 Nm) at 3,000 rpm; max engine rpm: 5,200; 38.8 hp/l (27.9 kW/l); cast iron block, wet liners, light alloy head; 5 crankshaft bearings; valves: overhead, slanted, push-rods and rockers; camshafts: 1, side; lubrication: gear pump, filter in sump, 5.3 imp pt, 6.3 US pt, 3 l; 1 Solex 32 SEIA or Zenith 32 IF 7 down- draught carburettor; fuel feed: mechanical pump; sealed circuit cooling, liquid, expansion tank, 8.8 imp pt, 10.6 US pt, 5 l.

TRANSMISSION driving wheels: front; clutch: single dry plate (diaphragm); gearbox: mechanical; gears: 4, fully synchronized; ratios: I 3.818, II 2.235, III 1.478, IV 1.036, rev 3.083; lever: central; final drive: hypoid bevel; axle ratio: 3.778; width of rims: 4.5''; tyres: 145 SR x 13.

PERFORMANCE max speeds: (I) 23 mph, 37 km/h; (II) 40 mph, 64 km/h; (III) 60 mph, 96 km/h; (IV) 85 mph, 137 km/h; power-weight ratio: 39.7 lb/hp (55.1 lb/kW), 18 kg/hp (25 kg/kW); carrying capacity: 882 lb, 400 kg; speed in top at 1,000 rpm: 16.4 mph, 26.4 km/h; consumption: 27.4 m/imp gal, 22.8 m/US gal, 10.3 l x 100 km.

CHASSIS integral; front suspension: independent, wishbones, anti-roll bar, coil springs/telescopic dampers; rear: rigid axle, trailing arms, A-bracket, anti-roll bar, coil springs/ telescopic dampers.

STEERING rack-and-pinion; turns lock to lock: 3.50.

BRAKES front disc (diameter 8.98 in, 22.8 cm), rear drum, rear compensator; lining area: front 22.2 sq in, 143 sq cm, rear 33.2 sq in, 214 sq cm, total 55.4 sq in, 357 sq cm.

ELECTRICAL EQUIPMENT 12 V; 36 Ah battery; 38 A alter- nator; 2 headlamps.

DIMENSIONS AND WEIGHT wheel base: 96.06 in, 244 cm; front and rear tracks: 51.57 in, 131 cm; length: 171.26 in, 435 cm; width: 63.78 in, 162 cm; height: 56.30 in, 143 cm; ground clearance: 4.41 in, 11.2 cm; weight: 1,985 lb, 900 kg; weight distribution: 58.3% front, 41.7% rear; turning circle: 35.4 ft, 10.8 m; fuel tank: 10.3 imp gal, 12.4 US gal, 47 l.

BODY saloon/sedan; 4 doors; 5 seats, separate front seats; heated rear window.

PRACTICAL INSTRUCTIONS fuel: 92 oct petrol; oil: engine 5.3 imp pt, 6.3 US pt, 3 l, SAE 10W-40, change every 4,650 miles, 7,500 km - gearbox and final drive 3.5 imp pt, 4.2 US pt, 2 l, SAE 80 EP, change every 9,300 miles, 15,000 km; greasing: none; tappet clearances: inlet 0.006 in, 0.15 mm, exhaust 0.908 in, 0.20 mm; valve timing: 22° 62° 60° 20°; tyre pressure: front 23 psi, 1.6 atm, rear 26 psi, 1.8 atm.

OPTIONALS luxury interior; metallic spray.

12 Break

See 12 Berline, except for:

PRICE EX WORKS: 28,500 francs**

TRANSMISSION tyres: 155 SR x 13.

12 BREAK

PERFORMANCE max speeds: (I) 24 mph, 38 km/h; (II) 40 mph, 65 km/h; (III) 61 mph, 98 km/h; (IV) 86 mph, 138 km/h; power-weight ratio: 42.3 lb/hp (58.8 lb/kW), 19.2 kg/hp (26.7 kg/kW); carrying capacity: 937 lb, 425 kg; speed in top at 1,000 rpm: 16.8 mph, 27 km/h.

BRAKES front disc, rear drum, servo; lining area: front 22.2 sq in, 143 sq cm, rear 38.3 sq in, 247 sq cm, total 60.5 sq cm, 390 sq cm.

ELECTRICAL EQUIPMENT 50 A alternator.

DIMENSIONS AND WEIGHT length: 172.09 in, 437 cm; height: 57.09 in, 145 cm; ground clearance: 5.12 in, 13 cm; weight: 2,117 lb, 960 kg.

BODY estate car/station wagon; 4 + 1 doors; folding rear seat.

12 TL Berline

See 12 Berline, except for:

PRICE IN GB: £ 2,980*
PRICE EX WORKS: 27,500 francs**

ENGINE compression ratio: 9.5:1; max power (DIN): 54 hp (39 kW) at 5,250 rpm; max torque (DIN): 65 lb ft, 9 kg m (88.3 Nm) at 3,500 rpm; max engine rpm: 5,500; 41.9 hp/l (30.2 kW/l).

PERFORMANCE max speed: 88 mph, 142 km/h; power-weight ratio: 36.8 lb/hp (50.9 lb/kW), 16.7 kg/hp (23.1 kg/kW); consumption: 28.8 m/imp gal, 24 m/US gal, 9.8 l x 100 km.

BRAKES front disc, rear drum, servo.

BODY reclining backrests, luxury equipment.

PRACTICAL INSTRUCTIONS fuel: 98-100 oct petrol.

OPTIONALS tinted glass.

12 Break TL

See 12 TL Berline, except for:

PRICE IN GB: £ 3,331*
PRICE EX WORKS: 30,200 francs**

TRANSMISSION tyres: 155 SR x 13.

PERFORMANCE max speed: 89 mph, 143 km/h; power-weight ratio: 39.2 lb/hp (54.3 lb/kW), 17.8 kg/hp (24.6 kg/kW); carrying capacity: 937 lb, 425 kg; speed in top at 1,000 rpm: 16.8 mph, 27 km/h.

BRAKES lining area: front 22.2 sq in, 143 sq cm, rear 38.3 sq in, 247 sq cm, total 60.5 sq in, 390 sq cm.

ELECTRICAL EQUIPMENT 50 A alternator.

DIMENSIONS AND WEIGHT length: 172.09 in, 437 cm; height: 57.09 in, 145 cm; ground clearance: 5.12 in, 13 cm; weight: 2,117 lb, 960 kg.

BODY estate car/station wagon; 4 + 1 doors; folding rear seat.

12 Break TS

See 12 Berline, except for:

PRICE EX WORKS: 32,300 francs**

ENGINE compression ratio: 9.5:1; max power (DIN): 60 hp (43.5 kW) at 5,500 rpm; max torque (DIN): 68 lb/ft, 9.4 kg m (92.2 Nm) at 3,500 rpm; max engine rpm: 5,700; 46.5 hp/l (33.7 kW/l); 1 Weber 32 DIR 21 downdraught twin barrel carburettor.

TRANSMISSION tyres: 155 SR x 13.

PERFORMANCE max speeds: (I) 29 mph, 47 km/h; (II) 45 mph, 72 km/h; (III) 68 mph, 110 km/h; (IV) 92 mph, 148 km/h; power-weight ratio: 36 lb/hp (49.7 lb/kW), 16.3 kg/hp (22.5 kg/kW); carrying capacity: 937 lb, 425 kg; speed in top at 1,000 rpm: 16.8 mph, 27 km/h.

BRAKES front disc, rear drum, servo; lining area: front 22.2 sq in, 143 sq cm, rear 38.3 sq in, 247 sq cm, total 60.5 sq in, 390 sq cm.

ELECTRICAL EQUIPMENT 50 A alternator; R 24C 34 distributor; iodine long-distance lights.

DIMENSIONS AND WEIGHT length: 172.09 in, 437 cm;

---

height: 57.09 in, 145 cm; ground clearance: 5,12 in, 13 cm; weight: 2,161 lb, 980 kg.

BODY estate car/station wagon; 4 + 1 doors; folding rear seat; rear window wiper-washer.

PRACTICAL INSTRUCTIONS fuel: 98-100 oct petrol; valve timing: 22° 62° 65° 25°; tyre pressure: front 23 psi, 1.6 atm, rear 26 psi, 1.8 atm.

OPTIONALS luxury interior; metallic spray; tinted glass.

12 Break Automatic

See 12 Break TS, except for:

PRICE EX WORKS: 33,600 francs**

ENGINE 1 Weber 32 DIR 39 downdraught twin barrel carburettor.

TRANSMISSION gearbox: automatic transmission, hydraulic torque converter and planetary gears with 3 ratios, max ratio of converter at stall 2.3, possible manual selection; ratios: I 2.600, II 1.609, III 1.114, rev 2.229; axle ratio: 3.555.

PERFORMANCE max speeds: (I) 37 mph, 60 km/h; (II) 60 mph, 97 km/h; (III) 89 mph, 144 km/h; power-weight ratio: 36 lb/hp (49.7 lb/kW), 16.3 kg/hp (22.5 kg/kW); speed in top at 1,000 rpm: 16.6 mph, 26.7 km/h.

RENAULT 12 Berline

RENAULT 12 Break Automatic

---

14 TL

PRICE IN GB: £ 2,927*
PRICE EX WORKS: 27,000 francs**

ENGINE front, transverse, slanted 72° to rear, 4 stroke; cylinders, vertical, in line; 74.3 cu in, 1,218 cc (2.95 2.72 in, 75 x 69 mm); compression ratio: 9.3:1; max power (DIN): 57 hp (41 kW) at 6,000 rpm; max torque (DIN): 67.4 lb ft, 9.3 kg m (91.3 Nm) at 3,000 rpm; max engine rpm: 6,000; 46.8 hp/l (33.7 kW/l); light alloy block and head, wet liners, hemispherical combustion chamber, 5 crankshaft bearings; valves: overhead, Vee-slanted, rockers; camshafts: 1, overhead; lubrication: gear pump, full flow filter, 7 imp pt, 8.3 US pt, 4 l; 1 Solex 32 SIE horizontal single barrel carburettor; sealed circuit cooling, liquid, expansion tank, 10.6 imp pt, 12.7 US pt, 6 l, electric thermostatic fan.

TRANSMISSION driving wheels: front; clutch: single dry plate (diaphragm); gearbox: mechanical, in unit with engine and final drive; gears: 4, fully synchronized; ratios: I 3.883, II 2.296, III 1.501, IV 1.042, rev 3.568; lever: central; final drive: spiral bevel; axle ratio: 3.867; width of rims: 4.5''; tyres: 145 SR x 13.

PERFORMANCE max speeds: (I) 26 mph, 42 km/h; (II) mph, 70 km/h; (III) 66 mph, 107 km/h; (IV) 89 mph, 1 km/h; power-weight ratio: 33.4 lb/hp (46.5 lb/kW), 1 kg/hp (21.1 kg/kW); carrying capacity: 882 lb, 400 kg; acceleration: standing ¼ mile 20 sec; speed in top

1,000 rpm: 15.9 mph, 25.6 km/h; consumption: 31 m/imp gal, 25.8 m/US gal, 9.1 l x 100 km.

CHASSIS integral; front suspension: independent, by McPherson, coil springs/telescopic damper struts, lower wishbones, anti-roll bar; rear: independent, swinging longitudinal trailing arms, transverse torsion bars, telescopic dampers.

STEERING rack-and-pinion; turns lock to lock: 4.

BRAKES front disc (diameter 9.49 in, 24.1 cm), rear drum, dual circuit, rear compensator, servo; lining area: front 22.2 sq in, 143 sq cm, rear 35.2 sq in, 227 sq cm, total 57.4 sq in, 378 sq cm.

ELECTRICAL EQUIPMENT 12 V; 32 Ah battery; 40 A alternator; 2 headlamps.

DIMENSIONS AND WEIGHT wheel base: 98.35 in, 250 cm (right), 99.61 in, 253 cm (left); tracks: 53.23 in, 135 cm front, 54.25 in, 138 cm rear; length: 158.46 in, 402 cm; width: 63.94 in, 162 cm; height: 55.31 in, 140 cm; ground clearance: 5.91 in, 15 cm; weight: 1,907 lb, 865 kg; turning circle: 34.8 ft, 10.6 m; fuel tank: 10.6 imp gal, 12.7 US gal, 48 l.

BODY saloon/sedan; 4 doors; 5 seats, separate front seats; folding rear seat; heated rear window.

PRACTICAL INSTRUCTIONS fuel: 98-100 oct petrol; oil: engine, gearbox and final drive 7 imp pt, 8.3 US pt, 4 l, change every 4,650 miles, 7,500 km; tappet clearances: inlet 0.004-0.006 in, 0.10-0.15 mm, exhaust 0.009-0.011 in, 0.23-0.28 mm; valve timing: 15° 45° 46° 15°; tyre pressure: front 24 psi, 1.7 atm, rear 27 psi, 1.9 atm.

OPTIONALS luxury interior; metallic spray; sunshine roof.

14 GTL

See 14, except for:

PRICE IN GB: £ 2,976*
PRICE EX WORKS: 28,900** francs

BODY luxury interior (standard); reclining backrests on front seats.

OPTIONALS tinted glass.

14 TS

See 14 TL, except for:

PRICE EX WORKS: 31,100** francs

ENGINE max power (DIN) 69 hp (50.5 kW) at 6,000 rpm; max torque (DIN): 71 lb/ft, 9.8 kg m (96.2 Nm) at 3,000 rpm; 1 Solex 32 MMI horizontal twin barrel carburettor.

PERFORMANCE max speed: 96 mph, 155 km/h; power-weight ratio: 28.1 lb/hp (38.4 lb/kW), 12.7 kg/hp (17.4 kg/kW); acceleration: standing 1/4 mile 18.7 sec; consumption: 27.4 m/imp gal, 22.8 m/US gal, 10.3 l x 100 km.

RENAULT 14 TL

CHASSIS rear suspension: anti-roll bar.

BRAKES lining area: front 19.8 sq in, 128.2 sq cm, rear 65.4 sq in, 422.2 sq cm, total 85.2 sq in, 550.4 sq cm.

ELECTRICAL EQUIPMENT 50 A alternator.

DIMENSIONS AND WEIGHT weight: 1,940 lb, 880 kg.

PRACTICAL INSTRUCTIONS valve timing: 19° 49° 49° 19°.

OPTIONALS tinted glass; rear window wiper-washer.

16 TL (55 hp)

PRICE IN GB: £ 3,594*
PRICE EX WORKS: 31,700** francs

ENGINE front, 4 stroke; 4 cylinders, vertical, in line; 95.5 cu in, 1,565 cc (3.03 x 3.31 in, 77 x 84 mm); compression ratio: 8:1; max power (DIN): 55 hp (40 kW) at 5,000 rpm; max torque (DIN): 79 lb ft, 10.9 kg m (106.9 Nm) at 2,500 rpm; max engine rpm: 5,200; 35.1 hp/l (25.6 kW/l); light alloy block and head, wet liners; 5 crankshaft bearings; valves: overhead, in line, slanted at 20°, push-rods and rockers; camshafts: 1, side; lubrication: eccentric pump, filter in sump, 7 imp pt, 8.5 US pt, 4 l; 1 Solex MIMAT downdraught carburettor; fuel feed: mechanical pump; sealed circuit cooling, liquid, expansion tank, 10.9 imp pt, 13.1 US pt, 6.2 l, electric thermostatic fan.

TRANSMISSION driving wheels: front; clutch: single dry plate (diaphragm); gearbox: mechanical; gears: 4, fully synchronized; ratios: I 3.818, II 2.235, III 1.478, IV 1.036, rev 3.083; lever: steering column; final drive: hypoid bevel; axle ratio: 3.778; width of rims: 4.5''; tyres: 145 SR x 14.

PERFORMANCE max speeds: (I) 24 mph, 39 km/h; (II) 41 mph, 66 km/h; (III) 63 mph, 101 km/h; (IV) 87 mph, 140 km/h; power-weight ratio: 40.5 lb/hp (55.7 lb/kW), 18.4 kg/hp (25.2 kg/kW); carrying capacity: 882 lb, 400 kg; speed in top at 1,000 rpm: 17.1 mph, 27.6 km/h; consumption: 27.4 m/imp gal, 22.8 m/US gal, 10.3 l x 100 km.

CHASSIS platform; front suspension: independent, wishbones, longitudinal torsion bars, anti-roll bar, telescopic dampers; rear: independent, swinging longitudinal trailing arms, transverse torsion bar, anti-roll bar, telescopic dampers.

STEERING rack-and-pinion; turns lock to lock: 4.11.

BRAKES front disc, rear drum, rear compensator, dual circuit, servo; lining area: front 22.2 sq in, 143 sq cm, rear 42.3 sq in, 273 sq cm, total 64.5 sq in, 416 sq cm.

ELECTRICAL EQUIPMENT 12 V; 36 Ah battery; 30/40 A alternator; 2 headlamps.

DIMENSIONS AND WEIGHT wheel base: 104.33 in, 265 cm (right), 107.09 in, 272 cm (left); tracks: 52.76 in, 134 cm front, 50.79 in, 129 cm rear; length: 166.93 in, 424 cm; width: 64.17 in, 163 cm; height: 57.09 in, 145 cm; ground clearance: 4.13 in, 10.5 cm; weight: 2,227 lb, 1,010 kg; weight distribution: 55.9% front, 44.1% rear; turning circle: 36.1 ft, 11 m; fuel tank: 11 imp gal, 13.2 US gal, 50 l.

BODY saloon/sedan; 4 + 1 doors; 5 seats, separate front seats, reclining backrests; folding rear seat; heated rear window.

PRACTICAL INSTRUCTIONS fuel: 85 oct petrol; oil: engine 7 imp pt, 8.5 US pt, 4 l, SAE 10W-40, change every 4,650 miles, 7,500 km - gearbox and final drive 2.8 imp pt, 3.4 US pt, 1.6 l, SAE 80 EP, change every 9,300 miles, 15,000 km; greasing: none; tappet clearances: inlet 0.008 in, 0.20 mm, exhaust 0.010 in, 0.25 mm; valve timing: 18° 54° 58° 18°; tyre pressure: front 23 psi, 1.6 atm, rear 28 psi, 2 atm.

OPTIONALS luxury interior; metallic spray.

16 TL (66 hp)

See 16 TL (55 hp), except for:

PRICE EX WORKS: 32,400** francs

ENGINE compression ratio: 8.6:1; max power (DIN): 66 hp (47.5 kW) at 5,000 rpm; max torque (DIN): 82 lb ft, 11.3 kg m (110.8 Nm) at 3,000 rpm; max engine rpm: 5,500; 42.2 hp/l (30.3 kW/l).

PERFORMANCE max speeds: (I) 25 mph, 41 km/h; (II) 43 mph, 70 km/h; (III) 66 mph, 106 km/h; (IV) 92 mph, 148 km/h; power-weight ratio: 33.7 lb/hp (46.9 lb/kW), 15.3 kg/hp (21.3 kg/kW); consumption: 26.9 m/imp gal, 22.4 m/US gal, 10.5 l x 100 km.

PRACTICAL INSTRUCTIONS fuel: 98-100 oct petrol.

OPTIONALS tinted glass; electrically-controlled sunshine roof.

16 TL Automatic

See 16 TL (55 hp), except for:

PRICE IN GB: £ 3,903*
PRICE EX WORKS: 34,900** francs

ENGINE 100.5 cu in, 1,647 cc (3.11 x 3.31 in, 79 x 84 mm); compression ratio: 8.6:1; max power (DIN): 68 hp (49 kW) at 5,000 rpm; max torque (DIN): 87 lb ft, 12 kg m (117.7 Nm) at 3,000 rpm; 41.3 hp/l (31.3 kW/l); valves: Vee-slanted.

TRANSMISSION gearbox: automatic transmission, hydraulic torque converter and planetary gears with 3 ratios, max ratio of converter at stall 2.3, possible manual selection; ratios: I 2.396, II 1.484, III 1.027, rev 2.054.

PERFORMANCE max speeds: (I) 37 mph, 59 km/h; (II) 60 mph, 96 km/h; (III) 90 mph, 145 km/h; power-weight ratio: 33.9 lb/hp (47 lb/kW), 15.4 kg/hp (21.3 kg/kW); speed in top at 1,000 rpm: 17.2 mph, 27.7 km/h; consumption: 26.4 m/imp gal, 22 m/US gal, 10.7 l x 100 km.

ELECTRICAL EQUIPMENT 50 A alternator.

DIMENSIONS AND WEIGHT weight: 2,304 lb, 1,045 kg; weight distribution: 56.9% front, 43.1% rear.

RENAULT 14 GTL

16 TL AUTOMATIC

PRACTICAL INSTRUCTIONS fuel: 98-100 oct petrol; oil: automatic transmission and final drive 10.6 imp pt, 12.7 US pt, 6 l, change every 18,600 miles, 30,000 km; tyre pressure: front 24 psi, 1.7 atm.

OPTIONALS tinted glass; electric sunshine roof.

16 TX

See 16 TL (55 hp), except for:

PRICE IN GB: £ 4,377*
PRICE EX WORKS: 37,100 francs**

ENGINE 100.5 cu in, 1,647 cc (3.11 x 3.31 in, 79 x 84 mm); compression ratio: 9.25:1; max power (DIN): 90 hp (65 kW) at 6,000 rpm; max torque (DIN): 95 lb ft, 13.1 kg m (128.5 Nm) at 4,000 rpm; max engine rpm: 6,300; 54.6 hp/l (39.5 kW/l); valves: Vee-slanted; lubrication: eccentric pump, full flow filter; 1 Weber 32 DAR 7 twin barrel carburettor; cooling system: 12 imp pt, 14.4 US pt, 6.8 l.

TRANSMISSION gears: 5, fully synchronized; ratios: I 3.818, II 2.235, III 1.478, IV 1.036, V 0.861, rev 3.083; axle ratio: 3.875; tyres: 155 SR x 14.

PERFORMANCE max speeds: (I) 28 mph, 45 km/h; (II) 48 mph, 77 km/h; (III) 72 mph, 116 km/h; (IV) 103 mph, 166 km/h; (V) 106 mph, 170 km/h; power-weight ratio: 26.1 lb/hp (36.1 lb/kW), 11.8 kg/hp (16.4 kg/kW); carrying capacity: 937 lb, 425 kg; acceleration: 0-50 mph (0-80 km/h) 8.1 sec; speed in top at 1,000 rpm: 20.7 mph, 33.3 km/h; consumption: 26.4 m/imp gal, 22 m/US gal, 10.7 l x 100 km.

ELECTRICAL EQUIPMENT 50 A alternator; 4 iodine headlamps.

DIMENSIONS AND WEIGHT ground clearance: 4.13 in, 10.5 cm; weight: 2,348 lb, 1,065 kg; weight distribution: 56.6% front, 43.4% rear.

BODY reclining backrests with built-in headrests; electric windows; rear window wiper-washer.

PRACTICAL INSTRUCTIONS fuel: 98-100 oct petrol; oil: gearbox and final drive 3 imp pt, 3.6 US pt, 1.7 l; valve timing: 24° 68° 68° 24°; tyre pressure: front 24 psi, 1.7 atm.

OPTIONALS luxury interior; metallic spray; leather upholstery; tinted glass; electric sunshine roof air-conditioning.

16 TX Automatic

See 16 TX, except for:

PRICE IN GB: £ 4,686*
PRICE EX WORKS: 40,300 francs**

ENGINE max torque (DIN): 96 lb ft, 13.2 kg m (129.5 Nm) at 3,500 rpm.

TRANSMISSION gearbox: automatic transmission, hydraulic torque converter and planetary gears with 3 ratios, max ratio of converter at stall 2.3, possible manual selection; ratios: I 2.459, II 1.523, III 1.054, rev 2.108; axle ratio: 3.556.

PERFORMANCE max speeds: (I) 47 mph, 76 km/h; (II) 76 mph, 123 km/h; (III) 103 mph, 165 km/h; power-weight ratio: 26.7 lb/hp (36.9 lb/kW), 12.1 kg/hp (16.8 kg/kW); carrying capacity: 882 lb, 400 kg; speed in top at 1,000 rpm: 18.5 mph, 29.7 km/h; consumption: 25.2 m/imp gal, 21 m/US gal, 11.2 l x 100 km.

DIMENSIONS AND WEIGHT weight: 2,403 lb, 1,090 kg.

PRACTICAL INSTRUCTIONS oil: automatic transmission and final drive 10.6 imp pt, 12.7 US pt, 6 l, change every 18,600 miles, 30,000 km; valve timing: 21° 59° 59° 21°.

18 TL

PRICE EX WORKS: 30,300 francs**

ENGINE front, 4 stroke 4 cylinders, vertical, in line; 85.2 cu in, 1,397 cc (2.99 x 3.03 in, 76 x 77 mm); compression ratio: 9.25:1; max power (DIN): 64 hp (46 kW) at 5,500 rpm; max torque (DIN): 76.1 lb ft, 10.5 kg m (103 Nm) at 3,000 rpm; max engine rpm: 6,000; 45.8 hp/l (32.9 kW/l); light alloy block and head, wet liners; 5 crankshaft bearings; valves: overhead, in line, push-rods and rockers; camshafts: 1, in side; lubrication: gear pump, filter in sump, 5.3 imp pt, 6.3 US pt, 3 l; 1 Solex 32 EITA downdraught single barrel carburettor; fuel feed: mechanical pump; sealed circuit cooling, liquid, expansion tank, 10.5 imp pt, 12.7 US pt, 6 l.

TRANSMISSION driving wheels: front; clutch: single dry plate (diaphragm); gearbox: mechanical; gears: 4, fully synchronized; ratios: I 3.818, II 2.235, III 1.478, IV 0.971, rev 3.083; lever: central; final drive: hypoid bevel; axle ratio: 3.778; width of rims: 5''; tyres: 155 SR x 13.

PERFORMANCE max speeds: (I) 25 mph, 40 km/h; (II) 42 mph, 68 km/h; (III) 64 mph, 103 km/h; (IV) 95 mph, 153 km/h; power-weight ratio: 31.7 lb/hp (44.1 lb/kW), 14.4 kg/hp (20 kg/kW); carrying capacity: 904 lb, 410 kg; acceleration: standing ¼ mile 19.3 sec; speed in direct drive/top at 1,000 rpm: 17.9 mph, 28.8 km/h; consumption: 26.9 m/imp gal, 22.4 m/US gal, 10.5 l x 100 km.

CHASSIS integral; front suspension: independent, wishbones, anti-roll bar, coil springs/telescopic dampers; rear: rigid axle, trailing arms, A-bracket, anti-roll bar, coil springs/telescopic dampers.

STEERING rack-and-pinion; turns lock to lock: 3.55.

BRAKES front disc, rear drum, dual circuit, rear compensator, servo; lining area: front 22.2 sq in, 143.2 sq cm, rear 66.4 - 70.4 sq in, 428 - 454 sq cm, total 88.6 - 92.6 sq in, 571.2 - 597.2 sq cm.

ELECTRICAL EQUIPMENT 12 V; 36 Ah battery; 50 A alternator; 2 headlamps.

DIMENSIONS AND WEIGHT wheel base: 96.1 in, 244 cm; tracks: 55.7 in, 142 cm front, 53.4 in, 136 cm rear; length: 172 in, 437 cm; width: 66.2 in, 168 cm; height: 55.3 in, 140 cm; weight: 2,028 lb, 920 kg; weight distribution: 60.3% front, 39.7% rear; turning circle between walls: 36.1 ft, 1 m; fuel tank: 11.7 imp gal, 14 US gal, 53 l.

BODY saloon/sedan; 4 doors; 5 seats, separate front seats, reclining backrests; heated rear window.

PRACTICAL INSTRUCTIONS fuel: 98-100 oct petrol; oil: engine 5.3 imp pt, 6.3 US pt, 3 l, SAE 15W-40 change every 4,650 miles, 7,500 km - gearbox and final drive 3.5 imp pt, 4.2 US pt, 2 l, SAE 80 EP, change every 18,600 miles, 30,000 km; greasing: none; tappet clearances: inlet 0.006 in, 0.15 mm, exhaust 0.008 in, 0.20 mm; valve timing: 22° 62° 65° 25°; tyre pressure: front 26 psi, 1. atm, rear 28 psi, 2 atm.

OPTIONALS luxury interior; tinted glass; metallic spray.

18 GTL

See 18 TL, except for:

PRICE EX WORKS: 32,500 francs**

ELECTRICAL EQUIPMENT: halogen headlamps.

BODY luxury interior (standard); headrests.

OPTIONALS sunshine roof.

RENAULT 18 GTS

RENAULT 16 TX

18 TS

See 18 TL, except for:

PRICE EX WORKS: 33,100 francs**

ENGINE 100.5 cu in, 1,647 cc (3.11 x 3.31 in, 79 x 84 mm); compression ratio: 9.3:1; max power (DIN): 79 hp (57.4 kW) at 5,500 rpm; max torque (DIN): 90.6 lb ft, 12.5 kg m (122.7 Nm) at 3,000 rpm; max engine rpm: 6,000; 47.9 hp/l (34.8 kW/l); lubrication: 7 imp pt, 8.5 US pt, 4 l; 1 Solex 35 EITA; cooling system: 11.1 imp pt, 13.3 US pt, 6.3 l

PERFORMANCE max speeds: (I) 27 mph, 43 km/h; (II) 4 mph, 73 km/h; (III) 68 mph, 110 km/h; (IV) 101 mph, 16 km/h; power-weight ratio: 26.2 lb/hp, (36.1 lb/kW), 11. kg/hp (16.4 kg/kW); acceleration: standing ¼ mile 18. sec; consumption: 28.5 m/imp gal, 23.8 m/US gal, 9. l x 100 km.

ELECTRICAL EQUIPMENT iodine headlamps.

DIMENSIONS AND WEIGHT weight: 2,072 lb, 940 kg.

PRACTICAL INSTRUCTIONS oil: engine 7 imp pt, 8.5 US pt, 4 l; valve timing: 22° 70° 70° 22°.

18 TS Automatic

See 18 TS, except for:

PRICE EX WORKS: 36,300 francs**

TRANSMISSION gearbox: automatic transmission, hydraulic torque converter and planetary gears with 3 ratios, max ratio of converter at stall 2.3, possible manual selection; ratios: I 2.396, II 1.484, III 1.027, rev 2.054; axle ratio: .556.

PERFORMANCE max speeds: (I) 40 mph, 65 km/h; (II) 66 mph, 106 km/h; (III) 98 mph, 157 km/h; power-weight ratio: 26.8 lb/hp (36.9 lb/kW), 12.1 kg/hp (16.7 kg/kW); acceleration: standing ¼ mile 20.4 sec; consumption: 26.6 m/imp gal, 22.2 m/US gal, 10.6 l x 100 km.

DIMENSIONS AND WEIGHT weight: 2,117 lb, 960 kg.

18 GTS

See 18 TS, except for:

PRICE EX WORKS: 37,100** francs

TRANSMISSION gears: 5, fully synchronized; ratios: I 3.818, II 2.235, III 1.478, IV 1.036, V 0.861, rev 3.083.

PERFORMANCE max speeds: (I) 27 mph, 43 km/h; (II) 46 mph, 74 km/h; (III) 69 mph, 111 km/h; (IV) 96 mph, 155 km/h; (V) 103 mph, 165 km/h; power-weight ratio: 26.5 lb/hp (36.5 lb/kW), 12 kg/hp (16.5 kg/kW); speed in top at 1,000 rpm: 20.1 mph, 32.4 km/h.

DIMENSIONS AND WEIGHT weight: 2,095 lb, 950 kg.

RENAULT 18 GTS

18 GTS Automatic

See 18 TS, except for:

PRICE EX WORKS: 39,400** francs

TRANSMISSION gearbox: automatic transmission, hydraulic torque converter and planetary gears with 3 ratios, max ratio of converter at stall 2.3, possible manual selection; ratios: I 2.396, II 1.485, III 1.027, rev 2.054; axle ratio: .556.

PERFORMANCE max speeds: (I) 40 mph, 65 km/h; (II) 66 mph, 106 km/h; (III) 98 mph, 157 km/h; power-weight ratio: 26.8 lb/hp (36.9 lb/kW), 12.1 kg/hp (16.7 kg/kW); acceleration: standing ¼ mile 20.4 sec; consumption: 26.6 m/imp gal, 22.2 m/US gal, 10.6 l x 100 km.

DIMENSIONS AND WEIGHT weight: 2,117 lb, 960 kg.

15 TL

PRICE EX WORKS: 31,600** francs

ENGINE front, 4 stroke; 4 cylinders, vertical, in line; 78.7 cu in, 1,289 cc (2.87 x 3.03 in, 73 x 77 mm); compression ratio: 9.5:1; max power (DIN): 60 hp (43 kW) at 5,500 rpm; max torque (DIN): 67 lb ft, 9.3 kg m (91.2 Nm) at 3,500 rpm; max engine rpm: 6,000; 46.5 hp/l (33.3 kW/l); cast iron block, light alloy head, wet liners; 5 crankshaft bearings; valves: overhead, in line, slanted, push-rods and rockers;

camshafts: 1, side; lubrication: gear pump, full flow filter, 5.3 imp pt, 6.3 US pt, 3 l; 1 Weber 32 DIR Z.I.T. downdraught twin barrel carburettor; fuel feed: mechanical pump; sealed circuit cooling, liquid, expansion tank, 8.8 imp pt, 10.6 US pt, 5 l, electric thermostatic fan.

TRANSMISSION driving wheels: front; clutch: single dry plate (diaphragm); gearbox: mechanical; gears: 4, fully synchronized; ratios: I 3.818, II 2.235, III 1.478, IV 1.036, rev 3.083; lever: central; final drive: hypoid bevel; axle ratio: 3.778; width of rims: 4.5''; tyres: 145 SR x 13.

PERFORMANCE max speeds: (I) 29 mph, 46 km/h; (II) 46 mph, 74 km/h; (III) 70 mph, 113 km/h; (IV) 93 mph, 150 km/h; power-weight ratio: 35.5 lb/hp (49.5 lb/kW), 16.1 kg/hp (22.4 kg/kW); carrying capacity: 761 lb, 345 kg; speed in top at 1,000 rpm: 16.4 mph, 26.4 km/h; consumption: 26.6 m/imp gal, 22.2 m/US gal, 10.6 l x 100 km.

CHASSIS integral; front suspension: independent, wishbones, anti-roll bar, coil springs/telescopic dampers; rear: rigid axle, trailing arms, A-bracket, anti-roll bar, coil springs/telescopic dampers.

STEERING rack-and-pinion; turns lock to lock: 3.50.

BRAKES front disc, rear drum, rear compensator, dual circuit, servo; swept area: front 157.2 sq in, 1,014 sq cm, rear 70.1 sq in, 452 sq cm, total 227.3 sq in, 1,466 sq cm.

ELECTRICAL EQUIPMENT 12 V; 36 Ah battery; 50 A alternator; 2 iodine headlamps.

DIMENSIONS AND WEIGHT wheel base: 96.06 in, 244 cm; front and rear tracks: 51.57 in, 131 cm; length: 167.72 in, 426 cm; width: 64.17 in, 163 cm; height: 51.57 in, 131 cm; ground clearance: 4.45 in, 11.3 cm; weight: 2,128 lb, 965 kg; weight distribution: 60.6% front, 39.4% rear; turning circle: 36.1 ft, 11 m; fuel tank: 12.1 imp gal, 14.5 US gal, 55 l.

BODY coupé; 2 doors; 4 seats, separate front seats, reclining backrests; heated rear window.

PRACTICAL INSTRUCTIONS fuel: 98-100 oct petrol; oil: engine 5.3 imp pt, 6.3 US pt, 3 l, change every 4,650 miles, 7,500 km - gearbox and final drive 3.5 imp pt, 4.2 US pt, 2 l, change every 9,300 miles, 15,000 km; greasing: none; tappet clearances: inlet 0.006-0.007 in, 0.15-0.18 mm, exhaust 0.007-0.009 in, 0.18-0.22 mm; valve timing: 22° 62° 65° 25°; tyre pressure: front 26 psi, 1.8 atm, rear 28 psi, 2 atm.

OPTIONALS metallic spray.

15 GTL

See 15 TL, except for:

PRICE IN GB: £ 3,766*
PRICE EX WORKS: 33,900** francs

BODY luxury equipment.

OPTIONALS metallic spray; tinted glass.

17 TS Cabriolet

PRICE IN GB: £ 4,682*
PRICE IN USA: $ 7,945*

ENGINE front, 4 stroke; 4 cylinders, vertical, in line; 100.5 cu in, 1,647 cc (3.11 x 3.31 in, 79 x 84 mm); compression ratio: 9.25:1; max power (DIN): 98 hp (70.5 kW) at 5,750 rpm; max torque (DIN): 98 lb ft, 13.5 kg m (132.4 Nm) at 3,500 rpm; max engine rpm: 6,000; 59.5 hp/l (42.8 kW/l); light alloy block and head, wet liners; 5 crankshaft bearings; valves: overhead, Vee-slanted, push-rods and rockers; camshafts: 1, side; lubrication: rotary pump, full flow filter, 7 imp pt, 8.5 US pt, 4 l; 1 Weber 32 DARA downdraught twin barrel carburettor; fuel feed: mechanical pump; sealed circuit cooling, liquid, expansion tank, 9.7 imp pt, 11.6 US pt, 5.5 l, electric thermostatic fan.

TRANSMISSION driving wheels: front; clutch: single dry plate (diaphragm); gearbox: mechanical; gears: 5, fully synchronized; ratios: I 3.818, II 2.235, III 1.478, IV 1.036, V 0.861, rev 3.083; lever: central; final drive: hypoid bevel; axle ratio: 3.778; width of rims: 5.5''; tyres: 175/70 SR x 13.

PERFORMANCE max speeds: (I) 26 mph, 42 km/h; (II) 45 mph, 72 km/h; (III) 68 mph, 109 km/h; (IV) 96 mph, 155 km/h; (V) 106 mph, 170 km/h; power-weight ratio: 24.3 lb/hp (33.8 lb/kW), 11 kg/hp (15.3 kg/kW); carrying capacity: 761 lb, 345 kg; speed in top at 1,000 rpm: 20.2 mph, 32.5 km/h; consumption: 26.2 m/imp gal, 21.8 m/US gal, 10.8 l x 100 km.

CHASSIS platform; front suspension: independent, wishbones, longitudinal torsion bars, anti-roll bar, telescopic dampers; rear: independent, swinging longitudinal trailing arms, transverse torsion bar, anti-roll bar, telescopic dampers.

STEERING rack-and-pinion; turns lock to lock: 3.50.

BRAKES front disc (diameter 8.98 in, 22.8 cm), internal radial fins, rear drum, rear compensator, dual circuit, servo; swept area: front 157.2 sq in, 1,014 sq cm, rear 89 sq in, 574 sq cm, total 246.2 sq in, 1,588 sq cm.

ELECTRICAL EQUIPMENT 12 V; 36 Ah battery; 50 A alternator; 4 iodine headlamps.

DIMENSIONS AND WEIGHT wheel base: 96.06 in, 244 cm; tracks: 52.76 in, 134 cm front, 51.57 in, 131 cm rear; length: 167.72 in, 426 cm; width: 64.17 in, 163 cm; height: 51.57 in, 131 cm; ground clearance: 4.72 in, 12 cm; weight: 2,381 lb, 1,080 kg; turning circle: 36.1 ft, 11 m; fuel tank: 12.1 imp gal, 14.5 US gal, 55 l.

BODY convertible; 2 doors; 4 seats, separate front seats, reclining backrests; heated rear window; electric windows; tinted glass.

PRACTICAL INSTRUCTIONS fuel: 98-100 oct petrol; oil: engine 7 imp pt, 8.5 US pt, 4 l, change every 4,650 miles, 7,500 km - gearbox and final drive 3.5 imp pt, 4.2 US pt, 2 l, change every 9,300 miles, 15,000 km; greasing: none; tappet clearances: inlet 0.008 in, 0.20 mm, exhaust 0.010 in, 0.25 mm; valve timing: 30° 72° 72° 30°; tyre pressure: front 26 psi, 1.8 atm, rear 27 psi, 1.9 atm.

OPTIONALS metallic spray; power steering; air-conditioning.

RENAULT 17 TS Cabriolet

RENAULT 20 TL

20 TL

PRICE IN GB: £ 4,296*
PRICE EX WORKS: 38,200 francs**

ENGINE front, 4 stroke; 4 cylinders, vertical, in line; 100.5 cu in, 1,647 cc (3.11 x 3.31 in, 79 x 84 mm); compression ratio: 9.3:1; max power (DIN): 96 hp (69 kW) at 5,750 rpm; max torque (DIN): 99 lb ft, 13.6 kg m (133.4 Nm) at 3.500 rpm; max engine rpm: 6,000; 58.3 hp/l (41.9 kW/l); light alloy block and head, wet liners, hemispherical combustion chambers; 5 crankshaft bearings; valves: overhead, Vee-slanted, push-rods and rockers; camshafts: 1, side; lubrication: gear pump, full flow filter, 7 imp pt, 8.5 US pt, 4 l; 1 Weber 32 DARA downdraught twin barrel carburettor; sealed circuit cooling, liquid, expansion tank, 12.3 imp pt, 14.8 US pt, 7 l, electric thermostatic fan.

TRANSMISSION driving wheels: front; clutch: single dry plate (diaphragm), hydraulically controlled; gearbox: mechanical, in unit with engine and final drive; gears: 4, fully synchronized; ratios: I 3.818, II 2.235, III 1.478, IV 1.036, rev 3.083; lever: central; final drive: hypoid bevel; axle ratio: 3.778; width of rims: 5.5''; tyres: 165 SR x 13.

PERFORMANCE max speeds: (I) 28 mph, 45 km/h; (II) 48 mph, 77 km/h; (III) 73 mph, 117 km/h; (IV) 103 mph, 165 km/h; power-weight ratio: 27.2 lb/hp (37.9 lb/kW), 12.3 kg/hp (17.2 kg/kW); carrying capacity: 882 lb, 400 kg; speed in top at 1,000 rpm: 17.2 mph, 27.7 km/h; consumption: 25.7 m/imp gal, 21.4 m/US gal, 11 l x 100 km.

CHASSIS integral; front suspension: independent, by McPherson, coil springs/telescopic damper struts, lower wishbones, anti-roll bar; rear: independent, oblique semi-trailing arms, coil springs, anti-roll bar, telescopic dampers.

STEERING rack-and-pinion; turns lock to lock: 4.

BRAKES front disc, internal radial fins, rear drum, rear compensator, dual circuit, servo; lining area: front 22.2 sq in, 143 sq cm, rear 42.3 sq in, 273 sq cm, total 64.5 sq in, 416 sq cm.

ELECTRICAL EQUIPMENT 12 V; 40 Ah battery; 50 A alternator; 2 headlamps.

DIMENSIONS AND WEIGHT wheel base: 104.68 in, 266 cm; tracks: 56.85 in, 144 cm front, 56.61 in, 144 cm rear; length: 177.95 in, 452 cm; width: 67.95 in, 173 cm; height: 56.50 in, 143 cm; weight: 2,613 lb, 1,185 kg; turning circle: 36.7 ft, 11.2 m; fuel tank: 13.2 imp gal, 15.8 US gal, 60 l.

BODY saloon/sedan; 4 doors; 5 seats, separate front seats, reclining backrests; heated rear window.

PRACTICAL INSTRUCTIONS fuel: 98-100 oct petrol; oil: engine 7 imp pt, 8.5 US pt, 4 l, SAE 10W-50, change every 4,650 miles, 7,500 km - gearbox 3.5 imp pt, 4.2 US pt, 2 l, SAE 20W-40, change every 9,300 miles, 15,000 km - final drive 2.8 imp pt, 3.4 US pt, 1.6 l, SAE 80, change every 9,300 miles, 15,000 km; tappet clearances: inlet 0.008 in, 0.20 mm, exhaust 0.010 in, 0.25 mm; valve timing: 30° 72° 72° 30°; tyre pressure: front and rear 27 psi, 1.9 atm.

OPTIONALS luxury interior; metallic spray; tinted glass; electric sunshine roof.

RENAULT 20 GTL

20 TL Automatic

See 20 TL, except for:

PRICE IN GB: £ 4,644*
PRICE EX WORKS: 41,400 francs**

TRANSMISSION gearbox: automatic transmission, hydraulic torque converter and planetary gears with 3 ratios, max ratio of converter at stall 2.3, possible manual selection; ratios: I 2.222, II 1.370, III 0.925, rev 1.777; axle ratio: 4.125.

PERFORMANCE max speeds: (I) 44 mph, 71 km/h; (II) 71 mph, 115 km/h; (III) 98 mph, 157 km/h; power-weight ratio: 28.1 lb/hp (39.1 lb/kW), 12.7 kg/hp (17.8 kg/kW); speed in top at 1,000 rpm: 17 mph, 27.4 km/h; consumption: 24.1 m/imp gal, 20.1 m/US gal, 11.7 l x 100 km.

DIMENSIONS AND WEIGHT weight: 2,701 lb, 1,225 kg.

PRACTICAL INSTRUCTIONS oil: automatic transmission 10.6 imp pt, 12.7 US pt, 6 l, change every 18,600 miles, 30,000 km.

20 GTL

See 20 TL, except for:

PRICE EX WORKS: 41,500 francs**

STEERING servo; turns lock to lock: 3.

DIMENSIONS AND WEIGHT turning circle (between walls) 38 ft, 11.6 m.

BODY luxury equipment; electric windows.

20 GTL Automatic

See 20 GTL, except for:

PRICE EX WORKS: 44,700 francs**

TRANSMISSION gearbox: automatic transmission, hydraulic torque converter and planetary gears with 3 ratios, max ratio of converter at stall 2.3, possible manual selection ratios: I 2.222, II 1.370, III 0.925, rev. 1.777; axle ratio 4.125.

PERFORMANCE max speeds: (I) 44 mph, 71 km/h; (II) mph, 115 km/h; (III) 98 mph, 157 km/h; power-weight ratio: 28.1 lb/hp (39.1 lb/kW), 12.7 kg/hp (17.8 kg/kW) speed in top at 1,000 rpm: 17 mph, 27.4 km/h; consumption: 24.1 m/imp gal, 20.1 m/US gal, 11.7 l x 100 km.

DIMENSIONS AND WEIGHT weight: 2,701 lb, 1,225 kg.

PRACTICAL INSTRUCTIONS oil: automatic transmission 1 imp pt, 12.7 US pt, 6 l, change every 18,600 miles, 30,0 km.

20 TS

See 20 TL, except for:

PRICE IN GB: £ 5,153*
PRICE EX WORKS: 43,200 francs**

ENGINE 121.7 cu in, 1,995 cc (3.46 x 3.23 in, 88 x 82 mm compression ratio: 9.2:1; max power (DIN): 109 hp (79 k at 5,550 rpm; max torque (DIN): 123 lb ft, 17.1 kg m (16 Nm) at 3,000 rpm; 54.6 hp/l (39.6 kW/l); camshafts: overhead, cogged belt.

TRANSMISSION gearbox ratios: I 3.364, II 2.059, III 1.31 IV 0.931, rev 3.182; axle ratio: 4.125; tyres: 165 SR x 1

PERFORMANCE max speed: 106 mph, 170 km/h; power weight ratio: 25.9 lb/hp (35.7 lb/kW), 11.7 kg/hp (16 kg/kW); speed in top at 1,000 rpm: 13 mph, 20.9 km/ consumption: 22.8 m/imp gal, 19 m/US gal, 12.4 l x 100 k

STEERING servo; turns lock to lock: 3.25.

BRAKES lining area: front 27.3 sq in, 176 sq cm, re 42.3 sq in, 273 sq cm, total 69.6 sq in, 449 sq cm.

DIMENSIONS AND WEIGHT weight: 2,822 lb, 1,280 kg; tur ing circle (between walls): 37.4 ft, 11.4 m.

BODY luxury equipment; electric windows.

PRACTICAL INSTRUCTIONS tappet clearances: inlet 0.0 0.012 in, 0.15-0.18 mm, exhaust 0.006-0.008 in, 0.25-0.30 m valve timing: 20° 60° 60° 20°; tyre pressure: front 27 p 1.9 atm, rear 28 psi, 2 atm.

OPTIONALS 5-speed mechanical gearbox (I 3.364, II 2.05 III 1.380, IV 1.060, V 0.820, rev 3.182); air-conditioning.

20 TS Automatic

See 20 TS, except for:

PRICE IN GB: £ 5,500*
PRICE EX WORKS: 46,400 francs**

TRANSMISSION gearbox: automatic transmission, hydraul torque converter and planetary gears with 3 ratios, m ratio of converter at stall 2.3, possible manual selectio ratios: I 2.222, II 1.370, III 0.926, rev 1.777.

PERFORMANCE max speed: 103 mph, 165 km/h; spee in top at 1,000 rpm: 18.5 mph, 29.7 km/h; consumptio 24.8 m/imp gal, 20.6 m/US gal, 11.4 l x 100 km.

DIMENSIONS AND WEIGHT weight: 2,822 lb, 1,280 kg.

PRACTICAL INSTRUCTIONS oil: automatic transmission 10 imp pt, 12.7 US pt, 6 l, change every 18,600 miles, 30,0 km; tyre pressure: front and rear 28 psi, 2 atm.

OPTIONALS air-conditioning.

30 TS

PRICE IN GB: £ 6,427*
PRICE EX WORKS: 47,200 francs**

ENGINE front, 4 stroke; 6 cylinders, Vee-slanted at 90 162.6 cu in, 2,664 cc (3.46 x 2.87 in, 88 x 73 mm); cor pression ratio: 9.2:1; max power (DIN): 128 hp (92.5 kW at 5,500 rpm; max torque (DIN): 149.3 lb ft, 20.6 kg

02.2 Nm) at 2,500 rpm; max engine rpm: 6,000; 48 hp/l
4.7 kW/l); light alloy block and head, wet liners, hemi-
erical combustion chambers; 4 crankshaft bearings;
lves: overhead; Vee-slanted, rockers; camshafts: 2, 1
r bank, overhead; lubrication: gear pump, full flow filter,
7 imp pt, 11.6 US pt, 5.5 l; 1 Weber 38-38 DGAR down-
aught twin barrel carburettor; fuel feed: mechanical
mp; water-cooled, expansion tank, 17.2 imp pt, 20.7 US
, 9.8 l, viscous coupling thermostatic fan.

ANSMISSION driving wheels: front; clutch: single dry
ate (diaphragm), hydraulically controlled; gearbox: me-
anical; gears: 4, fully synchronized; ratios: I 3.364, II
1.318, III 1.318, IV 0.931, rev 3.182; lever: central; final
ive: hypoid bevel; axle ratio: 3.889; width of rims: 5.5'';
es: 175 HR x 14.

RFORMANCE max speeds: (I) 31 mph, 50 km/h; (II) 50
ph, 81 km/h; (III) 79 mph, 127 km/h; (IV) 114 mph,
3 km/h; power-weight ratio: 22.7 lb/hp (31.5 lb/kW), 10.3
/hp (14.3 kg/kW); carrying capacity: 926 lb, 420 kg;
celeration: standing ¼ mile 17.4 sec, 0-50 mph (0-80
/h) 6.8 sec; speed in top at 1,000 rpm: 19.9 mph, 32
/h; consumption: 16.3 m/imp gal, 13.6 m/US gal, 17.3
x 100 km.

ASSIS integral; front suspension: independent, by Mc-
erson, coil springs/telescopic damper struts, lower wish-
nes, anti-roll bar; rear: independent, oblique semi-trail-
g arms, coil springs, anti-roll bar, telescopic dampers.

EERING rack-and-pinion, servo; turns lock to lock: 3.50.

RAKES disc (front diameter 9.92 in, 25.2 cm, rear 10 in,
.4 cm), front internal radial fins, rear compensator, dual
rcuit, servo; lining area: front 29.8 sq in, 192 sq cm,
ar 22.2 sq in, 143 sq cm, total 52 sq in, 335 sq cm.

ECTRICAL EQUIPMENT 12 V; 50 Ah battery; 50 A alter-
tor; dual ignition; 4 iodine headlamps, height adjustable
m driving seat.

MENSIONS AND WEIGHT wheel base: 105.12 in, 267 cm;
acks: 56.89 in, 144.5 cm front, 56.69 in, 144 cm rear; length:
7.95 in, 452 cm; width: 68.11 in, 173 cm; height: 56.30 in,
3 cm; weight: 2,911 lb, 1,320 kg; turning circle: 35.8
10.9 m; fuel tank: 14.7 imp gal, 17.7 US gal, 67 l.

DDY saloon/sedan; 4 doors; 5 seats, separate front seats,
clining backrests with adjustable built-in headrests; elec-
c front windows; heated rear window; headlamps with
per-washers; tinted glass.

RACTICAL INSTRUCTIONS fuel: 98-100 oct petrol; oil: en-
ne 9.7 imp pt, 11.6 US pt, 5.5 l, SAE 10W-50, change
ery 4,650 miles, 7,500 km - gearbox 6 imp pt, 7.2 US pt,
4 l, SAE 20W-40, change every 9,300 miles, 15,000 km -
nal drive 2.8 imp pt, 3.4 US pt, 1.6 l, SAE 80, change
ery 9,300 miles, 15,000 km; tappet clearances: inlet 0.004-
006 in, 0.10-0.15 mm, exhaust 0.010-0.012 in, 0.25-0.30
m; valve timing: 9º 45º 45º 9º (left), 7º 43º 43º 7º (right);
re pressure: front 26 psi, 1.8 atm, rear 28 psi, 2 atm.

PTIONALS metallic spray; electric sunshine roof; leather
holstery; air-conditioning.

30 TS Automatic

ee 30 TS, except for:

RICE IN GB: £ 6,774*
RICE EX WORKS: 50,400 francs**

RANSMISSION gearbox: automatic transmission, hydraulic
rque converter and planetary gears with 3 ratios, max
tio of converter at stall 2.3, possible manual selection;
tios: I 2.307, II 1.423, III 0.961, rev 1.846.

ERFORMANCE max speeds: (I) 45 mph, 72 km/h; (II) 70
ph, 113 km/h; (III) 110 mph, 177 km/h; power-weight
tio: 23.1 lb/hp (31.9 lb/kW), 10.4 kg/hp (14.5 kg/kW);
arrying capacity: 882 lb, 400 kg; speed in top at 1,000
m: 19.3 mph, 31 km/h; consumption: 17.1 m/imp gal,
4.3 m/US gal, 16.5 l x 100 km.

TEERING turns lock to lock: 3.25.

IMENSIONS AND WEIGHT weight: 2,955 lb, 1,340 kg; turn-
g circle: 37.4 ft, 11.4 m.

RACTICAL INSTRUCTIONS oil: automatic transmission
3.4 imp pt, 16.1 US pt, 7.6 l; tyre pressure: front 27 psi,
9 atm.

30 TX

ee 30 TS, except for:

RICE EX WORKS: 56,000 francs**

NGINE max power (DIN): 142 hp (102.5 kW) at 5,500 rpm;
ax torque (DIN): 161.6 lb ft, 22.3 kg m (218.8 Nm) at
,000 rpm; max engine rpm: 6,000; 53.3 hp/l (38.5 kW/l);
Bosch K-Jetronic electronic fuel injection.

RENAULT 30 TX

TRANSMISSION gears: 5, fully synchronized; ratios: I
3.360, II 2.060, III 1.380, IV 1.060, V 0.820, rev 3.182;
axle ratio: 3.150.

PERFORMANCE max speeds: (I) 33 mph, 53 km/h; (II)
53 mph, 86 km/h; (III) 80 mph, 129 km/h; (IV) 105 mph,
169 km/h; (V) 117 mph, 188 km/h; power-weight ratio:
20.8 lb/hp, (28.8 lb/kW), 9.4 kg/hp (13.1 kg/kW); acceleration: standing ¼ mile 17.3 sec; speed in top at 1,000
rpm: 22.5 mph, 36.3 km/h; consumption: 17.1 m/imp gal,
14.3 m/US gal, 16.5 l x 100 km.

STEERING turns lock to lock: 3.25.

ELECTRICAL EQUIPMENT 70 A alternator.

DIMENSIONS AND WEIGHT weight: 2,955 lb, 1,340 kg;
turning circle: 37.4 ft, 11.4 m.

OPTIONALS 150 TR x 390 or TRX 190/65 HR x 390 tyres.

30 TX Automatic

See 30 TX, except for:

PRICE EX WORKS: 59,200 francs**

TRANSMISSION gearbox: automatic transmission, hydraulic
torque converter and planetary gears with 3 ratios, max
ratio of converter at stall 2.3, possible manual selection;
ratios: I 2.307, II 1.423, III 0.961, rev 1.846.

PERFORMANCE max speeds: (I) 48 mph, 78 km/h; (II) 79
mph, 128 km/h; (III) 113 mph, 182 km/h; power-weight
ratio: 21.1 lb/hp (29.2 lb/kW), 9.6 kg/hp (13.2 kg/kW);
acceleration: standing ¼ mile 18.3 sec; speed in top at
1,000 rpm: 19.9 mph, 32.1 km/h; consumption: 18.5 m/imp
gal, 15.4 m/US gal, 15.3 l x 100 km.

DIMENSIONS AND WEIGHT weight: 2,999 lb, 1,360 kg.

PRACTICAL INSTRUCTIONS oil: automatic transmission
13.4 imp pt, 16.1 US pt, 7.6 l.

STIMULA　　　　　　　　　　　　　**FRANCE**

Bugatti 55

PRICE EX WORKS: 123,000 francs

ENGINE Opel, front, 4 stroke; 6 cylinders, in line; 169.9
cu in, 2,784 cc (3.62 x 2.75 in, 92 x 69.8 mm); compression
ratio: 9:1; max power (DIN): 155 hp (114.1 kW) at 5,600
rpm; max torque (DIN): 160 lb ft, 22.1 kg m (216 Nm)
at 4,200 rpm; max engine rpm: 6,000; 55.7 hp/l (41 kW/l);
cast iron block and head; 7 crankshaft bearings; valves:
overhead, in line, hydraulic tappets; camshafts: 1, overhead; lubrication: gear pump, full flow filter, 9.7 imp pt,
11.6 US pt, 5.5 l; Bosch electronic injection; fuel feed:
electric pump.

STIMULA Bugatti 55

BUGATTI 55

TRANSMISSION driving wheels: rear; clutch: single dry plate (diaphragm); gearbox: mechanical; gears: 4, fully synchronized; ratios: I 3.428, II 2.156, III 1.366, IV 1, rev 3.317; lever: central; final drive: hypoid bevel; axle ratio: 3.450; tyres: 165 SR x 15.

PERFORMANCE max speed: 124 mph, 200 km/h.

CHASSIS tubular and box-type; front suspension: independent, wishbones, lower trailing links, coil springs, anti-roll bar, telescopic dampers; rear: rigid axle, twin trailing radius arms, upper torque arms, transverse linkage bar, coil springs, anti-roll bar, telescopic dampers.

STEERING recirculating ball; turns lock to lock: 4.5.

BRAKES disc, servo.

ELECTRICAL EQUIPMENT 12 V; 44 Ah battery; 55 A alternator; Bosch distributor; 2 halogen headlamps.

DIMENSIONS AND WEIGHT tracks: 98.43 in, 250 cm; length: 145.67 in, 370 cm; width: 62.99 in, 160 cm.

BODY roadster, in plastic material; no doors; 2 seats.

PRACTICAL INSTRUCTIONS fuel: 98 oct petrol; oil: engine 8.8 imp pt, 10,6 US pt, 5 l, SAE 20W-30, change every 3,100 miles, 5,000 km - gearbox 1.9 imp pt, 2.3 US pt, 1.1 l, SAE 80, no change recommended - final drive 2.5 imp pt, 3 US pt, 1.4 l, SAE 90, no change recommended; greasing: none; sparking plug: 200°; valve timing: 30° 90° 70° 50°.

TRABANT 601 Limousine

TRABANT   GERMANY DDR

601 Limousine

ENGINE front, transverse, 2 stroke; 2 cylinders, in line; 36.2 cu in, 594.5 cc (2.83 x 2.87 in, 72 x 73 mm); compression ratio: 7.6:1; max power (DIN): 26 hp (19.1 kW) at 4,200 rpm; max torque (DIN): 40 lb ft, 5.5 kg m (53.9 Nm) at 3,000 rpm; max engine rpm: 4,500; 43.7 hp/l (32.1 kW/l); light alloy block and head, dry liners; 3 crankshaft bearings; valves: 1, per cylinder, rotary; lubrication: mixture; 1 BVF type 28 HB 2-8 horizontal single barrel carburettor; fuel feed: gravity; air-cooled.

TRANSMISSION driving wheels: front; clutch: single dry plate; gearbox: mechanical; gears: 4, fully synchronized; ratios: I 4.080, II 2.320, III 1.520, IV 1.103, rev 3.830; lever: on facia; final drive: conic bevel; axle ratio: 3.950; width of rims: 4''; tyres: 5.20 or 145 SR x 13.

PERFORMANCE max speeds: (I) 16 mph, 25 km/h; (II) 28 mph, 45 km/h; (III) 43 mph, 70 km/h; (IV) 62 mph, 100 km/h; power-weight ratio: 52.1 lb/hp (71 lb/kW), 23.6 kg/hp (32.2 kg/kW); carrying capacity: 849 lb, 385 kg; acceleration: 0-50 mph (0-80 km/h) 22.5 sec; speed in top at 1,000 rpm: 14.6 mph, 23.5 km/h; consumption: 40.4 m/imp gal, 33.6 m/US gal, 7 l x 100 km.

CHASSIS integral; front suspension: independent, wishbones, transverse leafspring upper arms, telescopic dampers; rear: independent, swinging semi-axles, transverse semi-elliptic leafspring, telescopic dampers.

STEERING rack-and-pinion; turns lock to lock: 2.60.

BRAKES drum, single circuit; swept area: front 38.9 sq in, 251 sq cm, rear 34.1 sq in, 220 sq cm, total 73 sq in, 471 sq cm.

ELECTRICAL EQUIPMENT 6 V; 56 Ah battery; 220 W dynamo; AKA distributor; 2 headlamps.

DIMENSIONS AND WEIGHT wheel base: 79.53 in, 202 cm; tracks: 47.64 in, 121 cm front, 49.21 in, 125 cm rear; length: 139.76 in, 355 cm; width: 59.06 in, 150 cm; height: 56.69 in, 144 cm; ground clearance: 6.10 in, 15.5 cm; weight: 1,356 lb, 615 kg; weight distribution: 45% front, 55% rear; turning circle: 32.8 ft, 10 m; fuel tank: 5.7 imp gal, 6.9 US gal, 26 l.

BODY saloon/sedan; 2 doors; 4 seats, separate front seats, reclining backrests.

PRACTICAL INSTRUCTIONS fuel: mixture 1:50, 88 oct petrol, SAE 20; oil: gearbox and final drive 2.6 imp pt, 3.2 US pt, 1.5 l, SAE 10W-30, change every 9,300 miles, 15,000 km; greasing: every 3,100 miles, 5,000 km, 9 points; sparking plug: M 14 x 225°; valve timing: 45° 45° 72°5' 72°5'; tyre pressure: front 20 psi, 1.4 atm, rear 20 psi, 1.4 atm.

OPTIONALS Hycomat automatic clutch.

601 Universal

See 601 Limousine, except for:

PERFORMANCE power-weight ratio: 55.1 lb/hp (75 lb/kW), 25 kg/hp (34 kg/kW); carrying capacity: 860 lb, 390 k

DIMENSIONS AND WEIGHT length: 140.16 in, 356 c width: 59.45 in, 151 cm; height: 57.87 in, 147 cm; weig 1,433 lb, 650 kg; weight distribution: 44% front, 56% re

BODY estate car/station; 2 + 1 doors; folding rear se

WARTBURG   GERMANY DD

353 W

ENGINE front, 2 stroke; 3 cylinders, vertical, in line; 6 cu in, 992 cc (2.89 x 3.07 in, 73.5 x 78 mm); compress ratio: 7.5:1; max power (DIN): 50 hp (36.8 kW) at 4,2 rpm; max torque (DIN): 72 lb ft, 10 kg m (98.1 Nm) 3,000 rpm; max engine rpm: 4,250; 50.4 hp/l (37.1 kW/ cast iron block, light alloy head; 4 crankshaft bearings; brication: mixture 1:50; 1 BVF 40F1-11 single barrel c burettor; fuel feed: mechanical pump; sealed circuit co ing, liquid, 13.2 imp pt, 15.9 US pt, 7.5 l.

TRANSMISSION driving wheels: front; clutch: single c plate; gearbox: mechanical; gears: 4, fully synchronize ratios: I 3.769, II 2.160, III 1.347, IV 0.906, rev 3.385; leve steering column; final drive: spiral bevel; axle ratio: 4.2 width of rims: 4.5''; tyres: 6.00 x 13 or 165 SR x 13.

PERFORMANCE max speeds: (I) 20 mph, 32 km/h; (I 35 mph, 57 km/h; (III) 56 mph, 90 km/h; (IV) 81 mp 130 km/h; power-weight ratio: 40.6 lb/hp (55.1 lb/kW 18.4 kg/hp (25 kg/kW); carrying capacity: 882 lb, 400 k acceleration: 0-50 mph (0-80 km/h) 14.5 sec; speed top at 1,000 rpm: 17.4 mph, 28 km/h; consumption: 28 m/imp gal, 24 m/US gal, 9.8 l x 100 km.

CHASSIS box-type ladder frame; front suspension: ind pendent, wishbones, coil springs, rubber elements, te scopic dampers; rear: independent, semi-trailing arms, c springs, rubber elements, anti-roll bar, telescopic damper

STEERING rack-and-pinion; turns lock to lock: 3.50.

BRAKES front disc, rear drum, rear compensator; linir area: front 20 sq in, 129 sq cm, rear 61.4 sq in, 396 sq cr total 81.4 sq in, 525 sq cm.

ELECTRICAL EQUIPMENT 12 V; 42 Ah battery; 588 W alte nator; FEK distributor; 2 headlamps.

DIMENSIONS AND WEIGHT wheel base: 96.46 in, 245 cr tracks: 50.39 in, 128 cm front, 51.18 in, 130 cm rear; lengt 166.14 in, 422 cm; width: 64.57 in, 164 cm; height: 58.66 i 149 cm; ground clearance: 6.10 in, 15.5 cm; weight: 2,0 lb, 920 kg; weight distribution: 51.5% front, 48.5% rea turning circle: 33.5 ft, 10.2 m; fuel tank: 9.7 imp gal, 11.6 US gal, 44 l.

BODY saloon/sedan; 4 doors; 5 seats, separate front seat reclining backrests.

WARTBURG 353 W De Luxe

PRACTICAL INSTRUCTIONS fuel: mixture 1:50, SAE 20-40; l: gearbox and final drive 3.2 imp pt, 3.8 US pt, 1.8 l, SAE 80 EP, change every 31,100 miles, 50,000 km; greasing: very 6,200 miles, 10,000 km, 3 points; sparking plug: 175°; ening timing: 62°17' 62°17' 78°2' 78°2'; tyre pressure: ont 23 psi, 1.6 atm, rear 24 psi, 1.7 atm.

OPTIONALS central lever; halogen headlamps; sunshine oof; luxury version.

353 W Tourist/De Luxe

ee 353 W, except for:

PERFORMANCE max speed: 78 mph, 125 km/h; power-weight tio: 42.8 lb/hp (58.1 lb/kW), 19.4 kg/hp (26.4 kg/kW); arrying capacity: 970 lb, 440 kg; consumption: 28.2 m/imp al, 23.5 m/US gal, 10 l x 100 km.

DIMENSIONS AND WEIGHT length: 172.44 in, 438 cm; eight: 2,139 lb, 970 kg.

ODY estate car/station wagon; 4 + 1 doors; folding rear at, De Luxe luxury equipment, sunshine roof.

RACTICAL INSTRUCTIONS tyre pressure: rear 27 psi, 1.9 m.

Audi 80 Series

RICES IN USA AND EX WORKS:	$	DM
2-dr Limousine	—	12,295*
4-dr Limousine	—	12,865*
L 2-dr Limousine	—	13,165*
L 4-dr Limousine	—	13,735*
S 2-dr Limousine	—	12,845*
S 4-dr Limousine	—	13,415*
LS 2-dr Limousine	6,295*	13,715*
LS 4-dr Limousine	6,445*	14,285*
GLS 2-dr Limousine	—	14,640*
GLS 4-dr Limousine	—	15,210*
GLE 2-dr Limousine	—	16,340*
GLE 4-dr Limousine	—	16,910*

wer team:	Standard for:	Optional for:
5 hp	1 to 4	—
5 hp	5 to 10	—
5 hp	—	7 to 10
0 hp	11,12	—

55 hp power team

NGINE front, 4 stroke; 4 cylinders, in line; 77.6 cu in, 272 cc (2.95 x 2.83 in, 75 x 72 mm); compression ratio: 2:1; max power (DIN): 55 hp (40.5 kW) at 5,800 rpm; ax torque (DIN): 66.7 lb ft, 9.2 kg m (90.3 Nm) at 3,400 m; max engine rpm: 6,200; 43.2 hp/l (31.8 kW); cast on block, light alloy head; 5 crankshaft bearings; valves: verhead, in line, thimble tappets; camshafts: 1, overhead, gged belt; lubrication: gear pump, full flow filter, 6.2 np pt, 7.4 US pt, 3.5 l; 1 Solex 30-35 PDSIT downdraught ngle barrel carburettor; fuel feed: mechanical pump; water-oled, 11.4 imp pt, 13.7 US pt, 6.5 l, electric thermo-atic fan.

RANSMISSION driving wheels: front; clutch: single dry ate (diaphragm); gearbox: mechanical; gears: 4, fully ynchronized; ratios: I 3.455, II 1.944, III 1.286, IV 0.969 v 3.166; lever: central; final drive: hypoid bevel; axle tio: 4.444; width of rims: 5''; tyres: 155 SR x 13.

ERFORMANCE max speeds: (I) 25 mph, 41 km/h; (II) 42 ph, 68 km/h; (III) 68 mph, 110 km/h; (IV) 90 mph, 145 n/h; power-weight ratio: 36.5 lb/hp (49.6 lb/kW), 16.5 /hp (22.5 kg/kW); carrying capacity: 1,014 lb, 460 kg; cceleration: 0-50 mph (0-80 km/h) 11 sec; speed in top 1,000 rpm: 14.9 mph, 24 km/h; consumption: 31.7 m/imp al, 26.4 m/US gal, 8.9 l x 100 km.

HASSIS integral, front auxiliary subframe; front suspen-on: independent, by McPherson, lower wishbones, coil rings/telescopic damper struts; rear: rigid axle, trailing dius arms, Panhard rod, telescopic damper struts.

TEERING rack-and-pinion; turns lock to lock: 3.94.

RAKES front disc (diameter 9.43 in, 23.9 cm), dual circuit, ear drum, servo.

ELECTRICAL EQUIPMENT 12 V; 36 Ah battery; 35 A alter-ator; Bosch distributor; 2 headlamps.

IMENSIONS AND WEIGHT wheel base: 100 in, 254 m; tracks: 55.1 in, 140 cm front, 55.9 in, 142 cm

---

rear; length: 172.6 in, 438 cm; width: 66.2 in, 168 cm; height: 53.54 in, 136 cm; ground clearance: 4.21 in, 10.7 cm; weight: 2,007 lb, 910 kg; turning circle: 34.1 ft, 10.4 m; fuel tank: 15 imp gal, 18 US gal, 68 l.

BODY saloon/sedan; 5 seats, separate front seats.

PRACTICAL INSTRUCTIONS fuel: 91 oct petrol; oil: engine 5.3 imp pt, 6.3 US pt, 3 l, SAE 20W-30, change every 4,700 miles, 7,500 km - gearbox and final drive 3.2 imp pt, 3.8 US pt, 1.8 l, SAE 80 or 90; greasing: none; spark-ing plug: 175°; tappet clearances: inlet 0.008-0.012 in, 0.20-0.30 mm, exhaust 0.016-0.020 in, 0.40-0.50 mm; tyre pres-sure: front 26 psi, 1.8 atm, rear 26 psi, 1.8 atm.

OPTIONALS 175/70 SR x 13 tyres; halogen headlamps; sun-shine roof; vinyl roof; metallic spray.

75 hp power team

See 55 hp power team, except for:

ENGINE 96.9 cu in, 1,588 cc (3.13 x 3.15 in, 79.5 x 80 mm); max power (DIN): 75 hp (55.2 kW) at 5,600 rpm; max torque (DIN): 88 lb ft, 12.1 kg m (118.7 Nm) at 3,200 rpm; max engine rpm: 6,000; 47.2 hp/l (34.8 kW/l); water-cooled, 12.3 imp pt, 14.8 US pt, 7 l.

TRANSMISSION gearbox ratios: IV 0.909; axle ratio: 4.111; tyres: 165 SR x 13.

AUDI NSU 80 GLS 4-dr Limousine

AUDI NSU 80 GLS Limousine

PERFORMANCE max speeds: (I) 27 mph, 44 km/h; (II) 47 mph, 75 km/h; (III) 70 mph, 112 km/h; (IV) 99 mph, 160 km/h; power-weight ratio: 27.9 lb/hp (37.9 lb/kW), 12.7 kg/hp (17.2 kg/kW); acceleration: 0-50 mph (0-80 km/h) 8.7 sec; speed in top at 1,000 rpm: 16.2 mph, 26 km/h.

CHASSIS front suspension: anti-roll bar.

DIMENSIONS AND WEIGHT weight: 2,095 lb, 950 kg.

PRACTICAL INSTRUCTIONS sparking plug: 200°; valve timing: 3° 47° 43° 7°.

OPTIONALS automatic transmission, hydraulic torque con-verter and planetary gears with 3 ratios (I 2.550, II 1.450, III 1, rev 2.460), max ratio of converter at stall 2.2, possible manual selection, 3.910 axle ratio, 5'' wide rims, max speed 97 mph, 156 km/h, consumption 29.7 m/imp gal, 24.8 m/US gal, 9.5 l x 100 km.

85 hp power team

See 55 hp power team, except for:

ENGINE 96.9 cu in, 1,588 cc (3.13 x 3.15 in, 79.5 x 80 mm); max power (DIN): 85 hp (62.6 kW) at 5,600 rpm; max torque (DIN): 92 lb ft, 12.7 kg m (124.5 Nm) at 3,200 rpm; max engine rpm: 6,000; 53.5 hp/l (39.4 kW/l); 1 Solex 32-35 TDID downdraught carburettor; water-cooled, 12.3 imp pt, 14.8 US pt, 7 l.

TRANSMISSION gearbox ratios: IV 0.909; axle ratio: 4.111; tyres: 175/70 SR x 13.

PERFORMANCE max speeds: (I) 29 mph, 46 km/h; (II) 48 mph, 78 km/h; (III) 73 mph, 117 km/h; (IV) 102 mph, 165 km/h; power-weight ratio: 24.6 lb/hp (33.5 lb/kW), 11.2 kg/hp (15.2 kg/kW); acceleration: 0-50 mph (0-80 km/h) 7.9 sec; speed in top at 1,000 rpm: 17.4 mph, 28 km/h; consumption: 32.8 m/imp gal, 27.3 m/US gal, 8.6 l x 100 km.

CHASSIS front suspension: anti-roll bar.

ELECTRICAL EQUIPMENT 45 Ah battery; 55 A alternator; halogen headlamps.

DIMENSIONS AND WEIGHT weight: 2,095 lb, 950 kg.

PRACTICAL INSTRUCTIONS sparking plug: 225°; valve timing: 3° 47° 43° 7°.

OPTIONALS automatic transmission with 3 ratios (I 2.550, II 1.450, III 1, rev 2.460), 3.909 axle ratio, 5'' wide rims, max speed 100 mph, 161 km/h, consumption 30.7 m/imp gal, 25.6 m/US gal, 9.2 l x 100 km; air-conditiong.

110 hp power team

See 55 hp power team, except for:

ENGINE 96.9 cu in, 1,588 cc (3.13 x 3.15 in, 79.5 x 80 mm); compression ratio: 9.5:1; max power (DIN): 110 hp (81 kW) at 6,100 rpm; max torque (DIN): 101 lb ft, 14 kg m (137.3 Nm) at 5,000 rpm; max engine rpm: 6,500; 59.3 hp/l

110 HP POWER TEAM

(51 kW/l); lubricating system: 6.2 imp pt, 7.4 US pt, 3.5 l; Bosch K-Jetronic fuel injection system; fuel feed: electric pump.

TRANSMISSION gearbox ratios: IV 0.909; axle ratio: 3.890; tyres: 175/70 HR x 13.

PERFORMANCE max speeds: (I) 31 mph, 50 km/h; (II) 52 mph, 83 km/h; (III) 80 mph, 128 km/h; (IV) 112 mph, 181 km/m; power-weight ratio: 19 lb/hp (25.9 lb/kW), 8.6 kg/hp (11.7 kg/kW); acceleration: 0-50 mph (0-80 km/h) 6.8 sec; speed in top at 1,000 rpm; 17.5 mph, 28.2 km/h; consumption: 33.6 m/imp gal, 28 m/US gal, 8.4 l x 100 km.

BRAKES lining area: front 16.3 sq in, 105 sq cm, rear 34.6 sq in, 223 sq cm, total 50.9 sq in, 328 sq cm.

CHASSIS front suspension: anti-roll bar.

ELECTRICAL EQUIPMENT 45 Ah battery; 55 A alternator; halogen headlamps.

DIMENSIONS AND WEIGHT weight: 2,095 lb, 950 kg.

BODY built-in headrests.

PRACTICAL INSTRUCTIONS fuel: 97 oct petrol; oil: engine 6.2 imp pt, 7.4 US pt, 3.5 l, SAE 20W-30, change every 4,700 miles, 7,500 km; sparking plug: 225°; valve timing: 4° 46° 44° 6°.

Audi 100 Series

PRICES IN GB, USA AND EX WORKS:

	£	$	DM
1 2-dr Limousine	—	—	15,615*
2 4-dr Limousine	—	—	16,220*
3 L 2-dr Limousine	—	—	16,520*
4 L 4-dr Limousine	—	—	17,125*
5 GL 4-dr Limousine	—	—	18,490*
6 5S 2-dr Limousine	—	—	16,440*
7 5S 4-dr Limousine	—	—	17,045*
8 L5S 2-dr Limousine	—	—	17,345*
9 L5S 4-dr Limousine	5,492*	—	17,950*
10 GL5S 4-dr Limousine	5,979*	—	19,315*
11 CD5S 4-dr Limousine	—	—	22,960*
12 5E 2-dr Limousine	—	—	17,305*
13 5E 4-dr Limousine	—	—	17,910*
14 L5E 2-dr Limousine	—	—	18,210*
15 L5E 4-dr Limousine	—	—	18,815*
16 GL5E 4-dr Limousine	6,589*	8,995*	20,180*
17 CD5E 4-dr Limousine	—	—	23,265*
18 5D 2-dr Limousine	—	—	18,095*
19 5D 4-dr Limousine	—	—	18,700*
20 L5D 2-dr Limousine	—	—	19,000*
21 L5D 4-dr Limousine	—	—	19,605*
22 GL5D 4-dr Limousine	—	—	20,970*
23 CD5D 4-dr Limousine	—	—	24,415*

Power team:	Standard for:	Optional for:
85 hp	1 to 5	—
115 hp	6 to 11	—
136 hp	12 to 17	—
70 hp (Diesel)	18 to 23	—

85 hp power team

ENGINE front, 4 stroke; 4 cylinders, in line; 96.9 cu in, 1,588 cc (3.13 x 3.15 in, 79.5 x 80 mm); compression ratio: 8.2:1; max power (DIN): 85 hp (62.6 kW) at 5,600 rpm; max torque (DIN): 90 lb ft, 12.4 kg m (121.6 Nm) at 3,200 rpm; max engine rpm: 6,200; 53.5 hp/l (39.4 kW/l); cast iron block, light alloy head; 5 crankshaft bearings; valves: overhead, in line, rockers; camshafts: 1, overhead, cogged belt; lubrication: gear pump, full flow filter, 6.2 imp pt, 7.4 US pt, 3.5 l; 1 Solex 2 B2 downdraught carburettor; fuel feed: mechanical pump; water-cooled, 12.3 imp pt, 14.8 US pt, 7 l.

TRANSMISSION driving wheels: front; clutch: single dry plate (diaphragm); gearbox: mechanical; gears: 4, fully synchronized; ratios: I 3.454, II 1.944, III 1.286, IV 0.909, rev 3.166; lever: central; final drive: hypoid bevel; axle ratio: 4.444; width of rims: 5.5''; tyres: 165 SR x 14.

PERFORMANCE max speeds: (I) 29 mph, 46 km/h; (II) 52 mph, 83 km/h; (III) 77 mph, 124 km/h; (IV) 99 mph, 160 km/h; power-weight ratio: 28.8 lb/hp (39.1 lb/kW), 13.1 kg/hp (17.7 kg/W); carrying capacity: 1,014 lb, 460 kg; acceleration: 0-50 mph (0-80 m/h) 8.6 sec; speed in top at 1,000 rpm: 17.6 mph, 28.3 km/h; consumption: 31.7 m/imp gal, 26.4 m/US gal, 8.9 l x 100 km.

CHASSIS integral, front auxiliary subframe; front suspension: independent, by McPherson, lower wishbones, anti-roll bar, coil springs/telescopic damper struts; rear: rigid axle, swinging longitudinal trailing radius arms, Panhard rod, anti-roll bar, telescopic dampers.

STEERING rack-and-pinion.

AUDI NSU 100 GL 4-dr Limousine

BRAKES front disc (diameter 10.24 in, 26 cm), rear drum, dual circuit, servo; lining area: front 20.2 sq in, 130 sq cm, rear 39.7 sq in, 256 sq cm, total 59.9 sq in, 386 sq cm.

ELECTRICAL EQUIPMENT 12 V; 45 Ah battery; 55 A alternator; Bosch distributor; 2 headlamps.

DIMENSIONS AND WEIGHT wheel base: 105.40 in, 268 cm; tracks: 57.90 in, 147 cm front, 56.90 in, 144 cm rear; length: 184.30 in, 468 cm - GL 185 in, 470 cm; width: 69.60 in, 177 cm; height: 54.80 in, 139 cm; ground clearance: 5.10 in, 13 cm; weight: 2,448 lb, 1,110 kg; weight distribution: 49% front, 51% rear; turning circle: 37.1 ft, 11.3 m; fuel tank: 13.2 imp gal, 15.8 US gal, 60 l.

BODY saloon/sedan; 5 seats, separate front seats, reclining backrests, heated rear window.

PRACTICAL INSTRUCTIONS fuel: 91 oct petrol; oil: engine 5.3 imp pt, 6.3 US pt, 3 l, SAE 10W-30, change every 4,700 miles, 7,500 km - gearbox and final drive 3 imp pt, 3.6 US pt, 1.7 l, SAE 80; greasing: none; tyre pressure: front 28 psi, 2 atm, rear 28 psi, 2 atm.

OPTIONALS automatic transmission, hydraulic torque converter and planetary gears with 3 ratios (I 2.552, II 1.448, III 1, rev 4.091), axle ratio, max speed 97 mph, 156 km/h, acceleration 0-50 mph ((0-80 km/h) 11.5 sec, consumption 29.7 m/imp gal, 24.8 m/US gal, 9.5 l x 100 km, 54 Ah battery; 185/70 SR x 14 tyres; sunshine roof; metallic spray; halogen headlamps (except for L and GL models).

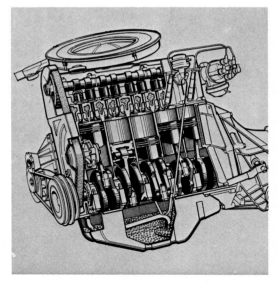

AUDI NSU 100 5S

115 hp power team

See 85 hp power team, except for:

ENGINE 5 cylinders, in line; 130.8 cu in, 2,144 cc (3.1 x 3.40 in, 74.5 x 86.4 mm); compression ratio: 8.3:1; max power (DIN): 115 hp (84.6 kW) at 5,500 rpm; max torque (DIN): 120 lb ft, 16.6 kg m (162.9 Nm) at 4,000 rpm; 53 hp/l (39.5 kW/l); 6 crankshaft bearings; lubrication: 8 imp pt, 10.6 US pt, 5 l; water-cooled: 14.3 imp pt, 17 US pt, 8.1 l.

TRANSMISSION gearbox ratios: I 3.600, II 2.125, III 1.36 IV 0.967, rev 3.500; axle ratio: 3.889.

PERFORMANCE max speed: 111 mph, 179 km/h; power-weight ratio: 22.4 lb/hp (30.5 lb/kW), 10.2 kg/hp (13.8 kg kW); consumption: 26.6 m/imp gal, 22.2 m/US gal, 10 l x 100 km.

BRAKES lining area: front 20.2 sq in, 130 sq cm, rear 44 sq in, 287 sq cm, total 64.7 sq in, 417 sq cm.

ELECTRICAL EQUIPMENT 63 Ah battery; electronic ignition

DIMENSIONS AND WEIGHT weight: 2,580 lb, 1,170 kg.

PRACTICAL INSTRUCTIONS oil: engine 7.9 imp pt, 9 US pt, 4.5 l.

OPTIONALS with automatic transmission 3.727 axle rati max speed 107 mph, 172 km/h, consumption 25.4 m/imp ga 21.2 m/US gal, 11.1 l x 100 km; power steering; air-co ditioning.

136 hp power team

See 85 hp power team, except for:

ENGINE 5 cylinders, in line; 130.8 cu in, 2,144 cc (3.13 3.40 in, 79.5 x 86.4 mm); compression ratio: 9.3:1; ma power (DIN): 136 hp (100.1 kW) at 5,700 rpm; max torqu (DIN): 134 lb ft, 18.5 kg m (181.4 Nm) at 4,200 rpm 63.4 hp/l (46.7 kW/l); 6 crankshaft bearings; lubricatio 8.8 imp pt, 10.6 US pt, 5 l; Bosch K-Jetronic injection sy tem;' water-cooled: 14.3 imp pt, 17.1 US pt, 8.1 l.

TRANSMISSION gearbox ratios: I 3.600, II 2.125, III 1.36 IV 0.967, rev 3.500; axle ratio: 3.889; tyres: 185/70 HR x 1

PERFORMANCE max speed: 118 mph, 190 km/h; power weight ratio: 19 lb/hp (25.8 lb/kW), 8.6 kg/hp (11.7 kg/kW consumption: 26.9 m/imp gal, 22.4 m/US gal, 10.5 l x 1 km.

BRAKES lining area: front 20.2 sq in, 130 sq cm, rear 44 sq in, 287 sq cm, total 64.7 sq in, 417 sq cm.

ELECTRICAL EQUIPMENT 63 Ah battery; 75 A alternato electronic ignition.

DIMENSIONS AND WEIGHT weight 2,580 lb, 1,170 kg.

PRACTICAL INSTRUCTIONS fuel: 98 oct petrol; oil: e gine 7.9 imp pt, 9.5 US pt. 4.5 l.

OPTIONALS with automatic transmission 3.727 axle rati max speed 115 mph, 185 km/h, consumption 25.4 m/im gal, 21.2 m/US gal, 11.1 l x 100 km; power steering; ai conditioning.

70 hp (Diesel) power team

See 85 hp power team, except for:

ENGINE Diesel; 5 cylinders, in line; 121.2 cu in, 1986 cc (3.01 x 3.40 in, 76.5 x 86.4 mm); compression ratio: 23.1; max power (DIN): 70 hp (51.5 kW) at 4,800 rpm; max torque (DIN): 91 lb ft, 12.5 kg m (122.7 Nm) at 3,000 rpm; max engine rpm: 5,000; 35.2 hp/l (25.9 kW/l); 6 crankshaft bearings; lubrication: 8.8 imp pt, 10.6 US pt, 5 l; Bosch injection system water-cooled: 14.3 imp pt, 17.1 US pt, 8.1 l.

TRANSMISSION gearbox ratios: I 3.600, II 1.941, III 1.231, IV 0.857, rev 3.500; axle ratio: 4.300; tyres: 185/70 SR x 14 (standard).

PERFORMANCE max speed: 93 mph, 150 km/h; power-weight ratio: 38.1 lb/hp (51.8 lb/kW), 17.3 kg/hp (23.5 kg/kW); speed in top at 1,000 rpm: 19.2 mph, 30.9 km/h; consumption: 34.4 m/imp gal, 28.7 m/US gal, 8.2 l x 100 km.

ELECTRICAL EQUIPMENT 88 Ah battery; 65 A alternator.

DIMENSIONS AND WEIGHT weight: 2,668 lb, 1,210 kg.

OPTIONALS automatic transmission not available.

Audi 100 Avant Series

PRICES IN GB AND EX WORKS:	£	DM
L 5-dr Limousine	5,340*	17,750*
GL 5-dr Limousine	—	19,115*
L5S 5-dr Limousine	—	18,575*
GL5S 5-dr Limousine	6,235*	19,940*
CD5S 5-dr Limousine	—	—
L5E 5-dr Limousine	—	19,440*
GL5E 5-dr Limousine	—	20,805*
CD5E 5-dr Limousine	8,446*	—
L5D 5-dr Limousine	—	20,230*
GL5D 5-dr Limousine	—	21,595*
CD5D 5-dr Limousine	—	—

Power team:	Standard for:	Optional for:
85 hp	1,2	—
115 hp	3 to 5	—
136 hp	6 to 8	—
70 hp (Diesel)	9 to 11	—

85 hp power team

ENGINE front, 4 stroke; 4 cylinders, in line; 96.9 cu in, 1,588 cc (3.13 x 3.15 in, 79.5 x 80 mm); compression ratio: 8.2:1; max power (DIN): 85 hp (62.6 kW) at 5,600 rpm; max torque (DIN): 90 lb ft, 12.4 kg m (121.6 Nm) at 3,200 rpm; max engine rpm: 6,200; 53.5 hp/l (39.4 kW/l); cast iron block, light alloy head; 5 crankshaft bearings; valves: overhead, in line, rockers; camshafts: 1, overhead, cogged belt; lubrication: gear pump, full flow filter, 6.2 imp pt, 7.4 US pt, 3.5 l; 1 Solex 2 B2 downdraught carburettor; fuel feed: mechanical pump; water-cooled, 12.3 imp pt, 14.8 US pt, 7 l, electric thermostatic fan.

TRANSMISSION driving wheels: front; clutch: single dry plate (diaphragm); gearbox: mechanical; gears: 4, fully synchronized; ratios: I 3.454, II 1.944, III 1.286, IV 0.909, rev 3.166; lever: central; final drive: hypoid bevel; axle ratio: 4.444; width of rims: 5.5''; tyres: 165 SR x 14.

PERFORMANCE max speeds: (I) 29 mph, 46 km/h; (II) 52 mph, 83 km/h; (III) 77 mph, 124 km/h; (IV) 99 mph, 160 km/h; power-weight ratio: 28.8 lb/hp (39.1 lb/kW), 13.1 kg/hp (17.7 kg/kW); carrying capacity: 1,014 lb, 460 kg; acceleration: 0-50 mph (0-80 km/h) 8.6 sec; speed in top at 1,000 rpm: 17.6 mph, 28.3 km/h; consumption: 31.7 m/imp gal, 26.4 m/US gal, 8.9 l x 100 km.

CHASSIS integral, front auxiliary subframe; front suspension: independent, by McPherson, lower wishbones, anti-roll bar, coil springs/telescopic damper struts; rear: rigid axle, swinging longitudinal trailing radius arms, Panhard rod, anti-roll bar, telescopic dampers.

STEERING rack-and-pinion.

BRAKES front disc (diameter 10.24 in, 26 cm), rear drum, dual circuit, 2 X circuits, servo; lining area: front 20.2 sq in, 130 sq cm, rear 39.7 sq in, 256 sq cm, total 59.9 sq in, 386 sq cm.

ELECTRICAL EQUIPMENT 12 V; 45 Ah battery; 55 A alternator; Bosch distributor; 2 headlamps.

DIMENSIONS AND WEIGHT wheel base: 105.40 in, 268 cm; tracks: 57.90 in, 147 cm front, 56.90 in, 144 cm rear; length: 180.59 in, 459 cm - GL 181.38 in, 461 cm; width: 69.60 in, 177 cm; height: 54.80 in, 139 cm; ground clearances: 5.10 in, 13 cm; weight: 2,448 lb, 1,110 kg; turning circle: 37.1 ft, 11.3 m; fuel tank: 13.2 imp gal, 15.8 gal, 60 l.

BODY 5 seats, separate seats, reclining backrests; heated rear window; folding rear seat.

PRACTICAL INSTRUCTIONS fuel: 91 oct petrol; oil: engine 5.3 imp pt, 6.3 US pt, 3 l, SAE 10W-30, change every 4,700 miles, 7,500 km - gearbox and final drive 3 imp pt, 3.6 US pt, 1.7 l, SAE 80; greasing: none; tyre pressure: front 28 psi, 2 atm, rear 28 psi, 2 atm.

OPTIONALS automatic transmission, hydraulic torque converter and planetary gears with 3 ratios (I 2.552, II 1.448, III 1, rev 2.462), 4.091 axle ratio, max speed 97 mph, 156 km/h, acceleration 0-50 mph (0-80 km/h) 11.5 sec, consumption 29.7 m/imp gal, 24.8 m/US gal, 9.5 l x 100 km, 54 Ah battery; 185/70 SR x 14 tyres; sunshine roof; metallic spray; rear window wiper-washer.

115 hp power team

See 85 hp power team, except for:

ENGINE 5 cylinders, in line; 130.8 cu in, 2,144 cc (3.13 x 3.40 in, 79.5 x 86.4 mm); compression ratio: 8.3:1; max power (DIN): 115 hp (84.6 kW) at 5,500 rpm; max torque (DIN): 120 lb ft, 16.6 kg m (162.9 Nm) at 4,000 rpm; 53.6 hp/l (39.5 kW/l); 6 crankshaft bearings; lubrication: 8.8 imp pt, 10.6 US pt, 5 l; water-cooled: 14.3 imp pt, 17.1 US pt, 8.1 l.

TRANSMISSION gearbox ratios: I 3.600, II 2.125, III 1.360, IV 0.967, rev 3.500; axle ratio: 3.889.

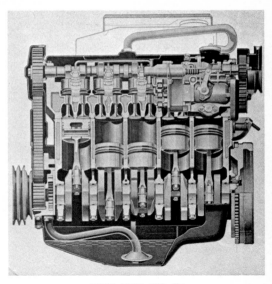

AUDI NSU 100 5D

PERFORMANCE max speed: 111 mph, 179 km/h; power-weight ratio: 22.4 lb/hp (30.5 lb/kW), 10.2 kg/hp (13.8 kg/kW); consumption: 26.6 m/imp gal, 22.2 m/US gal, 10.6 l x 100 km.

BRAKES lining area: front 20.2 sq in, 130 sq cm, rear 44.5 sq in, 287 sq cm, total 64.7 sq in, 417 sq cm.

ELECTRICAL EQUIPMENT 63 Ah battery; electronic ignition.

DIMENSIONS AND WEIGHT weight: 2,580 lb, 1,770 kg.

PRACTICAL INSTRUCTIONS oil: engine 7.9 imp pt, 9.5 US pt, 4.5 l.

OPTIONALS with automatic transmission 3.727 axle ratio, max speed 107 mph, 172 km/h, consumption 25.4 m/imp gal, 21.2 m/US gal, 11.1 l x 100 km; power steering; air-conditioning.

136 hp power team

See 85 hp power team, except for:

ENGINE 5 cylinders, in line; 130.8 cu in, 2,144 cc (3.13 x 3.40 in, 79.5 x 86.4 mm); compression ratio: 9.3:1; max power (DIN): 136 hp (100.1 kW) at 5,700 rpm; max torque (DIN): 134 lb ft, 18.5 kg m (181.4 Nm) at 4,200 rpm; 63.4 hp/l (46.7 kW/l); 6 crankshaft bearings; lubrication: 8.8 imp pt, 10.6 US pt, 5 l; Bosch K-Jetronic system; water-cooled: 14.3 imp pt, 17.1 US pt, 8.1 l.

TRANSMISSION gearbox ratios: I 3.600, II 2.125, III 1.360, IV 0.967, rev 3.500; axle ratio: 3.889; tyres: 185/70 HR x 14.

PERFORMANCE max speed: 118 mph, 190 km/h; power-weight ratio: 19 lb/hp (25.8 lb/kW), 8.6 kg/hp (11.7 kg/kW); acceleration: 0-50 mph (0-80 km/h) 6.3 sec; consumption: 26.9 m/imp gal, 22.4 m/US gal, 10.5 l x 100 km.

BRAKES lining area: front 20.2 sq in, 130 sq cm, rear 44.5 sq in, 287 sq cm, total 64.7 sq in, 417 sq cm.

ELECTRICAL EQUIPMENT 63 Ah battery; 75 A alternator; electronic ignition.

DIMENSIONS AND WEIGHT weight: 2,580 lb, 1,170 kg.

PRACTICAL INSTRUCTIONS fuel: 98 oct petrol; oil: engine 7.9 imp pt, 9.5 US pt, 4.5 l.

OPTIONALS with automatic transmission 3.727 axle ratio, max speed 115 mph, 185 km/h, acceleration 0-50 mph (0-80 km/h) 7.8 sec, consumption 25.4 m/imp gal, 21.2 m/US gal, 11.1 l x 100 km; power steering; air-conditioning.

70 hp (Diesel) power team

See 85 hp power team, except for:

ENGINE Diesel, 5 cylinders, in line; 121.2 cu in, 1,986 cc (3.01 x 3.40 in, 76.5 x 86.4 mm); compression ratio: 23.1; max power (DIN): 91 lb ft, 12.5 kg m (122.7 Nm) at 3,000 rpm; max engine rpm: 5,000; 35.2 hp/l (25.9 kW/l); 6 crankshaft bearings; lubrication: 8.8 imp pt, 10.6 US pt, 5 l; Bosch injection system; water-cooled: 14.3 imp pt, 17.1 US pt, 8.1 l.

AUDI NSU 100 Avant L 5-dr Limousine

70 HP (DIESEL) POWER TEAM

TRANSMISSION gearbox ratios: I 3.600, II 1.941, III 1.231, IV 0.857, rev 3.500; axle ratio: 4.300; tyres: 185/70 SR x 14 (standard).

PERFORMANCE max speed: 93 mph, 150 km/h; power-weight ratio: 38.1 lb/hp (51.8 lb/kW), 17.3 kg/hp (23.5 kg/kW); speed in top at 1,000 rpm: 19.2 mph, 30.9 km/h; consumption: 34.4 m/imp gal, 28.7 m/US gal, 8.2 l x 100 km.

ELECTRICAL EQUIPMENT 88 Ah battery; 65 A alternator.

DIMENSIONS AND WEIGHT weight: 2,668 lb, 1,210 kg.

OPTIONALS automatic transmission not available.

BMW   GERMANY FR

(For cars imported into the USA and Canada, exhaust system with thermal reactor and lower compression ratio).

316

PRICE IN GB: £ 4,399*
PRICE EX WORKS: 15,680* marks

ENGINE front, 4 stroke; 4 cylinders, slanted at 30°, in line; 96 cu in, 1,573 cc (3.31 x 2.80 in, 84 x 71 mm); compression ratio: 8.3:1; max power (DIN): 90 hp (66.2 kW) at 6,000 rpm; max torque (DIN): 91 lb ft, 12.5 kg m (122.6 Nm) at 4,000 rpm; max engine rpm: 6,000; 57.2 hp/l (42.1 kW/l); cast iron block, light alloy head, hemispherical combustion chambers; 5 crankshaft bearings; valves: overhead, Vee-slanted at 52°, rockers; camshafts: 1, overhead; lubrication: gear pump, full flow filter, 7.4 imp pt, 8.9 US pt, 4.2 l; 1 Solex DIDTA 32/32 downdraught twin barrel carburettor; fuel feed: mechanical pump; water-cooled, 12.3 imp pt, 14.8 US pt, 7 l.

TRANSMISSION driving wheels: rear; clutch: single dry plate (diaphragm), hydraulically controlled; gearbox: mechanical; gears: 4, fully synchronized; ratios: I 3.764, II 2.022, III 1.320, IV 1, rev 4.096; lever: central; final drive: hypoid bevel; axle ratio: 4.100; width of rims: 5''; tyres: 165 SR x 13.

PERFORMANCE max speeds: (I) 26 mph, 42 km/h; (II) 49 mph, 79 km/h; (III) 75 mph, 121 km/h; (IV) 99 mph, 160 km/h; power-weight ratio: 25 lb/hp (34 lb/kW), 11.3 kg/bp (15.4 kg/kW); carrying capacity: 926 lb, 420 kg; acceleration: standing ¼ mile 18.8 sec, 0-50 mph (0-80 km/h) 8.7 sec; speed in direct drive at 1,000 rpm: 16.3 mph, 26.3 km/h; consumption: 28.5 m/imp gal, 23.8 m/US gal, 9.9 l x 100 km.

CHASSIS integral; front suspension: independent, by McPherson, coil springs/telescopic damper struts, auxiliary rubber springs, lower wishbones, lower trailing links, anti-roll bar; rear: independent, oblique semi-trailing arms, auxiliary rubber springs, coil springs, telescopic dampers.

AUDI NSU 100 Avant GL5E (136 hp)

STEERING ZF, rack-and-pinion; turns lock to lock: 4.05.

BRAKES front disc (diameter 10.04 in, 25.5 cm), rear drum, dual circuit, servo; lining area: front 23.9 sq in, 154 sq cm, rear 51.5 sq in, 332 sq cm, total 75.4 sq in, 486 sq cm.

ELECTRICAL EQUIPMENT 12 V; 45 Ah battery; 630 W alternator; Bosch distributor; 2 headlamps.

DIMENSIONS AND WEIGHT wheel base: 100.79 in, 256 cm; tracks: 54.60 in, 139 cm front, 55.10 in, 140 cm rear; length: 171.26 in, 435 cm; width: 63.39 in, 161 cm; height: 54.33 in, 138 cm; ground clearance: 5.51 in, 14 cm; weight: 2,249 lb, 1,020 kg; turning circle: 33.5 ft, 10.2 m; fuel tank: 12.8 imp gal, 15.3 US gal, 58 l.

BODY saloon/sedan; 2 doors; 5 seats, separate front seats, reclining backrests, built-in adjustable headrests, heated rear window.

PRACTICAL INSTRUCTIONS fuel: 92 oct petrol; oil: engine 7.4 imp pt, 8.9 US pt, 4.2 l, SAE 20W-50, change every 3,700 miles, 6,000 km - gearbox 1.8 imp pt, 2.1 US pt, 1 l, SAE 80, change every 14,800 miles, 24,000 km - final drive 1.6 imp pt, 1.9 US pt, 0.9 l, SAE 90, no change recommended; greasing: none; sparking plug: 145°.

OPTIONALS limited slip differential; headlamps with wiper-washers; anti-roll bar on rear suspension; halogen headlamps; fog lamps; 55 Ah battery; 185/70 HR x 13 tyres; light alloy wheels; sunshine roof; metallic spray.

318

See 316, except for:

PRICE EX WORKS: 16,700* marks

ENGINE 107.8 cu in, 1,766 cc (3.50 x 2.80 in, 89 x 71 mm); max power (DIN): 98 hp (72.1 kW) at 5,800 rpm; max torque (DIN): 105 lb ft, 14.5 kg m (142.2 Nm) at 4,000 rpm; 55 hp/l (40.8 kW/l).

PERFORMANCE max speed: 103 mph, 165 km/h; power-weight ratio: 23.2 lb/hp (31.5 lb/kW), 10.5 kg/hp (14.3 kg/kW); acceleration: standing ¼ mile 17.9 sec, 0-50 mph (0-80 km/h) 7.6 sec; speed in direct drive at 1,000 rpm: 17 mph, 27.7 km/h.

ELECTRICAL EQUIPMENT halogen headlamps.

DIMENSIONS AND WEIGHT weight: 2,271 lb, 1,030 kg.

OPTIONALS ZF HP 22 automatic transmission, hydraulic torque converter and planetary gears with 3 ratios I 2.478, II 1.478, III 1, rev 2.090), 3.640 axle ratio, max ratio of converter at stall 2, possible manual selection, max speed 99 mph, 160 km/h, consumption 26.4 m/imp gal, 22 m/US gal, 10.7 l x 100 km.

320

See 316, except for:

PRICE IN GB: £ 5,549*
PRICE EX WORKS: 18,950* marks

ENGINE 6 cylinders, in line; 121.4 cu in, 1,990 cc (3.15 x 2.60 in, 80 x 66 mm); compression ratio: 9.2:1; max power (DIN): 122 hp (89.8 kW) at 6,000 rpm; max torque (DIN): 118 lb ft, 16.3 kg m (159.8 Nm) at 4,000 rpm; max engine rpm: 6,000; 61.3 hp/l (45.1 kW/l); 7 crankshaft bearings; valves: overhead, Vee-slanted, rockers; lubricating system 10 imp pt, 12 US pt, 5.7 l; 1 Solex 4A1 downdraught 4-barrel carburettor; cooling system: 21.1 imp pt, 25.4 US pt, 12 l.

TRANSMISSION axle ratio: 3.640; width of rims: 5.5''; tyres 185/70 HR x 13.

PERFORMANCE max speed: 112 mph, 181 km/h; power-weight ratio: 20.1 lb/hp (27.4 lb/kW), 9.1 kg/hp (12.4 kg/kW); acceleration: standing ¼ mile 17.4 sec, 0-50 mph (0-80 km/h) 7.2 sec; speed in direct drive at 1,000 rpm: 18 mph, 30.2 km/h; consumption: 29.7 m/imp gal, 24.8 m/US gal, 9.5 l x 100 km.

ELECTRICAL EQUIPMENT 65 A alternator; 4 halogen headlamps.

DIMENSIONS AND WEIGHT weight: 2,459 lb, 1,115 kg.

PRACTICAL INSTRUCTIONS fuel: 98 oct petrol; oil: engine 10 imp pt, 12 US pt, 5.7 l.

OPTIONALS ZF HP 22 automatic transmission, hydraulic torque converter and planetary gears with 3 ratios I 2.478, II 1.478, III 1, rev 2.090); 3.640 axle ratio, max ratio of converter at stall 2, possible manual selection, max speed 109 mph, 176 km/h, consumption 27.2 m/imp gal, 22.6 m/US gal, 10.4 l x 100 km.

BMW 316 - 318

320 i

[fo]r USA and Canada only).

[Se]e 316, except for:

[PR]ICE IN USA: $ 10,165*

[EN]GINE 121.4 cu in, 1,990 cc (3.50 x 3.15 in, 89 x 80 mm); [co]mpression ratio: 8.1:1; max power (DIN): 110 hp (79 kW) [at] 5,800 rpm; max torque (DIN): 112 lb ft, 15.5 kg m [(15]1.7 Nm) at 3,750 rpm; 55.3 hp/l (39.7 kW/l); Bosch K-[je]tronic injection system; fuel feed: electronic pump.

[TR]ANSMISSION axle ratio: 3.640; width of rims: 5.5''; tyres: [16]5/70 SR x 13.

[PE]RFORMANCE max speed: 106 mph, 171 km/h; power-weight [rat]io: 21 lb/hp (29.3 lb/kW), 9.5 kg/hp (13.3 kg/kW); [co]nsumption: 30.1 m/imp gal, 25 m/US gal, 9.4 l x 100 km.

[ST]EERING damper.

[BR]AKES front disc with internal radial fins.

[EL]ECTRICAL EQUIPMENT 55 Ah battery; 770 W alternator; [4] halogen headlamps.

[DI]MENSIONS AND WEIGHT length: 177.50 in, 451 cm; [we]ight: 2,315 lb, 1,050 kg.

[PR]ACTICAL INSTRUCTIONS fuel: 91 oct petrol.

[OP]TIONALS 105 hp power team (for California only); air-[co]nditioning.

323 i

[Se]e 316, except for:

[PR]ICE IN GB: £ 6,499*
[PRI]CE EX WORKS: 21,450* marks

[EN]GINE 6 cylinders, in line; 141 cu in, 2,315 cc (3.15 x 3.02 [in,] 80 x 76.8 mm); compression ratio: 9.5:1; max power [(DI]N): 143 hp (105.2 kW) at 6,000 rpm; max torque (DIN): [141] lb ft, 19.4 kg m (190.3 Nm) at 4,500 rpm; max engine [rp]m: 6,000; 61.8 hp/l (45.4 kW/l); 7 crankshaft bearings; [val]ves: overhead, Vee-slanted, rockers; lubricating system: [9.2] imp pt, 12 US pt, 5.7 l; Bosch K-Jetronic injection system; [coo]ling system: 21.1 imp pt, 25.4 US pt, 12 l.

[TR]ANSMISSION axle ratio: 3.450; width of rims: 5.5''; [tyr]es: 185/70 HR x 13.

[PE]RFORMANCE max speed: 118 mph, 190 km/h; power-[we]ight ratio: 17.5 lb/hp (23.8 lb/kW), 7.9 kg/hp (10.8 [kg/]kW); acceleration: standing 1/4 mile 16.7 sec, 0-50 mph [(80] km/h) 6.4 sec; speed in direct drive at 1,000 rpm: [17.]7 mph, 31.7 km/h; consumption: 30.7 m/imp gal, 25.6 [US] gal, 9.2 l x 100 km.

[EL]ECTRICAL EQUIPMENT 55 Ah battery; 65 A alternator; [tra]nsistorized ignition; 4 halogen headlamps.

[DI]MENSIONS AND WEIGHT weight: 2,503 lb, 1,135 kg.

[PR]ACTICAL INSTRUCTIONS fuel: 98 oct petrol; oil: engine [9.2] imp pt, 12 US pt, 5.7 l.

BMW 320

518

PRICE IN GB: £ 5,799*
PRICE EX WORKS: 18,780* marks

ENGINE front, 4 stroke; 4 cylinders, in line; 107.8 cu in, 1,766 cc (2.80 x 3.50 in, 71 x 89 mm); compression ratio: 8.3:1; max power (DIN): 90 hp (66.2 kW) at 5,500 rpm; max torque (DIN): 104 lb ft, 14.3 kg m (140.2 Nm) at 3,500 rpm; max engine rpm: 6,300; 51 hp/l (37.5 kW/l); cast iron block, light alloy head, hemispherical combustion chambers; 5 crankshaft bearings; valves: overhead, Vee-slanted at 52°, rockers; camshafts: 1, overhead; lubrication: rotary pump, full flow filter, 7.4 imp pt, 8.9 US pt, 4.2 l; 1 Solex DIDTA 32/32 downdraught twin barrel carburettor; fuel feed: mechanical pump; water-cooled, 12.3 imp pt, 14.8 US pt, 7 l.

TRANSMISSION driving wheels: rear; clutch: single dry plate; gearbox: mechanical; gears: 4, fully synchronized; ratios: I 3.764, II 2.022, III 1.320, IV 1, rev 4.096; lever: central; final drive: hypoid bevel; axle ratio: 4.440; width of rims: 5.5''; tyres: 175 SR x 14.

PERFORMANCE max speeds: (I) 27 mph, 43 km/h; (II) 49 mph, 79 km/h; (III) 76 mph, 122 km/h; (IV) 99 mph, 160 km/h; power-weight ratio: 30.4 lb/hp (41.3 lb/kW), 13.8 kg/hp (18.7 kg/kW); carrying capacity: 1,036 lb, 470 kg; speed in direct drive at 1,000 rpm: 15.8 mph, 25.5 km/h; consumption: 28.8 m/imp gal, 24 m/US gal, 9.8 l x 100 km.

CHASSIS integral; front suspension: independent, by Mc-
Pherson, coil springs/telescopic damper struts, auxiliary rubber springs, lower wishbones, lower trailing links, anti-roll bar; rear: independent, oblique semi-trailing arms, auxiliary rubber springs, coil springs, telescopic dampers.

STEERING ZF, worm and roller.

BRAKES front disc (diameter 11 in, 28 cm), rear drum, dual circuit, rear compensator, servo.

ELECTRICAL EQUIPMENT 12 V; 36 Ah battery; 630 W alternator; 4 halogen headlamps.

DIMENSIONS AND WEIGHT wheel base: 103.94 in, 264 cm; tracks: 56 in, 142 cm front, 57.70 in, 147 cm rear; length: 181.89 in, 462 cm; width: 66.54 in, 169 cm; height: 55.91 in, 142 cm; ground clearance: 5.51 in, 14 cm; weight: 2,734 lb, 1,240 kg; turning circle: 34.4 ft, 10.5 m; fuel tank: 15.4 imp gal, 18.5 US gal, 70 l.

BODY saloon/sedan; 4 doors; 5 seats, separate front seats, reclining backrests; heated rear window.

PRACTICAL INSTRUCTIONS fuel: 90 oct petrol; oil: engine 7.4 imp pt, 8.9 US pt, 4.2 l, SAE 20W-50, change every 3,700 miles, 6,000 km - gearbox 1.8 imp pt, 2.1 US pt, 1 l, SAE 80, change every 14,900 miles, 24,000 km - final drive 1.6 imp pt, 1.9 US pt, 0.9 l, SAE 90, no change recommended; greasing: none.

OPTIONALS limited slip differential; 195/70 HR x 14 tyres; light alloy wheels; power steering; manually-or electrically-controlled sunshine roof; fog lamps; metallic spray; 55 Ah battery; 770 W alternator; ZF 3 HP 22 automatic transmission, hydraulic torque converter and planetary gears with 3 ratios (I 2.478, II 1.478, III 1, rev 2.090), max ratio of converter at stall 2, possible manual selection, max speed 96 mph, 155 km/h, consumption 26.4 m/imp gal, 22 m/US gal, 10.7 l x 100 km.

520

See 518, except for:

PRICE IN GB: £ 6,749*
PRICE EX WORKS: 21,300* marks

ENGINE 6 cylinders, in line; 121.4 cu in, 1,990 cc (3.15 x 2.60 in, 80 x 66 mm); compression ratio: 9.2:1; max power (DIN): 122 hp (89.8 kW) at 6,000 rpm; max torque (DIN): 118 lb ft, 16.3 kg m (159.8 Nm) at 4,000 rpm; max engine rpm: 6,000; 61.3 hp/l (45.1 kW/l); 7 crankshaft bearings; valves: overhead, Vee-slanted, rockers; lubricating system: 10 imp pt, 12 US pt, 5.7 l; 1 Solex 4A1 downdraught 4-barrel carburettor; cooling system: 21.1 imp pt, 25.4 US pt, 12 l.

TRANSMISSION axle ratio: 3.900; tyres: 175 HR x 14.

PERFORMANCE max speed: 112 mph, 180 km/h; power-weight ratio: 23.7 lb/hp (32.2 lb/kW), 10.7 kg/hp (14.6 kg/kW); speed in direct drive at 1,000 rpm: 18.8 mph, 30.2 km/h; consumption: 27.4 m/imp gal, 22.8 m/US gal, 10.3 l x 100 km.

ELECTRICAL EQUIPMENT 44 Ah battery; 55 A alternator.

DIMENSIONS AND WEIGHT weight: 2,889 lb, 1,310 kg.

BMW 520

520

PRACTICAL INSTRUCTIONS fuel: 98 oct petrol; oil: engine 10 imp pt, 12 US pt, 5.7 l.

OPTIONALS ZF 3 HP 22 automatic transmission, hydraulic torque converter and planetary gears with 3 ratios (I 2.478 II 1.478, III 1, rev 2.090), max ratio of converter at stall 2, possible manual selection, 3.900 axle ratio, max speed 108 mph, 174 km/h, consumption 25.2 m/imp gal, 21 m/US gal, 11.2 l x 100 km.

525

See 520, except for:

PRICE IN GB: £ 7,779*
PRICE EX WORKS: 23,950* marks

ENGINE 152.2 cu in, 2,494 cc (3.39 x 2.82 in, 86 x 71.6 mm); compression ratio: 9:1; max power (DIN): 150 hp (110.4 kW) at 6,000 rpm; max torque (DIN): 154 lb ft, 21.2 kg m (207.9 Nm) at 4,000 rpm; 60.1 hp/l (44.2 kW/l).

TRANSMISSION gearbox ratios: I 3.855, II 2.203, III 1.402, IV 1, rev 4.300; axle ratio: 3.640.

PERFORMANCE max speeds: (I) 32 mph, 51 km/h; (II) 57 mph, 91 km/h; (III) 87 mph, 140 km/h; (IV) 120 mph, 193 km/h; power-weight ratio: 19.8 lb/hp (26.9 lb/kW), 9 kg/hp (12.2 kg/kW); carrying capacity: 1,014 lb, 460 kg; acceleration: standing ¼ mile 17.1 sec; consumption: 26.9 m/imp gal, 22.4 m/US gal, 10.5 l x 100 km.

CHASSIS front and rear suspension: anti-roll bar.

BRAKES rear disc (diameter 10.71 in, 27.2 cm).

ELECTRICAL EQUIPMENT 55 Ah battery.

DIMENSIONS AND WEIGHT weight: 2,977 lb, 1,350 kg.

OPTIONALS ZF 3 HP 22 automatic transmission, max speed 115 mph, 185 km/h, consumption 24.8 m/imp gal, 20.6 m/US gal, 11.4 l x 100 km.

528 i

See 525, except for:

PRICE IN USA: $ 15.895*
PRICE EX WORKS: 27,950* marks

ENGINE 170.1 cu in, 2,788 cc (3.39 x 3.15 in, 86 x 80 mm); max power (DIN): 177 hp (130 kW) at 5,800 rpm; max torque (DIN): 174 lb ft, 24 kg m (235.4 Nm) at 4,300 rpm; max engine rpm: 6,500; 63.5 hp/l (46.6 kW/l); Bosch L-Jetronic injection system.

TRANSMISSION width of rims: 6''; tyres: 195/70 VR x 1

PERFORMANCE max speed: 129 mph, 208 km/h; powe weight ratio: 17.6 lb/hp (23.9 lb/kW), 8 kg/hp (10.8 kg/k consumption: 26.6 m/imp gal, 22.2 m/US gal, 10.6 l x100 k

STEERING servo (standard).

DIMENSIONS AND WEIGHT weight: 3,109 lb, 1,410 kg.

OPTIONALS ZF 3 HP 22 automatic transmission, max spe 124 mph, 200 km/h, consumption 24.4 m/imp gal, 20 m/US gal, 11.6 l x 100 km.

728

PRICE IN GB: £ 9,849*
PRICE EX WORKS: 30,850* marks

ENGINE front, 4 stroke; 6 cylinders, in line; 170.1 cu 2,788 cc (3.39 x 3.15 in, 86 x 80 mm); compression rati 9:1; max power (DIN): 170 hp (125.1 kW) at 5,800 rp max torque (DIN): 172 lb ft, 23.8 kg m (233.4 Nm) 4,000 rpm; max engine rpm: 6,500; 61 hp/l (44.9 kW/ cast iron block, light alloy head, polispherical combusti chambers; 7 crankshaft bearings; valves: overhead, Ve slanted, rockers; camshafts: 1, overhead; lubrication: r tary pump, full flow filter, 10 imp pt, 12 US pt, 5.7 1 Solex 4A1 downdraught 4-barrel carburettor; fuel fee mechanical pump; water-cooled, 21.1 imp pt, 25.4 US 12 l.

TRANSMISSION driving wheels: rear; clutch: single d plate (diaphragm), hydraulically controlled; gearbox: mech nical; gears: 4, fully synchronized; ratios: I 3.855, II 2.20 III 1.402, IV 1, rev 4.300; lever: central; final drive: hypo bevel; axle ratio: 3.640; width of rims: 6''; tyres: 195/ HR x 14.

PERFORMANCE max speed: 119 mph, 192 km/h; powe weight ratio: 19.8 lb/hp (27 lb/kW), 9 kg/hp (12.2 kg/kW carrying capacity: 1,036 lb, 470 kg; speed in direct drive 1,000 rpm: 18.4 mph, 29.6 km/h; consumption: 24.6 m/in gal, 20.5 m/US gal, 11.5 l x 100 km.

CHASSIS integral; front suspension: independent, by M Pherson, coil springs/telescopic damper struts, auxilia rubber springs, lower wishbones (trailing links), anti-r bar; rear: independent, semi-trailing arms, auxiliary rubb springs, coil springs, telescopic dampers.

STEERING ZF, recirculating ball, variable ratio servo; tur lock to lock: 3.80.

BRAKES disc (diameter 11 in, 28 cm), front internal radi fins, 2 X circuits, servo.

ELECTRICAL EQUIPMENT 12 V; 55 Ah battery; 55 A alte nator; Bosch distributor; 4 halogen headlamps.

DIMENSIONS AND WEIGHT wheel base: 110 in, 279 cr tracks: 59.45 in, 151 cm front, 59.84 in, 152 cm rear; lengt 191.30 in, 486 cm; width: 70.90 in, 180 cm; height: 56.1 in, 143 cm; weight: 3,374 lb, 1,530 kg; turning circle: 37 ft, 11.4 m; fuel tank: 18.7 imp gal, 22.4 US gal, 85

BODY saloon/sedan; 4 doors; 5 seats, separate front seat reclining backrests, adjustable built-in headrests, heate rear window.

PRACTICAL INSTRUCTIONS fuel: 98 oct petrol; oil: engi 10 imp pt, 12 US pt, 5.7 l, SAE 20W-50, change every 3,7 miles, 6,000 km - gearbox 2.1 imp pt, 2.5 US pt, 1.2 SAE 20W-50, change every 14,800 miles, 24,000 km - fin drive 2.6 imp pt, 3.2 US pt, 1.5 l, SAE 90, no change r commended; greasing: none.

OPTIONALS limited slip differential; ZF automatic tran mission, hydraulic torque converter and planetary gea with 3 ratios (I 2.478, II 1.478, III 1, rev 2.090), ma ratio of converter at stall 2, possible manual selectio 3.640 axle ratio, max speed 116 mph, 186 km, consum tion 22.6 m/imp gal, 18.8 m/US gal, 12.5 l x 100 km; ant brake-locking system (ABS); light alloy wheels; sunshi roof; air-conditioning.

730

See 728, except for:

PRICE IN GB: £ 11,649*
PRICE EX WORKS: 34,850* marks

ENGINE 182 cu in, 2,986 cc (3.50 x 3.15 in, 89 x 80 mm max power (DIN): 184 hp (135.4 kW) at 5,800 rpm; m torque (DIN): 188 lb ft, 26 kg m (255 Nm) at 3,500 rp 61.6 hp/l (45.4 kW/l).

TRANSMISSION axle ratio: 3.450; width of rims: 6.5 tyres: 205/70 HR x 14.

PERFORMANCE max speed: 124 mph, 200 km/h; powe weight ratio: 18.9 lb/hp (25.7 lb/kW), 8.6 kg/hp (11 kg/kW); speed in direct drive at 1,000 rpm: 19.1 mph, 30

BMW 525

BMW 528 i

BMW 635 CSi

km - gearbox 2.1 imp pt, 2.5 US pt, 1.2 l, SAE 20W-50, change every 14,800 miles, 24,000 km - final drive 2.6 imp pt, 3.2 US pt, 1.5 l, SAE 90, no change recommended; greasing: none; sparking plug: 175° T30; tappet clearances: inlet 0.010 in, 0.25 mm, exhaust 0.012 in, 0.30 mm; valve timing: 6° 50° 50° 6°; tyre pressure: front 28 psi, 2 atm, rear 27 psi, 1.9 atm.

OPTIONALS ZF 3 HP 22 automatic transmission, hydraulic torque converter and planetary gears with 3 ratios + reverse (I 2.478, II 1.478, III 1, rev 2.090), max ratio of converter at stall 2, possible manual selection, max speed 126 mph, 202 km/h, consumption 22.8 m/imp gal, 19 m/US gal, 12.4 l x 100 km; limited slip differential; tyres with 7'' wide rims.

633 CSi

See 630 CS, except for:

PRICE IN GB: £ 15,379*
PRICE IN USA: $ 27,875*

ENGINE 195.81 cu in, 3,210 cc (3.50 x 3.39 in, 89 x 86 mm); max power (DIN): 200 hp (147.2 kW) at 5,500 rpm; max torque (DIN): 210 lb ft, 29 kg m (284.4 Nm) at 4,250 rpm; max engine rpm: 6,000; 62.3 hp/l (45.9 kW/l); Bosch L-Jetronic intermittent injection pump in inlet pipes and automatic starting device.

TRANSMISSION axle ratio: 3.250.

PERFORMANCE max speeds: (I) 35 mph, 56 km/h; (II) 61 mph, 98 km/h; (III) 95 mph, 153 km/h; (IV) 134 mph, 215 km/h; power-weight ratio: 16.1 lb/hp (22 lb/kW), 7.3 kg/hp (10 kg/kW); carrying capacity: 838 lb, 380 kg; acceleration: standing ¼ mile 15.8 sec, 0-50 mph (0-80 km/h) 5.6 sec; speed in direct drive at 1,000 rpm: 22.2 mph, 35.8 km/h; consumption: 25.7 m/imp gal, 21.4 m/US gal, 11 l x 100 km.

ELECTRICAL EQUIPMENT 910 W alternator.

DIMENSIONS AND WEIGHT weight: 3,241 lb, 1,470 kg.

OPTIONALS ZF 3 HP 22 automatic transmission, max speed 129 mph, 207 km/h.

635 CSi

See 630 CS, except for:

PRICE EX WORKS: 49,400* marks

ENGINE 210.7 cu in, 3,453 cc (3.68 x 3.31 in, 93.4 x 84 mm); compression ratio: 9.3:1; max power (DIN): 218 hp (160 kW) at 5,200 rpm; max torque (DIN): 223 lb ft, 31.6 kg m (310 Nm) at 4,000 rpm; max engine rpm: 5,600; 63.1 hp/l (46.3 kW/l); Bosch L-Jetronic intermittent injection pump in inlet pipes and automatic starking device.

TRANSMISSION gears: 5, fully synchronized; ratios: I 3.717, II 2.403, III 1.766, IV 1.263, V 1, rev 4.234; axle ratio: 3.070; width of rims: 6.5''.

/h; consumption: 23.7 m/imp gal, 19.8 m/US gal, 11.9 100 km.

MENSIONS AND WEIGHT weight: 3,484 lb, 1,580 kg.

TIONALS ZF automatic transmission, 3.450 axle ratio, × speed 121 mph, 194 km/h, consumption 21.9 m/imp , 18.2 m/US gal, 12.9 l x 100 km.

733 i

728, except for:

CE IN GB: £ 12,699*
CE IN USA: $ 24,575*

GINE 195.81 cu in, 3,210 cc (3.50 x 3.39 in, 89 x 86 mm); × power (DIN): 197 hp (145 kW) at 5,500 rpm; max torque N): 207 lb ft, 28.5 kg m (279.5 Nm) at 4,300 rpm; 61.4 l (45.2 kW/l); Bosch L-Jetronic electronic fuel injection tem.

ANSMISSION axle ratio: 3.450; width of rims: 6.5''; tyres: /70 VR x 14.

RFORMANCE max speed: 127 mph, 205 km/h; power-ght ratio: 17.9 lb/hp (24.3 lb/kW), 8.1 kg/hp (11 kg/kW); ed in direct drive at 1,000 rpm: 19.6 mph, 31.5 km/h; con-ption: 23.9 m/imp gal, 19.9 m/US gal, 11.8 l x 100 km.

CTRICAL EQUIPMENT 65 A alternator.

MENSIONS AND WEIGHT weight: 3,528 lb, 1,600 kg.

TIONALS ZF automatic transmission, 3.450 axle ratio, × speed 123 mph, 198 km/h, consumption 22.1 m/imp , 18.4 m/US gal, 12.8 l x 100 km.

630 CS

CE EX WORKS: 43,900* marks

GINE front, 4 stroke; 6 cylinders, in line; 182 cu in, 36 cc (3.50 x 3.15 in, 89 x 80 mm); compression ratio: ; max power (DIN): 185 hp (136.2 kW) at 5,800 rpm; × torque (DIN): 188 lb ft, 26 kg m (255 Nm) at 3,500 ; max engine rpm: 6,200; 62 hp/l (45.6 kW/l); cast iron ck, light alloy head, polispherical combustion cham-s; 7 crankshaft bearings; valves: overhead, Vee-slanted 52°, rockers; camshafts: 1, overhead, chain-driven; lu-cation: rotary pump, full flow filter, 10 imp pt, 12 US pt, l; 1 Solex 4A1 4-barrel carburettor with automatic ke and thermostatic by-pass starting device; fuel feed: ctric pump; water-cooled, 21.1 imp pt, 25.4 US pt, 12 l.

ANSMISSION driving wheels: rear; clutch: single dry te (diaphragm), hydraulically controlled; gearbox: mecha-al; gears: 4, fully synchronized; ratios: I 3.855, II 2.203, 1.402, IV 1, rev 4.300; lever: central; final drive: hy-d bevel; axle ratio: 3.450; width of rims: 6''; tyres: /70 VR x 14.

RFORMANCE max speeds: (I) 34 mph, 54 km/h; (II) mph, 95 km/h; (III) 93 mph, 150 km/h; (IV) 130 mph, km/h; power-weight ratio: 17.3 lb/hp (23.4 lb/kW), 7.8 hp (10.6 kg/kW); carrying capacity: 838 lb, 380 kg; eleration: standing ¼ mile 16.3 sec, 0-50 mph (0-80

---

km/h) 5.9 sec; speed in direct drive at 1,000 rpm: 20.9 mph, 33.7 km/h; consumption: 24.8 m/imp gal, 20.6 m/US gal, 11.4 l x 100 km.

CHASSIS integral; front suspension: independent, by Mc-Pherson, coil springs/telescopic damper struts, auxiliary rubber springs, anti-roll bar, lower wishbones; rear: inde-pendent, semi-trailing arms, auxiliary rubber springs, coil springs, telescopic dampers.

STEERING ZF, recirculating ball, variable ratio servo; turns lock to lock: 3.50.

BRAKES ventilated discs (diameter 11 in, 28 cm), twin dual-circuit system, servo, rear compensator.

ELECTRICAL EQUIPMENT 12 V; 66 Ah battery; 770 W al-ternator; Bosch distributor, 4 halogen headlamps.

DIMENSIONS AND WEIGHT wheel base: 103.15 in, 262 cm; tracks: 55.91 in, 142 cm front, 58.27 in, 148 cm rear; length: 187.01 in, 475 cm; width: 67.72 in, 172 cm; height: 53.54 in, 136 cm; ground clearance: 5.51 in, 14 cm; weight: 3,197 lb, 1,450 kg; turning circle: 36.7 ft, 11.2 m; fuel tank: 15.4 imp gal, 18.5 US gal, 70 l.

BODY coupé; 2 doors; 4 seats, separate front seats, re-clining backrests; tinted glass; heated rear window.

PRACTICAL INSTRUCTIONS fuel: 98 oct petrol; oil: engine 10 imp pt, 12 US pt, 5.7 l, change every 3,700 miles, 6,000

BMW 733 i

635 CSi

PERFORMANCE max speeds: (I) 37 mph, 60 km/h; (II) 58 mph, 94 km/h; (III) 79 mph, 127 km/h; (IV) 111 mph, 178 mph; (V) 140 mph, 225 km/h; power-weight ratio: 15.2 lb/hp, (20.7 lb/kW), 6.9 kg/hp (9.4 kg/kW); speed in direct drive at 1,000 rpm: 25 mph, 40.2 km/h; consumption: 28.2 m/imp gal, 23.5 m/US gal, 10 l x 100 km.

ELECTRICAL EQUIPMENT 910 W alternator.

DIMENSIONS AND WEIGHT weight: 3,307 lb, 1,500 kg.

M 1

PRICE EX WORKS: (on application)

ENGINE centre-rear, longitudinal, 4 stroke; 6 cylinders, in line, 210.7 cu in, 3,453 cc (3.68 x 3.31 in, 93.4 x 84 mm); compression ratio: 9:1; max power (DIN): 277 hp (204 kW) at 6,500 rpm; max torque (DIN): 239 lb ft, 32.9 kg m (330 Nm) at 5,000 rpm; max engine rpm: 7,000; 80.2 hp/l (59.1 kW/l); cast iron block, light alloy head, polispherical combustion chambers; 7 crankshaft bearings; valves: 4 per cylinder, overhead, Vee-slanted at 52°, rockers; camshafts: 2, overhead, chain driven; lubrication: gear pump, full flow filter, dry sump, 14.1 imp pt, 16.9 US pt, 8 l; Kugelfiseher-Bosch mechanical injection, 3 double intake

length: 171.7 in, 436 cm; width: 71.8 in, 182 cm; height: 44.9 in, 114 cm; ground clearance: 4.9 in, 12 cm; weight: 2,867 lb, 1,300 kg; turning circle (between walls): 42.7 ft, 13 m; fuel tanks: 25.5 imp gal, 30.6 US gal, 116 l (2 separate tanks).

BODY coupé, in plastic material; 2 doors; 2 seats; light alloy wheels.

PRACTICAL INSTRUCTIONS fuel: 98 oct petrol; oil: engine 14.1 imp pt, 16.9 US pt, 8 l, SAE 10W-50 change every 3,700 miles, 6,000 km - gearbox and final drive: 3 imp pt, 3.6 US pt, 1.7 l, SAE 90, change every 18,600 miles, 30,000 km, greasing: none; sparking plug: Bosch X4 CS; tyre pressure: front 34 psi, 2.4 atm, rear 37 psi, 2.6 atm.

VARIATIONS

(Competition version).
ENGINE 213.6 cu in, 3,500 cc (3.70 x 3.31 in, 94 x 84 mm), max power (DIN) 470 hp (345 kW) at 9,000 rpm, max torque (DIN) 282 lb ft, 38.9 kg m (390 Nm) at 7,000 rpm, 134.3 hp/l (98.6 kW/l), front-mounted oil cooler.
TRANSMISSION width of rims front 11'', rear 12.5'', 10/23.5 x 16 front, 12.5/25 x 16 rear tyres.
PERFORMANCE max speed 189 mph, 310 km/h, power-weight ratio 4.8 lb/hp (6.5 lb/kW), 2.2 kg/hp (2.9 kg/kW).
DIMENSIONS AND WEIGHT tracks 62.8 in, 159 cm front, 61.4 in, 156 cm rear, width 75.7 in, 192 cm, height 43.7 in, 111 cm, weight 2,249 lb, 1,020 kg.

Bugatti 35 B

ENGINE Volkswagen, rear, 4 stroke; 4 cylinders, horizontally opposed; 96.7 cu in, 1,584 cc (3.37 x 2.72 in, 85.5 x mm); compression ratio: 7.5:1; max power (DIN): 50 (36.8 kW) at 4,000 rpm; max torque (DIN): 78 lb ft, kg m (105.9 Nm) at 2,800 rpm; max engine rpm: 4,500; 3 hp/l (23.2 kW/l); block with cast iron liners and light al fins, light alloy head; 4 crankshaft bearings; valves: ov head, push-rods and rockers; camshafts: 1, central, low lubrication: gear pump, filter in sump, oil cooler, 5.3 i 6.3 US pt, 3 l; 1 Solex 34 PICT 2 downdraught car rettor; fuel feed: mechanical pump; air-cooled.

TRANSMISSION driving wheels: rear; clutch: single plate; gearbox: mechanical; gears: 4, fully synchronize ratios: I 3.780, II 2.060, III 1.260, IV 0.930, rev 4.010; le central; final drive: spiral bevel; axle ratio: 4.375; wi rims: 4.5''; tyres: 185/70 SR x 15.

PERFORMANCE max speed: about 100 mph, 161 km power-weight ratio: 35 lb/hp. (47.6 lb/kW), 15.9 kg/hp (2 kg/kW); carrying capacity: 442 lb, 200 kg; speed in top 1,000 rpm: 21.7 mph, 35 km/h; consumption: 30.7 m/i gal, 25.6 m/US gal, 9.2 l x 100 km.

CHASSIS backbone platform; front suspension: independent, twin swinging longitudinal trailing arms, transve laminated torsion bars, anti-roll bar, telescopic dampe rear: independent, semi-trailing arms, transverse comp sating torsion bar, telescopic dampers.

STEERING worm and roller, telescopic damper; turns l to lock: 2.60.

BRAKES front disc (diameter 10.91 in, 27.7 cm), r drum; lining area: front 12.4 sq in, 80 sq cm, rear 5 sq in, 358 sq cm, total 67.9 sq in, 438 sq cm.

ELECTRICAL EQUIPMENT 12 V; 36 Ah battery; 50 A ternator; Bosch distributor; 2 headlamps.

DIMENSIONS AND WEIGHT wheel base: 94.50 in, 240 c tracks: 56 in, 142 cm front, 57 in, 144 cm rear; leng 154 in, 391 cm; height: 58 in, 147 cm; ground clearan 9 in, 22.9 cm; weight: 1,750 lb, 793 kg; fuel tank: 8.8 i gal, 10.6 US gal, 40 l.

BODY sports in plastic material; no doors; 2 seats.

PRACTICAL INSTRUCTIONS fuel: 87 oct petrol; oil: eng 4.4 imp pt, 5.3 US pt, 2.5 l, SAE 10W-20 (winter) 20W (summer), change every 3,100 miles, 5,000 km - gearb and final drive 5.3 imp pt, 6.3 US pt, 3 l, SAE 90, char every 31,000 miles, 50,000 km; greasing: every 6,200 mil 10,000 km, 4 points; sparking plug: 175°; tappet clearan inlet 0.004 in, 0.10 mm, exhaust 0.004 in, 0.10 mm, va timing: 7°30' 37° 44°30' 4°.

OPTIONALS tonneau cover; wire wheels.

BMW M 1

pipes with 6 throttles; fuel feed: 2 electric pumps; water-cooled, 21.1 imp pt, 25.4 US pt, 12 l.

TRANSMISSION driving wheels: rear; clutch: F & S, 2-disc dry, hydraulically controlled; gearbox: ZF, mechanical; gears: 5, fully synchronized; ratios: I 2.420, II 1.610, III 1.140, IV 0.846, V 0.704, rev 2.860; lever: central; final drive: hypoid bevel, limited slip differential; axle ratio: 4.220; width of rims: 7'' front, 8'' rear; tyres: 205/55 VR x 16 front, 225/50 VR x 16 rear.

PERFORMANCE max speed: 163 mph, 262 km/h; power-weight ratio: 10.3 lb/hp, (14 lb/kW), 4.7 kg/hp (6.4 kg/kW); carrying capacity: 661 lb, 300 kg; speed in top at 1,000 rpm: 23.2 mph, 37.4 km/h; consumption: 14.4 m/imp gal, 12 m/US gal, 19.6 l x 100 km (ECE method A 70).

CHASSIS separate steel; front suspensions: independent, wishbones, anti-roll bar, coil springs/telescopic dampers (adjustable for height); rear: independent, wishbones, anti-roll bar, coil springs/telescopic dampers (adjustable for height).

STEERING rack-and-pinion.

BRAKES ventilated discs (front diameter 11.8 in, 30 cm, rear 11.7 in, 29.7 cm), dual circuit, servo, rear compensator.

ELECTRICAL EQUIPMENT 12 V; 55 Ah battery; 65 A alternator; Magneti-Marelli contactless fully electronic distributor; 2 halogen headlamps.

DIMENSIONS AND WEIGHT wheel base: 100.8 in, 256 cm; tracks: 61 in, 155 cm front, 62 in, 158 cm rear;

EL-KG Bugatti 35 B

lb, 570 kg; turning circle: 35.1 ft, 10.7 m; fuel tank: 4.4 imp gal, 5.3 US gal, 20 l.

BODY open in plastic material; 2 doors; 4 seats, separate front seats; built-in headrests on front seats.

VARIATIONS

ENGINE Citroën, front, 4 stroke, 2 cylinders, horizontally opposed, 36.7 cu in, 602 cc (2.91 x 2.76 in, 74 x 70 mm), max power (DIN) 26 hp (19.1 kW) at 5,500 rpm, max torque (DIN) 29 lb ft, 4 kg m (39.2 Nm) at 3,500 rpm, max engine rpm 6,000, 43.2 hp/l (31.7 kW/l), lubricating system 3.9 imp pt, 4.7 US pt, 2.2 l.

ENGINE Citroën, front, 4 stroke, 2 cylinders, horizontally opposed, 36.7 cu in, 602 cc (2.91 x 2.76 in, 74 x 70 mm), 9:1 compression ratio, max power (DIN) 32 hp (23.6 kW) at 5,750 rpm, max torque (DIN) 30 lb ft, 4.2 kg m (41.2 Nm) at 4,000 rpm, max engine rpm 6,000, 53.3 hp/l (39.2 kW/l), lubricating system 3.9 imp pt, 4.7 US pt, 2.2 l.

For further data, see Citroën.

FORD   GERMANY FR

Fiesta Series

PRICES EX WORKS:

1 3-dr Limousine	DM 9,095*
2 L 3-dr Limousine	DM 9,695*
3 S 3-dr Limousine	DM 10,995*
4 Ghia 3-dr Limousine	DM 11,750*

Power team:	Standard for:	Optional for:
40 hp	1,2,4	—
45 hp	—	1,2,4
53 hp	3	1,2,4
66 hp	—	3,4

40 hp power team

ENGINE front, transverse, 4 stroke; 4 cylinders, vertical, in line; 57.1 cu in, 935 cc (2.91 x 2.19 in, 74 x 55.7 mm); compression ratio: 8.3:1; max power (DIN) 40 hp (29.4 kW) at 5,500 rpm; max torque (DIN) 47 lb ft, 6.5 kg m (63.7 Nm) at 2,700 rpm; max engine rpm: 5,700; 42.8 hp/l (31.4 kW/l); cast iron block and head; 3 crankshaft bearings; valves: overhead, in line, push-rods and rockers; camshafts: 1, side, chain-driven; lubrication: gear pump, full flow filter (cartridge), 5.6 imp pt, 6.8 US pt, 3.2 l; 1 Ford downdraught single barrel carburettor; fuel feed: mechanical pump; semi-sealed circuit cooling expansion tank, 8.8 imp pt, 10.6 US pt, 5 l, electric fan.

TRANSMISSION driving wheels: front; clutch: single dry plate (diaphragm); gearbox: mechanical, in unit with final drive; gears: 4, fully synchronized; ratios: I 3.583, II 2.050, III 1.346, IV 0.959, rev 3.769; lever: central; final drive:

FIBERFAB Sherpa

spiral bevel; axle ratio: 4.060; width of rims: 4'' - Ghia 4.5''; tyres: 145 SR x 12.

PERFORMANCE max speed: 81 mph, 130 km/h; power-weight ratio: 40.2 lb/hp (54.7 lb/kW), 18.2 kg/hp (24.8 kg/kW); carrying capacity: 948 lb, 430 kg; acceleration: 0-50 mph (0-80 km/h) 14.2 sec; speed in top at 1,000 rpm: 15.8 mph, 25.4 km/h; consumption: 41.5 m/imp gal, 34.6 m/US gal, 6.8 l x 100 km.

CHASSIS integral; front suspension: independent, by McPherson, coil springs/telescopic damper struts, lower wishbones (trailing links); rear: rigid axle, swinging longitudinal trailing arms, upper oblique torque arms, Panhard rod, coil springs, telescopic dampers.

STEERING rack-and-pinion; turns lock to lock: 3.40.

BRAKES front disc (diameter 8.71 in, 22.1 cm), rear drum, rear compensator; lining area: front 18.6 sq in, 120 sq cm, rear 26.4 sq in, 169.9 sq cm, total 45 sq in, 289.9 sq cm; servo (standard for S and Ghia only).

ELECTRICAL EQUIPMENT 12 V; 35 Ah battery; 45 A alternator; Motorcraft distributor; 2 headlamps (2 halogen headlamps standard for Ghia only).

DIMENSIONS AND WEIGHT wheel base: 90.16 in, 229 cm; tracks: 52.36 in, 133 cm front, 51.97 in, 132 cm rear; length: 140.16 in, 356 cm; width: 61.81 in, 157 cm; height: 53.54 in, 136 cm; weight: ground clearance: 5.51 in, 14 cm; weight:

FIBERFAB Bonito

FIBERFAB   GERMANY FR

Bonito

ENGINE Volkswagen, rear, 4 stroke; 4 cylinders, horizontally opposed; 72.7 cu in, 1,192 cc (3.03 x 2.52 in, 77 x 64 mm); compression ratio: 7:1; max power (DIN): 34 hp (25 kW) at 3,600 rpm; max torque (DIN): 61 lb ft, 8.4 kg m (82.4 Nm) at 2,000 rpm; max engine rpm: 4,500; 28.5 hp/l (21 kW/l).

TRANSMISSION width of rims: 4'' or 6''; tyres: 165 x 15 or 175 x 14.

DIMENSIONS AND WEIGHT wheel base: 94.49 in, 240 cm; tracks: 51.18 in, 130 cm front, 53.54 in, 136 cm rear; length: 171.26 in, 435 cm; width: 66.14 in, 168 cm; height: 45.28 in, 115 cm; ground clearance: 5.91 in, 15 cm; weight: 1,499 lb, 680 kg; fuel tank: 9.2 imp gal, 11.1 US gal, 42 l.

BODY coupé in plastic material; 2 doors; 2 + 2 seats, separate front seats.

VARIATIONS

ENGINE Volkswagen, 78.4 cu in, 1,285 cc (3.03 x 2.72 in, 77 x 69 mm).

ENGINE Volkswagen, 91.1 cu in, 1,493 cc (3.27 x 2.72 in, 83 x 69 mm).

ENGINE Volkswagen, 96.7 cu in, 1,584 cc (3.37 x 2.72 in, 85.5 x 69 mm).

For further data, see Volkswagen.

Sherpa

ENGINE Citroën, front, 4 stroke; 2 cylinders, horizontally opposed; 26.5 cu in, 435 cc (2.70 x 2.32 in, 68.5 x 59 mm); compression ratio: 8.5:1; max power (DIN): 24 hp (17.7 kW) at 6,750 rpm; max torque (DIN): 21 lb ft, 2.9 kg m (28.4 Nm) at 4,500 rpm; max engine rpm: 6,750; 55.2 hp/l (40.7 kW/l); cast iron block, light alloy head, dry liners; light alloy sump, hemispherical combustion chambers; 2 crankshaft bearings; valves: overhead, Vee-slanted at 70°, push-rods and rockers; camshafts: 1, central, lower; lubrication: rotary pump, filter in sump, oil cooler, 3.5 imp pt, 4.2 US pt, 2 l; 1 Solex 34 PICS 6 downdraught carburettor; fuel feed: mechanical pump; air-cooled.

TRANSMISSION driving wheels: front (double homokinetic joints); clutch: single dry plate; gearbox: mechanical.

PERFORMANCE carrying capacity: 717 lb, 325 kg.

CHASSIS platform; front suspension: independent, swinging leading arms, 2 friction dampers, 2 inertia-type patter dampers; rear: independent, swinging longitudinal trailing arms linked to front suspension by longitudinal coil springs, 2 inertia-type patter dampers, 2 telescopic dampers.

DIMENSIONS AND WEIGHT wheel base: 94.49 in, 240 cm; tracks: 49.61 in, 126 cm front, 49.61 in, 126 cm rear; length: 138.58 in, 352 cm; width: 59.84 in, 152 cm; height: 55.51 in, 141 cm; ground clearance: 7.09 in, 18 cm; weight: 1,257

FORD Fiesta L 3-dr Limousine

40 HP POWER TEAM

1,610 lb, 730 kg; turning circle: 32.1 ft, 9.8 m; fuel tank: 7.5 imp gal, 9 US gal, 34 l.

BODY saloon/sedan; 3 doors; 5 seats, separate front seats; folding rear seat; light alloy wheels (standard for Ghia only).

PRACTICAL INSTRUCTIONS fuel: 90 oct petrol; oil: engine 4.8 imp pt, 5.7 US pt, 2.7 l, change every 6,200 miles, 10,000 km - gearbox and final drive 3.9 imp pt, 4.7 US pt, 2.2 l, change every 6,200 miles, 10,000 km; valve timing: 21° 55° 70° 22°.

OPTIONALS 155 SR x 12 tyres with 4.5" wide rims; servo brake; headrests on front seats; tinted glass; light alloy wheels; sunshine roof; rear window wiper-washer; head-lamps with wiper-washers; halogen headlamps; fog lamps; metallic spray; Touring equipment (except for Ghia).

45 hp power team

See 40 hp power team, except for:

ENGINE compression ratio: 9:1; max power (DIN): 45 hp (33.1 kW) at 6,000 rpm; max torque (DIN): 48 lb ft, 6.6 kg m (64.7 Nm) at 3,300 rpm; max engine rpm: 6,500; 48.1 hp/l (35.4 kW/l).

TRANSMISSION axle ratio: 4.290.

PERFORMANCE max speed: 85 mph, 137 km/h; power-weight ratio: 35.8 lb/hp (48.6 lb/kW), 16.2 kg/hp (22 kg/kW); speed in top at 1,000 rpm: 14.9 mph, 24 km/h; consumption: 37.7 m/imp gal, 31.4 m/US gal, 7.5 l x 100 km.

PRACTICAL INSTRUCTIONS fuel: 97 oct petrol.

53 hp power team

See 40 hp power team, except for:

ENGINE 66.3 cu in, 1,087 cc (2.91 x 2.56 in, 74 x 65 mm); compression ratio: 9:1; max power (DIN): 53 hp (39 kW) at 5,700 rpm; max torque (DIN): 59 lb ft, 8.2 kg m (80.4 Nm) at 3,000 rpm; max engine rpm: 6,000; 48.8 hp/l (35.9 kW/l); semi-sealed circuit cooling, expansion tank, 8.8 imp pt, 10.6 US pt, 5 l, electric thermostatic fan.

TRANSMISSION width of rims: 4.5".

PERFORMANCE max speed: 90 mph, 145 km/h; power-weight ratio: 30.4 lb/hp (41.3 lb/kW), 13.8 kg/hp (18.7 kg/kW); consumption: 35.8 m/imp gal, 29.8 m/US gal, 7.9 l x 100 km.

CHASSIS rear suspension: anti-roll bar.

PRACTICAL INSTRUCTIONS fuel: 97 oct petrol.

66 hp power team

See 40 hp power team, except for:

ENGINE 77.1 cu in, 1,263 cc (3.19 x 2.48 in, 81 x 63 mm); compression ratio: 9.2:1; max power (DIN): 66 hp (48.6 kW) at 5,600 rpm; max torque (DIN): 70 lb ft, 9.6 kg m (94.1 Nm) at 3,250 rpm; max engine rpm: 6,000; 52.2 hp/l (38.5 kW/l); 1 Weber downdraught single barrel carburettor; semi-sealed circuit cooling, expansion tank, 10.9 imp pt, 13.1 US pt, 6.2 l, electric thermostatic fan.

TRANSMISSION axle ratio: 3.840; width of rims: 4.5"; tyres: 155 SR x 12.

PERFORMANCE max speed: 98 mph, 158 km/h; power-weight ratio: 25.9 lb/hp (35.2 lb/kW), 11.7 kg/hp (15.9 kg/kW); speed in top at 1,000 rpm: 16.3 mph, 26.3 km/h; consumption: 36.2 m/imp gal, 30.2 m/US gal, 7.8 l x 100 km.

CHASSIS rear suspension: anti-roll bar.

DIMENSIONS AND WEIGHT weight: 1,709 lb, 775 kg.

PRACTICAL INSTRUCTIONS fuel: 97 oct petrol.

Escort Series

PRICES EX WORKS:

1 2-dr Limousine	DM	9,81*
2 4-dr Limousine	DM	10,35*
3 Turnier	DM	10,54*
4 L 2-dr Limousine	DM	10,38*
5 L 4-dr Limousine	DM	10,92*
6 L Turnier	DM	11,16*
7 GL 2-dr Limousine	DM	11,41*
8 GL 4-dr Limousine	DM	11,96*
9 GL Turnier	DM	12,18*
10 Ghia 2-dr Limousine	DM	13,52*
11 Ghia 4-dr Limousine	DM	14,06*
12 Sport 2-dr Limousine	DM	11,79*
13 Sport 4-dr Limousine	DM	12,34*
14 RS 2000 2-dr Limousine	DM	15,14*

Power team:	Standard for:	Optional for:
44 hp	—	1,3,4
54 hp	1 to 9	10,11
57 hp	—	1,2,4,5,7,8
70 hp	10,11	4,5,7,8
84 hp	12,13	10,11
110 hp	14	—

44 hp power team

ENGINE front, 4 stroke; 4 cylinders, vertical, in line; 65 cu in, 1,071 cc (3.19 x 2.10 in, 81 x 53.3 mm); compression ratio: 8:1; max power (DIN): 44 hp (32.4 kW) at 5,500 rpm; max torque (DIN): 52 lb ft, 7.2 kg m (70.6 Nm) at 3,000 rpm; max engine rpm: 6,000; 41.1 hp/l (30.2 kW/l); cast iron block and head; 5 crankshaft bearings; valves overhead, in line, push-rods and rockers; camshafts: 1, side; lubrication: gear pump, full flow filter (cartridge), 5.6 imp pt, 6.8 US pt, 3.2 l; 1 Ford downdraught single barrel carburettor; fuel feed: mechanical pump; water-cooled, 8.8 imp pt, 10.6 US pt, 5 l.

TRANSMISSION driving wheels: rear; clutch: single dry plate (diaphragm); gearbox: mechanical; gears: 4, fully synchronized; ratios: I 3.656, II 2.185, III 1.425, IV 1, rev 4.235; lever: central; final drive: hypoid bevel; axle ratio: 4.110; width of rims: 4.5"; tyres: 155 SR x 13.

PERFORMANCE max speeds: (I) 24 mph, 38 km/h; (II) 41 mph, 66 km/h; (III) 62 mph, 100 km/h; (IV) 79 mph, 127 km/h; power-weight ratio: 2-dr L limousines 44.1 hp/l (61.5 lb/kW), 20 kg/hp (28.1 kg/kW); carrying capacity: 970 lb, 440 kg; speed in direct drive at 1,000 rpm: 16 mph, 25.8 km/h; consumption: 35.3 m/imp gal, 29.4 m/US gal, 8 l x 100 km (Turnier 35.8 m/imp gal, 29.8 m/US gal, 7.9 l x 100 km).

CHASSIS integral; front suspension: independent, by Mc Pherson, coil springs/telescopic damper struts, anti-roll bar; rear: rigid axle, semi-elliptic leafsprings, torque trailing arms, anti-roll bar, telescopic dampers.

STEERING rack-and-pinion; turns lock to lock: 3.50.

BRAKES front disc (diameter 9.72 in, 24.7 cm), rear drum, lining area: front 23.4 sq in, 151.2 sq cm, rear 36.4 sq in, 235 sq cm, total 59.8 sq in, 386.2 sq cm; servo.

ELECTRICAL EQUIPMENT 12 V; 35 Ah battery; 45 A alternator (35 A for Turnier only); Motorcraft distributor; 2 headlamps.

DIMENSIONS AND WEIGHT wheel base: 94.88 in, 241 cm; tracks: 50.78 in, 129 cm front, 51.57 in, 131 cm rear; length: 156.69 in, 398 cm - Turnier 159.84 in, 406 cm; width: 62.2 in, 160 cm - Turnier 61.42 in, 156 cm; height: 55.12 in, 140 cm - Turnier 55.51 in, 141 cm; ground clearance: 4.72 in, 12 cm; weight: 2-dr limousines 1,940 lb, 880 kg - 2-dr L limousines 2,007 lb, 910 kg - Turnier 2,029 lb, 920 kg - turning

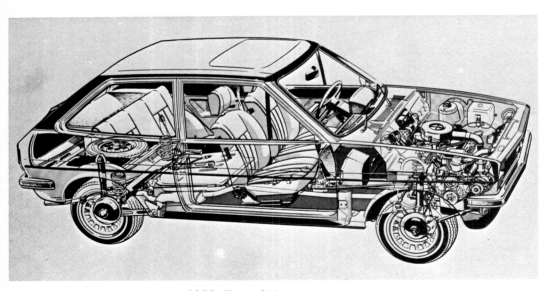

FORD Fiesta Ghia 3-dr Limousine

FORD Escort Ghia 4-dr Limousine

FORD Escort RS 2000 2-dr Limousine

ircle: 31.2 ft, 9.5 m; fuel tank: 9 imp gal, 10.8 US
al, 41 l.

ODY 4-5 seats, separate front seats.

RACTICAL INSTRUCTIONS fuel: 90 oct petrol; oil: engine
8 imp pt, 5.7 US pt, 2.7 l, SAE 10W-30, change every
200 miles, 10,000 km - gearbox 1.6 imp pt, 1.9 US pt,
9 l, SAE 80, no change recommended - final drive 2.6
mp pt, 3.2 US pt, 1.5 l, SAE 90, no change recommend-
d; greasing: none; tappet clearances: inlet 0.010 in, 0.25
m, exhaust 0.017 in, 0.43 mm; valve timing: 17° 51° 51°
7°; tyre pressure: front 24 psi, 1.7 atm, rear 24 psi, 1.7 atm.

OPTIONALS 5'' wide rims; 55 Ah battery; halogen head-
amps.

54 hp power team

ee 44 hp power team, except for:

NGINE 77.1 cu in, 1,263 cc (3.19 x 2.48 in, 81 x 63 mm);
ax power (DIN): 54 hp (39.7 kW) at 5,500 rpm; max torque
DIN): 63 lb ft, 8.7 kg m (85.3 Nm) at 3,000 rpm; 42.8
p/l (31.4 kW/l).

RANSMISSION axle ratio: 3.890; width of rims: 5''.

ERFORMANCE max speed: 85 mph, 137 km/h; power-
eight ratio: 4-dr. limousines 37.4 lb/hp (50.8 lb/kW), 16.9
g/hp (23 kg/kW) - Ghia 4-dr. Limousine 38.4 lb/hp (52.2
/kW), 17.4 kg/hp (23.7 kg/kW); carrying capacity: Ghia
37 lb, 425 kg; speed in direct drive at 1,000 rpm: 16.9 mph,
7.2 km/h; consumption: 33.2 m/imp gal, 27.7 m/US gal,
.5 l x 100 km.

LECTRICAL EQUIPMENT 45 A alternator and halogen head-
amps standard for GL Turnier and GL Limousines.

IMENSIONS AND WEIGHT weight: 2-dr. limousines 1,951
, 885 kg - 4-dr. limousines 2,018 lb, 915 kg - Turnier
,029 lb, 920 kg - Ghia 2-dr. Limousine 2,007 lb, 910 kg -
-dr. Limousine 2,073 lb, 940 kg.

57 hp power team

ee 54 hp power team, except for:

NGINE compression ratio: 9.2:1; max power (DIN): 57 hp
41.9 kW) at 5,500 rpm; max torque (DIN): 67 lb ft, 9.3
g m (91.2 Nm) at 3,000 rpm; 45.1 hp/l (33.2 kW/l); lubri-
ation: oil cooler.

RANSMISSION gearbox: Ford C3 automatic transmission,
ydraulic torque converter and planetary gears with 3 ratios,
ax ratio of converter at stall 2, possible manual selection:
atios: I 2.474, II 1.474, III 1, rev 2.111; axle ratio: 3.890;
idth of rims: 5.5''.

ERFORMANCE max speed: 84 mph, 135 km/h; power-weight
atio: 4-dr. limousines 35.4 lb/hp (48.2 lb/kW), 16 kg/hp
21.8 kg/kW) - Ghia 4-dr. Limousine 36.4 lb/hp (49.5
b/kW), 16.5 kg/hp (22.4 kg/kW); speed in direct drive
t 1,000 rpm: 15.3 mph, 24.6 km/h; consumption: 30.7
n/imp gal, 25.6 m/US gal, 9.2 l x 100 km.

LECTRICAL EQUIPMENT 44 Ah battery.

RACTICAL INSTRUCTIONS fuel: 97 oct petrol.

70 hp power team

See 44 hp power team, except for:

ENGINE 77.1 cu in, 1,263 cc (3.19 x 2.48 in, 81 x 63 mm);
compression ratio: 9.2:1; max power (DIN): 70 hp (51.5
kW) at 5,500 rpm; max torque (DIN): 68 lb ft, 9.4 kg m
(92.2 Nm) at 4,000 rpm; 55.4 hp/l (40.8 kW/l); 1 Weber
downdraught twin barrel carburettor.

TRANSMISSION gearbox ratios: I 3.337, II 1.995, III 1.418,
IV 1, rev 3.867; width of rims: 5.5''; tyres: Sport 175/70
SR x 13.

PERFORMANCE max speed: 93 mph, 150 km/h; power-weight
ratio: Ghia 4-dr. Limousine 30.1 lb/hp (40.9 lb/kW), 13.6
kg/hp (18.5 kg/kW) - Sport 4-dr. Limousine 28.8 lb/hp (39.2
lb/kW), 13.1 kg/hp (17.8 kg/kW); carrying capacity: Ghia
937 lb, 425 kg - Sport 970 lb, 440 kg; consumption: 29.7
m/imp gal, 24.8 m/US gal, 9.5 l x 100 km.

BRAKES servo (standard); lining area: front 23.4 sq in,
151.2 sq cm, rear 47.3 sq in, 305.2 sq cm, total 70.7 sq in,
456.4 sq cm.

ELECTRICAL EQUIPMENT 2 halogen headlamps.

DIMENSIONS AND WEIGHT length: Sport 160.63 in, 408
cm; height: Sport 54.33 in, 138 cm; weight: Ghia 2-dr.
Limousine 2,040 lb, 925 kg - 4-dr. Limousine 2,106 lb, 955
kg - Sport 2-dr. Limousine 1,951 lb, 885 kg - 4-dr. Limousine
2,018 lb, 915 kg.

PRACTICAL INSTRUCTIONS fuel: 97 oct petrol.

84 hp power team

See 70 hp power team, except for:

ENGINE 95.6 cu in, 1,566 cc (3.19 x 3.06 in, 81 x 77.6 mm);
compression ratio: 9:1; max power (DIN): 84 hp (61.8 kW)
at 5,500 rpm; max torque (DIN): 92 lb ft, 12.7 kg m (124.5
Nm) at 3,500 rpm; 53.6 hp/l (39.5 kW/l); cooling system:
9.5 imp pt, 11.4 US pt, 5.4 l.

TRANSMISSION axle ratio: 3.540.

PERFORMANCE max speed: 101 mph, 162 km/h; power-
weight ratio: Sport 4-dr. Limousine 24.4 lb/hp (33.2 lb/kW),
11.1 kg/hp (15 kg/kW) - Ghia 4-dr. Limousine 25.1 lb/hp
(34.1 lb/kW), 11.4 kg/hp (15.4 kg/kW); speed in direct
drive at 1,000 rpm: 18.5 mph, 29.8 km/h; consumption: 31
m/imp gal, 25.8 m/US gal, 9.1 l x 100 km.

DIMENSIONS AND WEIGHT weight: Sport 2-dr. Limousine
1,985 lb, 900 kg - 4-dr. Limousine 2,051 lb, 930 kg - Ghia
2-dr. Limousine 2,040 lb, 925 kg - 4-dr. Limousine 2,106 lb,
955 kg.

OPTIONALS Ford C3 automatic transmission, hydraulic
torque converter and planetary gears with 3 ratios (I 2.474
II 1.474, III 1, rev 2.111), max ratio of converter at stall
2, possible manual selection, 3.540 axle ratio, max speed
98 mph, 157 km/h, consumption 28.2 m/imp gal, 23.5 m/US
gal, 10 l x 100 km, oil cooler, 44 Ah battery.

110 hp power team

See 44 hp power team, except for:

ENGINE 121.6 cu in, 1,993 cc (3.57 x 3.03 in, 90.8 x 76.9 mm);
compression ratio: 9.2:1; max power (DIN): 110 hp (81
kW) at 5,500 rpm; max torque (DIN): 119 lb ft, 16.4 kg m
(160.8 Nm) at 3,750 rpm; max engine rpm: 6,500; 55.2 hp/l
(40.6 kW/l); valves: overhead, Vee-slanted, rockers; camshafts: 1, overhead, cogged belt; lubricating system: 6.7
imp pt, 8 US pt, 3.8 l; 1 Weber downdraught twin barrel
carburettor; water-cooled, 10.7 imp pt, 12.9 US pt, 6.1 l,
electric thermostatic fan.

TRANSMISSION gearbox ratios: I 3.656, II 1.970, III 1.370,
IV 1, rev 3.660; axle ratio: 3.540; width of rims: 5.5''; tyres:
175/70 HR x 13.

PERFORMANCE max speed: 112 mph, 180 km/h; power-
weight ratio: 18.6 lb/hp (25.2 lb/kW), 8.4 kg/hp (11.4
kg/kW); carrying capacity: 882 lb, 400 kg; consumption:
32.5 m/imp gal, 27 m/US gal, 8.7 l x 100 km.

BRAKES lining area: front 23.4 sq in, 151.2 sq cm, rear
47.3 sq in, 305.2 sq cm, total 70.07 sq in, 456.4 sq cm.

ELECTRICAL EQUIPMENT 55 Ah battery (standard); 55 A
alternator; 4 halogen headlamps.

DIMENSIONS AND WEIGHT length: 163.39 in, 415 cm;
height: 55.51 in, 141 cm; ground clearance: 5.51 in, 14
cm; weight: 2,040 lb, 925 kg; turning circle: 32.1 ft, 9.8 m.

BODY built-in headrests; heated rear window.

PRACTICAL INSTRUCTIONS fuel: 97 oct petrol; oil: engine
5.8 imp pt, 7 US pt, 3.3 l.

Taunus Series

PRICES EX WORKS:

1 2-dr Limousine	DM	11,430*
2 4-dr Limousine	DM	11,995*
3 Turnier	DM	12,630*
4 L 2-dr Limousine	DM	12,065*
5 L 4-dr Limousine	DM	12,630*
6 L Turnier	DM	13,265*
7 GL 2-dr Limousine	DM	13,745*
8 GL 4-dr Limousine	DM	14,310*
9 GL Turnier	DM	14,945*
10 Ghia 2-dr Limousine	DM	16,195*
11 Ghia 4-dr Limousine	DM	16,760*
12 S 2-dr Limousine	DM	15,308*
13 S 4-dr Limousine	DM	15,873*

Power team:	Standard for:	Optional for:
55 hp	1 to 6	—
68 hp	—	1 to 9
72 hp	7 to 11	1 to 6
90 hp	—	4 to 11
98 hp	12,13	—
108 hp	—	10 to 13

FORD Escort RS 2000 Limousine

55 hp power team

ENGINE front, 4 stroke; 4 cylinders, vertical, in line; 78.4 cu in, 1,285 cc (3.11 x 2.60 in, 79 x 66 mm); compression ratio: 8:1; max power (DIN): 55 hp (40.5 kW) at 5,500 rpm; max torque (DIN): 67 lb ft, 9.3 kg m (91.2 Nm) at 3,000 rpm; max engine rpm: 6,000; 42.8 hp/l (31.5 kW/l); cast iron block and head; 5 crankshaft bearings; valves: overhead, Vee-slanted, rockers; camshafts: 1, overhead, cogged belt; lubrication: gear pump, full flow filter (cartridge), 6.5 imp pt, 7.8 US pt, 3.7 l; 1 Ford downdraught carburettor; fuel feed: mechanical pump; water-cooled, 10.2 imp pt, 12.3 US pt, 5.8 l.

TRANSMISSION driving wheels: rear; clutch: single dry plate (diaphragm); gearbox: mechanical; gears: 4, fully synchronized; ratios: I 3.660, II 2.190, III 1.430, IV 1, rev 4.240; lever: central; final drive: hypoid bevel; axle ratio: 4.110 - Turniers 4.440; width of rims: 4.5''; tyres: 165 SR x 13.

PERFORMANCE max speed: 85 mph, 137 km/h; power-weight ratio: 4-dr. limousines 41.7 lb/hp (56.6 lb/kW), 18.9 kg/hp (25.7 kg/kW); speed in direct drive at 1,000 rpm: 14.2 mph, 22.8 km/h; consumption: 29.7 m/imp gal, 24.8 m/US gal, 9.5 l x 100 km - Turniers 28.5 m/imp gal, 23.8 m/US gal, 9.9 l x 100 km.

CHASSIS integral; front suspension: independent, wishbones (lower trailing links), coil springs/telescopic dampers, anti-roll bar; rear: rigid axle, lower trailing arms, upper oblique torque arms, coil springs, anti-roll bar, telescopic dampers.

STEERING rack-and-pinion.

BRAKES front disc (diameter 9.72 in, 24.7 cm), rear drum, rear compensator, servo; lining area: front 23.4 sq in, 151.2 sq cm, rear 40.9 sq in, 264.5 sq cm, total 64.3 sq in, 415.7 sq cm.

ELECTRICAL EQUIPMENT 12 V; 44 Ah battery; 45 A alternator; Bosch distributor; 2 headlamps (4 halogen headlamps standard for GL only).

DIMENSIONS AND WEIGHT wheel base: 102.57 in, 258 cm; front and rear tracks: 55.91 in, 142 cm; length: 172.44 in, 438 cm - Turniers 176.38 in, 448 cm; width: 66.93 in, 170 cm; height: 53.54 in, 136 cm - Turniers 53.94 in, 137 cm; ground clearance: 3.82 in, 9.7 cm; weight: 2-dr. limousines 2,249 lb, 1,020 kg - 4-dr. limousines 2,293 lb, 1,040 kg - Turniers 2,437 lb, 1,105 kg; turning circle: 34.8 ft, 10.6 m; fuel tank: 11.9 imp gal, 14.3 US gal, 54 l.

BODY 5 seats, separate front seats; heated rear wondow.

PRACTICAL INSTRUCTIONS fuel: 90 oct petrol; oil: engine 5.6 imp pt, 6.8 US pt, 3.2 l, SAE 10W-40, change every 6,200 miles, 10,000 km - gearbox 1.4 imp pt, 1.7 US pt, 0.8 l, SAE 80 EP, change every 12,400 miles, 20,000 km - final drive 1.8 imp pt, 2.1 US pt, 1 l, SAE 90, change every 12,400 miles, 20,000 km; greasing: every 31,100 miles, 50,000 km, 2 points; tyre pressure: front 24 psi, 1.7 atm, rear 24 psi, 1.7 atm.

OPTIONALS 4.440 axle ratio; 185/70 SR x 13 tyres with 5.5'' wide rims; halogen headlamps; built-in headrests on front seats; fog lamps; metallic spray; sunshine roof except for Turniers.

FORD Taunus S 2-dr Limousine

68 hp power team

See 55 hp power team, except for:

ENGINE 96.2 cu in, 1,576 cc (3.45 x 2.60 in, 87 x 66 mm); compression ratio: 8.2:1; max power (DIN): 68 hp (50 kW) at 5,200 rpm; max torque (DIN): 85 lb ft, 11.7 kg m (114.7 Nm) at 2,700 rpm; 43.1 hp/l (31.7 kW/l).

TRANSMISSION gearbox ratios: I 3.580, II 2.010, III 1.400, IV 1, rev 3.320; axle ratio: 3.890 - Turniers 4.110; width of rims: GL 5.5''.

PERFORMANCE max speed: 91 mph, 147 km/h; power-weight ratio: 4-dr. limousines 34.2 lb/hp (46.5 lb/kW), 15.5 kg/hp (21.1 kg/kW); speed in direct drive at 1,000 rpm: 15.2 mph, 24.5 km/h; consumption: 26.4 m/imp gal, 22 m/US gal, 10.7 l x 100 km.

DIMENSIONS AND WEIGHT weight: 2-dr. limousines 2,282 lb, 1,035 kg - 4-dr. limousines 2,326 lb, 1,055 kg - Turniers 2,459 lb, 1,115 kg.

OPTIONALS 4.110 axle ratio; Ford C3 automatic transmission, hydraulic torque converter and planetary gears with 3 ratios (I 2.474, II 1.474, III 1, rev 2.111), max ratio of converter at stall 2, possible manual selection, 55 Ah battery, max speed 88 mph, 142 km/h, consumption 24.6 m/imp gal, 20.5 m/US gal, 11.5 l x 100 km (Turniers 24.4 m/imp gal, 20.3 m/US gal, 11.6 l x 100 km), oil cooler.

72 hp power team

See 55 hp power team, except for:

ENGINE 96.2 cu in, 1,576 cc (3.45 x 2.60 in, 87.7 x 66 mm); compression ratio: 9.2:1; max power (DIN): 72 hp (53 kW) at 5,000 rpm; max torque (DIN): 87 lb ft, 12 kg m (117 Nm) at 2,700 rpm; 45.7 hp/l (33.6 kW/l).

TRANSMISSION gearbox ratios: I 3.580, II 2.010, III 1.400, IV 1, rev 3.320; axle ratio: 3.890 - Turniers 4.110; width of rims GL and Ghia 5.5''; tyres: Ghia 185/70 SR x 1

PERFORMANCE max speed: 94 mph, 152 km/h; power-weight ratio: 4-dr. limousines 32.3 lb/hp (43.9 lb/kW), 14.7 kg/kW (19.9 kg/kW); speed in direct drive at 1,000 rpm: 15.7 mp 25.3 km/h; consumption: 28.2 m/imp gal, 23.5 m/US ga 10 l x 100 km - Turniers 28 m/imp gal, 23.3 m/US ga 10.1 l x 100 km.

ELECTRICAL EQUIPMENT halogen headlamps (standard f GL and Ghia only).

DIMENSIONS AND WEIGHT weight: 2-dr. limousines 2,2 lb, 1,035 kg - 4-dr. limousines 2,326 lb, 1,055 kg - Turnie 2,459 lb, 1,115 kg.

PRACTICAL INSTRUCTIONS fuel: 97 oct petrol.

OPTIONALS 4.110 axle ratio; Ford C3 automatic transmi sion, hydraulic torque converter and planetary gears wi 3 ratios (I 2.474, II 1.474, III 1, rev 2.111), max ratio converter at stall 2, possible manual selection, 55 A battery, max speed 91 mph, 147 km/h, consumption 25 m/imp gal, 21.6 m/US gal, 10.9 l x 100 km (Turniers 25 m/imp gal, 21.4 m/US gal, 11 l x 100 km).

90 hp power team

See 55 hp power team, except for:

ENGINE 6 cylinders, Vee-slanted at 60°; 120.9 cu in, 1,981 c (3.31 x 2.37 in, 84 x 60.1 mm); compression ratio: 8.75: max power (DIN): 90 hp (66.2 kW) at 5,000 rpm; ma torque (DIN): 110 lb ft, 15.2 kg m (149.1 Nm) at 3,000 rpm 45.4 hp/l (33.4 kW/l); 4 crankshaft bearings; camshafts: at centre of Vee; lubricating system: 7.4 imp pt, 8.9 U pt, 4.2 l; 1 Solex 32/32 EEIT downdraught twin barre carburettor; cooling system: 12.1 imp pt, 14.6 US pt, 6.9

TRANSMISSION gearbox ratios: I 3.650, II 1.970, III 1.37 IV 1, rev 3.660; axle ratio: 3.440; width of rims: 4.5'' - G and Ghia 5.5''; tyres: Ghia 185/70 SR x 13.

PERFORMANCE max speed: 101 mph, 163 km/h; power-weigh ratio: 4-dr. limousines 27.7 lb/hp (37.6 lb/kW), 12.6 kg/h (17.1 kg/kW); speed in direct drive at 1,000 rpm: 16.9 mp 27.2 km/h; consumption: 27.7 m/imp gal, 23.1 m/US ga 10.2 l x 100 km - Turniers 28.5 m/imp gal, 23.8 m/US ga 9.9 l x 100 km.

BRAKES lining area: front 23.4 sq in, 151.2 sq cm, rear 58 sq in, 377.6 sq cm, total 82 sq in, 528.8 sq cm.

ELECTRICAL EQUIPMENT halogen headlamps (standard f GL and Ghia only).

DIMENSIONS AND WEIGHT weight: 2-dr. limousines 2,44 lb, 1,110 kg - 4-dr. limousines 2,492 lb, 1,130 kg - Turnier 2,591 lb, 1,175 kg.

PRACTICAL INSTRUCTIONS fuel: 97 oct petrol; oil: engin 7 imp pt, 8.5 US pt, 4 l.

OPTIONALS Ford C3 automatic transmission, hydrauli torque converter and planetary gears with 3 ratios (I 2.47 II 1.474, III 1, rev 2.111), max ratio of converter at sta 2, possible manual selection, 55 Ah battery, max spee 98 mph, 158 km/h, consumption 25.2 m/imp gal, 21 m/U gal, 11.2 l x 100 km (Turniers 25.9 m/imp gal, 21.6 m/U gal, 10.9 l x 100 km), oil cooler; power steering.

98 hp power team

See 55 hp power team, except for:

ENGINE 119.3 cu in, 1,955 cc (3.57 x 3.03 in, 90.8 x 76. mm); compression ratio: 9.2:1; max power (DIN): 98 h (72.1 kW) at 5,200 rpm; max torque (DIN): 112 lb ft, 15. kg m (151 Nm) at 3,500 rpm; 50.1 hp/l (36.9 kW/l); 1 We ber 32/36 DGAV downdraught twin barrel carburettor; coo ing system: 10.7 imp pt, 12.9 US pt, 6.1 l.

TRANSMISSION gearbox ratios: I 3.650, II 1.970, III 1.37 IV 1, rev 3.660; axle ratio: 3.750; width of rims: 5.5' tyres: 185/70 SR x 13.

PERFORMANCE max speed: 104 mph, 167 km/h; power weight ratio: 4-dr. Limousine 24.3 lb/hp (33 lb/kW), 11 kg/h (15 kg/kW); speed in direct drive at 1,000 rpm: 17.3 mp 27.8 km/h; consumption: 26.6 m/imp gal, 22.2 m/US ga 10.6 l x 100 km.

FORD Taunus GL 4-dr Limousine

BRAKES lining area: front 23.4 sq in, 151.2 sq cm, rear 58.6 sq in, 377.6 sq cm, total 82 sq in, 528.8 sq cm.

ELECTRICAL EQUIPMENT 4 halogen headlamps (standard).

DIMENSIONS AND WEIGHT weight: 2-dr. Limousine 2,337 lb, 1,060 kg - 4-dr. Limousine 2,381 lb, 1,080 kg.

PRACTICAL INSTRUCTIONS fuel: 97 oct petrol.

OPTIONALS Ford C3 automatic transmission, hydraulic torque converter and planetary gears with 3 ratios (I 2.474, II 1.474, III 1, rev 2.111), max ratio of converter at stall 2, possible manual selection, 55 Ah battery, max speed 101 mph, 162 km/h, consumption 24.1 m/imp gal, 20.1 m/US gal, 11.7 l x 100 km; oil cooler; power steering.

108 hp power team

See 55 hp power team, except for:

ENGINE 6 cylinders, Vee-slanted at 60°; 138.8 cu in, 2,274 cc (3.54 x 2.37 in, 90 x 60.1 mm); compression ratio: 8.75:1; max power (DIN): 108 hp (79.5 kW) at 5,000 rpm; max torque (DIN): 130 lb ft, 18 kg m (176.5 Nm) at 3,000 rpm; 47.5 hp/l (35 kW/l); 4 crankshaft bearings; camshafts: 1, at centre of Vee; lubricating system: 7.4 imp pt, 8.9 US pt, 4.2 l; 1 Solex 35/35 EEIT downdraught twin barrel carburettor; cooling system: 12.1 imp pt, 14.6 US pt, 6.9 l.

TRANSMISSION gearbox ratios: I 3.650, II 1.970, III 1.370, IV 1, rev 3.660; axle ratio: 3.440; width of rims: 5.5''; tyres: 185/70 SR x 13.

PERFORMANCE max speed: 107 mph, 173 km/h; power-weight ratio: 4-dr. limousines 23.1 lb/hp (31.3 lb/kW), 10.5 kg/hp (14.2 kg/kW); speed in direct drive at 1,000 rpm: 17.9 mph, 28.8 km/h; consumption: 28 m/imp gal, 23.3 m/US gal, 10.1 l x 100 km.

BRAKES lining area: front 23.4 sq in, 151.2 sq cm, rear 58.6 sq in, 377.6 sq cm, total 82 sq in, 528.8 sq cm.

ELECTRICAL EQUIPMENT 4 headlamps (standard).

DIMENSIONS AND WEIGHT weight: 2-dr. limousines 2,448 lb, 1,110 kg - 4-dr. limousines 2,492 lb, 1,130 kg.

PRACTICAL INSTRUCTIONS fuel: 97 oct petrol; oil: engine 7 imp pt, 8.5 US pt, 4 l.

OPTIONALS Ford C3 automatic transmission, hydraulic torque converter and planetary gears with 3 ratios (I 2.474, II 1.474, III 1, rev 2.111), max ratio of converter at stall 2, possible manual selection, 55 Ah battery, max speed 104 mph, 168 km/h, consumption 26.2 m/imp gal, 21.8 m/US gal, 10.8 l x 100 km; oil cooler; power steering.

Capri II Series

Power team:	Standard for:	Optional for:
68 hp	—	1,2
72 hp	1,2	—
90 hp	3	1,2
108 hp	4	3
138 hp	—	3,4

68 hp power team

ENGINE front, 4 stroke; 4 cylinders, vertical, in line; 96.2 cu in, 1,576 cc (3.45 x 2.60 in, 87.7 x 66 mm); compression ratio: 8.2:1; max power (DIN): 68 hp (50 kW) at 5,500 rpm; max torque (DIN): 85 lb ft, 11.7 kg m (114.7 Nm) at 2,700 rpm; max engine rpm: 6,000; 43.1 hp/l (31.7 kW/l); cast iron block and head; 5 crankshaft bearings; valves: overhead, Vee-slanted, rockers; camshafts: 1, overhead, cogged belt; lubrication: rotary pump, full flow filter (cartridge), 6.5 imp pt, 7.8 US pt, 3.7 l; 1 Ford downdraught carburettor; fuel feed: mechanical pump; water-cooled, 10.2 imp pt, 12.3 US pt, 5.8 l.

TRANSMISSION driving wheels: rear; clutch: single dry plate (diaphragm); gearbox: mechanical; gears: 4, fully synchronized; ratios: I 3.650, II 1.970, III 1.370, IV 1, rev 3.660; lever: central; final drive: hypoid bevel; axle ratio: 3.770; width of rims: 5''; tyres: 165 SR x 13.

PERFORMANCE max speeds: (I) 29 mph, 47 km/h; (II) 54 mph, 87 km/h; (III) 78 mph, 125 km/h; (IV) 96 mph, 155 km/h; power-weight ratio: 32.7 lb/hp (44.5 lb/kW), 14.8 kg/hp (20.2 kg/kW); carrying capacity 816 lb, 370 kg; speed in direct drive/top at 1,000 rpm: 17.8 mph, 28.6 km/h; consumption: 29.1 m/imp gal, 24.2 m/US gal, 9.7 l x 100 km.

CHASSIS integral; front suspension: independent, by Mc-Pherson, coil springs/telescopic damper struts, lower transverse arms, anti-roll bar; rear: rigid axle, semi-elliptic leafsprings, rubber springs, anti-roll bar, telescopic dampers.

STEERING rack-and-pinion.

BRAKES front disc (diameter 9.61 in, 24.4 cm), rear drum, servo; lining area: front 17.4 sq in, 151.2 sq cm, rear 45.4 sq in, 293.4 sq cm, total 62.8 sq in, 444.6 sq cm.

ELECTRICAL EQUIPMENT 35 Ah battery; 55 A alternator.

DIMENSIONS AND WEIGHT wheel base: 100.79 in, 256 cm; tracks: 53.15 in, 135 cm front, 54.33 in, 138 cm rear; length: 174.80 in, 444 cm; width: 66.93 in, 170 cm; height: 51.97 in, 132 cm; ground clearance: 4.92 in, 12.5 cm; weight: 2,227 lb, 1,010 kg; turning circle: 35.4 ft, 10.8 m; fuel tank: 12.8 imp gal, 15.3 US gal, 58 l.

BODY coupé; 2 + 1 doors; 5 seats, separate front seats, reclining backrests; folding rear seat.

PRACTICAL INSTRUCTIONS fuel: 90 oct petrol; oil: engine 5.6 imp pt, 6.8 US pt, 3.2 l, SAE 20W-40, change every 6,200 miles, 10,000 km - gearbox 2.3 imp pt, 2.7 US pt, 1.3 l, SAE 80, change every 12,400 miles, 20,000 km - final drive 1.9 imp pt, 2.3 US pt, 1.1 l, SAE 90, change every 12,400 miles, 20,000 km; greasing: none.

OPTIONALS servo brake; heated rear window; rear window wiper; headrests on front seats; sunshine roof; vinyl roof; halogen headlamps; metallic spray; 185/70 SR x 13 tyres; Ford C-3 automatic transmission, hydraulic torque converter and planetary gears with 3 ratios (I 2.474, II 1.474, III 1, rev 2.111), max ratio of converter at stall 2, possible manual selection, oil cooler, 55 Ah battery, max speed 93 mph, 150 km/h, consumption 27.7 m/imp gal, 21.4 m/US gal, 10.2 l x 100 km.

72 hp power team

See 68 hp power team, except for:

ENGINE compression ratio: 9.2:1; max power (DIN): 72 hp (53 kW) at 5,200 rpm; max torque (DIN): 87 lb ft, 12 kg m (117.7 Nm) at 2,700 rpm; 45.7 hp/l (33.6 kW/l).

PERFORMANCE max speed: 98 mph, 158 km/h; power-weight ratio: 30.9 lb/hp (42 lb/kW), 14 kg/hp (19 kg/kW); consumption: 30.7 m/imp gal, 25.6 m/US gal, 9.2 l x 100 km.

PRACTICAL INSTRUCTIONS fuel: 97 oct petrol.

OPTIONALS with Ford C-3 automatic transmission, max speed 95 mph, 153 km/h, consumption 29.1 m/imp gal, 24.2 m/US gal, 9.7 l x 100 km.

90 hp power team

See 68 hp power team, except for:

ENGINE 6 cylinders, Vee-slanted at 60°; 120.9 cu in, 1,981 cc (3.31 x 2.37 in, 84 x 60.1 mm); compression ratio: 8.75:1;

FORD Capri II S Coupé

max power (DIN): 90 hp (66.2 kW) at 5,000 rpm; max torque (DIN): 110 lb ft, 15.2 kg m (149.1 Nm) at 3,000 rpm; 45.4 hp/l (33.4 kW/l); 4 crankshaft bearings; valves: overhead, push-rods and rockers; camshafts: 1, at centre of Vee; lubricating system: 7.4 imp pt, 8.9 US pt, 4.2 l; 1 Solex 32/32 EEIT downdraught twin barrel carburettor; cooling system: 13.7 imp pt, 16.5 US pt, 7.8 l.

TRANSMISSION axle ratio: 3.440; width of rims: 5.5''.

PERFORMANCE max speed: 106 mph, 170 km/h - Capri S 107 mph, 173 km/h; power-weight ratio: 26.5 lb/hp (36.1 lb/kW), 12 kg/hp (16.4 kg/kW); consumption: 30 m/imp gal, 25 m/US gal, 9.4 l x 100 km - Capri S 31 m/imp gal, 25.8 m/US gal, 9.1 l x 100 km.

ELECTRICAL EQUIPMENT 44 Ah battery; 4 headlamps.

DIMENSIONS AND WEIGHT weight: 2,381 lb, 1,080 kg.

PRACTICAL INSTRUCTIONS fuel: 97 oct petrol.

OPTIONALS with Ford C-3 automatic transmission max speed 102 mph, 165 km/h (Capri S 104 mph, 168 km/h), consumption 27.7 m/imp gal, 23.1 m/US gal, 10.2 l x 100 km (Capri S 28.5 m/imp gal, 23.8 m/US gal, 9.9 l x 100 km); power steering.

108 hp power team

See 68 hp power team, except for:

ENGINE 6 cylinders, Vee-slanted at 60°; 138.8 cu in, 2,274 cc (3.54 x 2.37 in, 90 x 60.1 mm); compression ratio: 8.75:1; max power (DIN): 108 hp (79.5 kW) at 5,000 rpm; max torque (DIN): 130 lb ft, 18 kg m (176.5 Nm) at 3,000 rpm; max engine rpm: 5,600; 47.5 hp/l (35 kW/l); 4 crankshaft bearings; valves: overhead, push-rods and rockers; camshafts: 1, at centre of Vee; lubricating system: 7.4 imp pt, 8.9 US pt, 4.2 l; 1 Solex 35/35 EEIT downdraught twin barrel carburettor; cooling system: 13.7 imp pt, 16.5 US pt, 7.8 l.

TRANSMISSION axle ratio: 3.220; width of rims: 5.5''; tyres: 185/70 HR x 13 standard.

PERFORMANCE max speed: 112 mph, 180 km/h - Capri S 114 mph, 183 km/h; power-weight ratio: 22.7 lb/hp (30.8 lb/kW), 10.3 kg/hp (14 kg/kW); speed in direct drive at 1,000 rpm: 20.8 mph, 33.4 km/h consumption: 30.4 m/imp gal, 25.3 m/US gal, 9.3 l x 100 km - Capri S 31.4 m/imp gal, 26.1 m/US gal, 9 l x 100 km.

ELECTRICAL EQUIPMENT 44 Ah battery; halogen headlamps and fog lamps.

DIMENSIONS AND WEIGHT weight: 2,447 lb, 1,110 kg.

BODY light alloy wheels, headrest on front seats and heated rear window.

PRACTICAL INSTRUCTIONS fuel: 97 oct petrol.

OPTIONALS with Ford C-3 automatic transmission max speed 109 mph, 175 km/h (Capri S 111 mph, 178 km/h), consumption 28.2 m/imp gal, 23.5 m/US gal, 10 l x 100 km (Capri S 29.1 m/imp gal, 24.2 m/US gal, 9.7 l x 100 km); power steering.

FORD Capri II S Coupé

70 hp power team

ENGINE front, 4 stroke; 4 cylinders, Vee-slanted at 60°; 102.5 cu in, 1,680 cc (3.54 x 2.63 in, 90 x 66.8 mm); compression ratio: 7.75:1; max power (DIN): 70 hp (51.5 kW) at 5,000 rpm; max torque (DIN): 88 lb/ft, 12.2 kg m (119.6 Nm) at 3,000 rpm; max engine rpm: 5,500; 41.7 hp/l (30.6 kW/l); cast iron block and head; 3 crankshaft bearings; valves: overhead, in line, rockers; camshafts: 1, at centre of Vee; lubrication: gear pump, full flow filter, 6.5 imp pt, 7.8 US pt, 3.7 l; 1 Solex 32 TDID downdraught carburettor; fuel feed: mechanical pump; water-cooled, 10.6 imp pt, 12.7 US pt, 6 l.

TRANSMISSION driving wheels: rear; clutch: single dry plate (diaphragm); gearbox: mechanical; gears: 4, fully synchronized; ratios: I 3.650, II 1.970, III 1.370, IV 1, rev 3.660; lever: central; final drive: hypoid bevel; axle ratio: 4.110 - Turniers 4.440; width of rims: 5.5''; tyres: 175 SR x 14 - Turniers 185 SR x 14.

PERFORMANCE max speed: 89 mph, 144 km/h; power-weight ratio: 4-dr. limousines 39 lb/hp (53.1 lb/kW), 17.7 kg/hp (24.1 kg/kW); speed in direct drive at 1,000 rpm: 16.8 mph, 27.1 km/h; consumption: 26.4 m/imp gal, 22 m/US gal, 10.7 l x 100 km - Turniers 25.7 m/imp gal, 21.4 m/US gal, 11 l x 100 km.

CHASSIS integral, front and rear auxiliary frames; front suspension: independent, wishbones (lower trailing links), coil springs, anti-roll bar, telescopic dampers; rear: in-

138 hp power team

See 68 hp power team, except for:

ENGINE 6 cylinders, Vee-slanted at 60°; 179.7 cu in, 2,945 cc (3.69 x 2.85 in, 93.7 x 72.4 mm); compression ratio: 9:1; max power (DIN): 138 hp (101.6 kW) at 5,000 rpm; max torque (DIN): 174 lb ft, 24 kg m (235.4 Nm) at 3,000 rpm; 46.9 hp/l (34.5 kW/l); 4 crankshaft bearings; valves: overhead, push-rods and rockers; camshafts: 1, at centre of Vee; lubricating system: 8.8 imp pt, 10.6 US pt, 5 l; 1 Weber 38/38 EGAS downdraught twin barrel carburettor; cooling system: 16.4 imp pt, 19.7 US pt, 9.3 l.

TRANSMISSION gearbox ratios: I 3.163, II 1.940, III 1.412, IV 1, rev 3.346; axle ratio: 3.090; width of rims: 5.5''; tyres: 185/70 HR x 13.

PERFORMANCE max speed: 122 mph, 197 km/h - Capri S 124 mph, 200 km/h; power-weight ratio: 18.4 lb/hp (24.9 lb/kW), 8.3 kg/hp (11.3 kg/kW); speed in direct drive at 1,000 rpm: 21.8 mph, 35.1 km/h; consumption 26.2 m/imp gal, 21.8 m/US gal, 10.8 l x 100 km - Capri S 26.9 m/imp gal, 22.4 m/US gal, 10.5 l x 100 km.

BRAKES front disc (diameter 9.72 in, 24.7 cm), rear drum; lining area: front 17.4 sq in, 151.2 sq cm, rear 59.5 sq in, 384.4 cm, total 76.9 sq in, 535.6 sq cm.

ELECTRICAL EQUIPMENT 44 Ah battery; halogen headlamps and fog lamps.

DIMENSIONS AND WEIGHT weight: 2,535 lb, 1,150 kg.

BODY light alloy wheels, tinted glass, headrests on front seats and heated rear window.

PRACTICAL INSTRUCTIONS fuel: 97 oct petrol.

OPTIONALS with Ford C-3 automatic transmission, max speed 119 mph, 192 km/h (Capri S 121 mph, 195 km/h), consumption 24.6 m/imp gal, 20.5 m/US gal, 11.5 l x 100 km (Capri S 25.2 m/imp gal, 21 m/US gal, 11.2 l x 100 km); power steering.

Granada Series

PRICES EX WORKS:

1 2-dr Limousine	DM	14,535*
2 4-dr Limousine	DM	15,130*
3 Turnier	DM	15,705*
4 L 2-dr Limousine	DM	15,325*
5 4-dr Limousine	DM	15,825*
6 L Turnier	DM	16,755*
7 GL 2-dr Limousine	DM	19,875*
8 GL 4-dr Limousine	DM	20,470*
9 GL Turnier	DM	21,875*
10 Ghia 4-dr Limousine	DM	24,795*

Power team:	Standard for:	Optional for:
70 hp	1 to 6	—
73 hp	—	1 to 6
90 hp	7 to 9	1 to 6
108 hp	10	all except 10
135 hp	—	all except 1,2,3,6
160 hp	—	all except 1,2,3,6
63 hp (Diesel)	—	1,2,4,5

FORD Granada 2-dr Limousine

dependent, semi-trailing arms, coil springs, telescopic dampers.

STEERING rack-and-pinion.

BRAKES front disc (diameter 10.31 in, 26.2 cm), rear drum, servo; lining area: front 23.4 sq in, 151.2 sq cm, rear 58 sq in, 374.6 sq cm, total 81.4 sq in, 528.5 sq cm - Turniers rear 83.4 sq in, 538.5 sq cm, total 106.8 sq in, 689.7 sq cm.

ELECTRICAL EQUIPMENT 12 V; 35 Ah battery; 45 A (55 A for L limousines) alternator; Ford distributor; 2 headlamps.

DIMENSIONS AND WEIGHT wheel base: 109.05 in, 277 cm; tracks: 59.45 in, 151 cm front, 60.24 in, 153 cm rear; length: 185.83 in, 472 cm - Turniers 189.76 in, 482 cm; width: 70.47 in, 179 cm; height: 55.91 in, 142 cm; weight: 2-dr. limousines 2,701 lb, 1,225 kg - 4-dr. limousines 2,734 lb, 1,240 kg - Turniers 2,889 lb, 1,310 kg; turning circle: 36.7 ft, 11.2 m; fuel tank: 14.5 imp gal, 17.4 US gal, 66 l - Turniers 13.6 imp gal, 16.4 US gal, 62 l.

BODY 5 seats, separate front seats, reclining backrests; heated rear window.

PRACTICAL INSTRUCTIONS fuel: 90 oct petrol; oil: engine 5.6 imp pt, 6.8 US pt, 3.2 l, SAE 10W-40, change every 6,200 miles, 10,000 km - gearbox 3 imp pt, 3.6 US pt, 1.8 l, SAE 80, no change recommended - final drive 3.2 imp pt, 3.8 US pt, 1.8 l, SAE 90, no change recommended; greasing: none; tappet clearances: inlet 0.014 in, 0.35 mm, exhaust 0.016 in, 0.40 mm; valve timing: 24° 84° 65° 42°; tyre pressure: front 20 psi, 1.4 atm, rear 23 psi, 1.6 atm.

OPTIONALS 4.440 axle ratio; 185 SR x 14 tyres with 6'' wide rims; 66 Ah battery; 55 A alternator; halogen headlamps; power steering; built-in headrests; heated rear window; sunshine roof; metallic spray; S equipment with 190/65 HR 390 TRX tyres; rear window wiper-washer; headlamps with wiper-washers.

73 hp power team

See 70 hp power team, except for:

ENGINE compression ratio: 8.75:1; max power (DIN): 73 hp (53.7 kW) at 5,000 rpm; max torque (DIN): 93 lb ft, 12.8 kg m (125.5 Nm) at 3,000 rpm; 43.4 hp/l (32 kW/l).

PERFORMANCE max speed: 92 mph, 147 km/h; power-weight ratio: 4-dr. limousines 37.4 lb/hp (50.9 lb/kW), 17 kg/hp (23.1 kg/kW).

PRACTICAL INSTRUCTIONS fuel: 97 oct petrol.

OPTIONALS Ford C-3 automatic transmission, hydraulic torque converter and planetary gears with 3 ratios (I 2.474, II 1.474, III 1, rev 2.111), max ratio of converter at stall 2, possible manual selection, oil cooler, max speed 87 mph, 140 km/h, consumption 25.9 m/imp gal, 21.6 m/US gal, 10.9 l x 100 km - Turniers 25.4 m/imp gal, 21.2 m/US gal, 11.1 l x 100 km, 55 Ah battery.

90 hp power team

See 70 hp power team, except for:

ENGINE 6 cylinders, Vee-slanted at 60°; 120.9 cu in, 1,981 cc (3.31 x 2.37 in, 84 x 60.1 mm); compression ratio: 8.75:1; max power (DIN): 90 hp (66.2 kW) at 5,000 rpm; max torque (DIN): 110 lb ft, 15.2 kg m (149.1 Nm) at 3,000 rpm; 45.4 hp/l (33.4 kW/l); 4 crankshaft bearings; lubricating system: 7.4 imp pt, 8.9 US pt, 4.2 l; 1 Solex 32/32 EEIT downdraught twin barrel carburettor; cooling system: 12.1 imp pt, 14.6 US pt, 6.9 l.

TRANSMISSION axle ratio: 3.890; width of rims: GL limousines 6''; tyres: 185 SR x 14.

PERFORMANCE max speed: 98 mph, 158 km/h; power-weight ratio: GL 4-dr. Limousine 33.2 lb/hp (45.1 lb/kW), 15 kg/hp (20.5 kg/kW); speed in direct drive at 1,000 rpm: 17.3 mph, 27.9 km/h; consumption: 25.9 m/imp gal, 21.6 m/US gal, 10.9 l x 100 km - GL models 25.4 m/imp gal, 21.2 m/US gal, 11.1 l x 100 km.

STEERING servo (standard for GL only).

BRAKES lining area (except for Turniers): front 23.4 sq in, 151.2 sq cm, rear 75.3 sq in, 486 sq cm, total 98.7 sq in, 637.2 sq cm.

ELECTRICAL EQUIPMENT 44 Ah battery.

DIMENSIONS AND WEIGHT weight: GL 2-dr. Limousine 2,955 lb, 1,340 kg - GL 4-dr. Limousine 2,988 lb, 1,355 kg - GL Turnier 3,131 lb, 1,420 kg.

PRACTICAL INSTRUCTIONS fuel: 97 oct petrol; oil: engine 7 imp pt, 8.5 US pt, 4 l.

OPTIONALS Ford C-3 automatic transmission, hydraulic torque converter and planetary gears with 3 ratios (I 2.474, II 1.474, III 1, rev 2.111), max ratio of converter at stall 2, possible manual selection, 3.890 axle ratio. max speed 94 mph, 152 km/h, consumption 23.9 m/imp gal, 19.9 m/US gal, 11.8 l x 100 km - GL Limousines 23.5 m/imp gal, 19.6 m/US gal, 12 l x 100 km - GL Turnier 23.3 m/imp gal, 19.4 m/US gal, 12.1 l x 100 km, 55 Ah battery.

108 hp power team

See 70 hp power team, except for:

ENGINE 6 cylinders, Vee-slanted at 60°; 138.8 cu in, 2,274 cc (3.54 x 2.37 in, 90 x 60.1 mm); compression ratio: 8.75:1; max power (DIN): 108 hp (79.5 kW) at 5,000 rpm; max torque (DIN): 130 lb ft, 18 kg m (176.5 Nm) at 3,000 rpm; max engine rpm: 5,600; 47.5 hp/l (35 kW/l); 4 crankshaft bearings; lubricating system: 7.4 imp pt, 8.9 US pt, 4.2 l; 1 Solex 35/35 EEIT downdraught twin barrel carburettor; cooling system: 12.1 imp pt, 14.6 US pt, 6.9 l.

TRANSMISSION gearbox ratios (only for Turniers): I 3.360, II 1.810, III 1.260, IV 1, rev 3.370; axle ratio: 3.640; width of rims: Ghia and GL limousines 6''; tyres 185 SR x 14.

PERFORMANCE max speed: 104 mph, 167 km/h; power-weight ratio: Ghia 28.4 lb/hp (38.6 lb/kW), 12.9 kg/hp (17.5 kg/kW); speed in direct drive at 1,000 rpm: 18.5 mph, 29.8 km/h; consumption: 26.6 m/imp gal, 22.2 m/US gal, 10.6 l x 100 km - GL models 26.4 m/imp gal, 22 m/US gal, 10.7 l x 100 km - Ghia 26.2 m/imp gal, 21.8 m/US gal, 10.8 l x 100 km.

STEERING servo (standard only for GL and Ghia).

BRAKES lining area (except for Turniers): front 23.4 sq in, 151.2 sq cm, rear 75.3 sq in, 486 sq cm, total 98.7 sq in, 637.2 sq cm.

ELECTRICAL EQUIPMENT 44 Ah battery.

DIMENSIONS AND WEIGHT weight: L 2-dr. Limousine 2,889 lb, 1,310 kg - L 4-dr. Limousine 2,922 lb, 1,325 kg - L Turnier 3,076 lb, 1,395 kg - GL 2-dr. Limousine 2,988 lb, 1,355 kg - GL 4-dr. Limousine 3,021 lb, 1,370 kg - GL Turnier 3,131 lb, 1,420 kg - Ghia 4-dr. Limousine 3,065 lb, 1,390 kg.

BODY heated rear window (standard).

PRACTICAL INSTRUCTIONS fuel: 97 oct petrol; oil: engine 7 imp pt, 8.5 US pt, 4 l.

OPTIONALS Ford C-3 automatic transmission, hydraulic torque converter and planetary gears with 3 ratios (I 2.474, II 1.474, III 1, rev 2.111), max ratio of converter at stall 2, possible manual selection, oil cooler, max speed 100 mph, 161 km/h, consumption 25.4 m/imp gal, 21.2 m/US gal, 11.1 l x 100 km - GL and Ghia 24.8 m/imp gal, 20.6 m/US gal, 11.4 l x 100 km, 55 Ah battery; air-conditioning.

135 hp power team

See 70 hp power team, except for:

ENGINE 6 cylinders, Vee-slanted at 60°; 169.1 cu in, 2,772 cc (3.66 x 2.70 in, 93 x 68.5 mm); compression ratio: 9.2:1; max power (DIN): 135 hp (99.4 kW) at 5,200 rpm; max torque (DIN): 159 lb ft, 22 kg m (215.8 Nm) at 3,000 rpm; 48.7 hp/l (35.8 kW/l); 4 crankshaft bearings; lubricating system: 8 imp pt, 10.6 US pt, 5 l; 1 Solex downdraught twin barrel carburettor; cooling system: 18 imp pt, 21.6 US pt, 10.2 l.

TRANSMISSION gearbox ratios: I 3.160, II 1.940, III 1.410, IV 1, rev 3.350; axle ratio: 3.450; width of rims: GL and Ghia limousines 6''; tyres: 185 HR x 14.

PERFORMANCE max speed: 114 mph, 183 km/h; power-weight ratio: GL 4-dr. Limousine 22.8 lb/hp (31 lb/kW), 10.4 kg/hp (14.1 kg/kW) - Ghia 23.2 lb/hp (31.5 lb/kW), 10.5 kg/hp (14.3 kg/kW); speed in top at 1,000 rpm: 20.7 mph, 33.3 km/h; consumption: GL 25.7 m/imp gal, 21.4 m/US gal, 11 l x 100 km - Ghia 25.4 m/imp gal, 21.2 m/US gal, 11.1 l x 100 km.

STEERING servo (standard for GL and Ghia).

BRAKES front disc with internal radial fins; lining area (except for Turniers): front 29.3 sq in, 188.8 sq cm, rear 75.3 sq in, 486 sq cm, total 104.6 sq in, 674.8 sq cm.

ELECTRICAL EQUIPMENT 44 Ah battery.

DIMENSIONS AND WEIGHT (see 108 hp power team) weight: plus 66 lb, 30 kg - 2-dr. limousines plus 110 lb, 50 kg.

BODY heated rear window (standard).

PRACTICAL INSTRUCTIONS fuel: 97 oct petrol; oil: engine 9.4 imp pt, 8.9 US pt, 4.2 l.

FORD Granada GLS Turnier

OPTIONALS Ford C-2 automatic transmission, hydraulic torque converter and planetary gears with 3 ratios (I 2.474, II 1.474, III 1, rev 2.111), max ratio of converter at stall 2, possible manual selection, oil cooler, 3.450 axle ratio, max speed 109 mph, 176 km/h, consumption 23.9 m/imp gal, 19.9 m/US gal, 11.8 l x 100 km (GL 24.1 m/imp gal, 20.1 m/US gal, 11.7 l x 100 km); 55 Ah battery; air-conditioning.

160 hp power team

See 135 hp power team, except for:

ENGINE max power (DIN): 160 hp (117.8 kW) at 5,700 rpm; max torque (DIN): 163 lb ft, 22.5 kg m (220.7 Nm) at 4,300 rpm; max engine rpm: 5,700; 57.7 hp/l (42.5 kW/l); Bosch K-Jetronic fuel injection system.

PERFORMANCE max speed: 120 mph, 193 km/h; power-weight ratio: GL 4-dr. Limousine 19.3 lb/hp (26.2 lb/kW), 8.7 kg/hp (11.9 kg/kW) - Ghia 19.6 lb/hp (26.6 lb/kW), 8.9 kg/hp (12 kg/kW); speed in direct drive at 1,000 rpm: 21.1 mph, 33.9 km/h; consumption: GL 25.4 m/imp gal, 21.2 m/US gal, 11.1 l x 100 km - Ghia 25.2 m/imp gal, 21 m/US gal, 11.2 l x 100 km.

ELECTRICAL EQUIPMENT 70 A alternator.

OPTIONALS with Ford C-3 automatic transmission, max speed 117 mph, 188 km/h, consumption GL 23.7 m/imp gal, 19.8 m/US gal, 11.9 l x 100 km (Ghia 23.5 m/imp gal, 19.6 m/US gal, 12 l x 100 km).

63 hp (Diesel) power team

See 70 hp power team, except for:

ENGINE Diesel; 4 cylinders, in line; 127.9 cu in, 2,097 cc (3.54 x 3.27 in, 90 x 83 mm); compression ratio: 22.8:1; max power (DIN): 63 hp (46 kW) at 4,500 rpm; max torque (DIN): 89.8 lb ft, 12.4 kg m (122 Nm) at 2,000 rpm; max engine rpm: 4,700; 30 hp/l (21.9 kW/l); 5 crankshaft bearings; camshafts: 1, overhead; lubrication: 9.3 imp pt, 11.2 US pt, 5.3 l; Roto-Diesel injection system; cooling system: 17.6 imp pt, 21.1 US pt, 10 l.

TRANSMISSION ratios: I 3.980, II 2.330, III 1.420, IV 1, rev 3.990; axle ratio: 3.890.

PERFORMANCE max speed: 85 mph, 137 km/h; power-weight ratio: 4-dr. limousines 46.4 lb/hp (63.5 lb/kW), 21.3 kg/hp (28.8 kg/kW); consumption: 32.8 m/imp gal, 27.3 m/US gal, 8.6 l x 100 km.

ELECTRICAL EQUIPMENT 88 Ah battery.

DIMENSIONS AND WEIGHT weight: 2-dr. limousines 2,889 lb, 1,310 kg - 4-dr. limousines 2,922 lb, 1,325 kg.

PRACTICAL INSTRUCTIONS fuel: Diesel oil; oil: engine 9.3 imp pt, 11.2 US pt, 5.3 l.

FORD Granada Ghia 4-dr Limousine

MERCEDES-BENZ   GERMANY FR

200

PRICE IN GB: £ 6,964*
PRICE EX WORKS: 19,858* marks

ENGINE front, 4 stroke; 4 cylinders, vertical, in line; 121.3 cu in, 1,988 cc (3.43 x 3.29 in, 87 x 83.6 mm); compression ratio: 9:1; max power (DIN): 94 hp (69.2 kW) at 4,800 rpm; max torque (DIN): 117 lb ft, 16.1 kg m (157.9 Nm) at 3,000 rpm; max engine rpm: 6,000; 47.3 hp/l (34.8 kW/l); cast iron block, light alloy head; 5 crankshaft bearings; valves: overhead, in line, finger levers; camshafts: 1, overhead; lubrication: gear pump, oil-water heat exchanger, full flow filter (cartridge), 9.7 imp pt, 11.6 US pt, 5.5 l; 1 Stromberg 175 CD horizontal carburettor; fuel feed: mechanical pump; water-cooled, 18.8 imp pt, 22.6 US pt, 10.7 l.

TRANSMISSION driving wheels: rear; clutch: single dry plate, hydraulically controlled; gearbox: mechanical; gears: 4, fully synchronized; ratios: I 3.900, II 2.300, III 1.410, IV 1, rev 3.660; lever: steering column or central; final drive: hypoid bevel; axle ratio: 3.920; width of rims: 5.5''; tyres: 175 SR x 14.

PERFORMANCE max speeds: (I) 28 mph, 45 km/h; (II) 47 mph, 75 km/h; (III) 78 mph, 125 km/h; (IV) 99 mph, 160 km/h; power-weight ratio: 31.4 lb/hp (42.7 lb/kW), 14.3 kg/hp (19.4 kg/kW); carrying capacity: 1,145 lb, 520 kg; consumption: 25.4 m/imp gal, 21.2 m/US gal, 11.1 l x 100 km.

CHASSIS integral, front auxiliary frame; front suspension: independent, wishbones, coil springs, auxiliary rubber springs, anti-roll bar, telescopic dampers; rear: independent, oblique semi-trailing arms, coil springs, auxiliary rubber springs, anti-roll bar, telescopic dampers.

STEERING recirculating ball, damper.

BRAKES disc (front diameter 10.75 in, 27.3 cm, rear 10.98 in, 27.9 cm), dual circuit, servo; swept area: front 225.4 sq in, 1,454 sq cm, rear 195.8 sq in, 1,263 sq cm, total 421.2 sq in, 2,717 sq cm.

ELECTRICAL EQUIPMENT 12 V; 55 Ah battery; 770 W alternator; Bosch distributor; 4 headlamps.

DIMENSIONS AND WEIGHT wheel base: 110.04 in, 279 cm; tracks: 58.58 in, 149 cm front, 56.93 in, 145 cm rear; length: 186.02 in, 472 cm; width: 70.31 in, 179 cm; height: 56.69 in, 144 cm; ground clearance: 6.50 in, 16.5 cm; weight: 2,955 lb, 1,340 kg; turning circle: 37.1 ft, 11.3 m; fuel tank: 14.3 imp gal, 17.2 US gal, 65 l.

BODY saloon/sedan; 4 doors; 5 seats, separate front seats, reclining backrests.

PRACTICAL INSTRUCTIONS fuel: 98 oct petrol; oil: engine 9.7 imp pt, 11.6 US pt, 5.5 l, SAE 20W-30, change every 4,650 miles, 7,500 km - gearbox 2.8 imp pt, 3.4 US pt, 1.6 l, ATF, change every 12,400 miles, 20,000 km - final drive 1.9 imp pt, 2.3 US pt, 1.1 l, SAE 90, change every 12,400 miles, 20,000 km; greasing: none; tappet clearances: inlet 0.003 in, 0.08 mm, exhaust 0.008 in, 0.20 mm; valve timing: 11° 47° 48° 16°; tyre pressure: front 21 psi, 1.5 atm, rear 26 psi, 1.8 atm.

OPTIONALS MB automatic transmission, hydraulic torque converter and planetary gears with 4 ratios (I 3.980, II 2.390, III 1.460, IV 1, rev 5.480); possible manual selection, max speeds (I) 23 mph, 38 km/h, (II) 47 mph, 75 km/h, (III) 78 mph, 125 km/h, (IV) 96 mph, 155 km/h; automatic levelling control on rear suspension; power steering; halogen headlamps; fog lamps; electric or manual sunshine roof; heated rear window; heated seats; electric windows; tinted glass; headrests; air-conditioning; light alloy wheels; metallic spray.

230

See 200, except for:

PRICE IN GB: £ 7,981*
PRICE EX WORKS: 20,910* marks

ENGINE 140.8 cu in, 2,307 cc (3.69 x 3.29 in, 93.7 x 83.6 mm); max power (DIN): 109 hp (80.2 kW) at 4,800 rpm; max torque (DIN): 137 lb ft, 18.9 kg m (185.4 Nm) at 3,000 rpm; 47.2 hp/l (34.8 kW/l).

TRANSMISSION axle ratio: 3.690.

PERFORMANCE max speeds: (I) 30 mph, 48 km/h; (II) 50 mph, 80 km/h; (III) 83 mph, 134 km/h; (IV) 106 mph, 170 km/h; power-weight ratio: 27.3 lb/hp (37.1 lb/kW), 12.4

MERCEDES-BENZ 200

kg/hp (16.8 kg/kW); consumption: 24.1 m/imp gal, 20.1 m/US gal, 11.7 l x 100 km.

DIMENSIONS AND WEIGHT weight: 2,977 lb, 1,350 kg.

OPTIONALS with MB automatic transmission, max speeds (I) 25 mph, 40 km/h, (II) 50 mph, 80 km/h, (III) 83 mph, 134 km/h, (IV) 103 mph, 165 km/h.

230 C

See 230, except for:

PRICE IN GB: £ 9,750*
PRICE EX WORKS: 26,253* marks

TRANSMISSION width of rims: 6''; tyres: 195/70 HR x 14 or 195/70 SR x 14.

PERFORMANCE power-weight ratio: 27.8 lb/hp (37.8 lb/kW), 12.6 kg/hp (17.1 kg/kW).

STEERING servo (standard).

DIMENSIONS AND WEIGHT wheel base: 106.69 in, 271 cm; length: 182.68 in, 464 cm; height: 54.72 in, 139 cm; weight: 3,032 lb, 1,375 kg; turning circle: 36.1 ft, 11 m.

BODY coupé; 2 doors.

230 T

See 230, except for:

PRICE EX WORKS: 25,525* marks

TRANSMISSION width of rims: 6''; tyres: 195/70 SR x 14

PERFORMANCE power-weight ratio: 34.5 lb/hp (46.8 lb/kW), 15.6 kg/hp (21.2 kg/kW); carrying capacity: 1,235 lb, 560 kg.

CHASSIS rear suspension: automatic levelling control.

DIMENSIONS AND WEIGHT height: 56.10 in, 142 cm; weight: 3,241 lb, 1,470 kg; fuel tank: 15.4 imp gal, 18.5 US gal, 70 l.

BODY estate car/station wagon; 4 + 1 doors; folding rear seat; rear window wiper-washer.

OPTIONALS 185 HR x 15 tyres with 5.5'' wide rims.

250

See 200, except for:

PRICE IN GB: £ 9,200*
PRICE EX WORKS: 24,170* marks

MERCEDES-BENZ 300 D

ENGINE 6 cylinders; 154.1 cu in, 2,525 cc (3.39 x 2.85 in, 86 x 72.4 mm); compression ratio: 8.7:1; max power (DIN): 129 hp (94.9 kW) at 5,500 rpm; max torque (DIN): 145 lb ft, 20 kg m (196.1 Nm) at 3,500 rpm; 51.1 hp/l (37.3 kW/l); 4 crankshaft bearings; lubrication: 11.4 imp pt, 13.7 US pt, 6.5 l; 1 Solex 4 A 1 downdraught twin barrel carburettor.

TRANSMISSION gearbox ratios: I 3.980, II 2.290, III 1.450, IV 1, rev 3.740; axle ratio: 3.690.

PERFORMANCE max speeds: (I) 30 mph, 48 km/h; (II) 50 mph, 80 km/h; (III) 83 mph, 134 km/h; (IV) 112 mph, 180 km/h; power-weight ratio: 23.2 lb/hp (31.8 lb/kW), 10.5 kg/hp (14.4 kg/kW); consumption: 23.9 m/imp gal, 19.9 m/US gal, 11.8 l x 100 km.

STEERING servo (standard).

DIMENSIONS AND WEIGHT weight: 2,999 lb, 1,360 kg.

PRACTICAL INSTRUCTIONS oil: engine 11.4 imp pt, 13.7 US pt, 6.5 l.

OPTIONALS with MB automatic transmission, max speeds (I) 25 mph, 40 km/h, (II) 50 mph, 80 km/h, (II) 83 mph, 134 km/h, (IV) 109 mph, 175 km/h.

250 Long Wheelbase

See 250, except for:

PRICE EX WORKS: 36,333* marks

TRANSMISSION tyres: 185 SR x 15.

PERFORMANCE power-weight ratio: 26.3 lb/hp (36 lb/kW), 11.9 kg/hp (16.3 kg/kW); carrying capacity: 1,466 lb, 665 kg.

DIMENSIONS AND WEIGHT wheel base: 134.65 in, 342 cm; tracks: 58.27 in, 148 cm front. 56.30 in, 143 cm rear; length: 210.36 in, 535 cm; height: 58.27 in, 148 cm; weight: 3,396 lb, 1,540 kg; turning circle: 43.6 ft, 13.3 m.

250 T

See 250, except for:

PRICE EX WORKS: 28,784* marks

TRANSMISSION width of rims: 6''; tyres: 195/70 HR x 14.

PERFORMANCE power-weight ratio: 25.3 lb/hp (34.4 lb/kW), 1.5 kg/hp (15.6 kg/kW); carrying capacity: 1,235 lb, 560 kg.

CHASSIS rear suspension: automatic levelling control.

DIMENSIONS AND WEIGHT rear track: 57.20 in, 145 cm; height: 56.10 in, 142 cm; weight: 3,263 lb, 1,480 kg; fuel tank: 15.4 imp gal, 18.5 US gal, 70 l.

BODY estate car/station wagon; 4 + 1 doors; folding rear seat; rear window wiper-washer.

OPTIONALS 185 HR x 15 tyres 5.5'' wide rims.

200 D

See 200, except for:

PRICE IN GB: £ 7,121*
PRICE EX WORKS: 20,485* marks

ENGINE Diesel; compression ratio: 21:1; max power (DIN): hp (40.5 kW) at 4,200 rpm; max torque (DIN): 83 lb 11.5 kg m (112.8 Nm) at 2,400 rpm; max engine rpm: 200; 27.7 hp/l (20.4 kW/l); cast iron block and head; lubication: gear pump, full flow (cartridge) and by-pass ters, 11.4 imp pt, 13.7 US pt, 6.5 l; 4-cylinder Bosch inrect injection pump.

PERFORMANCE max speeds: (I) 21 mph, 33 km/h; (II) mph, 56 km/h; (III) 57 mph, 92 km/h; (IV) 81 mph, km/h; power-weight ratio: 55.1 lb/hp (74.9 lb/kW), kg/hp (33.9 kg/kW); consumption: 34 m/imp gal, 28.3 US gal, 8.3 l x 100 km.

ELECTRICAL EQUIPMENT 66 Ah battery.

DIMENSIONS AND WEIGHT weight: 3,032 lb, 1,375 kg.

PRACTICAL INSTRUCTIONS fuel: Diesel oil; oil: engine 4 imp pt, 13.7 US pt, 6,5 l, change every 3,100 miles, 00 km; tappet clearances: inlet 0.008 in, 0.10 mm; haust 0.016 in, 0.40 mm; valve timing: 12°30' 41°30' 45° 9°.

OPTIONALS with MB automatic transmission, max speeds 20 mph, 32 km/h, (II) 35 mph, 56 km/h, (III) 57 mph, km/h, (IV) 78 mph, 125 km/h.

MERCEDES-BENZ 280 TE

240 D

See 200 D, except for:

PRICE IN GB: £ 7,995*
PRICE IN USA: $ 14,245*
PRICE EX WORKS: 22,378* marks

ENGINE 146.7 cu in, 2,404 cc (3.58 x 3.64 in, 91 x 92.4 mm); max power (DIN): 65 hp (47.8 kW) at 4,200 rpm; max torque (DIN): 101 lb ft, 14 kg m (137.3 Nm) at 2,400 rpm; 27 hp/l (19.9 kW/l); oil cooler; cooling system: 17.6 imp pt, 21.1 US pt, 10 l.

TRANSMISSION axle ratio: 3.690.

PERFORMANCE max speeds: (I) 22 mph, 35 km/h; (II) 37 mph, 60 km/h; (III) 61 mph, 98 km/h; (IV) 86 mph, 138 km/h; power-weight ratio: 47 lb/hp (63.9 lb/kW), 21.3 kg/hp (29 kg/kW); consumption: 29.7 m/imp gal, 24.8 m/US gal, 9.5 l x 100 km.

ELECTRICAL EQUIPMENT 88 Ah battery.

DIMENSIONS AND WEIGHT weight: 3,054 lb, 1,385 kg.

OPTIONALS with MB automatic transmission, max speeds (I) 21 mph, 34 km/h, (II) 37 mph, 60 km/h, (III) 61 mph, 98 km/h, (IV) 83 mph, 133 km/h.

MERCEDES-BENZ 250

240 D Long Wheelbase

See 240 D, except for:

PRICE EX WORKS: 35,235* marks

TRANSMISSION tyres: 185 SR x 15.

PERFORMANCE power-weight ratio: 53.1 lb/hp (72.2 lb/kW), 24.1 kg/hp (32.7 kg/kW); carrying capacity: 1,466 lb, 665 kg.

STEERING servo (standard).

DIMENSIONS AND WEIGHT wheel base: 134.65 in, 342 cm; tracks: 58.27 in, 148 cm front, 56.30 in, 143 cm rear; length: 210.63 in, 535 cm; height: 58.27 in, 148 cm; weight: 3,451 lb, 1,565 kg; turning circle: 43.6 ft, 13.3 m.

240 TD

See 240 D, except for:

PRICE EX WORKS: 26,992* marks

TRANSMISSION width of rims: 6''; tyres: 195/70 SR x 14.

PERFORMANCE power-weight ratio: 51 lb/hp (69.4 lb/kW), 23.1 kg/hp (31.5 kg/kW); carrying capacity: 1,235 lb, 560 kg.

CHASSIS rear suspension: automatic levelling control.

DIMENSIONS AND WEIGHT rear track: 57.20 in, 145 cm; height: 56.10 in, 142 cm; weight: 3,318 lb, 1,505 kg; fuel tank: 15.4 imp gal, 18.5 US gal, 70 l.

BODY estate car/station wagon; 4 + 1 doors; folding rear seat; rear window wiper-washer.

OPTIONALS 185 SR x 15 tyres with 5.5'' wide rims.

300 D

See 200 D, except for:

PRICE IN GB: £ 9,923*
PRICE IN USA: $ 19,904* (automatic)
PRICE EX WORKS: 24,405* marks

ENGINE 5 cylinders, in line; 183.4 cu in, 3,005 cc (3.58 x 3.64 in, 91 x 92.4 mm); max power (DIN): 80 hp (58.9 kW) at 4,000 rpm; max torque (DIN): 127 lb ft, 17.5 kg m (171.6 Nm) at 2,400 rpm; max engine rpm: 5,100; 26.6 hp/l (19.6 kW/l); 6 crankshaft bearings; oil cooler; 5-cylinder Bosch indirect injection pump; cooling system: 19 imp pt, 22.8 US pt, 10.8 l.

TRANSMISSION axle ratio: 3.460.

PERFORMANCE max speed: (I) 24 mph, 38 km/h; (II) 40 mph, 64 km/h; (III) 65 mph, 104 km/h; (IV) 92 mph, 148 km/h; power-weight ratio: 39.8 lb/hp (54.1 lb/kW), 18.1 kg/hp (24.5 kg/kW); consumption: 26.2 m/imp gal, 21.8 m/US gal, 10.8 l x 100 km.

STEERING servo (standard).

300 D

ELECTRICAL EQUIPMENT 88 Ah battery.

DIMENSIONS AND WEIGHT weight: 3,186 lb, 1,445 kg.

OPTIONALS with MB automatic transmission, max speeds (I) 22 mph, 36 km/h, (II) 40 mph, 64 km/h, (III) 65 mph, 104 km/h, (IV) 89 mph, 143 km/h.

300 D Long Wheelbase

See 300 D, except for:

PRICE EX WORKS: 36,568* marks

TRANSMISSION tyres: 185 SR x 15.

PERFORMANCE power-weight ratio: 44.5 lb/hp (60.4 lb/kW), 20.2 kg/hp (27.4 kg/kW); carrying capacity: 1,466 lb, 665 kg.

DIMENSIONS AND WEIGHT wheel base: 134.65 in, 342 cm; tracks: 58.27 in, 148 cm front, 56.30 in, 143 cm rear; length: 210.63 in, 535 cm; height: 58.27 in, 148 cm; weight: 3,561 lb, 1,615 kg; turning circle: 43.6 ft, 13.3 m.

300 TD

See 300 D, except for:

PRICE EX WORKS: 29,019* marks

TRANSMISSION width of rims: 6''; tyres: 195/70 SR x 14.

PERFORMANCE power-weight ratio: 43.1 lb/hp (58.6 lb/kW), 19.6 kg/hp (26.6 kg/kW); carrying capacity: 1,235 lb, 560 kg.

CHASSIS rear suspension: automatic levelling control.

DIMENSIONS AND WEIGHT rear track: 57.20 in, 145 cm; height: 56.10 in, 142 cm; weight: 3,451 lb, 1,565 kg; fuel tank: 15.4 imp gal, 18.5 US gal, 70 l.

BODY estate car/station wagon; 4 + 1 doors; folding rear seat: rear window wiper-washer.

OPTIONALS 185 SR x 15 tyres with 5.5'' wide rims.

280

PRICE EX WORKS: 27,350* marks

ENGINE front, 4 stroke; 6 cylinders, vertical, in line; 167.6 cu in, 2,746 cc (3.39 x 3.10 in, 86 x 78.8 mm); compression ratio: 8.7:1; max power (DIN): 156 hp (114.8 kW) at 5,500 rpm; max torque (DIN): 164 lb ft, 22.7 kg m (222.6 Nm) at 4,000 rpm; max engine rpm: 6,500; 56.8 hp/l (41.8 kW/l); cast iron block, light alloy head; 7 crankshaft bearings; valves: overhead, Vee-slanted at 54°, finger levers; camshafts: 2, overhead; lubrication: gear pump, oil-water heat exchanger, filter (cartridge) on by-pass, oil cooler, 11.4 imp pt, 13.7 US pt, 6.5 l; 1 Solex 4 A 1 downdraught twin barrel carburettor; fuel feed: mechanical pump; water-cooled, 17.1 imp pt, 20.5 US pt, 9.7 l, magnetically-controlled fan.

TRANSMISSION driving wheels: rear; clutch: single dry plate, hydraulically controlled; gearbox: mechanical; gears: 4, fully synchronized; ratios: I 3.980, II 2.290, III 1.450, IV 1, rev 3.740; lever: steering column or central; final drive: hypoid bevel; axle ratio: 3.540; width of rims: 6''; tyres: 195/70 HR x 14.

PERFORMANCE max speeds: (I) 34 mph, 55 km/h; (II) 55 mph, 88 km/h; (III) 90 mph, 145 km/h; (IV) 118 mph, 190 km/h; power-weight ratio: 20.6 lb/hp (27.9 lb/kW), 9.3 kg/hp (12.7 kg/kW); carrying capacity: 1,147 lb, 520 kg; consumption: 22.6 m/imp gal, 18.8 m/US gal, 12.5 l x 100 km.

CHASSIS integral, front auxiliary frame; front suspension: independent, wishbones, coil springs, auxiliary rubber springs, anti-roll bar, telescopic dampers; rear: independent, oblique semi-trailing arms, coil springs, auxiliary rubber springs, anti-roll bar, telescopic dampers.

STEERING recirculating ball, damper, servo.

BRAKES disc (front diameter 10.94 in, 27.8 cm, rear 10.98 in, 27.9 cm), rear compensator, dual circuit, servo; swept area: front 255.5 sq in, 1,648 sq cm, rear 195.8 sq in, 1,263 sq cm, total 451.3 sq in, 2,911 sq cm.

ELECTRICAL EQUIPMENT 12 V; 55 Ah battery; 770 W alternator; Bosch distributor; 4 halogen headlamps.

DIMENSIONS AND WEIGHT wheel base: 110.04 in, 279 cm; tracks: 58.58 in, 149 cm front, 56.93 in, 145 cm rear; length: 186.02 in, 472 cm; width: 70.31 in, 179 cm; height:

56.69 in, 144 cm; ground clearance: 6.50 in, 16.5 cm; weight: 3,208 lb, 1,455 kg; turning circle: 37.1 ft, 11.3 m; fuel tank: 17.6 imp gal, 21.1 US gal, 80 l.

BODY saloon/sedan; 4 doors; 5 seats, separate front seats, reclining backrests with built-in headrests.

PRACTICAL INSTRUCTIONS fuel: 98 oct petrol; oil: engine 11.4 imp pt, 13.7 US pt, 6.5 l, SAE 20W-30, change every 4,650 miles, 7,500 km - gearbox 3.2 imp pt, 3.8 US pt, 1.8 l, ATF, change every 12,400 miles, 20,000 km - final drive 4.4 imp pt, 5.3 US pt, 2.5 l, SAE 90, change every 12,400 miles, 20,000 km; greasing: every 3,100 miles, 5,000 km, 20 points; tyre pressure: front 22 psi, 1.6 atm, rear 28 psi, 1.9 atm.

OPTIONALS MB automatic transmission hydraulic torque converter and planetary gears with 4 ratios (I 3.980, II 2.390, III 1.460, IV 1, rev 5.470), possible manual selection, max speeds (I) 26 mph, 42 km/h, (II) 55 mph, 88 km/h, (III) 90 mph, 145 km/h, (IV) 115 mph, 185 km/h; automatic levelling control on rear suspension; fog lamps; electric or manual sunshine roof; heated rear window; heated seats; electric windows; tinted glass; air- conditioning; light alloy wheels; metallic spray.

280 C

See 280, except for:

PRICE EX WORKS: 31,270* marks

PERFORMANCE power-weight ratio: 20.4 lb/hp (27.7 lb/kW), 9.3 kg/hp (12.6 kg/kW).

DIMENSIONS AND WEIGHT wheel base: 106.69 in, 271 cm; length: 182.68 in, 464 cm; height: 54.72 in, 139 cm; weight: 3,186 lb, 1,445 kg; turning circle (between walls): 36.1 ft, 11 m.

BODY coupé; 2 doors.

280 E

See 280, except for:

PRICE IN GB: £ 10,994*
PRICE IN USA: $ 20,775* (automatic)
PRICE EX WORKS: 29,422* marks

ENGINE compression ratio: 9:1; max power (DIN): 185 hp (136 kW) at 5,800 rpm; max torque (DIN): 177.5 lb ft, 24.5 kg m (240.4 Nm) at 4,500 rpm; 67.4 hp/l (49.5 kW/l); Bosch K-Jetronic injection system; fuel feed: electric pump.

PERFORMANCE max speeds: (I) 34 mph, 55 km/h; (II) 55 mph, 88 km/h; (III) 90 mph, 145 km/h; (IV) 124 mph, 200 km/h; power-weight ratio: 17.4 lb/hp (23.7 lb/kW), 7.9 kg/hp (10.7 kg/kW).

DIMENSIONS AND WEIGHT weight: 3,219 lb, 1,460 kg.

OPTIONALS with MB automatic transmission, max speeds (I) 26 mph, 42 km/h, (II) 55 mph, 88 km/h, (III) 90 mph, 145 km/h, (IV) 121 mph, 195 km/h.

MERCEDES-BENZ 280 CE

280 CE

See 280 E, except for:

PRICE IN GB: £ 11,950*
PRICE IN USA: $ 23,337* (automatic)
PRICE EX WORKS: 33,342* marks

PERFORMANCE power-weight ratio: 17,3 lb/hp (23.5 lb/kW), 7.8 kg/hp (10.7 kg/kW).

DIMENSIONS AND WEIGHT wheel base: 106.69 in, 271 cm; length: 182.68 in, 464 cm; height: 54.72 in, 139 cm; weight 3,197 lb, 1,450 kg; turning circle (between walls): 36.1 ft, 11 m.

BODY coupé; 2 doors.

280 TE

See 280 E, except for:

PRICE EX WORKS: 33,992* marks

PERFORMANCE power-weight ratio: 18.4 lb/hp (25 lb/kW), 8.3 kg/hp (11.4 kg/kW); carrying capacity: 1,235 lb, 560 kg.

CHASSIS rear suspension: automatic levelling control.

DIMENSIONS AND WEIGHT rear track: 57.20 in, 145 cm

MERCEDES-BENZ 280 CE

eight: 56.10 in, 142 cm; weight: 3,407 lb, 1,545 kg; fuel ank: 15.4 imp gal, 18.5 US gal, 70 l.

ODY estate car/station wagon; 4+1 doors; back seat folding down to luggage table; rear window wiper-washer.

280 S

RICE EX WORKS: 32,368* marks

NGINE front, 4 stroke; 6 cylinders, vertical, in line; 167.6 u in, 2,746 cc (3.39 x 3.10 in, 86 x 78.8 mm); compression tio: 8.7:1; max power (DIN): 156 hp (114.8 kW) at 5,500 m; max torque (DIN): 164 lb ft, 22.7 kg m (222.6 Nm) at 000 rpm; max engine rpm: 6,500; 54.6 hp/l (41.8 kW/l); ast iron block, light alloy head; 7 crankshaft bearings; valves: overhead, Vee-slanted at 54º, finger levers; camshafts: overhead; lubrication: gear pump, full flow filter, oil poler, 11.4 imp pt, 13.7 US pt, 6.5 l; 1 Solex, 4 A 1 downraught twin barrel carburettor; fuel feed: mechanical pump; ater-cooled, 19.4 imp pt, 23.3 US pt, 11 l, thermostatic fan.

RANSMISSION driving wheels: rear; clutch: single dry ate, hydraulically controlled; gearbox: mechanical; gears: fully synchronized; ratios I 3.980, II 2.290, III 1.450, IV rev 3.740; lever: central; final drive: hypoid bevel; axle tio: 3.690; width of rims: 6''; tyres: 185 HR x 14.

ERFORMANCE max speeds: (I) 32 mph, 52 km/h; (II) 55 ph, 88 km/h; (III) 90 mph, 145 km/h; (IV) 118 mph, 190

km/h; power-weight ratio: 22.7 lb/hp (30.9 lb/kW), 10.3 kg/hp (14 kg/kW); carrying capacity: 1,147 lb, 520 kg; speed in direct drive at 1,000 rpm: 19.8 mph, 31.8 km/h; consumption: 22.6 m/imp gal, 18.9 m/US gal, 12.5 l x 100 km.

CHASSIS integral; front suspension: independent, upper wishbones with single transverse rod, longitudinal leading arm in one with anti-roll bar, coil springs, telescopic dampers; rear: independent, oblique semi-trailing arms, coil springs, anti-roll bar, auxiliary rubber springs, telescopic dampers.

STEERING recirculating ball, damper, servo.

BRAKES disc (front diameter 10.94 in, 27.8 cm, rear 10.98 in, (27.9 cm), rear compensator, dual circuit, servo; swept area: front 255.5 sq in, 1,648 sq cm, rear 195.8 sq in, 1,263 sq in, total 451.3 sq in, 2,911 sq cm.

ELECTRICAL EQUIPMENT 12 V; 55 Ah battery; 770 W alternator; Bosch distributor; 4 headlamps.

DIMENSIONS AND WEIGHT wheel base: 112.60 in, 286 cm; tracks: 59.84 in, 152 cm front, 59.05 in, 150 cm rear; length: 195.28 in, 496 cm; width: 73.62 in, 187 cm; height: 55.90 in, 142 cm; ground clearance: 5.91 in, 15 cm; weight: 3,550 lb, 1,610 kg; turning circle: 37.4 ft, 11.4 m; fuel tank: 21.1 imp gal, 25.3 US gal, 96 l.

BODY saloon/sedan; 4 doors; 5 seats, separate front seats, reclining backrests.

MERCEDES-BENZ 280 S

PRACTICAL INSTRUCTIONS fuel: 98 oct petrol; oil: engine 11.4 imp pt, 13.7 US pt, 6.5 l, SAE 20W-30, change every 4,650 miles, 7,500 km - gearbox 3.2 imp pt, 3.8 US pt, 1.8 l, AFT, change every 12,400 miles, 20,000 km - final drive 4.4 imp pt, 5.3 US pt, 2.5 l, SAE 90, change every 12,400 miles, 20,000 km; tyre pressure: front 22 psi, 1.6 atm, rear 28 psi, 1.9 atm.

OPTIONALS MB automatic transmission, hydraulic torque converter and planetary gears with 4 ratios (I 3.980, II 2.390, III 1.460, IV 1, rev 5.480), max ratio of converter at stall 2.2, possible manual selection, steering column or central lever, max speeds (I) 25 mph, 40 km/h, (II) 55 mph, 88 km/h, (III) 90 mph, 145 km/h, (IV) 115 mph, 185 km/h; automatic levelling control; electric sunshine roof; heated rear window; electric windows; headrests; metallic spray; light alloy wheels; tinted glass; air-conditioning.

280 SE

See 280 S, except for:

PRICE IN GB: £ 12,749*
PRICE IN USA: $ 24,556* (automatic)
PRICE EX WORKS: 34,619* marks

ENGINE compression ratio: 9:1; max power (DIN): 185 hp (136 kW) at 5,800 rpm; max torque (DIN): 177.5 lb ft, 24.5 kg m (240 Nm) at 4,500 rpm; 67.4 hp/l (49.5 kW/l); Bosch K-Jetronic injection system; fuel feed: electric pump.

PERFORMANCE max speeds: (I) 34 mph, 55 km/h; (II) 55 mph, 88 km/h; (III) 90 mph, 145 km/h; (IV) 124 mph, 200

MERCEDES-BENZ 280 SL - 280 SLC

km/h; power-weight ratio: 19.2 lb/hp (26.1 lb/kW), 8.7 kg/hp (11.8 kg/kW).

ELECTRICAL EQUIPMENT transistorized ignition.

OPTIONALS with MB automatic transmission, max speeds (I) 26 mph, 42 km/h, (II) 55 mph, 88 km/h, (III) 90 mph, 145 km/h, (IV) 121 mph, 195 km/h; rev counter.

280 SEL

See 280 SE, except for:

PRICE EX WORKS: 36,870* marks

PERFORMANCE power-weight ratio: 19.6 lb/hp (26.7 lb/kW), 8.9 kg/hp (12.1 kW/kW).

DIMENSIONS AND WEIGHT wheel base: 116.73 in, 296 cm; length: 199.21 in, 506 cm; height: 56.30 in, 143 cm; weight: 3,627 lb, 1,645 kg; turning circle: 38.7 ft, 11.8 m.

280 SL

See 280 SE, except for:

PRICE EX WORKS: 37,150* marks

TRANSMISSION gearbox ratios: (II) 2.390; width of rims: 6.5''.

PERFORMANCE power-weight ratio: 17.9 lb/hp (24.3 lb/kW), 8.1 kg/hp (11 kg/kW); carrying capacity: 926 lb, 420 kg.

DIMENSIONS AND WEIGHT wheel base 96.85 in, 246 cm; tracks: 57.09 in, 145 cm front, 56.69 in, 144 cm rear; length: 172.83 in, 439 cm; width: 70.47 in, 179 cm; height: 51.18 in, 130 cm; ground clearance: 5.31 in, 13.5 cm; weight: 3,308 lb, 1,500 kg; turning circle: 33.8 ft, 10.3 m; fuel tank: 19.8 imp gal, 23.8 US gal, 90 l.

BODY convertible; 2 doors; 2 seats.

OPTIONALS hardtop.

280 SLC

See 280 SL, except for:

PRICE EX WORKS: 43,602* marks

PERFORMANCE power-weight ratio: 18.5 lb/hp (25.1 lb/kW), 8.4 kg/hp (11.4 kg/kW); carrying capacity: 1,080 lb, 490 kg.

DIMENSIONS AND WEIGHT wheel base: 111.02 in, 282 cm; length: 187.01 in, 475 cm; height: 52.36 in, 133 cm; weight: 3,418 lb, 1,550 kg; turning circle: 37.7 ft, 11.5 m.

BODY coupé; 5 seats.

350 SE

See 280 S, except for:

PRICE IN GB: £ 14,850* (automatic)
PRICE EX WORKS: 38,573* marks

ENGINE 8 cylinders, Vee-slanted at 90º; 213.5 cu in, 3,499 cc (3.62 x 2.59 in, 92 x 65.8 mm); compression ratio: 9:1; max power (DIN): 205 hp (151 kW) at 5,750 rpm; max torque (DIN): 210.1 lb ft, 29 kg m (285 Nm) at 4,000 rpm; max engine rpm: 6,300; 58.6 hp/l (43.2 kW/l); 5 crankshaft bearings; valves: overhead, finger levers; camshafts: 2,1 per bank, overhead; lubrication: 14.1 imp pt, 16.9 US pt, 8 l; Bosch electronic injection, injectors in inlet pipes; fuel feed: electric pump; cooling system: 23.8 imp pt, 28.5 US pt, 13.5 l.

TRANSMISSION gearbox ratios: I 3.960, II 2.340, III 1.430, IV 1, rev 3.720; axle ratio: 3.460; width of rims: 6.5''; tyres: 205/70 HR x 14.

PERFORMANCE max speeds: (I) 34 mph, 54 km/h; (II) 56 mph, 90 km/h; (III) 93 mph, 150 km/h; (IV) 127 mph, 205 km/h; power-weight ratio: 18 lb/hp (24.5 lb/kW), 8.2 kg/hp (11.1 kg/kW); speed in direct drive at 1,000 rpm: 21.1 mph, 33.9 km/h; consumption: 21.7 m/imp gal, 18.1 m/US gal, 13 l x 100 km.

ELECTRICAL EQUIPMENT 66 Ah battery; transistorized ignition.

DIMENSIONS AND WEIGHT weight: 3,693 lb, 1,675 kg.

PRACTICAL INSTRUCTIONS oil: engine 14.1 imp pt, 16.9 US pt, 8 l.

OPTIONALS MB automatic transmission, hydraulic torque converter and planetary gears with 3 ratios (I 2.310, II 1.460, III 1, rev 1.840), max ratio of converter at stall 2.2, possible manual selection, steering column or central lever, max speeds (I) 56 mph, 90 km/h, (II) 93 mph, 150 km/h, (III) 124 mph, 200 km/h; rev counter.

MERCEDES-BENZ 350 SL

350 SEL

See 350 SE, except for:

PRICE EX WORKS: 40,824* marks

PERFORMANCE power-weight ratio: 18.3 lb/hp (24.8 lb/kW), 8.3 kg/hp (11.3 kg/kW).

DIMENSIONS AND WEIGHT wheel base: 116.73 in, 296 cm; length: 199.21 in, 506 cm; height: 56.30 in, 143 cm; weight: 3,749 lb, 1,700 kg; turning circle: 38.7 ft, 11.8 m.

350 SL

PRICE IN GB: £ 14,495*
PRICE EX WORKS: 41,104* marks

ENGINE front, 4 stroke; 8 cylinders, Vee-slanted at 90°; 213 cu in, 3,499 cc (3.62 x 2.59 in, 92 x 65.8 mm); compression ratio: 9:1; max power (DIN): 195 hp (143.5 kW) at 5,500 rpm; max torque (DIN): 203 lb ft, 28 kg m (274.6 Nm) at 4,000 rpm; max engine rpm: 6,300; 55.7 hp/l (41 kW/l); cast iron block, light alloy head; 5 crankshaft bearings; valves: overhead, finger levers; camshafts: 1 per block, overhead; lubrication: gear pump, full flow filter, oil cooler, 14.1 imp pt, 16.9 US pt, 8 l; Bosch electronic injection; fuel feed: electric pump; water-cooled, fan with revolution limiting device (1,900 rpm), 25.2 imp pt, 30.2 US pt, 14.3 l.

TRANSMISSION driving wheels: rear; clutch: single dry plate, hydraulically controlled; gearbox: mechanical; gears: 4, fully synchronized; ratios: I 3.960, II 2.340, III 1.430, IV 1, rev 3.720; lever: central; final drive: hypoid bevel; axle ratio: 3.460; width of rims: 6.5''; tyres: 205/70 VR x 14.

PERFORMANCE max speeds: (I) 34 mph, 54 km/h; (II) 56 mph, 90 km/h; (III) 93 mph, 150 km/h; (IV) 127 mph, 205 km/h; power-weight ratio: 17.4 lb/hp (23.7 lb/kW), 7.9 kg/hp (10.7 kg/kW); carrying capacity: 926 lb, 420 kg; consumption: 21.7 m/imp gal, 18.1 m/US gal, 13 l x 100 km.

CHASSIS backbone platform with box-type ladder frame; front suspension: independent, wishbones, coil springs, auxiliary rubber springs, anti-roll bar, telescopic dampers; rear: independent, oblique semi-trailing arms, coil springs, auxiliary rubber springs, anti-roll bar, telescopic dampers.

STEERING recirculating ball, damper, servo.

BRAKES disc (front diameter 10.75 in, 27.3 cm, rear 10.98 in, 27.9 cm), front internal radial fins, rear compensator, dual circuit, servo.

ELECTRICAL EQUIPMENT 12 V; 66 Ah battery; 770 W alternator; Bosch (transistorized) distributor; 2 iodine headlamps.

DIMENSIONS AND WEIGHT wheel base: 96.85 in, 246 cm; tracks: 57.08 in, 145 cm front, 56.69 in, 144 cm rear; length: 172.83 in, 439 cm; width: 70.47 in, 179 cm; height:

51.18 in, 130 cm; ground clearance: 5.12 in, 13 c weight: 3,396 lb, 1,540 kg; turning circle: 33.8 ft, 10.3 fuel tank: 19.8 imp gal, 23.8 US gal, 90 l.

BODY convertible; 2 doors; 2 seats, reclining backres

PRACTICAL INSTRUCTIONS fuel: 96 oct petrol; oil: eng 14.1 imp pt, 16.9 US pt, 8 l, SAE 20W-40, change ev 4,650 miles, 7,500 km - gearbox 9.5 imp pt, 11.4 US 5.4 l; sparking plug: 215°; tyre pressure: front 30 psi, atm, rear 34 psi, 2.4 atm.

OPTIONALS MB automatic transmission hydraulic torc converter and planetary gears with 3 ratios (I 2.310, 1.460, III 1, rev 1.840), central lever, max speed 124 m 200 km/h; limited slip differential; hardtop; air-conditi ing; electric windows.

350 SLC

See 350 SL, except for:

PRICE EX WORKS: 47,555* marks

TRANSMISSION axle ratio: 3.640.

PERFORMANCE max speed: 130 mph, 210 km/h; pow weight ratio: 18 lb/hp (24.4 lb/kW), 8.2 kg/hp (11.1 kg/k carrying capacity: 1,080 lb, 490 kg.

DIMENSIONS AND WEIGHT wheel base: 111.02 in, 282 c length: 187.01 in, 475 cm; height: 52.36 in, 133 cm; weig 3,506 lb, 1,590 kg; turning circle: 37.7 ft, 11.5 m.

BODY coupé; 5 seats.

OPTIONALS with MB automatic transmission max sp 127 mph, 205 km/h.

450 SE

PRICE IN GB: £ 15,995*
PRICE EX WORKS: 43,310* marks

ENGINE front, 4 stroke; 8 cylinders, Vee-slanted at 9 275.8 cu in, 4,520 cc (3.62 x 3.35 in, 92 x 85 mm); compr sion ratio: 8.8:1; max power (DIN): 225 hp (165 kW) 5,000 rpm; max torque (DIN): 272 lb ft, 37.5 kg m (Nm) at 3,250 rpm; max engine rpm: 5,800; 49.8 hp/l (3 kW/l); cast iron block, light alloy head; 5 crankshaft be ings; valves: overhead, finger levers; camshafts: 2, 1 bank, overhead; lubrication: gear pump, full flow fil oil cooler, 14.1 imp pt, 16.9 US pt, 8 l; Bosch electro injection; fuel feed: electric pump; water-cooled, visc coupling thermostatic fan, 26.4 imp pt, 31.7 US pt, 15

TRANSMISSION driving wheels: rear; gearbox: MB automa transmission, hydraulic torque converter and planetary ge with 3 ratios, max ratio of converter at stall 2.5, possi manual selection; ratios: I 2.310, II 1.460, III 1, rev 1.8 lever: central or steering column; final drive: hypoid bev axle ratio: 3.070; width of rims: 6.5''; tyres: 205/70 VR x

PERFORMANCE max speeds: (I) 59 mph, 95 km/h; (II) mph, 155 km/h; (III) 130 mph, 210 km/h; power-we ratio: 16.9 lb/hp (23.1 lb/kW), 7.7 kg/hp (10.5 kg/kW); ca ing capacity: 1,147 lb, 520 kg; speed in direct drive 1,000 rpm: 21.9 mph, 35.3 km/h; consumption: 19.5 m/i gal, 16.2 m/US gal, 14.5 l x 100 km.

CHASSIS integral, front auxiliary frame (welded body); front suspension: independent, wishbones, springs, anti-roll bar, telescopic dampers; rear: independ oblique semi-trailing arms, coil springs, anti-roll auxiliary rubber springs, telescopic dampers.

STEERING recirculating ball, servo; turns lock to lock: 2

BRAKES disc (front diameter 10.94 in, 27.8 cm, rear 1 in, 27.9 cm), rear compensator, dual circuit, servo; sw area: front 255.5 sq in, 1,648 sq cm, rear 195.8 sq in, 7.9 sq cm, total 451.3 sq in, 2,911 sq cm.

ELECTRICAL EQUIPMENT 12 V; 66 Ah battery; 770 W a nator; Bosch (transistorized) distributor; 2 iodine he lamps.

DIMENSIONS AND WEIGHT wheel base: 112.60 in, 286 tracks: 59.84 in, 152 cm front, 59.06 in, 150 cm r length: 195.28 in, 496 cm; width: 73.62 in, 187 cm; hei 55.91 in, 142 cm; ground clearance: 5.31 in, 13.5 weight: 3,815 lb, 1,730 kg; turning circle: 37.4 ft, 11.4 fuel tank: 21.1 imp gal, 25.3 US gal, 96 l.

BODY saloon/sedan; 4 doors; 5 seats, separate front se reclining backrests, headrests; automatic safety belts.

PRACTICAL INSTRUCTIONS fuel: 98 oct petrol; oil: eng 14.1 imp pt, 16.9 US pt, 8 l, SAE 20W-40, change ev 4,650 miles, 7,500 km - automatic transmission 15.7 imp 18.8 US pt, 8.9 l, ATF, change every 12,400 miles, 20 km - final drive 2.3 imp pt, 2.7 US pt, 1.3 l, SAE 90, cha every 12,400 miles, 20,000 km; sparking plug: 200°; tap clearances (cold): inlet 0.003 in, 0.08 mm, exhaust 0.

MERCEDES-BENZ 450 SLC 5.0

20 mm; valve timing: 5° 21° 25° 5°; tyre pressure: front
psi, 2.1 atm, rear 34 psi, 2.4 atm.

OPTIONALS electric sunshine roof; electric windows; rev
#unter; heated rear window; headrests; metallic spray;
#ght alloy wheels; automatic levelling control; tinted glass;
#-conditioning.

450 SEL

#e 450 SE, except for:

#RICE IN GB: £ 16,995*
#RICE IN USA: $ 27,945*
#RICE EX WORKS: 48,496* marks

#RFORMANCE power-weight ratio: 17.3 lb/hp (23.6 lb/kW).
kg/hp (10.7 kg/kW).

#MENSIONS AND WEIGHT wheel base: 116.54 in, 296 cm;
#gth: 199.21 in, 506 cm; height: 56.30 in, 143 cm; weight:
#92 lb, 1,765 kg; turning circle: 38.7 ft, 11.8 m.

#DY electric windows (standard).

VARIATIONS

#RFORMANCE power-weight ratio 20.5 lb/hp (27.8 lb/kW).
kg/hp (12.6 kg/kW).

450 SL

#e 450 SE, except for:

#ICE IN GB: £ 15,495*
#ICE IN USA: $ 28,687*
#ICE EX WORKS: 45,841* marks

#NGINE max power (DIN): 217 hp (159.7 kW) at 5,000 rpm;
#ax torque (DIN): 266 lb ft, 36.7 kg m (359.9 Nm) at 3,250
#m; 48 hp/l (35.8 kW/l).

#RFORMANCE power-weight ratio: 16 lb/hp (21.8 lb/kW).
kg/hp (9.9 kg/kW); carrying capacity: 926 lb, 420 kg.

#EERING turns lock to lock: 3.

#MENSIONS AND WEIGHT wheel base: 96.46 in, 245 cm;
#cks: 57.09 in, 145 cm front, 56.69 in, 144 cm rear;
#gth: 177.83 in, 439 cm; width: 70.47 in, 179 cm; height:
#18 in, 130 cm; weight: 3,484 lb, 1,580 kg; turning
#cle: 33.8 ft, 10.3 m; fuel tank: 19.8 imp gal, 23.8 US
#l, 90 l.

#DY convertible; 2 doors; 2 seats.

VARIATIONS

#RFORMANCE 18.3 lb/hp (24.9 lb/kW), 8.3 kg/hp (11.3
#kW).

#TIONALS hardtop.

450 SLC

#e 450 SE, except for:

#ICE IN GB: £ 18,250*
#ICE IN USA: $ 34,760*
#ICE EX WORKS: 52,293* marks

#GINE max power (DIN): 217 hp (159.7 kW) at 5,000 rpm;
#x torque (DIN): 266 lb ft, 36.7 kg m (359.9 Nm) at 3,250
#m; 48 hp/l (35.8 kW/l).

#FORMANCE power-weight ratio: 16.6 lb/hp (22.5 lb/kW).
kg/hp (10.2 kg/kW); carrying capacity: 1,080 lb, 490 kg.

#ERING turns lock to lock: 3.

#MENSIONS AND WEIGHT wheel base: 110.63 in, 281 cm;
#cks: 57.09 in, 145 cm front, 56.69 in, 144 cm rear;
#gth: 187.01 in, 475 cm; width: 70.47 in, 179 cm; height:
#36 in, 133 cm; weight: 3,594 lb, 1,630 kg; turning
#cle: 37.7 ft, 11,5 m; fuel tank: 19.8 imp gal, 23.8 US
#, 90 l.

#DY coupé; 2 doors; 4-5 seats.

VARIATIONS

#FORMANCE power-weight ratio 18.9 lb/hp (25.7 lb/kW).
kg/hp (11.7 kg/kW).

450 SLC 5.0

#e 450 SLC, except for:

#CE EX WORKS: 62,272* marks

#GINE 304.5 cu in, 4,990 cc (3.82 x 3.35 in, 97 x 85 mm);
#x power (DIN): 240 hp (176.6 kW) at 5,000 rpm; max

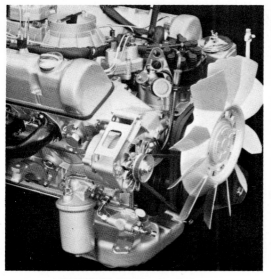

MERCEDES-BENZ 450 SLC 5.0

torque (DIN): 297 lb ft, 41 kg m (402.1 Nm) at 3,200 rpm;
48.1 hp/l (35.4 kW/l); light alloy block and head.

PERFORMANCE max speed: 140 mph, 225 km/h; power-
weight ratio: 13.9 lb/hp (18.9 lb/kW), 6.3 kg/hp (8.6 kg/kW);
speed in direct drive at 1,000 rpm: 24.1 mph, 38.8 km/h.

DIMENSIONS AND WEIGHT weight: 3,341 lb, 1,515 kg.

450 SEL 6.9

See 450 SE, except for:

PRICE IN GB: £ 26,501*
PRICE IN USA: $ 47,773*
PRICE EX WORKS: 77,392* marks

ENGINE 417 cu in, 6,834 cc (4.21 x 3.74 in, 107 x 95 mm);
max power (DIN): 286 hp (210.5 kW) at 4,250 rpm; max
torque (DIN): 406 lb ft, 56 kg m (549.2 Nm) at 3,000 rpm;
max engine rpm: 5,300; 41.8 hp/l (30.8 kW/l); lubrication:
gear pump, full flow filter, dry sump, oil cooler, 19.4 imp
pt, 23.2 US pt, 11 l; Bosch K-Jetronic injection.

TRANSMISSION final drive: limited slip differential; axle
ratio: 2.650; tyres: 215/70 VR x 14.

PERFORMANCE max speeds: (I) 59 mph, 95 km/h; (II) 96
mph, 155 km/h; (III) 140 mph, 225 km/h; power-weight
ratio: 14.9 lb/hp (20.3 lb/kW), 6.8 kg/hp (9.2 kg/kW); carry-

ing capacity: 1,069 lb, 485 kg; speed in direct drive at
1,000 rpm: 28.3 mph, 45.5 km/h; consumption: 17.7 m/imp
gal, 14.7 m/US gal, 16 l x 100 km.

CHASSIS front suspension: independent, wishbones, hydropneumatic suspension, anti-roll bar, automatic levelling
control, hydropneumatic telescopic dampers; rear: independent, oblique semi-trailing arms, hydropneumatic suspension, anti-roll bar, automatic levelling control, hydropneumatic telescopic dampers.

ELECTRICAL EQUIPMENT 88 Ah battery; 1,050 W alternator.

DIMENSIONS AND WEIGHT wheel base: 116.54 in, 296 cm;
length: 199.21 in, 506 cm; height: 56.69 in, 144 cm; weight:
4,267 lb, 1,935 kg; turning circle (between walls): 39.7 ft,
12.1 m.

BODY headrests, tinted glass with air-conditioning, heated
rear window, electric windows, headlamps wiper-washers
(standard).

PRACTICAL INSTRUCTIONS oil: engine 19.4 imp pt, 23.2
US pt, 11 l, change every 9,300 miles, 15,000 km.

VARIATIONS

None.

OPTIONALS ABS antilock braking system.

600

PRICE EX WORKS: 141,232* marks

ENGINE front, 4 stroke; 8 cylinders, Vee-slanted at 90°;
386.4 cu in, 6,332 cc (4.06 x 3.74 in, 103 x 95 mm); compression ratio: 9:1; max power (DIN): 250 hp (184 kW) at 4,000
rpm; max torque (DIN): 370 lb ft, 51 kg m (500.2 Nm)
at 2,800 rpm; max engine rpm: 4,800; 39.5 hp/l (29 kW/l);
cast iron block, light alloy head; 5 crankshaft bearings;
valves: overhead, finger levers; camshafts: 2, 1 per bank,
overhead; lubrication: gear pump, full flow and by-
pass filters, 14.1 imp pt, 16.9 US pt, 8 l; 8-cylinder Bosch
intermittent injection pump in inlet pipes; fuel feed: electric pump; water-cooled, 40.5 imp pt, 48.6 US pt, 23 l,
thermostatic fan.

TRANSMISSION driving wheels: rear; gearbox: MB automatic transmission, hydraulic coupling and twin planetary
gears with 4 ratios; ratios: I 3.980, II 2.460, III 1.580, IV 1,
rev 4.150; lever: steering column; final drive: hypoid bevel,
limited slip differential; axle ratio: 3.230; width of rims:
6.5''; tyres: 9.00 H x 15.

PERFORMANCE max speeds: (I) 31 mph, 50 km/h; (II)
50 mph, 80 km/h; (III) 81 mph, 130 km/h; (IV) 127 mph,
205 km/h; power-weight ratio: 21.8 lb/hp (29.6 lb/kW), 9.9
kg/hp (13.4 kg/kW); carrying capacity: 1,297 lb, 580 kg; acceleration: 0-50 mph (0-80 km/h) 6.9 sec; speed in direct
drive at 1,000 rpm: 26.4 mph, 42.5 km/h; consumption: 15.9
m/imp gal, 13.2 m/US gal, 17.8 l x 100 km.

CHASSIS integral, front auxiliary frame; front suspension:
independent, wishbones, air rubber springs, auxiliary rubber
springs, automatically- and manually-controlled levelling

MERCEDES-BENZ 600

600

system, anti-roll bar, telescopic dampers adjustable while running; rear: independent, single joint low pivot, swinging semi-axles, trailing lower radius arms, air rubber springs, auxiliary rubber springs, automatically and manually-controlled levelling system, anti-roll bar, telescopic dampers adjustable while running.

STEERING recirculating ball, damper, servo, adjustable height of steering wheel; turns lock to lock: 3.30.

BRAKES disc [front diameter (twin calipers) 11.46 in, 29.1 cm, rear 11.57 in, 29.4 cm], rear compensator, dual circuit, compressed-air servo; lining area: front 31.6 sq in, 204 sq cm, rear 24.7 sq in, 159 sq cm, total 56.3 sq in, 363 sq cm.

ELECTRICAL EQUIPMENT 12 V; 88 Ah battery; 2 490 W alternators; Bosch distributor; 2 headlamps.

DIMENSIONS AND WEIGHT wheel base: 125.98 in, 320 cm; tracks: 62.60 in, 159 cm front, 62.20 in, 158 cm rear; length: 218.11 in, 554 cm; width: 76.77 in, 195 cm; height: 58.26 in, 148 cm; ground clearance: 6.30 in, 16 cm; weight: 5,457 lb, 2,475 kg; weight distribution: 50.6% front, 49.4% rear; turning circle: 41.7 ft, 12.7 m; fuel tank: 24.6 imp gal, 29.6 US gal, 112 l.

BODY limousine; 4 doors; 6 seats, bench front seats; windows, locks, glass partition and front and rear seats (shifting horizontally and vertically) hydraulically controlled.

PRACTICAL INSTRUCTIONS fuel: 96 oct petrol; oil: engine 14.1 imp pt, 16.9 US pt, 8 l, SAE 20W-20, change every 4,650 miles, 7,500 km - automatic transmission 13.6 imp pt, 16.3 US pt, 7.7 l, ATF, change every 12,400 miles, 20,00 km - final drive 5.6 imp pt, 6.8 US pt, 3.2 l, SAE 90, change every 12,400 miles, 20,000 km; greasing: none; sparking plug: 215°; tappet clearances: inlet 0.004 in, 0.10 mm, exhaust 0.010 in, 0.25 mm; valve timing: 2°30' 52°30' 37°30' 18°; tyre pressure: front 28 psi, 2 atm, rear 33 psi, 2.3 atm.

OPTIONALS air-conditioning; sunshine roof.

600 Pullman

See 600, except for:

PRICE EX WORKS: 162,176* marks

PERFORMANCE power-weight ratio: 23.4 lb/hp (31.7 lb/kW), 10.6 kg/hp (14.4 kg/kW); carrying capacity: 1,544 lb, 700 kg.

DIMENSIONS AND WEIGHT wheel base: 153.54 in, 390 cm; length: 245.67 in, 624 cm; height: 59.06 in, 150 cm; weight: 5,843 lb, 2,650 kg; weight distribution: 51.5% front, 48.5% rear; turning circle: 49.2 ft, 15 m.

BODY 4 doors; 7-8 seats.

VARIATIONS

BODY 6 doors.

OPEL   GERMANY FR

City Series

PRICES IN GB AND EX WORKS:	DM
1 « J » Hatchback Coupé	**9,695***
2 Hatchback Coupé	**9,990***
3 L Hatchback Coupé	**10,520***
4 « Berlina » Hatchback Coupé	**11,195***

For 60 hp engine add DM 190; for 75 hp engine add DM 875.

Power team:	Standard for:	Optional for:
40 hp	—	all
48 hp	—	all
55 hp	all	—
60 hp	—	all
75 hp	—	all

40 hp power team

ENGINE front, 4 stroke; 4 cylinders, in line; 60.6 cu in, 993 cc (2.83 x 2.40 in, 72 x 61 mm); compression ratio: 7.9:1; max power (DIN): 40 hp (29.4 kW) at 5,400 rpm; max torque (DIN): 51 lb ft, 7 kg m (68.6 Nm) at 2,600-3,000 rpm; max engine rpm: 5,800; 40.3 hp/l (29.7 kW/l); cast iron block and head; 3 crankshaft bearings; valves: overhead, push-rods and rockers; camshafts: 1, side, chain-driven; lubrication: gear pump, full flow filter, 4.8 imp pt, 5.7 US pt, 2.7 l; 1 Solex 30 PDSI downdraught single barrel carburettor; fuel feed: mechanical pump; anti-freeze liquid cooled, 8.6 imp pt, 10.4 US pt, 4.9 l.

TRANSMISSION driving wheels: rear; clutch: single dry plate (diaphragm); gearbox: mechanical; gears: 4, fully synchronized; ratios: I 3.733, II 2.243, III 1.432, IV 1, rev 3.939; lever: central; final drive: hypoid bevel; axle ratio: 4.110; width of rims: 5''; tyres: 155 SR x 13.

PERFORMANCE max speed: 76 mph, 122 km/h; power-weight ratio: 43.8 lb/hp (59.6 lb/kW), 19.9 kg/hp (27 kg/kW); carrying capacity: 882 lb, 410 kg; acceleration: 0-50 mph (0-80 km/h) 15 sec; speed in direct drive at 1,000 rpm: 15.5 mph, 25 km/h; consumption: 36.7 m/imp gal, 30.5 m/US gal, 7.7 l x 100 km.

CHASSIS integral; front suspension: independent, wishbones, coil springs, anti-roll bar, telescopic dampers; rear: rigid axle (torque tube), longitudinal trailing radius arms, coil springs, transverse linkage bar, telescopic dampers.

STEERING rack-and-pinion; turns lock to lock: 3.75.

BRAKES front disc, rear drum; servo; lining area: total 49.2 sq in, 317 sq cm.

ELECTRICAL EQUIPMENT 12 V; 36 Ah battery; 45 A alternator; Bosch distributor; 2 headlamps.

DIMENSIONS AND WEIGHT wheel base: 94.09 in, 239 cm; tracks: 51.18 in, 130 cm front, 51.18 in, 130 cm rear; length: 153.27 in, 389 cm; width: 62.20 in, 158 cm; height: 54.13

---

in, 137 cm; ground clearance: 5.91 in, 15 cm; weight: 1,7█ lb, 795 kg; turning circle: 32.6 ft, 9.9 m; fuel tank: 8.1 i█ gal, 9.8 US gal, 37 l.

BODY hatchback coupé; 2 + 1 doors; 5 seats, separa█ front seats; heated rear window.

PRACTICAL INSTRUCTIONS fuel: 91 oct petrol; oil: engi█ 4.8 imp pt, 5.7 US pt, 2.7 l, SAE 20W-30, change eve█ 3,100 miles, 5,000 km - gearbox 1.2 imp pt, 1.5 US pt, █ l, SAE 80, no change recommended - final drive 1.2 i█ pt, 1.5 US pt, 0.7 l, SAE 90, no change recommende█ greasing: none; sparking plug: 200°; tappet clearances: in█ 0.006 in, 0.15 mm, exhaust 0.010 in, 0.25 mm; valve ti█ ing: 39° 93° 65° 45°.

OPTIONALS limited slip differential: 175/70 SR x 13 ty█ with 5.5'' wide rims; anti-roll bar on rear suspension. █ Ah battery; halogen headlamps; headrests; sunshine ro█ metallic spray; SR equipment for City L and City « Berlina█

48 hp power team

(Only for export).

See 40 hp power team, except for:

ENGINE compression ratio: 8.8:1; max power (DIN): █ hp (35.3 kW) at 5,600 rpm; max torque (DIN): 52 lb █ 7.2 kg m (70.6 Nm) at 3,400 rpm; max engine rpm: 6,0█ 48.3 hp/l (35.5 kW/l); cooling system: 8.1 imp pt, 9.7 █ pt, 4.6 l.

TRANSMISSION axle ratio: 4.375.

PERFORMANCE max speed: 80 mph, 128 km/h; power-wei█ ratio: 36.5 lb/hp (49.7 lb/kW), 16.6 kg/hp (22.5 kg/k█ acceleration: 0-50 mph (0-80 km/h) 13 sec; speed in di█ drive at 1,000 rpm: 14.6 mph, 23.5 km/h.

PRACTICAL INSTRUCTIONS fuel: 98 oct petrol; valve t█ ing: 44° 88° 78° 40°.

55 hp power team

See 40 hp power team, except for:

ENGINE 76 cu in, 1,196 cc (3.11 x 2.40 in, 79 x 61 m█ compression ratio: 7.8:1; max power (DIN): 55 hp (40.5 █ at 5,400 rpm; max torque (DIN): 62 lb ft, 8.5 kg m (83.4 █ at 3,400 rpm; max engine rpm: 6,000; 46 hp/l (33.9 kW/l█ Solex 35 PDSI downdraught single barrel carburettor; c█ ing system: 8.1 imp pt, 9.7 US pt, 4.6 l.

PERFORMANCE max speed: 84 mph, 136 km/h; power-wei█ ratio: 31.9 lb/hp (43.3 lb/kW), 14.4 kg/hp (19.6 kg/kW); a█ leration: 0-50 mph (0-80 km/h) 12.5 sec; consumption: █ m/imp gal, 26.1 m/US gal, 9 l x 100 km.

PRACTICAL INSTRUCTIONS valve timing: 46° 90° 70° **30°**█

60 hp power team

See 40 hp power team, except for:

ENGINE 76 cu in, 1,196 cc (3.11 x 2.40 in, 79 x61 mm); █ pression ratio: 9:1; max power (DIN): 60 hp (44.2 kW█ 5,400 rpm; max torque (DIN): 65 lb ft, 9 kg m (88.3 █ at 2,600-3,400 rpm; max engine rpm: 6,000; 50.2 hp/l (█ kW/l); 1 Solex 35 PDSI downdraught single barrel ca█ rettor; cooling system: 8.1 imp pt, 9.7 US pt, 4.6 l.

PERFORMANCE max speed: 87 mph, 140 km/h; power-wei█ ratio: 29.7 lb/hp (40.4 lb/kW), 13.5 kg/hp (18.3 kg/kW); a█ leration: 0-50 mph (0-80 km/h) 11.5 sec; consumption: █ m/imp gal, 26.1 m/US gal, 9 l x 100 km.

CHASSIS rear suspension: anti-roll bar (standard).

DIMENSIONS AND WEIGHT weight: 1,786 lb, 810 kg.

PRACTICAL INSTRUCTIONS fuel: 98 oct petrol; valve tim█ 46° 90° 70° 30°.

OPTIONALS Opel automatic transmission with 3 ratios█ 2.400, II 1.480, III 1, rev 1.920), max ratio of converter█ stall 2.2, possible manual selection, central lever, 4█ axle ratio, max speed 84 mph, 135 km/h, consumption █ m/imp gal, 24.2 m/US gal, 9.7 l x 100 km.

75 hp power team

See 40 hp power team, except for:

ENGINE 96.7 cu in, 1,584 cc (3.35 x 2.75 in, 85 x 69.8 █ compression ratio: 8.8:1; max power (DIN): 75 hp (55.2█ at 5,200 rpm; max torque (DIN): 83 lb ft, 11.5 kg m (█ Nm) at 3,800-4,200 rpm; 47.3 hp/l (34.8 kW/l); 5 cranks█ bearings; lubricating system: 6.7 imp pt, 8 US pt, 3.8█

OPEL City "Berlina" Hatchback Coupé

1 Solex 32/32 DIDTA-4 downdraught single barrel carburettor; cooling system: 11.6 imp pt, 14 US pt, 6.6 l.

TRANSMISSION gearbox ratios: I 3.640, II 2.120, III 1.336, IV 1, rev 3.522; axle ratio: 3.890.

PERFORMANCE max speed: 97 mph, 155 km/h; power-weight ratio: 26.8 lb/hp (36.3 lb/kW), 12.1 kg/hp (16.5 kg/kW); speed in direct drive at 1,000 rpm: 16.2 mph, 26 km/h; consumption: 26.9 m/imp gal, 22.4 m/US gal, 10.5 l x 100 km.

CHASSIS rear suspension: anti-roll bar (standard).

BRAKES lining area: total 85.7 sq in, 553 sq cm.

ELECTRICAL EQUIPMENT 44 Ah battery.

DIMENSIONS AND WEIGHT: 2,007 lb, 910 kg.

PRACTICAL INSTRUCTIONS fuel: 98 oct petrol; oil: engine 6.7 imp pt, 8 US pt, 3.8 l; tappet clearances: inlet 0.012 in, 0.30 mm, exhaust 0.012 in, 0.30 mm; valve timing: 44° 86° 84° 46°.

OPTIONALS Opel automatic transmission with 3 ratios (I 2.400, II 1.480, III 1, rev 1.920), max ratio of converter at stall 2.2, possible manual selection, central lever, 3.670 axle ratio, max speed 93 mph, 150 km/h, consumption 25.7 m/imp gal, 21.4 m/US gal, 11 l x 100 km.

OPEL Kadett 2-dr Limousine

Kadett Series

PRICES IN GB AND EX WORKS:

	£	DM
1 2-dr Limousine	2,348*	9,880*
2 4-dr Limousine	—	10,425*
3 Caravan	—	10,675*
4 L 2-dr Limousine	2,559*	10,410*
5 L 4-dr Limousine	—	10,955*
6 L Coupé	—	10,785*
7 L Caravan	2,975*	11,205*
8 « Berlina » 2-dr Limousine	3,043*	11,085*
9 « Berlina » 4-dr Limousine	—	11,535*
0 « Berlinetta » Coupé	—	11,460*
1 « Berlina » Caravan	—	11,785*
2 GT/E Coupé	—	17,470*

For 60 hp engine add DM 190; for 75 hp engine add DM 685.

Power team:	Standard for:	Optional for:
40 hp	—	1 to 11
48 hp	—	1 to 11
55 hp	1 to 11	
60 hp	—	1 to 11
75 hp	—	1 to 11
15 hp	12	

40 hp power team

ENGINE front, 4 stroke; 4 cylinders, in line; 60.6 cu in, 993 cc (2.83 x 2.40 in, 72 x 61 mm); compression ratio: 9.9:1; max power (DIN): 40 hp (29.4 kW) at 5,400 rpm; max torque (DIN): 51 lb ft, 7 kg (68.6 Nm) at 2,600-3,000 rpm; max engine rpm: 5,800; 40.3 hp/l (29.7 kW/l); cast iron block and head; 3 crankshaft bearings; valves: overhead, push-rods and rockers; camshafts: 1, side, chain-driven; lubrication: gear pump, full flow filter, 4.8 imp pt, 5.7 US pt, 2.7 l; 1 Solex 30 PDSI downdraught single barrel carburettor; fuel feed: mechanical pump; anti-freeze liquid cooled, 8.6 imp pt, 10.4 US pt, 4.9 l.

TRANSMISSION driving wheels: rear; clutch: single dry plate (diaphragm); gearbox: mechanical; gears: 4, fully synchronized; ratios: I 3.733, II 2.243, III 1.432, IV 1, rev 3.939; lever: central; final drive: hypoid bevel; axle ratio: 4.111; width of rims: 5''; tyres: 155 SR x 13.

PERFORMANCE max speed: 76 mph, 122 km/h - Coupé 78 mph, 125 km/h; power-weight ratio: 4-dr. limousines 44.4 lb/hp (60.4 lb/kW), 20.1 kg/hp (27.4 kg/kW); acceleration: 0-50 mph (0-80 km/h) 15 sec; speed in direct drive at 1,000 rpm: 15.5 mph, 25 km/h; consumption: 36.7 m/imp gal, 30.5 m/US gal, 7.7 l x 100 km.

CHASSIS integral; front suspension: independent, wishbones, coil springs, anti-roll bar, telescopic dampers; rear: rigid axle (torque tube), longitudinal trailing radius arms, coil springs, transverse linkage bar, telescopic dampers (anti-roll bar only for st. wagons).

STEERING rack-and-pinion; turns lock to lock: 3.75.

BRAKES front disc, rear drum; lining area: front 16.3 sq in, 105 sq cm, rear 32.9 sq in, 212 sq cm, total 49.2 sq in, 317 sq cm.

ELECTRICAL EQUIPMENT 12 V; 36 Ah battery; 45 A alternator; Bosch distributor; 2 headlamps.

DIMENSIONS AND WEIGHT wheel base: 94.09 in, 239 cm; tracks: 51.18 in, 130 cm front, 51.18 in, 130 cm rear; length: 162.36 in, 412 cm - Coupé, L and « Berlina » models 162.60 in, 413 cm - Caravan 162.91 in, 414 cm;

OPEL Kadett GT/E Coupé

width: 62.20 in, 158 cm; height: 54.13 in, 137 cm - Coupé 52.76 in, 134 cm - Caravan 54.33 in, 138 cm; ground clearance: 5.91 in, 15 cm; weight: 2-dr. limousines 1,731 lb, 785 kg - 4-dr. limousines 1,775 lb, 805 kg - Coupé 1,742 lb, 790 kg - Caravan 1,808 lb, 820 kg; turning circle: 32.6 ft, 9.9 m; fuel tank: 9.5 imp gal, 11.4 US gal, 43 l.

BODY 5 seats, separate front seats; heated rear window.

PRACTICAL INSTRUCTIONS fuel: 92 oct petrol; oil: engine 4.8 imp pt, 5.7 US pt, 2.7 l, SAE 20W-30, change every 3,100 miles, 5,000 km - gearbox 1.2 imp pt, 1.5 US pt, 0.7 l, SAE 80, no change recommended - final drive 1.2 imp pt, 1.5 US pt, 0.7 l, SAE 90, no change recommended; greasing: none; sparking plug: 200°; tappet clearances: inlet 0.006 in, 0.15 mm, exhaust 0.010 in, 0.25 mm; valve timing: 39° 93° 65° 45°.

OPTIONALS limited slip differential; 175/70 SR x 13 tyres with 5.5'' wide rims except for st. wagons; anti-roll bar on rear suspension; 44 Ah battery; halogen headlamps; headrests; sunshine roof except for st. wagons; metallic spray; rear window wiper-washer for st. wagons only.

48 hp power team

(only for export).

See 40 hp power team, except for:

ENGINE compression ratio: 8.8:1; max power (DIN): 48 hp (35.3 kW) at 5,600 rpm; max torque (DIN): 52 lb ft, 7.2 kg m (70.6 Nm) at 3,400 rpm; max engine rpm: 6,000; 48.3

hp/l (35.5 kW/l); cooling system: 8.1 imp pt. 9.7 US pt, 4.6 l.

TRANSMISSION axle ratio: 4.375.

PERFORMANCE max speed: 80 mph, 128 km/h - Coupé 82 mph, 132 km/h; power-weight ratio: 4-dr. limousines 37 lb/hp (50.3 lb/kW), 16.8 kg/hp (22.8 kg/kW); acceleration: 0-50 mph (0-80 km/h) 13 sec; speed in direct drive at 1,000 rpm: 14.6 mph, 23.5 km/h.

PRACTICAL INSTRUCTIONS fuel: 98 oct petrol; valve timing: 44° 88° 78° 40°.

55 hp power team

See 40 hp power team, except for:

ENGINE 76 cu in, 1,196 cc (3.11 x 2.40 in, 79 x 61 mm); compression ratio: 7.8:1; max power (DIN): 55 hp (40.5 kW) at 5,600 rpm; max torque (DIN): 62 lb ft, 8.5 kg m (83.4 Nm) at 3,400 rpm; max engine rpm: 6,000; 46 hp/l (33.9 kW/l); 1 Solex 35 PDSI downdraught single barrel carburettor; cooling system: 8.1 imp pt, 9.7 US pt, 4.6 l.

PERFORMANCE max speed: 86 mph, 138 km/h - Coupé 88 mph, 142 km/h; power-weight ratio: 4-dr. limousines 32.2 lb/hp (43.9 lb/kW), 14.6 kg/hp (19.9 kg/kW); acceleration: 0-50 mph (0-80 km/h) 12.5 sec; consumption: 31.4 m/imp gal, 26.1 m/US gal, 9 l x 100 km - Coupé 32.2 m/imp gal, 27.7 m/US gal, 8.5 l x 100 km.

PRACTICAL INSTRUCTIONS valve timing: 46° 90° 70° 30°.

60 hp power team

See 40 hp power team, except for:

ENGINE 76 cu in, 1,196 cc (3.11 x 2.40 in, 79 x 61 mm); compression ratio: 9:1; max power (DIN): 60 hp (44.2 kW) at 5,400 rpm; max torque (DIN): 65 lb ft, 9 kg m (88.3 Nm) at 2,600-3,400 rpm; max engine rpm: 6,000; 50.2 hp/l (32.5 kW/l); 1 Solex 35 PDSI downdraught single barrel carburettor; cooling system: 8.1 imp pt, 9.7 US pt, 4.6 l.

PERFORMANCE max speed: 88 mph, 142 km/h - Coupé 91 mph, 146 km/h; power-weight ratio: Kadett Aero and 4-dr. limousines 30.1 lb/hp (41 lb/kW), 13.6 kg/hp (18.6 kg/kW); acceleration: 0-50 mph (0-80 km/h) 11.5 sec; consumption: 33.2 m/imp gal, 27.7 m/US gal, 8.5 l x 100 km - Coupé 34.4 m/imp gal, 28.7 m/US gal, 8.2 l x 100 km.

CHASSIS rear suspension: anti-roll bar (standard).

DIMENSIONS AND WEIGHT weight: plus 33 lb, 15 kg - Coupé plus 66 lb, 30 kg.

PRACTICAL INSTRUCTIONS fuel: 98 oct petrol; valve timing: 46° 90° 70° 30°.

OPTIONALS Opel automatic transmission with 3 ratios (I 2.400, II 1.480, III 1, rev 1.920), max ratio of converter at stall 2.2, 4.110 axle ratio, max speed 85 mph, 137 km/h (Coupé 88 mph, 141 km/h), consumption 30.7 m/imp gal, 25.6 m/US gal, 9.2 l x 100 km - Coupé 31.4 m/imp gal, 26.1 m/US gal, 9 l x 100 km; SR equipment with 175/70 SR x 13 tyres except for st. wagons.

75 hp power team

See 40 hp power team, except for:

ENGINE 96.7 cu in, 1,584 cc (3.35 x 2.75 in, 85 x 69.8 mm); compression ratio: 8.8:1; max power (DIN): 75 hp (55.2 kW) at 5,200 rpm; max torque (DIN): 83 lb ft, 11.5 kg m (112.8 Nm) at 3,800-4,200 rpm; 47.3 hp/l (34.8 kW/l); 5 crankshaft bearings; lubricating system: 6.7 imp pt, 8 US pt, 3.8 l; 1 Solex 32/32 DIDTA-4 downdraught single barrel carburettor; cooling system: 11.6 imp pt, 14 US pt, 6.6 l.

TRANSMISSION gearbox ratios: I 3.640, II 2.120, III 1.336, IV 1, rev 3.522; axle ratio: 3.890.

PERFORMANCE max speed: 98 mph, 157 km/h - Coupé 99 mph, 160 km/h; power-weight ratio: 4-dr. limousines 27 lb/hp (36.7 lb/kW), 12.3 kg/hp (16.7 kg/kW); speed in direct drive at 1,000 rpm: 16.2 mph, 26 km/h; consumption: 27.7 m/imp gal, 23.1 m/US gal, 10.2 l x 100 km - Coupé 28.2 m/imp gal, 23.5 m/US gal, 10 l x 100 km.

CHASSIS rear suspension: anti-roll bar (standard).

BRAKES lining area: total 85.7 sq in, 553 sq cm.

ELECTRICAL EQUIPMENT 44 Ah battery.

DIMENSIONS AND WEIGHT weight: plus 253 lb, 115 kg - Coupé plus 286 lb, 130 kg.

OPEL Kadett Series (automatic transmission)

PRACTICAL INSTRUCTIONS fuel: 98 oct petrol; oil: engine 6.7 imp pt, 8 US pt, 3.8 l; tappet clearances: inlet 0.012 in, 0.30 mm, exhaust 0.012 in, 0.30 mm; valve timing: 44° 86° 84° 46°.

OPTIONALS Opel automatic transmission with 3 ratios (I 2.400, II 1.480, III 1, rev. 1.920), max ratio of converter at stall 2.2, possible manual selection, central lever, 3.670 axle ratio, max speed 94 mph, 152 km/h (Coupé 96 mph, 155 km/h), consumption 26.4 m/imp gal, 22 m/US gal, 10.7 l x 100 km - Coupé 27.7 m/imp gal, 23.1 m/US gal, 10.2 l x 100 km.

115 hp power team

See 40 hp power team, except for:

ENGINE 120.8 cu in, 1,979 cc (3.74 x 2.75 in, 95 x 69.8 mm); compression ratio: 9.6:1; max power (DIN): 115 hp (84.6 kW) at 5,600 rpm; max torque (DIN): 117 lb ft, 16.2 kg m (158.9 Nm) at 3,000 rpm; max engine rpm: 6,000; 58.1 hp/l (42.7 kW/l); 5 crankshaft bearings; valves: overhead, in line, rockers, hydraulic tappets; camshafts: 1, overhead; lubricating system: 6.7 imp pt, 8 US pt, 3.8 l; Bosch L-Jetronic electronic injection; fuel feed: electric pump; cooling system: 12 imp pt, 14.4 US pt, 6.8 l.

TRANSMISSION gears: 5, fully synchronized; ratios: I 2.991, II 1.763, III 1.301, IV 1, V 0.874, rev 3.663; axle ratio: 3.890; width of rims: 6''; tyres: 175/70 HR x 13.

PERFORMANCE max speed: 118 mph, 190 km/h; power-weight ratio: 17.6 lb/hp (24 lb/kW), 8 kg/hp (10.9 kg/kW); carrying capacity: 827 lb, 375 kg; speed in top at 1,000 rpm 19.7 mph, 31.7 km/h; consumption: 32.1 m/imp gal, 26 m/US gal, 8.8 l x 100 km.

CHASSIS rear suspension: anti-roll bar (standard).

STEERING turns lock to lock: 3.50

BRAKES front disc, rear drum, rear compensator, servo; lining area: total 85.7 sq in, 553 sq cm.

ELECTRICAL EQUIPMENT 55 Ah battery; halogen headlamps (standard).

DIMENSIONS AND WEIGHT tracks: 51.97 in, 132 cm front, 51.57 in, 131 cm rear; height: 52.76 in, 134 cm; ground clearance: 5 in, 12.7 cm; weight: 2,029 lb, 920 kg.

BODY coupé; 2 doors; 5 seats, separate front seats, built-in headrests, heated rear window.

PRACTICAL INSTRUCTIONS fuel: 98 oct petrol; oil: engine 6.7 imp pt, 8 US pt, 3.8 l - gearbox 1.9 imp pt, 2.3 US pt, 1.1 l - final drive 1.9 imp pt, 2.3 US pt, 1.1 l; tappet clearances: inlet 0.012 in, 0.30 mm, exhaust 0.012 in, 0.30 mm; valve timing: 44° 88° 84° 48°; tyre pressure: front 24 psi, 1.7 atm, rear 24 psi, 1.7 atm.

OPTIONALS 4.750 axle ratio; light alloy wheels.

Rallye Series

PRICES IN GB AND EX WORKS:	£	DM
1 1.6 S Coupé	—	12,43
2 E Coupé	3.688*	14,07

Power team:	Standard for:	Optional for:
75 hp	1	—
110 hp	2	—

75 hp power team

ENGINE front, 4 stroke; 4 cylinders, in line; 96.7 cu in, 1,584 cc (3.35 x 2.75 in, 85 x 69.8 mm); compression ratio: 8.8:1; max power (DIN): 75 hp (55.2 kW) at 5,200 rpm; max torque (DIN): 83 lb ft, 11.5 kg m (112.8 Nm) at 3,800-4,200 rpm; max engine rpm: 5,800; 47.3 hp/l (34.8 kW/l); cast iron block and head; 5 crankshaft bearings; valves: overhead, push-rods and rockers; camshafts: 1, side chain driven; lubrication: gear pump, full flow filter, 6.7 imp pt, 8 US pt, 3.8 l; 1 Solex 32/32 DIDTA-4 downdraught single barrel carburettor; fuel feed: mechanical pump; anti-freeze liquid cooled, 11.6 imp pt, 14 US pt, 6.6 l.

TRANSMISSION driving wheels: rear; clutch: single dry plate (diaphragm); gearbox: mechanical; gears: 4, fully synchronized; ratios: I 3.640, II 2.120, III 1.336, IV 1, rev 3.522; lever: central; final drive: hypoid bevel; axle ratio 3.890; width of rims: 5.5''; tyres 175/70 SR x 13.

PERFORMANCE max speed: 99 mph, 160 km/h; power-weight ratio: 26.6 lb/hp (36.1 lb/kW), 12.1 kg/hp (16 kg/kW); carrying capacity: 805 lb, 365 kg; speed in direct drive at 1,000 rpm: 17.1 mph, 27.6 km/h; consumption 28.2 m/imp gal, 23.5 m/US gal, 10 l x 100 km.

CHASSIS integral; front suspension: independent, wishbones, coil springs, anti-roll bar, telescopic dampers; rear: rigid axle (torque tube), longitudinal trailing radius arms, coil springs, transverse linkage bar, anti-roll bar, telescopic dampers.

STEERING rack-and-pinion.

BRAKES front disc, rear drum; lining area: total 85.7 sq in, 553 sq cm.

ELECTRICAL EQUIPMENT 12 V; 44 Ah battery; 45 A alternator; Bosch distributor; 2 halogen headlamps.

DIMENSIONS AND WEIGHT wheel base: 94.09 in, 239 cm; tracks: 51.18 in, 130 cm front, 51.18 in, 130 cm rear; length 162.36 in, 412 cm; width: 62.20 in, 158 cm; height: 52.76 in, 134 cm; ground clearance: 5.91 in, 15 cm; weight: 1,996 lb, 905 kg; turning circle: 32.6 ft, 9.9 m; fuel tank: 9.5 imp gal, 11.4 US gal, 43 l.

BODY coupé; 2 doors; 5 seats, separate front seats, reclining backrests with built-in headrests heated rear window.

PRACTICAL INSTRUCTIONS fuel: 98 oct petrol; oil: engine 6.7 imp pt, 8 US pt, 3.8 l, SAE 20W-30, change every 3,1 miles, 5,000 km - gearbox 1.9 imp pt, 2.3 US pt, 1.1 l, SAE 80, no change recommended - final drive 1.9 imp pt, 2.3 US pt, 1.1 l, SAE 90, no change recommended; greasing: none; tappet clearances: inlet 0.012 in, 0.30 mm, exhaust 0.012 in, 0.30 mm; valve timing: 46° 90° 70° 30°; tyre pressure: front 24 psi, 1.7 atm, rear 24 psi, 1.7 atm.

OPTIONALS limited slip differential; 3.670 axle ratio; light alloy wheels.

OPEL Kadett " Berlina " 4-dr Limousine

OPEL Kadett L Caravan

110 hp power team

e 75 hp power team, except for:

IGINE 120.8 cu in, 1,979 cc (3.74 x 2.75 in, 95 x 69.8 mm); mpression ratio: 9.4:1; max power (DIN): 110 hp (81 kW) 5,400 rpm; max torque (DIN): 117 lb ft, 16.2 kg m (158.9 n) at 3,400 rpm; max engine rpm: 6,000; 55.6 hp/l (40.9 /l); valves: hydraulic tappets; Bosch L-Jetronic electronic ection; fuel feed: electric pump; cooling system: 12 p pt, 14.4 US pt, 6.8 l.

ANSMISSION axle ratio: 3.440; tyres: 175/70 HR x 13.

RFORMANCE max speed: 117 mph, 189 km/h; power-eight ratio: 18.3 lb/hp (24.9 lb/kW), 8.3 kg/hp (11.3 kg/kW); rrying capacity: 827 lb, 375 kg; speed in direct drive at 00 rpm: 19.6 mph, 31.5 km/h; consumption: 29.7 m/imp l, 24.8 m/US gal, 9.5 l x 100 km.

MENSIONS AND WEIGHT weight: 2,018 lb, 915 kg.

ACTICAL INSTRUCTIONS valve timing: 34° 88° 74° 48°.

PTIONALS 5-speed fully synchronized mechanical gearbox 3.875, II 2.400, III 1.760, IV 1.260, V 1, rev. 3.670).

Ascona Series

ICES IN GB AND EX WORKS:	£	DM
1.2 2-dr Limousine	—	11,460*
1.2 4-dr Limousine	—	12,015*
1.2 L 2-dr Limousine	—	12,290*
1.2 L 4-dr Limousine	—	12,845*
1.2 « Berlina » 2-dr Limousine	—	13,110*
1.2 « Berlina » 4-dr Limousine	—	13,515*
1.6 2-dr Limousine	3,106*	11,900*
1.6 4-dr Limousine	3,210*	12,455*
1.6 L 2-dr Limousise	3,480*	12,730*
1.6 L 4-dr Limousine	3,583*	13,285*
1.6 « Berlina » 2-dr Limousine		13,550*
1.6 « Berlina » 4-dr Limousine		13,955*
2.0 D 2-dr Limousine		
2.0 D 4-dr Limousine		
2.0 LD 2-dr Limousine		
2.0 LD 4-dr Limousine		
2.0 D « Berlina » 2-dr Limousine		
2.0 D « Berlina » 4-dr Limousine		

r 75 hp engine add DM 715; for 90 hp engine add 935; for 100 hp engine add DM 1,075.

wer team:	Standard for:	Optional for:
5 hp	—	1 to 6
) hp	—	1 to 6
0 hp (1,584)	7 to 12	—
5 hp	—	7 to 12
) hp	—	7 to 12
) hp	—	7 to 12
3 hp (Diesel)	13 to 18	7 to 12

55 hp power team

GINE front, 4 stroke; 4 cylinders, in line; 76 cu in, 96 cc (3.11 x 2.40 in, 79 x 61 mm); compression ratio: 3:1; max power (DIN) 55 hp (40.5 kW) at 5,400 rpm; max rque (DIN) 62 lb ft, 8.5 kg m (83.4 Nm) at 3,400 rpm; max

engine rpm: 5,800; 50.2 hp/l (36.9 kW/l); cast iron block and head; 3 crankshaft bearings; valves: overhead, push-rods and rockers; camshafts: 1, side, chain-driven; lubri-cation: gear pump, full flow filter, 4.8 imp pt, 5.7 US pt, 2.7 l; 1 Solex 35 PDSI downdraught single barrel carburettor; fuel feed: mechanical pump; anti-freeze liquid cooled, 9.3 imp pt, 11.2 US pt, 5.3 l.

TRANSMISSION driving wheels: rear; clutch: single dry plate (diaphragm); gearbox: mechanical; gears: 4, fully synchronized; ratios: I 3.733, II 2.243, III 1.432, IV 1, rev 3.939; lever: central; final drive: hypoid bevel; axle ratio: 4.110; width of rims: 5''; tyres: 165 SR x 13.

PERFORMANCE max speed: 86 mph, 138 km/h; power-weight ratio: 4-dr. limousines 36.6 lb/hp (49.8 lb/kW), 16.6 kg/hp (22.6 kg/kW); carrying capacity: 937 lb, 425 kg - 4-dr. limousines 893 lb, 405 kg; acceleration: standing ¼ mile 21 sec, 0-50 mph (0-80 km/h) 12 sec; speed in direct drive at 1,000 rpm: 23.7 mph, 38.1 km/h; consumption: 31.4 m/imp gal, 26.1 m/US gal, 9 l x 100 km.

CHASSIS integral; front suspension: independent, wish-bones, coil springs, anti-roll bar, telescopic dampers; rear: rigid axle (torque tube), trailing radius arms, transverse linkage bar, coil springs, anti-roll bar, telescopic dampers.

STEERING rack-and-pinion; turns lock to lock: 4.

BRAKES front disc, rear drum, servo; lining area: front 22.9 sq in, 148 sq cm, rear 47.1 sq in, 304 sq cm, total 70 sq in, 452 sq cm.

ELECTRICAL EQUIPMENT 12 V; 36 Ah battery; 45 A alter-nator; Bosch or Delco Remy distributor; 2 headlamps.

DIMENSIONS AND WEIGHT wheel base: 99.21 in, 252 cm; front and rear tracks: 54.13 in, 137 cm; length: 170.12 in, 432 cm; width: 65.75 in, 167 cm; height: 54.33 in, 138 cm; ground clearance: 5.12 in, 13 cm; weight: 2-dr. limousines 1,973 lb, 895 kg - 4-dr. limousines 2,018 lb, 915 kg; turn-ing circle: 33.1 ft, 10.1 m; fuel tank: 11 imp gal, 13.2 US gal, 50 l.

BODY 5 seats, separate front seats, adjustable backrests.

PRACTICAL INSTRUCTIONS fuel: 98 oct petrol; oil: engine 4.8 imp pt, 5.7 US pt, 2.7 l, SAE 20W-30, change every 6,200 miles, 10,000 km - gearbox 1.1 imp pt, 1.3 US pt, 0.6 l, SAE 80, no change recommended - final drive 1.1 imp pt, 1.3 US pt, 0.6 l, SAE 90, no change recommended; greasing: none; sparking plug: 200°; tappet clearances (hot): inlet 0.006 in, 0.15 mm, exhaust 0.010 in, 0.25 mm; valve timing: 46° 90° 70° 30°; tyre pressure: front 24 psi, 1.7 atm, rear 24 psi, 1.7 atm.

OPTIONALS 185/70 SR x 13 tyres with 5.5'' wide rims; 44 Ah battery; 55 Ah battery; sunshine roof; heated rear window headrests; halogen headlamps; vinyl roof; head-lamps with wiper-washers; metallic spray; SR equipment.

60 hp power team

See 55 hp power team, except for:

ENGINE compression ratio: 9:1; max power (DIN): 60 hp (44.2 kW) at 5,400 rpm; max torque (DIN): 65 lb ft, 9 kg m (88.3 Nm) at 2,600-3,400 rpm; 50.2 hp/l (36.9 kW/l).

PERFORMANCE max speed: 88 mph, 142 km/h; power-weight ratio: 4-dr. limousines 33.5 lb/hp (45.6 lb/kW), 15.2 kg/hp (20.7 kg/kW); consumption: 33.2 m/imp gal, 27.7 m/US gal, 8.5 l x 100 km.

60 hp (1,584) power team

See 55 hp power team, except for:

ENGINE 96.7 cu in, 1,584 cc (3.35 x 2.75 in, 85 x 69.8 mm); compression ratio: 8:1; max power (DIN): 60 hp (44.2 kW) at 5,000 rpm; max torque (DIN): 76 lb ft, 10.5 kg m (103 Nm) at 3,000-3,400 rpm; max engine rpm: 6,000; 37.9 hp/l (27.9 kW/l); 5 crankshaft bearings; valves: overhead, in line, rockers; camshafts: 1, overhead; lubricating system: 6.7 imp pt, 8 US pt, 3.8 l; cooling system: 11.1 imp pt, 13.3 US pt, 6.3 l.

TRANSMISSION gearbox ratios: I 3.640, II 2.120, III 1.366, IV 1, rev 3.522; axle ratio: 3.700.

PERFORMANCE max speed: 90 mph, 145 km/h; power-weight ratio: 4-dr. limousines 35.6 lb/hp (48.3 lb/kW), 16.1 kg/hp (21.9 kg/kW); acceleration: standing ¼ mile 20 sec, 0-50 mph (0-80 km/h) 11 sec; speed in direct drive at 1,000 rpm: 21.3 mph, 34.3 km/h; consumption: 26.4 m/imp gal, 22 m/US gal, 10.7 l x 100 km.

DIMENSIONS AND WEIGHT weight: 2-dr. limousines 2,095 lb, 950 kg - 4-dr. limousines 2,139 lb, 970 kg.

OPEL Ascona 4-dr Limousine

60 HP POWER TEAM

PRACTICAL INSTRUCTIONS fuel: 92 oct petrol; oil: engine 6.7 imp pt, 8 US pt, 3.8 l, SAE 20W-30, change every 6,200 miles, 10,000 km - gearbox 1.9 imp pt, 2.3 US pt, 1.1 l, SAE 80, no change recommended - final drive 1,9 imp pt, 2.3 US pt, 1.1 l, SAE 90, no change recommended; tappet clearances (hot): inlet 0.012 in, 0.30 mm; exhaust 0.012 in, 0.30 mm; valve timing: 44° 86° 84° 46°.

OPTIONALS Opel automatic transmission with 3 ratios (I 2.400, II, 1.480, III 1, rev 1.920), max ratio of converter at stall 2.5, 3.670 axle ratio, max speed 87 mph, 140 km/h, consumption 24.6 m/imp gal, 20.5 m/US gal, 11.5 l x 100 km; 55 A alternator; air-conditioning.

75 hp power team

See 60 hp (1,584 cc) power team, except for:

ENGINE 115.8 cu in, 1,897 cc (3.66 x 2.75 in, 93 x 69.8 mm); compression ratio: 7.9:1; max power (DIN): 75 hp (55.2 kW) at 4,800 rpm; max torque (DIN): 98 lb ft, 13.5 kg m (132.4 Nm) at 2,200-3,400 rpm; max engine rpm: 5,200; 39.5 hp/l (29.1 kW/l); cooling system: 10.4 imp pt, 12.5 US pt, 5.9 l.

TRANSMISSION axle ratio: 3.670.

PERFORMANCE max speed: 98 mph, 157 km/h; power-weight ratio: 4-dr. limousines 29.4 lb/hp (39.9 lb/kW), 13.3 kg/hp (18.1 kg/kW).

ELECTRICAL EQUIPMENT 44 Ah battery.

DIMENSIONS AND WEIGHT weight: 2-dr. limousines 2,161 lb, 980 kg - 4-dr. limousines 2,205 lb, 1,000 kg.

OPTIONALS with Opel automatic transmission, max speed 95 mph, 152 km/h.

90 hp power team

See 60 hp (1,584 cc) power team, except for:

ENGINE 120.8 cu in, 1,979 cc (3.74 x 2.75 in, 95 x 69.8 mm); compression ratio: 8:1; max power (DIN): 90 hp (66.2 kW) at 5,200 rpm; max torque (DIN): 105 lb ft, 14.5 kg m (149 Nm) at 3,800 rpm; max engine rpm: 5,500; 45.4 hp/l (33.4 kW/l); 5 crankshaft bearings; valves: hydraulic tappets; 1 GMF Varajet II downdraught single barrel carburettor; cooling system: 10.9 imp pt, 13.1 US pt, 6.2 l.

TRANSMISSION axle ratio: 3.670.

PERFORMANCE max speed: 104 mph, 167 km/h; power-weight ratio: 4-dr. limousines 24.5 lb/hp (33.3 lb/kW), 11.1 kg/hp (15.1 kg/kW); carrying capacity: 970 lb, 400 kg - 4-dr. limousines 926 lb, 420 kg; acceleration: standing ¼ mile 18 sec, 0-50 mph (0-80 km/h) 8 sec; speed in direct drive at 1,000 rpm: 21.1 mph, 34 km/h; consumption: 28.2 m/imp gal, 23.5 m/US gal, 10 l x 100 km.

BRAKES rear compensator; lining area: front 22.9 sq in, 148 sq cm, rear 62.8 sq in, 405 sq cm, total 85.7 sq in, 553 sq cm.

ELECTRICAL EQUIPMENT 44 Ah battery.

DIMENSIONS AND WEIGHT weight: 2-dr. limousines 2,161 lb, 980 kg - 4-dr. limousines 2,205 lb, 1,000 kg.

PRACTICAL INSTRUCTIONS fuel: 98 oct petrol.

OPTIONALS with Opel automatic transmission; max speed 101 mph, 162 km/h, consumption 26.4 m/imp gal, 22 m/US gal, 10.7 l x 100 km; limited slip differential.

100 hp power team

See 60 hp (1,584 cc) power team, except for:

ENGINE 120.8 cu in, 1,979 cc (3.74 x 2.75 in, 95 x 69.8 mm); compression ratio: 9:1; max power (DIN): 100 hp (73.6 kW) at 5,400 rpm; max torque (DIN): 111 lb ft, 15.3 kg m (150 Nm) at 3,800 rpm; 50.5 hp/l (37.2 kW/l); valves: hydraulic tappets; 1 GMF Varajet II downdraught single barrel carburettor; cooling system: 10.9 imp pt, 13.1 US pt, 6.2 l.

TRANSMISSION axle ratio: 3.440.

PERFORMANCE max speed: 109 mph, 175 km/h; power-weight ratio: 4-dr. limousines 22 lb/hp (29.9 lb/kW), 10 kg/hp (13.6 kg/kW); speed in direct drive at 1,000 rpm: 18.1 mph, 29.2 km/h; consumption: 28.2 m/imp gal, 23.5 m/US gal, 10 l x 100 km.

BRAKES rear compensator; lining area: front 22.9 sq in, 148 sq cm, rear 62.8 sq in, 405 sq cm, total 85.7 sq in, 553 sq cm.

ELECTRICAL EQUIPMENT 44 Ah battery.

OPEL Ascona " Berlina " 4-dr Limousine

DIMENSIONS AND WEIGHT weight: 2-dr. limousines 2,161 lb, 980 kg - 4-dr. limousines 2,205 lb, 1,000 kg.

PRACTICAL INSTRUCTIONS fuel: 98 oct petrol; valve timing: 32° 90° 72° 50°.

OPTIONALS with Opel automatic transmission, max speed 106 mph, 170 km/h, consumption 26.4 m/imp gal, 22 m/US gal, 10.7 l x 100 km.

58 hp (Diesel) power team

See 60 hp (1,584) power team, except for:

ENGINE Diesel; 121.9 cu in, 1,998 cc (3.41 x 3.35 in, 86.5 x 85 mm); compression ratio: 22:1; max power (DIN): 58 hp (43 kW) at 4,200 rpm; max torque (DIN): 85 lb ft, 11.7 kg m (114.7 Nm) at 2,400 rpm; max engine rpm: 4,600; 29.0 hp/l (21.5 kW/l); lubrication: 9.7 imp pt, 11.6 US pt, 5.5 l; Bosch injection system; cooling system: 20.2 imp pt, 24.3 US pt, 11.5 l.

TRANSMISSION axle ratio: 3.670.

PERFORMANCE max speed: 84 mph, 135 km/h; power-weight ratio: 40.6 lb/hp, (54.8 lb/kW), 18.4 kg/hp (24.6 kg/kW); consumption: 31.4 m/imp gal, 26.1 m/US gal, 9 l x 100 km.

BRAKES lining area: total 85.7 sq in, 553 sq cm.

ELECTRICAL EQUIPMENT 44 Ah batery..

DIMENSIONS AND WEIGHT weight: 2,359 lb, 1,070 kg

BODY heated rear window.

PRACTICAL INSTRUCTIONS fuel: Diesel oil; oil: engine 9.7 imp pt, 11.6 US pt, 5.5 l; tappet clearances (hot): inlet 0.008 in, 0.20 mm, exhaust 0.012 in, 0.30 mm; valve timig: 24° 76° 48° 27°.

Manta Series

PRICES EX WORKS:

1 1.2 2-dr Coupé	DM	12.625
2 1.2 L 2-dr Coupé	DM	13.445
3 1.2 « Berlinetta » 2-dr Coupé	DM	14.265
4 1.6 2-dr Coupé	DM	13.065
5 1.6 L 2-dr Coupé	DM	13.885
6 1.6 « Berlinetta » 2-dr Coupé	DM	14.705
7 1.6 CC 2-dr Hatchback Coupé	DM	13.460
8 1.6 CC L 2-dr Hatchback Coupé	DM	14.280
9 1.6 CC « Berlinetta » 2-dr Hatchback Coupé	DM	15.100
10 2.0 E Coupé	DM	16.143
11 2.0 E « Berlinetta » Coupé	DM	16.930
12 2.0 CC E 2-dr Hatchback Coupé	DM	16.538
13 2.0 CC E « Berlinetta » 2-dr Hatchback Coupé	DM	17.325
14 2.0 GT/E Coupé	DM	16.149
15 2.0 CC GT/E 2-dr Hatchback Coupé	DM	16.544

OPEL Ascona 2.0 LD 4-dr Limousine

for GB prices, see price index.

power team:	Standard for:	Optional for:
55 hp	—	1 to 3
60 hp	1 to 3	—
60 hp (1,584)	4 to 9	—
75 hp	—	4 to 9
90 hp	—	4 to 9
100 hp	—	4 to 9
110 hp	10 to 15	—

55 hp power team

ENGINE front, 4 stroke; 4 cylinders, in line; 76 cu in, 1,196 cc (3.11 x 2.40 in, 79 x 61 mm); compression ratio: 7.8:1; max power (DIN): 55 hp (40.5 kW) at 5,400 rpm; max torque (DIN): 62 lb ft, 8.5 kg m (83.4 Nm) at 3,400 rpm; max engine rpm: 5,800; 50.2 hp/l (36.9 kW/l); cast iron block and head; 3 crankshaft bearings; valves: overhead, push-rods and rockers; camshafts: 1, side, chain-driven; lubrication: gear pump, full flow filter, 4.8 imp pt, 5.7 US pt, 2.7 l; 1 Solex 35 PDSI downdraught single barrel carburettor; fuel feed: mechanical pump; antifreeze liquid cooled, 9 imp pt, 10.8 US pt, 5.1 l.

TRANSMISSION driving wheels: rear; clutch: single dry plate (diaphragm); gearbox: mechanical; gears: 4, fully synchronized; ratios: I 3.733, II 2.243, III 1.432, IV 1, rev 3.939; lever: central; final drive: hypoid bevel; axle ratio: 4.110; width of rims: 5''; tyres: 165 SR x 13.

PERFORMANCE max speed: 89 mph, 143 km/h; power-weight ratio: 37.1 lb/hp (50.4 lb/kW), 16.8 kg/hp (22.8 kg/kW); carrying capacity: 816 lb, 370 kg; acceleration: standing ¼ mile 21 sec, 0-50 mph (0-80 km/h) 12 sec; speed in direct drive at 1,000 rpm: 23.7 mph, 38.1 km/h; consumption: 32.5 m/imp gal, 27 m/US gal, 8.7 l x 100 km.

CHASSIS integral; front suspension: independent, wishbones (lower trailing links), coil springs, anti-roll bar, telescopic dampers; rear: rigid axle (torque tube), trailing radius arms, transverse linkage bar, coil springs, anti-roll bar, telescopic dampers.

STEERING rack-and-pinion; turns lock to lock: 4.

BRAKES front disc, rear drum, rear compensator, servo; lining area: front 22.9 sq in, 148 sq cm, rear 47.1 sq in, 304 sq cm, total 70 sq in, 452 sq cm.

ELECTRICAL EQUIPMENT 12 V; 36 Ah battery; 45 A alternator; Bosch or Delco Remy distributor; 2 headlamps.

DIMENSIONS AND WEIGHT wheel base: 99.13 in, 252 cm; tracks: 54.33 in, 138 cm front, 54.13 in, 137 cm rear; length: 175.39 in, 444 cm; width: 65.75 in, 167 cm; height: 52.36 in, 133 cm; ground clearance: 5.12 in, 13 cm; weight: 2,040 lb, 925 kg; turning circle: 33.8 ft, 10.3 m; fuel tank: 11 imp gal, 13.2 US gal, 50 l.

BODY coupé; 2 doors; 5 seats, separate front seats, adjustable backrests.

PRACTICAL INSTRUCTIONS fuel: 91 oct petrol; oil: engine 4.8 imp pt, 5.7 US pt, 2.7 l, SAE 20W-30, change every 6,200 miles, 10,000 km - gearbox 1.1 imp pt, 1.3 US pt, 0.6 l, SAE 80, no change recommended - final drive 1.1 imp pt, 1.3 US pt, 0.6 l, SAE 90, no change recommended; greasing: none; sparking plug: 200°; tappet clearances (hot): inlet 0.006 in, 0.15 mm, exhaust 0.010 in, 0.25 mm; valve timing: 46° 90° 70° 30°; tyre pressure: front 24 psi, 1.7 atm, rear 24 psi, 1.7 atm.

OPTIONALS 185/70 SR x 13 tyres with 5.5'' wide rims; 44 or 55 Ah battery; heated rear window; sunshine roof; headrests; metallic spray; halogen headlamps; vinyl roof; headlamps with wiper-washers; air-conditioning; SR equipment.

60 hp power team

See 55 hp power team, except for:

ENGINE compression ratio: 9:1; max power (DIN): 60 hp (44.2 kW) at 5,400 rpm; max torque (DIN): 65 lb ft, 9 kg m (88.3 Nm) at 2,600-3,400 rpm; 50.2 hp/l (36.9 kW/l).

PERFORMANCE max speed: 91 mph, 147 km/h; power-weight ratio: 35 lb/hp (46.1 lb/kW), 15.4 kg/hp (20.9 kg/kW); consumption: 33.2 m/imp gal, 27.7 m/US gal, 8.5 l x 100 km.

PRACTICAL INSTRUCTIONS fuel: 98 oct petrol.

60 hp (1,584 cc) power team

See 55 hp power team, except for:

ENGINE 96.7 cu in, 1,584 cc (3.35 x 2.75 in, 85 x 69.8 mm); compression ratio: 8:1; max power (DIN): 60 hp (44.2 kW) at 5,000 rpm; max torque (DIN): 76 lb ft, 10.5 kg m (103 Nm) at 3,000-3,400 rpm; max engine rpm: 6,000; 37.9 hp/l (27.9 kW/l); 5 crankshaft bearings; valves: overhead, in

OPEL Manta CC L 2-dr Hatchback Coupé

line, rockers; camshafts: 1, overhead; lubricating system: 6.7 imp pt, 8 US pt, 3.8 l; cooling system: 11.4 imp pt, 13.7 US pt, 6.5 l.

TRANSMISSION gearbox ratios: I 3.640, II 2.120, III 1.336, IV 1, rev 3.522; axle ratio: 3.700.

PERFORMANCE max speed: 93 mph, 150 km/h; power-weight ratio: 36 lb/hp (48.9 lb/kW), 16.3 kg/hp (22.2 kg/kW); acceleration: standing ¼ mile 20 sec, 0-50 mph (0-80 km/h) 11 sec; speed in direct drive at 1,000 rpm: 21.3 mph, 34.3 km/h; consumption: 28.2 m/imp gal, 23.5 m/US gal, 10 l x 100 km.

DIMENSIONS AND WEIGHT weight: 2,161 lb, 980 kg.

PRACTICAL INSTRUCTIONS oil: engine 6.7 imp pt, 8 US pt, 3.8 l, SAE 20W-30, change every 6,200 miles, 10,000 km - gearbox 1.9 imp pt, 2.3 US pt, 1.1 l, SAE 90, no change recommended; tappet clearances (hot): inlet 0.012 in, 0.30 mm, exhaust 0.012 in, 0.30 mm; valve timing: 44° 86° 84° 46°.

OPTIONALS Opel automatic transmission with 3 ratios (I 2.400, II 1.480, III 1, rev 1.920), max ratio of converter at stall 2.5, 3.670 axle ratio, max speed 90 mph, 145 km/h, consumption 26.4 m/imp gal, 22 m/US gal, 10.7 l x 100 km.

75 hp power team

See 60 hp (1,584 cc) power team, except for:

ENGINE 115.8 cu in, 1,897 cc (3.66 x 2.75 in, 93 x 69.8 mm); compression ratio: 7.9:1; max power (DIN): 75 hp (55.2 kW) at 4,800 rpm; max torque (DIN): 98 lb ft, 13.5 kg m (132.4 Nm) at 2,200-3,400 rpm; max engine rpm: 5,200; 39.5 hp/l (29.1 kw/l); cooling system: 10.4 imp pt, 12.5 US pt, 5.9 l.

TRANSMISSION axle ratio: 3.670.

PERFORMANCE max speed: 101 mph, 162 km/h; power-weight ratio: 29.4 lb/hp (39.9 lb/kW), 13.3 kg/hp (18.1 kg/kW); consumption: 27.7 m/imp gal, 23.1 m/US gal, 10.2 l x 100 km.

BRAKES lining area: front 22.9 sq in, 148 sq cm, rear 62.8 sq in, 405 sq cm, total 85.7 sq in, 553 sq cm.

ELECTRICAL EQUIPMENT 44 Ah battery.

DIMENSIONS AND WEIGHT weight: 2,205 lb, 1,000 kg.

OPTIONALS with Opel automatic transmission, max speed 97 mph, 157 km/h, consumption 25.7 m/imp gal, 21.4 m/US gal, 11 l x 100 km.

90 hp power team

See 60 hp (1,584 cc) power team, except for:

ENGINE 115.8 cu in, 1,897 cc (3.74 x 2.75 in, 95 x 69.8 mm); compression ratio: 8:1; max power (DIN): 90 hp (66.2 kW) at 5,200 rpm; max torque (DIN): 109 lb ft, 15 kg m (147.1 Nm) at 2,600-3,800 rpm; 47.7 hp/l (34.9 kW/l); 1 GMF Vara Jet II downdraught carburettor; cooling system: 11.3 imp pt, 13.5 US pt, 6.4 l.

OPEL Manta GT/E Coupé

TRANSMISSION axle ratio: 3.670.

PERFORMANCE max speed: 107 mph, 172 km/h; power-weight ratio: 24.5 lb/hp (33.3 lb/kW), 11.1 kg/hp (15.1 kg/kW); acceleration: standing ¼ mile 18 sec, 0-50 mph (0-80 km/h) 8 sec; speed in direct drive at 1,000 rpm: 21.1 mph, 34 km/h; consumption: 31.4 m/imp gal, 26.1 m/US gal, 9 l x 100 km.

BRAKES lining area: front 22.9 sq in, 148 sq cm, rear 62.8 sq in, 405 sq cm, total 85.7 sq in, 553 sq cm.

ELECTRICAL EQUIPMENT 44 Ah battery.

DIMENSIONS AND WEIGHT weight: 2,205 lb, 1,000 kg.

PRACTICAL INSTRUCTIONS fuel: 98 oct petrol.

OPTIONALS with Opel automatic transmission, max speed 104 mph, 167 km/h, consumption 29.1 m/imp gal, 24.2 m/US gal, 9.7 x 100 km; limited slip differential.

100 hp power team

See 60 hp (1,584 cc) power team, except for:

ENGINE 120.8 cu in, 1,979 cc (3.74 x 2.75 in, 95 x 69.8 mm); compression ratio: 9:1; max power (DIN): 100 hp (73.6 kW) at 5,400 rpm; max torque (DIN): 111 lb ft, 15.3 kg m (150 Nm) at 3,800 rpm; 50.5 hp/l (37.2 kW/l); valves: hydraulic tappets; 1 GMF Varajet II downdraught single barrel carburettor; cooling system: 10.9 imp pt, 13.1 US pt, 6.2 l.

TRANSMISSION axle ratio: 3.440; tyres: 165 HR x 13.

PERFORMANCE max speed: 112 mph, 180 km/h; power-weight ratio: 22 lb/hp (29.9 lb/kW), 10 kg/hp (13.6 kg/kW); speed in direct drive at 1,000 rpm: 20.7 mph, 33.3 km/h; consumption: 31.4 m/imp gal, 26.1 m/US gal, 9 l x 100 km.

BRAKES lining area: front 22.9 sq in, 148 sq cm, rear 62.8 sq in, 405 sq cm, total 85.7 sq in, 553 sq cm.

ELECTRICAL EQUIPMENT 44 Ah battery.

DIMENSIONS AND WEIGHT weight: 2,205 lb, 1,000 kg.

PRACTICAL INSTRUCTIONS fuel: 98 oct petrol; valve timing: 32° 90° 72° 50°.

OPTIONALS with Opel automatic transmission, max speed 109 mph, 175 km/h, consumption 29.1 m/imp gal, 24.2 m/US gal, 9.7 l x 100 km; 185/70 HR x 13 tyres with 5.5'' wide rims.

110 hp power team

See 60 hp (1,584 cc) power team, except for:

ENGINE 120.8 cu in, 1,979 cc (3.74 x 2.75 in, 95 x 69.8 mm); compression ratio: 9.4:1; max power (DIN): 110 hp (81 kW) at 5,400 rpm; max torque (DIN): 117 lb ft, 16.2 kg m (158.9 Nm) at 3,400 rpm; max engine rpm: 6,000; 55.6 hp/l (40.9 kW/l); valves: hydraulic tappets; Bosch L-Jetronic electronic injection; cooling system: 10.9 imp pt, 13.1 US pt, 6.2 l.

TRANSMISSION axle ratio: 3.440; width of rims: E, cc E models S.S''-GT/E 6''; tyres: 185/70 HR x 13.

PERFORMANCE max speed: 116 mph, 187 km/h; power-weight ratio: 20 lb/hp (27.2 lb/kW) 9.1 kg/hp (12.3 kg/kW) - Manta GT/E 20.2 lb/hp (27.5 lb/kW), 9.2 kg/hp (12.5 kg/kW) - Manta cc E, cc GT/E 20.8 lb/hp (28.3 lb/kW), 9.4 kg/hp (12.8 kg/kW); speed in direct drive at 1,000 rpm: 19.6 mph, 31.5 km/h; consumption: 31.4 m/imp gal, 26.1 m/US gal, 9 l x 100 km.

BRAKES lining area: front 22.9 sq in, 148 sq cm, rear 62.8 sq in, 405 sq cm, total 85.7 sq in, 553 sq cm.

ELECTRICAL EQUIPMENT 44 Ah battery.

DIMENSIONS AND WEIGHT weight: Manta E 2,205 lb, 1,000 kg - Manta GT/E 2,227 lb, 1,010 kg - Manta cc E, cc GT/E 2,293 lb, 1,040 kg.

PRACTICAL INSTRUCTIONS fuel: 98 oct petrol; valve timing: 34° 88° 74° 48°.

OPTIONALS with Opel automatic transmission, max speed 113 mph, 182 km/h, consumption 29.1 m/imp gal, 24.2 m/US gal, 9.7 l x 100 km; 195/70 HR x 13 tyres.

Rekord Series

PRICES EX WORKS:

1	2-dr Limousine	DM	14,275*
2	4-dr Limousine	DM	14,865*
3	3-dr Caravan	DM	14,855*
4	5-dr Caravan	DM	15,445*
5	L 2-dr Limousine	DM	15,090*
6	L 4-dr Limousine	DM	15,525*
7	L 5-dr Caravan	DM	16,260*
8	« Berlina » 2-dr Limousine	DM	15,849*
9	« Berlina » 4-dr Limousine	DM	16,284*

For GB prices, see price index.

For 90 hp engine add DM 495; for 100 hp engine add DM 635; for 110 hp engine add DM 2,093; for 65 hp Diesel engine add DM 3,268.

Power team:	Standard for:	Optional for:
60 hp	—	all
75 hp	all	—
90 hp	—	all
100 hp	—	all
110 hp	—	all
65 hp (Diesel)	all	—

60 hp power team

ENGINE front, 4 stroke; 4 cylinders, in line; 103.6 cu in, 1,698 cc (3.46 x 2.75 in, 88 x 69.8 mm); compression ratio: 8:1; max power (DIN): 60 hp (44.2 kW) at 4,800 rpm; max torque (DIN): 83 lb ft, 11.4 kg m (111.8 Nm) at 2,200-3,000 rpm; max engine rpm: 5,000; 35.3 hp/l (26 kW/l); cast iron block and head; 5 crankshaft bearings; valves: overhead, in line, rockers; camshafts: 1, overhead; lubrication: gear pump, full flow filter, 6.7 imp pt, 8 US pt, 3.8 l; 1 Solex 35 PDSI downdraught carburettor; fuel feed: mechanical pump; anti-freeze liquid cooled, 11.1 imp pt, 13.3 US pt, 6.3 l.

TRANSMISSION driving wheels: rear; clutch: single dry plate (diaphragm); gearbox: mechanical; gears: 4, fully synchronized; ratios: I 3.640, II 2.120, III 1.336, IV 1, rev 3.522; lever: central; final drive: hypoid bevel; axle ratio: 3.890; width of rims: 5.5''; tyres: 175 SR x 14.

PERFORMANCE max speed: 91 mph, 146 km/h; st. wagons 89 mph, 143 km/h; power-weight ratio: 4-dr. limousines 41 lb/hp (55.6 lb/kW), 18.6 kg/hp (25.2 kg/kW); speed in direct drive at 1,000 rpm: 18.3 mph, 29.4 km/h; consumption: 26.9 m/imp gal, 22.4 m/US gal, 10.5 l x 100 km - st. wagons 24.6 m/imp gal, 20.5 m/US gal, 11.5 l x 100 km.

CHASSIS integral; front suspension: independent, wishbones, lower trailing links, coil springs, anti-roll bar, telescopic dampers; rear: rigid axle, trailing lower radius arms, upper torque arms, transverse linkage bar, coil springs, anti-roll bar, telescopic dampers.

STEERING recirculating ball; turns lock to lock: 4.

BRAKES front disc (diameter 9.37 in, 23.8 cm), rear drum, servo; lining area: total 85.7 sq in, 553 sq cm.

ELECTRICAL EQUIPMENT 12 V; 44 Ah battery; 45 A alternator; Bosch distributor; 2 headlamps.

DIMENSIONS AND WEIGHT wheel base: 105.04 in, 267 cm; tracks: 56.34 in, 143 cm front, 55.59 in, 141 cm rear; length: 108.75 in, 459 cm - st. wagons 181.81 in, 462 cm; width: 68.03 in, 173 cm; height: 55.71 in, 141 cm - st. wagons 56.69 in, 144 cm; ground clearance: 5.12 in, 13 cm; weight: 2-dr. limousines 2,414 lb, 1,095 kg - 4-d limousines 2,459 lb, 1,115 kg - 3-dr. Caravan 2,514 lb, 1,14 kg - 5-dr. Caravan 2,569 lb, 1,165 kg; turning circle: 37. ft, 11.4 m: fuel tank: 15.4 imp gal, 18.5 US gal, 70 l.

BODY 5 seats, separate front seats, reclining backrests heated rear window.

PRACTICAL INSTRUCTIONS fuel: 92 oct petrol; oil: engin 6.7 imp pt, 8 US pt, 3.8 l, SAE 20W-30, change ever 6,200 miles, 10,000 km - gearbox 1.9 imp pt, 2.3 US pt, 1.1 SAE 80, no change recommended - final drive 1.9 im pt, 2.3 US pt, 1.1 l, SAE 90, no change recommended greasing: none; sparking plug: 200°; tappet clearances (hot) inlet 0.012 in, 0.30 mm, exhaust 0.012 in, 0.30 mm; valv timing: 44° 86° 84° 46°; tyre pressure: front 24 psi, 1. atm, rear 25 psi, 1.8 atm.

OPTIONALS 185/70 SR x 14 tyres with 5.5'' wide rims sunshine roof: headrests: 55 Ah battery; 55 A alternator halogen headlamps; metallic spray; headlamps with wipe washers; rear window wiper-washer for st. wagons only

75 hp power team

See 60 hp power team, except for:

ENGINE 115.8 cu in, 1,897 cc (3.66 x 2.75 in, 93 x 69.8 mm) compression ratio: 7.9:1; max power (DIN): 75 hp (55 kW) at 4,800 rpm; max torque (DIN): 98 lb ft, 13.5 kg

OPEL Rekord " Berlina " Diesel

OPEL Rekord L 5-dr Caravan

OPEL Rekord (Diesel engine)

(132.4 Nm) at 2,200-3,400 rpm; 39.5 hp/l (29.1 kW/l); cooling system: 10.9 imp pt, 13.1 US pt, 6.2 l.

TRANSMISSION axle ratio: 3.890.

PERFORMANCE max speed: 96 mph, 155 km/h - st. wagons 94 mph, 152 km/h; power-weight ratio: 4-dr. limousines 32.8 lb/hp (44.5 lb/kW), 14.9 kg/hp (20.2 kg/kW); speed in direct drive at 1,000 rpm: 19.4 mph, 31.2 km/h; consumption: 25.7 m/imp gal, 21.4 m/US gal, 11 l x 100 km - st. wagons 24.6 m/imp gal, 20.5 m/US gal, 11.5 l x 100 km.

OPTIONALS Opel automatic transmission with 3 ratios (I 2.400, II 1.480, III 1, rev. 1.920), max ratio of converter at stall 2.5, possible manual selection, max speed 93 mph, 150 km/h (st. wagons 91 mph, 147 km/h), consumption 24.6 m/imp gal, 20.5 m/US gal, 11.5 l x 100 km - st. wagons 23.5 m/imp gal, 19.6 m/US gal, 12 l x 100 km.

90 hp power team

See 75 hp power team, except for:

ENGINE 120.8 cu in, 1,979 cc (3.74 x 2.75 in, 95 x 69.8 mm); compression ratio: 8:1; max power (DIN): 90 hp (66.2 kW) at 5,200 rpm; max torque (DIN): 105 lb ft, 14.5 kg m (142.2 Nm) at 3,000-3,800 rpm; 45.4 hp/l (33.4 kW/l); valves: hydraulic tappets; 1 varajet II downdraught carburettor; cooling system: 11.1 imp pt, 13.3 US pt, 6.3l.

PERFORMANCE max speed: 103 mph, 165 km/h - st. wagons 101 mph, 162 km/h; power-weight ratio: 4-dr. limousines 27.3 lb/hp (37 lb/kW), 12.4 kg/hp (16.8 kg/kW); speed in direct drive at 1,000 rpm: 20.4 mph, 32.8 km/h; consumption: 24.6 m/imp gal, 20.5 m/US gal, 11.5 l x 100 km - st. wagons 23.5 m/imp gal, 19.6 m/US gal, 12 l x 100 km.

BRAKES rear compensator (for st. wagons only).

PRACTICAL INSTRUCTIONS valve timing: 32° 90° 72° 50°.

OPTIONALS with Opel automatic transmission, max speed 99 mph, 160 km/h - st. wagons 97 mph, 157 km/h, consumption 23.2 m/imp gal, 19.3 m/US gal 12.2 l x 100 km - st. wagons 22.2 m/imp gal, 18.5 m/US gal, 12.7 l x 100 km; limited slip differential.

100 hp power team

See 75 hp power team, except for:

ENGINE 120.8 cu in, 1,979 cc (3.74 x 2.75 in, 95 x 69.8 mm); compression ratio: 9:1; max power (DIN): 100 hp (73.6 kW) at 5,200 rpm; max torque (DIN): 114 lb ft, 15.8 kg m (155 Nm) at 3,400-3,800 rpm; max engine rpm: 5,500; 50.5 hp/l (37.2 kW/l); valves: hydraulic tappets; 1 Zenith 35/40 INAT downdraught carburettor; cooling system: 11.1 imp pt, 13.3 US pt, 6.3 l.

PERFORMANCE max speed: 107 mph, 173 km/h - st. wagons 106 mph, 170 km/h; power-weight ratio: 4-dr. limousines 24.6 lb/hp (33.3 lb/kW), 11.1 kg/hp (15.1 kg/kW); speed in direct drive at 1,000 rpm: 19.8 mph, 31.8 km/h; consumption: 27.7 m/imp gal, 23.1 m/US gal, 10.2 l x 100 km - st. wagons 26.4 m/imp gal, 22 m/US gal, 10.7 l x 100 km.

BRAKES rear compensator (for st. wagons only).

PRACTICAL INSTRUCTIONS fuel: 98 oct petrol; valve timing: 32° 90° 72° 50°.

OPTIONALS with Opel automatic transmission, max speed 104 mph, 168 km/h - st. wagons 103 mph, 165 km/h, consumption 25.7 m/imp gal, 21.4 m/US gal, 11 l x 100 km - st. wagons 24.6 m/imp gal, 20.5 m/US gal, 11.5 l x 100 km; limited slip differential.

110 hp power team

See 75 hp power team, except for:

ENGINE 120.8 cu in, 1,979 cc (3.74 x 2.75 in, 95 x 69.8 mm); compression ratio: 9.4:1; max power (DIN): 110 hp (81 kW) at 5,400 rpm; max torque (DIN): 117 lb ft, 16.2 kg m (158.9 Nm) at 3,000 rpm; max engine rpm: 6,000; 55.6 hp/l (40.9 kW/l); valves: hydraulic tappets; Bosch L-Jetronic electronic injection; cooling system: 16 imp pt, 19.2 US pt, 9.1 l.

PERFORMANCE max speed: 111 mph, 179 km/h - st. wagons 109 mph, 176 km/h; power-weight ratio: 4-dr. limousines 22.3 lb/hp (30.3 lb/kW), 10.1 kg/hp (13.8 kg/kW); speed in direct drive at 1,000 rpm: 18.6 mph, 30 km/h; consumption: 27.7 m/imp gal, 23.1 m/US gal, 10.2 l x 100 km - st. wagons 26.4 m/imp gal, 22 m/US gal, 10.7 l x 100 km.

BRAKES rear compensator (for st. wagons only).

PRACTICAL INSTRUCTIONS fuel: 98 oct petrol; valve timing: 34° 88° 74° 48°.

65 hp (Diesel) power team

See 60 hp power team, except for:

ENGINE Diesel; 137.9 cu in, 2,260 cc (3.62 x 3.35 in, 92 x 85 mm); compression ratio: 22:1; max power (DIN): 65 hp (48 kW) at 4,200 rpm; max torque (DIN): 12 lb ft, 12.9 kg m (126.5 Nm) at 2,500 rpm; max engine rpm: 4,600; 28.7 hp/l (21.2 kW/l); lubrication: 9.7 imp pt, 11.6 US pt; 5.5 l; Bosch injection system; cooling system: 20.2 imp pt, 24.3 US pt, 11.5 l.

TRANSMISSION axle ratio: 3.670.

PERFORMANCE max speed: 84 mph, 135 km/h; power-weight ratio: 4-dr. limousines 42.4 lb/hp (57.4 lb/kW), 19.2 kg/hp (26 kg/kW); speed in direct drive at 1,000 rpm: 18 mph, 29 km/h; consumption: 31.4 m/imp gal, 26.1 m/US gal, 9 l x 100 km.

ELECTRICAL EQUIPMENT 88 Ah battery; 55 A alternator.

DIMENSIONS AND WEIGHT height: 56.50 in, 143 cm; weight: 2-dr. limousine 2,712 lb, 1,230 kg - 4-dr. limousines 2,756 lb, 1,250 kg - 3-dr. Caravan 2,789 lb, 1,265 kg - 5-dr. Caravan 2,844 lb, 1,290 kg.

PRACTICAL INSTRUCTIONS fuel: Diesel oil; oil: engine 9.7 imp pt, 11.6 US pt, 5.5 l; tappet clearances (hot): inlet 0.008 in, 0.20 mm, exhaust 0.008 in, 0.20 mm; valve timing: 24° 76° 48° 27°; tyre pressure: front 28 psi, 2 atm, rear 28 psi, 2 atm.

VARIATIONS

(Only for Italy).
ENGINE 121.9 cu in, 1,998 cc (3.41 x 3.35 in, 86.5 x 85 mm), max power (DIN) 57 hp (42 kW) at 4,400 rpm, max torque (DIN) 83 lb ft, 11.5 kg m (112.8 Nm) at 2,200 rpm, 28.5 hp/l (21 kW/l).
PERFORMANCE max speed 81 mph, 130 km/h, power-weight ratio 4-dr. limousines 48.3 lb/hp (65.7 lb/kW), 21.9 kg/hp (29.8 kg/kW), consumption 37.7 m/imp gal, 31.4 m/US gal, 7.5 l x 100 km.

OPTIONALS with Opel automatic transmission, max speed 81 mph, 130 km/h, consumption 29.1 m/imp gal, 24.2 m/US gal, 9.7 l x 100 km; power steering; 185/70 SR x 14 tyres not available.

Commodore Series

PRICES EX WORKS:

1	2-dr Limousine	DM 16,765*
2	4-dr Limousine	DM 17,200*
3	« Berlina » 2-dr Limousine	DM 17,415*
4	« Berlina » 4-dr Limousine	DM 17,850*

OPEL Commodore " Berlina " 4-dr Limousine

115 hp power team

ENGINE front, 4 stroke; 6 cylinders, in line; 151.9 cu in, 2,490 cc (3.43 x 2.75 in, 87 x 69.8 mm); compression ratio: 9.2:1; max power (DIN): 115 hp (85 kW) at 5,200 rpm; max torque (DIN): 130 lb ft, 17.9 kg m (176 Nm) at 3,800-4,200 rpm; max engine rpm: 6,000; 46.1 hp/l (34.1 kW/l); cost iron block and head; 7 crankshaft bearings; valves: overhead in line hydraulic tappets; camshafts: 1, overhead; lubrication: gear pump, full flow filter, 9.7 imp pt, 11.6 US pt, 5.5 l; 1 Zenith 35/40 INAT downdraught carburettor; fuel feed: mechanical pump; anti-freeze liquid cooled, 17.6 imp pt, 21.1 US pt, 10 l.

TRANSMISSION driving wheels: rear; clutch: single dry plate (diaphragm); gearbox: mechanical; gears: 4, fully synchronized; ratios: I 3.640, II 2.120, III 1.336, IV 1, rev 3.522; lever: central; final drive: hypoid bevel; axle ratio: 3.70; width of rims: 65 x 14; tyres: 175 HR 14.

PERFORMANCE max speed: 112 mph, 180 km/h; power-weight ratio: 23 lb/hp, (31.1 lb/kW), 10.4 kg/hp (14.1 kg/kW); carrying capacity: 1,169 lb, 530 kg; speed in direct drive/top at 1,000 rpm: 20.8 mph, 33.5 km/h; consumption: 26.4 m/imp gal, 22 m/US gal, 10.7 l x 100 km.

CHASSIS integral; front suspension: independent, wishbones, lower trailing links, coil springs, anti-roll bar, telescopic dampers; rear: rigid axle, twin trailing radius arms, upper torque arms transverse linkage bar, coil springs, anti-roll bar, telescopic dampers.

STEERING recirculating ball; turns lock to lock: 4.5.

115 HP POWER TEAM

BRAKES front disc, rear drum, rear compensator, servo; lining area: total 87.4 sq in, 564 sq cm.

ELECTRICAL EQUIPMENT 12 V; 44 Ah battery; 55 A alternator; 2 halogen headlamps.

DIMENSIONS AND WEIGHT wheel base: 105.12 in, 267 cm; tracks: 56.85 in, 144 cm front, 56.77 in, 142 cm rear; length: 185.04 in, 470 cm; width: 68.11 in, 173 cm; height: 55.71 in, 141 cm; ground clearance: 55.71 in, 14 cm; weight: 2.645 lb, 1,200 kg; turning circle: 36.1 ft, 11.5 m; fuel tank: 14.3 imp gal, 17.2 US gal, 65 l.

BODY 5 seats, separate front seats, reclining backrests with headrests; heated rear window.

PRACTICAL INSTRUCTIONS fuel: 98 oct petrol; oil: engine 9.7 imp pt, 11.6 US pt 5.5 l, SAE 20W-30 change every 3,100 miles, 5000 km - gearbox 1.9 imp pt, 2.3 US pt, 1.1 l, SAE 80 no change raccommended; final drive 2.5 imp pt, 3 US pt, 1.4 l, SAE 90, no change raccommended; greasing: none; sparking plug: 200°; valve timing: 40° 88° 80° 48°; tyre pressure: front 28 psi, 2 atm, rear 30 psi, 2.2 atm.

OPTIONALS Opel automatic transmission with 3 ratios (I 2.400, II 1.480, III 1, rev 1.920); limited slip differential; light alloy wheels; 195/70 HR x 14 tyres; power steering; 55 Ah battery; rear seat headrests; sunshine roof; metallic spray; headlight washer; vinyl roof.

Senator Series

	£	DM
1 4 dr Limousine	—	23,380*
2 C 4-dr Limousine	—	25,340*
3 CD Automatic 4-dr Limousine	9.500	37.325*

For 150 hp engine add DM 805; for 180 hp engine add DM 4,030 (DM 3,800 for C models); for Opel Automatic transmission add DM 1,590.

Power team:	Standard for:	Optional for:
140 hp	1,2	—
150 hp	—	1,2
180 hp	3	1,2

140 hp power team

ENGINE front, 4 stroke, 6 cylioders, in line, 169.9 cu in, 2,784 cc (3.62 x 2.75 in, 92 x 69.8 mm); compression ratio: 9:1; max power (DIN): 140 hp (103 kW) at 5,200 rpm; max torque (DIN): 158 lb ft, 21.8 kg m (218 Nm) at 3.400 rpm; max engine rpm: 6,000; 50.2 hp/l (36.9 kW/l); cast iran block and head; 7 crankshaft bearings; valves: overhead in line hydraulic tappets; camshafts: 1, overhead; lubrication: gear pump, full flow filter, 9.7 imp pt, 11.6 US pt, 5.5 l; 1 DVG 4 A1 4-barrel downdraught carburettor; fuel feed: mechanical pump; cooling system 17.2 imp pt, 207 US pt, 9.8 l.

TRANSMISSION driving wheels: rear; clutch: single dry plate (diaphragm); gearbox: mechanical; gears: 4, fully synchronized; ratios: I 3.640, II 2.120, III 1.336, IV 1, rev 3.522; lever: central; final drive: hypoid bevel; axle ratio: 3.45; width of rims: 6 J x 14; tyres: 175 HR 14.

PERFORMANCE max speed: 118 mph, 190 km/h; power-weight ratio: 21.6 lb/hp (29.4 lb/kW), 9.8 kg/hp (13.3 kg/kW); carrying capacity: 1,158 lb, 525 kg; acceleration: 0-62 mph (0-100 km/h) 10 sec; consumption: 26.4 m/imp gal, 22 m/US gal, 10.7 l x 100 km.

CHASSIS integral; front suspension: independent, by Mc-Pherson, wishbones lower trailing links, coil springs, anti-roll bar, telescopic dampers; rear: independent, with semi-trailing arms, coil spring, anti-roll bar, telescopic dampers.

STEERING recirculating ball, servo; turns lock to lock: 4.

BRAKES disc lining area: total 40.9 sq in, 264 sq cm.

ELECTRICAL EQUIPMENT 12 V; 44 Ah battery; 55 A alternator; 2 halogen headlamps, fog lamps.

DIMENSIONS AND WEIGHT wheel base: 105.12 in, 267 cm; tracks: 56.85 in, 144 cm front, 57.87 in, 147 cm rear; length: 189.37 in, 481 cm; width: 68.11 in, 173 cm; height: 55.51 in, 141 cm; ground clearance: 55.71 in, 14 cm; weight: 3.032 lb, 1.375 kg; turning circle 35.4 ft, 10.8 m; fuel tank: 16.5 imp gal, 19.8 US gal, 75 l.

BODY saloon/sedan, 5 seats, separate front seats, reclining backrests, with headrests.

PRACTICAL INSTRUCTIONS fuel: 98 oct petrol; oil: engine 9.7 imp pt, 11.6 US pt, 5.5 l, SAE 20W-30 change every 3,100 miles, 5,000 km - gearbox 1.9 imp pt, 2.3 US pt, 1.1 SAE 80 no change recommended - final drive 2.5

OPEL Senator C 4-dr Limousine

imp pt, 3 US pt, 1.4 l, SAE 90 no change recommended; greasing: none sparking plug: AC 42-6 FS; valve timing: 32° 90° 72° 50°; tyre ressure: front 28 psi, 2 atm, rear 30 psi, 2.2 atm.

OPTIONALS Opel automatic transmission with 3 ratios (I 2.400, II 1.480, III 1, rev 1.920); 195/70 HR 14 Tyres; 65 J x 15 wheels, 205/60 VR 15 tyres.

150 hp power team

See 140 hp power team, except for:

ENGINE 181.1 cu in, 2,968 cc (3.74 x 2.75 in, 95 x 69.8 mm); compression ratio: 9.2:1; max power (DIN): 150 hp (110 kW) at 5,200 rpm; max torque (DIN): 170 lb ft, 23.5 kg m (230 Nm) at 3,400 rpm; 50.3 hp/l (37 kW/l); cooling system 18 imp pt, 21.6 US pt, 10.2 l.

TRANSMISSION ratios: I 3.855, II 2.203, III 1.402, IV 1, rev 4.269.

PERFORMANCE max speed: 120 mph, 193 km/h; power-weight ratio: 20.2 lb/hp, (27.5 lb/kW), 9.1 kg/hp (12.5 kg/kW); consumption: 24.6 m/imp gal, 20.5 m/US gal, 11.5 l x 100 km.

180 hp power team

See 140 hp power team, except for:

ENGINE compression ratio: 9.4:1; max power (DIN): 180 hp (132 kW) at 5,800 rpm; max torque (DIN): 180 lb ft, 24.8 kg m (248 Nm) at 4,500 rpm; 60.6 hp/l (44.4 kW/l); lubrication: injection system; cooling system 18 imp pt, 21.6 US pt, 10.2 l.

TRANSMISSION tyres: 195/70 R 14.

PERFORMANCE max speed: 130 mph, 210 km/h; power-weight ratio: 17.4 lb/hp, (23.8 lb/kW), 7.9 kg/hp (10.7 kg/kW); acceleration: 0-62 mph (0-100 km/h) 8.5 sec.

DIMENSIONS AND WEIGHT weight: 3,142 lb, 1,425 kg.

Monza Series

	£	DM
1 2-dr Hatchback Coupé	—	25,325*
2 C 2-dr Hatchback Coupé	9,762	26,290*

For 150 hp engine add DM 805; for 180 hp engine add DM 4,030 (DM 3,800 for C models); for Opel Automatic transmission add DM 1,590).

Power team:	Standard for:	Optional for:
140 hp	both	—
150 hp	—	both
180 hp	—	both

140 hp power team

ENGINE front, 4 stroke; 6 cylinders, in line, 169.9 cu in, 2,784 cc (3.62 x 2.75 in, 92 x 69.8 mm); compression ratio:

9:1; max power (DIN): 140 hp (103 kW) at 5,200 rpm; max torque (DIN): 158 lb ft, 21.8 kg m (218 Nm) a 3,400 rpm; max engine rpm: 6,000; 50.2 hp/l (36.9 kW/l); cast iron block and head; 7 crankshaft bearings; valves Overheead in line hydraulic tappets; camshafts: 1, over head; lubrication: gear pump, full flow filter, 9.7 imp p 11.6 US pt, 5.5 l; 1 DVG 4 A1 4-barrel downdraugh carburettor; fuel feed: mechanical pump; cooling syste 17.2 imp pt, 20.7 US pt, 9.8 l.

TRANSMISSION driving wheels: rear; clutch: single dr plate (diaphragm); gearbox: mechanical; gears: 4, full synchronized; ratios: I 3.640, II 2.120, III 1.336, IV 1 rev 3.522; lever: central; final drive: hypoid bevel; axl ratio: 3.45; width of rims: 6 J x 14; tyres: 175 HR 14

PERFORMANCE max speed: 121 mph, 195 km/h; powe weight ratio: 21.6 lb/hp (29.4 lb/kW), 9.8 kg/hp (13. kg/kW); carrying capacity: 1,158 lb, 525 kg; acceleratio 0-62 mph (0-180 km/h) 10 sec; consumption: 26.4 m/im gal, 22 m/US gal, 10.7 l x 100 km.

CHASSIS integral; front suspension: independent, by Mc Pherson, wishbones, lower trailing links, coil spring anti-roll bar, telescopic dampers; rear: independent wit semi-trailing arms, coil spring, anti-roll bar, telescopi damper.

STEERING recirculating ball, servo; turns lock to lock: 4

BRAKES disc, lining area: total 40.9 sq in, 264 sq cm.

ELECTRICAL EQUIPMENT 12 V; 44 Ah battery; 55 A a ternator; 2 halogen headlamps, fog lamps.

DIMENSIONS AND WEIGHT wheel base: 105,12 in, 26 cm; tracks: 56.85 in, 144 cm front, 57.87 in, 147 c rear; length: 134.65 in, 469 cm; width: 68.11 in, 173 cm height: 54.33 in, 138 cm; ground clearance: 55.71 in, 14 cm weight: 3,032 lb, 1,375 kg; turning circle: 35.4 ft, 10.8 m fuel tank: 15.4 imp gal, 18.5 US gal, 70 l.

BODY coupé, 4 seats, separate front seats, reclinin backrests, with headrests.

PRACTICAL INSTRUCTIONS fuel: 98 oct petrol; oil: engin 9.7 imp pt, 11.6 US pt, 5.5 l, SAE 20W-30, change ever 3,100 miles, 5,000 km - gearbox 1.9 imp pt, 2.3 US p 1.1 l, SAE 80 no change recommended - final drive 2. imp pt, 3 US pt, 1.4 l, SAE 90 no change recommende greasing: none; sparking plug: AC42-6FS; valve timin 32° 90° 72° 50°; tyre pressure: front 28 psi, 2 atm rear 30 psi, 2.2 atm.

OPTIONALS Opel automatic transmission with 3 ratio (I 2.400, II 1.480, III 1, rev 1.920); 195/70 HR 14 tyre 65 x 15 wheels, 205/60 VR 15 tyres.

150 hp power team

See 140 hp power team, except for:

ENGINE 181.1 cu in, 2,968 cc (3.74 x 2.75 in, 95 x 69. mm); compression ratio: 9.2:1; max power (DIN): 150 h (110 kW) at 5,200 rpm; max torque (DIN): 170 lb ft, 23. kg m (230 Nm) at 3,400 rpm; 50.3 hp/l (37 kW/l); coolin system 18 imp pt, 21.6 US pt, 10.2 l.

TRANSMISSION ratios: I 3.855, II 2.203, III 1.402, IV 1 rev 4.269.

OPEL Monza C 2-dr Hatchback Coupé

PERFORMANCE max speed: 123 mph, 198 km/h; power-weight ratio: 20.2 lb/hp (27.5 lb/kW), 9.1 kg/hp (12.5 kg/kW); consumption: 24.6 m/imp gal, 20.5 m/US gal, 11.5 l x 100 km.

180 hp power team

See 140 hp power team, except for:

ENGINE compression ratio: 9.4:1; max power (DIN): 180 hp (132 kW) at 5,800 rpm; max torque (DIN): 180 lb ft, 24.8 kg m (248 Nm) at 4.500 rpm; 60.6 hp/l (44.4 kW/l); lubrication: injection system; cooling system 18 imp pt, 21.6 US pt, 10.2 l.

TRANSMISSION tyres: 195/70 VR 14.

PERFORMANCE max speed: 134 mph, 215 km/h; power-weight ratio: 16.8 lb/hp (23 lb/kW), 7.6 kg/hp (10.4 kg/kW); acceleration: 0-60 mph (0-100 km/h), 8.5 sec.

PORSCHE   GERMANY FR

924

PRICE IN GB: £ 8,199*
PRICE EX WORKS: 26,850* marks

ENGINE Audi, front, 4 stroke; 4 cylinders, vertical, in line; 121.1 cu in, 1,984 cc (3.41 x 3.32 in, 86.5 x 84.4 mm); compression ratio: 9.3:1; max power (DIN): 125 hp (92 kW) at 5,800 rpm; max torque (DIN): 122 lb ft, 16.8 kg m (164.8 Nm) at 3,500 rpm; max engine rpm: 6,500; 63 hp/l (46.3 kW/l); cast iron block, light alloy head: 5 crankshaft bearings; valves: overhead, in line, thimble tappets; camshafts: 1, overhead, cogged belt; lubrication: gear pump, full flow filter, 8.8 imp pt, 10.6 US pt, 5 l; Bosch K-Jetronic injection system; fuel feed: electric pump; water-cooled, 14.1 imp pt, 16.9 US pt, 8 l, electric thermostatic fan.

TRANSMISSION driving wheels: rear; clutch: single dry plate; gearbox: rear, mechanical, in unit with differential; gears: 4 fully synchronized; ratios: I 3.600, II 2.125, III 1.360, IV 0.966, rev 3.500; lever: central; final drive: hypoid bevel; axle ratio: 3.444; width of rims: 6''; tyres: 185/70 HR x 14.

PERFORMANCE max speeds: (I) 35 mph, 56 km/h; (II) 60 mph, 96 km/h; (III) 93 mph, 150 km/h; (IV) 124 mph, 200 km/h; power-weight ratio: 19 lb/hp (26 lb/kW), 8.6 kg/hp (11.7 kg/kW); carrying capacity: 706 lb, 320 kg; speed in top at 1,000 rpm: 19.5 mph, 31.4 km/h; consumption: 36.7 m/imp gal, 30.5 m/US gal, 7.7 l x 100 km.

CHASSIS integral; front suspension: independent, by McPherson, lower wishbones, coil springs/telescopic damper struts; rear: independent, semi-trailing arms, transverse torsion bars, coil springs/telescopic damper struts.

STEERING rack-and-pinion.

BRAKES front disc, rear drum, 2 X circuits, servo; lining area: total 72.9 sq in, 470 sq cm.

ELECTRICAL EQUIPMENT 12 V; 45 Ah battery; 1,050 W alternator; Bosch electronic ignition; 4 headlamps (2 retractable).

DIMENSIONS AND WEIGHT wheel base: 94.49 in, 240 cm; tracks: 55.83 in, 142 cm front, 54.02 in, 137 cm rear; length: 165.35 in, 420 cm; width: 66.34 in, 168 cm; height: 50 in, 127 cm; weight: 2,381 lb, 1,080 kg; fuel tank: 13.6 imp gal, 16.4 US gal, 62 l.

BODY coupé; 2 doors; 2 + 2 seats, separate front seats, reclining backrests with built-in headrests; heated rear window; light alloy wheels.

PRACTICAL INSTRUCTIONS fuel: 98 oct petrol; oil: engine 8.8 imp pt, 10.6 US pt, 5 l, SAE 30W (summer), 20W (winter), Change every 6,100 miles, 10,000 km - gearbox and final drive 4.6 imp pt, 5.5 US pt, 2.6 l, SAE 80; greasing: none; sparking plug: 225°.

OPTIONALS automatic transmission, hydraulic torque converter and planetary gears with 3 ratios (I 2.551, II 1.448, III 1, rev 2.461), max ratio of converter at stall 2.1, possible manual selection, 3.454 axle ratio, max speed 121 mph, 195 km/h, consumption 29.7 m/imp gal, 24.8 m/US gal, 9.5 l x 100 km; 5-speed fully synchronized mechanical gearbox (I 2.780, II 1.720, III 1.210, IV 0.930, V 0.700, rev 2.500), 4.714 axle ratio; anti-roll bar on front and rear suspensions; headlamps with wiper-washers; metallic spray; air-conditioning; sunshine roof; fog lamps; 63 Ah battery.

---

924 (USA)

See 924, except for:

PRICE IN USA: $ 13,950*

ENGINE compression ratio: 8.5:1; max power (DIN): 112 hp (82.4 kW) at 5,750 rpm; max torque (DIN): 115 lb ft, 15.9 kg m (156 Nm) at 3,500 rpm; 56.5 hp/l (41.5 kW/l).

PERFORMANCE max speed: 119 mph, 192 km/h; power-weight ratio: 23 lb/hp (31.3 lb/kW), 10.4 kg/hp (14.2 kg/kW); carrying capacity: 507 lb, 230 kg.

DIMENSIONS AND WEIGHT length: 170.08 in, 432 cm; weight: 2,580 lb, 1,170 kg.

PRACTICAL INSTRUCTIONS fuel: 91 oct petrol.

OPTIONALS automatic transmission with 3.727 axle ratio.

924 Turbo

See 924, except for:

PRICE EX WORKS: DM 37,000*

ENGINE turbocharged; compression ratio: 7.5:1; max power (DIN): 170 hp (125.1 kW) at 5,500 rpm; max torque (DIN): 181 lb ft, 25 kg m (245.2 Nm) at 3,500 rpm; 85.7 hp/l (63.1 kW/l); lubrication: gear pump, full flow filter, dry sump, oil cooler, 9.7 imp pt, 11.6 US pt, 5.5 l; Bosch K-Jetronic fuel injection system with KKK exhaust turbocharger.

TRANSMISSION clutch: single dry plate, hydraulically controlled; gears: 5, fully synchronized; ratios: I 3.167, II 1.778, III 1.217, IV 0.931, V 0.706, rev 3.167; tyres: 185/70 VR x 15.

PERFORMANCE max speed: 140 mph, 225 km/h; power-weight ratio: 15.3 lb/hp (20.8 lb/kW), 6.9 kg/hp (9.4 kg/kW); consumption: 30.7 m/imp gal, 25.6 m/US gal, 9.2 l x 100 km.

CHASSIS (standard) anti-roll bar on front and rear suspensions.

DIMENSIONS AND WEIGHT rear track: 54.80 in, 139 cm; length: 165.83 in, 421 cm; weight: 2,602 lb, 1,180 kg.

PRACTICAL INSTRUCTIONS oil: engine 9.7 imp pt, 11.6 US pt, 5.5 l.

OPTIONALS 205/55 VR x 16 tyres with aluminum wheels.

911 SC Coupé

PRICE IN GB: £ 13,849*
PRICE EX WORKS: 42,950* marks

ENGINE rear, 4 stroke; 6 cylinders, horizontally opposed; 182.7 cu in, 2,994 cc (3.74 x 2.77 in, 95 x 70.4 mm); compression ratio: 8.5:1; max power (DIN): 180 hp (132.5 kW) at 5,500 rpm; max torque (DIN): 196 lb ft, 27 kg m (264.8 Nm) at 4,200 rpm; max engine rpm: 7,000; 60.1 hp/l (42.3 kW/l); light alloy block with cast iron liners, light alloy head; 8 crankshaft bearings; valves: overhead, Vee-

PORSCHE 924 Turbo

911 SC COUPÉ

slanted, rockers; camshafts: 1 per block, overhead, double cogged belt; lubrication: gear pump, full flow filter, dry sump, thermostatically-controlled oil cooler, 22.9 imp pt, 27.5 US pt, 13 l; Bosch K-Jetronic fuel injection system; fuel feed: electric pump; air-cooled.

TRANSMISSION driving wheels: rear; clutch: single dry plate; gearbox: mechanical; gears: 5, fully synchronized; ratios: I 3.181, II 1.833, III 1.261, IV 1, V 0.821, rev 3.325; lever: central; final drive: spiral bevel; axle ratio: 3.875; width of rims: 6'' front, 7'' rear; tyres: 185/70 VR x 15 front, 215/60 VR x 15 rear.

PERFORMANCE max speed: over 140 mph, 225 km/h; power-weight ratio: 14.2 lb/hp (19.3 lb/kW), 6.4 kg/hp (8.7 kg/kW); carrying capacity: 750 lb, 340 kg; speed in top at 1,000 rpm: 25 mph, 40 km/h; consumption: 25.7 m/imp gal, 21.4 m/US gal, 11 l x 100 km.

CHASSIS integral; front suspension: independent, by McPherson, coil springs/telescopic damper struts, longitudinal torsion bars, lower wishbones, anti-roll bar; rear: independent, semi-trailing arms, transverse torsion bars, anti-roll bar, telescopic dampers.

STEERING ZF rack-and-pinion; turns lock to lock: 3.10.

BRAKES disc (front diameter 9.25 in, 23.5 cm, rear 9.61 in, 24.4 cm), internal radial fins; lining area: total 39.8 sq in, 257 sq cm.

ELECTRICAL EQUIPMENT 12 V; 66 Ah battery; 980 W alternator; Bosch electronic ignition; 2 iodine headlamps.

DIMENSIONS AND WEIGHT wheel base: 89.41 in, 227 cm; tracks: 54.02 in, 137 cm front, 54.33 in, 138 cm; length: 168.90 in, 429 cm; width: 64.96 in, 165 cm; height: 51.97 in, 132 cm; ground clearance: 4.72 in, 12 cm; weight: 2,558 lb, 1,160 kg; turning circle: 35.8 ft, 10.9 m; fuel tank: 17.6 imp gal, 21.1 US gal, 80 l.

BODY coupé; 2 doors; 2 + 2 seats, separate front seats, adjustable backrests, built-in headrests; heated rear window; light alloy wheels; automatic heating.

PRACTICAL INSTRUCTIONS fuel: 91 oct petrol; oil: engine 17.6 imp pt, 21.1 US pt, 10 l, SAE 30 (summer) 20 (winter), change every 6,200 miles, 10,000 km - gearbox and final drive 5.3 imp pt, 6.3 US pt, 3 l, SAE 90, change every 6,200 miles, 10,000 km; greasing: none; sparking plug: 225°; tappet clearances: inlet 0.004 in, 0.10 mm, exhaust 0.004 in, 0.10 mm; valve timing: 35° 50° 40° 20°; tyre pressure: front 29 psi, 2 atm, rear 34 psi, 2.4 atm.

OPTIONALS Sportomatic semi-automatic transmission with 3 ratios (I 2.400, II 1.429, rev 2.534), single dry plate clutch automatically operated by gear lever, hydraulic torque converter, max ratio of converter at stall 2.18, 3.375 axle ratio; Sportomatic transmission clutch; ZF limited slip differential (only with mechanical gearbox); air-conditioning; electric sunshine roof; electric windows; rear window wiper-washer; tinted glass; 88 Ah battery; 205/55 VR x 16 front tyres, 225/50 VR x 16 rear tyres; metallic spray; fog lamps.

911 SC Coupé (USA)

See 911 SC Coupé except for:

PRICE IN USA: $ 20,775*

ENGINE max power (DIN): 172 hp (126.6 kW) at 5,500 rpm; max torque (DIN): 189 lb ft, 26.1 kg m (256 Nm) at 4,200 rpm; 57.4 hp/l (42.3 kW/l).

PERFORMANCE power-weight ratio: 14.9 lb/hp (20.2 lb/kW), 6.7 kg/hp (9.2 kg/kW).

DIMENSIONS AND WEIGHT tracks: 53.60 in, 136 cm front, 53.80 in, 137 cm rear; height: 52.80 in, 134 cm; ground clearance: 5.60 in, 14.3 cm.

911 SC Targa

See 911 SC Coupé, except for:

PRICE IN GB: £ 15,498*
PRICE IN USA: $ 22,050³

BODY convertible; roll bar, detachable roof.

Turbo Coupé

See 911 SC Coupé, except for:

PRICE IN GB: £ 24,999*
PRICE EX WORKS: 79,900* marks

ENGINE turbocharged; 201.3 cu in, 3,299 cc (3.82 x 2.93 in, 97 x 74.4 mm); compression ratio: 7:1; max power (DIN): 300

PORSCHE Turbo Coupé

hp (220.1 kW) at 5,500 rpm; max torque (DIN): 304 lb ft, 42 kg m (411.9 Nm) at 4,000 rpm; max engine rpm: 6,800; 90.9 hp/l (66.7 kW/l); Bosch K-Jetronic fuel injection system with KKK exhaust turbocharger; fuel feed: 2 electric pumps.

TRANSMISSION gears: 4, fully synchronized; ratios: I 2.250, II 1.304, III 0.893, IV 0.656, rev 3.325; axle ratio: 4.222; width of rims: 7'' front, 8'' rear; tyres: 205/55 VR x 16 front, 225/50 VR x 16 rear.

PERFORMANCE max speed: over 162 mph, 260 km/h; power-weight ratio: 9.6 lb/hp (13 lb/kW), 4.3 kg/hp (5.9 kg/kW); carrying capacity: 838 lb, 380 kg; speed in top at 1,000 rpm: 29.3 mph, 47.2 km/h; consumption: 23.9 m/imp gal, 19.9 m/US gal, 11.8 l x 100 km.

BRAKES lining area: total 58.3 sq in, 376 sq cm.

DIMENSIONS AND WEIGHT tracks: 56.30 in, 143 cm front, 59.06 in, 150 cm rear; width: 69.68 in, 177 cm; height: 51.57 in, 131 cm; weight: 2,867 lb, 1,300 kg; turning circle: 35.1 ft, 10.7 m.

BODY rear window wiper-washer (standard).

PRACTICAL INSTRUCTIONS fuel: 96 oct petrol; oil: gearbox and final drive 6.5 imp pt, 7.8 US pt, 3.7 l; sparking plug: 280°.

OPTIONALS only limited slip differential, electric sunshine roof and air-conditioning.

Turbo Coupé (USA)

See Turbo Coupé, except for:

PRICE IN USA: $ 38,500*

ENGINE max power (DIN): 261 hp (192.1 kW) at 5,500 rpm; max torque (DIN): 291 lb ft, 40.1 kg m (393.3 Nm) at 4,000 rpm; 79.1 hp/l (58.2 kW/l).

PERFORMANCE max speed: 155 mph, 250 km/h; power-weight ratio: 10.9 lb/hp (14.9 lb/kW), 5 kg/hp (6.7 kg/kW); carrying capacity: 453 lb, 205 kg.

DIMENSIONS AND WEIGHT height: 52.30 in, 133 cm; ground clearance: 5.50 in, 14 cm; weight: 2,855 lb, 1,295 kg; turning circle: 34.8 ft, 10.6 m.

PRACTICAL INSTRUCTIONS fuel: 91 oct petrol.

928

PRICE IN GB: £ 19,499*
PRICE IN USA: $ 29,775*

ENGINE front, 4 stroke; 8 cylinders, Vee-slanted at 90°; 273 cu in, 4,474 cc (3.74 x 3.11 in, 95 x 78.9 mm); compression ratio: 8.5:1; max power (DIN): 240 hp (176.6 kW) at 5,250 rpm; max torque (DIN): 268 lb ft, 37 kg m (362.

PORSCHE 928

PORSCHE 928

m) at 3,600 rpm; 53.6 hp/l (39.5 kW/l); light alloy block
d head; 5 crankshaft bearings; valves: overhead, in line,
ydraulic tappets; camshafts: 1 per block, overhead, cogg-
d belt; lubrication: gear pump, full flow filter, 11.4 imp
t, 13.7 US pt, 6.5 l; Bosch K-Jetronic electronic injection;
el feed: electric pump; water-cooled, 28.2 imp pt, 33.8
S pt, 16 l.

RANSMISSION driving wheels: rear; clutch: single dry
ate; gearbox: mechanical, in unit with differential; gears:
fully synchronized; ratios: I 3.601, II 2.466, III 1.819, IV
343, V 1, rev 3.162; lever: central; final drive: hypoid
evel; axle ratio: 2.750; width of rims: 7''; tyres: 225/50
R x 16.

ERFORMANCE max speed: over 143 mph, 230 km/h; power-
eight ratio: 13.3 lb/hp, (18.1 lb/kW), 6 kg/hp (8.2 kg/kW);
arrying capacity: 926 lb, 420 kg; speed in direct drive at
000 rpm: 26.5 mph, 42.6 km/h; consumption: 21.7 m/imp
al, 18.1 m/US gal, 13 l x 100 km.

HASSIS integral; front suspension: independent, wishbones,
oil springs/telescopic damper struts, anti-roll bar; rear:
ndependent, Weissach axle, wishbones, semi-trailing arms,
ransverse torsion bars, coil springs/telescopic damper
truts.

TEERING rack-and-pinion, servo.

RAKES disc (front diameter 11.10 in, 28.2 cm, rear 11.38
n, 28.9 cm), internal radial fins, servo; lining area: total
9 sq in, 316 sq cm.

ELECTRICAL EQUIPMENT 12 V; 66 Ah battery; 1,260 W alternator; electronic ignition; 2 retractable headlamps.

DIMENSIONS AND WEIGHT wheel base: 98.43 in, 250 cm;
tracks: 60.63 in, 154 cm front, 59.45 in, 151 cm rear; length:
175.20 in, 445 cm; width: 72.44 in, 184 cm; height: 51.57 in,
131 cm; weight: 3,197 lb, 1,450 kg; turning circle: 37.7 ft,
11.5 m; fuel tank: 18.9 imp gal, 22.7 US gal, 86 l.

BODY coupé; 2 doors; 2 + 2 seats, separate front seats,
reclining backrest with built-in headrests; heated rear
window with wiper-washer.

PRACTICAL INSTRUCTIONS fuel: 91 oct petrol; oil: engine
11.4 imp pt, 13.7 US pt, 6.5 l, SAE 15W-50/20W-50 - gearbox and final drive 6.7 imp pt, 8 US pt, 3.8 l; sparking
plug: 145°.

OPTIONALS automatic transmission with 3 ratios (I 2.310,
II 1.460, III 1, rev 1.840), max ratio of converter at stall
2, possible manual selection; limited slip differential; 88
Ah battery; air-conditioning; metallic spray; sunshine roof.

VOLKSWAGEN GERMANY FR

Polo Series

PRICES IN GB AND EX WORKS:	£	DM
1 3-dr Limousine	2,535*	8,970*
2 3-dr L Limousine	2,810*	9,620*
3 3-dr GL Limousine	—	10,400*
4 3-dr S Limousine	—	9,290*
5 3-dr LS Limousine	—	9,940*
6 3-dr GLS Limousine	3,155*	10,720*

For 60 hp engine add DM 620.

Power team:	Standard for:	Optional for:
40 hp	1 to 3	—
50 hp	4 to 6	—
60 hp	—	5,6

40 hp power team

ENGINE front, transverse, slanted 15° to front, 4 stroke; 4
cylinders, in line; 54.6 cu in, 895 cc (2.74 x 2.32 in, 69.5 x 59
mm); compression ratio: 8:1; max power (DIN): 40 hp
(29.4 kW) at 5,900 rpm; max torque (DIN): 45 lb ft, 6.2 kg
m (60.8 Nm) at 3,500 rpm; max engine rpm; 6,000: 44.7
hp/l (32.8 kW/l); cast iron block, light alloy head; 5
crankshaft bearings; valves: overhead, in line, thimble
tappets; camshafts: 1, overhead, cogged belt; lubrication:
gear pump, full flow filter, 6.2 imp pt, 7.4 US pt, 3.5 l; 1
Solex 31 PICT-5 downdraught single barrel carburettor; fuel
feed: mechanical pump; water-cooled, 8.8 imp pt, 10.6 US
pt, 5 l, electric thermostatic fan.

TRANSMISSION driving wheels: front; clutch: single dry
plate; gearbox: mechanical; gears: 4, fully synchronized;
ratios: I 3.454, II 2.050, III 1.347, IV 0.963, rev 3.384;

lever: central; final drive: spiral bevel; axle ratio: 4.571;
width of rims: 4.5''; tyres: 135 SR x 13.

PERFORMANCE max speeds: (I) 27 mph, 43 km/h; (II) 46
mph, 74 km/h; (III) 62 mph, 110 km/h; (IV) 82 mph, 132
km/h; power-weight ratio: 37.7 lb/hp (51.4 lb/kW), 17.1
kg/hp (23.3 kg/kW); carrying capacity: 915 lb, 415 kg; acceleration: 0-50 mph (0-80 km/h) 12.7 sec; speed in top
at 1,000 rpm: 14.2 mph, 22.8 km/h; consumption: 38.7
m/imp gal, 32.2 m/US gal, 7.3 l x 100 km.

CHASSIS integral; front suspension: independent, by Mc-
Pherson, lower wishbones, anti-roll bar, coil springs/tele-
scopic damper struts; rear: independent, longitudinal trailing radius arms, coil springs/telescopic damper struts.

STEERING rack-and-pinion; turns lock to lock: 3.25.

BRAKES front disc, rear drum, 2 X circuits.

ELECTRICAL EQUIPMENT 12 V; 36 Ah battery; 35 A alternator; Bosch distributor; 2 headlamps.

DIMENSIONS AND WEIGHT wheel base: 91.93 in, 233 cm;
tracks: 51.02 in, 130 cm front, 51.65 in, 131 cm rear; length:
139.37 in, 354 cm; width: 61.38 in, 156 cm; height: 52.91
in, 134 cm; ground clearance: 4.72 in, 12 cm; weight: 1,510
lb, 685 kg; turning circle: 31.5 ft, 9.6 m; fuel tank: 7.9
imp gal, 9.5 US gal, 36 l.

BODY saloon/sedan; 4-5 seats, separate front seats, reclining backrests with built-in headrests; heated rear window;
folding rear seat.

PRACTICAL INSTRUCTIONS fuel: 91 oct petrol; oil: engine
5.3 imp pt, 6.3 US pt, 3 l, SAE 20W-30, change every
4,700 miles, 7,500 km - gearbox and final drive 4 imp pt,
4.9 US pt, 2.3 l, SAE 80 or 90; greasing: none; sparking
plug: 175°; tyre pressure: front 26 psi, 1.8 atm, rear 28
psi, 2 atm.

OPTIONALS rear window wiper-washer; halogen headlamps;
155/70 SR x 13 tyres; sunshine roof; metallic spray (for
L and GL models only).

50 hp power team

See 40 hp power team, except for:

ENGINE 66.7 cu in, 1,093 cc (2.74 x 2.83 in, 69.5 x 72 mm);
max power (DIN): 50 hp (36.8 kW) at 5,900 rpm; max torque
(DIN): 56 lb ft, 7.7 kg m (75.5 Nm) at 3,500 rpm; 47.5
hp/l (33.7 kW/l); cooling system: 10.9 imp pt, 13.1 US pt,
6.2 l.

TRANSMISSION tyres: 145 SR x 13.

PERFORMANCE max speed: 88 mph, 142 km/h; power-
weight ratio: 30.2 lb/hp (41 lb/kW), 13.7 kg/hp (18.6
kg/kW); acceleration: 0-50 mph (0-80 km/h) 9.6 sec; consumption: 37.2 m/imp gal, 30.9 m/US gal, 7.6 l x 100 km.

BRAKES servo.

60 hp power team

See 40 hp power team, except for:

ENGINE 77.6 cu in, 1,272 cc (2.95 x 2.83 in, 75 x 72 mm);
compression ratio: 8.2:1; max power (DIN): 60 hp (44.2 kW)
at 5,600 rpm; max torque (DIN): 70 lb ft, 9.7 kg m (95.1
Nm) at 3,400 rpm; 47.2 hp/l (34.7 kW/l); cooling system:
10.9 imp pt, 13.1 US pt, 6.2 l.

TRANSMISSION axle ratio: 4.063; tyres: 145 SR x 13.

PERFORMANCE max speed: 94 mph, 152 km/h; power-
weight ratio: 25.2 lb/hp (34.2 lb/kW), 11.4 kg/hp (15.5
kg/kW); acceleration: 0-50 mph (0-80 km/h) 8.3 sec; consumption: 34 m/imp gal, 28.3 m/US gal, 8.3 l x 100 km.

CHASSIS rear suspension: anti-roll bar.

BRAKES rear compensator, servo.

Derby Series

PRICES IN GB AND EX WORKS:	£	DM
1 2-dr Limousine	—	9,345*
2 2-dr L Limousine	—	9,995*
3 2-dr GL Limousine	—	10,605*
4 2-dr S Limousine	2,667*	9,665*
5 2-dr LS Limousine	2,995*	10,315*
6 2-dr GLS Limousine	3,295* (60 hp)	10,925*

For 60 hp engine add DM 620.

Power team:	Standard for:	Optional for:
40 hp	1 to 3	—
50 hp	4 to 6	—
60 hp	—	5,6

VOLKSWAGEN Polo 3-dr Limousine

VOLKSWAGEN Derby 2-dr LS Limousine

40 hp power team

ENGINE front, transverse, slanted 15° to front, 4 stroke; 4 cylinders, in line; 54.6 cu in, 895 cc (2.74 x 2.32 in, 69.5 x 59 mm); compression ratio: 8:1; max power (DIN): 40 hp (29.4 kW) at 5,900 rpm; max torque (DIN): 45 lb ft, 6.2 kg m (60.8 Nm) at 3,500 rpm; max engine rpm: 6,000; 44.7 hp/l (32.8 kW/l); cast iron block, light alloy head; 5 crankshaft bearings; valves: overhead, in line, thimble tappets; camshafts: 1, overhead, cogged belt; lubrication: gear pump, full flow filter, 6.2 imp pt, 7.4 US pt, 3.5 l; 1 Solex 35 PICT-5 downdraught single barrel carburettor; fuel feed: mechanical pump; water-cooled, 8.8 imp pt, 10.6 US pt, 5 l, electric thermostatic fan.

TRANSMISSION driving wheels: front; clutch: single dry plate; gearbox: mechanical; gears: 4, fully synchronized; ratios: I 3.454, II 2.050, III 1.347, IV 0.963, rev 3.384; lever: central; final drive: spiral bevel; axle ratio: 4.571; width of rims: 4.5''; tyres: 145 SR x 13.

PERFORMANCE max speeds: (I) 27 mph, 43 km/h; (II) 46 mph, 74 km/h; (III) 62 mph, 110 km/h; (IV) 82 mph, 132 km/h; power-weight ratio: 38.6 lb/hp (52.5 lb/kW), 17.5 kg/hp (23.8 kg/kW); carrying capacity: 948 lb, 430 kg; acceleration: 0-50 mph (0-80 km/h) 12.7 sec; speed in top at 1,000 rpm: 14.2 mph, 22.8 km/h; consumption: 38.7 m/imp gal, 32.2 m/US gal, 7.3 l x 100 km.

CHASSIS integral; front suspension: independent, by McPherson, lower wishbones, anti-roll bar, coil springs/tele-scopic damper struts; rear: independent, longitudinal trailing radius arms, coil springs/telescopic damper struts.

STEERING rack-and-pinion; turns lock to lock: 3.25.

BRAKES front disc (diameter 9.41 in, 23.9 cm), rear drum, 2 X circuits; lining area: front 16.3 sq in, 105 sq cm, rear 45.6 sq in, 189 sq cm, total 61.9 sq in, 294 sq cm.

ELECTRICAL EQUIPMENT 12 V; 36 Ah battery; 35 A alternator; Bosch distributor; 2 headlamps.

DIMENSIONS AND WEIGHT wheel base: 91.93 in, 233 cm; tracks: 51.02 in, 130 cm front, 51.65 in, 131 cm rear; length: 152.20 in, 387 cm; width: 61.38 in, 156 cm; height: 53.23 in, 135 cm; ground clearance: 3.74 in, 9.5 cm; weight: 1,544 lb, 700 kg; turning circle: 31.5 ft, 9.6 m; fuel tank: 7.9 imp gal, 9.5 US gal, 36 l.

BODY saloon/sedan; 2 doors; 4-5 seats, separate front seats, reclining backrests with built-in headrests; heated rear window.

PRACTICAL INSTRUCTIONS fuel: 91 oct petrol; oil: engine 5.3 imp pt, 6.3 US pt, 3 l, SAE 20W-30, change every 4,700 miles, 7,500 km - gearbox and final drive 4 imp pt, 4.9 US pt, 2.3 l, SAE 80 or 90; greasing: none; sparking plug: 175°; tyre pressure: front 26 psi, 1.8 atm, rear 28 psi, 2 atm.

OPTIONALS 155/70 SR x 13 tyres; sunshine roof; halogen headlamps; metallic spray (for L ad GL models only).

50 hp power team

See 40 hp power team, except for:

ENGINE 66.7 cu in, 1,093 cc (2.74 x 2.83 in, 69.5 x 72 mm); max power (DIN): 50 hp (36.8 kW) at 5,800 rpm; max torque (DIN): 56 lb ft, 7.7 kg m (75.5 Nm) at 3,500 rpm; 47.5 hp/l (33.7 kW/l); cooling system: 10.9 imp pt, 13.1 US pt, 6.2 l.

TRANSMISSION axle ratio: 4.267.

PERFORMANCE max speed: 88 mph, 142 km/h; power-weight ratio: 30.9 lb/hp (41.9 lb/kW), 14 kg/hp (19 kg/kW); acceleration: 0-50 mph (0-80 km/h) 9.6 sec; speed in top at 1,000 rpm: 15.7 mph, 25.2 km/h; consumption: 37.2 m/imp gal, 30.9 m/US gal, 7.6 l x 100 km.

BRAKES servo.

60 hp power team

See 40 hp power team, except for:

ENGINE 77.6 cu in, 1,272 cc (2.95 x 2.83 in, 75 x 72 mm); compression ratio: 8.2:1; max power (DIN): 60 hp (44.2 kW) at 5,600 rpm; max torque (DIN): 70 lb ft, 9.7 kg m (95 Nm) at 3,400 rpm; 47.2 hp/l (34.7 kW/l); cooling system 10.9 imp pt, 13.1 US pt, 6.2 l.

TRANSMISSION axle ratio: 4.063.

VOLKSWAGEN Derby 2-dr LS Limousine

PERFORMANCE max speed: 94 mph, 152 km/h; power-weight ratio: 25.7 lb/hp (34.9 lb/kW), 11.7 kg/hp (15.8 kg/kW); acceleration: 0-50 mph (0-80 km/h) 8.3 sec; speed in top at 1,000 rpm: 16.4 mph, 26.4 km/h; consumption: 3 m/imp gal, 28.3 m/US gal, 8.3 l x 100 km.

CHASSIS rear suspension: anti-roll bar.

BRAKES rear compensator, servo.

Golf Series

PRICES IN GB AND EX WORKS:	£	DM
1 3-dr Limousine	2,820*	9,965
2 5-dr Limousine	—	10,525
3 3-dr L Limousine	—	10,705
4 5-dr L Limousine	3,235*	11,265
5 3-dr GL Limousine	3,355*	11,515
6 5-dr GL Limousine	—	12,075*
7 3-dr S Limousine	—	10,820*
8 5-dr S Limousine	—	11,380*
9 3-dr LS Limousine	—	11,560
10 5-dr LS Limousine	—	12,120*
11 3-dr GLS Limousine	—	12,370*
12 5-dr GLS Limousine	3,740*	12,930*
13 3-dr GTI Limousine	—	15,085

Power team:	Standard for:	Optional for:
50 hp	1 to 6	—
70 hp	7 to 12	—
110 hp	13	

VOLKSWAGEN Golf GL 5-dr Limousine

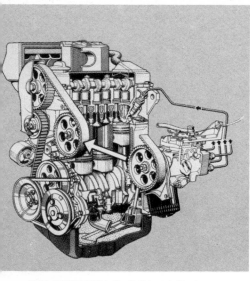

VOLKSWAGEN Golf Diesel Series

50 hp power team

ENGINE front, transverse, slanted 15° to front, 4 stroke; 4 cylinders, vertical, in line: 66.7 cu in, 1,093 cc (2.74 x 2.83 in, 69.5 x 72 mm); compression ratio: 8:1; max power (DIN): 50 hp (36.8 kW) at 6,000 rpm; max torque (DIN): 57 lb ft, 7.9 kg m (77.5 Nm) at 3,000 rpm; 45.7 hp/l (33.7 kW/l); cast iron block, light alloy head; 5 crankshaft bearings; valves: overhead, in line, thimble tappets; camshafts: 1, overhead, cogged belt; lubrication: gear pump, full flow filter, 5.3 imp pt, 6.3 US pt, 3 l; 1 Solex 35 PICT-5 downdraught single barrel carburettor; fuel feed: mechanical pump; liquid-cooled, expansion tank, 10.9 imp pt, 13.1 US pt, 6.2 l, electric thermostatic fan.

TRANSMISSION driving wheels: front; clutch: single dry plate, hydraulically controlled; gearbox: mechanical; gears: 4, fully synchronized; ratios: I 3.454, II 2.055, III 1.350, IV 0.960, rev 3.390; lever: central; final drive: spiral bevel; axle ratio: 4.570; width of rims: 4.5''; tyres: 145 SR x 13.

PERFORMANCE max speed: 87 mph, 140 km/h; power-weight ratio: 3-dr. limousines 33 lb/hp (44.9 lb/kW), 15 kg/hp (20.4 kg/kW) - 5-dr. limousines 34.2 lb/hp (46.4 lb/kW), 15.5 kg/hp (21.1 kg/kW); carrying capacity: 3-dr. limousines 992 lb, 450 kg - 5-dr. limousines 937 lb, 425 kg; acceleration: 0-50 mph (0-80 km/h) 10 sec; speed in top at 1,000 rpm: 14.9 mph, 24 km/h; consumption: 34 m/imp gal, 28.3 m/US gal, 8.3 l x 100 km.

CHASSIS integral; front suspension: independent, by McPherson, lower wishbones, coil springs/telescopic damper

struts; rear: independent, swinging longitudinal trailing arms linked by a T-section cross-beam, coil springs/telescopic damper struts.

STEERING rack-and-pinion.

BRAKES front disc, rear drum, 2 X circuits.

ELECTRICAL EQUIPMENT 12 V; 36 Ah battery; 36 A alternator; Bosch distributor; 2 headlamps.

DIMENSIONS AND WEIGHT wheel base: 94.49 in, 240 cm; tracks: 54.72 in, 139 cm front, 53.46 in, 136 cm rear; length: 150.20 in, 381 cm; width: 63.39 in, 161 cm; height: 55.51 in, 141 cm; ground clearance: 4.92 in, 12.5 cm; weight: 3-dr. limousines 1,654 lb, 750 kg - 5-dr. limousines 1,709 lb, 775 kg; turning circle: 33.8 ft, 10.3 m; fuel tank: 8.8 imp gal, 10 US gal, 40 l.

BODY saloon/sedan; 5 seats, separate front seats; folding rear seat; heated rear window.

PRACTICAL INSTRUCTIONS fuel: 90 oct petrol; oil: engine 5.3 imp pt, 6.3 US pt, 3 l, SAE 20W-30, change every 4,700 miles, 7,500 km - gearbox and final drive 3.2 imp pt, 3.8 US pt, 1.8 l, SAE 80 or 90; sparking plug: 175°; tyre pressure: front 26 psi, 1.8 atm, rear 26 psi, 1.8 atm.

OPTIONALS 5'' rim sports wheels: 175/70 SR x 13 tyres with 5'' wide rims; 155 SR x 13 tyres with 4.5'' wide rims; servo brake; halogen headlamps; sunshine roof; built-in headrests on front seats; rear window wiper-washer; metallic spray (for L and GL models only).

70 hp power team

See 50 hp power team, except for:

ENGINE front, transverse, slanted 15° to rear; 88.9 cu in, 1,457 cc (3.13 x 2.89 in, 79.5 x 73.4 mm); compression ratio: 8.2:1; max power (DIN): 70 hp (51.5 kW) at 5,600 rpm; max torque (DIN): 81 lb ft, 11.2 kg m (109.8 Nm) at 2,500 rpm; 48 hp/l (35.3 kW/l); 1 Solex 34 PICT-5 downdraught single barrel carburettor.

TRANSMISSION gearbox ratios: I 3.454, II 1.960, III 1.370, IV 0.970, rev 3.170; axle ratio: 3.900; width of rims: 5''; tyres: 155 SR x 13 (standard).

PERFORMANCE max speed: 98 mph, 158 km/h; power-weight ratio: 2-dr. limousines 24.6 lb/hp (33.4 lb/kW), 11.1 kg/hp (15.1 kg/kW) - 4-dr. limousines 25.4 lb/hp (34.5 lb/kW), 11.5 kg/hp (15.6 kg/kW); acceleration: 0-50 mph (0-80 km/h) 8.2 sec; speed in top at 1,000 rpm: 17.3 mph, 27.8 km/h; consumption: 32.8 m/imp gal, 27.3 m/US gal, 8.6 l x 100 km.

BRAKES front disc, rear drum, servo (standard).

DIMENSIONS AND WEIGHT weight: 3-dr. limousines 1,720 lb, 780 kg - 5-dr. limousines 1,775 lb, 805 kg.

OPTIONALS automatic transmission, hydraulic torque converter and planetary gears with 3 ratios (I 2.550, II 1.450, III 1, rev 2.410), max ratio of converter at stall 2.44, possible manual selection, central lever, 3.760 axle ratio, max speed 95 mph, 153 km/h, acceleration 0-50 mph (0-80 km/h) 9.4 sec, consumption 30.7 m/imp gal, 25.6 m/US gal, 9.2 l x 100 km.

110 hp power team

See 50 hp power team, except for:

ENGINE front, transverse, slanted 20° to rear; 96.9 cu in, 1,588 cc (3.13 x 3.15 in, 79.5 x 80 mm); compression ratio: 9.5:1; max power (DIN): 110 hp (81 kW) at 6,100 rpm; max torque (DIN): 101 lb ft, 14 kg m (137.3 Nm) at 5,000 rpm; max engine rpm: 6,900; 69.3 hp/l (51 kW/l); Bosch K-Jetronic electronic injection; fuel feed: electric pump.

TRANSMISSION gearbox ratios: I 3.454, II 1.960, III 1.370, IV 0.970, rev 3.170; axle ratio: 3.900; width of rims: 5.5''; tyres: 175/70 HR x 13.

PERFORMANCE max speed: 113 mph, 182 km/h; power-weight ratio: 16.2 lb/hp (22 lb/kW), 7.4 kg/hp (10 kg/kW); carrying capacity: 926 lb, 420 kg; acceleration: 0-50 mph (0-80 km/h) 6.1 sec; speed in top at 1,000 rpm: 18.5 mph, 29.8 km/h; consumption: 35.3 m/imp gal, 29.4 m/US gal, 8 l x 100 km.

BRAKES front disc, rear drum, rear compensator, servo (standard).

ELECTRICAL EQUIPMENT 55 A alternator; 2 halogen headlamps (standard).

DIMENSIONS AND WEIGHT tracks: 55.28 in, 140 cm front, 54.02 in, 137 cm rear; width: 64.09 in, 163 cm; height: 54.72 in, 139 cm; weight: 1,786 lb, 810 kg.

BODY built-in headrests on front seats (standard).

PRACTICAL INSTRUCTIONS fuel: 98-100 oct petrol.

Golf Diesel Series

PRICES IN GB, IN USA AND EX WORKS:

	£	$	DM
3-dr D Limousine	—	—	11,470*
5-dr D Limousine	—	—	12,030*
3-dr LD Limousine	—	5,199*	12,210*
5-dr LD Limousine	3,890*	5,339*	12,770*
3-dr GLD Limousine	—	5,585*	13,020*
5-dr GLD Limousine	—	5,725*	13,580*

50 hp power team

ENGINE Diesel, front, transverse, 4 stroke; 4 cylinders, vertical, in line: 89.8 cu in, 1,471 cc (3.01 x 3.15 in, 76.5 x 80 mm); compression ratio: 23.5:1; max power (DIN): 50 hp (36.8 kW) at 5,000 rpm; max torque (DIN): 59 lb ft, 8.2 kg m (80.4 Nm) at 3,000 rpm; max engine rpm: 5,000; 34 hp/l (25 kW/l); cast iron block, light alloy head; 5 crankshaft bearings; valves: overhead, in line, thimble tappets; camshafts: 1, overhead, cogged belt; lubrication: gear pump, full flow filter, 6.2 imp pt, 7.4 US pt, 3.5 l; Bosch injection pump; liquid-cooled, expansion tank, 10.9 imp pt, 13.1 US pt, 6.2 l, electric thermostatic fan.

TRANSMISSION driving wheels: front; clutch: single dry plate, hydraulically controlled; gearbox: mechanical; gears: 4, fully synchronized; ratios: I 3.454, II 2.055, III 1.350, IV 0.960, rev 3.390; lever: central; final drive: spiral bevel; axle ratio: 4.570; width of rims: 4.5''; tyres: 145 SR x 13.

PERFORMANCE max speed: 87 mph, 140 km/h; power-weight ratio: 3-dr. limousines 35.5 lb/hp (48.2 lb/kW), 16.1 kg/hp (21.9 kg/kW) - 5-dr. limousines 36.6 lb/hp (49.7 lb/kW), 16.6 kg/hp (22.6 kg/kW); carrying capacity: 3-dr. limousines 981 lb, 445 kg - 5-dr. limousines 926 lb, 420 kg; acceleration: 0-50 mph (0-80 km/h) 11.5 sec; speed in top at 1,000 rpm: 17.4 mph, 28 km/h; consumption: 43.5 m/imp gal, 36.2 m/US gal, 6.5 l x 100 km.

CHASSIS integral; front suspension: independent, by McPherson, lower wishbones, coil springs/telescopic damper struts; rear: independent, swinging longitudinal trailing arms linked by a T-section cross-beam, coil springs/telescopic damper struts.

STEERING rack-and-pinion.

BRAKES front disc, rear drum, 2 X circuits.

ELECTRICAL EQUIPMENT 12 V; 36 Ah battery; 35 A alternator; 2 headlamps.

DIMENSIONS AND WEIGHT wheel base: 94.49 in, 240 cm; tracks: 54.72 in, 139 cm front, 53.46 in, 136 cm rear; length: 150.20 in, 381 cm; width: 63.39 in, 161 cm; height: 55.51 in, 141 cm; ground clearance: 4.92 in, 12.5 cm; weight: 3-dr. limousines 1,775 lb, 805 kg - 5-dr. limousines 1,830 lb, 830 kg; turning circle: 33.8 ft, 10.3 m; fuel tank: 8.8 imp gal, 10.6 US gal, 40 l.

BODY saloon/sedan; 5 seats, separate front seats; built-in headrests; folding rear seat; heated rear window.

PRACTICAL INSTRUCTIONS fuel: Diesel oil; oil: engine 5.3 imp pt, 6.3 US pt, 3 l - gearbox and final drive 3.2

VOLKSWAGEN Golf GTI 3-dr Limousine

50 HP POWER TEAM

imp pt, 3.8 US pt, 1.8 l, SAE 80; tyre pressure: front 26 psi, 1.8 atm, rear 26 psi, 1.8 atm.

OPTIONALS 175/70 SR x 13 or 155 SR x 13 tyres with 5'' wide rims· servo brake; halogen headlamps; sunshine roof; metallic spray (for L and GL models only); rear window wiper-washer.

Scirocco Series

PRICES IN GB, IN USA AND EX WORKS:

	£	$	DM
1 Coupé	—	—	12,995*
2 L Coupé	—	—	14,020*
3 S Coupé	—	—	13,550*
4 LS Coupé	—	—	14,575*
5 GT Coupé	—	—	15,095*
6 GL Coupé	4,720*	6,545*	15,845*
7 GTI Coupé	—	—	17,595*
8 GLI Coupé	—	—	18,345*

For 85 hp engine add DM 975 (S and LS), add DM 420 (GT and GL).

Power team:	Standard for:	Optional for:
50 hp	1,2	—
70 hp	3 to 6	—
85 hp	—	3 to 6
110 hp	7,8	—

50 hp power team

ENGINE front, transverse, slanted 15° to front, 4 stroke; 4 cylinders, vertical, in line; 66.7 cu in, 1,093 cc (2.74 x 2.83 in, 69.5 x 72 mm); compression ratio: 8:1; max power (DIN): 50 hp (36.8 kW) at 6,000 rpm; max torque (DIN): 57 lb ft, 7.9 kg m (77.5 Nm) at 3,000 rpm; 45.7 hp/l (33.7 kW/l); cast iron block, light alloy head; 5 crankshaft bearings; valves: overhead, in line, thimble tappets; camshafts: 1, overhead, cogged belt; lubrication: gear pump, full flow filter, 6.2 imp pt, 7.4 US pt, 3.5 l; 1 Solex 35 PICT-5 downdraught single barrel carburettor; fuel feed: mechanical pump; liquid cooled, expansion tank, 10.9 imp pt, 13.1 US pt, 6.2 l, electric thermostatic fan.

TRANSMISSION driving wheels: front; clutch: single dry plate, hydraulically controlled; gearbox: mechanical; gears: 4, fully synchronized; ratios: I 3.454, II 2.055, III 1.370, IV 0.939, rev 3.166; lever: central; final drive: spiral bevel; axle ratio: 4.570; width of rims: 5''; tyres: 155 SR x 13.

PERFORMANCE max speed: 89 mph, 144 km/h; power-weight ratio: 34.4 lb/hp (46.7 lb/kW), 15.6 kg/hp (21.2 kg/kW); carrying capacity: 860 lb, 390 kg; acceleration: 0-50 mph (0-80 km/h) 9.9 sec; speed in top at 1,000 rpm: 14.9 mph, 24 km/h; consumption: 35.3 m/imp gal, 29.4 m/US gal, 8 l x 100 km.

CHASSIS integral; front suspension: independent, by McPherson, lower wishbones, coil springs/telescopic damper struts; rear: independent, swinging longitudinal trailing arms linked by a T-section cross beam, coil springs/telescopic damper struts.

STEERING rack-and-pinion.

BRAKES front disc (diameter 9.41 in, 23.9 cm), rear drum, servo; swept area: front 160 sq in, 1,032 sq cm, rear 90.9 sq in, 586 sq cm, total 250.9 sq in, 1,618 sq cm.

ELECTRICAL EQUIPMENT 12 V; 36 Ah battery; 35 A alternator; Bosch distributor; 2 headlamps.

DIMENSIONS AND WEIGHT wheel base: 94.49 in, 240 cm; tracks: 54.72 in, 139 cm front, 53.46 in, 136 cm rear; length: 152.95 in, 388 cm; width: 63.78 in, 162 cm; height: 50.98 in, 129 cm; ground clearance: 4.92 in, 12.5 cm; weight: 1,720 lb, 780 kg; turning circle: 33.8 ft, 10,3 m; fuel tank: 8.8 imp pt, 10.6 US pt, 40 l.

BODY coupé; 2+1 doors; 4 seats, separate front seats; heated rear window; folding rear seat; built-in headrests on front seats (standard for L only).

PRACTICAL INSTRUCTIONS fuel: 90 oct petrol; oil: engine 5.3 imp pt, 6.3 US pt, 3 l, SAE 20W-30, change every 4,700 miles, 7,500 km - gearbox and final drive 3.2 imp pt, 3.8 US pt, 1.8 l, SAE 80 or 90; sparking plug: 175°; tyre pressure: front 26 psi, 1.8 atm, rear 26 psi, 1.8 atm.

OPTIONALS 5'' rim sports wheels; 175/70 SR x 13 tyres; halogen headlamps; built-in headrests on front seats; reclining front seats; rear window wiper-washer; metallic spray.

VOLKSWAGEN Scirocco GLI Coupé

70 hp power team

See 50 hp power team, except for:

ENGINE front, transverse, slanted 20° to rear; 88.9 cu 1,457 cc (3.13 x 2.89 in, 79.5 x 73.4 mm); compression rat 8.2:1; max power (DIN): 70 hp (51.5 kW) at 5,600 rpm; n torque (DIN): 81 lb ft, 11.2 kg m (109.8 Nm) at 2,500 rp 48 hp/l (35.3 kW/l); 1 Solex 34 PICT-5 downdraught sin barrel carburettor.

TRANSMISSION gearbox ratios: I 3.454, II 1.960, III 1.3 IV 0.970, rev 3.170; axle ratio: 3.900.

PERFORMANCE max speed: 101 mph, 162 km/h; pow weight ratio: 25.2 lb/hp (34.2 lb/kW), 11.4 kg/hp (1 kg/kW); acceleration: 0-50 mph (0-80 km/h) 8.1 sec; spe in top at 1,000 rpm: 17.3 mph, 27.9 km/h; consumption: m/imp gal, 28.3 m/US gal, 8.3 l x 100 km.

ELECTRICAL EQUIPMENT 4 halogen headlamps.

DIMENSIONS AND WEIGHT weight: 1,764 lb, 800 kg.

BODY built-in headrests on front seats (standard); tin glass.

OPTIONALS automatic transmission, hydraulic torque c verter and planetary gears with 3 ratios (I 2.550, II 1.4 III 1, rev 2.410), max ratio of converter at stall 2.44, pos ble manual selection, central lever, 3.760 axle ratio, n speed 98 mph, 157 km/h, acceleration 0-50 mph (0-80 km 9.3 sec, carrying capacity 849 lb, 385 kg, consumption 3 m/imp gal, 26.4 m/US gal, 8.9 l x 100 km.

85 hp power team

See 70 hp power team, except for:

ENGINE 96.9 cu in, 1,588 cc (3.13 x 3.15 in, 79.5 x 80 m max power (DIN): 85 hp (62.6 kW) at 5,600 rpm; max tor (DIN): 92.4 lb/ft, 12.8 kg m (125 Nm) at 3,800 rpm; 5 hp/l (39.4 kW/l).

TRANSMISSION tyres: 175/70 SR x 13.

PERFORMANCE max speed: 107 mph, 172 km/h; pow weight ratio: 20.7 lb/hp (28.2 lb/kW), 9.4 kg/hp (1 kg/kW); acceleration: 0-50 mph (0-80 km/h) 7.5 sec; c sumption: 33.2 m/imp gal, 27.7 m/US gal, 8.5 l x 100

ELECTRICAL EQUIPMENT 55 A alternator.

OPTIONALS with automatic transmission max speed mph, 167 km/h, acceleration 0-50 mph (0-80 km/h) 8.6 s consumption 31 m/imp gal, 25.8 m/US gal, 9.1 l x 100

110 hp power team

See 50 hp power team, except for:

ENGINE front, transverse, slanted 20° to rear; 96.9 cu 1,588 cc (3.13 x 3.15 in, 79.5 x 80 mm); compression rat 9.5:1; max power (DIN): 110 hp (81 kW) at 6,100 rp max torque (DIN): 101 lb ft, 14 kg m (137.3 Nm) at 5, rpm; max engine rpm: 6,900; 69.3 hp/l (51 kW/l); Bo K-Jetronic electronic injection; fuel feed: electric pur

VOLKSWAGEN Passat Series

TRANSMISSION gearbox ratios: I 3.450, II 1.960, III 1.370, IV 0.970, rev 3.170; axle ratio: 3.900; width of rims: 5.5''; tyres: 175/70 HR x 13.

PERFORMANCE max speed: 115 mph, 185 km/h; power-weight ratio: 16 lb/hp (21.8 lb/kW), 7.3 kg/hp (9.9 kg/kW); carrying capacity: 904 lb, 410 kg; acceleration: 0-50 mph (0-80 km/h) 6 sec; speed in top at 1,000 rpm: 18.8 mph, 30.3 km/h; consumption: 36.2 m/imp gal, 30.2 m/US gal, 7.8 l x 100 km.

CHASSIS front and rear suspension: anti-roll bar.

ELECTRICAL EQUIPMENT 55 A alternator; 4 halogen head-lamps.

DIMENSIONS AND WEIGHT tracks: 55.28 in, 140 cm front, 54.02 in, 137 cm rear; weight: 1,764 lb, 800 kg.

BODY built-in headrests on front seats (standard); tinted glass.

PRACTICAL INSTRUCTIONS fuel: 98-100 oct petrol.

Passat Series

PRICES IN GB, IN USA AND EX WORKS:

	£	$	DM
1 3-dr Limousine	—	—	11,695*
2 5-dr Limousine	—	—	12,265*
3 Variant	—	—	12,645*
4 3-dr L Limousine	—	—	12,480*
5 5-dr L Limousine	—	—	13,050*
6 L Variant	—	—	13,430*
7 3-dr GL Limousine	—	—	13,435*
8 5-dr GL Limousine	—	—	14,005*
9 GL Variant	—	—	14,385*
10 3-dr S Limousine	—	—	12,195*
11 5-dr S Limousine	—	—	12,765*
12 S Variant	—	—	13,145*
13 3-dr LS Limousine	—	6,650*	12,980*
14 5-dr LS Limousine	4,155*	6,810*	13,550*
15 LS Variant	4,310*	7,080*	13,930*
16 3-dr GLS Limousine	—	—	13,935*
17 5-dr GLS Limousine	4,450*	—	14,505*
18 GLS Variant	—	—	14,885*

For 85 hp engine add DM 865.

Power team:	Standard for:	Optional for:
55 hp	1 to 9	—
75 hp	10 to 18	—
85 hp	—	13 to 18

55 hp power team

ENGINE front, slanted 20° to right, 4 stroke; 4 cylinders, in line; 77.6 cu in, 1,272 cc (2.95 x 2.83 in, 75 x 72 mm); compression ratio: 8.2:1; max power (DIN): 55 hp (40.5 kW) at 5,800 rpm; max torque (DIN): 68 lb ft, 9.4 kg m (92.2 Nm) at 3,400 rpm; max engine rpm: 6,500; 42.4 hp/l (31.2 kW/l); cast iron block, light alloy head; 5 crankshaft bearings; valves: overhead, in line, thimble tappets; camshafts: overhead, cogged belt; lubrication: gear pump, full flow

VOLKSWAGEN Passat Diesel Series

filter, 5.3 imp pt, 6.3 US pt, 3 l; 1 Solex 30-35 PDSI (T) downdraught single barrel carburettor; fuel feed: mechanical pump; water-cooled, 10.9 imp pt, 13.1 US pt, 6.2 l, electric thermostatic fan.

TRANSMISSION driving wheels: front; clutch: single dry plate (diaphragm); gearbox: mechanical; gears: 4, fully synchronized; ratios: I 3.454, II 2.055, III 1.370, IV 0.968, rev 3.166; lever: central; final drive: spiral bevel; axle ratio: 4.555; width of rims: 5''; tyres: 155 SR x 13.

PERFORMANCE max speeds: (I) 25 mph, 41 km/h; (II) 42 mph, 68 km/h; (III) 68 mph, 110 km/h; (IV) 93 mph, 150 km/h; power-weight ratio: 3-dr. limousines 34.4 lb/hp (46.8 lb/kW), 15.6 kg/hp (21.2 kg/kW); carrying capacity: 3-dr. limousines 1,036 lb, 470 kg - 5-dr. limousines 981 lb, 445 kg; acceleration: 0-50 mph (0-80 km/h) 10.5 sec; speed in top at 1,000 rpm: 14.9 mph, 24 km/h; consumption: 32.1 m/imp gal, 26.7 m/US gal, 8.8 l x 100 km.

CHASSIS integral, front auxiliary subframe; front suspension: independent, by McPherson, lower wishbones, anti-roll bar, coil springs/telescopic damper struts; rear: rigid axle, trailing radius arms, transverse linkage bar, coil springs, anti-roll bar, telescopic dampers.

STEERING rack-and-pinion, damper.

BRAKES front disc (diameter 9.41 in, 23.9 cm), rear drum, 2 X circuits; servo.

ELECTRICAL EQUIPMENT 12 V; 36 Ah battery; 35 A alternator; Bosch distributor; 2 headlamps.

DIMENSIONS AND WEIGHT wheel base: 97.24 in, 247 cm; tracks: 52.76 in, 134 cm front, 53.15 in, 135 cm rear; length: 168.90 in, 429 cm - Variants 167.91 in, 426 cm; width: 63.58 in, 161 cm; height: 53.54 in, 136 cm; ground clearance: 7.09 in, 18 cm; weight: 3-dr. limousines 1,896 lb, 860 kg - 5-dr. limousines 1,951 lb, 885 kg - Variants 2,029 lb, 920 kg; turning circle: 33.8 ft, 10.3 m; fuel tank: 9.9 imp gal, 11.9 US gal, 45 l.

BODY 5 seats, separate front seats, reclining backrests with headrests; heated rear window; folding rear seat (for Variant only).

PRACTICAL INSTRUCTIONS fuel: 86 oct petrol; oil: engine 4.4 imp pt, 5.3 US pt, 2.5 l, SAE 20W-30, change every 9,000 miles, 15,000 km - gearbox and final drive 3.2 imp pt, 3.8 US pt, 1.8 l, SAE 80, no change recommended; greasing: none; sparking plug: 175°; tappet clearances inlet 0.008-0.012 in, 0.20-0.30 mm; exhaust 0.016-0.020 in, 0.40-0.50 mm; tyre pressure: front 24 psi, 1.7 atm, rear 24 psi, 1.7 atm.

OPTIONALS 175/70 SR x 13 tyres; sport wheels; sunshine roof; halogen headlamps; metallic spray; tinted glass; tailgate with folding rear seat (for limousines only); rear window wiper-washer (for Variant only).

75 hp power team

See 55 hp power team, except for:

ENGINE 96.9 cu in, 1,588 cc (3.13 x 3.15 in, 79.5 x 80 mm); max power (DIN): 75 hp (55.2 kW) at 5,600 rpm; max torque (DIN): 88 lb ft, 12.1 kg m (118.7 Nm) at 3,200 rpm; 47.2 hp/l (34.8 kW/l); 1 Solex PDSIT downdraught single barrel carburettor.

TRANSMISSION axle ratio: 4.111.

PERFORMANCE max speed: 102 mph, 164 km/h; power-weight ratio: 3-dr. limousines 25.4 lb/hp (34.3 lb/kW), 11.5 kg/hp (15.6 kg/kW); acceleration: 0-50 mph (0-80 km/h) 8.4 sec; speed in top at 1,000 rpm: 16.3 mph, 26.3 km/h.

ELECTRICAL EQUIPMENT 4 halogen headlamps (standard for GLS only).

DIMENSIONS AND WEIGHT length: GLS 166.14 in, 422 cm.

OPTIONALS automatic transmission hydraulic torque converter and planetary gears with 3 ratios (I 2.650, II 1.580, III 1, rev 1.800), max ratio of converter at stall 2.2, possible manual selection, 4.091 axle ratio, max speed 99 mph, 159 km/h, acceleration 0-50 mph (0-80 km/h 9.6 sec, consumption 30.1 m/imp gal, 25 m/US gal, 9.4 l x 100 km.

85 hp power team

See 75 hp power team, except for:

ENGINE max power (DIN): 85 hp (62.6 kW) at 5,600 rpm; max torque (DIN): 92 lb ft, 12.7 kg m (124.5 Nm) at 3,200 rpm; 53.5 hp/l (39.4 kW/l); 1 Solex 32/35 TDID downdraught twin barrel carburettor.

TRANSMISSION tyres: 175/70 SR x 13.

PERFORMANCE max speed: 107 mph, 173 km/h; power-weight ratio 3-dr. limousines 22.3 lb/hp (30.3 lb/kW), 10.1 kg/hp (13.7 kg/kW); acceleration: 0-50 mph (0-80 km/h) 7.9 sec; speed in top at 1,000 rpm: 16.5 mph, 26.6 km/h; consumption: 32.8 m/imp gal, 27.3 m/US gal, 8.6 l x 100 km.

ELECTRICAL EQUIPMENT 45 Ah battery; 55 A alternator.

OPTIONALS automatic transmission with 3 ratios (I 2.590, II 1.590, III 1, rev 1.800), 3.909 axle ratio, max speed 104 mph, 168 km/h, acceleration 0-50 mph (0-80 km) 9.1 sec, consumption 30.7 m/imp gal, 25.6 m/US gal, 9.2 l x 100 km.

Passat Diesel Series

PRICES IN USA AND EX WORKS:

	$	DM
3-dr D Limousine	—	13,295*
5-dr D Limousine	—	13,865*
D Variant	—	14,245*
3-dr LD Limousine	6,950*	14,080*
5-dr LD Limousine	7,110*	14,650*
LD Variant	7,380*	15,030*
3-dr GLD Limousine	—	15,035*
5-dr GLD Limousine	—	15,605*
GLD Variant	—	15,985*

50 hp power team

ENGINE Diesel, front, 4 stroke; 4 cylinders, vertical, in line; 89.8 cu in, 1,471 cc (3.01 x 3.15 in, 76.5 x 80 mm); compression ratio: 23.5:1; max power (DIN): 50 hp (36.8

VOLKSWAGEN Passat Diesel 5-dr GLD Limousine

kW) at 5,000 rpm; max torque (DIN): 59 lb ft, 8.2 kg m (80.4 Nm) at 3,000 rpm; max engine rpm: 5,000; 34 hp/l (25 kW/l); cast iron block, light alloy head; 5 crankshaft bearings; valves: overhead, in line, thimble tappets; camshafts: 1, overhead, cogged belt; lubrication: gear pump, full flow filter, 6.2 imp pt, 7.4 US pt, 3.5 l; Bosch injection pump; liquid-cooled, espansion tank, 10.9 imp pt, 13.1 US pt, 6.2 l, electric thermostatic fan.

TRANSMISSION driving wheels: front; clutch: single dry plate (diaphragm); gearbox: mechanical; gears: 4, fully synchronized; ratios: I 3.454, II 1.944, III 1.286, IV 0.909, rev 3.167; lever: central; final drive: spiral bevel; axle ratio: 4.444; width of rims: 5''; tyres: 155 SR x 13.

PERFORMANCE max speed: (I) 24 mph, 38 km/h; (II) 42 mph, 67 km/h; (III) 63 mph, 102 km/h; (IV) 88 mph, 142 km; power-weight ratio: 3-dr limousines 39 lb/hp (53 lb/kW), 17.7 kg/hp (24 kg/kW); carrying capacity: 3-dr. Limousines 981 lb, 445 kg; acceleration: 0-50 mph (0-80 km/h) 13 sec; speed in top at 1,000 rpm: 16.2 mph, 26.1 km/h; consumption: 42.8 m/imp gal, 35.6 m/US gal, 6.6 l x 100 km.

CHASSIS integral, front auxiliary subframe; front suspension: independent by McPherson, lower wishbones, anti-roll bar, coil springs/telescopic damper struts; rear: rigid axle, trailing radius arms, transverse linkage bar, coil springs, anti-roll bar, telescopic dampers.

STEERING rack-and-pinion, damper.

BRAKES front disc (diameter 9.41 in, 23.9 cm), rear drum, 2 X circuits; servo.

ELECTRICAL EQUIPMENT 12 V; 63 Ah battery; 35 A alternator; 4 headlamps.

DIMENSIONS AND WEIGHT wheel base: 97.24 in, 247 cm; tracks: 52.76 in, 134 cm front, 53.15 in, 135 cm rear; length: 168.90 in, 429 cm - Variants 167.91 in, 426 cm; width: 63.58 in, 161 cm; height: 53.54 in, 136 cm; ground clearance: 7.09 in, 18 cm; weight: 3-dr. limousines 1,951 lb, 885 kg - 5-dr. limousines 2,007 lb, 910 kg - Variants 2,084 lb, 945 kg; turning circle: 33.8 ft, 10.3 m; fuel tank: 9.9 imp gal, 11.9 US gal, 45 l.

BODY 5 seats, separate front seats, reclining backrests with headrests; heated rear window; folding rear seat (for Variant only).

PRACTICAL INSTRUCTIONS fuel: Diesel oil; oil: engine 5.3 imp pt, 6.3 US pt, 3 l - gearbox and final drive 3.2 imp pt, 3.8 US pt, 1.8 l, SAE 80 no change recommended; tyre pressure: front 24 psi, 1.7 atm, rear 24 psi, 1.7 atm.

OPTIONALS 175/70 SR x 13 tyres; sport wheels; sunshine roof; halogen headlamps; metallic spray; tinted glass; tailgate with folding rear seat (for limousines only); rear window wiper-washer (for Variant only).

1200 L

PRICE EX WORKS: 8.145* marks

(For technical data, see Volkswagen Mexico).

1303 Cabriolet

PRICE IN USA: $ 6,245*
PRICE EX WORKS: 13,845* marks

ENGINE rear, 4 stroke; 4 cylinders, horizontally opposed; 96.7 cu in, 1,584 cc (3.37 x 2.72 in, 85.5 x 69 mm); compression ratio: 7.5:1; max power (DIN): 50 hp (36.8 kW) at 4,000 rpm; max torque (DIN): 78 lb ft, 10.8 kg m (105.9 Nm) at 2,800 rpm; max engine rpm: 4,600; 31.6 hp/l (23.2 kW/l); block with cast iron liners and light alloy fins, light alloy head; 4 crankshaft bearings; valves: overhead, push-rods and rockers; camshafts: 1, central, lower; lubrication: gear pump, filter in sump, oil cooler, 4.4 imp pt, 5.3 US pt, 2.5 l; 1 Solex 34 PICT 2 downdraught carburettor; fuel feed: mechanical pump; air-cooled.

TRANSMISSION driving wheels: rear; clutch: single dry plate; gearbox: mechanical; gears: 4, fully synchronized; ratios: I 3.780, II 2.060, III 1.260, IV 0.930, rev 4.010; lever: central; final drive: spiral bevel; axle ratio: 3.875; width of rims: 4.5''; tyres: 5.60 x 15.

PERFORMANCE max speeds: (1) 19 mph, 31 km/h; (II) 35 mph, 57 km/h; (III) 58 mph, 94 km/h; (IV) 81 mph, 130 km/h; weight ratio: 41.7 lb/hp (55.7 lb/kW), 18.6 kg/hp (25.3 kg/kW); carrying capacity: 794 lb, 360 kg; acceleration: 0-50 mph (0-80 km/h) 13 sec; speed in top at 1,000 rpm: 18,6 mph, 30 km/h; consumption: 30.7 m/imp gal, 25.6 m/US gal, 9.2 l x 100 km.

CHASSIS backbone platform; front suspension: independent, by McPherson, coil springs/telescopic damper struts, anti-roll bar, lower swinging trailing arms; rear: independent,

semi-trailing arms, transverse compensating torsion bar, telescopic dampers.

STEERING rack-and-pinion; turns lock to lock: 2.60.

BRAKES front disc (diameter 10.91 in, 27.7 cm), rear drum, dual circuit; lining area: front 12.4 sq in, 80 sq cm, rear 55.5 sq in, 358 sq cm, total 67.9 sq in, 438 sq cm.

ELECTRICAL EQUIPMENT 12 V; 36 Ah battery; 50 A alternator; Bosch distributor; 2 headlamps.

DIMENSIONS AND WEIGHT wheel base: 95.28 in, 242 cm; tracks: 54.72 in, 139 cm front, 53.15 in, 135 cm rear; length: 162.99 in, 414 cm; width: 62.20 in, 158 cm; height: 59.06 in, 150 cm; ground clearance: 5.90 in, 15 cm; weight: 2,051 lb, 930 kg; turning circle: 31.5 ft, 9.6 m; fuel tank: 9.2 imp gal, 11.1 US gal, 42 l.

BODY convertible; 2 doors; 4 seats, reclining backrests.

PRACTICAL INSTRUCTIONS fuel: 87 oct petrol; oil: engine 4.4 imp pt, 5.3 US pt, 2.5 l, SAE 10W-20 (winter) 20W-30 (summer), change every 3,100 miles, 5,000 km - gearbox and final drive 5.3 imp pt, 6.3 US pt, 3 l, SAE 90, change every 31,000 miles, 50,000 km; greasing: every 6,200 miles, 10,000 km, 4 points; sparking plug: 175°; tappet clearances: inlet 0.004 in, 0.10 mm, exhaust 0.004 in, 0.10 mm; valve timing: 7°30' 37° 44°30' 4°; tyre pressure: front 16 psi, 1.1 atm, rear 24 psi, 1.7 atm.

OPTIONALS 165 SR x 15 or sport wheels with 5.5'' rims and 175/70 SR x 15 tyres; metallic spray; independent heating; halogen headlamps; headrests.

VOLKSWAGEN 1303 Cabriolet

VOLKSWAGEN 181

181

PRICE EX WORKS: 14,345* marks

ENGINE rear, 4 stroke; 4 cylinders, horizontally opposed; 96.7 cu in, 1,584 cc (3.37 x 2.72 in, 85.5 x 69 mm); compression ratio: 7.5:1; max power (DIN): 48 hp (35.3 kW) at 4,000 rpm; max torque (DIN): 74 lb ft, 10.2 kg m (Nm) at 2,000 rpm; max engine rpm: 4,600; 30.3 hp/l (2. kW/l); block with cast iron liners and light alloy fir light alloy head; 4 crankshaft bearings; valves: overhead push-rods and rockers; camshafts: 1, central, lower; lubcation: gear pump, filter in sump, oil cooler, 4.4 imp 5.3 US pt, 2.5 l; 1 Solex 30 PICT 2 downdraught carburett fuel feed: mechanical pump; air-cooled.

TRANSMISSION driving wheels: rear; clutch: single plate; gearbox: mechanical; gears: 4, fully synchronize ratios: I 3.800, II 2.060, III 1.220, IV 0.820, rev 3.6 transfer box; lever: central; final drive: spiral bevel; a ratio: 4.880; width of rims: 5''; tyres: 185 SR x 14.

PERFORMANCE max speeds: (I) 15 mph, 24 km/h; (II) mph, 45 km/h; (III) 47 mph, 76 km/h; (IV) 71 mph, km/h; power-weight ratio: 41.3 lb/hp, (56.2 lb/kW), kg/hp (25.5 kg/kW); carrying capacity: 970 lb, 440 acceleration: 0-50 mph (0-80 km/h) 14.5 sec; speed in at 1,000 rpm: 18.3 mph, 29.5 m/h; consumption: 29.7 m/i gal, 24.8 m/US gal, 9.5 l x 100 km.

CHASSIS backbone platform; front suspension: independe by McPherson, coil springs/telescopic damper struts, a roll bar, lower swinging trailing arms, rubber cone sprin

rear: independent, semi-trailing arms, transverse compensating torsion bar, telescopic dampers.

STEERING worm and roller.

BRAKES drum, dual circuit; lining area: total 125.3 sq in, 808 sq cm.

ELECTRICAL EQUIPMENT 12 V; 36 Ah battery; 30 A alternator; Bosch distributor; 2 headlamps.

DIMENSIONS AND WEIGHT wheel base: 94.49 in, 240 cm; tracks: 53.35 in, 135 cm front, 54.53 in, 138 cm rear; length: 148.82 in, 378 cm; width: 64.57 in, 164 cm; height: 63.78 in, 162 cm; ground clearance: 8.07 in, 20.5 cm; weight: 1,985 lb, 900 kg; turning circle: 36.1 ft, 11 m; fuel tank: 8.8 imp gal, 10.6 US gal, 40 l.

BODY convertible; 4 doors; 5 seats, separate front seats.

PRACTICAL INSTRUCTIONS fuel: 87 oct petrol; oil: engine 4 imp pt, 5.3 US pt, 2.5 l, SAE 10W-30 (winter) 20W-30 (summer), change every 3,100 miles, 5,000 km - gearbox and final drive 4.4 imp pt, 5.3 US pt, 2.5 l, SAE 90, change every 31,000 miles, 50,000 km; greasing: every 6,200 miles, 10,000 km, 4 points; sparking plug: 175°; tappet clearances: inlet 0.004 in, 0.10 mm, exhaust 0.004 in, 0.10 mm; valve timing: 7°30' 37° 44°30' 4°; tyre pressure: front 16 psi, 1.1 atm, rear 24 psi, 1.7 atm.

OPTIONALS limited slip differential; 6.00 x 15 or 155 SR x 15 tyres.

AC 3000 ME

AC — GREAT BRITAIN

3000 ME

PRICE EX WORKS: £ 11,302*

ENGINE Ford, centre-rear, transverse, 4 stroke; 6 cylinders, vee-slanted at 60°; 182.7 cu in 2,994 cc (3.69 x 2.85 in, 93.7 x 72.4 mm); compression ratio: 9:1; max power (DIN): 138 hp (101.6 kW) at 5,000 rpm; max torque (DIN): 174 lb ft, 24 kg m (235.4 Nm) at 3,000 rpm; max engine rpm: 5,750; 46.1 hp/l (33.9 kW/l); cast iron block and head; 4 crankshaft bearings; valves: overhead, push-rods and rockers, camshafts: 1, at centre of Vee; lubrication: rotary pump, full flow filter, oil cooler, 10.9 imp pt, 13.1 US pt, 6.2 l; 1 Weber 38/38 EGAS downdraught twin barrel carburettor; fuel feed: mechanical pump; water-cooled, 18 imp pt, 21.6 US pt, 10.2 l, electric thermostatic fan.

TRANSMISSION driving wheels: rear; clutch: single dry plate; gearbox: mechanical; gears: 5, fully synchronized; ratios: I 3.242, II 1.947, III 1.403, IV 1, V 0.835, rev 2.901; lever: central; final drive: hypoid bevel; axle ratio: 3.167; width of rims: 7''; tyres: 205/60 HR x 14.

PERFORMANCE max speed: 125 mph, 201 km/h; power-weight ratio: 17.3 lb/hp (23.5 lb/kW), 7.9 kg/hp (10.7 kg/kW); speed in top at 1,000 rpm: 25.3 mph, 40.7 km/h; consumption: 26.9 m/imp gal, 22.4 m/US gal, 10.5 l x 100 km.

CHASSIS perimeter box-type frame; front suspension: independent, wishbones, vertical links, coil springs/telescopic dampers; rear: independent, wishbones, vertical link, coil springs/telescopic dampers.

STEERING rack-and-pinion, adjustable steering wheel; turns lock to lock: 3.

BRAKES disc (front diameter 10 in, 25.4 cm, rear 9.41 in, 23.9 cm), dual circuit; swept area: front 200.8 sq in, 1,295 sq cm, rear 172.1 sq in, 1,110 sq cm, total 372.9 sq in, 2,405 sq cm.

ELECTRICAL EQUIPMENT 12 V; 55 Ah battery; 35 A alternator; Lucas distributor; 2 retractable headlamps.

DIMENSIONS AND WEIGHT wheel base: 90.50 in, 230 cm; tracks: 55 in, 140 cm front, 56 in, 142 cm rear; length: 157 in, 399 cm; width: 65 in, 165 cm; height: 45 in, 114 cm; ground clearance: 5.25 in, 13.3 cm; weight: 2,387 lb, 1,085 kg; weight distribution: 40% front, 60 % rear; turning circle: 32 ft, 9.8 m; fuel tank: 14 imp gal, 16.8 US gal, 64 l.

BODY coupé in plastic material; 2 doors; 2 seats with built-in headrests; detachable roof; electric windows; light alloy wheels.

PRACTICAL INSTRUCTIONS fuel: 97 oct petrol; oil: engine 9.7 imp pt, 11.6 US pt, 5.5 l, SAE 20W-50, change every 6,200 miles, 10,000 km; greasing: every 6,200 miles, 10,000 km, 4 points; tappet clearances: inlet 0.012 in, 0.30 mm, exhaust 0.012 in, 0.30 mm; valve timing: 20° 56° 62° 14°.

OPTIONALS servo brake.

AC 3000 ME

ARGYLL — GREAT BRITAIN

Turbo GT

PRICES EX WORKS: £ 10,500 (turbocharged engine)
£ 9,300

ENGINE Rover, turbocharged, central, transverse, 4 stroke; V8 cylinders; 215 cu in, 3,528 cc (3.50 x 2.80 in, 88.9 x 71.1 mm); compression ratio: 8.5:1; max power (DIN): 250 hp (184 kW) at 5,200-6,200 rpm; max torque (DIN): 310 lb ft, 42.8 kg m (419.7 Nm) at 3,500-4,500 rpm; max engine rpm: 6,200; 70.9 hp/l (52.2 kW/l): light alloy block and head, dry liners; 5 crankshaft bearings; valves: overhead, in line, push-rods and rockers, hydraulic tappets; camshaft: 1, at centre of Vee; lubrication: gear pump, full flow filter, oil cooler, 15 imp pt, 18 US pt, 8.5 l; 1 Minnow Fish TM7 carburettor; turbocharger; fuel feed: electric pump; water-cooled, 30 imp pt, 35.9 US pt, 17 l.

TRANSMISSION driving wheels: rear; clutch: single dry plate; gearbox: ZF mechanical; gears: 5, fully synchronized; ratios: I 2.580, II 1.520, III 1.040, IV 0.850, V 0.740, rev 2.860; lever: central; final drive: hypoid bevel, limited slip differential; width of rims: 7'' front, 8'' rear; tyres: 205 x 15.

PERFORMANCE max speed: over 150 mph, 241 km/h; power-weight ratio: 9.3 lb/hp (12.6 lb/kW), 4.2 kg/hp (5.7

ARGYLL Turbo GT

TURBO GT

kg/kW); carrying capacity: 353 lb, 160 kg; consumption: not declared.

CHASSIS box-section with integral roll cage; front suspension: independent, coil springs, telescopic dampers, double wishbone, anti-roll bar; rear: independent, semi-trailing arms, coil springs, telescopic dampers.

STEERING rack-and-pinion; turns lock to lock: 2.50.

BRAKES disc (diameter 10.30 in, 26 cm).

ELECTRICAL EQUIPMENT 12 V; 60 Ah battery; alternator; Lucas distributor; 4 headlamps.

DIMENSIONS AND WEIGHT wheel base: 118 in, 300 cm; tracks: 59.50 in, 151 cm front, 59.50 in, 151 cm rear; length: 183 in, 465 cm; width: 72 in, 183 cm; height: 48 in, 122 cm; ground clearance: 6 in, 15 cm; weight: 2,300 lb, 1,043 kg; weight distribution: 48% front, 52% rear; fuel tank: 20 imp gal, 24 US gal, 91 l.

BODY coupé, in plastic material; 2 doors; 2 seats.

PRACTICAL INSTRUCTIONS fuel: 97 oct petrol; oil: engine 15 imp pt, 18 US pt, 8.5 l, SAE 20W-30, change every 3,100 miles, 5,000 km - gearbox and final drive 5.8 imp pt, 7 US pt, 3.3 l, SAE 90, change every 12,400 miles, 20,000 km; tyre pressure: front 22 psi, 1.5 atm, rear 24 psi, 1.7 atm.

VARIATIONS

ENGINE 4 cylinders, in line, 121.1 cu in, 1,985 cc (3.54 x 3.07 in, 90 x 78 mm), 7.5:1 compression ratio, max power (DIN) 175 hp (128.8 kW) at 5,500-6,500 rpm, max torque (DIN) 220 lb ft, 30.3 kg m (297.2 Nm) at 3,500-4,500 rpm, max engine rpm 6,500, 88.2 hp/l (64.9 kW/l), cast iron block, light alloy head, 1 overhead camshafts, 1 Minnow Fish TB7 carburettor.
TRANSMISSION 4-speed fully synchronized mechanical gearbox, 185 x 15 tyres.
PERFORMANCE max speed 130 mph, 209 km/h, power-weight ratio 13.2 lb/hp (17.9 lb/kW), 6 kg/hp (8.1 kg/kW), carrying capacity 706 lb, 320 kg.
ELECTRICAL EQUIPMENT Bosch distributor.
BODY 4 seats.

OPTIONALS power steering; servo brake.

ARKLEY   GREAT BRITAIN

SS

PRICE EX WORKS: £ 2,658

ENGINE Triumph, front, 4 stroke; 4 cylinders, vertical, in line; 91.1 cu in, 1,493 cc (2.90 x 3.44 in, 73.7 x 87.5 mm); compression ratio: 9:1; max power (DIN): 65 hp (47.8 kW) at 5,500 rpm; max torque (DIN): 84 lb ft, 11.6 kg m (113.8 Nm) at 3,000 rpm; max engine rpm: 6,000; 43.5 hp/l (32 kW/l); cast iron block and head; 3 crankshaft bearings; valves: overhead, in line, push-rods and rockers; camshafts: 1, side; lubrication: eccentric pump, full flow filter, 7 imp pt, 8.5 US pt, 4 l; 2 SU type HS4 horizontal carburettors; fuel feed: electric pump; sealed circuit cooling, water, 6 imp pt, 7.2 US pt, 3.4 l.

TRANSMISSION driving wheels: rear; clutch: single dry plate (diaphragm); gearbox: mechanical; gears: 4, fully synchronized; ratios: I 3.412, II 2.112, III 1.433, IV 1, rev 3.753; lever: central; final drive: hypoid bevel; axle ratio: 3.900; width of rims: 7''; tyres: 195/70 x 13.

PERFORMANCE max speeds: (I) 35 mph, 57 km/h; (II) 59 mph, 96 km/h; (III) 85 mph, 137 km/h; (IV) 95 mph, 137 km/h; power-weight ratio: 19.8 lb/hp (26.9 lb/kW), 9 kg/hp (12.2 kg/kW); carrying capacity: 353 lb, 160 kg; acceleration: standing ¼ mile 17.5 sec, 0-50 mph (0-80 km/h) 8.2 sec; speed in direct drive at 1,000 rpm: 19.8 mph, 31.8 km/h; consumption: 38 m/imp gal, 31.8 m/US gal, 7.4 l x 100 km.

CHASSIS integral; front suspension: independent, wishbones, coil springs, anti-roll bar, telescopic dampers; rear: rigid axle, semi-elliptic leafsprings, telescopic dampers.

STEERING rack-and-pinion; turns lock to lock: 2.25.

BRAKES front disc (diameter 8.25 in, 21 cm), rear drum

ELECTRICAL EQUIPMENT 12 V; 40 Ah battery; 34 A alternator; Lucas distributor; 2 headlamps.

DIMENSIONS AND WEIGHT wheel base: 79.92 in, 203 cm;

---

tracks: 46.46 in, 118 cm front, 44.88 in, 114 cm rear; length: 123 in, 312 cm; width: 60 in, 152 cm; height: 47.50 in, 121 cm; ground clearance: 4.50 in, 10.3 cm; weight: 1,288 lb, 584 kg; weight distribution: 52.4% front, 47.6% rear; turning circle: 32 ft, 9.8 m; fuel tank: 7 imp gal, 8.4 US gal, 32 l.

BODY convertible; 2 doors; 2 seats, reclining backrests with built-in headrests.

PRACTICAL INSTRUCTIONS fuel: 98 oct petrol; oil: engine 6.5 imp pt, 7.8 US pt, 3.7 l, CAE 10W-30 (winter) 20W-50 (summer), change every 6,000 miles, 9,700 km - gearbox 2.3 imp pt, 2.7 US pt, 1.3 l, SAE 10W-30 (winter) 20W-50 (summer) - final drive 1.4 imp pt, 1.7 US pt, 0.8 l, SAE 90, change every 6,000 miles, 9,700 km; greasing: every 3,000 miles, 4,800 km, 8 points; tappet clearances: inlet 0.010 in, 0.25 mm, exhaust 0.010 in, 0.25 mm, exhaust 0.010 in, 0.25 mm; valve timing: 18° 58° 58° 19°; tyre pressure: front 18 psi, 1.3 atm, rear 20 psi, 1.4 atm.

ASTON MARTIN   GREAT BRITAIN

V8

PRICE IN USA: $ 47,875*
PRICE EX WORKS: £ 23,999*

ENGINE front, 4 stroke; 8 cylinders, Vee-slanted at 90°; 325.8 cu in, 5,340 cc (3.94 x 3.35 in, 100 x 85 mm); compression ratio: 9:1; max engine rpm: 6,000; light alloy block and head, wet liners, hemispherical combustion chambers; 5 crankshaft bearings; valves: overhead, Vee-slanted at 64°, thimble tappets; camshafts: 2 per block, overhead; lubrication: rotary pump, full flow filter, 2 oil coolers, 24 imp pt, 28.8 US pt, 13.6 l; 4 Weber 42 DCNF downdraught twin barrel carburettors; fuel feed; 2 electric pumps; water-cooled, 32 imp pt, 38.5 US pt, 18.2 l, viscous coupling fan drive.

TRANSMISSION driving wheels: rear; clutch: single dry plate (diaphragm), hydraulically controlled; gearbox: mechanical; gears: 5, fully synchronized; ratios: I 2.900, II 1.780, III 1.220, IV 1, V 0.845, rev 2.630; lever: central; final drive: hypoid bevel, limited slip differential; axle ratio: 3.310; width of rims: 7''; tyres: GR 70 VR x 15.

PERFORMANCE max speeds: (I) 47 mph, 75 km/h; (II) 77 mph, 124 km/h; (III) 112 mph, 180 km/h; (IV) 136 mph, 219; (V) 160 mph, 257 km/h; acceleration: standing ¼ mile 14 sec, 0-50 mph (0-80 km/h) 4.5 sec; speed in top at 1,000 rpm: 27 mph, 43.5 km/h; consumption: 15 m/imp gal, 12.5 m/US gal, 18.8 l x 100 km.

CHASSIS box-type platform; front suspension: independent, wishbones, coil springs, anti-roll bar, telescopic dampers; rear: de Dion rigid axle, parallel trailing arms, transverse Watt linkage, coil springs, telescopic dampers.

STEERING rack-and-pinion, adjustable height of steering wheel, servo; turns lock to lock: 2.90.

BRAKES disc (front diameter 11.50 in, 29.2 cm, rear 10.8 in, 27.4 cm), internal radial fins, rear compensator, dual circuit, dual servo; swept area: front 259 sq in, 1,670 sq cm, rear 209 sq in, 1,348 sq cm, total 468 sq in, 3,01 sq cm.

ELECTRICAL EQUIPMENT 12 V; 73 Ah battery; 75 A alternator; Lucas transistorized ignition; 2 halogen headlamps.

DIMENSIONS AND WEIGHT wheel base: 102.75 in, 261 cm; front and rear tracks: 59 in, 150 cm; length: 182 in, 462 cm; width: 72 in, 183 cm; height: 52.25 in, 133 cm; ground clearance: 5.50 in, 14 cm; weight: 3,900 lb, 1,769 kg; weight distribution: 52% front, 48% rear; turning circle: 43 ft, 13.1 m; fuel tank: 23 imp gal, 27.5 US gal, 104 l.

BODY coupé; 2 doors; 4 seats, separate front seats, reclining backrests; adjustable two-position clutch, brake and accelerator pedals; leather upholstery; heated rear window, electric windows; air-conditioning.

PRACTICAL INSTRUCTIONS fuel: 98 oct petrol; oil: engine 22 imp pt, 26.4 US pt, 12.5 l, SAE 10W-50, change every 5,000 miles, 8,000 km; greasing: every 5,000 miles, 8,00 km, 6 points; tappet clearances: inlet 0.010 in, 0.25 mm, exhaust 0.012 in, 0.30 mm; valve timing: 30° 66° 68° 28°; tyre pressure: front 35 psi, 2.4 atm, rear 35 psi, 2.4 atm.

OPTIONALS Chrysler-Torqueflite automatic transmission, hydraulic torque converter and planetary gears with 3 ratios (I 2.450, II 1.450, III 1, rev 2.200), max ratio of converter at stall 2.1, possible manual selection, 3.0 axle ratio; sunshine roof; headlamps with wiper-washers.

V8 Vantage

See V8, except for:

PRICE IN USA: $ 50,550*
PRICE EX WORKS: £ 25,999*

ENGINE compression ratio: 9.3:1; max engine rpm: 6,50 4 Weber 48IDF downdraught twin barrel carburettors.

TRANSMISSION tyres: 255/60 VR x 15.

PERFORMANCE max speeds: (I) 46 mph, 74 km/h; (II) mph, 120 km/h; (III) 109 mph, 175 km/h; (IV) 133 mph, 214 km/h; (V) 170 mph, 273 km/h; acceleration: 0-50 m (0-80 km/h) 3.8 sec.

ELECTRICAL EQUIPMENT 4 headlamps.

V8 Volante

See V8, except for:

PRICE IN USA: $ 73,000*
PRICE EX WORKS: £ 32,500*

TRANSMISSION tyres: 235/70 HR x 15.

PERFORMANCE max speeds: (I) 45 mph, 72 km/h; (II 73 mph, 116 km/h; (III) 104 mph, 166 km/h; (IV) 120 mp

ARKLEY SS

ASTON MARTIN V8 Volante

ASTON MARTIN Lagonda

2 km/h; (V) 130 mph, 209 km/h; acceleration: 0-50 mph
-80 km/h) 4.8 sec.

IMENSIONS AND WEIGHT fuel tank: 21.6 imp gal, 26
S gal, 98 l.

ODY convertible.

Lagonda

RICE EX WORKS: £ 32,620*

NGINE front, 4 stroke; 8 cylinders, Vee-slanted at 90°;
25.8 cu in, 5,340 cc (3.94 x 3.35 in, 100 x 85 mm); com-
ression ratio: 9:1; max engine rpm: 6,000; light alloy block
nd head; 5 crankshaft bearings; valves: overhead, Vee-
lanted at 64°, thimble tappets; camshafts: 2 per block,
verhead; lubrication: rotary pump, full flow filter, 2 oil
olers, 24 imp pt, 28.8 US pt, 13.6 l; 4 Weber 42 DCNF
owndraught twin barrel carburettors; fuel feed: 2 electric
umps; water-cooled, 32 imp pt, 38.5 US pt, 18.2 l, hydro-
tatic fan drive.

RANSMISSION driving wheels: rear; gearbox: Chrysler
orqueflite automatic transmission, hydraulic torque con-
erter and planetary gears with 3 ratios, max ratio of
onverter at stall 2.1, possible manual selection: ratios: I
2.450, II 1.450, III 1, rev 2.200; lever: central; final
rive: hypoid bevel, limited slip differential; axle ratio:
.070; width of rims: 6''; tyres: 235/70 HR x 15.

ERFORMANCE max speed: 140 mph, 225 km/h; speed in

ASTON MARTIN V8 Vantage

direct drive at 1,000 rpm: 24.4 mph, 39.3 km/h; consumption:
15 m/imp gal, 12.5 m/US gal, 18.8 l x 100 km.

CHASSIS box-type platform; front suspension: independent,
wishbones, coil springs, anti-roll bar, telescopic dampers;
rear: de Dion rigid axle, parallel trailing arms, transverse
Watt linkage, coil springs, telescopic dampers, self-level-
ing system.

STEERING rack-and-pinion, variable ratio servo; turns lock
to lock: 2.3.

BRAKES disc, internal radial fins, rear compensator, dual
circuit, dual servo.

ELECTRICAL EQUIPMENT 12 V; 73 Ah battery; 75 A alternator; Lucas transistorized ignition; 4 halogen headlamps.

DIMENSIONS AND WEIGHT wheel base: 114.02 in, 290 cm;
tracks: 58.27 in, 148 cm front, 59.06 in, 150 cm rear; length:
207.99 in, 528 cm; width: 70 in, 178 cm; height: 50.98 in,
129 cm; ground clearance: 9.84 in, 25 cm; weight: 4,400 lb,
2,000 kg; weight distribution: 52% front, 48% rear; turning circle: 38 ft, 11.6 m; fuel tank: 28 imp gal, 33.8 US
gal, 128 l.

BODY saloon/sedan; 4 doors; 4 seats, separate front seats,
reclining backrests, headrests; adjustable two-position clutch,
brake and accelerator pedals; leather upholstery; heated
rear window; electric windows; air-conditioning; cruise
control; laminated windscreen; glass panel in roof above
rear compartment.

PRACTICAL INSTRUCTIONS fuel: 98 oct petrol; oil: engine
22 imp pt, 26.4 US pt, 12.5 l, SAE 10W-50, change every
5,000 miles, 8,000 km; greasing: every 5,000 miles, 8,000
km, 6 points; tappet clearances: inlet 0.010 in, 0.25 mm,
exhaust 0.012 in, 0.30 mm; valve timing: 30° 66° 68° 28°;
tyre pressure: front 35 psi, 2.4 atm, rear 35 psi, 2.4 atm.

AUSTIN   GREAT BRITAIN

Allegro Series

PRICES EX WORKS:

1 1100 De Luxe 2-dr Saloon	£	2,601*
2 1100 De Luxe 4-dr Saloon	£	2,704*
3 1300 Super 2-dr Saloon	£	2,918*
4 1300 Super 4-dr Saloon	£	3,021*
5 1300 Super 2+1-dr Estate Car	£	3,199*
6 1500 Super 4-dr Saloon	£	3,119*
7 1500 Super 2+1-dr Estate Car	£	3,324*
8 1500 Special 4-dr Saloon	£	3,459*
9 1750 HL 4-dr Saloon	£	3,669*

Power team:	Standard for:	Optional for:
45 hp	1,2	—
54 hp	3 to 5	—
68 hp	6 to 8	—
90 hp	9	—

45 hp power team

ENGINE front, transverse, 4 stroke, in unit with gearbox
and final drive; 4 cylinders, vertical, in line; 67 cu in,
1,098 cc (2.54 x 3.29 in, 64.4 x 83.5 mm); compression ratio:
8.5:1; max power (DIN): 45 hp (33.1 kW) at 5,250 rpm;
max torque (DIN): 57 lb ft, 7.9 kg m (77.5 Nm) at 2,600
rpm; max engine rpm: 6,000; 41 hp/l (30.1 kW/l); cast
iron block and head; 3 crankshaft bearings; valves: overhead,
in line, push-rods and rockers; camshafts: 1, side; lubrication: rotary pump, full flow filter by cartridge, 8.5 imp
pt, 10.1 US pt, 4.8 l; 1 SU type HS4 single barrel carburettor; fuel feed: mechanical pump; sealed circuit cooling,
liquid, 7.2 imp pt, 8.7 US pt, 4.1 l, electric thermostatic fan.

TRANSMISSION driving wheels: front; clutch: single dry
plate (diaphragm); gearbox: mechanical; gears: 4, fully
synchronized; ratios: I 3.525, II 2.218, III 1.433, IV 1, rev
3.544; lever: central; final drive: helical spur gears; axle
ratio: 4.130; width of rims: 4'' or 4.5''; tyres: 145 x 13.

PERFORMANCE max speeds: (I) 26 mph, 42 km/h; (II) 41
mph, 66 km/h; (III) 64 mph, 103 km/h; (IV) 80 mph, 128
km/h; power-weight ratio: 4-dr. Saloon 41 lb/hp (55.8
lb/kW), 18.6 kg/hp (25.3 kg/kW); carrying capacity: 710
lb, 320 kg; acceleration: standing ¼ mile 22.1 sec; speed
in direct drive at 1,000 rpm: 15.5 mph, 24.9 km/h; consumption: 38.2 m/imp gal, 31.8 m/US gal, 7.4 l x 100 km.

CHASSIS integral; front suspension: independent, wishbones, hydragas (liquid and gas) rubber cone springs,
hydraulic connecting pipes to rear wheels; rear: independent, swinging longitudinal trailing arms, hydragas (liquid
and gas) rubber cone springs, hydraulic connecting pipes
to front wheels.

STEERING rack-and-pinion; turns lock to lock: 3.50.

45 HP POWER TEAM

BRAKES front disc (diameter 9.68 in, 24.6 cm), rear drum; swept area: front 178 sq in, 1,148 sq cm, rear 75.6 sq in, 487 sq cm, total 253.6 sq in, 1,635 sq cm.

ELECTRICAL EQUIPMENT 12 V; 40 Ah battery; 34 A alternator; Lucas distributor; 2 headlamps.

DIMENSIONS AND WEIGHT wheel base: 96.14 in, 244 cm; tracks: 54.33 in, 138 cm front, 54.41 in, 138 cm rear; length: 151.67 in, 385 cm; width: 63.52 in, 161 cm; height: 54.75 in, 139 cm; ground clearance: 7.48 in, 19 cm; weight: 2-dr Saloon 1,815 lb, 823 kg - 4-dr Saloon 1,847 lb, 838 kg; turning circle: 33.2 ft, 10.1 m; fuel tank: 10.5 imp gal, 12.7 US gal, 48 l.

BODY 4-5 seats, separate front seats, reclining backrests; heated rear window.

PRACTICAL INSTRUCTIONS fuel: 97 oct petrol; oil: engine, gearbox and final drive 8.5 imp pt, 10.1 US pt, 4.8 l, SAE 20W-50, change every 6,000 miles, 9,700 km; greasing: every 6,000 miles, 9,700 km, 4 points; tappet clearances (cold): inlet 0.012 in, 0.30 mm, exhaust 0.012 in, 0.30 mm; valve timing: 5° 45° 51° 21°; tyre pressure: front 26 psi, 1.8 atm, rear 24 psi, 1.7 atm.

OPTIONALS servo brake.

54 hp power team

See 45 hp power team, except for:

ENGINE 77.8 cu in, 1,275 cc (2.78 x 3.20 in, 70.5 x 81.2 mm); compression ratio: 8.8:1; max power (DIN): 54 hp (39.7 kW) at 5,250 rpm; max torque (DIN): 68 lb ft, 9.4 kg m (92.2 Nm) at 2,700 rpm; max engine rpm: 6,000; 42.3 hp/l (31.1 kW/l).

TRANSMISSION axle ratio: 3.940.

PERFORMANCE max speeds: (I) 30 mph, 48 km/h; (II) 48 mph, 77 km/h; (III) 74 mph, 119 km/h; (IV) 87 mph, 140 km/h; power-weight ratio: 4-dr Saloon 35.1 lb/hp (47.8 lb/kW), 15.9 kg/hp (21.7 kg/kW); acceleration: standing ¼ mile 21.4 sec, 0-50 mph (0-80 km/h) 14 sec; speed in direct drive at 1,000 rpm: 16.4 mph, 26.4 km/h; consumption: 37 m/imp gal, 30.9 m/US gal, 7.6 l x 100 km.

DIMENSIONS AND WEIGHT length: Estate Car 155.22 in, 394 cm; height: Estate Car 55.80 in, 141 cm; weight: 2-dr Saloon 1,830 lb, 830 kg - 4-dr Saloon 1,896 lb, 860 kg - Estate Car 1,929 lb, 875 kg.

BODY rear window wiper-washer (Estate Car only).

OPTIONALS servo brake (except for Estate Car); metallic spray.

68 hp power team

See 45 hp power team, except for:

ENGINE 90.6 cu in, 1,485 cc (3 x 3.20 in, 76.1 x 81.2 mm); compression ratio: 9:1; max power (DIN): 68 hp (50 kW) at 5,500 rpm; max torque (DIN): 80 lb ft, 11.1 kg m (108.9 Nm) at 3,100 rpm; max engine rpm: 6,500; 45.8 hp/l (33.7 kW/l); 5 crankshaft bearings; valves: overhead, Vee-slanted, thimble tappets; camshafts: 1, overhead, chain-driven; lubrication: 9.7 imp pt, 11.6 US pt, 5.5 l; 1 SU type HS6 carburettor; cooling: 9.7 imp pt, 11.6 US pt, 5.5 l.

TRANSMISSION gears: 5, fully synchronized; ratios: I 3.202, II 2.004, III 1.372, IV 1, V 0.869, rev 3.467; axle ratio: 3.647.

PERFORMANCE max speeds: (I) 33 mph, 53 km/h; (II) 54 mph, 87 km/h; (III) 78 mph, 125 km/h; (IV) 92 mph, 148 km/h; (V) 90 mph, 145 km/h; power-weight ratio: 4-dr saloons 28.2 lb/hp (38.4 lb/kW), 12.8 kg/hp (17.4 kg/kW); acceleration: standing ¼ mile 20 sec, 0-50 mph (0-80 km/h) 10 sec; speed in top at 1,000 rpm: 19 mph, 30.5 km/h; consumption: 32.1 m/imp gal, 26.7 m/US gal, 8.8 l x 100 km.

BRAKES servo (standard).

DIMENSIONS AND WEIGHT length: Estate Car 155.22 in, 394 cm; height: Estate Car 55.80 in, 141 cm; weight: 4-dr saloons 1,918 lb, 870 kg - Estate Car 1,996 lb, 905 kg.

BODY vinyl roof (1500 Special only); rear window wiper-washer (Estate Car only).

PRACTICAL INSTRUCTIONS oil: engine, gearbox and final drive 9.7 imp pt, 11.6 US pt, 5.5 l; tappet clearances: inlet 0.012-0.018 in, 0.30-0.45 mm, exhaust 0.012-0.022 in, 0.30-0.55 mm; valve timing: 9° 50° 48° 11°.

OPTIONALS automatic transmission with 4 ratios (I 2.612, II 1.807, III 1.446, IV 1, rev 2.612), max ratio of converter

AUSTIN Allegro 1100 De Luxe 2-dr Saloon

at stall 2, possible manual selection, 3.800 axle ratio, max speed 87 mph, 140 km/h; metallic spray.

90 hp power team

See 45 hp power team, except for:

ENGINE 106.7 cu in, 1,748 cc (3 x 3.77 in, 76.1 x 95.7 mm); compression ratio: 9.5:1; max power (DIN): 90 hp (66.2 kW) at 5,500 rpm; max torque (DIN): 104 lb ft, 14.3 kg m (140.2 Nm) at 3,100 rpm; max engine rpm: 6,500; 51.5 hp/l (37.9 kW/l); 5 crankshaft bearings; valves: overhead, Vee-slanted, thimble tappets; camshafts: 1, overhead, chain-driven; lubrication: 9.7 imp pt, 11.6 US pt, 5.5 l; 2 SU type HS6 carburettors; cooling: 9.7 imp pt, 11.6 US pt, 5.5 l.

TRANSMISSION gears: 5, fully synchronized; ratios: I 3.202, II 2.004, III 1.372, IV 1, V 0.869, rev 3.467; axle ratio: 3.647; tyres: 155 x 13.

PERFORMANCE max speeds: (I) 34 mph, 54 km/h; (II) 54 mph, 87 km/h; (III) 80 mph, 128 km/h; (IV) 94 mph, 151 km/h; (V) 94 mph, 151 km/h; power-weight ratio: 22.7 lb/hp (30.8 lb/kW), 10.3 kg/hp (14 kg/kW); acceleration: standing ¼ mile 19.1 sec, 0-50 mph (0-80 km/h) 9.2 sec; speed in top at 1,000 rpm: 19.4 mph, 31.2 km/h; consumption: 32 m/imp gal, 27.3 m/US gal, 8.6 l x 100 km.

BRAKES servo (standard).

ELECTRICAL EQUIPMENT 50 Ah battery; fog lamps.

DIMENSIONS AND WEIGHT weight: 2,040 lb, 925 kg.

BODY built-in headrests.

PRACTICAL INSTRUCTIONS oil: engine, gearbox and final drive 9.7 imp pt, 11.6 US pt, 5.5 l; tappet clearances: inlet 0.012-0.018 in, 0.30-0.45 mm, exhaust 0.012-0.022 in, 0.30-0.55 mm; valve timing: 9° 51° 49° 11°.

OPTIONALS metallic spray; laminated windscreen.

Maxi Series

PRICES EX WORKS:

1 1500 Saloon	£	3,462*
2 1750 Saloon	£	3,621*
3 1750 HL Saloon	£	3,936*

Power team:	Standard for:	Optional for:
68 hp	1	—
72 hp	2	—
91 hp	3	—

68 hp power team

ENGINE front, transverse, 4 stroke, in unit with gearbox and final drive; 4 cylinders, in line; 90.6 cu in, 1,485 cc (3 x 3.20 in, 76.2 x 81.3 mm); compression ratio: 9:1; max power (DIN): 68 hp (50 kW) at 5,500 rpm; max torque (DIN): 82 lb/ft, 11.3 kg m (110.8 Nm) at 3,200 rpm; max engine rpm: 6,000; 45.8 hp/l (33.7 kW/l); cast iron block and head; 5 crankshaft bearings; valves: overhead, Vee-slanted, thimble tappets; camshafts: 1, overhead, chain-

driven; lubrication: rotary pump, full flow filter, 9.5 imp pt, 11.4 US pt, 5.4 l; 1 SU type HS6 horizontal carburettor, fuel feed: mechanical pump; water-cooled, 9.5 imp pt, 11 US pt, 5.4 l.

TRANSMISSION driving wheels: front; clutch: single dry plate (diaphragm), hydraulically controlled; gearbox: mechanical; gears: 5, fully synchronized; ratios: I 3.202, II 2.004; III 1.372, IV 1, V 0.795, rev 3.467; lever: central; final drive: helical spur gears; axle ratio: 3.938; width of rims: 4.5''; tyres: 155 x 13.

PERFORMANCE max speeds: (I) 30 mph, 48 km/h; (II) 50 mph, 80 km/h; (III) 70 mph, 112 km/h; (IV) 90 mph, 145 km/h; (V) 85 mph, 136 km/h; power-weight ratio: 32.4 lb/hp (44.1 lb/kW), 14.7 kg/hp (20 kg/kW); carrying capacity: 882 lb, 400 kg; speed in 4th gear at 1,000 rpm: 15.6 mph, 25.2 km/h; consumption: 32.1 m/imp gal, 26 m/US gal, 8.8 l x 100 km.

CHASSIS integral; front suspension: independent, wishbones, hydragas (liquid and gas) rubber cone springs, hydraulic connecting pipes to rear wheels; rear: independent, swinging longitudinal trailing arms, hydragas (liquid and gas) rubber cone springs, hydraulic connecting pipes to front wheels.

STEERING rack-and-pinion; turns lock to lock: 3.90.

BRAKES front disc (diameter 9.68 in, 24.6 cm), rear drum, servo; swept area: front 182 sq in, 1,174 sq cm, rear 75 sq in, 486 sq cm, total 257.3 sq in, 1,660 sq cm.

AUSTIN Allegro 1300 Super

ELECTRICAL EQUIPMENT 12 V; 40 Ah battery; 34 A alternator; Lucas distributor; 2 headlamps.

DIMENSIONS AND WEIGHT wheel base: 104 in, 264 cm; tracks: 53.80 in, 137 cm front, 53.20 in, 135 cm rear; length: 158.33 in, 402 cm; width: 64.12 in, 163 cm; height: 55.28 in, 140 cm; ground clearance: 5.50 in, 14 cm; weight: 2,204 lb, 999 kg; weight distribution: 62.3% front, 37.7% rear; turning circle: 33.9 ft, 10.3 m; fuel tank: 9 imp gal, 10.8 US gal, 41 l.

BODY saloon/sedan; 4 + 1 doors; 4-5 seats, separate front seats, reclining backrests; heated rear window.

PRACTICAL INSTRUCTIONS fuel: 98-100 oct petrol; oil: engine, gearbox and final drive 9.5 imp pt, 11.4 US pt, 5.4 l, SAE 10W-30 (winter) 20W-50 (summer), change every 6,000 miles, 9,700 km; greasing: none; tappet clearances: inlet 0.016-0.018 in, 0.40-0.45 mm, exhaust 0.020-0.022 in, 0.50-0.55 mm; valve timing: 9°4' 50°56' 48°56' 11°4'; tyre pressure: front 26 psi, 1.8 atm, rear 24 psi, 1.7 atm.

72 hp power team

See 68 hp power team, except for:

ENGINE 106.7 cu in, 1,748 cc (3 x 3.77 in, 76.2 x 95.7 mm); compression ratio: 8.75:1; max power (DIN): 72 hp (53 kW) at 4,900 rpm; max torque (DIN): 97 lb ft, 13.4 kg m (131.4 Nm) at 2,600 rpm; 41.2 hp/l (30.3 kW/l).

TRANSMISSION gearbox ratio: V 0.869; axle ratio: 3.647.

PERFORMANCE max speeds: (I) 34 mph, 54 km/h; (II) 56 mph, 90 km/h; (III) 78 mph, 125 km/h; (IV) 92 mph, 148 km/h; (V) 86 mph, 138 km/h; power-weight ratio: 30.6 lb/hp (41.6 lb/kW), 13.9 kg/hp (18.8 kg/kW); speed in 4th gear at 1,000 rpm: 16.8 mph, 27 km/h; consumption: 24.6 m/imp gal, 20.5 m/US gal, 11.5 l x 100 km.

PRACTICAL INSTRUCTIONS tappet clearances: inlet 0.012 in, 0.30 mm, exhaust 0.012 in, 0.30 mm; valve timing: 9° 51' 49° 11°.

OPTIONALS AP automatic transmission, hydraulic torque converter with 2 conic bevel gears (twin concentric differential-like gear clusters) with 4 ratios (I 2.612, II 1.807, III 1.446, IV 1, rev 2.612), operated by 3 brake bands and 2 multi-disc clutches, max ratio of converter at stall 2, possible manual selection, max speeds (I) 41 mph, 66 km/h, (II) 59 mph, 95 km/h, (III) 73 mph, 118 km/h, (IV) 88 mph, 141 km/h.

91 hp power team

See 68 hp power team, except for:

ENGINE 106.7 cu in, 1,748 cc (3 x 3.77 in, 76.2 x 95.7 mm); compression ratio: 9.5:1; max power (DIN): 91 hp (67 kW) at 5,250 rpm; max torque (DIN): 104 lb ft, 14.4 kg m (141.2 Nm) at 3,400 rpm; 52.1 hp/l (38.3 kW/l); 2 SU type HS6 semi-downdraught carburettors.

TRANSMISSION gearbox ratio: V 0.869; axle ratio: 3.647; tyres: 165 x 13.

PERFORMANCE max speeds: (I) 35 mph, 56 km/h; (II) 56 mph, 90 km/h; (III) 82 mph, 132 km/h; (IV) 98 mph, 158 km/h; (V) 96 mph, 155 km/h; power-weight ratio: 24.3 lb/hp (33.1 lb/kW), 11 kg/hp (15 kg/kW); speed in top at 1,000 rpm: 19.9 mph, 32 km/h; consumption: 23.2 m/imp gal, 19.3 m/US gal, 12.2 l x 100 km.

STEERING turns lock to lock: 4.20.

DIMENSIONS AND WEIGHT weight: 2,216 lb, 1,005 kg.

PRACTICAL INSTRUCTIONS tappet clearances: inlet 0.012 in, 0.30 mm, exhaust 0.012 in, 0.30 mm; valve timing: 9° 51' 49° 11°.

OPTIONALS metallic spray.

BENTLEY GREAT BRITAIN

T2 Saloon

PRICE EX WORKS: £ 26,740*

ENGINE front, 4 stroke; 8 cylinders, Vee-slanted at 90°; 441.9 cu in, 6,750 cc (4.10 x 3.90 in, 104.1 x 99.1 mm); compression ratio: 8:1; aluminium alloy block and head, cast iron wet liners; 5 crankshaft bearings; valves: overhead, in line, slanted, push-rods and rockers, hydraulic tappets; camshafts: 1, at centre of Vee; lubrication: gear pump, full flow filter (cartridge), 14.5 imp pt, 17.5 US pt, 8.3 l; 2 SU type HIF7 horizontal carburettors; dual exhaust system; fuel feed: 2 electric pumps; sealed circuit cooling, expansion tank, 28.5 imp pt, 34.2 US pt, 16.2 l, viscous coupling thermostatic fan.

TRANSMISSION driving wheels: rear; gearbox: Turbo-Hydramatic 400 automatic transmission, hydraulic torque converter and planetary gears with 3 ratios, max ratio of converter at stall 2, possible manual selection; ratios: I 2.500, II 1.500, III 1, rev 2; lever: steering column; final drive: hypoid bevel; axle ratio: 3.080; width of rims: 6''; tyres: 235/70 HR x 15.

PERFORMANCE max speeds: (I) 47 mph, 76 km/h; (II) 79 mph, 126 km/h; (III) 118 mph, 190 km/h; carrying capacity: 1,014 lb, 460 kg; speed in direct drive at 1,000 rpm: 26.2 mph, 42.2 km/h; consumption: 14.1 m/imp gal, 11.8 m/US gal, 20 l x 100 km.

CHASSIS integral, front and rear auxiliary frames; front suspension: independent, lower wishbones, coil springs, anti-roll bar, telescopic dampers; rear: independent, semi-trailing arms, coil springs, anti-roll bar, automatic levelling control, telescopic dampers.

STEERING rack-and-pinion, progressive servo, right or left-hand drive; turns lock to lock: 3.20.

BRAKES disc (diameter 11 in, 27.9 cm), front internal radial fins, servo; swept area: front 227 sq in, 1,464 sq cm, rear 286 sq in, 1,845 sq cm, total 513 sq in, 3,309 sq cm.

ELECTRICAL EQUIPMENT 12 V; 68 Ah battery; 75 A alternator; Lucas transistorized distributor; 4 headlamps, 2 front and 2 rear fog lamps.

DIMENSIONS AND WEIGHT wheel base: 120.10 in, 305 cm; tracks: 60 in, 152 cm front, 59.60 in, 151 cm rear; length: 204.50 in, 519 cm; width: 71 in, 180 cm; height: 59.75 in, 152 cm; ground clearance 6.50 in, 16.5 cm; weight: 4,930 lb, 2,236 kg; turning circle: 38.5 ft, 11.7 m; fuel tank: 23.5 imp gal, 28.2 US gal, 107 l.

BODY saloon/sedan; 4 doors; 5 seats, separate front seats, adjustable and reclining backrests; headrests; automatic air-conditioning; heated rear window, electric windows; seat adjustment and gear range selector.

PRACTICAL INSTRUCTIONS fuel: 98 oct petrol; oil: engine 14.5 imp pt, 17.5 US pt, 8.3 l, SAE 20W-50, change every 6,000 miles, 9,700 km - automatic transmission 18.6 imp pt, 22.2 US pt, 10.5 l, Dexron, change every 24,000 miles, 38,600 km - final drive 4.5 imp pt, 5.3 US pt, 2.5 l, SAE 90 EP, change every 24,000 miles, 38,600 km - power steering and automatic levelling control change every 20,000 miles, 32,000 km; greasing: every 12,000 miles, 19,300 km, 5 points; valve timing: 26° 52° 68° 10°; tyre pressure: front 28 psi, 2 atm, rear 28 psi, 2 atm.

OPTIONALS iodine headlamps; tinted glass.

VARIATIONS

(For USA, Japan and Australia only).
ENGINE 7.3:1 compression ratio, catalytic converter (except for Japan).

AUSTIN Maxi 1750 HL Saloon

BENTLEY T2 Saloon

Corniche Saloon

See T2 Saloon, except for:

PRICE EX WORKS: £ 38,879*

ENGINE 1 Solex 4A1 4-barrel carburettor.

DIMENSIONS AND WEIGHT width: 72 in, 183 cm; height: 58.75 in, 149 cm; ground clearance: 6 in, 15.2 cm; weight: 5,045 lb, 2,288 kg.

ELECTRICAL EQUIPMENT 55 A alternator.

BODY 2 doors; 4 seats.

Corniche Convertible

See T2 Saloon, except for:

PRICE EX WORKS: £ 41,289*

ENGINE 1 Solex 4A1 4-barrel carburettor.

DIMENSIONS AND WEIGHT width: 72 in, 183 cm; ground clearance: 6 in, 15.2 cm; weight: 5,200 lb, 2,358 kg.

ELECTRICAL EQUIPMENT 55 A alternator.

BODY convertible; 2 doors; 4 seats.

BENTLEY T2 Saloon

CHASSIS box type ladder frame with cross members; fron suspension: independent, wishbones, coil springs, ant roll bar, adjustable telescopic dampers; rear: rigid axle longitudinal torsion bars, trailing lower radius arms, uppe torque link, transverse Watt linkage, automatic levellin control, adjustable telescopic dampers.

STEERING recirculating ball, servo; turns lock to lock:

BRAKES disc (front diameter 10.91 in, 27.7 cm, rear 10.6 in, 26.9 cm), dual circuit, servo, swept area: front 22 sq in, 1,445 sq cm, rear 196 sq in, 1,264 sq cm, total 42 sq in, 2,709 sq cm.

ELECTRICAL EQUIPMENT 12 V; 71 Ah battery; 65 A alte nator; Chrysler electronic ignition; 4 headlamps.

DIMENSIONS AND WEIGHT wheel base: 114 in, 290 cm tracks: 54.5 in, 138 cm front, 55 in, 139 cm rear; lengt 193 in, 491 cm; width: 69.5 in, 177 cm; height: 56.65 in 144 cm; ground clearance: 5 in, 13 cm; weight: 3,951 lI 1,792 kg; weight distribution: 53% front, 47% rear; tur ing circle: 39.4 ft, 12 m; fuel tank: 18 imp gal, 21.6 U gal, 82 l.

BODY saloon/sedan; 2 doors; 4 seats, reclining backrest detachable headrests front and rear; leather upholster electric windows; heated rear window; air-conditionin electric seats; laminated windscreen.

PRACTICAL INSTRUCTIONS fuel: 91 oct petrol; oil: engir 8.4 imp pt, 10.1 US pt, 4.8 l, SAE 20W-50 change eve 3,100 miles, 5,000 km - gearbox 13.9 imp pt, 16.7 US p 7.9 l, Dexron II, change every 20,000 miles, 32,000 km final drive 3.5 imp pt, 4.2 US pt, 2 l, change every 20,0 miles, 32,000 km; greasing: every 20,000 miles, 32,000 kr 4 points; valve timing: 18° 54° 57° 15°; tyre pressur front 28 psi, 2 atm, rear 28 psi, 2 atm.

OPTIONALS light alloy wheels: 3.070 axle ratio.

VARIATIONS

ENGINE Chrysler, 318 cu in, 5,211 cc (3.91 x 3.31 in, 99 x 84.1 mm); compression ratio: 8.5:1; 1 Carter downdraug twin barrel carburettor.
PERFORMANCE max speed: about 118 mph, 190 km/h.

412 S2

See 603 S2, except for:

PRICE EX WORKS: £ 27,097*

ELECTRICAL EQUIPMENT 2 headlamps.

DIMENSIONS AND WEIGHT length: 192.5 in, 490 cr weight: 3,859 lb, 1,750 kg.

BODY convertible.

OPTIONALS air-conditioning; electrically-controlled sea

BRISTOL 603 S2

BRISTOL   GREAT BRITAIN

603 S2

PRICE EX WORKS: £ 29,984*

ENGINE Chrysler, front, 4 stroke; 8 cylinders, Vee-slanted at 90°; 360 cu in, 5,900 cc (4 x 3.58 in, 101.6 x 90.9 mm); compression ratio: 8:1; cast iron block and head; 5 crank-shaft bearings; valves: overhead, hydraulic tappets, push-rods and rockers; camshafts: 1, at centre of Vee, chain driven; lubrication: rotary pump, full flow filter, 8.4 imp pt, 10.1 US pt, 4.8 l; 1 Carter downdraught 4-barrel carbu-rettor; fuel feed: mechanical pump; water-cooled, 29 imp pt, 34.9 US pt, 16.5 l, 2 electric thermostatic fans.

TRANSMISSION driving wheels: rear; gearbox: Torqueflite automatic transmission, hydraulic torque converter and planetary gears with 3 ratios, max ratio of converter at stall 2.2, possible manual selection; ratios: I 2.450, II 1.450, III 1, rev 2.200; lever: central; final drive: hypoid bevel, limited slip differential; axle ratio: 2.880; width of rims: 6''; tyres: 205 VR x 15.

PERFORMANCE max speeds: (I) 54 mph, 87 km/h; (II) 92 mph, 148 km/h; (III) 132 mph, 212 km/h; speed in direct drive/top at 1,000 rpm: 28.4 mph, 45.7 km/h; consumption at 56 mph (90 km/h): 21 m/imp gal, 17.6 m/US gal, 13.4 l x 100 km.

BRISTOL 412 S2

CHRYSLER   GREAT BRITAIN

Sunbeam Series

PRICES EX WORKS:

1.0 LS Hatchback Saloon	£ 2,499*
1.0 GL Hatchback Saloon	£ 2,732*
1.3 LS Hatchback Saloon	£ 2,603*
1.3 GL Hatchback Saloon	£ 2,836*
1.6 GL Hatchback Saloon	£ 2,944*
1.6 GLS Hatchback Saloon	£ 3,283*

Power team:	Standard for:	Optional for:
42 hp	1,2	—
59 hp	3,4	—
69 hp	5	—
80 hp	6	—

42 hp power team

ENGINE front, 4 stroke; 4 cylinders, in line; 56.6 cu in, 928 cc (2.76 x 2.37 in, 70 x 60.3 mm); compression ratio: 9.6:1; max power (DIN): 42 hp (30.9 kW) at 5,000 rpm; max torque (DIN): 51 lb ft, 7 kg m (68.6 Nm) at 2,600 rpm; max engine rpm: 6,000; 45.3 hp/l (33.3 kW/l); light alloy block and head; 3 crankshaft bearings; valves: overhead; camshafts: 1, overhead; lubrication: rotary pump, full flow filter, 5.3 imp pt, 6.3 US pt, 3 l; 1 Zenith 150 DC3 downdraught single barrel carburettor; fuel feed: mechanical pump; water-cooled, 9 imp pt, 10.8 US pt, 5.1 l, electric thermostatic fan.

TRANSMISSION driving wheels: rear; clutch: single dry plate (diaphragm); gearbox: mechanical; gears: 4, fully synchronized; ratios: I 3.894, II 2.382, III 1.527, IV 1, rev 3.050; lever: central; final drive: hypoid bevel; axle ratio: 4.375; width of rims: 4.5''; tyres: 145 x 13.

PERFORMANCE max speeds: (I) 22.6 mph, 36 km/h; (II) 37 mph, 60 km/h; (III) 57.6 mph, 93 km/h; (IV) 80 mph, 128 km/h; power-weight ratio: LS 40.7 lb/hp (55.3 lb/kW), 18.4 kg/hp (25 kg/kW) - GL 41 lb/hp (55.8 lb/kW), 18.6 kg/hp (25.3 kg/kW); carrying capacity: 980 lb, 445 kg; acceleration: 0-50 mph (0-80 km/h) 14.3 sec; speed in direct drive top at 1,000 rpm: 14.7 mph, 23.6 km/h; consumption: 35.4 m/imp gal, 42 m/US gal, 5.6 l x 100 km.

CHASSIS integral; front suspension: independent, by McPherson, coil springs/telescopic damper struts, wishbones, anti-roll bar; rear: rigid axle, swinging longitudinal trailing arms, upper oblique torque arms, coil springs, telescopic dampers.

STEERING rack-and-pinion; turns lock to lock: 3.66.

BRAKES front disc (diameter 9.50 in, 24.1 cm), rear drum, servo; swept area: front 177.8 sq in, 1,147 sq cm, rear 74 sq in, 477 sq cm, total 251.8 sq in, 1,624 sq cm.

ELECTRICAL EQUIPMENT 12 V; 40 Ah battery; 35 A alternator; Lucas distributor; 2 headlamps.

DIMENSIONS AND WEIGHT wheel base: 95 in, 241 cm; tracks: 51.80 in, 132 cm front, 51.30 in, 130 cm rear; length: 150.70 in, 383 cm; width: 63.10 in, 160 cm; height: 54.90 in, 139 cm; ground clearance: 6.50 in, 16.6 cm; weight: LS 1,709 lb, 775 kg - GL 1,725 lb, 782 kg; weight distribution: 52% front, 48% rear; turning circle: 33.5 ft, 10.2 m; fuel tank: 9 imp gal, 10.8 US gal, 41 l.

BODY hatchback saloon; 2+1 doors; 4 seats, separate front seats; reclining backrests; folding rear seat; heated rear window; headrests (GL models).

PRACTICAL INSTRUCTIONS fuel: 97 oct petrol; oil: engine 5.3 imp pt, 6.3 US pt, 3 l, SAE 20W-50, change every 5,000 miles, 8,000 km - gearbox 3 imp pt, 3.6 US pt, 1.7 l, SAE 80W-50, no change recommended; final drive 1.5 imp pt, 1.9 US pt, 0.9 l, SAE 90 EP, no change recommended; greasing: none; tappet clearances: inlet 0.007 in, 0.17 mm, exhaust 0.009 in, 0.22 mm; valve timing: 27° 61° 55° 9°; tyre pressure: front 21 psi, 1.5 atm, rear 26 psi, 1.8 atm.

OPTIONALS tinted glass; laminated windscreen; halogen headlamps; metallic spray; rear window wiper-washer.

59 hp power team

See 42 hp power team, except for:

ENGINE 79 cu in, 1,295 cc (3.09 x 2.62 in, 78.6 x 66.7 mm); compression ratio: 8.8:1; max power (DIN): 59 hp (43.4 kW) at 5,000 rpm; max torque (DIN): 69 lb ft, 9.5 kg m (93.2 Nm) at 2,600 rpm; max engine rpm: 5,900; 45.5 hp/l (33.5 kW/l); cast iron block and head; 5 crankshaft bearings; valves: overhead, push-rods and rockers; camshafts: 1, side; lubricating system: 7 imp pt, 8.5 US pt, 4 l; cooling system: 13.9 imp pt, 16.7 US pt, 7.9 l.

CHRYSLER Sunbeam GL Hatchback Saloon

CHRYSLER Sunbeam 1.6 GLS Hatchback Saloon

TRANSMISSION axle ratio: 3.890; tyres: 155 x 13.

PERFORMANCE max speeds: (I) 27 mph, 43 km/h; (II) 44 mph, 71 km/h; (III) 69 mph, 111 km/h; (IV) 89 mph, 143 km/h; power-weight ratio: LS 31.4 lb/hp (42.7 lb/kW), 14.3 kg/hp (19.4 kg/kW) - GL 31.7 lb/hp (43 lb/kW), 14.4 kg/hp (19.5 kg/kW); carrying capacity: 960 lb, 435 kg; acceleration: 0-50 mph (0-80 km/h) 12.6 sec; speed in direct drive at 1,000 rpm: 16.8 mph, 27 km/h; consumption: 41.5 m/imp gal, 34.6 m/US gal, 6.8 l x 100 km.

DIMENSIONS AND WEIGHT weight: LS 1,853 lb, 840 kg - GL 1,868 lb, 847 kg; weight distribution: 55.5% front, 44.5% rear.

PRACTICAL INSTRUCTIONS oil: engine 7 imp pt, 8.5 US pt, 4 l; tappet clearances: inlet 0.008 in, 0.20 mm, exhaust 0.016 in, 0.40 mm; valve timing: 38° 66° 72° 20°; tyre pressure: front 22 psi, 1.6 atm, rear 22 psi, 1.6 atm.

OPTIONALS Borg-Warner 45 automatic transmission with 4 ratios.

69 hp power team

See 42 hp power team, except for:

ENGINE 97.5 cu in, 1,598 cc (3.44 x 2.62 in, 87.3 x 66.7 mm); compression ratio: 8.8:1; max power (DIN): 69 hp (50.8 kW) at 4,800 rpm; max torque (DIN): 91 lb ft, 12.5 kg m (122.6 Nm) at 2,900 rpm; max engine rpm: 5,700; 43.2 hp/l (31.8 kW/l); cast iron block and head; 5 crankshaft bearings; valves: overhead, push-rods and rockers; camshafts: 1, side;

lubricating system: 7 imp pt, 8.5 US pt, 4 l; cooling system: 13.9 imp pt, 16.7 US pt, 7.9 l.

TRANSMISSION gearbox ratios: I 3.538, II 2.165, III 1.387, IV 1, rev 3.680; axle ratio: 3.540; tyres: 155 x 13.

PERFORMANCE max speeds: (I) 30 mph, 48 km/h; (II) 49 mph, 79 km/h; (III) 76 mph, 122 km/h; (IV) 95 mph, 153 km/h; power-weight ratio: 27 lb/hp (36.8 lb/kW), 12.3 kg/hp (16.7 kg/kW); carrying capacity: 920 lb, 416 kg; acceleration: 0-50 mph (0-80 km/h) 9.4 sec; speed in direct drive at 1,000 rpm: 18.4 mph, 29.6 km/h; consumption: 40.9 m/imp gal, 34.1 m/US gal, 6.9 l x 100 km.

DIMENSIONS AND WEIGHT weight: 1,868 lb, 847 kg; weight distribution: 55% front, 45% rear.

PRACTICAL INSTRUCTIONS oil: engine 7 imp pt, 8.5 US pt, 4 l; tappet clearances: inlet 0.008 in, 0.20 mm, exhaust 0.016 in, 0.40 mm; valve timing: 38° 66° 72° 20°; tyre pressure: front 22 psi, 1.6 atm, rear 22 psi, 1.6 atm.

OPTIONALS Borg-Warner 45 automatic transmission with 4 ratios.

80 hp power team

See 69 hp power team, except for:

ENGINE max power (DIN): 80 hp (58.9 kW) at 5,400 rpm; max torque (DIN): 86 lb ft, 11.9 kg m (116.7 Nm) at 4,400 rpm; max engine rpm: 6,500; 50 hp/l (36.9 kW/l); 1 Zenith-Stromberg 175 CD3 VX horizontal carburettor.

80 HP POWER TEAM

TRANSMISSION axle ratio: 3.700.

PERFORMANCE max speeds: (I) 30 mph, 48 km/h; (II) 51 mph, 82 km/h: (III) 79 mph, 127 km/h; (IV) 100 mph, 161 km/h; power-weight ratio: 23.8 lb/hp (32.4 lb/kW), 10.8 kg/hp (14.7 kg/kW); acceleration: 0-50 mph (0-80 km/h) 8.5 sec; speed in direct drive at 1,000 rpm: 17.7 mph, 28.5 km/h; consumption: 36.2 m/imp gal, 30.2 m/US gal, 7.8 l x 100 km.

ELECTRICAL EQUIPMENT halogen headlamps (standard).

DIMENSIONS AND WEIGHT weight: 1,910 lb, 866 kg.

BODY tinted glass and rear window wiper-washer (standard).

PRACTICAL INSTRUCTIONS tappet clearances: inlet 0.010 in, 0.25 mm; valve timing: 44° 78° 69° 23°.

OPTIONALS Borg-Warner 45 automatic transmission, hydraulic torque converter and planetary gears with 4 ratios (I 3, II 1.937, III 1.351, IV 1, rev 4.692), max ratio of converter at stall 2.43, possible manual selection, max speed 95 mph, 153 km/h, acceleration 0-50 mph (0-80 km/h) 10 sec, consumption 33.5 m/imp gal, 28 m/US gal, 8.4 l x 100 km.

Avenger Series

PRICES EX WORKS:

1 1.3 LS Saloon	£	2,953*
2 1.3 LS Estate Car	£	2,992*
3 1.3 GL Saloon	£	3,084*
4 1.3 GL Estate Car	£	3,414*
5 1.6 LS Saloon	£	2,789*
6 1.6 LS Estate Car	£	3,099*
7 1.6 GL Saloon	£	3,192*
8 1.6 GL Estate Car	£	3,522*
9 1.6 GLS Saloon	£	3,503*

Power team:	Standard for:	Optional for:
59 hp	1 to 4	—
69 hp	5 to 8	—
80 hp	9	—

59 hp power team

ENGINE front, 4 stroke; 4 cylinders, in line; 79 cu in, 1,295 cc (3.09 x 2.62 in, 78.6 x 66.7 mm); compression ratio: 8.8:1; max power (DIN): 59 hp (43.4 kW) at 5,000 rpm; max torque (DIN): 69 lb ft, 9.5 kg m (93.2 Nm) at 2,600 rpm; max engine rpm: 5,900; 45.6 hp/l (33.5 kW/l); cast iron block and head; 5 crankshaft bearings; valves: overhead, in line, push-rods and rockers; camshafts: 1, side chain driven; lubrication: rotary pump, full flow filter, 7 imp pt, 8.5 US pt, 4 l; 1 Zenith-Stromberg 150 CD3 horizontal carburettor; fuel feed: mechanical pump; water-cooled, 13.9 imp pt, 16.7 US pt, 7.9 l, thermostatically-controlled electric fan.

TRANSMISSION driving wheels: rear; clutch: single dry plate (diaphragm); gearbox: mechanical; gears: 4, fully synchronized; ratios: I 3.894, II 2.382, III 1.527, IV 1, rev 4.050; lever: central; final drive: hypoid bevel; axle ratio: saloons 3.890 - station wagons 4.110, width of rims: 4.5''; tyres: 155 SR x 13.

PERFORMANCE max speed: (I) 27 mph, 43 km/h; (II) 43 mph, 69 km/h; (III) 68 mph, 109 km/h; (IV) 89 mph, 143 km/h; power-weight ratio: LS saloons 33.1 lb/hp (44.9 lb/kW), 15 kg/hp (20.4 kg/kW) - GL saloons 33.8 lb/hp (45.9 lb/kW), 15.3 kg/hp (20.8 kg/kW); carrying capacity: 948 lb, 430 kg; acceleration: 0-50 mph (0-80 km/h) 12.2 sec; speed in direct drive at 1,000 rpm: 16.8 mph, 27 km/h; consumption: 41 m/imp gal, 34.1 m/US gal, 6.9 l x 100 km.

CHASSIS integral; front suspension: independent, by McPherson, coil springs/telescopic damper struts, wishbones, anti-roll bar; rear: rigid axle, swinging longitudinal trailing arms, upper oblique torque arms, coil springs. telescopic dampers (transverse linkage bar for station wagons only).

STEERING rack-and-pinion; turns lock to lock: 3.66.

BRAKES front disc (diameter 9.50 in, 24.1 cm), rear drum, servo; swept area: front 177.8 sq in, 1,147 sq cm, rear 74 sq in, 477 sq cm, total 251.8 sq in, 1,624 sq cm.

ELECTRICAL EQUIPMENT 12 V; 40 Ah battery; 34 A alternator; Lucas distributor; 2 headlamps.

DIMENSIONS AND WEIGHT wheel base: 98 in, 248 cm; tracks: 51.80 in, 132 cm front, 51.30 in, 130 cm rear; length: 164 in, 416 cm - LS saloons 163.10 in, 414 cm; width: 63.50 in, 161 cm; height: 55.30 in, 140 cm - estate cars 55.60 in, 141 cm; ground clearance: 5.60 in, 14,4 cm - estate cars 6.75 in, 17.2 cm; weight: LS saloons 1,951 lb, 885 kg - estate cars 2,072 lb, 940 kg - GL saloons 1,993

CHRYSLER Avenger 1.6 GLS 4-dr Saloon

CHRYSLER Avenger 1.6 GLS 4-dr Saloon

lb, 904 kg - estate cars 2,114 lb, 959 kg; turning circle 31.9 ft, 9.7 m; fuel tank: 9.8 imp gal, 11.6 US gal, 44

BODY 4-5 seats, separate front seats (reclining backrest on GL models); headrests; heated rear window.

PRACTICAL INSTRUCTIONS fuel: 97 oct petrol; oil: engine 7 imp pt, 8.5 US pt, 4 l, SAE 20W-50, change every 5,0 miles, 8,000 km - gearbox 3 imp pt, 3.6 US pt, 1.7 l, SA 20W-50, no change recommended - final drive 1.5 in pt, 1.9 US pt, 0.9 l, SAE 90 EP, no change recommende greasing: none; tappet clearances: inlet 0.008 in, 0.20 mr exhaust 0.016 in, 0.40 mm; valve timing: 38° 66° 72° 20 tyre pressure saloons: front and rear 24 psi, 1.7 atm estate cars; front and rear 22 psi, 1.5 atm.

OPTIONALS Borg-Warner 45 automatic transmission; tinte glass; metallic spray; reclining backrests (on LS models vinyl roof (on saloons).

69 hp power team

See 59 hp power team, except for:

ENGINE 97.5 cu in, 1,598 cc (3.44 x 2.62 in, 87.3 x 66.5 mm max power (DIN): 69 hp (50.8 kW) at 4,800 rpm; ma torque (DIN): 91 lb ft, 12.6 kg m (123.6 Nm) at 2,900 rpm 43.2 hp/l (31.8 kW/l).

TRANSMISSION gearbox ratios: I 3.538, II 2.165, III 1.38 IV 1, rev 3.680; axle ratio: 3.540.

CHRYSLER Alpine S

PERFORMANCE max speeds: (I) 30 mph, 48 km/h; (II) 48
ph, 77 km/h; (III) 75 mph, 120 km/h; (IV) 95 mph, 153
n/h; power-weight ratio: LS saloons 28.3 lb/hp (38.4 lb/
V), 12.8 kg/hp (17.4 kg/kW); acceleration: 0-50 mph
-80 km/h) 9.4 sec; speed in direct drive at 1,000 rpm:
5 mph, 29.8 km/h; consumption: 39.2 m/imp gal, 32.7
/US gal, 7.2 l x 100 km.

PTIONALS Borg-Warner 45 automatic transmission, hy-
aulic torque converter and planetary gears with 4 ratios
3, II 1.937, III 1.351, IV 1, rev 4.692), max ratio of con-
rter at stall 2.43, possible manual selection, max speed
mph, 145 km/h, acceleration 0-50 mph (0-80 km/h) 10.3
c, consumption 33.5 m/imp gal, 28 m/US gal, 8.4 l x 100
n.

80 hp power team

e 59 hp power team, except for:

IGINE 97.5 cu in, 1,598 cc (3.44 x 2.62 in, 87.3 x 66.5
n); max power (DIN): 80 hp (58.9 kW) at 5,400 rpm;
ax torque (DIN): 86 lb ft, 11.9 kg m (116.7 Nm) at 4,400
m; max engine rpm: 6,500; 50 hp/l (36.9 kW/l); 1 Zenith-
romberg 175 CD3 VX horizontal carburettor.

ANSMISSION axle ratio: 3.700.

RFORMANCE max speeds: (I) 30 mph, 48 km/h; (II) 51
ph, 82 km/h; (III) 79 mph, 127 km/h; (IV) 100 mph, 161
n/h; power-weight ratio: 25.6 lb/hp (34.7 lb/kW), 11.6
/hp (15.7 kg/kW); acceleration: 0-50 mph (0-80 km/h)
5 sec; speed in direct drive at 1,000 rpm: 17.7 mph, 28.5
n/h; consumption: 36.2 m/imp gal, 30.2 m/US gal, 7.8
x 100 km.

MENSIONS AND WEIGHT weight: 2,044 lb, 927 kg.

IDY reclining backrests; vinyl roof (standard).

ACTICAL INSTRUCTIONS tappet clearances: inlet 0.010
0.25 mm; valve timing: 44° 78° 69° 23°

PTIONALS Borg-Warner 45 automatic transmission, hydrau-
; torque converter and planetary gears with 4 ratios (I
II 1.937, III 1.351, IV 1, rev 4.692), max ratio of con-
rter at stall 2.43, possible manual selection, max speed
mph, 153 km/h, acceleration 0-50 mph (0-80 km/h) 10
c, consumption 33.5 m/imp gal, 28 m/US gal, 8.4 l x 100
n.

Alpine GL

ICE EX WORKS: £ 3,304*

IGINE front, transverse, slanted 45° to rear, 4 stroke, 4
linders, in line; 79 cu in, 1,294 cc (3.02 x 2.76 in, 76.7 x
mm); compression ratio: 9.5:1; max power (DIN): 68
(50 kW) at 5,600 rpm; max torque (DIN): 78 lb ft,
7 kg m (104.9 Nm) at 2,800 rpm; max engine rpm: 5,800;
6 hp/l (38.6 kW/l); cast iron block, light alloy head; 4
crankshaft bearings; valves: overhead, in line, push-
ds and rockers; camshafts: 1, side; lubrication: gear
mp, full flow filter, 5.3 imp pt, 6.1 US pt, 3 l; 1 Solex
BISA downdraught single barrel carburettor; fuel feed:
echanical pump; sealed circuit cooling, expansion tank,
uid, 11.4 imp pt, 13.7 US pt, 6.5 l, electric thermostatic
n.

ANSMISSION driving wheels: front; clutch: single dry
ate (diaphragm), hydraulically controlled; gearbox: me-
anical; gears: 4, fully synchronized; ratios: I 3.900, II
312, III 1.524, IV 1.080, rev 3.769; lever: central; final
ive: cylindrical gears; axle ratio: 3.706; width of rims:
; tyres: 155 SR x 13.

RFORMANCE max speed: 94 mph, 151 km/h; power-weight
tio: 33.5 lb/hp (45.6 lb/kW) 15.2 kg/hp (20.7 kg/kW);
rrying capacity: 882 lb, 400 kg; speed in top at 1,000
m: 16.3 mph, 26.2 km/h; consumption: about 38.5 m/imp
l, 32.2 m/US gal, 7.3 l x 100 km.

IASSIS integral; front suspension: independent, wish-
nes, longitudinal torsion bars, anti-roll bar, telescopic
mpers; rear: independent, swinging longitudinal trailing
ms, coil springs, anti-roll bar, telescopic dampers.

EERING rack-and-pinion; turns lock to lock: 4.15.

AKES front disc (diameter 9.45 in, 24 cm), rear drum,
ar compensator, servo; swept area: front 169.3 sq in,
092 sq cm, rear 90.2 sq in, 582 sq cm, total 259.5 sq
, 1,674 sq cm.

ECTRICAL EQUIPMENT 12 V; 40 Ah battery; 35 A alter-
tor; Chrysler transistorized ignition; 2 headlamps.

MENSIONS AND WEIGHT wheel base: 102.36 in, 260 cm;
icks: 55.51 in, 141 cm front, 54.72 in, 139 cm rear; length:
9 cm; ground clearance: 7.87 in, 20 cm; weight: 2,282
, 1,035 kg; turning circle: 36.1 ft, 11 m; fuel tank: 13.2
p gal, 15.8 US gal, 60 l.

CHRYSLER Alpine GLS

BODY saloon/sedan; 4 doors; 5 seats, separate front seats,
reclining backrests; heated rear window; folding rear seat.

PRACTICAL INSTRUCTIONS fuel: 98-100 oct petrol; oil:
engine 5.3 imp pt, 6.3 US pt, 3 l, SAE 20W-50, change
every 5,000 miles, 8,000 km - gearbox and final drive 1.9
imp pt, 2.3 US pt, 1.1 l, SAE 90 EP, no change recommended; greasing: none.

VARIATIONS

ENGINE 88 cu in, 1,442 cc (3.02 x 3.07, 76.7 x 78 mm);
max power (DIN) 85 hp (62.6 kW) at 5,600 rpm; max
torque (DIN) 92 lb ft, 12.7 kg m (124.5 Nm) at 3,000 rpm,
6,000 max engine rpm, 58.9 hp/l (43.4 kW/l), 1 Weber 36
DCNV downdraught twin barrel carburettor.
TRANSMISSION 3.588 axle ratio.
PERFORMANCE max speed 102 mph, 164 km/h, power-
weight ratio 26.9 lb/hp (36.4 lb/kW), 12.2 kg/hp (16.5
kg/kW), speed in top at 1,000 rpm 16.8 mph, 27.1 km/h,
consumption about 37.5 m/imp gal, 31.4 m/US gal, 7.5
l x 100 m.

OPTIONALS halogen headlamps; headrests on front seats;
tinted glass; headlamps with wiper-washers; metallic spray.

Alpine S

See Alpine GL, except for:

PRICE EX WORKS: £ 3,797*

ENGINE 88 cu in, 1,442 cc (3.02 x 3.07, 76.7 x 78 mm);
max power (DIN): 85 hp (62.6 kW) at 5,600 rpm; max torque
(DIN): 92 lb ft, 12.7 kg m (124.5 Nm) at 3,000 rpm; max
engine rpm: 6,000; 58.9 hp/l (43.4 kW/l); 1 Weber 36 DCNV
downdraught twin barrel carburettor.

TRANSMISSION axle ratio: 3.588.

PERFORMANCE max speed: 102 mph, 164 km/h; power-
weight ratio: 27.2 lb/hp (36.8 lb/kW), 12.3 kg/hp (16.7
kg/kW); speed in top at 1,000 rpm: 16.8 mph, 27.1 km/h;
consumption: about 37.5 m/imp gal, 31.4 m/US gal, 7.5
l x 100 km.

ELECTRICAL EQUIPMENT halogen headlamps.

DIMENSIONS AND WEIGHT weight: 2,304 lb, 1,045 kg.

BODY headlamps with wiper-washers (standard).

Alpine GLS

See Alpine S, except for:

PRICE EX WORKS: £ 4,328*

PERFORMANCE power-weight ratio: 27.6 lb/hp (37.3 lb/kW),
12.5 kg/hp (16.9 kg/kW).

DIMENSIONS AND WEIGHT weight: 2,335 lb, 1,059 kg.

BODY laminated windscreen; vinyl roof; electric windows;
tinted glass; headrests on front seats and headlamps with
wiper-washer (standard).

DAIMLER　　　　　**GREAT BRITAIN**

Sovereign 4.2

PRICE EX WORKS: £ 10,733*

ENGINE front, 4 stroke; 6 cylinders, vertical, in line; 258.4
cu in, 4,235 cc (3.63 x 4.17 in, 92 x 106 mm); compression
ratio: 7.8:1; max power (DIN): 166 hp (122.2 kW) at 4,750
rpm; max torque (DIN): 222 lb ft, 30.7 kg m (301.1 Nm) at
3,000 rpm; max engine rpm: 5,500; 39.2 hp/l (28.9 kW/l);
cast iron dry liners, light alloy head, hemispherical combustion chambers; 7 crankshaft bearings; valves: overhead,
Vee-slanted, thimble tappets; camshafts: 2, overhead; lubrication: rotary pump, full flow filter, oil cooler, 14.5
imp pt, 17.3 US pt, 8.2 l; 2 SU type HIF7 horizontal carburettors; fuel feed: 2 electric pumps; water-cooled, 32.5
imp pt, 38.9 US pt, 18.4 l, viscous coupling thermostatic
fan.

TRANSMISSION driving wheels: rear; gearbox: Borg-Warner
65 automatic transmission, hydraulic torque converter and
planetary gears with 3 ratios, max ratio of converter at
stall 2, possible manual selection; ratios: I 2.400, II 1.460,
III 1, rev 2; lever: central; final drive: hypoid bevel; axle
ratio: 3.540; width of rims: 6''; tyres: E 70 VR x 15.

PERFORMANCE max speeds: (I) 49 mph, 79 km/h; (II) 81
mph, 130 km/h; (III) 118 mph, 190 km/h; power-weight
ratio: 23.8 lb/hp, (32.3 lb/kW), 10.8 kg/hp (14.6 kg/kW);
carrying capacity: 904 lb, 410 kg; acceleration: standing ¼
mile 17.5 sec; speed in direct drive at 1,000 rpm: 22 mph,
35.4 km/h; consumption: 15.3 m/imp gal, 12.7 m/US gal,
18.5 l x 100 km.

CHASSIS integral, front and rear auxiliary frames; front
suspension: independent, wishbones, coil springs, anti-roll
bar, telescopic dampers; rear: independent, lower wishbones,
semi-axles as upper arms, trailing lower radius arms, 4
coil springs, 4 telescopic dampers.

STEERING rack-and-pinion, adjustable steering wheel, servo;
turns lock to lock: 3.30.

BRAKES disc (front diameter 11.18 in, 28.4 cm, rear 10.38
in, 26.4 cm), front internal radial fins, servo; swept area:
front 234.5 sq in, 1,512 sq cm, rear 213.7 sq in, 1,378 sq
cm, total 448.2 sq in, 2,890 sq cm.

ELECTRICAL EQUIPMENT 12 V; 66 Ah battery: 45 A alternator; Lucas distributor; 4 headlamps.

DIMENSIONS AND WEIGHT wheel base: 112.80 in, 286 cm;
tracks: 57.99 in, 147 cm front, 58.58 in, 149 cm rear; length:
194.68 in, 494 cm; width: 69.68 in, 177 cm; height: 54.13 in,
137 cm; ground clearance: 7.09 in, 18 cm; weight: 3,947
lb, 1,790 kg; turning circle: 40 ft, 12.2 m; fuel tank: 20
imp gal, 24 US gal, 91 l (2 separate tanks).

BODY saloon/sedan; 4 doors; 5 seats, separate front seats,
reclining backrests; headrests; heated rear window.

PRACTICAL INSTRUCTIONS fuel: 97 oct petrol; oil: engine
14.5 imp pt, 17.3 US pt, 8.2 l, SAE 20W-50, change every
6,000 miles, 9,700 km - gearbox 4.5 imp pt, 6.3 US pt, 2.5
l, SAE 90 EP, change every 12,000 miles, 19,400 km - final

SOVEREIGN 4.2

drive 2.7 imp pt, 3.2 US pt, 1.5 l, SAE 90 EP, change every 12,000 miles, 19,400 km; greasing: every 6,000 miles, 9,700 km, 17 points; tappet clearances: inlet 0.012-0.014 in, 0.30-0.35 mm, exhaust 0.012-0.014 in, 0.30-0.35 mm; tyre pressure: front 25 psi, 1.7 atm, rear 26 psi, 1.8 atm.

OPTIONALS 4-speed fully synchronized mechanical gearbox + overdrive/top (I 3.320, II 2.090, III 1.400, IV 1, overdrive 0.830, rev 3.428) 3.310 axle ratio; max speed 121 mph, 195 km/h, acceleration standing ¼ mile 16.4 sec, consumption 16 m/imp gal, 13.4 m/US gal, 17.6 l x 100 km; limited slip differential; air-conditioning; light alloy wheels; tinted glass; fog lamps; halogen headlamps.

Vanden Plas 4.2

See Sovereign 4.2, except for:

PRICE EX WORKS: £ 14,300*

PERFORMANCE power-weight ratio: 28.7 lb/hp (39 lb/kW), 13 kg/hp (17.7 kg/kW).

ELECTRICAL EQUIPMENT halogen headlamps (standard).

DIMENSIONS AND WEIGHT weight: 4,763 lb, 2,160 kg.

BODY fog lamps and air-conditioning (standard).

Double-Six 5.3

PRICE EX WORKS: £ 12,991*

ENGINE front, 4 stroke; 12 cylinders, Vee-slanted at 60°; 326 cu in, 5,343 cc (3.54 x 2.76 in, 90 x 70 mm); compression ratio: 9:1; max power (DIN): 284 hp (209 kW) at 5,750 rpm; max torque (DIN): 294 lb ft, 40.7 kg m (399.1 Nm) at 3,500 rpm; max engine rpm: 6,500; 53.2 hp/l (39.1 kW/l); light alloy block and head, wet liners; 7 crankshaft bearings; valves: overhead in line, thimble tappets; camshafts: 1 per block, overhead; lubrication: rotary pump, full flow filter, oil cooler, 19 imp pt, 22.8 US pt, 10.8 l; Lucas-Bosch electronic injection; fuel feed: electric pump; water-cooled, 36 imp pt, 43.3 US pt, 20.5 l, 1 viscous coupling thermostatic and 1 electric thermostatic fan.

TRANSMISSION driving wheels: rear; gearbox: Turbo-Hydramatic 400 automatic transmission, hydraulic torque converter and planetary gears with 3 ratios, max ratio of converter at stall 2, possible manual selection; ratios: I 2.480, II 1.480, III 1, rev 2.070; lever: central; final drive: hypoid bevel, limited slip differential; axle ratio: 3.310; width of rims: 6''; tyres: 205/70 VR x 15.

PERFORMANCE max speeds: (I) 58 mph, 94 km/h; (II) 96 mph, 155 km/h; (III) 140 mph, 225 km/h; power-weight ratio: 14.6 lb/hp (20 lb/kW), 6.6 kg/hp (9 kg/kW); carrying capacity: 904 lb, 410 kg; acceleration: standing ¼ mile 15.7 sec, 0-50 mph (0-80 km/h) 6.1 sec; speed in direct drive at 1,000 rpm: 24.3 mph, 39.1 km/h; consumption: 14.1 m/imp gal, 11.8 m/US gal, 20 l x 100 km.

DAIMLER Double-Six 5.3

CHASSIS integral, front and rear auxiliary frames; front suspension: independent, wishbones, coil springs, anti-roll bar, telescopic dampers; rear: independent, wishbones, semi-axles as upper arms, trailing lower radius arms, 4 coil springs, 4 telescopic dampers.

STEERING rack-and-pinion, adjustable steering wheel, servo; turns lock to lock: 3.30.

BRAKES disc (front diameter 11.18 in, 28.4 cm, rear 10.38 in, 26.4 cm), front internal radial fins, servo; swept area: front 234.5 sq in, 1,512 sq cm, rear 213.7 sq in, 1,378 sq cm, total 448.2 sq in, 2,890 sq cm.

ELECTRICAL EQUIPMENT 12 V; 68 Ah battery; 60 A alternator; Lucas electronic distributor; 4 headlamps.

DIMENSIONS AND WEIGHT wheel base: 112.80 in, 286 cm; tracks: 57.99 in, 147 cm front, 58.58 in, 149 cm rear; length: 194.68 in, 494 cm; width: 69.68 in, 177 cm; height: 54.13 in, 137 cm; ground clearance: 7.09 in, 18 cm; weight: 4,156 lb, 1,885 kg; turning circle: 40 ft, 12.2 m; fuel tanks: 20 imp gal, 24 US gal, 91 l (2 separate tanks).

BODY saloon/sedan; 4 doors; 5 seats, separate front seats, reclining backrests with built-in headrests; heated rear window; electric windows.

PRACTICAL INSTRUCTIONS fuel: 97 oct petrol; oil: engine 19 imp pt, 22.8 US pt, 10.8 l, SAE 10W-40 (winter) 20W-50 (summer), change every 6,000 miles, 9,700 km; final drive 2.7 imp pt, 3.2 US pt, 1.5 l, SAE 90 EP, change every

12,000 miles, 19,400 km; greasing: every 6,000 miles, 9,700 km, 17 points; tappet clearances: inlet 0.012-0.014 in, 0.... 0.35 mm, exhaust 0.012-0.014 in, 0.30-0.35 mm; tyre pressure: front 25 psi, 1.7 atm, rear 26 psi, 1.8 atm.

OPTIONALS air-conditioning; fog lamps; light alloy wheels; halogen headlamps.

Double-Six Vanden Plas 5.3

See Double-Six 5.3, except for:

PRICE EX WORKS: £ 16,791*

PERFORMANCE power-weight ratio: 14.5 lb/hp (19.7 lb/kW), 6.6 kg/hp (8.9 kg/kW).

ELECTRICAL EQUIPMENT halogen headlamps (standard).

DIMENSIONS AND WEIGHT weight: 4,116 lb, 1,866 kg.

BODY luxury equipment; fog lamps and air-conditioning (standard).

Limousine

PRICE EX WORKS: £ 16,486*

ENGINE front, 4 stroke; 6 cylinders, vertical, in line; 2... cu in, 4,235 cc (3.63 x 4.17 in, 92.1 x 106 mm); compression ratio: 7.5:1; max power (DIN): 162 hp (119.2 kW) at 4... rpm; max torque (DIN): 222 lb ft, 30.7 kg m (301.1 N...) at 3,000 rpm; max engine rpm: 5,500; 38.2 hp/l (28.1 kW/...) cast iron block, dry liners, light alloy head, hemispheri... combustion chambers; 7 crankshaft bearings; valves: ov... head, Vee-slanted at 70°, thimble tappets; camshafts: ... overhead; lubrication: mechanical pump, full flow filter, ... imp pt, 14.4 US pt, 6.8 l; 2 SU type HIF 7 horizontal ... burettors; fuel feed: 2 electric pumps; water-cooled, 2... imp pt, 30.7 US pt, 14.5 l, viscous coupling thermosta... fan.

TRANSMISSION driving wheels: rear; gearbox: Borg-War... automatic transmission, hydraulic torque converter and ... netary gears with 3 ratios, max ratio of converter at stal... possible manual selection; ratios: I 2.401, II 1.458, III... rev 2; lever: steering column; final drive: hypoid bev... axle ratio: 3.540; tyres 205/70 HR x 15.

PERFORMANCE max speeds: (I) 48 mph, 78 km/h; ... 79 mph, 127 km/h; (III) 115 mph, 185 km/h; power-wei... ratio: 29 lb/hp (39.7 lb/kW), 13.2 kg/hp (17.9 kg/k... carrying capacity: 1,235 lb, 560 kg; acceleration: stan... ¼ mile 19.5 sec; speed in direct drive at 1,000 rpm: 2... mph, 33.6 km/h; consumption: 17.6 m/imp gal, 14.7 m/... gal, 16 l x 100 km.

CHASSIS integral, front and rear auxiliary frames; fr... suspension: independent, wishbones, coil springs, anti-... bar, telescopic dampers; rear: independent, wishbon... semi-axle as upper arm, trailing lower radius arms, 4 '... springs, 4 telescopic dampers.

STEERING recirculating ball, adjustable steering wheel, v... able ratio gearing servo; turns lock to lock: 2.75.

BRAKES disc (front diameter 10.90 in, 27.7 cm, rear 10... in, 26.1 cm), internal radial fins, servo; swept area: fr...

DAIMLER Limousine

[...] sq in, 1,509 sq cm, rear 212 sq in, 1,367 sq cm, total [...] sq in, 2,876 sq cm.

[...]ECTRICAL EQUIPMENT 12 V; 60 Ah battery: 45 A alter-[...]or; Lucas distributor; 4 headlamps.

[...]MENSIONS AND WEIGHT wheel base: 141 in, 358 cm; [...]nt and rear tracks: 58 in, 147 cm; length: 226 in, 574 cm; [...]dth: 77.56 in, 197 cm; height: 63.39 in, 161 cm; ground [...]arance: 7.09 in, 18 cm; weight: 4,705 lb, 2,134 kg; [...]ning circle: 46 ft, 14 m; fuel tank: 20 imp gal, 24 US [...], 91 l (2 separate tanks).

[...]DY limousine; 4 doors; 8 seats, bench front seats; [...]ss partition.

[...]ACTICAL INSTRUCTIONS fuel: 97 oct petrol; oil: engine [...] imp pt, 14.4 US pt, 6.8 l, multigrade, change every [...]00 miles, 5,000 km; tappet clearances: inlet 0.012-0.014 [...]0.31-0.36 mm, exhaust 0.012-0.014 in, 0.31-0.36 mm.

[...]TIONALS air-conditioning; electric glass partition; elec-[...]c windows; tinted glass; heated rear window; halogen [...]adlamps.

[D]UTTON   GREAT BRITAIN

Malaga

[...]GINE Ford Cortina 1600, front, 4 stroke; 4 cylinders, [...]rtical, in line; 97.2 cu in, 1,593 cc (3.45 x 2.60 in, 87.6 [...]6 mm); compression ratio: 9:1; max power (DIN): 72 [...](53 kW) at 5,500 rpm; max torque (DIN): 87 lb ft, 12 [...]m (117.7 Nm) at 3,000 rpm; max engine rpm: 6,000; 45.2 [...]/l (33.3 kW/l); cast iron block and head; 5 crankshaft [...]arings; valves: overhead; camshafts: 1, overhead; [...]tion: rotary pump, full flow filter, 6 imp pt, 7.2 US pt. [...] l; 1 Weber downdraught twin barrel carburettor; fuel [...]d: mechanical pump; water-cooled, 11.4 imp pt, 13.7 [...] pt, 6.5 l.

[...]ANSMISSION driving wheels: rear; clutch: single dry [...]te (diaphragm); gearbox: mechanical; gears: 4, fully [...]nchronized; ratios: I 3.580, II 2.010, III 1.400, IV 1, rev [...]20; lever: central; final drive: hypoid bevel; axle ratio: [...]00; width of rims: 5.5'' or 6''.

[...]RFORMANCE power-weight ratio: 15.6 lb/hp (21.2 lb/kW), [...] kg/hp (9.6 kg/kW).

[...]ASSIS multi-tubular space frame; front suspension: in-[...]pendent, lower wishbones, coil springs/telescopic damper [...]its, anti-roll bar; rear: rigid axle, twin trailing radius [...]ns, A-bracket, coil springs/telescopic damper units.

[...]EERING rack-and-pinion; turns lock to lock: 3.50.

[...]AKES front disc, rear drum.

[...]ECTRICAL EQUIPMENT 12 V; 2 headlamps.

[...]MENSIONS AND WEIGHT wheel base: 86 in, 218 cm; [...]cks: 52 in, 132 cm front, 52 in, 132 cm rear; length: [...]8 in, 351 cm; width: 61 in, 155 cm; height: 42.50 in, [...]3 cm; ground clearance: 6 in, 15 cm; weight: about [...]25 lb, 510 kg.

[...]DY roadster, in plastic material; 2 seats; 2 side screens; [...]l bar.

VARIATIONS

[...]NGINE Ford Capri II 3000 GT, 6 cylinders, Vee-slanted at [...]°, 182.7 cu in, 2,994 cc (3.69 x 2.85 in, 93.7 x 72.4 mm), [...]ax power (DIN) 142 hp (104.5 kW) at 5,100 rpm, max [...]rque (DIN) 174 lb ft, 24 kg m (235.4 Nm) at 3,000 rpm, [...]4 hp/l (34.9 kW/l). [...]RFORMANCE power-weight ratio 7.9 lb/hp (10.8 lb/kW), [...] kg/hp (4.9 kg/kW).

B Plus

[...]NGINE Ford Cortina 1600, front, 4 stroke; 4 cylinders, [...]rtical, in line; 97.2 cu in, 1,593 cc (3.45 x 2.60 in, 87.6 [...]6 mm); compression ratio: 9:1; max power (DIN): 72 [...](53 kW) at 5,500 rpm; max torque (DIN): 87 lb ft, 12 [...]m (117.7 Nm) at 3,000 rpm; max engine rpm: 6,000; [...]2 hp/l (33.3 kW/l); cast iron block and head; 5 crank-[...]aft bearings; valves: overhead; camshafts: 1, overhead; [...]brication: rotary pump, full flow filter, 6 imp pt, 7.2 [...]S pt, 3.4 l; 1 Weber downdraught twin barrel carburettor; [...]el feed: mechanical pump; water-cooled, 11.4 imp pt, 13.7 [...]S pt, 6.5 l.

[...]RANSMISSION driving wheels: rear; clutch: single dry [...]te (diaphragm); gearbox: mechanical; gears: 4, fully [...]nchronized; ratios: I 3.580, II 2.010, III 1.400, IV 1, rev [...]320; lever: central; final drive: hypoid bevel; axle ratio: [...]700; width of rims: 5.5'' or 6''.

PERFORMANCE power-weight ratio: 15.6 lb/hp (21.2 lb/kW), 7.1 kg/hp (9.6 kg/kW).

CHASSIS multi-tubular space frame; front suspension: in-dependent, lower wishbones, coil springs/telescopic damper units, anti-roll bar; rear: rigid axle, twin trailing radius arms, A-bracket, coil springs/telescopic damper units.

STEERING rack-and-pinion; turns lock to lock: 3.50.

BRAKES front disc, rear drum.

ELECTRICAL EQUIPMENT 12 V; 2 headlamps.

DIMENSIONS AND WEIGHT wheel-base: 86 in, 218 cm; tracks: 52 in, 132 cm front, 52 in, 132 cm rear; length: 135 in, 343 cm; width: 61 in, 155 cm; height: 42.50 in, 108 cm; ground clearance: 6 in, 15 cm; weight: about 1,125 lb, 510 kg.

BODY roadster, in plastic material; 2 seats; 2 side screens; roll bar.

VARIATIONS

ENGINE Ford Capri II 3000 GT, 6 cylinders, Vee-slant-ed at 60°, 182.7 cu in, 2,994 cc (3.69 x 2.85 in, 93.7 x 72.4 mm), max power (DIN) 142 hp (104.5 kW) at 5,100 rpm, max torque (DIN) 174 lb ft, 24 kg m (235.4 Nm) at 3,000 rpm, 47.4 hp/l (34.9 kW/l).
PERFORMANCE power-weight ratio 7.9 lb/hp (10.8 lb/kW), 3.6 kg/hp (4.9 kg/kW).

DAIMLER Double-Six Vanden Plas

DUTTON Malaga

DUTTON B Plus

FAIRTHORPE   GREAT BRITAIN

TX-S 1500

PRICE EX WORKS: £ 3,087

ENGINE front, 4 stroke; 4 cylinders, in line; 91.1 cu in, 1,493 cc (2.90 x 3.44 in, 73.7 x 87.5 mm); compression ratio: 9.5:1; max power (SAE): 71 hp (52.3 kW) at 5,000 rpm; max torque (SAE): 82 lb ft, 11.3 kg m (110.8 Nm) at 3,000 rpm; max engine rpm: 6,000; 47.6 hp/l (35 kW/l); cast iron block and head; 5 crankshaft bearings; valves: overhead, in line, push-rods and rockers; camshafts: 1, side; lubrication: gear pump, full flow filter, 8 imp pt, 9.5 US pt, 4.5 l; 2 SU type HS 4 semi-downdraught carburettors; fuel feed: mechanical pump; water-cooled, 6 imp pt, 7.2 US pt, 3.4 l.

TRANSMISSION driving wheels: rear; clutch: single dry plate (diaphragm), hydraulically controlled; gearbox: mechanical; gears: 4, fully synchronized; ratios: I 3.500, II 2.160, III 1.390, IV 1, rev 3.990; lever: central; final drive: hypoid bevel; axle ratio: 3.890; width of rims: 5''; tyres: 165 SR x 13.

PERFORMANCE max speed: 105 mph, 169 km/h; power-weight ratio: 21.3 lb/hp (28.9 lb/kW), 9.6 kg/hp (13.1 kg/kW); carrying capacity: 672 lb, 304 kg; speed in direct drive at 1,000 rpm: 17.2 mph, 27.7 km/h; consumption: 33 m/imp gal, 27.7 m/US gal, 8.5 l x 100 km.

CHASSIS double backbone, box section with outriggers; front suspension: independent, wishbones, coil springs, telescopic dampers; rear: independent, wishbones, transverse leafspring as upper arms, lower trailing links, telescopic dampers.

STEERING rack-and-pinion; turns lock to lock: 3.50.

BRAKES front disc (diameter 9 in, 22.3 cm), rear drum; swept area: front 197 sq in, 1,270 sq cm, rear 63 sq in, 406 sq cm, total 260 sq in, 1,676 sq cm.

ELECTRICAL EQUIPMENT 12 V; 52 Ah battery; 17 A alternator; Lucas distributor; 2 headlamps.

DIMENSIONS AND WEIGHT wheel base: 83 in, 211 cm; tracks: 49.50 in, 126 cm front, 49.50 in, 126 cm rear; length: 146.46 in, 372 cm; width: 58 in, 147 cm; height: 44.49 in, 113 cm; ground clearance: 5 in, 12.7 cm; weight: 1,512 lb, 685 kg; turning circle: 25.3 ft, 7.7 m; fuel tank: 9.7 imp gal, 11.6 US gal, 44 l.

BODY coupé, in reinforced plastic material; 2 doors; 2 seats.

PRACTICAL INSTRUCTIONS fuel: 97 oct petrol; oil: engine 6.5 imp pt, 7.8 US pt, 3.7 l, SAE 20W-30, change every 6,000 miles, 9,700 km - gearbox 1.4 imp pt, 1.7 US pt, 0.8 l, SAE 90, no change recommended - final drive 1.6 imp pt, 1.9 US pt, 0.9 l, SAE 90, no change recommended; greasing: every 6,000 miles, 9,700 km, 3 points; tappet clearances: inlet 0.010 in, 0.25 mm, exhaust 0.010 in, 0.25

FAIRTHORPE TX-S 1500 - TX-S 2000

mm; valve timing: 18° 58° 58° 18°; tyre pressure: front 23 psi, 1.6 atm, rear 23 psi, 1.6 atm.

TX-S 2000

See TX-S 1500, except for:

PRICE EX WORKS: £ 3,892

ENGINE 121.9 cu in, 1,998 cc (3.56 x 3.07 in, 90.3 x 78 mm); max power (SAE): 127 hp (93.5 kW) at 5,700 rpm; max torque (SAE): 122 lb ft, 16.8 kg m (164.8 Nm) at 4,500 rpm; 63.6 hp/l (46.8 kW/l); cast iron block, light alloy head; valves: overhead, in line, thimble tappets; camshafts: 1, overhead; 2 Stromberg 175 CD SEV horizontal carburettors; cooling system: 12.8 imp pt, 15.4 US pt, 7.3 l.

PERFORMANCE max speed: 118 mph, 190 km/h; power-weight ratio: 12.8 lb/hp (17.4 lb/kW), 5.8 kg/hp (7.9 kg/kW); carrying capacity: 728 lb, 330 kg; speed in direct drive at 1,000 rpm: 19.7 mph, 31.7 km/h; consumption: 24 m/imp gal, 19.9 m/US gal, 11.8 l x 100 km.

DIMENSIONS AND WEIGHT weight: 1,624 lb, 736 kg.

PRACTICAL INSTRUCTIONS tappet clearances: inlet 0.008 in, 0.20 mm, exhaust 0.008 in, 0.20 mm; valve timing: 16° 56° 56° 16°.

FORD   GREAT BRITAIN

Fiesta Series

PRICES EX WORKS:

		£
1 3-dr Saloon		2,26
2 L 3-dr Saloon		2,52
3 S 3-dr Saloon		2,95
4 Ghia 3-dr Saloon		3,32

Power team:	Standard for:	Optional for:
40 hp	1	—
45 hp	2	—
53 hp	3,4	1,2
66 hp	—	3,4

40 hp power team

ENGINE front, transverse, 4 stroke; 4 cylinders, vertical, line; 58.4 cu in, 957 cc (2.91 x 2.19 in, 74 x 55.7 mm); compression ratio: 8.3:1; max power (DIN): 40 hp (29.4 kW) at 5,500 rpm; max torque (DIN): 47 lb ft, 6.5 kg m (63.7 Nm) at 2,700 rpm; max engine rpm: 5,700; 41.8 hp/l (30.7 kW/l); cast iron block and head; 3 crankshaft bearings; valves: overhead, in line, push-rods and rockers; camshafts: 1, side, chain driven; lubrication: gear pump, full flow filter (cartridge), 6.2 imp pt, 7.4 US pt, 3.5 l; 1 Ford downdraught single barrel carburettor; fuel feed: mechanical pump; semi-sealed circuit cooling, expansion tank, 8.8 imp pt, 10 US pt, 5 l, electric fan.

TRANSMISSION driving wheels: front; clutch: single dry plate (diaphragm); gearbox: mechanical, in unit with final drive; gears: 4, fully synchronized; ratios: I 3.583, II 2.05, III 1.346, IV 0.959, rev 3.769; lever: central; final drive: spiral bevel; axle ratio: 4.060; width of rims: 4''; tyres: 135 SR x 12.

PERFORMANCE max speed: 81 mph, 130 km/h; power-weight ratio: 38.6 lb/hp (52.5 lb/kW), 17.5 kg/hp (23.8 kg/kW); carrying capacity: 948 lb, 430 kg; acceleration: 0-50 mph, 0-80 km/h 14.2 sec; speed in top at 1,000 rpm: 15 mph, 25.4 km/h; consumption: 35.8 m/imp gal, 29.8 m/US gal, 7.9 l x 100 km.

CHASSIS integral; front suspension: independent, by McPherson, coil springs/telescopic damper struts, lower wishbones (trailing links); rear: rigid axle, swinging longitudinal trailing arms, upper oblique torque arms, Panhard rod, coil springs, telescopic dampers.

STEERING rack-and-pinion; turns lock to lock: 3.40.

BRAKES front disc (diameter 8.71 in, 22.1 cm), rear drum, dual circuit, rear compensator; lining area: front 18.6 sq in, 120 sq cm, rear 26.4 sq in, 169.9 sq cm, total 45 sq in, 289.9 sq cm.

ELECTRICAL EQUIPMENT 12 V; 35 Ah battery; 45 A alternator; Motorcraft distributor; 2 headlamps.

DIMENSIONS AND WEIGHT wheel base: 90.16 in, 229 cm; tracks: 52.36 in, 133 cm front, 51.97 in, 132 cm rear; length

FORD Fiesta Ghia 3-dr Saloon

0.16 in, 356 cm; width: 61.81 in, 157 cm; height: 53.54
, 136 cm; weight: ground clearance: 5.51 in, 14 cm; weight:
544 lb, 700 kg; turning circle: 32.1 ft, 9.8 m; fuel tank:
5 imp gal, 9 US gal, 34 l.

ODY saloon/sedan; 3 doors; 5 seats, separate front seats;
lding rear seat.

RACTICAL INSTRUCTIONS fuel: 90 oct petrol; oil: engine
8 imp pt, 5.7 US pt, 2.7 l, change every 6,200 miles, 10,000
n - gearbox and final drive 3.9 imp pt, 4.7 US pt, 2.2 l.
ange every 6,200 miles, 10,000 km; valve timing: 21°
o 70° 22°.

PTIONALS 155 SR x 12 tyres with 4.5'' wide rims; servo
ake; headrests on front seats; tinted glass; light alloy
heels; sunshine roof; rear window wiper-washer; head-
mp washers; halogen headlamps; fog lamps; metallic
ray; Touring equipment.

45 hp power team

e 40 hp power team, except for:

GINE compression ratio: 9:1; max power (DIN): 45 hp
3.1 kW) at 6,000 rpm; max torque (DIN): 48 lb ft, 6.6
m (64.7 Nm) at 3,300 rpm; max engine rpm: 6,500; 47
/l (34.6 kW/l).

ANSMISSION axle ratio: 4.290; tyres: 145 SR x 12.

RFORMANCE max speed: 85 mph, 137 km/h; power-
eight ratio: 34.3 lb/hp (46.6 lb/kW), 15.6 kg/hp (21.1
/kW); speed in top at 1,000 rpm: 14.9 mph, 24 km/h;
nsumption: 34.4 m/imp gal, 28.7 m/US gal, 8.2 l x 100 km.

RACTICAL INSTRUCTIONS fuel: 97 oct petrol.

53 hp power team

e 40 hp power team, except for:

GINE 68.2 cu in, 1,117 cc (2.91 x 2.56 in, 74 x 65 mm);
mpression ratio: 9:1; max power (DIN): 53 hp (39 kW)
5,700 rpm; max torque (DIN): 59 lb ft, 8.2 kg m (80.4
n) at 3,000 rpm; max engine rpm: 6,000; 47.4 hp/l (34.9
/l); electric thermostatic fan.

ANSMISSION width of rims: 4.5''.

RFORMANCE max speed: 90 mph, 145 km/h; power-
eight ratio: S 30.1 lb/hp (40.9 lb/kW), 13.6 kg/hp (18.5
/kW) - Ghia 30.4 lb/hp (41.2 lb/kW), 13.8 kg/hp (18.7
/kW); consumption: 32.1 m/imp gal, 26.7 m/US gal, 8.8
100 km.

ASSIS rear suspension: anti-roll bar.

AKES servo (standard).

MENSIONS AND WEIGHT weight: S 1,594 lb, 723 kg -
ia 1,610 lb, 730 kg.

FORD Fiesta S 3-dr Saloon

BODY Ghia light alloy wheels.

PRACTICAL INSTRUCTIONS fuel: 97 oct petrol.

66 hp power team

See 40 hp power team, except for:

ENGINE 79.2 cu in, 1,298 cc (3.19 x 2.48 in, 81 x 63 mm);
compression ratio: 9.2:1; max power (DIN): 66 hp (49.2 kW)
at 5,600 rpm; max torque (DIN): 68 lb ft, 9.4 kg m (92.1 Nm)
at 3,250 rpm; max engine rpm: 6,000; 50.8 hp/l (37.9 kW/l);
1 Ford downdraught twin barrel carburettor.

TRANSMISSION axle ratio: 3.842; width of rims: 4.5'';
tyres: 155 SR x 12.

PERFORMANCE max speed: 98 mph, 158 km/h; power-weight
ratio: 25.7 lb/hp (34.5 lb/kW), 11.7 kg/hp (15.6 kg/kW);
consumption: 31.4 m/imp gal, 26.1 m/US gal, 9 l x 100 km.

CHASSIS front and rear suspension: anti-roll bar and
adjustable telescopic dampers.

BRAKES servo (standard).

DIMENSIONS AND WEIGHT weight: 1,698 lb, 770 kg.

FORD Fiesta L 3-dr Saloon

FORD Escort GL 4-dr Saloon

Escort Series

PRICES EX WORKS:

	£
1 Popular 1100 2-dr Saloon	2,253*
2 Popular 1100 Plus 2-dr Saloon	2,366*
3 Popular 1100 4-dr Saloon	2,469*
4 1100 Estate Car	2,526*
5 1100 L 2-dr Saloon	2,587*
6 1100 L 4-dr Saloon	2,690*
7 1300 Popular 2-dr Saloon	2,328*
8 Popular 1300 Plus 2-dr Saloon	2,453*
9 Popular 1300 Plus 4-dr Saloon	2,556*
10 1300 Estate Car	2,657*
11 1300 L 2-dr Saloon	2,661*
12 1300 L 4-dr Saloon	2,764*
13 1300 L Estate Car	2,973*
14 1300 GL 2-dr Saloon	2,934*
15 1300 GL 4-dr Saloon	3,038*
16 1300 GL Estate Car	3,311*
17 1300 Sport 2-dr Saloon	3,108*
18 1300 Ghia 2-dr Saloon	3,468*
19 1300 Ghia 4-dr Saloon	3,571*
20 1600 Sport 2-dr Saloon	3,201*
21 1600 Ghia 4-dr Saloon	3,664*
22 RS 2000 2-dr Saloon	3,902*
23 RS 2000 Custom 2-dr Saloon	4,416*

Power team:	Standard for:	Optional for:
45 hp (economy)	1 to 6	—
48 hp (economy)	1 to 6	—
57 hp	7 to 16	—
70 hp	17 to 19	—
84 hp	20,21	—
110 hp	22,23	—

41 hp power team (economy)

ENGINE front, 4 stroke; 4 cylinders, vertical, in line; 67 cu in, 1,098 cc (3.19 x 2.10 in, 81 x 53.3 mm); compression ratio: 9:1; max power (DIN): 41 hp (30.2 kW) at 5,300 rpm; max torque (DIN): 52 lb ft, 7.2 kg m (70.6 Nm) at 3,000 rpm; max engine rpm: 6,000; 37.3 hp/l (27.5 kW/l); cast iron block and head; 5 crankshaft bearings; valves: overhead, in line, push-rods and rockers; camshafts: 1, side, chain driven; lubrication: rotary or vane-type pump, full flow filter, 5.7 imp pt, 6.8 US pt, 3.2 l; 1 Ford GPD downdraught single barrel carburettor; fuel feed: mechanical pump; water-cooled, 8.8 imp pt, 10.6 US pt, 5 l.

TRANSMISSION driving wheels: rear; clutch: single dry plate (diaphragm); gearbox: mechanical; gears: 4, fully synchronized; ratios: I 3.656, II 2.185, III 1.425, IV 1, rev 4.235; lever: central; final drive: hypoid bevel; axle ratio: 3.890; width of rims: 4.5''; tyres: 155 SR x 12.

PERFORMANCE max speed: 77 mph, 124 km/h; power-weight ratio: 43.9 lb/hp (59.6 lb/kW), 19.9 kg/hp (27 kg/kW); carrying capacity: 939 lb, 426 kg; speed in direct drive at 1,000 rpm: 16 mph, 25.8 km/h; consumption: 30.4 m/imp gal, 25.3 m/US gal, 9.3 l x 100 km.

CHASSIS integral; front suspension: independent, by McPherson, coil springs/telescopic damper struts, anti-roll bar; rear: rigid axle, semi-elliptic leafsprings, telescopic dampers.

STEERING rack-and-pinion; turns lock to lock: 3.50.

BRAKES front disc (diameter 9.60 in, 24.4 cm), rear drum (drum front and rear on Popular models), dual circuit.

ELECTRICAL EQUIPMENT 12 V; 38 Ah battery; 35 A alternator; Motorcraft distributor; 2 headlamps.

DIMENSIONS AND WEIGHT wheel base: 94.50 in, 240 cm; tracks: 49.50 in, 126 cm front, 50.60 in, 128 cm rear; length: 156.80 in, 398 cm; width: 61.80 in, 157 cm; height: 54.50 in, 138 cm; ground clearance: 4.92 in, 12.5 cm; weight: 1,799 lb, 816 kg; turning circle: 29.2 ft, 8.9 m; fuel tank: 9 imp gal, 10.8 US gal, 41 l.

BODY 5 seats, separate front seats; reclining backrests and heated rear window (standard for L models only).

PRACTICAL INSTRUCTIONS fuel: 97 oct petrol; oil: engine 5.8 imp pt, 7 US pt, 3.3 l, SAE 10W-30, change every 6,000 miles, 9,700 km - gearbox 1.6 imp pt, 1.9 US pt, 0.9 l, SAE 80, no change recommended - final drive 1.7 imp pt, 2.1 US pt, 1 l, SAE 90, no change recommended; greasing: none; tappet clearances: inlet 0.010 in, 0.25 mm, exhaust 0.017 in, 0.43 mm; valve timing: 21° 55° 70° 22°; tyre pressure: front 24 psi, 1.7 atm, rear 24 psi, 1.7 atm.

OPTIONALS laminated windscreen; heated rear window; halogen headlamps; rear fog lamps; headrests; metallic spray; servo brake (for Estate Car only); reclining backrests; 155 SR x 12 tyres (for L models only); tinted glass; vinyl roof; sports road wheels.

48 hp power team (standard)

See 41 hp power team, except for:

ENGINE max power (DIN): 48 hp (35.3 kW) at 5,500 rpm; max torque (DIN): 54 lb ft, 7.5 kg m (73.6 Nm) at 3,000 rpm; 43.7 hp/l (32.1 kW/l).

PERFORMANCE max speed: 82 mph, 132 km/h; power-weight ratio: 37.4 lb/hp (50.9 lb/kW), 17 kg/hp (23.1 kg/kW); consumption: 27.7 m/imp gal, 23.1 m/US gal, 10.2 l x 100 km.

57 hp power team

See 41 hp power team, except for:

ENGINE 79.2 cu in, 1,298 cc (3.19 x 2.48 in, 81 x 63 mm); compression ratio: 9.2:1; max power (DIN): 57 hp (41.9 kW) at 5,500 rpm; max torque (DIN): 67 lb ft, 9.3 kg m (91.2 Nm) at 3,000 rpm; max engine rpm: 5,700; 43.9 hp/l (32.3 kW/l).

TRANSMISSION tyres: 155 SR x 13.

PERFORMANCE max speed: 88 mph, 141 km/h; power-weight ratio: Escort 1300 GL saloons 32.6 lb/hp (44.4 lb/kW), 14.8 kg/hp (20.1 kW/kW); acceleration: 0-50 mph (0-80 km/h) 16.5 sec; consumption: 38.2 m/imp gal, 31.8 m/US gal, 7.4 l x 100 km.

CHASSIS rear suspension: anti-roll bar.

ELECTRICAL EQUIPMENT halogen headlamps (standard for GL models only).

DIMENSIONS AND WEIGHT length: 1300 GL saloons 159.50 in, 405 cm; weight: 1300 GL saloons 1,859 lb, 843 kg.

OPTIONALS Ford C3 automatic transmission, hydraulic torque converter and planetary gears with 3 ratios (I 2.474, II

FORD Escort 1600 Sport 2-dr Saloon

1.474, III 1, rev 2.111), max ratio of converter at stall 2.3, possible manual selection, max speed 84 mph, 135 km/h.

70 hp power team

See 41 hp power team, except for:

ENGINE 79.2 cu in, 1,298 cc (3.19 x 2.48 in, 81 x 63 mm); compression ratio: 9.2:1; max power (DIN): 70 hp (51.5 kW) at 5,500 rpm; max torque (DIN): 68 lb ft, 9.4 kg m (92.2 Nm) at 4,000 rpm; max engine rpm: 6,500; 53.9 hp/l (39.7 kW/l); 1 Weber 32/32 DGV downdraught twin barrel carburettor.

TRANSMISSION ratios: I 3.337, II 1.995, III 1.418, IV 1, rev 3.876; axle ratio: 4.125; width of rims: 5''; tyres: 155 SR x 13 - 1300 Sport 175/70 SR x 13.

PERFORMANCE max speed: 94 mph, 151 km/h - 1300 Ghia saloons 95 mph, 153 km/h; power-weight ratio: 1300 Sport 27.1 lb/hp (36.8 lb/kW), 12.3 kg/hp (16.7 kg/kW) - 1300 Ghia saloons 27.7 lb/hp (37.7 lb/kW), 12.6 kg/hp (17.1 kg/kW); consumption: 29.1 m/imp gal, 24.2 m/US gal, 9.7 l x 100 km.

CHASSIS rear suspension: anti-roll bar.

BRAKES servo.

ELECTRICAL EQUIPMENT halogen headlamps.

DIMENSIONS AND WEIGHT weight: 1300 Sport 1,896 860 kg - 1300 Ghia saloons 1,940 lb, 880 kg.

PRACTICAL INSTRUCTIONS valve timing: 29° 63° 71° 2

84 hp power team

See 41 hp power team, except for:

ENGINE 95.6 cu in, 1,599 cc (3.19 x 3.06 in, 81 x 77.6 mm max power (DIN): 84 hp (61.8 kW) at 5,500 rpm; m torque (DIN): 92 lb ft, 12.7 kg m (124.5 Nm) at 3,500 rp max engine rpm: 6,600; 52.5 hp/l (38.6 kW/l); 1 Web 32/36 DGV downdraught twin barrel carburettor; cool system: 9.5 imp pt, 11.4 US pt, 5.4 l.

TRANSMISSION ratios: I 3.337, II 1.995, III 1.418, IV rev 3.876; axle ratio: 3.540; width of rims: 5''; tyres: SR x 13 - 1600 Sport 175/70 SR x 13.

PERFORMANCE max speed: 102 mph, 164 km/h; power-wei ratio: Sport 23.6 lb/hp (32 lb/kW), 10.7 kg/hp (14.5 kg/k - Ghia 24.2 lb/hp (32.9 lb/kW), 11 kg/hp (14.9 kg/kV speed in direct drive at 1,000 rpm: 18.5 mph, 29.7 km consumption: 25.7 m/imp gal, 21.4 m/US gal, 11 l x 100 k

CHASSIS rear suspension: anti-roll bar.

BRAKES servo.

ELECTRICAL EQUIPMENT halogen headlamps.

FORD Escort RS 2000 2-dr Saloon

...MENSIONS AND WEIGHT weight: Sport 1,980 lb, 898 kg - ...Ghia 2,035 lb, 923 kg.

...DY reclining backrests with built-in headrests; sports ...d wheels; heated rear window.

...ACTICAL INSTRUCTIONS valve timing: 29° 63° 71° 21°.

...TIONALS (for Ghia only) Ford C3 automatic transmission, ...draulic torque converter and planetary gears with 3 ratios ...2.474, II 1.474, III 1, rev 2.111), max ratio of converter ...stall 2.3, possible manual selection.

110 hp power team

...e 41 hp power team, except for:

...GINE 121.6 cu in, 1,993 cc (3.57 x 3.03 in, 90.8 x 76.9 ...n); compression ratio: 9.2:1; max power (DIN): 110 hp ...kW) at 5,500 rpm; max torque (DIN): 118 lb ft, 16.3 ...m (159.8 Nm) at 3,750 rpm; max engine rpm: 6,600; 55.2 ...I (40.6 kW/I); valves: overhead, Vee-slanted, rockers; ...mshafts: 1, overhead, cogged belt; lubrication: gear or ...ne-type pump, full flow filter, oil cooler, 6.7 imp pt, 8 ...pt, 3.8 l; 1 Weber 32/36 DGAV downdraught twin barrel ...rburettor; cooling system: 12.5 imp pt, 15 US pt, 7.1 l, ...ctric thermostatic fan.

...ANSMISSION ratios: I 3.656, II 1.970, III 1.370, IV 1, ...3.660; axle ratio: 3.540; width of rims: 6''; tyres: 175/70 ...x 13.

FORD Cortina 1600 L Estate Car

FORD Escort 1600 Sport 2-dr Saloon

...RFORMANCE max speeds: (I) 32 mph, 52 km/h; (II) 60 ...h, 96 km/h; (III) 86 mph, 138 km/h; (IV) 110 mph, 177 ...h; power-weight ratio: 18.7 lb/hp (25.5 lb/kW), 8.5 ...hp (11.5 kg/kW); speed in direct drive at 1,000 rpm: ...6 mph, 29.9 km/h; consumption: 27.6 m/imp gal, 23.1 ...US gal, 10.2 l x 100 km.

...HASSIS rear suspension: trailing radius arms.

...EERING turns lock to lock: 3.30.

...AKES front disc (diameter 9.60 in, 24.4 cm), rear drum, ...rvo; swept area: front 195 sq in, 1,258 sq cm, rear 99 ...in, 639 sq cm, total 294 sq in, 1,897 sq cm.

...ECTRICAL EQUIPMENT 55 Ah battery; 45 A alternator; ...ogen headlamps.

...MENSIONS AND WEIGHT wheel base: 94 in, 239 cm; ...cks: 50.30 in, 128 cm front, 51.10 in, 130 cm rear; length: ...1.80 in, 411 cm; width: 61.60 in, 156 cm; height: 55 in, ...0 cm; weight: 2,062 lb, 935 kg; weight distribution: 54% ...nt, 46% rear.

...ACTICAL INSTRUCTIONS oil: engine 6.7 imp pt, 8 US pt, ...8 l, SAE 10W-30, change every 6,000 miles, 9,700 km - ...arbox 2.4 imp pt, 2.7 US pt, 1.3 l - final drive 2 imp ...2.3 US pt, 1.1 l; tappet clearances: inlet 0.008 in, 0.20 ...n, exhaust 0.010 in, 0.25 mm; valve timing: 18° 70° 64° 24°.

...PTIONALS competition equipment; sports road wheels; ...etallic spray; tinted glass with laminated windscreen; ...nyl roof.

Cortina Series

PRICES EX WORKS:

1	1300 2-dr Saloon	£ 2,767*
2	1300 4-dr Saloon	£ 2,878*
3	1300 L 2-dr Saloon	£ 2,960*
4	1300 L 4-dr Saloon	£ 3,071*
5	1600 4-dr Saloon	£ 3,049*
6	1600 Estate Car	£ 3,398*
7	1600 L 4-dr Saloon	£ 3,242*
8	1600 L Estate Car	£ 3,624*
9	1600 GL 4-dr Saloon	£ 3,557*
10	1600 GL Estate Car	£ 3,939*
11	1600 Ghia 4-dr Saloon	£ 4,233*
12	1600 Ghia Estate Car	£ 4,615*
13	2000 GL 4-dr Saloon	£ 3,762*
14	2000 GL Estate Car	£ 4,144*
15	2000 S 4-dr Saloon	£ 4,009*
16	2000 Ghia 4-dr Saloon	£ 4,356*
17	2000 Ghia Estate Car	£ 4,738*
18	2300 GL 4-dr Saloon	£ 4,251*
19	2300 GL Estate Car	£ 4,633*
20	2300 S 4-dr Saloon	£ 4,497*
21	2300 Ghia 4-dr Saloon	£ 4,844*
22	2300 Ghia Estate Car	£ 5,226*

Power team:	Standard for:	Optional for:
50 hp (economy)	1 to 4	—
57 hp (standard)	1 to 4	—
59 hp (economy)	5,6	7,8
72 hp (standard)	7 to 10	—
88 hp	11,12	—
98 hp	13 to 17	—
108 hp	18 to 22	—

50 hp power team (economy)

ENGINE front, 4 stroke; 4 cylinders, vertical, in line; 79.2 cu in, 1,298 cc (3.19 x 2.48 in, 81 x 63 mm); compression ratio: 9.2:1; max power (DIN): 50 hp (36.8 kW) at 5,000 rpm; max torque (DIN): 64 lb ft, 8.8 kg m (86.3 Nm) at 3,000 rpm; max engine rpm: 6,000; 38.6 hp/l (28.4 kW/l); cast iron block and head; 5 crankshaft bearings; valves: overhead, push-rods and rockers; camshafts: 1, side, chain driven; lubrication: rotary pump, full flow filter, 6 imp pt, 7.2 US pt, 3.4 l; 1 Motorcraft GPD downdraught single barrel carburettor; fuel feed: mechanical pump; water-cooled, 8.7 imp pt, 10.4 US pt, 4.9 l.

TRANSMISSION driving wheels: rear; clutch: single dry plate (diaphragm); gearbox: mechanical; gears: 4, fully synchronized; ratios: I 3.580, II 2.010, III 1.400, IV 1, rev 3.320; lever: central; final drive: hypoid bevel; axle ratio: 4.110; width of rims: 4.5''; tyres: 165 SR x 13.

PERFORMANCE max speeds: (I) 24 mph, 38 km/h; (II) 37 mph, 59 km/h; (III) 63 mph, 101 km/h; (IV) 82 mph, 132 km/h; power-weight ratio: 44.1 lb/hp (59.9 lb/kW), 20 kg/hp (27.2 kg/kW); carrying capacity: 1,049 lb, 475 kg; speed in direct drive at 1,000 rpm: 16.3 mph, 26.2 km/h; consumption: 26.6 m/imp gal, 22.2 m/US gal, 10.6 l x 100 km.

CHASSIS integral, front auxiliary frame; front suspension: independent, wishbones, anti-roll bar, coil springs/telescopic dampers; rear: rigid axle, lower longitudinal trailing arms, upper oblique torque arms, coil springs, anti-roll bar, telescopic dampers.

STEERING rack-and-pinion; turns lock to lock: 3.70.

BRAKES front disc (diameter 9.72 in, 24.7 cm), rear drum, dual circuit, servo.

ELECTRICAL EQUIPMENT 12 V; 38 Ah battery; 35 A alternator; Ford distributor; 2 headlamps.

DIMENSIONS AND WEIGHT wheel base: 101.50 in, 258 cm; tracks: 56.90 in, 144 cm front, 56 in, 142 cm rear; length: 170.35 in, 433 cm; width: 66.90 in, 170 cm; height: 52 in, 132 cm; ground clearance: 5.12 in, 13 cm; weight: 2,205 lb, 1,000 kg; weight distribution: 53% front, 47% rear; turning circle: 32 ft, 9.8 m; fuel tank: 12 imp gal, 14.3 US gal, 54 l.

BODY saloon/sedan; 5 seats, separate front seats.

PRACTICAL INSTRUCTIONS fuel: 97 oct petrol; oil: engine 6 imp pt, 7.2 US pt, 3.4 l, SAE 10W-30, change every 6,000 miles, 9,700 km - gearbox 1.6 imp pt, 1.9 US pt, 0.9 l, SAE 80 EP, no change recommended - final drive 1.8 imp pt, 2.1 US pt, 1 l, SAE 90 EP, no change recommended; greasing: none; tappet clearances: inlet 0.004 in, 0.10 mm, exhaust 0.007 in, 0.17 mm; valve timing: 21° 55° 70° 22°; tyre pressure: front 24 psi, 1.7 atm, rear 24 psi, 1.7 atm.

OPTIONALS laminated windscreen; metallic spray; rear fog lamp; reclining backrests; headrests (for L models only); sunshine roof; tinted glass; vinyl roof; 185/70 SR x 13 tyres only with sports road wheels.

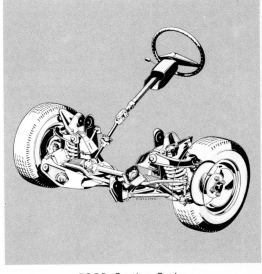

FORD Cortina Series

57 hp power team (standard)

See 50 hp power team, except for:

ENGINE max power (DIN): 57 hp (41.9 kW) at 5,500 rpm; max torque (DIN): 67 lb/ft, 9.3 kg m (91.3 Nm) at 3,000 rpm; 43.9 hp/l (33.3 kW/l).

PERFORMANCE max speed: 86 mph, 138 km/h; power-weight ratio: 38.7 lb/hp (52.6 lb/kW), 17.5 kg/hp (23.9 kg/kW); consumption: 26.4 m/imp gal, 22 m/US gal, 10.7 l x 100 km.

59 hp power team (economy)

See 50 hp power team, except for:

ENGINE 97.2 cu in, 1,593 cc (3.45 x 2.60 in, 87.6 x 66 mm); max power (DIN): 59 hp (43.4 kW) at 4,500 rpm; max torque (DIN): 82 lb ft, 11.7 kg m (114.7 Nm) at 2,600 rpm; max engine rpm: 5,200; 37 hp/l (27.2 kW/l); valves: overhead, Vee-slanted, rockers; camshafts: 1, overhead, cogged belt.

TRANSMISSION axle ratio: 3.780.

PERFORMANCE max speed: 88 mph, 141 km/h; power-weight ratio: 39.4 lb/hp (53.6 lb/kW), 17.9 kg/hp (24.3 kg/kW); speed in direct drive at 1,000 rpm: 17.8 mph, 28.6 km/h; consumption: 26.4 m/imp gal, 22 m/US gal, 10.7 l x 100 km.

DIMENSIONS AND WEIGHT length: station wagons 174.30 in, 443 cm; height: station wagons 52.10 in, 132 cm; weight: 2,326 in, 1,055 kg; weight distribution: 54% front, 46% rear.

OPTIONALS rear window wiper-washer for 1600 L Estate Car only.

72 hp power team (standard)

See 59 hp power team, except for:

ENGINE max power (DIN): 72 hp (53 kW) at 5,000 rpm; max torque (DIN): 87 lb ft, 12 kg m (117.7 Nm) at 2,700 rpm; max engine rpm: 5,500; 45.2 hp/l (33.3 kW/l).

TRANSMISSION axle ratio: 3.890.

PERFORMANCE max speed: 94 mph, 151 km/h; power-weight ratio: 32.3 lb/hp (43.9 lb/kW), 14.6 kg/hp (19.9 kg/kW); carrying capacity: 977 lb, 443 kg; speed in direct drive at 1,000 rpm: 17.3 mph, 27.8 km/h; consumption: 25.7 m/imp gal, 21.4 m/US gal, 11 l x 100 km.

OPTIONALS Ford C3 automatic transmission, hydraulic torque converter and planetary gears with 3 ratios (I 2.474, II 1.474, III 1, rev 2.111), max ratio of converter at stall 2, possible manual selection, max speed 89 mph, 143 km/h.

FORD Cortina 1600 GL 4-dr Saloon

88 hp power team

See 59 hp power team, except for:

ENGINE max power (DIN): 88 hp (64.8 kW) at 5,700 rpm; max torque (DIN): 92 lb ft, 12.7 kg m (124.5 Nm) at 4,000 rpm; max engine rpm: 6,000; 55.2 hp/l (40.7 kW/l).

TRANSMISSION axle ratio: 3.890.

PERFORMANCE max speed: 101 mph, 163 km/h; power-weight ratio: 26.5 lb/hp (35.9 lb/kW), 12 kg/hp (16.3 kg/kW); carrying capacity: 977 lb, 443 kg; speed in direct drive at 1,000 rpm: 17.3 mph, 27.8 km/h; consumption: 25.9 m/imp gal, 21.5 m/US gal, 10.9 l x 100 km.

OPTIONALS Ford C3 automatic transmission, hydraulic torque converter and planetary gears with 3 ratios (I 2.474, II 1.474, III 1, rev 2.111), max ratio of converter at stall 2, possible manual selection, max speed 94 mph, 151 km/h.

98 hp power team

See 59 hp power team, except for:

ENGINE 121.6 cu in, 1,993 cc (3.89 x 3.03 in, 90.8 x 76.9 mm); max power (DIN): 98 hp (72.1 kW) at 5,200 rpm; max torque (DIN): 112 lb ft, 15.4 kg m (151 Nm) at 3,500 rpm; max engine rpm: 6,500; 49.2 hp/l (36.2 kW/l); Weber 32/36 DGAV downdraught twin barrel carburett cooling system: 13.7 imp pt, 16.5 US pt, 7.8 l.

TRANSMISSION ratios: I 3.650, II 1.970, III 1.370, IV rev 3.660; axle ratio: 3.750; width of rims: 5.5''.

PERFORMANCE max speed: 103 mph, 166 km/h; pow weight ratio: 24.2 lb/hp (33 lb/kW), 11 kg/hp (15 kg/kV carrying capacity: 977 lb, 443 kg; speed in direct drive 1,000 rpm: 18.3 mph, 29.5 km/h; consumption: 24.1 m/i gal, 20.1 m/US gal, 11.7 l x 100 km.

ELECTRICAL EQUIPMENT halogen headlamps.

DIMENSIONS AND WEIGHT weight: 2,381 lb, 1,080 kg.

BODY sports road wheels; reclining backrests; light al wheels and headrests (except for GL models); tinted gla and vinyl roof (for Ghia models only); rear window wip washer (for estate cars only).

PRACTICAL INSTRUCTIONS tappet clearances: inlet 0. in, 0.20 mm; exhaust 0.010 in, 0.25 mm; valve timi 18° 70° 64° 24°.

OPTIONALS Ford C3 automatic transmission, hydrau torque converter and planetary gears with 3 ratios (I 2.4 II 1.474, III 1, rev 2.111), max ratio of converter at st 2, possible manual selection, max speed 100 mph, 161 km 66 Ah battery; sunshine roof; 185/70 SR x 13 tyres (for and Ghia models only).

108 hp power team

See 59 hp power team, except for:

ENGINE 6 cylinders, Vee-slanted at 60°; 140.1 cu in, 2,2 cc (3.54 x 2.37 in, 90 x 60.1 mm); max power (DIN): 108 (79.5 kW) at 5,000 rpm; max torque (DIN): 138 lb ft, 19 m (186.3 Nm) at 3,000 rpm; max engine rpm: 5,500; 47 h (34.6 kW/l); 1 Solex 35/35 downdraught twin barrel c burettor; cooling system: 13.7 imp pt, 16.5 US pt, 7.8

TRANSMISSION ratios: I 3.650, II 1.970, III 1.370, IV 1, 3.660; axle ratio: 3.440; width of rims: 5.5''.

PERFORMANCE max speed: 106 mph, 171 km/h; pow weight ratio: 23.1 lb/hp (31.3 lb/kW), 10.5 kg/hp (14.2 kW); carrying capacity: 977 lb, 443 kg; speed in direct dr at 1,000 rpm: 19.6 mph, 31.6 km/h; consumption: 21.4 m/i gal, 17.8 m/US gal, 13.2 l x 100 km.

DIMENSIONS AND WEIGHT weight: 2,496 lb, 1,132 kg.

BODY sports road wheels; reclining backrests; light al wheels and headrests (except for GL models); tinted gla and vinyl roof (for Ghia models only); rear window wip washer (for estate cars only).

PRACTICAL INSTRUCTIONS tappet clearances: inlet 0.0 in, 0.35 mm; exhaust 0.016 in, 0.40 mm; valve timing: 56° 62° 14°.

OPTIONALS Ford C3 automatic transmission, hydrau torque converter and planetary gears with 3 ratios (I 2.4 II 1.474, III 1, rev 2.111), max ratio of converter at st 2, possible manual selection, max speed 103 mph, 166 k 66 Ah battery; sunshine roof; 185/70 SR x 13 tyres (for and Ghia models only).

FORD Cortina 2000 S 4-dr Saloon

Capri II Series

PRICES EX WORKS:

1	1300 Coupé	£	2,959*
2	1300 L Coupé	£	3,180*
3	1600 L Coupé	£	3,359*
4	1600 GL Coupé	£	3,581*
5	1600 Coupé	£	4,088*
6	2000 GL Coupé	£	3,786*
7	2000 S Coupé	£	4,211*
8	2000 Ghia Coupé	£	4,980*
9	3000 S Coupé	£	4,613*
10	3000 Ghia Coupé	£	5,644*

Power team:	Standard for:	Optional for:
57 hp	1,2	—
72 hp	3,4	—
88 hp	5	—
98 hp	6 to 8	—
138 hp	9,10	—

57 hp power team

ENGINE front, 4 stroke; 4 cylinders, vertical, in line; 79.2 cu in, 1,298 cc (3.19 x 2.48 in, 81 x 63 mm); compression ratio: 9.2:1; max power (DIN): 57 hp (41.9 kW) at 5,500 rpm; max torque (DIN): 67 lb/ft, 9.3 kg m (91.3 Nm) at 3,000 rpm; max engine rpm: 6,000; 43.9 hp/l (33.3 kW/l); cast iron block and head; 5 crankshafts bearings; valves: overhead, in line, push-rods and rockers; camshafts: 1, side, chain driven; lubrication: rotary or vane-type pump, full flow filter, 5.7 imp pt, 6.8 US pt, 3.2 l; 1 Motorcraft GPD downdraught single barrel carburettor; fuel feed: mechanical pump; water-cooled, 8.2 imp pt, 9.7 US pt, 4.6 l.

TRANSMISSION driving wheels: rear; clutch: single dry plate (diaphragm); gearbox: mechanical; gears: 4, fully synchronized; ratios: I 3.580, II 2.010, III 1.400, IV 1, rev 4.320; lever: central; final drive: hypoid bevel; axle ratio: 3.890; width of rims: 5''; tyres: 165 SR x 13.

PERFORMANCE max speeds: (I) 27 mph, 43 km/h; (II) 33 mph, 53 km/h; (III) 69 mph, 111 km/h; (IV) 91 mph, 146 km/h; power-weight ratio: 39.1 lb/hp 53.1 lb/kW), 17.7 kg/hp (24.1 kg/kW); carrying capacity: 750 lb, 340 kg; speed in direct drive at 1,000 rpm: 17.3 mph, 27.9 km/h; consumption: 27.2 m/imp gal, 22.6 m/US gal, 10.4 l x 100 km.

CHASSIS integral; front suspension: independent, by McPherson, coil springs/telescopic damper struts, lower wishbones (trailing arms), anti-roll bar; rear: rigid axle, semi-elliptic leafsprings, anti-roll bar (acting as torque radius arms), telescopic dampers.

STEERING rack-and-pinion.

BRAKES front disc (diameter 9.60 in, 24.4 cm), rear drum, dual circuit, servo.

ELECTRICAL EQUIPMENT 12 V; 38 Ah battery; 45 A alternator; Motorcraft distributor; 4 headlamps.

DIMENSIONS AND WEIGHT wheel base: 100.80 in, 256 cm; tracks: 53.30 in, 135 cm front, 54.40 in, 138 cm rear; length:

FORD Capri II GL Coupé

FORD Capri II S Coupé

168 in, 427 cm; width: 66.90 in, 170 cm; height: 51.10 in, 130 cm; ground clearance: 4.50 in, 11 cm; weight: 2,227 lb, 1,010 kg; weight distribution: 52.5% front, 47.5% rear; turning circle: 32 ft, 9.8 m; fuel tank: 12.7 imp gal, 15.3 US gal, 58 l.

BODY coupé; 2 doors; 4 seats, separate front seats, reclining backrests.

PRACTICAL INSTRUCTIONS fuel: 97 oct petrol; oil: engine 5.3 imp pt, 6.3 US pt, 3 l, SAE 10W-30, change every 6,000 miles, 9,700 km - gearbox 1.7 imp pt, 1.9 US pt, 0.9 l, SAE 80, no change recommended - final drive 2 imp pt, 2.3 US pt, 1.1 l, SAE 90, no change recommended; greasing: none; tappet clearances: inlet 0.010 in, 0.25 mm, exhaust 0.017 in, 0.44 mm; valve timing: 21° 55° 70° 22°; tyre pressure: front 24 psi, 1.7 atm, rear 27 psi, 1.9 atm.

OPTIONALS 4.444 axle ratio; sunshine roof; vinyl roof; sports road wheels; tinted glass with laminated windscreen; halogen headlamps; metallic spray; rear window wiper-washer.

72 hp power team

See 57 hp power team, except for:

ENGINE 97.2 cu in, 1,593 cc (3.45 x 2.60 in, 87.6 x 66 mm); max power (DIN): 72 hp (53 kW) at 5,200 rpm; max torque (DIN): 87 lb ft, 12 kg m (117.7 Nm) at 2,700 rpm; 45.2 hp/l (33.3 kW/l); valves: overhead, Vee-slanted, rockers; camshafts: 1, overhead, cogged belt; lubrication: 6.5 imp pt, 7.8 US pt, 3.7 l.

TRANSMISSION axle ratio: 3.770.

PERFORMANCE max speed: 98 mph, 157 km/h; power-weight ratio: 31.7 lb/hp (43.3 lb/kW), 14.4 kg/hp (19.6 kg/kW); acceleration: standing ¼ mile 18.9 sec, 0-50 mph (0-80 km/h) 9 sec; speed in direct drive at 1,000 rpm: 17.8 mph, 28.6 km/h; consumption: 25.4 m/imp gal, 21.2 m/US gal, 11.1 l x 100 km.

DIMENSIONS AND WEIGHT weight: 2,293 lb, 1,040 kg; weight distribution: 52.6% front, 47.4% rear.

PRACTICAL INSTRUCTIONS oil: engine 6.5 imp pt, 7.8 US pt, 3.7 l.

OPTIONALS Ford C3 automatic transmission hydraulic torque converter and planetary gears with 3 ratios (I 2.474, II 1.474, III 1, rev 2.111), max ratio of converter at stall 2.3, possible manual selection, max speed 95 mph, 153 km/h, 55 Ah battery.

88 hp power team

See 57 hp power team, except for:

ENGINE 97.2 cu in, 1,593 cc (3.45 x 2.60 in, 87.6 x 66 mm); max power (DIN): 88 hp (64.8 kW) at 5,700 rpm; max torque (DIN): 92 lb ft, 12.7 kg m (124.5 Nm) at 4,000 rpm; max engine rpm: 6,500; 55.2 hp/l (40.7 kW/l); valves: overhead, Vee-slanted, rockers; camshafts: 1, overhead, cogged belt; lubrication: 6.5 imp pt, 7.8 US pt, 3.7 l; 1 Weber 32/36 DGV downdraught twin barrel carburettor.

FORD Capri II 3000 S Coupé

---

88 HP POWER TEAM

TRANSMISSION axle ratio: 3.750.

PERFORMANCE max speed: 108 mph, 174 km/h; power-weight ratio: 26.5 lb/hp (35.8 lb/kW), 12 kg/hp (16.3 kg/kW); speed in direct drive at 1,000 rpm: 18 mph, 28.9 km/h; consumption: 24.8 m/imp gal, 20.6 m/US gal, 11.4 l x 100 km.

ELECTRICAL EQUIPMENT 44 Ah battery.

DIMENSIONS AND WEIGHT weight: 2,326 lb, 1,055 kg; weight distribution: 52.6% front, 47.4% rear.

PRACTICAL INSTRUCTIONS oil: engine 6.5 imp pt, 7.8 US pt, 3.7 l; tappet clearances: inlet 0.008 in, 0.20 mm, exhaust 0.010 in, 0.25 mm; valve timing: 18° 70° 69° 24°.

OPTIONALS Ford C3 automatic transmission, hydraulic torque converter and planetary gears with 3 ratios (I 2.474, II 1.474, III 1, rev 2.111), max ratio of converter at stall 2.3, possible manual selection, max speed 102 mph, 164 km/h, 55 Ah battery; sports equipment.

98 hp power team

See 57 hp power team, except for:

ENGINE 121.6 cu in, 1,993 cc (3.89 x 3.03 in, 90.8 x 76.9 mm); max power (DIN): 98 hp (72.1 kW) at 5,200 rpm; max torque (DIN): 112 lb ft, 15.4 kg m (151 Nm) at 3,500 rpm; max engine rpm: 6,500; 49.2 hp/l (36.2 kW/l); valves: overhead, Vee-slanted, rockers; camshafts: 1, overhead, cogged belt; 1 Weber 32/36 DGAV downdraught twin barrel carburettor; cooling system: 13.7 imp pt, 16.5 US pt, 7.8 l.

TRANSMISSION ratios: I 3.650, II 1.970, III 1.370, IV 1, rev 3.160; axle ratio: 3.440.

PERFORMANCE max speed: 111 mph, 179 km/h; power-weight ratio: 22.5 lb/hp (30.4 lb/kW), 10.2 kg/hp (13.8 kg/kW); acceleration: standing ¼ mile 18.2 sec, 0-50 mph (0-80 km/h) 7.5 sec; speed in direct drive at 1,000 rpm: 19.5 mph, 31.4 km/h; consumption: 24.6 m/imp gal, 20.5 m/US gal, 11.5 l x 100 km.

ELECTRICAL EQUIPMENT 44 Ah battery.

DIMENSIONS AND WEIGHT weight: 2,194 lb, 995 kg; weight distribution: 55.1% front, 44.9% rear.

PRACTICAL INSTRUCTIONS tappet clearances: inlet 0.008 in, 0.20 mm, exhaust 0.010 in, 0.25 mm; valve timing: 18° 70° 64° 24°.

OPTIONALS Ford C3 automatic transmission hydraulic torque converter and planetary gears with 3 ratios (I 2.474, II 1.474, III 1, rev 2.111), max ratio of converter at stall 2, possible manual selection, max speed 105 mph, 169 km/h, 55 Ah battery; sports equipment.

138 hp power team

See 57 hp power team, except for:

ENGINE 6 cylinders, Vee-slanted at 60°; 182.7 cu in, 2,994 cc (3.69 x 2.85 in, 93.7 x 72.4 mm); compression ratio: 9:1; max power (DIN): 138 hp (101.6 kW) at 5,000 rpm; max torque (DIN): 174 lb ft, 24 kg m (235.4 Nm) at 3,000 rpm; max engine rpm: 5,500; 46.1 hp/l (33.9 kW/l); 4 crankshaft bearings; camshafts: 1, at centre of Vee; lubrication: 7.6 imp pt, 9.1 US pt, 4.3 l; 1 Weber 38/38 EGAS downdraught twin barrel carburettor; cooling system: 16.4 imp pt, 19.7 US pt, 9.3 l.

TRANSMISSION ratios: I 3.160, II 1.940, III 1.412, IV 1, rev 3.346; axle ratio: 3.090; tyres: 185/70 HR x 13.

PERFORMANCE max speed: 124 mph, 200 km/h; power-weight ratio: 18.7 lb/hp (25.4 lb/kW), 8.5 kg/hp (11.5 kg/kW); acceleration: standing ¼ mile 16.6 sec, 0-50 mph (0-80 km/h) 6 sec; speed in direct drive at 1,000 rpm: 21.9 mph, 35.2 km/h; consumption: 20 m/imp gal, 16.7 m/US gal, 14.1 l x 100 km.

BRAKES front disc (diameter 9.72 in, 24.7 cm).

DIMENSIONS AND WEIGHT weight: 2,580 lb, 1,170 kg.

PRACTICAL INSTRUCTIONS oil: engine 6.7 imp pt, 8 US pt, 3.8 l - gearbox 3.2 imp pt, 3.8 US pt, 1.8 l; tappet clearances: inlet 0.012 in, 0.30 mm, exhaust 0.012 in, 0.30 mm; valve timing: 20° 56° 62° 14°.

OPTIONALS Ford C3 automatic transmission, hydraulic torque converter and planetary gears with 3 ratios (I 2.474, II 1.474, III 1, rev 2.111), max ratio of converter at stall 2.2, possible manual selection, max speed 118 mph, 190 km/h, 55 Ah battery

FORD Granada 2000 L Saloon

FORD Granada 2800i Ghia Saloon

Granada Series

PRICES EX WORKS:

1 2000 L Saloon	£	4,517*
2 2000 L Estate Car	£	5,286*
3 2100 Diesel Saloon	£	5,087*
4 2300 L Saloon	£	4,785*
5 2300 L Estate Car	£	5,555*
6 2300 GL Saloon	£	5,734*
7 2300 GLS Saloon	£	6,087*
8 2800 GL Saloon (Automatic)	£	6,143*
9 2800 GL Estate Car (Automatic)	£	6,960*
10 2800 GLS Saloon (Automatic)	£	6,496*
11 2800 GLS Estate Car (Automatic)	£	7,079*
12 2800i GLS Saloon	£	6,390*
13 2800i GLS Estate Car	£	7,207*
14 2800 Ghia Saloon (Automatic)	£	7,354*
15 2800i Ghia Saloon	£	7,601*

Power team:		Standard for:	Optional for:
99 hp		1,2	—
63 hp	(Diesel)	3	—
108 hp		4 to 7	—
135 hp		8 to 11, 14	—
160 hp		12,13,15	—

99 hp power team

ENGINE front, 4 stroke; 4 cylinders, vertical, in line; 121.6 cu in, 1,993 cc (3.89 x 3.03 in, 90.8 x 76.9 mm); compression ratio: 9.2:1; max power (DIN): 99 hp (72.9 kW) at 5,200 rpm; max torque (DIN): 111 lb ft, 15.3 kg m (150 Nm) at 3,500 rpm; max engine rpm: 6,500; 49.7 hp/l (36.6 kW/l); cast iron block and head; 5 crankshaft bearings; valves: overhead, Vee-slanted, rockers; camshafts: 1, overhead, cogged belt; lubrication: rotary pump, full flow filter, 6 imp pt, 7.8 US pt, 3.7 l; 1 Weber 32/36 DGAV downdraught carburettor; fuel feed: mechanical pump; water-cooled, 10 imp pt, 12.9 US pt, 6.1 l.

TRANSMISSION driving wheels: rear; clutch: single dry plate (diaphragm); gearbox: mechanical; gears: 4, fully synchronized; ratios: I 3.650, II 1.970, III 1.370, IV 1, rev 3.660; lever: central; final drive: hypoid bevel; axle ratio 3.890; width of rims: 6''; tyres: 175 SR x 14.

PERFORMANCE max speeds: (I) 29 mph, 47 km/h; (II) mph, 87 km/h; (III) 78 mph, 125 km/h; (IV) 103 mph, 1 km/h; power-weight ratio: 26.4 lb/hp (35.8 lb/kW), kg/hp (16.3 kg/kW); speed in direct drive at 1,000 rpm: mph, 29 km/h; consumption: 21.6 m/imp gal, 18 m/ gal, 13.1 l x 100 km.

CHASSIS integral, front and rear auxiliary frames; fro suspension: independent, wishbones (lower trailing links coil springs, anti-roll bar, telescopic dampers; rear: dependent, semi-trailing arms, coil springs, telescop dampers.

STEERING rack-and-pinion; turns lock to lock: 4.39.

BRAKES front disc (diameter 10.31 in, 26.2 cm), rear dru dual circuit, servo.

ELECTRICAL EQUIPMENT 12 V; 44 Ah battery; 45 A alt nator; Motorcraft distributor; 2 halogen headlamps.

DIMENSIONS AND WEIGHT wheel base: 109.05 in, 277 cm; tracks: 59.45 in, 151 cm front, 60.63 in, 154 cm rear; length: 182.28 in, 463 cm; width: 70.47 in, 179 cm; height: 53.94 in, 137 cm; ground clearance: 5.12 in, 13 cm; weight: 2,613 lb, 1,185 kg; turning circle: 34.1 ft, 10.4 m; fuel tank: 14.3 imp gal, 17.2 US gal, 65 l.

BODY 4 doors; 5 seats, separate front seats, reclining backrests; headrests.

PRACTICAL INSTRUCTIONS fuel: 97 oct petrol; oil: engine 6 imp pt, 7.2 US pt, 3.4 l, SAE 20W-50, change every 6,200 miles, 10,000 km - gearbox 3 imp pt, 3.6 US pt, 1.7 l, SAE 80, no change recommended - final drive 3.2 imp pt, 3.8 US pt, 1.8 l, SAE 90, no change recommended; greasing: none; tappet clearances: inlet 0.008 in, 0.20 mm; exhaust 0.010 in, 0.25 mm; valve timing: 18° 70° 64° 24°; tyre pressure: front 24 psi, 1.7 atm, rear 26 psi, 1.8 atm.

OPTIONALS Ford C3 automatic transmission, hydraulic torque converter and planetary gears with 3 ratios (I 2.474, II 1.474, III 1, rev 2.111), max ratio of converter at stall 2.34, possible manual selection, max speed 95 mph, 153 km/h, consumption 25.7 m/imp gal, 21.4 m/US gal, 11 l x 100 km; 185 SR x 14 tyres with 6'' wide rims; power steering; sunshine roof; metallic spray; fog lamps.

63 hp (Diesel) power team

See 99 hp power team, except for:

ENGINE Diesel; 128.9 cu in, 2,112 cc (3.54 x 3.27 in, 90 x 83 mm); compression ratio: 22.2:1; max power (DIN): 63 hp (46.4 kW) at 4,500 rpm; max torque (DIN): 90 lb ft, 12.4 kg m (121.7 Nm) at 2,500 rpm; max engine rpm: 4,700; 29.8 hp/l (22 kW/l); lubrication: 8.8 imp pt, 10.6 US pt, 5 l; Bosch injection system; water-cooled, 17.6 imp pt, 21.1 US pt, 10 l.

PERFORMANCE max speed: 84 mph, 135 km/h; power-weight ratio: 43.6 lb/hp (59.2 lb/kW), 19.8 kg/hp (26.8 kg/kW); consumption: 31 m/imp gal, 25.8 m/US gal, 9.1 l x 100 km.

DIMENSIONS AND WEIGHT weight: 2,745 lb, 1,245 kg.

108 hp power team

See 99 hp power team, except for:

ENGINE 6 cylinders, Vee-slanted at 60°; 139.9 cu in, 2,293 cc (3.54 x 2.37 in, 90 x 60.1 mm); compression ratio: 8.75:1; max power (DIN): 108 hp (79.5 kW) at 5,000 rpm; max torque (DIN): 130 lb ft, 18 kg m (176.5 Nm) at 3,000 rpm; max engine rpm: 5,600; 47.1 hp/l (34.7 kW/l); 4 crankshaft bearings; lubrication: 7.4 imp pt, 8.9 US pt, 4.2 l; 1 Solex 35/35 EEIT downdraught twin barrel carburettor; cooling system: 15.3 imp pt, 18.4 US pt, 8.7 l.

PERFORMANCE max speed: 105 mph, 169 km/h; power-weight ratio: 26.5 lb/hp (35.9 lb/kW), 12 kg/hp (16.3 kg/kW); speed in direct drive at 1,000 rpm: 19.6 mph, 31.6 km/h; consumption: 20.9 m/imp gal, 17.4 m/US gal, 13.5 l x 100 km.

GINETTA G21 "S"

STEERING servo (standard for GL-GLS and Ghia models).

BRAKES front disc, internal radial fins; lining area: front 23.3 sq in, 150 sq cm, rear 75 sq in, 484 sq cm, total 98.3 sq in, 634 sq cm.

ELECTRICAL EQUIPMENT 55 Ah battery; 55 A alternator.

DIMENSIONS AND WEIGHT weight: 2,855 lb, 1,295 kg.

PRACTICAL INSTRUCTIONS oil: engine 7 imp pt, 8.5 US pt, 4 l.

135 hp power team

See 99 hp power team, except for:

ENGINE 6 cylinders, Vee-slanted at 60°; 170.4 cu in, 2,792 cc (3.66 x 2.70 in, 93 x 68.5 mm); max power (DIN): 135 hp (99.4 kW) at 5,200 rpm; max torque (DIN): 159 lb ft, 22 kg m (215.8 Nm) at 3,000 rpm; max engine rpm: 5,600; 48.4 hp/l (35.6 kW/l); 4 crankshaft bearings; lubrication: 7.4 imp pt, 8.9 US pt, 4.2 l; 1 Solex 35/35 EEIT downdraught twin barrel carburettor; cooling system: 15.3 imp pt, 18.4 US pt, 8.7 l.

TRANSMISSION ratios: I 3.160, II 1.950, III 1.410, IV 1, rev 3.350; axle ratio: 3.450; width of rims: Ghia 6''; tyres: Ghia 185 SR x 14.

PERFORMANCE max speed: 113 mph, 182 km/h; power-weight ratio: 21.2 lb/hp (28.7 lb/kW), 9.6 kg/hp (13 kg/kW); speed in direct drive at 1,000 rpm: 20.8 mph, 33.4 km/h; consumption: 19 m/imp gal, 15.8 m/US gal, 14.9 l x 100 km.

STEERING servo (standard).

BRAKES front disc, internal radial fins; lining area: front 23.3 sq in, 150 sq cm, rear 75 sq in, 484 sq cm; total 98.3 sq in, 634 sq cm.

ELECTRICAL EQUIPMENT 55 Ah battery; 55 A alternator.

DIMENSIONS AND WEIGHT weight: 2,855 lb, 1,295 kg.

PRACTICAL INSTRUCTIONS oil: engine 7 imp pt, 8.5 US pt, 4 l.

160 hp power team

See 135 hp power team, except for:

ENGINE max power (DIN): 160 hp (117.8 kW) at 5,700 rpm; max torque (DIN): 162 lb ft, 22.4 kg m (219.7 Nm) at 4,300 rpm; max engine rpm: 6,000; 57.3 hp/l (42.2 kW/l); Bosch K-Jetronic fuel injection system.

TRANSMISSION tyres: 190/65 HR x 390.

PERFORMANCE max speed: 120 mph, 193 km/h; power-weight ratio: 17.9 lb/hp (24.3 lb/kW), 8.1 kg/hp (11 kg/kW); consumption: 18.7 m/imp gal, 15.6 m/US gal, 15.1 l x 100 km.

ELECTRICAL EQUIPMENT 70 A alternator.

GINETTA G21

G21

PRICE EX WORKS: £ 3,959*

ENGINE Chrysler, front, 4 stroke; 4 cylinders, vertical, in line, 105.3 cu in, 1,725 cc (3.21 x 3.25 in, 81.5 x 82.5 mm); compression ratio: 9.2:1; max power (DIN): 85 hp (62.6 kW) at 5,200 rpm; max torque (DIN): 91 lb ft, 12.5 kg m (122.6 Nm) at 3,800 rpm; max engine rpm: 6,200; 49.3 hp/l (36.3 kW/l); cast iron block, light alloy head; 5 crankshaft bearings; valves: overhead, in line, push-rods and rockers; camshafts: 1, in side; lubrication: rotary pump, full flow filter, 7.5 imp pt, 8.9 US pt, 4.2 l; 2 Stromberg semi-downdraught carburettors; fuel feed: mechanical pump; water-cooled 13.7 imp pt, 16.5 US pt, 7.8 l.

TRANSMISSION driving wheels: rear; clutch: single dry plate (diaphragm); gearbox: mechanical; gears: 4, fully synchronized; ratios: I 2.970, II 2.000, III 1.290, IV 1, rev 3.300; lever: central; final drive: hypoid bevel; axle ratio: 3.700; width of rims: 5.5''; tyres: 165 x 13.

PERFORMANCE max speeds: (I) 35 mph 56 km/h; (II) 55 mph, 89 km/h; (III) 82 mph, 132 km/h; (IV) 108 mph, 174 km/h; power-weight ratio: 19.1 lb/hp, (25.9 lb/kW), 8.7 kg/hp (11.8 kg/kW); carrying capacity: 420 lb, 168 kg; acceleration: standing ¼ mile 17 sec; speed in direct drive/top at 1,000 rpm: 19.3 mph, 31 km/h; consumption: 25.7 m/imp gal, 21.4 m/US gal, 11 l x 100 km.

CHASSIS tubular; front suspension: independent, wishbones, coil springs, anti-roll bar, telescopic dampers; rear: rigid axle, longitudinal radius arms, transverse linkage bar, coil springs, telescopic dampers.

STEERING rack-and-pinion; turns lock to lock: 2.75.

BRAKES front disc, rear drum.

ELECTRICAL EQUIPMENT 12 V; 42 Ah battery; 450 W alternator; Lucas distributor; 2 headlamps.

DIMENSIONS AND WEIGHT wheel base: 91 in, 231 cm; tracks: 50.75 in, 128 cm front, 51 in, 129 cm rear; length: 156.5 in, 397 cm; width: 63 in, 160 cm; height: 46 in, 117 cm; ground clearance: 4.75 in, 12 cm; weight: 1,624 lb, 737 kg; weight distribution: 52% front, 48% rear; turning circle: 35 ft, 10.5 m; fuel tank: 10 imp gal, 11.9 US gal, 45 l.

BODY coupé, in plastic material; 2 doors; 2 seats, separate front seats, reclining backrests.

PRACTICAL INSTRUCTIONS fuel: 97 oct petrol; oil: engine 7.5 imp pt, 8.9 US pt, 4.2 l, SAE 20W-50, change every 3,000 miles, 4,800 km - gearbox 3.5 imp pt, 4.2 US pt, 2 l, SAE 80 EP, change every 12,000 miles, 20,000 km - final drive 1.7 imp pt, 2.1 US pt, 1 l, SAE 90 EP, change every 12,000 miles, 20,000 km; greasing: every 6,000 miles, 10,000 km, 2 points; valve timing: 38° 72° 72° 38°; tyre pressure: front 20 psi, 1.4 atm, rear 22 psi, 1.6 atm.

OPTIONALS « S » version with 2 Weber 40 DCDE horizontal carburettors; Laycock-de Normanville overdrive/top (0.820 ratio); sunshine roof.

JAGUAR GREAT BRITAIN

XJ 3.4

PRICE EX WORKS: £ 9,662*

ENGINE front, 4 stroke; 6 cylinders, vertical, in line; 210 cu in, 3,442 cc (3.28 x 4.17 in, 83 x 106 mm); compression ratio: 8.5:1; max power (DIN): 161 hp (118.5 kW) at 5,250 rpm; max torque (DIN): 184 lb ft, 25.4 kg m (249.1 Nm) at 4,000 rpm; max engine rpm: 5,500; 46.8 hp/l (34.4 kW/l); cast iron dry liners, light alloy head, hemispherical combustion chambers; 7 crankshaft bearings; valves: overhead, Vee-slanted, thimble tappets; camshafts: 2, overhead; lubrication: rotary pump, full flow filter, oil cooler, 14.5 imp pt, 17.3 US pt, 8.2 l; 2 SU type HIF7 horizontal carburettors; fuel feed: 2 electric pumps; water-cooled, 32.5 imp pt, 38.9 US pt, 18.4 l, viscous coupling thermostatic fan.

TRANSMISSION driving wheels: rear; gearbox: Borg-Warner 65 automatic transmission, hydraulic torque converter and planetary gears with 3 ratios, max ratio of converter at stall 2, possible manual selection; ratios: I 2.400, II 1.460, III 1, rev 2; lever: central; final drive: hypoid bevel; axle ratio: 3.070 or 3.310; width of rims: 6''; tyres: E70 VR x 15.

PERFORMANCE max speeds: (I) 48 mph, 77 km/h; (II) 79 mph, 127 km/h; (III) 115 mph, 185 km/h; power-weight ratio: 23.1 lb/hp (31.5 lb/kW), 10.5 kg/hp (14.2 kg/kW); carrying capacity: 904 lb, 410 kg; acceleration: standing ¼ mile 18.6 sec; speed in direct drive at 1,000 rpm: 21.4 mph, 34.4 km/h; consumption: 19 m/imp gal, 15.8 m/US gal, 14.9 l x 100 km.

CHASSIS integral, front and rear auxiliary frames; front suspension: independent, wishbones, coil springs, anti-roll bar, telescopic dampers; rear: independent, lower wishbones, semi-axles as upper arms, trailing lower radius arms, 4 coil springs, 4 telescopic dampers.

STEERING rack-and-pinion, adjustable steering wheel, servo; turns lock to lock: 3.30.

BRAKES disc (front diameter 11.18 in, 28.4 cm, rear 10.36 in, 26.4 cm), front internal radial fins, servo; swept area: front 234.5 sq in, 1,512 sq cm, rear 213.7 sq in, 1,378 sq cm, total 448.2 sq in, 2,890 sq cm.

ELECTRICAL EQUIPMENT 12 V; 66 Ah battery; 60 A alternator; Lucas distributor; 4 headlamps.

DIMENSIONS AND WEIGHT wheel base: 112.83 in, 287 cm; tracks: 57.99 in, 147 cm front, 58.58 in, 149 cm rear; length: 194.68 in, 494 cm; width: 69.68 in, 177 cm; height: 54.13 in, 137 cm; ground clearance: 7.09 in, 18 cm; weight: 3,715 lb, 1,685 kg; turning circle: 40 ft, 12.2 m; fuel tanks: 20 imp gal, 24 US gal, 91 l (2 separate tanks).

BODY saloon/sedan; 4 doors; 5 seats; separate front seats, reclining backrests; heated rear window.

PRACTICAL INSTRUCTIONS fuel: 97 oct petrol; oil: engine 14.5 imp pt, 17.3 US pt, 8.2 l, SAE 20W-50, change every 6,000 miles, 9,700 km - gearbox 4.5 imp pt, 6.3 US pt, 2.5 l, SAE 90 EP, change every 12,000 miles, 19,400 km - final drive 2.7 imp pt, 3.2 US pt, 1.5 l, SAE 90 EP, change every 12,000 miles, 19,400 km; greasing: every 6,000 miles, 9,700 km, 17 points; tappet clearances: inlet 0.012-0.014 in, 0.30-0.35 mm, exhaust 0.012-0.014 in, 0.30-0.35 mm; tyre pressure: front 25 psi, 1.7 atm, rear 26 psi, 1.8 atm.

OPTIONALS 4-speed fully synchronized mechanical gearbox + overdrive/top (I 3.320, II 2.090, III 1.400, IV 1, overdrive 0.830, rev 3.428) 3.540 axle ratio; max speed 117 mph, 188 km/h, acceleration standing ¼ mile 18 sec, consumption 21.7 m/imp gal, 18.1 m/US gal, 13 l x 100 km; halogen headlamps; fog lamps; headrests; tinted glass; limited slip final drive; light alloy wheels.

XJ 4.2

See XJ 3.4, except for:

PRICE IN USA: $ 20,000*
PRICE EX WORKS: £ 10,209*

ENGINE 258.4 cu in, 4,235 cc (3.63 x 4.17 in, 92 x 106 mm); compression ratio: 7.8:1; max power (DIN): 166 hp (122.2 kW) at 4,750 rpm; max torque (DIN): 222 lb ft, 30.7 kg m (301.1 Nm) at 3,000 rpm; 39.2 hp/l (28.9 kW/l).

TRANSMISSION axle ratio: 3.540.

PERFORMANCE max speeds: (I) 49 mph, 79 km/h; (II) 81 mph, 130 km/h; (III) 118 mph, 190 km/h; power-weight ratio: 23.8 lb/hp (32.3 lb/kW), 10.8 kg/hp (14.6 kg/kW); acceleration: standing ¼ mile 17.5 sec; speed in direct drive at 1,000 rpm: 22 mph, 35.4 km/h; consumption: 15.3 m/imp gal, 12.7 m/US gal, 18.5 l x 100 km.

DIMENSIONS AND WEIGHT weight: 3,947 lb, 1,790 kg.

JAGUAR XJ 4.2

JAGUAR XJ 5.3

BODY 4 doors; electric windows; headrests (standard).

OPTIONALS with 4-speed mechanical gearbox and 3.31 axle ratio, max speed 121 mph, 195 km/h, acceleration standing ¼ mile 16.4 sec, consumption 16 m/imp gal, 13 m/US gal, 17.6 l x 100 km; air-conditioning.

XJ 5.3

PRICE IN USA: $ 22,000*
PRICE EX WORKS: £ 12,436*

ENGINE front, 4 stroke; 12 cylinders, Vee-slanted at 60°, 326 cu in, 5,343 cc (3.54 x 2.76 in, 90 x 70 mm); compression ratio: 9:1; max power (DIN): 284 hp (209 kW) at 5,750 rpm; max torque (DIN): 294 lb ft, 40.7 kg m (399 Nm) at 4,500 rpm; max engine rpm: 6,500; 53.2 hp/l (39 kW/l); light alloy block and head, wet liners; 7 crankshaft bearings; valves: overhead, in line, thimble tappets; camshafts: 1 per block, overhead; lubrication: rotary pump, full flow filter, oil cooler, 19 imp pt, 22.8 US pt, 10.8 l, Lucas-Bosch electronic injection; fuel feed: electric pump; water-cooled, 36 imp pt, 43.3 US pt, 20.5 l, 1 viscous coupling thermostatic fan and 1 electric thermostatic fan.

TRANSMISSION driving wheels: rear; gearbox: Turbo-Hydramatic 400 automatic transmission, hydraulic torque converter and planetary gears with 3 ratios, max ratio of converter at stall 2, possible manual selection; ratios: I 2.480, II 1.48, III 1, rev 2.070; lever: central; final drive: hypoid bevel;

JAGUAR XJ 5.3

...ted slip differential; axle ratio: 3.310; width of rims: ...''; tyres: 205/70 VR x 15.

...RFORMANCE max speeds: (I) 58 mph, 94 km/h; (II) 96 ...ph, 155 km/h; (III) 140 mph, 225 km/h; power-weight ratio: ....6 lb/hp (20 lb/kW), 6.6 kg/hp (9 kg/kW); carrying ...apacity: 904 lb, 410 kg; acceleration: standing ¼ mile ....7 sec, 0-50 mph (0-80 km/h) 6.1 sec; speed in direct ...ive at 1,000 rpm: 24.3 mph, 39.1 km/h; consumption: ....1 m/imp gal, 11.8 m/US gal, 20 l x 100 km.

...HASSIS integral, front and rear auxiliary frames; front ...spension: independent, wishbones, coil springs, anti-roll ...ar, telescopic dampers; rear: independent, wishbones, ...mi-axles as upper arms, trailing lower radius arms, 4 coil ...rings, 4 telescopic dampers.

...TEERING rack-and-pinion, adjustable steering wheel, servo; ...rns lock to lock: 3.30.

...RAKES disc (front diameter 11.18 in, 28.4 cm, rear 10.38 ..., 26.4 cm), front internal radial fins, servo; swept area: ...ont 234.5 sq in, 1,512 sq cm, rear 213.7 sq in, 1,378 sq ...n, total 448.2 sq in, 2,890 sq cm.

...ECTRICAL EQUIPMENT 12 V; 68 Ah battery; 60 A alter-...nator; Lucas electronic distributor; 4 headlamps.

...IMENSIONS AND WEIGHT wheel base: 112.83 in, 287 cm; ...acks: 57.99 in, 147 cm front, 58.27 in, 148 cm rear; ...ngth: 194.68 in, 494 cm; width: 69.68 in, 177 cm; height: ....13 in, 137 cm; ground clearance: 7.09 in, 18 cm; weight: ...156 lb, 1,885 kg; turning circle: 40 ft, 12.2 m; fuel tanks: ... imp gal, 24 US gal, 91 l (2 separate tanks).

...ODY saloon/sedan; 4 doors; 5 seats, separate front seats, ...clining backrests with built-in headrests; heated rear ...indow; electric windows; vinyl roof; tinted glass.

...RACTICAL INSTRUCTIONS fuel: 97 oct petrol; oil: engine ... imp pt, 22.8 US pt, 10.8 l, SAE 10W-40 (winter) 20W-50 ...ummer), change every 6,000 miles, 9,700 km - final ...ive 2.7 imp pt, 3.2 US pt, 1.5 l, SAE 90 EP, change every ...,000 miles, 19,400 km; greasing: every 6,000 miles, 9,700 ...m, 17 points; tappet clearances: inlet 0.012-0.014 in, 0.30-0.35 ...m, exhaust 0.012-0.014 in, 0.30-0.35 mm; tyre pressure: ...ont 25 psi, 1.7 atm, rear 26 psi, 1.8 atm.

...PTIONALS air-conditioning; light alloy wheels; halogen ...eadlamps; fog lamps.

XJ-S

PRICE IN USA: $ 25,000*
PRICE EX WORKS: £ 15,149*

...NGINE front, 4 stroke; 12 cylinders, Vee-slanted at 60°; ...26 cu in, 5,343 cc (3.54 x 2.76 in, 90 x 70 mm); compres-...ion ratio: 9:1; max power (DIN): 284 hp (209 kW) at ...750 rpm; max torque (DIN): 294 lb ft, 40.7 kg m (399.1 ...m) at 4,500 rpm; max engine rpm: 6,500; 53.2 hp/l (39.1 ...W/l); light alloy block and head, wet liners; 7 crankshaft ...earings; valves: overhead, in line, thimble tappets; cam-...hafts: 1 per block, overhead; lubrication: rotary pump, ...ll flow filter, oil cooler, 19 imp pt, 22.8 US pt, 10.8 l; ...ucas-Bosch electronic injection; fuel feed: electric pump;

water-cooled, 37.5 imp pt, 47.2 US pt, 21.3 l, 1 viscous coupling thermostatic fan and 1 electric thermostatic fan.

TRANSMISSION driving wheels: rear; gearbox: Turbo-Hy-dramatic 400 automatic transmission, hydraulic torque con-verter and planetary gears with 3 ratios, max ratio of con-verter at stall 2, possible manual selection; ratios: I 2.480, II 1.480, III 1, rev 2.070; lever: central; final drive: hypoid bevel, limited slip differential; axle ratio: 3.070; width of rims: 6''; tyres: 205/70 VR x 15.

PERFORMANCE max speeds: (I) 60 mph, 97 km/h; (II) 101 mph, 163 km/h; (III) 150 mph, 241 km/h; power-weight ratio: 13.6 lb/hp (18.5 lb/kW), 6.2 kg/hp (8.4 kg/kW); carrying capacity: 990 lb, 408 kg; acceleration: standing ¼ mile 14.5 sec, 0-50 mph (0-80 km/h) 4.8 sec; speed in direct drive at 1,000 rpm: 24.8 mph, 39.9 km/h; consump-tion: 14 m/imp gal, 11.6 m/US gal, 20.2 l x 100 km.

CHASSIS integral, front and rear auxiliary frames; front suspension: independent, wishbones, coil springs, anti-roll bar, telescopic dampers; rear: independent, lower wishbones, semi-axles as upper arms, trailing lower radius arms, 4 coil springs, 4 telescopic dampers, anti-roll bar.

STEERING rack-and-pinion, servo; turns lock to lock: 3.25.

BRAKES disc (front diameter 11.18 in, 28.4 cm, rear 10.38 in, 26.4 cm), front internal radial fins, servo; swept area: front 252 sq in, 1,624 sq cm, rear 148 sq in, 956 sq cm, total 400 sq in, 2,580 sq cm.

ELECTRICAL EQUIPMENT 12 V; 68 Ah battery; 60 A alter-nator; Lucas electronic distributor; 2 halogen headlamps.

DIMENSIONS AND WEIGHT wheel base: 102 in, 259 cm; tracks: 58 in, 147 cm front, 58.60 in, 149 cm rear; length: 191.70 in, 487 cm; width: 70.60 in, 179 cm; height: 49.65 in, 126 cm; ground clearance: 5.50 in, 14 cm; weight: 3,859 lb, 1,750 kg; turning circle: 36 ft, 11 m; fuel tank: 20 imp gal, 24 US gal, 91 l.

BODY coupé; 2 doors; 4 seats, separate front seats, reclin-ing backrests with built-in headrests; heated rear window; leather upholstery; tinted glass; air-conditioning; electric windows.

PRACTICAL INSTRUCTIONS fuel: 98 oct petrol; oil: engine 16 imp pt, 19.2 US pt, 9.1 l, SAE 20W-50, change every 6,000 miles, 9,700 km - gearbox 2.8 imp pt, 3.4 US pt, 1.6 l - final drive 1.7 imp pt, 2.1 US pt, 1 l; greasing: every 12,000 miles, 19,400 km, 17 points; tappet clearances: inlet 0.014-0.016 in, 0.36-0.38 mm, exhaust 0.014-0.016 in, 0.36-0.38 mm; valve timing: 17° 59° 59° 17°; tyre pressure: front 26 psi, 1.8 atm, rear 24 psi, 1.7 atm.

VARIATIONS

(For USA only).
ENGINE 7.8:1 compression ratio, max power (DIN) 247 hp (181.8 kW) at 5,250 rpm, max torque (DIN) 270 lb ft, 37.2 kg m (364.8 Nm) at 4,500 rpm, 46.2 hp/l (34 kW/l).
TRANSMISSION 3.310 axle ratio.
PERFORMANCE power-weight ratio 15 lb/hp (20.5 lb/kW), 6.8 kg/hp (9.3 kg/kW).
PRACTICAL INSTRUCTIONS 91 oct petrol.

OPTIONALS 4-speed mechanical gearbox (I 3.238, II 1.905, III 1.389, IV 1, rev 3.428).

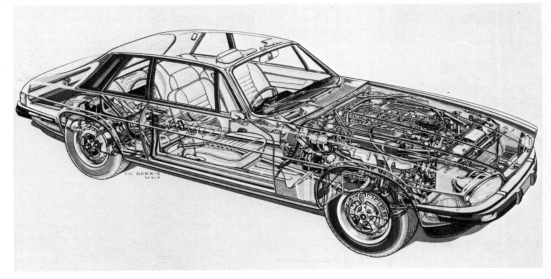

JAGUAR XJ-S

JAGUAR XJ-S

JAGUAR XJ-S

JOHNARD VINTAGE CAR
GREAT BRITAIN

Bentley Donington

PRICE EX WORKS: $ 15,500*

ENGINE Rolls-Royce or Bentley, front, 4 stroke; V8 cylinders; 380.2 cu in, 6,230 cc (4.10 x 3.60 in, 104.1 x 91.4 mm); compression ratio: 9:1; light alloy block and head, cast iron wet liners; 5 crankshaft bearings; valves: overhead, in line, slanted, push-rods and rockers, hydraulic tappets; camshafts: 1, at centre of Vee: lubrication: gear pump, full flow filter (cartridge), 14.4 imp pt, 17.3 US pt, 8.2 l; 2 SU type HD8 horizontal carburettors; fuel feed: mechanical pump; sealed circuit cooling, expansion tank, 28.2 imp pt, 33.8 US pt, 16 l, viscous coupling thermostatic fan.

TRANSMISSION driving wheels: rear; clutch: single dry plate; gearbox: mechanical; gears: 4, II, III and IV synchronized; ratios: I 2.990, II 2.050, III 1.330, IV 1; lever: central; final drive: hypoid bevel, limited slip differential; axle ratio: 2.880; width of rims: 7.5''; tyres: ER 70 VR x 15.

PERFORMANCE max speed: 140 mph, 225 km/h; speed in direct drive at 1,000 rpm: 28 mph, 45 km/h; consumption: 12 m/imp gal, 10 m/US gal, 23.5 l x 100 km.

CHASSIS channel section ladder frame; front suspension: independent, wishbones, coil springs, anti-roll bar, telescopic dampers; rear: rigid axle, semi-elliptic leafsprings, radius arms, adjustable telescopic dampers.

STEERING cam and roller, adjustable height.

BRAKES drum.

ELECTRICAL EQUIPMENT 12 V; 71 Ah battery; 55 A alternator; Lucas distributor; 2 headlamps.

DIMENSIONS AND WEIGHT wheel base: 109 in, 277 cm; tracks: 58 in, 147 cm front, 58 in, 147 cm rear; height: 52 in, 132 cm; weight: 2,271 lb, 1,030 kg; fuel tank: 20 imp gal, 24 US gal, 91 l.

BODY sports, in plastic material; no doors; 2 seats.

PRACTICAL INSTRUCTIONS fuel: 98-100 oct petrol; oil: engine 14.1 imp pt, 16.9 US pt, 8 l, SAE 20W-50, change every 6,000 miles, 9,700 km.

VARIATIONS

ENGINE 6 cylinders, in line, 262.4 cu in, 4,300 cc.

ENGINE 6 cylinders, in line, 280.7 cu in, 4,600 cc.

ENGINE 6 cylinders, in line, 299 cu in, 4,900 cc.

ENGINE V8 cylinders, 441.9 cu in, 6,750 cc.

OPTIONALS 3.770, 3.310 or 3.540 axle ratio; Turbo-Hydramatic 400 automatic transmission, hydraulic torque converter and planetary gears with 3 ratios (I 2.480, II 1.480, III 1, rev 2.080), max ratio of converter at stall 2.1, possible manual selection; servo brake; left-hand drive; adjustable clutch, brake and accelerator pedals.

K.M.B.
GREAT BRITAIN

GTM Mk 1-3

ENGINE British Leyland, central, transverse, 4 stroke; 4 cylinders, vertical, in line; 77.8 cu in, 1,275 cc (2.78 x 3.20 in, 70.7 x 81.4 mm); compression ratio: 9.9:1; max power (SAE): 90 hp (66.2 kW) at 5,800 rpm; max torque (SAE): 83 lb ft, 11.4 kg m (111.8 Nm) at 3,200 rpm; max engine rpm: 7,600; 70.6 hp/l (51.9 kW/l); cast iron block and head; 3 crankshaft bearings; valves: overhead, in line, push-rods and rockers; camshafts: 1, side; lubrication: rotary pump, full flow filter, oil cooler, 8 imp pt, 9.5 US pt, 4.5 l; 2 SU carburettors; fuel feed: electric pump; water-cooled, 7 imp pt, 8.5 US pt, 4 l, rear mounted radiator.

TRANSMISSION driving wheels: rear; clutch: single dry plate (diaphragm); gearbox: mechanical; gears: 4, fully synchronized; ratios: I 3.203, II 1.919, III 1.358, IV 1, rev 3.350; lever: central; final drive: helical spur gears; axle ratios: from 2.900 to 4.300; width of rims: 5''; tyres: 145 x 10 or 165 x 10.

PERFORMANCE max speeds: (I) 39 mph, 62 km/h; (II) 61 mph, 98 km/h; (III) 90 mph, 145 km/h; (IV) 120 mph, 193 km/h; power-weight ratio: 13 lb/hp (17.9 lb/kW), 5.9 kg/hp (8.1 kg/hp); carrying capacity: 953 lb, 432 kg; acceleration: standing ¼ mile 17.5 sec, 0-50 mph (0-80 km/h) 7

sec; speed in direct drive at 1,000 rpm: 16 mph, 25.7 km/h; consumption: 38 m/imp gal, 31.8 m/US gal, 7.4 l x 100 km.

CHASSIS integral with front and rear tubular frame sections; front suspension: independent, wishbones, coil springs, telescopic dampers; rear: independent, wishbones, rubber elements, telescopic dampers.

STEERING rack-and-pinion; turns lock to lock: 3.20.

BRAKES front disc, rear drum, servo.

ELECTRICAL EQUIPMENT 12 V; 75 Ah battery; dynamo or alternator; Lucas distributor; 2 headlamps.

DIMENSIONS AND WEIGHT wheel base: 84 in, 213 cm; front and rear tracks: 48 in, 122 cm; length: 128 in, 325 cm; width: 56 in, 142 cm; height: 43 in, 109 cm; ground clearance: 5 in, 13 cm; weight: 1,175 lb, 533 kg; weight distribution: 45% front, 55% rear; fuel tank: 10 imp gal, 11.9 US gal, 45 l.

BODY coupé in plastic material; 2 doors; 2 seats.

PRACTICAL INSTRUCTIONS oil: engine, gearbox and final drive 8 imp pt, 9.5 US pt, 4.5 l, SAE 20W-50, change every 6,000 miles, 9,600 km; greasing: every 6,000 miles, 9,600 km, 12 points; tyre pressure: front 20 psi, 1.3 atm, rear 30 psi, 2.1 atm.

VARIATIONS

ENGINE 51.7 cu in, 848 cc.

LAND ROVER
GREAT BRITAIN

88" Regular

PRICE EX WORKS: £ 4,101*

ENGINE front, 4 stroke; 4 cylinders, vertical, in line; 139 cu in, 2,286 cc (3.56 x 3.50 in, 90.5 x 88.9 mm); compression ratio: 8:1; max power (DIN): 70 hp (51.5 kW) at 4,000 rpm; max torque (DIN): 120 lb ft, 16.5 kg m (161.8 Nm) 1,500 rpm; max engine rpm: 5,000; 30.6 hp/l (22.5 kW/l); cast iron block and head; 3 crankshaft bearings; valves: overhead, in line, roller tappets, push-rods and rockers; camshafts: 1, side; lubrication: gear pump, full flow filter, 12.5 imp pt, 14.8 US pt, 7 l; 1 Zenith 36 IV downdraught single barrel carburettor; fuel feed: mechanical pump; water-cooled, 15.2 imp pt, 18.3 US pt, 8.7 l.

TRANSMISSION driving wheels: front (automatically engaged with transfer box low ratio) and rear; clutch: single dry plate, hydraulically controlled; gearbox: mechanical; gears: 4, fully synchronized and 2-ratio transfer box (high 1.15, low 2.350); ratios: I 3.680, II 2.220, III 1.500, IV 1, rev 4.020; gear and transfer levers: central; final drive front and rear: spiral bevel; axle ratio front and rear: 4.70; width of rims: 5''; tyres: 6.00 x 16.

PERFORMANCE max speeds: (I) 21 mph, 33 km/h; (II)

JOHNARD VINTAGE CAR Bentley Donington

K.M.B. GTM Mk 1-3

LAND ROVER Range Rover

...ph, 54 km/h; (III) 50 mph, 80 km/h; (IV) 66 mph, 106 ...m/h; power-weight ratio: 42.2 lb/hp (57.3 lb/kW), 19.1 ...g/hp (26 kg/kW); carrying capacity: 1,499 lb, 680 kg; ...cceleration: 0-50 mph (0-80 km/h) 16.3 sec; speed in ...rect drive at 1,000 rpm: 15 mph, 24.1 km/h; consump-...on: 19.1 m/imp gal, 15.9 m/US gal, 14.8 l x 100 km.

...HASSIS box-type ladder frame; front suspension: rigid axle, ...emi-elliptic leafsprings, telescopic dampers; rear: rigid ...xle, semi-elliptic leafsprings, telescopic dampers.

...TEERING recirculating ball; turns lock to lock: 3.35.

...RAKES drum; swept area: total 189 sq in, 1,219 sq cm.

...LECTRICAL EQUIPMENT 12 V, 58 Ah battery; 408 W alterna-...r; Lucas distributor; 2 headlamps.

...IMENSIONS AND WEIGHT wheel base: 88 in, 223 cm; ...ront and rear tracks: 51.50 in, 131 cm; length: 142.35 in, ...62 cm; width: 66 in, 168 cm; height: 77.85 in, 198 cm; ...round clearance: 7 in, 17.8 cm; weight: 2,953 lb, 1,339 ...g; weight distribution: 52.5% front, 47.5% rear; turning ...rcle 38 ft, 11.6 m; fuel tank: 10 imp gal, 12 US gal, 45 l.

...ODY estate car/station wagon; 2+1 doors; 7-8 seats, ...eparate front seats.

...RACTICAL INSTRUCTIONS fuel: 91 oct petrol; oil: engine ...2.5 imp pt, 14.8 US pt, 7 l, SAE 20W, change every ...200 miles, 10,000 km - gearbox 2.5 imp pt, 3 US pt, ...4 l - transfer box 4.4 imp pt, 5.3 US pt, 2.5 l, SAE ...0 EP, change every 24,000 miles, 39,000 km - final drive ...imp pt, 3.6 US pt, 1.7 l, SAE 90 EP, change every ...4,000 miles, 39,000 km; greasing: every 6,200 miles, 10,000 ...m, 1 point; tappet clearances: inlet 0.010 in, 0.25 mm, ...xhaust 0.010 in, 0.25 mm; valve timing: 6° 52° 34° 24°; ...yre pressure: front 25 psi, 1.7 atm, rear 25 psi, 1.7 atm.

VARIATIONS

...NGINE Diesel, 23:1 compression ratio, max power (DIN) ...2 hp (45.6 kW) at 4,000 rpm, max torque (DIN) 103 lb ft, ...4.2 kg m (139.3 Nm) at 1,800 rpm, max engine rpm 4,000, ...7.1 hp/l (19.9 kW/l), cast iron head with precombustion ...hambers.
...ERFORMANCE power-weight ratio 47.6 lb/hp (64.8 lb/kW), ...1.6 hp/hp (29.4 kg/kW).

...PTIONALS oil cooler; front and rear power take-off; ...7.50 x 16 tyres; servo brake; 45 A alternator; hardtop; ...pecial equipment.

109" Estate Car

...ee Land Rover 88" Regular, except for:

...RICE EX WORKS: £ 4,810*

...RANSMISSION width of rims: 5.5"; tyres: 7.50 x 16.

...ERFORMANCE power-weight ratio 53.6 lb/hp (72.9 lb/kW), ...4.3 kg/hp (33 kg/kW).

...IMENSIONS AND WEIGHT wheel base: 109 in, 277 cm; ...ength: 175 in, 444 cm; height: 81.35 in, 207 cm; ground ...learance: 8.25 in, 21 cm; weight: 3,752 lb, 1,702 kg; weight

LAND ROVER 88" Regular

distribution: 46.5% front, 53.5% rear; turning circle: 48 ft, 14.6 m; fuel tank: 16 imp gal, 19.3 US gal, 73 l.

BODY 10-12 seats.

VARIATIONS

ENGINE Diesel (62 hp).

ENGINE 6 cylinders, 160.2 cu in, 2,625 cc (3.06 x 3.63 in, 77.8 x 92.1 mm), 7.8:1 compression ratio, max power (DIN) 86 hp (63.3 kW) at 4,500 rpm, max torque (DIN) 132 lb ft, 18.2 kg m (178.5 Nm) at 1,500 rpm, 32.8 hp/l (24.1 kW/l), 1 Zenith 175-CD2S carburettor.
PERFORMANCE max speed 72 mph, 116 km/h, power-weight ratio 45.5 lb/hp (61.8 lb/kW), 20.6 kg/hp (28 kg/kW).
DIMENSIONS AND WEIGHT weight 3,910 lb, 1,774 kg.

Range Rover

PRICE EX WORKS: £ 9,151*

ENGINE front, 4 stroke; 8 cylinders, Vee-slanted at 90°; 215 cu in, 3,528 cc (3.50 x 2.80 in, 88.9 x 71.1 mm); compression ratio: 8.13:1; max power (DIN): 132 hp (97.1 kW) at 5,000 rpm; max torque (DIN): 186 lb ft, 25.6 kg m (251.1 Nm) at 2,500 rpm; max engine rpm: 5,200; 37.4 hp/l (27.5 kW/l); light alloy block and head, dry liners; 5 crankshaft bearings; valves: overhead, in line, push-rods and rockers, hydraulic tappets; camshafts: 1, at centre of Vee; lubrication: gear pump, full flow filter, 10 imp pt, 12 US pt, 5.7 l; 2 Zenith-Stromberg CD2 semi-downdraught carburettors; fuel feed: electric pump; water-cooled, 20 imp pt, 23.9 US pt, 11.3 l.

TRANSMISSION driving wheels: 4, with lockable differential in transfer box; clutch: single dry plate (diaphragm), hydraulically controlled; gearbox: mechanical; gears: 4, fully synchronized, and 2-ratio transfer box (high 1.174, low 3.321); ratios: I 4.069, II 2.448, III 1.505, IV 1, rev 3.664; gear and transfer levers: central; final drive front and rear: spiral bevel; axle ratio front and rear: 3.540; width of rims: 6"; tyres: 205 x 16.

PERFORMANCE max speeds: (I) 24 mph, 39 km/h; (II) 41 mph, 66 km/h; (III) 68 mph, 109 km/h; (IV) 96 mph, 154 km/h; power-weight ratio: 28.8 lb/hp (39.1 lb/kW), 13.1 kg/hp (17.8 kg/kW); carrying capacity: 1,720 lb, 780 kg; acceleration: standing ¼ mile 19.3 sec, 0-50 mph (0-80 km/h) 11.1 sec; speed in direct drive at 1,000 rpm: 20 mph, 32.2 km/h; consumption: 18.2 m/imp gal, 15.1 m/US gal, 15.5 l x 100 km.

CHASSIS box-type ladder frame; front suspension: rigid axle, longitudinal radius arms, transverse linkage bar, coil springs/telescopic dampers units; rear: rigid axle, longitudinal radius arms, upper A bracket, Boge Hydromat self-energizing levelling device, coil springs, telescopic dampers.

STEERING Burman, recirculating ball, worm and nut; turns lock to lock: 4.75.

BRAKES disc (front diameter 11.75 in, 29.8 cm, rear 11.42 in, 29 cm); swept area: front 261 sq in, 1,683 sq cm, rear 235 sq in, 1,516 sq cm, total 496 sq in, 3,199 sq cm.

ELECTRICAL EQUIPMENT 12 V; 60 Ah battery; 540 W alternator; Lucas distributor; 2 headlamps.

DIMENSIONS AND WEIGHT wheel base: 100 in, 254 cm; front and rear tracks: 58.50 in, 149 cm; length: 175.98 in, 447 cm; width: 70 in, 178 cm; height: 70 in, 178 cm; ground clearance: 7.50 in, 19 cm; weight: 3,800 lb, 1,724 kg; weight distribution: 50% front, 50% rear; turning circle: 37 ft, 11.3 m; fuel tank: 18 imp gal, 21.6 US gal, 82 l.

BODY estate car/station wagon; 2 + 1 doors; 5 seats, separate front seats, reclining backrests; heated rear window with wiper-washer.

PRACTICAL INSTRUCTIONS fuel: 91-93 oct petrol; oil: engine 10 imp pt, 12 US pt, 5.7 l, SAE 20W, change every 6,200 miles, 10,000 km - gearbox 4.5 imp pt, 5.5 US pt, 2.6 l, SAE 80 EP, change every 24,000 miles, 39,000 km - transfer box 5.5 imp pt, 6.6 US pt, 3.1 l, SAE 80 EP, change every 6,200 miles, 10,000 km - final drive rear 2.7 imp pt, 3.2 US pt, 1.5 l, SAE 80 EP, change every 24,000 miles, 39,000 km, front 3 imp pt, 3.6 US pt, 1.7 l, SAE 80 EP, change every 24,000 miles, 39,000 km; greasing: every 6,200 miles, 10,000 km, 6 points; valve timing: 30° 75° 68° 37°; tyre pressure: front 25 psi, 1.7 atm, rear 25 psi, 1.7 atm.

OPTIONALS power steering; headrests; tinted glass.

LENHAM   GREAT BRITAIN

Austin-Healey 3000

PRICE EX WORKS: £ 6,300

ENGINE Austin-Healey, front, 4 stroke; 6 cylinders, in line; 178.1 cu in, 2,912 cc (3.28 x 3.50 in, 83.3 x 88.9 mm); compression ratio: 8.5:1; max power (DIN): 124 hp (91.3 kW) at 4,600 rpm; max torque (DIN): 167 lb ft, 23 kg m (225.6 Nm) at 2,700 rpm; max engine rpm: 5,000; 42.6 hp/l (31.4 kW/l); cast iron block and head; 4 crankshaft bearings valves: overhead, push-rods and rockers; camshafts: 1, side; lubrication: rotary pump, full flow filter, 12 imp pt, 14.4 US pt, 6.8 l; 2 SU type HD6 or HS6 semi-downdraught carburettors; fuel feed: electric pump; water-cooled, 30 imp pt, 35.9 US pt, 17 l.

TRANSMISSION driving wheels: rear; clutch: single dry plate; gearbox: mechanical; gears: 4 + overdrive; ratios: I 2.930, II 2.053, III 1.309, IV 1; lever: central; final drive: hypoid bevel; axle ratio: 4.100; width of rims: 6"; tyres: 185 x 15.

PERFORMANCE max speeds: (I) 28 mph, 45 km/h; (II) 45 mph, 72 km/h; (III) 80 mph, 128 km/h; (IV) 100 mph, 161 km/h; (overdrive-top) 120 mph, 193 km/h; power-weight ratio: 12.6 lb/hp (17.2 lb/kW), 5.7 kg/hp (7.8 kg/kW); carrying capacity: 353 lb, 160 kg; acceleration: 0-50 mph (0-80 km/h) 6 sec; speed in direct drive at 1,000 rpm: 20 mph, 32.2 km/h; consumption: 25 m/imp gal, 20.8 m/US gal, 11.3 l x 100 km.

CHASSIS box section frame; front suspension: independent, unequal length wishbones, coil springs, anti-roll bar, lever dampers; rear: rigid axle, two longitudinal leaf-springs, lever dampers.

STEERING cam and peg; turns lock to lock: 2.75.

AUSTIN-HEALEY 3000

BRAKES front disc (diameter 11.25 in, 28.6 cm), rear drum.

ELECTRICAL EQUIPMENT 12 V; 50 Ah battery; dynamo; Lucas distributor; 2 headlamps.

DIMENSIONS AND WEIGHT wheel base: 92.13 in, 234 cm; tracks: 50.50 in, 128 cm front, 52.50 in, 133 cm rear; length: 151 in, 383 cm; width 63 in, 160 cm; height: 47 in, 119 cm; ground clearance: 6 in, 15 cm; weight: 1,568 lb, 711 kg; weight distribution: 60% front 40% rear; turning circle: 36 ft, 11 m; fuel tank: 12 imp gal, 14.3 US gal, 54 l.

BODY open, in composite aluminum and fibreglass material; no doors; 2 seats; folding windscreen; outside handbrake; country hide trim; stainless steel exhaust system; screen washers and wipers; tonneau cover; wood rim steering wheel.

PRACTICAL INSTRUCTIONS fuel: 98 oct petrol; oil: engine 12 imp pt, 14.4 US pt, 6.8 l, SAE 20/50, change every 3,000 miles, 4,800 km - gearbox 6 imp pt, 7.2 US pt, 3.4 l, SAE 20/50 - final drive 3 imp pt, 3.6 US pt, 1.7 l; greasing: every 2,000 miles, 3,200 km, 10 points; tappet clearances (bot): inlet and exhaust 0.012 in, 0.30 mm; valve timing: 5° 45° 40 10°; tyre pressure: front 24 psi, 1.7 atm, rear 20 psi, 1.4 atm.

OPTIONALS 3.900 axle ratio without overdrive; side-mounted spare wheel; hood; heater.

LENHAM Austin-Healey 3000

LOTUS   GREAT BRITAIN

Elite 501

PRICE EX WORKS: £ 11,503*

ENGINE front, 4 stroke; 4 cylinders, in line, slanted 45° to left; 120.4 cu in, 1,973 cc (3.75 x 2.72 in, 95.2 x 69.2 mm); compression ratio: 9.5:1; max power (DIN): 155 hp (114.1 kW) at 6,500 rpm; max torque (DIN): 135 lb ft, 18.6 kg m (182.4 Nm) at 5,000 rpm; max engine rpm: 7,000; 78.6 hp/l (57.8 kW/l); light alloy block and head, wet liners; 5 crankshaft bearings; valves: 4 per cylinder, overhead, slanted at 38°, thimble tappets; camshafts: 2, overhead, cogged belt; lubrication: rotary pump, full flow filter, 10 imp pt, 12 US pt, 5.7 l; 2 Dell'Orto DHLA 45E horizontal twin barrel carburettors; fuel feed: electric pump; water-cooled, 12 imp pt, 14.4 US pt, 6.8 l, electric thermostatic fan.

TRANSMISSION driving wheels: rear; clutch: single dry plate (diaphragm); gearbox: mechanical; gears: 5, fully synchronized; ratios: I 3.200, II 2.010, III 1.370, IV 1, V 0.800, rev 3.467; lever: central; final drive: hypoid bevel; axle ratio: 4.100; width of rims: 7''; tyres: 205/60 VR x 14.

PERFORMANCE max speeds: (I) 40 mph, 64 km/h; (II) 64 mph, 103 km/h; (III) 93 mph, 149 km/h; (IV) 128 mph, 206 km/h; (V) 125 mph, 201 km/h; power-weight ratio: 15 lb/hp (20.5 lb/kW), 6.8 kg/hp (9.3 kg/kW); carrying capacity: 860 lb, 390 kg; speed in top at 1,000 rpm: 20.7 mph, 33.3 km/h; consumption: 26.4 m/imp gal, 22 m/US gal. 10.7 l x 100 km.

CHASSIS box-type backbone; front suspension: independent, wishbones, coil springs, anti-roll bar, telescopic dampers; rear: independent, lower wide-based wishbones, semi-axles as upper arms, coil springs/telescopic struts.

STEERING rack-and-pinion; turns lock to lock: 3.50.

BRAKES disc (diameter 10.40 in, 26.4 cm), rear drum, servo.

ELECTRICAL EQUIPMENT 12 V; 50 Ah battery; 60 A alternator; Lucas distributor; 2 retractable headlamps .

DIMENSIONS AND WEIGHT wheel base: 97.64 in, 248 cm; tracks: 58.50 in, 149 cm front, 58.50 in, 149 cm rear; length: 175.50 in, 446 cm; width: 71.50 in, 182 cm; height: 47.65 in, 121 cm; ground clearance: 5.50 in, 14 cm; weight: 2,338 lb, 1,060 kg; turning circle: 34.5 ft, 10.5 m; fuel tank: 14.7 imp gal, 17.7 US gal, 67 l.

BODY coupé, in reinforced plastic material; 2 doors; 4 seats, separate front seats, reclining backrests, built-in front and rear headrests; electric windows; heated rear window; light alloy wheels; rear window wiper-washer.

PRACTICAL INSTRUCTIONS fuel: 98-100 oct petrol; oil engine 9.2 imp pt, 11 US pt, 5.2 l, SAE 20W-50, change every 3,000 miles, 4,800 km - gearbox 2 imp pt, 2.3 US pt, 1.1 l, SAE 80 EP, change every 6,000 miles, 9,700 km - final drive 2 imp pt, 2.3 US pt, 1.1 l, SAE 90 EP, change every 12,000 miles, 20,000 km; greasing: every 3,000 miles, 4,800 km, 2 points; tappet clearances: inlet 0.010 in, 0.[...] mm, exhaust 0.010 in, 0.25 mm; valve timing: 25° 65° 6[...] 25°; tyre pressure: front 22 psi, 1.6 atm, rear 22 psi, 1[...] atm.

VARIATIONS

(For USA only).

ENGINE 8.4:1 compression ratio, max power (DIN) 142 (104.5 kW) at 6,500 rpm, max torque (DIN) 130 lb ft, kg m (176.5 Nm) at 5,000 rpm, 72 hp/l (53 kW/l), 2 Zenit Stromberg 175 CD 2SE horizontal carburettors.
PERFORMANCE max speed 118 mph, 190 km/h, powe weight ratio 16.1 lb/hp (22.4 lb/kW), 7.3 kg/hp (10.1 kg/kW)
PRACTICAL INSTRUCTIONS valve timing 26° 66° 66° 26°.

OPTIONALS automatic transmission, hydraulic torque co verter and planetary gears with 3 ratios (I 2.390, II 1.45 III 1, rev 2.090), max ratio of converter at stall 2, possib manual selection, 3.730 axle ratio (only for 501); powe steering (only for 501); metallic spray; vinyl roof.

Elite 502

See Elite 501, except for:

PRICE EX WORKS: £ 12,518*

ELECTRICAL EQUIPMENT halogen headlamps.

BODY tinted glass; air-conditioning.

Elite 503

See Elite 501, except for:

PRICE IN USA: $ 30,746*
PRICE EX WORKS: £ 12,989*

STEERING servo.

ELECTRICAL EQUIPMENT halogen headlamps.

BODY tinted glass; air-conditioning.

Elite 504

See Elite 501, except for:

PRICE IN USA: $ 31,236*
PRICE EX WORKS: £ 13,150*

TRANSMISSION gearbox: automatic transmission hydraul[...] torque converter and planetary gears with 3 ratios, ma ratio of converter at stall 2, possible manual selection ratios: I 2.390, II 1.450, III 1, rev 2.090; axle ratio: 3.73[...]

STEERING servo.

LOTUS Elite 501

ECTRICAL EQUIPMENT halogen headlamps.

ODY tinted glass; air-conditioning.

Eclat 520

RICE EX WORKS: £ 10,232*

NGINE front, 4 stroke; 4 cylinders, in line; 120.4 cu in, 973 cc (3.75 x 2.72 in, 95.2 x 69.2 mm); compression ratio: 5:1; max power (DIN): 160 hp (117.8 kW) at 6,200 rpm; ax torque (DIN): 140 lb ft, 19.3 kg m (189.3 Nm) at 900 rpm; max engine rpm: 7,300; 81.1 hp/l (59.7 kW/l); ght alloy block and head, wet liners; 5 crankshaft bear-gs; valves: 4 per cylinder, overhead, slanted at 38°, imble tappets; camshafts: 2, overhead, cogged belt; lu-ication: rotary pump, full flow filter, 10.5 imp pt, 12.5 S pt, 5.9 l; 2 Dell'Orto DHLA 45E horizontal twin barrel arburettors; fuel feed: electric pump; water-cooled, 12 np pt, 14.4 US pt, 6.8 l, electric thermostatic fan.

RANSMISSION driving wheels: rear; clutch: single dry ate (diaphragm); gearbox: mechanical; gears: 4, fully nchronized; ratios: I 3.160, II 1.950, III 1.410, IV 1, v 3.350; lever: central; final drive: hypoid bevel; axle tio: 3.730; width of rims: 5.5''; tyres: 185/70 HR x 13.

ERFORMANCE max speeds: (I) 40 mph, 65 km/h; (II) mph, 106 km/h; (III) 92 mph, 148 km/h; (IV) 130 mph, 9 km/h; power-weight ratio: 13.5 lb/hp (18.3 lb/kW); kg/hp (8.3 kg/kW); carrying capacity: 706 lb, 320 kg; cceleration: standing ¼ mile 15.8 sec, 0-50 mph (0-80 m/h) 6 sec; speed in direct drive at 1,000 rpm: 17.9 mph, 8 km/h; consumption: 28 m/imp gal, 23.3 m/US gal, 0.1 l x 100 km.

HASSIS box-type backbone; front suspension: independent, ishbones, coil springs, anti-roll bar, telescopic dampers; ar: independent, lower wide-based wishbones, semi-axles upper arms, coil springs, telescopic dampers.

TEERING rack-and-pinion; turns lock to lock: 3.50.

RAKES front disc, rear drum, servo.

LECTRICAL EQUIPMENT 12 V; 48 Ah battery; 45 A alterna-r; Lucas distributor; 2 retractable headlamps.

IMENSIONS AND WEIGHT wheel base: 97.75 in, 248 cm; acks: 58.50 in, 149 cm front, 59 in, 150 cm rear; length: 75.50 in, 446 cm; width: 71.50 in, 182 cm; height: 47.25 , 120 cm; ground clearance: 5.40 in, 13.7 cm; weight: 160 lb, 979 kg; fuel tank: 14.7 imp gal, 17.7 US gal, l.

ODY coupé, in reinforced plastic material; 2 doors; 2+2 ats, separate front seats, reclining backrests with built-headrests; electric windows; heated rear window.

RACTICAL INSTRUCTIONS fuel: 98 oct petrol; oil: engine .5 imp pt, 12.5 US pt, 5.9 l, SAE 20W-50, change every 000 miles, 4,800 km - gearbox 2 imp pt, 2.3 US pt, 1.1 l, AE 80 EP, change every 6,000 miles, 9,700 km - final ive 2 imp pt, 2.3 US pt, 1.1 l, SAE 90 EP, change every ,000 miles, 20,000 km; greasing: every 3,000 miles, 4,800 n, 4 points; tappet clearances: inlet 0.004-0.006 in, 11-0.14 mm, exhaust 0.008-0.10 in, 0.20-0.25 mm; valve ming: 30° 50° 50° 30°; tyre pressure: front 20 psi, 1.4 m, rear 22 psi, 1.6 atm.

LOTUS Eclat 520

LOTUS Esprit S2

Eclat 521

e Eclat 520, except for:

RICE EX WORKS: £ 10,990*

RANSMISSION gears: 5, fully synchronized; ratios: I 200, II 2.010, III 1.370, IV 1, V 0.800, rev 3.467; axle tio: 4.100; width of rims: 7''; tyres: 205/60 VR x 14.

ERFORMANCE max speeds: (I) 42 mph, 67 km/h; (II) mph, 106 km/h; (III) 97 mph, 156 km/h; (IV) 105 mph, 9 km/h; (V) 132 mph, 212 km/h; acceleration: standing mile 16 sec, 0-50 mph (0-80 km/h) 6.1 sec; speed in p at 1,000 rpm: 22.9 mph, 36.8 km/h.

ODY light alloy wheels.

PTIONALS automatic transmission, hydraulic torque con-erter and planetary gears with 3 ratios (I 2.390, II 1.450, I 1, rev 2.090), max ratio of converter at stall 2, possi-le manual selection, 3.730 axle ratio (only for 521); power teering (only for 521).

Eclat 522

ee Eclat 521, except for:

RICE EX WORKS: £ 11,991*

LECTRICAL EQUIPMENT halogen headlamps.

ODY air-conditioning; tinted glass.

Eclat 523

See Eclat 522, except for:

PRICE IN USA: $ 29,609*
PRICE EX WORKS: £ 12,429*

STEERING servo.

Eclat 524

See Eclat 523, except for:

PRICE IN USA: $ 30,138*
PRICE EX WORKS: £ 12,590*

TRANSMISSION gearbox: automatic transmission, hydraulic torque converter and planetary gears with 3 ratios, max ratio of converter at stall 2, possible manual selection; ratios: I 2.390, II 1.450, III 1, rev 2.090; axle ratio: 3.730.

Esprit S2

PRICE EX WORKS: £ 11,236*

ENGINE centre-rear, longitudinal, 4 stroke; 4 cylinders, in line; 120.4 cu in, 1,973 cc (3.75 x 2.72 in, 95.2 x 69.2 mm); compression ratio: 9.5:1; max power (DIN): 160 hp (117.8 kW) at 6,200 rpm; max torque (DIN): 140 lb ft, 19.3 kg m (189.3 Nm) at 4,900 rpm; max engine rpm: 7,300; 81.1 hp/l (59.7 kW/l); light alloy block and head, wet liners; 5 crank-shaft bearings; valves: 4 per cylinder, overhead, slanted at 38°, thimble tappets; camshafts: 2, overhead, cogged belt; lu-brication: rotary pump, full flow filter, 10.5 imp pt, 12.5 US pt, 5.9 l; 2 Dell'Orto DHLA 45 horizontal twin barrel carburettors; fuel feed: electric pump; water-cooled, 15.8 imp pt, 19 US pt, 9 l, front radiator, electric thermostatic fans.

TRANSMISSION driving wheels: rear; clutch: single dry plate (diaphragm), hydraulically controlled; gearbox: mechanical; gears: 5, fully synchronized; ratios: I 2.920, II 1.940, III 1.320, IV 0.970, V 0.760, rev 4.375; lever: central; final drive: hypoid bevel, in unit with gearbox; axle ratio: 4.375; width of rims: 6'' front, 7'' rear; tyres: 195/70 HR x 14 front, 205/70 HR x 14 rear.

PERFORMANCE max speeds: (I) 36 mph, 58 km/h; (II) 54 mph, 87 km/h; (III) 79 mph, 127 km/h; (IV) 108 mph, 174 km/h; (V) 138 mph, 222 km/h; power-weight ratio: 12.4 lb/hp (16.8 lb/kW), 5.6 kg/hp (7.6 kg/kW); carrying ca-pacity: 500 lb, 227 kg; acceleration: standing ¼ mile 15 sec, 0-50 mph (0-80 km/h) 4.9 sec; speed in top at 1,000 rpm: 21.8 mph, 35.1 km/h; consumption: 28 m/imp gal, 23.3 m/US gal, 10.1 l x 100 km.

CHASSIS box type backbone with space-frame section; front suspension: independent, wishbones, coil springs, anti-roll bar, telescopic dampers; rear: independent, wishbones, diagonal trailing arm and lateral link with fixed length driveshaft, coil springs, telescopic dampers.

STEERING rack-and-pinion.

ESPRIT S2

BRAKES disc (front diameter 9.7 in, 24.6 cm, rear 10.6 in, 25.6 cm).

ELECTRICAL EQUIPMENT 12 V; 48 Ah battery; 45 A alternator; Lucas distributor; 4 retractable halogen headlamps.

DIMENSIONS AND WEIGHT wheel base: 96 in, 244 cm; front and rear tracks: 59.50 in, 151 cm; length: 165 in, 419 cm; width: 73.25 in, 186 cm; height: 43.70 in, 111 cm; ground clearance: 5.50 in, 14 cm; weight: 1,980 lb, 898 kg; fuel tank: 15 imp gal, 18 US gal, 68 l.

BODY coupé, in reinforced plastic material; 2 doors; 2 seats with built-in headrests; electric windows; light alloy wheels; heated rear window; tinted glass.

PRACTICAL INSTRUCTIONS fuel: 98 oct petrol; oil: engine 10.5 imp pt, 12.5 US pt, 5.9 l, SAE 20W-50, change every 3,000 miles, 4,800 km - gearbox and final drive 4.4 imp pt, 5.3 US pt, 2.5 l, SAE 80 EP, change every 12,000 miles, 20,000 km; greasing: every 3,000 miles, 4,800 km, 4 points; tappet clearances: inlet 0.004-0.006 in, 0.11-0.14 mm, exhaust 0.008-0.10 in, 0.20-0.25 mm; valve timing: 30° 50° 50° 30°; tyre pressure: front 18 psi, 1.3 atm, rear 28 psi, 2 atm.

OPTIONALS metallic spray.

LOTUS Esprit S2

LYNX   GREAT BRITAIN

D Type

PRICE EX WORKS: £ 17,500

ENGINE Jaguar XKE, front, 4 stroke; 6 cylinders, in line; 258.4 cu in, 4,235 cc (3.63 x 4.17 in, 92.1 x 106 mm); compression ratio: 9:1; max power (DIN): 171 hp (125.9 kW) at 4,500 rpm; max torque (DIN): 230 lb ft, 31.8 kg m (311.9 Nm) at 2,500 rpm; max engine rpm: 5,500; 40.4 hp/l (29.7 kW/l); block with chrome iron dry liners, head with aluminium alloy hemispherical combustion chambers; 7 crankshaft bearings; valves: overhead, Vee-slanted at 70°, thimble tappets; camshafts: 2, 1 per bank, overhead; lubrication: rotary pump, full flow filter, 15 imp pt, 18 US pt, 8.5 l; 3 Weber semi-downdraught carburettors; fuel feed: electric pump; water-cooled, 32,9 imp pt, 39.5 US pt, 18.7 l, automatic thermostatic fan.

TRANSMISSION driving wheels: rear; clutch: single dry plate (diaphragm), hydraulically controlled; gearbox: mechanical; gears: 4, fully synchronized; ratios: I 2.933, II 1.905, III 1.389, IV 1, rev 3.378; lever: central; final drive: hypoid bevel, limited slip differential; axle ratio: 3.070; width of rims: 6''; tyres: E70 VR x 15.

PERFORMANCE max speeds: (I) 48 mph, 77 km/h; (II) 73 mph, 117 km/h; (III) 108 mph, 174 km/h; (IV) 150 mph, 241

LYNX D Type

LYNX D Type

km/h; power-weight ratio: 12.8 lb/hp (17.4 lb/kW), 5.8 kg/hp (7.9 kg/kW); carrying capacity: 408 lb, 185 kg; acceleration standing ¼ mile 16 sec, 0-50 mph (0-80 km/h) 5.4 se consumption: 18.8 m/imp gal, 15.7 m/US gal, 15 l x 100 k

CHASSIS integral, front and rear tubular auxiliary frame front suspension: independent, wishbones, swinging lo gitudinal torsion bars, anti-roll bar, telescopic damper rear: independent, wide-based wishbones, semi-axles upper arms, trailing lower radius arms, 4 coil springs, telescopic dampers.

STEERING rack-and-pinion.

BRAKES disc (front diameter 11.18 in, 28.4 cm, rear 10. in, 26.4 cm), twin master cylinder; swept area: front 234 sq in, 1,512 sq cm, rear 213.7 sq in, 1,378 sq cm, tot 448.2 sq in, 2,890 sq cm.

ELECTRICAL EQUIPMENT 12 V; 68 Ah battery; 60 A alte nator; Lucas distributor; 2 headlamps.

DIMENSIONS AND WEIGHT wheel base: 90.50 in, 230 c tracks: 50.25 in, 128 cm front, 51 in, 129 cm rear; leng 159 in, 404 cm; width: 63 in, 160 cm; height: 45.50 116 cm; ground clearance: 5 in, 12.7 cm; weight: 2,184 990 kg; weight distribution: 51% front, 49% rear; turn circle: 32 ft, 9.8 m; fuel tank: 21 imp gal, 25.1 US gal, 95

BODY sports; 2 doors; 2 seats.

PRACTICAL INSTRUCTIONS fuel: 97 oct petrol; oil: engi 15 imp pt, 18 US pt, 8.5 l, SAE 20W-50, change every 6,0 miles, 9,700 km - gearbox 2.5 imp pt, 3 US pt, 1.4 l, S 90 EP, change every 12,000 miles, 19,300 km - final dri 2.7 imp pt, 3.2 US pt, 1.5 l, SAE 90 EP, change every 12,0 miles, 19,300 km; greasing: every 6,000-12,000 miles, 9,7 19,300 km; tappet clearances: inlet 0.012-0.014 in, 0.30-0 mm, exhaust 0.012-0.014 in, 0.30-0.35 mm; valve timin 17° 59° 59° 17°; tyre pressure: front 24 psi, 1.7 atm, re 28 psi, 2 atm.

VARIATIONS

ENGINE Jaguar, tuned, max power (DIN) 285 hp (209.8 kW

ENGINE Jaguar, tuned, max power (DIN) 320 hp (234.8 kW

OPTIONALS 8:1 compression ratio; XKSS model; sh nose body-work; dry sump lubrication with oil tank; cooler; light alloy peg-drive wheels; 6.50L x 15 tyres; m dified suspension; headrests; side exit exhaust; weath equipment.

MG   GREAT BRITAI

Midget

PRICE IN USA: $ 5,200*
PRICE EX WORKS: £ 2,971*

ENGINE front, 4 stroke; 4 cylinders, vertical, in line; cu in, 1,491 cc (2.90 x 3.44 in, 73.7 x 87.4 mm); compress ratio: 9:1; max power (DIN): 65 hp (47.8 kW) at 5,500 rp max torque (DIN): 84 lb ft, 10.6 kg m (104 Nm) at 3,0 rpm; max engine rpm: 6,000; 43.6 hp/l (32.1 kW/l); ca iron block and head; 3 crankshaft bearings; valves: overhea push-rods and rockers; camshafts: 1, side; lubrication: centric pump, full flow filter, 7 imp pt, 8.5 US pt, 4 l; SU type HS4 semi-downdraught carburettors; fuel fee electric pump; water-cooled, 6 imp pt, 7.2 US pt, 3.4

TRANSMISSION driving wheels: rear; clutch: single plate (diaphragm), hydraulically controlled; gearbox: m chanical; gears: 4, fully synchronized; ratios: I 3.412, 2.112, III 1.433, IV 1, rev 3.753; lever: central; final dri hypoid bevel; axle ratio: 3.720; width of rims: 4''; tyre 145 x 13.

PERFORMANCE max speeds: (I) 29 mph, 46 km/h; (47 mph, 75 km/h; (III) 69 mph, 111 km/h; (IV) 95 mp 153 km/h; power-weight ratio: 27.3 lb/hp (37.1 lb/kW 12.4 kg/hp (16.8 kg/kW); carrying capacity: 353 lb, 160 k speed in direct drive at 1,000 rpm: 16.4 mph, 26.4 km/ consumption: 35.3 m/imp gal, 29.4 m/US gal, 8 l x 100 k

CHASSIS integral; front suspension: independent, wis bones, coil springs, anti-roll bar, telescopic dampers; re rigid axle, semi-elliptic leafsprings, telescopic dampers

STEERING rack-and-pinion; turns lock to lock: 2.25.

BRAKES front disc (diameter 8.25 in, 21 cm), rear dru

ELECTRICAL EQUIPMENT 12 V; 40 Ah battery; 34 A alte nator; Lucas distributor; 2 headlamps.

DIMENSIONS AND WEIGHT wheel base: 79.92 in, 203 c tracks: 46.46 in, 118 cm front, 44.88 in, 114 cm rear; leng 141 in, 358 cm; width: 60.24 in, 153 cm; height: 48.23

cm; ground clearance: 5.12 in, 13 cm; weight: 1,774 lb.
4 kg; weight distribution: 52.4% front, 47.6% rear; turn-
g circle: 32 ft, 9.8 m; fuel tank: 7 imp gal, 8.4 US gal.
l.

ODY convertible; 2 doors; 2 seats, built-in headrests;
nneau cover.

ACTICAL INSTRUCTIONS fuel: 97 oct petrol; oil: engine
5 imp pt, 7.8 US pt, 3.7 l. SAE 20W-50, change every
000 miles, 9,700 km - gearbox 2 imp pt, 2.3 US pt, 1.1 l.
AE 90, change every 3,000 miles, 4,800 km - final drive
7 imp pt, 1.9 US pt, 0,9 l, SAE 90, change every 3,000
les, 4,800 km; greasing: every 3,000 miles, 4,800 km,
points; tappet clearances: inlet 0.010 in, 0.25 mm, exhaust
010 in, 0.25 mm; valve timing: 18° 58° 58° 18°; tyre
essure: front 22 psi, 1.5 atm, rear 24 psi, 1.7 atm.

VARIATIONS

NGINE 8:1 compression ratio.
ANSMISSION (only for export) 5.20 x 13 tyres.

PTIONALS oil cooler; wire wheels; hardtop.

MGB GT

ICE EX WORKS: £ 4,559*

NGINE front, 4 stroke; 4 cylinders, in line; 109.7 cu in,
798 cc (3.16 x 3.50 in, 80.3 x 88.9 mm); compression ratio:
1; max power (DIN): 97 hp (71.4 kW) at 5,500 rpm; max
rque (DIN): 104 lb ft, 14.5 kg m (142.2 Nm) at 2,500
m; max engine rpm: 6,200; 53.9 hp/l (39.7 kW/l); cast
on block and head; 5 crankshaft bearings; valves: overhead,
sh-rods and rockers; camshafts: 1, side; lubrication: ec-
ntric pump, full flow filter (cartridge), oil cooler, 6.5
p pt, 7.8 US pt, 3.7 l; 2 SU type HIFA semi-downdraught
rburettors; fuel feed: electric pump; sealed circuit cool-
g, liquid, expansion tank, 10 imp pt, 12 US pt, 5.7 l,
ermostatically-controlled electric fan.

ANSMISSION driving wheels: rear; clutch: single dry
ate (diaphragm), hydraulically controlled; gearbox: me-
anical; gears: 4, fully synchronized, and Laycock-de
ormanville overdrive on III and IV; ratios: I 3.036, II
66, III 1.381 (overdrive 1.132), IV 1 (overdrive 0.820);
v 3.095; lever: central; final drive: hypoid bevel; axle
tio: 3.909; width of rims: 5''; tyres: 165 SR x 14.

RFORMANCE max speeds: (I) 32 mph, 51 km/h; (II)
mph, 82 km/h; (III) 81 mph, 130 km/h; (IV) 107 mph,
2 km/h; power-weight ratio: 24.4 lb/hp (33.2 lb/kW),
.1 kg/hp (15 kg/kW); carrying capacity: 529 lb, 240 kg;
eed in direct drive at 1,000 rpm: 18 mph, 28.9 km/h;
nsumption: 25.4 m/imp gal, 21.2 m/US gal, 11.1 l x 100 km.

HASSIS integral; front suspension: independent, wish-
nes, coil springs, anti-roll bar, lever dampers as upper
ms; rear: rigid axle, semi-elliptic leafsprings, anti-roll
r, lever dampers.

TEERING rack-and-pinion; turns lock to lock: 3.57.

RAKES front disc (diameter 10.75 in, 27.3 cm), rear drum,
rvo; lining area: front 20 sq in, 129 sq cm, rear 67.3 sq
, 434 sq cm, total 87.3 sq in, 563 sq cm.

ECTRICAL EQUIPMENT 12 V; 66 Ah battery; 45 A alter-
tor; Lucas distributor; 2 halogen headlamps.

MENSIONS AND WEIGHT wheel base: 91 in, 231 cm;
acks: 49 in, 124 cm front, 49.25 in, 125 cm rear; length:
8.25 in, 402 cm; width: 61.75 in, 157 cm; height: 50.79
, 129 cm; ground clearance: 4.19 in, 10.6 cm; weight:
370 lb, 1,075 kg; turning circle: 32.6 ft, 9.9 m; fuel tank:
imp gal, 14.5 US gal, 55 l.

ODY coupé; 2 doors; 2+2 seats, separate front seats,
ilt-in headrests; tinted glass; heated rear window.

ACTICAL INSTRUCTIONS fuel: 98-100 oct petrol; oil:
ngine 6 imp pt, 7.2 US pt, 3.4 l, SAE 10W-30 (winter)
W-50 (summer), change every 3,000 miles, 4,800 km -
earbox 4.6 imp pt, 5.5 US pt, 2.6 l, SAE 20W-50 - final
ive 1.5 imp pt, 1.9 US pt, 0.9 l, SAE 90; greasing:
ery 3,000 miles, 4,800 km, 8 points; tappet clearances:
let 0.015 in, 0.38 mm, exhaust 0.015 in, 0.38 mm; valve
ming: 16° 56° 51° 21°; tyre pressure: front 21 psi, 1.5
m, rear 24 psi, 1.7 atm.

PTIONALS wire wheels.

MGB Sports

e MGB GT, except for:

RICE IN USA: £ 6,550*
RICE EX WORKS: £ 3,996*

ERFORMANCE power-weight ratio: 23.8 lb/hp (32.3 lb/kW),
.8 kg/hp (14.7 kg/kW).

MG Midget

MG Midget

DIMENSIONS AND WEIGHT weight: 2,310 lb, 1,047 kg.

BODY sports; 2 seats; tonneau cover; tinted glass and heated rear window not available.

OPTIONALS hardtop.

MINI   GREAT BRITAIN

850 Saloon

PRICE EX WORKS: £ 2,157*

ENGINE front, transverse, in unit with gearbox and final
drive, 4 stroke; 4 cylinders, vertical, in line; 51.7 cu in,
848 cc (2.48 x 2.69 in, 62.9 x 68.2 mm); compression ratio:
8.3:1; max power (DIN): 33 hp (24.3 kW) at 5,300 rpm;
max torque (DIN): 40 lb ft, 5.5 kg m (53.9 Nm) at 2,500
rpm; max engine rpm: 5,500; 38.9 hp/l (28.7 kW/l); cast
iron block and head; 3 crankshaft bearings; valves: overhead,
in line, push-rods and rockers; camshafts: 1, side; lubrication: rotary pump, full flow filter by cartridge, 8.4 imp pt,
10.1 US pt, 4.8 l; 1 SU type HS4 semi-downdraught carburettor; fuel feed: mechanical pump; water-cooled, 6.2
imp pt, 7.4 US pt, 3.5 l.

MG MGB GT

850 SALOON

TRANSMISSION driving wheels: front; clutch: single dry plate (diaphragm), hydraulically controlled; gearbox: mechanical; gears: 4, fully synchronized; ratios: I 3.525, II 2.218, III 1.433, IV 1, rev 3.544; lever: central; final drive: helical spur gears; axle ratio: 3.765; width of rims: 3.5''; tyres: 145 SR x 10 (5.20 x 10 only for export).

PERFORMANCE max speeds: (I) 22 mph, 35 km/h; (II) 35 mph, 56 km/h; (III) 54 mph, 87 km/h; (IV) 73 mph, 117 km/h; power-weight ratio: 39.9 lb/hp (54.2 lb/kW), 18.1 kg/hp (24.6 kg/kW); carrying capacity: 706 lb, 320 kg; acceleration: standing ¼ mile 23.6 sec, 0-50 mph (0-80 km/h) 18.3 sec; speed in direct drive at 1,000 rpm: 15.9 mph, 25.6 km/h; consumption: 42.8 m/imp gal, 35.6 m/US gal, 6.6 l x 100 km.

CHASSIS integral, front and rear auxiliary frames; front suspension: independent, wishbones, rubber cone springs, telescopic dampers; rear: independent, swinging longitudinal trailing arms, rubber cone springs, telescopic dampers.

STEERING rack-and-pinion; turns lock to lock: 2.33.

BRAKES drum, single circuit, 2 front leading shoes; swept area: front 66 sq in, 426 sq cm, rear 55 sq in, 355 sq cm, total 121 sq in, 781 sq cm.

ELECTRICAL EQUIPMENT 12 V; 30 Ah battery; 34 A alternator; Lucas distributor; 2 headlamps.

DIMENSIONS AND WEIGHT wheel base: 80.16 in, 204 cm; tracks: 47.82 in, 121 cm front, 46.40 in, 118 cm rear; length: 120.25 in, 305 cm; width: 55.50 in, 141 cm; height: 53 in, 135 cm; ground clearance: 5.75 in, 14.7 cm; weight: 1,318 lb, 598 kg; weight distribution: 61% front, 39% rear; turning circle: 29.5 ft, 9 m; fuel tank: 7.5 imp gal, 9 US gal, 34 l.

BODY saloon/sedan; 2 doors; 4 seats, separate front seats; heated rear window.

PRACTICAL INSTRUCTIONS fuel: 94 oct petrol; oil: engine, gearbox and final drive 9 imp pt, 10.8 US pt, 5.1 l, SAE 20W-50, change every 6,000 miles, 9,700 km; greasing: every 6,000 miles, 9,700 km, 8 points; tappet clearances: inlet 0.012 in, 0.30 mm, exhaust 0.012 in, 0.30 mm; valve timing: 5° 45° 40° 10°; tyre pressure: front 24 psi, 1.7 atm, rear 21 psi, 1.5 atm.

1000 Saloon

See 850 Saloon, except for:

PRICE EX WORKS: £ 2,278*

ENGINE 60.9 cu in, 998 cc (2.54 x 3 in, 64.6 x 76.2 mm); max power (DIN): 39 hp (28.7 kW) at 4,750 rpm; max torque (DIN): 51 lb ft, 7.1 kg m (69.6 Nm) at 2,000 rpm; 39 hp/l (28.8 kW/l).

TRANSMISSION axle ratio: 3.444.

PERFORMANCE max speeds: (I) 26 mph, 42 km/h; (II) 49 mph, 79 km/h; (III) 62 mph, 100 km/h; (IV) 77 mph,

MINI 1000 Saloon

123 km/h; power-weight ratio: 33.8 lb/hp (45.9 lb/kW), 15.3 kg/hp (20.8 kg/kW).

OPTIONALS AP automatic transmission, hydraulic torque converter with 2 conic bevel gears (twin concentric differential-like gear clusters) with 4 ratios (I 2.690, II 1.845, III 1.460, IV 1.269, rev 2.690), operated by 3 brake bands and 2 multi-disc clutches, max ratio of converter at stall 2, possible manual selection.

Clubman Saloon

See 1000 Saloon, except for:

PRICE EX WORKS: £ 2,537*

ENGINE 67 cu in, 1,098 cc (2.54 x 3.29 in, 64.4 x 83.5 mm); compression ratio: 8.5:1; max power (DIN): 45 hp (33.1 kW) at 5,250 rpm; max torque (DIN): 56 lb ft, 7.7 kg m (75.5 Nm) at 2,700 rpm; 41 hp/l (30.1 kW/l).

PERFORMANCE max speed: 81 mph, 130 km/h; power-weight ratio: 31.6 lb/hp (43 lb/kW), 14.4 kg/hp (19.5 kg/kW); consumption: 48.7 m/imp gal, 40.6 m/US gal, 5.8 l x 100 km at steady 50 mph, 80 km/h.

DIMENSIONS AND WEIGHT wheel base: 80.20 in, 204 cm; tracks: 48.77 in, 124 cm front, 47.43 in, 120 cm rear; length: 124.64 in, 317 cm; ground clearance: 6.55 in, 16.6 cm; weight: 1,424 lb, 646 kg; turning circle: 30 ft, 9.2 m.

MINI 1275 GT

BODY tinted glass; heated rear window.

PRACTICAL INSTRUCTIONS fuel: 97 oct petrol; valve timing 5° 45° 51° 21°.

OPTIONALS metallic spray (only with 998 cc engine); AP automatic transmission, hydraulic torque converter with 2 conic bevel gears (twin concentric differential-like gear clusters) with 4 ratios (I 2.690, II 1.845, III 1.460, IV 1.269, rev 2.690), operated by 3 brake bands and 2 multi-disc clutches, max ratio of converter at stall, possible manual selection.

Clubman Estate Car

See Clubman Saloon, except for:

PRICE EX WORKS: £ 2,742*

PERFORMANCE power-weight ratio: 32.4 lb/hp (44 lb/kW), 14.7 kg/hp (20 kg/kW).

ELECTRICAL EQUIPMENT 36 Ah battery.

DIMENSIONS AND WEIGHT wheel base: 84.20 in, 214 cm; tracks: 47.82 in, 121 cm front, 46.40 in, 118 cm rear; length: 133.92 in, 340 cm; height: 53.50 in, 136 cm; ground clearance: 6.30 in, 16 cm; weight: 1,458 lb, 661 kg; turning circle: 30.5 ft, 9.3 m; fuel tank: 6 imp gal, 7.1 US gal, 27 l.

BODY estate car/st. wagon; 2+2 doors; folding rear seat; heated rear window not available.

OPTIONALS metallic spray not available.

MINI Clubman Estate Car

1275 GT

...e 850 Saloon, except for:

...ICE EX WORKS: £ 2,854*

...NGINE 77.8 cu in, 1,275 cc (2.78 x 3.20 in, 70.6 x 81.3 mm); ...mpression ratio: 8.8:1; max power (DIN): 54 hp (39.7 ...V) at 5,250 rpm; max torque (DIN): 67 lb ft, 9.2 kg m ...0.2 Nm) at 2,500 rpm; 42.4 hp/l (31.1 kW/l).

...RANSMISSION ratios: I 3.330, II 2.090, III 1.350, IV 1. ...V 3.350; axle ratio: 3.440; width of rims: 4.5''; tyres: ...5/65 R x 310.

...RFORMANCE max speeds: (I) 28 mph, 45 km/h; (II) 44 ...ph, 71 km/h; (III) 68 mph, 110 km/h; (IV) 87 mph, 140 ...h/h; power-weight ratio: 26.4 lb/hp (35.9 lb/kW), 12 ...hp (16.3 kg/kW); acceleration: 0-50 mph (0-80 km/h) ...5 sec; speed in direct drive at 1,000 rpm: 16.8 mph, 27 ...h/h; consumption: 40.4 m/imp gal, 33.6 m/US gal, 7 ...x 100 km.

...RAKES front disc (diameter 8.50 in, 21.6 cm), rear drum, ...rvo; swept area: front 134.5 sq in, 867 sq cm, rear 55 sq ...355 sq cm, total 189.5 sq in, 1,222 sq cm.

...ECTRICAL EQUIPMENT 40 Ah battery.

...MENSIONS AND WEIGHT wheel base: 80.20 in, 204 cm; ...cks: 48.77 in, 124 cm front, 47.43 in, 120 cm rear; ...ngth: 124.64 in, 317 cm; height: 53.55 in, 136 cm; ground ...earance: 6.55 in, 16.6 cm; weight: 1,424 lb, 646 kg; turning ...rcle: 30 ft, 9.1 m; fuel tank: 7.5 imp gal, 9 US gal, 34 l.

...DY heated rear window.

...ACTICAL INSTRUCTIONS fuel: 97 oct petrol.

...TIONALS metallic spray.

...ORGAN   GREAT BRITAIN

4/4 1600 2-seater

...ICE EX WORKS: £ 4,347*

...NGINE Ford, front, 4 stroke; 4 cylinders, vertical, in line; ...6 cu in, 1,599 cc (3.19 x 3.06 in, 81 x 77.6 mm); com...ession ratio: 9:1; max power (DIN): 84 hp (61.8 kW) at ...600 rpm; max torque (DIN): 92 lb ft, 12.7 kg m (124.5 Nm) ...3,500 rpm; max engine rpm: 6,000; 52.5 hp/l (38.6 kW/l); ...st iron block and head; 5 crankshaft bearings; valves: ...erhead, push-rods and rockers; camshafts: 1, side; lu...cation: rotary pump, full flow filter, 7.5 imp pt, 8.9 US ..., 4.2 l; 1 Weber 32/36 downdraught twin barrel carbu...tor; fuel feed: mechanical pump; water-cooled, 12 imp ...14.4 US pt, 6.8 l.

...ANSMISSION driving wheels: rear; clutch: single dry ...ate, hydraulically controlled; gearbox: mechanical; gears: ...fully synchronized; ratios: I 2.976, II 2.024, III 1.390, ...1, rev 3.317; lever: central; final drive: hypoid bevel; ...le ratio: 4.100; tyres: 165 x 15.

...RFORMANCE max speeds: (I) 37 mph, 59 km/h; (II) 55 ...h, 88 km/h; (III) 80 mph, 128 km/h; (IV) 105 mph, 169 ...; power-weight ratio: 19.3 lb/hp (26.3 lb/kW), 8.8 kg/hp ...9 kg/kW); carrying capacity: 353 lb, 160 kg; speed in ...rect drive at 1,000 rpm: 18.5 mph, 29.7 km/h; consumption: ...3 m/imp gal, 29.4 m/US gal, 8 l x 100 km.

...HASSIS ladder frame, Z-section long members, tubular ...d box-type cross members; front suspension: indepen...nt, vertical sliding pillars, coil springs, telescopic dam...rs; rear: rigid axle, semi-elliptic leafsprings, lever dam...rs.

...EERING cam and peg; turns lock to lock: 2.25.

...RAKES front disc (diameter 11 in, 27.9 cm), rear drum, ...al circuit; swept area: total 325.1 sq in, 2,097 sq cm.

...ECTRICAL EQUIPMENT 12 V; 38 Ah battery; alternator; ...headlamps.

...MENSIONS AND WEIGHT wheel base: 96 in, 244 cm; ...cks: 47 in, 119 cm front, 49 in, 124 cm rear; length: 144 ...366 cm; width: 56 in, 142 cm; height: 51 in, 129 cm; ...ound clearance: 7 in, 17.8 cm; weight: 1,624 lb, 736 kg. ...ight distribution: 48% front, 52% rear; turning circle: ...ft, 9.8 m; fuel tank: 8.5 imp gal, 10.3 US gal, 39 l.

...DY roadster; 2 doors; 2 seats.

...ACTICAL INSTRUCTIONS fuel: 98 oct petrol; oil: engine ...imp pt, 8.5 US pt, 4 l, SAE 10W-30, change every 6,000 ...les, 9,700 km - gearbox 1.8 imp pt, 2.1 US pt, 1 l, SAE ...- final drive 1.9 imp pt, 2.3 US pt, 1.1 l, SAE 90; greas-

MORGAN 4/4 1600 4-seater

MORGAN Plus 8

ing: every 3,000 and 9,000 miles, 4,800 and 14,500 km, 10 points; tyre pressure: front 17 psi, 1.2 atm, rear 17 psi, 1.2 atm.

OPTIONALS wire wheels; tonneau cover; reclining backrests.

4/4 1600 4-seater

See 4/4 1600 2-seater, except for:

PRICE EX WORKS: £ 4,785*

PERFORMANCE power-weight ratio: 20 lb/hp (27.2 lb/kW), 9.1 kg/hp (12.3 kg/kW).

DIMENSIONS AND WEIGHT weight: 1,680 lb, 762 kg; fuel tank: 10 imp gal, 12.1 US gal, 46 l.

BODY 4 seats.

Plus 8

See 4/4 1600 2-seater, except for:

PRICE EX WORKS: £ 6,499*

ENGINE Rover, 8 cylinders, Vee-slanted at 90°; 215.3 cu in, 3,528 cc (3.50 x 2.80 in, 89 x 71 mm); compression ratio: 9.35: 1; max power (DIN): 155 hp (114.1 kW) at 5,250 rpm; max torque (DIN): 199 lb, 27.5 kg m (269.7 Nm) at 2,500 rpm; max engine rpm: 5,800; 43.9 hp/l (32.3 kW/l); light alloy block and head; valves: hydraulic tappets; camshafts: 1, at centre of Vee; lubrication: gear pump, full flow filter, 9.5 imp pt, 11.4 US pt, 5.4 l; 2 SU type HIF6 semi-down-draught carburettors; water-cooled, 15 imp pt, 18 US pt, 8.5 l, electric thermostatic fan.

TRANSMISSION clutch: single dry plate (diaphragm), hydraulically controlled; gears: 5, fully synchronized; ratios: I 3.320, II 2.080, III 1.390, IV 1, V 0.860, rev 3.110; final drive: hypoid bevel, limited slip differential; axle ratio: 3.310; width of rims: 6''; tyres: 195 x 14.

PERFORMANCE max speeds: (I) 40 mph, 64 km/h; (II) 64 mph, 103 km/h; (III) 95 mph, 153 km/h; (IV) 132 mph, 212 km/h; (V) 150 mph, 241 km/h; power-weight ratio: 11.8 lb/hp (16 lb/kW), 5.3 kg/hp (7.3 kg/kW); acceleration: standing ¼ mile 14.5 sec, 0-50 mph (0-80 km/h) 5.1 sec; speed in direct drive at 1,000 rpm: 27.4 mph, 44.1 km/h; consumption: 24 m/imp gal, 20.1 m/US gal, 11.7 l x 100 km.

BRAKES servo.

ELECTRICAL EQUIPMENT 58 Ah battery; 4 headlamps.

DIMENSIONS AND WEIGHT wheel base: 98 in, 249 cm; tracks: 52 in, 132 cm front, 53 in, 135 cm rear; length: 147 in, 373 cm; width: 62 in, 158 cm; height: 52 in, 132 cm; weight: 1,826 lb, 828 kg; turning circle: 38 ft, 11.5 m; fuel tank: 13.5 imp gal, 16.1 US gal, 61 l.

OPTIONALS 185 x 15 tyres; headrests.

MORRIS — GREAT BRITAIN

Marina Series

PRICES EX WORKS:

1	1300 2-dr Coupé	£ 2,847*
2	1300 4-dr Saloon	£ 2,967*
3	1300 4+1-dr Estate Car	£ 3,385*
4	1300 L 2-dr Coupé	£ 3,078*
5	1300 L 4-dr Saloon	£ 3,163*
6	1300 HL 4-dr Saloon	£ 3,501*
7	1700 4-dr Saloon	£ 3,201*
8	1700 4+1-dr Estate Car	£ 3,553*
9	1700 L 4-dr Saloon	£ 3,412*
10	1700 L 4+1-dr Estate Car	£ 3,801*
11	1700 HL 4-dr Saloon	£ 3,774*

Power team:	Standard for:	Optional for:
57 hp	1 to 6	—
78 hp	7 to 11	—

57 hp power team

ENGINE front, 4 stroke; 4 cylinders, in line; 77.8 cu in, 1,275 cc (2.78 x 3.20 in, 70.6 x 81.3 mm); compression ratio: 8.8:1; max power (DIN): 57 hp (41.9 kW) at 5,500 rpm; max torque (DIN): 68 lb ft, 9.5 kg m (93.2 Nm) at 2,450 rpm; max engine rpm: 6,500; 44.7 hp/l (32.9 kW/l); cast iron block and head; 3 crankshaft bearings; valves: overhead, in line, push-rods and rockers; camshafts: 1, side, chain-driven; lubrication: rotary pump, full flow filter. 7.6 imp pt, 9.1 US pt, 4.3 l; 1 SU type HS4 semi-downdraught carburettor; fuel feed: mechanical pump; water-cooled, 7.4 imp pt, 8.9 US pt, 4.2 l.

TRANSMISSION driving wheels: rear; clutch: single dry plate (diaphragm), hydraulically controlled; gearbox: mechanical; gears: 4, fully synchronized; ratios: I 3.412, II 2.112, III 1.433, IV 1, rev 3.753; lever: central; final drive: hypoid bevel; axle ratio: 4.111; width of rims: 4.5''; tyres: 145/165 SR x 13 - Estate Car 155 SR x 13.

PERFORMANCE max speeds: (I) 30 mph, 48 km/h; (II) 49 mph, 79 km/h; (III) 72 mph, 116 km/h; (IV) 86 mph, 138 km/h; power-weight ratio: 4-dr saloons 34.6 lb/hp (47.2 lb/kW), 15.7 kg/hp (21.4 kg/kW); carrying capacity: 882 lb, 400 kg; acceleration: standing 1/4 mile 22 sec; speed in direct drive at 1,000 rpm: 15.7 mph, 25.2 km/h; consumption: 31.3 m/imp gal, 26.1 m/US gal, 9 l x 100 km - Estate Car 29.5 m/imp gal, 24.5 m/US gal, 9.6 l x 100 km.

CHASSIS integral; front suspension: independent, wishbones, lower trailing links, longitudinal torsion bars, lever dampers as upper arms, telescopic dampers, anti-roll bar; rear: rigid axle, semi-elliptic leafsprings, telescopic dampers, anti-roll bar.

STEERING rack-and-pinion; turns lock to lock: 4.

BRAKES front disc (diameter 9.78 in, 24.8 cm), rear drum, servo; swept area: front 182.2 sq in, 1,175 sq cm, rear 76 sq in, 490 sq cm, total 258.1 sq in, 1.665 sq cm.

MORRIS Marina 1700 L

MORRIS Marina 1300 L 2-dr Coupé

ELECTRICAL EQUIPMENT 12 V; 40 44 or 50 Ah batte 34 A alternator; Lucas distributor; 4 headlamps, 2 haloge

DIMENSIONS AND WEIGHT wheel base: 96.16 in, 244 c front and rear track: 52 in, 132 cm; length: 2-dr coup 165.75 in, 421 cm - 4-dr saloons 169 in, 429 cm - Est Car 170.09 in, 432 cm; width: 64.57 in, 164 cm; heig 55.91 in, 142 cm - Estate Car 56.60 in, 144 cm; grou clearance: 6.10-6.30 in, 15.5-16 cm; weight: 2-dr coup 1,951 lb, 885 kg - 4-dr saloons 1,973 lb, 895 kg - Esta Car 2,139 lb, 970 kg; turning circle: 33.1 ft, 10.1 fuel tank: 11.5 imp gal, 13.7 US gal, 52 l.

BODY 5 seats, separate front seats, reclining backres heated rear window; (for HL model only) tinted gla

PRACTICAL INSTRUCTIONS fuel: 97 oct petrol; oil: eng 7.6 imp pt, 9.1 US pt, 4.3 l, SAE 20W-50, change every 6,0 miles, 9,700 km - gearbox 2.2 imp pt, 2.5 US pt, 1.2 change every 6,000 miles, 9,700 km - final drive 1.2 imp 1.5 US pt, 0.7 l, change every 6,000 miles, 9,700 k greasing: every 3,000 miles, 4,800 km, 4 points; spark plug: 225º; tappet clearances: inlet 0.012 in, 0.30 m exhaust 0.012 in, 0.30 mm; valve timing: 5º 45º 51º 2 tyre pressure: front 26 psi, 1.8 atm, rear 28 psi, 2 at

OPTIONALS 8:1 compression ratio; (only for L 4-dr HL models) Borg-Warner 65 automatic transmission, hydr lic torque converter and planetary gears with 3 ratios 2.393, II 1.450, III 1, rev 2.094), max ratio of conver at stall 2, possible manual selection; servo brake 165 SR x 13 tyres; (only for L and HL models) metallic spr

tinted glass; (for L 4-dr model only) vinyl roof; laminat windscreen.

78 hp power team

See 57 hp power team, except for:

ENGINE 103.6 cu in, 1,698 cc (3.33 x 2.98 in, 84.5 x 7 mm); compression ratio: 9:1; max power (DIN): 78 (57.4 kW) at 5,150 rpm; max torque (DIN): 93 lb ft, 1 kg m (126.5 Nm) at 3,400 rpm; max engine rpm: 5,6 45.9 hp/l (33.8 kW/l); cast iron block light alloy he 5 crankshaft bearings; camshafts: 1, overhead, chain-dri lubrication: 9.1 imp pt, 9.7 US pt, 4.6 l; 1 SU type H semi-downdraught carburettor; cooling: 10 imp pt, 12 pt, 5.7 l.

TRANSMISSION ratios: I 3.111, II 1.926, III 1.307, IV rev 3.422; axle ratio: 3.636; tyres: 155 SR x 13.

PERFORMANCE max speeds: (I) 33 mph, 53 km/h; 53 mph, 85 km/h; (III) 78 mph, 125 km/h; (IV) 95 m 153 km/h; power-weight ratio: saloons 26.2 lb/hp (3 lb/kW), 11.9 kg/hp (16.1 kg/kW); speed in direct dr at 1,000 rpm: 18.1 mph, 29.2 km/h; consumption: 3 m/imp gal, 25 m/US gal, 9.4 l x 100 km.

ELECTRICAL EQUIPMENT 55 Ah battery; 4 headlam 2 halogen.

DIMENSIONS AND WEIGHT weight: saloons 2,040 lb, kg - st. wagons 2,194 lb, 995 kg.

BODY (for st. wagons only) rear window wiper-washe

MORRIS Marina 1700 L 4-dr Saloon

NOVA   GREAT BRITAIN

Sports

PRICE IN GB: £ 4,800

ENGINE Volkswagen, rear, 4 stroke; 4 cylinders, horizontally opposed; 96.7 cu in, 1,584 cc (3.37 x 2.72 in, 85.5 x 69 mm); compression ratio: 7.5:1; max power (DIN): 50 hp (36.8 kW) at 4,000 rpm; max torque (DIN): 78 lb ft, 10.8 kg m (105.9 Nm) at 2,800 rpm; max engine rpm: 4,500; 31.6 hp/l (23.2 kW/l); block with cast iron liners and light alloy fins, light alloy head; 4 crankshaft bearings; valves: overhead, push-rods and rockers; camshafts: 1, central, lower; lubrication: gear pump, filter in sump, oil cooler, 4.4 imp pt, 5.3 US pt, 2.5 l; 1 Nikki downdraught carburettor; fuel feed: mechanical pump; air-cooled.

TRANSMISSION driving wheels: rear; clutch: single dry plate, heavy-duty; gearbox: mechanical; gears: 4, fully synchronized; ratios: I 3.780, II 2.060, III 1.260, IV 0.930, rev 4.010; lever: central; final drive: spiral bevel; axle ratio: 4.375; width of rims: 7''; tres: 205 x 14.

PERFORMANCE max speed: 110 mph, 177 km/h; power-weight ratio: 31.3 lb/hp (42.6 lb/kW), 14.2 kg/hp (19.3 kg/kW); carrying capacity: 353 lb, 160 kg; consumption: 35 m/imp gal, 29 m/US gal, 8.1 l x 100 km.

CHASSIS backbone platform; front suspension: independent, twin swinging longitudinal trailing arms, transverse laminated torsion bars, anti-roll bar, lowered and uprated telescopic dampers; rear; independent, semi-trailing arms, transverse compensating torsion bar, lowered telescopic dampers.

STEERING worm and roller, telescopic damper.

BRAKES front disc, rear drum.

ELECTRICAL EQUIPMENT 12 V; 12 V heavy-duty battery; dynamo; Bosch distributor; 2 headlamps.

DIMENSIONS AND WEIGHT length: 174 in, 442 cm width: 66 in, 168 cm; height: 45 in, 114 cm; ground clearance: 5 in, 13 cm; weight: 1,568 lb, 711 kg; weight distribution: 40% front, 60% rear; fuel tank: 9 imp gal, 10.8 US gal, 41 l.

BODY sports, in plastic material with lift up roof section; 1 door; 2 seats.

PRACTICAL INSTRUCTIONS fuel: 87 oct petrol; oil: engine 4.4 imp pt, 5.3 US pt, 2.5 l, SAE 10W-20 (winter) 20W-30 (summer), change every 3,100 miles, 5,000 km - gearbox and final drive 5.3 imp pt, 6.3 US pt, 3 l, SAE 90, change every 31,000 miles, 50,000 km; greasing: every 6,200 miles, 10,000 km, 4 points; sparking plug: 175°; tappet clearances: inlet 0.004 in, 0.10 mm, exhaust 0.004 in, 0.10 mm; valve timing: 7°30' 37° 43°30' 4°.

OPTIONALS electric roof; air-conditioning; tinted glass; sunshine roof; halogen headlamps.

NOVA Sports

STEERING rack-and-pinion; turns lock to lock: 3.16.

BRAKES disc (front diameter 10.03 in, 25.5 cm, rear 9 in, 22.9 cm), servo.

ELECTRICAL EQUIPMENT 12 V; 39 Ah battery; 28 A alternator; Lucas distributor; 2 headlamps.

DIMENSIONS AND WEIGHT wheel base: 97 in, 246 cm; tracks: 52.30 in, 133 cm front, 52 in, 132 cm rear; length: 142.13 in, 361 cm; width: 63.39 in, 161 cm; height: 48.03 in, 122 cm; ground clearance: 4.53 in, 11.5 cm; weight: 1,800 lb, 816 kg; weight distribution: 50% front, 50% rear; turning circle: 32.2 ft, 9.8 m; fuel tank: 10 imp gal, 12.1 US gal, 46 l.

BODY roadster, in plastic material; 2 doors; 2 seats; leather upholstery.

PRACTICAL INSTRUCTIONS fuel: 98 oct petrol; oil: engine 8.5 imp pt, 10.1 US pt, 4.8 l, SAE 20W-50, change every 6,000 miles, 9,700 km - gearbox and final drive 2.5 imp pt, 3 US pt, 1.4 l, SAE 90 EP; greasing: none; tappet clearances: inlet 0.007-0.010 in, 0.17-0.25 mm, exhaust 0.015-0.019 in, 0.37-0.45 mm; valve timing: 31°36' 63°36' 63°36' 31°36'; tyre pressure: front 24 psi, 1.7 atm, rear 24 psi, 1.7 atm.

OPTIONALS automatic transmission, hydraulic torque converter and planetary gears with 3 ratios (I 2.400, II 1.480, III 1, rev 1.920), max ratio of converter at stall 2.25, possible manual selection; wire wheels: laminated glass; metallic

spray: tonneau cover; front spoiler; tuned engine with max speed 125 mph, 200 km/h; hardtop; luggage rack.

VARIATIONS

ENGINE 1 Holley-Weber carburettor with airesearch turbocharger.
TRANSMISSION 6'' wide rims, 205/60 VR x 14 tyres.

J 72 4.2-litre

PRICE EX WORKS: £ 16,556*

ENGINE Jaguar, front, 4 stroke; 6 cylinders, vertical, in line; 258.4 cu in, 4,235 cc (3.63 x 4.17 in, 92 x 106 mm): compression ratio: 8:1; max power (DIN): 190 hp (139.8 kW) at 5,000 rpm; max torque (DIN): 200 lb ft, 27.6 kg m (270.7 Nm) at 2,000 rpm; max engine rpm: 6,000; 44.9 hp/l (33 kW/l); cast iron block, light alloy head, hemispherical combustion chambers; 7 crankshaft bearings; valves: overhead, Vee-slanted at 70°, thimble tappets; camshafts: 2, overhead; lubrication: rotary pump, full flow filter, 14.5 imp pt, 17.3 US pt, 8.2 l; 2 SU type AED horizontal carburettors; fuel feed: 2 electric pumps; water-cooled, 20 imp pt, 23.9 US pt, 11.3 l.

TRANSMISSION driving wheels: rear; clutch: single dry plate (diaphragm); gearbox: mechanical; gears: 4, fully synchronized with overdrive/top; ratios: I 3.040, II 1.970, III 1.330, IV 1, overdrive 0.780, rev 3.490; lever: central;

PANTHER   GREAT BRITAIN

Lima

PRICE EX WORKS: £ 6,067*

ENGINE Vauxhall, front, slanted at 45°, 4 stroke; 4 cylinders, in line; 139.2 cu in, 2,279 cc (3.84 x 3 in, 97.5 x 76.2 mm); compression ratio: 8.5:1; max power (DIN): 108 hp (79.5 kW) at 5,000 rpm; max torque (DIN): 138 lb ft, 19 kg m (186.2 Nm) at 3,000 rpm; max engine rpm: 5,500; 47.4 hp/l (34.9 kW/l); cast iron block and head; 5 crankshaft bearings; valves: overhead, in line, push-rods; camshafts: 1, overhead, cogged belt; lubrication: gear pump, full flow filter, 8.5 imp pt, 10.1 US pt, 4.8 l; 1 Zenith-Stromberg 175 CD2 downdraught single barrel carburettor; fuel feed: mechanical pump; water-cooled, 13.5 imp pt, 16.1 US pt, 7.6 l, viscous coupling thermostatic fan.

TRANSMISSION driving wheels: rear; clutch: single dry plate (diaphragm); gearbox: mechanical; gears: 4, fully synchronized; ratios: I 3.300, II 2.145, III 1.414, IV 1, rev 3.063; lever: central; final drive: hypoid bevel; axle ratio: 3.730; width of rims: 5.5''; tyres: 185/70 HR x 13.

PERFORMANCE max speed: 110 mph, 177 km/h; power-weight ratio: 16.7 lb/hp (22.6 lb/kW), 7.6 kg/hp (10.3 kg/kW); carrying capacity: 353 lb, 160 kg; speed in direct drive at 1,000 rpm: 18.9 mph, 30.4 km/h; consumption: 25 m/imp gal, 20.8 m/US gal, 11.3 l x 100 km.

CHASSIS integral; front suspension: independent, wishbones, coil springs, anti-roll bar, telescopic dampers; rear: rigid axle, twin trailing radius arms, transverse linkage bar, coil springs, anti-roll bar, telescopic dampers.

PANTHER Lima

J 72 4.2-LITRE

final drive: hypoid bevel, limited slip differential; axle ratio: 3.540; width of rims: 6''; tyres: 225/70VR x 15.

PERFORMANCE max speeds: (I) 43 mph, 69 km/h; (II) 66 mph, 106 km/h; (III) 94 mph, 151 km/h; (IV) 114 mph, 183 km/h; power-weight ratio: 13.6 lb/hp (18.4 lb/kW), 6.2 kg/hp (8.3 kg/kW); carrying capacity: 420 lb, 190 kg; acceleration: standing ¼ mile 15.3 sec; speed in direct drive at 1,000 rpm: 20.2 mph, 32.5 km/h; consumption: 15 m/imp gal, 12.5 m/US gal, 18.8 l x 100 km.

CHASSIS square section ladder frame; front suspension: independent, wishbones, coil springs, anti-roll bar, telescopic dampers; rear: rigid axle, trailing arms, Panhard rod, adjustable coil springs/telescopic damper units.

STEERING recirculating ball; turns lock to lock: 2.8.

BRAKES front disc, rear drum, servo.

ELECTRICAL EQUIPMENT 12 V; 57 Ah battery; 45 A alternator; Lucas distributor; 2 headlamps.

DIMENSIONS AND WEIGHT wheel base: 111 in, 282 cm; tracks: 58.50 in, 149 cm front, 58.50 in, 149 cm rear; length: 165 in, 419 cm; width: 68.50 in, 174 cm; height: 49 in 124 cm; ground clearance: 5 in, 12.7 cm; weight: 2,576 lb, 1,166 kg; weight distribution: 53.5% front, 46.5% rear; turning circle: 40 ft, 9.3 m; fuel tank: 26 imp gal, 31.2 US gal, 118 l.

BODY roadster in light alloy; 2 doors; 2 seats; leather upholstery; laminated windscreen.

PRACTICAL INSTRUCTIONS fuel: 98 oct petrol; oil: engine 13 imp pt, 15.6 US pt, 7.4 l, SAE 20W-50, change every 6,000 miles, 9,700 km - gearbox and overdrive 4 imp pt, 4.9 US pt, 2.3 l, SAE 90 EP, change every 12,000 miles, 20,000 km - final drive 2.7 imp pt, 3.2 US pt, 1.6 l, SAE 90, change every 12,000 miles, 20,000 km; greasing: every 6,000 miles, 10,000 km, 4 points; tyre pressure: front 22 psi, 1.5 atm, rear 19 psi, 1.3 atm.

OPTIONALS Borg-Warner 65 automatic transmission, hydraulic torque converter and planetary gears with 3 ratios (I 2.400, II 1.450, III 1, rev 2.100), max ratio of converter at stall 2, possible manual selection; headrests; air-conditioning; metallic spray; tonneau cover; power steering; hardtop.

De Ville Saloon

PRICE EX WORKS: £ 44,825*

ENGINE Jaguar, front, 4 stroke; 12 cylinders, Vee-slanted at 60°; 326 cu in, 5,343 cc (3.54 x 2.76 in, 90 x 70 mm); compression ratio: 9:1; cast iron block with light alloy wet liners, aluminium alloy head with hemisperical combustion chambers; 7 crankshaft bearings; valves: overhead, in line, thimble tappets; camshafts: 1 per block, overhead; lubrication: rotary pump, full flow filter, 17.6 imp pt, 21.1 US pt, 10 l; electronic fuel injection; fuel feed: 2 electric pumps; water-cooled, 36 imp pt, 43.3 US pt, 20.5 l.

PANTHER J 72 4.2-litre

TRANSMISSION driving wheels: rear; gearbox: GM 400 automatic transmission, hydraulic torque converter and planetary gears with 3 ratios, max ratio of converter at stall 2, possible manual selection; ratios: I 2.460, II 1.460, III 1, rev 2.090; lever: central; final drive: hypoid bevel, limited slip differential; axle ratio: 3.310; width of rims: 6''; tyres: 235/70 HR x 15.

PERFORMANCE max speed: 128 mph, 206 km/h; carrying capacity: 925 lb, 419 kg; acceleration: speed in direct drive at 1,000 rpm: 21.1 mph, 31.7 km/h; consumption: not declared.

CHASSIS ladder tube; front suspension: independent, wishbones, coil springs, anti-roll bar, telescopic dampers; rear: independent, wishbones (trailing links), 4 coil springs, transverse linkage bar, 4 telescopic dampers.

STEERING rack-and-pinion, servo.

BRAKES disc (front diameter 11.2 in, 28.4 cm, rear 10.4 in, 26.4 cm), front internal radial fins, servo; swept area: total 448 sq in, 2,890 sq cm.

ELECTRICAL EQUIPMENT 12 V; 68 Ah battery; 67 A alternator; Lucas distributor; 2 headlamps.

DIMENSIONS AND WEIGHT wheel base: 142 in, 361 cm; tracks: 58 in, 147 cm front, 58 in, 147 cm rear; length: 204 in, 519 cm; width: 71 in, 180 cm; height: 61 in, 155 cm; weight: 4,360 lb, 1,973 kg; fuel tank: 22 imp gal, 26.4 US gal, 100 l.

BODY saloon/sedan; 4 doors; 4 seats; separate front sea reclining backrests with built-in headrests; leather uph stery tinted glass; heated rear window; electric window air-conditioning; laminated windscreen; chrome wire whee

PRACTICAL INSTRUCTIONS fuel: 97 oct petrol; oil: eng 16 imp pt, 19.2 US pt, 9.1 l, SAE 20W-50, change ev 6,000 miles, 9,700 km - automatic transmission 16 imp 19.2 US pt, 9.1 l, TQF no change recommended - final dr 2.7 imp pt, 3.4 US pt, 1.6 l, SAE 90, change every 12, miles, 20,000 km; greasing: every 6,000 miles, 9,700 k 17 points; tappet clearances: inlet 0.012-0.014 in, 0.30-0 mm, exhaust 0.012-0.014 in, 0.30-0.35 mm; type pressu front 30 psi, 2.1 atm, rear 32 psi, 2.2 atm.

VARIATIONS

ENGINE Jaguar, 6 cylinders, vertical, in line, 258.4 cu 4,235 cc (3.63 x 4.17 in, 92 x 106 mm), 8:1 compress ratio, 7 crankshaft bearings, Vee-slanted valves, 2 overh camshafts, lubricating system 14.5 imp pt, 17.3 US 8.2 l, 2 SU type AED horizontal carburettors, cooling syst 20 imp pt, 23.9 US pt, 11.3 l.
TRANSMISSION Borg-Warner 65 automatic transmissi hydraulic torque converter and planetary gears with 3 rat (I 2.390, II 1.450, III 1, rev 2.090).

OPTIONALS 4-speed fully synchronized mechanical gearb electric sunshine roof; metallic spray.

De Ville Convertible

PRICE EX WORKS: £ 50,895*

BODY convertible; 2 doors; tonneau cover.

OPTIONALS detachable hardtop; electric sunshine r not available.

6

PRICE EX WORKS: £ 39,950*

ENGINE Cadillac, centre-rear, 4 stroke; 8 cylinders, V slanted at 90°; 500 cu in, 8,194 cc (4.30 x 4.30 in, 109. 109.1 mm); compression ratio: 8.5:1; cast iron block a head; 5 crankshaft bearings; valves: overhead, in line, pus rods and rockers, hydraulic tappets; camshafts: 1, at cen of Vee; lubrication: gear pump, full flow filter, oil cool 10 imp pt, 12 US pt, 5.7 l; 2 Airesearch TO4 turbocharge with 1 Holley downdraught 4-barrel carburettor; water-co ed, 43.1 imp pt, 51.8 US pt, 24.5 l, 2 electric fans.

TRANSMISSION driving wheels: rear; gearbox: Turbo-H dramatic 425 automatic transmission, hydraulic torque c verter and planetary gears with 3 ratios, max ratio converter at stall 2, possible manual selection; ratio I 2.480, II 1.480, III 1, rev 2.090; lever: steering colum final drive: spiral bevel; axle ratio: 1.800; width of rim 6'' front, 9'' rear; tyres: P7 205/40 VR x 13 front, 265/50 VR x 16 rear.

PERFORMANCE max speed: over 200 mph, 322 km/h.

CHASSIS tubular; front suspension: independent, wishbon coil springs, anti-roll bar, telescopic dampers; rear: in

PANTHER De Ville Convertible

TRANSMISSION driving wheels: front; clutch: single dry plate (diaphragm), hydraulically controlled; gearbox: mechanical, in unit with engine; gears; 4, fully synchronized; ratios: I 3.292, II 2.059, III 1.384, IV 1, rev 3.075; lever: central; final drive: spiral bevel; axle ratio: 3.720; width of rims: 4.5''; tyres: 185/70 SR x 14.

PERFORMANCE max speeds: (I) 35 mph, 56 km/h; (II) 55 mph, 88 km/h; (III) 82 mph, 132 km/h; (IV) 99 mph, 159 km/h; power-weight ratio: 28.9 lb/hp (39.2 lb/kW) 13.1 kg/hp (17.8 kg/kW); carrying capacity: 882 lb, 400 kg; speed in direct drive at 1,000 rpm: 18.8 mph, 30.3 km/h; consumption: 29.7 m/imp gal, 24.8 m/US gal, 9.5 l x 100 km.

CHASSIS integral; front suspension: independent, wishbones, hydragas (liquid and gas) rubber cone springs, hydraulic connecting pipes to rear wheels; rear: independent, swinging longitudinal trailing arms, hydragas (liquid and gas) rubber cone springs, hydraulic connecting pipes to front wheels.

STEERING rack-and-pinion; turns lock to lock: 4.57.

BRAKES front disc (diameter 10.63 in, 27 cm), rear drum, dual circuit, servo; lining area: front 26.4 sq in, 170 sq cm, rear 47.9 sq in, 309 sq cm, total 74.3 sq in, 479 sq cm.

ELECTRICAL EQUIPMENT 12 V; 55 Ah battery; 45 A alternator; Lucas distributor; 4 headlamps.

DIMENSIONS AND WEIGHT wheel base: 105.24 in, 267 cm; tracks: 58 in, 147 cm front, 57.36 in, 146 cm rear; length: 175.41 in, 445 cm; width: 68.11 in, 173 cm; height: 55.48 in, 141 cm; ground clearance: 6.45 in, 16.4 cm; weight: 2,514 lb, 1,140 kg; weight distribution: 63.5% front, 36.5% rear; turning circle: 40 ft, 12.2 m; fuel tank: 16 mp gal, 19.3 US gal, 73 l.

BODY saloon/sedan; 4 doors; 5 seats, separate front seats, reclining backrests; heated rear window; laminated windscreen.

PRACTICAL INSTRUCTIONS fuel: 96-98 oct petrol; oil: engine, gearbox and final drive 10.2 imp pt, 12.3 US pt, 5.8 l, SAE 20W-50, change every 6,000 miles, 9,700 km; greasing: every 6,000 miles, 9,700 km; tappet clearances: inlet 0.015 in, 0.38 mm, exhaust 0.015 in, 0.38 mm; valve timing: 5° 45° 40° 10°; tyre pressure: front 23 psi, 1.6 atm, rear 21 psi, 1.5 atm.

OPTIONALS Borg-Warner automatic transmission, hydraulic torque converter and planetary gears with 3 ratios (I 2.388, II 1.449, III 1, rev 2.090), max ratio of converter at stall 2, on facia lever, 3.880 axle ratio, max speed 96 mph, 155 km/h; power steering; tinted glass; headrests; 195/65 SR x 350 tyres; Denovo wheels and tyres; metallic spray; (for HL models only) vinyl roof.

93 hp power team

See 87 hp power team, except for:

ENGINE 121.6 cu in, 1,993 cc (3.32 x 3.50 in, 84.4 x 89 mm); max power (DIN): 93 hp (68.4 kW) at 4,900 rpm; max torque (DIN): 112 lb ft, 15.4 kg m (151 Nm) at 3,400 rpm; 46.7 hp/l (34.3 kW/l).

PANTHER 6

PANTHER De Ville Saloon

dent, wishbones, coil springs, anti-roll bar, telescopic ...pers.

...ERING rack-and-pinion, servo; turns lock to lock: 2.80.

...AKES disc (front diameter 10 in, 25.4 cm, rear 11 in, ... cm), 3 circuits; swept area: front 400 sq in, 2,580 sq ... rear 224 sq in, 1,445 sq cm, total 624 sq in, 4,025 ... cm.

...CTRICAL EQUIPMENT 12 V; 66 Ah battery; 100 A alter-...or; 4 halogen headlamps.

...MENSIONS AND WEIGHT wheel base: 105 in, 267 cm; ...ks: 61.50 in, 156 cm front, 64.50 in, 164 cm rear; length: ... in, 487 cm; width: 80 in, 203 cm; height: 48 in, 122 ... ground clearance: 7 in, 17.8 cm; weight: 2,870 lb, ...2 kg; fuel tank: 30 imp gal, 36.2 US gal, 137 l (2 ...arate tanks).

...DY convertible; 2 doors; 3 seats; leather upholstery, air-...ditioning, tinted glass.

...ACTICAL INSTRUCTIONS fuel: 98 oct petrol; oil: engine; ... imp pt, 12 US pt, 5.7 l, - automatic transmission 10.3 ... pt, 12.3 US pt, 5.8 l - final drive 3.3 imp pt, 4 US pt, ... l.

...IONALS electrically-controlled seats; hardtop; metallic ...ay.

...INCESS GREAT BRITAIN

1700-2000-2200 Series

...CES EX WORKS:

...700 L Saloon	£ 4,193*
...700 HL Saloon	£ 4,480*
...000 HL Saloon	£ 4,666*
...200 HL Saloon	£ 5,011*
...200 HLS Saloon	£ 5,535*

...er team:	Standard for:	Optional for:
...hp	1,2	—
...hp	3	—
...hp	4,5	—

87 hp power team

...INE front, transverse, in unit with gearbox and final ...e, 4 stroke; 4 cylinders, vertical, in line; 103.6 cu in, ...8 cc (3.33 x 2.98 in, 84.5 x 75.8 mm); compression ratio: ...; max power (DIN): 87 hp (64 kW) at 5,200 rpm; max ...que (DIN): 97 lb ft, 13.4 kg m (131.4 Nm) at 3,800 rpm; ... engine rpm: 5,600; 51.2 hp/l (37.7 kW/l); cast iron ...ck, light alloy head; 5 crankshaft bearings; valves: ...rhead, push-rods and rockers; camshafts: 1, overhead, ...in-driven; lubrication: rotary pump, magnetic metal ...ze filter in sump and full flow, 10.2 imp pt, 12.3 US ... 5.8 l; 1 SU type HIF6 semi-downdraught carburettor; ... feed: electric pump; sealed circuit cooling, liquid, ...ansion tank, 10.6 imp pt, 12.7 US pt, 6 l, thermostati-...y-controlled electric fan.

PRINCESS 2000 HL Saloon

93 HP POWER TEAM

PERFORMANCE power-weight ratio: 27.1 lb/hp (36.8 lb/kW), 12.3 kg/hp (16.7 kg/kW); acceleration: standing ¼ mile 19.4 sec; consumption: 27.2 m/imp gal, 22.6 m/US gal, 10.4 l x 100 km.

STEERING servo (standard); turns lock to lock: 3.30.

DIMENSIONS AND WEIGHT tracks: 58.50 in, 149 cm front, 58 in, 147 cm rear; length: 177.50 in, 451 cm; width: 67.75 in, 172 cm; ground clearance: 7.50 in, 19 cm; weight: 2,525 lb, 1,145 kg; weight distribution: 61,5% front, 38,5% rear.

PRACTICAL INSTRUCTIONS tappet clearances (cold): inlet 0.012 in, 0.30 mm, exhaust 0.012 in, 0.30 mm; tyre pressure: front 26 psi, 1.8 atm, rear 24 psi, 1.7 atm.

110 hp power team

See 87 hp power team, except for:

ENGINE 6 cylinders; 135.9 cu in, 2,227 cc (3 x 3.20 in, 76.2 x 81.3 mm); max power (DIN): 110 hp (81 kW) at 5,250 rpm; max torque (DIN): 124 lb ft, 17.1 kg m (167.7 Nm) at 3,500 rpm; 49.4 hp/l (36.4 kW/l); cast iron block and head; 7 crankshaft bearings; lubrication: 13 imp pt, 15.6 US pt, 7.4 l; 2 SU type HIF6 horizontal carburettors; cooling: 15 imp pt, 18 US pt, 8.5 l.

PERFORMANCE max speed: 106 mph, 170 km/h; power-weight ratio: 24.3 lb/hp (33.1 lb/kW), 11 kg/hp (15 kg/kW); consumption: 22.1 m/imp gal, 18.4 m/US gal, 12.8 l x 100 km.

STEERING servo (standard).

ELECTRICAL EQUIPMENT 2 headlamps.

DIMENSIONS AND WEIGHT length: HLS 176.37 in, 448 cm; weght: 2,679 lb, 1,215 kg.

BODY headrests and tinted glass (standard HLS only).

PRACTICAL INSTRUCTIONS oil: engine, gearbox and final drive 13 imp pt, 15.6 US pt, 7.4 l; tappet clearances: inlet 0.015-0.016 in, 0.38-0.40 mm, exhaust 0.015-0.016 in, 0.38-0.40 mm.

RELIANT   GREAT BRITAIN

Kitten DL Saloon

PRICE EX WORKS: £ 2,235*

ENGINE front, 4 stroke; 4 cylinders, in line; 51.7 cu in, 848 cc (2.46 x 2.72 in, 62.5 x 69.1 mm); compression ratio: 9.5:1; max power (DIN): 40 hp (29.4 kW) at 5,500 rpm; max torque (DIN): 46 lb ft, 6.3 kg m (61.8 Nm) at 3,500 rpm; max engine rpm: 5,500; 47.2 hp/l (34.7 kW/l); light alloy block and head, wet liners; 3 crankshaft bearings; valves: overhead, in line, push-rods and rockers; camshafts: 1, side; lubrication: rotary pump, full flow filter, 5.5 imp pt, 6.6 US pt, 3.1 l; 1 SU HS2 1¼ semi-downdraught single barrel carburettor; fuel feed: mechanical pump; sealed circuit cooling, anti-freeze liquid, 6.5 imp pt, 7.8 US pt, 3.7 l.

TRANSMISSION driving wheels: rear; clutch: single dry plate; gearbox: mechanical; gears: 4, fully synchronized; ratios: I 3.876, II 2.046, III 1.319, IV 1, rev 3.250; lever: central; final drive: spiral bevel; axle ratio: 3.230; width of rims: 3.5''; tyres: 145 x 10.

PERFORMANCE max speeds: (I) 24 mph, 39 km/h; (II) 45 mph, 73 km/h; (III) 71 mph, 114 km/h; (IV) 80 mph, 128 km/h; power-weight ratio: 29.4 lb/hp (40 lb/kW), 13.3 kg/hp (18.1 kg/kW); carrying capacity: 700 lb, 317 kg; acceleration: standing ¼ mile 20.4 sec, 0-50 mph (0-80 km/h) 11.1 sec; speed in direct drive at 1,000 rpm: 17 mph, 27.3 km/h; consumption: 38.9 m/imp gal, 32.2 m/US gal, 7.3 l x 100 km.

CHASSIS box-section side members and channel section diagonal reinforcements; front suspension: independent, wishbones, anti-roll bar, coil springs/telescopic damper units; rear: rigid axle, semi-elliptic leafsprings, telescopic dampers.

STEERING rack-and-pinion; turns lock to lock: 3.50.

BRAKES drum (diameter 7 in, 17.8 cm); swept area: front 66 sq in, 426 sq cm, rear 55 sq in, 355 sq cm, total 121 sq in, 781 sq cm.

ELECTRICAL EQUIPMENT 12 V; 30 Ah battery; 28 A alternator; Lucas distributor; 2 headlamps.

RELIANT Kitten DL Saloon

RELIANT Scimitar GTE

DIMENSIONS AND WEIGHT wheel base: 84.50 in, 215 cm; tracks: 48.5 in, 123 cm front, 49 in, 124 cm rear; length: 131 in, 333 cm; width: 56 in, 142 cm; height: 55 in, 140 cm; ground clearance: 5 in, 12.7 cm; weight: 1,175 lb, 533 kg; turning circle: 24 ft, 7.3 m; fuel tank: 6 imp gal, 7.1 US gal, 27 l.

BODY saloon/sedan in plastic material; 2 doors; 4 seats, separate front seats, reclining driver's seat; heated rear window; folding rear seat.

PRACTICAL INSTRUCTIONS fuel: 97 oct petrol; oil: engine 5.5 imp pt, 6.6 US pt, 3.1 l, SAE 20W-50, change every 6,000 miles, 9,700 km - gearbox 1.1 imp pt, 1.3 US pt, 0.6 l, SAE 80 EP, change every 12,000 miles, 19,400 km - final drive 2.2 imp pt, 2.5 US pt, 1.2 l, SAE 90 EP, change every 6,000 miles, 9,700 km; greasing: every 6,000 miles, 9,700 km, 7 points; tappet clearances: inlet 0.010 in, 0.25 mm, exhaust 0.010 in, 0.25 mm; valve timing: 13° 72° 54° 29°; tyre pressure: front 20 psi, 14 atm, rear 22 psi, 1.6 atm.

OPTIONALS light alloy wheels; laminated windscreen.

Kitten DL Estate Car

See Kitten DL Saloon, except for:

PRICE EX WORKS: £ 2,353*

PERFORMANCE power-weight ratio: 29.7 lb/hp (40.4 lb/kW), 13.5 kg/hp (18.3 kg/kW).

DIMENSIONS AND WEIGHT length: 131.75 in, 335 cm; weight: 1,189 lb, 539 kg.

BODY estate car/station wagon; 2+1 doors.

OPTIONALS rear window wiper-washer.

Robin 850 Saloon

PRICE EX WORKS: £ 1,883*

ENGINE front, 4 stroke; 4 cylinders, in line; 51.7 cu in, 848 cc (2.46 x 2.72 in, 62.5 x 69.1 mm); compression ratio: 9.5:1; max power (DIN): 40 hp (29.4 kW) at 5,500 rpm; max torque (DIN): 46 lb ft, 6.3 kg m (61.8 Nm) at 3,500 rpm; max engine rpm: 5,500; 47.2 hp/l (34.7 kW/l); light alloy block and head; 3 crankshaft bearings; valves: overhead, push-rods and rockers; camshafts: 1, side; lubrication: rotary pump, full flow filter, 5.5 imp pt, 6.6 US pt, 3.1 l; 1 SU type HS2 1¼ semi-downdraught carburettor; fuel feed: mechanical pump; water-cooled, 5 imp pt, US pt, 2.8 l.

TRANSMISSION driving wheels: rear; clutch: single dry plate; gearbox: mechanical; gears: 4, fully synchronized; ratios: I 3.880, II 2.050, III 1.320, IV 1, rev 3.250; lever: central; final drive: spiral bevel; axle ratio: 3.230; width of rims: 3.5''; tyres: 5.20 x 10.

PERFORMANCE max speeds: (I) 25 mph, 40 km/h; (II) mph, 75 km/h; (III) 73 mph, 117 km/h; (IV) 80 mph, km/h; power-weight ratio: 24 lb/hp (32.7 lb/kW),

kg/hp (14.8 kg/kW); carrying capacity: 788 lb, 357 kg; acceleration: standing ¼ mile 20.9 sec, 0-50 mph (0-80 km/h) 11.4 sec; speed in direct drive at 1,000 rpm: 17 mph, 27.3 km/h; consumption: 60 m/imp gal, 50 m/US gal, 4.7 l x 100 km.

CHASSIS box-section ladder frame, tubular cross members; front suspension: single wheel, swinging leading arm, coil spring, telescopic damper; rear: rigid axle, semi-elliptic leafsprings, anti-roll bar, telescopic dampers.

STEERING worm and peg; turns of steering wheel lock to lock: 2.25.

BRAKES drum, single circuit; swept area: front 33 sq in, 213 sq cm, rear 55 sq in, 355 sq cm, total 88 sq in, 568 sq cm.

ELECTRICAL EQUIPMENT 12 V; 30 Ah battery; 28 A alternator; Lucas distributor; 4 headlamps.

DIMENSIONS AND WEIGHT wheel base: 85 in, 216 cm, front and rear tracks: 49 in, 124 cm; length: 131 in, 333 cm; width: 56 in, 142 cm; height: 54 in, 137 cm; ground clearance: 5 in, 12.7 cm; weight: 962 lb, 436 kg; weight distribution: 44% front, 56% rear; turning circle: 27 ft, 8.2 m; fuel tank: 6 imp gal, 7.1 US gal, 27 l.

BODY saloon/sedan in plastic material; 2 doors; 4 seats, separate front seats.

PRACTICAL INSTRUCTIONS fuel: 97 oct petrol; oil: engine

5.5 imp pt, 6.6 US pt, 3.1 l, SAE 20W-50, change every 6,000 miles, 9,700 km - gearbox 1.1 imp pt, 1.3 US pt, 0.6 l, SAE 80 EP, change every 12,000 miles, 19,400 km - final drive 2.2 imp pt, 2.5 US pt, 1.2 l, SAE 90 EP, change every 6,000 miles, 9,700 km; greasing: every 6,000 miles 9,700 km, 4 points; tappet clarances: inlet 0.010 in, 0.25 mm hot, exhaust 0.010 in, 0.25 mm hot; valve timing: 13° 72° 54° 29°; tyre pressure: front 30 psi, 2.1 atm, rear 24 psi, 1.7 atm.

OPTIONALS heated rear window.

Robin 850 Super Saloon

See Robin 850 Saloon, except for:

PRICE EX WORKS: £ 2,190*

OPTIONALS rear window wiper-washer; light alloy wheels.

Robin 850 Super Estate Car

See Robin 850 Saloon, except for:

PRICE EX WORKS: £ 2,285*

BODY estate car/station wagon; 2 + 1 doors.

OPTIONALS rear window wiper-washer; light alloy wheels.

Scimitar GTE

PRICE EX WORKS: £ 7,014*

ENGINE Ford, front, 4 stroke; 6 cylinders, Vee-slanted at 60°; 182.7 cu in, 2,994 cc (3.69 x 2.85 in, 93.7 x 72.4 mm); compression ratio: 8.9:1; max power (DIN): 135 hp (99.4 kW) at 5,500 rpm; max torque (DIN): 172 lb ft, 23.7 kg m (232.4 Nm) at 3,000 rpm; max engine rpm: 6,400; 45.1 hp/l (33.2 kW/l); cast iron block and head; 4 crankshaft bearings; valves: overhead, push-rods and rockers; camshafts: 1, at centre of Vee; lubrication: rotary pump, full flow filter, 9.9 imp pt, 11.8 US pt, 5.6 l; 1 Weber 38 DGAS/3A downdraught twin barrel carburettor; fuel feed: mechanical pump; water-cooled, 21.5 imp pt, 26 US pt, 12.2 l, electric thermostatic fan.

TRANSMISSION driving wheels: rear; clutch: single dry plate (diaphragm); gearbox: mechanical; gears: 4+overdrive on III and IV; ratios: I 3.163, II 1.950, III 1.412 (overdrive 1.160), IV 1 (overdrive 0.780), rev 3.350; lever: central; final drive: hypoid bevel; axle ratio: 3.310; width of rims: 5.5''; tyres: 135 HR x 14.

PERFORMANCE max speeds: (I) 38 mph, 6\ km/h; (II) 62 mph, 100 km/h; (III) 85 mph, 136 km/h; (IV) 120 mph, 193 km/h; (overdrive/top) 112 mph, 180 km/h; power-weight ratio: 20.7 lb/hp (28.1 lb/kW), 9.4 kg/hp (12.8 kg/kW); carrying capacity: 850 lb, 385 kg; speed in direct drive at 1,000 rpm; 21.9 mph, 35.2 km/h; consumption: 18.2 m/imp gal, 15.1 m/US gal, 15.6 l x 100 km.

CHASSIS box-type ladder frame, tubular cross members; front suspension: independent, wishbones, anti-roll bar, coil

springs/telescopic damper units; rear: rigid axle, twin trailing arms, transverse Watt linkage, coil springs/telescopic damper units.

STEERING rack-and-pinion; turns lock to lock: 4.30.

BRAKES front disc (diameter 10.51 in, 26.6 cm), rear drum, rear compensator, servo; swept area: front 237 sq in, 1,529 sq cm, rear 110 sq in, 710 sq cm, total 347 sq in, 2,239 sq cm.

ELECTRICAL EQUIPMENT 12 V; 55 Ah battery; 36 A alternator; Motorcraft distributor; 4 headlamps.

DIMENSIONS AND WEIGHT wheel base: 103.81 in, 264 cm; tracks: 58.14 in, 148 cm front, 56.13 in, 143 cm rear; length: 174.50 in, 443 cm; width: 67.75 in, 172 cm; height: 52 in, 132 cm; ground clearance: 5.50 in, 14 cm; weight: 2,797 lb, 1,269 kg; turning circle: 38.5 ft, 1.7 m; fuel tank: 20 imp gal, 24 US gal, 91 l.

BODY coupé in plastic material; 2 doors; 4 seats, separate front seats, reclining backrests with built-in headrests; folding rear seat; heated rear window.

PRACTICAL INSTRUCTIONS fuel: 97 oct petrol; oil: engine 9.9 imp pt, 11.8 US pt, 5.6 l, SAE 20W-50, change every 6,000 miles, 9,700 km - gearbox 5 imp pt, 6 US pt, 2.8 l, SAE 80, change every 6,000 miles, 9,700 km - final drive 3.5 imp pt, 4.2 US pt, 2 l, SAE 90, change every 6,000 miles, 9,700 km; greasing: every 6,000 miles, 9,700 km, 4 points; tappet clearances: inlet 0.012 in, 0.30 mm, exhaust 0.020 in, 0.50 mm; valve timing: 29° 67° 70° 14°; tyre pressure: front 24 psi, 1.6 atm, rear 24 psi, 1.6 atm.

OPTIONALS Ford C3 automatic transmission, hydraulic torque converter and planetary gears with 3 ratios (I 2.474, II 1.474, III 1, rev. 2.111), max ratio of converter at stall 2, possible manual selection, oil cooler, 3.310 axle ratio; power steering; light alloy wheels; electric windows; rear window wiper-washer; laminated windscreen; tinted glass; fog lamps; leather upholstery.

RELIANT Robin 850 Saloon

ROLLS-ROYCE   GREAT BRITAIN

Silver Shadow II

PRICE IN USA: $ 65,400*
PRICE EX WORKS: £ 26,740*

ENGINE front, 4 stroke; 8 cylinders, Vee-slanted at 90°; 411.9 cu in, 6,750 cc (4.10 x 3.90 in, 104.1 x 99.1 mm); compression ratio: 8:1; aluminium alloy block and head, cast iron wet liners; 5 crankshaft bearings; valves: overhead, in line, slanted, push-rods and rockers, hydraulic tappets; camshafts: 1, at centre of Vee; lubrication: gear pump, full flow filter (cartridge), 14.5 imp pt, 17.5 US pt, 8.3 l; 2 SU type HIF7 horizontal carburettors; dual exhaust system; fuel feed: 2 electric pumps; sealed circuit cooling, expansion tank, 28.5 imp pt, 34.2 US pt, 16.2 l, viscous coupling thermostatic fan.

TRANSMISSION driving wheels: rear; gearbox: Turbo-Hydramatic 400 automatic transmission, hydraulic torque converter and planetary gears with 3 ratios, max ratio of converter at stall 2, possible manual selection; ratios: I 2.500, II 1.500, III 1, rev 2; lever: steering column; final drive: hypoid bevel; axle ratio: 3.080; width of rims: 6''; tyres: 235/70 HR x 15.

PERFORMANCE max speeds: (I) 47 mph, 76 km/h; (II) 79 mph, 126 km/h; (III) 118 mph, 190 km/h; carrying capacity: 1,014 lb, 460 kg; speed in direct drive at 1,000 rpm: 26.2 mph, 42.2 km/h; consumption: 14.1 m/imp gal, 11.8 m/US gal, 20 l x 100 km.

CHASSIS integral, front and rear auxiliary frames; front suspension: independent, lower wishbones, coil springs, anti-roll bar, telescopic dampers; rear: independent, semi-trailing arms, coil springs, anti-roll bar, automatic levelling control, telescopic dampers.

STEERING rack-and-pinion, progressive servo, right or left-hand drive; turns lock to lock: 3.20.

BRAKES disc (diameter 11 in, 27.9 cm), front internal radial fins, servo; swept area: front 227 sq in, 1,464 sq cm, rear 286 sq in, 1,845 sq cm, total 513 sq in, 3,309 sq cm.

ELECTRICAL EQUIPMENT 12 V; 68 Ah battery; 75 A alternator; Lucas transistorized distributor; 4 headlamps, 2 front and 2 rear fog lamps.

DIMENSIONS AND WEIGHT wheel base: 120.10 in, 305 cm; tracks: 60 in, 152 cm front, 59.60 in, 151 cm rear; length: 204.50 in, 519 cm; width: 71 in, 180 cm; height: 59.75 in, 152 cm; ground clearance: 6.50 in, 16.5 cm; weight: 4,930 lb, 2,236 kg; turning circle: 38.5 ft, 11.7 m; fuel tank: 23.5 imp gal, 28.2 US gal, 107 l.

ROLLS-ROYCE Silver Shadow II

SILVER SHADOW II

BODY saloon/sedan; 4 doors; 5 seats, separate front seats, adjustable and reclining backrests; headrests; automatic air-conditioning; heated rear window; electric windows; seat adjustment and gear range selector.

PRACTICAL INSTRUCTIONS fuel: 98 oct petrol; oil: engine 14.5 imp pt, 17.5 US pt, 8.3 l, SAE 20W-50, change every 6,000 miles, 9,700 km - automatic transmission 18.6 imp pt, 22.2 US pt, 10.5 l, Dexron, change every 24,000 miles, 38,600 km - final drive 4.5 imp pt, 5.3 US pt, 2.5 l, SAE 90 EP, change every 24,000 miles, 38,600 km - power steering and automatic levelling control change every 20,000 miles, 32,000 km; greasing: every 12,000 miles 19,300 km, 5 points; valve timing: 26° 52° 68° 10°; tyre pressure: front 28 psi, 2 atm, rear 28 psi, 2 atm.

OPTIONALS iodine headlamps; tinted glass.

VARIATIONS

(For USA, Japan and Australia only).
ENGINE 7.3:1 compression ratio, catalytic converter (except for Japan).

Silver Wraith II

See Silver Shadow II, except for:

PRICE IN USA: $ 74,500*
PRICE EX WORKS: £ 31,484*

DIMENSIONS AND WEIGHT wheel base: 124.10 in, 315 cm; length: 208.50 in, 530 cm; weight: 5,020 lb, 2,277 kg; turning circle (between walls): 40 ft, 12.2 m.

PRACTICAL INSTRUCTIONS tyre pressure: rear 30 psi, 2.1 atm.

Silver Wraith II with division

See Silver Shadow II, except for:

PRICE EX WORKS: £ 32,841*

DIMENSIONS AND WEIGHT wheel base: 124.10 in, 315 cm; length: 208.50 in, 530 cm; weight: 5,260 lb, 2,386 kg; turning circle (between walls): 40 ft, 12.2 m.

BODY glass partition.

PRACTICAL INSTRUCTIONS tyre pressure: rear 30 psi, 2.1 atm.

Corniche Saloon

See Silver Shadow II, except for:

PRICE IN USA: $ 102,900*
PRICE EX WORKS: £ 38,879*

ENGINE 1 Solex 4A1 4-barrel carburettor.

DIMENSIONS AND WEIGHT width: 72 in, 183 cm; height: 58.75 in, 149 cm; ground clearance: 6 in, 15.2 cm; weight: 5,045 lb, 2,285 kg.

ELECTRICAL EQUIPMENT 55 A alternator.

BODY 2 doors; 4 seats.

Corniche Convertible

See Silver Shadow II, except for:

PRICE IN USA: $ 109,800*
PRICE EX WORKS: £ 41,289*

ENGINE 1 Solex 4A1 4-barrel carburettor.

DIMENSIONS AND WEIGHT width: 72 in, 183 cm; ground clearance: 6 in, 15.2 cm; weight: 5,200 lb, 2,358 kg.

ELECTRICAL EQUIPMENT 55 A alternator.

BODY convertible; 2 doors; 4 seats.

Phantom VI

PRICE EX WORKS: quotation on request.

ENGINE front, 4 stroke; 8 cylinders, Vee-slanted at 90°; 411.9 cu in, 6,750 cc (4.10 x 3.90 in, 104.1 x 99.1 mm); compression ratio: 8:1; aluminium alloy block and head, cast iron wet liners; 5 crankshaft bearings; valves: overhead, in line, slanted, push-rods and rockers, hydraulic tappets:

camshafts: 1, at centre of Vee; lubrication: gear pump, full flow filter (cartridge), 14.5 imp pt, 17.5 US pt, 8.3 l; 2 SU type HIF 7 horizontal carburettors; fuel feed: 2 electric pumps; sealed circuit cooling, expansion tank, 28.5 imp pt, 34.2 US pt, 16.2 l, viscous coupling thermostatic fan.

TRANSMISSION driving wheels: rear; gearbox: Turbo-Hydramatic 400 automatic transmission, hydraulic torque converter and planetary gears with 3 ratios, max ratio of converter at stall 2, possible manual selection; ratios: I 2.500, II 1.500, III 1, rev 2; lever: steering column; final drive: hypoid bevel; axle ratio: 3.890; width of rims: 6''; tyres: 8.90 x 15.

PERFORMANCE max speeds: (I) 29 mph, 47 km/h; (II) 42 mph, 68 km/h; (III) 77 mph, 124 km/h; (IV) 112 mph, 180 km/h; carrying capacity: 1,235 lb, 560 kg; acceleration: standing ¼ mile 19.4 sec, 0-50 mph (0-80 km/h) 9.7 sec; speed in direct drive at 1,000 rpm: 22.5 mph, 36.2 km/h; consumption: 14 m/imp gal, 11.6 m/US gal, 20.2 l x 100 km.

CHASSIS box-type ladder frame; front suspension: independent, wishbones, coil springs, anti-roll bar, lever dampers; rear: rigid axle, asymmetrical semi-elliptic leafsprings, Z-type transverse linkage bar, electrically-adjustable lever dampers.

STEERING worm and roller, progressive servo (50%-80%); turns lock to lock: 4.25.

BRAKES drum, 2 independent power hydraulic circuits;

ROLLS-ROYCE Silver Shadow II

ROLLS-ROYCE Corniche Saloon

ROLLS-ROYCE Phantom VI

swept area: front 211.92 sq in, 1,361 sq cm, rear 211.92
sq in, 1,361 sq cm, total 423.84 sq in, 2,722 sq cm.

ELECTRICAL EQUIPMENT 12 V; 68 Ah battery; 75 A alternator; AC Delco distributor; 4 headlamps.

DIMENSIONS AND WEIGHT wheel base: 145 in, 368 cm;
tracks: 60.87 in, 155 cm front, 64 in, 162 cm rear;
length: 238 in, 604 cm; width: 79 in, 201 cm; height:
69 in, 175 cm; ground clearance: 7.25 in, 18.4 cm; weight:
5,994 lb, 2,718 kg; weight distribution: 48% front, 52%
rear; turning circle (between walls): 48.7 ft, 14.9 m; fuel
tank: 23 imp gal, 27.5 US gal, 104 l.

BODY limousine; 4 doors; 7 seats, separate front seats;
glass partition; air-conditioning; electric windows; heated
rear window.

PRACTICAL INSTRUCTIONS fuel: 98 oct petrol; oil: engine
14.5 imp pt, 17.5 US pt, 8.3 l, SAE 20W-50, change every
6,000 miles, 9,700 km - automatic transmission 21 imp pt.
25.2 US pt, 11.9 l, change every 24,000 miles, 38,600 km -
final drive 1.7 imp pt, 1.9 US pt, 0.9 l, SAE 90 EP, change
every 24,000 miles, 38,600 km; greasing: every 12,000 miles,
19,300 km, 21 points; valve timing: 20° 61° 62° 19°; tyre
pressure: front 24 psi, 1.7 atm, rear 30 psi, 2.1 atm.

OPTIONALS Landaulette version.

Camargue

PRICE IN USA: $ 115,000*
PRICE EX WORKS: £ 47,367*

ENGINE front, 4 stroke; 8 cylinders, Vee-slanted at 90°;
411.9 cu in, 6,750 cc (4.10 x 3.90 in, 104.1 x 99.1 mm);
compression ratio: 8:1; aluminium alloy block and head, cast
iron wet liners; 5 crankshaft bearings; valves: overhead,
in line, push-rods and rockers, hydraulic tappets; camshafts: 1, at centre of Vee; lubrication: gear pump, full
flow filter (cartridge), 14.5 imp pt, 17.5 US pt, 8.3 l;
1 Solex 4A1 horizontal 4-barrel carburettor; dual exhaust
system; fuel feed: 2 electric pumps; sealed circuit cooling,
expansion tank, 28.5 imp pt, 34.2 US pt, 16.2 l, viscous
coupling thermostatic fan.

TRANSMISSION driving wheels: rear; gearbox: Turbo-Hydramatic 400 automatic transmission, hydraulic torque converter
and planetary gears with 3 ratios, max ratio of converter
at stall 2, possible manual selection; ratios: I 2.500, II
1.500, III 1, rev 2; lever: steering column; final drive:
hypoid bevel; axle ratio: 3.080; width of rims: 6''; tyres
GR70 x 15 or 235/70 HR x 15.

PERFORMANCE max speeds: (I) 47 mph, 76 km/h; (II)
79 mph, 127 km/h; (III) 118 mph, 190 km/h; carrying
capacity: 882 lb, 400 kg; speed in direct drive at 1,000
rpm: 26.2 mph, 42.2 km/h; consumption: 14.1 m/imp
gal, 11.8 m/US gal, 20 l x 100 km.

CHASSIS integral, front and rear auxiliary frame; front
suspension: independent, lower wishbones, coil springs,
anti-roll bar, telescopic dampers; rear: independent, semi-
trailing arms, coil springs, anti-roll bar, automatic levelling
control, telescopic dampers.

STEERING rack-and-pinion, servo; turns lock to lock: 3.20.

BRAKES disc [diameter (twin calipers) 11 in, 27.9 cm], front
internal radial fins, servo; swept area: front 227 sq in,
1,464 sq cm, rear 286 sq in, 1,845 sq cm. total 513 sq in,
3,309 sq cm.

ELECTRICAL EQUIPMENT 12 V; 68 Ah battery; 75 A alternator; Lucas Opus electronic ignition; 4 headlamps, 2 front
and 2 rear fog lamps.

DIMENSIONS AND WEIGHT wheel base: 120.10 in, 305 cm;
tracks: 60 in, 152 cm front, 59.60 in, 151 cm rear; length:
203.50 in, 517 cm; width: 75.59 in, 192 cm; height: 57.87
in, 147 cm; ground clearance: 6.50 in, 16.5 cm; weight:
5,135 lb, 2,329 kg; turning circle (between walls): 38.5 ft,
11.7 m; fuel tank: 23.5 imp gal, 28.2 US gal, 107 l.

BODY saloon/sedan; 2 doors; 5 seats, separate front seats,
adjustable and reclining backrests; built-in headrests;
leather upholstery; automatic air-conditioning; electric
windows; seat adjustment and gear range selector; heated
rear window.

PRACTICAL INSTRUCTIONS fuel: 98 oct petrol; oil:
engine 14.5 imp pt, 17.5 US pt, 8.3 l, SAE 20W-50, change
every 6,000 miles, 9,700 km - automatic transmission 18.6
imp pt, 10.5 US pt, 22.2 l, Dexron, change every 24,000
miles, 38,600 km - final drive 4.5 imp pt, 5.3 US pt, 2.5 l,
SAE 90 EP, change every 24,000 miles, 38,600 km -
automatic levelling control 4 imp pt, 4.9 US pt, 2.3 l -
power steering 3 imp pt, 3.6 US pt, 1.7 l; greasing:
every 12,000 miles, 19,300 km; type pressure: front 28 psi,
2 atm, rear 28 psi, 2 atm.

VARIATIONS

(for USA, Japan and Australia only).
ENGINE 7.3:1 compression ratio, 2 SU type HIF 7 horizontal
carburettors, catalytic converter (except for Japan).

ROLLS-ROYCE Camargue

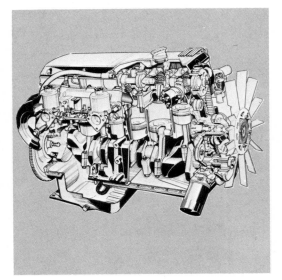
ROVER 2600

ROVER   GREAT BRITAIN

3500

PRICE EX WORKS: £ 7,511*

ENGINE front, 4 stroke; 8 cylinders, Vee-slanted at 90°;
215 cu in, 3,528 cc (3.50 x 2.80 in, 88.9 x 71.1 mm); compression ratio: 9.25:1; max power (DIN): 155 hp (114.1 kW)
at 5,250 rpm; max torque (DIN): 198 lb ft, 27.3 kg m
(267.7 Nm) at 2,500 rpm; max engine rpm: 6,000; 43.9
hp/l (32.3 kW/l); light alloy block and head, dry liners;
5 crankshaft bearings; valves: overhead, in line, push-rods
and rockers, hydraulic tappets; camshafts: 1, at centre of
Vee; lubrication: gear pump, full flow filter, 9.5 imp pt,
11.4 US pt, 5.4 l; 2 SU type HIF6 semi-downdraught carburettors; fuel feed: electric pump; water-cooled, 19.5 imp
pt, 23.5 US pt, 11.1 l, viscous-coupling thermostatic fan.

TRANSMISSION driving wheels: rear; clutch: single dry
plate (diaphragm), hydraulically controlled; gearbox: mechanical; gears: 5, fully synchronized; ratios: I 3.321, II
2.087, III 1.396, IV 1, V 0.833, rev 3.428; lever: central;
final drive: hypoid bevel; axle ratio: 3.080; width of rims:
6''; tyres: 185 HR x 14.

PERFORMANCE max speed: 126 mph, 202 km/h; power-
weight ratio: 18.7 lb/hp (25.4 lb/kW), 8.5 kg/hp (11.5

ROVER 3500

3500

kg/kW); carrying capacity: 1,235 lb, 560 kg; acceleration: 0-50 mph (0-80 km/h) 6.4 sec; speed in top at 1,000 rpm: 28.8 mph, 46.4 km/h; consumption: 28 m/imp gal, 23.3 m/US gal, 10.1 l x 100 km.

CHASSIS integral with front cross members; front suspension: independent, by McPherson, wishbones (lower trailing links), coil spring/telescopic damper struts, anti-roll bar; rear: rigid axle (torque tube), coil springs with combined telescopic dampers and self-levelling struts, transverse Watt linkage.

STEERING rack-and-pinion, adjustable steering column, servo; turns lock to lock: 2.70.

BRAKES front disc (diameter 10.15 in, 25.8 cm), rear drum, rear compensator, servo.

ELECTRICAL EQUIPMENT 12 V; 68 Ah battery; 55 A alternator; Lucas electronic ignition; 2 halogen headlamps, plus 2 fog lamps.

DIMENSIONS AND WEIGHT wheel base: 111 in, 282 cm; tracks: 59 in, 150 cm front, 59 in, 150 cm rear; length: 185 in, 469 cm; width: 69.60 in, 177 cm; height: 53.3 in, 135 cm; weight: 2,895 lb, 1,313 kg; turning circle: 34.2 ft, 10.4 m; fuel tank: 14.5 imp gal, 17.4 US gal, 66 l.

BODY saloon/sedan; 5 doors; 5 seats, separate front seats, reclining backrests with adjustable built-in headrests; electric windows; laminated windscreen with tinted glass; heated rear window; metallic spray; folding rear seat.

PRACTICAL INSTRUCTIONS fuel: 100 oct petrol; oil: engine 8.2 imp pt, 9.9 US pt, 4.7 l, SAE 20W-30, change every 6,000 miles, 9,700 km - gearbox 2.8 imp pt, 3.4 US pt, 1.6 l, SAE 90 EP, change every 6,000 miles, 9,700 km - final drive 1.6 imp pt, 1.9 US pt, 0.9 l, SAE 90 EP, change every 6,000 miles, 9,700 km; valve timing: 10° 75° 68° 37°; tyre pressure: front 26 psi, 1.8 atm, rear 26 psi, 1.8 atm.

OPTIONALS Borg-Warner 65 automatic transmission, hydraulic torque converter and planetary gears with 3 ratios (I 2.390, II 1.450, III 1, rev 2.090), max ratio of converter at stall 2.1, possible manual selection, 3.080 axle ratio; max speed 123 mph, 198 km/h, speed in direct drive at 1,000 rpm 23.5 mph, 37.8 km/h, consumption 24 m/imp gal, 19.9 m/US gal, 11.8 l x 100 km; Dunlop Denovo wheels and tyres; 195/70 HR x 14 tyres with light alloy wheels; sunshine roof; leather upholstery.

2600

See 3500, except for:

PRICE EX WORKS: £ 6,272*

ENGINE 6 cylinders, in line; 158.3 cu in, 2,597 cc (3.19 x 3.31 in, 81 x 84 mm); max power (DIN): 136 hp (100.1 kW) at 5,000 rpm; max torque (DIN): 152 lb ft, 21 kg m (206 Nm) at 3,750 rpm; 52.4 hp/l (38.5 kW/l); cast iron block, light alloy head; 4 crankshaft bearings; valves: overhead, Vee-slanted, thimble tappets; camshafts: 1, overhead, cogged belt; lubrication: rotary pump, full flow filter, 11.1 imp pt,

ROVER 2600

13.3 US pt, 6.3 l; 2 SU type HS6 horizontal carburettors; cooling system: 15.5 imp pt, 18.6 US pt, 8.8 l.

TRANSMISSION axle ratio: 3.450; width of rims: 5.5''; tyres: 175 HR x 14.

PERFORMANCE max speed: 117 mph, 188 km/h; power-weight ratio: 21.8 lb/hp (29.8 lb/kW), 9.9 kg/hp (13.5 kg/kW); speed in top at 1,000 rpm: 25 mph, 40.2 km/h; consumption: 30.1 m/imp gal, 25 m/US gal, 9.4 l x 100 km.

STEERING rack-and-pinion; turns lock to lock: 4.50.

DIMENSIONS AND WEIGHT weight: 2,978 lb, 1,351 kg.

PRACTICAL INSTRUCTIONS fuel: 97 oct petrol; oil: engine 11.1 imp pt, 13.3 US pt, 6.3 l.

OPTIONALS power steering; electric windows; fog lamps; tinted glass; metallic spray.

2300

See 3500, except for:

PRICE EX WORKS: £ 5,910*

ENGINE 6 cylinders, in line; 143.4 cu in, 2,350 cc (3.19 x 2.99 in, 81 x 76 mm); max power (DIN): 123 hp (90.5 kW) at 5,000 rpm; max torque (DIN): 134 lb ft, 18.5 kg m (181.4

Nm) at 4,000 rpm; 52.3 hp/l (38.5 kW/l); cast iron block, light alloy head; 4 crankshaft bearings; valves: overhead, Vee-slanted, thimble tappets; camshafts: 1, overhead, cogged belt; lubrication: rotary pump, full flow filter, 11.1 imp pt, 13.3 US pt, 6.3 l; 2 SU type HS6 horizontal carburettors; cooling system: 15.5 imp pt, 18.6 US pt, 8.8 l.

TRANSMISSION gears: 4, fully synchronized; ratios: I 3.321, II 2.087, III 1.396, IV 1, rev 3.428; axle ratio: 3.450; width of rims: 5.5''; tyres: 175 HR x 14.

PERFORMANCE max speed: 114 mph, 183 km/h; power-weight ratio: 22.7 lb/hp (30.8 lb/kW), 10.3 kg/hp (14 kg/kW); speed in direct drive at 1,000 rpm: 21 mph, 33.8 km/h; consumption: 27.4 m/imp gal, 22.8 m/US gal, 10.3 l x 100 km.

STEERING rack-and-pinion; turns lock to lock: 4.50.

DIMENSIONS AND WEIGHT weight: 2,787 lb, 1,264 kg.

PRACTICAL INSTRUCTIONS fuel: 97 oct petrol; oil: engine 11.1 imp pt, 13.3 US pt, 6.3 l; tappet clearances: inlet 0.018 in, 0.46 mm, exhaust 0.018 in, 0.46 mm; valve timing 16° 56° 56° 16°; tyre pressure: front 26 psi, 1.8 atm, rear 28 psi, 2 atm.

OPTIONALS 5-speed fully synchronized mechanical gearbox (I 3.321, II 2.087, III 1.396, IV 1, V 0.833, rev 3.428), power steering; halogen headlamps; fog lamps; tinted glass; metallic spray; 195/70 HR x 14 tyres and leather upholstery not available.

Super 7

PRICE EX WORKS: £ 4,134*

ENGINE Lotus front, 4 stroke; 4 cylinders, vertical, in line; 95.1 cu in, 1,558 cc (3.25 x 2.87 in, 82.6 x 72.8 mm); compression ratio: 10.3:1; max power (DIN): 126 hp (92.7 kW) at 6,500 rpm; max torque (DIN): 113 lb ft, 15.6 kg m (153 Nm) at 5,500 rpm; max engine rpm: 6,800; 80.9 hp/l (59.5 kW/l); cast iron block, light alloy head; 5 crankshaft bearings; valves: overhead, Vee-slanted, thimble tappets; camshafts: 2, overhead; lubrication: rotary pump, full flow filter by cartridge, 7.5 imp pt, 8.9 US pt, 4.2 l; 2 Dell'Orto 40 DHL twin barrel carburettors; fuel feed: mechanical pump; water cooled, 12 imp pt, 14.4 US pt, 6.8 l.

TRANSMISSION driving wheels: rear; clutch: single dry plate (diaphragm), hydraulically controlled; gearbox: mechanical; gears: 4, fully synchronized; ratios: I 2.972, II 2.010, III 1.400, IV 1, rev 3.325; lever: central; final drive: hypoid bevel; axle ratio: 3.540; width of rims: 5.5''; tyres: 165 SR x 13.

PERFORMANCE max speeds: (I) 42 mph, 68 km/h; (II) 62 mph, 100 km/h; (III) 89 mph, 143 km/h; (IV) 112 mph, 180 km/h; power-weight ratio: 8.7 lb/hp (11.9 lb/kW), 4 kg/hp (5.4 kg/kW); carrying capacity: 450 lb, 204 kg; acceleration: standing ¼ mile 14.6 sec, 0-50 mph (0-80 km/h) 4.4 sec; speed in direct drive at 1,000 rpm: 19.1 mph, 30 km/h; consumption: 25 m/imp gal, 20.8 m/US gal, 11 l x 100 km.

SEVEN Super 7

CHASSIS tubular space-frame with aluminium panels; front suspension: independent, lower wishbones, anti-roll bar, coil springs/telescopic dampers units; rear: rigid axle, twin trailing radius arms, A-bracket, coil spring/telescopic dampers units.

STEERING rack-and-pinion; turns lock to lock: 2.75.

BRAKES front disc, rear drum.

ELECTRICAL EQUIPMENT 12 V; 39 Ah battery; dynamo, Lucas distributor; 2 headlamps.

DIMENSIONS AND WEIGHT wheel base: 88 in, 223 cm; tracks: 49 in, 124 cm front, 51.50 in, 131 cm rear; length: 133 in, 338 cm; width: 65.50 in, 159 cm; height: 43.50 in, 110 cm; ground clearance: 4 in, 10 cm; weight: 1,100 lb, 499 kg; turning circle: 29.6 ft, 9 m; fuel tank: 8 imp gal, 9.5 US gal, 36 l.

BODY sports; no doors; 2 seats.

PRACTICAL INSTRUCTIONS fuel: 98-100 oct petrol; oil: engine 6.5 imp pt, 7.8 US pt, 3.7 l, SAE 20W-50, change every 6,000 miles, 9,700 km - gearbox 2 imp pt, 2.3 US pt, 1.1 l, SAE 80 EP, no change recommended - final drive 2 imp pt, 2.3 US pt, 1.1 l, SAE 90 EP, no change recommended; greasing: every 6,000 miles, 9,700 km, 5 points; tappet clearances: inlet 0.005-0.007 in, 0.12-0.17 mm, exhaust 0.009-0.011 in, 0.22-0.27 mm; valve timing: 26º 66º 66º 26º; tyre pressure: front 20 psi, 1.4 atm, rear 20 psi, 1.4 atm.

SPARTAN CARS　　　　GREAT BRITAIN

2-seater Sports

PRICE EX WORKS: £ 3,900

ENGINE Ford, front, 4 stroke; 4 cylinders, vertical, in line; 97.5 cu in, 1,598 cc (3.19 x 3.06 in, 81 x 77.6 mm); compression ratio: 9:1; max power (DIN): 84 hp (61.8 kW) at 5,500 rpm; max torque (DIN): 92 lb ft, 12.7 kg m (124.5 Nm) at 3,500 rpm; max engine rpm: 6,600; 52.6 hp/l (38.7 kW/l); cast iron block and head; 5 crankshaft bearings; valves: overhead, in line, push-rods and rockers; camshafts: 1, side, chain-driven; lubrication: rotary or vane-type pump, full flow filter, 5.7 imp pt, 6.8 US pt, 3.2 l; 1 Weber 32/32 DGV downdraught twin barrel carburettor; fuel feed: mechanical pump; water-cooled, 9.5 imp pt, 11.4 US pt, 5.4 l.

TRANSMISSION driving wheels: rear; clutch: single dry plate (diaphragm); gearbox: mechanical; gears: 4, fully synchronized; ratios: I 3.337, II 1.995, III 1.418, IV 1, rev 3.876; lever: central; final drive: hypoid bevel; axle ratio: 3.770; width of rims: 5.5''; tyres: 175/70 SR x 13.

PERFORMANCE max speed: 108 mph, 174 km/h; power-weight ratio: 18.7 lb/hp (25.4 lb/kW), 8.5 kg/hp (11.5 kg/kW); carrying capacity: 353 lb, 160 kg; acceleration: standing ¼ mile 17.3 sec; consumption: 33 m/imp gal, 27.7 m/US gal, 8.5 l x 100 km.

SPARTAN CARS 2-seater Sports

SYD LAWRENCE Mk 2 Sports

CHASSIS tubular space-frame with aluminium panels; front suspension: independent, by McPherson, coil springs/telescopic damper struts, anti-roll bar; rear: rigid axle, trailing lower radius arms, upper oblique torque arms, coil springs, telescopic dampers.

STEERING rack-and-pinion, turns lock to lock: 3.50.

BRAKES front disc (diameter 9.60 in, 24.4 cm), rear drum.

ELECTRICAL EQUIPMENT 12 V; 38 Ah battery; 35 A alternator; Motorcraft distributor; 4 headlamps.

DIMENSIONS AND WEIGHT length: 150 in, 381 cm; width: 62.60 in, 159 cm; height: 49.61 in, 126 cm; weight: 1,568 lb, 711 kg; fuel tank: 9 imp gal, 10.8 US gal, 41 l.

BODY sports; 2 doors; 2 seats; built-in headrests.

PRACTICAL INSTRUCTIONS fuel: 97 oct petrol; oil: engine 5.8 imp pt, 7 US pt, 3.3 l, SAE 10W-30, change every 6,000 miles, 9,700 km - gearbox 1.6 imp pt, 1.9 US pt, 0.9 l, SAE 80, no change recommended - final drive 1.7 imp pt, 2.1 US pt, 1 l, SAE 90, no change recommended; greasing: every 6,000 miles, 9,700 km, 2 points; tappet clearances: inlet 0.010 in, 0.25 mm, exhaust 0.017 in, 0.43 mm; valve timing: 29º 63º 71º 21º; tyre pressure: front 24 psi, 1.7 atm, rear 24 psi, 1.7 atm.

OPTIONALS light alloy wheels; reclining backrests; leather upholstery; halogen headlamps; rear fog lamps; tonneau cover; metallic spray.

2+2-seater Sports

See 2-seater Sports, except for:

PRICE EX WORKS: £ 4,196

PERFORMANCE power-weight ratio: 20.2 lb/hp (27.5 lb/kW), 9.2 kg/hp (12.5 kg/kW); carrying capacity: 706 lb, 320 kg.

DIMENSIONS AND WEIGHT length: 156 in, 396 cm; height: 52.11 in, 132 cm; weight: 1,700 lb, 771 kg.

BODY 2+2 seats.

SYD LAWRENCE　　　　GREAT BRITAIN

Mk 2 Sports

PRICE EX WORKS: £ 16,500

ENGINE front, 4 stroke; 6 cylinders, in line; 259.8 cu in, 4,257 cc (3.50 x 4.50 in, 88.9 x 114.3 mm); compression ratio: 6.4:1; max engine rpm: 4,750; cast iron block, light alloy head; 7 crankshaft bearings; valves: overhead inlet, side exhaust, push-rods and rockers; camshafts: 1, lateral; lubrication: gear pump, full flow filter, 20 imp pt, 23.9 US pt, 11.3 l; 4 SU type H1-F carburettors; fuel feed: electric pump; water-cooled, 46 imp pt, 56 US pt, 26 l.

TRANSMISSION driving wheels: rear; clutch: single dry plate; gearbox: mechanical; gears: 4, II, III and IV synchronized; ratios: I 2.981, II 2.018, III 1.342, V 1, rev 3.155; lever: at driver's right; final drive: hypoid bevel; axle ratio: 3.727; width of rims: 6''; tyres: 8.15 x 15.

PERFORMANCE max speed: 120 mph, 193 km/h; speed in direct drive at 1,000 rpm: 30 mph, 48.2 km/h; consumption: about 17 m/imp gal, 14.2 m/US gal, 16.6 l x 100 km.

CHASSIS box-type ladder frame; front suspension: independent, wishbones, coil springs, lever dampers; rear: rigid axle, semi-elliptic leafsprings, telescopic dampers.

STEERING worm and roller; turns lock to lock: 3.

BRAKES drum, servo; lining area: total 186.6 sq in, 1,203 sq cm.

ELECTRICAL EQUIPMENT 12 V; 77 Ah battery; dynamo; Delco-Remy distributor; 4 headlamps.

DIMENSIONS AND WEIGHT wheel base: 114 in, 289 cm; tracks: 55.75 in, 144 cm front, 58.62 in, 149 cm rear; length: 165 in, 419 cm; width: 67 in, 170 cm; height: 43 in, 109 cm; ground clearance: 6 in, 15 cm; weight: 2,549 lb, 1,156 kg; fuel tank: 12 imp gal, 14.3 US gal, 54 l.

BODY sports, in fibreglass material; no doors; 2 seats; leather upholstery.

PRACTICAL INSTRUCTIONS fuel: 98-100 oct petrol; oil: engine 16 imp pt, 19.2 US pt, 9.1 l, SAE 20W-50, change every 5,000 miles, 8,000 km - gearbox 6 imp pt, 7.2 US pt, 3.4 l, SAE 20W-50, change every 10,000 miles, 16,100 km - final drive 1.7 imp pt, 2.1 US pt, 1 l, SAE 90, change every 10,000 miles, 16,100 km; greasing: every 5,000 miles, 8,000

Mk 2 SPORTS

km, 10 points; tappet clearances (cold): inlet 0.006 in, 0.15 mm, exhaust 0.012 in, 0.30 mm; valve timing: 3° 43° 40° 1°; tyre pressure: front 23 psi, 1.6 atm, rear 25 psi, 1.7 atm.

OPTIONALS 8.15 x 16 tyres; long wheelbase 120 in, 305 cm.

TECHNICAL EXPONENTS
GREAT BRITAIN

TX Tripper 1500/De Luxe

PRICES EX WORKS: 1500   £ 3,150
1500 De Luxe £ 3,350

ENGINE Triumph, front, 4 stroke; 4 cylinders, vertical, in line; 91.1 cu in, 1,493 cc (2.90 x 3.44 in, 73.7 x 87.5 mm); compression ratio: 9:1; max power (DIN): 71 hp (52.3 kW) at 5,500 rpm; max torque (DIN): 82 lb ft, 11.3 kg m (110.8 Nm) at 3,000 rpm; max engine rpm: 6,000; 47.6 hp/l (35 kW/l); cast iron block and head; 5 crankshaft bearings; valves: overhead, in line, push-rods and rockers; camshafts: 1, side; lubrication: gear pump, full flow filter, 8 imp pt, 9.5 US pt, 4.5 l; 2 SU type HS 4 semi-down-draught carburettors; fuel feed: mechanical pump; water-cooled, 6 imp pt, 7.2 US pt, 3.4 l.

TRANSMISSION driving wheels: rear; clutch: single dry plate (diaphragm); gearbox: mechanical; gears: 4, II, III and IV synchronized; ratios: I 3.750, II 2.160, III 1.390, IV 1, rev 3.750; lever: central; final drive: hypoid bevel; axle ratio: 3.690; width of rims: 5.5''; tyres: 165 x 13.

PERFORMANCE max speeds: (I) 35 mph, 56 km/h; (II) 52 mph, 83 km/h; (III) 81 mph, 130 km/h; (IV) 108 mph, 174 km/h; power-weight ratio: 15 lb/hp (20.4 lb/kW), 6.8 kg/hp (9.3 kg/kW); carrying capacity: 784 lb, 356 kg; acceleration: standing ¼ mile 7.6 sec; speed in direct drive at 1,000 rpm: 18.5 mph, 29.7 km/h; consumption: 40 m/imp gal, 33.1 m/US gal, 7.1 l x 100 km.

CHASSIS box-type double backbone with outriggers; front suspension: independent, wishbones, coil springs, telescopic dampers; rear: independent, wishbones, transverse leafspring as upper arms, telescopic dampers.

STEERING rack-and-pinion; turns lock to lock: 3.50.

BRAKES front disc (diameter 9 in, 22.9 cm), rear drum; swept area: total 197 sq in, 1,271 sq cm.

ELECTRICAL EQUIPMENT 12 V; 45 Ah battery; 15 W alternator; Lucas distributor; 2 headlamps.

DIMENSIONS AND WEIGHT wheel base: 83.07 in, 211 cm; tracks: 50.12 in, 127 cm front, 49.61 in, 126 cm rear; length: 145.08 in, 368 cm; width: 57.05 in, 145 cm; height: 47.17 in, 120 cm; ground clearance: 6.50 in, 16.5

TECHNICAL EXPONENTS TX Tripper 1500 - 2000 Sprint

cm; weight: 1,067 lb, 484 kg; weight distribution: 52% front, 48% rear; turning circle: 25.3 ft, 7.7 m; fuel tank: 8.2 imp gal, 9.8 US gal, 37 l.

BODY open, in plastic material; no doors; 2 seats; De Luxe: luxury equipment, folding rear seat.

PRACTICAL INSTRUCTIONS fuel: 97-100 oct petrol; oil: engine 7 imp pt, 8.5 US pt, 4 l, SAE 20, change every 6,000 miles, 9,700 km - gearbox 1.5 imp pt, 1.9 US pt, 0.9 l, SAE 90 - final drive 1.1 imp pt, 1.3 US pt, 0.6 l, SAE 90; greasing: every 6,000 miles, 9,700 km, 3 points, every 12,000 miles, 19,300 km, 2 points; tappet clearances: inlet 0.010 in, 0.25 mm; valve timing: 18° 58° 58° 18°; tyre pressure: front 21 psi, 1.5 atm, rear 26 psi, 1.8 atm.

OPTIONALS 3.270 or 4.110 axle ratio; overdrive, 0.797 ratio; oil cooler; left-hand drive; servo brake larger fuel tank; halogen headlamps; laminated windscreen; hardtop with heated rear window; tonneau cover; reclining backrests with built-in headrests.

TX Tripper 2000 Sprint

See TX Tripper 1500, except for:

PRICE EX WORKS: £ 3,955

ENGINE Triumph, front, 4 stroke; 121.9 cu in, 1,998 cc (3.56 x 3.07 in, 90.3 x 78 mm); compression ratio: 9.5:1;

max power (DIN): 127 hp (93.5 kW) at 5,700 rpm; max torque (DIN): 122 lb ft, 16.9 kg m (165.7 Nm) at 4,500 rpm; max engine rpm: 6,500; 63.6 hp/l (46.8 kW/l); cast iron block, light alloy head; valves: 4 per cylinder overhead, in line, thimble tappets; camshafts: 1, overhead, 2 SU type HS 6 horizontal carburettors.

TRANSMISSION gearbox ratios: I 2.995, II 2.100, III 1.380 (overdrive 1.100), IV 1 (overdrive 0.797), rev 3.370; axle ratio: 3.450; width of rims: 5.5''; tyres: 175/70 HR x 13.

PERFORMANCE max speed: 125 mph, 201 km/h; power weight ratio: 8.4 lb/hp (11.4 lb/kW), 3.8 kg/hp (5.2 kg/kW); speed in direct drive at 1,000 rpm: 20.6 mph, 33.1 km/h; consumption: 30 m/imp gal, 25 m/US gal, 9.4 l x 100 km.

CHASSIS anti-roll bar on front and rear suspension.

BRAKES servo.

PRACTICAL INSTRUCTIONS tappet clearances: inlet 0.018 in, 0.45 mm, exhaust 0.018 in, 0.45 mm; valve timing 10° 50° 50° 10°.

TRIUMPH   GREAT BRITAIN

Dolomite 1300

PRICE EX WORKS: £ 3,140*

ENGINE front, 4 stroke; 4 cylinders, vertical, in line; 79 cu in, 1,296 cc (2.90 x 2.99 in, 73.7 x 76 mm); compression ratio: 8.5:1; max power (DIN): 58 hp (42.7 kW) at 5,500 rpm; max torque (DIN): 68 lb ft, 9.4 kg m (92.2 Nm) at 3,300 rpm; max engine rpm: 6,000; 44.8 hp/l (32.9 kW/l) cast iron block and head; 3 crankshaft bearings; valves overhead, in line, push-rods and rockers; camshafts: 1 side; lubrication: rotary pump, full flow filter, 7.5 imp pt 8.9 US pt, 4.2 l; 1 SU type HS4 E semi-downdraught carburettor; fuel feed: mechanical pump; water-cooled, 9. imp pt, 11.4 US pt, 5.4 l.

TRANSMISSION driving wheels: rear; clutch: single dry plate (diaphragm), hydraulically controlled; gearbox: mechanical; gears: 4, fully synchronized; ratios: I 3.504, II 2.158, III 1.394, IV 1, rev 3.988; lever: central; final drive hypoid bevel; axle ratio: 4.110; width of rims: 4.5''; tyres 155 SR x 13.

PERFORMANCE max speed: 85 mph, 136 km/h; power weight ratio: 35.8 lb/hp (48.7 lb/kW), 16.3 kg/hp (22. kg/kW); carrying capacity: 882 lb, 400 kg; speed in direct drive at 1,000 rpm: 15.9 mph, 25.6 km/h; consumption 27.2 m/imp gal, 22.6 m/US gal, 10.4 l x 100 km.

CHASSIS integral; front suspension: independent, wishbones lower trailing links, coil springs, anti-roll bar, telescopic dampers; rear: rigid axle, lower trailing arms, upper oblique torque arms, coil springs, telescopic dampers.

STEERING rack-and-pinion; turns lock to lock: 3.50.

BRAKES front disc (diameter 8.75 in, 22.2 cm), rear drum

TRIUMPH Dolomite 1300

dual circuit, servo swept area: total 240.6 sq in, 1,552 sq cm.

ELECTRICAL EQUIPMENT 12 V; 40 Ah battery; 34 A alternator; Lucas distributor; 2 headlamps.

DIMENSIONS AND WEIGHT wheel base: 96.61 in, 245 cm; tracks: 53 in, 135 cm front, 50 in, 127 cm rear; length: 162.4 in, 412 cm; width: 65.4 in, 166 cm; height: 54 in, 137 cm; ground clearance: 4.25 in, 10.8 cm; weight: 2,079 lb, 943 kg; weight distribution: 48% front, 52% rear; turning circle: 30.5 ft, 9.3 m; fuel tank: 12.5 imp gal, 15 US gal, 57 l.

BODY saloon/sedan; 4 doors; 4 seats, separate front seats, reclining backrests with headrests; laminated windscreen; heated rear window.

PRACTICAL INSTRUCTIONS fuel: 97 oct petrol; oil: engine 7.5 imp pt, 8.9 US pt, 4.2 l, SAE 20W-50, change every 6,000 miles, 9,700 km - gearbox 1.3 imp pt, 1.7 US pt, 0.8 l, SAE 90, change every 6,000 miles, 9,700 km - final drive 1.5 imp pt, 1.9 US pt, 0.8 l, SAE 90, change every 6,000 miles, 9,700 km; tappet clearances: inlet 0.010 in, 0.25 mm, exhaust 0.010 in, 0.25 mm; valve timing: 18° 58° 58° 18°; tyre pressure: front 26 psi, 1.8 atm, rear 30 psi, 2.1 atm.

OPTIONALS tinted glass.

Dolomite 1500

See Dolomite 1300, except for:

PRICE EX WORKS: £ 3,358*

ENGINE 91 cu in, 1,493 cc (2.90 x 3.44 in, 73.7 x 87.5 mm); compression ratio: 9:1; max power (DIN): 71 hp (52.3 kW) at 5,500 rpm; max torque (DIN): 82 lb ft, 11.3 kg m (110.8 Nm) at 3,000 rpm; 47.6 hp/l (35 kW/l); 2 SU type HS4 E semi-downdraught carburettors.

TRANSMISSION gearbox ratios: I 3.500, II 2.160, III 1.390, IV 1, rev 3.990; axle ratio: 3.630.

PERFORMANCE max speed: 94 mph, 151 km/h; power-weight ratio: 29.3 lb/hp (39.7 lb/kW), 13.3 kg/hp (18 kg$kW); speed in direct drive at 1,000 rpm: 18 mph, 29 km/h; consumption: 26.6 m/imp gal, 22.2 m/US gal, 10.6 l x 100 km at steady 50 mph, 80 km/h.

OPTIONALS Borg-Warner automatic transmission with oil cooler, hydraulic torque converter and planetary gears with 3 ratios (I 2.390, II 1.450, III 1, rev 2.100), max ratio of converter at stall 1.91, possible manual selection, 3.270 axle ratio; overdrive; tinted glass.

Dolomite 1500 HL

See Dolomite 1500, except for:

PRICE EX WORKS: £ 3,735*

ELECTRICAL EQUIPMENT 36 A alternator; 4 headlamps.

BODY luxury equipment.

Dolomite 1850 HL

See Dolomite 1300, except for:

PRICE EX WORKS: £ 4,165*

ENGINE 4 cylinders, slanted at 45°, in line; 113.2 cu in, 1,854 cc (3.42 x 3.07 in, 87 x 78 mm); compression ratio: 9:1; max power (DIN): 91 hp (67 kW) at 5,200 rpm; max torque (DIN): 105 lb ft, 14.5 kg m (142.2 Nm) at 3,500 rpm; 49.1 hp/l (36.1 kW/l); cast iron block, light alloy head; 5 crankshaft bearings; valves: overhead, in line, thimble tappets; camshafts: 1, overhead; lubricating system: 8 imp pt, 9.5 US pt, 4.5 l; 2 SU tyre HS4 horizontal carburettors; fuel feed: mechanical pump; water-cooled, 9.5 imp pt, 11.4 US pt, 5.4 l.

TRANSMISSION gearbox ratios: I 2.646, II 1.779, III 1.254, IV 1, rev 3.011; axle ratio: 3.630; width of rims: 4.5''.

PERFORMANCE max speed: 102 mph, 164 km/h; power-weight ratio: 23.5 lb/hp (31.9 lb/kW), 10.6 kg/hp (14.5 kg/kW); speed in direct drive at 1,000 rpm: 18 mph, 29 km/h; consumption: 30.4 m/imp gal, 25.3 m/US gal, 9.3 l x 100 km.

CHASSIS integral, front subframe; rear suspension: anti-roll bar.

STEERING rack-and-pinion, adjustable steering wheel; turns lock to lock: 3.50.

BRAKES lining area: front 17.4 sq in, 112 sq cm, rear 37.8 sq in, 245 sq cm, total 55.2 sq in, 357 sq cm.

ELECTRICAL EQUIPMENT 36 A alternator; AC Delco distributor; 4 headlamps.

TRIUMPH Dolomite Sprint

DIMENSIONS AND WEIGHT tracks: 53.10 in, 135 cm front, 49.90 in, 127 cm rear; ground clearance: 4.25 in, 10.8 cm; weight: 2,136 lb, 969 kg.

BODY tinted glass (standard).

PRACTICAL INSTRUCTIONS oil: engine 8 imp pt, 9.5 US pt, 4.5 l, SAE 20W-30, change every 6,000 miles, 9,700 km - gearbox 1.8 imp pt, 2.1 US pt, 1 l, SAE 90, change every 6,000 miles, 9,700 km - final drive 1.5 imp pt, 1.9 US pt, 0.9 l, SAE 90, change every 6,000 miles, 9,700 km; greasing: every 6,000 miles, 9,700 km, 3 points; tappet clearances: inlet 0.008 in, 0.21 mm, exhaust 0.018 in, 0.45 mm; valve timing: 16° 56° 56° 16°; tyre pressure: front 26 psi, 1.8 atm, rear 30 psi, 2.1 atm.

OPTIONALS Borg-Warner automatic transmission with oil cooler; overdrive.

Dolomite Sprint

See Dolomite 1850 HL, except for:

PRICE EX WORKS: £ 5,078*

ENGINE 121.9 cu in, 1,998 cc (3.56 x 3.07 in, 90.3 x 78 mm); compression ratio: 9.5:1; max power (DIN): 127 hp (93.5 kW) at 5,700 rpm; max torque (DIN): 122 lb ft, 16.9 kg m (165.7 Nm) at 4,500 rpm; max engine rpm: 6,500; 63.6 hp/l (46.8 kW/l); valves: 4 per cylinder; 2 SU type HS6 horizontal carburettors; fuel feed: electric pump.

TRANSMISSION gearbox ratios: I 2.995, II 2.100, III 1.386 (overdrive 1.110), IV 1 (overdrive 0.797), rev 3.370; axle ratio: 3.450; width of rims: 5.5''; tyres: 175/70 HR x 13.

PERFORMANCE max speed: 116 mph, 186 km/h; power-weight ratio: 18.1 lb/hp (24.5 lb/kW), 8.2 kg/hp (11.1 kg/kW); consumption: 23.3 m/imp gal, 19.4 m/US gal, 12.1 l x 100 km.

STEERING steering wheel adjustable in height and distance.

BRAKES lining area: front 17.4 sq in, 112 sq cm, rear 49.5 sq in, 319 sq cm, total 66.9 sq in, 431 sq cm.

DIMENSIONS AND WEIGHT tracks: 53.40 in, 135.6 cm front, 50.8 in, 129 cm rear; weight: 2,295 lb, 1,041 kg.

BODY vinyl roof; light alloy wheels.

PRACTICAL INSTRUCTIONS tappet clearances: inlet 0.018 in, 0.45 mm, exhaust 0.018 in, 0.45 mm; valve timing: 14° 50° 50° 14°; tyre pressure: front 22 psi, 1.5 atm, rear 24 psi, 1.7 atm.

OPTIONALS limited slip differential; Borg-Warner automatic transmission with oil cooler.

Spitfire 1500

PRICE IN USA: $ 5,795*
PRICE EX WORKS: £ 3,246*

ENGINE front, 4 stroke; 4 cylinders, vertical, in line; 91.1 cu in, 1,493 cc (2.90 x 3.44 in, 73.7 x 87.5 mm); compression ratio: 9:1; max power (DIN): 71 hp (52.3 kW) at 5,500 rpm; max torque (DIN): 82 lb ft, 11.3 kg m (110.8 Nm) at 3,000 rpm; max engine rpm: 6,000; 47.6 hp/l (35 kW/l); cast iron block and head; 3 crankshaft bearings; valves: overhead, in line, push-rods and rockers; camshafts: 1, side; lubrication: rotary pump, full flow filter, 8 imp pt, 9.5 US pt, 4.5 l; 2 SU type HS4 horizontal carburettors; fuel feed: mechanical pump; sealed circuit cooling, liquid, 8 imp pt, 9.5 US pt, 4.5 l; viscous coupling thermostatic fan.

TRANSMISSION driving wheels: rear; clutch: single dry plate (diaphragm), hydraulically controlled; gearbox: mechanical; gears: 4, fully synchronized; ratios: I 3.500, II 2.160, III 1.390, IV 1, rev 3.990; lever: central; final drive: hypoid bevel; axle ratio: 3.630; width of rims: 4.5''; tyres: 155 SR x 13.

PERFORMANCE max speeds: (I) 31 mph, 50 km/h; (II) 50 mph, 81 km/h; (III) 77 mph, 124 km/h; (IV) 100 mph, 161 km/h; power-weight ratio: 24.6 lb/hp (33.5 lb/kW), 11.2 kg/hp (15.2 kg/kW); carrying capacity: 534 lb, 242 kg; speed in direct drive at 1,000 rpm: 18 mph, 29 km/h; consumption: 29.4 m/imp gal, 24.5 m/US gal, 9.6 l x 100 km.

CHASSIS double backbone, channel section with outriggers; front suspension: independent, wishbones, coil springs, anti-roll bar, telescopic dampers; rear: independent, swinging semi-axles, transverse leafspring swinging longitudinal trailing arms, telescopic dampers.

STEERING rack-and-pinion; turns lock to lock: 3.75.

BRAKES front disc (diameter 9 in, 22.9 cm), rear drum,

TRIUMPH Dolomite Sprint

SPITFIRE 1500

dual circuit; lining area: front 14.8 sq in, 95 sq cm, rear 34 sq in, 220 sq cm, total 48.8 sq in, 315 sq cm.

ELECTRICAL EQUIPMENT 12 V; 40 Ah battery; 34 A alternator; Lucas distributor; 2 headlamps.

DIMENSIONS AND WEIGHT wheel base: 83 in, 211 cm; tracks: 49 in, 124 cm front, 50 in, 127 cm rear; length: 149 in, 378 cm; width: 58.58 in, 149 cm; height: 45.80 in, 116 cm; ground clearance: 4.6 in, 11.8 cm; weight: 1,750 lb, 794 kg; weight distribution: 56% front, 44% rear; turning circle; 24 ft, 7.3 m; fuel tank: 7.2 imp gal, 8.7 US gal, 33 l.

BODY convertible; 2 doors; 2 seats; headrests; laminated windscreen.

PRACTICAL INSTRUCTIONS fuel: 97 oct petrol; oil: engine 7 imp pt, 8.5 US pt, 4 l, SAE 20, change every 6,000 miles, 9,700 km - gearbox 1.5 imp pt, 1.9 US pt, 0.9 l, SAE 90 - final drive 1.1 imp pt, 1.3 US pt, 0.6 l, SAE 90; greasing: every 6,000 miles, 9,700 km, 3 points, every 12,000 miles, 19,300 km, 2 points; tappet clearances: inlet 0.010 in, 0.25 mm, exhaust 0.010 in, 0.25 mm; valve timing: 18° 58° 58° 18°; tyre pressure: front 21 psi, 1.5 atm, rear 26 psi, 1.8 atm.

VARIATIONS

(For USA only).
ENGINE 7.5:1; compression ratio, max power (DIN) 52.5 hp (38.6 kW) at 5,000 rpm, max torque (DIN) 68.7 lb ft, 9.5 kg m (93.1 Nm) at 2,500 rpm, 35.2 hp/l (25.9 kW/l), 1 Stromberg 1.50 CD4T horizontal carburettor, water-cooled 9.3 imp pt, 11.2 US pt, 5.3 l.
TRANSMISSION 3.890 axle ratio, 5'' width of rims.
PERFORMANCE max speeds (I) 29 mph, 47 km/h, (II) 47 mph, 76 km/h, (III) 72 mph, 116 km/h, (IV) 92 mph, 148 km/h, power-weight ratio 33.3 lb/hp (45.3 lb/kW), 15.1 kg/hp (20.6 kg/kW), speed in direct drive at 1,000 rpm 16.8 mph, 27 km/h, consumption 40.9 m/imp gal, 34.1 m/US gal, 6.8 l x 100 km.
ELECTRICAL EQUIPMENT Lucas electronic ignition.
DIMENSIONS AND WEIGHT length 157.56 in, 400 cm.
PRACTICAL INSTRUCTIONS 91 oct petrol.

OPTIONALS Laycock-de Normanville overdrive on III and IV, 0.797 ratio; hardtop.

TR 7

PRICE IN USA: $ 6,750*
PRICE EX WORKS: £ 4,268*

ENGINE front, 4 stroke; 4 cylinders, vertical in line; 121.9 cu in, 1,998 cc (3.56 x 3.07 in, 90.3 x 78 mm); compression ratio: 9.25:1; max power (DIN): 105 hp (77.3 kW) at 5,500 rpm; max torque (DIN): 119 lb ft, 16.4 kg m (160.8 Nm) at 3,500 rpm; max engine rpm: 6,000. 52.6 hp/l (38.7 kW/l); cast iron block, light alloy head; 5 crankshaft bearings; valves: overhead, in line, thimble tappets; camshafts: 1,

TRIUMPH Spitfire 1500

overhead; lubrication. rotary pump, full flow filter, 8 imp pt, 9.5 US pt, 4.5 l; 2 SU type HS6 carburettors; fuel feed mechanical pump; water-cooled, 13 imp pt, 15.6 US pt 7.4 l.

TRANSMISSION driving wheels: rear; clutch: single dr plate (diaphragm), hydraulically controlled; gearbox mechanical; gears: 4, fully synchronized; ratios: I 2.646 II 1.779, III 1.254, IV 1, rev 3.050; lever: central; fina drive: hypoid bevel; axle ratio: 3.630; width of rims 5.5''; tyres: 175/70 SR x 13.

PERFORMANCE max speed: 110 mph, 177 km/h; power weight ratio: 20.3 lb/hp (27.5 lb/kW), 9.2 kg/hp (12. kg/kW); consumption: 25.4 m/imp gal, 21.2 m/US ga 11.1 l x 100 km.

CHASSIS integral, front subframe; front suspension: inde pendent, by McPherson, coil springs/telescopic dampe struts, lower wishbones (leading arm), anti-roll bar; rear rigid axle, lower trailing arms, upper oblique torque arms coil springs, anti-roll bar, telescopic dampers.

STEERING rack-and-pinion; turns lock to lock: 3.87.

BRAKES front disc (diameter 9.75 in, 24.8 cm), rear drum dual circuit; servo; swept area: front 183.5 sq in, 1,183 s cm, rear 75.4 sq in, 487 sq cm, total 258.9 sq in, 1,67 sq cm.

ELECTRICAL EQUIPMENT 12 V; 40 Ah battery; 36 A alter nator; AC Delco distributor; 2 retractable headlamps.

TRIUMPH Spitfire 1500

DIMENSIONS AND WEIGHT wheel base: 85 in, 216 cm tracks: 55.50 in, 141 cm front, 55.30 in, 140 cm rear length: 160 in, 406 cm; width: 66.20 in, 168 cm; height 49.40 in, 125 cm; ground clearance: 3.50 in, 9 cm weight: 2,127 lb, 965 kg; weight distribution. 53% fron 47% rear. turning circle: 29 ft, 8.8 m; fuel tank: 12 im gal, 14.4 US gal, 55 l.

BODY coupé; 2 doors; 2 seats; reclining backrests wit headrests; laminated windscreen; heated rear window.

PRACTICAL INSTRUCTIONS fuel: 97 oct petrol; oil: engin 8 imp pt, 9.5 US pt, 4.5 l, SAE 20W-30, change every 6,00 miles, 9,700 km - gearbox 2.1 imp pt, 2.5 US pt, 1.2 l, SA 90, no change recommended - final drive 2.2 imp pt, 2. US pt, 1.3 l, SAE 90, no change recommended; greasing none; tappet clearances: inlet 0.008 in, 0.20 mm, exhaus 0.018 in, 0.50 mm; valve timing: 16° 56° 56° 16°; tyr pressure: front 24 psi, 1.7 atm, rear 28 psi, 2 atm.

VARIATIONS

(For USA only).
ENGINE 8:1 compression ratio, max power (DIN) 88.5 h (65.1 kW) at 5,250 rpm, max torque (DIN) 100 lb ft, 13. kg m (135.4 Nm) at 2,500 rpm, max engine rpm 6,500 44.3 hp/l (32.6 kW/l), 2 Stromberg 175 CDFVX horizonta carburettors.
TRANSMISSION 5-speed mechanical gearbox (I 3.320, I 2.090, III 1.400, IV 1, V 0.830, rev 3.430), 3.900 axle ratio 185/70SR x 13.
PERFORMANCE max speeds (I) 34 mph, 55 km/h, (II) 5 mph, 85 km/h, (III) 80 mph, 129 km/h, (IV) 107 mph, 17 km/h, (V) 107 mph, 172 km/h, power-weight ratio 25 lb/hp (35.1 lb/kW), 11.7 kg/hp (15.9 kg/kW), speed i direct drive (IV) at 1,000 rpm 17.3 mph, 27.8 km/h.

TRIUMPH TR 7

TVR Convertible 3000 S

SAE 90, change every 6,000 miles, 9,700 km - final drive 2 imp pt, 2.5 US pt, 1.2 l, SAE 90, change every 6,000 miles, 9,700 km; greasing: every 6,000 miles, 9,700 km, 10 points; tappet clearances: inlet 0.013 in, 0.32 mm, exhaust 0.020 in, 0.50 mm; valve timing: 29° 67° 70° 14°; tyre pressure: front 22 psi, 1.6 atm, rear 24 psi, 1.7 atm.

OPTIONALS halogen headlamps; sunshine roof; vinyl roof; leather upholstery; light alloy wheels.

230 hp power team

See 142 hp power team, except for:

ENGINE with Holset 3LD turbocharger; compression ratio: 8:1; max power (DIN): 230 hp (169.3 kW) at 5,500 rpm; max torque (DIN): 273 lb ft, 37.7 kg m (369.7 Nm) at 3,500 rpm; max engine 76.8 hp/l (56.5 kW/l).

TRANSMISSION final drive: limited slip differential; tyres: 195 VR x 14.

PERFORMANCE max speeds: (I) 45 mph, 72 km/h; (II) 72 mph, 116 km/h; (III) 105 mph, 169 km/h; (IV) 140 mph, 225 kh/h; power-weight ratio: Turbo Coupé 10.1 lb/hp (13.8 lb/kW), 4.6 kg/hp (6.2 kg/kW); speed in direct drive at 1,000 rpm: 25 mph, 40.2 km/h.

DIMENSIONS AND WEIGHT weight: Turbo Coupé 2,333 lb, 1,058 kg - Convertible Turbo 2,270 lb, 1,030 kg - Taimar Turbo Hatchback Coupé 2,426 lb, 1,100 kg.

ELECTRICAL EQUIPMENT 50 Ah battery, Lucas electronic ignition.
DIMENSIONS AND WEIGHT length 164.29 in, 417 cm, weight 2,287 lb, 1,037 kg.
PRACTICAL INSTRUCTIONS 91 oct petrol.

OPTIONALS Borg-Warner automatic transmission with oil cooler, hydraulic torque converter and planetary gears with 3 ratios (I 2.390, II 1.450, III 1, rev 2.090), max ratio of converter at stall 1.9, possible manual selection; 3.270 axle ratio; 5-speed fully synchronized mechanical gearbox with 185/70 HR x 13 and 3.900 axle ratio; sunshine roof; light alloy wheels; halogen headlamps; metallic spray.

TVR — GREAT BRITAIN

3000, Turbo and Taimar Series

PRICES IN USA AND EX WORKS:

	$	£
1 3000 M Coupé	—	6,707*
2 Convertible 3000 S	16,000*	7,029*
3 Turbo Coupé	—	10,112*
4 Convertible Turbo	—	10,597*
5 Taimar Hatchback Coupé	16,000*	7,302*
6 Taimar Turbo Hatchback Coupé	—	10,844*

Power team:	Standard for:	Optional for:
142 hp	1, 2, 5	—
230 hp	3, 4, 6	—

142 hp power team

ENGINE Ford, front, 4 stroke; 6 cylinders, Vee-slanted at 60°; 182.7 cu in, 2,994 cc (3.70 x 2.85 in, 94 x 72.4 mm); compression ratio: 8.9:1; max power (DIN): 142 hp (104.5 kW) at 5,000 rpm; max torque (DIN): 172 lb ft, 23.7 kg m (232.4 Nm) at 3,000 rpm; max engine rpm: 6,000; 47.4 hp/l (34.9 kW/l); cast iron block and head; 4 crankshaft bearings; valves: overhead, in line, push-rods and rockers; camshafts: 1, at centre of Vee; lubrication: eccentric pump, full flow filter, 9.8 imp pt, 11.6 US pt, 5.5 l; 1 Weber 40 DFA-1 downdraught twin barrel carburettor; fuel feed: mechanical pump; water-cooled, 19.9 imp pt, 23.9 US pt, 11.3 l, thermostatically-controlled electric fan.

TRANSMISSION driving wheels: rear; clutch: single dry plate (diaphragm), hydraulically controlled; gearbox: mechanical; gears: 4, fully synchronized; ratios: I 3.163, II 2.950, III 1.412, IV 1, rev 3.346; lever: central; final drive: hypoid bevel; axle ratio: 3.310; width of rims: 6''; tyres: 185 HR x 14.

PERFORMANCE max speeds: (I) 42 mph, 67 km/h; (II) 68 mph, 109 km/h; (III) 94 mph, 151 km/h; (IV) 133 mph, 214 km/h; power-weight ratio: 3000 M Coupé 15.5 lb/hp (21 lb/kW), 7 kg/hp (9.6 kg/kW); carrying capacity: 620 lb, 281 kg; acceleration: standing ¼ mile 16 sec, 0-50 mph 0-80 km/h) 5.6 sec; speed in direct drive at 1,000 rpm: 16 mph, 34.7 km/h; consumption: 22 m/imp gal, 18.4 m/US gal, 12.8 l x 100 km.

CHASSIS multi-tubular backbone with outriggers; front suspension: independent, wishbones, coil springs, anti-roll bar, telescopic dampers; rear: independent, wishbones, coil springs, anti-roll bar, coil springs, 4 telescopic dampers.

STEERING rack-and-pinion.

BRAKES front disc (diameter 10.87 in, 27.6 cm), rear drum, servo; swept area: front 233 sq in, 1,503 sq cm, rear 99 sq in, 639 sq cm, total 332 sq in, 2,142 sq cm.

ELECTRICAL EQUIPMENT 12 V; 58 Ah battery; 34 A alternator; 2 headlamps.

DIMENSIONS AND WEIGHT wheel base: 90 in, 229 cm; front and rear tracks: 53.75 in, 136 cm; length: 155.12 in, 394 cm; width: 63.78 in, 162 cm; height: coupés 44.88 in, 114 cm - convertible 44.09 in, 112 cm; ground clearance: coupés 5 in, 12.7 cm - convertible 5.51 in, 14 cm; weight: 3000 M Coupé 2,200 lb, 998 kg - Convertible 3000 S 2,137 lb, 969 kg - Taimar Hatchback Coupé 2,293 lb, 1,040 kg; turning circle: 35.7 ft, 10.9 m; fuel tank: 12 imp gal, 14.5 US gal, 55 l.

BODY 2 doors; 2 seats, reclining backrests with built-in headrests; laminated windows; heated rear window; aluminium alloy wheels; leather steering wheel; for convertible only fully detachable hood.

PRACTICAL INSTRUCTIONS fuel: 98 oct petrol; oil: engine 9.8 imp pt, 11.6 US pt, 5.5 l, SAE 20W-50, change every 6,000 miles, 9,700 km - gearbox 2.5 imp pt, 3 US pt, 1.4 l,

VANDEN PLAS — GREAT BRITAIN

1500

PRICE EX WORKS: £ 4,545*

ENGINE front, transverse, in unit with gearbox and final drive, 4 stroke; 4 cylinders, vertical, in line; 90.6 cu in, 1,485 cc (3 x 3.20 in, 76.2 x 81.3 mm); compression ratio: 9.1; max power (DIN): 68 hp (50 kW) at 5,500 rpm; max torque (DIN): 80 lb ft, 11.1 kg m (108.9 Nm) at 2,900 rpm; max engine rpm: 5,900; 45.8 hp/l (33.7 kW/l); cast iron block and head; 5 crankshaft bearings; valves: overhead, Vee-slanted, thimble tappets; camshafts: 1, overhead, chain-driven; lubrication: mechanical pump, full flow filter (cartridge), 9.7 imp pt, 11.6 US pt, 5.5 l; 1 SU type HS6 single barrel carburettor; fuel feed: mechanical pump; sealed circuit cooling, liquid, expansion tank, 11.5 imp pt, 13.7 US pt, 6.5 l, electric thermostatic fan.

TRANSMISSION driving wheels: front; clutch: single dry plate (diaphragm); gearbox: mechanical; gears: 5, fully synchronized; ratios: I 3.202, II 2.004, III 1.372, IV 1, V 0.869, rev 3.467; lever: central; final drive: helical spur gears; axle ratio: 3.800; width of rims: 4''; tyres 155 SR x 13.

PERFORMANCE max speeds: (I) 33 mph, 53 km/h; (II) 54 mph, 87 km/h; (III) 78 mph, 125 km/h; (IV) 92 mph, 148

VANDEN PLAS 1500

1500

km/h; (V) 90 mph, 145 km/h; power-weight ratio: 29.2 lb/hp (39.7 lb/kW), 13.2 kg/hp (18 kg/kW); carrying capacity: 710 lb, 320 kg; acceleration: standing ¼ mile 20.2 sec, 0-50 mph (0-80 km/h) 10.4 sec; speed in top at 1,000 rpm: 20.1 mph, 32.3 km/h; consumption: 28.2 m/imp gal, 23.5 m/US gal, 10 l x 100 km.

CHASSIS integral; front suspension: independent, wishbones, hydragas (liquid and gas) rubber cone springs, hydraulic connecting pipes to rear wheels; rear: independent, swinging longitudinal trailing arms, hydragas (liquid and gas) rubber cone springs, hydraulic connecting pipes to front wheels.

STEERING rack-and-pinion; turns lock to lock: 3.50.

BRAKES front disc (diameter 9.68 in, 24.6 cm), rear drum, vacuum servo; swept area: front 178 sq in, 1,148 sq cm, rear 75.6 sq in, 487 sq cm, total 253.6 sq in, 1,635 sq cm.

ELECTRICAL EQUIPMENT 12 V; 40 Ah battery; 34 A alternator; Lucas distributor; 4 headlamps (2 fog lamps).

DIMENSIONS AND WEIGHT wheel base: 96.14 in, 244 cm; tracks: 54.33 in, 138 cm front, 54.41 in, 138 cm rear; length: 154.25 in, 392 cm; width: 63.52 in, 161 cm; height: 55.80 in 142 cm; ground clearance: 7.48 in, 19 cm; weight: 1,984 lb, 900 kg turning circle: 33.2 ft, 10.1 m; fuel tank: 10.5 imp gal, 12.7 US gal, 48 l.

BODY saloon/sedan; 4 doors; 4 seats, separate front seats, reclining backrests; picnic tables behind front seats; heated rear window.

PRACTICAL INSTRUCTIONS fuel: 97 oct petrol; oil: engine, gearbox and final drive 9.7 imp pt, 11.6 US pt, 5.5 l, SAE 20W-50, change every 6,000 miles, 9,700 km; greasing: every 6,000 miles, 9,700 km, 4 points; tappet clearances: inlet 0.012-0.018 in, 0.30-0.45 mm, exhaust 0.012-0.022 in, 0.30-0.55 mm; valve timing: 9° 51° 49° 11°; tyre pressure: front 26 psi, 1.8 atm, rear 24 psi, 1.7 atm.

OPTIONALS headrests; automatic transmission with 4 ratios (I 2.612, II 1.807, III 1.446, IV 1, rev 2.612), 3.800 axle ratio; metallic spray.

VAUXHALL　　　　GREAT BRITAIN

Chevette Series

PRICES EX WORKS:

1 E 2-dr Saloon	£	2,341*
2 E 4-dr Saloon	£	2,444*
3 E 3-dr Hatchback	£	2,380*
4 L 2-dr Saloon	£	2,576*
5 L 4-dr Saloon	£	2,679*
6 L 3-dr Hatchback	£	2,615*
7 L Estate Car	£	2,888*
8 GL 3-dr Hatchback	£	2,918*
9 GLS 4-dr Saloon	£	2,982*
10 2300 HS Hatchback	£	5,312*

Power team:	Standard for:	Optional for:
57.7 hp	1 to 9	—
135 hp	10	—

57.7 hp power team

ENGINE front, 4 stroke; 4 cylinders, vertical, in line; 76.6 cu in, 1,256 cc (3.19 x 2.40 in, 81 x 61 mm); compression ratio: 8.7:1 (7.3:1 only for export); max power (DIN): 57.7 hp (42.7 kW) at 5,600 rpm; max torque (DIN): 66.4 lb ft, 9.2 kg m (90 Nm) at 2,600 rpm; max engine rpm: 6,000; 45.9 hp/l (34 kW/l); chromium cast iron block and head; 3 crankshaft bearings; valves: overhead, in line, push-rods and rockers; camshafts: 1, side; lubrication: gear pump, full flow filter, 5.5 imp pt, 6.6 US pt, 3.1 l; 1 Zenith-Stromberg 150 CDS downdraught single barrel carburettor; fuel feed: mechanical pump; water-cooled, 10.2 imp pt, 12.3 US pt, 5.8 l, viscous coupling fan.

TRANSMISSION driving wheels: rear; clutch: single dry plate (diaphragm); gearbox: mechanical; gears: 4, fully synchronized; ratios: I 3.760, II 2.213, III 1.404, IV 1, rev 3.707; lever: central; final drive: hypoid bevel; axle ratio: 4.111; width of rims: 5''; tyres: 5.60 x 13 - L and GL models 155 SR x 13.

PERFORMANCE max speeds: (I) 31 mph, 50 km/h; (II) 49 mph, 79 km/h; (III) 77 mph, 124 km/h; (IV) 91 mph, 146 km/h; power-weight ratio: E 4-dr. Saloon 32.7 lb/hp (44.1 lb/kW), 14.8 kg/hp (20 kg/kW) - L 4-dr. Saloon 33 lb/hp (44.6 lb/kW), 15 kg/hp (20.2 kg/kW) - GLS 4-dr. Saloon 33.4 lb/hp (45.2 lb/kW), 15.2 kg/hp (20.5 kg/kW); carrying capacity: 1,076 lb, 488 kg; acceleration: standing ¼ mile 19.6 sec, 0-50 mph (0-80 km/h)9.6 sec; speed in direct drive at 1,000 rpm: 15.9 mph, 25.6 km/h; consumption: 28.8 m/imp gal, 24 m/US gal, 9.8 l x 100 km.

VAUXHALL Chevette GL 3-dr Hatchback

CHASSIS integral; front suspension: independent, wishbones, coil springs, anti-roll bar, telescopic dampers; rear: rigid axle (torque tube), longitudinal trailing radius arms, coil springs, Panhard rod, anti-roll bar, telescopic dampers.

STEERING rack-and-pinion; turns lock to lock: 3.50.

BRAKES front disc (diameter 9.37 in, 23.8 cm), self-adjusting rear drum, rear compensator, dual circuit, servo; swept area: front 157.5 sq in, 1,016 sq cm, rear 73.8 sq in, 476 sq cm, total 231.3 sq in, 1,492 sq cm.

ELECTRICAL EQUIPMENT 12 V; 40 Ah battery; 504 or 630 W alternator; AC Delco distributor; 2 headlamps.

DIMENSIONS AND WEIGHT wheel base: 94.30 in, 239 cm; front and rear tracks: 51.20 in, 130 cm; length: 164.40 in, 417 cm - hatchbacks 155.20 in, 394 cm - Estate Car 164.9 in, 419 cm; width: 61.80 in, 157 cm; height: 2-dr. saloons and hatchbacks 51.5 in, 131 cm - 4-dr. saloons 51.3 in, 130 cm - Estate Car 52.1 in, 132 cm; ground clearance: 4.70 in, 11.9 cm; weight: E 2-dr. Saloon 1,821 lb, 826 kg - E 4-dr. Saloon 1,885 lb, 855 kg - E Hatchback 1,865 lb, 846 kg - L 2-dr. Saloon 1,841 lb, 835 kg - L 4-dr. Saloon 1,903 lb, 863 kg - L Hatchback 1,885 lb, 855 kg - L Estate Car 1,951 lb, 885 kg - GL Hatchback 1,916 lb, 869 kg - GL 4-dr. Saloon 1,929 lb, 875 kg; turning circle: 32.8 ft, 10 m; fuel tank: saloons 9.9 imp gal, 11.9 US gal, 45 l - Estate Car 9.5 imp gal, 11.4 US gal, 43 l - hatchbacks 8.4 imp gal, 10 US gal, 38 l.

BODY 5 seats, separate front seats.

PRACTICAL INSTRUCTIONS fuel: 98 oct petrol; oil: engine 5.5 imp pt, 6.6 US pt, 3.1 l, SAE 10W-30, change every 6,000 miles, 9,700 km - gearbox 1.1 imp pt, 1.3 US pt 0.6 l, SAE 90, change every 6 months - final drive 1.2 imp pt, 1.5 US pt, 0.7 l, SAE 90, no change recommended; greasing: every 6 months, 4 points; tappet clearances: inlet 0.008 in, 0.20 mm, exhaust 0.008 in, 0.20 mm; valve timing: 37° 71° 69° 39°; tyre pressure: front 21 psi, 1 atm, rear 25 psi, 1.7 atm.

OPTIONALS 155 SR x 13 tyres; metallic spray except for E models.

135 hp power team

ENGINE 139.1 cu in, 2,279 cc (3.84 x 3 in, 97.5 x 76.2 mm); compression ratio: 8.2:1; max power (DIN): 135 hp (99 kW) at 5,500 rpm; 59.2 hp/l (43.6 kW/l); valves: 4 per cylinder; 2 Stromberg 175 CD carburettors.

TRANSMISSION gears: 5, fully synchronized; ratios: I 3.370, II 2.160, III 1.580, IV 1.240, V 1; axle ratio: 3.440; width of rims: 6''; tyres: 205/60 HR x 13.

PERFORMANCE max speed: 115 mph, 185 km/h; power-weight ratio: 14.5 lb/hp (19.7 lb/kW), 6.6 kg/hp (8. kg/kW).

DIMENSIONS AND WEIGHT weight: 1,960 lb, 889 kg.

VAUXHALL Viva 1300 GLS 4-dr Saloon

Viva Series

CES EX WORKS:

2-dr Saloon	£ 2,423*
4-dr Saloon	£ 2,526*
300 L 2-dr Saloon	£ 2,658*
300 L 4-dr Saloon	£ 2,761*
300 L Estate Car	£ 2,969*
300 GLS 2-dr Saloon	£ 3,021*
300 GLS 4-dr Saloon	£ 3,124*
300 GLS Estate Car	£ 3,332*
800 GLS 4-dr Saloon	£ 3,294*

ver team:	Standard for:	Optional for:
' hp	1 to 8	—
hp	9	—

57.7 hp power team

GINE front, 4 stroke; 4 cylinders, vertical, in line; 76.6 in, 1,256 cc (3.19 x 2.40 in, 81 x 61 mm); compression o: 8.7:1 (7.3:1 only for export); max power (DIN): ' hp (42.7 kW) at 5,600 rpm; max torque (DIN): 66.4 lb ft, kg m (90 Nm) at 2,600 rpm; max engine rpm: 6,000; hp/l (34 kW/l); chromium cast iron block and head; rankshaft bearings; valves: overhead, in line, push-rods rockers; camshafts: 1, side; lubrication: gear pump, flow filter, 5.5 imp pt, 6.6 US pt, 3.1 l; 1 Zenith-

omberg 150 CDS downdraught single barrel carburettor; feed: mechanical pump; water-cooled, 10.2 imp pt, 3 US pt, 5.8 l, viscous coupling fan.

ANSMISSION driving wheels: rear; clutch: single dry te (diaphragm); gearbox: mechanical; gears: 4, fully chronized; ratios: I 3.760, II 2.213, III 1.404, IV 1, rev 07; lever: central; final drive: hypoid bevel; axle ratio: 25; width of rims: 4.5'' - GLS models 5''; tyres: 5.60 x 13 iva 1300 L and Viva 1300 GLS models 155 SR x 13.

RFORMANCE max speeds: (I) 29 mph, 47 km/h; (II) mph, 72 km/h; (III) 70 mph, 113 km/h; (IV) 86 mph, km/h; power-weight ratio: Viva 1300 L 4-dr. Saloon lb/hp (46 lb/kW), 15.4 kg/hp (21 kg/kW) - 1300 S 4-dr. Saloon 34.8 lb/hp (47 lb/kW), 15.8 kg/hp 3 kg/kW); speed in direct drive at 1,000 rpm: 16.1 mph, 9 km/h; consumption: 27.6 m/imp gal, 22.9 m/US gal, 2 l x 100 km.

ASSIS integral; front suspension: independent, wish-es, coil springs, telescopic dampers; rear: rigid axle, ling lower radius arms, upper oblique radius arms, coil ings, telescopic dampers.

ERING rack-and-pinion; turns lock to lock: 3.16.

AKES front disc (diameter 8.50 in, 21.6 cm), self-adjust-rear drum, dual circuit, servo; swept area: front 154.6 in, 997 sq cm, rear 63 sq in, 406 sq cm, total 217.6 n, 1,403 sq cm.

ECTRICAL EQUIPMENT 12 V; 33 Ah battery; 336 W ernator; AC Delco distributor; 2 headlamps (4 on GLS dels)

DIMENSIONS AND WEIGHT wheel base: 97 in, 246 cm; tracks: 51.80 in, 13.2 cm front, 51.50 in, 131 cm rear; length: 162.90 in, 414 cm; width: 64.70 in, 164 cm; height: 53.20 in, 135 cm; ground clearance: 5.40 in, 13.7 cm; weight: E 2-dr. and 1300 L 2-dr. 1,927 lb, 828 kg - E 4-dr. 1,951 lb, 885 kg - 1300 L 4-dr. 1,964 lb, 891 kg - 1300 L Estate Car 2,030 lb, 920 kg - 1300 GLS 2-dr. 1,969 lb, 893 kg - 1300 GLS 4-dr. 2,006 lb, 910 kg - 1300 GLS Estate Car 2,072 lb, 940 kg; turning circle: 32.2 ft, 9.8 m; fuel tank: 8 imp gal, 9.5 US gal, 36 l.

BODY 4-5 seats, separate front seats, reclining backrests; heated rear window (except for Viva E models); luxury equipment (only for GLS models).

PRACTICAL INSTRUCTIONS fuel: 98 oct petrol; oil: engine 4.9 imp pt, 5.9 US pt, 2.8 l, SAE 10W-30, change every 6,000 miles, 9,700 km - gearbox 0.9 imp pt, 1.1 US pt, 0.5 l, SAE 90, change every 6 months - final drive 1.2 imp pt, 1.5 US pt, 0.7 l, SAE 90, no change recommended; greasing: every 6 months, 4 points; tappet clearances: inlet 0.008 in, 0.20 mm, exhaust 0.008 in, 0.20 mm; valve timing: 39° 73° 71° 41°; tyre pressure: front 24 psi, 1.7 atm, rear 24 psi, 1.7 atm.

OPTIONALS 155 SR x 13 tyres (only for Viva E); metallic spray (except for Viva E); vinyl roof (only for GLS saloons).

88 hp power team

See 57.7 hp power team, except for:

ENGINE 107.3 cu in, 1,759 cc (3.37 x 3 in, 85.7 x 76.1 mm); compression ratio: 8.5:1; max power (DIN): 88 hp (64.8 kW) at 5,800 rpm; max torque (DIN): 99 lb ft, 13.7 kg m (134.4 Nm) at 3,500 rpm; max engine rpm: 6,250; 50 hp/l (36.8 kW/l); 5 crankshaft bearings; valves: overhead, in line; camshafts: 1, overhead, cogged belt; lubricating system: 8.5 imp pt, 10.1 US pt, 4.8 l; 1 Zenith 36 IV downdraught single barrel carburettor; cooling system: 14 imp pt, 16.9 US pt, 8 l.

TRANSMISSION gearbox ratios: I 3.300, II 2.145, III 1.414, IV 1, rev 3.063; axle ratio: 3.727; tyres: 175 SR x 13.

PERFORMANCE max speed: 93 mph, 149 km/h; power-weight ratio: 25.8 lb/hp (35.1 lb/kW), 11.7 kg/hp (15.9 kg/kW); speed in direct drive at 1,000 rpm: 17.8 mph, 28.6 km/h; consumption: 21.1 m/imp gal, 17.6 m/US gal, 13.4 l x 100 km.

CHASSIS front suspension: anti-roll bar.

BRAKES front disc (diameter 10.03 in, 25.5 cm).

DIMENSIONS AND WEIGHT weight: 2,273 lb, 1,031 kg; fuel tank: 12 imp gal, 14.5 US gal, 55 l.

PRACTICAL INSTRUCTIONS oil: engine 8 imp pt, 9.5 US pt, 4.5 l; tappet clearances: inlet 0.005-0.010 in, 0.12-0.25 mm, exhaust 0.015-0.018 in, 0.37-0.45 mm; valve timing: 33°26' 65°26' 65°26' 33°26'.

OPTIONALS G.M. automatic transmission, hydraulic torque converter and planetary gears with 3 ratios (I 2.390, II 1.480, III 1, rev 1.920), max ratio of converter at stall 2, possible manual selection.

VAUXHALL Cavalier GLS Coupé

Cavalier Series

PRICES EX WORKS:

1	1300 L 2-dr Saloon	£ 2,984*
2	1300 L 4-dr Saloon	£ 3,088*
3	1600 L 2-dr Saloon	£ 3,154*
4	1600 L 4-dr Saloon	£ 3,257*
5	1600 GL 4-dr Saloon	£ 3,579*
6	1600 GLS Sports Hatchback	£ 4,175*
7	2000 GL 4-dr Saloon	£ 3,778*
8	2000 GLS Coupé	£ 4,335*
9	2000 GLS Sport Hatchback	£ 4,373*

Power team:	Standard for:	Optional for:
57.7 hp	1,2	—
75 hp	3 to 6	—
100 hp	7 to 9	—

57.7 hp power team

ENGINE front, 4 stroke; 4 cylinders, vertical, in line; 76.6 cu in, 1,256 cc (3.19 x 2.40 in, 81 x 61 mm); compression ratio: 8.7:1; max power (DIN): 57.7 hp (42.7 kW) at 5,600 rpm; max torque (DIN): 66.4 lb ft, 9.2 kg m (90 Nm) at 2,600 rpm; max engine rpm: 6,000; 45.9 hp/l (34 kW/l); chromium cast iron block and head; 3 crankshaft bearings; valves: overhead, in line, push-rods and rockers; camshafts: 1, side; lubrication: gear pump, full flow filter, 5.5 imp pt, 6.6 US pt, 3.1 l; 1 Zenith-Stromberg 150 CDS downdraught single barrel carburettor; fuel feed: mechanical pump; water-cooled, 10.2 imp pt, 12.3 US pt, 5.8 l, viscous coupling thermostatic fan.

TRANSMISSION driving wheels: rear; clutch: single dry plate (diaphragm); gearbox: mechanical; gears: 4, fully synchronized; ratios: I 3.760, II 2.213, III 1.404, IV 1, rev 3.707; lever: central; final drive: hypoid bevel; axle ratio: 4.111; width of rims: 5''; tyres: 165 SR x 13.

PERFORMANCE max speed: (I) 31 mph, 50 km/h; (II) 49 mph, 79 km/h; (III) 77 mph, 124 km/h; (IV) 91 mph, 146 km/h; power-weight ratio: 4-dr. Saloon 37.5 lb/hp (50.7 lb/kW), 17 kg/hp (23 kg/kW); carrying capacity: 906 lb, 411 kg; acceleration: standing 1/4 mile 19.6 sec, 0-50 mph (0-80 km/h) 9.6 sec; speed in direct drive at 1,000 rpm: 16.4 mph, 26.4 km/h; consumption: 28.2 m/imp gal, 23.5 m/US gal, 10 l x 100 km.

CHASSIS integral; front suspension: independent, wishbones, coil springs, anti-roll bar, telescopic dampers; rear: rigid axle (torque tube), trailing radius arms, transverse linkage bar, coil springs, anti-roll bar, telescopic dampers.

STEERING rack-and-pinion; turns lock to lock: 4.

BRAKES front disc (diameter 9.70 in, 24.6 cm), rear drum, rear compensator, dual circuit, servo.

ELECTRICAL EQUIPMENT 12 V; 36 Ah battery; 45 A alternator; Bosch or Delco-Remy distributor; 2 headlamps.

DIMENSIONS AND WEIGHT wheel base: 99.10 in, 252 cm; tracks: 54.10 in, 137 cm front, 54.10 in, 137 cm rear; length: 175.5 in, 446 cm; width: 64.70 in, 164 cm; height: 52 in, 132 cm; ground clearance: 5 in, 12.7 cm; weight: 2-dr. Saloon 1,989 lb, 902 kg - 4-dr. Saloon 2,163 lb, 981 kg; turning circle: 31.1 ft, 9.5 m; fuel tank: 11 imp gal, 13.2 US gal, 50 l.

VAUXHALL Cavalier 1300 L 4-dr Saloon

57.7 HP POWER TEAM

BODY saloon/sedan; 5 seats, separate front seats, reclining backrests, heated rear window.

PRACTICAL INSTRUCTIONS fuel 98 oct petrol; oil: engine 5.5 imp pt, 6.6 US pt, 3.1 l, SAE 10W-30, change every 6,000 miles, 9,700 km - gearbox 0.9 imp pt, 1.1 US pt, 0.5 l, SAE 90, change every 6 months - final drive 1.2 imp pt, 1.5 US pt, 0.7 l, SAE 90, no change recommended; greasing: none; tappet clearances: inlet 0.008 in, 0.20 mm, exhaust 0.008 in, 0.20 mm; valve timing: 37° 71° 69° 39°; tyre pressure: front 28 psi, 2 atm, rear 28 psi, 2 atm.

75 hp power team

See 57.7 hp power team, except for:

ENGINE 96.7 cu in, 1,584 cc (3.35 x 2.75 in, 85 x 69.8 mm); compression ratio: 8.8:1; max power (DIN): 75 hp (55.2 kW) at 5,000 rpm; max torque (DIN): 81 lb ft, 11.2 kg m (109.8 Nm) at 3,800 rpm; max engine rpm: 6,000; 47.3 hp/l (34.8 kW/l); cast iron block, chromium cast iron head; 5 crankshaft bearings; camshafts: 1, overhead; lubricating system: 8.7 imp pt, 10.4 US pt, 4.9 l; 1 Solex 32 DIDTA-4 downdraught single barrel carburettor; fuel feed: electric pump; cooling system: 13.8 imp pt, 16.5 US pt, 7.8 l.

TRANSMISSION gearbox ratios: I 3.640, II 2.120, III 1.336, IV 1, rev 3.522; axle ratio: 3.670; width of rims: 5.5'' (for Hatchback); tyres: 185 SR x 13 (for Hatchback).

PERFORMANCE max speed: 98 mph, 158 km/h; power-weight ratio: 1600 L 4-dr. Saloon 29.4 lb/hp (40 lb/kW), 13.4 kg/hp (18.2 kg/kW) - 1600 GL 4-dr. Saloon 29.6 lb/hp (40.2 lb/kW), 13.4 kg/hp (18.2 kg/kW); carrying capacity: 937 lb, 425 kg; speed in direct drive at 1,000 rpm: 18.3 mph, 29.4 km/h; consumption: 25.7 m/imp gal, 21.4 m/US gal, 11 l x 100 km.

ELECTRICAL EQUIPMENT 44 Ah battery.

DIMENSIONS AND WEIGHT length: Hatchback 171.8 in, 436 cm; weight: 1600 L 2-dr. Saloon 2,165 lb, 982 kg - 4-dr. Saloon 2,209 lb, 1,002 kg - 1600 GL 4-dr. Saloon 2,220 lb, 1,007 kg - Hatchback 2,172 lb, 985 kg.

BODY 5 seats, separate front seats, reclining backrests; heated rear window.

PRACTICAL INSTRUCTIONS oil: engine 6.7 imp pt, 8 US pt, 3.8 l, SAE 20W-30, change every 6,000 miles, 9,700 km - gearbox 2.3 imp pt, 2.7 US pt, 1.3 l, SAE 80, no change recommended - final drive 2.3 imp pt, 2.7 US pt, 1.3 l, SAE 90, no change recommended; tappet clearances: inlet 0.012 in, 0.30 mm, exhaust 0.012 in, 0.30 mm; valve timing: 44° 86° 84° 46°.

OPTIONALS G.M. automatic transmission, hydraulic torque converter and planetary gears with 3 ratios (I 2.400, II 1.480, III 1, rev 1.920), max ratio of converter at stall 2.5, possible manual selection, 3.670 axle ratio, max speed 95 mph, 153 km/h, consumption 25.9 m/imp gal, 21.6 m/US gal, 10.9 l x 100 km; metallic spray.

100 hp power team

See 75 hp power team, except for:

ENGINE 120.8 cu in, 1,979 cc (3.74 x 2.75 in, 95 x 69.8 mm); compression ratio: 9:1; max power (DIN): 100 hp (73.6 kW) at 5,400 rpm; max torque (DIN): 113 lb/ft, 15.6 kg m (153.1 Nm) at 3,800 rpm; 50.5 hp/l (37.2 kW/l); valves: hydraulic tappets: 1 GMF Varajet II downdraught single barrel carburettor.

TRANSMISSION axle ratio: 3.440; width of rims: 5.5'' (for Coupé and Hatchback); tyres: 185 HR x 13 (for Coupé and Hatchback).

PERFORMANCE max speed: 109 mph, 175 km/h; power-weight ratio: Saloon and Coupé 22 lb/hp (29.9 lb/kW), 10 kg/hp (13.6 kg/kW) - Hatchback 22.5 lb/hp (30.6 lb/kW), 10.2 kg/hp (13.8 kg/kW); speed in direct drive at 1,000 rpm: 19.5 mph, 31.4 km/h; consumption: 23.7 m/imp gal, 19.8 m/US gal, 11.9 l x 100 km.

ELECTRICAL EQUIPMENT 44 Ah battery.

DIMENSIONS AND WEIGHT length: Coupé 175 in, 444 cm; weight: Saloon and Coupé 2,205 lb, 1,000 kg - Hatchback 2,249 lb, 1,020 kg.

OPTIONALS G.M. automatic transmission, hydraulic torque converter and planetary gears with 3 ratios (I 2.400, II 1.480, III 1, rev 1.920), max ratio of converter at stall 2.5, possible manual selection; metallic spray.

Carlton 2000 Saloon

PRICE EX WORKS: £ 4,600*

ENGINE front, 4 stroke; 4 cylinders vertical, in line; 120.7 cu in, 1,979 cc (3.74 x 2.75 in, 95 x 69.8 mm); compression ratio: 9:1; max power (DIN): 100 hp (73.6 kW) at 5,200 rpm; max torque (DIN): 116.5 lb ft, 16.1 kg m (158 Nm) at 3,600 rpm; max engine rpm: 6,000; 50.5 hp/l (37.9 kW/l); cast iron block and head; 5 crankshaft bearings; valves: overhead, hydraulic tappets; camshafts: 1, overhead; lubrication: 6.7 imp pt, 8 US pt, 3.8 l; 1 Zenith INAT 35/40 downdraught carburettor; fuel feed: mechanical pump; water-cooled, 11 imp pt, 13.1 US pt, 6.2 l.

TRANSMISSION driving wheels: rear; clutch: single dry plate; gearbox: mechanical; gears: 4, fully synchronized; ratios: I 3.640, II 2.120, III 1.336, IV 1, rev 3.522; lever: central; final drive: hypoid bevel; axle ratio: 3.670; width of rims: 5.5''; tyres: 175 SR x 14.

PERFORMANCE max speeds: (I) 29 mph, 48 km/h; (II) 51 mph, 82 km/h; (III) 80 mph, 129 km/h; (IV) 107 mph, 172 km/h; power-weight ratio: 33.7 lb/hp, (32.4 lb/kW), 11.4 kg/hp (14.7 kg/kW); carrying capacity: 1,036 lb, 470 kg; acceleration: standing ¼ mile 18.5 sec, 0-50 mph, (0-80 km/h) 8.5 sec; speed in direct drive at 1,000 rpm: 19.5 mph, 31.4 km/h; consumption: 24.4 m/imp gal, 20.3 m/US gal, 11.6 l x 100 km.

CHASSIS integral; front suspension: independent, by McPherson, coil springs/telescopic damper struts, anti-roll bar;

VAUXHALL Carlton 2000 Saloon

rear: rigid axle, trailing lower radius arms, upper torque arms, transverse linkage bar, coil springs, anti-roll bar, telescopic dampers.

STEERING recirculating ball; turns lock to lock: 4.

BRAKES front disc (diameter 9.6 in, 24.4 cm), internal radial fins, self-adjusting rear drum, rear compensator, dual circuit, servo; swept area: front 22.9 sq in, 148 sq cm, rear 62.8 sq in, 405 sq cm, total 85.7 sq in, 553 sq cm.

ELECTRICAL EQUIPMENT 12 V; 44 Ah battery; 45 A alternator; AC Delco distributor; 2 halogen headlamps.

DIMENSIONS AND WEIGHT wheel base: 105 in, 267 cm; tracks: 56.5 in, 144 cm front, 55.6 in, 141 cm rear; length: 186.7 in, 474 cm; width: 69.9 in, 173 cm; height: 53.6 in, 136 cm; ground clearance: 5.2 in, 13 cm; weight: 2,384 lb, 1,081 kg; weight distribution: 55.5% front, 44.5% rear; turning circle: 35.5 ft, 10.8 m; fuel tank: 14.3 imp gal, 17.2 US gal, 65 l.

BODY saloon/sedan; 4 doors; 5 seats, separate front seats, reclining backrests, headrests; heated rear window.

PRACTICAL INSTRUCTIONS fuel: 98-100 oct petrol; oil: engine 6.7 imp pt, 8 US pt, 3.8 l, SAE 10W-50 change every 6,000 miles, 9,700 km - gearbox 1.9 imp pt, 2.3 US pt, 1.1 l, SAE 80, change every 18,300 miles, 30,000 km - final drive 2.1 imp pt, 2.5 US pt, 1.2 l, SAE 90 no change recommend; greasing: none; valve timing: 32° 90° 72° 50°; tyre pressure: front 24 psi, 1.7 atm, rear 25 psi, 1.8 atm.

OPTIONALS metallic spray; sports wheels.

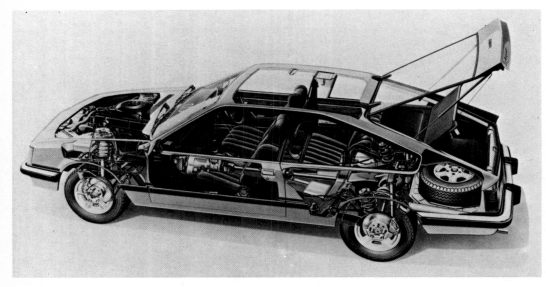

VAUXHALL Royale Coupé

Carlton 2000 Estate

Carlton 2000 Saloon, except for:

CE EX WORKS: £ 5,068*

FORMANCE power-weight ratio: 24.8 lb/hp (33.8 lb/kW), kg/hp (15.3 kg/kW); carrying capacity: 1,290 lb, 585 consumption: 23.7 m/imp gal, 19.8 m/US gal, 11.9 l) km.

ENSIONS AND WEIGHT lenght: 186.2 in, 473 cm; height: in, 143 cm; ground clearance: 6.4 in, 16 cm; weight: 5 lb, 1,127 kg; weight distribution: 53% front, 47% fuel tank: 15.4 imp gal, 18.5 US gal, 70 l.

Y estate car/station wagon; 5 doors.

Royale Saloon

CE EX WORKS: £ 7,956*

INE front, 4 stroke; 6 cylinders, vertical, in line; 169.9 n, 2,784 cc (3.62 x 2.75 in, 92 x 69.8 mm); compression : 9:1; max power (DIN): 140 hp (103 kW) at 5,200 rpm; max torque (DIN): 161 lb ft, 22.2 kg m (218 Nm) at rpm; max engine rpm: 6,150; 50.3 hp/l (37.4 kW/l); iron block and head; 7 crankshaft bearings; valves: head, hydraulic tappets; camshafts: 1, overhead; lubri-n: 9.8 imp pt, 11.6 US pt, 5.5 l; 1 DVG 4AI down-ght carburettor; fuel feed: mechanical pump; water-ed, 17.2 imp pt, 20.7 US pt, 9.8 l.

ISMISSION driving wheels: rear; gearbox: automatic smission, hydraulic torque converter and planetary s with 3 ratios, max ratio of converter at stall 2, ible manual selection; ratios: I 2.400, II 1.480, III 1, 1.920; lever: central; final drive: hypoid bevel; axle : 3.450; width of rims: 6''; tyres: 195/70 HR x 14.

ORMANCE max speed: 115 mph, 185 km/h; power-ht ratio: 20.8 lb/hp, (28.3 lb/kW), 9.5 kg/hp (12.8 W); carrying capacity: 1,169 lb, 530 kg; acceleration: ding ¼ mile 19 sec, 0-50 mph (0-80 km/h) 8.5 sec; d in direct drive/top at 1,000 rpm: 20.8 mph, 33.5 ; consumption: 22.6 m/imp gal, 18.8 m/US gal, 12.5 00 km.

SSIS integral; front suspension: independent, by Mc-son, coil springs/telescopic damper struts, anti-roll rear: independent, two semi-trailing arms, coil springs, oll bar, telescopic dampers.

RING recirculating ball, servo; turns lock to lock: 4.

KES disc (diameter front 10.6 in, 27.1 cm, rear 10.9 7.7 cm), dual circuit, servo.

TRICAL EQUIPMENT 12 V; 55 Ah battery; 55 A al-tor; Bosch distributor; 2 halogen headlamps.

ENSIONS AND WEIGHT wheel base: 105.6 in, 268 cm; s: 56.8 in, 144 cm front, 57.7 in, 146 cm rear; length: in, 481 cm; width: 68 in, 173 cm; height: 55.7 in, cm; ground clearance: 5.1 in, 13 cm; weight: 2,919 ,324 kg; weight distribution: 55% front, 45% rear; ng circle: 35.4 ft, 10.8 m; fuel tank: 16.5 imp gal, US gal, 75 l.

VAUXHALL Royale Saloon

BODY saloon/sedan; 4 doors; 4 seats, separate front seats, reclining backrests, headrests; tinted glass, electric glass, heated rear window.

PRACTICAL INSTRUCTIONS fuel: 98-100 oct petrol; oil: engine 9.8 imp pt, 11.6 US pt, 5.5 l, SAE 10W-50 change every 6,000 miles, 9,700 km - automatic transmission 10.6 imp pt, 12.7 US pt, 6 l, Dexron, change every 24,000 miles, 38,600 km - final drive 2.1 imp pt, 2.5 US pt, 1.2 l, SAE 90 no change recommended; greasing: none; valve timing: 32° 90° 72° 50°; tyre pressure: front 25 psi, 1.8 atm, rear 28 psi, 2 atm.

OPTIONALS mechanical gearbox; air-conditioning.

Royale Coupé

See Royale Saloon, except for:

PRICE EX WORKS: £ 8,248*

PERFORMANCE max speed: 121 mph, 194 km/h; power-weight ratio: 21 lb/hp (28.5 lb/kW), 9.5 kg/hp (12.9 kg/kW); carrying capacity: 1,158 lb, 525 kg; acceleration: 0-50 mph (0-80 km/h) 8 sec.

DIMENSIONS AND WEIGHT wheel base: 105 in, 267 cm; length: 184.7 in, 469 cm; width: 68.3 in, 173 cm; height: 54.3 in, 138 cm; ground clearance: 4.6 in, 12 cm; weight: 2,937 lb, 1,332 kg; weight distribution: 53.5% front, 46.5% rear; fuel tank: 15.4 imp gal, 18.5 US gal, 70 l.

BODY coupé; 3 doors.

VOLVO 66

VOLVO   HOLLAND

66 DL 2-door/3-door

ENGINE front, 4 stroke; 4 cylinders, vertical, in line; 67.6 cu in, 1,108 cc (2.76 x 2.83 in, 70 x 72 mm); compression ratio: 8.5:1; max power (DIN): 47 hp (34.6 kW) at 5,000 rpm; max torque (DIN): 54 lb ft, 7.6 kg m (74.5 Nm) at 2,700 rpm; max engine rpm: 6,200; 42.4 hp/l (31.2 kW/l); cast iron block, light alloy head; 5 crankshaft bearings; valves: overhead, in line, push-rods and rockers; camshafts: 1, side; lubrication: gear pump, full flow filter, 5.6 imp pt, 6.8 US pt, 3.2 l; 1 Solex 32 EHSAREN 577 carburettor; fuel feed: mechanical pump; water-cooled, 8.4 imp pt, 10.1 US pt, 4.8 l.

TRANSMISSION driving wheels: rear; clutch: automatic, centrifugal; transmission: C.V.T./transaxle automatic; gears: continuously variable ratio between 14.22:1 and 3.86:1; lever: central; width of rims: 4''; tyres: 135 SR x 14.

PERFORMANCE max speed: 85 mph, 136 km/h; power-weight ratio: 38.1 lb/hp (51.9 lb/kW), 17.3 kg/hp (23.6 kg/kW); carrying capacity: 849 lb, 385 kg; acceleration: 0-50 mph (0-80 km/h) 12.9 sec; consumption: 31.4 m/imp gal, 26.1 m/US gal, 9 l x 100 km.

CHASSIS integral; front suspension: independent, longitudinal torsion bars, telescopic damper struts, lower wishbones (trailing links), anti-roll bar; rear: de Dion rigid axle, semi-elliptic leafsprings, upper torque ams, telescopic dampers.

STEERING rack-and-pinion; turns lock to lock: 3.40.

BRAKES front disc, rear drum, servo; swept area: front 151.9 sq in, 980 sq cm, rear 74.4 sq in, 480 sq cm, total 226.3 sq in, 1,460 sq cm.

ELECTRICAL EQUIPMENT 12 V; 36 Ah battery; 500 W alternator; Ducellier distributor; 2 headlamps.

DIMENSIONS AND WEIGHT wheel base: 88.58 in, 225 cm; tracks: 51.57 in, 131 cm front, 48.82 in, 124 cm rear; length: 153.54 in, 390 cm; width: 59.84 in, 152 cm; height: 56.69 in, 144 cm; ground clearance: 4.72 in, 12 cm; weight: 1,797 lb, 815 kg; weight distribution: 56.2% front, 43.8% rear; turning circle: 32.1 ft, 9.8 m; fuel tank: 9.2 imp gal, 11.1 US gal, 42 l.

BODY saloon/sedan; 4-5 seats, separate front seats, reclining backrests, built-in headrests.

PRACTICAL INSTRUCTIONS fuel: 98 oct petrol; oil: engine 5.6 imp pt, 6.8 US pt, 3.2 l, SAE 10W-30 (summer) 20W-40 (winter), change every 3,100 miles, 5,000 km - C.V.T. automatic transmission 1.4 imp pt, 1.7 US pt, 0.8 l, SAE 80 EP, change every 12,400 miles, 20,000 km; greasing: none; tappet clearances: 0.006 in, 0.15 mm, exhaust 0.008 in, 0.20 mm; valve timing: 0°30' 36° 38°30' 5°; tyre pressure: front 22 psi, 1.6 atm, rear 26 psi, 1.8 atm.

OPTIONALS 155 SR x 13 tyres only with 4.5'' wide rims; sunshine roof.

66 GL 2-door/3-door

See 66 DL 2-door, except for:

ENGINE 78.7 cu in, 1,289 cc (2.87 x 3.03 in, 73 x 77 mm); max power (DIN): 57 hp (41.9 kW) at 5,200 rpm; max torque (DIN): 61 lb ft, 9.6 kg m (94.1 Nm) at 2,800 rpm; 44.2 hp/l (32.5 kW/l); 1 Solex 32 EHSAREN 596 carburettor.

TRANSMISSION width of rims: 4.5''; tyres: 155 SR x 13.

PERFORMANCE max speed: 90 mph, 145 km/h; power-weight ratio: 32.5 lb/hp (44.1 lb/kW), 14.7 kg/hp (20 kg/kW); carrying capacity: 915 lb, 415 kg; acceleration: 0-50 mph (0-80 km/h) 10.8 sec; consumption: 28.2 m/imp gal, 23.5 m/US gal, 10 l x 100 km.

ELECTRICAL EQUIPMENT 4 headlamps, 2 halogen.

DIMENSIONS AND WEIGHT width: 60.63 in, 154 cm; height: 54.33 in, 138 cm; weight: 1,846 lb, 837 kg; weight distribution: 56.3% front, 43.7% rear; turning circle: 31.2 ft, 9.5 m.

PRACTICAL INSTRUCTIONS tyre pressure: front 20 psi, 1.4 atm, rear 23 psi, 1.6 atm.

OPTIONALS metallic spray.

343 L/DL

PRICE IN GB: DL (manual) £ 3,350*
DL (automatic) £ 3,550*

ENGINE front, 4 stroke; 4 cylinders, vertical, in line; 85.2

VOLVO 343 DL

343 L/DL

cu in, 1,397 cc (2.99 x 3.03 in, 76 x 77 mm); compression ratio: 9.5:1; max power (DIN): 70 hp (51.5 kW) at 5,500 rpm; max torque (DIN): 80 lb ft, 11 kg m (107.9 Nm) at 3,500 rpm; max engine rpm: 6,000; 50.1 hp/l (36.9 kW/l); cast iron block, wet liners, light alloy head; 5 crankshaft bearings; valves: overhead, in line, slanted, push-rods and rockers; camshafts: 1, side; lubrication: gear pump, full flow filter, 6.2 imp pt, 7.4 US pt, 3.5 l; 1 Weber 32 DIR 57-8400 downdraught carburettor; fuel feed: mechanical pump; sealed circuit cooling, 10.6 imp pt, 12.7 US pt, 6 l, electric fan.

TRANSMISSION driving wheels: rear; clutch: single dry plate (diaphragm), or automatic, centrifugal; gearbox: mechanical, or C.V.T./transaxle automatic; gears: 4, fully synchronized; ratios: I 3.705, II 2.159, III 1.369, IV 1 or, continuously variable between 14.22:1 and 3.86:1; lever: central; final drive: hypoid bevel; axle ratio: 3.909; width of rims: 5''; tyres: 155 SR x 13.

PERFORMANCE max speed: 90 mph, 145 km/h; power-weight ratio: 30.8 lb/hp (41.9 lb/kW), 14 kg/hp (19 kg/kW); carrying capacity: 931 lb, 422 kg; acceleration: 0-50 mph (0-80 km/h) 10.5 sec; consumption: 31.4 m/imp gal, 26.1 m/US gal, 9 l x 100 km.

CHASSIS integral; front suspension: independent, by McPherson, lower wishbones, coil springs/telescopic damper struts, anti-roll bar; rear: De Dion rigid axle, single leaf semi-elliptic springs, swinging longitudinal trailing arm, telescopic dampers.

STEERING rack-and-pinion; turns lock to lock: 4.10.

BRAKES front disc, rear drum, servo; lining area: front 17.4 sq in, 112 sq cm, rear 37.7 sq in, 243 sq cm, total 55.1 sq in, 355 sq cm.

ELECTRICAL EQUIPMENT 12 V; 36 Ah battery; 700 W alternator; Ducellier distributor; 2 headlamps.

DIMENSIONS AND WEIGHT wheel base: 94.09 in, 239 cm; tracks: 53.15 in, 135 cm front, 54.33 in, 138 cm rear; length: 164.96 in, 419 cm; width: 65.35 in, 166 cm; height: 54.72 in, 139 cm; ground clearance: 5.31 in, 13.5 cm; weight: 2,156 lb, 978 kg; weight distribution: 53.7% front, 46.3% rear; turning circle: 30.2 ft, 9.2 m; fuel tank 9.9 imp gal, 11.9 US gal, 45 l.

BODY saloon/sedan; 2 + 1 doors; 4-5 seats, separate front seats, reclining backrests with built-in headrests; detachable back seat; folding rear seat; heated rear window.

PRACTICAL INSTRUCTIONS fuel: 98 oct petrol; oil: engine 6.2 imp pt, 7.4 US pt, 3.5 l, SAE 10W-30 (summer) SAE 20W-40 (winter), change every 6,200 miles, 10,000 km - gearbox: 3.7 imp pt, 4.4 US pt, 2.1 l, ATF Type; final drive: 2.5 imp pt, 3.0 US pt, 1.45 l, API - GL - 5; C.V.T. automatic transmission 1.4 imp pt, 1.7 US pt, 0.8 l, SAE 80 EP, change every 12,400 miles, 20,000 km; greasing: none; tappet clearances: inlet 0.006 in, 0.15 mm, exhaust 0.006 in, 0.15 mm; tyre pressure: front 24 psi, 1.7 atm, rear 28 psi, 2 atm.

OPTIONALS (for DL models only) 175/70 SR x 13 tyres; sunshine roof: tinted glass; metallic spray; halogen headlamps; headlamps with wiper/washers; vinyl upholstery.

VOLVO 343 (mechanical gearbox)

ALFA ROMEO   ITAL

Alfasud Series

PRICES IN GB AND EX WORKS:

		£	liras
1	4-dr Berlina	—	4,154,0*
2	Super 4-dr Berlina	—	4,685,0*
3	Super 1.3 4-dr Berlina	3,100*	4,873,0*
4	Giardinetta 1.3 3-dr		5,168,0*
5	ti 1.3 2-dr Berlina	3,349*	4,865,0*
6	ti 1.5 2-dr Berlina	3,499*	5,481,0*
7	Sprint 1.3 Coupé		6,431,0*
8	Sprint 1.5 Coupé	4,299*	6,708,0*

Power team:	Standard for:	Optional for:
63 hp	1,2	—
71 hp	3,4	—
79 hp	5,7	—
84 hp	6,8	—

63 hp power team

ENGINE front, 4 stroke; 4 cylinders, horizontally oppos 72.4 cu in, 1,186 cc (3.15 x 2.32 in, 80 x 59 mm); compr sion ratio: 8.8:1; max power (DIN): 63 hp (46.4 kW) 6,000 rpm; max torque (DIN): 65 lb ft, 9 kg m (88.3 N at 3,200 rpm; max engine rpm: 6,000; 53.1 hp/l (3 kW/l); cast iron block, light alloy head; 3 crankshaft be ings; valves: overhead, in line, thimble tappets, new va adjustment patented by Alfa Romeo; camshafts: 2, 1 bank, overhead, cogged belt; lubrication: gear pump, flow filter (cartridge), 7 imp pt, 8.5 US pt, 4 l; 1 So C32 DIS/40 or Dell'Orto FRDA 32F downdraught single ba carburettor; fuel feed: mechanical pump; water-cooled, 1 imp pt, 15.4 US pt, 7.3 l, electric thermostatic fan.

TRANSMISSION driving wheels: front; clutch: single plate (diaphragm), hydraulically controlled; gearbox: r chanical; gears: 4 (for Super 5), fully synchronized; rati I 3.545, II 1.941, III 1.292, IV 0.966, rev 3.091 (for Su I 3.545, II 2.062, III 1.434, IV 1.115, V 0.931, rev 3.091); lev central; final drive: hypoid bevel; axle ratio: 4.111 - Su 3.888; width of rims: 5''; tyres: 165/70 SR x 13.

PERFORMANCE max speeds: (I) 26 mph, 42 km/h; 48 mph, 77 km/h; (III) 71 mph, 115 km/h; (IV) over mph, 150 km/h; power-weight ratio: 30.1 lb/hp (40.8 lb/k 13.6 kg/hp (18.5 kg/kW); carrying capacity: 882 lb, 400 speed in top at 1,000 rpm: 16 mph, 25.7 km/h; consur tion at 62 mph, 100 km/h: 39.2 m/imp gal, 32.7 m/US 7.2 l x 100 km - Super 41.5 m/imp gal, 34.6 m/US 6.8 l x 100 km.

CHASSIS integral; front suspension: independent, McPherson, coil springs/telescopic damper struts, lov trailing links, anti-roll bar; rear: rigid axle, longitudi Watt linkage, Panhard transverse linkage bar, coil sprin telescopic dampers.

STEERING rack-and-pinion, adjustable height of steer wheel; turns lock to lock: 3.40.

ALFA ROMEO Alfasud Super 1.3 4-dr Berlina

BRAKES disc (front diameter 10.16 in, 25.8 cm, rear 9.17 in, 23.3 cm), rear compensator, servo; swept area: front 193 sq in, 1,245 sq cm, rear 155.5 sq in, 1,003 sq cm, total 348.5 sq in, 2,248 sq cm.

ELECTRICAL EQUIPMENT 12 V; 43 Ah battery; 600 W alternator; 2 headlamps.

DIMENSIONS AND WEIGHT wheel base: 96.65 in, 245 cm; tracks: 54.49 in, 138 cm front, 53.19 in, 135 cm rear; length: 153.15 in, 389 cm; width: 62.48 in, 159 cm; height: 53.15 in, 137 cm; ground clearance: 5.91 in, 15 cm; weight: 1,896 lb, 860 kg; turning circle: 30.8 ft, 9.4 m; fuel tank: 11 imp gal, 13.2 US gal, 50 l.

BODY 5 seats, separate front seats, reclining backrests; heated rear window.

PRACTICAL INSTRUCTIONS fuel: 98-100 oct petrol; oil: engine 7 imp pt, 8.5 US pt, 4 l, SAE 20W-50, change every 6,200 miles, 10,000 km - gearbox and final drive 6 imp pt, 7.2 US pt, 3.4 l, SAE 90, change every 24,900 miles, 40,000 km; greasing: none; tappet clearances: inlet 0.014-0.016 in, 0.35-0.40 mm, exhaust 0.018-0.020 in, 0.45-0.50 mm; valve timing: 12° 48° 45° 7°; tyre pressure: front 28 psi, 1.9 atm, rear 21 psi, 1.5 atm.

OPTIONALS antitheft.

71 hp power team

See 63 hp powre team, except for:

ENGINE 82.4 cu in, 1,351 cc (3.15 x 2.65 in, 80 x 67.2 mm); compression ratio: 9:1; max power (DIN): 71 hp (52.2 kW) at 5,800 rpm; max torque (DIN): 77.5 lb ft, 10.7 kg m (104.9 Nm) at 3,000 rpm; 52.6 hp/l (38.7 kW/l); 1 Solex C32 DIS/41 or Dell'Orto FRDA 32 G downdraught single barrel carburettor.

TRANSMISSION gears: 5, fully synchronized; ratios: I 3.545, II 2.062, III 1.434, IV 1.115, V 0.931, rev 3.091; axle ratio: 3.888.

PERFORMANCE max speed: over 96 mph, 155 km/h; power-weight ratio: Super 27 lb/hp (36.7 lb/kW), 12.2 kg/hp (16.7 kg/kW) - Giardinetta 28.4 lb/hp (38.6 lb/kW), 12.9 kg/hp (17.7 kg/kW); consumption at 62 mph, 100 km/h: Super 40.9 m/imp gal, 34.1 m/US gal, 6.9 l x 100 km - Giardinetta 40.4 m/imp gal, 33.6 m/US gal, 7 l x 100 km.

DIMENSIONS AND WEIGHT length: Super 154.72 in, 393 cm - Giardinetta 156.30 in, 397 cm; weight: Super 1,918 lb, 870 kg - Giardinetta 2,018 lb, 915 kg.

OPTIONALS (for Super only) light alloy wheels; metallic spray.

79 hp power team

See 63 hp power team, except for:

ENGINE 82.4 cu in, 1,351 cc (3.15 x 2.65 in, 80 x 67.2 mm); compression ratio: 9:1; max power (DIN): 79 hp (58.1 kW) at 6,000 rpm; max torque (DIN): 89.1 lb ft, 12.3 kg m

ALFA ROMEO Alfasud ti 1.3 - 1.5 2-dr Berlina

ALFA ROMEO Alfasud Sprint 1.3 - 1.5 Coupé

FA ROMEO Alfasud Sprint 1.3 - 1.5 Coupé

(110.8 Nm) at 3,500 rpm; 58.5 hp/l (43 kW/l); 1 Weber 32 DIR 81/250 downdraught twin barrel carburettor.

TRANSMISSION gears: 5, fully synchronized; ratios: I 3.545, II 2.062, III 1.434, IV 1.115, V 0.931, rev 3.091; axle ratio: 3.888.

PERFORMANCE max speed: 103 mph, 165 km/h; power-weight ratio: ti 24.3 lb/hp (33 lb/kW), 11 kg/hp (15 kg/kW) - Sprint 24.8 lb/hp (33.8 lb/kW), 11.3 kg/hp (15.3 kg/kW); speed in top at 1,000 rpm: 17.9 mph, 28.8 km/h; consumption at 62 mph, 100 km/h: ti 42.1 m/imp gal, 35.1 m/US gal, 6.7 l x 100 km - Sprint 41.5 m/imp gal, 34.6 m/US gal, 6.8 l x 100 km.

ELECTRICAL EQUIPMENT 4 iodine headlamps.

DIMENSIONS AND WEIGHT length: ti 154.72 in, 393 cm - Sprint 158.27 in, 402 cm; width: Sprint 63.39 in, 161 cm; height: Sprint 49.61 in, 126 cm; ground clearance: Sprint 6.30 in, 16 cm; weight: ti 1,918 lb, 870 kg - Sprint 1,962 lb, 890 kg.

OPTIONALS light alloy wheels; metallic spray; adjustable headrests.

84 hp power team

See 63 hp power team, except for:

ENGINE 90.9 cu in, 1,490 cc (3.31 x 2.65 in, 84 x 67.2 mm); compression ratio: 9:1; max power (DIN): 84 hp (61.8 kW) at 5,800 rpm; max torque (DIN): 89.1 lb ft, 12.3 kg m (120.6

Nm) at 3,500 rpm; max engine rpm: 5,800; 57 hp/l (41.5 kW/l); 1 Weber 32 DIR 71/250 downdraught twin barrel carburettor.

TRANSMISSION gears: 5, fully synchronized; ratios: I 3.545, II 2.048, III 1.452, IV 1.114, V 0.921, rev 3.091; axle ratio: 3.888.

PERFORMANCE max speed: 105 mph, 170 km/h; power-weight ratio: ti 22.8 lb/hp (31 lb/kW) - Sprint 23.3 lb/hp (31.7 lb/kW); speed in top at 1,000 rpm: 17.9 mph, 28.8 km/h; consumption at 62 mph, 100 km/h: ti 40.9 m/imp gal, 34.1 m/US gal, 6.9 l x 100 km - Sprint 40.3 m/imp gal, 33.6 m/US gal, 7 l x 100 km.

ELECTRICAL EQUIPMENT 4 iodine headlamps.

DIMENSIONS AND WEIGHT length: ti 154.72 in, 393 cm - Sprint 158.27 in, 402 cm; width: Sprint 63.39 in, 161 cm; height: Sprint 49.61 in, 126 cm; ground clearance: Sprint 6.30 in, 16 cm; weight: ti 1,940 lb, 880 kg - Sprint 1,984 lb, 900 kg.

OPTIONALS light alloy wheels; metallic spray.

Spider Junior 1300

PRICE EX WORKS: 6,927,000* liras

ENGINE front, 4 stroke; 4 cylinders, vertical, in line; 78.7 cu in, 1,290 cc (2.91 x 2.95 in, 74 x 75 mm); compression ratio: 9:1; max power (SAE): 103 hp (75.8 kW) at 6,000 rpm; max torque (SAE): 101 lb ft, 14 kg m (137.3 Nm)

SPIDER JUNIOR 1300

at 3,200 rpm; max engine rpm: 6,000; 79.8 hp/l (58.7 kW/l); light alloy block and head, wet liners, hemispherical combustion chambers; 5 crankshaft bearings; valves: overhead, Vee-slanted at 80°, thimble tappets; camshafts: 2, overhead; lubrication: gear pump, full flow filter (cartridge), 12.7 imp pt, 15.2 US pt, 7.2 l; 2 Weber (or Solex or Dell'Orto) 40 DCOE 28 horizontal twin barrel carburettors; fuel feed: mechanical pump; water-cooled, 13.2 imp pt, 15.9 US pt, 7.5 l.

TRANSMISSION driving wheels: rear; clutch: single dry plate (diaphragm), hydraulically controlled; gearbox: mechanical; gears: 5, fully synchronized; ratios: I 3.300, II 1.990, III 1.350, IV 1, V 0.860, rev 3.010; lever: central; final drive: hypoid bevel; axle ratio: 4.555; width of rims: 4.5''; tyres: 155 SR x 15.

PERFORMANCE max speeds: (I) 27 mph, 44 km/h; (II) 46 mph, 74 km/h; (III) 67 mph, 108 km/h; (IV) 91 mph, 146 km/h; (V) over 106 mph, 170 km/h; power-weight ratio: 21.2 lb/hp (28.9 lb/kW), 9.6 kg/hp (13.1 kg/kW); carrying capacity: 706 lb, 320 kg; acceleration: standing ¼ mile 19.1 sec; speed in top at 1,000 rpm: 18.2 mph, 29.3 km/h; consumption: 28.5 m/imp gal, 23.8 m/US gal, 9.9 l x 100 km.

CHASSIS integral; front suspension: independent, wishbones, coil springs, anti-roll bar, telescopic dampers; rear: rigid axle, trailing lower radius arms, upper transverse

Spider Junior 1600

See Spider Junior 1300, except for:

PRICE EX WORKS: 7,257,000* liras

ENGINE 95.8 cu in, 1,570 cc (3.07 x 3.28 in, 78 x 82 mm); max power (SAE): 116 hp (85.4 kW) at 5,500 rpm; max torque (SAE): 120 lb ft, 16.5 kg m (161.8 Nm) at 2,900 rpm; 73.8 hp/l (54.3 kW/l); 2 Weber (or Solex or Dell'Orto) 40 DCOE 33 horizontal twin barrel carburettors.

PERFORMANCE max speed: over 109 mph, 175 km/h; power-weight ratio: 19.4 lb/hp (26.2 lb/kW), 8.8 kg/hp (11.9 kg/kW); acceleration: standing ¼ mile 18 sec; speed in top at 1,000 rpm: 19.8 mph, 31.8 km/h; consumption: 33.2 m/imp gal, 27.7 m/US gal, 8.5 l x 100 km.

DIMENSIONS AND WEIGHT weight: 2,249 lb, 1,020 kg.

Giulietta 1.3

PRICE EX WORKS: 7,074,000* liras

ENGINE front, 4 stroke; 4 cylinders, vertical, in line; 82.8 cu in, 1,357 cc (3.15 x 2.66 in, 80 x 67.5 mm); compression ratio: 9:1; max power (DIN): 95 hp (69.9 kW) at 6,000 rpm; max torque (DIN): 89 lb ft, 12.3 kg m (120.6 Nm) at 4,500 rpm; max engine rpm: 6,100; 70 hp/l (51.5 kW/l); light

ALFA ROMEO Giulietta 1.3 - 1.6

alloy block and head, wet liners, hemispherical combustion chambers; 5 crankshaft bearings; valves: overhead, Vee-slanted at 80°; camshafts: 2, overhead, chain drive; lubrication: gear pump, full flow filter (cartridge), 11.4 imp pt, 13.7 US pt, 6.5 l; 2 Solex Cho ADDHE downdraught twin barrel carburettors; fuel feed: mechanical pump; water-cooled, 14.1 imp pt, 16.9 US pt, 8 l.

TRANSMISSION driving wheels: rear; clutch: single plate (diaphragm), hydraulically controlled; gearbox: mechanical, in unit with differential; gears: 5 fully synchronized; ratios: I 3.307, II 1.956, III 1.345, IV 1.026, V 0.833, rev 2.615; lever: central; final drive: hypoid bevel; axle ratio: 4.778; width of rims: 5''; tyres: 165 SR x 13.

PERFORMANCE max speed: (I) 25 mph, 41 km/h; (II) 43 mph, 70 km/h; (III) 63 mph, 101 km/h; (IV) 83 mph, 134 km/h; (V) 103 mph, 165 km/h; power-weight ratio: 24.9 lb/hp (33.7 lb/kW), 11.3 kg/hp (15.3 kg/kW); carrying capacity: 882 lb, 400 kg; acceleration: standing ¼ mile 18 sec; speed in top at 1,000 rpm: 16.9 mph, 27.2 km/h; consumption: 37.7 m/imp gal, 31.4 m/US gal, 7.5 l x 100 km.

CHASSIS integral; front suspension: independent, wishbones (upper trailing links), torsion bars, anti-roll bar, telescopic dampers; rear: de Dion rigid axle, oblique trailing arms, transverse Watt linkage, coil springs, anti-roll bar, telescopic dampers.

STEERING rack-and-pinion, adjustable height of steering wheel; turns lock to lock: 3.50

ALFA ROMEO Giulietta 1.6

Vee radius arms, coil springs, anti-roll bar, telescopic dampers.

STEERING recirculating ball or worm and roller; turns lock to lock: 3.70.

BRAKES disc (diameter 10.51 in, 26.7 cm), rear compensator, servo; swept area: front 184.5 sq in, 1,190 sq cm, rear 167.1 sq in, 1,078 sq cm, total 351.6 sq in, 2,268 sq cm.

ELECTRICAL EQUIPMENT 12 V; 50 Ah battery; 540 W alternator; Bosch distributor; 2 headlamps.

DIMENSIONS AND WEIGHT wheel base: 88.58 in, 225 cm; tracks: 52.13 in, 132 cm front, 50.16 in, 127 cm rear; length: 162.20 in, 412 cm; width: 64.17 in, 163 cm; height: 50.79 in, 129 cm; ground clearance: 4.72 in, 12 cm; weight: 2,183 lb, 990 kg; turning circle: 34.4 ft, 10.5 m; fuel tank: 10.1 imp gal, 12.1 US gal, 46 l.

BODY convertible; 2 doors; 2+2 seats. separate front seats.

PRACTICAL INSTRUCTIONS fuel: 98-100 oct petrol; oil: engine 12.7 imp pt, 15.2 US pt, 7.2 l, SAE 20W-40, change every 6,200 miles, 10,000 km - gearbox 3.2 imp pt, 3.8 US pt, 1.8 l, SAE 90 EP, change every 18,600 miles, 30,000 km - final drive 2.5 imp pt, 3 US pt, 1.4 l, SAE 90 EP, change every 18,600 miles, 30,000 km; greasing: every 7,500 miles, 12,000 km, 1 point; tappet clearances: inlet 0.019-0.020 in, 0.48-0.50 mm, exhaust 0.021-0.022 in, 0.53-0.55 mm; valve timing: 36°50' 60°50' 54°10' 30°10'; tyre pressure: front 24 psi, 1.7 atm, rear 26 psi, 1.8 atm.

OPTIONALS 165 SR x 14 tyres with 5'' wide rims; adjustable headrests; hardtop; metallic spray; sport steering wheel.

ALFA ROMEO Giulietta 1.6

BRAKES disc (diameter 9.84 in, 25 cm), rear compensator, servo; swept area: front 173.3 sq in, 1,118 sq cm, rear 156.6 sq in, 1,010 sq cm, total 329.9 sq in, 2,128 sq cm.

ELECTRICAL EQUIPMENT 12 V; 50 Ah battery; 540 W alternator; Bosch or Marelli distributor; 2 iodine headlamps.

DIMENSIONS AND WEIGHT wheel base: 98.82 in, 251 cm; front and rear track: 53.54 in, 136 cm; length: 165.75 in, 421 cm; width: 64.96 in, 165 cm; height: 55.12 in, 140 cm; ground clearance: 5.51 in, 14 cm; weight: 2,359 lb, 1,070 kg; weight distribution: 50% front, 50% rear; turning circle: 35.8 ft, 10.9 m; fuel tank: 11 imp gal, 13.2 US gal, 50 l.

BODY saloon/sedan; 4 doors; 5 seats, separate front seats, reclining backrests, adjustable headrests; heated rear window.

PRACTICAL INSTRUCTIONS fuel: 98 oct petrol; oil: engine 11.4 imp pt, 13.7 US pt, 6.5 l, SAE 10W-50, change every 6,200 miles, 10,000 km - gearbox 4.9 imp pt, 5.9 US pt, 2.8 l, SAE 90, change every 24,900 miles, 40,000 km; tappet clearances: inlet 0.019-0.020 in, 0.47-0.50 mm, exhaust 0.020-0.022 in, 0.52-0.55 mm; valve timing: 33°54′ 57°54′ 51°14′ 21°14′; tyre pressure: front 26 psi, 1.8 atm, rear 28 psi, 2 atm.

OPTIONALS metallic spray; light alloy wheels; tinted glass.

Giulietta 1.6

See Giulietta 1.3, except for:

PRICE IN GB: £ 4,499*
PRICE EX WORKS: 7,428,000* liras

ENGINE 95.8 cu in, 1,570 cc (3.07 x 3.23 in, 78 x 82 mm); max power (DIN): 109 hp (80.2 kW) at 5,600 rpm; max torque (DIN): 105 lb ft, 14.5 kg m (142.2 Nm) at 4,300 rpm; max engine rpm: 5,800; 69.4 hp/l (51.1 kW/l); 2 Dell'Orto DHLA 40H downdraught twin barrel carburettors.

TRANSMISSION axle ratio: 4.300.

PERFORMANCE max speeds: (I) 26 mph, 42 km/h; (II) 45 mph, 72 km/h; (III) 65 mph, 105 km/h; (IV) 86 mph, 138 km/h; (V) 109 mph, 175 km/h; power-weight ratio: 21.6 lb/hp (29.3 lb/kW), 9.8 kg/hp (13.3 kg/kW); acceleration: standing ¼ mile 17.6 sec; speed in top at 1,000 rpm: 18.8 mph, 30.2 km/h; consumption: 36.2 m/imp gal, 30.2 m/US gal, 7.8 l x 100 km.

OPTIONALS air-conditioning.

Alfetta 1.6

PRICE EX WORKS: 7,599,000* liras

ENGINE front, 4 stroke; 4 cylinders, vertical, in line; 95.8 cu in, 1,570 cc (3.07 x 3.23 in, 78 x 82 mm); compression ratio: 9:1; max power (DIN): 108 hp (79.5 kW) at 5,600 rpm; max torque (DIN): 105 lb ft, 14.5 kg m (142.2 Nm) at 4,300 rpm; max engine rpm: 5,600; 68.8 hp/l (50.6 kW/l); light alloy block and head, wet liners, hemispherical combustion chambers; 5 crankshaft bearings; valves: overhead, Vee-slanted at 80°, thimble tappets; camshafts: 2, overhead; lubrication: gear pump, full flow filter (cartridge), 11.4 imp pt, 13.7 US pt, 6.5 l; 2 Dell'Orto DHLA 40F horizontal twin barrel carburettors; fuel feed: mechanical pump; water-cooled, 14.1 imp pt, 16.9 US pt, 8 l, electric thermostatic fan.

TRANSMISSION driving wheels: rear; clutch: single dry plate (diaphragm), hydraulically controlled; gearbox: mechanical, in unit with differential; gears: 5, fully synchronized; ratios: I 3.300, II 2.000, III 1.370, IV 1.040, V 0.830, rev 3.620; lever: central; final drive: hypoid bevel; axle ratio: 4.300; width of rims: 5.5''; tyres: 165 SR x 14.

PERFORMANCE max speeds: (I) 28 mph, 45 km/h; (II) 47 mph, 75 km/h; (III) 68 mph, 109 km/h; (IV) 90 mph, 145 km/h; (V) 109 mph, 175 km/h; power-weight ratio: 21.2 lb/hp (28.9 lb/kW), 9.6 kg/hp (13.1 kg/kW); carrying capacity: 882 lb, 400 kg; acceleration: standing ¼ mile 18 sec; speed in top at 1,000 rpm: 19.4 mph, 31.2 km/h; consumption: 33.6 m/imp gal, 28 m/US gal, 8.4 l x 100 km.

CHASSIS integral; front suspension: independent, wishbones (upper trailing links), torsion bars, anti-roll bar, telescopic dampers; rear: de Dion rigid axle, oblique trailing arms, transverse Watt linkage, coil springs, anti-roll bar, telescopic dampers.

STEERING rack-and-pinion, adjustable height of steering wheel; turns lock to lock: 3.50.

BRAKES disc, rear compensator, servo; swept area: front 182.3 sq in, 1,176 sq cm, rear 156.6 sq in, 1,010 sq cm, total 338.9 sq in, 2,186 sq cm.

ELECTRICAL EQUIPMENT 12 V; 50 Ah battery; 540 W alternator; Bosch or Marelli distributor; 4 iodine headlamps.

ALFA ROMEO Alfetta 1.6 - 1.8

ALFA ROMEO Alfetta 2000 L

DIMENSIONS AND WEIGHT wheel base: 98.82 in, 251 cm; tracks: 53.54 in, 136 cm front, 53.15 in, 135 cm rear; length: 168.50 in, 428 cm; width: 63.78 in, 162 cm; height: 56.30 in, 143 cm; ground clearance: 4.92 in, 12.5 cm; weight: 2,293 lb, 1,040 kg; weight distribution: 50% front, 50% rear; turning circle: 33.1 ft, 10.1 m; fuel tank: 10.8 imp gal, 12.9 US gal, 49 l.

BODY saloon/sedan; 4 doors; 5 seats, separate front seats, reclining backrests; heated rear window.

PRACTICAL INSTRUCTIONS fuel: 98 oct petrol; oil: engine 10.4 imp pt, 12.5 US pt, 5.9 l, SAE 20W-50, change every 6,200 miles, 10,000 km - gearbox and final drive 4.9 imp pt, 5.9 US pt, 2.8 l, SAE 90, change every 18,600 miles, 30,000 km; greasing: none; tappet clearances: inlet 0.019-0.020 in, 0.47-0.50 mm, exhaust 0.020-0.022 in, 0.52-0.55 mm; valve timing: 41°20′ 60°20′ 62°40′ 25°40′; tyre pressure: front 22 psi, 1.6 atm, rear 26 psi, 1.8 atm.

OPTIONALS adjustable headrests; Texalfa interior; light alloy wheels; metallic spray; tinted glass; adjustable headrests.

Alfetta GT 1.6

See Alfetta 1.6, except for:

PRICE IN GB: £ 4,999*
PRICE EX WORKS: 8,077,000* liras

PERFORMANCE max speeds: 112 mph, 180 km/h; power-weight ratio: 20.3 lb/hp (27.6 lb/kW), 9.2 kg/hp (12.5

kg/kW); consumption: 34 m/imp gal, 28.3 m/US gal, 8.3 l x 100 km.

DIMENSIONS AND WEIGHT wheel base: 94.49 in, 240 cm; rear track: 53.54 in, 136 cm; length: 164.96 in, 419 cm; width: 65.35 in, 166 cm; height: 52.36 in, 133 cm; ground clearance: 4.80 in, 12 cm; weight: 2,183 lb, 990 kg.

BODY coupé; 2 doors; 4 seats, separate front seats, reclining backrests.

OPTIONALS 185/70 HR x 14 tyres.

Alfetta 1.8

See Alfetta 1.6, except for:

PRICE EX WORKS: 7,953,000* liras

ENGINE 108.6 cu in, 1,779 cc (3.15 x 3.48 in, 80 x 88.5 mm); compression ratio: 9.5:1; max power (DIN): 118 hp (86.8 kW) at 5,300 rpm; max torque (DIN): 123 lb ft, 17 kg m (166.7 Nm) at 4,400 rpm; max engine rpm: 5,300; 66.3 hp/l (48.8 kW/l); 2 Dell'Orto DHLA 40 (or Solex C40 DDHE or Weber 40 DCOE 32) horizontal twin barrel carburettors.

TRANSMISSION axle ratio: 4.100.

PERFORMANCE max speeds: (I) 29 mph, 46 km/h; (II) 48 mph, 77 km/h; (III) 70 mph, 112 km/h; (IV) 92 mph, 148 km/h; (V) 112 mph, 180 km/h; power-weight ratio:

ALFETTA 1.8

19.8 lb/hp (26.9 lb/kW), 9 kg/hp (12.2 kg/kW); acceleration: standing ¼ mile 17.3 sec; speed in top at 1,000 rpm: 20.8 mph, 33.5 km/h; consumption: 32.1 m/imp gal, 26.7 m/US gal, 8.8 l x 100 km.

DIMENSIONS AND WEIGHT weight: 2,337 lb, 1,060 kg.

OPTIONALS air-conditioning with tinted glass.

Alfetta 2000 L

See Alfetta 1.6, except for:

PRICE IN GB: £ 4,999*
PRICE EX WORKS: 9,192.000* liras

ENGINE 119.7 cu in, 1,962 cc (3.31 x 3.48 in, 84 x 88.5 mm); max power (DIN): 130 hp (95.6 kW) at 5,400 rpm; max torque (DIN): 131.1 lb ft, 18.1 kg m (177.5 Nm) at 4,000 rpm; max engine rpm: 5,400; 66.2 hp/l (48.7 kW/l); 2 Dell'Orto DHLA 40 horizontal twin barrel carburettors.

TRANSMISSION axle ratio: 4.100; tyres: 165 HR x 14.

PERFORMANCE max speeds: (I) 28 mph, 45 km/h; (II) 46 mph, 74 km/h; (III) 68 mph, 109 km/h; (IV) 89 mph, 143 km/h; (V) 115 mph, 185 km/h; power-weight ratio: 18.5 lb/hp, (24.1 lb/kW), 8.4 kg/hp (11.4 kg/kW); acceleration: standing ¼ mile 16.4 sec; speed in top at 1,000 rpm: 20.6 mph, 33.2 km/h; consumption: 29.7 m/imp gal, 24.8 m/US gal, 9.5 l x 100 km.

ELECTRICAL EQUIPMENT 60 Ah battery.

DIMENSIONS AND WEIGHT rear track: 53.46 in, 136 cm; length: 172.64 in, 438 cm; width: 64.57 in, 164 cm; ground clearance: 5.51 in, 14 cm; weight: 2,403 lb, 1,090 kg.

PRACTICAL INSTRUCTIONS valve timing: 41°20' 60°20 53°40' 34°40'; tyre pressure: front 26 psi, 1.8 atm, rear 26 psi, 1.8 atm.

OPTIONALS ZF automatic transmission; limited slip differential; automatic levelling system; 185/70 HR x 14 tyres; light alloy wheels; metallic spray; air-conditioning. sunshine roof.

Alfetta GTV 2000

See Alfetta 1.6, except for:

PRICE IN GB: £ 5,999*
PRICE IN USA: $ 10,495*

ENGINE 119.7 cu in, 1,962 cc (3.31 x 3.48 in, 84 x 88.5 mm); max power (DIN): 130 hp (95.6 kW) at 5,400 rpm; max torque (DIN): 131.1 lb ft, 18.1 kg m (177.5 Nm) at 4,000 rpm; max engine rpm: 5,400; 66.2 hp/l (48.7 kW/l); 2 twin barrel carburettors.

ALFA ROMEO Alfetta 2000 L

ALFA ROMEO Alfetta GTV 2000

TRANSMISSION axle ratio: 4,100; tyres: 165 HR x 14.

PERFORMANCE max speed: 121 mph, 194 km/h; power-weight ratio: 16.8 lb/hp, (22.8 lb/kW), 7.6 kg/hp (10.3 kg/kW); speed in top at 1,000 rpm: 20.8 mph, 33.5 km/h; consumption: 31.4 m/imp gal, 26.1 m/US gal, 9 l x 100 km.

ELECTRICAL EQUIPMENT 60 Ah battery.

DIMENSIONS AND WEIGHT wheel base: 94.49 in, 240 cm; rear track: 53.54 in, 136 cm; length: 165.35 in, 420 cm; width: 65.35 in, 166 cm; height: 52.36 in, 133 cm; ground clearance: 4.80 in, 12 cm; weight: 2,183 lb, 990 kg.

BODY coupé; 2 doors; 4 seats, separate front seats, reclining backrests.

PRACTICAL INSTRUCTIONS valve timing: 41°20' 60°20 53°40' 34°40'.

OPTIONALS 185/70 HR x 14 tyres; light alloy wheels; metallic spray; air-conditioning.

2000 Spider Veloce

PRICE IN GB: £ 7,499*
PRICE IN USA: $ 11,195*

ENGINE front, 4 stroke; 4 cylinders, vertical, in line; 119. cu in, 1,962 cc (3.31 x 3.48 in, 84 x 88.5 mm); compression ratio: 9:1; max power (SAE): 147 hp (108.2 kW) at 5,30 rpm; max torque (SAE): 151 lb ft, 20.9 kg m (205 Nm at 4,400 rpm; max engine rpm: 5,300; 74.9 hp/l (55.1 kW/l) light alloy block and head, wet liners, hemispherical com bustion chambers; 5 crankshaft bearings; valves: overhead Vee-slanted at 80°, thimble tappets; camshafts: 2, overhead lubrication: gear pump, full flow filter (cartridge), 12.7 im pt, 15.2 US pt, 7.2 l; 2 Solex C 40 DDH5 or Dell'Orto DHL 40 horizontal twin barrel carburettors; fuel feed: mechanica pump; water-cooled, 17.1 imp pt, 20.5 US pt, 9.7 l.

TRANSMISSION driving wheels: rear; clutch: single dr plate, hydraulically controlled; gearbox: mechanical; gears 5, fully synchronized; ratios: I 3.300, II 1.990, III 1.350, I 1, V 0.790, rev 3.010; lever: central; final drive: hypo bevel, limited slip differential; axle ratio: 4.100; width rims: 5.5''; tyres: 165 HR x 14.

PERFORMANCE max speeds: (I) 29 mph, 47 km/h; (II) 4 mph, 77 km/h; (III) 71 mph, 114 km/h; (IV) 96 mph, 15 km/h; (V) over 121 mph, 195 km/h; power-weight rati 15.7 lb/hp (21.2 lb/kW), 7.1 kg/hp (9.6 kg/kW); carryir capacity: 772 lb, 350 kg; acceleration: standing ¼ mi 16.8 sec; speed in top at 1,000 rpm: 20.9 mph, 33.7 km/ consumption: 23.7 m/imp gal, 19.8 m/US gal, 11.9 l x 100 km.

CHASSIS integral; front suspension: independent, wishbone (lower trailing links), coil springs, anti-roll bar, telescop dampers; rear: rigid axle, trailing lower radius arms, upp transverse Vee radius arm, coil springs, anti-roll ba telescopic dampers.

STEERING recirculating ball or worm and roller; turns lo to lock: 3.70.

BRAKES disc, rear compensator, servo; swept area: fro 229.8 sq in, 1,482 sq cm, rear 167.1 sq in, 1,078 sq c total 396.9 sq in, 2,560 sq cm.

ALFA ROMEO Alfetta GTV 2000

ELECTRICAL EQUIPMENT 12 V; 50 Ah battery; 540 W alternator; Bosch or Marelli distributor; 4 iodine headlamps.

DIMENSIONS AND WEIGHT wheel base: 88.58 in, 225 cm; tracks: 52.13 in, 132 cm front, 50.16 in, 127 cm rear; length: 162.20 in, 412 cm; width: 64.17 in, 163 cm; height: 50.79 in, 129 cm; ground clearance: 4.72 in, 12 cm; weight: 2,293 lb, 1,040 kg; turning circle: 34.4 ft, 10.5 m; fuel tank: 11.2 imp gal, 13.5 US gal, 51 l.

BODY convertible; 2 doors; 2 + 2 seats, separate front seats, reclining backrests; heated rear window.

PRACTICAL INSTRUCTIONS fuel: 98-100 oct petrol; oil: engine 11.8 imp pt, 14.2 US pt, 6.7 l, SAE 20W-50, change every 6,200 miles, 10,000 km - gearbox 3.2 imp pt, 3.8 US pt, 1.8 l, SAE 90 EP, change every 11,200 miles, 18,000 km - final drive 2.5 imp pt, 3 US pt, 1.4 l, SAE 90 EP, change every 11,200 miles, 18,000 km; greasing: every 18,600 miles, 30,000 km, 1 point; tappet clearances: inlet 0.019-0.020 in, 0.47-0.50 mm, exhaust 0.020-0.022 in, 0.52-0.55 mm; valve timing: 41°20' 62°20' 53°40' 34°40'; tyre pressure: front 24 psi, 1.7 atm, rear 26 psi, 1.8 atm.

OPTIONALS hardtop; adjustable headrests; light aloy wheels; metallic spray.

AUTOBIANCHI A 112 Elegant

AUTOBIANCHI   ITALY

A 112

PRICE EX WORKS: 3,604,900** liras

ENGINE front, transverse, 4 stroke; 4 cylinders, in line; 55.1 cu in, 903 cc (2.56 x 2.68 in, 65 x 68 mm); compression ratio: 9:1; max power (DIN): 42 hp (30.9 kW) at 5,400 rpm; max torque (DIN): 51 lb ft, 7 kg m (68.6 Nm) at 2,800 rpm; max engine rpm: 6,400; 46.5 hp/l (34.2 kW/l); cast iron cylinder block, light alloy head; 3 crankshaft bearings; valves: overhead, push-rods and rockers; camshafts: 1, side; lubrication: gear pump, cartridge filter, 6.0 imp pt, 8.2 US pt, 3.9 l; 1 Weber 32 IBA 23 downdraught single barrel carburettor; fuel feed: mechanical pump; water-cooled, 8.8 imp pt, 10.6 US pt, 5 l, electric thermostatic fan.

TRANSMISSION driving wheels: front; clutch: single dry plate; gearbox: mechanical; gears: 4, fully synchronized; ratios: I 3.909, II 2.055, III 1.348, IV 0.963, rev 3.615; lever: central; final drive: cylindrical gears; axle ratio: 4.460; width of rims: 4''; tyres: 135 SR x 13.

PERFORMANCE max speeds: (I) 23 mph, 37 km/h; (II) 43 mph, 70 km/h; (III) 66 mph, 107 km/h; (IV) 84 mph, 135 km/h; power-weight ratio: 34.4 lb/hp (46.7 lb/kW), 15.6 kg hp (21.2 kg/kW); carrying capacity: 882 lb, 400 kg; speed in top at 1,000 rpm: 13.8 mph, 22.2 km/h; consumption: 44.8 m/imp gal, 37.3 m/US gal, 6.3 l x 100 km.

CHASSIS integral; front suspension: independent, by Mc-Pherson, coil springs/telescopic damper struts, lower wish-

bones (trailing links), anti-roll bar; rear: independent, wishbones, transverse anti-roll leafspring lower arms, telescopic dampers.

STEERING rack-and-pinion; turns lock to lock: 3.40.

BRAKES front disc, rear drum, dual circuit, rear compensator; lining area: front 19.2 sq in, 124 sq cm, rear 33.5 sq in, 216 sq cm, total 52.7 sq in, 340 sq cm.

ELECTRICAL EQUIPMENT 12 V; 34 Ah battery; 400 W alternator; Marelli distributor; 2 headlamps.

DIMENSIONS AND WEIGHT wheel base: 80.24 in, 204 cm; tracks: 49.21 in, 125 cm front, 48.03 in, 122 cm rear; length: 125.98 in, 320 cm; width: 58.27 in, 148 cm; height: 53.54 in, 136 cm; ground clearance: 5.59 in, 14.2 cm; weight: 1,444 lb, 655 kg; weight distribution: 60% front, 40% rear; turning circle: 29.2 ft, 8.9 m; fuel tank: 6.6 imp gal, 7.9 US gal, 30 l.

BODY saloon/sedan; 2 + 1 doors; 5 seats, separate front seats, reclining backrests; folding rear seat.

PRACTICAL INSTRUCTIONS fuel: 98 oct petrol; oil: engine 6.2 imp pt, 7.4 US pt, SAE 10W-20 (winter) 30W-40 (summer), change every 6,200 miles, 10,000 km - gearbox and final drive 4.2 imp pt, 5.1 US pt, 2.4 l, ZC 90, change every 18,600 miles, 30,000 km; greasing: none; tappet clearances: inlet 0.006 in, 0.15 mm, exhaust 0.008 in, 0.20

mm; valve timing: 11° 43° 43° 11°; tyre pressure: front 24 psi, 1.7 atm, rear 27 psi, 1.9 atm.

OPTIONALS heated rear window; reclining backrests; front vents, rear opening vents.

A 112 Elegant

See A 112 Normale, except for:

PRICE EX WORKS: 4,118,200** liras

ENGINE 58.9 cu in, 965 cc (2.65 x 2.68 in, 67.2 x 68 mm); compression ratio: 9.2:1; max power (DIN): 48 hp (35.3 kW) at 5,600 rpm; max torque (DIN): 53 lb ft, 7.3 kg m (71.6 Nm) at 3,300 rpm; 49.7 hp/l (36.5 kW/l); 1 Weber 32 IBA 22 downdraught single barrel carburettor.

PERFORMANCE max speed: 87 mph, 140 km/h; power-weight ratio: 31 lb/hp (42.2 lb/kW), 14 kg/hp (19.1 kg/kW); consumption: 40.9 m/imp gal, 34.1 m/US gal, 6.9 l x 100 km.

DIMENSIONS AND WEIGHT weight: 1,488 lb, 675 kg.

BODY special luxury interior.

PRACTICAL INSTRUCTIONS tappet clearances: inlet 0.006 in, 0.15 mm, exhaust 0.006 in, 0.15 mm; valve timing: 17° 43° 57° 3°.

OPTIONALS light alloy wheels; metallic spray; built-in headrests; rev counter; tinted glass and heated rear window; headrests; iodine headlamps; rear window wiper-washer.

A 112 Abarth

See A 112 Berlina Normale, except for:

PRICE EX WORKS: 4,543,000** liras

ENGINE 64.1 cu in, 1,050 cc (2.65 x 2.91 in, 67.2 x 74 mm); compression ratio: 10.4:1; max power (DIN): 70 hp (51.5 kW) at 6,660 rpm; max torque (DIN): 63 lb ft, 8.7 kg m (85.3 Nm) at 4,200 rpm; max engine rpm: 7,000; 66.7 hp/l (49.1 kW/l); lubricating system: 7.9 imp pt, 9.5 US pt, 4.5 l; 1 Weber 32 DMTR 3 vertical twin barrel carburettor.

PERFORMANCE max speed: 99 mph, 160 km/h; power-weight ratio: 22.1 lb/hp (30 lb/kW), 10 kg/hp (13.6 kg/kW); consumption: 36.7 m/imp gal, 30.5 m/US gal, 7.7 l x 100 km.

BRAKES servo.

ELECTRICAL EQUIPMENT 2 iodine headlamps (standard).

DIMENSIONS AND WEIGHT weight: 1,544 lb, 700 kg; weight distribution: 62% front, 38% rear.

BODY built-in headrests (standard); rev counter (standard).

PRACTICAL INSTRUCTIONS oil: engine 7.9 imp pt, 9.5 US pt, 4.5 l; tappet clearances: inlet 0.010 in, 0.25 mm, exhaust 0.012 in, 0.30 mm; valve timing: 16° 56° 56° 16°.

AUTOBIANCHI A 112 Abarth

DE TOMASO   ITALY

Pantera L

PRICE IN GB: £ 16,146*
PRICE EX WORKS: 21,330,000 liras**

ENGINE Ford, centre-rear, 4 stroke; 8 cylinders, Vee-slanted at 90°; 351.7 cu in, 5,763 cc (4 x 3.50 in, 101.6 x 89 mm); compression ratio: 8.5:1; max power (SAE): 330 hp (243 kW) at 5,400 rpm; max torque (SAE): 326 lb ft, 45 kg m (441.3 Nm) at 3,400 rpm; max engine rpm: 6,000; 53.8 hp/l (42.2 kW/l); cast iron block and head; 5 crankshaft bearings; valves: overhead, slanted, push-rods and rockers, hydraulic tappets; camshafts: 1, at centre of Vee; lubrication: rotary pump, full flow filter, 9.7 imp pt, 11.6 US pt, 5.5 l; 1 Motorcraft downdraught 4-barrel carburettor; fuel feed: mechanical pump; water-cooled, 42.2 imp pt, 50.7 US pt, 24 l, electric fan.

TRANSMISSION driving wheels: rear; clutch: single dry plate, hydraulically controlled; gearbox: ZF mechanical; gears: 5, fully synchronized; ratios: I 2.230, II 1.475, III 1.040, IV 0.846, V 0.705, rev 2.865; lever: central; final drive: spiral bevel, limited slip differential; axle ratio: 4.220; width of rims: 7'' front, 8'' rear; tyres: 185/70 VR x 15 front, 215/70 VR x 15 rear.

PERFORMANCE max speed: 158 mph, 254 km/h; power-weight ratio: 9.5 lb/hp (12.9 lb/kW), 4.3 kg/hp (5.8 kg/kW); speed in top at 1,000 rpm: 27 mph, 43.5 km/h; consumption: 14.1 m/imp gal, 11.8 m/US gal, 20 l x 100 km.

CHASSIS integral; front and rear suspension: independent, wishbones, coil springs, anti-roll bar, telescopic dampers.

STEERING rack-and-pinion; turns lock to lock: 3.40.

BRAKES disc (front diameter 11.18 in, 28.4 cm, rear 11.10 in, 28.2 cm), dual circuit, internal radial fins, servo.

ELECTRICAL EQUIPMENT 12 V; 72 Ah battery; 55 A alternator; 4 retractable iodine headlamps.

DIMENSIONS AND WEIGHT wheel base: 98.82 in, 251 cm; tracks: 57.09 in, 145 cm front, 57.48 in, 146 cm rear; length: 168.11 in, 427 cm; width: 72.05 in, 183 cm; height: 43.31 in, 110 cm; ground clearance: 4.72 in, 12 cm; dry weight: 3,131 lb, 1,420 kg; turning circle: 39.4 ft, 12 m; fuel tank: 17.6 imp gal, 21.1 US gal, 80 l.

BODY coupé; 2 doors; 2 seats, built-in headrests; electric windows; tinted glass; heated rear window; air-conditioning; light alloy wheels.

PRACTICAL INSTRUCTIONS fuel: 98-100 oct petrol; oil: engine 9.2 imp pt, 11 US pt, 5.2 l, SAE 10W-40 (winter) 20W-50 (summer), change every 3,100 miles, 5,000 km - gearbox and final drive 6 imp pt, 7.2 US pt, 3.4 l, SAE 90, change every 3,700 miles, 6,000 km; greasing: every 3,700 miles, 6,000 km, 2 points; valve timing: 14° 72° 70° 20°.

OPTIONALS 225/50 VR x 15 P7 front and 285/50 VR x 15 P7 rear tyres with 10'' wide rims; right-hand drive; metallic spray; leather interior.

Pantera GTS

See Pantera L, except for:

PRICE IN GB: £ 16,556*
PRICE EX WORKS: 2,100,000 liras**

ENGINE max power (SAE): 350 hp (257.6 kW) at 6,000 rpm; max torque (SAE): 333 lb ft, 46 kg m (451 Nm) at 3,800 rpm; 60.7 hp/l (44.7 kW/l).

PERFORMANCE max speed: about 174 mph, 280 km/h; power-weight ratio: 9 lb/hp (12.2 lb/kW), 4.1 kg/hp (5.5 kg/kW).

BODY front and rear spoiler.

Deauville

See Pantera L, except for:

PRICES IN GB: £ 21,645*
PRICE EX WORKS: 28,823,000 liras**

ENGINE front; cooling system capacity: 31.7 imp pt, 38.1 US pt, 18 l.

TRANSMISSION gearbox: Select-Shift Cruise-o-matic automatic transmission, hydraulic torque converter and planetary gears with 3 ratios + reverse, max ratio of converter at stall 2.05, possible manual selection; ratios: I 2.460, II 1.460, III 1, rev 2.100; axle ratio: 3.070; width of rims: 7''; tyres: 215/70 VR x 15.

DE TOMASO Pantera L

DE TOMASO Pantera L

PERFORMANCE max speed: over 143 mph, 230 km/h; power-weight ratio: 13 lb/hp (17.6 lb/kW), 5.9 kg/hp (8 kg/kW); carrying capacity: 1,169 lb, 530 kg; acceleration: standing ¼ mile 16 sec; speed in direct drive at 1,000 rpm: 23 mph, 38.4 km/h; fuel consumption: 16 m/imp gal, 13 m/US gal, 17.6 l x 100 km.

CHASSIS rear suspension: trailing radius arms, 4 coil springs, 4 telescopic dampers.

STEERING servo.

DIMENSIONS AND WEIGHT wheel base: 109.05 in, 277 cm; tracks: 59.84 in, 152 cm front, 59.84 in, 152 cm rear; length: 195.52 in, 489 cm; width: 73.94 in, 188 cm; height: 53.86 in, 137 cm; ground clearance: 5.12 in, 13 cm; dry weight: 4,278 lb, 1,940 kg; turning circle: 42.6 ft, 13 m; fuel tank: 26.4 imp gal, 31.7 US gal, 120 l.

BODY saloon/sedan; 4 doors; 5 seats, separate front seats, reclining backrests; air-conditioning; electric windows; tinted glass; electric rear view mirror; roll safety belts; adjustable steering wheel; halogen headlamps; light alloy wheels; headrests; leather upholstery; heated rear window; front spoiler.

PRACTICAL INSTRUCTIONS oil: engine 7 imp pt, 8.5 US pt, 4 l - automatic transmission 17.6 imp pt, 21.1 US pt, 10 l, final drive 3.2 imp pt, 3.8 US pt, 1.8 l.

OPTIONALS oil cooler; right hand drive; metallic spray.

DE TOMASO Deauville

Longchamp 2 + 2

See Deauville, except for:

PRICE IN GB: £ 19,480*
PRICE EX WORKS: 27,000,000** liras

PERFORMANCE max speed: 149 mph, 240 km/h; power-weight ratio: 11.6 lb/hp (16.3 lb/kW), 5.3 kg/hp (7.2 kg/kW); speed in direct drive at 1,000 rpm: 24.9 mph, 40 km/h; consumption: 16.6 m/imp gal, 13.8 m/US gal, 17 l x 100 km.

ELECTRICAL EQUIPMENT 61 A alternator.

DIMENSIONS AND WEIGHT wheel base: 102.36 in, 260 cm; length: 177.95 in, 452 cm; width: 72.44 in, 184 cm; height: 50.79 in, 129 cm; ground clearance: 5.91 in, 15 cm; dry weight: 3,858 lb, 1,750 kg; turning circle: 37.7 ft, 11.5 m; fuel tank: 22 imp gal, 26.4 US gal, 100 l.

BODY coupé; 2 doors; 2 + 2 seats.

OPTIONALS 5-speed mechanical gearbox.

ENNEZETA   ITALY

Nuova Lele Iso Rivolta

PRICE EX WORKS: 15,000,000* liras

ENGINE Ford, front, 4 stroke; V8 cylinders; 351.6 cu in, 5.762 cc (4 x 3.50 in, 101.6 x 88.9 mm); compression ratio: 8.6:1; max power (SAE): 325 hp (239.2 kW) at 5,800 rpm; max torque (SAE): 349 lb ft, 48.3 kg m (473.7 Nm) at 3,800 rpm; max engine rpm: 5,800; 56.4 hp/l (82.2 kW/l); cast iron block and head; 5 crankshaft bearings; valves: 8, overhead, in line, push-rods and rockers, hydraulic tappets; camshafts: 1, at centre of Vee; lubrication: gear pump, full flow filter (cartridge), 11.4 imp pt, 13.7 US pt, 6.5 l; fuel feed: electric pump; water-cooled, 31.7 imp pt, 38.1 US pt, 18 l.

TRANSMISSION driving wheels: rear; automatic transmission, hydraulic torque converter and planetary gears with 3 ratios, max ratio of converter at stall 2.10, possible manual selection; ratios: I 2.460, II 1.460, III 1, rev 2.180; lever: central; final drive: hypoid bevel, limited slip differential; axle ratio: 3.310; width of rims: 7''; tyres: 215/70 VR x 15.

PERFORMANCE max speeds: (I) 57 mph, 91 km/h; (II) 95 mph, 153 km/h; (III) 149 mph, 240 km/h; power-weight ratio: 11.7 lb/hp (16.1 lb/kW), 5.3 kg/hp (7.3 kg/kW); carrying capacity: 882 lb, 400 kg; acceleration: standing ¼ mile 13.8 sec, 0-50 mph (0-80 km/h) 6 sec; speed in direct drive at 1,000 rpm: 26.1 mph, 42 km/h; consumption: 14.9 m/imp gal, 12.4 m/US gal, 19 l x 100 km.

CHASSIS integral; front suspension: independent, wishbones, coil springs, anti-roll bar, telescopic dampers; rear:

De Dion rigid axle, twin trailing radius arms, transverse linkage bar, coil springs, telescopic dampers.

STEERING recirculating ball, servo; turns lock to lock: 4.

BRAKES disc, servo; lining area: front 36.7 sq in, 237 sq cm, rear 21.1 sq in, 136 sq cm, total 57.8 sq in, 373 sq cm.

ELECTRICAL EQUIPMENT 12 V; 80 Ah battery; 630 W alternator; Motorcraft distributor; electronic ignition; 4 iodine headlamps.

DIMENSIONS AND WEIGHT wheel base: 106.30 in, 270 cm; front and rear track: 56.69 in, 144 cm; length: 183.58 in, 466 cm; width: 69.90 in, 175 cm; height: 52.36 in, 133 cm; ground clearance: 4.72 in, 12 cm; weight: 3,837 lb, 1,740 kg; weight distribution: 55% front, 45% rear; turning circle: 39.4 ft, 12 m; fuel tank: 24.6 imp gal, 22 US gal, 100 l.

BODY saloon/sedan; 2 doors; 5 seats, built-in headrest.

PRACTICAL INSTRUCTIONS fuel: 88-100 oct petrol; oil: engine 11.4 imp pt, 13.7 US pt, 6.5 l, SAE 20W-50, change every 6,200 miles, 10,000 km - gearbox 16.7 imp pt, 4.6 US pt, 9.5 l, Castrol TQF - final drive 3.2 imp pt, 3.8 US pt, 1.8 l, SAE 90, change every 12,400 miles, 20,000 km; greasing: every 9,300 miles, 15,000 km, 12 points; tyre pressure: front 31 psi, 2.2 atm, rear 34 psi, 2.4 atm.

OPTIONALS leather upholstery; tinted glass; electric windows; adjustable steering wheel; adjustable speed wiper; brake warning light; electromagnetic bonnet and boot clips.

DE TOMASO Longchamp 2 + 2

FERRARI   ITALY

Dino 208 GT 4

PRICE EX WORKS: 20,178,000* liras

ENGINE centre-rear, transverse, 4 stroke; 8 cylinders, Vee-slanted at 90°; 121.5 cu in, 1,991 cc (2.63 x 2.80 in, 66.8 x 71 mm); compression ratio: 9:1; max power (DIN): 160 hp 117.7 kW) at 6,600 rpm; max torque (DIN): 134.5 lb ft, 18.5 kg m (182.5 Nm) at 5,400 rpm; max engine rpm: 7,700 85.4 hp/l (62.8 kW/l); light alloy block and head, wet liners; 5 crankshaft bearings; valves: overhead, Vee-slanted, thimble tappets; camshafts: 2,1 per bank, overhead, cogged belt; lubrication: gear pump, full flow filter, oil cooler; 4 Weber 34 DCNF downdraught twin barrel carburettors; fuel feed: electric pump; water-cooled, front radiator, 2 electric automatic fans.

TRANSMISSION driving wheels: rear; clutch: single dry plate; gearbox: mechanical; gears: 5, fully synchronized; ratios: I 3.419, II 2.353, III 1.693, IV 1.244, V 0.881, rev 3.200; lever: central; final drive: hypoid bevel, limited slip differential; axle ratio: 4.600; width of rims: 6.5''; tyres: 195/70 VR x 14 XDX.

PERFORMANCE max speed: 132 mph, 213 km/h; speeds at 7,000 rpm: (I) 32 mph, 52 km/h; (II) 47 mph, 76 km/h; (III) 65 mph, 105 km/h; (IV) 89 mph, 143 km/h; (V) 125 mph, 202 km/h; power-weight ratio: 17.5 lb/hp (23.7 lb/kW), 7.9 kg/hp (10.8 kg/kW); acceleration: standing ¼ mile 16 sec; speed in top at 1,000 rpm: 17.9 mph, 28.8 km/h; consumption: 17.7/15.7 m/imp gal, 14.7/13.1 m/US gal, 16/18 l x 100 km.

CHASSIS tubular; front suspension: independent, wishbones, anti-roll bar, coil springs/telescopic dampers; rear: independent, wishbones, anti-roll bar, coil springs/telescopic dampers.

STEERING rack-and-pinion.

BRAKES disc, internal radial fins, dual circuit, servo.

ELECTRICAL EQUIPMENT 12 V; alternator Marelli distributor; 4 retractable iodine headlamps.

DIMENSIONS AND WEIGHT wheel base: 100.39 in, 255 cm; front and rear track: 57.48 in, 146 cm; length: 169.29 in, 430 cm; width: 70.47 in, 179 cm; height: 47.64 in, 121 cm; ground clearance: 4.72 in, .12 cm; wieght: 2,793 lb, 1,267 kg; turning circle: 40.3 ft, 12.3 m; fuel tank: 17.6 imp gai, 21.1 US gal, 80 l (2 separate tanks).

BODY coupé; 2 doors; 2 + 2 seats, separate front seats, reclining backrests; built-in headrests; tinted glass; heated rear window; light alloy wheels; quartz clock.

PRACTICAL INSTRUCTIONS fuel: 98-100 oct petrol.

OPTIONALS electric windows; air-conditioning.

ENNEZETA Nuova Lele Iso Rivolta

Dino 308 GT 4

See Dino 208 GT 4, except for:

PRICE IN GB: £ 15,250*
PRICE IN USA: $ 34,670*

ENGINE 178.5 cu in, 2,926 cc (3.19 x 2.80 in, 81 x 71 mm); compression ratio: 8.8:1; max power (DIN): 230 hp (169.2 kW) at 6,600 rpm; max torque (DIN): 203.1 lb/ft, 28.1 kg m (275 Nm) at 4,600 rpm; 78.6 hp/l (57.8 kW/l); 4 Weber 40 DCNF downdraught twin barrel carburettors.

TRANSMISSION ratios: V 0.952; axle ratio: 3.706; width of rims: 6.5'' or 7.5''; tyres: 205/70 VR x 14 XWX.

PERFORMANCE max speed: 148 mph, 238 km/h; speeds at 7,000 rpm: (I) 41 mph, 66 km/h; (II) 59 mph, 95 km/h; (III) 83 mph, 133 km/h; (IV) 112 mph, 180 km/h; (V) 147 mph, 236 km/h; power-weight ratio: 12.1 lb/hp (16.5 lb/kW), 5.5 kg/hp (7.5 kg/kW); acceleration: standing ¼ mile 14.8 sec; speed in top at 1,000 rpm: 20.9 mph, 33.6 km/h; consumption: 14.9 m/imp gal, 12.4 m/US gal, 19 l x 100 km.

ELECTRICAL EQUIPMENT electronic ignition.

OPTIONALS leather upholstery; metallic spray; factory fitted sunshine roof; air-conditioning; electric windows.

308 GTB

See Dino 308 GT 4, except for:

PRICE IN GB: £ 16,499*
PRICE IN USA: $ 35,950*

ENGINE lubrication: dry sump.

TRANSMISSION ratios: V 0.920.

PERFORMANCE max speed: 152 mph, 244 km/h; power-weight ratio: 12.1 lb/hp (16.5 lb/kW), 5.5 kg/hp (7.5 kg/kW); speed in top at 1,000 rpm: 21.7 mph, 34.8 km/h.

DIMENSIONS AND WEIGHT wheel base: 92.13 in, 234 cm; front and rear track: 57.48 in, 146 cm; length: 166.54 in, 423 cm; width: 67.72 in, 172 cm; height: 44.09 in, 112 cm; weight: 2,788 lb, 1,265 kg; turning circle: 39.4 ft, 12 m; fuel tank: 16.3 imp gal, 19.6 US gal, 74 l.

BODY in light alloy; 2 seats; electric windows (standard).

308 GTS

See 308 GTB, except for:

PRICE IN GB: £ 17,300*
PRICE IN USA: $ 37,950*

ENGINE lubrication: wet sump.

TRANSMISSION ratios: V 0.952.

PERFORMANCE max speed: 147 mph, 236 km/h; power-

FERRARI Dino 308 GT 4

FERRARI 308 GTS

weight ratio: 12.4 lb/hp (16.9 lb/kW), 5.6 kg/hp (7.7 kg/kW); speed in top at 1,000 rpm: 20.9 mph, 33.6 km/h.

DIMENSIONS AND WEIGHT weight: 2,859 lb, 1,297 kg.

BODY spider.

400 Automatic

PRICE IN GB: £ 27,000*
PRICE EX WORKS: 42,390,000* liras

ENGINE front, 4 stroke; 12 cylinders, Vee-slanted at 60°; 294.3 cu in, 4,823 cc (3.19 x 3.07 in, 81 x 78 mm); compression ratio: 8.8:1; max power (DIN): 325 hp (239 kW) at 6,000 rpm; max torque (DIN): 347 lb ft, 48 kg m (471 Nm) at 3,600 rpm; max engine rpm: 6,500; 67.4 hp/l 49. kW/l); light alloy block and head, wet liners; 7 crankshaft bearings; valves: overhead, Vee-slanted at 46°, thimble tappets; camshafts: 2, 1 per bank, overhead; lubrication gear pump, 31.7 imp pt, 38.1 US pt, 18 l; 6 Weber 3 DCOE 110/111 carburettors; fuel feed: 2 electric pump water-cooled, 22.9 imp pt, 27.5 US pt, 13 l, 2 electri automatic fans.

TRANSMISSION driving wheels: rear; gearbox: GM auto matic transmission, hydraulic torque converter and pla netary gears with 3 ratios, max ratio of converter at sta 2.20, possible manual selection; gears: ratios: I 2.520, 1.520, III 1, rev 1.940; lever: central; final drive: spira bevel, limited slip differential; axle ratio: 3.250; width rims: 7.5''; tyres: 215/70 VR x 15.

FERRARI 400 Automatic

PERFORMANCE max speeds: (I) 61 mph, 98 km/h; (II) 101 mph, 164 km/h; (III) 152 mph, 245 km/h; power-weight ratio: 12.2 lb/hp (16.6 lb/kW), 5.5 kg/hp (7.5 kg/kW); speed in direct drive at 1,000 rpm: 23.4 mph, 37.6 km/h; consumption: 14.1 m/imp gal, 11.8 m/US gal, 20 l x 100 km.

CHASSIS tubular; front suspension: independent, wishbones, anti-roll bar, coil springs/telescopic dampers; rear: independent, wishbones, anti-roll bar, coil springs/telescopic dampers.

STEERING recirculating ball, ZF servo; turns lock to lock: 3.80.

BRAKES discs (front diameter 11.89 in, 30.2 cm, rear 11.69 in, 29.7 cm), internal radial fins, dual circuit, servo; lining area: front 28.8 sq in, 186 sq cm, rear 19.5 sq in, 126 sq cm, total 48.3 sq in, 312 sq cm.

ELECTRICAL EQUIPMENT 12 V; 77 Ah battery; 960 W alternator; 2 Marelli S 138 C distributors; 4 retractable iodine headlamps.

DIMENSIONS AND WEIGHT wheel base: 106.30 in, 270 cm; tracks: 57.87 in, 147 cm front, 59.06 in, 150 cm rear; length: 189.37 in, 481 cm; width: 70.87 in, 180 cm; height: 51.57 in, 131 cm; ground clearance: 5.12 in, 13 cm; weight: 3,979 lb, 1,805 kg; turning circle: 40 ft, 12.2 m; fuel tank: 23 imp gal, 28 US gal, 105 l.

BODY coupé; 2 doors; 2 + 2 seats, separate front seats, reclining backrests with built-in headrests; folding rear seat; air-conditioning; electric windows; heated rear window.

PRACTICAL INSTRUCTIONS fuel: 98-100 oct petrol; oil: engine 31.7 imp pt, 38.1 US pt, 18 l, SAE 20W-40, change every 6,200 miles, 10,000 km - gearbox 7.9 imp pt, 9.5 US pt, 4.5 l, SAE 80 EP, change every 6,200 miles, 10,000 km - final drive 4.4 imp pt, 5.3 US pt, 2.5 l, change every 6,200 miles, 10,000 km; greasing: every 6,200 miles, 10,000 km, 8 points; tappet clearances: inlet 0.004-0.006 in, 0.10-0.15 mm, exhaust 0.010-0.012 in, 0.25-0.30 mm; tyre pressure: front 34 psi, 2.4 atm, rear 38 psi, 2.7 atm.

OPTIONALS 5 speed mechanical gearbox, ratios (I 2.590, II 1.700, III 1.254, IV 1, V 0.795, rev 2.240), axle ratio 4.300.

BB 512

PRICE IN GB: £ 28,750*
PRICE EX WORKS: 45,630,000* liras

ENGINE centre-rear, 4 stroke; 12 cylinders, horizontally opposed; 301.6 cu in, 4,942 cc (3.23 x 3.07 in, 82 x 78 mm); compression ratio: 9.2:1; max power (DIN): 340 hp (250 kW) at 6,200 rpm; max engine rpm: 6,800; 68.8 hp/l (50.6 kW/l); light alloy block and head, cast iron liners; 7 crankshaft bearings; valves: overhead, Vee-slanted, thimble tappets; camshafts: 2, 1 per bank, cogged belt; lubrication: gear pump, full flow filter, dry sump, 17.6 imp pt, 2.1 US pt, 10 l; 4 Weber 40 IF3 C three-barrel carburettors; fuel feed: electric pumps; water-cooled, 24.6 imp pt, 29.6 US pt, 14 l, 3 electric automatic fans.

TRANSMISSION driving wheels: rear; clutch: single dry plate; gearbox: mechanical, in unit with final drive; gears: 5, fully synchronized; ratios: I 2.937, II 2.099, III 1.587, IV 1.200, V 0.913, rev 2.620; lever: central; final drive: hypoid bevel, limited slip differential; axle ratio: 3.214; width of rims: 7.5'' front, 9'' rear; tyres: 215/70 VR x 15 front, 225/70 VR x 15 rear.

PERFORMANCE max speed: 176 mph, 283 km/h; speeds at 6,200 rpm: (I) 53 mph, 85 km/h; (II) 73 mph, 118 km/h; (III) 97 mph, 156 km/h; (IV) 129 mph, 207 km/h; (V) 169 mph, 272 km/h; power-weight ratio: 9.8 lb/hp (13.4 lb/kW), 4.4 kg/hp (6 kg/kW); speed in top at 1,000 rpm: 27.4 mph, 44 km/h; consumption: 13.5 m/imp gal, 11.2 m/US gal, 21 l x 100 km.

CHASSIS tubular; front suspension: independent, wishbones, anti-roll bar, coil springs/telescopic dampers; rear: independent, wishbones, coil springs/telescopic dampers, 4 telescopic dampers.

STEERING worm and roller.

BRAKES discs, internal radial fins, servo.

ELECTRICAL EQUIPMENT 12 V; 74 Ah battery; 780 W alternator; Marelli distributor; electronic ignition; 2 retractable headlamps.

DIMENSIONS AND WEIGHT wheel base: 98.43 in, 250 cm; tracks: 59.06 in, 150 cm front, 61.42 in, 156 cm rear; length: 173.23 in, 440 cm; width: 72.05 in, 183 cm; height: 44.09 in, 112 cm; ground clearance: 4.92 in, 12.5 cm; weight: 3,340 lb, 1,515 kg; turning circle (between walls): 39 ft, 11.9 m; fuel tank: 24 imp gal, 29 US gal, 110 l.

BODY coupé; 2 doors; 2 seats; light alloy wheels; electric windows; air-conditioning.

PRACTICAL INSTRUCTIONS fuel: 98-100 oct petrol.

FERRARI Dino 308 GT4 - 308 GTB - 308 GTS

FERRARI BB 512

FIAT   ITALY

126 Berlina Base

PRICE IN GB: £ 1,640*
PRICE EX WORKS: 2,507,500** liras

ENGINE rear, 4 stroke; 2 cylinders, vertical, in line; 39.8 cu in, 652 cc (3.03 x 2.76 in, 77 x 70 mm); compression ratio: 7.5:1; max power (DIN): 24 hp (17.7 kW) at 4,500 rpm; max torque (DIN): 30 lb ft, 4.2 kg m (41.2 Nm) at 3,000 rpm; max engine rpm: 5,200; 36.8 hp/l (27.1 kW/l); light alloy block and head; 2 crankshaft bearings; valves: overhead, in line, push-rods and rockers; camshafts: 1, side; lubrication: gear pump, centrifugal filter, 4.4 imp pt, 5.3 US pt, 2.5 l; 1 Weber 28 IMB downdraught carburettor; fuel feed: mechanical pump; air-cooled.

TRANSMISSION driving wheels: rear; clutch: single dry plate; gearbox: mechanical; gears: 4, II, III and IV silent claw coupling; ratios: I 3.250, II 2.067, III 1.300, IV 0.872, rev 4.024; lever: central; final drive: spiral bevel; axle ratio: 4.875; width of rims: 4''; tyres: 135 SR x 12.

PERFORMANCE max speeds: (I) 19 mph, 30 km/h; (II) 31 mph, 50 km/h; (III) 50 mph, 80 km/h; (IV) over 65 mph, 105 km/h; power-weight ratio: 53.3 lb/hp (72.2 lb/kW); 24.2 kg/hp (33.4 kg/kW); carrying capacity: 706 lb, 320 kg; speed in top at 1,000 rpm: 14 mph, 22.6 km/h; consumption: 55.3 m/imp gal, 46.1 m/US gal, 5.1 l x 100 km.

CHASSIS integral; front suspension: independent, wishbones, transverse leafspring lower arms, telescopic dampers; rear: independent, oblique semi-trailing arms, coil springs, telescopic dampers.

STEERING screw and sector; turns lock to lock: 2.90.

BRAKES drum; lining area: front 33.3 sq in, 215 sq cm, rear 33.3 sq in, 215 sq cm, total 66.6 sq in, 430 sq cm.

ELECTRICAL EQUIPMENT 12 V; 34 Ah battery; 230 W dynamo; Marelli distributor; 2 headlamps.

DIMENSIONS AND WEIGHT wheel base: 72.44 in, 184 cm; tracks: 44.96 in, 114 cm front, 47.36 in, 120 cm rear; length: 120.24 in, 305 cm; width: 54.21 in, 138 cm; height: 52.56 in, 133 cm; ground clearance: 4.92 in, 12.5 cm; weight: 1,279 lb, 580 kg; weight distribution: 40% front, 60% rear; turning circle: 28.2 ft, 8.6 m; fuel tank: 4.6 imp gal, 5.5 US gal, 21 l.

BODY saloon/sedan; 2 doors; 4 seats, separate front seats.

PRACTICAL INSTRUCTIONS fuel: 80-85 oct petrol; oil: engine 4.4 imp pt, 5.3 US pt, 2.5 l, SAE 30W (summer) 20W (winter), change every 6,200 miles, 10,000 km - gearbox and final drive 1.9 imp pt, 2.3 US pt, 1.1 l, FIAT ZC 90, change every 18,600 miles, 30,000 km; greasing: every 3,100 miles, 5,000 km, 2 points; tappet clearances: inlet 0.008 in, 0.20 mm, exhaust 0.010 in, 0.25 mm; valve timing: 26° 57' 66° 17'; tyre pressure: front 22 psi, 1.4 atm, rear 28 psi, 2 atm.

OPTIONALS reclining backrests; luxury interior; opening rear windows; sunshine roof; folding rear seat; antitheft.

126 Personal

See 126 Berlina Base, except for:

PRICE IN GB: £ 1,799*
PRICE EX WORKS: 2,690,400** liras

PERFORMANCE power-weight ratio: 53.7 lb/hp (72.8 lb/kW), 24.4 kg/hp (33 kg/kW).

ELECTRICAL EQUIPMENT 33 A alternator.

DIMENSIONS AND WEIGHT length: 123.19 in, 313 cm; width: 54.33 in, 138 cm; weight: 1,289 lb, 585 kg.

127 Series

PRICES IN GB AND EX WORKS:

		£	liras
1	L 2-dr Berlina	2,138*	3,551,800**
2	L 3-dr Berlina	—	3,658,000**
3	C 2-dr Berlina	—	3,899,900**
4	C 3-dr Berlina	—	4,006,100**
5	CL 2-dr Berlina	—	4,088,700**
6	CL 3-dr Berlina	2,471*	4,194,900**
7	Sport	2,775*	4,672,800**

Power team:	Standard for:	Optional for:
45 hp	1 to 4	—
50 hp	5,6	—
70 hp	7	—

FIAT 126 Personal

FIAT 127 L 3-dr Berlina

45 hp power team

ENGINE front, transverse, 4 stroke; 4 cylinders, vertical, in line; 55.1 cu in, 903 cc (2.56 x 2.68 in, 65 x 68 mm); compression ratio: 9:1; max power (DIN): 45 hp (33.1 kW) at 5,600 rpm; max torque (DIN): 47 lb ft, 6.5 kg m (63.7 Nm) at 3,000 rpm; max engine rpm: 6,400; 49.8 hp/l (36.7 kW/l); cast iron block, light alloy head; 3 crankshaft bearings; valves: overhead, in line, push-rods and rockers; camshafts: 1, side; lubrication: gear pump, full flow filter (cartridge), 6.7 imp pt, 8 US pt, 3.8 l; 1 Weber 30 IBA 22 single barrel carburettor; fuel feed: mechanical pump; water-cooled, 8.8 imp pt, 10.6 US pt, 5 l, electric thermostatic fan.

TRANSMISSION driving wheels: front; clutch: single dry plate; gearbox: mechanical; gears: 4, fully synchronized; ratios: I 3.910, II 2.055, III 1.348, IV 0.963, rev 3.615; lever: central; final drive helical cylindrical; axle ratio: 4.071; width of rims: 4''; tyres: 135 SR x 13.

PERFORMANCE max speeds: (I) 25 mph, 40 km/h; (II) 43 mph, 70 km/h; (III) 65 mph, 105 km/h; (IV) over 84 mph, 135 km/h; power-weight ratio: 33.7 lb/hp (45.8 lb/kW), 15.3 kg/hp (20.8 kg/kW); carrying capacity: 882 lb, 400 kg; acceleration: standing ¼ mile 20.4 sec; speed in top at 1,000 rpm: 15.8 mph, 25.4 km/h; consumption: 40.9 m/imp gal, 34.1 m/US gal, 6.9 l x 100 km.

CHASSIS integral; front suspension: independent, by McPherson, coil springs/telescopic damper struts, lower wishbones, transverse anti-roll bar; rear: independent, single widebased wishbone, transverse anti-roll leafspring, telescopic dampers.

STEERING rack-and-pinion; turns lock to lock: 3.50.

BRAKES front disc (diameter 8.94 in, 22.7 cm), rear drum, dual circuit, rear compensator; lining area: front 19.2 sq in, 124 sq cm, rear 33.3 sq in, 215 sq cm, total 52.6 sq in, 339 sq cm.

ELECTRICAL EQUIPMENT 12 V; 34 Ah battery; 33 A alternator; Marelli S 146 A distributor; 2 headlamps.

DIMENSIONS AND WEIGHT wheel base: 87.60 in, 222 cm; tracks: 50.39 in, 128 cm front, 50.79 in, 129 rear; length: 143.5 in, 364 cm; width: 60.12 in, 153 cm; height: 53.54 in, 136 cm; ground clearance: 5.12 in, 13 cm; weight: 1,517 lb, 688 kg; weight distribution: 62% front, 38% rear; turning circle: 31.5 ft, 9.6 m; fuel tank: 6.6 imp gal, 7.9 US gal, 30 l.

BODY saloon/sedan; 5 seats, separate front seats; folding rear seat (for 3-dr models only).

PRACTICAL INSTRUCTIONS fuel: 98 oct petrol; oil: engine 6.3 imp pt, 7.6 US pt, 3.6 l, SAE 20 W (winter) 30 (summer), change every 6,200 miles, 10,000 km - gearbox and final drive 4.2 imp pt, 5.1 US pt, 2.4 l, SAE 90, change every 18,600 miles, 30,000 km; greasing: homokinetic joints, every 18,600 miles, 30,000 km; sparking plug: 260°; tappet clearances: inlet 0.006 in, 0.15 mm, exhaust 0.008 in, 0.20 mm; valve timing: 17° 43° 57° 3°; tyre pressure: front 24 psi, 1.7 atm, rear 27 psi, 1.9 atm.

OPTIONALS headrests; reclining backrests; luxury interior; opening rear windows; heated rear window; antitheft; metallic spray.

50 hp power team

See 45 hp power team, except for:

ENGINE 64 cu in, 1,049 cc (2.99 x 2.27 in, 76 x 57.8 mm); compression ratio: 9.3:1; max power (DIN): 50 hp (36.8 kW) at 5,600 rpm; max torque (DIN): 57.2 lb ft, 7.9 kg m (77. Nm) at 4,000 rpm; 55.4 hp/l (40.7 kW/l); 5 crankshaft bearings; camshafts: 1, overhead; lubrication: four-lobe rotary pump, 6.2 imp pt, 7.4 US pt, 3.5 l; 1 Weber 3. ICEV 16 or Solex C32 TDI/4 downdraught carburettor; cooling system 9.7 imp pt, 11.6 US pt, 5.5 l.

PERFORMANCE max speed: 87 mph, 140 km/h; power-weight ratio: 31.2 lb/hp (42.4 lb/kW), 14.2 kg/hp (19.2 kg/kW); acceleration: standing ¼ mile 19.9 sec; consumption: 36.2 m/imp gal, 30.2 m/US gal, 7.8 l x 100 km.

DIMENSIONS AND WEIGHT weight: 1,561 lb, 708 kg.

PRACTICAL INSTRUCTIONS oil: engine 5.5 imp pt, 6.6 US pt, 3.1 l; valve timing: 2° 42° 42° 2°.

70 hp power team

See 50 hp power team, except for:

ENGINE compression ratio: 9.8:1; max power (DIN): 70 hp (51.5 kW) at 6,500 rpm; max torque (DIN): 61.6 lb ft, 8.5 kg m (83.4 Nm) at 4,500 rpm; 66.7 hp/l (49.1 kW/l); 1 Weber 34 DMTR downdraught twin barrel carburettor.

TRANSMISSION axle ratio: 4.462; width of rims: 4.5''.

PERFORMANCE max speed: about 99 mph, 160 km/h; power-weight ratio: 23.8 lb/hp (32.3 lb/kW), 10.8 kg/hp (14.6 kg/kW); acceleration: standing ¼ mile 18.5 sec; speed in top at 1,000 rpm: 14.3 mph, 23 km/h; consumption: 31.7 m/imp gal, 26.4 m/US gal, 8.9 l x 100 km.

ELECTRICAL EQUIPMENT 45 A alternator.

DIMENSIONS AND WEIGHT tracks: 50.78 in, 129 cm front 51.18 in, 130 cm rear; weight: 1,665 lb, 755 kg.

PRACTICAL INSTRUCTIONS valve timing: 6° 46° 47° 7°.

128 CL 1100

PRICE EX WORKS: 4,826,200** liras

ENGINE front, transverse, 4 stroke; 4 cylinders, in line; 68.1 cu in, 1,116 cc (3.15 x 2.19 in, 80 x 55.5 mm); compression ratio: 9.2:1; max power (DIN): 55 hp (40.4 kW) at 6,000 rpm; max torque (DIN): 60 lb ft, 8.3 kg m (81.4 Nm) at 2,800 rpm; max engine rpm: 6,500; 49.3 hp/l (36.2 kW/l); cast iron block, light alloy head; 5 crankshaft bearings; valves: overhead, thimble tappets; camshafts: 1, overhead, cogged belt; lubrication: gear pump, cartridge filter, 8.8 imp pt, 10.6 US pt, 5 l; 1 Weber 32 ICEV 14 or Solex C 32 DISA 41 downdraught carburettor; fuel feed: mechanical pump; water-cooled, expansion tank, 11.4 imp pt, 13.7 US pt, 6.5 l, electric thermostatic fan.

TRANSMISSION driving wheels: front; clutch: single dry plate; gearbox: mechanical; gears: 4, fully synchronized;

...os: I 3.583, II 2.235, III 1.454, IV 1.042, rev 3.714; lever:
...tral; final drive: helical cylindrical; axle ratio: 3.765 -
...th of rims: 4.5''; tyres: 145 SR x 13.

...FORMANCE max speeds: (I) 31 mph, 50 km/h; (II)
...mph, 80 km/h; (III) 75 mph, 120 km/h; (IV) 87 mph, 140
.../h; power-weight ratio: 30 lb/hp (40.9 lb/kW), 13.6
...hp (18.6 kg/kW); carrying capacity: 882 lb, 400 kg;
...eleration: standing ¼ mile 19.7 sec; speed in top at
...0 rpm: 16.3 mph, 26.3 km/h; consumption: 35.3 m/
... gal, 29.4 m/US gal, 8 l x 100 km.

...ASSIS integral; front suspension: independent, by
...Pherson, coil springs/telescopic damper struts, lower
...hbones, anti-roll bar; rear: independent, single wide-
...ed wishbones, transverse anti-roll leafspring, telescopic
...pers.

...ERING rack-and-pinion; turns lock to lock: 3.50.

...AKES front disc (diameter 8.94 in, 22.7 cm), rear drum,
... circuit, rear compensator, servo; lining area: front
... sq in, 124 sq cm, rear 33.3 sq in, 215 sq cm, total
... sq in, 339 sq cm.

...CTRICAL EQUIPMENT 12 V; 34 Ah battery; 33 A
...rnator; Marelli distributor; 2 headlamps.

...ENSIONS AND WEIGHT wheel base: 96.38 in, 245 cm;
...cks: 51.50 in, 131 cm front, 51.69 in, 131 cm rear;
...gth: 151.18 in, 384 cm; width: 62.60 in, 159 cm; height:
...1 in, 142 cm; ground clearance: 5.71 in, 14.5 cm;
...ght: 1,698 lb, 770 kg; weight distribution: 64% front,
... rear; turning circle: 33.8 ft, 10.3 m; fuel tank: 8.4
... gal, 10 US gal, 38 l.

...Y saloon/sedan; 4 doors; 5 seats, separate front seats;
...ining backrests.

...CTICAL INSTRUCTIONS fuel: 98 oct petrol; oil: engine
...imp pt, 8.9 US pt, 4.2 l, SAE 20W (winter) 30 (summer),
...nge every 6,200 miles, 10,000 km - gearbox and final
...e 5.5 imp pt, 6.6 US pt, 3.1 l, SAE 90, change every
...0 miles, 30,000 km; greasing: homokinetic joints, every
...0 miles, 30,000 km; sparking plug: 240°; tappet
...arances: inlet 0.012 in, 0.30 mm, exhaust 0.016 in, 0.40
...; valve timing: 12° 52° 52° 12°; tyre pressure: front 26
...1.8 atm, rear 24 psi, 1.7 atm.

...IONALS headrests; tinted glass with heated rear window;
...theft; light alloy wheels; heated rear window; metallic
...ay.

128 Panorama Base 1100

128 CL 1100, except for:

...CE EX WORKS: 4,602,000** liras

...NSMISSION axle ratio: 4.077.

...FORMANCE power-weight ratio: 31.7 lb/hp (43.1 lb/kW),
... kg/hp (19.6 kg/kW); carrying capacity: 948 lb, 430
... speed in top at 1,000 rpm: 15.1 mph, 24.3 km/h.

...ENSIONS AND WEIGHT weight: 1,742 lb, 790 kg.

FIAT Ritmo 60 - 65 CL 5-dr Berlina

FIAT 127 Sport

FIAT 128 CL 1100

BODY 2 + 1 doors; olding rear seat.

PRACTICAL INSTRUCTIONS tyre pressure: front 27 psi, 1.9 atm, rear 24 psi, 1.7 atm.

Ritmo Series

PRICES EX WORKS: liras

		liras
1	60 L 3-dr Berlina	4,436,800**
2	60 L 5-dr Berlina	4,637,400**
3	60 CL 3-dr Berlina	4,708,200**
4	60 CL 5-dr Berlina	4,908,800**
5	65 L 5-dr Berlina	4,755,400**
6	65 CL 3-dr Berlina	4,826,200**
7	65 CL 5-dr Berlina	5,026,800**
8	75 CL 3-dr Berlina	5,439,800**
9	75 CL 5-dr Berlina	5,640,400**

Power team:	Standard for:	Optional for:
60 hp	1 to 4	—
65 hp	5 to 7	—
75 hp	8,9	—

60 hp power team

ENGINE front transverse, 4 stroke; 4 cylinders, in line; 68.1 cu in, 1,116 cc (3.15 x 2.19 in, 80 x 55.5 mm); compression ratio: 9.2:1; max power (DIN): 60 hp (44.1 kW) at 5,800 rpm; max torque (DIN): 60 lb ft, 8.3 kg m (81.4 Nm) at 3,500 rpm; 53.8 hp/l (39.5 kW/l); cast iron block, light alloy head; 5 crankshaft bearings; valves: overhead, thimble tappets; camshafts: 1, overhead, cogged belt; lubrication: gear pump, cartridge filter, 8.3 imp pt, 9.9 US pt, 4.7 l; 1 Weber 32 ICEV 21 or Solex C32 DISA/1 downdraught single barrel carburettor; fuel feed: mechanical pump; water-cooled, expansion tank, 12.5 imp pt, 15 US pt, 7.1 l; electric thermostatic fan.

TRANSMISSION driving wheels: front; clutch: single dry plate; gearbox: mechanical; gears: 4, fully synchronized; ratios: I 3.583, II 2.235, III 1.454, IV 1.042, rev 3.714; lever: central; final drive: helical cylindrical; axle ratio: 4.077; width of rims: 4.5''; tyres: 145SR x 13.

PERFORMANCE max speeds: 90 mph, 145 km/h; power-weight ratio: L 3-dr 30.1 lb/hp (41 lb/kW), 13.7 kg/hp (18.6 kg/kW) - CL 5-dr and L 3-dr 30.9 lb/hp (42 lb/kW), 14 kg/hp (19 kg/kW) - CL 5-dr 31.4 lb/hp (42.7 lb/kW), 14.2 kg/hp (19.4 kg/kW); carrying capacity: 882 lb, 400 kg; speed in top at 1,000 rpm: 15 mph, 24.2 km/h; consumption: 32.4 m/imp gal, 27 m/US gal, 8.7 l x 100 km.

CHASSIS integral; front suspension: independent, by McPherson, lower wishbones, trailing links, coil springs/telescopic damper struts; rear: independent, by McPherson, lower wishbones, transverse anti-roll leafspring, telescopic dampers.

STEERING rack-and-pinion; turns lock to lock: 3.5.

BRAKES front disc (diameter 8.94 in, 22.7 cm), rear drum dual circuit, rear compensator, lining area: front 19.2 sq in, 124 sq cm, rear 33.3 sq in, 215 sq cm, total 52.5 sq in, 339 sq cm.

199

60 HP POWER TEAM

ELECTRICAL EQUIPMENT 12 V; 34 Ah battery; 45 A alternator; 2 headlamps.

DIMENSIONS AND WEIGHT wheel base: 96.38 in, 245 cm; tracks: 55.12 in, 140 cm front, 55.51 in, 141 cm rear; length: 155.12 in, 394 cm; width: 65 in, 165 cm; height: 55.12 in, 140 cm; weight: L 3-dr 1,808 lb, 820 kg - CL 3-dr and - L 5-dr 1,852 lb, 840 kg - CL 5-dr 1,885 lb, 855 kg; weight distribution: 62.5% front, 37.5% rear; turning circle: 33.8 ft, 10.3 m; fuel tank: 11.2 imp gal, 13.5 US gal, 51 l.

BODY saloon/sedan; 5 seats, separate front seats; folding rear seat.

PRACTICAL INSTRUCTIONS fuel: 98 oct petrol; oil: engine 7.7 imp pt, 9.3 US pt, 4.4 l, gearbox and final drive: 5.3 imp pt, 6.3 US pt, 3 l; valve timing: 12° 52° 52° 12° tyre pressure: front 27 psi, 1.9 atm, rear 26 psi, 1.8 atm.

OPTIONALS 5-speed fully synchronized mechanical gearbox (V 0.863); tyres: 165/70 SR x 13; sunshine roof; heated rear window; rear window with wiper-washer, headrests; metallic spray

65 hp power team

See 60 hp power team, except for:

ENGINE 79.39 cu in, 1,301 cc (3.40 x 2.18 in, 86.4 x 55.5 mm); compression ratio: 9.1:1; max power (DIN): 65 hp (47.8 kW) at 5,800 rpm; max torque (DIN): 72.5 lb ft, 10 kg m (98 Nm) at 3,500 rpm; 49.9 hp/l (36.7 kW/l); 1 Weber 32 ICEV 22 or Solex C 32 DISA/2 downdraught single barrel carburettor; cooling system: 13.9 imp pt, 16.7 US pt, 7.9.

TRANSMISSION axle ratio: 3.765.

PERFORMANCE max speed: 93 mph, 150 km/h; power-weight ratio: L 3-dr 27.8 lb/hp (37.8 lb/kW), 12.6 kg/hp (17.1 kg/kW) - CL 3-dr and L 5-dr 28.5 lb/hp (38.7 lb/kW), 12.9 kg/hp (17.6 kg/hp) - CL 5-dr 29 lb/hp (39.4 lb/kW), 13.1 kg/hp (17.9 kg/kW); speed in top at 1,000 rpm: 16.3 mph, 26.2 km/h; consumption: 32.1 m/imp gal, 26.7 m/US gal, 8.8 l x 100 km.

ELECTRICAL EQUIPMENT 45 Ah battery.

OPTIONALS air-conditioning.

75 hp power team

See 60 hp power team, except for:

ENGINE 91.41 cu in, 1,498 cc (3.40 x 2.51 in, 86.4 x 63.9 mm); compression ratio: 9:1; max power (DIN): 75 hp (55 kW) at 5,800 rpm; max torque (DIN): 86.9 lb ft, 12 kg m (118 Nm) at 3,000 rpm; 1 Weber 34 ICEV 23/250 downdraught single barrel carburettor; cooling system: 14.1 imp pt, 16.9 US pt, 8 l.

TRANSMISSION axle ratio: 3.588.

FIAT Ritmo 60 CL 5-dr Berlina

PERFORMANCE max speed: 99 mph, 160 km/h; power-weight ratio: L 3-dr 24.4 lb/hp (33.3 lb/kW), 11.1 kg/hp (15.1 kg/kW) - CL 3-dr and L 5-dr 25 lb/hp (34.1 lb/kW), 11.3 kg/hp (15.4 kg/kW) - CL 5-dr 25.4 lb/hp (34.7 lb/kW), 11.5 kg/hp (15.7 kg/kW); speed in top at 1,000 rpm: 17.1 mph, 27.5 km/h; consumption: 33 m/imp gal, 27.7 m/US gal, 8.5 l x 100 km.

BRAKES servo

DIMENSIONS AND WEIGHT weight: L 3-dr 1,830 kg - CL 3-dr and L 5-dr 1,875 lb, 850 kg - CL 5-dr 1,907 lb, 865 kg.

OPTIONALS automatic transmission, hydraulic torque converter and planetary gears with 3 ratios (I 2.550, II 1.450, III 1, rev 2.460), max ratio of converter at stall 2.47, axle ratio 3.565, anti-roll bar on front suspension, max speed mph, 155 km/h; power-weight ratio L 3-dr 25.3 lb/hp (34.5 lb/kW), 11.5 kg/hp (15.6 kg/kW), consumption 28.5 m/imp gal, 23.7 m/US gal, 9.9 l x 100 km, weight L 3-dr 1,896 lb, 860 kg, weight distribution 64.5% front, 35.5% rear; air-conditioning.

X1/9 five speed

PRICE IN GB: £ 4,275*
PRICE EX WORKS: 6,500,000 liras**

ENGINE centre-rear, transverse, 4 stroke; 4 cylinders, vertical, in line; 91.4 cu in, 1,498 cc (3.40 x 2.52 in, 86.4 x 63.9 mm); compression ratio: 9.2:1; max power (DIN): 8 hp (62.5 kW) at 6,000 rpm; max torque (DIN): 87 lb ft, kg m (118 Nm) at 3,200 rpm; max engine rpm: 6,500; 56 hp/l (41.7 kW/l); cast iron block, light alloy head; crankshaft bearings; valves: overhead, in line, thimble tappets; camshafts: 1, overhead, cogged belt; lubrication 7.9 imp pt, 9.5 US pt, 4.5 l; 1 Weber 34 DATR 7/250 downdraught twin barrel carburettor; fuel feed: mechanical pump; water-cooled, 20.4 imp pt, 24.5 US pt, 11.6 l, electr thermostatic fan.

TRANSMISSION driving wheels: rear; clutch: single dry plate (diaphragm), hydraulically controlled; gearbox: mechanical; gears: 5, fully synchronized; ratios: I 3.583, II 2.23 III 1.454, IV 1.042, V 0.863, rev 3.714; lever: central; final drive: helical cylindrical; axle ratio: 4.076; width of rim 5''; tyres: 165/70 SR x 13.

PERFORMANCE max speeds: (I) 31 mph, 50 km/h; (II) mph, 80 km/h; (III) 77 mph, 124 km/h; (IV) 102 mph, 1 km/h; (V) 112 mph, 180 km/h; power-weight ratio: 23 lb/hp, (32.5 lb/kW), 10.8 kg/hp (14.7 kg/kW); carrying c pacity: 441 lb, 200 kg; acceleration: standing ¼ mile 17 sec; speed in top at 1,000 rpm: 17.2 mph, 27.7 km/h; consumption: 36.2 m/imp gal, 30.2 m/US gal, 7.8 l x 100 km

CHASSIS integral; front suspension: independent, McPherson (lower trailing links), coil springs/telescopic damper struts, lower wishbones; rear: independent, low wishbones, each with articulated transverse control ba coil springs/telescopic damper struts.

STEERING rack-and-pinion; turns lock to lock: 3.05.

BRAKES disc (diameter 8.94 in, 22.7 cm), dual circuit servo; lining area: front 19.2 sq in, 124 sq cm, rear 19 sq in, 124 sq cm, total 38.4 sq in, 248 sq cm.

ELECTRICAL EQUIPMENT 12 V; 45 Ah battery; 45 A alternator; 2 retractable headlamps.

DIMENSIONS AND WEIGHT wheel base: 86.69 in, 220 cm tracks: 53.35 in, 135.5 cm front, 53.15 in, 135 cm rea length: 156.26 in, 397 cm; width: 61.81 in, 157 cm; height 46.46 in, 118 cm; ground clearance: 4.92 in, 12.5 cm weight: 2,029 lb, 920 kg; weight distribution: 40.2% front 59.8% rear; turning circle: 32.8 ft, 10 m; fuel tank: 10 imp gal, 12.9 US gal, 49 l.

BODY sports; 2 doors; 2 seats, built-in headrests; rollbar; detachable roof.

PRACTICAL INSTRUCTIONS fuel: 98-100 oct petrol; oil engine 7.9 imp pt, 9.5 US pt, 4.5 l, SAE 10W-50, change every 6,200 miles, 10,000 km - gearbox and final drive 4.9 imp pt, 5.9 US pt, 2.8 l, change every 18,600 mile 30,000 km; greasing: none; valve timing: 24° 68° 64° 28° tyre pressure: front 26 psi, 1.8 atm, rear 28 psi, 2 atm.

OPTIONALS light alloy wheels; heated rear window; tinted glass with heated rear window.

VARIATIONS

(For USA only).
ENGINE 8.5 compression ratio, max power (DIN) 67 (49.3 kW) at 5,250 rpm, 44.7 hp/l (32.9 kW/l).
PERFORMANCE max speed 106 mph, 170 km/h, power-weight ratio 31.6 lb/hp (43 lb/kW), 14.4 kg/hp (19.5 kg/kW).
DIMENSIONS AND WEIGHT weight 2,120 lb, 962 kg.

OPTIONALS air-conditioning, metallic spray.

FIAT X1/9 five speed

131 Series

PRICES IN GB AND EX WORKS:

	£	liras
Mirafiori 1300 L 4-dr Berlina	2,858*	5,168,400**
Mirafiori 1300 L 5-dr Panorama	—	5,593,200**
Mirafiori 1300 CL 2-dr Berlina	—	5,516,500**
Mirafiori 1300 CL 4-dr Berlina	—	5,782,000**
Mirafiori 1600 CL 4-dr Berlina	3,365*	5,923,600**
Mirafiori 1600 CL 5-dr Panorama	3,691*	6,348,400**
Supermirafiori 1300 4-dr Berlina	—	6,590,300**
Supermirafiori 1600 4-dr Berlina	3,748*	6,731,900**
Supermirafiori 1600 5-dr Panorama	—	—
Racing 2000 2-dr Berlina	4,395*	7,221,600**
Diesel 2000 L 4-dr Berlina	—	6,832,200**
Diesel 2000 CL 4-dr Berlina	—	7,162,600**
Diesel 2000 CL 5-dr Panorama	—	7,587,400**
Diesel 2500 Super 4-dr Berlina	—	8,460,000**
Diesel 2500 5-dr Panorama Super	—	8,944,000**

Power team:	Standard for:	Optional for:
65 hp	1 to 4	—
75 hp	5,6	—
78 hp	7	—
96 hp	8,9	—
55 hp (Diesel)	10	—
70 hp (Diesel)	11 to 13	—
72 hp (Diesel)	14,15	—

65 hp power team

ENGINE front, 4 stroke; 4 cylinders, vertical, in line; 79.1 cu in, 1,297 cc (2.99 x 2.81 in, 76 x 71.5 mm); compression ratio: 9.2:1; max power (DIN): 65 hp (47.8 kW) at 5,200 rpm; max torque (DIN): 75 lb ft, 10.4 kg m (102 Nm) at 3,000 rpm; 50.2 hp/l (36.9 kW/l); cast iron block, light alloy head; 5 crankshafts bearings; valves: overhead, in line, slanted at 10°, push-rods and rockers; camshafts: 1, side, in crankcase, cogged belt; lubrication: gear pump, full flow filter (cartridge), 7.6 imp pt, 9.1 US pt, 4.3 l; 1 Weber 32 ADF/7 or Solex C32 TEIE/42 downdraught twin barrel carburettor; fuel feed: mechanical pump; water-cooled, 13.4 imp pt, 16.1 US pt, 7.6 l, electric thermostatic fan.

TRANSMISSION driving wheels: rear; clutch: single dry plate (diaphragm); gearbox: mechanical; gears: 4, fully synchronized; ratios: I 3.612, II 2.045, III 1.357, IV 1, rev 3.244; lever: central; final drive: hypoid bevel; axle ratio: 4.100; width of rims: 5''; tyres: 155 SR x 13 - CL 2-dr, CL 4-dr and L Panorama 165 SR x 13.

PERFORMANCE max speed: 93 mph, 150 km/h; power-weight ratio: 2-dr models 32.2 lb/hp (43.8 lb/kW), 14.6 kg/hp (19.9 kg/kW); carrying capacity: 882 lb, 400 kg - Panorama 948 lb, 430 kg; acceleration: standing ¼ mile 19.3 sec; speed in direct drive at 1,000 rpm: 16.4 mph, 26.4 km/h; consumption: 31.7 m/imp gal, 26.4 m/US gal, 8.9 l x 100 km.

CHASSIS integral; front suspension: independent, by McPherson, coil springs/telescopic damper struts, lower wishbones, anti-roll bar; rear: rigid axle, twin trailing lower radius arms, transverse linkage bar, coil springs, telescopic dampers.

STEERING rack-and-pinion, adjustable height of steering wheel (for CL models only); turns lock to lock: 3.50.

FIAT 131 Racing 2000

BRAKES front disc (diameter 8.94 in, 22.7 cm), rear drum (diameter 8.97 in, 22.8 cm), dual circuit, rear compensator, servo; lining area: front sq in, 124 sq cm, rear sq in, 270 sq cm, total sq in, 394 sq cm.

ELECTRICAL EQUIPMENT 12 V; 45 Ah battery 45 A alternator; Marelli distributor; headlamps: 2.

DIMENSIONS AND WEIGHT wheel base: 98.03 in, 249 cm; tracks: 54.33 in, 138 cm front, 51.97 in, 132 cm rear; length: 167.72 in, 426 cm; width: 64.96 in, 165 cm; height: 54.33 in, 138 cm - Panorama models 54.72 in, 139 cm; weight: 2-dr models 2,095 lb, 950 kg - 4-dr models 2,128 lb, 965 kg - Panorama models 2,172 lb, 985 kg; turning circle: 34 ft, 10.3 m; fuel tank: 11 imp gal, 13.2 US gal, 50 l.

BODY saloon/sedan 5 seats, separate front seats; folding rear seat (for Panorama only); reclining backrests.

PRACTICAL INSTRUCTIONS fuel: 98-100 oct petrol; oil: engine 7 imp pt, 8.4 US pt, 4 l, SAE 10W-30 (winter) 20W-40 (summer), change every 6,200 miles, 10,000 km - gearbox 3.2 imp pt, 3.8 US pt, 1.8 l, SAE 90 EP, change every 18,600 miles, 30,000 km - final drive 1.8 imp pt, 2.1 US pt, 1 l, SAE 90 EP, change every 18,600 miles, 30,000 km; sparking plug: 200°; valve timing: 3° 45° 43° 5°; tyre pressure: front 26 psi, 1.8 atm, rear 26 psi, 1.8 atm (Panorama 31 psi, 2.2 atm).

OPTIONALS 5-speed fully synchronized mechanical gearbox (I 3.612, II 2.045, III 1.357, IV 1, V 0.870, rev 3.244), speed in top at 1,000 rpm 18 mph, 29 km/h (Panorama 18.9 mph, 30.4 km/h), consumption 32.8 m/imp gal, 27.3 m/US gal, 8.6 l x 100 km; light alloy wheels; heated rear window; tinted glass with heated rear window; reclining backrests; reclining backrests with built-in headrests; antitheft; shock absorbing bumpers; opening rear window (for 2-dr models only); metallic spray; vinyl roof; air-conditioning; tyres 175/70 SR x 13; wiper-washers on rear window (for Panorama models only).

75 hp power team

See 65 hp power team, except for:

ENGINE 96.7 cu in, 1,585 cc (3.31 x 2.81 in, 84 x 71.5 mm); max power (DIN): 75 hp (55.2 kW) at 5,200 rpm; max torque (DIN): 91 lb ft, 12.6 kg m (123.6 Nm) at 3,000 rpm; 47.4 hp/l (34.8 kW/l); cooling system: 13 imp pt, 15.6 US pt, 7.4 l.

TRANSMISSION axle ratio: 3.900.

PERFORMANCE max speed: 99 mph, 160 km/h; power-weight ratio: 2-dr models 27.9 lb/hp (37.9 lb/kW), 12.7 kg/hp (17.2 kg/kW); acceleration: standing ¼ mile 18.2 sec; speed in direct drive at 1,000 rpm: 16.8 mph, 27 km/h - Panorama models 17.3 mph, 27.8 km/h; consumption 30.7 m/imp gal, 25.6 m/US gal, 9.2 l x 100.

PRACTICAL INSTRUCTIONS valve timing: 10° 49° 50° 9°.

OPTIONALS limited slip differential; with 5-speed fully synchronized mechanical gearbox, 3.900 axle ratio, speed in top at 1,000 rpm 19 mph, 30.6 km/h (Panorama models 19.9 mph, 32 km/h), consumption 31.7 m/imp gal, 26.4 m/US gal, 8.9 l x 100 km; G.M.S. automatic transmission, hydraulic torque converter and planetary gears with 3 ratios (I 2.400, II 1.480, III 1, rev 1.920), max ratio of converter at stall 2.4, possible manual selection, 3.900 axle ratio, acceleration standing ¼ mile 19 sec, consumption 28 m/imp gal, 23.3 m/US gal, 10.1 l x 100 km.

78 hp power team

See 65 hp power team, except for:

ENGINE compression ratio: 8.9:1; max power (DIN): 78 hp (57.4 kW) at 6,000 rpm; max torque (DIN): 76.1 lb ft, 10.5 kg m (103 Nm) at 4,000 rpm; 60.1 hp/l (44.2 kW/l); camshafts: 2, overhead; lubrication: 8.4 imp pt, 10.1 US pt, 4.8 l; 1 Weber 32 ADF13 downdraught twin barrel carburettor; cooling system: 14.1 imp pt, 16.9 US pt, 8 l.

TRANSMISSION gears: 5, fully synchronized; ratios: I 3.612, II 2.045, III 1.357, IV 1, V 0.870; tyres: 165 SR x 13.

PERFORMANCE max speeds: 99 mph, 160 km/h; power-weight ratio: 28.3 lb/hp (38.4 lb/kW), 12.8 kg/hp (17.4 kg/kW); acceleration: standing ¼ mile 18.7 sec; consumption: 34 m/imp gal, 28.3 m/US gal, 8.3 l x 100 km.

ELECTRICAL EQUIPMENT 2 halogen headlamps.

DIMENSIONS AND WEIGHT length: in, 423 cm; weight: 2,205 lb, 1,000 kg; weight distribution: 52.4% front, 47.6% rear.

BODY built-in headrests on front and rear seats.

FIAT 131 Mirafiori 1300 L 4-dr Berlina

78 HP POWER TEAM

PRACTICAL INSTRUCTIONS oil: engine 7.2 imp pt, 8.7 US pt, 4.1 l; valve timing: 17° 37° 48° 6°.

OPTIONALS G.M.S. automatic transmission, hydraulic torque converter and planetary gears with 3 ratios (I 2.400, II 1.480, III 1, rev 1.920).

96 hp power team

See 78 hp power team, except for:

ENGINE 96.72 cu in, 1,585 cc (3.31 x 2.81 in, 84 x 71.5 mm); compression ratio: 9:1; max power (DIN): 96 hp (70.6 kW) at 6,000 rpm; max torque (DIN): 94.2 lb/ft, 13 kg m (127.5 Nm) at 3,800 rpm; 60.1 hp/l (44.5 kW/l); 1 Weber 32 ADF 14 downdraught twin barrel carburettor.

TRANSMISSION axle ratio: 3.900.

PERFORMANCE max speed: 106 mph, 170 km/h; power-weight ratio: 22.9 lb/hp (31.2 lb/kW), 10.4 kg/hp (14.2 kg/kW); acceleration: standing ¼ mile 17.5 sec; speed in direct drive at 1,000 rpm: 17.3 mph, 27.8 km/h; consumption: 32.8 m/imp gal, 27.3 m/US gal, 8.6 l x 100 km.

PRACTICAL INSTRUCTIONS valve timing: 12° 53° 54° 11°.

115 hp power team

See 78 hp power team, except for:

ENGINE 121.7 cu in, 1,995 cc (3.31 x 3.54 in, 84 x 90 mm); max power (DIN): 115 hp (84 kW) at 5,800 rpm; max torque (DIN): 123.2 lb ft, 17 kg m (167 Nm) at 3,600 rpm; 57.6 hp/l (42.1 kW/l); 1 Weber 34 ADF 15 downdraught twin barrel carburettor; cooling system: 14.4 imp pt, 17.3 US pt, 8.2 l.

TRANSMISSION axle ratio: 3.900; width of rims: 5.5''; tyres: 185/70 SR x 13.

PERFORMANCE max speed: 112 mph, 180 km/h; power-weight ratio: 19.6 lb/hp (26.8 lb/kW), 8.9 kg/hp (12.1 kg/kW); acceleration: standing ¼ mile 16.5 sec; speed in direct drive at 1,000 rpm: 19.9 mph, 32.1 km/h; consumption: 28.8 m/imp gal, 24 m/US gal, 9.8 l x 100 km.

ELECTRICAL EQUIPMENT 4 headlamps.

DIMENSIONS AND WEIGHT tracks: 52.36 in, 133 cm rear; width: 65.35 in, 166 cm; height: 55.12 in, 140 cm; weight: 22.50 lb, 1,020 kg; weight distribution: 54% front, 46% rear.

PRACTICAL INSTRUCTIONS valve timing: 15° 55° 57° 13°.

60 hp (Diesel) power team

See 65 hp power team, except for:

ENGINE Diesel; 121.7 cu in, 1,995 cc (3.46 x 3.23 in, 88 x 82 mm); compression ratio: 22:1; max power (DIN): 60 hp (44.1 kW) at 4,400 rpm; max torque (DIN): 83.3 lb ft, 11.5 kg m (112.8 Nm) at 2,400 rpm; 30.1 hp/l (22.1 kW/l); camshafts: 1, overhead; lubrication: 11.6 imp pt, 13.9 US pt, 6.6 l; Bosch indirect injection pump; liquid cooled, expansion tank, 19.4 imp pt, 23.3 US pt, 11 l, electromagnetic thermostatic fan.

TRANSMISSION gears: 5, fully synchronized; ratios: I 3.612, II 2.045, III 1.357, IV 1, V 0.870, rev 3.244; axle ratio: 3.900; tyres: 165 SR x 13.

PERFORMANCE max speed: 87 mph, 140 km/h; power-weight ratio: 40.8 lb/hp, (55.5 lb/kW), 18.5 kg/hp (25.2 kg/kW) - Panorama 41.5 lb/hp (56.5 lb/kW), 18.8 kg/hp (25.6 kg/kW); acceleration: standing ¼ mile 22.8 sec; speed in direct drive at 1,000 rpm: 17.3 mph, 27.8 km/h; consumption: 35.7 m/imp gal, 29.8 m/US gal, 7.9 l x100 km.

STEERING turns lock to lock: 4.08.

ELECTRICAL EQUIPMENT 77 Ah battery; 4 iodine headlamps.

DIMENSIONS AND WEIGHT height: 54.72 in, 139 cm; weight: 2,447 lb, 1,110 kg - Panorama 2,492 lb, 1,130 kg; weight distribution: 58.3% front, 41.4% rear - Panorama 56.4% front, 43.6% rear.

PRACTICAL INSTRUCTIONS fuel: Diesel oil; oil: engine 9.7 imp pt, 11.6 US pt, 5.5 l; valve timing: 8° 48° 48° 8°; tyre pressure: front 30 psi, 2.1 atm, rear 28 psi, 2 atm.

FIAT 131 Diesel 2500 Super

72 hp (Diesel) power team

See 60 hp power team (Diesel), except for:

ENGINE 149.2 cu in, 2,445 cc (3.66 x 3.54 in, 93 x 90 m max power (DIN): 72 hp (53 kW) at 4,200 rpm; max tor (DIN): 108.7 lb ft, 15 kg m (147.2 Nm) at 2,400 r 29.4 hp/l (21.7 kW/l).

PERFORMANCE max speed: over 93 mph, 150 km/h; pow weight ratio: 34 lb/hp (46.2 lb/kW), 15.4 kg/hp (kg/kW); acceleration: standing ¼ mile: 20.5 sec; sumption: 34.4 m/imp gal, 28.7 m/US gal, 8.2 l x 100

BODY built-in headrests on front and rear seats.

124 Sport Spider 2000

(Only for USA).

**PRICE IN USA: $ 7,090*

ENGINE front, 4 stroke; 4 cylinders, vertical, in line; 1 cu in, 1,995 cc (3.31 x 3.54 in, 84 x 90 mm); compres ratio: 8:1; max power (DIN): 86 hp (63.3 kW) at 5,100 max torque (DIN): 104.3 lb ft, 14.4 kg m (141.3 Nm) 3,000 rpm; max engine rpm: 5,600; 43.1 hp/l (31.7 kW cast iron block, light alloy head; 5 crankshaft bearin valves: overhead, Vee-slanted at 63°30', thimble tapp camshafts: 2, overhead, cogged belt; lubrication: gear pu full flow filter (cartridge), 8.3 imp pt, 9.9 US pt, 4.7 Weber or Solex downdraught twin barrel carburettor; feed: electric pump; water-cooled, 14.1 imp pt, 16.9 pt, 8 l.

TRANSMISSION driving wheels: rear; clutch: single plate; gearbox: mechanical; gears: 5, fully synchroni ratios: I 3.667, II 2.100, III 1.361, IV 1, V 0.881, rev 3. lever: central; final drive: hypoid bevel: axle ratio: 3. width of rims: 5''; tyres: 165 HR x 13.

PERFORMANCE max speeds: (I) 30 mph, 48 kn (II) 52 mph, 83 km/h; (III) 78 mph, 125 km/h; (IV) 103 165 km/h; (V) 109 mph, 175 km/h; power-weight ra 26.9 lb/hp, (36.5 lb/kW), 12.2 kg/hp (16.6 kg/kW); ca ing capacity: 706 lb, 320 kg; acceleration: standing ¼ 18 sec; speed in top at 1,000 rpm: 19.4 mph, 31.2 kn consumption: 32.8 m/imp gal, 27.3 m/US gal, 8.6 l x 100

CHASSIS integral; front suspension: independent, wishbor coil springs, anti-roll bar, telescopic dampers; rear: r axle, twin trailing radius arms, transverse linkage coil springs, telescopic dampers.

STEERING worm and roller; turns lock to lock: 2.75.

BRAKES disc (diameter 8.94 in, 22.7 cm), dual cir servo; lining area: total 38.4 sq in, 248 sq cm.

ELECTRICAL EQUIPMENT 12 V; 35 Ah battery; 42 A a nator; Marelli electronic ignition; 2 halogen headlar

DIMENSIONS AND WEIGHT wheel base: 89.76 in, 228 tracks: 52.99 in, 135 cm front, 51.82 in, 132 cm rear; 163 in, 414 cm; width: 63.50 in, 161 cm; height: 48.20 122 cm; ground clearance: 4.92 in, 12.5 cm; 2

FIAT 124 Sport Spider 2000

1,048 kg; weight distribution: 56% front, 44% rear;
ning circle: 34.1 ft, 10.4 m; fuel tank: 9.9 imp gal, 11.9
gal, 45 l.

DY sports; 2 doors; 2 + 2 seats, separate front seats,
clining backrests, headrests, tinted glass.

ACTICAL INSTRUCTIONS fuel: 100 oct petrol; oil: engine
mp pt, 8.5 US pt, 4 l, SAE 30W (summer) 20W (winter)
ange every 6,200 miles, 10,000 km - gearbox 2.3 imp pt,
US pt, 1.3 l, FIAT ZC 90, change every 18,600 miles,
000 km - final drive 2.5 imp pt, 3 US pt, 1.4 l, FIAT
0/W, change every 18,600 miles, 30,000 km; greasing:
ery 18,600 miles, 30,000 km, 4 points; tyre pressure:
nt 26 psi, 1.8 atm rear 26 psi, 1.8 atm.

TIONALS G.M. automatic transmission, hydraulic torque
nverter and planetary gears with 3 ratios (I 2.400, II
80, III 1, rev 1.920), max ratio of converter at stall 2.4,
ssible manual selection, 3.583 axle ratio; electric win-
ws; hardtop; light alloy wheels; metallic spray.

132 1600 Berlina

ICE EX WORKS: **7,198,000** ** liras

GINE front, 4 stroke; 4 cylinders, vertical, in line; 96.7
in, 1,585 cc (3.31 x 2.81 in, 84 x 71.5 mm); compression
io: 9:1; max power (DIN): 98 hp (72.1 kW) at 5,600 rpm;
x torque (DIN): 97 lb ft, 13.4 kg m (131.4 Nm) at 4,000
n; max engine rpm: 6,500; 61.8 hp/l (45.5 kW/l); cast
n block, light alloy head; 5 crankshaft bearings; valves:
erhead, Vee slanted, thimble tappets; camshafts:
overhead, cogged belt; lubrication: gear pump, full flow
er (cartridge), 8.3 imp pt, 9.9 US pt, 4.7 l; 1 Weber
ADF2 downdraught twin barrel carburettor; fuel feed: me-
anical pump; water-cooled, 14.1 imp pt, 16.9 US pt, 8
electric thermostatic fan.

ANSMISSION driving wheels: rear; clutch: single dry
te; gearbox: mechanical; gears: 5, fully synchronized
ios: I 3.612, II 2.045, III 1.357, IV 1, V 0.870, rev 3.244;
er: central; final drive: hypoid bevel axle ratio: 3.727;
dth of rims: 5.5''; tyres: 175 SR x 14.

RFORMANCE max speeds: (I) 28 mph, 45 km/h; (II) 50
h, 80 km/h; (III) 78 mph, 125 km/h; (IV) 103 mph,
km/h; (V) about 99 mph, 160 km/h; power-weight ratio:
9 lb/hp (32.5 lb/kW), 10.8 kg/hp (14.8 kg/kW); carrying
acity: 882 lb, 400 kg; acceleration: standing ¼ mile
sec; speed in direct drive at 1,000 rpm: 18.3 mph, 29.4
/h; consumption: 30 m/imp gal, 25 m/US gal, 9.4
100 km.

ASSIS integral; front suspension: independent, wish-
nes (lower trailing links), coil springs, anti-roll bar,
escopic dampers; rear: rigid axle, lower longitudinal
iling radius arms, upper oblique torque arms, coil
rings, telescopic dampers.

EERING worm and roller; turns lock to lock: 3.05.

AKES front disc (diameter 9.88 in, 25.1 cm), rear drum,
ar compensator, dual circuit, servo; lining area: front
2 sq in, 124 sq cm, rear 41.8 sq in, 270 sq cm, total
1 sq in, 394 sq cm.

ECTRICAL EQUIPMENT 12 V; 45 Ah battery; 45 A alter-
tor; Marelli distributor; 4 headlamps.

MENSIONS AND WEIGHT wheel base: 100.67 in, 256 cm;
cks: 51.97 in, 132 cm front, 52.36 in, 133 cm rear;
ngth: 172.83 in, 439 cm; width: 64.57 in, 164 cm; height:
30 in, 143 cm; ground clearance: 4.92 in, 12.5 cm;
ight: 2,348 lb, 1,065 kg; weight distribution: 53% front,
% rear; turning circle: 35.4 ft, 10.8 m; fuel tank: 12.3
p gal, 14.8 US gal, 56 l.

DY saloon/sedan; 4 doors; 5 seats, separate front seats,
clining backrests.

ACTICAL INSTRUCTIONS fuel: 98-100 oct petrol; oil:
gine 7.2 imp pt, 8.7 US pt, 4.1 l, SAE 30W (summer) 20W
inter), change every 6.200 miles, 10,000 km - gearbox
imp pt, 3.8 US pt, 1.8 l, FIAT ZC 90, change every
.600 miles, 30,000 km - final drive 2.3 imp pt, 2.7 US pt,
l, FIAT W90/M, change every 18,600 miles, 30,000 km;
easing: every 18,600 miles, 30,000 km, 4 points; tappet
arances: inlet 0.018 in, 0.45 mm, exhaust 0.024 in,
60 mm; valve timing: 12° 53° 54° 11°; tyre pressure:
nt 26 psi, 1.8 atm, rear 27 psi, 1.9 atm.

PTIONALS G.M. automatic transmission with 3 ratios (I
400, II 1.480, III 1, rev 1.920), hydraulic torque converter
d planetary gears, possible manual selection, max speeds
43 mph, 70 km/h, (II) 71 mph, 115 km/h, (III) 99
mph, 160 km/h, power-weight ratio 24.7 lb/hp (33.3 lb/
W), 11.2 kg/hp (15.1 kg/kW), acceleration standing ¼
le 19.2 sec, consumption 25.4 m/imp gal, 21.2 m/US
l, 11.1 l x 100 km, weight 2,403 lb, 1,090 kg, gearbox oil
imp pt, 5.9 US pt, 2.8 l; limited slip differential; light
oy wheels; electronic ignition; headrests; heated rear
ndow; tinted glass with heated rear window; rev counter;
-conditioning; metallic spray; antitheft.

FIAT 132 2000 Berlina

FIAT 132 Diesel 2000 - 2500

132 2000 Berlina

See 132 1600 Berlina except for:

PRICE IN GB: £ 4,595*
PRICE EX WORKS: 8,177,400 ** liras

ENGINE 121.7 cu in, 1,995 cc (3.31 x 3.54 in, 84 x 90 mm);
compression ratio: 8.9:1; max power (DIN): 112 hp (82.4 kW)
at 5,600 rpm; max torque (DIN): 117 lb ft, 16.1 kg m (157.9
Nm) at 3,000 rpm; 56.1 hp/l (41.3 kW/l); 1 Weber 34 ADF
downdraught twin barrel carburettor.

PERFORMANCE max speed: 105 mph, 169 km/h; power-
weight ratio: 21.6 lb/hp (29.4 lb/kW), 9.8 kg/hp (13.3 kg/kW);
acceleration: standing ¼ mile 17 sec; speed in top at
1,000 rpm: 20 mph, 32.2 km/h; consumption: 17.2 m/imp gal,
20.7 m/US gal, 9.8 l x 100 km.

DIMENSIONS AND WEIGHT weight: 2,425 lb, 1,100 kg.

PRACTICAL INSTRUCTIONS valve timing: 15° 55° 57° 13°.

132 Diesel 2000

See 132 1600 Berlina, except for:

PRICE EX WORKS: 8,850,000 ** liras

ENGINE Diesel; 121.7 cu in, 1,995 cc (3.46 x 3.23 in, 88 x 82
mm); compression ratio: 22:1; max power (DIN): 60 hp
(44.1 kW) at 4,400 rpm; max torque (DIN): 83.3 lb ft, 11.5

kg m (112.8 Nm) at 2,400 rpm; 30.1 hp/l (22.1 kW/l); valves:
overhead, in line; camshafts: 1, overhead; lubrication: 11.6
imp pt, 13.9 US pt, 6.6 l; Bosch indirect injection pump;
liquid cooled, expansion tank, 19.4 imp pt, 23.3 US pt, 11
l, electromagnetic thermostatic fan.

TRANSMISSION axle ratio: 4.100.

PERFORMANCE max speed: (I) 84 mph, 135 km/h; power-
weight ratio: 44.8 lb/hp, (61 lb/kW), 20.3 kg/hp (27.7 kg/
kW); acceleration: standing ¼ mile 23 sec, speed in direct
drive at 1,000 rpm: 16.7 mph, 26.9 km/h; consumption: 33.2
m/imp gal, 27.7 m/US gal, 8.5 l x 100 km.

STEERING recirculating ball, servo: turns lock to lock: 2.9.

ELECTRICAL EQUIPMENT 77 Ah battery.

DIMENSIONS AND WEIGHT weight: 2,690 lb, 1,220 kg;
weight distribution: 58% front, 42% rear.

PRACTICAL INSTRUCTIONS fuel: Diesel oil; oil: engine
9.7 imp pt, 11.6 US pt, 5.5 l; valve timing: 8° 48° 48° 8°;
tyre pressure: front 30 psi, 2.1 atm, rear 27 psi, 1.9 atm.

132 Diesel 2500

See 132 Diesel 2000, except for:

PRICE EX WORKS: 9,274,800 ** liras

ENGINE 149.2 cu in, 2,445 cc (3.66 x 3.54 in, 93 x 90 mm);
max power (DIN): 72 hp (53 kW) at 4,200 rpm; max torque

132 DIESEL 2500

(DIN): 108.7 lb ft, 15 kgm (147.2 Nm) at 2,400 rpm; 29.4 hp/l (21.7 kW/l).

TRANSMISSION axle ratio: 3.727.

PERFORMANCE max speed: 93 mph, 150 km/h; power-weight ratio: 37.7 lb/hp (51.7 lb/kW), 17.1 kg/hp (23.2 kg/kW); acceleration: standing ¼ mile 20.8 sec; speed in direct drive at 1,000 rpm: 18.4 mph, 29.6 km/h; consumption: 31.7 m/imp gal, 26.4 m/US gal, 8.9 l x 100 km.

DIMENSIONS AND WEIGHT weight: 2,712 lb, 1,230 kg.

Campagnola

PRICE EX WORKS: 9,936,000** liras

ENGINE front, 4 stroke; 4 cylinders, vertical, in line; 121.7 cu in, 1,995 cc (3.31 x 3.54 in, 84 x 90 mm); compression ratio: 8.6:1; max power (DIN): 80 hp (58.9 kW) at 4,600 rpm; max torque (DIN): 112 lb ft, 15.4 kg m (151 Nm) at 2,800 rpm; 40.1 hp/l (29.5 kW/l); cast iron block, light alloy head; 5 crankshaft bearings; valves: overhead, slanted at 10°, push-rods and rockers; camshafts: 1, side, cogged belt; lubrication: gear pump, full flow filter (cartridge), 8.4 imp pt, 10.1 US pt, 4.8 l; 1 Solex C 32 PHHE-1 horizontal twin barrel carburettor; fuel feed: mechanical pump; water-cooled, 15.7 imp pt, 18.8 US pt, 8.9 l.

TRANSMISSION driving wheels: front and rear; clutch: single dry plate; gearbox: mechanical, in unit with engine; gears: 4, fully synchronized; high ratios: I 3.667, II 2.100, III 1.361, IV 1, rev 3.444; low ratios: 1.120 and 3.333; gear and transfer levers: central; final drive: hypoid bevel, rear limited slip differential; axle ratio (front and rear): 5.375; width of rims: 4.5 K; tyres: 7.00 x 16 C 6PR.

PERFORMANCE max speeds (high ratio): (I) 20 mph, 33 km/h; (II) 35 mph, 57 km/h; (III) 55 mph, 88 km/h; (IV) over 71 mph, 115 km/h - (low ratios): (I) 7 mph, 11 km/h; (II) 12 mph, 19 km/h; (III) 18 mph, 29 km/h; (IV) 25 mph, 40 km/h; power-weight ratio: 44.3 lb/hp (60.2 lb/kW), 20.1 kg/hp (27.3 kg/kW); carrying capacity: 1,103 lb, 500 kg; speed in direct drive at 1,000 rpm: 14 mph, 22.5 km/h; consumption: 18.8 m/imp gal, 15.7 m/US gal, 15 l x 100 km.

CHASSIS integral; front suspension: independent, by McPherson, coil springs/telescopic damper struts, lower wishbones, anti-roll bar; rear: independent, by McPherson, coil springs, 4 telescopic dampers, lower wishbones, anti-roll bar.

STEERING worm and roller; turns lock to lock: 4.60.

BRAKES drum, dual circuit; swept area: front 91.5 sq in, 590 sq cm, rear 91.5 sq in, 590 sq cm, total 183 sq in, 1,180 sq cm.

ELECTRICAL EQUIPMENT 12 V; 45 Ah battery; 44 A alternator; Marelli distributor; 2 headlamps.

DIMENSIONS AND WEIGHT wheel base: 90.55 in, 230 cm; tracks: 53.54 in, 136 cm front, 55.91 in, 142 cm rear; length: 148.42 in, 377 cm; width: 62.20 in, 158 cm; height: 76.77 in, 195 cm; ground clearance: 10.16 in, 25.8 cm; weight: 3.550 lb, 1.610 kg; turning circle: 35.4 ft, 10.8 m; fuel tank: 12.5 imp gal, 15 US gal, 57 l.

BODY open; 2 doors; 7 seats, separate front seats.

PRACTICAL INSTRUCTIONS fuel: 99 oct petrol; oil: engine 7.4 imp pt, 8.9 US pt, 4.2 l, SAE 10W-40, change every 3,100 miles, 5,000 km - gearbox 2.5 imp pt, 3 US pt, 1.4 l, SAE 90 EP, change every 12,400 miles, 20,000 km - transfer box 3.9 imp pt, 4.7 US pt, 2.2 l, SAE 90 EP, change every 12,400 miles, 20,000 km - final drive 3.2 imp pt, 3.8 US pt, 1.8 l front, 3.2 imp pt, 3.8 US pt, 1.8 l rear, SAE 90 EP, change every 12,400 miles, 20,000 km; valve timing: 10° 49° 50° 9°; tyre pressure: front 26 psi, 1.8 atm, rear 36 psi, 2.5 atm.

OPTIONALS hardtop; front limited slip differential.

Campagnola Lunga

See Campagnola, except for:

PRICE EX WORKS: 10,242,000** liras

TRANSMISSION axle ratio (front and rear): 5.625; width of rims: 5K or 5.00 F.

PERFORMANCE max speeds (hight ratios): (I) 19 mph, 31 km/h; (II) 34 mph, 54 km/h; (III) 52 mph, 84 km/h; (IV) over 68 mph, 110 km/h - (low ratios): (I) 6 mph, 10 km/h; (II) 11 mph, 18 km/h; (III) 17 mph, 28 km/h; (IV) 24 mph, 38 km/h; power-weight ratio: 46.8 lb/hp (63.6 lb/kW), 21.3 kg/hp (28.9 kg/kW); carrying capacity: 1,433 lb, 650 kg.

DIMENSIONS AND WEIGHT length: 158.46 in, 403 cm; weight: 3,748 lb, 1,700 kg.

FIAT Campagnola

GIANNINI ITALY

Fiat Giannini 126 Series

PRICES EX WORKS:

1 GP Base	2,665,000* liras
2 GP Personal	2,845,000* liras
3 GP S Base	2,820,000* liras
4 GP S Personal	2,990,000* liras
5 Sport Base DC	3,010,000* liras
6 Sport Personal DC	3,180,000* liras

Power team:	Standard for:	Optional for:
30 hp	1,2	—
35 hp	3,4	—
36.8 hp	5,6	—

30 hp power team

ENGINE rear, 4 stroke; 2 cylinders, vertical in line; 39.8 cu in, 652 cc (3.03 x 2.76 in, 77 x 70 mm); compression ratio: 8.8:1; max power (DIN): 30 hp (22 kW) at 5,000 rpm; max torque (DIN): 34 lb ft, 4.9 kg m (47.7 Nm) at 3,850 rpm; max engine rpm: 5,300; 46 hp/l (33.7 kW/l); light alloy block and head; 2 crankshaft bearings; valves: overhead, in line, push-rods and rockers; camshafts: 1, side; lubricat[ed] gear pump, centrifugal filter, 6.2 imp pt, 7.4 US pt, 3.5 [l] Weber 28 IMB downdraught carburettor; fuel feed: mec[ha]nical pump; air-cooled.

TRANSMISSION driving wheels: rear; clutch: single [dry] plate; gearbox: mechanical; gears: 4, II, III and IV si[n]claw coupling; ratios: I 3.250, II 2.067, III 1.300, IV 0.[?] rev 4.024; lever: central; final drive: spiral bevel; axle ra[tio] 4.875; width of rims: 4''; tyres: 135 SR x 12.

PERFORMANCE max speed: 75 mph, 120 km/h; pow[er] weight ratio: 43 lb/hp (58.6 lb/kW), 19.5 kg/hp (26.5 kg/k[W]) carrying capacity: 706 lb, 320 kg; speed in top at 1,000 r[pm] 14.3 mph, 23 km/h; consumption: 56.5 m/imp gal, 47 m[/US] gal, 5 l x 100 km.

CHASSIS integral; front suspension: independent, wishbo[nes] transverse leafspring lower arms, telescopic dampers; re[ar] independent, oblique semi-trailing arms, coil springs, [te]lescopic dampers.

STEERING screw and sector; turns lock to lock: 2.90.

BRAKES drum; lining area: front 33.5 sq in, 216 sq c[m] rear 33.5 sq in, 216 sq cm, total 67 sq in, 432 sq cm.

ELECTRICAL EQUIPMENT 12 V; 34 Ah battery; 230 W [al]ternator; Marelli distributor; 2 headlamps.

DIMENSIONS AND WEIGHT wheel base: 72.44 in, 184 [cm] tracks: 44.96 in, 114 cm front, 47.36 in, 120 cm rear; len[gth]

GIANNINI 126 GP Personal

120.24 in, 305 cm; width: 54.21 in, 138 cm; height: 52.56 in, 133 cm; ground clearance: 5.51 in, 14 cm; weight: 1,290 lb, 585 kg; weight distribution: 40% front, 60% rear; turning circle: 28.2 ft, 8.6 m; fuel tank: 4.6 imp gal, 5.5 US gal, 21 l.

BODY saloon/sedan; 2 doors; 4 seats, separate front seats.

PRACTICAL INSTRUCTIONS fuel: 98-100 oct petrol; oil: engine 6.2 imp pt, 7.4 US pt, 3.5 l, SAE 20W-50, change every 3,700 miles, 6,000 km - gearbox and final drive pt, 2.3 US pt, 1.1 l, Fiat ZC 90, change every 18,600 miles, 30,000 km; greasing: every 3,100 miles, 5,000 km, 2 points; sparking plug: 240°; tappet clearances: inlet 0.008 in, 0.20 mm, exhaust 0.010 in, 0.25 mm; valve timing: 28° 72° 66° 32°; tyre pressure rear 22 psi, 1.4 atm, rear 28 psi, 2 atm.

OPTIONALS light alloy wheels; electronic injection; roll-bar; twin barrel carburettor.

35 hp power team

See 30 hp power team, except for:

ENGINE 42.3 cu in, 694 cc (3.13 x 2.76 in, 79.5 x 70 mm); compression ratio: 8.5:1; max power (DIN): 35 hp (25.7 kW) at 5,400 rpm; max torque (DIN): 37 lb ft, 5.1 kg m (49.8 Nm) at 3,500 rpm; max engine rpm: 5,800; 50.4 hp/l (37 kW/l).

58 hp power team

ENGINE front, transverse, 4 stroke; 4 cylinders, vertical, in line; 55.1 cu in, 903 cc (2.56 x 2.68 in, 65 x 68 mm); compression ratio: 9.6:1; max power (DIN): 58 hp (42.6 kW) at 6,400 rpm; max torque (DIN): 49 lb ft, 6.8 kg m (66.6 Nm) at 4,600 rpm; max engine rpm: 7,000; 64.2 hp/l (47.1 kW/l); cast iron block, light alloy head; 3 crankshaft bearings; valves: overhead, in line, push-rods and rockers; camshafts: 1, side; lubrication: gear pump, full flow filter (cartridge), 7.7 imp pt, 9.3 US pt, 4.4 l; 1 Weber 30 DIC twin barrel carburettor; fuel feed: mechanical pump; water-cooled, 8.8 imp pt, 10.6 US pt, 5 l, electric thermostatic fan.

TRANSMISSION driving wheels: front; clutch: single dry plate; gearbox: mechanical; gears: 4, fully synchronized; ratios: I 3.910, II 2.055, III 1.348, IV 0.963, rev 3.615; lever: central; final drive: cylindrical gears; axle ratio: 4.071; width of rims: 4''; tyres: 135 SR x 13.

PERFORMANCE max speed: 93 mph, 150 km/h; power-weight ratio: 26.5 lb/hp (35.6 lb/kW), 11.8 kg/hp (16.1 kg/kW); carrying capacity: 882 lb, 400 kg; speed in top at 1,000 rpm: 14 mph, 22 km/h; consumption: 44.8 m/imp gal, 37.3 m/US gal, 6.3 l x 100 km.

CHASSIS integral; front suspension: independent, by Mc-Pherson, coil springs/telescopic damper struts, lower wishbones, anti-roll bar; rear: independent, single wide-based wishbone, transverse anti-roll leafspring, telescopic dampers.

STEERING rack-and-pinion; turns lock to lock: 3.50.

BRAKES front disc (diameter 8.94 in, 22.7 cm), rear drum, dual circuit, rear compensator; lining area: front 19.2 sq in, 124 sq cm, rear 33.5 sq in, 216 sq cm, total 52.7 sq in, 340 sq cm.

ELECTRICAL EQUIPMENT 12 V; 34 Ah battery; 33 A alternator; Marelli distributor; 2 headlamps.

DIMENSIONS AND WEIGHT wheel base: 87.60 in, 222 cm; tracks: 50.39 in, 128 cm front, 50.98 in, 129 cm rear; length: 142.91 in, 363 cm; width: 60.12 in, 153 cm; height: 53.94 in, 137 cm; ground clearance: 5.12 in, 13 cm; weight: 1,517 lb, 688 kg; turning circle: 31.5 ft, 9.6 m; fuel tank: 6.6 imp gal, 7.9 US gal, 30 l.

BODY saloon/sedan; 5 seats, separate front seat; folding rear seat (for 3-door models only).

PRACTICAL INSTRUCTIONS fuel: 98 oct petrol; oil: engine 6.9 imp pt, 8.2 US pt, 3.9 l, SAE 20W (winter) 30 (summer), change every 6,200 miles, 10,000 km - gearbox and final drive 4.2 imp pt, 5.1 US pt, 2.4 l, SAE 90, change every 18,600 miles, 30,000 km; greasing: every 18,600 miles, 30,000 km; sparking plug: 260°; tappet clearances: inlet 0.006 in, 0.15 mm, exhaust 0.008 in, 0.20 mm; valve timing: 25° 51° 64° 12°; tyre pressure: front 24 psi, 1.7 atm, rear 27 psi, 1.9 atm.

OPTIONALS light alloy wheels; iodine fog lamps; electronic injection; special instrument panel with rev counter.

Fiat Giannini 128 Series

PRICES EX WORKS:

1 NP 2-dr Berlina Confort L	4,385,000*	liras
2 NP 4-dr Berlina Confort L	5,350,000*	liras
3 NP S 2-dr Berlina Confort L	4,695,000*	liras
4 NP S 4-dr Berlina Confort L	5,595,000*	liras
5 5M 2-dr Autostrada Confort L	5,265,000*	liras
6 5M 4-dr Autostrada Confort L	6,085,000*	liras

Power team:	Standard for:	Optional for:
66.2 hp	1,2	—
80 hp	3 to 6	—

66.2 hp power team

ENGINE front, transverse, 4 stroke; 4 cylinders, vertical, in line; 68.1 cu in, 1,116 cc (3.15 x 2.19 in, 80 x 55.5 mm); compression ratio: 9.8:1; max power (DIN): 66.2 hp (48.7 kW) at 6,500 rpm; max torque (DIN): 62 lb ft, 8.6 kg m (84.3 Nm) at 4,000 rpm; max engine rpm: 6,500; 59.3 hp/l (43.6 kW/l); cast iron block, light alloy head; 5 crankshaft bearings; valves: overhead, thimble tappets; camshafts: 1, overhead, cogged belt; lubrication: gear pump, cartridge, 8.8 imp pt, 10.6 US pt, 5 l; 1 Weber 32 ICEV downdraught carburettor; fuel feed: mechanical pump; water-cooled, 11.4 imp pt, 13.7 US pt, 6.5 l, electric thermostatic fan.

TRANSMISSION driving wheels: front; clutch: single dry plate; gearbox: mechanical; gears: 4, fully synchronized; ratios: I 3.583, II 2.235, III 1.454, IV 1.042, rev 3.714; lever: central; final drive: cylindrical gears; axle ratio: 3.764; width of rims: 4.5''; tyres: 145 SR x 13.

GIANNINI 127 NP 2-dr Berlina

PERFORMANCE max speed: 81 mph, 130 km/h; power-weight ratio: 41.5 lb hp (56.6 lb/kW), 18.8 kg/hp (25.6 kg/kW); consumption: 52.3 m/imp gal, 43.6 m/US gal, 5.4 l x 100 km.

DIMENSIONS AND WEIGHT weight: 1,455 lb, 660 kg.

36.8 hp power team

See 35 hp power team, except for:

ENGINE compression ratio: 8.8:1; max power (DIN): 36.8 hp (27.1 kW) at 5,400 rpm; max torque (DIN): 41 lb ft, kg m (55.8 Nm) at 4,000 rpm; max engine rpm: 6,000; hp/l (39 kW/l); 1 Weber 28 IMB downdraught twin barrel carburettor.

PERFORMANCE max speed: 84 mph, 135 km/h; power-weight ratio: 35.9 lb hp (48.7 lb/kW), 16.3 kg/hp (22.1 kg/kW); consumption: 51.4 m/imp gal, 42.8 m/US gal, 5.5 l x 100 km.

DIMENSIONS AND WEIGHT weight: 1,323 lb, 600 kg.

Fiat Giannini 127 Series

PRICES EX WORKS:

2-dr Berlina Base	3,810,000*	liras
3-dr Berlina Base	3,930,000*	liras
2-dr Berlina Confort	4,160,000*	liras
3-dr Berlina Confort	4,280,000*	liras

GIANNINI 128 Series

66.2 HP POWER TEAM

PERFORMANCE max speed: 96 mph, 155 km/h; power-weight ratio: 2-dr models 25 lb/hp (34.1 lb/kW), 11.3 kg/hp (15.4 kg/kW); carrying capacity: 882 lb, 400 kg; speed in top at 1,000 rpm: 15.1 mph, 24.3 km/h; consumption: 31 m/imp gal, 25.8 m/US gal, 9.1 l x 100 km.

CHASSIS integral; front suspension: independent, by McPherson, coil springs/telescopic damper struts, lower wishbones, anti-roll bar; rear: independent, single wide-based wishbones, transverse anti-roll leafspring, telescopic dampers.

STEERING rack-and-pinion; turns lock to lock: 3.50.

BRAKES front disc (diameter 8.94 in, 22.7 cm), rear drum, dual circuit, rear compensator, servo; lining area: front 19.2 sq in, 124 sq cm, rear 33.5 sq in, 216 sq cm, total 52.7 sq in, 340 sq cm.

ELECTRICAL EQUIPMENT 12 V; 34 Ah battery; 33 A alternator; Marelli distributor; 2 headlamps.

DIMENSIONS AND WEIGHT wheel base: 96.38 in, 245 cm; tracks: 51.50 in, 131 cm front, 51.69 in, 131 cm rear; length: 151.18 in, 384 cm; width: 62.60 in, 159 cm; height: 55.91 in, 142 cm; ground clearance: 5.71 in, 14.5 cm; weight: 2-dr models 1,654 lb, 750 kg - 4-dr models 1,698 lb, 770 kg; weight distribution: 61.5% front, 38.5% rear; turning circle: 33.8 ft, 10.3 m; fuel tank: 8.4 imp gal, 10 US gal, 38 l.

BODY saloon/sedan; 5 seats, separate front seats, reclining backrests.

PRACTICAL INSTRUCTIONS fuel: 98 oct petrol; oil: engine 7.4 imp pt, 8.9 US pt, 4.2 l, SAE 20W (winter) 30 (summer), change every 6,200 miles, 10,000 km - gearbox and final drive 5.5 imp pt, 6.6 US pt, 3.1 l, SAE 90, change every 18,600 miles, 30,000 km; greasing: every 18,600 miles, 30,000 km; sparking plug: 240°; tappet clearances: inlet 0.012 in, 0.30 mm, exhaust 0.016 in, 0.40 mm; valve timing: 12° 52° 52° 12°; tyre pressure: front 26 psi, 1.8 atm, rear 24 psi, 1.7 atm.

OPTIONALS 5-speed fully synchronized mechanical gearbox; light alloy wheels; iodine fog lamps; electronic injection.

80 hp power team

See 66.2 hp power team, except for:

ENGINE max power (DIN): 80 hp (58 kW) at 6,800 rpm; max torque (DIN): 67 lb ft, 9.2 kg m (90.2 Nm) at 4,800 rpm; max engine rpm: 7,200; 71.7 hp/l (52 kW/l); electronic injection (only for Autostrada models); 2 Weber 40 DCNF twin barrel carburettors.

TRANSMISSION (only for Autostrada models) 5-speed fully synchronized mechanical gearbox.

PERFORMANCE max speed: 103 mph, 165 km/h - Autostrada models about 109 mph, 175 km/h; power-weight ratio: 2-dr models 20.6 lb/hp (28.5 lb/kW), 9.3 kg/hp (12.9 kg/kW).

LAMBORGHINI   ITALY

Urraco P 200

PRICE EX WORKS: 20,532,000* liras

ENGINE centre-rear, transverse, 4 stroke; 8 cylinders, Vee-slanted at 90°; 121.7 cu in, 1,994 cc (3.05 x 2.09 in, 77.4 x 53 mm); compression ratio: 9.8:1; max power (DIN): 182 hp (134 kW) at 7,500 rpm; max torque (DIN): 109 lb ft, 15 kg m (147.1 Nm) at 3,800 rpm; max engine rpm: 7,900; 91.3 hp/l (67.2 kW/l); light alloy block and head, wet liners; 5 crankshaft bearings; valves: overhead, in line, thimble tappets; camshafts: 2, 1 per bank, Vee-slanted at 70°, overhead, cogged belt; lubrication: gear pump, full flow filter, 13.2 imp pt, 15.9 US pt, 7.5 l; 4 Weber IDF 40 downdraught twin barrel carburettors; fuel feed: electric pump; water-cooled, 21.1 imp pt, 25.4 US pt, 12 l, 2 front fans, 1 electric and 1 thermostatic.

TRANSMISSION driving wheels: rear; clutch: single dry plate (diaphragm), hydraulically controlled; gearbox: mechanical; gears: 5, fully synchronized; ratios: I 2.935, II 2.105, III 1.565, IV 1.185, V 0.900, rev 2.540; lever: central; final drive: helical spur gears; axle ratio: 4.350; width of rims: 7.5; tyres: 195/70 VR x 14 front, 205/70 VR x 14 rear.

PERFORMANCE max speed: 127 mph, 205 km/h; power-weight ratio: 15.1 lb/hp (20.6 lb/kW), 6.9 kg/hp (kg/kW); carrying capacity: 882 lb, 400 kg; speed in top 1,000 rpm: 18.8 mph, 30.2 km/h; consumption: 20.5 m/i gal, 17 m/US gal, 13.8 l x 100 km.

CHASSIS integral, rear auxiliary frame; front suspensi independent, by McPherson, coil springs/telescopic damp struts, lower wishbones (trailing links), anti-roll bar; re independent, by McPherson, coil springs/telescopic damp struts, lower wishbones, anti-roll bar.

STEERING rack-and-pinion; turns lock to lock: 4.25.

BRAKES disc (diameter 10.94 in, 27.8 cm), internal rad fins, dual circuit, each with servo.

ELECTRICAL EQUIPMENT 12 V; 55 Ah battery; 770 alternator; Marelli distributor; 2 iodine retractable hea lamps.

DIMENSIONS AND WEIGHT wheel base: 96.46 in, 245 c front and rear track: 57.48 in, 146 cm; length: 168.50 in, cm; width: 68.50 in, 174 cm; height: 44.88 in, 114 c ground clearance: 4.72 in, 12 cm; weight: 2,756 lb, 1,250 turning circle: 35.1 ft, 10.7 m; fuel tank: 17.6 imp gal, 2 US gal, 80 l.

BODY coupé; 2 doors; 4 seats, separate front seats.

PRACTICAL INSTRUCTIONS fuel: 98-100 oct petrol; c

LAMBORGHINI Urraco P 250

engine 13.2 imp pt, 15.9 US pt, 7.5 l, SAE 20W-50, chan every 2,500 miles, 4,000 km - gearbox and final dri 10.6 imp pt, 12.7 US pt, 6 l, SAE 90, change every 6,2 miles, 10,000 km; sparking plug: 235°; tappet clearance inlet 0.018 in, 0.45 mm, exhaust 0.018 in, 0.45 mm; val timing: 40° 60° 58° 38°; tyre pressure: front 28 psi, atm, rear 31 psi, 2.2 atm.

OPTIONALS leather upholstery; metallic spray; electric ti ed windows; air-conditioning.

Urraco P 250

See Urraco P 200, except for:

PRICE EX WORKS: 23,490,000* liras

ENGINE 150 cu in, 2,463 cc (3.39 x 2.09 in, 86 x 53 mm compression ratio: 10.4:1; max power (DIN): 220 hp (16 kW) at 7,500 rpm; max torque (DIN): 167 lb ft, 23 kg (225.6 Nm) at 5,600 rpm; 89.3 hp/l (65.7 kW/l).

PERFORMANCE max speed: over 149 mph, 240 km/h; pow weight ratio: 13.7 lb/hp (18.6 lb/kW), 6.2 kg/hp (8.5 kg/kV speed in top at 1,000 rpm: 19.2 mph, 30.9 km/h; consum tion: 18.8 m/imp gal, 15.7 m/US gal, 15 l x 100 km.

DIMENSIONS AND WEIGHT weight: 3,021 lb, 1,370 kg.

BODY (standard) leather upholstery, metallic spray, elect tinted windows.

LAMBORGHINI Urraco P 300

Urraco P 300

e Urraco P 200, except for:

ICE EX WORKS: 25,650,000* liras

GINE 128.8 cu in, 2,996 cc (3.39 x 2.54 in, 86 x 64.5 mm); mpression ratio: 10.1:1; max power (DIN): 265 hp (195) at 7,500 rpm; max torque (DIN): 203 lb ft, 28 kg m 4.6 Nm) at 3,500 rpm; 88.5 hp/l (65.1 kW/l); valves: e-slanted at 45°; camshafts: 4, 2 per bank, chain driven; Weber 40 DCNF downdraught twin barrel carburettors.

RFORMANCE max speed: 165 mph, 265 km/h; power-ight ratio: 10.8 lb/hp (14.7 lb/kW), 4.9 kg/hp (67 kg/kW); eed in top at 1,000 rpm: 19.9 mph, 32 km/h; consumpn: 17.7 m/imp gal, 14.7 m/US gal, 16 l x 100 km.

MENSIONS AND WEIGHT weight: 2,867 lb, 1,300 kg.

ACTICAL INSTRUCTIONS valve timing: 32° 60° 60° 32°.

Silhouette

e Urraco P 200, except for:

ICE EX WORKS: 31,050,000* liras

GINE 182.8 cu in, 2,996 cc (3.39 x 2.54 in, 86 x 64.5 mm); mpression ratio: 10.1:1; max power (DIN): 265 hp (195 kW) 7,500 rpm; max torque (DIN): 203 lb ft, 28 kg m (274.6) at 3,500 rpm; 88.5 hp/l (65.1 kW/l); valves: Vee-nted at 45°; camshafts: 4, 2 per bank, chain driven; 4 eber 40 DCNF downdraught twin barrel carburettors.

ANSMISSION axle ratio: 4; width of rims: 8'' front, 11'' r; tyres: 195/50 VR x 15 P7 front, 285/40 VR x 15 P7 rear.

RFORMANCE max speeds: (I) 47 mph, 75 km/h; (II) 62 h, 100 km/h; (III) 89 mph, 143 km/h; (IV) 111 mph, 178 /h; (V) over 155 mph, 250 km/h; power-weight ratio: lb/hp (14.8 lb/kW), 4.5 kg/hp (6.7 kg/kW); speed in at 1,000 rpm: 19.9 mph, 32 km/h; consumption: 17.7 /imp gal, 14.7 m/US gal, 16 l x 100 km.

MENSIONS AND WEIGHT tracks: 58.66 in, 149 cm front, .02 in, 155 cm rear; length: 170.08 in, 432 cm; width: 74.02 188 in, height: 44.09 in, 112 cm; ground clearance: 51 in, 14 cm; weight: 2,867 lb, 1,300 kg.

DY sports; 2 seats.

ACTICAL INSTRUCTIONS oil: engine 21.1 imp pt, 25.4 S pt, 12 l - gearbox and final drive 6.7 imp pt, 8 US pt, l; valve timing: 32° 60° 60° 32°; tyre pressure: front psi, 2.5 atm, rear 40 psi, 2.8 atm.

Espada 400 GT

ICE EX WORKS: 41,175,000* liras

GINE front, 4 stroke; 12 cylinders, Vee-slanted at 60°; .7 cu in, 3,929 cc (3.23 x 2.44 in, 82 x 62 mm); com-

LAMBORGHINI Silhouette

LAMBORGHINI Espada 400 GT

pression ratio: 9.55:1; max power (DIN): 350 hp (257.6 kW) at 7,500 rpm; max torque (DIN): 290 lb ft, 40 kg m (392.3 Nm) at 5,500 rpm; max engine rpm: 7,900; 89.1 hp/l (65.6 kW/l); light alloy block and head, wet liners; 7 crankshaft bearings; valves: overhead, Vee-slanted at 70°, thimble tappets; camshafts: 4, per bank, overhead, chain driven lubrication: gear pump, full flow filter, 25.2 imp pt, 30.2 US pt, 14.3 l; 6 Weber 40 DCOE 20/21 hori-zontal twin barrel carburettors; fuel feed: electric pump; water-cooled, 24.6 imp pt, 29.6 US pt, 14 l, 2 electric thermo-static fans.

TRANSMISSION driving wheels: rear; clutch: single dry plate (diaphragm), hydraulically controlled; gearbox: me-chanical; gears: 5, fully synchronized; ratios: I 2.520, II 1.735, III 1.225, IV 1, V 0.815, rev 2.765; lever: central; final drive: hypoid bevel; axle ratio: 4.100; width of rims: 7'' ; tyres: 215/70 VR x 15.

PERFORMANCE max speeds: (I) 47 mph, 75 km/h; (II) 68 mph, 110 km/h; (III) 93 mph, 150 km/h; (IV) 124 mph, 200 km/h; (V) 155 mph, 250 km/h; power-weight ratio: 10.3 lb/hp (13.1 lb/kW), 4.7 kg/hp (6.3 kg/kW); carrying capacity: 937 lb, 425 kg; acceleration: standing ¼ mile 15.5 sec; speed in top at 1,000 rpm: 21.6 mph, 34.8 km/h; consumption: 14.9 m/imp gal, 12.4 m/US gal, 19 l x 100 km.

CHASSIS integral; front suspension: independent, wish-bones, coil springs, anti-roll bar, telescopic dampers; rear: independent, wishbones, coil springs, anti-roll bar, tele-scopic dampers.

STEERING ZF screw and sector; turns lock to lock: 3.80.

BRAKES disc (front diameter 11.81 in, 30 cm, rear 11.02 in, 28 cm), internal radial fins, dual circuit, each with servo; swept area: front 285.3 sq in, 1,840 sq cm, rear 206.2 sq in, 1,330 sq cm, total 491.5 sq in, 3,170 sq cm.

ELECTRICAL EQUIPMENT 12 V; 72 Ah battery; 2 x 770 W alternators; Marelli distributor; 2 iodine headlamps, 2 iodine fog lamps.

DIMENSIONS AND WEIGHT wheel base: 104.33 in, 265 cm; tracks: 58.66 in, 149 cm front, 58.66 in, 149 cm rear; length: 186.54 in, 474 cm; width: 73.23 in, 186 cm; height: 46.65 in, 118 cm; ground clearance: 4.92 in, 12.5 cm; weight: 3,605 lb, 1,635 kg; weight distribution: 49.5% front, 50.5% rear; turning circle: 39.4 ft. 12 m; fuel tank: 20.9 imp gal, 25.1 US gal, 95 l (2 separate tanks).

BODY coupé; 2 doors; 4 seats, separate front seats, reclin-ing backrests; leather upholstery; air-conditioning; tinted glass; electric windows; heated rear window.

PRACTICAL INSTRUCTIONS fuel: 98-100 oct petrol; oil: engine 25.2 imp pt, 30.2 US pt, 14.3 l, SAE 20W-50, change every 2,500 miles, 4,000 km - gearbox 7 imp pt, 8.5 US pt, 4 l, SAE 90, change every 6,200 miles, 10,000 km - final drive 2.6 imp pt, 3.2 US pt, 1.5 l, SAE 90, change every 6,200 miles, 10,000 km; greasing: every 6,200 miles, 10,000 km, 2 points, every 12,400 miles, 20,000 km, 2 points; sparking plug: 235°; tappet clearances: inlet 0.010 in, 0.25 mm, exhaust 0.010 in, 0.25 mm; valve timing: 32° 76° 64° 32°; tyre pressure: front 34 psi, 2.4 atm, rear 37 psi, 2.6 atm.

OPTIONALS right-hand drive; 4.090 axle ratio; power steer-ing; metallic spray; special spray.

LAMBORGHINI Espada 400 GT

LAMBORGHINI Countach "S"

Countach « S »

PRICE EX WORKS: 54,000,000* liras

ENGINE centre-rear, longitudinal, 4 stroke; 12 cylinders, Vee-slanted at 60º; 239.7 cu in, 3,929 cc (3.23 x 2.44 in, 82 x 62 mm); compression ratio: 10.5:1; max power (DIN): 375 hp (276 kW) at 8,000 rpm; max torque (DIN): 267 lb ft, 36.8 kg m (360.9 Nm) at 5,500 rpm; max engine rpm: 8,000; 95.4 hp/l (70.2 kW/l); light alloy block and head, wet liners; 7 crankshaft bearings; valves: overhead Vee-slanted at 70º, thimble tappets; camshafts: 4, 2 per bank overhead, chain driven lubrication: gear pump, full flow filter, oil cooler, 30.8 imp pt, 37 US pt, 17.5 l; 6 Weber 45 DCOE 104-105 horizontal twin barrel carburettors; fuel feed: 2 electric pumps; water-cooled, 29.9 imp pt, 35.9 US pt, 17 l, 2 radiators, 2 electric fans (1 thermostatic).

TRANSMISSION driving wheels: rear; clutch: single dry plate (diaphragm), hydraulically controlled: gearbox: mounted ahead of engine, mechanical; gears: 5, fully synchronized; ratios: I 2.256, II 1.769, III 1.310, IV 0.990, V 0.755, rev 2.134; lever: central; final drive: hypoid bevel, limited slip differential; axle ratio: 4.090; width of rims: 8.5'' front 12'' rear; tyres: 205/50 VR x 15 P7 front, 345/35 VR x 15 P7 rear.

PERFORMANCE max speeds: (I) 65 mph, 105 km/h; (II) 84 mph, 135 km/h; (III) 113 mph, 182 km/h; (IV) 150 mph, 241 km/h; (V) 196 mph, 315 km/h; power-weight ratio: 7.4 lb/hp (10 lb/kW), 3.4 kg/hp (4.6 kg/kW); carrying capacity:

397 lb, 180 kg; acceleration: 0-50 mph, 0-80 km/h) 6 sec; speed in top at 1,000 rpm: 23.2 mph, 37.3 km/h; consumption: 19.8 m/imp gal, 16.4 m/US gal, 14.3 l x 100 km.

CHASSIS tubular; front suspension: independent, wishbones, coil springs, anti-roll bar, telescopic dampers; rear: independent, wishbones (trailing links), coil springs, anti-roll bar, 4 telescopic dampers.

STEERING rack-and-pinion; turns lock to lock: 3.

BRAKES disc (diameter 11.81 in, 30 cm front, 11.02 in, 28 cm rear), internal radial fins, dual circuit, rear compensator, servo; lining area: front 27.9 sq in, 180 sq cm, rear 26.5 sq in, 171 sq cm, total 54.4 sq in, 351 sq cm.

ELECTRICAL EQUIPMENT 12 V; 72 Ah battery; 840 W alternator; 2 Marelli distributors; 4 iodine retractable headlamps.

DIMENSIONS AND WEIGHT wheel base: 96.46 in, 245 cm; tracks: 58.66 in, 149 cm front, 63.39 in, 161 cm rear; length: 162.99 in, 414 cm; width: 78.74 in, 200 cm; height: 42.13 in, 107 cm; ground clearance: 4.92 in, 12.5 cm; weight: 2,778 lb, 1,260 kg; weight distribution: 42% front axle, 58% rear axle; turning circle: 42.6 ft, 13 m; fuel tank: 26.4 imp gal, 31.7 US gal, 120 l (2 separate tanks).

BODY coupé; 2 doors; 2 seats; leather upholstery; tinted glass; heated rear window; light alloy wheels.

PRACTICAL INSTRUCTIONS fuel: 98-100 oct petrol; oil: engine 30.8 imp pt, 37 US pt, 17.5 l, SAE 20W-50, change every 3,100 miles, 5,000 km - gearbox 5.6 imp pt, 6.8 pt, 3.2 l, SAE 90, change every 9,300 miles, 15,000 km, final drive 11.3 imp pt, 13.5 US pt, 6.4 l, SAE 90, change every 9,300 miles, 15,000 km; greasing: none; sparking plu 235º; tappet clearances: inlet 0.010 in, 0.25 mm, exhau 0.010 in, 0.25 mm; valve timing: 42º 70º 64º 40º; ty pressure: front 34 psi, 2.4 atm, rear 34 psi, 2.4 atm.

OPTIONALS right-hand drive; air-conditioning.

LANCIA   ITAL

Beta Berlina 1300

PRICE IN GB: £ 3,457*
PRICE EX WORKS: 7,032,800** liras

ENGINE front, transverse, slanted 20º to rear, 4 stroke; cylinders, in line; 79.4 cu in, 1,301 cc (3 x 2.81 76.1 x 71.5 mm); compression ratio: 8.9:1; max power (DII 82 hp (60.3 kW) at 5,800 rpm; max torque (DIN): 80 lb 11 kg m (107.8 Nm) at 3,300 rpm; max engine rpm: 6,40 63 hp/l (46.3 kW/l); cast iron block, light alloy hea hemispherical combustion chambers; 5 crankshaft bearing valves: overhead, Vee-slanted at 65º, thimble tappe camshafts: 2, overhead, cogged belt; lubrication: gear pum full flow filter, 7.4 imp pt, 8.9 US pt, 4.2 l; 1 Weber DAT 3 downdraught twin barrel carburettor with pow valve and thermostatic filter; fuel feed: mechanical pum liquid-cooled, 13.4 imp pt, 16.1 US pt, 7.6 l, electr thermostatic fan.

TRANSMISSION driving wheels: front; clutch: single d plate; gearbox: mechanical; gears: 5, fully synchronize ratios: I 3.500, II 2.235, III 1.522, IV 1.152, V 0.925, r 3.071; lever: central; final drive: cylindrical gears, in u with gearbox; axle ratio: 4.466; width of rims: 5''; tyre 155 SR x 14.

PERFORMANCE max speeds: (I) 28 mph, 45 km/h; (II) mph, 71 km/h; (III) 65 mph, 105 km/h; (IV) 85 mph, 1 km/h; (V) 99 mph, 160 km/h; power-weight ratio: 29 lb/ (39.5 lb/kW), 13.2 kg/hp (17.9 kg/kW); carrying capaci 992 lb, 450 kg; acceleration: standing ¼ mile 19 sec; spe in top at 1,000 rpm: 16.7 mph, 26.8 km/h; consumptio 33.6 m/imp gal, 28 m/US gal, 8.4 l x 100 km.

CHASSIS integral; front suspension: independent, low wide-based wishbones, coil springs, telescopic damp struts, anti-roll bar; rear: independent, wishbones, c springs, telescopic dampers struts, anti-roll bar acting longitudinal torque arm.

STEERING rack-and-pinion; turns lock to lock: 3.80.

BRAKES disc (diameter 9.88 in, 25.1 cm), rear compensatc Superduplex circuit, servo; lining area: front 24.8 sq 160 sq cm, rear 22 sq in, 142 sq cm, total 46.8 sq in, 3 sq cm.

ELECTRICAL EQUIPMENT 12 V; 45 Ah battery; 600 W alte nator; Bosch or Marelli electronic ignition; 4 iodine hea lamps.

DIMENSIONS AND WEIGHT wheel base: 100 in, 254 cr tracks: 55.35 in, 141 cm front, 54.80 in, 139 cm rea length: 168.90 in, 429 cm; width: 66.93 in, 170 cm; heigh 55.12 in, 140 cm; ground clearance: 5.51 in, 14 cm; weigh 2,381 lb, 1,080 kg; turning circle: 34.8 ft, 10.6 m; fu tank: 10.8 imp gal, 12.9 US gal, 49 l.

BODY saloon/sedan; 4 doors; 5 seats, separate front seat reclining backrests; heated rear window.

PRACTICAL INSTRUCTIONS fuel: 98-100 oct petrol; oi engine 7.4 imp pt, 8.9 US pt, 4.2 l, SAE 10W-50, chan every 3,100 miles, 5,000 km - gearbox and final dri 3 imp pt, 3.6 US pt, 1.7 l, SAE 90, change every 18,6 miles, 30,000 km; greasing: none; tappet clearances: inl 0.015-0.018 in, 0.39-0.45 mm, exhaust 0.018-0.020 in, 0. 0.51 mm; valve timing: 17º 37º 48º 6º; tyre pressur front 24 psi, 1.7 atm, rear 24 psi, 1.7 atm.

OPTIONALS light alloy wheels with 175/70 SR x 14 tyre fog lamps; manually-controlled sunshine roof; tinted glas metallic spray; headrests.

Beta Coupé 1300

See Beta Berlina 1300, except for:

PRICE IN USA: £ 3,949*
PRICE EX WORKS: 7,640,500** liras

PERFORMANCE max speed: over 103 mph, 165 km/h; powe weight ratio: 26.5 lb/hp (35.9 lb/kW), 12 kg/hp (16 kg/kW); carrying capacity: 794 lb, 360 kg; acceleratio

LANCIA Beta Coupé 1600 - 2000

anding ¼ mile 18 sec; consumption: 34.4 m/imp gal,
.7 m/US gal, 8.2 l x 100 km.

IMENSIONS AND WEIGHT wheel base: 92.52 in, 235 cm;
ngth: 157.09 in, 399 cm; width: 64.96 in, 165 cm; height:
.39 in, 128 cm; ground clearance: 5.31 in, 13.5 cm; weight:
161 lb, 980 kg; turning circle: 33.5 ft, 10.2 m.

ODY coupé; 2 doors; 4 seats.

PTIONALS heated rear window; rear red fog lamp.

Beta Berlina 1600

ee Beta Berlina 1300, except for:

RICE IN GB: £ 4,015*
RICE IN USA: $ 8,217

NGINE 96.7 cu in, 1,585 cc (3.31 x 2.81 in, 84 x 71.5 mm);
ompression ratio: 9.4:1; max power (DIN): 100 hp (73.6
V) at 5,800 rpm; max torque (DIN): 99 lb ft, 13.7 kg m
34.4 Nm) at 3,000 rpm; 63.1 hp/l (46.4 kW/l); 1 Weber 34
AT 1 downdraught twin barrel carburettor with power-
alve and thermostatic filter.

RANSMISSION axle ratio: 4.071; width of rims: 5.5''; tyres:
5/70 SR x 14 (standard).

RFORMANCE max speeds: (I) 31 mph, 50 km/h; (II)
mph, 78 km/h; (III) 71 mph, 114 km/h; (IV) 94 mph,
1 km/h; (V) 106 mph, 170 km/h; power-weight ratio:
.3 lb/hp (32.8 lb/kW), 11 kg/hp (14.9 kg/kW); accelera-
on: standing ¼ mile 18 sec; speed in top at 1,000 rpm:
.2 mph, 29.3 km/h; consumption: 34 m/imp gal, 28.3 m/US
al, 8.3 l x 100 km.

LECTRICAL EQUIPMENT 750 W alternator; 4 iodine head-
mps with automatic adjustable height.

IMENSIONS AND WEIGHT weight: 2,420 lb, 1,097 kg.

ODY luxury interior; built-in headrests (standard).

PTIONALS Lancia/AP automatic transmission, hydraulic
rque converter and planetary gears with 3 ratio (I 2.346,
1.402, III 1, rev 2.346), max ratio of converter at stall
05, possible manual selection, 4.380 axle ratio, max
eeds (I) 38 mph, 61 km/h, (II) 76 mph, 123 km/h, (III)
98 mph, 158 km/h; air-conditioning; ZF progressive power
eering; light alloy wheels; leather upholstery.

Beta Coupé 1600

ee Beta Berlina 1600, except for:

RICE IN GB: £ 4,595*
RICE IN USA: $ 8,803

RFORMANCE max speed: 111 mph, 178 km/h; power-
eight ratio: 21.8 lb/hp (29.6 lb/kW), 9.9 kg/hp (13.4
/kW); carrying capacity: 794 lb, 360 kg; acceleration:
anding ¼ mile 17.1 sec; consumption: 35.3 m/imp gal,
.4 m/US gal, 8 l x 100 km.

ANCIA Beta 1600 - 2000 (automatic gearbox)

LANCIA Beta HPE 1600 - 2000

LANCIA Beta Berlina 2000

STEERING turns lock to lock: 3.75.

ELECTRICAL EQUIPMENT 4 iodine headlamps.

DIMENSIONS AND WEIGHT wheel base: 92.52 in, 235 cm;
length: 157.09 in, 399 cm; width: 64.96 in, 165 cm; height:
50.39 in, 128 cm; ground clearance: 5.31 in, 13.5 cm;
weight: 2,180 lb, 988 kg; weight distribution: 61% front,
39% rear; turning circle: 33.5 ft, 10.2 m.

BODY coupé; 2 doors; 4 seats.

Beta HPE 1600

See Beta Coupé 1600, except for:

PRICE IN GB: £ 5,277*
PRICE IN USA: $ 9,868

PERFORMANCE max speed: 108 mph, 174 km/h; power-
weight ratio: 23.4 lb/hp (31.7 lb/kW), 10.6 kg/hp (14.4
kg/kW); carrying capacity: 992 lb, 450 kg; acceleration:
standing ¼ mile 17.5 sec; consumption: 34 m/imp gal,
28.3 m/US gal, 8.3 l x 100 km.

STEERING turns lock to lock: 4.

DIMENSIONS AND WEIGHT wheel base: 100 in, 254 cm;
length: 168.50 in, 428 cm; height: 51.57 in, 131 cm; weight:
2,337 lb, 1,060 kg.

BODY 5 seats; rear window wiper.

Beta Spider 1600

See Beta Coupé 1600, except for:

PRICE EX WORKS: 8,454,700** liras

PERFORMANCE power-weight ratio: 23.1 lb/hp (31.4 lb/kW),
10.5 kg/hp (14.2 kg/kW); acceleration: standing ¼ mile
17.3 sec.

DIMENSIONS AND WEIGHT length: 159.05 in, 404 cm;
height: 49.61 in, 126 cm; weight: 2,315 lb, 1,050 kg.

BODY convertible; detachable roof; heated rear window not
available.

OPTIONALS only ZF progressive power steering, light
alloy wheels and metallic spray.

Beta Berlina 2000

See Beta Berlina 1300, except for:

PRICE IN GB: £ 4,285*
PRICE EX WORKS: 7,917,800** liras

ENGINE 121.7 cu in, 1,995 cc (3.31 x 3.54 in, 84 x 90 mm);
max power (DIN): 115 hp (84.6 kW) at 5,500 rpm; max
torque (DIN): 129 lb ft, 17.8 kg m (174.6 Nm) at 2,800
rpm; 57.6 hp/l (42.4 kW/l); lubrication: 7.9 imp pt, 9.5 US
pt, 4.5 l; 1 Weber 34 DAT 2 downdraught twin barrel carburettor with power-valve and thermostatic filter.

BETA BERLINA 2000

TRANSMISSION axle ratio: 3.785; width of rims: 5.5''; tyres: 175/70 SR x 14 (standard).

PERFORMANCE max speeds: (I) 33 mph, 53 km/h; (II) 52 mph, 83 km/h; (III) 76 mph, 123 km/h; (IV) 101 mph, 162 km/h; (V) 112 mph, 180 km/h; power-weight ratio: 21.2 lb/hp (28.7 lb/kW), 9.6 kg/hp (13 kg/kW); acceleration: standing ¼ mile 17 sec; speed in top at 1,000 rpm: 19.6 mph, 31.5 km/h; consumption: 32.8 m/imp gal, 27.3 m/US gal, 8.6 l x 100 km.

STEERING ZF progressive servo.

ELECTRICAL EQUIPMENT 750 W alternator; 4 iodine headlamps with automatically adjustable height (standard).

DIMENSIONS AND WEIGHT weight: 2,426 lb, 1,100 kg.

BODY luxury interior; built-in headrests (standard).

PRACTICAL INSTRUCTIONS valve timing: 13° 45° 49° 9°.

OPTIONALS Lancia/AP automatic transmission, hydraulic torque converter and planetary gears with 3 ratio (I 2.346, II 1.402, III 1, rev 2.346), max ratio of converter at stall 1.95, possible manual selection, 4.380 axle ratio, max ratio, max speeds (I) 40 mph, 64 km/h, (II) 81 mph, 130 km/h, (III) 101 mph, 162 km/h; air-conditioning; light alloy wheels; leather upholstery.

Beta Coupé 2000

See Beta Berlina 2000, except for:

PRICE IN GB: £ 5,029*
PRICE EX WORKS: 9,056,500** liras

TRANSMISSION tyres: 175/70 HR x 14.

PERFORMANCE max speed: 117 mph, 188 km/h; power-weight ratio: 19 lb/hp (25.8 lb/kW), 8.6 kg/hp (11.7 kg/kW); carrying capacity: 794 lb, 360 kg; acceleration: standing ¼ mile 16.2 sec; consumption: 33.6 m/imp gal, 28.6 m/US gal, 8.4 l x 100 km.

STEERING turns lock to lock: 3.75.

DIMENSIONS AND WEIGHT wheel base: 92.52 in, 235 cm; length: 157.09 in, 399 cm; width: 64.96 in, 165 cm; height: 50.39 in, 128 cm; ground clearance: 5.31 in, 13.5 cm; weight: 2,180 lb, 988 kg; weight distribution: 61% front, 39% rear; turning circle: 33.5 ft, 10.2 m.

BODY coupé; 2 doors; 4 seats.

Beta HPE 2000

See Beta 2000 Coupé, except for:

PRICE IN GB: £ 5,710*
PRICE EX WORKS: 9,056,500** liras

TRANSMISSION tyres: 175/70 SR x 14.

PERFORMANCE max speed: 112 mph, 180 km/h; power-weight ratio: 20.3 lb/hp (27.6 lb/kW), 9.2 kg/hp (12.5 kg/kW); carrying capacity: 992 lb, 450 kg; acceleration: standing ¼ mile 16.8 sec; consumption: 32.8 m/imp gal, 27.3 m/US gal, 8.6 l x 100 km.

STEERING turns lock to lock: 4.

DIMENSIONS AND WEIGHT wheel base: 100 in, 254 cm; length: 168.50 in, 428 cm; height: 51.57 in, 131 cm; weight: 2,337 lb, 1,060 kg.

BODY 5 seats; heated rear window (standard); rear window wiper.

Beta Spider 2000

See Beta 2000 Coupé, except for:

PRICE IN GB: £ 5,384*
PRICE EX WORKS: 8,879,500** liras

PERFORMANCE max speed: 116 mph, 186 km/h; power-weight ratio: 20.1 lb/hp (27.3 lb/kW), 9.1 kg/hp (12.4 kg/kW); acceleration: standing ¼ mile 16.4 sec.

DIMENSIONS AND WEIGHT length: 159.05 in, 404 cm; height: 49.61 in, 126 cm; weight: 2,315 lb, 1,050 kg.

LANCIA Beta Coupé 1600

BODY convertible: detachable roof; light alloy wheel (standard).

OPTIONALS only ZF progressive power steering and metalli spray.

Beta ES 2000

(Only for Great Britain).

See Beta Berlina 2000, except for:

PRICE IN GB: £ 4,680*

BODY (standard) manually-controlled sunshine roof, electri windows, tinted glass, built-in headrests and light allo wheels.

Beta Montecarlo

PRICE IN GB: £ 5,927*
PRICE EX WORKS: 9,634,700** liras

ENGINE centre-rear, transverse, in unit with gearbox ar final drive, 4 stroke; 4 cylinders, in line; 121.7 cu i 1,995 cc (3.31 x 3.54 in, 84 x 90 mm); compression rati 9.35:1; max power (DIN): 120 hp (88.3 kW) at 6,000 rpr max torque (DIN): 126 lb ft, 17.4 kg m (170.6 Nm) 3,400 rpm; max engine rpm: 6,400; 60.1 hp/l (44.3 kW/ cast iron block, light alloy head, hemispherical combu tion chambers; 5 crankshaft bearings; valves: overhea Vee-slanted at 65°, thimble tappets; camshafts: 2, overhea cogged belt; lubrication: gear pump, full flow filter (ca tridge), 7.9 imp pt, 9.5 US pt, 4.5 l; 1 Weber 34 DATR 4/2 downdraught twin barrel carburettor; fuel feed: mechanic pump; liquid-cooled, 13.4 imp pt, 16.1 US pt, 7.6 l, electr thermostatic fan.

TRANSMISSION driving wheels: rear; clutch: single dry plat (diaphragm), hydraulically controlled; gearbox: mechanica gears: 5, fully synchronized; ratios: I 3.750, II 2.235, I 1.522, IV 1.152, V 0.925, rev 3.071; lever: central; fina drive: helical spur gears; axle ratio: 3.714; width of rim 5.5''; tyres: 185/70 HR x 13.

PERFORMANCE max speeds: (I) 30 mph, 49 km/h; (II) 5 mph, 84 km/h; (III) 80 mph, 128 km/h; (IV) 101 mph, 1 km/h; (V) over 118 mph, 190 km/h; power-weight rati 19.1 lb/hp (25.9 lb/kW), 8.7 kg/hp (11.8 kg/kW); carryi capacity: 463 lb, 210 kg; acceleration: standing ¼ mile sec; speed in top at 1,000 rpm: 19.6 mph, 31.6 km/h; co sumption: 29.7 m/imp gal, 24.8 m/US gal, 9.5 l x 100 kr

CHASSIS integral; front suspension: independent, McPherson, coil springs/telescopic damper struts, low wishbones, anti-roll bar; rear: independent, by McPherso coil springs/telescopic damper struts, lower wishbone anti-roll bar.

STEERING rack-and-pinion.

BRAKES disc (diameter 8.94 in, 22.7 cm), dual circuit, serv

ELECTRICAL EQUIPMENT 12 V; 45 Ah battery; 460 alternator; Bosch or Marelli electronic ignition; 2 iodi headlamps.

DIMENSIONS AND WEIGHT wheel base: 90.55 in, 230 cr tracks: 55.59 in, 141 cm front, 57.32 in, 146 cm rea length: 150.12 in, 381 cm; width: 66.77 in, 170 cm; heigh 46.85 in, 119 cm; ground clearance: 5.20 in, 13.2 cr weight: 2,293 lb, 1,040 kg; turning circle: 34.1 ft, 10.4 m fuel tank: 13 imp gal, 15.6 US gal, 59 l.

BODY coupé; 2 doors; 2 seats; detachable roof; built-headrests.

PRACTICAL INSTRUCTIONS fuel: 98 oct petrol; oil: engir 10.9 imp pt, 13.1 US pt, 6.2 l, SAE 10W-50, change eve 3,100 miles, 5,000 km - gearbox and final drive 3 imp p 3.6 US pt, 1.7 l, SAE 90, change every 18,600 mile 30,000 km; greasing: none; sparking plug: 200°; tapp clearances: inlet 0.016-0.020 in, 0.40-0.50 mm, exhau 0.022-0.026 in, 0.55-0.65 mm; valve timing: 15° 55° 57° 13 tyre pressure: front 24 psi, 1.7 atm, rear 27 psi, 1.9 atr

OPTIONALS air-conditioning with tinted glass; metallic spra leather upholstery; heated rear window; tinted glass wi heated rear window; electric windows.

Gamma Berlina 2000

PRICE EX WORKS: 11,440,100** liras

ENGINE front, 4 stroke; 4 cylinders, horizontally oppose 122 cu in, 1,999 cc (3.60 x 2.99 in, 91.5 x 76 mm); con pression ratio: 9:1; max power (DIN): 120 hp (88.3 kW) 5,500 rpm; max torque (DIN): 127 lb ft, 17.5 kg m (171 Nm) at 3,500 rpm; max engine rpm: 6,200; 60 hp/l (44 kW/l); 3 crankshaft bearings; valves: overhead; camshaft 2, 1 per bank, overhead; lubrication: rotary pump, full flo filter (cartridge), 10.7 imp pt, 12.9 US pt, 6.1 l; 1 Web

LANCIA Gamma Berlina 2000 - 2500

LANCIA Gamma Coupé 2000 - 2500

36 ADLD/150 twin barrel carburettor, automatic starter; fuel feed: electric pump; liquid, 15.8 imp pt, 19 US pt, 9 l.

TRANSMISSION driving wheels: front; clutch: single dry plate (diaphragm); gearbox: mechanical; gears: 5, fully synchronized; ratios: I 3.462, II 2.105, III 1.458, IV 1.129, V 0.897, rev 3.214; lever: central; final drive: hypoid bevel, in unit with gearbox; axle ratio: 4.100; width of rims: 6''; tyres: 185/70 HR x 14 tubeless.

PERFORMANCE max speeds: (I) 31 mph, 50 mph; (II) 51 mph, 82 km/h; (III) 73 mph, 118 km/h; (IV) 94 mph, 152 km/h; (V) 115 mph, 185 km/h; power-weight ratio: 24 lb/hp (32.9 lb/kW), 11 kg/hp (14.9 kg/kW); carrying capacity: 992 lb, 450 kg; acceleration: standing ¼ mile 17.4 sec; consumption: 30.1 m/imp gal, 25 m/US gal, 9.4 l x 100 km.

CHASSIS integral; front and rear suspension: independent, wishbones, coil springs, telescopic damper struts, anti-roll bar.

STEERING rack-and-pinion, ZF progressive servo; adjustable height and tilt; turns lock to lock: 3.

BRAKES ventilated disc, Superduplex circuit, servo.

ELECTRICAL EQUIPMENT 12 V; 60 Ah battery; 770 W alternator; Bosch or Marelli distributor; 4 iodine headlamps with automatically adjustable height.

DIMENSIONS AND WEIGHT wheel base: 105.12 in, 267 cm; tracks: 57.09 in, 145 cm front, 56.69 in, 144 cm rear; length: 180.31 in, 458 cm; width: 68.11 in, 173 cm; height: 55.51 in, 141 cm; weight: 2,911 lb, 1,320 kg; fuel tank: 13.9 imp gal, 16.6 US gal, 63 l.

BODY saloon/sedan; 4 doors; 5 seats, separate front seats, 4 built-in headrests, reclining backrests; front electric windows.

PRACTICAL INSTRUCTIONS fuel: 98 oct petrol; oil: engine 10.7 imp pt, 12.9 US pt, 6.1 l, 15W-50, change every 6,200 miles, 10,000 km - gearbox and final drive 5.8 imp pt, 7 US pt, 3.3 l, 85W-90, change every 18,600 miles, 30,000 km; greasing: none; sparking plug: Bosch W200 T 30 OV Champion N 7 y; tappet clearances: inlet 0.016 in, 0.40 mm, exhaust 0.014 in, 0.35 mm; valve timing: 15° 47° 53° 9°; front and rear tyre pressure: 26 psi, 1.8 atm.

OPTIONALS air-conditioning; metallic spray; tinted glass; rear electric windows; leather upholstery; light alloy wheels; front and rear (wrap-round) belts; rear red fog lamp.

Gamma Coupé 2000

See Gamma Berlina 2000, except for:

PRICE EX WORKS: 14,543,500** liras

PERFORMANCE power-weight ratio: 23.3 lb/hp (31.7 lb/kW), 10.6 kg/hp (14.4 kg/kW).

DIMENSIONS AND WEIGHT wheel base: 100.59 in, 255 cm; length: 176.38 in, 448 cm; height: 52.36 in, 133 cm; weight: 2,800 lb, 1,270 kg.

BODY coupé; 2 doors; 4 seats.

Gamma Berlina 2500

See Gamma Berlina 2000, except for:

PRICE IN GB: £ 7,136*
PRICE EX WORKS: 13,722,750** liras

ENGINE 151.6 cu in, 2,484 cc (4.02 x 2.99 in, 102 x 76 mm); max power (DIN): 140 hp (103 kW) at 5,400 rpm; max torque (DIN): 154 lb ft, 21.2 kg m (208 Nm) at 3,000 rpm; max engine rpm: 6,000; 56.4 hp/l (41.5 kW/l); 1 Weber 38 ADLD/150 twin barrel carburettor.

TRANSMISSION axle ratio: 3.700.

PERFORMANCE max speeds: (I) 33 mph, 53 km/h; (II) 55 mph, 88 km/h; (III) 79 mph, 127 km/h; (IV) 101 mph, 163 km/h; (V) 121 mph, 195 km/h; power-weight ratio: 20.7 lb/hp (28.2 lb/kW), 9.4 kg/hp (12.8 kg/kW); consumption: 29.4 m/imp gal, 24.5 m/US gal, 9.6 l x 100 km.

BODY light alloy wheels (standard).

Gamma Coupé 2500

See Gamma Berlina 2500, except for:

PRICE IN GB: £ 9,186*
PRICE EX WORKS: 17,286,750** liras

LAWIL   ITALY

S3 Varzina

PRICE EX WORKS: 1,971,000* liras

ENGINE front, 2 stroke; 2 cylinders, in line; 15 cu in, 246 cc (2.05 x 2.28 in, 52 x 58 mm); compression ratio: 7.5:1; max power (SAE): 14 hp (10.3 kW) at 4,400 rpm; max torque (SAE): 14 lb ft, 1.9 kg m (18.6 Nm) at 3,000 rpm; max engine rpm: 4,500; 56.9 hp/l (41.8 kW/l); cast iron block, light alloy head; 3 crankshaft bearings; lubrication: mixture; 1 Dell'Orto WHB horizontal carburettor; fuel feed: gravity; air-cooled.

TRANSMISSION driving wheels: rear; clutch: single dry plate; gearbox: mechanical; gears: 4, silent claw coupling; ratios: I 2.449, II 1.492, III 0.986, IV 0.674, rev 2.760; lever: central; final drive: spiral bevel; axle ratio: 3.083; width of rims: 3''; tyres: 4.00 x 10.

PERFORMANCE max speeds: (I) 12 mph, 20 km/h; (II) 19 mph, 30 km/h; (III) 29 mph, 47 km/h; (IV) 39 mph, 63 km/h; power-weight ratio: 50.5 lb/hp (68.6 lb/kW), 22.9 kg/hp (31.1 kg/kW); carrying capacity: 353 lb, 160 kg; consumption: 70.6 m/imp gal, 58.8 m/US gal, 4 l x 100 km.

CHASSIS tubular; front suspension: independent, wishbones, transverse semi-elliptic leafsprings, telescopic dampers; rear: rigid axle, semi-elliptic leafsprings, telescopic dampers.

STEERING rack-and-pinion; turns lock to lock: 3.50.

BRAKES drum, single circuit.

ELECTRICAL EQUIPMENT 12 V; 35 Ah battery; 160 W alternator; Ducati (electronic) distributor; 2 headlamps.

DIMENSIONS AND WEIGHT wheel base: 46.06 in, 117 cm; tracks: 40.94 in, 104 cm front, 42.32 in, 107 cm rear; length: 81.50 in, 207 cm; width: 50 in, 127 cm; height: 53.54 in, 136 cm; ground clearance: 4.72 in, 12 cm; weight: 706 lb, 320 kg; weight distribution: 55% front, 45% rear; turning circle: 19.7 ft, 6 m; fuel tank: 2.4 imp gal, 2.9 US gal, 11 l.

BODY sport; 2 doors; 2 seats, bench front seats.

PRACTICAL INSTRUCTIONS fuel: mixture 1:50; oil: gearbox 1.8 imp pt, 2.1 US pt, 1 l, SAE 90 EP, change every 3,100 miles, 5,000 km - final drive 1.1 imp pt, 1.3 US pt, 0.6 l.

LAWIL S3 Varzina

S3 VARZINA

SAE 90 EP, change every 6,200 miles, 10,000 km; greasing: every 3,100 miles, 5,000 km, 3 points; sparking plug: 240°; tyre pressure: front 18 psi, 1.3 atm, rear 20 psi, 1.4 atm.

OPTIONALS tonneau cover; roll-bar.

A4 City

See S3 Varzina, except for:

PRICE EX WORKS: 1,947,000* liras

PERFORMANCE power-weight ratio: 55.1 lb/hp (75 lb/kW), 25 kg/hp (34 kg/kW).

DIMENSIONS AND WEIGHT length: 80.71 in, 205 cm; width: 50.39 in, 128 cm; height: 56.69 in, 144 cm; weight: 772 lb, 350 kg.

BODY saloon/sedan.

OPTIONALS none.

MASERATI   ITALY

MASERATI Merak

Merak

PRICE EX WORKS: 19,296,500* liras

ENGINE centre-rear, 4 stroke; 6 cylinders, Vee-slanted at 90°; 122 cu in, 1,999 cc (3.15 x 2.61 in, 80 x 66.3 mm); compression ratio: 9:1; max power (DIN): 170 hp (125.1 kW) at 7,000 rpm; max torque (DIN): 138 lb ft, 19 kg m (186.3 Nm) at 5,000 rpm; max engine rpm: 7,300; 86 hp/l (93.2 kW/l); light alloy block and head, wet liners, hemispherical combustion chambers; 4 crankshaft bearings; valves: overhead, Vee-slanted, thimble tappets; camshafts: 4, 2 per bank, overhead, chain driven; lubrication: gear pump, full flow filter, oil cooler, 13 imp pt, 16 US pt, 7 l; 3 Weber 44 DCNF downdraught twin barrel carburettors; fuel feed: 1 electric pump; water-cooled, 23 imp pt, 28 US pt, 14 l, front radiator, 2 electric fans.

TRANSMISSION driving wheels: rear; clutch: single dry plate (diaphragm), hydraulically controlled; gearbox: mechanical; gears: 5, fully synchronized; ratios: I 2.920, II 1.940, III 1.320, IV 0.940, V 0.730, rev 3.150; lever: central; final drive: hypoid bevel, limited slip differential; axle ratio: 5.500; width of rims: 7.5''; tyres: 185/70 VR x 15 front, 205/70 VR x 15 rear.

PERFORMANCE max speed: 137 mph, 220 km/h; power-weight ratio: 15 lb/hp (18.2 lb/kW), 6.8 kg/hp (9.3 kg/kW); carrying capacity: 706 lb, 320 kg; speed in top at 1,000 rpm: 18.7 mph, 29.7 km/h; consumption: 30.7 m/imp gal, 25.6 m/US gal, 9.2 l x 100 km.

MASERATI Merak

CHASSIS integral; front and rear suspension: independent, wishbones, coil springs, anti-roll bar, telescopic dampers.

STEERING rack-and-pinion, adjustable tilt and height, turns lock to lock: 3.

BRAKES ventilated discs, independent circuit for each axle, servo; swept area: front 244.2 sq in, 1,575 sq cm, rear 209 sq in, 1,348 sq cm, total 453.2 sq in, 2,923 sq cm.

ELECTRICAL EQUIPMENT 12 V; 60 Ah battery; 780 W alternator; Bosch electronic ignition; 2 retractable iodine headlamps.

DIMENSIONS AND WEIGHT wheel base: 102.30 in, 260 cm; front and rear track: 58 in, 147.40 cm; length: 170 in, 433 cm; width: 69.60 in, 177 cm; height: 44.60 in, 113 cm; ground clearance: 5.12 in, 13 cm; weight: 2,550 lb, 1,160 kg; turning circle: 34.4 ft, 10.5 m; fuel tank: 18.7 imp gal, 22.4 US gal, 85 l.

BODY coupé; 2 doors; 2 + 2 seats, separate front seats, reclining backrests, headrests; tinted glass; electric windows; heated rear window; air-conditioning; light alloy wheels.

PRACTICAL INSTRUCTIONS fuel: 98-100 oct petrol; oil: engine 12.3 imp pt, 14.8 US pt, 7 l, SAE 10W/50, change every 3,100 miles, 5,000 km - gearbox 1.8 imp pt, 2.3 US pt, 1.1 l, SAE 90, change every 12,400 miles, 20,000 km - final drive 2.5 imp pt, 3 US pt, 1.4 l, change every 12,400 miles, 20,000 km; greasing: 2 points, every 3,100 miles, 5000 km; sparking plug type: Bosch 200 T 30; tappet clearances: inlet 0.011 in, 0.25 mm, exhaust 0.024 in, 0.50 mm; valve timing: 42° 80° 56° 20°; tyre pressure: front 31 psi, 2.5 atm, rear 34 psi, 2.4 atm.

OPTIONALS metallic spray.

Merak SS

See Merak 2000, except for:

PRICE IN GB: £ 14,888*
PRICE IN USA: $ 29,800

ENGINE 108.9 cu in, 2,965 cc (3.61 x 2.95 in, 91.6 x 75 mm); max power (DIN): 220 hp (162 kW) at 6,500 rpm; max torque (DIN): 199 lb ft, 27.5 kg m (269.7 Nm) at 4,500 rpm; max engine rpm: 7,000; 74.2 hp/l (54.6 kW/l).

TRANSMISSION axle ratio: 4.370; tyres: 195/70 VR x 15 front, 215/70 VR x 15 rear.

PERFORMANCE max speed: 155 mph, 250 km/h; power-weight ratio: 11.8 lb/hp (16 lb/kW), 5.4 kg/hp (7.3 kg/kW); speed in top at 1,000 rpm: 24 mph, 38.5 km/h; consumption: 26.6 m/imp gal, 22.2 m/US gal, 10.6 l x 100 km.

BRAKES swept area: front 244.2 sq in, 1,575 sq cm, rear 254.3 sq in, 1,640 sq cm, total 498.5 sq in, 3,215 sq cm.

DIMENSIONS AND WEIGHT weight: 2,601 lb, 1,180 kg.

PRACTICAL INSTRUCTIONS oil: gearbox and final drive 4.3 imp pt, 5.5 US pt, 2.5 l.

OPTIONALS right-hand drive; leather upholstery.

MASERATI Quattroporte

Quattroporte

ENGINE front, 4 stroke; 8 cylinders, Vee-slanted at 90°; 252.3 cu in, 4,136 cc (3.46 x 3.35 in, 88 x 85 mm); compression ratio: 8.5:1; max power (DIN): 270 hp (198.7 kW) at 6,000 rpm; max torque (DIN): 289 lb ft, 40 kg m (392.3 Nm) at 3,800 rpm; max engine rpm: 6,000; 65 hp/l (48 kW/l); light alloy block and head, wet liners, hemispherical combustion chambers; 5 crankshaft bearings; valves: overhead; camshafts: 4, 2 per bank, overhead, chain driven; lubrication: gear pump, full flow filter, 17 imp pt, 4 US pt, 9 l; 4 Weber 42 DCNF downdraught twin barrel carburettors; fuel feed: electric pump; water-cooled, 28 imp pt, 33.5 US pt, 16 l, 2 electric fans.

TRANSMISSION driving wheels: rear; gearbox: automatic transmission, hydraulic torque converter and planetary gears with 3 ratios, max ratio of converter at stall 2.75, possible manual selection; ratios: I 2.400, II 1.470, III 1, rev 2.700; lever: central; final drive: hypoid bevel, limited slip differential; axle ratio: 3.310; width of rims: 7''; tyres: 215/70 VR x 15 XDX tubeless.

PERFORMANCE max speed: 143 mph, 230 km/h; power-weight ratio: 14.5 lb/hp (19.7 lb/kW), 6.6 kg/hp (8.9 kg/kW); carrying capacity: 1,103 lb, 500 kg; speed in top at 1,000 rpm: 24.2 mph, 39.5 km/h; consumption: 21.4 m/imp gal, 17.8 m/US gal, 13.2 l x 100 km.

CHASSIS integral; front and rear suspension: independent, wishbones, coil springs, anti-roll bar, telescopic dampers.

STEERING rack-and-pinion, adjustable height and distance, servo; turns lock to lock: 2.50.

BRAKES ventilated disc, dual circuit, servo; swept area: front 245.4 sq in, 1,583 sq cm, rear 188.5 sq in, 1,216 sq cm, total 433.9 sq in, 2,799 sq cm.

ELECTRICAL EQUIPMENT 12 V; 60 Ah battery; 650 W alternator; Bosch electronic ignition; 4 iodine headlamps.

DIMENSIONS AND WEIGHT wheel base: 110.20 in, 280 cm; front and rear track: 60.03 in, 152 cm; length: 196 in, 498 cm; width: 70.47 in, 179 cm; height: 53.14 in, 135 cm; ground clearance: 5.55 in, 14 cm; weight: 3,924 lb, 1,780 kg; turning circle: 35 ft, 11.5 m; fuel tank: 22 imp gal, 26.4 US gal, 100 l.

BODY saloon/sedan; 4 doors; 5 seats, separate and reclining front seats; air-conditioning; tinted glass; electric windows; heated rear window; leather upholstery.

PRACTICAL INSTRUCTIONS fuel: 98-100 oct petrol; oil: engine 17.6 imp pt, 21.1 US pt, 10 l, SAE 10W/50, change every 3,000 miles, 5,000 km - automatic transmission 13.6 imp pt, 16.3 US pt, 7.7 l - final drive 2.5 imp pt, 3 US pt, 1.4 l, SAE 90, change every 12,400 miles, 20,000 km; greasing: every 3,100 miles, 5,000 km; sparking plug type: Bosch 200 T 30; tappet clearances: inlet 0.011 in, 0.25 mm, exhaust 0.024 in, 0.50 mm; valve timing: 40° 80° 55° 25°; tyre pressure: front 31 psi, 2.2 atm, rear 34 psi, 2.4 atm.

OPTIONALS right hand drive; metallic spray.

MASERATI Kyalami

MASERATI Kyalami

MASERATI Khamsin

VARIATIONS

ENGINE 300.8 cu in, 4,930 cc (3.70 x 3.50 in, 93.9 x 89 mm), max power (DIN) 280 hp (206 kW) at 5,600 rpm, max torque (DIN) 289 lb/ft, 40 kg/m (392.3 Nm) at 3.000 rpm, 56.8 hp/l, 41.8 kW/l.

Kyalami

See Quattroporte, except for:

PRICE IN GB: £ 21,996*
PRICE EX WORKS: 30,535,000* liras

TRANSMISSION clutch: single dry plate (diaphragm), hydraulically controlled; gearbox: ZF mechanical; gears: 5, fully synchronized; ratios: I 2,990, II 1.900, III 1.320, IV 1, V 0.890, rev 2.700; axle ratio: 3.540; width of rims: 7.5''; tyres: 205/70 VR x 15, tubeless.

PERFORMANCE max speed: 149 mph, 240 km/h; power-weight ratio: 126 lb/hp (17.2 lb/kW), 5.7 kg/hp (7.8 kg/kW); speed in top at 1,000 rpm: 24.5 mph, 39.7 km/h.

STEERING turns lock to lock: 2.

DIMENSIONS AND WEIGHT wheel base: 102.30 in, 260 cm; front and rear track: 60.20 in, 153 cm; length: 180 in, 458 cm; width: 72.80 in, 185 cm; height: 50 in, 127 cm; weight: 3,421 lb, 1,550 kg.

BODY coupé; 2 doors; 4 seats.

Khamsin

PRICE IN GB: £ 23,975*
PRICE IN USA: $ 41,450

ENGINE front, 4 stroke; 8 cylinders, Vee-slanted at 90°; 300.8 cu in, 4,930 cc (3.70 x 3.50 in, 93.9 x 89 mm); compression ratio: 8.5:1; max power (DIN): 320 hp (235.5 kW) at 5,500 rpm; max torque (DIN): 355 lb ft, 49 kg m (480.5 Nm) at 4,000 rpm; max engine rpm: 6,000; 64.9 hp/l (47.8 kW/l); light alloy cylinder block and head, wet liners, hemispherical combustion chambers; 5 crankshaft bearings; valves: overhead, Vee-slanted at 30°, thimble tappets; camshafts: 4, 2 per bank, overhead, driven by chain; lubrication: gear pump, full flow filter, dry sump, separate oil tank, 21.1 imp pt, 25.4 US pt, 12 l; 4 Weber 42 DCNF 6 downdraught twin barrel carburettors; fuel feed: 2 electric pumps; water-cooled, 28.2 imp pt, 33.8 US pt, 16 l, 2 electric fans.

TRANSMISSION driving wheels: rear; clutch: single dry plate, hydraulically controlled; gearbox: ZF mechanical; ratios: I 2.990, II 1.900, III 1.320, IV 1, V 0.890, rev 2.700; lever: central; final drive: hypoid bevel; axle ratio: 3.310; width of rims: 7.5''; tyres: 215/70 VR x 15.

PERFORMANCE max speed: 171 mph, 275 km/h; power-weight ratio: 10.4 lb/hp (14.3 lb/kW), 4.7 kg/hp (6.5 kg/kW); carrying capacity: 706 lb, 320 kg; speed in top at 1,000 rpm: 26.1 mph, 42 km/h; fuel consumption: 19.3 m/imp gal, 16.1 m/US gal, 14.6 l x 100 km.

CHASSIS tubular; front suspension: independent, wish-

KHAMSIN

bones, coil springs, anti-roll bar, telescopic dampers; rear: independent, wishbones, coil springs, anti-roll bar, 4 telescopic dampers.

STEERING rack-and-pinion, adjustable height and distance, variable ratio, servo; turns lock to lock: 2.

BRAKES disc (front diameter 10.75 in, 27.3 cm, rear 10.28 in, 26.1 cm), internal radial fins, dual circuit, servo: swept area: front 245.4 sq in, 1,583 sq cm, rear 188.5 sq in, 1,216 sq cm, total 423.9 sq in, 2,799 sq cm.

ELECTRICAL EQUIPMENT 12 V; 72 Ah battery; 650 W alternator; Bosch electronic ignition; 4 retractable iodine headlamps.

DIMENSIONS AND WEIGHT wheel base: 100.39 in, 255 cm; tracks: 56.69 in, 144 cm front, 57.87 in, 147 cm rear; length: 173.23 in, 440 cm; width: 70.87 in, 180 cm; height: 44.88 in, 114 cm; ground clearance: 5.51 in, 14 cm; dry weight: 3,374 lb, 1,530 kg; turning circle: 34.4 ft, 10.5 m; fuel tank: 19.8 imp gal, 23.8 US gal, 90 l.

BODY coupé; 2 doors; 2 + 2 seats, separate front seats, reclining backrest, built-in headrests; heated rear window; tinted glass; electric windows; leather upholstery; light alloy wheels; air-conditioning.

PRACTICAL INSTRUCTIONS fuel: 98-100 oct petrol; oil: engine 21.1 imp pt, 25.4 US pt, 12 l, SAE 20W-50, change every 3,100 miles, 5,000 km - gearbox 2.5 imp pt, 3 US pt, 1.4 l, SAE 90, change every 12,400 miles, 20,000 km - final drive 2.5 imp pt, 3 US pt, 1.4 l, SAE 90, change every 12,400 miles, 20,000 km; greasing: every 3,100 miles, 5,000 km, 4 points; sparking plug: 240°; tappets clearances: inlet 0.010 in, 0.25 mm, exhaust 0.020 in, 0.50 mm; valve timing: 40° 80° 55° 25°; tyre pressure: front 31 psi, 2.2 atm, rear 34 psi, 2.4 atm.

OPTIONALS right-hand drive; limited slip differential; Borg-Warner automatic transmission, hydraulic torque converter and planetary gears with 3 ratios (I 2.400, II 1.470, III 1, rev 2.700), max ratio of converter at stall 2.75, possible manual selection; metallic spray.

Bora

PRICE IN GB: £ 22,991*
PRICE IN USA: $ 38,790

ENGINE centre-rear, 4 stroke; 8 cylinders, Vee-slanted at 90°; 308.8 cu in, 4930 cc (3.70 x 3.50 in, 93.9 x 89 mm); compression ratio: 8.5:1; max power (DIN): 320 hp (235.5 kW) at 5,500 rpm; max torque (DIN): 335 lb ft, 49 kg m (480.5 Nm) at 4,000 rpm; max engine rpm: 6,000; 64.9 hp/l (47.8 kW/l); light alloy block and head, wet liners, hemispherical combustion chambers; 5 crankshaft bearings; valves: overhead, Vee-slanted at 30°, thimble tappets; camshafts: 4, 2 per bank, overhead, driven by chain; lubrication: gear pump, full flow filter, dry sump, separate oil tank, 21 imp pt, 25.4 US pt, 12 l; 4 Weber 42 DCNF 6 downdraught twin

MASERATI Bora

barrel carburettors; fuel feed: 2 electric pumps; water-cooled, 28.2 imp pt, 33.8 US pt, 16 l, 2 electric fans.

TRANSMISSION driving wheels: rear; clutch: single dry plate (diaphragm), hydraulically controlled; gearbox: mechanical; gears: 5, fully synchronized; ratios: I 2.580, II 1.520, III 1.040, IV 0.850, V 0.740, rev 2.860; lever: central; final drive: hypoid bevel, limited slip differential; axle ratio: 3.770; width of rims: 7.5''; tyres: 215/70 x 15.

PERFORMANCE max speeds: (I) 49 mph, 79 km/h; (II) 83 mph, 133 km/h; (III) 121 mph, 194 km/h; (IV) 148 mph, 238 km/h; (V) 174 mph, 280 km/h; power-weight ratio: 9.5 lb/hp (13.5 lb/kW), 4.4 kg/hp (6.1 kg/kW); carrying capacity: 662 lb, 300 kg; acceleration: standing ¼ mile 14.4 sec, 0-50 mph (0-80 km/h) 4.4 sec; speed in top at 1,000 rpm: 28.9 mph, 46.5 km/h; fuel consumption: 17.8 m/imp gal, 14.8 m/US gal, 15.9 l x 100 km.

CHASSIS integral; front suspension: independent, wishbones, coil springs, anti-roll bar, telescopic dampers; rear: independent, wishbones, coil springs, anti-roll bar, telescopic dampers.

STEERING rack-and-pinion, adjustable height and distance; turns lock to lock: 3.

BRAKES disc (front diameter 9.45 in, 24 cm, rear 9.76 in, 24.8 cm), internal radial fins, rear compensator, dual circuit, servo; swept area: front 244.2 sq in, 1,575 sq cm, rear 209 sq in, 1,348 sq cm, total 453.2 sq in, 2,923 sq cm.

ELECTRICAL EQUIPMENT 12 V; 66 Ah battery; 650 W alternator; Bosch electronic ignition; 2 retractable iodine headlamps.

DIMENSIONS AND WEIGHT wheel base: 102.36 in, 260 cm; tracks: 58.03 in, 147 cm front, 53.03 in, 145 cm rear; length: 170.67 in, 433 cm; width: 69.61 in, 177 cm; height: 44.49 in, 113 cm; ground clearance: 5.12 in, 13 cm; dry weight: 3,087 lb, 1,400 kg; distribution of weight: 42% front, 58% rear; turning circle: 36.1 ft, 11 m; fuel tank: imp gal, 26.4 US gal, 100 l.

BODY coupé; 2 doors; 2 seats; adjustable pedals; air-conditioning; tinted glass; electric windows; heated rear window; leather upholstery.

PRACTICAL INSTRUCTIONS fuel: 98-100 oct petrol; oil: engine 17.6 imp pt, 21.1 US pt, 10 l, SAE 20W-50, change every 3,100 miles, 5,000 km - gearbox and final drive 5.8 imp pt, 7 US pt, 3.3 l, SAE 90, change every 12,400 miles, 20,000 km; greasing: every 3,100 miles, 5,000 km, 5 points; sparking plug: 240°; tappet clearances: inlet 0.011-0.012 in, 0.28-0.30 mm, exhaust 0.019-0.020 in, 0.47-0.50 mm; valve timing: 40° 80° 54° 22°; tyre pressure: front 36 psi, 2.5 atm, rear 38 psi, 2.7 atm.

OPTIONALS right-hand drive; metallic spray.

NUOVA INNOCENTI   ITALY

Mini 90N/90SL

PRICES EX WORKS: Mini 90N 3,160,000* liras
                   Mini 90SL 3,510,000* liras

ENGINE front, transverse, 4 stroke; 4 cylinders, vertical, in line; 60.9 cu in, 998 cc (2.54 x 3 in, 64.6 x 76.2 mm); compression ratio: 9:1; max power (DIN): 49 hp (36.1 kW) at 5,600 rpm; max torque (DIN): 51 lb ft, 7 kg m (68.6 Nm) at 2,600 rpm; max engine rpm: 6,000; 49.1 hp/l (36.2 kW/l); cast iron block and head; 3 crankshaft bearings; valves: overhead, in line, push-rods and rockers; camshafts: side; lubrication: eccentric pump, full flow filter (cartridge), 8.8 imp pt, 10.6 US pt, 5 l; 1 SU type HS 4 semi-downdraught carburettor; fuel feed: mechanical pump; water-cooled, 6.7 imp pt, 8 US pt, 3.8 l, electric thermostatic fan.

TRANSMISSION driving wheels: front; clutch: single dry plate (diaphragm), hydraulically controlled; gearbox: mechanical, in unit with engine; gears: 4, fully synchronized; ratios: I 3.525, II 2.217, III 1.433, IV 1, rev 3.544; lever: central; final drive: spiral bevel; axle ratio: 3.937; width of rims: 4.5''; tyres: 135 SR x 12.

PERFORMANCE max speeds: (I) 25 mph, 40 km/h; (II) 39 mph, 63 km/h; (III) 61 mph, 98 km/h; (IV) about 87 mph, 140 km/h; power-weight ratio: 32.4 lb/hp (44 lb/kW), 14.7 kg/hp (20 kg/kW); carrying capacity: 882 lb, 400 kg; speed in direct drive at 1,000 rpm: 14.6 mph, 23 km/h; consumption: 36.7 m/imp gal, 30.5 m/US gal, 7.7 l x 100 km.

CHASSIS integral, front and rear auxiliary frames; front suspension: independent, wishbones (lower trailing links), rubber cone springs, telescopic dampers; rear: independent, swinging longitudinal trailing arms, rubber cone springs, telescopic dampers.

STEERING rack-and-pinion; turns lock to lock: 2.75.

BRAKES front disc (diameter 8.38 in, 21.3 cm), rear drum, dual circuit; lining area: front 17.7 sq in, 114 sq cm, rear 33.8 sq in, 218 sq cm, total 51.5 sq in, 332 sq cm.

ELECTRICAL EQUIPMENT 12 V; 43 Ah battery; 385 W alternator; Lucas or Bosch distributor; 2 headlamps.

DIMENSIONS AND WEIGHT wheel base: 80.16 in, 204 cm; front and rear tracks: 49.21 in, 125 cm; length: 122.83 in, 312 cm; width: 59.06 in, 150 cm; height: 54.33 in, 138 cm; ground clearance: 4.92 in, 12.5 cm; weight: 1,588 lb, 720 kg; turning circle: 28.2 ft, 8.6 m; fuel tank: 8.4 imp gal, 10 US gal, 38 l.

BODY saloon/sedan; 2 + 1 doors; 5 seats, separate front seats, reclining backrests; heated rear window folding rear seat; rear window wiper-washer, tinted glass and headrests (for 90 SL only).

PRACTICAL INSTRUCTIONS fuel: 98-100 oct petrol; oil: engine, gearbox and final drive 8.8 imp pt, 10.6 US pt, 5 l, SAE 20W-50, change every 3,100 miles, 5,000 km; greasing: every 3,100 miles, 5,000 km, 7 points; sparking plug: 175°; tappet clearances: inlet 0.012 in, 0.30 mm, exhaust 0.012 in, 0.30 mm; valve timing: 5° 45° 51° 21°; tyre pressure: front 30 psi, 2.1 atm, rear 28 psi, 2 atm.

OPTIONALS headrests (for 90 N only); metallic spray (for 90 SL only).

MASERATI Bora

Mini 120 SL

See Mini 90N/90SL, except for:

PRICE EX WORKS: 3,781,000* liras

ENGINE 77.8 cu in, 1,275 cc (2.78 x 3.20 in, 70.6 x 81.3 mm); compression ratio: 9.75:1; max power (DIN): 65 hp (47.8 kW) at 5,600 rpm; max torque (DIN): 72 lb ft, 10 kg m (98.1 Nm) at 2,600 rpm; 51 hp/l (37.5 kW/l); oil cooler; 1 SU type HS 6 semi-downdraught carburettor; fuel feed: electric pump.

TRANSMISSION gearbox ratios: I 3.329, II 2.094, III 1.353, IV 1, rev 3.347; axle ratio: 3.647; tyres: 155/70 SR x 12.

PERFORMANCE max speeds: (I) 29 mph, 46 km/h; (II) 45 mph, 73 km/h; (III) 70 mph, 113 km/h; (IV) about 96 mph, 155 km/h; power-weight ratio: 24.8 lb/hp (33.7 lb/kW), 11.2 kg/hp (15.3 kg/kW); speed in direct drive at 1,000 rpm: 16 mph, 25.7 km/h; consumption: 33.6 m/imp gal, 28 m/US gal, 8.4 l x 100 km.

ELECTRICAL EQUIPMENT iodine headlamps.

DIMENSIONS AND WEIGHT weight: 1,610 lb, 730 kg.

BODY rear window wiper-washer; tinted glass; headrests.

PRACTICAL INSTRUCTIONS tappet clearances: inlet 0.014 in, 0.35 mm, exhaust 0.014 in, 0.35 mm; valve timing: 10° 50° 51° 21°.

Mini De Tomaso

See Mini 90N/90SL, except for:

PRICE EX WORKS: 4,090,000* liras

ENGINE 77.8 cu in, 1,275 cc (2.78 x 3.20 in, 70.6 x 81.3 mm); compression ratio: 9.75:1; max power (SAE): 77 hp (56.7 kW) at 6,050 rpm; max torque (SAE): 77 lb ft, 10.6 kg m (104 Nm) at 3,200 rpm; max engine rpm: 6,100; 60.4 hp/l (44.5 kW/l); oil cooler; 1 SU type HS 6 semi-downdraught carburettor; fuel feed: electric pump.

TRANSMISSION gearbox ratios: I 3.329, II 2.094, III 1.353, IV 1, rev 3.347; axle ratio: 3.647; tyres: 155/70 SR x 12.

PERFORMANCE max speeds: (I) 30 mph, 48 km/h; (II) 47 mph, 76 km/h; (III) 73 mph, 118 km/h; (IV) over 99 mph, 160 km/h; power-weight ratio: 21.4 lb/hp (29.1 lb/kW), 9.7 kg/hp (13.2 kg/kW); consumption: 33.6 m/imp gal, 28 m/US gal, 8.4 l x 100 km.

ELECTRICAL EQUIPMENT iodine headlamps.

DIMENSIONS AND WEIGHT length: 123.23 in, 313 cm; width: 59.84 in, 152 cm; height: 54.33 in, 138 cm; ground clearance: 4.72 in, 12 cm; weight: 1,654 lb, 750 kg.

BODY headrests; tinted glass; halogen fog lamps; rear window wiper-washer; light alloy wheels.

PRACTICAL INSTRUCTIONS tappet clearances: inlet 0.014 in, 0.35 mm, exhaust 0.014 in, 0.35 mm; valve timing: 10° 50° 51° 21°.

OPTIONALS special version.

NUOVA INNOCENTI Mini 120 SL

NUOVA INNOCENTI Mini De Tomaso

POLSKI-FIAT 126 P/650K

POLSKI-FIAT POLAND

126 P/650

ENGINE rear, 4 stroke; 2 cylinders, vertical, in line; 39.8 cu in, 652 cc (3 x 2.7 in, 77 x 70 mm); compression ratio: 7.5:1; max power (DIN): 24 hp (17.6 kW) at 4,500 rpm; max torque (DIN): 30 lb ft, 4.2 kg m (41.2 Nm) at 3,000 rpm; max engine rpm: 5,400; 36.8 hp/l (27 kW/l); light alloy block and head; 2 crankshaft bearings; valves: overhead, in line, push-rods and rockers; camshafts: 1, side, chain-driven; lubrication: gear pump, centrifugal filter, 4.8 imp pt, 5.7 US pt, 2.7 l; 1 Fos 28 IMB 5/250 downdraught carburettor; fuel feed: mechanical pump; air-cooled.

TRANSMISSION driving wheels: rear; clutch: single dry plate (diaphragm); gearbox: mechanical; gears: 4, II, III and IV silent claw coupling; ratios: I 3.250, II 2.067, III 1.300, IV 0.872, rev 4.024; lever: central; final drive: spiral bevel; axle ratio: 4.875; width of rims: 4''; tyres: 135 SR x 12.

PERFORMANCE max speeds: (I) 19 mph, 30 km/h; (II) 31 mph, 50 km/h; (III) 50 mph, 80 km/h; (IV) 65 mph, 105 km/h; power-weight ratio: 55.6 lb/hp (75.7 lb/kW), 25.2 kg/hp (34.3 kg/kW); carrying capacity: 750 lb, 340 kg; speed in direct drive at 1,000 rpm: 14.7 mph, 23.6 km/h; consumption: 49.5 m/imp gal, 41.3 m/US gal, 5.7 l x 100 km.

CHASSIS integral; front suspension: independent, wishbones, transverse leafspring lower arms, telescopic dampers;

POLSKI-FIAT 125 P 1300 - 1500

direct drive at 1,000 rpm: 15.8 mph, 25.9 km/h; consumption: 29.7 m/imp gal, 24.8 m/US gal, 9.5 l x 100 km.

CHASSIS integral; front suspension: independent, wishbone coil springs, anti-roll bar acting as lower trailing arm telescopic dampers; rear: rigid axle, semi-elliptic leaf springs, telescopic dampers.

STEERING worm and roller; turns lock to lock: 3.

BRAKES disc (diameter 8.94 in, 22.7 mm), servo; lining area: total 38.4 sq in, 248 sq cm.

ELECTRICAL EQUIPMENT 12 V; 45 Ah battery; 1,500 alternator; Marelli distributor; 4 headlamps.

DIMENSIONS AND WEIGHT wheel base: 98.62 in, 250 cm; tracks: 51.10 in, 130 cm front, 50.39 in, 128 cm rear; length 166.65 in, 423 cm; width: 63.98 in, 162 cm; height: 56 in, 144 cm; ground clearance: 5.51 in, 14 cm; weight: 2,1 lb, 970 kg; turning circle: 35.4 ft, 10.8 m; fuel tank: 9.9 imp gal, 11.9 US gal, 45 l.

BODY saloon/sedan; 4 doors; 5 seats, separate front seat reclining backrests, built-in headrests.

PRACTICAL INSTRUCTIONS fuel: 92 oct petrol; oil: engine 6.2 imp pt, 7.4 US pt, 3.5 l, SAE 20W-30, change ever 6,200 miles, 10,000 km - gearbox 2.3 imp pt, 2.7 US 1.3 l, SAE 90 EP, change every 18,600 miles, 30,000 km final drive 3.5 imp pt, 4.2 US pt, 2 l, SAE 90 EP, chang

126 P/650

rear: independent, semi-trailing arms, coil springs, telescopic dampers.

STEERING screw and sector; turns lock to lock: 2.90.

BRAKES drum; swept area: front 32.4 sq in, 208 sq cm. rear 32.4 sq in, 208 sq cm, total 64.7 sq in, 418 sq cm.

ELECTRICAL EQUIPMENT 12 V; 34 Ah battery; 400 W alternator; Zelmot distributor; 2 headlamps.

DIMENSIONS AND WEIGHT wheel base: 72.44 in, 184 cm; tracks: 44.88 in, 114 cm front, 47.24 in, 120 cm rear; length: 120.08 in, 305 cm; width: 54.33 in, 138 cm; height: 51.18 in, 130 cm; ground clearance: 5.51 in, 14 cm; weight: 1,323 lb, 600 kg; weight distribution: 39.5% front, 60.5% rear; turning circle: 28.2 ft, 8.6 m; fuel tank: 4.6 imp gal, 5.5 US gal, 21 l.

BODY saloon/sedan; 2 doors; 4 seats, separate front seats.

PRACTICAL INSTRUCTIONS fuel: 94 oct petrol; oil: engine 4.4 imp pt, 5.3 US pt, 2.5 l, SAE 10W-30, change every 6,200 miles, 10,000 km - gearbox and final drive 1.9 imp pt, 2.3 US pt, 1.1 l, SAE 90, change every 18,600 miles, 30,000 km; greasing: every 6,200 miles, 10,000 km, 2 points; tappet clearances: inlet 0.008 in, 0.20 mm, exhaust 0.010 in, 0.25 mm; valve timing: 26° 56° 66° 16°; tyre pressure: front 22 psi, 1.4 atm, rear 29 psi, 2 atm.

OPTIONALS I version: manual clutch, brake and accelerator controls; fastenings for folding wheel chair; grab handle over left hand door; heated rear window. S version: reclining backrest; tinted windscreen; heated rear window. K version: retractable seat belts; rear side windows opening half way down; heavy-duty brakes.

125 P 1300

ENGINE front, 4 stroke; 4 cylinders, in line; 79 cu in, 1,295 cc (2.83 x 3.13 in, 72 x 79.5 mm); compression ratio: 9:1; max power (DIN): 65 hp (47.8 kW) at 5,200 rpm; max torque (DIN): 69 lb ft, 9.5 kg m (93.2 Nm) at 4,000 rpm; max engine rpm: 6,000; 50.2 hp/l (36.9 kW/l); cast iron block, light alloy head, polispherical combustion chambers; 3 crankshaft bearings; valves: overhead, pushrods and rockers; camshafts: 1, side, in crankcase; lubrication: gear pump, centrifugal filter (cartridge), 6.2 imp pt, 7.4 US pt, 3.5 l; 1 Weber 34 DCHD 1-17 downdraught twin barrel carburettor; fuel feed: mechanical pump; watercooled, 11.8 imp pt, 14.2 US pt, 6.7 l.

TRANSMISSION driving wheels: rear; clutch: single dry plate, hydraulically controlled; gearbox: mechanical; gears: 4, fully synchronized; ratios: I 3.750, II 2.300, III 1.490, IV 1, rev 3.870; lever: central; final drive: hypoid bevel; axle ratio: 4.100; width of rims: 4.5''; tyres: 165 SR x 13.

PERFORMANCE max speeds: (I) 25 mph, 40 km/h; (II) 40 mph, 65 km/h; (III) 62 mph, 100 km/h; (IV) over 90 mph, 145 km/h; power-weight ratio: 32.9 lb/hp (44.7 lb/kW), 14.9 kg/hp (20.3 kg/kW); carrying capacity: 882 lb, 400 kg; acceleration: 0-50 mph (0-80 km/h) 13 sec; speed in

POLSKI-FIAT 125 P 1300 - 1500 Estate

POLSKI-FIAT Polonez

every 18,600 miles, 30,000 km; greasing: none; sparking plug: 240°; tappet clearances: inlet 0.008 in, 0.20 mm exhaust 0.010 in, 0.25 mm; valve timing: 5° 44° 47° 2°; tyre pressure: front 23 psi, 1.6 atm, rear 27 psi, 1.9 atm.

OPTIONALS luxury interior; sunshine roof.

125 P 1300 Estate

See 125 P 1300, except for:

PERFORMANCE power-weight ratio: 36.1 lb/hp (49.1 lb/kW) 16.4 kg/hp (22.3 kg/kW); carrying capacity: 992 lb, 450 kg

DIMENSIONS AND WEIGHT length: 166.92 in, 424 cm width: 66.34 in, 168 cm; height: 57.99 in, 147 cm; ground clearance: 6.06 in, 15.4 cm: weight: 2,348 lb, 1,065 kg.

BODY estate car/st. wagon; 4 + 1 doors; folding rear seat

125 P 1500

See 125 P 1300, excpet for:

PRICE IN GB: £ 2,029*

ENGINE 90.4 cu in, 1,481 cc (3.03 x 3.13 in, 77 x 79.5 mm) max power (DIN): 75 hp (55.2 kW) at 5,400 rpm; max torque (DIN): 83 lb ft, 11.5 kg m (112.8 Nm) at 3,800 rpm max engine rpm: 6,000; 50.6 hp/l (37.2 kW/l); electric thermostatic fan.

POLAND

POLSKI-FIAT Polonez

POLSKI-FIAT Polonez

iron block and light alloy head; 3 crankshaft bearings; valves: 2 per cylinder, overhead, push-rods and rockers; camshafts: 1, side; lubrication: gear pump, full flow filter, 7 imp pt, 8.4 US pt, 4 l; 1 Weber 34 DCMPI/250, down-draught, twin barrel carburettors; fuel feed: mechanical pump; water-cooled, 13.2 imp pt, 15.8 US pt, 7.5 l.

TRANSMISSION driving wheels: rear; clutch: single dry plate; gearbox: mechanical; gears: 4, fully synchronized; ratios: I 3.753, II 2.132, III 1.378, IV 1; lever: central; final drive: hypoid bevel; axle ratio: 4.100; width of rims: 5J x 13''; tyres: 175 SR x 13''.

PERFORMANCE max speeds: (I) 26 mph, 42 km/h; (II) 47 mph, 75 km/h; (III) 71 mph, 115 km/h; (IV) 90 mph, 145 km/h; power-weight ratio: 32 lb/hp, (43.4 lb/kW), 14.5 kg/hp (19.7 kg/kW); carrying capacity: 882 lb, 400 kg; acceleration: standing ¼ mile 19.8 sec, 0-50 mph, (0-80 km/h) 12.5 sec; speed in direct drive at 1,000 rpm: 16.8 mph, 27 km/h; consumption: 34.4 m/imp gal, 28.7 m/US gal, 8.2 l x 100 km.

CHASSIS integral; front suspension: independent, wishbones, coil springs, anti-roll bar acting as lower trailing arms, telescopic dampers, distance rods; rear: rigid axle, 2 semi-elliptic leaf springs, 2 telescopic shock absorbers, 2 distance rods.

STEERING worm and roller; turns lock to lock: 3.05.

BRAKES disc, servo; swept area: front 19.2 sq in, 124 sq cm, rear 19.2 sq in, 124 sq cm, total 38.4 sq in, 248 sq cm.

ELECTRICAL EQUIPMENT 12 V; 45 Ah battery; 840 W alternator; Marelli distributor; 4 headlamps.

DIMENSIONS AND WEIGHT wheel base: 98.78 in, 251 cm; tracks: 51.73 in, 131 cm front, 50.87 in, 129 cm rear; length: 168.20 in, 427 cm; width: 64.96 in, 165 cm; height: 55.90 in, 142 cm; ground clearance: 5.51 in, 14 cm; weight: 2,403 lb, 1,090 kg; weight distribution: 45% front, 55% rear; turning circle: 35.4 ft, 10.8 m; fuel tank: 9.9 imp gal, 11.9 US gal, 45 l.

BODY saloon/sedan; 4 + 1 doors; 5 seats, separate front seats, reclining backrests with adjustable headrests.

PRACTICAL INSTRUCTIONS fuel. 94 oct petrol; oil: engine 7 imp pt, 8.5 US pt, 4 l, SAE 20W-30, change every 6,200 miles, 10,000 km - gearbox 2.7 imp pt, 3.3 US pt, 1.5 l, SAE 90 EP, change every 18,600 miles, 30,000 km - final drive 2.1 imp pt, 2.5 US pt, 1.2 l, change every 18,600 miles, 30,000 km; tappet clearances: inlet 0.008 in, 0.20 mm, exhaust 0.009 in, 0.25 mm; valve timing: 25° 51° 64° 12°; tyre pressure: front 26 psi, 1.8 atm, rear 27 psi, 1.9 atm.

SYRENA **POLAND**

105

ENGINE front, 2 stroke; 3 cylinders, vertical, in line; 51.4 cu in, 842 cc (2.76 x 2.87 in, 70 x 73 mm); compression ratio: 7-7.2:1; max power (DIN): 40 hp (29.4 kW) at 4,300 rpm; max torque (DIN): 58 lb ft, 8 kg m (78.5 Nm) at 2,750 rpm; max engine rpm: 5,200; 47.5 hp/l (34.9 kW/l); cast iron block, dry liners, light alloy head; 4 crankshaft bearings on ball bearings; lubrication: mixture; 1 Jikov 35POH/048 horizontal carburettor; fuel feed: mechanical pump; water-cooled, 12.3 imp pt, 14.8 US pt, 7 l.

TRANSMISSION driving wheels: front; clutch: single dry plate; gearbox: mechanical; gears: 4, free wheel, fully synchronized; ratios: I 3.900, II 2.357, III 1.474, IV 0.958, rev 3.273; lever: steering column; final drive: spiral bevel; axle ratio: 4.875; width of rims: 4''; tyres: 5.60 x 15.

PERFORMANCE max speeds: (I) 19 mph, 31 km/h; (II) 32 mph, 51 km/h; (III) 50 mph, 81 km/h; (IV) 75 mph, 120 km/h; power-weight ratio: 47.8 lb/hp (65 lb/kW), 21.7 kg/hp (29.5 kg/kW); carrying capacity: 706 lb, 320 kg; acceleration: 0-50 mph (0-80 km/h) 21 sec; speed in top at 1,000 rpm: 14.9 mph, 24 km/h; consumption: 32.1 m/imp gal, 26.7 m/US gal, 8.8 l x 100 km.

CHASSIS box-type ladder frame; front suspension: independent, wishbones, tranverse leafspring lower arms, telescopic dampers; rear: rigid axle, transverse upper leafspring, trailing radius arms, telescopic dampers.

STEERING worm and roller; turns lock to lock: 2.80.

BRAKES drum; swept area: front 76.3 sq in, 492 sq cm, rear 45 sq in, 290 sq cm, total 121.3 sq in, 782 sq cm.

ELECTRICAL EQUIPMENT 12 V; 42 Ah battery; 300 W dynamo; 2 headlamps.

DIMENSIONS AND WEIGHT wheel base: 90.55 in, 230 cm;

RFORMANCE max speed: 96 mph, 155 km/h; power-ight ratio: 28.4 lb/hp (38.8 lb/kW), 12.9 kg/hp (17.6 kW); acceleration: 0-50 mph (0-80 km/h) 11 sec; carbption: 26.9 m/imp gal, 22.4 m/US gal, 10.5 l x 100 km.

125 P 1500 Estate

125 P 1300 Estate, except for:

CE IN GB: £ 2,349*

GINE 90.4 cu in, 1,481 cc (3.03 x 3.13 in, 77 x 79.5 mm); x power (DIN): 75 hp (55.2 kW) at 5,400 rpm; max que (DIN): 83 lb ft, 11.5 kg m (112.8 Nm) at 3,800 rpm; x engine rpm: 6,000; 50.6 hp/l (37.2 kW/l); electric ther-static fan.

RFORMANCE max speed: 96 mph, 155 km/h; power-ight ratio: 31.3 lb/hp (42.6 lb/kW), 14.2 kg/hp (19.3 kW); acceleration: 0-50 mph (0-80 km/h) 12 sec; conption: 26.9 m/imp gal, 22.4 m/US gal, 10.5 l x 100 km.

Polonez

CE IN GB: £ 2,999*

GINE front, 4 stroke; 4 cylinders, in line; 90.4 cu in, 31 cc (3.03 x 3.13 in, 77 x 79.5 mm); compression ratio: ; max power (DIN): 75 hp (55.2 kW) at 5,200 rpm; max que (DIN): 85 lb ft, 11.7 kg m (114.7 Nm) at 3,200 ; max engine rpm: 6,000; 50.6 hp/l 37.2 kW/l); cast

SYRENA 105

105

tracks: 47.24 in, 120 cm front, 48.82 in, 124 cm rear; length: 159.05 in, 404 cm; width: 61.42 in, 156 cm; height: 59.65 in, 151 cm; ground clearance: 7.87 in, 20 cm; weight: 1,912 lb, 867 kg; weight distribution: 48% front, 52% rear; turning circle: 34.1 ft, 10.4 m; fuel tank: 7 imp gal, 9.2 US gal, 35 l.

BODY saloon/sedan; 2 doors; 5 seats, separate front seats.

PRACTICAL INSTRUCTIONS fuel: mixture 1:30; oil: gearbox and final drive 4 imp pt, 4.9 US pt, 2.3 l, SAE 90, change every 7,500 miles, 12,000 km; greasing: every 7,500 miles, 12,000 km, 29 points; sparking plug: 175° or 225°; tyre pressure: front 23 psi, 1.6 atm, rear 23 psi, 1.6 atm.

PORTARO   PORTUGAL

250

ENGINE Daihatsu Diesel; front, 4 cylinders, in line; 154.4 cu in, 2,530 cc (3.46 x 4.09 in, 88 x 104 mm); compression ratio: 20:1; max power (DIN): 80 hp (58.9 kW) at 3,800 rpm; max torque (DIN): 127 lb ft, 17.5 kg m (171.6 Nm) at 2,200 rpm; max engine rpm: 3,800; 31.6 hp/l (23.2 kW/l); cast iron block and head; 4 crankshaft bearings; valves: 8, overhead; camshafts: 1, overhead; lubrication: rotary pump, 11.4 imp pt, 13.7 US pt, 6.5 l; 1 Nippon Deuso injection pump; fuel feed: mechanical pump; water-cooled, 23.4 imp pt, 28.1 US pt, 13.3 l.

TRANSMISSION driving wheels: rear, or front and rear; clutch: single dry plate; gearbox: mechanical; gears: 4, fully synchronized and 2 ratios transfer box; ratios: I 4.921, II 2.781, III 1.654, IV I, rev 5.080; transfer box ratios: high 1, low 2.18; lever: central; final drive: spiral bevel; axle ratio: 4.714; tyres: 6.50 x 16.

PERFORMANCE max speed: 70 mph, 112 km/h; power-weight ratio: 46.1 lb/hp, (62.6 lb/kW), 20.9 kg/hp (28.4 kg/kW); carrying capacity: 2,977 lb, 1,350 kg; speed in direct drive at 1,000 rpm: 17.4 mph, 28 km/h; consumption: 28.2 m/imp gal, 23.5 m/US gal, 10 l x 100 km.

CHASSIS ladder frame; front suspension: independent, swinging arms, coil springs, telescopic dampers; rear: rigid axle, semi-elliptic leafsprings with rubber elements, telescopic dampers.

STEERING worm and roller; turns lock to lock: 2.25.

BRAKES drum.

ELECTRICAL EQUIPMENT 12 V; 120 Ah battery; 35 A alternator; 2 headlamps.

DIMENSIONS AND WEIGHT wheel base: 92.51 in, 235 cm; tracks: 56.89 in, 144 cm front, 56.89 in, 144 cm rear; length: 156.81 in, 398 cm; width: 70.24 in, 178 cm; height: 75.98 in, 193 cm; ground clearance: 9.05 in, 23 cm; weight: 3,682 lb, 1,670 kg; weight distribution: 52% front, 48% rear; turning circle: 39.4 ft, 12 m; fuel tank: 19.8 imp gal, 23.8 US gal, 90 l.

BODY estate car/station wagon; 2 + 1 doors; 9 seats.

PRACTICAL INSTRUCTIONS fuel: Diesel oil; oil: engine 11.4 imp pt, 13.7 US pt, 6.5 l, SAE 90 EP - gearbox 3.5 imp pt, 4.2 US pt, 2 l, SAE 90 EP - final drive 2.1 imp pt, 2.5 US pt, 1.2 l, SAE 90 EP, greasing: 6 points, every 3,100 miles, 5,000 km; tappet clearances: inlet 0.0010 in, 0.25 mm, exhaust 0.0010 in, 0.25 mm; valve timing: 25° 55° 60° 20°; tyre pressure: front 54 psi, 3.8 atm, rear 54 psi, 3.8 atm.

ARO   ROMANIA

240/241/243/244

ENGINE front, 4 stroke; 4 cylinders, vertical, in line; 152.2 cu in, 2,495 cc (3.82 x 3.32 in, 97 x 84.4 mm); compression ratio: 8:1; max power (DIN): 83 hp (61.1 kW) at 4,200 rpm; max torque (DIN): 125 lb ft, 17.3 kg m (169.7 Nm) at 2,800 rpm; 33.3 hp/l (24.5 kW/l); cast iron block, light alloy head; 5 crankshaft bearings; valves: overhead, Vee-slanted, push-rods and rockers; camshafts: 1, side; lubrication: gear pump; 1 Weber twin barrel carburettor; fuel feed: mechanical pump; water-cooled.

TRANSMISSION driving wheels: rear and front; clutch: single dry plate, hydraulically-controlled; gearbox: mecha-

PORTARO 250

ARO 240

ARO 244

nical; gears: 4, fully synchronized and 2 ratios trans box; ratios: I 4.921, II 2.781, III 1.654, IV 1, rev 5.0. transfer box ratios: high 1, low 2.180; lever: central; fi drive: spiral bevel; axle ratio: 4.714; tyres: 6.50 x 16.

PERFORMANCE max speed: 240 and 243 models 68 m 110 km/h - 241 and 244 models 71 mph, 115 km/h; pow weight ratio: 240 models 41.2 lb/hp, (56 lb/kW), 18.7 kg (25.4 kg/kW); carrying capacity: 240 model 1,433 lb, kg; consumption: 18.2 m/imp gal, 15.2 m/US gal, 15.5 100 km.

CHASSIS box-type ladder frame; front suspension: in pendent, swinging semi-axles, coil springs, telesco dampers; rear: rigid axle, leafsprings with rubber elemen telescopic dampers.

STEERING worm and double roller.

BRAKES drum.

ELECTRICAL EQUIPMENT 12 V; 500 W alternator; 2 he lamps.

DIMENSIONS AND WEIGHT wheel base: 92.52 in, 235 c front and rear track: 56.69 in, 144 cm; length: 158.66 403 cm - for 243 model only 161.42 in, 410 cm; wid 69.68 in, 177 cm; height: 240 model 78.35 in, 199 cm 241 model 74.41 in, 189 cm - 243 model 79.13 in, 201 - 244 model 74.02 in, 188 cm; ground clearance: 8.66 22 cm; weight: 240 model 3,418 lb, 1,550 kg - 241 mo 3,506 lb, 1,590 kg - 243 model 3,572 lb, 1,620 kg - model 3,660 lb, 1,660 kg; turning circle (between wal 39.4 ft, 12 m; fuel tank: 20.9 imp gal, 25.1 US gal, 95

BODY 240 and 241 models open with canvas top - 243 and 244 models hardtop; 240 and 243 models 2 doors, 8 seats, folding rear seat - 241 and 244 models 4 doors, 5 seats.

VARIATIONS

ENGINE Diesel, 190.4 cu in, 3,120 cc (3.74 x 4.33 in, 95 x 110 mm), 17:1 compression ratio, max power (DIN) 65 hp (47.8 kW), max torque (DIN) 138 lb ft, 19 kg m (186.3 Nm).
PERFORMANCE max speed 65 mph, 105 km/h, power-weight ratio 240 model 58 lb/hp (78.9 lb/kW), 26.3 kg/hp (35.8 kg/kW), consumption 25.7 m/imp gal, 21.4 m/US gal, 11 l x 100 km.
DIMENSIONS AND WEIGHT weight 240 model 3,770 lb, 1,710 kg - 241 model 3,881 lb, 1,760 kg - 243 model 3,903 lb, 1,770 kg - 244 model 4,013 lb, 1,820 kg.

DACIA ROMANIA

1300 Saloon

ENGINE front, 4 stroke; 4 cylinders, vertical, in line; 78.7 cu in, 1,289 cc (2.87 x 3.03 in, 73 x 77 mm); compression ratio: 8.5:1; max power (DIN): 54 hp (39.7 kW) at 5,250 rpm; max torque (DIN): 65 lb ft, 9 kg m (88.3 Nm) at 3,500 rpm; max engine rpm: 5,500; 41.8 hp/l (30.8 kW/l); cast iron block, wet liners, light alloy head; 5 crankshaft bearings; valves: overhead, slanted, push-rods and rockers; camshafts: 1, side; lubrication: gear pump, filter in sump, 5.3 imp pt, 6.3 US pt, 3 l; 1 Solex 32 EISA downdraught carburettor; fuel feed: mechanical pump; sealed circuit cooling, liquid, 8.8 imp pt, 10.6 US pt, 5 l.

TRANSMISSION driving wheels: front; clutch: single dry plate (diaphragm); gearbox: mechanical; gears: 4, fully synchronized; ratios: I 3.615, II 2.263, III 1.480, IV 1.030, rev 3.080; lever: central; final drive: hypoid bevel; axle ratio: 3.780; width of rims: 4.5''; tyres: 155 SR x 13.

PERFORMANCE max speeds: (I) 30 mph, 48 km/h; (II) 45 mph, 73 km/h; (III) 68 mph, 110 km/h; (IV) 90 mph, 145 km/h; power-weight ratio: 36.8 lb/hp (50 lb/kW), 16.7 kg/hp (22.7 kg/kW); carrying capacity: 882 lb, 400 kg; speed in top at 1,000 rpm: 16.8 mph, 27 km/h; consumption: 33.2 m/imp gal, 27.7 m/US gal, 8.5 l x 100 km.

CHASSIS integral; front suspension: independent, wishbones, anti-roll bar, coil springs, telescopic dampers; rear: rigid axle, trailing arms, A-bracket, anti-roll bar, coil springs, telescopic dampers.

STEERING rack-and-pinion; turns lock to lock: 3.50.

BRAKES front disc (diameter 8.98 in, 22.8 cm), rear drum, rear compensator; swept area: front 157.2 sq in, 1,014 sq cm, rear 70.1 sq in, 452 sq cm, total 241.3 sq in, 1,466 sq cm.

ELECTRICAL EQUIPMENT 12 V; 36 Ah battery; 30-40 A alternator; 2 headlamps.

CHRYSLER Simca 1200

DACIA 1300 Saloon

DIMENSIONS AND WEIGHT wheel base: 96.06 in, 244 cm; front and rear track: 51.57 in, 131 cm; length: 170.87 in, 434 cm; width: 64.57 in, 164 cm; height: 56.30 in, 143 cm; ground clearance: 4.33 in, 11 cm; weight: 1,985 lb, 900 kg; weight distribution: 58.3% front, 41.7% rear; turning circle: 35.4 ft, 10.8 m; fuel tank: 11 imp gal, 13.2 US gal, 50 l.

BODY saloon/sedan; 4 doors; 4-5 seats, separate front seats.

1300 Break

See 1300 Saloon, except for:

ENGINE 1 Zenith 32 IF8 downdraught carburettor.

PERFORMANCE power-weight ratio: 39.2 lb/hp (53.4 lb/kW), 17.8 kg/hp (24.2 kg/kW).

DIMENSIONS AND WEIGHT length: 173.23 in, 440 cm; height: 57.28 in, 145 cm; weight: 2,117 lb, 960 kg.

CHRYSLER SPAIN

Simca 1200 Series

PRICES EX WORKS:

1 L	292,200	pesetas
2 LS	306,800	pesetas
3 LS Break	343,600	pesetas
4 LX	319,500	pesetas
5 GLS	331,400	pesetas
6 GLS Confort	345,700	pesetas
7 Special TI	375,200	pesetas
8 Special TI Break	389,100	pesetas

Power team:	Standard for:	Optional for:
52 hp	1 to 3	—
65 hp	4 to 6	—
85 hp	7,8	—

52 hp power team

ENGINE front, transverse, 4 stroke; 4 cylinders, in line; 68.2 cu in, 1,118 cc (2.91 x 2.56 in, 74 x 65 mm); compression ratio: 8.2:1; max power (DIN): 52 hp (38.2 kW) at 5,900 rpm; max torque (DIN): 55 lb ft, 7.6 kg m (74.5 Nm) at 3,000 rpm; max engine rpm: 6,000; 46.5 hp/l (34.2 kW/l); 5 crankshaft bearings; valves: overhead, in line, push-rods and rockers; camshafts: 1, side; lubrication: gear pump, full flow filter, 5.3 imp pt, 6.3 US pt, 3 l; 1 Bressel 32 IBS 7 downdraught single barrel carburettor; fuel feed: mechanical pump; sealed circuit cooling, liquid, expansion tank, 10.6 imp pt, 12.7 US pt, 6 l, electric thermostatic fan.

TRANSMISSION driving wheels: front; clutch: single dry plate (diaphragm), hydraulically controlled; gearbox: mechanical; gears: 4, fully synchronized; ratios: I 3.900, II 2.312,

CHRYSLER Simca 1200 LX

52 HP POWER TEAM

III 1.524, IV 1.080, rev 3.769; lever: central; final drive: cylindrical gears; axle ratio: 3.937; width of rims: 4.5''; tyres: 145 SR x 13 - LS Break 155 SR x 13.

PERFORMANCE max speed: 86 mph, 138 km/h; power-weight ratio: 39.4 lb/hp, (53.7 lb/kW), 17.9 kg/hp (24.3 kg/kW) - L 38.1 lb/hp (51.9 lb/kW), 17.3 kg/hp (23.5 kg/kW); carrying capacity: L 882 lb, 400 kg - LS 948 lb, 430 kg - LS Break 1,058 lb, 480 kg; speed in top at 1,000 rpm: 15 mph, 24 km/h; consumption: 37.6 m/imp gal, 31.3 m/US gal, 7.5 l x 100 km.

CHASSIS integral; front suspension: independent, wishbones, longitudinal torsion bars, anti-roll bar, telescopic dampers; rear: independent, longitudinal trailing arms, transverse torsion bars, anti-roll bar, telescopic dampers.

STEERING rack-and-pinion; turns lock to lock: 3.25.

BRAKES front disc (diameter 9.21 in, 23.4 cm), rear drum, dual circuit, rear compensator, servo; swept area: front 146.2 sq in, 943 sq cm, rear 73.8 sq in, 476 sq cm, total 220 sq in, 1,419 sq cm.

ELECTRICAL EQUIPMENT 12 V; 36 Ah battery; 35 A alternator; 2 headlamps.

DIMENSIONS AND WEIGHT wheel base: 99.21 in, 252 cm; tracks: 54.33 in, 138 cm front, 52.36 in, 133 cm rear; length: 155.12 in, 394 cm; width: 62.60 in, 159 cm; height: 57.48 in, 146 cm - LS Break 58.26 in, 148 cm; ground clearance: 5.50 in, 14 cm; weight: 2,051 lb, 930 kg - L 1,984 lb, 900 kg; turning circle: 34.1 ft, 10.4 m; fuel tank: 9.2 imp gal, 11.1 US gal, 42 l.

BODY saloon/sedan - LS Break estate car/station wagon; 4 doors - LS Break 4+1 doors; 5 seats, separate front seats; folding rear seat.

65 hp power team

See 52 hp power team, except for:

ENGINE 79 cu in, 1,294 cc (3.02 x 2.76 in, 76.7 x 70 mm); compression ratio: 9.5:1; max power (DIN): 65 hp (47.8 kW) at 6,000 rpm; max torque (DIN): 78 lb ft, 10.7 kg m (104.9 Nm) at 2,800 rpm; max engine rpm: 6,300; 50.2 hp/l (36.9 kW/l); 1 Bresel 32 IBS 6 downdraught single barrel carburettor.

TRANSMISSION width of rims: for LX only 5.5''.

PERFORMANCE max speed: 93 mph, 150 km/h; power-weight ratio: 31.5 lb/hp (42.9 lb/kW), 14.3 kg/hp (19.4 kg/kW) - LX 30.8 lb/hp (41.9 lb/kW), 14 kg/hp (19 kg/kW); carrying capacity: 904 lb, 410 kg - LX 926 lb, 420 kg; consumption: 35.3 m/imp gal, 29.4 m/US gal, 8 l x 100 km.

DIMENSIONS AND WEIGHT weight: LX 2,006 lb, 910 kg - GLS and GLS Confort 2,051 lb, 930 kg.

BODY LX 2 + 1 doors; GLS Confort heated rear window.

CHRYSLER Simca 1200 Special TI Break

CHRYSLER 150 GT

CHRYSLER 150 GT

85 hp power team

See 52 hp power team, except for:

ENGINE 88 cu in, 1,442 cc (3.02 x 3.07 in, 76.7 x 78 mm); max power (DIN): 85 hp (62.6 kW) at 5,600 rpm; max torque (DIN): 92 lb ft, 12.7 kg m (124.5 Nm) at 3,000 rpm; max engine rpm: 7,200; 58.9 hp/l (43.4 kW/l); 1 Weber DCNV downdraught twin barrel carburettor.

TRANSMISSION axle ratio: 3.588; width of rims: 5''; tyres Special TI 155 SR x 13.

PERFORMANCE max speed: 106 mph, 170 km; power-weight ratio: 25.5 lb/hp (34.7 lb/kW), 11.6 kg/hp (15.7 kW); carrying capacity: Special TI 1,058 lb, 480 kg; consumption: 24.6 m/imp gal, 20.5 m/US gal, 11.5 l x 100 km.

ELECTRICAL EQUIPMENT 2 halogen headlamps.

DIMENSIONS AND WEIGHT length: 154.70 in, 393 cm; height: 58.20 in, 148 cm; weight: 2,172 lb, 985 kg.

BODY Special TI 4 + 1 doors; heated rear window.

Chrysler 150 Series

PRICES EX WORKS:

1 GLS	406,900	pesetas
2 GLS Confort	412,700	pesetas
3 S	445,300	pesetas
4 GT	476,500	pesetas

Power team:	Standard for:	Optional for:
68 hp	1,2	—
85 hp	3,4	—

68 hp power team

ENGINE front, transverse, slanted 41° to rear, 4 stroke; 4 cylinders, in line; 79 cu in, 1,294 cc (3.02 x 2.76 in, 76.7 x 70 mm); compression ratio: 9.5:1; max power (DIN): 68 hp (50 kW) at 5,600 rpm; max torque (DIN): 78 lb ft, 10.7 kg m (104.9 Nm) at 2,800 rpm; max engine rpm: 5,800; 52.6 hp/l (38.6 kW/l); cast iron block, light alloy head, 5 crankshaft bearings; valves: overhead, in line, push rods and rockers; camshafts: 1, side; lubrication: gear pump, full flow filter, 5.3 imp pt, 6.3 US pt, 3 l; 1 Solex 32 BISA 5 A or Weber 32 IBSA 9 downdraught single barrel carburettor; fuel feed: mechanical pump; sealed circuit cooling, expansion tank, liquid, 11.4 imp pt, 13.7 US pt, 6.5 l, electric thermostatic fan.

TRANSMISSION driving wheels: front; clutch: single dry plate (diaphragm), hydraulically controlled; gearbox: mechanical; gears: 4, fully synchronized; ratios: I 3.900, II 2.312, III 1.524, IV 1.080, rev 3.769; lever: central; final drive: cylindrical gears; axle ratio: 3.706; width of rims: 5'' tyres: 155 SR x 13.

PERFORMANCE max speed: 94 mph, 152 km/h; power-weight ratio: 34 lb/hp, (46.3 lb/kW), 15.4 kg/hp (21 kg/kW); carrying capacity: 882 lb, 400 kg; acceleration: standing 1/4 mile 19.8 sec, 0-50 mph (0-80 km/h) 10.7 sec; speed in top at 1,000 rpm: 16.3 mph, 26.2 km/h; consumption: 31 m/imp gal, 25.8 m/US gal, 9.1 l x 100 km.

CHASSIS integral; front suspension: independent, wishbones, longitudinal torsion bars, anti-roll bar, telescopic dampers; rear: independent, swinging longitudinal trailing arms, coil springs, anti-roll bar, telescopic dampers.

STEERING rack-and-pinion; turns lock to lock: 4.15.

BRAKES front disc (diameter 9.45 in, 24 cm), rear drum, rear compensator, servo; swept area: front 169.3 sq in, 1,092 sq cm, rear 90.2 sq in, 582 sq cm, total 259.5 sq in, 1,674 sq cm.

ELECTRICAL EQUIPMENT 12 V; 40 Ah battery; 40 A alternator; Chrysler transistorized ignition; 2 headlamps.

DIMENSIONS AND WEIGHT wheel base: 102.36 in, 260 cm; tracks: 55.51 in, 141 cm front, 54.72 in, 139 cm rear; length: 166.93 in, 424 cm; width: 66.14 in, 168 cm; height: 54.72 in, 139 cm; ground clearance: 5.12 in, 13 cm; weight: 2,315 lb, 1,050 kg; turning circle 36.1 ft, 11 m; fuel tank: 13.2 imp gal, 15.8 US gal, 60 l.

BODY saloon/sedan; 4 doors; 5 seats, separate front seats, reclining backrests; heated rear window; folding rear seat - Confort, luxury equipment.

PRACTICAL INSTRUCTIONS fuel: 98-100 oct petrol; oil: engine 5.3 imp pt, 6.3 US pt, 3 l, SAE 20W-40 change every 4,650 miles, 7,500 km - gearbox and final drive 1.9 imp pt, 2.3 US pt, 1.1 l, SAE 90 EP, change every 9,300 miles, 15,000 km; greasing: none.

OPTIONALS iodine long-distance lights; headrests on front seats; tinted glass; headlamps with wiper-washers; rear window wiper-washer.

85 hp power team

See 68 hp power team, except for:

ENGINE 88 cu in, 1442 cc (3.02 x 3.07 in, 76.7 x 78 mm); max power (DIN): 85 hp (62.6 kW) at 5,600 rpm; max torque (DIN): 92 lb ft, 12.7 kg m (124.5 Nm) at 3,000 rpm; max engine rpm: 6,000; 58.9 hp/l (43.4 kW/l); 1 Weber 36 DCNVA downdraught twin barrel carburettor.

TRANSMISSION axle ratio: 3.588.

PERFORMANCE max speed: 102 mph, 164 km/h; power-weight ratio: 27.9 lb/hp (37.9 lb/kW), 12.6 kg/hp (17.2 kg/kW); acceleration: standing ¼ mile 19 sec, 0-50 mph (0-80 km/h) 8.9 sec; speed in top at 1,000 rpm: 16.8 mph, 27.1 km/h; consumption: 26.2 m/imp gal, 21.8 m/US gal, 10.8 l x 100 km.

ELECTRICAL EQUIPMENT iodine long-distance lights (standard).

DIMENSIONS AND WEIGHT weight: 2,370 lb, 1,075 kg.

BODY (standard) tinted glass, headlamps with wiper-washers, electric windows.

CHRYSLER 180 Series

CHRYSLER 2-litros

Chrysler 180 Series

PRICES EX WORKS:

1 180		
2 Automatico		
3 Diesel		
4 Diesel De Luxe		

1 180	537,600	pesetas
2 Automatico	581,700	pesetas
3 Diesel	599,800	pesetas
4 Diesel De Luxe	636,600	pesetas

Power team:	Standard for:	Optional for:
100 hp	1,2	—
60 hp	3,4	—

For prices in GB, see price index.

100 hp power team

ENGINE front, slanted 15° to right, 4 stroke; 4 cylinders, in line; 110.6 cu in, 1,812 cc (3.45 x 2.95 in, 87.7 x 75 mm); compression ratio: 9.45:1; max power (DIN): 100 hp (73.6 kW) at 5,800 rpm; max torque (DIN): 107 lb ft, 14.7 kg m (144.2 Nm) at 3,800 rpm; max engine rpm: 5,800; 55.2 hp/l (40.6 kW/l); cast iron block, light alloy head; 5 crankshaft bearings; valves: overhead, rockers; camshafts: 1, overhead; lubrication: gear pump, full flow filter, 7 imp pt, 8.5 US pt, 4 l; 1 Weber 34 ADS-D downdraught twin barrel carburettor; fuel feed: mechanical pump; water-cooled, 17.6 imp pt, 21.1 US pt, 10 l, electric thermostatic fan.

TRANSMISSION driving wheels: rear; clutch: single dry plate (diaphragm), hydraulically controlled; gearbox: mechanical; gears: 4, fully synchronized; ratios: I 3.546, II 2.175, III 1.418, IV 1, rev 3.226; automatic transmission, hydraulic torque converter and planetary gear with 3 ratios (I 2.450, II 1.450, III 1, rev 2.200) for Automatico; lever: central; final drive: hypoid bevel; axle ratio: 3.909 - 3.727 for Automatico; width of rims: 5.5''; tyres: 175 SR x 14.

PERFORMANCE max speeds: (I) 27 mph, 44 km/h; (II) 45 mph, 73 km/h; (III) 70 mph, 113 km/h; (IV) 106 mph, 170 km/h; power-weight ratio: 24.3 lb/hp, (33 lb/kW), 11 kg/hp (14.9 kg/kW); carrying capacity: 915 lb, 415 kg; acceleration: standing 1/4 mile 18.1; speed in direct drive at 1,000 rpm: 18 mph, 29 km/h; consumption: 25.7 m/imp gal, 21.4 m/US gal, 11 l x 100 km.

CHASSIS integral; front suspension: independent, by Mc Pherson, coil springs/telescopic damper struts, lower wishbones, anti-roll bar; rear: rigid axle, lower longitudinal trailing arms, upper torque arms, transverse linkage bar, coil springs, anti-roll bar, telescopic dampers.

STEERING rack-and-pinion; turns lock to lock: 4.

BRAKES disc (front diameter 9.80 in, 24.9 cm, rear 9.02 in, 22.3 cm), rear compensator, servo; swept area: front 186 sq in, 1,200 sq cm, rear 145.1 sq in, 936 sq cm, total 331 sq in, 2,136 sq cm.

ELECTRICAL EQUIPMENT 12 V; 40 Ah batery; 490 W alternator; Chrysler transistorized ignition; 2 headlamps, iodine long-distance lights.

DIMENSIONS AND WEIGHT wheel base: 105.12 in, 267 cm; tracks: 55.12 in, 140 cm front, 55.12 in, 140 cm rear; length: 178.35 in, 453 cm; width: 68.11 in 173 cm; height: 57.09 in, 145 cm; ground clearance: 4.72 in, 12 cm; weight: 2,426 lb, 1,100 kg; weight distribution: 53.8% front, 46.2% rear; turning circle: 33.8 ft, 10.3 m; fuel tank: 14.3 imp gal, 17.2 US gal, 65 l.

BODY saloon/sedan; 4 doors; 5 seats, separate front seats; built-in headrests; vinyl roof; heated rear window.

PRACTICAL INSTRUCTIONS fuel: 98-100 oct petrol; oil: engine 7 imp pt, 8.5 US pt, 4 l, SAE 10W-50, change every 3,100 miles, 5,000 km - gearbox 2.6 imp pt, 3.2 US pt, 1.5 l, SAE 90 EP, change every 12,400 miles, 20,000 km - final drive 2.3 imp pt, 2.7 US pt, 1.3 l, SAE 90 EP, change every 12,400 miles, 20,000 km; greasing: none; sparking plug: 225°; tappet clearances: inlet 0.010 in, 0.25 mm, exhaust 0.014 in, 0.35 mm; tyres pressure: front 24 psi, 1.7 atm, rear 27 psi, 1.9 atm.

OPTIONALS tinted glass; metallic spray.

60 hp power team

See 100 hp power team, except for.

ENGINE Diesel front; 117.0 cu in, 1,918 cc (3.23 x 3.57 in, 82 x 90.8 mm); compression ratio: 20:1; max power (DIN): 60 hp (44.2 kW) at 4,000 rpm; max torque (DIN): 93 lb ft, 12.8 kg m (125.5 Nm) at 2,100 rpm; max engine rpm: 4,000; 31.3 hp/l (23.0 kW/l).

PERFORMANCE max speed: 81 mph, 130 km/h; power-weight ratio: 45.0 lb/hp, (61.1 lb/kW), 20.4 kg/hp (25.4 kg/kW); consumption: 35.3 m/imp gal, 29.4 m/US gal, 8 l x 100 km.

60 HP POWER TEAM

BRAKES front disc, rear drum.

ELECTRICAL EQUIPMENT 90 Ah battery; 700 W alternator.

DIMENSIONS AND WEIGHT weight: 2,701 lb, 1,225 kg.

BODY Luxe, luxury equipment.

Chrysler 2-litros

See Chrysler 180 100 hp power team, except for:

PRICE EX WORKS: 561,200 pesetas

ENGINE 120.9 cu in, 1981 cc (3.61 x 2.95 in, 91.7 x 75 mm); max power (DIN): 110 hp (81 kW) at 5,800 rpm; max torque (DIN): 117 lb ft, 16.1 kg m (157.9 Nm) at 3,400 rpm; 55.5 hp/l (40.9 kW/l).

TRANSMISSION gearbox: Torqueflite Chrysler A 904 automatic transmission, hydraulic torque converter and planetary gears with 3 ratios, max ratio of converter at stall 2.2, possible manual selection: ratios: I 2.450, II 1.450, III 1, rev 2.200; axle ratio: 3.727.

PERFORMANCE max speed: 106 mph, 170 km/h; power-weight ratio: 22.6 lb/hp (30.6 lb/kW), 10.2 kg/hp (13.9 kg/kW); carrying capacity: 904 lb, 410 kg; acceleration: standing 1/4 mile 18.7 sec; speed in direct drive at 1,000 rpm: 18.3 mph, 29.5 km/h; consumption: 23.7 m/imp gal, 19.8 m/US gal, 11.9 l x 100 km.

STEERING turns lock to lock: 4.50.

DIMENSIONS AND WEIGHT weight: 2,481 lb, 1,125 kg.

RENAULT   SPAIN

4

PRICE EX WORKS: 205,600 pesetas

ENGINE front, 4 stroke; 4 cylinders, vertical, in line; 52 cu in, 852 cc (2.42 x 2.83 in, 61.4 x 72 mm); compression ratio: 8:1; max power (DIN): 32 hp (23.5 kW) at 5,000 rpm; max torque (DIN): 40.6 lb ft, 5.6 kg m (54.9 Nm) at 2,750 rpm; 37.5 hp/l (27.6 kW/l); 5 crankshaft bearings; valves: overhead, in line, push-rods and rockers; camshafts: 1, side; lubrication: gear pump, filter in sump, 5.3 imp pt, 6.3 US pt, 3 l; 1 Zenith 28 downdraught single barrel carburettor; fuel feed: mechanical pump; sealed circuit cooling, liquid, expansion tank, 10.2 imp pt, 12.2 US pt, 5.8 l.

TRANSMISSION driving wheels: front; clutch: single dry plate (diaphragm); gearbox: mechanical; gears: 4, fully synchronized; ratios: I 3.833, II 2.235, III 1.458, IV 1.026, rev 3.545; lever: on facia; final drive: spiral bevel; axle ratio: 4.125; width of rims: 4''; tyres: 135 SR x 13.

PERFORMANCE max speed: 71 mph, 115 km/h; power-weight ratio: 46.8 lb/hp (63.8 lb/kW), 21.2 kg/hp (28.9 kg/kW); carrying capacity: 860 lb, 390 kg; speed in top at 1,000 rpm: 14.7 mph, 23.7 km/h; consumption: 43.5 m/imp gal, 36.2 m/US gal, 6.5 l x 100 km.

CHASSIS platform; front suspension: independent, wishbones, longitudinal torsion bars, anti-roll bar, telescopic dampers; rear: independent, swinging longitudinal trailing arms, transverse torsion bars, telescopic dampers.

STEERING rack-and-pinion.

BRAKES drum, rear compensator; lining area: front 44.5 sq in, 287 sq cm, rear 19.4 sq in, 125 sq cm, total 63.9 sq in, 412 sq cm.

ELECTRICAL EQUIPMENT 12 V; 30 Ah battery; dynamo; 2 headlamps.

DIMENSIONS AND WEIGHT wheel base: 94.46 in, 245 cm (right), 94.49 in, 240 cm (left); tracks: 50.39 in, 128 cm front, 48.82 in, 124 cm rear; length: 144.49 in, 367 cm; width: 58.27 in, 148 cm; height: 61.02 in, 155 cm; weight: 1,499 lb, 680 kg; turning circle: 31.8 ft, 9.7 m; fuel tank: 5.7 imp gal, 6.8 US gal, 26 l.

BODY estate car/st. wagon; 4+1 doors; 4 seats, bench front seats; folding rear seat.

OPTIONALS metallic spray; luxury interior; heated rear window.

CHRYSLER 2-litros

4 TL

See 4, except for:

PRICE EX WORKS: 231,700 pesetas

PERFORMANCE power-weight ratio 48.2 lb/hp (65.6 lb/kW), 21.8 kg/hp (29.8 kg/kW).

DIMENSIONS AND WEIGHT weight: 1,543 lb, 700 kg.

BODY luxury interior.

OPTIONALS sunshine roof; separate front seats with reclining backrests.

5 Series

PRICES EX WORKS:

1 TL	275,400 pesetas
2 GTL	294,800 pesetas
3 Copa	451,500 pesetas

Power team:	Standard for:	Optional for:
44 hp	1	—
50 hp	2	—
93 hp	3	—

RENAULT 4

RENAULT 5 Copa

44 hp power team

ENGINE front, 4 stroke; 4 cylinders, vertical, in line; 58.3 cu in, 956 cc (2.56 x 2.83 in, 65 x 72 mm); compression ratio: 9.25:1; max power (DIN): 44 hp (32.4 kW) at 5,500 rpm; max torque (DIN): 47.8 lb ft, 6.6 kg m (64.7 Nm) at 3,500 rpm; max engine rpm: 5,800; 46 hp/l (33.9 kW/l); cast iron block, wet liners, light alloy head; 5 crankshaft bearings; valves: overhead, in line, push-rods and rockers; camshafts: 1, side; lubrication: gear pump, 5.3 imp pt, 6.3 US pt, 3 l; 1 Solex 32 SEIA downdraught single barrel carburettor; fuel feed: mechanical pump; sealed circuit cooling, liquid, expansion tank, 11 imp pt, 13.3 US pt, 6.3 l.

TRANSMISSION driving wheels: front; clutch: single dry plate (diaphragm); gearbox: mechanical; gears: 4, fully synchronized; ratios: I 3.383, II 2.235, III 1.458, IV 1.026, rev 3.545; lever: central; final drive: spiral bevel; axle ratio: 4.125; width of rims: 4''; tyres: 135 SR x 13.

PERFORMANCE max speeds: (I) 24 mph, 39 km/h; (II) 40 mph, 64 km/h; (III) 62 mph, 100 km/h; (V) 84 mph, 135 km/h; power-weight ratio: 38.8 lb/hp (52.7 lb/kW), 17.6 kg/hp (23.9 kg/kW); carrying capacity: 882 lb, 400 kg; speed in top at 1,000 rpm: 14.6 mph, 23.6 km/h; consumption: 31.4 m/imp gal, 26.1 m/US gal, 9 l x 100 km.

CHASSIS integral; front suspension: independent, wishbones, longitudinal torsion bar, anti-roll bar, telescopic dampers; rear: independent, swinging longitudinal trailing arms, transverse torsion bars, telescopic dampers.

STEERING rack-and-pinion.

BRAKES front disc, rear drum, rear compensator; lining area: front 78.6 sq in, 507 sq cm, rear 26.2 sq in, 169 sq cm, total 104.8 sq in, 676 sq cm.

ELECTRICAL EQUIPMENT 12 V; 28 Ah battery; dynamo - TL alternator; 2 headlamps.

DIMENSIONS AND WEIGHT wheel base: 94.49 in, 240 cm (right), 95.67 in, 243 cm (left); tracks: 50.71 in, 129 cm front, 48.82 in, 124 cm rear; length: 138.19 in, 351 cm; width: 59.84 in, 152 cm; height: 55.12 in, 140 cm; weight: 1,709 lb, 775 kg; turning circle: 32.1 ft, 9.8 m; fuel tank: 8.4 imp gal, 10 US gal, 38 l.

BODY saloon/sedan; 2+1 doors; 4 seats, separate front seats.

50 hp power team

See 44 hp power team, except for:

ENGINE 63.27 cu in, 1,037 cc (2.66 x 2.83 in, 67.7 x 72 mm); compression ratio: 9.5:1; max power (DIN): 50 hp (36.7 kW) at 5,500 rpm; max torque (DIN): 54 lb ft, 7.4 kg m (72.5 Nm) at 3,000 rpm; max engine rpm: 6,000; 48.2 hp/l (35.4 kW/l).

PERFORMANCE max speed: 86 mph, 138 km/h; power-weight ratio: 34.6 lb/hp (47.1 lb/kW), 15.7 kg/hp (21.4 kg/hp).

CHASSIS rear suspension: anti-roll bar.

ELECTRICAL EQUIPMENT alternator.

DIMENSIONS AND WEIGHT weight: 1,730 lb, 785 kg.

BODY reclining front seats; built-in headrests.

93 hp power team

See 44 hp power team, except for:

ENGINE 85.2 cu in, 1,397 cc (2.99 x 3.03 in, 76 x 77 mm); compression ratio: 10:1; max power (DIN): 93 hp (68.3 kW) at 6,400 rpm; max torque (DIN): 84 lb ft, 11.6 kg m (113.7 Nm) at 4,000 rpm; max engine rpm: 6,400; 66.5 hp/l (48.9 kW/l); 1 Weber 32 DIR 58 T twin barrel carburettor.

TRANSMISSION ratios: I 3.810, II 2.230, III 1.470, IV 1.030, rev 3.500; axle ratio: 4.125; width of rims: 5.5''; tyres: 175 SR x 13.

PERFORMANCE max speed: 106 mph, 170 km/h; power-weight ratio: 20.1 lb/hp (27.4 lb/kW), 9.1 kg/hp (12.4 kg/kW); speed in top at 1,000 rpm: 17.5 mph, 28.2 km/h; consumption: 28.2 m/imp gal, 23.5 m/US gal, 10 l x 100 km.

CHASSIS rear suspension: anti-roll bar, telescopic dampers.

BRAKES servo.

ELECTRICAL EQUIPMENT 36 Ah battery; 55 A alternator; 2 halogen headlamps.

DIMENSIONS AND WEIGHT length: 139.30 in, 354 cm; weight: 1,874 lb, 850 kg.

BODY heated rear window; rear window wiper-washer.

6 TL

PRICE EX WORKS: 285,900 pesetas

ENGINE front, 4 stroke; 4 cylinders, vertical, in line; 63.3 cu in, 1,037 cc (2.66 x 2.83 in, 67.7 x 72 mm); compression ratio: 9.5:1; max power (DIN): 50 hp (36.7 kW) at 5,500 rpm; max torque (DIN): 54 lb ft, 7.4 kg m (72.6 Nm) at 3,000 rpm; max engine rpm: 6,000; 48.2 hp/l (35.4 kW/l); cast iron block, wet liners, light alloy head; 5 crankshaft bearings; valves: overhead, push-rods and rockers; camshafts: 1, side, chain driven; lubrication: gear pump, 5.3 imp pt, 6.3 US pt, 3 l; 1 Zenith 32 IF or Solex 32 DIS downdraught carburettor; fuel feed: mechanical pump; sealed circuit cooling, liquid, 11.1 imp pt, 13.3 US pt, 6.3 l.

TRANSMISSION driving wheels: front; clutch: single dry plate; gearbox: mechanical; gears: 4, fully synchronized; ratios: I 3.660, II 2.230, III 1.450, IV 1.030, rev 3.230; lever: on facia; final drive: spiral bevel; axle ratio: 4.125; width of rims: 4.5''; tyres: 145 SR x 13.

PERFORMANCE max speed: 83 mph, 133 km/h; power-weight ratio: 36.6 lb/hp (49.8 lb/kW), 16.6 kg/hp (22.6 kg/kW); carrying capacity: 860 lb, 390 kg; speed in top at 1,000 rpm:

14.1 mph, 22.7 km/h; consumption: 43.4 m/imp gal, 36.2 m/US gal, 6.5 l x 100 km.

CHASSIS integral; front suspension: independent, swinging arms, longitudinal torsion bars, anti-roll bar, telescopic dampers; rear independent, swinging longitudinal leading arms, transverse torsion bars, anti-roll bar, telescopic dampers.

STEERING rack-and-pinion.

BRAKES front disc, rear drum, rear compensator; lining area: front 78.6 sq in, 507 sq cm, rear 26.3 sq in, 169 sq cm, total 104.9 sq in, 676 sq cm.

ELECTRICAL EQUIPMENT 12 V; 28 Ah battery; 35 A alternator; 2 headlamps.

DIMENSIONS AND WEIGHT wheel base: 96.46 in, 245 cm (right); 94.49 in, 240 cm (left); tracks: 50.39 in, 128 cm front, 48.82 in, 124 cm rear; length: 151.97 in, 386 cm; width: 59.06 in, 150 cm; height: 56.69 in, 144 cm; ground clearance: 4.92 in, 12.5 cm; weight: 1,830 lb, 830 kg; turning circle: 32.5 ft, 9.9 m; fuel tank: 8.8 imp gal, 10.5 US gal, 40 l.

BODY saloon/sedan; 4+1 doors; 4 seats, separate front seats; folding rear seat.

Siete TL

See 6 TL, except for:

PRICE EX WORKS: 291,600 pesetas

TRANSMISSION ratios: I 3.830, II 2.230, III 1.450, IV 1.020, rev 3.540.

PERFORMANCE power-weight ratio: 35.9 lb/hp (48.9 lb/kW), 16.3 kg/hp (22.2 kg/kW); speed in top at 1,000 rpm: 15.2 mph, 24.4 km/h; consumption: 40.3 m/imp gal, 33.5 m/US gal, 7 l x 100 km.

ELECTRICAL EQUIPMENT 38 A alternator.

DIMENSIONS AND WEIGHT wheel base: 99.60 in, 253 cm (right), 98.40 in, 250 cm (left); tracks: 50.78 in, 129 cm front, 49.21 in, 125 cm rear; length: 153.15 in, 389 cm; width: 59.80 in, 152 cm; height: 55 in, 140 cm; ground clearance: 5.50 in, 14 cm; weight: 1,797 lb, 815 kg; turning circle: 32.8 ft, 10 m; fuel tank: 8.4 imp gal, 10 US gal, 38 l.

12 Series

PRICES EX WORKS:

1 12		331,700 pesetas
2 Familiar		354,100 pesetas
3 TL		349,200 pesetas
4 TL Familiar		368,200 pesetas
5 TS		386,200 pesetas
6 TS Familiar		402,900 pesetas

Power team:	Standard for:	Optional for:
57 hp	1 to 4	—
70 hp	5,6	—

57 hp power team

ENGINE front, 4 stroke; 4 cylinders, vertical, in line; 78.7 cu in, 1,289 cc (2.87 x 3.03 in, 73 x 77 mm); compression ratio: 8.5:1; max power (DIN): 57 hp (41.9 kW) at 5,300 rpm; max torque (DIN): 69 lb ft, 9.5 kg m (93.2 Nm) at 3,000 rpm; max engine rpm: 5,300; 44.2 hp/l (32.5 kW/l); cast iron block, wet liners, light alloy head; 5 crankshaft bearings; valves: overhead, slanted, push-rods and rockers; camshafts: 1, side; lubrication: gear pump, filter in sump, 5.3 imp pt, 6.3 US pt, 3 l; 1 Solex 32 downdraught single barrel carburettor; fuel feed: mechanical pump; sealed cooling, liquid, 3.5 imp pt, 4.2 US pt, 2 l.

TRANSMISSION driving wheels: front; clutch: single dry plate; gearbox: mechanical; gears: 4, fully synchronized; ratios: I 3.818, II 2.235, III 1.478, IV 1.036, rev 3.083; lever: central; final drive: hypoid bevel; axle ratio: 3.778; width of rims: 5''; tyres: 155 x 330.

PERFORMANCE max speed: 87 mph, 140 km/h; power-weight ratio: saloons 35 lb/hp (47.6 lb/kW), 15.8 kg/hp (21.6 kg/kW) - station wagons 37.1 lb/hp (50.5 lb/kW), 16.8 kg/hp (22.9 kg/kW); carrying capacity: saloons 882 lb, 400 kg - station wagons 937 lb, 425 kg; speed in top at 1,000 rpm: 16.6 mph, 26.7 km/h; consumption: 35.3 m/imp gal, 29.4 m/US gal, 8 l x 100 km.

CHASSIS integral; front suspension: independent, wishbones, anti-roll bar, coil springs/telescopic dampers; rear: rigid axle, trailing arms, A-bracket, anti-roll bar, coil springs/telescopic dampers.

STEERING rack-and-pinion.

RENAULT Siete TL

RENAULT 12 TL Familiar

57 HP POWER TEAM

BRAKES front disc, rear drum, rear compensator - 12 TL and station wagons servo; lining area: front 78.6 sq in, 507 sq cm, rear 35 sq in, 226 sq cm, total 113.6 sq in, 733 sq cm.

ELECTRICAL EQUIPMENT 12 V; dynamo - TL models alternator; 36 Ah battery; 2 headlamps.

DIMENSIONS AND WEIGHT wheel base: 96.06 in, 244 cm; front and rear track: 51.96 in, 132 cm; length: saloons 172.44 in, 438 cm - station wagons 173.23 in, 440 cm; width: 63.78 in, 162 cm; height: saloons 55.90 in, 142 cm - station wagons 57.08 in, 145 cm; ground clearance: 5.12 in, 13 cm; weight: saloons 1,995 lb, 905 kg - station wagons 2,117 lb, 960 kg; turning circle: 33 ft, 10.1 m; fuel tank: 11 imp gal, 13.2 US gal, 50 l.

BODY saloons 5 seats - station wagons 5/7 seats, separate front seats; heated rear window (for TL models only).

70 hp power team

See 57 hp power team, except for:

ENGINE 85.2 cu in, 1,397 cc (2.99 x 3.03 in, 76 x 77 mm); compression ratio: 9.2:1; max power (DIN): 70 hp (51.5 kW) at 5,500 rpm; max torque (DIN): 80 lb ft, 11 kg m (107.8 Nm) at 3,500 rpm; max engine rpm: 5,600; 50.1 hp/l (36.9 kW/l); 1 Weber 32 DIR 40 T downdraught twin barrel carburettor.

PERFORMANCE max speed: 92 mph, 148 km/h; power-weight ratio: 28.9 lb/hp (39.3 lb/kW), 13.1 kg/hp (17.8 kg/kW) - Familiar 30.7 lb/hp (41.7 lb/kW), 13.9 kg/hp (18.9 kg/kW).

BRAKES servo.

ELECTRICAL EQUIPMENT alternator; 4 headlamps, 2 iodine.

DIMENSIONS AND WEIGHT weight: 2,028 lb, 920 kg - Familiar 2,149 lb, 975 kg.

BODY built-in headrests.

SEAT   SPAIN

133 Lujo

PRICE EX WORKS: 225,000* pesetas

ENGINE rear, longitudinal, 4 stroke; 4 cylinders, vertical, in line; 51.4 cu in, 843 cc (2.56 x 2.50 in, 65 x 63.5 mm); compression ratio: 8:1; max power (DIN): 34 hp (25 kW) at 4,800 rpm; max torque (DIN): 40 lb ft, 5.5 kg m (53.9 Nm) at 3,200 rpm; max engine rpm: 5,500; 40.3 hp/l (29.7 kW/l); cast iron block, light alloy head; 3 crankshaft bearings; valves: overhead, in line, push-rods and rockers; camshafts: 1, side; lubrication: gear pump, full flow filter, 6 imp pt, 7.2 US pt, 3.4 l; 1 Bressel 30 ICF-3 or Solex 30 PIB-5 downdraught single barrel carburettor; fuel feed: mechanical pump; sealed circuit cooling, liquid, 13.2 imp pt, 15.9 US pt, 7.5 l.

TRANSMISSION driving wheels: rear; clutch: single dry plate; gearbox: mechanical; gears: 4, fully synchronized; ratios: I 3.636, II 2.055, III 1.409, IV 0.963, rev 3.615; lever: central; final drive: hypoid bevel; axle ratio: 4.625; width of rims: 4''; tyres: 5.50 x 12.

PERFORMANCE max speeds: (I) 20 mph, 32 km/h; (II) 35 mph, 56 km/h; (III) 52 mph, 83 km/h; (IV) about 75 mph, 120 km/h; power-weight ratio: 44.7 lb/hp (60.8 lb/kW), 20.3 kg/hp (27.6 kg/kW); carrying capacity: 706 lb, 320 kg; speed in top at 1,000 rpm: 13.7 mph, 22.1 km/h; consumption: 40.9 m/imp gal, 34.1 m/US gal, 6.9 l x 100 km.

CHASSIS integral; front suspension: independent, wishbone, transverse leafspring lower arms, transverse torsion bar, telescopic dampers; rear: independent, semi-trailing arms, coil springs, torsion bar, telescopic dampers.

STEERING rack-and-pinion; turns lock to lock: 2.80.

BRAKES drum, dual circuit; lining area: front 33.5 sq in, 216 sq cm, rear 33.5 sq in, 216 sq cm, total 67 sq in, 432 sq cm.

ELECTRICAL EQUIPMENT 12 V; 34 Ah battery; 230 W dynamo; Femsa DI 4-7 distributor; 2 headlamps.

DIMENSIONS AND WEIGHT wheel base: 79.92 in, 203 cm; tracks: 45.28 in, 115 cm front, 48.03 in, 122 cm rear;

length: 135.83 in, 345 cm; width: 55.91 in, 142 cm; height: 52.36 in, 133 cm; ground clearance: 5.30 in, 13 cm; weight: 1,521 lb, 690 kg; weight distribution: 39% front, 61% rear; turning circle: 31.5 ft, 9.6 m; fuel tank: 6.6 imp gal, 7.9 US gal, 30 l.

BODY saloon/sedan; 2 doors; 4-5 seats, separate front seats; luxury equipment.

PRACTICAL INSTRUCTIONS fuel: 85 oct petrol; oil: engine 5.8 imp pt, 7 US pt, 3.3 l, SAE 40W (winter) 30 (summer), change every 6,200 miles, 10,000 km - gearbox and final drive 3.7 imp pt, 4.4 US pt, 2.1 l, SAE 90 EP, change every 18,600 miles, 30,000 km; greasing: every 1,600 miles, 2,500 km, 2 points; sparking plug: 175°; tappet clearances: inlet 0.006 in, 0.15 mm, exhaust 0.006 in, 0.15 mm; valve timing: 16° 56° 56° 16°; tyre pressure: front 20 psi, 1.4 atm, rear 28 psi, 2 atm.

133 Especial Lujo

See 133 Lujo, except for:

PRICE EX WORKS: 232,000* pesetas

ENGINE compression ratio: 9:1; max power (DIN): 44 hp (32.4 kW) at 6,400 rpm; max torque (DIN): 41 lb ft, 5.6 kg m (54.9 Nm) at 3,700 rpm; max engine rpm: 6,400; 52.2 hp/l (38.4 kW/l); 1 Bressel 30 DIC-10 downdraught twin barrel carburettor.

SEAT 133 Lujo

TRANSMISSION axle ratio: 5.125; tyres: 145 SR x 13.

PERFORMANCE max speeds: (I) 22 mph, 36 km/h; (II) 40 mph, 64 km/h; (III) 58 mph, 94 km/h; (IV) about 84 mph, 135 km/h; power-weight ratio: 35.1 lb/hp (47.7 lb/kW), 15.9 kg/hp (21.6 kg/kW); carrying capacity: 882 lb, 400 kg.

BRAKES front disc (diameter 8.94 in, 22.7 cm), rear drum; lining area: front 19.2 sq in, 124 sq cm, rear 33.5 sq in, 216 sq cm, total 52.7 sq in, 340 sq cm.

DIMENSIONS AND WEIGHT rear track: 47.91 in, 122 cm; length: 136.81 in, 347 cm; weight: 1,544 lb, 700 kg.

PRACTICAL INSTRUCTIONS fuel: 96 oct petrol; tappet clearances: inlet 0.006-0.008 in, 0.15-0.20 mm, exhaust 0.008-0.010 in, 0.20-0.25 mm; valve timing: 25° 51° 64° 12°.

127 Series

Power team:	Standard for:	Optional for:
43 hp	1 to 6	—
52 hp	7 to 9	—

43 hp power team

ENGINE front, transverse, 4 stroke; 4 cylinders, vertical in line; 55.1 cu in, 903 cc (2.56 x 2.68 in, 65 x 68 mm); compression ratio: 8.7:1; max power (DIN): 43 hp (31.6 kW) at 5,600 rpm; max torque (DIN): 44.2 lb ft, 6.1 kg m (59 Nm) at 3,000 rpm; max engine rpm: 6,200; 47.6 hp/l (3 kW/l); cast iron block, light alloy head; 3 crankshaft bearings; valves: overhead, in line, push-rods and rockers; camshafts: 1, side; lubrication: gear pump, full flow filter (cartridge), 6 imp pt, 7.2 US pt, 3.4 l; 1 Bressel 30 IBA 22/350 downdraught single barrel carburettor; fuel feed: mechanical pump; sealed circuit cooling, 8.8 imp pt, 10 US pt, 5 l.

TRANSMISSION driving wheels: front; clutch: single dry plate; gearbox: mechanical; gears: 4, fully synchronized; ratios: I 3.909, II 2.055, III 1.348, IV 0.963, rev 3.615; lever: central; final drive: cylindrical gears; axle ratio: 4.692; width of rims: 4''; tyres: 135 SR x 13.

PERFORMANCE max speeds: (I) 21.7 mph, 35 km/h; (II) 4 mph, 65 km/h; (III) 62 mph, 100 km/h; (IV) over 84 mph, 135 km/h; power-weight ratio: 36.4 lb/hp (49.5 lb/kW), 16 kg/hp (22.4 kg/kW); carrying capacity: 882 lb, 400 kg; acceleration: standing ¼ mile 20.9 sec; consumption: 40.9 m/imp gal, 36.2 m/US gal, 6.5 l x 100 km.

SEAT 127 900 4 Puertas Confort Lujo

SEAT 128/3P 1430

CHASSIS integral; front suspension: independent, by McPherson, coil springs/telescopic damper struts, lower swinging arms, anti-roll bar; rear: independent, lower swinging arms, transverse anti-roll leafsprings, telescopic dampers.

STEERING rack-and-pinion; turns lock to lock: 3.40.

BRAKES front disc (diameter 8.94 in, 22.7 cm), rear drum, rear compensator, dual circuit; lining area: front 19.2 sq in, 124 sq cm, rear 33.5 sq in, 216 sq cm, total 52.7 sq in, 340 sq cm.

ELECTRICAL EQUIPMENT 12 V; 45 Ah battery; 33 A alternator; Femsa distributor; 2 headlamps.

DIMENSIONS AND WEIGHT wheel base: 87.40 in, 222 cm; tracks: 50.39 in, 128 cm front, 50.79 in, 129 cm rear; length: 142.90 in, 364 cm; width: 60.24 in, 153 cm; height: 53.50 in, 136 cm; ground clearance: 5.12 in, 13 cm; weight: 1,565 lb, 710 kg; weight distribution: 48% front, 52% rear; turning circle: 31.5 ft, 9.6 m; fuel tank: 6.6 imp gal, 7.9 US gal, 30 l.

BODY saloon/sedan; 2 doors; 4 seats, separate front seats; for Confort Lujo models luxury equipment.

PRACTICAL INSTRUCTIONS fuel: 90 oct petrol; oil: engine 6.9 imp pt, 8.2 US pt, 3.9 l, SAE 30W-40, change every 6,200 miles, 10,000 km - gearbox and final drive 4.2 imp pt, 5.1 pt, 2.4 l, SAE 50, change every 18,600 miles, 30,000 km; greasing: none; tappet clearances: inlet 0.006 in, 0.15 mm, exhaust 0.008 in, 0.20 mm; valve timing: 17° 43° 57° 3°; tyre pressure: front 24 psi, 1.7 atm, rear 27 psi, 1.9 atm.

52 hp power team

ENGINE 61.6 cu in, 1,010 cc (2.62 x 2.86 in, 66.5 x 72.7 mm); compression ratio: 9.4:1; max power (DIN): 52 hp (38.3 kW) at 5,800 rpm; max torque (DIN): 55 lb ft, 7.6 kg m (74.5 Nm) at 3,100 rpm; 51.5 hp/l (37.9 kW/l); 1 Bressel 32 DMTR-45/250 downdraught twin barrel carburettor.

TRANSMISSION axle ratio: 4.461.

PERFORMANCE max speeds: (I) 21 mph, 35 km/h; (II) 43 mph, 70 km/h; (III) 65 mph, 105 km/h; (IV) 90 mph, 145 km/h; power-weight ratio: 30.1 lb/hp, (40.9 lb/kW), 13.6 kg/hp (18.5 kg/kW); acceleration: standing ¼ mile 19.7 sec.

ELECTRICAL EQUIPMENT 22 A alternator.

PRACTICAL INSTRUCTIONS fuel: 96 oct petrol; valve timing: 9° 48° 45° 10°.

128/3P 1200

PRICE EX WORKS: 382,000* pesetas

ENGINE front, transverse, slanted at 16°, 4 stroke; 4 cylinders, vertical, in line; 73 cu in, 1,197 cc (2.87 x 2.81 in, 73 x 71.5 mm); compression ratio: 8.8:1; max power (DIN): 67 hp (49.3 kW) at 5,600 rpm; max torque (DIN): 67 lb ft, 9.2 kg m (90.2 Nm) at 3,700 rpm; max engine rpm: 5,600; 56 hp/l (41.2 kW/l); cast iron block, light alloy head; 3 crankshaft bearings; valves: overhead, push-rods and rockers; camshafts: 1, side, in crankcase; lubrication: gear pump, full flow filter (cartridge), 7.7 imp pt, 9.3 US pt,

4.4 l; 1 Bressel 32 DMTR downdraught twin barrel carburettor; fuel feed: mechanical pump; water-cooled, 13.2 imp pt, 15.9 US pt, 7.5 l.

TRANSMISSION driving wheels: front; clutch: single dry plate; gearbox: mechanical; gears: 4, fully synchronized; ratios: I 3.583, II 2.235, III 1.454, IV 1.042, rev 3.714; lever: central; final drive: cylindrical gears; axle ratio: 3.765; width of rims: 4.5''; tyres: 145 SR x 13.

PERFORMANCE max speeds: (I) 25 mph, 40 km/h; (II) 47 mph, 75 km/h; (III) 71 mph, 115 km/h; (IV) 99 mph, 160 km/h; power-weight ratio: 27.9 lb/hp (38 lb/kW), 12.7 kg/hp (17.2 kg/kW); carrying capacity: 794 lb, 360 kg; acceleration: standing ¼ mile 19 sec; speed in top at 1,000 rpm: 17.8 mph, 28.6 km/h; consumption: 35.3 m/imp gal, 29.4 m/US gal, 8 l x 100 km.

CHASSIS integral; front suspension: independent, by McPherson, coil springs/telescopic damper struts, lower wishbones, anti-roll bar; rear: independent, single wide-based wishbone, transverse anti-roll leafsprings, telescopic dampers.

STEERING rack-and-pinion; turns lock to lock: 3.50.

BRAKES front disc (diameter 8.94 in, 22.7 cm), rear drum, dual circuit; lining area: front 19.2 sq in, 124 sq cm, rear 33.5 sq in, 216 sq cm, total 52.7 sq in, 340 sq cm.

ELECTRICAL EQUIPMENT 12 V; 45 Ah battery; 480 W alternator; Femsa distributor; 4 headlamps.

DIMENSIONS AND WEIGHT wheel base: 87.60 in, 222 cm; front and rear track: 52.36 in, 133 cm; length: 150.78 in, 383 cm; width: 61.18 in, 155 cm; height: 51.57 in, 131 cm; ground clearance: 5.12 in, 13 cm; weight: 1,874 lb, 850 kg; weight distribution: 51.7% front, 48.3% rear; turning circle: 31.5 ft, 9.6 m; fuel tank: 11 imp gal, 13.2 US gal, 50 l.

BODY coupé; 2 doors; 4 seats, separate front seats.

PRACTICAL INSTRUCTIONS fuel: 96 oct petrol; oil: engine 6.5 imp pt, 7.8 US pt, 3.7 l, SAE 40W (winter) 30 (summer), change every 6,200 miles, 10,000 km - gearbox and final drive 2.3 imp pt, 2.7 US pt, 1.3 l, SAE 90 EP, change every 12,400 miles, 20,000 km; greasing: homokinetic joints, every 18,600 miles, 30,000 km; sparking plug: 145°; tappet clearances: inlet and exhaust 0.010-0.012 in, 0.25-0.30 mm; valve timing: 10° 49° 50° 9°; tyre pressure: front 27 psi, 1.9 atm, rear 26 psi, 1.8 atm.

128/3P 1430

See 128/3 P 1200, except for:

PRICE EX WORKS: 400,000* pesetas

ENGINE 87.74 cu in, 1,438 cc (3.15 x 2.81 in, 80 x 71.5 mm); compression ratio: 9:1; max power (DIN): 77 hp (56.6 kW) at 5,600 rpm; max torque (DIN): 82 lb ft, 11.3 kg m (110 Nm) at 2,800 rpm; 53.5 hp/l (39.3 kW/l).

PERFORMANCE max speeds: (I) 28 mph, 45 km/h; (II) 46 mph, 75 km/h; (III) 71 mph, 115 km/h; (IV) over 99 mph, 160 km/h; power-weight ratio: 24.5 lb/hp (33.3 lb/kW), 11.1 kg/hp (15.1 kg/kW); carrying capacity: 882 lb, 400 kg.

DIMENSIONS AND WEIGHT weight: 1,885 lb, 855 kg.

Sport 1430

See 128/3 P 1430, except for:

PRICE EX WORKS: 425,000* pesetas

ENGINE max engine rpm: 5,800.

TRANSMISSION tyres: 165/70 SR x 13.

PERFORMANCE max speed: over 103 mph, 165 km/h; power-weight ratio: 23.2 lb/hp (31.5 lb/kW), 10.5 kg/hp (14.3 kg/kW); consumption: 40 m/imp gal, 33.6 m/US gal, 7 l x 100 km.

CHASSIS swinging leading arms on front and rear suspension.

ELECTRICAL EQUIPMENT 2 headlamps.

DIMENSIONS AND WEIGHT tracks: 50.78 in, 129 cm front, 51.57 in, 131 cm rear; length: 144.49 in, 367 cm; height: 49.21 in, 125 cm; weight: 1,786 lb, 810 kg.

BODY built-in headrests.

SEAT Sport 1430

124-D/124-D LS

PRICE EX WORKS: 124-D 325,000* pesetas
124-D LS 362,000* pesetas

ENGINE front, 4 stroke; 4 cylinders, in line; 73 cu in, 1,197 cc (2.87 x 2.81 in, 73 x 71.5 mm); compression ratio: 8.8:1; max power (DIN): 65 hp (47.8 kW) at 5,600 rpm; max torque (DIN): 65 lb ft, 9 kg m (88.3 Nm) at 3,400 rpm; max engine rpm: 5,600, 54.3 hp/l (39.9 kW/l); cast iron block, light alloy head; 5 crankshaft bearings; valves: overhead, push-rods and rockers; camshafts: 1, side, in crankcase; lubrication: gear pump, full flow filter (cartridge), 7.7 imp pt, 9.3 US pt, 4.4 l; 1 Bressel 32 DHS-20 downdraught twin barrel carburettor; fuel feed: mechanical pump; water-cooled, 13.2 imp pt, 15.9 US pt, 7.5 l.

TRANSMISSION driving wheels: rear; clutch: single dry plate; gearbox: mechanical; gears: 4, fully synchronized; ratios: I 3.750, II 2.300, III 1.490, IV 1, rev 3.870; lever: central; final drive: hypoid bevel; axle ratio: 4.300; width of rims: 4.5''; tyres: 150 SR x 13 or 155 SR x 13.

PERFORMANCE max speeds: (I) 22 mph, 35 km/h; (II) 37 mph, 60 km/h; (III) 59 mph, 95 km/h; (IV) about 93 mph, 150 km/h; power-weight ratio: 29.7 lb/hp (40.3 lb/kW), 13.4 kg/hp (18.3 kg/kW); carrying capacity: 882 lb, 400 kg; speed in direct drive at 1,000 rpm: 16.7 mph, 26.8 km/h; consumption: 35.3 m/imp gal, 29.4 m/US gal, 8 l x 100 km.

CHASSIS integral; front suspension: independent, wishbones, coil springs, anti-roll bar, telescopic dampers; rear: rigid axle, twin trailing radius arms, transverse linkage bar, coil springs, telescopic dampers.

STEERING worm and roller; turns lock to lock: 2.75.

BRAKES disc (diameter 8.94 in, 22.7 cm), rear compensator, servo; lining area: front 19.2 sq in, 124 sq cm, rear 19.2 sq in, 124 sq cm, total 38.4 sq in, 248 sq cm.

ELECTRICAL EQUIPMENT 12 V; 45 Ah battery; 540 W alternator; Femsa DI 4-8 distributor; 2 headlamps.

DIMENSIONS AND WEIGHT wheel base: 95.28 in, 242 cm; tracks: 52.36 in, 133 cm front, 51.18 in, 130 cm rear; length: 159.05 in, 404 cm; width: 63.39 in, 161 cm; height: 55.91 in, 142 cm; ground clearance: 5.12 in, 13 cm; weight: 1,929 lb, 875 kg; weight distribution: 43% front, 57% rear; turning circle: 35.1 ft, 10.7 m; fuel tank: 8.6 imp gal, 10.3 US gal, 39 l.

BODY saloon/sedan; 4 doors; 5 seats, separate front seats; heated rear window; for 124-D LS tinted glass, built-in headrests and luxury equipment.

PRACTICAL INSTRUCTIONS fuel: 96 oct petrol; oil: engine 6.5 imp pt, 7.8 US pt, 3.7 l, SAE 30W (summer) 40 (winter), change every 6,200 miles, 10,000 km - gearbox 2.3 imp pt, 2.7 US pt, 1.3 l, ZC 90, change every 12,400 miles, 20,000 km - final drive 2.3 imp pt, 2.7 US pt, 1.3 l, SAE 90, change every 12,400 miles, 20,000 km; greasing: every 3,100 miles, 5,000 km, 4 points; sparking plug: 145°; tappet clearances: inlet and exhaust 0.010-0.012 in, 0.25-0.30 mm; valve timing: 10° 49° 50° 9°; tyre pressure: front 24 psi, 1.7 atm, rear 26 psi, 1.8 atm.

SEAT 124-D Especial

124-D Especial

See 124-D/124-D LS, except for.

PRICE EX WORKS: 375,000* pesetas

ENGINE 87.7 cu in, 1,438 cc (3.15 x 2.81 in, 80 x 71.5 mm); compression ratio: 9:1; max power (DIN): 75 hp (55.2 kW) at 5,400 rpm; max torque (DIN): 82 lb ft, 11.3 kg m (110.8 Nm) at 3,400 rpm; max engine rpm: 6,000; 52.2 hp/l (38.4 kW/l); 1 Bressel 32 DHS-21 downdraught twin barrel carburettor.

TRANSMISSION gearbox ratios: I 3.797, II 2.175, III 1.410, IV 1, rev 3.655.

PERFORMANCE max speeds: (I) 25 mph, 40 km/h; (II) 43 mph, 70 km/h; (III) 68 mph, 110 km/h; (IV) about 96 mph, 155 km/h; power-weight ratio: 26.8 lb/hp (36.4 lb/kW), 12.1 kg/hp (16.5 kg/kW); speed in direct drive at 1,000 rpm: 16 mph, 25.8 km/h; consumption: 32.1 m/imp gal, 26.7 m/US gal, 8.8 l x 100 km.

DIMENSIONS AND WEIGHT weight: 2,007 lb, 910 kg; weight distribution: 44% front, 56% rear.

PRACTICAL INSTRUCTIONS sparking plug: 175°.

OPTIONALS 5-speed mechanical gearbox (I 3.667, II 2.100, III 1.361, IV 1, V 0.881).

131 1430/Supermirafiori

PRICE EX WORKS: 131 1430 381,000* pesetas
131 Supermirafiori 415,000* pesetas

ENGINE front, 4 stroke; 4 cylinders, vertical, in line; 87 cu in, 1,438 cc (3.15 x 2.81 in, 80 x 71.5 mm); compression ratio: 9:1; max power (DIN): 75 hp (55.2 kW) at 5,400 rpm; max torque (DIN): 82 lb ft, 11.3 kg m (110.8 Nm) at 3,4 rpm; max engine rpm: 6,300; 52.2 hp/l (38.4 kW/l); cast iron block, light alloy head; 5 crankshaft bearings; valves: overhead, push-rods and rockers; camshafts: 1, side, crankcase; lubrication: gear pump, full flow filter (cartridge), 7.7 imp pt, 9.3 US pt, 4.4 l; 1 Bressel 32 DHS-2 or Solex 32EIES-4 downdraught twin barrel carburetto, fuel feed: mechanical pump; sealed circuit cooling, ant freeze liquid, 13.2 imp pt, 15.9 US pt, 7.5 l.

TRANSMISSION driving wheels: rear; clutch: single d plate; gearbox: mechanical; gears: 4, fully synchronize ratios: I 3.667, II 2.100, III 1.361, IV 1, rev 3.526; leve central; final drive: hypoid bevel; axle ratio: 3.900; wid of rims: 4.5''; tyres: 155 SR x 13.

PERFORMANCE max speeds: (I) 28 mph, 45 km/h; (I 47 mph, 75 km/h; (III) 75 mph, 120 km/h; (IV) abo 96 mph, 155 km/h; power-weight ratio: 28.5 lb/hp (38 lb/kW), 12.9 kg/hp (17.6 kg/kW); carrying capacity: 8 lb, 400 kg; acceleration: standing ¼ mile 19 sec; speed direct drive at 1,000 rpm: 16.8 mph, 27.1 km/h; consum tion: 36 m/imp gal, 30 m/US gal, 7.8 l x 100 km.

CHASSIS integral; front suspension: independent, by M Pherson, coil springs/telescopic damper struts, lower wis bones, anti-roll bar; rear: rigid axle, twin trailing low radius arms, transverse linkage bar, coil springs, telescop dampers.

STEERING rack-and-pinion; turns lock to lock: 3.40.

BRAKES front disc (diameter 8.94 in, 22.7 cm), rear drum rear compensator, dual circuit, vacuum servo; lining are front 19.2 sq in, 124 sq cm, rear 41.7 sq n, 269 sq cm total 60.9 sq in, 393 sq cm.

ELECTRICAL EQUIPMENT 12 V; 45 Ah battery; 540 W alte nator; Femsa distributor; 2 headlamps.

DIMENSIONS AND WEIGHT wheel base: 98.03 in, 249 cm tracks: 53.94 in, 137 cm front, 51.57 in, 131 cm rea length: 166.93 in, 424 cm; width: 64.17 in, 163 cm; heigh 53.54 in, 136 cm; weight: 2,139 lb, 970 kg; weight distrib tion: 44.4% front, 55.6% rear; turning circle: 34.8 ft, 10 m; fuel tank: 11 imp gal, 13.2 US gal, 50 l.

BODY saloon/sedan; 4 doors; 5 seats, separate front seat reclining backrests; (for Supermirafiori only) tinted glas heated rear window, front and rear headrests, halogen hea lamps.

PRACTICAL INSTRUCTIONS fuel: 96 oct petrol; oil: engin 6.7 imp pt, 8 US pt, 3.8 l, SAE 30W (winter) 40 (summer change every 6,200 miles, 10,000 km - gearbox and fin drive 1.6 imp pt, 1.9 US pt, 0.9 l, SAE 50 VS type Z greasing: none; sparking plug: 175°; tappet clearance inlet and exhaust 0.010-0.012 in, 0.25-0.30 mm; valve timin 10° 49° 50° 9°; tyre pressure: front 24 psi, 1.7 atm rea 26 psi, 1.8 atm.

SEAT 131 Supermirafiori 1430

SEAT 131 Supermirafiori 1430 - 1600

131 CL 1430 5 Puertas

e 131 1430/Supermirafiori, except for:

ICE EX WORKS: 431,000* pesetas

ANSMISSION axle ratio: 4.100; tyres: 165 SR x 13.

RFORMANCE max speeds: (I) 25 mph, 40 km/h; (II) mph, 70 km/h; (III) 71 mph, 115 km/h; (IV) about mph, 150 km/h; power-weight ratio: 29.5 lb/hp (40.1 kW), 13.4 kg/hp (18.2 kg/kW); carrying capacity: 1,058 480 kg; acceleration: standing ¼ mile 19.1 sec.

MENSIONS AND WEIGHT tracks: 54.17 in, 138 cm front, 93 in, 132 cm rear; height: 55.12 in, 140 cm; weight: 16 lb, 1,005 kg.

DY estate car/st. wagon; 4+1 doors; folding rear seat.

ACTICAL INSTRUCTIONS tyre pressure: front 26 psi, atm, rear 31 psi, 2.2 atm.

131 Supermirafiori 1600

e 131 1430/Supermirafiori, except for:

ICE EX WORKS: 458,000* pesetas

GINE 97.1 cu in, 1,592 cc (3.15 x 3.12 in, 80 x 79.2 mm); mpression ratio: 8.98:1; max power (DIN): 95 hp (69.9) at 6,000 rpm; max torque (DIN): 93 lb ft, 12.8 kg m 25.5 Nm) at 4,000 rpm; max engine rpm: 6,700; 59.7 hp/l 3.9 kW/l); valves: overhead, Vee-slanted at 65°15', thim- e tappets; camshafts: 2, overhead, cogged belt; 1 Bressel DMS-1 downdraught twin barrel carburettor; sealed cuit cooling, anti-freeze liquid, 13.4 imp pt, 16.1 US 7.6 l, electric thermostatic fan.

ANSMISSION gears: 5, fully synchronized; ratios: I 3.667, 2.100, III 1.361, IV 1, V 0.881, rev 3.526; tyres: 160 x 13.

RFORMANCE max speeds: (I) 31 mph, 50 km/h; (II) 56 h, 90 km/h; (III) 84 mph, 135 km/h; (IV) 106 mph, 0 km/h; (V) 103 mph, 165 km/h; power-weight ratio: 2 lb/hp (31.5 lb/kW), 10.5 kg/hp (14.3 kg/kW); acce- ration: standing ¼ mile 17.4 sec; speed in top at 1,000 m: 19.1 mph, 30.8 km/h; consumption: 31.7 m/imp gal, 4 m/US gal, 8.9 l x 100 km.

EERING adjustable height of steering wheel.

ECTRICAL EQUIPMENT 4 halogen headlamps.

MENSIONS AND WEIGHT length: 167.72 in, 426 cm; dth: 64.57 in, 164 cm; weight: 2,205 lb, 1,000 kg; weight stribution: 44.6% front, 55.4% rear.

DY front and rear headrests; tinted glass; heated rear ndow; bumper.

ACTICAL INSTRUCTIONS sparking plug: 215°; tappet clear- ces: inlet 0.018-0.020 in, 0.45-0.50 mm, exhaust 0.024-0.026 0.60-0.65 mm; valve timing: 12° 53° 52° 13°; front tyre essure 23 psi, 1.6 atm.

OPTIONALS G.M.S. type Z. M. automatic transmission, hydraulic torque converter and planetary gears with 3 ratios (I 2.400, II 1.480, III 1, rev 1.920), max ratio of converter at stall 2.4, possible manual selection, 3.700 axle ratio; air-conditioning.

131 CL 1600 5 Puertas

See 131 Supermirafiori 1600, except for:

PRICE EX WORKS: 475,000* pesetas

TRANSMISSION tyres: 165 SR x 13.

PERFORMANCE max speeds: (I) 31 mph, 50 km/h; (II) 56 mph, 90 km/h; (III) 84 mph, 135 km/h; (IV) about 103 mph, 165 km/h; (V) about 99 mph, 160 km/h; power- weight ratio: 24 lb/hp (32.6 lb/kW), 10.9 kg/hp (14.8 kg/kW); carrying capacity: 1,058 lb, 480 kg; acceleration: standing ¼ mile 17.7 sec.

DIMENSIONS AND WEIGHT tracks: 54.17 in, 138 cm front, 51.93 in, 132 cm rear; height: 55.12 in, 140 cm; weight: 2,282 lb, 1,035 kg.

BODY estate car/st. wagon; 4 + 1 doors; folding rear seat.

PRACTICAL INSTRUCTIONS valve timing: 12° 53° 54° 11°; tyre pressure: front 26 psi, 1.8 atm, rear 31 psi, 2.2 atm.

---

131 Diesel 1760

See 131 1430/Supermirafiori, except for:

PRICE EX WORKS: 464,000* pesetas

ENGINE Diesel Perkins; 107.4 cu in, 1,760 cc (3.13 x 3.50 in, 79.4 x 88.9 mm); compression ratio: 22:1; max power (DIN): 49 hp (36.1 kW) at 4,000 rpm; max torque (DIN): 77 lb ft, 10.6 kg m (104 Nm) at 2,200 rpm; 27.8 hp/l (20.5 kW/l); 3 crankshaft bearings.

TRANSMISSION axle ratio: 3.700; tyres: 165 SR x 13.

PERFORMANCE max speeds: (I) 22 mph, 35 km/h; (II) 38 mph, 61 km/h; (III) 57 mph, 92 km/h; (IV) 81 mph, 130 km/h; power-weight ratio: 48.1 lb/hp (65.3 lb/kW), 21.8 kg/hp (29.6 kg/kW); consumption: 34.4 m/imp gal, 28.7 m/US gal, 8.2 l x 100 km.

ELECTRICAL EQUIPMENT 68 Ah battery; halogen head- lamps.

DIMENSIONS AND WEIGHT weight 2,359 lb, 1,070 kg.

131 Diesel 1760 5 Puertas

See 131 Diesel 1760, except for:

PRICE EX WORKS: 482,000* pesetas

SEAT 131 CL 1430 5 Puertas

SEAT 132 2000 Lujo

131 DIESEL 1760 5 PUERTAS

PERFORMANCE max speed: 78 mph, 125 km/h; power-weight ratio: 49.8 lb/hp (67.5 lb/kW), 22.6 kg/hp (30.6 kg/kW); carrying capacity: 1,058 lb, 480 kg.

DIMENSIONS AND WEIGHT tracks: 54.17 in, 138 cm front, 51.93 in, 132 cm rear; height: 55.12 in, 140 cm; weight: 2,437 lb, 1,105 kg.

BODY estate car/st. wagon; 4 + 1 doors; folding rear seat.

PRACTICAL INSTRUCTIONS tyre pressure: front 26 psi, 1.8 atm, rear 31 psi, 2.2 atm.

132 2000 Lujo

PRICE EX WORKS: 588,000* pesetas

ENGINE front, 4 stroke; 4 cylinders, vertical, in line; 117.1 cu in, 1,919 cc (3.31 x 3.41 in, 84 x 86.6 mm); compression ratio: 8.9:1; max power (DIN): 109 hp (80.2 kW) at 5,800 rpm; max torque (DIN): 112 lb ft, 15.4 kg m (151 Nm) at 3,000 rpm; max engine rpm: 6.300; 56.8 hp/l (41.8 kW/l); cast iron block, light alloy head; 5 crankshaft bearings; valves: overhead, Vee-slanted at 65°, thimble tappets; camshafts: 2, overhead, cogged belt; lubrication: gear pump, full flow filter (cartridge), 7.7 imp pt, 9.3 US pt, 4.4 l; 1 Weber 34 DMS/4 or Bressel 34 DMS 4-250 downdraught twin barrel carburettor; fuel feed: mechanical pump; sealed circuit cooling, anti-freeze liquid, 14.1 imp pt, 16.9 US pt, 8 l, electric thermostatic fan.

TRANSMISSION driving wheels: rear; clutch: single dry plate; gearbox: mechanical; gears: 5, fully synchronized; ratios: I 3.667, II 2.100, III 1.361, IV 1, V 0.881, rev 3.526; lever: central; final drive: hypoid bevel; axle ratio: 4.100; width of rims: 5.5''; tyres: 175 SR x 14.

PERFORMANCE max speeds: (I) 28 mph, 45 km/h; (II) 47 mph, 75 km/h; (III) 71 mph, 115 km/h; (IV) 99 mph, 160 km/h; (V) 106 mph, 170 km/h; power-weight ratio: 23.1 lb/hp (31.3 lb/kW), 10.5 kg/hp (14.2 kg/kW); carrying capacity: 882 lb, 400 kg; consumption: 33.2 m/imp gal 27.7 m/US gal, 8.5 l x 100 km.

CHASSIS integral; front suspension: independent, wishbones (lower trailing links), coil springs, anti-roll bar, telescopic dampers; rear: rigid axle, lower longitudinal trailing radius arms, upper oblique torque arms, coil springs, telescopic dampers.

STEERING screw and sector, recirculating ball, servo; adjustable height of steering wheel; turns lock to lock: 3.05.

BRAKES front disc, rear drum, rear compensator, dual circuit, servo; lining area: front 19.2 sq in, 124 sq cm, rear 41.7 sq in, 269 sq cm, total 60.9 sq in, 393 sq cm.

ELECTRICAL EQUIPMENT 12 V; 55 Ah battery; 770 W alternator; Marelli distributor; transistorized ignition; 4 halogen headlamps.

DIMENSIONS AND WEIGHT wheel base: 100.67 in, 256 cm; tracks: 51.97 in, 132 cm front, 52.36 in, 133 cm rear; length: 172.83 in, 439 cm; width: 64.57 in, 164 cm; height: 56.29 in, 143 cm; ground clearance: 4.72 in, 12 cm; weight: 2,514 lb, 1,140 kg; turning circle: 36.1 ft, 11 m; fuel tank: 12.3 imp gal, 14.8 US gal, 56 l.

BODY saloon/sedan; 4 doors; 5 seats, separate front seats, reclining backrests with built-in headrests; heated rear window; electric windows; bumpers.

PRACTICAL INSTRUCTIONS fuel: 96 oct petrol; oil: engine 7 imp pt, 8.5 US pt, 4 l, SAE 30W (summer) 40 (winter), change every 6,200 miles, 10,000 km - gearbox 2.3 imp pt. 2.7 US pt, 1.3 l, ZC 90, change every 18,600 miles, 30,000 km - final drive 2.8 imp pt, 3.4 US pt, 1.6 l, SAE 90 EP, change every 18,600 miles, 30,000 km; greasing: none; tappet clearances: inlet 0.018 in, 0.45 mm, exhaust 0.024 in, 0.60 mm; valve timing: 15° 55° 53° 17°; tyre pressure: front 27 psi, 1.9 atm, rear 28 psi, 2 atm.

OPTIONALS air-conditioning; metallic spray; GMS type ZR-T2 automatic transmission, hydraulic torque converter and planetary gears with 3 ratios (I 2.400, II 1.480, III 1, rev 1,920), max ratio of converter at stall 2.4; possible manual selection, max speed 103 mph, 165 km/h.

132 Diesel 2200/Lujo

See 132 2000 Lujo, except for:

PRICES EX WORKS: 132 Diesel 2200 602,000* pesetas
132 Diesel 2200 Lujo 659,000* pesetas

ENGINE Mercedes-Benz, Diesel, front, 4 stroke; 134.1 cu in, 2,197 cc (3.43 x 3.63 in, 87 x 92.4 mm); compression ratio: 21:1; max power (DIN): 60 hp (44.1 kW) at 4,200 rpm; max torque (DIN): 92.7 lb ft, 12.8 kg m (125.5 Nm) at 2,200

rpm; max engine rpm: 4,350; 27.3 hp/l (20.1 kW/l); valves: overhead, in line, finger levers; camshafts: 1, overhead; lubrication: gear pump, oil-water heat exchanger, full flow filter, 9.7 imp pt, 11.6 US pt, 5.5 l; Bosch injection pump.

TRANSMISSION width of rims: 5''.

PERFORMANCE max speeds: (I) 22 mph, 35 km/h; (II) 37 mph, 60 km/h; (III) 59 mph, 95 km/h; (IV) 81 mph, 130 km/h; (V) 84 mph, 135 km/h; power-weight ratio: 44.6 lb/hp (60.7 lb/kW), 20.2 kg/hp (27.5 kg/kW); acceleration: standing ¼ mile 22.8 sec; speed in top at 1,000 rpm: 19.3 mph, 30 km/h; consumption: 34.9 m/imp gal, 29 m/US gal, 8.1 l x 100 km.

ELECTRICAL EQUIPMENT 66 Ah battery.

DIMENSIONS AND WEIGHT weight: 2,679 lb, 1,215 kg.

PRACTICAL INSTRUCTIONS fuel: Diesel oil; oil: engine 7.9 imp pt, 9.5 US pt, 4.5 l, SAE 30W-40, change every 6,200 miles, 10,000 km; tappet clearances: inlet 0.008 in, 0.10 mm, exhaust 0.012 in, 0.30 mm; valve timing: 12°30' 41°30' 45° 9°.

SAAB SWEDEN

96 GL

ENGINE Ford, front, 4 stroke; 4 cylinders, Vee-slanted at 60°; 91.4 cu in, 1,498 cc (3.54 x 2.32 in, 90 x 58.9 mm); compression ratio: 9:1; max power (DIN): 68 hp (50 kW) at 5,500 rpm; max torque (DIN): 72 lb ft, 10 kg m (98.1 Nm) at 3,000 rpm; max engine rpm: 5,500; 45.4 hp/l (33.4 kW/l); cast iron block and head, 3 crankshaft bearings; valves: overhead, push-rods and rockers; camshafts: 1, at centre of Vee; lubrication: rotary pump, full flow filter, 5.8 imp pt, 7 US pt, 3.3 l; 1 Solex 77 TF 9510 SA downdraught carburettor; fuel feed: mechanical pump; liquid-cooled, expansion tank, 10.2 imp pt, 12.3 US pt, 5.8 l.

TRANSMISSION driving wheels: front; clutch: single dry plate, hydraulically controlled; gearbox: mechanical, in unit with differential; gears: 4, fully synchronized; ratios: I 3.479, II 2.088, III 1.296, IV 0.838, rev 3.182; lever: steering column; final drive: spiral bevel; axle ratio: 4.875; width of rims: 4.5''; tyres: 155 SR x 15.

PERFORMANCE max speeds: (I) 23 mph, 37 km/h; (II) 39 mph, 62 km/h; (III) 62 mph, 99 km/h; (IV) 93 mph, 150 km/h; power-weight ratio: 30.2 lb/hp (41 lb/kW), 13.7 kg/hp (18.6 kg/kW); carrying capacity: 925 lb, 420 kg; acceleration: standing ¼ mile 19.5 sec, 0-50 mph (0-80 km/h) 10.5 sec; speed in top at 1,000 rpm: 17.3 mph, 27.9 km/h; consumption: 32.1 m/imp gal, 26.7 m/US gal, 8.8 l x 100 km.

CHASSIS integral; front suspension: independent, wishbones, coil springs, telescopic dampers; rear: U-shaped tubular rigid axle (swept-back ends), swinging trailing lower radius levers, coil springs, telescopic dampers.

SAAB 96 GL

STEERING rack-and-pinion; turns lock to lock: 2.60.

BRAKES front disc (diameter 10.51 in, 26.7 cm), rear drum, 2 separate X hydraulic circuits, servo; swept area: front 182.2 sq in, 1,175 sq cm, rear 73.6 sq in, 475 sq cm, total 255.8 sq in, 1,650 sq cm.

ELECTRICAL EQUIPMENT 12 V; 60 Ah battery; 55 A alternator; Bosch distributor; 2 halogen headlamps.

DIMENSIONS AND WEIGHT wheel base: 98.35 in, 250 cm; tracks: 48.82 in, 124 cm front, 48.50 in, 123 cm rear; length: 169.29 in, 430 cm; width: 62.60 in, 159 cm; height: 57.87 in, 147 cm; ground clearance: 5.90 in, 15 cm; weight: 2,050 lb, 930 kg; weight distribution: 61.7% front, 38.3% rear; turning circle: 36.1 ft, 11 m; fuel tank: 8.4 imp gal, 10 US gal, 38 l.

BODY saloon/sedan; 2 doors; 5 seats, separate front seats, adjustable backrests, built-in headrests; heated rear window; heated driving seat; impact-absorbing bumpers; headlamps with wiper-washers.

PRACTICAL INSTRUCTIONS fuel: 97 oct petrol; oil: engine 5.8 imp pt, 7 US pt, 3.3 l, SAE 10W-30 (winter) 10W-40 (summer), change every 6,200 miles, 10,000 km - gearbox and final drive 3 imp pt, 3.6 US pt, 1.7 l, SAE 80 change every 12,400 miles, 20,000 km; greasing: none; tappet clearances: inlet 0.014 in, 0.35 mm, exhaust 0.016 in, 0.40 mm; valve timing: 21° 82° 63° 40°; tyre pressure: front 24 psi, 1.7 atm, rear 24 psi, 1.7 atm.

SAAB 96 GL

SAAB 99 GL 2-dr Sedan

99 Series

ICES IN GB AND USA:	£	$
GL 2-dr Sedan	4,495*	6,398*
GL 4-dr Sedan	4,905*	—
EMS 2-dr Sport Sedan	6,580*	—
Turbo 2-dr Sport Sedan	—	—

wer team:	Standard for:	Optional for:
0 hp	1,2	—
8 hp	—	1,2
8 hp	3	—
5 hp	4	—

100 hp power team

NGINE front, 4 stroke; 4 cylinders, slanted at 45°, in line; 1.1 cu in, 1,985 cc (3.54 x 3.07 in, 90 x 78 mm); compres- on ratio: 9.2:1; max power (DIN): 100 hp (73.6 kW) at 200 rpm; max torque (DIN): 120 lb ft, 16.5 kg m (161.8 n) at 3,500 rpm; max engine rpm: 6,000; 50.4 hp/l (37.1 V/l); cast iron block, light alloy head; 5 crankshaft bear- gs; valves: overhead, thimble tappets; camshafts: 1, erhead, driven by double chain; lubrication: rotary pump, l flow filter, 6.2 imp pt, 7.4 US pt, 3.5 l; 1 Zenith- romberg 175 CDSEVX horizontal carburettor; fuel feed: me- anical pump; liquid-cooled, expansion tank, 14.1 imp pt, 9 US pt, 8 l, thermostatic fan.

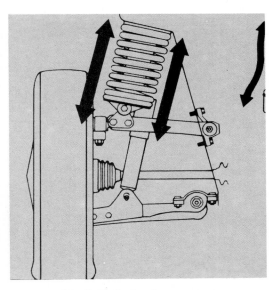

SAAB 99 Series (suspension)

SAAB 99 Turbo 2-dr Sport Sedan

TRANSMISSION driving wheels: front; clutch: single dry plate, hydraulically controlled; gearbox: mechanical, in unit with differential and engine, transfer chain in front of engine ratio 0.968:1; gears: 4, fully synchronized; ratios: I 3.316, II 2.005, III 1.337, IV 1, rev 3.650; lever: central; final drive: spiral bevel; axle ratio: 3.890; width of rims: 5''; tyres: 165 SR x 15.

PERFORMANCE max speeds: (I) 34 mph, 55 km/h; (II) 57 mph, 91 km/h; (III) 84 mph, 135 km/h; (IV) 102 mph, 164 km/h; power-weight ratio: 2-dr sedan 24.9 lb/hp (34 lb/kW), 11.3 kg/hp (15.4 kg/kW); carrying capacity: 970 lb, 440 kg; speed in direct drive at 1,000 rpm: 19.3 mph, 31 km/h; consumption: 26.6 m/imp gal, 22.2 m/US gal, 10.6 l x 100 km.

CHASSIS integral; front suspension: independent, double wishbones, progressive action coil springs, telescopic dampers; rear: rigid axle, twin longitudinal leading arms, twin swinging trailing radius arms, transverse linkage bar, coil springs, telescopic dampers.

STEERING rack-and-pinion; turns lock to lock: 4.11.

BRAKES disc (front diameter 11.02 in, 28 cm, rear 10.61 in, 27 cm), 2 separate X hydraulic circuits, servo; swept area: total 388.2 sq in, 2,504 sq cm.

ELECTRICAL EQUIPMENT 12 V; 60 Ah battery; 790 W alter- nator; Bosch distributor; 2 halogen headlamps with wiper- washers.

DIMENSIONS AND WEIGHT wheel base: 97.36 in, 247 cm; tracks: 55.12 in, 140 cm front, 56.30 in, 143 cm rear; length: 174.02 in, 442 cm; width: 66.54 in, 169 cm; height: 57 in, 144 cm; ground clearance: 6.90 in, 17.5 cm; weight: 2-dr sedan 2,492 lb, 1,130 kg - 4-dr sedan 2,558 lb, 1,160 kg; weight distribution: 61.1% front, 38.9% rear; turning circle: 34.4 ft, 10.5 m; fuel tank: 12.8 imp gal, 15.3 US gal, 58 l.

BODY 5 seats, separate front seats, adjustable backrests; heated driving seat; folding rear seat; impact-absorbing bumpers; hazard lights; heated rear window.

PRACTICAL INSTRUCTIONS fuel: 97 oct petrol; oil: engine 6.2 imp pt, 7.4 US pt, 3.5 l, SAE 10W-40, change every 9,300 miles, 15,000 km - gearbox 4.4 imp pt, 5.3 US pt, 2.5 l, SAE 10W-30/40, change every 18,600 miles, 30,000 km; greasing: every 6,200 miles, 10,000 km; tappet clearances: inlet 0.006-0.012 in, 0.15-0.30 mm, exhaust 0.014-0.020 in, 0.35-0.50 mm; valve timing: 10° 54° 54° 10°; tyre pressure: front 31 psi, 2.2 atm, rear 34 psi, 2.4 atm.

108 hp power team

See 100 hp power team, except for:

ENGINE max power (DIN): 108 hp (79.5 kW) at 5,200 rpm; max torque (DIN): 121 lb ft, 16.7 kg m (163.8 Nm) at 3,300 rpm; 54.4 hp/l (40 kW/l); 2 Zenith-Stromberg 150 CDSEVX carburettors.

PERFORMANCE max speed: 106 mph, 171 km/h; power- weight ratio: 2-dr sedan 23.1 lb/hp (31.3 lb/kW), 10.5 kg/hp (14.2 kg/kW); consumption: 28.2 m/imp gal, 23.5 m/US gal, 10 l x 100 km.

OPTIONALS Borg-Warner 35 automatic transmission, hy- draulic torque converter and planetary gears with 3 ratios (I 2.390, II 1.450, III 1, rev 2.090), max ratio of converter at stall 1.91, max speed 102 mph, 164 km/h, consumption 26.2 m/imp gal, 21.8 m/US gal, 10.8 l x 100 km.

118 hp power team

See 100 hp power team, except for:

ENGINE max power (DIN): 118 hp (86.8 kW) at 5,500 rpm; max torque (DIN): 123 lb ft, 17 kg m (166.7 Nm) at 3,700 rpm; 59.4 hp/l (43.7 kW/l); Bosch CI injection system; fuel feed: electric pump.

TRANSMISSION tyres: 175/70 HR x 15.

PERFORMANCE max speed: 108 mph, 174 km/h; power- weight ratio: 21.4 lb/hp (29.1 lb/kW), 9.7 kg/hp (13.2 kg/kW); consumption: 26.2 m/imp gal, 21.8 m/US gal, 10.8 l x 100 km.

STEERING turns lock to lock: 3.40.

DIMENSIONS AND WEIGHT weight: 2,536 lb, 1,150 kg; weight distribution: 60.9% front, 39.1% rear.

BODY 5 seats, separate front seats, adjustable backrests; heated driving seat; folding rear seat; impact-absorbing bumpers; hazard lights; heated rear window; luxury equipment; rev counter; light alloy wheels; front spoiler.

OPTIONALS sunshine roof.

145 hp power team

See 100 hp power team, except for:

ENGINE compression ratio: 7.2:1; max power (DIN): 145 hp (106.7 kW) at 5,000 rpm; max torque (DIN): 174 lb ft, 24 kg m (235.4 Nm) at 3,000 rpm; 73 hp/l (53.8 kW/l); Bosch CI fuel injection system; centrifugal compressor, mounted coaxially with exhaust driven Garret Airresearch turbine; fuel feed: electric pump; water-cooled.

TRANSMISSION transfer chain in front of engine ratio 0.839:1; gearbox ratios: I 3.053, II 1.841, III 1.235, IV 0.839, rev 3.358; width of rims: 5.5''! tyres: 175/70 HR x 15.

PERFORMANCE max speeds: (I) 36 mph, 58 km/h; (II) 59 mph, 95 km/h; (III) 88 mph, 142 km/h; (IV) 121 mph, 195 km/h; power-weight ratio: 17.9 lb/hp (24.3 lb/kW), 8.1 kg/hp (11 kg/kW); speed in top at 1,000 rpm: 21.9 mph, 35.3 km/h; consumption: 24.6 m/imp gal, 20.5 m/US gal, 11.5 l x 100 km.

STEERING turns lock to lock: 3.40.

ELECTRICAL EQUIPMENT 840 W alternator.

DIMENSIONS AND WEIGHT tracks: 55.51 in, 141 cm front 56.69 in, 144 cm rear; weight: 2,580 lb, 1,170 kg; weight distribution: 59.1% front, 40.9% rear.

BODY 5 seats, separate front seats, adjustable backrests; heated driving seat; front spoiler; sport steering wheel; tinted glass; folding rear seat; impact-absorbing bumpers; hazard lights; heated rear window.

PRACTICAL INSTRUCTIONS engine oil: change every 4,700 miles, 7,500 km; valve timing: 12° 40° 62° 2°.

SAAB 900 GL 3-dr Hatchback Sedan

900 Series

PRICES IN GB AND USA:	£	$
1 GL 3-dr Hatchback Sedan	—	7,798*
2 GLs 3-dr Hatchback Sedan	—	—
3 GLs 5-dr Hatchback Sedan	—	—
4 GLE 5-dr Hatchback Sedan	6,845*	8,948*
5 EMS 3-dr Hatchback Sedan	—	9,073*
6 Turbo 3-dr Hatchback Sedan	7,950*	—
7 Turbo 5-dr Hatchback Sedan	8,350*	11,968*

Power team:	Standard for:	Optional for:
100 hp	1	—
108 hp	2,3	—
118 hp	4,5	—
145 hp	6,7	—

100 hp power team

ENGINE front, 4 stroke; 4 cylinders, slanted at 45°, in line; 121.1 cu in, 1,985 cc (3.54 x 3.07 in, 90 x 78 mm); compression ratio: 9.2:1; max power (DIN): 100 hp (73.6 kW) at 5,200 rpm; max torque (DIN): 120 lb ft, 16.5 kg m (161.8 Nm) at 3,500 rpm; max engine rpm: 6,000; 50.4 hp/l

SAAB 900 GLs 5-dr Hatchback Sedan

(37.1 kW/l); cast iron block, light alloy head; 5 crank shaft bearings; valves: overhead, thimble tappets; camshafts: 1, overhead, driven by double chain; lubrication rotary pump, full flow filter, 6.2 imp pt, 7.4 US pt, 3 l; 1 Zenith-Stromberg 175 CDSEVX horizontal carburettor fuel feed: mechanical pump; liquid-cooled, expansion tank 17.6 imp pt, 21.1 US pt, 10 l, thermostatic fan.

TRANSMISSION driving wheels: front; clutch: single d plate, hydraulically controlled; gearbox: mechanical, unit with differential and engine, transfer chain in fro of engine ratio 0.968:1; gears: 4, fully synchronized; ratio I 3.437, II 2.072, III 1.391, IV 1, rev 3.781; lever: centra final drive: spiral bevel; axle ratio: 3.890; width of rim 5''; tyres: 165 SR x 15.

PERFORMANCE max speeds: (I) 34 mph, 55 km/h; (II) mph, 91 km/h; (III) 84 mph, 135 km/h; (IV) 102 mph, 1 km/h; power-weight ratio: 26.5 lb/hp (35.9 lb/kW), kg/hp (16.3 kg/kW); carrying capacity: 970 lb, 440 k speed in direct drive at 1,000 rpm: 19.4 mph, 31.3 km/ consumption: 26.6 m/imp gal, 22.2 m/US gal, 10.6 l x 100 k

CHASSIS integral; front suspension: independent, doub wishbones, progressive action coil springs, telescop dampers; rear: rigid axle twin longitudinal leading arm twin swinging trailing radius arms, transverse linkage ba coil springs, telescopic dampers.

STEERING rack-and-pinion; turns lock to lock: 4.11.

BRAKES disc (front diameter 11.02 in, 28 cm, rear 10. in, 27 cm), 2 separate X hydraulic circuits, servo; swe area: total 388.2 sq in, 2,504 sq cm.

SAAB 900 Turbo 5-dr Hatchback Sedan

ELECTRICAL EQUIPMENT 12 V; 60 Ah battery; 790 W alter-
[na]tor; Bosch distributor; 2 halogen headlamps with wiper-
[wa]shers.

DIMENSIONS AND WEIGHT wheel base: 99.21 in, 252 cm;
[tra]cks: 55.91 in, 142 cm front, 56.30 in, 143 cm rear; length:
[18]6.61 in, 474 cm; width: 66.54 in, 169 cm; height: 55.91 in,
[14]2 cm; ground clearance: 5.91 in, 15 cm; weight: 2,646 lb,
[12]00 kg; turning circle: 33.8 ft, 10.3 m; fuel tank: 12.8
[im]p gal, 15.3 US gal, 58 l.

BODY 5 seats, separate front seats, adjustable backrests;
[im]pact-absorbing bumpers; hazard lights; heated rear
[wi]ndow; front spoiler.

PRACTICAL INSTRUCTIONS fuel: 97 oct petrol; oil: engine
[6.1] imp pt, 7.4 US pt, 35 l, SAE 10W-40, change every
[9,3]00 miles, 15,000 km - gearbox 4.4 imp pt, 5.3 US pt, 2.5
[l,]SAE 10W-30/40, change every 18,600 miles, 30,000 km;
[gre]asing: every 6,200 miles, 10,000 km; tappet clearances:
[inl]et 0.006-0.012 in, 0.15-0.30 mm, exhaust 0.014-0.020 in,
[0.3]5-0.50 mm; valve timing: 10° 54° 54° 10°; tyre pressure:
[fro]nt 31 psi, 2.2 atm, rear 34 psi, 2.4 atm.

OPTIONALS sunshine roof; power steering.

108 hp power team

[Se]e 100 hp power team, except for:

ENGINE max power (DIN): 108 hp (79.5 kW) at 5,200 rpm;
[rp]m; max torque (DIN): 121 lb ft, 16.7 kg m (163.8 Nm) at
[3,8]00 rpm; 54.4 hp/l (40.1 kW/l); 2 Zenith-Stromberg 150
[CD]SEVX horizontal carburettors.

PERFORMANCE max speed: 106 mph, 171 km/h; power-
[w]eight ratio: 3-dr model 24.5 lb/hp (33.3 lb/kW), 11.1
[lb/]hp (15.1 kg/kW); consumption: 28.2 m/imp gal, 23.5
[m/]US gal, 10 l x 100 km.

DIMENSIONS AND WEIGHT weight: 3-dr model 2,646 lb,
[1,2]00 kg - 5-dr model 2,822 lb, 1,280 kg.

OPTIONALS sunshine roof; power steering; Borg-Warner 35
[au]tomatic transmission, hydraulic torque converter and
[pl]anetary gears with 3 ratios (I 2.390, II 1.450, III 1, rev
[2.0]90), max ratio of converter at stall 2.37, power steering.
[m]ax speed 102 mph, 164 km/h, consumption 26.2 m/imp
[ga]l, 21.8 m/US gal, 10.8 l x 100 km.

118 hp power team

[Se]e 100 hp power team, except for:

ENGINE max power (DIN): 118 hp (86.8 kW) at 5,500 rpm;
[m]ax torque (DIN): 123 lb ft, 17 kg m (166.7 Nm) at 3,700
[rp]m; 59.4 hp/l (43.7 kW/l); Bosch CI injection system;
[fu]el feed: electric pump.

TRANSMISSION (for GLE only) gearbox: Borg-Warner 35
[au]tomatic transmission, hydraulic torque converter and pla-
[ne]tary gears with 3 ratios, max ratio of converter at stall
[2.3]7; ratios: I 2.390, II 1.450, III 1, rev 2.090; (for EMS
[on]ly) tyres: 175/70 HR x 15.

PERFORMANCE max speed: GLE 105 mph, 169 km/h - EMS
[10]8 mph, 174 km/h; power-weight ratio: EMS 22.7 lb/hp
[(30].6 lb/kW), 10.3 kg/hp (13.9 kg/kW); consumption: EMS
[23].2 m/imp gal, 21.8 m/US gal, 10.8 l x 100 km - GLE 25.2
[m/]imp gal, 21 m/US gal, 11.2 l x 100 km.

STEERING (for GLE only) servo; turns lock to lock: 3.65.

ELECTRICAL EQUIPMENT 840 W alternator.

DIMENSIONS AND WEIGHT weight: EMS 2,668 lb, 1,210
[kg] - GLE 2,822 lb, 1,280 kg.

BODY 5 seats, separate front seats, adjustable backrests;
[im]pact-absorbing bumper; hazard lights; heated rear window;
[fr]ont spoiler; tinted glass; (for EMS only) heated driving
[se]at; (for GLE only) heated front seats; (for GLE only)
[su]nshine roof.

OPTIONALS (for EMS only) sunshine roof; power steering.

145 hp power team

[Se]e 100 hp power team, except for:

ENGINE compression ratio: 7.2:1; max power (DIN): 145
[hp] (106.7 kW) at 5,000 rpm; max torque (DIN): 174 lb ft,
[24] kg m (235.4 Nm) at 3,000 rpm; 73 hp/l (53.8 kW/l);
[Bo]sch CI fuel injection system; centrifugal compressor,
[m]ounted coaxially with exhaust driven Garrett Airresearch
[tu]rbine; fuel feed: electric pump.

TRANSMISSION transfer chain in front of engine ratio
[0.]839:1; gearbox ratios: I 3.053, II 1.841, III 1.235, IV 0.839,
[re]v 3.358; width of rims: 5.5''; tyres: 3-dr model 195/60
[H]R x 15 - 5-dr model 180/65 HR x 390.

SAAB 900 EMS 3-dr Hatchback Sedan

VOLVO 240 Series

PERFORMANCE max speeds: (I) 36 mph, 58 km/h; (II) 59
mph, 95 km/h; (III) 88 mph, 142 km/h; (IV) 123 mph, 198
km/h; power-weight ratio: 3-dr model 18.7 lb/hp (25.4
lb/kW), 8.5 kg/hp (11.5 kg/kW); speed in top at 1,000 rpm:
21.9 mph, 35.3 km/h; consumption: 24.6 m/imp gal, 20.5
m/US gal, 11.5 l x 100 km.

STEERING servo.

ELECTRICAL EQUIPMENT 950 W alternator; electronic
ignition.

DIMENSIONS AND WEIGHT (for 3-dr model only) tracks:
56.30 in, 143 cm front, 56.69 in, 144 cm rear; weight: 3-dr
model 2,712 lb, 1,230 kg - 5-dr model 2,822 lb, 1,280 kg;
fuel tank: 12.1 imp gal, 14.5 US gal, 55 l.

BODY 5 seats, separate front seats, adjustable backrests;
heated driving seat; front and rear spoiler; sport steering
wheel; impact-absorbing bumpers; hazard lights; heated rear
window; tinted glass; light alloy wheels; (for 5-dr model
only) sunshine roof.

PRACTICAL INSTRUCTIONS engine oil: engine every 4,700
miles, 7,500 km; valve timing: 12° 40° 62° 2°.

OPTIONALS (for 3-dr model only) sunshine roof.

VOLVO   SWEDEN

240 Series

PRICES IN GB AND USA:	£	$
1 244 DL 4-dr Sedan	5,285*	7,485*
2 244 GL 4-dr Sedan	6,469*	—
3 244 GLE 4-dr Sedan	7,036*	—
4 245 DL 5-dr Station Wagon	5,903*	7,935*
5 245 GL 5-dr Station Wagon	—	—
6 245 GLE 5-dr Station Wagon	7,036*	—
7 242 GT 2-dr Sedan	—	8,585*

Power team:	Standard for:	Optional for:
97 hp	1,2,4,5	—
100 hp	3,6	1,2,4,5
140 hp	7	—

97 hp power team

ENGINE front, 4 stroke; 4 cylinders, in line; 121.2 cu in,
1,986 cc (3.50 x 3.15 in, 88.9 x 80 mm); compression ratio:
8.5:1; max power (DIN): 97 hp (71.4 kW) at 5,400 rpm;
max torque (DIN): 116 lb ft, 16 kg m (157 Nm) at 3,200
rpm; max engine rpm: 6,000; 48.8 hp/l (35.9 kW/l); cast
iron block, light alloy head; 5 crankshaft bearings; valves:
overhead, push-rods and rockers; camshafts: 1, side; lubrication: gear pump, full flow filter, 6.5 imp pt, 7.8 US pt, 3.7
l; 1 SU type HIF 6 horizontal carburettor; fuel feed: mecha-

VOLVO 244 GL 4-dr Sedan

nical pump; sealed circuit cooling, liquid, 16.7 imp pt, 20.1 US pt, 9.5 l.

TRANSMISSION driving wheels: rear; clutch: single dry plate (diaphragm); gearbox: mechanical; gears: 4, fully synchronized; ratios: I 3.790, II 2.160, III 1.370, IV 1, rev 3.680; lever: central; final drive: hypoid bevel; axle ratio: 3.910; width of rims: sedans 5'' - st. wagons 5.5''; tyres: 244 DL Sedan 165 SR x 14 - 244 GL Sedan 175 SR x 14 - 245 DL and GL models 185 SR x 14.

PERFORMANCE max speed: 103 mph, 165 km/h; power weight ratio: 244 DL Sedan 28.8 lb/hp (39.1 lb/kW), 13.1 kg/hp (17.8 kg/kW); carrying capacity: 1,191 lb, 540 kg; consumption: 28.2 m/imp gal, 23.5 m/US gal, 10 l x 100 km.

CHASSIS integral; front suspension: independent, lower wishbones, coil springs, damper struts, anti-roll bar; rear: rigid axle, twin trailing radius arms, transverse linkage bar, coil springs, anti-roll bar, telescopic dampers.

STEERING rack-and-pinion; turns lock to lock: 4.30.

BRAKES disc (front diameter 10.71 in, 27.2 cm, rear 11.61 in, 29.5 cm), dual circuit, rear compensator, servo.

ELECTRICAL EQUIPMENT 12 V; 60 Ah battery; 55 A alternator; Bosch distributor; 2 halogen headlamps.

DIMENSIONS AND WEIGHT wheel base: 103.94 in, 264 cm; tracks: 55.91 in, 142 cm front, 53.15 in, 135 cm rear; length: 192.91 in, 490 cm; width: 67.32 in, 171 cm; height: 56.30 in, 143 cm; ground clearance: 5.51 in, 14 cm; weight: 244 DL Sedan 2,794 lb, 1,270 kg - 244 GL Sedan 2,833 lb, 1,285 kg - 245 DL St. Wagon 2,911 kg - 245 GL St. Wagon 2,944 lb, 1,335 kg; turning circle: 32.1 ft, 9.8 m; fuel tank: 13.2 imp gal, 15.8 US gal, 60 l.

BODY 5 seats, separate front seats, reclining backrests, built-in adjustable headrests; heated rear window.

PRACTICAL INSTRUCTIONS fuel: 93 oct petrol; oil: engine 5.6 imp pt, 6.8 US pt, 3.2 l, SAE 10W-40, change every 6,200 miles, 10,000 km - gearbox 1.2 imp pt, 1.5 US pt, 0.7 l, SAE 80-90, change every 24,900 miles, 40,000 km - final drive 2.3 imp pt, 2.7 US pt, 1.3 l, SAE 90; greasing: none; sparking plug: 175°; tappet clearances: inlet and exhaust 0.016-0.018 in, 0.40-0.45 mm; tyre pressure: front 26 psi, 1.8 atm, rear 28 psi, 1.9 atm.

OPTIONALS limited slip differential; Borg-Warner 35 automatic transmission, hydraulic torque converter and planetary gears with 3 ratios (I 2.390, II 1.450, III 1, rev 2.090), max ratio of converter at stall 2; 100 hp engine.

100 hp power team

See 97 hp power team, except for:

ENGINE 129.8 cu in, 2,127 cc (3.62 x 3.15 in, 92 x 80 mm); max power (DIN): 100 hp (74 kW) at 5,250 rpm; max torque (DIN): 124 lb ft, 17.1 kg m (167.7 Nm) at 3,200 rpm;

VOLVO 245 GL 5-dr Station Wagon

47 hp/l (34.6 kW/l); camshafts: 1, overhead; Bosch CI fuel injection system.

TRANSMISSION width of rims: 5.5''; tyres: 185/70 SR x 14.

PERFORMANCE max speeds: (I) 35 mph, 56 km/h; (II) 55 mph, 88 km/h; (III) 80 mph, 128 km/h; (IV) 109 mph, 175 km/h; power-weight ratio: 244 GLE 29.5 lb/hp (40.1 lb/kW), 13.4 kg/hp (18.2 kg/kW).

STEERING servo.

ELECTRICAL EQUIPMENT transistorized Bosch ignition.

DIMENSIONS AND WEIGHT weight: 244 GLE 2,950 lb, 1,338 kg - 245 GLE 3,043 lb, 1,385 kg.

PRACTICAL INSTRUCTIONS oil: engine 5.8 imp pt, 7 US pt, 3.3 l; tappet clearances: inlet and exhaust 0.012-0.020 in, 0.30-0.50 mm; front tyre pressure: 28 psi, 1.9 atm.

140 hp power team

See 97 hp power team, except for:

ENGINE 141.3 cu in, 2,316 cc (3.78 x 3.15 in, 96 x 80 mm); compression ratio: 10:1; max power (DIN): 140 hp (103 kW) at 5,500 rpm; max torque (DIN): 144 lb ft, 19.9 kg m (195 Nm) at 4,500 rpm; 60.4 hp/l (44.5 kW/l); camshafts: 1, overhead; Bosch K-Jetronic fuel injection system.

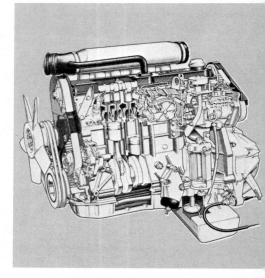

VOLVO 240 Diesel Series

TRANSMISSION gears: 4 overdrive; ratios: I 3.710, II 2.160, III 1.370, IV 1, overdrive 0.797, rev 3.680; axle ratio 3.730; width of rims: 5.5''; tyres: 185/70 HR x 14.

PERFORMANCE max speed: 115 mph, 185 km/h; power weight ratio: 20.7 lb/hp (28.1 lb/kW), 9.4 kg/hp (12.8 kg/kW); consumption: 25.9 m/imp gal, 21.6 m/US gal, 10 l x 100 km.

STEERING servo.

DIMENSIONS AND WEIGHT weight: 2,911 lb, 1,320 kg.

240 Diesel Series

1 244 DL D6 4-dr Sedan
2 244 GL D6 4-dr Sedan
3 245 DL D6 5-dr Station Wagon
4 245 GL D6 5-dr Station Wagon
5 244 GL D5 4-dr Sedan
6 245 GL D5 5-dr Station Wagon

Power team:	Standard for:	Optional for:
82 hp	1 to 4	—
70 hp	5,6	—

82 hp power team

ENGINE Volkswagen, Diesel; 6 cylinders, in line; 145 cu in, 2,383 cc (3.01 x 3.40 in, 76.5 x 86.4 mm); compression ratio: 23.5:1; max power (DIN): 82 hp (60.5 kW) at 4,8

VOLVO 244 GL D6 4-dr Sedan

; max torque (DIN): 104 lb ft, 14.3 kg m (140 Nm) at
00 rpm; 34.4 hp/l (25.4 kW/l); cast iron block, light
by head; 7 crankshaft bearings; valves: overhead; cam-
fts: 1, overhead, cogged belt; lubrication: full flow
er, 10.6 imp pt, 12.7 US pt, 6 l; Bosch VE fuel injection
tem; water-cooled, 16.7 imp pt, 20.1 US pt, 9.5 l.

ANSMISSION driving wheels; rear; clutch: single dry
te diaphragm; gearbox: mechanical; gears: 4, fully syn-
onized and overdrive; ratios: I 4.030, II 2.160, III 1.370,
1, overdrive 0.798 rev 3.680; lever: central; final drive:
oid bevel; axle ratio: 3.730; width of rims: sedans 5''
t. wagons 5.5''; tyres: sedans 175 SR x 14 - st. wagons
SR x 14.

RFORMANCE max speed: 92 mph, 148 km/h; power-
ight ratio: 244 DL D6 36.6 lb/hp (49.6 lb/kW), 16.6
hp (22.5 kg/kW); max speed in overdrive/top at 1,000
n: 24 mph, 38.7 km/h; consumption: 33.2 m/imp gal,
7 m/US gal, 8.5 l x 100 km.

ASSIS integral; front suspension: independent, Mc-
erson lower wishbones, coil springs, damper struts, anti-
bar; rear: rigid axle, twin trailing radius arms trans-
se linkage bar, coil springs, anti-roll bar; telescopic
npers.

EERING rack-and-pinion, servo; turns lock to lock: 3.50.

AKES disc, dual circuit, rear compensator, servo.

ECTRICAL EQUIPMENT 12 V; 90 Ah battery; 55 A alter-
or; 2 halogen headlamps.

MENSIONS AND WEIGHT wheel base: 104.33 in, 2.65 cm;
cks: sedans 55.91 in, 142 cm front, 53.15 in, 135 cm
r - st. wagons 56.30 in, 143 cm front, 53.54 in, 136
, rear; length: 192.13 in, 488 cm; width: 67.32 in, 171
; height: sedans 56.30 in, 143 cm - st. wagons 57.09 in,
cm; ground clearance: 5.51 in, 14 cm; weight: sedans
99 lb, 1,360 kg - st. wagons 3,131 lb, 1,420 kg; turning
cle: 32.1 ft, 9.8 m; fuel tank: 13.2 imp gal, 15.8 US gal,
l.

DY 5 seats, separate front seats, reclining backrests,
lt-in adjustable headrests; heated rear window; heated
ving seat.

ACTICAL INSTRUCTIONS fuel: Diesel oil; oil: engine
6 imp pt, 12.7 US pt, 6 l.

TIONALS Borg-Warner automatic transmission, hydraulic
que converter and planetary gears with 3 ratios (I 2.450,
1.450, III 1, rev 2.210), 3.540 axle ratio, max speed 90
h, 145 km/h.

70 hp power team

e 82 hp power team, except for:

GINE Audi, Diesel; 5-cylinders, in line: 121.2 cu in,
86 cc (3.01 x 3.40 in, 76.5 x 86.4 mm); compression ratio:
1; max power (DIN): 70 hp (51.5 kW) at 4,800 rpm;
x torque (DIN): 87 lb ft, 12 kg m (117.7 Nm) at 3,200
; max engine rpm: 5,000; 35.2 hp/l (25.9 kW/l); 6
nkshaft bearings.

ANSMISSION gearbox ratios: I 3.600, II 1.941, III 1.231,
0.857, rev 3.500; axle ratio: 4.300.

RFORMANCE max speed: 87 mph, 140 km/h; power-
ight ratio: 244 GL D5 42.4 lb/hp (57.6 lb/kW), 19.2 kg/hp
.1 kg/kW); consumption: 34.4 m/imp gal, 28.7 m/US
, 8.2 l x 100 km.

EERING rack-and-pinion.

ECTRICAL EQUIPMENT 70 A battery.

TIONALS 4-speed mechanical gearbox (I 4.030, II 2.160,
1.370, IV 1, rev 3.680).

260 Series

wer team	Standard for:	Optional for:
hp	1,4	—
hp	2,3,5,6	—

125 hp power team

GINE front, 4 stroke; 6 cylinders, Vee-slanted at 90°;
.6 cu in, 2,664 cc (3.46 x 2.87 in, 88 x 73 mm); compres-

---

sion ratio: 8.7:1; max power (DIN): 125 hp (92 kW) at
5,250 rpm; max torque (DIN): 145 lb ft, 20 kg m (196.1 Nm)
at 3,500 rpm; max engine rpm: 6,000; 46.9 hp/l (34.5 kW/l);
light alloy block and head; 4 crankshaft bearings; valves:
overhead, Vee-slanted, rockers; camshafts: 1, per cylinder
block, overhead; lubrication: gear pump, full flow filter, oil
cooler, 11.4 imp pt, 13.7 US pt, 6.5 l; 1 SU type HIF 6
horizontal carburettor; fuel feed: electric pump; sealed
circuit cooling, liquid, 19.2 imp pt, 23 US pt, 10.9 l.

TRANSMISSION driving wheels: rear; clutch: single dry
plate (diaphragm); gearbox: mechanical; gears: 4, fully
synchronized; ratios: I 3.710, II 2.160, III 1.370, IV 1,
rev 3.680; lever: central; final drive: hypoid bevel; axle
ratio: 3.730; width of rims: 5''; tyres: 175 HR x 14.

PERFORMANCE max speed: 106 mph, 170 km/h; weight
ratio: Sedan 24.2 lb/hp (32.9 lb/kW), 11 kg/hp (14.9 kg/kW);
carrying capacity: 1,103 lb, 500 kg; consumption: 25.7
m/imp gal, 21.4 m/US gal, 11 l x 100 km.

CHASSIS integral; front suspension: independent, lower
wishbones, coil springs, telescopic damper struts, anti-
roll bar; rear: rigid axle, twin trailing radius arms, transverse linkage bar, coil springs, telescopic dampers, anti-
roll bar.

STEERING rack-and-pinion, servo; turns lock to lock: 4.30.

BRAKES disc, servo.

VOLVO 244 GL D6

ELECTRICAL EQUIPMENT 12 V; 70 Ah battery; 770 W alternator; Bosch transistorized ignition; 2 halogen headlamps.

DIMENSIONS AND WEIGHT wheel base: 103.94 in, 264
cm; tracks: 56.30 in, 143 cm front, 53.54 in, 136 cm
rear; length: 192.91 in, 490 cm; width: 67.32 in, 171 cm;
height: 56.30 in, 143 cm; ground clearance: Sedan 5.51 in,
14 cm - St. Wagon 4.09 in, 10.4 cm; weight: Sedan 3,032
lb, 1,375 kg - St. Wagon 3,164 lb, 1,435 kg; turning circle:
32.1 ft, 9.8 m; fuel tank: 13.2 imp gal, 15.8 US gal, 60 l.

BODY 5 seats, separate front seats, reclining backrests,
built-in adjustable headrests; heated rear window; heated
driving rear.

PRACTICAL INSTRUCTIONS fuel: 93 oct petrol; oil: engine
10.6 imp pt, 12.7 US pt, 6 l, SAE 10W-40, change every
6,200 miles, 10,000 km - gearbox 1.9 imp pt, 2.3 US pt,
1.1 l, SAE 90, change every 24,900 miles, 40,000 km -
final drive 2.8 imp pt, 3.4 US pt, 1.6 l, SAE 90 EP, change
every 24,900 miles, 40,000 km; greasing: none; tappet
clearances: inlet 0.006 in, 0.15 mm, exhaust 0.012 in,
0.30 mm; valve timing: 32° 72° 20° 32°; tyre pressure:
front 26 psi, 1.8 atm, rear 27 psi, 1.9 atm.

OPTIONALS limited slip differential; 5-speed mechanical
gearbox; Borg-Warner 55 automatic transmission, hydraulic
torque converter and planetary gears with 3 ratios (I 2.390,
II 1.450, III 1, rev 2.090), max ratio of converter at stall 2,
3.540 axle ratio; air-conditioning.

140 hp power team

See 125 hp power team, except for:

ENGINE max power (DIN): 140 hp (103 kW) at 6,000 rpm;
max torque (DIN): 150 lb ft, 20.7 kg m (203 Nm) at 3,000
rpm; 52.6 hp l (38.7 kW/l); Bosch electronic fuel injection
system.

TRANSMISSION gears: 4 and overdrive, fully synchronized; ratios: I 3.710, II 2.160, III 1.370, IV 1, overdrive
0.797, rev 3.680; (for 264 TE only Borg-Warner automatic
transmission, hydraulic torque converter and planetary gears
with 3 ratios: I 2.450, II 1.450, III 1, rev 2.810); axle ratio:
3.730 - 264 TE 3.540; width of rims: 5.5'' tyres: 185/70
HR x 14.

PERFORMANCE max speed: 109 mph, 175 km/h; power-
weight ratio: 264 GLE 21.6 lb/hp (29.4 lb/kW), 9.8 kg/hp
(13.3 kg/kW).

STEERING for 264 TE only turns lock to lock: 3.50.

DIMENSIONS AND WEIGHT wheel base: 264 TE 131.49 in,
334 cm; length: 264 TE 220.47 in, 560 cm - 262 C 192.12 in,
488 cm; height: 262 C 53.54 in, 136 cm; weight: 264 TE
3,605 lb, 1,635 kg - 262 C 3,197 lb, 1,450 kg.

BODY for 264 TE 6 seats; air-conditioning; electric windows.

OPTIONALS for 264 GLE, 265 GL and 262 C Borg-Warner
automatic transmission, hydraulic torque converter and planetary gears with 3 ratios (I 2.450, II 1.450, III 1, rev
2.810), 3.540 axle ratio.

VOLVO 262 C 2-dr Coupé

FELBER · SWITZERLAND

Excellence Coupé/Roadster

PRICES EX WORKS: Excellence Coupé 53,000 francs
Excellence Roadster 57,000 francs

ENGINE Pontiac, front, 4 stroke; 8 cylinders, Vee-slanted at 90°; 400 cu in, 6,555 cc (4.12 x 3.75 in, 104.6 x 95.2 mm); compression ratio: 8:1; max power (DIN): 225 hp (161.7 kW) at 4,000 rpm; max torque (DIN): 320 lb ft, 44.1 kg m (432.3 Nm) at 2,800 rpm; max engine rpm: 4,400; 34.3 hp/l (24.7 kW/l); cast iron block and head; 5 crankshaft bearings; valves: overhead, in line, push-rods and rockers, hydraulic tappets; camshafts: 1, at centre of Vee; lubrication: gear pump, full flow filter, 10 imp pt, 12 US pt, 5.7 l; 1 Rochester downdraught 4-barrel carburettor; cleaner air system; exhaust system with catalytic converter; fuel feed: mechanical pump; water-cooled, 30.6 imp pt, 36.8 US pt, 17.4 l.

TRANSMISSION driving wheels: rear; Turbo-Hydramatic automatic transmission, hydraulic torque converter and planetary gears with 3 ratios, max ratio of converter at stall 2.5, possible manual selection; ratios: I 2.520, II 1.520, III 1, rev 1.920; lever: central; final drive: hypoid bevel, limited slip differential; axle ratio: 3.230; width of rims: 7''; tyres: GR70 x 15.

PERFORMANCE max speed: about 118 mph, 190 km/h; power-weight ratio 17.1 lb/hp (23.9 lb/kW), 7.8 kg/hp (10.8 kg/kW); carrying capacity: 926 lb, 420 kg; consumption: 15.7 m/imp gal, 13.1 m/US gal, 18 l x 100 km.

CHASSIS integral with separate partial frame; front suspension: independent, wishbones (lower trailing links), coil springs, anti-roll bar, telescopic dampers; rear: rigid axle, semi-elliptic leafsprings, anti-roll bar, telescopic dampers.

STEERING recirculating ball, variable ratio servo; turns lock to lock: 2.41.

BRAKES front disc, internal radial fins, rear drum, dual circuit, servo.

ELECTRICAL EQUIPMENT 12 V; 3,200 W battery; 42 A alternator; Delco-Remy transistorized ignition; 4 headlamps.

DIMENSIONS AND WEIGHT wheel base: 108.20 in, 275 cm; tracks: 61.30 in, 156 cm front, 60 in, 152 cm rear; length: 196.80 in, 500 cm; width: 73.40 in, 186 cm; height: 49.30 in, 125 cm; ground clearance: 5.20 in, 13.2 cm; weight: 3,859 lb, 1,750 kg; turning circle: 41.3 ft, 12.6 m; fuel tank: 17.6 imp gal, 21 US gal, 80 l.

BODY coupé or roadster; 2 doors; 2+2 seats; electric windows; tinted glass; air-conditioning; sport wheels.

PRACTICAL INSTRUCTIONS fuel: 100 oct petrol.

OPTIONALS electric sunshine roof; leather upholstery; metallic spray.

FELBER Excellence Coupé

Oasis

PRICE EX WORKS: 46,500 francs

ENGINE International, front, 4 stroke; 8 cylinders, Vee-slanted at 90°; 345 cu in, 5,654 cc (3.88 x 3.66 in, 98.5 x 92.9 mm); compression ratio: 8.05; max power (DIN): 165 hp (121.5 kW) at 3,600 rpm; max torque (DIN): 293 lb ft, 40.4 kg m (396 Nm) at 2,000 rpm; max engine rpm: 3,800; 29.2 hp/l (21.5 kW/l); cast iron block and head; 5 crankshaft bearings; valves: overhead, in line, push-rods and rockers, hydraulic tappets; camshafts: 1, at centre of Vee; lubrication: rotary pump, full flow filter, 13.2 imp pt, 15.9 US pt, 7.5 l; 1 downdraught twin barrel carburettor; dual exhaust system; fuel feed: mechanical pump; water-cooled, 34.3 imp pt, 41.2 US pt, 19.5 l.

TRANSMISSION driving wheels: front and rear with lockable front differential in transfer box; Torqueflite automatic transmission, hydraulic torque converter and planetary gears with 3 ratios, max ratio of converter at stall 2.16, possible manual selection; ratios: I 2.450, II 1.450, III 1, rev 2.200; lever: central; final drive: hypoid bevel, limited slip differential; axle ratio: 3.070; width of rims: 8.5''; tyres: LR78 x 15.

PERFORMANCE max speed: about 106 mph, 170 km/h; power-weight ratio: 21.8 lb/hp (29.6 lb/kW), 9.9 kg/hp (13.4 kg/kW); carrying capacity: 1,632 lb, 740 kg; consumption: 17.7 m/imp gal, 14.7 m/US gal, 16 l x 100 km.

FELBER Oasis

CHASSIS box type perimeter frame; front and rear suspension: rigid axle, semi-elliptic leafsprings, telescopic dampers.

STEERING worm and roller, servo.

BRAKES front disc (diameter 11.81 in, 30 cm), rear drum, dual circuit, servo.

ELECTRICAL EQUIPMENT 12 V; 65 Ah battery; 65 A alternator; 2 headlamps.

DIMENSIONS AND WEIGHT wheel base: 100 in, 254 cm; tracks: 57 in, 145 cm front and rear; length: 166.20 in, 422 cm; width: 70 in, 178 cm; height: 65.70 in, cm; ground clearance: 7.60 in, 19.5 cm weight: 3,598 lb, 1,632 kg; turning circle: 36.4 ft, 11.1 m; fuel tank: imp gal, 19 US gal, 72 l.

BODY estate car/station wagon; 2+1 doors; 5 seat separate front seats, reclining backrests; built-in he rests; tinted glass; rear window wiper-washer; hea rear window.

PRACTICAL INSTRUCTIONS fuel: 91 oct petrol.

OPTIONALS air-conditioning; sunshine roof; leather uph stery; sport wheels; hydropneumatic suspension: meta spray.

MONTEVERDI · SWITZERLAN

Sierra

PRICE EX WORKS: 69,200 francs

ENGINE Chrysler, front, 4 stroke; 8 cylinders, Vee-slan at 90°; 359.9 cu in, 5,898 cc (4 x 3.58 in, 101.6 x 90.9 m compression ratio: 8.5:1; max power (DIN): 180 hp (13 kW) at 4,000 rpm; max torque (DIN): 287 lb ft, 39.6 kg (388 Nm) at 2,400 rpm; 30.5 hp/l (22.5 kW/l); 5 cranks bearings; valves: overhead, in line, hydraulic tappe camshafts: 1, at centre of Vee; lubrication: rotary pu full flow filter, 13.2 imp pt, 15.8 US pt, 7.5 l; 1 Ca downdraught twin barrel carburettor; fuel feed: mechan pump; water-cooled, 28.2 imp pt, 33.8 US pt, 16 l.

TRANSMISSION driving wheels: rear; gearbox: Torquef automatic transmission, hydraulic torque converter and netary gears with 3 ratios, max ratio of converter stall 2.3, possible manual selection; ratios: I 2.450, 1.450, III 1, rev 2.200; lever: central; final drive: hyp bevel, limited slip differential; axle ratio: 2.710; wi of rims: 6''; tyres: 215/70 VR x 14.

PERFORMANCE max speed: about 124 mph, 200 km power-weight ratio: 19.6 lb/hp (26.6 lb/kW), 8.9 kg (12 kg/kW); carrying capacity: 1,554 lb, 750 kg; speed direct drive at 1,000 rpm: 28.6 mph, 46 km/h; consu tion: 20.2 m/imp gal, 16.8 m/US gal, 14 l x 100 km.

CHASSIS integral; front suspension: upper wishbones lower horizontal arms combined with trailing radius ro coil springs, anti-roll bar, adjustable telescopic dampe rear: de Dion rigid axle, semi-elliptic leafsprings, adj able telescopic dampers.

STEERING worm and roller, servo.

BRAKES front disc (diameter 11.8 in, 30 cm), rear dr dual circuit, servo; lining area: total 139.5 sq in, sq cm.

ELECTRICAL EQUIPMENT 12 V; 65 Ah battery; 55 A ternator; 4 halogen headlamps.

DIMENSIONS AND WEIGHT wheel base: 112.20 in, cm; tracks: 59.44 in, 151 cm front, 58.66 in, 149 cm re length: 192.12 in, 488 cm; width: 71.65 in, 182 cm; heig 55.12 in, 140 cm; ground clearance: 5.9 in, 15 cm; weig 3,528 lb, 1,600 kg; turning circle: 41.9 ft, 12.8 m; f tank: 18 imp gal, 21.6 US gal, 82 l.

BODY saloon/sedan; 4 doors; 5 seats, separate front sea air-conditioning; automatic speed control.

VARIATIONS

ENGINE 317.9 cu in, 5,210 cc (3.91 x 3.31 in, 99.3 x 8 mm), max power (DIN) 160 hp (117.8 kW) at 3,500 r max torque (DIN) 287 lb ft, 39.6 kg m (388.4 Nm) at 2, rpm, 30.7 hp/l (22.6 kW/l).
PERFORMANCE power-weight ratio 22 lb/hp (30 lb/k 10 kg/hp (13.6 kg/kW).

OPTIONALS 2.450 axle ratio.

Monteverdi

MONTEVERDI Sierra

lubrication: rotary pump, full flow filter, 13.2 imp pt, 15.9 US pt, 7.5 l; 1 downdraught twin barrel carburettor; dual exhaust system; fuel feed: mechanical pump; water-cooled. 34.3 imp pt, 41.2 US pt, 19.5 l.

TRANSMISSION driving wheels: front and rear with lockable front differential in transfer box; Torqueflite automatic transmission, hydraulic torque converter and planetary gears with 3 ratios, max ratio of converter at stall 2.16, possible manual selection; ratios: I 2.450, II 1.450, III 1 (transfer box 2.030 ratio), rev 2.200; lever: central; final drive: hypoid bevel, limited slip differential; axle ratio: 3.070; width of rims: 8.5''; tyres: LR 78 x 15.

PERFORMANCE max speed: about 106 mph, 170 km/h; power-weight ratio: 26.7 lb/hp (36.3 lb/kW), 12.1 kg/hp (16.5 kg/kW); carrying capacity: 1,632 lb, 740 kg; acceleration: 0-50 mph (0-80 km/h) 9.8 sec; consumption: 17.7 m/imp gal, 14.7 m/US gal, 16 l x 100 km.

CHASSIS box-type perimeter frame; front and rear suspension: rigid axle, semi-elliptic leafsprings, telescopic dampers.

STEERING worm and roller, servo.

BRAKES front disc (diameter 11.81 in, 30 cm), rear drum, dual circuit, servo.

ELECTRICAL EQUIPMENT 12 V; 65 Ah battery; 65 A alternator; 4 hedalamps.

DIMENSIONS AND WEIGHT wheel base: 100 in, 254 cm; tracks: 58.27 in, 148 cm front and rear; length: 170.87 in, 434 cm; width: 70.47 in, 179 cm; height: 68.11 in, 173 cm; ground clearance: 7.48 in, 19 cm; weight: 4,410 lb, 2,000 kg; turning circle: 36.4 ft, 11.1 m; fuel tank: 18 imp gal, 21.6 US gal, 82 l.

BODY estate car/station wagon; 2+1 doors; 5 seats, separate front seats, reclining backrests; built-in headrests on front and rear seats; folding rear seat; tinted glass; air-conditioning.

PRACTICAL INSTRUCTIONS fuel: oct petrol.

VARIATIONS

ENGINE Nissan, Diesel, 6 cylinders vertical in line, 198 cu in, 3,245 cc (3.27 x 3.94 in, 83 x 100 mm), 22:1 compression ratio, max power (DIN) 82 hp (60.5 kW) at 3,800 rpm, max torque (DIN) 138 lb ft, 19.1 kg m (187 Nm) at 1,200-1,600 rpm, 25.3 hp/l (18.7 kW/l), 7 crankshaft bearings, indirect injection system.
TRANSMISSION 3.540 axle ratio.
PERFORMANCE max speed 90 mph, 145 km/h, power-weight ratio 53.8 lb/hp (72.9 lb/kW), 24.4 kg/hp (33.1 kg/kW), consumption 28.2 m/imp gal, 23.5 m/US gal, 10 l x 100 km.
ELECTRICAL EQUIPMENT 85 Ah battery.
PRACTICAL INSTRUCTIONS fuel Diesel oil.

OPTIONALS 4-speed mechanical gearbox; oil cooler.

MONTEVERDI Sierra Cabriolet

Sierra Cabriolet

e Sierra, except for:

ICE EX WORKS: 89,000 francs

ANSMISSION axle ratio: 2.450 (standard).

RFORMANCE max speed: 130 mph, 210 km/h; power-eight ratio: 17.2 lb/hp (23.3 lb/kW), 7.8 kg/hp (10.6 /kW).

MENSIONS AND WEIGHT wheel base: 107.87 in, 274 cm; ngth: 184.25 in, 468 cm; height: 50.39 in, 128 cm; turning cle: 39.7 ft, 12.1 m.

DY convertible; 2 doors; 5 seats; separate front seats.

Sahara

ICE EX WORKS: 37,300 francs

NGINE international, front, 4 stroke; 8 cylinders, Vee-anted at 90°; 345 cu in, 5,654 cc (3.88 x 3.66 in, 98.5 x 92.9 n); compression ratio: 8.05; max power (DIN): 165 hp 21.5 kW) at 3,600 rpm; max torque (DIN): 293 lb ft, .4 kg m (396 Nm) at 2,000 rpm; max engine rpm: 3,800; .2 hp/l (21.5 kW/l); cast iron block and head; 5 crank-aft bearings; valves: overhead, in line, push-rods and ckers, hydraulic tappets; camshafts: 1, at centre of Vee;

MONTEVERDI Sahara

Safari

PRICE EX WORKS: 54,900 francs

ENGINE International front, 4 stroke; 8 cylinders, Vee-slanted at 90°; 345 cu in, 5,654 cc (3.88 x 3.66 in, 98.5 x 92.9 mm); compression ratio: 8.05; max power (DIN): 165 hp (121.5 kW) at 3,600 rpm; max torque (DIN): 293 lb ft, 40.4 kg m (396 Nm) at 2,000 rpm; max engine rpm: 3,800; 29.2 hp/l (21.5 kW/l); cast iron block and head; 5 crankshaft bearings; valves: overhead, in line, push-rods and rockers, hydraulic tappets; camshafts: 1, at centre of Vee; lubrication: rotary pump, full flow filter, 13.2 imp pt, 15.9 US pt, 7.5 l; downdraught twin barrel carburettor; fuel feed: mechanical pump; water-cooled, 34.3 imp pt, 41.2 US pt, 19.5 l.

TRANSMISSION driving wheels: front and rear with lockable front differential in transfer box; gearbox: Torqueflite automatic transmission, hydraulic torque converter and planetary gears with 3 ratios, max ratio of converter at stall 2.16, possible manual selection; ratios: I 2.450, II 1.450, III 1 (transfer box 2.030 ratio), rev 2.200; lever: central; final drive: hypoid bevel, limited slip differential; axle ratio: 3.070; width of rims: 7''; tyres: 225/235 x 15.

PERFORMANCE max speed: about 93 mph, 150 km/h; power-weight ratio: 25.4 lb/hp (34.5 lb/kW), 11.5 kg/hp (15.6 kg/kW); carrying capacity: 1,632 lb, 740 kg; consumption: 17.7 m/imp gal, 14.7 m/US gal, 16 l x 100 km.

CHASSIS box-type perimeter frame; front and rear suspension: rigid axle, semi-elliptic leafsprings, anti-roll bar, adjustable telescopic dampers.

STEERING ZF, recirculating ball, servo.

BRAKES front disc (diameter 11.81 in, 30 cm), front internal radial fins, rear drum, dual circuit, servo.

ELECTRICAL EQUIPMENT 12 V; 65 Ah battery; 55 A alternator; 4 headlamps.

DIMENSIONS AND WEIGHT wheel base: 100 in, 254 cm; front and rear track: 58.27 in, 148 cm; length: 179.50 in, 456 cm; width: 70.87 in, 180 cm; height: 68.50 in, 174 cm; ground clearance: 7.48 in, 19 cm; weight: 4,189 lb, 1,900 kg; turning circle (between walls): 35.8 ft, 10.9 m; fuel tank: 18 imp gal, 21.6 US gal, 82 l.

BODY estate car/station wagon; 2 + 1 doors; 5 seats, separate front seats, reclining backrests; built-in headrests on front and rear seats; folding rear seat; air-conditioning.

PRACTICAL INSTRUCTIONS fuel: 91 oct petrol.

VARIATIONS

ENGINE Chrysler, 439.7 cu in, 7,206 cc (4.32 x 3.75 in, 109.7 x 95.2 mm), 9.7:1 compression ratio, max power (DIN) 305 hp (224.5 kW) at 4,200 rpm, max torque (DIN) 450 lb ft, 62.1 kg m (609 Nm) at 3,300 rpm, 42.3 hp/l (31.2 kW/l).
PERFORMANCE max speed 124 mph, 200 km/h, power-weight ratio 13.7 lb/hp (18.6 lb/kW), 6.2 kg/hp (8.5 kg/kW), consumption 11.3 m/imp gal, 9.4 m/US gal, 25 l x 100 km.

OPTIONALS 3.310 3.730 4.270 axle ratios; 4-speed mechanical gearbox.

MONTEVERDI Safari

kg/hp (11.3 kg/kW); carrying capacity: 353 lb, 160 kg; speed in direct drive at 1,000 rpm: 18 mph, 29 km/h; consumption: 29.4 m/imp gal, 24.5 m/US gal, 9.6 l x 100 km.

CHASSIS integral, box-type reinforced platform; front suspension: independent, coil springs/telescopic damper struts, auxiliary rubber springs, lower wishbones, lower links; rear: independent, oblique semi-trailing arms, auxiliary rubber springs, coil springs, telescopic dampers.

STEERING rack-and-pinion.

BRAKES disc (diameter 10.71 in, 27.2 cm), dual circuit, servo.

ELECTRICAL EQUIPMENT 12 V; 36 Ah battery; 630 W alternator; Bosch distributor; 2 headlamps.

DIMENSIONS AND WEIGHT wheel base: 99.21 in, 252 cm; tracks: 63.78 in, 162 cm front, 61.02 in, 155 cm rear; length: 145.67 in, 370 cm; width: 61.42 in, 156 cm; ground clearance: 7.90 in, 18 cm; weight: 1,654 lb, 750 kg; turning circle: 29.5 ft, 9 m; fuel tank: 11 imp gal, 13.2 US gal, 50 l.

BODY roadster, in plastic material; 2 doors; 2 seats.

PRACTICAL INSTRUCTIONS fuel: 92 oct petrol; oil: engine 7.4 imp pt, 8.9 US pt, 4.2 l, SAE 20W-50, change every 3,700 miles, 6,000 km - gearbox 1.8 imp pt, 2.1 US pt, 1 l, SAE 80, change every 14,800 miles, 24,000 km - final drive 1.6 imp pt, 1.9 US pt, 0.9 l, SAE 90, no change recommended; greasing: none; sparking plug: 145°.

VARIATIONS

ENGINE BMW, 107.8 cu in, 1,766 cc (3.50 x 2.80 in, 89 x 71 mm), max power (DIN) 98 hp (72.1 kW) at 5,800 rpm, max torque (DIN) 105 lb ft, 14.5 kg m (142.2 Nm) at 4,000 rpm, 55.5 hp/l (40.8 kW/l).
TRANSMISSION 3.900 axle ratio.
PERFORMANCE power-weight ratio 17 lb/hp (22.9 lb/kW), 7.7 kg/hp (10.4 kg/kW), consumption 28.5 m/imp gal, 23.7 m/US gal, 9.9 l x 100 km.

ENGINE BMW, 121.4 cu in, 1,990 cc (3.50 x 3.15 in, 89 x 80 mm), 8.1:1 compression ratio, max power (DIN) 109 hp (80.2 kW) at 5,800 rpm, max torque (DIN) 116 lb ft, 16 m (156.9 Nm) at 3,700 rpm, 54.8 hp/l (40.3 kW/l).
TRANSMISSION 3.900 axle ratio.
PERFORMANCE power-weight ratio 15.2 lb/hp (20.7 lb/kW), 6.9 kg/hp (9.4 kg/kW), consumption 28.2 m/imp gal, 23.5 m/US gal, 10 l x 100 km.

ENGINE BMW, 121.4 cu in, 1,990 cc (3.50 x 3.15 in, 89 x 80 mm), 9.3:1 compression ratio, max power (DIN) 125 hp (92 kW) at 5,700 rpm, max torque (DIN) 127 lb ft, 17.5 kg m (171.6 Nm) at 4,350 rpm, 62.8 hp/l (46.2 kW/l), Bosch K-Jetronic injection system, electric pump.
TRANSMISSION 3.640 axle ratio.
PERFORMANCE max speed 137 mph, 220 km/h, power-weight ratio 13.2 lb/hp (18.1 lb/kW), 6 kg/hp (8.2 kg/kW), consumption 32.1 m/imp gal, 26.7 m/US gal, 8.8 l x 100 km.

OPTIONALS 5-speed fully synchronized mechanical gearbox (I 3.368, II 2.160, III 1.579, IV 1.241, V 1, rev 4); 3.64 or 3.450 axle ratio; 6'' or 7'' wide rims.

SBARRO   SWITZERLAND

Replica BMW 328 Standard

PRICE EX WORKS: 33,000 francs

ENGINE BMW, front, 4 stroke; 4 cylinders, slanted at 30°, in line; 96 cu in, 1,573 cc (3.31 x 2.80 in, 84 x 71 mm); compression ratio: 8.3:1; max power (DIN): 90 hp (66.2 kW) at 6,000 rpm; max torque (DIN): 91 lb ft, 12.5 kg m (122.6 Nm) at 4,000 rpm; max engine rpm: 6,200; 57.2 hp/l (42.1 kW/l); cast iron block, light alloy head; hemispherical combustion chambers; 5 crankshaft bearings; valves: overhead, Vee-slanted at 52°, rockers; camshafts: 1, overhead; lubrication: gear pump, full flow filter, 7.4 imp pt, 8.9 US pt, 4.2 l; 1 Solex DIDTA 32/32 downdraught twin barrel carburettor; fuel feed: mechanical pump; water-cooled, 12.3 imp pt, 14.8 US pt, 7 l.

TRANSMISSION driving wheels: rear; clutch: single dry plate (diaphragm), hydraulically controlled; gearbox: mechanical; gears: 4, fully synchronized; ratios: I 3.764, II 2.022, III 1.320, IV 1, rev 4.096; lever: central; final drive: hypoid bevel; axle ratio: 4.100; width of rims: 5''.

PERFORMANCE max speeds: (I) 30 mph, 48 km/h; (II) 55 mph, 89 km/h; (III) 85 mph, 136 km/h; (IV) 112 mph, 180 km/h; power-weight ratio: 18.3 lb/hp (24.9 lb/kW), 8.3

SBARRO Replica BMW 328 Standard

Replica BMW 328 America

e Replica BMW 328 Standard, except for:

RICE EX WORKS: 42,000 francs

NGINE 6 cylinders, in line; 152.2 cu in, 2,494 cc (3.39 x 2.82 , 86 x 71.6 mm); compression ratio: 9:1; max power DIN): 150 hp (110.4 kW) at 6,000 rpm; max torque (DIN): 4 lb ft, 21.2 kg m (207.9 Nm) at 4,000 rpm; 60.1 hp/l 4.2 kW/l); polispherical combustion chambers; 7 crank- aft bearings; lubrication: 10 imp pt, 12 US pt, 5.7 l; 1 lex 4A1 downdraught twin barrel carburettor; cooling stem: 21.1 imp pt, 25.4 US pt, 12 l.

RFORMANCE max speed: 132 mph, 212 km/h; power- eight ratio: 13.3 lb/hp (18 lb/kW), 6 kg/hp (8.2 kg/kW); eed in direct drive at 1,000 rpm: 21.3 mph, 34.2 km/h; nsumption: 25.9 m/imp gal, 21.6 m/US gal, 10.9 l x 100 .

LECTRICAL EQUIPMENT 55 Ah battery; 770 W alternator.

MENSIONS AND WEIGHT wheel base: 100.39 in, 255 cm; ont and rear track: 64.17 in, 163 cm; length: 149.61 in, 0 cm; width: 67.32 in, 171 cm; weight: 1,989 lb, 902 kg.

RACTICAL INSTRUCTIONS oil: engine 10 imp pt, 12 US , 5.7 l; tappet clearances: inlet 0.010 in, 0.25 mm, exhaust 012 in, 0.30 mm; valve timing: 6° 50° 50° 6°.

VARIATIONS

NGINE 170.1 cu in, 2,788 cc (3.39 x 3.15 in, 86 x 80 mm); 3:1 compression ratio, max power (DIN) 170 hp (125.1 V) at 5,800 rpm, max torque (DIN) 172 lb ft, 23.8 kg m 23.4 Nm) at 4,000 rpm, 6,500 max engine rpm, 61 hp/l 4.9 kW/l).
RFORMANCE power-weight ratio 11.7 lb/hp (15.9 lb/kW), 3 kg/hp (7.2 kg/kW), consumption 25.7 m/imp gal, 21.4 /US gal, 11 l x 100 km.

NGINE 182 cu in, 2,982 cc (3.50 x 3.15 in, 89 x 80 mm), 1 compression ratio, max power (DIN) 175 hp (128.8 kW) 5,500 rpm, max torque (DIN) 185 lb ft, 25.5 kg m (250.1 m) at 4,500 rpm, 6,500 max engine rpm, 58.7 hp/l (43.2 ectric thermostatic fan.
RFORMANCE power-weight ratio 11.5 lb/hp (15.4 lb/kW), 2 kg/hp (7 kg/kW), consumption 24.8 m/imp gal, 20.6 /US gal, 11.4 l x 100 m.
RACTICAL INSTRUCTIONS valve timing 14° 54° 54° 14°.

NGINE 195.6 cu in, 3,205 cc (3.50 x 3.39 in, 89 x 86 mm), ax power (DIN) 200 hp (147.2 kW) at 5,500 rpm, max rque (DIN) 210 lb ft, 29 kg m (284.4 Nm) at 4,250 rpm, .4 hp/l (45.9 kW/l), Bosch L-Jetronic electronic injection, ectric pump.
RFORMANCE power-weight ratio 9.9 lb/hp (13.4 lb/kW), 5 kg/hp (6.1 kg/kW).

Stash HS Cabriolet

RICE EX WORKS: 100,000 francs

NGINE Mercedes-Benz, centre-rear, 4 stroke; 8 cylinders,

SBARRO Stash HS Cabriolet

Vee-slanted at 90°; 417 cu in, 6,834 cc (4.21 x 3.74 in, 107 x 95 mm); compression ratio: 8.8:1; max power (DIN): 286 hp (210,5 kW) at 4,250 rpm; max torque (DIN): 406 lb ft, 56 kg m (549.2 Nm) at 3,000 rpm; max engine rpm: 5,300; 41.8 hp/l (30.8 kW/l); cast iron block, light alloy head; 5 crankshaft bearings; valves: overhead, finger levers; camshafts: 2, 1 per bank, overhead; lubrication: gear pump, full flow filter, dry sump, oil cooler, 21.1 imp pt, 25.4 US pt, 12 l; Bosch K-Jetronic injection; fuel feed: electric pump; water-cooled, viscous coupling thermostatic fan, 26.4 imp pt, 31.7 US pt, 15 l.

TRANSMISSION driving wheels: rear; clutch: MB automa- tic transmission, hydraulic torque converter and planetary gears with 3 ratios, max ratio of converter at stall 2.5, possible manual selection; ratios: I 2.310, II 1.460, III 1, rev 1.840; lever: central or steering column; final drive: hypoid bevel; axle ratio: 2.650; width of rims: 9'' front, 13'' rear; tyres: 9'' x 15 front, 13'' x 15 rear.

PERFORMANCE max speed: about 149 mph, 240 km/h; power-weight ratio: 10.8 lb/hp (14.7 lb/kW), 4.9 kg/hp (6.6 kg/kW); carrying capacity: 926 lb, 420 kg; speed in direct drive/top at 1,000 rpm: 28.3 mph, 45.5 km/h; con- sumption: 47.7 m/imp gal, 14.7 m/US gal, 16 l x 100 km.

CHASSIS integral, box-type reinforced platform; front suspension: independent, wishbones, coil springs/telescopic dampers struks; rear: independent, wishbones, coil springs, telescopic dampers, anti-roll bar.

STEERING recirculating ball.

BRAKES disc, dual circuit, rear compensator, servo.

ELECTRICAL EQUIPMENT 12 V; 88 Ah battery; 1,050 W alternator; Bosch (transistorized) distributor; 2 iodine headlamps.

DIMENSIONS AND WEIGHT wheel base: 104.33 in, 265 cm; tracks: 55.90 in, 142 cm front, 62.99 in, 160 cm rear; length: 181.10 in, 460 cm; width: 74.80 in, 190 cm; height: 45.67 in, 116 cm; ground clearance: 5.91 in, 15 cm; weight: 3,087 lb, 1,400 kg; fuel tank: 11 imp gal, 13.2 US gal, 50 l.

BODY convertible, in plastic material; 2 doors; 2+2 seats; detachable roof.

PRACTICAL INSTRUCTIONS fuel: 98 oct petrol.

OPTIONALS limited slip differential.

SBARRO Stash HS Cabriolet

Windhound 4 x 4

PRICE EX WORKS: 60,000 francs

ENGINE BMW, front, 4 stroke; 6 cylinders, in line; 182 cu in, 2,982 cc (3.58 x 3.15 in, 89 x 80 mm); compression ratio: 8:1; max power (DIN): 175 hp (128.8 kW) at 5,500 rpm; max torque (DIN): 185 lb ft, 25.5 kg m (250.1 Nm) at 4,500 rpm; max engine rpm: 6,500; 58.7 hp/l (43.2 kW/l); cast iron block, light alloy head, polispherical combustion chambers; 7 crankshaft bearings; valves: overhead, Vee- slanted, rockers; camshafts: 1, overhead; lubrication: rotary pump, full flow filter, 10 imp pt, 12 US pt, 5.7 l; Bosch electronic injection, exhaust thermal reactor; fuel feed: mechanical pump; water-cooled, 21.1 imp pt, 25.4 US pt, 12 l.

SBARRO Replica BMW 328

SBARRO Windhound 4 x 4

WINDHOUND 4 x 4

TRANSMISSION driving wheels: front and rear; clutch: single dry plate; gearbox: mechanical; gears: 4, fully synchronized; ratios: I 3,855, II 2.203, III 1.402, IV 1, rev 4.030; gear and transfer levers: central; final drive: hypoid bevel; axle ratio (front and rear): 3.640; tyres: 9 x 15 front, 11 x 15 rear.

PERFORMANCE max speeds: (I) 118 mph, 190 km/h; power-weight ratio: 23.3 lb/hp (31.7 lb/kW), 10.6 kg/hp (14.4 kg/kW); consumption: 15.4 m/imp gal, 18.5 m/US gal, 14.4 l x 100 km.

CHASSIS integral, box-type reinforced platform; front suspension: independent, by Mc Pherson, coil springs/telescopic damper struts, lower wishbones, torsion bar, automatic levelling control; rear: independent, oblique semi-trailing arms, coil springs, torsion bar, automatic levelling control.

STEERING rack and pinion.

BRAKES drum, dual circuit, servo.

ELECTRICAL EQUIPMENT 12 V; 65 Ah battery; 55 A alternator; 4 headlamps.

DIMENSIONS AND WEIGHT wheel base: 106.30 in, 270 cm; tracks: 58.66 in, 149 cm front, 59.45 in, 151 cm rear; length: 177.16 in, 450 cm; width: 71.26 in, 181 cm; height: 66.93 in, 170 cm; ground clearance: 9.84-16.54 in, 25-42 cm; weight: 4,079 lb, 1,850 kg; fuel tank: 15.4 imp gal, 18.5 US gal, 70 l.

BODY estate car/station wagon, in plastic material; 2+1 doors; 4-6 seats.

PRACTICAL INSTRUCTIONS fuel: 98 oct petrol; oil: engine 10 imp pt, 12 US pt, 5.7 l, SAE 20W-50, change every 3,700 miles, 6,000 km - gearbox 1.8 imp pt, 2.1 US pt, 1 l, SAE 80, change every 14,900 miles, 24,000 km - final drive (front and rear) 1.6 imp pt, 1.9 US pt, 0.9 l, SAE 90, no change recommended; greasing: none; tyre pressure: front 36 psi, 2.5 atm, rear 36 psi, 2.5 atm.

VARIATIONS

ENGINE 4 cylinders - 6 cylinders - 8 cylinders - 12 cylinders.

OPTIONALS 5-speed mechanical gearbox; ZF automatic transmission; front disc brakes.

AZLK   USSR

Moskvich 2138

ENGINE front, 4 stroke; 4 cylinders, in line; 82.8 cu in, 1,357 cc (2.99 x 2.95 in, 76 x 75 mm); compression ratio: 7:1; max power (DIN): 50 hp (36.8 kW) at 4,750 rpm; max torque (DIN): 67 lb ft, 9.3 kg m (91.2 Nm) at 2,750 rpm; max engine rpm: 4,750; 36.8 hp/l (27.1 kW/l); cast iron block, light alloy head; 3 crankshaft bearings; valves: overhead; camshafts: 1, side; lubrication: gear pump, filter on by-pass, 7.9 imp pt, 9.5 US pt, 4.5 l; 1 downdraught twin barrel carburettor; fuel feed: mechanical pump; water-cooled, 12.3 imp pt, 14.8 US pt, 7 l.

TRANSMISSION driving wheels: rear; clutch: single dry plate, hydraulically controlled; gearbox: mechanical; gears: 4, II, III and IV synchronized; ratios: I 3.810, II 2.242, III 1.450, IV 1, rev 4.710; lever: steering column; final drive: hypoid bevel; axle ratio: 4.220; width of rims: 4''; tyres: 5.90/6.00 x 13.

PERFORMANCE max speed: 75 mph, 120 km/h; power-weight ratio: 46.7 lb/hp (63.5 lb/kW), 21.2 kg/hp (28.8 kg/kW); carrying capacity: 882 lb, 400 kg; speed in direct drive at 1,000 rpm: 16.2 mph, 26 km/h; consumption: 26.9 m/imp gal, 22.4 m/US gal, 10.5 l x 100 km.

CHASSIS integral; front suspension: independent, wishbones, coil springs, anti-roll bar, telescopic dampers; rear: rigid axle, semi-elliptic leafsprings, telescopic dampers.

STEERING worm and roller.

BRAKES drum; lining area: front 59.5 sq in, 384 sq cm, rear 59.5 sq in, 384 sq cm, total 119 sq in, 768 sq cm.

ELECTRICAL EQUIPMENT 12 V; 42 or 55 Ah battery; 250 W dynamo; R 107 distributor; 2 headlamps.

DIMENSIONS AND WEIGHT wheel base: 94.49 in, 240 cm; tracks: 48.82 in, 124 cm front, 48.43 in, 123 cm rear; length:

AZLK Moskvich 2138 Diesel

AZLK Moskvich 2140 Combi IZh

AZLK Moskvich 2138 Diesel

167.32 in, 425 cm; width: 61.02 in, 155 cm; height: 58.48 in, 146 cm; ground clearance: 7.09 in, 18 cm; weight: 2,337 lb, 1,060 kg; turning circle: 37.7 ft, 11.5 m; fuel tank: 10 imp gal, 12.1 US gal, 46 l.

BODY saloon/sedan; 4 doors; 5 seats.

PRACTICAL INSTRUCTIONS fuel: 85 oct petrol; sparking plug: 175°.

VARIATIONS

(For export only).
ENGINE Diesel Perkins, 4 cylinders, in line with, fre-combustion chamber, 107.4 cu in, 1,760 cc (3.13 x 3.50 in, 79.4 x 88.9 mm), 22:1 compression ratio, max power (DIN) 50 hp (36.8 kW) at 4,000 rpm, max torque (DIN) 80 lb ft, 11 kg m (107.9 Nm) at 2,200 rpm, 28.4 hp/l (20.9 kW/l) 1 camshaft in crankcase, lubrication 10.6 imp pt, 12.7 US pt, 6 l, sealed circuit cooling, water, 17.6 imp pt, 21 US pt, 10 l.
TRANSMISSION 4-speed mechanical fully synchronized gearbox, ratios (I 3.490, II 2.040, III 1.330, IV 1, rev 3.390), central lever, 4.5'' wide rims, 165/175 SR x 13 tyres.
PERFORMANCE max speed 75 mph, 120 km/h, power-weight ratio 46.7 lb/hp (63.5 lb/kW), 21.2 kg/hp (28.8 kg/kW), consumption 33.6 m-imp gal, 28 m/US gal, 8 l x 100 km.
BRAKES fron disc, rear drum, servo.
ELECTRICAL EQUIPMENT 66 Ah battery, 480 W alternator.

OPTIONALS 4.5'' wide rims; front disc brakes; front and rear track 50 in, 127 cm.

Moskvich 2136

See Moskvich 2138, except for:

TRANSMISSION tyres: 175 x 13.

PERFORMANCE power-weight ratio: 50.5 lb/hp (68.6 lb/kW), 22.9 kg/hp (31.1 kg/kW).

DIMENSIONS AND WEIGHT height: 59.45 in, 151 cm; weight: 2,525 lb, 1,145 kg.

BODY estate car/st. wagon; 4 + 1 doors.

Moskvich 2140/Moskvich 2140 IZh

ENGINE front, slanted at 20°, 4 stroke; 4 cylinders, in line; 90.2 cu in, 1,479 cc (3.23 x 2.76 in, 82 x 70 mm); compression ratio: 8.8:1; max power (DIN): 75 hp (55.2 kW) at 5,800 rpm; max torque (DIN): 83 lb ft, 11.4 kg m (111.8 Nm) at 3,400 rpm; max engine rpm: 6,500; 50.7 hp/l (37.3 kW/l); light alloy block and head, wet liners; 5 crankshaft bearings; valves: overhead, Vee-slanted at 52°, rockers; camshafts: 1, overhead, chain driven; lubrication: gear pump, full flow filter, 8.8 imp pt, 10.6 US pt, 5 l; 1 K-126 H downdraught twin barrel carburettor; fuel feed: mechanical pump; sealed circuit cooling, liquid, 13.2 imp pt, 15.9 US pt, 7.5 l.

TRANSMISSION driving wheels: rear; clutch: single dry plate (diaphragm), hydraulically controlled; gearbox: mechanical; gears: 4, fully synchronized; ratios: I 3.490, II 2.040, III 1.330, IV 1, rev 3.390; lever: central; final drive: hypoid bevel; axle ratio: 4.220; width of rims: 4.5''; tyres: 165/6.95 x 13.

PERFORMANCE max speeds: (I) 27 mph, 43 km/h; (II) 45 mph, 73 km/h; (III) 70 mph, 113 km/h; (IV) 93 mph, 150 km/h; power-weight ratio: 31.7 lb/hp (43.2 lb/kW), 14.4 kg/hp (19.6 kg/kW); carrying capacity: 882 lb, 400 kg; speed in direct drive at 1,000 rpm: 16.9 mph, 27.2 km/h; consumption: 32.1 m/imp gal, 26.7 m/US gal, 8.8 l x 100 km.

CHASSIS integral; front suspension: independent, wishbones, coil springs, anti-roll bar, telescopic dampers; rear: rigid axle, semi-elliptic leafsprings, telescopic dampers.

STEERING worm and double roller; turns lock to lock: 3.50.

BRAKES front disc, rear drum, servo.

ELECTRICAL EQUIPMENT 12 V; 42 Ah battery; 40 A alternator; R 107 distributor; 2 headlamps.

DIMENSIONS AND WEIGHT wheel base: 94.49 in, 240 cm; tracks: 48.82 in, 124 cm front, 48.43 in, 123 cm rear; length: 167.32 in, 425 cm; width: 61.02 in, 155 cm; height: 57.27 in, 148 cm; ground clearance: 7.87 in, 20 cm; weight: 2,381 lb, 1,080 kg; turning circle: 37.7 ft, 11.5 m; fuel tank: 10.1 imp gal, 12.1 US gal, 46 l.

BODY saloon/sedan; 4 doors; 5 seats, separate front seats, reclining backrests with adjustable headrests; headlamps with wiper-washers.

OPTIONALS 165/175 SR x 13 tyres; cooling system 17.6 imp pt, 21.1 US pt, 10 l; front and rear track 50 in, 127 cm.

AZLK Moskvich 2136

GAZ Volga 24

Moskvich 2137/Moskvich 2140 Combi IZh

See Moskvich 2140/Moskvich 2140 IZh, except for:

TRANSMISSION axle ratio: 4.550; tyres: 6.40 x 13.

PERFORMANCE max speed: 84 mph, 135 km/h; power-weight ratio: 32.8 lb/hp (44.8 lb/kW), 14.9 kg/hp (20.3 kg/kW).

DIMENSIONS AND WEIGHT height: 59.45 in, 151 cm; weight: 2,470 lb, 1,120 kg.

BODY estate car/st. wagon; 4 + 1 doors.

GAZ   USSR

Volga 24

ENGINE front, 4 stroke; 4 cylinders, in line; 149.3 cu in, 2,446 cc (3.62 x 3.62 in, 92 x 92 mm); compression ratio: 8.2:1; max power (SAE): 110 hp (80.9 kW) at 4,500 rpm; max torque (SAE): 152 lb ft, 21 kg m (205.9 Nm) at 2,400 rpm; max engine rpm: 4,500; 45 hp/l (33 kW/l); light alloy block and head, wet liners; 5 crankshaft bearings; valves: overhead, in line, push-rods and rockers; camshafts: 1, side; lubrication: gear pump, filter on by-pass, 10.4 imp pt, 12.5 US pt, 5.9 l; 1 K-126 G downdraught twin barrel carburettor; fuel feed: mechanical pump; water-cooled, 20.2 imp pt, 24.3 US pt, 11.5 l.

TRANSMISSION driving wheels: rear; clutch: single dry plate, hydraulically controlled; gearbox: mechanical; gears: 4, fully synchronized; ratios: I 3.500, II 2.260, III 1.450, IV 1, rev 3.540; lever: central; final drive: hypoid bevel; axle ratio: 4.100; width of rims: 5''; tyres: 7.35/185 x 14.

PERFORMANCE max speeds: (I) 25 mph, 41 km/h; (II) 40 mph, 64 km/h; (III) 62 mph, 100 km/h; (IV) 90 mph, 145 km/h; power-weight ratio: 29.1 lb/hp (39.7 lb/kW), 13.2 kg/hp (18 kg/kW); carrying capacity: 1,058 lb, 480 kg; speed in direct drive at 1,000 rpm: 18 mph, 29 km/h; consumption: 22.6 m/imp gal, 18.8 m/US gal, 12.5 l x 100 km.

CHASSIS integral; front suspension: independent, wishbones, coil springs, anti-roll bar, telescopic dampers; rear: rigid axle, semi-elliptic leafsprings, telescopic dampers.

STEERING worm and roller; turns lock to lock: 3.50.

BRAKES drum, servo; swept area: front 87.6 sq in, 565 sq cm, rear 87.6 sq in, 565 sq cm, total 175.2 sq in, 1,130 sq cm.

ELECTRICAL EQUIPMENT 12 V; 54 Ah battery; 40 A alternator; R 119-B distributor; 2 headlamps.

DIMENSIONS AND WEIGHT wheel base: 110.24 in, 280 cm; tracks: 57.87 in, 147 cm front, 55.91 in, 142 cm rear; length: 186.22 in, 473 cm; width: 70.87 in, 180 cm; height: 58.66 in, 149 cm; ground clearance: 7.09 in, 18 cm; weight: 3,208 lb, 1,455 kg; turning circle: 40.7 ft, 12.4 m; fuel tank: 12.1 imp gal, 14.5 US gal, 55 l.

BODY saloon/sedan; 4 doors; 5-6 seats, separate front seats, reclining backrests.

PRACTICAL INSTRUCTIONS fuel: 94 oct petrol; oil: engine 10.4 imp pt, 12.5 US pt, 5.9 l - gearbox 1.6 imp pt, 1.9 US pt, 0.9 l - final drive 0.2 imp pt, 0.2 US pt, 0.1 l; greasing: 9 points; sparking plug: 175°; tappet clearances: inlet 0.014 in, 0.35 mm, exhaust 0.014 in, 0.35 mm; tyre pressure: front 24 psi, 1.7 atm, rear 24 psi, 1.7 atm.

VARIATIONS

ENGINE 6.7:1 compression ratio, max power (SAE) 95 hp (69.9 kW) at 4,700 rpm, max torque (SAE) 141 lb ft, 19.5 kg m (191.2 Nm) at 2,400 rpm, 38.8 hp/l (28.5 kW/l).
PERFORMANCE power-weight ratio 33.7 lb/hp (45.9 lb/kW), 15.3 kg/hp (20.8 kg/kW).

ENGINE 7.8:1 compression ratio, max power (SAE) 105 hp (77.3 kW) at 4,700 rpm, max torque (SAE) 145 lb ft, 20 kg m (196.1 Nm) at 2,400 rpm, 43 hp/l (31.6 kW/l).
PERFORMANCE power-weight ratio 30.6 lb/hp (41.4 lb/kW), 13.9 kg/hp (18.8 kg/kW).

Volga 24-02

See Volga 24, except for:

PERFORMANCE power-weight ratio: 31.5 lb/hp (43 lb/kW), 14.3 kg/hp (19.5 kg/kW); carrying capacity: 1,235 lb, 550 kg.

DIMENSIONS AND WEIGHT height: 60.63 in, 154 cm; weight: 3,473 lb, 1,575 kg.

BODY estate car/st. wagon; 4 + 1 doors; 7 seats; folding rear seat.

Volga 24 Indenor Diesel

(Only for export).

See Volga 24, except for:

ENGINE Diesel; 4 cylinders, in line, slanted at 20° to right; 128.9 cu in, 2,112 cc (3.54 x 3.27 in, 90 x 83 mm); compression ratio: 22.2:1; max power (DIN): 59 hp (43.4 kW) at 4,500 rpm; max torque (DIN): 86 lb ft, 11.9 kg m (116.7 Nm) at 2,500 rpm; 27.9 hp/l (20.5 kW/l); injection pump.

PERFORMANCE max speed: 84 mph, 135 km/h; power-weight ratio: 54.5 lb/hp (73.9 lb/kW), 24.7 kg/hp (33.5 kg/kW); consumption: 35.3 m/imp gal, 29.4 m/US gal, 8 l x 100 km.

ELECTRICAL EQUIPMENT 65 Ah battery.

PRACTICAL INSTRUCTIONS fuel: Diesel oil.

VARIATIONS

ENGINE 118.9 cu in, 1,948 cc (3.46 x 3.15 in, 88 x 80 mm); 21.8:1 compression ratio, max power (DIN) 50 hp (36.8 kW) at 4,500 rpm, max torque (DIN) 79 lb ft, 10.9 kg m (106.9 Nm) at 2,250 rpm, 25.7 hp/l (18.9 kW/l).
PERFORMANCE power-weight ratio 64.2 lb/hp (87.1 lb/kW), 29.1 kg/hp (39.5 kg/kW).

Chaika

ENGINE front, 4 stroke; V8 cylinders; 337 cu in, 5,522 cc (3.94 x 3.46 in, 100 x 88 mm); compression ratio: 8.5:1; max power (DIN): 207 hp (152.4 kW) at 4,000 rpm; max torque (DIN): 297 lb ft, 41 kg m (402.1 Nm) at 2,300 rpm; max engine rpm: 4,400; 37.5 hp/l (27.6 kW/l); cast iron block, light alloy head; 5 crankshaft bearings; valves: overhead, in line; camshafts: 1, side; lubrication: gear pump, full flow filter, 11.4 imp pt, 13.7 US pt, 6.5 l; 2 LK3 type K113 downdraught 4-barrel carburettors; fuel feed: mechanical pump; water-cooled, thermostatic fan.

TRANSMISSION driving wheels: rear; gearbox: automatic transmission, hydraulic torque converter and planetary gears with 3 ratios; ratios: I 2.840, II 1.680, III 1; lever: push-button control; final drive: hypoid bevel; axle ratio: 3.540; tyres: 8.20 x 15.

PERFORMANCE max speed: about 112 mph, 180 km/h; power-weight ratio: 27.6 lb/hp (37.5 lb/kW), 12.5 kg/hp (17 kg/kW); carrying capacity: 1,235 lb, 560 kg; consumption: about 14.1 m/imp gal, 11.8 m/US gal, 20 l x 100 km.

CHASSIS integral; front suspension: independent, wishbones, coil springs, anti-roll bar, telescopic dampers; rear: rigid axle, semi-elliptic springs, telescopic dampers.

STEERING roller and sector, servo.

BRAKES front disc, rear drum, servo.

ELECTRICAL EQUIPMENT 12 V; 68 Ah battery; 300 W dynamo; P13 distributor; 4 headlamps.

DIMENSIONS AND WEIGHT wheel base: 135.80 in, 345 cm; tracks: 60.65 in, 154 cm front, 60.25 in, 153 cm rear; length: 240.70 in, 611 cm; width: 79.50 in, 202 cm; height: 60 in, 152 cm; ground clearance: 7.10 in, 18 cm; weight: 5,698 lb, 2,584 kg; turning circle: 26.2 ft, 8 m; fuel tank: 17.6 imp gal, 21.1 US gal, 80 l.

BODY saloon/sedan; 4 doors; 7 seats; folding rear seat; headlamps with wiper-washers.

GAZ Chaika

UAZ   USSR

469 B

ENGINE front, 4 stroke; 4 cylinders, vertical, in line; 149.2 cu in, 2,445 cc (3.62 x 3.62 in, 92 x 92 mm); compression ratio: 6.7:1; max power (SAE): 78 hp (57.4 kW) at 4,000 rpm; max torque (SAE): 125 lb ft, 17.2 kg m (168.6 Nm) at 2,200-2,500 rpm; max engine rpm: 4,500; 31.9 hp/l (23.4 kW/l); cast iron block and head; 4 crankshaft bearings; valves: overhead, in line, push-rods and rockers; camshafts: 1, side; lubrication: gear pump, full flow filter, oil cooler, 10.6 imp pt, 12.7 US pt, 6 l; 1 downdraught 4-barrel carburettor; fuel feed: mechanical pump; water-cooled, 22.9 imp pt, 27.5 US pt, 13 l.

TRANSMISSION driving wheels: front (automatically engaged with transfer box low ratio) and rear; clutch: single dry plate; gearbox: mechanical; gears: 4, III and IV synchronized; ratios: I 4.120, II 2.640, III 1.580, IV 1, rev 3.738; lever: central; final drive: spiral bevel; axle ratio: 5.125; tyres: 8.40 x 15.

PERFORMANCE max speed: about 71 mph, 115 km/h; power-weight ratio: 43.5 lb/hp (59.2 lb/kW), 19.7 kg/hp (26.8 kg/kW); carrying capacity: 1,654 lb, 750 kg; speed in direct drive at 1,000 rpm: 15.9 mph, 25.6 km/h; consumption: 23.5 m/imp gal, 19.6 m/US gal, 12 l x 100 km.

CHASSIS box-type ladder frame; front and rear suspension: rigid axle, semi-elliptic leafsprings, telescopic dampers.

STEERING worm and double roller.

BRAKES drum; lining area: total 153.5 sq in, 990 sq cm.

ELECTRICAL EQUIPMENT 12 V; 54 Ah battery; 350 W alternator; 2 headlamps.

DIMENSIONS AND WEIGHT wheel base: 93.70 in, 238 cm; front and rear track: 56.69 in, 144 cm; length: 158.27 in, 402 cm; width: 70.08 in, 178 cm; height: 79.13 in, 201 cm; ground clearance: 8.66 in, 22 cm; weight: 3,396 lb, 1,540 kg; turning circle: 39.4 ft, 12 m; fuel tank: 15.8 imp gal, 19 US gal, 72 l (2 separate tanks).

BODY open; 4 doors; 7 seats, separate front seats.

PRACTICAL INSTRUCTIONS fuel: 72 oct petrol.

VARIATIONS

ENGINE Peugeot Diesel, 128.9 cu in, 2,112 cc (3.54 x 3.27 in, 90 x 83 mm), 22.8:1 compression ratio, max power (DIN) 65 hp (47.8 kW) at 4,500 rpm, max torque (DIN) 89

UAZ 469 B

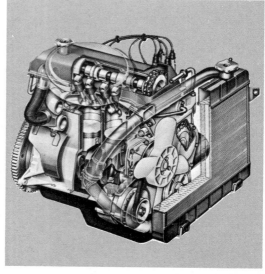

VAZ Lada 1200

lb ft, 12.3 kg m (120.6 Nm) at 2,200 rpm, max engine rpm 4,750, 30.8 hp/l (22.6 kW/l).
PERFORMANCE max speed 62 mph, 100 km/h, power-weight ratio 55.2 lb/hp (71 lb/kW), 23.7 kg/hp (32.2 kg/kW), consumption 31.7 m/imp gal, 26.4 m/US gal, 8.9 l x 100 km.

OPTIONALS independent heating; hardtop: fabric top.

VAZ   USSR

Lada Series

PRICES IN GB:

1 1200 4-dr Sedan	£	2,056
2 1200 5-dr Combi	£	2,340
3 1300 ES 4-dr Sedan	£	2,404
4 1500 4-dr Sedan	£	2,511
5 1500 5-dr Combi	£	2,461
6 1500 ES 5-dr Combi	£	2,826
7 1600 4-dr Sedan	£	2,666
8 1600 ES 4-dr Sedan	£	2,999

Power team:	Standard for:	Optional for:
60 hp	1,2	—
68 hp	3	—
75 hp	4 to 6	—
78 hp	7,8	—

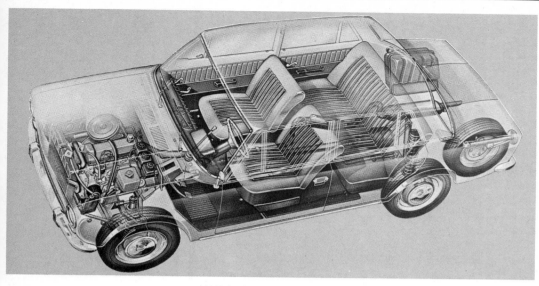

VAZ Lada 1200 4-dr Sedan

60 hp power team

ENGINE front, 4 stroke; 4 cylinders, in line; 73.1 cu in, 1,198 cc (2.99 x 2.60 in, 76 x 66 mm); compression ratio: 8.8:1; max power (DIN): 60 hp (44.2 kW) at 5,600 rpm; max torque (DIN): 64 lb ft, 8.9 kg m (87.3 Nm) at 3,400 rpm; max engine rpm: 6,000; 50.1 hp/l (36.9 kW/l); cast iron block, light alloy head; 5 crankshaft bearings; valves: overhead, in line, rockers; camshafts: 1, overhead, chain driven; lubrication: gear pump, full flow filter, 6.5 imp pt, 7.8 US pt, 3.7 l; 1 Weber 32 DCR downdraught twin barrel carburettor; fuel feed: mechanical pump; sealed circuit cooling, liquid, 15 imp pt, 18 US pt, 8.5 l.

TRANSMISSION driving wheels: rear; clutch: single dry plate (diaphragm), hydraulically controlled; gearbox: mechanical; gears: 4, fully synchronized; ratios: I 3.753, II 2.303, III 1.493, IV 1, rev 3.867; lever: central; final drive: hypoid bevel; axle ratio: saloon 4.300, st. wagon 4.440; width of rims: 4.5''; tyres: saloon 155 SR/6.15 x 13 - st. wagon 165 SR/6.45 x 13.

PERFORMANCE max speeds: (I) 25 mph, 40 km/h; (II) 40 mph, 65 km/h; (III) 62 mph, 100 km/h; (IV) 87 mph, 140 km/h; power-weight ratio: saloon 35.7 lb/hp (48.3 lb/kW), 16.2 kg/hp (21.9 kg/kW) - st. wagon 37 lb/hp (50.5 lb/kW), 16.8 kg/hp (22.9 kg/kW); carrying capacity: 882 lb, 400 kg; acceleration: 0-50 mph (0-80 km/h) 12 sec; speed in direct drive at 1,000 rpm: 15.2 mph, 24.5 km/h; consumption: 31.4 m/imp gal, 26.1 m/US gal, 9 l x 100 km.

CHASSIS integral; front suspension: independent, wishbones, coil springs, anti-roll bar, telescopic dampers; rear: rigid axle, twin trailing radius arms, transverse linkage bar, coil springs, telescopic dampers.

STEERING worm and roller; turns lock to lock: 3.

BRAKES front disc (diameter 9.96 in, 25.3 cm), dual circuit, rear drum, rear compensator; lining area: front 20.9 sq in, 135 sq cm, rear 76.9 sq in, 496 sq cm, total 97.8 sq in, 631 sq cm.

ELECTRICAL EQUIPMENT 12 V; 55 Ah heavy-duty battery; 40 A alternator; R 125 distributor; 2 headlamps.

DIMENSIONS AND WEIGHT wheel base: 95.47 in, 242 cm; tracks: 52.76 in, 134 cm front, 51.38 in, 130 cm rear; length: saloon 160.43 in, 407 cm - st. wagon 159.84 in, 406 cm; width: 63.43 in, 161 cm; height: saloon 54.33 in, 138 cm - st. wagon 57.48 in, 146 cm; ground clearance: 6.69 in, 17 cm; weight: saloon 2,139 lb, 970 kg - st. wagon 2,227 lb, 1,010 kg; turning circle: 34.1 ft, 10.4 m; fuel tank: saloon 8.6 imp gal, 10.3 US gal, 39 l - st. wagon 9.9 imp gal, 11.9 US gal, 45 l.

BODY 5 seats, separate front seats, reclining backrests, adjustable headrests.

68 hp power team

See 60 hp power team, except for:

ENGINE 79 cu in, 1,294 cc (3.11 x 2.60 in, 79 x 66 mm); max power (SAE): 68 hp (50 kW) at 5,400 rpm; max torque (SAE): 78 lb ft, 10.8 kg m (105.9 Nm) at 3,500 rpm; 52.6 hp/l (38.6 kW/l).

VAZ Lada 1500 4-dr Sedan

TRANSMISSION tyres: 155 x 13.

PERFORMANCE max speed: 92 mph, 148 km/h; power-weight ratio: 31.5 lb/hp (42.8 lb/kW), 14.3 kg/hp (19.4 kg/kW).

BODY vinyl roof; heated rear window; hazard lights.

75 hp power team

See 60 hp power team, except for:

ENGINE 88.6 cu in, 1,452 cc (2.99 x 3.15 in, 76 x 80 mm); max power (DIN): 75 hp (55.2 kW) at 5,600 rpm; max torque (DIN): 78 lb ft, 10.8 kg m (105.9 Nm) at 3,500 rpm; max engine rpm: 6,500; 51.6 hp/l (38 kW/l).

TRANSMISSION axle ratio: 4.100; width of rims: 5''; tyres: 165 SR x 13.

PERFORMANCE max speed: 93 mph, 150 km/h; power-weight ratio: 30.2 lb/hp (41.2 lb/kW), 13.7 kg/hp (18.7 kg/kW); acceleration: 0-50 mph (0-80 km/h) 10.7 sec.

BRAKES servo.

ELECTRICAL EQUIPMENT 53 A alternator; 4 headlamps.

DIMENSIONS AND WEIGHT wheel base: 94.88 in, 241 cm; tracks: 52.95 in, 135 cm front, 50.79 in, 129 cm rear; length: saloon 162.20 in, 412 cm - st. wagons 159.84 in, 406 cm; height: st. wagons 55.12 in, 140 cm; ground clearance: 6.89 in, 17.5 cm; weight: 2,271 lb, 1,030 kg.

BODY (for 1500 ES 5-door Combi only) heated rear window wiper-washer, vinyl roof and hazard lights.

78 hp power team

See 60 hp power team, except for:

ENGINE 95.7 cu in, 1,568 cc (3.11 x 3.15 in, 79 x 80 mm); max power (DIN): 78 hp (57.4 kW) at 5,200 rpm; max torque (DIN): 91 lb ft, 12.5 kg m (122.6 Nm) at 3,400 rpm; max engine rpm: 6,500; 49.7 hp/l (36.6 kW/l).

TRANSMISSION axle ratio: 4.100; width of rims: 5''; tyres: 165 SR x 13.

PERFORMANCE max speed: 96 mph, 155 km/h; power-weight ratio: 29.1 lb/hp (39.5 lb/kW), 13.2 kg/hp (17.9 kg/kW).

BRAKES servo.

ELECTRICAL EQUIPMENT 53 A alternator; 4 headlamps.

DIMENSIONS AND WEIGHT tracks: 53.54 in, 136 cm front, 51.97 in, 132 cm rear; length: 161.81 in, 411 cm; ground clearance: 6.88 in, 17.5 cm; weight: 2,271 lb, 1,030 kg.

BODY (for ES 4-dr saloon only) alloy sports wheels, vinyl roof and cloth upholstery.

VAZ Lada 1300 ES 4-dr Sedan

VAZ Lada Niva 2121 4 x 4

dampers; rear: rigid axle, coil springs, transverse (Panhard) arm, 4, longitudinal arms, telescopic double action dampers.

STEERING worm and roller; turns lock to lock: 3.

BRAKES front disc (diameter 10.75 in, 27.3 cm), dual circuit, rear drum (diameter 9.80 in, 24.9 cm), vacuum servo.

ELECTRICAL EQUIPMENT 12 V; 55 Ah heavy-duty battery; 42 A alternator; 2 headlamps.

DIMENSIONS AND WEIGHT wheel base: 86.61 in, 220 cm; tracks: 55.91 in, 142 cm front, 55.12 in, 140 cm rear; length: 146.06 in, 371 cm; width: 66.14 in, 168 cm; height: 64.57 in, 164 cm; ground clearance: 9.05 in, 23 cm; weight: 2,611 lb, 1,184 kg weight distribution: 60% front, 40% rear; turning circle: 36 ft, 11 m; fuel tank: 9.9 imp gal, 11.9 US gal, 45 l.

BODY estate car/st. wagon; 2+1 doors; 5 seats, separate front seats, reclining backrests, adjustable headrests; heated rear window wiper-washer; impact absorbing bumpers.

PRACTICAL INSTRUCTIONS fuel: 93 oct petrol; oil: engine 6.5 imp pt, 7.8 US pt, 3.7 l, change every 6,000 miles, 9,700 km - gearbox 2.3 imp pt, 2.7 US pt, 1.3 l, change every 6,000 miles, 9,700 km - final drive 2.3 imp pt, 2.7 US pt, 1.3 l; tyre pressure: front 24 psi, 1.7 atm, rear 24 psi, 1.7 atm.

VAZ Lada Niva 2121 4 x 4

Lada Niva 2121 4 x 4

PRICE IN GB: £ 4,098*

ENGINE front, 4 stroke; 4 cylinders, in line; 95.7 cu in, 1,568 cc (3.11 x 3.15 in, 79 x 80 mm); compression ratio: 8.5:1; max power (DIN): 78 hp (57.4 kW) at 5,400 rpm; max torque (DIN): 88 lb ft, 12.1 kg m (118.7 Nm) at 3,000 rpm; max engine rpm: 6,000; 49.7 hp/l (38.6 kW/l); cast iron block, light alloy head; 5 crankshaft bearings; valves: overhead, in line, rockers; camshafts: 1, overhead, chain driven; lubrication: gear pump, full flow filter, 6.5 imp pt, 7.8 US pt, 3.7 l; 1 double Venturi multijet twin barrel carburettor; fuel feed: mechanical pump; sealed circuit cooling, water, 18.8 imp pt, 22.6 US pt, 10.7 l.

TRANSMISSION driving wheels: front and rear; clutch: single dry plate (diaphragm), hydraulically controlled; gearbox: mechanical; gears: 4, fully synchronized and 2-ratio transfer box; ratios: I 3.242, II 1.989, III 1.289, IV 1, rev 3.340; transfer box ratios: I 1.200, II 2.135; lever: central; final drive: hypoid bevel; axle ratio: 4.300; width of rims: 5''; tyres: 6.95/175 x 16.

PERFORMANCE max speeds: (I) 25 mph, 40 km/h; (II) 41 mph, 66 km/h; (III) 63 mph, 101 km/h; (IV) 82 mph, 132 km/h; power-weight ratio: 33.5 lb/hp (45.4 lb/kW), 15.2 kg/hp (20.6 kg/kW); carrying capacity: 882 lb, 400 kg; acceleration: standing 1/4 mile 22.2 sec; consumption: about 25.9 m/imp gal, 21.6 m/US gal, 10.9 l x 100 km.

CHASSIS integral; front suspension: independent, wishbones, coil springs, anti-roll bar telescopic double action

968-A

ENGINE rear, 4 stroke; 4 cylinders, Vee-slanted at 90°; 73 cu in, 1,196 cc (2.99 x 2.60 in, 76 x 66 mm); compression ratio: 8.4:1; max power (DIN): 45 hp (33.1 kW) at 4,500 rpm; max torque (DIN): 59 lb ft, 8.2 kg m (80.4 Nm) at 3,200 rpm; max engine rpm: 4,600; 37.6 hp/l (27.6 kW/l); cast iron block, light alloy head; 3 crankshaft bearings; valves: overhead, push-rods and rockers; camshafts: 1, at centre of Vee; lubrication: gear pump, full flow filter, 5.8 imp pt, 7 US pt, 3.3 l; 1 K 127 downdraught carburettor; fuel feed: mechanical pump; air-cooled.

TRANSMISSION driving wheels: rear; clutch: single dry plate, hydraulically controlled; gearbox: mechanical; gears: 4, fully synchronized; ratios: I 3.800, II 2.120, III 1.410, IV 0.964, rev 4.165; lever: central; final drive: hypoid bevel; axle ratio: 4.125; tyres: 6.15 x 13 or 5.20/5.60 x 13 or 145 SR x 13.

PERFORMANCE max speed: 78 mph, 125 km/h; power-weight ratio: 38.7 lb/hp (52.6 lb/kW), 17.5 kg/hp (23.9 kg/kW); carrying capacity: 882 lb, 400 kg; speed in top at 1,000 rpm: 16.5 mph, 26.5 km/h; consumption: 35.3 m/imp gal, 29.4 m/US gal, 8 l x 100 km.

CHASSIS integral; front suspension: independent, swinging longitudinal trailing arms, transverse torsion bars, telescopic dampers; rear: independent, semi-trailing arms, coil springs, telescopic dampers.

STEERING worm and double roller.

BRAKES drum, dual circuit; lining area: total 78.9 sq in, 509 sq cm.

ELECTRICAL EQUIPMENT 12 V; 42 Ah battery; 250 W alternator; 2 headlamps.

DIMENSIONS AND WEIGHT wheel base: 85.04 in, 216 cm; tracks: 48.03 in, 122 cm front, 47.24 in, 120 cm rear; length: 146.85 in, 373 cm; width: 61.81 in, 157 cm; height: 55.12 in, 140 cm; ground clearance: 7.48 in, 19 cm; weight: 1,742 lb, 790 kg; turning circle: 36.1 ft, 11 m; fuel tank: 6.6 imp gal, 7.9 US gal, 30 l.

BODY saloon/sedan; 2 doors; 5 seats, separate front seats, front and rear reclining backrests; independent heating; antitheft; hazard lights.

OPTIONALS 155 SR x 13 tyres.

969-A 4 x 4

See 968-A, except for:

ENGINE front, 4 stroke; compression ratio: 7.2:1; max power (DIN): 38 hp (28 kW) at 4,400 rpm; 31.8 hp/l (23.4 kW/l).

ZAZ 969-A 4 x 4

ZIL 114 Limousine

RANSMISSION driving wheels: front and rear; gears: 4,
ully synchronized and low ratio: 5.90 x 13 tyres.

PERFORMANCE max speed: 56 mph, 90 km/h; power-weight
atio: 55.8 lb/hp (75.6 lb/kW), 25.3 kg/hp (34.3 kg/kW).

DIMENSIONS AND WEIGHT wheel base: 70.87 in, 180 cm;
ront and rear track: 51.97 in, 132 cm; length: 132.68 in,
37 cm; width: 63.39 in, 161 cm; height: 69.68 in, 177 cm;
veight: 2,117 lb, 960 kg.

ODY open.

114 Limousine

NGINE front, 4 stroke; V8 cylinders; 424.8 cu in, 6,962 cc
4.25 x 3.74 in, 108 x 95 mm); compression ratio: 9:1; max
ower (SAE): 300 hp (220.8 kW) at 4,400 rpm; max torque
SAE): 420 lb ft, 58 kg m (568.8 Nm) at 2,900 rpm; max
engine rpm: 4,500; 43.1 hp/l (31.7 kW/l); cast iron block,
ight alloy head; 5 crankshaft bearings; valves: overhead,
ush-rods and rockers camshafts: 1, at centre of Vee;
ubrication: gear pump, full flow filter, 12.3 imp pt, 14.8
IS pt, 7 l; 1 K 85 downdraught 4-barrel carburettor; fuel
eed: electric pump; water-cooled, 39.9 imp pt, 48 US pt,
2.7 l.

RANSMISSION driving wheels: rear; gearbox: automatic
ransmission, hydraulic torque converter and planetary gears
vith 2 ratios, max ratio of converter at stall 2.5; ratios:
1.720, II 1, rev 2.930; lever: push button control; final
rive: hypoid bevel; axle ratio: 3.540; width of rims: 6.5'';
yres: 8.90 x 15 or 9.35 x 15.

PERFORMANCE max speed: 124 mph, 200 km/h; power-
weight ratio: 23.4 lb/hp (31.7 lb/kW), 10.6 kg/hp (14.4
g/kW); carrying capacity: 1,411 lb, 640 kg; consumption:
.4 m/imp gal, 7.8 m/US gal, 30 l x 100 km.

CHASSIS box-type ladder frame and X cross members; front
uspension: independent, wishbones, coil springs, anti-roll
ar, lever dampers; rear: rigid axle, semi-elliptic leafsprings,
elescopic dampers.

STEERING recirculating ball, servo; turns lock to lock: 4.30.

BRAKES disc, servo.

LECTRICAL EQUIPMENT 12 V; 2 x 54 Ah batteries; 500 W
ynamo; R-4 distributor; 4 headlamps; 2 fog lamps.

DIMENSIONS AND WEIGHT wheel base: 148.03 in, 376
cm; tracks: 61.81 in, 157 cm front, 63.78 in, 162 cm
ear; length: 247.44 in, 628 cm; width: 81.50 in, 207
cm; height: 59.45 in, 151 cm; ground clearance: 7.09 in,
8 cm; weight: 7,001 lb, 3,175 kg; turning circle: 52.4 ft,
6 m; fuel tank: 26.4 imp gal, 31.7 US gal, 120 l.

BODY limousine; 4 doors; 7 seats, separate front seats;
air-conditioning; electric windows.

117 Limousine

See 114 Limousine, except for:

PERFORMANCE power-weight ratio: 21.4 lb/hp (28.9 lb/kW),
9.7 kg/hp (13.1 kg/kW).

DIMENSIONS AND WEIGHT wheel base: 128.35 in, 326
cm; length: 227.56 in, 578 cm; weight: 6,395 lb, 2,900
kg; turning circle: 45.9 ft, 14 m.

BODY 5 seats.

Zastava 750/750 Luxe

PRICE EX WORKS: 750: 39,337 dinara

ENGINE rear, 4 stroke; 4 cylinders, vertical, in line; 46.8
cu in, 767 cc (2.44 x 2.50 in, 62 x 63.5 mm); compression
ratio: 7.5:1; max power (DIN): 25 hp (18.4 kW) at 4,800 rpm;
max torque (DIN): 32.8 lb ft, 4.7 kg m (46 Nm) at 3000 rpm
max engine rpm: 4,800; 32.6 hp/l (23.9 kW/l); cast iron

block, light alloy head; 3 crankshaft bearings; valves:
overhead, in line, push-rods and rockers; camshafts:
1, side; lubrication: gear pump, centrifugal filter, 6.5 imp
pt, 7.8 US pt, 3.7 l; 1 Weber 28 ICP 3 or Holley Europa
28 ICP downdraught single barrel carburettor; fuel feed:
mechanical pump; water-cooled, 7.9 imp pt, 9.5 US pt, 4.5 l.

TRANSMISSION driving wheels: rear; clutch: single dry
plate; gearbox: mechanical; gears: 4, II, III and IV synchronized; ratios: I 3.385, II 2.055, III 1.333, IV 0.896, rev
4.275; lever: central; final drive: spiral bevel; axle ratio:
4.875; width of rims: 3.5''; tyres: 5.20 x 12.

PERFORMANCE max speeds: (I) 19 mph, 30 km/h; (II) 28
mph, 45 km/h; (III) 43 mph, 70 km/h; (IV) about 68 mph,
110 km/h; power-weight ratio: 54.2 lb/hp (73.7 lb/kW), 24.6
kg/hp (33.4 kg/kW); carrying capacity: 706 lb, 320 kg; acceleration: standing ¼ mile 26.7 sec, 0-50 mph (0-80 km/h)
24 sec; speed in top at 1,000 rpm: 14.1 mph, 22.7 km/h;
consumption: 40.3 m/imp gal, 40.6 m/US gal, 7 l x 100 km.

CHASSIS integral; front suspension: independent, wishbones, transverse leafspring lower arms, telescopic dampers; rear: independent, oblique semi-trailing arms, coil
springs, telescopic dampers.

STEERING screw and sector; turns lock to lock: 2.12.

BRAKES drum, single circuit; lining area: front 33.5 sq in,
216 sq cm, rear 33.5 sq in, 216 sq cm, total 67 sq in,
432 sq cm.

ELECTRICAL EQUIPMENT 12 V; 32 Ah battery; 230 W
dynamo; Marelli distributor: 2 headlamps.

DIMENSIONS AND WEIGHT wheel base: 78.74 in, 200 cm;
tracks: 45.28 in, 115 cm front, 45.67 in, 116 cm rear:
length: 129.72 in, 329 cm; width: 54.25 in, 138 cm; height:
55.12 in, 140 cm; ground clearance: 5.71 in, 14.5 cm;
weight: 1,334 lb, 605 kg; weight distribution: 46% front,
54% rear; turning circle: 28.5 ft, 8.7 m; fuel tank: 6.6
imp gal, 7.9 US gal, 30 l.

BODY saloon/sedan; 2 doors; 4 seats, separate front seats;
folding rear seat - Luxe, reclining backrests and luxury
interior.

PRACTICAL INSTRUCTIONS fuel: 86 : 88 oct petrol; oil:
engine 5.3 imp pt, 6.3 US pt, 3 l, change every 6,210 miles,
10,000 km - gearbox and final drive 2.6 imp pt, 3.2 US pt,
1.5 l, SAE 90, change every 31,000 miles, 50,000 km;
tappet clearances (cold): inlet and exhaust 0.006 in, 0.15
mm; tyre pressure: front 14 psi, 1 atm, rear 22 psi,
1.6 atm.

Zastava 750 S

See Zastava 750 except for:

PRICE EX WORKS: 46,047 dinara

ENGINE compression ratio 8.5:1; max power (DIN): 30 hp
(22 kW) at 5,400 rpm; max torque (DIN): 37 lb ft,
5.2 kg m (51 Nm) at 3,600 rpm; max engine rpm: 5,400;
39.1 hp/l (28.8 kW/l) 1 Holley 30 ICV-6 or Solex C 30
PIP-4 or IPM 30 MGV-1 single barrel carburettor.

ZCZ Zastava 750 S

ZASTAVA 750 S

TRANSMISSION tyres: 145 SR-12;

PERFORMANCE max speeds: (I) 20 mph, 32 km/h; (II) 33 mph, 53 km/h; (III) 51 mph, 82 km/h; (IV) 75 mph, 120 km/h; power-weight ratio: 47 lb/hp (63.8 lb/kW), 21.3 kg/hp (29 kg/kW).

DIMENSIONS AND WEIGHT weight: 1,411 lb, 640 kg.

PRACTICAL INSTRUCTIONS futl: 98 oct petrol; tyre pressure: front 18 psi, 1.3 atm, rear 22 psi, -1.6 atm.

Zastava 101/101 Luxe

PRICES EX WORKS: 101   65,563 dinara
              101 Luxe 68,032 dinara

ENGINE front, transverse, slanted 20° to front, 4 stroke; 4 cylinders, in line; 68.1 cu in, 1,116 cc (3.15 x 2.19 in, 80 x 55.5 mm); compression ratio: 8.8:1; max power (DIN): 55 hp (40.4 kW) at 6,000 rpm; max torque (DIN): 59 lb ft, 8,2 kg m (80.3 Nm) at 3,500 rpm; max engine rpm: 6,000; 49.3 hp/l (36.2 kW/l); cast iron block, light alloy head; 5 crankshaft bearings; valves: overhead, thimble tappets; camshafts: 1, overhead; lubrication: gear pump, cartridge filter, 8.8 imp pt, 10.6 US pt, 5 l; 1 Weber 32 ICEV or IPM 32 MGV-10 carburettor; fuel feed: mechanical pump; water-cooled, 11.4 imp pt, 13.7 US pt, 6.5 l, electric thermostatic fan.

TRANSMISSION driving wheels: front; clutch: single dry plate; gearbox: mechanical; gears: 4, fully synchronized; ratios: I 3.583, II 2.235, III 1.454, IV 1.042, rev 3.714; lever: central; final drive: cylindrical gears; axle ratio: 4.077; width of rims: 4.5"; tyres: 145 SR x 13.

PERFORMANCE max speeds: (I) 28 mph, 45 km/h; (II) 47 mph, 75 km/h; (III) 71 mph, 115 km/h; (IV) 85 mph, 136 km/h; power-weight ratio: 33.5 lb/hp (45.5 lb/kW), 15.2 kg/hp (20.7 kg/kW); carrying capacity: 882 lb, 400 kg; acceleration: standing ¼ mile 21 sec, 0-50 mph (0-80 km/h) 12.7 sec; speed in top at 1,000 rpm: 15.2 mph, 24.4 km/h; consumption: 33.2 m/imp gal, 27.7 m/US gal, 8.5 l x 100 km.

CHASSIS integral; front suspension: independent, by McPherson, coil springs/telescopic damper struts, lower wishbones, anti-roll bar; rear: independent, single wide-based wishbone, transverse leafspring, telescopic dampers.

STEERING rack-and-pinion; turns lock to lock: 3.40.

BRAKES front disc (diameter 8.94 in, 22.7 cm), rear drum, rear compensator; lining area: front 19.2 sq in, 124 sq cm, rear 33.5 sq in, 216 sq cm, total 52.7 sq in, 340 sq cm.

ELECTRICAL EQUIPMENT 12 V; 34 Ah battery; 400 W alternator; Marelli distributor; 2 headlamps.

DIMENSIONS AND WEIGHT wheel base: 96.42 in, 245 cm; front and rear track: 51.34 in, 130 cm; length: 151.02 in, 384 cm; width: 62.60 in, 159 cm; height: 54.02 in, 137 cm; ground clearance: 5.71 in, 14.5 cm; weight:

1,841 lb, 835 kg; weight distribution: 61.5% front, 38.5% rear; turning circle: 33.8 ft, 10.3 m; fuel tank: 8.4 imp gal, 10 US gal, 38 l.

BODY saloon/sedan; 4 + 1 doors; 5 seats, separate front seats - Luxe, luxury equipment.

PRACTICAL INSTRUCTIONS fuel: 98 oct petrol; oil: engine 7.5 imp pt, 9 US pt, 4.2 l, change every 3,100 miles, 5,000 km - gearbox and final drive 5.5 imp pt, 6.6 US pt, 3.1 l, HIP 90 CZ or UMOL 90 CZ (SAE 90), change every 12,500 miles, 20,000 km; tappet camshaft operating clearances (cold): inlet 0.015 in, 0.4 mm, exhaust 0.020 in, 0.5 mm; tyre pressure: front 26 psi, 1.8 atm, rear 24 psi, 1.7 atm.

Zastava 101 Super

See Zastava 101 except for:

PRICE EX WORKS: 73,723 dinara

ENGINE compression ratio: 9.2:1; max power (DIN): 64 hp (47 kW) at 6,000 rpm; max torque (DIN): 61 lb ft, 8.4 kg m (82.3 Nm) at 3,800 rpm; 57.3 hp/l (42.1 kW/l).

PERFORMANCE max speeds: (I) 29 mph, 47 km/h; (II) 45 mph, 74 km/h; (III) 72 mph, 117 km/h; (IV) 91 mph, 146 km/h; power-weight ratio: 29.5 lb/hp (40.1 lb/kW), 13.4 kg/hp (18.2 kg/kW); consumption: 29.4 m/imp gal, 24.7 m/US gal, 9.5 l x 100 km.

DIMENSIONS AND WEIGHT weight: 1,887 lb, 856 kg.

Zastava 1300/1300 Luxe

PRICES EX WORKS: 1300   62,248 dinara
             1300 Luxe 65,768 dinara

ENGINE front, 4 stroke; 4 cylinders, vertical, in line; 79 cu in, 1,295 cc (2.83 x 3.13 in, 72 x 79.5 mm); compression ratio: 9:1; max power (DIN): 60 hp (44.1 kW) at 5,400 rpm; max torque (DIN): 69 lb ft, 9.5 kg m (93.1 Nm) at 3,100 rpm; max engine rpm: 5,400; 46.3 hp/l (34 kW/l); cast iron block, light alloy head, 3 crankshaft bearings; valves: overhead, Vee-slanted, push-rods and rockers; camshafts: 1, side; lubrication: gear pump, centrifugal filter, cartridge on by-pass, 7.6 imp pt, 9.1 US pt, 4.3 l; 1 Weber 34 DCHD or Solex C 34 PAIA 2 downdraught twin barrel carburettor; fuel feed: mechanical pump; water-cooled, 11.8 imp pt, 14.2 US pt, 6.7 l.

TRANSMISSION driving wheels: rear; clutch: single dry plate, hydraulically controlled; gearbox: mechanical; gears: 4, fully synchronized; ratios: I 3.750, II 2.300, III 1.490, IV 1, rev 3.870; lever: central; final drive: hypoid bevel; axle ratio: 4.100; width of rims: 4.5"; tyres: 5.60 S x 13.

PERFORMANCE max speeds: (I) 25 mph, 40 km/h; (II) 40 mph, 65 km/h; (III) 62 mph, 100 km/h; (IV) over 87 mph, 140 km/h; power-weight ratio: 1300 35.3 lb/hp (40 lb/kW), 16 kg/hp (21.8 kg/kW) - 1300 Luxe 35.5 lb/hp (48.5 lb/kW), 16.1 kg/hp (22 kg/kW); carrying capacity: 882 lb, 400 kg; acceleration: standing ¼ mile 23.1 sec, 0-50 mph (0-80 km/h) 13.9 sec; speed in direct drive at 1,000 rpm: 16.1

ZCZ Zastava 1300

mph, 25.9 km/h; consumption: 26.9 m/imp gal, 22.4 m/US gal, 10.5 l x 100 km.

CHASSIS integral; front suspension: independent, wishbones, lower trailing links, coil springs, anti-roll bar, telescopic dampers; rear: rigid axle, semi-elliptic leaf springs, telescopic dampers.

STEERING worm and roller; turns lock to lock: 3.

BRAKES disc, servo.

ELECTRICAL EQUIPMENT 12 V; 48 Ah battery; 400 W dynamo, Marelli distributor; 4 headlamps.

DIMENSIONS AND WEIGHT wheel base: 95.37 in, 242 cm; tracks: 50.98 in, 129 cm front, 50.08 in, 127 cm rear; length: 158.66 in, 403 cm; width: 60.83 in, 154 cm; height: 56.69 in, 144 cm; ground clearance: 5.12 in, 1 cm; weight: 1300 2,117 lb, 960 kg - 1300 Luxe 2,139 lb 970 kg; weight distribution: 56% front, 44% rear; turning circle: 33.5 ft, 10.2 m; fuel tank: 9.9 imp gal, 11.9 US gal 45 l.

BODY saloon/sedan; 4 doors; 5 seats, separate front seats reclining backrests - Luxe, luxury equipment.

PRACTICAL INSTRUCTIONS fuel: 98 oct petrol; oil: engine change every 6,200 miles, 10,000 km - gearbox and final drive change every 18,600 miles, 30,000 km; tappet clearances (cold): inlet and exhaust 0.007 in, 0.20 mm; tyre pressure: front 20 : 23 psi, 1.4 : 1.6 atm, rear 24 : 2 psi, 1.7 : 2.0 atm.

Zastava 1500/1500 Luxe

See Zastava 1300/1300 Luxe, except for:

PRICES EX WORKS: 1500   64,579 dinara
             1500 Luxe 70,190 dinara

ENGINE 90 cu in, 1,481 cc (3.03 x 3.13 in, 77 x 79.5 mm) compression ratio: 9:1; max power (DIN): 75 hp (55.2 kW at 5,400 rpm; max torque (DIN): 83 lb ft, 11.5 kg m (112. Nm) at 3,200 rpm; 50.6 hp/l (37.3 kW/l).

PERFORMANCE max speeds: (I) 25 mph, 40 km/h; (II 40 mph, 65 km/h; (III) 62 mph, 100 km/h; (IV) 96 mph 155 km/h; power-weight ratio: 1500 28.2 lb/hp (38.3 lb-kW) 12.8 kg/hp (17.4 kg/kW) - 1500 Luxe 28.5 lb/hp (38. lb/kW), 12.9 kg/hp (17.6 kg/kW); speed in direct drive at 1,000 rpm: 17.8 mph, 28.7 km/h; consumption: 22. m/imp gal, 18.8 m/US gal, 12.5 l x 100 km.

Zastava 1500 Familiare

See Zastava 1500 except for:

TRANSMISSION tyres: 5.90 x 13.

PERFORMANCE carrying capacity: 1,058 lb, 480 kg.

DIMENSIONS AND WEIGHT weight: 2,293 lb, 1,040 kg.

BODY estate car/st. wagon.

PRACTICAL INSTRUCTIONS tyre pressure: front 24 psi, 1.7 atm, rear 33 psi, 2.3 atm.

ZCZ Zastava 101 Luxe

The Americas

Models now in production

Illustrations and technical information

CHEVROLET CANADA

Bel Air Series

PRICES EX WORKS (Canadian $):

1 Coupé	$ 6,424
2 Sedan	$ 6,561
3 6-pass. St. Wagon	$ 7,197
4 9-pass. St. Wagon	$ 7,366

Power team:	Standard for:	Optional for:
115 hp	1,2	—
130 hp	3,4	1,2
170 hp	—	all

115 hp power team

ENGINE front, 4 stroke; 6 cylinders, vertical, in line; 250 cu in, 4,097 cc (3.87 x 3.53 in, 98.2 x 89.6 mm); compression ratio: 8:1; max power (DIN): 115 hp (84.6 kW) at 3,800 rpm; max torque (DIN): 200 lb ft, 27.6 kg m (270.7 Nm) at 1,600 rpm; max engine rpm: 4,400; 28.1 hp/l (20.6 kW/l); cast iron block and head; 7 crankshaft bearings; valves: overhead, in line, push-rods and rockers, hydraulic tappets; camshafts: 1, side; lubrication: gear pump, full flow filter, 8.3 imp pt, 9.9 US pt, 4.7 l; 1 Rochester 17059014 downdraught single barrel carburettor; cleaner air system; exhaust system with catalytic converter; fuel feed: mechanical pump; water-cooled, 23.6 imp pt, 28.3 US pt, 13.4 l.

TRANSMISSION driving wheels: rear; gearbox: Turbo-Hydramatic 350 automatic transmission, hydraulic torque converter and planetary gears with 3 ratios, max ratio of converter at stall 2, possible manual selection; ratios: I 2.520, II 1.520, III 1, rev 1.930; lever: steering column; final drive: hypoid bevel; axle ratio: 2.560; width of rims: 6''; tyres: FR78 x 15.

PERFORMANCE max speed: about 99 mph, 159 km/h; power-weight ratio: Sedan 30.4 lb/hp (41.4 lb/kW), 13.8 kg/hp (18.8 kg/kW); speed in direct drive at 1,000 rpm: 24.9 mph, 40 km/h; consumption: 18 m/imp gal, 15 m/US gal, 15.7 l x 100 km.

CHASSIS perimeter box-type with 2 cross members; front suspension: independent, wishbones, coil springs, anti-roll bar, telescopic dampers; rear: rigid axle, lower trailing radius arms, upper oblique torque arms, coil springs, anti-roll bar, telescopic dampers.

STEERING recirculating ball, servo; turns lock to lock: 3.16.

BRAKES front disc (diameter 11 in, 27.9 cm), front internal radial fins, rear drum, servo; swept area: total 329.8 sq in, 2,127 sq cm.

ELECTRICAL EQUIPMENT 12 V; 2,500 W battery; 37 A alternator; Delco-Relmy high energy ignition system; 4 headlamps.

DIMENSIONS AND WEIGHT wheel base: 116 in, 295 cm; tracks: 61.80 in, 157 cm front, 60.80 in, 154 cm rear; length: 212.10 in, 538 cm; width: 76 in, 193 cm; height: Coupé 55.30 in, 141 cm - Sedan 56 in, 142 cm; ground clearance: 5.80 in, 14.7 cm; weight: Coupé 3,485 lb, 1,580 kg - Sedan 3,500 lb, 1,587 kg; turning circle: 44.6 ft, 13.6 m; fuel tank: 17.6 imp gal, 21 US gal, 80 l.

OPTIONALS central lever; limited slip differential; electric windows; heavy-duty suspension; GR78 x 15 or GR 70 x 15 tyres with 7'' wide rims; automatic speed control; heated rear window; tilt of steering wheel; electric sunshine roof; vinyl roof; tinted glass; air-conditioning.

130 hp power team

See 115 hp power team, except for:

ENGINE 8 cylinders; 305 cu in, 4,999 cc (3.74 x 3.48 in, 94.9 x 88.4 mm); compression ratio: 8.4:1; max power (DIN): 130 hp (95.7 kW) at 3,200 rpm; max torque (DIN): 245 lb ft, 33.9 kg m (332.5 Nm) at 2,000 rpm; max engine rpm: 3,600; 26 hp/l (19.1 kW/l); 5 crankshaft bearings; camshafts: 1, at centre of Vee; 1 Rochester 17059134 downdraught twin barrel carburettor; cooling system: 27.6 imp pt, 33.2 US pt, 15.7 l.

TRANSMISSION axle ratio: 2.410 - st. wagons 2.560; width of rims: st. wagons 7''; tyres: st. wagons HR78 x 15.

PERFORMANCE max speed: about 106 mph, 170 km/h; power-weight ratio: 6-pass. St. Wagon 30.7 lb/hp (41.8 lb/kW), 13.9 kg/hp (18.9 kg/kW); speed in direct drive at 1,000 rpm: 29.3, mph 47.2 km/h; consumption: 16.8 m/imp gal, 14 m/US gal, 16.8 l x 100 km.

CHEVROLET Bel Air Coupé

STEERING turns lock to lock: st. wagons 3.30.

BRAKES (for st. wagons only) front disc (diameter 11.86 in, 30.1 cm); swept area: total 375.1 sq in, 2,420 sq cm.

ELECTRICAL EQUIPMENT 3,200 W battery.

DIMENSIONS AND WEIGHT (for st. wagons only) tracks: 62.20 in, 158 cm front, 64.10 in, 163 cm rear; length: 214.70 in, 545 cm; width: 79.10 in, 201 cm; height: 58 in, 147 cm; ground clearance: 5.90 in, 15 cm; weight: 6-pass. St. Wagon 3,997 lb, 1,812 kg; turning circle: 45.1 ft, 13.8 m; fuel tank: 18.3 imp gal, 22 US gal, 83 l.

OPTIONALS Turbo-Hydramatic 200 automatic transmission with 3 ratios (I 2.740, II 1.570, III 1, rev 2.070), max ratio of converter at stall 2.35, possible manual selection, 2.410 axle ratio.

170 hp power team

See 115 hp power team, except for:

ENGINE 8 cylinders; 350 cu in, 5,736 cc (4 x 3.48 in, 101.6 x 88.4 mm); compression ratio: 8.2:1, max power (DIN): 170 hp (125.1 kW) at 3,800 rpm; max torque (DIN): 270 lb ft, 37.2 kg m (364.8 Nm) at 2,400 rpm; max engine rpm: 3,600; 29.6 hp/l (21.8 kW/l); 5 crankshaft bearings; camshafts: 1, at centre of Vee; 1 Rochester 17059202 downdraught 4-barrel carburettor; cooling system: 27 imp pt, 33.2 US pt, 15.7 l.

TRANSMISSION axle ratio: 2.410 - st. wagons 2.560; width of rims: st. wagons 7''; tyres: st. wagons HR78 x 15.

PERFORMANCE max speed: about 109 mph, 175 km/h; power-weight ratio: Sedan 21.3 lb/hp (29 lb/kW), 9. kg/hp (13.1 kg/kW); consumption: 19.2 m/imp gal, 1 m/US gal, 14.7 l x 100 km.

STEERING turns lock to lock: st. wagons 3.30.

BRAKES (for st. wagons only) front disc (diameter 11.8 in, 30.1 cm); swept area: total 375.1 sq in, 2,420 sq cm.

ELECTRICAL EQUIPMENT 3,200 W battery.

DIMENSIONS AND WEIGHT tracks: st. wagons 62.20 in 158 cm front, 64.10 in, 163 cm rear; length: st. wagon 214.70 in, 545 cm; width: st. wagons 79.10 in, 201 cm height: st. wagons 58 in, 147 cm; ground clearance: st wagons 5.90 in, 15 cm; weight: Coupé 3,609 lb, 1,636 kg Sedan 3,624 lb, 1,643 kg - 6-pass. St. Wagon 4,010 lb 1,818 kg; turning circle: st. wagons 45.1 ft, 13.8 m; fue tank: st. wagons 18.3 imp gal, 22 US gal, 83 l.

OPTIONALS Turbo-Hydramatic 200 automatic transmissio with 3 ratios (I 2.740, II 1.570, III 1, rev 2.070), ma ratio of converter at stall 2.35, possible manual selection 3.080 axle ratio.

CHEVROLET Bel Air Sedan

FORD   CANADA

Granada Special Edition Series

PRICES EX WORKS (Canadian $):

2-dr Sedan	$ 4,901
4-dr Sedan	$ 5,047

97 hp power team

ENGINE front, 4 stroke; 6 cylinders, in line; 250 cu in, 4,097 cc (3.68 x 3.91 in, 93.5 x 99.3 mm); compression ratio: 8.6:1; max power (DIN): 97 hp (71.4 kW) at 3,200 rpm; max torque (DIN): 210 lb ft, 29 kg m (284.4 Nm) at 1,400 rpm; max engine rpm: 3,800; 23.7 hp/l (17.4 kW/l); cast iron block and head; 7 crankshaft bearings; valves: overhead, in line, push-rods and rockers, hydraulic tappets; camshafts: 1, side; lubrication: rotary pump, full flow filter, 8.3 imp pt, 9.9 US pt, 4.7 l; 1 Carter YFA 9510 D9DE-EA downdraught single barrel carburettor; cleaner air system; exhaust system with catalytic converter; fuel feed: mechanical pump; water-cooled, 17.4 imp pt, 21 US pt, 9.9 l.

TRANSMISSION driving wheels: rear; clutch: single dry plate, semi-centrifugal; gearbox: mechanical; gears: 4, fully synchronized with overdrive/top; ratios: I 3.290, II 1.840, III 1, IV 0.810, rev 3.290; lever: central; final drive: hypoid bevel; axle ratio: 3; width of rims: 6''; tyres: DR78 x 14.

PERFORMANCE max speed: about 93 mph, 149 km/h; power-weight ratio: 4-dr 31.9 lb/hp (43,3 lb/kW), 14.4 kg/hp (19.6 kg/kW); speed in top at 1,000 rpm: 25.5 mph, 41 km/h; consumption: 21.6 m/imp gal, 18 m/US gal, 13.1 l x 100 km.

CHASSIS integral; front suspension: independent, wishbones, coil springs, anti-roll bar, telescopic dampers; rear: rigid axle, semi-elliptic leafsprings, telescopic dampers.

STEERING recirculating ball; turns lock to lock: 5.18.

BRAKES front disc (diameter 11,03 in, 28 cm), front internal radial fins, rear compensator, rear drum; swept area: total 348.2 sq in, 2,247 sq cm.

ELECTRICAL EQUIPMENT 12 V; 36 Ah battery; 40 A alternator; Motorcraft transistorized ignition; 2 headlamps.

DIMENSIONS AND WEIGHT wheel base: 109.90 in, 279 cm; tracks: 59 in, 150 cm front, 57.70 in, 147 cm rear; length: 197.80 in, 502 cm; width: 74 in, 188 cm; height: 53.20 in, 135 cm - 4-dr 53.30 in, 135 cm; ground clearance: 4.41 in, 11.2 cm; weight: 2-dr 3,054 lb, 1,384 kg - 4-dr 3,093 lb, 1,401 kg; turning circle: 39 ft, 11.9 m; fuel tank: 15 imp gal, 18 US gal, 68 l.

BODY saloon/sedan; 5 seats, separate front seats, reclining backrests.

OPTIONALS heavy-duty cooling system; Select-Shift Cruise-O-Matic automatic transmission with 3 ratios (I 2.460, II 1.460, III 1, rev 2.800), max ratio of converter at stall 2.3, possible manual selection, steering column or central lever, 2,790 axle ratio; aluminum wheels; ER78 x 14 or FR78 x 14 tyres; tilt of steering wheel; power steering; servo brake; heavy-duty suspension; automatic speed control; 54 Ah heavy-duty battery; metallic spray; vinyl roof; electric windows; heated rear window; tinted glass; vinyl roof; air-conditioning.

Custom 500 Series

PRICES EX WOKS (Canadian $):

2-dr Sedan	$ 6,538
4-dr Sedan	$ 6,672

129 hp power team

ENGINE front, 4 stroke; 8 cylinders; 302 cu in, 4,950 cc (4 x 3 in, 101.6 x 76.2 mm); compression ratio: 8.4:1; max power (DIN): 129 hp (94.9 kW) at 3,600 rpm; max torque (DIN): 223 lb ft, 30.8 kg m (302.1 Nm) at 2,600 rpm; max engine rpm: 4,000; 26.1 hp/l (19.2 kW/l); cast iron block and head; 5 crankshaft bearings; valves: overhead, in line, push-rods and rockers, hydraulic tappets; camshafts: 1, at centre of Vee; lubrication: rotary pump, full flow filter, 8.3 imp pt, 9.9 US pt, 4.7 l; 1 Ford 2700A D9AE-YB-JB downdraught carburettor with variable Venturi; cleaner air system; exhaust system with 2 catalytic converters; fuel

FORD Granada Special Edition 4-dr Sedan

MERCURY Bobcat 3-dr Runabout

feed: mechanical pump; water-cooled, 22.2 imp pt, 62.6 US pt, 12.6 l.

TRANSMISSION driving wheels: rear; gearbox: Select-Shift Cruise-O-Matic automatic transmission, hydraulic torque converter and planetary gears with 3 ratios, max ratio of converter at stall 1.97, possible manual selection; ratios: I 2.400, II 1.470, III 1, rev 2; lever: steering column; final drive: hypoid bevel; axle ratio: 2.260; width of rims: 5.5''; tyres: FR78 x 14.

PERFORMANCE max speed: about 96 mph, 154 km/h; power-weight ratio: 4-dr 26.7 lb/hp (36.2 lb/kW), 12.1 kg/hp (16.4 kg/kW); speed in direct drive at 1,000 rpm: 25.4 mph, 40.8 km/h; consumption: 18 m/imp gal, 15 m/US gal, 15.7 l x 100 km.

CHASSIS perimeter box-type frame; front suspension: independent, wishbones, coil springs, anti-roll bar, telescopic dampers; rear: rigid axle, lower trailing radius arms, upper oblique torque arms, coil springs, telescopic dampers.

STEERING recirculating ball, servo; turns lock to lock: 3.29.

BRAKES front disc (diameter 11.08 in, 28.1 cm), front internal radial fins, rear compensator, rear drum, servo; swept area: front 228.7 sq in, 1,475 sq cm, rear 157.1 sq in, 1,013 sq cm, total 385.8 sq in, 2,488 sq cm.

ELECTRICAL EQUIPMENT 12 V; 36 A battery; 60 A alternator; Motorcraft transistorized ignition; 4 headlamps.

DIMENSIONS AND WEIGHT wheel base: 114.30 in, 290 cm;

tracks: 62.20 in, 158 cm front, 62 in, 157 cm rear; length: 209 in, 531 cm; width: 77.50 in, 197 cm; height: 54.50 in, 138 cm; ground clearance: 4.87 in, 12.4 cm; weight: 2-dr Sedan 3,411 lb, 1,547 kg - 4-dr Sedan 3,439 lb, 1,560 kg; fuel tank: 15.8 imp gal, 19 US gal, 72 l.

BODY saloon/sedan; 6 seats, bench front seats with built in headrests.

OPTIONALS heavy-duty cooling system: 2.730 axle ratio; GR78 x 14 tyres with 6.5'' wide rims; heavy-duty suspension with rear anti-roll bar; tilt of steering wheel; 71 Ah heavy-duty battery; heated rear window; tinted glass; automatic speed control; luxury interior; vinyl roof; electric windows; air-conditioning.

MERCURY   CANADA

Bobcat Series

PRICES EX WORKS (Canadian $):

2-dr '' Special ''	$ 3,683
2-dr Sedan	$ 4,102
3-dr Runabout	$ 4,253
2-dr St. Wagon '' Special ''	$ 4,245
2-dr St. Wagon	$ 4,685

88 hp power team

ENGINE front, 4 stroke; 4 cylinders, in line, 140 cu in, 2,300 cc (3.78 x 3.13 in, 95.9 x 79.5 mm); compression ratios: 9:1; max power (DIN): 88 hp (64.8 kW) at 4,800 rpm; max torque (DIN): 118 lb ft, 16.3 kg m (159.8 Nm) at 2,800 rpm; max engine rpm: 5,200; cast iron block and head; 5 crankshaft bearings; valves: overhead, Vee-slanted, rockers, hydraulic tappets; camshafts: 1, overhead, cogged belt; lubrication: gear pump, full flow filter, 8.3 imp pt, 9.9 US pt, 4.7 l; 1 Holley-Weber D9EE-ALA/AMA downdraught twin barrel carburettor; cleaner air system; exhaust system with catalytic converter; fuel feed: mechanical pump; water-cooled, 14.4 imp pt, 17.3 US pt, 8.2 l.

TRANSMISSION driving wheels: rear; clutch: single dry plate; gearbox: mechanical; gears: 4, fully synchronized; ratios: I 3.980, II 2.140, III 1.420, IV 1, rev 3.990; lever: central; final drive: hypoid bevel; axle ratio: 2.730 - st. wagons 3.080; width of rims: 5''; tyres: BR78 x 13.

PERFORMANCE max speed: about 96 mph, 154 km/h; power-weight ratio: 27.4 lb/hp (37.3 lb/kW), 12.4 kg/hp (16.9 kg/kW) - st. wagons 29.1 lb/hp (39.6 lb/kW), 13.2 kg/hp (17.9 kg/kW); speed in direct drive at 1,000 rpm: 19.3 mph, 31 km/h; consumption: 26.4 m/imp gal, 22 m/US gal, 10.7 l x 100 km.

CHASSIS integral; front suspension: independent, wish-

bones, coil springs, telescopic dampers; rear: rigid axle, semi-elliptic leafsprings, telescopic dampers.

STEERING rack-and-pinion; turns lock to lock: 4.15.

BRAKES front disc (diameter 9.30 in, 23.6 cm), front internal radial fins, rear drum, rear compensator; swept area: front 145.5 sq in, 939 sq cm, rear 99 sq in, 639 sq cm, total 244.5 sq in, 1,578 sq cm.

ELECTRICAL EQUIPMENT 12 V; 45 Ah battery; 40 A alternator; Motorcraft transistorized ignition; 2 headlamps.

DIMENSIONS AND WEIGHT wheel base: 94.50 sq in, 240 cm - st. wagons 94.80 in, 241 cm; tracks: 55 in, 140 cm front, 55.80 in, 142 cm rear; length: 168.80 in, 429 cm - st. wagons 178.60 in, 454 cm; width: 69.40 in, 176 cm - st. wagons 69.70 in, 177 cm; height: 50.50 in, 128 cm - st. wagons 52 in, 132 cm; ground clearance: 5.30 in, 13.5 cm - st. wagons 5.11 in, 13 cm; weight: 2,416 lb, 1,095 kg - st. wagons 2,565 lb, 1,163 kg; turning circle: 35.9 ft, 10.9 m; fuel tank: 10.8 imp gal, 13 US gal, 49 l - st. wagons 11.7 imp gal, 14 US gal, 53 l.

BODY 4 seats, separate front seats; folding rear seat.

OPTIONALS heavy-duty cooling system; limited slip differential; 3.080 axle ratio (except for st. wagons); Select-shift automatic transmission with 3 ratios (I 2.470, II 1.470, III 1, rev. 2.110), max ratio of converter at stall 2.9, possible manual selection, central lever, 3.080 axle ratio; aluminum wheels; BR70 x 13 or A70 x 13 tyres with 5'' wide rims; anti-roll bar on front suspension; power steering; tilt of steering wheel; servo brake; 54 Ah heavy-duty battery; heated rear window; tinted glass; luxury interior; Sports equipment; air-conditioning; sunshine roof (except for st. wagons).

Monarch Special Edition Series

PRICES EX WORKS (Canadian $):

2-dr Sedan	$ 4,931
4-dr Sedan	$ 5,078

97 hp power team

ENGINE front, 4 stroke; 6 cylinders, in line; 250 cu in, 4,097 cc (3.68 x 3.91 in, 93.5 x 99.3 mm); compression ratio: 8.6:1; max power (DIN): 97 hp (71.4 kW) at 3,200 rpm; max torque (DIN): 210 lb ft, 29 kg m (284.4 Nm) at 1,400 rpm; max engine rpm: 3,800; 23.7 hp/l (17.4 kW/l); cast iron block and head; 7 crankshaft bearings; valves: overhead, in line, push-rods and rockers, hydraulic tappets camshafts: 1, side; lubrication: rotary pump, full flow filter, 8.3 imp pt, 9.9 US pt, 4.7 l; 1 Carter YFA9510 D9DE-EA downdraught single barrel carburettor; cleaner air system; exhaust system with catalytic converter; fuel feed: mechanical pump; water-cooled, 17.4 imp pt, 21 US pt, 9.9 l.

TRANSMISSION driving wheels: rear; clutch: single dry plate, semi-centrifugal; gearbox: mechanical; gears: 4, fully synchronized with overdrive/top; ratios: I 3.290, II 1.840, III 1, IV 0.810, rev 3.290; lever: central; final drive: hypoid bevel; axle ratio: 3; width of rims: 6''; tyres: DR78 x 14.

PERFORMANCE max speed: about 93 mph, 149 km/h; power-weight ratio: 4-dr 31.9 lb/hp (43.4 lb/kW), 13.7 kg/hp (18.6 kg/kW); speed in top at 1,000 rpm: 25.5 mph, 41 km/h; consumption: 21.6 m/imp gal, 18 m/US gal, 13.1 l x 100 km.

CHASSIS integral; front suspension: independent, wishbones, coil springs, anti-roll bar, telescopic dampers; rear: rigid axle, semi-elliptic leafsprings, telescopic dampers.

STEERING recirculating ball; turns lock to lock: 5.18.

BRAKES front disc (diameter 11.03 in, 28 cm), front internal radial fins, rear compensator, rear drum; swept area: total 348.2 sq in, 2,247 sq cm.

ELECTRICAL EQUIPMENT 12 V; 36 Ah battery; 40 A alternator; Motorcraft transistorized ignition; 2 headlamps.

DIMENSIONS AND WEIGHT wheel base: 109.90 in, 279 cm; tracks: 59 in, 150 cm front, 57.70 in, 147 cm rear; length: 197.80 in, 502 cm; width: 74 in, 188 cm; height: 2-dr 53.20 in, 135 cm - 4-dr 53.30 in, 135 cm; ground clearance: 4.41 in, 11.2 cm; weight: 2-dr 3,056 lb, 1,311 kg - 4-dr 3,098 lb, 1,330 kg; turning circle: 39 ft, 11.9 m; fuel tank: 15 imp gal, 18 US gal, 68 l.

MERCURY Bobcat 3-dr Runabout

BODY saloon/sedan; 5 seats, bench front seats with built-in headrests.

OPTIONALS heavy-duty cooling system; Select-Shift Cruise-O-Matic automatic transmission with 3 ratios (I 2.460, II 1.460, III 1, rev 2.800), max ratio of converter at stall 2.3, possible manual selection, steering column or central lever, 2.790 axle ratio; aluminum wheels; ER78 x 14 or FR78 x 14 tyres with 6'' wide rims; heavy-duty suspension; power steering; tilt of steering wheel; servo brake; automatic speed control; electric windows; tinted glass, heated rear window; 54 Ah heavy-duty battery; metallic spray; vinyl roof; separate front seats with reclining backrests; electric sunshine roof; ESS equipment; Ghia equipment; air-conditioning.

Cougar 'S' Series

PRICES EX WORKS (Canadian $):

2-dr Hardtop	$ 6,149
4-dr Pillared Hardtop	$ 6,256

133 hp power team

ENGINE front, 4 stroke; 8 cylinders; 302 cu in, 4,590 cc (4 x 3 in, 101.6 x 76.2 mm); compression ratio: 8.4:1;

MERCURY Monarch Special Edition 4-dr Sedan

MERCURY Monarch Special Edition 2-dr Sedan

max power (DIN): 133 hp (97.9 kW) at 3,400 rpm; max torque (DIN): 245 lb ft, 33.8 kg m (331.5 Nm) at 1,600 rpm; max engine rpm: 4,000; 26.9 hp/l (19.8 kW/l); cast iron block and head; 5 crankshaft bearings; valves: overhead, in line, push-rods and rockers, hydraulic tappets; camshafts: 1, at centre of Vee; lubrication: rotary pump, full flow filter, 8.3 imp pt, 9.9 US pt, 4.7 l; 1 Ford 2150A D84E-TA/UA downdraught twin barrel carburettor; cleaner air system; exhaust system with 2 catalytic converters; fuel feed: mechanical pump; water-cooled, 23.8 imp pt, 28.5 US pt, 13.5 l.

TRANSMISSION driving wheels: rear; gearbox: Select-Shift automatic transmission, hydraulic torque converter and planetary gears with 3 ratios, max ratio of converter at stall 1.97, possible manual selection: ratios: I 2.460, II 1 460, III 1, rev 2.200; lever: steering column; final drive: hypoid bevel; axle ratio: 2.750; width of rims: 5.5''; tyres: HR78 x 14.

PERFORMANCE max speed: about 103 mph, 165 km/h; power-weight ratio: 4-dr Pillared Hardtop 28.6 lb/hp (38.8 lb/kW), 13 kg/hp (17.6 kg/kW); speed in direct drive at 1,000 rpm: 25.6 mph, 41.2 km/h; consumption: 16.8 m/imp gal, 14 m/US gal, 16.8 l x 100 km.

CHASSIS perimeter box-type frame; front suspension: independent, wishbones, coil springs, anti-roll bar, telescopic dampers; rear: rigid axle, lower trailing radius arms, upper oblique torque arms, coil springs, telescopic dampers.

STEERING recirculating ball, servo; turns lock to lock: 4.

BRAKES front disc (diameter 10.72 in, 27.2 cm), front internal radial fins, rear compensator, rear drum, servo; swept area: front 212 sq in, 1,368 sq cm, rear 155.9 sq in, 1,006 sq cm, total 367.9 sq in, 2,374 sq cm

ELECTRICAL EQUIPMENT 12 V; 36 Ah battery; 40 A alternator; Motorcraft transistorized ignition; 4 headlamps.

DIMENSIONS AND WEIGHT wheel base: 2-dr 113.90 in, 289 cm - 4-dr 117.90 in, 299 cm; tracks: 63.60 in, 161 cm front, 63.50 in, 161 cm rear; length: 2-dr 217.20 in, 552 cm - 4-dr 221.20 in, 562 cm; width: 78.60 in, 200 cm; height: 2-dr 52.60 in, 134 cm - 4-dr 53.30 in, 135 cm; ground clearance: 2-dr 4.76 in, 12.1 cm - 4-dr 4.73 in, 12 cm; weight: 2-dr Hardtop 3,732 lb, 1,693 kg - 4-dr Pillared Hardtop 3,802 lb, 1,725 kg; turning circle: 42.4 ft, 12.9 m; fuel tank: 17.6 imp gal, 21 US gal, 80 l.

BODY hardtop; 6 seats, bench front seats with built-in headrests.

OPTIONALS heavy-duty cooling system; limited slip differential; GR78 x 15 tyres with 6'' wide rims or HR70 x 15 tyres with 6.5'' wide rims; Cross Country suspensions with rear anti-roll bar; central lever; tilt of steering wheel; 77 Ah heavy-duty battery; electric windows; heated rear window; tinted glass; air-conditioning; separate front seats with reclining backrests; automatic speed control sunshine roof; larger fuel tank; vinyl roof; Brougham equipment.

Marquis Meteor Series

PRICES EX WORKS (Canadian $):

2-dr Sedan	$ 6,655
4-dr Sedan	$ 6,789

129 hp power team

ENGINE front, 4 stroke; 8 cylinders; 302 cu in, 4,950 cc (4 x 3 in, 101.6 x 76.2 mm); compression ratio: 8.4:1; max power (DIN): 129 hp (94.9 kW) at 3,600 rpm; max torque (DIN): 223 lb ft, 30.8 kg m (302.1 Nm) at 2,600 rpm; max engine rpm: 4,000; 26.1 hp/l (19.2 kW/l); cast iron block and head; 5 crankshaft bearings; valves: overhead, in line, push-rods and rockers, hydraulic tappets; camshafts: 1, at centre of Vee; lubrication: rotary pump, full flow filter, 8.3 imp pt, 9.9 US pt, 4.7 l; 1 Ford 2700 D9AE-YB-JB downdraught carburettor with variable Venturi; cleaner air system; exhaust system with 2 catalytic converters; fuel feed: mechanical pump; water-cooled, 22.2 imp pt, 26.6 US pt, 12.6 l.

TRANSMISSION driving wheels: rear; gearbox: Select-Shift Cruise-O-Matic automatic transmission, hydraulic torque converter and planetary gears with 3 ratios, max ratio of converter at stall 1.97, possible manual selection; ratios: I 2.400, II 1.470, III 1, rev 2; lever: steering column; final drive: hypoid bevel; axle ratio: 2.260; width of rims: 5.5''; tyres: FR78 x 14.

PERFORMANCE max speed: about 96 mph, 154 km/h; power-weight ratio: 4-dr 27 lb/hp (36.8 lb/kW), 12.3 kg/hp (16.7 kg/kW); speed in direct drive at 1,000 rpm: 25.4 mph, 40.8 km/h; consumption: 18 m/imp gal, 15 m/US gal, 15.7 l x 100 km.

MERCURY Cougar Brougham 4-dr Pillared Hardtop

MERCURY Cougar Brougham
4-dr Pillared Hardtop

CHASSIS perimeter box-type frame; front suspension: independent, wishbones, coil springs, anti-roll bar, telescopic dampers; rear: rigid axle, lower trailing radius arms, upper oblique torque arms, coil springs, telescopic dampers.

STEERING recirculating ball, servo; turns lock to lock: 3.40.

BRAKES front disc (diameter 11.08 in, 28.1 cm), front internal radial fins, rear compensator, rear drum; servo; swept area: front 228.7 sq in, 1,475 sq cm, rear 157.1 sq in, 1,013 sq cm, total 385.8 sq in, 2,488 sq cm.

ELECTRICAL EQUIPMENT 12 V; 36 Ah battery; 60 A alternator; Motorcraft transistorized ignition; 4 headlamps.

DIMENSIONS AND WEIGHT wheel base: 114.30 in, 290 cm; tracks: 62.20 in, 158 cm front, 62 in, 157 cm rear; length: 212 in, 538 cm; width: 77.50 in, 197 cm; height: 54.50 in, 138 cm; ground clearance: 4.87 in, 12.4 cm; weight: 2-dr Sedan 3,442 lb, 1,561 kg - 4-dr Sedan 3,489 lb, 1,583 kg; fuel tank: 15.8 imp gal, 19 US gal, 72 l.

BODY saloon/sedan; 6 seats, bench front seats with built-in headrests.

OPTIONALS heavy-duty cooling system; 2.730 axle ratio; GR78 x 14 tyres with 6.5'' wide rims; heavy-duty suspension with rear anti-roll bar; tilt of steering wheel; 71 Ah heavy-duty battery; electric windows; heated rear window;

MERCURY Marquis Meteor 4-dr Sedan

129 HP POWER TEAM

tinted glass; automatic speed control; luxury interior; separate front seats with reclining backrests; vinyl roof; leather upholstery; air-conditioning.

PONTIAC   CANADA

Acadian Series

PRICES EX WORKS (Canadian $):

S Hatchback Coupé	$ 3,879
Hatchback Coupé	$ 4,360
Hatchback Sedan	$ 4,492

Power team:	Standard for:	Optional for:
70 hp	all	—
74 hp	—	all

70 hp power team

ENGINE front, 4 stroke; 4 cylinders, vertical, in line; 97.6 cu in, 1,599 cc (3.23 x 2.98 in, 82 x 75.6 mm); compression ratio: 8.6:1; max power (DIN): 70 hp (51.5 kW) at 5,200 rpm; max torque (DIN): 82 lb ft, 11.3 kg m (110.8 Nm) at 2,400 rpm; max engine rpm: 5,600; 43.8 hp/l (32.2 kW/l); cast iron block and head; 5 crankshaft bearings; valves: overhead, hydraulic tappets; camshafts: 1, overhead, cogged belt; lubrication: gear pump, full flow filter, 8.3 imp pt, 9.9 US pt, 4.7 l; 1 Holley 466336 downdraught twin barrel carburettor; cleaner air system; exhaust system with catalytic converter; fuel feed: mechanical pump; water-cooled, 15 imp pt, 18 US pt, 8.5 l.

TRANSMISSION driving wheels: rear; clutch: single dry plate (diaphragm); gearbox: mechanical; gears: 4, fully synchronized; ratios: I 3.750, II 2.160, II 1.380, IV 1, rev 3.820; lever: central; final drive: hypoid bevel; axle ratio: 3.700; width of rims: 5''; tyres: P155/80R x 13.

PERFORMANCE max speed: about 93 mph, 149 km/h; power-weight ratio: Hatchback Sedan 29.3 lb/hp (39.8 lb/kW), 13.3 kg/hp (18.1 kg/kW); speed in direct drive at 1,000 rpm: 17.2 mph, 27.7 km/h; consumption: 34.9 m/imp gal, 29 m/US gal, 8.1 l x 100 km.

CHASSIS integral with cross member reinforcements; front suspension: independent, wishbones, coil springs, anti-roll bar, telescopic dampers; rear: rigid axle (torque tube), longitudinal trailing radius arms, coil springs, transverse linkage bar, anti-roll bar, telescopic dampers.

STEERING rack-and-pinion; turns lock to lock: 3.60.

BRAKES front disc (diameter 9.68 in, 24.6 cm), rear drum; swept area: total 297.7 sq in, 1,920 sq cm.

ELECTRICAL EQUIPMENT 12 V; 2,500 W battery; 32 A alternator; Delco-Remy high energy ignition system; 2 headlamps.

DIMENSIONS AND WEIGHT wheel base: 94.30 in, 239 cm - Hatchback Sedan 97.30 in, 247 cm; tracks: 51.20 in, 130 cm front, 51.20 in, 130 cm rear; length: S Hatchback Coupé 158.80 in, 403 cm - Hatchback Coupé 159.70 in, 406 cm - Hatchback Sedan 162.60 in, 443 cm; width: 61.80 in, 157 cm; height: 52.30 in, 133 cm; ground clearance: 5.30 in, 13.5 weight: S Hatchback Coupé 1,925 lb, 873 kg - Hatchback Coupé 1,972 lb, 894 kg - Hatchback Sedan 2,052 lb, 931 kg; turning circle: 34.3 ft, 10.5 m - Hatchback Sedan 34.9 ft, 10.6 m; fuel tank: 10.3 imp gal, 12.5 US gal, 47 l.

OPTIONALS 4.110 axle ratio; Turbo-Hydramatic automatic transmission, hydraulic torque converter and planetary gears with 3 ratios (I 2.400, II 1.480, III 1, rev 1.920), max ratio of converter at stall 2.20, possible manual selection, central lever, 3.700 or 4.110 axle ratio; heavy-duty radiator; heavy-duty battery; tilt of steering wheel; servo brake; heated rear window; air-conditioning.

74 hp power team

See 70 hp power team, except for:

ENGINE max power (DIN): 74 hp (54.5 kW) at 5,200 rpm; max torque (DIN): 88 lb ft, 12.1 kg m (118.7 Nm) at 2,800 rpm; 46.3 hp/l (34.1 kW/l); 1 Holley 466371 downdraught twin barrel carburettor.

PERFORMANCE max speed: about 96 mph, 155 km/h; power-weight ratio: Hatchback Sedan 27.7 lb/hp (37.7 lb/kW), 12.6 kg/hp (17.1 kg/kW).

OPTIONALS 4.110 axle ratio not available.

Laurentian - Parisienne Series

PRICES EX WORKS (Canadian $):

1 Laurentian Coupé	$ 6,618
2 Laurentian Sedan	$ 6,755
3 Laurentian Safari St. Wagon	$ 7,435
4 Parisienne Coupé	$ 7,239
5 Parisienne Sedan	$ 7,376
6 Parisienne Safari St. Wagon	$ 8,195

Power team:	Standard for:	Optional for:
115 hp	1,2	—
130 hp	4,5	1,2
135 hp	3,6	—
150 hp	—	all
155 hp	—	all

115 hp power team

ENGINE front, 4 stroke; 6 cylinders, Vee-slanted at 90°; 231 cu in, 3,785 cc (3.80 x 3.40 in, 96.5 x 86.4 mm); compression ratio: 8:1; max power (DIN): 115 hp (84.6 kW) at 3,800 rpm; max torque (DIN): 190 lb ft, 26.2 kg m (257 Nm) at 2,000 rpm; max engine rpm: 4,400; 30.4 hp/l (22.4 kW/l); cast iron block and head; 4 crankshaft bearings; valves: overhead, in linee, push-rods and rockers, hydraulic tappets; camshafts: 1, at centre of Vee; lubrication: gear pump, full flow filter, 8.3 imp pt, 9.9 US pt, 4.7 l; 1 Rochester 2GE downdraught twin barrel carburettor; cleaner air system; exhaust system with catalytic converter; fuel feed: mechanical pump; water-cooled, 22. imp pt, 26.6 US pt, 12.6 l.

TRANSMISSION driving wheels: rear; gearbox: Turbo Hydramatic automatic transmission, hydraulic torque converter and planetary gear with 3 ratios, max ratio of converter at stall 2, possible manual selection; ratios I 2.520, II 1.520, III 1, rev 1.940; lever: steering column; final drive: hypoid bevel; axle ratio: 2.730; width of rims: 6''; tyres: FR78 x 15.

PERFORMANCE max speed: about 93 mph, 149 km/h; power-weight ratio: Sedan 30.5 lb/hp (41.5 lb/kW), 13. kg/hp (18.8 kg/kW); speed in direct drive at 1,000 rpm: 23.3 mph, 37.5 km/h; consumption: 21.6 m/imp gal, 1 m/US gal, 13.1 l x 100 km.

CHASSIS perimeter; front suspension: independent, wishbones, coil springs, anti-roll bar, telescopic dampers; rear: rigid axle, lower trailing radius arms, upper oblique torque arms, coil springs, telescopic dampers.

STEERING recirculating ball, variable ratio servo; turn lock to lock: 3.30.

BRAKES front disc (diameter 11 in, 27.9 cm), front internal radial fins, rear drum, servo; swept area: total 337. sq in, 2,175 sq cm.

PONTIAC Acadian S Hatchback Coupé

PONTIAC Laurentian Coupé

CTRICAL EQUIPMENT 12 V; 2,500 W battery; 42 A rnator; Delco-Remy transistorized ignition; 4 headlamps.

MENSIONS AND WEIGHT wheel base: 116 in, 295 cm; ks: 61.70 in, 157 cm front, 60.70 in, 154 cm rear; gth: 214.30 in, 544 cm; width: 76.40 in, 194 cm; height: pé 54.20 in, 138 cm - Sedan 54.90 in, 139 cm; ground arance: 5.60 in, 14.2 cm; weight: Coupé 3,475 lb, 7 kg - Sedan 3,507 lb, 1,591 kg; turning circle: 41.6 ft, m; fuel tank: 17.2 imp gal, 20.6 US gal, 78 l.

TIONALS limited slip differential; 3.230 axle ratio; 78 x 15 or HR78 x 15 tyres with 6'' wide rims; GR70 x 15 es with 7'' wide rims; automatic levelling control; tilt steering wheel; heavy-duty battery; heavy-duty alterna- reclining backrests; speed control device; electric dows; heated rear window; air-conditioning.

130 hp power team

115 hp power team, except for:

GINE 8 cylinders; 301 cu in, 4,932 cc (4 x 3 in, 101.6 x 76.2); compression ratio: 8.1; max power (DIN): 130 hp 7 kW) at 3,200 rpm; max torque (DIN): 245 lb ft, kg m (331.5 Nm) at 2,000 rpm; max engine rpm: 4,000; hp/l (19.4 kW/l); 5 crankshaft bearings; lubricating tem: 10 imp pt, 12 US pt, 5.7 l; 1 Rochester M2MC ndraught twin barrel carburettor; cooling system: 34.8 pt, 41.9 US pt, 19.8 l.

ANSMISSION axle ratio: 2.290.

FORMANCE max speed: about 99 mph, 160 km/h; power- ght ratio: Laurentian Sedan 27.9 lb/hp (37.9 lb/kW), kg/hp (17.2 kg/kW) - Parisienne Sedan 28.2 lb/hp 4 lb/kW), 12.8 kg/hp (17.4 kg/k W); speed in direct ve at 1,000 rpm: 25 mph, 40 km/h; consumption: 20.5 mp gal, 17 m/US gal, 13.8 l x 100 km.

CTRICAL EQUIPMENT 3,200 W battery.

MENSIONS AND WEIGHT weight: Laurentian Coupé 3,593 1,629 kg - Sedan 3,625 lb, 1,644 kg - Parisienne Coupé 6 lb, 1,640 kg - Sedan 3,672 lb, 1,665 kg.

TIONALS 2.410 axle ratio.

135 hp power team

115 hp power team, except for:

GINE 8 cylinders; 301 cu in, 4,932 cc (4 x 3 in, 101.6 x 76.2); compression ratio: 8.1:1; max power (DIN): 135 hp 4 kW) at 3,800 rpm; max torque (DIN): 240 lb ft, kg m (324.6 Nm) at 1,600 rpm; 27.4 hp/l (20.2 kW/l); crankshaft bearings; lubricating system: 10 imp pt, 12 pt, 5.7 l; 1 Rochester M2MC downdraught twin barrel burettor; cooling system: 34.8 imp pt, 41.9 US pt, 19.8 l.

ANSMISSION axle ratio: 2.560; tyres: HR78 x 15.

RFORMANCE max speed: about 99 mph, 160 km/h; power- ight ratio: Laurentian Safari 29.6 lb/hp (40.2 lb/kW), 4 kg/hp (18.2 kg/kW) - Parisienne Safari 29.8 lb/hp .5 lb/kW), 13.5 kg/hp (18.4 kg/kW); speed in direct ve at 1,000 rpm: 25 mph, 40 km/h; consumption: 18 imp gal, 15 m/US gal, 15.7 l x 100 km.

AKES swept area: total 362.58 sq in, 2,339 sq cm.

ECTRICAL EQUIPMENT 3,200 W batery.

MENSIONS AND WEIGHT tracks: 62 in, 158 cm front, 10 in, 163 cm rear; length: 215.10 in, 546 cm; width: 90 in, 203 cm; height: 57.30 in, 146 cm; ground clear- ce: 6 in, 15.2 cm; weight: Laurentian Safari St. Wagon 97 lb, 1,813 kg - Parisienne Safari St. Wagon 4,023 lb, 25 kg; turning circle: 42.3 ft, 12.9 m; fuel tank: 18.3 p gal, 22 US gal, 83 l.

DY estate car/st. wagon; 4+1 doors; 6 seats; folding r seat.

150 hp power team

e 115 hp power team, except for:

GINE 8 cylinders; 301 cu in, 4,932 cc (4 x 3 in, 101.6x76.2 n); compression ratio: 8.1:1; max power (DIN): 150 hp 0.4 kW) at 4,000 rpm; max torque (DIN): 240 lb ft, kg m (324.6 Nm) at 1,600 rpm; 30.4 hp/l (22.4 kW/l); crankshaft bearings; lubricating system: 10 imp pt, 12 pt, 5.7 l; 1 Rochester M4MC downdraught 4-barrel rburettor; cooling system: 34.8 imp pt, 41.9 US pt, 19.8 l.

ANSMISSION axle ratio: 2.560 - st. wagons 2.730; tyres: wagons HR78 x 15.

RFORMANCE max speed: about 103 mph, 165 km/h; wer-weight ratio: Laurentian Sedan 24.2 lb/hp (32.8

PONTIAC Parisienne Sedan

lb/kW), 11 kg/hp (14.9 kg/kW) - Parisienne Sedan 24.5 lb/hp (33.3 lb/kW), 11.1 kg/hp (15.1 kg/kW); speed in direct drive at 1,000 rpm: 25.6 mph, 41.2 km/h; consump- tion: 19.2 m/imp gal, 16 m/US gal, 14.7 l x 100 km.

BRAKES swept area: st. wagons total 362.58 sq in, 2,339 sq cm.

ELECTRICAL EQUIPMENT 3,200 W battery.

DIMENSIONS AND WEIGHT tracks: st. wagons 62 in, 158 cm front, 64.10 in, 163 cm rear; length: st. wagons 215.10 in, 546 cm; width: st. wagons 79.90 in, 203 cm; height: st. wagons 57.30 in, 146 cm; ground clearance: st. wagons 6 in, 15.2 cm; weight: Laurentian Coupé 3,593 lb, 1, 631 kg - Sedan 3,625 lb, 1,645 kg - Safari St. Wagon 3,997 lb, 1,813 kg - Parisienne Coupé 3,616 lb, 1,640 kg - Sedan 3,672 lb, 1,665 kg - Safari St. Wagon 4,023 lb, 1,825 kg; turning circle: st. wagons 42.3 ft, 12.9 m; fuel tank: st. wagons 18.3 imp gal, 22 US gal, 83 l.

155 hp power team

See 115 hp power team, except for:

ENGINE 8 cylinders; 350 cu in, 5,736 cc (3.80 x 3.85 in, 96.5 x 97.8 mm); max power (DIN): 155 hp (114.1 kW) at 3,400 rpm; max torque (DIN): 280 lb ft, 38.6 kg m (378.6 Nm) at 1,800 rpm; max engine rpm: 4,200; 27 hp/l (19.9 kW/l); 5 crankshaft bearings; 1 Rochester M4MC down-

draught 4-barrel carburettor; cooling system: 25.2 imp pt, 30.2 US pt, 14.3 l.

TRANSMISSION axle ratio: 2.410 - st. wagons 2.730; tyres: st. wagons HR78 x 15.

PERFORMANCE max speed: about 106 mph, 170 km/h; power-weight ratio: Laurentian Sedan 24 lb/hp (32.7 lb/kW), 10.9 kg/hp (14.8 kg/kW) - Parisienne Sedan 24.3 lb/hp (33 lb/kW), 11 kg/hp (15 kg/kW); speed in direct drive at 1,000 rpm: 25.2 mph, 40.5 km/h; consumption: 18 m/imp gal, 15 m/US gal, 15.7 l x 100 km.

BRAKES swept area: st. wagons total 362.58 sq in, 2,339 sq cm.

ELECTRICAL EQUIPMENT 3,200 W battery.

DIMENSIONS AND WEIGHT (see 150 hp power team) weight: plus 96 lb, 44 kg - Laurentian Coupé and Sedan plus 101 lb, 46 kg.

OPTIONALS 2.730 or 3.080 axle ratio (st. wagons 3.080).

AMERICAN MOTORS USA

Spirit Series

PRICES EX WORKS:

1 Sedan	$ 3,899
2 Liftback	$ 3,999

Power team:	Standard for:	Optional for:
80 hp	both	—
90 hp	—	both
100 hp	—	1
110 hp	—	both
125 hp	—	2

80 hp power team

ENGINE front, 4 stroke; 4 cylinders, in line; 121 cu in, 1,983 cc (3.41 x 3.23 in, 86.5 x 82 mm); compression ratio: 8.1:1; max power (DIN): 80 hp (58.9 kW) at 5,000 rpm; max torque (DIN): 105 lb ft, 14.5 kg m (142.2 Nm) at 2,800 rpm; max engine rpm: 5,400; 40.3 hp/l (29.7 kW/l); cast iron block, light alloy head; 5 crankshaft bearings; valves: overhead, in line, rockers; camshafts: 1, overhead, cogged belt; lubrication: eccentric pump, full flow filter, 7.6 imp pt, 9.1 US pt, 4.3 l; 1 Holley 5210 downdraught twin barrel carburettor; cleaner air system; exhaust system with ca- talytic converter; fuel feed: mechanical pump; water- cooled, 10.7 imp pt, 12.9 US pt, 6.1 l.

TRANSMISSION driving wheels: rear; clutch: single dry plate; gearbox: mechanical (Torque-Command automatic transmission standard in California); ratios: I 3.980, II 2.140, III 1.420, IV 1, rev 3.990; lever: central; final drive: hypoid bevel; axle ratio: 3.080 (3.310 California only); width of rims: 4.5''; tyres: C78 x 14.

AMERICAN MOTORS Spirit Limited Sedan

AMERICAN MOTORS *Spirit D/L Liftback*

80 HP POWER TEAM

PERFORMANCE max speed: about 85 mph, 136 km/h; power-weight ratio: Sedan 31.3 lb/hp (42.5 lb/kW), 14.2 kg/hp (19.3 kg/kW); speed in direct drive at 1,000 rpm: 16 mph, 27.2 km/h; consumption: 26.4 m/imp gal, 22 m/US gal, 10.7 l x 100 km.

CHASSIS integral; front suspension: independent, wishbones, coil springs, anti-roll bar (except for Sedan), telescopic dampers; rear: rigid axle, torque tube, semi-elliptic leaf-springs, telescopic dampers.

STEERING recirculating ball; turns lock to lock: 5.

BRAKES front disc (diameter 10.27 in, 26.1 cm), front internal radial fins, rear drum; swept area: total 265.78 sq in, 1,714 sq cm.

ELECTRICAL EQUIPMENT 12 V; 45 Ah battery; 42 A alternator; Bosch distributor; 4 headlamps.

DIMENSIONS AND WEIGHT wheel base: 96 in, 244 cm; tracks: 58.08 in, 147 cm front, 57.50 in, 146 cm rear; length: Sedan 166.82 in, 424 cm - Liftback 168.46 in, 428 cm; width: Sedan 71.96 in, 183 cm - Liftback 71.88 in, 183 cm; height: Sedan 51.66 in, 131 cm - Liftback 51.55 in, 131 cm; ground clearance: 4.20 in, 10.7 cm; weight: Sedan 2,506 lb, 1,137 kg - Liftback 2,570 lb, 1,166 kg; turning circle: 35.3 ft, 10.8 m; fuel tank: Sedan 11 imp gal, 13 US gal, 50 l - Liftback 17.6 imp gal, 21 US gal, 80 l.

BODY 2 doors; 4 seats, separate front seats, reclining backrests; folding rear seat.

OPTIONALS Torque-Command automatic transmission, hydraulic torque converter and planetary gears with 3 ratios (I 2.450, II 1.450, III 1, rev 2.200), max ratio of converter at stall 2, possible manual selection, steering column or central lever, 3.310 axle ratio; limited slip differential; D78 x 14 or P195/75R x 14 tyres with 5'' wide rims; DR70 x 14 tyres with 6'' wide rims; light alloy wheels; anti-roll bar on front suspension (Sedan only); anti-roll bar on rear suspension; heavy-duty cooling system; heavy-duty battery; power steering; servo brake; heated rear window; tinted glass; sunshine roof; air-conditioning; D/L equipment; Limited equipment.

90 hp power team

(not available in California).

See 80 hp power team, except for:

ENGINE 6 cylinders, in line; 232 cu in, 3,802 cc (3.75 x 3.50 in, 95.2 x 88.8 mm); compression ratio: 8:1; max power (DIN): 90 hp (66.2 kW) at 3,400 rpm; max torque (DIN): 168 lb ft, 23.2 kg m (227.5 Nm) at 1,600 rpm; max engine rpm: 3,800; 23.7 hp/l (17.4 kW/l); cast iron block and head; 7 crankshaft bearings; valves: push-rods and rockers, hydraulic tappets; camshafts: 1, side; lubrication: gear pump, full flow filter, 8.3 imp pt, 9.9 US pt, 4.7 l; 1 Carter YF downdraught single barrel carburettor; cooling system: 18.3 imp pt, 22 US pt, 10.4 l.

TRANSMISSION gearbox: mechanical; gears: 3, fully synchronized; ratios: I 2.990, II 1.750, III 1, rev 3.170; axle ratio: 2.730.

PERFORMANCE max speed: about 90 mph, 145 km/h; power-weight ratio: Sedan 30.9 lb/hp (42 lb/kW), 14 kg/hp (19.1 kg/kW); speed in direct drive at 1,000 rpm: 23.7 mph, 38.2 km/h; consumption: 24.1 m/imp gal, 20 m/US gal, 11.7 l x 100 km.

CHASSIS (standard) anti-roll bar on front suspension.

BRAKES front disc (diameter 10.80 in, 27.4 cm), front internal radial fins, rear drum; swept area: total 310.65 sq in, 2,004 sq cm.

ELECTRICAL EQUIPMENT 50 Ah battery; Motorcraft electronic distributor.

DIMENSIONS AND WEIGHT weight: Sedan 2,783 lb, 1,262 kg - Liftback 2,797 lb, 1,268 kg; fuel tank: 17.6 imp gal, 21 US gal, 80 l.

OPTIONALS 4-speed fully synchronized mechanical gearbox (I 3.980, II 2.140, III 1.420, IV 1, rev 3.990), 2.530 axle ratio; Torque-Command automatic transmission with 2.530 axle ratio; ER60 x 14 tyres with 7'' wide rims.

100 hp power team

(for California only).

See 80 hp power team, except for:

ENGINE 6 cylinders, in line; 258 cu in, 4,228 cc (3.75 x 3.90

in, 95.2 x 99 mm); compression ratio: 8:1; max power (DIN): 100 hp (73.6 kW) at 3,400 rpm; max torque (DIN): 200 lb ft, 27.7 kg m (271.7 Nm) at 1,600 rpm; max engine rpm: 3,800; 23.6 hp/l (17.4 kW/l); cast iron block head; 7 crankshaft bearings; valves: push-rods and rocker, hydraulic tappets; camshafts: 1, side; lubrication: gear pump, full flow filter, 8.3 imp pt, 9.9 US pt, 4.7 l; 1 Carter BBD downdraught single barrel carburettor; cooling system: 18.3 imp pt, 22 US pt, 10.4 l.

TRANSMISSION gearbox: Torque-Command automatic transmission (standard), hydraulic torque converter and planetary gears with 3 ratios, max ratio of converter at stall 2, possible manual selection; ratios: I 2.450, II 1.450, III 1, rev 2.200; axle ratio: 3.080.

PERFORMANCE max speed: about 93 mph, 150 km/h; power-weight ratio: Sedan 28.1 lb/hp (38.1 lb/kW), 12.7 kg/hp (17.3 kg/kW); speed in direct drive at 1,000 rpm: 24.5 mph, 39.5 km/h; consumption: 16.8 m/imp gal, 14 m/US gal 16.8 l x 100 km.

CHASSIS (standard) anti-roll bar on front suspension.

BRAKES front disc (diameter 10.80 in, 27.4 cm), front internal radial fins, rear drum; swept area: total 310.65 sq in, 2,004 sq cm.

ELECTRICAL EQUIPMENT 50 Ah battery; Motorcraft electronic distributor.

DIMENSIONS AND WEIGHT weight: Sedan 2,806 lb, 1,273 kg; fuel tank: 17.6 imp gal, 21 US gal, 80 l.

OPTIONALS ER60 x 14 tyres with 7'' wide rims.

110 hp power team

See 80 hp power team, except for:

ENGINE 6 cylinders, in line; 258 cu in, 4,228 cc (3.75 x 3.90 in, 95.2 x 99 mm); compression ratio: 8.3:1; max power (DIN): 110 hp (81 kW) at 3,200 rpm; max torque (DIN): 210 lb ft, 29 kg m (284.4 Nm) at 1,800 rpm; max engine rpm: 3,800; 26 hp/l (19.2 kW/l); cast iron block and head 7 crankshaft bearings; valves: push-rods and rockers hydraulic tappets; camshafts: 1, side; lubrication: gear pump, full flow filter, 8.3 imp pt, 9.9 US pt, 4.7 l; 1 Carter BBD downdraught twin barrel carburettor; cooling system: 18.3 imp pt, 22 US pt, 10.4 l.

TRANSMISSION axle ratio: 2.530 (2.730 California only).

PERFORMANCE max speed: about 99 mph, 160 km/h; power-weight ratio: Sedan 25.2 lb/hp (34.2 lb/kW), 11.4 kg/hp 15.5 kg/kW); speed in direct drive at 1,000 rpm: 26.2 mph, 42.1 km/h; consumption: 20.5 m/imp gal, 17 m/US gal, 13.8 l x 100 km.

CHASSIS (standard) anti-roll bar on front suspension.

BRAKES front disc (diameter 10.80 in, 27.4 cm), front internal radial fins, rear drum; swept area: total 310.65 sq in, 2,004 sq cm.

ELECTRICAL EQUIPMENT 50 Ah battery; Motorcraft electronic distributor.

AMERICAN MOTORS *AMX Liftback*

DIMENSIONS AND WEIGHT weight: Sedan 2,770 lb, 1,256 - Liftback 2,784 lb, 1,262 kg; fuel tank: 17.6 imp gal, 21 gal, 80 l.

OPTIONALS Torque-Command automatic transmission with 80 axle ratio (2.730 California only); ER60 x 14 tyres with wide rims.

125 hp power team

(not available in California).

80 hp power team, except for:

ENGINE 8 cylinders; 304 cu in, 4,982 cc (3.75 x 3.44 in, 2 x 87.3 mm); compression ratio: 8.4:1; max power (DIN): 125 hp (92 kW) at 3,200 rpm; max torque (DIN): lb ft, 30.3 kg m (297.2 Nm) at 2,400 rpm; max engine : 3,800, 25.1 hp/l (18.5 kW/l); cast iron block and head; ves: push-rods and rockers, hydraulic tappets; camshafts: at centre of Vee; lubrication: gear pump, full flow filter, imp pt, 9.9 US pt, 4.7 l; 1 Ford 2100 downdraught twin rel carburettor; cooling system: 29.9 imp pt, 35.9 US pt, l.

TRANSMISSION axle ratio: 2.870.

PERFORMANCE max speed: about 103 mph, 165 km/h; ver-weight ratio: Liftback 23.6 lb/hp (32.1 lb/kW), 10.7 hp (14.6 kg/kW); speed in direct drive at 1,000 rpm: mph, 43.4 km/h; consumption: 15.6 m/imp gal, 13 m/US , 18.1 l x 100 km.

BRAKES front disc (diameter 10.80 in, 27.4 cm), front ernal radial fins, rear drum; swept area: total 310.65 in, 2,004 sq cm.

ELECTRICAL EQUIPMENT 36 Ah battery; 45 A alternator; torcraft electronic distributor.

DIMENSIONS AND WEIGHT weight: Liftback 2,952 lb, 39 kg.

OPTIONALS Torque-Command automatic transmission with 60 axle ratio; ER60 x 14 tyres with 7'' wide rims.

AMX

PRICE EX WORKS: $ 5,899

110 hp power team

(standard).

ENGINE front, 4 stroke; 6 cylinders, in line; 258 cu in, 28 cc (3.75 x 3.90 in, 95.2 x 99 mm); compression ratio: :1; max power (DIN): 110 hp (81 kW) at 3,200 rpm; x torque (DIN): 210 lb ft, 29 kg m (284.4 Nm) at 1,800 ; max engine rpm: 3,800, 26 hp/l (19.2 kW/l); cast n block and head; 7 crankshaft bearings; valves: over- ad, in line, push-rods and rockers, hydraulic tappets; nshafts: 1, side; lubrication: gear pump, full flow filter,

8.3 imp pt, 9.9 US pt, 4.7 l; 1 Carter BBD downdraught twin barrel carburettor; cleaner air system; exhaust system with catalytic converter; fuel feed: mechanical pump; water-cooled, 18.3 imp pt, 22 US pt, 10.4 l.

TRANSMISSION driving wheels: rear; clutch: single dry plate; gearbox: mechanical; gears: 4, fully synchronized; ratios: I 3.980, II 2.140, III 1.420, IV 1, rev 3.990; lever: central; final drive: hypoid bevel; axle ratio: 2.530 (2.730 California only); width of rims: 7''; tyres: ER60 x 14.

PERFORMANCE max speed: about 99 mph, 159 km/h; power-weight ratio: 26.4 lb/hp (35.9 lb/kW), 12 kg/hp (16.3 kg/kW); speed in direct drive at 1,000 rpm: 26.2 mph, 42.1 km/h; consumption: 20.5 m/imp gal, 17 m/US gal, 13.8 l x 100 km.

CHASSIS integral; front suspension: independent, wish-bones, coil springs, anti-roll bar, telescopic dampers; rear: rigid axle, torque tube, semi-elliptic leafsprings, telescopic dampers.

STEERING recirculating ball; turns lock to lock: 5.

BRAKES front disc (diameter 10.80 in, 27.4 cm), front internal radial fins, rear drum; swept area: total 310.65 sq in, 2,004 sq cm.

ELECTRICAL EQUIPMENT 12 V; 50 Ah batery; 42 A alternator; Motorcraft electronic distributor; 4 headlamps.

DIMENSIONS AND WEIGHT wheel base: 96 in, 244 cm;

TRANSMISSION axle ratio: 2.870.

PERFORMANCE max speed: about 103 mph, 165 km/h; power-weight ratio: 24.6 lb/hp (33.4 lb/kW), 11.2 kg/hp (15.2 kg/kW); speed in direct drive at 1,000 rpm: 27 mph, 43.4 km/h; consumption: 15.6 m/imp gal, 13 m/US gal, 18.1 l x 100 km.

ELECTRICAL EQUIPMENT 36 Ah battery; 45 A alternator.

DIMENSIONS AND WEIGHT weight: plus 166 lb, 75 kg.

OPTIONALS Torque-Command automatic transmission with central lever and 2.560 axle ratio.

Concord Series

PRICES EX WORKS:

1 2-dr Sedan	$ 4,049
2 4-dr Sedan	$ 4,149
3 2-dr Hatchback	$ 4,149
4 4+1-dr St. Wagon	$ 4,349

Power team:	Standard for:	Optional for:
90 hp	all	—
80 hp	—	1,2,3
100 hp	—	all
110 hp	—	all
125 hp	—	all

AMERICAN MOTORS Concord Limited 2-dr Sedan

tracks: 58.08 in, 147 cm front, 57.50 in, 146 cm rear; length: 168.46 in, 428 cm; width: 71.88 in, 183 cm; height: 51.55 in, 131 cm; ground clearance: 4.20 in, 10.7 cm; weight: 2,908 lb, 1,319 kg; turning circle: 35.3 ft, 10.8 m; fuel tank: 17.6 imp gal, 21 US gal, 80 l.

BODY liftback; 2 doors; 4 seats, separate front seats, reclining backrests; folding rear seat; light alloy wheels.

OPTIONALS Torque-Command automatic transmission, hydraulic torque converter and planetary gears with 3 ratios (I 2.450, II 1.450, III 1, rev 2.200), max ratio of converter at stall 2, possible manual selection, steering column or central lever, 2.530 axle ratio (2.730 California only); limited slip differential; anti-roll bar on rear suspension; heavy-duty cooling system; heavy-duty battery; power steering; tilt of steering wheel; servo brake; tinted glass; sunshine roof; heated rear window; air-conditioning.

125 hp power team

(optional, not available in California).

See 110 hp power team, except for:

ENGINE 8 cylinders; 304 cu in, 4,982 cc (3.75 x 3.44 in, 95.2 x 87.3 mm); compression ratio: 8.4:1; max power (DIN): 125 hp (92 kW) at 3,200 rpm; max torque (DIN): 220 lb ft, 30.3 kg m (297.2 Nm) at 2,400 rpm; 25.1 hp/l (18.5 kW/l); 5 crankshaft bearings; camshafts: 1, at centre of Vee; 1 Ford 2100 downdraught twin barrel carburettor; cooling system: 29.9 imp pt, 35.9 US pt, 17 l.

90 hp power team

(not available in California).

ENGINE front, 4 stroke; 6 cylinders, in line; 232 cu in, 3,802 cc (3.75 x 3.50 in, 95.2 x 88.8 mm); compression ratio: 8:1; max power (DIN): 90 hp (66.2 kW) at 3,400 rpm; max torque (DIN): 168 lb ft, 23.2 kg m (227.5 Nm) at 1,600 rpm; max engine rpm: 3,800; 23.7 hp/l (17.4 kW/l); cast iron block and head; 7 crankshaft bearings; valves: overhead, in line, push-rods and rockers, hydraulic tappets; camshafts: 1, side; lubrication: gear pump, full flow filter, 8.3 imp pt, 9.9 US pt, 4.7 l; 1 Carter YF downdraught single barrel carburettor; cleaner air system; exhaust system with catalytic converter; fuel feed: mechanical pump; water-cooled, 18.3 imp pt, 22 US pt, 10.4 l.

TRANSMISSION driving wheels: rear; clutch: single dry plate; gearbox: mechanical; gears: 4, fully synchronized; ratios: I 3.980, II 2.140, III 1.420, IV 1, rev 3.990; lever: central; final drive: hypoid bevel; axle ratio: 2.530; width of rims: 5''; tyres: D78 x 14.

PERFORMANCE max speed: about 90 mph, 145 km/h; power-weight ratio: 4-dr. Sedan 32.8 lb/hp (44.5 lb/kW), 14.9 kg/hp (20.2 kg/kW); speed in direct drive at 1,000 rpm: 23.7 mph, 38.2 km/h; consumption: 21.6 m/imp gal, 18 m/US gal, 13.1 l x 100 km.

CHASSIS integral; front suspension: independent, wishbones coil springs, anti-roll bar, telescopic dampers; rear: rigid axle, torque tube, semi-elliptic leafsprings, telescopic dampers.

AMERICAN MOTORS AMX Liftback

90 HP POWER TEAM

STEERING recirculating ball; turns lock to lock: 6.

BRAKES front disc (diameter 10.80 in, 27.4 cm), front internal radial fins, rear drum; swept area: total 310.65 sq in, 2,004 sq cm.

ELECTRICAL EQUIPMENT 12 V; 50 Ah battery; 42 A alternator; Motorcraft electronic distributor; 4 headlamps.

DIMENSIONS AND WEIGHT wheel base: 108 in, 274 cm; front track: 57.64 in, 146 cm - 4-dr Sedan and St. Wagon 57.66 in, 146 cm; rear track: 57.06 in, 146 cm; length: 186 in, 472 cm; width: 71 in, 181 cm - St. Wagon 71.16 in, 181 cm; height: 51.62 in, 131 cm - 4-dr Sedan 51.10 in, 130 cm - St. Wagon 51.34 in, 130 cm; ground clearance: 2-dr Sedan and Hatchback 3.98 in, 10.1 cm - 4-dr Sedan 3.47 in, 8.8 cm - St. Wagon 3.64 in, 9.2 cm; weight: 2-dr Sedan 2,878 lb, 1,305 kg - 4-dr Sedan 2,948 lb, 1,337 kg - Hatchback 2,906 lb, 1,318 kg - St. Wagon 2,977 lb, 1,350 kg; turning circle: 38.6 ft, 11.8 m; fuel tank: 18.3 imp gal, 22 US gal, 83 l.

BODY 4 seats (4-dr Sedan and St. Wagon 5), separate front seats.

OPTIONALS Torque-Command automatic transmission, hydraulic torque converter and planetary gears with 3 ratios (I 2.450, II 1.450, III 1, rev 2.200), max ratio of converter at stall 2, possible manual selection, steering column lever. 2.530 axle ratio (2.730 St. Wagon only); limited slip differential; P195/75R x 14 tyres; DR70 x 14 tyres with 6'' wide rims; anti-roll bar on rear suspension; heavy-duty suspension; heavy-duty cooling system; heavy-duty battery; power steering; tilt of steering wheel; servo brake; reclining backrests; tinted glass; heated rear window; sunshine roof; light alloy wheels; air-conditioning; D/L equipment; Limited equipment except for Hatchback.

80 hp power team

See 90 hp power team, except for:

ENGINE 4 cylinders, in line; 121 cu in, 1,983 cc (3.41 x 3.23 in, 86.5 x 82 mm); compression ratio: 8.1:1; max power (DIN): 80 hp (58.9 kW) at 5,000 rpm; max torque (DIN): 105 lb ft, 14.5 kg m (142.2 Nm) at 2,800 rpm; max engine rpm: 5,400; 40.3 hp/l (29.7 kW/l); cast iron block, light alloy head; 5 crankshaft bearings; valves: overhead, in line, rockers; camshafts: 1, overhead; lubrication: eccentric pump, full flow filter, 7.6 imp pt, 9.1 US pt, 4.3 l; 1 Holley 5210 downdraught twin barrel carburettor; cooling system: 10.7 imp pt, 12.9 US pt, 6.1 l.

TRANSMISSION gearbox: mechanical (Torque-Command automatic transmission standard in California); axle ratio: 3.310 (3.580 California only).

PERFORMANCE max speed: about 85 mph, 136 km/h; power-weight ratio: 4-dr, Sedan 34.5 lb/hp (46.8 lb/kW), 15.6 kg/hp (21.2 kg/kW); speed in direct drive at 1,000 rpm: 16 mph, 27.2 km/h; consumption: 26.4 m/imp gal, 22 m/US gal, 10.7 l x 100 km.

BRAKES front disc (diameter 10.27 in, 26.1 cm), front internal radial fins, rear drum; swept area: total 262.14 sq in, 1,690 sq cm.

ELECTRICAL EQUIPMENT 45 Ah battery; Bosch distributor.

DIMENSIONS AND WEIGHT weight: 2-dr Sedan 2,688 lb, 1,219 kg - 4-dr Sedan 2,758 lb, 1,251 kg - Hatchback 2,716 lb, 1,231 kg.

OPTIONALS Torque-Command automatic transmission with 3.580 axle ratio.

100 hp power team

(for California only).

See 90 hp power team, except for:

ENGINE 258 cu in, 4,228 cc (3.75 x 3.90 in, 95.2 x 99 mm); max power (DIN): 100 hp (73.6 kW) at 3,400 rpm; max torque (DIN): 200 lb ft, 27.7 kg m (271.7 Nm) at 1,600 rpm; 23.6 hp/l (17.4 kW/l); 1 Carter BBD downdraught single barrel carburettor.

TRANSMISSION gearbox: Torque-Command automatic transmission (standard), hydraulic torque converter and planetary gears with 3 ratios, max ratio of converter at stall 2, possible manual selection: ratios: I 2.450, II 1.450, III 1, rev 2.200; lever: steering column; axle ratio: 3.080.

PERFORMANCE max speed: about 93 mph, 150 km/h; power-weight ratio: 4-dr Sedan 30 lb/hp (40.7 lb/kW), 13.6 kg/hp (18.4 kg/kW); speed in direct drive at 1,000 rpm: 24.5 mph, 39.5 km/h; consumption: 16.8 m/imp gal, 14 m/US gal, 16.8 l x 100 km.

AMERICAN MOTORS Concord Limited

DIMENSIONS AND WEIGHT weight: 2-dr Sedan 2,926 lb, 1,327 kg - 4-dr Sedan 2,996 lb, 1,358 kg - Hatchback 2,954 lb, 1,340 kg - St. Wagon 3,025 lb, 1,372 kg.

110 hp power team

See 90 hp power team, except for:

ENGINE 258 cu in, 4,228 cc (3.75 x 3.90 in, 95.2 x 99 mm); compresion ratio: 8.3:1; max power (DIN): 110 hp (81 kW) at 3,200 rpm; max torque (DIN): 210 lb ft, 29 kg m (284.4 Nm) at 1,800 rpm; 26 hp/l (19.2 kW/l); 1 Carter BBD downdraught twin barrel carburettor.

TRANSMISSION axle ratio: 2.530 (2.730 California only).

PERFORMANCE max speed: about 96 mph, 155 km/h; power-weight ratio: 4-dr Sedan 26.9 lb/hp (36.5 lb/kW), 12.2 kg/hp (16.6 kg/kW); speed in direct drive at 1,000 rpm: 25.4 mph, 40.8 km/h; consumption: 20.5 m/imp gal, 17 m/US gal, 13.8 l x 100 km.

DIMENSIONS AND WEIGHT weight: 2-dr Sedan 2,890 lb, 1,310 kg - 4-dr Sedan 2,960 lb, 1,343 kg - Hatchback 2,918 lb, 1,323 kg - St. Wagon 2,989 lb, 1,355 kg.

OPTIONALS Torque-Command automatic transmission with steering column lever and 2.530 axle ratio (2.730 California only).

125 hp power team

(not available in California).

See 90 hp power team, except for:

ENGINE 8 cylinders; 304 cu in, 4,982 cc (3.75 x 3.44 95.2 x 87.3 mm); compression ratio: 8.4:1; max pow (DIN): 125 hp (92 kW) at 3,200 rpm; max torque (DI 220 lb ft, 30.3 kg m (297.2 Nm) at 2,400 rpm; 25.1 h (18.5 kW/l); 5 crankshaft bearings; camshafts: 1, at cer of Vee; 1 Ford 2100 downdraught twin barrel carburet cooling system: 31.7 imp pt, 38 US pt, 18 l.

TRANSMISSION gearbox: Torque-Command automatic tra mission (standard), hydraulic torque converter and pla tary gears with 3 ratios, max ratio of converter at stall possible manual selection; ratios: I 2.450, II 1.450, III rev 2.200; lever: steering column; axle ratio: 2.560; tyr D78 x 14.

PERFORMANCE max speed: about 99 mph, 160 km$h; pow weight ratio: 4-dr Sedan 25.3 lb/hp (34.4 lb/kW), 1 kg/hp (15.6 kg/kW); speed in direct drive at 1,000 r 26.2 mph, 32.1 km/h; consumption: 18 m/imp gal, m/US gal, 15.7 l x 100 km.

ELECTRICAL EQUIPMENT 36 Ah battery; 45 A alternat

DIMENSIONS AND WEIGHT weight: 2-dr Sedan 3,092 1,402 kg - 4-dr Sedan 3,162 lb, 1,434 kg - Hatchback 3, lb, 1,415 kg - St. Wagon 3,191 lb, 1,447 kg.

OPTIONALS 2,870 axle ratio.

Pacer Series

PRICES EX WORKS:

2-dr Hatchback	$ 4,
2+1-dr St. Wagon	$ 4,

Power team:	Standard for:	Optional for:
110 hp	both	—
100 hp	—	both
125 hp	—	both

110 hp power team

ENGINE front, 4 stroke; 6 cylinders, in line; 258 cu 4,228 cc (3.75 x 3.90 in, 95.2 x 99 mm); compression rat 8.3:1; max power (DIN): 110 hp (81 kW) at 3,200 rp max torque (DIN): 210 lb ft, 29 kg m (284.4 Nm) at 1,8 rpm; max engine rpm: 3,800; 26 hp/l (19.2 kW/l); cast block and head; 7 crankshaft bearings; valves: overhead, line, push-rods and rockers, hydraulic tappets; camshaf 1, side; lubrication: gear pump, full flow filter, 8.3 i pt, 9.9 US pt, 4.7 l; 1 Carter BBD downdraught twin bar carburettor; cleaner air system; exhaust system with ca lytic converter; fuel feed: mechanical pump; water-cool 24.6 imp pt, 29.6 US pt, 14 l.

TRANSMISSION driving wheels: rear; clutch: single dry p te; gearbox mechanical; gears: 4, fully synchronized;

AMERICAN MOTORS Pacer Limited 2-dr Hatchback

AMERICAN MOTORS Pacer D/L Station Wagon

I 3.980, II 2.140, III 1.420, IV 1, rev 3.990; lever: central; final drive: hypoid bevel; axle ratio: 2.530 (2.730 California only); width of rims: 5''; tyres: P195/75R x 14.

PERFORMANCE max speed: about 96 mph, 154 km/h; power-weight ratio: Hatchback 28.6 lb/hp (38.8 lb/kW), 12.9 kg/hp (17.6 kg/kW) - St. Wagon 29 lb/hp (39.4 lb/kW), 13.1 kg/hp (17.9 kg/kW); speed in direct drive at 1,000 rpm: 25.4 mph, 40.8 km/h; consumption: 20.5 m/imp gal, 17 m/US gal, 13.8 l x 100 km.

CHASSIS integral; front suspension: independent, wishbones, coil springs, anti-roll bar, telescopic dampers; rear: rigid axle, semi-elliptic leafsprings, telescopic dampers.

STEERING rack-and-pinion; turns lock to lock: 5.80.

BRAKES front disc (diameter 10.80 in 27.4 cm), front internal radial fins, rear drum; swept area: total 310.65 sq in, 2,004 sq cm.

ELECTRICAL EQUIPMENT 12 V; 50 Ah battery; 42 A alternator; Motorcraft electronic distributor; 2 headlamps.

DIMENSIONS AND WEIGHT wheel base: 100 in, 254 cm; tracks: 61.20 in, 155 cm front, 60 in, 152 cm rear; length: Hatchback 172.73 in, 439 cm - St. Wagon 177.65 in, 451 cm; width: 77 in, 196 cm; height: Hatchback 52.80 in, 134 cm - St. Wagon 53.13 in, 135 cm; ground clearance: Hatchback 4.67 in, 11.8 cm - St. Wagon 4.90 in, 12.5 cm; weight: Hatchback 3,142 lb, 1,425 kg - St. Wagon 3,188 lb, 1,446 kg; turning circle: 39 ft, 11.9 m; fuel tank: 17.6 imp gal, 21 US gal, 80 l.

BODY 4 seats, separate front seats.

OPTIONALS Torque-Command automatic transmission, hydraulic torque converter and planetary gears with 3 ratios (I 2.450, II 1.450, III 1, rev 2.200), max ratio of converter at stall 2, possible manual selection, steering column or central lever, 2.530 axle ratio (2.730 California only); limited slip differential; light alloy wheels; heavy-duty cooling system; heavy-duty-battery; power steering; tilt of steering wheel; servo brake; electric windows; tinted glass; sunshine roof; heated rear window; rear window wiper-washer; reclining backrests; air-conditioning; Limited equipment; D/L equipment.

100 hp power team

(for California only).

See 110 hp power team, except for:

ENGINE compression ratio: 8:1; max power (DIN): 100 hp (73.6 kW) at 3,400 rpm; max torque (DIN): 200 lb ft, 27.7 kg m (271.7 Nm) at 1,600 rpm; 23.6 hp/l (17.4 kW/l); 1 Carter BBD downdraught single barrel carburettor.

TRANSMISSION gearbox: Torque-Command automatic transmission (standard), hydraulic torque converter and planetary gears with 3 ratios, max ratio of converter at stall 2, possible manual selection; ratios: I 2.450, II 1.450, III 1, rev 2.200; lever: steering column or central; axle ratio: 3.080.

PERFORMANCE max speed: about 93 mph, 150 km/h; power-weight ratio: Hatchback 31.8 lb/hp (43.2 lb/kW), 14.4 kg/hp (19.6 kg/kW) - St. Wagon 32.3 lb/hp (43.8 lb/kW), 14.6 kg/hp (19.9 kg/kW); speed in direct drive at 1,000 rpm:

24.5 mph, 39.5 km/h; consumption: 16.8 m/imp gal, 14 m/US gal, 16.8 l x 100 km.

DIMENSIONS AND WEIGHT weight: Hatchback 3,180 lb, 1,442 kg - St. Wagon 3,226 lb, 1,463 kg.

125 hp power team

(not available in California).

See 110 hp power team, except for:

ENGINE 8 cylinders; 304 cu in, 4,982 cc (3.75 x 3.44 in, 95.2 x 87.3 mm); compression ratio: 8.4:1; max power (DIN): 125 hp (92 kW) at 3,200 rpm; max torque (DIN): 220 lb ft, 30.3 kg m (297.2 Nm) at 2,400 rpm; 25.1 hp/l (18.5 kW/l); 5 crankshaft bearings; camshafts: 1, at centre of Vee; 1 Ford 2100 downdraught twin barrel carburettor; cooling system: 31.7 imp pt, 38.1 US pt, 18 l.

TRANSMISSION gearbox: Torque-Command automatic transmission (standard), hydraulic torque converter and planetary gears with 3 ratios, max ratio of converter at stall 2, possible manual selection; ratios: I 2.450, II 1.450, III 1, rev 2.200; lever: central; axle ratio: 2.560.

PERFORMANCE max speed: about 99 mph, 160 km/h; power-weight ratio: Hatchback 27.1 lb/hp (36.8 lb/kW), 12.3 kg/hp (16.7 kg/kW) - St. Wagon 27.4 lb/hp (37.3 lb/kW), 12.4 kg/hp (16.9 kg/kW); speed in direct drive at 1,000 rpm: 26.2 mph, 42.1 km/h; consumption: 16.8 m/imp gal, 14 m/US gal, 16.8 l x 100 km.

BRAKES servo (standard).

ELECTRICAL EQUIPMENT 36 Ah battery; 45 A alternator.

DIMENSIONS AND WEIGHT weight: Hatchback 3,385 lb, 1,535 kg - St. Wagon 3,431 lb, 1,556 kg.

OPTIONALS 2.870 axle ratio.

ANTIQUE & CLASSIC AUTOMOTIVE USA

Frazer Nash TT Interceptor

PRICES EX WORKS: $ 9,550 (complete car)
               $ 3,595 (kit only)

ENGINE Volkswagen, rear, 4 stroke; 4 cylinders, horizontally opposed; 96.7 cu in, 1,584 cc (3.37 x 2.72 in, 85.5 x 69 mm); compression ratio: 8.5:1; max power (DIN): 50 hp (36.8 kW) at 4,000 rpm; max torque (DIN): 78 lb ft, 10.8 kg m (105.9 Nm) at 2,800 rpm; max engine rpm: 4,600; 31.6 hp/l (23.2 kW/l); block with cast iron liners and light alloy fins, light alloy head; crankshaft bearings; valves: overhead, push-rods and rockers; camshafts: 1, central, lower; lubrication: gear pump, filter in sump, oil cooler, 4.4 imp pt, 5.3 US pt, 2.5 l; 1 Solex 34 PICT 2 downdraught carburettor; fuel feed: mechanical pump; air-cooled.

TRANSMISSION driving wheels: rear; clutch: single dry plate; gearbox: mechanical; gears: 4, fully synchronized; ratios: I 3.780, II 2.060, III 1.260, IV 0.930, rev 4.010; lever: central; final drive: spiral bevel; axle ratio: 3.875; width of rims: 4''; tyres: 5.60 x 15.

PERFORMANCE max speed: 90 mph, 145 km/h; power-weight ratio: 32.6 lb/hp, (44.3 lb/kW), 14.8 kg/hp (20.1 kg/kW); consumption: 30.7 m/imp gal, 25.6 m/US gal, 9.2 l x 100 km.

CHASSIS backbone platform; front suspension: independent, twin swinging longitudinal trailing arms, transverse laminated torsion bars, anti-roll bar, telescopic dampers; rear: independent, swinging semi-axles, swinging longitudinal trailing arms, transverse torsion bars, telescopic dampers.

STEERING worm and roller.

BRAKES drum; lining area: total 111 sq in, 716 sq cm.

ELECTRICAL EQUIPMENT 12 V; 36 Ah battery; alternator; Bosch distributor; 4 headlamps.

DIMENSIONS AND WEIGHT wheel base: 108.50 in, 276 cm; tracks: 51.50 in, 131 cm front, 53.10 in, 135 cm rear; length: 159.50 in, 405 cm; height: 52 in, 132 cm; ground clearance: 7.20 in, 18.3 cm; weight: 1,630 lb, 739 kg; weight distribution: 35% front, 65% rear; fuel tank: 9.7 imp gal, 11.6 US gal, 44 l.

BODY roadster in plastic material; 2 doors; 2 seats.

Jaguar SS 100

PRICES EX WORKS: $ 12,995 (complete car)
               $ 4,489 (kit only)

ENGINE Volkswagen, rear, 4 stroke; 4 cylinders, horizontally opposed; 96.7 cu in, 1,584 cc (3.37 x 2.72 in, 85.5 x 69 mm); compression ratio: 8.5:1; max power (DIN): 50 hp (36.8 kW) at 4,000 rpm; max torque (DIN): 78 lb ft, 10.8 kg m (105.9 Nm) at 2,800 rpm; max engine rpm: 4,600; 31.6 hp/l (23.2 kW/l); block with cast iron liners, and light alloy fins, light alloy head; 4 crankshaft bearings; valves: overhead, push-rods and rockers; camshafts: 1, central, lower; lubrication: gear pump, filter in sump, oil cooler, 4.4 imp pt, 5.3 US pt, 2.5 l; 1 Solex 34 PICT 2 downdraught carburettor; fuel feed: mechanical pump; air-cooled.

TRANSMISSION driving wheels: rear; clutch: single dry plate; gearbox: mechanical; gears: 4, fully synchronized; ratios: I 3.780, II 2.060, III 1.260, IV 0.930, rev 4.010; lever: central; final drive: spiral bevel; axle ratio: 3.875; width of rims: 4''; tyres: 5.60 x 15.

PERFORMANCE max speed: 90 mph, 145 km/h; power-weight ratio: 32.6 lb/hp, (44.3 lb/kW), 14.8 kg/hp (20.1 kg/kW); consumption: 30.7 m/imp gal, 25.6 m/US gal, 9.2 l x 100 km.

CHASSIS backbone platform; front suspension: independent, twin swinging longitudinal trailing arms, transverse laminated torsion bars, anti-roll bar, telescopic dampers; rear: independent, swinging semi-axles, swinging longi-

ANTIQUE & CLASSIC AUTOMOTIVE Frazer Nash TT Interceptor Roadster

JAGUAR SS 100

tudinal trailing arms, transverse torsion bars, telescopic dampers.

STEERING worm and roller.

BRAKES drum; lining area: total 111 sq in, 716 sq cm.

ELECTRICAL EQUIPMENT 12 V; 36 Ah battery; alternator; Bosch distributor; 2 headlamps.

DIMENSIONS AND WEIGHT wheel base: 108.50 in, 276 cm; tracks: 51.50 in, 131 cm front, 53.10 in, 135 cm rear; length: 159.50 in, 405 cm; height: 52 in, 132 cm; ground clearance: 7.20 in, 18.3 cm; weight: 1,630 lb, 739 kg; weight distribution: 35% front, 65% rear; fuel tank: 9.7 imp gal, 11.6 US gal, 44 l.

BODY roadster in plastic material; 2 doors; 2 seats.

ANTIQUE & CLASSIC AUTOMOTIVE Jaguar SS 100 Roadster

AUBURN   USA

Speedster

PRICE EX WORKS: $ 24,900

ENGINE Lincoln Continental, front, 4 stroke; 8 cylinders; 460 cu in, 7,539 cc (4.36 x 3.85 in, 110.7 x 97.8 mm); compression ratio: 8:1; max power (DIN): 208 (153.1 kW) at 4,000 rpm; max torque (DIN): 356 lb ft, 49.1 kg m (481.5 Nm) at 2,000 rpm; max engine rpm: 4,400; 27.6 hp/l (20.3 kW/l); cast iron block and head; 5 crankshafts bearings; valves: overhead, in line, pushrods and rockers, hydraulic tappets; camshafts: 1, at centre of Vee; lubrication: rotary pump, full flow filter, 8.3 imp pt, 9.9 US pt, 4.7 l; 1 Motorcraft 9510 D7VE-AA downdraught 4-barrel carburettor; cleaner air system; dual exhaust system with catalytic converter; fuel feed: mechanical pump; water-cooled, 30.8 imp pt, 37 US pt, 17.5 l.

TRANSMISSION driving wheels: rear; gearbox: Select-Shift Merc-O-Matic automatic transmission, hydraulic torque converter and planetary gears with 3 ratios, max ratio of converter at stall 2.03, possible manual selection; ratios: I 2.460, II 1.460, III 1, rev 2.180; lever: central; final drive: hypoid bevel, limited slip differential; axle ratio: 2.750; width of rims: 6''; tyres: JR78 x 15.

PERFORMANCE not declared; power-weight ratio: 15.4 lb/hp (20.9 lb/kW), 7 kg/hp (9.5 kg/kW); carrying capacity: 353 lb, 160 kg.

CHASSIS box-type ladder frame; front suspension: independent, wishbones, lower trailing arms, coil springs, anti-roll bar, telescopic dampers; rear: rigid axle, lower trailing radius arms, upper torque arms, transverse linkage bar, coil springs, telescopic dampers.

STEERING recirculating ball, tilt of steering wheel, servo.

BRAKES front disc, front internal radial fins, rear drum.

ELECTRICAL EQUIPMENT 12 V; 68 Ah battery; 60 A alternator; Motorcraft transistorized ignition; 2 headlamps.

DIMENSIONS AND WEIGHT wheel base: 127 in, 323 cm; tracks: 63 in, 160 cm front, 65 in, 165 cm rear; length: 191 in, 485 cm; height: 58 in, 147 cm; ground clearance: 7 in, 17.8 cm; weight: 3,200 lb, 1,451 kg; weight distribution: 50% front, 50% rear; fuel tank: 15 imp gal, 18 US gal, 68 l.

BODY convertible in plastic material; 2 doors; 2 seats; leather interior.

OPTIONALS tonneau cover; wire wheels; air-conditioning.

Dual Cowl Phaeton

PRICE EX WORKS: $ 60,000

ENGINE Lincoln Continental, front, 4 stroke; 8 cylinders; 460 cu in, 7,539 cc (4.36 x 3.85 in, 110.7 x 97.8 mm); compression ratio: 8:1; max power (DIN): 208 hp (153.1 kW) at 4,000 rpm; max torque (DIN): 356 lb ft, 49.1 kg m (481.5 Nm) at 2,000 rpm; max engine rpm: 4,400; 27.6 hp/l (20.3 kW/l); cast iron block and head; 5 crankshaft bearings; valves: overhead, in line, push-rods and rockers, hydraulic tappets; camshafts: 1, at centre of Vee; lubrication: rotary pump, full flow filter, 8.3 imp pt, 9.9 US pt, 4.7 l; 1 Motorcraft 9510 D7VE-AA downdraught 4-barrel carburettor; cleaner air system; dual exhaust system with catalytic converter; fuel feed: mechanical pump; water-cooled, 30.8 imp pt, 37 US pt, 17.5 l.

TRANSMISSION driving wheels: rear; gearbox: Select-Shift Merc-O-Matic automatic transmission, hydraulic torque con-

AUBURN Dual Cowl Phaeton

verter and planetary gears with 3 ratios, max ratio of converter at stall 2.03, possible manual selection; ratios: I 2.460, II 1.460, III 1, rev 2.180; lever: central; final drive: hypoid bevel, limited slip differential; axle ratio: 2.750; width of rims: 6''; tyres: JR78 x 15.

PERFORMANCE not declared; power-weight ratio: 19.6 lb/hp (26.7 lb/kW), 8.9 kg/hp (12.1 kg/kW); carrying capacity: 706 lb, 320 kg.

CHASSIS box-type ladder frame; front suspension: independent, wishbones, lower trailing arms, coil springs, anti-roll bar, telescopic dampers; rear: rigid axle, lower trailing radius arms, upper torque arms, transverse linkage bar, coil springs, telescopic dampers.

STEERING recirculating ball, tilt of steering wheel, servo.

BRAKES front disc, front internal radial fins, rear drum.

ELECTRICAL EQUIPMENT 12 V; 68 Ah battery; 60 A alternator; Motorcraft transistorized ignition; 2 headlamps.

DIMENSIONS AND WEIGHT wheel base: 140 in, 356 cm; tracks: 63 in, 160 cm front, 65 in, 165 cm rear; length: 204 in, 518 cm; height: 58 in, 147 cm; ground clearance: 7 in, 17.8 cm; weight: 4,100 lb, 1,860 kg; weight distribution: 50% front, 50% rear; fuel tank: 20.9 imp gal, 25 US gal, 95 l.

BODY convertible in plastic material; 4 doors; 4 seats, bench front seats; leather interior; tonneau cover; air-conditioning.

OPTIONALS wire wheels.

AVANTI   USA

Avanti II

PRICE EX WORKS: $ 17,670

ENGINE Chevrolet, front, 4 stroke; 8 cylinders; 350 cu in, 5,736 cc (4 x 3.48 in, 101.6 x 88.3 mm); compression ratio: 8.2:1; max power (DIN): 195 hp (143.5 kW) at 4,000 rpm; max torque (DIN): 285 lb ft, 39.3 kg m (385.4 Nm) at 3,200 rpm; max engine rpm: 4,400; 34 hp/l (25 kW/l); cast iron block and head; 5 crankshaft bearings; valves: overhead, in line, push-rods and rockers, hydraulic tappets; camshafts: 1, at centre of Vee; lubrication: gear pump, full flow filter, 8.3 imp pt, 9.9 US pt, 4.7 l; 1 Rochester 17059202 (17059502 for California only) downdraught 4-barrel carburettor; cleaner air system; dual exhaust system with catalytic converter; fuel feed: mechanical pump; water-cooled, 34.5 imp pt, 41.4 US pt, 19.6 l, viscous-coupling thermostatic fan.

TRANSMISSION driving wheels: rear; gearbox: Turbo-Hydramatic 350 automatic transmission, hydraulic torque converter and planetary gears with 3 ratios, max ratio of converter at stall 2, possible manual selection; ratios: I 2.520, II 1.520, III 1, rev 1.930; lever: central; final drive: hypoid bevel, limited slip differential; axle ratio: 3.550; width of rims: 8''; tyres: P225/70R x 15.

PERFORMANCE max speed: about 120 mph, 193 km/h; power-weight ratio: 18.3 lb/hp (24.9 lb/kW), 8.3 kg/hp

.3 kg/kW); speed in direct drive at 1,000 rpm: 28 mph,
km/h; consumption: 19.2 m/imp gal, 16 m/US gal,
7 l x 100 km.

HASSIS box-type ladder frame, X cross members; front
spension: independent, wishbones, coil springs, anti-
l bar, telescopic dampers; rear: rigid axle, semi-elliptic
afsprings, upper torque arms, anti-roll bar, telescopic
mpers.

EERING cam and lever, tilt of steering wheel, servo.

AKES front disc with internal radial fins, rear drum,
rvo.

ECTRICAL EQUIPMENT 12 V; 61 Ah battery; 37 A alter-
tor; Delco-Remy high energy ignition system; 2 head-
mps.

MENSIONS AND WEIGHT wheel base: 109 in, 277 cm;
cks: 57.37 in, 146 cm front, 56.56 in, 144 cm rear;
igth: 197.80 in, 502 cm; width: 70.40 in, 179 cm; height:
40 in, 138 cm; ground clearance: 6.19 in, 15.7 cm;
ight: 3,570 lb, 1,619 kg; turning circle: 37.5 ft, 11.4 m;
el tank: 15.8 imp gal, 19 US gal, 72 l.

DY coupé, in plastic material; 2 doors; 4 seats, sepa-
e front seats, built-in headrests; heated rear window;
ted glass; air-conditioning.

TIONALS electric sunroof; electric moonroof; electric
ndows; luxury equipment; leather upholstery; fog lamps;
tomatic speed control; reclining front seats; genuine
od veneer dash and console panels; Recaro front seats;
re wheels; magnum '' 500 '' wheels.

AVANTI II Coupé

LAKELY   **USA**

Bearcat 'S'

ICE EX WORKS: $ 8,500 (complete car)

GINE Ford Pinto, front, 4 stroke; 4 cylinders, in line;
) cu in, 2,300 cc (3.78 x 3.13 in, 95.9 x 79.5 mm); comession ratio: 9.5:1; max power (DIN): 125 hp (92 kW)
4,800 rpm; max torque (DIN): 134 lb ft, 18.5 kg m
1.4 Nm) at 3,200 rpm; max engine rpm: 5,200; 54.3 hp/l
kW/l); cast iron block and head; 5 crankshaft bearings;
ves: overhead, Vee-slanted, rockers, hydraulic tappets;
mshafts: 1, overhead, cogged belt; lubrication: gear
mp, full flow filter, 8.3 imp pt, 9.9 US pt, 4.7 l; 1 Holley
) C.F.M. downdraught 4-barrel carburettor; cleaner air
stem; exhaust system with catalytic converter; fuel
d: mechanical pump; water-cooled, 15.8 imp pt, 19 US
9 l.

ANSMISSION driving wheels: rear; clutch: single dry
te; gearbox: mechanical; gears: 4, fully synchronized;
ios: I 2.460, II 1.460, III 1.240, IV 1, rev 2.460; lever:
ntral; final drive: hypoid bevel; axle ratio: 2.730; width
rims: 5.5''; tyres: 175 R x 13.

PERFORMANCE max speed: 100 mph, 161 km/h; power-
weight ratio: 14.4 lb/hp, (19.6 lb/kW), 6.5 kg/hp (8.9 kg/kW);
consumption: 31.4 m/imp gal, 26 m/US gal, 9 l x 100 km.

CHASSIS tubular; front suspension: independent, unequal-
length upper; A arms, coil springs, telescopic dampers;
rear: rigid axle, three-link cantilever leafspring with central
trailing arm, telescopic dampers.

STEERING rack-and-pinion; turns lock to lock: 4.

BRAKES front disc (diameter 9.30 in, 23.6 cm), front internal radial fins, rear drum; swept area: front 145.5 sq
in, 938 sq cm, rear 99 sq in, 639 sq cm, total 244.5 sq
in, 1,577 sq cm.

ELECTRICAL EQUIPMENT 12 V; 70 Ah battery; 42 A alternator; Ford distributor; 2 headlamps.

DIMENSIONS AND WEIGHT wheel base: 93 in, 236 cm;
tracks: 56 in, 142 cm front, 56.80 in, 144 cm rear; length:
145 in, 368 cm; width: 65 in, 165 cm; height: 46 in, 117
cm; ground clearance: 7 in, 17.8 cm; weight: 1,800 lb,
816 kg; turning circle: 30.6 ft, 9.3 m; fuel tank: 9.9 imp
gal, 12 US gal, 45 l.

BODY roadster in plastic material; 2 doors; 2 seats.

OPTIONALS Cruise-O-Matic automatic transmission with
3 ratios (I 2.470, II 1.470, III 1, rev 2.110), max ratio of
converter at stall 2.9, possible manual selection, central
lever; 61 A alternator; hardtop; sunshine roof installed
in hardtop; wire wheels.

BUICK   **USA**

Skyhawk Series

PRICES EX WORKS:

S Hatchback Coupé	$ 4,480
Hatchback Coupé	$ 4,698

115 hp power team

ENGINE front, 4 stroke; 6 cylinders, Vee-slanted at 90°;
231 cu in, 3,785 cc (3.80 x 3.40 in, 96.5 x 86.4 mm); compression ratio: 8:1; max power (DIN): 115 hp (84.6 kW) at
3,800 rpm; max torque (DIN): 190 lb ft, 26.2 kg m (257 Nm)
at 2,000 rpm; max engine rpm: 4,200; 30.4 hp/l (22.3 kW/l);
cast iron block and head; 4 crankshaft bearings; valves:
overhead, in line, push-rods and rockers, hydraulic tappets;
camshafts: 1, at centre of Vee; lubrication: gear pump, full
flow filter, 8.3 imp pt, 9.9 US pt, 4.7 l; 1 Rochester 2ME
downdraught twin barrel carburettor; cleaner air system;
exhaust system with catalytic converter; fuel feed: electric
pump; water-cooled, 21.6 imp pt, 26 US pt, 12.3 l.

TRANSMISSION driving wheels: rear; clutch: single dry
plate; gearbox: mechanical; gears: 4, fully synchronized;
ratios: I 3.500, II 2.480, III 1.660, IV 1, rev 3.500; lever:
central; final drive: hypoid bevel; axle ratio: 2.930; width
of rims: 6'' - Skyhawk S 5''; tyres: BR78 x 13 - Skyhawk
S B78 x 13.

PERFORMANCE max speed: about 109 mph, 175 km/h;
power-weight ratio: 24.9 lb/hp (33.8 lb/kW), 11.3 kg/hp
(15.3 kg/kW); speed in direct drive at 1,000 rpm: 26.2
mph, 42.2 km/h; consumption: 22.8 m/imp gal, 19 m/US
gal, 12.4 l x 100 km.

CHASSIS integral; front suspension: independent, wishbones (lower trailing links), coil springs, anti-roll bar,
telescopic dampers; rear: rigid axle, lower trailing radius
arms, upper torque arms, transverse linkage bar, coil
springs, telescopic dampers.

STEERING recirculating ball; turns lock to lock: 4.40.

BRAKES front disc (diameter 9.74 in, 24.7 cm), front internal
radial fins, rear drum; swept area: total 264.7 sq in, 1,707
sq cm.

ELECTRICAL EQUIPMENT 12 V; 2,500 W battery; 37 A alternator; Delco-Remy transistorized ignition; 4 headlamps.

DIMENSIONS AND WEIGHT wheel base: 97 in, 246 cm;
tracks: 54.70 in, 139 cm front, 53.60 in, 136 cm rear; length:
179.30 in, 455 cm; width: 65.40 in, 166 cm; height: 50.20
in, 127 cm; ground clearance: 4.90 in, 12.4 cm; weight:
Skyhawk 2,861 lb, 1,297 kg - Skyhawk 2,855 lb, 1,295 kg;
turning circle: 38.5 ft, 11.7 m; fuel tank: 15.4 imp gal, 18.5
US gal, 70 l.

BODY hatchback coupé; 2 + 1 doors; 2 + 2 seats, separate front seats; folding rear seat.

OPTIONALS Turbo-Hydramatic 350 automatic transmission
with 3 ratios (I 2.520, II 1.520, III 1, rev 1.930), max ratio
of converter at stall 2.50, possible manual selection, central

BLAKELY Bearcat 'S' Roadster

lever, 2.560 or 2.930 axle ratio; 5-speed fully synchronized mechanical gearbox (I 3.400, II 2.080, III 1.390, IV 1, V 0.800, rev 3.360), central lever, 2.930 axle ratio; limited slip differential; BR70 x 13 tyres with 6'' wide rims; power steering; tilt of steering wheel; servo brake; heavy-duty radiator; heavy-duty battery; reclining backrests; tinted glass; heated rear window; air-conditioning; sunshine roof; Road Hawk equipment.

Skylark Series

PRICES EX WORKS:

Skylark 2-dr Hatchback Coupé	$ 4,357
Skylark 2-dr Thin Pillar Coupé	$ 4,208
Skylark S 2-dr Thin Pillar Coupé	$ 4,082
Skylark 4-dr Thin Pillar Sedan	$ 4,308
Skylark S/R 2-dr Thin Pillar Coupé	$ 4,462
Skylark S/R 4-dr Thin Pillar Sedan	$ 4,562

For V8 130 hp engine add $ 195; for V8 160 hp engine add $ 320.

Power team:	Standard for:	Optional for:
115 hp	all	—
130 hp	—	all
160 hp	—	all

115 hp power team

(not available in California).

ENGINE front, 4 stroke; 6 cylinders, Vee-slanted at 90°; 231 cu in, 3,785 cc (3.80 x 3.40 in, 96.5 x 86.4 mm); compression ratio: 8:1; max power (DIN): 115 hp (84.6 kW) at 3,800 rpm; max torque (DIN): 190 lb ft, 26.2 kg m (257 Nm) at 2,000 rpm; max engine rpm: 4,200; 30.4 hp/l (22.3 kW/l); cast iron block and head; 4 crankshaft bearings; valves: overhead, in line, pushrods and rockers, hydraulic tappets; camshafts: 1, at centre of Vee; lubrication: gear pump, full flow filter, 8.3 imp pt, 9.9 US pt, 4.7 l; 1 Rochester 2ME downdraught twin barrel carburettor; cleaner air system; exhaust system with catalytic converter; fuel feed: mechanical pump; water-cooled, 24.1 imp pt, 29 US pt, 13.7 l.

TRANSMISSION driving wheels: rear; clutch: single dry plate; gearbox: mechanical; gears: 3, fully synchronized; ratios: I 3.500, II 1.810, III 1, rev 3.620; lever: steering column; final drive: hypoid bevel; axle ratio: 3.080; width of rims: 5''; tyres: E78 x 14 - Skylark SR ER78 x 14.

PERFORMANCE max speed: about 96 mph, 154 km/h; power-weight ratio: Thin Pillar Sedan 28.4 lb/hp (38.6 lb/kW), 12.9 kg/hp (17.5 kg/kW) - S/R Thin Pillar Sedan 28.6 lb/hp (38.8 lb/kW), 13 kg/hp (17.6 kg/kW); speed in direct drive at 1,000 rpm: 24.2 mph, 39 km/h; consumption: 22.8 m/imp gal, 19 m/US gal, 12.4 l x 100 km.

CHASSIS integral with separate partial front box-type frame; front suspension: independent, wishbones (lower trailing links), coil springs, anti-roll bar, telescopic dampers; rear: rigid axle, semi-elliptic leafsprings, telescopic dampers.

BUICK Skyhawk Hatchback Coupé

BUICK Skylark Hatchback Coupé

STEERING recirculating ball; turns lock to lock: 4.99.

BRAKES front disc (diameter 11 in, 27.9 cm), front ternal radial fins, rear drum; swept area: total 344 sq 2,219 sq cm.

ELECTRICAL EQUIPMENT 12 V; 2,500 W battery; 37 A ternator; Delco-Remy transistorized ignition; 2 headlam

DIMENSIONS AND WEIGHT wheel base: 111 in, 282 c tracks: 59.10 in, 150 cm front, 59.70 in, 152 cm re length: 200.20 in, 508 cm; width: 72.70 in, 185 cm; heig 52.20 in, 133 cm - sedans 53.10 in, 135 cm; ground cl rance: 5.20 in, 13.2 cm; weight: Hatchback Coupé 3,307 1,500 kg - Thin Pillar Coupé 3,225 lb, 1,462 kg - S T Pillar Coupé 3,212 lb, 1,457 kg - Thin Pillar Sedan 3,2 lb, 1,482 kg - S/R Thin Pillar Coupé 3,234 lb, 1,466 kg - S Thin Pillar Sedan 3,287 lb, 1,490 kg; turning circle: 41.7 12.7 m; fuel tank: 17.6 imp gal, 21 US gal, 80 l.

OPTIONALS Turbo-Hydramatic 350 automatic transmissi with 3 ratios (I 2.520, II 1.520, III 1, rev 1.930), m ratio of converter at stall 2.2, possible manual selecti 2.560, 2.930 or 3.230 axle ratio; limited slip differential; EF x 14 tyres; FR78 x 14 tyres with 6'' wide rims; anti-roll bar rear suspension; heavy-duty radiator; heavy-duty batte power steering; tilt of steering wheel; servo brake; rec ing backrests; electric windows; air-conditioning.

130 hp power team

(not available in California).

See 115 hp power team, except for:

ENGINE 8 cylinders; 305 cu in, 4,999 cc (3.80 x 3.40 in, 96. 86.4 mm); compression ratio: 8.4:1; max power (DIN): 130 (95.7 kW) at 3,200 rpm; max torque (DIN): 245 lb ft, 33.8 kg (331.5 Nm) at 2,000 rpm; 26 hp/l (19.1 kW/l); 5 cranksh bearings.

TRANSMISSION gearbox: Turbo-Hydramatic 350 automa transmission (standard), hydraulic torque converter a planetary gears with 3 ratios, max ratio of converter stall 2.20, possible manual selection; ratios: I 2.520, 1.520, III 1, rev 1.930; axle ratio: 2.410.

PERFORMANCE max speed: about 106 mph, 170 km, power-weight ratio: Thin Pillar Sedan 26.3 lb/hp (3. lb/kW), 11.9 kg/hp (16.2 kg/kW) - S/R Thin Pillar Sed 26.4 lb/hp (35.9 lb/kW), 12 kg/hp (16.3 kg/kW); speed direct drive at 1,000 rpm: 27.5 mph, 44.2 km/h; consum tion: 19.2 m/imp gal, 16 m/US gal, 14.7 l x 100 km.

DIMENSIONS AND WEIGHT weight: plus 150 lb, 60

OPTIONALS 3.080 axle ratio.

160 hp power team

(for California only).

See 115 hp power team, except for:

ENGINE 8 cylinders; 350 cu in, 5,736 cc (4 x 3.48 in, 101. 88.3 mm); compression ratio: 8.2:1; max power (DIN): hp (117.8 kW) at 3,800 rpm; max torque (DIN): 260 lb

BUICK Skyhawk Road Hawk Hatchback Coupé

35.9 kg m (352.1 Nm) at 2,400 rpm; max engine rpm: 4,600; 27.9 hp/l (20.5 kW/l); 5 crankshaft bearings; 1 Rochester M4MC downdraught 4-barrel carburettor; cooling system: 24.8 imp pt, 29.8 US pt, 14.1 l.

TRANSMISSION gearbox: Turbo-Hydramatic 350 automatic transmission (standard), hydraulic torque converter and planetary gears with 3 ratios, max ratio of converter at stall 2.20, possible manual selection; ratios: I 2.520, II 1.520, III 1, rev 1.930; axle ratio: 2.410.

PERFORMANCE max speed: about 112 mph, 180 km/h; power-weight ratio: Thin Pillar Sedan 21.6 lb/hp (29.3 lb/kW), 9.7 kg/hp (13.3 kg/kW) - S/R Thin Pillar Sedan 21.7 lb/hp (29.5 lb/kW), 9.8 kg/hp (13.4 kg/kW); speed in direct drive at 1,000 rpm: 27.5 mph, 44.2 km/h; consumption: 18 m/imp gal, 15 m/US gal, 15.7 l x 100 km.

DIMENSIONS AND WEIGHT weight: plus 184 lb, 83 kg.

OPTIONALS 3.080 axle ratio.

Century Series

PRICES EX WORKS:

1 Special 2-dr Coupé	$ 4,716
2 Special 4-dr Sedan	$ 4,816
3 Special 4+1-dr St. Wagon	$ 5,363
4 2-dr Sport Coupé	$ 5,268
5 Custom 2-dr Coupé	$ 4,960
6 Custom 4-dr Sedan	$ 5,085
7 Custom 4+1-dr St. Wagon	$ 5,677
8 Limited 2-dr Coupé	
9 Limited 4-dr Sedan	$ 5,453

For 115 hp engine add $40; for V8 140 hp engine add $256 (for Sport Coupé add $235); for V8 150 and 155 hp engines add $316 (for Sport Coupé add $295).

Power team:	Standard for:	Optional for:
105 hp	all except 3,7	—
115 hp	3,7	all except 3,7
140 hp	—	all
150 hp	—	all
155 hp	—	all
165 hp	—	3,7

105 hp power team

(not available in California).

ENGINE front, 4 stroke; 6 cylinders, Vee-slanted at 90°; 196 cu in, 3,212 cc (3.50 x 3.40 in, 88.9 x 86.4 mm); compression ratio: 8:1; max power (DIN): 105 hp (77.3 kW) at 4,000 rpm; max torque (DIN): 160 lb ft, 22.1 kg m (216.7 Nm) at 2,000 rpm; max engine rpm: 4,400; 32.7 hp/l (24.1 kW/l); cast iron block and head; 4 crankshaft bearings; valves: overhead, in line, push-rods and rockers, hydraulic tappets; camshafts: 1, at centre of Vee; lubrication: gear pump, full flow filter, 8.3 imp pt, 9.9 US pt, 4.7 l; 1 Rochester 2ME downdraught twin barrel carburettor; cleaner air system; exhaust system with catalytic converter; fuel feed: mechanical pump; water-cooled, 22.2 imp pt, 26.6 US pt, 12.6 l.

BUICK Century Custom 2-dr Coupé

TRANSMISSION driving wheels: rear; clutch: single dry plate; gearbox: mechanical; gears: 3, fully synchronized; ratios: I 3.504, II 1.895, III 1, rev 3.625; lever: central; final drive: hypoid bevel; axle ratio: 2.930; width of rims: 6''; tyres: P185/75 x 14.

PERFORMANCE max speed: about 90 mph, 145 km/h; power-weight ratio: Special Sedan 30 lb/hp (40.8 lb/kW), 13.6 kg/hp (18.5 kg/kW) - Custom Sedan 30.2 lb/hp (41 lb/kW), 13.7 kg/hp (18.6 kg/kW) - Limited Sedan 30.5 lb/hp (41.4 lb/kW), 13.8 lb/hp (18.8 kg/kW); speed in direct drive at 1,000 rpm: 20.4 mph, 32.9 km/h; consumption: 21.6 m/imp gal, 18 m/US gal, 13.1 l x 100 km.

CHASSIS perimeter box-type frame; front suspension: independent, wishbones (lower trailing links), coil springs, anti-roll bar, telescopic dampers; rear: rigid axle, lower trailing radius arms, upper oblique torque arms, coil springs, telescopic dampers.

STEERING recirculating ball; turns lock to lock: 6.14.

BRAKES front disc (diameter 10.50 in, 26.7 cm), front internal radial fins, rear drum, rear compensator; swept area: total 312.68 sq in, 2,017 sq cm.

ELECTRICAL EQUIPMENT 12 V; 2,500 W battery; 42 A alternator; Delco-Remy transistorized ignition; 2 headlamps.

DIMENSIONS AND WEIGHT wheel base: 108.10 in, 274 cm; tracks: 58.50 in, 149 cm front, 57.80 in, 147 cm rear; length: 196 in, 498 cm; width: 72.20 in, 183 cm; height: 54.10 in,

137 cm - sedans 55 in, 140 cm; ground clearance: 6.10 in; 15.4 cm; weight: Special Coupé 3,130 lb, 1,420 kg - Special Sedan 3,153 lb, 1,430 kg - Sport Coupé 3,201 lb, 1,452 kg - Custom Coupé 3,148 lb, 1,428 kg - Custom Sedan 3,172 lb, 1,439 kg - Limited Coupé 3,172 lb, 1,439 kg - Limited Sedan 3,199 lb, 1,451 kg; turning circle: 43.3 ft, 13.2 m - coupés 42.2 ft, 12.9 m; fuel tank: 15 imp gal, 18.1 US gal, 68 l.

OPTIONALS Turbo-Hydramatic 350 automatic transmission with 3 ratios (I 2.520, II 1.520, III 1, rev 1.930), max ratio of converter at stall 2.50, possible manual selection, steering column or central lever, 2.560 axle ratio; limited slip differential; P195/75 x 14 or P205/70 x 14 tyres; automatic levelling control; anti-roll bar on rear suspension; tilt of steering wheel; power steering; servo brake; heavy-duty cooling system; heavy-duty battery; heated rear window; reclining backrests; electric windows; air-conditioning; electric sunshine roof except for sedans.

115 hp power team

See 105 hp power team, except for:

ENGINE 231 cu in, 3,785 cc (3.80 x 3.40 in, 96.5 x 86.4 mm); max power (DIN): 115 hp (84.6 kW) at 3,800 rpm; max torque (DIN): 190 lb ft, 26.2 kg m (257 Nm) at 2,000 rpm; max engine rpm: 4,200; 30.4 hp/l (22.3 kW/l).

TRANSMISSION gearbox: Turbo-Hydramatic 350 automatic transmission (standard), hydraulic torque converter and planetary gears with 3 ratios, max ratio of converter at stall 2.50, possible manual selection; ratios: I 2.520, II 1.520, III 1, rev 1.930; lever: steering column; axle ratio: 2.730; tyres: st. wagons P195/75 x 14.

PERFORMANCE max speed: about 93 mph, 150 km/h; power-weight ratio: Special St. Wagon 28.6 lb/hp (38.9 lb/kW), 13 kg/hp (17.6 kg/kW) - Custom St. Wagon 28.9 lb/hp (39.3 lb/kW), 13.1 kg/hp (17.8 kg/kW); speed in direct drive at 1,000 rpm: 24.5 mph, 39.5 km/h; consumption: 22.8 m/imp gal, 19 m/US gal, 12.4 l x 100 km.

DIMENSIONS AND WEIGHT height: st. wagons 55.70 in, 142 cm; ground clearance: st. wagons 6.90 in, 17.6 cm; weight: Special St. Wagon 3,287 lb, 1,491 kg - Custom St. Wagon 3,329 lb, 1,510 kg.

OPTIONALS 2.410 or 3.230 axle ratio.

140 hp power team

(not available in California).

See 105 hp power team, except for:

ENGINE 8 cylinders; 301 cu in, 4,932 cc (4 x 3 in, 101.6 x 76.2 mm); compression ratio: 8.1:1; max power (DIN): 140 hp (103 kW) at 3,600 rpm; max torque (DIN): 235 lb ft, 32.4 kg m (317.7 Nm) at 2,000 rpm; 28.4 hp/l (20.9 kW/l); 5 crankshaft bearings.

TRANSMISSION gearbox: Turbo-Hydramatic 350 automatic transmission (standard), hydraulic torque converter and planetary gears with 3 ratios, max ratio of converter at stall 2.50, possible manual selection; ratios: I 2.520, II 1.520, III 1, rev 1.930; lever: steering column; axle ratio: 2.290; tyres: st. wagons P195/75 x 14.

BUICK Century Limited 4-dr Sedan

BUICK Century Turbo Coupé

140 HP POWER TEAM

PERFORMANCE max speed: about 99 mph, 160 km/h; power-weight ratio: Special Sedan 23.3 lb/hp (31.6 lb/kW), 10.5 kg/hp (14.3 kg/kW) - Custom Sedan 23.4 lb/hp (31.8 lb/kW), 10.6 kg/hp (14.4 kg/kW) - Limited Sedan 23.6 lb/hp (32.1 lb/kW), 10.7 kg/hp (14.5 kg/kW); speed in direct drive at 1,000 rpm: 27.6 mph, 44.4 km/h; consumption: 21.6 m/imp gal, 18 m/US gal, 13.1 l x 100 km.

DIMENSIONS AND WEIGHT height: st. wagons 55.70 in, 142 cm; ground clearance: st. wagons 6.90 in, 17.6 cm; weight: Special Coupé 3,234 lb, 1,466 kg - Special Sedan 3,257 lb, 1,477 kg - Special St. Wagon 3,391 lb, 1,538 kg - Sport Coupé 3,305 lb, 1,499 kg - Custom Coupé 3,252 lb, 1,475 kg - Custom Sedan 3,276 lb, 1,485 kg - Custom St. Wagon 3,433 lb, 1,557 kg - Limited Coupé 3,276 lb, 1,485 kg - Limited Sedan 3,303 lb, 1,498 kg.

150 hp power team

(not available in California).

See 105 hp power team, except for:

ENGINE 8 cylinders; 301 cu in, 4,932 cc (4 x 3 in, 101.6 x 76.2 mm); compression ratio: 8.1:1; max power (DIN): 150 hp (110.4 kW) at 4,000 rpm; max torque (DIN): 240 lb ft, 33.1 kg m (324.6 Nm) at 2,000 rpm; 30.4 hp/l (22.4 kW/l); 5 crankshaft bearings; 1 Rochester M4MC downdraught 4-barrel carburettor.

TRANSMISSION gearbox: Turbo-Hydramatic 350 automatic transmission (standard), hydraulic torque converter and planetary gears with 3 ratios, max ratio of converter at stall 2.50, possible manual selection: ratios: I 2.520, II 1.520, III 1, rev 1.930; lever: steering column; axle ratio: 2.290; tyres: st. wagons P195/75 x 14.

PERFORMANCE max speed: about 103 mph, 165 km/h; power-weight ratio: Special Sedan 21.8 lb/hp (29.6 lb/kW), 9.9 kg/hp (13.4 kg/kW) - Custom Sedan 21.9 lb/hp (29.8 lb/kW), 9.9 kg/hp (13.5 kg/kW) - Limited Sedan 22.1 lb/hp (30 lb/kW), 10 kg/hp (13.6 kg/kW); speed in direct drive at 1,000 rpm: 25.6 mph, 41.2 km/h; consumption: 20.5 m/imp gal, 17 m/US gal, 13.8 l x 100 km.

DIMENSIONS AND WEIGHT height: st. wagons 55.70 in, 142 cm; ground clearance: st. wagons 6.90 in, 17.6 cm; weight: Special Coupé 3,248 lb, 1,473 kg - Special Sedan 3,271 lb, 1,483 kg - Special St. Wagon 3,405 lb, 1,544 kg - Sport Coupé 3,319 lb, 1,505 kg - Custom Coupé 3,266 lb, 1,481 kg - Custom Sedan 3,290 lb, 1,492 kg - Custom St. Wagon 3,447 lb, 1,563 kg - Limited Coupé 3,290 lb, 1,492 kg - Limited Sedan 3,317 lb, 1,504 kg.

OPTIONALS 2.560 axle ratio.

155 hp power team

See 105 hp power team, except for:

ENGINE 8 cylinders; 305 cu in, 4,999 cc (3.80 x 3.40 in, 96.5

BUICK Century Turbo Coupé

x 86.4 mm); compression ratio: 8.4:1; max power (DIN): 155 hp (114.1 kW) at 4,000 rpm; max torque (DIN): 225 lb ft, 31 kg m (304 Nm) at 2,400 rpm; 31 hp/l (22.8 kW/l); 5 crankshaft bearings; 1 Rochester M4MC downdraught 4-barrel carburettor.

TRANSMISSION gearbox: Turbo-Hydramatic 350 automatic transmission (standard), hydraulic torque converter and planetary gears with 3 ratios, max ratio of converter at stall 2.50, possible manual selection: ratios: I 2.520, II 1.520, III 1, rev 1.930; lever: steering column; axle ratio: 2.410 (2.730 California only); tyres: st. wagons P195/75 x 14.

PERFORMANCE max speed: about 106 mph, 170 km/h; power-weight ratio: Special Sedan 21.1 lb/hp (28.7 lb/kW), 9.6 kg/hp (13 kg/kW) - Custom Sedan 21.2 lb/hp (28.8 lb/kW), 9.6 kg/hp (13.1 kg/kW) - Limited Sedan 21.4 lb/hp (29.1 lb/kW), 9.7 kg/hp (13.2 kg/kW); speed in direct drive at 1,000 rpm: 26.4 mph, 42.5 km/h; consumption: 20.5 m/imp gal, 17 m/US gal, 13.8 l x 100 km.

DIMENSIONS AND WEIGHT height: st. wagons 55.70 in, 142 cm; ground clearance: st. wagons 6.90 in, 17.6 cm; weight: Special Coupé 3,248 lb, 1,473 kg - Special Sedan 3,271 lb, 1,483 kg - Special St. Wagon 3,405 lb, 1,544 kg - Sport Coupé 3,319 lb, 1,505 kg - Custom Coupé 3,266 lb, 1,481 kg - Custom Sedan 3,290 lb, 1,492 kg - Custom St. Wagon 3,447 lb, 1,563 kg - Limited Coupé 3,290 lb, 1,492 kg - Limited Sedan 3,317 lb, 1,504 kg.

OPTIONALS 2.730 axle ratio except for st. wagons.

165 hp power team

See 105 hp power team, except for:

ENGINE 8 cylinders; 350 cu in, 5,736 cc (4.06 x 3.38 in, 103.1 x 85.8 mm); compression ratio: 8.2:1; max power (DIN): 165 hp (121.4 kW) at 3,800 rpm; max torque (DIN): 260 lb ft, 35.9 kg m (352.1 Nm) at 2,400 rpm; 28.8 hp/l (21.2 kW/l); 5 crankshaft bearings; 1 Rochester M4MC downdraught 4-barrel carburettor; cooling system: 24.8 imp pt, 29.8 US pt, 14.1 l.

TRANSMISSION gearbox: Turbo-Hydramatic 350 automatic transmission (standard), hydraulic torque converter and planetary gears with 3 ratios, max ratio of converter at stall 2.50, possible manual selection: ratios: I 2.520, II 1.520, III 1, rev 1.930; lever: steering column; axle ratio: 2.730; tyres: P195/75 x 14.

PERFORMANCE max speed: about 109 mph, 175 km/h; power-weight ratio: Special St. Wagon 20.6 lb/hp (28 lb/kW), 9.4 kg/hp (12.7 kg/kW) - Custom St. Wagon 20.9 lb/hp (28.4 lb/kW), 9.5 kg/hp (12.9 kg/kW); speed in direct drive at 1,000 rpm: 28.6 mph, 46 km/h; consumption: 19.2 m/imp gal, 16 m/US gal, 14.7 l x 100 km.

DIMENSIONS AND WEIGHT height: 55.70 in, 142 cm; ground clearance 6.90 in, 17.6 cm; weight: Special St. Wagon 3,405 lb, 1,544 kg - Custom St. Wagon 3,447 lb, 1,563 kg.

BODY estate car/st. wagon; 4 + 1 doors; 6 seats, bench front seats, folding rear seat.

Century Turbo Coupé

PRICE EX WORKS: $ 5,738

175 hp power team

(standard).

ENGINE turbocharged, front, 4 stroke; 6 cylinders, Vee-slanted at 90°; 231 cu in, 3,785 cc (3.80 x 3.40 in, 96.5 x 86.4 mm); compression ratio: 8:1; max power (DIN): 175 hp (128.8 kW) at 4,000 rpm; max torque (DIN): 275 lb ft, 37.5 kg m (371.7 Nm) at 2,600 rpm; max engine rpm: 4,400; 46.2 hp/l (34 kW/l); cast iron block and head; 4 crankshaft bearings; valves: overhead, in line, push-rods and rockers, hydraulic tappets; camshafts: 1, at centre of Vee; lubrication: gear pump, full flow filter, 8.3 imp pt, 9.9 US pt, 4.7 l; 1 RDP 1705243 (RDP 17059543 for California only) downdraught 4-barrel carburettor; cleaner air system; dual exhaust system with catalytic converter; fuel feed: mechanical pump; water-cooled, 22.2 imp pt, 26.6 US pt, 12.6 l.

TRANSMISSION driving wheels: rear; gearbox: Turbo-Hydramatic 350 automatic transmission, hydraulic torque converter and planetary gears with 3 ratios, max ratio of converter at stall 2.50, possible manual selection: ratios: I 2.520, II 1.520, III 1, rev 1.930; lever: steering column; final drive: hypoid bevel; axle ratio: 3.080; width of rims: 6''; tyres: P185/75 x 14.

PERFORMANCE max speed: about 112 mph, 180 km/h; power-weight ratio: 18.4 lb/hp (24.9 lb/kW), 8.3 kg/hp (11.3 kg/kW); speed in direct drive at 1,000 rpm: 28 mph, 45 km/h; consumption: 20.5 m/imp gal, 17 m/US gal, 13.8 l x 100 km.

CHASSIS perimeter box-type frame; front suspension: independent, wishbones (lower trailing links), coil springs, anti-roll bar, telescopic dampers; rear: rigid axle, lower trailing radius arms, upper oblique torque arms, coil springs, telescopic dampers.

STEERING recirculating ball; turns lock to lock: 6.14.

BRAKES front disc (diameter 10.50 in, 26.7 cm), front internal radial fins, rear drum; swept area: total 312.68 sq in, 2,017 sq cm.

ELECTRICAL EQUIPMENT 12 V; 2,500 W battery; 42 A alternator; Delco-Remy transistorized ignition; 2 headlamps.

DIMENSIONS AND WEIGHT wheel base: 108.10 in, 274 cm; tracks: 58.50 in, 149 cm front, 57.80 in, 147 cm rear; length: 196 in, 498 cm; width: 70 in, 178 cm; height: 54.10 in, 137 cm; ground clearance: 6.10 in, 15.4 cm; weight: 3,212 lb, 1,456 kg; turning circle 42.2 ft, 12.9 m; fuel tank: 15 imp gal, 18.1 US gal, 68 l.

BODY coupé; 2 doors; 6 seats, separate front seats.

OPTIONALS central lever; limited slip differential; P195/75 x 14 or P205/70 x 14 tyres; automatic levelling control; anti-roll bar on rear suspension; tilt of steering wheel; power steering; servo brake; heavy-duty cooling system; heavy-duty battery; heated rear window; reclining backrests; electric windows; electric sunshine roof; air-conditioning.

Regal Series

PRICES EX WORKS:

1 Coupé	$ 5,189
2 Limited Coupé	$ 5,596
3 Sport Coupé	$ 6,355

For 115 hp engine add $ 40; for V8 140 hp engine add $ 235; for V8 150 and 155 hp engines add $ 295; for 170 hp engine add $ 470.

Power team:	Standard for:	Optional for:
105 hp	1,2	—
115 hp	—	1,2
140 hp	—	1,2
150 hp	—	1,2
155 hp	—	1,2
170 hp	3	—

105 hp power team

(not available in California).

ENGINE front, 4 stroke; 6 cylinders, Vee-slanted at 90°; 196 cu in, 3,212 cc (3.50 x 3.40 in, 88.9 x 96.4 mm); compression ratio: 8:1; max power (DIN): 105 hp (77.3 kW) at 4,000 rpm; max torque (DIN): 160 lb ft, 22.1 kg m (216.7 Nm) at 2,000 rpm; max engine rpm: 4,400; 32.7 hp/l (24.1 kW/l); cast iron block and head; 4 crankshaft bearings; valves: overhead, in line, push-rods and rockers, hydraulic tappets; camshafts: 1, at centre of Vee; lubrication: gear pump, full flow filter, 8.3 imp pt, 9.9 US pt, 4.7 l; 1 Rochester 2ME downdraught twin barrel carburettor; cleaner air system; exhaust system with catalytic converter; fuel feed: mechanical pump; water-cooled, 22.2 imp pt, 26.6 US pt, 12.6 l.

TRANSMISSION driving wheels: rear; clutch: single dry plate; gearbox: mechanical; gears: 3, fully synchronized; ratios: I 3.504, II 1.895, III 1, rev 3.625; lever: central; final drive: hypoid bevel; axle ratio: 2.930; width of rims: 6''; tyres: P185/75 x 14.

PERFORMANCE max speed: about 90 mph, 145 km/h; power-weight ratio: Coupé 30.2 lb/hp (41 lb/kW), 13.7 kg/hp (18.6 kg/kW) - Limited Coupé 30.5 lb/hp (41.4 lb/kW), 13.8 kg/hp (18.8 kg/kW); speed in direct drive at 1,000 rpm: 20.4 mph, 32.9 km/h; consumption: 21.6 m/imp gal, 18 m/US gal, 13.1 l x 100 km.

CHASSIS perimeter box-type frame; front suspension: independent, wishbones (lower trailing links), coil springs, anti-roll bar, telescopic dampers; rear: rigid axle, lower trailing radius arms, upper oblique torque arms, coil springs, telescopic dampers.

STEERING recirculating ball; turns lock to lock: 6.14.

BRAKES front disc (diameter 10.50 in, 26.7 cm), front internal radial fins, rear drum, rear compensator; swept area: total 312.68 sq in, 2,017 sq cm.

ELECTRICAL EQUIPMENT 12 V; 2,500 W battery; 42 A alternator; Delco-Remy transistorized ignition; 2 headlamps.

DIMENSIONS AND WEIGHT wheel base: 108.10 in, 274 cm;

BUICK Regal Sport Coupé

tracks: 58.50 in, 149 cm front, 57.80 in, 147 cm rear; length: 200 in, 508 cm; width: 72.20 in, 183 cm; height: 53.40 in, 136 cm; ground clearance: 6.10 in, 15.4 cm; weight: Coupé 3,171 lb, 1,438 kg - Limited Coupé 3,201 lb, 1,452 kg; turning circle: 42.2 ft, 12.9 m; fuel tank: 15 imp gal, 18.1 US gal, 68 l.

BODY coupé; 2 doors; 6 seats, separate front seats.

OPTIONALS Turbo-Hydramatic 350 automatic transmission with 3 ratios (I 2.520, II 1.520, III 1, rev 1.930), max ratio of converter at stall 2.50, possible manual selection, steering column or central lever, 2.560 axle ratio; limited slip differential; P195/75 x 14 or P205/70 x 14 tyres; automatic levelling control; anti-roll bar on rear suspension; tilt of steering wheel; power steering; servo brake; heavy-duty cooling system; heavy-duty battery; heated rear window; reclining backrests; electric windows; air-conditioning; electric sunshine roof.

115 hp power team

See 105 hp poewr team, except for:

ENGINE 231 cu in, 3,785 cc (3.80 x 3.40 in, 96.5 x 86.4 mm); max power (DIN): 115 hp (84.6 kW) at 3,800 rpm; max torque (DIN): 190 lb ft, 26.2 kg m (257 Nm) at 2,000 rpm; max engine rpm: 4,200; 30.4 hp/l (22.3 kW/l).

TRANSMISSION gearbox: mechanical (Turbo-Hydramatic 350

BUICK Regal Limited Coupé

automatic transmission standard in California); gears: 4, fully synchronized; ratios: I 3.504, II 2.480, III 1.655, IV 1, rev 3.504; axle ratio: 2.930 (2.410 California only).

PERFORMANCE max speed: about 93 mph, 150 km/h; power-weight ratio: Coupé 27.6 lb/hp (37.5 lb/kW), 12.5 kg/hp (17 kg/kW) - Limited Coupé 27.8 lb/hp (37.8 lb/kW), 12.6 kg/hp (17.2 kg/kW); speed in direct drive at 1,000 rpm: 24.5 mph, 39.5 km/h; consumption: 22.8 m/imp gal, 19 m/US gal, 12.4 l x 100 km.

OPTIONALS 2.730 or 3.230 axle ratio.

140 hp power team

(not available in California).

See 105 hp power team, except for:

ENGINE 8 cylinders; 301 cu in, 4,932 cc (4 x 3 in, 101.6 x 76.2 mm); compression ratio: 8.1:1; max power (DIN): 140 hp (103 kW) at 3,600 rpm; max torque (DIN): 235 lb ft, 32.4 kg m (317.7 Nm) at 2,000 rpm; 28.4 hp/l (20.9 kW/l); 5 crankshaft bearings.

TRANSMISSION gearbox: Turbo-Hydramatic 350 automatic transmission (standard), hydraulic torque converter and planetary gears with 3 ratios, max ratio of converter at stall 2.50, possible manual selection; ratios: I 2.520, II 1.520, III 1, rev 1.930; lever: steering column; axle ratio: 2.290.

PERFORMANCE max speed: about 99 mph, 160 km/h; power-weight ratio: Coupé 23.4 lb/hp (31.8 lb/kW), 10.6 kg/hp (14.4 kg/kW) - Limited Coupé 23.6 lb/hp (32.1 lb/kW), 10.7 kg/hp (14.6 kg/kW); speed in direct drive at 1,000 rpm: 27.6 mph, 44.4 km/h; consumption: 21.6 m/imp gal, 18 m/US gal, 13.1 l x 100 km.

DIMENSIONS AND WEIGHT weight: Coupé 3,275 lb, 1,485 kg - Limited Coupé 3,305 lb, 1,499 kg.

150 hp power team

(not available in California).

See 105 hp power team, except for:

ENGINE 8 cylinders; 301 cu in, 4,932 cc (4 x 3 in, 101.6 x 76.2 mm); compression ratio: 8.1:1; max power (DIN): 150 hp (110.4 kW) at 4,000 rpm; max torque (DIN): 240 lb ft, 33.1 kg m (324.6 Nm) at 2,000 rpm; 30.4 hp/l (22.4 kW/l); 5 crankshaft bearings; 1 Rochester M4MC downdraught 4-barrel carburettor.

TRANSMISSION gearbox: Turbo-Hydramatic 350 automatic transmission (standard), hydraulic torque converter and planetary gears with 3 ratios, max ratio of converter at stall 2.50, possible manual selection; ratios: I 2.520, II 1.520, III 1, rev 1.930; lever: steering column; axle ratio: 2.290.

PERFORMANCE max speed: about 103 mph, 165 km/h; power-weight ratio: Coupé 21.9 lb/hp (29.8 lb/kW), 9.9 kg/hp (13.5 kg/kW) - Limited Coupé 22.1 lb/hp (30.1 lb/kW), 10 kg/hp (13.6 kg/kW); speed in direct drive at 1,000 rpm: 25.6 mph, 41.2 km/h; consumption: 20.5 m/imp gal, 17 m/US gal, 13.8 l x 100 km.

DIMENSIONS AND WEIGHT weight: Coupé 3,289 lb, 1,491 kg - Limited Coupé 3,319 lb, 1,505 kg.

OPTIONALS 2.560 axle ratio.

155 hp power team

See 105 hp power team, except for:

ENGINE 8 cylinders; 305 cu in, 4,999 cc (3.80 x 3.40 in, 96.5 x 86.4 mm); compression ratio: 8.4:1; max power (DIN): 155 hp (114.1 kW) at 4,000 rpm; max torque (DIN): 225 lb ft, 31 kg m (304 Nm) at 2,400 rpm; 31 hp/l (22.8 kW/l); 5 crankshaft bearings; 1 Rochester M4MC downdraught 4-barrel carburettor.

TRANSMISSION gearbox: Turbo-Hydramatic 350 automatic transmission (standard), hydraulic torque converter and planetary gears with 3 ratios, max ratio of converter at stall 2.50, possible manual selection; ratios: I 2.520, II 1.520, III 1, rev 1.930; lever: steering column; axle ratio: 2.290 (2.730 California only).

PERFORMANCE max speed: about 106 mph, 170 km/h; power-weight ratio: Coupé 21.2 lb/hp (28.8 lb/kW), 9.6 kg/hp (13.1 kg/kW) - Limited Coupé 21.4 lb/hp (29.1 lb/kW), 9.7 kg/hp (13.2 kg/W); speed in direct drive at 1,000 rpm: 26.4 mph, 42.5 km/h; consumption: 20.5 m/imp gal, 17 m/US gal, 13.8 l x 100 km.

DIMENSIONS AND WEIGHT weight: Coupé 3,289 lb, 1,491 kg - Limited Coupé 3,319 lb, 1,505 kg.

OPTIONALS 2.730 axle ratio.

170 hp power team

See 105 hp power team, except for:

ENGINE turbocharged; 231 cu in, 3.785 cc (3.80 x 3.40 in, 96.5 x 86.4 mm); max power (DIN): 170 hp (125.1 kW) at 4,000 rpm; max torque (DIN): 265 lb ft, 36.6 kg m (358.9 Nm) at 2,400 rpm; 44.9 hp/l (33.1 kW/l); 1 RDP 1705243 (RDP 17059543 for California only) downdraught 4-barrel carburettor.

TRANSMISSION gearbox: Turbo-Hydramatic 350 automatic transmission (standard), hydraulic torque converter and planetary gears with 3 ratios, max ratio of converter at stall 2.50, possible manual selection; ratios: I 2.520, II 1.520, III 1, rev 1.930; lever: steering column; axle ratio: 2.410 (2.730 California only).

PERFORMANCE max speed: about 112 mph, 180 km/h; power-weight ratio: 19.5 lb/hp (26.4 lb/kW), 8.8 kg/hp (12 kg/kW); speed in direct drive at 1,000 rpm: 28 mph, 45 km/h; consumption: 20.5 m/imp gal, 17 m/US gal, 13.8 l x 100 km.

DIMENSIONS AND WEIGHT weight: 3,309 lb, 1,501 kg.

OPTIONALS 2.730 or 3.080 axle ratio (3.080 California only).

Le Sabre Series

PRICES EX WORKS:

1 2-dr Hardtop Coupé	$ 5,788
2 4-dr Thin Pillar Sedan	$ 5,888
3 2-dr Limited Hardtop Coupé	$ 6,252
4 4-dr Limited Thin Pillar Sedan	$ 6,377
5 2-dr Sport Coupé	$ 6,762

For V8 140 hp engine add $ 246; for V8 155 and 160 hp engines add $ 371; for 170 hp engine add $ 470.

Power team:	Standard for:	Optional for:
115 hp	1 to 4	—
140 hp	—	1 to 4
155 hp	—	1 to 4
160 hp	—	1 to 4
170 hp	5	—

115 hp power team

ENGINE front, 4 stroke; 6 cylinders, Vee-slanted at 90°; 231. cu in, 3,785 cc (3.80 x 3.40 in, 96.5 x 86.4 mm); compression ratio: 8:1; max power (DIN): 115 hp (84.6 kW) at 3,800 rpm; max torque (DIN): 190 lb ft, 26.2 kg m (257 Nm) at 2,000 rpm; max engine rpm: 4,200; 30.4 hp/l (22.3 kW/l); cast iron block and head; 4 crankshaft bearings; valves: overhead, in line, push-rods and rockers, hydraulic tappets; camshafts: 1, at centre of Vee; lubrication: gear pump, full flow filter, 8.3 imp pt, 9.9 US pt, 4.7 l; 1 Rochester 2ME downdraught twin barrel carburettor; cleaner air system; exhaust system with catalytic converter; fuel feed: mechanical pump; water-cooled, 22.2 imp pt, 26.6 US pt, 12.6 l.

TRANSMISSION driving wheels: rear; gearbox: Turbo-Hy-

BUICK Le Sabre 2-dr Sport Coupé

dramatic 350 automatic transmission, hydraulic torque converter and planetary gears with 3 ratios, max ratio of converter at stall 2.50, possible manual selection; ratios: I 2.520, II 1.520, III 1, rev 1.930; lever: steering column; final drive: hypoid bevel; axle ratio: 2.730; width of rims: 6''; tyres FR78 x 15.

PERFORMANCE max speed: about 93 mph, 149 km/h; power-weight ratio: Thin Pillar Sedan 31.3 lb/hp (42.6 lb/kW), 14.2 kg/hp (19.3 kg/kW) - Limited Thin Pillar Sedan 31.7 lb/hp (43.1 lb/kW), 14.4 kg/hp (19.6 kg/kW); speed in direct drive at 1,000 rpm: 24.5 mph, 39.5 km/h; consumption: 21.6 m/imp gal, 18 m/US gal, 13.1 l x 100 km.

CHASSIS perimeter box-type frame; front suspension: independent, wishbones (lower trailing links), coil springs, anti-roll bar, telescopic dampers; rear: rigid axle, lower trailing radius arms, upper oblique torque arms, coil springs, telescopic dampers.

STEERING recirculating ball, variable ratio servo; turns lock to lock: 3.37.

BRAKES front disc (diameter 11 in, 27.9 cm), front internal radial fins, rear drum, servo; swept area: total 344 sq in, 2,219 sq cm.

ELECTRICAL EQUIPMENT 12 V; 2,500 W battery; 42 A alternator; Delco-Remy transistorized ignition; 4 headlamps.

DIMENSIONS AND WEIGHT wheel base: 115.90 in, 294 cm; tracks: 61.80 in, 157 cm front, 60.70 in, 154 cm rear;

length: 218.20 in, 554 cm; width: 77.20 in, 196 cm; height: 55 in, 140 cm - sedans 55.70 in, 141 cm; ground clearance: 6.70 in, 17 cm; weight: Hardtop Coupé 3,571 lb, 1,620 kg - Thin Pillar Sedan 3,600 lb, 1,633 kg - Limited Hardtop Coupé 3,598 lb, 1,632 kg - Limited Thin Pillar Sedan 3,646 lb, 1,654 kg; turning circle: 43 ft, 13.1 m; fuel tank: 21.1 imp gal, 25.3 US gal, 96 l.

OPTIONALS limited slip differential; 3.230 axle ratio: anti-roll bar on rear suspension; automatic levelling control; GR78 x 15 tyres with 6'' or 7'' wide rims; GR70 x 15 tyres with 7'' wide rims; heavy-duty cooling system; tilt of steering wheel; heated rear window; electric windows; vinyl roof; sunshine roof; air-conditioning.

140 hp power team

(not available in California).

See 115 hp power team, except for:

ENGINE 8 cylinders; 301 cu in, 4,932 cc (4 x 3 in, 101.6 x 76.2 mm); compression ratio: 8.1:1; max power (DIN): 140 hp (103 kW) at 3,600 rpm; max torque (DIN): 235 lb ft, 32.4 kg m (317.7 Nm) at 2,000 rpm; 28.4 hp/l (20.9 kW/l); 5 crankshaft bearings.

TRANSMISSION axle ratio: 2.290.

PERFORMANCE max speed: about 99 mph, 160 km/h; power-weight ratio: Thin Pillar Sedan 26.5 lb/hp (36 lb/kW), 12 kg/hp (16.3 kg/kW) - Limited Thin Pillar Sedan 26.8 lb/hp (36.5 lb/kW), 12.2 kg/hp (16.5 kg/kW); speed in direct drive at 1,000 rpm: 27.6 mph, 44.4 km/h; consumption: 20.5 m/imp gal, 17 m/US gal, 13.8 l x 100 km.

ELECTRICAL EQUIPMENT 3,200 W battery.

DIMENSIONS AND WEIGHT weight: plus 111 lb, 50 kg.

OPTIONALS 2.410 axle ratio.

155 hp power team

(not available in California).

See 115 hp power team, except for:

ENGINE 8 cylinders; 350 cu in, 5,736 cc (4.06 x 3.38 in, 103.1 x 85.8 mm); max power (DIN): 155 hp (114.1 kW) at 3,400 rpm; max torque (DIN): 280 lb ft, 38.6 kg m (378.6 Nm) at 1,800 rpm; 27 hp/l (19.9 kW/l); 5 crankshaft bearings; 1 Rochester M4MC downdraught 4-barrel carburettor; cooling system: 24.8 imp pt, 29.8 US pt, 14.1 l.

TRANSMISSION axle ratio: 2.410.

PERFORMANCE max speed: about 106 mph, 170 km/h; power-weight ratio: Thin Pillar Sedan 24.3 lb/hp (33 lb/kW), 11 kg/hp (15 kg/kW) - Limited Thin Pillar Sedan 24.6 lb/hp (33.4 lb/kW), 11.2 kg/hp (15.2 kg/kW); speed in direct drive at 1,000 rpm: 26.4 mph, 42.5 km/h; consumption: 18 m/imp gal, 15 m/US gal, 15.7 l x 100 km.

ELECTRICAL EQUIPMENT 3,200 W battery.

BUICK Le Sabre 4-dr Limited Thin Pillar Sedan

DIMENSIONS AND WEIGHT weight: plus 169 lb, 76 kg.

OPTIONALS 2.730 3.080 or 3.230 axle ratio.

160 hp power team

(California only).

See 115 hp power team, except for:

ENGINE 8 cylinders; 350 cu in, 5,736 cc (4.06 x 3.38 in, 101.1 x 85.8 mm); max power (DIN): 160 hp (117.8 kW) at 3,800 rpm; max torque (DIN): 270 lb ft, 37.3 kg m (365.8 Nm) at 2,000 rpm; 27.9 hp/l (20.5 kW/l); 5 crankshaft bearings; 1 Rochester M4MC downdraught 4-barrel carburettor; cooling system: 24.9 imp pt, 29.8 US pt, 14.1 l.

TRANSMISSION axle ratio: 2.410.

PERFORMANCE max speed: about 106 mph, 170 km/h; power-weight ratio: Thin Pillar Sedan 23.6 lb/hp (32 lb/kW), 10.7 kg/hp (14.5 kg/kW) - Limited Thin Pillar Sedan 23.8 lb/hp (32.4 lb/kW), 10.8 kg/hp (14.7 kg/kW); speed in direct drive at 1,000 rpm: 26.4 mph, 42.5 km/h; consumption: 18 m/imp gal, 15 m/US gal, 15.7 l x 100 km.

ELECTRICAL EQUIPMENT 3,200 W battery.

DIMENSIONS AND WEIGHT weight: plus 169 lb, 76 kg.

170 hp power team

See 115 hp power team, except for:

ENGINE turbocharged; max power (DIN): 170 hp (125.1 kW) at 4,000 rpm; max torque (DIN): 265 lb ft, 36.6 kg m (358.9 Nm) at 2,400 rpm; 44.9 hp/l (33.1 kW/l); 1 RDP 17059240 (RDP 17059540 for California only) downdraught 4-barrel carburettor.

TRANSMISSION axle ratio: 2.730 (3.080 California only).

PERFORMANCE max speed: about 112 mph, 180 km/h; power-weight ratio: 21.7 lb/hp (29.4 lb/kW), 9.8 kg/hp (13.3 kg/kW); speed in direct drive at 1,000 rpm: 28 mph, 45 km/h; consumption: 20.5 m/imp gal, 17 m/US gal, 13.8 l x 100 km.

DIMENSIONS AND WEIGHT weight: 3,684 lb, 1,671 kg.

OPTIONALS 3.080 or 3.230 axle ratio.

Estate Wagon Series

Estate St. Wagon	$ 6,958
Estate St. Wagon	$ 7,152

For 175 hp engine add $ 70.

Power team:	Standard for:	Optional for:
155 hp	both	—
160 hp	—	both
175 hp	—	both

155 hp power team

(not available in California).

ENGINE front, 4 stroke; 8 cylinders; 350 cu in, 5,736 cc (3.80 x 3.85 in, 96.5 x 97.8 mm); compression ratio: 8:1; max power (DIN): 155 hp (114.1 kW) at 3,400 rpm; max torque (DIN): 280 lb ft, 38.6 kg m (378.6 Nm) at 1,800 rpm; max engine rpm: 4,200; 27 hp/l (19.9 kW/l); cast iron block and head; 5 crankshaft bearings; valves: overhead, in line, push-rods and rockers, hydraulic tappets; camshafts: 1, at centre of Vee; lubrication: gear pump, full flow filter, 8.3 imp pt, 9.9 US pt, 4.7 l; 1 Rochester M4MC downdraught 4-barrel carburettor; cleaner air system; exhaust system with catalytic converter; fuel feed: mechanical pump; water-cooled, 24.3 imp pt, 29.2 US pt, 13.8 l.

TRANSMISSION driving wheels: rear; gearbox: Turbo-Hydramatic 350 automatic transmission, hydraulic torque converter and planetary gears with 3 ratios, max ratio of converter at stall 2, possible manual selection; ratios: I 2.520, II 1.520, III 1, rev 1.930; lever: steering column; final drive: hypoid bevel; axle ratio: 2,730; width of rims: 7''; tyres: GR78 x 15.

PERFORMANCE max speed: about 106 mph, 170 km/h; power-weight ratio: 26.7 lb/hp (36.3 lb/kW), 12.1 kg/hp (16.4 kg/kW); speed in direct drive at 1,000 rpm: 26.7 mph, 43 km/h; consumption: 18 m/imp gal, 15 m/US gal, 15.7 l x 100 km.

CHASSIS perimeter box-type frame; front suspension: independent, wishbones (lower trailing links), coil springs, anti-roll bar, telescopic dampers; rear: rigid axle, semi-elliptic leafsprings, telescopic dampers.

STEERING recirculating ball, variable ratio servo; turns lock to lock: 3.37.

BRAKES front disc (diameter 11.86 in, 30 cm), front internal radial fins, rear drum, rear compensator, servo; swept area: total 396.58 sq in, 2,559 sq cm.

ELECTRICAL EQUIPMENT 12 V; 3,200 W battery; 42 A alternator; Delco-Remy transistorized ignition; 4 headlamps.

DIMENSIONS AND WEIGHT wheel base: 115.90 in, 294 cm; tracks: 62.20 in, 158 cm front, 64 in, 163 cm rear; length: 216.70 in, 550 cm; width: 79.90 in, 203 cm; height: 56.50 in, 143 cm; ground clearance: 6.50 in, 16.5 cm; weight: 4,138 lb, 1,877 kg; turning circle: 42.9 ft, 13.1 m; fuel tank: 18.7 imp gal, 22.5 US gal, 85 l.

BODY estate car/st. wagon; 4+1 doors; 6-8 seats; folding rear seat.

OPTIONALS limited slip differential; 3.080 axle ratio; automatic levelling control; tilt of steering wheel; heavy-duty battery; electric windows; heated rear window; electric sunshine roof; reclining backrests; speed control device; vinyl roof; air-conditioning.

160 hp power team

(for California only).

See 155 hp power team, except for:

ENGINE max power (DIN): 160 hp (117.8 kW) at 3,800 rpm; max torque (DIN): 270 lb ft, 37.3 kg m (365.8 Nm) at 2,000 rpm; max engine rpm: 4,600; 27.9 hp/l (20.5 kW/l).

TRANSMISSION axle ratio: 2.410.

PERFORMANCE power-weight ratio: 25.9 lb/hp (35.1 lb/kW), 11.7 kg/hp (15.9 kg/kW).

OPTIONALS 2.730 axle ratio.

175 hp power team

See 155 hp power team, except for:

ENGINE 403 cu in, 6,604 cc (4.35 x 3.38 in, 110.4 x 85.8 mm); max power (DIN): 175 hp (128.8 kW) at 3,600 rpm; max torque (DIN): 310 lb ft, 42.8 kg m (419.7 Nm) at 2,000 rpm; 26.5 hp/l (19.5 kW/l).

TRANSMISSION axle ratio: 2.410.

PERFORMANCE max speed: about 112 mph, 180 km/h; power-weight ratio: 23.7 lb/hp (32.3 lb/kW), 10.8 kg/hp (14.6 kg/kW); speed in direct drive at 1,000 rpm: 31.1 mph, 50 km/h; consumption: 16.8 m/imp gal, 14 m/US gal, 16.8 l x 100 km.

DIMENSIONS AND WEIGHT weight: plus 18 lb, 8 kg.

OPTIONALS 3.080 or 3.230 axle ratio.

Electra Series

225 2-dr Coupé	$ 7,827
225 4-dr Sedan	$ 8,002
Limited 2-dr Coupé	$ 8,227
Limited 4-dr Sedan	$ 8,402
Park Avenue 2-dr Coupé	$ 8,669
Park Avenue 4-dr Sedan	$ 8,844

For 175 hp engine add $ 70.

Power team:	Standard for:	Optional for:
155 hp	all	—
160 hp	—	all
175 hp	—	all

155 hp power team

(not available in California).

ENGINE front, 4 stroke; 8 cylinders; 350 cu in, 5,736 cc (3.80 x 3.85 in, 96.5 x 97.8 mm); compression ratio: 8:1; max power (DIN): 155 hp (114.1 kW) at 3,400 rpm; max torque (DIN): 280 lb ft, 38.6 kg m (378.6 Nm) at 1,800 rpm; max engine rpm: 4,200; 27 hp/l (19.9 kW/l); cast iron block and head; 5 crankshaft bearings; valves: overhead, in line, push-rods and rockers, hydraulic tappets; camshafts: 1, at centre of Vee; lubrication: gear pump, full flow filter, 8.3 imp pt, 9.9 US pt, 4.7 l; 1 Rochester M4MC downdraught 4-barrel carburettor; cleaner air system; exhaust system with catalytic converter; fuel feed: mechanical pump; water-cooled, 24.3 imp pt, 29.2 US pt, 13.8 l.

TRANSMISSION driving wheels: rear; gearbox: Turbo-Hydramatic 400 automatic transmission, hydraulic torque converter and planetary gears with 3 ratios, max ratio of converter at stall 2, possible manual selection; ratios: I 2.480, II 1.480, III 1, rev 2.080; lever: steering column; final drive: hypoid bevel; axle ratio: 2.410; width of rims: 6''; tyres: GR78 x 15.

PERFORMANCE max speed: about 106 mph, 170 km/h; power-weight ratio: 225 Sedan 25.7 lb/hp (34.9 lb/kW), 11.6 kg/hp (15.8 kg/kW) - Limited Sedan and Park Avenue Sedan 25.8 lb/hp (35 lb/kW), 11.7 kg/hp (15.9 kg/kW); speed in direct drive at 1,000 rpm: 26.7 mph, 43 km/h; consumption: 18 m/imp gal, 15 m/US gal, 15.7 l x 100 km.

CHASSIS perimeter box-type frame; front suspension: independent, wishbones (lower trailing links), coil springs, anti-roll bar, telescopic dampers; rear: rigid axle, lower trailing radius arms, upper oblique torque arms, coil springs, telescopic dampers.

STEERING recirculating ball, variable ratio servo; turns lock to lock: 3.37.

BRAKES front disc (diameter 11.86 in, 30 cm), front internal radial fins, rear drum, rear compensator, servo; swept area: total 384.18 sq in, 2,479 sq cm.

ELECTRICAL EQUIPMENT 12 V; 3,200 W battery; 42 A alternator; Delco-Remy transistorized ignition; 4 headlamps.

DIMENSIONS AND WEIGHT wheel base: 118.90 in, 302 cm; tracks: 61.80 in, 157 cm front, 60.70 in, 154 cm rear;

BUICK Electra Limited 2-dr Coupé

BUICK Electra Park Avenue 4-dr Sedan

CHASSIS perimeter box-type frame; front suspension: in
pendent, wishbones, longitudinal torsion bars, anti-roll b
telescopic dampers; rear: independent, swinging longi
dinal trailing arms, transverse linkage bar, coil sprin
telescopic dampers; automatic levelling control.

STEERING recirculating ball, variable ratio servo; tu
lock to lock: 2.99.

BRAKES front disc (diameter 10.50 in, 26.7 cm), fro
internal radial fins, rear drum, rear compensator, ser
swept area: total 307.69 sq in, 1,985 sq cm.

ELECTRICAL EQUIPMENT 12 V; 3,200 W battery; 42 A alt
nator; Delco-Remy transistorized ignition; 4 headlamps.

DIMENSIONS AND WEIGHT wheel base: 114 in, 289 c
tracks: 59.30 in, 151 cm front, 60 in, 152 cm rear; leng
206.60 in, 525 cm; width: 70.40 in, 179 cm; height: 54
in, 138 cm; groung clearance: 6.20 in, 15.8 cm; weig
Coupé 3,862 lb, 1,752 kg - Sport Coupé 3,878 bl, 1,759
turning circle: 42.7 ft, 13 m; fuel tank 16.7 imp gal,
US gal, 76 l.

BODY coupé; 2 doors; 4 seats, separate front seats; elect
windows; air-conditioning.

OPTIONALS central lever; 2.190 axle ratio; GR70 x
tyres; heavy-duty battery; heated rear window; elect
sunshine roof; vinyl roof; Landau top.

155 HP POWER TEAM

length: 222.10 in, 564 cm; width: 77.20 in, 196 cm; height: coupés 55 in, 140 cm - sedans 55.90 in, 142 cm; ground clearance: 6.90 in, 17.5 cm; weight: 225 Coupé 3.911 lb, 1,774 kg - 225 Sedan 3,977 lb, 1,804 kg - Limited Coupé 3,926 lb, 1,781 kg - Limited Sedan 3,995 lb, 1,812 kg - Park Avenue Coupé 3,933 lb, 1,784 kg - Park Avenue Sedan 3,999 lb, 1,814 kg; turning circle: 42.9 ft, 13.1 m; fuel tank: 21.1 imp gal, 25.3 US gal, 96 l.

OPTIONALS limited slip differential; 2.730 or 3.080 axle ratio automatic levelling control; tilt of steering wheel; heavy-duty battery; heated rear window; electric windows; electric sunshine roof; speed control device; reclining backrests; vinyl roof; air-conditioning; Landau top (coupés only).

160 hp power team

(for California only).

See 155 hp power team, except for:

ENGINE max power (DIN): 160 hp (117.8 kW) at 3,800 rpm; max torque (DIN): 270 lb ft, 37.3 kg m (365.8 Nm) at 2,000 rpm; max engine rpm: 4,600; 27.9 hp/l (30.5 kW/l).

PERFORMANCE power-weight ratio: 225 Sedan 24.9 lb/hp (33.8 lb/kW), 11.2 kg/hp (15.3 kg/kW) - Limited Sedan and Park Avenue Sedan 25 lb/hp (33.9 lb/kW), 11.3 kg/hp (15.4 kg/kW).

OPTIONALS 2.730 axle ratio.

175 hp power team

See 155 hp power tema, except for:

ENGINE 403 cu in, 6,604 cc (4.35 x 3.38 in, 110.4 x 85.8 mm); max power (DIN): 175 hp (128.8 kW) at 3,600 rpm; max torque (DIN): 310 lb ft, 42.8 kg m (419.7 Nm) at 2,000 rpm; 26.5 hp/l (19.5 kW/l).

PERFORMANCE max speed: about 112 mph, 180 km/h; power-weight ratio: 225 Sedan 22.7 lb/hp (31 lb/kW), 10.3 kg/hp (14 kg/kW) - Limited Sedan and Park Avenue Sedan 22.9 lb/hp (31 lb/kW), 10.4 kg/hp (14.1 kg/kW); speed in direct drive at 1,000 rpm: 31.1 mph, 50 km/h; consumption: 16.8 m/imp gal, 14 m/US gal, 16.8 l x 100 km.

DIMENSIONS AND WEIGHT weight: plus 4 lb, 2 kg.

OPTIONALS 3.080 3.230 or 2.560 axle ratio.

Riviera Series

PRICES EX WORKS:

1 Coupé	$	10,371
2 Sport Coupé	$	10,648

Power team:	Standard for:	Optional for:
160 hp	1	2
185 hp	2	1

160 hp power team

ENGINE front, 4 stroke; 8 cylinders; 350 cu in, 5,736 cc (4.06 x 3.38 in, 103.1 x 86 mm); compression ratio: 8:1; max power (DIN): 160 hp (117.8 kW) at 3,800 rpm; max torque (DIN): 270 lb ft, 37.3 kg m (365.8 Nm) at 2,000 rpm; max engine rpm: 4,200; 27.9 hp/l (20.5 kW/l); cast iron block and head; 5 crankshaft bearings; valves: overhead, in line, push-rods and rockers, hydraulic tappets; camshafts: 1, at centre of Vee; lubrication: gear pump, full flow filter, 8.3 imp pt, 9.9 US pt, 4.7 l; 1 Rochester M4MC downdraught 4-barrel carburettor; cleaner air system; exhaust system with catalytic converter; fuel feed: mechanical pump; water-cooled, 24.3 imp pt, 29.2 US pt, 13.8 l.

TRANSMISSION driving wheels: front; gearbox: Turbo-Hydramatic 325 automatic transmission, hydraulic torque converter and planetary gears with 3 ratios, max ratio of converter at stall 2.20, possible manual selection: ratios: I 2.740, II 1.570, III 1, rev 2.570; lever: steering column; final drive: hypoid bevel; axle ratio: 2.410; width of rims: 6''; tyres: P205/75R x 15.

PERFORMANCE max speed: about 112 mph, 180 km/h; power-weight ratio: Coupé 24.1 lb/hp (32.8 lb/kW), 10.9 kg/hp (14.9 kg/kW) - Sport Coupé 24.2 lb/hp (32.9 lb/kW), 11 kg/hp (14.9 kg/kW); speed in direct drive at 1,000 rpm: 29.5 mph, 47.4 km/h; consumption: 19.2 m/imp gal, 16 m/US gal, 14.7 l x 100 km.

BUICK Riviera Sport Coupé

BUICK Riviera Sport Coupé

185 hp power team

See 160 hp power team, except for:

ENGINE turbocharged; 6 cylinders, Vee-slanted at 90°; 231 cu in, 3,785 cc (3.80 x 3.40 in, 96.5 x 86.4 mm); max power (DIN): 185 hp (136.2 kW) at 4,200 rpm; max torque (DIN): 280 lb ft, 38.6 kg m (378.6 Nm) at 2,400 rpm; max engine rpm: 4,600; 48.9 hp/l (36 kW/l); 4 crankshaft bearings; RDP 17059242 (RDP 17059542 for California only) downdraught 4-barrel carburettor; cooling system: 22.2 imp pt, 26.6 US pt, 12.6 l.

TRANSMISSION axle ratio: 2.930.

PERFORMANCE max speed: about 115 mph, 185 km/h; power-weight ratio: 21 lb/hp (28.5 lb/kW), 9.5 kg/hp (12.9 kg/kW); consumption: 20.5 m/imp gal, 17 m/US gal, 13.8 l x 100 km.

CADILLAC   USA

Seville

170 hp power team

(standard).

ENGINE front, 4 stroke; 8 cylinders; 350 cu in, 5,736 cc (4.06 x 3.38 in, 103 x 85.8 mm); compression ratio: 8:1; max power (DIN): 170 hp (125.1 kW) at 4,200 rpm; max torque (DIN): 270 lb, ft, 37.2 kg m (364.8 Nm) at 2,000 rpm; max engine rpm: 4,800; 29.6 hp/l (21.8 kW/l); cast iron block and head; 5 crankshaft bearings; valves: overhead, in line, push-rods and rockers, hydraulic tappets; camshafts: 1, at centre of Vee; lubrication: gear pump, full flow filter, 8.3 imp pt, 9.9 US pt, 4.7 l; electronic fuel injection system; cleaner air system; exhaust system with catalytic converter; fuel feed: 2 electric pumps; water-cooled, 28.7 imp pt, 34.5 US pt, 16.3 l.

TRANSMISSION driving wheels: rear; gearbox: Turbo-Hydramatic 400 automatic transmission, hydraulic torque converter and planetary gears with 3 ratios, max ratio of converter at stall 2, possible manual selection; ratios: I 2.480, II 1.480, III 1, rev 2.070; lever: steering column; final drive: hypoid bevel; axle ratio: 2.240 (2.560 California only); width of rims: 6''; tyres: GR78 x 15.

PERFORMANCE max speed: about 115 mph, 185 km/h; power-weight ratio: 24.6 lb/hp (33.4 lb/kW), 11.2 kg/hp (15.2 kg/kW); speed in direct drive at 1,000 rpm: 30.4 mph, 49 km/h; consumption: 16.8 m/imp gal, 14 m/US gal, 16.8 l x 100 km.

CHASSIS integral, front auxiliary frame; front suspension: independent, wishbones, coil springs, anti-roll bar, telescopic dampers; rear: rigid axle, semi-elliptic leafsprings, anti-roll bar, automatic levelling control, telescopic dampers.

STEERING recirculating ball, tilt of steering wheel, variable ratio servo; turns lock to lock: 3.

BRAKES disc (front diameter 11.74 in, 29.8 cm, rear 11.14 in, 28.3 cm), internal radial swept area: front 236 sq in, 1,528 sq cm, rear 237.24 sq in, 1,530 sq cm, total 473.24 sq in, 3,058 sq cm.

ELECTRICAL EQUIPMENT 12 V; 465 A battery; 80 A alternator; high energy ignition system; 4 headlamps.

DIMENSIONS AND WEIGHT wheel base: 114.30 in, 290 cm; tracks: 61.30 in, 156 cm front, 59 in, 150 cm rear; length: 204 in, 518 cm; width: 71.80 in, 182 cm; height: 54.60 in, 139 cm; ground clearance: 5.40 in, 13.7 cm; weight: 4,180 lb, 1,896 kg; turning circle: 42.3 ft, 12.9 m; fuel tank: 17.4 imp gal, 21 US gal, 79 l.

BODY saloon/sedan; 4 doors; 5 seats, separate front seats with built-in headrests; electric windows; air-conditioning.

OPTIONALS limited slip differential; 3.080 axle ratio; 478 x 15 tyres; heavy-duty cooling system; reclining backrests; speed control device; heated rear window; electric sunshine roof; leather upholstery; trip computer; Elegante equipment.

---

125 hp (Diesel) power team

(optional).

See 170 hp power team, except for:

ENGINE Diesel, 4 stroke; compression ratio: 22.5:1; max power (DIN): 125 hp (92 kW) at 3,600 rpm; max torque (DIN): 225 lb ft, 31 kg m (304 Nm) at 1,600 rpm; max engine rpm: 4,200; 21.8 hp/l (16 kW/l); lubricating system: 14.1 imp pt, 16.9 US pt, 8 l; Diesel fuel injection pump; fuel feed: mechanical pump.

TRANSMISSION gearbox: Turbo-Hydramatic 200 automatic transmission, hydraulic torque converter and planetary gears with 3 ratios, max ratio of converter at stall 2.2, possible manual selection; ratios, max ratio of converter at stall 2.2, possible manual selection; ratios: I 2.740, II 1.570, III 1, rev 2.070; axle ratio: 2.560.

PERFORMANCE max speed: about 96 mph, 155 km/h; power-weight ratio: 34.1 lb/hp (46.4 lb/kW), 15.5 kg/hp (21 kg/kW); speed in direct drive at 1,000 rpm: 26.7 mph, 43 km/h; consumption: 25.2 m/imp gal, 21 m/US gal, 11.2 l x 100 km.

ELECTRICAL EQUIPMENT 540 A battery.

DIMENSIONS AND WEIGHT weight: 4,268 lb, 1,936 kg.

OPTIONALS 3.080 axle ratio not available.

CADILLAC Seville Elegante

De Ville - Fleetwood Series

Power team:	Standard for:	Optional for:
180 hp	all	—
195 hp	—	1 to 3

180 hp power team

ENGINE front, 4 stroke; 8 cylinders; 425 cu in, 6,964 cc (4.08 x 4.06 in, 104 x 103 mm); compression ratio: 8.2:1; max power (DIN): 180 hp (132.5 kW) at 4,000 rpm; max torque (DIN): 320 lb ft, 44.2 kg m (433.5 Nm) at 2,000 rpm; max engine rpm: 4,400; 25.8 hp/l (19 kW/l); cast iron block and head; 5 crankshaft bearings; valves: overhead, in line, push-rods and rockers, hydraulic tappets; camshafts: 1, at centre of Vee; lubrication: gear pump, full flow filter, 8.3 imp pt, 9.9 US pt, 4.7 l; 1 Rochester M4ME downdraught 4-barrel carburettor; cleaner air system; exhaust system with catalytic converter; fuel feed: mechanical pump; water-cooled, 34.7 imp pt, 41.6 US pt, 19.7 l.

TRANSMISSION driving wheels: rear; gearbox: Turbo-Hydramatic 400 automatic transmission, hydraulic torque

CADILLAC Fleetwood Brougham d'Elegance

180 HP POWER TEAM

converter and planetary gears with 3 ratios, max ratio of converter at stall 2, possible manual selection; ratios: I 2.480, II 1.480, III 1, rev 2.070; lever: steering column; final drive: hypoid bevel; axle ratio: 2.280 - limousines 3.080; width of rims: 6''; tyres: HR78 x 15 - De Ville GR78 x 15.

PERFORMANCE max speed: about 112 mph, 180 km/h; power-weight ratio: De Ville Sedan 23.4 lb/hp (31.8 lb/kW), 10.6 kg/hp (14.4 kg/kW) - Brougham 23.6 lb/hp (32.1 lb/kW), 10.7 kg/hp (14.6 kg/kW) - Limousine 26.6 lb/hp (36.1 lb/kW), 12 kg/hp (16.4 kg/kW) - Formal Limousine 27 lb/hp (36.7 lb/kW), 12.3 kg/hp (16.7 kg/kW); speed in direct drive at 1,000 rpm: 28 mph, 45 km/h; consumption: 16.8 m/imp gal, 14 m/US gal, 16.8 l x 100 km.

CHASSIS ladder frame with cross members; front suspension: independent, wishbones, coil springs, automatic levelling control (except for De Ville), anti-roll bar, telescopic dampers; rear: rigid axle, lower trailing radius arms, upper oblique torque arms, coil springs, automatic levelling control (except for De Ville), anti-roll bar, telescopic dampers.

STEERING recirculating ball, tilt of steering wheel, variable ratio servo; turns lock to lock: 3.20.

BRAKES front disc (diameter 11.74 in, 29.8 cm) internal radial fins, rear drum (disc Brougham only), rear compensator, servo; swept area: total 474.04 sq in, 3,057 sq cm - Brougham 375.03 sq in, 2,419 sq cm - limousines 425.3 sq in, 2,743 sq cm.

ELECTRICAL EQUIPMENT 12 V; 365 A battery; 63 A alternator (80 A standard for limousines); Delco-Remy electronic ignition; 4 headlamps.

DIMENSIONS AND WEIGHT wheel base: 121.50 in, 308 cm - Limousine and Formal Limousine 144.50 in, 367 cm; tracks: 61.70 in, 157 cm front, 60.70 in, 154 cm rear; length: 221.20 in, 562 cm - Limousine and Formal Limousine 244.20 in, 620 cm; width: 76.40 in, 194 cm; height: Brougham 56.70 in, 144 cm - De Ville Coupé 54.40 in, 138 cm - De Ville Sedan 55.30 in, 140 cm - Limousine and Formal Limousine 56.90 in, 145 cm; ground clearance: Brougham 5.50 in, 14 cm - De Ville 5.70 in, 14.5 cm - Limousine and Formal Limousine 6.10 in, 15.6 cm; weight: De Ville Coupé 4,143 lb, 1,879 kg - De Ville Sedan 4,212 lb, 1,911 kg - Brougham 4,250 lb, 1,928 kg - Limousine 4,782 lb, 2,169 kg - Formal Limousine 4,866 lb, 2,207 kg; turning circle: De Ville 44.1 ft, 13.4 m - Brougham 51.2 ft, 15.6 m - Limousine and Formal Limousine 57.2 ft, 17.4 m; fuel tank: 20.9 imp gal, 25 US gal, 95 l.

BODY 4 doors (Coupé 2); bench front seats; electric windows; air-conditioning.

OPTIONALS heavy-duty cooling system; limited slip differential; 2.730 axle ratio (except for limousines); H78 x 15 tyres; 478 x 15 tyres with 5'' wide rims (De Ville only); wire wheels; automatic levelling control (De Ville only); speed control device; 80 A alternator (except for limousines); heated rear window; reclining backrests; vinyl roof; electric sunshine roof; leather upholstery; Cabriolet equipment (Coupé only); d'Elegance equipment; Custom Phaeton equipment (De Ville only).

CADILLAC Fleetwood Brougham

CADILLAC Fleetwood Eldorado

195 hp power team

See 180 hp power team, except for:

ENGINE max power (DIN): 195 hp (143.5 kW) at 3,800 rpm; max torque (DIN): 320 lb ft, 44.2 kg m (433.5 Nm) at 2,400 rpm; 28 hp/l (20.6 kW/l); electronic fuel injection system; fuel feed: 2 electric pumps.

TRANSMISSION axle ratio: 2.280.

PERFORMANCE max speed: about 115 mph, 185 km/h; power-weight ratio: De Ville Sedan 21.6 lb/hp (29.4 lb/kW), 9.8 kg/hp (13.3 kg/kW) - Brougham 21.8 lb/hp (29.6 lb/kW), 9.9 kg/hp (13.4 kg/kW); consumption: 14.4 m/imp gal, 12 m/US gal, 19.6 l x 100 m.

ELECTRICAL EQUIPMENT 80 A alternator.

Fleetwood Eldorado

PRICE EX WORKS: $ 14,240

170 hp power team

(standard).

ENGINE front, 4 stroke; 8 cylinders; 350 cu in, 5,736 cc (4.06 x 3.38 in, 103 x 85.8 mm); compression ratio: 8:1; max power (DIN): 170 hp (125.1 kW) at 4,200 rpm; max torque (DIN): 270 lb ft, 31 kg m (364.8 Nm) at 2,000 rpm; max engine rpm: 4,800; 29.6 hp/l (21.8 kW/l); cast iron block and head; 5 crankshaft bearings; valves: overhead, in line, push-rods and rockers, hydraulic tappets; camshafts: 1, at centre of Vee; lubrication: gear pump, full flow filter, 8.3 imp pt, 9.9 US pt, 4.7 l; electronic fuel injection system; cleaner air system; exhaust system with catalytic converter; fuel feed: 2 electric pumps; water-cooled, 28.7 imp pt, 34.5 US pt, 16.3 l.

TRANSMISSION driving wheels: front; gearbox: Turbo-Hydramatic 325 automatic transmission, hydraulic torque converter and planetary gears with 3 ratios, max ratio of converter at stall 2, possible manual selection; ratios: I 2.740, II 1.570, III 1, rev 2.070; lever: steering column; final drive: spiral bevel; axle ratio: 2.190; width of rims: 6''; tyres: P205/75R x 15.

PERFORMANCE max speed: about 115 mph, 185 km/h; power-weight ratio: 22.3 lb/hp, (30.3 lb/kW), 10.1 kg/hp (13.7 kg/kW); speed in direct drive at 1,000 rpm: 35.5 mph, 57.2 km/h; consumption: 16.8 m/imp gal, 14 m/US gal, 16.8 l x 100 km.

CHASSIS ladder frame with cross members; front suspension, independent, wishbones, longitudinal torsion bars, anti-roll bar, telescopic dampers; rear: independent, swinging longitudinal trailing arms, coil springs, automatic levelling control, telescopic dampers.

STEERING recirculating ball, tilt of steering wheel, variable ratio servo; turns lock to lock: 2.90.

BRAKES disc (diameter 10.40 in, 26.5 cm), internal radial fins, rear swept area: compensator, servo; front 198 sq in, 1,277 sq cm, rear 198 sq in, 1,277 sq cm, total 396 sq in, 2,554 sq cm.

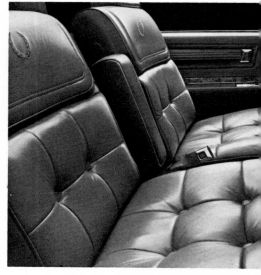

CADILLAC Fleetwood Eldorado

ELECTRICAL EQUIPMENT 12 V; 465 A battery; 80 A alternator; high energy ignition system; 4 headlamps.

DIMENSIONS AND WEIGHT wheel base: 113.90 in, 289 cm; tracks: 59.30 in, 151 cm front, 60.50 in, 154 cm rear; length: 204 in, 518 cm; width: 71.40 in, 182 cm; height: 54.20 in, 138 cm; ground clearance: 5.50 in, 14 cm; weight: 3,792 lb, 1,720 kg; turning circle: 42.2 ft, 12.8 m; fuel tank: 16.3 imp gal, 19.6 US gal, 74 l.

BODY hardtop coupé; 2 doors; 4 seats, separate front seats with built-in headrests; electric windows; air conditioning.

OPTIONALS heavy-duty cooling system; 2.410 axle ratio; P205/75D x 15 tyres with light alloy wheels; reclining backrests; speed control device; heated rear window; sunshine roof; trip computer; electric sunshine roof; leather upholstery; Biaritz equipment.

125 hp (Diesel) power team

(optional).

See 170 hp power team, except for:

ENGINE Diesel, 4 stroke; compression ratio: 22.5:1; max power (DIN): 125 hp (92 kW) at 3,600 rpm; max torque (DIN): 225 lb ft, 31 kg m (304 Nm) at 1,600 rpm; max engine rpm: 4,200; 21.8 hp/l (16 kW/l); lubricating system: 14.1 imp pt, 16.9 US pt, 8 l; Diesel fuel injection pump; fuel feed: mechanical pump.

TRANSMISSION gearbox: Turbo-Hydramatic 200 automatic transmission, hydraulic torque converter and planetary gears with 3 ratios, max ratio of converter at stall 2.2, possible manual selection; ratios: I 2.740, II 1.570, III 1, rev 2.070; axle ratio: 2.560.

PERFORMANCE max speed: about 96 mph, 155 km/h; power-weight ratio: 32 lb/hp (43.4 lb/kW), 14.5 kg/hp (19.7 kg/kW); speed in direct drive at 1,000 rpm: 26.7 mph, 43 km/h; consumption: 25.2 m/imp gal, 21 m/US gal, 11.2 l x 100 km.

ELECTRICAL EQUIPMENT 540 A battery.

DIMENSIONS AND WEIGHT weight: 3,994 lb, 1,812 kg; fuel tank: 18.7 imp gal, 22.4 US gal, 85 l.

OPTIONALS 2.410 axle ratio not available.

CHECKER   USA

Marathon Series

PRICES EX WORKS:

Sedan	$ 6,814
De Luxe Sedan	$ 7,867

Power team:	Standard for:	Optional for:
110 hp	1	—
90 hp	1	—
145 hp	2	1
160 hp	—	both

110 hp power team

(not available in California).

ENGINE front, 4 stroke; 6 cylinders, vertical, in line; 250 cu in, 4,097 cc (3.87 x 3.53 in, 98.2 x 89.6 mm); compression ratio: 8.1:1; max power (DIN): 110 hp (82 kW) at 3,800 rpm; max torque (DIN): 190 lb ft, 26.2 kg m (256.9 Nm) at 1,600 rpm; max engine rpm: 4,400; 26.8 hp/l (19.7 kW/l); cast iron block and head; 7 crankshaft bearings; valves: overhead, in line, push-rods and rockers; camshafts: 1, side; lubrication: gear pump, full flow filter, 8.3 imp pt, 9.9 US pt, 4.7 l; 1 Rochester 17058020 downdraught single barrel carburettor; cleaner air system; exhaust system with catalytic converter; fuel feed: mechanical pump; water-cooled, 24.3 imp pt, 29.2 US pt, 13.8 l.

TRANSMISSION driving wheels: rear; gearbox: Turbo-Hydramatic 400 automatic transmission, hydraulic torque converter and planetary gears with 3 ratios, max ratio of converter at stall 2.2, possible manual selection; ratios: I 2.480, II 1.480, III 1, rev 2.070; lever: steering column; final drive: hypoid bevel; axle ratio: 3.070; width of rims: 6"; tyres: G78 x 15.

PERFORMANCE max speed: about 90 mph, 145 km/h; power-weight ratio: 34.2 lb/hp (45.9 lb/kW), 15.5 kg/hp (20.8 kg/kW); speed in direct drive at 1,000 rpm: 24.2 mph, 38.9 km/h; consumption: 22.8 m/imp gal, 19 m/US gal, 12.4 l x 100 km.

CHASSIS box-type ladder frame with X reinforcements; front suspension: independent, wishbones, coil springs, anti-roll bar, telescopic dampers; rear: rigid axle, semi-elliptic leafsprings, telescopic dampers.

STEERING recirculating ball, variable ratio servo; turns lock to lock: 3.46.

BRAKES front disc (diameter 11.75 in, 29.8 cm), front internal radial fins, rear drum, servo; swept area: total 374.7 sq in, 2,417 sq cm.

ELECTRICAL EQUIPMENT 12 V; 80 Ah battery; 63 A alternator; Delco-Remy high energy ignition system; 4 headlamps.

DIMENSIONS AND WEIGHT wheel base: 120 in, 305 cm; tracks: 64.45 in, 164 cm front, 63.31 in, 161 cm rear; length: 204.75 in, 520 cm; width: 76 in, 193 cm; height: 62.75 in, 159 cm; ground clearance: 7.50 in, 19 cm; weight: 3,765 lb, 1,707 kg; turning circle: 43.3 ft, 13.2 m; fuel tank: 17.9 imp gal, 21.6 US gal, 82 l.

OPTIONALS limited slip differential; HR78 x 15 tyres; auxiliary rear seats; air-conditioning; heavy-duty telescopic dampers; tinted glass.

90 hp power team

(for California only).

See 110 hp power team, except for:

ENGINE max power (DIN): 90 hp (66.2 kW) at 3,600 rpm; max torque (DIN): 175 lb ft, 24.1 kg m (236.3 Nm) at 1,600 rpm; 22 hp/l (16.2 kW/l); 1 Rochester 17058314 C dofndraught single barrel carburettor.

PERFORMANCE power-weight ratio: 42.1 lb/hp (57.3 lb/kW), 19.1 kg/hp (26 kg/kW).

DIMENSIONS AND WEIGHT weight: 3,793 lb, 1,720 kg.

145 hp power team

See 110 hp power team, except for:

ENGINE 8 cylinders; 305 cu in, 4,998 cc (3.74 x 3.48 in, 94.9 x 88.3 mm); compression ratio: 8.4:1; max power (DIN): 145 hp (106.7 kW) at 3,800 rpm; max torque (DIN): 245 lb ft, 33.8 kg m (331.5 Nm) at 2,400 rpm; 29 hp/l (21.3 kW/l); 5 crankshaft bearings; camshafts: 1, at centre of Vee; 1 Rochester 17058108B downdraught twin barrel carburettor; cooling system: 28.7 imp pt, 34.5 US pt, 16.3 l.

TRANSMISSION axle ratio: 2.720.

PERFORMANCE max speed: about 103 mph, 165 km/h; power-weight ratio: Marathon 26.6 lb/hp (36.2 lb/kW), 12.1 kg/hp (16.4 kg/kW) - Marathon De Luxe 28 lb/hp (38.1 lb/kW), 12.7 kg/hp (17.3 kg/kW); speed in direct drive at 1,000 rpm: 26.7 mph, 43 km/h; consumption: 20.5 m/imp gal, 17 m/US gal, 13.8 l x 100 km.

DIMENSIONS AND WEIGHT wheel base: Marathon De Luxe 129 in, 328 cm; length: Marathon De Luxe 213.75 in, 543 cm; weight: Marathon 3,862 lb, 1,751 kg - Marathon De Luxe 4,062 lb, 1,842 kg.

160 hp power team

See 110 hp power team, except for:

ENGINE 8 cylinders; 350 cu in, 5,736 cc (4 x 3.48 in, 101.6 x 88.3 mm); compression ratio: 8.2:1; max power (DIN): 160 hp (117.8 kW) at 3,800 rpm; max torque (DIN): 260 lb ft, 35.9 kg m (352.1 Nm) at 2,400 rpm; 27.9 hp/l (20.5 kW/l); 5 crankshaft bearings; camshafts: 1, at centre of Vee; 1 Rochester 17058504A downdraught 4-barrel carburettor; cooling system: 28.7 imp pt, 34.5 US pt, 16.3 l.

TRANSMISSION axle ratio: 2.720.

PERFORMANCE max speed: about 106 mph, 170 km/h; power-weight ratio: Marathon 24.2 lb/hp (32.8 lb/kW), 11 kg/hp (14.9 kg/kW) - Marathon De Luxe 25.4 lb/hp (34.5 lb/kW), 11.5 kg/hp (15.6 kg/kW); speed in direct drive at 1,000 rpm: 26.7 mph, 43 km/h; consumption: 19.2 m/imp gal, 16 m/US gal, 14.7 l x 100 km.

DIMENSIONS AND WEIGHT (see 145 hp power team) weight: Marathon 3,865 lb, 1,753 kg - Marathon De Luxe 4,065 lb, 1,843 kg.

CHEVROLET   USA

Chevette Series

PRICES EX WORKS:

Scooter Hatchback Coupé	$ 3,299
Hatchback Coupé	$ 3,794
Hatchback Sedan	$ 3,914

For 74 hp engine add $ 60.

Power team:	Standard for:	Optional for:
70 hp	all	—
74 hp	—	all

70 hp power team

ENGINE front, 4 stroke; 4 cylinders, vertical, in line; 97.6 cu in, 1,599 cc (3.23 x 2.98 in, 82 x 75.6 mm); compression ratio: 8.6:1; max power (DIN): 70 hp (51.5 kW) at 5,200 rpm; max torque (DIN): 82 lb ft, 11.3 kg m (110.8 Nm) at 2,400 rpm; max engine rpm: 5,600; 43.8 hp/l (32.2 kW/l); cast iron block and head; 5 crankshaft bearings; valves: overhead, hydraulic tappets; camshafts: 1, overhead, cogged belt; lubrication: gear pump, full flow filter, 8.3 imp pt, 9.9 US pt, 4.7 l; Holley 466363 (466367 for California only) downdraught twin barrel carburettor; cleaner air system; exhaust system with catalytic converter; fuel feed: mechanical pump; water-cooled, 15.3 imp pt, 18.4 US pt, 8.7 l.

TRANSMISSION driving wheels: rear; clutch: single dry plate (diaphragm); gearbox: mechanical; gears: 4, fully synchronized; ratios: I 3.750, II 2.160, III 1.380, IV 1, rev 3.820; lever: central; final drive: hypoid bevel; axle ratio: 3.700; width of rims: 5"; tyres: P155/80 R x 13.

PERFORMANCE max speed: about 90 mph, 145 km/h; power-weight ratio: Hatchback Sedan 29.3 lb/hp (39.8 lb/kW), 13.3 kg/hp (18.1 kg/kW); speed in direct drive at 1,000 rpm: 17.9 mph, 28.8 km/h; consumption: 34.9 m/imp gal, 29 m/US gal, 8.1 l x 100 km.

CHASSIS integral with cross member reinforcement; front suspension: independent, wishbones, coil springs, anti-roll bar, telescopic dampers; rear: rigid axle (torque tube), longitudinal trailing radius arms, coil springs, transverse linkage bar, anti-roll bar, telescopic dampers.

STEERING rack-and-pinion; turns lock to lock: 3.60.

BRAKES front disc (diameter 9.68 in, 24.6 cm), rear drum; swept area: total 297.7 sq in, 1,920 sq cm.

ELECTRICAL EQUIPMENT 12 V; 2,500 W battery; 32 A alternator; Delco-Remy high energy ignition system; 2 headlamps.

DIMENSIONS AND WEIGHT wheel base: 94.30 in, 239 cm - Hatchback Sedan 97.30 in, 247 cm; tracks: 51.20 in, 130 cm

CHECKER Marathon Sedan

CHEVROLET Chevette Hatchback Coupé

CHEVROLET Monza 2 + 2 Hatchback Coupé

rpm; max torque (DIN): 128 lb ft, 17.6 kg m (172.6 N) at 2,400 rpm; max engine rpm: 4,800; 36.4 hp/l (26 kW/l); cast iron block and head; 5 crankshaft bearing valves: overhead, in line, push-rods and rockers, hydraul tappets; camshafts: 1, side; lubrication: gear pump, fu flow filter, 7.6 imp pt, 9.1 US pt, 4.3 l; 1 Holley 52 downdraught twin barrel carburettor; cleaner air syste exhaust system with catalytic converter; fuel feed: mech nical pump; water-cooled, 19.9 imp pt, 23.9 US pt, 11.3

TRANSMISSION driving wheels: rear; clutch: single d plate (diaphragm); gearbox: mechanical; gears: 4, ful synchronized; ratios: I 3.500, II 2.480, III 1.660, IV 1, r 3.500; lever: central; final drive: hypoid bevel; axle rati 2.730; width of rims: 5''; tyres: A78 x 13 - St. Wag B78 x 13.

PERFORMANCE max speed: about 96 mph, 154 km/h; powe weight ratio: Coupé 28.9 lb/hp (39.3 lb/kW), 13.1 kg/l (17.8 kg/kW); speed in direct drive at 1,000 rpm: 24 mp 38.7 km/h; consumption: 28/8 m/imp gal, 24 m/US ga 9.8 l x 100 km.

CHASSIS integral; front suspension: independent, wishbone coil springs, anti-roll bar, telescopic dampers; rear: rig axle, lower trailing radius arms, upper oblique torque arm coil springs, telescopic dampers.

STEERING recirculating ball; turns lock to lock: **4.40.**

BRAKES front disc (diameter 9.74 in, 24.7 cm), rear drum swept area; total 264.8 sq in, 1,708 sq cm.

ELECTRICAL EQUIPMENT 12 V; 3,200 W battery; 37 A a ternator; Delco-Remy high energy ignition system; 2 hea lamps.

DIMENSIONS AND WEIGHT wheel base: 97 in, 246 c tracks: 54.80 in, 139 cm front, 53.60 in, 136 cm rea length: 179.20 in, 455 cm - Sport Hatchback Coupé 179. in, 455 cm - St. Wagon 178 in, 452 cm; width: 65.40 in 166 cm; height: 50.20 in, 127 cm - Coupé 49.80 in, 126 c - St. Wagon 51.80 in, 132 cm; ground clearance: 4.80 i 12.2 cm; weight: Coupé 2,599 lb, 1,179 kg - St. Wago 2,669 lb, 1,210 kg - 2+2 Hatchback Coupé 2,656 lb, 1,2 kg - 2+2 Sport Hatchback Coupé 2,699 lb, 1,224 kg; tur ing circle: 38.4 ft, 11.7 m; fuel tank: 15.4 imp gal, 18 US gal, 70 l - St. Wagon 12.5 imp gal, 15 US gal, 57

BODY 4 seats, separate front seats with built-in headrest

OPTIONALS limited slip differential; 2.930 axle ratio; speed fully synchronized mechanical gearbox (I 3.400, 2.080, III 1.390, IV 1, V 0.800, rev 3.360), 3.080 axle rati Turbo-Hydramatic 200 automatic transmission with 3 ratio (I 2.740, II 1.570, III 1, rev 2.070), max ratio of convert at stall 2, possible manual selection, central lever, 2.7 axle ratio; BR 70 x 13 tyres with 6'' wide rims; pow steering; tilt of steering wheel; servo brake; heavy-du radiator; heavy-duty battery; reclining backrests; foldi rear seat (for Coupé only); heated rear window; sunshi roof (for Coupé only); anti-roll bar on rear suspensio « Spider » equipment (for 2 + 2 Sport Hatchback Coup only); air-conditioning.

85 hp power team

(for California only).

See 90 hp power team, except for:

ENGINE compression ratio: 8.3:1; max power (DIN): 85 h (62.6 kW) at 4,400 rpm; max torque (DIN): 123 lb ft, 1 kg m (166.7 Nm) at 2,800 rpm; 34.4 hp/l (25.3 kW/l).

TRANSMISSION axle ratio: 2.930.

PERFORMANCE max speed: about 93 mph, 150 km/h; powe weight ratio: Coupé 31.2 lb/hp (42.4 lb/kW), 14.2 kg/h (19.2 kg/kW).

DIMENSIONS AND WEIGHT weight: plus 56 lb, 26 kg.

OPTIONALS 5-speed fully synchronized mechanical gearbo not available.

105 hp power team

(not available in California).

See 90 hp power team, except for:

ENGINE 6 cylinders, Vee-slanted at 90°; 196 cu in, 3,21 cc (3.50 x 3.40 in, 88.8 x 86.4 mm); max power (DIN): 10 hp (77.3 kW) at 4,000 rpm; max torque (DIN): 160 lb ft, 22. kg m (216.7 Nm) at 2,000 rpm; max engine rpm: 4,400; 32. hp/l (24.1 kW/l); 4 crankshaft bearings; camshafts: 1, a centre of Vee; lubricating system: 8.3 imp pt, 9.9 US p 4.7 l; 1 Rochester 2ME downdraught twin barrel carburetto fuel feed: electric pump; cooling system: 20.4 imp pt 24.5 US pt, 11.6 l.

TRANSMISSION tyres: B78 x 13.

---

70 HP POWER TEAM

front, 51.20 in, 130 cm rear; length: Scooter Hatchback Coupé 158.80 in, 403 cm - Hatchback Coupé 159.70 in, 406 cm - Hatchback Sedan 162.60 in, 413 cm; width: 61.80 in, 157 cm; height: 52.30 in, 133 cm; ground clearance: 5.30 In, 13.5 cm; weight: Scooter Hatchback Coupé 1,925 lb, 873 kg - Hatchback Coupé 1,972 lb, 894 kg - Hatchback Sedan 2,052 lb, 931 kg; turning circle: 34.3 ft, 10.5 m - Hatchback Sedan 34.9 ft, 10.6 m; fuel tank: 10.3 imp gal, 12.5 US gal, 47 l.

OPTIONALS Turbo-Hydramatic 180 automatic transmission, hydraulic torque converter and planetary gears with 3 ratios (I 2.400, II 1.480, III 1, rev 1.920), max ratio of converter at stall 2.20, possible manual selection, central lever; 4.110 axle ratio; heavy-duty battery; servo brake; vinyl roof; heavy-duty radiator; tilt of steering wheel; heated rear window; air-conditioning

74 hp power team

(not available in California).

See 70 hp power team, except for:

ENGINE max power (DIN): 74 hp (54.5 kW) at 5,200 rpm; max torque (DIN): 88 lb ft, 12.1 kg m (118.7 Nm) at 2,800 rpm; 46.3 hp/l (34.1 kW/l); 1 Holley 466371 downdraught twin barrel carburettor.

PERFORMANCE max speed: about 93 mph, 150 km/h; power-weight ratio: Hatchback Sedan 27.7 lb/hp (37.6 lb/kW), 12.6 kg/hp (17.1 kg/kW).

Monza Series

PRICES EX WORKS:

1 Coupé	$	3,617
2 St. Wagon	$	3,974
3 2+2 Hatchback Coupé	$	3,844
4 2+2 Sport Hatchback Coupé	$	4,291

For 105 hp engine add $ 160; for 115 hp engine add $ 200; for V8 engines add $ 395.

Power team:	Standard for:	Optional for:
90 hp	all	—
85 hp	all	—
105 hp	—	all
115 hp	—	all
125 hp	—	all except 2
130 hp	—	all except 2

90 hp power team

(not available in California).

ENGINE front, 4 stroke; 4 cylinders, vertical, in line; 151 cu in, 2,474 cc (4 x 3 in, 101.5 x 76.1 mm); compression ratio: 8:1; max power (DIN): 90 hp (66.2 kW) at 4,000

PERFORMANCE max speed: about 99 mph, 160 km/h; power-weight ratio: Coupé 25.9 lb/hp (35.2 lb/kW), 11.7 kg/hp (15.9 kg/kW) - 2 + 2 Sport Hatchback Coupé 26.7 lb/hp (36.2 lb/kW), 12.1 kg/hp (16.4 kg/kW); speed in direct drive at 1,000 rpm: 24.9 mph, 40 km/h; consumption: 27.7 m/imp gal, 23 m/US gal, 10.2 l x 100 km.

ELECTRICAL EQUIPMENT 2,500 W battery.

DIMENSIONS AND WEIGHT weight: plus 119 lb, 54 kg - 2 + 2 Sport Hatchback Coupé plus 103 lb, 47 kg.

OPTIONALS 5-speed fully synchronized mechanical gearbox with 2.930 axle ratio; Turbo Hydramatic 350 automatic transmission with 3 ratios (I 2.520; II 1.520, III 1, rev 1.930), max ratio of converter at stall 2.35, possible manual selection, 2.730 axle ratio.

115 hp power team

(for California only).

See 90 hp power team, except for:

ENGINE 6 cylinders, Vee-slanted at 90°; 231 cu in, 3,785 cc (3.80 x 3.40 in, 96.5 x 86.4 mm); max power (DIN): 115 hp (84.6 kW) at 3,800 rpm; max torque (DIN): 190 lb ft, 26.2 kg m (257 Nm) at 2,000 rpm; max engine rpm: 4,200; 49.4 hp/l (22.3 kW/l); 4 crankshaft bearings; camshafts: 1 at centre of Vee; lubricating system: 8.3 imp pt, 9.9 US pt, 4.7 l; 1 Rochester 2ME downdraught twin barrel carburettor; fuel feed: electric pump; cooling system: 20.4 imp pt, 24.5 US pt, 11.6 l.

TRANSMISSION axle ratio: 2.930; tyres: B78 x 13.

PERFORMANCE max speed: about 103 mph, 165 km/h; power-weight ratio: Coupé 23.9 lb/hp (32.4 lb/kW), 10.8 kg/hp (14.7 kg/kW) - 2 + 2 Sport Hatchback Coupé 24.6 lb/hp (33.4 lb/kW), 11.1 kg/hp (15.2 kg/kW); speed in direct drive at 1,000 rpm: 27 mph, 43.4 km/h; consumption: 24.1 m/imp gal, 20 m/US gal, 11.7 l x 100 km.

ELECTRICAL EQUIPMENT 2,500 W battery.

DIMENSIONS AND WEIGHT weight: plus 145 lb, 66 kg - 2 + 2 Sport Hatchback Coupé plus 128 lb, 58 kg.

OPTIONALS 5-speed fully synchronized mechanical gearbox with 2.930 axle ratio; Turbo-Hydramatic 350 automatic transmission with 3 ratios (I 2.520, II 1.520, III 1, rev 1.930), max ratio of converter at stall 2.35, possible manual selection, 2.560 or 2.930 axle ratio.

125 hp power team

(for California only).

See 90 hp power team, except for:

ENGINE 8 cylinders; 305 cu in, 4,999 cc (3.74 x 3.48 in, 94.9 x 88.3 mm); compression ratio: 8.4:1; max power (DIN): 125 hp (92 kW) at 3,200 rpm; max torque (DIN): 235 lb ft, 32.4 kg m (317.7 Nm) at 2,000 rpm; max engine rpm: 3,600; 25 hp/l (18.4 kW/l); camshafts: 1, at centre of Vee; lubricating system: 8.3 imp pt, 9.9 US pt, 4.7 l; 1 Rochester 17059434 downdraught twin barrel carburettor; fuel feed: electric pump; cooling system: 28.7 imp pt, 34.5 US pt, 16.3 l.

TRANSMISSION gearbox: Turbo-Hydramatic 350 automatic transmission (standard), hydraulic torque converter and planetary gears with 3 ratios, max ratio of converter at stall 2.35, possible manual selection: ratios: I 2.520, II 1.520, III 1, rev 1.930; axle ratio: 2.290; width of rims: 6''; tyres: BR70 x 13 (standard).

PERFORMANCE max speed: about 106 mph, 170 km/h; power-weight ratio: Coupé 22.9 lb/hp (31.2 lb/kW), 10.4 kg/hp (14.2 kg/kW) - 2 + 2 Sport Hatchback Coupé 23.7 lb/hp (32.3 lb/kW), 10.8 kg/hp (14.7 kg/kW); speed in direct drive at 1,000 rpm: 29.3 mph, 47.2 km/h; consumption: 21.6 m/imp gal, 18 m/US gal, 13.1 l x 100 km.

DIMENSIONS AND WEIGHT weight: plus 269 lb, 125 kg.

OPTIONALS 5-speed fully synchronized mechanical gearbox not available.

130 hp power team

(not available in California).

See 90 hp power team, except for:

ENGINE 8 cylinders; 305 cu in, 4,999 cc (3.74 x 3.48 in, 94.9 x 88.3 mm); compression ratio: 8.4:1; max power (DIN): 130 hp (95.7 kW) at 3,200 rpm; max torque (DIN): 245 lb ft, 33.8 kg m (331.5 Nm) at 2,000 rpm; max engine rpm: 3,600; 26 hp/l (19.1 kW/l); camshafts: 1, at centre of Vee; lubricating system: 8.3 imp pt, 9.9 US pt, 4.7 l; 1 Roche-

ster 17059135 downdraught twin barrel carburettor; fuel feed: electric pump; cooling system: 28.7 imp pt, 34.5 US pt, 16.3 l.

TRANSMISSION clutch: single dry plate (diaphragm), centrifugal; gearbox ratios: I 2.850, II 2.020, III 1.350, IV 1, rev 2.850; axle ratio: 3.080; width of rims: 6''; tyres: BR70 x 13 (standard).

PERFORMANCE max speed: about 109 mph, 175 km/h; power-weight ratio: Coupé 22.1 lb/hp (30 lb/kW), 10 kg/hp (13.6 kg/kW) - 2 + 2 Sport Hatchback Coupé 22.8 lb/hp (31 lb/kW), 10.4 kg/hp (14.1 kg/kW); speed in direct drive at 1,000 rpm: 30.2 mph, 48.6 km/h; consumption: 21.6 m/imp gal, 18 m/US gal, 13.1 l x 100 km.

DIMENSIONS AND WEIGHT weight: plus 269 lb, 125 kg.

OPTIONALS Turbo-Hydramatic 350 automatic transmission with 3 ratios (I 2.520, II 1.520, III 1, rev 1.930), max ratio of converter at stall 2.35, possible manual selection, 2.290 axle ratio.

Nova Series

PRICES EX WORKS:

Hatchback Coupé	$ 4,118
Coupé	$ 3,955
Sedan	$ 4,055
Custom Coupé	$ 4,164
Custom Sedan	$ 4,264

For V8 engines add $ 235 (for 165 hp engine add $ 360).

Power team:	Standard for:	Optional for:
90 hp	all	—
115 hp	all	—
125 hp	—	all
130 hp	—	all
165 hp	—	all

90 hp power team

(for California only).

ENGINE front, 4 stroke; 6 cylinders, in line; 250 cu in, 4,097 cc (3.87 x 3.53 in, 98.2 x 89.6 mm); compression ratio: 8.2:1; max power (DIN): 90 hp (66.2 kW) at 3,600 rpm; max torque (DIN): 175 lb ft, 24.1 kg m (236.3 Nm) at 1,600 rpm; max engine rpm: 4,400; 22 hp/l (16.2 kW/l); cast iron block and head; 7 crankshaft bearings; valves: overhead in line, push-rods and rockers, hydraulic tappets; camshafts: 1, side; lubrication: gear pump, full flow filter, 8.3 imp pt, 9.9 US pt, 4.7 l; 1 Rochester 17059314 downdraught single barrel carburettor; cleaner air system; exhaust system with catalytic converter; fuel feed: mechanical pump; water-cooled, 23.9 imp pt, 28.8 US pt, 13.6 l.

TRANSMISSION driving wheels: rear; gearbox: Turbo-Hydramatic 350 automatic transmission, hydraulic torque converter and planetary gears with 3 ratios, max ratio of converter at stall 2, possible manual selection: ratios: I 2.520, II 1.520, III 1, rev 1.930; lever: steering column; final drive:

CHEVROLET Monza 2+2 Hatchback Coupé

hypoid bevel; axle ratio: 2.730; width of rims: 6''; tyres: E78 x 14.

PERFORMANCE max speed: about 93 mph, 149 km/h; power-weight ratio: Sedan 35.4 lb/hp (48.2 lb/kW), 16.1 kg/hp (21.9 kg/kW) - Custom Sedan 35.9 lb/hp (48.8 lb/kW), 16.3 kg/hp (22.1 kg/kW); speed in direct drive at 1,000 rpm: 25.9 mph, 41.7 km/h; consumption: 19.2 m/imp gal, 16 m/US gal, 14.7 l x 100 km.

CHASSIS integral with separate partial front box-type frame; front suspension: independent, wishbones, coil springs, anti-roll bar, telescopic dampers; rear: rigid axle, semi-elliptic leafsprings, telescopic dampers.

STEERING recirculating ball; turns lock to lock: 4.99.

BRAKES front disc (diameter 11 in, 27.9 cm), front internal radial fins, rear drum; swept area: total 326.4 sq in, 2,105 sq cm.

ELECTRICAL EQUIPMENT 12 V; 2,500 W battery; 37 A alternator; Delco-Remy high energy ignition system; 2 headlamps.

DIMENSIONS AND WEIGHT wheel base: 111 in, 282 cm; tracks: 61.30 in, 156 cm front, 59 in, 150 cm rear; length: 196.70 in, 500 cm; width: 72.20 in, 183 cm; height: 52.70 in, 134 cm - sedans 53.60 in, 136 cm; ground clearance: 4.60 in, 11.7 cm; weight: Hatchback Coupé 3,272 lb, 1,484 kg - Coupé 3,152 lb, 1,429 kg - Sedan 3,190 lb, 1,447 kg -

CHEVROLET Nova Hatchback Coupé

90 HP POWER TEAM

Custom Coupé 3,197 lb, 1,450 kg - Custom Sedan 3,232 lb, 1,466 kg; turning circle: 39.9 ft, 12.2 m; fuel tank: 17.6 imp gal, 21 US gal, 80 l.

OPTIONALS limited slip differential; heavy-duty radiator; central lever; heavy-duty suspension with rear anti-roll bar; FR78 x 14 tyres; automatic speed control; power steering; tilt of steering wheel; servo brake; heavy-duty battery; air-conditioning; vinyl roof; electric windows.

115 hp power team

(not available in California).

See 90 hp power team, except for:

ENGINE compression ratio: 8:1; max power (DIN): 115 hp (84.6 kW) at 3,800 rpm; max torque (DIN): 200 lb ft, 27.6 kg m (270.7 Nm) at 1,600 rpm; 28.1 hp/l (20.6 kW/l); 1 Rochester 17059013 downdraught single barrel carburettor.

TRANSMISSION clutch: single dry plate (diaphragm), centrifugal; gearbox: mechanical; gears: 3, fully synchronized; ratios: I 3.500, II 1.890, III 1, rev 3.620; lever: steering column; axle ratio: 2.560.

PERFORMANCE max speed: about 99 mph, 160 km/h; power-weight ratio: Sedan 27.7 lb/hp (37.7 lb/kW), 12.6 kg/hp (17.1 kg/kW) - Custom Sedan 28.1 lb/hp (38.2 lb/kW), 12.7 kg/hp (17.3 kg/kW); speed in direct drive at 1,000 rpm: 22.6 mph, 36.4 km/h; consumption: 22.8 m/imp gal, 19 m/US gal, 12.4 l x 100 km.

OPTIONALS Turbo-Hydramatic 350 automatic transmission with 3 ratios (I 2.520, III 1.520, III 1, rev 1.930), max ratio of converter at stall 2, possible manual selection, 2.560 axle ratio.

125 hp power team

(for California only).

See 90 hp power team, except for:

ENGINE 8 cylinders; 305 cu in, 4,999 cc (3.74 x 3.48 in, 94.9 x 88.3 mm); compression ratio: 8.4:1; max power (DIN): 125 hp (92 kW) at 3,200 rpm; max torque (DIN): 235 lb ft, 32.4 kg m (317.7 Nm) at 2,000 rpm; max engine rpm: 3,600; 25 hp/l (18.4 kW/l); 5 crankshaft bearings; camshafts: 1, at centre of Vee; 1 Rochester 17059434 downdraught twin barrel carburettor; cooling system: 28.2 imp pt, 33.8 US pt, 16 l.

TRANSMISSION axle ratio: 2.410.

PERFORMANCE max speed: about 103 mph, 165 km/h; power-weight ratio: Sedan 26.6 lb/hp (36.1 lb/kW), 12 kg/hp (16.4 kg/kW) - Custom Sedan 26.9 lb/hp (36.5 lb/kW), 12.2 kg/hp (16.6 kg/kW); consumption: 19.2 m/imp gal, 16 m/US gal, 14.7 l x 100 km.

BRAKES servo (standard).

ELECTRICAL EQUIPMENT 3,200 W battery.

DIMENSIONS AND WEIGHT weight: plus 130 lb, 59 kg.

OPTIONALS 3.080 axle ratio.

130 hp power team

(not available in California).

See 90 hp power team, except for:

ENGINE 8 cylinders; 305 cu in, 4,999 cc (3.74 x 3.48 in, 94.9 x 88.3 mm); compression ratio: 8.4:1; max power (DIN): 130 hp (95.7 kW) at 3,200 rpm; max torque (DIN): 245 lb ft, 33.8 kg m (331.5 Nm) at 2,000 rpm; max engine rpm: 3,600; 26 hp/l (19.1 kW/l); 5 crankshaft bearings; camshafts: 1, at centre of Vee; 1 Rochester 17059135 downdraught twin barrel carburettor; cooling system: 28.2 imp pt, 33.8 US pt, 16 l.

TRANSMISSION clutch: single dry plate (diaphragm), centrifugal; gearbox: mechanical; gears: 4, fully synchronized; ratios: I 2.850, II 2.020, III 1.350, IV 1, rev 2.850; lever: central; axle ratio: 3.080.

PERFORMANCE max speed: about 106 mph, 170 km/h; power-weight ratio: Sedan 25.5 lb/hp (34.7 lb/kW), 11.6 kg/hp (15.7 kg/kW) - Custom Sedan 25.9 lb/hp (35.1 lb/kW), 11.7 kg/hp (15.9 kg/kW); speed in direct drive at 1,000 rpm: 29.3 mph, 47.2 km/h; consumption: 18 m/imp gal, 15 m/US gal, 15.7 l x 100 km.

BRAKES servo (standard).

CHEVROLET Nova Custom Sedan

ELECTRICAL EQUIPMENT 3,200 W battery.

DIMENSIONS AND WEIGHT weight: plus 130 lb, 59 kg.

OPTIONALS Turbo-Hydramatic 350 automatic transmission with 3 ratios (I 2.520, II 1.520, III 1, rev 1.930), max ratio of converter at stall 2, possible manual selection, 2.410 or 3.080 axle ratio.

165 hp power team

See 90 hp power team, except for:

ENGINE 8 cylinders; 350 cu in, 5,736 cc (4 x 3.48 in, 101.6 x 88 mm); max power (DIN): 165 hp (121.4 kW) at 3,800 rpm; max torque (DIN): 260 lb ft, 35.9 kg m (352.1 Nm) at 2,400 rpm; max engine rpm: 4,200; 28.8 hp/l (21.2 kW/l); 5 crankshaft bearings; camshafts: 1, at centre of Vee; 1 Rochester 17059582 (17059502 for California only) downdraught 4-barrel carburettor; cooling system: 28.2 imp pt, 33.8 US pt, 16 l.

TRANSMISSION axle ratio: 2.410.

PERFORMANCE max speed: about 109 mph, 175 km/h; power-weight ratio: Sedan 20.1 lb/hp (27.3 lb/kW), 9.1 kg/hp (12.4 kg/kW) - Custom Sedan 20.4 lb/hp (27.7 lb/kW), 9.2 kg/hp (12.6 kg/kW); consumption: 19.2 m/imp gal, 16 m/US gal, 14.7 l x 100 km.

BRAKES servo (standard).

ELECTRICAL EQUIPMENT 3,200 W battery.

DIMENSIONS AND WEIGHT weight: plus 129 lb, 59 kg.

OPTIONALS 3.080 axle ratio.

Camaro Series

PRICES EX WORKS:

1 Sport Coupé	$ 4,67
2 Rally Sport Coupé	$ 5,07
3 Berlinetta Coupé	$ 5,39
4 Z28 Sport Coupé	$ 6,11

For V8 engines add $ 235 or $ 360.

Power team:	Standard for:	Optional for:
90 hp	1,2,3	—
115 hp	1,2,3	—
125 hp	—	1,2,3
130 hp	—	1,2,3
165 hp	—	1,2,3
170 hp A	—	1,2,3
175 hp	4	—
170 hp	4	—

CHEVROLET Camaro Z28 Sport Coupé

90 hp power team

(for California only).

ENGINE front, 4 stroke; 6 cylinders, vertical, in line; 250 cu in, 4,097 cc (3.87 x 3.53 in, 98.2 x 89.6 mm); compression ratio: 8.2:1; max power (DIN): 90 hp (66.2 kW) at 3,600 rpm; max torque (DIN): 175 lb ft, 24.1 kg m (236.3 Nm) at 1,600 rpm; max engine rpm: 4,400; 22 hp/l (16.2 kW/l); cast iron block and head; 7 crankshaft bearings; valves: overhead, in line, push-rods and rockers, hydraulic tappets; camshafts: 1, side; lubrication: gear pump, full flow filter, 8.3 imp pt, 9.9 US pt, 4.7 l; 1 Rochester 17059314 downdraught single barrel carburettor; cleaner air system; exhaust system with catalytic converter; fuel feed: mechanical pump; water-cooled, 25.7 imp pt, 30.9 US pt, 14.6 l.

TRANSMISSION driving wheels: rear; gearbox: Turbo-Hyramatic 350 automatic transmission, hydraulic torque converter and planetary gears with 3 ratios, max ratio of converter at stall 2, possible manual selection; ratios: I 2.520, II 1.520, III 1, rev 1.930; lever: steering column; final drive: hypoid bevel; axle ratio: 2.730; width of rims: 6'' - Berlinetta 7''; tyres: FR78 x 14.

PERFORMANCE max speed: about 96 mph, 154 km/h; power-weight ratio: Sport Coupé and Rally Sport Coupé 36.5 lb/hp (49.6 lb/kW), 16.5 kg/hp (22.5 kg/kW) - Berlinetta 37 lb/hp (50.3 lb/kW), 16.8 kg/hp (22.8 kg/kW); speed in direct drive at 1,000 rpm: 25.9 mph, 41.7 km/h; consumption: 19.2 m/imp gal, 16 m/US gal, 14.7 l x 100 km.

CHASSIS integral with separate partial front box-type frame; front suspension: independent, wishbones, coil springs, anti-roll bar, telescopic dampers; rear: rigid axle, semi-elliptic leafsprings, anti-roll bar, telescopic dampers.

STEERING recirculating ball, servo; turns lock to lock: 2.41.

BRAKES front disc (diameter 11 in, 27.9 cm), front internal radial fins, rear drum; swept area: total 326.4 sq in, 2,105 sq cm.

ELECTRICAL EQUIPMENT 12 V; 2,500 W battery; 37 A alternator; Delco-Remy high energy ignition system; 4 headlamps.

DIMENSIONS AND WEIGHT wheel base: 108 in, 274 cm; front track: 61.30 in, 156 cm - Berlinetta 61.60 in, 156 cm; rear track: 60 in, 152 cm - Berlinetta 60.30 in, 153 cm; length: 197.60 in, 502 cm; width: 74.50 in, 189 cm; height: 49.20 in, 125 cm; ground clearance: 4.90 in, 12.4 cm; weight: Sport Coupé and Rally Sport Coupé 3,282 lb, 1,488 kg - Berlinetta 3,327 lb, 1,509 kg; turning circle: 41.1 ft, 12.5 m; fuel tank 17.6 imp gal, 21 US gal, 80 l.

BODY coupé; 2 doors; 4 seats, separate front seats.

OPTIONALS limited slip differential; central lever; E78 x 14 tyres with 6'' or 7'' wide rims; tilt of steering wheel; servo brake; electric windows; heavy-duty battery; heavy-duty radiator; reclining front seats; removable glass roof panels; tinted glass; air-conditioning.

115 hp power team

(not available in California).

See 90 hp power team, except for:

ENGINE compression ratio: 8:1; max power (DIN): 115 hp (84.6 kW) at 3,800 rpm; max torque (DIN): 200 lb ft, 27.6 kg m (270.7 Nm) at 1,600 rpm; 28.1 hp/l (20.6 kW/l); 1 Rochester 17059013 downdraught single barrel carburettor.

TRANSMISSION clutch: single dry plate (diaphragm), centrifugal; gearbox: mechanical; gears: 3, fully synchronized; ratios: I 3.500, II 1.890, III 1, rev 3.620; lever: central; axle ratio: 2.560.

PERFORMANCE max speed: about 99 mph, 160 km/h; power-weight ratio: Sport Coupé and Rally Sport Coupé 28.5 lb/hp (38.8 lb/kW), 12.9 kg/hp (17.6 kg/kW) - Berlinetta 28.9 lb/hp (39.3 lb/kW), 13.1 kg/hp (17.8 kg/kW); speed in direct drive at 1,000 rpm: 24.2 mph, 30 km/h; consumption: 21.6 m/imp gal, 18 m/US gal, 13.1 l x 100 km.

OPTIONALS Turbo-Hydramatic 350 automatic transmission with 3 ratios (I 2.520, II 1.520, III 1, rev 1.930), max ratio of converter at stall 2, possible manual selection, steering column lever, 2.560 axle ratio.

125 hp power team

(for California only).

See 90 hp power team, except for:

ENGINE 8 cylinders; 305 cu in, 4,999 cc (3.74 x 3.48 in, 94.9 x 88.3 mm); compression ratio: 8.4:1; max power (DIN): 125 hp (92 kW) at 3,200 rpm; max torque (DIN): 235 lb ft, 32.4 kg m (317.7 Nm) at 2,000 rpm; max engine rpm:

3,600; 25 hp/l (18.4 kW/l); 5 crankshafts bearings; camshafts: 1, at centre of Vee; 1 Rochester 17059434 downdraught twin barrel carburettor; cooling system: 30.4 imp pt, 36.6 US pt, 17.3 l.

TRANSMISSION axle ratio: 2.410.

PERFORMANCE max speed: about 103 mph, 165 km/h; power-weight ratio: Sport Coupé and Rally Sport Coupé 27.3 lb/hp (37.1 lb/kW), 12.4 kg/hp (16.8 kg/kW) - Berlinetta 27.7 lb/hp (37.6 lb/kW), 12.5 kg/hp (17 kg/kW); consumption: 19.2 m/imp gal, 16 m/US gal, 14.7 l x 100 km.

BRAKES servo (standard).

ELECTRICAL EQUIPMENT 3,200 W battery.

DIMENSIONS AND WEIGHT weight: plus 130 lb, 59 kg.

OPTIONALS automatic speed control.

130 hp power team

(not available in California)

See 90 hp power team, except for:

ENGINE 8 cylinders; 305 cu in, 4,999 cc (3.74 x 3.48 in, 94.9 x 88.3 mm); compression ratio: 8.4:1; max power (DIN): 130 hp (95.7 kW) at 3,200 rpm; max torque (DIN): 245 lb ft, 33.8 kg m (331.5 Nm) at 2,000 rpm; max engine rpm: 3,600; 26 hp/l (19.1 kW/l); 5 crankshaft bearings; camshafts: 1, at centre of Vee; 1 Rochester 17059135 downdraught twin barrel carburettor; cooling system: 30.4 imp pt, 36.6 US pt, 17.3 l.

TRANSMISSION clutch: single dry plate (diaphragm), centrifugal; gearbox: mechanical; gears: 4, fully synchronized; ratios: I 2.850, II 2.020, III 1.350, IV 1, rev 2.850; lever: central; axle ratio: 3.080.

PERFORMANCE max speed: about 106 mph, 170 km/h; power-weight ratio: Rally Sport Coupé and Sport Coupé 26.2 lb/hp (35.7 lb/kW), 11.9 kg/hp (16.2 kg/kW) - Berlinetta 26.6 lb/hp (36.1 lb/kW), 12.1 kg/hp (16.4 kg/kW); speed in direct drive at 1,000 rpm: 29.3 mph, 47.2 km/h; consumption: 18 m/imp gal, 15 m/US gal, 15.7 l x 100 km.

BRAKES servo (standard).

ELECTRICAL EQUIPMENT 3,200 W battery.

DIMENSIONS AND WEIGHT weight: plus 130 lb, 59 kg.

OPTIONALS Turbo-Hydramatic 350 automatic transmission with 3 ratios (I 2.520, II 1.520, III 1, rev 1.930), max ratio of converter at stall 2, possible manual selection, steering column lever, 2.410 axle ratio; automatic speed control.

165 hp power team

(for California only).

See 90 hp power team, except for:

ENGINE 8 cylinders; 350 cu in, 5,736 cc (4 x 3.48 in, 101.6 x 88 mm); max power (DIN): 165 hp (121.4 kW) at 3,800 rpm; max torque (DIN): 260 lb ft, 35.9 kg m (352.1 Nm) at 2,400 rpm; max engine rpm: 4,200; 28.8 hp/l (21.2 kW/l); 5 crankshaft bearings; camshafts: 1, at centre of Vee; 1 Rochester 17059202 downdraught 4-barrel carburettor; cooling system: 30.6 imp pt, 36.8 US pt, 17.4 l.

TRANSMISSION axle ratio: 2.410.

PERFORMANCE max speed: about 112 mph, 180 km/h; power-weight ratio: Sport Coupé and Rally Sport Coupé 20.7 lb/hp (28.1 lb/kW), 9.4 kg/hp (12.8 kg/kW) - Berlinetta 21 lb/hp (28.5 lb/kW), 9.5 kg/hp (12.9 kg/kW); speed in direct drive at 1,000 rpm: 26.7 mph, 43 km/h; consumption: 19.2 m/imp gal, 16 m/US gal, 14.7 l x 100 km.

BRAKES servo (standard).

ELECTRICAL EQUIPMENT 3,200 W battery.

DIMENSIONS AND WEIGHT weight: plus 134 lb, 61 kg.

OPTIONALS 3.080 axle ratio; automatic speed control.

170 hp A power team

(not available in California).

See 90 hp engine, except for:

ENGINE 8 cylinders; 350 cu in, 5,736 cc (4 x 3.48 in, 101.6 x 88 mm); max power (DIN): 170 hp (125.1 kW) at 3,800 rpm; max torque (DIN): 270 lb ft, 37.2 kg m (364.8 Nm) at 2,400 rpm; 29.6 hp/l (21.8 kW/l); 5 crankshaft bearings;

CHEVROLET Camaro Berlinetta Coupé

camshafts: 1, at centre of Vee; 1 Rochester 17059203 downdraught 4-barrel carburettor; cooling system: 30.6 imp pt, 36.8 US pt, 17.4 l.

TRANSMISSION clutch: single dry plate (diaphragm), centrifugal; gearbox: mechanical; gears: 4, fully synchronized; ratios: I 2.850, II 2.020, III 1.350, IV 1, rev 2.850; lever: central; axle ratio: 3.080.

PERFORMANCE max speed: about 115 mph, 185 km/h; power-weight ratio: Sport Coupé and Rally Sport Coupé 20.1 lb/hp (27.3 lb/kW), 9.1 kg/hp (12.4 kg/kW) - Berlinetta 20.4 lb/hp (27.7 lb/kW), 9.2 kg/hp (12.5 kg/kW); speed in direct drive at 1,000 rpm: 26.7 mph, 43 km/h; consumption: 18 m/imp gal, 15 m/US gal, 15.7 l x 100 km.

BRAKES servo (standard).

ELECTRICAL EQUIPMENT 3,200 W battery.

DIMENSIONS AND WEIGHT weight: plus 134 lb, 61 kg.

OPTIONALS Turbo-Hydramatic 350 automatic transmission with 3 ratios (I 2.520, II 1.520, III 1, rev 1.930), max ratio of converter at stall 2, possible manual selection, steering column lever, 2.410 or 3.080 axle ratio; automatic speed control.

175 hp power team

(not available in California).

See 90 hp power team, except for:

ENGINE 8 cylinders; 350 cu in, 5,736 cc (4 x 3.48 in, 101.6 x 88 mm); max power (DIN): 175 hp (128.8 kW) at 4,000 rpm; max torque (DIN): 270 lb ft, 37.2 kg m (364.8 Nm) at 2,400 rpm; 30.5 hp/l (22.5 kW/l); 5 crankshaft bearings; camshafts: 1, at centre of Vee; 1 Rochester 17059203 downdaught 4-barrel carburettor; dual exhaust system; cooling system: 30.6 imp pt, 36.8 US pt, 17.4 l.

TRANSMISSION clutch: single dry plate (diaphragm), centrifugal; gearbox: mechanical; gears: 4, fully synchronized; ratios: I 2.640, II 1.750, III 1.340, IV 1, rev 2.550; lever: central; axle ratio: 3.730; width of rims: 7''; tyres: P225/70R x 15.

PERFORMANCE max speed: about 118 mph, 190 km/h; power-weight ratio: Z28 Sport Coupé 20.8 lb/hp (28.2 lb/kW), 9.4 kg/hp (12.8 kg/kW); speed in direct drive at 1,000 rpm: 26.8 mph, 43.2 km/h; consumption: 18 m/imp gal, 15 m/US gal, 15.7 l x 100 km.

BRAKES servo (standard).

ELECTRICAL EQUIPMENT 3,200 W battery.

DIMENSIONS AND WEIGHT weight: Z28 Sport Coupé 3,636 lb, 1,649 kg.

OPTIONALS Turbo-Hydramatic 350 automatic transmission with 3 ratios (I 2.520, II 1.520, III 1, rev 1.930), max ratio of converter at stall 2, possible manual selection, steering column lever, 3.420 axle ratio; automatic speed control.

CHEVROLET Malibu Classic Sedan

170 hp power team

(for California only).

See 175 hp power team, except for:

ENGINE max power (DIN): 170 hp (125.1 kW) at 4,000 rpm; max torque (DIN): 265 lb ft, 36.6 kg m (358.9 Nm) at 2,400 rpm; 29.6 hp/l (21.8 kW/l); 1 Rochester 17059202 downdraught 4-barrel carburettor.

TRANSMISSION gearbox: Turbo-Hydramatic 350 automatic transmission (standard), hydraulic torque converter and planetary gears with 3 ratios, max ratio of converter at stall 2, possible manual selection: ratios: I 2.520, II 1.520, III 1, rev 1.930; lever: steering column; axle ratio: 3.420.

PERFORMANCE max speed: about 115 mph, 185 km/h; power-weight ratio: Z28 Sport Coupé 21.4 lb/hp (29.1 lb/kW), 9.7 kg/hp (13.2 kg/kW); speed in direct drive at 1,000 rpm: 28.7 mph, 46.2 km/h.

Malibu Series

PRICES EX WORKS:

1 Coupé	$ 4,398
2 Sedan	$ 4,498
3 St. Wagon	$ 4,745
4 Classic Coupé	$ 4,676
5 Classic Landau Coupé	$ 4,915
6 Classic Sedan	$ 4,801
7 Classic St. Wagon	$ 4,955

For 3.8-litre engines add $ 40; for 4.4-litre add $ 190; for 5-litre add $ 295; for 5.7-litre add $ 360.

Power team:	Standard for:	Optional for:
94 hp	all	—
115 hp	—	all
125 hp	—	all
160 hp	—	all
165 hp	—	3,7

94 hp power team

(not available in California).

ENGINE front, 4 stroke; 6 cylinders, Vee-slanted at 90°; 200 cu in, 3,227 cc (3.50 x 3.48 in, 88.9 x 88.4 mm); compression ratio: 8.2:1; max power (DIN): 94 hp (69.2 kW) at 4,000 rpm; max torque (DIN): 154 lb ft, 21.2 kg m (208 Nm) at 2,000 rpm; max engine rpm: 4,400; 28.1 hp/l (21.1 kW/l); cast iron block and head; 4 crankshaft bearings; valves: overhead, in line, push-rods and rockers, hydraulic tappets; camshafts: 1, at centre of Vee; lubrication: gear pump, full flow filter, 8.3 imp pt, 9.9 US pt, 4.7 l; 1 Rochester 17059131 downdraught twin barrel carburettor; cleaner air system; exhaust system with catalytic converter; fuel feed: mechanical pump; water-cooled, 31.3 imp pt, 37.6 US pt, 17.8 l.

TRANSMISSION driving wheels: rear; clutch: single dry plate (diaphragm); gearbox: mechanical; gears: 3, fully synchronized; ratios: I 3.500, II 1.890, III 1, rev 3.620; lever: central; final drive: hypoid bevel; axle ratio: 2.730; width of rims: 6''; tyres: P185/75R x 14 - st. wagons P195/75R x 14.

PERFORMANCE max speed: about 93 mph, 149 km/h; power-weight ratio: Sedan 31.8 lb/hp (43.2 lb/kW), 14.4 kg/hp (19.6 kg/kW) - Classic Sedan 32.2 lb/hp (43.7 lb/kW), 14.6 kg/hp (19.8 kg/kW); speed in direct drive at 1,000 rpm: 23.3 mph, 37.5 km/h; consumption: 26.4 m/imp gal, 22 m/US gal, 10.7 l x 100 km.

CHASSIS perimeter box-type with front and rear cross members; front suspension: independent, wishbones, coil springs, anti-roll bar, telescopic dampers; rear: rigid axle, lower trailing radius arms, upper oblique torque arms, coil springs, telescopic dampers.

STEERING recirculating ball; turns lock to lock: 5.30.

BRAKES front disc (diameter 10.50 in, 26.7 cm) front internal radial fins, rear drum, servo (standard st. wagons only); swept area: total 307.77 sq in, 1,986 sq cm.

ELECTRICAL EQUIPMENT 12 V; 3,200 W battery; 37 A alternator; Delco-Remy high energy ignition system; 4 headlamps.

DIMENSIONS AND WEIGHT wheel base: 108.10 in, 274 cm; tracks: 58.50 in, 149 cm front, 57.80 in, 147 cm rear; length: 192.70 in, 489 cm - st. wagons 193.40 in, 491 cm; width: 71.50 in, 182 cm - st. wagons 71.20 in, 181 cm; height: coupés 53.30 in, 135 cm - sedans 54.20 in, 138 cm - st. wagons 54.50 in, 138 cm; ground clearance: 5.40 in, 13.7 cm - st. wagons 5.70 in, 14.5 cm; weight: Coupé 2,986 lb, 1,355 kg - Sedan 2,992 lb, 1,357 kg - St. Wagon 3,147 lb, 1,427 kg - Classic Coupé and Landau Coupé 3,014 lb, 1,367 kg - Classic Sedan 3,024 lb, 1,372 kg - Classic St. Wagon

CHEVROLET Malibu Classic Sedan

3,172 lb, 1,439 kg: turning circle: 40 ft, 12 m; fuel tank: 15 imp gal, 18 US gal, 68 l - st. wagons 15.2 imp gal, 18.2 US gal, 69 l.

OPTIONALS limited slip differential; Turbo-Hydramatic 200 or 350 automatic transmission with 3 ratios (I 2.520, II 1.520, III 1, rev 1.930 or I 2.740, II 1.570, III 1, rev 2.070), max ratio of converter at stall 2 or 2.35, possible manual selection, 2.730 axle ratio; P195/75R x 14 or P205/70R x 14 tyres; anti-roll bar on rear suspension; power steering; tilt of steering wheel; servo brake; vinyl roof; heated rear window; electric windows; air-conditioning; electric sunshine roof; automatic speed control.

115 hp power team

(for California only).

See 94 hp power team, except for:

ENGINE 231 cu in, 3,785 cc (3.80 x 3.40 in, 96.5 x 86.4 mm); compression ratio: 8:1; max power (DIN): 115 hp (84.6 kW) at 3,800 rpm; max torque (DIN): 190 lb ft, 26.2 kg m (257 Nm) at 2,000 rpm; max engine rpm: 4,200; 30.4 hp/l (22.3 kW/l); 1 Rochester 2ME downdraught twin barrel carburettor; cooling system: 25.7 imp pt, 30.9 US pt, 14.6 l.

TRANSMISSION gearbox: Turbo-Hydramatic 350 (st. wagons 200) automatic transmission (standard), hydraulic torque converter and planetary gears with 3 ratios, max ratio of converter at stall 2 (st. wagons 2.35), possible manual selection; ratios: I 2.520, II 1.520, III 1, rev 1.930 (st. wagons I 2.740, II 1.570, III 1, rev 2.070); lever: steering column.

PERFORMANCE max speed: about 96 mph, 155 km/h; power-weight ratio: Sedan 26 lb/hp (35.4 lb/kW), 11.8 kg/hp (16.3 kg/kW) - Classic Sedan 26.3 lb/hp (35.7 lb/kW), 11.9 kg/hp (16.6 kg/kW); speed in direct drive at 1,000 rpm: 25.4 mph, 40.8 kb/h; consumption: 22.8 m/imp gal, 19 m/US gal, 12.4 l x 100 m.

ELECTRICAL EQUIPMENT 42 A alternator.

125 hp power team

(not available in California).

See 94 hp power team, except for:

ENGINE 8 cylinders; 267 cu in, 4,375 cc (3.50 x 3.48 in, 88.8 x 88.3 mm); max power (DIN): 125 hp (92 kW) at 3,800 rpm; max torque (DIN): 215 lb ft, 29.7 kg m (291.3 Nm) at 2,400 rpm; max engine rpm: 4,200; 28.6 hp/l (21 kW/l); 5 crankshaft bearings; 1 Rochester 17059138 downdraught twin barrel carburettor; cooling system: 35.5 imp pt, 42.7 US pt, 20.2 l.

TRANSMISSION gearbox: Turbo-Hydramatic 350 automatic transmission (standard), hydraulic torque converter and planetary gears with 3 ratios, max ratio of converter at stall 2, possible manual selection: ratios: I 2.520, II 1.520, III 1, rev 1.930; lever: steering column; axle ratio: 2.290 - st. wagons 2.560.

PERFORMANCE max speed: about 99 mph, 160 km/h; power-weight ratio: Sedan 25 lb/hp (34 lb/kW), 11.4 kg/hp (15.4 kg/kW) - Classic Sedan 25.3 lb/hp (34.4 lb/kW), 11.5 kg/hp (15.6 kg/kW); speed in direct drive at 1,000 rpm: 25.4 mph, 40.8 km/h; consumption: 21.6 m/imp gal, 18 m/US gal, 13.1 l x 100 km.

DIMENSIONS AND WEIGHT weight: plus 138 lb, 63 kg - st. wagons 142 lb, 64 kg.

OPTIONALS 4-speed fully synchronized mechanical gearbox (I 3.110, II 2.200, III 1.470, IV 1, rev 3.110), central lever, 2.730 axle ratio (st. wagons 3.080).

160 hp power team

See 94 hp power team, except for:

ENGINE 8 cylinders; 305 cu in, 4,999 cc (3.74 x 3.48 in, 94.9 x 88.3 mm); compression ratio: 8.4:1; max power (DIN): 160 hp (117.8 kW) at 4,000 rpm; max torque (DIN): 235 lb ft, 32.4 kg m (317.7 Nm) at 2,400 rpm; 32 hp/l (23.5 kW/l); 5 crankshaft bearings; 1 Rochester 17059202 (17059502 for California only) downdraught 4-barrel carburettor; cooling system: 31.7 imp pt, 38.1 US pt, 18 l.

TRANSMISSION gearbox: Turbo-Hydramatic 350 automatic transmission (standard), hydraulic torque converter and planetary gears with 3 ratios, max ratio of converter at stall 2, possible manual selection: ratios: I 2.520, II 1.520, III 1, rev 1.930; lever: steering column; axle ratio: 2.290 - st. wagons 2.410.

PERFORMANCE max speed: about 106 mph, 170 km/h; power-weight ratio: Sedan 19.6 lb/hp (26.7 lb/kW), 8.9 kg/hp (12.1 kg/kW) - Classic Sedan 19.8 lb/hp (26.9 lb/kW), 9 kg/hp (12.2 kg/kW); speed in direct drive at 1,000 rpm: 26.4 mph, 42.5 m/h; consumption: 19.2 m/imp gal, 16 m/US gal, 14.7 l x 100 km.

DIMENSIONS AND WEIGHT weight: plus 147 lb, 66 kg - wagons 151 lb, 68 kg.

OPTIONALS 4-speed fully synchronized mechanical gearbox (I 2.850, II 2.020, III 1.350, IV 1, rev 2.850), central lever, 3.080 axle ratio.

165 hp power team

(not available in California).

See 94 hp power team, except for:

ENGINE 8 cylinders; 350 cu in, 5,736 cc (4 x 3.48 in, 101.6 x 88.3 mm); max power (DIN): 165 hp (121.4 kW) at 3,800 rpm; max torque (DIN): 260 lb ft, 35.9 kg m (352.1 Nm) at 2,400 rpm; max engine rpm: 4,200; 28.8 hp/l (21.2 kW/l); 5 crankshaft bearings; 1 Rochester 17059582 downdraught 4-barrel carburettor; cooling system: 31.7 imp pt, 38.1 US pt, 18 l.

TRANSMISSION gearbox: Turbo-Hydramatic 350 automatic transmission (standard), hydraulic torque converter and planetary gears with 3 ratios, max ratio of converter at stall 2, possible manual selection; ratios: I 2.520, II 1.520, III 1, rev 1.930; lever: steering column; axle ratio: 2.730.

PERFORMANCE max speed: about 109 mph, 175 km/h; power-weight ratio: St. Wagon 20.2 lb/hp (27.5 lb/kW), 9.2 kg/hp (12.4 kg/kW) - Classic St. Wagon 20.4 lb/hp (27.7 lb/kW), 9.2 kg/hp (12.5 kg/kW); speed in direct drive at 1,000 rpm: 28.6 mph, 46 m/h; consumption: 18 m/imp gal, 15 m/US gal, 15.7 l x 100 km.

DIMENSIONS AND WEIGHT weight: St. Wagon 3,335 lb, 1,512 kg - Classic St. Wagon 3,360 lb, 1,523 kg.

Monte Carlo Series

PRICES IN GB AND EX WORKS:

	£	$
Sport Coupé	7,467*	4,995
Landau Coupé	—	5,907

For 3.8-litre engine add $ 40; for 4.4-litre engine add $ 190; for 5-litre engine add $ 295.

Power team:	Standard for:	Optional for:
94 hp	both	—
115 hp	—	both
125 hp	—	both
145 hp	—	both
160 hp	—	both

94 hp power team

(not available in California).

ENGINE front, 4 stroke; 6 cylinders, Vee-slanted at 90°; 200 cu in, 3,227 cc (3.50 x 3.48 in, 88.9 x 88.4 mm); compression ratio: 8.2:1; max power (DIN): 94 hp (69.2 kW) at 4,000 rpm; max torque (DIN): 154 lb ft, 21.2 kg m (208 Nm) at 2,000 rpm; max engine rpm: 4,400; 28.7 hp/l (21.1

CHEVROLET Malibu Classic Station Wagon

CHEVROLET Monte Carlo Landau Coupé

kW/l); cast iron block and head; 4 crankshaft bearings; valves: overhead, in line, push-rods and rockers, hydraulic tappets; camshafts: 1, at centre of Vee; lubrication: gear pump, full flow filter, 8.3 imp pt, 9.9 US pt, 4.7 l; 1 Rochester 17059131 or 17059130 downdraught twin barrel carburettor; fuel feed: mechanical pump; water-cooled, 31.3 imp pt, 37.6 US pt, 17.8 l.

TRANSMISSION driving wheels: rear; clutch: single dry plate (diaphragm); gearbox: mechanical (Turbo-Hydramatic 350 standard on Landau Coupé); gears: 3, fully synchronized; ratios: I 3.500, II 1.890, III 1, rev 3.620; lever: central; final drive: hypoid bevel; axle ratio: 2.730; width of rims: 6''; tyres: P205/70R x 14.

PERFORMANCE max speed: about 93 mph, 149 km/h; power-weight ratio: 32.2 lb/hp, (43.7 lb/kW), 14.9 kg/hp (19.8 kg/kW); speed in direct drive at 1,000 rpm: 23.3 mph, 37.5 km/h; consumption: 26.4 m/imp gal, 22 m/US gal, 10.7 l x 100 km.

CHASSIS perimeter; front suspension: independent, wishbones, coil springs, anti-roll bar, telescopic dampers; rear: rigid axle, lower trailing radius arms, upper oblique torque arms, coil springs, anti-roll bar, telescopic dampers.

STEERING recirculating ball (servo standard on Landau Coupé); turns lock to lock: 5.30 - Landau Coupé 3.30.

BRAKES front disc (diameter 10.50 in, 26.7 cm), front internal radial fins, rear drum (servo standard on Landau Coupé); total 307.77 sq in, 1,986 sq cm.

ELECTRICAL EQUIPMENT 12 V; 2,500 W battery; 37 A alternator; Delco-Remy high energy ignition system; 2 head-lamps.

DIMENSIONS AND WEIGHT wheel base: 108.10 in, 274 cm; tracks: 58.50 in, 149 cm front, 57.80 in, 147 cm rear; length: 200.40 in, 509 cm; width: 71.50 in, 182 cm; height: 53.90 in, 137 cm; ground clearance: 4.80 in, 12.2 cm; weight: 3,027 lb, 1,373 kg; turning circle: 40.5 ft, 12.4 m; fuel tank: 15 imp gal, 18.1 US gal, 68 l.

BODY coupé; 2 doors; 6 seats, separate front seats, reclining backrests with built-in headrests; vinyl roof standard on Landau Coupé.

OPTIONALS limited slip differential; Turbo-Hydramatic 350 automatic transmission with 3 ratios (I 2.520, II 1.520, III 1, rev 1.930), max ratio of converter at stall 2, possible manual selection, steering column or central lever, 2.730 axle ratio; power steering; tilt of steering wheel; servo brake; heated rear window; electric windows; electric sunshine roof; automatic speed control; tinted glass; removable glass roof panels (not available on Landau or with fully vinyl roof); heavy-duty suspension; heavy-duty radiator; air-conditioning.

115 hp power team

See 94 hp power team, except for:

ENGINE 231 cu in, 3,785 cc (3.80 x 3.40 in, 96.5 x 86.4 mm); compression ratio: 8:1; max power (DIN): 115 hp (84.6 kW) at 3,800 rpm; max torque (DIN): 190 lb ft, 26.2 kg m (257 Nm) at 2,000 rpm; max engine rpm: 4,200; 30.4 hp/l (22.3 kW/l); 1 Rochester 2ME downdraught twin barrel carburettor; cooling system: 25.7 imp pt, 30.9 US pt, 14.6 l.

CHEVROLET Monte Carlo Landau Coupé

115 HP POWER TEAM

TRANSMISSION gearbox: Turbo-Hydramatic 350 automatic transmission (standard), hydraulic torque converter and planetary gears with 3 ratios, max ratio of converter at stall 2, possible manual selection; ratios: I 2.520, II 1.520, III 1, rev 1.930; lever: steering column; axle ratio: 2.410 (2.730 for California only).

PERFORMANCE max speed: about 96 mph, 155 km/h; power-weight ratio: 26.3 lb/hp (35.8 lb/kW), 12 kg/hp (16.2 kg/kW); speed in direct drive at 1,000 rpm: 25.4 mph, 40.8 km/h; consumption: 22.8 m/imp gal, 19 m/US gal, 12.4 l x 100 km.

ELECTRICAL EQUIPMENT 42 A alternator.

OPTIONALS central lever.

125 hp power team

(not available in California).

See 94 hp power team, except for:

ENGINE 8 cylinders; 267 cu in, 4,375 cc (3.50 x 3.48 in, 88.9 x 88.4 mm); max power (DIN): 125 hp (92 kW) at 3,800 rpm; max torque (DIN): 215 lb ft, 29.7 kg m (291.3 Nm) at 2,400 rpm; max engine rpm: 4,200; 28.6 hp/l (21 kW/l); 5 crankshaft bearings; 1 Rochester 17059138 downdraught twin barrel carburettor; cooling system: 34.3 imp pt, 41.2 US pt, 19.5 l.

TRANSMISSION gearbox: Turbo-Hydramatic 350 automatic transmission (standard), hydraulic torque converter and planetary gears with 3 ratios, max ratio of converter at stall 2, possible manual selection; ratios: I 2.520, II 1.520, III 1, rev 1.930; steering column; axle ratio: 2.290.

PERFORMANCE max speed: about 103 mph, 165 km/h; power-weight ratio: 25.3 lb/hp (34.3 lb/kW), 11.5 kg/hp (15.6 kg/kW); speed in direct drive at 1,000 rpm: 27 mph, 43.4 km/h; consumption: 21.6 m/imp gal, 18 m/US gal, 13.1 l x 100 km.

STEERING servo (standard); turns lock to lock: 3.30.

BRAKES servo (standard).

ELECTRICAL EQUIPMENT 3,200 W battery.

DIMENSIONS AND WEIGHT weight: plus 130 lb, 59 kg.

OPTIONALS central lever.

155 hp power team

(for California only).

See 94 hp power team, except for:

ENGINE 8 cylinders; 305 cu in, 4,999 cc (3.74 x 3.48 in, 94.9 x 88.4 mm); compression ratio: 8.4:1; max power (DIN): 155 hp (114.1 kW) at 4,000 rpm; max torque (DIN): 225 lb ft, 31 kg m (304 Nm) at 2,400 rpm; max engine rpm: 4,400; 31 hp/l (22.8 kW/l); 5 crankshaft bearings; 1 Rochester 17059502 downdraught 4-barrel carburettor; cooling system: 31.7 imp pt, 38.1 US pt, 18 l.

TRANSMISSION gearbox: Turbo-Hydramatic 200 automatic transmission, hydraulic torque converter and planetary gears with 3 ratios, max ratio of converter at stall 2.35, possible manual selection; ratios: I 2.740, II 1.570, III 1, rev 2.070; lever: steering column; axle ratio: 2.290.

PERFORMANCE max speed: about 109 mph, 175 km/h; power-weight ratio: 20.4 lb/hp (27.7 lb/kW), 9.3 kg/hp (12.6 kg/kW); speed in direct drive at 1,000 rpm: 27.2 mph, 43.7 km/h; consumption: 20.5 m/imp gal, 17 m/US gal, 13.8 l x 100 km.

STEERING servo (standard); turns lock to lock: 3.30.

BRAKES servo (standard).

ELECTRICAL EQUIPMENT 3,200 W battery.

DIMENSIONS AND WEIGHT weight: plus 139 lb, 63 kg.

OPTIONALS central lever; 2.730 axle ratio.

160 hp power team

(not available in California).

See 155 hp power team, except for:

ENGINE max power (DIN): 160 hp (117.8 kW) at 4,000 rpm; max torque (DIN): 235 lb ft, 32.4 kg m (317.7 Nm) at 2,400 rpm; 32 hp/l (23.6 kW/l); 1 Rochester 17059202 downdraught 4-barrel carburettor.

CHEVROLET Impala Coupé

PERFORMANCE power-weight ratio: 19.8 lb/hp (26.9 lb/kW), 9 kg/hp (12.2 kg/kW).

Impala - Caprice Classic Series

PRICES EX WORKS:

1 Impala Coupé	$ 5,497
2 Impala Landau Coupé	$ 5,961
3 Impala Sedan	$ 5,597
4 Impala 6-pass. St. Wagon	$ 6,109
5 Impala 9-pass. St. Wagon	$ 6,239
6 Caprice Classic Coupé	$ 5,837
7 Caprice Classic Landau Coupé	$ 6,234
8 Caprice Classic Sedan	$ 5,962
9 Caprice Classic 6-pass. St. Wagon	$ 6,389
10 Caprice Classic 9-pass. St. Wagon	$ 6,544

For 5-litre engine add $ 235; for 5.7-litre engine add $ 360 (st. wagons add $ 125).

Power team:	Standard for:	Optional for:
90 hp	1,2,3,6,7,8	—
115 hp	1,2,3,6,7,8	—
125 hp	4,5,9,10	1,2,3,6,7,8
130 hp	4,5,9,10	1,2,3,6,7,8
165 hp	—	all
170 hp	—	all

90 hp power team

(for California only).

ENGINE front, 4 stroke; 6 cylinders, vertical, in line; 2? cu in, 4,097 cc (3.87 x 3.53 in, 98.2 x 89.6 mm); compressio ratio: 8.2:1; max power (DIN): 90 hp (66.2 kW) at 3,600 rpm max torque (DIN): 175 lb ft, 24.1 kg m (236.3 Nm) at 1,60 rpm; max engine rpm: 4,400; 22 hp/l (16.2 kW/l); cast iro block and head; 7 crankshaft bearings; valves: ove head, in line, push-rods and rockers, hydraulic tappet camshafts: 1, side; lubrication: gear pump, full flow filte 8.3 imp pt, 9.9 US pt, 4.7 l; 1 Rochester 17059314 dow draught single barrel carburettor; cleaner air syster exhaust system with catalytic converter; fuel feed: m chanical pump; water-cooled, 23.6 imp pt, 28.3 US p 13.4 l.

TRANSMISSION driving wheels: rear; gearbox: Turbo-H dramatic 350 automatic transmission, hydraulic torque co verter and planetary gears with 3 ratios, max ratio of conve ter at stall 2, possible manual selection; ratios: I 2.520, 1.520, III 1, rev 1.930; lever: steering column; final driv hypoid bevel; axle ratio: 2.730; width of rims: 6''; tyre FR78 x 15.

PERFORMANCE max speed: about 99 mph, 159 km/h; powe weight ratio: Impala Sedan 38.9 lb/hp (52.9 lb/kW), 17 kg/hp (24 kg/kW) - Caprice Classic Sedan 39.5 lb/hp (53 lb/kW), 17.9 kg/hp (24.3 kg/kW); speed in direct drive 1,000 rpm: 24.9 mph, 40 km/h; consumption: 18 m/imp ga 15 m/US gal, 15.7 l x 100 km.

CHEVROLET Caprice Classic Sedan

CHASSIS perimeter box-type with 2 cross members; front suspension: independent, wishbones, coil springs, anti-roll bar, telescopic dampers; rear: rigid axle, lower trailing radius arms, upper oblique torque arms, coil springs, anti-roll bar, telescopic dampers.

STEERING recirculating ball, servo; turns lock to lock: 3.16.

BRAKES front disc (diameter 11 in, 27.9 cm), front internal radial fins, rear drum, servo; swept area: total 329.8 sq in, 2,127 sq cm.

ELECTRICAL EQUIPMENT 12 V; 2,500 W battery; 37 A alternator; Delco-Remy high energy ignition system; 4 headlamps.

DIMENSIONS AND WEIGHT wheel base: 116 in, 295 cm; tracks: 61.80 in, 157 cm front, 60.80 in, 154 cm rear; length: 212.10 in, 538 cm; width: 76 in, 193 cm; height: sedans 56 in, 142 cm - coupés 55.30 in, 141 cm; ground clearance: 5.80 in, 14.7 cm; weight: Impala Coupé 3,485 lb, 1,580 kg - Sedan 3,500 lb, 1,587 kg - Caprice Classic Coupé 3,528 lb, 1,600 kg - Sedan 3,553 lb, 1,611 kg; turning circle: 44.6 ft, 13.6 m; fuel tank: 17.6 imp gal, 21 US gal, 80 l.

OPTIONALS central lever; limited slip differential; electric windows; heavy-duty suspension; GR78 x 15 or GR70 x 15 tyres with 7'' wide rims; automatic speed control; heated rear window; tilt of steering wheel; electric sunshine roof; vinyl roof; tinted glass; air-conditioning.

115 hp power team

(not available in California).

See 90 hp power team, except for:

ENGINE compression ratio: 8:1; max power (DIN): 115 hp (84.6 kW) at 3,800 rpm; max torque (DIN): 200 lb ft, 27.6 kg m (270.7 Nm) at 1,600 rpm; 28.1 hp/l (20.6 kW/l); 1 Rochester 17059014 downdraught single barrel carburettor.

TRANSMISSION axle ratio: 2.560.

PERFORMANCE power-weight ratio: Impala Sedan 30.4 lb/hp (41.4 lb/kW), 13.8 kg/hp (18.8 kg/kW) - Caprice Classic Sedan 30.9 lb/hp (42 lb/kW), 14 kg/hp (19 kg/kW).

125 hp power team

(for California only).

See 90 hp power team, except for:

ENGINE 8 cylinders; 305 cu in, 4,999 cc (3.74 x 3.48 in, 94.9 x 88.4 mm); compression ratio: 8.4:1; max power (DIN): 125 hp (92 kW) at 3,200 rpm; max torque (DIN): 235 lb ft, 32.4 kg m (317.7 Nm) at 2,000 rpm; max engine rpm: 3,600; 25 hp/l (18.4 kW/l); 5 crankshaft bearings; camshafts: 1, at centre of Vee; 1 Rochester 17059434 downdraught twin barrel carburettor; cooling system: 27.6 imp pt, 33.2 US pt, 15.7 l.

TRANSMISSION axle ratio: 2.410 - st. wagons 2.560; width of rims: st. wagons 7''; tyres: st. wagons HR78 x 15.

CHEVROLET Caprice Classic Coupé

CHEVROLET Caprice Classic Station Wagon

PERFORMANCE max speed: about 106 mph, 170 km/h; power-weight ratio: Impala 6-pass. St. Wagon 32 lb/hp (43.4 lb/kW), 14.5 kg/hp (19.7 kg/kW) - Caprice Classic 6-pass. St. Wagon 32.3 lb/hp (43.9 lb/kW), 14.7 kg/hp (19.9 kg/kW); speed in direct drive at 1,000 rpm: 29.3 mph, 47.2 km/h; consumption: 16.8 m/imp gal, 14 m/US gal, 16.8 l x 100 km.

STEERING turns lock to lock: st. wagons 3.30.

BRAKES (for st. wagons only) front disc (diameter 11.86 in, 30.1 cm); swept area: total 375.1 sq in, 2,420 sq cm.

ELECTRICAL EQUIPMENT 3,200 W battery.

DIMENSIONS AND WEIGHT (for st. wagons only) tracks: 62.20 in, 158 cm front, 64.10 in, 163 cm rear; length: 214.70 in, 545 cm; width: 79.10 in, 201 cm; height: 58 in, 147 cm; ground clearance: 5.90 in, 15 cm; weight: Impala 6-pass. St. Wagon 3,997 lb, 1,812 kg - Caprice Classic 6-pass. St. Wagon 4,041 lb, 1,832 kg; turning circle: 45.1 ft, 13.8 m; fuel tank: 18.3 imp gal, 22 US gal, 83 l.

OPTIONALS Turbo-Hydramatic 200 automatic transmission with 3 ratios (I 2.740, II 1.570, III 1, rev 2.070), max ratio of converter at stall 2.35, possible manual selection, 2.410 axle ratio.

130 hp power team

(not available in California).

See 125 hp power team, except for:

ENGINE max power (DIN): 130 hp (95.7 kW) at 3,200 rpm; max torque (DIN): 245 lb ft, 33.8 kg m (331.5 Nm) at 2,000 rpm; 26 hp/l (19.1 kW/l); 1 Rochester 17059134 downdraught twin barrel carburettor.

PERFORMANCE power-weight ratio: Impala 6-pass. St. Wagon 30.7 lb/hp (41.8 lb/kW), 13.9 kg/hp (18.9 kg/kW) - Caprice Classic 6-pass. St. Wagon 31.1 lb/hp (42.2 lb/kW), 14.1 kg/hp (19.1 kg/kW).

165 hp power team

(for California only).

See 125 hp power team, except for:

ENGINE 350 cu in, 5,736 cc (4 x 3.48 in, 101.6 x 88.4 mm); compression ratio: 8.2:1; max power (DIN): 165 hp (121.4 kW) at 3,800 rpm; max torque (DIN): 260 lb ft, 35.9 lb ft (352.1 Nm) at 2,400 rpm; 28.8 hp/l (21.2 kW/l); 1 Rochester 17059502 downdraught 4-barrel carburettor.

PERFORMANCE max speed: about 109 mph, 175 km/h; power-weight ratio: Impala Sedan 22 lb/hp (29.8 lb/kW), 10 kg/hp (13.5 kg/kW) - Caprice Classic Sedan 22.3 lb/hp (30.3 lb/kW), 10.1 kg/hp (13.7 kg/kW); consumption: 19.2 m/imp gal, 16 m/US gal, 14.7 l x 100 km.

DIMENSIONS AND WEIGHT weight: coupés and sedans plus 124 lb, 56 kg - st. wagons plus 13 lb, 6 kg.

OPTIONALS 3.080 axle ratio.

170 hp power team

(not available in California).

See 165 hp power team, except for:

ENGINE max power (DIN): 170 hp (125.1 kW) at 3,800 rpm; max torque (DIN): 270 lb ft, 37.2 kg m (364.8 Nm) at 2,400 rpm; 29.6 hp/l (21.8 kW/l); 1 Rochester 17059202 downdraught 4-barrel carburettor.

PERFORMANCE power-weight ratio: Impala Sedan 21.3 lb/hp (29 lb/kW), 9.7 kg/hp (13.1 kg/kW) - Caprice Classic Sedan 21.6 lb/hp (29.4 lb/kW), 9.8 kg/hp (13.3 kg/kW).

Corvette

PRICE IN GB: £ 11,362*
PRICE EX WORKS: $ 10,220

For 225 hp engine add $ 565.

195 hp power team

(standard).

ENGINE front, 4 stroke; 8 cylinders; 350 cu in, 5,736 cc (4 x 3.48 in, 101.6 x 88.4 mm); compression ratio: 8.2:1; max power (DIN): 195 hp (143.5 kW) at 4,000 rpm; max torque (DIN): 285 lb ft, 39.3 kg m (385.4 Nm) at 3,200 rpm; max engine rpm: 4,400; 34 hp/l (25 kW/l); cast iron block and head; 5 crankshaft bearings; valves: overhead, in line, push-rods and rockers, hydraulic tappets; camshafts: 1, at centre of Vee; lubrication: gear pump, full flow filter, 8.3 imp pt, 9.9 US pt, 4.7 l; 1 Rochester 17059203 (17059502 for California only) downdraught 4-barrel carburettor; cleaner air system; dual exhaust system with catalytic converter; fuel feed: mechanical pump; water-cooled, 34.5 imp pt, 41.4 US pt, 19.6 l, viscous-coupling thermostatic fan.

TRANSMISSION driving wheels: rear; clutch: single dry plate, semi-centrifugal; gearbox: mechanical (Turbo-Hydramatic 350 automatic transmission standard for California only); gears: 4, fully synchronized; ratios: I 2.850, II 2.020, III 1.350, IV 1, rev 2.850; lever: central; final drive: hypoid bevel, limited slip differential; axle ratio: 3.360 (3.550 for California only); width of rims: 8''; tyres: P225/70R x 15.

PERFORMANCE max speed: about 118 mph, 190 km/h; power-weight ratio: 17.3 lb/hp (23.5 lb/kW), 7.8 kg/hp (10.7 kg/kW); speed in direct drive at 1,000 rpm: 28 mph, 45 km/h; consumption: 19.2 m/imp gal, 16 m/US gal, 14.7 l x 100 km.

CHASSIS ladder frame with cross members; front suspension: independent, wishbones, coil springs, anti-roll bar, telescopic dampers; rear: independent, wishbones, semi-axles as upper arms, transverse semi-elliptic leaf-spring, trailing radius arms, telescopic dampers.

STEERING recirculating ball, servo; turns lock to lock: 2.92.

BRAKES disc (diameter 11.75 in, 30 cm), internal radial fins, servo; swept area: total 498.30 sq in, 3,214 sq cm.

195 HP POWER TEAM

ELECTRICAL EQUIPMENT 12 V; 3,500 W battery; 42 A alternator; Delco-Remy high energy ignition system; 4 retractable headlamps.

DIMENSIONS AND WEIGHT wheel base: 98 in, 249 cm; tracks: 58.70 in, 149 cm front, 59.50 in, 151 cm rear; length: 185.20 in, 470 cm; width: 69 in, 175 cm; height: 48 in, 122 cm; ground clearance: 4.30 in, 10.9 cm; weight: 3,374 lb, 1,530 kg; turning circle: 38.6 ft, 11.8 m; fuel tank: 20 imp gal, 24 US gal, 91 l.

BODY coupé, in plastic material; 2 doors; 2 seats, built-in headrests.

OPTIONALS Turbo-Hydramatic 350 automatic transmission with 3 ratios (I 2.520, II 1.520, III 1, rev 1.930), max ratio of converter at stall 2, possible manual selection, central lever, 3.550 axle ratio; Gymkhana suspension; tilt of steering wheel; heavy-duty battery; electric windows; heated rear window; tinted glass; removable tinted glass roof panels; automatic speed control; aluminum wheels; air-conditioning.

225 hp power team

(optional, not available in California).

See 195 hp power team, except for:

ENGINE compression ratio: 8.9:1; max power (DIN): 225 hp (165.6 kW) at 5,200 rpm; max torque (DIN): 270 lb ft, 37.2 kg m (364.8 Nm) at 3,600 rpm; max engine rpm: 5,600; 39.2 hp/l (28.9 kW/l); 1 Rochester 17059211 downdraught 4-barrel carburettor.

TRANSMISSION gearbox ratios: I 2.640, II 1.750, III 1.340, IV 1, rev 2.550; axle ratio: 3.700.

PERFORMANCE max speed: about 131 mph, 211 km/h; power-weight ratio: 15 lb/hp (20.4 lb/kW), 6.8 kg/hp (9.2 kg/kW).

OPTIONALS 3.360 axle ratio; 4-speed fully synchronized mechanical gearbox (I 2.430, II 1.610, III 1.230, IV 1, rev 2.350), 3.700 axle ratio; Turbo-Hydramatic 350 automatic transmission with 3 ratios (I 2.520, II 1.520, III 1, rev 1.930), max ratio of converter at stall 2, possible manual selection, central lever, 3.550 axle ratio.

CHEVROLET Corvette Coupé

CHRYSLER   USA

Le Baron Series

PRICES EX WORKS:

Coupé	$ 5,024
Sedan	$ 5,122
Town and Country St. Wagon	$ 5,955
Salon Coupé	$ 5,261
Salon Sedan	$ 5,489
Medallion Coupé	$ 5,735
Medallion Sedan	$ 5,963

Power team:	Standard for:	Optional for:
100	all	—
90	all	—
110	—	all
135	—	all
150	—	all
155	—	all
170	—	all
190	—	all
195	—	all

100 hp power team

(not available in California).

ENGINE front, 4 stroke; 6 cylinders, vertical, in line; 225 cu in, 3,687 cc (3.40 x 4.12 in, 86.4 x 104.6 mm); compression ratio: 8.4:1; max power (DIN): 100 hp (73.6 kW) at 3,600 rpm; max torque (DIN): 165 lb ft, 22.8 kg m (223.6 Nm) at 1,600 rpm; max engine rpm: 4,400; 27.1 hp/l (20 kW/l); cast iron block and head; 4 crankshaft bearings; valves: overhead, in line, push-rods and rockers; camshafts: 1, side; lubrication: rotary pump, full flow filter, 8.3 imp pt, 9.9 US pt, 4.7 l; 1 Holley R8523A downdraught single barrel carburettor; cleaner air system; exhaust system with catalytic converter; fuel feed: mechanical pump; water-cooled, 19.2 imp pt, 23 US pt, 10.9 l.

TRANSMISSION driving wheels: rear; clutch: single dry plate; gearbox: mechanical; gears: 4, fully synchronized

with overdrive/top; ratios: I 3.090, II 1.670, III 1, IV 0.710, rev 3.000; lever: central; final drive: hypoid bevel; axle ratio: 3.230 - St. Wagon 3.210; width of rims: 5.5''; tyres: FR78 x 15.

PERFORMANCE max speed: about 90 mph, 145 km/h; power-weight ratio: Sedan 33.3 lb/hp (45.2 lb/kW), 15.1 kg/hp (20.5 kg/kW) - Salon Sedan 33.5 lb/hp (45.5 lb/kW), 15.2 kg/hp (20.7 kg/kW) - Medallion Sedan 34.2 lb/hp (46.5 lb/kW), 15.5 kg/hp (21.1 kg/kW); speed in direct drive at 1,000 rpm: 25.5 mph, 41 km/h; consumption: 21.6 m/imp gal, 18 m/US gal, 13.1 l x 100 km.

CHASSIS integral with isolated front cross member; front suspension: independent, wishbones, transverse torsion bars, anti-roll bar, telescopic dampers; rear: rigid axle, semi-elliptic leafsprings, telescopic dampers.

STEERING recirculating ball, servo; turns lock to lock: 3.50.

BRAKES front disc (diameter 10.82 in, 27.5 cm),) front internal radial fins, rear drum, rear compensator, servo; swept area: total 355.24 sq in, 2,292 sq cm.

ELECTRICAL EQUIPMENT 12 V; 375 A battery; 60 A alternator; Essex or Prestalite transistorised ignition with electronic spark control; 4 headlamps.

DIMENSIONS AND WEIGHT wheel base: 112.70 in, 286 cm; tracks: 60 in, 152 cm front, 58,50 in, 149 cm rear; length: coupés 204.10 in, 518 cm - sedans 206.10 in, 523 cm - St. Wagon 202.80 in, 515 cm; width: 72.80 in, 185 cm - coupés 73.50 in, 187 cm; height: coupés 53 in,

CHRYSLER Le Baron Medallion Coupé

135 cm - sedans 55.30 in, 140 cm - St. Wagon 55.70 in 141 cm; ground clearance: 590 in, 15 cm - St. Wagor 6.20 in, 15.7 cm; weight: Coupé 3,269 lb, 1,482 kg Sedan 3,329 lb, 1,510 kg - Town and Country St. Wago 3,584 lb, 1,626 kg - Salon Coupé 3,286 lb, 1,491 kg Salon Sedan 3,351 lb, 1,520 kg - Medallion Coupé 3,34 lb, 1,516 kg - Medallion Sedan 3,425 lb, 1,554 kg; turnin circle: 43.5 ft, 13.2 m; fuel tank: 16.3 imp gal, 19.5 US gal, 74 l.

OPTIONALS heavy-duty cooling system; limited slip differential; 3.210 axle ratio; Torqueflite automatic trans mission with 3 ratios (I 2.450, II 1.450, III 1, re 2.220) max ratio of converter at stall 2.01, possible manua selection, steering column or central lever, 2.760 or 2.71 axle ratio; heavy-duty suspension; tilt of steering wheel automatic speed control; 500 A battery; heated rear win dow with 65 A alternator; electric windows; electri sunshine roof; tinted glass; vinyl roof; halogen head lamps; leather upholstery; air-conditioning; T-Bar roo (coupés only).

90 hp power team

(for California only).

See 100 hp power team, except for:

ENGINE max power (DIN): 90 hp (66.2 kW) at 3,600 rpm max torque (DIN): 160 lb ft, 22.1 kg m (216.7 Nm) a 1,600 rpm; 24.4 hp/l (18 kW/l); 1 Holley R8680A down draught single barrel carburettor.

TRANSMISSION gearbox: Torqueflite automatic transmission (standard), hydraulic torque converter and planetary gears with 3 ratios, max ratio of converter at stall 2.01, possible manual selection; ratios: I 2.450, II 1.450, III rev 2.220; lever: steering column or central; axle ratio: 3.230 - St. Wagon 3.210.

PERFORMANCE max speed: about 87 mph, 140 km/h; power-weight ratio: Sedan 37 lb/hp (50.3 lb/kW), 16.8 kg/hp (22.8 kg/kW) - Salon Sedan 37.2 lb/hp (50.6 lb/kW), 16.9 kg/hp (23 kg/kW) - Medallion Sedan 38 lb/hp (51.7 lb/kW), 17.3 kg/hp (23.5 kg/kW); speed in direct drive at 1,000 rpm: 24.2 mph, 38.9 km/h; consumption: 16.8 m/imp gal, 14 m/US gal, 16.8 l x 100 km.

OPTIONALS 3.210 axle ratio (except for St. Wagon).

110 hp power team

(not available in California).

See 100 hp power team, except for:

ENGINE max power (DIN): 110 hp (81 kW) at 3,600 rpm; max torque (DIN): 180 lb ft, 24.8 kg m (243.2 Nm) at 2,000 rpm; 29.8 hp/l (22 kW/l); 1 Carter BBD81995 downdraught twin barrel carburettor.

TRANSMISSION gearbox: Torqueflite automatic transmission (standard), hydraulic torque converter and planetary gears with 3 ratios, max ratio of converter at stall 2.01, possible manual selection; ratios: I 2.450, II 1.450, III 1, rev 2.220; lever: steering column or central; axle ratio: 2.940.

PERFORMANCE max speed: about 93 mph, 150 km/h; power-weight ratio: Sedan 30.6 lb/hp (41.6 lb/kW), 13.9 kg/hp (18.9 kg/kW) - Salon Sedan 30.8 lb/hp (41.9 lb/kW), 14 kg/hp (19 kg/kW) - Medallion Sedan 31.5 lb/hp (42.8 lb/kW), 14.3 kg/hp (19.4 kg/kW); speed in direct drive at 1,000 rpm: 25.9 mph, 41.7 km/h; consumption: 20.5 m/imp gal, 17 m/US gal, 13.8 l x 100 km.

DIMENSIONS AND WEIGHT weight: Coupé 3,271 lb, 1,484 kg - Sedan 3,370 lb, 1,529 kg - Town and Country St. Wagon 3,595 lb, 1,631 kg - Salon Coupé 3,288 lb, 1,491 kg - Salon Sedan 3,392 lb, 1,539 kg - Medallion Coupé 3,383 lb, 1,535 kg - Medallion Sedan 3,466 lb, 1,572 kg.

135 hp power team

(not available in California).

See 100 hp power team, except for:

ENGINE 8 cylinders; 318 cu in, 5,211 cc (3.91 x 3.31 in, 99.2 x 84 mm); compression ratio: 8.5:1; max power (DIN): 135 hp (99.4 kW) at 4,000 rpm; max torque (DIN): 250 lb ft, 34.5 kg m (338.3 Nm) at 1,600 rpm; 25.9 hp/l (19.1 kW/l); 5 crankshaft bearings; valves: hydraulic tappets; camshafts: 1, at centre of Vee; 1 Holley R8448A downdraught twin barrel carburettor; cooling system: 25 imp pt, 30 US pt, 14.2 l.

TRANSMISSION gearbox: Torqueflite automatic transmission (standard), hydraulic torque converter and planetary gears with 3 ratios, max ratio of converter at stall 1.90, possible manual selection; ratios: I 2.450, II 1.450, III 1, rev 2.220; lever: steering column or central; axle ratio: 2.470 - St. Wagon 2.450.

PERFORMANCE max speed: about 102 mph, 164 km/h; power-weight ratio: Sedan 25.4 lb/hp (34.5 lb/kW), 11.5 kg/hp (15.6 kg/kW) - Salon Sedan 25.5 lb/hp (34.7 lb/kW), 11.6 kg/hp (15.7 kg/kW) - Medallion Sedan 26.1 lb/hp (35.4 lb/kW), 11.8 kg/hp (16.1 kg/kW); speed in direct drive at 1,000 rpm: 25.5 mph, 41 km/h; consumption: 19.2 m/imp gal, 16 m/US gal, 14.7 l x 100 km.

ELECTRICAL EQUIPMENT 325 A battery.

DIMENSIONS AND WEIGHT weight: Coupé 3,365 lb, 1,526 kg - Sedan 3,425 lb, 1,554 kg - Town and Country St. Wagon 3,673 lb, 1,666 kg - Salon Coupé 3,382 lb, 1,534 kg - Salon Sedan 3,447 lb, 1,564 kg - Medallion Coupé 3,438 lb, 1,559 kg - Medallion Sedan 3,521 lb, 1,597 kg.

OPTIONALS 2.710 axle ratio.

150 hp power team

(not available in California).

See 100 hp power team, except for:

ENGINE 8 cylinders; 360 cu in, 5,900 cc (4 x 3.58 in, 101.6 x 89.6 mm); max power (DIN): 150 hp (110.4 kW) at 3,600 rpm; max torque (DIN): 265 lb ft, 36.6 kg m (358.9 Nm) at 2,400 rpm; 25.4 hp/l (18.7 kW/l); 5 crankshaft bearings; valves: hydraulic tappets; camshafts: 1, at

CHRYSLER Le Baron Medallion Coupé

centre of Vee; 1 Holley R8450A downdraught twin barrel carburettor; cooling system: 25 imp pt, 30 US pt, 14.2 l.

TRANSMISSION gearbox: Torqueflite automatic transmission (standard), hydraulic torque converter and planetary gears with 3 ratios, max ratio of converter at stall 1.90, possible manual selection; ratios: I 2.450, II 1.450, III 1, rev 2.220; lever: steering column or central; axle ratio: 2.450.

PERFORMANCE max speed: about 106 mph, 170 km/h; power-weight ratio: Sedan 23.3 lb/hp (31.6 lb/kW), 10.6 kg/hp (14.3 kg/kW) - Salon Sedan 23.4 lb/hp (31.8 lb/kW), 10.6 kg/hp (14.4 kg/kW) - Medallion Sedan 23.9 lb/hp (32.5 lb/kW), 10.8 kg/hp (14.7 kg/kW); speed in direct drive at 1,000 rpm: 29.3 mph, 47.2 km/h; consumption: 16.8 m/imp gal, 14 m/US gal, 16.8 l x 100 km.

ELECTRICAL EQUIPMENT 430 A battery.

DIMENSIONS AND WEIGHT weight: Coupé 3,431 lb, 1,556 kg - Sedan 3,491 lb, 1,584 kg - Town and Country St. Wagon 3,706 lb, 1,681 kg - Salon Coupé 3,448 lb, 1,564 kg - Salon Sedan 3,513 lb, 1,594 kg - Medallion Coupé 3,504 lb, 1,589 kg - Medallion Sedan 3,587 lb, 1,627 kg.

OPTIONALS 2.710 axle ratio.

155 hp power team

(for California only).

See 100 hp power team, except for:

ENGINE 8 cylinders; 318 cu in, 5,211 cc (3.91 x 3.31 in, 99.2 x 84 mm); compression ratio: 8.5:1; max power (DIN): 155 hp (114.1 kW) at 4,000 rpm; max torque (DIN): 245 lb ft, 33.8 kg m (331.5 Nm) 1,600 rpm; 29.7 hp/l (21.9 kW/l); 5 crankshaft bearings; valves: hydraulic tappets; camshafts: 1, at centre of Vee; 1 Carter TQ9156S downdraught 4-barrel carburettor; cooling system: 25 imp pt, 30 US pt, 14.2 l.

TRANSMISSION gearbox: Torqueflite automatic transmission (standard), hydraulic torque converter and planetary gears with 3 ratios, max ratio of converter at stall 1.90, possible manual selection; ratios: I 2.450, II 1.450, III 1, rev 2.220; lever: steering column or central; axle ratio: 2.470 - St. Wagon 2.450.

PERFORMANCE max speed: about 106 mph, 170 km/h; power-weight ratio: Sedan 22.1 lb/hp (30 lb/kW), 10 kg/hp (13.6 kg/kW) - Salon Sedan 22.2 lb/hp (30.2 lb/kW), 10.1 kg/hp (13.7 kg/kW) - Medallion Sedan 22.7 lb/hp (30.9 lb/kW), 10.3 kg/hp (14 kg/kW); speed in direct drive at 1,000 rpm: 29.3 mph, 47.2 km/h; consumption: 16.8 m/imp gal, 14 m/US gal, 16.8 l x 100 km.

ELECTRICAL EQUIPMENT 325 A battery.

DIMENSIONS AND WEIGHT weight: Coupé 3,365 lb, 1,526 kg - Sedan 3,425 lb, 1,554 kg - Town and Country St. Wagon 3,673 lb, 1,666 kg - Salon Coupé 3,382 lb, 1,534 kg - Salon Sedan 3,447 lb, 1,564 kg - Medallion Coupé 3,438 lb, 1,559 kg - Medallion Sedan 3,521 lb, 1,597 kg.

OPTIONALS 2.450 axle ratio (except for St. Wagon).

170 hp power team

(for California only).

See 100 hp power team, except for:

ENGINE 8 cylinders; 360 cu in, 5,900 cc (4 x 3.58 in, 101.6 x 89.6 mm); max power (DIN): 170 hp (125.1 kW) at 4,000 rpm; max torque (DIN): 270 lb ft, 37.2 kg m (364.8 Nm) at 1,600 rpm; 28.8 hp/l (21.2 kW/l); 5 crankshaft bearings; valves: hydraulic tappets; camshafts: 1, at centre of Vee; 1 Carter TQ9198S downdraught 4-barrel carburettor; cooling system: 25 imp pt, 30 US pt, 14.2 l.

TRANSMISSION gearbox: Torqueflite automatic transmission (standard), hydraulic torque converter and planetary gears with 3 ratios, max ratio of converter at stall 1.90, possible manual selection; ratios: I 2.450, II 1.450, III 1, rev 2.220; lever: steering column or central; axle ratio: 2.710.

PERFORMANCE max speed: about 109 mph, 175 km/h; power-weight ratio: Sedan 21 lb/hp (28.5 lb/kW), 9.5 kg/hp (12.9 kg/kW) - Salon Sedan 21.1 lb/hp (28.7 lb/kW), 9.6 kg/hp (13 kg/kW) - Medallion Sedan 21.5 lb/hp (29.3 lb/kW), 9.8 kg/hp (13.3 kg/kW); speed in direct drive at 1,000 rpm: 27.2 mph, 43.7 km/h; consumption: 16.8 m/imp gal, 14 m/US gal, 16.8 l x 100 km.

ELECTRICAL EQUIPMENT 430 A battery.

DIMENSIONS AND WEIGHT weight: Coupé 3,504 lb, 1,589 kg - Sedan 3,564 lb, 1,617 kg - Town and Country St. Wagon 3,770 lb, 1,710 kg - Salon Coupé 3,521 lb, 1,597 kg - Salon Sedan 3,586 lb, 1,627 kg - Medallion Coupé 3,577 lb, 1,623 kg - Medallion Sedan 3,660 lb, 1,660 kg.

190 hp power team

(for California only).

See 100 hp power team, except for:

ENGINE 8 cylinders; 360 cu in, 5,900 cc (4 x 3.58 in, 101.6 x 89.6 mm); compression ratio: 8:1; max power (DIN): 190 hp (139.8 kW) at 4,000 rpm; max torque (DIN): 275 lb ft, 37.9 kg m (371.7 Nm) at 2,000 rpm; 32.2 hp/l (23.7 kW/l); 5 crankshaft bearings; valves: hydraulic tappets; camshafts: 1, at centre of Vee; 1 Carter TQ9198S downdraught 4-barrel carburettor; dual exhaust system with catalytic converter; cooling system: 25 imp pt, 30 US pt, 14.2 l.

TRANSMISSION gearbox: Torqueflite automatic transmission (standard), hydraulic torque converter and planetary gears with 3 ratios, max ratio of converter at stall 1.90, possible manual selection; ratios: I 2.450, II 1.450, III 1, rev 2.220; lever: steering column or central; axle ratio: 3.210.

PERFORMANCE max speed: about 112 mph, 180 km/h; power-weight ratio: Sedan 18.8 lb/hp (25.5 lb/kW), 8.5 kg/hp (11.6 kg/kW) - Salon Sedan 18.9 lb/hp (25.6 lb/kW), 8.6 kg/hp (11.6 kg/kW) - Medallion Sedan 19.3 lb/hp (26.2 lb/kW), 8.7 kg/hp (11.9 kg/kW);speed in direct drive at 1,000 rpm: 28 mph, 45 km/h; consumption: 16.8 m/imp gal, 14 m/US gal, 16.8 l x 100 km.

ELECTRICAL EQUIPMENT 430 A battery.

DIMENSIONS AND WEIGHT weight: Coupé 3,504 lb, 1,589 kg - Sedan 3,564 lb, 1,617 kg - Town and Country St. Wagon 3,770 lb, 1,710 kg - Salon Coupé 3,521 lb, 1,597 kg - Salon Sedan, 3,586 lb, 1,627 kg - Medallion Coupé 3,577 lb, 1,623 kg - Medallion Sedan 3,660 lb, 1,660 kg.

195 hp power team

(not available in California).

See 100 hp power team, except for:

ENGINE 8 cylinders; 360 cu in, 5,900 cc (4 x 3.58 in, 101.6 x 89.6 mm); compression ratio: 8:1; max power (DIN): 195 hp (143.5 kW) at 4,000 rpm; max torque (DIN): 280 lb ft, 38.6 kg m (378.6 Nm) at 2,400 rpm; 33 hp/l (24.3 kW/l); 5 crankshaft bearings; valves: hydraulic tappets; camshafts: 1, at centre of Vee; 1 Carter TQ9196S downdraught 4-barrel carburettor; dual exhaust system with catalytic converter; cooling system: 25 imp pt, 30 US pt, 14.2 l.

TRANSMISSION gearbox: Torqueflite automatic transmission (standard), hydraulic torque converter and planetary gears with 3 ratios, max ratio of converter at stall 1.90, possible manual selection; ratios: I 2.450, II 1.450, III 1, rev 2.220; lever: steering column or central; axle ratio: 3.210.

PERFORMANCE max speed: about 115 mph, 185 km/h; power-weight ratio: Sedan 18.3 lb/hp (24.8 lb/kW), 8.3 kg/hp (11.3 kg/kW) - Salon Sedan 18.4 lb/hp (25 lb/kW),

195 HP POWER TEAM

8.3 kg/hp (11.3 kg/kW) - Medallion Sedan 18.7 lb/hp (25.5 lb/kW), 8.5 kg/hp (11.6 kg/kW); speed in direct drive at 1,000 rpm: 28.7 mph, 46.2 km/h; consumption: 16.8 m/imp gal, 14 m/US gal, 16.8 l x 100 km.

ELECTRICAL EQUIPMENT 430 A battery.

DIMENSIONS AND WEIGHT weight: Coupé 3,504 lb, 1,589 kg - Sedan 3,564 lb, 1,617 kg - Town and Country St. Wagon 3,770 lb, 1,710 kg - Salon Coupé 3,521 lb, 1,597 kg - Salon Sedan 3,586 lb, 1,627 kg - Medallion Coupé 3,577 lb, 1,623 kg - Medallion Sedan, 3,660 lb, 1,660 kg.

Cordoba

PRICE EX WORKS: $ 5,995

135 hp power team

(optional, not available in California).

ENGINE front, 4 stroke; 8 cylinders; 318 cu in, 5,211 cc (3.91 x 3.31 in, 99.2 x 84 mm); compression ratio: 8.5:1; max power (DIN): 135 hp (99.4 kW) at 4,000 rpm; max torque (DIN): 250 lb ft, 34.5 kg m (338.3 Nm) at 1,600 rpm; max engine rpm: 4,400; 25.9 hp/l (19.1 kW/l); cast iron block and head; 5 crankshaft bearings; valves: overhead, in line, push-rods and rockers, hydraulic tappets; camshafts: 1, at centre of Vee; lubrication: rotary pump, full flow filter, 8.3 imp pt, 9.9 US pt, 4.7 l; 1 Holley R8448A downdraught twin barrel carburettor; cleaner air system; exhaust system with catalytic converter; fuel feed: mechanical pump; water-cooled, 25 imp pt, 30 US pt, 14.2 l.

TRANSMISSION driving wheels: rear; gearbox: Torqueflite automatic transmission, hydraulic torque converter and planetary gears with 3 ratios, max ratio of converter at stall 1.90, possible manual selection; ratios: I 2.450, II 1.450, III 1, rev 2.220; lever: steering column; final drive: hypoid bevel; axle ratio: 2.710; width of rims: 5.5''; tyres: FR78 x 15.

PERFORMANCE max speed: about 103 mph, 165 km/h; power-weight ratio: 27.2 lb/hp (36.9 lb/kW), 12.3 kg/hp (16.7 kg/kW); speed in direct drive at 1,000 rpm: 28.5 mph, 45.8 km/h; consumption: 19.2 m/imp gal, 16 m/US gal, 14.7 l x 100 km.

CHASSIS integral with isolated front cross member; front suspension: independent, wishbones, longitudinal torsion bars, anti-roll bar, telescopic dampers; rear: rigid axle, semi-eeliptic leafsprings, anti-roll bar, telescopic dampers.

STEERING recirculating ball, servo; turns lock to lock: 3.50.

BRAKES front disc (diameter 11.58 in, 29.4 cm), front internal radial fins, rear drum, rear compensator, servo; swept area: total 375.3 sq in, 2,421 sq cm.

CHRYSLER Cordoba

CHRYSLER Cordoba

ELECTRICAL EQUIPMENT 12 V; 325 A battery; 60 A alternator; Essex or Prestolite transistorized ignition with electronic spark control; 4 headlamps.

DIMENSIONS AND WEIGHT wheel base: 114.90 in, 292 cm; tracks: 61.90 in, 157 cm front, 62 in, 157 cm rear; length: 215.80 in, 548 cm; width: 77.10 in, 196 cm; height: 52.10 in, 135 cm; ground clearance: 5.20 in, 13.2 cm; weight: 3,668 lb, 1,664 kg; turning circle: 44.9 ft, 13.7 m; fuel tank: 17.6 imp gal, 21 US gal, 80 l.

BODY hardtop; 2 doors; 6 seats, separate front seats with built-in headrests.

OPTIONALS heavy-duty cooling system; central lever; limited slip differential; GR78 x 15 or HR78 x 15 tyres; GR60 x 15 tyres with 7'' wide rims; heavy-duty suspension; tilt of steering wheel; speed control device; reclining backrests; electric windows; tinted glass; heated rear window with 100 A alternator; electric sunshine roof; Landau vinyl roof; T-Bar roof; air-conditioning; Special Appearance equipment.

150 hp power team

(standard, not available in California).

See 135 hp power team, except for:

ENGINE 360 cu in, 5,900 cc (4 x 3.58 in, 101.6 x 89.6 mm); compression ratio: 8.4:1; max power (DIN): 150 hp (110.4 kW) at 3,600 rpm; max torque (DIN): 265 lb ft 36.6 kg m (358.9 Nm) at 2,400 rpm; 25.4 hp/l (18.7 kW/l); 1 Holley R8450A downdraught twin barrel carburettor; cooling system: 26.6 imp pt, 31.9 US pt, 15.1 l.

TRANSMISSION axle ratio: 2.450; tyres: GR78 x 15 (standard).

PERFORMANCE max speed: about 106 mph, 170 km/h; power-weight ratio: 24.7 lb/hp (33.6 lb/kW), 11.2 kg/hp (15.2 kg/kW); consumption: 16.8 m/imp gal, 14 m/US gal, 16.8 l x 100 km.

ELECTRICAL EQUIPMENT 430 A battery.

DIMENSIONS AND WEIGHT weight: 3,709 lb, 1,682 kg.

OPTIONALS 2.710 axle ratio.

155 hp power team

(optional for California only).

See 135 hp power team, except for:

ENGINE max power (DIN): 155 hp (114.1 kW) at 4,000 rpm max torque (DIN): 245 lb ft, 33.8 kg m (331.5 Nm) at 1,600 rpm; 29.7 hp/l (21.9 kW/l); 1 Carter TQ9195S downdraught 4-barrel carburettor.

PERFORMANCE max speed: about 108 mph, 174 km/h; power-weight ratio: 23.7 lb/hp (32.1 lb/kW), 10.7 kg/hp (14.6 kg/kW); consumption: 15.6 m/imp gal, 13 m/US gal, 18.1 l x 100 km.

170 hp power team

(optional for California only).

See 135 hp power team, except for:

ENGINE 360 cu in, 5,900 (4 x 3.58 in, 101.6 x 89.6 mm) compression ratio: 8.4:1; max power (DIN): 170 hp (125 kW) at 4,000 rpm; max torque (DIN): 270 lb ft, 37.2 kg (364.8 Nm) at 1,600 rpm; 28.8 hp/l (21.2 kW/l); 1 Carter TQ9198S downdraught 4-barrel carburettor; cooling system 26.6 imp pt, 31.9 US pt, 15.1 l.

TRANSMISSION tyres: GR78 x 15 (standard).

PERFORMANCE max seped: about 112 mph, 180 km/ power-weight ratio: 22.4 lb/hp (30.5 lb/kW), 10.2 kg/h (13.8 kg/kW); consumption: 15.6 m/imp gal, 13 m/U gal, 18.1 l x 100 km.

ELECTRICAL EQUIPMENT 430 A battery.

DIMENSIONS AND WEIGHT weight: 3,816 lb, 1,731 kg.

190 hp power team

(optional for California only).

See 135 hp power team, except for:

ENGINE 360 cu in, 5,900 cc (4 x 3.58 in, 101.6 x 89.6 mm compression ratio: 8:1; max power (DIN): 190 hp (139 kW) at 4,000 rpm; max torque (DIN): 275 lb ft, 37.9 m (371.7 Nm) at 2,000 rpm; 32.2 hp/l (23.7 kW/l); Carter TQ9198S downdraught 4-barrel carburettor; du exhaust system with catalytic converter; cooling system 26.6 imp pt, 31.9 US pt, 15.1 l.

TRANSMISSION axle ratio: 3.210; tyres: GR78 x 15 (standard).

PERFORMANCE max speed: about 115 mph, 185 km/ power-weight ratio: 20.1 lb/hp (27.3 lb/kW), 9.1 kg/h (12.4 kg/kW); speed in direct drive at 1,000 rpm: 30 mph, 49 km/h; consumption: 15.6 m/imp gal, 13 m/U gal, 18.1 l x 100 km.

ELECTRICAL EQUIPMENT 430 A battery.

DIMENSIONS AND WEIGHT weight: 3,816 lb, 1,731 kg

195 hp power team

(optional, not available in California).

See 135 hp power team, except for:

ENGINE 360 cu in, 5,900 cc (4 x 3.58 in, 101.6 x 89.6 mm compression ratio: 8:1; max power (DIN): 195 hp (143 kW) at 4,000 rpm; max torque (DIN): 280 lb ft, 38.6 kg (378.6 Nm) at 2,400 rpm; 33 hp/l (24.3 kW/l); 1 Carte TQ9196S downdraught 4-barrel carburettor; dual exhaus system with catalytic converter; cooling system: 26.6 i pt, 31-9 US pt, 15.1 l.

TRANSMISSION tyres: GR78 x 15 (standard).

RFORMANCE max speed: about 118 mph, 190 km/h; wer-weight ratio: 19.6 lb/hp (26.6 lb/kW), 8.9 kg/hp 2.1 kg/kW); speed in direct drive at 1,000 rpm: 30.4 ph, 49 km/h; consumption: 15.6 m/imp gal, 13 m/US l, 18.1 l x 100 km.

ECTRICAL EQUIPMENT 430 A battery.

MENSIONS AND WEIGHT weight: 3,816 lb, 1,731 kg.

TIONALS 3.210 axle ratio.

Newport - New Yorker

ICES EX WORKS:

Newport 4-dr Pillared Hardtop	$ 6.089
New Yorker 4-dr Pillared Hardtop	$ 8.631

wer team:	Standard for:	Optional for:
0 hp	1	—
5 hp	—	both
0 hp	2	1
5 hp	—	1
0 hp	—	both
0 hp	—	2
5 hp	—	2

110 hp power team

ot available in California).

GINE front, 4 stroke; 6 cylinders, vertical, in line; 5 cu in, 3,687 cc (3.40 x 4.12 in, 86.4 x 104.6 mm); comession ratio: 8.4:1; max power (DIN): 110 hp (81 kW) 3,600 rpm; max torque (DIN): 180 lb ft, 24.8 kg m 43.2 Nm) at 2,000 rpm; max engine rpm: 4,400; 29.8 /l (22 kW/l); 4 crankshaft bearings; valves: overhead, line, push-rods and rockers; camshafts: 1, side; lucation: rotary pump, full flow filter, 8.3 imp pt, 9.9 pt, 4.7 l; 1 Carter BBD8199S downdraught twin barrel rburettor; cleaner air system; exhaust system with talytic converter; fuel feed: mechanical pump; wateroled, 19.2 imp pt, 23 US pt, 10.9 l.

RANSMISSION driving wheels: rear; gearbox: Torqueflite tomatic transmission, hydraulic torque converter and anetary gears with 3 ratios, max ratio of converter at all 1.90, possible manual selection; ratios: I 2.450, II 450, III 1, rev 2.220; lever: steering column; final drive: poid bevel; axle ratio: 2.940; width of rims: 5.5''; tyres: 95/75R x 15.

ERFORMANCE max speed: about 93 mph, 149 km/h; wer-weight ratio: 32 lb/hp (43.5 lb/kW), 14.5 kg/hp 9.7 kg/kW); speed in direct drive at 1,000 rpm: 25.9 ph, 41.7 km/h; consumption: 20.5 m/imp gal, 17 m/US l, 13.8 l x 100 km.

HASSIS integral with isolated front cross member; front spension: independent, wishbones, longitudinal torsion

CHRYSLER Newport 4-dr Pillared Hardtop

bars, anti-roll bar, telescopic dampers; rear: rigid axle, semielliptic leafsprings, telescopic dampers.

STEERING recirculating ball, servo; turns lock to lock: 3.50.

BRAKES front disc (diameter 11.58 in, 29.4 cm), front internal radial fins, rear drum, rear compensator, servo; swept area: total 375.3 sq in, 2,421 sq cm.

ELECTRICAL EQUIPMENT 12 V; 375 A battery; 65 A alternator; Essex or Prestolite transistorized ignition with electronic spark control; 4 headlamps.

DIMENSIONS AND WEIGHT wheel base: 118.50 in, 301 cm; tracks: 61.90 in, 157 cm front, 62 in, 157 cm rear; length: 220.20 in, 559 cm; width: 77.10 in, 196 cm; height: 54.50 in, 138 cm; ground clearance: 5.30 in, 13.5 cm; weight: 3,522 lb, 1,598 kg; turning circle: 45.8 ft, 13.9 m; fuel tank: 17.6 imp gal, 21 US gal, 80 l.

BODY hardtop; 4 doors; 6 seats, bench front seats with built-in headrests.

OPTIONALS heavy-duty cooling system; limited slip differential; P205/75R x 15 tyres; P225/70R x 15, FR70 x 15 or GR70 x 15 tyres with 7'' wide rims; heavy-duty suspension; tilt of steering wheel heavy-duty battery; halogen headlamps; heated rear window with 100 A alternator; electric windows; electric sunshine roof; speed control device; reclining backrests; Landau vinyl roof; air-conditioning.

CHRYSLER Newport 4-dr Pillared Hardtop

135 hp power team

(not available in California).

See 110 hp power team, except for:

ENGINE 8 cylinders; 318 cu in, 5,211 cc (3.91 x 3.31 in, 99.2 x 84 mm); compression ratio: 8.5:1; max power (DIN): 135 hp (99.4 kW) at 4,000 rpm; max torque (DIN): 250 lb ft, 34.5 kg m (338.3 Nm) at 1,600 rpm; 25.9 hp/l (19.1 kW/l); 5 crankshaft bearings; valves: hydraulic tappets; camshafts: 1, at centre of Vee; 1 Holley R8448A downdraught twin barrel carburettor; cooling system: 25 imp pt, 30 US pt, 14.2 l.

TRANSMISSION axle ratio: 2.450; width of rims: New Yorker 6''; tyres: New Yorker P205/75R x 15.

PERFORMANCE max speed: about 96 mph, 155 km/h; power-weight ratio: Newport 26.6 lb/hp (36.1 lb/kW), 12.1 kg/hp (16.4 kg/kW) - New Yorker 27.3 lb/hp (37.1 lb/kW), 12.4 kg/hp (16.8 kg/kW); consumption: 19.2 m/imp gal, 16 m/US gal, 14.7 l x 100 km.

BRAKES (New Yorker only) swept area: total 390.37 sq in, 2,518 sq cm.

ELECTRICAL EQUIPMENT 325 A battery.

DIMENSIONS AND WEIGHT length: New Yorker 221.50 in, 563 cm; weight: New Yorker 3,689 lb, 1,673 kg - Newport 3,593 lb, 1,630 kg; turning circle: New Yorker 45.4 ft, 13.8 m.

BODY electric windows (standard for New Yorker only).

CHRYSLER New Yorker Fifth Avenue Edition 4-dr Pillared Hardtop

279

135 HP POWER TEAM

OPTIONALS 2.710 axle ratio; Fifth Avenue Edition equipment (New Yorker only).

150 hp power team

(not available in California).

See 110 hp power team, except for:

ENGINE 8 cylinders; 360 cu in, 5,900 cc (4 x 3.58 in, 101.6 x 89.6 mm); max power (DIN): 150 hp (110.4 kW) at 3,600 rpm; max torque (DIN): 265 lb ft, 36.6 kg m (358.9 Nm) at 2,400 rpm; 25.4 hp/l (18.7 kW/l); 5 crankshaft bearings; valves: hydraulic tappets; camshafts: 1, at centre of Vee; 1 Holley R8450A downdraught twin barrel carburettor; cooling system: 26.6 imp pt, 31.9 US pt, 15.1 l.

TRANSMISSION axle ratio: 2.450; width of rims: New Yorker 6''; tyres: New Yorker P205/75R x 15.

PERFORMANCE max speed: about 99 mph, 160 km/h; power-weight ratio: New Yorker 25.3 lb/hp (34.3 lb/kW), 11.5 kg/hp (15.6 kg/kW) - Newport 24.4 lb/hp (33.1 lb/kW), 11 kg/hp (15 kg/kW); speed in direct drive at 1,000 rpm: 27.6 mph, 44.4 km/h; consumption: 16.8 m/imp gal, 14 m/US gal, 16.8 l x 100 km.

BRAKES (New Yorker only) swept area: total 390.37 sq in, 2,518 sq cm.

ELECTRICAL EQUIPMENT 430 A battery; 4 retractable headlamps.

DIMENSIONS AND WEIGHT length: New Yorker 221.50 in, 563 cm; weight: New Yorker 3,790 lb, 1,719 kg - Newport 3,656 lb, 1,658 kg; turning circle: New Yorker 45.4 ft, 13.8 m.

BODY electric windows (standard for New Yorker only).

OPTIONALS 2.710 axle ratio; Fifth Avenue Edition equipment (New Yorker only).

155 hp power team

(for California only).

See 110 hp power team, except for:

ENGINE 8 cylinders; 318 cu in, 5,211 cc (3,91 x 3,31 in, 99.2 x 84 mm); compression ratio: 8.5:1; max power (DIN): 155 hp (114.1 kW) at 4,000 rpm; max torque (DIN): 245 lb ft, 33.8 kg m (331.5 Nm) at 1,600 rpm; 29.7 hp/l (21.9 kW/l); 5 crankshaft bearings; valves: hydraulic tappets; camshafts: 1, at centre of Vee; 1 Carter TQ9156S downdraught 4-barrel carburettor; cooling system: 25 imp pt, 30 US pt, 14.2 l.

TRANSMISSION axle ratio: 2.710.

PERFORMANCE max speed: about 103 mph, 165 km/h; power-weight ratio: 23.1 lb/hp (31.5 lb/kW), 10.5 kg/hp (14.3 kg/kW); speed in direct drive at 1,000 rpm: 25.6 mph, 41.2 km/h; consumption: 15.6 m/imp gal, 13 m/US gal, 18.1 l x 100 km.

ELECTRICAL EQUIPMENT 325 A battery.

DIMENSIONS AND WEIGHT weight: Newport 3,593 lb, 1,630 kg.

170 hp power team

(for California only).

See 110 hp power team, except for:

ENGINE 8 cylinders; 360 cu in, 5,900 cc (4 x 3.58 in, 101.6 x 89.6 mm); max power (DIN): 170 hp (125.1 kW) at 4,000 rpm; max torque (DIN): 270 lb ft, 37.2 kg m (364.8 Nm) at 1,600 rpm; 28.8 hp/l (21.2 kW/l); 5 crankshaft bearings; valves: hydraulic tappets; camshafts: 1, at centre of Vee; 1 Carter TQ9198S downdraught 4-barrel carburettor; cooling system: 26.6 imp pt, 31.9 US pt, 15.1 l.

TRANSMISSION axle ratio: 2.710; width of rims: New Yorker 6''; tyres: New Yorker P205/75R x 15.

PERFORMANCE max speed: about 106 mph, 170 km/h; power-weight ratio: Newport 22.1 lb/hp (30.1 lb/kW), 10 kg/hp (13.6 kg/kW) - New Yorker 22.9 lb/hp (31.2 lb/kW), 10.4 kg/hp (14.1 kg/kW); speed in direct drive at 1,000 rpm: 26.4 mph, 42.5 km/h; consumption: 15.6 m/imp gal, 13 m/US gal, 18.1 l x 100 km.

BRAKES (New Yorker only) swept area: total 390.37 sq in, 2,518 sq cm.

ELECTRICAL EQUIPMENT 430 A battery.

DIMENSIONS AND WEIGHT length: New Yorker 221.50 in, 563 cm; weight: Newport 3,763 lb, 1,707 kg - New Yorker 3,897 lb, 1,768 kg; turning circle: New Yorker 45.4 ft, 13.8 m.

BODY electric windows (standard for New Yorker only).

OPTIONALS Fifth Avenue Edition equipment (New Yorker only).

190 hp power team

(for California only).

See 110 hp power team, except for:

ENGINE 8 cylinders; 360 cu in, 5,900 cc (4 x 3.58 in, 101.6 x 89.6 mm); compression ratio: 8:1; max power (DIN): 190 hp (139.8 kW) at 4,000 rpm; max torque (DIN): 275 lb ft, 37.9 kg m (371.7 Nm) at 2,000 rpm; 32.2 hp/l (23.7 kW/l); 5 crankshaft bearings; valves: hydraulic tappets; camshafts: 1, at centre of Vee; 1 Carter TQ9196S downdraught 4-barrel carburettor; dual exhaust system with catalytic converter; cooling system: 26.6 imp pt, 31.9 US pt, 15.1 l.

TRANSMISSION axle ratio: 3.210; width of rims: 6''; tyres: P205/75R x 15.

PERFORMANCE max speed: 109 mph, 175 km/h; power-weight ratio: 20.5 lb/hp (27.9 lb/kW), 9.3 kg/hp (12.6 kg/kW); speed in direct drive at 1,000 rpm: 27.2 mph, 43.7 km/h; consumption: 15.6 m/imp gal, 13 m/US gal, 18.1 l x 100 km.

BRAKES swept area: total 390.37 sq in, 2,518 sq cm.

ELECTRICAL EQUIPMENT 430 A battery.

DIMENSIONS AND WEIGHT length: 221.50 in, 563 cm; weight: 3,897 lb, 1,768 kg; turning circle: 45.4 ft, 13.8 m.

BODY electric windows (standard).

OPTIONALS Fifth Avenue Edition equipment.

195 hp power team

(not available in California).

See 110 hp power team, except for:

ENGINE 8 cylinders; 360 cu, in 5,900 cc (4 x 3.58 in, 101.6 x 89.6 mm); compression ratio: 8:1; max power (DIN): 195 hp (143.5 kW) at 4,000 rpm; max torque (DIN): 280 lb ft, 38.6 kg m (378.6 Nm) at 2,400 rpm; 33 hp/l (24.3 kW/l); 5 crankshaft bearings; valves: hydraulic tappets; camshafts: 1, at centre of Vee; 1 Carter TQ9196S downdraught 4-barrel carburettor; dual exhaust system with catalytic converter; cooling system: 26.6 imp pt, 31.9 US pt, 15.1 l.

TRANSMISSION axle ratio: 3.210; width of rims: 6''; tyres: P205/75R x 15.

CHRYSLER New Yorker Fifth Avenue Edition 4-dr Pillared Hardtop

PERFORMANCE max speed: about 112 mph, 180 km/h; power-weight ratio: 20 lb/hp (27.2 lb/kW), 9.1 kg/hp (1 kg/kW); speed in direct drive at 1,000 rpm: 28 mph, km/h; consumption: 15.6 m/imp gal, 13 m/US gal, l x 100 km.

BRAKES swept area: total 390.37 sq in, 2,518 sq cm.

ELECTRICAL EQUIPMENT 430 A battery.

DIMENSIONS AND WEIGHT length: 221.50 in, 563 c weight: 3,897 lb, 1,768 kg; turning circle: 45.4 ft, 13.8

BODY electric windows (standard).

OPTIONALS Fifth Avenue Edition equipment.

CLÉNET   US

Roadster

PRICE EX WORKS: $ 65,000

ENGINE Lincoln, front, 4 stroke; 8 cylinders; 351 cu 5,732 cc (4 x 3.50 in, 101.6 x 88.8 mm); compression rat

CLÉNET Roadster

CLÉNET 4-passeger Convertible

:1; cast iron block and head; 5 crankshaft bearings; alves: overhead, in line, push-rods and rockers, hydrauc tappets; camshafts: 1, at centre of Vee; lubrication: tary pump, full flow filter, 8.3 imp pt, 9.9 US pt, 4.7 l; 1 Ford 2150 A D8WE-CA downdraught twin barrel carurettor; cleaner air system; exhaust system with cataytic converter; fuel feed: mechanical pump; water-cooled, 2 imp pt, 38.5 US pt, 18.2 l.

RANSMISSION driving wheels: rear; gearbox: Ford MX or C4 automatic transmission, hydraulic torque conerter and planetary gears with 3 ratios, max ratio of onverter at stall 2.17, possible manual selection: ratios: 2.400, II 1.470, III 1, rev 2; lever: on facia; final drive: ypoid bevel; axle ratio: 2.750; width of rims: 7''; tyres: R78 x 15.

ERFORMANCE max speed: 121 mph, 194 km/h; consumpon: 16.8 m/imp gal, 14 m/US gal, 16.8 l x 100 km.

HASSIS perimeter box-type; front suspension: independ-ent, wishbones (lower trailing links), coil springs, anti-oll bar, telescopic dampers; rear: rigid axle, lower trail-ng radius arms, upper oblique torque arms, coil springs, elescopic dampers.

TEERING recirculating ball, servo; turns lock to lock: 4.

RAKES front disc (diameter 10.72 in, 27.2 cm), front nternal radial fins, rear drum, rear compensator, servo.

LECTRICAL EQUIPMENT 12 V; 77 Ah battery; 40 A al-ernator; Motorcraft transistorized ignition; 4 headlamps.

IMENSIONS AND WEIGHT wheel base: 120.40 in, 306 m; tracks: 62.90 in, 160 cm front, 62.60 in, 159 cm ear; length: 192 in, 488 cm; width: 73.62 in, 187 cm; eight: 73.50 in, 187 cm; ground clearance: 4.59 in, 11.7 m; weight: 3,908 lb, 1,772 kg; weight distribution: 46% ont, 54% rear; fuel tank: 17.6 imp gal, 21 US gal, 80 l.

ODY roadster; 2 doors; 2 seats; adjustable and reclining ackrests; headrests; leather upholstery; tinted glass; onneau cover; automatic speed control; adjustable steer-g column; air-conditioning.

PTIONALS limited slip differential with 3.000 axle ratio; nti-roll bar on rear suspension; 235/60 VR x 15 tyres; ilstein telescopic dampers; metallic spray; hardtop.

4-passenger Convertible

NGINE Lincoln, front, 4 stroke; 8 cylinders; 351 cu in, ,732 cc (4 x 3.50 in, 101.6 x 88.8 mm)); compression atio: 8:1; cast iron block and head; 5 crankshaft bearings: alves: overhead, in line, push-rods and rockers, hydraulic appets; camshafts: 1, at centre of Vee; lubrication: rotary ump, full flow filter, 8.3 imp pt, 9.9 US pt, 4.7 l; 1 lotorcraft downdraught twin barrel carburettor; cleaner ir system; exhaust system with 2 catalytic converters; uel feed: mechanical pump; water-cooled, 28.2 imp pt, 3.8 US pt, 16 l.

RANSMISSION driving wheels: rear; gearbox: Select-hift Merc-O-Matic automatic transmission, hydraulic tor-ue converter and planetary gears with 3 ratios, max ratio

of converter at stall 2.17, possible manual selection; ratios: I 2.400, II 1.470, III 1, rev 2; lever: steering column; final drive: hypoid bevel; axle ratio: 3.080; width of rims: 7''; tyres: LR78 x 15.

PERFORMANCE not declared.

CHASSIS box-type ladder frame; front suspension: inde-pendent, wishbones (lower trailing links), coil springs, anti-roll bar, telescopic dampers; rear: rigid axle, lower trailing radius arms, upper oblique torque arms, trans-verse linkage bar, coil springs, telescopic dampers.

STEERING recirculating ball, servo; turns lock to lock: 3.40.

BRAKES front disc (diameter 11.03 in, 28 cm), front inter-nal radial fins, rear drum, servo.

ELECTRICAL EQUIPMENT 12 V; 63 Ah battery; 60 A al-ternator; Motorcraft transistorized ignition; 4 headlamps.

DIMENSIONS AND WEIGHT wheel base: 136 in, 345 cm; tracks: 62.20 in, 159 cm front, 62 in, 157 cm rear; length: 221 in, 561 cm; width: 73 in, 185 cm; height: 62.50 in, 159 cm; weight: 3,774 lb, 1,711 kg; weight distribution: 50.9% front, 49.1% rear.

BODY convertible; 2 doors; 4 seats, separate front seats.

OPTIONALS LR70 x 15 tyres

DAYTONA   USA

Migi

PRICE EX WORKS: $ 7,000

ENGINE Volkswagen, rear, 4 stroke; 4 cylinders, horizon-tally opposed; 96.7 cu in, 1,584 cc (3.37 x 2.72 in, 85.5 x 69 mm); compression ratio: 7.2:1; max power (DIN): 56 hp (41.2 kW) at 4,200 rpm; max torque (DIN): 80 lb ft, 11 kg m (107.9 Nm) at 3,000 rpm; max engine rpm: 4,600; 35.4 hp/l (26 kW/l); cylinder block with cast iron liners and light alloy fins, light alloy head; 4 crankshaft bearings; valves: overhead, push-rods and rockers; cam-shafts: 1, central, lower; lubrication: gear pump, filter in sump, oil cooler, 4.4 imp pt, 5.3 US pt, 2.5 l; 2 Solex H 32 twin barrel carburettors; fuel feed: mechanical pump; air-cooled.

TRANSMISSION driving wheels: rear; clutch: single dry plate; gearbox: mechanical; gears: 4, fully synchronized; ratios: I 3.800, II 2.060, III 1.320, IV 0.880, rev 3.880; lever: central; final drive: spiral bevel; axle ratio: 4.125; width of rims: 5''; tyres: 5.60 x 15.

PERFORMANCE max speed: about 90 mph, 145 km/h; power-weight ratio: 24.6 lb/hp (33.4 lb/kW), 11.1 kg/hp (15.1 kg/kW); speed in top at 1,000 rpm: 21.2 mph, 34.2 km/h; consumption: 37.2 m/imp gal, 31 m/US gal, 7.6 l x 100 km.

CHASSIS backbone platform; front suspension: indepen-dent, twin swinging longitudinal trailing arms, transverse laminated torsion bars, anti-roll bar, telescopic dampers; rear: independent, swinging semi-axles, swinging longi-tudinal trailing arms, transverse torsion bars, telescopic dampers.

STEERING worm and roller; turns lock to lock: 2.60.

BRAKES front disc (diameter 10.94 in, 27.8 cm), rear drum; linig area: front 11.8 sq in, 76 sq cm, rear 56.4 sq in, 364 sq cm, total 68.2 sq in, 440 sq cm.

ELECTRICAL EQUIPMENT 12 V; 36 Ah battery; 350 W dynamo; Bosch distributor; 4 headlamps.

DIMENSIONS AND WEIGHT wheel base: 94.50 in, 240 cm; tracks: 51.50 in, 131 cm front, 53 in, 134 cm rear; length: 137 in, 348 cm; width: 60 in, 152 cm; ground clearance: 5.91 in, 15 cm; weight: 1,375 lb, 624 kg; turning circle: 36.1 ft, 11 m; fuel tank: 9 imp gal, 10.8 US gal, 41 l.

BODY roadster in plastic material; 2 doors; 2 seats; tonneau cover.

OPTIONALS luxury interior; wire wheels; wooden steer-ing wheel.

DAYTONA Migi

DODGE   USA

Omni Series

PRICES EX WORKS:

.024 2-dr Hatchback	$ 4,482
4-dr Hatchback	$ 4,122

Power team:	Standard for:	Optional for:
70 hp	both	—
65 hp	both	—

70 hp power team

(not available in California).

ENGINE front, transverse, slanted 15° to front, 4 stroke; 4 cylinders, in line; 104.7 cu in, 1,714 cc (3.13 x 3.40 in, 79.5 x 86.4 mm); compression ratio: 8.2:1; max power (DIN): 70 hp (51.5 kW) at 5,200 rpm; max torque (DIN): 85 lb ft, 11.7 kg m (114.7 Nm) at 2,800 rpm; max engine rpm: 6,500; 40.8 hp/l (30 kW/l); cast iron block, light alloy head; 5 crankshaft bearings; valves: overhead, in line, thimble tappets; camshafts: 1, overhead, cogged belt; lubrication: gear pump, full flow filter, 6.7 imp pt, 8 US pt, 3.8 l; 1 Holley R8525A downdraught twin barrel carburettor; cleaner air system; exhaust system with catalytic converter; fuel feed: mechanical pump; water-cooled, 10 imp pt, 12 US pt, 5.7 l.

TRANSMISSION driving wheels: front; clutch: single dry plate (diaphragm); gearbox: mechanical; gears: 4, fully synchronized; ratios: I 3.450, II 1.940, III 1.290, IV 0.970, rev 3.170; lever: central; final drive: spiral bevel; axle ratio: 3.370; width of rims: 4.5''; tyres: 2-dr P165/75R x 13 - 4-dr P155/80R x 13.

PERFORMANCE max speed: about 91 mph, 146 km/h; power-weight ratio: 2-dr 31.4 lb/hp (42.6 lb/kW), 14.2 kg/hp (19.3 kg/kW) - 4-dr 30.5 lb/hp (41.5 lb/kW), 13.9 kg/hp (18.9 kg/kW); speed in top at 1,000 rpm: 16.7 mph, 26.9 km/h; consumption: 30.1 m/imp gal, 25 m/US gal, 9.4 l x 100 km.

CHASSIS integral; front suspension: independent, by Mc Pherson, lower wishbones, anti-roll bar, coil springs/telescopic damper struts; rear: independent, semi-trailing arms, coil springs, telescopic dampers.

STEERING rack-and-pinion; turns lock to lock: 4.

BRAKES front disc (diameter 8.98 in, 22.8 cm), front internal radial fins, rear drum; swept area: total 197.5 sq in, 1,274 sq cm.

ELECTRICAL EQUIPMENT 12 V; 325 A battery; 65 A alternator; Essex or Prestolite transistorized ignition with electronic spark control; 2 headlamps.

DIMENSIONS AND WEIGHT wheel base: 2-dr 96.70 in, 246 cm - 4-dr 99.20 in, 252 cm; tracks: 56 in, 142 cm front, 55.60 in, 141 cm rear; length: 2-dr 172.70 in, 439 cm - 4-dr 164.80 in, 419 cm; width: 2-dr 66 in, 168 cm - 4-dr 66.20 in, 168 cm; height: 2-dr 51.40 in, 131 cm - 4-dr 53.70 in, 136 cm; ground clearance: 2-dr 5.10 in, 13 cm - 4-dr 5 in, 12.7 cm; weight: 2-dr 2,196 lb, 996 kg - 4-dr 2,136 lb, 971 kg; turning circle: 2-dr 36.1 ft, 11 m - 4 dr 36.2 ft, 11.04 m; fuel tank: 10.8 imp gal, 13 US pt, 49 l.

BODY hatchback; 4 seats, separate front seats with built-in headrests; heated rear window.

OPTIONALS Torqueflite automatic transmission, hydraulic torque converter and planetary gears with 3 ratios (I 2.470, II 1.470, III 1, rev 2.100), max ratio of converter at stall 1.97, possible manual selection, central lever, 3.480 axle ratio; P165/75R x 13 tyres; P175/75R x 13 tyres with 5'' wide rims; P185/70R x 13 tyres with 5'' wide rims (2-dr only); heavy-duty suspension; power steering; servo brake; reclining backrests; rear window wiper-washer; vinyl roof; sunshine roof; air-conditioning; Custom or Premium equipment for 4-dr; Premium or Sport equipment for 2-dr.

65 hp power team

(for California only).

See 70 hp power team, except for:

ENGINE max power (DIN): 65 hp (47.8 kW) at 5,200 rpm; 37.9 hp/l (27.9 kW/l); 1 Holley R8527A downdraught twin barrel carburettor.

TRANSMISSION axle ratio: 3.580.

PERFORMANCE power-weight ratio: 2-dr. 33.8 lb/hp (45.9 lb/kW), 15.3 kg/hp (20.8 kg/kW) - 4-dr 32.9 lb/hp (44.7

DODGE Omni 024 2-dr Hatchback

lb/kW), 14.9 kg/hp (20.3 kg/kW); consumption: 28.8 m/imp gal, 24 m/US gal, 9.8 l x 100 km.

OPTIONALS Torqueflite automatic transmission with 3.740 axle ratio.

Aspen Series

PRICES EX WORKS:

Coupé	$ 3,968
Sedan	$ 4,069
St. Wagon	$ 4,445

Power team:	Standard for:	Optional for:
100 hp	all	—
90 hp	all	—
110 hp	—	all
135 hp	—	all
155 hp	—	all
170 hp	—	1
195 hp	—	1

100 hp power team

(not available in California).

ENGINE front, 4 stroke; 6 cylinders, vertical, in line; 225 cu in, 3,687 cc (3.40 x 4.12 in, 86.4 x 104.6 mm); compression ratio: 8.4:1; max power (DIN): 100 hp (73.6 kW) at 3,600 rpm; max torque (DIN): 165 lb ft, 22.8 kg m (223.6 Nm) at 1,600 rpm; max engine rpm: 4,400; 27.1 hp/l (20 kW/l); cast iron block and head; 4 crankshaft bearings; valves: overhead, in line; push-rods and rockers; camshafts: 1, side; lubrication: rotary pump, full flow filter, 8.3 imp pt, 9.9 US pt, 4.7 l; 1 Holley R8523A downdraught single barrel carburettor; cleaner air system; exhaust system with catalytic converter; fuel feed: mechanical pump; water-cooled, 19.2 imp pt, 23 US pt, 10.9 l.

TRANSMISSION driving wheels: rear; clutch: single dry plate; gearbox: mechanical; gears: 3, fully synchronized; ratios: I 3.080, II 1.700, III 1, rev 2.900; lever: central; final drive: hypoid bevel; axle ratio: 3.230 - St. Wagon 3.210; width of rims: 5'' - St. Wagon 5.5''; tyres: D78 x 14 - St. Wagon ER78 x 14.

PERFORMANCE max speed: about 90 mph, 145 km/h; power-weight ratio: Sedan 31.1 lb/hp (42.3 lb/kW), 14.1 kg/hp (19.2 kg/kW); speed in direct drive at 1,000 rpm: 20.4 mph, 32.9 km/h; consumption: 21.6 m/imp gal, 18 m/US gal, 13.1 l x 100 km.

CHASSIS integral with front cross members; front suspension: independent, wishbones, transverse torsion bars, anti-roll bar, telescopic dampers; rear: rigid axle, semi-elliptic leafsprings, anti-roll bar, telescopic dampers.

STEERING recirculating ball; turns lock to lock: 5.30.

BRAKES front disc (diameter 10.82 in, 27.5 cm), front internal radial fins, rear drum, rear compensator; swept area: total 355.24 sq in, 2,292 sq cm.

ELECTRICAL EQUIPMENT 12 V; 325 A battery; 41 A alternator; Essex or Prestolite transistorized ignition with electronic spark control; 4 headlamps.

DIMENSIONS AND WEIGHT wheel base: 112.70 in, 286 cm - Coupé 108.70 in, 276 cm; tracks: 60 in, 152 cm front, 58.5 in, 149 cm rear; length: 201.20 in, 511 cm - Coupé 197.20 in 501 cm; width: 72.80 in, 185 cm; height: Coupé 53.30 in 135 cm - Sedan 55.30 in, 140 cm - St. Wagon 55.70 in, 14 cm; ground clearance: 5.90 in, 15 cm - St. Wagon 6.20 in 15.7 cm; weight: Coupé 3,050 lb, 1,383 kg - Sedan 3,114 lb 1,413 kg - St. Wagon 3,323 lb, 1,507 kg - turning circle 43.5 ft, 13.2 m - Coupé 42.1 ft, 12.8 m; fuel tank: 15 gal, 18 US gal, 68 l - St. Wagon 16.3 imp gal, 19.5 US gal 74 l.

OPTIONALS limited slip differential; 3.210 axle ratio: Torque flite automatic transmission with 3 ratios (I 2.450, II 1.450 III 1, rev 2.220), max ratio of converter at stall 2.01, possi ble manual selection, steering column or central lever 2.760 or 2.710 axle ratio; 4-speed fully synchronized mecha nical gearbox with overdrive/top (I 3.090, II 1.670, III 1 IV 0.710, rev 3), central lever, 3.230 or 3.210 axle ratio heavy-duty cooling system; DR78 x 14, ER78 x 14 or FR78 14 tyres with 5.5'' wide rims; FR70 x 14 tyres with 6'' wide rims; heavy-duty suspension; power steering; tilt of steer ing wheel; servo brake; heavy-duty battery; tinted glass electric windows; heated rear window; automatic speed control; vinyl roof; luxury equipment; air-conditioning Custom equipment; Special Edition equipment; R/T equip ment (Coupé only); Sunrise equipment (Coupé only); Sport equipment (St. Wagon only).

90 hp power team

(for California only).

See 100 hp power team, except for:

ENGINE max power (DIN): 90 hp (66.2 kW) at 3,600 rpm max torque (DIN): 160 lb ft, 22.1 kg m (216.7 Nm) a 1,600 rpm; 24.4 hp/l (18 kW/l); 1 Holley R8680A down draught single barrel carburettor.

TRANSMISSION gearbox: Torqueflite automatic transmission (standard), hydraulic torque converter and planetary gears with 3 ratios, max ratio of converter at stall 2.01, possible manual selection; ratios: I 2.450, II 1.450, III 1, rev 2.220 lever: steering column or central; axle ratio: 3.230 - St Wagon 3.210.

PERFORMANCE power-weight ratio: Sedan 34.6 lb/hp (47. lb/kW), 15.7 kg/hp (21.3 kg/kW); consumption: 18 m/imp gal, 15 m/US gal, 15.7 l x 100 km.

OPTIONALS 3.210 axle ratio; 4-speed fully synchronize mechanical gearbox with overdrive/top not available.

110 hp power team

(not available in California).

See 100 hp power team, except for:

ENGINE max power (DIN): 110 hp (81 kW) at 3,600 rpm max torque (DIN): 180 lb ft, 24.8 kg m (243.2 Nm) at 2,00 rpm; 29.8 hp/l (22 kW/l); 1 Carter BBD8198S downdraugh twin barrel carburettor.

TRANSMISSION gearbox: Torqueflite automatic transmis sion (standard), hydraulic torque converter and planetar

gears with 3 ratios, max ratio of converter at stall 2.01, possible manual selection; ratios: I 2.450, II 1.450, III 1, rev 2.220; lever: steering column or central; axle ratio: 2.760 - St. Wagon 2.940.

PERFORMANCE max speed: about 93 mph, 150 km/h; power-weight ratio: Sedan 28.4 lb/hp (38.6 lb/kW), 12.9 kg/hp (17.5 kg/kW); speed in direct drive at 1,000 rpm: 25.9 mph, 41.7 km/h; consumption: 18 m/imp gal, 15 m/US gal, 15.7 l x 100 km.

DIMENSIONS AND WEIGHT weight: Coupé 3,059 lb, 1,388 kg - Sedan 3,123 lb, 1,417 kg - St. Wagon 3,355 lb, 1,522 kg.

OPTIONALS 4-speed fully synchronized mechanical gearbox with overdrive/top not available.

135 hp power team

(not available in California).

See 100 hp power team, except for:

ENGINE 8 cylinders; 318 cu in, 5,211 (3.91 x 3.31 in, 99.2 x 84 mm); compression ratio: 8.5:1; max power (DIN): 135 hp (99.4 kW) at 4,000 rpm; max torque (DIN): 250 lb ft, 34.5 kg m (338.3 Nm) at 1,600 rpm; 25.9 hp/l (19.1 kW/l); 5 crankshaft bearings; valves: hydraulic tappets; camshafts: 1 at centre of Vee; 1 Holley R8448A downdraught twin barrel carburettor; cooling system: 25 imp pt, 30 US pt, 14.2 l.

DODGE Aspen Sunrise Coupé

1, at centre of Vee; 1 Carter TQ9156S downdraught 4-barrel carburettor; cooling system: 25 imp pt, 30 US pt, 14.2 l.

TRANSMISSION gearbox: Torqueflite automatic transmission (standard), hydraulic torque converter and planetary gears with 3 ratios, max ratio of converter at stall 1.90, possible manual selection; ratios: I 2.450, II 1.450, III 1, rev 2.220; lever: steering column or central; axle ratio: 2.470 - St. Wagon 2.450.

PERFORMANCE max speed: about 103 mph, 165 km/h; power-weight ratio: Sedan 20.9 lb/hp (28.3 lb/kW), 9.5 kg/hp (12.8 kg/kW); speed in direct drive at 1,000 rpm: 25.6 mph, 41.2 km/h; consumption: 16.8 m/imp gal, 14 m/US gal, 16.8 l x 100 km.

ELECTRICAL EQUIPMENT 60 A alternator.

DIMENSIONS AND WEIGHT weight: Coupé 3,168 lb, 1,383 kg - Sedan 3,232 lb, 1,466 kg - St. Wagon 3,433 lb, 1,557 kg; fuel tank: 16.3 imp gal, 19.5 US gal, 74 l.

OPTIONALS 2.450 axle ratio; 4-speed fully synchronized mechanical gearbox with overdrive/top not available.

170 hp power team

(for California only).

See 100 hp power team, except for:

DODGE Aspen Station Wagon

TRANSMISSION gearbox: Torqueflite automatic transmission (standard), hydraulic torque converter and planetary gears with 3 ratios, max ratio of converter at stall 1.90, possible manual selection; ratios: I 2.450, II 1.450, III 1, rev 2.220; lever: steering column or central; axle ratio: 2.470 - St. Wagon 2.450.

PERFORMANCE max speed: about 102 mph, 164 km/h; power-weight ratio: Sedan 23.9 lb/hp (32.5 lb/kW), 10.9 kg/hp (14.7 kg/kW); speed in direct drive at 1,000 rpm: 25.5 mph, 41 km/h; consumption: 19.2 m/imp gal, 16 m/US gal, 14.7 x 100 km.

ELECTRICAL EQUIPMENT 60 A alternator.

DIMENSIONS AND WEIGHT weight: Coupé 3,168 lb, 1,383 kg - Sedan 3,232 lb, 1,466 kg - St. Wagon 3,433 lb, 1,557 kg; fuel tank: 16.3 imp gal, 19.5 US gal, 74 l.

OPTIONALS 2.710 axle ratio; 4-speed fully synchronized mechanical gearbox with overdrive/top not available.

155 hp power team

(for California only).

See 100 hp power team, except for:

ENGINE 8 cylinders; 318 cu in, 5,211 cc (3.91 x 3.31 in, 99.2 x 84 mm); compression ratio: 8.5:1; max power (DIN): 155 hp (114.1 kW) at 4,000 rpm; max torque (DIN): 245 lb ft, 33.8 kg m (331.5 Nm) at 1,600 rpm; 29.7 hp/l (21.9 kW/l); 5 crankshaft bearings; valves: hydraulic tappets; camshafts:

ENGINE 8 cylinders; 360 cu in, 5,900 cc (4 x 3.58 in, 101.6 x 89.6 mm); compression ratio: 8:1; max power (DIN): 170 hp (125.1 kW) at 4,000 rpm; max torque (DIN): 270 lb ft, 37.2 kg m (364.8 Nm) at 1,600 rpm; 28.8 hp/l (21.2 kW/l); 5 crankshaft bearings; valves: hydraulic tappets; camshafts: 1, at centre of Vee; 1 Carter TQ9198S downdraught 4-barrel carburettor; dual exhaust system with catalytic converter; cooling system: 25 imp pt, 30 US pt, 14.2 l.

TRANSMISSION gearbox: Torqueflite automatic transmission (standard), hydraulic torque converter and planetary gears with 3 ratios, max ratio of converter at stall 1.90, possible manual selection; ratios: I 2.450, II 1.450, III 1, rev 2.220; lever: steering column or central; axle ratio: 2.710.

PERFORMANCE max speed: about 106 mph, 170 km/h; power-weight ratio: Coupé 19.7 lb/hp (26.8 lb/kW), 8.9 kg/hp (12.1 kg/kW); speed in direct drive at 1,000 rpm: 29.3 mph, 47.2 km/h; consumption: 15.6 m/imp gal, 13 m/US gal, 18.1 l x 100 km.

ELECTRICAL EQUIPMENT 430 A battery; 60 A alternator.

DIMENSIONS AND WEIGHT weight: Coupé 3,347 lb, 1,518 kg; fuel tank: 16.3 imp gal, 19.5 US gal, 74 l.

BODY coupé; 2 doors.

OPTIONALS 3.210 axle ratio; 4-speed fully synchronized mechanical gearbox with overdrive/top not available.

195 hp power team

(not available in California).

See 100 hp power team, except for:

ENGINE 8 cylinders; 360 cu in, 5,900 cc (4 x 3.58 in, 101.6 x 89.6 mm); compression ratio: 8:1; max power (DIN): 195 hp (143.5 kW) at 4,000 rpm; max torque (DIN): 280 lb ft, 38.6 kg m (378.6 Nm) at 2,400 rpm; 33 hp/l (24.3 kW/l); 5 crankshaft bearings; valves: hydraulic tappets; camshafts: 1, at centre of Vee; 1 Carter TQ9196S downdraught 4-barrel carburettor; dual exhaust system with catalytic converter; cooling system: 25 imp pt, 30 US pt, 14.2 l.

TRANSMISSION gearbox: Torqueflite automatic transmission (standard), hydraulic torque converter and planetary gears with 3 ratios, max ratio of converter at stall 1.90, possible manual selection; ratios: I 2.450, II 1.450, III 1, rev 2.220; lever: steering column or central; axle ratio: 2.710.

PERFORMANCE max speed: about 112 mph, 180 km/h; power-weight ratio: Coupé 17.2 lb/hp (23.3 lb/kW), 7.8 kg/hp (10.6 kg/kW); speed in direct drive at 1,000 rpm: 29.5 mph, 47.5 km/h; consumption: 16.8 m/imp gal, 14 m/US gal, 16.8 l x 100 km.

ELECTRICAL EQUIPMENT 430 A battery; 60 A alternator.

DIMENSIONS AND WEIGHT weight: Coupé 3,347 lb, 1,518 kg; fuel tank: 16.3 imp gal, 19.5 US gal, 74 l.

BODY coupé; 2 doors.

OPTIONALS 3.210 axle ratio; 4-speed fully synchronized mechanical gearbox with overdrive/top not available.

DODGE Aspen Sport Station Wagon

DODGE Diplomat Coupé

Diplomat Series

PRICES EX WORKS:

Coupé	$ 4,901
Sedan	$ 4,999
St. Wagon	$ 5,769
Salon Coupé	$ 5,138
Salon Sedan	$ 5,366
Medallion Coupé	$ 5,612
Medallion Sedan	$ 5,840

Power team:	Standard for:	Optional for:
100 hp	all	—
90 hp	all	—
110 hp	—	all
135 hp	—	all
150 hp	—	all
155 hp	—	all
170 hp	—	all
190 hp	—	all
195 hp	—	all

100 hp power team

(not available in California).

ENGINE front, 4 stroke; 6 cylinders, vertical, in line; 225 cu in, 3,687 cc (3.40 x 4.12 in, 86.4 x 104.6 mm); compression ratio: 8.4:1; max power (DIN): 100 hp (73.6 kW) at 3,600 rpm; max torque (DIN): 165 lb ft, 22.8 kg m (223.6 Nm) at 1,600 rpm; max engine rpm: 4,400; 27.1 hp/l (20 kW/l); cast iron block and head; 4 crankshaft bearings; valves: overhead, in line, push-rods and rockers; camshafts: 1, side; lubrication: rotary pump, full flow filter, 8.3 imp pt, 9.9 US pt, 4.7 l; 1 Holley R8523A downdraught single barrel carburettor; cleaner air system; exhaust system with catalytic converter; fuel feed: mechanical pump; water-cooled, 19.2 imp pt, 23 US pt, 10.9 l.

TRANSMISSION driving wheels: rear; clutch: single dry plate; gearbox: mechanical; gears: 4, fully synchronized with overdrive/top; ratios: I 3.090, II 1.670, III 1, IV 0.710, rev 3.000; lever: steering column; final drive: hypoid bevel; axle ratio: 3.230 - St. Wagon 3.210; width of rims: 5.5''; tyres: FR78 x 15.

PERFORMANCE max speed: about 90 mph, 145 km/h; power-weight ratio: Sedan 33.3 lb/hp (45.2 lb/kW), 15.1 kg/hp (20.5 kg/kW) - Salon Sedan 33.5 lb/hp (45.5 lb/kW), 15.2 kg/hp (20.7 kg/kW) - Medallion Sedan 34.2 lb/hp (46.5 lb/kW), 15.5 kg/hp (21.1 kg/kW); speed in direct drive at 1,000 rpm: 25.5 mph, 41 km/h; consumption: 21.6 m/imp gal, 18 m/US gal, 13.1 l x 100 km.

CHASSIS integral with isolated front cross member; front suspension: independent, wishbones, transverse torsion bars, anti-roll bar, telescopic dampers; rear: rigid axle, semi-elliptic leafsprings, teelscopic dampers.

STEERING recirculating ball, servo; turns lock to lock: 3.50.

BRAKES front disc (diameter 10.82 in, 27.5 cm), front internal radial fins, rear drum, rear compensator, servo; swept area: total 355.24 sq in, 2,292 sq cm.

ELECTRICAL EQUIPMENT 12 V; 375 A battery; 60 A alternator; Essex or Prestolite transistorized ignition with electronic spark control; 4 headlamps.

DIMENSIONS AND WEIGHT wheel base: 112.70 in, 286 cm; tracks: 60 in, 152 cm front, 58.50 in, 149 cm rear; length: coupés 204.10 in, 518 cm - sedans 206.10 in, 523 cm - St. Wagon 202.80 in, 515 cm; width: 72.80 in, 185 cm - coupés 73.50 in, 187 cm; height: coupés 53 in, 135 cm - sedans 55.30 in, 140 cm - St. Wagon 55.70 in, 141 cm; ground clearance: 5.90 in, 15 cm - St. Wagon 6.20 in, 15.7 cm; weight: Coupé 3,267 lb, 1,482 kg - Sedan 3,327 lb, 1,509 kg - St. Wagon 3,542 lb, 1,607 kg - Salon Coupé 3,286 lb, 1,491 kg - Salon Sedan 3,351 lb, 1,520 kg - Medallion Coupé 3,342 lb, 1,516 kg - Medallion Sedan 3,425 lb, 1,554 kg; turning circle: 43.5 ft, 13.2 m; fuel tank: 16.3 imp gal, 19.5 US gal, 74 l.

OPTIONALS limited slip differential; 3.210 axle ratio; Torqueflite automatic transmission with 3 ratios (I 2.450, II 1.450, III 1, rev 2.220), max ratio of converter at stall 2.01, possible manual selection, steering column or central lever, 2.760 or 2.710 axle ratio; heavy-duty suspension; tilt of steering wheel; automatic speed control; 500 A battery; heated rear window with 65 A alternator; electric windows; electric sunshine roof; halogen headlamps; tinted glass; vinyl roof; air-conditioning; T-bar roof (coupés only).

90 hp power team

(for California only)

See 100 hp power team, except for:

ENGINE max power (DIN): 90 hp (66.2 kW) at 3,600 rpm; max torque (DIN): 160 lb ft, 22.1 kg m (216.7 Nm) at 1,600 rpm; 24.4 hp/l (18 kW/l); 1 Holley R8680A downdraught single barrel carburettor.

TRANSMISSION gearbox: Torqueflite automatic transmission (standard), hydraulic torque converter and planetary gears with 3 ratios, max ratio of converter at stall 2.01, possible manual selection; ratios: I 2.450, II 1.450, III 1, rev 2.220; lever: steering column or central; axle ratio: 3.230 - St. Wagon 3.210.

PERFORMANCE max speed: about 87 mph, 140 km/h; power-weight ratio: Sedan 37 lb/hp (50.3 lb/kW), 16.8 kg/hp (22.8 kg/kW) - Salon Sedan 37.2 lb/hp (50.6 lb/kW), 16.9 kg/hp (23 kg/kW) - Medallion Sedan 38 lb/hp (51.7 lb/kW), 17.3 kg/hp (23.5 kg/kW); consumption: 16.8 m/imp gal, 14 m/US gal, 16.8 l x 100 km.

OPTIONALS 3.210 axle ratio (except for St. Wagon).

110 hp power team

(not available in California).

See 100 hp power team, except for:

ENGINE max power (DIN): 110 hp (81 kW) at 3,600 rpm; max torque (DIN): 180 lb ft, 24.8 kg m (243.2 Nm) at 2,000 rpm; 29.8 hp/l (22 kW/l); 1 Carter BBD8199S downdraught twin barrel carburettor.

TRANSMISSION gearbox: Torqueflite automatic transmission (standard), hydraulic torque converter and planetary gears with 3 ratios, max ratio of converter at stall 2.01, possible manual selection; ratios: I 2.450, II 1.450, III 1, rev 2.220; lever: steering column or central; axle ratio: 2.940.

PERFORMANCE max speed: about 93 mph, 150 km/h; power-weight ratio: Sedan 30.6 lb/hp (41.6 lb/kW), 13.9 kg/hp (18? kg/kW) - Salon Sedan 30.8 lb/hp (41.9 lb/kW), 14 kg/h? (19 kg/kW) - Medallion Sedan 31.5 lb/hp (42.8 lb/kW? 14.3 kg/hp (19.4 kg/kW); speed in direct drive at 1,00? rpm; 25.9 mph, 41.7 km/h; consumption: 20.5 m/imp ga? 17 m/US gal, 13.8 l x 100 km.

DIMENSIONS AND WEIGHT weight: Coupé 3,269 lb, 1,48? kg - Sedan 3,368 lb, 1,528 kg - St. Wagon 3,553 lb, 1,61? kg - Salon Coupé 3,288 lb, 1,491 kg - Salon Sedan 3,39? lb, 1,539 kg; Medallion Coupé 3,383 lb, 1,535 kg - Medallio? Sedan 3,466 lb, 1,572 kg.

135 hp power team

(not available in California).

See 100 hp power team, except for:

ENGINE 8 cylinders; 318 cu in, 5,211 cc (3.91 x 3.31 in? 99.2 x 84 mm); compression ratio: 8.5:1; max power (DIN? 135 hp (99.4 kW) at 4,000 rpm; max torque (DIN): 250 ? ft, 34.5 kg m (338.3 Nm) at 1,600 rpm; 25.9 hp/l (19.1 kW/l? 5 crankshaft bearings; valves: hydraulic tappets; camshaft? 1, at centre of Vee; 1 Holley R8448A downdraught tw? barrel carburettor; cooling system: 25 imp pt, 30 US p? 14.2 l.

TRANSMISSION gearbox: Torqueflite automatic transmissio? (standard), hydraulic torque converter and planetary gea? with 3 ratios, max ratio of converter at stall 1.90, poss? ible manual selection; ratios: I 2.450, II 1.450, III 1, IV 2.220; lever: steering column or central; axle ratio: 2.47? - St. Wagon 2.450.

PERFORMANCE max speed: about 102 mph, 164 km/h; powe? -weight ratio: Sedan 25.4 lb/hp (34.5 lb/kW), 11.5 kg/h? (15.6 kg/kW) - Salon Sedan 25.5 lb/hp (34.7 lb/kW), 11? kg/hp (15.7 kg/kW) - Medallion Sedan 26.1 lb/hp (35? lb/kW), 11.8 kg/hp (16.1 kg/kW); speed in direct drive ? 1,000 rpm: 25.5 mph, 41 km/h; consumption: 19.2 m/im? gal, 16 m/US gal, 14.7 l x 100 km.

ELECTRICAL EQUIPMENT 325 A battery.

DIMENSIONS AND WEIGHT weight: Coupé 3,363 lb, 1,52? kg - Sedan 3,423 lb, 1,553 kg - St. Wagon 3,631 lb, 1,64? kg - Salon Coupé 3,382 lb, 1,534 kg - Salon Sedan 3,44? lb, 1,564 kg - Medallion Coupé 3,438 lb, 1,559 kg - Me? dallion Sedan 3,521 lb, 1,597 kg.

OPTIONALS 2.710 axle ratio.

150 hp power team

(not available in California).

See 100 hp power team, except for:

ENGINE 8 cylinders; 360 cu in, 5,900 cc (4 x 3.58 in, 101.? x 89.6 mm); max power (DIN): 150 hp (110.4 kW) at 3,60? rpm; max torque (DIN): 265 lb ft, 36.6 kg m (358.9 Nm at 2,400 rpm; 25.4 hp/l (18.7 kW/l); 5 crankshaft bearings valves: hydraulic tappets; camshafts: 1, at centre of Vee?

DODGE Diplomat Coupé

Holley R8450A downdraught twin barrel carburettor; cooling system: 25 imp pt, 30 US pt, 14.2 l.

TRANSMISSION gearbox: Torqueflite automatic transmission (standard), hydraulic torque converter and planetary gears with 3 ratios, max ratio of converter at stall 1.90, possible manual selection; ratios: I 2.450, II 1.450, III 1, rev 2.220; lever: steering column or central; axle ratio: 2.450.

PERFORMANCE max speed: about 106 mph, 170 km/h; power-weight ratio: Sedan 23.3 lb/hp (31.6 lb/kW), 10.6 kg/hp (14.3 kg/kW) - Salon Sedan 23.4 lb/hp (31.8 lb/kW), 10.6 kg/hp (14.4 kg/kW) - Medallion Sedan 23.9 lb/hp (32.5 lb/kW), 10.8 kg/hp (14.7 kg/kW); speed in direct drive at 1,000 rpm: 29.3 mph, 47.2 km/h; consumption: 16.8 m/imp gal, 14 m/US gal, 16.8 l x 100 km.

ELECTRICAL EQUIPMENT 430 A battery.

DIMENSIONS AND WEIGHT weight: Coupé 3,429 lb, 1,555 kg - Sedan 3,489 lb, 1,583 kg - St. Wagon 3,664 lb, 1,662 kg - Salon Coupé 3,448 lb, 1,564 kg - Salon Sedan 3,513 lb, 1,594 kg - Medallion Coupé 3,504 lb, 1,589 kg - Medallion Sedan 3,587 lb, 1,627 kg.

OPTIONALS 2.710 axle ratio.

155 hp power team

(for California only).

See 100 hp power team, except for:

ENGINE 8 cylinders; 318 cu in, 5,211 cc (3.91 x 3.31 in, 99.2 x 84 mm); compression ratio: 8.5:1; max power (DIN): 155 hp (114.1 kW) at 4,000 rpm; max torque (DIN): 245 lb ft, 33.8 kg m (331.5 Nm) at 1,600 rpm; 29.7 hp/l (21.9 kW/l); 5 crankshaft bearings; valves: hydraulic tappets; camshafts: 1, at centre of Vee; 1 Carter TQ9156S downdraught 4-barrel carburettor; cooling system: 25 imp pt, 30 US pt, 14.2 l.

TRANSMISSION gearbox: Torqueflite automatic transmission (standard), hydraulic torque converter and planetary gears with 3 ratios, max ratio of converter at stall 1.90, possible manual selection; ratios: I 2.450, II 1.450, III 1, rev 2.220; lever: steering column or central; axle ratio: 2.470 - St. Wagon 2.450.

PERFORMANCE max speed: about 106 mph, 170 km/h; power-weight ratio: Sedan 22.1 lb/hp (30 lb/kW), 10 kg/hp (13.6 kg/kW) - Salon Sedan 22.2 lb/hp (30.2 lb/kW), 10.1 kg/hp (13.7 kg/kW) - Medallion Sedan 22.7 lb/hp (30.9 lb/kW), 10.3 kg/hp (14 kg/kW); speed in direct drive at 1,000 rpm: 29.3 mph, 47.2 km/h; consumption: 16.8 m/imp gal, 14 m/US gal, 16.8 l x 100 km.

ELECTRICAL EQUIPMENT 325 A battery.

DIMENSIONS AND WEIGHT weight: Coupé 3,363 lb, 1,525 kg - Sedan 3,423 lb, 1,553 kg - St. Wagon 3,631 lb, 1,647 kg - Salon Coupé 3,382 lb, 1,534 kg - Salon Sedan 3,447 lb, 1,564 kg - Medallion Coupé 3,438 lb, 1,559 kg - Medallion Sedan 3,521 lb, 1,597 kg.

OPTIONALS 2.450 axle ratio (except for St. Wagon).

DODGE Diplomat Station Wagon

DODGE Magnum XE 2-dr Hardtop

170 hp power team

(for California only).

See 100 hp power team, except for:

ENGINE 8 cylinders; 360 cu in, 5,900 cc (4 x 3.58 in, 101.6 x 89.6 mm); max power (DIN): 170 hp (125.1 kW) at 4,000 rpm; max torque (DIN): 270 lb ft, 37.2 kg m (364.8 Nm) at 1,600 rpm; 28.8 hp/l (21.2 kW/l); 5 crankshaft bearings; valves: hydraulic tappets; camshafts: 1, at centre of Vee; 1 Carter TQ9198S downdraught 4-barrel carburetor; cooling system: 25 imp pt, 30 US pt, 14.2 l.

TRANSMISSION gearbox: Torqueflite automatic transmission (standard), hydraulic torque converter and planetary gears with 3 ratios, max ratio of converter at stall 1.90, possible manual selection; ratios: I 2.450, II 1.450, III 1, rev 2.220; lever: steering column or central; axle ratio: 2.710.

PERFORMANCE max speed: about 109 mph, 175 km/h; power-weight ratio: Sedan 21 lb/hp (28.5 lb/kW), 9.5 kg/hp (12.9 kg/kW) - Salon Sedan 21.1 lb/hp (28.7 lb/kW), 9.6 kg/hp (13 kg/kW) - Medallion Sedan 21.5 lb/hp (29.3 lb/kW), 9.8 kg/hp (13.3 kg/kW); speed in direct drive at 1,000 rpm: 27.2 mph, 43.7 km/h; consumption: 16.8 m/imp gal, 14 m/US gal, 16.8 l x 100 km.

ELECTRICAL EQUIPMENT 430 A battery.

DIMENSIONS AND WEIGHT weight: Coupé 3,502 lb, 1,589 kg - Sedan 3,562 lb, 1,616 kg - St. Wagon 3,728 lb, 1,691 kg - Salon Coupé 3,521 lb, 1,597 kg - Salon Sedan 3,586 lb, 1,627 kg - Medallion Coupé 3,577 lb, 1,623 kg - Medallion Sedan 3,660 lb, 1,660 kg.

190 hp power team

(for California only).

See 100 hp power team, except for:

ENGINE 8 cylinders; 360 cu in, 5,900 cc (4 x 3.58 in, 101.6 x 89.6 mm); compression ratio: 8:1; max power (DIN): 190 hp (139.8 kW) at 4,000 rpm; max torque (DIN): 275 lb ft, 37.9 kg m (371.7 Nm) at 2,000 rpm; 32.2 hp/l (23.7 kW/l); 5 crankshaft bearings; valves: hydraulic tappets; camshafts: 1, at centre of Vee; 1 Carter TQ9198S downdraught 4-barrel carburettor; dual exhaust system with catalytic converter; cooling system: 25 imp pt, 30 US pt, 14.2 l.

TRANSMISSION gearbox: Torqueflite automatic transmission (standard), hydraulic torque converter and planetary gears with 3 ratios, max ratio of converter at stall 1.90, possible manual selection; ratios: I 2.450, II 1.450, III 1, rev 2.220; lever: steering column or central; axle ratio: 3.210.

PERFORMANCE max speed: about 112 mph, 180 km/h; power-weight ratio: Sedan 18.8 lb/hp (25.5 lb/kW), 8.5 kg/hp (11.6 kg/kW) - Salon Sedan 18.9 lb/hp (25.6 lb/kW), 8.6 kg/hp (11.6 kg/kW) - Medallion Sedan 19.3 lb/hp (26.2 lb/kW), 8.7 kg/hp (11.9 kg/kW); speed in direct drive at 1,000 rpm: 28 mph, 45 km/h; consumption: 16.8 m/imp gal, 14 m/US gal, 16.8 l x 100 km.

ELECTRICAL EQUIPMENT 430 A battery.

DIMENSIONS AND WEIGHT weight: Coupé 3,502 lb, 1,589

kg - Sedan 3,562 lb, 1,616 kg - St. Wagon 3,728 lb, 1,691 kg - Salon Coupé 3,521 lb, 1,597 kg - Salon Sedan 3,586 lb, 1,627 kg - Medallion Coupé 3,577 lb, 1,623 kg - Medallion Sedan 3,660 lb, 1,660 kg.

195 hp power team

(not available in California).

See 100 hp power team, except for:

ENGINE 8 cylinders; 360 cu in, 5,900 cc (4 x 3.58 in, 101.6 x 89.6 mm); compression ratio: 8:1; max power (DIN): 195 hp (143.5 kW) at 4,000 rpm; max torque (DIN): 280 lb ft, 38.6 kg m (378.6 Nm) at 2,400 rpm; 33 hp/l (24.3 kW/l); 5 crankshaft bearings; valves: hydraulic tappets; camshafts: 1, at centre of Vee; 1 Carter TQ9196S downdraught 4-barrel carburettor; dual exhaust system with catalytic converter; cooling system: 25 imp pt, 30 US pt, 14.2 l.

TRANSMISSION gearbox: Torqueflite automatic transmission (standard), hydraulic torque converter and planetary gears with 3 ratios, max ratio of converter at stall 1.90, possible manual selection; ratios: I 2.450, II 1.450, III 1, rev 2.220; lever: steering column or central; axle ratio: 3.210.

PERFORMANCE max speed: about 115 mph, 185 km/h; power-weight ratio: Sedan 18.3 lb/hp (24.8 lb/kW), 8.3 kg/hp (11.3 kg/kW) - Salon Sedan 18.4 lb/hp (25 lb/kW), 8.3 kg/hp (11.3 kg/kW) - Medallion Sedan 18.7 lb/hp (25.5 lb/kW), 8.5 kg/hp (11.6 kg/kW); speed in direct drive at 1,000 rpm: 28.7 mph, 46.2 km/h; consumption: 16.8 m/imp gal, 14 m/US gal, 16.8 l x 100 km.

ELECTRICAL EQUIPMENT 430 A battery.

DIMENSIONS AND WEIGHT weight: Coupé 3,502 lb, 1,589 kg - Sedan 3,562 lb, 1,616 kg - St. Wagon 3,728 lb, 1,691 kg - Salon Coupé 3,521 lb, 1,597 kg - Salon Sedan 3,586 lb, 1,627 kg - Madallion Coupé 3,577 lb, 1,623 kg - Medallion Sedan 3,660 lb, 1,660 kg.

Magnum XE

PRICE EX WORKS: $ 5,709

135 hp power team

(standard, not available in California).

ENGINE front, 4 stroke; 8 cylinders; 318 cu in, 5,211 (3.91 x 3.31 in, 99.2 x 84 mm); compression ratio: 8.5:1; max power (DIN): 135 hp (99.4 kW) at 4,000 rpm; max torque (DIN): 250 lb ft, 34.5 kg m (338.3 Nm) at 1,600 rpm; max engine rpm: 4,400; 25.9 hp/l (19.1 kW/l); cast iron block and head; 5 crankshaft bearings; valves: overhead, in line, push-rods and rockers, hydraulic tappets; camshafts: 1, at centre of Vee; lubrication: rotary pump, full flow filter, 8.3 imp pt, 9.7 US pt, 4.7 l; 1 Holley R8448A downdraught twin barrel carburettor cleaner air system; exhaust system with catalytic converter; fuel feed: mechanical pump; water-cooled, 25 imp pt, 30 US pt, 14.2 l.

TRANSMISSION driving wheels: rear; gearbox: Torqueflite automatic transmission, hydraulic torque converter and planetary gears with 3 ratios, max ratio of converter at

DODGE Magnum XE 2-dr Hardtop

135 HP POWER TEAM

stall 1.90, possible manual selection; ratios: I 2.450, II 1.450, III 1, rev 2.220; lever: steering column; final drive: hypoid bevel; axle ratio: 2.710; width of rims: 5.5''; tyres: FR78 x 15.

PERFORMANCE max speed: about 103 mph, 165 km/h; power-weight ratio: 27.2 lb/hp, (36.9 lb/kW), 12.3 kg/hp (16.7 kg/kW); speed in direct drive at 1,000 rpm: 28.5 mph, 45.8 km/h; consumption: 19.2 m/imp gal, 16 m/US gal, 14.7 l x 100 km.

CHASSIS integral with isolated front cross member; front suspension: independent, wishbones (lower trailing links), longitudinal torsion bars, anti-roll bar, telescopic dampers; rear: rigid axle, semi-elliptic leafsprings, anti-roll bar, telescopic dampers.

STEERING recirculating ball, servo; turns lock to lock: 3.50.

BRAKES front disc (diameter 11.58 in, 29.4 cm), front internal radial fins, rear drum, rear compensator, servo; swept area: total 375.3 sq in, 2,421 sq cm.

ELECTRICAL EQUIPMENT 12 V; 325 A battery; 60 A alternator; Essex or Prestolite transistorized ignition with electronic spark control; 4 headlamps.

DIMENSIONS AND WEIGHT wheel base: 114.90 in, 292 cm; tracks: 61.90 in, 157 cm front, 62 in, 157 cm rear; length: 215.80 in, 548 cm; width: 77.10 in, 196 cm; height: 53.10 in, 135 cm; ground clearance: 5.20 in, 13.2 cm; weight: 3,667 lb, 1,663 kg; turning circle: 44.9 ft, 13.7 m; fuel tank: 17.6 imp gal, 21 US gal, 80 l.

BODY hardtop; 2 doors; 6 seats, separate front seats with built-in headrests.

OPTIONALS heavy-duty cooling system; central lever; limited slip differential; light alloy wheels; GR78 x 15 or HR78 x 15 tyres; GR60 x 15 tyres with 7'' wide rims; heavy-duty suspension; tilt of steering wheel; speed control device; reclining backrests; electric windows; tinted glass; heated rear window with 100 A alternator; electric sunshine roof; Landau vinyl roof; T-Bar roof; air-conditioning; Gran Touring equipment.

150 hp power team

(optional, not available in California).

See 135 hp power team, except for:

ENGINE 360 cu in, 5,900 cc (4 x 3.58 in, 101.6 x 89.6 mm); compression ratio: 8.4:1; max power (DIN): 150 hp (110.4 kW) at 3,600 rpm; max torque (DIN): 265 lb ft, 36.6 kg m (358.9 Nm) at 2,400 rpm; 25.4 hp/l (18.7 kW/l); 1 Holley R8450A downdraught twin barrel carburettor; cooling system: 26.6 imp pt, 31.9 US pt, 15.1 l.

TRANSMISSION axle ratio: 2.450; tyres: GR78 x 15 (standard).

PERFORMANCE max speed: about 106 mph, 170 km/h; power-weight ratio: 24.7 lb/hp (33.6 lb/kW), 11.2 kg/hp (15.2 kg/kW); consumption: 16.8 m/imp gal, 14 m/US gal, 16.8 l x 100 km.

ELECTRICAL EQUIPMENT 430 A battery.

DIMENSIONS AND WEIGHT weight: 3,708 lb, 1,682 kg.

OPTIONALS 2.710 axle ratio.

155 hp power team

(optional for California only).

See 135 hp power team, except for:

ENGINE max power (DIN): 155 hp (114.1 kW) at 4,000 rpm; max torque (DIN): 245 lb ft, 33.8 kg m (331.5 Nm) at 1,600 rpm; 29.7 hp/l (31.9 kW/l); 1 Carter TQ9195S downdraught 4-barrel carburettor.

PERFORMANCE max speed: about 108 mph, 174 km/h; power-weight ratio: 23.7 lb/hp (32.1 lb/kW), 10.7 kg/hp (14.6 kg/kW); consumption: 15.6 m/imp gal, 13 m/US gal, 18.1 l x 100 km.

170 hp power team

(optional for California only).

See 135 hp power team, except for:

ENGINE 360 cu in, 5,900 cc (4 x 3.58 in, 101.6 x 89.6 mm); compression ratio: 8.4:1; max power (DIN): 170 hp (125.1 kW) at 4,000 rpm; max torque (DIN): 270 lb ft, 37.2 kg m (364.8 Nm) at 1,600 rpm; 28.8 hp/l (21.2 kW/l); 1 Carter TQ9198S downdraught 4-barrel carburettor; cooling system: 26.6 imp pt, 31.9 US pt, 15.1 l.

TRANSMISSION tyres: GR78 x 15 (standard).

PERFORMANCE max speed: about 112 mph, 180 km/h; power-weight ratio: 22.4 lb/hp (30.5 lb/kW), 10.2 kg/hp (13.8 kg/kW); consumption: 15.6 m/imp gal, 13 m/US gal, 18.1 l x 100 km.

ELECTRICAL EQUIPMENT 430 A battery.

DIMENSIONS AND WEIGHT weight: 3,815 lb, 1,731 kg.

190 hp power team

(optional for California only).

See 135 hp power team, except for:

ENGINE 360 cu in, 5,900 cc (4 x 3.58 in, 101.6 x 89.6 mm); compression ratio: 8:1; max power (DIN): 190 hp (139.8 kW) at 4,000 rpm; max torque (DIN): 275 lb ft, 37.9 kg m (371.7 Nm) at 2,000 rpm; 32.2 hp/l (23.7 kW/l); 1 Carter TQ9198S downdraught 4-barrel carburettor; dual exhaust system with catalytic converter; cooling system: 26.6 imp pt, 31.9 US pt, 15.1 l.

TRANSMISSION axle ratio: 3.210; tyres: GR78 x 15 (standard).

PERFORMANCE max speed: about 115 mph, 185 km/h;

DODGE Magnum XE 2-dr Hardtop

---

power-weight ratio: 20.1 lb/hp (27.3 lb/kW), 9.1 kg/hp (12.4 kg/kW); speed in direct drive at 1,000 rpm: 30.4 mph, 49 km/h; consumption: 15.6 m/imp gal, 13 m/US gal, 18.1 l x 100 km.

ELECTRICAL EQUIPMENT 430 A battery.

DIMENSIONS AND WEIGHT weight: 3,815 lb, 1,731 kg.

195 hp power team

(optional, not available in California).

See 135 hp power team, except for:

ENGINE 360 cu in, 5,900 cc (4 x 3.58 in, 101.6 x 89.6 mm); compression ratio: 8:1; max power (DIN): 195 hp (143 kW) at 4,000 rpm; max torque (DIN): 280 lb ft, 38.6 kg m (378.6 Nm) at 2,400 rpm; 33 hp/l (24.3 kW/l); 1 Carter TQ9196S downdraught 4-barrel carburettor; dual exhaust system with catalytic converter; cooling system: 26.6 imp pt, 31.9 US pt, 15.1 l.

TRANSMISSION tyres: GR78 x 15 (standard).

PERFORMANCE max speed: about 118 mph, 190 km/h; power-weight ratio: 19.6 lb/hp (26.6 lb/kW), 8.9 kg/h (12.1 kg/kW); speed in direct drive at 1,000 rpm: 30, mph, 49 km/h; consumption: 15.6 m/imp gal, 13 m/US ga, 18.1 l x 100 km.

ELECTRICAL EQUIPMENT 430 A battery.

DIMENSIONS AND WEIGHT weight: 3,815 lb, 1,731 kg.

OPTIONALS 3.210 axle ratio.

St. Regis

PRICE EX WORKS: $ 6,216

110 hp power team

(standard, not available in California).

ENGINE front, 4 stroke; 6 cylinders, vertical, in line; 22 cu in, 3,687 cc (3.40 x 4.12 in, 86.4 x 104.6 mm); compression ratio: 8.4:1; max power (DIN): 110 hp (81 kW) a 3,600 rpm; max torque (DIN): 180 lb ft, 24.8 kg m (243 Nm) at 2,000 rpm; max engine rpm: 4,400; 29.8 hp/l (2 kW/l); cast iron block and head; 4 crankshaft bearings valves: overhead, in line, push-rods and rockers; camshafts 1, side; lubrication: rotary pump, full flow filter, 8.3 im pt, 9.9 US pt, 4.7 l; 1 Carter BBD8199S downdraught tw barrel carburettor; cleaner air system; exhaust syste with catalytic converter; fuel feed: mechanical pump water-cooled, 19.2 imp pt, 23 US pt, 10.9 l.

TRANSMISSION driving wheels: rear; gearbox: Torqueflit automatic transmission, hydraulic torque converter and pla netary gears with 3 ratios, max ratio of converter at sta 1.90, possible manual selection; ratios: I 2.450, II 1.450 III 1, rev 2.220; lever: steering column; final drive: hy poid bevel; axle ratio: 2.940; width of rims: 5.5''; tyres P195/75R x 15.

PERFORMANCE max speed: about 93 mph, 149 km/h; powe -weight ratio: 32.3 lb/hp, (43.9 lb/kW), 14.7 kg/hp (19. kg/kW); speed in direct drive at 1,000 rpm: 25.9 mph, 41. km/h; consumption: 20.5 m/imp gal, 17 m/US gal, 13. l x 100 km.

CHASSIS integral with isolated front cross member; fron suspension: independent, wishbones (lower trailing links) longitudinal torsion bars, anti-roll bar, telescopic dampers rear: rigid axle, semi-elliptic leafsprings, telescopic dam pers.

STEERING recirculating ball, servo; turns lock to lock: 3.50

BRAKES front disc (diameter 11.58 in, 29.4 cm), fron internal radial fins, rear drum, rear compensator, servo swept area: total 375.3 sq in, 2,421 sq cm.

ELECTRICAL EQUIPMENT 12 V; 375 A battery; 65 A a ternator; Essex or Prestolite transistorized ignition wit electronic spark control; 4 headlamps.

DIMENSIONS AND WEIGHT wheel base: 118.50 in, 301 cm tracks: 61.90 in, 157 cm front, 62 in, 157 cm rear; length 220.20 in, 559 cm; width: 77.10 in, 196 cm; height: 54.5 in, 138 cm; ground clearance: 5.30 in, 13.5 cm; weight 3,557 lb, 1,613 kg; turning circle: 45.8 ft, 13.9 m; fue tank: 17.6 imp gal, 21 US gal, 80 l.

BODY hardtop; 4 doors; 6 seats, separate front seats wit built-in headrests.

OPTIONALS heavy-duty cooling system; limited slip diffe rential; light alloy wheels; P205/75R x 15 tyres; P225/7 R x 15, FR70 x 15 or GR70 x 15 tyres with 7'' wide rims heavy-duty suspension; tilt of steering wheel; automati speed control; reclining backrests; anti-roll bar on rea

DODGE St. Regis 4-dr Hardtop

suspension; electric windows; tinted glass; heated rear window with 100 A alternator; electric sunshine roof; vinyl roof; halogen headlamps; air-conditioning.

135 hp power team

(optional, not available in California).

See 110 hp power team, except for:

ENGINE 8 cylinders; 318 cu in, 5,211 cc (3.91 x 3.31 in, 99.2 x 84 mm); compression ratio: 8.5:1; max power (DIN): 135 hp (99.4 kW) at 4,000 rpm; max torque (DIN): 250 lb ft, 34.5 kg m (338.3 Nm) at 1,600 rpm; 25.9 hp/l (19.1 kW/l); 5 crankshaft bearings; valves: hydraulic tappets; camshafts: 1, at centre of Vee; 1 Holley R8448A downdraught twin barrel carburettor; cooling system: 25 imp pt, 30 US pt, 14.2 l.

TRANSMISSION axle ratio: 2.450.

PERFORMANCE max speed: about 96 mph, 155 km/h; power-weight ratio: 26.9 lb/hp (36.5 lb/kW), 12.2 kg/hp (16.6 kg/kW); consumption: 19.2 m/imp gal, 16 m/US gal, 14.7 l x 100 km.

ELECTRICAL EQUIPMENT 325 A battery.

DIMENSIONS AND WEIGHT weight: 3,628 lb, 1,646 kg.

OPTIONALS 2.710 axle ratio.

150 hp power team

(optional, not available in California).

See 110 hp power team, except for:

ENGINE 8 cylinders; 360 cu in, 5,900 cc (4 x 3.58 in, 101.6 x 89.6 mm); max power (DIN): 150 hp (110.4 kW) at 3,600 rpm; max torque (DIN): 265 lb ft, 36.6 kg m (358.9 Nm) at 2,400 rpm; 25.4 hp/l (18.7 kW/l); 5 crankshaft bearings; valves: hydraulic tappets; camshafts: 1, at centre of Vee; 1 Holley R8450A downdraught twin barrel carburettor; cooling system: 26.6 imp pt, 31.9 US pt, 15.1 l.

TRANSMISSION axle ratio: 2.450.

PERFORMANCE max speed: about 99 mph, 160 km/h; power-weight ratio: 24.6 lb/hp (33.4 lb/kW), 11.2 kg/hp (15.2 kg/kW); speed in direct drive at 1,000 rpm: 27.6 mph, 44.4 km/h; consumption: 16.8 m/imp gal, 14 m/US gal, 16.8 l x 100 km.

ELECTRICAL EQUIPMENT 430 A battery.

DIMENSIONS AND WEIGHT weight: 3,691 lb, 1,674 kg.

OPTIONALS 2.710 axle ratio.

155 hp power team

(optional for California only).

See 110 hp power team, except for:

DODGE St. Regis 4-dr Hardtop

ENGINE 8 cylinders; 318 cu in, 5,211 cc (3.91 x 3.31 in, 99.2 x 84 mm); compression ratio: 8.5:1; max power (DIN): 155 hp (114.1 kW); max torque (DIN): 245 lb ft, 33.8 kg m (331.5 Nm) at 1,600 rpm; 29.7 hp/l (21.9 kW/l); 5 crankshaft bearings; valves: hydraulic tappets; camshafts: 1, at centre of Vee; 1 Carter TQ9195S downdraught 4-barrel carburettor; cooling system: 25 imp pt, 30 US pt, 14.2 l.

TRANSMISSION axle ratio: 2.710.

PERFORMANCE max speed: about 103 mph, 165 km/h; power-weight ratio: 23.4 lb/hp (31.8 lb/kW), 10.6 kg/hp (14.4 kg/kW); speed in direct drive at 1,000 rpm: 25.6 mph, 41.2 km/h; consumption: 15.6 m/imp gal, 13 m/US gal, 18.1 l x 100 km.

ELECTRICAL EQUIPMENT 325 A battery.

DIMENSIONS AND WEIGHT weight: 3,628 lb, 1,646 kg.

170 hp power team

(optional for California only).

See 110 hp power team, except for:

ENGINE 8 cylinders; 360 cu in, 5,900 cc (4 x 3.58 in, 101.6 x 89.6 mm); max power (DIN): 170 hp (125.1 kW) at 4,000 rpm; max torque (DIN): 270 lb ft, 37.2 kg m (364.8 Nm) at 1,600 rpm; 28.8 hp/l (21.2 kW/l); 5 crankshaft bearings; valves: hydraulic tappets; camshaft: 1, at centre of Vee; 1 Carter TQ9198S downdraught 4-barrel carburettor; cooling system: 26.6 imp pt, 31.9 US pt, 15.1 l.

TRANSMISSION axle ratio: 2.710.

PERFORMANCE max speed: about 106 mph, 170 km/h; power-weight ratio: 21.7 lb/hp (29.5 lb/kW), 9.8 kg/hp (13.4 kg/kW); speed in direct drive at 1,000 rpm: 26.4 mph, 42.5 km/h; consumption: 15.6 m/imp gal, 13 m/US gal, 18.1 l x 100 km.

ELECTRICAL EQUIPMENT 430 A battery.

DIMENSIONS AND WEIGHT weight: 3,691 lb, 1,674 kg.

DUESENBERG   USA

SSJ

PRICE EX WORKS: $ 60,000

ENGINE Chrysler, front, 4 stroke; 8 cylinders; 440 cu in, 7,210 cc (4.32 x 3.75 in, 109.7 x 95.2 mm); compression ratio: 8.2:1; max power (DIN): 215 hp (158.2 kW) at 4,000 rpm; max torque (DIN): 330 lb ft, 45.5 kg m (446.2 Nm) at 3,200 rpm; max engine rpm: 4,400; 29.8 hp/l (21.9 kW/l); cast iron block and head; 5 crankshaft bearings; valves: overhead, in line; push-rods and rockers, hydraulic tappets; camshafts: 1, at centre of Vee; lubrication: rotary pump,

DUESENBERG SSJ Roadster

SSJ

full flow filter, 8.3 imp pt, 9.9 US pt, 4.7 l; 1 Carter TQ9009S (TQ9010S for California only) downdraught 4-barrel carburettor; cleaner air system; exhaust system with catalytic converter; fuel feed: mechanical pump; water-cooled, 28.3 imp pt, 34 US pt, 16.1 l.

TRANSMISSION driving wheels: rear; gearbox: Torqueflite automatic transmission, hydraulic torque converter and planetary gears with 3 ratios, max ratio of converter at stall 2.02, possible manual selection: ratios: I 2.450, II 1.450, III 1, rev 2.200; lever: central; final drive: hypoid bevel; axle ratio: 3.540; tyres: 7.00/7.50 x 18.

PERFORMANCE max speed: about 110 mph, 177 km/h; power-weight ratio: 16.7 lb/hp, (22.8 lb/kW), 7.6 kg/hp (10.3 kg/kW); speed in direct drive at 1,000 rpm: 25 mph, 40.2 km/h; consumption: 12.3 m/imp gal, 10.2 m/US gal, 23 l x 100 km.

CHASSIS channel section ladder frame; front suspension: rigid axle, semi-elliptic leafsprings, friction dampers; rear: rigid axle, semi-elliptic leafsprings, telescopic dampers.

STEERING recirculating ball, servo.

BRAKES drum (diameter 12.50 in, 31.8 cm), servo.

ELECTRICAL EQUIPMENT 12 V; 500 A battery; 65 A alternator; Chrysler distributor; 4 headlamps.

DIMENSIONS AND WEIGHT wheel base: 128 in, 325 cm; tracks: 63.30 in, 161 cm front, 64.58 in, 164 cm rear; length: 166.50 in, 423 cm; width: 78.50 in, 199 cm; height: 60 in, 152 cm; weight: 3,600 lb, 1,633 kg; fuel tank: 17.6 imp gal, 21 US gal, 80 l.

BODY roadster; 2 doors; 2 seats; tonneau cover; wire wheels.

OPTIONALS air-conditioning.

DUESENBERG BROS.   USA

Four-door Town Sedan

PRICE EX WORKS: $ 100,000

ENGINE GM, front, 4 stroke; 8 cylinders; 425 cu in, 6,964 cc (4.08 x 4.06 in, 104 x 103 mm); compression ratio: 8.2:1; max power (DIN): 195 hp (143.5 kW) at 3,800 rpm; max torque (DIN): 320 lb ft, 44.2 kg m (433.5 Nm) at 2,400 rpm; max engine rpm: 4,200; 28 hp/l (20.6 kW/l); cast iron block and head; 5 crankshaft bearings; valves: overhead, in line, push-rods and rockers, hydraulic tappets; camshafts: 1, at centre of Vee; lubrication: gear pump, full flow filter, 8.3 imp pt, 9.9 US pt, 4.7 l; electronic fuel injection; cleaner air system; exhaust system with catalytic converter; fuel feed: 2 electric pumps; water-cooled, 34.7 imp pt, 41.7 US pt, 19.7 l.

TRANSMISSION driving wheels: rear; gearbox: Turbo-Hydramatic 400 automatic transmission, hydraulic torque converter and planetary gears with 3 ratios, max ratio of converter at stall 2, possible manual selection: ratios: I 2.480, II 1.480, III 1, rev 2.070; lever: steering column; final drive: hypoid bevel, limited slip differential; axle ratio: 3.080; width of rims: 6''; tyres: GR78 x 15.

PERFORMANCE max speed: about 115 mph, 185 km/h; power-weight ratio: 23.3 lb/hp, (31.6 lb/kW), 10.6 kg/hp (14.3 kg/kW); speed in direct drive at 1,000 rpm: 28 mph, 45 km/h; consumption: 16.8 m/imp gal, 14 m/US gal, 16.8 l x 100 km.

CHASSIS ladder frame with cross members; front suspension: independent, wishbones, coil springs, anti-roll bar, telescopic dampers; rear: rigid axle, lower trailing radius arms, upper oblique torque arms, automatic levelling control, coil springs, telescopic dampers.

STEERING recirculating ball, servo.

BRAKES disc.

ELECTRICAL EQUIPMENT 12 V; 3,500 W battery; 80 A alternator; Delco-Renny high energy ignition system; 4 headlamps.

DIMENSIONS AND WEIGHT wheel base: 133 in, 338 cm; tracks: 61.70 in, 157 cm front, 60.70 in, 154 cm rear; length: 233 in, 592 cm; width: 79 in, 207 cm; height: 57.40 in, 146 cm; weight: 4,540 lb, 2,059 kg.

BODY saloon/sedan; 4 doors; wire wheels.

OPTIONALS 2 turbochargers.

DUESENBERG BROS. Four-door Town Sedan

ELEGANT MOTORS Elegantè 2+2 Sports Phaeton

ELEGANT MOTORS   USA

898 Phaeton

PRICE EX WORKS: $ 50,000

ENGINE Jaguar, front, 4 stroke; 12 cylinders, Vee-slanted at 60°; 326 cu in, 5,343 cc (3.54 x 2.76 in, 90 x 70 mm); compression ratio: 8:1; max power (DIN): 288 hp (212 kW) at 5,750 rpm; max torque (DIN): 295 lb ft, 40.7 kg m (399.1 Nm) at 3,500 rpm; max engine rpm: 6,500; 53.9 hp/l (39.7 kW/l); light alloy block and head, wet liners, hemispherical combustion chambers; 7 crankshaft bearings; valves: overhead, in line, thimble tappets; camshafts: 1, per block, overhead; lubrication: rotary pump, full flow filter, oil cooler, 19 imp pt, 22.8 US pt, 10.8 l; Lucas-Bosch electronic injection; fuel feed: electric pump; water-cooled, 36 imp pt, 43.3 US pt, 20.5 l, 1 viscous coupling thermostatic fan and 1 electric thermostatic fan.

TRANSMISSION driving wheels: rear; clutch: single dry plate (diaphragm), hydraulically controlled; gearbox: mechanical; gears: 4, fully synchronized; ratios: I 3.238, II 1.905, III 1.389, IV 1, rev 3.428; lever: central; final drive: hypoid bevel, limited slip differential; axle ratio: 3.070; width of rims: 6''; tyres: 205/70VR x 15.

PERFORMANCE max speed: about 150 mph, 241 km/h power-weight ratio: 10.4 lb/hp (14.1 lb/kW), 4.7 kg/hp (6.4 kg/kW); speed in direct drive at 1,000 rpm: 24.8 mph, 39.9 km/h; consumption: 14 m/imp gal, 11.6 m/US gal, 20.2 l x 100 km.

CHASSIS box-type ladder frame with cross members; front suspension: independent, wishbones, coil springs, anti-roll bar, telescopic dampers; rear: independent, wishbones, semi-axles as upper arms, transverse semi-elliptic leafsprings, trailing radius arms, telescopic dampers.

STEERING recirculating ball, servo; turns lock to lock: 4.10.

BRAKES front disc, rear drum.

ELECTRICAL EQUIPMENT 12 V; 2 headlamps.

DIMENSIONS AND WEIGHT wheel base: 128 in, 325 cm; length: 203.94 in, 518 cm; height: 57.09 in, 145 cm; ground clearance: 10 in, 25.4 cm; weight: 3,000 lb, 1,360 kg; fuel tank: 16.7 imp gal, 20 US gal, 76 l.

BODY phaeton in plastic material; 2 doors; 2 + 2 seats, separate front seats.

OPTIONALS leather upholstery; tonneau cover; electric windows; dual exhaust system; supercharger; air-conditioning.

856 Speedster

See 898 Phaeton, except for:

PRICE EX WORKS: $ 40,000

BODY roadster; 2 seats.

Eleganté 2+2 Sports Phaeton

See 898 Phaeton, except for:

PRICE EX WORKS: $ 60,000

TRANSMISSION width of rims: front 7''.

DIMENSIONS AND WEIGHT length: 207.13 in, 526 cm; width: 78 in, 198 cm; height: 56 in, 142 cm; ground clearance: 7 in, 17.8 cm.

ELITE USA

Laser 917

PRICES EX WORKS: $ 7,500 (body only)
$ 4,595 (kit only)

ENGINE Volkswagen, rear, 4 stroke; 4 cylinders, horizontally opposed; 96.7 cu in, 1,584 cc (3.37 x 2.72 in, 85.5 x 69 mm); compression ratio: 8.5:1; max power (DIN): 50 hp (36.8 kW) at 4,000 rpm; max torque (DIN): 78 lb ft, 10.8 kg m (105.9 Nm) at 2,800 rpm; max engine rpm: 4,600; 31.6 hp/l (23.3 kW/l); block with cast iron liners and light alloy fins, light alloy

ELITE Laser 917

6.50 in, 16.5 cm; weight: 1,950 lb, 884 kg; weight distribution: 40% front, 60% rear; fuel tank: 12.5 imp gal, 15 US gal, 57 l.

BODY sports in plastic material; 2 doors; 2 seats.

EXCALIBUR USA

Series III

PRICES EX WORKS:
SS Roadster $ 27,600
SS Phaeton $ 27,600

215 hp power team

(not available in California).

ENGINE Chevrolet, front, 4 stroke; 8 cylinders; 454 cu in, 7,440 cc (4.25 x 4 in, 107.9 x 101.6 mm); compression ratio: 7.9:1; max power (DIN): 215 hp (158.2 kW) at 4,000 rpm; max torque (DIN): 350 lb ft, 48.3 kg m (473.7 Nm) at 2,400 rpm; max engine rpm: 4,400; 28.9 hp/l (21.3 kW/l); cast iron block and head; 5 crankshaft bearings; valves: overhead, in line, push-rods and rockers, hydraulic tappets; camshafts: 1, at centre of Vee; lubrication: gear pump, full flow filter, 8.3 imp pt, 9.9 US pt, 4.7 l; 1 Rochester 7045200 downdraught 4-barrel carburettor; cleaner air system; dual exhaust system; water-cooled, 52.8 imp pt, 63.4 US pt, 30 l.

EXCALIBUR Series III SS Phaeton

head; 4 crankshaft bearings; valves: overhead, push-rods and rockers; camshaft: 1, central, lower; lubrication: gear pump, filter in sump, oil cooler, 4.4 imp pt, 5.3 US pt, 2.5 l; 1 Solex 34 PICT 2 downdraught carburettor; fuel feed: mechanical pump; air-cooled.

TRANSMISSION driving wheels: rear; clutch: single dry plate; gearbox: mechanical; gears: 4, fully synchronized; ratios: I 3.780, II 2.060, III 1.260, IV 0.930, rev 4.010; lever: central; final drive: spiral bevel; axle ratio: 3.875; width of rims: 4''; tyres: 5.60 x 15.

PERFORMANCE max speed: about 100 mph, 161 km/h; power-weight ratio: 39 lb/hp (52.9 lb/kW), 17.6 kg/hp (24 kg/ kW); carrying capacity: 353 lb, 160 kg, consumption: 30.7 m/imp gal, 25.6 m/US gal, 9.2 l x 100 km.

CHASSIS backbone platform; front suspension: independent, twin swinging longitudinal trailing arms, transverse laminated torsion bars, anti-roll bar, telescopic dampers; rear: independent, swinging semi-axles, swinging longitudinal trailing arms, transverse torsion bars, telescopic dampers.

STEERING worm and roller.

BRAKES front disc (diameter 10.91 in, 27.7 cm), rear drum; lining area: front 12.4 sq in, 80 sq cm, rear 55.5 sq in, 358 sq cm, total 67.9 sq in, 438 sq cm.

ELECTRICAL EQUIPMENT 12 V; 36 Ah battery; 50 A alternator; Bosch distributor; 4 headlamps.

DIMENSIONS AND WEIGHT wheel base: 94.50 in, 240 cm; tracks: 58 in, 147 cm front, 59 in, 150 cm rear; length: 174 in, 442 cm; height: 43.50 in, 110 cm; ground clearance:

EXCALIBUR Series III SS Roadster

TRANSMISSION driving wheels: rear; gearbox: Turbo-Hydramatic 400 automatic transmission, hydraulic torque converter and planetary gears with 3 ratios, max ratio of converter at stall 2.2, possible manual selection; ratios: I 2.480, II 1.480, III 1, rev 2.080; lever: steering column or central; final drive: hypoid bevel, limited slip differential; axle ratio: 2.730; width of rims: 7.5''; tyres: GR78 x 15.

PERFORMANCE max speed: 110 mph, 177 km/h; power-weight ratio: 20.2 lb/hp (27.6 lb/kW), 9.2 kg/hp (12.5 kg/kW); speed in direct drive at 1,000 rpm: 25 mph, 40.2 km/h; consumption: 12.3 m/imp gal, 10.2 m/US gal, 23 l x 100 km.

CHASSIS box-type ladder frame; front suspension: independent, wishbones, coil springs, anti-roll bar, telescopic dampers; rear: independent, semi-axle as upper pivoting arm and angular strut rod as lower pivoting arm, transverse semi-elliptic leafspring, trailing radius arms, anti-roll bar, telescopic dampers adjustable while running.

STEERING recirculating ball, variable ratio, tilt and telescopic, servo; turns lock to lock: 3.

BRAKES disc, internal radial fins, servo; swept area: total 461 sq in, 2,973 sq cm.

ELECTRICAL EQUIPMENT 12 V; 73 Ah battery; 61 A alternator; Delco-Remy high energy ignition system; 4 headlamps.

DIMENSIONS AND WEIGHT wheel base: 112 in, 284 cm; front and rear track: 62.50 in, 159 cm; length: 175 in, 444 cm; width: 72 in, 183 cm; height: 58 in, 147 cm; ground clearance: 5.70 in, 14.4 cm; weight: 4,350 lb, 1,973 kg;

215 HP POWER TEAM

weight distribution: 48% front, 52% rear; turning circle: 35 ft, 10.7 m; fuel tank: 20.9 imp gal, 25 US gal, 95 l.

BODY 2 doors; 2 or 4 seats, separate front seats; leather upholstery; wire wheels; all-weather removable hardtop; tonneau cover; air-conditioning; heating and defrosting system; luggage rack; two side mounted spare wheels.

FORD   USA

Pinto Series

PRICES EX WORKS:

Sedan	$ 3,629
Runabout	$ 3,744
St. Wagon	$ 4,028

For 2.8-litre engine add $ 273.

Power team:	Standard for:	Optional for:
88 hp	all	—
88 hp (2,800 cc)	—	all
102 hp	—	all

88 hp power team

ENGINE front, 4 stroke; 4 cylinders, in line; 140 cu in, 2,300 cc (3.78 x 3.13 in, 95.9 x 79.5 mm); compression ratio: 9:1; max power (DIN): 88 hp (64.8 kW) at 4,800 rpm; max torque (DIN): 118 lb ft, 16.3 kg m (159.8 Nm) at 2,800 rpm; max engine rpm: 5,200; 38.3 hp/l (28.2 kW/l); cast iron block and head; 5 crankshaft bearings; valves: overhead, Vee-slanted, rockers, hydraulic tappets; camshafts: 1, overhead, cogged belt; lubrication: gear pump, full flow filter, 8.3 imp pt, 9.9 US pt, 4.7 l; 1 Holley-Weber D9DEE-ALA/AMA (D9EE-AGC/AHC or AEC/AFC for California only) downdraught twin barrel carburettor; cleaner air system; exhaust system with catalytic converter; fuel feed: mechanical pump; water-cooled, 14.4 imp pt, 17.3 US pt, 8.2 l.

TRANSMISSION driving wheels: rear; clutch: single dry plate; gearbox: mechanical; gears: 4, fully synchronized; ratios: I 3.980, II 2.140, III 1.420, IV 1, rev 3.990; lever: central; final drive: hypoid bevel; axle ratio: 2.730 - St. Wagon 3.080; width of rims: 5''; tyres: A78 x 13.

PERFORMANCE max speed: about 96 mph, 154 km/h; power-weight ratio: Sedan 26.7 lb/hp (36.2 lb/kW), 12.1 kg/hp (16.4 kg/kW) - Runabout 27.2 lb/hp (36.9 lb/kW), 12.3 kg/hp (16.7 kg/kW) - St. Wagon 28.8 lb/hp (39.1 lb/kW), 13 kg/hp (17.7 kg/kW); speed in direct drive at 1,000 rpm: 19.3 mph, 31 km/h; consumption: 26.4 m/imp gal, 22 m/US gal, 10.7 l x 100 km.

CHASSIS integral; front suspension: independent, wishbones, coil springs, telescopic dampers; rear: rigid axle, semi-elliptic leafsprings, telescopic dampers.

STEERING rack-and-pinion; turns lock to lock: 4.15.

BRAKES front disc (diameter 9.30 in, 23.6 cm), front internal radial fins, rear drum, rear compensator; swept area: front 145.5 sq in, 939 sq cm, rear 99 sq cm, 639 sq cm, total 244.5 sq in, 1,578 sq cm.

ELECTRICAL EQUIPMENT 12 V; 45 Ah battery; 40 A alternator; Motorcraft transistorized ignition; 2 headlamps.

DIMENSIONS AND WEIGHT wheel base: 94.50 in, 240 cm - St. Wagon 94.80 in, 241 cm; tracks: 55 in, 140 cm front, 55.80 in, 142 cm rear; length: 170.80 in, 434 cm - St. Wagon 180.60 in, 459 cm; width: 69.40 in, 176 cm - St. Wagon 69.70 in, 177 cm; height: 50.60 in, 128 cm - St. Wagon 52.10 in, 132 cm; ground clearance: 4.52 in, 11.5 cm - St. Wagon 5.04 in, 12.8 cm; weight: Sedan 2,346 lb, 1,064 kg - Runabout 2,392 lb, 1,085 kg - St. Wagon 2,532 lb, 1,148 kg; turning circle: 35.9 ft, 10.9 m; fuel tank: 10.8 imp gal, 13 US gal, 49 l - St. Wagon 11.7 imp gal, 14 US gal, 53 l.

BODY 4 seats, separate front seats; folding rear seat (standard for Runabout and St. Wagon only).

OPTIONALS heavy-duty cooling system; limited slip differential; 3.080 axle ratio (except for St. Wagon); Select-Shift automatic transmission with 3 ratios (I 2.470, II 1.470, III 1, rev 2.110), max ratio of converter at stall 2.9, possible manual selection, central lever, 3.080 axle ratio; aluminum wheels; BR78 x 13, BR70 x 13 or A70 x 13 tyres; anti-roll bar on front suspension; power steering; servo brake; 54 Ah heavy-duty battery; heated rear window; tinted glass; air-conditioning; sunshine roof (except for St. Wagon); Sports equipment; Pony or ESS equipment (except for St. Wagon); Cruising equipment (except for Sedan); Squire equipment (for St. Wagon only).

FORD Pinto Runabout

88 hp (2,800 cc) power team

(for California only).

See 88 hp power team, except for:

ENGINE 6 cylinders, Vee-slanted at 60°; 170.8 cu in, 2,800 cc (3.66 x 2.70 in, 92.9 x 68.5 mm); max power (DIN): 88 hp (64.8 kW) at 4,800 rpm; max torque (DIN): 118 lb ft, 16.3 kg m (159.8 Nm) at 2,800 rpm; 31.4 hp/l (23.1 kW/l); 4 crankshaft bearings; valves: overhead, in line, push-rods and rockers; camshafts: 1, at centre of Vee; 1 Motorcraft 2700 D9ZE-LB downdraught carburettor with variable Venturi; cooling system: 14.1 imp pt, 16.9 US pt, 8 l.

TRANSMISSION gearbox: SelectShift automatic transmission (standard), hydraulic torque converter and planetary gears with 3 ratios, max ratio of converter at stall 2.05, possible manual selection: ratios: I 2.460, II 1.460, III 1, rev 2.190; lever: central; axle ratio: 3.080.

PERFORMANCE max speed: about 99 mph, 160 km/h; power-weight ratio: Sedan 28 lb/hp (38 lb/kW), 12.7 kg/hp (17.2 kg/kW) - Runabout 28.5 lb/hp (38.7 lb/kW), 12.9 kg/hp (17.6 kg/kW) - St. Wagon 30.1 lb/hp (40.9 lb/kW), 13.7 kg/hp (18.5 kg/kW); speed in direct drive at 1,000 rpm: 23.5 mph, 37.9 km/h; consumption: 21.6 m/imp gal, 18 m/US gal, 13.1 l x 100 km.

CHASSIS (standard) anti-roll bar on front suspension.

DIMENSIONS AND WEIGHT weight: plus 116 lb, 53 kg - St. Wagon plus 119 lb, 54 kg.

OPTIONALS 3.400 axle ratio.

102 hp power team

(not available in California).

See 88 hp power team, except for:

ENGINE 6 cylinders, Vee-slanted at 60°; 170.8 cu in, 2,800 cc (3.66 x 2.70 in, 92.9 x 68.5 mm); compression ratio: 8.7:1; max power (DIN): 102 hp (75.1 kW) at 4,400 rpm; max torque (DIN): 138 lb ft, 19 kg m (186.3 Nm) at 3,200 rpm; 36.4 hp/l (26.8 kW/l); 4 crankshaft bearings; valves: overhead, in line, push-rods and rockers; camshafts: 1, at centre of Vee; 1 Motorcraft D9YE-AB downdraught twin barrel carburettor; cooling system: 14.1 imp pt, 16.9 US pt, 8 l.

TRANSMISSION gearbox: SelectShift automatic transmission (standard), hydraulic torque converter and planetary gears with 3 ratios, max ratio of converter at stall 2.05, possible manual selection: ratios: I 2.460, II 1.460, III 1, rev 2.190; lever: central; axle ratio: 3.080.

PERFORMANCE max speed: about 103 mph, 165 km/h; power-weight ratio: Sedan 24.1 lb/hp (32.8 lb/kW), 10.9 kg/hp (14.9 kg/kW) - Runabout 24.6 lb/hp (33.4 lb/kW), 11.2 kg/hp (15.2 kg/kW) - St. Wagon 26 lb/hp (35.3 lb/kW), 11.8 kg/hp (16 kg/kW); speed in direct drive at 1,000 rpm: 23.5 mph, 37.9 km/h; consumption: 21.6 m/imp gal; 18 m/US gal, 13.1 l x 100 km.

CHASSIS (standard) anti-roll bar on front suspension.

DIMENSIONS AND WEIGHT weight: plus 116 lb, 53 kg - St. Wagon plus 119 lb, 54 kg.

Mustang Series

PRICES EX WORKS:

2-dr Sedan	$ 4,07
3-dr Sedan	$ 4,43
Ghia 2-dr Sedan	$ 4,64
Ghia 3-dr Sedan	$ 4,82

For 2.8-litre engine add $ 273; for 5.0-litre engine add 514. For 2.3-litre turbocharged engine add $ 542.

Power team:	Standard for:	Optional for:
88 hp	all	—
109 hp	—	all
140 hp	—	all
143 hp	—	all
150 hp	—	all

88 hp power team

ENGINE front, 4 stroke; 4 cylinders, in line; 140 cu in, 2,300 cc (3.78 x 3.13 in, 95.9 x 79.5 mm); compression ratio 9:1; max power (DIN): 88 hp (64.8 kW) at 4,800 rpm; max torque (DIN): 118 lb ft, 16.3 kg m (159.8 Nm) at 2,800 rpm; max engine rpm: 5,200; 38.3 hp/l (28.2 kW/l); cast iron block and head; 5 crankshaft bearings; valves: overhead, Vee-slanted, rockers, hydraulic tappets; camshafts: 1, overhead, coged belt; lubrication: rotary pump, full flow filter, 8.3 imp pt, 9.9 US pt, 4.7 l; 1 Holley-Weber D9BE-AAA/ADA (D9BE-ABA/ACA for California only) downdraught twin barrel carburettor; cleaner air system; exhaust system with catalytic converter; fuel feed: mechanical pump; water-cooled, 14.4 imp pt, 17.3 US pt, 8.2 l.

TRANSMISSION driving wheels: rear; clutch: single dry plate; gearbox: mechanical; gears: 4, fully synchronized; ratios: I 3.980, II 2.140, III 1.420, IV 1, rev 3.990; lever: central; final drive: hypoid bevel; axle ratio: 3.080; width of rims: 5''; tyres: B78 x 13.

PERFORMANCE max speed: about 96 mph, 154 km/h; power-weight ratio: 2-dr Sedan 27.7 lb/hp (37.6 lb/kW), 12.5 kg/hp (17 kg/kW) - Ghia 2-dr Sedan 29 lb/hp (39.4 lb/kW), 13.2 kg/hp (17.9 kg/kW); speed in direct drive at 1,000 rpm: 19.3 mph, 31 km/h; consumption: 25.2 m/imp gal, 21 m/US gal, 11.2 l x 100 km.

CHASSIS platform with front subframe; front suspension: independent, by McPherson, wishbones (lower control arms) coil springs/telescopic damper struts, anti-roll bar; rear: rigid axle, lower trailing radius arms, upper oblique torque arms, transverse linkage bar, coil springs, telescopic dampers.

STEERING rack-and-pinion; turns lock to lock: 4.08.

BRAKES front disc (diameter 9.31 in, 23.6 cm), front internal radial fins, rear compensator, rear drum; swept area: total 249.7 sq in, 1,611 sq cm.

ELECTRICAL EQUIPMENT 12 V; 45 Ah battery; 40 A alternator; Motorcraft transistorized ignition; 4 headlamps.

DIMENSIONS AND WEIGHT wheel base: 100.40 in, 255 cm; tracks: 56.60 in, 144 cm front, 57 in, 145 cm rear; length: 179.10 in, 455 cm; width: 69.10 in, 176 cm; height: 51.50 in, 131 cm; ground clearance: 5.67 in, 14.5 cm; weight: 2-dr Sedan 2,436 lb, 1,104 kg - 3-dr Sedan 2,518 lb, 1,142

g - Ghia 2-dr Sedan 2,554 lb, 1,158 kg - Ghia 3-dr Sedan
,578 lb, 1,169 kg; turning circle: 37.4 ft, 11.4 m; fuel
ank: 9.5 imp pt, 11.5 US pt, 43 l.

ODY saloon/sedan; 4 seats, separate front seats, reclin-
g backrests with built-in headrests.

PTIONALS heavy-duty cooling system; SelectShift auto-
atic transmission with 3 ratios (I 2.470, II 1.470, III 1,
ev 2.110), max ratio of converter at stall 2.9, possible
anual selection, central lever, 3.080 axle ratio; heavy-
uty suspension with rear anti-roll bar; aluminum wheels;
78 x 13, B78 x 14 or BR78 x 14 tyres; CR78 x 14 tyres with
5'' wide rims; 190/65R x 390 tyres with TRX forged alu-
inum wheels; power steering; tilt of steering wheel; servo
rake; 54 Ah heavy-duty battery; heated rear window; tint-
d glass; air-conditioning; sunshine roof; vinyl roof; speed
ontrol device; rear window wiper-washer (except for 2-dr
odels); metallic spray; Cobra equipment (for 3-dr Sedan
nly); Sport equipment; leather upholstery (for Ghia models
nly).

109 hp power team

ee 88 hp power team, except for:

NGINE 6 cylinders, Vee-slanted at 60°; 170.8 cu in, 2,800
c (3.66 x 2.70 in, 92.9 x 68.5 mm); compression ratio: 8.7:1;
ax power (DIN): 109 hp (80.2 kW) at 4,800 rpm; max
orque (DIN): 142 lb ft, 19.6 kg m (192.2 Nm) at 2,800
m; 38.9 hp/l (28.6 kW/l); 4 crankshaft bearings; valves:
verhead, in line, push-rods and rockers; camshafts: 1, at
entre of Vee; 1 Ford 2150 D9YE-BB (Motorcraft 2700
9ZE-LB with variable Venturi for California only) downraught twin barrel carburettor; cooling system: 15.3 imp
t, 18.4 US pt, 8.7 l.

RANSMISSION gearbox: SelectShift automatic transmis-
ion (standard) hydraulic torque converter and planetary
ears with 3 ratios, max ratio of converter at stall 2.05,
ossible manual selection; ratios: I 2.460, II 1.460, III 1,
ev 2.180; lever: central; axle ratio: 3.080.

ERFORMANCE max speed: about 99 mph, 160 km/h;
ower-weight ratio: 2-dr Sedan 23.1 lb/hp (31.4 lb/kW), 10.5
g/hp (14.2 kg/kW) - Ghia 2-dr Sedan 24.2 lb/hp (32.9
b/kW), 11 kg/hp (14.9 kg/kW); speed in direct drive at
,000 rpm: 26.4 mph, 42.5 km/h; consumption: 21.6 m/imp
al, 18 m/US gal, 13.1 l x 100 km.

RAKES servo (standard).

IMENSIONS AND WEIGHT weight: plus 85 lb, 38 kg;
uel tank: 10.1 imp gal, 12.2 US gal, 46 l.

140 hp power team

not available in California).

ee 88 hp power team, except for:

NGINE 8 cylinders; 302 cu in, 4,950 cc (4 x 3 in, 101.6 x
6.2 mm); compression ratio: 8.4:1; max power (DIN): 140
p (103 kW) at 3,600 rpm; max torque (DIN): 250 lb ft, 34.5
g m (338.3 Nm) at 1,800 rpm; max engine rpm: 4,000; 28.3

FORD Mustang Cobra 3-dr Sedan

hp/l (20.8 kW/l); valves: overhead, in line, push-rods and
rockers, hydraulic tappets; camshafts: 1, at centre of Vee;
1 Ford 2150 D9BE-YB downdraught twin barrel carburettor;
cooling system: 23.1 imp pt, 27.7 US pt, 13.1 l.

TRANSMISSION gearbox ratios: I 3.070, II 1.720, III 1,
IV 0.700, rev 3.070; axle ratio: 3.080.

PERFORMANCE max speed: about 105 mph, 169 km/h;
power-weight ratio: 2-dr Sedan 18.9 lb/hp (25.7 lb/kW),
8.6 kg/hp (11.6 kg/kW) - Ghia 2-dr Sedan 19.7 lb/hp (26.8
lb/kW), 8.9 kg/hp (12.2 kg/kW); speed in top at 1,000 rpm:
26.2 mph, 42.2 km/h; consumption: 19.2 m/imp gal, 16
m/US gal, 14.7 l x 100 km.

CHASSIS (standard) anti-roll bar on rear suspension.

STEERING servo (standard); turns lock to lock: 3.05:

BRAKES front disc (diametr 10 in, 25.5 cm), front internal
radial fins, rear compensator, rear drum, servo (standard),
swept area: total 275.5 sq in, 1,777 sq cm.

ELECTRICAL EQUIPMENT 36 Ah battery; 60 A alternator.

DIMENSIONS AND WEIGHT weight: plus 210 lb, 95 kg;
fuel tank: 10.1 imp gal, 12.2 US gal, 46 l.

OPTIONALS SelectShift automatic transmission with 3
ratios (I 2.460, II 1.460, III 1, rev 2.180), max ratio of
converter at stall 2.05, possible manual selection, central
lever, 2.470 axle ratio.

143 hp power team

(for California only).

See 88 hp power team, except for:

ENGINE 8 cylinders; 302 cu in, 4,950 cc (4 x 3 in, 101.6 x
76.2 mm); compression ratio: 8.4:1; max power (DIN): 143
hp (105.2 kW) at 3,600 rpm; max torque (DIN): 243 lb ft,
33.5 kg m (328.5 Nm) at 2,200 rpm; max engine rpm: 4,000;
28.9 hp/l (21.3 kW/l); valves: overhead, in line, push-
rods and rockers, hydraulic tappets; camshafts: 1, at centre of Vee; 1 Motorcraft 2700 D9ZE-BEA downdraught carburettor with variable Venturi; cooling system: 23.1 imp
pt, 27.7 US pt, 13.1 l.

TRANSMISSION gearbox: SelectShift automatic transmission (standard), hydraulic torque converter and planetary
gears with 3 ratios, max ratio of converter at stall 2.05,
possible manual selection; ratios: I 2.460, II 1.460, III 1,
rev 2.180; lever: central; axle ratio: 2.470.

PERFORMANCE max speed: about 103 mph, 165 km/h;
power-weight ratio: 2-dr Sedan 18.6 lb/hp (25.3 lb/kW),
8.4 kg/hp (11.5 kg/kW) - Ghia 2-dr Sedan 19.4 lb/hp (26.4
lb/kW), 8.8 kg/hp (12 kg/kW); speed in direct drive at
1,000 rpm: 25.6 mph, 41.2 km/h; consumption: 18 m/imp
gal, 15 m/US gal, 15.7 l x 100 km.

CHASSIS (standard) anti-roll bar on rear suspension.

STEERING servo (standard); turns lock to lock: 3.05.

BRAKES front disc (diameter 10 in, 25.5 cm), front internal
radial fins, rear compensator, servo (standard); swept area:
total 275.5 sq in, 1,777 sq cm.

ELECTRICAL EQUIPMENT 36 Ah battery; 60 A alternator.

DIMENSIONS AND WEIGHT weight: plus 227 lb, 103 kg;
fuel tank: 10.1 imp gal, 12.2 US gal, 46 l.

150 hp power team

See 88 hp power team, except for:

ENGINE turbocharged; max power (DIN): 150 hp (110.4
kW) at 4,800 rpm; 65.2 hp/l (48 kW/l); lubricating system:
9.2 imp pt, 11 US pt, 5.2 l; 1 Holley-Weber D9ZE-MD/ND
(D9ZE-SB/TB for California only) downdraught twin barrel
carburettor; exhaust system with turbocharger; cooling
system: 17.1 imp pt, 20.5 US pt, 9.7 l.

TRANSMISSION gearbox ratios: I 4.070, II 2.570, III 1.660,
IV 1, rev 3.950; lever: central; axle ratio: 3.450.

PERFORMANCE max speed: about 109 mph, 175 km/h;
power-weight ratio: 2-dr Sedan 16.7 lb/hp (22.7 lb/kW), 7.6
kg/hp (10.3 kg/kW) - Ghia 2-dr Sedan 17.5 lb/hp (23.8
lb/kW), 7.9 kg/hp (10.8 kg/kW); speed in direct drive at
1,000 rpm: 22.7 mph, 36.5 km/h; consumption: 26.4 m/imp
gal, 22 m/US gal, 10.7 l x 100 km.

DIMENSIONS AND WEIGHT weight: plus 71 lb, 32 kg; fuel
tank: 10.3 imp gal, 12.5 US gal, 47 l.

OPTIONALS SelectShift automatic transmission not available.

FORD Mustang 2-dr Sedan

Fairmont Series

PRICES EX WORKS:

2-dr Sedan	$ 3,710
4-dr Sedan	$ 3,810
St. Wagon	$ 4,157
Futura Coupé	$ 4,071

For 6-cylinder engine add $ 241. For V8 add $ 524.

Power team:	Standard for:	Optional for:
88 hp	all	—
85 hp	—	all
140 hp	—	all
143 hp	—	all

88 hp power team

ENGINE front, 4 stroke; 4 cylinders, in line; 140 cu in, 2,300 cc (3.78 x 3.13 in, 95.9 x 79.5 mm); compression ratio: 9:1; max power (DIN): 88 hp (64.8 kW) at 4,800 rpm; max torque (DIN): 118 lb ft, 16.3 kg m (159.8 Nm) at 2,800 rpm; max engine rpm: 5,200; 38.3 hp/l (28.2 kW/l); cast iron block and head; 5 crankshaft bearings; valves: overhead, Vee-slanted, rockers; camshafts: 1, overhead, cogged belt; lubrication: gear pump, full flow filter, 8.3 imp pt, 9.9 US pt, 4.7 l; 1 Holley-Weber D9BE-AAA (D9BE-ABA for California only) downdraught twin barrel carburettor; cleaner air system; exhaust system with catalytic converter;

FORD Fairmont ES 2-dr Sedan

fuel feed: mechanical pump; water-cooled, 14.4 imp pt, 17.3 US pt, 8.2 l.

TRANSMISSION driving wheels: rear; clutch: single dry plate; gearbox: mechanical; gears: 4, fully synchronized; ratios: I 3.980, II 2.140, III 1.420, IV 1, rev 3.990; lever: central; final drive: hypoid bevel; axle ratio: 3.080; width of rims: 5'' - St. Wagon 5.5''; tyres: B78 x 14 - St. Wagon CR78 x 14.

PERFORMANCE max speed: about 96 mph, 154 km/h; power-weight ratio: 4-dr. Sedan 29.3 lb/hp (39.8 lb/kW), 13.3 kg/hp (18 kg/kW); speed in direct drive at 1,000 rpm: 19.3 mph, 31 km/h; consumption: 23.9 m/imp gal, 20 m/US gal, 11.8 l x 100 km.

CHASSIS integral with 2 cross members; front suspension: independent, by McPherson, wishbones (lower control arms), coil springs/telescopic damper struts, anti-roll bar; rear: rigid axle, lower trailing radius arms, upper oblique torque arms, coil springs, telescopic dampers.

STEERING rack-and-pinion; turns lock to lock: 4.10.

BRAKES front disc (diameter 10.06 in, 25.4 cm), front internal radial fins, rear compensator, rear drum; swept area: front 176.6 sq in, 1,140 sq cm, rear 98.9 sq in, 638 sq cm - St. Wagon 110 sq in, 710 sq cm, total 275.5 sq in, 1,778 sq cm - St. Wagon 286.6 sq in, 1,850 sq cm.

ELECTRICAL EQUIPMENT 12 V; 45 Ah battery; 40 A alternator; Motorcraft transistorized ignition; 4 headlamps.

DIMENSIONS AND WEIGHT wheel base: 105.50 in, 268 cm; tracks: 56.60 in, 144 cm front, 57 in, 145 cm rear; length: 194.90 in, 495 cm - Futura 196.80 in, 500 cm; width: 71 in, 180 cm; height: 53.60 in, 136 cm - St. Wagon 54.40 in, 138 cm - Futura 52.30 in, 133 cm; ground clearance: 4.38 in, 11.1 cm - St. Wagon 4.75 in, 12.1 cm; weight: 2-dr Sedan 2,551 lb, 1,157 kg - 4-dr Sedan 2,576 lb, 1,168 kg - St. Wagon 2,685 lb, 1,218 kg - Futura 2,598 lb, 1,178 kg; turning circle: 39 ft, 11.9 m; fuel tank: 13.4 imp gal, 16 US gal, 61 l.

OPTIONALS heavy-duty cooling system; alluminum wheels; BR78 x 14, C78 x 14, CR78 x 14 or DR78 x 14 tyres; heavy-duty suspension with rear anti-roll bar; power steering; tilt of steering wheels; servo brake; 54 Ah heavy-duty battery; heated rear window; tinted glass; air-conditioning; electric windows; rear window wiper-washer (St. Wagon only); metallic spray; vinyl roof; speed control device; luxury interior; sunshine roof (sedans only); Ghia equipment (except for St. Wagon); Squire equipment (St. Wagon only); Sports equipment (Futura only); ES equipment (sedans only). (For sedans and Futura only) SelectShift automatic transmission with 3 ratios (I 2.470, II 1.470, III 1, rev 2.110), max ratio of converter at stall 2.9, possible manual selection, steering column lever, 3.080 axle ratio.

85 hp power team

See 88 hp power team, except for:

ENGINE 6 cylinders, in line; 200 cu in, 3,277 cc (3.68 x 3.13 in, 95.3 x 79.5 mm); compression ratio: 8.5:1; max power (DIN): 85 hp (62.6 kW) at 3,600 rpm; max torque (DIN): 154 lb ft, 21.2 kg m (208 Nm) at 1,600 rpm; max engine rpm: 4,000; 25.9 hp/l (19.1 kW/l); 7 crankshaft bearings; valves: overhead, in line, push-rods and rockers, hydraulic tappets; camshafts: 1, side; 1 Carter YFA (Holley 1946 for California only) downdraught single barrel carburettor; cooling system: 15 imp pt, 18 US pt, 8.5 l.

TRANSMISSION gearbox: mechanical (SelectShift automatic transmission standard for California only); gears: 4, fully synchronized with overdrive/top; ratios: I 3.290, II 1.840, III 1, IV 0.810, rev 3.290.

PERFORMANCE max speed: about 99 mph, 160 km/h; power-weight ratio: 4-dr Sedan 31.3 lb/hp (42.5 lb/kW), 14.2 kg/hp (19.2 kg/kW); speed in top at 1,000 rpm: 24.9 mph, km/h; consumption: 22.8 m/imp gal, 19 m/US gal, 12 l x 100 km.

ELECTRICAL EQUIPMENT 36 Ah battery.

DIMENSIONS AND WEIGHT weight: plus 82 lb, 37 kg.

OPTIONALS SelectShift automatic transmission with 3 ratios (I 2.460, II 1.460, III 1, rev 2.190), max ratio of converter at stall 2, possible manual selection, steering column or central lever, 2.730 axle ratio.

140 hp power team

(not available in California).

See 88 hp power team, except for:

ENGINE 8 cylinders; 302 cu in, 4,950 cc (4 x 3 in, 101.6 x 76.2 mm); compression ratio: 8.4:1; max power (DIN): 140 hp (103 kW) at 3,600 rpm; max torque (DIN): 250 lb ft, 34.5 kg m (338.3 Nm) at 1,800 rpm; max engine rpm 4,000; 28.3 hp/l (20.8 kW/l); valves: overhead, in line, push-rods and rockers, hydraulic tappets; camshafts: 1, at centre of Vee; 1 Ford 2150 D9BE-YB downdraught twin barrel carburettor; cooling system: 23.1 imp pt, 27.7 US pt, 13.1 l.

TRANSMISSION gears: 4, fully synchronized with overdrive/top; ratios: I 3.070, II 1.720, III 1, IV 0.700, rev 3.070; axle ratio: 2.730.

PERFORMANCE max speed: about 109 mph, 175 km/h; power-weight ratio: 4-dr Sedan 20.4 lb/hp (27.7 lb/kW), 9.2 kg/hp (12.6 kg/kW); speed in top at 1,000 rpm: 27 mph, 43.7 km/h; consumption: 19.2 m/imp gal, 16 m/US gal, 14.7 l x 100 km.

ELECTRICAL EQUIPMENT 36 Ah battery.

DIMENSIONS AND WEIGHT weight: plus 277 lb, 126 kg.

OPTIONALS SelectShift automatic transmission with ratios (I 2.460, II 1.460, III 1, rev 2.190), max ratio of converter at stall 2, possible manual selection, steering column or central lever, 2.260 axle ratio.

FORD Granada Ghia 4-dr Sedan

138 hp power team

(for California only).

See 97 hp power team, except for:

ENGINE 8 cylinders; 302 cu in, 4,950 cc (4 x 3 in, 101.6 x 76.2 mm); compression ratio: 8.4:1; max power (DIN): 138 hp (101.6 kW) at 3,800 rpm; max torque (DIN): 239 lb ft, 33 kg m (323.6 Nm) at 2,200 rpm; max engine rpm: 4,200; 27.9 hp/l (20.5 kW/l); 5 crankshaft bearings; camshafts: 1, at centre of Vee; 1 Ford 2700 9510 D9DE-HA downdraught carburettor with variable Venturi; cooling system: 23.6 imp pt, 28.3 US pt, 13.4 l.

TRANSMISSION gearbox: SelectShift Cruise-O-Matic automatic transmission (standard), hydraulic torque converter and planetary gears with 3 ratios, max ratio of converter at stall 2, possible manual selection; ratios: I 2.460, II 1.460, III 1, rev 2.800; lever: steering column; axle ratio: 2.790.

PERFORMANCE max speed: about 99 mph, 160 km/h; power-weight ratio: 4-dr 23 lb/hp (31.2 lb/kW), 10.4 kg/hp (14.1 kg/kW); speed in direct drive at 1,000 rpm: 26.1 mph, 42 km/h; consumption: 16.8 m/imp gal, 14 m/US gal, 16.8 l x 100 km.

DIMENSIONS AND WEIGHT weight: plus 80 lb, 36 kg.

OPTIONALS central lever.

FORD Granada ESS 4-dr Sedan

143 hp power team

[f]or California only).

[S]ee 88 hp power team, except for:

[E]NGINE 8 cylinders; 302 cu in, 4,950 cc (4 x 3 in, 101.6 x [7]6.2 mm); compression ratio: 8.4:1; max power (DIN): 143 [hp] (105.2 kW) at 3,600 rpm; max torque (DIN): 243 lb ft, [33].5 kg m (328.5 Nm) at 2,200 rpm; max engine rpm: 4,000; [2]8.9 hp/l (21.3 kW/l); valves: overhead, in line, push-rods [an]d rockers, hydraulic tappets; camshafts: 1, at centre [of] Vee; 1 Ford 2700 D9DE-HA downdraught carburettor with [va]riable Venturi; cooling system: 23.1 imp pt, 27.7 US pt, [13].1 l.

[T]RANSMISSION gearbox: SelectShift automatic transmission [(s]tandard), hydraulic torque converter and planetary gears [wi]th 3 ratios, max ratio of converter at stall 2, possible [m]anual selection; ratios: I 2.460, II 1.460, III 1, rev 2.190; [le]ver: steering column or central; axle ratio: 2.730.

[P]ERFORMANCE max speed: about 106 mph, 170 km/h; [p]ower-weight ratio: 4-dr Sedan 20 lb/hp (27.1 lb/kW), 9 [kg]/hp (12.3 kg/kW); speed in direct drive at 1,000 rpm: [2]9.3 mph, 47.2 km/h; consumption: 18 m/imp gal, 15 m/US [ga]l, 15.7 l x 100 km.

[E]LECTRICAL EQUIPMENT 36 Ah battery.

[D]IMENSIONS AND WEIGHT weight: plus 278 lb, 126 kg.

Granada Series

[P]RICES EX WORKS:

[2-]dr Sedan	$ 4,342
[4-]dr Sedan	$ 4,445
[G]hia 2-dr Sedan	$ 4,728
[G]hia 4-dr Sedan	$ 4,830
[E]SS 2-dr Sedan	$ 4,888
[E]SS 4-dr Sedan	$ 4,990

[f]or V8 engines add $ 283.

Power team:	Standard for:	Optional for:
[9]7 hp	all	—
[9]7 hp	—	all
[8]8 hp	—	all

97 hp power team

[E]NGINE front, 4 stroke; 6 cylinders, in line; 250 cu in, [4],097 cc (3.68 x 3.91 in, 93.5 x 99.3 mm); compression ratio: [8].6:1; max power (DIN): 97 hp (71.4 kW) at 3,200 rpm; [m]ax torque (DIN): 210 lb ft, 29 kg m (284.4 Nm) at 1,400 [rp]m; max engine rpm: 3,800; 23.7 hp/l (17.4 kW/l); cast [ir]on block and head; 7 crankshaft bearings; valves: over-[h]ead, in line, push-rods and rockers, hydraulic tappets; [c]amshafts: 1, side; lubrication: rotary pump, full flow filter, [8].3 imp pt, 9.9 US pt, 4.7 l; 1 Carter YFA 9510 D9DE-EA [D]9DE-BA for California only) downdraught single barrel [c]arburettor; cleaner air system; exhaust system with cata-[ly]tic converter; fuel feed: mechanical pump; water-cooled, [1]7.4 imp pt, 21 US pt, 9.9 l (California only 17.8 imp [p]t, 21.4 US pt, 10.1 l).

[T]RANSMISSION driving wheels: rear; clutch: single dry

plate, semi-centrifugal; gearbox: mechanical; (SelectShift Cruise-O-Matic automatic transmission standard for California only); gears: 4, fully synchronized with overdrive/top; ratios: I 3.290, II 1.840, III 1, IV 0.810, rev 3.290; lever: central; final drive: hypoid bevel; axle ratio: 3.000 (2.790 for California only); width of rims: 6''; tyres: DR78 x 14.

PERFORMANCE max speed: about 93 mph, 149 km/h; power-weight ratio: 4-dr 31.9 lb/hp (43.3 lb/kW), 14.4 kg/hp (19.6 kg/kW); speed in top at 1,000 rpm: 25.5 mph, 41 km/h; consumption: 21.6 m/imp gal, 18 m/US gal, 13.1 l x 100 km.

CHASSIS integral; front suspension: independent, wishbones, coil springs, anti-roll bar, telescopic dampers; rear: rigid axle, semi-elliptic leafsprings, telescopic dampers.

STEERING recirculating ball; turns lock to lock: 5.18.

BRAKES front disc (diameter 11.03 in, 28 cm), front internal radial fins, rear compensator, rear drum; swept area: total 348.2 sq in, 2,247 sq cm.

ELECTRICAL EQUIPMENT 12 V; 36 Ah battery; 40 A alternator; Motorcraft transistorized ignition; 2 headlamps.

DIMENSIONS AND WEIGHT wheel base: 109.90 in, 279 cm; tracks: 59 in, 150 cm front, 57.70 in, 147 cm rear; length: 197.80 in, 502 cm; width: 74 in, 188 cm; height: 53.20 in, 135 cm - 4-dr 53.30 in, 135 cm; ground clearance: 4.41 in, 11.2 cm; weight: 2-dr 3,054 lb, 1,384 kg - 4-dr 3,093 lb, 1,401 kg; turning circle: 39 ft, 11.9 m; fuel tank: 15 imp gal, 18 US gal, 68 l.

BODY saloon/sedan; 5 seats, separate front seats, reclining backrests.

OPTIONALS heavy-duty cooling system; SelectShift Cruise-O-Matic automatic transmission with 3 ratios (I 2.460, II 1.460, III 1, rev 2.800), max ratio of converter at stall 2.3, possible manual selection, steering column or central lever, 2.790 axle ratio; ER78 x 14 or FR78 x 14 tyres; aluminum wheels; heavy-duty suspension; powersteering; tilt of steering wheel; servo brake; automatic speed control; heated rear dindow; electric windows; 54 Ah heavy-duty battery; tinted glass; metallic spray; vinyl roof; air-conditioning.

137 hp power team

(not available in California).

See 97 hp power team, except for:

ENGINE 8 cylinders; 302 cu in, 4,950 cc (4 x 3 in, 101.6 x 76.2 mm); compression ratio: 8.4:1; max power (DIN): 137 hp (100.8 kW) at 3,600 rpm; max torque (DIN): 243 lb ft, 33.5 kg m (328.5 Nm) at 2,000 rpm; max engine rpm: 4,200; 27.7 hp/l (20.4 kW/l); 5 crankshaft bearings; camshafts: 1, at centre of Vee; 1 Ford 2150A 9510 D9DE-KA downdraught twin barrel carburettor; cooling system: 23.6 imp pt, 28.3 US pt, 13.4 l.

PERFORMANCE max speed: about 103 mph, 165 km/h; power-weight ratio: 4-dr 23.1 lb/hp (31.4 lb/kW), 10.5 kg/hp (14.2 kg/kW); consumption: 19.2 m/imp gal, 16 m/US gal, 14.7 l x 100 km.

DIMENSIONS AND WEIGHT weight: plus 71 lb, 32 kg.

OPTIONALS SelectShift Cruise-O-Matic automatic transmission with max ratio of converter at stall 2.

Thunderbird Series

PRICES EX WORKS:

Hardtop	$ 5,877
Town Landau Hardtop	$ 8,866
Heritage Hardtop	$ 10,687

For 5.8-litre engines add $ 263.

Power team:	Standard for:	Optional for:
133 hp	all	—
129 hp	—	all
135 hp	—	all
149 hp	all	—
151 hp	—	all

133 hp power team

(not available in California).

ENGINE front, 4 stroke; 8 cylinders; 302 cu in, 4,950 cc (4 x 3 in, 101.6 x 76.2 mm); compression ratio: 8.4:1; max power (DIN): 133 hp (97.9 kW) at 3,400 rpm; max torque (DIN): 245 lb ft, 33.8 kg m (331.5 Nm) at 1,600 rpm; max engine rpm: 4,000; 26.9 hp/l (19.8 kW/l); cast iron block and head; 5 crankshaft bearings; valves: overhead, in line, push-rods and rockers, hydraulic tappets; camshafts: 1, at centre of Vee; lubrication: rotary pump, full flow filter, 8.3 imp pt, 9.9 US pt, 4.7 l; 1 Ford 2150A D84E-TA/UA downdraught twin barrel carburettor; cleaner air system; exhaust system with 2 catalytic converters; fuel feed: mechanical pump; water-cooled, 23.8 imp pt, 28.5 US pt, 13.5 l.

TRANSMISSION driving wheels: rear; gearbox: SelectShift automatic transmission, hydraulic torque converter and planetary gears with 3 ratios, max ratio of converter at stall 1.97, possible manual selection; ratio: I 2.460, II 1.460, III 1, rev 2.200; lever: steering column; final drive: hypoid bevel; axle ratio: 2.750; width of rims: 6''; tyres: GR78 x 15.

PERFORMANCE max speed: about 103 mph, 165 km/h; power-weight ratio: 29 lb/hp (39.4 lb/kW), 13.1 kg/hp (17.9 kg/kW); speed in direct drive at 1,000 rpm: 25.6 mph, 41.2 km/h; consumption: 16.8 m/imp gal, 14 m/US gal, 16.8 l x 100 km.

CHASSIS perimeter box-type frame; front suspension: independent, wishbones, coil springs, anti-roll bar, telescopic dampers; rear: rigid axle, lower trailing radius arms, upper oblique torque arms, coil springs, anti-roll bar, telescopic dampers.

STEERING recirculating ball, tilt of steering wheel (standard on Town Landau and Heritage models), servo; turns lock to lock: 4.10.

BRAKES front disc (diameter 10.72 in, 27.2 cm), front internal radial fins, rear compensator, rear drum, servo; swept area: front 212 sq in, 1,368 sq cm, rear 155.9 sq in, 1,006 sq cm, total 367.9 sq in, 2,374 sq cm.

ELECTRICAL EQUIPMENT 12 V; 36 Ah battery; 40 A alternator; Motorcraft transistorized ignition; 4 headlamps.

DIMENSIONS AND WEIGHT wheel base: 113.90 in, 289 cm; tracks: 63.20 in, 160 cm front, 63.10 in, 160 cm rear; length: 217.20 in, 552 cm; width: 78.50 in, 199 cm; height: 52.80 in, 134 cm; ground clearance: 5.06 in, 12.8 cm; weight: 3,856 lb, 1,749 kg; fuel tank: 17.6 imp gal, 21 US gal, 80 l.

133 HP POWER TEAM

BODY hardtop; 2 doors; 6 seats, bench front seats, built-in headrests; heated rear window; electric windows, tinted glass and air-conditioning (standard on Town Landau and Heritage); leather upholstery (standard for Heritage only).

OPTIONALS heavy-duty cooling system; limited slip differential; H78 x 15 tyres; HR70 x 15 tyres with 6.5'' wide rims; central lever; tilt of steering wheel (except for Town Landau and Heritage); heavy-duty suspension; 77 Ah heavy-duty battery; heated rear window; electric windows, tinted glass and air-conditioning (except for Town Landau and Heritage); separate front seats; automatic speed control; sunshine roof; leather upholstery (except for Heritage); larger fuel tank.

129 hp power team

(only for export).

See 133 hp power team, except for:

ENGINE max power (DIN): 129 hp (94.9 kW) at 3,400 rpm; max torque (DIN): 234 lb ft, 32.3 kg m (316.8 Nm) at 1,600 rpm; 26.1 hp/l (19.2 kW/l).

PERFORMANCE power-weight ratio: 29.9 lb/hp (40.6 lb/kW), 13.6 kg/hp (18.4 kg/kW).

135 hp power team

(not available in California).

See 133 hp power team, except for:

ENGINE 351 cu in, 5,732 cc (4 x 3.50 in, 101.6 x 88.8 mm); compression ratio: 8.3:1; max power (DIN): 135 hp (99.4 kW) at 3,200 rpm; max torque (DIN): 286 lb ft, 39.4 kg m (386.4 Nm) at 1,400 rpm; 23.6 hp/l (17.3 kW/l); 1 Ford 2150A D9WE-EA downdraught twin barrel carburettor; cooling system: 25.7 imp pt, 30.9 US pt, 14.6 l.

TRANSMISSION gearbox: automatic transmission with max ratio of converter at stall 1.85; ratios: I 2.400, II 1.470, III 1, rev 2; axle ratio: 2.470.

PERFORMANCE power-weight ratio: 29.6 lb/hp (40.2 lg/kW), 13.4 kg/hp (18.2 kg/kW); consumption: 15.6 m/imp gal, 13 m/US gal, 18.1 l x 100 km.

ELECTRICAL EQUIPMENT 45 Ah battery.

DIMENSIONS AND WEIGHT weight: plus 142 lb, 64 kg.

149 hp power team

(for California only).

See 133 hp power team, except for:

ENGINE 351 cu in, 5,732 cc (4 x 3.50 in, 101.6 x 88.8 mm); compression ratio: 8:1; max power (DIN): 149 hp (109.7 kW) at 3,800 rpm; max torque (DIN): 258 lb ft, 35.6 kg m (349.1 Nm) at 2,200 rpm; max engine rpm: 4,400; 26 hp/l (19.1 kW/l); 1 Ford 2150A D9AE-AHA downdraught twin barrel carburettor; cooling system: 27.5 imp pt, 33 US pt, 15.6 l.

TRANSMISSION gearbox: automatic transmission with max ratio of converter at stall 1.85; ratios: I 2.400, II 1.470, III 1, rev 2; axle ratio: 2.470.

PERFORMANCE max speed: about 106 mph, 170 km/h; power-weight ratio: 26.8 lb/hp (36.4 lb/kW), 12.2 kg/hp (16.5 kg/kW); speed in direct drive at 1,000 rpm: 27.8 mph, 44.7 km/h; consumption: 13.2 m/imp gal, 11 m/US gal, 21.4 l x 100 km.

ELECTRICAL EQUIPMENT 45 Ah battery.

DIMENSIONS AND WEIGHT weight: plus 142 lb, 64 kg.

151 hp power team

(not available in California).

See 133 hp power team, except for:

ENGINE 351 cu in, 5,732 cc (4 x 3.50 in, 101.6 x 88.8 mm); compression ratio: 8:1; max power (DIN): 151 hp (111.1 kW) at 3,600 rpm; max torque (DIN): 270 lb ft, 37.2 kg m (364.8 Nm) at 2,200 rpm; 26.3 hp/l (19.3 kW/l); 1 Ford 2150A D90E-CB or D8WE-CA downdraught twin barrel carburettor; cooling system: 27.5 imp pt, 33 US pt, 15.6 l.

TRANSMISSION gearbox: automatic transmission with max

FORD Thunderbird Hardtop

ratio of converter at stall 1.85; ratios: I 2.400, II 1.470, III 1, rev 2; axle ratio: 2.470.

PERFORMANCE max speed: about 109 mph, 175 km/h; power-weight ratio: 26.5 lb/hp (36 lb/kW), 12 kg/hp (16.3 kg/kW); speed in direct drive at 1,000 rpm: 27.2 mph, 43.7 km/h; consumption: 15.6 m/imp gal, 13 m/US gal, 18.1 l x 100 km.

DIMENSIONS AND WEIGHT weight: plus 142 lb, 64 kg.

OPTIONALS 3.000 axle ratio.

LTD II Series

PRICES EX WORKS:

S 2-dr Hardtop	$ 5,198
S 4-dr Pillared Hardtop	$ 5,298
2-dr Hardtop	$ 5,445
4-dr Pillared Hardtop	$ 5,569
Brougham 2-dr Hardtop	$ 5,780
Brougham 4-dr Pillared Hardtop	$ 5,905

For 5.8-litre engines add $ 263.

Power team:	Standard for:	Optional for:
133 hp	all	—
129 hp	—	all
149 hp	all	—
151 hp	—	all

133 hp power team

(not available in California).

ENGINE front, 4 stroke; 8 cylinders; 302 cu in, 4,950 cc (4 x 3 in, 101.6 x 76.2 mm); compression ratio: 8.4:1; max power (DIN): 133 hp (97.9 kW) at 3,400 rpm; max torque (DIN): 245 lb ft, 33.8 kg m (331.5 Nm) at 1,600 rpm; max engine rpm: 4,000; 26.9 hp/l (19.8 kW/l); cast iron block and head; 5 crankshaft bearings; valves: overhead, in line, push-rods and rockers, hydraulic tappets; camshafts: 1, at centre of Vee; lubrication: rotary pump, full flow filter, 8.3 imp pt, 9.9 US pt, 4.7 l; 1 Ford 2150A D84E-TA-UA downdraught twin barrel carburettor; cleaner air system; exhaust system with 2 catalytic converters; fuel feed: mechanical pump; water-cooled, 23.8 imp pt, 28.5 US pt, 13.5 l.

TRANSMISSION driving wheels: rear; gearbox: SelectShift automatic transmission, hydraulic torque converter and planetary gears with 3 ratios, max ratio of converter at stall 2.04, possible manual selection; ratios: I 2.460, II 1.460, III 1, rev 2.180; lever: steering column; final drive: hypoid bevel; axle ratio: 2.750; width of rims: 5.5''; HR78 x 14.

PERFORMANCE max speed: about 96 mph, 154 km/h; power-weight ratio: S 4-dr Pillared Hardtop 28.5 lb/hp (38.7 lb/kW), 12.9 kg/hp (17.6 kg/kW); speed in direct drive at 1,000 rpm: 26.1 mph, 42 km/h; consumption: 16.8 m/imp gal, 14 m/US gal, 16.8 l x 100 km.

CHASSIS perimeter box-type frame; front suspension: inde-

FORD Thunderbird Heritage Hardtop

...ndent, wishbones, coil springs, anti-roll bar, telescopic ...mpers; rear: rigid axle, lower trailing radius arms, upper ...lique torque arms, coil springs, telescopic dampers.

...TEERING recirculating ball, servo; turns lock to lock: 4.10.

...RAKES front disc (diameter 10.72 in, 27.2 cm), front in-...rnal radial fins, rear compensator, rear drum, servo: ...ept area: front 212 sq in, 1,368 sq cm, rear 155.9 sq ..., 1,006 sq cm, total 367.9 sq in, 2,374 sq cm.

...ECTRICAL EQUIPMENT 12 V; 36 Ah battery; 40 A alter-...tor; Motorcraft transistorized ignition; 4 headlamps.

...IMENSIONS AND WEIGHT wheel base: 2-dr 113.90 in. ...9 cm - 4-dr 117.90 in, 299 cm; tracks: 63.60 in, 161 cm ...ont, 63.50 in, 161 cm rear; length: 2-dr 217.20 in, 552 ...n - 4-dr 221.20 in, 562 cm; width: 78.60 in, 200 cm: ...eight: 2-dr 52.60 in, 134 cm - 4-dr 53.30 in, 135 cm: ...ound clearance: 2-dr 4.76 in, 12.1 cm -4-dr 4.73 in, ...1 cm; weight: S 2-dr Hardtop 3,717 lb, 1,686 kg - S ...dr Pillared Hardtop 3,796 lb, 1,722 kg - 2-dr Hardtop ...732 lb, 1,693 kg - 4-dr Pillared Hardtop 3,793 lb, 1,721 ..., turning circle: 42.4 ft, 12.9 m; fuel tank: 17.6 imp ...l, 21 US gal, 80 l.

...ODY hardtop; 6 seats, bench front seats with built-in ...adrests.

...PTIONALS heavy-duty cooling system; central lever; limit-...-slip differential; H78 x 14 tyres; GR78 x 15 tyres with ... wide rims; heavy-duty suspension with rear anti-roll ...r; tilt of steering wheel; 77 Ah heavy-duty battery; heated ...ar window; tinted glass; electric windows; separate front ...ats; automatic speed control; vinyl roof; metallic spray; ...rger fuel tank; air-conditioning.

129 hp power team

...nly for export).

...e 133 hp power team, except for:

...NGINE max power (DIN): 129 hp (94.9 kW) at 3,400 rpm; ...ax torque (DIN): 234 lb ft, 32.3 kg m (316.8 Nm) at ...600 rpm; 26.1 hp/l (19.2 kW/l).

...ERFORMANCE power-weight ratio: S 4-dr Pillared Hardtop ....4 lb/hp (40 lb/kW), 13.3 kg/hp (18.1 kg/kW).

149 hp power team

...or California only).

...e 133 hp power team, except for:

...NGINE 351 cu in, 5,732 cc (4 x 3.50 in, 101.6 x 88.8 mm); ...ompression ratio: 8:1; max power (DIN): 149 hp (109.7 kW) ... 3,800 rpm; max torque (DIN): 258 lb ft, 35.6 kg m (349.1 ...m) at 2,200 rpm; max engine rpm: 4,400; 26 hp/l (19.1 ...W/l); 1 Ford 2150 A D9AE-AHA downdraught twin barrel ...rburettor; cooling system: 27.5 imp pt, 33 US pt, 15.6 l.

...RANSMISSION gearbox: automatic transmission with max ...tio of converter at stall 1.83; ratios: I 2.400, II 1.400, III ... rev 2.200; axle ratio: 2.470.

...ERFORMANCE max speed: about 104 mph, 167 km/h; power ...weight ratio: S 4-dr Pillared Hardtop 26.7 lb/hp (36.3 lb/ ...V), 12.1 kg/hp (16.4 kg/kW); consumption: 13.2 m/imp gal, ... m/US gal, 21.4 l x 100 km.

...ECTRICAL EQUIPMENT 45 Ah battery.

...IMENSIONS AND WEIGHT weight: plus 181 lb, 82 kg.

151 hp power team

...ot available in California).

...e 133 hp power team, except for:

...NGINE 351 cu in, 5,732 cc (4 x 3.50 in, 101.6 x 88.8 mm); ...ompression ratio: 8:1; max power (DIN): 151 hp (111.1 ...W) at 3,600 rpm; max torque (DIN): 270 lb ft, 37.2 kg m ...64.8 Nm) at 2,200 rpm; 26.3 hp/l (19.3 kW/l); 1 Ford ...50A D90E-CB or D8WE-CA downdraught twin barrel car-...rettor; cooling system: 27.5 imp pt, 33 US pt, 15.6 l.

...RANSMISSION gearbox: automatic transmission with max ...tio of converter at stall 1.83; ratios: I 2.400, II 1.400, ...I 1, rev 2.200; axle ratio: 2.470.

...ERFORMANCE max speed: about 106 mph, 170 km/h; ...wer-weight ratio: S 4-dr Pillared Hardtop 26.3 lb/hp ...5.8 lb/kW), 11.9 kg/hp (16.2 kg/kW); speed in direct ...ive at 1,000 rpm: 29.3 mph, 47.2 km/h; consumption: ...6 m/imp gal, 13 m/US gal, 18.1 l x 100 km.

...ECTRICAL EQUIPMENT 45 Ah battery.

...PTIONALS 3.000 axle ratio.

FORD LTD II S 2-dr Hardtop

LTD Series

PRICES EX WORKS:

1 2-dr Sedan		$ 5,813
2 4-dr Sedan		$ 5,913
3 St. Wagon		$ 6,122
4 Landau 2-dr Sedan		$ 6,349
5 Landau 4-dr Sedan		$ 6,474
6 Country Squire St. Wagon		$ 6,615

For 5.8-litre engines add $ 263.

Power team:	Standard for:	Optional for:
129 hp	all	—
130 hp	1,2,4,5	—
138 hp	—	all
142 hp	—	all

129 hp power team

(not available in California).

ENGINE front, 4 stroke; 8 cylinders; 302 cu in, 4,950 cc (4 x 3 in, 101.6 x 76.2 mm); compression ratio: 8.4:1; max power (DIN): 129 hp (94.9 kW) at 3,600 rpm; max torque (DIN): 223 lb ft, 30.8 kg m (302.1 Nm) at 2,600 rpm; max engine rpm: 4,000; 26.1 hp/l (19.2 kW/l); cast iron block and head; 5 crankshaft bearings; valves: overhead, in line, push-rods and rockers, hydraulic tappets; camshafts:

1, at centre of Vee; lubrication: rotary pump, full flow filter, 8.3 imp pt, 9.9 US pt, 4.7 l; 1 Ford 2700 A D9AE-YB-JB downdraught carburettor with variable Venturi; cleaner air system; exhaust system with 2 catalytic converters; fuel feed: mechanical pump; water-cooled, 22.2 imp pt, 26.6 US pt, 12.6 l.

TRANSMISSION driving wheels: rear; gearbox: SelectShift Cruise-O-Matic automatic transmission, hydraulic torque converter and planetary gears with 3 ratios, max ratio of converter at stall 1.97, possible manual selection; ratios: I 2.400, II 1.470, III 1, rev 2; lever: steering column; final drive: hypoid bevel; axle ratio: 2.260 - st. wagons 2.730; width of rims: 5.5'' - st. wagons 6.5''; tyres: FR78 x 14 - st. wagons GR78 x 14.

PERFORMANCE max speed: about 96 mph, 154 km/h; power -weight ratio: 4-dr Sedan 26.7 lb/hp (36.2 lb/kW), 12.1 kg/hp (16.4 kg/kW) - Landau 4-dr Sedan 27 lb/hp (36.7 lb/kW, 12.2 kg/hp (16.6 kg/kW); speed in direct drive at 1,000 rpm: 25.4 mph, 40.8 km/h; consumption: 18 m/imp gal, 15 m/US gal, 15.7 l x 100 km.

CHASSIS perimeter box-type frame; front suspension: inde-pendent, wishbones, coil springs, anti-roll bar, telescopic dampers; rear: rigid axle, lower trailing radius arms, upper oblique torque arms, coil springs, telescopic dampers.

STEERING recirculating ball, servo; turns lock to lock: 3.29 - st. wagons 3.99.

BRAKES front disc (diameter 11.08 in, 28.1 cm), front inter-

FORD LTD 2-dr Sedan

129 HP POWER TEAM

nal radial fins, rear compensator, rear drum, servo; swept area: front 228.7 sq in, 1,475 sq cm, rear 157.1 sq in, 1,013 sq cm - st. wagons 155.9 sq in, 1,006 sq cm, total 385.8 sq in, 2,488 sq cm - st. wagons 384.6 sq in, 2,481 sq cm.

ELECTRICAL EQUIPMENT 12 V; 36 A battery; 60 A alternator; Motorcraft transistorized ignition; 4 headlamps.

DIMENSIONS AND WEIGHT wheel base: 114.30 in, 290 cm; tracks: 62.20 in, 158 cm front, 62 in, 157 cm rear; length: sedans 290 in, 531 cm - st. wagons 214.70 in, 545 cm; width: sedans 77.50 in, 197 cm - st. wagons 79.10 in, 201 cm; height: sedans 54.50 in, 138 cm - st. wagons 56.80 in, 144 cm; ground clearance: sedans 4.87 in, 12.4 cm - st. wagons 4.75 in, 12.1 cm; weight: 2-dr Sedan 3,411 lb, 1,547 kg - 4-dr Sedan 3,439 lb, 1,560 kg - St. Wagon 3,682 lb, 1,670 kg - Landau 2-dr Sedan 3,445 lb, 1,563 kg - Landau 4-dr Sedan 3,484 lb, 1,580 kg - Squire St. Wagon 3,707 lb, 1,682 kg; fuel tank: sedans 15.8 imp gal, 19 US gal, 72 l - st. wagons 16.7 imp gal, 20 US gal, 76 l.

BODY 6 seats, bench front seats with built-in headrests.

OPTIONALS heavy-duty cooling system; 2.730 axle ratio (except for st. wagons); GR78 x 14 tyres with 6.5'' wide rims (sedans only); HR78 x 14 tyres with 6.5'' wide rims (st. wagons only); heavy-duty suspension with rear anti-roll bar; tilt of steering wheel; 71 Ah heavy-duty battery; heated rear window; tinted glass; automatic speed control; luxury interior; vinyl roof; electric windows; air-conditioning.

130 hp power team

(for California only).

See 129 hp power team, except for:

ENGINE max power (DIN): 130 hp (95.7 kW) at 3,600 rpm; max torque (DIN): 226 lb ft, 31.2 kg m (306 Nm) at 2,200 rpm; 26.3 hp/l (19.3 kW/l); 1 Ford 2700 D9AE-ZB-CB downdraught carburettor with variable Venturi.

TRANSMISSION axle ratio: 2.260.

PERFORMANCE power-weight ratio: 4-dr Sedan 26.4 lb/hp (35.9 lb/kW), 12 kg/hp (16.3 kg/kW) - Landau 4-dr Sedan 26.8 lb/hp (36.4 lb/kW), 12.1 kg/hp (16.5 kg/kW); consumption: 16.8 m/imp gal, 14 m/US gal, 16.8 l x 100 km.

OPTIONALS 2.730 axle ratio not available.

138 hp power team

(for California only).

See 129 hp power team, except for:

ENGINE 351 cu in, 5,732 cc (4 x 3.50 in, 101.6 x 88.8 mm); compression ratio: 8.3:1; max power (DIN): 138 hp (101.6 kW) at 3,200 rpm; max torque (DIN): 260 lb ft, 35.9 kg m (352.1 Nm) at 2,200 rpm; 24.1 hp/l (17.7 kW/l); 1 Ford 7200 D9AE-CA downdraught carburettor with variable Venturi; cooling system: 23.9 imp pt, 28.8 US pt, 13.6 l.

TRANSMISSION gearbox: automatic transmission with max ratio of converter at stall 1.85; ratios: I 2.460, II 1.460, III 1, rev 2.200.

PERFORMANCE max speed: about 99 mph, 160 km/h; power-weight ratio: 4-dr Sedan 25.3 lb/hp (34.4 lb/kW), 11.5 kg/hp (15.6 kg/kW) - Landau 4-dr Sedan 25.7 lb/hp (34.9 lb/kW), 11.6 kg/hp (15.8 kg/kW); consumption: 15.6 m/imp gal, 13 m/US gal, 18.1 l x 100 km.

ELECTRICAL EQUIPMENT 45 Ah battery.

DIMENSIONS AND WEIGHT weight: plus 59 lb, 27 kg.

OPTIONALS 3.080 axle ratio.

142 hp power team

(not available in California).

See 129 hp power team, except for:

ENGINE 351 cu in, 5,732 cc (4 x 3.50 in, 101.6 x 88.8 mm); compression ratio: 8.3:1; max power (DIN): 142 hp (104.5 kW) at 3,200 rpm; max torque (DIN): 286 lb ft, 39.4 kg m (386.4 Nm) at 1,400 rpm; 24.8 hp/l (18.2 kW/l); 1 Ford 2150A D9AE-APB or Ford 2150 TBD downdraught twin barrel carburettor; cooling system: 23.9 imp pt, 28.8 US pt, 13.6 l.

TRANSMISSION gearbox: automatic transmission with max ratio of converter at stall 1.85; ratio: I 2.460, II 1.460, III 1, rev 2.200; axle ratio: 2.260.

FORD LTD Landau 4-dr Sedan

PERFORMANCE max speed: about 103 mph, 165 km/h; power-weight ratio: 4-dr Sedan 24.6 lb/hp (33.5 lb/kW), 11.2 kg/hp (15.2 kg/kW) - Landau 4-dr Sedan 24.9 lb/hp (33.9 lb/kW), 11.3 kg/hp (15.4 kg/kW); speed in direct drive at 1,000 rpm: 28.5 mph, 45.8 km/h; consumption: 16.8 m/imp gal, 14 m/US gal, 16.8 l x 100 km.

ELECTRICAL EQUIPMENT 45 Ah battery.

DIMENSIONS AND WEIGHT weight: plus 59 lb, 27 kg.

OPTIONALS 3.080 axle ratio.

GREENWOOD   USA

Turbo

PRICE EX WORKS: $ 28,000

ENGINE Chevrolet Corvette, turbocharged, front, 4 stroke; 8 cylinders; 350 cu in, 5,736 cc (4 x 3.48 in, 101.6 x 88.3 mm); compression ratio: 8.5:1; cast iron block and head; 5 crankshaft bearings; valves: overhead, in line, push-rods and rockers, hydraulic tappets; camshafts: 1, at centre of Vee; lubrication: gear pump, full flow filter, 8.3 imp pt, 9.9 US pt, 4.7 l; 1 downdraught 4-barrel carburettor with turbocharger; cleaner air system; exhaust system with catalytic converter; fuel feed: mechanical pump; water-cooled, 34.5 imp pt, 41.4 US pt, 19.6 l.

TRANSMISSION driving wheels: rear; gearbox: Turbo Hydramatic automatic transmission, hydraulic torque converter and planetary gears with 3 ratios; lever: central; final drive: hypoid bevel, limited slip differential; axle ratio: 3.550; width of rims: 8''; tyres: HR60 x 15 front, LR60 x 15 rear.

PERFORMANCE max speed: about 130 mph, 209 km/h; speed in direct drive at 1,000 rpm: 28 mph, 45 km/h; consumption: not declared.

CHASSIS ladder frame with cross members; front suspension: independent, wishbones, coil springs, anti-roll bar, adjustable telescopic dampers; rear: independent, wishbones, coil springs, anti-roll bar, adjustable telescopic dampers.

STEERING recirculating ball, servo.

BRAKES disc (diameter 11.75 in, 30 cm), internal radial fins, servo.

ELECTRICAL EQUIPMENT 12 V; 3500 W battery; 42 A alternator; Delco-Remy high energy ignition system; retractable headlamps.

DIMENSIONS AND WEIGHT wheel base: 98 in, 249 cm;

GREENWOOD Turbo

racks: 61 in, 155 cm front, 62 in, 157 cm rear; length: 85.20 in, 470 cm; width: 72 in, 183 cm front, 75 in, 190 m rear; height: 48 in, 122 cm; weight: 3,320 lb, 1,505 kg; uel tank: 20 imp gal, 24 US gal, 91 l.

ODY coupé, in plastic material; 2 doors; 2 seats.

OPTIONALS 3.360 axle ratio; special spray.

NTERMECCANICA   USA

Speedster

RICE EX WORKS: $ 10,250

NGINE Volkswagen, rear, 4 stroke; 4 cylinders, horizontally pposed; 96.7 cu in, 1,584 cc (3.37 x 2.72 in, 85.5 x 69 mm); ompression ratio: 8.5:1; max power (DIN): 50 hp (36.8 kW) t 4,000 rpm; max torque (DIN): 78 lb ft, 10.8 kg m (105.9 m) at 2,800 rpm; max engine rpm: 4,600; 31.6 hp/l (23.3 W/l); block with cast iron liners and light alloy fins, light lloy head; 4 crankshaft bearings; valves: overhead, push-ods and rockers; camshafts: 1, central, lower; lubrication: ear pump, filter in sump, oil cooler, 4.4 imp pt, 5.3 US t, 2.5 l; 1 Solex 1661 downdraught single barrel carbu-ettor; fuel feed: mechanical pump; air-cooled.

RANSMISSION driving wheels: rear; clutch: single dry late; gearbox: mechanical; gears: 4, fully synchronized; atios: I 3.780, II 2.060, III 1.260, IV 0.930, rev 4.010; lever: entral; final drive: spiral bevel; axle ratio: 3.875; width of ims: 4''; tyres: 5.60 x 15.

PERFORMANCE max speed: 110 mph, 177 km/h; power-weight atio: 31.6 lb/hp (43 lb/kW), 14.3 kg/hp (19.5 kg/kW); carry-ing capacity: 353 lb, 160 kg; consumption: 33.6 m/imp gal, 8 m/US gal, 8.4 l x 100 km.

CHASSIS box-section perimeter frame; front suspension: in-lependent, twin swinging longitudinal trailing arms, trans-erse laminated torsion bars, anti-roll bar, telescopic lampers; rear: independent, swinging semi-axles, swinging ongitudinal trailing arms, transverse torsion bars, tele-scopic dampers.

STEERING worm and roller.

RAKES drum; lining area: total 111 sq in, 716 sq cm.

ELECTRICAL EQUIPMENT 12 V; 36 Ah battery; alternator; osch distributor; 2 headlamps.

DIMENSIONS AND WEIGHT wheel base: 82.70 in, 210 cm; racks: 51.57 in, 131 cm front, 53.15 in, 135 cm rear; weight: ,580 lb, 716 kg; weight distribution: 41% front, 59% rear; uel tank: 5.9 imp gal, 7 US gal, 27 l.

BODY roadster in plastic material; 2 doors; 2 seats; ton-neau cover.

OPTIONALS turbocharger.

INTERMECCANICA Speedster

INTERNATIONAL HARVESTER   USA

Scout Series

PRICES EX WORKS:

1 II 4 x 2	$ 5,884
2 II 4 x 4	$ 6,604
3 II Diesel 4 x 2	$ 8,465
4 II Diesel 4 x 4	$ 9,241
5 Traveler 4 x 2	$ 6,481
6 Traveler 4 x 4	$ 7,248
7 Traveler Diesel 4 x 2	$ 8,869
8 Traveler Diesel 4 x 4	$ 9,696
9 SS-II 4 x 4	$ 5,825

For 122.3 hp V8 engines add $ 203. For 148 hp V8 engines add $ 359.

Power team:	Standard for:	Optional for:
76.5 hp	1,2,5,6,9	—
81 hp (Diesel)	3,4,7,8	—
122.3 hp	5,6	1,2,9
148 hp	—	1,2,5,6,9

76.5 hp power team

ENGINE front, 4 stroke; 4 cylinders, in line; 196 cu in, 3,212 cc (4.13 x 3.66 in, 104.8 x 92.9 mm); compression ratio: 8.02:1; max power (DIN): 76.5 hp (56.3 kW) at 3,600 rpm, max torque (DIN): 153 lb ft, 21.2 kg m (207.9 Nm) at 2,000 rpm; max engine rpm: 4,000; 23.9 hp/l (17.6 kW/l); cast iron block and head; 5 crankshaft bearings; valves: overhead, in line, push-rods and rockers, hydraulic tappets; cam-shafts: 1, side; lubrication: gear pump, full flow filter, 11.6 imp pt, 14 US pt, 6.6 l; 1 Holley 1940 downdraught single barrel carburettor; cleaner air system; fuel feed: mechanical pump; water-cooled, 23.2 imp pt, 27.9 US pt, 13.2 l.

TRANSMISSION driving wheels: rear or front and rear; clutch: single dry plate; gearbox: mechanical; gears: 3, fully synchronized; ratios: I 2.997, II 1.550, III 1, rev 2.997; lever: central; final drive: hypoid bevel; axle ratio: 4.090; width of rims: 5.5''; tyres H78 x 15.

PERFORMANCE max speed: 80 mph, 128 km/h; power-weight ratio: 45.9 lb/hp (62.4 lb/kW), 20.8 kg/hp (28.3 kg/kW); speed in direct drive at 1,000 rpm: 20.1 mph, 32.3 km/h; consumption: 18 m/imp gal, 15 m/US gal, 15.7 l x 100 km.

CHASSIS perimeter box-type frame; front and rear suspen-sion: rigid axle, semi-elliptic leafsprings, telescopic dampers.

STEERING worm and roller.

BRAKES front disc (diameter 11.75 in, 29.8 cm), rear drum; swept area: front 226 sq in, 1,458 sq cm, rear 101.8 sq in, 656 sq cm, total 327.8 sq in, 2,114 sq cm.

ELECTRICAL EQUIPMENT 12 V; 62 Ah battery; 37 A alter-nator; Prestolite electronic ignition; 2 headlamps.

DIMENSIONS AND WEIGHT wheel base: 100 in, 254 cm - Travelers 118 in, 300 cm; front and rear track: 57 in, 145 cm; length: 166.20 in, 422 cm - Travelers 184.20 in, 468 cm; width: 70 in, 178 cm; height: 65.70 in, 167 cm - Travelers 66 in, 168 cm; ground clearance: 7.60 in, 19.3 cm; weight: 3,511 lb, 1,592 kg - Travelers 3,711 lb, 1,683 kg; turning circle: 36.4 ft, 11.1 m - Travelers 40.5 ft, 12.3 m; fuel tank: 15.8 imp gal, 19 US gal, 72 l.

BODY estate-car/station wagon; 2 + 1 doors; 5 seats, se-parate front seats.

OPTIONALS 4-speed fully synchronized mechanical gearbox (I 4.020, II 2.410, III 1.410, IV 1, rev 4.730 or I 6.320, II 3.090, III 1.680, IV 1, rev 6.960); gearbox with transfer box; 3-speed automatic transmission; 3.540, or 3.730 axle ratio; HR78 x 15 tyres; limited slip differential; power steering; tilt of steering wheel; front bucket seats with console; folding rear seat; 61 A alternator; 72 Ah battery; heavy-duty front and rear suspension; air-conditioning; Rallye equipment.

81 hp (Diesel) power team

See 76.5 hp power team, except for:

ENGINE Diesel, 4 stroke; 6 cylinders, vertical, in line; 198 cu in, 3,245 cc (3.27 x 3.94 in, 83 x 100 mm); compres-sion ratio: 22:1; max power (DIN): 81 hp at 4,000 rpm; max torque (DIN): 137 lb ft, 18.9 kg m at 2,000 rpm; max engine rpm: 4,400; 25 hp/l; 7 crankshaft bearings.

INTERNATIONAL HARVESTER SS II 4 x 4

81 HP (DIESEL) POWER TEAM

PERFORMANCE power-weight ratio: 43.3 lb/hp (58.8 lb/kW), 19.7 kg/hp (26.8 kg/kW).

PRACTICAL INSTRUCTIONS fuel: Diesel oil.

122.3 hp power team

See 76.5 hp power team, except for:

ENGINE 8 cylinders; 304 cu in, 4,982 cc (3.88 x 3.22 in, 98.5 x 81.7 mm); compression ratio: 8.19:1; max power (DIN): 122.3 hp (90 kW) at 3,400 rpm; max torque (DIN): 226 lb ft, 31 kg m (304 Nm) at 2,000 rpm; 24.5 hp/l (18 kW/l); camshafts: 1, at centre of Vee; dual exhaust system.

TRANSMISSION axle ratio: 3.540.

PERFORMANCE max speed: 90 mph, 145 km/h; power-weight ratio: 30 lb/hp (40.8 lb/kW), 13.6 kg/hp (18.5 kg/kW) - Travelers 31.6 lb/hp (42.9 lb/kW), 14.3 kg/hp (19.4 kg/kW); speed in direct drive at 1,000 rpm: 20.3 mph, 36.2 km/h; consumption: 16.8 m/imp gal, 14 m/US gal, 16.8 l x 100 km.

DIMENSIONS AND WEIGHT weight: 3,666 lb, 1,663 kg - Travelers 3,866 lb, 1,754 kg.

148 hp power team

See 76.5 hp power team, except for:

ENGINE 8 cylinders; 345 cu in, 5,654 cc (3.88 x 3.66 in, 98.5 x 92.9 mm); compression ratio: 8.05:1; max power (DIN): 148 hp at 3,600 rpm; max torque (DIN): 265 lb ft, 35.9 kg m (352 Nm) at 2,000 rpm; max engine rpm: 3,800; 26.1 hp/l (19.2 kW/l); camshafts: 1, at centre of Vee; dual exhaust system; cooling system: 33.3 imp pt, 40 US pt, 18.9 l.

TRANSMISSION axle ratio: 3.540.

PERFORMANCE max speed: 90 mph, 145 km/h; power-weight ratio: 24.9 lb/hp (33.8 lb/kW), 11.3 kg/hp (15.3 kg/kW) - Travelers 26.3 lb/hp (35.7 lb/kW), 11.9 kg/hp (16.2 kg/kW); speed in direct drive at 1,000 rpm: 25 mph, 40.3 km/h; consumption: 14.4 m/imp gal, 12 m/US gal, 19.6 l x 100 km.

DIMENSIONS AND WEIGHT weight: 3,686 lb, 1,672 kg - Travelers 3,891 lb, 1,765 kg.

JEEP CORPORATION USA

Jeep Series

PRICES IN GB AND EX WORKS:	£	$
CJ-5 Roadster		5,488
CJ-7 Roadster	4,989*	5,582

Power team:	Standard for:	Optional for:
98 hp	both	—
126 hp	—	both

98 hp power team

ENGINE front, 4 stroke; 6 cylinders, in line; 258 cu in, 4,228 cc (3.75 x 3.50 in, 95.2 x 99 mm); compression ratio: 8:1; max power (DIN): 98 hp (72.1 kW) at 3,200 rpm; max torque (DIN): 193 lb ft, 26.6 kg m (261 Nm) at 1,600 rpm; max engine rpm: 4,000; 23.2 hp/l (17.1 kW/l); cast iron block and head; 7 crankshaft bearings; valves: overhead, in line, push-rods and rockers, hydraulic tappets; camshafts: 1, side; lubrication: gear pump, full flow filter, 10 imp pt, 12 US pt, 5.7 l; 1 Carter downdraught single barrel carburettor; fuel feed: mechanical pump; water-cooled, 17.4 imp pt, 21 US pt, 9.9 l.

TRANSMISSION driving wheels: front (automatically-engaged with transfer box low ratio) and rear; clutch: single dry plate; gearbox: mechanical; gears: 3, with high and low ratios, fully synchronized; ratios: I 2.990, II 1.750, III 1, rev 3.170; low ratios: I 2.030, II 1; lever: central; final drive: hypoid bevel; axle ratio: 3.540; width of rims 5.5''; tyres: H78 x 15.

PERFORMANCE max speed: about 78 mph, 125 km/h; power-weight ratio: 26.9 lb/hp (36.5 lb/kW), 12.2 kg/hp (16.6 kg/kW); speed in direct drive at 1,000 rpm: 23.6 mph, 38 km/h; consumption: 21.6 m/imp gal, 18 m/US gal, 13.1 l x 100 km.

INTERNATIONAL HARVESTER Scout II Series (Diesel engine)

CHASSIS perimeter box-type with cross members; front and rear suspension: rigid axle, semi-elliptic leafsprings, telescopic dampers.

STEERING recirculating ball.

BRAKES drum; swept area: front 138 sq in, 890 sq cm, rear 138 sq in, 890 sq cm, total 276 sq in, 1,780 sq cm.

ELECTRICAL EQUIPMENT 12 V; 50 Ah battery; 37 A alternator; electronic ignition; 2 headlamps.

DIMENSIONS AND WEIGHT wheel base: CJ-5 83.50 in, 212 cm - CJ-7 93.50 in, 237 cm; tracks: 51.50 in, 131 cm front, 50 in, 127 cm rear; length: CJ-5 138.40 in, 351 cm - CJ-7 147.90 in, 376 cm; width: 68.60 in, 174 cm; height: 67.60 in, 172 cm; ground clearance: 6.90 in, 17.5 cm; weight: CJ-5 2,665 lb, 1,209 kg - CJ-7 2,708 lb, 1,228 kg; turning circle: CJ-5 36.7 ft, 11.2 m - CJ-7 40.9 ft, 12.5 m; fuel tank: 12.5 imp gal, 15 US gal, 57 l.

OPTIONALS rear limited slip differential; 4-speed fully synchronized mechanical gearbox (I 4.020, II 2.410, III 1.410, IV 1, rev 4.730); sports steering wheel; power steering; servo brake; all or half metal top; rear bench seats; heavy-duty suspension; light alloy wheels; Levi's interior; Renegade equipment with luxury interior, racing style roll bar, heavy-duty cooling system and L78 x 15 tyres; Golden Eagle equipment with luxury interior, styled steel wheels, roll bar, rear bench seats, 9 x 15 tyres; Turbo-Hydramatic automatic transmission with 4-wheel drive Quadra-Trac system; full plastic top.

126 hp power team

See 98 hp power team, except for:

ENGINE 8 cylinders; 304 cu in, 4,982 cc (3.75 x 3.44 in, 95.2 x 87.3 mm); compression ratio: 8.4:1; max power (DIN): 126 hp (92.7 kW) at 3,600 rpm; max torque (DIN): 219 ft, 30.2 kg m (296.2 Nm) at 2,000 rpm; 25.3 hp/l (18 kW/l); 5 crankshaft bearings; camshafts: 1, at centre of Vee; lubrication: 8.3 imp pt, 9.9 US pt, 4.7 l; 1 downdraught twin barrel carburettor; exhaust system with catalytic converter; cooling system: 23.2 imp pt, 28 US pt, 13.2 l.

PERFORMANCE max speed: about 84 mph, 135 km/h; power-weight ratio: 21 lb/hp (28.5 lb/kW), 9.5 kg/hp (12.9 kW); consumption: 19.2 m/imp gal, 16 m/US gal, 14 l x 100 km.

Cherokee Series

PRICES IN GB AND EX WORKS:	£	$
2-dr Station Wagon	7,799*	6,82
Wide Wheel 2-dr Station Wagon	—	7,17
4-dr Station Wagon	7,899*	6,94

Power team:	Standard for:	Optional for:
114 hp	all	—
129 hp	—	all

114 hp power team

(not available in California).

ENGINE front, 4 stroke; 6 cylinders, in line; 258 cu in, 4,228 cc (3.75 x 3.90 in, 95.2 x 99 mm); compression ratio: 8:1; max power (DIN): 114 hp (83.9 kW) at 3,600 rpm; max torque (DIN): 192 lb ft, 26.5 kg m (259.9 Nm) at 2,00 rpm; max engine rpm: 4,000; 27 hp/l (19.9 kW/l); cast iron block and head; 7 crankshaft bearings; valves: overhead, in line, push-rods and rockers, hydraulic tappets; camshafts: 1, side; lubrication: gear pump, full flow filter 10 imp pt, 12 US pt, 5.7 l; 1 Carter downdraught twin barrel carburettor; fuel feed: mechanical pump; water-cooled, 17 imp pt, 21 US pt, 9.9 l.

TRANSMISSION driving wheels: front (automatically engaged with transfer box low ratio) and rear; clutch: single dry plate; gearbox: mechanical; gears: 3, with high and low ratios, fully synchronized; ratios: I 3.000, II 1.830, III 1, rev 3.100; low ratios: I 2.030, II 1; lever: central; final drive: hypoid bevel; axle ratio: 4.090 width of rims: 5.5' tyres: H78 x 15 - Wide Wheel 10 x 15.

PERFORMANCE max speed: about 90 mph, 145 km/h; power-weight ratio: 4-dr. 36 lb/hp (48.9 lb/kW), 16.3 kg/hp (22. kg/kW); speed in direct drive at 1,000 rpm: 22.5 mph, 36. km/h; consumption: 21.6 m/imp gal, 18 m/US gal, 13. l x 100 km.

CHASSIS perimeter box-type with cross members; fron and rear suspension: rigid axle, semi-elliptic leafsprings telescopic dampers.

STEERING recirculating ball.

JEEP CORPORATION Jeep CJ-7 Renegade Roadster

BRAKES front disc (diameter 12 in, 30.5 cm), rear drum, servo.

ELECTRICAL EQUIPMENT 12 V; 50 Ah battery; 37 A alternator; electronic ignition; 2 headlamps.

DIMENSIONS AND WEIGHT wheel base: 108.70 in, 276 cm; front track: 59.40 in, 151 cm - Wide Wheel 65.40 in, 166 cm; rear track: 57.80 in, 147 cm - Wide Wheel 62.30 in, 158 cm; length: 183.50 in, 466 cm; width: 75.60 in, 192 cm - Wide Wheel 78.90 in, 200 cm; height: 66.90 in, 170 cm - Wide Wheel 67.60 in, 172 cm; ground clearance: 7.70 in, 19.6 cm - Wide Wheel 8.60 in, 21.8 cm; weight: 2-dr. 3,971 lb, 1,801 kg - Wide Wheel 3,991 lb, 1,810 kg - 4-dr. 4,106 lb, 1,862 kg; turning circle: 37.7 ft, 11.5 m - Wide Wheel 39.4 ft, 12 m; fuel tank: 17.8 imp gal, 21.5 US gal, 81 l.

OPTIONALS 4-speed fully synchronized mechanical gearbox; Turbo-Hydramatic automatic transmission with 4-wheel drive Quadra-Trac system and 3.540 axle ratio; rear limited slip differential; light alloy wheels; power steering with variable ratio; sports steering wheel; tilt of steering wheel; de luxe interior; heavy-duty cooling system; 70 Ah battery; 63 A alternator; anti-roll bar on front suspension; heavy-duty suspension; tinted glass; heated rear window; air-conditioning; S equipment, Chief equipment and Golden Eagle equipment (for Wide Wheel only).

129 hp power team

(standard in California).

See 114 hp power team, except for:

ENGINE 8 cylinders; 360 cu in, 5,899 cc (4.08 x 3.44 in, 103.6 x 87.3 mm); compression ratio: 8.25:1; max power (DIN): 129 hp (94.9 kW) at 3,700 rpm; max torque (DIN): 245 lb ft, 33.8 kg m at 1,600 rpm; max engine rpm: 4,200; 21.9 hp/l (16.1 kW/l); 5 crankshaft bearings; camshafts: 1, at centre of Vee; lubrication: 8.3 imp pt, 9.9 US pt, 4.7 l; 1 downdraught twin barrel carburettor; cleaner air system; cooling system: 21.6 imp pt, 26 US pt, 12.3 l.

TRANSMISSION ratios: I 2.997, II 1.832, III 1, rev 2.997.

PERFORMANCE max speed: about 99 mph, 160 km/h; power-weight ratio: 4-dr. 31.8 lb/hp (43.2 lb/kW), 14.4 kg/hp (19.6 kg/kW); speed in direct drive at 1,000 rpm: 24.9 mph, 40 km/h; consumption: 16.8 m/imp gal, 14 m/US gal, 16.8 l x 100 km.

ELECTRICAL EQUIPMENT 60 Ah battery; 40 A alternator.

OPTIONALS 3.540 axle ratio; Turbo-Hydramatic automatic transmission with 4-wheel drive Quadra-Trac system and 3.540 axle ratio.

Wagoneer Series

PRICES EX WORKS:

Standard	$ 8,375
Limited	$ 11,688

129 hp power team

ENGINE front, 4 stroke; 8 cylinders; 360 cu in, 5,899 cc (4.08 x 3.44 in, 103.6 x 87.3 mm); compression ratio: 8.25:1; max power (DIN): 129 hp at 3,700 rpm; max torque (DIN): 245 lb ft, 33.8 kg m at 1,600 rpm; max engine rpm: 4,200; 21.9 hp/l; cast iron block and head; 5 crankshaft bearings; valves: overhead, in line, push-rods and rockers; hydraulic tappets; camshafts: 1, at centre of Vee; lubrication: gear pump, full flow filter, 8.3 imp pt, 9.9 US pt, 4.7 l; 1 downdraught twin barrel carburettor; cleaner air system; fuel feed: mechanical pump; water-cooled, 21.6 imp pt, 26 US pt, 12.3 l.

TRANSMISSION driving wheels: front and rear (Quadra-Trac system with central limited slip differential); gearbox: Turbo-Hydramatic automatic transmission, hydraulic torque converter and planetary gears with 3 ratios, max ratio of converter at stall 2.3, possible manual selection; ratios: I 2.480, II 1.480, III 1, rev 2.080; lever: central; final drive: hypoid bevel; axle ratio: 3.070; width of rims: 5.5''; tyres: H78 x 15.

PERFORMANCE max speed: about 99 mph, 159 km/h; power-weight ratio: 33.7 lb/hp, 15.3 kg/hp; speed in direct drive at 1,000 rpm: 26.4 mph, 42.5 km/h; consumption: 16.8 m/imp gal, 14 m/US gal, 16.8 l x 100 km.

CHASSIS perimeter box-type with cross members; front and rear suspension: rigid axle, semi-elliptic leafsprings, telescopic dampers.

STEERING recirculating ball, variable ratio, servo.

BRAKES front disc (diameter 12 in, 30 cm), rear drum, servo.

JEEP CORPORATION Wagoneer Limited

ELECTRICAL EQUIPMENT 12 V; 60 Ah battery; 40 A alternator; electronic ignition; 2 headlamps.

DIMENSIONS AND WEIGHT wheel base: 108.70 in, 276 cm; tracks: 59.40 in, 151 cm front, 57.80 in, 147 cm rear; length: 183.50 in, 466 cm; width: 75.60 in, 192 cm; height: 66.70 in, 169 cm; ground clearance: 7.70 in, 19.6 cm; weight: 4,118 lb, 1,868 kg; turning circle: 37.7 ft, 11.5 m; fuel tank: 17.8 imp gal, 21.5 US gal, 81 l.

BODY estate car/station wagon; 4 + 1 doors; 6 seats; bench front seats; folding rear seat; for Limited only luxury equipment, light alloy wheels and HR78 x 15 tyres.

OPTIONALS 3.540 axle ratio; anti-roll bar on front suspension; light alloy wheels; tilt of steering wheel; 70 Ah battery; 63 A alternator; heavy-duty cooling system; heavy-duty suspension; tinted glass; heated rear window; air-conditioning.

KELMARK   USA

GT Mark II

ENGINE Volkswagen-Porsche, rear, 4 stroke; 4 cylinders, horizontally opposed; 102.4 cu in, 1,679 cc (3.54 x 2.60 in, 90 x 66 mm); compression ratio: 8.5:1; max power (DIN): 100 hp (73.6 kW) at 5,000 rpm; max torque (DIN): 110 lb ft, 13.8 kg m (135.3 Nm) at 3,500 rpm; max engine rpm: 5,500; 59.6 hp/l (43.8 kW/l); light alloy block and head, separate cylinders with Ferral chromium walls; 4 crankshaft bearings; valves: overhead, in line, push-rods and rockers; camshafts: 1, central, lower; lubrication: gear pump, filter in sump, oil cooler, 6.2 imp pt, 7.4 US pt, 3.5 l; 2 Weber downdraught carburettors; fuel feed: electric pump; air-cooled.

TRANSMISSION driving wheels: rear; clutch: single dry plate (diaphragm), hydraulically controlled; gearbox: mechanical; gears: 4, fully synchronized; ratios: I 3.560, II 2.060, III 1.250, IV 0.890; lever: central; final drive: hypoid bevel; width of rims: front 7'', rear 8.5''; tyres: ER60 x 14 front, GR50 x 15 rear.

PERFORMANCE max speed: about 125 mph, 201 km/h; power-weight ratio: 17 lb/hp (23.1 lb/kW), 7.7 kg/hp (10.5 kg/kW); speed in top at 1,000 rpm: 24.9 mph, 40 km/h; consumption: 42.2 m/imp gal, 35 m/US gal, 6.7 l x 100 km.

CHASSIS backbone platform; front suspension: independent, twin swinging longitudinal trailing arms, transverse laminated torsion bars, anti-roll bar, telescopic dampers; rear: independent, swinging semi-axles, swinging longitudinal trailing arms, transverse torsion bars, telescopic dampers.

STEERING rack-and-pinion.

BRAKES front disc, rear drum.

KELMARK GT Mark II

GT MARK II

ELECTRICAL EQUIPMENT 12 V; 43 Ah battery; alternator; Bosch distributor; 2 headlamps.

DIMENSIONS AND WEIGHT wheel base: 95 in, 241 · cm; tracks: 58 in, 147 cm front, 60 in, 152 cm rear; length: 174 in, 442 cm; width: 73 in, 185 cm; height: 45 in, 114 cm; ground clearance: 7 in, 17.8 cm; weight: 1,700 lb. 771 kg; weight distribution: 40% front, 60% rear; fuel tank: 8.4 imp gal, 10 US gal, 38 l.

BODY coupé in plastic material; 2 doors; 2 seats.

OPTIONALS light alloy wheels; air-conditioning; sunshine roof.

LINCOLN   USA

Versailles

PRICE EX WORKS: $ 12,939

130 hp power team

(standard).

ENGINE front, 4 stroke; 8 cylinders; 302 cu in, 4,950 cc (4 x 3 in, 101.6 x 76.2 mm); compression ratio: 8.4:1; max power (DIN): 130 hp (95.7 kW) at 3,600 rpm; max torque (DIN): 237 lb ft, 32.7 kg m (320.7 Nm) at 1,600 rpm; max engine rpm: 4,000; 26.3 hp/l (19.3 kW/l); cast iron block and head; 5 crankshaft bearings; valves: overhead, in line, push-rods and rockers, hydraulic tappets; camshafts: 1, at centre of Vee; lubrication: rotary pump, full flow filter, 8.3 imp pt, 9.9 US pt, 4.7 l; 1 Ford 2700 D94E-KA downdraught carburettor with variable Venturi; cleaner air system; exhaust system with catalytic converter; fuel feed: mechanical pump; water-cooled, 23.9 imp pt, 28.8 US pt, 13.6 l.

TRANSMISSION driving wheels:rear; gearbox: SelectShift automatic transmission, hydraulic torque converter and planetary gears with 3 ratios, max ratio of converter at stall 2, possible manual selection; ratios: I 2.460, II 1.460, III 1, rev 2.180; lever: steering column; final drive: hypoid bevel, limited slip differential; axle ratio: 2.470; width of rims: 6''; tyres: FR78 x 14.

PERFORMANCE max speed: about 108 mph, 174 km/h; power-weight ratio: 28.3 lb/hp, (38.5 lb/kW), 12.8 kg/hp (17.4 kg/kW); speed in direct drive at 1,000 rpm: 30 mph, 48.3 km/h; consumption: 16.8 m/imp gal, 14 m/US gal, 16.8 l x 100 km.

CHASSIS integral; front suspension: independent, wishbones, coil springs, anti-roll bar, telescopic dampers; rear: rigid axle, semi-elliptic leafsprings, telescopic dampers.

STEERING recirculating ball, servo; turns lock to lock: 3.70.

LINCOLN Versailles

BRAKES disc (front diameter 11.03 in, 28 cm, rear 10.66 in, 27.1 cm), internal radial fins, rear compensator, servo; swept area: front 222.50 sq in, 1,435 sq cm, rear 211.20 sq in, 1,363 sq cm, total 433.70 sq in, 2,798 sq cm.

ELECTRICAL EQUIPMENT 12 V; 53 Ah battery; 60 A alternator; Motorcraft transistorized ignition; 4 halogen headlamps.

DIMENSIONS AND WEIGHT wheel base: 109.90 in, 279 cm; tracks: 59 in, 150 cm front, 57.70 in, 147 cm rear; length: 201 in, 510 cm; width: 74.50 in, 189 cm; height: 54.10 in, 137 cm; ground clearance: 4.94 in, 12.6 cm; weight: 3,682 lb, 1,668 kg; fuel tank: 16.1 imp gal, 19.2 US gal, 73 l.

BODY saloon/sedan; 4 doors; 5 seats, bench front seats with built-in headrests; electric windows; tinted glass; speed control device; air-conditioning; vinyl roof.

OPTIONALS central lever; tilt of steering wheel; heated rear window; separate front seats with reclining backrests; sunshine roof.

133 hp power team

(optional, for California only).

See 130 hp power team, except for:

ENGINE max power (DIN): 133 hp (97.9 kW) at 3,600 rpm;

max torque (DIN): 236 lb ft, 32.5 kg m (318.7 Nm) at 1,4[...] rpm; 26.9 hp/l (19.8 kW/l); 1 Ford 2700 D9DE-HA dow[...] draught carburettor with variable Venturi.

PERFORMANCE power-weight ratio: 27.7 lb/hp (37.6 lb/kW[...] 12.5 kg/hp (17 kg/kW).

Continental Series

PRICES EX WORKS:

Coupé	$ 10,98[...]
Sedan	$ 11,20[...]

159 hp power team

(standard).

ENGINE front, 4 stroke; 8 cylinders; 400 cu in, 6,555 c[...] (4 x 4 in, 101.6 x 101.6 mm); compression ratio: 8:1; ma[...] power (DIN): 159 hp (117 kW) at 3,400 rpm; max torqu[...] (DIN): 315 lb ft, 43.5 kg m (426.6 Nm) at 1,800 rpm; ma[...] engine rpm: 4,000; 24.3 hp/l (17.8 kW/l); cast iron bloc[...] and head; 5 crankshaft bearings; valves: overhead, in lin[...] push-rods and rockers, hydraulic tappets; camshafts: 1[...] at centre of Vee; lubrication: rotary pump, full flow filte[...] 8.3 imp pt, 9.9 US pt, 4.7 l; 1 Ford 2150A 9510 D9VE-L[...] (9510 D9VE-UA for California only) downdraught twin barre[...] carburettor; cleaner air system; exhaust system with 2 c[...] talytic converters; fuel feed: mechanical pump; water-coole[...] 28.9 imp pt, 34.7 US pt, 16.4 l.

TRANSMISSION driving wheels: rear; gearbox: Selec[...] Shift automatic transmission, hydraulic torque converte[...] and planetary gears with 3 ratios, max ratio of converte[...] at stall 1.87, possible manual selection; ratios: I 2.460, [...] 1.460, III 1, rev 2.180; lever: steering column; final driv[...] hypoid bevel; axle ratio: 2.470 (2.750 California only[...] width of rims: 6''; tyres: 225 x 15.

PERFORMANCE max speed: about 109 mph, 175 km/h[...] power-weight ratio: 29.3 lb/hp (39.8 lb/kW), 13.2 kg/h[...] (18.1 kg/kW); speed in direct drive at 1,000 rpm: 29 mp[...] 46.6 km/h; consumption: 14.4 m/imp gal, 12 m/US ga[...] 19.6 l x 100 km.

CHASSIS box-type ladder frame, front suspension: inde[...] pendent, wishbones, coil springs, anti-roll bar, telescopi[...] dampers; rear: rigid axle, lower trailing radius arms, uppe[...] oblique torque arms, transverse linkage bar, coil spring[...] telescopic dampers.

STEERING recirculating ball, servo; turns lock to lock: 4.08[...]

BRAKES front disc (diameter 11.80 in, 30 cm), front interna[...] radial fins, rear compensator, rear drum, servo; swept are[...] front 242 sq in, 1,561 sq cm, rear 173.2 sq in, 1,117 sq c[...] total 415.2 sq in, 2,678 sq cm.

ELECTRICAL EQUIPMENT 12 V; 54 Ah battery; 65 A alter[...] nator; Motorcraft transistorized ignition; 4 headlamps.

DIMENSIONS AND WEIGHT wheel base: 127.20 in, 323 cm[...] tracks: 64.30 in, 163 cm front, 64.30 in, 163 cm rear; length[...] 233 in, 592 cm; width: Sedan 79.90 in, 203 cm - Coupé 79.6[...] in, 202 cm; height: Sedan 55.40 in, 141 cm - Coupé 55.2[...] in, 140 cm; ground clearance: 4.83 in, 12.3 cm; weight[...]

LINCOLN Continental Collector's Edition Sedan

Coupé 4,655 lb, 2,113 kg - Sedan 4,652 lb, 2,112 kg; turning circle: 51.5 ft, 15.7 m; fuel tank: 20 imp gal, 24.2 US gal, 92 l.

BODY 6 seats, bench front seats with built-in headrest; tinted glas; electric windows; air-conditioning.

OPTIONALS limited slip differential; 2.750 axle ratio (except for California); LR78 x 15 or L78 x 15 tyres with 6'' wide rims; J78 x 15 tyres with 5.5'' wide rims; aluminium wheels; tilt of steering wheel; 4-wheel disc brakes, total swept area 465.9 sq in, 3,006 sq cm; anti-skid brakes; 63 Ah or 68 Ah batteries; 70 A alternator; heated rear window; automatic speed control; separate front seats with reclining backrests; sunshine roof; Williamsburg Edition equipment (Sedan only); Town Car equipment (Sedan only); Town Coupé equipment (Coupé only); Collector's Series equipment.

Continental Mark V

PRICE EX WORKS: $ 13,067

159 hp power team

(standard).

ENGINE front, 4 stroke; 8 cylinders; 400 cu in, 6,555 cc

STEERING recirculating ball, servo; turns lock to lock: 3.99.

BRAKES disc (front diameter 11.80 in, 30 cm, rear 11.50 in, 29.2 cm), internal radial fins, rear compensator, servo; swept area: front 242 sq in, 1,561 sq cm, rear 224 sq in, 1,445 sq cm, total 468 sq in, 3,006 sq cm.

ELECTRICAL EQUIPMENT 12 V; 63 Ah battery; 60 A alternator; Motorcraft transistorized ignition; 4 headlamps.

DIMENSIONS AND WEIGHT wheel base: 120.30 in, 306 cm; tracks: 63.20 in, 160 cm front, 62.60 in, 159 cm rear; length: 230.30 in, 585 cm; width: 79.70 in, 202 cm; height: 53.10 in, 135 cm; ground clearance: 5.08 in, 12 cm; weight: 4,515 lb, 2,045 kg; turning circle: 46.7 ft, 14.2 m; fuel tank: 20.9 imp gal, 25 US gal, 95 l.

BODY hardtop; 2 doors; 6 seats, bench front seats with built-in headrests; tinted glass; electric windows; air-conditioning.

OPTIONALS limited slip differential; 2.750 axle ratio (except for California); LR78 x 15 or L78 x 15 tyres with 6'' wide rims; aluminium wheels; tilt of steering wheel; anti-skid brakes; 68 Ah battery; 65 A alternator; 70 A alternator; heated rear window; automatic speed control; separate front seats with reclining backrests; sunshine roof; leather upholstery; Collector's Edition Series equipment; Pucci Edition equipment; Givenchy Edition equipment; Cartier Edition equipment; Bill Blass Edition equipment; luxury equipment.

LINCOLN Continental Mark V

4 x 4 in, 101.6 x 101.6 mm); compression ratio: 8:1; max power (DIN): 159 hp (117 kW) at 3,400 rpm; max torque (DIN): 315 lb ft, 43.5 kg m (426.6 Nm) at 1,800 rpm; max engine rpm: 4,000; 24.3 hp/l (17.8 kW/l); cast iron block and head; 5 crankshaft bearings; valves: overhead, in line, push-rods and rockers, hydraulic tappets; camshafts: 1, at centre of Vee; lubrication: rotary pump, full flow filter, 8.3 imp pt, 9.9 US pt, 4.7 l; 1 Ford 2150A 9510 D9VE-LB 9510 D9VE-UA for California only) downdraught twin barrel carburettor; cleaner air system; exhaust system with 2 catalytic converters; fuel feed: mechanical pump; water-cooled, 28.9 imp pt, 34.7 US pt 16.4 l.

TRANSMISSION driving wheels: rear; gearbox: SelectShift automatic transmission, hydraulic torque converter and planetary gears with 3 ratios, max ratio of converter at stall 1.87, possible manual selection; ratios: I 2.460, II 1.460, III 1, rev 2.180; lever: steering column; final drive: hypoid bevel; axle ratio: 2.470 (2.750 California only); width of rims: 6''; tyres: 225 x 15.

PERFORMANCE max speed: about 109 mph, 175 km/h; power-weight ratio: 28.4 lb/hp, (38.6 lb/kW), 12.9 kg/hp 17.5 kg/kW); speed in direct drive at 1,000 rpm: 29 mph, 46.6 km/h; consumption: 14.4 m/imp gal, 12 m/US gal, 19.6 l x 100 km.

CHASSIS box-type ladder frame; front suspension: independent, wishbones, coil springs, anti-roll bar, telescopic dampers; rear: rigid axle, lower trailing radius arms, upper oblique torque arms, coil springs, anti-roll bar, telescopic dampers.

MERCURY   USA

Bobcat Series

PRICES EX WORKS:

Runabout	$ 3,797
St. Wagon	$ 4,099
Villager St. Wagon	$ 4,212

For 2.8-litre engine add $ 273.

Power team	Standard for:	Optional for:
88 hp	all	—
102 hp	—	102

88 hp power team

ENGINE front, 4 stroke; 4 cylinders, in line, 140 cu in, 2,300 cc (3.78 x 3.13 in, 95.9 x 79.5 mm); compression ratio: 9:1; max power (DIN): 88 hp (64.8 kW) at 4,800 rpm; max torque (DIN): 118 lb ft, 16.3 kg m (159.8 Nm) at 2,800 rpm; max engine rpm: 5,200; 38.3 hp/l (28.2 kW/l); cast iron block and head; 5 crankshaft bearings; valves: overhead, Vee-slanted, rockers, hydraulic tappets; camshafts: 1, overhead, cogged belt; lubrication: gear pump, full flow filter, 8.3 imp pt, 9.9 US pt, 4.7 l; 1 Holley-Weber D9EE-ALA/AMA (D9EE-AGC/AHC or AEC/AFC for California only) downdraught twin barrel carburettor; cleaner air system; exhaust system with catalytic converter; fuel feed: mechanical pump; water-cooled, 14.4 imp pt, 17.3 US pt, 8.2 l.

TRANSMISSION driving wheels: rear; clutch: single dry plate; gearbox: mechanical; gears: 4, fully synchronized; ratios: I 3.980, II 2.140, III 1.420, IV 1, rev 3.990; lever: central; final drive: hypoid bevel; axle ratio: 2.730 - st. wagons 3.080; width of rims: 5''; tyres: BR78 x 13.

PERFORMANCE max speed: about 96 mph, 154 km/h; power-weight ratio: Runabout 27.4 lb/hp (37.3 lb/kW), 12.4 kg/hp (16.9 kg/kW) - st. wagons 29.1 lb/hp (39.6 lb/kW), 13.2 kg/hp (17.9 kg/kW); speed in direct drive at 1,000 rpm: 19.3 mph, 31 km/h; consumption: 26.4 m/imp gal, 22 m/US gal, 10.7 l x 100 km.

CHASSIS integral; front suspension: independent, wishbones, coil springs, telescopic dampers; rear: rigid axle, semi-elliptic leafsprings, telescopic dampers.

STEERING rack-and-pinion; turns lock to lock: 4.15.

BRAKES front disc (diameter 9.30 in, 23.6 cm), front internal radial fins, rear drum, rear compensator; swept area: front 145.5 sq in, 939 sq cm, rear 99 sq in, 639 sq cm, total 244.5 sq in, 1,578 sq cm.

ELECTRICAL EQUIPMENT 12 V; 45 Ah battery; 40 A alternator; Motorcraft transistorized ignition; 2 headlamps.

DIMENSIONS AND WEIGHT wheel base: Runabout 94.50 in, 240 cm - st. wagons 94.80 in, 241 cm; tracks: 55 in, 140 cm front, 55.80 in, 142 cm rear; length: Runabout 168.80 in, 429 cm - st. wagons 178.60 in, 454 cm; width: Runabout 69.40 in, 176 cm - st. wagons 69.70 in, 177 cm; height: Runabout 50.50 in, 128 cm - st. wagons 52 in, 132

MERCURY Bobcat Villager Station Wagon

88 HP POWER TEAM

cm; ground clearance: Runabout 5.30 in, 13.5 cm - st. wagons 5.11 in, 13 cm; weight: Runabout 2,416 lb, 1,095 kg - st. wagons 2,565 lb, 1,163 kg; turning circle: 35.9 ft, 10.9 m; fuel tank: Runabout 10.8 imp gal, 13 US gal, 49 l - st. wagons 11.7 imp gal, 14 US gal, 53 l.

BODY 4 seats, separate front seats; folding rear seat.

OPTIONALS heavy-duty cooling system; limited slip differential; 3.080 axle ratio (except for st. wagons); Select-Shift automatic transmission with 3 ratios (I 2.470, II 1.470, III 1, rev 2.110) max ratio of converter at stall 2.9, possible manual selection, central lever, 3.080 axle ratio; aluminium wheels; BR70 x 13 or A70 x 13 tyres with 5'' wide rims; anti-roll bar on front suspension; power steering; tilt of steering wheel; servo brake; 54 Ah heavy-duty battery; heated rear window; tinted glass; sunshine roof (except for st. wagons); air-conditioning; luxury interior; Sports equipment.

102 hp power team

(not available in California).

See 88 hp power team, except for:

ENGINE 6 cylinders, Vee-slanted at 60°; 170.8 cu in, 2,800 cc (3.66 x 2.70 in, 92.9 x 68.5 mm); compression ratio: 8.7:1; max power (DIN): 102 hp (75.1 kW) at 4,400 rpm; max torque (DIN): 138 lb ft, 19 kg m (186.3 Nm) at 3,200 rpm; 36.4 hp/l (26.8 kW/l); 4 crankshaft bearings; valves: overhead, in line, push-rods and rockers; camshafts: 1, at centre of Vee; 1 Motorcraft 2700 D9ZE-LB downdraught carburettor with variable Venturi; cooling system: 14.1 imp pt, 16.9 US pt, 8 l.

TRANSMISSION gearbox: SelectShift automatic transmission (standard), hydraulic torque converter and planetary gears with 3 ratios, max ratio of converter at stall 2.05, possible manual selection; ratios: I 2.460, II 1.460, III 1, rev 2.190; lever: central; axle ratio: 3.080.

PERFORMANCE max speed: about 103 mph, 165 km/h; power-weight ratio: Runabout 24.7 lb/hp (33.5 lb/kW), 11.2 kg/hp (15.2 kg/kW) - st. wagons 26 lb/hp (35.3 lb/kW), 11.8 kg/hp (16 kg/kW); speed in direct drive at 1,000 rpm: 23.5 mph, 37.9 km/h; consumption: 21.6 m/imp gal, 18 m/US gal, 13.1 l x 100 km.

CHASSIS (standard) anti-roll bar on front suspension.

DIMENSIONS AND WEIGHT weight: Runabout plus 100 lb, 45 kg - st. wagons plus 87 lb, 39 kg.

Zephyr Series

PRICES EX WORKS:

2-dr Sedan	$ 3,870
4-dr Sedan	$ 3,970
St. Wagon	$ 4,317
Z-7 Sports Coupé	$ 4,122

For 6-cylinder engine add $ 241. For V8 add $ 524.

Power team:	Standard for:	Optional for:
88 hp	all	—
85 hp	—	all
140 hp	—	all
143 hp	—	all

88 hp power team

ENGINE front, 4 stroke; 4 cylinders, in line; 140 cu in, 2,300 cc (3.78 x 3.13 in, 95.9 x 79.5 mm); compression ratio: 9:1; max power (DIN): 88 hp (64.8 kW) at 4,800 rpm; max torque (DIN): 118 lb ft, 16.3 kg m (159.8 Nm) at 2,800 rpm; max engine rpm: 5,200; 38.3 hp/l (28.2 kW/l); cast iron block and head; 5 crankshaft bearings; valves: overhead, Vee-slanted, rockers, hydraulic tappets; camshafts: 1, overhead, Vee-slanted, rockers, hydraulic tappets; camshafts: 1, overhead, cogged belt; lubrication: gear pump, full flow filter, 8.3 imp pt, 9.9 US pt, 4.7 l; 1 Holley-Weber D9BE-AAA (D9BE-ABA for California only) downdraught twin barrel carburettor; cleaner air system; exhaust system with catalytic converter; fuel feed: mechanical pump; water-cooled, 14.4 imp pt, 17.3 US pt, 8.2 l.

TRANSMISSION driving wheels: rear; clutch: single dry plate; gearbox: mechanical; gears: 4, fully synchronized; ratios: I 3.980, II 2.140, III 1.420, IV 1, rev 3.990; lever: central; final drive: hypoid bevel; axle ratio: 3.080; width of rims: 5'' - St. Wagon 5.5''; tyres: B78 x 14 - St. Wagon CR78 x 14.

PERFORMANCE max speed: about 96 mph, 154 km/h; power-weight ratio: 4-dr Sedan 29.6 lb/hp (40.1 lb/kW), 13.4 kg/hp (18.2 kg/kW); speed in direct drive at 1,000 rpm: 19.3 mph,

MERCURY Zephyr ES 2-dr Sedan

31 km/h; consumption: 23.9 m/imp gal, 20 m/US gal, 11.8 l x 100 km.

CHASSIS integral with 2 cross members; front suspension: independent, by McPherson, wishbones (lower control arms), coil springs/telescopic damper struts, anti-roll bar; rear: rigid axle, lower trailing radius arms, upper oblique torque arms, coil springs, telescopic dampers.

STEERING rack-and-pinion; turns lock to lock: 4.10.

BRAKES front disc (diameter 10.06 in, 25.4 cm), front internal radial fins, rear compensator, rear drum; swept area: front 176.6 sq in, 1,140 sq cm, rear 98.9 sq in, 638 sq cm - St. Wagon 110 sq in, 710 sq cm, total 275.5 sq in, 1,778 sq cm - St. Wagon 286.6 sq in, 1,850 sq cm.

ELECTRICAL EQUIPMENT 12 V; 45 Ah battery; 40 A alternator; Motorcraft transistorized ignition; 4 headlamps.

DIMENSIONS AND WEIGHT wheel base: 105.50 in, 268 cm; tracks: 56.60 in, 144 cm front, 57 in, 145 cm rear; length: 194.90 in, 495 cm - Z-7 Sports Coupé 196.80 in, 500 cm; width: 71 in, 180 cm; height: sedans 53.60 in, 136 cm - Z-7 Sports Coupé 52.30 in, 133 cm - St. Wagon 54.40 in, 138 cm; ground clearance: 4.38 in, 11.1 cm - St. Wagon 4.75 in, 12.1 cm; weight: 2-dr Sedan 2,573 lb, 1,167 kg - 4-dr Sedan 2,601 lb, 1,180 kg - St. Wagon 2,715 lb, 1,232 kg - Z-7 Sports Coupé 2,599 lb, 1,179 kg; turning circle: 39 ft, 11.9 m; fuel tank: 13.4 imp gal, 16 US gal, 61 l.

BODY 5 seats, bench front seats with built-in headrests.

MERCURY Zephyr Z-7 Sports Coupé

OPTIONALS heavy-duty cooling system; aluminium wheels; BR78 x 14, C78 x 14, CR78 x 14 or DR78 x 14 tyres with 5'' wide rims; heavy-duty suspension with rear anti-roll bar; power steering; tilt of steering wheel; servo brake; 54 Ah heavy-duty battery; heated rear window; tinted glass; electric windows; metallic spray; vinyl roof; luxury interior; speed control device; air-conditioning; rear window wiper-washer (St. Wagon only); sunshine roof (sedans only); ES equipment (sedans only); Ghia equipment; separate front seats with reclining backrests. (For sedans and Z-7 Sports Coupé only) SelectShift automatic transmission with 3 ratios (I 2.470, II 1.470, III 1, rev 2.110), max ratio of converter at stall 2.9, possible manual selection, steering column lever, 3.080 axle ratio.

85 hp power team

See 88 hp power team, except for:

ENGINE 6 cylinders, in line; 200 cu in, 3,277 cc (3.68 x 3.13 in, 95.3 x 79.5 mm); compression ratio: 8.5:1; max power (DIN): 85 hp (62.6 kW) at 3,600 rpm; max torque (DIN): 154 lb ft, 21.2 kg m (208 Nm) at 1,600 rpm; max engine rpm: 4,000; 25.9 hp/l (19.1 kW/l); 7 crankshaft bearings; valves: overhead, in line, push-rods and rockers, hydraulic tappets; camshafts: 1, side; 1 Carter YFA (Holley 1946 for California only) downdraught single barrel carburettor; cooling system: 15 imp pt, 18 US pt, 8.5 l.

TRANSMISSION gearbox: mechanical (SelectShift automatic transmission standard for California only); gears: 4, fully synchronized with overdrive/top; ratios: I 3.290, II 1.840, III 1, IV 0.810, rev 3.290.

PERFORMANCE max speed: about 99 mph, 160 km/h; power-weight ratio: 4-dr Sedan 31.6 lb/hp (42.9 lb/kW), 14.3 kg/hp (19.4 kg/kW); speed in top at 1,000 rpm: 24.9 mph, 40 km/h; consumption: 22.8 m/imp gal, 19 m/US gal, 12.4 l x 100 km.

ELECTRICAL EQUIPMENT 36 Ah battery.

DIMENSIONS AND WEIGHT weight: plus 82 lb, 37 kg.

OPTIONALS SelectShift automatic transmission with 3 ratios (I 2.460, II 1.460, III 1, rev 2.190), max ratio of converter at stall 2, possible manual selection, steering column or central lever, 2.730 axle ratio.

140 hp power team

(not available in California).

See 88 hp power team, except for:

ENGINE 8 cylinders; 302 cu in, 4,950 cc (4 x 3 in, 101.6 x 76.2 mm); compression ratio: 8.4:1; max power (DIN): 140 hp (103 kW) at 3,600 rpm; max torque (DIN): 250 lb ft, 34.5 kg m (338.3 Nm) at 1,800 rpm; max engine rpm: 4,000; 28.3 hp/l (20.8 kW/l); valves: overhead, in line, push-rods and rockers, hydraulic tappets; camshafts: 1, at centre of Vee; 1 Ford 2150 D9BE-YB downdraught twin barrel carburettor; cooling system: 23.1 imp pt, 27.7 US pt, 13.1 l.

TRANSMISSION gears: 4, fully synchronized with overdrive/top; ratios: I 3.070, II 1.720, III 1, IV 0.700, rev 3.070; axle ratio: 2.730.

PERFORMANCE max speed: about 109 mph, 175 km/h; power-weight ratio: 4-dr Sedan 20.6 lb/hp (27.9 lb/kW), 9.3 g/hp (12.7 kg/kW); speed in top at 1,000 rpm: 27.2 mph, 43.7 km/h; consumption: 19.2 m/imp gal, 16 m/US gal, 14.7 l x 100 km.

ELECTRICAL EQUIPMENT 36 Ah battery.

DIMENSIONS AND WEIGHT weight: plus 277 lb, 126 kg.

OPTIONALS SelectShift automatic transmission with 3 ratios (I 2.460, II 1.460, III 1, rev 2.190), max ratio of converter at stall 2, possible manual selection, steering column or central lever, 2.260 axle ratio.

143 hp power team

(for California only).

See 88 hp power team, except for:

ENGINE 8 cylinders; 302 cu in, 4,950 cc (4 x 3 in, 101.6 x 76.2 mm); compression ratio: 8.4:1; max power (DIN): 143 hp (105.2 kW) at 3,600 rpm; max torque (DIN): 243 lb ft, 33.5 kg m (328.5 Nm) at 2,200 rpm; max engine rpm: 4,000; 28.9 hp/l (21.3 kW/l); valves: overhead, in line, push-rods and rockers, hydraulic tappets; camshafts: 1, at centre of Vee; 1 Ford 2700 D9DE-HA downdraught carburettor with variable Venturi; cooling system: 23.1 imp pt, 27.7 US pt, 13.1 l.

TRANSMISSION gearbox: SelectShift automatic transmission (standard), hydraulic torque converter and planetary gears with 3 ratios, max ratio of converter at stall 2, possible manual selection; ratios: I 2.460, II 1.460, III 1, rev 2.190; lever: steering column or central; axle ratio: 2.730.

PERFORMANCE max speed: about 106 mph, 170 km/h; power-weight ratio: 4-dr Sedan 20.1 lb/hp (27.4 lb/kW), 9.1 kg/hp (12.4 kg/kW); speed in direct drive at 1,000 rpm: 29.3 mph, 47.2 km/h; consumption: 18 m/imp gal, 15 m/US gal, 15.7 l x 100 km.

ELECTRICAL EQUIPMENT 36 Ah battery.

DIMENSIONS AND WEIGHT weight: plus 278 lb, 126 kg.

Capri Series

PRICES EX WORKS:

Coupé	$ 4,481
Ghia Coupé	$ 4,845

For 2.8-litre engine add $ 273; for 5.0-litre engine add $ 514. For 2.3-litre turbocharged engine add $ 542.

Power team:	Standard for:	Optional for:
88 hp	both	—
109 hp	—	both
140 hp	—	both
143 hp	—	both
150 hp	—	both

MERCURY Capri Series
(2.3-litre turbocharged engine)

MERCURY Capri RS Coupé

88 hp power team

ENGINE front, 4 stroke; 4 cylinders, in line; 140 cu in, 2,300 cc (3.78 x 3.13 in, 95.9 x 79.5 mm); compression ratio: 9:1; max power (DIN): 88 hp (64.8 kW) at 4,800 rpm; max torque (DIN): 118 lb ft, 16.3 kg m (159.8 Nm) at 2,800 rpm; max engine rpm: 5,200; 38.3 hp/l (28.2 kW/l); cast iron block and head; 5 crankshaft bearings; valves: overhead, Vee-slanted, rockers, hydraulic tappets; camshafts: 1, overhead, cogged belt; lubrication: rotary pump, full flow filter, 8.3 imp pt, 9.9 US pt, 4.7 l; 1 Holley-Weber D9BE-AAA/ADA (D9BE-ABA/ACA for California only) downdraught twin barrel carburettor; cleaner air system; exhaust system with catalytic converter; fuel feed: mechanical pump; water-cooled, 14.4 imp pt, 17.3 US pt, 8.2 l.

TRANSMISSION driving wheels: rear; clutch: single dry plate; gearbox: mechanical; gears: 4, fully synchronized; ratios: I 3.980, II 2.140, III 1.420, IV 1, rev 3.990; lever: central; final drive: hypoid bevel; axle ratio: 3.080; width of rims: 5''; tyres: B78 x 13.

PERFORMANCE max speed: about 96 mph, 154 km/h; power-weight ratio: Coupé 28.6 lb/hp (38.9 lb/kW), 13 kg/hp (17.6 kg/kW) - Ghia Coupé 29.4 lb/hp (39.9 lb/kW), 13.3 kg/hp (18.1 kg/kW); speed in direct drive at 1,000 rpm: 19.3 mph, 31 km/h; consumption: 23.9 m/imp gal, 20 m/US gal, 11.8 l x 100 m.

CHASSIS platform with front subframe; front suspension: independent, by McPherson, wishbones (lower control arms), coil springs/telescopic damper struts, anti-roll bar; rear: rigid axle, lower trailing radius arms, upper oblique torque arms, transverse linkage bar, coil springs, telescopic dampers.

STEERING rack-and-pinion; turns lock to lock: 4.08.

BRAKES front disc (diameter 9.31 in, 23.6 cm), front internal radial fins, rear compensator, rear drum; swept area: total 249.7 sq in, 1,611 sq cm.

ELECTRICAL EQUIPMENT 12 V; 45 Ah battery; 40 A alternator; Motorcraft transistorized ignition; 4 headlamps.

DIMENSIONS AND WEIGHT wheel base: 100.40 in, 255 cm; tracks: 56.60 in, 144 cm front, 57 in, 145 cm rear; length: 179.10 in, 455 cm; width: 69.10 in, 176 cm; height: 51.50 in, 131 cm; ground clearance: 5.67 in, 14.5 cm; weight: Coupé 2.519 lb, 1,142 kg - Ghia Coupé 2,586 lb, 1,173 kg; turning circle: 37.4 ft, 11.4 m; fuel tank: 9.5 imp gal, 11.5 US gal, 43 l.

BODY coupé; 3 doors; 4 seats, separate front seats, reclining backrests with built-in headrests.

OPTIONALS heavy-duty cooling system; SelectShift automatic transmission with 3 ratios (I 2.470, II 1.470, III 1, rev 2.110), max ratio of converter at stall 2.9, possible manual selection, central lever, 3.080 axle ratio; aluminium wheels; C78 x 13, B78 x 14 or BR78 x 14 tyres with 5'' wide rims; CR78 x 14 tyres with 5,5'' wide rims; 190/65R x 390 tyres with TRX forged aluminum wheels; heavy-duty suspension with rear anti-roll bar; power steering; tilt of steering wheel; servo brake; 54 Ah heavy-duty battery; heated rear window; tinted glass; air-conditioning; sunshine roof; vinyl roof; speed control device; metallic spray; rear window wiper-washer; leather upholstery (Ghia only); RS equipment.

109 hp power team

See 88 hp power team, except for:

ENGINE 6 cylinders, Vee-slanted at 60°; 170.8 cu in, 2,800 cc (3.66 x 2.70 in, 92.9 x 68.5 mm); compression ratio: 8.7:1; max power (DIN): 109 hp (80.2 kW) at 4,800 rpm; max torque (DIN): 142 lb ft, 19.6 kg m (192.2 Nm) at 2,800 rpm; max engine rpm: 4,800; 38.9 hp/l (28.6 kW/l); 4 crankshaft bearings; valves: overhead, in line, push-rods and rockers; camshafts: 1, at centre of Vee; 1 Ford 2700 D9ZE-BB (Motorcraft 2700 D9ZE-LB with variable Venturi for California only) downdraught twin barrel carburettor; cooling system: 15.3 imp pt, 18.4 US pt, 8.7 l.

TRANSMISSION gearbox: SelectShift automatic transmission (standard), hydraulic torque converter and planetary gears with 3 ratios, max ratio of converter at stall 2.05, possible manual selection; ratios: I 2.460, II 1.460, III 1, rev 2.180; lever: central; axle ratio: 3.080.

PERFORMANCE max speed: about 99 mph, 160 km/h; power-weight ratio: Coupé 23.9 lb/hp (32.4 lb/kW), 10.8 kg/hp (14.7 kg/kW) - Ghia Coupé 24.5 lb/hp (33.3 lb/kW), 11.1 kg/hp (15.1 kg/kW); speed in direct drive at 1,000 rpm: 26.4 mph, 42.5 km/h; consumption: 21.6 m/imp gal, 18 m/US gal, 13.1 l x 100 km.

BRAKES servo (standard).

DIMENSIONS AND WEIGHT weight: plus 85 lb, 38 kg; fuel tank: 10.1 imp gal, 12.2 US gal, 46 l.

140 hp power team

(not available in California).

See 88 hp power team, except for:

ENGINE 8 cylinders; 302 cu in, 4,950 cc (4 x 3 in, 101.6 x 76.2 mm); compression ratio: 8.4:1; max power (DIN): 140 hp (103 kW) at 3,600 rpm; max torque (DIN): 250 lb ft, 34.5 g m (338.3 Nm) at 1,800 rpm; max engine rpm: 4,000; 28.3 hp/l (20.8 kW/l); valves: overhead, in line, push-rods and rockers, hydraulic tappets; camshafts: 1, at centre of Vee; 1 Ford 2150 D9BE-YB downdraught twin barrel carburettor; cooling system: 23.1 imp pt, 27.7 US pt, 13.1 l.

TRANSMISSION gears: 4, fully synchronized with overdrive/top; ratios: I 3.070, II 1.720, III 1, IV 0.700, rev 3.070; axle ratio: 3.080.

PERFORMANCE max speed: about 105 mph, 169 km/h; power-weight ratio: Coupé 19.5 lb/hp (26.5 lb/kW), 8.8 kg/hp (12 kg/kW) - Ghia Coupé 20 lb/hp (27.1 lb/kW), 9.1 kg/hp (12.3 kg/kW); speed in top at 1,000 rpm: 26.2 mph, 42.2 km/h; consumption: 19.2 m/imp gal, 16 m/US gal, 14.7 l x 100 km.

CHASSIS (standard) anti-roll bar on rear suspension.

STEERING servo (standard); turns lock to lock: 3.05.

BRAKES front disc (diameter 10 in, 25.5 cm), front internal radial fins, rear compensator, rear drum, servo (standard); swept area: total 275.5 sq in, 1,777 sq cm.

ELECTRICAL EQUIPMENT 36 Ah battery; 60 A alternator.

MERCURY Monarch 2-dr Sedan

140 HP POWER TEAM

DIMENSIONS AND WEIGHT weight: plus 210 lb, 95 kg; fuel tank: 10.1 imp gal, 12.2 US gal, 46 l.

OPTIONALS SelectShift automatic transmission with 3 ratios (I 2.460, II 1.460, III 1, rev 2.180), max ratio of converter at stall 2.05, possible manual selection, central lever, 2.470 axle ratio.

143 hp power team

(for California only).

See 88 hp power team, except for:

ENGINE 8 cylinders; 302 cu in, 4,950 cc (4 x 3 in, 101.6 x 76.2 mm); compression ratio: 8.4:1; max power (DIN): 143 hp (105.2 kW) at 3,600 rpm; max torque (DIN): 243 lb ft, 33.5 kg m (328.5 Nm) at 2,200 rpm; max engine rpm: 4,000; 28.9 hp/l (21.3 kW/l); valves: overhead, in line, push-rods and rockers, hydraulic tappets; camshafts: 1, at centre of Vee; 1 Motorcraft 2700 D9ZE-BEA downdraught carburettor with variable Venturi; cooling system: 23.1 impt pt, 27.7 US pt, 13.1 l.

TRANSMISSION gearbox: SelectShift automatic transmission (standard), hydraulic torque converter and planetary gears with 3 ratios, max ratio of converter at stall 2.05, possible manual selection; ratios: I 2.460, II 1.460, III 1, rev 2.180; lever: central; axle ratio: 2.470.

PERFORMANCE max speed: about 103 mph, 165 km/h; power-weight ratio: Coupé 19.2 lb/hp (26.1 lb/kW), 8.7 kg/hp (11.8 kg/kW) - Ghia Coupé 19.7 lb/hp (26.7 lb/kW), 8.9 kg/hp (12.1 kg/kW); speed in direct drive at 1,000 rpm: 25.6 mph, 41.2 km/h; consumption: 18 m/imp gal, 15 m/US gal, 15.7 l x 100 km.

CHASSIS (standard) anti-roll bar on rear suspension.

STEERING servo (standard); turns lock to lock: 3.05.

BRAKES front disc (diameter 10 in, 25.5 cm), front internal radial fins, rear compensator, rear drum, servo (standard); swept area: total 275.5 sq in, 1,777 sq cm.

ELECTRICAL EQUIPMENT 36 Ah battery; 60 A alternator.

DIMENSIONS AND WEIGHT weight: plus 227 lb, 103 kg; fuel tank: 10.1 imp gal, 12.2 US gal, 46 l.

OPTIONALS 3.080 axle ratio.

150 hp power team

See 88 hp power team, except for:

ENGINE turbocharged; max power (DIN): 150 hp (110.4 kW) at 4,800 rpm; 65.2 hp/l (48 kW/l); lubricating system: 9.2 imp pt, 11 US pt, 5.2 l; 1 Holley-Weber D9ZE-MD/ND (D9ZE-SB/TB for California only) downdraught twin barrel carburettor; exhaust system with turbocharger; cooling system: 17.1 imp pt, 20.5 US pt, 9.7 l.

TRANSMISSION gearbox ratios: I 4.070, II 2.570, III 1.660, IV 1, rev 3.950; lever: central; axle ratio: 3.450.

PERFORMANCE max speed: about 109 mph, 175 km/h; power-weight ratio: Coupé 17.3 lb/hp (23.5 lb/kW), 7.8 kg/hp (10.6 kg/kW) - Ghia Coupé 17.7 lb/hp (24.1 lb/kW), 8 kg/hp (10.9 kg/kW); speed in direct drive at 1,000 rpm: 22.7 mph, 36.5 km/h; consumption: 26.4 m/imp gal, 22 m/US gal, 10.7 l x 100 km.

DIMENSIONS AND WEIGHT weight: plus 71 lb, 32 kg; fuel tank: 10.3 imp gal, 12.5 US gal, 47 l.

OPTIONALS SelectShift automatic transmission not available.

Monarch Series

PRICES EX WORKS:

2-dr Sedan	$ 4,412
4-dr Sedan	$ 4,515

For V8 engines add $ 283.

Power team:	Standard for:	Optional for:
97 hp	both	—
137 hp	—	both
138 hp	—	both

97 hp power team

ENGINE front, 4 stroke; 6 cylinders, in line; 250 cu in, 4,097 cc (3.68 x 3.91 in, 93.5 x 99.3 mm); compression ratio: 8.6:1; max power (DIN): 97 hp (71.4 kW) at 3,200 rpm; max torque (DIN): 210 lb ft, 29 kg m (284.4 Nm) at 1,400 rpm; max engine rpm: 3,800; 23.7 hp/l (17.4 kW/l); cast iron block and head; 7 crankshaft bearings; valves: overhead, in line, push-rods and rockers, hydraulic tappets; camshafts: 1, side; lubrication: rotary pump, full flow filter, 8.3 imp pt, 9.9 US pt, 4.7 l; 1 Carter YFA 9510 D9DE-EA (D9DE-BA for California only) downdraught single barrel carburettor; cleaner air system; exhaust system with catalytic converter; fuel feed: mechanical pump; water-cooled, 17.4 imp pt, 21 US pt, 9.9 l (California only 17.8 imp pt, 21.4 US pt, 10.1 l).

TRANSMISSION driving wheels: rear; clutch: single dry plate, semi-centrifugal; gearbox: mechanical (SelectShift Cruise-O-Matic automatic transmission standard for California only); gears: 4, fully synchronized with overdrive/top; ratios: I 3.290, II 1.840, III 1, IV 0.810, rev 3.290; lever: central; final drive: hypoid bevel; axle ratio: 3.000 (2.790 for California only); width of rims: 6''; tyres: DR78 x 14.

PERFORMANCE max speed: about 93 mph, 149 km/h; power-weight ratio: 4-dr 31.9 lb/hp (43.4 lb/kW), 13.7 kg/hp (18.6 kg/kW); speed in top at 1,000 rpm: 25.5 mph, 41 km/h; consumption: 21.6 m/imp gal, 18 m/US gal, 13.1 l x 100 km.

CHASSIS integral; front suspension: independent, wishbones, coil springs, anti-roll bar, telescopic dampers; rear: rigid axle semi-elliptic leafsprings, telescopic dampers.

STEERING recirculating ball; turns lock to lock: 5.18.

BRAKES front disc (diameter 11.03 in, 28 cm), front internal fins, rear compensator, rear drum; swept area: total 348.2 sq in, 2,247 sq cm.

ELECTRICAL EQUIPMENT 12 V; 36 Ah battery; 40 A alternator; Motorcraft transistorized ignition; 4 headlamps.

DIMENSIONS AND WEIGHT wheel base: 109.90 in, 279 cm; tracks: 59 in, 150 cm front, 57.70 in, 147 cm rear; length: 197.80 in, 502 cm; width: 74 in, 188 cm; height: 2-dr 53.20 in, 135 cm - 4-dr 53.30 in, 135 cm; ground clearance: 4.4 in, 11.2 cm; weight: 2-dr 3,056 lb, 1,311 kg - 4-dr 3,098 lb, 1,330 kg; turning circle: 39 ft, 11.9 m; fuel tank: 15 imp gal, 18 US gal, 68 l.

BODY saloon/sedan; 5 seats, bench front seats with built-in headrests.

OPTIONALS heavy-duty cooling system; SelectShift Cruise-O-Matic automatic transmission with 3 ratios (I 2.460, II 1.460, III 1, rev 2.800), max ratio of converter at stall 2.300, possible manual selection, steering column or central lever, 2.790 axle ratio; aluminium wheels; ER78 x 14 or FR78 x 14 tyres with 6'' wide rims; heavy-duty suspension; power steering; tilt of steering wheel; servo brake; automatic speed control; electric windows; tinted glass; 54 Ah heavy duty battery; metallic spray; vinyl roof; separate front seats with reclining backrests; electric sunshine roof; air-conditioning; ESS equipment; Ghia equipment; heated rear window.

137 hp power team

(not available in California)

See 97 hp power team, except for:

ENGINE 8 cylinders; 302 cu in, 4,950 cc (4 x 3 in, 101.6 x 76.2 mm); compression ratio: 8.4:1; max power (DIN): 137 hp (100.8 kW) at 3,600 rpm; max torque (DIN): 243 lb ft, 33.5 kg m (328.5 Nm) at 2,000 rpm; max engine rpm: 4,200; 27.7 hp/l (20.4 kW/l); 5 crankshaft bearings; camshafts: 1, at centre of Vee; 1 Ford 2150A D9DE-KA downdraught twin barrel carburettor; cooling system: 23.6 imp pt, 28.3 US pt, 13.4 l.

PERFORMANCE max speed: about 103 mph, 165 km/h; power-weight ratio: 4-dr 23.1 lb/hp (31.4 lb/kW), 9.9 kg/hp (13.5 kg/kW); consumption: 19.2 m/imp gal, 16 m/US gal, 14.7 l x 100 km.

DIMENSIONS AND WEIGHT weight: plus 71 lb, 32 kg.

OPTIONALS SelectShift Cruise-O-Matic automatic transmission with max ratio of converter at stall. 2.

138 hp power team

(for California only).

See 97 hp power team, except for:

ENGINE 8 cylinders; 302 cu in, 4,950 cc (4 x 3 in, 101.6 x 76.2 mm); compression ratio: 8.4:1; max power (DIN): 138 hp (101.6 kW) at 3,800 rpm; max torque (DIN): 239 lb ft, 33 kg m (323.6 Nm) at 2,000 rpm; max engine rpm: 4,200; 27.9 hp/l (20.5 kW/l); 5 crankshaft bearings; camshafts: 1 at centre of Vee; 1 Ford 2700 9510 D9DE-HA downdraught carburettor with variable Venturi; cooling system: 23.6 imp pt, 28.3 US pt, 13.4 l.

TRANSMISSION gearbox: SelectShift Cruise-O-Matic automatic transmission (standard), hydraulic torque converter and planetary gears with 3 ratios, max ratio of converter at stall 2, possible manual selection; ratios: I 2.460, II 1.460, III 1, rev 2.800; lever: steering column; axle ratio: 2.790.

PERFORMANCE max speed: about 99 mph, 160 km/h; power-weight ratio: 4-dr 23 lb/hp (31.3 lb/kW), 9.9 kg/hp (13.4 kg/kW); speed in direct drive at 1,000 rpm: 26.1 mph, 42 km/h; consumption: 16.8 m/imp gal, 14 m/US gal, 16.8 l x 100 km.

DIMENSIONS AND WEIGHT weight: plus 80 lb, 36 kg.

OPTIONALS central lever.

Cougar Series

PRICES EX WORKS:

1 2-dr Hardtop	$ 5,379
2 4-dr Pillared Hardtop	$ 5,524
3 XR-7 2-dr Hardtop	$ 5,994

For 5.8-litre engines add $ 263.

Power team:	Standard for:	Optional for:
133 hp	all	—
129 hp	—	all
135 hp	—	3
149 hp	all	—
151 hp	—	all

133 hp power team

(not available in California).

ENGINE front, 4 stroke; 8 cylinders; 302 cu in, 4,950 cc (4 x 3 in, 101.6 x 76.2 mm); compression ratio: 8.4:1; max power (DIN) 133 hp (97.9 kW) at 3,400 rpm; max torque (DIN): 245 lb ft, 33.8 kg m (331.5 Nm) at 1,600 rpm; max engine rpm: 4,000; 26.9 hp/l (19.8 kW/l); cast iron block and head; 5 crankshaft bearings; valves: overhead, in line, push-rods and rockers, hydraulic tappets; camshafts: 1, at centre of Vee; lubrication: rotary pump, full flow filter, 8.3 imp pt, 9.9 US pt, 4.7 l; 1 Ford 2150A D84E-TA/UA downdraught twin barrel carburettor; cleaner air system; exhaust system with 2 catalytic converters; fuel feed: mechanical pump; water-cooled, 23.8 imp pt, 28.5 US pt, 13.5 l.

TRANSMISSION driving wheels: rear; gearbox: SelectShift automatic transmission, hydraulic torque converter and planetary gears with 3 ratios, max ratio of converter at stall 1.97, possible manual selection; ratios: I 2.460, II 1.460, III 1, rev 2.200; lever: steering column; final drive: hypoid bevel; axle ratio: 2.750; width of rims: 5.5'' - XR-7 6''; tyres: HR78 x 14 - XR-7 GR78 x 15.

PERFORMANCE max speed: about 103 mph, 165 km/h; power-weight ratio: 2-dr Hardtop 28.1 lb/hp (38.1 lb/kW), 12.7 kg/hp (17.3 kg/kW) - XR-7 2-dr Hardtop 28.6 lb/hp (38.9 lb/kW), 13 kg/hp (17.6 kg/kW); speed in direct drive at 1,000 rpm: 25.6 mph, 41.2 km/h; consumption: 16.8 m/imp gal, 14 m/US gal, 16.8 l x 100 km.

CHASSIS perimeter box-type frame; front suspension: independent, wishbones, coil springs, anti-roll bar, telescopic dampers; rear: rigid axle, lower trailing radius arms, upper oblique torque arms, coil springs, telescopic dampers.

STEERING recirculating ball, servo; turns lock to lock: 4.

BRAKES front disc (diameter 10.72 in, 27.2 cm), front internal radial fins, rear compensator, rear drum, servo; swept area: front 212 sq in, 1,368 sq cm, rear 155.9 sq in, 1,006 sq cm, total 367.9 sq in, 2,374 sq cm.

ELECTRICAL EQUIPMENT 12 V; 36 Ah battery; 40 A alternator; Motorcraft transistorized ignition; 4 headlamps.

DIMENSIONS AND WEIGHT wheel base: 113.90 in, 289 cm - 4-dr Pillared Hardtop 117.90 in, 299 cm; front track: 63.60 in, 161 cm - XR-7 63.20 in, 160 cm; rear track: 63.50 in, 161 cm - XR-7 63.10 in, 160 cm; length: 217.20 in, 552 cm - 4-dr Pillared Hardtop 221.20 in, 562 cm; width: 78.60 in, 200 cm; height: 2-dr Hardtop 52.60 in, 134 cm - 4-dr Pillared Hardtop 53.30 in, 135 cm - XR-7 52.80 in, 134 cm; ground clearance: 2-dr Hardtop 4.76 in, 12.1 cm - 4-dr Pillared Hardtop 4.73 in, 12 cm - XR-7 5.06 in, 12.8 cm; weight: 4-dr Hardtop 3,732 lb, 1,693 kg - 4-dr Pillared Hardtop 3,802 lb, 1,725 kg - XR-7 2-dr Hardtop 3,809 lb, 1,728 kg; turning circle: 42.4 ft, 12.9 m; fuel tank: 17.6 imp gal, 21 US gal, 80 l.

BODY hardtop; 6 seats, bench front seats with built-in headrests.

OPTIONALS heavy-duty cooling system; limited slip differential; GR78 x 15 tyres with 6'' wide rims or HR70 x 15 tyres with 6.5'' wide rims (except for XR-7); GR78 x 15 tyres with 6.5'' wide rims, HR70 x 15 tyres with 6.5'' wide rims or H78 x 15 tyres with 6'' wide rims (XR-7 only); Cross Country suspension with rear anti-roll bar; central lever; tilt of steering wheel; 77 Ah heavy-duty battery; heated rear window; electric windows; tinted glass; air-conditioning; separate front seats with reclining backrests; automatic speed control; sunshine roof; larger fuel tank; vinyl roof; leather upholstery (XR-7 only); Brougham equipment (except for XR-7).

129 hp power team

(only for export).

See 133 hp power team, except for:

ENGINE max power (DIN): 129 hp (94.9 kW) at 3,400 rpm; max torque (DIN): 234 lb ft, 32.3 kg m (316.8 Nm) at 1,600 rpm; 26.1 hp/l (19.2 kW/l).

PERFORMANCE power-weight ratio: 2-dr Hardtop 28.9 lb/hp (39.3 lb/kW), 13.1 kg/hp (17.8 kg/kW) - XR-7 2-dr Hardtop 29.5 lb/hp (40.1 lb/kW), 13.4 kg/hp (18.2 kg/kW).

135 hp power team

(not available in California).

See 133 hp power team, except for:

ENGINE 351 cu in, 5,732 cc (4 x 3.50 in, 101.6 x 88.8 mm); compression ratio: 8.3:1; max power (DIN): 135 hp (99.4 kW) at 3,200 rpm; max torque (DIN): 286 lb ft, 39.4 kg m (386.4 Nm) at 1,400 rpm; 23.6 hp/l (17.3 kW/l); 1 Ford 2150A D9WE-EA downdraught twin barrel carburettor; cooling system: 25.7 imp pt, 30.9 US pt, 14.6 l.

TRANSMISSION gearbox: automatic transmission with max ratio of converter at stall 1.85; ratios: I 2.400, II 1.470, III 1, rev 2; axle ratio: 2.470.

PERFORMANCE power-weight ratio: 29.2 lb/hp (39.6 lb/kW), 13.3 kg/hp (18 kg/kW); consumption: 15.6 m/imp gal, 13 m/US gal, 18.1 l x 100 km.

ELECTRICAL EQUIPMENT 45 Ah battery.

DIMENSIONS AND WEIGHT weight: plus 142 lb, 64 kg.

149 hp power team

(for California only).

See 133 hp power team, except for:

ENGINE 351 cu in, 5,732 cc (4 x 3.50 in, 101.6 x 88.8 mm); compression ratio: 8:1; max power (DIN) 149 hp (109.7 kW) at 3,800 rpm; max torque (DIN): 258 lb ft, 35.6 kg m (349.1 Nm) at 2,200 rpm; max engine rpm: 4,400; 26 hp/l (19.1 kW/l); 1 Ford 2150A D9AE-AHA downdraught twin barrel carburettor; cooling system: 27.5 imp pt, 33 US pt, 15.6 l.

TRANSMISSION gearbox: automatic transmission with max ratio of converter at stall 1.85; ratios: I 2.400, II 1.470, III 1, rev 2; axle ratio: 2.470.

PERFORMANCE max speed: about 106 mph, 170 km/h; power-weight ratio: 2-dr Hardtop 26 lb/hp (35.3 lb/kW), 11.8 kg/hp (16 kg/kW) - XR-7 2-dr Hardtop 26.4 lb/hp (35.9 lb/kW), 12 kg/hp (16.3 kg/kW); speed in direct drive at 1,000 rpm: 27.8 mph, 44.7 km/h; consumption: 13.2 m/imp gal, 11 m/US gal, 21.4 l x 100 km.

ELECTRICAL EQUIPMENT 45 Ah battery.

DIMENSIONS AND WEIGHT weight: plus 142 lb, 64 kg.

151 hp power team

(not available in California).

See 133 hp power team, except for:

ENGINE 351 cu in, 5,732 cc (4 x 3.50 in, 101.6 x 88.8 mm); compression ratio: 8:1; max power (DIN): 151 hp (111.1 kW) at 3,600 rpm; max torque (DIN): 270 lb ft, 37.2 kg m (364.8 Nm) at 2,200 rpm; 26.3 hp/l (19.3 kW/l); 1 Ford 2150A D90E-CB or D8WE-CA downdraught twin barrel carburettor; cooling system: 27.5 imp pt, 33 US pt, 15.6 l.

TRANSMISSION gearbox: automatic transmission with max ratio of converter at stall 1.85; ratios: I 2.400, II 1.470, III 1, rev 2; axle ratio: 2.470.

PERFORMANCE max speed: about 109 mph, 175 km/h; power-weight ratio: 2-dr Hardtop 25.7 lb/hp (34.9 lb/kW), 11.6 kg/hp (15.8 kg/kW) - XR-7 2-dr Hardtop 26.1 lb/hp (35.5 lb/kW), 11.9 kg/hp (16.1 kg/kW); speed in direct drive at 1,000 rpm: 27.2 mph, 43.7 km/h; consumption: 15.6 m/imp gal, 13 m/US gal, 18.1 l x 100 km.

ELECTRICAL EQUIPMENT 45 Ah battery.

DIMENSIONS AND WEIGHT weight: plus 142 lb, 64 kg.

OPTIONALS 3.000 axle ratio.

Marquis - Grand Marquis Series

PRICES EX WORKS:

1 Marquis 2-dr Sedan		$ 5,984
2 Marquis 4-dr Sedan		$ 6,079
3 Marquis St. Wagon		$ 6,315
4 Marquis Colony Park St. Wagon		$ 7,100
5 Marquis Brougham 2-dr Sedan		$ 6,643
6 Marquis Brougham 4-dr Sedan		$ 6,831
7 Grand Marquis 2-dr Sedan		$ 7,321
8 Grand Marquis 4-dr Sedan		$ 7,510

For 5.8-litre engine add $ 263.

Power team:	Standard for:	Optional for:
129 hp	all	—
130 hp	1,2,5,6,7,8	—
138 hp	—	all

129 hp power team

(not available in California).

ENGINE front, 4 stroke; 8 cylinders; 302 cu in, 4,950 cc (4 x 3 in, 101.6 x 76.2 mm); compression ratio: 8.4:1; max power (DIN) 129 hp (94.9 kW) at 3,600 rpm; max torque (DIN) 223 lb ft, 30.8 kg m (302.1 Nm) at 2,600 rpm; max engine rpm: 4,000; 26.1 hp/l (19.2 kW/l); cast iron block and head; 5 crankshaft bearings; valves: overhead, in line, push-rods and rockers, hydraulic tappets; camshafts: 1, at centre of Vee; lubrication: rotary pump, full flow filter, 8.3 imp pt, 9.9 US pt, 4.7 l; 1 Ford 2700 D9AE-YB-JB downdraught carburettor with variable Venturi; cleaner air system; exhaust system with 2 catalytic converter; fuel feed: mechanical pump; water-cooled, 22.2 imp pt, 26.6 US pt, 12.6 l.

TRANSMISSION driving wheels: rear; gearbox: SelectShift Cruise-O-Matic automatic transmission, hydraulic torque converter and planetary gears with 3 ratios, max ratio of converter at stall 1.97, possible manual selection; ratios: I 2.400, II 1.470, III 1, rev 2; lever: steering column; final drive: hypoid bevel; axle ratio: 2.260 - st. wagons 2.730; width of rims: 5.5'' - st. wagons 6.5''; tyres: FR78 x 14 - st. wagons GR78 x 14.

PERFORMANCE max speed: about 96 mph, 154 km/h; power-weight ratio: Marquis 4-dr Sedan 27 lb/hp (36.8 lb/kW), 12.3 kg/hp (16.7 kg/kW) - Marquis Brougham 4-dr Sedan 27.3 lb/hp (37.1 lb/kW), 12.4 kg/hp (16.8 kg/kW) - Grand Marquis 4-dr Sedan 27.6 lb/hp (37.5 lb/kW), 12.5 kg/hp (17 kg/kW); speed in direct drive at 1,000 rpm: 25.4 mph, 40.8 km/h; consumption: 18 m/imp gal, 15 m/US gal, 15.7 l x 100 km.

CHASSIS perimeter box-type frame; front suspension: independent, wishbones, coil springs, anti-roll bar, telescopic

MERCURY Cougar XR-7 2-dr Hardtop

129 HP POWER TEAM

dampers; rear: rigid axle, lower trailing radius arms, upper oblique torque arms, coil springs, telescopic dampers.

STEERING recirculating ball, servo; turns lock to loc: 3.40.

BRAKES front disc (diameter 11.08 in, 28.1 cm), front internal radial fins, rear compensator, rear drum, servo; swept area: front 228.7 sq in, 1,475 sq cm, rear 157.1 sq in, 1,013 sq cm - st. wagons 155.9 sq in, 1,006 sq cm, total 385.8 sq in, 2,488 sq cm - st. wagons 384.6 sq in, 2,481 sq cm.

ELECTRICAL EQUIPMENT 12 V; 36 Ah battery; 60 A alternator; Motorcraft transistorized ignition; 4 headlamps.

DIMENSIONS AND WEIGHT wheel base: 114.30 in, 290 cm; tracks: 62.20 in, 158 cm front, 62 in, 157 cm rear; length: sedans 212 in, 538 cm - st. wagons 217.70 in, 553 cm; width: sedans 77.50 in, 197 cm - st. wagons 79.30 in, 201 cm; height: sedans 54.50 in, 138 cm - st. wagons 56.80 in, 144 cm; ground clearance: sedans 4.87 in, 12.4 cm - st. wagons 4.75 in, 12.1 cm; weight: Marquis 2-dr Sedan 3,442 lb, 1,561 kg - Marquis 4-dr Sedan 3,489 lb, 1,583 kg - Marquis Brougham 2-dr Sedan 3,471 lb, 1,574 kg - Marquis Brougham 4-dr Sedan 3,523 lb, 1,598 kg - Grand Marquis 2-dr Sedan 3,510 lb, 1,592 kg - Grand Marquis 4-dr Sedan 3,555 lb, 1,613 kg - Marquis St. Wagon 3,730 lb, 1,692 kg - Marquis Colony Park St. Wagon 3,756 lb, 1,704 kg; fuel

tank: sedans 15.8 imp gal, 19 US gal, 72 l - st. wagons 16.7 imp gal, 20 US gal, 76 l.

BODY 6 seats, bench front seats with built-in headrests.

OPTIONALS heavy-duty cooling system; 2.730 axle ratio (except for st. wagons); GR78 x 14 tyres with 6.5'' wide rims (sedans only); HR78 x 14 tyres with 6.5'' wide rims (st. wagons only); heavy-duty suspension with rear anti-roll bar; tilt of steering wheel; 71 Ah heavy-duty battery; electric windows; heated rear window air-conditioning; tinted glass; automatic speed control; luxury interior; separate front seats; with reclining backrests; vinyl roof; leather upholstery.

130 hp power team

(for California only).

See 129 hp power team, except for:

ENGINE max power (DIN): 130 hp (95.7 kW) at 3,600 rpm; max torque (DIN): 226 lb ft, 31.2 kg m (306 Nm) at 2,200 rpm; 26.3 hp/l (19.3 kW/l); 1 Ford 2700 D9AE-ZB-CB downdraught carburettor with variable Venturi.

TRANSMISSION axle ratio: 2.260.

PERFORMANCE power-weight ratio: Marquis 4-dr Sedan 26.8 lb/hp (36.5 lb/kW), 12.2 kg/hp (16.5 kg/kW) - Marquis

Brougham 4-dr Sedan 27.1 lb/hp (36.8 lb/kW), 12.3 kg/h (16.7 kg/kW) - Grand Marquis 4-dr Sedan 27.3 lb/hp (37. lb/kW), 12.4 kg/hp (16.9 kg/kW); consumption: 16.8 m/im gal, 14 m/US gal, 16.8 l x 100 km.

OPTIONALS 2.730 axle ratio not available.

138 hp power team

See 129 hp power team, except for:

ENGINE 351 cu in, 5,732 cc (4 x 3.50 in, 101.6 x 88.8 mm) compression ratio: 8.3:1; max power (DIN): 138 hp (101. kW) at 3,200 rpm; max torque (DIN): 260 lb ft, 35.9 kg r (352.1 Nm) at 2,200 rpm; 24.1 hp/l (17.7 kW/l); 1 For 7200 D9ME-AA (D7AE-CA for California only) downdraugh carburettor with variable Venturi; cooling system: 23.9 im pt, 28.8 US pt, 13.6 l.

TRANSMISSION gearbox: automatic transmission with ma ratio of converter at stall 1.85; ratios: I 2.460, II 1.460 III 1, rev 2.200.

PERFORMANCE max speed: about 103 mph, 165 km/h; powe -weight ratio: Marquis 4-dr Sedan 25.7 lb/hp (34.9 lb/kW) 11.7 kg/hp (15.8 kg/kW) - Marquis Brougham 4-dr Sedan 2 lb/hp (35.3 lb/kW), 11.8 kg/hp (16 kg/kW) - Grand Marqui 4-dr Sedan 26.2 lb/hp (35.6 lb/kW), 11.9 kg/hp (16.1 kg/kW) speed in direct drive at 1,000 rpm: 28.5 mph, 45.8 km/h consumption: 16.8 m/imp gal, 14 m/US gal, 16.8 l x 10 km (California only 15.6 m/imp gal, 13 m/US gal, 15.6 l l x 100 km).

ELECTRICAL EQUIPMENT 45 Ah battery.

DIMENSIONS AND WEIGHT weight: plus 59 lb, 27 kg.

OPTIONALS 3.080 axle ratio.

MONOCOQUE   USA

Box

PRICE EX WORKS: $ 18,000

ENGINE Honda Accord, rear, transverse, 4 stroke, stratifi ed charge; 4 cylinders, in line; 97.6 cu in, 1,599 cc (2.91 x 3,66 in, 74 x 93 mm); compression ratio: 8:1; max power (JIS): 68 hp (50 kW) at 5,000 rpm; max torque (JIS): 85 lb ft, 11.7 kg m (114.7 Nm) at 3,000 rpm; max engine rpm: 5,800; 42.5 hp/l (31.3 kW/l); cast iron block, light alloy head; 5 crankshaft bearings; valves: 3 per cylinder (one intake and one exhaust in main combustion chamber, one intake in auxiliary chamber), overhead, Vee-slanted, rockers; camshafts: 1, overhead, cogged belt; lubrication: rotary pump, full flow filter, 5.3 imp pt, 6.3 US pt, 3 l; 1 Keihin-Honda downdraught 3-barrel CVCC carburettor; fuel feed: electric pump; water-cooled, 8.8 imp pt, 10.6 US pt, 5 l.

TRANSMISSION driving wheels: front and rear with amphi-bious drive gear; clutch: single dry plate (diaphragm), hydraulically controlled; gearbox: mechanical; gears: 5, fully synchronized ratios: I 3.181, II 1.823, III 1.181, IV 0.846, V 0.714, rev 2.916; lever: central; final drive: hypoid bevel, front and rear limited slip differentials; axle ratio: 4.933; width of rims: 8''; tyres: HR70 x 15.

PERFORMANCE max speed: 125 mph, 201 km/h; power-weight ratio: 14.7 lb/hp, (20 lb/kW), 6.7 kg/hp (9.1 kg/kW); acceleration: standing ¼ mile 14 sec; consumption: 35.3 m/imp gal, 29.4 m/US gal, 8 l x 100 km.

CHASSIS monocoque unit construction; front suspension: independent, wishbones (swinging semi-axles), coil springs, telescopic dampers; rear: independent, wishbones (swinging semi-axles), coil springs, telescopic dampers.

STEERING (front and rear wheels) rack-and-pinion; turns lock to lock: 3.

BRAKES disc.

ELECTRICAL EQUIPMENT 12 V; 35 Ah battery; 50 A alternator; Mitsubishi distributor; 4 headlamps.

DIMENSIONS AND WEIGHT wheel base: 77 in, 196 cm; tracks: 68 in, 173 cm front, 68 in, 173 cm rear; length: 129 in, 328 cm; width: 80 in, 203 cm; height: 44 in, 112 cm; ground clearance: 13.50 in, 34.3 cm; weight: 1,000 lb, 454 kg; weight distribution: 50% front, 50% rear; turning circle: 30 ft, 9.2 m; fuel tank: 8.4 imp gal, 10 US gal, 38 l.

BODY in plastic material; 1 front opening door; 2 seats, reclining backrests with built-in headrests; aluminium wheels.

OPTIONALS air-oil suspensions; larger fuel tank.

MERCURY Grand Marquis 4-dr Sedan

MONOCOQUE Box

OLDSMOBILE Starfire Sport Coupé

OLDSMOBILE · USA

Starfire Series

PRICES EX WORKS:

Sport Coupé	$ 4,095
SX Sport Coupé	$ 4,295

For V6 engine add $ 200; for V8 engine add $ 395.

Power team:	Standard for:	Optional for:
85 hp	both	—
115 hp	—	both
130 hp	—	both

85 hp power team

(not available in California).

ENGINE front, 4 stroke; 4 cylinders, in line; 151 cu in, 2,474 cc (4 x 3 in, 101.6 x 76.1 mm); compression ratio: 8.3:1; max power (DIN): 85 hp (62.6 kW) at 4,400 rpm; max torque (DIN): 123 lb ft, 17 kg m (166.7 Nm) at 2,800 rpm; max engine rpm: 4,800; 34.4 hp/l (25.3 kW/l); cast iron block and head; 5 crankshaft bearings; valves: overhead, in line, push-rods and rockers, hydraulic tappets; camshafts: 1, side; lubrication: gear pump, full flow filter, 8.3 imp pt, 9.9 US pt, 4.7 l; 1 Holley 5210 downdraught twin barrel carburettor; cleaner air system; exhaust system with catalytic converter; fuel feed: mechanical pump; water-cooled, 18.3 imp pt, 22 US pt, 10.4 l.

TRANSMISSION driving wheels: rear; clutch: single dry plate; gearbox: mechanical; gears: 4, fully synchronized; ratios: I 3.500, II 2.480, III 1.660, IV 1, rev 3.500; lever: central; final drive: hypoid bevel; axle ratio: 2.730; width of rims: 6''; tyres: B78 x 13.

PERFORMANCE max speed: about 93 mph, 149 km/h; power-weight ratio: Starfire 30.9 lb/hp (42 lb/kW), 14.3 kg/hp 19.4 kg/kW); speed in direct drive at 1,000 rpm: 21.2 mph, 34.1 km/h; consumption: 28.8 m/imp gal, 24 m/US gal, 9.8 l x 100 km.

CHASSIS integral; front suspension: independent, wishbones (lower trailing links), coil springs, anti-roll bar, telescopic dampers; rear: rigid axle, lower trailing radius arms, upper oblique torque arms, transverse linkage bar, coil springs, anti-roll bar, telescopic dampers.

STEERING recirculating ball; turns lock to lock: 4.40.

BRAKES front disc (diameter 9.74 in, 24.7 cm), front internal radial fins, rear drum, rear compensator; swept area: total 264.7 sq in, 1,707 sq cm.

ELECTRICAL EQUIPMENT 12 V; 2,500 W battery; 37 A alternator; Delco-Remy transistorized ignition; 2 headlamps.

DIMENSIONS AND WEIGHT wheel base: 97 in, 246 cm; tracks: 54.70 in, 139 cm front, 53.60 in, 136 cm rear; length: 179.60 in, 456 cm; width: 65.40 in, 166 cm; height: 50.20 in, 127 cm; ground clearance: 4.90 in, 12.4 cm; weight: Starfire 2,627 lb, 1,212 kg - Starfire SX 2,641 lb, 1,198 kg; turning circle: 41 ft, 12.5 m; fuel tank: 15.4 imp gal, 18.5 US gal, 70 l.

BODY coupé; 2 doors; 4 seats, separate front seats with built-in headrests; folding rear seats.

OPTIONALS limited slip differential; 5-speed fully synchronized mechanical gearbox (I 3.400, II 2.080, III 1.390, IV 1, V 0.800, rev 3.360), 3.080 axle ratio; Turbo-Hydramatic automatic transmission, hydraulic torque converter and planetary gears with 3 ratios (I 2.520, II 1.520, III 1, rev 1.930), max ratio of converter at stall 2.25, possible manual selection, 2.730 axle ratio; BR78 x 13 tyres; heavy-duty battery; power steering; tilt of steering wheel; servo brake; heated rear window; air-conditioning; sunshine roof; Firenza Sport equipment (except for Starfire SX).

115 hp power team

See 85 hp power team, except for:

ENGINE 6 cylinders, Vee-slanted at 90°; 231 cu in, 3,785 cc (3.80 x 3.40 in, 96.5 x 86.4 mm); compression ratio: 8:1; max power (DIN): 115 hp (84.6 kW) at 3,600 rpm; max torque (DIN): 190 lb ft, 26.2 kg m (257 Nm) at 2,000 rpm; max engine rpm: 4,200; 30.4 hp/l (22.4 kW/l); 4 crankshaft bearings; camshafts: 1, at centre of Vee; 1 Rochester 2ME rear window; air-conditioning; sunshine roof; Firenza Sport equipment (except for Starfire SX).

TRANSMISSION clutch: centrifugal; axle ratio: 2.930.

PERFORMANCE max speed: about 103 mph, 165 km/h; power-weight ratio: Starfire 23.9 lb/hp (50.2 lb/kW), 11 kg/hp (15 kg/kW); speed in direct drive at 1,000 rpm: 25.6 mph, 41.2 km/h; consumption: 22.8 m/imp gal, 19 m/US gal, 12.4 l x 100 km.

ELECTRICAL EQUIPMENT 3,200 W battery.

DIMENSIONS AND WEIGHT weight: plus 116 lb, 53 kg.

OPTIONALS 5-speed fully synchronized mechanical gearbox with 2.930 axle ratio; Turbo-Hydramatic automatic transmission with 2.560 or 2.930 axle ratio; GT equipment.

130 hp power team

See 85 hp power team, except for:

ENGINE 8 cylinders; 305 cu in, 4,999 cc (3.74 x 3.48 in, 94.9 x 88.4 mm); compression ratio: 8.5:1; max power (DIN): 130 hp (95.7 kW) at 3,200 rpm; max torque (DIN): 245 lb ft, 33.8 kg m (331.5 Nm) at 2,400 rpm; max engine rpm: 4,000; 26 hp/l (19.1 kW/l); camshafts: 1, at centre of Vee; 1 Rochester 17057107 (17057404 for California only) downdraught twin barrel carburettor; fuel feed: electric pump; cooling system: 27.5 imp pt, 33.1 US pt, 15.4 l.

TRANSMISSION clutch: centrifugal; gearbox: mechanical (Turbo-Hydramatic automatic transmission standard for California only); ratios: I 2.850, II 2.020, III 1.350, IV 1, rev 2.850; axle ratio: 3.080 (2.290 California only).

PERFORMANCE max speed: about 106 mph, 170 km/h; power-weight ratio: Starfire 22.5 lb/hp (30.6 lb/kW), 10.4 kg/hp (14.1 kg/kW); speed in direct drive at 1,000 rpm: 26.4 mph, 42.5 km/h; consumption: 18 m/imp gal, 15 m/US gal, 15.7 l x 100 km.

ELECTRICAL EQUIPMENT 3,200 W battery; Delco-Remy high energy ignition system.

DIMENSIONS AND WEIGHT weight: plus 297 lb, 135 kg.

OPTIONALS Turbo-Hydramatic automatic transmission with 2.290 axle ratio; heavy-duty cooling system.

Omega Series

PRICES EX WORKS:

Coupé	$ 4,181
Hatchback Coupé	$ 4,346
Sedan	$ 4,281
Brougham Coupé	$ 4,387
Brougham Sedan	$ 4,487

For 130 hp engine add $ 195; for 160 hp engine add $ 320.

Power team:	Standard for:	Optional for:
115 hp	all	—
130 hp	—	all
160 hp	—	all

OLDSMOBILE Omega Brougham Sedan

115 hp power team

ENGINE front, 4 stroke; 6 cylinders, Vee-slanted at 90°; 231 cu in, 3,785 cc (3.80 x 3.40 in, 96.5 x 86.4 mm); compression ratio: 8:1; max power (DIN): 115 hp (84.6 kW) at 3,600 rpm; max torque (DIN): 190 lb ft, 26.2 kg m (257 Nm) at 2,000 rpm; max engine rpm: 4,200; 30.4 hp/l (22.4 kW/l); cast iron block and head; 4 crankshaft bearings; valves: overhead, in line, push-rods and rockers, hydraulic tappets; camshafts: 1, at centre of Vee; lubrication gear pump, full flow filter, 8.3 imp pt, 9.9 US pt, 4.7 l; 1 Rochester 2ME downdraught twin barrel carburettor; cleaner air system; exhaust system with catalytic converter; fuel feed: mechanical pump; water-cooled, 21.3 imp pt, 25.6 US pt, 12.1 l.

TRANSMISSION driving wheels: rear; clutch: single dry plate; gearbox: mechanical (Turbo-Hydramatic automatic transmission standard for California only); gears: 3, fully synchronized; ratios: I 3.500, II 1.810, III 1, rev 3.620; lever: steering column; final drive: hypoid bevel; axle ratio: 3.080 (2.560 California only); width of rims: 5; tyres: E78 x 14.

PERFORMANCE max speed: about 96 mph, 154 km/h; power-weight ratio: Sedan 27.1 lb/hp (36.8 lb/kW), 12.3 kg/hp (16.7 kg/kW) - Brougham Sedan 27.4 lb/hp (37.2 lb/kW), 12.4 kg/hp (16.9 kg/kW); speed in direct drive at 1,000 rpm: 24.2 mph, 39 km/h; consumption: 22.8 m/imp gal, 19 m/US gal, 12.4 l x 100 km.

CHASSIS integral with front separate partial frame; front suspension: independent, wishbones, coil springs, anti-roll bar, telescopic dampers; rear: rigid axle, semi-elliptic leafsprings, telescopic dampers.

STEERING recirculating ball; turns lock to lock: 6.11.

BRAKES front disc (diameter 10.88 in, 27.6 cm), front internal radial fins, rear drum, rear compensator.

ELECTRICAL EQUIPMENT 12 V; 2,500 W battery; 37 A alternator; Delco-Remy transistorized ignition; 2 headlamps.

DIMENSIONS AND WEIGHT wheel base: 111 in, 282 cm; tracks: 61.90 in, 157 cm front, 59.60 in, 151 cm rear; length: 199.60 in, 507 cm; width: 72.90 in, 185 cm; height: 53.20 in, 135 cm - sedans 54.10 in, 140 cm; ground clearance: 4.86 in, 12.3 cm; weight: Omega Coupé 3,079 lb, 1,396 kg - Hatchback Coupé 3,156 lb, 1,431 kg - Sedan 3,117 lb, 1,413 kg - Omega Brougham Coupé 3,090 lb, 1,401 kg - Sedan 3,147 lb, 1,427 kg; turning circle: 41.3 ft, 12.6 m; fuel tank: 17.6 imp gal, 21 US gal, 80 l.

OPTIONALS limited slip differential; Turbo-Hydramatic automatic transmission, hydraulic torque converter and planetary gears with 3 ratios (I 2.740, II 1.570, III 1, rev 2.070), max ratio of converter at stall 2.25, possible manual selection, 2.560, 2.930 or 3.230 axle ratio, steering column or central lever; FR78 x 14 tyres; heavy-duty cooling system; power steering; tilt of steering wheel; servo brake; electric windows; vinyl roof; air-conditioning; LS equipment; SX equipment.

130 hp power team

(not available in California).

See 115 hp power team, except for:

ENGINE 8 cylinders; 305 cu in, 4,999 cc (3.74 x 3.48 in, 94.9 x 88,4 mm); compression ratio: 8.5:1; max power (DIN): 130 hp (95.7 kW) at 3,200 rpm; max torque (DIN): 245 lb ft, 33.8 kg m (331.5 Nm) at 2,000 rpm; max engine rpm: 4,000; 26 hp/l (19.1 kW/l); 5 crankshaft bearings; 1 Rochester 17057107 downdraught twin barrel carburettor; cooling system: 26.2 imp pt, 31.5 US pt, 14.9 l.

TRANSMISSION gears: 4, fully synchronized; ratios: I 3.500, II 2.480, III 1.660, IV 1, rev 3.500; axle ratio: 3.080.

PERFORMANCE max speed: about 103 mph, 165 km/h; power-weight ratio: Sedan 25.2 lb/hp (34.2 lb/kW), 11.4 kg/hp (15.5 kg/kW) - Brougham Sedan 25.4 lb/hp (34.5 lb/kW), 11.5 kg/hp (15.7 kg/kW); speed in direct drive at 1,000 rpm: 25.7 mph, 41.3 km/h; consumption: 18 m/imp gal, 15 m/US gal, 15.7 l x 100 km.

ELECTRICAL EQUIPMENT 3,200 W battery; Delco-Remy high energy ignition system.

DIMENSIONS AND WEIGHT weight: plus 157 lb, 71 kg.

OPTIONALS Turbo-Hydramatic automatic transmission with 3 ratios (I 2.520, II 1.520, III 1, rev 1.930), 3.080 or 2.410 axle ratio.

160 hp power team

(for California only).

See 115 hp power team, except for:

ENGINE 8 cylinders; 350 cu in, 5,736 cc (4 x 3.48 in, 101.6

x 88.4 mm); compression ratio: 8.5:1; max power (DIN): 160 hp (117.8 kW) at 3,800 rpm; max torque (DIN): 260 lb ft, 35.9 kg m (352.1 Nm) at 2,400 rpm; 27.9 hp/l (20.5 kW/l); 5 crankshaft bearings; 1 Rochester downdraught 4-barrel carburettor; cooling system: 26.6 imp pt, 31.9 US pt, 15.1 l.

TRANSMISSION gearbox: Turbo-Hydramatic automatic transmission (standard), hydraulic torque converter and planetary gears with 3 ratios, max ratio of converter at stall 2.25, possible manual selection: ratios: I 2.520, II 1.520, III 1, rev 1.930; lever: steering column or central; axle ratio: 2.410.

PERFORMANCE max speed: about 106 mph, 170 km/h; power-weight ratio: Sedan 20.6 lb/hp (28 lb/kW), 9.3 kg/hp (12.7 kg/kW) - Brougham Sedan 20.8 lb/hp (28.3 lb/kW), 9.4 kg/hp (12.8 kg/kW); speed in direct drive at 1,000 rpm: 27.8 mph, 44.7 km/h; consumption: 15.6 m/imp gal, 13 m/US gal, 18.1 l x 100 km.

ELECTRICAL EQUIPMENT 3,200 W battery; Delco-Remy high energy ignition system.

DIMENSIONS AND WEIGHT weight: plus 184 lb, 83 kg.

OPTIONALS 3.080 axle ratio.

Cutlass Series

PRICES EX WORKS:

1 Salon Sedan	$ 4,723
2 Salon Coupé	$ 4,623
3 Salon Brougham Sedan	$ 5,032
4 Salon Brougham Coupé	$ 4,907
5 Supreme Coupé	$ 5,063
6 Calais Coupé	$ 5,491
7 Supreme Brougham Coupé	$ 5,492
8 Cruiser St. Wagon	$ 4,980
9 Cruiser Brougham St. Wagon	$ 5,517

For 105 hp engine add $ 140. For 160 hp engine add $ 255; for 160 hp 5.7-litre engine add $ 320. For 90 hp Diesel engine add $ 735; for 125 hp Diesel engine add $ 895.

Power team:	Standard for:	Optional for:
115 hp	all	—
105 hp	—	all
160 hp	—	all
160 hp (5.7-litre)	—	8
90 hp (Diesel)	—	all except 8
125 hp (Diesel)	—	8

115 hp power team

ENGINE front, 4 stroke; 6 cylinders, Vee-slanted at 90°; 231 cu in, 3,785 cc (3.80 x 3.40 in, 96.5 x 86.4 mm); compression ratio: 8:1; max power (DIN): 115 hp (84.6 kW) at 3,600 rpm; max torque (DIN): 190 lb ft, 26.2 kg m (257 Nm) at 2,000 rpm; max engine rpm: 4,200; 30.4 hp/l (22.4 kW/l); cast iron block and head; 4 crankshaft bearings; valves: overhead, in line, push-rods and rockers, hydraulic tappets; camshafts: 1, at centre of Vee; lubrication: gear pump, full flow filter, 8.3 imp pt, 9.9 US pt, 4.7 l; 1 Rochester 2ME downdraught twin barrel carburettor; cleaner

air system; exhaust system with catalytic converter; fuel feed: mechanical pump; water-cooled, 22.2 imp pt, 26. US pt, 12.6 l.

TRANSMISSION driving wheels: rear; clutch: single dr plate (diaphragm), centrifugal; gearbox: mechanical (Turbo Hydramatic automatic transmission standard for Californi only); gears: 3 (Calais 4), fully synchronized; ratios: I 3.500 II 1.895, III 1, rev 3.620 (Calais I 3.500, II 2.480, III 1.660 IV 1, rev 3.500); lever: central; final drive: hypoid bevel axle ratio: 2.930 (2.730 California only); width of rims: 6' tyres: P185/75R x 14 - st. wagons P195/75R x 14.

PERFORMANCE max speed: about 99 mph, 159 km/h; power weight ratio: Salon Sedan 26.8 lb/hp (36.4 lb/kW), 12. kg/hp (16.5 kg/kW) - Salon Brougham Sedan 27.1 lb/h (36.8 lb/kW), 12.3 kg/hp (16.7 kg/kW); speed in direc drive at 1,000 rpm: 24.2 mph, 38.9 km/h; consumption: 22. m/imp gal, 19 m/US gal, 12.4 l x 100 km.

CHASSIS channel section perimeter type frame; front sus pension: independent, wishbones, coil springs, anti-roll ba telescopic dampers; rear: rigid axle, lower trailing radiu arms, upper oblique torque arms, coil springs, telescopi dampers.

STEERING recirculating ball; turns lock to lock: 3.90 - st wagons 4.13.

BRAKES front disc (diameter 10.50 in, 26.7 cm), fron internal radial fins, rear drum, rear compensator; swep area: total 312.7 sq in, 2,017 sq cm.

ELECTRICAL EQUIPMENT 2,500 W battery; 42 A alternator Delco-Remy transistorized ignition; 2 headlamps.

DIMENSIONS AND WEIGHT wheel base: 108.10 in, 274 cm tracks: 58.50 in, 149 cm front, 57.80 in, 147 cm rear length: 197.70 in, 502 cm - Supreme Coupé, Calais Coupé and Supreme Brougham Coupé 200.10 in, 508 cm - st wagons 197.60 in, 502 cm; width: 71.90 in, 183 cm - Suprem Coupé, Calais Coupé and Supreme Brougham Coupé 71.3 in, 181 cm - st. wagons 71.70 in, 182 cm; height: 53.50 in 136 cm - sedans 54.50 in, 138 cm - Salon Coupé 53.70 in 136 cm - st. wagons 54.90 in, 139 cm; ground clearance 5.20 in, 13.1 cm - st. wagons 7.42 in, 18.8 cm; weight Salon Sedan 3,077 lb, 1,396 kg - Coupé 3,057 lb, 1,387 kg Salon Brougham Sedan 3,114 lb, 1,415 kg - Coupé 3,09 lb, 1,405 kg - Supreme Coupé 3,088 lb, 1,401 kg - Calais Coupé 3,110 lb, 1,411 kg - Supreme Brougham Coupé 3,11 lb, 1,412 kg - Cruiser St. Wagon 3,199 lb, 1,451 kg - Cruise Brougham St. Wagon 3,233 lb, 1,467 kg; turning circle: Coupé 40.2 ft, 12.2 m - sedans 40.6 ft, 12.5 m - st. wagons 40. ft, 12.3 m; fuel tank: 15.2 imp gal, 18.2 US gal, 69 l.

OPTIONALS limited slip differential; Turbo-Hydramatic au tomatic transmission with 3 ratios (I 2.740, II 1.567, III 1, rev 2.006), max ratio of converter at stall 2.10, possibl manual selection, steering column or central lever, 2.73 or 3.230 axle ratio; 4-speed fully synchronized mechanica gearbox (I 3.500, II 2.480, III 1.660, IV 1, rev 3.500), centra lever; P195/75R x 14 or P205/75R x 14 tyres; automati levelling control; heavy-duty suspension; heavy-duty coolin system; power steering; tilt of steering wheel; servo brake heavy-duty battery; heavy-duty alternator; heated rea window; electric windows; automatic speed control; elec tric sunshine roof; air-conditioning; 4-4-2 equipment; Re minder equipment.

OLDSMOBILE Cutlass Salon Brougham Coupé

OLDSMOBILE Cutlass Calais Coupé

105 hp power team

ee 115 hp power team, except for:

NGINE 8 cylinders; 260 cu in, 4,261 cc (3.50 x 3.38 in, 8.8 x 85.8 mm); compression ratio: 7.5:1; max power (DIN): 5 hp (77.3 kW) at 3,600 rpm; max torque (DIN): 205 lb , 28.3 kg m (277.5 Nm) at 1,800 rpm; 24.6 hp/l (18.1 W/l); 5 crankshaft bearings; 1 Rochester 2MC down- aught twin barrel carburettor; cooling system: 26.9 imp , 32.3 US pt, 15.3 l.

RANSMISSION gearbox: Turbo-Hydramatic automatic trans- ission (standard), hydraulic torque converter and plane- ry gears with 3 ratios, max torque of converter at stall 10, possible manual selection; ratios: I 2.470, II 1.567, 1, rev 2.006; lever: steering column or central; axle tio: 2.290.

ERFORMANCE max speed: about 96 mph, 155 km/h; power- eight ratio: Salon Sedan 30.6 lb/hp (41.5 lb/kW), 13.9 /hp (18.8 kg/kW) - Salon Brougham Sedan 30.9 lb/hp (42 /kW), 14 kg/hp (19.1 kg/kW); consumption: 22.8 m/imp l, 19 m/US gal, 12.4 l x 100 km.

TEERING servo (standard); turns lock to lock: 3.60.

RAKES servo (standard).

LECTRICAL EQUIPMENT 61 A alternator.

IMENSIONS AND WEIGHT weight: plus 131 lb, 59 kg - . wagons 177 lb, 80 kg.

PTIONALS 2.930 axle ratio; 5-speed fully synchronized me- hanical gearbox (I 3.400, II 2.080, III 1.390, IV 1, V 0.800, v 3.060), central lever, 2.560 axle ratio.

160 hp power team

ee 115 hp power team, except for:

NGINE 8 cylinders; 305 cu in, 4,999 cc (3.74 x 3.48 in, 4.9 x 88.4 mm); compression ratio: 8.5:1; max power (DIN): 50 hp (117.8 kW) at 4,000 rpm; max torque (DIN): 235 lb ft, 2.4 kg m (317.7 Nm) at 2,400 rpm; max engine rpm: 4,000; 2 hp/l (23.6 kW/l); 5 crankshaft bearings; 1 Rochester owndraught 4-barrel carburettor; cooling system: 26 imp t, 31.3 US pt, 14.8 l.

RANSMISSION gearbox: mechanical (Turbo-Hydramatic au- matic transmission standard for st. wagons only); gears: , fully synchronized; ratios: I 3.500, II 2.480, III 1.660, IV 1, v 3.500; lever: central; axle ratio: 3.080 - st. wagons 2.410.

ERFORMANCE max speed: about 103 mph, 165 km/h; power- eight ratio: Salon Sedan 20 lb/hp (27.2 lb/kW), 9.1 kg/hp 2.3 kg/kW) - Salon Brougham Sedan 20.3 lb/hp (27.5 /kW), 9.2 kg/hp (12.5 kg/kW); speed in direct drive at ,000 rpm: 25.6 mph, 41.2 km/h; consumption: 18 m/imp al, 15 m/US gal, 15.7 l x 100 km.

TEERING servo (standard); turns lock to lock: 3.60.

RAKES servo (standard).

LECTRICAL EQUIPMENT 3,200 W battery; 63 A alternator.

DIMENSIONS AND WEIGHT weight: plus 128 lb, 58 kg - st. wagons plus 193 lb, 88 kg.

OPTIONALS Turbo-Hydramatic automatic transmission with 3 ratios (I 2.520, II 1.520, III 1, rev 1.930), max ratio of converter at stall 2, possible manual selection, steering column or central lever, 2.290 or 2.730 axle ratio.

160 hp (5.7 litre) power team

(not available in California).

See 115 hp power team, except for:

ENGINE 8 cylinders; 350 cu in, 5,736 cc (4.06 x 3.38 in, 103 x 85.8 mm); compression ratio: 8.5:1; max power (DIN): 160 hp (117.8 kW) at 3,600 rpm; max torque (DIN): 260 lb ft, 35.9 kg m (352.1 Nm) at 2,400 rpm; 27.9 hp/l (20.5 kW/l); 5 crankshaft bearings; 1 Rochester downdraught 4- barrel carburettor; cooling system: 29.9 imp pt, 35.9 US pt, 17 l.

TRANSMISSION gearbox: Turbo-Hydramatic automatic trans- mission (standard), hydraulic torque converter and plane- tary gears with 3 ratios, max ratio of converter at stall 2, possible manual selection; ratios: I 2.520, II 1.520, III 1, rev 1.930; lever: steering column or central; axle ratio: 2.730.

PERFORMANCE max speed: about 106 mph, 170 km/h; power-weight ratio: Cruiser St. Wagon 21.5 lb/hp (29.2 lb/kW), 9.7 kg/hp (13.2 kg/kW); speed in direct drive at 1,000 rpm: 29.3 mph, 47.2 km/h; consumption: 20.5 m/imp gal, 17 m/US gal, 13.8 l x 100 km.

STEERING servo (standard); turns lock to lock: 3.60.

BRAKES servo (standard).

ELECTRICAL EQUIPMENT 3,200 W battery; 63 A alternator.

DIMENSIONS AND WEIGHT weight: plus 240 lb, 109 kg.

BODY estate car/st. wagon; 4 + 1 doors; 6 seats, separate front seats; folding rear seat.

OPTIONALS 4-speed fully synchronized mechanical gearbox not available.

90 hp (Diesel) power team

See 115 hp power team, except for:

ENGINE Diesel; 8 cylinders; 260 cu in, 4,261 cc (3.50 x 3.38 in, 88.8 x 85.8 mm); compression ratio: 22.5:1; max power (DIN): 90 hp (66.2 kW) at 3,600 rpm; max torque (DIN): 160 lb ft, 22.1 kg m (216.7 Nm) at 1,600 rpm; 21.1 hp/l (15.5 kW/l); 5 crankshaft bearings; lubricating system: 15 imp pt, 18 US pt, 8.5 l; Diesel injection pump; cooling system: 26.9 imp pt, 32.3 US pt, 15.3 l.

TRANSMISSION gearbox: mechanical; gears: 5, fully syn- chronized; ratios: I 3.400, II 2.080, III 1.390, IV 0.800, V 3.060; lever: central; axle ratio: 3.060.

PERFORMANCE max speed: about 87 mph, 140 km/h; power-weight ratio: Salon Sedan 35.6 lb/hp (48.5 lb/kW), 16.2

kg/hp (22 kg/kW) - Salon Brougham Sedan 36.1 lb/hp (49 lb/kW), 16.4 kg/hp (22.3 kg/kW); speed in direct drive at 1,000 rpm: 24.2 mph, 38.9 km/h; consumption: 30.1 m/imp gal, 25 m/US gal, 9.4 l x 100 km.

STEERING servo (standard); turns lock to lock: 3.60.

BRAKES servo (standard).

ELECTRICAL EQUIPMENT 61 A alternator.

DIMENSIONS AND WEIGHT weight: plus 131 lb, 59 kg - Cruiser Brougham St. Wagon plus 177 lb, 80 kg.

OPTIONALS Turbo-Hydramatic automatic transmission with 2.410 axle ratio.

125 hp (Diesel) power team

See 115 hp power team, except for:

ENGINE Diesel; 8 cylinders; 350 cu in, 5,736 cc (4.06 x 3.38 in, 103 x 85.8 mm); compression ratio: 22.5:1; max power (DIN): 125 hp (92 kW) at 3,600 rpm; max torque (DIN): 225 lb ft, 31 kg m (304 Nm) at 1,600 rpm; 21.8 hp/l (16 kW/l); 5 crankshaft bearings; lubricating system: 15 imp pt, 18 US pt, 8.5 l; Diesel injection pump; cooling system: 29.9 imp pt, 35.9 US pt, 17 l.

TRANSMISSION gearbox: Turbo-Hydramatic automatic trans- mission (standard), hydraulic torque converter and plane- tary gears with 3 ratios, max ratio of converter at stall 2, possible manual selection; ratios: I 2.520, II 1.520, III 1, rev 1.930; lever: steering column or central; axle ratio: 2.290.

PERFORMANCE max speed: about 99 mph, 160 km/h; power-weight ratio: Cruiser St. Wagon 27.5 lb/hp (37.4 lb/kW), 12.5 kg/hp (16.9 kg/kW); speed in direct drive at 1,000 rpm: 27.6 mph, 44.4 km/h; consumption: 26.4 m/imp gal, 22 m/US gal, 10.7 l x 100 km.

STEERING servo (standard); turns lock to lock: 3.60.

BRAKES servo (standard).

ELECTRICAL EQUIPMENT 3,200 W battery; 63 A alternator.

DIMENSIONS AND WEIGHT weight: Cruiser St. Wagon 3,439 lb, 1,559 kg.

BODY estate car/st. wagon; 4 + 1 doors; 6 seats, separate front seats; folding rear seat.

OPTIONALS 4-speed fully synchronized mechanical gearbox not available.

Delta 88 - Delta 88 Royale - Ninety-Eight - Custom Cruiser Series

PRICES EX WORKS:

1 Delta 88 Hardtop Coupé	$ 5,782
2 Delta 88 Sedan	$ 5,882
3 Delta 88 Royale Hardtop Coupé	$ 6,029
4 Delta 88 Royale Sedan	$ 6,154
5 Ninety-Eight Luxury Coupé	$ 7,492
6 Ninety-Eight Luxury Sedan	$ 7,673
7 Ninety-Eight Regency Coupé	$ 7,875
8 Ninety-Eight Regency Sedan	$ 8,063
9 Custom Cruiser St. Wagon	$ 6,742

For 105 hp engine add $ 140. For 135 hp engine add $ 195; for 160 hp engine add $ 320; for 175 hp engine add $ 80. For 125 hp Diesel engine add $ 895 (Ninety-Eights and Custom Cruiser add $ 785).

Power team:	Standard for:	Optional for:
115 hp	1 to 4	—
105 hp	—	1 to 4
135 hp	—	1 to 4
160 hp	5 to 9	1 to 4
175 hp	—	5 to 9
125 hp (Diesel)	—	all

115 hp power team

ENGINE front, 4 stroke; 6 cylinders, Vee-slanted at 90°; 231 cu in, 3,785 cc (3.80 x 3.40 in, 96.5 x 86.4 mm); com- pression ratio: 8:1; max power (DIN): 115 hp (84.6 kW) at 3,600 rpm; max torque (DIN): 190 lb ft, 26.2 kg m (257 Nm) at 2,000 rpm; max engine rpm: 4,200; 30.4 hp/l (22.4 kW/l); cast iron block and head; 4 crankshaft bearings; valves: overhead, in line, push-rods and rockers, hydraulic tappets; camshafts: 1, at centre of Vee; lubrication: gear pump, full flow filter, 8.3 imp pt, 9.9 US pt, 4.7 l; 1 Rochester 2 downdraught twin barrel carburettor; cleaner air system; exhaust system with catalytic converter; fuel

OLDSMOBILE Ninety-Eight Regency Sedan

115 HP POWER TEAM

feed: mechanical pump; water-cooled, 22.2 imp pt, 26.6 US pt, 12.6 l.

TRANSMISSION driving wheels: rear; gearbox: Turbo-Hydramatic automatic transmission, hydraulic torque converter and planetary gears with 3 ratios, max ratio of converter at stall 2.25, possible manual selection; ratios: I 2.520, II 1.520, III 1, rev 1.930; lever: steering column; final drive: hypoid bevel; axle ratio: 2.730; width of rims: 6''; tyres: FR78 x 15.

PERFORMANCE max speed: about 96 mph, 154 km/h; power-weight ratio: Sedan 30.4 lb/hp (41.3 lb/kW), 13.8 kg/hp (18.7 kg/kW) - Royale 30.6 lb/hp (41.5 lb/kW), 13.9 kg/hp (18.8 kg/kW); speed in direct drive at 1,000 rpm: 27.4 mph, 44.1 km/h; consumption: 21.6 m/imp gal, 18 m/US gal, 13.1 l x 100 km.

CHASSIS channel section perimeter type frame; front suspension: independent, wishbones, coil springs, anti-roll bar, telescopic dampers; rear: rigid axle, lower trailing radius arms, upper oblique torque arms, coil springs, telescopic dampers.

STEERING recirculating ball, variable ratio servo; turns lock to lock: 3.50.

BRAKES front disc (diameter 11 in, 27.9 cm), front internal radial fins, rear drum, rear compensator, servo; swept area: total 384.2 sq in, 2,478 sq cm.

ELECTRICAL EQUIPMENT 12 V; 2,500 W battery; 42 alternator; Delco-Remy transistorized ignition; 4 headlamps.

DIMENSIONS AND WEIGHT wheel base: 116 in, 295 cm; tracks: 61.70 in, 157 cm front, 60.70 in, 154 cm rear; length: 217.50 in, 552 cm; width: 76.80 in, 195 cm; height: coupés 54.50 in, 138 cm - sedans 55.20 in, 140 cm; ground clearance: 5.93 in, 15 cm; weight: Hardtop Coupé 3,464 lb, 1,571 kg - Sedan 3,491 lb, 1,583 kg - Royale Hardtop Coupé 3,473 lb, 1,575 kg - Sedan 3,515 lb, 1,594 kg; turning circle: 42.6 ft, 13 m; fuel tank: 20.9 imp gal, 25 US gal, 95 l.

OPTIONALS limited slip differential; automatic levelling control; heavy-duty suspension; heavy-duty cooling system; heavy-duty battery; Reminder equipment 3.230 axle ratio; GR78 x 15 or HR78 x 15 tyres; tilt of steering wheel; electric windows; heated rear window; vinyl roof; air-conditioning.

105 hp power team

See 115 hp power team, except for:

ENGINE 8 cylinders; 260 cu in, 4,261 cc (3.50 x 3.38 in, 88.8 x 85.8 mm); compression ratio: 7.5:1; max power (DIN): 105 hp (77.3 kW) at 3,600 rpm; max torque (DIN): 205 lb ft, 28.3 kg m (277.5 Nm) at 1,800 rpm; 24.6 hp/l (18.1 kW/l); 5 crankshaft bearings; cooling system: 26.9 imp pt, 32.3 US pt, 15.3 l.

TRANSMISSION axle ratio: 2.560.

PERFORMANCE max speed: about 93 mph, 150 km/h; power-weight ratio: Sedan 34.8 lb/hp (47.2 lb/kW), 15.8 kg/hp

OLDSMOBILE Delta 88 Royale Sedan

(21.4 kg/kW) - Royale Sedan 35 lb/hp (47.6 lb/kW), 15.9 kg/hp (21.6 kg/kW); consumption: 20.5 m/imp gal, 17 m/US gal, 13.8 l x 100 km.

ELECTRICAL EQUIPMENT 3,200 W battery; 61 A alternator.

DIMENSIONS AND WEIGHT weight: plus 161 lb, 73 kg.

135 hp power team

See 115 hp power team, except for:

ENGINE 8 cylinders; 301 cu in, 4,932 cc (4 x 3 in, 101.6 x 76.2 mm); compression ratio: 8.2:1; max power (DIN): 135 hp (99.4 kW) at 3,800 rpm; max torque (DIN): 240 lb ft, 33.1 kg m (324.6 Nm) at 1,600 rpm; 27.4 hp/l (20.2 kW/l); 5 crankshaft bearings; lubricating system: 10 imp pt, 12 US pt, 5.7 l; 1 Rochester M2MC downdraught twin barrel carburettor; cooling system: 34.8 imp pt, 41.9 US pt, 19.8 l.

TRANSMISSION axle ratio: 2.290.

PERFORMANCE max speed: about 99 mph, 160 km/h; power-weight ratio: Sedan 25.9 lb/hp (35.1 lb/kW), 11.7 kg/hp (15.9 kg/kW) - Royale Sedan 26 lb/hp (35.4 lb/kW), 11.8 kg/hp (16 kg/kW); consumption: 20.5 m/imp gal, 17 m/US gal, 13.8 l x 100 km.

ELECTRICAL EQUIPMENT 3,200 W battery; 61 A alternator.

OPTIONALS 2.410 axle ratio.

160 hp power team

See 115 hp power team, except for:

ENGINE 8 cylinders; 350 cu in, 5,736 cc (4.06 x 3.38 in, 103 x 85.8 mm); max power (DIN): 160 hp (117.8 kW) at 3,6 rpm; max torque (DIN): 270 lb ft, 37.2 kg m (364.8 N at 2,000 rpm; 27.9 hp/l (20.5 kW/l); 5 crankshaft bearing 1 Rochester downdraught 4-barrel carburettor; cooli system: 24.3 imp pt, 29.2 US pt, 13.8 l.

TRANSMISSION axle ratio: 2.410; width of rims: Custo Cruiser 7''; tyres: Ninety-Eights GR78 x 15 - Custom Cruis HR78 x 15.

PERFORMANCE max speed: about 103 mph, 165 km/h; pow weight ratio: Luxury Sedan 24.1 lb/hp (32.7 lb/kW), 10 kg/hp (14.8 kg/kW) - Regency Sedan 24.3 lb/hp (33 lb/kW 11 kg/hp (15 kg/kW) - Custom Cruiser 25.1 lb/hp (3 lb/kW), 11.4 kg/hp (15.5 kg/kW); speed in direct drive 1,000 rpm: 28.5 mph, 45.8 km/h; consumption: 18 m/im gal, 15 m/US gal, 15.7 l x 100 km.

BRAKES (Ninety-Eights and Custom Cruiser) front disc (d meter 11.88 in, 30.2 cm); swept area: total 396.58 in, 2,5 sq cm.

ELECTRICAL EQUIPMENT 3,200 W battery; 63 A alternat

DIMENSIONS AND WEIGHT wheel base: Ninety-Eights 1 in, 302 cm; tracks: Custom Cruiser 62.10 in, 158 cm fro 64.10 in, 163 cm rear; length: Ninety-Eights 220.40 in, 5 cm - Custom Cruiser 217.10 in, 551 cm; width: Custo Cruiser 79.80 in, 203 cm; height: Ninety-Eights 55.50 in 141 cm - Custom Cruiser 57.20 in, 145 cm; ground clearanc Ninety-Eights 5.97 in, 15.2 cm - Custom Cruiser 5.80 in 14.7 cm; weight: Luxury Coupé 3,808 lb, 1,727 kg - Luxu Sedan 3,852 lb, 1,747 kg - Regency Coupé 3,812 lb, 1,7 kg - Regency Sedan 3,887 lb, 1,763 kg - Custom Cruis 4,020 lb, 1,823 kg; turning circle: Ninety-Eights: 43.3 13.2 m; fuel tank: Custom Cruiser 18.3 imp gal, 22 US g 83 l.

OPTIONALS 2.730 axle ratio (Custom Cruiser 2.730 or 3.0 axle ratio).

175 hp power team

See 160 hp power team, except for:

ENGINE 403 cu in, 6,604 cc (4.35 x 3.38 in, 110.4 x 85.8 compression ratio: 7.8:1; max power (DIN): 175 hp (128 kW) at 3,800 rpm; max torque (DIN): 310 lb ft, 42.8 kg (419.7 Nm) at 2,000 rpm; 26.5 hp/l (19.5 kW/l); cooli system: 26.2 imp pt, 31.4 US pt, 14.9 l.

PERFORMANCE max speed: about 109 mph, 175 km/h; pow weigrt ratio: Luxury Sedan 23.4 lb/hp (31.8 lb/kW), 10 kg/hp (14.4 kg/kW) - Regency Sedan 23.6 lb/hp (32.1 lb/kW 10.7 kg/hp (14.6 kg/kW) - Custom Cruiser 24.4 lb/hp (33 lb/kW), 11.1 kg/hp (15 kg/kW); consumption: 16.8 m/imp ga 14 m/US gal, 16.8 l x 100 km.

ELECTRICAL EQUIPMENT 3,500 W battery.

DIMENSIONS AND WEIGHT weight: plus 250 lb, 114 k

OPTIONALS 3.080 or 3.230 axle ratio.

125 hp (Diesel) power team

See 115 hp power team, except for:

ENGINE Diesel; 8 cylinders; 350 cu in, 5,736 cc (4.06 3.38 in, 103 x 85.8 mm); compression ratio: 2.5:1; ma power (DIN): 125 hp (92 kW) at 3,600 rpm; max torqu (DIN): 225 lb ft, 31 kg m (304 Nm) at 1,600 rpm; 21 hp/l (16 kW/l); 5 crankshaft bearings; lubricating system 15 imp pt, 18 US pt, 8.5 l; Diesel injection pump; cooli system: 29.9 imp pt, 35.9 US pt, 17 l.

TRANSMISSION axle ratio: 2.410 - Custom Cruiser 2,73 width of rims: Custom Cruiser 7''; tyres: Ninety-Eight GR78 x 15 - Custom Cruiser HR78 x 15.

PERFORMANCE max speed: about 96 mph, 155 km/h; powe weight ratio: 88 Sedan 30.8 lb/hp (41.9 lb/kW), 14 kg/h (19 kg/kW) - Royale Sedan 31 lb/hp (42.1 lb/kW), 14 kg/h (19.1 kg/kW) - Luxury Sedan 32 lb/hp (43.5 lb/kW), 14. kg/hp (19.7 kg/kW) - Regency Sedan 32.3 lb/hp (43.8 lb/kW 14.6 kg/hp (19.9 kg/kW); speed in direct drive at 1,00 rpm: 28.5 mph, 45.8 km/h; consumption: 25.2 m/imp ga 21 m/US gal, 11.2 l x 100 km.

BRAKES (Ninety-Eights and Custom Cruiser) front dis (diameter 11.88 in, 30.2 cm); swept area: total 396.58 sq in 2,559 sq cm.

ELECTRICAL EQUIPMENT 3,200 W battery; 63 A alternato

DIMENSIONS AND WEIGHT (see 160 hp power team) weigh 88 Hardtop Coupé 3,826 lb, 1,735 kg - 88 Sedan 3,854 l

,748 kg - Royale Hardtop Coupé 3,830 lb, 1,737 kg - Royale
edan 3,872 lb, 1,756 kg - Luxury Coupé 3,954 lb, 1,793 kg -
Luxury Sedan 3,998 lb, 1,813 kg - Regency Coupé 3,958
°, 1,795 kg - Regency Sedan 4,033 lb, 1,829 kg - Custom
ruiser St. Wagon 4,203 lb, 1,906 kg; fuel tank: 22.4 imp
al, 27 US gal, 102 l - Custom Cruiser 18.3 imp gal, 22
S gal, 83 l.

Toronado Brougham Coupé

RICE EX WORKS: $ 10,371

165 hp power team

standard).

NGINE front, 4 stroke; 8 cylinders; 350 cu in, 5,736 cc
.06 x 3.38 in, 103 x 85.8 mm); compression ratio: 8:1;
ax power (DIN): 165 hp (121.4 kW) at 3,600 rpm; max
rque (DIN): 275 lb ft, 37.9 kg m (371.7 Nm) at 2,000 rpm;
ax engine rpm: 4,200; 28.8 hp/l (21.2 kW/l); cast iron
ock and head; 5 crankshaft bearings; valves: overhead, in
ne, push-rods and rockers, hydraulic tappets; camshafts:
 at centre of Vee; lubrication: gear pump, full flow
lter, 8.3 imp pt, 9.9 US pt, 4.7 l; 1 Rochester M4MC
owndraught 4-barrel carburettor; cleaner air system;
xhaust system with catalytic converter; fuel feed: mecha-
cal pump; water-cooled, 24.8 imp pt, 29.8 US pt, 14.1 l.

OLDSMOBILE Toronado Diesel Brougham Coupé

PLYMOUTH Horizon TC 3 2-dr Hatchback

RANSMISSION driving wheels: front; gearbox: Turbo-Hyramatic automatic transmission, hydraulic torque converter
nd planetary gears (chain torque engine-mounted conver-
r), with 3 ratios, max ratio of converter at stall 2, possi-
le manual selection; ratios: I 2.740, II 1.570, III 1, rev
.070; lever: steering column; final drive: spiral bevel;
xle ratio: 2.410; width of rims: 6''; tyres: P205/75R x 15.

ERFORMANCE max speed: about 112 mph, 180 km/h; power-
eight ratio: 22.7 lb/hp (30.9 lb/kW), 10.3 kg/hp (14
g/kW); speed in direct drive at 1,000 rpm: 31.1 mph, 50
m/h; consumption: 19.2 m/imp gal, 16 m/US gal, 14.7
 x 100 km.

HASSIS channel section perimeter type frame; front sus-
ension: independent, wishbones, longitudinal torsion bars,
nti-roll bar, telescopic dampers; rear: independent, swing-
ng longitudinal trailing arms, coil springs, automatic level-
ng control, telescopic dampers.

TEERING recirculating ball, servo; turns lock to lock: 3.

RAKES front disc (diameter 10.50 in, 26.7 cm), front
internal radial fins, rear drum, rear compensator, servo;
wept area: total 307.8 sq in, 1,985 sq cm.

LECTRICAL EQUIPMENT 12 V; 80 Ah battery; 63 A alter-
ator; Delco-Remy transistorized ignition; 4 headlamps.

IMENSIONS AND WEIGHT wheel base: 114 in, 289 cm;
racks: 59.30 in, 151 cm front, 60 in, 152 cm rear; length:
05.60 in, 522 cm; width: 80 in, 203 cm; height: 54.20 in,
38 cm; ground clearance: 5.11 in, 13 cm; weight: 3,749 lb,
700 kg; turning circle: 44.2 ft, 13.5 m; fuel tank: 16.7
mp gal, 20 US gal, 76 l.

BODY coupé; 2 doors; 4 seats, separate front seats with
built-in headrests; electric tinted windows; air-conditioning.

OPTIONALS 2.190 axle ratio; heavy-duty cooling system;
heavy-duty battery; heavy-duty alternator; tilt of steering
wheel; speed control device; heated rear window; electric
sunshine roof; heavy-duty suspension; Reminder equipment;
reclining backrests.

125 hp (Diesel) power team

(optional).

See 165 hp power team, excpet for:

ENGINE Diesel; compression ratio: 22.5:1; max power (DIN):
125 hp (92 kW) at 3,600 rpm; max torque (DIN): 225 lb
ft, 31 kg m (304 Nm) at 1,600 rpm; 21.8 hp/l (16 kW/l);
lubricating system: 15 imp pt, 18 US pt, 8.5 l; Diesel
injection pump; cooling system: 30.6 imp pt, 36.8 US pt,
17.4 l.

PERFORMANCE max speed: about 96 mph, 155 km/h; power-
weight ratio: 31.2 lb/hp (42.5 lb/kW), 14.2 kg/hp (19.2
kg/kW); speed in direct drive at 1,000 rpm: 28.5 mph,
45.8 km/h; consumption: 25.2 m/imp gal, 21 m/US gal,
11.2 l x 100 km.

ELECTRICAL EQUIPMENT 125 Ah battery.

DIMENSIONS AND WEIGHT weight: plus 157 lb, 71 kg; fuel
tank: 18.9 imp gal, 22.8 US gal, 86 l.

PLYMOUTH   USA

Horizon Series

PRICES EX WORKS:

TC3 2-dr Hatchback	$ 4,482
4-dr Hatchback	$ 4,122

Power team:	Standard for:	Optional for:
70 hp	both	—
65 hp	both	—

70 hp power team

(not available in California).

ENGINE front, transverse, slanted 15° to front, 4 stroke;
4 cylinders, in line; 104.7 cu in, 1,714 cc (3.13 x 3.40 in,
79.5 x 86.4 mm); compression ratio: 8.2:1; max power (DIN):
70 hp (51.5 kW) at 5,200 rpm; max torque (DIN): 85 lb ft,
11.7 kg m (114.7 Nm) at 2,800 rpm; max engine rpm: 6,500;
40.8 hp/l (30 kW/l); cast iron block, light alloy head; 5
crankshaft bearings; valves: overhead, in line, thimble
tappets; camshafts: 1, overhead, cogged belt; lubrication:
gear pump, full flow filter, 6.7 imp pt, 8 US pt, 3.8 l; 1
Holley R8525A downdraught twin barrel carburettor; cleaner
air system; exhaust system with catalytic converter; fuel
feed: mechanical pump; water-cooled, 10 imp pt, 12 US
pt, 5.7 l.

TRANSMISSION driving wheels: front; clutch: single dry
plate (diaphragm); gearbox: mechanical; gears: 4, fully synchronized; ratios I 3.450, II 1.940, III 1.290, IV 0.970, rev
3.170; lever: central; final drive: spiral bevel; axle ratio:
3.370; width of rims: 4.5''; tyres: 2-dr P165/75R x 13 - 4-dr
P155/80R x 13.

PERFORMANCE max speed: about 91 mph, 146 km/h; power-
weight ratio: 2-dr 31.4 lb/hp (42.6 lb/kW), 14.2 kg/hp (19.3
kg/kW) - 4-dr 30.5 lb/hp (41.5 lb/kW), 13.9 kg/hp (18.9
kg/kW); speed in top at 1,000 rpm: 16.7 mph, 26.9 km/h;
consumption: 30.1 m/imp gal, 25 m/US gal, 9.4 l x 100 km.

CHASSIS integral; front suspension: independent, by Mc-
Pherson, lower wishbones, anti-roll bar, coil springs/tele-
scopic dampers struts; rear: independent, semi-trailing arms,
coil springs, telescopic dampers.

STEERING rack-and-pinion; turns lock to lock: 4.

BRAKES front disc (diameter 8.98 in, 22.8 cm), front internal
radial fins, rear drum; swept area: total 197.5 sq in, 1,274
sq cm.

ELECTRICAL EQUIPMENT 12 V; 325 A battery; 65 A alternator; Essex or Prestolite transistorized ignition with electronic spark control; 2 headlamps.

DIMENSIONS AND WEIGHT wheel base: 2-dr 96.70 in,
246 cm - 4-dr 99.20 in, 252 cm; tracks: 56 in, 142 cm front,
55.60 in, 141 cm; length: 2-dr 172.70 in, 439 cm - 4-dr
164.80 in, 419 cm; width: 2-dr 66 in, 168 cm - 4-dr 66.20
in, 168 cm; height: 2-dr 51.40 in, 131 cm - 4-dr 53.70 in,
136 cm; ground clearance: 2-dr 5.10 in, 13 cm - 4-dr 5
in, 12.7 cm; weight: 2-dr 2,196 lb, 996 kg - 4-dr 2,136 lb,

70 HP POWER TEAM

971 kg; turning circle: 2-dr 36.1 ft, 11 m - 4-dr 36.2 ft, 11.04 m; fuel tank: 10.8 imp pt, 13 US pt, 49 l.

BODY hatchback; 4 seats, separate front seats with built-in headrests; heated rear window.

OPTIONALS Torqueflite automatic transmission, hydraulic torque converter and planetary gears with 3 ratios (I 2.470, II 1.470, III 1, rev 2.100), max ratio of converter at stall 1.97, possible manual selection, central lever, 3.480 axle ratio; P165/75R x 13 tyres; P175/75R x 13 tyres with 5'' wide rims; P185/70R x 13 tyres with 5'' wide rims (2-dr only); power steering; servo brake; reclining backrests; heavy-duty suspension; rear window wiper-washer; vinyl roof; sunshine roof; air-conditioning; Custom or Premium equipment for 4-dr; Premium or Sport equipment for 2-dr.

65 hp power team

(for California only).

See 70 hp power team, except for:

ENGINE max power (DIN): 65 hp (47.8 kW) at 5,200 rpm; 37.9 hp/l (27.9 kW/l); 1 Holley R8527A downdraught twin barrel carburettor.

TRANSMISSION axle ratio: 3.580.

PERFORMANCE power-weight ratio: 2-dr 33.8 lb/hp (45.9 lb/kW), 15.3 kg/hp (20.8 kg/kW) - 4-dr 32.9 lb/hp (44.7 lb/kW), 14.9 kg/hp (20.3 kg/kW); consumption: 28.8 m/imp gal, 24 m/US gal, 9.8 l x 100 km.

OPTIONALS Torqueflite automatic transmission with 3.740 axle ratio.

Volaré Series

PRICES EX WORKS:

1 2-dr Coupé		$ 3,956
2 4-dr Sedan		$ 4,057
3 St. Wagon		$ 4,433

Power team:	Standard for:	Optional for:
100 hp	all	—
90 hp	all	—
110 hp	—	all
135 hp	—	all
155 hp	—	all
170 hp	—	1
195 hp	—	1

100 hp power team

(not available in California).

ENGINE front, 4 stroke; 6 cylinders, vertical, in line; 225 cu in, 3,687 cc (3.40 x 4.12 in, 86.4 x 104.6 mm); compression ratio: 8.4:1; max power (DIN): 10 hp (73.6 kW) at 3,600 rpm; max torque (DIN): 165 lb ft, 22.8 kg m (223.6 Nm) at 1,600 rpm; max engine rpm: 4,400; 27.1 hp/l (20 kW/l); cast iron block and head; 4 crankshaft bearings; valves: overhead, in line, push-rods and rockers; camshafts: 1, side; lubrication: rotary pump, full flow filter, 8.3 imp pt, 9.9 US pt, 4.7 l; 1 Holley R8523A downdraught single barrel carburettor; cleaner air system; exhaust system with catalytic converter; fuel feed: mechanical pump; water-cooled, 19.2 imp pt, 23 US pt, 10.9 l.

TRANSMISSION driving wheels: rear; clutch: single dry plate; gearbox: mechanical; gears: 3, fully synchronized; ratios: I 3.080, II 1.700, III 1, rev 2.900; lever: central; final drive: hypoid bevel; axle ratio: 3.230 - St. Wagon 3.210; width of rims: 5'' - St. Wagon 5.5''; tyres: D78 x 14 - St. Wagon ER78 x 14.

PERFORMANCE max speed: about 90 mph, 145 km/h; power-weight ratio: Sedan 31.1 lb/hp (42.3 lb/kW), 14.1 kg/hp (19.2 kg/kW); speed in direct drive at 1,000 rpm: 20.4 mph, 32.9 km/h; consumption: 21.6 m/imp gal, 18 m/US gal, 13.1 l x 100 km.

CHASSIS integral with front cross members; front suspension: independent, wishbones, transverse torsion bars, anti-roll bar, telescopic dampers; rear: rigid axle, semi-elliptic leafsprings, anti-roll bar, telescopic dampers.

STEERING recirculating ball; turns lock to lock: 5.30.

BRAKES front disc (diameter 10.82 in, 27.5 cm), front internal radial fins, rear drum, rear compensator; swept area: total 355.24 sq in, 2,292 sq cm.

ELECTRICAL EQUIPMENT 12 V; 325 A battery; 41 A alternator; Essex or Prestolite transistorized ignition with electronic spark control; 4 headlamps.

DIMENSIONS AND WEIGHT wheel base: 112.70 in, 286 cm Coupé 108.70 in, 276 cm; tracks: 60 in, 152 cm front, 58.50 in, 149 cm rear; length: 201.20 in, 511 cm - Coupé 197.20 in, 501 cm; width: 72.80 in, 185 cm; height: Coupé 53.30 in, 135 cm - Sedan 55.30 in, 140 cm - St. Wagon 55.70 in, 141 cm; ground clearance: 5.90 in, 15 cm - St. Wagon 6.20 in, 15.7 cm; weight: Coupé 3,050 lb, 1,383 kg - Sedan 3,114 lb, 1,413 kg - St. Wagon 3,323 lb, 1,507 kg; turning circle: 43.5 ft, 13.2 m - Coupé 42.1 ft, 12.8 m; fuel tank: 15 imp gal, 18 US gal, 68 l - St. Wagon 16.3 imp gal, 19.5 US gal, 74 l.

OPTIONALS limited slip differential; 3.210 axle ratio; Torqueflite automatic transmission with 3 ratios (I 2.450, II 1.450, III 1, rev 2.220), max ratio of converter at stall 2.01, possible manual selection, steering column or central lever, 2.760 or 2.710 axle ratio; 4-speed fully synchronized mechanical gearbox with overdrive/top (I 3.090, II 1.670, III 1, IV 0.710, rev 3), central lever, 3.230 or 3.210 axle ratio; DR78 x 14, ER78 x 14 or FR78 x 14 tyres with 5.5'' wide rims; FR70 x 14 tyres with 6'' wide rims; power steering; tilt of steering wheel; servo brake; heavy-duty battery; heavy-duty suspension; heavy-duty cooling system; tinted glass; electric windows; heated rear window; vinyl roof; automatic speed control air-conditioning; Premier equipment; Road Runner equipment (Coupé only); « Duster » equipment (Coupé only); Sport equipment (St. Wagon only).

90 hp power team

(for California only).

See 100 hp power team, except for:

ENGINE max power (DIN): 90 hp (66.2 kW) at 3,600 rpm; max torque (DIN): 160 lb ft, 22.1 kg m (216.7 Nm) at 1,600 rpm; 24.4 hp/l (18 kW/l); 1 Holley R8680A downdraught single barrel carburettor.

TRANSMISSION gearbox: Torqueflite automatic transmission (standard), hydraulic torque converter and planetary gears with 3 ratios, max ratio of converter at stall 2.01, possible manual selection; ratios: I 2.450, II 1.450, III 1, rev 2.200; lever: steering column or central; axle ratio: 3.230 - St. Wagon 3.210.

PERFORMANCE power-weight ratio: Sedan 34.6 lb/hp (47.5 lb/kW), 15.7 kg/hp (21.3 kg/kW); consumption: 18 m/imp gal, 15 m/US gal, 15.7 l x 100 km.

OPTIONALS 3.210 axle ratio; 4-speed fully synchronized mechanical gearbox with overdrive/top not available.

110 hp power team

(not available in California).

See 100 hp power team, except for:

ENGINE max power (DIN): 110 hp (81 kW) at 3,600 rpm; max torque (DIN): 180 lb ft, 24.8 kg m (243.2 Nm) at 2,000 rpm; 29.8 hp/l (22 kW/l); 1 Carter BBD8198S downdraught twin barrel carburettor.

TRANSMISSION gearbox: Torqueflite automatic transmission (standard), hydraulic torque converter and planetary gears

with 3 ratios, max ratio of converter at stall 2.01, possible manual selection; ratios: I 2.450, II 1.450, III 1, rev 2.22 lever: steering column or central; axle ratio: 2.760 - Wagon 2.940.

PERFORMANCE max speed: about 93 mph, 150 km/h; power weight ratio: Sedan 28.4 lb/hp (38.6 lb/kW), 12.9 kg/k (17.5 kg/kW); speed in direct drive at 1,000 rpm: 25.9 mp 41.7 km/h; consumption: 18 m/imp gal, 15 m/US gal, 15 l x 100 km.

DIMENSIONS AND WEIGHT weight: Coupé 3,059 lb, 1,3 kg - Sedan 3,123 lb, 1,417 kg - St. Wagon 3,355 lb, 1,522 k

OPTIONALS 4-speed fully synchronized mechanical gearb with overdrive/top not available.

135 hp power team

(not available in California).

See 100 hp power team, except for:

ENGINE 8 cylinders; 318 cu in, 5,211 cc (3.91 x 3.31 in, 99.2 84 mm); compression ratio: 8.5:1; max power (DIN): 135 (99.4 kW) at 4,000 rpm; max torque (DIN): 250 lb ft, 34 kg m (338.3 Nm) at 1,600 rpm; 25.9 hp/l (19.1 kW/l); crankshaft bearings valves: hydraulic tappets; camshafts: at centre of Vee; 1 Holley R8448A downdraught twin barr carburettor; cooling system: 25 imp pt, 30 US pt, 14.2 l.

TRANSMISSION gearbox: Torqueflite automatic transmissi (standard), hydraulic torque converter and planetary gea with 3 ratios, max ratio of converter at stall 1.90, possib manual selection; ratios: I 2.450, II 1.450, III 1, rev 2.20 lever: steering column or central; axle ratio: 2.470 - Wagon 2.450.

PERFORMANCE max speed: about 102 mph, 164 km/h; power weight ratio: Sedan 23.9 lb/hp (32.5 lb/kW), 10.9 kg/ (14.7 kg/kW); speed in direct drive at 1,000 rpm: 25.5 mp 41 km/h; consumption: 19.2 m/imp gal, 16 m/US gal, l x 100 km.

ELECTRICAL EQUIPMENT 60 A alternator.

DIMENSIONS AND WEIGHT weight: Coupé 3,168 lb, 1,3 kg - Sedan 3,232 lb, 1,466 kg - St. Wagon 3,433 lb, 1,5 kg; fuel tank: 16.3 imp gal, 19.5 US gal, 74 l.

OPTIONALS 2.710 axle ratio; 4-speed fully synchroniz mechanical gearbox with overdrive/top not available.

155 hp power team

(for California only).

See 100 hp power team, except for:

ENGINE 8 cylinders; 318 cu in, 5,211 cc (3.91 x 3.31 99.2 x 84 mm); compression ratio: 8.5:1; max power (DI 155 hp (114.1 kW) at 4,000 rpm; max torque (DIN): 245 ft, 33.8 kg m (331.5 Nm) at 1,600 rpm; 29.7 hp/l (21.9 kW/ 5 crankshaft bearings; valves: hydraulic tappets; camshaf 1, at centre of Vee; 1 Carter TQ9156S downdraught barrel carburettor; cooling system: 25 imp pt, 30 US 14.2 l.

PLYMOUTH Volaré Premier 4-dr Sedan

PLYMOUTH Volaré Road Runner 2-dr Coupé

TRANSMISSION gearbox: Torqueflite automatic transmission (standard), hydraulic torque converter and planetary gears with 3 ratios, max ratio of converter at stall 1.90, possible manual selection: ratios: I 2.450, II 1.450, III 1, IV 2.220; lever: steering column or central; axle ratio: 2.470 - St. Wagon 2.450.

PERFORMANCE max speed: about 103 mph, 165 km/h; power-weight ratio: Sedan 20.9 lb/hp (28.3 lb/kW), 9.5 kg/hp (12.8 kg/kW); speed in direct drive at 1,000 rpm: 25.6 mph, 41.2 km/h; consumption: 16.8 m/imp gal, 14 m/US gal, 16.8 l x 100 km.

ELECTRICAL EQUIPMENT 60 A alternator.

DIMENSIONS AND WEIGHT weight: Coupé 3,168 lb, 1,383 kg - Sedan 3,232 lb, 1,466 kg - St. Wagon 3,433 lb, 1,557 kg; fuel tank: 16.3 imp gal, 19.5 US gal, 74 l.

OPTIONALS 2.450 axle ratio; 4-speed fully synchronized mechanical gearbox with overdrive/top not available.

170 hp power team

(for California only).

(see 100 hp power team, except for:)

ENGINE 8 cylinders; 360 cu in, 5,900 cc (4 x 3.58 in, 101.6 x 89.6 mm); compression ratio: 8:1; max power (DIN): 170 hp (125.1 kW) at 4,000 rpm; max torque (DIN): 270 lb ft, 37.2 kg m (364.8 Nm) at 1,600 rpm; 28.8 hp/l (21.2 kW/l); 5 crankshaft bearings; valves: hydraulic tappets; camshafts: 1, at centre of Vee; 1 Carter TQ9198S downdraught 4-barrel carburettor; dual exhaust system with catalytic converter; cooling system: 25 imp pt, 30 US pt, 14.2 l.

TRANSMISSION gearbox: Torqueflite automatic transmission (standard), hydraulic torque converter and planetary gears with 3 ratios, max ratio of converter at stall 1.90, possible manual selection; ratios: I 2.450, II 1.450, III 1, IV 2.220; lever: central of steering column; axle ratio: 2.710.

PERFORMANCE max speed: about 106 mph, 170 km/h; power-weight ratio: Coupé 19.7 lb/hp (26.8 lb/kW), 8.9 kg/hp (12.1 kg/kW); speed in direct drive at 1,000 rpm: 29.3 mph, 47.2 km/h; consumption: 15.6 m/imp gal, 13 m/US gal, 18.1 l x 100 km.

ELECTRICAL EQUIPMENT 430 A battery; 60 A alternator.

DIMENSIONS AND WEIGHT weight: Coupé 3,347 lb, 1,518 kg; fuel tank: 16.3 imp gal, 19.5 US gal, 74 l.

BODY coupé; 2 doors.

OPTIONALS 3.210 axle ratio; 4-speed fully synchronized mechanical gearbox with overdrive/top not available.

195 hp power team

(not available in California).

(see 100 hp power team, except for:)

ENGINE 8 cylinders; 360 cu in, 5,900 cc (4 x 3.58 in, 101.6 x 89.6 mm); compression ratio: 8:1; max power (DIN): 195 hp (143.5 kW) at 4,000 rpm; max torque (DIN): 280 lb ft, 38.6 kg m (378.6 Nm) at 2,400 rpm; 33 hp/l (24.3 kW/l); 5 crankshaft bearings; valves: hydraulic tappets; camshafts: 1, at centre of Vee; 1 Carter TQ9196S downdraught 4-barrel carburettor; dual exhaust system with catalytic converter; cooling system: 25 imp pt, 30 US pt, 14.2 l.

TRANSMISSION gearbox: Torqueflite automatic transmission (standard), hydraulic torque converter and planetary gears with 3 ratios, max ratio of converter at stall 1.90, possible manual selection; ratios: I 2.450, II 1.450, III 1, rev 2.220; lever: central or steering column; axle ratio: 2.710.

PERFORMANCE max speed: about 112 mph, 180 km/h; power-weight ratio: Coupé 17.2 lb/hp (23.3 lb/kW), 7.8 kg/hp (10.6 kg/kW); speed in direct drive at 1,000 rpm: 29.5 mph, 47.5 km/h; consumption: 16.8 m/imp gal, 14 m/US gal, 16.8 l x 100 km.

ELECTRICAL EQUIPMENT 430 A battery; 60 A alternator.

DIMENSIONS AND WEIGHT weight: Coupé 3,347 lb, 1,518 kg; fuel tank: 16.3 imp gal, 19.5 US gal, 74 l.

BODY coupé; 2 doors.

OPTIONALS 3.210 axle ratio; 4-speed fully synchronized mechanical gearbox with overdrive/top not available.

PONTIAC   USA

Sunbird Series

PRICES EX WORKS:

1 Coupé	$ 3,781
2 Sport Coupé	$ 3,964
3 Sport Hatchback Coupé	$ 4,064
4 Sport Safari St. Wagon	$ 4,138

For V6 engine add $ 200; for V8 engines add $ 395.

Power team:	Standard for:	Optional for:
90 hp	all	—
85 hp	—	all
115 hp	—	all
125 hp	—	1,2,3
130 hp	—	1,2,3

90 hp power team

(not available in California).

ENGINE front, 4 stroke; 4 cylinders, in line; 151 cu in, 2,475 cc (4 x 3 in, 101.6 x 76.2 mm); compression ratio: 8.2:1; max power (DIN): 90 hp (66.2 kW) at 4,400 rpm; max torque (DIN): 128 lb ft, 17.6 kg m (172.6 Nm) at 2,400 rpm; max engine rpm: 5,200; 36.4 hp/l (26.7 kW/l); cast iron block and head; 5 crankshaft bearings; valves: overhead, in line, push-rods and rockers, hydraulic tappets; camshafts: 1, side; lubrication: gear pump, full flow filter, 6.7 imp pt, 8 US pt, 3.8 l; 1 Holley 5210 downdraught twin barrel carburettor; cleaner air system; exhaust system with catalytic converter; fuel feed: mechanical pump; water-cooled, 17.8 imp pt, 21.4 US pt, 10.1 l.

TRANSMISSION driving wheels: rear; clutch: single dry plate; gearbox: mechanical; gears: 4, fully synchronized; ratios: I 3.500, II 2.480, III 1.660, IV 1, rev 3.500; lever: central; final drive: hypoid bevel; axle ratio: 2.730; width of rims: 5''; tyres: A78 x 13.

PERFORMANCE max speed: about 87 mph, 140 km/h; power-weight ratio: Coupé 28.9 lb/hp (39.3 lb/kW), 13.1 kg/hp (17.8 kg/kW) - Sport Hatchback Coupé 29.5 lb/hp (40.1 lb/kW), 13.4 kg/hp (18.2 kg/kW); speed in direct drive at 1,000 rpm: 19.8 mph, 31.8 km/h; consumption: 28.8 m/imp gal, 24 m/US gal, 9.8 l x 100 km.

CHASSIS integral; front suspension: independent, wishbones, coil springs, telescopic dampers; rear: rigid axle lower trailing radius arms, upper oblique torque arms, coil springs, telescopic dampers.

STEERING recirculating ball; turns lock to lock: 4.40.

BRAKES front disc (diameter 9.74 in, 24.7 cm), rear drum; swept area: total 264.7 sq in, 1,707 sq cm.

ELECTRICAL EQUIPMENT 12 V; 3,200 W battery; 37 A alternator; Delco-Remy transistorized ignition; 4 headlamps.

PONTIAC Sunbird Formula Sport Hatchback Coupé

90 HP POWER TEAM

DIMENSIONS AND WEIGHT wheel base: 97 in, 246 cm; tracks: 55.30 in, 140 cm front, 54.10 in, 137 cm rear; length: 179.20 in, 455 cm - St. Wagon 178 in, 452 cm; width: 65.40 in, 166 cm; height: 49.60 in, 126 cm - St. Wagon 51.80 in, 132 cm; ground clearance: 4.90 in, 12.4 cm; weight: Coupé 2,599 lb, 1,178 kg - Sport Coupé 2,605 lb, 1,181 kg - Sport Hatchback Coupé 2,653 lb, 1,203 kg - Sport St. Wagon 2,641 lb, 1,197 kg; turning circle: 38.4 ft, 11.7 m; fuel tank: 15.4 imp gal, 18.5 US gal, 70 l.

BODY 4 seats, separate front seats.

OPTIONALS limited slip differential; 2.930 axle ratio; 5-speed fully synchronized mechanical gearbox (I 3.400, II 2.080, III 1.390, IV 1, V 0.800, rev 3.360), 3.080 or 2.730 axle ratio; Turbo-Hydramatic automatic transmission with 3 ratios (I 2.740, II 1.570, III 1, rev 2.070), max ratio of converter at stall 2.15, possible manual selection, central lever, 2.560 or 2.730 axle ratio; B78 x 13 tyres; BR78 x 13 or BR70 x 13 tyres with 6'' wide rims; heavy-duty suspension; anti-roll bar on front and rear suspensions; power steering; tilt of steering wheel; servo brake; heated rear window; air-conditioning; Formula equipment for Hatchback only; heavy-duty battery; heavy-duty alternator.

85 hp power team

(for California only).

See 90 hp power team, except for:

ENGINE compression ratio: 8.3:1; max power (DIN): 85 hp (62.6 kW) at 4,400 rpm; max torque (DIN): 123 lb ft, 17 kg m (166.7 Nm) at 2,800 rpm; 34.3 hp/l (25.3 kW/l); 1 Holley 6510 downdraught twin barrel carburettor.

TRANSMISSION gearbox: Turbo-Hydramatic automatic transmission (standard), hydraulic torque converter and planetary gears with 3 ratios, max ratio of converter at stall 2.15, possible manual selection: ratios: I 2.740, II 1.570, III 1, rev 2.070; lever: central; axle ratio: 2.730.

PERFORMANCE power-weight ratio: Coupé 31.2 lb/hp (42.4 lb/kW), 14.2 kg/hp (19.2 kg/kW) - Sport Hatchback Coupé 31.9 lb/hp (43.3 lb/kW), 14.4 kg/hp (19.6 kg/kW); consumption: 26.4 m/imp gal, 22 m/US gal, 10.7 l x 100 km.

DIMENSIONS AND WEIGHT weight: plus 56 lb, 25 kg.

OPTIONALS 4-speed fully synchronized mechanical gearbox (I 3.500, II 2.480, III 1.660, IV 1, rev 3.500), central lever, 2.930 axle ratio; 5-speed fully synchronized mechanical gearbox not available.

115 hp power team

See 90 hp power team, except for:

ENGINE 6 cylinders, Vee-slanted at 90°; 231 cu in, 3,785 cc (3.80 x 3.40 in, 96.5 x 86.4 mm); compression ratio: 8:1; max power (DIN): 115 hp (84.6 kW) at 3,800 rpm; max torque (DIN): 190 lb ft, 26.2 kg m (257 Nm) at 2,000 rpm; max engine rpm: 4,400; 30.4 hp/l (22.4 kW/l); 4 crankshaft bearings; camshafts: 1, at centre of Vee; lubricating system: 8.3 imp pt, 9.9 US pt, 4.7 l; 1 Rochester 2GE downdraught twin barrel carburettor; fuel feed: electric pump; cooling system: 22.2 imp pt, 26.6 US pt, 12.6 l.

TRANSMISSION axle ratio: 2.930; tyres: B78 x 13 (standard).

PERFORMANCE max speed: about 99 mph, 160 km/h; power-weight ratio: Coupé 23.9 lb/hp (32.5 lb/kW), 10.8 kg/hp (14.7 kg/kW) - Sport Hatchback Coupé 24.4 lb/hp (33.2 lb/kW), 11.1 kg/hp (15 kg/kW); speed in direct drive at 1,000 rpm: 26.1 mph, 42 km/h; consumption: 16.8 m/imp gal, 14 m/US gal, 16.8 l x 100 km.

ELECTRICAL EQUIPMENT 2,500 W battery.

DIMENSIONS AND WEIGHT weight: plus 152 lb, 69 kg.

OPTIONALS 5-speed fully synchronized mechanical gearbox with 2.930 axle ratio; Turbo-Hydramatic automatic transmission with 3 ratios (I 2.520, II 1.520, III 1, rev 1.920), max ratio of converter at stall 2.50, 2.560 or 2.930 axle ratio.

125 hp power team

(for California only).

See 90 hp power team, except for:

ENGINE 8 cylinders; 305 cu in, 4,999 cc (3.74 x 3.48 in, 95 x 88.4 mm); compression ratio: 8.4:1; max power (DIN): 125 hp (92 kW) at 3,200 rpm; max torque (DIN): 235 lb ft, 32.4 kg m (317.7 Nm) at 2,000 rpm; max engine rpm: 4,000; 25 hp/l (18.4 kW/l); camshafts: 1, at centre of Vee; lubricating system: 8.3 imp pt, 9.9 US pt, 4.7 l; 1 Rochester

PONTIAC Sunbird Formula Sport Hatchback Coupé

17059434 downdraught twin barrel carburettor; cooling system: 27.6 imp pt, 33.2 US pt, 15.7 l.

TRANSMISSION gearbox: Turbo-Hydramatic automatic transmission (standard), hydraulic torque converter and planetary gears with 3 ratios, max ratio of converter at stall 2, possible manual selection: ratios: I 2.520, II 1.520, III 1, rev 1.920; lever: central; axle ratio: 2.290.

PERFORMANCE max speed: about 103 mph, 165 km/h; power-weight ratio: Coupé 23.6 lb/hp (32.1 lb/kW), 10.7 kg/hp (14.6 kg/kW) - Sport Hatchback Coupé 24.1 lb/hp (32.7 lb/kW), 10.9 kg/hp (14.8 kg/kW); speed in direct drive at 1,000 rpm: 27.3 mph, 44 km/h; consumption: 16.8 m/imp gal, 14 m/US gal, 16.8 l x 100 km.

DIMENSIONS AND WEIGHT weight: plus 355 lb, 161 kg.

OPTIONALS 5-speed fully synchronized mechanical gearbox not available.

130 hp power team

(not available in California).

See 90 hp power team, except for:

ENGINE 8 cylinders; 305 cu in, 4,999 cc (3.74 x 3.48 in, 95 x 88.4 mm); compression ratio: 8.4:1; max power (DIN): 130 hp (95.7 kW) at 3,200 rpm; max torque (DIN): 245 lb ft, 33.8 kg m (331.5 Nm) at 2,000 rpm; max engine rpm: 4,000; 26 hp/l (19.1 kW/l); camshafts: 1, at centre of Vee; lubricating system: 8.3 imp pt, 9.9 US pt, 4.7 l; 1 Roche-

ster 17059134 downdraught twin barrel carburettor; cooling system: 27.6 imp pt, 33.2 US pt, 15.7 l.

TRANSMISSION axle ratio: 3.080.

PERFORMANCE max speed: about 109 mph, 170 km/h; power-weight ratio: Coupé 22.5 lb/hp (30.6 lb/kW), 1 kg/hp (13.8 kg/kW) - Sport Hatchback Coupé 22.9 lb/hp (31.1 lb/kW), 10.4 kg/hp (14.1 kg/kW); speed in direct drive at 1,000 rpm: 26.4 mph, 42.5 km/h; consumption: m/imp gal, 15 m/US gal, 15.7 l x 100 km.

DIMENSIONS AND WEIGHT weight: plus 325 lb, 147 l

OPTIONALS Turbo-Hydramatic automatic transmission w 3 ratios (I 2.520, II 1.520, III 1, rev 1.920), max ratio converter at stall 2, possible manual selection, cent lever. 2.290 axle ratio; 5-speed fully synchronized mecl nical gearbox not available.

Phoenix Series

PRICES EX WORKS:

Hatchback Coupé	$ 4,2
Coupé	$ 4,1
Sedan	$ 4,
LJ Coupé	$ 4,3
LJ Sedan	$ 4,4

For 5-litre engines add $ 195; for 5.7-litre engine add $ 3

PONTIAC Phoenix LJ Sedan

Power team:	Standard for:	Optional for:
115 hp	all	—
125 hp	—	all
130 hp	—	all
165 hp	—	all

115 hp power team

ENGINE front, 4 stroke; 6 cylinders, Vee-slanted at 9 231 cu in, 3,785 cc (3.80 x 3.40 in, 96.5 x 86.4 mm); co pression ratio: 8:1; max power (DIN): 115 hp (84.6 k at 3,800 rpm; max torque (DIN): 190 lb ft, 26.2 kg (257 Nm) at 2,000 rpm; max engine rpm: 4,400; 30.4 h (22.4 kW/l); cast iron block and head; 4 crankshaft be ings; valves: overhead, in line, push-rods and rocke hydraulic tappets; camshafts: 1, at centre of Vee; lub cation: gear pump, full flow filter, 8.3 imp pt, 9.9 US 4.7 l; 1 Rochester 2GE downdraught twin barrel carburett cleaner air system; exhaust system with catalytic c verter; fuel feed: mechanical pump; water-cooled, 2 imp pt, 26.6 US pt, 12.6 l.

TRANSMISSION driving wheels: rear; clutch: single plate; gearbox: mechanical; gears: 3, fully synchroniz ratios: I 3.500, II 1.890, III 1, rev 3.500; lever: steer column; final drive: hypoid bevel, axle ratio: 3.080; wi of rims: 5'' - Phoenix LJ 6''; tyres: E78 x 14.

PERFORMANCE max speed: about 93 mph, 149 km power-weight ratio: Sedan 27.6 lb/hp (37.6 lb/kW), 1 kg/hp (17 kg/kW) - LJ Sedan 28.6 lb/hp (38.8 lb/kW), kg/hp (17.6 kg/kW); speed in direct drive at 1,000 rp

4.5 mph, 39.5 km/h; consumption: 22.8 m/imp gal, 19 ·/US gal, 12.4 l x 100 km.

·HASSIS integral with separate partial frame; front sus-·ension: independent, wishbones, coil springs, anti-roll ·ar, telescopic dampers; rear: rigid axle, semi-elliptic leaf-·prings, telescopic dampers.

·TEERING recirculating ball; turns lock to lock: 4.99.

·RAKES front disc (diameter 11 in, 27.9 cm), front internal ·adial fins, rear drum; swept area (total 337.3 sq in, 2,175 ·q cm.

·LECTRICAL EQUIPMENT 12 V; 2,500 W battery; 37 A alter-·ator; Delco-Remy transistorized ignition; 2 headlamps.

·IMENSIONS AND WEIGHT wheel base: 111.10 in, 282 ·m; tracks: 61.90 in, 157 cm front, 59.60 in, 151 cm rear ·ngth: 203.40 in, 517 cm; width: 72.40 in, 184 cm; height: ·2.30 in, 133 cm - sedans 53.20 in, 135 cm; ground clear-·nce: 4.20 in, 10.7 cm; weight: Hatchback Coupé 3,277 lb, ·486 kg - Coupé 3,127 lb, 1,418 kg - Sedan 3,178 lb, 1,441 ·g - LJ Coupé 3,236 lb, 1,467 kg - LJ Sedan 3,286 lb, 1,490 ·g; turning circle: 39.1 ft, 11.9 m; fuel tank: 17.6 imp gal, ·| US gal, 80 l.

·ODY 6 seats.

·PTIONALS central lever; limited slip differential; Turbo-·ydramatic automatic transmission with 3 ratios (I 2.520, ·.1.520, III 1, rev 1.920), max ratio of converter at stall ·50, possible manual selection, steering column or central ·ver, 2.560 or 3.230 axle ratio; FR78 x 14 tyres with 7'' ·ide rims; heavy-duty suspension with rear anti-roll bar; ·wer steering; tilt of steering wheel; servo brake; heavy-·ty battery; heavy-duty alternator; electric windows; speed ·ontrol device; heated rear window except for Hatchback; ·r-conditioning.

125 hp power team

·or California only).

·ee 115 hp power team, except for:

·NGINE 8 cylinders; 305 cu in, 4,999 cc (3.74 x 3.48 in, ·5 x 88.4 mm); compression ratio: 8.4:1; max power (DIN): ·25 hp (92 kW) at 3,200 rpm; max torque (DIN): 235 lb ft, ·2.4 kg m (317.7 Nm) at 2,000 rpm; max engine rpm: 4,000; ·5 hp/l (18.4 kW/l); 5 crankshaft bearings; 1 Rochester ·GC downdraught twin barrel carburettor; cooling system: ·7.6 imp pt, 33.2 US pt, 15.7 l.

·RANSMISSION gearbox: Turbo-Hydramatic automatic trans-·ission (standard), hydraulic torque converter and plane-·ry gears with 3 ratios, max ratio of converter at stall 2, ·ossible manual selection; ratios: I 2.520, II 1.520, III 1, ·v 1.920; lever: steering column or central; axle ratio: ·290.

·ERFORMANCE max speed: about 96 mph, 155 km/h; ·wer-weight ratio: Sedan 27.2 lb/hp (37 lb/kW), 12.3 kg/hp ·6.7 kg/kW) - LJ Sedan 28.1 lb/hp (38.1 lb/kW), 12.7 ·g/hp (17.3 kg/kW); speed in direct drive at 1,000 rpm: ·0.1 mph, 48.4 km/h; consumption: 15.6 m/imp gal, 13 ·/US gal, 18.1 l x 100 km.

BRAKES servo (standard).

ELECTRICAL EQUIPMENT 3,200 W battery.

DIMENSIONS AND WEIGHT weight: plus 222 lb, 100 kg.

130 hp power team

(not available in California).

See 115 hp power team, except for:

ENGINE 8 cylinders; 305 cu in, 4,999 cc (3.74 x 3.48 in, 95 x 88.4 mm); compression ratio: 8.4:1; max power (DIN): 130 hp (95.7 kW) at 3,200 rpm; max torque (DIN): 245 lb ft, 33.8 kg m (331.5 Nm) at 2,000 rpm; max engine rpm: 4,000; 26 hp/l (19.1 kW/l); 5 crankshaft bearings; 1 Roche-ster 2GC downdraught twin barrel carburettor; cooling system: 27.6 imp pt, 33.2 US pt, 15.7 l.

TRANSMISSION gears: 4, fully synchronized; ratios: I 2.850, II 2.020, III 1.350, IV 1, rev 2.850; lever: central; axle ratio: 3.080.

PERFORMANCE max speed: about 103 mph, 165 km/h; power-weight ratio: Sedan 26.2 lb/hp (35.6 lb/kW), 11.9 kg/hp (16.2 kg/kW) - LJ Sedan 27.1 lb/hp (36.8 lb/kW), 12.3 kg/hp (16.7 kg/kW); speed in direct drive at 1,000 rpm: 25.6 mph, 41.2 km/h; consumption: 18 m/imp gal, 15 m/US gal, 15.7 l x 100 km.

BRAKES servo (standard).

ELECTRICAL EQUIPMENT 3,200 W battery.

DIMENSIONS AND WEIGHT weight: plus 233 lb, 105 kg.

OPTIONALS Turbo-Hydramatic automatic transmission with 3 ratios (I 2.520, II 1.520, III 1, rev 1.920), max ratio of converter at stall 2, possible manual selection, central or steering column lever, 2.410 or 3.080 axle ratio.

165 hp power team

(for California only).

See 115 hp power team, except for:

ENGINE 8 cylinders; 350 cu in, 5,736 cc (4 x 3.48 in, 101.6 x 88.4 mm); compression ratio: 8.2:1; max power (DIN): 165 hp (121.4 kW) at 3,800 rpm; max torque (DIN): 260 lb ft, 35.9 kg m (352.1 Nm) at 2,400 rpm; 28.8 hp/l (21.2 kW/l); 5 crankshaft bearings; 1 Rochester M4MC downdraught 4-barrel carburettor; cooling system: 27.6 imp pt, 33.2 US pt, 15.7 l.

TRANSMISSION gearbox: Turbo-Hydramatic automatic trans-mission (standard), hydraulic torque converter and planetary gears with 3 ratios, max ratio of converter at stall 2, possible manual selection; ratios: I 2.520, II 1.520, III 1, rev 1.920; lever: steering column or central; axle ratio: 2.410.

PERFORMANCE max speed: about 109 mph, 170 km/h;

power-weight ratio: Sedan 20.6 lb/hp (28 lb/kW), 9.4 kg/hp (12.7 kg/kW) - LJ Sedan 21.3 lb/hp (28.9 lb/kW), 9.6 kg/hp (13.1 kg/kW); speed in direct drive at 1,000 rpm: 27.8 mph, 44.7 km/h; consumption: 15.6 m/imp gal, 13 m/US gal, 18.1 l x 100 km.

BRAKES servo (standard).

ELECTRICAL EQUIPMENT 3,200 W battery.

DIMENSIONS AND WEIGHT weight: plus 225 lb, 102 kg.

OPTIONALS 3.080 axle ratio.

Firebird Series

Power team:	Standard for:	Optional for:
115 hp	1,2	—
125 hp	—	1 to 3
135 hp	3	1,2
150 hp	—	all
165 hp	—	1 to 3
185 hp	4	3
220 hp	—	3,4

115 hp power team

ENGINE front, 4 stroke; 6 cylinders, Vee-slanted at 90°; 231 cu in, 3,785 cc (3.80 x 3.40 in, 96.5 x 86.4 mm); com-pression ratio: 8:1; max power (DIN): 115 hp (84.6 kW) at 3,800 rpm; max torque (DIN): 185 lb ft, 25.5 kg m (250.1 Nm) at 2,000 rpm; max engine rpm: 4,400; 30.4 hp/l (22.4 kW/l); cast iron block and head; 4 crankshaft bearings; valves: overhead, in line, push-rods and rockers, hydraulic tappets; camshafts: 1, at centre of Vee; lubrication: gear pump, full flow filter, 8.3 imp pt, 9.9 US pt, 4.7 l; 1 Roche-ster 2GE downdraught twin barrel carburettor; cleaner air system; exhaust system with catalytic converter; fuel feed: mechanical pump; water-cooled, 22.2 imp pt, 26.6 US pt, 12.6 l.

TRANSMISSION driving wheels: rear; clutch: single dry plate; gearbox: mechanical (Turbo-Hydramatic automatic transmission standard for California only); gears: 3, fully synchronized; ratios: I 3.110, II 1.840, III 1, rev 3.220; lever: central; final drive: hypoid bevel; axle ratio: 3.080; width of rims: 6''; tyres: FR78 x 15.

PERFORMANCE max speed: about 93 mph, 149 km/h; power-weight ratio: Firebird 28.3 lb/hp (38.5 lb/kW), 12.8 kg/hp (17.5 kg/kW); speed in direct drive at 1,000 rpm: 27.4 mph, 44.1 km/h; consumption: 21.6 m/imp gal, 18 m/US gal, 13.1 l x 100 km.

CHASSIS integral with separate partial frame; front sus-pension: independent, wishbones (lower trailing links), coil springs, anti-roll bar, telescopic dampers; rear: rigid axle, semi-elliptic leafsprings, anti-roll bar, telescopic dampers.

STEERING recirculating ball, variable ratio servo; turns lock to lock: 2.41.

BRAKES front disc (diameter 11 in, 27.9 cm), front internal radial fins, rear drum; swept area: total 326.49 sq in, 2,106 sq cm.

ELECTRICAL EQUIPMENT 12 V; 2,500 W battery; 42 A alternator; Delco-Remy transistorized ignition; 4 headlamps.

DIMENSIONS AND WEIGHT wheel base: 108.20 in, 275 cm; tracks: 61.30 in, 156 cm front, 60 in, 152 cm rear; length: 198.10 in, 503 cm; width: 73 in, 185 cm; height: 49.30 in, 125 cm; ground clearance: 4.60 in 11.7 cm; weight: Firebird 3,258 lb, 1,477 kg - Esprit 3,266 lb, 1,481 kg; turning circle: 41.3 ft, 12.6 m; fuel tank: 17.6 imp gal, 21 US gal, 80 l.

BODY hardtop coupé; 2 doors; 4 seats, separate front seats, built-in headrests.

OPTIONALS limited slip differential; Turbo-Hydramatic auto-matic transmission with 3 ratios (I 2.520, II 1.520, III 1, rev 1.920), max ratio of converter at stall 2.25, possible manual selection, steering column or central lever; 2.560 or 3.230 axle ratio; G78 x 14 tyres, F78 x 14 tyres with 5'' wide rims; heavy-duty radiator; tilt of steering wheel; servo brake; heavy-duty battery; heavy-duty alternator; electric windows; heated rear window; removable roof panels; air-conditioning; Red Bird equipment (Esprit only); Special Edition equipment (Trans Am only); Special Per-formance equipment (Trans Am only).

PONTIAC Firebird Formula Hardtop Coupé

125 hp power team

(for California only).

See 115 hp power team, except for:

ENGINE 8 cylinders; 305 cu in, 4,999 cc (3.74 x 3.48 in, 95 x 88.4 mm); compression ratio: 8.4:1; max power (DIN): 125 hp (92 kW) at 3,200 rpm; max torque (DIN): 245 lb ft, 33.8 kg m (331.5 Nm) at 2,000 rpm; max engine rpm: 4,000; 25 hp/l (18.4 kW/l); 5 crankshaft bearings; 1 Rochester 2GC downdraught twin barrel carburettor; cooling system: 29.2 imp pt, 35.1 US pt, 16.6 l.

TRANSMISSION gearbox: Turbo-Hydramatic automatic transmission (standard), hydraulic torque converter and planetary gears with 3 ratios, max ratio of converter at stall 2, possible manual selection; ratios: I 2.520, II 1.520, III 1, rev 1.920; lever: steering column or central; axle ratio: 2.410; width of rims: Formula 7''; tyres: Formula P225/70R x 15.

PERFORMANCE max speed: about 96 mph, 155 km/h; power-weight ratio: Esprit 26.9 lb/hp (36.5 lb/kW), 12.3 kg/hp (16.6 kg/kW) - Formula 26.8 lb/hp (36.4 lb/kW), 12.2 kg/hp (16.5 kg/kW); speed in direct drive at 1,000 rpm: 25.4 mph, 40.8 km/h; consumption: 15.6 m/imp gal, 13 m/US gal, 18.1 l x 100 km.

BRAKES servo (standard).

PONTIAC Firebird Trans Am Hardtop Coupé

ELECTRICAL EQUIPMENT 3,200 W battery.

DIMENSIONS AND WEIGHT weight: Firebird 3,358 lb, 1,523 kg - Esprit 3,366 lb, 1,527 kg - Formula 3,356 lb, 1,522 kg.

135 hp power team

(not available in California).

See 115 hp power team, except for:

ENGINE 8 cylinders; 301 cu in, 4,932 cc (4 x 3 in, 101.6 x 76.2 mm); compression ratio: 8.1:1; max power (DIN): 135 hp (99.4 kW) at 3,800 rpm; max torque (DIN): 240 lb ft, 33.1 kg m (324.6 Nm) at 1,600 rpm; 27.4 hp/l (20.2 kW/l); 5 crankshaft bearings; 1 Rochester M2MC downdraught twin barrel carburettor; cooling system: 38.4 imp pt, 46.1 US pt, 21.8 l.

TRANSMISSION gearbox: Turbo-Hydramatic automatic transmission (standard), hydraulic torque converter and planetary gears with 3 ratios, max ratio of converter at stall 2, possible manual selection; ratios: I 2.520, II 1.520, III 1, rev 1.920; lever: steering column or central; axle ratio: 2.410; width of rims: Formula 7''; tyres: Formula P225/70R x 15.

PERFORMANCE max speed: about 99 mph, 160 km/h; power-weight ratio: Esprit 24.9 lb/hp (33.9 lb/kW), 11.3 kg/hp (15.4 kg/kW) - Formula 24.9 lb/hp (33.8 lb/kW), 11.3 kg/hp (15.3 kg/kW); speed in direct drive at 1,000 rpm: 26.2 mph, 42.1 km/h; consumption: 20.5 m/imp gal, 17 m/US gal, 13.8 l x 100 km.

BRAKES servo (standard).

ELECTRICAL EQUIPMENT 3,200 W battery.

DIMENSIONS AND WEIGHT weight: Firebird 3,358 lb, 1,523 kg - Esprit 3,366 lb, 1,527 kg - Formula 3,356 lb, 1,522 kg.

150 hp power team

(not available in California).

See 115 hp power team, except for:

ENGINE 8 cylinders; 301 cu in, 4,932 cc (4 x 3 in, 101.6 x 76.2 mm); compression ratio: 8.1:1; max power (DIN): 150 hp (110.4 kW) at 4,000 rpm; max torque (DIN): 240 lb ft, 33.1 kg m (324.6 Nm) at 2,400 rpm; 30.4 hp/l (22.4 kW/l); 5 crankshaft bearings; 1 Rochester M4MC downdraught 4-barrel carburettor; cooling system: 38.4 imp pt, 46.1 US pt, 21.8 l.

TRANSMISSION gears: 4, fully synchronized; ratios: I 2.850, II 2.020, III 1.350, IV 1, rev 2.850; lever: central; axle ratio: 3.080; width of rims: Formula and Trans Am 7''; tyres: Formula and Trans Am P225/70R x 15.

PERFORMANCE max speed: about 103 mph, 165 km/h; power-weight ratio: Formula 22.4 lb/hp (30.4 lb/kW), 10.1 kg/hp (13.8 kg/kW) - Trans Am 23.3 lb/hp (31.6 lb/kW), 10.6 kg/hp (14.3 kg/kW); speed in direct drive at 1,000 rpm: 25.6 mph, 41.2 m/h; consumption: 18 m/imp gal, 15 m/US gal, 15.7 l x 100 km.

BRAKES servo (standard).

ELECTRICAL EQUIPMENT 3,200 W battery.

DIMENSIONS AND WEIGHT weight: Firebird 3,358 lb, 1,523 kg - Esprit 3,366 lb, 1,527 kg - Formula 3,356 lb, 1,522 kg - Trans Am 3,490 lb, 1,583 kg.

OPTIONALS Turbo-Hydramatic automatic transmission with 3 ratios (I 2.520, II 1.520, III 1, rev 1.920), max ratio of converter at stall 2, possible manual selection, steering column or central lever, 2.730 axle ratio.

165 hp power team

See 115 hp power team, except for:

ENGINE 8 cylinders; 350 cu in, 5,736 cc (4 x 3.48 in, 101.6 x 88.4 mm); compression ratio: 8.2:1; max power (DIN): 165 hp (121.4 kW) at 3,800 rpm; max torque (DIN): 260 lb ft, 35.9 kg m (352.1 Nm) at 2,400 rpm; 28.8 hp/l (21.2 kW/l); 5 crankshaft bearings; 1 Rochester M4MC downdraught 4-barrel carburettor; cooling system: 29.2 imp pt, 35.1 US pt, 16.6 l.

TRANSMISSION gearbox: Turbo-Hydramatic automatic transmission (standard), hydraulic torque converter and planetary gears with 3 ratios, max ratio of converter at stall 2, possible manual selection; ratios: I 2.520, II 1.520, III 1, rev 1.920; lever: steering column or central; axle ratio: 3.080; width of rims: Formula 7''; tyres: Formula P225/70 R x 15.

BRAKES servo (standard).

ELECTRICAL EQUIPMENT 3,200 W battery.

DIMENSIONS AND WEIGHT weight: Firebird 3,358 lb, 1,523 kg - Esprit 3,366 lb, 1,527 kg - Formula 3,356 lb, 1,522 kg.

PERFORMANCE max speed: about 103 mph, 165 km/h; power-weight ratio: Esprit 20.6 lb/hp (27.9 lb/kW), 9.3 kg/l (12.7 kg/kW) - Formula 20.5 lb/hp (27.8 lb/kW), 9.3 kg/l (12.6 kg/kW); speed in direct drive at 1,000 rpm: 27 mp 43.4 km/h; consumption: 19.2 m/imp gal, 16 m/US gal, 14 l x 100 km.

BRAKES servo (standard).

ELECTRICAL EQUIPMENT 3,200 W battery.

DIMENSIONS AND WEIGHT weight: Firebird 3,385 lb, 1,5 kg - Esprit 3,393 lb, 1,539 kg - Formula 3,383 lb, 1,534 k

185 hp power team

See 115 hp power team, except for:

ENGINE 8 cylinders; 403 cu in, 6,604 cc (4.35 x 3.38 110.4 x 85.8 mm); compression ratio: 7.9:1; max pow (DIN): 185 hp (136.2 kW) at 3,600 rpm; max torque (DIN 315 lb ft, 43.5 kg m (426.6 Nm) at 2,000 rpm; 28 hp (20.6 kW/l); 5 crankshaft bearings; 1 Rochester M4N downdraught 4-barrel carburettor; dual exhaust syste cooling system: 34 imp pt, 40.8 US pt, 19.3 l.

TRANSMISSION gearbox: Turbo-Hydramatic automatic trar mission (standard), hydraulic torque converter and plar tary gears with 3 ratios, max ratio of converter at st 2, possible manual selection; ratios: I 2.520, II 1.520, 1, rev 1.920; lever: steering column or central; axle rat 2.410; width of rims: 7''; tyres: P225/70R x 15.

PERFORMANCE max speed: about 112 mph, 180 km power-weight ratio: Trans Am 18.9 lb/hp (25.6 lb/kV 8.6 kg/hp (11.6 kg/kW) - Formula 19 lb/hp (25.8 lb/kV 8.6 kg/hp (11.7 kg/kW); speed in direct drive at 1,000 rp 30.6 mph, 49.2 km/h; consumption: 16.8 m/imp gal, m/US gal, 16.8 l x 100 km.

BRAKES servo (standard).

ELECTRICAL EQUIPMENT 3,500 W battery.

DIMENSIONS AND WEIGHT weight: Trans Am 3,490 1,583 kg - Formula 3,518 lb, 1,595 kg.

OPTIONALS 3.230 or 3.080 axle ratio.

220 hp power team

(not available in California).

See 115 hp power team, except for:

ENGINE 8 cylinders; 400 cu in, 6,555 cc (4.12 x 3.75 104.6 x 95.2 mm); compression ratio: 8.1:1; max pov (DIN): 220 hp (161.9 kW) at 4,000 rpm; max torque (DI 320 lb ft, 44.1 kg m (432.5 Nm) at 2,800 rpm; 33.6 h (24.7 kW/l); 5 crankshaft bearings; lubrication: 10 imp 12 US pt, 5.7 l; 1 Rochester M4MC downdraught 4-bar carburettor; dual exhaust system; cooling system: 30.6 pt, 36.8 US pt, 17.4 l.

PONTIAC Grand Le Mans Sedan

TRANSMISSION gears: 4, fully synchronized; ratios: I 2.430, II 1.610, III 1.230, IV 1, rev 2.350; lever: central; axle ratio: 3.230; width of rims: 7'' tyres: P225/70R x 15.

PERFORMANCE max speed: about 118 mph, 190 km/h; power-weight ratio: Trans Am 16.3 lb/hp (22.1 lb/kW), 7.4 kg/hp (10 kg/kW) - Formula 16.4 lb/hp (22.3 lb/kW), 7.4 kg/hp (10.1 kg/kW); speed in direct drive at 1,000 rpm: 28 mph, 45 m/h; consumption: 14.4 m/imp gal, 12 m/US gal, 19.6 l x 100 km.

BRAKES servo (standard).

ELECTRICAL EQUIPMENT 3,500 W battery.

DIMENSIONS AND WEIGHT weight: Trans Am 3,580 lb, 1,623 kg - Formula 3,608 lb, 1,636 kg.

OPTIONALS Turbo-Hydramatic automatic transmission not available.

Le Mans - Grand Le Mans - Grand Am Series

PRICES EX WORKS:

Le Mans Coupé	$ 4,608
Le Mans Sedan	$ 4,708
Le Mans Safari St. Wagon	$ 5,216
Grand Le Mans Coupé	$ 4,868
Grand Le Mans Sedan	$ 4,993
Grand Le Mans Safari St. Wagon	$ 5,560
Grand Am Coupé	$ 5,084
Grand Am Sedan	$ 5,209

For 135 engine add $ 195; for 150 hp engine add $ 255; for 155 hp engine add $ 255; for 165 hp engine add $ 320.

Power team:	Standard for:	Optional for:
115 hp	all	—
135 hp	—	all
150 hp	—	all
155 hp	—	1 to 6
165 hp	—	3,6

115 hp power team

ENGINE front, 4 stroke; 6 cylinders, Vee-slanted at 90°; 231 cu in, 3,785 cc (3.80 x 3.40 in, 96.5 x 86.4 mm); compression ratio: 8:1; max power (DIN): 115 hp (84.6 kW) at 3,800 rpm; max torque (DIN): 190 lb ft, 26.2 kg m (257 Nm) at 2,000 rpm; max engine rpm: 4,400; 30.4 hp/l (22.4 kW/l); cast iron block and head 4 crankshaft bearings; valves: overhead, in line, push-rods and rockers, hydraulic tappets; camshafts: 1, at centre of Vee; lubrication: gear pump, full flow filter, 8.3 imp pt, 9.9 US pt, 4.7 l; 1 Rochester 2ME downdraught twin barrel carburettor; cleaner air system; exhaust system with catalytic converter; fuel feed: mechanical pump; water-cooled, 27.6 imp pt, 33.2 US pt, 15.7 l.

TRANSMISSION driving wheels: rear; clutch: single dry plate; gearbox: mechanical (Turbo-Hydramatic transmission standard for st. wagons); gears: 3, fully synchronized; ratios: I 3.500, II 1.890, III 1, rev 3.500; lever: steering column; final drive: hypoid bevel; axle ratio: 2.930 - st. wagons 2.730; width of rims: 6''; tyres: P185/75R x 14 - st. wagons P195/75R x 14 - Grand Am P205/70R x 14.

PERFORMANCE max speed: about 93 mph, 149 km/h; power-weight ratio: Le Mans Sedan 26.4 lb/hp (36 lb/kW), 12 kg/hp (16.3 kg/kW) - Grand Le Mans Sedan 26.9 lb/hp 26.5 lb/hp, 12.2 kg/hp (16.5 kg/kW); speed in direct drive at 1,000 rpm: 27.4 mph, 44.1 km/h; consumption: 22.8 m/imp gal, 19 m/US gal, 12.4 l x 100 km.

CHASSIS perimeter; front suspension: independent, wishbones (lower trailing links), coil springs, anti-roll bar, telescopic dampers; rear: rigid axle, lower trailing radius arms, upper oblique torque arms, coil springs, telescopic dampers.

STEERING recirculating ball (variable ratio servo standard for Grand Am and st. wagons); turns lock to lock: 5.60 - Grand Am and st. wagons 3.30.

BRAKES front disc (diameter 11 in, 27.9 cm), front internal radial fins, rear drum, rear compensator (servo standard for st. wagons); swept area: total 307.73 sq in, 1,984 sq cm.

ELECTRICAL EQUIPMENT 12 V; 2,500 W battery; 42 A alternator; Delco-Remy transistorized ignition; 2 headlamps.

DIMENSIONS AND WEIGHT wheel base: 108.10 in, 274 cm; front tracks: 58.50 in, 149 cm; rear tracks: 57.80 in, 147 cm - st. wagons 58 in, 147 cm; length: 198.60 in, 504 cm - st. wagons 197.80 in, 502 cm; width: 72.40 in, 184 cm - st. wagons 72.60 in, 184 cm; height: coupés 53.50 in, 136 cm - sedans 54.40 in, 138 cm - st. wagons 54.40 in, 139 cm; ground clearance: 5.60 in, 14.2 cm - st. wagons 5.90 in, 15 cm; weight: Le Mans Coupé 3,037 lb, 1,377 kg - Sedan 3,042 lb, 1,379 kg - Safari 3,206 lb, 1,454 kg - Grand Le Mans Coupé 3,061 lb, 1,388 kg - Sedan 3,088 lb, 1,400 kg - Safari 3,239 lb, 1,469 kg - Grand Am Coupé 3,082 lb, 1,397

PONTIAC Grand Am Coupé

kg - Sedan 3,086 lb, 1,399 kg; fuel tank: 15.2 imp gal, 18.2 US gal, 69 l.

OPTIONALS limited slip differential; Turbo-Hydramatic automatic transmission with 3 ratios (I 2.740, II 1.570, III 1, rev 2.070), max ratio of converter at stall 2, possible manual selection, steering column lever, 2.410 or 3.230 axle ratio; 4-speed fully synchronized mechanical gearbox (I 3.500, II 2.480, III 1.660, IV 1, rev 3.500), steering column lever, 2.930 axle ratio; P205/70R x 14 tyres; tilt of steering wheel; power steering (except for Grand Am and st. wagons); servo brake (except for st. wagons); electric windows; speed control device; heated rear window; electric sunshine roof; air-conditioning; heavy-duty battery; heavy-duty cooling system.

135 hp power team

(not available in California).

See 115 hp power team, except for:

ENGINE 8 cylinders; 301 cu in, 4,932 cc (4 x 3 in, 101.6 x 76.2 mm); compression ratio: 8.1:1; max power (DIN): 135 hp (99.4 kW) at 3,800 rpm; max torque (DIN): 240 lb ft, 33.1 kg m (324.6 Nm) at 1,600 rpm; 27.4 hp/l (20.2 kW/l); 5 crankshaft bearings; 1 Rochester 17059160 downdraught twin barrel carburettor; cooling system 34.8 imp pt, 41.9 US pt, 19.8 l.

TRANSMISSION gearbox: Turbo-Hydramatic automatic trans-

PONTIAC Grand Le Mans Safari Station Wagon

mission (standard), hydraulic torque converter and planetary gears with 3 ratios, max ratio of converter at stall 2, possible manual selection; ratios: I 2.740, II 1.570, III 1, rev 2.070; lever: steering column; axle ratio: 2.140 - st. wagons 2.290.

PERFORMANCE max speed: about 103 mph, 165 km/h; power-weight ratio: Le Mans Sedan 23.6 lb/hp (32.1 lb/kW), 10.7 kg/hp (14.5 kg/kW) - Grand Le Mans Sedan 23.9 lb/hp (32.5 lb/kW), 10.9 kg/hp (14.7 kg/kW); speed in direct drive at 1,000 rpm: 27 mph, 43.4 km/h; consumption: 21.6 m/imp gal, 18 m/US gal, 13.1 l x 100 km.

ELECTRICAL EQUIPMENT 3,200 W battery; 63 A alternator.

DIMENSIONS AND WEIGHT weight: plus 145 lb, 66 kg - st.wagons plus 159 lb, 73 kg.

OPTIONALS 2.290 axle ratio (except for st. wagons); 4-speed fully synchronized mechanical gearbox not available.

150 hp power team

(not available in California).

See 115 hp power team, except for:

ENGINE 8 cylinders; 301 cu in, 4,392 cc (4 x 3 in, 101.6 x 76.2 mm); compression ratio: 8.1:1; max power (DIN): 150 hp (110.4 kW) at 4,000 rpm; max torque (DIN): 240 lb ft, 33.1 kg m (324.6 Nm) at 1,600 rpm; 30.4 hp/l (22.4 kW/l); 5 crankshaft bearings; 1 Rochester 17059271 downdraught 4-barrel carburettor; cooling system: 34.8 imp pt, 41.9 US pt, 19.8 l.

TRANSMISSION gearbox: Turbo-Hydramatic automatic transmission (standard), hydraulic torque converter and planetary gears with 3 ratios, max ratio of converter at stall 2, possible manual selection; ratios: I 2.740, II 1.570, III 1, rev 2.070; lever: steering column; axle ratio: 2.290.

PERFORMANCE max speed: about 106 mph, 170 km/h; power-weight ratio: Le Mans Sedan 21.5 lb/hp (29.3 lb/kW), 9.8 kg/hp (13.3 kg/kW) - Grand Le Mans Sedan 21.9 lb/hp (29.7 lb/kW), 9.9 kg/hp (13.5 kg/kW); speed in direct drive at 1,000 rpm: 26.4 mph, 42.5 km/h; consumption: 20.5 m/imp gal, 17 m/US gal, 13.8 l x 100 km.

ELECTRICAL EQUIPMENT 3,200 W battery; 63 A alternator.

DIMENSIONS AND WEIGHT weight: Le Mans and Grand Le Mans plus 190 lb, 86 kg - Grand Am 194 lb, 88 kg - st. wagons 154 lb, 70 kg.

OPTIONALS (except for st. wagons) 4-speed fully synchronized mechanical gearbox with 2.730 axle ratio.

155 hp power team

(for California only).

See 115 hp power team, except for:

ENGINE 8 cylinders; 305 cu in, 4,999 cc (3.74 x 3.48 in, 95 x 88.4 mm); compression ratio: 8.4:1; max power (DIN): 155 hp (114.1 kW) at 4,000 rpm; max torque (DIN): 225 lb ft, 31 kg m (304 Nm) at 2,400 rpm; 31 hp/l (22.8 kW/l);

155 HP POWER TEAM

5 crankshaft bearings; 1 Rochester M4MC downdraught 4-barrel carburettor; cooling system: 29.9 imp pt, 35.9 US pt, 17 l.

TRANSMISSION gearbox: Turbo-Hydramatic automatic transmission (standard), hydraulic torque converter and planetary gears with 3 ratios, max ratio of converter at stall 2, possible manual selection; ratios: I 2.740, II 1.570, III 1, rev 2.070; lever: steering column; axle ratio: 2.290 - st. wagons 2.410.

PERFORMANCE max speed: about 109 mph, 175 km/h; power-weight ratio: Le Mans Sedan 20.7 lb/hp (28.2 lb/kW), 9.4 kg/hp (12.8 kg/kW) - Grand Le Mans Sedan 21 lb/hp (28.6 lb/kW), 9.5 kg/hp (13 kg/kW); speed in direct drive at 1,000 rpm: 27.2 mph, 43.7 km/h; consumption: 19.2 m/imp gal, 16 m/US gal, 14.7 l x 100 km.

ELECTRICAL EQUIPMENT 3,200 W battery; 63 A alternator.

DIMENSIONS AND WEIGHT weight: plus 172 lb, 78 kg - st. wagons plus 189 lb, 86 kg.

OPTIONALS 2.730 axle ratio; 4-speed fully synchronized mechanical gearbox not available.

165 hp power team

See 115 hp power team, except for:

ENGINE 8 cylinders; 350 cu in, 5,736 cc (4 x 3.48 in, 101.6 x 88.4 mm); compression ratio: 8.2:1; max power (DIN): 165 hp (121.4 kW) at 3,800 rpm; max torque (DIN): 260 lb ft, 35.9 kg m (352.1 Nm) at 2,400 rpm; 28.8 hp/l (21.2 kW/l); 5 crankshaft bearings; 1 Rochester M4MC downdraught 4-barrel carburettor; cooling system: 29.9 imp pt, 35.9 US pt, 17 l.

TRANSMISSION gearbox: Turbo-Hydramatic automatic transmission (standard), hydraulic torque converter and planetary gears with 3 ratios, max ratio of converter at stall 2, possible manual selection; ratios: I 2.740, II 1.570, III 1, rev 2.070; lever: steering column; axle ratio: 2.730.

PERFORMANCE max speed: about 112 mph, 180 km/h; power-weight ratio: Le Mans Safari 20.7 lb/hp (28.2 lb/kW), 9.4 kg/hp (12.8 kg/kW) - Grand Le Mans Safari 20.9 lb/hp (28.5 lb/kW), 9.5 kg/hp (12.9 kg/kW); speed in direct drive at 1,000 rpm: 29.5 mph, 47.4 km/h; consumption: 19.2 m/imp gal, 16 m/US gal, 14.7 l x 100 km.

ELECTRICAL EQUIPMENT 3,200 W battery; 63 A alternator.

DIMENSIONS AND WEIGHT weight: plus 216 lb, 98 kg.

BODY estate car/st. wagon; 4 + 1 doors; folding rear seat.

OPTIONALS 4-speed fully synchronized mechanical gearbox not available.

Grand Prix Series

PRICES EX WORKS:

1 Hardtop Coupé	$ 5,113
2 LJ Hardtop Coupé	$ 6,192
3 SJ Hardtop Coupé	$ 6,438

For 135 hp engine add $ 195; for 150 hp or 155 hp engines add $ 225 (LJ add $ 60).

Power team:	Standard for:	Optional for:
115 hp	1	2
135 hp	2	1
150 hp	3	1,2
155 hp	—	all

115 hp power team

(not available in California).

ENGINE front, 4 stroke; 6 cylinders, Vee-slanted at 90°; 231 cu in, 3,785 cc (3.80 x 3.40 in, 96.5 x 86.4 mm); compression ratio: 8:1; max power (DIN): 115 hp (84.6 kW) at 3,800 rpm; max torque (DIN): 190 lb ft, 26.2 kg m (257 Nm) at 2,000 rpm; max engine rpm: 4,400; 30.4 hp/l (22.4 kW/l); cast iron block and head; 4 crankshaft bearings; valves: overhead, in line, push-rods and rockers, hydraulic tappets; camshafts: 1, at centre of Vee; lubrication: gear pump, full flow filter, 8.3 imp pt, 9.9 US pt, 4.7 l; 1 Rochester 2GE downdraught twin barrel carburettor; cleaner air system; exhaust system with catalytic converter; fuel feed: mechanical pump; water-cooled, 22.2 imp pt, 26.6 US pt, 12.6 l.

TRANSMISSION driving wheels: rear; clutch: single dry plate; gearbox: mechanical; gears: 3, fully synchronized; ratios: I 3.500, II 1.890, III 1, rev 3.500; lever: steering

column; final drive: hypoid bevel; axle ratio: 2.930; width of rims: 6''; tyres: P195/75R x 14.

PERFORMANCE max speed: about 96 mph, 154 km/h; power-weight ratio: Hardtop Coupé 26.7 lb/hp (36.4 lb/kW), 12.1 kg/hp (16.5 kg/kW) - LJ Hardtop Coupé 27.4 lb/hp (37.3 lb/kW), 12.4 kg/hp (16.9 kg/kW); speed in direct drive at 1,000 rpm: 28.3 mph, 45.6 km/h; consumption: 22.8 m/imp gal, 19 m/US gal, 12.4 l x 100 km.

CHASSIS perimeter; front suspension: independent, wishbones, coil springs, anti-roll bar, telescopic dampers; rear: rigid axle, lower trailing radius arms, upper oblique torque arms, coil springs, telescopic dampers.

STEERING recirculating ball (variable ratio servo standard on LJ); turns lock to lock: 3.30.

BRAKES front disc (diameter 10.50 in, 26.7 cm), front internal radial fins, rear drum, rear compensator.

ELECTRICAL EQUIPMENT 12 V; 2,500 W battery; 42 A alternator; Delco-Remy transistorized ignition; 4 headlamps.

DIMENSIONS AND WEIGHT wheel base 108.10 in, 275 cm; tracks: 58.50 in, 149 cm front, 57.80 in, 147 cm rear; length: 201.40 in, 512 cm; width: 72.70 in, 185 cm; height: 53.30 in, 135 cm; ground clearance 5.30 in, 13.5 cm; weight: Hardtop Coupé 3,076 lb, 1,395 kg - LJ Hardtop Coupé 3,154 lb, 1,430 kg; fuel tank: 15.2 imp gal, 18.2 US gal, 69 l.

BODY hardtop coupé; 2 doors; 6 seats, separate front seats with built-in headrests.

OPTIONALS limited slip differential; Turbo-Hydramatic automatic transmission with 3 ratios (I 2.520, II 1.520, III 1, rev 1.940), max ratio of converter at stall 2.3, possible manual selection, central lever, 2.730 or 3.230 axle ratio; P205/70R x 14 or P205/75R x 14 tyres; power steering; tilt of steering wheel; servo brake; heavy-duty battery; heavy-duty alternator; heavy-duty radiator; electric windows; automatic levelling control speed control device; heated rear window; electric sunshine roof; reclining backrests; air-conditioning; leather upholstery.

135 hp power team

(not available in California).

See 115 hp power team, except for:

ENGINE 8 cylinders; 301 cu in, 4,932 cc (4 x 3 in, 101.6 x 76.2 mm); compression ratio: 8.1:1; max power (DIN): 135 hp (99.4 kW) at 3,800 rpm; max torque (DIN): 240 lb ft, 33.1 kg m (324.6 Nm) at 1,600 rpm; 27.4 hp/l (20.2 kW/l); 5 crankshaft bearings; 1 Rochester M2MC downdraught twin barrel carburettor; cooling system: 34.8 imp pt, 41.9 US pt, 19.8 l.

TRANSMISSION gearbox: turbo-Hydramatic automatic transmission (standard), hydraulic torque converter and planetary gears with 3 ratios, max ratio of converter at stall 2, possible manual selection; ratios: I 2.520, II 1.520, III 1, rev 1.940; lever: central; axle ratio: 2.140.

PERFORMANCE max speed: about 106 mph, 170 km/h;

PONTIAC Grand Prix LJ Hardtop Coupé

power-weight ratio: Hardtop Coupé 23.6 lb/hp (32.1 lb/kW), 10.7 kg/hp (14.5 kg/kW) - LJ Hardtop Coupé 24 lb/hp (32.6 lb/kW), 10.9 kg/hp (14.8 kg/kW); speed in direct drive at 1,000 rpm: 27.8 mph, 44.7 km/h; consumption: 21.6 m/imp gal, 18 m/US gal, 13.1 l x 100 km.

BRAKES servo (standard).

ELECTRICAL EQUIPMENT 3,200 W battery.

DIMENSIONS AND WEIGHT weight: Hardtop Coupé 3,189 lb, 1,446 kg - LJ Hardtop Coupé 3,240 lb, 1,471 kg.

OPTIONALS 2.290 axle ratio.

150 hp power team

(not available in California).

See 115 hp power team, except for:

ENGINE 8 cylinders; 301 cu in, 4,932 cc (4 x 3 in, 101.6 x 76.2 mm); compression ratio: 8.1:1; max power (DIN): 150 hp (110.4 kW) at 4,000 rpm; max torque (DIN): 240 lb ft, 33.1 kg m (324.6 Nm) at 1,600 rpm; 30.4 hp/l (22.4 kW/l); 5 crankshaft bearings; 1 Rochester M4MC downdraught 4-barrel carburettor; cooling system: 34.8 imp pt, 41.9 US pt, 19.8 l.

TRANSMISSION gearbox: Turbo-Hydramatic automatic trans-

PONTIAC Grand Prix SJ Hardtop Coupé

ission (standard), hydraulic torque converter and plane-
ry gears with 3 ratios, max ratio of converter at stall 2.3,
ossible manual selection; ratios: I 2.740, II 1.570, III 1,
v 2.070; lever: central; axle ratio: 2.290.

PERFORMANCE max speed: about 109 mph, 175 km/h;
wer-weight ratio: SJ Hardtop Coupé 22.5 lb/hp (30.5
/kW), 10.2 kg/hp (13.8 kg/kW); speed in direct drive at
000 rpm: 27.2 mph, 43.7 km/h; consumption: 20.5 m/imp
al, 17 m/US gal, 13.8 l x 100 km.

RAKES servo (standard).

LECTRICAL EQUIPMENT 3,200 W battery.

IMENSIONS AND WEIGHT weight: Hardtop Coupé 3,155
, 1,431 kg - LJ Hardtop Coupé 3,312 lb, 1,502 kg - SJ
ardtop Coupé 3,368 lb, 1,527 kg.

OPTIONALS 2.560 axle ratio; 4-speed fully synchronized
echanical gearbox with 3.080 axle ratio.

155 hp power team

or California only).

ee 115 hp power team, except for:

NGINE 8 cylinders; 305 cu in, 4,999 cc (3.74 x 3.48 in, 95 x
.4 mm); compression ratio: 8.4:1; max power (DIN): 155

PONTIAC Bonneville Safari Station Wagon

---

hp (114.1 kW) at 4,000 rpm; max torque (DIN): 225 lb ft,
31 kg m (304 Nm) at 2,400 rpm; 31 hp/l (22.8 kW/l); 5
crankshaft bearings; 1 Rochester M4MC downdraught 4-
barrel carburettor; cooling system: 28.3 imp pt, 34 US pt,
16.1 l.

TRANSMISSION gearbox: Turbo-Hydramatic automatic transmission (standard), hydraulic torque converter and planetary
gears with 3 ratios, max ratio of converter at stall 2.3,
possible manual selection; ratios: I 2.740, II 1.570, III 1,
rev 2.070; lever: central; axle ratio: 2.290.

PERFORMANCE max speed: about 112 mph, 180 km/h; power-
weight ratio: Hardtop Coupé 20.6 lb/hp (27.9 lb/kW), 9.3
kg/hp (12.7 kg/kW) - LJ Hardtop Coupé 21.1 lb/hp (28.6
lb/kW), 9.6 kg/hp (13 kg/kW) - SJ Hardtop Coupé 21.5
lb/hp), 9.6 kg/hp (13 kg/kW) - SJ Hardtop Coupé 21.5 lb/hp
(29.1 lb/kW), 9.7 kg/hp (13.2 kg/kW); speed in direct drive
at 1,000 rpm: 28 mph, 45 km/h; consumption: 19.2 m/imp
gal, 16 m/US gal, 14.7 l x 100 km.

BRAKES servo (standard).

ELECTRICAL EQUIPMENT 3,200 W battery.

DIMENSIONS AND WEIGHT weight: Hardtop Coupé 3,188 lb,
1,446 kg - LJ Hardtop Coupé 3,268 lb, 1,482 kg - SJ Hardtop
Coupé 3,325 lb, 1,508 kg.

OPTIONALS 2.730 or 2.560 axle ratio.

Catalina - Bonneville - Bonneville Brougham Series

PRICES EX WORKS:

1 Catalina Coupé	$ 5,690
2 Catalina Sedan	$ 5,746
3 Catalina Safari St. Wagon	$ 6,273
4 Bonneville Coupé	$ 6,205
5 Bonneville Sedan	$ 6,330
6 Bonneville Safari St. Wagon	$ 6,632
7 Bonneville Brougham Coupé	$ 6,960
8 Bonneville Brougham Sedan	$ 7,149

For 130 hp engine add $ 195. For 150 hp engine add $ 60
(Catalina Coupé and Sedan add $ 255). For 155 hp or 160 hp
engines add $ 125 (Catalina Coupé and Sedan add $ 320).
For 175 hp engine add $ 195.

Power team:	Standard for:	Optional for:
115 hp	1,2	—
130 hp	4,5,7,8	1,2
135 hp	3,6	—
150 hp	—	all
155 hp	—	all
160 hp	—	all
175 hp	—	all

115 hp power team

ENGINE front, 4 stroke; 6 cylinders, Vee-slanted at 90°;
231 cu in, 3,785 cc (3.80 x 3.40 in, 96.5 x 86.4 mm); compression ratio: 8:1; max power (DIN): 115 hp (84.6 kW) at

---

3,800 rpm; max torque (DIN): 190 lb ft, 26.2 kg m (257
Nm) at 2,000 rpm; max engine rpm: 4,400; 30.4 hp/l (22.4
kW/l); cast iron block and head; 4 crankshaft bearings;
valves: overhead, in line, push-rods and rockers, hydraulic
tappets; camshafts: 1, at centre of Vee; lubrication: gear
pump, full flow filter, 8.3 imp pt, 9.9 US pt, 4.7 l; 1
Rochester 2GE downdraught twin barrel carburettor; cleaner
air system; exhaust system with catalytic converter; fuel
feed: mechanical pump; water-cooled, 22.2 imp pt, 26.6 US
pt, 12.6 l.

TRANSMISSION driving wheels: rear; gearbox: Turbo-Hydramatic automatic transmission, hydraulic torque converter
and planetary gears with 3 ratios, max ratio of converter at
stall 2, possible manual selection; ratios: I 2.520, II 1.520,
III 1, rev 1.940; lever: steering column; final drive: hypoid
bevel; axle ratio: 2.730; width of rims: 6''; tyres: FR78 x 15.

PERFORMANCE max speed: about 93 mph, 149 km/h;
power-weight ratio: Sedan 30.5 lb/hp (41.5 lb/kW), 13.8
kg/hp (18.8 kg/kW); speed in direct drive at 1,000 rpm: 23.3
mph, 37.5 km/h; consumption: 21.6 m/imp gal, 18 m/US
gal, 13.1 l x 100 km.

CHASSIS perimeter; front suspension: independent, wishbones, coil springs, anti-roll bar, telescopic dampers; rear:
rigid axle, lower trailing radius arms, upper oblique torque
arms, coil springs, telescopic dampers.

STEERING recirculating ball, variable ratio servo; turns
lock to lock. 3.30.

BRAKES front disc (diameter 11 in, 27.9 cm), front internal
radial fins, rear drum, servo; swept area: total 337.3 sq
in, 2,175 sq cm.

ELECTRICAL EQUIPMENT 12 V; 2,500 W battery; 42 A alternator; Delco-Remy transistorized ignition; 4 headlamps.

DIMENSIONS AND WEIGHT wheel base: 116 in, 295 cm;
tracks: 61.70 in, 157 cm front, 60.70 in, 154 cm rear; length:
214.30 in, 544 cm; width: 76.40 in, 194 cm; height: Coupé
54.20 in, 138 cm - Sedan 54.90 in, 139 cm; ground clearance: 5.60 in, 14.2 cm; weight: Coupé 3,475 lb, 1,577 kg -
Sedan 3,507 lb, 1,591 kg; turning circle: 41.6 ft, 12.7 m;
fuel tank: 17.2 imp gal, 20.6 US gal, 78 l.

OPTIONALS limited slip differential; 3.230 axle ratio; GR78 x
15 or HR78 x 15 tyres with 6'' wide rims; GR70 x 15 tyres
with 7'' wide rims; tilt of steering wheel; automatic levelling control; electric windows; reclining backrests; speed
control device; heated rear window; heavy-duty battery;
heavy-duty alternator; air-conditioning.

130 hp power team

(not available in California).

See 115 hp power team, except for:

ENGINE 8 cylinders; 301 cu in, 4,932 cc (4 x 3 in, 101.6 x
76.2 mm); compression ratio: 8.1:1; max power (DIN): 130
hp (95.7 kW) at 3,200 rpm; max torque (DIN): 245 lb ft,
33.8 kg m (331.5 Nm) at 2,000 rpm; max engine rpm: 4,000;
26.4 hp/l (19.4 kW/l); 5 crankshaft bearings; lubricating
system: 10 imp pt, 12 US pt, 5.7 l; 1 Rochester M2MC
downdraught twin barrel carburettor; cooling system: 34.8
imp pt, 41.9 US pt, 19.8 l.

TRANSMISSION axle ratio: 2.290.

PERFORMANCE max speed: about 99 mph, 160 km/h; power-
weight ratio: Catalina Sedan 27.9 lb/hp (37.9 lb/kW), 12.6
kg/hp (17.2 kg/kW) - Bonneville Sedan 28.2 lb/hp (38.4
lb/kW), 12.8 kg/hp (17.4 kg/kW) - Bonneville Brougham
Sedan 28.8 lb/hp (39.1 lb/kW), 13 kg/hp (17.7 kg/kW);
speed in direct drive at 1,000 rpm: 25 mph, 40 km/h; consumption: 20.5 m/imp gal, 17 m/US gal, 13.8 l x 100 km.

ELECTRICAL EQUIPMENT 3,200 W battery.

DIMENSIONS AND WEIGHT weight: Catalina Coupé 3,593
lb, 1,629 kg - Sedan 3,625 lb, 1,644 kg - Bonneville Coupé
3,616 lb, 1,640 kg - Sedan 3,672 lb, 1,665 kg - Bonneville
Brougham Coupé 3,729 lb, 1,691 kg - Sedan 3,740 lb, 1,696 kg.

OPTIONALS 2.410 axle ratio.

135 hp power team

(not available in California).

See 115 hp power team, except for:

ENGINE 8 cylinders; 301 cu in, 4,932 cc (4 x 3 in, 101.6 x
76.2 mm); compression ratio: 8.1:1; max power (DIN):
135 hp (99.4 kW) at 3,800 rpm; max torque (DIN): 240 lb
ft, 33.1 kg m (324.6 Nm) at 1,600 rpm; 27.4 hp/l (20.2 kW/l);
5 crankshaft bearings; lubricating system: 10 imp pt, 12
US pt, 5.7 l; 1 Rochester M2MC downdraught twin barrel
carburettor; cooling system: 34.8 imp pt, 41.9 US pt, 19.8 l.

TRANSMISSION axle ratio: 2.560; tyres: HR78 x 15.

PONTIAC Bonneville Sedan

135 HP POWER TEAM

PERFORMANCE max speed: about 99 mph, 160 km/h; power-weight ratio: Catalina Safari 29.6 lb/hp (40.2 lb/kW), 13.4 kg/hp (18.2 kg/kW) - Bonneville Safari 29.8 lb/hp (40.5 lb/kW), 13.5 kg/hp (18.4 kg/kW); speed in direct drive at 1,000 rpm: 25 mph, 40 km/h; consumption: 18 m/imp gal, 15 m/US gal, 15.7 l x 100 km.

BRAKES swept area: total 362.58 sq in, 2,339 sq cm.

ELECTRICAL EQUIPMENT 3,200 W battery.

DIMENSIONS AND WEIGHT tracks: 62 in, 158 cm front, 64.10 in, 163 cm rear; length: 215.10 in, 546 cm; width: 79.90 in, 203 cm; height: 57.30 in, 146 cm; ground clearance: 6 in, 15.2 cm; weight: Catalina Safari St. Wagon 3,997 lb, 1,813 kg - Bonneville Safari St. Wagon 4,023 lb, 1,825 kg; turning circle: 42.3 ft, 12.9 m; fuel tank: 18.3 imp gal, 22 US gal, 83 l.

BODY estate car/st. wagon; 4 + 1 doors; 6 seats; folding rear seat.

150 hp power team

(not available in California).

See 115 hp power team, except for:

ENGINE 8 cylinders; 301 cu in, 4,932 cc (4 x 3 in, 101.6 x 76.2 mm); compression ratio: 8.1:1; max power (DIN): 150 hp (110.4 kW) at 4,000 rpm; max torque (DIN): 240 lb ft, 33.1 kg m (324.6 Nm) at 1,600 rpm; 30.4 hp/l (22.4 kW/l); 5 crankshaft bearings; lubricating system: 10 imp pt, 12 US pt, 5.7 l; 1 Rochester M4MC downdraught 4-barrel carburettor; cooling system: 34.8 imp pt, 41.9 US pt, 19.8 l.

TRANSMISSION axle ratio: 2.560 - st. wagons 2.730; tyres: st. wagons HR78 x 15.

PERFORMANCE max speed: about 103 mph, 165 km/h; power-weight ratio: Catalina Sedan 24.2 lb/hp (32.8 lb/kW), 11 kg/hp (14.9 kg/kW) - Bonneville Sedan 24.5 lb/hp (33.3 lb/kW), 11.1 kg/hp (15.1 kg/kW) - Bonneville Brougham Sedam 24.9 lb/hp (33.9 lb/kW), 11.3 kg/hp (15.4 kg/kW); speed in direct drive at 1,000 rpm: 25.6 mph, 41.2 km/h; consumption: 19.2 m/imp gal, 16 m/US gal, 14.7 l x 100 km.

BRAKES swept area: st. wagons total 362.58 sq in, 2,339 sq cm.

ELECTRICAL EQUIPMENT 3,200 W battery.

DIMENSIONS AND WEIGHT tracks: st. wagons 62 in, 158 cm front, 64.10 in, 163 cm rear; length: st. wagons 215.10 in, 546 cm; width: st. wagons 79.90 in, 203 cm; height: st. wagons 57.30 in, 146 cm; ground clearance: st. wagons 6 in, 15.2 cm; weight: Catalina Coupé 3,593 lb, 1,631 kg - Sedan 3,625 lb, 1,645 kg - Safari St. Wagon 3,997 lb, 1,813 kg - Bonneville Coupé 3,616 lb, 1,640 kg - Sedan 3,672 lb, 1,665 kg - Safari St. Wagon 4,023 lb, 1,825 kg - Bonneville Brougham Coupé 3,729 lb, 1,691 kg - Sedan 3,740 lb, 1,696 kg; turning circle: st. wagons 42.3 ft, 12.9 m; fuel tank: st. wagons 18.3 imp gal, 22 US gal, 83 l.

155 hp power team

(not available in California).

See 115 hp power team, except for:

ENGINE 8 cylinders; 350 cu in, 5,736 cc (3.80 x 3.85 in, 96.5 x 97.8 mm); max power (DIN): 155 hp (114.1 kW) at 3,400 rpm; max torque (DIN): 280 lb ft, 38.6 kg m (378.6 Nm) at 1,800 rpm; max engine rpm: 4,200; 27 hp/l (19.9 kW/l); 5 crankshaft bearings; 1 Rochester M4MC downdraught 4-barrel carburettor; cooling system: 25.2 imp pt, 30.2 US pt, 14.3 l.

TRANSMISSION axle ratio: 2.410 - st. wagons 2.730; tyres: st. wagons HR78 x 15.

PERFORMANCE max speed: about 106 mph, 170 km/h; power-weight ratio: Catalina Sedan 24 lb/hp (32.7 lb/kW), 10.9 kg/hp (14.8 kg/kW) - Bonneville Sedan 24.3 lb/hp (33 lb/kW), 11 kg/hp (15 kg/kW) - Bonneville Brougham Sedan 24.7 lb/hp (33.6 lb/kW), 11.2 kg/hp (15.2 kg/kW); speed in direct drive at 1,000 rpm: 25.2 mph, 40.5 km/h; consumption: 18 m/imp gal, 15 m/US gal, 15.7 l x 100 km.

BRAKES swept area: st. wagons total 362.58 sq in, 2,339 sq cm.

ELECTRICAL EQUIPMENT 3,200 W battery.

DIMENSIONS AND WEIGHT (see 150 hp engine) weight: plus 96 lb, 44 kg - Catalina Coupé and Sedan plus 101 lb, 46 kg.

OPTIONALS 2.730 or 3.080 axle ratio (st. wagons 3.080).

REPLICARS Phaeton

160 hp power team

(for California only).

See 115 hp power team, except for:

ENGINE 8 cylinders; 350 cu in, 5,736 cc (4.06 x 3.38 in, 103.8 x 85.8 mm); compression ratio: 7.9:1; max power (DIN): 160 hp (117.8 kW) at 3,600 rpm; max torque (DIN): 270 lb ft, 37.2 kg m (364.8 Nm) at 2,000 rpm; 27.9 hp/l (20.5 kW/l); 5 crankshaft bearings; 1 Rochester M4MC downdraught 4-barrel carburettor; cooling system: 25.2 imp pt, 30.2 US pt, 14.3 l.

TRANSMISSION axle ratio: 2.410 - st. wagons 2.730; tyres: st. wagons HR78 x 15.

PERFORMANCE max speed: about 106 mph, 170 km/h; power-weight ratio: Catalina Sedan 23 lb/hp (31.2 lb/kW), 10.4 kg/hp (14.2 kg/kW) - Bonneville Sedan 23.3 lb/hp (31.7 lb/kW), 10.6 kg/hp (14.4 kg/kW) - Bonneville Brougham Sedan 23.7 lb/hp (32.2 lb/kW), 10.8 kg/hp (14.6 kg/kW); speed in direct drive at 1,000 rpm: 25.2 mph, 40.5 km/h; consumption: 16.8 m/imp gal, 14 m/US gal, 16.8 l x 100 km.

BRAKES swept area: st. wagons total 362.58 sq in, 2,339 sq cm.

ELECTRICAL EQUIPMENT 3,200 W battery.

DIMENSIONS AND WEIGHT (see 150 hp power team) weight: plus 53 lb, 24 kg - Bonneville plus 57 lb, 26 kg.

175 hp power team

(for California only).

See 115 hp power team, except for:

ENGINE 8 cylinders; 403 cu in, 6.604 cc (4.35 x 3.38 in, 110.4 x 85.8 mm); compression ratio: 7.9:1; max power (DIN): 175 hp (128.8 kW) at 3,600 rpm; max torque (DIN): 310 lb ft, 42.8 kg m (419.7 Nm) at 2,000 rpm; 26.5 hp/l (19.5 kW/l); 5 crankshaft bearings; 1 Rochester M4MC downdraught 4-barrel carburettor; cooling system: 27.1 imp pt, 32.6 US pt, 15.4 l.

TRANSMISSION axle ratio: 2.410 - st. wagons 2.560; tyres: st. wagons HR78 x 15.

PERFORMANCE max speed: about 112 mph, 180 km/h; power-weight ratio: Catalina Sedan 21.3 lb/hp (28.9 lb/kW), 9.6 kg/hp (13.1 kg/kW) - Bonneville Sedan 21.5 lb/hp (29.2 lb/kW), 9.8 kg/hp (13.3 kg/kW) - Bonneville Brougham Sedan 21.9 lb/hp (29.8 lb/kW), 9.9 kg/hp (13.5 kg/kW); speed in direct drive at 1,000 rpm: 31.1 mph, 50 km/h; consumption: 16.8 m/imp gal, 14 m/US gal, 16.8 l x 100 km.

BRAKES swept area: st. wagons total 362.58 sq in, 2,339 sq cm.

ELECTRICAL EQUIPMENT 3,500 W battery.

DIMENSIONS AND WEIGHT (see 150 hp power team) weight: plus 95 lb, 43 kg.

OPTIONALS 3.230 axle ratio (st. wagons 3.230 or 2.080 axle ratio).

Phaeton/Roadster

PRICES EX WORKS: Phaeton $ 14,750
Roadster $ 14,750

ENGINE Ford, front, 4 stroke; 8 cylinders; 302 cu in, 4,950 cc (4 x 3 in, 101.6 x 76.2 mm); compression ratio: 8.4:1; max power (DIN): 135 hp (99.4 kW) at 3,600 rpm; max torque (DIN): 240 lb ft, 33.1 kg m (324.6 Nm) at 2,000 rpm; max engine rpm: 4,000; 27.3 hp/l (20.1 kW/l); cast iron block and head; 5 crankshaft bearings; valves: overhead, in line, push-rods and rockers, hydraulic tappets; camshafts: 1, at centre of Vee; lubrication: 8.3 imp pt, 9.9 US pt, 4.7 l; 1 Ford 2150 D9BE-YB downdraught twin barrel carburettor; cleaner air system; exhaust system with catalytic converter; fuel feed: mechanical pump; water-cooled, 23.1 imp pt, 27.7 US pt, 13.1 l.

TRANSMISSION driving wheels: rear; gearbox: SelectShift automatic transmission, hydraulic torque converter and planetary gears with 3 ratios, max ratio of converter at stall 2, possible manual selection; ratios: I 2.460, II 1.460, III 1, rev 2.180; lever: steering column; final drive: hypoid bevel; axle ratio: 2.260; width of rims: 5''; tyres: E78 x 14.

PERFORMANCE max speed: about 106 mph, 170 km/h; power-weight ratio: 18.5 lb/hp (25.1 lb/kW), 8.4 kg/hp (11.4 kg/kW); speed in direct drive at 1,000 rpm: 29.3 mph, 47.2 km/h; consumption: 18 m/imp gal, 15 m/US gal, 15.7 l x 100 km.

CHASSIS box-type ladder frame with cross members; front suspension: independent, by McPherson, wishbones (lower control arms), coil springs/telescopic damper struts, anti-roll bar; rear: rigid axle, lower trailing radius arms, upper oblique torque arms, coil springs, telescopic dampers.

STEERING rack-and-pinion, tilt of steering wheel, variable ratio servo; turns lock to lock: 3.05.

BRAKES front disc (diameter 10.06 in, 25.4 cm), front internal radial fins, rear compensator, rear drum, servo; swept area: front 176.6 sq in, 1,140 sq cm, rear 98.9 sq in, 638 sq cm, total 275.5 sq in, 1,778 sq cm.

ELECTRICAL EQUIPMENT 12 V; 36 Ah battery; 40 A alternator; Motorcraft transistorized ignition; 2 headlamps.

DIMENSIONS AND WEIGHT wheel base: 102 in, 259 cm; tracks: 65.50 in, 166 cm front, 65.50 in, 166 cm rear; length: 160 in, 406 cm; width: 65 in, 165 cm; height: 54.50 in, 138 cm; ground clearance: 7 in, 17.8 cm; weight: 2,500 lb, 1,134 kg; weight distribution: 60% front, 40% rear; fuel tank: 10.6 imp gal, 12.6 US gal, 48 l.

BODY in plastic material; 2 doors; 4 seats, separate front seats; tinted glass; air-conditioning; wire wheels.

OPTIONALS metallic spray.

6.6 S

PRICE EX WORKS: $ 50,000

ENGINE Lincoln-Mercury, front, 4 stroke; 8 cylinders; 400 cu in, 6,555 cc (4 x 4 in, 101.6 x 101.6 mm); compression ratio: 8:1; max power (DIN): 168 hp (123.6 kW) at 4,000 rpm; max engine rpm: 4,400; 25.6 hp/l (18.9 kW/l); cast iron block and head; 5 crankshaft bearings; valves: overhead, in line, push-rods and rockers, hydraulic tappets; camshafts: 1, at centre of Vee; lubrication: rotary pump, full flow filter, 8.3 imp pt, 9.9 US pt, 4.7 l; 1 downdraught 4-barrel carburettor; fuel feed: mechanical pump; water-cooled, 34.1 imp pt, 41 US pt, 19.4 l, electric thermostatic fan.

TRANSMISSION driving wheels: rear; gearbox: SelectShift automatic transmission, hydraulic torque converter and planetary gears with 3 ratios, max ratio of converter at stall 2, possible manual selection; ratios: I 2.460, II 1.460, III 1, rev 2.180; lever: central; final drive: hypoid bevel; axle ratio: 3.000; width of rims: 6''; tyres: GR70 x 15.

PERFORMANCE max speed: about 125 mph, 201 km/h; power-weight ratio: 18.1 lb/hp (24.6 lb/kW), 8.2 kg/hp (11.2 kg/kW); acceleration: 0-50 mph (0-80 km/h) 7.2 sec; speed in direct drive at 1,000 rpm: 31.1 mph, 50 km/h; consumption: 19.2 m/imp gal, 16 m/US gal, 14.7 l x 100 km.

CHASSIS box-type ladder frame; front suspension: independent, wishbones, coil springs, anti-roll bar, 4 telescopic dampers; rear: rigid axle, lower trailing radius arms, upper oblique torque arms, coil springs, 4 telescopic dampers.

SCEPTRE 6.6 S

STUTZ Blackhawk

STEERING recirculating ball, servo; turns lock to lock: 3.90.

BRAKES front disc, rear drum, servo.

ELECTRICAL EQUIPMENT 12 V; 77 Ah battery; 770 W alternator; Motorcraft transistorized ignition; 2 headlamps.

DIMENSIONS AND WEIGHT wheel base: 118.40 in, 301 cm; tracks: 65 in, 165 cm front, 65 in, 165 cm rear; length: 188.50 in, 479 cm; width: 74.50 in, 189 cm; height: 54 in, 137 cm; ground clearance: 6. in, 15.2 cm; weight: 3,045 lb, 1,381 kg; turning circle: 31.2 ft, 9.5 m; fuel tank: 16.3 imp gal, 19.5 US gal, 74 l.

BODY roadster in plastic material; 2 separate front seats; leather upholstery; automatic speed control; wire wheels; air-conditioning.

OPTIONALS mouton lambswool overlay; halogen headlamps; tonneau cover; hardtop.

STUTZ   USA

IV Porte - Blackhaw K VI - Bearcat

PRICES EX WORKS:
IV Porte 4-dr Sedan	$ 69,500
Blackhawk VI 2-dr Coupé	$ 69,500
Bearcat 2-dr Convertible	$ 107,000

ENGINE front, 4 stroke; V8 cylinders; 403 cu in, 6,605 cc (4.35 x 3.38 in, 110.5 x 85.8 mm); compression ratio: 7.9:1; max power (DIN): 185 hp (136.2 kW) at 3,600 rpm; max torque (DIN): 320 lb ft, 44.1 kg m (432.5 Nm) at 2,000 rpm; max engine rpm: 3,800; 28 hp/l (20.6 kW/l); cast iron block and head; 5 crankshaft bearings; valves: overhead, in line, push-rods and rockers, hydraulic tappets; camshafts: 1, at centre of Vee; lubrication: gear pump, 8.3 imp pt, 9.9 US pt, 4.7 l; 1 4-barrel carburettor; fuel feed: mechanical pump; water-cooled, 31.7 imp pt, 38.1 US pt, 18 l.

TRANSMISSION driving wheels: rear; gearbox: Turbo-Hydramatic automatic transmission, hydraulic torque converter and planetary gears with 3 ratios.

PERFORMANCE power-weight ratio: sedan 24.3 lb/hp (33.1 lb/kW), 11 kg/hp (15 kg/kW).

CHASSIS box-type perimeter frame; front suspension: independent, wishbones, coil springs, anti-roll bar, adjustable telescopic dampers; rear: rigid axle, lower trailing radius arms, upper oblique arms, coil springs, adjustable telescopic dampers.

STEERING recirculating ball, adjustable steering wheel, servo.

BRAKES front disc, rear drum.

ELECTRICAL EQUIPMENT 12 V; alternator; Delco-Remy distributor; electronic ignition; 2 headlamps.

DIMENSIONS AND WEIGHT wheel base: 116 in, 295 cm; tracks: 61.60 in, 156 cm front, 61.10 in, 155 cm rear; length: 227 in, 577 cm - sedan 224 in, 569 cm; width: 79 in, 201 cm; height: 54 in, 137 cm; weight: sedan 4,500 lb, 2,041 kg - coupé 4,450 lb, 2,018 kg - convertible 4,550 lb, 2,063 kg; fuel tank: 20.9 imp gal, 25 US gal, 95 l.

BODY 5-6 seats, bench or separate front seats.

OPTIONALS air-conditioning; tinted glass; electric sun roof (except for convertible); electric windows; electrically-controlled seats; leather upholstery.

STUTZ Bearcat 2-dr Convertible

TOTAL REPLICA   USA

Ford « B » Roadster

PRICE EX WORKS: $ 19,500

ENGINE Chevrolet, front, 4 stroke; V8 cylinders; 350 cu in, 5,736 cc (4 x 3.48 in, 101.6 x 88.3 mm); compression ratio: 8:1; max power (DIN): 250 hp (184 kW); 43.6 hp/l (32.1 kW/l); cast iron block and head; 5 crankshaft bearings; valves: overhead, in line, push-rods and rockers, hydraulic tappets; camshafts: 1, at centre of Vee; lubrication: gear pump, full flow filter, 8.3 imp pt, 10 US pt, 4.7 l; 1 Holley 450 CFM 4-barrel carburettor; fuel feed: mechanical pump; water-cooled, 19.9 imp pt, 24 US pt, 11.3 l.

TRANSMISSION driving wheels: rear; gearbox: Turbo-Hydramatic automatic transmission, hydraulic torque converter and planetary gears with 3 ratios + reverse; lever: central; final drive: hypoid bevel.

TOTAL REPLICA Ford « B » Roadster

FORD « B » ROADSTER

PERFORMANCE max speed: about 100 mph, 161 km/h; power-weight ratio: 11.5 lb/hp, (15.4 lb/kW), 5.2 kg/hp (7 kg/kW); consumption: 23.9 m/imp gal, 20 m/US gal, 11.8 l x 100 km.

CHASSIS perimeter box-type with front and rear cross members; front suspension: rigid axle, semi-elliptic leafsprings, telescopic dampers; rear: rigid axle, lower trailing radius arms, upper oblique torque arms, coil springs, telescopic dampers.

STEERING recirculating ball.

BRAKES front disc, rear drum, twin master cylinder.

ELECTRICAL EQUIPMENT 12 V; alternator; Delco-Remy high energy ignition system; 2 headlamps.

DIMENSIONS AND WEIGHT wheel base: 106 in, 269 cm; length: 186 in, 472 cm; width: 68 in, 173 cm; height: 64.50 in, 164 cm; ground clearance: 5.50 in, 14 cm; weight: 2,850 lb, 1,292 kg; fuel tank: 9,9 imp gal, 12 US gal, 45 l.

BODY roadster, in fibreglass material; 2 doors; 2 + 2 seats in rumble seat, bench front seats; chrome windshield frame with tinted glass and stainless posts; heater; luggage rack with matching chrome bumpers; wire wheels.

OPTIONALS rear mounted spare tyre without luggage rack; side curtains.

VOLKSWAGEN USA

Rabbit Series

PRICES EX WORKS:

3-dr Hatchback	$ 4,499
3-dr Custom	$ 4,899
5-dr Custom	$ 5,039
3-dr De Luxe	$ 5,349
5-dr De Luxe	$ 5,489

71 hp power team

ENGINE front, transverse, slanted 15° to front, 4 stroke; 4 cylinders, vertical, in line; 88.9 cu in, 1,457 cc (3.13 x 2.89 in, 79.5 x 73.4 mm); compression ratio: 8:1; max power (DIN): 71 hp (52.3 kW) at 5,800 rpm; max torque (DIN): 73 lb ft, 10.1 kg m (102.2 Nm) at 3,500 rpm; max engine rpm: 6,000; 48.7 hp/l (35.9 kW/l); cast iron block, light alloy head; 5 crankshaft bearings; valves: overhead, in line, thimble tappets; camshafts: 1, overhead, cogged belt; lubrication: gear pump, full flow filter, 5.3 imp pt, 6.3 US pt, 3 l; CIS injection; liquid-cooled, expansion tank, 10.9 imp pt, 13.1 US pt, 6.2 l, electric thermostatic fan.

TRANSMISSION driving wheels: front; clutch: single dry plate, hydraulically controlled; gearbox: mechanical; gears: 4, fully synchronized; ratios: I 3.450, II 1.940, III 1.370, IV 0.970, rev 3.170; lever: central; final drive: spiral bevel; axle ratio: 3.900; width of rims: 4.5''; tyres: 155 SR x 13.

PERFORMANCE max speed: 93 mph, 149 km/h; power-weight ratio: 3-dr models 25 lb/hp, (34 lb/kW), 1.4 kg/hp (15.4 kg/kW); carrying capacity: 3-dr models 992 lb, 450 kg; consumption: 30.1 m/imp gal, 25 m/US gal, 9.4 l x 100 km.

CHASSIS integral; front suspension: independent, by McPherson, lower wishbones, coil springs/telescopic damper struts; rear: independent, swinging longitudinal trailing arms linked by a T-section cross-beam, coil springs/telescopic damper struts.

STEERING rack-and-pinion; turns lock to lock: 3.85.

BRAKES front disc, rear drum, 2 X circuits.

ELECTRICAL EQUIPMENT 12 V; 45 Ah battery; 36 A alternator; Bosch distributor; 2 headlamps.

DIMENSIONS AND WEIGHT wheel base: 94.49 in, 240 cm; tracks: 54.72 in, 139 cm front, 53.46 in, 136 cm rear; length: 155.3 in, 394 cm; width: 63.39 in, 161 cm; height: 55.51 in, 141 cm; ground clearance: 4.92 in, 12.5 cm; weight: 3-dr models 1,779 lb, 807 kg; turning circle: 33.8 ft, 10.3 m; fuel tank: 8.8 imp gal, 10.6 US gal, 40 l.

BODY saloon/sedan; 5 seats, separate front seats, built-in headrests; folding rear seats; heated rear window.

PRACTICAL INSTRUCTIONS fuel: 100 oct petrol; oil: engine 5.3 imp pt, 6.3 US pt, 3 l, SAE 20W-30, change every 4,700 miles, 7,500 km - gearbox and final drive 3.2 imp pt, 3.8 US pt, 1.8 l, SAE 80 or 90, change every 12,400 miles, 20,000 km; greasing: none; tyre pressure: front 26 psi, 1.8 atm, rear 26 psi, 1.8 atm.

OPTIONALS 5-speed mechanical gearbox (V 0.760) with 4.170 axle ratio; automatic transmission, hydraulic torque converter and planetary gears with 3 ratios (I 2.550, II 1.450, III 1, rev 2.460), max ratio of converter at stall 2.44, possible manual selection, 3.760 axle ratio; 70 hp engine only for California.

VOLKSWAGEN MEXICO

1200 L

ENGINE rear, 4 stroke; 4 cylinders, horizontally opposed; 72.7 cu in, 1,192 cc (3.03 x 2.52 in, 77 x 64 mm); compression ratio: 7.3:1; max power (DIN): 34 hp (25 kW) at 3,800 rpm; max torque (DIN): 55 lb ft, 7.6 kg m (74.6 Nm) at 1,700 rpm; max engine rpm: 4,500; 28.5 hp/l (21 kW/l); block with cast iron liners and light alloy fins, light alloy head; 4 crankshaft bearings; valves: overhead, push-rods and rockers; camshafts: 1, central, lower; lubrication: gear pump, filter in sump, oil cooler, 4.4 imp pt, 5.3 US pt, 2.5 l; 1 Solex 30 PICT downdraught single barrel carburettor; fuel feed: mechanical pump; air-cooled.

TRANSMISSION driving wheels: rear; clutch: single dry plate; gearbox: mechanical; gears: 4, fully synchronized; ratios: I 3.780, II 2.060, III 1.260, IV 0.890, rev 4.010; lever: central; final drive: spiral bevel; axle ratio: 4.375; width of rims: 4.5''; tyres: 155 SR x 15.

PERFORMANCE max speeds: (I) 18 mph, 31 km/h; (II) 35 mph, 57 km/h; (III) 58 mph, 94 km/h; (IV) 71 mph, 115 km/h; power-weight ratio: 50.6 lb/hp (68.8 lb/kW), 22.9 kg/hp (31.2 kg/kW); carrying capacity: 838 lb, 380 kg; acceleration: standing ¼ mile 23 sec, 0-50 mph (0-80 km/h) 18 sec; speed in top at 1,000 rpm: 18.6 mph, 30 km/h; consumption: 37.7 m/imp gal, 31.4 m/US gal, 7.5 l x 100 km.

CHASSIS backbone platform; front suspension: independent, twin swinging longitudinal trailing arms, transverse laminated torsion bars, anti-roll bar, telescopic dampers; rear: independent, swinging semi-axles, swinging longitudinal trailing arms, transverse torsion bars, telescopic dampers.

STEERING worm and roller, telescopic damper; turns lock to lock: 2.60.

BRAKES drum, dual circuit; lining area: total 111 sq in 716 sq cm.

ELECTRICAL EQUIPMENT 12 V; 36 Ah battery; 270 W dynamo; Bosch distributor; 2 headlamps.

DIMENSIONS AND WEIGHT wheel base: 94.49 in, 240 cm; tracks: 51.57 in, 131 cm front, 53.15 in, 135 cm rear; length: 159.84 in, 406 cm; width: 61.02 in, 155 cm

VOLKSWAGEN Rabbit 3-dr De Luxe

VOLKSWAGEN 1200 L

FIAT 600 S

eight: 59.06 in, 150 cm; ground clearance: 5.90 in, 15 m; weight: 1,720 lb, 780 kg; weight distribution: 43% summer), change every 3,100 miles, 5,000 km - gearbox 1 m; fuel tank: 8.8 imp gal, 10.6 US gal, 40 l.

ODY saloon/sedan; 2 doors; 5 seats, separate front seats, djustable backrests.

RACTICAL INSTRUCTIONS fuel: 87 oct petrol; oil: engine .4 imp pt, 5.3 US pt, 2.5 l, SAE 10W-20 (winter) 20W-30 nd final drive 5.3 imp pt, 6.3 US pt, 3 l, SAE 90 change very 31,000 miles, 50,000 km; greasing: every 6,200 iles, 10,000 km, 4 points; sparking plug: 175°; tappet learances: inlet 0.004 in, 0.10 mm, exhaust 0.004 in, 0.10 nm; valve timing: 6° 35°5' 42°5' 3°; tyre pressure: front 6 psi, 1.1 atm, rear 24 psi, 1.7 atm.

IAT   URUGUAY

600 S

RICE EX WORKS: **47,500 pesos**

NGINE rear, 4 stroke; 4 cylinders, vertical, in line; 51.4 u in, 843 cc (2.56 x 2.50 in, 65 x 63.5 mm); compression

ratio: 7.4:1; max power (DIN): 32 hp (24 kW) at 4,800 rpm; 37.9 hp/l (28.5 kW/l); cast iron block, light alloy head; 3 crankshaft bearings; valves: overhead, in line, push-rods and rockers; camshafts: 1, side; lubrication: gear pump, full flow filter (cartridge), 6.5 imp pt, 7.8 US pt, 3.7 l; 1 Galileo 285 CP 10 or Bressel 285 CP 10 downdraught single barrel carburettor; fuel feed: mechanical pump; sealed circuit cooling liquid, 7.9 imp pt, 9.5 US pt, 4.5 l.

TRANSMISSION driving wheels: rear; clutch: single dry plate; gearbox: mechanical; gears: 4 fully synchronized; ratios: I 3.385, II 2,055, III 1.333, IV 0.896, rev 4.275; lever: central; final drive: spiral bevel; axle ratio: 4.875; width of rims: 4''; tyres: 5.20 x 12.

PERFORMANCE max speeds: (I) 19 mph, 30 km/h; (II) 28 mph, 45 km/h; (III) 43 mph, 70 km/h; (IV) 68 mph, 110 km/h; power-weight ratio: 43 lb/hp (57.4 lb/kW), 19.5 kg/hp (26 kg/kW); carrying capacity: 706 lb, 320 kg; acceleration: standing 1/4 mile 26.7 sec, 0-50 mph (0-80 km/h) 26 sec; speed in top at 1,000 rpm: 14.1 mph, 22.7 km/h; consumption: 48.7 m/imp gal, 40.6 m/US gal, 5.8 l x 100 km.

CHASSIS integral; front suspension: independent, upper swinging arms, anti-roll bar, telescopic dampers; rear: independent, swinging arms, coil springs, telescopic dampers.

STEERING screw and sector; turns lock to lock: 2.12.

BRAKES drum; lining area: front 33.5 sq in, 216 sq cm, rear 33.5 sq in, 216 sq cm, total 67 sq in, 432 sq cm.

ELECTRICAL EQUIPMENT 12 V; 32 Ah battery; 475 W alternator; Garef-Marelli distributor; 2 headlamps.

DIMENSIONS AND WEIGHT wheel base: 78.74 in, 200 cm; tracks: 45.28 in, 115 cm front, 45.67 in, 116 cm rear; length: 131.89 in, 335 cm; width: 54.33 in, 138 cm; height: 55.12 in, 140 cm; ground clearance: 5.71 in, 14.5 cm; weight: 1,378 lb, 625 kg; weight distribution: 46% front, 54% rear; turning circle: 29.5 ft, 9 m; fuel tank: 5.9 imp gal, 7.1 US gal, 27 l.

BODY saloon/sedan; 2 doors; 4 seats, separate front seats.

PRACTICAL INSTRUCTIONS fuel: 90 oct petrol; oil: engine 5.3 imp pt, 6.3 US pt, 3 l, 20W-40, change every 3,100 miles, 5,000 km - gearbox 2.6 imp pt, 3.2 US pt, 1.5 l, SAE 90 EP, change every 18,600 miles, 30,000 km; tappet clearances: inlet 0.0059 in, 0.15 mm, exhaust 0.0059 in, 0.15 mm; valve timing: 4° 26° 29° 1°; tyre pressure: front 14 psi, 1 atm, rear 23 psi, 1.6 atm.

AVALLONE   BRAZIL

A 11

ENGINE front, 4 stroke; 4 cylinders, in line; 85.3 cu in, 1,398 cc (3.23 x 2.61 in, 82 x 66.2 mm); compression ratio: 7.8:1; max power (DIN): 60 hp (44.2 kW) at 5,400 rpm; max torque (DIN): 67 lb ft, 9.2 kg m (90 Nm) at 3,600 rpm; max engine rpm: 6,000; 42.9 hp/l (31.6 kW/l); cast iron block, light alloy head; 5 crankshaft bearings; valves: overhead, rockers; camshafts: 1, overhead, cogged belt; lubrication: gear pump, full flow filter, 6.2 imp pt, 7.4 US pt, 3.5 l; 1 Solex H 32/34 PDSI downdraught carburettor; fuel feed: mechanical pump; water-cooled, 12.3 imp pt, 14.8 US pt, 7 l.

TRANSMISSION driving wheels: rear; clutch: single dry plate (diaphragm); gearbox: mechanical; gears: 4, fully synchronized; ratios: I 3.746, II 2.157, III 1.378, IV 1, rev 3.815; lever: central; final drive: hypoid bevel; axle ratio: 4.100; width of rims: 5''; tyres: 165 x 13.

PERFORMANCE max speed: 90 mph, 145 km/h; power-weight ratio: 28.7 lb/hp (38.9 lb/kW), 13 kg/hp (17.6 kg/kW); speed in direct drive at 1,000 rpm: 16 mph, 25.7 km/h; consumption: 37.7 m/imp gal, 31.4 m/US gal, 7.5 l x 100 km.

CHASSIS integral; front suspension: independent, wishbones, coil springs, anti-roll bar, telescopic dampers; rear: rigid axle, twin trailing radius arms, transverse linkage bar, coil springs, anti-roll bar, telescopic dampers.

STEERING rack-and-pinion; turns lock to lock: 3.25.

BRAKES front disc (diameter 9.37 in, 23.8 cm), rear drum, dual circuit; lining area: front 17.1 sq in, 110 sq cm, rear 46.8 sq in, 302 sq cm, total 63.9 sq in, 412 sq cm.

ELECTRICAL EQUIPMENT 12 V; 36 Ah battery; 32 A alternator; Arno distributor; 2 headlamps.

DIMENSIONS AND WEIGHT wheel base: 94.09 in, 239 cm; front and rear track: 51.18 in, 130; length: 151.97 in, 386 cm; width: 61.42 in, 156 cm; height: 49.21 in, 125 cm; ground clearance: 5.51 in, 14 cm; weight: 1,720 lb, 780 kg; turning circle: 32.1 ft, 9.8 m; fuel tank: 9.9 imp gal, 11.9 US gal, 45 l.

BODY sports, in plastic material; 2 doors; 2 seats.

OPTIONALS 185/70 SR x 13 tyres; servo brake; 1.6-litre engine with 2 Weber carburettors.

CHEVROLET   BRAZIL

Chevette Series

PRICES EX WORKS:

2-dr Sedan	92,752	cruzeiros
L 2-dr Sedan	100,495	cruzeiros
SL 2-dr Sedan	104,759	cruzeiros
Jeans 2-dr Sedan	—	
4-dr Sedan	—	
SL 4-dr Sedan	—	

60 hp power team

ENGINE front, 4 stroke; 4 cylinders, in line; 85.3 cu in, 1,398 cc (3.23 x 2.61 in, 82 x 66.2 mm); compression ratio: 7.8:1; max power (DIN): 60 hp (44.1 kW) at 5,400 rpm; max torque (DIN): 67 lb ft, 9.2 kg m (90.2 Nm) at 3,600 rpm; max engine rpm: 6,000; 42.9 hp/l (31.5 kW/l); cast iron block, light alloy head; 5 crankshaft bearings; valves:

AVALLONE A 11

CHEVROLET Chevette L 2-dr Sedan

60 HP POWER TEAM

overhead, rockers; camshafts: 1, overhead, cogged belt; lubrication: gear pump, full flow filter, 6.2 imp pt, 7.4 US pt, 3.5 l; 1 Solex DFV 1861 downdraught carburettor; fuel feed: mechanical pump; water-cooled, 12.3 imp pt, 14.8 US pt, 7 l.

TRANSMISSION driving wheels: rear; clutch: single dry plate (diaphragm); gearbox: mechanical; gears: 4, fully synchronized; ratios: I 3.746, II 2.157, III 1.378, IV 1, rev 3.815; lever: central; final drive: hypoid bevel; axle ratio: 4.100; width of rims: 5''; tyres: 165 x 13.

PERFORMANCE max speed: 83 mph, 134 km/h; power-weiht ratio: 30.6 lb/hp (41.7 lb/kW), 13.9 kg/hp (18.1 kg/kW); carrying capacity: 915 lb, 415 kg; speed in direct drive at 1,000 rpm: 16 mph, 25.7 km/h; consumption: 37.7 m/imp gal, 31.4 m/US gal, 7.5 l x 100 km.

CHASSIS integral; front suspension: independent, wishbones, coil springs, anti-roll bar, telescopic dampers; rear: rigid axle, twin trailing radius arms, transverse linkage bar, coil springs, anti-roll bar, telescopic dampers.

STEERING rack-and-pinion; turns lock to lock: 3.25.

BRAKES front disc (diameter 9.37 in, 23.8 cm), rear drum, servo; swept area: total 240.2 sq in, 1549 sq cm.

ELECTRICAL EQUIPMENT 12 V; 36 Ah battery; 28 A alternator; Arno distributor; 2 headlamps.

DIMENSIONS AND WEIGHT wheel base: 94.09 in, 239 cm; front and rear track: 51.18 in, 130 cm; length: 165.35 in, 420 cm; width: 61.81 in, 157 cm; height: 51.97 in, 132 cm; ground clearance: 5.51 in, 14 cm; weight: 1,843 lb, 836 kg; turning circle: 32.1 ft, 9.8 m; fuel tank: 9.9 imp gal, 11.9 US gal, 45 l.

BODY 5 seats, separate front seats; luxury equipment; reclining backrests with built-in headrests.

PRACTICAL INSTRUCTIONS fuel: 73 oct petrol; oil: engine 6.2 imp pt, 7.4 US pt, 3.5 l, SAE 20W-40, change every 3,100 miles, 5,000 km - gearbox 2.5 imp pt, 3.0 US pt, 1.4 l, SAE 90, change every 15,500 miles, 25,000 km - final drive 1.4 imp pt, 1.7 US pt, 0.8 l, SAE 90 change every 31,000 miles, 50,000 km; greasing: none; tappet clearances: inlet 0.010 in, 0.25 mm, exhaust 0.010 in, 0.25 mm; valve timing: 34° 86° 66° 54° tyre pressure: front 20 psi, 1.4 atm, rear 24 psi, 1.7 atm.

OPTIONALS tinted glass; brakes: servo.

Opala Sedan/Coupé

PRICES EX WORKS: Opala Sedan 127,991 cruzeiros
Opala Coupé 128,897 cruzeiros

ENGINE front, 4 stroke; 4 cylinders, in line; 152.2 cu in, 2,494 cc (4 x 3 in, 101.6 x 76.2 mm); compression ratio: 7.5:1; max power (DIN): 80 hp (58.8 kW) at 4,400 rpm; max torque (DIN): 120 lb ft, 16.5 kg m (161.8 Nm) at 2,400-2,800 rpm; max engine rpm: 5.200; 32.3 hp/l (23.7 kW/l); cast iron block and head; 5 crankshaft bearings; valves: overhead, push-rods and rockers, hydraulic tappets; camshafts: 1, side; lubrication: gear pump, full flow filter, 6.2 imp pt, 7.4 US pt, 3.5 l; 1 DFV or Brosol-Sole Bbl downdraught single barrel carburettor; fuel feed: mechanical pump; water-cooled, 15 imp pt, 18 US pt, 8.5 l.

TRANSMISSION driving wheels: rear; clutch: single dry plate; gearbox: mechanical; gears: 3, fully synchronized; ratios: I 3.070, II 1.680, III 1, rev 3.570; lever: steering column; final drive: hypoid bevel; axle ratio: 3.540; width of rims: 5''; tyres: 6.45 x 14.

PERFORMANCE max speed: 96 mph, 154 km/h; power-weight ratio: 30.0 lb/hp (40.8 lb/kW), 13.6 kg/hp (18.5 kg/kW); carrying capacity: 1,091 lb, 495 kg; speed in direct drive at 1,000 rpm: 22.6 mph, 36.4 km/h; consumption: 22.6 m/imp gal, 18.8 m/US gal, 12.5 l x 100 km.

CHASSIS integral; front suspension: independent, wishbones, coil springs, anti-roll bar, telescopic dampers; rear: rigid axle, longitudinal torsion bars, transverse linkage bar, coil springs, anti-roll bar, telescopic dampers.

STEERING worm and roller; turns lock to lock: 3.75.

BRAKES front disc, rear drum, servo.

ELECTRICAL EQUIPMENT 12 V; 45 Ah battery; 32 A alternator; Arno distributor; 2 headlamps.

DIMENSIONS AND WEIGHT wheel base: 105.12 in, 267 cm; tracks: 55.51 in, 141 cm front, 55.12 in, 140 cm rear; length:

183.86 in, 467 cm; width: 68.11 in, 173 cm; height: Sedan 54.72 in, 139 cm - Coupé 53.54 in, 136 cm; ground clearance: 5.79 in, 14.7 cm; weight: Sedan 2,401 lb, 1,089 kg - Coupé 2,379 lb, 1,079 kg; turning circle: 37.7 ft, 11.5 m; fuel tank: 11.9 imp gal, 14.3 US gal, 54 l.

BODY saloon/sedan, 4 doors - coupé, 2 doors; 6 seats, bench front seats - 5 seats, separate front seats.

PRACTICAL INSTRUCTIONS fuel: 73 oct petrol; oil: engine 6.2 imp pt, 7.4 US pt, 3.5 ,l, SAE 20W-40; change every 3,100 miles, 5,000 km - gearbox 2.1 imp pt, 2.5 US pt, 1,2 l, SAE 90, change every 15,500 miles, 25,000 km - final drive 1.3 imp pt, 2.1 US pt, 0,98 l, change every 31,000 miles, 50,000 km; greasing: none; valve timing: 33° 81° 76° 38° tyre pressure: front 20 psi, 1.4 atm, rear 22 psi, 1.6 atm.

VARIATIONS

ENGINE 6 cylinders, in line, 249.8 cu in, 4.093 cc (3.87 x 3.53 in, 98.4 x 89.6 mm), 8:1 compression ratio, max power (DIN): 153 hp (112.6 kW) at 4,600 rpm, max torque (DIN) 215 lb ft, 29.7 kg m at (291.3 Nm) 2,400 rpm, 37.4 hp/l (27.5 kW/l); 7 crankshaft bearings, lubrication 8.8 imp pt, 10.6 US pt, 5 l, 1 DFV 446052 downdraught twin barrel carburettor, cooling system 18 imp pt, 21.6 US pt, 10.2 l.
TRANSMISSION 3.080 axle ratio, 7.35 S x 14 tyres.
PERFORMANCE max speed about 118 mph, 190 km/h, power-weight ratio 15.6 lb/hp (21.3 lb/kW) 7.1 kg/hp (9.7 kg/kW) speed in direct drive at 1,000 rpm 23.6 mph, 38 km/h, fuel consumption 18.2 m/imp gal, 15.2 m/US gal, 15.5 l x 100 km.

OPTIONALS 4-speed fully synchronized mechanical gearbox (I 3.070, II 2.020, III 1.390, IV 1, rev 3.570), 3.080 axle ratio, central lever: "Automatic" automatic transmission, hydraulic torque converter and planetary gears with 3 ratios (I 2.310, II 1.460, III 1, rev 1.850), max ratio of converter at stall 2.4, possible manual selection, steering column or central lever; power-assisted steering (only with 6-cylinder engine); separate front seats with reclining backrests; air-conditioning (only with 6-cylinder engine); halogen headlamps; fog lamps; vinyl roof; tinted glass; metallic spray.

Opala Caravan

See Opala Sedan/Coupé, except for:

PRICE EX WORKS: 141,473 cruzeiros

TRANSMISSION tyres: 6.95 x 14.

PERFORMANCE power-weight ratio: 31.7 lb/hp (42.7 lb/kW), 14.4 kg/hp (19.4 kg/kW).

DIMENSIONS AND WEIGHT length: 182.28 in, 463 cm; height: 54.72 in, 139 cm; weight: 2,514 lb, 1,140 kg.

BODY estate car/station wagon; 2 + 1 doors; folding rear seat.

OPTIONALS 6.45 S x 14 tyres.

Opala SS-4 Coupé

See Opala Sedan/Coupé, except for:

PRICE EX WORKS: 148,409 cruzeiros

ENGINE max power (DIN): 88 hp (64.8 kW) at 4,600 rpm; max torque (DIN): 135 lb ft, 18.6 kg m (182.4 Nm) at 2,600 rpm; 35.6 hp/l; 1 Zenith WW 4 downdraught twin barrel carburettor.

TRANSMISSION gears: 4, fully synchronized; ratios: I 3.070, II 2.020, III 1.390, IV 1, rev 3.570; lever: central; tyres: 7.35 S x 14.

PERFORMANCE max speed: 99 mph, 159 km/h; power-weight ratioq 27.3 lb/hp (38.3 lb/kW), 12.4 kg/hp (17.4 kg/kW) speed in direct drive at 1,000 rpm: 20.5 mph, 33 km/h.

DIMENSIONS AND WEIGHT height: 53.54 in, 136 cm; weight 2,485 lb, 1,127 kg.

BODY coupé; 2 doors; 5 seats, separate front seats reclining backrests.

Opala SS-4 Caravan

See Opala SS-4 Coupé, except for:

PRICE EX WORKS: 157,571 cruzeiros

TRANSMISSION tyres: 6.95 S x 14.

PERFORMANCE power-weight ratio: 29.1 lb/hp (39.1 lb/kW), 13.2 kg/hp (17.7 kg/kW).

CHEVROLET Opala Coupé

DIMENSIONS AND WEIGHT length: 182.28 in, 463 cm; height: 54.72 in, 139 cm; weight: 2,536 lb, 1,150 kg.

BODY estate car/st. wagon; 2 + 1 doors.

Opala SS-6 Coupé

See Opala SS-4 Coupé, except for:

PRICE EX WORKS: 186,366 cruzeiros

ENGINE 6 cylinders; 250 cu in, 4,097 cc (3.87 x 3.53 in, 98.4 x 89.7 mm); compression ratio: 7.8:1; max power (DIN): 149 hp (26.8 kW/l); at 4,600 rpm; max torque (DIN): 209 lb ft, 28.8 kg m (282.4 Nm) at 2,400 rpm; max hp/l (26.8 kW/l) 7 crankshaft bearings; lubrication: 8.8 imp pt, 10.6 US pt, 5 l; cooling system: 17.2 imp pt, 20.7 US pt, 9.8 l.

TRANSMISSION axle ratio: 3.070; tyres: 7.35H x 14.

PERFORMANCE max speed: about 106 mph, 170 km/h; power-weight ratio: 17.2 lb/hp (23.8 lb/kW), 7.8 kg/hp (10.8 kg/kW) speed in direct drive at 1,000 rpm: 23.6 mph, 38 km/h; consumption: 18.2 m/imp gal, 15.2 m/US gal, 15.5 l x 100 km.

DIMENSIONS AND WEIGHT weight: 2,615 lb, 1,186 kg.

Opala SS-6 Caravan

See Opala SS-6 Coupé, except for:

PRICE EX WORKS: 177,775 cruzeiros

ENGINE lubrication: 7.9 imp pt, 9.5 US pt, 4.5 l; cooling system: 15 imp pt, 18 US pt, 8.5 l.

TRANSMISSION tyres: 6.95S x 14.

PERFORMANCE power-weight ratio: 18.3 lb/hp (24.3 lb/kW), 8.3 kg/hp (11.0 kg/kW).

DIMENSIONS AND WEIGHT length: 182.28 in, 463 cm; height: 54.72 in, 139 cm; weight: 2,666 lb, 1,209 kg.

BODY estate car/st. wagon; 2 + 1 doors.

Comodoro 4 Sedan/4 Coupé

PRICES EX WORKS: Comodoro 4 Sedan 144,233 cruzeiros
Comodoro 4 Coupé 143,565 cruzeiros

ENGINE front, 4 stroke; 4 cylinders, in line; 152.2 cu in, 2,494 cc (4 x 3 in, 101.6 x 76.2 mm); compression ratio: 7.5:1; max power (DIN): 88 hp (64.7 kW) at 4,600 rpm; max torque (DIN): 135 lb ft, 18.6 kg m (182.4 Nm) at 2,600 rpm; max engine rpm: 5,000; 35.6 hp/l (25.9 kW/l) cast iron block and head; 5 crankshaft bearings; valves: overhead in line, push-rods and rockers, hydraulic tappets; camshafts: 1, side; lubrication: gear pump, full flow filter, 6.2 imp pt, 7.4 US pt, 3.5 l; 1 Brosol - Solex H 40/41 DIS or DVF/Zenith 2285 downdraught twin barrel carburettor; fuel feed: mechanical pump; sealed circuit cooling, liquid, 15 imp pt, 18 US pt, 8.5 l.

TRANSMISSION driving wheels: rear; clutch: single dry plate; gearbox: mechanical; gears: 3, fully synchronized; ratios: I 3.070, II 1.680, III 1, rev 3.570; lever: steering column; final drive: hypoid bevel; axle ratio: 3.540; width of rims: 5''; tyres: 6.95 x 14.

PERFORMANCE max speeds: (I) 34 mph, 55 km/h; (II) 63 mph, 101 km/h; (III) 106 mph, 170 km/h; power-weight ratio: 28.2 lb/hp (37.6 lb/kW), 12.8 kg/hp (17.0 kg/kW); carrying capacity: 882 lb, 400 kg; speed in direct drive at 1,000 rpm: 23.6 mph, 38 km/h; consumption: 18.2 m/imp gal, 15.2 m/US gal, 15.5 l x 100 km.

CHASSIS integral; front suspension: independent, wishbones, coil springs, anti-roll bar, telescopic dampers; rear: rigid axle, longitudinal torsion bars, transverse linkage bar, coil springs, anti-roll bar, telescopic dampers.

STEERING worm and roller.

BRAKES front disc, rear drum, servo.

ELECTRICAL EQUIPMENT 12 V; 45 Ah battery; 32 A alternator; Arno distributor; 2 headlamps.

DIMENSIONS AND WEIGHT wheel base: 105.12 in, 267 cm; tracks: 55.51 in, 141 cm front, 55.12 in, 140 cm rear; length: 185.12 in, 470 cm; width: 69.29 in, 176 cm; height: Sedan 54.72 in, 139 cm - Coupé 53.54 in, 136 cm; ground clearance: 5.79 in, 14.7 cm; weight: Sedan 2,434 lb, 1,104 kg - Coupé 2,417 lb, 1,096 kg, turning circle: 37.7 ft, 11.5 m; fuel tank: 11.9 imp gal, 14.3 US gal, 54 l.

BODY saloon/sedan, 4 doors - 4 coupé, 2 doors; 5 seats, separate front seats; vinyl roof.

PRACTICAL INSTRUCTIONS fuel: 73 oct petrol; oil: engine 6.2 imp pt, 7.4 US pt, 3.5 l. SAE 20W-40 change every

3,100 miles, 5,000 km - gearbox 2.1 imp pt, 2.5 US pt, 1,2 l, change every 15,500 miles, 25,000 km - final drive 1.3 imp pt, 2.1 US pt, 0.98 l, change every 31,000 miles 50,000 km; greasing: none; valve timing: 33° 81° 76° 38° tyre pressure: front 20 psi, 1.4 atm, rear 22 psi, 1.6 atm.

OPTIONALS « Automatic » automatic transmission; reclining backrests; halogen headlamps; fog lamps; tinted glass; air-conditioning.

Comodoro 6 Sedan/6 Coupé

See Comodoro 4 Sedan/4 Coupé, except for:

PRICES EX WORKS: Comodoro 6 Sedan 160,827 cruzeiros
Comodoro 6 Coupé 159,316 cruzeiros

ENGINE 6 cylinders; 250 cu in, 4,097 cc (3.87 x 3.53 in, 98.4 x 89.7 mm); max power (DIN): 127 hp (93.4 kW) at 3,800 rpm; max torque (DIN): 201 lb ft, 27.8 kg m (272.6 Nm) at 2,200 rpm; max engine rpm: 4,400; 31 hp/l (22.7 kW/l); 7 crankshaft bearings; lubrication: 8.8 imp pt, 10.6 US pt, 5 l; cooling system: 17.2 imp pt, 20.7 US pt, 9.8 l.

TRANSMISSION gears: 4, fully synchronized; ratios: I 3.070, II 2.020, III 1.390, IV 1, rev 3.570; lever: central; axle ratio: 3.080; tyres: 7.35 S x 14.

PERFORMANCE max speeds: (I) 34 mph, 55 km/h; (II) 52 mph, 84 km/h; (III) 76 mph, 122 km/h; (IV) 106 mph, 170 km/h; power-weight ratio: 20.8 lb/hp (27.6 lb/kW), 9.4 kg/hp (12.5 kg/kW).

DIMENSIONS AND WEIGHT weight: 2,589 lb, 1,174 kg.

VARIATIONS

ENGINE 8:1 compression ratio, max power (DIN) 153 hp (112.6 kW) at 4,600 rpm, max torque (DIN) 215 lb ft, 29.7 kg m (291.2 Nm) at 2,400 rpm, 37.4 hp/l, 1 DFV 44 6052 downdraught twin barrel carburettor.
PERFORMANCE max speed 118 mph, 190 km/h, power-weight ratio 17.2 lb/hp (22.9 lb/kW) 7.8 kg/hp (10.4 kg/kW).

Veraneio Series

PRICES EX WORKS:

Standard	174,621	cruzeiros
De Luxo	182,439	cruzeiros
Super Luxo	215,081	cruzeiros

151 hp power team

ENGINE front, 4 stroke; 6 cylinders, vertical in line; 261.2 cu in, 4,280 cc (3.75 x 3.94 in, 95.2 x 100.1 mm); compression ratio: 7.8:1; max power (SAE): 151 hp (111.1 kW) at 3,800 rpm; max torque (SAE): 233 lb ft, 32.1 kg m (314.8 Nm) at 2,400 rpm; max engine rpm: 4,200; 35.3 hp/l (25.9 kW/l); cast iron block and head; 3 crankshaft bearings; valves: overhead, in line, push-rods and rockers; camshafts: 1, side; lubrication: gear pump, full flow filter, 8.3 imp pt, 9.9 US pt, 4.7 l; 1 DFV-Zenith 228 downdraught single barrel

carburettor; fuel feed: mechanical pump; water-cooled, 28.2 imp pt, 33.8 US pt, 16 l.

TRANSMISSION driving wheels: rear; clutch: single dry plate (diaphragm); gearbox: mechanical; gears: 3, fully synchronized; ratios: I 3.167, II 1.753, III 1, rev 3.761; lever: steering column; final drive: hypoid bevel, limited slip differential; axle ratio: 3.900; width of rims: 5.5''; tyres 7.10 x 15.

PERFORMANCE max speed: 90 mph, 145 km/h; power-weight ratio: 28.7 lb/hp (39.4 lb/kW), 13.0 kg/hp (17.7 kg/kW); carrying capacity: 1,058 lb, 480 kg; speed in direct drive at 1,000 rpm: 20.9 mph, 33.6 km/h; consumption: 17.7 m/imp gal, 14.7 m/US gal, 16 l x 100 km.

CHASSIS box-type ladder frame; front suspension: independent, wishbones, coil springs, telescopic dampers; rear: rigid axle, longitudinal trailing arms, coil springs, anti-roll bar, telescopic dampers.

STEERING worm and roller.

BRAKES drum; swept area: total 276.4 sq in, 1,783 sq cm.

ELECTRICAL EQUIPMENT 12 V; 45 Ah battery; 37 A alternator; Arno distributor; 2 headlamps.

DIMENSIONS AND WEIGHT wheel base: 114.96 in, 292 cm; tracks: 63.39 in, 161 cm front, 64.96 in, 155 cm rear; length: 203.15 in, 516 cm - De Luxo 207.87 in, 528 cm; width: 77.95 in, 198 cm; height: 68.11 in, 173 cm; ground clearance: 7.87 in, 20 cm; weight: 4,344 lb, 1,970 kg; turning circle: 42.6 ft, 13 m; fuel tank: 15.4 imp gal, 18.5 US gal, 70 l.

BODY estate car/st. wagon; 4 + 1 doors; 6 seats, bench front seats; folding rear seat - De Luxo, luxury equipment.

PRACTICAL INSTRUCTIONS fuel: 73 oct petrol; oil: engine 8.3 imp pt, 9.9 US pt, 4.7 l, SAE 10W-50 multi change every miles, 3,000 km - gearbox 2.1 imp pt, 2.5 US pt, 1.3 l, SAE 90, change every 15,500 miles, 25,000 km - final drive 3.5 imp pt, 4.2 US pt, 2 l, change every 31,000 miles, 50,000 km; greasing: none; valve timing: 11°30' 52°30' 51° 13°; tyre pressure: front 30 psi, 2.1 atm, rear 30 psi, 2.1 atm.

OPTIONALS power-steering.

DODGE   BRAZIL

Polara/Gran Luxo

PRICES EX WORKS: Polara   90,600 cruzeiros
Polara Gran Luxo 102,400 cruzeiros

ENGINE front, 4 stroke; 4 cylinders, vertical, in line; 109.8 cu in, 1,799 cc (3.39 x 3.04 in, 86 x 77.1 mm); compression ratio: 7.7:1; max power (SAE): 85 hp (62.6 kW) at 5,000 rpm; max torque (SAE): 103 lb ft, 14.2 kg m

CHEVROLET Comodoro Sedan

POLARA/GRAN LUXO

(139.3 Nm) at 3,500 rpm; max engine rpm: 6,400; 47.2 hp/l (34.8 kW/l); cast iron block and head; 5 crankshaft bearings valves: overhead, in line, push-rods and rockers; camshafts: 1, side; lubrication: rotary pump, full flow filter, 7.2 imp pt, 8.7 US pt, 4 l; 1 SU HS-6 horizontal single barrel carburettor; fuel feed: mechanical pump; water-cooled, 10.6 imp pt, 12.7 US pt, 6 l.

TRANSMISSION driving wheels: rear; clutch: single dry plate (diaphragm); gearbox: mechanical; gears: 4, fully synchronized; ratios: I 3.538, II 2.165, III 1.387, IV 1, rev 3.680; lever: central; final drive: hypoid bevel; axle ratio: 3,890; width of rims: 5''; tyres: 6.45 x 13.

PERFORMANCE max speeds: (I) 30 mph, 49 km/h; (II) 50 mph, 81 km/h; (III) 78 mph, 120 km/h; (IV) 95 mph, 153 km/h; power-weight ratio: 24 lb/hp (32.8 lb/kW), 10.9 kg/hp (14.9 kg/kW) - Gran Luxo 24.9 lb/hp (34.0 lb.kW), 11.3 kg/hp (15.4 kg/kW); carrying capacity: 882 lb, 400 kg; acceleration: standing ¼ mile 18.2 sec, 0-50 mph (0-80 km/h) 8.2 sec; speed in direct drive at 1,000 rpm: 17.4 mph, 28 km/h; consumption: 33.2 m/imp gal, 27.7 m/US gal, 8.5 l x 100 km.

CHASSIS integral; front suspension: independent, by Mc-Pherson, coil springs/telescopic damper struts, wishbones (lower trailing links), anti-roll bar; rear: rigid axle, swinging longitudinal trailing arms, upper oblique torque arms, coil springs, telescopic dampers.

STEERING rack-and-pinion; turns lock to lock: 3.60.

BRAKES front disc, rear drum, servo; swept area: front 22 sq in, 142 sq cm, rear 60.1 sq in, 387 sq cm, total 82.1 sq in, 529 sq cm.

ELECTRICAL EQUIPMENT 12 V; 40 Ah battery; 360 W alternator; Bosch or Wapsa distributor; 2 headlamps.

DIMENSIONS AND WEIGHT wheel base: 98 in, 249 cm; tracks: 52 in, 132 cm front, 52 in, 132 cm rear; length: 162.40 in, 412 cm; width: 62.50 in, 159 cm; height: 54.20 in, 138 cm; ground clearance: 5.50 in, 14 cm; weight: 2,051 lb, 930 kg - Gran Luxo 2,126 lb, 964 kg; turning circle: 30.8 ft, 9.4 m; fuel tank: 9.2 imp gal, 11.1 US gal, 42 l.

BODY coupé; 2 doors; 5 seats, separate front seats.

OPTIONALS 165 SR x 13 tyres.

Dart De Luxo Sedan/Gran Sedan

PRICES EX WORKS: Dart De Luxo Sedan 140,810 cruzeiros
Dart Gran Sedan 181,680 cruzeiros

ENGINE front, 4 stroke; 8 cylinders; 318 cu in, 5,212 cc (3.91 x 3.31 in, 99.3 x 84.1 mm); compression ratio: 7.5:1; max power (SAE): 149 hp (109.7 kW) at 4,400 rpm; max torque (SAE): 248 lb ft, 34.2 kg m (335.4 Nm) at 2,400 rpm; max engine rpm: 4,800 28.6 hp/l (21.1 kW/l); cast iron block and head; 5 crankshaft bearings; valves: overhead, in line, push-rods and rockers, hydraulic tappets; camshafts: 1, at centre of Vee; lubrication: rotary pump, full flow filter, 8.3 imp pt, 9.9 US pt, 4.7 l; 1 DFV downdraught twin barrel carburettor; fuel feed: mechanical pump; water-cooled, 33.4 imp pt, 40.2 US pt, 19 l.

TRANSMISSION driving wheels: rear; clutch: single dry plate; gearbox: mechanical; gears: 3, fully synchronized; ratios: I 2.670, II 1.600, III 1, rev 3.440; lever: steering column; final drive: hypoid bevel; axle ratio: 3.150; width of rims: 5.5''; tyres: 185 SR 14.

PERFORMANCE max speeds: (I) 48 mph, 78 km/h; (II) 71 mph, 115 km/h; (III) 102 mph, 164 km/h; power-weight ratio: 22.1 lb/hp (30.1 lb/kW), 10.1 kg/hp (13.6 kg/kW) - Gran Sedan 16.6 lb/hp (29.9 lb/kW), 7.5 kg/hp (13.5 kg/kW) carrying capacity: 882 lb, 400 kg; acceleration: standing ¼ mile 19 sec, 0-50 mph (0-80 km/h) 9.8 sec; speed in direct drive at 1,000 rpm: 23 mph, 37 km/h; consumption: 17.4 m/imp gal, 4.3 m/US gal, 16.5 l x 100 km.

CHASSIS integral; front suspension: independent, wishbones (lower trailing links), longitudinal torsion bars, anti-roll bar, telescopic dampers; rear: rigid axle, semi-elliptic leafsprings, telescopic dampers.

STEERING recirculating ball, servo; turns lock to lock: 6.50.

BRAKES front disc, rear drum, servo; swept area: total 354.3 sq in, 2.285 sq cm.

ELECTRICAL EQUIPMENT 12 V; 50 Ah battery; 480 W alternator; Chrysler electronic distributor; 2 headlamps.

DIMENSIONS AND WEIGHT wheel base: 111 in, 282 cm; tracks: 58.27 in, 148 cm front, 56.30 in, 143 cm rear; length: 195.30 in, 496 cm; width: 71.30 in, 181 cm; height: 54.70 in, 139 cm; ground clearance: 6.30 in, 16 cm; weight: 3,301 lb, 1,497 kg - Gran Sedan 3,285 lb, 1,490 kg; turning circle: 40.3 ft, 12.3 m; fuel tank: 23.5 imp gal, 28.2 US gal, 107 l.

DODGE Dart De Luxo Coupé

BODY saloon/sedan; 4 doors; 6 seats, bench front seats.

OPTIONALS Torqueflite automatic transmission with 3 ratios (I 2.540, II 1.450, III 1, rev 2.200), max ratio of converter at stall 2.4, possible manual selection; 4-speed fully synchronized mechanical gearbox (I 2.670, II 1.860, III 1.300, IV 1, rev 3.140); 3.070 axle ratio; dual exhaust system; metallic spray; air-conditioning.

Dart De Luxo Coupé

See Dart De Luxo Sedan/Gran Sedan, except for:

PRICE EX WORKS: 139.670 cruzeiros

PERFORMANCE power-weight ratio: 16.6 lb/hp, 7.5 kg/hp.

DIMENSIONS AND WEIGHT weight: 3,285 lb, 1,490 kg.

BODY coupé; 2 doors.

Le Baron - Charger R/T - Magnum

PRICE EX WORKS: Carger R/T 203,610 cruzeiros

ENGINE front, 4 stroke; 8 cylinders; 318 cu in, 5,212 cc (3.91 x 3.31 in, 99.3 x 84.1 mm); compression ratio: 7.5:1; max power (SAE): 149 hp (109.7 kW) at 4,400 rpm Le Baron - 165 hp (121.4 kW) at 4,400 rpm Charger and Magnum; max torque (SAE): 248 lb ft, 34.2 kg m (335.4 Nm) at 2,400 rpm Le Baron - 263 lb ft, 36.3 kg m (356.0 Nm) Charger and Magnum; max engine rpm: 4,800; 28.6 hp/l (21.0 kW/l) Le Baron - 31.7 hp/l (23.3 kW/l) Charger and Magnum; cast iron block and head; 5 crankshaft bearings; valves: overhead, in line, pushrods and rockers, hydraulic tappets; camshafts: 1 at centre of Vee; lubrication: rotary pump, full flow filter, 8.3 imp pt, 9.9 US pt, 4.7 l; 1 DFV downdraught twin barrel carburettor; dual exhaust system; fuel feed: mechanical pump; water-cooled, 33.4 imp pt, 40.2 US pt, 19 l.

TRANSMISSION driving wheels: rear; clutch: single dry plate; gearbox: mechanical; gears: 3, fully synchronized; ratios: I 2.670, II 1.60, III 1, rev 3.44; lever: steering column Le Baron - gears 4; ratios: I 2.670, II 1.860, III 1.30, IV 1, rev 3.140 lever: central Charger and Magnum; axle ratio: 3.150; width of rims: S.S'' Le Baron and Magnum - 6'' Charger; tyres: 7.35 S x 14.

PERFORMANCE max speeds: (I) 39 mph, 62 km/h; (II) 56 mph, 90 km/h; (III) 81 mph, 130 km/h; (IV) 112 mph, 180 km/h; power-weight ratio: 16.3 lb/hp (30.4 lb/kW), 7.4 kg/hp (13.8 kg/kW); carrying capacity: 882 lb, 400 kg; consumption: 20.2 m/imp gal, 16.8 m/US gal, 14 l x 100 km.

CHASSIS integral; front suspension: independent, wishbones (lower trailing links), longitudinal torsion bars, anti-roll bar, telescopic dampers; rear: rigid axle, semi-elliptic leafsprings, telescopic dampers.

STEERING recirculating ball, servo; turns lock to lock: 6.50.

DODGE Le Baron

BRAKES front disc, rear drum, servo; swept area: total 354.3 sq in, 2,285 sq cm.

ELECTRICAL EQUIPMENT 12 V; 50 Ah battery; 480 W alternator; Chrysler electronic distributor: 4 headlamps.

DIMENSIONS AND WEIGHT wheel base: 111 in, 282 cm; tracks: 58,27 in, 148 cm front, 56.30 in, 143 cm rear; length: 195.30 in, 496 cm; width: 71.30 in, 181 cm; height: 54.70 in, 139 cm; ground clearance: 6.30 in, 16 cm; weight: 3.341 lb, 1,515 kg; turning circle: 40.3 ft, 12.3 m; fuel tank: 23.5 imp gal, 28.2 US gal, 107 l.

BODY saloon/sedan; 4 doors; 6 seats, bench front seats Le Baron - coupé; 2 doors; 5 seats, separate front seats Magnum and Charger.

OPTIONALS Torqueflite automatic transmission, hydraulic torque converter and planetary gears with 3 ratios (I 2.540, II 1.450, III 1, rev 2.200), max ratio of converter at stall 2.4, possible manual selection, 3.070 axle ratio; air-conditioning.

FIAT   BRAZIL

147 Series

PRICES EX WORKS:

1 147	**86,385**	**cruzeiros**
2 147 L	**90,920**	**cruzeiros**
3 147 GL	**99,145**	**cruzeiros**
4 147 GLS	—	
5 147 Rallye	—	

Power team:	Standard for:	Optional for:
57 hp	1 to 3	—
61 hp	4	—
72 hp	5	—

57 hp power team

ENGINE front, 4 stroke; 4 cylinders, transverse; 64 cu in, 1,049 cc (2.99 x 2.23 in, 76 x 57.8 mm); compression ratio: 7.2:1; max power (SAE): 57 hp (42 kW) at 5,800 rpm; max torque (SAE): 57 lb ft, 7.9 kg m (77.5 Nm) at 3,600 rpm; max engine rpm: 6,000; 54.3 hp/l (40 kW/l); light alloy block; 5 crankshaft bearings; valves: overhead; camshafts: 1, overhead; lubrication: gear pump, full flow filter (cartridge), 7 imp pt, 8.5 US pt, 4 l; 1 downdraught carburettor; fuel feed: mechanical pump; water-cooled, 10.2 imp pt, 12.3 US pt, 5.8 l.

TRANSMISSION driving wheels: front; clutch: single dry plate (diaphragm); gearbox: mechanical; gears: 4, fully synchronized; ratios: I 4.091, II 2.235, III 1.455, IV 0.957, rev 3.714; lever: central; final drive: cylindrical gears; axle ratio: 4.417; width of rims: 4''; tyres: 145 SR x 13.

PERFORMANCE max speed: 84 mph, 135 km/h; power-weight ratio: 30.9 lb/hp (42 lb/kW), 14 kg/hp (19.1 kg/kW); carrying capacity: 882 lb, 400 kg; acceleration: standing ¼ mile 20.4 sec; consumption: 36.7 m/imp gal, 30.5 m/US gal, 7.7 l x 100 km.

CHASSIS integral; front suspension: independent, by McPherson, coil springs/telescopic damper struts, lower wishbones, anti-roll-bar; rear: independent, single wide-based wishbone, transverse anti-roll leafspring, telescopic dampers.

STEERING rack-and-pinion; turns lock to lock: 3.40.

BRAKES front disc, rear drum; lining area: front 12 sq in, 77 sq cm, rear 16.7 sq in, 108 sq cm, total 28.7 sq in, 185 sq cm.

ELECTRICAL EQUIPMENT 12 V; 36 Ah battery; 35 A alternator; 2 headlamps.

DIMENSIONS AND WEIGHT tracks: 50 in, 127 cm front, 50.79 in, 129 cm rear; length: 142.91 in, 363 cm; width: 60.83 in, 154 cm; height: 53.15 in, 135 cm; weight: 1,764 lb, 800 kg; weight distribution: 49.6% front, 50.4% rear; turning circle: 39 ft, 9.1 m; fuel tank 8.4 imp gal, 10 US gal, 38 l.

BODY saloon/sedan; 2 + 1 doors; 5 seats, separate front seats; folding rear seat.

61 hp power team

See 57 hp power team, except for:

ENGINE 79 cu in, 1,297.4 cc (2.99 x 2.81 in, 76 x 71.5 mm); compression ratio: 7.5:1; max power (SAE): 61 hp (44.9 kW) at 5,400 rpm; max torque (SAE): 71.7 lb ft, 9.9 kg m (97 Nm) at 3,000 rpm; 47 hp/l (34.6 kW/l).

TRANSMISSION axle ratio: 4.080.

PERFORMANCE max speed: about 87 mph, 140 km/h; power-weight ratio: 29.3 lb/hp (39.8 lb/kW), 13.3 kg/hp (18 kg/kW).

DIMENSIONS AND WEIGHT weight: 1,786 lb, 810 kg.

72 hp power team

See 57 hp power team except for:

ENGINE 79 cu in, 1,297.4 cc (2.99 x 2.81 in, 76 x 71.5 mm); compression ratio: 7.5:1; max power (SAE): 72 hp (53 kW) at 5,800 rpm; max torque (SAE): 78.3 lb ft, 10.8 kg m (105.9 Nm) at 4,000 rpm; 55.5 hp/l (40.8 kW/l); 1 downdraught twin barrel carburettor.

TRANSMISSION axle ratio: 4.080.

PERFORMANCE max speed: over 93 mph, 150 km/h; power-weight ratio: 24.8 lb/hp (33.7 lb/kW), 11.2 kg/hp (15.2 kg/kW).

DIMENSIONS AND WEIGHT weight: 1,786 lb, 810 kg.

Alfa Romeo 2300 B

PRICE EX WORKS: 243,760 cruzeiros

ENGINE front, 4 stroke; 4 cylinders, vertical, in line; 141 cu in, 2,310 cc (3.46 x 3.74 in, 88 x 95 mm); compression ratio: 7.5:1; max power (SAE): 141 hp (103.8 kW) at 5,700 rpm; max torque (SAE): 156 lb ft, 21.5 kg m (210.8 Nm) at 3,500 rpm; max engine rpm: 5,700; 61 hp/l (44.9 kW/l); light alloy block and head; 5 crankshaft bearings; valves: overhead, Vee-slanted at 90º, thimble tappets; camshafts: 2, overhead; lubrication: gear pump, filter on by-pass, 12.3 imp pt, 14.8 US pt, 7 l; 1 Solex C-34 EIES downdraught twin barrel carburettor; fuel feed: mechanical pump; water-cooled, 16 imp pt, 19.2 US pt, 9.1 l, electric thermostatic fan.

TRANSMISSION driving wheels: rear; clutch: single dry plate (diaphragm), hydraulically controlled; gearbox: mechanical; gears: 5, fully synchronized; ratios: I 3.303, II 1.985, III 1.353, IV 1, V 0.790, rev 3.008; lever: central; final drive: hypoid bevel; axle ratio: 4.770; width of rims: 6''; tyres: 185 SR x 14.

PERFORMANCE max speeds: (I) 25 mph, 41 km/h; (II) 42 mph, 68 km/h; (III) 62 mph, 100 km/h; (IV) 84 mph, 135 km/h; (V) 106 mph, 170 km/h; power-weight ratio: 18.9 lb/hp (25.7 lb/kW), 8.6 kg/hp (11.7 kg/kW); carrying capacity: 1,180 lb, 535 kg; speed in top at 1,000 rpm: 19.3 mph, 31 km/h; consumption: 27.6 m/imp gal, 23 m/US gal, 10.2 l x 100 km.

CHASSIS integral; front suspension: independent, wishbones (lower trailing links), coil springs, anti-roll bar, telescopic dampers; rear: rigid axle, trailing lower radius arms, upper transverse Vee radius arms, twin transverse linkage bar, coil springs/telescopic damper struts.

STEERING worm and roller; turns lock to lock: 4.50.

BRAKES disc (front diameter 11.02 in, 28 cm, rear 11.06 in, 28.1 cm), dual circuit, rear compensator, servo; swept area: front 207.1 sq in, 1,336 sq cm, rear 207.1 sq in, 1,336 sq cm, total 414.2 sq in, 2,672 sq cm.

ELECTRICAL EQUIPMENT 12 V; 54 Ah battery; 420 W alternator; Bosch distributor; 4 headlamps.

DIMENSIONS AND WEIGHT wheel base: 107.48 in, 273 cm; tracks: 55.12 in, 140 cm front, 55.12 in, 140 cm rear; length: 185.82 in, 472 cm; width: 66.54 in, 169 cm; height: 59.69 in, 144 cm; ground clearance: 5.91 in, 15 cm; weight: 2,668 lb, 1,210 kg; turning circle: 41 ft, 12.6 m; fuel tank: 22 imp gal, 26.4 US gal, 100 l.

BODY saloon/sedan; 4 doors; 5 seats, separate front seats, reclining backrests.

OPTIONALS air-conditioning; tinted glass; metallic spray.

Alfa Romeo 2300 TI

See Alfa Romeo 2300 B, except for:

PRICE EX WORKS: 311,260 cruzeiros

ENGINE max power (SAE): 149 hp at 5,700 rpm; max torque (SAE): 167 lb ft, 23 kg m at 3,500 rpm; 64.5 hp/l; 2 Solex C-40 DHE downdraught twin barrel carburettor.

PERFORMANCE max speed 109 mph, 175 km/h; power-weight ratio: 18.2 lb/hp, 8.2 kg/hp; consumption: 25.4 m/imp gal, 21 m/US gal, 11.1 l x 100 km.

ELECTRICAL EQUIPMENT 540 W alternator; 4 iodine headlamps.

FIAT 147 GL

ALFA ROMEO 2300 TI

DIMENSIONS AND WEIGHT length: 185.82 in, 472 cm; height: 59.69 in, 144 cm; weight: 2,712 lb, 1,230 kg.

BODY luxury equipment; built-in headrests on rear seats; air-conditioning; tinted glass.

OPTIONALS only metallic spray.

FORD   BRAZIL

Corcel II Base/L/LDO

PRICES EX WORKS: Corcel II Base 115,977 cruzeiros
Corcel II L   129,229 cruzeiros
Corcel II LDO 154,229 cruzeiros

ENGINE front, 4 stroke; 4 cylinders, vertical, in line; 83.7 cu in, 1,372 cc (2.96 x 3.03 in, 75.3 x 77 mm); compression ratio: 8:1; max power (SAE): 71 hp (52.3 kW) at 5,400 rpm; max torque (SAE): 83 lb ft, 11.5 kg m (156.4 Nm) at 3,600 rpm; max engine rpm: 5,800; 51.7 hp/l (38.1 kW/l); cast iron block, light alloy head; 5 crankshaft bearings; valves: overhead, push-rods and rockers; camshafts: 1, in crankcase; lubrication: gear pump, full flow filter, 5.3 imp pt, 6.3 US pt, 3 l; 1 DFV 228 downdraught carburettor; fuel feed: mechanical pump; sealed circuit cooling, water, 7.6 imp pt, 9.1 US pt, 4.3 l.

CORCEL II BASE/L/LDO

TRANSMISSION driving wheels: front; clutch: single dry plate; gearbox: mechanical; gears: 4, fully synchronized; ratios: I 3.460, II 2.210, III 1.420, IV 0.970, rev 3.080; lever: central; final drive: hypoid bevel; axle ratio: 4.125; width of rims: 4.5''; tyres: 6.45 x 13.

PERFORMANCE max speeds: (I) 27 mph, 44 km/h; (II) 43 mph, 69 km/h; (III) 66 mph, 107 km/h; (IV) 88 mph, 141 km/h; power-weight ratio: Base 26.7 lb/hp (36.4 lb/kW), 12.1 kg/hp (16.5 kg/kW); carrying capacity: 873 lb, 396 kg; speed in top at 1,000 rpm: 17 mph, 27 km/h; consumption: 32.8 m/imp gal, 27.3 m/US gal, 8.6 l x 100 km.

CHASSIS integral; front suspension: independent, wishbones, upper trailing arms, coil springs, anti-roll bar, telescopic dampers; rear: rigid axle, upper and lower trailing arms, coil springs, telescopic dampers.

STEERING rack-and-pinion; turns lock to lock: 3.39.

BRAKES front disc, rear drum; lining area: total 150 sq in, 968 sq cm.

ELECTRICAL EQUIPMENT 12 V; 36 Ah battery; alternator; Bosch distributor; 2 headlamps.

DIMENSIONS AND WEIGHT wheel base: 96.06 in, 244 cm; tracks: 53.50 in, 136 cm front, 53.14 in, 135 cm rear; length: 175.98 in, 447 cm - LDO 177.16 in, 450 cm; width: 65.35 in, 166 cm; height: 53.14 in, 135 cm; ground clearance: 5.50 in, 14 cm; weight: Base 2,013 lb, 913 kg - L 2,033 lb, 922 kg - LDO 2,115 lb, 959 kg; weight distribution: 59% front, 41% rear; turning circle: 36.7 ft, 11.2 m; fuel tank: 12.5 imp gal, 15 US gal, 57 l.

BODY saloon/sedan; 2 doors; 5 seats, separate front seats.

OPTIONALS 5-speed mechanical gearbox; servo brake; 5'' wide rims; 5.00 x 13 tyres.

Corcel II Belina Base/L/LDO

See Corcel II Base/L/LDO, except for:

PRICES EX WORKS: Corcel II Belina Base 134,053 cruzeiros
Corcel II Belina L 141,982 cruzeiros
Corcel II Belina LDO 160,368 cruzeiros

PERFORMANCE power-weight ratio: Base 27.8 lb/hp (37.7 lb/kW), 12.6 kg/hp (17.1 kg/kW); carrying capacity: 1,005 lb, 456 kg; acceleration: 0-50 mph (0-80 km/h) 20.6 sec; consumption: 30 m/imp gal, 25.1 US gal, 9.4 l x 100 km.

DIMENSIONS AND WEIGHT length: 176.77 in, 449 cm - LDO 177.95 in, 452 cm; height: 53.54 in, 136 cm; weight: Base 1,967 lb, 892 kg - L 1,986 lb, 901 kg - LDO 2,022 lb, 917 kg; fuel tank: 13.8 imp gal, 16.6 US gal, 63 l.

BODY estate car/st. wagon; 2+1 doors.

Corcel II GT

See Corcel II Base/L/LDO, except for:

PRICE EX WORKS: 97,031 cruzeiros

ENGINE max power (SAE): 89 hp (65.5 kW) at 5,600 rpm; max torque (SAE): 83 lb ft, 11.5 kg m (156.4 Nm) at 4,000 rpm; 64.9 hp/l (47.8 kW/l); 1 Solex 34 SIE - 2V downdraught carburettor.

PERFORMANCE power-weight ratio: 23.4 lb/hp (31.7 lb/kW), 10.6 kg/hp (14.4 kg/kW).

DIMENSIONS AND WEIGHT weight: 2,073 lb, 940 kg.

Maverick Sedan Super/ Super Luxo/LDO

		cruzeiros
PRICES EX WORKS: Maverick Sedan Super		138,699
Maverick Sedan Super Luxo		148,565
Maverick Sedan LDO		166,777

ENGINE front, 4 stroke; 4 cylinders, in line; 140.4 cu in, 2,301 cc (3.78 x 3.13 in, 96 x 79.4 mm); compression ratio: 7.8:1; max power (SAE): 99 hp (72.9 kW) at 5,400 rpm; max torque (SAE): 122 lb ft, 16.9 kg m (165.7 Nm) at 3,200 rpm; max engine rpm: 5,700; 43 hp/l (31.7 kW/l); cast iron block and head; 5 crankshaft bearings; valves: overhead, push-rods and rockers; camshafts: 1, overhead; lubrication: rotary pump, full flow filter, 8.3 imp pt, 9.9 US pt, 4.7 l; 1 Solex downdraught single barrel carburettor; fuel feed: mechanical pump; water-cooled, 13.4 imp pt, 16.1 US pt, 7.6 l.

FORD Corcel II Belina LDO

TRANSMISSION driving wheels: rear; clutch: single dry plate; gearbox: mechanical; gears: 4, fully synchronized; ratios: I 3.569, II 2.378, III 1.531, IV 1, rev 4.229; lever: steering column; final drive: hypoid bevel; axle ratio: 3.920; width of rims: 5''; tyres: 6.95 S x 14 or D 70 S x 14.

PERFORMANCE max speed: 96 mph, 154 km/h; power-weight ratio: 29.1 lb/hp (39.7 lb/kW), 13.2 kg/hp (18 kg/kW); carrying capacity: 882 lb, 400 kg; speed in direct drive at 1,000 rpm: 18 mph, 29 km/h; consumption: 28.8 m/imp gal, 24 m/US gal, 9.8 l x 100 km.

CHASSIS integral; front suspension: independent, wishbones (lower trailing links), coil springs, anti-roll bar, telescopic dampers; rear: rigid axle, semi-elliptic leafsprings, telescopic dampers.

STEERING worm and roller; turns lock to lock: 6.50.

BRAKES front disc, internal radial fins, rear drum; lining area: total 91.6 sq in, 591 sq cm.

ELECTRICAL EQUIPMENT 12 V; 54 Ah battery; 30 A alternator; Motorcraft distributor; 2 headlamps.

DIMENSIONS AND WEIGHT wheel base: 103.15 in, 262 cm; front and rear track: 56.30 in, 143 cm; length: 186.22 in, 473 cm; width: 70.47 in, 179 cm; height: 53.54 in, 136 cm; ground clearance: 6.81 in, 17.3 cm; weight: 3,889 lb, 1,310 kg; turning circle: 37.4 ft, 11.4 m; fuel tank: 14.3 imp gal, 17.2 US gal, 65 l.

BODY saloon/sedan; 4 doors; 6 seats, bench front seats (for Super Luxo only) luxury equipment.

VARIATIONS

ENGINE V8 cylinders, 302 cu in 4,950 cc (4 x 3 in, 101.6 76.2 mm), 7.5:1 compression ratio, max power (SAE) 19 hp (145 kW) at 4,600 rpm, max torque (SAE) 286 lb ft 39.5 kg m (387.4 Nm) at 2,400 rpm, max engine rpm 4,900 39.8 hp/l (29.3 kW/l), 5 crankshaft bearings, overhead valves with hydraulic tappets, 1 camshaft at cenrte of Vee 1 Motorcraft D20F-KB downdraught twin barrel carburetto cooling system 20.1 imp pt, 24.1 US pt, 11.4 l.
PERFORMANCE max speed 112 mph, 180 km/h, power-weigh ratio 15.4 lb/hp (19.8 lb/kW), 7 kg/hp (9 kg/kW), consump tion 21.6 m/imp gal, 18 m/US gal, 13.1 l x 100 km.
STEERING recirculating ball, 5.80 turns lock to lock.
ELECTRICAL EQUIPMENT 40 A alternator.

OPTIONALS gearbox ratios (I 2.920, II 2.030, III 1.420, I 1, rev 3.430), 3.070 axle ratio; Select-Shift Cruise-o-Mati automatic transmission, hydraulic torque converter an planetary gears with 3 ratios (I 2.460, II 1.460, III 1, re 2.200), max ratio of converter at stall 2, possible manua selection, 3.070 axle ratio; 3-speed fully synchronized mecha nical gearbox (I 2.920, II 1.750, III 1, rev 3.760), 3.07 axle ratio; recirculating ball steering gear; power-assiste steering; total swept area 338 sq in, 2,180 sq cm; separat front seats; vinyl roof; metallic spray; air-conditionin only with V8 engine.

FORD Maverick Coupé GT-4

Maverick Coupé Super/Super Luxo/LDO/GT-4

See Maverick Sedan Super/Super Luxo/LDO, except for:

PRICES EX WORKS:

	cruzeiros
Maverick Coupé Super	139,624
Maverick Coupé Super Luxo	149,427
Maverick Coupé LDO	169,214

PERFORMANCE power-weight ratio: 28.7 lb/hp (39.7 lb/kW), 13 kg/hp (18 kg/kW).

DIMENSIONS AND WEIGHT length: 179.13 in, 455 cm; weight: 2,833 lb, 1,285 kg; weight distribution: 53.3% front, 44.7% rear turning circle: 35.1 ft, 10.7 m.

BODY coupé; 2 doors; 5 seats; (for Super Luxo only) luxury equipment.

Maverick Coupé GT

See Maverick Sedan Super/Super Luxo/LDO, except for:

PRICE EX WORKS: 166,966 cruzeiros

ENGINE V8 cylinders; 302 cu in, 4,950 cc (4 x 3 in, 101.6 x 76.2 mm); compression ratio: 7.5:1; max power (SAE): 197 hp (145 kW) at 4,600 rpm; max torque (SAE): 286 lb ft, 39.5 kg m (387.4 Nm) at 2,400 rpm; max engine rpm: 4,900; 39.8 hp/l (29.3 kW/l); valves: overhead, in line, push-rods and rockers, hydraulic tappets; camshafts: 1, at centre of Vee; 1 Motorcraft D20F-KB downdraught twin barrel carburettor cooling system: 20.1 imp pt, 24.1 US pt, 11.4 l.

TRANSMISSION ratios: I 2.920, II 2.030, III 1.420, IV 1, rev 3.430; lever: central; axle ratio: 3.070; width of rims: 6''; tyres: D70 S x 14.

PERFORMANCE max speeds: (I) 39 mph, 62 km/h; (II) 56 mph, 90 km/h; (III) 81 mph, 130 km/h; (IV) 114 mph, 183 km/h; power-weight ratio: 15 lb/hp (20.3 lb/kW), 6.8 kg/hp (9.2 kg/kW); speed in direct drive at 1,000 rpm: 23.6 mph, 38 km/h; consumption: 21.6 m/imp gal, 18 m/US gal, 13.1 l x 100 km.

STEERING recirculating ball, servo; turns lock to lock: 5.80.

BRAKES swept area: total 338 sq in, 2,180 sq cm.

ELECTRICAL EQUIPMENT 40 A alternator.

DIMENSIONS AND WEIGHT length: 180.71 in, 459 cm; height: 53.94 in, 137 cm; weight: 2,955 lb, 1,340 kg; weight distribution: 53.3% front, 44.7% rear; turning circle: 35.1 ft, 10.7 m.

BODY coupé; 2 doors; 5 seats, separate front seats; air-conditioning.

VARIATIONS

None.

Galaxie 500/LTD/Landau

PRICES EX WORKS:

Galaxie 500	305,494 cruzeiros
Galaxie LTD	331,737 cruzeiros
Galaxie Landau	378,617 cruzeiros

ENGINE front, 4 stroke; V8 cylinders; 302 cu in, 4,950 cc (4 x 3 in, 101.6 x 76.2 mm); compression ratio: 7.8:1; max powre (SAE): 197 hp (145 kW) at 4,600 rpm; max torque (SAE): 288 lb ft, 39.8 kg m (390.3 Nm) at 2,400 rpm; max engine rpm: 4,800; 40.2 hp/l (29.3 kW/l); cast iron block and head; 5 crankshaft bearings; valves: overhead, push-rods and rockers; camshafts: 1, at centre of Vee; lubrication: gear pump, full flow filter, 8.3 imp pt, 9.9 US pt, 4.7 l; 1 Motorcraft downdraught twin barrel carburettor; fuel feed: mechanical pump; water-cooled, 19.4 imp pt, 23.3 US t, 11 l.

TRANSMISSION driving wheels: rear; clutch: single dry plate; gearbox: mechanical; gears: 3, fully synchronized; ratios: I 2.920, II 1.750, III 1, rev 3.760; lever: steering column; final drive: hypoid bevel; axle ratio: 3.540; width of rims: 5''; tyres: 7.75 x 15.

PERFORMANCE max speeds: (I) 37 mph, 59 km/h; (II) 61 mph, 98 km/h; (III) 103 mph, 165 km/h; power-weight ratio: 19.4 lb/hp (26.7 lb/kW), 8.6 kg/hp (12.1 kg/kW); carrying capacity: 1,069 lb, 485 kg; speed in direct drive at 1,000 rpm: 22.2 mph, 35.7 km/h; consumption: 19.6 m/imp gal, 16.3 m/US gal, 14.4 l x 100 km.

CHASSIS box-type ladder frame; front suspension: independent, wishbones, lower trailing arms, coil springs, anti-roll bar, telescopic dampers; rear: rigid axle, lower trailing arms, upper torque arms, coil springs, telescopic dampers.

STEERING recirculating ball, servo; turns lock to lock: 4.

BRAKES front disc, internal radial fins, rear drum, servo; lining area: total 103.7 sq in, 669 sq cm.

ELECTRICAL EQUIPMENT 12 V; 54 Ah battery; 50 A alternator; 4 headlamps.

DIMENSIONS AND WEIGHT wheel base: 119.02 in, 302 cm; front and rear track: 62.42 in, 158 cm; length: 212.99 in, 541 cm; width: 78.74 in, 200 cm; height: 55.51 in, 141 cm; ground clearance: 5.51 in, 14 cm; weight: 3,859 lb, 1,750 kg; turning circle: 44 ft, 13.4 m; fuel tank: 16.7 mp gal, 20.1 US gal, 76 l.

BODY saloon/sedan; 4 doors; 6 seats, bench front seats; (for LTD only) luxury equipment.

OPTIONALS Ford-o-Matic automatic transmission, hydraulic torque converter and planetary gears with 3 ratios (I 2.460, II 1.460, III 1, rev 2.200), max ratio of converter at stall 2.1, possible manual selection, 3.310 axle ratio; air-conditioning.

GURGEL   BRAZIL

X-12/X-12 TR

PRICES EX WORKS:

X-12	105,750 cruzeiros
X-12TR	114,809 cruzeiros

ENGINE Volkswagen, rear, 4 stroke; 4 cylinders, horizontally opposed; 96.7 cu in, 1,584 cc (3.37 x 2.72 in, 85.5 x 69 mm); compression ratio: 7.2:1; max power (DIN): 50 hp (36.8 kW) at 4,200 rpm; max torque (DIN): 80 lb ft, 11 kg m (108 Nm) at 2,200 rpm; max engine rpm: 4,600; 31.6 hp/l (23.2 kW/l); block with cast iron liners and light alloy fins, light alloy head; 4 crankshaft bearings; valves: overhead, push-rods and rockers; camshafts: 1, central, lower; lubrication: gear pump, oil cooler, 4.4 imp pt, 5.3 US pt, 2.5 l; 1 Solex H 30 Pic downdraught single barrel carburettor; fuel feed: mechanical pump; air-cooled.

TRANSMISSION driving wheels: rear; clutch: single dry plate; gearbox: mechanical; gears: 4, fully synchronized; ratios: I 3.800, II 2.060, III 1.320, IV 0.890, rev 3.880; lever: central; final drive: spiral bevel; axle ratio: 4.375; width of rims: 5.5''; tyres: 7.35 x 15.

PERFORMANCE max speeds: (I) 17 mph, 27 km/h; (II) 32 mph, 51 km/h; (III) 50 mph, 80 km/h; (IV) 73 mph, 118 km/h; power-weight ratio: 33.5 lb/hp (45.5 lb/kW), 15.2 kg/hp (20.6 kg/kW); carrying capacity: 772 lb, 350 kg; speed in top at 1,000 rpm: 19.3 mph, 31 km/h; consumption: 28.2 m/imp gal, 23.5 m/US gal, 10 l x 100 km.

CHASSIS backbone platform; front suspension: independent, twin swinging longitudinal trailing arms, transverse laminated torsion bars, telescopic dampers; rear: independent, swinging semi-axles, swinging longitudinal trailing arms, transverse torsion bars, telescopic dampers.

GURGEL X-12 TR

STEERING worm and roller; turns lock to lock: 2.50.

BRAKES drum; swept area: front 20.5 sq in, 132 sq cm, rear 20.8 sq in, 134 sq cm, total 41.2 sq in, 266 sq cm.

ELECTRICAL EQUIPMENT 12 V; 36 Ah battery; 350 W dynamo; Bosch distributor; 2 headlamps.

DIMENSIONS AND WEIGHT wheel base: 81.50 in, 207 cm; tracks: 52.36 in, 133 cm front, 55.12 in, 140 cm rear: length: 128.74 in, 328 cm; width: 62.99 in, 160 cm; height: 59.45 in, 151 cm; ground clearance: 9.84 in, 25 cm; weight: 1,676 lb, 760 kg; turning circle: 31.2 ft, 9.5 m; fuel tank: 8.8 imp gal, 10.6 US gal, 40 l.

BODY in plastic material; 2 doors; 4 seats, separate front seats (X-12 open in plastic material, no doors).

OPTIONALS limited slip differential; anti-roll bar on front and rear suspension.

X-20

See X-12/X-12TR except for:

PRICE EX WORKS: 142,363 cruzeiros

TRANSMISSION axle ratio: 4.125; tyres: 7.75 x 15.

PERFORMANCE max speeds: (I) 16 mph, 25 km/h; (II) 30 mph, 48 km/h; (III) 47 mph, 75 km/h; (IV) 62 mph, 100 km/h; power-weight ratio: 44.1 lb/hp (59.9 lb/kW), 20 kg/hp (27.2 kg/kW); consumption: 23.5 m/imp gal, 19.6 m/US gal, 12 l x 100 km.

DIMENSIONS AND WEIGHT wheel base: 88.19 in, 224 cm; front and rear track: 56.69 in, 144 cm; length: 144.88 in, 368 cm; width: 70.87 in, 180 cm; height: 74.80 in, 190 cm; ground clearance: 13.78 in, 35 cm; weight: 2,205 lb, 1,000 kg; fuel tank: 17.6 imp gal, 21.1 US gal, 80 l.

BODY 8 seats.

LAFER   BRAZIL

MP

ENGINE Volkswagen, rear, 4 stroke; 4 cylinders, horizontally opposed; 96.7 cu in, 1,584 cc (3.37 x 2.72 in, 85.5 x 69 mm); compression ratio: 7.2:1; max power (SAE): 65 hp (47.8 kW) at 4,600 rpm; max torque (SAE): 85 lb ft, 12 kg m (118 Nm) at 3,200 rpm; max engine rpm: 4,800; 41 hp/l (30.2 kW/l); block with cast iron liners and light alloy fins, light alloy head; 4 crankshaft bearings; valves: overhead, in line, push-rods and rockers; camshafts: 1, central, lower; lubrication: gear pump, filter in sump, oil cooler, 4.4 imp pt, 5.3 US pt, 2.5 l; 2 Solex H 32 twin barrel carburettors; fuel feed: mechanical pump; air-cooled.

TRANSMISSION driving wheels: rear; clutch: single dry plate; gearbox: mechanical; gears: 4, fully synchronized; ratios: I 3.800, II 2.060, III 1.320, IV 0.890, rev 3.880; lever: central; final drive: spiral bevel; axle ratio: 4.125; width of rims: 4.5''; tyres: 5.60 x 15.

PERFORMANCE max speeds: (I) 25 mph, 41 km/h; (II) 48 mph, 77 km/h; (III) 71 mph, 115 km/h; (IV) 86 mph, 138 km/h; power-weight ratio: 25.8 lb/hp (35.1 lb/kW), 11.7 kg/hp (15.9 kg/kW); acceleration: standing ¼ mile 22.5 sec, 0-50 mph (0-80 km/h) 9.9 sec; speed in direct drive at 1,000 rpm: 19.6 mph, 31.6 km/h; consumption: 32.8 m/imp gal, 27.3 m/US gal, 8.6 l x 100 km.

CHASSIS backbone platform, rear auxiliary frame; front suspension: independent, twin swinging longitudinal trailing arms, transverse laminated torsion bars, anti-roll bar, telescopic dampers; rear: independent, semi-trailing arms, transverse compensating torsion bars, anti-roll bar, telescopic dampers.

STEERING worm and roller; turns lock to lock: 2.60.

BRAKES front disc (diameter 10.94 in, 27.8 cm), rear drum; lining area: front 11.7 sq in, 76 sq cm, rear 56.4 sq in, 364 sq cm, total 68.2 sq in, 440 sq cm.

ELECTRICAL EQUIPMENT 12 V; 36 Ah battery; 350 W alternator; Bosch distributor; 2 headlamps.

DIMENSIONS AND WEIGHT wheel base: 94.49 in, 240 cm; tracks: 51.57 in, 131 cm front, 53.15 in, 135 cm rear; length: 153.94 in, 391 cm; width: 61.81 in, 157 cm; height: 53.15 in, 135 cm; ground clearance: 5.9 in, 15 cm; weight: 1,676 lb, 760 kg; weight distribution: 40% front, 60% rear; turning circle: 36.1 ft, 11 m; fuel tank: 10.1 imp gal, 12.1 US gal, 46 l.

BODY roadster; 2 doors; 2 seats.

LAFER MP

MP

PRACTICAL INSTRUCTIONS fuel: 70.75 oct petrol; oil: engine 4.4 imp pt, 5.3 US pt, 2.5 l, change every 3,100 miles, 5,000 km - gearbox 4.4 imp pt, 5.3 US pt, 2.5 l; greasing: every 6,200 miles, 10,000 km; tyre pressure: front 15 psi, 1.1 atm, rear 18 psi, 1.3 atm.

OPTIONALS 175 SR x 14 tyres with light alloy wheels; hardtop; 3 auxiliary halogen headlamps; leather upholstery.

LL

ENGINE front, 4 stroke; 6 cylinders, in line; 250 cu in, 4,097 cc (3.87 x 3.53 in, 98.4 x 89.6 mm); compression ratio: 8:1; max power (SAE): 169 hp (124 kW) at 4,800 rpm; max torque (SAE): 261 lb ft, 36 kg m (353 Nm) at 2,400 rpm; max engine rpm: 5,200; 42.2 hp/l (30.3 kW/l) cast iron block and head; 7 crankshaft bearings; valves: overhead, in line, push-rods and rockers; camshafts: 1, side; lubrication: gear pump, full flow filter, 7 imp pt, 8.5 US pt, 4 l; 1 Solex H 40 EIS downdraught single barrel carburettor; fuel feed: mechanical pump; water-cooled, 33.4 imp pt, 40.2 US pt, 19 l.

TRANSMISSION driving wheels: rear; clutch: single dry plate; gearbox: mechanical; gears: 4, fully synchronized; ratios: I 2.790, II 2.020, III 1.390, IV 1, rev 3.570; lever: central; final drive: hypoid bevel; axle ratio: 3.080; width of rims: 8''; tyres: 70 HR x 14.

PERFORMANCE max speeds: (I) 45 mph, 73 km/h; (II) 63 mph, 101 km/h; (III) 91 mph, 147 km/h; (IV) 137 mph, 220 km/h; power-weight ratio: 17.6 lb/hp (24 lb/kW), 7.9 kg/hp (10.9 kg/kW); carrying capacity: 706 lb, 320 kg; acceleration: standing ¼ mile 18.3 sec, 0-50 mph (0-80 km/h) 7.5 sec; speed in direct drive at 1,000 rpm: 25 mph, 41 km/h; consumption: 19.5 m/imp gal, 16.2 m/US gal, 14.5 l x 100 km.

CHASSIS integral; front suspension: independent, wishbones, coil springs, anti-roll bar, telescopic dampers; rear: rigid axle, longitudinal trailing arms, coil springs, telescopic dampers.

STEERING recirculating ball, servo; turns lock to lock: 3.75.

BRAKES front disc, rear drum, servo; swept area: front 114.4 sq in, 738 sq cm, rear 58.9 sq in, 380 sq cm, total 173.3 sq in, 1,118 sq cm.

ELECTRICAL EQUIPMENT 12 V; 60 Ah battery; 55 A alternator; Bosch distributor; 4 headlamps.

DIMENSIONS AND WEIGHT wheel base: 105.12 in, 267 cm; tracks: 57.09 in, 145 cm front, 58.66 in, 149 cm rear; length: 177.95 in, 452 cm; width: 69.68 in, 177 cm; height: 50.79 in, 129 cm; ground clearance: 7.09 in, 18 cm; weight: 2,977 lb, 1,350 kg; weight distribution: 53% front, 47% rear; turning circle: 41 ft, 12.5 m; fuel tank: 18.9 imp gal, 22.7 US gal, 86 l.

BODY coupé; 2 doors; 2 + 2 seats, separate front seats.

PRACTICAL INSTRUCTIONS fuel: 80 oct petrol; oil: engine 8.3 imp pt, 9.9 US pt, 4.7 l, change every 7,500 miles, 12,000 km - gearbox 6.2 imp pt, 7.4 US pt, 3.5 l, change

every 3,100 miles, 5,000 km - final drive 2.1 imp pt, 2.5 US pt, 1.2 l, SAE 90, change every 5,000 miles, 8,000 km; tyre pressure: front 24 psi, 1.7 atm, rear 22 psi, 1.6 atm.

OPTIONALS 0.930 gearbox ratio in IV, automatic transmission.

PUMA   BRAZIL

GTE 1600 Coupé - GTS 1600 Sport

ENGINE Volkswagen, rear, 4 stroke; 4 cylinders, horizontally opposed; 96.7 cu in, 1,584 cc (3.37 x 2.72 in, 85.5 x 69 mm); compression ratio: 9:1 max power (SAE): 90 hp (66.2 kW) at 5,800 rpm; max torque (SAE): 96 lb ft, 13.2 kg m (129.4 Nm) at 3,000 rpm; max engine rpm: 6,000; 56.8 hp/l (41.8 kW/l); block with cast iron liners and light alloy fins, light alloy head; 4 crankshaft bearings; valves: overhead, push-rods and rockers; camshafts: 1, central, lower; lubrication: gear pump, filter in sump, oil cooler, 4.4 imp pt, 5.3 US pt, 2.5 l; 2 Solex-Brosol H40 EIS downdraught single barrel carburettors; fuel feed: mechanical pump; air-cooled.

TRANSMISSION driving wheels: rear; clutch: single dry plate; gearbox: mechanical; gears: 4, fully synchronized;

ratios: I 3.800, II 2.060, III 1.320, IV 0.890, rev 3.880; lever: central; final drive: spiral bevel; axle ratio: 4.125; width of rims: 6''; tyres: front 185/70HR x 14, rear 195/70HR x 14.

PERFORMANCE max speeds: (I) 26 mph, 42 km/h; (II) 47 mph, 76 km/h; (III) 75 mph, 120 km/h; (IV) 113 mph, 182 km/h; power-weight ratio: 18.4 lb/hp (25.0 lb/kW), 8.3 kg/hp (11.3 kg/kW); carrying capacity: 507 lb, 230 kg; acceleration: 0-50 mph (0-80 km/h) 12.5 sec; speed in top at 1,000 rpm: 19.9 mph, 32 km/h; consumption: 35.3 m/imp gal, 29.4 m/US gal, 8 l x 100 km.

CHASSIS backbone, rear auxiliary frame; front suspension: independent, twin swinging longitudinal trailing arms, transverse torsion bars, anti-roll bar, telescopic dampers; rear: independent, semi-trailing arms, transverse linkage by oblique swinging trailing arms, transverse torsion bars, telescopic dampers.

STEERING worm and roller; turns lock to lock: 2.70.

BRAKES front disc (diameter 10.94 in, 27.8 cm), rear drum; lining area: front 11.2 sq in, 72 sq cm, rear 52.6 sq in, 339 sq cm, total 63.8 sq in, 441 sq cm.

ELECTRICAL EQUIPMENT 12 V; 36 Ah battery; 350 W alternator; Bosch distributor; 2 headlamps.

DIMENSIONS AND WEIGHT wheel base: 84.65 in, 215 cm; tracks: 54.33 in, 138 cm front, 55.11 in, 140 cm rear; length: 157.48 in, 400 cm; width: 65.55 in, 166 cm; height: 47.24 in, 120 cm; ground clearance: 5.98 in, 15.2 cm; weight: 1,654 lb, 750 kg; weight distribution: 40% front, 60% rear; turning circle: 32.5 ft, 9.9 m; fuel tank: 8.8 imp gal, 10.6 US gal, 40 l.

BODY in plastic material; 2 doors; 2 seats, reclining backrests, built-in headrests; light alloy wheels.

VARIATIONS

ENGINE 109.8 cu in, 1,800 cc; 115.9 cu in, 1,900 cc; 122 cu in, 2,000 cc; 128.1 cu in, 2,100 cc.

OPTIONALS 4-speed fully synchronized mechanical gearbox (I 2.570, II 1.610, III 1.240, IV 0.960, rev 3.880), 4.375 axle ratio; 4-speed fully synchronized mechanical gearbox (I 1.740, II 1.320, III 1.120, IV 0.960, rev. 3.880), 3.880 axle ratio; ZF limited slip differential; anti-roll bar on rear suspension; (for GTS 1600 only) hardtop.

GTB

ENGINE front, 4 stroke; 6 cylinders, in line; 250 cu in, 4,097 cc (3.87 x 3.52 in, 98.4 x 89.5 mm); compression ratio: 7.8:1; max power (SAE): 171 hp (125.9 kW) at 4,800 rpm; max torque (SAE): 236 lb ft, 32.5 kg m (318.7 Nm) at 2,600 rpm; max engine rpm: 5,000; 41.7 hp/l (30.7 kW/l); cast iron block and head; 7 crankshaft bearings; valves: overhead, in line, push-rods and rockers, hydraulic tappets; camshafts: 1, side; lubrication: gear pump, full flow filter, 7 imp pt, 8.5 US pt, 4 l; 1 DFV or Solex-Brosol 40 downdraught single barrel carburettor; fuel feed: mechanical pump; water-cooled, 18 imp pt, 21.6 US pt,10.2 l.

PUMA GTS 1600 Sport

TRANSMISSION driving wheels: rear; clutch: single dry plate (diaphragm), hydraulically controlled; gearbox: mechanical; gears: 4, fully synchronized; ratios: I 3.070, II 2.020, III 1.390, IV 1, rev 3.570; lever: central; final drive: hypoid bevel; axle ratio: 3.080; width of rims: front 7'', rear 8''; tyres: front 205/70HR x 14, rear 215/70HR x 14.

PERFORMANCE max speeds: (I) 40 mph, 64 km/h; (II) 61 mph, 98 km/h; (III) 88 mph, 142 km/h; (IV) 123 mph, 198 km/h; power-weight ratio: 12.6 lb/hp (17.2 lb/kW), 5.7 kg/hp (7.8 kg/kW); carrying capacity: 617 lb, 280 kg; speed in direct drive at 1,000 rpm: 24.6 mph, 39.6 km/h; consumption: 11.4 m/imp gal, 17.8 m/US gal, 13.2 l x 100 km.

CHASSIS box-type perimeter frame with cross members; front suspension: independent, wishbones (lower trailing links), coil springs, telescopic dampers; rear: rigid axle, twin upper longitudinal leading arms, lower transverse arms, telescopic dampers.

STEERING worm and roller.

BRAKES front disc, rear drum, servo.

ELECTRICAL EQUIPMENT 12 V; 44 Ah battery; 32 A alternator; Bosch distributor; 2 iodine headlamps.

DIMENSIONS AND WEIGHT wheel base: 95.28 in, 242 cm; front and rear track: 55.51 in, 141 cm; length: 169.29 in, 430 cm; width: 68.50 in, 174 cm; height: 49.61 in, 126 cm; ground clearance: 5.91 in, 15 cm; weight: 2,161 lb, 980 kg; turning circle: 33.8 ft, 10.3 m; fuel tank: 11.9 imp gal, 14.3 US gal, 54 l.

BODY coupé; 2 doors; 2 + 2 seats, separate front seats, reclining backrests; light alloy wheels; tinted glass; air-conditioning.

VOLKSWAGEN **BRAZIL**

1300/1300 L

PRICES EX WORKS: 1300 66,164 cruzeiros
1300 L 69,099 cruzeiros

ENGINE rear, 4 stroke; 4 cylinders, horizontally opposed; 78.4 cu in, 1,285 cc (3.03 x 2.72 in, 77 x 69 mm); compression ratio: 6.8:1; max power (DIN): 38 hp (28 kW) at 4,000 rpm; max torque (DIN): 62 lb ft, 8.5 kg m (83 Nm) at 2,200 rpm; max engine rpm: 4,600; 29.6 hp/l (21.8 kW/l); cylinder block with cast iron liners and light alloy fins, light alloy head; 4 crankshaft bearings; valves: overhead, push-rods and rockers; camshafts: 1, central, lower; lubrication: gear pump, filter in sump, oil cooler, 4.4 imp pt, 5.3 US pt, 2.5 l; 1 Solex H 30 PIC downdraught single barrel carburettor; fuel feed: mechanical pump; air-cooled.

TRANSMISSION driving wheels: rear; clutch: single dry plate; gearbox: mechanical; gears: 4, fully synchronized; ratios: I 3.800, II 2.060, III 1.320, IV 0.880, rev 3.880; lever: central; final drive: spiral bevel; axle ratio: 4.375; width of rims: 4.5''; tyres: 5.60 x 15.

PERFORMANCE max speeds: (I) 17.4 mph, 28 km/h; (II) 32 mph, 52 km/h; (III) 50 mph, 80 km/h; (IV) 75 mph, 120 km/h; power-weight ratio: 45.2 lb/hp (61.4 lb/kW), 20.5 kg/hp (27.8 kg/kW); carrying capacity: 838 lb, 380 kg; acceleration: 0-50 mph (0-80 km/h) 14.3 sec; speed in top at 1,000 rpm: 18.6 mph, 30 km/h; consumption: 39.8 m/imp gal, 33.1 m/US gal, 7.1 l x 100 km.

CHASSIS backbone platform; front suspension: independent, twin swinging longitudinal trailing arms, transverse laminated torsion bars, anti-roll bar, telescopic dampers; rear: independent, swinging semi-axles, swinging longitudinal trailing arms, transverse torsion bars, telescopic dampers.

STEERING worm and roller, telescopic damper; turns lock to lock: 2.60.

BRAKES drum; lining area front: 56.43 sq in, 364 sq cm; rear: 56.43 sq in, 364 sq cm; total: 112.87 sq in, 728 sq cm.

ELECTRICAL EQUIPMENT 12 V; 36 Ah battery; 350 W dynamo; Bosch distributor; 2 headlamps.

DIMENSIONS AND WEIGHT wheel base: 94.49 in, 240 cm; tracks: 51.18 in, 130 cm front, 50.79 in, 129 cm rear; length: 158.66 in, 403 cm; width: 60.63 in, 154 cm; height: 59.06 in, 150 cm; ground clearance: 5.91 in, 15 cm; weight: 1,720 lb, 780 kg; turning circle: 36.1 ft, 11 m; fuel tank: 9 imp gal, 10.8 US gal, 41 l.

BODY saloon/sedan; 2 doors; 5 seats, separate front seats, adjustable backrests - 1300 L, luxury equipment.

PRACTICAL INSTRUCTIONS fuel: 73 oct petrol; oil: engine 4.4 imp pt, 5.3 US pt, 2.5 l, SAE 20W-40, change every 3,100 miles, 5,000 km - gearbox 4.4 imp pt, 5.3 US pt, 2.5 l, SAE 90 EP, change every 9,300 miles, 15,000 km; greasing: every 6,200 miles, 10,000 km, 8 points; valve

---

timing: 9°48' 35°02' 44°28' 4°14'; tyre pressure: front 16 psi, 1.1 atm, rear 20 psi, 1.4 atm.

OPTIONALS heating.

1600 Limousine

See 1300 L Limousine, except for:

PRICE EX WORKS: 71,408 cruzeiros

ENGINE 96.7 cu in, 1,584 cc (3.37 x 2.72 in, 85.5 x 69 mm); compression ratio: 7.2:1; max power (DIN): 56 hp (41.2 kW) at 4,200 rpm; max torque (DIN): 80 lb ft, 11 kg m (107.9 Nm) at 3,000 rpm; 35.3 hp/l (26 kW/l); 2 Solex 32 PDSIT downdraught single barrel carburettors.

TRANSMISSION axle ratio: 4.125; width of rims: 5''; tyres: 5.90 x 14.

PERFORMANCE max speed: 86 mph, 138 km/h; power-weight ratio: 31.4 lb/hp (42.7 lb/kW), 14.3 kg/hp (19.4 kg/kW); acceleration: 0-50 mph (0-80 km/h) 10.2 sec; consumption: 32.1 m/imp gal, 26.7 m/US gal, 8.8 l x 100 km.

BRAKES front disc (diameter 10.94 in, 27.8 cm); rear drum; lining area: front 11.8 sq in, 76 sq cm, rear 56.4 sq in, 364 sq cm, total 68.2 sq in, 440 sq cm.

DIMENSIONS AND WEIGHT tracks: 51.97 in, 132 cm front, 53.15 in, 135 cm rear.

BODY luxury equipment.

VOLKSWAGEN Passat TS 2-dr Limousine

Passat Series

PRICES EX WORKS:

1 2-dr Limousine	105,793	cruzeiros
2 LS 2-dr Limousine	112,426	cruzeiros
3 LS 3-dr Limousine	115,137	cruzeiros
4 LS 4-dr Limousine	115,450	cruzeiros
5 TS 2-dr Limousine	124,845	cruzeiros
6 LSE 4-dr Limousine	136,757	cruzeiros

Power team:	Standard for:	Optional for:
65 hp	1 to 4	—
80 hp	5,6	—

65 hp power team

ENGINE front, slanted 20° to right, 4 stroke; 4 cylinders, in line; 89.8 cu in, 1,471 cc (3.01 x 3.15 in, 76.5 x 80 mm); compression ratio: 7.4:1; max power (DIN): 65 hp (47.8 kW) at 5,600 rpm; max torque (DIN): 75 lb ft, 10.3 kg m (101 Nm) at 3,000 rpm; max engine rpm: 6,500; 44.2 hp/l (32.5 kW/l); cast iron block, light alloy head; 5 crankshaft bearings; valves: overhead, in line, thimble tappets; camshafts: 1, overhead, cogged belt; lubrication: gear pump, full flow filter, 5.3 imp pt, 6.3 US pt, 3 l; 1 Solex H 35 PDSI (T) downdraught single barrel carburettor; fuel feed: mechanical pump; water-cooled, 10.9 imp pt, 13.1 US pt, 6.2 l, electric thermostatic fan.

TRANSMISSION driving wheels: front; clutch: single dry plate (diaphragm); gearbox: mechanical; gears: 4, fully

---

synchronized; ratios: I 3.454, II 1.940, III 1.290, IV 0.910, rev 3.170; lever: central; final drive: spiral bevel; axle ratio: 4.111; width of rims: 4.5''; tyres: 155 SR x 13.

PERFORMANCE max speed: 90 mph, 145 km/h; power-weight ratio: 29.2 lb/hp (39.7 lb/kW), 13.2 kg/hp (17.9 kg/kW) - LS 4-dr 30 lb/hp (40.8 lb/kW), 13.6 kg/h (18.5 kg/kW); carrying capacity: 992 lb, 450 kg - LS 4-dr 937 lb, 425 kg; speed in top at 1,000 rpm: 16.5 mph, 26.6 km/h; consumption: 34 m/imp gal, 28.3 m/US gal, 8.3 l x 100 km.

CHASSIS integral, front auxiliary subframe; front suspension: independent, by McPherson, lower wishbones, anti-roll bar, coil springs/telescopic damper struts; rear: **rigid axle,** trailing radius arms, transverse linkage bar, coil springs, anti-roll bar, telescopic dampers.

STEERING rack-and-pinion, telescopic damper.

BRAKES front disc (diameter 9.41 in, 23.9 cm), rear drum, servo.

ELECTRICAL EQUIPMENT 12 V; 36 Ah battery; 35 A alternator; Bosch distributor; 2 headlamps.

DIMENSIONS AND WEIGHT wheel base: 97.24 in, 247 cm; tracks: 52.76 in, 134 cm front, 52.36 in, 133 cm rear; length: 168.5 in, 428 cm; width: 62.99 in, 160 cm; height: 53.35 in, 135 cm; ground clearance: 5.12 in, 13 cm; weight: 1,896 lb, 860 kg LS 4-dr 1,951 lb, 885 kg; turning circle: 33.8 ft, 10.3 m; fuel tank: 9.9 imp gal, 11.9 US gal, 45 l.

BODY saloon/sedan; 5 seats, separate front seats, reclining backrests - LS, luxury equipment.

PRACTICAL INSTRUCTIONS fuel: 73 oct petrol; oil: engine 5.3 imp pt, 6.3 US pt, 3 l SAE 20 W 40, change every 4,600 miles, 7,500 km - gearbox 2.6 imp pt, 3.2 US pt, 1.5 l, SAE 80, change every 2,800 miles, 4,500 km; valve timing: 4°, 46° 44° 6°; tyre pressure: front 26 psi, 1.8 atm, rear 26 psi, 1.8 atm.

80 hp power team

See 65 hp power team, except for:

ENGINE 96.9 cu in, 1,588 cc (3.13 x 3.15 in, 79.5 x 80 mm); compression ratio: 7.5:1; max power (DIN): 80 hp (58.9 kW) at 5,600 rpm; max torque (DIN): 87 lb ft, 12 kgm (117.7 Nm) at 3,000 rpm; 50.4 hp/l (37.1 kW/l); 1 Solex H 32/35 TDID (T) downdraught single barrel carburettor.

TRANSMISSION gearbox ratios: I 3.454, II 1.950, III 1.290 IV 0.910, rev 3.170; tyres: 175 SR x 13 or 175 HR x 13.

PERFORMANCE max speed: 99 mph, 160 km/h; power-weight ratio: 23.7 lb/hp (32.2 lb/kW), 10.7 kg/hp (14.5 kg/kW) - LSE 24.4 lb/hp (33.1 lb/kW), 11.1 kg/hp (15.1 kg/kW); carrying capacity: LSE 937 lb, 425 kg; consumption: 34.9 m/imp gal, 28 m/US gal, 8.1 l x 100 km.

ELECTRICAL EQUIPMENT 42 Ah battery.

DIMENSIONS AND WEIGHT weight: LSE 1,951 lb, 885 kg.

80 HP POWER TEAM

BODY built-in headrests - LSE, executive equipment.

OPTIONALS metallic spray; heating; air-conditioning; heated rear window.

Brasilia 2-door/4-door/LS

PRICE EX WORKS: 86,500 cruzeiros

ENGINE rear, 4 stroke; 4 cylinders, horizontally opposed; 96.7 cu in, 1,584 cc (3.37 x 2.72 in, 85.5 x 69 mm); compression ratio: 7.2:1; max power (DIN): 54 hp (39.7 kW) at 4,200 rpm; max torque (DIN): 78 lb ft, 10.8 kg m (105.9 Nm) at 3,000 rpm; max engine rpm: 4,600; 34.1 hp/l (25.1 kW/l); cylinder block with cast iron liners and light alloy fins, light alloy head; 4 crankshaft bearings; valves: overhead, push-rods and rockers; camshafts: 1, central, lower; lubrication: gear pump, filter in sump, oil cooler, 4.4 imp pt, 5.3 US pt, 2.5 l; 2 Solex H 32 PDSI downdraught single barrel carburettors; fuel feed: mechanical pump; air-cooled.

TRANSMISSION driving wheels: rear; clutch: single dry plate; gearbox: mechanical; gears: 4, fully synchronized; ratios: I 3.800, II 2.060, III 1.320, IV 0.880, rev 3.880; lever: central; final drive: spiral bevel; axle ratio: 4.125; width of rims: 5''; tyres: 5.90 x 14.

PERFORMANCE max speeds: (I) 20 mph, 32 km/h; (II) 36 mph, 58 km/h; (III) 57 mph, 92 km/h; (IV) 86 mph, 138 km/h; power-weight ratio: 36.3 lb/hp (49.3 lb/kW), 16.5 kg/hp (22.4 kg/kW); carrying capacity: 926 lb, 420 kg; speed in top at 1,000 rpm: 19.3 mph, 31 km/h; consumption: 32.5 m/imp gal, 27 m/US gal, 8.7 l x 100 km.

CHASSIS backbone platform, rear auxiliary frame; front suspension: independent, twin swinging longitudinal trailing arms, transverse torsion bars, anti-roll bar, telescopic dampers; rear: independent, semi-trailing arms, transverse compensating torsion bar, anti-roll bar, telescopic dampers.

STEERING worm and roller, telescopic damper; turns lock to lock: 2.70.

BRAKES front disc (diameter 10.94 in, 27.8 cm), rear drum; lining area: total 38.4 sq in, 248 sq cm.

ELECTRICAL EQUIPMENT 12 V; 36 Ah battery; 35 A alternator; Bosch distributor; 4 headlamps.

DIMENSIONS AND WEIGHT wheel base: 94.49 in, 240 cm; tracks: 51.97 in, 132 cm front, 53.54 in, 136 cm rear; length: 157.87 in, 401 cm; width 63.39 in, 161 cm; height: 56.30 in, 143 cm; weight: 1,962 lb, 890 kg; turning circle: 36.1 ft, 11 m; fuel tank: 10.1 imp gal, 12.1 US gal, 46 l.

BODY saloon/sedan; 2 doors; 4 doors; 5 seats, separate front seats, adjustable backrests - LS, luxury equipment.

PRACTICAL INSTRUCTIONS fuel: 73 oct petrol; oil: engine 4.4 imp pt, 5.3 US pt, 2.5 l, SAE 20W-40, change every 3,100 miles, 5,000 km; gearbox and final drive 5.3 imp pt, 6.3 US pt, 3 l, SAE 90, change every 9,300 miles, 15,000

VOLKSWAGEN Brasilia LS

VOLKSWAGEN Variant II

km; greasing: every 6,200 miles, 10,000 km, 4 points; sparking plug: 145°; tappet clearances: inlet 0.004 in, 0.10 mm, exhaust 0.004 in, 0.10 mm; valve timing: 9°48' 35°02' 44°28' 4°14'; tyre pressure: front 17 psi, 1.2 atm, rear 26 psi, 1.8 atm.

OPTIONALS heating; heated rear window; metallic spray.

Variant II/II Luxe

PRICES EX WORKS: Variant II   109,181 cruzeiros
Variant II Luxe 121,697 cruzeiros

ENGINE rear, 4 stroke; 4 cylinders, horizontally opposed; 196.7 cu in, 1,584 cc (3.36 x 2.71 in, 85.5 x 69 mm); compression ratio: 7.2:1; max power (DIN): 56 hp (41.2 kW) at 4,200 rpm; max torque (DIN): 80 lb ft, 11 kg m (107.9 Nm) at 2,800 rpm; max engine rpm: 4,600; 35.3 hp/l (26 kW/l); cylinder block with cast iron liners and light alloy fins, light alloy head; 4 crankshaft bearings; valves: overhead, push-rods and rockers; camshafts: 1, central, lower lubrication: gear pump, filter in sump, oil cooler, 4.4 imp pt, 5.3 US pt, 2.5 l; 2 Solex 32 PDSIT carburettors; fuel feed: mechanical pump; air-cooled.

TRANSMISSION driving wheels: rear; clutch: single dry plate; gearbox: mechanical; gears: 4, fully synchronized; ratios: I 3.800, II 2.060, III 1.320, IV 0.880, rev 3.880; lever: central; final drive: spiral bevel; axle ratio: 4.375; width of rims: 5''; tyres: 175 x 14.

PERFORMANCE max speeds: (I) 19 mph, 31 km/h; (II) 36 mph, 58 km/h; (III) 59 mph, 95 km/h; (IV) 86 mph, 138 km/h; power-weight ratio: 38.2 lb/hp (51.9 lb/kW), 17.3 kg/hp (23.5 kg/kW); carrying capacity: 1,102 lb, 500 kg; acceleration: 0-50 mph (0-80 km/h) 12.5 sec; speed in top at 1,000 rpm: 19.9 mph, 32 km/h; consumption: 30.4 m/imp gal, 25.3 m/US gal, 9.3 l x 100 km.

CHASSIS backbone platform, rear auxiliary frame; front suspension: independent, by McPherson, lower wishbones, anti-roll bar, coil springs/telescopic damper struts; rear: independent, transverse torsion bars, semi-axles with homokinetic joints, telescopic dampers.

STEERING rack-and-pinion; turns lock to lock: 3.94.

BRAKES front disc, rear drum; swept area: front 16.3 sq in, 105 sq cm, rear 70.1 sq in, 452 sq cm, total 86.4 sq in, 557 sq cm.

ELECTRICAL EQUIPMENT 12 V; 36 Ah battery; 490 W dynamo; Bosch distributor; 4 headlamps.

DIMENSIONS AND WEIGHT wheel base: 98.20 in, 249 cm; tracks: 53.74 in, 136 cm front, 55.20 in, 140 cm rear; length: 170.31 in, 433 cm; width: 64.17 in, 163 cm; height: 56.29 in, 143 cm; ground clearance: 5.90 in, 15 cm; weight: 2,138 lb, 970 kg; weight distribution: 36.4% front, 63.6% rear; turning circle: 34.4 ft, 10.5 m; fuel tank: 11 imp gal, 13.2 US gal, 50 l.

BODY estate car/st. wagon; 2 + 1 doors; 5 seats, separate front seats, adjustable backrests; folding rear seat - II Luxe, luxury equipment.

PRACTICAL INSTRUCTIONS fuel: 73 oct petrol; oil: engine 4.4 imp pt, 5.3 US pt, 2.5 l, SAE 20W-30, change every 3,100 miles, 5,000 km; gearbox and final drive: 4.4 imp pt, 5.3 US pt, 2.5 l, SAE 90, change every 9,300 miles,

15,000 km; tappet clearances: inlet and exhaust 0.006 in 0.15 mm; valve timing: 9°18' 35°02' 51°18' 11°; tyre pressure: front 17 psi, 1.2 atm, rear 26 psi, 1.8 atm.

OPTIONALS metallic spray; heating; built-in headrest heated rear window; rear window wiper-washer.

DODGE   ARGENTIN

1500

PRICE EX WORKS: 7,584 pesos

ENGINE front, 4 stroke; 4 cylinders, vertical, in line; 91 cu in, 1,498 cc (3.39 x 2.53 in, 86.1 x 64.3 mm); compression ratio: 8:1; max power (SAE): 72 hp (54 kW) at 5,4 rpm; max torque (SAE): 88 lb ft, 12.2 kg m (119 Nr at 3,200 rpm; max engine rpm: 5,400; 48 hp/l (35.3 kW/l; cast iron block and head; 5 crankshaft bearings; valve overhead, in line, push-rods and rockers; camshafts: side; lubrication: rotary pump, full flow filter, 7 imp p 8.5 US pt, 4 l; 1 Holley A-RX-7034A single barrel carb rettor; fuel feed: mechanical pump; water-cooled, 13 im pt, 15.6 US pt, 7.4 l.

TRANSMISSION driving wheels: rear; clutch: single d plate (diaphragm); gearbox: mechanical; gears: 4, full synchronized; ratios: I 3.317, II 2.029, III 1.366, IV, re 3.450; lever: central; final drive: hypoid bevel; axle rati 3.890; width of rims: 5''; tyres: 5.60 x 13.

PERFORMANCE max speeds: (I) 29 mph, 46 km/h; (I 48 mph, 77 km/h; (III) 71 mph, 114 km/h; (IV) 90 mpl 145 kmh; power-weight ratio: 28.2 lb/hp (38.3 lb/kW), 12 kg/hp (17.4 kg/kW); carrying capacity: 882 lb, 400 kç acceleration: 0-50 mph (0-80 km/h) 9.5 sec; speed i direct drive at 1,000 rpm: 18.6 mph, 30 km/h; consum tion: 25.7 m/imp gal, 21.4 m/US gal, 11 l x 100 km.

CHASSIS integral; front suspension: independent, t McPherson, lower trailing links, coil springs, anti-roll ba telescopic dampers; rear: rigid axle, lower trailing radiu arms, upper oblique torque arms, coil springs, telescopi dampers.

STEERING rack-and-pinion; turns lock to lock: 3.66.

BRAKES front disc, rear drum; lining area: front 15.7 s in, 100.1 sq cm, rear 53.5 sq in, 345 sq cm, total 69 sq in, 446 sq cm.

ELECTRICAL EQUIPMENT 12 V; 48 Ah battery; 32 A alterna tor; Chrysler-TRIA distributor; 2 headlamps.

DIMENSIONS AND WEIGHT wheel base: 97.99 in, 249 cm tracks: 50.98 in, 129 cm front, 51.26 in, 130 cm rea length: 162.99 in, 414 cm; width: 62.52 in, 159 cm height: 53.15 in, 135 cm; ground clearance: 5.59 i 14 cm; weight: 2,029 lb, 920 kg; weight distribution: 54.2% front, 45.8% rear; turning circle: 31.8 ft, 9.7 m; fue tank: 9.9 imp gal, 11.9 US gal, 45 l.

BODY saloon/sedan; 4 doors; 5 seats, separate front seat reclining backrests.

PRACTICAL INSTRUCTIONS fuel: 89-100 oct petrol; oi engine 7 imp pt, 8.5 US pt, 4 l, change every 3,700 mile 6,000 km; gearbox 3 imp pt, 3.6 US pt, 1.7 l; final driv 2.3 imp pt, 2.7 us pt, 1.3 l; greasing: 2 points; tyr pressure: front 24 psi, 1.7 atm, rear 26 psi, 1.8 atm.

OPTIONALS servo, dual circuit.

1500 M 1.8

PRICE EX WORKS: 8,660 pesos

ENGINE front, 4 stroke; 4 cylinders, vertical, in line 109.7 cu in, 1,798 cc (3.39 x 3.04 in, 86.1 x 77.2 mm compression ratio: 8.6:1; max power (SAE): 92 hp (69 kW at 4,900 rpm; max torque (SAE): 116 lb ft, 16 kg m (15 Nm) at 3,400 rpm; max engine rpm: 5,800; 51.2 hp/l (37. kW/l); cast iron block and head; 5 crankshaft bearings valves: overhead, in line, push-rods and rockers; cam shafts: 1, side; lubrication: rotary pump, full flow filte 7 imp pt, 8.5 US pt, 4 l; 1 Holley A-RX-7035A single barre carburettor; fuel feed: mechanical pump; water-coole 11.4 imp pt, 13.7 US pt, 6.5 l.

TRANSMISSION driving wheels: rear; clutch: single d plate (diaphragm); gearbox: mechanical; gears: 4, full synchronized; ratios: I 3.317, II 2.029, III 1.366, IV rev 3.450; lever: central; final drive: hypoid bevel; axl ratio: 3.890; width of rims: 5''; tyres: 5.60 x 13.

PERFORMANCE max speeds: (I) 31 mph, 50 km/h; (II) mph, 75 km/h; (III) 78 mph, 125 km/h; (IV) 93 mph, 14 km/h; power-weight ratio: 22.9 lb/hp (31.1 lb/kW), 10. kg/hp (14.1 kg/kW); carrying capacity: 882 lb, 400 kg acceleration: 0-50 mph (0-80 km/h) 9.5 sec; speed

direct drive at 1,000 rpm: 21.7 mph, 35 km/h; consumption: 11.4 m/imp gal, 26.1 m/US gal, 9 l x 100 km.

CHASSIS integral; front suspension: independent, by McPherson, lower trailing links, coil springs, anti-roll bar, telescopic dampers; rear: rigid axle, lower trailing radius arms, upper oblique torque arms, coil springs, telescopic dampers.

STEERING rack-and-pinion; turns lock to lock: 3.66.

BRAKES front disc, rear drum, servo, dual circuit; lining area: front 15.7 sq in, 100.1 sq cm, rear 53.5 sq in, 345 sq cm, total 69.2 sq in, 446 sq cm.

ELECTRICAL EQUIPMENT 12 V; 48 Ah battery; 32 A alternator; Chrysler-TRIA distributor; 2 iodine headlamps.

DIMENSIONS AND WEIGHT wheel base: 97.99 in, 249 cm; tracks: 50.98 in, 129 cm front, 51.26 in, 130 cm rear; length: 162.99 in, 414 cm; width: 62.52 in, 159 cm; height: 53.15 in, 135 cm; ground clearance: 5.59 in, 14 cm; weight: 2,110 lb, 957 kg; weight distribution: 54.2% front, 45.8% rear; turning circle: 31.8 ft, 9.7 m; fuel tank: 9.9 imp gal, 11.9 US gal, 45 l.

BODY saloon/sedan; 4 doors; 5 seats, separate front seats, reclining backrests with built-in headrests.

PRACTICAL INSTRUCTIONS see 1500 except for: tyre pressure: rear 24 psi, 1.7 atm.

OPTIONALS Borg-Warner 45 automatic transmission; 155 x 13 tyres; heated rear window.

TRANSMISSION driving wheels: rear; clutch: single dry plate; gearbox: mechanical; gears: 3, fully synchronized; ratios: I 2.830, II 1.560, III 1, rev 2.660; lever: steering column; final drive: hypoid bevel; axle ratio: 3.070; width of rims: 5.5''; tyres: 135 x 14.

PERFORMANCE max speeds: (I) 34 mph, 55 km/h; (II) 71 mph, 115 km/h; (III) 99 mph, 159 km/h; power-weight ratio: 21.4 lb/hp (29 lb/kW), 9.7 kg/hp (13.2 kg/kW); carrying capacity: 1,213 lb, 550 kg; acceleration: 0-50 mph (0-80 km/h) 9 sec; speed in direct drive at 1,000 rpm: 24.9 mph, 40 km/h; consumption: 21.7 m/imp gal, 18.1 m/US gal, 13 l x 100 km.

CHASSIS integral; front suspension: independent, wishbones, lower trailing links, longitudinal torsion bars, telescopic dampers; rear: rigid axle, semi-elliptic leaf-springs, telescopic dampers.

STEERING recirculating ball; turns lock to lock: 5.30.

BRAKES front disc, rear drum, servo, dual circuit; lining area: front 60.5 sq in, 390 sq cm, rear 32.4 sq in, 209 sq cm, total 92.9 sq in, 599 sq cm.

ELECTRICAL EQUIPMENT 12 V; 59 Ah battery; 40 A alternator; Chrysler electronic ignition; 2 iodine headlamps.

DIMENSIONS AND WEIGHT wheel base: 110.63 in, 281 cm; tracks: 56.30 in, 143 cm front, 57.48 in, 146 cm rear; length: 197.24 in, 501 cm; width: 70.87 in, 180 cm; height: 55.51 in, 141 cm; ground clearance: 6.38 in,

---

16 cm; weight: 3,175 lb, 1,440 kg; weight distribution: 55% front, 45% rear; turning circle: 38.7 ft, 11.8 m; fuel tank: 15 imp gal, 18 US gal, 68 l.

BODY saloon/sedan; 4 doors; 6 seats, bench front seats.

PRACTICAL INSTRUCTIONS fuel 89-100 oct petrol; oil: engine 7 imp pt, 8.4 US pt, 4 l, change every 3,700 miles, 6,000 km; gearbox 3.5 imp pt, 4.2 US pt, 2 l, change every 22,400 miles, 36,000 km; final drive 1.75 imp pt, 2.1 US pt, 1 l, change every 22,400 miles, 36,000 km; greasing: 2 points; valve timing: 10° 50° 6°; tyre pressure: front 26 psi, 1.8 atm, rear 26 psi, 1.8 atm.

OPTIONALS power steering.

Coronado Automatic

See Coronado, except for:

PRICE EX WORKS: 13,748 pesos

TRANSMISSION gearbox: Torqueflite automatic transmission, hydraulic torque converter and planetary gears with 3 ratios + reverse, max ratio of converter at stall 2.1, possible manual selection; ratios: I 2.450, II 1.450, III 1, rev 2.200; tyres: 7.35 x 14.

PERFORMANCE max speeds: (I) 32 mph 52 km/h; (II) 68 mph, 110 km/h; (III) 96 mph, 154 km/h; acceleration 0-50 mph (0-80 km/h) 10 sec; consumption: 20.2 m/imp gal, 16.8 m/US gal, 14 l x 100 km.

CHASSIS front suspension: anti-roll bar.

STEERING servo: turns lock to lock: 3.50.

BRAKES front disc with internal radial fins.

BODY vinyl roof.

FIAT　　　　　　　　　　　**ARGENTINA**

600 S

ENGINE rear, 4 stroke; 4 cylinders, vertical, in line; 51.4 cu in, 843 cc (2.56 x 2.50 in, 65 x 63.5 mm); compression ratio: 7.4:1; max power (DIN): 32 hp (24 kW) at 4,800 rpm; 37.9 hp/l (28.5 kW/l); cast iron block, light alloy head; 3 crankshaft bearings; valves: overhead, in line, push-rods and rockers; camshafts: 1, side; lubrication: gear pump, full flow filter (cartridge), 6.5 imp pt, 7.8 US pt, 3.7 l; 1 Galileo 285 CP 10 or Bressel 285 CP 10 downdraught single barrel carburettor; fuel feed: mechanical pump; sealed circuit cooling, liquid, 7.9 imp pt, 9.5 US pt, 4.5 l.

TRANSMISSION driving wheels: rear; clutch: single dry plate; gearbox: mechanical; gears: 4, fully synchronized; ratios: I 3.385, II 2.055, III 1.333, IV 0.896, rev 4.275;

DODGE 1500 M 1.8 Rural

1500 M 1.8 Rural

See 1500 M 1.8, except for:

PRICE EX WORKS: 10,313 pesos

PERFORMANCE power-weight ratio: 31.5 lb/hp (42.8 lb/kW), 14.3 kg/hp (19.4 kg/kW).

CHASSIS rear suspension: 4 swinging links.

DIMENSIONS AND WEIGHT length: 165.35 in, 420 cm; height: 53.54 in, 136 cm; weight: 2,910 lb, 1,320 kg; weight distribution: 45.8% front, 54.2% rear.

BODY estate car/station wagon; 4 + 1 doors.

Coronado

PRICE EX WORKS: 12,062 pesos

ENGINE front, 4 stroke; 6 cylinders, vertical, in line; 225 cu in, 3,688 cc (3.40 x 4.13 in, 86.4 x 104.8 mm); compression ratio: 8.4:1; max power (SAE): 145 hp (108 kW) at 4,400 rpm; max torque (SAE): 215 lb ft, 29.7 kg m (294 Nm) at 2,400 rpm; max engine rpm 4,600; 39.3 hp/l (28.9 kW/l); cast iron block and head; 4 crankshaft bearings; valves: overhead, in line, push-rods and rockers camshafts: 1, side; lubrication: rotary pump, full flow filter, 7 imp pt, 8.4 US pt, 4 l; 1 Holley R 2535A downdraught single barrel carburettor; fuel feed: mechanical pump; water-cooled 21.6 imp pt, 26 US pt, 12.3 l.

DODGE Coronado

600 S

lever: central; final drive: spiral bevel; axle ratio: 4.875; width of rims: 4''; tyres: 5.20 x 12.

PERFORMANCE max speeds: (I) 19 mph, 30 km/h; (II) 28 mph, 45 km/h; (III) 43 mph, 70 km/h; (IV) 68 mph, 110 km/h; power-weight ratio: 43 lb/hp (57.4 lb/kW), 19.5 kg/hp (26 kg/kW); carrying capacity: 706 lb, 320 kg; acceleration: standing ¼ mile 26.7 sec, 0-50 mph (0-80 km/h) 26 sec; speed in top at 1,000 rpm: 14.1 mph, 22.7 km/h; consumption: 48.7 m/imp gal, 40.6 m/US gal, 5.8 l x 100 km.

CHASSIS integral; front suspension: independent, upper swinging arms, anti-roll bar, telescopic dampers; rear: independent, swinging arms, coil springs, telescopic dampers.

STEERING screw and sector; turns lock to lock: 2.12.

BRAKES drum; lining area: front 33.5 sq in, 216 sq cm, rear 33.5 sq in, 216 sq cm, total 67 sq in, 432 sq cm.

ELECTRICAL EQUIPMENT 12 V; 32 Ah battery; 475 W alternator; Garef-Marelli distributor; 2 headlamps.

DIMENSIONS AND WEIGHT wheel base: 78.74 in, 200 cm; tracks: 45.28 in, 115 cm front, 45.67 in, 116 cm rear; length: 131.89 in, 335 cm; width: 54.33 in, 138 cm; height: 55.12 in, 140 cm; ground clearance: 5.71 in, 14.5 cm; weight: 1,378 lb, 625 kg; weight distribution: 46% front, 54% rear; turning circle: 29.5 ft, 9 m; fuel tank: 5.9 imp gal, 7.1 US gal, 27 l.

BODY saloon/sedan; 2 doors; 4 seats, separate front seats.

PRACTICAL INSTRUCTIONS fuel: 90 oct petrol; oil: engine 5.3 imp pt, 6.3 US pt, 3 l, 20W-40, change every 3,100 miles, 5,000 km - gearbox 2.6 imp pt, 3.2 US pt, 1.5 l, SAE 90 EP, change every 18,600 miles, 30,000 km; tappet clearances: inlet 0.0059 in, 0.15 mm, exhaust 0.0059 in, 0.15 mm; valve timing: 4° 26° 29° 1°; tyre pressure: front 14 psi, 1 atm, rear 23 psi, 1.6 atm.

133

ENGINE rear, longitudinal, 4 stroke; 4 cylinders, vertical, in line; 55.1 cu in, 903 cc (2.56 x 2.68 in, 65 x 68 mm); compression ratio: 7.8:1; max power (DIN): 40 hp (29.4 kW) at 5,600 rpm; max torque (DIN): 42 lb ft, 5.8 kg m (56.9 Nm) at 3,400 rpm; max engine rpm: 6,200; 44.3 hp/l; cast iron block, light alloy head; 3 crankshaft bearings; valves: overhead, in line, push-rods and rockers; camshafts: 1, side; lubrication: gear pump, full flow filter (cartridge), 6 imp pt, 7.2 US pt, 3.4 l; 1 Weber 30 IGF 19 vertical single barrel carburettor; exhaust gas recirculation; fuel feed: mechanical pump; water-cooled, 8.8 imp pt, 10.6 US pt, 5 l.

TRANSMISSION driving wheels: rear; clutch: single dry plate (diaphragm); gearbox: mechanical; gears: 4, fully synchronized; ratios: I 3.636, II 2.055, III 1.409, IV 0.963, rev 3.615; lever: central; final drive: hypoid bevel; axle ratio: 4.625; width of rims: 4.5''; tyres: 145 R x 13.

PERFORMANCE max speed: 81 mph, 130 km/h; carrying capacity: 706 lb, 320 kg; consumption: 40.9 m/imp gal, 34.1 m/US gal, 6.9 l x 100 km.

CHASSIS integral; front suspension: independent, wishbones, transverse leafspring lower arms, transverse torsion bar, anti-roll bar, telescopic dampers; rear: independent, semi-trailing arms, coil springs, torsion bar, anti-roll bar, telescopic dampers.

STEERING screw and sector; turns lock to lock: 2.26.

BRAKES front disc, rear drum.

ELECTRICAL EQUIPMENT 12 V; 34 Ah battery; 475 W dynamo; 2 headlamps.

DIMENSIONS AND WEIGHT wheel base: 79.53 in, 202 cm; tracks: 45.28 in, 115 cm front, 47.64 in, 121 cm rear; length: 137.40 in, 349 cm; width: 55.91 in, 142 cm; height: 52.36 in, 133 cm; turning circle: 31.5 ft, 9.6 m; fuel tank: 6.6 imp gal, 7.9 US gal, 30 l.

BODY saloon/sedan; 2 doors; 4 seats, separate front seats.

PRACTICAL INSTRUCTIONS fuel: 90-92 oct petrol; oil: engine 5.8 imp pt, 6.9 US pt, 3.3 l, SAE 20W-40, change every 3,100 miles, 5,000 km - gearbox 3.7 imp pt, 4.4 US pt, 2.1 l, SAE 90 EP, change every 18,600 miles, 30,000 km; valve timing: 25° 51° 64° 12°; tyre pressure: front 20 psi, 1.4 atm, rear 28 psi, 2 atm.

FIAT 600 S

133 L

See 133, except for:

ENGINE compression ratio: 8.4:1; max torque (DIN): 43 lb ft, 6 kg m (58.8 Nm) at 3,600 rpm.

128 Berlina

ENGINE front, transverse, 4 stroke; 4 cylinders, in line; 68.1 cu in, 1,116 cc (3.15 x 2.19 in, 80 x 55.5 mm); compression ratio: 8.8:1; max power (SAE): 63 hp at 6,00 rpm; max torque (DIN): 59 lb ft, 8.1 kg m at 3,000 rpm; max engine rpm: 6,500; 56.4 hp/l; cast iron block, light alloy head; 5 crankshaft bearings; valves: overhead, thimble tappets; camshafts: 1, overhead, cogged belt; lubrication: gear pump, full flow filter (cartridge), 7.9 imp pt, 9.5 US pt, 4.5 l; 1 Weber 32 ICEV 14 or Solex C 3 DISA 24 downdraught single barrel carburettor; fuel feed: mechanical pump; water-cooled, 11.4 imp pt, 13.7 US pt, 6.5 l, electric thermostatic fan.

TRANSMISSION driving wheels: front; clutch: single dry plate; gearbox: mechanical; gears: 4, fully synchronized; ratios: I 3.583, II 2.235, III 1.454, IV 1.042, rev 3.714; lever: central; final drive: cylindrical gears; axle ratio 4.077; width of rims: 4.5''; tyres: 145 SR x 13.

PERFORMANCE max speeds: (I) 28 mph, 45 km/h; (II) 4 mph, 75 km/h; (III) 71 mph, 115 km/h; (IV) 87 mph, 14

FIAT 133

km/h; power-weight ratio: 28.2 lb/hp, 12.8 kg/hp; carrying capacity: 882 lb, 400 kg; acceleration: standing ¼ mil 19.7 sec, 0-50 mph (0-80 km/h) 11.6 sec; speed in top at 1,000 rpm: 15.2 mph, 24.4 km/h; consumption: 35. m/imp gal, 29.4 m/US gal, 8 l x 100 km.

CHASSIS integral; front suspension: independent, by Mc Pherson, coil springs/telescopic damper struts, lowe wishbones, anti-roll bar; rear: independent, single wide based wishbones, transverse anti-roll leafsprings, telescopi dampers.

STEERING rack-and-pinion; turns lock to lock: 3.40.

BRAKES front disc (diameter 8.94 in, 22.7 cm), rear drum rear compensator, servo; lining area: front 19.2 sq in 124 sq cm, rear 33.5 sq in, 216 sq cm, total 52.7 sq in 340 sq cm.

ELECTRICAL EQUIPMENT 12 V; 34 Ah battery; 38 A alter nator; Garef-Marelli distributor; 2 headlamps.

DIMENSIONS AND WEIGHT wheel base: 96.06 in, 244 cm tracks: 51.57 in, 131 cm front, 51.57 in, 131 cm rear length: 152.76 in, 388 cm; width: 62.60 in, 159 cm; heigh 55.91 in, 142 cm; ground clearance: 7.60 in, 19.3 cm weight: 1,775 lb, 805 kg; weight distribution: 61.5% front, 38.5% rear; turning circle: 33.8 ft, 10.3 m; fue tank: 8.44 imp gal, 10 US gal, 38 l.

BODY saloon/sedan; 4 doors; 5 seats, separate front seats

PRACTICAL INSTRUCTIONS fuel: 92 oct petrol; oil: engine 7 imp pt, 8.4 US pt, 4 l, SAE 20W-40, change every 3,10

FIAT 128 Familiar 5 Puertas

miles, 5,000 km - gearbox 5.6 imp pt, 6.7 US pt, 3.2 l,
SAE 90 EP, change every 18,600 miles, 30,000 km; valve
timing: 12º 52º 52º 12º; tyre pressure: front 25 psi, 1.8
atm, rear 24 psi, 1.7 atm.

128 L Berlina

See 128 Berlina, except for:

ENGINE 78.7 cu in, 1,290 cc (3.39 x 2.19 in, 86 x 55.5 mm);
compression ratio: 8.9:1; max power (SAE): 70 hp at 6,250
rpm; max torque (DIN): 67 lb ft, 9.2 kg m at 3,250 rpm;
max engine rpm: 7,000; 54.3 hp/l; 1 Weber 32 ICEV 10
downdraught single barrel carburettor.

TRANSMISSION gearbox ratio: IV 1.030; tyres: 155 SR x 13.

PERFORMANCE max speeds: (I) 28 mph, 45 km/h; (II) 47
mph, 75 km/h; (III) 73 mph, 118 km/h; (IV) over 90 mph, 145
km/h; power-weight ratio: 26.1 lb/hp, 11.9 kg/hp; speed in
top at 1,000 rpm: 15.5 mph, 25 km/h; consumption:
33.2 m/imp gal, 27.7 m/US gal, 8.5 l x 100 km.

STEERING turns lock to lock: 3.50.

DIMENSIONS AND WEIGHT weight: 1,841 lb, 835 kg; turning circle: 35.8 ft, 10.9 m.

BODY luxury equipment; reclining front seats.

1300 TV lava

See 128 L Berlina, except for:

ENGINE compression ratio: 8.9:1; max power (SAE): 90 hp
at 6,250 rpm; 69.8 hp/l; 1 Solex C 34 EIES downdraught
twin barrel carburettor; exhaust gas recirculation.

TRANSMISSION width of rims: 5''.

PERFORMANCE max speed: over 99 mph, 160 km/h.

DIMENSIONS AND WEIGHT tracks: 52.76 in, 134 cm front,
53.15 in, 135 cm rear.

128 Familiar 5 Puertas

See 128 L Berlina, except for:

PERFORMANCE max speed: over 87 mph, 140 km/h; power-
weight ratio: 26.9 lb/hp, 12.2 kg/hp; acceleration: standing
¼ mile 20 sec, 0-50 mph (0-80 km/h) 12 sec.

DIMENSIONS AND WEIGHT length: 153.15 in, 389 cm;
weight: 1,885 lb, 855 kg; weight distribution: 60% front,
40% rear.

BODY estate car/station wagon; 4+1 doors; 5 seats,
separate front seats, reclining backrests; folding rear seat.

125 S

ENGINE front, 4 stroke; 4 cylinders, vertical, in line; 98.1
cu in, 1,608 cc (3.15 x 3.15 in, 80 x 80 mm); compression
ratio: 8.8:1; max power (DIN): 100 hp at 6,200 rpm; max
torque (DIN): 96 lb ft, 13.3 kg m at 4,000 rpm; max engine
rpm: 6,200; 62 hp/l; cast iron block, light alloy head;
5 crankshaft bearings; valves: overhead; camshafts:
2, overhead, cogged belt; lubrication: gear pump, full flow
filter, 8.6 imp pt, 10.4 US pt, 4.9 l; 1 Weber 34 DCHE 20
or Solex C34 PAIA/33 downdraught twin barrel carburettor;
exhaust gas recirculation; fuel feed: mechanical pump; water-
cooled, 13.2 imp pt, 15.9 US pt, 7.5 l, electric thermostatic
fan.

TRANSMISSION driving wheels: rear; clutch: single dry
plate; gearbox: mechanical; gears: 4, fully synchronized;
ratios: I 3.670, II 2.110, III 1.360, IV 1, rev 3.570; lever:
central; final drive: hypoid bevel; axle ratio: 3.900; width
of rims: 5''; tyres: 175 S x 13.

PERFORMANCE max speeds: (I) 28 mph, 45 km/h; (II) 50
mph, 80 km/h; (III) 78 mph, 125 km/h; (IV) 106 mph,
170 km/h; power-weight ratio: 23.1 lb/hp, 10.5 kg/hp;
carrying capacity: 882 lb, 400 kg; acceleration: standing
¼ mile 18.6 sec, 0-50 mph (0-80 km/h) 9 sec; speed in
direct drive at 1,000 rpm: 17.5 mph, 28.2 km/h; consumption:
28.5 m/imp gal, 23.8 m/US gal, 9.9 l x 100 km.

CHASSIS integral; front suspension: independent, wishbones, coil springs, anti-roll bar, telescopic dampers; rear:
rigid axle, upper torque arms, semi-elliptic leafsprings,
telescopic dampers.

STEERING worm and roller; turns lock to lock: 3.

BRAKES front disc, rear drum, servo.

ELECTRICAL EQUIPMENT 12 V; 48 Ah battery; 38 A alternator; Garef Marelli distributor; 4 headlamps.

DIMENSIONS AND WEIGHT wheel base: 98.82 in, 251 cm;
tracks: 51.57 in, 131 cm front, 50.79 in, 129 cm rear;
length: 167.32 in, 425 cm; width: 63.39 in, 161 cm; height:
56.69 in, 144 cm; ground clearance: 7.28 in, 18.5 cm;
weight: 2,326 lb, 1,055 kg; turning circle: 35.4 ft, 10.8 m;
fuel tank: 9.9 imp gal, 11.9 US gal, 45 l.

BODY saloon/sedan; 4 doors; 5 seats, separate front seats,
reclining backrests.

PRACTICAL INSTRUCTIONS fuel: 92 oct petrol; oil: engine
6.2 imp pt, 7.4 US pt, 3.5 l - gearbox 2.5 imp pt, 2.9
US pt, 1.4 l, SAE 90 EP, change every 18,600 miles,
30,000 km - final drive 2.6 imp pt, 3.2 US pt, 1.5 l, SAE
90 EP, change every 18,600 miles, 30,000 km; valve timing:
26º 66º 66º 26º; tyre pressure: front 21 psi, 1.5 atm, rear
24 psi, 1.7 atm.

OPTIONALS 175 SR x 13 tyres with 5.5'' wide rims.

125 SL

See 125 S, except for:

ENGINE compression ratio: 9:1; max power (DIN): 110
hp (80.9 kW) at 6,200 rpm; 68.4 hp/l (50.3 kW/l).

PERFORMANCE power-weight ratio: 21.1 lb/hp (28.7 lb/kW),
9.6 kg/hp (13 kg/kW).

PRACTICAL INSTRUCTIONS valve timing: 24º 66º 64º 26º.

125 Familiar

See 125 S, except for:

PERFORMANCE max speed: 103 mph, 165 km/h; power-
weight ratio: 24 lb/hp, 10.9 kg/hp; acceleration: standing
¼ mile 19 sec, 0-50 mph (0-80 km/h) 9.5 sec.

DIMENSIONS AND WEIGHT length: 168.11 in, 427 cm; weight:
2,043 lb, 1,090 kg; weight distribution: 50% front, 50% rear.

BODY estate car/station wagon; 4 + 1 doors; 5 seats,
separate front seats, reclining backrests; folding rear seat.

FORD   ARGENTINA

Taunus L 2000 Sedan/GXL Sedan

ENGINE front, 4 stroke; 4 cylinders, in line; 121.4 cu in,
1,990 cc (3.52 x 3.13 in, 89.3 x 79.4 mm); compression ratio:
8:1; max power (SAE): 92 hp (67.7 kW) at 5,500 rpm;
max torque (SAE): 109 lb ft, 15.1 kg m (148 Nm) at 3,000
rpm; max engine rpm: 6,000 46.2 hp/l (34 kW/l); cast
iron block and head; 5 crankshaft bearings; valves: overhead, push-rods and rockers; camshafts: 1, overhead, cogg-

FIAT 125 S

FORD Taunus L 2000 Sedan

TAUNUS L 2000 SEDAN/GXL SEDAN

ed belt; lubrication: gear pump, full flow filter, 7.9 imp pt, 9.5 US pt, 4.5 l; 1 Galileo Argentina downdraught single barrel carburettor; fuel feed: mechanical pump; water-cooled, 13.9 imp pt, 16.7 US pt, 7.9 l.

TRANSMISSION driving wheels: rear; clutch: single dry plate; gearbox: mechanical; gears: 4, fully synchronized; ratios: I 3.360, II 1.810, III 1.260, IV 1, rev 3.360; lever: central; final drive: hypoid bevel; axle ratio: 3.540; width of rims: 5.5''; tyres: 6.95 S x 13.

PERFORMANCE max speed: 95 mph, 153 km/h; power-weight ratio: 27.1 lb/hp (36.8 lb/kW), 12.3 kg/hp (16.7 kg/kW); speed in direct drive at 1,000 rpm: 18.5 mph, 29.7 km/h; consumption: 26.6 m/imp gal, 22.2 m/US gal, 10.6 l x 100 km.

CHASSIS integral; front suspension: independent, wishbones. coil springs/telescopic dampers, anti-roll bar; rear: rigid axle, lower trailing arms, upper oblique trailing arms, coil springs, telescopic dampers.

STEERING rack-and-pinion.

BRAKES front disc (diameter 9.75 in, 24.8 cm), rear drum; lining area: front 28.5 sq in, 184 sq cm, rear 59.8 sq in, 386 sq cm, total 88.3 sq in, 570 sq cm.

ELECTRICAL EQUIPMENT 12 V; 45 Ah battery; 540 W alter-nator; 2 headlamps.

DIMENSIONS AND WEIGHT wheel base: 101.57 in, 258 cm; front and rear track: 55.91 in, 142 cm; length: 171.26 in, 435 cm; width: 66.93 in, 170 cm; height: 52.76 in, 134 cm; ground clearance: 4.61 in, 11.7 cm; weight: 2,496 lb, 1,132 kg; turning circle: 35.1 ft, 10.7 m; fuel tank: 11.9 imp gal, 14.3 US gal, 54 l.

BODY saloon/sedan; 4 doors; 5 seats - GXL, luxury equip-ment.

OPTIONALS servo brake; 175 SR x 13 tyres; anti-roll bar on rear suspension.

Taunus GXL 2300 Sedan/GT Coupé

See Taunus L 2000 Sedan GXL Sedan, except for:

ENGINE 140.3 cu in, 2,299 cc (3.78 x 3.13 in, 96 x 79.4 mm); compression ratio: 9:1; max power (SAE): 122 hp (89.8 kW) at 5,000 rpm; max torque (SAE): 142 lb ft, 19.6 kg m (192.2 Nm) at 3,500 rpm; max engine rpm: 5,500; 53 hp/l (39 kW/l); 1 Argelite downdraught twin barrel carburettor; cooling system: 13.7 imp pt, 16.5 US pt, 7.8 l.

PERFORMANCE max speed: 106 mph, 170 km/h; power-weight ratio: 20.5 lb/hp (27.8 lb/kW), 9.3 kg/hp (12.6 kg/kW); consumption: 28.5 m/imp gal, 23.8 m/US gal, 9.9 l x 100 km.

ELECTRICAL EQUIPMENT 38 A alternator.

FORD Taunus GT Coupé

FORD Fairlane LTD-V8 Sedan

DIMENSIONS AND WEIGHT height: coupé 51.97 in, 132 cm.

BODY coupé; 2 doors.

OPTIONALS air conditioning; automatic transmission: 3 gears; ratios: I 2.47, II 1.47, III 1; axle ratio 3.31.

Fairlane LTD 3600 Sedan

ENGINE front, 4 stroke; 6 cylinders in line; 221 cu in, 3,620 cc (3.68 x 3.46 in, 93.5 x 87.9 mm); compression ratio: 8.2:1; max power (SAE): 132 hp (97.1 kW) at 4,000 rpm; max torque (SAE): 201.4 lb ft, 27.8 kg m (272.6 Nm) at 1,800 rpm; 36.6 hp/l (26.9 kW/l); cast iron block and head; 7 crankshaft bearings; valves: overhead, push-rods and rockers camshafts: 1, side, timing chain; lubrication: gear pump, full flow filter, 7.9 imp pt, 9.5 US pt, 4.5 l; 1 Argelite downdraught twin barrel carburettor; fuel feed: mechanical pump; water-cooled 14.7 imp pt, 17.6 US pt, 8.3 l.

TRANSMISSION driving wheels: rear; clutch: single dry plate; gearbox: mechanical; gears: 3, fully synchronized; ratios: I 2.99, II 1.75, III 1, rev 3.17; lever: steering column; axle .ratio: 3.31; tyres: 7.35 x 14.

PERFORMANCE max speed: 96 mph, 154 km/h; power-weight ratio: 25.9 lb/hp (35.2 lb/kW), 11.7 kg/hp (15.9 kg/kW); acceleration: standing ¼ mile 20 sec., 0-50 mph (0-80 km/h) 10.5 sec; consumption: 19.4 m/imp gal, 16.2 m/US gal, 14.5 l x 100 km.

CHASSIS integral; front suspension: independent, coil springs/telescopic dampers, anti-roll bar; rear: rigid axle, long leafsprings/telescopic dampers.

STEERING recirculating ball; power steering.

BRAKES front disc (diameter 10.9 in, 27.7 cm), rear drum, servo; lining area: front 28 sq in, 181 sq cm, rear 85 sq in, 548 sq cm, total 113 sq in, 729 sq cm.

ELECTRICAL EQUIPMENT 12 V; 55 Ah battery; 725 W alter-nator; 4 headlamps.

DIMENSIONS AND WEIGHT wheel base: 116 in, 294.6 cm; tracks: 58.5 in, 148.6 cm front, 58.5 in, 148.6 cm rear; length: 205 in, 520 cm; width: 74.8 in, 190 cm; height: 55 in, 140 cm; ground clearance: 6.7 in, 17 cm; weight: 3,418 lb, 1,550 kg; fuel tank: 16.5 imp gal, 19.8 US gal, 75 l.

BODY saloon/sedan; 4 doors; 5 seats.

OPTIONALS air conditioning; twin drive rear axle; « Elite » luxury equipment.

Fairlane LTD-V8 Sedan

See Fairlane LTD 3600, except for:

ENGINE 8 cylinders Vee-slanted 292 cu in, 4,785 cc (3.75 x 3.30 in, 95.2 x 83.8 mm); compression ratio: 8:1; max power (SAE) 180 hp (132.5 kW) at 4,500 rpm; max torque (SAE): 270 lb ft, 37.3 kg m (367 Nm) at 2,500 rpm; 37.6 hp/l (27.7 kW/l); cast iron block and head; 5 crank-shafts bearings; valves: overhead, push-rods and rockers;

camshaft: 1; lubrication: full flow filter, 9.7 imp pt, 11.6 US pt, 5.5 l; water-cooled, 28.2 imp pt, 33.8 US pt, 16 l.

TRANSMISSION tyres: 7.75 x 14.

PERFORMANCE max speed: 109 mph, 175 km/h; power weight ratio: 20.4 lb/hp (27.7 lb/kW), 9.6 kg/hp (12.6 kg/kW); acceleration: standing ¼ mile 19.5 sec, 0-50 mph (0-80 km/h) 9.8 sec; consumption: 18.4 m/imp gal, 15.4 m/US gal, 15.3 l x 100 km.

BRAKES front disc (diameter 11.3 in, 28.7 km), rear drum; lining area: front 38.5 sq in, 248.5 sq cm, rear 84.8 sq in, 548 sq cm; total 123.3 sq in, 797 sq cm.

DIMENSIONS AND WEIGHT weight: 3.667 lb, 1,663 kg.

Falcon Sedan Standard/De Luxe

ENGINE front, 4 stroke; 6 cylinders, in line; 188 cu in, 3,080 cc (3.68 x 2.94 in, 93.5 x 74.7 mm); compression ratio: 7.4:1; max power (SAE): 116 hp (85.4 kW) at 4,000 rpm; max torque (SAE): 176 lb ft, 24.3 kg m (238.3 Nm) at 2,300 rpm; 37.7 hp/l (27.7 kW/l); 7 crankshaft bearings; valves: overhead, push-rods and rockers; camshafts: 1, side, timing chain; lubrication: gear pump, full flow filter, 7.9 imp pt, 9.5 US pt, 4.5 l; 1 Galileo or Argelite down-draught single barrel carburettor; fuel feed: mechanical pump; water-cooled, 15.2 imp pt, 18.3 US pt, 8.6 l.

TRANSMISSION driving wheels: rear; clutch: single dry plate; gearbox: mechanical; gears: 3, fully synchronized; ratios: I 2.99, II 1.75, III 1, rev 3.17 lever: steering column; axle ratio: 3.31; tyres: 6.95 x 14.

PERFORMANCE max speed: 95 mph, 153 km/h; power-weight ratio: 23.6 lb/hp (32 lb/kW), 10.7 kg/hp (14.5 kg/kW); acceleration: standing ¼ mile 20.9 sec, 0-50 mph (0-80 km/h) 11.5 sec; consumption: 23.7 m/imp gal, 19.7 m/US gal, 11.9 l x 100 km.

CHASSIS integral; front suspension: independent, coil springs/telescopic dampers; suspension arms mounted on silent blocks, anti-roll bar; rear suspension: rigid axle, leafsprings/telescopic dampers.

STEERING recirculating ball.

BRAKES front disc (diameter 10.9 in, 27.7 cm), rear drum; lining area: front 28 sq in, 180.6 sq cm, rear 67.3 sq in, 434 sq cm, total 95.3 sq in, 614.6 sq cm.

ELECTRICAL EQUIPMENT 12 V; 45 Ah battery; 540 W alter-nator; 2 headlamps.

DIMENSIONS AND WEIGHT wheel base: 109.5 in, 278 cm; tracks: 55.6 in, 141 cm front, 54.5 in, 138 cm rear; length: 186.3 in, 473 cm; width: 70.6 in, 179 cm; height: 55.2 in, 140 cm; ground clearance: 7.04 in, 18 cm; weight: 2,740 lb, 1243 kg; fuel tank: 11.6 imp gal, 14 US gal, 53 l.

BODY saloon/sedan; 4 doors; 5 seats - Deluxe, luxury equipment.

OPTIONALS power steering; twin drive rear axle. Deluxe only: air-conditioning; 3.6 cc engine; 4-speed transmission halogen headlamps.

Falcon Station Wagon Standard/De Luxe

See Falcon Sedan except for:

TRANSMISSION axle ratio: 3.54.

PERFORMANCE power weight ratio: 26 lb/hp (35.3 kg/kW), 11.8 kg/hp (16 kg/kW).

DIMENSIONS AND WEIGHT weight: 3,013 lb, 1,367 kg; fuel tank: 14.4 imp gal, 17.3 US gal, 65.5 l.

BODY estate car/st. wagon.

Falcon Sedan Futura

See Falcon Sedan Standard and Deluxe except for:

ENGINE 221 cu in, 3,621 cc (3.68 x 3.46 in, 93.5 x 87.9 mm); compression ratio: 8.2:1; max power (SAE): 132 hp (97.1 kW) at 4,000 rpm; max torque (SAE): 201.4 lb ft, 27.8 kgm (272.6 Nm) at 1,800 rpm; 36.6 hp/l (26.9 kW/l).

TRANSMISSION gears: 4, fully synchronized; ratios: I 2.85, II 2.02, III 1.26, IV 1, rev 2.85; lever: central.

PERFORMANCE max speed: 97 mph, 156 km/h; power-weight ratio: 21.3 lb/hp (28.9 lb/kW), 9.7 lb/kW (13.2 kg/kW); acceleration: standing ¼ mile 19 sec, 0-50 mph (0-80 km/h) 13.8 sec; consumption 21.5 m/imp gal, 17.9 m/US gal, 13.1 l x 100 km.

DIMENSIONS AND WEIGHT weight: 2,811 lb, 1,275 kg.

BODY luxury equipment.

Falcon Sedan Sprint

See Falcon Sedan Futura except for:

ENGINE compression ratio: 8.1:1; max power (SAE): 166 hp (122.2 kW) at 4,500 rpm; max torque (SAE): 224.6 lb ft, 31 kgm (304 Nm) at 3,000 rpm; 46.1 hp/l (33.9 kW/l); 1 Argelite downdraught twin barrel carburettor.

PERFORMANCE max speed: 112 mph, 180 km/h; power-weight ratio: 17.3 lb/hp (23.5 lb/kW), 7.8 kg/hp (10.6 kg/kW); acceleration: standing ¼ mile 16.6 sec, 0-50 mph (0-80 km/h) 6.5 sec; consumption: 21.4 m/imp gal, 17.8 m/US gal, 13.2 l x 100 km.

TRANSMISSION axle ratio: 3.07; radial tyres: 175 R x 14.

RENAULT   ARGENTINA

4 S

ENGINE front, 4 stroke; 4 cylinders, vertical, in line; 62.24 cu in, 1,020 cc (2.56 x 2.64 in, 65 x 77 mm); compression ratio: 8.2:1; max power (SAE): 48 hp (35.3 kW) at 5,200 rpm; max torque (SAE): 60 lb ft, 8 kg m (78.5 Nm) at 3,000 rpm; 47 hp/l (34.6 kW/l); cast iron block, wet liners, light alloy head; 5 crankshaft bearings; valves: overhead, in line, push-rods and rockers; camshafts: 1, side; 1 weber 28 ICP downdraught single barrel carburettor; fuel feed: mechanical pump; water cooled.

TRANSMISSION driving wheels: front; clutch: single dry plate (diaphragm); gearbox: mechanical; gears: 4, fully synchronized; lever: on facia; final drive: hypoid bevel; axle ratio: 3.875; width of rims: 4''; tyres: 145 x 13.

PERFORMANCE max speed: over 75 mph, 120 km/h; power-weight ratio: 34.1 lb/hp (46.3 lb/kW), 15.4 kg/hp 21 kg/kW); consumption: 40.9 m/imp gal, 34.1 m/US gal, 6.9 l x 100 km.

CHASSIS platform; front suspension: independent, wishbones, longitudinal torsion bars, anti-roll bar, telescopic dampers; rear: independent, swinging longitudinal trailing arms, transverse torsion bars, telescopic dampers.

STEERING rack-and-pinion; turns lock to lock: 3.1.

BRAKES drum, rear compensator.

ELECTRICAL EQUIPMENT 12 V; 40 Ah battery; 28 A alternator; 2 headlamps.

DIMENSIONS AND WEIGHT wheel base: 96.06 in, 244 cm (right), 94.09 in, 239 cm (left); tracks: 50.39 in, 128 cm front, 49.21 in, 125 cm rear; length: 149.21 in, 379 cm; width: 58.27 in, 148 cm; height: 60.23 in, 153 cm; ground clearance: 8.07 in, 20.5 cm weight: 1,636 lb, 742 kg; turning circle: 33 ft, 10 m; fuel tank: 5.72 imp gal, 6.86 US gal, 26 l.

FORD Falcon De Luxe Sedan

BODY estate car/st. wagon; 4+1 doors; 4 seats, separate front seats; folding rear seat.

PRACTICAL INSTRUCTIONS fuel: 85 oct petrol.

6

ENGINE front, 4 stroke; 4 cylinders, vertical, in line; 85.43 cu in, 1,397 cc (2.99 x 3.03 in, 76 x 77 mm); compression ratio: 9:1; max power (SAE): 60 hp (44.1 kW) at 4,500 rpm; max torque (SAE): 79.7 lb ft, 11 kg m (108 Nm) at 2,000 rpm; 42.8 hp/l (31.5 kW/l); cast iron block, wet liners, light alloy head; 5 crankshaft bearings; valves: overhead, in line, push-rods and rockers; camshafts: 1, side; 1 Weber 30 ICF downdraught single barrel carburettor; fuel feed: mechanical pump; water-cooled, electric fan.

TRANSMISSION driving wheels: front; clutch: single dry plate (diaphragm); gearbox: mechanical; gears: 4, fully synchronized; lever: on facia; final drive: hypoid bevel; axle ratio: 3.180; width of rims: 4''; tyres: 145 x 13.

PERFORMANCE power-weight ratio: 31.2 lb/hp (42.5 lb/kW), 14.2 kg/hp (19.3 kg/kW).

CHASSIS platform front suspension: independent, wishbones, longitudinal torsion bars, anti-roll bar, telescopic dampers; rear: independent, swinging longitudinal trailing arms, transverse torsion bars, anti-roll bar, telescopic dampers.

STEERING rack-and-pinion; turns lock to lock: 3.1.

BRAKES drum, rear compensator.

ELECTRICAL EQUIPMENT 12 V; 40 Ah battery; 28 A alternator; 2 headlamps.

DIMENSIONS AND WEIGHT wheel base: 96.06 in, 244 cm (right), in, 239 cm (left); tracks: 50.39 in, 128 cm front, 49.21 in, 125 cm rear; length: 157.08 in, 399 cm; width: 59.05 in, 150 cm; height: 59.05 in, 150 cm; ground clearance: 7.9 in, 20 cm; weight: 1,874 lb, 850 kg; fuel tank: 7.9 imp gal, 9.5 US gal, 36 l.

BODY saloon/sedan; 4+1 doors; 4-5 seats, separate front seats; folding rear seat.

PRACTICAL INSTRUCTIONS fuel: 92 oct petrol.

12 TL

ENGINE front, 4 stroke; 4 cylinders, vertical in line; 78.65 cu in, 1,289 cc (2.87 x 3.03 in, 73 x 77 mm); compression ratio: 8.7:1; max power (SAE): 68 hp (50 kW) at 5,500 rpm; max torque (SAE): 79.7 lb ft, 11 kg m (107.9 Nm) at 3,000 rpm; 52.7 hp/l (38.8 kW/l); cast iron block, wet liners, light alloy head; 5 crankshaft bearings; valves: overhead; 1 Solex 32 EISA-3 downdraught carburettors; fuel feed: mechanical pump; water-cooled.

TRANSMISSION driving wheels: front; clutch: single dry

RENAULT 6

12 TL

plate (diaphragm); gearbox: mechanical gearbox; gears: 4, fully synchronized; lever: central; final drive: hypoid bevel; axle ratio: 3.770; width of rims: 4.5''; tyres: 175 S x 13.

PERFORMANCE max speed: 87 mph, 140 km/h; power-weight ratio: 29.9 lb/hp (40.6 lb/kW), 13.5 kg/kW (18.4 kg/kW); consumption: 27.4 m/imp gal, 22.8 m/US gal, 10.3 l x 100 km.

CHASSIS integral; front suspension: independent, wishbones, anti-roll bar, coil springs/telescopic dampers; rear: rigid axle, trailing arms, A-bracket, anti-roll bar, coil springs/telescopic dampers.

STEERING rack and pinion.

BRAKES front disc, rear drum.

ELECTRICAL EQUIPMENT 12 V; 40 Ah battery; 28 A alternator; 2 headlamps.

DIMENSIONS AND WEIGHT wheel base: 96.06 in, 244 cm; front and rear tracks, 51.57 in, 131 cm; length: 172.05 in, 473 cm; width: 64.56 in, 164 cm; height: 56.69 in, 144 cm; ground clearance: 6.7 in, 17 cm; weight: 2,033 lb, 922 kg; turning circle: 33 ft, 10 m fuel tank: 9.9 imp gal, 11.9 US gal, 45 l.

BODY saloon/sedan; 4 doors; 5 seats, separate front seats.

PRACTICAL INSTRUCTIONS fuel: 92 oct petrol.

12 TS

See 12 TL, except for:

ENGINE 85.24 cu in, 1,397 cc (2.99 x 3.03 in, 76 x 77 mm); compression ratio: 9.5:1; max power (SAE): 90 hp (66.2 kW) at 5,500 rpm; max torque (SAE): 92 lb ft, 12.7 kg m (124 Nm) at 3,500 rpm; 64.4 hp/l (47.4 kW/l); 1 Solex C 34 EIES2 downdraught twin barrel carburettor.

TRANSMISSION tyres: 155 SR x 13.

PERFORMANCE max speed: 96 mph, 155 km/h; power-weight ratio: 22.6 lb/hp (30.7 lb/kW), 10.2 kg/hp (13.9 kg/kW).

BRAKES dual circuit, servo.

BODY built-in headrests; air-conditioning.

12 TS Break

See 12 TS, except for:

TRANSMISSION tyres: 165 SR x 13.

PERFORMANCE power-weight ratio: 23.9 lb/hp (32.6 lb/kW), 10.9 kg/hp (14.8 kg/kW).

DIMENSIONS AND WEIGHT length 174,80 in, 444 cm; height: 59.45 in, 151 cm; ground clearance: 7.5 in, 19 cm; weight: 2,158 lb, 979 kg.

BODY 4+1 doors; folding rear seat.

12 Alpine

See 12 TS, except for:

ENGINE max power (SAE): 110 hp (80.9 kW) at 6,200 rpm; max torque (SAE): 99.3 lb ft, 13.7 kg-m (134 Nm) 5,000 rpm; 78.7 hp/l (57.9 kW/l).

TRANSMISSION ratios: I 3.615, II 2.263, III 1.480, IV 1.032, rev 3.076.

PERFORMANCE max speed: over 109 mph, 175 km/h; power-weight ratio: 19.2 lb/hp (26.1 lb/kW), 8.7 kg/hp (11.8 kg/kW); consumption: 23.5 m/imp gal, 19.6 m/US gal, 12 l x 100 km.

STEERING turns lock to lock: 3.5.

ELECTRICAL EQUIPMENT 38 A alternator; 4 headlamps.

DIMENSIONS AND WEIGHT length 171.26 in, 435 cm; height: 56.30 in, 143 cm; weight: 2,108 lb, 956 kg.

Torino Grand Routier

ENGINE front, 4 stroke; 6 cylinders, in line; 230 cu in, 3,770 cc (3.34 x 4.37 in, 84.9 x 111.1 mm); compression ratio: 8.3:1; max power (SAE): 180 hp (132.3 kW) at 4,700 rpm, max torque (SAE): 225 lb ft, 31 kgm (304 Nm) at 2,500 rpm;

RENAULT 12TS

RENAULT Torino Grand Routier

max engine rpm: 5,000; 47.7 hp/l (35.1 kW/l); 7 crankshaft bearings; valves: overhead; camshafts: 1, overhead; lubrication: gear pump, full flow filter, 7.9 imp pt, 9.5 US pt, 4.5 l; 1 Carter ABD downdraught twin barrel carburettor; fuel feed: mechanical pump; water-cooled, 20.4 imp pt, 24.5 US pt, 11.6 l.

TRANSMISSION driving wheels: rear; clutch: single dry plate; gearbox: mechanical; gears: 4, fully synchronized; ratios: I 2.830, II 1.850, III 1.380, IV 1, rev 3.150; lever: central; final drive: hypoid bevel; axle ratio: 3.310; width of rims: 6''; tyres: 185 HR x 15.

PERFORMANCE max speed: 115 mph, 185 km/h; power-weight ratio: 17.4 lb/hp, 7.9 kg/hp; consumption: 21.7 m/imp gal, 18.1 m/US gal, 13 l x 100 km.

CHASSIS integral; front suspension: independent, wishbones, anti-roll bar, coil springs, telescopic dampers; rear: rigid axle, 4 linkage bars, coil springs, telescopic dampers.

STEERING recirculating ball.

BRAKES front disc, rear drum, dual circuit, servo; swept area: total 202.8 sq in, 1,308 sq cm.

ELECTRICAL EQUIPMENT 12 V; 55 Ah battery; 40 A alternator; 4 headlamps.

DIMENSIONS AND WEIGHT wheel base: 107.09 in, 272 cm; tracks: 57.48 in, 146 cm front, 55.51 in, 141 cm rear; length: 185.83 in, 472 cm; width: 70.08 in, 178 cm; height: 56.69 in, 144 cm; ground clearance: 6.69 in, 17 cm; weight: 3,138 lb, 1,423 kg; turning circle: 41 ft, 12.5 m; fuel tank: 14.1 imp gal, 16.9 US gal, 64 l.

BODY saloon/sedan; 4 doors; 5/6 seats.

PRACTICAL INSTRUCTIONS fuel: 90 oct petrol; oil: engine 7.9 imp pt, 9.5 US pt, 4.5 l, SAE 30 HD, change every 3,100 miles, 5,000 km - gearbox 2.1 imp pt, 2.5 US pt, 1.2 l, SAE 90, change every 18,600 miles, 30,000 km, final drive 2.3 imp pt, 2.7 US pt, 1.3 l, SAE 90; greasing every 6,200 miles, 10,000 km, 12 points, valve timing 18° 26° 13° 21°; tyre pressur: front 28 psi, 2 at, rear 2 psi, 2 atm.

Torino TSX

See Torino Grand Routier, except for:

ENGINE compression ratio: 8.2:1; max power (SAE): 200 hp (147 kW) at 4,500 rpm; max torque (SAE): 239 lb ft, 3 kg m (324 Nm) at 3,000 rpm; 53 kg/l (39 kW/l); 1 Carter ABD 2053-6 downdraught twin barrel carburettor; cooling system: 21.6 imp pt, 26 US pt, 12.3 l.

TRANSMISSION ratios: I 3.540, II 2.310, III 1.500, IV 1, rev 3.150.

PERFORMANCE max speed: 124 mph, 200 km/h; power-weight ratio: 15.3 lb/hp, 6.9 kg/hp; consumption: 18.8 m/imp gal, 15.7 m/US gal, 15 l x 100 km.

ELECTRICAL EQUIPMENT 42 A alternator.

DIMENSIONS AND WEIGHT height: 55.91 in, 142 cm; ground clearance: 6.30 in, 16 cm; weight: 3,076 lb, 1,395 kg.

BODY hardtop; 2 doors; 5 seats.

Middle East
Africa
Asia
Australasia

Models now in production

Illustrations and technical information

OTOSAN   TURKEY

Anadol SL

PRICE EX WORKS: 185,000 liras

ENGINE Ford, front, 4 stroke; 4 cylinders, vertical, in line; 79.1 cu in, 1,298 cc (3.19 x 2.48 in, 81 x 63 mm); compression ratio: 8:1; max power (DIN): 54 hp at 5,500 rpm; max torque (DIN): 63 lb ft, 8.7 kg m at 3,000 rpm; max engine rpm: 5,700; 41.6 hp/l; cast iron block and head; 5 crankshaft bearings; valves: overhead, in line, push-rods and rockers; camshafts: 1, side; lubrication: rotary or vane-type pump, full flow filter, 6.3 imp pt, 7.6 US pt, 3.6 l; 1 Ford GPD downdraught single barrel carburettor; fuel feed: mechanical pump; water-cooled, 10 imp pt, 12 US pt, 5.7 l.

TRANSMISSION driving wheels: rear; clutch: single dry plate (diaphragm); gearbox: mechanical; gears: 4, fully synchronized; ratios: I 3.580, II 2.010, III 1.397, IV 1, rev 3.963; lever: central; final drive: hypoid bevel; axle ratio: 4.125; width of rims: 4.5''; tyres: 5.60/5.90 x 13.

PERFORMANCE max speeds: (I) 22 mph, 35 km/h; (II) 36 mph, 58 km/h; (III) 56 mph, 90 km/h; (IV) 87 mph, 140 km/h; power-weight ratio: 37.6 lb/hp, 17 kg/hp; carrying capacity: 1.102 lb, 500 kg; speed in direct drive at 1,000 rpm: 16.3 mph, 26.3 km/h; consumption: 33.2 m/imp gal, 27.7 m/US gal ,8.5 l x 100 km.

CHASSIS box-type perimeter frame with cross members; front suspension: independent, wishbones, coil springs, anti-roll bar, telescopic dampers; rear: rigid axle, semi-elliptic leafsprings, telescopic dampers.

STEERING rack-and-pinion; turns lock to lock: 3.90.

BRAKES front disc (diameter 9.13 in, 23.2 cm), rear drum; lining area: front 15.7 sq in, 101 sq cm, rear 46 sq in, 297 sq cm, total 61.7 sq in, 398 sq cm.

ELECTRICAL EQUIPMENT 12 V; 45 Ah battery; 42 A alternator; Ford distributor; 2 headlamps.

DIMENSIONS AND WEIGHT wheel base: 100.98 in, 256 cm; tracks: 51.97 in, 132 cm front, 50.39 in, 128 cm rear; length: 174.80 in, 444 cm; width: 64.76 in, 164 cm; height: 55.91 in, 142 cm; ground clearance: 6.30 in, 16 cm; weight: 2,073 lb, 940 kg; weight distribution: 52% front, 48% rear; turning circle: 31.5 ft, 9.6 m; fuel tank: 8.6 imp gal, 10.3 US gal, 39 l.

BODY saloon/sedan, in reinforced plastic material: 4 doors; 5 seats, bench front seats; vinyl roof.

Anadol SV-1600

PRICE EX WORKS: 219,000 liras

ENGINE front, 4 stroke; 4 cylinders, in line; 97.6 cu in, 1.599 cc (3.18 x 3.05 in, 81 x 77.6 mm); compression ratio: 8:1; max power (DIN): 65 hp (47.8 kW) at 5,200 rpm; max torque (DIN): 82 lb ft, 11.2 kg m (110.3 Nm) at 2,600 rpm; max engine rpm: 5,700; 40 hp/l (29.4 kW/l); 5 crankshaft bearings; valves: overhead, in line, pushrods and rockers; camshaft: 1, side; lubrication: rotary or vane-pump type, full flow filter, 7.2 imp pt, 8.7 US pt, 4.1 l; 1 Ford GPD downdraught single barrel carburettor; fuel feed: mechanical pump; water-cooled, 13.7 imp pt, 16.5 US pt, 7.8 l.

TRANSMISSION driving wheels: rear; clutch: single dry plate (diaphragm); gearbox: mechanical; gears: 4, fully synchronized; ratios: I 2.972, II 2.010, III 1.397, IV 1, rev 3.324; lever: central; final drive: hypoid; axle ratio: 4.125; width of rims: 5.5; tyres: 165 SR 13.

PERFORMANCE max speed: (IV) 90 mph, 145 kh/h; power-weight ratio: 30.4 lb/hp, 13.8 kg/hp; carrying capacity: 1,433 lb, 650 kg; consumption: 21.6 m/imp gal, 18 m/US gal, 13.1 l x 100 km.

CHASSIS box-type perimeter frame with cross members; front suspension: independent, wishbones, coil springs, anti-roll bar, telescopic dampers; rear: rigid axle, semi-elliptic leafsprings, telescopic dampers.

STEERING rack and pinion; turns lock to lock: 3.34.

BRAKES front disc, rear drum, servo; swept area: front 15.7 sq in, 101 sq cm, rear 46 sq in, 297 sq cm, total 61.7 sq in, 398 sq cm.

ELECTRICAL EQUIPMENT 12 V; 45 Ah battery; 42 A alternator; Autolite distributor; 2 headlamps.

DIMENSIONS AND WEIGHT wheel base: 100.79 in, 256 cm; tracks: 51.97 in, 132 cm front, 50.39 in, 128 cm rear; length: 174.80 in, 444 cm; width: 64.57 in, 164 cm; height: 55.51 in, 141 cm; ground clearance: 6.69 in, 17 cm; weight:

OTOSAN Anadol SV-1600 Station Wagon

2.073 lb, 940 kg; turning circle: 35.1 ft, 10.7 m; fuel tank: 8.6 imp gal, 10.3 US gal, 39 l.

BODY estate car/station wagon in plastic material; 4+1 doors; 5 seats, separate front seats.

TOFAS   TURKEY

Murat 131

ENGINE Fiat, front, 4 stroke; 4 cylinders, vertical, in line; 79.1 cu in, 1,297 cc (2.99 x 2.81 in, 76 x 71.5 mm); compression ratio: 7.8:1; max power (SAE): 70 hp at 5,250 rpm; max torque (SAE): 72 lb ft, 10 kg m at 3,400 rpm; max engine rpm: 5,750; 54 hp/l; cast iron block, light alloy head; 5 crankshaft bearings; valves: overhead, in line, slanted at 10°, push-rods and rockers; camshafts: 1, side, in crankcase, cogged belt; lubrication: gear pump, full flow filter (cartridge), 7.4 imp pt, 8.9 US pt, 4.2 l; 1 Solex 32 TEIE 42 downdraught twin barrel carburettor; fuel feed: mechanical pump; water-cooled, 13.4 imp pt, 16.1 US pt, 7.6 l, electric thermostatic fan.

TRANSMISSION driving wheels: rear; clutch: single dry plate (diaphragm); gearbox: mechanical; gears: 4, fully synchronized; ratios: I 3.667, II 2.100, III 1.361, IV 1, rev 3.526; lever: central; final drive: hypoid bevel; axle ratio: 4.100; width of rims: 4.5''; tyres: 165 SR x 13.

PERFORMANCE max speed: 93 mph, 150 km/h; power-weight ratio: 31 lb/hp, 14.1 kg/hp; carrying capacity: 882 lb, 400 kg; acceleration: standing ¼ mile 19.2 sec; speed in direct drive at 1,000 rpm: 15.7 mph, 25.3 km/h; consumption: 31.7 m/imp gal, 26.4 m/US gal, 8.9 l x 100 km.

CHASSIS integral; front suspension: independent, by McPherson, coil springs/telescopic damper struts, lower wishbones, anti-roll bar; rear: rigid axle, twin trailing lower radius arms, transverse linkage bar, coil springs, telescopic dampers.

STEERING rack-and-pinion; turns lock to lock: 3.40.

BRAKES front disc (diameter 8.94 in, 22.7 cm), rear drum (diameter 8.97 in, 22.8 cm), rear compensator, servo; lining area: front 19.2 sq in, 124 sq cm, rear 36.9 sq in, 238 sq cm, total 56.1 sq in, 362 sq cm.

ELECTRICAL EQUIPMENT 12 V; 45 Ah battery; 44 A alternator; Marelli distributor; 2 headlamps.

DIMENSIONS AND WEIGHT wheel base: 98.03 in, 249 cm; tracks: 53.94 in, 137 cm front, 51.57 in, 131 cm rear; length: 166.93 in, 424 cm; width: 64.17 in, 163 cm; height: 55.12 in, 140 cm; ground clearance: 5.51 in, 14 cm; weight: 2,172 lb, 985 kg; weight distribution: 53% front, 47% rear; turning circle: 34.8 ft, 10.6 m; fuel tank: 11 imp gal, 13.2 US gal, 50 l.

BODY saloon/sedan; 4 doors; 5 seats, separate front seats.

TOFAS Murat 131

ROM CARMEL ISRAEL

Rom 1300

ENGINE front, 4 stroke, 4 cylinders, in line; 79.2 cu in, 1,297 cc (3.19 x 2.48 in, 81 x 63 mm); compression ratio: 8:1; max power (DIN): 54 hp at 5,500 rpm; max torque (DIN): 63 lb ft, 8.7 kg m at 3,000 rpm; max engine rpm: 5,800; 41.6 hp/l; cast iron block and head; 5 crankshaft bearings; valves: 8, overhead, roller chain; camshafts: 1, overhead; lubrication: rotary pump, full flow filter, 5.8 imp pt, 7 US pt, 3.3 l; 1 Solex downdraught carburettor; fuel feed: mechanical pump; water-cooled, 8.8 imp pt, 10.6 US pt, 5 l.

TRANSMISSION driving wheels: rear; clutch: single dry plate (diaphragm); gearbox: mechanical; gears: 4, fully synchronized; ratios: I 3.660, II 2.190, III 1.430, IV 1, rev 4.240; lever: central; final drive: hypoid bevel; axle ratio: 4.110; width of rims: 4.5''; tyres: 5.60 x 13.

PERFORMANCE max speeds: (I) 24 mph, 38 km/h; (II) 40 mph, 64 km/h; (III) 61 mph, 98 km/h; (IV) 87 mph, 140 km/h; power-weight ratio: 36.8 lb/hp, 16.6 kg/hp; carrying capacity: 882 lb, 400 kg; speed in direct drive at 1,000 rpm: 14.5 mph, 23.3 km/h; consumption: 34.4 m/imp gal, 28.7 m/US gal, 8.2 l x 100 m.

CHASSIS separate steel frame, boxed side-members, arc welded; front suspension: independent, wishbones, coil springs, anti-roll bar, telescopic dampers; rear: rigid axle, semi-elliptic leafsprings, telescopic dampers.

STEERING rack-and-pinion; turns lock to lock: 3.

BRAKES front disc, rear drum, servo; swept area: front 142.2 sq in, 917 sq cm, rear 62.8 sq in, 405 sq cm, total 205 sq in, 1,322 sq cm.

ELECTRICAL EQUIPMENT 12 V; 40 Ah battery; 336 W alternator; Motorcraft distributor; 2 headlamps.

DIMENSIONS AND WEIGHT wheel base: 98.43 in, 250 cm; front and rear track: 49.21 in, 125 cm; length: 162.99 in, 414 cm; width: 61.42 in, 156 cm; height: 59.06 in, 150 cm; ground clearance: 6.50 in, 16.5 cm; weight: 1,985 lb, 900 kg; turning circle: 31.8 ft, 9.7 m; fuel tank: 9.2 imp gal, 11.1 US gal, 42 l.

BODY saloon/sedan, in plastic material; 4 doors; 5 seats, separate front seats.

ROM CARMEL Rom 1300

EL NASR EGYPT

Nasr 128

ENGINE front, transverse, 4 stroke; 4 cylinders, in line; 68.1 cu in, 1,116 cc (3.15 x 2.19 in, 80 x 55.5 mm); compression ratio: 7.8:1; max power (DIN): 51 hp at 6,000 rpm; max torque (DIN): 55 lb ft, 7.6 kg m at 3,500 rpm; max engine rpm: 6.500; 45.7 hp/l; cast iron block, light alloy head; 5 crankshaft bearings; valves: overhead, thimble tappets; camshafts: 1, overhead; lubrication: gear pump, full flow filter (cartridge), 8.8 imp pt, 10.6 US pt, 5 l; 1 Weber 32 ICEV 17 downdraught carburettor; fuel feed: mechanical pump; water-cooled, 11.4 imp pt, 13.7 US pt, 6.5 l, electric thermostatic fan.

TRANSMISSION driving wheels: front; clutch: single dry plate; gearbox: mechanical; gears: 4, fully synchronized; ratios: I 3.583, II 2.235, III 1.454, IV 1.042, rev 3.714; lever: central; final drive: cylindrical gears; axle ratio: 3.765; width of rims: 4.5''; tyres: 145 SR x 13.

PERFORMANCE max speeds: (I) 30 mph, 48 km/h; (II) 50 mph, 80 km/h; (III) 75 mph, 120 km/h; (IV) 84 mph, 135 km/h; power-weight ratio: 34.8 lb/hp, 15.8 kg/hp; carrying capacity: 882 lb, 400 kg; acceleration: standing ¼ mile 21 sec, 0-50 mph (0-80 km/h) 15.8 sec; speed in top at 1,000 rpm: 14.9 mph, 24 km/h; consumption: 35.3 m/imp gal, 29.4 m/US gal, 8 l x 100 km.

CHASSIS integral; front suspension: independent, by McPherson, coil springs, telescopic damper struts, lower wishbones, anti-roll bar; rear: independent, single wide-based wishbone, transverse leafspring, telescopic dampers.

STEERING rack-and-pinion; turns lock to lock: 3.50.

BRAKES front disc (diameter 8.94 in, 22.7 cm), rear drum, rear compensator, servo; lining area: front 19.2 sq in, 124

sq cm, rear 33.5 sq in, 216 sq cm, total 52.7 sq in, 340 sq cm.

ELECTRICAL EQUIPMENT 12 V; 34 Ah battery; 33 A alternator; Marelli distributor; 2 headlamps.

DIMENSIONS AND WEIGHT wheel base: 96.38 in, 245 cm; tracks: 51.50 in, 131 cm front, 51.69 in, 131 cm rear; length: 151.18 in, 384 cm; width: 62.60 in, 159 cm; height: 55.91 in, 142 cm; ground clearance: 5.71 in, 14.5 cm; weight: 1,775 lb, 805 kg; weight distribution: 61.5% front, 38.5% rear; turning circle: 35.8 ft, 10.9 m; fuel tank: 8.4 imp gal, 10 US gal, 38 l.

BODY saloon/sedan; 4 doors; 5 seats, separate front seats.

Nasr 125

ENGINE front, 4 stroke; 4 cylinders, vertical, in line; 90.4 cu in, 1,481 cc (3.03 x 3.13 in, 77 x 79.5 mm); compression ratio: 9:1; max power (DIN): 70 hp at 5,400 rpm; max torque (DIN): 83 lb ft, 11.5 kg m at 3,200 rpm; max engine rpm: 5,500; 45.2 hp/l; cast iron block, light alloy head; 3 crankshaft bearings; valves: overhead, in line, pushrods and rockers; camshafts: 1, side; lubrication: gear pump, centrifugal filter, cartridge on by-pass, 7.5 imp pt, 9 US pt, 4.3 l; 1 Weber 34 DCHD 1 downdraught twin barrel carburettor; fuel feed: mechanical pump; water-cooled, 11.8 imp pt, 14.2 US pt, 6.7 l.

TRANSMISSION driving wheels: rear; clutch: single dry plate, hydraulically controlled; gearbox: mechanical; gears:

EL NASR Nasr 128

4, fully synchronized; ratios: I 3.750, II 2.300, III 1.490, IV 1, rev 3.870; lever: central; final drive: hypoid bevel; axle ratio: 4.100; width of rims: 4.5''; tyres: 5.60 S x 13.

PERFORMANCE max speeds: (I) 25 mph, 40 km/h; (II) 40 mph, 65 km/h; (III) 62 mph, 100 km/h; (IV) 93 mph, 150 km/h; power-weight ratio: 31.1 lb/hp, 14.1 kg/hp; carrying capacity: 882 lb, 400 kg; acceleration: 0-50 mph (0-80 km/h) 13 sec; speed in direct drive at 1,000 rpm: 16.1 mph, 25.9 km/h; consumption: 29.7 m/imp gal, 24.8 m/US gal, 9.5 l x 100 km.

CHASSIS integral; front suspension: independent, wishbones, lower trailing links, coil springs, anti-roll bar, telescopic dampers; rear: rigid axle, semi-elliptic leafsprings, telescopic dampers.

STEERING worm and roller; turns lock to lock: 3.

BRAKES disc, servo.

ELECTRICAL EQUIPMENT 12 V; 53 Ah battery; 770 W alternator; Marelli distributor; 4 headlamps.

DIMENSIONS AND WEIGHT wheel base: 98.43 in, 250 cm; tracks: 51.18 in, 130 cm front, 51.18 in, 130 cm rear; length: 166.65 in, 423 cm; width: 63.98 in, 162 cm; height: 56.69 in, 144 cm; ground clearance: 5.51 in, 14 cm; weight: 2,183 lb, 990 kg; turning circle: 36.1 ft, 11 m; fuel tank: 9.9 imp gal, 11.9 US gal, 45 l.

BODY saloon/sedan; 4 doors; 5 seats, separate front seats, reclining backrests.

VOLKSWAGEN   NIGERIA

1200

ENGINE rear, 4 stroke; 4 cylinders, horizontally opposed; 72.7 cu in, 1,192 cc (3.03 x 2.52 in, 77 x 64 mm); compression ratio: 7.3:1; max power (DIN): 34 hp at 3,800 rpm; max torque (DIN): 55 lb ft, 7.6 kg m at 1,700 rpm; max engine rpm: 4,500; 28.5 hp/l; block with cast iron liners and light alloy fins, light alloy head; 4 crankshaft bearings; valves: overhead, push-rods and rockers; camshafts: 1, central, lower; lubrication: gear pump, filter in sump, oil cooler, 4.4 imp pt, 5.3 US pt, 2.5 l; 1 Solex 30 PICT downdraught single barrel carburettor; fuel feed: mechanical pump; air-cooled.

TRANSMISSION driving wheels: rear; clutch: single dry plate; gearbox: mechanical; gears: 4, fully synchronized; ratios: I 3.780, II 2.060, III 1.260, IV 0.890, rev 4.010; lever: central; final drive: spiral bevel; axle ratio: 4.375; width of rims: 4.5''; tyres: 155 SR x 15.

PERFORMANCE max speeds: (I) 19 mph, 31 km/h; (II) 35 mph, 57 km/h; (III) 58 mph, 94 km/h; (IV) 71 mph, 115 km/h; power-weight ratio: 50.6 lb/hp; 22.9 kg/hp; carrying capacity: 838 lb, 380 kg; acceleration: standing ¼ mile 23 sec, 0-50 mph (0-80 km/h) 18 sec; speed in top at 1,000 rpm: 18.6 mph, 30 km/h; consumption: 37.7 m/imp gal, 31.4 m/US gal, 7.5 l x 100 km.

CHASSIS backbone platform; front suspension: independent, twin swinging longitudinal trailing arms, transverse laminated torsion bars, anti-roll bar, telescopic dampers; rear: independent, swinging semi-axles, swinging longitudinal trailing arms, transverse torsion bars, telescopic dampers.

STEERING worm and roller telescopic damper; turns lock to lock: 2.60.

BRAKES drum, dual circuit; lining area: total 111 sq in, 716 sq cm.

ELECTRICAL EQUIPMENT 12 V; 36 Ah battery; 270 W dynamo; Bosch distributor; 2 headlamps.

DIMENSIONS AND WEIGHT wheel base: 94.49 in, 240 cm; tracks: 51.57 in, 131 cm front, 53.15 in, 135 cm rear; length: 159.84 in, 406 cm; width: 61.02 in, 155 cm; height: 59.06 in, 150 cm; ground clearance: 5.90 in, 15 cm; weight: 1,720 lb, 780 kg; weight distribution: 43% front, 57% rear; turning circle (between walls): 36.1 ft, 11 m; fuel tank: 8.8 imp gal, 10.6 US gal, 40 l.

BODY saloon/sedan; 2 doors; 5 seats, separate front seats, adjustable backrests.

BMW   SOUTH AFRICA

520

ENGINE front, 4 stroke; 4 cylinders, in line; 121.4 cu in, 1,990 cc (3.50 x 3.15 in, 89 x 80 mm); compression ratio: 9:1; max power (DIN): 115 hp at 5,800 rpm; max torque (DIN): 122 lb ft, 16.8 kg m at 3,700 rpm; max engine rpm: 5,800; 57.8 hp/l cast iron block, light alloy head, swirl-action combustion chambers; 5 crankshafts bearings; valves: overhead, Vee-slanted, rockers; camshafts: 1, overhead; lubrication: rotary pump, full flow filter, 7.5 imp pt, 9 US pt, 4.2 l; 2 Stromberg 175 CDE7 downdraught carburettors; fuel feed: mechanical pump; water-cooled, 12.7 imp pt, 15.2 US pt, 7.2 l.

TRANSMISSION driving wheels: rear; clutch: single dry plate, hydraulically-controlled; gearbox: mechanical; gears: 4, fully synchronized; ratios: I 3.764, II 2.022, III 1.320, IV 1, rev 4.096; lever: central; final drive: hypoid bevel; axle ratio: 4.100; width of rims: 5.5''; tyres: 185 SR x 14.

PERFORMANCE max speed: 109 mph, 175 km/h; power-weight ratio: 23.8 lb/hp, 10.8 kg/hp; carrying capacity: 1,014 lb, 460 kg; acceleration: standing ¼ mile 17.4 sec, 0-50 mph (0-80 km/h) 7.3 sec; speed in direct drive at 1,000 rpm: 17.1 mph, 27.5 km/h; consumption: 26.4 m/imp gal, 22 m/US gal, 10.7 l x 100 km.

CHASSIS integral; front suspension: independent, by McPherson, coil springs/telescopic damper struts, auxiliary rubber springs, lower wishbones, lower trailing links, anti-roll bar; rear: independent, oblique semi-trailing arms, auxiliary rubber springs, coil springs, telescopic dampers.

STEERING ZF, worm and roller.

BRAKES front disc (diameter 11 in, 28 cm), rear drum, dual circuit, rear compensator, servo.

VOLKSWAGEN 1200

ELECTRICAL EQUIPMENT 12 V; 45 Ah battery; 55 A alternator; 4 halogen headlamps.

DIMENSIONS AND WEIGHT wheel base: 103.94 in, 264 cm; tracks: 55.35 in, 141 cm front, 56.76 in, 144 cm rear; length: 181.89 in, 462 cm; width: 66.54 in, 169 cm; height: 55.91 in, 142 cm; weight: 2,734 lb, 1,240 kg; turning circle: 34.4 ft, 10.5 m; fuel tank: 14.5 imp gal, 17.4 US gal, 66 l.

BODY saloon/sedan; 4 doors; 5 seats, separate front seats, reclining backrests.

OPTIONALS ZF 3 HP 22 automatic transmission, hydraulic torque converter and planetary gears with 3 ratios (I 2.478, II 1.478, III 1, rev 2.090), max ratio of converter at stall 2.1, possible manual selection, 4.100 axle ratio, max speed 106 mph, 170 km/h, weight 2,778 lb, 1,260 kg.

528

See 520, except for:

ENGINE 6 cylinders, in line; 170.1 cu in, 2,788 cc (3.39 x 3.15 in, 86 x 80 mm); compression ratio: 9:1; max power (DIN): 170 hp at 5,800 rpm; max torque (DIN): 176 lb ft, 24.3 kg m at 4,000 rpm; 61.2 hp/l; 7 crankshaft bearings; lubrication: 10.1 imp pt, 12.1 US pt, 5.7 l; 1 Solex 4 A1 4-barrel downdraught carburettor; water-cooled, 20.6 imp pt, 25.4 US pt, 12 l.

TRANSMISSION gearbox: ZF 3HP 22 automatic transmission, hydraulic torque converter and planetary gears with 3 ratios, max ratio of converter at stall 2, possible manual selection; ratios: I 2.478, II 1.478, III 1, rev 2.090; axle ratio: 3.640; width of rims: 6''; tyres: 195/70 HR x 14.

PERFORMANCE max speed: 118 mph, 190 km/h; power-weight ratio: 18.5 lb/hp, 8.4 kg/hp carrying capacity: 91 lb, 415 kg; consumption: 26.3 m/imp gal, 21.9 m/US gal, 10.7 l x 100 km.

CHASSIS anti-roll bar on rear suspension.

BRAKES disc (front diameter 11 in, 28 cm, rear 10.7 in, 27.2 cm).

ELECTRICAL EQUIPMENT 55 Ah battery; 60 A alternator.

DIMENSIONS AND WEIGHT tracks: 55.90 in, 142 cm front, 57.48 in, 146 cm rear; weight: 3,142 lb, 1,425 kg; fuel tank: 15 imp gal, 17.9 US gal, 68 l.

530

See 520, except for:

ENGINE 6 cylinders, in line; 182 cu in, 2,986 cc (3.50 x 3.1 in, 89 x 80 mm); compression ratio: 9:1; max power (DIN): 177 hp at 5,800 rpm; max torque (DIN): 188 lb ft, 26 kg m

BMW 520

3,500 rpm; 59.1 hp/l; 7 crankshaft bearings; lubrication:
.1 imp pt, 12.1 US pt, 5.7 l; 1 Solex 4A1 4-barrel down-
aught carburettor; water-cooled, 20.6 imp pt, 25.4 US
, 12 l.

TRANSMISSION gearbox ratios: I 3.855, II 2.202, III 1.401,
1, rev 4.300; axle ratio: 3.450; width of rims: 7''; tyres:
5 HR x 14.

PERFORMANCE max speed: 124 mph, 200 km/h; power-
eight ratio: 17.8 lb/hp, 8.1 kg/hp; speed in direct drive
1,000 rpm: 21.7 mph, 35 km/h; consumption: 26.1 m/imp
l, 21.8 m/US gal, 10.8 l x 100 km.

CHASSIS anti-roll bar on rear suspension.

STEERING servo.

BRAKES disc (front and rear diameter 11 in, 28 cm).

ELECTRICAL EQUIPMENT 55 Ah battery; 60 A alternator.

DIMENSIONS AND WEIGHT tracks: 55.90 in, 142 cm front,
.48 in, 146 cm rear; weight: 3,142 lb, 1,425 kg; fuel
nk: 15 imp gal, 17.9 US gal, 68 l.

BMW 530

CHEVROLET — SOUTH AFRICA

Ascona Series

4-dr Sedan	4,550 rand
« S » 4-dr Sedan	4,845 rand

Power team:	Standard for:	Optional for:
hp	1	—
hp	2	—

54 hp power team

ENGINE front, 4 stroke; 4 cylinders, vertical, in line; 76.6
in, 1,256 cc (3.18 x 2.40 in, 81 x 61 mm); compression
tio: 9.2:1; max power (DIN): 54 hp at 5,400 rpm; max
rque (DIN): 61 lb ft, 8.4 kg m at 2,400 rpm; max
gine rpm: 5,800; 43 hp/l; cast iron block and head;
crankshaft bearings; valves: overhead, in line, push-rods
d rockers; camshafts: 1, side; lubrication: gear pump,
ll flow filter, 5.1 imp pt, 6.1 US pt, 2.9 l; 1 Stromberg
DS 1.50 downdraught carburettor; fuel feed: mechanical
mp; water-cooled, 10.2 imp pt, 12.3 US pt, 5.8 l.

TRANSMISSION driving wheels: rear; clutch: single dry
ate (diaphragm); gearbox: mechanical gears: 4, fully
nchronized; ratios: I 3.760, II 2.213, III 1.404, IV 1,
v 3.707; lever: central; final drive: hypoid bevel; axle
tio: 4.440; width of rims: 5'' tyres: 155 SR x 13.

PERFORMANCE max speed: 86 mph, 138 km/h; power-
weight ratio: 37.4 lb/hp, 17 kg/hp; carrying capacity: 937
lb, 425 kg; acceleration: standing ¼ mile 21 sec, 0-50
mph (0-80 km/h) 12 sec; speed in direct drive at 1,000
rpm: 23.7 mph, 38.1 km/h; consumption: 31.4 m/imp gal,
26.1 m/US gal, 9 l x 100 km.

CHASSIS integral; front suspension: independent, wishbones coil springs, anti-roll bar, telescopic dampers; rear:
rigid axle (torque tube), trailing radius arms, transverse
linkage bar, coil springs, anti-roll bar, telescopic dampers.

STEERING rack-and-pinion; turns lock to lock: 4.

BRAKES front disc, rear drum, servo; lining area: front
22.9 sq in, 148 sq cm, rear 47.1 sq in, 304 sq cm, total
70 sq in, 452 sq cm.

ELECTRICAL EQUIPMENT 12 V; 32 Ah battery; 45 A alternator, 2 headlamps.

DIMENSIONS AND WEIGHT wheel base: 99.21 in, 252 cm;
front and rear tracks: 54.13 in, 137 cm; length: 170.12 in,
432 cm; width: 65.75 in, 167 cm; height: 54.33 in, 138 cm;
ground clearance: 5.12 in, 13 cm; weight: 2,018 lb, 915
kg; turning circle ft, 9.5 m; fuel tank: 12.3 imp gal, 14.8 US
gal, 56 l.

BODY 5 seats, separate front seats with headrests, adjustable backrests.

OPTIONALS metallic spray.

57 hp power team

See 54 hp power team, except for:

ENGINE max power (DIN): 57 hp (42.1 kW) at 5,400 rpm;
45.4 hp/l (33.5 kW/l).

PERFORMANCE max speed: about 87 mph, 140 km/h;
power-weight ratio: 35.4 lb/hp, (48 lb/kW), 16 kg/hp (21.7
kg/kW).

Chevair Series

2300 De Luxe 4-dr Sedan	5,340 rand
2300 GL 4-dr Sedan	5,740 rand
2300 Automatic Berlina 4-dr Sedan	6,420 rand

For De Luxe and GL models with automatic transmission
add rand 385.

105 hp power team

ENGINE front, 4 stroke; 4 cylinders, vertical in line; 141.6
cu in, 2.320 cc (3.87 x 3 in, 98.4 x 76.2 mm); compression
ratio: 9:1; max power (SAE): 105 hp at 5,100 rpm; max
torque (SAE): 136 lb ft, 18.7 kg m at 3,300 rpm; max
engine rpm: 5,800; 45.3 hp/l; cast iron block and head;
5 crankshaft bearings; valves: overhead; 1 Rochester/
Monojet carburettor.

TRANSMISSION driving wheels: rear; clutch: single dry
plate; gearbox: mechanical; gears: 4, fully synchronized;
ratios: I 3.428, II 2.156, III 1.366, IV 1, rev 3.317; lever:
central; final drive: hypoid bevel; axle ratio: 3.420; width
of rims: 5.5''; tyres: 165 SR x 13.

PERFORMANCE max speed: 110 mph, 177 km/h; acceleration: 0-50 mph (0-80 km/h) 8.4 sec; speed in direct
drive at 1,000 rpm: 20 mph, 32 km/h; consumption: 37.2
m/imp gal, 30.9 m/US gal, 7.6 l x 100 km.

CHASSIS integral; front suspension: independent, wishbones, coil springs, telescopic dampers; rear: rigid axle,
trailing lower radius arms, coil springs, telescopic dampers.

STEERING rack-and-pinion; turns lock to lock: 4.

BRAKES front disc, rear drum.

ELECTRICAL EQUIPMENT 12 V; 32 Ah battery; 37 A alternator; 2 headlamps.

DIMENSIONS AND WEIGHT wheel base: 99.13 in, 252
cm; front and rear track: 54.13 in, 137 cm; length: 177.17
in, 450 cm; width: 64.96 in, 165 cm; height: 51.97 in, 132
cm; ground clearance: 5 in, 12.7 cm; turning circle: 31.2
ft, 9.5 m; fuel tank: 12.3 imp gal, 14.8 US gal, 56 l.

BODY 5 seats, separate front seats, reclining backrests
with headrests.

OPTIONALS (Standard for Berlina) Tri-Matic automatic
transmission, hydraulic torque converter and planetary
gears with 3 ratios (I 2.310, II 1.460, III 1, rev 1.860),
max ratio of converter at stall 2.33, possible manual selection; metallic spray; vinyl roof; tinted glass.

CHEVROLET Ascona "S" 4-dr Sedan

Rekord Series

PRICES EX WORKS:

4-dr Sedan	6,120	rand
Automatic 4-dr Sedan	6,475	rand
GL 4-dr Sedan	6,420	rand
Automatic GL 4-dr Sedan	6,720	rand
4 + 1-dr St. Wagon	6,545	rand
Automatic 4 + 1-dr St. Wagon	6,930	rand

90 hp power team

ENGINE front, 4 stroke; 4 cylinders, vertical in line; 141,5 cu in, 2,319 cc (3.87 x 3 in, 98.4 x 76.2 mm); compression ratio: 9:1; max power (DIN): 90 hp at 4,800 rpm; max torque (DIN): lb ft, 17 kg m at 2,800 rpm; max engine rpm: 5,000; 39 hp/l; cast iron block and head; 5 crankshaft bearings; valves: overhead, hydraulic tappets; 1 Rochester/Monojet carburettor; camshafts: 1, overhead; lubrication: gear pump, full flow filter, 6.7 imp pt, 8 US pt, 3.8 l; fuel feed: mechanical pump; cooling system: 11.1 imp pt, 13.3 US pt, 6.3 l.

TRANSMISSION driving wheels: rear; clutch: single dry plate gearbox: mechanical; gears: 4, fully synchronized; ratios: I 3.640, II 2.120, III 1.336, IV 1, rev 3.317; lever: central; final drive: hypoid bevel; axle ratio: 3.500; width of rims: 5.5'', tyres: 175 SR x 14.

PERFORMANCE max speed: 103 mph, 165 km/h - st. wagons 101 mph, 162 km/h; power-weight ratio: 4-dr sedans 27.3 lb/hp, 12.4 kg/hp; speed in direct drive at 1,000 rpm: 20.4 mph, 32.8 km/h; consumption: 24.6 m/imp gal, 20.5 m/US gal, 11.5 l x 100 km - st. wagons 23.5 m/imp gal, 19.6 m/US gal, 12 l x 100 km.

CHASSIS integral; front suspension: independent, wishbones, lower trailing links, coil springs, anti-roll bar, telescopic dampers; rear: rigid axle, trailing lower radius arms, upper torque arms, transverse linkage bar, coil springs, anti-roll bar, telescopic dampers.

STEERING recirculating ball; turns lock to lock: 4.

BRAKES front disc (diameter 9.37 in, 23.8 cm), rear drum, servo; lining area: total 85.7 sq in, 553 sq cm.

ELECTRICAL EQUIPMENT 12 V; 32 Ah battery; 37 A alternator; 2 headlamps.

DIMENSIONS AND WEIGHT wheel base: 105.4 in, 267 cm; tracks: 56.34 in, 143 cm front, 55.59 in, 141 cm rear; length: 108.75 in, 459 cm - st. wagons 181.81 in, 462 cm; width: 68.03 in, 173 cm; height: 55.71 in, 141 cm - st. wagons 56.69 in, 144 cm; ground clearance: 5.12 in, 13 cm; weight: 2,459 lb, 1,115 kg - St. wagons 2,569 lb, 1,165 kg; turning circle: 32.6 ft, 9.9 m; fuel tank: 15.4 imp gal, 18.5 US gal, 70 l.

BODY 5 seats, separate front seats, reclining backrests with headrests.

OPTIONALS Opel automatic transmission with 3 ratios (I 2.400, II 1.480, III 1, rev 1.920), max ratio of converter at

CHEVROLET Rekord 4-dr Sedan

stall 2.5, possible manual selection, max speed 99 mph, 160 km/h - St. wagons 97 mph, 157 km/h, consumption: 23.2 m/imp gal, 19.3 m/US gal, 12.2 l x 100 km - St. wagons 22.2 m/imp gal, 18.5 m/US gal, 12.7 l x 100 km; limited slip differential.

Commodore Series

PRICES EX WORKS:

1	3800 4-dr Sedan	6,755	rand
2	3800 Automatic 4-dr Sedan	7,185	rand
3	3800 GL 4-dr Sedan	8,495	rand
4	3800 GL Automatic 4 + 1-dr St. Wagon	7,995	rand
5	4100 GL Automatic 4-dr Sedan	—	

Power team:	Standard for:	Optional for:
121 hp	1,2,3,4	—
132 hp	5	—

120 hp power team

ENGINE front, 4 stroke; 6 cylinders, vertical in line; 230 cu in, 3,769 cc (3.87 x 3.26 in, 98.4 x 82.5 mm); compression ratio: 8.8:1; max power (DIN): 120 hp at 4,300 rpm; max torque (DIN): 189 lb ft, 26.1 kg m at 2,200 rpm; max engine rpm: 4,600; 31.8 hp/l; cast iron block and head; 7 crankshaft bearings; valves: overhead, in line, push rods and rockers, hydraulic tappets; camshafts: 1, side; lubrication: 7.6 imp pt, 9.1 US pt, 4.3 l; 1 Rochester Monojet carburettor; fuel feed: mechanical pump; cooling system: 21.6 imp pt, 26 US pt, 12.3 l.

TRANSMISSION driving wheels: rear; clutch: single dry plate (diaphragm), hydraulically controlled; gearbox: mechanical; gears: 4, fully synchronized; ratios: I 3.500, II 2.480, III 1.660, IV 1, rev 3.500; lever: central; final drive: hypoid bevel; axle ratio: 2.920; width of rims: 6''; tyres 175 SR x 14.

PERFORMANCE max speed: 103 mph, 165 km/h; power-weight ratio: 22.3 lb/hp, 10 kg/hp - St. wagons 22.8 lb/hp, 10.4 kg/hp.

CHASSIS integral; front suspension: independent, wishbones, lower trailing links, coil springs, anti-roll bar, telescopic dampers; rear: rigid axle, trailing lower radius arms, upper torque arms, transverse linkage bar, coil springs, anti-roll bar, telescopic dampers.

STEERING recirculating ball; turns lock to lock: 4.

BRAKES front disc (diameter 9.37 in, 23.8 cm), rear drum, servo; lining area: total 85.7 sq in, 553 sq cm.

ELECTRICAL EQUIPMENT 12 V; 32 Ah battery; 37 A alternator; 2 headlamps.

DIMENSIONS AND WEIGHT wheel base: 105.4 in, 267 cm; tracks: 56.34 in, 143 cm front, 55.59 in, 141 cm rear; length: 184.88 in, 469 cm - st. wagons 185.83 in, 472 cm; width: 68.03 in, 173 cm; height: 56.69 in, 144 cm - st. wagons 58.66 in, 149 cm; ground clearance: 5.12 in, 13 cm; weight: 2,683 lb, 1,217 kg - st. wagons 2,741 lb, 1,243 kg; turning circle: 32.6 ft, 9.9 m; fuel tank: 15.4 imp gal, 18.5 US gal, 70 l.

BODY 5 seats, separate front seats, reclining backrests with headrests.

OPTIONALS (Standard for St. Wagons) Tri-Matic automatic transmission with 3 ratios (I 2.520, II 1.520, III 1, rev 1.940), max ratio of converter at stall 2, possible manual selection; power steering; metallic spray; tinted glass.

132 hp power team

See 120 hp power team, except for:

ENGINE 249.7 cu in, 4,093 cc (3.87 x 3.53 in, 98.4 x 89 mm); max power (DIN): 132 hp at 4,400 rpm; max torque (DIN): 198 lb ft, 27.3 kg m at 1,500 rpm; max engine rpm: 4,800; 32.2 hp/l; lubrication: 7.6 imp pt, 9.1 US pt, 4.3 l; cooling system: 21.6 imp pt, 26 US pt, 12.3 l.

TRANSMISSION gearbox: Tri-Matic automatic transmission with 3 ratios, max ratio of converter at stall 2, possible manual selection; ratios: I 2.520, II 1.520, III 1, rev 1.940.

PERFORMANCE max speed: over 103 mph, 165 km/h; power-weight ratio: 20.5 lb/hp, 9 kg/hp.

STEERING servo.

DIMENSIONS AND WEIGHT weight: 2,712 lb, 1,230 kg.

CHEVROLET Commodore GL Automatic Station Wagon

Nomad

PRICE EX WORKS: 3,845 rand

ENGINE front, 4 stroke; 4 cylinders, vertical, in line; 153 cu in, 2,507 cc (3.87 x 3.25 in, 98.4 x 82.5 mm); compression ratio: 8.5:1; max power (DIN): 86 hp at 4,300 rpm; max torque (DIN): 128 lb ft, 17.7 kg m at 2,300 rpm; max engine rpm: 4,600; 34.3 hp/l; 5 crankshaft bearings; valves: overhead, hydraulic tappets; camshafts: 1, side; lubrication: gear pump, full flow filter, 5.8 imp pt, 7 US pt. 3.3 l; 1 Rochester Monojet downdraught twin barrel carburettor; fuel feed: mechanical pump; water-cooled, 13 imp pt, 15.6 US pt, 7.4 l.

TRANSMISSION driving wheels: rear; clutch: single dry plate (diaphragm), hydraulically controlled; gearbox: mechanical; gears: 4, fully synchronized; ratios: I 4.258, II 2.567, III 1.531, IV 1, rev 4.121; lever: central; final drive: hypoid bevel; axle ratio: 4.000; width of rims: 5''; tyres: 6.95 x 14.

PERFORMANCE max speed: about 74 mph, 119 km/h; power-weight ratio: 26 lb/hp, 11.8 kg/hp; carrying capacity: 1,235 lb, 560 kg; speed in direct drive at 1,000 rpm: 17.8 mph, 28.7 km/h; consumption: 23.5 m/imp gal, 19.6 m/US gal, 12 l x 100 km.

CHASSIS integral; front suspension: wishbones, coil springs, heavy-duty double-acting telescopic dampers; rear: rigid axle, twin longitudinal trailing arms, leafspring, heavy-duty double-acting telescopic dampers.

STEERING rack-and-pinion.

BRAKES front disc, rear drum, dual circuit, servo; lining area: front 24.6 sq in, 159 sq cm, rear 77.5 sq in, 500 sq cm, total 102.1 sq in, 659 sq cm.

ELECTRICAL EQUIPMENT 12 V; 55 Ah battery; 37 A alternator; 2 headlamps.

DIMENSIONS AND WEIGHT wheel base: 81.89 in, 208 cm; front and rear track: 51.57 in, 131 cm; length: 137.01 in, 348 cm; width: 61.81 in, 157 cm; height: 60.23 in, 153 cm; weight: 2,260 lb, 1,025 kg; turning circle: 34.1 ft, 10.4 m; fuel tank: 13.2 imp gal, 15.8 US gal, 60 l.

BODY estate car/st. wagon; 2-dr; 3-7 seats; separate front seats.

OPTIONALS nylon roof with perspex windows; fibreglass canopy; removable door windows; 175SR x 14 tyres.

FORD   SOUTH AFRICA

Escort 1300 L 4-door Sedan

PRICE EX WORKS: 4,260 rand

ENGINE front, 4 stroke; 4 cylinders, vertical, in line; 79.1 cu in, 1,297 cc (3.19 x 2.48 in, 81 x 63 mm); compression ratio: 9.2:1; max power (DIN): 57 hp at 5,500 rpm; max torque (DIN): 67 lb ft, 9.3 kg m at 3,000 rpm; max engine rpm: 5,700; 43.9 hp/l; cast iron block and head; 5 crankshaft bearings; valves: overhead, in line, push-rods and rockers; camshafts: 1, side, chain driven; lubrication: rotary pump, full flow filter, 6.5 imp pt, 7.8 US pt, 3.7 l; 1 Ford GPD downdraught single barrel carburettor; fuel feed: mechanical pump; water-cooled, 8.8 imp pt, 10.6 US pt, 5 l.

TRANSMISSION driving wheels: rear; clutch: single dry plate (diaphragm); gearbox: mechanical; gears: 4, fully synchronized; ratios: I 3.656, II 2.185, III 1.425, IV 1, rev 4.235; lever: central; final drive: hypoid bevel; axle ratio: 4.110; width of rims: 4.5''; tyres: 155 SR x 13.

PERFORMANCE max speed: 88 mph, 141 km/h; power-weight ratio: 35.4 lb/hp, 16 kg/hp; carrying capacity: 939 lb, 426 kg; acceleration: 0-50 mph (0-80 km/h) 12.5 sec; speed in direct drive at 1,000 rpm: 15.5 mph, 24.9 km/h; consumption: 42.2 m/imp gal, 35.1 m/US gal, 6.7 l x 100 km at 50 mph, 80 km/h.

CHASSIS integral; front suspension: independent, by McPherson, coil springs/telescopic damper struts, anti-roll bar; rear: rigid axle, semi-elliptic leafsprings, telescopic dampers.

STEERING rack-and-pinion; turns lock to lock: 3.50

BRAKES front disc, rear drum, servo.

ELECTRICAL EQUIPMENT 12 V; 40 Ah battery; 45 Alternator; Motorcraft distributor; 2 headlamps.

DIMENSIONS AND WEIGHT wheel base: 94.76 in, 241 cm; tracks: 49.72 in, 126 cm front, 50.75 in, 129 cm rear; length:

CHEVROLET Nomad

157.40 in, 400 cm; width: 62.83 in, 160 cm; height: 55.04 in, 140 cm; ground clearance: 3.94 in, 10 cm; weight: 2,018 lb, 915 kg; turning circle: 29.2 ft, 8.9 m; fuel tank: 12.1 imp gal, 14.5 US gal, 55 l.

BODY saloon/sedan; 4 doors; 5 seats, separate front seats, reclining backrests.

Escort 1600 GL 4-door Sedan

See Escort 1300 L 4-door Sedan, except for:

PRICE EX WORKS: 4,810 rand

ENGINE 97.5 cu in, 1,598 cc (3.19 x 3.06 in, 81 x 77.6 mm); compression ratio: 9:1; max power (DIN): 84 hp at 5,500 rpm; max torque (DIN): 92 lb ft, 12.7 kg m at 3,500 rpm; 52.6 hp/l; lubrication: 6.7 imp pt, 8 US pt, 3.8 l; 1 Weber 32/32 DGV downdraught twin barrel carburettor; cooling system: 9.5 imp pt, 11.4 US pt, 5.4 l.

TRANSMISSION gearbox ratios: I 3.337, II 1.995, III 1.418, IV 1, rev 3.867; axle ratio: 3.890.

PERFORMANCE max speed: 100 mph, 161 km/h; power-weight ratio: 24 lb/hp, 10.9 kg/hp; acceleration: 0-50 mph (0-80 km/h) 8.4 sec; speed in direct drive at 1,000 rpm: 18.5 mph, 29.8 km/h; consumption: 46.3 m/imp gal, 38.6 m/US gal, 6.1 l x 100 km at 50 mph, 80 km/h.

ELECTRICAL EQUIPMENT halogen headlamps.

DIMENSIONS AND WEIGHT weight: 2,073 lb, 940 kg.

BODY vinyl roof.

OPTIONALS Bordeaux C 3 automatic transmission, hydraulic torque converter and planetary gears with 3 ratios (I 2.474, II 1.474, III 1, rev 2.111), max ratio of converter at stall 2, possible manual selection, max speed 98 mph, 157 km/h, power-weight ratio 24.9 lb/hp, 11.3 kg/hp, acceleration 0-50 mph (0-80 km/h) 9.9 sec, consumption 41.5 m/imp gal, 34.6 m/US gal, 6.8 l x 100 km at 50 mph, 80 km/h, 55 Ah battery; weight 2,095 lb, 950 kg.

Escort RS 2000 2-door Sedan

See Escort 1300 L 4-door Sedan, except for:

PRICE EX WORKS: 5,965 rand

ENGINE 121.6 cu in, 1,993 cc (3.57 x 3.03 in, 90.8 x 76.9 mm); max power (DIN): 110 hp at 5,500 rpm; max torque (DIN): 120 lb ft, 16.6 kg m at 4,000 rpm; max engine rpm: 6,600; 55.2 hp/l; valves: overhead, Vee-slanted, rockers; camshafts: 1, overhead, cogged belt; 1 Weber 32/36 DGAV downdraught twin barrel carburettor; cooling system: 12.5 imp pt, 15 US pt, 7.1 l.

TRANSMISSION gearbox ratios: I 3.651, II 1.968, III 1.368, IV 1, rev 3.660; axle ratio: 3.700; width of rims: 5.5''; tyres: 175/70 SR x 13.

PERFORMANCE max speed: 112 mph, 180 km/h; power-weight ratio: 19.6 lb/hp, 8.9 kg/hp; carrying capacity: 750 lb, 340 kg; acceleration: 0-50 mph (0-80 km/h) 6.9 sec; speed in direct drive at 1,000 rpm: 17.7 mph, 28.5 km/h; consumption: 42.8 m/imp gal, 35.6 m/US gal, 6.6 l x 100 km at 50 mph, 80 km/h.

CHASSIS anti-roll bar on rear suspension.

BRAKES swept area: total 289.6 sq in, 1,868 sq cm.

ELECTRICAL EQUIPMENT 4 headlamps.

DIMENSIONS AND WEIGHT length: 162.99 in, 414 cm; ground clearance: 3.66 in, 9.3 cm; weight: 2,161 lb, 980 kg; turning circle: 28.2 ft, 8.6 m; fuel tank: 12.1 imp gal, 14.5 US gal, 55 l.

BODY 2 doors.

OPTIONALS tinted glass; limited slip differential; 3.770 axle ratio.

Cortina 1600 L Sedan

PRICE EX WORKS: 5,450 rand

ENGINE front, 4 stroke; 4 cylinders, vertical, in line; 97.5 cu in, 1,598 cc (3.19 x 3.06 in, 81 x 77.6 mm); compression

---

FORD Escort RS 2000 2-dr Sedan

FORD Cortina 3000 S Sedan

CORTINA 1600 L SEDAN

ratio: 9:1; max power (DIN): 84 hp at 5,500 rpm; max torque (DIN): 92 lb ft, 12.7 kg m at 3,500 rpm; max engine rpm: 6,300; 52.5 hp/l; cast iron block and head; 5 crankshaft bearings; valves: overhead, in line, push-rods and rockers; camshafts: 1, overhead; lubrication: rotary pump, full flow filter, 7.6 imp pt, 9.1 US pt, 4.3 l; 1 Weber downdraught twin barrel carburettor; fuel feed: mechanical pump; water-cooled, 11.4 imp pt, 13.7 US pt, 6.5 l.

TRANSMISSION driving wheels: rear; clutch: single dry plate, semi-centrifugal; gearbox: mechanical; gears: 4, fully synchronized; ratios: I 3.580, II 2.010, III 1.397, IV 1, rev 3.320; lever: central; final drive: hypoid bevel; axle ratio: 3.890; width of rims: 5.5''; tyres 165 SR x 13.

PERFORMANCE max speeds: (I) 31 mph, 50 km/h; (II) 53 mph, 86 km/h; (III) 74 mph, 119 km/h; (IV) 99 mph, 159 km/h; power-weight ratio: 27.6 lb/hp, 12.5 kg/hp; carrying capacity: 948 lb, 430 kg; acceleration: standing ¼ mile 19.2 sec, 0-50 mph (0-80 km/h) 9.1 sec; speed in direct drive at 1,000 rpm: 17 mph, 27.8 km/h; consumption: 37 m/imp gal, 31 m/US gal, 7.6 l x 100 km.

CHASSIS integral, front auxiliary frame; front suspension: independent, coil springs, telescopic dampers; rear: rigid axle, trailing radius arms, 4 linkage bars, coil springs, telescopic dampers.

STEERING rack-and-pinion; turns lock to lock: 4.40.

BRAKES front disc, rear drum, servo; swept area: front 194.6 sq in, 1,255 sq cm, rear 96.1 sq in, 620 sq cm, total 290.7 sq in, 1,875 sq cm.

ELECTRICAL EQUIPMENT 12 V; 40 Ah battery; 45 A alternator; 2 headlamps.

DIMENSIONS AND WEIGHT wheel base: 101.57 in, 258 cm; tracks: 56.69 in, 144 cm front, 55.90 in, 142 cm rear; length: 170.87 in, 434 cm; width: 66.90 in, 170 cm; height: 53.93 in, 137 cm; ground clearance: 6.69 in, 17 cm; weight: 2,315 lb, 1,050 kg; weight distribution: 53% front, 47% rear; turning circle: 32 ft, 9.9 m; fuel tank: 14.3 imp gal, 17.1 US gal, 65 l.

BODY saloon/sedan; 4 doors; 5 seats, separate front seats, reclining backrests.

OPTIONALS metallic spray; tinted glass; cloth seats; vinyl roof.

Cortina 1600 L Station Wagon

See Cortina 1600 L Sedan, except for:

PRICE EX WORKS: 5,815 rand

PERFORMANCE power-weight ratio: 29.1 lb/hp, 13.2 kg/hp.

DIMENSIONS AND WEIGHT length: 174.80 in, 444 cm; weight: 2,447 lb, 1,110 kg.

BODY st. wagon/estate car; 4 + 1 doors; folding rear seat.

Cortina 2000 GL Sedan

See Cortina 1600 L Sedan, except for:

PRICE EX WORKS: 6,330 rand

ENGINE 121.6 cu in, 1,993 cc (3.58 x 3.03 in, 91 x 77 mm); compression ratio: 9.2:1; max power (DIN): 98 hp at 5,200 rpm; max torque (DIN): 112 lb ft, 15.4 kg m at 3,500 rpm; max engine rpm: 5,800; 49 hp/l; lubrication: 6.5 imp pt, 7.8 US pt, 3.7 l.

TRANSMISSION gearbox ratios: I 3.650, II 1.970, III 1.370, IV 1, rev 3.660; axle ratio: 3.700.

PERFORMANCE max speeds: (I) 30 mph, 48 km/h; (II) 55 mph, 89 km/h; (III) 75 mph, 121 km/h; (IV) 104 mph, 167 km/h; power-weight ratio: 24 lb/hp, 10.9 kg/hp; acceleration: standing ¼ mile 18.2 sec, 0-50 mph (0-80 km/h) 7.8 sec; speed in direct drive at 1,000 rpm: 18 mph, 29 km/h; consumption: 36 m/imp gal, 30 m/US gal, 7.9 l x 100 km.

DIMENSIONS AND WEIGHT weight: 2,359 lb, 1,070 kg.

OPTIONALS Ford C3 automatic transmission hydraulic torque converter and planetary gears with 3 ratios (I 2.474, II 1.474, III 1, rev 2.111), max ratio of converter at stall 2, possible manual selection, max speed 101 mph, 162 km/h, power-weight ratio 24.2 lb/hp, 11 kg/hp, consumption 35 m/imp gal, 29 m/US gal, 8.1 l x 100 km, weight 2,370 lb, 1,075 kg.

Cortina 2000 GL Station Wagon

See Cortina 2000 GL Sedan, except for:

PRICE EX WORKS: 6,330 rand

PERFORMANCE power-weight ratio: 25.9 lb/hp, 11.7 kg/hp.

DIMENSIONS AND WEIGHT length: 174.80 in, 444 cm; weight: 2,536 lb, 1,150 kg.

BODY st. wagon/estate car; 4 + 1 doors; folding rear seat.

OPTIONALS with Ford C3 automatic transmission, power-weight ratio 26 lb/hp, 11.8 kg/hp, weight 2,547 lb, 1,155 kg.

Cortina 3000 S Sedan

See Cortina 1600 L Sedan, except for:

PRICE EX WORKS: 6,780 rand

ENGINE 6 cylinders, Vee-slanted at 60°; 182.7 cu in, 2,994 cc (3.69 x 2.83 in, 93.7 x 72 mm); compression ratio: 8.9:1; max power (DIN): 138 hp at 5,000 rpm; max torque (DIN): 174 lb ft, 24 kg m at 3,000 rpm; max engine rpm: 5,700; 46 hp/l; 4 crankshaft bearings; lubrication: 9.8 imp pt, 11.8 US pt, 5.6 l; cooling system: 18.8 imp pt, 22.6 US pt, 10.7 l.

TRANSMISSION gearbox ratios: I 3.160, II 1.950, III 1.410, IV 1, rev 3.350; axle ratio: 3.080; tyres: 185/70 SR x 13.

PERFORMANCE max speeds: (I) 41 mph, 66 km/h; (II) 65 mph, 105 km/h; (III) 87 mph, 140 km/h; (IV) 88 mph, 14 km/h; power-weight ratio: 19.2 lb/hp, 8.7 kg/hp; acceleration: standing ¼ mile 16.9 sec, 0-50 mph (0-80 km/h) 6.4 sec; speed in direct drive at 1,000 rpm: 22.6 mph, 36.4 km/h; consumption: 32.8 m/imp gal, 27.3 m/US gal, 8.6 l x 100 km.

BRAKES swept area: front 194.6 sq in, 1,255 sq cm, rear 122.8 sq in, 792 sq cm, total 317.4 sq in, 2,047 sq cm.

ELECTRICAL EQUIPMENT 4 headlamps.

DIMENSIONS AND WEIGHT height: 53.15 in, 135 cm; ground clearance: 5.90 in, 15 cm; weight: 2,657 lb, 1,205 kg; weight distribution: 56% front, 44% rear.

Cortina 3000 Ghia Sedan

See Cortina 3000 S Sedan, except for:

PRICE EX WORKS: 7,660 rand

TRANSMISSION gearbox: Ford C3 automatic transmission, hydraulic torque converter and planetary gears; ratios: I 2.474, II 1.474, III 1, rev 2.110; tyres: 175 SR x 13.

PERFORMANCE max speed: (I) 48 mph, 78 km/h; (II) 81 mph, 131 km/h; (III) 114 mph, 183 km/h; acceleration: standing ¼ mile 17.8 sec, 0-50 mph (0-80 km/h) 7.2 sec; speed in direct drive at 1,000 rpm: 21.7 mph, 35 km/h.

DIMENSIONS AND WEIGHT length: 172.44 in, 438 cm; ground clearance: 6.69 in, 17 cm.

FORD Cortina Station Wagon

Cortina 3000 Ghia Station Wagon

See Cortina 3000 Ghia Sedan, except for:

PRICE EX WORKS: 8,205 rand

PERFORMANCE power-weight ratio: 20.4 lb/hp, 9.2 kg/hp.

DIMENSIONS AND WEIGHT length: 176.38 in, 448 cm; weight: 2,811 lb, 1,275 kg.

BODY st. wagon/estate car; 4 + 1 doors; folding rear seat.

Granada 2000 GL Sedan

PRICE EX WORKS: 6,855 rand

ENGINE front, 4 stroke; 4 cylinders, in line; 121.6 cu in, 1,993 cc (3.57 x 3.03 in, 90.8 x 76.9 mm); compression ratio: 9.2:1; max power (DIN): 99 hp at 5,500 rpm; max torque (DIN): 112 lb ft, 15.4 kg m at 4,000 rpm; max engine rpm: 5,600; 49.7 hp/l cast iron block and head; 5 crankshaft bearings; valves: overhead, Vee-slanted, rockers; camshafts: 1, overhead, cogged belt; lubrication: rotary pump, full flow filter, 6.6 imp pt, 7.8 US pt, 3.7 l; 1 Weber downdraught carburettor; fuel feed; mechanical pump; water-cooled, 12.3 imp pt, 14.8 US pt, 7 l.

TRANSMISSION driving wheels: rear; clutch: single dry plate (diaphragm); gearbox: mechanical; gears: 4, fully syn-

FORD Granada 2000 GL Sedan

FORD Granada 3000 Ghia Sedan

chronized; ratios: I 3.650, II 1.970, III 1.370, IV 1, rev 3.666; lever: central; final drive: hypoid bevel; axle ratio: 4; width of rims: 5.5''; tyres: 175 SR x 14.

PERFORMANCE max speed: 102 mph, 164 km/h; power-weight ratio: 29.3 lb/hp, 13.3 kg/hp; carrying capacity: 992 lb, 450 kg; acceleration: 0-50 mph (0-80 km/h) 8.8 sec; speed in direct drive at 1,000 rpm: 17.9 mph, 28.8 km/h; consumption: 36.2 m/imp gal, 30.1 m/US gal, 7.8 l x 100 km at 50 mph, 80 km/h.

CHASSIS integral; front suspension: independent, wishbones (lower trailing links), coil springs, anti-roll bar, telescopic dampers; rear: independent, semi-trailing arms, coil springs, telescopic dampers.

STEERING rack-and-pinion; turns lock to lock: 4.40.

BRAKES front disc (diameter 10.31, 26.2 cm) rear drum, servo; swept area: total 334.3 sq in, 2,156 sq cm.

ELECTRICAL EQUIPMENT 12 V; 40 Ah battery; 45 A alternator; 2 headlamps.

DIMENSIONS AND WEIGHT wheel base: 109.01 in, 277 cm; tracks: 59.64 in, 151 cm front, 60.31 in, 153 cm rear; length: 183.07 in, 465 cm; width: 70.51 in, 179 cm; height: 56.10 in, 142 cm; ground clearance: 5.24 in, 13.3 cm; weight: 2,911 lb, 1,320 kg; weight distribution: 48.9% front, 51.1% rear; turning circle: 33.8 ft, 10.3 m; fuel tank: 22 imp gal, 26 US gal, 100 l.

BODY saloon/sedan; 4 doors; 5 seats, separate front seats, reclining backrests.

OPTIONALS metallic spray; tinted glass; Ford C3 automatic transmission, hydraulic torque converter and planetary gears with 3 ratios (I 2.470, II 1.470, III 1, rev 2.111), max speed 97 mph, 156 km/h, acceleration (0-50 mph, 0-80 km/h), 10.9 sec.

Granada 3000 GL Sedan

See Granada 2000 GL Sedan, except for:

PRICE EX WORKS: 8,360 rand

ENGINE front, 4 stroke; 6 cylinders, Vee-slanted at 60°; 182.7 cu in, 2,994 cc (3.69 x 2.85 in, 93.7 x 72.4 mm); compression ratio: 8.9:1; max power (SAE): 159 hp at 5,200 rpm; max torque (SAE): 191 lb ft, 26.4 kg m at 3,000 rpm; max engine rpm: 5,500; 53.1 hp/l; 4 crankshaft bearings; valves: overhead, push-rods and rockers; camshafts: 1, at centre of Vee; lubrication: 9.9 imp pt, 11.8 US pt, 5.6 l; 1 Weber 38/38 EGAS downdraught twin barrel carburettor; fuel feed: mechanical pump; water-cooled, 20.1 imp pt, 24.1 US pt, 11.4 l.

TRANSMISSION gearbox ratios: I 3.160, II 1.940, III 1.410, IV 1, rev 3.346; axle ratio: 3.450.

PERFORMANCE max speed: about 114 mph, 183 km/h; power-weight ratio: 18 lb/hp, 8.2 kg/hp; speed in direct drive at 1,000 rpm: 20.8 mph, 33.4 km/h; consumption: 24 m/imp gal, 20.1 m/US gal, 11.7 l x 100 km.

STEERING servo; turns lock to lock: 3.50.

BRAKES front internal radial fins.

ELECTRICAL EQUIPMENT 12 V; 45 Ah battery; 55 A alternator.

DIMENSIONS AND WEIGHT weight: 3,120 lb, 1,415 kg.

OPTIONALS air conditioning; halogen headlamps; vinyl roof.

Granada 3000 Ghia Sedan

See Granada 3000 GL Sedan, except for:

PRICE EX WORKS: 12,850 rand

TRANSMISSION Ford C3 automatic gearbox (standard); width of rims: 6''; tyres: 185 SR x 14.

PERFORMANCE max speed: 110 mph, 177 km/h; power-weight ratio: 24.4 lb/hp, 11 kg/hp; carrying capacity: 882 lb, 400 kg; acceleration: 0-50 mph (0-80 km/h) 8.4 sec; speed in direct drive at 1,000 rpm: 20.2 mph, 32.5 km/h; consumption: 27.7 m/imp gal, 23.1 m/US gal, 10.2 l x 100 km.

ELECTRICAL EQUIPMENT halogen headlamps (standard).

DIMENSIONS AND WEIGHT weight: tracks: 62.13 in, 158 cm front, 60.83 in, 154 cm rear; length: 183.54 in, 466 cm.

BODY luxury equipment; reclining backrests with adjustable built-in headrests; tinted glass (standard); air-conditioning (standard).

PAYKAN   IRAN

Saloon

ENGINE front, 4 stroke; 4 cylinders, slanted 10°, in line; 105.3 cu in, 1,725 cc (3.21 x 3.25 in, 81.5 x 82.5 mm); compression ratio: 7.5:1; max power (DIN): 64 hp at 4,500 rpm; max torque (DIN): 90 lb ft, 12.4 kg m at 2,500 rpm; max engine rpm: 5,600; 37.1 hp/l; cast iron block, light alloy head; 5 crankshaft bearings; valves: overhead, in line, push-rods and rockers; camshafts: 1, side; lubrication: rotary pump, full flow filter, 7.5 imp pt, 8.9 US pt, 4.2 l; 1 Zenith-Stromberg 150 CDS horizontal carburettor; fuel feed: mechanical pump; water-cooled, 12.3 imp pt, 14.8 US pt, 7 l.

TRANSMISSION driving wheels: rear; clutch: single dry plate (diaphragm), hydraulically controlled; gearbox: mechanical; gears: 4, fully synchronized; ratios: I 3.353, II 2.141, III 1.392, IV 1, rev 3.569; lever: central; final drive: hypoid bevel; axle ratio: 3.890; width of rims: 4.5''; tyres: 5.60 x 13.

PERFORMANCE max speed: 87 mph, 140 km/h; power-weight ratio: 32 lb/hp, 14.5 kg/hp; carrying capacity: 882 lb, 400 kg; speed in direct drive at 1,000 rpm: 17.4 mph, 28 km/h; consumption: 28.2 m/imp gal, 23.5 m/US gal, 10 l x 100 km.

PAYKAN Saloon

SALOON

CHASSIS integral; front suspension: independent, by Mc-Pherson, coil springs/telescopic damper struts, anti-roll bar; rear: rigid axle, semi-elliptic leafsprings, telescopic dampers.

STEERING recirculating ball; turns lock to lock: 3.75.

BRAKES front disc (diameter 9.61 in, 24.4 cm), rear drum, servo; swept area: total 278 sq in, 1,793 sq cm.

ELECTRICAL EQUIPMENT 12 V; 54 Ah battery; 24 A alternator; Lucas distributor; 2 headlamps.

DIMENSIONS AND WEIGHT wheel base: 98.43 in, 250 cm; front and rear track: 51.97 in, 132 cm; length: 169.29 in, 430 cm; width: 63.39 in, 161 cm; height: 55.51 in, 141 cm; ground clearance: 6.69 in, 17 cm; weight: 2,051 lb, 930 kg; turning circle: 33.5 ft, 10.2 m; fuel tank: 9.9 imp gal, 11.9 US gal, 45 l.

BODY saloon/sedan; 4 doors; 5 seats, separate front seats.

OPTIONALS Laycock overdrive on III and IV (0.803 ratio), 4.220 or 3.890 axle ratio; Borg-Warner 35 automatic transmission, hydraulic torque converter and planetary gears with 3 ratios (I 2.393, II 1.450, III 1, rev 2.094), max ratio of converter at stall 2, possible manual selection, steering column lever, 3.890 or 4.220 axle ratio.

Saloon GT

See Saloon, except for:

ENGINE compression ratio: 9.2:1; max power (DIN): 79 hp at 5,200 rpm; max torque (DIN): 91 lb ft, 12.6 kg m at 4,000 rpm; max engine rpm: 6,400; 45.8 hp/l; 2 Stromberg semi-downdraught carburettors.

TRANSMISSION gearbox ratios: I 3.120, II 1.990, III 1.295, IV 1, rev 3.320; axle ratio: 3.700; tyres: 165 SR x 13.

PERFORMANCE max speed: 96 mph, 155 km/h; power-weight ratio: 28 lb/hp, 12.7 kg/hp; speed in direct drive at 1,000 rpm: 18.3 mph, 29.5 km/h; consumption: 25.7 m/imp gal, 21.4 m/US gal, 11 l x 100 km.

ELECTRICAL EQUIPMENT 30 A alternator.

DIMENSIONS AND WEIGHT weight: 2,205 lb, 1,000 kg.

OPTIONALS Laycock overdrive on III and IV (0.803 ratio), 3.890 axle ratio; Borg-Warner 35 automatic transmission with 3.700 axle ratio.

HINDUSTAN   INDIA

Ambassador Mark 3

ENGINE front, 4 stroke; 4 cylinders, vertical, in line; 90.88 cu in, 1,489 cc (2.87 x 3.50 in, 73 x 88.9 mm); compression ratio: 7.2:1; max power (SAE): 50 hp at 4,200 rpm; max torque (SAE): 74 lb ft, 10.2 kg m at 3,000 rpm; max engine rpm: 4,800; 33.6 hp/l; cast iron block and head; 3 crankshaft bearings; valves: overhead, in line, push-rods and rockers; camshafts: 1, side; lubrication: gear pump, full flow filter, 8 imp pt, 9.6 US pt, 4.5 l; 1 SU type HS 2 semi-downdraught carburettor; fuel feed: electric pump; water-cooled, 14.1 imp pt, 16.9 US pt, 8 l.

TRANSMISSION driving wheels: rear; clutch: single dry plate; gearbox: mechanical; gears: 4, II, III and IV synchronized; ratios: I 3.807, II 2.253, III 1.506, IV 1, rev 3.807; lever: steering column; final drive: hypoid bevel; axle ratio: 4.875; width of rims: 4''; tyres: 5.90 x 15.

PERFORMANCE max speeds: (I) 20 mph, 32 km/h; (II) 33 mph, 53 km/h; (III) 49 mph, 79 km/h; (IV) 74 mph, 119 km/h; power-weight ratio: 49.1 lb/hp, 22.3 kg/hp; carrying capacity: 850 lb, 386 kg; acceleration: standing ¼ mile 25 sec, 0-50 mph (0-80 km/h) 19.8 sec; speed in direct drive at 1,000 rpm: 15.5 mph, 25 km/h; consumption: 26.9 m/imp gal, 22.4 m/US gal, 10.5 l x 100 km.

CHASSIS integral; front suspension: independent, wishbones, longitudinal torsion bars, telescopic dampers; rear: rigid axle, semi-elliptic leafsprings, telescopic dampers.

STEERING rack-and-pinion; turns lock to lock: 3.75.

BRAKES drum, rear compensator; lining area: front 48.1 sq in, 310 sq cm, rear 48.1 sq in, 310 sq cm, total 96.2 sq in, 620 sq cm.

HINDUSTAN Ambassador Mark 3

ELECTRICAL EQUIPMENT 12 V; 60 Ah battery; 20 A dynamo; Lucas distributor; 2 headlamps.

DIMENSIONS AND WEIGHT wheel base: 97 in, 246 cm; tracks: 53.50 in, 136 cm front, 53 in, 135 cm rear; length: 170.87 in, 434 cm; width: 65 in, 165 cm; height: 63 in, 160 cm; ground clearance: 7.87 in, 20 cm; weight: 2,456 lb, 1,114 kg; turning circle: 35.4 ft, 10.8 m; fuel tank: 12 imp gal, 14.4 US gal, 55 l.

BODY saloon/sedan; 4 doors; 5 seats, bench front seats.

PREMIER   INDIA

Padmini

PRICE EX WORKS: 32,975* Rs

ENGINE front, 4 stroke; 4 cylinders, vertical, in line; 66.5 cu in, 1,089 cc (2.68 x 2.95 in, 68 x 75 mm); compression ratio: 7.3:1; max power (SAE): 40 hp at 4,800 rpm; max torque (SAE): 57 lb ft, 7.9 kg m at 2,400 rpm; max engine rpm: 4,800; 36.7 hp/l; cast iron block, light alloy head; 3 crankshaft bearings; valves: overhead, in line, push-rods and rockers; camshafts: 1, side; lubrication: 5.3 imp pt, 6. US pt, 3 l; 32 BIC type IBX downdraught single barrel ca burettor; fuel feed: mechanical pump; water-cooled, 7. imp pt, 9.5 US pt, 4.5 l.

TRANSMISSION driving wheels: rear; clutch: single d plate; gearbox: mechanical; gears: 4, II, III and IV sy chronized; ratios: I 3.860, II 2.380, III 1.570, V 1, re 3.860; lever: steering column; final drive: hypoid beve axle ratio: 4.300; width of rims: 3.5''; tyres: 5.20 x 14.

PERFORMANCE max speeds: (I) 19 mph, 30 km/h; (II) 3 mph, 50 km/h; (III) 47 mph, 75 km/h; (IV) 75 mph, 120 km/ power-weight ratio: 49.3 lb/hp, 22.4 kg/hp; carrying capacit 882 lb, 400 kg; acceleration: standing ¼ mile 26.9 sec, 0-5 mph, (0-80 km/h) 20.3 sec; speed in direct drive at 1,00 rpm: 15.6 mph, 25 km/h; consumption: 42.2 m/imp gal, 35 m/US gal, 6.7 l x 100 km.

CHASSIS integral; front suspension: independent, wishbone anti-roll bar, coil springs, telescopic dampers; rear: rigi axle, anti-roll bar, semi-elliptic leafsprings, telescopi dampers.

STEERING worm and roller; turns lock to lock: 4.80.

BRAKES drum; lining area: front 76.9 sq in, 496 sq cm rear 76.9 sq in, 496 sq cm, total 153.8 sq in, 992 sq cm

ELECTRICAL EQUIPMENT 12 V; 45 Ah battery; 22 A dynam Lucas distributor; 2 headlamps.

PREMIER Padmini

DIMENSIONS AND WEIGHT wheel base: 92.13 in, 234 cm; tracks: 48.50 in, 123 cm front, 47.83 in, 121 cm rear; length: 155.12 in, 394 cm; width: 57.40 in, 146 cm; height: 57.40 in, 146 cm; ground clearance: 5.04 in, 13 cm; weight: 1,973 lb, 895 kg; turning circle: 34.7 ft, 10.9 m; fuel tank: 8.4 imp gal, 10 US gal, 38 l.

BODY saloon/sedan; 4 doors; 5 seats, bench front seats.

Padmini De Luxe

See Padmini, except for:

PRICE EX WORKS: 38,169* Rs

ENGINE compression ratio: 8:1; max power (SAE): 47 hp at 5,000 rpm; max torque (SAE): 58 lb ft, 8 kg m at 3,000 rpm; max engine rpm: 5,000; 43.6 hp/l.

TRANSMISSION lever: central.

PERFORMANCE max speeds: (I) 21 mph, 33 km/h; (II) 34 mph, 54 km/h; (III) 51 mph, 81 km/h; (IV) 80 mph, 128 km/h; power-weight ratio: 42 lb/hp, 19 kg/hp.

BODY separate front seats, safety belts.

STANDARD Gazel

STANDARD INDIA

Gazel

ENGINE front, 4 stroke; 4 cylinders, vertical, in line; 57.85 cu in, 948 cc (2.48 x 2.99 in, 63 x 76 mm); compression ratio: 7.2:1; max power (DIN): 35 hp at 4,800 rpm; max torque (DIN): 48 lb ft, 6.6 kg m at 2,400 rpm; max engine rpm: 4,800; 36.9 hp/l; cast iron block and head; 3 crankshaft bearings; valves: overhead, push-rods and rockers; camshafts: 1, side; lubrication: full flow filter, 7 imp pt, 8.4 US pt, 4 l; 1 Solex B30 PSEI downdraught single barrel carburettor; fuel feed: mechanical pump; water-cooled, 8.4 imp pt, 10.1 US pt, 4.8 l.

TRANSMISSION driving wheels: rear; clutch: single dry plate; gearbox: mechanical; gears: 4, fully synchronized; ratios: I 4.271, II 2.460, III 1.454, IV 1, rev 4.271; lever: central; final drive: hypoid bevel; axle ratio: 4.870; tyres: 5.20 x 13.

PERFORMANCE max speed: 71 mph, 115 km/h; power-weight ratio: 57.3 lb/hp, 26 kg/hp; consumption: 28.2 m/imp gal, 23.5 m/US gal, 10 l x 100 km.

CHASSIS central steel backbone, box-type ladder frame; front suspension: independent, wishbones, anti-roll bar, coil springs, telescopic dampers; rear: trailing radius arms, anti-roll bar, coil springs, telescopic dampers.

STEERING rack-and-pinion.

ELECTRICAL EQUIPMENT 12 V; 40 Ah battery; 264 W dynamo; 2 headlamps.

DIMENSIONS AND WEIGHT wheel base: 91.33 in, 232 cm; front and rear track: 48.03 in, 122 cm; length: 156.29 in, 397 cm; width: 59.84 in, 152 cm; height: 57.87 in, 147 cm; ground clearance: 6.30 in, 16 cm; weight: 2,006 lb, 910 kg; turning circle: 26.9 ft, 8.2 m.

BODY saloon/sedan; 4 doors; 5 seats, separate front seats.

HONGQI CHINA (People's Republic)

9-pass. Limousine/6-pass. Limousine

ENGINE front, 4 stroke; V8 cylinders; 344.9 cu in, 5,652 cc (3.94 x 3.54 in, 100 x 90 mm); compression ratio: 8.5:1; max power (SAE): 220 hp at 4,400 rpm; max torque (SAE): 304 lb ft, 42 kg m at 2,800-3,000 rpm; max engine rpm: 4,400; 38.9 hp/l; cast iron block and head; 5 crankshaft bearings; valves: overhead, in line, push-rods and rockers; camshafts: 1, at centre of Vee; lubrication: gear pump, full flow filter, 9.7 imp pt, 11.6 US pt, 5.5 l; 1 type 241 downdraught twin barrel carburettor; fuel feed: mechanical pump; water-cooled, 9-pass. 52,8 imp pt, 63.4 US pt, 30 l - 6-pass. 44 imp pt, 52.9 US pt, 25 l.

TRANSMISSION driving wheels: rear: gearbox: automatic transmission, hydraulic torque converter and planetary gears with 2 ratios, max ratio of converter at stall 2.5; ratios: I 1.720, II 1, rev 2.390; lever: steering column; final drive: hypoid bevel; axle ratio: 9-pass. 3.900 - 6-pass. 3.540; width of rims: 6''; tyres: 9-pass. 8.90 x 15 - 6-pass. 8.20 x 15.

PERFORMANCE max speed: 9-pass. 99 mph, 160 km/h; - 6-pass. 112 mph, 180 km/h; power-weight ratio: 9-pass. 27.3 lb/hp, 12.4 kg/hp - 6-pass. 22.7 lb/hp, 10.3 kg/hp; carrying capacity: 9-pass. 1,588 lb, 720 kg; - 6-pass. 1,058 lb, 480 kg; consumption: 9-pass. 14.1 m/imp gal, 11.8 m/US gal, 20 l x 100 km - 6-pass. 15.7 m/imp gal, 13.1 m/US gal, 18 l x 100 km.

CHASSIS box-type ladder frame; front suspension: independent, wishbones, coil springs, horizontal torsion bars, telescopic dampers; rear: rigid axle, semi-elliptic leaf-springs, telescopic dampers.

STEERING recirculating ball, servo.

BRAKES drum.

ELECTRICAL EQUIPMENT 12 V; 68 Ah battery (2 for 9-pass.); 36 Ah dinamo; 2 headlamps.

DIMENSIONS AND WEIGHT wheel base: 9-pass. 146.46 in, 372 cm - 6-pass. 120.87 in, 307 cm; tracks: 62.20 in, 158 cm front, 61.02 in, 155 cm rear; length: 9-pass. 235.43 in, 598 cm - 6-pass. 209.84 in, 533 cm; width: 78.35 in, 199 cm; height: 64.57 in, 164 cm; ground clearance: 7.09 in, 18 cm; weight: 9-pass. 6,020 lb, 2,730 kg - 6-pass. 5,005 lb, 2,270 kg; weight distribution: 9-pass. 52.2% front, 47.8% rear - 6-pass. 54% front, 46% rear; turning circle: 9-pass. 49.2 ft, 15 m - 6-pass. 42 ft, 12.8 m; fuel tank: 17.6 imp gal, 21.1 US gal, 80 l.

BODY limousine; 4 doors; 9 seats in three rows or 6 seats, bench front seats; electrically-controlled rear seat; electric windows; air-conditioning.

PEKING CHINA (People's Republic)

BJ 212

ENGINE front, 4 stroke; 4 cylinders, vertical, in line; 149.2 cu in, 2,445 cc (3.62 x 3.62 in, 92 x 92 mm); compression ratio: 6.6:1; max power (SAE): 75 hp at 3,500 - 4,000 rpm; max torque (SAE): 127 lb ft, 17.5 kg m at 2,000 - 2,500 rpm; max engine rpm: 4,000; 30.7 hp/l; cast iron block, light alloy head; 5 crankshaft bearings; valves: overhead,

HONGQI 9-pass. Limousine

BJ 212

Vee-slanted, push-rods and rockers; camshafts: 1, side; lubrication: gear pump, full flow filter, 10.9 imp pt, 13.1 US pt, 6.2 l; 1 type K-22D downdraught single barrel carburettor; fuel feed: mechanical pump; water-cooled, 18.5 imp pt, 22.2 US pt, 10.5 l.

TRANSMISSION driving wheels: front (automatically engaged with transfer box low ratio) and rear; clutch: single dry plate, hydraulically controlled; gearbox: mechanical; gears: 3, II and III synchronized; ratios: I 3.115, II 1.772, III 1, rev 3.738; transfer box ratios: high 1.200, low 2.648; lever: central; final drive: spiral bevel; axle ratio: 4.550; width of rims: 4.5''; tyres: 6.50 x 16.

PERFORMANCE max speeds: (I) 20 mph, 32 km/h; (II) 35 mph, 56 km/h; (III) 61 mph, 98 km/h; power-ewight ratio: 4.5 lb/hp, 20.4 kg/hp; carrying capacity: 882 lb, 400 kg; consumption: 16.6 m/imp gal, 13.8 m/US gal, 17 l x 100 km.

CHASSIS box-type ladder frame; front and rear suspension: rigid axle, semi-elliptic leafsprings, telescopic dampers.

STEERING worm and double roller.

BRAKES drum; lining area: total 153.5 sq in, 990 sq cm.

ELECTRICAL EQUIPMENT 12 V; 54 Ah battery; 250 W dynamo; 2 headlamps.

DIMENSIONS AND WEIGHT wheel base: 90.55 in, 230 cm; front and rear tracks: 56.69 in, 144 cm; length: 151.97 in, 386 cm; width: 68.90 in, 175 cm; height: 73.62 in, 187 cm; ground clearance: 8.66 in, 22 cm; weight: 3,374 lb, 1,530 kg; weight distribution: 52% front, 48% rear; turning circle 39.4 ft, 12 m; fuel tank: 13.2 imp gal, 15.8 US gal, 60 l - (separate tank) 5.5 imp gal, 6.6 US gal, 25 l.

BODY open; 4 doors; 5 seats, separate front seats; canvas roof.

PEKING BJ 212

SHANGHAI CHINA (People's Republic)

Sedan

ENGINE front, 4 stroke; 6 cylinders, in line; 136.2 cu in, 2,232 cc (3.15 x 2.91 in, 80 x 74 mm); compression ratio: 7.7:1; max power (SAE): 90 hp at 4,800 rpm; max torque (SAE): 109 lb ft, 15 kg m at 3,500 rpm; max engine rpm: 5,000; 40.3 hp/l; cast iron block, light alloy head; 4 crankshaft bearings; valves: overhead, in line; camshafts: 1, side; lubrication: gear pump, full flow filter, 10.8 imp pt, 12.7 US pt, 6 l; 1 Shangfu 593 downdraught twin barrel carburettor; fuel feed: mechanical pump; water-cooled, 19.4 imp pt, 23.3 US pt, 11 l.

TRANSMISSION driving wheels: rear; clutch: single dry plate; gearbox: mechanical; gears: 4, fully synchronized; ratios: I 3.520, II 2.320, III 1.520, IV 1, rev 3.290; lever: steering column; final drive: hypoid bevel; axle ratio: 4.110; width of rims: 5''; tyres: 6.70 x 13.

PERFORMANCE max speed: 81 mph, 130 km/h; power-weight ratio: 35.3 lb/hp, 16 kg/hp; carrying capacity: 882 lb, 400 kg.

CHASSIS integral; front and rear suspension: independent, coil springs, telescopic dampers.

STEERING recirculating ball.

BRAKES drum.

ELECTRICAL EQUIPMENT 12 V; 54 Ah battery; 220 W dynamo; 2 headlamps.

DIMENSIONS AND WEIGHT wheel base: 111.42 in, 283 cm; tracks: 56.69 in, 144 cm front, 58.27 in, 148 cm rear; length: 188.19 in, 478 cm; width: 69.68 in, 177 cm; height: 62,20 in, 158 cm; ground clearance: 5.12 in, 13 cm; weight: 3,175 lb, 1,440 kg; turning circle: 36.7 ft, 11.2 m; fuel tank: 14.1 imp gal, 16.9 US gal, 64 l.

BODY saloon/sedan; 4 doors; 5 seats, bench front seats.

SHANGHAI Sedan

HYUNDAI   KOREA

Pony Sedan

ENGINE Mitsubishi, front, 4 stroke; 4 cylinders, vertical, in line; 75.5 cu in, 1,238 cc (2.87 x 2.91 in, 73 x 74 mm); compression ratio: 8:1; max power (DIN): 55 hp at 5,000 rpm; max torque (DIN): 62.3 lb ft, 8.6 kg m at 4,000 rpm; 44.4 hp/l; light alloy head; 5 crankshaft bearings; valves: overhead, rockers; camshafts: 1, overhead; lubrication: trochoid pump, cartridge filter, 7 imp pt, 8.4 US pt, 4 l; 1 Mikuni Kogyo (Stromberg type) downdraught twin barrel carburettor; water-cooled, 10.5 imp pt, 12.7 US pt, 6 l.

TRANSMISSION driving wheels: rear; clutch: single dry plate (diaphragm), mechanically controlled; gearbox: mechanical; gears: 4, fully synchronized; ratios: I 3.523, II 2.193, III 1.442, IV 1, rev 3.867; lever: central; final drive: hypoid bevel; axle ratio: 4.222.

PERFORMANCE max speed: about 97 mph, 156 km/h; power-weight ratio: 35.3 lb/hp, 16 kg/hp; carrying capacity: 714 lb, 324 kg speed in direct drive at 1,000 rpm: 15.3 mph, 24.6 km/h; consumption: 37.4 m/imp gal, 31.2 m/US gal, 7.5 l x 100 km.

CHASSIS integral; front suspension: independent, by McPherson, coil springs/telescopic damper struts, lower wishbones (trailing links), anti-roll bar; rear: rigid axle, semi-elliptic leafsprings, telescopic dampers.

STEERING recirculating ball; turns lock to lock: 4.2.

BRAKES front disc (diameter 8.0 in, 20.2 cm) rear drum, servo.

ELECTRICAL EQUIPMENT 12 V; 40 Ah battery; 40 A alternator; Mitsubishi distributor; 4 headlamps.

DIMENSIONS AND WEIGHT wheel base: 92.13 in, 234 cm; tracks: 50 in, 127 cm front, 49.21 in, 125 cm rear; length: 156.69 in, 398 cm; width: 61.42 in, 156 cm; height: 53.54 in, 136 cm; ground clearance: 6.89 in, 17.5 cm; weight: 1,940 lb, 880 kg; turning circle: 29.5 ft, 9 m; fuel tank: 9.9 imp gal, 11.9 US gal, 45 l.

BODY saloon/sedan; 4 doors; 4 seats, separate front seats, reclining backrests.

VARIATIONS

ENGINE 87.80 cu in, 1,439 cc (2.87 x 3.38 in, 73 x 86 mm); max power (DIN): 68 hp at 5,000 rpm; max torque (DIN): 76.8 lb ft, 10.6 kg m at 3,000 rpm; max engine rpm: 6,300; 47.3 hp/l.

Pony Coupé

See Pony Sedan except for:

PERFORMANCE: power-weight ratio: 22.9 lb/hp, 10.4 kg/hp

DIMENSIONS AND WEIGHT wheel base 92.12 in, 234 cm front tracks 50.98 in, 129 cm, rear 50.20 in, 127 cm; length

HYUNDAI Pony Sedan

PERFORMANCE max speeds: (I) 25 mph, 40 km/h; (II) 40 mph, 65 km/h; (III) 65 mph, 105 km/h; (V) 87 mph, 140 km/h; power-weight ratio: 31.7 lb/hp, 14.4 kg/hp; carrying capacity: 882 lb, 400 kg; acceleration: standing ¼ mile 21 sec, 0-50 mph (0-80 km/h) 14 sec; speed in direct drive at 1,000 rpm: 14.9 mph, 24 km/h; consumption: 35.3 m/imp gal, 29.4 m/US gal, 8 l x 100 km.

CHASSIS integral; front suspension: independent, by Mc-Pherson, coil springs/telescopic damper struts, lower wishbones (trailing links), anti-roll bar; rear: rigid axle, semi-elliptic leafsprings, telescopic dampers.

STEERING recirculating ball; turns lock to lock: 3.40.

BRAKES drum, dual circuit; lining area: front 39.7 sq in, 256 sq cm, rear 39.7 sq in, 256 sq cm, total 79.4 sq in, 512 sq cm.

ELECTRICAL EQUIPMENT 12 V; 45 Ah battery; 420 W alternator; Mitsubishi distributor; 4 headlamps.

DIMENSIONS AND WEIGHT wheel base: 88.98 in, 226 cm; tracks: 49.61 in, 126 cm front, 48.82 in, 124 cm rear; length: 151.57 in, 385 cm; width: 60.63 in, 154 cm; height: 54.72 in, 139 cm; ground clearance: 6.70 in, 17 cm; weight: 1,742 lb, 790 kg; weight distribution: 54% front, 46% rear; turning circle: 27.6 ft, 8.4 m; fuel tank: 8.8 imp gal, 10.6 US gal, 40 l.

BODY saloon/sedan; 4 doors: 5 seats, separate front seats.

161.41 in, 410 cm; width 61.41 in, 156 cm; height, 47.63 in, 121 cm; weight: 1,830 lb, 830 kg.

BODY coupé; 2 doors; 4 seats.

KIA   KOREA

Brisa 1000

ENGINE front, 4 stroke; 4 cylinders, in line; 60.1 cu in, 985 cc (2.76 x 2.52 in, 70 x 64 mm); compression ratio: 8.8:1; max power (DIN): 55 hp at 6,000 rpm; max torque (DIN): 51 lb ft, 7 kg m at 3,500 rpm; max engine rpm: 6,000; 55.8 hp/l; cast iron block, light alloy head; 5 crankshaft bearings; valves: overhead, rockers; camshafts: 1, overhead; lubrication: rotary pump, full flow filter, 5.3 imp pt, 6.3 US pt, 3 l; NIKKI downdraught twin barrel carburettor; fuel feed: mechanical pump; water-cooled, 10.4 imp pt, 12.5 US pt, 5.9 l.

TRANSMISSION driving wheels: rear; clutch: single dry plate (diaphragm); gearbox: mechanical; gears: 4, fully synchronized; ratios: I 3.655, II 2.185, III 1.425, IV 1, rev 3.655; lever: central; final drive: hypoid bevel; axle ratio: 4.375; tyres: 6.15 x 13.

KIA Brisa 1300

Brisa 1300

See Brisa 1000 except for:

ENGINE 77.6 cu in, 1,272 cc (2.87 x 2.99 in, 73 x 76 mm); compression ratio: 9.2:1; max power (DIN): 65 hp at 6,000 rpm; max torque (DIN): 68.1 lb ft, 9.4 kg m at 3,500 rpm; 51.1 hp/l.

TRANSMISSION axle ratio: 4.111.

PERFORMANCE max speed: 93 mph, 150 km/h; power-weight ratio: 28.7 lb/hp, 13 kg/hp; acceleration: standing ¼ mile 18.1 sec; speed in direct drive at 1,000 rpm: 15.8 mph, 25.5 km/h.

DIMENSIONS AND WEIGHT weight: 1,863 lb, 845 kg.

YLN   TAIWAN

902 SD

ENGINE front, 4 stroke; 6 cylinders, in line; 121.9 cu in, 1,998 cc (3.07 x 2.74 in, 78 x 69.7 mm); compression ratio: 8.6:1; max power (SAE): 115 hp at 5,600 rpm; max torque (SAE): 120 lb ft, 16.6 kg m at 4,000 rpm; max engine rpm:

YLN 902 SD

YLN 803 SD

902 SD

5,600; 57.6 hp/l cast iron block and light alloy head; 7 crankshaft bearings; valves: 2 per cylinder, overhead, rockers; camshafts: 1, overhead; lubrication: trochoid pump, cartridge filter, 8.8 imp pt, 10.6 US pt, 5 l; 1 Hitachi DAF 342-22 downdraught twin barrel carburettor; fuel feed: mechanical pump; water-cooled, 15.6 imp pt, 18.8 US pt, 8.9 l.

TRANSMISSION driving wheels: rear; clutch: single dry plate (diaphragm); gearbox: mechanical; gears: 4, fully synchronized; ratios: I 3.592, II 2.246, III 1.415, IV 1, rev 3.657; lever: central; final drive: hypoid bevel; axle ratio: 3.910; width of rims: 5''; tyres: 175 SR x 14.

PERFORMANCE max speeds: (I) 28 mph, 45 km/h; (II) 47 mph, 75 km/h; (III) 71 mph, 115 km/h; (IV) 103 mph, 165 km/h; power-weight ratio: 23 lb/hp, 10.4 kg/hp; speed in direct drive at 1,000 rpm: 17.4 mph, 28 km/h; consumption: 35.3 m/imp gal, 29.4 m/US gal, 8 l x 100 km.

CHASSIS integral; front suspension: independent, coil springs/telescopic damper struts, stabilizer torsion bar; rear: rigid axle, 4 link coil springs, telescopic dampers.

STEERING recirculating ball.

BRAKES front disc, rear drum, vacuum booster servo; swept area: front 22.9 sq in, 1.48 sq cm, rear 53.9 sq in, 348 sq cm, total 76.9 sq in, 496 sq cm.

ELECTRICAL EQUIPMENT 12 V; 50 Ah battery; 600 W alternator; Shih-Lin distributor; 4 headlamps.

DIMENSIONS AND WEIGHT wheel base: 105.11 in, 267 cm; tracks: 54.33 in, 138 cm front, 53.93 in, 137 cm rear; length: 178.14 in, 452 cm; width: 66.33 in, 168 cm; height: 55.31 in, 140 cm; ground clearance: 6.69 in, 17 cm; weight: 2,646 lb, 1,200 kg; turning circle: 36 ft, 11 m; fuel tank: 13.2 imp gal, 15.8 US gal, 60 l.

BODY saloon/sedan; 4 doors; 5 seats, separate front seats, reclining backrests, built-in headrests.

803 DL

ENGINE Diesel, front, 4 stroke; 4 cylinders, vertical, in line; 132 cu in, 2,164 cc (3.26 x 3.93 in, 83 x 100 mm); compression ratio: 20:1; max power (SAE): 66 hp at 4,000 rpm; max torque (SAE): 104 lb ft, 14.4 kg m at 1,800 rpm; max engine rpm: 30.5 hp/l; cast iron block and head; 3 crankshaft bearings; valves: overhead, push-rods and rockers; camshafts: 1, side; lubrication: gear pump, full flow filter, 10.4 imp pt, 12.5 US pt, 5.9 l; fuel injection system; fuel feed: mechanical pump; water-cooled, 14.1 imp pt, 16.9 US pt, 8 l.

TRANSMISSION driving wheels: rear; clutch: single dry plate (diaphragm); gearbox: mechanical; gears: 4, fully synchronized; ratios: I 3.592, II 2.246, III 1.415, IV 1, rev 3.657; lever: steering column; final drive: hypoid bevel; axle ratio: 4.100; width of rims: 5''; tyres: 175 SR x 14.

PERFORMANCE max speed: 78 mph, 125 km/h; power-weight ratio: 21.1 lb/hp, 46.6 kg/hp.

CHASSIS integral; front suspension: independent, double

wishbones, coil springs, anti-roll bar; rear: rigid axle, semi-elliptic leafspring, telescopic double acting dampers.

STEERING recirculating ball.

BRAKES front disc, rear drum; swept area: front 227 sq in, 1,464 sq cm, rear 117.4 sq in, 757 sq cm, total 344.3 sq in, 2,221 sq cm.

ELECTRICAL EQUIPMENT 12 V; 70 Ah battery; 40 A alternator; 4 headlamps.

DIMENSIONS AND WEIGHT wheel base: 105.90 in, 269 cm; tracks: 54.53 in, 139 cm front, 54.33 in, 138 cm rear; length: 184.64 in, 469 cm; width: 66.53 in, 169 cm; height: 56.89 in, 144 cm; ground clearance: 7.48 in, 19 cm; weight: 3,076 lb, 1,395 kg; turning circle: 36.1 ft, 11 m; fuel tank: 14.7 imp gal, 17.7 US gal, 67 l.

BODY saloon/sedan; 4 doors; 6 seats, bench front seats.

803 SD

ENGINE front, 4 stroke; 6 cylinders, in line; 146 cu in, 2,393 cc (3.27 x 2.90 in, 83 x 73.7 mm); compression ratio: 8.6:1; max power (SAE): 130 hp at 5,600 rpm; max torque (SAE): 145 lb ft, 20 kg m at 3,600 rpm; max engine rpm: 5,600; 54.3 hp/l; cast iron block, light alloy head; 7 crankshaft bearings; valves: 2 per cylinder, overhead, rockers; camshafts: 1, overhead; lubrication: trochoid pump, cartridge filter, 7.2 imp pt, 8.7 US pt, 4.1 l; 1 Hitachi DAF 342-14B downdraught twin barrel carburettor; fuel feed: electric pump; water-cooled, 16.7 imp pt, 20.1 US pt, 9.5 l.

TRANSMISSION driving wheels: rear; clutch: single dry plate (diaphragm); gearbox: mechanical; gears: 4, fully synchronized; ratios: I 3.592, II 2.246, III 1.415, IV 1, rev 3.657; lever: central; final drive: hypoid bevel; axle ratio: 4.100; width of rims: 5''; tyres: 175 SR x 14.

PERFORMANCE max speeds: (I) 31 mph, 50 km/h; (II) 47 mph, 75 km/h; (III) 71 mph, 115 km/h; (IV) 106 mph, 170 power-weight ratio 23.7 lb/hp, 10.7 kg/hp; speed in direct drive at 1,000 rpm: 17.4 mph, 28 km/h; consumption: 25.7 m/imp gal, 21.4 m/US gal, 11 l x 100 km.

CHASSIS integral; front suspension: independent, coil springs, telescopic dampers, stabilizer torsion bar; rigid axle, semi-elliptic leafsprings, telescopic dampers, stabilizer torsion bar.

STEERING servo.

BRAKES front disc, rear drum, vacuum booster servo; swept area: front 24.8 sq in, 160 sq cm, rear 71.9 sq in, 464 sq cm, total 96.7 sq in, 624 sq cm.

ELECTRICAL EQUIPMENT 12 V; 60 Ah battery; 600 W alternator; Shih Lin distributor; 4 headlamps.

DIMENSIONS AND WEIGHT wheel base: 105.90 in, 269 cm; tracks: 54.53 in, 138 cm front, 54.33 in, 138 cm rear; length: 188.38 in, 478 cm; width: 66.53 in, 169 cm; height: 56.70 in, 144 cm; ground clearance: 7.08 in, 18 cm; weight: 3,076 lb, 1,395 kg; turning circle: 42.6 ft, 13 m; fuel tank: 14.7 imp gal, 17.7 US gal, 67 l.

BODY saloon/sedan; 4 doors; 5 seats, separate front seats.

DAIHATSU   JAPAN

Max Cuore Series

PRICES (Tokyo):

Standard 2-dr Sedan	547,000 yen
De Luxe 4-dr Sedan	618,000 yen
Custom 2-dr Sedan	611,000 yen
Custom 4-dr Sedan	645,000 yen
Custom EX 2-dr Sedan	637,000 yen
Custom EX 4-dr Sedan	671,000 yen
Hi-Custom 4-dr Sedan	671,000 yen
Hi-Custom EX 4-dr Sedan	697,000 yen

28 hp power team

ENGINE front, transverse, 4 stroke; 2 cylinders, in line; 33.4 cu in, 547 cc (2.82 x 2.68 in, 71.6 x 68 mm); compression ratio: 8.7:1; max power (JIS): 28 hp at 6,000 rpm; max torque (JIS): 28 lb ft, 3.9 kg m at 3,500 rpm; max engine rpm: 7,800; 51.2 hp/l; cast iron block, light alloy head; 3 crankshaft bearings; valves: overhead, rockers; camshafts: 1 overhead, cogged belt; lubrication: rotary pump, full flow filter, 5.1 imp pt, 6.1 US pt, 2.9 l; 1 Aisan downdraught twin barrel carburettor; fuel feed: mechanical pump; emission control by Daihatsu lean-burn system with turbulence generating pot in each combustion chamber and catalytic converter; water-cooled, 5.3 imp pt, 6.3 US pt, 3 l.

TRANSMISSION driving wheels: front; clutch: single dry plate (diaphragm); gearbox: mechanical; gears: 4, fully synchronized; ratios: I 4.727, II 2.823, III 1.809, IV 1.269, rev 4.865; lever: central; final drive: hypoid bevel; axle ratio: 3.955; width of rims: 3.5''; tyres: 5.20 x 10.

PERFORMANCE max speeds: (I) 18 mph, 29 km/h; (II) 31 mph, 50 km/h; (III) 47 mph, 75 km/h; (IV) 68 mph, 110 km/h; power-weight ratio: 2-dr. sedans 42.6 lb/hp, 19.3 kg/hp - 4-dr. sedans 44.1 lb/hp, 20 kg/hp; carrying capacity: 706 lb, 320 kg; acceleration: standing 1/4 mile 21.8 sec; speed in top at 1,000 rpm: 8.8 mph, 14.2 km/h; fuel consumption: 52.3 m/imp gal, 43.6 m/US gal, 5.4 l x 100 km at 37 mph, 60 km/h.

CHASSIS integral; front suspension: independent, by McPherson, coil springs/telescopic damper struts, lower wishbones (trailing links); rear: independent, semi-trailing arms, coil springs, telescopic dampers.

STEERING rack-and-pinion; turns lock to lock: 3.30.

BRAKES drum, single circuit; lining area: front 18.6 sq in, 120 sq cm, rear 18.6 sq in, 120 sq cm, total 37.2 sq in, 240 sq cm.

ELECTRICAL EQUIPMENT 12 V; 26 Ah battery; 35 A alternator; 2 headlamps.

DIMENSIONS AND WEIGHT wheel base: 82.28 in, 209 cm; front and rear tracks: 48.03 in, 122 cm; length: 124.40 in,

DAIHATSU Max Cuore Hi-Custom 4-dr Sedan

DAIHATSU Charade Coupé XTE

316 cm; width: 54.72 in, 139 cm; height: 51.97 in, 132 cm; ground clearance: 7.09 in, 18 cm; weight: 2-dr. sedans 1,191 lb, 540 kg - 4-dr. sedans 1,235 lb, 560 kg; weight distribution: 64% front, 36% rear; turning circle: 30.2 ft, 9.2 m; fuel tank: 5.7 imp gal, 6.9 US gal, 26 l.

BODY saloon/sedan; 4 seats, separate front seats.

OPTIONALS 145 SR x 10 tyres.

Charade Sedan Series

PRICES (Tokyo):

Sedan XO	653,000 yen
Sedan XG	698,000 yen
Sedan XT	748,000 yen
Sedan XTE	798,000 yen
Sedan XGE	768,000 yen

55 hp power team

ENGINE front, transverse, 4 stroke; 3 cylinders, in line; 60.6 cu in, 993 cc (2.99 x 2.87 in, 76 x 73 mm); compression ratio: 8.7:1; max power (JIS): 55 hp at 5,500 rpm; max torque (JIS): 57 lb ft, 7.8 kg m at 2,800 rpm; max engine rpm: 6,000; 55.4 hp/l; cast iron block, light alloy head; 4 crankshaft bearings; valves: overhead, push-rods and rockers; camshafts: 1, overhead; lubrication: rotary pump, full flow filter, 5.1 imp pt, 6.1 US pt, 2.9 l; 1 Aisan-Stromberg downdraught twin barrel carburettor; fuel feed: mechanical pump; water-cooled, 7 imp pt, 8.5 US pt, 4 l.

TRANSMISSION driving wheels: front; clutch: single dry plate (diaphragm); gearbox: mechanical; gears: 4, fully synchronized; ratios: I 3.666, II 2.150, III 1.464, IV 0.971, rev 3.529; lever: central; final drive: helical spur gears; axle ratio: 4.588; width of rims: 5''; tyres: 6.00 x 12 (XT and XTE 155 SR x 12).

PERFORMANCE max speeds: (I) 25 mph, 40 km/h; (II) 40 mph, 64 km/h; (III) 58 mph, 94 km/h; (IV) 84 mph, 135 km/h; power-weight ratio: XO 25.4 lb/hp, 11.5 kg/hp; carrying capacity: 882 lb, 400 kg; consumption: 53.3 m/imp gal, 44.4 m/US gal, 5.3 l x 100 km at 37 mph, 60 km/h.

CHASSIS integral; front suspension: independent, by McPherson, coil springs/telescopic dampers struts; rear: independent, upper and lower trailing links, Panhard rod, coil spring, telescopic dampers.

STEERING rack-and-pinion; turns lock to lock: 3.40.

BRAKES drum (front disc on XTE, XTG and XT); lining area: front 47.1 sq in, 304 sq cm (disc 16.7 sq in, 108 sq cm), rear 37.2 sq in, 240 sq cm, total 84.3 sq in, 544 sq cm.

ELECTRICAL EQUIPMENT 12 V; 30 Ah battery; 40 A alternator; 2 headlamps.

DIMENSIONS AND WEIGHT wheel base: 90.55 in, 230 cm; tracks: 51.18 in, 130 cm front, 50.39 in, 128 cm rear; length: 136.22 in, 346 cm; width: 59.45 in, 151 cm; height: 53.54 in, 136 cm; ground clearance: 7.09 in, 18 cm; weight: XO 1,389 lb, 630 kg - XG 1,411 lb, 640 kg - XT 1,433 lb, 650 kg - XGE 1,444 lb, 655 kg - XTE 1,455 lb, 660 kg; weight distribution: 63% front, 37% rear; turning circle: 32.8 ft, 10 m; fuel tank: 7.5 imp gal, 9 US gal, 34 l.

BODY saloon/sedan; 4 + 1 doors; 5 seats; separate front seats, reclining backrests, headrests.

OPTIONALS 5-speed mechanical gearbox, V 0.971; max speed 87 mph, 140 km/h.

Charade Coupé Series

See Charade Sedan Series, except for:

PRICES (Tokyo):

Coupé XG	698,000 yen
Coupé XT	758,000 yen
Coupé XTE	813,000 yen

55 hp power team

TRANSMISSION gears: 5, fully synchronized; ratios: V 0.971; axle ratio: 4.277; tyres: XG 6.00 x 12 - XT and XTE 155 SR x 12.

PERFORMANCE max speed: 87 mph, 140 km/h; power-weight ratio: XG 36.7 lb/hp, 16.6 kg/hp - XT 37.1 lb/hp, 16.8 kg/hp - XTE 37.5 lb/hp, 17 kg/hp.

BRAKES front disc, rear drum.

DIMENSIONS AND WEIGHT weight: XG 2,018 lb, 915 kg - XT 2,040 lb, 925 kg - XTE 2,062 lb, 935 kg.

BODY coupé; 2 + 1 doors.

Charmant 1300 Series

PRICES (Tokyo):

De Luxe Sedan	815,000	yen
Custom Sedan	853,000	yen
Hi-Custom Sedan	887,000	yen

72 hp power team

ENGINE front, 4 stroke; 4 cylinders, in line; 78.7 cu in, 1,290 cc (2.95 x 2.87 in, 75 x 73 mm); compression ratio: 9:1; max power (JIS): 72 hp at 5,600 rpm; max torque (JIS): 76 lb ft, 10.5 kg m at 3,600 rpm; max engine rpm: 6,000; 55.8 hp/l; cast iron block, light alloy head; 5 crankshaft bearings; valves: overhead, push-rods and rockers; camshafts: 1, side; lubrication: trochoid pump, full flow filter, 6.2 imp pt, 7.4 US pt, 3.5 l; 1 Aisan 4 K-U downdraught twin barrel carburettor; secondary air induction, EGR, catalytic converter; fuel feed: mechanical pump; water-cooled, 10.8 imp pt, 12.7 US pt, 6 l.

TRANSMISSION driving wheels: rear; clutch: single dry plate (diaphragm); gearbox: mechanical; gears: 4, fully synchronized; ratios: I 3.789, II 2.220, III 1.435, IV 1, rev 4.316; lever: central; final drive: hypoid bevel; axle ratio: 3.909; width of rims: 4.5''; tyres: 6.00 x 12.

PERFORMANCE max speed: (I) 25 mph, 40 km/h; (II) 43 mph, 70 km/h; (III) 75 mph, 110 km/h; (IV) 93 mph, 150 km/h; power-weight ratio: De Luxe Sedan 24.5 lb/hp, 11.1 kg/hp; carrying capacity: 882 lb, 400 kg; consumption: 43.5 m/imp gal, 36.2 m/US gal, 6.5 l x 100 km.

CHASSIS integral; front suspension: independent, by McPherson, coil springs/telescopic dampers struts, lower transverse l arms, trailing locating rods, anti-roll bar; rear: rigid axle, semi-elliptic leafsprings, telescopic dampers.

STEERING recirculating ball; turns lock to lock: 3.40.

BRAKES drum, dual circuit, servo; swept area: front 47.1 sq in, 304 sq cm, rear 41.6 sq in, 268 sq cm, total 88.7 sq in, 672 sq cm.

ELECTRICAL EQUIPMENT 12 V; 32 Ah battery; 30 A alternator; contactless fully transistorized distributor; 2 headlamps.

DIMENSIONS AND WEIGHT wheel base: 91.93 in, 233.5 cm; tracks: 49.21 in, 125 cm front, 49.02 in, 124.5 cm rear; length: 161.81 in, 411 cm; width: 60.24 in, 153 cm; height: 54.33 in, 138 cm; ground clearance 6.69 in, 17 cm; weight: De Luxe 1,764 lb, 800 kg - Custom 1,786 lb, 810 kg - Hi-Custom 1,797 lb, 815 kg; weight distribution: 56% front, 44% rear; turning circle: 33.5 ft, 10.2 m; fuel tank: 9.5 imp gal, 11.4 US gal, 43 l.

BODY saloon/sedan; 4 doors; 5 seats; separate front seats.

DAIHATSU Charmant 1600 GC Sedan

72 HP POWER TEAM

OPTIONALS 5-speed mechanical gearbox, V 0.865 (for Hi-Custom only).

Charmant 1600 Series

See Charmant 1300 series, except for:

PRICES (Tokyo):

Custom Sedan	923,000 yen
Hi-Custom Sedan	957,000 yen
SC Sedan	973,000 yen
GC Sedan	1,007,000 yen

88 hp power team

ENGINE 96.9 cu in, 1,588 cc (3.35 x 2.76 in, 85 x 70 mm); max power (JIS): 88 hp at 5,600 rpm; max torque (JIS): 96 lb ft, 13.3 kg m at 3,400 rpm; 55.4 hp/l; lubrication: 7.4 imp pt, 8.9 US pt, 4.2 l; 1 12T-U downdraught twin barrel carburettor; 12T-U low emission engine with TGP high turbulence cylinder head; water-cooled: 12.7 imp pt, 15.2 US pt, 7.2 l.

TRANSMISSION ratios: I 3.587, II 2.022, III 1.384, IV 1, rev 3.484; axle ratio: 3.727; tyres: 6.15 x 13 - SC 155 SR x 13.

PERFORMANCE max speeds: (I) 31 mph, 50 km/h; (II) 53 mph, 85 km/h; (III) 78 mph, 125 km/h; (IV) 99 mph, 160 km/h; power-weight ratio: Custom 22.3 lb/hp, 10.1 kg/hp; consumption: 35.3 m/imp gal, 29.4 m/US gal, 8 l x 100 km.

ELECTRICAL EQUIPMENT 35 Ah battery; 40 A alternator; 4 headlamps.

DIMENSIONS AND WEIGHT tracks: 49.61 in, 126 cm front; weight: Custom 1,962 lb, 890 kg - Hi-Custom and SC 1,973 lb, 895 kg - GC 1,984 lb, 900 kg.

OPTIONALS 5-speed fully synchronized mechanical gearbox, V 0.861, 3.909 axle ratio (for Hi-Custom, SC and GC), automatic transmission with 3 ratios (I 2.450, II 1.450, III 1, rev 2.222) and 3.909 axle ratio (for Hi-Custom and GC).

Delta Wagon Series

Standard Wagon
De Luxe Wagon
Custom Wagon
Custom EX Wagon

92 hp power team

ENGINE front, 4 stroke; 4 cylinders, in line; 108 cu in, 1,770 cc (3.35 x 3.07 in, 85 x 78 mm); compression ratio: 8.5:1; max power (JIS): 92 hp at 5,000 rpm; max torque

(JIS): 109 lb ft, 15 kg m at 3,400 rpm; max engine rpm: 5,400; 52 hp/l cast iron block, light alloy head; 5 crankshaft bearings; valves: overhead, push-rods and rockers; camshafts: 1, side; lubrication: rotary pump, full flow filter, 7.4 imp pt, 8.9 US pt, 4.2 l; 1 Aisan 13T downdraught twin barrel carburettor; TGP high turbulence cylinder head, secondary air induction, exhaust gas recirculation and catalytic converter; fuel feed: mechanical pump; water-cooled, 14.1 imp pt, 16.9 US pt, 8 l.

TRANSMISSION driving wheels: rear; clutch: single dry plate (diaphragm); gearbox: mechanical; gears: 4, fully synchronized; ratios: I 3.674, II 2.114, III 1.403, IV 1, rev 4.183; lever: steering column; final drive: hypoid bevel; axle ratio: 4.100; width of rims: 4'' - Custom and Custom EX 4.5''; tyres: 5.50 x 13 - Custom and Custom EX 165 SR x 14.

PERFORMANCE max speeds: (I) 23 mph, 37 km/h; (II) 40 mph, 65 km/h; (III) 61 mph, 98 km/h; (IV) 87 mph, 140 km/h; power-weight ratio: standard 26 lb/hp, 11.8 kg/hp consumption: 29.7 m/imp gal, 24.8 m/US gal, 9.5 l x 100 km.

CHASSIS integral; front suspension: independent, double wishbones, coil springs, telescopic dampers; rear: rigid axle, semi-elliptic leafsprings, telescopic dampers.

STEERING recirculating ball.

BRAKES drum - Custom and Custom EX front disc, dual circuit, servo; swept area: front 67.6 sq in, 436 sq cm, rear 54.6 sq in, 353 sq cm, total 122.2 sq in, 788 sq cm.

ELECTRICAL EQUIPMENT 12 V; 33 Ah battery; 40 A alternator; Denso distributor; 2 headlamps.

DIMENSIONS AND WEIGHT wheel base: 86.42 in, 219 cm; tracks: 56.30 in, 143 cm front, 52.95 in, 134 cm rear; length: 157.09 in, 399 cm; width: 64.96 in, 165 cm; height: 68.70 in, 174 cm - Custom EX 78.35 in, 199 cm; ground clearance: 6.89 in, 17.5 cm; weight: Standard and De Luxe 2,392 lb, 1,085 kg - Custom 2,414 lb, 1,095 kg - Custom EX 2,503 lb, 1,135 kg; weight distribution: 57.8% front, 42.2% rear; fuel tank: 12.1 imp gal, 14.5 US gal, 55 l.

BODY estate car/station wagon; 3 doors; 8 seats, separate front seats.

Taft Series

1 Gran 1600 H-F20S (canvas doors)
2 Gran 1600 H-F20SK (steel doors)
3 Gran 1600 H-F20J (6-pass., canvas doors)
4 Gran 1600 H-F20JK (6-pass., steel doors)
5 Gran 1600 H-F20V (4-pass., steel body)
6 Diesel F50S (canvas doors)
7 Diesel F50SK (steel doors)
8 Diesel F50J (6-pass., canvas doors)
9 Diesel F50JK (6-pass., steel doors)
10 Diesel F50V (4-pass., steel body)

Power team:	Standard for:	Optional for:
80 hp	1 to 5	—
75 hp (Diesel)	6 to 10	—

DAIHATSU Taft Diesel F50 Series

80 hp power team

ENGINE front, 4 stroke; 4 cylinders, in line; 96.8 cu in, 1,587 cc (3.17 x 3.07 in, 80.5 x 78 mm); compression ratio 8.5:1; max power (JIS): 80 hp at 5,200 rpm; torque (JIS) 91 lb ft, 12.5 kg m at 3,000 rpm; max engine rpm: 5,700; 50.4 hp/l; cast iron block, light alloy head; 3 crankshaft bearings; valves: overhead, push-rods and rockers; camshafts: 1, side; lubrication: trochoid pump, full flow filter 7.4 imp pt, 8.9 US pt, 4.2 l; 1 Aisan 12 R-J downdraught twin barrel carburettor; fuel feed: mechanical pump; water-cooled, 12.3 imp pt, 14.8 US pt, 7 l.

TRANSMISSION driving wheels: rear, or front and rear; clutch: single dry plate (diaphragm); gearbox: mechanical; gears: 4, fully synchronized and 2-ratio transfer box; ratios: I 3.717, II 2.177, III 1.513, IV 1, rev 4.434; transfer box ratios: high 1.300, lowe 2.407; lever: central; final drive: hypoid bevel; axle ratio: 4.777 front and rear; width of rims: 4.5''; tyres: 6.00 x 16.

PERFORMANCE max speeds: (rear drive only) (I) 20 mph, 33 km/h; (II) 35 mph, 57 km/h; (III) 50 mph, 80 km/h; (IV) 71 mph, 115 km/h; power-weight ratio: H-F20S 29.2 lb/hp, 13.2 kg/hp; carrying capacity: 882 lb, 400 kg; consumption: 28.2 m/imp gal, 23.5 m/US gal, 10 l x 100 km at 37 mph, 60 km/h.

CHASSIS box section ladder frame; front and rear suspension: rigid axle, semi-elliptic leafsprings, telescopic dampers.

STEERING recirculating ball; turns lock to lock: 2.70.

BRAKES drum; lining area: front 72.6 sq in, 468 sq cm, rear 72.6 sq in, 468 sq cm, total 145.2 sq in, 936 sq cm.

ELECTRICAL EQUIPMENT 12 V; 35 Ah battery; 35 A alternator; Denso distributor; 2 headlamps.

DIMENSIONS AND WEIGHT wheel base: 79.53 in, 202 cm; tracks front and rear: 47.24 in, 120 cm; length: H-F20S and H-F20SK 130.71 in, 332 cm - H-F20J, H-F20JK and H-F20V 137.2 in, 348.5 cm; width: 57.48 in, 146 cm; height: H-F20S and H-F20SK 73.20 in, 186 cm - H-F20J and H-F20JK 73.03 in, 185 cm - H-F20V 73.42 in, 186.5 cm; ground clearance: 8.46 in, 21.5 cm; weight: H-F20S 2,337 lb, 1,060 kg - H-F20SK 2,370 lb, 1,075 kg - H-F20J 2,381 lb, 1,080 kg - H-F20JK 2,414 lb, 1,095 kg - H-F20V 2,492 lb, 1,130 kg; weight distribution: 56% front, 44% rear; turning circle: 35.4 ft, 10.8 m; fuel tank: 8.8 imp gal, 10.6 US gal, 40 l.

BODY open, canvas top, canvas or steel doors, steel hardtop; 4 or 6 seats, separate front seats, built-in headrests.

75 hp (Diesel) power team

See 80 hp power team, except for:

ENGINE Diesel; 154.4 cu in, 2,530 cc (3.46 x 4.94 in, 88 x 104 mm); max power (JIS): 75 hp at 3,600 rpm; max torque (JIS): 127 lb ft, 17.5 kg m at 2,200 rpm; max engine rpm: 3,600; 29.6 hp/l; Ricardo Comet swirl chamber type; lubrication: 9.7 imp pt, 11.6 US pt, 5.5 l; Denso plunger type mechanical fuel injection; water-cooled: 17.6 imp pt, 21.1 US pt, 10 l.

TRANSMISSION ratios: II 2.276; axle ratio: 3.545.

DAIHATSU Delta Custom Wagon

PERFORMANCE max speeds: (rear drive only) (I) 16 mph, 26 km/h, (II) 29 mph, 46 km/h, (III) 43 mph, 70 km/h, (IV) 65 mph, 105 km/h; power-weight ratio: F50S 34.8 lb/hp, 15.8 kg/hp; consumption: 42.2 m/imp gal, 35.1 m/US gal, 6.7 l x 100 km at 37 mph, 60 km/h.

DIMENSIONS AND WEIGHT length: F50S and F50SK 130.71 in, 332 cm - F50J, F50JK and F50V 137.2 in, 348.5 cm; height: F50S and F50SK 73.20 in, 186 cm - F50J and F50JK 73.03 in, 185.5 cm - F50V 73.42 in, 186.5 cm; weight: F50S 2,612 lb, 1,185 kg - F50CK 2,646 lb, 1,200 kg - F50J 2,657 lb, 1,205 kg - F50JK 2,690 lb, 1,220 kg - F50V 2,767 lb, 1,255 kg.

OPTIONALS power take-off; front wheel freewheelling hub.

DAIHATSU Taft Diesel F50S

HONDA   JAPAN

Civic CVCC Series

PRICES (Tokyo):

1 1300 Standard 2-dr Sedan	666,000	yen
2 1300 De Luxe 3-dr Sedan	721,000	yen
3 1300 GL 3-dr Sedan	807,000	yen
4 1300 GL-II-5 3-dr Sedan	842,000	yen
5 1300 De Luxe 5-dr Sedan	764,000	yen
6 1300 Hi-De Luxe 5-dr Sedan	818,000	yen
7 1300 GF 5-dr Sedan	845,000	yen
8 1300 GF-5 5-dr Sedan	870,000	yen
9 1500 RSL 3-dr Sedan	911,000	yen
10 1500 GTL-II 3-dr Sedan	897,000	yen
11 1500 GF-II 5-dr Sedan	892,000	yen
12 1500 GF-II-5 5-dr Sedan	912,000	yen

Power team:	Standard for:	Optional for:
68 hp	1 to 8	—
75 hp	9 to 12	—

68 hp power team

ENGINE front, transverse, 4 stroke, stratified charge; 4 cylinders, vertical, in line; 81.5 cu in, 1,335 cc (2.83 x 3.23 in, 72 x 82 mm); compression ratio: 7.9:1; max power (JIS): 68 hp at 5,500 rpm; max torque (JIS): 73 lb ft, 10 kg m at 3,500 rpm; max engine rpm: 6,000; 50.9 hp/l; light alloy cylinder block with cast iron liners, light alloy head; 5 crankshaft bearings; valves: 3 per cylinder (one intake and one exhaust in main combustion chamber, one intake in auxiliary chamber), overhead, Vee-slanted, rockers; camshafts: 1, overhead, cogged belt; lubrication: rotary pump, full flow filter, 5.3 imp pt, 6.3 US pt, 3 l; 1 Keihin-Honda downdraught 3-barrel CVCC carburettor; fuel feed: mechanical pump; water-cooled, 7 imp pt, 8.5 US pt, 4 l.

TRANSMISSION driving wheels: front; clutch: single dry plate (diaphragm); gearbox: mechanical; gears: 4 (5 for GL II-5 and GF-5 only), fully synchronized; ratios: I 3.181, II

HONDA Civic CVCC 1300 GF-5 5-dr Sedan

1.823, III 1.181, IV 0.846, rev 2.916 (for GL II-5 and GF-5 V 0.714; lever: central; final drive: helical spur gears; axle ratio: 4.624; width of rims: 4''; tyres: 6.000 x 12 - GL II-5 155 SR x 12.

PERFORMANCE max speeds: (I) 26 mph, 42 km/h; (II) 45 mph, 72 km/h; (III) 70 mph, 112 km/h; (IV) 93 mph, 150 km/h; power-weight ratio: Standard 2-dr. Sedan 21.7 lb/hp, 9.8 kg/hp; carrying capacity: 882 lb, 400 kg; consumption: 36.7 m/imp gal, 30.5 m/US gal, 7.7 l x 100 km.

CHASSIS integral, front auxiliary frame; front suspension: independent, by McPherson, coil springs/telescopic damper struts, lower wishbones (trailing links), anti-roll bar; rear: independent, by McPherson, coil springs/telescopic damper struts, lower wishbones (torque arms).

STEERING rack-and-pinion; turns lock to lock: 3.10 2-dr. Sedan - 3.50 5-dr. Sedan.

BRAKES front disc, rear drum, dual circuit; lining area: front 15.2 sq in, 98 sq cm, rear 34.7 sq in, 224 sq cm, total 49.9 sq in, 322 sq cm.

ELECTRICAL EQUIPMENT 12 V; 30 Ah battery; 35 A alternator; Mitsubishi distributor; 2 headlamps.

DIMENSIONS AND WEIGHT wheel base: 2- and 3-dr. models 86.61 in, 220 cm, 5-dr. models 89.76 in, 228 cm; tracks: 51.18 in, 130 cm front, 50.39 in, 128 cm rear; length: 2- and 3-dr. models 140.16 in, 356 cm, GL II-5 143.50 in, 364 cm,

5-dr. models 143.90 in, 366 cm, GF-5 147.24 in, 374 cm; width: 59.25 in, 150 cm; height: 52.17 in, 132 cm; ground clearance: 6.69 in, 17 cm; weight: Standard 2-dr. 1,477 lb, 670 kg - De Luxe 3-dr. 1,521 lb, 690 kg - GL 3-dr. 1,532 lb, 695 kg - GL-II-5 3-dr. 1,543, 700 kg - De Luxe 5-dr. 1,621 lb, 735 kg - Hi-De Luxe 5-dr. 1,632 lb, 740 kg - GF 5-dr. 1,643 lb, 745 kg - GF-5 5-dr. 1,654 lb, 750 kg; weight distribution: Standard 2-dr. 63% front, 37% rear; turning circle: 33.8 ft, 10.3 m (5-dr. models 35.1 ft, 10.7 m); fuel tank: 8.4 imp gal, 10 US gal, 38 l (5-dr. models 8.8 imp gal, 10.6 US gal, 40 l).

OPTIONALS semi-automatic transmission with 2 ratios: (I 1.636, II 1.034, rev 2.045). 4.117 axle ratio; air-conditioning.

75 hp power team

See 68 hp power team, except for:

ENGINE 90.8 cu in, 1,488 cc (2.91 x 3.41 in, 74 x 86.5 mm); max power (JIS): 75 hp at 5,500 rpm; max torque (JIS): 80.4 lb ft, 11.1 kg m at 3,000 rpm; 50.4 hp/l.

TRANSMISSION gears: 4 for GF-II 5-dr. only (5 for RSL, GTL-II and GF-II-5); axle ratio: RSL 4.642 - GTL-II and 5-dr. models 4.428; tyres: RSL 155 SR x 13.

PERFORMANCE max speeds: RSL (I) 26 mph, 42 km/h, (II) 45 mph, 73 km/h, (III) 70 mph, 113 km/h, (IV) 98 mph, 158 km/h, (V) 99 mph, 160 km/h - GF-II-5 (I) 29 mph, 46 km/h, (II) 51 mph, 82 km/h, (III) 78 mph, 126 km/h, (IV) 93 mph, 150 km/h, (V) 93 mph, 150 km/h; power-weight ratio: RSL 3-dr. Sedan 22.5 lb/hp, 10.2 kg/hp; consumption: 40.9 m/imp gal, 34.1 m/US gal, 6.9 l x 100 km.

DIMENSIONS AND WEIGHT length: GTL-II 143.50 in, 364 cm, RSL and 5-dr. models 146.85 in, 373 cm; height: RSL 59.65 in, 151 cm, other models 59.06 in, 150 cm; weight: RSL 1,687 lb, 765 kg - GTL-II 1,643 lb, 745 kg - GF-II and GF-II-5 1,731 lb, 785 kg; fuel tank: 8.8 imp gal, 10.6 US gal, 40 l.

OPTIONALS semi-automatic transmission with 2 ratios (I 1.565, II 0.966, rev 2.045), 4.117 axle ratio, max speed 90 mph, 145 km/h (except for RSL).

Civic Wagon Series

1 Civic CVCC 1500 Station Wagon
2 Civic 1500 Van Custom

Power team:	Standard for:	Optional for:
70 hp	1	—
75 hp	2	—

70 hp power team

(for USA only).

ENGINE front, transverse, 4 stroke, stratified charge; 4 cylinders, vertical, in line; 90.8 cu in, 1,488 cc (2.91 x 3.41 in, 74 x 86.5 mm); compression ratio: 7.9:1; max power (JIS): 70 hp at 5,500 rpm; max torque (JIS): 78 lb ft, 10.7 kg m at 3,000 rpm; max engine rpm: 6,000;

70 HP POWER TEAM

47 hp/l; cast iron cylinder block, light alloy head; 5 crankshaft bearings; valves: 3 per cylinder (intake in auxiliary combustion chamber, intake and exhaust in main chamber), overhead, Vee-slanted, rockers; camshafts: 1, overhead, cogged belt; lubrication: rotary pump, full flow filter, 5.3 imp pt, 6.3 US pt, 3 l; 1 Keihin-Honda downdraught 3-barrel CVCC carburettor; fuel feed: electric pump; water-cooled, 7 imp pt, 8.5 US pt, 4 l.

TRANSMISSION driving wheels: front; clutch: single dry plate (diaphragm); gearbox: mechanical; gears: 4, fully synchronized; ratios: I 3.181, II 1.823, III 1.181, IV 0.846, rev 2.916; lever: central; final drive: helical spur gears; axle ratio: 4.642; width of rims: 4''; tyres: 6.00S x 12.

PERFORMANCE max speeds: (I) 25 mph, 41 km/h; (II) 45 mph, 72 km/h; (III) 68 mph, 110 km/h; (IV) 93 mph, 150 km/h; power-weight ratio: 28.3 lb/hp, 12.8 kg/hp; carrying capacity: 882 lb, 400 kg; speed in top at 1,000 rpm: 15 mph, 24.1 km/h; fuel consumption: 58.8 m/imp gal, 49 m/US gal, 4.8 l x 100 km at 37 mph, 60 km/h.

CHASSIS integral, front auxiliary frame; front suspension: independent, by McPherson, coil springs/telescopic damper struts, lower wishbones (trailing links), anti-roll bar; rear: rigid axle, semi-elliptic leafsprings, telescopic dampers

STEERING rack-and-pinion; turns lock to lock: 3.10.

BRAKES front disc, rear drum, dual circuit, servo; lining area: front 15.2 sq in, 98 sq cm, rear 34.7 sq in, 224 sq cm, total 49.9 sq in, 322 sq cm.

ELECTRICAL EQUIPMENT 12 V; 30 Ah battery; 35 alternator; CVCC distributor; 2 headlamps.

DIMENSIONS AND WEIGHT wheel base: 89.76 in, 228 cm; tracks: 51.18 in, 130 cm front, 50.39 in, 128 cm rear; length: 159.72 in, 406 cm; width: 59.06 in, 150 cm; height: 54.09 in, 137 cm; ground clearance: 6.69 in, 17 cm; dry weight: 1,985 lb, 900 kg; distribution of weight: 63.7% front, 36.3% rear; turning circle: 32.1 ft, 9.8 m; fuel tank: 9.7 imp gal, 11.6 US gal, 44 l.

BODY estate car/station wagon; 4+1 doors; 5 seats, separate front seats, built-in headrests.

OPTIONALS semi-automatic transmission with 2 ratios (I 1.565, II 0.966, rev 2.045), 4.117 axle ratio, max speed 90 mph, 145 km/h; air-conditioning.

75 hp power team

(domestic version).

See 70 hp power team, except for:

ENGINE max power (JIS): 75 hp at 5,500 rpm; max torque (JIS): 80.4 lb ft, 11.1 kg m at 3,300 rpm; 50.4 hp/l; valves: 2 per cylinder.

TRANSMISSION axle ratio: 4.428; tyres: 5.00 x 12.

PERFORMANCE max speeds: (I) 27 mph, 43 km/h, (II) 47 mph, 75 km/h; (III) 71 mph, 115 km/h; (IV) 90 mph, 145 km/h; power-weight ratio: 26.5 lb/hp, 12 kg/hp; fuel consumption: 53.3 m/imp gal, 44.4 m/US gal, 5.3 l x 100 km at 37 mph, 60 km/h.

DIMENSIONS AND WEIGHT length: 151.97 in, 386 cm.

Accord 1800 Series

PRICES (Tokyo):

GL 3-dr Hatchback	1,033,000	yen
LX 3-dr Hatchback	1,093,000	yen
EX 3-dr Hatchback	1,200,000	yen
EX-L 3-dr Hatchback	1,340,000	yen
SL 4-dr Sedan	998,000	yen
GF 4-dr Sedan	1,108,000	yen
EX 4-dr Sedan	1,225,000	yen
EX-L 4-dr Sedan	1,385,000	yen

90 hp power team

ENGINE front, transverse, 4 stroke, stratified charge; 4 cylinders, in line; 106.8 cu in, 1,750 cc (3.03 x 3.70 in, 77 x 94 mm); compression ratio: 8:1; max power (JIS): 90 hp at 5,300 rpm; max torque (JIS): 98 lb ft, 13.5 kg m at 3,000 rpm; max engine rpm: 5,700; 51.4 hp/l; cast iron block, light alloy head; 5 crankshaft bearings; valves: 3 per cylinder (one intake and one exhaust in main combustion chamber, one intake in auxiliary chamber), overhead, rockers; camshafts: 1, overhead, cogged belt; lubrication: trochoid pump, full flow filter, 7 imp pt, 8.5 US pt, 4 l; 1 Keihin downdraught 3-barrel CVCC carburettor; fuel feed: electric pump; water-cooled, 10.6 imp pt, 12.7 US pt, 6 l.

TRANSMISSION driving wheels: front; clutch: single dry plate (diaphragm) hydraulically controlled; gearbox: mechanical; gears: 5, fully synchronized; ratios: I 3.181, II 1.842, III 1.200, IV 0.896, V 0.718, rev 3.000; lever: central; final drive: helical spur gears; axle ratio: 4.615; width of rims: 5''; tyres: 6.45 x 13 - EX and EX-L 165 SR x 13.

PERFORMANCE max speeds: (I) 27 mph, 43 km/h; (II) 45 mph, 73 km/h; (III) 71 mph, 115 km/h; (IV) 93 mph, 150 km/h; (V) 93 mph, 150 km/h; power-weight ratio: 22 lb/hp, 10 kg/hp; consumption: 29.7 m/imp gal, 24.8 m/US gal, 9.5 l x 100 km.

CHASSIS integral, front auxiliary frame; front suspension: independent, by McPherson, coil springs/telescopic damper struts, lower transverse arms, diagonal links, anti-roll bar; rear: independent, by McPherson, coil springs/telescopic damper struts, lower transverse arms, radius rods.

STEERING rack-and-pinion - EX and EX-L servo; turns lock to lock: 3.50 - EX and EX-L 2.90.

BRAKES front disc, rear drum, dual circuit, rear compensator, servo; lining area: front 19.4 sq in, 125 sq cm, rear 34.7 sq in, 224 sq cm, total 54.1 sq in, 349 sq cm.

ELECTRICAL EQUIPMENT 12 V; 35 Ah battery; 50 A alternator; transistorized ignition; 4 headlamps.

DIMENSIONS AND WEIGHT wheel base: 93.70 in, 238 cm; tracks: 55.51 in, 141 cm front, 55.12 in, 140 cm rear; length: GL, LX, EX 3-dr. 162.40 in, 412 cm - EX-L 3-dr. 166.54, 423 cm - SL 4-dr. 170.28 in, 432 cm - GF and EX 4-dr. 171.06 in, 434 cm - EX-L 4-dr. 175.20 in, 445 cm; width: 63.78 in, 162 cm; height: 3-dr. models 52.76 in, 134 cm - 4-dr. models 53.54 in, 136 cm; ground clearance: 6.50 in, 16.5 cm; weight: GL 3-dr. 1,984 lb, 900 kg - LX 3-dr. 2,007 lb, 910 kg - EX 3-dr. 2,040 lb, 925 kg - EX-L 3-dr. 2,062 lb, 935 kg - SL 4-dr. 2,051 lb, 930 kg - GF 4-dr. 2,062 lb, 935 kg - EX 4-dr. 2,117 lb, 960 kg - EX-L 4-dr. 2,128 lb, 965 kg; weight distribution: 61% front, 39% rear; turning circle: 36.1 ft, 11 m; fuel tank: 11 imp gal, 13.2 US gal, 50 l.

OPTIONALS Hondamatic semi-automatic transmission, hydraulic torque converter and constant mesh with 2 ratios: (I 1.565, II 0.903, rev 2.045), possible manual selection, 4.117 axle ratio, only with 85 hp power team.

HONDA Accord 1800 EX 3-dr Hatchback

Prelude Series

PRICES (Tokyo):

XT Coupé	1,160,000	yen
E Coupé	1,260,000	yen
XE Coupé	1,400,000	yen
XR Coupé	1,380,000	yen

90 hp power team

ENGINE front, transverse, 4 stroke, stratified charge; 4 cylinders, in line; 106.8 cu in, 1,750 cc (3.03 x 3.70 in, 77 x 94 mm); compression ratio: 8:1; max power (JIS): 90 hp at 5,300 rpm; max torque (JIS): 98 lb ft, 13.5 kg m at 3,000 rpm; max engine rpm: 5,700; 51.4 hp/l; cast iron block, light alloy head; 5 crankshaft bearings; valves: 3 per cylinder (one intake and one exhaust in main combustion chamber, one intake in auxiliary chamber), overhead, rockers; camshafts: 1, overhead, cogged belt; lubrication: trochoid pump, full flow filter, 7 imp pt, 8.5 US pt, 4 l; 1 Keihin downdraught 3-barrel CVCC carburettor; fuel feed: electric pump; water-cooled, 9.8 imp pt, 11.8 US pt, 5.6 l.

TRANSMISSION driving wheels: front; clutch: single dry plate (diaphragm), hydraulically controlled; gearbox: mechanical; gears: 5, fully synchronized; ratios: I 3.181, II 1.842, III 1.200, IV 0.896, V 0.718, rev 3.000; lever: central; final drive: helical spur gears; axle ratio: 4.615; width of rims: 4.5'' - XR 5''; tyres: 155 SR x 13 - XR 175/70 SR x 13.

PERFORMANCE max speeds: (I) 27 mph, 43 km/h; (II) 45 mph, 73 km/h; (III) 63 mph, 102 km/h; (IV) 93 mph, 150 km/h; (V) 106 mph, 170 km/h; power-weight ratio: 21.8 lb/hp, 9.9 kg/hp; consumption: 29.7 m/imp gal, 24.8 m/US gal, 9.5 l x 100 km.

CHASSIS integral; front suspension: independent, by McPherson, coil springs/telescopic damper struts, lower transverse I arms, anti-roll bar; rear: independent, by McPherson, coil springs/telescopic damper struts, trailing arms and transverse arms, anti-roll bar.

STEERING rack-and-pinion; turns lock to lock: 3.20.

BRAKES front disc (diameter 7.36 in, 187 mm), rear drum, dual circuit, servo.

HONDA Accord 1800 EX-L 4-dr Sedan

HONDA Prelude XR Coupé

ELECTRICAL EQUIPMENT 12 V; 35 Ah battery; 50 A alternator; transistorized ignition; 2 headlamps.

DIMENSIONS AND WEIGHT wheel base: 91.34 in, 232 cm; tracks: 55.12 in, 140 cm front, 55.51 in, 141 cm rear; length: 161.02 in, 409 cm; width: 64.35 in, 163.5 cm; height: 51.97 in, 132 cm; ground clearance: 6.30 in, 16 cm; weight: XT 1,962 lb, 890 kg - E 1,973 lb, 895 kg - XE 2,017 lb, 915 kg - XR 1,984 lb, 900 kg; weight distribution: 63.5% front, 36.5% rear; turning circle: 36.1 ft, 11 m; fuel tank: 11 imp gal, 13.2 US gal, 50 l.

BODY coupé; 2 doors; 2 + 2 seats, separate front seats.

OPTIONALS Hondamatic semi-automatic transmission, hydraulic torque converter and constant mesh with 2 ratios: (I 1.565, II 0.903, rev 2.045), possible manual selection, 4.117 axle ratio, only with 85 hp power team; air-conditioning.

ISUZU   JAPAN

Gemini Series

PRICES (Tokyo):

1 1600 LD 4-dr Sedan	904,000	yen
2 1600 LD 2-dr Coupé	934,000	yen
3 1600 LT 4-dr Sedan	943,000	yen
4 1600 LT 2-dr Coupé	973,000	yen
5 1600 LS 4-dr Sedan	1,001,000	yen
6 1600 LS 2-dr Coupé	1,073,000	yen
7 1600 Minx 4-dr Sedan	983,000	yen
8 1600 Minx 2-dr Coupé	1,013,000	yen
9 1800 LT 4-dr Sedan	998,000	yen
10 1800 LT 2-dr Coupé	1,028,000	yen
11 1800 LS 4-dr Sedan	1,056,000	yen
12 1800 LS 2-dr Coupé	1,103,000	yen
13 1800 Minx 4-dr Sedan	1,093,000	yen
14 1800 LS/G 2-dr Coupé	1,178,000	yen

Power team:	Standard for:	Optional for:
100 hp	1 to 8	—
110 hp	9 to 14	—

100 hp power team

ENGINE front, 4 stroke; 4 cylinders, in line; 97.6 cu in, 1,584 cc (3.23 x 2.95 in, 82 x 75 mm); compression ratio: 8.7:1; max power (JIS): 100 hp at 6,000 rpm; max torque (JIS): 101 lb ft, 14 kg m at 4,000 rpm; max engine rpm: 6,500; 63.1 hp/l; cast iron block, light alloy head; 5 crankshaft bearings; valves: overhead, rockers; camshafts: 1, overhead; lubrication: rotary pump, full flow filter, 8.8 imp pt, 10.6 US pt, 5 l; 1 Nikki-Stromberg downdraught twin barrel carburettor, catalytic converter, secondary air injection and exhaust gas recirculation; fuel feed: electric pump; water-cooled, 10.8 imp pt, 12.7 US pt, 6 l.

TRANSMISSION driving wheels: rear; clutch: single dry plate (diaphragm); gearbox: mechanical; gears: 4, fully synchronized - for LS models 5; ratios: I 3.506, II 2.174, III 1.417, IV 1, rev 3.826 (for LS models I 3.506, II 2.174, III 1.471, IV 1, V 0.855, rev 3.759); lever: central; final drive: hypoid bevel; axle ratio: 3.909; width of rims: 5''; tyres: 6.15 x 13 - 1600 LS 4-dr Sedan Z78 x 13 - 1600 LS 2-dr Coupé SR x 13.

PERFORMANCE max speeds: (I) 29 mph, 47 km/h; (II) 48 mph, 78 km/h; (III) 73 mph, 117 km/h; (IV) 103 mph, 165 km/h; power-weight ratio: 1600 LD 4-dr Sedan 20.3 lb/hp, 9.2 kg/hp; carrying capacity: 882 lb, 400 kg; speed in direct drive at 1,000 rpm: 16.2 mph, 26.1 km/h; consumption: 39.8 m/imp gal, 33.1 m/US gal, 7.1 l x 100 km.

CHASSIS integral; front suspension: independent, wishbones, coil springs, anti-roll bar, telescopic dampers; rear: rigid axle, lower radius arms, torque tube, Panhard rod, coil springs, telescopic dampers.

STEERING rack-and-pinion; turns lock to lock: 4.20.

BRAKES front disc, rear drum, servo; lining area: front 17.4 sq in, 112 sq cm, rear 49 sq in, 316 sq cm, total 66.4 sq in, 428 sq cm.

ELECTRICAL EQUIPMENT 12 V; 35 Ah battery; alternator; Hitachi distributor; 2 headlamps.

DIMENSIONS AND WEIGHT wheel base: 94.49 in, 240 cm; tracks: 51.18 in, 130 cm front, 51.38 in, 130 cm rear; length: 162.60 in, 413 cm; width: 61.81 in, 157 cm; height: sedans 53.54 in, 136 cm - coupés 52.36 in, 133 cm; ground clearance: 5.71 in, 14.5 cm; weight: 1600 LD 4-dr Sedan 2,040

lb, 925 kg - 1600 LD 2-dr Coupé 1,996 lb, 905 kg - 1600 LT, LS and Minx sedans 2,051 lb, 930 kg - 1600 LT ,LS and Minx coupés 2,007 lb, 910 kg; weight distribution: 54.5% front, 45.5% rear; turning circle: 32.8 ft, 10 m; fuel tank: 11.4 imp gal, 13.7 US gal, 52 l.

BODY 5 seats, separate front seats.

OPTIONALS 5-speed mechanical gearbox (V 0.855); Borg-Warner automatic transmission, hydraulic torque converter and planetary gears with 3 ratios (I 2.450, II 1.450, III 1, rev 2.222), with max power (DIN) 94 hp at 5,400 rpm, max torque (DIN) 99 lb ft, 13.6 kg m at 3,800 rpm, 59.3 hp/l, power-weight ratio 22.5 lb/hp, 10.2 kg/hp, max speed 99 mph, 160 km/h; for 1600 LS 2-dr Coupé air-conditioning.

110 hp power team

See 100 hp power team, except for:

ENGINE 110.9 cu in, 1,817 cc (3.31 x 3.23 in, 84 x 82 mm); compression ratio: 8.5:1; max power (JIS): 110 hp at 5,600 rpm; max torque (JIS): 112 lb ft, 15.5 kg m at 4,000 rpm; 60.5 hp/l.

TRANSMISSION gears: 4, fully synchronized; ratios: I 3.207, II 1.989, III 1.356, IV 1, V 0.855, rev 3.438; axle ratio: 3.909; tyres: LS models 155 SR x 13 - 1800 LS/G 2-dr Coupé 175/ 70 SR x 13.

PERFORMANCE max speed: 106 mph, 170 km/h; power-weight ratio: sedans 19.2 lb/hp, 8.7 kg/hp.

DIMENSIONS AND WEIGHT weight: sedans 2,106 lb, 955 kg - coupés 2,062 lb, 935 kg.

OPTIONALS with 3-speed automatic transmission engine max power (JIS) 105 hp at 5,400 rpm, 57.8 hp/l, power-weight ratio sedans 20.1 lb/hp, 9.1 hp/hp.

Florian SII Series

PRICES (Tokyo):

1 1800 De Luxe 4-dr Sedan	1,211,000	yen
2 1800 Super De Luxe 4-dr Sedan	1,383,000	yen
3 Diesel 2000 Semi-De Luxe 4-dr Sedan	1,253,000	yen
4 Diesel 2000 De Luxe 4-dr Sedan	1,298,000	yen
5 Diesel 2000 Super De Luxe 4-dr Sedan	1,470,000	yen

Power team:	Standard for:	Optional for:
105 hp	1,2	—
62 hp	3 to 5	—

105 hp power team

ENGINE front, 4 stroke; 4 cylinders, vertical, in line; 110.9 cu in, 1,817 cc (3.31 x 3.23 in, 84 x 82 mm); compression ratio: 8.7:1; max power (JIS): 105 hp at 5,400 rpm; max torque (JIS): 109 lb ft, 15 kg m at 3,800 rpm; max engine rpm: 6,300; 57.8 hp/l; cast iron block, light alloy head; 5 crankshaft bearings; valves: overhead, Vee-slanted, rockers; camshafts: 1, overhead; lubrication: rotary pump,

ISUZU Gemini 1800 LS 2-dr Coupé

105 HP POWER TEAM

full flow filter, 6.3 imp pt, 7.6 US pt, 3.6 l; 1 Stromberg downdraught twin barrel carburettor, catalytic converter, secondary air injection and exhaust gas recirculation; fuel feed: mechanical pump; water-cooled, 10.6 imp pt, 12.7 US pt, 6 l.

TRANSMISSION driving wheels: rear; clutch: single dry plate (diaphragm); gearbox: mechanical; gears: 5, fully synchronized; ratios: I 3.207, II 1.989, III 1.356, IV 1, V 0.855, rev 3.438; lever: central; final drive: hypoid bevel; axle ratio: 3.727; width of rims: 4.5''; tyres: 6.45 x 13.

PERFORMANCE max speed: 99 mph, 160 km/h; power-weight ratio: 21.6 lb/hp, 9.8 kg/hp; consumption: not declared.

CHASSIS integral; front suspension: independent, wishbones, coil springs, anti-roll bar, telescopic dampers; rear: rigid axle, semi-elliptic leafsprings, telescopic dampers.

STEERING worm and roller; turns lock to lock: 3.50.

BRAKES front disc, rear drum, servo; lining area: front 16.7 sq in, 108 sq cm, rear 57.5 sq in, 371 sq cm, total 74.2 sq in, 479 sq cm.

ELECTRICAL EQUIPMENT 12 V; 35 Ah battery; 40 A alternator; Hitachi distributor; 4 headlamps.

DIMENSIONS AND WEIGHT wheel base: 98.43 in, 250 cm; tracks: 52.56 in, 133 cm front, 51.77 in, 131 cm rear; length: 174.41 in, 443 cm; width: 63.78 in, 162 cm; height: 56.89 in, 144 cm; ground clearance: 6.69 in, 17 cm; weight: 2,260 lb, 1,025 kg; weight distribution: 55% front, 45% rear; turning circle: 34.1 ft, 10.4 m; fuel tank: 9.7 imp gal, 11.6 US gal, 44 l.

BODY 5 seats, separate front seats.

62 hp power team

See 105 hp power team, except for:

ENGINE Diesel; 119.1 cu in, 1,951 cc (3.39 x 3.31 in, 86 x 84 mm); compression ratio: 20:1; max power (JIS): 62 hp at 4,400 rpm; max torque (JIS): 91 lb ft, 12.5 kg m at 2,200 rpm; valves: overhead, Vee-slanted, push-rods and rockers; lubrication: 11.4 imp pt, 13.7 US pt, 6.5 l; Bosch fuel injection; cooling: 13.2 imp pt, 15.9 US pt, 7.5 l.

TRANSMISSION gears: 5 (Semi-De Luxe 4), fully synchronized; ratios: I 3.467, II 1.989, III 1.356, IV 1, V 0.855, rev 3.438 (Semi-De Luxe I 3.467, II 1.989, III 1.356, IV 1, rev 3.499); axle ratio: 4.100.

PERFORMANCE max speeds: (I) 22 mph, 35 km/h; (II) 39 mph, 62 km/h; (III) 59 mph, 95 km/h; (IV) 75 mph, 120 km/h; (V) 81 mph, 131 km/h; power-weight ratio: Semi-De Luxe 39 lb/hp, 17.7 kg/hp; consumption: 58.8 m/imp gal, 49 m/US gal, 4.8 l x 100 km at 37 mph, 60 km/h.

DIMENSIONS AND WEIGHT weight: Semi-De Luxe 2,426 lb, 1,100 kg - De Luxe and Super De Luxe 2,492 lb, 1,130 kg.

117 1950 Series

PRICES (Tokyo):

1 XT 2-dr Coupé	1,539,000	yen
2 XT-L 2-dr Coupé	1,764,000	yen
3 XC 2-dr Coupé	1,745,000	yen
4 XC-J 2-dr Coupé	1,832,000	yen
5 XE 2-dr Coupé	2,533,000	yen
6 XG 2-dr Coupé	2,022,000	yen

Power team:	Standard for:	Optional for:
105 hp	1,2	—
115 hp	3,4	—
135 hp	5,6	—

105 hp power team

ENGINE front, 4 stroke; 4 cylinders, vertical, in line; 118.9 cu in, 1,949 cc (3.43 x 2.23 in, 87 x 82 mm); compression ratio: 8.7:1; max power (JIS): 105 hp at 5,400 rpm; max torque (JIS): 109 lb ft, 15 kg m at 3,800 rpm; max engine rpm: 6,600; 53.9 hp/l; cast iron block, light alloy head; 5 crankshaft bearings; valves: overhead, rockers; camshafts: 1, overhead; lubrication: rotary pump, full flow filter, 14.1 imp pt, 16.9 US pt, 8 l; 1 Stromberg downdraught twin barrel carburettor; fuel feed: mechanical pump; water-cooled, 15.8 imp pt, 19 US pt, 9 l.

ISUZU Florian SII De Luxe 4-dr Sedan

TRANSMISSION driving wheels: rear; clutch: single dry plate (diaphragm); gearbox: mechanical; gears: 5, fully synchronized; ratios: I 3.207, II 1.989, III 1.355, IV 1, V 0.855, rev 3.438; lever: central; final drive: hypoid bevel; axle ratio: 4.100; tyres: 6.45 x 13.

PERFORMANCE max speed: 106 mph, 170 km/h; power-weight ratio: 22.7 lb/hp, 10.3 kg/hp; consumption: not declared.

CHASSIS integral with platform; front suspension: independent, wishbones, coil springs, anti-roll bar, telescopic dampers; rear: rigid axle, semi-elliptic leafsprings, telescopic dampers.

STEERING recirculating ball; turns lock to lock: 3.50.

BRAKES front disc, rear drum, servo; lining area: front 16.7 sq in, 108 sq cm, rear 57.5 sq in, 371 sq cm, total 74.2 sq in, 479 sq cm.

ELECTRICAL EQUIPMENT 12 V; 35 Ah battery; 40 A alternator; Hitachi D408-53 alternator; 4 headlamps.

DIMENSIONS AND WEIGHT wheel base: 98.43 in, 250 cm; tracks: 53.15 in, 135 cm front, 51.57 in, 131 cm rear; length: 170.08 in, 432 cm; width: 62.99 in, 160 cm; height: 51.97 in, 132 cm; ground clearance: 70.87 in, 18 cm; weight: 2,381 lb, 1,080 kg; weight distribution: 55% front, 45% rear; turning circle: 37.4 ft, 11.4 m; fuel tank: 12.3 imp gal, 14.8 US gal, 56 l.

ISUZU 117 1950 XE 2-dr Coupé

BODY coupé; 2 doors; 4 seats, separate front seats, reclining backrests, built-in headrests.

OPTIONALS Borg-Warner automatic transmission, hydraulic torque converter and planetary gears with 3 ratios (I 2.450, II 1.450, III 1, rev 2.222).

115 hp power team

See 105 hp power team, except for:

ENGINE compression ratio: 9:1; max power (JIS): 115 hp at 5,800 rpm; max torque (JIS): 116 lb ft, 16 kg m at 3,800 rpm; max engine rpm: 6,800; 59 hp/l.

TRANSMISSION tyres: for 117 1950 XC 2-dr Coupé only 165 SR x 13.

PERFORMANCE max speed: 109 mph, 175 km/h power-weight ratio: 20.7 lb/hp, 9.4 kg/hp.

135 hp power team

See 105 hp power team, except for:

ENGINE compression ratio: 9:1; max power (JIS): 135 hp at 6,200 rpm; max torque (JIS): 123 lb ft, 17 kg m at 5,000 rpm; max engine rpm: 6,800; 69.3 hp/l; valves: overhead, thimble tappets; camshafts: 2, overhead, 1 per bank; lubrication: rotary pump, full flow filter, 8.8 imp pt, 10.6 US pt, 5 l; Bosch electronic fuel injection system;

...mission control 3-way catalyst with oxygen sensor, ...xhaust gas recirculation.

...RANSMISSION 3.909 axle ratio.

...ERFORMANCE max speeds: (I) 35 mph, 57 km/h; (II) 58 ...ph, 93 km/h; (III) 72 mph, 116 km/h; (IV) 112 mph, 180 ...n/h; power-weight ratio: XE 18.7 lb/hp, 8.5 kg/hp; con-...umption: 26.9 m/imp gal, 22.4 m/US gal, 10.5 l x 100 km.

...HASSIS rear suspension: rigid axle, semi-elliptic leaf-...orings, torque arms, anti-roll bar, telescopic dampers.

...TEERING XG recirculating ball, variable ratio - XE servo.

...RAKES disc.

...IMENSIONS AND WEIGHT weight: XG 2,459 lb, 1,115 kg - ...E 2,525 lb, 1,145 kg.

...PTIONALS Borg-Warner automatic transmission, hydraulic ...rque converter and planetary gears with 3 ratios (I 2.450, ...1.450, III 1, rev 2.222); air-conditioning.

MAZDA Familia AP 1400 Touring Custom 3-dr Sedan

MAZDA

JAPAN

Familia AP Series

1300 Standard 3-dr Sedan	665,000	yen
1300 De Luxe 3-dr Sedan	735,000	yen
1300 GF 3-dr Sedan	790,000	yen
1300 Super Custom 3-dr Sedan	830,000	yen
1300 Standard 5-dr Sedan	700,000	yen
1300 De Luxe 5-dr Sedan	770,000	yen
1300 GL 5-dr Sedan	825,000	yen
1300 Super Custom 5-dr Sedan	865,000	yen
1400 GF 3-dr Sedan	825,000	yen
1400 Super Custom 3-dr Sedan	865,000	yen
1400 Touring Custom 3-dr Sedan	890,000	yen
1400 GL 5-dr Sedan	860,000	yen
1400 Super Custom 5-dr Sedan	900,000	yen
1400 Elegant Custom 5-dr Sedan	940,000	yen

...wer team:	Standard for:	Optional for:
...2 hp	1 to 8	—
...2 hp	9 to 14	—

72 hp power team

...NGINE front, 4 stroke, (1978 emission models, Mazda con-...olled combustion engine with secondary air induction, ...xhaust gas recirculation and three elements catalyst); 4 ...ylinders, in line; 77.6 cu in, 1,272 cc (2.87 x 2.99 in, 73 x ...6 mm); compression ratio: 9.2:1; max power (JIS) 72 hp ... 5,700 rpm; max torque (JIS): 76 lb ft, 10.5 kg m at ...,500 rpm; max engine rpm: 6,000; 56.6 hp/l; cast iron ...ock, light alloy head; 5 crankshaft bearings; valves: over-...ead, rockers; camshafts: 1, overhead; lubrication: rotary ...ump, full flow filter, 6.5 imp pt, 7.8 US pt, 3.7 l; 1 2-stage ...owndraught twin barrel carburettor; fuel feed: mechanical ...ump; water-cooled, 9.7 imp pt, 11.6 US pt, 5.5 l.

...RANSMISSION driving wheels: rear; clutch: single dry ...ate (diaphragm); gearbox: mechanical; gears: 4, fully syn-...hronized (Super Custom models 5); ratios: I 3.337, II ...995, III 1.301, IV 1 (Super Custom models V 0.831), rev ...337; lever: central; final drive: hypoid bevel; axle ratio: ...909; width of rims: 4.5''; tyres: 6.00 x 12.

...ERFORMANCE max speeds: (I) 28 mph, 45 km/h; (II) 47 ...ph, 76 km/h; (III) 72 mph, 116 km/h; (IV) 90 mph, 145 ...n/h; power-weight ratio: Standard 3-dr. Sedan 23.8 lb/hp, ...0.8 kg/hp; acceleration: standing 1/4 mile 20.2 sec, 0-50 ...ph (0-80 km/h) 11 sec; speed in direct drive at 1,000 rpm: ...6.3 mph, 24.6 km/h; consumption: 40.9 m/imp gal, 34.1 ...US gal, 6.9 l x 100 km (1978 emission models 39.8 m/imp ...al, 33.1 m/US gal, 7.1 l x 100 km).

...HASSIS integral; front suspension: independent, by Mc-...herson, coil springs/telescopic damper struts, lower wish-...ones (trailing links), anti-roll bar; rear: rigid axle, lower ...railing arms, upper torque rods, coil springs, telescopic ...ampers.

...TEERING recirculating ball; turns lock to lock: 3.50.

...RAKES drum, dual circuit (Super Custom models front disc, ...ervo); lining area: front 39.7 sq in, 256 sq cm, rear 39.7 ...q in, 256 sq cm, total 79.4 sq in, 512 sq cm (Super Custom ...odels front 18 sq in, 116 sq cm, rear 39.7 sq in, 256 sq ..., total 57.7 sq in, 372 sq cm).

...LECTRICAL EQUIPMENT 12 V; 32 Ah battery; 35 A alter-...or; 2 headlamps.

DIMENSIONS AND WEIGHT wheel base: 91.14 in, 231 cm; tracks: 50.98 in, 129 cm front, 51.57 in, 131 cm rear; length: 150.39 in, 382 cm - Super Custom models 150.79 in, 383 cm; width: 63.19 in, 160 cm; height: 53.94 in, 137 cm; ground clearance: 6.30 in, 16 cm; weight: Standard and De Luxe 3-dr. sedans 1,720 lb, 780 kg - GF 3-dr. Sedan 1,742 lb, 790 kg - Super Custom 3-dr. sedans 1,764 lb, 800 kg - Standard and De Luxe 5-dr. sedans 1,753 lb, 795 kg - GF Super Custom 5-dr. sedans 1,775 lb, 805 kg - weight distribution: 56% front, 44% rear; fuel tank: 8.8 imp gal, 10.6 US gal, 40 l.

BODY 4 seats, separate front seats, built-in headrests, re-clining front and rear seats.

OPTIONALS 5-speed fully synchronized mechanical gearbox (I 3.337, II 1.995, III 1.301, IV 1, V 0.831, rev 3.337); 155 SR x 13 tyres; air-conditioning.

82 hp power team

See 72 hp power team, except for:

ENGINE 86.3 cu in, 1,415 cc (3.03 x 2.99 in, 77 x 76 mm); compression ratio: 9:1; max power (JIS): 82 hp at 5,700 rpm; max torque (JIS): 85 lb ft, 11.7 kg m at 3,500 rpm; 57.9 hp/l.

TRANSMISSION (gears: 5, for Touring Custom only); axle ratio: 3.727; tyres: 6.15 x 13 (Touring Custom 155 SR x 13).

MAZDA Familia AP 1400

PERFORMANCE max speeds: (I) 32 mph, 52 km/h; (II) 52 mph, 83 km/h; (III) 79 mph, 127 km/h; (IV) 96 mph, 155 km/h; power-weight ratio: GF 3-dr Sedan 21.5 lb/hp, 9.8 kg/hp.

BRAKES front disc.

DIMENSIONS AND WEIGHT length: 153.94 in, 391 cm; weight: GF 3-dr 1,764 lb, 800 kg - Super Custom 3-dr and Elegant Custom 3-dr 1,786 lb, 810 kg - Touring Custom 3-dr 1,797 lb, 815 kg - GL 5-dr 1,808 lb, 820 kg - Super Custom 5-dr and Elegant Custom 5-dr 1,819 lb, 825 kg.

OPTIONALS 5-speed mechanical gearbox (V 0.831); JATCO 3N 71B automatic transmission, hydraulic torque converter and planetary gears with 3 ratios (I 2.458, II 1.458, III 1, rev 2.181), 3.909 axle ratio (for Super Custom and Elegant Custom only).

Familia (USA) Series

PRICES IN USA:

1	GLC Regular 3-dr Sedan	$	3,895*
2	GLC De Luxe 3-dr Sedan	$	4,195*
3	GLC De Luxe 5-dr Sedan	$	4,395*
4	GLC De Luxe Station Wagon	$	4,595*

Power team:	Standard for:	Optional for:
52 hp	1 to 3	—
65 hp	4	—

52 hp power team

See Familia AP Series, 72 hp power team, except for:

ENGINE catalytic converter air induction, EGR (catalytic converter air injection, EGR for California only); max power (DIN): 52 hp (49 hp for California only) at 5,000 rpm; max torque (DIN): 64 lb ft, 8.8 kg m (63 lb ft, 8.7 kg m for California only) at 3,000 rpm; 40.9 hp/l (38.5 hp/l for California only).

TRANSMISSION gearbox ratios: I 3.655, II 2.185, III 1.425, IV 1, rev 3.655; axle ratio: 3.727; tyres: 6.15 x 13.

PERFORMANCE max speed: 86 mph, 138 km/h; power-weight ratio: 37.8 lb/hp, 17.1 kg/hp (40.4 lb/hp, 17.3 kg/hp for California only).

BRAKES front disc, rear drum.

ELECTRICAL EQUIPMENT 45 Ah battery (35 Ah for California only).

DIMENSIONS AND WEIGHT length: 154.33 in, 392 cm; weight: 1,965 lb, 891 kg (1,980 lb, 898 kg for California only).

OPTIONALS 5-speed fully synchronized mechanical gearbox (I 3.655, II 2.185, III 1.425, IV 1, V 0.827); JATCO 3N 71B automatic transmission, hydraulic torque converter and planetary gears with 3 ratios (I 2.458, II 1.458, III 1, rev 2.181), 4.100 axle ratio; 155 SR x 13 tyres; air-conditioning.

65 hp power team

See Familia AP Series, 82 hp power team, except for:

ENGINE max power (DIN): 65 hp at 5,000 rpm; max torque (DIN): 76 lb ft, 10.5 kg m at 3,000 rpm; 45.9 hp/l.

TRANSMISSION gears: 5; ratios: V 0.831; tyres: 155 SR x 13.

PERFORMANCE power-weight ratio: 32.6 lb/hp, 14.8 kg/hp.

CHASSIS rear suspension: rigid axle, semi-elliptic leaf-springs, telescopic dampers.

DIMENSIONS AND WEIGHT length: 163.19 in, 414.5 cm; height: 56.10 in, 142.5 cm; weight: 2,117 lb, 960 kg.

BODY estate car/station wagon; doors: 4 + 1.

Capella Series

PRICES (Tokyo):

1 1600 Standard Sedan	850,000	yen
2 1600 De Luxe Sedan	910,000	yen
3 1600 GL Sedan	960,000	yen
4 1600 Super Custom	1,030,000	yen
5 1600 De Luxe Hardtop	945,000	yen
6 1600 GL Hardtop	995,000	yen
7 1600 Super Custom Hardtop	1,065,000	yen
8 1800 GL Sedan	1,040,000	yen
9 1800 GL Hardtop	1,100,000	yen
10 1800 Super Custom Sedan	1,110,000	yen
11 1800 Super Custom Hardtop	1,170,000	yen

Power team:	Standard for:	Optional for:
90 hp	1 to 7	—
100 hp	8 to 11	—

90 hp power team

ENGINE front, 4 stroke; 4 cylinders, in line; 96.8 cu in, 1,586 cc (3.07 x 3.27 in, 78 x 83 mm); compression ratio: 8.6:1; max power (JIS): 90 hp at 5,700 rpm; max torque (JIS): 94 lb ft, 13 kg m at 3,500 rpm; max engine rpm: 6,000; 56.7 hp/l; cast iron block, light alloy head; 5 crankshaft bearings; valves: overhead, rockers; camshafts: 1, overhead; lubrication: rotary pump, full flow filter, 7.2 imp pt, 8.7 US pt, 4.1 l; 1 Nikki 242302 downdraught twin barrel carburettor with automatic air-fuel ratio adjustment; Mazda stabilized combustion system, secondary air induction, EGR, 3-way catalytic; fuel feed: electric pump; water-cooled: 12.3 imp pt, 14.8 US pt, 7 l.

TRANSMISSION driving wheels: rear; clutch: single dry plate (diaphragm); gearbox: mechanical; gears: 4, fully synchronized; ratios: I 3.403, II 1.925, III 1.373, IV 1, rev 3.665; lever: central; final drive: hypoid bevel; axle ratio: 3.909; width of rims: 4.5'' (Super Custom 5''); tyres: 6.45 x 13 (Super Custom 165 SR x 13).

PERFORMANCE max speeds: (I) 30 mph, 48 km/h; (II) 50 mph, 80 km/h; (III) 73 mph, 117 km/h; (IV) 99 mph, 160 km/h; power-weight ratio: Standard Sedan 24 lb/hp, 10.9

MAZDA Capella 1800 Super Custom Sedan

kg/hp; consumption: 40.9 m/imp gal, 34.1 m/US gal, 6.9 l x 100 km.

CHASSIS integral; front suspension: independent by McPherson, coil springs/telescopic dampers struts, transverse I arms, trailing locating rods, anti-roll bar; rear: rigid axle, lower trailing arms, upper torque rods, Panhard rod, coil springs, telescopic dampers.

STEERING recirculating ball; turns lock to lock: 4.50.

BRAKES front disc, rear drum, dual circuit, servo; lining/area: front 22.9 sq in, 148 sq cm, rear 39.7 sq in, 256 sq cm, total 62.6 sq in, 404 sq cm.

ELECTRICAL EQUIPMENT 12 V; 33 Ah battery; 50 A alternator; IC high energy ignition; 2 headlamps.

DIMENSIONS AND WEIGHT wheel base: 98.82 in, 251 cm; tracks: 53.94 in, 137 cm front, 54.33 in, 138 cm rear; length: 169.49 in, 430.5 cm; width: 65.35 in, 166 cm; height: sedans 54.33 in, 138 cm - hardtops 53.35 in, 135.5 cm; ground clearance: 6.10 in, 15.5 cm; weight: Standard Sedan 2,161 lb, 980 kg - De Luxe Sedan and Hardtop 2,172 lb, 985 kg - GL Sedan and Hardtop 2,183 lb, 990 kg - Super Custom Sedan 2,205 lb, 1,000 kg - Super Custom Hardtop 2,194 lb, 995 kg; weight distribution: 53.5% front, 46.5% rear; turning circle: 34.7 ft, 10.6 m; fuel tank: 12.1 imp gal, 14.5 US gal, 55 l.

BODY 5 seats, separate front seats, reclining backrests, built-in headrests.

100 hp power team

See 90 hp power team, except for:

ENGINE 107.9 cu in, 1,769 cc (3.15 x 3.46 in, 80 x 88 mm); max power (JIS): 100 hp at 5,500 rpm; max torque (JIS) 100 lb ft, 15.2 kg m at 3,300 rpm; 56.5 hp/l.

TRANSMISSION gears: 5 (for Super Custom and GL Hardtop only); ratios: V 0.854; axle ratio: 3.727.

PERFORMANCE max speed: 103 mph, 165 km/h; power-weight ratio: GL Sedan 21.9 lb/hp, 9.9 kg/hp; consumption 35.3 m/imp gal, 29.4 m/US gal, 8 l x 100 km.

DIMENSIONS AND WEIGHT weight: GL Sedan 2,194 lb, 995 kg - GL Hardtop 2,205 lb, 1,000 kg - Super Custom Sedan 2,227 lb, 1,010 kg - Super Custom 2,238 lb, 1,015 kg.

OPTIONALS JATCO automatic transmission with 3 ratios (I 2.458, II 1.458, III 1, rev 2.181) for Super Custom Sedan only; light alloy wheels with 5.5'' wide rims; 185/70 SR x 13 tyres; air-conditioning.

626 Series (for Europe)

See Capella Series, 100 hp power team, except for:

90 hp power team

ENGINE 120.2 cu in, 1,970 cc (3.15 x 3.86 in 80 x 98 mm); max power (DIN): 90 hp at 4,800 rpm; max torque (DIN) 115 lb ft, 15.9 kg m at 2,500 rpm; 45.7 hp/l; lubrication 7.7 imp pt, 9.3 US pt, 4.4 l; water-cooled: 13.2 imp pt 15.8 US pt, 7.5 l.

TRANSMISSION gears: 4; ratios: I 3.214, II 1.818, III 1.296 IV 1, rev 3.461; axle ratio: 3.636; tyres: 165 SR x 13.

PERFORMANCE max speed: sedans 106 mph, 170 km/h hardtops 109 mph, 175 km/h; power-weight ratio: sedans 26 lb/hp, 11.8 kg/hp; consumption: 31 m/imp gal, 25.8 m/US gal, 9.1 l x 100 km.

ELECTRICAL EQUIPMENT 45 Ah battery; 50 A alternator

DIMENSIONS AND WEIGHT weight: sedans 2,337 lb, 1,060 kg - hardtops 2,348 lb, 1,065 kg.

OPTIONALS 5-speed mechanical gearbox (V 0.860); JATCO 3-speed automatic transmission; light alloy wheels with 5.5'' wide rims; 185/70 SR x 13 tyres.

Luce Series

PRICES (Tokyo):

1 1800 Custom Special Sedan	996,000	yen
2 1800 Custom Sedan	1,100,000	yen
3 2000 Custom Sedan	1,165,000	yen
4 2000 Super Custom Sedan	1,230,000	yen
5 2000 Custom Special 4-dr Hardtop	1,105,000	yen
6 2000 Custom 4-dr Hardtop	1,230,000	yen
7 2000 Super Custom 4-dr Hardtop	1,345,000	yen
8 2000 Super Custom SE 4-dr Hardtop	1,420,000	yen
9 RE Custom Special 4-dr Hardtop	1,250,000	yen
10 RE Super Custom 4-dr Hardtop	1,620,000	yen
11 RE Limited 4-dr Hardtop	2,005,000	yen

Power team:	Standard for:	Optional for:
100 hp	1,2	—
110 hp	3 to 8	—
135 hp	9 to 11	—

100 hp power team

ENGINE front, 4 stroke; 4 cylinders, in line; 107.9 cu in 1,769 cc (3.15 x 3.46 in, 80 x 88 mm); compression ratio 8.6:1; max power (JIS): 100 hp at 5,500 rpm; max torque (JIS): 110 lb ft, 15.2 kg m at 3,300 rpm; max engine rpm 6,000; 56.5 hp/l; cast iron block, light alloy head; 5 crankshaft bearings; valves: overhead, rockers; camshafts: 1 overhead; lubrication: rotary pump, full flow filter, 7.2 imp pt, 8.7 US pt, 4.1 l; 1 downdraught twin barrel carburettor with automatic air-fuel ratio adjustment; Mazda stabilized combustion system, secondary air induction, EGR, 3-way catalyst; fuel feed: electric pump; water-cooled, 12.3 imp pt, 14.8 US pt, 7 l.

TRANSMISSION driving wheels: rear; clutch: single dry plate (diaphragm); gearbox: mechanical; gears: 4, fully synchronized; ratios: I 3.403, II 2.005, III 1.373, IV 1, rev 3.900; lever: central; final drive: hypoid bevel; axle ratio: 4.100; width of rims: 5''; tyres: 6.45 x 13.

PERFORMANCE max speeds: (I) 29 mph, 46 km/h; (II) 50 mph, 80 km/h; (III) 68 mph, 110 km/h; (IV) 96 mph, 154 km/h; power-weight ratio: Custom Special 24 lb/hp, 10.9

MAZDA Capella 1800 Super Custom Sedan

kg/hp; carrying capacity: 882 lb, 400 kg; acceleration: standing ¼ mile 17.1 sec; speed in direct drive/top at 1,000 rpm: 19.5 mph, 31.4 km/h; consumption: 31 m/imp gal, 25.8 m/US gal, 9.1 l x 100 km.

CHASSIS integral; front suspension: independent, by McPherson, coil springs/telescopic dampers struts, lower wishbones, anti-roll bar; rear: rigid axle, lower trailing arms, upper torque rods, Panhard rod, coil springs, telescopic dampers.

STEERING recirculating ball; turns lock to lock: 4.70.

BRAKES front disc, rear drum, dual circuit, servo; lining area: front 26.7 sq in, 172 sq cm, rear 59.5 sq in, 384 sq cm, total 86.2 sq in, 556 sq cm.

ELECTRICAL EQUIPMENT 12 V; 35 Ah battery; 55 A alternator; fully transistorized ignition with pointless contact breaker; 4 headlamps.

DIMENSIONS AND WEIGHT wheel base: 102.76 in, 261 cm; tracks: 56.30 in, 143 cm front, 55.12 in, 140 cm rear; length: Custom Special 179.33 in, 455.5 cm - Custom 180.12 in, 457.5 cm; width: 66.54 in, 169 cm; height: 55.71 in, 141.5 cm; ground clearance: 6.89 in, 17.5 cm; weight: Custom Special 2,403 lb, 1,090 kg - Custom 2,414 lb, 1,095 kg; turning circle: 36.7 ft, 11.2 m; fuel tank: 14.3 imp gal, 17.2 US gal 65 l.

BODY 5 seats, separate front seats, reclining backrests, built-in headrests.

135 hp power team

See 100 hp power team, except for:

ENGINE front, 4 stroke, Wankel rotary type with Mazda REAPS emission control system (thermal reactor, air injection, EGR and ignition control); 2 co-axial 3-lobe rotors; 39.9 x 2 cu in, 654 x 2 cc; max power (JIS): 135 hp at 6,000 rpm; max torque (JIS): 138 lb ft, 19 kg m at 4,000 rpm; lubrication: trochoid pump, full flow filter, forced lubrication/cooling of rotors, 11 imp pt, 13.3 US pt, 6.3 l; 1 downdraught 4-barrel carburettor; cooling: water-cooled housings, 17.6 imp pt, 21.1 US pt, 10 l, oil-cooled rotors.

TRANSMISSION gearbox: mechanical with hydraulic fluid coupling; gears: 5, fully synchronized; ratios: I 3.380, II 2.077, III 1.390, IV 1, V 0.841, rev 3.389; axle ratio: 3.727; width of rims: 5.5''; tyres: 175 SR x 14.

PERFORMANCE max speeds: (I) 36 mph, 58 km/h; (II) 59 mph, 95 km/h; (III) 90 mph, 145 km/h; (IV) 109 mph, 175 km/h; (V) 109 mph, 175 km/h; power-weight ratio: 20 lb/hp, 9.1 kg/hp; consumption: 17.8 m/imp gal, 14.9 m/US gal, 15.8 l x 100 km.

STEERING servo; turns lock to lock: 4.

DIMENSIONS AND WEIGHT length: 181.89 in, 462 cm; height: 54.33 in, 138 cm; weight: 2,723 lb, 1,235 kg.

OPTIONALS with JATCO automatic transmission max speed 106 mph, 170 km/h.

Cosmo Series

PRICES (Tokyo):

1 1800 AP Custom Special Coupé	1,055,000	yen
2 1800 AP Custom Coupé	1,190,000	yen
3 1800 AP Super Custom Coupé	1,355,000	yen
4 2000 AP Custom Coupé	1,280,000	yen
5 2000 AP Super Custom Coupé	1,420,000	yen
6 L 2000 AP Custom Special Coupé	1,205,000	yen
7 L 2000 AP Custom Coupé	1,340,000	yen
8 L 2000 AP Super Custom Coupé	1,480,000	yen
9 RE Custom Special Coupé	1,200,000	yen
10 RE Custom Coupé	1,330,000	yen
11 RE Super Custom Coupé	1,538,000	yen
12 L RE Custom Special Coupé	1,285,000	yen
13 L RE Custom Coupé	1,415,000	yen
14 L RE Super Custom Coupé	1,590,000	yen
15 RE Limited Coupé	1,795,000	yen
16 L RE Limited Coupé	1,855,000	yen

Power team:	Standard for:	Optional for:
100 hp	1 to 3	—
110 hp	4 to 8	—
125 hp	9 to 14	—
135 hp	15,16	—

100 hp power team

ENGINE front, 4 stroke, Mazda low emission system with secondary air induction, exhaust gas recirculation and three-elements catalyst; 4 cylinders, vertical, in line; 107.9 cu in, 1,769 cc (3.15 x 3.46 in, 80 x 88 mm); compression ratio: 8.6:1; max power (JIS): 100 hp at 5,500 rpm; max torque (JIS): 110 lb ft, 15.2 kg m at 3,300 rpm; max engine rpm: 6,000; 56.5 hp/l; cast iron block, light alloy head; 5 crankshaft bearings; valves: overhead, rockers; camshafts: 1, overhead; lubrication: rotary pump, full flow filter, 6.3 imp pt, 7.6 US pt, 3.6 l; 1 Nikki downdraught twin barrel carburettor; fuel feed: electric pump; water-cooled, 12.3 imp pt, 14.8 US pt, 7 l.

TRANSMISSION driving wheels: rear; clutch: single dry plate (diaphragm); gearbox: mechanical; gears: 5, fully synchronized; ratios: I 3.403, II 2.005, III 1.373, IV 1, V 0.854, rev 3.665; lever: central; final drive: hypoid bevel; axle ratio: 4.100; width of rims: 5.5''; tyres: B78 x 14.

PERFORMANCE max speeds: (I) 31 mph, 50 km/h; (II) 50 mph, 80 km/h; (III) 75 mph, 120 km/h; (IV) 103 mph, 165 km/h; (V) 106 mph, 170 km/h; power-weight ratio: 24.7 lb/hp, 11.2 kg/hp; carrying capacity: 882 lb, 400 kg; acceleration: standing ¼ mile 18.8 sec, 0-50 mph (0-80 km/h) 9.2 sec; speed in direct drive at 1,000 rpm: 17.1 mph, 27.5 km/h; consumption: 28.2 m/imp gal, 23.5 m/US gal, 10 l x 100 km.

CHASSIS integral with front and rear auxiliary frames; front suspension: independent, by McPherson, coil springs/telescopic damper struts, lower wishbones (trailing links), anti-roll bar; rear: rigid axle, lower trailing arms, upper oblique torque arms, Panhard rod, coil springs, telescopic dampers.

STEERING recirculating ball, variable ratio; turns lock to lock: 4.30.

MAZDA Luce 2000 Super Custom 4-dr Hardtop

OPTIONALS power steering, turns lock to lock 4.0

110 hp power team

See 100 hp power team, except for:

ENGINE 120.2 cu in, 1,970 cc (3.15 x 3.86 in, 80 x 98 mm); max power (JIS): 110 hp at 5,300 rpm; max torque (JIS): 123 lb ft, 17 kg m at 3,000 rpm; max engine rpm: 5,600; 55.8 hp/l; lubrication: 7.7 imp pt, 9.3 US pt, 4.4 l.

TRANSMISSION gears: 5 (for Custom Special 4-dr. Hardtop 4); ratios: I 3.403, II 1.925, III 1.373, IV 1, V 0.854, rev 3.665; axle ratio: 3.909; tyres: Custom and Custom Special 6.45 x 14 - others 175 SR x 14 with 5.5'' wide rims.

PERFORMANCE max speed: 99 mph, 160 km/h; power-weight ratio: Custom Sedan 22.3 lb/hp, 10.1 kg/hp; consumption: 29.7 m/imp gal, 24.7 m/US gal, 9.5 l x 100 km.

DIMENSIONS AND WEIGHT length: Custom Special 4-dr Hardtop 179.33 in, 455.5 cm - all other models 180.12 in, 457.5 cm; height: hardtops 54.72 in, 139 cm; weight: Custom Sedan and Custom Special 2,459 lb, 1,115 kg - Custom Hardtop 2,470 lb, 1,120 kg - Super Custom and Super Custom SE 2,514 lb, 1,140 kg.

BODY adjustable headrests.

OPTIONALS JATCO automatic transmission, hydraulic torque converter and planetary gears with 3 ratios (I 2.458, II 1.458, III 1, rev 2.181).

MAZDA Cosmo L 2000 AP Custom Coupé

100 HP POWER TEAM

BRAKES front disc, rear drum, dual circuit, servo; lining area: front 26.7 sq in, 172 sq cm, rear 18.6 sq in, 120 sq cm, total 45.3 sq in, 292 sq cm.

ELECTRICAL EQUIPMENT 12 V; 35 Ah battery; 50 A alternator; Mitsubishi distributor; 4 headlamps.

DIMENSIONS AND WEIGHT wheel base: 98.82 in, 251 cm; tracks: 54.33 in, 138 cm front, 53.94 in, 137 cm rear; length: 176.18 in, 447 cm; width: 66.34 in, 168 cm; height: 52.36 in, 133 cm; ground clearance: 6.50 in, 16.5 cm; weight: 2,470 lb, 1,120 kg; weight distribution; 56.7% front, 43.3% rear; turning circle: 36.7 ft, 11.2 m; fuel tank: 14.3 imp gal, 17.2 US gal, 65 l.

BODY coupé; 2 doors; 5 seats, separate front seats.

110 hp power team

See 100 hp power team, except for:

ENGINE 120.2 cu in, 1,970 cc (3.15 x 3.86 in, 80 x 98 mm); max power (JIS): 110 hp at 5,300 rpm; max torque (JIS): 123 lb ft, 17 kg m at 3,000 rpm; 55.8 hp/l; lubrication: 7.7 imp pt, 9.3 US pt, 4.4 l.

TRANSMISSION gears: 5, fully synchronized; ratios: I 3.403, II 1.925, III 1.373, IV 1, V 0.854, rev 3.665; axle ratio: 3.909; tyres: L models 6.45 x 14 - Super Custom Coupé 185/70 SR x 14.

PERFORMANCE power-weight ratio: Custom Coupé 22.4 lb/hp, 10.2 kg/hp; consumption: 28.2 m/imp gal, 23.5 m/US gal, 10 l x 100 km.

DIMENSIONS AND WEIGHT length: L models 177.16 in, 450 cm; height: L models 52.75 in, 134 cm; weight: Custom Coupé 2,470 lb, 1,120 kg - Super Custom Coupé 2,481 lb, 1,125 kg - L Custom and Custom Special coupés 2,547 lb, 1,155 kg - L Super Custom Coupé 2,558 lb, 1,160 kg.

125 hp power team

See 100 hp power team, except for:

ENGINE front, 4 stroke, Wankel type with Mazda REAPS emission control system (thermal reactor and air injection); 2 co-axial 3-lobe rotors; 35 x 2 cu in, 573 x 2 cc; compression ratio: 9.4:1; max power (JIS): 125 hp at 6,500 rpm; max torque (JIS): 120 lb ft, 16.5 kg m at 4,000 rpm; max engine rpm: 7,000; light alloy engine block, dual ignition, cast iron rotors; 2 crankshaft bearings; lubrication: rotary pump, full flow filter, oil cooler, 9.2 imp pt, 11 US pt, 5.2 l; 1 Nikki 2-10284 downdraught 4-barrel carburettor; water-cooled: 15.8 imp pt, 19 US pt, 9 l.

TRANSMISSION gears: 4, fully synchronized - L models 5; ratios: I 3.683, II 2.263, III 1.397, IV 1 - L models V 0.862, rev 3.692; axle ratio: 3.909.

PERFORMANCE max speeds: (I) 35 mph, 56 km/h; (II) 56 mph, 90 km/h; (III) 89 mph, 144 km/h; (IV) 115 mph, 185 km/h; power-weight ratio: Custom Special Coupé 20.5 lb/hp, 9.3 kg/hp; acceleration: standing ¼ mile 16.3 sec, 0-50 mph (0-80 km/h) 6.4 sec; speed in direct drive at 1,000 rpm: 16.4 mph, 26.4 km/h; consumption: 36.7 m/imp gal, 30.5 m/US gal, 7.7 l x 100 km.

ELECTRICAL EQUIPMENT 63 A alternator.

DIMENSIONS AND WEIGHT weight: 2,558 lb, 1,160 kg - Custom Coupé and L Custom Special Coupé 2,547 lb, 1,155 kg; weight distribution: 57.3% front, 42.7% rear.

OPTIONALS 5-speed fully synchronized mechanical gearbox (I 3.683, II 2.263, III 1.397, IV 1, V 0.862, rev 3.692); automatic transmission with 3 ratios (only for Super Custom Coupé): 185/70 SR x 14 tyres.

135 hp power team

See 125 hp power team, except for:

ENGINE 39.9 x 2 cu in, 654 x 2 cc; max power (JIS): 135 hp at 6,000 rpm; max torque (JIS): 138 lb ft, 19 kg m at 4,000 rpm; lubrication: 11.1 imp pt, 13.3 US pt, 6.3 l; 1 Hitachi KCH 348 downdraught 4-barrel carburettor.

TRANSMISSION gearbox: mechanical with hydraulic fluid coupling; gears: 5, fully synchronized; ratios: I 3.380, II 2.077, III 1.390, IV 1, V 0.841, rev 3.389; axle ratio: 3.636; tyres: 185/70 SR x 14.

PERFORMANCE max speeds: (I) 39 mph, 63 km/h; (II) 65 mph, 104 km/h; (III) 96 mph, 155 km/h; (IV) 121 mph, 195 km/h; (V) 118 mph, 190 km/h; power-weight ratio: RE Limited Coupé 19.9 lb/hp, 9 kg/hp; acceleration: standing ¼ mile 15.9 sec, 0-50 mph (0-80 km/h) 6.2 sec; speed in top at 1,000 rpm: 17.3 mph, 27.9 km/h.

CHASSIS rear suspension: anti-roll bar.

STEERING servo; turns lock to lock: 3.50.

ELECTRICAL EQUIPMENT 45 Ah battery.

DIMENSIONS AND WEIGHT length: RE Limited Coupé 178.94 in, 454 cm - L RE Limited Coupé 177.16 in, 450 cm; weight: RE Limited Coupé 2,690 lb, 1,220 kg - L RE Limited Coupé 2,646 lb, 1,200 kg; weight distribution: 57.8% front, 42.2% rear.

OPTIONALS JATCO automatic transmission with 3 ratios (I 2.458, II 1.458, III 1, rev 2.181), max ratio of converter at stall 2, max speeds (I) 53 mph, 85 km/h, (II) 90 mph, 145 km/h, (III) 118 mph, 190 km/h, acceleration standing ¼ mile 17.7 sec, consumption 31 m/imp gal, 25.8 m/US gal, 9.1 l x 100 km; air-conditioning.

Roadpacer Sedan

PRICE (Tokyo): 3,835,000 yen

ENGINE front, 4 stroke, Wankel type with emission control system (thermal reactor, air injection and exhaust gas recirculation); 2 co-axial 3-lobe rotors; 39.9 x 2 cu in, 654 x 2 cc; compression ratio: 9.4:1; max power (JIS): 135

MAZDA Roadpacer Sedan

hp at 6,000 rpm; max torque (JIS): 138 lb ft, 19 kg m at 4,000 rpm; max engine rpm: 6,000; light alloy engine block, dual ignition, cast iron rotors; 2 crankshaft bearings; lubrication: rotary pump, full flow filter, oil cooler, 11.1 imp pt, 13.3 US pt, 6.3 l; 1 Hitachi downdraught 4-barrel carburettor; fuel feed: electric pump; water-cooled, 15.8 imp pt, 19 US pt, 9 l.

TRANSMISSION driving wheels: rear; gearbox: JATCO automatic transmission, hydraulic torque converter and planetary gears with 3 ratios, max ratio of converter at stall 2, possible manual selection; ratios: I 2.458, II 1.458, III 1, rev 2.181; lever: steering column; final drive: hypoid bevel; axle ratio: 4.444; width of rims: 5''; tyres: 7.50 x 14.

PERFORMANCE max speed: 103 mph, 165 kmh; power-weight ratio: 25.7 lb/hp, 11.7 kg/hp; carrying capacity: 1,058 lb, 480 kg; speed in direct drive at 1,000 rpm: 17.1 mph, 27.5 km/h; consumption: not declared.

CHASSIS integral, front auxiliary frame; front suspension: independent, wishbones, coil springs, anti-roll bar, telescopic dampers; rear: rigid axle, lower trailing arms, upper oblique torque arms, coil springs, telescopic dampers.

STEERING worm and roller, variable ratio, servo; turns lock to lock: 2.60.

BRAKES front disc, internal radial fins, rear drum, dual circuit, servo.

ELECTRICAL EQUIPMENT 12 V; 45 Ah battery; 63 A alternator; 4 headlamps.

DIMENSIONS AND WEIGHT wheel base: 111.42 in, 283 cm; front and rear track: 60.24 in, 153 cm; height: 190.94 in, 485 cm; width: 74.21 in, 188 cm; height: 57.68 in, 146 cm; ground clearance: 6.30 in, 16 cm; weight: 3,473 lb, 1,575 kg; turning circle: 41.3 ft, 12.6 m; fuel tank: 16.5 imp gal, 19.8 US gal, 75 l.

BODY saloon/sedan; 4 doors; 5-6 seats, bench front seats.

OPTIONALS separate front seats.

Savanna RX7 Series

PRICES (Tokyo):

Custom Coupé	1,230,000 yen
Super Custom Coupé	1,370,000 yen
GT Coupé	1,440,000 yen
Limited Coupé	1,690,000 yen

For USA prices, see price index.

130 hp power team

ENGINE front, 4 stroke, Wankel rotary type with Mazda REAPS emission control system (thermal reactor, EGR and secondary air injection); 2 co-axial 3-lobe rotors; 35 x 2 cu in, 573 x 2 cc; compression ratio: 9.4; max power (JIS): 130 hp at 7,000 rpm; max torque (JIS): 120 lb ft, 16.5 kg m at 4,000 rpm; max engine rpm: 7,000; cast iron side-housing, light alloy trochoid housings, cast iron rotors; 2 crankshaft bear-

MAZDA Savanna RX7 GT Coupé

gs; lubrication: trochoid pump, full flow filter, forced
brication/cooling of rotors, 9.2 imp pt, 11 US pt, 5.2 l;
Nikki downdraught 4-barrel carburettor; fuel feed: electric
ump; cooling: water-cooled housings, 15.8 imp pt, 19 US
, 9 l, oil-cooled rotors.

RANSMISSION driving wheels: rear; clutch: single dry plate
iaphragm), hydraulically controlled; gearbox: mechanical;
ears: 5, fully synchronized; ratios: I 3.674, II 2.217, III
432, IV 1, V 0.825, rev 3.542; lever: central; final drive:
ypoid bevel; axle ratio: 3.909; width of rims: 5'' - Limited
oupé 5.5''; tyres: 165 SR x 13 - GT and Limited Coupé
5/70 SR x 13.

ERFORMANCE max speeds: (I) 32 mph, 52 km/h; (II) 54
ph, 87 km/h; (III) 82 mph, 132 km/h; (IV) 112 mph, 180
n/h; (V) 112 mph, 180 km/h; power-weight ratio: Custom
oupé 16.7 lb/hp, 7.6 kg/hp; carrying capacity: accele-
tion: standing ¼ mile 15.8 sec; consumption: 18.3 m/imp
al, 15.3 m/US gal, 15.4 l x 100 km.

HASSIS integral; front suspension: independent, by Mc-
erson, coil springs/telescopic damper struts, transverse
arms, trailing locating rods, anti-roll bar; rear: rigid axle,
wer trailing links, upper torque rods, Watts linkage, coil
rings, telescopic dampers (for GT and Limited Coupé
ti-roll bar).

TEERING recirculating ball; turns lock to lock: 3.70.

RAKES front disc, internal radial fins, rear drum, dual
rcuit, servo; lining area: front 24.8 sq in, 160 sq cm,
ar 39.7 sq in, 256 sq cm, total 64.5 sq cm.

LECTRICAL EQUIPMENT 12 V; 35 Ah battery; 63 A alter-
ator; 2 retractable headlamps.

IMENSIONS AND WEIGHT wheel base: 94.88 in, 241 cm;
acks: 55.90 in, 142 cm front, 55.12 in, 140 cm rear;
ngth: 168.70 in, 428.5 cm; width: 65.94 in, 167.5 cm;
eight: 49.60 in, 126 cm; ground clearance: 6.10 in, 15.5
; weight: Custom Coupé 2,172 lb, 985 kg - GT and Limited Coupé
ustom Coupé 2,194 lb, 995 kg - GT and Limited Coupé
216 lb, 1,005 kg; weight distribution: 54% front, 46%
ar; turning circle: 34.8 ft, 10.6 m; fuel tank: 12.1 imp
al, 14.5 US gal, 55 l.

ODY coupé; 2 + 1 doors; 2 + 2 seats; separate front seats.

PTIONALS JATCO automatic transmission with 3 ratios
2.458, II 1.458, III 1, rev 2.181), max speed 112 mph,
0 km/h, acceleration standing ¼ mile 17.4 sec; air-con-
tioning.

MITSUBISHI   JAPAN

Minica Ami 55 Series

RICES (Tokyo):

De Luxe 2-dr Sedan	563,000	yen
uper De Luxe 2-dr Sedan	629,000	yen
2-dr Sedan	653,000	yen
L 2-dr Sedan	676,000	yen

31 hp power team

NGINE front, 4 stroke; 2 cylinders, in line; 33.3 cu in,
6 cc (2.75 x 2.79 in, 70 x 71 mm); compression ratio: 9:1;
ax power (JIS): 31 hp at 6,000 rpm; max torque (JIS):
lb ft, 4.1 kg m at 3,000 rpm; max engine rpm: 6,500;
.7 hp/l; cast iron block, light alloy head; 3 crankshaft
earings; valves: overhead, rockers; camshafts: 1, overhead;
brication: rotary pump, full flow filter, 5.1 imp pt, 6.1 US
, 2.9 l; 1 Mikuni 24-30 DIDS downdraught twin barrel
arburettor; fuel feed: electric pump; emission control
atalytic converter, secondary air injection, exhaust gas re-
rculation; water-cooled, 5.3 imp pt, 6.3 US pt, 3 l.

RANSMISSION driving wheels: rear; clutch: single dry
ate (diaphragm); gearbox: mechanical; gears: 4, fully
nchronized; ratios: I 3.882, II 2.265, III 1.473, IV 1, rev
271; lever: central; final drive: hypoid bevel; axle ratio:
625; width of rims: 3.5''; tyres: 5.20 x 10.

ERFORMANCE max speeds: (I) 20 mph, 32 km/h; (II) 34
ph, 55 km/h; (III) 53 mph, 85 km/h; (IV) 68 mph, 110 km/h;
ower-weight ratio: except XL 40.2 lb/hp, 18/2 kg/hp; con-
mption: 54 m/imp gal, 45 m/US gal, 5.2 l x 100 km.

HASSIS integral; front suspension: independent, by Mc-
erson, coil springs/telescopic damper struts, anti-roll bar,
wer wishbones (trailing links); rear: rigid axle, twin
ngitudinal trailing radius arms, transverse linkage bar,
il springs, telescopic dampers.

TEERING recirculating ball.

RAKES drum dual circuit; lining area: total 67 sq in,
2 sq cm.

MAZDA Savanna RX7

ELECTRICAL EQUIPMENT 12 V; 24 Ah battery; 25 A alternator; Mitsubishi distributor; 2 headlamps.

DIMENSIONS AND WEIGHT wheel base: 78.84 in, 200 cm;
tracks: 48.03 in, 122 cm front, 46.85 in, 119 cm rear; length:
124.41 in, 316 cm - XL 125.19 in, 318 cm; width: 55.12
in, 140 cm; height: 51.96 in, 132 cm; ground clearance:
5.51 in, 14 cm; weight: 1,245 lb, 565 kg - XL 1,257 lb, 570
kg; fuel tank: 6.6 imp gal, 7.9 US gal, 30 l.

BODY 4 seats, separate front seats, reclining backrests,
built-in headrests; folding rear seat.

Mirage Series

PRICES EX WORKS:

1 1200 EL 2-dr Sedan	728,000	yen
2 1200 EL 4-dr Sedan	766,000	yen
3 1200 TL 4-dr Sedan	826,000	yen
4 1200 GL 2-dr Sedan	828,000	yen
5 1200 GL 4-dr Sedan	871,000	yen
6 1400 GL 2-dr Sedan	865,000	yen
7 1400 GL 4-dr Sedan	913,000	yen
8 1400 GLX 2-dr Sedan	922,000	yen
9 1400 GLX 4-dr Sedan	965,000	yen
10 1400 GLS 2-dr Sedan	1,030,000	yen

Power team:	Standard for:	Optional for:
72 hp	1 to 5	—
82 hp	6 to 10	—

---

72 hp power team

ENGINE front, transverse, 4 stroke; 4 cylinders, in line; 75.9
cu in, 1,244 cc (2.74 x 3.23 in, 69.5 x 82 mm); compression
ratio: 9:1; max power (JIS): 72 hp at 5,500 rpm; max torque
(JIS): 77 lb ft, 10.7 kg m at 3,000 rpm; max engine rpm:
6,000; 56.3 hp/l; cast iron block, light alloy head; 5 crankshaft bearings; valves: 3 per cylinder, overhead, Vee-slanted, rockers; camshafts: 1, overhead; lubrication: gear
pump, full flow filter, 6.2 imp pt, 7.4 US pt, 3.5 l; 1
Stromberg 26-30 DIDTA-11 downdraught twin barrel carburettor; Mitsubishi MCA-Jet super lean-burn low emission engine with third air inlet valve, exhaust gas recirculation and oxidizing catalyst; fuel feed: mechanical pump;
water-cooled, 8.8 imp pt, 10.6 US pt, 5 l.

TRANSMISSION driving wheels: rear; clutch: single dry
plate (diaphragm); gearbox: mechanical; gears: TL and GL models
4, fully synchronized - TL and GL models 4 and Super-
Shift 2-speed transfer box; ratios: I 4.225, II 2.365, III
1.466, IV 1.163, rev 4.108; for TL and GL models, transfer
box: high 0.774, low 1; lever: central - two levers for TL and
GL models; final drive: spiral bevel; axle ratio: EL models
3.166 - TL and GL models 3.687; width of rims: 4.5'';
tyres: 6.00 x 12.

PERFORMANCE max speeds: EL models (I) 27 mph, 43
km/h; (II) 47 mph, 75 km/h; (III) 75 mph, 120 km/h; (IV)
93 mph, 150 km/h; power-weight ratio: EL 2-dr Sedan 23.3
lb/hp, 10.6 kg/hp; carrying capacity: 882 lb, 400 kg; consumption: EL models 43.7 m/imp gal, 36.4 m/US gal, 6.4
l x 100 km.

CHASSIS integral; front suspension: independent, by Mc-
Pherson, coil springs/telescopic damper struts, lower wishbones (trailing links), anti-roll bar; rear: independent, coil
springs, telescopic dampers, trailing radius arms.

STEERING rack-and-pinion; turns lock to lock: 3.90.

BRAKES front disc, rear drum, servo.

ELECTRICAL EQUIPMENT 12 V; 45 A alternator; Mitsubishi
distributor; 2 headlamps.

DIMENSIONS AND WEIGHT wheel base: 2-dr models 90.55
in, 230 cm - 4-dr models 93.70 in, 238 cm; tracks: 53.94
in, 137 cm front, 52.75 in, 134 cm rear; length: 2-dr
models 149.21 in, 379 cm - 4-dr models 153.35 in, 389 cm;
width: 2-dr models 62.40 in, 158 cm - 4-dr models 62.60
in, 159 cm; ground clearance: 6.69 in, 17 cm; weight: EL
2-dr Sedan 1,676 lb, 760 kg - EL 4-dr Sedan 1,742 lb, 790 kg - TL 4-dr Sedan 1,764 lb, 800
kg - GL 2-dr Sedan 1,709 lb, 775 kg - GL 4-dr Sedan 1,775
lb, 805 kg; weight distribution: 62% front, 38% rear; turning circle: 4-dr models 35.4 ft, 10.8 m; fuel tank: 8.8
imp gal, 10.6 US gal, 40 l.

BODY 5 seats, separate front seats.

82 hp power team

See 72 hp power team, except for:

ENGINE 86 cu in, 1,410 cc (2.91 x 3.23 in, 74 x 82 mm);
max power (JIS): 82 hp at 5,500 rpm; max torque (JIS):
88 lb ft, 12.1 kg m at 3,500 rpm; 58.1 hp/l.

MITSUBISHI Minica Ami 55 XL 2-dr Sedan

82 HP POWER TEAM

TRANSMISSION gears: 4, fully synchronized and Super-Shift 2-speed transfer box; axle ratio: 3.470; tyres: 155 SR x 13.

PERFORMANCE power-weight ratio: GL 2-dr Sedan 20.8 lb/hp, 9.4 kg/hp; consumption: 42.3 m/imp gal, 35.3 m/US gal, 6.7 l x 100 km.

DIMENSIONS AND WEIGHT weight: GL 2-dr Sedan 1,709 lb, 775 kg - GLX 2-dr Sedan 1,753 lb, 795 kg - GLS 2-dr Sedan 1,764 lb, 800 kg - GL 4-dr Sedan 1,786 lb, 810 kg - GLX 4-dr Sedan 1,830 lb, 830 kg.

Lancer Series

PRICES (Tokyo):

1 1200 Standard 2-dr Sedan	714,000	yen
2 1200 Populaire 2-dr Sedan	778,000	yen
3 1200 Populaire 4-dr Sedan	800,000	yen
4 1200 GL 2-dr Sedan	817,000	yen
5 1200 GL 4-dr Sedan	839,000	yen
6 1200 GL-EX 4-dr Sedan	879,000	yen
7 1200 SL-5 2-dr Sedan	863,000	yen
8 1200 SL-5 4-dr Sedan	885,000	yen
9 1400 GL 2-dr Sedan	875,000	yen
10 1400 GL 4-dr Sedan	900,000	yen
11 1400 GL-EX 4-dr Sedan	940,000	yen
12 1400 SL-5 2-dr Sedan	934,000	yen
13 1400 SL-5 4-dr Sedan	956,000	yen
14 1600 GL-EX 4-dr Sedan	990,000	yen
15 1600 GSL 4-dr Sedan	1,014,000	yen
16 1600 GSR 2-dr Sedan	1,078,000	yen

Power team:	Standard for:	Optional for:
70 hp	1 to 8	—
80 hp	9 to 13	—
86 hp	14,15	—
100 hp	16	—

70 hp power team

ENGINE front, 4 stroke; 4 cylinders, vertical, in line; 75.91 cu in, 1,244 cc (2.74 x 3.23 in, 69.5 x 82 mm); compression ratio: 9:1; max power (JIS): 70 hp at 5,500 rpm; max torque (JIS): 77 lb ft, 10.7 kg m at 3,000 rpm; max engine rpm: 6,000; 56.3 hp/l; cast iron block, light alloy head; 5 crankshaft bearings; valves: overhead, Vee-slanted, rockers; camshafts: 1, overhead; lubrication: rotary pump, full flow filter, 6.2 imp pt, 7.4 US pt, 3.5 l; 1 Stromberg 28-32 DIDTA downdraught twin barrel carburettor; Mitsubishi MCA-Jet super lean-burn low emission engine with third air inlet valve, exhaust gas recirculation and small capacity catalyst in exhaust manifold; fuel feed: mechanical pump; water-cooled, 10.6 imp pt, 12.7 US pt, 6 l.

TRANSMISSION driving wheels: rear; clutch: single dry plate (diaphragm); gearbox: mechanical; gears: 4 (5 for SL-5 models only), fully synchronized; ratios: I 3.525, II 2.193, III 1.442, IV 1, rev 3.867 - SL-5 models I 3.215, II 2, III 1.316, IV 1, V 0.853, rev 3.667; lever: central; final drive: hypoid bevel; axle ratio: 4.222 - 3.909 for Standard 2-dr Sedan; tyres: 6.15 x 13 - 6.00 X12 for Standard 2-dr Sedan.

PERFORMANCE max speeds: (I) 26 mph, 42 km/h; (II) 42 mph, 68 km/h; (III) 65 mph, 105 km/h; (IV) 93 mph, 150 km/h; power-weight ratio: 1200 Populaire 2-dr Sedan 26.1 lb/hp, 11.8 kg/hp; consumption: 39.8 m/imp gal, 33.1 m/US gal, 7.1 l x 100 km.

CHASSIS integral; front suspension: independent, by McPherson, coil springs/telescopic damper struts, lower wishbones (trailing links), anti-roll bar; rear: rigid axle, semi-elliptic leafsprings, telescopic dampers.

STEERING recirculating ball, variable ratio.

BRAKES drum (front disc for GL and SL-5 models only); lining area: front 60.3 sq in, 389 sq cm, rear 47.8 sq in, 308 sq cm, total 108.1 sq in, 697 sq cm.

ELECTRICAL EQUIPMENT 12 V; 32 Ah battery; 35 A alternator; Mitsubishi distributor; 2 headlamps.

DIMENSIONS AND WEIGHT wheel base: 92.13 in, 234 cm; tracks: Populaire models 50 in, 127 cm - GL and SL-5 models 50.59 in, 128 cm front, 49.21 in, 125 cm rear; length: 157.28 in, 399 cm; width: 60.43 in, 153 cm; height: 53.74 in, 136 cm; ground clearance: 6.50 in, 16.5 cm; weight: Populaire 2-dr Sedan 1,830 lb, 830 kg - Populaire 4-dr Sedan 1,885 lb, 855 kg - GL 2-dr Sedan 1,841 lb, 835 kg - GL 4-dr Sedan 1,896 lb, 860 kg - SL-5 2-dr Sedan 1,852 lb, 840 kg - SL-5 4-dr Sedan 1,907 lb, 865 kg; weight distribution: 56% front, 44% rear; turning circle: 31.5 ft, 9.6 m; fuel tank: 11 imp gal, 13.2 US gal, 50 l.

BODY 5 seats, separate front seats, reclining backrests, built-in headrests.

80 hp power team

See 70 hp power team, except for:

ENGINE 86 cu in, 1,410 cc (2.91 x 3.23 in, 74 x 82 mm); max power (JIS): 80 hp at 5,500 rpm; max torque (JIS): 88 lb ft, 12.1 kg m at 3,500 rpm; 58.1 hp/l; 1 Stromberg 28-32 DIDSA downdraught twin barrel carburettor.

TRANSMISSION axle ratio: 3.909 - SL-5 models 4.222.

PERFORMANCE max speed: 96 mph, 155 km/h; power-weight ratio: GL 4-dr Sedan 23.3 lb/hp, 10.5 kg/hp; consumption: SL-5 models 36.6 m/imp gal, 30.5 m/US gal, 7.7 l x 100 km.

BRAKES front disc, rear drum; lining area: front 19.8 sq in, 128 sq cm, rear 47.8 sq in, 308 sq cm, total 67.6 sq in, 436 sq cm.

DIMENSIONS AND WEIGHT front track: 50.59 in, 128 cm; weight: GL 4-dr Sedan 1,907 lb, 865 kg - GL-E 4-dr Sedan 1,929 lb, 875 kg - SL-5 models 1,918 lb, 870 kg.

OPTIONALS (for GL 4-dr Sedan only) Borg-Warner 35 automatic transmission with 3 ratios (I 2.450, II 1.450, III 1, rev 2.222).

86 hp power team

See 70 hp power team, except for:

ENGINE 97.4 cu in, 1,597 cc (3.03 x 3.39 in, 76.9 x 86 mm); compression ratio: 8.5:1; max power (JIS): 86 hp at 5,000 rpm; max torque (JIS): 98 lb ft, 13.5 kg m at 3,000 rpm; Mitsubishi twin contra-rotating omni-phase balancing shafts; 1 Stromberg 28-32 DIDSA downdraught twin barrel carburettor.

TRANSMISSION gears: 5, fully synchronized; ratios: I 3.215, II 2, III 1.316, IV 1, V 0.853, rev 3.667; axle ratio: 3.909.

PERFORMANCE max speed: 96 mph, 155 km/h; power-weight ratio: 22.9 lb/hp, 10.4 kg/hp; speed in top at 1,000 rpm: 14.8 mph, 23.8 km/h; consumption: 38.1 m/imp gal, 31.8 m/US gal, 7.4 l x 100 km.

BRAKES front disc, rear drum; lining area: front 19.8 sq in, 128 sq cm, rear 47.8 sq in, 308 sq cm, total 67.6 sq in, 436 sq cm.

DIMENSIONS AND WEIGHT front track: 50.59 in, 128 cm; weight: 1,973 lb, 895 kg.

100 hp power team

See 70 hp power team, except for:

ENGINE 97.4 cu in, 1,597 cc (3.03 x 3.39 in, 76.9 x 86 mm); compression ratio: 9.5:1; max power (JIS): 100 hp at 6,300 rpm; max torque (JIS): 98 lb ft, 13.5 kg m at 4,000 rpm; max engine rpm: 7,000; 62.6 hp/l; Mitsubishi twin contra-rotating balancing shafts incorporated with crankshaft;

camshafts: cogged belt; 2 Stromberg 28-32 DIDSA dow draught twin barrel carburettors; emission control therm reactor, secondary air injection and exhaust gas recir lation.

TRANSMISSION gears: 5, fully synchronized; ratios: I 3.2 II 2, III 1.316, IV 1, V 0.853, rev 3.667; final drive: limi slip; tyres: 155 SR x 13.

PERFORMANCE max speed: 103 mph, 165 km/h; pow weight ratio: 19.6 lb/hp, 8.9 kg/hp.

BRAKES front disc, rear drum; lining area: front 19.8 in, 128 sq cm, rear 47.8 sq in, 308 sq cm, total 67.6 sq 436 sq cm.

DIMENSIONS AND WEIGHT tracks: 51.18 in, 130 cm fro 50 in, 127 cm rear; weight: 1,962 lb, 890 kg.

Celeste Series

PRICES (Tokyo):

1 1400 SR Coupé	935,000	y
2 1400 GL Coupé	975,000	y
3 1400 GSL Coupé	1,031,000	y
4 1600 GL Coupé	1,117,000	y
5 1600 XL Coupé	1,115,000	y
6 1600 GT Coupé	1,117,000	y
7 1600 GSR Coupé	1,136,000	y

Power team:	Standard for:	Optional for:
80 hp	1 to 3	—
86 hp	4 to 6	—
100 hp	7	—

80 hp power team

ENGINE front, 4 stroke; 4 cylinders, vertical, in line; cu in, 1,410 cc (2.91 x 3.23 in, 74 x 82 mm); compress ratio: 9:1; max power (JIS): 80 hp at 5,400 rpm; m torque (JIS): 88 lb ft, 12.1 kg m at 3,000 rpm; max eng rpm: 6,000; 56.7 hp/l; cast iron block, light alloy hea 5 crankshaft bearings; valves: overhead, Vee-slanted, ckers; camshafts: 1, overhead; lubrication: rotary pun full flow filter, 7 imp pt, 8.5 US pt, 4 l; 1 Stromberg 28 DIDTA downdraught twin barrel carburettor; Mitsubishi MC Jet super lean-burn low emission engine with third air in valve, exhaust gas recirculation and small capacity cataly in exhaust manifold; fuel feed: mechanical pump; wat cooled, 10.6 imp pt, 12.7 US pt, 6 l.

TRANSMISSION driving wheels: rear; clutch: single plate (diaphragm); gearbox: mechanical; gears: 4 (5 GSL only), fully synchronized; ratios: I 3.525, II 2.193, 1.442, IV 1, rev 3.867 - GSL I 3.215, II 2, III 1.316, IV V 0.853, rev 3.667; lever: central; final drive: hypoid bev axle ratio: 3.909 - GSL 4.222; width of rims: 4.5''; ty 155 SR x 13.

PERFORMANCE max speeds: (I) 28 mph, 45 km/h; (II) mph, 72 km/h; (III) 67 mph, 108 km/h; (IV) 96 mph, km/h; power-weight ratio: GL and SR models 25.1 lb/ 11.4 kg/hp; carrying capacity: 882 lb, 400 kg; consumpti 39.8 m/imp gal, 33.1 m/US gal, 7.1 l x 100 km.

MITSUBISHI Mirage 1400 GLX 2-dr Sedan

MITSUBISHI Lancer 1600 GL-EX 4-dr Sedan

8.5:1; max power (JIS): 86 hp at 5,000 rpm; max torque (JIS): 98 lb ft, 13.5 kg m at 3,000 rpm; max engine rpm: 5,700; 53.8 hp/l; cast iron block, light alloy head; 5 crankshaft bearings; Mitsubishi Saturn 80 omni-phase balancing shafts; valves: overhead, Vee-slanted, rockers; camshafts: 1, overhead; lubrication· rotar pump, full flow filter, 7 imp pt, 8.5 US pt, 4 l; 1 Stromberg 28-32 DIDTA downdraught twin barrel carburettor; Mitsubishi MCA-Jet super lean-burn low emission engine, with third air inlet valve, exhaust gas recirculation and catalyst in exhaust manifold; fuel feed: mechanical pump; water-cooled, 10.6 imp pt, 12.7 US pt, 6 l.

TRANSMISSION driving wheels: rear; clutch: single dry plate (diaphragm); gearbox: mechanical; gears: 4 (5 for SL only), fully synchronized; ratios: I 3.525, II 2.193, III 1.442, IV 1, rev 3.867 - SL I 3.215, II 2, III 1.316, IV 1, V 0.853, rev 3.667; lever: central; final drive: hypoid bevel; axle ratio: 3.909 - SL 4.222; width of rims: 4.5'' (5'' for SL only); tyres: 6.45 x 13 - SL 165 SR x 13.

PERFORMANCE max speeds: (I) 28 mph, 45 km/h; (II) 45 mph, 72 km/h; (III) 68 mph, 110 km/h; (IV) 96 mph, 155 km/h - SL (V) 96 mph, 155 km/h; power-weight ratio: L and GL models 22.4 lb/hp, 10.1 kg/hp; carrying capacity: 882 lb, 400 kg; consumption: 59.3 m/imp gal, 49.4 m/US gal, 4.8 l x 100 km at 37 mph, 60 km/h.

CHASSIS integral; front suspension: independent, by McPherson, coil springs/telescopic damper struts, lower wishbones (trailing links), anti-roll bar; rear: rigid axle, semi-elliptic leafsprings, telescopic dampers.

CHASSIS integral; front suspension: independent, by McPherson, coil springs/telescopic damper struts, lower wishbones (trailing links), anti-roll bar; rear: rigid axle, semi-elliptic leafsprings, telescopic dampers.

STEERING recirculating ball, variable ratio.

BRAKES front disc, rear drum, rear compensator.

ELECTRICAL EQUIPMENT 12 V; 32 Ah battery; 35 A alternator; Mitsubishi distributor; 2 headlamps.

DIMENSIONS AND WEIGHT wheel base: 92.13 in, 234 cm; tracks: 52.17 in, 132 cm front, 50.98 in, 129 cm rear; length: 163.58 in, 415 cm; width: 63.39 in, 161 cm; height: 52.17 in, 132 cm; ground clearance: 6.30 in, 16 cm; weight: SR and GL models 2,007 lb, 910 kg - GSL 2,018 lb, 915 kg; weight distribution: 55.4% front, 44.6% rear; fuel tank: 11 imp gal, 13.2 US gal, 50 l.

BODY 2 + 1 doors; 5 seats, separate front seats.

OPTIONALS (for GL only) Borg-Warner 35 automatic transmission with 3 ratios (I 2.680, II 1.508, III 1, rev 2.310).

86 hp power team

See 80 hp power team, except for:

ENGINE 97.4 cu in, 1,597 cc (3.03 x 3.39 in, 76.9 x 86 mm); compression ratio: 8.5:1; max power (JIS): 86 hp at 5,000 rpm; max torque (JIS): 98 lb ft, 13.5 kg m at 3,000 rpm; 53.6 hp/l; Mitsubishi twin contra-rotating balancing shafts incorporated with crankshaft; camshafts: cogged belt.

TRANSMISSION gearbox: for GL automatic transmission, hydraulic torque converter and planetary gears with 3 ratios - for XL and GT models 5-speed fully synchronized mechanical gearbox; ratios: GL I 2.680,, II 1.508, III 1, rev 2.310 - XL and GT models I 3.215, II 2, III 1.316, IV 1, V 0.853, rev 3.667; axle ratio: 3.909; tyres: for GT only 175/70 HR x 13.

PERFORMANCE max speed: GL 93 mph, 150 km/h - XL and GT models 99 mph, 160 km/h; power-weight ratio: GL 24.5 lb/hp, 11.1 kg/hp; consumption: 38.2 m/imp gal, 31.8 m/US gal, 7.4 l x 100 km.

DIMENSIONS AND WEIGHT length: GT 166.54 in, 423 cm; weight: XL 2,073 lb, 940 kg - GT 2,084 lb, 945 kg - GL 2,106 lb, 955 kg.

100 hp power team

See 80 hp power team, except for:

ENGINE 97.4 cu in, 1,597 cc (3.03 x 3.39 in, 76.9 x 86 mm); compression ratio: 9.5:1; max power (JIS): 100 hp at 6,300 rpm; max torque (JIS): 98 lb ft, 13.5 kg m at 4,000 rpm; 62.6 hp/l; 2 Stromberg 28-32 DIDTA downdraught twin barrel carburettors; emission control thermal reactor, secondary air injection and exhaust gas recirculation.

TRANSMISSION gears: 5, fully synchronized; ratios: I 3.215, II 2, III 1.316, IV 1, V 0.853, rev 3.667; axle ratio: 4.222; tyres: 175/70 HR x 13.

PERFORMANCE max speeds: (I) 31 mph, 50 km/h; (II) 51 mph, 82 km/h; (III) 79 mph, 127 km/h; (IV) 103 mph, 165 km/h; (V) 103 mph, 165 km/h; power-weight ratio: 28.8 lb/hp, 9.4 kg/hp.

DIMENSIONS AND WEIGHT weight: 2,084 lb, 945 kg.

MITSUBISHI Celeste 1600 GT Coupé

Galant Sigma Series

PRICES (Tokyo):

1 1600 L 4-dr Sedan	1,012,000	yen
2 1600 GL 4-dr Sedan	1,087,000	yen
3 1600 SL 4-dr Sedan	1,132,000	yen
4 1600 SL Super 4-dr Sedan	1,222,000	yen
5 Eterna 1600 GL 4-dr Sedan	1,077,000	yen
6 Eterna 1600 SL Super 4-dr Sedan	1,202,000	yen
7 2000 GL 4-dr Sedan	1,210,000	yen
8 2000 GSL 4-dr Sedan	1,329,000	yen
9 2000 GSL Super 4-dr Sedan	1,415,000	yen
10 Eterna 2000 GSL 4-dr Sedan	1,309,000	yen
11 Eterna 2000 GSL Super 4-dr Sedan	1,395,000	yen
12 2000 Super Saloon 4-dr Sedan	1,540,000	yen

Power team:	Standard for:	Optional for:
86 hp	1 to 6	—
105 hp	7 to 12	—

86 hp power team

ENGINE front, 4 stroke; 4 cylinders, in line; 97.4 cu in, 1,597 cc (3.03 x 3.39 in, 76.9 x 86 mm); compression ratio:

STEERING recirculating ball, variable ratio.

BRAKES front disc, rear drum, servo; lining area: front 19.2 sq in, 124 sq cm, rear 47.8 sq in, 308 sq cm, total 67 sq in, 432 sq cm.

ELECTRICAL EQUIPMENT 12 V; 35 Ah battery; 40 A alternator; Mitsubishi distributor; 4 headlamps - 2 for Eterna models.

DIMENSIONS AND WEIGHT wheel base: 99.02 in, 251 cm; tracks: 53.15 in, 135 cm front, 52.76 in, 134 cm rear; length: 172.44 in, 438 cm - SL Super 175.20 in, 445 cm; width: 65.16 in, 165 cm - SL Super 65.75 in, 167 cm; height: 53.54 in, 136 cm; ground clearance: 6.30 in, 16 cm; weight: L and GL models 2,172 lb, 985 kg - SL 2,194 lb, 995 kg - SL Super 2,227 lb, 1,010 kg; turning circle: 36.1 ft, 11 m; fuel tank: 13.2 imp gal, 15.8 US gal, 60 l.

BODY 5 seats, separate front seats.

OPTIONALS (for GL only) Borg-Warner 35 automatic transmission with 3 ratios (I 2.450, II 1.450, III 1, rev 2.222).

105 hp power team

See 86 hp power team, except for:

ENGINE 121.7 cu in, 1,995 cc (3.31 x 3.54 in, 84 x 90 mm); max power (JIS): 105 hp at 5,400 rpm; max torque (JIS): 119 lb ft, 16.5 kg m at 3,500 rpm; 52.6 hp/l; Mitsubishi Astron 80 twin contra-rotating balancing shafts incorporated

105 HP POWER TEAM

with crankshaft; lubrication: gear pump, full flow filter, 7.6 imp pt, 9.1 US pt, 4.3 l; 1 Stromberg 30-32 DIDTA down-draught twin barrel carburettor; cooling: 13.6 imp pt, 16.3 US pt, 7.7 l.

TRANSMISSION gears: 5, fully synchronized; ratios: I 3.369, II 2.035, III 1.360, IV 1, V 0.856, rev 3.635; width of rims: 5''; tyres: GL 6.45 x 13 - GSL models 165 SR x 14 - GSL Super models and Super Saloon 185/70 HR x 13.

PERFORMANCE max speeds: (I) 28 mph, 45 km/h; (II) 45 mph, 73 km/h; (III) 68 mph, 110 km/h; (IV) 92 mph, 148 km/h; (V) 102 mph, 165 km/h; power-weight ratio: GL 22.5 lb/hp, 10.2 kg/hp; consumption: 32.4 m/imp gal, 27 m/US gal, 8.7 l x 100 km.

BRAKES disc (for GSL Super models and Super Saloon).

DIMENSIONS AND WEIGHT length: 175.20 in, 445 cm - Eterna models 172.83 in, 439 cm; GL and GSL models 2,359 lb, 1,070 kg - GSL Super 2,425 lb, 1,100 kg - Eterna GSL Super 2,414 lb, 1,095 kg - Super Saloon 2,503 lb, 1,135 kg.

OPTIONALS (for GSL Super and Super Saloon only) Borg-Warner 35 automatic transmission with 3 ratios (I 2.450, II 1.450, III 1, rev 2.222), 3.545 axle ratio; (for Super Saloon only) power-steering.

Galant Lambda Series

PRICES (Tokyo):

1 1600 SL 2-dr Coupé	1,195,000	yen
2 1600 SL Super 2-dr Coupé	1,275,000	yen
3 Eterna 1600 SR 2-dr Coupé	1,225,000	yen
4 2000 GL 2-dr Coupé	1,277,000	yen
5 2000 GSL 2-dr Coupé	1,376,000	yen
6 2000 GSL Super 2-dr Coupé	1,475,000	yen
7 2000 Super Touring 2-dr Coupé	1,641,000	yen
8 Eterna 2000 XL 2-dr Coupé	1,460,000	yen

Power team	Standard for:	Optional for:
86 hp	1 to 3	—
105 hp	4 to 8	—

86 hp power team

ENGINE front, 4 stroke; 4 cylinders, in line; 97.45 cu in, 1,597 cc (3.03 x 3.38 in, 77 x 86 mm); compression ratio: 8.5:1; max power (JIS): 86 hp at 5,000 rpm; max torque (JIS): 98 lb ft, 13.5 kg m at 3,000 rpm; max engine rpm: 5,700; 53.9 hp/l; cast iron block, light alloy head; Mitsubishi twin contra-rotating balancing shafts incorporated with crankshaft; valves: overhead, rockers; camshafts: 1, overhead; lubrication: rotary pump, full flow filter, 7 imp pt, 8.4 US pt, 4 l; 1 Stromberg 30-32 DIDTA downdraught twin barrel carburettor; Mitsubishi MCA-Jet super lean-burn low emission engine with third air inlet valve, exhaust gas recirculation and small capacity catalyst in exhaust

MITSUBISHI Galant Sigma 2000 Super Saloon 4-dr Sedan

manifold; fuel feed: mechanical pump; water-cooled, 10.6 imp pt, 12.7 US pt, 6 l.

TRANSMISSION driving wheels: rear; clutch: single dry plate (diaphragm); gearbox: mechanical; gears: 5, fully synchronized; ratios: I 3.215, II 2, III 1.316, IV 1, V 0.853, rev 3.667; lever: central; final drive: hypoid bevel; axle ratio: 4.222; width of rims: 5''; tyres: 165 SR x 13.

PERFORMANCE max speed: 96 mph, 155 km/h; power-weight ratio: SL and SL Super models 26.5 lb/hp, 12.6 kg/hp; consumption: 32.4 m/imp gal, 27 m/US gal, 8.7 l x 100 km.

CHASSIS integral; front suspension: independent, by McPherson, coil springs/telescopic damper struts, anti-roll bar, lower wishbones; rear: rigid axle, semi-elliptic leaf-springs, telescopic dampers.

STEERING recirculating ball, variable ratio.

BRAKES front disc, rear drum.

ELECTRICAL EQUIPMENT 12 V; 35 Ah battery; 45 A alternator; Mitsubishi distributor; 4 headlamps.

DIMENSIONS AND WEIGHT wheel base: 99.02 in, 251 cm; tracks: 53.94 in, 137 cm front, 53.54 in, 136 cm rear; length: 174.41 in, 443 cm; width: 65.94 in, 167 cm; height: 52.36 in, 133 cm; ground clearance: 6.30 in, 16 cm; weight: SL and SL Super models 2,282 lb, 1,035 kg - Eterna SR 2,293 lb, 1,040 kg; turning circle: 36.1 ft, 11 m; fuel tank: 13.2 imp gal, 15.8 US gal, 60 l.

BODY 5 seats, separate front seats

OPTIONALS Borg-Warner 35 automatic transmission with ratios (I 2.450, II 1.450, III 1, rev 2.222).

105 hp power team

See 86 hp power team, except for:

ENGINE 121.7 cu in, 1,995 cc (3.31 x 3.54 in, 84 x 90 mm); max power (JIS): 105 hp at 5,400 rpm; max torque (JIS): 120 lb ft, 16.5 kg m at 3,500 rpm; lubrication: 7.6 imp pt, 9.1 US pt, 4.3 l; cooling: 12.3 imp pt, 14.8 US pt, 7 l.

TRANSMISSION gearbox ratios: I 3.369, II 2.035, III 1.360, IV 1, V 0.856, rev 3.650; axle ratio: 3.889; tyres: 165 SR x 13 - Super Touring 195/70 HR x 14.

PERFORMANCE max speeds: (I) 30 mph, 48 km/h; (II) 48 mph, 77 km/h; (III) 73 mph, 117 km/h; (IV) 98 mph, 158 km/h; (V) 103 mph, 165 km/h; power-weight ratio: GL 22.9 lb/hp, 10.4 kg/hp.

BRAKES disc, servo; lining area: front 32.9 sq in, 219 sq cm, rear 19.8 sq in, 128 sq cm, total 52.7 sq in, 340 sq cm.

DIMENSIONS AND WEIGHT length: GL, GSL and GSL Super models 177.56 in, 451 cm - Super Touring and Eterna XL models 177.16 in, 450 cm; weight: GL 2,403 lb, 1,090 kg, GSL 2,447 lb, 1,110 kg - GSL Super 2,481 lb, 1,125 kg - Eterna XL 2,492 lb, 1,130 kg - Super Touring 2,580 lb, 1,170 kg.

OPTIONALS for GSL, Eterna XL and Super Touring models 3-speed automatic transmission, hydraulic torque converter with 3 ratios (I 2.450, II 1.450, III 1, rev 2.222), 3.545 axle ratio.

Debonair Series

PRICES (Tokyo):

De Luxe 4-dr Sedan	2,280,000	y
Super De Luxe 4-dr Sedan	2,420,000	y
Super De Luxe 5-pass. 4-dr Sedan	2,480,000	y

120 hp power team

ENGINE front, 4 stroke; 4 cylinders, in line; 155.9 cu in, 2,555 cc (3.59 x 3.86 in, 91.1 x 98 mm); compression ratio: 8.2:1; max power (JIS): 120 hp at 5,000 rpm; max torque (JIS): 152 lb ft, 21 kg m at 3,000 rpm; max engine rpm: 5,500; 47 hp/l; cast iron block, light alloy head; Mitsubishi twin contra-rotating balancing shafts; 5 crankshaft bearings; valves: overhead, rockers; camshafts: 1, overhead; lubrication: rotary pump, full flow filter, 8.8 imp pt, 10.6 US pt, 5 l; 1 Stromberg 30-32 DIDTA downdraught twin barrel carburettor; emission control with thermal reactor and exhaust gas recirculation; fuel feed: mechanical pump; water-cooled, 13.2 imp pt, 15.9 US pt, 7.5 l.

TRANSMISSION driving wheels: rear; gearbox: automatic transmission, hydraulic torque converter and planetary gears with 3 ratios; ratios: I 2.680, II 1.508, III 1, rev 2.31; lever: steering column; final drive: hypoid bevel; axle ratio: 3.889; tyres: 175 SR x 14.

MITSUBISHI Galant Lambda Eterna 2000 XL 2-dr Coupé

PERFORMANCE max speeds: (I) 35 mph, 57 km/h; (II) 65 mph, 105 km/h; (III) 96 mph, 155 km/h; power-weight ratio: 25.5 lb/hp, 11.6 kg/hp; consumption: not declared.

CHASSIS integral; front suspension: independent, double wishbones, coil springs/telescopic dampers, anti-roll bar; rear: rigid axle, semi-elliptic leafsprings, telescopic dampers.

STEERING recirculating ball, servo.

BRAKES front disc, rear drum, servo.

ELECTRICAL EQUIPMENT 12 V; 60 Ah battery; 55 A alternator; Mitsubishi distributor; 4 headlamps.

DIMENSIONS AND WEIGHT wheel base: 105.91 in, 269 cm; front and rear track: 54.72 in, 139 cm; length: 183.86 in, 467 cm; width: 66.54 in, 169 cm; height: 57.48 in, 146 cm; ground clearance: 6.69 in, 17 cm; weight: 3,065 lb, 1,390 kg; weight distribution: 56% front, 44% rear; fuel tank: 15.4 imp gal, 18.5 US gal, 70 l.

BODY 5 seats, separate front seats.

Jeep Series

PRICES (Tokyo):

1 H-J58	1,208,000	yen
2 H-J56	1,248,000	yen
3 H-J26	1,332,000	yen
4 J54	1,343,000	yen
5 J24	1,427,000	yen

Power team:	Standard for:	Optional for:
100 hp	1	—
110 hp	2,3	—
80 hp (Diesel engine)	4,5	—

100 hp power team

ENGINE front, 4 stroke; 4 cylinders, vertical, in line; 121.7 cu in, 1,995 cc (3.31 x 3.54 in, 84 x 90 mm); compression ratio: 8.5:1; max power (JIS): 100 hp at 5,000 rpm; max torque (JIS): 123 lb ft, 17 kg m at 3,000 rpm; max engine rpm: 5,400; 50.1 hp/l; cast iron block, light alloy head; 5 crankshaft bearings; valves: overhead, Vee-slanted, rockers; camshafts: 1, overhead; lubrication: rotary pump, full flow filter, 7.6 imp pt, 9.1 US pt, 4.3 l; 1 Stromberg 30-32 DIDTA downdraught twin barrel carburettor; fuel feed: mechanical pump; water-cooled, 14 imp pt, 17 US pt, 8 l.

TRANSMISSION driving wheels: front (automatically-engaged with transfer box) and rear; clutch: single dry plate (diaphragm), hydraulically controlled; gearbox: mechanical; gears: 4, fully synchronized; ratios: I 2.971, II 1.795, III 1.345, IV 1, rev 3.157; transfer box: high 1, low 2.465; lever: central; final drive: hypoid bevel; axle ratio: 5.375; width of rims: 4.5''; tyres: 6.00 x 16.

PERFORMANCE max speeds: (I) 27 mph, 43 km/h; (II) 47 mph, 75 km/h; (III) 58 mph, 94 km/h; (IV) 75 mph, 120 km/h; power-weight ratio: 23.8 lb/hp, 10.8 kg/hp; carrying capacity: 551 lb, 250 kg; speed in direct drive at 1,000 rpm: 13.8 mph, 22.2 km/h; consumption: not declared.

MITSUBISHI Debonair Series

MITSUBISHI Jeep H-J58

CHASSIS ladder frame; front and rear suspension: rigid axle, semi-elliptic leafsprings, telescopic dampers.

STEERING cam and lever, variable ratio.

BRAKES drum.

ELECTRICAL EQUIPMENT 12 V; 35 Ah battery; 35 A alternator; Mitsubishi distributor; 2 headlamps.

DIMENSIONS AND WEIGHT wheel base: 79.92 in, 203 cm; front and rear track: 48.62 in, 123 cm; length: 133.46 in, 339 cm; width: 65.55 in, 166 cm; height: 75 in, 190 cm; ground clearance: 8.27 in, 21 cm; weight: 2,381 lb, 1,080 kg; weight distribution: 55% front, 45% rear; turning circle: 40 ft, 12.2 m; fuel tank: 9.7 imp gal, 11.6 US gal, 44 l.

BODY open; 2 detachable doors; 4 seats, separate front seats.

110 hp power team

See 100 hp power team, except for:

ENGINE 145.5 cu in, 2,384 cc (3.46 x 3.86 in, 88 x 98 mm); compression ratio: 8:1; max power (JIS): 110 hp at 5,000 rpm; max torque (JIS): 145 lb ft, 20 kg m at 3,000 rpm; 46.1 hp/l.

TRANSMISSION (for H-J26 only) lever: steering column.

PERFORMANCE power-weight ratio: H-J56 21.7 lb/hp, 9.9 kg/hp.

STEERING (for H-J26 only) recirculating ball.

ELECTRICAL EQUIPMENT 50 Ah battery.

DIMENSIONS AND WEIGHT wheel base: H-J26 87.60 in, 222 cm; front and rear track: H-J26 50.79 in, 129 cm; length: H-J26 145.08 in, 368 cm; width: H-J26 65.75 in, 167 cm; height: H-J26 76.77 in, 195 cm; weight: H-J56 2,392 lb, 1,085 kg - H-J26 2,844 lb, 1,290 kg.

BODY (for H-J26 only) 7 seats.

80 hp power team

See 100 hp power team, except for:

ENGINE Diesel, 4 stroke; 162.3 cu in, 2,659 cc (3.62 x 3.94 in, 92 x 100 mm); compression ratio: 20:1; max power (JIS): 80 hp at 3,700 rpm; max torque (JIS): 130 lb ft, 18 kg m at 2,200 rpm; 30.1 hp/l.

TRANSMISSION transfer box ratios: high 0.933, low 2.384; (for J24 only) lever: steering column.

PERFORMANCE power-weight ratio: J54 29.9 lb/hp, 13.6 kg/hp.

STEERING (for J24 only) recirculating ball.

ELECTRICAL EQUIPMENT 24 V; 70 Ah x 2 batteries.

DIMENSIONS AND WEIGHT wheels base: J24 87.60 in, 222 cm; front and rear track: J24 50.79 in, 129 cm; length: J24

145.08 in, 368 cm; width: J24 65.75 in, 167 cm; height: J24 76.77 in, 195 cm; weight: J54 2,392 lb, 1,085 kg - J24 2,844 lb, 1,290 kg; fuel tank: 9.9 imp gal, 11.9 US gal, 45 l.

BODY (for J24 only) 7 seats.

NISSAN   JAPAN

Pulsar Series

PRICES (Tokyo):

1 1200 Custom 4-dr Sedan	774,000	yen
2 1200 Custom D 4-dr Sedan	804,000	yen
3 1200 TS 4-dr Sedan	870,000	yen
4 1200 TS Coupé	918,000	yen
5 1200 Standard Hatchback	740,000	yen
6 1200 Custom Hatchback	766,000	yen
7 1200 Custom D Hatchback	796,000	yen
8 1200 TS Hatchback	860,000	yen
9 1400 TS 4-dr Sedan	945,000	yen
10 1400 TS-G 4-dr Sedan	1,013,000	yen
11 1400 TS Coupé	993,000	yen
12 1400 TS Hatchback	925,000	yen
13 1400 TS-X Hatchback	1,010,000	yen
14 1400 TS-GE 4-dr Sedan	1,108,000	yen
15 1400 TS-XE 4-dr Sedan	1,070,000	yen
16 1400 TS-XE Coupé	1,106,000	yen
17 1400 TS-XE Hatchback	1,080,000	yen

Power team:	Standard for:	Optional for:
70 hp	1 to 8	—
80 hp	9 to 13	—
92 hp	14 to 17	—

70 hp power team

ENGINE front, transverse, 4 stroke; 4 cylinders, in line; 75.5 cu in, 1,237 cc (2.95 x 2.75 in, 75 x 70 mm); compression ratio: 9:1; max power (JIS): 70 hp at 6,000 rpm; max torque (JIS): 74 lb ft, 10.2 kg m at 3,600 rpm; max engine rpm: 6,000; 56.6 hp/l; cast iron cylinder block, light alloy head; 5 crankshaft bearings; valves: overhead, push-rods and rockers; camshafts: 1, side; lubrication: rotary pump, full flow filter, 5.8 imp pt, 7 US pt, 3.3 l; 1 Hitachi DCH 306-42 downdraught twin barrel carburettor; emission control with catalytic converter, secondary air induction and exhaust gas recirculation; fuel feed: mechanical pump; water-cooled, 8.8 imp pt, 10.6 US pt, 5 l.

TRANSMISSION driving wheels: front; clutch: single dry plate (diaphragm); gearbox: mechanical; gears: 4, fully synchronized; ratios: I 3.673, II 2.217, III 1.433, IV 1, rev 4.093; lever: central; final drive: helical spur gears; axle ratio: 3.933 (for Standard only 3.471); width of rims: 4''; tyres: 6.00 x 12.

PERFORMANCE max speeds: (I) 27 mph, 43 km/h; (II) 43 mph, 70 km/h; (III) 68 mph, 110 km/h; (IV) 90 mph, 145 km/h; power-weight ratio: Custom 4-dr Sedan 24.9 lb/hp, 11.3 kg/hp; carrying capacity: 882 lb, 400 kg; consumption: 42.1 m/imp gal, 35.1 m/US gal, 6.7 l x 100 km.

NISSAN Pulsar 1400 TS-G 4-dr Sedan

70 HP POWER TEAM

CHASSIS integral; front suspension: independent, by Mc-Pherson, coil springs/telescopic damper struts, lower wishbones; rear: independent, trailing arms, coil springs, telescopic dampers.

STEERING rack-and-pinion; turns lock to lock: 3.30.

BRAKES drum (front disc for TS models only), servo; swept area: front 42.2 sq in, 272 sq cm, rear 42.2 sq cm, 272 sq cm, total 84.4 sq in, 544 sq cm - for TS models front 14.3 sq in, 92 sq cm, rear 42.2 sq in, 272 sq cm, total 56.5 sq in, 364 sq cm.

ELECTRICAL EQUIPMENT 12 V; 40 Ah battery; 35 A alternator; Hitachi distributor; 2 headlamps.

DIMENSIONS AND WEIGHT wheel base: 94.29 in, 239 cm; tracks: 54.13 in, 137 cm (for TS and Custom D models 53.74 in, 136 cm) front, 52.86 in, 133 cm rear; length: 153.15 in, 389 cm; width: 62.99 in, 160 cm; height: sedans 53.54 in, 136 cm - hatchbacks 53.54 in, 136 cm - coupés 52.16 in, 132 cm; ground clearance: 6.69 in, 17 cm; weight: Custom models 1,742 lb, 790 kg - TS 4-dr Sedan 1,764 lb, 800 kg - TS Coupé 1,775 lb, 805 kg - Standard Hatchback 1,720 lb, 780 kg; weight distribution: 63% front, 37% rear; turning circle: 36.6 ft, 10.8 m; fuel tank: 11 imp gal, 13.2 US gal, 50 l.

BODY 5 seats separate front seats.

OPTIONALS (only for hatchbacks and coupés) 5-speed fully synchronized gearbox (I 4.018, II 2.475, III 1.720, IV 1.254, V 1, rev 4.093), axle ratio 3.471.

80 hp power team

See 70 hp power team, except for:

ENGINE 85.2 cu in, 1,397 cc (2.99 x 3.03 in, 76 x 77 mm); max power (JIS): 80 hp at 6,000 rpm; max torque (JIS): 83 lb ft, 11.5 kg m at 3,600 rpm; 1 Hitachi DCH 306-53 downdraught twin barrel carburettor.

TRANSMISSION gearbox ratios: I 3.275, II 1.977, III 1.383, IV 1, rev 3.649 (for Coupé only gears: 5; ratios: I 4.018, II 2.475, III 1.720, IV 1.254, V 1, rev 4.093); axle ratio: 3.933 (for Coupé, only 3.471; width of rims: 4.5''; tyres: 155 SR x 13 - Coupé TS-X Hatchback 165/70 SR x 13.

CHASSIS front suspension: anti-roll bar.

PERFORMANCE max speeds: (I) 27 mph, 43 km/h; (II) 50 mph, 80 km/h; (III) 73 mph, 117 km/h; (IV) 93.2 mph, 150 km/h (for Coupé only: (I) 29 mph, 47 km/h; (II) 46 mph, 74 km/h; (III) 71 mph, 114 km/h; (IV) 89 mph, 143 km/h; (V) 93 mph, 150 km/h); power-weight ratio: TS 4-dr Sedan 22.9 lb/hp, 10.4 kg/hp; consumption: 38.1 m/imp gal, 31/7 m/US gal, 7.4 l x 100 km.

DIMENSIONS AND WEIGHT tracks: 54.13 in, 137 cm front, 52.95 in, 134 cm rear; length: 155.11 in, 394 cm; width: 63.78 in, 162 cm; weight: TS 4-dr Sedan, TS Coupé and TS Hatchback 1,830 lb, 830 kg - TS-G 4-dr Sedan, and TS-X Hatchback 1,852 lb, 840 kg.

OPTIONALS 5-speed fully synchronized mechanical gearbox (except for Coupé); Nissan Sportsmatic semi-automatic transmission, hydraulic torque converter with 3 ratios (I 1.603, II 1, III 0.726, rev 1.846), solenoid operated clutch, 4.629 axle ratio; 5'' wide rims with light alloy wheels.

92 hp power team

See 80 hp power team except for:

ENGINE max power (JIS): 92 hp at 6,400 rpm; max torque (JIS): 85 lb ft, 11.7 kg m at 3,600 rpm; max engine rpm: 6,800; 65.8 hp/l: Nissan EGI (Bosch L-Jetronic) electronic injection; fuel feed: electric pump.

TRANSMISSION tyres: 165/70 SR x 13.

PERFORMANCE max speed: 99 mph, 160 km/h; power-weight ratio: TS-GE 4-dr Sedan 20.4 lb/hp, 9.2 kg/hp; consumption: 36.7 m/imp gal, 30.6 m.US gal, 7.7 l x 100 km.

DIMENSIONS AND WEIGHT weight: TS-GE 4-dr Sedan, TS-XE Coupé and TS-XE Hatchback 1,874 lb, 850 kg - TS-XE 4-dr Sedan, 1,863 lb, 845 kg.

Sunny Series

PRICES (Tokyo):

1 1200 CT 2-dr Sedan	737,000	yen
2 1200 CT 4-dr Sedan	757,000	yen
3 1200 City De Luxe 2-dr Sedan	760,000	yen
4 1200 City De Luxe 4-dr Sedan	780,000	yen
5 1200 De Luxe 2-dr Sedan	788,000	yen
6 1200 De Luxe 4-dr Sedan	808,000	yen
7 1200 De Luxe Coupé	838,000	yen
8 1200 GL 2-dr Sedan	850,000	yen
9 1200 GL 4-dr Sedan	870,000	yen
10 1200 GL Coupé	910,000	yen
11 1400 De Luxe 2-dr Sedan	833,000	yen
12 1400 De Luxe 4-dr Sedan	853,000	yen
13 1400 De Luxe Coupé	883,000	yen
14 1400 GL 2-dr Sedan	902,000	yen
15 1400 GL 4-dr Sedan	917,000	yen
16 1400 GL Coupé	947,000	yen
17 1400 SGL 4-dr Sedan	975,000	yen
18 1400 SGL Coupé	1,010,000	yen
19 1400 GX 4-dr Sedan	962,000	yen
20 1400 GX Coupé	1,001,000	yen
21 1400 SGX 4-dr Sedan	1,020,000	yen
22 1400 SGX Coupé	1,089,000	yen
23 1400 GX-E 4-dr Sedan	1,032,000	yen
24 1400 GX-E Coupé	1,071,000	yen
25 1400 SGX-E 4-dr Sedan	1,090,000	yen
26 1400 SGX-E Coupé	1,134,000	yen

For USA prices, see price index.

Power team:	Standard for:	Optional for:
70 hp	1 to 10	—
80 hp	11 to 22	—
92 hp	23 to 26	—

70 hp power team

ENGINE front, 4 stroke; 4 cylinders, vertical, in line; 75.48

cu in, 1,237 cc (2.95 x 2.76 in, 75 x 70 mm); compression ratio: 9:1; max power (JIS): 70 hp at 6,000 rpm; max torque (JIS): 73.9 lb ft, 10.2 kg m at 3,600 rpm; max engine rpm: 6,250; 56.6 hp/l; cast iron cylinder block, light alloy head; 5 crankshaft bearings; valves: overhead, push-rods and rockers; camshafts: 1, side; lubrication: rotary pump, full flow filter, 6 imp pt, 7.2 US pt, 3.4 l; 1 Hitachi DCH 306-41 downdraught twin barrel carburettor; emission control with catalytic converter, secondary air injection and exhaust gas recirculation; fuel feed: mechanical pump; water-cooled, 7 imp pt, 8.4 US pt, 4 l.

TRANSMISSION driving wheels: rear; clutch: single dry plate (diaphragm); gearbox: mechanical; gears: 4, fully synchronized; ratios: I 3.757, II 2.169, III 1.404, IV 1, rev 3.640; lever: central; final drive: hypoid bevel; axle ratio: 3.889; width of rims: 4''; tyres: 6.00 x 12.

PERFORMANCE max speeds: (I) 25 mph, 40 km/h; (II) 44 mph, 70 km/h; (III) 70 mph, 112 km/h; (IV) 90 mph, 145 km/h; power-weight ratio: CT 2-dr Sedan 24.9 lb/hp, 11.3 kg/hp; speed in direct drive at 1,000 rpm: 16.4 mph, 26.4 km/h; consumption: 40.9 m/imp gal, 34.1 m/US gal, 6.9 l x 100 km.

CHASSIS integral; front suspension: independent by Mc-Pherson, coil springs/telescopic damper struts, lower wishbones (trailing links); rear: rigid axle, lower trailing rods, upper torque rods, coil springs, telescopic dampers.

STEERING recirculating ball; turns lock to lock: 3.50.

BRAKES drum (front disc for GL Coupé only); lining area: front 42.2 sq in, 272 sq cm, rear 42.2 sq in, 272 sq cm, total 84.4 sq in, 544 sq cm - GL Coupé front 13.3 sq in, 85.6 sq cm, total 55.5 sq in, 357.6 sq cm.

ELECTRICAL EQUIPMENT 12 V; 32 Ah battery; alternator; Hitachi distributor; 2 headlamps.

DIMENSIONS AND WEIGHT wheel base: 92.13 in, 234 cm; tracks: 51.18 in, 130 cm front, 51.18 in, 130 cm rear; length: 155.12 in, 394 cm - GL models 157.28 in, 399 cm; width: 62.20 in, 158 cm; height: 53.94 in, 137 cm - coupés 52.76 in, 134 cm; ground clearance: 6.50 in, 16 cm; weight: CT 2-dr 1,742 lb, 790 kg - CT 4-dr 1,764 lb, 800 kg - De Luxe 2-dr 1,753 lb, 795 kg - De Luxe 4-dr, coupé and GL 2-dr 1,775 lb, 805 kg - GL 4-dr and coupé 1,797 lb, 815 kg; turning circle: 31.5 ft, 9.6 m; fuel tank: 11 imp gal, 13.2 US gal, 50 l.

OPTIONALS 5-speed fully synchronized mechanical gearbox (I 3.513, II 2.710, III 1.378, IV 1, V 0.846), rev 3.464.

80 hp power team

See 70 hp power team, except for:

ENGINE 85.2 cu in, 1,397 cc (2.99 x 3.03 in, 76 x 77 mm); max power (JIS): 80 hp at 6,000 rpm; max torque (JIS): 83 lb ft, 11.5 kg m at 3,600 rpm; max engine rpm: 6,600; 57.3 hp/l; 1 Hitachi DCH 306-51 or 52 downdraught twin barrel carburettor.

TRANSMISSION gearbox ratios: I 3.513, II 2.170, III 1.378, IV 1, rev 3.764; tyres: GX and SGX sedans 155 SR x 13 - GX and SGX coupés 165/70 HR x 13.

PERFORMANCE max speeds: (I) 27 mph, 44 km/h; (II) 45 mph, 72 km/h; (III) 70 mph, 112 km/h; (IV) 93 mph, 150 km/h; power-weight ratio: De Luxe 2-dr Sedan 22.6 lb/hp, 10.2 kg/hp; consumption: 38.1 m/imp gal, 31.8 m/US gal, 7.4 l x 100 km.

BRAKES front disc, rear drum; lining area: front 13.3 sq in, 85.6 sq cm, rear 42.2 sq in, 272 sq cm, total 55.5 sq in, 357.6 sq cm.

DIMENSIONS AND WEIGHT tracks: 52.36 in, 133 cm front; width: 62.60 in, 159 cm (except for De Luxe models); weight: De Luxe sedans and Coupé 1,808 lb, 820 kg - GL and SGL sedans and coupés 1,852 lb, 840 kg - GX and SGX sedans and coupés 1,895 lb, 865 kg.

OPTIONALS 5-speed fully synchronized mechanical, gearbox (I 3.513, II 2.170, III 1.378, IV 1, V 0.846, rev 3.464); JATCO automatic transmission with 3 ratios (I 2.458, II 1.458, III 1, rev 2.182).

92 hp power team

See 80 hp power team, except for:

ENGINE max power (JIS): 92 hp at 6,400 rpm; max torque (JIS): 85 lb ft, 11.7 kg m at 3,600 rpm; max engine rpm: 6,800; 65.8 hp/l; Nissan EGI (Bosch L-jetronic) electronic injection; fuel feed: electric pump.

TRANSMISSION tyres: 165/70 HR x 13.

PERFORMANCE max speed: 99 mph, 160 km/h.

NISSAN Sunny 1400 SGL 4-dr Sedan

NISSAN Violet 1600 GL 4-dr Sedan

Violet - Auster - Stanza Series

PRICES EX WORKS:

1 Violet 1400 Standard Sedan	858,000	yen
2 Violet 1400 De Luxe Sedan	926,000	yen
3 Violet 1400 De Luxe Hatchback Coupé	956,000	yen
4 Auster 1400 De Luxe Sedan	926,000	yen
5 Auster 1400 De Luxe Hatchback Coupé	956,000	yen
6 Violet 1400 GL Sedan	969,000	yen
7 Violet 1400 GL Hatchback Coupé	999,000	yen
8 Violet 1600 De Luxe Sedan	951,000	yen
9 Auster 1600 De Luxe Sedan	951,000	yen
10 Violet 1600 GL Sedan	999,000	yen
11 Violet 1600 GL Hatchback Coupé	1,029,000	yen
12 Violet 1600 GL-L Sedan	1,037,000	yen
13 Auster 1600 CS Sedan	1,042,000	yen
14 Auster 1600 CS Hatchback Coupé	1,072,000	yen
15 Violet 1600 GL-L Hatchback Coupé	1,067,000	yen
16 Violet 1600 GX Sedan	1,035,000	yen
17 Violet 1600 GX Hatchback Coupé	1,065,000	yen
18 Auster 1600 CS-L Sedan	1,094,000	yen
19 Auster 1600 CS-L Hatchback Coupé	1,124,000	yen
20 Stanza 1600 Luxury Sedan	976,000	yen
21 Stanza 1600 Extra Sedan	1,032,000	yen
22 Stanza 1600 Maxima Sedan	1,106,000	yen
23 Violet 1600 GX-EL Sedan	1,181,000	yen
24 Violet 1600 GX-EL Hatchback Coupé	1,211,000	yen
25 Auster 1600 CS-E Sedan	1,112,000	yen
26 Auster 1600 CS-EL Sedan	1,168,000	yen
27 Auster 1600 CS-E Hatchback Coupé	1,142,000	yen
28 Auster 1600 CS-EL Hatchback Coupé	1,198,000	yen
29 Stanza 1600 GT-E Sedan	1,172,000	yen
30 Stanza 1600 Maxima GT-E Sedan	1,222,000	yen
31 Stanza 1800 Extra Sedan	1,057,000	yen
32 Stanza 1800 Maxima Sedan	1,141,000	yen
33 Stanza 1800 Maxima GT-E Sedan	1,262,000	yen

For USA prices, see price index.

Power team:	Standard for:	Optional for:
80 hp	1 to 7	—
95 hp	8 to 22	—
105 hp	23 to 30	—
105 hp (1,770 cc)	31 to 32	—
115 hp	33	—

80 hp power team

ENGINE front, 4 stroke; 4 cylinders, vertical, in line; 85.2 cu in, 1,397 cc (2.99 x 3.03 in, 76 x 77 mm); compression ratio: 9:1; max power (JIS): 80 hp at 6,000 rpm; max torque (JIS): 83.3 lb ft, 11.5 kg m at 3,600 rpm; max engine rpm: 6,250; 57.3 hp/l; cast iron cylinder block; light alloy head; 5 crankshaft bearings; valves: overhead, in line, push-rods and rockers; camshafts: 1, side; lubrication: rotary pump, full flow filter, 6 imp pt, 7.2 US pt, 3.4 l; 1 Hitachi DCH 306-32 downdraught twin barrel carburettor; emission control with catalytic converter, secondary air induction and exhaust gas recirculation; fuel feed: mechanical pump; water-cooled, 7 imp pt, 8.4 US pt, 4 l.

TRANSMISSION driving wheels: rear; clutch: single dry plate (diaphragm); gearbox: mechanical; gears: 4, fully synchronized; ratios: I 3.513, II 2.170, III 1.378, IV 1, rev

3.764; lever: central; final drive: hypoid bevel; axle ratio: 3.889; width of rims: 4.5''; tyres: 5.60 x 13.

PERFORMANCE max speeds: (I) 28 mph, 45 km/h; (II) 47 mph, 75 km/h; (III) 75 mph, 120 km/h; (IV) 93 mph, 150 km/h; power-weight ratio: De Luxe Sedan 24.1 lb/hp, 10.9 kg/hp; consumption: 38.1 m/imp gal, 31.7 m/US gal, 7.4 l x 100 km.

CHASSIS integral; front suspension: independent, by McPherson, coil springs/telescopic dampers struts, lower wishbones (trailing links), anti-roll bar; rear: rigid axle, lower trailing rods, upper torque rods, coil springs, telescopic dampers.

STEERING recirculating ball; turns lock to lock: 3.70.

BRAKES front disc, rear drum; lining area: front 17.4 sq in, 112 sq cm, rear 54 sq in, 348 sq cm, total 71.4 sq in, 460 sq cm.

ELECTRICAL EQUIPMENT 12 V; 32 Ah battery; 50 A alternator; Hitachi distributor; 4 headlamps.

DIMENSIONS AND WEIGHT wheel base: 94.49 in, 240 cm; tracks: 52.36 in, 133 cm; length: 167.72 in, 426 cm; width: 62.99 in, 160 cm; height: sedans 54.72 in, 139 cm - coupés 53.15 in, 135 cm; ground clearance: 6.30 in, 16 cm; weight: De Luxe Sedan 1,929 lb, 875 kg - De Luxe Hatchback Coupé 1,985 lz, 900 kg - Violet 1400 GL Hatchback Coupé 1,996 lb, 905 kg; weight distribution: 55% front, 45% rear; turning circle: 32.8 ft, 10 m; fuel tank: 11 imp gal, 13.2 US gal, 50 l.

95 hp power team

See 80 hp power team, except for:

ENGINE 97.3 cu in, 1,595 cc (3.27 x 2.90 in, 83 x 73.7 mm); compression ratio: 8.5:1; max power (JIS): 95 hp at 6,000 rpm; max torque (JIS): 98 lb ft, 13.5 kg m at 3,600 rpm; 59.6 hp/l; Nissan NAPS-Z fast burn cylinder head with two spark plugs per cylinder; valves: overhead, Vee-slanted, rockers; camshafts: 1, overhead; lubrication: 8.1 imp pt, 9.7 US pt, 4.6 l; 1 Hitachi 21A 304-201 downdraught twin barrel carburettor; cooling system: 10.6 imp pt, 12.7 US pt, 6 l.

TRANSMISSION gearbox ratios: I 3.657, II 2.177, III 1.419, IV 1, rev 3.638; axle ratio: 3.700; tyres: De Luxe, GL and Luxury models 5.60 x 13 - Extra and Maxima sedans 6.45 x 13 - GX, CS and CS-L models 165 SR x 13.

PERFORMANCE max speeds: (I) 27 mph, 43 km/h; (II) 60 mph, 80 km/h; (III) 78 mph, 126 km/h; (IV) 99 mph, 160 km/h; power-weight ratio: De Luxe Sedan 21.5 lb/hp, 9.7 kg/hp; consumption: 38.1 m/imp gal, 31.7 m/US gal, 7.4 l x 100 km.

CHASSIS rear suspension: anti-roll bar.

DIMENSIONS AND WEIGHT length: Stanza models 168.31 in, 427 cm; weight: De Luxe sedans 2,040 lb, 925 kg - GL Sedan 2,051 lb, 930 kg - Luxury Sedan 2,062 lb, 935 kg - GX, CS, Extra and Maxima sedans 2,073 lb, 940 kg - GL Hatchback Coupé 2,095 lb, 950 kg - GX and CS Hatchback Coupé 2,117 lb, 960 kg.

OPTIONALS 5-speed fully synchronized mechanical gearbox (I 3.657, II 2.177, III 1.419, IV 1, V 0.852, rev 3.860); automatic transmission with 3 ratios (I 2.458, II 1.458, III 1, rev 2.182), 3.889 axle ratio, max speed 93 mph, 150 km/h.

105 hp power team

See 80 hp power team, ecept for:

ENGINE 97.3 cu in, 1,595 cc (3.27 x 2.90 in, 83 x 73.7 mm); max power (JIS): 105 hp at 6,000 rpm; max torque (JIS): 100 lb ft, 13.8 kg m at 4,000 rpm; 65.8 hp/l; Nissan NAPS-Z fast burn cylinder head with two spark plugs per cylinder; valves: overhead, Vee-slanted, rockers; camshafts: 1, overhead; lubrication: 8.1 imp pt, 9.7 US pt, 4.6 l; Bosch electronically-controlled injection system; fuel feed: electric pump; cooling system: 10.6 imp pt, 12.7 US pt, 6 l.

TRANSMISSION gearbox ratios: I 3.657, II 2.177, III 1.419, IV 1, 3.638; axle ratio: 3.700; tyres: Auster coupés and Stanza Maxima GT-E Sedan 165 SR x 13 - Stanza GT-E Sedan 6.45 x 13.

PERFORMANCE max speed: 103 mph, 165 km/h; power-weight ratio: Violet GX-EL Sedan 20.2 lb/hp, 9.1 kg/hp.

CHASSIS rear suspension: anti-roll bar.

DIMENSIONS AND WEIGHT length: Stanza models 168.31 in, 427 cm; weight Violet and Auster sedans 2,117 lb, 960 kg - Violet and Auster coupés 2,161 lb, 980 kg - Stanza models 2,128 lb, 965 kg.

OPTIONALS 5-speed fully synchronized mechanical gearbox (I 3.657, II 2.117, III 1.419, IV 1, V 0.852, rev 3.860); automatic transmission with 3 ratios (I 2.458, II 1.458, III 1, rev 2.182), 3.889 axle ratio.

105 hp power team (1,770 cc)

See 80 hp power team, except for:

ENGINE 108 cu in, 1,770 cc (3.35 x 3.07 in, 85 x 78 mm); max power (JIS): 105 hp at 6,000 rpm; max torque (JIS): 109 lb ft, 15 kg m at 3,600 rpm; 59.3 hp/l; Nissan NAPS-Z fast burn cylinder head with two spark plugs per cylinder; valves: overhead, Vee-slanted, rockers; camshafts: 1, overhead; lubrication: 8.1 imp pt, 9.7 US pt, 4.6 l; 1 Hitachi 21A 304-20 downdraught twin barrel carburettor; cooling system: 10.6 imp pt, 12.7 US pt, 6 l.

TRANSMISSION gearbox; ratios: I 3.382, II 2.013, III 1.312, IV 1, rev 3.665; axle ratio: 3.700; tyres: Extra 6.45 x 13 - Maxima 165 SR x 13.

PERFORMANCE max speeds: (I) 29 mph, 46 km/h; (II) 54 mph, 87 km/h; (II) 81 mph, 130 km/h; (IV) 106 mph, 170 km/h; power-weight ratio: 19 lb/hp, 9 kg/hp; consumption: 36.7 m/imp gal, 30.6 m/US gal, 7.7 l x 100 km.

DIMENSIONS AND WEIGHT length: 168.31 in, 427 cm; weight: 2,095 lb, 950 kg.

OPTIONALS 5-speed fully synchronized mechanical gearbox (I 3.382, II 2.013, III 1.312, IV 1, V 0.854, rev 3.570); automatic transmission with 3 ratios (I 2.458, II 1.458, III 1, rev 2.182), 3.889 axle ratio, max speed 102 mph, 165 km/h.

115 hp power team

See 105 hp (1,770 cc) power team, except for:

ENGINE max power (JIS): 115 hp at 6,000 rpm; max torque (JIS): 112 lb ft, 15.5 kg m at 3,600 rpm; 65 hp/l; Bosch electronic fuel injection; fuel feed: electric pump.

PERFORMANCE max speed: 109 mph, 175 km/h; power-weight ratio: 18.7 lb/hp, 8.5 kg/hp; consumption: 35.3 m/imp gal, 29.4 m/US gal, 8 l x 100 km.

CHASSIS rear suspension: anti-roll bar.

DIMENSIONS AND WEIGHT weight: 2,150 lb, 975 kg.

Datsun Bluebird Series

PRICES (Tokyo):

1 1600 De Luxe Sedan	994,000	yen
2 1600 GL Sedan	1,071,000	yen
3 1600 GL-L Sedan	1,114,000	yen
4 1600 GL-L Hardtop	1,149,000	yen
5 1800 De Luxe Sedan	1,017,000	yen
6 1800 GL Sedan	1,127,000	yen
7 1800 GL Hardtop	1,162,000	yen
8 1800 GF Sedan	1,284,000	yen
9 1800 GF Hardtop	1,319,000	yen
10 1800 SSS Sedan	1,193,000	yen
11 1800 SSS Hardtop	1,228,000	yen
12 1800 G4 Sedan	1,156,000	yen
13 1800 G4 Hardtop	1,192,000	yen
14 1800 GF-E Sedan	1,364,000	yen
15 1800 GF-E Hardtop	1,399,000	yen
16 1800 SSS-E Sedan	1,301,000	yen
17 1800 SSS-E Hardtop	1,336,000	yen
18 1800 SSS-ES Sedan	1,451,000	yen
19 1800 SSS-ES Hardtop	1,451,000	yen
20 2000 G6-L Sedan	1,366,000	yen
21 2000 G6-L Hardtop	1,402,000	yen
22 2000 G6-F Sedan	1,508,000	yen
23 2000 G6-F Hardtop	1,544,000	yen
24 2000 G6-E Sedan	1,446,000	yen
25 2000 G6-E Hardtop	1,482,000	yen
26 2000 G6-EL Sedan	1,580,000	yen
27 2000 G6-EL Hardtop	1,616,000	yen
28 2000 G6-EF Sedan	1,718,000	yen
29 2000 G6-EF Hardtop	1,754,000	yen

For USA prices, see price index.

Power team:	Standard for:	Optional for:
95 hp	1 to 4	—
105 hp	5 to 13	—
115 hp	14 to 19	—
115 hp (1,998 cc)	20 to 23	—
130 hp	24 to 29	—

95 hp power team

ENGINE front, 4 stroke; 4 cylinders, in line; 97.3 cu in, 1,595 cc (3.27 x 2.90 in, 83 x 73.7 mm); compression ratio: 8.5:1; max power (JIS): 95 hp at 6,000 rpm; max torque (JIS): 98 lb ft, 13.5 kg m at 3,600 rpm; 59.6 hp/l; cast iron cylinder block, light alloy head; 5 crankshaft bearings; valves: ovehread, Vee-slanted, rockers; camshafts: 1, overhead; lubrication: rotary pump, full flow filter, 8.1 imp pt, 9.7 US pt, 4.6 l; Nissan NAPS-Z fast burn engine with two spark plugs per cylinder; Nikki downdraught twin barrel

carburettor; emission control with catalytic converter, secondary air injection and exhaust gas recirculation; fuel feed: mechanical pump; water-cooled, 10.6 imp pt, 12.7 US pt, 6 l.

TRANSMISSION driving wheels: rear; clutch: single dry plate (diaphragm); gearbox: mechanical; gears: 4, fully synchronized; ratios: I 3.657, II 2.177, III 1.419, IV 1, rev 3.638; lever: central; final drive: hypoid bevel; axle ratio: 3.889; width of rims: 4.5''; tyres: 6.45 x 14 - GL-L models 165 SR x 13.

PERFORMANCE max speeds: (I) 28 mph, 45 km/h; (II) 49 mph, 79 km/h; (III) 75 mph, 120 km/h; (IV) 103 mph, 165 km/h; power-weight ratio: De Luxe Sedan 23.4 lb/hp, 10.6 kg/hp; carrying capacity: 882 lb, 400 kg; consumption: 39.5 m/imp gal, 32.9 m/US gal, 7.1 l x 100 km.

CHASSIS integral; front suspension: independent, by McPherson, coil springs/telescopic damper struts, lower wishbones (trailing links), anti-roll bar; rear: rigid axle, lower trailing arms, upper torque rods, coil springs, telescopic dampers.

STEERING recirculating ball; turns lock to lock: 3.40.

BRAKES front disc, rear drum, servo; lining area: front 15.5 sq in, 100 sq cm, rear 54 sq in, 348 sq cm, total 69.5 sq in, 448 sq cm.

ELECTRICAL EQUIPMENT 12 V; 35 Ah battery; 50 A alternator; Hitachi distributor; 4 headlamps.

NISSAN Datsun Bluebird 1800 SSS-ES Sedan

DIMENSIONS AND WEIGHT wheel base: 98.43 in, 250 cm; tracks: 52.76 in, 134 cm front, 53.15 in, 135 cm rear; length: De Luxe Sedan 169.88 in, 431 cm - GL and GL-L models 171.06 in, 434 cm; width: 64.17 in, 163 cm; height: sedans 54.72 in, 139 cm - hardtop 54.33 in, 138 cm; ground clearance: 6.89 in, 17.5 cm; weight: De Luxe Sedan 2,227 lb, 1,010 kg - GL and GL-L models 2,249 lb, 1,020 kg; weight distribution: 55.5% front, 44.5% rear; turning circle: 36.1 ft, 11 m; fuel tank: 13.2 imp gal, 15.8 US gal, 60 l.

BODY 5 seats, separate front seats, reclining backrests, built-in headrests.

105 hp power team

See 95 hp power team, except for:

ENGINE 108 cu in, 1,770 cc (3.35 x 3.07 in, 85 x 78 mm); max power (JIS): 105 hp at 6,000 rpm; max torque (JIS): 109 lb ft, 15 kg m at 3,600 rpm; 59.3 hp/l.

TRANSMISSION gearbox ratios: I 3.382, II 2.013, III 1.312, IV 1, rev 3.365; axle ratio: 3.889 - SSS models 4.111; tyres: GL and GF models 165 SR x 13 - SSS models 165 SR x 14.

PERFORMANCE power-weight ratio: De Luxe Sedan 21.7 lb/hp, 9.8 kg/hp.

CHASSIS (for SSS models only) rear suspension: independent; semi-trailing arms, coil springs, telescopic dampers.

DIMENSIONS AND WEIGHT wheel base: G4 models 104.33

in, 265 cm; tracks: SSS models 53.15 in 135 cm fro... 52.95 in, 134 cm rear; length: G4 models 177.95 in, 4.. cm; weight: De Luxe Sedan 2,282 lb, 1,035 kg - ... models 2,304 lb, 1,045 kg - GF and G4 models 2,392 .. 1,085 kg - SSS models 2,370 lb, 1,075 kg.

OPTIONALS 3-speed automatic transmission; (for SSS mode... only) 5-speed fully synchronized mechanical gearbox 3.382, II 2.013, III 1.312, IV 1, V 0.854, rev 3.570).

115 hp power team

See 95 hp power team, except for:

ENGINE max power (JIS): 115 hp at 6,200 rpm; max torqu... (JIS): 112 lb ft, 15.5 kg m at 3,600 rpm; 65 hp/l; lub... cation: Bosch electronic fuel injection; fuel feed: electri... pump.

TRANSMISSION (for SSS-ES models only) gears: 5, ful... synchronized; ratios: I 3.382, II 2.013, III 1.312, IV 1, ... 0.854, rev 3.570; axle ratio: 4.111; width of rims: 5... tyres: 185/70 HR x 14.

PERFORMANCE power-weight ratio: GF-E models 21 lb/hp 9.5 kg/hp.

CHASSIS rear suspension: independent, semi-trailing arm... coil springs, telescopic dampers - SSS-ES models anti-ro...

bar - GF-E models rigid axle, lower radius arms, uppe... torque rods, coil springs, and telescopic dampers.

BRAKES (for SSS-ES models only) rear disc; lining area... front 15.5 sq in, 100 sq cm, rear 14.3 sq in, 92 sq cm total 29.8 sq in, 192 sq cm.

DIMENSIONS AND WEIGHT length: 175.79 in, 446 cm weigth: GF-E models 2,414 lb, 1,095 kg - SSS-ES model... 2,470 lb, 1,120 kg.

115 hp power team (1,998 cc)

See 95 hp power team, except for:

ENGINE 6 cylinders, vertical, in line; 121.9 cu in, 1,99... cc (3.07 x 2.74 in, 78 x 69.7 mm); compression ratio: 8.6:1 max power (JIS): 115 hp at 5,600 rpm; max torque (JIS) 120 lb ft, 16.5 kg m at 3,600 rpm; max engine rpm 6,000; 57.6 hp/l; 7 crankshaft bearings; valves: in line lubrication: 10 imp pt, 12 US pt, 5.7 l; 1 downdraugh twin barrel carburettor; 1 ECC automatic air-fuel ratio adjusting; cooling system: 15.8 imp pt, 19 US pt, 9 l.

TRANSMISSION gears: 5, fully synchronized; ratios: 3.592, II 2.246, III 1.415, IV 1, V 0.882, rev 3.657; axle ratio: 4.111; width of rims: 5''; tyres: 165 SR x 14.

PERFORMANCE max speeds: (I) 28 mph, 45 km/h; (II) 4.. mph, 73 km/h; (III) 73 mph, 117 km/h; (IV) and (V) 10... mph, 165 km/h; power-weight ratio: G6-L models 22...

lb/hp, 10.1 kg/hp; consumption: 24.4 m/imp gal, 20.3 m/US gal, 11.6 l x 100 km.

CHASSIS rear suspension: independent, semi-trailing arms, coil springs, telescopic dampers.

STEERING recirculating ball, variable ratio; turns lock to lock: 3.90.

BRAKES lining area: front 22.3 sq in, 144 sq cm, rear 54 sq in, 348 sq cm, total 76.3 sq in, 492 sq cm.

DIMENSIONS AND WEIGHT wheel base: 104.33 in, 265 cm; tracks: 53.15 in, 135 cm front, 52.95 in, 134 cm rear; length: G6-L models 177.95 in, 452 cm - G6-F models 183.86 in, 467 cm; width: 64.17 in, 163 cm; height: sedans 54.53 in, 138 cm - hardtops 54.13 in, 137 cm; ground clearance: 66.93 in, 17 cm; weight G6-L models 2,569 lb, 1,165 kg - G6-F models 2,635 lb, 1,195 kg; weight distribution: 57% front, 43% rear; turning circle: 38 ft, 11.6 m.

OPTIONALS automatic transmission with 3 ratios (I 2.458, II 1.458, III 1, rev 2.182).

130 hp power team

See 95 hp power team, except for:

ENGINE 6 cylinders, vertical, in line; 121.9 cu in, 1,998 cc (3.07 x 2.74 in, 78 x 69.7 mm); compression ratio: 8.6:1; max power (JIS): 130 hp at 6,000 rpm; max torque (JIS): 123 lb ft, 17 kg m at 4,400 rpm; max engine rpm: 6,000; 65.1 hp/l; 7 crankshaft bearings; lubrication: 10 imp pt, 12 US pt, 5.7 l; Bosch L-Jetronic electronic fuel injection; emission control with catalytic converter, exhaust gas recirculation; fuel feed: electric pump; cooling system: 15.8 imp pt, 19 US pt, 9 l.

TRANSMISSION gears: 5, fully synchronized; ratios: I 3.321, II 2.077, III 1.308, IV 1, V 0.864, rev 3.382; tyres: (for G6-EF models only) 185/70 HR x 14.

PERFORMANCE max speed: 109 mph, 175 km/h; power-weight ratio: G6-E Sedan 19.8 lb/hp, 9 kg/hp.

STEERING recirculating ball, variable ratio; turns lock to lock: 3.90.

BRAKES (for G6-EL and EF models only) rear disc; lining area: front 22.3 sq in, 144 sq cm, rear 15.2 sq in, 98 sq cm, total 76.3 sq in, 492 sq cm.

DIMENSIONS AND WEIGHT wheel base: 104.33 in, 2.65 cm; tracks: 53.15 in, 135 cm front, 52.76 in, 134 cm rear; length: G6-E and EL models 177.95 in 452 cm - G6-F models 183.86 in, 467 cm; width: 64.57 in, 164 cm; height: sedans 54.33 in, 138 cm - hardtops 53.90 in, 137 cm; ground clearance: 7.09 in, 18 cm; weight: G6-E models 2,591 lb, 1,175 kg - G6-EL models 2,635 lb, 1,195 kg - G6-EF models 2,723 lb, 1,235 kg; weight distribution: 58% front, 42% rear; turning circle: 38 ft, 11.6 m.

OPTIONALS automatic transmission with 3 ratios (I 2.458, II 1.458, III 1, rev 2.182); 5½'' x 14 alloy wheels 185/70 HR x 14 tyres, 195/HR x 14 tyres; power steering, turns lock to lock 3.20.

Skyline Series

Power team:	Standard for:	Optional for:
95 hp	1 to 3	—
105 hp	4 to 6	—
115 hp	7 to 12	—
115 hp (1,998 cc)	13 to 16	—
130 hp	17 to 24	—

95 hp power team

ENGINE front, 4 stroke; 4 cylinders, in line; 97.3 cu in, 1,595 cc (3.27 x 2.90 in, 83 x 73.7 mm); compression ratio: 8.5:1; max power (JIS): 95 hp at 6,000 rpm; max torque (JIS): 98 lb ft, 13.5 kg m at 3,600 rpm; max engine rpm: 6,300; 62.7 hp/l; cast iron block, light alloy head; 5 crankshaft bearings; valves: overhead, Vee-slanted, rockers; camshafts: 1, overhead; lubrication: rotary pump, full flow filter, 8.1 imp pt, 9.7 US pt, 4.6 l; Nissan NAPS-Z fast burn engine with two spark plugs per cylinder; 1 Nikki 21A-304-20 downdraught twin barrel carburettor; emission control with catalytic converter, secondary air induction and exhaust gas recirculation; fuel feed: mechanical pump; water-cooled, 10.6 imp pt, 12.7 US pt, 6 l.

TRANSMISSION driving wheels: rear; clutch: single dry plate (diaphragm); gearbox: mechanical; gears: 4, fully synchronized; ratios: I 3.657, II 2.177, III 1.419, IV 1, rev 3.638; lever: central; final drive: hypoid bevel; axle ratio: 4.111; width of rims: 4.5''; tyres: 6.45 x 13.

PERFORMANCE max speeds: (I) 25 mph, 40 km/h; (II) 47 mph, 75 km/h; (III) 68 mph, 110 km/h; (IV) 96 mph, 155 km/h; power-weight ratio: TI Sedan 24.2 lb/hp, 11 kg/hp; consumption: 35.3 m/imp gal, 29.4 m/US gal, 8 l x 100 km.

CHASSIS integral; front suspension: independent, by McPherson, coil springs/telescopic damper struts, lower wishbones (trailing links), anti-roll bar; rear: rigid axle, lower

NISSAN Datsun Bluebird 115 hp (1,998 cc) (electronic low emission carburettor)

trailing links, upper torque rods, coil springs, telescopic dampers.

STEERING recirculating ball; turns lock to lock: 3.60.

BRAKES front disc, rear drum, servo; lining area: front 15.5 sq in, 100 sq cm, rear 54 sq in, 348 sq cm, total 69.5 sq in, 448 sq cm.

ELECTRICAL EQUIPMENT 12 V; 35 Ah battery; 50 A alternator; Hitachi distributor; 4 headlamps.

DIMENSIONS AND WEIGHT wheel base: 98.82 in, 251 cm; tracks: 53.54 in, 136 cm front, 53.15 in, 135 cm rear; length: 173.23 in, 440 cm; width: 63.78 in, 162 cm; height: sedans 54.72 in, 139 cm - Hardtop 54.13 in, 137 cm; ground clearance: 6.30 in, 16 cm; weight: TI Sedan 2,304 lb, 1,045 kg - TI-L Sedan 2,337 lb, 1,060 kg - TI-L Hardtop 2,348 lb, 1,065 kg; turning circle: 36.1 ft, 11 m; fuel tank: 13.2 imp gal, 15.8 US gal, 60 l.

105 hp power team

See 95 hp power team, except for:

ENGINE 108 cu in, 1,770 cc (3.35 x 3.07 in, 85 x 78 mm); max power (JIS): 105 hp at 6,000 rpm; max torque (JIS): 109 lb ft, 15 kg m at 3,600 rpm; 59.3 hp/l.

TRANSMISSION gearbox ratios: I 3.382, II 2.013, III 1.312, IV 1, rev 3.365; axle ratio: 3.889; tyres: (for TI-L models only) 165 SR x 13.

PERFORMANCE max speeds: (I) 27 mph, 44 km/h; (II) 45 mph, 73 km/h; (III) 68 mph, 110 km/h; (IV) 103 mph, 165 km/h; power-weight ratio: TI Sedan 22.3 lb/hp, 10.1 kg/hp; consumption: 36.7 m/imp gal, 30.6 m/US gal, 7.7 l x100 km.

DIMENSIONS AND WEIGHT weight TI Sedan 2,337 lb, 1,060 kg - TI-L Sedan 2,359 lb, 1,070 kg - TI-L Hardtop 2,370 lb, 1,075 kg.

OPTIONALS 5-speed mechanical gearbox, ratio V 0.854, rev 3.570; automatic transmission with 3 ratios (I 2.458, II 1.458, III 1, rev 2.182).

115 hp power team

ENGINE 108 cu in, 1,770 cc (3.35 x 3.07 in, 85 x 78 mm); max power (JIS): 115 hp at 6,200 rpm; max torque (JIS): 112 lb ft, 15.5 kg m at 3,600 rpm; 65 hp/l; Bosch L-Jetronic electronic fuel injection.

TRANSMISSION gearbox ratios: I 3.382, II 2.013, III 1.312, IV 1, rev 3.365; axle ratio: 4.111; tyres: TI-EL and TI-EX models 165 SR x 14 - TI-ES models 185/70 HR x 14.

PERFORMANCE max speed: 103 mph, 165 km/h; power-weight ratio: TI-ES Sedan 20.8 lb/hp, 9.4 kg/hp; consumption: 33.9 m/imp gal, 28.2 m/US gal, 8.3 l x 100 km.

CHASSIS (for TI-ES models only) anti-roll bar on rear suspension.

BRAKES (for TI-ES models only) disc.

NISSAN Skyline 1800 TI-EL Hardtop

115 HP POWER TEAM

DIMENSIONS AND WEIGHT height: TI-EL and TI-ES sedans 55.31 in, 140 cm - TI-EL and TI-ES hardtops 54.92 in, 139 cm; weight: TI-EL Sedan 2,392 lb, 1,085 kg - TI-EL Hardtop 2,403 lb, 1,090 kg - TI-EX Sedan 2,425 lb, 1,100 kg - TI-EX Hardtop 2,436 lb, 1,105 kg - TI-ES Sedan 2,447 lb, 1,110 kg - TI-ES Hardtop 2,458 lm, 1,115 kg.

115 hp power team (1,998 cc)

See 95 hp power team, except for:

ENGINE 6 cylinders, in line; 121.9 cu in, 1,998 cc (3.07 x 2.74 in, 78 x 69.7 mm); compression ratio: 8.6:1; max power (JIS): 115 hp at 5,600 rpm; max torque (JIS): 120 lb ft, 16.5 kg m at 3,600 rpm; 57.6 hp/l; 7 crankshaft bearings; valves: in line; lubrication: rotary pump, full flow filter, 10 imp pt, 12 US pt, 5.7 l; 1 Hitachi ECC air-fuel ratio adjusting downdraught twin barrel carburettor; emission control with 3-way catalytic converter; water-cooled, 15.8 imp pt, 19 US pt, 9 l.

TRANSMISSION gearbox ratios: I 3.592, III 2.246, III 1.415, IV 1, rev 3.657; tyres: 185/70 HR x 14.

PERFORMANCE max speeds: (I) 26 mph, 42 km/h; (II) 43 mph, 70 km/h; (III) 58 mph, 110 km/h; (IV) 99 mph, 160 km/h; power-weight ratio: GT Sedan 22.7 lb/hp, 10.3 kg/hp; consumption: 26.5 m/imp gal, 22.1 m/US gal, 10.6 l x 100 km.

CHASSIS rear suspension: independent, semi-trailing arms, coil springs, telescopic dampers.

STEERING recirculating ball, variable ratio; turns lock to lock: 4.

BRAKES rear compensator; lining area: front 22.3 sq in, 144 sq cm, rear 54 sq in, 348 sq cm, total 89.3 sq in, 576 sq cm.

DIMENSIONS AND WEIGHT wheel base: 102.76 in, 261 cm; tracks: 53.94 in, 137 cm front; length: 181.10 in, 460 cm; weight: GT Sedan 2,613 lb, 1,185 kg - GT Hardtop and GT-L Sedan 2,624 lb, 1,190 kg - GT-L Hardtop 2,635 lb, 1,195 kg - turning circle: 38 ft, 11.6 m.

OPTIONALS 5-speed fully synchronized mechanical gearbox (I 3.321, II 2.077, III 1.308, IV 1, V 0.864, rev 3.382), 4.111 axle ratio, max speed 106 mph, 170 km/h; automatic transmission with 3 ratios (I 2.458, II 1.458, III 1, rev 2.182); power steering, turns lock to lock 3.60.

130 hp power team

See 95 hp power team, except for:

ENGINE 6-cylinders, in line; 121.9 cu in, 1,998 cc (3.07 x 2.74 in, 78 x 69.7 mm); compression ratio: 8.6:1; max power (JIS): 130 hp at 6,000 rpm; max torque (JIS): 123 lb ft, 17 kg m at 4,000 rpm; 65.1 hp/l; 7 crankshaft

bearings; lubrication: 10 imp pt, 12 US pt, 5.7 l; Bosch L-Jetronic electronic fuel injection; emission control with 3-way catalytic converter exhaust gas recirculation; fuel feed: electric pump; water-cooled, 15.8 imp pt, 19 US pt, 9 l.

TRANSMISSION gears: 5, fully synchronized; ratios: I 3.592, II 2.246, III 1.415, IV 1, V 0.882, rev 3.657; axle ratio: 4.111; width of rims: 5''; tyres: 185/70HR x 14.

PERFORMANCE max speeds: (I) 28 mph, 45 km/h; (II) 47 mph, 76 km/h; (III) 71 mph, 115 km/h; (IV) and (V) 109 mph, 175 km/h; power-weight ratio: GT-EL Sedan 20.2 lb/hp, 9.1 kg/hp; consumption: 26.5 m/imp gal, 22.1 m/US gal, 10.6 l x 100 km.

CHASSIS rear suspension: independent, semi-trailing arms, coil springs, telescopic dampers (for GT-EX and GT-ES models only) anti-roll bar.

STEERING recirculating ball, variable ratio; turns lock to lock: 4.

BRAKES rear compensator (for GT-EX and GT-ES models only) rear disc; lining area: front 22.3 sq in, 144 sq cm; rear 54 sq in, 348 sq cm, total 89.3 sq in, 576 sq cm (for GT-EX and GT-ES models only) rear lining area 14.3 sq in, 92 sq cm.

DIMENSIONS AND WEIGHT wheel base: 102.76 in, 261 cm; tracks: 53.94 in, 137 cm front, 53.15 in, 135 cm rear; length: 181.10 in, 460 cm; width: GT-EX models 64.37 in, 163 cm;

NISSAN Skyline 2000 GT-ES Hardtop

NISSAN Skyline 2000 GT-EL Sedan

weight: GT-EL Sedan 2,624 lb, 1,190 kg - GT-EL Hardtop 2,635 lb, 1,195 kg - GT-EX Sedan 2,690 lb, 1,220 kg - GT-EX Hardtop 2,701 lb, 1,225 kg - GT-ES Sedan 2,668 lb, 1,210 kg - GT-ES Hardtop 2,679 lb, 1,215 kg; turning circle: 38 ft, 11.6 m.

OPTIONALS automatic transmission with 3 ratios (I 2.458, II 1.458, III, rev 2.182), 4.111 axle ratio, max speed 106 mph, 170 km/h; power steering, turns lock to lock 3.60; 5.5'' cast alloy wheels.

Laurel Series

PRICES (Tokyo).

1	1800 Standard 4-dr Sedan	1,098,000 yen
2	1800 Custom 4-dr Sedan	1,138,000 yen
3	1800 GL 4-dr Sedan	1,212,000 yen
4	1800 GL 2-dr Hardtop	1,241,000 yen
5	1800 GL 4-dr Hardtop	1,289,000 yen
6	1800 SGL 4-dr Sedan	1,344,000 yen
7	2000 Diesel Standard 4-dr Sedan	1,190,000 yen
8	2000 Diesel De Luxe 4-dr Sedan	1,284,000 yen
9	2000 Diesel GL 4-dr Sedan	1,406,000 yen
10	2000 Custom 6 4-dr Sedan	1,263,000 yen
11	2000 GL 6 4-dr Sedan	1,390,000 yen
12	2000 GL 6 2-dr Hardtop	1,448,000 yen
13	2000 GL 6 4-dr Hardtop	1,512,000 yen
14	2000 SGL 4-dr Sedan	1,498,000 yen
15	2000 SGL-E 4-dr Sedan	1,603,000 yen
16	2000 SGL-E 2-dr Hardtop	1,659,000 yen
17	2000 SGL-E 4-dr Hardtop	1,717,000 yen
18	2000 GL6-E 4-dr Hardtop	1,617,000 yen
19	2000 Medalist 4-dr Sedan	1,888,000 yen
20	2000 Medalist 2-dr Hardtop	1,965,000 yen
21	2000 Medalist 4-dr Hardtop	2,032,000 yen
22	2800 Medalist 4-dr Sedan	2,011,000 yen
23	2800 Medalist 2-dr Hardtop	2,063,000 yen
24	2800 Medalist 4-dr Hardtop	2,138,000 yen

Power team:	Standard for:	Optional for:
105 hp	1 to 6	—
60 hp Diesel	7 to 9	—
115 hp	10 to 14	—
130 hp	15 to 21	—
140 hp	22 to 24	—

105 hp power team

ENGINE front, 4 stroke; 4 cylinders, in line; 108 cu in, 1,770 cc (3.35 x 3.07 in, 85 x 78 mm); compression ratio: 8.5:1; max power (JIS): 105 hp at 6,000 rpm; max torque (JIS): 109 lb ft, 15 kg m at 3,600 rpm; max engine rpm: 6,400; 59.3 hp/l; cast iron block, light alloy head; 5 crankshaft bearings; valves: overhead, Vee-slanted, rockers; camshafts: 1, overhead; lubrication: rotary pump full flow filter, 8.1 imp pt, 9.7 US pt, 4.6 l; Nissan NAPS-Z fast burn engine with two spark plugs per cylinder; 1 Hitachi DCR 340-1 downdraught twin barrel carburettor; emission control with catalytic converter, secondary air induction and exhaust gas recirculation; fuel feed: mechanical pump; water-cooled, 14 imp pt, 16.9 US pt, 8 l.

TRANSMISSION driving wheels: rear; clutch: single dry plate (diaphragm); gearbox: mechanical; gears: 4, fully synchronized; ratios: I 3.382, II 2.013, III 1.312, IV 1, rev 3.365; lever: central; final drive: hypoid bevel; axle ratio: 4.111; width of rims: 5''; tyres: 6.45 x 14.

PERFORMANCE max speeds: (I) 30 mph, 48 km/h; (II) 52 mph, 83 km/h; (III) 77 mph, 124 km/h; (IV) 99 mph, 160 km/h; power-weight ratio: Custom 4-dr Sedan 23.6 lb/hp, 10.7 kg/hp; consumption: 28.2 m/imp gal, 23.5 m/US gal, 10 l x 100 km.

CHASSIS integral; front suspension: independent, by McPherson, coil springs/telescopic damper struts, lower wishbones (trailing links), anti-roll bar; rear: rigid axle, lower trailing links, upper torque rods, coil springs, telescopic dampers.

STEERING recirculating ball; turns lock to lock: 4; (for SGL 4-dr Sedan only) servo, turns lock to lock 3.20.

BRAKES front disc, rear drum, servo; lining area: front 22.3 sq in, 144 sq cm, rear 54 sq in, 348 sq cm, total 76.3 sq in, 492 sq cm.

ELECTRICAL EQUIPMENT 12 V; 35 Ah battery; 50 A alternator; Hitachi distributor; 4 headlamps.

DIMENSIONS AND WEIGHT wheel base: 105.12 in, 267 cm; tracks: 54.33 in, 138 cm front, 53.94 in, 137 cm rear; length: 182.09 in, 462 cm; width: 66.53 in, 169 cm; height: sedans 55.31 in, 140 cm - hardtops 54.92 in, 139 cm; ground clearance: 6.69 in, 17 cm; weight: Custom 4-dr Sedan 2,481 lb, 1,125 kg - GL 4-dr Sedan 2,514 lb, 1,140 kg - GL 2-dr Hardtop 2,536 lb, 1,150 kg - GL 4-dr Hardtop 2,602 lb, 1,180 kg - SGL 4-dr Sedan 2,569 lb, 1,165 kg; turning circle: 38 ft, 11.6 m; fuel tank: 13.2 imp gal, 15.8 US gal, 60 l.

OPTIONALS 5-speed mechanical gearbox (V 0.854); automatic transmission with 3 ratios (I 2.458, II 1.458, III 1, rev

NISSAN Laurel 2000 SGL-E 4-dr Sedan

2.182), central lever; 5.5'' light alloy wheels with 185/70 HR x 14 tyres.

60 hp power team

See 105 hp power team, except for:

ENGINE Diesel, Ricardo Comet swirl chamber type; 121.5 cu in, 1,991 cc (3.27 x 3.62 in, 83 x 92 mm); compression ratio: 20:1; max power (JIS): 60 hp at 4,000 rpm; max torque (JIS): 94 lb ft, 13 kg m at 3,600 rpm; valves: overhead, Vee-slanted, push-rods and rockers; camshafts: 1, side; lubrication: gear pump, 11.4 imp pt, 13.7 US pt, 6.5 l; plunger type in line injection pump; water-cooled, 17.6 imp pt, 21.1 US pt, 10 l.

TRANSMISSION gears: 5, fully synchronized; ratios: I 3.592, II 2.246, III 1.415, IV 1, V 0.882, rev 3.657; lever: central; axle ratio: 3.889.

PERFORMANCE max speed: 81 mph, 130 km/h; power-weight ratio: De Luxe 4-dr Sedan 44.1 lb/hp, 20 kg/hp; consumption: 59.3 m/imp gal, 49.4 m/US gal, 4.8 l x 100 km at 37 mph, 60 km/h.

DIMENSIONS AND WEIGHT weight: De Luxe 4-dr Sedan 2,646 lb, 1,200 kg - GL 4-dr Sedan 2,679 lb, 1,215 kg.

115 hp power team

See 105 hp power team, except for:

ENGINE 6 cylinders, in line; 121.9 cu in, 1,998 cc (3.07 x 2.74 in, 78 x 69.7 mm); compression ratio: 8.6:1; max power (JIS): 115 hp at 5,600 rpm; max torque (JIS): 120 lb ft, 16.5 kg m at 3,600 rpm; max engine rpm: 6,000; 60 hp/l; 7 crankshaft bearing; lubrication: 10 imp pt, 12 US pt, 5.7 l; 1 Hitachi DCR 340-11 with ECC air-fuel ratio adjusting system downdraught twin barrel carburettor; emission control with 3-way catalytic converter; water-cooled, 15.8 imp pt, 19 US pt, 9 l.

TRANSMISSION gearbox ratios: I 3.592, II 2.246, III 1.415, IV 1, rev 3.657; axle ratio: 4.100; tyres: (for SGL 4-dr Sedan only) 185/70 SR x 14.

PERFORMANCE max speed: 102 mph, 165 km/h; power-weight ratio: Custom 6 4-dr Sedan 22.9 lb/hp, 10.4 kg/hp; consumption: 24 m/imp gal, 20 m/US gal, 11.8 l x 100 km.

CHASSIS (for hardtops only) rear suspension: independent, semi-trailing arms, coil springs, telescopic dampers.

STEERING servo; turns lock to lock: 3.20 - (for Custom 6 4-dr Sedan only) manual, turns lock to lock 4.

BRAKES rear compensator.

DIMENSIONS AND WEIGHT rear track: hardtops 53.54 in, 136 cm; length: 182.09 in, 426 cm; weight: Custom 6 4-dr Sedan 2,635 lb, 1,195 kg - GL 6 4-dr Sedan 2,701 lb, 1,225 kg - GL 6 2-dr Hardtop 2,756 lb, 1,250 kg - GL 6 4-dr Hardtop 2,789 lb, 1,265 kg - SGL 4-dr Sedan 2,712 lb, 1,230 kg; weight distribution: 55.7% front, 44.3% rear.

OPTIONALS 5-speed mechanical gearbox (V 0.882).

130 hp power team

See 105 hp power team, except for:

ENGINE 6 cylinders in line; 121.9 cu in, 1,998 cc (3.07 x 2.74 in, 78 x 69.7 mm); compression ratio: 8.6:1; max power (JIS): 130 hp at 6,000 rpm; max torque (JIS): 126 lb ft, 17 kg m at 4,000 rpm; max engine rpm: 6,000; 65.1 hp/l; 7 crankshafts bearings; lubrication: 10 imp pt, 12 US pt, 5.7 l; Bosch electronic fuel injection; emission control with 3-way catalytic converter; fuel feed: electric pump; water-cooled, 15.8 imp pt, 19 US pt, 9 l.

TRANSMISSION gearbox ratios: I 3.592, II 2.246, III 1.415, IV 1, rev 3.657; axle ratio: 4.100; tyres: 185/70 SR x 14 - (for Medalist models only) 185/70 HR x 14.

PERFORMANCE max speed: 109 mph, 175 km/h; power-weight ratio: SGL-E 4-dr Sedan 20.9 lb/hp, 9.5 kg/hp; consumption: 24 m/imp gal, 20 m/US gal, 11.8 l x 100 km.

CHASSIS (for hardtops only) rear suspension: independent, semi-trailing arms, coil springs, telescopic dampers.

STEERING servo; turns lock to lock: 3.20.

BRAKES rear compensator - (for Medalist hardtops only) rear disc.

DIMENSIONS AND WEIGHT rear track; hardtops 53.54 in, 136 cm; length: 182.09 in, 426 cm; width: 66.53 in, 169 cm; weight: SGL-E 4-dr Sedan 2.712 lb, 1,230 kg - SGL-E 2-dr Hardtop 2,778 lb, 1,260 kg - SGL-E 4-dr Sedan 2,811 lb, 1,275 kg - Medalist 4-dr Sedan 2,800 lb, 1,270 kg - Medalist 2-dr Hardtop 2,88 lb, 1,310 kg - Medalist 4-dr Hardtop 2,922 lb, 1,325 kg.

OPTIONALS 5-speed mechanical gearbox (V 0.882): 3-speed automatic transmission: 5.5'' light alloy wheels with 185/70 HR x 14 tyres.

140 hp power team

See 105 hp power team, except for:

ENGINE 6 cylinders, in line; 168 cu in, 2,753 cc (3.39 x 3.11 in, 86 x 79 mm); compression ratio: 8.6:1; max power (JIS): 140 hp at 5,200 rpm; max torque (JIS): 163 lb ft, 22.5 kg m at 3,600 rpm; max engine rpm: 6,200; 50.1 hp/l; 7 crankshaft bearings; lubrication: 10 imp pt, 12 US pt, 5.7 l; 1 Hitachi DCR 360-1 downdraught twin barrel carburettor with electronic air-fuel ratio adjustment system; water-cooled, 17.6 imp pt, 21.1 US pt, 10 l.

TRANSMISSION gears: 5, fully synchronized; ratios: I 3.321, II 2.077, III 1.308, IV 1, V 0.864, rev 3.382; axle ratio: 3.700; tyres: 185/70 HR x 14.

PERFORMANCE max speeds: (I) 36 mph, 58 km/h; (II) 52 mph, 83 km/h; (III) 89 mph, 144 km/h; IV 104 mph, 168 km/h; V 112 mph, 180 km/h; power-weight ratio: Medalist 4-dr Sedan 20.3 lb/hp, 9.2 kg/hp; consumption: 23.1 m/imp gal, 19.3 m/US gal, 12.2 l x 100 km.

CHASSIS (for hardtops only) rear suspension: independent, semi-trailing arms, coil springs, telescopic dampers.

STEERING servo; turns lock to lock: 3.60.

BRAKES front disc, rear drum, rear compensator, servo; lining area: front 20.5 sq in, 132 sq cm.

DIMENSIONS AND WEIGHT tracks: hardtops 53.54 in, 136 cm rear; length: 182.09 in, 462 cm; width: 66.34 in, 168 cm; weight: Medalist 4-dr Sedan 2,844 lb, 1,290 kg - Medalist 2-dr Hardtop 2,944 lb, 1,335 kg - Medalist 4-dr Hardtop 2,977 lb, 1,350 kg.

OPTIONALS 3-speed automatic transmission.

Silvia Series

PRICES (Tokyo):

1 LS Coupé	1,075,000	yen
2 LS Type S Coupé	1,125,000	yen
3 LS Type L Coupé	1,114,000	yen
4 LS Type X Coupé	1,205,000	yen
5 LS Type G Coupé	1,305,000	yen
6 LS-E Type S Coupé	1,209,000	yen
7 LS-E Type L Coupé	1,225,000	yen
8 LS-E Type X Coupé	1,283,000	yen
9 LS-E Type G Coupé	1,383,000	yen

For USA prices, see price index.

Power team:	Standard for:	Optional for:
105 hp	1 to 5	—
115 hp	6 to 9	—

105 hp power team

ENGINE front, 4 stroke; 4 cylinders, in line; 108 cu in, 1,770 cc (3.35 x 3.07 in, 85 x 78 mm); compression ratio: 8.5:1; max power (JIS): 105 hp at 6,000 rpm; max torque (JIS): 109 lb ft, 15 kg m at 3,600 rpm; max engine rpm: 6,000; 59.3 hp/l; cast iron block, light alloy head; 5 crankshaft bearings; valves: overhead, in line, rockers; camshafts: 1, overhead; lubrication: rotary pump, full flow filter, 8.1 imp pt, 9.7 US pt, 4.6 l; 1 Hitachi DCH340 downdraught twin barrel carburettor; emission control with catalytic converter, secondary air injection and exhaust gas recirculation; fuel feed: mechanical pump; water-cooled, 10.6 imp pt, 12.7 US pt, 6 l.

TRANSMISSION driving wheels: rear; clutch: single dry plate (diaphragm); gearbox: mechanical; gears: 4, fully synchronized; ratios: I 3.382, II 2.013, III 1.312, IV 1, rev 3.365; lever: central; final drive: hypoid bevel; axle ratio 3.700; width of rims: 4.5''; tyres: LS and LS-L Z78 x 13 - LS-S, LS-X and LS-G 175/70 HR x 13.

PERFORMANCE max speeds: (I) 31 mph, 50 km/h; (II) 51 mph, 82 km/h; (III) 81 mph, 130 km/h; (IV) 106 mph, 170 km/h; power-weight ratio: 20.8 lb/hp, 9.4 kg/hp; carrying capacity: 882 lb, 400 kg; speed in direct drive at 1,000 rpm: 17.6 mph, 28.3 km/h; consumption: 26.4 m/imp gal, 22 m/US gal, 10.7 l x 100 km.

CHASSIS integral; front suspension: independent, by McPherson, coil springs/telescopic damper struts, lower wishbones (trailing links), anti-roll bar; rear: rigid axle, semi-elliptic leafsprings, telescopic dampers.

STEERING recirculating ball; turns lock to lock: 2.90.

NISSAN Laurel 2000 Diesel GL

105 HP POWER TEAM

BRAKES front disc, rear drum, servo; lining area: front 15.5 sq in, 100 sq cm, rear 54 sq in, 348 sq cm, total 69.5 sq in, 448 sq cm.

ELECTRICAL EQUIPMENT 12 V; 35 Ah battery; 50 A alternator; Hitachi distributor; 2 headlamps.

DIMENSIONS AND WEIGHT wheel base: 92.13 in, 234 cm; tracks: 50.39 in, 128 cm front, 49.80 in, 126 cm rear; length: 162.79 in, 413 cm; width: 62.99 in, 160 cm; height: 51.18 in, 130 cm; ground clearance: 6.50 in, 16.5 cm; weight: 2,183 lb, 990 kg; weight distribution: 55% front, 45% rear; turning circle: 35.4 ft, 10.8 m; fuel tank: 13.2 imp gal, 15.8 US gal, 60 l.

BODY coupé; 2 doors; 5 seats, separate front seats.

OPTIONALS 5-speed fully synchronized mechanical gearbox (I 3.382, II 2.013, III 1.312, IV 1, V 0.854, rev 3.570), 3.889 axle ratio, max speed 109 mph, 175 km/h; JATCO automatic transmission with 3 ratios (I 2.458, II 1.458, III 1, rev 2.182), max speed 103 mph, 165 km/h.

115 hp power team

See 105 hp power team, except for:

ENGINE max power (JIS): 115 hp at 6,200 rpm; max torque (JIS): 112 lb ft, 15.5 kg m at 3,600 rpm; max engine rpm: 6,200; 65 hp/l; Bosch L-Jetronic electronic fuel injection, exhaust gas recirculation.

TRANSMISSION tyres: 175/HR x 13.

PERFORMANCE max speed: 109 mph, 175 km/h; power-weight ratio: 19.2 lb/hp, 8.7 kg/hp; consumption: 29.7 m/imp gal, 24.8 m/US gal, 9.5 l x 100 km.

DIMENSIONS AND WEIGHT weight: 2,205 lb, 1,000 kg.

OPTIONALS only 5-speed fully synchronized mechanical gearbox.

Cedric - Gloria Series

Power team:	Standard for:	Optional for:
115 hp	1 to 7	—
130 hp	8 to 15	—
80 hp Diesel	—	1 to 7
60 hp Diesel	16	—
65 hp	17 to 19	—
145 hp	20 to 24	—

115 hp power team

ENGINE front, 4 stroke; 6 cylinders, in line; 121.9 cu in, 1,998 cc (3.07 x 2.74 in, 78 x 69.7 mm); compression ratio: 8.6:1; max power (JIS): 115 hp at 5,600 rpm; max torque (JIS): 120 lb ft, 16.5 kg m at 3,600 rpm; 57.6 hp/l; cast iron block, light alloy head; 7 crankshaft bearings; valves: overhead, in line, rockers; camshafts: 1, overhead; lubrication: rotary pump, full flow filter, 8.3 imp pt, 9.9 US pt, 4.7 l; 1 Hitachi DCR 340 downdraught twin barrel carburettor; with air-fuel ratio adjusting system; emission control with 3-way catalytic converter, secondary air induction and exhaust gas recirculation; fuel feed: mechanical pump; water-cooled, 17.6 imp pt, 21.1 US pt, 10 l.

TRANSMISSION driving wheels: rear; clutch: single dry plate (diaphragm); gearbox: mechanical; gears: 4, fully synchronized; ratios: I 3.592, II 2.246, III 1.415, IV 1,

rev 3.657; lever: central; final drive: hypoid bevel; axle ratio: 4.375; width of rims: 5''; tyres: 6.95 x 14.

PERFORMANCE max speeds: (I) 25 mph, 40 km/h; (II) 53 mph, 85 km/h; (III) 87 mph, 140 km/h; (IV) 99 mph, 160 km/h; power-weight ratio: Standard 4-dr Sedan 25/8 lb/hp, 11.7 kg/hp; carrying capacity: 882 lb, 400 kg; consumption: 23.4 m/imp gal, 19.5 m/US gal, 12 l x 100 km.

CHASSIS integral; front suspension: independent, wishbones, coil springs, anti-roll bar, telescopic dampers; rear: rigid axle, semi-elliptic leafsprings, telescopic dampers.

STEERING recirculating ball, servo; turns lock to lock: 4.70 - (for GL and SGL models only) servo, turns lock to lock 3.80.

BRAKES front disc, rear drum, servo; lining area: front 23.6 sq in, 152 sq cm, rear 71.9 sq in, 464 sq cm, total 95.5 sq in, 616 sq cm.

ELECTRICAL EQUIPMENT 12 V; 35 Ah battery; 50 A alternator; 4 headlamps.

DIMENSIONS AND WEIGHT wheel base: 105.91 in, 269 cm; front and rear track: 54.33 in, 138 cm; length: 184.65 in, 469 cm; width: 66.54 in, 169 cm; height: sedans 56.69 in, 144 cm - hardtops 56.30 in, 143 cm; ground clearance: 7.09 in, 18 cm; weight Standard 4-dr Sedan 2,966 lb, 1,345 kg - De Luxe 4-dr Sedan 2,977 lb, 1,350 kg - Custom De Luxe 4-dr Sedan 2,999 lb, 1,360 kg - Custom De Luxe 4-dr Hardtop 3,043 lb, 1,380 kg - GL 4-dr Sedan 3,076 lb, 1,395 kg - GL 4-dr Hardtop 3,120 lb, 1,415 kg - SGL 4-dr Hardtop 3,208 lb, 1,455 kg; turning circle: 39.4 ft, 12 m; fuel tank: 14.7 imp gal, 17.7 US gal, 67 l.

BODY 5 seats, separate front seats, reclining backrests, built-in headrests.

OPTIONALS 4-speed fully synchronized mechanical gearbox (I 3.143, II 1.641, III 1, IV 0.784, rev 3.657), steering column lever, 4.625 axle ratio; Nissan automatic transmission with 3 ratios (I 2.458, II 1.458, III 1, rev 2.182), steering column lever, 4.625 axle ratio; 5-speed mechanical gearbox (V 0.882), 4.625 axle ratio.

130 hp power team

See 115 hp power team, except for:

ENGINE max power (JIS): 130 hp at 6,000 rpm; max torque (JIS): 123 lb ft, 17 kg m at 4,400 rpm; 65.1 hp/l; Bosch electronic fuel injection; emission control with 3-way catalytic converter; fuel feed: electric pump.

PERFORMANCE max speed: 106 mph, 170 km/h; power-weight ratio: GL-E 4-dr Sedan 23.6 lb/hp, 10.7 kg/hp; consumption: 23.4 m/imp gal, 19.5 m/US gal, 12 l x 100 km.

STEERING servo; turns lock to lock: 3.80.

DIMENSIONS AND WEIGHT weight: GL-E 4-dr Sedan 3,065 lb, 1,390 kg - GL-E 2-dr Hardtop 3,054 lb, 1,385 kg - GL-E

NISSAN Silvia LS Coupé

NISSAN Cedric 2000 SGL-E Extra 4-dr Sedan

dr Hardtop 3,120 lb, 1,415 kg - SGL-E 4-dr Sedan 3,153
, 1,430 kg - SGL-E 2-dr Hardtop 3,142 lb, 1,425 kg - SGL-E
dr Hardtop 3,208 lb, 1,455 kg - SGL-E Extra 4-dr Sedan
153 lb, 1,430 kg - SGL-E Extra 4-dr Hardtop 3,252 lb,
475 kg.

80 hp power team

ee 115 hp power team, except for:

NGINE 4 cylinders, in line; 120.9 cu in, 1,982 cc (3.43
3.27 in, 87.2 x 83 mm); compression ratio: 9:1; max power
IIS): 80 hp at 4,800 rpm; max torque (JIS): 109 lb ft,
kg m at 2,800 rpm; 40.4 hp/l; 3 crankshaft bearings;
lves: overhead, in line, push-rods and rockers; cam-
afts: 1, side; 1 245304 LPG carburettor; emission control
ith catalytic converter; cooling system: 12.3 imp pt, 14.8
S pt, 7 l.

RANSMISSION gears: 3, fully synchronized; ratios: I
143, II 1.641, III 1, rev 3.657; lever: steering column;
res: 6.40 x 14.

RFORMANCE max speed: 81 mph, 130 km/h; power-
eight ratio: Standard 4-dr Sedan 37 lb/hp, 168 kg/hp.

RAKES drum, servo.

60 hp power team

ee 115 hp power team, except for:

NGINE Diesel, 4 cylinders, in line; 121.5 cu in, 1,991 cc
27 x 3.62 in, 83 x 92 mm); compression ratio: 20:1; max
wer (JIS): 60 hp at 4,000 rpm; max torque (JIS): 94
ft, 13 kg m at 1,800 rpm; 30.1 hp/l 3 crankshaft bearings;
lves: overhead, in line, push-rods and rockers; camshafts:
side; lubrication: 9.9 imp pt, 11.8 US pt, 5.6 l; 1 245304
PG carburettor; plunger type in line injection pump;
icardo Comet swirl chamber type.

RANSMISSION gears: 3, fully synchronized; ratios: I
143, II 1.641, III 1, rev 3.657; lever: steering column;
res: 6.40 x 14.

RFORMANCE max speed: 68 mph, 110 km/h; power-
eight ratio: 50.7 lb/hp, 23 kg/hp; 52.3 m/imp gal, 43.6
/US gal, 5.4 l x 100 km at 37 mph, 60 km/h.

RAKES drum, servo.

IMENSIONS AND WEIGHT weight: 3.043 lb, 1,380 kg.

PTIONALS 4-speed fully synchronized mechanical gearbox
ith steering column lever.

65 hp power team

ee 60 hp power team, except for:

NGINE Diesel; 132 cu in, 2,164 cc (3.27 x 3.94 in, 83 x 100
m); compression ratio: 20.8:1; max power (JIS): 65 hp at
000 rpm; max torque (JIS): 105 lb ft, 14.5 kg m at 1,800
m; 30 hp/l.

NISSAN Cedric SGL-E 2-dr Hardtop

TRANSMISSION tyres: Standard 4-dr Sedan 6.40 x 14 - De
Luxe and GL models 6.95 x 14.

PERFORMANCE max speed: 81 mph, 130 km/h; power-
weight ratio: Standard 4-dr Sedan 46.3 lb/hp, 21 kg/hp.

STEERING (for GL 4-dr Sedan only) servo; turns lock to
lock: 3.80.

BRAKES (for GL 4-dr Sedan only) front disc.

DIMENSIONS AND WEIGHT weight: Standard 4-dr Sedan
3.010 lb, 1,365 kg - De Luxe 4-dr Sedan 3,021 lb, 1,370 kg
- GL 4-dr Sedan 3,120 lb, 1,415 kg.

OPTIONALS 4-speed mechanical gearbox with overdrive
(I 3.143, II 1.641, III 1, overdrive 0.784), steering column
lever, 4.625 axle ratio; 5-speed mechanical gearbox (I
3.592, II 2.246, III 1.415, IV 1, V 0.882), 4.111 axle ratio.

145 hp power team

See 115 hp power team, except for:

ENGINE 168 cu in, 2,753 cc (3.39 x 3.11 in, 86 x 79 mm);
compression ratio: 8.3:1; max power (JIS): 145 hp at 5,200
rpm; max torque (JIS): 166.7 lb ft, 23 kg m at 4,000 rpm;
52.7 hp/l; Bosch L-Jetronic fuel injection; fuel feed:
electric pump.

TRANSMISSION gears: 5 fully synchronized; ratios: I 3.321,
II 2.077, III 1.308, IV 1, V 0.864, rev 3.382; axle ratio:
3.889; tyres: 7.35 S x 14.

PERFORMANCE power-weight ratio: Brougham 4-dr Sedan
22.6 lb/hp, 10.2 kg/hp; consumption: 20.3 m/imp gal, 16.9
m/US gal, 13.9 l x 100 km.

DIMENSIONS AND WEIGHT length: 188.38 in, 478 cm; weight:
Brougham 4-dr Sedan 3,274 lb, 1,485 kg - Brougham 2-dr
Hardtop 3,175 lb, 1,440 kg - Brougham 4-dr. Hardtop 3,330
lb, 1,510 kg.

OPTIONALS 4-speed fully synchronized mechanical gearbox,
4.375 axle ratio; JATCO automatic transmission with 3
ratios (I 2.458, II 1.458, III 1, rev 2.182), max speed 96
mph, 155 km/h, 4.111 axle ratio.

Fairlady Series

PRICES (Tokyo):

1 Fairlady Z Sports	1,460,000	yen
2 Fairlady ZL Sports	1,625,000	yen
3 Fairlady ZT Sports	1,795,000	yen
4 Fairlady Z 2 + 2 Sports	1,598,000	yen
5 Fairlady ZL 2 + 2 Sports	1,793,000	yen
6 Fairlady ZT 2 + 2 Sports	1,988,000	yen
7 Fairlady 280 ZL Sports	1,800,000	yen
8 Fairlady 280 ZT Sports	2,155,000	yen
9 Fairlady 280 ZL 2 + 2 Sports	1,965,000	yen
10 Fairlady 280 ZT 2 + 2 Sports	2,373,000	yen

Power team:	Standard for:	Optional for:
130 hp	1 to 6	—
145 hp	7 to 10	—

130 hp power team

ENGINE front, 4 stroke; 6 cylinders, in line; 121.9 cu in,
1,998 cc 3.07 x 2.74 in, 78 x 69.7 mm); compression ratio:
8.8:1; max power (JIS): 130 hp at 6,000 rpm; max torque
(JIS): 123 lb ft, 17 kg m at 4,000 rpm; max engine rpm:
6,400; 65.1 hp/l; cast iron block, light alloy head; 7 crankshaft bearings; valves: overhead, in line, rockers; camshafts:
1, overhead; lubrication: rotary pump, full flow filter, 8.3
imp pt, 9.9 US pt, 4.7 l; Bosch electronic fuel injection;
emission control with 3-way catalytic converter and exhaust
gas recirculation; fuel feed: electric pump; water-cooled,
17.6 imp pt, 21.1 US pt, 10 l.

TRANSMISSION driving wheels: rear; clutch: single dry
plate, hydraulically controlled; gearbox: mechanical; gears:
mechanical; gears; 5, fully synchronized; ratios: I 3.592,
II 2.246, III 1.415, IV 1, V 0.822, rev 3.657; lever: central;
final drive: hypoid bevel; axle ratio: 4.375; width of rims:
5.5''; tyres: 175 SR x 14 - ZL and ZT models 195/70 HR x 14.

PERFORMANCE max speeds: (I) 27 mph, 44 km/h; (II) 43
mph, 70 km/h; (III) 68 mph, 110 km/h; (IV) 99 mph, 160
km/h; (V) 112 mph, 180 km/h; power-weight ratio: Z 19.9
lb/hp, 9 kg/hp; carrying capacity: 397 lb, 180 kg; consumption: 25.7 m/imp gal, 21.4 m/US gal, 11 l x 100 km; Z
2 + 2 models 24 m/imp gal, 20 m/US gal, 11.8 l x 100 km.

CHASSIS integral; front suspension: independent, by Mc-
Pherson, coil springs/telescopic damper struts, lower wish-

NISSAN Fairlady 280 ZL 2 + 2 Sports

130 HP POWER TEAM

bones (trailing links), anti-roll bar; rear: independent, semi-trailing arms, coil springs, telescopic dampers, anti-roll bar.

STEERING rack-and-pinion; turns lock to lock: 3.50.

BRAKES disc, servo; lining area: front 28.5 sq in, 184 sq cm, rear 14.3 sq in, 92 sq cm, total 42.8 sq in, 276 sq cm.

ELECTRICAL EQUIPMENT 12 V; 35 Ah battery; 50 A alternator; contactless distributor; 2 headlamps.

DIMENSIONS AND WEIGHT wheel base: 91.34 in, 232 cm - 2+2 models 99.21 in, 252 cm; tracks: 54.52 in, 138 cm front, 54.52 in, 138 cm rear; length: 170.86 in, 434 cm - 2+2 models 178.74 in, 454 cm; width: 66.53 in, 169 cm; height: 50.98 in, 129 cm - 2 + 2 models 51.38 in, 130 cm; ground clearance: 5.90 in, 15 cm; weight: Z 2,591 lb, 1,175 kg - ZL 2,624 lb, 1,190 kg - ZT 2,635 lb, 1,195 kg - Z 2 + 2 2,657 lb, 1,205 kg - ZL 2 + 2 2,701 lb, 1,225 kg - ZT 2 + 2 2,712 lb, 1,230 kg; turning circle: 34.1 ft, 10.4 m - 2 + 2 models 38 ft, 11.6 m; fuel tank: 17.6 imp gal, 21.1 US gal, 80 l.

BODY coupé; 2 + 1 doors; 2 seats (4 for 2 + 2 models), separate front seats.

OPTIONALS recirculating ball steering wheel with servo, 2.70 turns lock to lock; 3-speed automatic transmission (I 2.458, II 1.458, III 1, rev 2.182), 4.111 axle ratio; 6'' light alloy wheels; air-conditioning.

145 hp power team

See 130 hp power team, except for:

ENGINE 168 cu in, 2,754 cc (3.39 x 3.11 in, 86 x 79 mm); compression ratio: 8.3:1; max power (JIS): 145 hp at 5,200 rpm; max torque (JIS): 167 lb ft, 23 kg m at 4,000 rpm.

TRANSMISSION gearbox ratios: I 3.321, II 2.077, III 1.308, IV 1, V 0.864, rev 3.382; axle ratio: 3.700; tyres 195/70 HR x 14.

PERFORMANCE max speeds: (I) 31 mph, 50 km/h; (II) 48 mph, 78 km/h; (III) 73 mph, 118 km/h; (IV) 102 mph, 165 km/h; (V) 112 mph, 180 km/h; power-weight ratio: ZL 18.6 lb/hp, 8.4 kg/hp; consumption: (for 2-seater models only) 38.1 m/imp gal, 31.7 m/US gal, 7.4 l x 100 km.

ELECTRICAL EQUIPMENT 60 Ah battery; 60 A alternator.

DIMENSIONS AND WEIGHT length: 2-seater models 174.01 in, 442 cm - 2 + 2 models 181.89 in, 462 cm; weight: ZL 2,701 lb, 1,225 kg - ZT 2,800 lb, 1,270 kg - ZL 2 + 2 2,778 lb, 1,260 kg - ZT 2 + 2 2,877 lb, 1,305 kg.

President Series

PRICES (Tokyo):

President C Sedan	3,846,000 yen
President D Sedan	4,238,000 yen
President Sovereign Sedan	4,627,000 yen

200 hp power team

ENGINE front, 4 stroke; V8 cylinders; 269.3 cu in, 4,414 cc (3.62 x 3.27 in, 92 x 83 mm); compression ratio: 8.6:1; max power (JIS): 200 hp at 4,800 rpm; max torque (JIS): 250 lb ft, 34.5 kg m at 3,200 rpm; max engine rpm: 5,200; 45.1 hp/l; cast iron block, light alloy head; 5 crankshaft bearings; valves: overhead. Vee-slanted, push-rods and rockers, hydraulic tappets; camshafts: 1, at centre of Vee; lubrication: gear pump, full flow filter, 8.3 imp pt, 9.9 US pt, 4.7 l; Bosch L-Jetronic fuel injection; emission control with 2 catalytic converters and exhaust gas recirculation; fuel feed: electric pump; water-cooled, 28.2 imp pt, 33.8 US pt, 16 l.

TRANSMISSION driving wheels: rear; gearbox: automatic transmission, hydraulic torque converter and planetary gears with 3 ratios; ratios: I 2.458, II 1.458, III 1, rev 2.182; lever: steering column; final drive: hypoid bevel; axle ratio: 3.364; width of rims: 5''; tyres: 7.75S x 14.

PERFORMANCE max speeds: (I) 42 mph, 68 km/h; (II) 65 mph, 115 km/h; (III) 112 mph, 180 km/h; power-weight ratio: C Sedan 20.3 lb/hp, 9.2 kg/hp; consumption: 14.7 m/imp gal, 12.2 m/US gal, 19.2 l x 100 km.

CHASSIS integral; front suspension: independent, wishbones, coil springs, anti-roll bar, telescopic dampers; rear: rigid axle, semi-elliptic leafsprings, telescopic dampers.

STEERING recirculating ball, servo; turns lock to lock: 4.10.

BRAKES front disc, rear drum, servo; lining area: front 26.7 sq in, 172 sq cm, rear 71.9 sq in, 464 sq cm, total 98.6 sq in, 636 sq cm.

NISSAN President Sovereign Sedan

ELECTRICAL EQUIPMENT 12 V; 60 Ah battery; 600 W alternator; Hitachi distributor; 4 headlamps.

DIMENSIONS AND WEIGHT wheel base: 112.20 in, 285 cm; front and rear track: 58.66 in, 149 cm; length: C 206.69 in, 525 cm - D and Sovereign 207.87 in, 528 cm; width: 72.05 in, 183 cm; height: 58.27 in, 148 cm; ground clearance: 7.28 in, 18 cm; weight: C Sedan 4,057 lb, 1,850 kg - D Sedan 4,123 lb, 1,870 kg - Sovereign Sedan 4,134 lb, 1,875 kg; weight distribution: 54% front, 46% rear; turning circle: 42 ft, 12.8 m; fuel tank: 16.5 imp gal, 19.8 US gal, 7.5 l.

BODY saloon/sedan; 4 doors; 6 seats, bench front seats, reclining backrests, built-in headrests; electric windows.

OPTIONALS air-conditioning; separate front seats.

Patrol 4WD

PRICE (Tokyo): 1,302,000 yen

ENGINE front, 4 stroke; 6 cylinders, vertical, in line; 241.4 cu in, 3,956 cc (3.37 x 4.50 in, 85.7 x 114.3 mm); compression ratio: 7.6:1; max power (JIS): 130 hp at 3,600 rpm; max torque (JIS): 217 lb ft, 30 kg m at 1,600 rpm; max engine rpm: 3,600; 32.9 hp/l; cast iron block and head; 7 crankshaft bearings; valves: overhead, in line, push-rods and rockers; camshafts: 1, side; lubrication: gear pump, full flow filter, oil cooler; 9.3 imp pt, 11.2 US pt, 5.3 l; 1 Hitachi VC 42-4A downdraught carburettor; fuel

feed: mechanical pump; water-cooled, 32.2 imp pt, 38 US pt, 18.3 l.

TRANSMISSION driving wheels: front (automatically engaged with transfer box low ratio) and rear; clutch: single dry plate; gearbox: mechanical; gears: 3, with high and low ratios, II and III synchronized; ratios: I 2.900, 1.562, III 1, rev 4.015; low ratios: I 6.565, II 3.536, 2.264, rev 9.089; levers: 3, central; final drive: hypoid bevel; axle ratio: 4.100; tyres: 6.50 x 16.

PERFORMANCE max speed: 78 mph, 125 km/h; power-weight ratio: 28.2 lb/hp, 12.8 kg/hp; carrying capacity 1,654 lb, 750 kg; speed in direct drive at 1,000 rpm: 21 mph, 34.7 km/h; consumption: not declared.

CHASSIS ladder frame; front and rear suspension: rigid axle, semi-elliptic leafsprings, telescopic dampers.

STEERING worm and roller.

BRAKES drum, servo.

ELECTRICAL EQUIPMENT 12 V; 60 Ah battery; 35 A alternator; Hitachi distributor; 2 headlamps.

DIMENSIONS AND WEIGHT wheel base: 98.43 in, 250 cm; tracks: 54.57 in, 139 cm front, 55.28 in, 140 cm rear; length: 160.24 in, 407 cm; width: 67.52 in, 171 cm; height 79.33 in, 201 cm; ground clearance: 8.46 in, 21.5 cm; weight: 3,660 lb, 1,660 kg; turning circle: 38.7 ft, 11.9 m; fuel tank: 14.3 imp gal, 17.2 US gal, 65 l.

BODY open; 2 doors; 3 seats, bench front seats.

NISSAN Patrol 4WD

SUBARU   JAPAN

Rex 550 SEEC-T Series

PRICES (Tokyo):

Standard 2-dr Sedan	551,000	yen
A I 2-dr Sedan	618,000	yen
A I 4-dr Sedan	643,000	yen
A I 3-dr Swingback	638,000	yen
A II 4-dr Sedan	682,000	yen
A II 3-dr Swingback	677,000	yen
A II G 4-dr Sedan	709,000	yen
A II G 3-dr Swingback	704,000	yen

31 hp power team

ENGINE rear, low emission SEEC-T type, transverse, 4 stroke; 2 cylinders, in line; 33.2 cu in, 544 cc (2.99 x 2.36 in, 76 x 60 mm); compression ratio: 8.5:1; max power (JIS): 31 hp at 6,200 rpm; max torque (JIS): 30.4 lb ft, 4.2 kg m at 3,500 rpm; max engine rpm: 7,000; 56.9 hp/l; cast iron block, light alloy head; 3 crankshaft bearings; valves: overhead, Vee-slanted, rockers; camshafts: 1, overhead; lubrication: rotary pump, full flow filter, 4.4 imp pt, 5.3 US pt, 2.5 l; 1 Hitachi DCG306 downdraught twin barrel carburettor; fuel feed: mechanical pump; water-cooled, 10.6 imp pt, 12.7 US pt, 6 l.

TRANSMISSION driving wheels: rear; clutch: single dry plate (diaphragm); gearbox: mechanical; gears: 4, fully synchronized; ratios: I 4.363, II 2.625, III 1.809, IV 1.269, rev 4.272; lever: central; final drive: helical spur gears; axle ratio: 4.315; width of rims: 3.5''; tyres: 5.20 x 10.

PERFORMANCE max speeds: (I) 21 mph, 34 km/h; (II) 34 mph, 55 km/h; (III) 50 mph, 80 km/h; (IV) 65 mph, 105 km/h; power-weight ratio: Standard 2-dr Sedan 38 lb/hp, 17.3 kg/hp; carrying capacity: 706 lb, 320 kg; consumption: 58.8 m/imp gal, 48 m/US gal, 4.8 l x 100 km.

CHASSIS integral; front and rear suspension: independent, semi-trailing arms, torsion bars, telescopic dampers.

STEERING rack-and-pinion; turns lock to lock: 3.20.

BRAKES drum (for AII and AIIG models, front disc brakes); lining area: front 37.2 sq in, 240 sq cm, rear 33.5 sq in, 216 sq cm, total 70.7 sq in, 456 sq cm.

ELECTRICAL EQUIPMENT 12 V; 30 Ah battery; 35 A alternator; Hitachi distributor; 2 headlamps.

DIMENSIONS AND WEIGHT wheel base: 75.59 in, 192 cm; tracks: 48.43 in, 123 cm front, 47.83 in, 121 cm rear; length: 125.39 in, 318 cm; height: 52.17 in, 132 cm; width: 54.92 in, 139 cm; ground clearance: 6.89 in, 17.5 cm; weight: Standard 2-dr 1,180 lb, 535 kg - AI 2-dr 1,202 lb, 545 kg - AI 4-dr 1,246 lb, 565 kg - AI 3-dr 1,235 lb, 560 kg - AII 2-dr 1,213 lb, 550 kg - AII 4-dr 1,257 lb, 570 kg - AII 3-dr 1,246 lb, 565 kg - AIIG 4-dr 1,257 lb, 570 kg; weight distribution: 37% front, 63% rear; turning circle 30.2 ft, 9.2 m; fuel tank: 5.5 imp gal, 6.6 US gal, 25 l.

BODY saloon/sedan; 4 seats, separate front seats, reclining backrests, built-in headrests.

Leone SEEC-T Series

PRICES (Tokyo):

1	1400 Standard 2-dr Sedan	749,000	yen
2	1400 De Luxe 2-dr Sedan	836,000	yen
3	1400 De Luxe 4-dr Sedan	861,000	yen
4	1400 GL 2-dr Sedan	908,000	yen
5	1400 GL 4-dr Sedan	933,000	yen
6	1600 De Luxe 4-dr Sedan	886,000	yen
7	1600 GL 4-dr Sedan	958,000	yen
8	1600 Custom 4-dr Sedan	1,008,000	yen
9	1600 Super Custom 4-dr Sedan	1,130,000	yen
10	1600 GL Coupé	1,016,000	yen
11	1600 GF Hardtop	1,050,000	yen
12	1600 Grand Am 4-dr Sedan	1,122,000	yen
13	1600 Grand Am Hardtop	1,185,000	yen
14	1600 Super Touring 4-dr Sedan	1,135,000	yen
15	1600 RX Coupé	1,153,000	yen
16	1600 GFT Hardtop	1,149,000	yen
17	1600 Grand Am T Hardtop	1,307,000	yen
18	1600 4WD 4-dr Sedan	1,366,000	yen
19	1600 4WD Station Wagon L	1,130,000	yen
20	1600 4WD Station Wagon LG	1,185,000	yen

For GB and USA prices, see price index.

Power team:	Standard for:	Optional for:
72 hp	1 to 5	—
82 hp	6 to 13	—
95 hp	14 to 17	—
82 hp 4x4	18	—
87 hp	19,20	—

72 hp power team

ENGINE front, SEEC-T type, low emission system with secondary air injection by suction valve, 4 stroke; 4 cylinders, horizontally opposed; 83 cu in, 1,361 cc (3.35 x 2.36 in, 85 x 60 mm); compression ratio: 8.5:1; max power (JIS): 72 hp at 6,000 rpm; max torque (JIS): 74 lb ft, 10.2 kg m at 3,600 rpm; max engine rpm: 6,400; 52.9 hp/l; light alloy cylinder block and head; 3 crankshaft bearings; valves: overhead, push-rods and rockers; camshafts: 1, side; lubrication: rotary pump, full flow filter, 5.8 imp pt, 7 US pt, 3.3 l; 1 Hitachi-Zenith-Stromberg DCJ306 downdraught twin barrel carburettor; fuel feed: electric pump; water-cooled, 10.6 imp pt, 12.7 US pt, 6 l.

TRANSMISSION driving wheels: front; clutch: single dry plate (diaphragm); gearbox: mechanical; gears: 4, fully synchronized; ratios: I 3.666, II 2.157, III 1.464, IV 1.029, rev 4.100; lever: central; final drive: hypoid bevel; axle ratio: 4.125; width of rims: 4.5''; tyres: 6.15 x 13.

PERFORMANCE max speeds: (I) 27 mph, 44 km/h; (II) 45 mph, 73 km/h; (III) 67 mph, 108 km/h; (IV) 93 mph, 150 km/h; power-weight ratio: Standard 2-dr Sedan 25.1 lb/hp, 11.4 kg/hp; carrying capacity: 882 lb, 400 kg; consumption: 34 m/imp gal, 28.3 m/US gal, 8.3 l x 100 km.

CHASSIS integral; front suspension: independent, by McPherson, coil springs/telescopic damper struts, lower wishbones (trailing links), anti-roll bar; rear: independent, semi-trailing arms, torsion bars, telescopic dampers.

STEERING rack-and-pinion; turns lock to lock: 3.80.

BRAKES drum (for GL models front disc brakes); lining area: front 65.1 sq in, 420 sq cm - GL models 24.2 sq in, 156 sq cm, rear 26 sq in, 168 sq cm, total 91.1 sq in, 588 sq cm - GL models 50.2 sq in, 324 sq cm.

ELECTRICAL EQUIPMENT 12 V; 35 Ah battery; 50 A alternator; Hitachi distributor; 2 headlamps.

DIMENSIONS AND WEIGHT wheel base: 96.85 in, 246 cm; tracks: 49.80 in, 126.5 cm front, 49.60 in, 126 cm rear; length: 157.09 in, 399 cm; width: 61.02 in, 155 cm; height: 54.92 in, 139 cm; ground clearance: 6.69 in, 17 cm; weight: Standard 2-dr Sedan 1,808 lb, 820 kg - De Luxe 2-dr Sedan 1,874 lb, 850 kg - De Luxe 4-dr Sedan 1,896 lb, 860 kg - GL 2-dr Sedan 1,852 lb, 840 kg - GL 4-dr Sedan 1,918 lb, 870 kg; turning circle: 35.4 ft, 10.8 m; fuel tank: 11 imp gal, 13.2 US gal, 50 l.

BODY 5 seats, separate front seats, reclining backrests, built-in headrests.

82 hp power team

See 72 hp power team, except for:

ENGINE 97.3 cu in, 1,595 cc (3.62 x 2.36 in, 92 x 60 mm); max power (JIS): 82 hp at 5,600 rpm; max torque (JIS): 87 lb ft, 12 kg m at 3,600 rpm; 51.4 hp/l; 1 Hitachi DCG 306 downdraught twin barrel carburettor.

SUBARU Rex 550 SEEC-T A II G Sedan

SUBARU Leone SEEC-T 1600 Super Custom Sedan

82 HP POWER TEAM

TRANSMISSION gears: Custom, Super Custom and Grand Am models 5 fully synchronized; ratios: V 0.789; axle ratio: 3700; tyres: Grand Am models 155 SR x 13.

PERFORMANCE max speeds: (I) 31 mph, 50 km/h; (II) 50 mph, 80 km/h; (III) 75 mph, 120 km/h; (IV) 99 mph, 160 km/h; power-weight ratio: De Luxe 4-dr Sedan 23.1 lb/hp, 10.5 kg/hp; consumption: 31 m/imp gal, 25.8 m/US gal, 9.1 l x 100 km.

BRAKES front disc, rear drum; lining area: front 24.2 sq in, 156 sq cm, rear 26 sq in, 168 sq cm, total 50.2 sq in, 324 sq cm.

ELECTRICAL EQUIPMENT (for GL and Custom sedans, and GF Hardtop) 4 headlamps.

DIMENSIONS AND WEIGHT length: GL Coupé and Super Custom Sedan 158.07 in, 401 cm - Grand Am models 164.17 in, 417 cm; height: Coupé 53.35 in, 135 cm - Hardtop 53.54 in, 136 cm; weight: De Luxe 4-dr Sedan 1,896 lb, 860 kg - GL 4-dr Sedan 1,918 lb, 870 kg - Custom 4-dr Sedan 1,929 lb, 875 kg - Super Custom 4-dr Sedan 1,940 lb, 880 kg - GL Coupé 1,852 lb, 840 kg - GF Hardtop 1,918 lb, 870 kg - Grand Am 4-dr Sedan and Hardtop 1,984 lb, 900 kg.

OPTIONALS automatic transmission with 3 ratios (I 2.600, II 1.505, III 1, rev 2.167) 3.811 axle ratio.

SUBARU Leone SEEC-T 1600 4WD Station Wagon LG

95 hp power team

See 72 hp power team, except for:

ENGINE 97.3 cu in, 1,595 cc (3.62 x 2.36 in, 92 x 60 mm); compression ratio: 9.5:1; max power (JIS): 95 hp at 6,400 rpm; max torque (JIS): 89 lb ft, 12.3 kg m at 4,000 rpm; 59.6 hp/l; 2 Hitachi DCG306 downdraught twin barrel carburettors.

TRANSMISSION gears: 5, fully synchronized; ratios: I 3.666, II 2.157, III 1.518, IV 1.156, V 0.942, rev 4.110; axle ratio: 3.700; tyres: 155 SR x 13 - RX Coupé 165/70 HR x 13.

PERFORMANCE max speeds: (I) 34 mph, 55 km/h; (II) 55 mph, 88 km/h; (III) 79 mph, 127 km/h; (IV) 102 mph, 165 km/h; (V) 105 mph, 170 km/h; power-weight ratio: Super Touring Sedan 20.6 lb/hp, 9.4 kg/hp; consumption: 29.7 m/imp gal, 24.7 m/US gal, 9.5 l x 100 km.

STEERING turns lock to lock: 2.90.

BRAKES front disc, rear drum, servo; lining area: front 24.2 sq in, 156 sq cm, rear 26 sq in, 168 sq cm, total 50.2 sq in, 324 sq cm (Super Touring Sedan and RX Coupé rear disc brakes).

ELECTRICAL EQUIPMENT Super Touring Sedan and GFT Hardtop 4 headlamps.

DIMENSIONS AND WEIGHT front track: RX Coupé 50.39 in, 128 cm - Grand Am T 50.98 in, 129.5 cm; rear track: RX Coupé 50.19 in, 127.5 cm - Grand Am T 50.78 in, 129 cm; length: Grand Am T Hardtop 164.17 in, 417 cm; height: RX Coupé 53.35 in, 135.5 cm - GFT and Grand Am T Hardtop 53.54 in, 136 cm; weight: Super Touring Sedan 1,962 lb, 890 kg - RX Coupé 1,951 lb, 885 kg - GFT Hardtop 1,929 lb, 875 kg - Grand Am T Hardtop 1,984 lb, 900 kg.

OPTIONALS automatic transmission with 3 ratios (I 2.600, II 1.505, III 1, rev 2.167), 3.811 axle ratio.

82 hp power team 4 x 4

See 72 hp power team, except for:

ENGINE 97.3 cu in, 1,595 cc (3.62 x 2.36 in, 92 x 60 mm); max power (JIS): 82 hp at 5,600 rpm; max torque (JIS): 87 lb ft, 12 kg m at 3,600 rpm; 51.4 hp/l.

TRANSMISSION driving wheels: front and rear with transfer box; ratios: I 4.090, II 2.312, III 1.464, IV 1.029, rev 4.100; axle ratios: front 3.889, rear 3.900; tyres: 155SR x 13.

PERFORMANCE max speeds: (I) 25 mph, 40 km/h; (II) 45 mph, 72 km/h; (III) 72 mph, 116 km/h; (IV) 93 mph, 150 km/h; power-weight ratio: 26.7 lb/hp, 12.1 kg/hp.

BRAKES front disc, rear drum; lining area: front 24.2 sq in, 156 sq cm, rear 26 sq in, 168 sq cm, total 50.2 sq in, 324 sq cm.

DIMENSIONS AND WEIGHT tracks: 49.61 in, 126 cm front, 49.41 in, 125.5 cm rear; height: 56.10 in, 142.5 cm; ground clearance: 7.68 in, 19.5 cm; weight: 2,194 lb, 995 kg; fuel tank: 9.9 imp gal, 11.9 US gal, 45 l.

BODY saloon/sedan; 4 doors.

87 hp power team

See 72 hp power team, except for:

ENGINE not SEEC-T type: 97.3 cu in, 1,595 cc (3.62 x 2.36 in 92 x 60 mm); max power (JIS): 87 hp at 5,600 rpm; max torque (JIS): 89 lb ft, 12.3 kg m at 3,600 rpm; 54.5 hp/l; 1 Hitachi DCG306 downdraught twin barrel carburettor.

TRANSMISSION driving wheels: front and rear with transfer box; ratios: I 4.090, II 2.312, III 1.464, IV 1.029, rev 4.100; axle ratio: front 3.889, rear 3.900; tyres: 155 SR x 13.

PERFORMANCE max speeds: (I) 25 mph, 40 km/h; (II) 45 mph, 72 km/h; (III) 72 mph, 116 km/h; (IV) 93 mph, 150 km/h; power-weight ratio: 24.6 lb/hp, 11.2 kg/hp; consumption: 29.7 m/imp pt, 24.7 m/US pt, 9.5 l x 100 km.

BRAKES front disc, rear drum; lining area: front 24.2 sq in, 156 sq cm, rear 26 sq in, 168 sq cm, total 50.2 sq in, 324 sq cm.

DIMENSIONS AND WEIGHT wheel base: 96.06 in, 244 cm; tracks: 49.41 in, 125 cm front, 47.44 in, 120 cm rear; length: L 158.86 in, 403 cm - LG 164.96 in, 419 cm; height: 57.48 in, 146 cm; ground clearance: 8.27 in, 21 cm; weight: L 2,129 lb, 965 kg - LG 2,172 lb, 985 kg; turning circle: 40 ft, 12.2 m; fuel tank: 9.9 imp gal, 11.9 US gal, 45 l.

BODY estate car/station wagon; 4 + 1 doors.

SUZUKI SC100 CXG Coupé

Fronte 7-S Series

PRICES (Tokyo) yen:	2-stroke	4-stroke
1 Standard 2-dr Sedan	527,000	556,000
2 De Luxe 2-dr Sedan	576,000	604,000
3 De Luxe 4-dr Sedan	599,000	627,000
4 Super De Luxe 4-dr Sedan	662,000	662,000
5 Custom 2-dr Sedan	658,000	658,000
6 Custom 4-dr Sedan	698,000	698,000
7 Cervo Coupé CX	608,000	—
8 Cervo Coupé CXG	698,000	—
9 SC 100 CXG Coupé	—	—

Power team:	Standard for:	Optional for:
28 hp (2-stroke)	1 to 8	—
28 hp (4-stroke)	1 to 6	—
47 hp	9	—

28 hp power team

(2-stroke engine)

ENGINE rear, transverse, 2 stroke; 3 cylinders, in line; 32.9 cu in, 539 cc (2.40 x 2.42 in, 61 x 61.5 mm); compression ratio: 7; max power (JIS): 28 hp at 5,000 rpm; max torque (JIS): 38.4 lb ft, 5.3 kg m at 3,000 rpm; max engine rpm: 6,400; 51.9 hp/l; cast iron block, light alloy head; 4 crankshaft bearings on ball bearings; lubrication: mechanical pump, injection to cylinders and crankshaft bearings, total loss system, 7 imp pt, 8.5 US pt, 4 l; 1 Mikuni-Solex downdraught carburettor; fuel feed: mechanical pump emission control 2-3 stage catalyst; water-cooled, 9.5 imp pt, 11.4 US pt, 5.4 l.

TRANSMISSION driving wheels: rear; clutch: single dry plate (diaphragm); gearbox: mechanical; engine-gearbox ratio: 1.471; gears: 4, fully synchronized; ratios: I 3.182, II 1.875, III 1.238, IV 0.880, rev 2.727; lever: central; final drive: helical spur gears; axle ratio: 4.385; width of rims: 3.5''; tyres: 5.20 x 10 (Cervo Coupé CXG 145 SR x 10).

PERFORMANCE max speeds: (I) 18 mph, 30 km/h; (II) 32 mph, 52 km/h; (III) 49 mph, 79 km/h; (IV) 65 mph, 105 km/h; power-weight ratio: Standard 2-dr Sedan 41.7 lb/hp, 18.9 kg/hp; consumption: 49.5 m/imp gal, 41.3 m/US gal, 5.7 l x 100 km.

CHASSIS integral; front suspension: independent, wishbones, coil springs, anti-roll bar, telescopic dampers; rear: independent, semi-trailing arms, coil springs, telescopic dampers.

STEERING rack-and-pinion; turns lock to lock: 2.75.

BRAKES drum (front disc on Cervo Coupé CXG); lining area: front 31.6 sq in, 204 sq cm, rear 31.6 sq in, 204 sq cm total 63.2 sq in, 408 sq cm.

ELECTRICAL EQUIPMENT 12 V; 24 Ah battery; 35 A alternator; 2 headlamps.

DIMENSIONS AND WEIGHT wheel base: 79.92 in, 203 cm

tracks: 47.64 in, 121 cm front (Cervo Coupé 48.03 in, 122 cm), 46.65 in, 118 cm rear (Cervo Coupé 46.85 in, 119 cm); length: 125.59 in, 319 cm; width: 54.92 in, 139 cm; height: 51.18 in, 130 cm (Cervo Coupé 47.64 in, 121 cm); weight: Standard and De Luxe 2-dr sedans 1,169 lb, 530 kg - Cervo Coupé CX 1,180 lb, 535 kg - Custom 2-dr Sedan 1,191 lb, 540 kg - De Luxe 4-dr Sedan 1,202 lb, 545 kg - Cervo Coupé CXG 1,212 lb, 550 kg - Super De Luxe and Custom 4-dr sedans 1,224 lb, 555 kg; turning circle: 26.9 ft, 8.2 m; fuel tank: 5.7 imp gal, 6.9 US gal, 26 l.

BODY 4 seats, separate front seats, reclining backrests, built-in headrests.

28 hp power team

(4-stroke engine)

See 28 hp power team (2-stroke engine), except for:

ENGINE rear, transverse, 4 stroke; 2 cylinders, in line; 33.4 cu in, 547 cc (2.82 x 2.68 in, 71.6 x 68 mm); compression ratio: 8.7; max power (JIS): 28 hp at 6,000 rpm; max torque (JIS): 28.3 lb ft, 3.9 kg m at 3,500 rpm; max engine rpm: 6,300; 51.2 hp/l; 3 crankshaft bearings; valves: 2, overhead, rocker arms; camshafts: 1, overhead; lubrication: rotary pump, full flow filter, 5.1 imp pt, 6.1 US pt, 2.9 l; 1 downdraught twin barrel carburettor; Daihatsu lean-burn system turbulence generating pot in the combustion chamber and catalytic converter.

TRANSMISSION engine - gearbox ratio: direct; ratios: I 3.583, II 2.176, III 1.375, IV 0.965, rev 3.363; axle ratio: 5.285.

PERFORMANCE max speeds: (I) 18 mph, 30 km/h; (II) 31 mph, 50 km/h; (III) 50 mph, 80 km/h; (IV) 68 mph, 110 km/h; power-weight ratio: Standard 2-dr Sedan 43.2 lb/hp, 19.6 kg/hp.

DIMENSIONS AND WEIGHT weight: Standard 2-dr Sedan 1,212 lb, 550 kg - De Luxe and Custom 2-dr sedans 1,224 lb, 555 kg - De Luxe and Custom 4-dr sedans 1,257 lb, 570 kg.

47 hp power team

See 28 hp power team (2-stroke engine), except for:

ENGINE rear, transverse, 4 stroke; 4 cylinders, in line; 59.2 cu in, 970 cc (2.58 x 2.83 in, 65.5 x 72 mm); compression ratio: 8.7:1; max power (JIS): 47 hp at 5,000 rpm; max torque (JIS): 61 lb ft, 8.4 kg m at 2,500 rpm; 48.4 hp/l; valves: overhead, rockers; camshafts: 1, overhead; lubrication: gear pump, full flow filter; 1 Mikuni - Solex downdraught carburettor.

TRANSMISSION tyres: 145/70 SR x 12.

PERFORMANCE power-weight ratio: 29.3 lb/hp, 13.3 kg/hp.

BRAKES front disc, rear drum.

DIMENSIONS AND WEIGHT tracks: 48.03 in, 122 cm front, 46.85 in, 119 cm rear; height: 48.42 in, 123 cm; weight: 1,378 lb, 625 kg.

Fronte Hatch 55 Series

PRICES (Tokyo):

Hatch 55B Station Wagon	507,000 yen
Hatch 55D Station Wagon	537,000 yen
Hatch 55T Station Wagon	567,000 yen

25 hp power team

ENGINE front, 2 stroke; 3 cylinders, in line; 32.8 cu in, 539 cc (2.40 x 2.42 in, 61 x 61.5 mm); compression ratio: 6.4:1; max power (JIS): 25 hp at 4,500 rpm; max torque (JIS): 37 lb ft, 5.1 kg m at 3,000 rpm; max engine rpm: 6,000; 46.4 hp/l; cast iron block, light alloy head; 4 crankshaft bearings; lubrication: mechanical pump, injection to cylinders and crankshaft bearings, total loss system, 6.2 imp pt, 7.4 US pt, 3.5 l; 1 Solex downdraught carburettor; fuel feed: mechanical pump; water-cooled, 7.2 imp pt, 8.7 US pt, 4.1 l.

TRANSMISSION driving wheels: rear; clutch: single dry plate (diaphragm); gearbox: mechanical; engine-gearbox ratio 1.600; gears: 4, fully synchronized; ratios: I 3.428, II 2.109, III 1.307, IV 1, rev 3.600; lever: central; final drive: hypoid bevel; axle ratio: 5.125; tyres: 5.00 x 10.

PERFORMANCE max speeds: (I) 21 mph, 33 km/h; (II) 32 mph, 52 km/h; (III) 48 mph, 77 km/h; (IV) 67 mph, 108 km/h; power-weight ratio: 55 B 48.5 lb/hp, 22 kg/hp - 55 D and 55 T lb/hp, 22.2 kg/hp; carrying capacity: 662 lb, 300 kg; consumption: 70.6 m/imp gal, 58.8 m/US gal, 4 l x 100 km at 37 mph, 60 km/h.

CHASSIS integral; front suspension: independent, by Mc-

Pherson, coil springs/telescopic damper struts, anti-roll bar, lower wishbones; rear: rigid axle, semi-elliptic leafsprings, telescopic dampers.

STEERING recirculating ball.

BRAKES drum.

ELECTRICAL EQUIPMENT 12 V; 24 Ah battery; 35 Ah alternator; 2 headlamps.

DIMENSIONS AND WEIGHT wheel base: 82.68 in, 210 cm; tracks: 46.46 in, 118 cm front, 42.52 in, 108 cm rear; length: 123.59 in, 319 cm; width: 53.74 in, 136 cm; height: 54.13 in, 137 cm; ground clearance: 5.91 in, 15 cm; weight: 55 B 1,213 lb, 550 kg - 55D and 55 T 1,224 lb, 555 kg; turning circle: 28.2 ft, 8.6 m; fuel tank: 5.7 imp gal, 6.9 US gal, 26 l.

BODY estate car/station wagon; 2 + 1 doors; 2 + 2 seats, separate front seats, reclining backrests; built-in headrests; folding rear seat.

Jimny 55 - Jimny 8 Series

PRICES (Tokyo):

1 Jimny 55 Softtop	748,000	yen
2 Jimny 55 Steelbody Wagon	797,000	yen
3 Jimny 8 Softtop	859,000	yen
4 Jimny 8 Steelbody Wagon	908,000	yen

Power team:	Standard for:	Optional for:
26 hp	1,2	—
41 hp	3,4	—

26 hp power team

ENGINE front, 2 stroke; 3 cylinders, in line; 32.8 cu in, 539 cc (2.40 x 2.42 in, 61 x 61.5 mm); compression ratio: 6.2:1; max power (JIS): 26 hp at 4,500 rpm; max torque (JIS): 38 lb ft, 5.3 kg m at 3,000 rpm; max engine rpm: 6,000; 48.2 hp/l; cast iron block, light alloy head; 4 crankshaft bearings, on ball bearings; lubrication: mechanical pump, injection to cylinders and crankshaft bearings, total system, 4.9 imp pt, 5.9 US pt, 2.8 l; 1 Solex downdraught carburettor; fuel feed: mechanical pump; water-cooled, 7.2 imp pt, 8.7 US pt, 4.1 l.

TRANSMISSION driving wheels: front and rear; clutch: single dry plate; gearbox: mechanical; gears: 4, fully synchronized and 2-ratio transfer box; ratios: I 3.855, II 2.359, III 1.543, IV 1, rev 4.026; transfer box ratios: Softtop I 3.012, II 1.714 - Steelbody I 2.571, II 1.562; levers: central; final drive: hypoid bevel; axle ratio: 4.875; width of rims: 4.5''; tyres: 6.00 x 16 - Steelbody 5.60 x 15.

PERFORMANCE max speeds: (I) 15 mph, 24 km/h; (II) 20 mph, 38 km/h; (III) 37 mph, 60 km/h; (IV) 55 mph, 88 km/h; power-weight ratio: Softtop 57.2 lb/hp, 26 kg/hp - Steelbody 60.2 lb/hp, 27.3 kg/hp; carrying capacity: Softtop 551 lb, 250 kg - Steelbody 441 lb, 200 kg; consumption: 47.9 m/imp gal, 39.9 m/US gal, 5.9 l x 100 km at 37 mph, 60 km/h.

SUZUKI Fronte Hatch 55T Station Wagon

CHASSIS box-type ladder frame; front suspension: rigid axle, semi-elliptic leafsprings, telescopic dampers; rear: rigid axle, semi-elliptic leafspring, telescopic dampers.

STEERING recirculating ball; turns lock to lock: 3.20.

BRAKES drum.

ELECTRICAL EQUIPMENT 12 V; 24 Ah battery; 35 A alternator; Nihon Denso distributor; 2 headlamps.

DIMENSIONS AND WEIGHT wheel base: 75.98 in, 193 cm; tracks: 42.91 in, 109 cm front, 43.31 in, 110 cm rear; length: 124.80 in, 317 cm; width: 50.98 in, 129 cm; height: Softtop 72.64 in, 184 cm - Steelbody 64.96 in, 165 cm; ground clearance: Softtop 9.45 in, 24 cm - Steelbody 8.07 in, 20.5 cm; weight: Softtop 1,488 lb, 675 kg - Steelbody 1,566 lb, 710 kg; turning circle: 28.9 ft, 8.8 m; fuel tank: 5.7 imp gal, 6.9 US gal, 26 l.

OPTIONALS (for Steelbody only) 2-ratio transfer box (I 1.714, II 3.012) with 6.00 x 16 tyres.

41 hp power team

See 26 hp power team, except for:

ENGINE front, 4 stroke; 4 cylinders, in line; 48.6 cu in, 797 cc (2.44 x 2.60 in, 62 x 66 mm); compression ratio: 8.7; max power (JIS): 41 hp at 5,500 rpm; max torque (JIS): 44

SUZUKI Jimny 55 Softtop

41 HP POWER TEAM

lb ft, 6.1 kg m at 3,500 rpm; 51.4 hp/l; valves: 2, overhead, rocker arms; camshafts: 1, overhead; lubrication: gear pump, full flow filter, 6.2 imp pt, 7.4 US pt, 3.5 l; 1 Mikuni-Solex sidedraught carburettor; water-cooled 6.7 imp pt, 8 US pt, 3.8 l.

TRANSMISSION final drive: 4.556.

PERFORMANCE max speeds: (I) 17 mph, 28 km/h; (II) 26 mph, 42 km/h; (III) 26 mph, 64 km/h; (IV) 60 mph, 97 km/h; power-weight ratio: Softtop 38.4 lb/hp, 17.4 kg/hp; consumption: 45.5 m/imp gal, 37.9 m/US gal, 6.2 l x 100 km at 37 mph, 60 km/h.

DIMENSIONS AND WEIGHT weight: Softtop 1,576 lb, 715 kg - Steelbody 1,676 lb, 760 kg.

TOYOTA   JAPAN

Starlet Series

PRICES (Tokyo):

DX 3-dr Sedan	705,000 yen
DX 5-dr Sedan	730,000 yen
XL 3-dr Sedan	745,000 yen
XL 5-dr Sedan	770,000 yen
S 3-dr Sedan	798,000 yen
S 5-dr Sedan	823,000 yen
SE 3-dr Sedan	813,000 yen
SE 5-dr Sedan	838,000 yen

72 hp power team

ENGINE front, 4 stroke; 4 cylinders, in line; 78.7 cu in, 1,290 cc (2.95 x 2.87 in, 75 x 73 mm); max power (JIS): 72 hp at 5,600 rpm; max torque (JIS): 76 lb ft, 10.5 kg m at 3,600 rpm; max engine rpm: 6,000; 58.9 hp/l; cast iron block, light alloy head; 5 crankshaft bearings; valves: overhead, push-rods and rockers; camshafts: 1, side; lubrication: rotary pump, full flow filter, 6.2 imp pt, 7.4 US pt, 3.5 l; 1 Aisan 4K-U downdraught twin barrel carburettor; emission control with oxidizing catalist, secondary air induction and exhaust gas recirculation; fuel feed: mechanical pump; water-cooled, 8.8 imp pt, 10.6 US pt, 5 l.

TRANSMISSION driving wheels: rear; clutch: single dry plate (diaphragm); gearbox: mechanical; gears: 4, fully synchronized; ratios: I 3.789, II 2.220, III 1.435, IV 1, rev 4.316; lever: central; final drive: hypoid bevel; axle ratio: 3.417 -S models 3.583; width of rims: 4'' - S models 4.5''; tyres: 6.00 x 12 - S models 145 SR x 13 - SE models 155 SR x 12.

PERFORMANCE max speeds: (I) 29 mph, 46 km/h; (II) 51 mph, 82 km/h; (III) 79 mph, 127 km/h; (IV) 103 mph, 165 km/h; power-weight ratio: DX 3-dr Sedan 21.3 lb/hp, 9.6 kg/hp; carrying capacity: 882 lb, 400 kg; consumption: 46.6 m/imp gal, 38.8 m/US gal, 6.1 l x 100 km.

CHASSIS integral; front suspension: independent, by McPherson, coil springs/telescopic dampers, lower wishbones, anti-roll bar; rear: rigid axle, coil springs/telescopic dampers, trailing lower radius arms, upper torque arms.

STEERING rack-and-pinion; turns lock to lock: 3.10.

BRAKES front disc, rear drum, servo; lining area: front 19.8 sq in, 128 sq cm, rear 31.6 sq in, 204 sq cm, total 51.4 sq in, 332 sq cm.

ELECTRICAL EQUIPMENT 12 V; 32 Ah battery; 45 A alternator; Denso distributor; 2 headlamps.

DIMENSIONS AND WEIGHT wheel base: 90.55 in, 230 cm; tracks: 50.79 in, 129 cm front, 50.19 in, 127 cm rear; length: DX and XL models 144.88 in, 368 cm - S models 146.65 in, 372 cm - SE models 147.44 in, 374 cm; width: 60.04 in, 152 cm - SE models 60.43 in, 152 cm; height: 54.33 in, 138 cm - S models 53.94 in, 137 cm; ground clearance: 6.50 in, 16.5 cm - S models 6.30 in, 16 cm; weight: DX 3-dr Sedan 1,532 lb, 695 kg - DX 5-dr and S 3-dr sedans 1,565 lb, 710 kg - XL 3-dr Sedan 1,543 lb, 700 kg - XL 5-dr and SE 3-dr Sedans 1,576 lb, 715 kg - S 5-dr Sedan 1,599 lb, 725 kg - SE 5-dr Sedan 1,609 lb, 730 kg; weight distribution: 55% front, 45% rear; turning circle: 32.1 ft, 9.8 m; fuel tank: 8.8 imp gal, 10.6 US gal, 40 l.

BODY saloon/sedan; 5 seats, separate front seats.

OPTIONALS 5-speed mechanical gearbox, V ratio 0.865, max speed 103 mph, 165 km/h; Toyoglide automatic transmission, hydraulic torque converter and planetary gears with 2 ratios (I 1.820, II 1, rev 1.820), axle ratio 3.583.

Corsa - Tercel Series

PRICES (Tokyo):

1	Corsa Standard 2-dr Sedan	711,000 yen
2	Corsa De Luxe 2-dr Sedan	770,000 yen
3	Corsa De Luxe 4-dr Sedan	795,000 yen
4	Corsa De Luxe 3-dr Coupé	790,000 yen
5	Corsa GL 2-dr Sedan	822,000 yen
6	Corsa GL 4-dr Sedan	847,000 yen
7	Corsa GL 3-dr Coupé	842,000 yen
8	Corsa S 3-dr Coupé	912,000 yen
9	Corsa GSL 4-dr Sedan	931,000 yen
10	Corsa GSL 3-dr Coupé	926,000 yen
11	Tercel Standard 2-dr Sedan	705,000 yen
12	Tercel De Luxe 2-dr Sedan	764,000 yen
13	Tercel De Luxe 4-dr Sedan	789,000 yen
14	Tercel De Luxe 3-dr Coupé	784,000 yen
15	Tercel Hi-De Luxe 2-dr Sedan	810,000 yen
16	Tercel Hi-De Luxe 4-dr Sedan	835,000 yen
17	Tercel Hi-De Luxe 3-dr Coupé	830,000 yen
18	Tercel S 3-dr Coupé	904,000 yen
19	Tercel SE 4-dr Sedan	918,000 yen
20	Tercel SE 3-dr Coupé	918,000 yen

80 hp power team

ENGINE front, 4 stroke; 4 cylinders, in line; 88.6 cu in, 1,452 cc (3.05 x 3.03 in, 77.5 x 77 mm); compression ratio: 9:1; max power (JIS): 80 hp at 5,600 rpm; max torque (JIS): 83 lb ft, 11.5 kg m at 3,600 rpm; max engine rpm 6,000; 55.1 hp/l; cast iron block, light alloy head; 5 crankshaft bearings; valves: overhead, rockers; camshafts: 1 overhead; lubrication: gear pump, full flow filter, 6.5 imp pt, 7.8 US pt, 3.7 l; 1 Aisan 1A-U downdraught twin barrel carburettor; emission ocntrol with catalytic converter, secondary air induction and exhaust gas recirculation; fuel feed: mechanical pump; water-cooled, 8.8 imp pt, 10.6 US pt, 5 l.

TRANSMISSION driving wheels: front; clutch: single dry plate (diaphragm); gearbox: mechanical; gears: 4, fully synchronized; ratios: I 3.467, II 2.076, III 1.380, IV 1, rev 3.377; lever: central; final drive: hypoid bevel; axle ratio 3.727; width of rims: 4''; tyres: De Luxe models 6.00 x 13 - Hi De Luxe and GL models 6.15 x 13 - GSL and SE models 145 SR x 13 - S models 165/70 SR x 13.

PERFORMANCE max speeds: (I) 29 mph, 46 km/h; (II) 49 mph, 79 km/h; (III) 74 mph, 120 km/h; (IV) 99 mph, 160 km/h; power-weight ratio: De Luxe 2-dr Sedan 21.2 lb/hp, 9.6 kg/hp; consumption: 45.2 m/imp gal, 37.6 m/US gal, 6.2 l x 100 km.

CHASSIS integral; front suspension: independent, by McPherson, coil springs/telescopic damper struts, transverse trailing arms, trailing links, anti-roll bar; rear: independent, coil springs, telescopic dampers, trailing arms.

STEERING rack-and-pinion; turns lock to lock: 3.60.

BRAKES front disc, rear drum, servo; lining area: front 19.8

TOYOTA Starlet S 3-dr Sedan

TOYOTA Corsa S 3-dr Coupé

sq in, 128 sq cm, rear 31.6 sq in, 204 sq cm, total 51.4 sq in, 332 sq cm.

ELECTRICAL EQUIPMENT 12 V; 33 Ah battery; 40 A alternator; Denso distributor; 2 headlamps.

DIMENSIONS AND WEIGHT wheel base: 98.42 in, 250 cm; tracks: 52.36 in, 133 cm front, 51.77 in, 131 cm rear; length: 155.90 in, 396 cm - Corsa S 3-dr, GSL, Tercel S 3-dr and SE models 157.10 in, 399 cm; width: 61.22 in, 17 cm; height: 54.13 in, 137 cm; ground clearance: 6.89 in, 17 cm; weight: De Luxe 2-dr 1,698 lb, 770 kg - De Luxe 4-dr 1,742 lb, 790 kg - Hi De Luxe and GL 2-dr models 1,720 lb, 780 kg - Hi De Luxe and GL 4-dr models 1,764 lb, 800 kg - GSL and SE 4-dr sedans and coupés 1,797 lb, 815 kg - De Luxe Coupés 1,731 lb, 785 kg - Hi De Luxe and GL coupés 1,753 lb, 795 kg - S Coupé 1,786 lb, 810 kg; weight distribution: 61% front, 39% rear; turning circle: 34.8 ft, 10.6 m; fuel tank: 9.9 imp gal, 11.9 US gal, 45 l.

BODY 5 seats, separate front seats.

OPTIONALS 5-speed mechanical gearbox, V ratio 0.827, 3.583 axle ratio, max speeds (I) 31 mph, 50 km/h, (II) 52 mph, 83 km/h, (III) 79 mph, 127 km/h, (IV) and (V) 102 mph, 165 km/h.

Corolla Series

PRICES (Tokyo):

1	1300 Standard 2-dr Sedan	698,000 yen
2	1300 Standard 4-dr Sedan	723,000 yen
3	1300 De Luxe 2-dr Sedan	743,000 yen
4	1300 De Luxe 4-dr Sedan	768,000 yen
5	1300 De Luxe 2-dr Hardtop	798,000 yen
6	1300 De Luxe 2-dr Coupé	811,000 yen
7	1300 De Luxe 3-dr Liftback	836,000 yen
8	1300 Hi-De Luxe 2-dr Sedan	800,000 yen
9	1300 Hi-De Luxe 4-dr Sedan	825,000 yen
10	1300 Hi-De Luxe 2-dr Hardtop	851,000 yen
11	1300 Hi-De Luxe 2-dr Coupé	863,000 yen
12	1300 Hi-De Luxe 3-dr Liftback	892,000 yen
13	1300 SL 4-dr Sedan	856,000 yen
14	1300 SL 2-dr Hardtop	888,000 yen
15	1300 SL 2-dr Coupé	892,000 yen
16	1300 SL 3-dr Liftback	935,000 yen
17	1300 SR 2-dr Coupé	898,000 yen
18	1400 De Luxe 2-dr Sedan	779,000 yen
19	1400 De Luxe 4-dr Sedan	804,000 yen
20	1400 De Luxe 2-dr Hardtop	834,000 yen
21	1400 De Luxe 2-dr Coupé	848,000 yen
22	1400 De Luxe 3-dr Liftback	873,000 yen
23	1400 Hi-De Luxe 2-dr Sedan	824,000 yen
24	1400 Hi-De Luxe 4-dr Sedan	849,000 yen
25	1400 Hi-De Luxe 2-dr Hardtop	875,000 yen
26	1400 Hi-De Luxe 2-dr Coupé	886,000 yen
27	1400 Hi-De Luxe 3-dr Liftback	924,000 yen
28	1400 SL 4-dr Sedan	894,000 yen
29	1400 SL 2-dr Hardtop	925,000 yen
30	1400 SL 2-dr Coupé	929,000 yen
31	1400 SL 3-dr Liftback	961,000 yen
32	1600 Hi-De Luxe 4-dr Sedan	884,000 yen
33	1600 Hi-De Luxe 2-dr Hardtop	910,000 yen
34	1600 Hi-De Luxe 2-dr Coupé	919,000 yen
35	1600 Hi-De Luxe 3-dr Liftback	978,000 yen
36	1600 GSL 4-dr Sedan	970,000 yen
37	1600 GSL 2-dr Hardtop	1,003,000 yen
38	1600 GSL 2-dr Coupé	1,003,000 yen
39	1600 GSL 3-dr Liftback	1,058,000 yen
40	1600 SR 2-dr Coupé	1,011,000 yen
41	1600 Levin 2-dr Coupé	1,227,000 yen
42	1600 Levin GT 2-dr Coupé	1,282,000 yen
43	1600 GT 3-dr Liftback	1,332,000 yen

Power team	Standard for:	Optional for:
72 hp	1 to 17	—
82 hp	18 to 31	—
88 hp	32 to 40	—
115 hp	41 to 43	—

72 hp power team

ENGINE front, 4 stroke; 4 cylinders, in line; 78.72 cu in, 1,290 cc (2.95 x 2.87 in, 75 x 73 mm); compression ratio: 9:1; max power (JIS): 72 hp at 5,600 rpm; max torque (JIS): 76 lb ft, 10.5 kg m at 3,600 rpm; max engine rpm: 6,000; 55.8 hp/l; cast iron block, light alloy head; 5 crankshaft bearings; valves: overhead, push-rods and rockers; camshafts: 1, side; lubrication: rotary pump, full flow filter, 6.2 impt pt, 7.4 US pt, 3.5 l; 1 Aisan 4K-U downdraught twin barrel carburettor; emission control with catalytic converter, secondary air induction and exhaust gas recirculation; fuel feed: mechanical pump; water-cooled, 10.6 imp pt, 12.7 US pt, 6 l.

TRANSMISSION driving wheels: rear; clutch: single dry plate (diaphragm); gearbox: mechanical; gears: 4, fully synchronized; ratios: I 3.789, II 2.220, III 1.435, IV 1, rev 4.316; lever: central; final drive: hypoid bevel; axle ratio: 3.909; width of rims: 4''; tyres: 6.00 x 12 - Hi De Luxe and SL models 6.15 x 13 - SR Coupé 155 SR x 13.

TOYOTA Corolla 1600 Hi-De Luxe 4-dr Sedan

PERFORMANCE max speeds: (I) 25 mph, 40 km/h; (II) 46 mph, 74 km/h; (III) 67 mph, 108 km/h; (IV) 93 mph, 150 km/h; power-weight ratio: Standard 2-dr. Sedan 24.5 lb/hp, 11.1 kg/hp; consumption: 40 m/imp gal, 33 m/US gal, 7.1 l x 100 km.

CHASSIS integral; front suspension: independent, by McPherson, coil springs/telescopic damper struts, lower wishbones (trailing links), anti-roll bar; rear: rigid axle, semi-elliptic leafsprings, telescopic dampers.

STEERING recirculating ball, variable ratio; turns lock to lock: 3.60.

BRAKES drum (for Hi-De Luxe, SL and SR models front disc); lining area: front 47.1 sq in, 304 sq cm, rear 41.6 sq in, 268 sq cm, total 88.7 sq in, 572 sq cm.

ELECTRICAL EQUIPMENT 12 V; 32 Ah battery; 40 A alternator; Nihon-Denso distributor; 2 headlamps.

DIMENSIONS AND WEIGHT wheel base: 93.31 in, 237 cm; tracks: 50.98 in, 129 cm front, 50.59 in, 128 cm rear; length: Standard models 157.28 in, 399 cm - sedans and hardtops 163.98 in, 416 cm - coupés 167.12 in, 424 cm - liftbacks 168.90 in 429 cm; width: 61.81 in, 157 cm - coupés and liftbacks 62.99 in, 160 cm; height: sedans 54.33 in, 138 cm - hardtops 53.54 in, 136 cm - coupés and liftbacks 51.97 in, 132 cm - SR Coupé 51.57 in, 131 cm; ground clearance: 6.30 in, 16 cm; weight: Standard and De Luxe 2-dr sedans 1,764 lb, 800 kg; Standard 4-dr Sedan 1,808 lb, 820 kg - De Luxe 4-dr Sedan 1,830 lb, 830 kg - De Luxe

Hardtop and Coupé 1,841 lb, 835 kg - Hi-De Luxe 4-dr Sedan, Hardtop and Coupé 1,863 lb, 845 kg - SL 4-dr Sedan, Hardtop and Coupé 1,885 lb, 855 kg - De Luxe Liftback 1,896 lb, 860 kg - SR Coupé 1,907 lb, 865 kg - Hi-De Luxe Liftback 1,918 lb, 870 kg - SL Liftback 1,929 lb, 875 kg; turning circle: 33.5 ft, 10.2 m; fuel tank: 11 imp gal, 13.2 US gal, 50 l.

BODY 5 seats, separate front seats, reclining backrests, built-in headrests.

OPTIONALS (for Hi-De Luxe and SL models and SR Coupé) 5-speed fully synchronized mechanical gearbox (I 3.789, II 2.220, III 1.435, IV 1, V 0.865, rev 4.136); (for sedans and hardtops) Toyoglide automatic transmission with 2 ratios (I 1.820, II 1, rev 1.820), 4.100 axle ratio.

82 hp power team

See 72 hp power team, except for:

ENGINE 85.9 cu in, 1,407 cc (3.15 x 2.76 in, 80 x 70 mm); compression ratio: 9:1; max power (JIS): 82 hp at 5,800 rpm; max torque (JIS): 84 lb ft, 11.6 kg m at 3,400 rpm; max engine rpm: 6,300; 58.3 hp/l; valves: overhead, Vee-slanted, push-rods and rockers; lubrication: 7.9 imp pt, 9.5 US pt, 4.5 l; 1 Aisan T-U downdraught twin barrel carburettor; cooling system: 14.1 imp pt, 16.9 US pt, 8 l.

TRANSMISSION gearbox ratios: I 3.587, II 2.022, III 1.384, IV 1, rev 3.484; axle ratio: 3.727 - SL models 3.909; tyres: 6.15 x 13 - SL models 155 SR x 13.

PERFORMANCE max speeds: (I) 29 mph, 47 km/h; (II) 51 mph, 82 km/h; (III) 75 mph, 120 km/h; (IV) 99 mph, 160 km/h; power-weight ratio: De Luxe 2-dr. Sedan 24 lb/hp, 10.9 kg/hp; consumption: 35 m/imp gal, 29 m/US gal, 8 l x 100 km.

BRAKES lining area: total 114.8 sq in, 740 sq cm (for Hi-De Luxe and SL models front disc brakes, rear drum, total lining area 78.2 sq in, 504 sq cm).

ELECTRICAL EQUIPMENT 35 Ah battery.

DIMENSIONS AND WEIGHT front track: 51.18 in, 130 cm; weight: De Luxe 2-dr Sedan 1,962 lb, 890 kg - Hi-De Luxe 2-dr Sedan 1,973 lb, 895 kg - De Luxe 4-dr Sedan 2,017 lb, 915 kg - Hi-De Luxe 4-dr Sedan, Hardtop, Coupé and SL Coupé 2,029 lb, 920 kg - SL 4-dr Sedan and Hardtop 2,040 lb, 925 kg - Hi-De Luxe Liftback 2,106 lb, 955 kg - SL Liftback 2,117 lb, 960 kg.

OPTIONALS 5-speed fully synchronized mechanical gearbox (I 3.587, II 2.022, III 1.384, IV 1, V 0.861, rev 3.484), 3.909 axle ratio (SL models 4.100).

88 hp power team

See 82 hp power team, except for:

ENGINE 96.9 cu in, 1,588 cc (3.35 x 2.76 in, 85 x 70 mm); max power (JIS): 88 hp at 5,600 rpm; max torque (JIS): 96 lb ft, 13.3 kg m at 3,400 rpm; 55.4 hp/l; 1 Aisan 12 T-U downdraught twin barrel carburettor; low emission control TGP lean-burn type with auxiliary combustion chambers, secondary air induction, exhaust gas recirculation and catalytic converter.

TOYOTA Corolla 1600 Hi-De Luxe Sedan

TOYOTA Corolla 1300 SL 2-dr Hardtop

88 HP POWER TEAM

TRANSMISSION axle ratio: 3.909 - (for Hi-De Luxe Coupé and Liftback and, GSL Coupé) 3.727; tyres: Hi-De Luxe Sedan and Hardtop 6.15 x 13 - GSL models 155 SR x 13 - Hi-De Luxe Coupé and Liftback Z 78 x 13 - SR Coupé 175/70 HR x 13.

PERFORMANCE max speed: 99 mph, 160 km/h; power-weight ratio: Hi-De Luxe 4-dr Sedan 22.8 lb/hp, 10.3 kg/hp consumption: 34 m/imp gal, 28 m/US gal, 8.3 l x 100 km.

DIMENSIONS AND WEIGHT weight: Hi-De Luxe models 2,006 lb, 910 kg - GSL 4-dr Sedan and Hardtop 2,051 lb, 930 kg - GSL and SR Coupé 2,040 lb, 925 kg - Hi-De Luxe Liftback 2,084 lb, 945 kg - GSL Liftback 2,106 lb, 955 kg.

OPTIONALS 5-speed fully synchronized mechanical gearbox (I 3.587, II 2.022, III 1.384, IV 1, V 0.861, rev 3.484), 4.100 axle ratio (Hi-De Luxe Coupé and Liftback 3.909), Toyoglide automatic transmission, hydraulic torque converter with 3 ratios (I 2.450, II 1.450, III 1, rev 2.222), 4.100 axle ratio (Hi-De Luxe Coupé and Liftback 3.909).

115 hp power team

See 82 hp power team, except for:

ENGINE 96.9 cu in, 1,588 cc (3.35 x 2.76 in, 85 x 70 mm); compression ratio: 8.4:1; max power (JIS): 115 hp at 6,000 rpm; max torque (JIS): 109 lb ft, 15 kg m at 4,800 rpm; max engine rpm: 6,400; 72.4 hp/l; camshafts: 2, overhead; Bosch-Denso L-jetronic electronic fuel jniection.

TRANSMISSION gears: 5; fully synchronized; ratios: I 3.587, II 2.022, III 1.384, IV 1, V 0.861, rev 3.484; axle ratio: 4.100; width of rims: 5''; tyres - coupés 185/70 HR x 13 - Liftback 175/70 HR x 13.

PERFORMANCE power-weight ratio: Levin Coupé 18.4 lb/hp, 8.3 kg/hp.

DIMENSIONS AND WEIGHT width: 63.58 in, 161 cm; height: 51.57 in, 131 cm; weight: Levin Coupé 2,117 lb, 960 kg - Levin GT Coupé 2,128 lb, 965 kg - Levin GT Liftback 2,172 lb, 985 kg.

Corolla (USA) Series

PRICES IN USA:

Corolla 2-dr Sedan	$ 3,748
Corolla Custom 2-dr Sedan	$ 4,133
Corolla Custom 4-dr Sedan	$ 4,253
Corolla De Luxe 2-dr Sedan	$ 4,338
Corolla De Luxe 4-dr Sedan	$ 4,563
Corolla De Luxe 4-dr Station Wagon	$ 4,933
Corolla De Luxe Sport Coupé	$ 4,758
Corolla De Luxe Liftback	$ 4,928
Corolla SR-5 Sport Coupé	$ 5,248
Corolla SR-5 Liftback	$ 5,388

75 hp power team

ENGINE front, 4 stroke; 4 cylinders, in line; 96.9 cu in, 1,588 cc (3.35 x 2.76 in, 85 x 70 mm); compression ratio:

8.5:1; max power (SAE): 75 hp at 5,800 rpm; max torque (SAE): 83 lb ft, 11.4 kg m at 3,800 rpm; max engine rpm: 6,300; 47.2 hp/l; cast iron block and head; 5 crankshaft bearings; valves: overhead, push-rods and rockers; camshafts: 1, side; lubrication: rotary pump, full flow filter, 7.7 imp pt, 9.3 US pt, 4.4 l; 1 Aisan downdraught twin barrel carburettor; fuel feed: mechanical pump; water-cooled, 13.7 imp pt, 16.5 US pt, 7.8 l.

TRANSMISSION driving wheels: rear; clutch: single dry plate (diaphragm); gearbox: mechanical; gears: 4 (5 for SR-5 only), fully synchronized; ratios: I 3.587, II 2.022, III 1.384, IV 1, rev 3.484 (SR-5 I 3.587, II 2.022, III 1.384, IV 1, V 0.861, rev 3.484); lever: central; final drive: hypoid bevel; axle ratio: 4.100 - SR-5 4.300; width of rims: 4.5''; tyres: 6.45S x 13 - liftback 165SR x 13 - SR-5 180/70HR x 13.

PERFORMANCE max speed: 99 mph, 160 km/h; power-weight ratio: 4-dr. Sedan 30.3 lb/hp, 13.7 kg/hp; consumption: not declared.

CHASSIS integral; front suspension: independent, by McPherson, coil springs/telescopic damper struts, lower wishbones (trailing links), anti-roll bar; rear: rigid axle, semi-elliptic leafsprings, telescopic dampers.

STEERING recirculating ball, variable ratio; turns lock to lock: 3.60 - SR-5 3.

BRAKES front disc, rear drum, servo; lining area: total 60.2 sq in, 388 sq cm.

TOYOTA Corolla 1400 SL 2-dr Coupé

ELECTRICAL EQUIPMENT 12 V; 35 Ah battery; 40 A alternator; Nihon-Denso distributor; 2 headlamps.

DIMENSIONS AND WEIGHT wheel base: 93.31 in, 237 cm; front track: 50.98 in, 129 cm - SR-5 52 in, 132 cm; rear track: 50.59 in, 128 cm - SR-5 52.60 in, 134 cm; length: 165.20 in, 420 cm - st. wagon 167.70 in, 426 cm; width: 61.80 in, 157 cm - SR-5 65 in, 165 cm; height: 53.94 in, 137 cm - liftback 53.15 in, 135 cm; ground clearance: 6.69 in, 17 cm; weight: 4-dr sedans 2.270 lb, 1,029 kg - liftback 2,280 lb, 1,034 kg - SR-5 Coupé 2,360 lb, 1,070 kg - 4-dr Station Wagon 2,325 lb, 1,054 kg; turning circle: 33.5 ft, 10.2 m; fuel tank: 11 imp gal, 13.2 US gal, 50 l.

BODY 5 seats, separate front seats, reclining backrests, built-in headrests.

OPTIONALS 5-speed fully synchronized mechanical gearbox (I 3.587, II 2.022, III 1.384, IV 1, V 0.861, rev 3.484), 4,300 axle ratio; automatic transmission with 3 ratios (I 2.450, II 1.450, III 1, rev 2.222).

Sprinter Series

PRICES (Tokyo):

1	1300 DX 4-dr Sedan	785,000 yen
2	1300 DX Hardtop	819,000 yen
3	1300 DX Coupé	831,000 yen
4	1300 DX Liftback	857,000 yen
5	1300 XL 4-dr Sedan	842,000 yen
6	1300 XL Hardtop	867,000 yen
7	1300 XL Coupé	879,000 yen
8	1300 XL Liftback	916,000 yen
9	1300 ST 4-dr Sedan	873,000 yen
10	1300 ST Hardtop	904,000 yen
11	1300 ST Coupé	908,000 yen
12	1300 ST Liftback	956,000 yen
13	1400 DX 4-dr Sedan	830,000 yen
14	1400 DX Hardtop	859,000 yen
15	1400 DX Coupé	864,000 yen
16	1400 DX Liftback	891,000 yen
17	1400 XL 4-dr Sedan	861,000 yen
18	1400 XL Hardtop	891,000 yen
19	1400 XL Coupé	904,000 yen
20	1400 XL Liftback	943,000 yen
21	1400 ST 4-dr Sedan	909,000 yen
22	1400 ST Hardtop	939,000 yen
23	1400 ST Coupé	943,000 yen
24	1400 ST Liftback	982,000 yen
25	1600 XL 4-dr Sedan	900,000 yen
26	1600 XL Hardtop	930,000 yen
27	1600 XL Coupé	941,000 yen
28	1600 XL Liftback	992,000 yen
29	1600 GS 4-dr Sedan	991,000 yen
30	1600 GS Hardtop	1,023,000 yen
31	1600 GS Coupé	1,023,000 yen
32	1600 GS Liftback	1,078,000 yen
33	1600 SR Coupé	1,033,000 yen
34	1600 Trueno GT	1,302,000 yen
35	1600 Liftback GT	1,352,000 yen

Power team:	Standard for:	Optional for:
72 hp	1 to 12	—
82 hp	13 to 24	—
88 hp	25 to 33	—
115 hp	34,35	—

TOYOTA Sprinter 1600 GS 4-dr Sedan

72 hp power team

ENGINE front, 4 stroke; 4 cylinders, in line; 78.7 cu in, 1,290 cc (2.95 x 2.87 in, 75 x 73 mm); compression ratio: 9:1; max power (JIS): 72 hp at 5,600 rpm; max torque (JIS): 76 lb ft, 10.5 kg m at 3,600 rpm; max engine rpm: 6,000; 55.8 hp/l; cast iron block, light alloy head; 5 crankshaft bearings; valves: overhead, push-rods and rockers; camshafts: 1, side; lubrication: rotary pump, full flow filter, 6.2 imp pt, 7.4 US pt, 3.5 l; 1 Aisan 4K-U downdraught twin barrel carburettor; emission control with catalytic converter, secondary air induction and exhaust gas recirculation; fuel feed: mechanical pump; water-cooled, 10.6 imp pt, 12.7 US pt, 6 l.

TRANSMISSION driving wheels: rear; clutch: single dry plate (diaphragm); gearbox: mechanical; gears: 4, fully synchronized; ratios: I 3.789, II 2.220, III 1.435, IV 1, rev 4.316; lever: central; final drive: hypoid bevel; axle ratio: 3.909; width of rims: 4'' - ST models 4.5''; tyres: 6.00 x 12 - XL and ST models 6.15 x 13.

PERFORMANCE max speeds: (I) 25 mph, 40 km/h; (II) 46 mph, 74 km/h; (II) 67 mph, 108 km/h; (IV) 93 mph, 150 km/h; power-weight ratio: DX 4-dr Sedan 25.6 lb/hp, 11.6 kg/hp; consumption: 40 m/imp gal, 33 m/US gal, 7.1 l x 100 km.

CHASSIS integral; front suspension: independent, by Mc-Pherson, coil springs/telescopic damper struts, lower wishbones (trailing links), anti-roll bar; rear: rigid axle, semi-elliptic leafsprings, telescopic dampers.

STEERING recirculating ball, variable ratio; turns lock to lock: 3.60.

BRAKES drum (for XL and ST models front disc); lining area: front 47.1 sq in, 304 sq cm, rear 41.6 sq in, 268 sq cm, total 88.7 sq in, 572 sq cm.

ELECTRICAL EQUIPMENT 12 V; 32 Ah battery; 40 A alternator; Nihon-Denso distributor; 2 headlamps.

DIMENSIONS AND WEIGHT wheel base: 93.31 in, 237 cm; tracks: 50.98 in, 129 cm front, 50.59 in, 128 cm rear; length: sedans and hardtops 163.98 in, 416 cm - coupés 167.12 in, 424 cm - liftbacks 168.90 in, 429 cm; width: 62.99 in, 160 cm - sedans and hardtops 61.81 in, 157 cm; height: 51.97 in, 132 cm - sedans and hardtops 53.54 in, 136 cm; ground clearance: 6.30 in, 16 cm - sedans 6.69 in, 17 cm; weight: DX 4-dr Sedan and Hardtop 1,841 lb, 835 kg - DX Coupé, XL Hardtop and Coupé 1,863 lb, 845 kg - XL 4-dr Sedan 1,874 lb, 850 kg - ST Sedan, Hardtop and Coupé 1,885 lb, 855 kg - DX and XL liftbacks 1,918 lb, 870 kg - ST Liftback 1,928 lb, 875 kg; turning circle: 33.5 ft, 10.2 m; fuel tank: 11 imp gal, 13.2 US gal, 50 l.

BODY 5 seats, separate front seats, reclining backrests, built-in headrests.

OPTIONALS 5-speed fully synchronized mechanical gearbox (I 3.789, II 2.220, III 1.453, IV 1, V 0.865, rev 4.316), 3.909 axle ratio; for sedans and hardtops only Toyoglide automatic transmission, hydraulic torque converter with 2 ratios (I 1.820, II 1, rev 1.820), 4.100 axle ratio.

82 hp power team

See 72 hp power team, except for:

ENGINE 85.9 cu in, 1,407 cc (3.15 x 2.76 in, 80 x 70 mm); max power (JIS): 82 hp at 5,800 rpm; max torque (JIS): 84 lb ft, 11.6 kg m at 3,400 rpm; max engine rpm: 6,300; 58.3 hp/l; valves: overhead, Vee-slanted, push-rods and rockers; 1 Aisan T-U downdraught twin barrel carburettor; cooling system: 14.1 imp pt, 16.8 US pt, 8 l.

TRANSMISSION gearbox ratios: I 3.587, II 2.022, III 1.384, IV 1, rev 3.484; axle ratio: 3.727 - ST models 3.909; width of rims: 4.5''; tyres: 6.15 x 13 - ST models 155 SR x 13.

PERFORMANCE max speeds: (I) 29 mph, 47 km/h; (II) 51 mph, 82 km/h; (III) 75 mph, 120 km/h; (IV) 99 mph, 160 km/h; power-weight ratio: XL 4-dr Sedan 24.7 lb/hp, 11.2 kg/hp; consumption: 32 m/imp gal, 29 m/US gal, 8 l x 100 km.

BRAKES front disc, rear drum; lining area: total 78.2 sq in, 504 sq cm.

ELECTRICAL EQUIPMENT 35 Ah battery.

DIMENSIONS AND WEIGHT front track: 51.18 in, 130 cm; weight: XL 4-dr Sedan, Hardtop, Coupé and ST Coupé 2,029 lb, 920 kg - ST Hardtop 2,040 lb, 925 kg - ST 4-dr Sedan 2,051 lb, 930 kg - XL Liftback 2,106 lb, 955 kg - ST Liftback 2,117 lb, 960 kg.

OPTIONALS 5-speed fully synchronized mechanical gearbox (I 3.587, II 2.022, III 1.384, IV 1, V 0.861, rev 3.484), 3.909 axle ratio (for ST models only 4.100).

88 hp power team

See 82 hp power team, except for:

ENGINE TTC-L low emission lean-burn type with auxiliary combustion chambers; 96.9 cu in, 1,588 cc (3.35 x 2.76 in, 85 x 70 mm); max power (JIS): 88 hp at 5,600 rpm; max torque (JIS): 96 lb ft, 13.3 kg m at 3,400 rpm: 55.4 hp/l; 1 Aisan 12T-U downdraught twin barrel carburettor; emission control turbulence generating pot auxiliary combustion chambers, exhaust gas recirculation, secondary air induction and catalytic converter.

TRANSMISSION axle ratio: 3.909; tyres: 6.15 x 13 - XL Coupé and Liftback Z18 x 13 - GS models 155 SR x 13 - SR Coupé 175/70 HR x 13.

PERFORMANCE max speed: 99 mph, 160 km/h; power-weight ratio: XL 4-dr Sedan 22.9 lb/hp, 10.4 kg/hp; consumption: 34 m/imp gal, 28 m/US gal, 8.3 l x 100 km.

DIMENSIONS AND WEIGHT weight: XL 4-dr Sedan 2,017 lb, 915 kg - XL Hardtop and Coupé 2,007 lb, 910 kg - GS 4-dr Sedan 2,061 lb, 935 kg - GS and SR Coupé 2,040 lb, 925 kg - GS Hardtop 2,051 lb, 930 kg - XL Liftback 2,084 lb, 945 kg - GS Liftback 2,106 lb, 955 kg.

OPTIONALS 5-speed fully synchronized mechanical gearbox (I 3.587, II 2.022, III 1.384, IV 1, V 0.861, rev 3.484), 4.100 axle ratio; for sedans and hardtops only Toyoglide automatic transmission hydraulic torque converter with 3 ratios (I 2.450, II 1.450, III 1, rev 2.222), 3.909 axle ratio.

115 hp power team

See 82 hp power team, except for:

ENGINE 96.9 cu in, 1,588 cc (3.35 x 2.76 in, 85 x 70 mm); compression ratio: 8.4:1; max power (JIS): 115 hp at 6,000 rpm; max torque (JIS): 109 lb ft, 15 kg m at 4,800 rpm; max engine rpm: 6,400; 69.3 hp/l; camshafts: 2, overhead; Bosch-Denso L-jetronic electronic fuel jniection.

TRANSMISSION gears: 5, fully synchronized; ratios: I 3.587, II 2.022, III 1.384, IV 1, V 0.861, rev 3.484; axle ratio: 4.100; width of rims: 5''; tyres Trueno GT 185/70 HR x 13 - Liftback GT 175/70 HR x 13.

PERFORMANCE power-weight ratio: Trueno GT 18.5 lb/hp, 8.4 kg/hp - Liftback GT 18.9 lb/hp, 8.6 kg/.hp.

DIMENSIONS AND WEIGHT height: 51.57 in, 131 cm; weight: Trueno GT 2,128 lb, 965 kg - Liftback GT 2,172 lb, 985 kg.

Carina Series

PRICES (Tokyo):

1	1600 Standard 2-dr Sedan	845,000 yen
2	1600 Standard 4-dr Sedan	865,000 yen
3	1600 De Luxe 2-dr Sedan	903,000 yen
4	1600 De Luxe 4-dr Sedan	923,000 yen
5	1600 De Luxe Hardtop	958,000 yen
6	1600 Super De Luxe 4-dr Sedan	961,000 yen
7	1600 Super De Luxe Hardtop	996,000 yen
8	1600 ST 4-dr Sedan	1,026,000 yen
9	1600 ST Hardtop	1,061,000 yen
10	1600 SR Hardtop	1,076,000 yen
11	1600 GT 4-dr Sedan	1,377,000 yen
12	1600 GT Hardtop	1,412,000 yen
13	1800 De Luxe 4-dr Sedan	989,000 yen
14	1800 De Luxe Hardtop	1,024,000 yen
15	1800 Super De Luxe 4-dr Sedan	1,046,000 yen
16	1800 Super De Luxe Hardtop	1,087,000 yen
17	1800 ST 4-dr Sedan	1,117,000 yen
18	1800 ST Hardtop	1,152,000 yen
19	1800 SE 4-dr Sedan	1,171,000 yen
20	1800 SE Hardtop	1,206,000 yen
21	1800 SR Hardtop	1,167,000 yen
22	1800 EFI ST 4-dr Sedan	1,177,000 yen
23	1800 EFI ST Hardtop	1,212,000 yen
24	1800 EFI SR Hardtop	1,217,000 yen
25	2000 SE 4-dr Sedan	1,224,000 yen
26	2000 SE Hardtop	1,259,000 yen
27	2000 GT 4-dr Sedan	1,487,000 yen
28	2000 GT Hardtop	1,522,000 yen

Power team:	Standard for:	Optional for:
88 hp	1 to 10	—
110 hp	11,12	—
95 hp	13 to 21	—
105 hp	22 to 24	—
105 hp (1,972 cc)	25,26	—
135 hp	27,28	—

88 hp power team

ENGINE TTC-L lean-burn low emission type with turbulence generating pot auxiliary combustion chambers; front, 4 stroke; 4 cylinders, in line; 96.9 cu in, 1,588 cc (3.35 x 2.76 in, 85 x 70 mm); compression ratio: 9:1; max power (JIS): 88 hp at 5,600 rpm; max torque (JIS): 96 lb ft, 13.3 kg m at 3,400 rpm; max engine rpm: 6,000; cast iron block, light alloy head; 5 crankshaft bearings; valves: overhead, Vee-slanted, push-rods and rockers; camshafts: 1, side; lubrication: rotary pump, full flow filter, 7.4 imp pt, 8.9 US pt, 4.2 l; 1 Aisan 12T-U downdraught twin barrel carburettor; emission control with catalytic converter, secondary air induction and exhaust gas recirculation; fuel feed: mechanical pump; water-cooled, 14.1 imp pt, 16.9 US pt, 8 l.

TRANSMISSION driving wheels: rear; clutch: single dry plate (diaphragm); gearbox: mechanical; gears: 4, fully synchronized; ratios: I 3.587, II 2.022, III 1.384, IV 1, rev 3.484; (for ST and SR models gears 5, V 0.861); lever: central; final drive: hypoid bevel; axle ratio: 4.100; width of rimss: Standard models 4'' - De Luxe, Super De Luxe and ST models and SR Hardtop 4.5''; tyres: Standard models 5.60 x 13 - De Luxe and Super De Luxe models 6.45 x 13 - ST models and SR Hardtop 165 SR x 13.

PERFORMANCE max speeds: (I) 29 mph, 46 km/h; (II) 52 mph, 83 km/h; (III) 75 mph, 120 km/h; (IV) 103 mph, 165 km/h; power-weight ratio: Standard 2-dr Sedan 23.4 lb/hp, 10.6 kg/hp; consumption: 34 m/imp gal, 28 m/US gal, 8.3 l x 100 km.

CHASSIS integral; front suspension: independent, by Mc-Pherson, coil springs/telescopic damper struts, lower wish-

TOYOTA Carina 1800 EFI-ST 4-dr Sedan

88 HP POWER TEAM

bones (trailing links), anti-roll bar; rear: rigid axle, twin trailing radius arms, transverse linkage bar, coil springs, telescopic dampers.

STEERING recirculating ball; turns lock to lock: 3.80 - SR Hardtop 3.50.

BRAKES drum (for De Luxe, Super De Luxe and ST models and SR Hardtop front disc): lining area: front 60.8 sq in, 392 sq cm, rear 54 sq in, 384 sq cm, total 114.8 sq in, 740 sq cm.

ELECTRICAL EQUIPMENT 12 V; 35 Ah battery: 45 A alternator; Nihon-Denso distributor; 4 headlamps.

DIMENSIONS AND WEIGHT wheel base: 98.42 in, 250 cm; tracks: 52.56 in, 133 cm front; 53.15 in, 135 cm rear; length: Standard and De Luxe models 165.75 in, 421 cm - Super De Luxe and ST models 166.54 in, 423 cm - SR Hardtop 169.88 in, 431 cm; width: 64.17 in, 163 cm; height: sedans 54.72 in, 139 cm - De Luxe, Super De Luxe and ST hardtops 52.76 in, 134 cm - SR Hardtop 52.36 in, 133 cm; ground clearance: 6.30 in, 16 cm weight: Standard 2-dr Sedan 2,062 lb, 935 kg - De Luxe 2-dr Sedan 2,073 lb, 940 kg - Standard 4-dr Sedan 2,084 lb, 945 kg - De Luxe 4-dr Sedan 2,095 lb, 950 kg - Super De Luxe and ST Sedan, De Luxe Hardtop 2,106 lb, 955 kg - ST Hardtop 2,117 lb, 960 kg - SR Hardtop 2,161 lb, 980 kg; weight distribution: 57.3% front, 42.7% rear; turning circle: 35.4 ft, 10.8 m; fuel tank: 13.4 imp gal, 16.1 US gal, 61 l.

BODY 5 seats, separate front seats, reclining backrests, built-in headrests.

OPTIONALS 5-speed fully synchronized mechanical gearbox (I 3.587, II 2.022, III 1.384, IV 1, V 0.861, rev 3.484), 4.100 axle ratio.

110 hp power team

See 88 hp power team, except for:

ENGINE compression ratio: 8.4:1; max power (JIS): 110 hp at 6,000 rpm; max torque (JIS): 109 lb ft, 15 kg m at 4,800 rpm; max engine rpm: 6,400; 69.3 hp/l; camshafts: 2, overhead; Bosch-Denso L-jetronic electronic injection.

TRANSMISSION gears: 5, fully synchronized; ratios: I 3.587, II 2.022, III 1.384 IV 1, V 0.861, rev 3.484; axle ratio: 4.100; width of rims: 5''; tyres: 185/70 HR x 13.

PERFORMANCE max speeds: (I) 29 mph, 47 km/h; (II) 52 mph, 83 km/h; (III) 76 mph, 122 km/h; (IV) 106 mph, 170 km/h; (V) 106 mph, 170 km/h; power-weight ratio: Sedan 19.8 lb/hp, 9 kg/hp; consumption: 29.7 m/imp gal, 24.8 m/US gal, 9.5 l x 100 km.

STEERING turns lock to lock: 3.50.

BRAKES rear disc.

CHASSIS rear suspension: anti-roll bar.

DIMENSIONS AND WEIGHT height: Sedan 54.33 in, 138 cm - Hardtop 52.36 in, 133 cm; tracks: 53.15 in, 135 cm front, 53.54 in, 136 cm rear; ground clearance: 6.10 in, 15.5 cm; weight: Sedan 2,183 lb, 990 kg - Hardtop 2,194 lb, 995 kg.

95 hp power team

See 88 hp power team, except for:

ENGINE 108 cu in, 1,770 cc (3.35 x 3.01 in, 85 x 78 mm); max power (JIS): 95 hp at 5,400 rpm; max torque (JIS): 109 lb ft, 15 kg m at 3,400 rpm; 53.7 hp/l; 1 13T-U downdraught twin barrel carburettor.

TRANSMISSION (for ST models and SR Hardtop only gears: 5, fully synchronized; ratios: I 3.587, II 2.022, III 1.384, IV 1, V 0.861, rev 3.484; axle ratio: 3.909) axle ratio: 3.727; width of rims: (for SR Hardtop only) 5''; tyres: De Luxe and Super De Luxe models 6.45 x 13 - SE and ST models 165 SR x 13 - SR Hardtop 185/70 HR x 13.

PERFORMANCE max speed: 106 mph, 170 km/h; power-weight ratio: De Luxe 4-dr Sedan 22.3 lb/hp, 10.1 kg/hp; consumption: 32 m/imp gal, 27 m/US gal, 8.7 l x 100 km.

DIMENSIONS AND WEIGHT weight: De Luxe 4-dr Sedan 2,117 lb, 960 kg - De Luxe Hardtop, Super De Luxe and ST sedans 2,128 lb, 965 kg - Super De Luxe and ST hardtops and SE 4-dr Sedan 2,139 lb, 970 kg - SE 4-dr Sedan 2,139 lb, 970 kg - SE Hardtop 2,150 lb, 975 kg - SR Hardtop 2,194 lb, 995 kg.

OPTIONALS 5-speed mechanical gearbox (except ST models and SR Hardtop), 3.909 axle ratio; Toyoglide automatic transmission with 3 ratios (I 2.450, II 1.450, III 1, rev 2.222).

TOYOTA Carina 2000 SE Hardtop

105 hp power team

See 88 hp power team, except for:

ENGINE 108 cu in, 1,770 cc (3.35 x 3.01 in, 85 x 78 mm); max power (JIS): 105 hp at 5,400 rpm; max torque (JIS): 119 lb ft, 16.5 kg m at 3,600 rpm; 59.3 hp/l; Bosch-Denso L-Jetronic electronic fuel injection; emission control: (without TTC-L and TGP cylinder head), 3-way catalytic converter.

TRANSMISSION gears: 5, fully synchronized; ratios: I 3.587, II 2.022, III 1.384, IV 1, V 0.861, rev 3.484; axle ratio: ST models 3.909 - SR 4.100; tyres: ST models 165 SR x 13 - SR 185/70 HR x 13.

PERFORMANCE max speeds (with 3.909 axle ratio): (I) 29 mph, 46 km/h; (II) 48 mph, 78 km/h; (III) 71 mph, 114 km/h; (IV) 99 mph, 160 km/h; (V) 106 mph, 170 km/h; power-weight ratio: ST 4-dr Sedan 20.7 lb/hp, 9.4 kg/hp; consumption: 33.9 m/imp gal, 28.2 m/US gal, 8.3 l x 100 km.

BRAKES front disc, rear drum, servo.

STEERING recirculating ball, variable ratio; turns lock to lock: 3.50.

DIMENSIONS AND WEIGHT weight: ST 4-dr Sedan 2,172 lb, 985 kg - ST Hardtop 2,194 lb, 995 kg - SR Hardtop 2,238 lb, 1,015 kg.

OPTIONALS Toyoglide automatic transmission with 3 ratios (I 2.450, II 1.450, III 1, rev 2.222).

105 hp power team (1,972 cc)

See 88 hp power team, except for:

ENGINE 120.3 cu in, 1,972 cc (3.30 x 3.50 in, 84 x 89 mm); compression ratio: 8.5:1; max power (JIS): 105 hp at 5,200 rpm; max torque (JIS): 120 lb ft, 16.5 kg m at 3,600 rpm; max engine rpm: 5,600; 53.2 hp/l; valves: overhead, rockers; camshafts: 1, overhead; lubrication: 8.8 imp pt, 10.6 US pt, 5 l; 1 Aisan 21R-U downdraught twin barrel carburettor; emission control: (without TGP cylinder head), 3-way catalytic converter, secondary air induction, exhaust gas recirculation.

TRANSMISSION gears: 5, fully synchronized; ratios: I 3.287, II 2.043, III 1.394, IV 1, V 0.853, rev 4.039; axle ratio: 3.909; width of rims: 4.5''; tyres: 165 SR x 13.

PERFORMANCE max speeds: (I) 29 mph, 46 km/h; (II) 46 mph, 74 km/h; (III) 71 mph, 114 km/h; (IV) 96 mph, 155 km/h; (V) 109 mph, 175 km/h; power-weight ratio: SE 4-dr Sedan 21.6 lb/hp, 9.8 kg/hp; consumption: 28 m/imp gal, 23 m/US gal, 10 l x 100 km.

STEERING variable ratio.

BRAKES front disc, rear drum, servo.

DIMENSIONS AND WEIGHT length: 166.53 in, 423 cm; height: Sedan 54.72 in, 139 cm - Hardtop 52.95 in, 134 cm; weight: Sedan 2,271 lb, 1,030 kg - Hardtop 2,282 lb, 1,035 kg.

OPTIONALS Toyoglide automatic transmission, hydraulic torque converter with 3 ratios (I 2.450, II 1.450, III 1, rev 2.222), 3.909 axle ratio; power assisted steering, turn lock to lock 3.40.

135 hp power team

See 88 hp power team, except for:

ENGINE 120.1 cu in, 1,968 cc (3.48 x 3.15 in, 88.5 x 80 mm); compression ratio: 8.3:1; max power (JIS): 135 hp at 5,800 rpm; max torque (JIS): 127 lb ft, 17.5 kg m at 4,400 rpm; max engine rpm: 6,300; 66 hp/l; valves: overhead, Vee-slanted, thimble tappets; camshafts: 2, overhead; lubrication: 8.2 imp pt, 9.9 US pt, 4.7 l; Bosch-Denso L-Jetronic electronic fuel injection; emission control: 3-way catalytic converter; cooling system: 16 imp pt, 19.2 US pt, 9.1 l.

TRANSMISSION gears: 5, fully synchronized; ratios: I 3.525, II 2.054, III 1.396, IV 1, V 0.858, rev 3.755; axle ratio: 3.909; width of rims: 5''; tyres: 185/70 HR x 13.

PERFORMANCE max speed: 112 mph, 180 km/h; power-weight ratio: Sedan 17.2 lb/hp, 7.8 kg/hp; consumption: 28 m/imp gal, 23 m/US gal, 10 l x 100 km.

CHASSIS rear suspension: anti-roll bar.

STEERING variable ratio, servo; turns lock to lock: 3.50.

BRAKES disc, servo.

ELECTRICAL EQUIPMENT transistorized ignition.

DIMENSIONS AND WEIGHT tracks: 53.15 in, 135 cm front, 53.54 in, 136 cm rear; height: Sedan 54.33 in, 138 cm - Hardtop 52.36 in, 133 cm; ground clearance: 5.91 in, 15 cm; weight: Sedan 2,326 lb, 1,055 kg - Hardtop 2,337 lb, 1,060 kg.

Celica Series

PRICES EX WORKS:

1 1600 ET Coupé	985,000	yen
2 1600 LT Coupé	1,045,000	yen
3 1600 LT Liftback	1,125,000	yen
4 1600 ST Coupé	1,080,000	yen
5 1600 ST Liftback	1,160,000	yen
6 1600 XT Coupé	1,130,000	yen
7 1600 XT Liftback	1,226,000	yen
8 1600 GT Coupé	1,467,000	yen
9 1600 GT Liftback	1,563,000	yen
10 1800 ST Coupé	1,110,000	yen
11 1800 ST Liftback	1,190,000	yen
12 1800 XT Coupé	1,160,000	yen
13 1800 XT Liftback	1,256,000	yen
14 1800 SE Coupé	1,251,000	yen
15 1800 SE Liftback	1,347,000	yen
16 1800 EFI ST Coupé	1,193,000	yen
17 1800 EFI ST Liftback	1,273,000	yen
18 2000 XT Coupé	1,213,000	yen
19 2000 XT Liftback	1,309,000	yen
20 2000 SE Coupé	1,304,000	yen
21 2000 SE Liftback	1,400,000	yen
22 2000 XX-L Liftback	1,466,000	yen
23 2000 XX-S Liftback	1,576,000	yen
24 2000 XX-G Liftback	1,696,000	yen
25 2000 GT Rally Coupé	1,440,000	yen
26 2000 GT Rally Liftback	1,536,000	yen
27 2000 GT Coupé	1,577,000	yen
28 2000 GT Liftback	1,673,000	yen
29 2600 XX-S Liftback	1,713,000	yen
30 2600 XX-G Liftback	1,839,000	yen

For GB prices, see price index.

Power team:	Standard for:	Optional for:
88 hp	1 to 7	—
115 hp	8,9	—
95 hp	10 to 15	—
105 hp	16,17	—
135 hp	25 to 28	—
105 hp (1,972 cc)	18 to 21	—
125 hp	22 to 24	—
140 hp	29,30	—

88 hp power team

ENGINE Toyota TTC-L lean-burn low emissione engine with turbulence generating pot auxiliary combustion chamber; front, 4 stroke; 4 cylinders, in line; 96.9 cu in, 1,588 cc (3.35 x 2.76 in, 85 x 70 mm); compression ratio: 9:1; max power (JIS): 88 hp at 5,600 rpm; max torque (JIS): 96 lb ft, 13.3 kg ·m at 3,400 rpm; max engine rpm: 6,000; 55 hp/l; cast iron block, light alloy head; 5 crankshaft bearings; valves: overhead, Vee-slanted, push-rods and rockers; camshafts: 1, side; lubrication: rotary pump, full flow filter, 7.4 imp pt, 8.9 US pt, 4.2 l; 1 Aisan 12T-U downdraught twin barrel carburettor; emission control with catalytic converter, secondary air injection and exhaust gas recirculation; fuel feed: mechanical pump; water-cooled, 14.1 imp pt, 16.9 US pt, 8 l.

TRANSMISSION driving wheels: rear; clutch: single dry plate (diaphragm); gearbox: mechanical; gears: 4, fully synchronized; ratios: I 3.587, II 2.022, III 1.384, IV 1, rev 3.484; lever: central; final drive: hypoid bevel; axle ratio: 4.100; width of rims: 4.5''; tyres: 6.45 x 13 - ST and XT models 165 SR x 13.

PERFORMANCE max speeds: (I) 29 mph, 46 km/h; (II) 52 mph, 83 km/h; (III) 75 mph, 120 km/h; (IV) 103 mph, 165 km/h; power-weight ratio: ET and LT coupés 23 lb/hp, 10.5 kg/hp; consumption: 34 m/imp gal, 28.3 m/US gal, 8.3 l x 100 km.

CHASSIS integral; front suspension: independent, by McPherson, coil springs/telescopic damper struts, lower wishbones (trailing links), anti-roll bar; rear: rigid axle, twin trailing radius arms, transverse linkage bar, coil springs, telescopic dampers.

STEERING recirculating ball; turns lock to lock; 3.80.

BRAKES front disc, rear drum; lining area: front 24.2 sq in, 156 sq cm, rear 54 sq in, 348 sq cm, total 78.2 sq in, 504 sq cm.

ELECTRICAL EQUIPMENT 12 V; 35 Ah battery; 45 A alternator; Nihon-Denso distributor; 4 headlamps.

DIMENSIONS AND WEIGHT wheel base: 98.43 in, 250 cm; tracks: 52.56 in, 133 cm front, 53.15 in, 135 cm rear; length: 170.47 in, 433 cm; width: 64.17 in, 163 cm; height: 51.57 in, 131 cm; ground clearance: ET Coupé and LT models 6.30 in, 16 cm - ST and XT models 5.90 in, 15 cm; weight: ET and LT coupés 2,084 lb, 945 kg - LT Liftback and ST Coupé 2,095 lb, 950 kg - ST Liftback and XT Coupé 2,106 lb, 955 kg - XT Liftback 2,117 lb, 960 kg; weight distribution:

56.7% front, 43.3% rear; turning circle: 36.1 ft, 11 m; fuel tank: 13.4 imp gal, 16.1 US gal, 61 l.

BODY 5 seats, separate front seats, reclining backrests, built-in headrests.

OPTIONALS 5-speed fully synchronized mechanical gearbox (I 3.587, II 2.022, III 1.384, IV 1, V 0.861, rev 3.484), 4.100 axle ratio, max speed 106 mph, 170 km/h; Toyoglide automatic transmission, hydraulic torque converter with 3 ratios (I 2.450, II 1.450, III 1, rev 2.222).

115 hp power team

See 88 hp power team, except for:

ENGINE (without TTC-L engine); compression ratio: 8.4:1; max power (JIS): 115 hp at 6,000 rpm; max torque (JIS): 109 lb ft ,15 kg m at 4800 rpm, max engine rpm: 6,400; 69 hp/l; camshafts: 2, overhead; lubrication: 6.7 imp pt, 8 US pt, 3.8 l; Bosch-Denso L-Jetronic electronic injection.

TRANSMISSION gears: 5, fully synchronized; ratios: I 3.587, II 2.022, III 1.384, IV 1, 0.861, rev 3.484; axle ratio: 4.100; width of rims: 5''; tyres: 185/70 HR x 13.

PERFORMANCE max speeds: (I) 29 mph, 47 km/h; (II) 51 mph, 83 km/h; (III) 76 mph, 122 km/h; (IV) 106 mph, 170 km/h; (V) 109 mph, 175 km/h; power-weight ratio: GT Coupé 19.2 lb/hp, 8.7 kg/hp.

CHASSIS rear suspension: anti-roll bar.

STEERING turns lock to lock: 3.50.

BRAKES rear disc.

DIMENSIONS AND WEIGHT tracks: 53.15 in, 135 cm front, 53.54 in, 136 cm rear; length: 173.62 in, 441 cm; width: Coupé 64.57 in, 164 cm - Liftback 62.99 in, 160 cm; height: Coupé 51.38 in, 131 cm - Liftback 51.18 in, 130 cm; weight: Coupé 2,205 lb, 1,000 kg - Liftback 2,216 lb, 1,005 kg.

95 hp power team

See 88 hp power team, except for:

ENGINE 108 cu in, 1,770 cc (3.35 x 3.07 in, 85 x 78 mm); max power (JIS): 95 hp at 5,400 rpm; max torque (JIS): 109 lb ft, 15 kg m at 3,400 rpm; 54 hp/l; 1 Aisan 13T-U downdraught twin barrel carburettor.

TRANSMISSION axle ratio: 3.909; tyres: 165 SR x 13.

PERFORMANCE max speed: 106 mph, 170 km/h; power-weight ratio: ST Coupé 22.3 lb/hp, 10.1 kg/hp; consumption: 32.4 m/imp gal, 27 m/US gal, 8.7 l x 100 km.

DIMENSIONS AND WEIGHT width: SE models 64.57 in, 164 cm; weight: ST Coupé 2,117 lb, 960 kg - ST Liftback and XT Coupé 2,128 lb, 965 kg - XT Liftback and SE Coupé 2,139 lb, 970 kg - SE Liftback 2,150 lb, 975 kg.

TOYOTA Celica 1600 GT Coupé

OPTIONALS 5-speed fully synchronized gearbox (V 0.861); Toyoglide automatic transmission, hydraulic torque converter with 3 ratios (I 2.450, II 1.450, III 1, rev 2.222).

105 hp power team

See 88 hp power team, except for:

ENGINE (without TTC-L engine); 108 cu in, 1,770 cc (3.35 x 3.07 in, 85 x 78 mm); max power (JIS): 105 hp at 5,400 rpm; max torque (JIS): 120 lb ft, 16.5 kg m at 3,600 rpm; 59.3 hp/l; Bosch-Denso L-jetronic electronic fuel injection; emission control: 3-way catalytic converter.

TRANSMISSION gears: 5, fully synchronized; ratios: I 3.287, II 2.043, III 1.394, IV 1, V 0.853, rev 4.039; axle ratio: 3.909; tyres: 165 SR x 13.

PERFORMANCE max speeds: (I) 29 mph, 47 km/h; (II) 47 mph, 76 km/h; (III) 71 mph, 114 km/h; (IV) 99 mph, 160 km/h; (V) 109 mph, 175 km/h; power-weight ratio: ST Coupé 20.6 lb/hp, 9.3 kg/hp; consumption: 33.9 m/imp gal, 28.2 m/US gal, 8.3 l x 100 km.

STEERING turns lock to lock: 3.50.

DIMENSIONS AND WEIGHT weight: ST Coupé 2,161 lb, 980 kg - ST Liftback 2,172 lb, 985 kg.

135 hp power team

See 88 hp power team, except for:

ENGINE 120.1 cu in, 1,968 cc (3.48 x 3.15 in, 88.5 x 80 mm); compression ratio: 8.3:1; max power (JIS): 135 hp at 5,800 rpm; max torque (JIS): 127 lb ft, 17.5 kg m at 4,800 rpm; 68.6 hp/l; cast iron block and head; valves: thimble tappets; camshafts: 2, overhead; Bosch-Denso L-jetronic electronic fuel injection.

TRANSMISSION gears: 5, fully synchronized; ratios: I 3.287, II 2.043, III 1.394, IV 1, V 0.853, rev 4.039; axle ratio: 3.909; width of rims: 5''; tyres: 185/70HR x 13.

PERFORMANCE max speeds: (I) 37 mph, 60 km/h; (II) 55 mph, 88 km/h; (III) 79 mph, 127 km/h; (IV) and (V) 112 mph, 180 km/h; power-weight ratio: GT Rally Coupé 17.2 lb/hp, 7.8 kg/hp; consumption: 28.2 m/imp gal, 23.5 m/US gal, 10 l x 100 km.

CHASSIS rear suspension: anti-roll bar.

STEERING variable ratio, servo; turns lock to lock: 3.50.

BRAKES rear disc, servo.

DIMENSIONS AND WEIGHT tracks: 53.13 in, 135 cm front, 53.54 in, 136 cm rear; length: 173.62 in, 441 cm; width: Rally models 64.37 in, 163 cm - GT models 64.57 in, 164 cm; weight: GT Rally Coupé 2,326 lb, 1,055 kg - GT Rally Liftback and GT Coupé 2,337 lb, 1,060 kg - GT Liftback 2,348 lb, 1,065 kg.

OPTIONALS tyres: 185/70 HR x 14.

TOYOTA Celica 2000 GT Rally Liftback

105 hp power team (1,972 cc)

See 88 hp power team, except for:

ENGINE (not TTC-L engine); 120.3 cu in, 1,972 cc (3.31 x 3.50 in, 84 x 89 mm); compression ratio: 8.5:1; max power (JIS): 105 hp at 5,200 rpm; max torque (JIS): 120 lb ft, 16.5 kg m at 3,600 rpm; 53.2 hp/l; cast iron block and light alloy head; valves: overhead, in line, rockers; camshafts: 1, overhead; 1 Aison 21R-U downdraught twin barrel carburettor; emission control: 3-way catalytic converter.

TRANSMISSION gears: 5, fully synchronized; ratios: I 3.287, II 2.043, III 1.394, IV 1, V 0.853, rev 4.039; axle ratio: 3.909; tyres: 165 SR x 13.

PERFORMANCE max speeds: (I) 29 mph, 46 km/h; (II) 47 mph, 75 km/h; (III) 70 mph, 112 km/h; (IV) 97 mph, 157 km/h; (V) 109 mph, 175 km/h; power-weight ratio: XT Coupé 21.5 lb/hp, 9.8 kg/hp; consumption: 28.2 m/imp gal, 23.5 m/US gal, 10 l x 100 km.

STEERING variable ratio.

BRAKES servo.

DIMENSIONS AND WEIGHT width: SE models 64.57 in, 164 cm; weight: XT Coupé 2,260 lb, 1,025 kg - XT Liftback and SE Coupé 2,271 lb, 1,030 kg - SE Liftback 2,282 lb, 1,035 kg.

OPTIONALS Toyoglide automatic transmission, hydraulic torque converter with 3 ratios (I 2.400, II 1.479, III 1, rev 1.920), max speed 103 mph, 165 km/h.

125 hp power team

ENGINE front, 4 stroke; 6 cylinders, in line; 121.3 cu in, 1,988 cc (2.95 x 2.95 in, 75 x 75 mm); compression ratio: 8.6:1; max power (JIS): 125 hp at 6,000 rpm; max torque (JIS): 123 lb ft, 17 kg m at 4,400 rpm; max engine rpm: 6,200; 62.9 hp/l; cast iron block and light alloy head; 7 crankshaft bearings; valves: overhead, rockers; camshafts: 1, overhead; lubrication: gear pump, full flow filter, 9.1 imp pt, 11 US pt, 5.2 l; Bosch-Denso electronic fuel injection; emission control: 3-way catalytic converter, exhaust gas recirculation; fuel feed: electric pump; water-cooled, 19.3 imp pt, 23.2 US pt, 11 l.

TRANSMISSION driving wheels: rear; clutch: single dry plate (diaphragm); gearbox: mechanical; gears: 5, fully synchronized; ratios: I 3.287, II 2.043, III 1.394, IV 1, V 0.853, rev 4.039; lever: central; final drive: hypoid bevel; axle ratio: 3.909; width of rims: 5.5''; tyres: L and S 185/70 HR x 14 - G 195/70 HR x 14.

PERFORMANCE max speeds: (I) 33 mph, 54 km/h; (II) 54 mph, 87 km/h; (III) 85 mph, 137 km/h; (IV) and (V) 112 mph, 180 km/h; power-weight ratio: L 20.3 lb/hp, 9.2 kg/hp; carrying capacity: 882 lb, 400 kg; consumption: 26.2 m/imp gal, 21.9 m/US gal, 10.7 l x 100 km.

TOYOTA Corona 1800 GL 4-dr Sedan

CHASSIS integral; front suspension: independent, by McPherson, coil springs/telescopic damper struts, lower wishbones (trailing links), anti-roll bar; rear: rigid axle, twin trailing radius arms, transverse linkage bar, coil springs, telescopic dampers, anti-roll bar.

STEERING recirculating ball; turns lock to lock: 4.30.

BRAKES disc, servo.

ELECTRICAL EQUIPMENT 12 V; 35 Ah battery; 55 A alternator; Denso distributor; 4 headlamps.

DIMENSIONS AND WEIGHT wheel base: 103.54 in, 263 cm; front and rear track: 53.74 in, 136 cm; length: 181.10 in, 460 cm; width: 64.96 in, 165 cm; height: 51.57 in, 131 cm; ground clearance: 6.30 in, 16 cm; weight: L 2,536 lb, 1,150 kg - S and G 2,580 lb, 1,170 kg; weight distribution: 54% front, 46% rear; turning circle: 38 ft, 11.6 m; fuel tank: 13.4 imp gal, 16.1 US gal, 61 l.

OPTIONALS Toyoglide automatic transmission, hydraulic torque converter with 4 ratios (I 2.450, II 1.450, III 1, IV 0.689, rev 2.222), 4.300 axle ratio, max speed 109 mph, 175 km/h, consumption 23.1 m/imp gal, 19.3 m/US gal, 12.2 l x 100 km; automatic speed control; power-assisted steering, turns lock to lock 3.30; air-conditioning; sunshine roof.

140 hp power team

See 125 hp power team, except for:

ENGINE 156.4 cu in, 2,563 cc (3.15 x 3.35 in, 80 x 85 mm); max power (JIS): 140 hp at 5,400 rpm; max torque (JIS): 156 lb ft, 21.5 kg m at 3,600 rpm; max engine rpm: 5,600; 54.6 hp/l.

TRANSMISSION tyres: S 185/70 HR x 14 — G 195/70 HR x 14.

PERFORMANCE max speeds: (I) 33 mph, 54 km/h; (II) 53 mph, 85 km/h; (III) 73 mph, 117 km/h; (IV) 107 mph, 173 km/h; (V) 112 mph, 180 km/h; power-weight ratio: 18.6 lb/hp, 8.4 kg/hp; consumption: 23.1 m/imp gal, 19.3 m/US gal, 12.2 l x 100 km.

STEERING servo; turns lock to lock: 3.30.

DIMENSIONS AND WEIGHT weight: 2,602 lb, 1,180 kg.

OPTIONALS Toyoglide automatic transmission, hydraulic torque converter with 4 ratios (I 2.450, II 1.450, III 1, IV 0.689, rev 2.222), 3.909 axle ratio, max speed 109 mph, 175 km/h, consumption 23.1 m/imp gal, 19.3 m/US gal, 12.2 l x 100 km; automatic speed control; air-conditioning; sunshine roof.

Celica (USA) Series

PRICES IN USA:

ST Hardtop	$ 5,899*
GT Hardtop	$ 6,329*
GT Liftback	$ 6,559*

96 hp power team

ENGINE front, 4 stroke; 4 cylinders, vertical, in line; 139.7 cu in, 2,289 cc; compression ratio: 8.4:1; max power (SAE): 96 hp at 4,800 rpm; max torque (SAE): 120 lb ft, 16.5 kg m at 2,800 rpm; max engine rpm: 5,600; 41.9 hp/l; cast iron block, light alloy head; 5 crankshaft bearings; valves: overhead, Vee-slanted, rockers; camshafts: 1, overhead; lubrication: rotary pump, full flow filter, 6.5 imp pt, 7.8 US pt, 3.7 l; 1 Aisan downdraught twin barrel carburettor; fuel feed: mechanical pump; water-cooled, 11.4 imp pt, 13.7 US pt, 6.5 l.

TRANSMISSION driving wheels: rear; clutch: single dry plate (diaphragm); gearbox: mechanical; gears: 4 (5 for GT models only), fully synchronized; ratios: I 3.579, II 2.081, III 1.397, IV 1, rev 4.399 - GT models I 3.287, II 2.043, III 1.394, IV 1, V 0.853, rev 4.039; lever: central; final drive: hypoid bevel; axle ratio: 3.727 - GT models 3.909; width of rims: 5''; tyres: ST 175SR x 14 - GT models 185/70HR x 14.

PERFORMANCE max speed: 109 mph, 175 km/h; consumption: not declared.

CHASSIS integral; front suspension: independent, by McPherson, coil springs/telescopic damper struts, lower wishbones (trailing links), anti-roll bar; rear: rigid axle, twin trailing radius arms, transverse linkage bar, coil springs, telescopic dampers.

STEERING recirculating ball; turns lock to lock: 3.50.

BRAKES front disc, rear drum, servo; lining area: front 24.2 sq in, 156 sq cm, rear 54 sq in, 348 sq cm, total 78.2 sq in, 504 sq cm.

ELECTRICAL EQUIPMENT 12 V; 35 Ah battery; 40 A alternator; Nihon-Denso distributor; 4 headlamps.

BODY 5 seats, separate front seats, reclining backrests, built-in headrests.

OPTIONALS Toyoglide automatic transmission, hydraulic torque converter with 3 ratios (I 2.400, II 1.479, III 1, rev 1.920), 3.900 axle ratio, max speed 103 mph, 165 km/h, acceleration standing ¼ mile 19 sec.

Corona Series

PRICES (Tokyo):

1	1600 Standard 4-dr Sedan	897,000 yen
2	1600 De Luxe 4-dr Sedan	989,000 yen
3	1600 De Luxe Hardtop	1,024,000 yen
4	1600 De Luxe Liftback	1,039,000 yen
5	1600 GL 4-dr Sedan	1,046,000 yen
6	1600 GL Hardtop	1,081,000 yen
7	1600 GL Liftback	1,096,000 yen
8	1600 SL 4-dr Sedan	1,107,000 yen
9	1600 SL Hardtop	1,145,000 yen
10	1600 SL Liftback	1,157,000 yen
11	1800 De Luxe 4-dr Sedan	1,022,000 yen
12	1800 De Luxe Hardtop	1,057,000 yen
13	1800 De Luxe Liftback	1,072,000 yen
14	1800 GL 4-dr Sedan	1,107,000 yen

TOYOTA Corona 1800 GL 4-dr Sedan

15	1800 GL Hardtop	1,142,000	yen
16	1800 GL Liftback	1,169,000	yen
17	1800 SL 4-dr Sedan	1,169,000	yen
18	1800 SL Hardtop	1,207,000	yen
19	1800 SL Liftback	1,231,000	yen
20	1800 SL Touring 4-dr Sedan	1,291,000	yen
21	1800 SL Touring Hardtop	1,329,000	yen
22	1800 SL Touring Liftback	1,355,000	yen
23	2000 GL 4-dr Sedan	1,162,000	yen
24	2000 GL Hardtop	1,197,000	yen
25	2000 GL Liftback	1,224,000	yen
26	2000 SL 4-dr Sedan	1,219,000	yen
27	2000 SL Hardtop	1,257,000	yen
28	2000 SL Liftback	1,281,000	yen
29	2000 CX 4-dr Sedan	1,307,000	yen
30	2000 CX Hardtop	1,342,000	yen
31	2000 CX Liftback	1,371,000	yen
32	2000 GT 4-dr Sedan	1,528,000	yen
33	2000 GT Hardtop	1,571,000	yen
34	2000 GT Liftback	1,592,000	yen

Power team:	Standard for:	Optional for:
88 hp	1 to 10	—
95 hp	11 to 19	—
105 hp	20 to 22	—
135 hp	32 to 34	—
105 hp (1,972 cc)	23 to 31	—

TOYOTA Corona 1800 SL Touring Liftback

88 hp power team

ENGINE TTC-L lean-burn system with turbulence generating pot combustion chambers; front, 4 stroke; 4 cylinders, vertical, in line; 96.9 cu in, 1,588 cc (3.35 x 2.76 in, 85 x 70 mm); compression ratio: 9:1; max power (JIS): 88 hp at 5,600 rpm; max torque (JIS): 96 lb ft, 13.3 kg m at 3,400 rpm; max engine rpm: 6,000; 55 hp/l; cast iron block, light alloy head; 5 crankshaft bearings; valves: overhead, push-rods and rockers; camshafts: 1, side; lubrication: rotary pump, full flow filter, 7.4 imp pt, 8.9 US pt, 4.2 l; 1 Aisan 12 T-U downdraught twin barrel carburettor; emission control with catalytic converter, secondary air induction and exhaust gas recirculation fuel feed: mechanical pump; water-cooled, 14.1 imp pt, 16.9 US pt, 8 l.

TRANSMISSION driving wheels: rear; clutch: single dry plate (diaphragm); gearbox: mechanical; gears: 4, fully synchronized; ratios: I 3.587, II 2.022, III 1.384, IV 1, rev 3.484; lever: central; (for Standard 3-speed mechanical gearbox, ratios I 3.368, II 1.644, III 1, rev 4.079, steering column lever - for SL models 5-speed mechanical gearbox, V 0.861); final drive: hypoid bevel; axle ratio: 3.909 - SL models 4.100; width of rims: 4.5''; tyres: 6.45 x 13 - SL models 165 SR x 13.

PERFORMANCE max speeds: (I) 29 mph, 46 km/h; (II) 52 mph, 83 km/h; (III) 75 mph, 120 km/h; (IV) 103 mph, 165 km/h; power-weight ratio: De Luxe 4-dr Sedan 24.3 lb/hp, 11 kg/hp; carrying capacity: 882 lb, 400 kg; consumption: 33.9 m/imp gal, 28.2 m/US gal, 8.3 l x 100 km.

CHASSIS integral; front suspension: independent, by Mc-Pherson, coil springs/telescopic damper struts, lower wishbones (trailing links), anti-roll bar; rear: rigid axle, twin trailing radius arms, transverse linkage bar, coil springs, telescopic dampers.

STEERING recirculating ball, variable ratio; turns lock to lock: 3.80.

BRAKES front disc, rear drum, servo; lining area: front 22.3 sq in, 144 sq cm, rear 53.9 sq in, 348 sq cm, total 76.2 sq in, 492 sq cm.

ELECTRICAL EQUIPMENT 12 V; 33 Ah battery; 55 A alternator; 4 headlamps.

DIMENSIONS AND WEIGHT wheel base: 99.41 in, 252 cm; front and rear track: 53.15 in, 135 cm; - SL models 53.74 in, 136 cm; length: 167.72 in, .426 cm - GL and SL models 168.90 in, 429 cm; width: 64.76 in, 164 cm; height: sedans 55.12 in, 140 cm - hardtops 53.94 in, 137 cm - liftbacks 54.14 in, 138 cm; ground clearance: 6.50 in, 16.5 cm; weight: De Luxe 4-dr Sedan 2,139 lb, 970 kg - GL 4-dr Sedan 2,183 lb, 990 kg - De Luxe Hardtop 2,172 lb, 985 kg - De Luxe Liftback, GL Hardtop and SL 4-dr Sedan 2,194 lb, 995 kg - GL Liftback and SL Hardtop 2,216 lb, 1,005 kg - SL Liftback 2,227 lb, 1,010 kg; weight distribution: 55% front, 45% rear; turning circle: 35.4 ft, 10.8 m; fuel tank: 13.4 imp gal, 16.1 US gal, 61 l.

BODY 5 seats, separate front seats, reclining backrests, built-in headrests.

OPTIONALS (except SL models) 5-speed mechanical gearbox (V 0.861); Toyoglide automatic transmission, hydraulic torque converter with 3 ratios (I 2.450, II 1.450, III 1, rev 2.222).

TOYOTA Corona 2000 CX Liftback

95 hp power team

See 88 hp power team, except for:

ENGINE 108 cu in, 1,770 cc (3.35 x 3.07 in, 85 x 78 mm); compression ratio 8.5:1; max power (JIS): 95 hp at 5,400 rpm; max torque (JIS): 109 lb ft, 15 kg m at 3,400 rpm; 54 hp/l; 1 Aisan 13T-U downdraught twin barrel carburettor.

TRANSMISSION gears: (for SL models only) 5, fully synchronized; ratios: I 3.587, III 2.022, III 1.384, IV 1, V 0.861, rev 0.861; tyres: SL models 165 SR x 14.

PERFORMANCE max speeds: (I) 28 mph, 45 km/h; (II) 50 mph, 80 km/h; (III) 75 mph, 120 km/h; (IV) 102 mph 165 km/h; power-weight ratio: De Luxe 4-dr Sedan 22.9 lb/hp, 10.4 kg/hp; consumption: 33.9 m/imp gal, 28.2 m/US gal, 8.3 l x 100 km.

DIMENSIONS AND WEIGHT length: SL models 175 in, 444 cm; weight: De Luxe 4-dr Sedan 2,172 lb, 985 kg - De Luxe Hardtop 2,183 lb, 990 kg - GL 4-dr Sedan 2,194 lb, 995 kg - GL Hardtop 2,205 lb, 1,000 kg - De Luxe Liftback 2,227 lb, 1,010 kg - GL Liftback 2,249 lb, 1,020 kg - SL 4-dr Sedan 2,293 lb, 1,040 kg - SL Hardtop 2,315 lb, 1,050 kg - SL Liftback 2,337 lb, 1,060 kg.

105 hp power team

See 88 hp power team, except for:

ENGINE (without TTC-L engine); 108 cu in, 1,770 cc (3.35 x 3.07 in, 85 x 78 mm); max power (JIS): 105 hp at

TOYOTA Corona 2000 SL Hardtop

105 HP POWER TEAM

5,400 rpm; max torque (JIS): 120 lb ft, 16.5 kg m at 3,600 rpm; max engine rpm: 5,800; 59.3 hp/l; Bosch-Denso electronic fuel injection; emission control with 3-way catalytic converter; fuel feed: electronic pump.

TRANSMISSION gears: 5, fully synchronized; ratios: I 3,287, II 2.043, III 1.394, IV 1, V 0.853, rev 4.039; axle ratio: 3.909; width of rims: 5''; tyres: 185/70 HR 14.

PERFORMANCE max speeds: (I) 33 mph, 53 km/h; (II) 51 mph, 83 km/h; (III) 75 mph, 120 km/h; (IV) and (V) 109 mph, 175 km/h; power-weight ratio: 4-dr Sedan 22.7 lb/hp, 10.3 kg/hp; consumption: 28.2 m/imp gal, 23.5 m/US gal, 10 l x 100 km.

CHASSIS rear suspension: anti-roll bar.

BRAKES rear disc; lining area: front 22.3 sq in, 144 cm, rear 18 sq in, 116 sq cm, total 40.3 sq in, 260 sq cm.

DIMENSIONS AND WEIGHT front and rear track: 53.54 in, 136 cm; length: 175 in, 444 cm; height: 4-dr Sedan 55.31 in, 140 cm - Hardtop 54.13 in, 137 cm - Liftback 54.33 in, 138 cm; weight: 4-dr Sedan 2,381 lb, 1,080 kg - Hardtop and Liftback 2,403 lb, 1,090 kg.

OPTIONALS 4.100 axle ratio.

TOYOTA Corona 2000 CX 4-dr Sedan

135 hp power team

See 88 hp power team, except for:

ENGINE hemispherical combustion chambers without TTC-L lean-burn system; 120.1 cu in, 1,968 cc (3.48 x 3.15 in, 88.5 x 80 mm); compression ratio: 8.3:1; max power (JIS): 135 hp at 5,800 rpm; max torque (JIS): 127 lb ft, 17.5 kg m at 4,800 rpm; max engine rpm: 6,600; 68.6 hp/l; valves: overhead, Vee-slanted, thimble tappets; camshafts: 2, overhead; lubrication: 8.3 imp pt, 9.9 US pt, 4.7 l; Bosch-Denso electronic fuel injection; emission control with 3-way catalytic converter; cooling system: 14.4 imp pt, 17.3 US pt, 8.2 l.

TRANSMISSION gears: 5, fully synchronized; ratios: I 3,287, II 2.043, III 1.394, IV 1, V 0.853; axle ratios: 4.100; width of rims: 5''; tyres: 185/70 HR x 14.

PERFORMANCE max speed: 112 mph, 180 km/h; power-weight ratio: Sedan 18.3 lb/hp, 8.3 kg/hp; consumption: 28.2 m/imp gal, 23.5 m/US gal, 10 l x 100 km.

CHASSIS rear suspension: anti-roll bar.

STEERING turns lock to lock: 3.90.

BRAKES rear disc, servo.

DIMENSIONS AND WEIGHT length: 175 in, 444 cm; height: Sedan 55.11 in, 140 cm - Hardtop 53.94 in, 137 cm - Liftback 54.33 in, 138 cm; weight: Sedan 2,470 lb, 1,120 kg - Hardtop 2,492 lb, 1,130 kg - Liftback 2,514 lb, 1,140 kg.

TOYOTA Mark II 2600 Grande 4-dr Sedan

OPTIONALS power-steering, 3.60 turns lock to lock; limited slip differential.

105 hp power team (1,972 cc)

See 88 hp power team, except for:

ENGINE (not TTC-L engine); 120 cu in, 1,972 cc (3.31 x 3.50 in, 84 x 89 mm); compression ratio: 8.5:1; max power (JIS): 105 hp at 5,200 rpm; max torque (JIS): 120 lb ft, 16.5 kg m at 3,600 rpm; 53.2 hp/l; camshafts: 1, overhead; lubrication: 8.8 imp pt, 10.6 US pt, 5 l; emission control with 3-way catalytic converter, secondary air induction, exhaust gas recirculation.

TRANSMISSION gears: 5, fully synchronized; ratios: I 3,287, II 2.043, III 1.394, IV 1, V 0.853, rev 4.039; axle ratio: GL and CX models 3.727 - SL models 4.100; tyres: GL models 6.45 x 13 - SL models 165 SR x 14 - CX models 165 SR x 13.

PERFORMANCE max speeds: (I) 30 mph, 48 km/h; (II) 50 mph, 80 km/h; (III) 71 mph, 115 km/h; (IV) 102 mph, 164 km/h; (V) 109 mph, 175 km/h; power-weight ratio: GL 4-dr Sedan 22.1 lb/hp, 10 kg/hp; consumption: 29.6 m/imp gal, 24.7 m/US gal, 9.5 l x 100 km.

BRAKES (for SL models only) rear disc.

DIMENSIONS AND WEIGHT length: GL and CX models 168.90 in, 429 cm - SL models 175 in, 444 cm; height: GL and CX Sedans 55.11 in, 140 cm - SL Sedan 55.31 in, 141 cm - GL and CX hardtops 53.94 in, 137 cm - SL Hardtop, GL, CX and SL Liftbacks 54.33 in, 138 cm; width: CX models 65.16 in, 165 cm; weight: GL 4-dr Sedan, 2,326 lb, 1,055 kg - SL 4-dr Sedan 2,414 lb, 1,095 kg - CX 4-dr Sedan 2,392 lb, 1,085 kg - GL Hardtop 2,337 lb, 1,060 kg - SL Hardtop and CX Liftback 2,436 lb, 1,105 kg - CX Hardtop 2,403 lb, 1,090 kg - GL Liftback 2,370 lb, 1,075 kg - SL Liftback 2,447 lb, 1,110 kg.

OPTIONALS Toyoglide automatic transmission, hydraulic torque converter with 3 ratios (I 2.450, II 1.450, III 1, rev 2.222); (only for CX models) Toyoglide automatic transmission, hydraulic torque converter with 4 ratios (I 2.450, II 1.450, III 1, IV 0.689), 3.909 axle ratio.

Mark II - Chaser Series

PRICES (Tokyo):

1 Mark II 1800 Standard 4-dr Sedan	990,000	yen
2 Mark II 1800 De Luxe 4-dr Sedan	1,066,000	yen
3 Mark II 1800 De Luxe 2-dr Hardtop	1,107,000	yen
4 Chaser 1800 De Luxe 4-dr Sedan	1,072,000	yen
5 Chaser 1800 De Luxe 2-dr Hardtop	1,113,000	yen
6 Mark II 1800 GL 4-dr Sedan	1,127,000	yen
7 Mark II 1800 GL 2-dr Hardtop	1,169,000	yen
8 Chaser 1800 XL 4-dr Sedan	1,133,000	yen
9 Chaser 1800 XL 2-dr Hardtop	1,174,000	yen
10 Mark II 2000 De Luxe 4-dr Sedan	1,096,000	yen
11 Mark II 2000 De Luxe 2-dr Hardtop	1,137,000	yen
12 Chaser 2000 De Luxe 4-dr Sedan	1,102,000	yen
13 Chaser 2000 De Luxe 4-dr Hardtop	1,143,000	yen
14 Mark II 2000 GL 4-dr Sedan	1,157,000	yen

TOYOTA Mark II 2600 Grande 4-dr Sedan

TOYOTA Mark II 2600 Grande Hardtop

TOYOTA Chaser 2000 SGS 2-dr Hardtop

15 Mark II 2000 GL 2-dr Hardtop	1,198,000	yen
16 Chaser 2000 XL 4-dr Sedan	1,163,000	yen
17 Chaser 2000 XL 4-dr Hardtop	1,204,000	yen
18 Chaser 2000 GS 4-dr Sedan	1,284,000	yen
19 Chaser 2000 GS 4-dr Hardtop	1,362,000	yen
20 Mark II 2000 GSL 4-dr Sedan	1,278,000	yen
21 Mark II 2000 GSL 2-dr Hardtop	1,354,000	yen
22 Chaser 2000 SXL 4-dr Sedan	1,366,000	yen
23 Chaser 2000 SXL 2-dr Hardtop	1,438,000	yen
24 Mark II 2000 LG 4-dr Sedan	1,459,000	yen
25 Mark II 2000 LG 2-dr Hardtop	1,531,000	yen
26 Chaser 2000 SGS 4-dr Sedan	1,482,000	yen
27 Chaser 2000 SGS 2-dr Hardtop	1,554,000	yen
28 Mark II 2000 LG Touring 4-dr Sedan	1,516,000	yen
29 Mark II 2000 LG Touring 2-dr Hardtop	1,588,000	yen
30 Chaser 2000 SG Touring 4-dr Sedan	1,608,000	yen
31 Chaser 2000 SG Touring 2-dr Hardtop	1,645,000	yen
32 Mark II 2000 Grande 4-dr Sedan	1,835,000	yen
33 Mark II 2000 Grande 2-dr Hardtop	1,872,000	yen
34 Mark II 2600 Grande 4-dr Sedan	—	yen
35 Mark II 2600 Grande 2-dr Hardtop	2,092,000	yen

Power team:	Standard for:	Optional for:
95 hp	1 to 9	—
105 hp	10 to 21	—
125 hp	22 to 33	—
140 hp	34,35	—

95 hp power team

ENGINE TTC-L lean-burn low emission engine with turbulence generating pot auxiliary combustion chamber; front, 4 stroke; 4 cylinders, in line; 108 cu in, 1,770 cc (3.35 x 3.07 in, 85 x 78 mm); compression ratio: 9:1; max power (JIS): 95 hp at 5,700 rpm; max torque (JIS): 109 lb ft, 15 kg m at 3,400 rpm; max engine rpm: 6,000; 53.7 hp/l; cast iron block, light alloy head; 5 crankshaft bearings; valves: overhead, rockers; camshafts: 1, overhead; lubrication: rotary pump, full flow filter, 7.4 imp pt, 8.9 US pt, 4.2 l; 1 Aisan 13T-U downdraught twin barrel carburettor; emission control with catalytic converter, secondary air injection and exhaust gas recirculation; fuel feed: mechanical pump; water-cooled, 14.1 imp pt, 16.9 US pt, 8 l.

TRANSMISSION driving wheels: rear; clutch: single dry plate (diaphragm); gearbox: mechanical; gears: 4, fully synchronized; ratios: I 3.579, II 2.081, III 1.397, IV 1, rev 4.399; lever: central; final drive: hypoid bevel; axle ratio: 3.909; width of rims: 5''; tyres: 6.45 x 14.

PERFORMANCE max speeds: (I) 29 mph, 47 km/h; (II) 52 mph, 83 km/h; (III) 76 mph, 123 km/h; (IV) 103 mph, 165 km/h; power-weight ratio: De Luxe sedans 24.5 lb/hp, 11.1 kg/hp; consumption: 31.4 m/imp gal, 26.1 m/US gal, 9 l x 100 km.

CHASSIS integral; front suspension: independent, by McPherson, lower transverse arms, diagonal trailing locating rods, anti-roll bar, coil springs, telescopic damper struts; rear: rigid axle, lower trailing links, upper torque rods, coil springs, telescopic dampers.

STEERING recirculating ball, variable ratio; turns lock to lock: 4.30.

BRAKES front disc, rear drum, servo; lining area: front 22.3 sq in, 144 sq cm, rear 54.6 sq in, 352 sq cm, total 76.9 sq in, 496 sq cm.

ELECTRICAL EQUIPMENT 12 V; 35 Ah battery; 55 A alternator; Nihon Denso distributor; 2 headlamps.

DIMENSIONS AND WEIGHT wheel base: 103.94 in, 264 cm; tracks: 53.94 in, 137 cm front, 53.15 in, 135 cm rear; length: De Luxe models 177.17 in, 450 cm - GL and XL models 178.35 in, 453 cm; width: 65.75 in, 167 cm; height: sedans 55.51 in, 141 cm - hardtops 54.72 in, 139 cm; ground clearance: 6.69 in, 17 cm; weight: Standard and De Luxe 4-dr sedans 2,326 lb, 1,055 kg - De Luxe hardtops 2,337 lb, 1,060 kg - GL and XL sedans 2,359 lb, 1,070 kg - GL and XL hardtops 2,370 lb, 1,075 kg; weight distribution: 54% front, 46% rear; turning circle: 37 ft, 11.4 m.

BODY 5 seats, separate front seats, reclining backrests, built-in headrests.

OPTIONALS 5-speed fully synchronized mechanical gearbox (I 3.287, II 2.043, II 1.394, IV 1, V 0.853).

105 hp power team

See 95 hp power team, except for:

ENGINE (not TTC-L engine); 120.3 cu in, 1.972 cc (3.30 x 3.50 in, 84 x 89 mm); compression ratio: 8.5:1; max power (JIS): 105 hp at 5,200 rpm; max torque (JIS): 120 lb ft, 16.5 kg m at 3,600 rpm; 53.2 hp/l; cast iron block, light alloy head; lubrication: gear pump, 8.8 imp pt, 10.6 US pt, 5 l; 1 Aisan 21R-U downdraught twin barrel carburettor; emission control with 3-way catalytic converter.

TRANSMISSION gears: 4 (5 for GSL and GS models), fully synchronized; ratios: De Luxe, GL and XL models (I 3.579, II 2.081, III 1.397, IV 1, rev 4.399) - GSL and GS models (I 3.287, II 2.043, III 1.394, IV 1, V 0.853, rev 4.039); axle ratio: 3.909 - GSL and GS models 4,100; tyres: 6.45 x 14 - GSL and GS models 175 SR x 14.

PERFORMANCE max speeds: (I) 31 mph, 50 km/h; (II) 53 mph, 86 km/h; (III) 78 mph, 126 km/h; (IV) 103 mph, 165 km/h; power-weight ratio: Mark II De Luxe Sedan 22.5 lb/hp, 10.2 kg/hp; consumption: 28.2 m/imp gal, 23.5 m/US gal, 10 l x 100 km.

BRAKES (for GSL and GS models only) disc; lining area: front 22.3 sq in, 144 sq cm, rear 18 sq in, 116 sq cm, total 40.3 sq in, 260 sq cm.

ELECTRICAL EQUIPMENT 50 A alternator.

DIMENSIONS AND WEIGHT rear tracks: GSL and GS models 54.33 in, 138 cm; length: De Luxe models 177.17 in, 450 cm - GL, GSL and GS models 178.35 in, 453 cm; height: sedans 55.71 in, 141 cm - hardtops 54.72 in, 139 cm; weight: Mark II De Luxe Sedan 2,370 lb, 1,075 kg - Chaser De Luxe Sedan 2,381 lb, 1,080 kg - De Luxe hardtops 2,392 lb, 1,085 kg - Mark II GL Sedan 2,403 lb, 1,090 kg - Chaser XL Sedan 2,414 lb, 1,095 kg - XL hardtops 2,425 lb, 1,100 kg - Mark II GSL and Chaser GS sedans 2,525 lb, 1,145 kg - GSL and GS hardtops 2,536 lb, 1,150 kg.

OPTIONALS steering column lever; Toyoglide automatic transmission, hydraulic torque converter and planetary gears with 3 ratios (I 2.450, II 1.450, III 1, rev 2.222).

125 hp power team

See 95 hp power team, except for:

ENGINE (without TTC-L engine); 6 cylinders, in line; 121.3 cu in, 1,988 cc (2.95 x 2.95 in, 75 x 75 mm); compression ratio: 8.5:1; max power (JIS): 125 hp at 6,000 rpm; max torque (JIS): 123 lb ft, 17 kg m at 4,400 rpm; 62.9 hp/l; cast iron block, light alloy head; 7 crankshaft bearings; valves: overhead, Vee-slanted, rockers; lubrication: gear pump, 9.2 imp pt, 11 US pt, 5.2 l; Bosch-Denso L-jetronic electronic fuel injection; 3-way catalytic converter with oxygen sensor; cooling system: 19.4 imp pt, 23.3 US pt, 11 l.

TRANSMISSION gears: 5, fully synchronized; ratios: I 3.287, II 2.043, III 1.394, IV 1, V 0.853, rev 4.039; tyres: 175 SR x 14 - SXL models 6.45 x 14 - SGS, SG Touring and Grande models 185/70 HR x 14.

PERFORMANCE max speeds: (I) 32 mph, 52 km/h; (II) 52 mph, 83 km/h; (III) 76 mph, 123 km/h; (IV) 109 mph, 175 km/h; (V) 109 mph, 175 km/h; power-weight ratio: SXL 4-dr Sedan 20 lb/hp, 9.1 kg/hp; consumption: 25.4 m/imp gal, 21.2 m/US gal, 11.1 l x 100 km.

CHASSIS rear suspension: (except for SXL models) independent, semi-trailing arms, coil springs, telescopic dampers, anti-roll bar.

STEERING (except for SXL and SGS models) servo; turns lock to lock: 3.40.

125 HP POWER TEAM

BRAKES (except for SXL and LG models) rear disc.

DIMENSIONS AND WEIGHT tracks: Grande and SG Touring 54.72 in, 139 cm front, Grande and SG Touring 54.72 in, 139 cm rear - SGS models 54.33 in, 138 cm; width: 66.14 in, 168 cm; weight: SXL 4-dr Sedan 2,503 lb, 1,135 kg - SXL 2-dr Hardtop 2,514 lb, 1,140 kg - LG 4-dr Sedan 2,536 lb, 1,150 kg - LG 2-dr Hardtop 2,547 lb, 1,155 kg - SGS 4-dr Sedan, 2,580 lb, 1,170 kg - SGS 2-dr Hardtop 2,591 lb, 1,175 kg - LG and SG Touring sedans 2,613 lb, 1,185 kg - LG and SG Touring hardtops 2,624 lb, 1,190 kg - Grande 4-dr Sedan 2,767 lb, 1,255 kg - Grande 2-dr Hardtop 2,712 lb, 1,230 kg.

OPTIONALS automatic transmission with 3 ratios (I 2.400, II 1.479, III 1, rev 1.920), 3.909 axle ratio; (only for Grande, LG Touring and SG Touring models) Toyoglide automatic transmission with 4 ratios (I 2.450, II 1.450, III 1, IV 0.689).

140 hp power team

See 95 hp power team, except for:

ENGINE (without TTC-L engine); 6 cylinders, in line; 156.4 cu in, 2,563 cc (3.15 x 3.35 in, 80 x 85 mm); compression ratio: 8.5:1; max power (JIS): 140 hp at 5,400 rpm; max torque (JIS): 156 lb ft, 21.5 kg m at 3,600 rpm; 54.6 hp/l; cast iron block, light alloy head; 7 crankshaft bearings; valves: overhead, Vee-slanted, rockers; lubrication: gear pump, 9.2 imp pt, 11 US pt, 5.2 l; Bosch-Denso electronic fuel injection; emission control with 3-way catalytic converter and oxygen sensor; cooling system: 19.4 imp pt, 23.3 US pt, 11 l.

TRANSMISSION automatic transmission, hydraulic torque converter and planetary gears; ratios: I 2.450, II 1.450, III 1, IV 0.689, rev 2.222; axle ratio: 3.909; tyres: 185/70 HR x 14.

PERFORMANCE power-weight ratio: Grande 4-dr Sedan 19.4 lb/hp, 8.8 kg/hp; consumption: 22 m/imp gal, 18.3 m/US gal, 12.8 l x 100 km.

CHASSIS rear suspension: independent, semi-trailing arms, coil springs, telescopic dampers, anti-roll bar.

STEERING servo.

BRAKES rear disc.

DIMENSIONS AND WEIGHT front and rear track: 54.72 in, 139 cm; length: 181.69 in, 461 cm; width: 66.14 in, 168 cm; weight: Grande 4-dr Sedan 2,679 lb, 1,235 kg - Grande 2-dr Hardtop 2,734 lb, 1,240 kg.

Crown Series

PRICES (Tokyo):

1 2000 De Luxe A 4-dr Sedan	1,370,000	yen
2 2000 De Luxe 4-dr Sedan	1,508,000	yen
3 2000 De Luxe 2-dr Hardtop	1,454,000	yen
4 2000 De Luxe 4-dr Hardtop	1,489,000	yen
5 2000 De Luxe Custom 2-dr Hardtop	—	
6 2000 De Luxe Custom 4-dr Hardtop	—	
7 2000 Super De Luxe 4-dr Sedan	1,690,000	yen
8 2000 Super De Luxe 4-dr Hardtop	1,800,000	yen
9 2000 Super Saloon 4-dr Sedan	1,828,000	yen
10 2000 Super Saloon 4-dr Hardtop	1,976,000	yen
11 2000 EFI De Luxe A 4-dr Sedan	1,453,000	yen
12 2000 EFI De Luxe 4-dr Sedan	1,621,000	yen
13 2000 EFI De Luxe 4-dr Hardtop	1,577,000	yen
14 2000 EFI De Luxe Custom 2-dr Hardtop	—	
15 2000 EFI De Luxe Custom 4-dr Hardtop	—	
16 2000 EFI Super De Luxe 4-dr Sedan	1,803,000	yen
17 2000 EFI Super De Luxe 2-dr Hardtop	1,896,000	yen
18 2000 EFI Super De Luxe 4-dr Hardtop	1,936,000	yen
19 2000 EFI Super Saloon 4-dr Sedan	1,941,000	yen
20 2000 EFI Super Saloon 2-dr Hardtop	2,161,000	yen
21 2000 EFI Super Salon 4-dr Hardtop	2,131,000	yen
22 2200 Diesel Standard 4-dr Sedan	1,372,000	yen
23 2200 Diesel De Luxe A 4-dr Sedan	1,447,000	yen
24 2200 Diesel De Luxe 4-dr Sedan	1,585,000	yen
25 2200 Diesel Super De Luxe 4-dr Sedan	1,765,000	yen
26 2600 Super Saloon 4-dr Sedan	2,243,000	yen
27 2600 Super Saloon 2-dr Hardtop	2,626,000	yen
28 2600 Super Saloon 4-dr Hardtop	2,341,000	yen
29 2600 Royal Saloon 4-dr Sedan	2,597,000	yen
30 2600 Royal Saloon 2-dr Hardtop	2,626,000	yen

Power team:	Standard for:	Optional for:
110 hp	1 to 10	—
125 hp	11 to 21	—
72 hp	22 to 25	—
140 hp	26 to 30	—

TOYOTA Crown 2200 Diesel Super De Luxe 4-dr Sedan

TOYOTA Crown 2600 Royal Saloon 4-dr Sedan

TOYOTA Crown 2000 De Luxe Hardtop

110 hp power team

ENGINE front, 4 stroke; 6 cylinders, vertical, in line; 121.3 cu in, 1,988 cc (2.95 x 2.95 in, 75 x 75 mm); compression ratio: 8.6:1; max power (JIS): 110 hp at 5,600 rpm; max torque (JIS): 116 lb ft, 16 kg m at 3,800 rpm; max engine rpm: 6,200; 55.3 hp/l; cast iron block, light alloy head; 7 crankshaft bearings; valves: overhead, Vee-slanted, rockers; camshafts: 1, overhead; lubrication: rotary pump, full flow filter, 9.9 imp pt, 11.8 US pt, 5.6 l; 1 Aisan M-U type downdraught twin barrel carburettor; emission control with catalytic converter, secondary air injection and exhaust gas recirculation; fuel feed: mechanical pump; water-cooled, 19.4 imp pt, 23.3 US pt, 11 l.

TRANSMISSION driving wheels: rear; clutch: single dry plate (diaphragm), hydraulically controlled; gearbox: mechanical; gears: 4, fully synchronized (5 for Super De Luxe 4-dr Hardtop only); ratios: I 3.579, II 2.081, III 1.397, IV 1, rev 4.399 - Super De Luxe 4-dr Hardtop I 3.287, II 2.043, III 1.394, IV 1, V 0.853, rev 4.039; lever: central; final drive: hypoid bevel; axle ratio: 4.556; width of rims: 5"; tyres: 6.95 x 14 - De Luxe Custom 2-dr Hardtop 185 SR x 14 - Super Saloon 4-dr Hardtops D78 x 14.

PERFORMANCE max speeds: (I) 27 mph, 44 km/h; (II) 47 mph, 76 km/h; (III) 70 mph, 112 km/h; (IV) 99 mph, 160 km/h; power-weight ratio: De Luxe-A 4-dr Sedan 27.1 lb/hp, 12.3 kg/hp; carrying capacity: 882 lb, 400 kg; speed in direct drive at 1,000 rpm: 15.5 mph, 25 km/h; consumption: 36.7 m/imp gal, 30.5 m/US gal, 7.7 l x 100 km.

CHASSIS box-type perimeter frame; front suspension: inde-

pendent, double wishbones, coil springs, anti-roll bar, telescopic dampers; rear: rigid axle, lower radius arms, upper
torque arm, coil springs, telescopic dampers.

STEERING recirculating ball; turns lock to lock: 4.60.

BRAKES front disc, rear drum, servo; lining area: front
22.8 sq in, 147.6 sq cm, rear 75.7 sq in, 488 sq cm, total
98.5 sq in, 635.6 sq cm.

ELECTRICAL EQUIPMENT 12 V; 45 Ah battery; 50 A alternator; Denso distributor; 4 headlamps.

DIMENSIONS AND WEIGHT wheel base: 105.91 in, 269 cm;
tracks: 55.51 in, 141 cm front, 54.33 in, 138 cm rear;
length: hardtops 184.25 in, 468 cm - sedans 184.65 in, 469 cm;
width: 66.49 in, 169 cm; height: sedans 56.69 in, 144
cm - De Luxe 2-dr Hardtop 55.51 in, 141 cm - 4-dr hardtops
55.91 in, 142 cm; ground clearance: 6.89 in, 17.5 cm; weight:
De Luxe-A 4-dr Sedan 2,977 lb, 1,350 kg - De Luxe 4-dr
Sedan, De Luxe and Custom 2-dr hardtops 3,010 lb, 1,365
kg - De Luxe 4-dr Hardtop 3,054 lb, 1,385 kg - Super De
Luxe 4-dr Sedan and De Luxe Custom 4-dr Hardtop 3,076
lb, 1,395 kg - Super Saloon 4-dr Sedan 3,087 lb, 1,400 kg -
Super De Luxe 4-dr Hardtop 3,131 lb, 1,420 kg - Super
Saloon 4-dr Hardtop 3,153 lb, 1,430 kg; turning circle: 40 ft.
12.2 m; fuel tank: 13.2 imp gal, 15.8 US gal, 60 l.

BODY 5 seats, separate front seats, reclining backrests,
built-in headrests.

TOYOTA Crown 2200 Diesel

TOYOTA Crown 2600 Royal Saloon 4-dr Sedan

OPTIONALS 5-speed fully synchronized mechanical gearbox
(I 3.287, II 2.043, III 1.394, IV 1, V 0.853, rev 4.039), 4.778
axle ratio (except for Super De Luxe 4-dr Hardtop); automatic transmission with 3 ratios (I 2.400, II 1.479, III 1,
rev 1.920), 4.556 axle ratio; power steering with 3.90 turns
lock to lock; air-conditioning.

125 hp power team

See 110 hp power team, except for:

ENGINE max power (JIS): 125 hp at 6,000 rpm; max torque
(JIS): 123 lb ft, 17 kg m at 4,400 rpm; 62.9 hp/l; Bosch-
Denso electronic fuel injection system; emission control
with 3-way catalytic converter with oxygen sensor and
exhaust gas recirculation; fuel feed: electric pump.

TRANSMISSION gears: (for De Luxe 4-dr Sedan and 4-dr
Hardtop, Super De Luxe hardtops and Super Saloon 2-dr
Hardtop only) 5, fully synchronized; ratios: I 3.287, II 2.043,
III 1.394, IV 1, V 0.853, rev 4.039; axle ratio: 4.778; tyres:
sedans 6.95 x 14 - hardtops D78 x 14 - De Luxe Custom
models 185 SR x 14.

PERFORMANCE max speed: 106 mph, 170 km/h; power-
weight ratio: De Luxe-A 4-dr Sedan 23.9 lb/hp, 10.8 kg/hp;
consumption: 21.2 m/imp gal, 17.6 m/US gal, 13.3 l x 100 km.

STEERING servo; turns lock to lock: 3.90.

DIMENSIONS AND WEIGHT weight: De Luxe A 4-dr Sedan
2,988 lb, 1,355 kg - De Luxe 4-dr Sedan 3,021 lb, 1.370 kg

- De Luxe 4-dr Hardtop 3,054 lb, 1,385 kg - De Luxe
Custom 2-dr Hardtop 3,065 lb, 1,390 kg - De Luxe Custom
4-dr Hardtop 3,098 lb, 1,405 kg - Super De Luxe 4-dr Sedan
3,087 lb, 1,400 kg - Super De Luxe 2-dr Hardtop and Super
Saloon 4-dr Sedan 3,109 lb, 1,410 kg - Super De Luxe 4-dr
Hardtop 3.153 lb, 1,430 kg - Super Saloon 2-dr Hardtop 3,142
lb, 1,425 kg - Super Saloon 4-dr Hardtop 3,186 lb, 1,445 kg.

OPTIONALS automatic transmission with 3 ratios (I 2.400,
II 1.479, III 1, rev 1.920), 4.556 axle ratio.

72 hp power team

See 110 hp power team, except for:

ENGINE front, Diesel, 4 stroke; 4 cylinders, vertical, in
line; 133.5 cu in, 2,188 cc (3.54 x 3.39 in, 90 x 86 mm);
compression ratio: 21.5:1; max power (JIS): 72 hp at 4,200
rpm; max torque (JIS): 105 lb ft, 14.5 kg m at 2,000 rpm;
max engine rpm: 4,500; 32.9 hp/l; Ricardo Comet precombustion chamber type; camshafts: 1, overhead, cogged belt; Bosch-Denso VE distributor type fuel injection
pump; lubrication: 11.4 imp pt, 13.7 US pt, 6.5 l; cooling
system: 14.1 imp pt, 16.9 US pt, 8 l.

TRANSMISSION gears: 5; ratios: I 3.287, II 2.043, III 1.394,
IV 1, V 0.853, rev 4.039; axle ratio: 4.300 (for Standard
4-dr Sedan only gears: 4; ratios: I 3.579, II 2.081, III 1.397,
IV 1, rev 4.399; axle ratio: 3.909); width of rims: 4.5'';
tyres: 6.95 x 14 - Standard 4-dr Sedan 6.40 x 14.

PERFORMANCE max speed: 81 mph, 130 km/h; power-weight
ratio: Standard 4-dr Sedan 41.3 lb/hp, 18.7 kg/hp; consumption: 55.4 m/imp gal, 46.1 m/US gal, 5.1 l x 100 km at 37
mph, 60 km/h.

BRAKES (for Standard 4-dr Sedan only) drum.

DIMENSIONS AND WEIGHT length: 184.65 in, 469 cm -
Standard 4-dr Sedan 184.25 in, 468 cm; weight: Standard
4-dr Sedan 2,977 lb, 1,350 kg - De Luxe A 4-dr Sedan
3,010 lb, 1,365 kg - De Luxe 4-dr Sedan 3,043 lb, 1,380
kg - Super De Luxe 4-dr Sedan 3,098 lb, 1,405 kg.

140 hp power team

See 110 hp power team, except for:

ENGINE 156.4 cu in, 2,563 cc (3.15 x 3.35 in, 80 x 85 mm);
compression ratio: 8.5:1; max power (JIS): 140 hp at 5,400
rpm; max torque (JIS): 156 lb ft, 21.5 kg m at 3,600 rpm;
54.6 hp/l; Bosch-Denso electronic fuel injection system.

TRANSMISSION gearbox: mechanical; gears: 4, fully synchronized (5 for Super Saloon 2-dr Hardtop and Royal
Saloon 4-dr Hardtop); ratios: I 3.368, II 1.644, III 1, IV
0.813, rev 4.079 - Super Saloon 2-dr Hardtop and Royal
Saloon 4-dr Hardtop I 3.287, II 2.043, III 1.394, IV 1, V
0.853, rev 4.039; (for Royal Saloon and Super Saloon sedans
only automatic transmission, hydraulic torque converter and
planetary gears; ratios: I 2.450, II 1.450, III 1, rev 2.222);
axle ratio: 4.100; width of rims: 5.5''; tyres: sedans D78 x
14 - hardtops 185 SR x 14.

TOYOTA Crown 2600 Royal Saloon 2-dr Hardtop

TOYOTA Century D Sedan

140 HP POWER TEAM

PERFORMANCE max speed: hardtops 109 mph, 175 km/h - sedans 99 mph, 160 km/h; power-weight ratio: Super Saloon 4-dr Sedan 22.4 lb/hp, 10.1 kg/hp

STEERING servo; turns lock to lock: 3.90.

BRAKES (for sedans only) disc, front internal radial fins, servo; lining area: front 28.2 sq in, 182 sq cm, rear 18.1 sq in, 117.2 sq cm, total 46.3 sq in, 299.2 sq cm.

DIMENSIONS AND WEIGHT tracks: 56.30 in, 143 cm front. 55.12 in, 140 cm rear; length: sedans 187.40 in, 476 cm - hardtops 188.61 in, 474 cm; ground clearance: 7.09 in, 18 cm; weight: Super Saloon 4-dr Sedan 3,131 lb, 1,420 kg - Super Saloon 2-dr Hardtop and Royal Saloon 4-dr Sedan 3,274 lb. 1,485 kg - Super Saloon 4-dr Hardtop 3,208 lb, 1,455 kg - Royal aloon 4-dr Hardtop 3,318 lb, 1,505 kg.

OPTIONALS 5-speed mechanical gearbox (I 3.287, II 2.043, III 1.394, IV 1, V 0.853, rev 4.039) (except for Super Saloon 2-dr Hardtop and Royal Saloon 4-dr Hardtop); 3-speed automatic transmission, hydraulic torque converter and planetary gears with 3 ratios (I 2.450, II 1.450, III 1, rev 2.222) (except for Royal Saloon and Super Saloon sedans); electronic skid control brakes.

Century Series

PRICES EX WORKS:

Century D Sedan	4,276,000 yen
Century C Sedan	3,876,000 yen

180 hp power team

ENGINE front, 4 stroke; V8 cylinders; 206 cu in, 3,376 cc (3.27 x 3.07 in, 83 x 78 mm); compression ratio: 8.5:1; max power (JIS): 180 hp at 5,200 rpm; max torque (JIS): 199 lb ft, 27.5 kg m at 4,400 rpm; max engine rpm: 6,000; 53.3 hp/l; light alloy block and head; 5 crankshaft bearings; valves: overhead, push-rods and rockers; camshafts: 1, at centre of Vee; lubrication: gear pump, full flow filter, 8.8 imp pt, 10.6 US pt, 5 l; Bosch-Denso L jetronic electronic fuel injection system; emission control with 3-way catalytic converter and oxygen sensor secondary air injection and exhaust gas recirculation; fuel feed: electric pump water-cooled, 23.6 imp pt, 28.3 US pt, 13.4 l.

TRANSMISSION driving wheels: rear; gearbox: Toyoglide automatic transmission, hydraulic torque converter and planetary gears with 3 ratios, max ratio of converter at stall 2; ratios: I 2.400, II 1.479, III 1, rev 1.920; lever: steering column; final drive: hypoid bevel; axle ratio: 3.727; tyres: F78 x 14.

PERFORMANCE max speed: 112 mph, 180 km/h; power-weigth ratio: Century D 22.6 lb/hp, 10.2 kg/hp - Century C 22.1 lb/hp, 10 kg/hp; carrying capacity: 1,058 lb, 480 kg; consumption: 15.5 m/imp gal, 12.9 m/US gal, 18.2 l x 100 km.

CHASSIS integral; front suspension: independent, by Mc-Pherson, air bellows/telescopic damper struts, lower wishbones (trailing links), anti-roll bar; rear: rigid axle, lower radius arms, upper torque arm, transverse linkage bar, coil springs, telescopic dampers.

TOYOTA Landcruiser BJ40-KC

STEERING recirculating ball, servo; turns lock to lock: 3.9◊

BRAKES front disc, rear drum, servo; swept area: fro◊ 92.7 sq in, 598 sq cm, rear 75 sq in, 484 sq cm, tot◊ 167.7 sq in, 1,082 sq cm.

ELECTRICAL EQUIPMENT 12 V; 45 Ah battery; 780 W alterna◊ tor; Nihon Denso distributor; 2 iodine headlamps.

DIMENSIONS AND WEIGHT wheel base: 112.60 in, 28◊ cm; tracks: 60.24 in, 153 cm front, 60.63 in, 154 c◊ rear; length: 196.06 in, 498 cm; width: 74.41 in, 189 cm◊ height: 57.48 in, 146 cm; ground clearance: 6.89 in, 1◊ cm; weight: Century D 4,068 lb, 1,845 kg - Century C 3,98◊ lb, 1,805 kg; weight distribution: 53.9% front; 46.1% rea◊ turning circle: 37.4 ft, 11.4 m; fuel tank: 19.8 imp gal, 23◊ US gal, 90 l.

BODY saloon/sedan; 4 doors; 6 seats, bench front seats◊

OPTIONALS limited slip differential; separate front seats◊ semi-separate front seats.

Landcruiser FJ56V-K

PRICE IN USA: $ 8,998*

ENGINE front, 4 stroke; 6 cylinders, vertical, in line◊ 258.1 cu in, 4,230 cc (3.70 x 4 in, 94 x 101.6 mm); compres◊ sion ratio: 7.8:1; max power (SAE): 140 hp at 3,600 rpm◊ max torque (SAE): 217 lb ft, 30 kg m at 1,800 rpm; ma◊ engine rpm: 4,000; 33.1 hp/l; cast iron block and head; crankshaft bearings; valves: overhead, in line, push-rods an◊ rockers; camshafts: 1, side; lubrication: rotary pump, filte◊ on by-pass, oil cooler, 15 imp pt, 18 US pt, 8.5 l; 1 Aisa◊ downdraught twin barrel carburettor; fuel feed: mechanica◊ pump; water-cooled, 26.8 imp pt, 32.1 US pt, 15.2 l.

TRANSMISSION driving wheels: front (automatically engag◊ ed with transfer box low ratio) and rear; clutch: single◊ dry plate (diaphragm); gearbox: mechanical; gears: 4◊ with high and low ratios, fully synchronized; ratios: 4.925, II 2.643, III 1.519, IV 1, rev 4.925; low ratios: high◊ 1, low 1.992; lever: central; final drive: hypoid bevel◊ axle ratio: 3.700; tyres: 7.00 x 15.

PERFORMANCE max speed: 87 mph, 140 km/h; power-weigh◊ ratio: 30.4 lb/hp, 13.8 kg/hp; carrying capacity: 1,103 lb◊ 500 kg; speed in direct drive at 1,000 rpm: 21.7 mph, 3◊ km/h; consumption: not declared.

CHASSIS ladder frame; front and rear suspension: rigi◊ axle, semi-elliptic leafsprings, telescopic dampers.

STEERING recirculating ball and nut.

BRAKES drum.

ELECTRICAL EQUIPMENT 12 V; 50 Ah battery; 40 A alter◊ nator; Nihon Denso distributor; 2 headlamps.

DIMENSIONS AND WEIGHT wheel base: 106.30 in, 27◊ cm; tracks: 55.71 in, 141 cm front, 55.12 in, 140 cm rear◊ length: 184.05 in, 467 cm; width: 68.31 in, 173 cm; height◊ 73.43 in, 186 cm; ground clearance: 8.27 in, 21 cm◊ weight: 4,256 lb, 1,930 kg; turning circle: 40.7 ft, 12.4 m◊ fuel tank: 18 imp gal, 21.6 US gal, 82 l.

TOYOTA Landcruiser BJ40-KC

BODY estate car/st. wagon; 4 + 1 doors; 2 or 5 seats.

Landcruiser BJ40-KC

See Landcruiser FJ56V-K, except for:

PRICE IN USA: $ 7,768*

ENGINE Diesel, 4 stroke; 4 cylinders, vertical, in line; 181.7 cu in, 2,977 cc (3.74 x 4.13 in, 95 x 105 mm); compression ratio: 20:1; max power (SAE): 85 hp at 3,600 rpm; max torque (SAE): 145 lb ft, 20 kg m at 2,200 rpm; 28.6 hp/l; 5 crankshaft bearings; fuel injection pump.

TRANSMISSION axle ratio: 4.111.

PERFORMANCE max speed: 75 mph, 120 km/h; power-weight ratio: 42.1 lb/hp, 19.1 kg/hp; speed in direct drive at 1,000 rpm: 18.6 mph, 30 km/h.

DIMENSIONS AND WEIGHT wheel base: 89.96 in, 228 cm; length: 152.36 in, 387 cm; width: 65.55 in, 166 cm; height: 77.17 in, 196 cm; weight: 3,583 lb, 1,625 kg.

BODY open, fully opening canvas sunshine roof; 2 doors; 2 or 6 seats.

GENERAL MOTORS   MALAYSIA

Harimau/Amigo

ENGINE Vauxhall Viva, front, 4 stroke; 4 cylinders, vertical, in line; 76.6 cu in, 1,256 cc (3.19 x 2.40 in, 81 x 61 mm); compression ratio: 7.3:1; max power (SAE): 59 hp at 5,400 rpm; max torque (SAE): 64 lb ft, 8.8 kg m at 3,200 rpm; max engine rpm: 5,800; 47 hp/l; cast iron block and head; 3 crankshaft bearings; valves: overhead, in line, push-rods and rockers; camshafts: 1, side; lubrication: gear pump, full flow filter, 5.5 imp pt, 6.6 US pt, 3.1 l; 1 Zenith 150 CDS downdraught carburettor; fuel feed: mechanical pump; water-cooled, 10.2 imp pt, 12.3 US pt, 5.8 l.

TRANSMISSION driving wheels: rear; clutch: single dry plate (diaphragm); gearbox: mechanical; gears: 4, fully synchronized; ratios: I 3.460, II 2.213, III 1.404, IV 1, rev 3.707; lever: central; final drive: hypoid bevel; axle ratio: 4.125; width of rims: 4.5''; tyres: 6.15 x 13.

PERFORMANCE max speed: 75 mph, 120 km/h; power-weight ratio: 23.1 lb/hp, 10.5 kg/hp; carrying capacity: 1,521 lb, 690 kg; speed in direct drive at 1,000 rpm: 12.9 mph, 20.7 km/h; consumption: 33 m/imp gal, 27.7 m/US gal, 8.5 l x 100 km.

CHASSIS perimeter box-type with cross members; front suspension: independent, wishbones, transverse anti-roll bar leafsprings, telescopic dampers; rear: rigid axle, semi-elliptic leafspring, telescopic dampers.

STEERING rack-and-pinion.

BRAKES drum, dual circuit.

ELECTRICAL EQUIPMENT 12 V; 32 Ah battery; 336 W alternator; AC Delco distributor; 2 headlamps.

DIMENSIONS AND WEIGHT wheel base: 91.50 in, 232 cm; front and rear track: 51.18 in, 130 cm; length: 141.42 in, 359 cm; width: 63.39 in, 161 cm; height: 67.72 in, 172 cm; ground clearance: 6.69 in, 17 cm; weight: 1,367 lb, 620 kg; turning circle: 29.8 ft, 9.1 m; fuel tank: 9.9 imp gal, 11.9 US gal, 45 l.

BODY open; 2 doors; 2-10 seats.

Gemini 1.6 Sedan/Coupé

ENGINE Isuzu, front, 4 stroke; 4 cylinders; 97 cu in, 1,584 cc (3.20 x 3 in, 82 x 75 mm); compression ratio: 8.7:1; max torque (DIN): 101 lb ft, 14 kg m at 4,000 rpm; camshafts: 1, overhead, in line; lubrication: full flow filter, 8.8 imp pt, 10.6 US pt, 5 l; 1 Nikki-Stromberg downdraught twin barrel carburettor; fuel feed: mechanical pump; water-cooled, 11.4 imp pt, 13.7 US pt, 6.5 l.

TRANSMISSION driving wheels: rear; clutch: single dry plate (diaphragm); gearbox: mechanical; gears: 4, fully synchronized; ratios: I 3.057, II 2.175, III 1.418, IV 1, rev 3.826; axle ratio: 3.889; width of rims: 5''; tyres: 155 SR x 13.

PERFORMANCE max speed: 106 mph, 170 km/h.

CHASSIS front suspension: independent, wishbones, coil spring, anti-roll bar, telescopic dampers; rear: torque tube, coil springs, telescopic dampers.

STEERING rack-and-pinion.

GENERAL MOTORS Amigo

BRAKES front disc, rear drum, dual circuit, servo.

ELECTRICAL EQUIPMENT 12 V; 35 Ah battery; 2 headlamps.

DIMENSIONS AND WEIGHT wheel base: 95 in, 240 cm; tracks: 51.20 in, 130 cm front, 51.40 in, 130 cm rear; length: 163 in, 413 cm; width: 62 in, 157 cm; height: Sedan 54 in, 136 cm - Coupé 53 in, 133 cm; ground clearance: 5.7 in, 14 cm; weight: Sedan 1,962 lb, 890 kg - Coupé 1,918 lb, 870 kg; turning circle: 30.2 ft, 9.2 m; fuel tank: 11.4 imp gal, 14 US gal, 52 l.

BODY Sedan 4 doors - Coupé 2 doors; separate front seats.

OPTIONALS tinted glass.

TORO   PHILIPPINES

1300

ENGINE Volkswagen, rear, 4 stroke; 4 cylinders, horizontally opposed; 74.8 cu in, 1,285 cc (3.03 x 2.72 in, 77 x 69 mm); compression ratio: 7.5:1; max power (DIN): 44 hp at 4,100 rpm; max torque (DIN): 64 lb ft, 8.8 kg m at 3,000 rpm; max engine rpm: 4,600; 34.2 hp/l; block with cast iron liners and light alloy fins, light alloy head; 4 crank-

GENERAL MOTORS Gemini 1.6 4-dr Sedan

TORO 1300

1300

shaft bearings; valves: overhead, push-rods and rockers; camshafts: 1, central, lower; lubrication: gear pump, filter in sump, oil cooler, 4.4 imp pt, 5.3 US pt, 2.5 l; 1 Solex 31 PICT- downdraught single barrel carburettor; fuel feed: mechanical pump; air-cooled.

TRANSMISSION driving wheels: rear; clutch: single dry plate; gearbox: mechanical; gears: 4, fully synchronized; ratios: I 3.780, II 2.060, III 1.260, IV 0.890, rev 4.010; lever: central; final drive: spiral bevel; axle ratio: 4.375; width of rims: 4''; tyres: 5.60 x 15.

PERFORMANCE max speeds: (I) 25 mph, 41 km/h; (II) 47 mph, 75 km/h; (III) 76 mph, 123 km/h; (IV) 96 mph, 155 km/h; power-weight ratio: 44.6 lb/hp, 20.2 kg/hp; carrying capacity: 882 lb, 400 kg; speed in top at 1,000 rpm: 18.6 mph, 29.9 km/h; consumption: 32.1 m/imp gal, 26.7 m/US gal, 8.8 l x 100 km.

CHASSIS backbone platform; front suspension: independent, twin swinging longitudinal trailing arms, transverse laminated torsion bars, anti-roll bar, telescopic dampers; rear: independent, swinging semi-axles, swinging longitudinal trailing arms, transverse torsion bars, telescopic dampers.

STEERING worm and roller, telescopic damper.

BRAKES drum; lining area: total 125.3 sq in, 808 sq cm.

ELECTRICAL EQUIPMENT 12 V; 36 Ah battery; 260 W dynamo; Bosch distributor; 2 headlamps.

DIMENSIONS AND WEIGHT wheel base: 94.49 in, 240 cm; tracks: 51.97 in, 132 cm front, 53.15 in, 135 cm rear; length: 169.29 in, 430 cm; width: 64.37 in, 163 cm; height: 52.95 in, 134 cm; weight: 1,962 lb, 890 kg; turning circle: 37.1 ft, 11.3 m; fuel tank: 9 imp gal, 10.8 US gal, 41 l.

BODY coupé, in plastic material; 2 doors; 2+2 seats, separate front seats.

CHRYSLER   AUSTRALIA

Valiant CL Series

PRICES EX WORKS (Australian $):

1 Sedan	$ 6,850
2 Station Wagon	$ 7,209
3 Regal Sedan	$ 8,538
4 Regal Station Wagon	$ 8,848
5 Regal SE Sedan	$ 12,202

Power team:	Standard for:	Optional for:
138 hp	1,2,3	—
146 hp	—	1,2,3
143 hp	4,5	all

138 hp power team

ENGINE front, 4 stroke; 6 cylinders, vertical, in line; 245 cu in, 4,015 cc (3.76 x 3.68 in, 95.4 x 93.4 mm); compression ratio: 9:1; max power (SAE): 138 hp at 4,400 rpm; max torque (SAE): 201 lb ft, 27.7 kg m at 1,800 rpm; max engine rpm: 4,800; 34.4 hp/l; cast iron block and head, hemispherical combustion chambers; 7 crankshaft bearings; valves: overhead, in line, push-rods and rockers, hydraulic tappets; camshafts: 1, side; lubrication: gear pump, full flow filter, 8.3 imp pt, 9.9 US pt, 4.7 l; 1 downdraught single barrel carburettor; cleaner air system; fuel feed: mechanical pump; water-cooled, 23.2 imp pt, 27.9 US pt, 13.2 l.

TRANSMISSION driving wheels: rear; clutch: single dry plate (diaphragm); gearbox: mechanical; gears: 3, fully synchronized; ratios: I 2.950, II 1.690, III 1, rev 3.670; lever: central; final drive: hypoid bevel; axle ratio: 2.920; width of rims: 5.5''; tyres: 6.95 x 14 - St. Wagon 7.35 x 14.

PERFORMANCE max speed: about 109 mph, 175 km/h; power-weight ratio: Sedan 22.7 lb/hp, 10.3 kg/hp; carrying capacity: 1,058 lb, 480 kg; speed in direct drive at 1,000 rpm: 23 mph, 37 km/h; consumption: not declared.

CHASSIS integral; front suspension: independent, wishbones, longitudinal torsion bars, telescopic dampers, anti-roll bar; rear: rigid axle, semi-elliptic leafsprings, telescopic dampers.

STEERING recirculating ball.

BRAKES front disc (diameter 11 in, 27.9 cm), front internal radial fins, rear drum, servo; swept area: total 327 sq in, 2,113 sq cm.

ELECTRICAL EQUIPMENT 12 V; 45 Ah battery; 35 A alternator; Chrysler electronic ignition; 4 headlamps.

CHRYSLER Valiant CL Sedan

DIMENSIONS AND WEIGHT wheel base: 115 in, 292 cm; tracks: 58.32 in, 148 cm front, 58.72 in, 149 cm rear; length: 198.40 in, 504 cm; width: 74.20 in, 188 cm; height: 55.80 in, 142 cm; weight: Sedan 3,127 lb, 1,418 kg - St. Wagon 3,367 lb, 1,527 kg - Regal Sedan 3,158 lb, 1,432 kg; turning circle: 38.6 ft, 11.8 m; fuel tank: 17.5 imp gal, 20.9 US gal, 79 l.

BODY 4 doors; 6 seats, separate front seats, reclining backrests.

OPTIONALS Torqueflite automatic transmission, hydraulic torque converter and planetary gears with 3 ratios (I 2.390, II 1.450, III 1, rev 2.090), max ratio of converter at stall 2, possible manual selection, steering column; 4-speed fully synchronized mechanical gearbox (I 3.320, II 2.600, III 1.430, IV 1, rev 3), central lever; limited slip differential; light alloy wheels; F78S x 14 tyres; 185SR x 14 or ER70H x 14 tyres with 6.5'' wide rims; heavy-duty suspension; vinyl roof; heated rear window; Sports equipment; anti-roll bar on front suspension; power steering only with automatic transmission; electric windows; air-conditioning; tinted glass; 3.230 axle ratio.

146 hp power team

See 138 hp power team, except for:

ENGINE 265.1 cu in, 4,345 cc (3.91 x 3.68 in, 99.2 x 93.4 mm);

max power (SAE): 146 hp at 4,800 rpm; max torque (SAE): 212 lb ft, 29.2 kg m at 2,000 rpm; max engine rpm: 5,200; 33.6 hp/l; 1 downdraught twin barrel carburettor.

PERFORMANCE max speed: about 112 mph, 180 km/h; power-weight ratio: Sedan 21.4 lb/hp, 9.7 kg/hp.

OPTIONALS 3.230 axle ratio.

143 hp power team

See 138 hp power team, except for:

ENGINE V 8 cylinders; 318 cu in, 5,211 cc (3.91 x 3.31 in, 99.2 x 84 mm); compression ratio: 8.2:1; max power (SAE): 143 hp at 4,400 rpm; max torque (SAE): 253 lb ft, 35 kg m at 2,400 rpm; 27.4 hp/l; 5 crankshaft bearings; camshafts: 1 at centre of Vee; 1 downdraught twin barrel carburettor; cooling: 26 imp pt, 31.3 US pt, 14.8 l.

TRANSMISSION gearbox: Torqueflite automatic transmission, hydraulic torque converter and planetary gears with 3 ratios, max ratio of converter at stall 2, possible manual selection; ratios: I 2.450, II 1.450, III 1, rev 2.200; axle ratio: 2.920.

PERFORMANCE max speed: about 115 mph, 185 km/h; power-weight ratio: Sedan 21.8 lb/hp, 9.9 kg/hp; speed in direct drive at 1,000 rpm: 26.7 mph, 43 km/h.

CHRYSLER Valiant CL Regal SE Sedan

FORD Escort GL 4-dr Sedan

FORD Cortina TE GL Sedan

ELECTRICAL EQUIPMENT 50 Ah battery.

DIMENSIONS AND WEIGHT weight: Regal St. Wagon 3,535 lb, 1,603 kg - Regal SE Sedan 3,592 lb, 1,629 kg.

FORD   AUSTRALIA

Escort Series

PRICES EX WORKS (Australian $):

1 L 2-dr Sedan	$ 4,438
2 GL 2-dr Sedan	$ 4,859
3 GL 4-dr Sedan	$ 4,938
4 Ghia 4-dr Sedan	$ 5,793

Power team:	Standard for:	Optional for:
98 hp	1 to 3	—
112 hp	4	—

98 hp power team

ENGINE front, 4 stroke; 4 cylinders, vertical in line; 97.5 cu in, 1,598 cc (3.19 x 3.06 in, 87 x 77.6 mm); compression ratio: 9:1; max power (SAE): 98 hp at 6,000 rpm; max torque (SAE): 101 lb ft, 14 kg m at 4,000 rpm; max engine rpm:

6,500; 61.3 hp/l; cast iron block and head; 5 crankshaft bearings; valves: overhead, in line, push-rods and rockers; camshafts: 1, side, chain-driven; lubrication: rotary or vane type pump, full flow filter, 5.7 imp pt, 6.8 US pt, 3.2 l; 1 Weber 32/32 DGV downdraught twin barrel carburettor; fuel feed: mechanical pump; water-cooled, 9.5 imp pt, 11.4 US pt, 5.4 l.

TRANSMISSION driving wheels: rear; clutch: single dry plate (diaphragm); gearbox: mechanical; gears: 4, fully synchronized; ratios: I 3.337, II 1.995, III 1.418, IV 1, rev 3.876; lever: central; final drive: hypoid bevel; axle ratio: 4.125; width of rims: 4.5''; tyres: 155 SR x 13.

PERFORMANCE max speed: 101 mph, 162 km/h; power-weight ratio: L 2-dr 19.7 lb/hp, 8.9 kg/hp - GL 2-dr 20 lb/hp, 9 kg/hp - GL 4-dr 20.4 lb/hp, 9.3 kg/hp; carrying capacity: 939 lb, 426 kg; acceleration: 0-50 mph (0-80 km/h) 16.5 sec; speed in direct drive at 1,000 rpm: 16 mph, 25.8 km/h; consumption: 37.8 m/imp gal, 31.4 m/US gal, 7.5 l x 100 km.

CHASSIS integral; front suspension: independent, by McPherson, coil springs/telescopic dampers struts, anti-roll bar; rear: rigid axle, semi-elliptic leafsprings, anti-roll bar, telescopic dampers.

STEERING rack-and-pinion; turns lock to lock: 3.50.

BRAKES front disc (diameter 9.60 in, 24.4 cm), rear drum, servo.

ELECTRICAL EQUIPMENT 12 V; 38 Ah battery; 35 A alternator; Motorcraft distributor; 4 headlamps.

DIMENSIONS AND WEIGHT wheel base: 94.50 in, 240 cm; tracks: 49.50 in, 126 cm front, 50.60 in, 128 cm rear; length: 156.80 in, 398 cm; width: 62.80 in, 159 cm; height: 54.50 in, 138 cm; ground clearance: 4.92 in, 12.5 cm; weight: L 2-dr 1,936 lb, 878 kg - GL 2-dr 1,959 lb, 884 kg - GL 4-dr 2,004 lb, 909 kg; turning circle: 29.5 ft, 9 m; fuel tank: 9 imp gal, 10.8 US gal, 41 l.

BODY saloon/sedan; 5 seats, separate front seats.

OPTIONALS Ford C3 automatic transmission, hydraulic torque converter and planetary gears with 3 ratios (I 2.474, II 1.474, III 1, rev 2.111), max ratio of converter at stall 2.3, possible manual selection.

112 hp power team

See 98 hp power team, except for:

ENGINE 121.9 cu in, 1,998 cc (3.56 x 3.02 in, 90.4 x 76.7 mm); compression ratio: 9.2:1; max power (SAE): 112 hp at 6,000 rpm; max torque (SAE): 122 lb ft, 16.8 kg m at 3,500 rpm; 56 hp/l; valves: overhead, Vee-slanted, rockers; camshafts: 1, overhead, cogged belt; lubrication: 6.2 imp pt, 7.4 US pt, 3.5 l; 1 Autolite downdraught twin barrel carburettor; cooling: 12.5 imp pt, 15 US pt, 7.1 l.

TRANSMISSION axle ratio: 3.540; width of rims: 5''; tyres: YR 78S x 13.

PERFORMANCE max speed: about 110 mph, 177 km/h; power-weight ratio: 18.7 lb/hp, 8.5 kg/hp; speed in direct drive at 1,000 rpm: 18.5 mph, 29.7 km/h; consumption: 36.7 m/imp gal, 30.5 m/US gal, 7.7 l x 100 km.

DIMENSIONS AND WEIGHT weight: 2,095 lb, 950 kg.

Cortina TE Series

PRICES EX WORKS (Australian $):

1 L Sedan	$ 5,467
2 L Station Wagon	$ 6,033
3 GL Sedan	$ 5,907
4 GL Station Wagon	$ 6,531
5 Ghia Sedan	$ 6,496

Power team:	Standard for:	Optional for:
112 hp	all	—
130 hp	—	1 to 4
155 hp	—	all

112 hp power team

ENGINE front, 4 stroke; 4 cylinders, vertical, in line; 121.9 cu in, 1,998 cc (3.56 x 3.02 in, 90.4 x 76.7 mm); compression ratio: 9.2:1; max power (SAE): 112 hp at 6,000 rpm; max torque (SAE): 122 lb ft, 16.8 kg m at 3,500 rpm; max engine rpm: 6,500; 56 hp/l; cast iron block and head; 5 crankshaft bearings; valves: overhead, Vee-slanted, rockers; camshafts: 1, overhead, cogged belt; lubrication: rotary pump, full flow filter, 6.2 imp pt, 7.4 US pt, 3.5 l; 1 Autolite downdraught twin barrel carburettor; fuel feed: mechanical pump; water-cooled, 12.5 imp pt, 15 US pt, 7.1 l.

FORD Cortina TE GL Sedan

FORD Falcon 500 4-dr Sedan

112 HP POWER TEAM

TRANSMISSION driving wheels: rear; clutch: single dry plate (diaphragm); gearbox: mechanical; gears: 4, fully synchronized; ratios: I 3.650, II 1.970, III 1.370, IV 1, rev 3.660; lever: central; final drive: hypoid bevel; axle ratio: 3.700; width of rims: 4.5'' - Cortina TE Ghia 5.5''; tyres: 165 SR x 13 - Cortina TE Ghia 175 SR x 13 (standard).

PERFORMANCE max speed: about 103 mph, 165 km/h; power-weight ratio: sedans 22.4 lb/hp, 10.2 kg/hp; carrying capacity: 882 lb, 400 kg; speed in direct drive at 1,000 rpm: 18.3 mph, 29.5 km/h; consumption: 29.7 m/imp gal, 24.8 m/US gal, 9.5 l x 100 km.

CHASSIS integral, front auxiliary frame; front suspension: independent, wishbones, coil springs, anti-roll bar, telescopic dampers; rear: rigid axle, lower longitudinal trailing radius arms, upper oblique torque arms, coil springs, anti-roll bar, telescopic dampers.

STEERING rack-and-pinion; turns lock to lock: 3.70.

BRAKES front disc (diameter 9.80 in, 24.9 cm), rear drum, servo.

ELECTRICAL EQUIPMENT 12 V; 55 Ah battery; 22 A alternator; Autolite distributor; 4 headlamps.

DIMENSIONS AND WEIGHT wheel base: 101.50 in, 258 cm; front and rear track: 56 in, 142 cm; length: sedans 167.70 in, 426 cm - st. wagons 171.70 in, 436 cm; width: 67.20 in, 171 cm; height: sedans 51.80 in, 131 cm - st. wagons 52.60 in, 134 cm; ground clearance: sedans 5.80 in, 14.7 cm - st. wagons 5.90 in, 14.8 cm; weight: sedans 2,510 lb, 1,138 kg - st. wagons 2,640 lb, 1,197 kg; turning circle: 31.8 ft, 9.7 m; fuel tank: 12 imp gal, 14.3 US gal, 54 l.

BODY 4 doors; 5 seats, separate front seats, reclining backrests; heated rear window (standard for Cortina TE Ghia only).

OPTIONALS automatic transmission with 3 ratios (I 2.393, II 1.450, III 1, rev 2.094), 3.500 axle ratio; 175 SR x 13 tyres with 5.5'' wide rims; BR 704 x 13 tyres; Rally equipment; sports steering wheel; sports road wheel; vinyl roof, heated rear window and sunshine roof (except for st. wagons).

130 hp power team

See 112 hp power team, except for:

ENGINE 6 cylinders, vertical, in line; 200 cu in, 3,277 cc (3.68 x 3.13 in, 93.4 x 79.4 mm); compression ratio: 9.1:1; max power (SAE): 130 hp at 4,600 rpm; max torque (SAE): 190 lb ft, 26.2 kg m at 2,000 rpm; max engine rpm: 4,800; 39.7 hp/l; 7 crankshaft bearings; valves: overhead, in line, push-rods and rockers and rockers, hydraulic tappets; camshafts: 1, side; lubrication: 7 imp pt, 8.5 US pt, 4 l; 1 Autolite downdraught single barrel carburettor; cooling: 15.5 imp pt, 18.6 US pt, 8.8 l.

TRANSMISSION gears: 3, fully synchronized; ratios: I 2.950, II 1.690, III 1, rev 3.670; axle ratio: 2.920.

PERFORMANCE max speed: about 106 mph, 170 km/h;

power-weight ratio: sedans 19.3 lb/hp, 8.7 kg/hp; speed in direct drive at 1,000 rpm: 22 mph, 35.4 km/h; consumption: 23.5 m/imp gal, 19.6 m/US gal, 12 l x 100 km.

ELECTRICAL EQUIPMENT 38 A alternator.

OPTIONALS 4-speed fully synchronized mechanical gearbox (I 2.820, II 1.840, III 1.320, IV 1, rev 2.560), 2.920 axle ratio; automatic transmission with 3 ratios (I 2.393, II 1.450, III 1, rev 2.094), 2.920 axle ratio.

155 hp power team

See 130 hp power team, except for:

ENGINE 250 cu in, 4,097 cc (3.68 x 3.91 in, 93.4 x 99.2 mm); compression ratio: 9.3:1; max power (SAE): 155 hp at 4,000 rpm; max torque (SAE): 240 lb ft, 33.1 kg m at 1,600 rpm; max engine rpm: 4,600; 37.8 hp/l.

TRANSMISSION axle ratio: 2.770.

PERFORMANCE max speed: about 109 mph, 175 km/h; power-weight ratio: sedans 16.1 lb/hp, 7.3 kg/hp; speed in direct drive at 1,000 rpm: 23.6 mph, 38 km/h; consumption: 22.6 m/imp gal, 18.8 m/US gal, 12.5 l x 100 km.

OPTIONALS 4-speed fully synchronized mechanical gearbox with 2.770 axle ratio; automatic transmission with 2.770 axle ratio.

Falcon - Falcon 500 - Fairmont Series

PRICES EX WORKS (Australian $):

1 Falcon 4-dr Sedan	$ 5,837
2 Falcon Station Wagon	$ 6,176
3 Falcon 500 4-dr Sedan	$ 6,403
4 Falcon 500 2-dr Hardtop	$ 7,198
5 Fairmont 4-dr Sedan	$ 7,956
6 Fairmont 2-dr Coupé	$ 8,092
7 Fairmont Station Wagon	$ 8,447
8 Fairmont GXL Sedan	$ 9,183

Power team:	Standard for:	Optional for:
130 hp	1 to 3	—
155 hp	4,5	3
240 hp	6 to 8	3 to 5
260 hp	—	3,4

130 hp power team

ENGINE front, 4 stroke; 6 cylinders, in line; 200 cu in, 3,277 cc (3.68 x 3.13 in, 93.4 x 79.4 mm); compression ratio: 8.8:1; max power (SAE): 130 hp at 4,600 rpm; max torque (SAE): 190 lb ft, 26.2 kg m at 2,000 rpm; max engine rpm: 4,800; 39.7 hp/l; cast iron block and head; 7 crankshaft bearings; valves: overhead, push-rods and rockers, hydraulic tappets; camshafts: 1, side; lubrication: gear pump, full flow filter, 7 imp pt, 8.5 US pt, 4 l; 1 Autolite downdraught single barrel carburettor; fuel feed: mechanical pump; water-cooled, 15.5 imp pt, 18.6 US pt, 8.8 l.

TRANSMISSION driving wheels: rear; clutch: single dry plate (diaphragm), hydraulically controlled; gearbox: mechanical; gears: 3, fully synchronized; ratios: I 2.950, II 1.690, III 1, rev 3.670; lever: steering column; final drive: hypoid bevel; axle ratio: 3.230; width of rims: 5''; tyres: 6.95 L x 14 - Station Wagon 7.35 x 14.

PERFORMANCE max speed: about 96 mph, 154 km/h; speed in direct drive at 1,000 rpm: 20.5 mph, 33 km/h; consumption: 19.9 m/imp gal, 16.6 m/US gal, 14.2 l x 100 km.

CHASSIS integral; front suspension: independent, wishbones, lower trailing links, coil springs, anti-roll bar, telescopic dampers; rear: rigid axle, semi-elliptic leafsprings, telescopic dampers.

STEERING recirculating ball.

BRAKES front disc (diameter 11.25 in, 28.6 cm), rear drum; swept area: total 297.2 sq in, 1,917 sq cm.

ELECTRICAL EQUIPMENT 12 V; 45 Ah battery; 38 A alternator; Autolite distributor; 2 headlamps.

DIMENSIONS AND WEIGHT wheel base: 110 in, 279 cm - Station Wagon 116 in, 295 cm; tracks: 60.50 in, 154 cm front, 60 in, 152 cm rear; length: 189.30 in, 481 cm - Station Wagon 198.90 in, 505 cm; width: 74.80 in, 190 cm; height: 53.90 in, 137 cm - Station Wagon 55.40 in, 141 cm; ground clearance: 5.40 in, 13.7 cm - Station Wagon 6.40 in, 16.2 cm; turning circle: 39.4 ft, 12 m - Station Wagon 41.2 ft,

FORD Fairlane 500 Sedan

FORD LTD 4-dr Sedan

12.6 m; fuel tank: 14.5 imp gal, 17.4 US gal, 66 l - Station Wagon 16 imp gal, 19.3 US gal, 73 l.

OPTIONALS Select-Shift Cruise-o-Matic automatic transmission with 3 ratios (I 2.390, II 1.450, III 1, rev 2.090), max ratio of converter at stall 2, possible manual selection; 7.35 L x 14, 7.35 S x 14, 185 SR x 14 or ER 70H x 14 tyres with 6'' wide rims; power steering; servo brake: disc brakes; heated rear window; tinted glass; vinyl roof; GS Rally equipment; reclining backrests: sunshine roof (not available for Station Wagon).

155 hp power team

See 130 hp power team, except for:

ENGINE 250 cu in, 4,097 cc (3.68 x 3.91 in, 93.4 x 99.2 mm); compression ratio: 9.1:1; max power (SAE): 155 hp at 4,000 rpm; max torque (SAE): 240 lb ft, 33.1 kg m at 1,600 rpm; max engine rpm: 4,600; 37.8 hp/l.

PERFORMANCE max speed: about 99 mph, 159 km/h; speed in direct drive at 1,000 rpm: 22 mph, 35.4 km/h; consumption: 19.5 m/imp gal, 16.2 m/US gal, 14.5 l x 100 km.

BRAKES front disc, internal radial fins, servo.

OPTIONALS Select-Shift Cruise-o-Matic automatic transmission, steering column or central lever, 2.920 axle ratio; 4-speed fully synchronized mechanical gearbox (I 2.820, II 1.840, III 1.320, IV 1, rev 2.560), central lever, 3.230 axle ratio; air-conditioning; electric windows.

240 hp power team

See 130 hp power team, except for:

ENGINE V8 cylinders; 302 cu in, 4,950 cc (4 x 3 in, 101.6 x 76.1 mm); compression ratio: 9.4:1; max power (SAE): 240 hp at 5,000 rpm; max torque (SAE): 305 lb ft, 42.1 kg m at 2,600 rpm; max engine rpm: 5,200; 48.5 hp/l; 5 crankshaft bearings; camshafts: 1, at centre of Vee; 1 Autolite downdraught twin barrel carburettor; cooling: 22.5 imp pt, 27.1 US pt, 12.8 l.

TRANSMISSION gearbox ratios: I 2.710, II 1.690, III 1, rev 3.370; axle ratio: 2.920; width of rims: 6''; tyres: 7.35 S x 14.

PERFORMANCE max speed: about 112 mph, 180 km/h; speed in direct drive at 1,000 rpm: 25 mph, 40 km/h; consumption: 17.2 m/imp gal, 14.3 m/US gal, 16.4 l x 100 km.

BRAKES front disc, internal radial fins, servo.

DIMENSIONS AND WEIGHT (for Fairmont Coupé only) wheel base: 111 in, 282 cm; rear track: 60.50 in, 154 cm; width: 77.50 in, 197 cm; height: 51.90 in, 132 cm; fuel tank: 17.5 imp gal, 20.9 US gal, 79 l.

OPTIONALS Select-Shift Cruise-o-Matic automatic transmission with 3 ratios (I 2.460, II 1.460, III 1, rev 2.200), max ratio of converter at stall 2, steering column or central lever, 2.920 axle ratio; 4-speed fully synchronized mechanical gearbox (I 2.820, II 1.840, III 1.320, IV 1, rev 2.560), central or steering column lever; 85 x 14 or ER 70 HR x 14 conditioning; electric windows.

260 hp power team

See 130 hp power team, except for:

ENGINE V8 cylinders; 351 cu in, 5,752 cc (4 x 3.50 in, 101.6 x 88.8 mm); compression ratio: 9.1:1; max power (SAE): 260 hp at 4,600 rpm; max torque (SAE): 355 lb ft, 49 kg m at 2,600 rpm; max engine rpm: 4,900; 45.2 hp/l; 5 crankshaft bearings: camshafts: 1, at centre of Vee; 1 Autolite downdraught twin barrel carburettor; cooling: 24.6 imp pt, 29.6 US pt, 14 l.

TRANSMISSION clutch: 2 dry plates (diaphragm), hydraulically controlled; gears: 4, fully synchronized; ratios: I 2.820, II 1.840, III 1.320, IV 1, rev 2.560; lever: central; axle ratio: 3; width of rims: 6''; tyres: 7.35 H x 14.

PERFORMANCE max speed: about 118 mph, 190 km/h; speed in direct drive at 1,000 rpm: 25 mph, 40 km/h; consumption: 16.6 m/imp gal, 13.8 m/US gal, 17 l x 100 km.

BRAKES front disc, internal radial fins, servo.

OPTIONALS Select-Shift Cruise-o-Matic automatic transmission with 3 ratios (I 2.460, II 1.460, III 1, rev 2.200), max ratio of converter at stall 2, steering column or central lever, 2.750 axle ratio; limited slip differential; dual exhaust system; air-conditioning: electric windows.

Fairlane Series

PRICES EX WORKS (Australian $):

1 500 Sedan	$ 11,340
2 Marquis Sedan	$ 13,150

Power team:	Standard for:	Optional for:
240 hp	1	—
260 hp	2	1

240 hp power team

ENGINE front, 4 stroke; V8 cylinders; 302 cu in, 4,950 cc (4 x 3 in, 101.6 x 76.1 mm); compression ratio: 9.4:1; max power (SAE): 240 hp at 5,000 rpm; max torque (SAE): 305 lb ft, 42.1 kg m at 2,600 rpm: max engine rpm: 5,200; 48.5 hp/l; cast iron block and head; 5 crankshaft bearings; valves: overhead, push-rods and rockers, hydraulic tappets; camshafts: 1, at centre of Vee; lubrication: gear pump, full flow filter, 7.6 imp pt, 9.1 US pt, 4.3 l; 1 Stromberg downdraught twin barrel carburettor; fuel feed: mechanical pump; water-cooled, 22.5 imp pt, 27.1 US pt, 12.8 l.

TRANSMISSION driving wheels: rear; clutch: single dry plate (diaphragm), hydraulically controlled; gearbox: mechanical; gears: 3, fully synchronized; ratios: I 2.710, II 1.690, II 1, rev 3.370; lever: steering column; final drive: hypoid bevel; axle ratio: 2.920; width of rims: 5''; tyres: 7.35 I x 14.

PERFORMANCE max speed: about 102 mph, 164 km/h; power-weight ratio: 14.3 lb/hp, 6.5 kg/hp; speed in direct drive at 1,000 rpm: 22 mph, 35.4 km/h; consumption: 16.8 m/imp gal, 14 m/US gal, 16.8 l x 100 km.

CHASSIS integral; front suspension: independent, wishbones, lower trailing links, coil springs, anti-roll bar, telescopic

dampers; rear: rigid axle, semi-elliptic leafsprings, telescopic dampers.

STEERING recirculating ball, servo.

BRAKES front disc (diameter 11.25 in, 28.6 cm), internal radial fins, rear drum, servo; swept area: total 296.9 sq in, 1,915 sq cm.

ELECTRICAL EQUIPMENT 12 V; 45 Ah battery; 38 A alternator; Autolite distributor: 4 headlamps.

DIMENSIONS AND WEIGHT wheel base: 116 in, 295 cm; tracks: 60.50 in, 154 cm front, 60 in, 152 cm rear; length: 198.90 in, 505 cm; width: 74.60 in, 189 cm; height: 53.90 in, 137 cm; ground clearance: 5.40 in, 13.7 cm; weight: 3.415 lb, 1,549 kg; turning circle: 41.2 ft, 12.6 m; fuel tank: 17.5 imp gal, 20.9 US gal, 79 l.

BODY saloon/sedan; 4 doors; 5-6 seats, separate front seats.

OPTIONALS Select-Shift Cruise-o-Matic automatic transmission with 3 ratios (I 2.460, II 1.460, III 1, rev 2.200), max ratio of converter at stall 2, possible manual selection, central or steering column lever; 185 x 14 or ER 70 HR x 14 tyres with 6'' wide rims; bench front seats; sunshine roof; air-conditioning.

260 hp power team

See 240 hp power team, except for:

ENGINE 351 cu in, 5,752 cc (4 x 3.50 in, 101.6 x 88.8 mm); max power (SAE): 260 hp at 4,600 rpm; max torque (SAE): 335 lb ft, 49 kg m at 2,600 rpm; max engine rpm: 4,900; 45.2 hp/l; cooling: 24.6 imp pt, 29.6 US pt, 14 l.

TRANSMISSION (standard) gearbox: Select-Shift Cruise-o-Matic automatic transmission, hydraulic torque converter and planetary gears with 3 ratios, max ratio of converter at stall 2.40, possible manual selection; ratios: I 2.460, II 1.460, III 1, rev 2.200; lever: central; axle ratio: 2.750.

PERFORMANCE max speed: about 106 mph, 171 km/h; power-weight ratio: 13.2 lb/hp, 6 kg/hp; consumption: 16 m/imp gal, 13.3 m/US gal, 17.7 l x 100 km.

OPTIONALS limited slip differential.

LTD 4-door Sedan

PRICE EX WORKS (Australian $): $ 16,602

ENGINE front, 4 stroke; V8 cylinders; 351 cu in, 5,752 cc (4 x 3.50 in, 101.6 x 88.8 mm); compression ratio: 11:1; max power (SAE): 290 hp at 5,000 rpm: max torque (SAE): 380 lb ft, 52.4 kg m at 3,200 rpm; max engine rpm: 5,400; 50.4 hp/l; cast iron block and head; 5 crankshaft bearings; valves: overhead, in line, push-rods and rockers, hydraulic tappets; camshafts: 1, at centre of Vee: lubrication: gear pump, full flow filter, 8.3 imp pt, 9.9 US pt, 4.7 l; 1 Autolite downdraught 4-barrel carburettor; fuel feed: mechanical pump; water-cooled, 24.6 imp pt, 29.6 US pt, 14 l.

TRANSMISSION driving wheels: rear; gearbox: Select-Shift Cruise-o-Matic automatic transmission, hydraulic torque converter and planetary gears with 3 ratios, max ratio of converter at stall 2, possible manual selection; ratios: I 2.400, II 1.470, III 1, rev 2; lever: central; final drive: hypoid bevel, limited slip differential; axle ratio: 2.750; width of rims: 6''; tyres: ER 70 H x 15.

PERFORMANCE max speed: 124 mph, 200 km/h; power-weight ratio: 13.7 lb/hp, 6.2 kg/hp; carrying capacity: 1,103 lb, 500 kg; speed in direct drive at 1,000 rpm: 23.6 mph, 38 km/h; consumption: 14.9 m/imp gal, 12.4 m/US gal, 19 l x 100 km.

CHASSIS perimeter box-type with cross members; front suspension: independent, wishbones (lower trailing links), coil springs, anti-roll bar, telescopic dampers; rear: rigid axle, semi-elliptic leafsprings, telescopic dampers.

STEERING recirculating ball, variable ratio, servo.

BRAKES disc (diameter 11.25 in, 28.6 cm), internal radial fins, rear compensator, servo.

ELECTRICAL EQUIPMENT 12 V; 55 Ah battery; 42 alternator Autolite distributor; 4 headlamps.

DIMENSIONS AND WEIGHT wheel base: 121 in, 307 cm; tracks: 60.50 in, 154 cm front, 60 in, 152 cm rear; length: 203.80 in, 518 cm; width: 74.80 in, 190 cm; height: 54.30 in, 138 cm; ground clearance: 6.50 in, 16.5 cm; weight: 3,950 lb, 1,971 kg; turning circle: 42.2 ft, 12.9 m; fuel tank: 17.5 imp gal, 20.9 US gal, 79 l.

BODY 6 seats, separate front seats, reclining backrests; tinted glass; vinyl roof; heated rear window; air-conditioning; electric windows.

OPTIONALS leather upholstery.

HOLDEN   AUSTRALIA

Gemini TD Series

PRICES EX WORKS (Australian $):

4-dr Sedan	$ 4,881
SL 4-dr Sedan	$ 5,121
SL Coupé	$ 5,340
SL/E 4-dr Sedan	$ 5,930
SL/E Coupé	$ 6,065
3 + 1 dr St. Wagon	$ 5,664

83 hp power team

ENGINE front, 4 stroke; 4 cylinders, in line; 97.6 cu in, 1,584 cc (3.23 x 2.95 in, 82 x 75 mm); compression ratio: 8.7:1; max power (DIN): 83 hp at 5,200 rpm; max torque (DIN): 93 lb ft, 12.9 kg m at 3,600 rpm; max engine rpm: 6,500; 52.4 hp/l; cast iron block, light alloy head; 5 crankshaft bearings, valves: overhead, rockers; camshafts: 1, overhead; lubrication: rotary pump, full flow filter, 8.8 imp pt, 10.6 US pt, 5 l; 1 Nikki-Stromberg downdraught twin barrel carburettor; fuel feed: electric pump; water-cooled, 10.8 imp pt, 12.7 US pt, 6 l.

TRANSMISSION driving wheels: rear; clutch: single dry plate (diaphragm); gearbox: mechanical; gears: 4, fully synchronized; ratios: I 3.507, II 2.157, III 1.418, IV 1, rev 3.927; lever: central; final drive: hypoid bevel; axle ratio: 3.889; width of rims: 5''; tyres: YR 78 S 13 - ZR 70 S 13 - ZR 78 S 13.

PERFORMANCE max speeds: (I) 31 mph, 50 km/h; (II) 50 mph, 81 km/h; (III) 76 mph, 123 km/h; (IV) 96 mph, 154 km/h; power-weight ratio: 25 lb/hp, 11.3 kg/hp; carrying capacity: 882 lb, 400 kg; acceleration: standing ¼ mile 19.4 sec, 0-62 mph (0-100 km/h) 14.2 sec; speed in direct drive at 1,000 rpm: 16.2 mph, 26.1 km/h; consumption: 30.1 m/imp gal, 25 m/US gal, 9.4 l x 100 km.

CHASSIS integral; front suspension: independent, wishbones, coil springs, anti-roll bar, telescopic dampers; rear: rigid axle, lower radius arms, torque tube, Panhard rod, coil springs, telescopic dampers, anti-roll bar.

STEERING rack-and-pinion; turns lock to lock: 4.2.

BRAKES front disc (diameter 9.41 in, 23.9 cm), rear drum (9.02 in, 22.9 cm); swept area: total 266.5 sq in, 1,718.8 sq cm.

ELECTRICAL EQUIPMENT 12 V; 40 Ah battery, 40 A alternator - 50 A alternator for SL-SL/E wagon models; 2 headlamps.

DIMENSIONS AND WEIGHT wheel base: 94.49 in, 240 cm; tracks: 51.18 in, 130 cm front, 51.57 in, 131 cm rear; length: 162.60 in, 413 cm; width: 61.81 in, 157 cm; height: 53.15 in, 135 cm; ground clearance: 5.71 in, 14.5 cm; weight: Sedan 2,037 lb, 924 kg - SL Sedan 2,075 lb, 941 kg - SL Coupé 2,031 lb, 921 kg - SL/E Sedan 2,117 lb, 960 kg - SL/E Coupé 2,066 lb, 937 kg - St. Wagon 2,123 lb, 963 kg; turning circle: 30.8 ft, 9.4 m; fuel tank: 11.4 imp gal, 13.7 US gal, 52 l.

BODY 5 seats, separate front seats.

OPTIONALS 5, fully synchronized gears; ratios: I 3.510, II 2.170, III 1.420, IV 1, V 0.850, rev 3.760; Trimatic automatic transmission with 3 ratios (I 2.310, III 1.460, III 1) with central lever and 3.890 axle ratio; air-conditioning.

Sunbird Series

PRICES EX WORKS (Australian $):

4-dr Sedan	$ 5,567
4-dr Hatchback	$ 5,907
SL 4-dr Sedan	$ 5,977
SL Hatchback	$ 6,319
SL/E 4-dr Sedan	$ 6,589
SL/E Hatchback	$ 6,929

81 hp power team

ENGINE front, 4 stroke; 4 cylinders, vertical, in line; 115.4 cu in, 1,892 cc (3.50 x 3 in, 88.9 x 76.2 mm); compression ratio: 8.7:1; max power (DIN): 81 hp at 4,800 rpm; max torque (DIN): 104 lb ft, 14.3 kg m at 2,600 rpm; max engine rpm: 5,200; 43 hp/l; cast iron block and head; 5 crankshaft bearings; valves: 8, overhead, push-rods and rockers, hydraulic lifters; camshafts: 1, side; lubrication: gear pump; 1 Varajet twin barrel carburettor fuel feed: mechanical pump; water-cooled, 15 imp pt, 18 US pt, 8.5 l.

TRANSMISSION driving wheels: rear; clutch: single dry plate (diaphragm); gearbox: mechanical; gears: 4, fully synchronized; ratios: I 3.050, II 2.020, III 1.410, IV 1, rev 1.850; lever: central; final drive: hypoid bevel; axle ratio: 3.900; width of rims: 6''; tyres: BR 78 S x 13.

PERFORMANCE max speed: 99 mph, 159 km/h; power-weight ratio: 31.5 lb/hp, 14.3 kg/hp; carrying capacity: 1,091 lb, 495 kg; speed in direct drive at 1,000 rpm: 15.5 mph, 25 km/h; consumption: 28.2 m/imp gal, 23.5 m/US gal, 10 l x 100 km.

CHASSIS integral; front suspension: independent, wishbones, coil springs, telescopic dampers, anti-roll bar; rear: rigid axle, trailing lower radius arms, upper oblique radius arms, coil springs, telescopic dampers, anti-roll bar.

STEERING rack-and-pinion; turns lock to lock: 3.8.

BRAKES front disc (diameter 10 in, 25.4 cm), rear drum (9.02 in, 22.8 cm); servo.

ELECTRICAL EQUIPMENT 12 V; 48 Ah battery; 250 W-40 A alternator; AC Delco or Bosch distributor; 2 headlamps.

DIMENSIONS AND WEIGHT wheel base: 101.97 in, 259 cm; tracks: 55.71 in, 141.5 cm front, 54.40 in, 138 cm rear; length: 177.76 in, 451.5 cm; width: 66.93 in, 170 cm; height: sedans 52.76 in, 134 cm - hatchbacks 52.36 in, 133 cm; ground clearance: 4.80 in, 12.2 cm; weight: sedans 2,551 lb, 1,157 kg - hatchbacks 2,556 lb, 1,159; turning circle: 36 ft, 11 m; fuel tank: 12.1 imp gal, 14.5 US gal, 55 l.

BODY saloon/sedan; 4-dr; 4 seats, separate front seats, reclining backrests.

HOLDEN Gemini TD SL/E 4-dr Sedan

HOLDEN Sunbird Series

OPTIONALS Trimatic automatic transmission with 3 ratios (I 2.310, II 1.460, III 1, rev 1.850); heated rear window.

Torana UC Series

PRICES EX WORKS (Australian $):

1 S 4-dr Sedan	$ 6,098
2 SL 4-dr Sedan	$ 6,706
3 SL Hatchback	$ 7,046

Power team	Standard for:	Optional for:
105 hp	1,2	—
110 hp	3	1,2

105 hp power team

ENGINE 6 cylinders, in line; 173.2 cu in, 2,838 cc (3.50 x 3 in, 88.9 x 76.2 mm); compression ratio: 9.4:1; max power (SAE): 105 hp at 4,000 rpm; max torque (SAE): 165 lb ft, 22.2 kg m at 2,400 rpm; max engine rpm: 5,500; 37 hp/l; cast iron block and head; 7 crankshaft bearings; valves: overhead, push-rods and rockers; camshafts: 1, side; lubrication: gear pump, full flow filter, 7.5 imp pt, 8.9 US pt, 4.2 l; 1 Stromberg BXUV-3 downdraught single barrel carburettor; fuel feed: mechanical pump; water-cooled, 15 imp pt, 18 US pt, 8.5 l.

TRANSMISSION driving wheels: rear; clutch: single dry plate (diaphragm); gearbox: mechanical; gears: 3, fully synchronized; ratios: I 3.070, II 1.680, III 1, rev 3.590; lever: steering column; final drive: hypoid bevel; axle ratio: 3.360; width of rims: 4.5''; tyres: A78L x 13.

PERFORMANCE max speed: about 103 mph, 165 km/h; power-weight ratio: S 24 lb/hp, 10.9 kg/hp - SL 24.7 lb/hp, 11.2 kg/hp; carrying capacity: S 1,080 lb, 490 kg - SL 900 lb, 408 kg; speed in direct drive at 1,000 rpm: 20.1 mph, 32.3 km/h; consumption: 23.2 m/imp gal, 19.3 m/US gal, 12.2 l x 100 km.

CHASSIS integral; front suspension: independent, wishbones, coil springs, telescopic dampers; rear: rigid axle, trailing lower radius arms, upper oblique radius arms, coil springs, telescopic dampers.

STEERING rack-and-pinion; turns lock to lock: 3.30.

BRAKES front disc, rear drum, servo; swept area: front 99 sq in, 638 sq cm, rear 99 sq in, 638 sq cm, total 198 sq in, 1,276 sq cm - SL total 275.4 sq in, 1,776 sq cm.

ELECTRICAL EQUIPMENT 12 V; 48 Ah battery; 520 W alternator; AC Delco or Bosch distributor; 2 headlamps.

DIMENSIONS AND WEIGHT wheel base: 101.80 in, 259 cm; tracks: 54.90 in, 139 cm front, 54 in, 137 cm rear; length: S 176.90 in, 449 cm - SL 177.50 in, 451 cm; width: 67.10 in, 170 cm; height: 52.40 in, 133 cm; ground clearance: 4.80 in, 12.2 cm; weight: S 2,520 lb, 1,143 kg - SL 2,951 lb, 1,175 kg; turning circle: 36 ft, 11 m; fuel tank: 12 imp gal, 14.3 US gal, 54 l.

HOLDEN Torana UC SL Hatchback

BODY saloon/sedan; 4-dr; 4 seats, separate front seats; reclining backrests.

OPTIONALS Trimatic automatic transmission with 3 ratios (I 2.310, II 1.460, III 1, rev 1.850); 4-speed fully synchronized mechanical gearbox (I 3.050, II 2.190, III 1.510, IV 1, rev 3.050); 3.080 or 2.780 axle ratio; limited slip differential; dual exhaust system; vinyl roof; air-conditioning.

110 hp power team

See 105 hp power team, except for:

ENGINE 201.2 cu in, 3,298 cc (3.62 x 3.25 in, 92.1 x 82.5 mm); max power (SAE): 110 hp at 4,000 rpm; max torque (SAE): 191 lb ft, 26.4 kg m at 1,600 rpm; 33.3 hp/l.

TRANSMISSION gears: 4, fully synchronized; gearbox ratios: I 3.050, II 2.190, III 1.510, IV 1, rev 3.050; axle ratio: 3.080; width of rims: 5.5''; tyres: 175 SR x 13.

PERFORMANCE max speed: about 109 mph, 175 km/h; power-weight ratio: SL Hatchback 24.1 lb/hp, 10.9 kg/hp; speed in direct drive at 1,000 rpm: 22.1 mph, 35.6 km/h.

CHASSIS front and rear suspension: anti-roll bar.

BRAKES swept area: front 99 sq in, 638 sq cm, rear 176.4 sq in, 1,138 sq cm, total 275.4 sq in, 1,776 sq cm.

DIMENSIONS AND WEIGHT length: 177.50 in, 451 cm; height: SL Hatchback 52.20 in, 133 cm; ground clearance: 4.90 in, 12.4 cm; weight: SL Hatchback 2,654 lb, 1,204 kg.

OPTIONALS Trimatic automatic transmission with 2.780 axle ratio.

Commodore Series

PRICES EX WORKS (Australian $):

1 S 4-dr Sedan	$	6,710
2 SL 4-dr Sedan	$	8,047
3 SL/E 4-dr Sedan	$	10,828

Power team:	Standard for:	Optional for:
110 hp	1,2	—
161 hp	—	1,2,3
216 hp	3	1,2

110 hp power team

ENGINE front, 4 stroke; 6 cylinders, vertical, in line; 201.2 cu in, 3,298 cc (3.62 x 3.25 in, 91.9 x 82.5 mm); compression ratio: 9.4:1; max power (DIN): 110 hp at 4,000 rpm; max torque (DIN): 190 lb ft, 26.2 kg m at 1,600 rpm; max engine rpm: 5,000; 33.3 hp/l; cast iron block and head; 7 crankshaft bearings; valves: 8, overhead, in line, push-rods and rockers, hydraulic tappets; camshafts: 1, overhead; lubrication: gear pump, full flow filter, 7.5 imp pt, 8.9 US pt, 4.2 l; 1, Bendix - Stromberg BXV-2 downdraught single barrel carburettor; fuel feed: mechanical pump; water-cooled, 14 imp pt, 16.7 US pt, 7.9 l.

TRANSMISSION driving wheels: rear; clutch: single dry plate (diaphragm) gearbox: mechanical; gears: 3, fully

synchronized; ratios: I 3.070, II 1.680, III 1, rev 3.590; lever: steering column; final drive: hypoid bevel; axle ratio: 3.550; width of rims: 6'' tyres: C 78 L x 14.

PERFORMANCE max speed: 102 mph, 164 km/h; power weight ratio: 24.5 lb/hp, 11.1 kg/hp - SL 25.1 lb/hp, 11.4 kg/hp; carrying capacity: 882 lb, 400 kg; speed in direct drive at 1,000 rpm: 20 mph, 32.2 km/h; consumption: 22.2 m/imp gal, 18.5 m/US gal, 12.7 l x 100 km.

CHASSIS integral; front suspension: independent, wishbones, coil springs, anti-roll bar, telescopic dampers; rigid axle, trailing lower radius arms, upper oblique radius arms, coil springs, telescopic dampers.

STEERING rack-and-pinion turns lock to lock: 4.1.

BRAKES front disc, rear drum, servo; swept area: front 17.7 sq in, 113.6 sq cm, rear 11.1 sq in, 71.6 sq cm, total 23.7 sq in, 185.2 sq cm.

ELECTRICAL EQUIPMENT 12 V; 48 Ah battery; 40 A alternator; Bosch or Lucas distributor; 2 halogen headlamps.

DIMENSIONS AND WEIGHT wheel base: 105.04 in, 267 cm; tracks: 57.09 in, 145 cm front, 55.91 in, 142 cm rear; length: 185.24 in, 470.5 cm; width: 67.72 in, 172 cm; height: 53.94 in, 137 cm; weight: 2,690 lb, 1,220 kg - SL 2,767 lb, 1,255 kg; turning circle: 33.5 ft, 10.2 m; fuel tank: 13.9 imp gal, 16.6 US gal, 63 l.

BODY saloon/sedan, 5 seats, separate front seats with buchrests.

OPTIONALS Trimatic automatic transmission with 3 ratios (I 2.310, II 1.460, III 1, rev 1.850), 3.360 axle ratio; 4-speed fully synchronized mechanical gearbox (I 3.740, II 2.190, III 1.510, IV 1, rev 3.050); limited slip differential; central lever; power steering; electric windows; tinted glass sunshine roof air-conditioning.

161 hp power team

See 110 hp power team, except for:

ENGINE 8 cylinders; 253 cu in, 4,146 cc (3.62 x 3.06 in, 91.9 x 77.6 mm); max power (SAE): 161 hp at 4,550 rpm; max torque (SAE): 240 lb ft, 33.1 kg m at 2,600 rpm; 38.8 hp/l; 5 crankshaft bearings; camshafts: 1, at centre of Vee; lubrication: 8.5 imp pt, 10.1 US pt, 4.8 l; 1 Bendix-Stromberg BXV-2 downdraught twin barrel carburettor; cooling system: 21 imp pt, 25.2 US pt, 11.9 l.

PERFORMANCE max speed: about 109 mph, 175 km/h; power-weight ratio: 18.7 lb/hp, 8.5 kg/hp.

DIMENSIONS AND WEIGHT weight: 3,010 lb, 1,365 kg.

216 hp power team

See 110 hp power team, except for:

ENGINE 8 cylinders; 307.8 cu in, 5,044 cc (4 x 306 in, 101.6 x 77.7 mm); compression ratio: 9.7:1; max power

(SAE): 216 hp at 4,800 rpm; max torque (SAE): 295 lb ft, 40.7 kg m at 3,100 rpm; max engine rpm: 5,400; 42.8 hp/l; 5 crankshaft bearings; camshafts: 1, at centre of Vee; lubrication: 8.5 imp pt, 10.1 US pt, 4.8 l; 1 Rochester 4MV downdraught 4-barrel carburettor; cooling system: 20 imp pt, 23.9 US pt, 11.3 l.

TRANSMISSION gearbox: Turbo Hydramatic automatic transmission; ratios: I 2.480, II 1.480, III 1, rev 2.080; lever: central; axle ratio: 3.360; tyres: BR 60 H x 15.

PERFORMANCE max speed: about 115 mph, 185 km/h; power-weight ratio: 14.1 lb/hp, 6.4 kg/hp.

STEERING servo.

ELECTRICAL EQUIPMENT 55 A alternator.

DIMENSIONS AND WEIGHT weight; 3,043 lb, 1,380 kg.

HZ Series

PRICES EX WORKS: (Australian $):

1 Kingswood SL 4-dr Sedan	$ 6,760
2 Kingswood SL Station Wagon	$ 7,065
3 Premier 4-dr Sedan	$ 8,815
4 Premier Station Wagon	$ 9,116
5 GTS 4-dr Sedan	$ 9,584
6 Statesman De Ville 4-dr Sedan	$ 11,586
7 Statesman Caprice 4-dr Sedan	$ 16,640

Power team:	Standard for:	Optional for:
110 hp	1 to 4	—
161 hp	5	1 to 4
216 hp	6,7	1 to 5

110 hp power team

ENGINE front, 4 stroke; 6 cylinders, vertical, in line; 201.2 cu in, 3,298 cc (3.62 x 3.25 in, 91.9 x 82.5 mm); compression ratio: 9.4:1; max power (SAE): 110 hp at 4,000 rpm; max torque (SAE): 190 lb ft, 26.2 kg m at 1,600 rpm; max engine rpm: 5,000; 33.3 hp/l; cast iron block and head; 7 crankshaft bearings; valves: overhead, in line, push-rods and rockers, hydraulic tappets; camshafts: 1, side; lubrication: gear pump, full flow filter, 7.5 imp pt, 8.9 US pt, 4.2 l; 1 Bendix-Stromberg BXV-2 downdraught single barrel carburettor; fuel feed: mechanical pump; water-cooled, 14 imp pt, 16.7 US pt, 7.9 l.

TRANSMISSION driving wheels: rear; clutch: single dry plate (diaphragm); gearbox: mechanical (Trimatic automatic transmission standard for Premier models); gears: 3, fully synchronized; ratios: I 3.070, II 1.680, III 1, rev 3.590 (Premier models I 2.310, II 1.460, III 1, rev 1.850); lever: steering column; final drive: hypoid bevel; axle ratio: 3.550 - Premier models 3.080 or 3.360; width of rims: 5''; tyres: Kingswood models C78L x 14 - Premier models E78L x 14.

PERFORMANCE max speed: about 96 mph, 154 km/h; power-weight ratio: Kingswood SL 4-dr. Sedan 26.9 lb/hp, 12.2 kg/hp - Premier 4-dr. Sedan 27.8 lb/hp, 12.6 kg/hp; carrying capacity: 882 lb, 400 kg; speed in direct drive at 1,000 rpm: 20 mph, 32.2 km/h.

HOLDEN Commodore SL/E 4-dr Sedan

HOLDEN HZ GTS 4-dr Sedan

110 HP POWER TEAM

CHASSIS integral, front auxiliary box-type frame; front suspension: independent, wishbones, coil springs, anti-roll bar, telescopic dampers; rear: rigid axle, trailing lower radius arms, upper oblique radius arms, coil springs, telescopic dampers.

STEERING recirculating ball; turns lock to lock: 3.68.

BRAKES front disc, internal radial fins (diameter 10.8 in, 27.6 cm), rear drum.

ELECTRICAL EQUIPMENT 12 V; 48 Ah battery; 35 A alternator; Bosch or Lucas distributor; 4 headlamps.

DIMENSIONS AND WEIGHT wheel base: sedans 111 in, 282 cm - station wagons 114 in, 289 cm; tracks: 59.50 in, 151 cm front, 60.20 in, 153 cm rear; length: Kingswood SL 4-dr. Sedan 190.30 in, 483 cm - Station Wagon 192.30 in, 488 cm - Premier 4-dr. Sedan 190.80 in, 485 cm - Station Wagon 192.80 in, 490 cm; width: 74.30 in, 189 cm; height: Kingswood SL 4-dr. Sedan 54.10 in, 137 cm - Station Wagon 55.30 in, 140 cm - Premier 4-dr. Sedan 54.40 in, 138 cm - Station Wagon 55.10 in, 140 cm; ground clearance: 5.60 in, 14.2 cm; weight: Kingswood SL 4-dr. Sedan 2,960 lb, 1,342 kg - Station Wagon 3,145 lb, 1,426 kg - Premier 4-dr. Sedan 3,062 lb, 1,389 kg - Station Wagon 3,242 lb, 1,470 kg; turning circle: sedans 39.7 ft, 12.1 m - station wagons 40.5 ft, 12.3 m; fuel tank: 16.5 imp gal, 19.8 US gal, 75 l.

BODY 5 seats, separate front seats.

OPTIONALS Trimatic automatic transmission with 3 ratios (I 2.310, II 1.460, III 1, rev 1.850), 3.360 axle ratio; 4-speed fully synchronized mechanical gearbox (I 3.740, II 2.190, III 1.510, IV 1, rev 3.050); limited slip differential; 3.900 or 3.360 axle ratio; central lever; power steering; front disc brakes with servo; electric windows; tinted glass; sunshine roof; vinyl roof; air-conditioning.

161 hp power team

See 110 hp power team, except for:

ENGINE 8 cylinders; 253 cu in, 4,146 cc (3.62 x 3.06 in, 91.9 x 77.6 mm); max power (SAE): 161 hp at 4,550 rpm; max torque (SAE): 240 lb ft, 33.1 kg m at 2,600 rpm; 38.8 hp/l; 5 crankshaft bearings; camshafts: 1, at centre of Vee; lubrication: 8.5 imp pt, 10.1 US pt, 4.8 l; 1 Bendix-Stromberg BXV-2 downdraught twin barrel carburettor; cooling system: 21 imp pt, 25.2 US pt, 11.9 l.

TRANSMISSION gears: 4, fully synchronized; ratios: I 3.050, II 2.190, III 1.510, IV 1, rev 3.050; width of rims: 6''; tyres: ER 70H x 14.

PERFORMANCE max speed: about 109 mph, 175 km/h; power-weight ratio: 20.2 lb/hp, 9.2 kg/hp.

STEERING turns lock to lock: 3.07.

ELECTRICAL EQUIPMENT Bosch distributor.

DIMENSIONS AND WEIGHT tracks: 59.80 in, 152 cm front, 60.50 in, 154 cm rear; length: 190.30 in, 483 cm; width: 73.90 in, 188 cm; height: 53.70 in, 136 cm; weight: 3,253 lb, 1,475 kg.

OPTIONALS Trimatic automatic transmission with 2.780 axle ratio; 4-speed fully synchronized mechanical gearbox (I 2.540, II 1.830, III 1.380, IV 1, rev 2.540), central lever, 3.360 axle ratio.

216 hp power team

See 110 hp power team, except for:

ENGINE 8 cylinders; 307.8 cu in, 5,044 cc (4 x 3.06 in, 101.6 x 77.7 mm); compression ratio: 9.7:1; max power (SAE): 216 hp at 4,800 rpm; max torque (SAE): 295 lb ft, 40.7 kg m at 3,100 rpm; max engine rpm: 5,400; 42.8 hp/l; 5 crankshaft bearings; camshafts: 1, at centre of Vee; lubrication: 8.5 imp pt, 10.1 US pt, 4.8 l; 1 Rochester 4MV downdraught 4-barrel carburettor; cooling system: 20 imp pt, 23.9 US pt, 11.3 l.

TRANSMISSION gearbox: Turbo-Hydramatic automatic transmission; ratios: I 2.480, II 1.480, III 1, rev 2.080; lever: central; axle ratio: 3.360; width of rims: 6''; tyres: De Ville E78S x 14 - Caprice FR78S x 14.

PERFORMANCE max speed: about 115 mph, 185 km/h; power-weight ratio: De Ville 15.7 lb/hp, 7.1 kg/hp - Caprice 16.8 lb/hp, 7.6 kg/hp.

STEERING servo; turns lock to lock: 3.07.

BRAKES servo.

ELECTRICAL EQUIPMENT 55 A alternator; Bosch distributor.

DIMENSIONS AND WEIGHT length: De Ville 203.10 in, 516 cm - Caprice 904.10 in, 518 cm; width: 74.30 in, 189 cm; height: De Ville 54.60 in, 139 cm - Caprice 54.80 in, 139 cm; weight: De Ville 3,406 lb, 1,545 kg - Caprice 3,635 lb, 1,649 kg.

OPTIONALS 4-speed fully synchronized mechanical gearbox (I 2.540, II 1.830, III 1.380, IV 1, rev 2.540).

LEYLAND   AUSTRALIA

Mini-Moke Californian

PRICE EX WORKS (Australian $): $ 3,775

ENGINE front, transverse, 4 stroke; 4 cylinders, in line; 60.9 cu in 998 cc (2.54 x 2.86 in, 64.5 x 72.6 mm); compression ratio: 8.3:1; max power (DIN): 39 hp at 5,200 rpm; max torque (DIN): 51 lb ft, 7 kg m at 2,500 rpm; max engine rpm: 6,000; 39.1 hp/l; cast iron block and head; 3 crankshaft bearings; valves: 8, overhead, pushrods and rockers; camshafts: 1, overhead; lubrication: gear pump, full flow filter, 8.8 imp pt, 10.6 US pt, 5 l; 1 SU hype HS4 carburettor; fuel feed; mechanical pump; water-cooled, 6.2 imp pt, 7.4 US pt, 3.5 l.

TRANSMISSION driving wheels: front; clutch: single dry plate; gearbox: mechanical; gears: 4, fully synchronized; ratios: I 3.530, II 2.200, III 1.030, IV 1, rev 3.540; lever: central; axle ratio: 3.440; width of rims: 5.5''; tyres: 175 R x 13.

PERFORMANCE max speed: 81 mph, 130 km/h; power-weight ratio: 35.7 lb/hp, 16.2 kg/hp; carrying capacity: 353 lb, 160 kg; consumption: 42 m/imp gal, 35.1 m/US gal, 6.7 l x 100 km.

CHASSIS integral, front and rear auxiliary frames; front suspension: independent, wishbones, rubber springs, telescopic dampers; rear independent, swinging longitudinal trailing arms, rubber springs, telescopic dampers.

STEERING rack-and-pinion; turns lock to lock: 2.30.

BRAKES drum.

ELECTRICAL EQUIPMENT 12 V; 40 Ah battery; 40 W alternator; 2 headlamps.

DIMENSIONS AND WEIGHT wheel base: 82.48 in, 209 cm; tracks: 49.02 in, 124 cm front, 49.76 in, 126 cm rear; length: 127.17 in, 323 cm; width: 57.09 in, 145 cm; height: 62.99 in, 160 cm; ground clearance: 7.99 in, 20 cm; weight: 1,394 lb, 632 kg; turning circle: 32.1 ft, 9.8 m; fuel tank: 5.9 imp gal, 7.1 US gal, 27 l.

BODY open; no doors; 2 seats, separate front seats.

OPTIONALS 77.8 cu in, 1,275 cc engine, front disc brakes.

LEYLAND Mini-Moke Californian

Car manufacturers and coachbuilders

An outline of their history, structure and activities

CAR MANUFACTURERS

A.C. CARS Ltd — Great Britain

Founded in 1900 by Portwine & Weller, assumed title Auto-carriers (A.C.) Ltd in 1907, moved from London to Thames Ditton in 1911. Present title since 1930. Chairman: W.D. Hurlock. Managing Director: A.D. Turner. Works Director: R. Alsop. Secretary/Financial Director: A. Wilson. Head office press office and works: The High Street, Thames Ditton, Surrey. 170 employees. Models: ACE Bristol 2 l Le Mans (1959); ACE Cobra Le Mans (1963). Entries and wins in numerous competitions (Monte Carlo Rally, Le Mans, etc.).

ADAM OPEL AG — Germany (Federal Republic)

Founded in 1862. Owned by General Motors Corp. USA since 1929. Chairman: J.F. Waters jr. Members of the board: W. Schlotfeldt, H. Zincke, K. Kartzke, F. Beickler, E. Rohde, F. Schwenger, J.E. Rhame, J.M. Fleming. Head office and press office: 6090 Rüsselsheim/Main. Works: Bochum, Kaiserslautern, Rüsselsheim. 60,869 employees. 925,167 cars produced 1977. Car production begun in 1898. Most important models: 10/18 (1908); 4/8 (1909); 6/16 (1910); 8/25 (1920); 4/12 (1924); 4/14 (1925-29); Olympia (1935); Super Six, Admiral (1938); Kapitän (1939); Rekord (1961); Kadett (1962); Admiral, Diplomat, Commodore (1968); GT (1969); Ascona, Manta (1970); Senator, Monza (1978).

ASSEMBLY IN OTHER COUNTRIES — **Belgium:** GM Continental S.A. (associated company), Noorderlaan 75, Antwerp (assem. Kadett, Rekord, Commodore, Ascona, Manta). **Korea:** V.P. GM Overseas Corp. (concessionaire), Shinjn Motor Co. Ltd., 62-10, 2-ka Choong Moo Ro, Coong-ku, Seoul (assem. Rekord). **Malaysia:** Capital Motor Assembly Corp. Sdn, P.O.B. 204, Yohore Bahru (assem. Kadett, Rekord). **Morocco:** Société Marocaine de Mécanique Industrielle et Automobile, Blod Moulay Ismael 22, Casablanca (assem. Rekord). **Portugal:** GM de Portugal Ltda (associated company), Rua Particular n. 1 de Rafinaria Colonial 26, Lisbon (assem. Kadett, Rekord). **South Africa:** GM South Africa Pty Ltd (associated company), Kempston Rd, Port Elizabeth (assem. Ascona, Rekord). **Thailand:** GM Thailand Ltd, Catlay Trust Bldg, 4th Fl. 1016 Rama IV Rd, Bangkok (assem. Rekord). **Uruguay:** GM Uruguaya S.A. (associated company), C.C. 234, Montevideo (assem. Kadett, Rekord). **Zaire:** GM Zaire (associated company), Boulevard Patrice Lumumba, Masina 1, Kinshasa (assem. Kadett, Commodore). 315,123 cars produced outside Federal Republic in 1976.

ALFA ROMEO S.p.A. — Italy

Founded in 1910 as Anonima Lombarda Fabbrica Automobili, became Accomandita Semplice Ing. Nicola Romeo in 1915, Società Anonima Italiana Ing. Nicola Romeo & C. in 1918, S.A. Alfa Romeo in 1930. Became part of IRI group in 1933 and assumed name of S.A. Alfa Romeo Milano-Napoli in 1939. Present title since 1946. For volume of production it holds second place in Italian motor industry. President: E. Massacesi. Vice-President: E. Peracchi. Vice-President and Managing Director: C. Innocenti. Managing Director and General Manager: A. Lingiardi. Head office and press office: Arese (Milan), Works: Arese (Milan), Pomigliano d'Arco (Naples). 44,000 employees. 220,000 vehicles produced in 1978. Most important models: 24 hp (1910); 40-60 hp (1913); RL Targa Florio (1923); P2 (1924); 6C-1500 (1926); 6C-1750 (1929); 8C-2300 (1930); P3 (1932); 8C-2600 (1933); 8C-2900 (1935); 158 (1938); 6C-2500 SS (1939); 2500 Freccia d'Oro (1947); 1900 (1950); Giulietta Sprint (1954); Giulietta Berlina (1955); Giulietta Spider (1956); Giulietta TI (1957); 2000 (1958); Giulia TI, Giulia Sprint, Giulia Spider, 2600 (1962); Giulia Sprint GT, Giulia TZ (1963); Giulia 1300, Giulia Spider Veloce (1964); Giulia 1300 TI, Giulia Super, GTA (1965); Junior (1966); 1750, 1300 Spider Junior, GTA 1300 Junior, "33" Coupé (1968); Giulia 1600 S, 1300 Junior Z (1969); Giulia 1300 Super, Montreal (1970); 2000 Berlina, 2000 GT Veloce, 2000 Spider Veloce (1971); Alfasud (1972); Alfetta (1973), Giulietta (1977). Entries and wins in numerous competitions. European Mountain Championship and European Touring Challenge Cup in 1967, in 1968 the 33/2 l was classified first at Daytona, in Targa Florio and Nürburgring 1000 km. In 1969 Alfa Romeo won European Touring Challenge Cup, National Championship for Makes in Brazil, three American National Drivers Championships and numerous national championships. In 1970, first place in European Championship for Touring Cars and many national championships. In 1971, in Makers' International Championship, a 33-3 was placed outright first in Brands Hatch 1000 km, in Targa Florio and Watkins Glen 6 Hour. It won European Touring Car Makers' Championship, coming first and second in final classification. In 1971 it also won a series of international championships, including Austrian Mountain Championship and Belgian Touring Drivers' Championship, Dutch Touring Championship for Touring Cars up to 1300 cc, Italian Absolute Championship for Special Touring Cars, American National Championship for SCCA Drivers, class C Sedan and Class C Sports Racing, and finally Venezuelan National Championship outright. In 1973 2000 GTV won Coupe du Roi and in 1974 2000 GTV won Coupe du Roi and 33 TT 12 finished 1, 2 and 3 in Monza 1000 km. 1975 holders of World Championship for Makes and 1977 of World Sports Car Championship.

ASSEMBLY IN OTHER COUNTRIES — **Indonesia:** Alfa Delta Motors (concessionaire), Jalon P. Arena; Pekan Raya IKt, P.O.B. 2126, Djakarta (assem. Alfasud 1.3, 1.5, Alfetta 1.8, 2.0. **Malaysia:** City Motors SDN BHD (concessionaire), Foo yet Kai Building 270 Hugh how Street, Ipoh Perak (assem. Alfasud 1.3, 1.5, Alfetta 1.8, 2.0); Swedish Motor Assemblies (concessionaire), Kuala Lumpur (assem. Alfasud 1.3, 1.5, Alfetta 1.8, 2.0). **South Africa:** Alfa Romeo Sudafrica (Pty) Ltd (associated company), P.O.B. 78438, Johannesburg (assem. Alfasud 1.3, 1.5, Giulietta 1.8, Alfetta 1.8, 2.0, Alfetta GTV). **Thailand:** Siam Europe Motors (concessionaire), 404 Phayatha Rd, Bangkok (assem. Alfasud 1.3, Giulietta 1.6, Alfetta 2.0). **Uruguay:** Alfa Automotors SA (concessionaire) Av. 18 de Julio 1077, P.2 Montevideo (assem. Alfasud 1.3).

ALPINE - see AUTOMOBILES ALPINE S.A.

AMERICAN MOTORS CORPORATION — USA

(Makes: Gremlin, Pacer, Concord, Matador, Jeep vehicles)

Established in 1954 as result of merger between Nash-Kelvinator Corp. and Hudson Motor Car Co.; acquired Jeep Corp., Feb. 1970. Chairman: G.C. Meyers. President: W.P. Tippett, Jr. Central office and press office: American Center Building, P.O. Box 442, Southfield, Mich. 48034. Technical center: 14250 Plymouth Rd., Detroit, Mich. 48232. Passenger car works: 5626, 25th Ave., Kenosha, Wisc. 53140; 3880 N. Richards, Milwaukee, Wisc. 53201, Jeep plant: Toledo, Ohio. Plastics operations: Windsor Plastics, Inc., 601 N. Congress Ave, Evansville, Ind., 47711; Mercury Plastics Co., Inc., 34501 Harper, Mt Clemens, Mich. 48043; Evart Products Co., Evart, Mich. 49631 (subsidiaries-injection moulding); AM General Corp., 32500 Van Born Rd., Wayne, Mich. 48184 (subsidiary). Works: 701 W. Chippewa Ave, South Bend, Ind., 46623; 13200 E. McKinley Hwy, Mishawaka, Ind., 46544; 1428 West Henry St, Indianapolis, Ind. 46221 (military trucks, post-office delivery trucks and transit buses). 28,500 employees. 156,994 cars and 155,960 Jeep vehicles produced in 1977.

MANUFACTURE AND ASSEMBLY IN OTHER COUNTRIES — **Argentina:** Renault S.A., Sarmiento 1230, Buenos Aires (assem. Classic, Torino, Jeep CJ-5 and trucks). **Australia:** Australian Motor Industries Ltd (associated company), G.P.O.B. 2006S, 155 Bertie St, Port Melbourne (Matador). **Canada:** American Motors (Canada) Ltd (subsidiary), Brampton, Ont. (Concord, Gremlin). **Costa Rica:** Motorizada de Costa Rica S.A., San José (assem. Jeep CJ-5, Wagoneer). **India:** Mahindra & Mahindra Ltd, Gateway Bldg, Apollo Bunder, Bombay (assem. Jeep CJ-4 and Wagoneer). **Indonesia:** N.V. Indonesian Service Co. Ltd, P.O.B. 121, Djakarta-Kota (assem. Jeep CJ-5). **Iran:** Sherkate Sahami Jeep, Ekbatan Ave, Jeep Bldg, Teheran (assem. Arya, Shahin, Jeep CJ-5 and Wagoneer). **Israel:** Matmar Industries Ltd, P.O.B. 1007, Haifa (assem. Jeep CJ-5). **Japan:** Mitsubishi Heavy-Industries Ltd, No. 10, 2-chome, Marunouchi, Chiyoda-ku, Tokyo (manuf. Jeep CJ-5). **Korea:** Shinjin Jeep Co., 62-7 Ika Choong Mu-Ro Choòng Ku, Seoil (assem. Jeep CJ-5). **Mexico:** Vehiculos Automotores Mexicanos S.A., Poniente 150, num. 837, Industrial Vallejo, Mexico City 16, D.F. (assem. American, Pacer, Jeep CJ-5 and Wagoneer). **Morocco:** Société d'Importation & Distribution Automobile, 84 av. Lalla Yacoute, Casablanca (assem. Jeep CJ-5). **Pakistan:** Naya Daur Motors Ltd., State Life Building, Dr. Ziauddin Ahmed Rd, Karachi 3 (assem. Jeep trucks, Jeep station wagons and CJ-5). **Philippines:** Jeep Philippines, Guevent Bldg, 49 Libertad St., Mandaluyong, Rizal (assem. Jeep CJ-5, CJ-6). **South Africa:** Jeep South Africa, P.O.B. 80, Uitenhage (assem. Jeep CJ-5, CJ-7). **Spain:** Construcciones y Auxiliar de Ferrocarriles S.A., V.I.A.S.A. Division, Apdo 279, Zaragoza (manuf. Jeep CJ-5). **Taiwan:** Yue Loong Motor Co. Ltd, 150 Nanking East Rd, Sec. II, Taipei (assem. Jeep CJ-5). **Thailand:** Thai Yarnyon Co. Ltd, 388/3 Petchburi Rd, Bangkok (assem. Jeep CJ-5). **Turkey:** Genoto General Otomotive Sanyi, ve Ticaret AS, Takisim la Martin Cad. No. 8/1, Istanbul (assem. CJ-6, trucks). **Venezuela:** Constructora Venezolana de Vehiculos C.A., P.O.B. 61033, Caracas (assem. Hornet); Jeep de Venezuela S.A., Apdo 41-42, Tejerias, Edo Uragua (assem. Jeep CJ-5 and Wagoneer). 16,928 passengers cars and 22,555 Jeep vehicles produced outside USA in 1977.

ANTIQUE & CLASSIC AUTOMOTIVE Inc. — USA

Established in 1973 as Antique & Classic Cars, Inc. Present title since 1977. Chairman: S.J. Wilson, President: K.L. Malick. Directors: R. Paulus, Nancy Wilson, S. Wilson. Head office, showroom: 100 Sonwil Industrial Park, Buffalo, N.Y. 14225. Works: 8000 Rein Rd, Buffalo, N.Y. 1425. 28 employees. Over 3,000 cars in kit form produced. Most important models: 1937 Jaguar SS-100, 1930 Bentley Phaeton, 1934 Frazer Nash, 1927 Bugatti 35B, 1930 Alfa Romeo.

ARGYLL TURBO CARS Ltd — Great Britain

Founded in 1977. Directors: R.M. Henderson, A. Smith, H. Crow, J. Hughes. Head office and works: Minnow House, Lochgilphead, Argyll, Scotland.

● The information given in these descriptions refers specifically to cars and therefore does not cover the activities in which any of the car manufacturers are engaged in other fields of industry.

402

ARKLEY - see JOHN BRITTEN GARAGES Ltd.

ARO INTREPRINDEREA MECANICA MUSCEL **Rumania**

General Manager: V. Naghi. Head office, press office and works: Str. Vasile Roaità 173. Cimpulung Muscel Jud. Arges. 53,600 cars produced in 1974.

ASTON MARTIN LAGONDA (1975) Ltd **Great Britain**

Founded in 1913 as Bamford & Martin, it is one of the greatest names in the world of touring and competition cars. The name "Aston Martin" recalls the many successes in the Aston Clinton Hill Climb. In 1947, when it was taken over by David Brown, the title was changed to Aston Martin Lagonda Ltd. In January 1975 the company went into voluntary liquidation and since June 1975 has been owned by a consortium headed by P. Sprague and G. Minden, with the title Aston Martin Lagonda (1975) Ltd. Directors: P. Sprague (USA), A.G. Curtis, D.G. Flather (U.K.). Works: Tickford St., Newport Pagnell. Bucks MK16 9AN. 350 employees. 243 cars produced in 1977. Most important models: Lionel Martin series (1921-25); first 1.5 l series (1927-32); second 1.5 l series (1932-34); third 1.5 l series (1934-36); 2 l series with single overhead camshaft (1936-40); 2 l DB1 series (1948-50); 2.6 l DB2 series (1950-1953); 2.6 and 2.9 l DB3 series (1952-53); 2.6 and 2.9 l DB2/4 series (1953-55); 2.9 l DB3S series (1955-56); 2.9 l DB2/4 Mk II series (1955-57); 2.6 l, 2.9 l Lagonda Saloon, Convertible (1949-1956); 2.9 l DB Mk III series (1957-59); 3.7 l DB4 series (1959-63); 3.7 l DB4 GT series (1959-63); 4 l Lagonda Rapide (1961-63); 4 l DB5 series (1963-65); 4 l DB6 Saloon and Volante Convertible (1965-69); DB6 Mk 2 Saloon with electronic fuel injection or carburettor induction (1969-70); DBS 4 l Saloon (1967); DBS V8 Saloon 5.35 l 4 O.H.C. fuel injection engine (1969); V8 (1973); Lagonda 4-door (1974); V8 Vantage (1977); Volante (1978). Entries in numerous competitions (Le Mans, Spa, Tourist Trophy, Nürburgring, Aintree). Won Le Mans and World Sports Car Championship in 1959.

AUBURN-CORD-DUESENBERG Co. **USA**

President: G.A. Pray. Head office, press office and works: 122 South Elm Place, Broken Arrow, Oklahoma 74012. 15 employees, 12 cars produced in 1977.

AUDI NSU AUTO UNION AG **Germany (Federal Republic)**

Established in 1969 as result of merger between Auto Union GmbH (founded in Zwickau in 1932 and transferred to Ingolstadt in 1949 when Zwickau company was nationalized) and NSU Motorenwerke AG (founded in 1873 at Riedlingen, moved to Neckarsulm in 1880; changed its name to Neckarsulmer Fahrzeugwerke AG in 1919 and became NSU Motorenwerke AG in 1960). Board of Directors: W. Habbel, F. Piëch, H. Kialka, W. Neuwald. Head office and press office: Postfach 220, D-8070 Ingolstadt. Works: as above, Neckarsulm. 28,349 employees. 339,883 cars produced in 1977. Most important models: NSU Ro 80 (1967); Audi 100 and 100 LS (1969); Audi 100 Coupé S (1970); Audi 100 GL (1971); Audi 80, 80 L, 80 S, 80 LS, 80 GL (1972).

ASSEMBLY IN OTHER COUNTRIES — **South Africa:** VW of South Africa Ltd (associated company), P.O.B. 80, Uitenhage (assem. Audi 100 range). 116.249 cars produced outside Federal Republic in 1976.

AUSTIN - see BL Ltd

AUTOBIANCHI **Italy**

Created in 1955 in collaboration between Edoardo Bianchi firm and Fiat and Pirelli. Incorporated into Fiat in 1968 as Autobianchi, retaining, however, own maker's marks but incorporating sales organisation and maintenance services into Lancia. Office: Lancia, v. V. Lancia 27, 10141 Turin. About 4,000 employees. 88,400 cars produced in 1978.

AUTOMOBILES ALPINE S.A. **France**

Founded in 1955. President: J. Rédélé. Head office and press office: 3 bd. Foch, Epinay s/Seine. Works: 40 av. Pasteur, Dieppe. 563 employees. 3,746 cars produced in 1977. Most important models: Mille Miles (1955); Coupé Sport and Sport Convertible (1959-60); Berlinette Tour de France (1961); A110 956 and 1108 cc series (1962); M. 63 (1963); M. 64 and F2 (1964); A 310 (1971). Alpine Renault, A 310 (1977). Entries and wins in numerous competitions (rallies, Le Mans, Montecarlo, etc.).

MANUFACTURE IN OTHER COUNTRIES — **Brazil:** Willys Overland do Brasil (associated company), São Paulo (manuf. Interlagos). **Bulgaria:** Bullet (associated company), Sofia. **Mexico:** Diesel Nacional (associated company), Mexico City. **Spain:** Fasa (associated company), Valladolid.

AUTOMOBILES MONTEVERDI Ltd **Switzerland**

Founded in 1967. Chairman and Managing Director: P. Monteverdi. Vice-Chairman: R. Jenzer. General Manager: P. Berger. Head office, press office and works: Oberwilerstr. 14-20, 4102 Binningen/Basel. 170 employees. 1300 cars produced in 1976. Most important models: 2-seater (1968); High Speed 375 L 2+2 (1969); Hal 450 SS (1970); High Speed 375/4 Limousine (1971); Berlinetta (1972); Hai 450 GTS (1973); Palm Beach (1975); Sierra (1977).

AUTOMOBILES PEUGEOT S.A. **France**

Founded in 1890 as Les Fils Peugeot Fres. Present title since 1966. In December 1974 acquired 38.2% of Citroën stock and in May 1976 take over full control of Citroën. In 1978 it acquired a controlling interest in the three Chrysler European companies, in U.K. France and Spain. Directorate: J. Baratte (President), J. Boilot (General Manager), L. Collaine. Head office and press office: 75 av. de la Grande-Armée, Paris. Works: Dijon, Lille, Montbéliard, Mulhouse, Sochaux, St. Etienne, Vesoul. About 70,000 employees. 782,000 cars produced in 1977. Most important models: Bebé Peugeot (1911); 201, 301, 302, 402, 203 (1929-60); 403 (1955); 404 (1960); 204 (1965); 504 (1968); 304 (1969); 604 (1975). First place in ACF (1912-13, 1923-24).

MANUFACTURE AND ASSEMBLY IN OTHER COUNTRIES — **Argentina:** Safrar (subsidiary), Buenos Aires (manuf. 404, 504). **Chile:** Automotores San Cristobal S.A.I.C., Santiago (assem. 404). **Madagascar:** Somacoa, Tananarive (assem. 304, 404). **Malaysia:** Asia Automobiles Industries, Petaling-Jaya (assem. 204, 504). **Nigeria:** Scoa, Lagos (assem. 404). **Paraguay:** Automotores y Maquinaria, C.C. 1160, Asuncion (assem. 404, 504). **Portugal:** Movauto, Setubal (assem. 204, 304, 404, 504). **South Africa:** National Motors Assemblies (subsidiary), Johannesburg (assem. 404, 504). **Uruguay:** S.A.D.A.R., Montevideo (assem. 404).

AUTOMOBILE STIMULA **France**

Manufacturer of replicars in small series. Head office, press office and works: 79 av. du 8 Mai 1945, 69500 Bron. Production of Bugatti 55 began in 1978.

AUTOMOBILI FERRUCCIO LAMBORGHINI S.p.A. **Italy**

Founded in 1962 as Automobili Ferruccio Lamborghini Sas. Present title since 1965. President and General Manager: R. Leimer. Head office, press office and works: v. Modena 1b, 40019 S. Agata Bolognese (Bologna). About 200 employees. 170 cars produced in 1977. Models: 350 GT (1963); 400 GT (1966); Miura (1967); Espada, Islero (1968); Jarama (1970); Urraco (1971); Countach (1974); Countach S (1978).

AUTOMOBILI INTERMECCANICA **USA**

President: F. Reisner. Vice President and General Manager: A.E.T. Baumgartner. Head office, press office and works: 2421 S. Susan St. Santa Ana, California. 38 employees. 314 cars produced in 1977.

AVALLONE - ACIEI Ltda **Brazil**

Specializes in the production of sports cars. Head office, press office and works: Av. Friburgo 61, 04781 São Paulo.

AVANTI MOTOR CORPORATION **USA**

Founded in 1965. Chairman: L. Newman. President: A.D. Altman. Vice-Presidents: F. Baer, E. Harding. Secretary and Treasurer: F. Baer. Head office and works: P.O.B. 1916, South Bend, Ind. 46634. 100 employees. 180 cars produced in 1977.

AZLK - AVTOMOBILNY ZAVOD IMENI LENINSKOGO KOMSOMOLA **USSR**

Press office: Avtoexport, Ul. Volkhonka 14, Moscow 119902. Works: Moscow, Izhevsk. 27,000 employees. About 390,000 cars produced in 1976.

BAYERISCHE MOTOREN WERKE AG **Germany (Federal Republic)**

Established in 1916 as Bayerische Flugzeugwerke AG. Present title since 1918. Chairman: E. von Kuenheim. Members of the board: H. Koch, H. Schäfer, K. Radermacher, H.E. Schönbeck, E. Sarfert, E. Haiber. Head office and press office: P.O.B. 400240, 8 Munich 40. Works: Munich, Landshut, Dingolfing. 33,398 employees. 290,236 cars produced in 1977. Most important models: 3/15 hp Saloon (1928); 326, 327, 328 (1936); 501 6 cyl, (1951); V8 (1954); 503 and 507 Sport (1955); 700 (1959); 1500 (1962); 1800 (1963); 2000 (1966); 2002, 2500, 2800 (1968); 3,0, CS (1971); 520, 520 i (1972); 2002 Turbo (1973); 518 (1974); 320 (1975); 633 CSi (1976); 323i (1977). Entries and wins in numerous competitions (Mille Miglia, Monza 12 hour, Hockenheim, Nürburgring, Friburg Mountain Record, Brands Hatch, European Mountain Championship, Salzburgring, Rally TAP; winner 1968, 1969, 1973, 1976 and 1978 European Touring Cars Championship; 1973, 1974, 1975 and 1978 European F2 Championship; 1977, 1978 World Championship for Makes (under 2000 cc).

ASSEMBLY IN OTHER COUNTRIES — **South Africa:** BMW (South Africa) (Pty) Ltd, 6 Frans de Toit St, Rosslyn, Pretoria (assem. 518, 520, 528, 528i, 728, 730, 733i). 6,100 cars assembled outside Federal Republic in 1977.

BENTLEY MOTORS Ltd **Great Britain**

Founded in 1920, taken over by Rolls-Royce Ltd in 1931, specializing in high-class vehicles. Head office and works: Crewe, Ches. Press office: 14-15 Conduit St., London W1. Most important models: first Bentley 3.5 l manufactured by Rolls-Royce (1933); 4.5 l (1936); 4.5 l MK VI (1946); Continental (1951); "R" Type (1952); S1 (1955); S2 (1959); S3 (1962) "T" series 1965); Corniche (1971); T2 (1977).

BL Ltd **Great Britain**

(Makes: Austin, Daimler, Jaguar, Land Rover, MG, Mini, Morris, Princess, Rover, Triumph, Vanden Plas).

BL Ltd, 99% of whose shares are now held by British Government, is Britains largest producer of motor vehicles. Formed in May 1968, following merger between British Motor Holdings (BMC and Jaguar) and Leyland Motor Corporation (Leyland Motors, Rover and Triumph), it employs 188,300 throughout the world and current annual sales exceed £ 2,600 million. In July 1978 BL Cars was split into three companies: Austin Morris Ltd (Austin Morris House, Bickenhill, Birmingham. General Manager: R. Horrocks; makes: Austin, Mini, Morris, MG, Princess) Jaguar Rover Triumph Ltd (Coventry House, Eaton Square, Coventry. General Manager: W.P. Thompson; makes: Daimler, Jaguar, Land Rover, Rover, Triumph, Vanden Plas) BL Components Ltd (Unipart House, Cowley, Oxford. General Manager: P.W. McGranth) Head office BL Ltd: 174 Marylebone Rd, London NW1 5AA. Hon. President: Lord Stokes. Chairman: M. Edwardes. Deputy Chairman: J. McGregor. In 1977 629,000 passenger cars were produced and a total of 785,000 vehicles at home and abroad.

MANUFACTURE AND ASSEMBLY IN OTHER COUNTRIES — The Company sells its vehicles in 175 countries. The major manufacturing and assembly plants are at Seneffe in Belgium (cars), Madras in India (commercial vehicles), Sydney in Australia (mainly commercial vehicles but also Mini-Mokes), and Cape Town and Durban in South Africa (cars and commercial vehicles). There are many smaller factories in other parts of the world, including Turkey, Zaire, Zambia, Malaysia, New Zealand and Hong Kong. For specific details apply to BL Ltd, 174 Marylebone Rd, London NW1 5AA.

BLAKELY AUTO WORKS Ltd **USA**

Founded by D. Blakely in 1972. Chief Marketing Director: A. Herschberger. Head office and press office: 124 B Fulton St., Princeton, WI 54968. Works: 203 Pacific St., Davis Junction, Illinois 61020. 36 employees. 126 cars produced in 1977. Most important models: Bantam (1972); Bearcat (1973); Bearcat 'S' (1976).

BMW (South Africa) (Pty) Ltd **South Africa**

A privatly owned company began assembly of Glas bodies, BMW 1800 and 2000 version in 1968. In 1974 BMW AG, West Germany, took control and Series 5 was introduced that year and Series 7 in 1978. BMW 530 model raced in Group 2 FORM in 1976/77/78 in 40 races, 38 wins and 2 Championship wins. Managing Director: E. von Koerber. Directors: W. Jones, R. Meatchem, D. Balfour, H. Doeg. Head office, press office and works: 6 Frans du Toit St, Rosslyn.

BRISTOL CARS Partnership **Great Britain**

Established in 1946 as Car Division of Bristol Aeroplane Co., became affiliated company of Bristol Aeroplane Co. in 1955, and subsidiary of Bristol Siddeley Engines in 1959. Became privately owned company in 1960 and owned by partnership from 1966. Partners: Bristol Cars Ltd T.A.D. Crook, F.S. Derham. Head office, press office 368-370 Kensington High St, London. Works: Filton, Bristol.

Most important models: 400 (1947); 401 and 402 (1949); 403 and 404 (1953-55); 405 (1954-58); 406 (1958); 407 (1961); 408 (1963); 409 (1965); 410 (1967); 411 (1969); 412 (1975); 603 (1976). Entries and first places in numerous competitions with Bristol cars or Bristol-engined cars (Monte Carlo Rally, Targa Florio, Mille Miglia) with F1 and F2 (British GP, GP of Europe, Sebring, Reims, Montlhéry, Le Mans, etc.), from 1946 until 1955.

BUICK - see GENERAL MOTORS CORPORATION

CADILLAC - see GENERAL MOTORS CORPORATION

CATERHAM CAR Sales Ltd **Great Britain**

(Make: Seven)

In 1973 took over manufacture of Lotus Seven Series III introduced by Lotus Cars Ltd in 1957. Managing Director: G.B. Nearn. Director: D.S. Wakefield. Head office, press office and works: 36/40 Town End, Caterham Hill, Surrey GR3 5UG. 18 employees. 163 cars produced in 1977. Models: Super Seven Series III powered by Lotus big valve twin cam engine.

CHECKER MOTORS CORPORATION **USA**

Founded in 1922. Chairman and President: D. Markin. Executive Vice-President: R.E. Oakland. Vice-President Marketing: J.J. Love. Head office, press office and works: 2016 N. Pitcher St. Kalamazoo, Mich. 49007. 1,000 employees. 4,800 cars produced in 1977.

CHEVROLET - see GENERAL MOTORS CORPORATION
GENERAL MOTORS OF CANADA Ltd and
GENERAL MOTORS SOUTH AFRICA (Pty) Ltd

CHRYSLER AUSTRALIA Ltd **Australia**

Founded in 1951. Affiliated with Chrysler Corporation USA. Chairman: T.D. Anderson. Directors: I. Webber, R. Smith, W. Bivens, D.B. Coleman, J.M. Hill, J.W. Wiley. Head office, press office and works: South Rd, Clovelly Park, South Australia. 5,803 employees. 33,570 cars produced in 1977.

CHRYSLER CORPORATION **USA**

(Makes: Chrysler, Dodge, Plymouth)

Founded in 1925 as successor to Maxwell Motors Corp. It holds third place in U.S. motor industry. Chrysler Corp. American operations are made up of a U.S. Automotive Sales Division selling Chrysler, Dodge, Plymouth cars and trucks. President and Chief Operating Officer: L. Iacocca. Vice Chairman: E. A. Cafiero. Vice President South America: H. Leshinsky. Vice President Europe: D.H. Lander. Head office and press office Chrysler Corp.: 12000 Lynn Townsend Dr., Mich. 48288. Mailing address: Chrysler Corp., P.O. Box 1919, Detroit, Mich. 48288. Works: eight vehicle assembly plants and 35 supporting manufacturing plants throughout the U.S. Over 259,800 employees. 2,374,113 cars produced in 1977. Most important models: Chrysler (1924); Plymouth and Dodge (1928). In 1978, the Chrysler UK, Chrysler France and Chrysler España holdings it had acquired over the previous 20 years passed to PSA Peugeot-Citroën of France. The Chrysler names and distribution networks remain unchanged.

MANUFACTURE AND ASSEMBLY IN OTHER COUNTRIES — **Argentina:** Chrysler Fevre Argentina S.A.I.C. (subsidiary), Casilla de Correo 444, 1000 - Buenos Aires (manuf. Dodge Polara, Coronado, GTX, 1500). **Australia:** Chrysler Australia Ltd (subsidiary), South Rd, Clovelly Park, South Australia (manuf. Valiant Regal, Centura, Sigma, Lancer). **Columbia:** Chrysler Colmotores (subsidiary), Apdo Aéreo 7329, Bogotà (assem. Simca, Dodge, Dodge Dart, Dart). **Perù:** Chrysler Perù S.A. (subsidiary), Apdo 5037, Lima (assem. Dodge Coronet. Hillman Hunter). **South Africa:** Sigma Motor Corp. Ltd (associated company), P.O.B. 411, Pretoria (manuf. Valiant, Hillman, Chrysler, Colt Fastback). **Venezuela:** Chrysler de Venezuela S.A. (subsidiary), Apdo 62362, Caracas 106 (assem. Dodge Aspen, Chrysler Le Baron). 813,314 cars produced outside USA and Canada in 1977.

CHRYSLER CORPORATION DO BRASIL **Brazil**

(Make: Dodge)

Founded in 1967 as Chrysler do Brasil S.A. Ind. e Comércio, it began producing Dodge trucks and Dodge Dart in May 1969. In 1971 it became Chrysler Corporation do Brasil and started production of Dodge 1800 in November 1972. Managing Director: D.W. Dancey. Head office, press office and works: Av. Dr. José Fornari 715, B. Ferrazopolis, São Bernardo do Campo, São Paulo. 3.762 employees. 17,380 cars produced in 1976. At present it produces Dodge trucks and Dodge, Polara, Dart Charger and Magnum models.

CHRYSLER ESPAÑA S.A. **Spain**

(Makes: Chrysler, Simca)

Founded in 1951 as Barreiros Diesel S.A., 40% of shares were brought in 1963 by Chrysler Motor Corporation which became majority shareholder in 1967 eventually owning 99% of shares. Present title since 1970. In 1978 a controlling interest was acquired by PSA Peugeot-Citroën. President: E. Chaves. Vice President and Managing Director: W. Storen. Head office and press office: Apdo 140, Madrid 21. Works: Villaverde, Madrid. 16,800 employees. 98,000 cars produced in 1977.

CHRYSLER FEVRE ARGENTINA S.A.I.C. **Argentina**

(Make: Dodge)

Founded in 1959 as Fevre y Basset Ltda. Present title since 1965. Chairman: C.M. Hollis. Head office and press office: Florencio Varela 1903, San Justo, Buenos Aires. Works: as above; Charcas 4200, Monte Chingolo, Lanús, Buenos Aires. 5,000 employees. 16,440 cars produced in 1977. Most important models: Valiant I (1962); Valiant II (1963); Valiant III (1964-65); Valiant IV (1966); Valiant V (1967-68); Dodge Polara, Coronado, GT (1969); Dodge Polara, Coronado, GT, GTX (1970); Polara, Coronado, GTX, Polara Coupé, 1500 (1971-72); Polara, Coronado, GTX, Polara Coupé, 1500, GT90 (1972-73); GTX, Polara, Polara RT, Coronado, 1500, GT90 (1974); Polara, Coronado, Polara RT, GTX, 1500, 1500 1.8 engine, 1500 Automatic (1975); Polara, Coronado, Polara RT, GTX, 1500, 1500 Automatic, 1500 1.8 engine (1977-78).

CHRYSLER FRANCE **France**

(Makes: Chrysler, Simca)

Founded in 1934 as Sté Industrielle de Mécanique et de Carrosserie Automobile. Assumed title Société Simca Automobiles in 1960. In 1971 controlling interest passed to Chrysler Corp. and then in 1978 to PSA Peugeot-Citroën. Present title since 1970. Watch Committee: F. Gautier (President). P. Perrin (Vice President). Management Board: F. Perrin-Pelletier (President). J. Peronnin (General Manager). D. Savey. Head office and press office: 136 av. des Champs Elysées, 75008, Paris. Works: Poissy; La Rochelle-Perigny; Sully-sur-Loire; Sept Fons; Vieux Condé; Bondy; Valenciennes. 38,141 employees. 568,872 cars produced in 1977. Most important models: Simca 5 (1936); Simca 8-1100 (1938); Simca 6, 8-1100 (1948); Simca 8-1200, 8 Sport (1949); 9 Aronde (1951); Aronde, Coupé de Ville (1953); Aronde Week-End, Vedette (1955); Aronde 1300, Ocean, Plein Ciel (1956); Ariane 4 (1957); Aronde Montlhéry, Ariane 8, Vedette (1958); Aronde 6, 7, P.60 (1959); Aronde Etoile 6 and 7, P.60, Ocean, Plein Ciel (1960); Ariane (1961); Aronde Montlhéry and Monaco Spéciale, Simca 1000 (1962); Simca 900, 1300, 1500 (1963); Simca 1000 and 1500 A (1966); Simca 1301, 1501, 1200 S (1967); Simca 1100 (1968); Simca 4 CV, 1000 Special, 1100 5 CV, 1501 Special (1969); Simca 1301 Special, 1000 Rallye (1970); Chrysler 160, 160 GT, 180, Simca 1100 Special (1971); Simca 1000, 1000 Rallye 1 (1972); Simca 1000 Rallye 2, 1100 VF2, Chrysler 2 litres (1973); Simca 1100 S, 1501 S, 1100 TI, 1100 LX (1974); Simca 1100 GLX, 1000 SR, 1307 GLS, 1307 S, 1308 GT (1975), Simca 1000 Extra, 1005 GLS, 1100 AS (1976); Simca 1005 LS, 1006 GLS, 1100 LE, 1100 GLX, 1100 ES, Rallye, 1307 GLS, 1308 GT, Chrysler Simca 1610, 2-litres (1977); Horizon (1978).

CHRYSLER UNITED KINGDOM Ltd **Great Britain**

Founded in 1917 as Rootes Motors Ltd. In 1967 became a member of Chrysler Group but in 1978 a controlling interest was acquired by PSA Peugeot-Citroën. Present title since 1970. Chairman: G. Turnbull. President: G. Hunt. Managing Director: G. Lacy. Deputy Managing Director: P. Griffiths. Directors: D. Lander, L.B. Warren, R. Grantham, G. Hereil, A. Murray, Lord Roll, F. Perrin-Pelletier, D. Savey, R. Parham. Head office: Bowater House, 68 Knightsbridge, London SW1 7LH. Press office: Whitley, Conventry. Works: Chrysler Scotland Ltd, Linwood, nr. Paisley, Renfrewshire, Scotland; Ryton on Dunsmore, Stoke, nr. Coventry, Warwick.; Dunstable, Luton, Beds. 23,600 employees. 203,549 cars produced in 1977.

MANUFACTURE AND ASSEMBLY IN OTHER COUNTRIES — **Colombia:** Chrysler Colmotores S.A. (subsidiary). Apdo Aereo 7329, Bogotà I (assem. Avenger, Estate). **Eire:** Chrysler Ireland Ltd (subsidiary), Shanowen Rd, Whitehall, Dublin 9 (assem. Hunter). **Indonesia:** N.V. Jakarta Motor C. (Concessionaire), DJL Tijkini Raya 58, Tromol Pos 251, Djakarta (assem. Avenger). **Iran:** I.N.I.M., P.O.B. 14/1637 km 18, Industrial Manufacturing Co. Ltd (associated company), Karadj Rd, Teheran (manuf. and assem. Hunter, Paykan, Avenger). **Malaysia:** Associated Motor Industries (concessionaire), P.O.B. 763, Kuala Lumpur (assem. Avenger). **Malta:** Industrial Motor Co. Ltd (concessionaire), National Rd, Blata 1-Bajda (assem. Hunter, Estate). **New Zealand:** Todd Motors Ltd LMVD (concessionaire), P.O.B. 50-349 « Todd Park », Heriot Drive, Porirua (assem. Hunter, Estate, Avenger). **Peru:** Chrysler Perú S.A. (associated company), Apdo 5037, Carretera Pau Norte, km 6.5, Lima (assem. Hunter). **Portugal:** Representateos Automoveis Chrysler Sarl (associated company), Avda de Roma 15B, Apdo 1208, Lisbon I (assem. Avenger). **Thailand:** Han Co (concessionaire), 98 Soi Aree, Sukhumvit 26, Bangkok (assem. Hunter, Avenger). **Trinidad:** H.E. Robinson Co. (concessionaire), B.O.B. 641, 82/84 Queen St, Port of Spain (assem. Hunter, Estate, Avenger). 89,234 cars produced outside U.K. in 1976.

CITROEN - see S.A. AUTOMOBILES CITROËN

CLÉNET COACHWORKS Inc.

Established in 1976. President: A.J.M. Clénet. Vice President and General Manager: T.L. Cadle. Vice President: J.W. Whitman. Head office, press office and works: 495 South Fairview, Goleta, Cal. 93017. 85 employees. 65 cars produced in 1977.

CUSTOCA **Austria**

Proprietor: G. Höller. Head office and works: 8714 Kraubath/Mur 55.

DACIA - see RÉGIE NATIONALE DES USINES RENAULT

DAIHATSU KOGYO COMPANY Ltd **Japan**

Established in 1907 as Hatsudoki Seizo Kabushiki Kaisha, assumed title of Daihatsu Kogyo Co. Ltd in 1951. Now consists of Daihatsu Motor Co. Ltd and Daihatsu Motor Sales Co. Ltd, and belongs to Toyota Group. Chairman: M. Yamamoto. President: S. Ohhara. Senior Managing. Directors: T. Eguchi, A. Makino, J. Ono. Head office and works: 1-1 Daihatsu-cho, Ikeda-shi, Osaka. Press office: Daihatsu Motor Sales Co. Ltd, 2-7 Ninonbashi-Honcho, Chuoku, Tokyo. 8,063 employees. 900,030 vehicles produced in 1977. Production of 4-wheeled vehicles begun in 1958. Most important models: Compagno Station Wagon (1963); Compagno 800 Sedan (1964); Compagno Spider and Sedan (1965); Fellow 360 (1966); Consorte Berlina (1969); Fellow Max (1970): Charmant (1974); Charade (1977); Charade Runabout (1978).

MANUFACTURE IN OTHER COUNTRIES — **Indonesia:** P.T. Astra International Inc., Jl. Ir. H. Jaunda No. 22, Djakarta. **Portugal:** Assistauto Sociedade de Assistencia Tecnica de Automoveis Ltda, Avda. de Igreja, Lote 1278, 1.°-D Lisboa-5. **Singapore:** Sin Tien Seng PTE Ltd, 8 Hamilton Rd, Singapore 8. 880 vehicles produced outside Japan in 1977.

DAIMLER - see BL Ltd

DAIMLER-BENZ AG **Germany (Federal Republic)**

(Make: Mercedes-Benz)

Established in 1926 as a result of merger between Daimler-Motorengesellschaft and Benz & Cie; it is the best-known German manufacturer of highclass cars. Board of Directors: J. Zahn (chairman); G. Prinz, W. Breitschwerdt, H. Schmidt, W. Niefer, R. Osswald, H.C. Hoppe, E. Reuter (members). Head office and press office: Mercedes-Strasse 136, 7 Stuttgart. Works: as above, Sindelfingen, Mannheim, Gaggenau, Berlin-Marienfelde, Düsseldorf, Bad Homburg, Wörth/Rhein. 131,807 employees. 401,255 cars produced in 1977. Most important models: Stuttgart 200, Mannheim (1926); Stuttgart 260, Mannheim 350 and Sport-Wagen SSK (1928); Grosser Mercedes (1930); Nürburg 500 (1931); 170 V (1935); 260 D, first Diesel car (1935); Grosser Mercedes (1938); 170 V (1946); 300 SL (1954); 190 SL 1955); 180 b/Db and 220 Sb (1959); 190 c/Dc and 300 Se (1961); 230 SL and 600 (1963); 250 (1966); 200, 220, 230, 250, 280 S, 280 SE, 300 SEL 6.3, 250 C, 250 SE (1968); 280 SE 3.5, 300 SEL 3.5 (1969); 350 SL, 450 SL (1971); 280 SE, 350 SE, 450 SE (1972); 240 D, 230/4 (1973); 240 D 3.0 (1974); 450 SEL 6.9 (1975); 200 D, 280 E(1976); 230 - 280 C, 280 CE (1977); 300 SD, 450 SLC, 240 - 300 TD, 230 - 250 T, 280 TE (1978). First places in numerous international competitions (1894-1955).

DAYTONA AUTOMOTIVE FIBERGLASS Inc. **USA**

Established in 1976. President: LaVerne Martincic. Vice President: M. Zimmerman. Production Manager and Treasurer: E. Kuhel. 15 employees.

DE TOMASO MODENA S.p.A. AUTOMOBILI **Italy**

Founded in 1959. President: A. de Tomaso. General Manager: A. Bertocchi. Head office, press office and works: v. Emilia Ovest 1250, Modena. 60 employees. 150 cars produced in 1977. Most important models: Berlinetta Vallelunga with Ford Cortina 1500 engine (two-seater). Sport Prototype 5 litre (1965); Mangusta with V8 4700 engine (1966); Pantera with V8 5700 engine, 310 hp (1970); Deauville 4-door with 5700 engine (1971); Longchamp 2 + 2 with V8 5700 engine (1973).

DODGE - see CHRYSLER CORPORATION, CHRYSLER CORPORATION DO BRASIL, CHRYSLER FEVRE ARGENTINA SAIC

Dr. Ing. h.c. F. PORSCHE A.G. **Germany (Federal Republic)**

Founded in 1948. Owned by Porsche Holding Co. (co-chairmen: F. Porsche, L. Piëch). Managing Directors: E. Fuhrmann, H. Branitzki, L.R. Schmidt, H. Bott, K. Kalkbrenner, H. Kurtz. Head office and press office: Porschestr. 42, 7 Stuttgart-Zuffenhausen. Works: Schwieberdingerstr., 7 Stuttgart-Zuffenhausen. 4,970 employees. 36,130 cars produced in 1977. Most important models: type 356/1100, 1300, 1300 S, 1500 S (1950-1955); 356 A/1300, 1300 S, 1600, 1600 S, Carrera (1955-1959); 356 B/1600, 1600 S, 1600 S-90, Carrera (1959-1963); 356 C/1600 C, 1600 SC (1963-1965); 911, 912 (1965-1966); 911, 911 S, 912 (1967); 911 T, S, 912 (1968); 911 T, E, S, Carrera (1969-1976). 924, Turbo (1975); 928 (1977). First places in numerous international competitions: Le Mans 24 hour with 1100 Coupé (1951), Sebring (1958-59), European Mountain Championship (1960-68), Targa Florio and Nürburgring (1959-1967-68-69-70-73), Constructors' Cup for F2 cars (1960), European Rally Championship with Carrera (1961). GT World Championship up to 2000 cc (1962-63-64-65), World Cup for speed and endurance European Touring Car Trophy, 32 national championships. Overall wins in Le Mans 24 hours (1970-71-76-77), Rallye Monte Carlo winners (1968-69-70), International Rallye Championship (1968-69-70), International Grand Touring Car Championship and International Manufacturers Championship (1969-70-71-76-77).

DUESENBERG **USA**

The company started building cars in 1970. After extensive reorganization in 1972-73 under the direction and ownership of E.W. Rose the company started a program of increased production. Head office, press office and works: 604 1/2 Manchester Terrace, Inglewood, Cal. 90301. 25 employecs. 15 cars produced in 1977.

DUESENBERG BROS. Inc. **USA**

President: H. Duesenberg. Vice President: K.W. Duesenberg. Head office, press office and works: 888 Tower Rd, Mundelein, Illinois 60060.

DUTTON SPORTS Ltd **Great Britain**

First Dutton built in 1968. Chairman and Managing Director: T. Dutton-Woolley. Head office, press office and works: Newcroft Tangmere, West Sussex, POZO 6HB, 8 employees. 201 cars produced in 1977. Most important models: B Type (1971); B plus (1974); Malaga and Cantera (1975).

ELEGANT MOTORS Inc. **USA**

Founded in 1971. Owner: D.O. Amy. Head office and press office: P.O.B. 20188, Indianapolis Ind. 46220. Works: 5335 Winthrop St, Indianapolis, Ind. 46220, 10 employees.

ELITE ENTERPRISES Inc. **USA**

Established in 1969. President: G.W. Knapp. Head office, works: 690 E. 3rd St., Cokato, Minn. 55321. Press office: 210 E. 3rd St, Cokato, Minn. 55321. 8 employees. 95 cars produced in 1977.

EL-KG BUGATTIBAU **Germany (Federal Republic)**

Head office and works: Hanauer Str. 51, 6360 Friedberg (Hessen) 1.

EL-NASR AUTOMOTIVE MANUFACTURING COMPANY **Egypt**

Founded in 1959. Directors: A. Gazarin, A. Shawky, O. Amin. Head office and works: Wadi-Hof, Helwan. Press office: 1081 Cornish El-Nil St. Cairo.

ENNEZETA S.d.f. **Italy**

Proprietors: R. Negri, M. Zanisi. Head office, press office and works: v. Einaudi 1, 20037 Paderno Dugnano, Milan.

EXCALIBUR AUTOMOBILE CORPORATION **USA**

Founded in 1964 as SS Automobiles Inc. Present title since 1976. President: D.B. Stevens. Executive Vice-President: W.C. Stevens. Head office and works: 1735 South 106th St, Milwaukee, Wisc. 53214. 90 employees. 250 cars produced in 1977. Models: Roadster SS, Phaeton SS.

FABRYKA SAMOCHODÓW MALOLITRAZOWYCH **Poland**

(Makes: Fiat 126, Syrena)

Founded in 1972. State-owned company. Director: R. Wosatka. Press office: ul. Stalingradzka 50, Warsaw. Works: Bielsko-Biala. 180 cars produced in 1978.

FABRYKA SAMOCHODÓW OSOBOWYCH **Poland**

(Make: Polski-Fiat)

Founded in 1949. State-owned Company. Chairman: J. Bielecki. Vice-Presidents: M. Karwas, S. Tyminski, Z. Sokalski, W. Komendarek, J. Burchard, Z. Chorazy, E. Pietrzak. Head office, press office and works: ul. Stalingradzka 50, Warsaw. 42,000 employees. About 127,000 cars produced in 1977. Most important models: Warszawa 223 and 224 (1964); Syrena 104 (1958); Polski-Fiat 125 P (1968). Entries in Rallies (Monte Carlo, Acropolis, Jadransky, Semperit, Peace and Friedship, etc.).

FAIRTHORPE Ltd **Great Britain**

Founded in 1957. Proprietor: D.C.T. Bennett. General Manager: T. Bennett. Head office: Deepwood House, Farnham Royal, Bucks. Press office and works: Denham Green Lane, Denham, Bucks. Most important models: Electron, Zeta, Mk VI EM, TXI, TX-GT, TX-S, TX-SS.

FELBER - see HAUTE PERFORMANCE MORGES

FERRARI S.p.A. **Italy**

Founded in 1929 as Scuderia Ferrari, became Società Auto-Avio Costruzioni Ferrari in 1940 and Ferrari S.p.A.-SEFAC in 1960. Since 1-7-1969, Fiat has been associated on joint venture basis and company has used its present title. Its name is bound up with superb technical achievements in field of racing and GT cars. Hon. President: E. Ferrari. President: N. Tufarelli. Managing Director: G. Sguazzini. General Manager: P. Fusaro. Directors: L. Montezemolo, C. Pelloni, S. Pininfarina, P. Lardi. Head office: vl. Trento Trieste 31, 41100 Modena. Press. office and works: v. Abetone Inferiore 2. 41053 Maranello (Modena). 1,350 employees (including Scaglietti, Modena). Over 2,000 cars produced in 1978. Most important GT models: 125 (1947); 166 inter (1949); 340 America (1952); 250 GT, V12 250 GT, Superfast (1961); 275 GTB 4 Berlinetta (1963); Dino 206 GT Berlinetta, 365 Coupé GT 2+2 (1967): 365 GTB 4 Berlinetta, 246 GT Dino (1969); 308 GTB (1975). Entries and wins in various world competitions and championships. 22 times world champion.

FIAT (Brazil) - see FIAT S.p.A.

FIAT (Uruguay) - see FIAT S.p.A.

FIAT S.p.A. **Italy**

President: G. Agnelli. Vice President and Managing Director: U. Agnelli. Managing Directors: C. Romiti, N. Tufarelli. Founded in July 1899 as Società Anonima Fabbrica Italiana di Automobili Torino. With the statutary modification of the shareholders' meeting in 1918, it assumed the title Fiat written either with capital or small letters. In 1968, FIAT incorporated Autobianchi which is still produced as separate make. In 1969 it took over Lancia and acquired 50% of Ferrari shares and in 1971 took over Abarth. In 1976, the reorganisation of the Fiat Group was practically completed. The new Fiat Holding is a structure in which all the sectors are now organized with their own design, production and marketing responsibilities, some of them as individual legal entities and other with Fiat S.p.A. but with similar management autonomy. Among these is Fiat Auto S.p.A. (incorporating Lancia-Autobianchi) Head office: c.so Agnelli 200, Turin. Press office: c.so Marconi 10, 10125 Turin. Works: Mirafiori, Rivalta, Lingotto (Turin), Vado Ligure, Termoli, Villar Perosa, Cassino, Florence, Bari. President: B. Beccaria. Vice-Presidents: U. Agnelli, C. Romiti. Managing Director: V. Ghidella. 151,540 employees. 1,182,800 cars produced in 1978. Most important models: Fiat 3½ HP (1899-1900); 6 HP and 8 HP, 12 HP, 24-32 HP (1900-04); 16-24 HP (1903-04); Brevetti e 60 HP (1905-09); 18-24 (1908); Fiacre mod. 1 (1908-10); Fiat 1,2,3,4,5, (1910-18); Zero e 3 ter (1912-15); 2B e 3A (1912-21); 70 (1915-20); 501 (1919-26); 505 and 510 (1919-25); Superflat (1921-22); 519 (1922-24); 502 (1923-26); 509 (1925-27); 503 and 507 (1926-27); 512 (1926-28); 520 (1927-29); 521 (1928-31); 525 (1928-29); 525 S (1929-31); 514 and 514 MM (1929-32); 515, 522 C and 524 C (1931-34); 508 Balilla and 508 S Balilla Sport (1932-37); 518 Ardita (1933-38); 527 Ardita 2500 (1934-36); 1500 (1935-48); 500 (1936-48); 508 C Balilla 1100 (1937-39); 2800 (1938-44); 1100 (1939-48); 500 B and Giardiniera (1948-49); 1100 B and 1500 D (1948-49); 1500 E (1949-50); 1100 E (1949-53); 500 C (1949-54); 500 C Giardiniera (1949-52); 1100 ES (1950-51); 1400, 1400 A and 1400 B (1950-58); 500 C Belvedere (1951-55); 1900 A and 1900 B (1952-58); 8V (1952-54); Nuova 1100 and Nuova 1100 Familiare (1953-56); 1100 TV (1953-56); 600 (1955-60); 1100/103 E (1956-57); Nuova 500 Trasformabile (1957-60); 1100/103 D (1957-60); Nuova 500 Sport (1958-60); 1200 Gran Luce (1957-60); 1200 Trasformabile (1958-59); 1100/103 H (1959-60); 1800 and 1800 Familiare (1959-61); 1100 Special (1960-62); 500 D (1960-65); 600 D Multipla, 500 Giardiniera (1960-68); 1300, 1500, 1300 Familiare, 2300 Coupé, 2300 S Coupé (1961-68); 1600 S Cabriolet (1962-66); 850 (1964-71); 124 and 124 Sport Spider (1966); Dino Spider (1966); 125, Dino Coupé, 124 Sport Coupé, 850 Idroconvert (1967); 850 Special, Sport Coupé, Sport Spider, 500 L, 124 Special, 125 Special (1968); 128, 128 Familiare, 124 Sport Coupé 1600, 124 Sport Spider 1600, Dino Coupé 2400, Dino Spider 2400, 130 (1969); 124 Special T (1970); 127, 128 Rally, 128 Coupé, 130 3200, 130 Coupé (1971); 126, 127 3 Porte, X 1/9, 124 Spider Rally, 124 Coupé e Spider 1600 e 1800, 132 (1972); 126 Tetto Apribile, 132 GLS, 128 Special, 127 Special, 131 Mirafiori (1974); 128 3P (1975); 126 Personal (1976); 132 1600-2000, 127 900-1050 CL (1972). It has been entering competitions since 1900, when true racing car was not yet born. First national wins, followed by many others, in Automobile Tour of Italy with 6-8 HP, a car with two horizontal rear cylinders. Since 1904 numerous first places in international field. In 1927 officially retired from motor racing. Since 1970 works competition in rallies. In 1977 and 1978 World Rally Championship with Fiat 131 Abarth.

MANUFACTURE AND ASSEMBLY IN OTHER COUNTRIES — **Argentina:** Fiat Concord S.A.I.C. (affiliated company) Cerrito 740, Buenos Aires (manuf. 600, 128, 125). **Brazil:** Fiat Automoveis (affiliated company), Avda São Luiz 50, 28º Andar, São Paulo (manuf. 147). **Chile:** Fiat Chile S.A. (affiliated company), Carmen 8, Santiago (assem. 600, 125). **Colombia:** Compania Colombiana Automotriz S.A. (associated company), Calle 13 n. 38-54, Bogotà (asem. 128, 125). **Costa Rica:** S.A.V.A. (licensee company), Apdo 10042, San José (assem. 131, 127). **Egypt:** El-Nasr Automotive Mfg Co. Ltd (licensee company), Wadi-Hof, Helwan, Cairo (assem. 128, 131, Polmot 125). **Eire:** Fiat Ireland Ltd (affiliated company), Industrial Garden Estate, Chapelizod, Dublin (assem. 127, 128). **Indonesia:** Daha Motors (licensee company), Medan Merkeda Selatan 2, Djakarta (assem. 131, 127, 132 S). **Malaysia:** Sharikat Fiat Distributors (licensee company), Tanglin Rd. 99/101, Singapore (assem. 127, 128, 131, 132). **Morocco:** Somaca (associated company), km 12 Autoroute de Rabat, Casablanca (assem. 127, 131, 132). **New Zealand:** Torino Motors Ltd (licensee company), 19/29 Nelson St, Auckland (assem. 128). **Poland:** Pol-Mot (licensee company), Stalingradzka 23, Warszawa (manuf. 126, 125 P). **Portugal:** Fiat Portuguesa Sarl (affiliated company), Av. Eng. Duarte Pacheco 15, Lisbon (assem. 127, 128, 131). **South Africa:** Fiat South Africa Pty Ltd, 2 Bosworth St. Alrode Extension, Alberton (assem. 128, 131, 132). **Spain:** Seat (associated company), av. del Generalisimo 146, Madrid (manuf. 133, 127, 128 3P, 1200/1400 Sport, 124, 131, 132). **Thailand:** Karnasuta General Assembly Co. (licensee company), P.O.B. 1421, Bangkok (assem. 128, 131, 132 S). **Turkey:** Tofas (associated company), K. 57 Mecidiyekoy, Istanbul (manuf. 131). **Uruguay:** Ayax S.A. (licensee company), Av. Rondeau 1751, Montevideo (assem. 125, 600, 128); Mar y Sierra (concessionaire), 8 de Octubre 3381, Montevideo (assem. 125). **Venezuela:** Fiav (associated company), Alcabala de Candelaria à Urapal 8, Caracas (assem. 131, 132). **Yugoslavia:** Zavodi Crvena Zastava (associated company), Span, Boraca 2, Kragujevac (manuf. Zastava 750, 128, 1300, 1500, 125 PZ, 126 P, 132 GLS). **Zambia:** Livingstone Motor Assemblers Ltd (associated company), P.O.B. 2718, Lusaka (assem. 127, 128, 131, 132 S). 900,000 cars produced outside Italy in 1978.

FIAT AUTOMOVEIS S.A.I.C. **Argentina**

Head office: Cerrito 740, Buenos Aires. Press office: as above; División Automoviles, Juramento 750, Buenos Aires. Works: Humberto I - 1001, Palomar - Pcia Buenos Aires. About 12,000 employees. 44,400 cars produced in 1977.

FIBERFAB - KAROSSERIE **Germany (Federal Republic)**

Proprietor: J. Kuhnle. Head office, press office and works: 7141 Auenstein b. Heilbronn. About 120 cars produced in 1976.

FORD BRASIL S.A. — Brazil

Established in 1919 merged with Willys Overland do Brasil. President and General Manager: R.C. Graham. Directors: A.S. Kuchta, V.J. Trivison, J.P. Dias, N. Chiaparini, W.F. Paul, R.B. Stevenson, M. Borghetti. Head office and press office: Av. Rudge Ramos 1501, São Bernardo do Campo. Works: Av. Henry Ford 1787, São Paulo; Av. do Taboão 899, São Bernardo do Campo, Parque das Indústrias, Tambaté, SP; Av. Henry Ford 17, Osasco, SP. 21,000 employees. About 134,000 vehicles produced in 1977. Most important models: Ford T (1924); Willys Jeep (1954); Rural Jeep (1958); Renault Dauphine (1959); Aero Willys (1960); Itamaraty (1965); Ford Galaxie 500 (1967); Corcel Sedan and Ford LTD Landau (1968); Corcel Coupé (1969); Corcel Belina Station Wagon (1970); Maverick (1973); Corcel II, Corcel II Belina (1977). Entries in numerous competitions from 1962 to 1968. Brazilian Makers Championship in 1972-73 with Corcel. Brazilian Touring Car Championship (Group 1) in 1973-74 with Maverick. Brazilian Makers Championship with Avallone-Ford in 1974 and with Hollywood-Berta-Ford in 1975. Formula Ford-Corcel main sponsor in 1974-75-76-77-78.

FORD MOTOR ARGENTINA S.A. — Argentina

Incorporated 1959. President: J.M. Courad. Head office and press office: cc Central 696, Buenos Aires. Works: Pacheco. 6,520 employees. 36,759 cars produced in 1977.

FORD MOTOR COMPANY — USA

(Makes: Ford, Lincoln, Mercury)

Founded in 1903, is the second largest of the American motor manufacturers. Chairman and Chief Executive Officer: Henry Ford II. Vice-Chairman and President: P. Caldwell. Executive Vice-President International Automotive Operations: D.E. Petersen. Executive Vice-President North American Automotive Operations. W.O. Bourke. Components include Ford Division (300 Renaissance Center, P.O.B. 43303, Detroit, Mich. 48243. Vice-President and General Manager W.S. Walla) and Lincoln-Mercury Division (300 Renaissance Centre, P.O.B. 43322, Detroit, Mich. 48243. Vice-President and General Manager W.G. Oben). World headquarters: The American Rd, Dearborn, Mich. Assembly plants: Atlanta, Ga.: Chicago, Ill.; Dearborn Wayne (2) and Wixom, Mich.; Kansas City and St. Louis, Mo.; Lorain and Avon Lake, Ohio; Los Angeles and San José, Calif.; Louisville, Ky. (2); Mahwah and Metuchen, N.J.; Norfolk, Va.; St. Paul, Minn. 253,000 employees. 2,559,438 cars produced in 1977.

MANUFACTURE AND ASSEMBLY IN OTHER COUNTRIES (excluding models of Ford Motor Company Ltd, Great Britain, of Ford Motor Company of Canada Ltd, Canada, of Ford Werke AG, Germany, of Ford Brasil S.A., Brazil and of Ford Motor Company of Australia Ltd, Australia) — **Argentina:** Ford Motor Argentina S.A. (subsidiary), C.C. Central 696, Buenos Aires 32/1 (manuf. and assem. Fairlane, Falcon, Taunus). **Ireland:** Henry Ford & Sons Ltd (subsidiary), Marina Cork (assem. Cortina, Escort, Capri, Granada, Fiesta). **Mexico:** Ford Motor Co. Branch S.A. (subsidiary), Apdo 39 bis, Mexico City (manuf. and assem. Ford, Fairmont, LTD, Maverick, Mustang). **Netherlands:** Ford Nederland N.V. (subsidiary), Hemweg 201, Postbus 795, Amsterdam (assem. Fiesta, Taunus, Capri, Granada, Escort). **New Zealand:** Ford Motor Co. of New Zealand Ltd (subsidiary), P.O.B. 30012. Lower Hutt (assem. Falcon, Escort, Cortina, Fairlane, LTD). **Portugal:** Ford Lusitana Sarl (subsidiary), Apdo 2248 R. Rosa/Aranjo 2, Lisbon (assem. Cortina, Escort). **Singapore:** Ford Motor Co. Private Ltd (subsidiary), P.O.B. 4047, Bukit Timah, Singapore (assem. Cortina, Escort). **Spain:** Ford Espana S.A. (subsidiary), Edificio Cuzco III/Avda Generalisimo 59, Madrid 16 (manuf. and assem. Fiesta). **South Africa:** Ford Motor Co. of South Africa (Pty) Ltd (subsidiary), P.O.B. 788, Port Elizabeth (assem. Granada, Cortina, Fairlane, Escort). **Taiwan:** Ford Lio Ho Motor Co. Ltd (subsidiary). Taipei (assem. Escort, Cortina, Granada). **Uruguay:** Ford (Uruguay) S.A. (subsidiary), C.C. 296, Montevideo (assem. Falcon, Escort). **Venezuela:** Ford Motor de Venezuela S.A. (subsidiary), Apdo 61131 del Este, Caracas (assem. Fairlane, Ford, Fairmont). 1,744,900 cars produced outside USA in 1977.

FORD MOTOR COMPANY Ltd — Great Britain

Founded in 1911, owned by Ford Motor Company USA, it had its first head office at Trafford Park (Manchester). In 1925, construction of Dagenham works was begun where production was started in 1931. Chairman and Managing Director: Sir Terence Beckett. Head office and press office: Eagle Way, Warley Brentwood, Essex. Works: Dagenham, Essex; Halewood, nr. Liverpool, and others. 70,000 employees. 406,923 cars produced in 1977. Most important models: 8 hp "Y", 10 hp "C", 14.9 hp "B.F.", 24 hp "B", 30 hp "V8" (all prior to 2nd World War); Prefect (1938); Anglia (1939); Pilot (1947); Consul, Zephyr (1951); Anglia 100E, Popular, Zodiac (1953); Mk II Consul, Zephyr, Zodiac 1956); Anglia 105E (1959); Consul Classic 315, Capri (1961); Mk III Zephyr, Zodiac, Cortina (1962); Corsair (1963); Mk IV Zephyr, Zodiac (1966); Mk II Cortina (1966); Escort (1968); Capri (1969); Mk III Cortina (1970); Granada (1972); Fiesta (1977). Entries and wins in numerous competitions.

ASSEMBLY IN OTHER COUNTRIES — **Costa Rica:** Anglofores Ltda. (concessionaire), Apdo 1768, San José (assem. Escort). **Eire:** Henry Ford and Son Ltd (associated company), Cork (assem. Cortina). **Holland:** N.V. Nederlandsche Ford Automobiel Fabriek (associated company), P.O.B. 795, Amsterdam (assem. Cortina). **Israel:** Palestina Automobile Corp. Ltd (concessionaire), P.O.B. 975, Tel Aviv (assem. Escort). **Korea:** Hyundai Motor Co. (concessionaire), 55 Chrongro 3KA, Seoul (assem. Cortina). **Malaysia:** Associated Motor Industries, Malaysian Sdn Bhd (concessionaire), 109 Jalan Pudu, Kuala Lumpur (assem. Cortina, Escort). **New Zealand:** Ford Motor Co. of New Zealand Ltd (associated company), P.O.B. 30012, Lower Hutt (assem. Escort, Cortina, Zephyr, Zodiac). **Pakistan:** Ali Autos Ltd (concessionaire), P.O.B. 4206, Karachi (assem. Cortina). **Peru:** Ford Motor Co. Perú S.A. (associated company), Apdo 4130, Lima (assem. Escort). **Philippines:** Ford Philipp. Inc. (associated company), P.O.B. 415, Makati Commercial Centre, Makati Rizal (assem. Cortina, Escort). **Portugal:** Ford Lusitana (associated company), Apdo 2248, R. Rosa Arajo 2, Lisbon (assem. Escort, Cortina). **Singapore:** Ford Motor Co. Private Ltd (associated company), P.O.B. 4047, Bukit Timah, Singapore (assem. Cortina, Escort, Capri). **South Africa:** Ford Motor Co. of South Africa (Pty) Ltd (associated company), P.O.B. 788, Port Elizabeth (assem. Escort, Cortina, Capri). **Venezuela:** Ford Motor Co. Venezuela S.A. (associated company), Apdo 61131 Del Este, Caracas (assem. Cortina). 59,230 cars produced outside U.K. in 1977.

FORD MOTOR COMPANY OF AUSTRALIA Ltd — Australia

Founded in 1925. Directors: B.S. Inglis, R.F. Bennett, B.L. Burton, W.L. Dise, F.A. Erdman, E.T. Gardner, W.F. Grandsden, K.A. Horner, D.C. Jacobi, R.M. Lamb, R.J. Marshall, J. Sagovac, E.A. Witts. Head office and press office: Private Bag, 6 Campbellfield, Victoria 3061 Works: Broadmeadows, Campbellfield, Geelong, Victoria. 14,738 employees. 129,617 cars produced in 1977.

FORD MOTOR COMPANY OF CANADA Ltd — Canada

(Makes: Ford, Mercury)

Founded in 1904 in Windsor, Ont. Has always built a large percentage of all cars and trucks produced by Canadian automotive industry. President and Chief Executive Officer: R.F. Bennett. Vice-Presidents: K. Hallsworth, W. Mitchell, W.L. Hawkins, K.W. Harrigan, C.J. Roberts, Head office and press office: The Canadian Road, Oakville, Ont. 16J 5E4. Works: Oakville, St. Thomas, Windsor, Niagara Falls, Ont. 17,900 employees. 319,000 cars produced in 1977.

FORD MOTOR COMPANY OF SOUTH AFRICA — South Africa

Established in 1923. Now leader in South African motor industry. Managing Director: D.B. Pitt. Directors: N.G. Cohen, J.C. Dill, F.H. Ferreira, D.M. Morris, W.F. Rautenbach, G. Simpson. Head office and press office: 187 Main St., Port Elizabeth, 6001. Works: Neave Township, Struandale, Deal Party (Port Elizabeth). 5,581 employees. 27,555 cars produced in 1977. Company competes in rallying and the « works » Escorts were champions in 1977 and 1978.

FORD WERKE AG — Germany (Federal Republic)

Founded in 1925. Owned by Ford Motor Company USA. Chairman and Managing Director: P. Weiher. Directors: P.A. Guckel, H. Dederichs, H.W. Gäb, H. Bergemann, H.J. Lehmann, W. Inden, W. Ebers, A. Langer, D.M. Schultz, D. Uilsperger. Head office and press office: Ottoplatz 2, Köln-Deutz. Works: Henry Ford-Strasse 1, Köln-Niehl, Saarlouis. 56,332 employees. 878,468 cars produced in 1977. Most important models: Köln 1 l, Rheinland 3 l (1933); Eifel 1.2 l (1935); Taunus (1938); Taunus (since 1948); 12M (1952); 15M (1955); 17M (1960); 12M (1962); 17M and 20M (1964); 12M and 15M (1966); 17M, 20M and 20M 2.3 l (1967); Escort (1968); Capri (1969); Taunus (1970); Consul, Granada (1972); Capri II (1974); Escort (1975); Fiesta (1976); Granada (1978). Winner of East African Safari in 1969. European Saloon Car Championship 1971, 1972, 1974.

MANUFACTURE AND ASSEMBLY IN OTHER COUNTRIES — **Belgium:** Ford Werke AG Fabrieken (subsidiary), Genk. **South Africa:** Ford Motor Co. of South Africa Pty (associated company), P.O.B. 788, Port Elizabeth (assem. Granada). **Taiwan:** Ford Lio Ho Motors Co. Ltd, Taipei (asem. Granada). 3,975 cars assembled outside F.R. in 1977 (South Africa and Taiwan).

FUJI HEAVY INDUSTRIES Ltd — Japan

(Make: Subaru)

A part of former Nakajima Aircraft Co. Reorganized after the end of World War II and named Fuji Sangyo Co. in August 1945. Disbanded and divided into 12 smaller companies by order of occupying Allied Forces in 1950. Five of smaller companies reunited as Fuji Heavy Industries Ltd in 1953. Manufacturer of cars and commercial vehicles, aircraft and industrial power units. Joined Nissan Group in 1968. Member of Nissan Group. Chairman: E. Ohhara. President: S. Sasaki. Executive Vice President: N. Sakata. Senior Managing Directors: S. Nagashima, S. Irie. Managing Directors: K. Kawabata, K. Ogawa, I. Shibuya. Y. Suzuki, H. Yamamoto. Head office and press office: 1-7-2 Subaru Bldg, Nishi-Shinjuku, Shinjukuku, Tokyo. Works: Gumma, 10-1 Higashi Hon-cho, Ohta City; Mitaka, 3-9-6 Oshawa, Mitakashi. 13,467 employees. 223,492 vehicles produced in 1977. Most important models: 360 Sedan (1958); 1000 (1966); 1000 Sport (1967); 1300 G, R2 (1970); Leone (1971).

GAZ - GORKOVSKI AVTOMOBILNY ZAVOD — USSR

Press office: Avtoexport, Ul. Volkhonka 14, Moscow 119902. Works: Gorki. About 70,000 cars produced in 1976.

GENERAL MOTORS CORPORATION — USA

(Makes: Buick, Cadillac, Chevrolet, Oldsmobile, Pontiac)

Founded in 1908, is largest motor manufacturer in world with production range extending from the most economical and popular cars to the most costly. Chairman: T.A. Murphy. President: E.M. Estes. Executive Vice-Presidents: J.F. McDonald, R.R. Jensen, H.L. Kehrl, R.B. Smith. GM has brought together five American motor manufacturing factories, transforming them into following divisions: Buick Motor Division (902 East Hamilton Ave, Flint, Mich. 48550), General Manager D.H. McPherson, 19,250 employees, 801,202 cars produced in 1977; Cadillac Motor Car Division (2860 Clark Ave, Detroit, Mich. 48232), General Manager E.C. Kennard, 11,000 employees, 369,254 cars produced in 1977; Chevrolet Motor Division (3044 West Grand Blvd, Detroit, Mich. 48202), General Manager R.D. Lund, 97,500 employees, 2,133,394 cars produced in 1977; Oldsmobile Division (920 Townsend St, Lansing, Mich. 48921), General Manager R.J. Cook, 17,000 employees, 1,079,842 cars produced in 1977; Pontiac Motor Division (One Pontiac Plaza, Pontiac, Mich. 48053), General Manager R.C. Stempel, 17,400 employees, 875,955 cars produced in 1977. GM also owns General Motors - Holden's Pty Ltd (Australia), Adam Opel AG (Germany) and Vauxhall Motors Ltd (Great Britain). Head Office: 3044 West Grand Blvd, Detroit, Mich. 48202.

MANUFACTURE AND ASSEMBLY IN OTHER COUNTRIES (excluding: non-American GM makes) — **Belgium:** GM Continental (subsidiary), 75 Norderlaan, Antwerp (assem. imported vehicles). **Brazil:** GM do Brasil S.A. (subsidiary), Avda Goias 1805, Rio de Janeiro (manuf. Chevrolet Chevette, Opala). **Chile:** GM Chile S.A. (subsidiary), Piloto Lazo 99, P.O.B. 14370, Santiago (assem. imported vehicles). **Iran:** GM Joran Ltd. (associated company), P.O. Box 8-6173, Teheran (manuf. Chevrolet Royale). **Kenya:** GM Kenya Ltd (associated company), P.O.B. 30527, Nairobi (assem. imported vehicles). **Malaysia:** GM Malaysia SDN.BHD (subsidiary). Batu Dua. Jalan Tampoi. P.O. Box 204, Johone Bahru (manuf. Harimau). **Mexico:** G.M. de Mexico S.A. de C.V. (subsidiary), Av. Ejercito Nacional 843, Mexico 59F (manuf. Chevrolet). **New Zealand:** GM New Zealand, Ltd (subsidiary), Trentham Assembly Plant, Alexander Rd, Upper Hutt (assem. imported vehicles). **Philippines:** GM Philippines Inc. (subsidiary), P.O. Box 1497 MCC, Makati, Rizal 3117 (manuf. BTV vehicles). **Portugal:** GM de Portugal Ltda (subsidiary), Av. Marechal Gomes da Costa 3, Lisbon 6 (assem. imported vehicles). **South Africa:** GM South African (Pty) Ltd (subsidiary, Kempston Rd, P.O.B. 1137, Port Elizabeth (manuf. Chevrolet; assem. imported vehicles). **Thailand:** Bangchan General Assembly Co. Ltd (associated company), 4th Floor, Cathay Trust Bldg, 1016 Rama IV Rd, Bangkok (assem. imported vehicles). **Uruguay:** GM Uruguaya S.A. (subsidiary), Av. Sayago 1385, Montevideo (assem. imported vehicles). **Venezuela:** GM de Venezuela C.A. (subsidiary), Carapa, Carretera de Antimano, Caracas (assem. imported vehicles). **Zaire:** GM Zaire S.E.R.L. (subsidiary), Boulevard Patrice Lumumba, Kinshasa (assem. imported vehicles). Cars produced outside USA in 1977 1,595,975.

GENERAL MOTORS DO BRASIL — Brazil

(Make: Chevrolet)

Subsidiary of GM Corporation. Managing Director: J.J. Sanchez. Head office, press office and works: Avda Goiás 1805, São Caetano do Sul, São Paulo. 18,488 employees. 154,411 cars produced in 1977.

GENERAL MOTORS - HOLDEN'S Pty Ltd — Australia

Established in 1931 as result of merger between General Motors (Australia) Pty Ltd and Holden's Motor Body Builder Ltd. Affiliate of GM Corp. USA. Managing Director: C. Chapman. Head office and press office: 241 Salmon St, Fishermans Bend, Melbourne, Victoria. Works: as above; Dandenong, Victoria; Woodville, Elizabeth, S. Australia; Page-

wood, N.S.W., Acacia Ridge, Queensland. 21,255 employees. 140,269 cars produced in 1977.

ASSEMBLY IN OTHER COUNTRIES — **New Zealand:** GM New Zealand Ltd, Trentham Plant No. 1, Private Bag, Upper Hutt (assem. Sedan, Premier). **South Africa:** GM South African (Pty) Ltd, Kempston Rd, Port Elizabeth (assem. Sedan).

GENERAL MOTORS (Malaysia) - see GENERAL MOTORS CORPORATION

GENERAL MOTORS OF CANADA Ltd   Canada

(Make: Chevrolet, Pontiac)

Established in 1918 as result of merger between McLaughlin Motor Car Company and Chevrolet Motor Car Company. It is a wholly owned subsidiary of General Motors Corp. President and General Manager: F.A. Smith. Vice-President and General Manufacturing Manager: R.C. Walter. Vice-President and General Sales Manager: R.M. Colcomb. Vice-President and Finance Manager: W.R. Waugh. Vice-President and General Manager, Diesel Division: A. Grant Warner. Head office and press office: 215 William St. Oshawa, Ontario L1G IKZ. Works: as above, Ste. Therese, P.Q., St. Catharines, London, Windsor and Scarborough. 40,654 employees. 464,733 cars produced in 1977.

GENERAL MOTORS SOUTH AFRICAN (Pty) Ltd   South Africa

(Make: Chevrolet)

Founded in 1926. Managing Director: L.H. Wilking. Directors: K.P. Klayton, J.L. Fry, W.F. Kohl, C.R. von zur Gathen, J.B. Watson, R.J. Ironside, D. Martin, Jr. Head office and press office: Kempston Rd, Port Elizabeth. Works: as above; Aloes (Engine Plant), nr. Port Elizabeth. 4,516 employees. 16,675 cars produced in 1977.

GIANNINI AUTOMOBILI S.p.A.   Italy

Founded in 1920 as F.lli Giannini A. & D., it later became Giannini Automobili S.p.A. President and Managing Director: V. Polverelli. Head office, press office and works: v. Idrovore della Magliana 57, Rome. 35 employees. 1,500 cars produced in 1977. Most important models: 750 Berlinetta San Remo (1949); Fiat 750 TV and 850 GT (1963); 850 Coupé Gazzella, Fiat 500 TV and TVS, 590 GT and GTS (1964); Fiat Berlina 850 S, 850 SL and 950, Fiat Coupé 850 and 1000, Fiat 1300 Super and 1500 GL, Fiat 500 TVS Montecarlo (1965); Fiat 650 NP, 128 NPS (1970); 650 NPL, 650 NP Modena, 128 NP-S, 128 NP Rally (1972). It is engaged above all in producing variations of Fiat cars. Entries in various competitions and first places in category in various Italian championships.

GINETTA CARS Ltd   Great Britain

Founded in 1958. Chairman and Managing Director: K.R. Walklett. Directors: T.G. Walklett, D.J. Walklett, I.A. Walklett. Head office, press office and works: West End Works, Witham, Essex GM8 1BE. 18 employees. 46 cars produced in 1977. Most important model: G 21.

GREENWOOD WORLD HEADQUARTERS CORPORATION   USA

Division of American Custom Shop, Inc. Specializes in race cars. Frist Turbo Corvettes produced in 1975. President: R. Schuller. Head office, press office and works: 5035 Alexis Rd, Sylvania, Ohio 43560. 30 employees.

GROUP LOTUS CARS COMPANIES Ltd   Great Britain

Founded in 1952. Chairman: A.C.B. Chapman. Group Board: A.C.B. Chapman, F.R. Bushell, P.R. Kirwan-Taylor. Managing Director: M.J. Kimberley. Sales Director: R.G. Putnam. Head office, press office and works: Norwich, NR14 8EZ. 550 employees. 1,070 cars produced in 1977. Most important models: Mk Six (1952); Mk Eight, Mk Nine, Mk Ten, Elite (1957); Eleven (1960); Elan (1962); Cortina (1963); Elan + 2 (1967); Europa (1968); Elan Sprint, Elan + 2 'S' 130, Europa Twin Cam (1971); Europa Special (1972). Entries and first places in numerous international competitions with F1, F2, F3, F5 cars; seven F1 World Champion Constructors victories in last 10 years (Indianapolis, Le Mans, Monte Carlo GP, Pacific GP at Laguna Seca. etc.). May 1975 Elite design won European Don Safety Trophy.

GURGEL S.A INDUSTRIA E COMERCIO DE VEHICULOS   Brazil

Chairman and Managing Director: J.A.C. do Amaral Gurgel. Head office and works: Rod. Washington Luiz, km 171, Rio Claro 13500, S.P. Press office: Avda do Cursino 2518, Jardim de Saude, São Paulo. 300 employees. 1,334 cars produced in 1977.

HAUTE PERFORMANCE MORGES   Switzerland

(Make: Felber)

Founded in 1975. Proprietor: W.H. Felber. Special versions of high-class cars in small series. 42 cars produced in 1978. Head office, press office and works: route Suisse, Morges.

HINDUSTAN MOTORS Ltd   India

Founded in 1942. Chairman: B.M. Birla. Vice-Chairman: G.P. Birla. Directors: R.N. Mafatlal, B.P. Khaitan, G.D. Kothari, M.R. Damle, N.L. Hingorani, S.M. Ghosh, M.V. Arunachalam. Head office and press office: Birla Bldg, 9/1 R.N. Mukherjee Rd, Calcutta 1. Works: P.O. Hind Motor, Hooghly, West Bengal. Car production begun in 1951. About 16,000 employees. 28,000 cars produced in 1976. Most important models: Hindustan 10, Hindustan 14, Baby Hindustan, Landmaster (1954); Ambassador (1957); Ambassador Mk II (1963); Ambassador Mark III (1975).

HOLDEN - see GENERAL MOTORS - HOLDEN'S Pty Ltd

HONDA MOTOR COMPANY Ltd   Japan

Founded in 1949 as Honda Giyitsu Kenkunjo. Present title since 1948. Manufacturer and exporter of motorcycles from 50 to 750 cc, automobiles, trucks, portable generators, general-purpose engines, power tillers, water pumps and outboard motors. President: K. Kawashima. Executive Vice-Presidents: K. Kawashima, M. Nishida. Senior Managing Directors: H. Sugiura, S. Shinomiya, N. Okamura, M. Suzuki. Directors and advisors: S. Honda (founder), T. Fujisawa (cofounder). Head office and press office: 6-27-8 Jingumae, Shibuyaku, Tokyo, Japan 150. Works: Saitama, 8-1 Honcho, Wako-shi, Saitama-ken; Suzuka, 1907 Mirata-cho, Suzuka-shi, Mie-ken; Hamamatsu, 34 Oi-machi, Hamamatsushi, Shizuoka-ken; Sayama, 1-10 Shinsayama, Sayama-shi, Saltama-ken. 21,715 employees including Honda R & D Co. 581,799 vehicles produced in 1977. Models: Sports 500 (1962); Sports 600 (1964); L 700, L 800 (1966); N360, LN360 (1967); N600 (1968); 1300 (1969); 1300 Coupé, NIII Sedan, Z Coupé (1970); Life (1971); Civic (1972); Civic CVCC 4-dr. Sedan (1973); Accord (1976). Wins in F1 racings: Mexican GP (1965), Italian GP (1967). French GP and GP USA (1968) and entries in F1, F2, GP Racings.

MANUFACTURE AND ASSEMBLY IN OTHER COUNTRIES — **Costa Rica:** Coopesa (affiliated company), Anexo Aeroplierto, Jan St. Maria, Acajufla. **Indonesia:** P.T. Prospect Motor (associated company), Jt. Jossubarso, P.O.B. TPK 31, Djakarta. **Malaysia:** Kah Motor (associated company), 24-C Farqumar St, Penang. **New Zealand:** N.Z.M.C. (associated company), 89 Courtney Place, Wellington. **Portugal:** Santomar S.A. (associated company), Av. Casal Ribeiro, 46-C, Lisbon. **Taiwan:** San Yang Industries Co. Ltd (affiliated company), No. 124 Hsing-Ning Rd, Neihu, Taipei. 14,060 cars produced outside Japan in 1977.

HONGQI   China (People's Republic)

Public Relations office: China National Machinery Import & Export Corp., P.O.B. 49, Peking. Works: Chang-Chun, Kirin.

HYUNDAI MOTOR Co.   Korea

Founded in 1967. Chairman: Jung, Se Young. Vice-Chairman: Yun, Joo Won. Managing Director: Jun, Sung Won. General Manager: Shin, Hang Soo. Head office and press office: 140-2, Ke-Dong, Jong Ro-Ku, Seoul. Works: 700, Yang Jung-Dong, Ulsan. 10,000 employees. 30,000 cars produced in 1977. Most important models: Ford Cortina (1968); Pony Sedan (1976).

INTERMECCANICA - see AUTOMOBILI INTERMECCANICA

INTERNATIONAL HARVESTER INTERNATIONAL TRUCKS   USA

Founded in 1902. Principal products trucks, agricultural equipment, construction equipment and gas turbine engines sold in 168 countries. Chairman and Chief Executive Officer: Brooks McCormick. President and Chief Operating Officer: A.R. McCardell. President Truck Group: J.P. Kaine. World Headquarters: 401 North Michigan Avenue, Chicago, Illinois 60611. 93,160 employees worldwide. 129,656 trucks produced in 1977.

MANUFACTURE IN OTHER COUNTRIES — **Australia:** International Harvester Australia (subsidiary), Melbourne, Victoria. **Canada:** International Harvester Canada (subsidiary), Hamilton, Ontario. **Mexico:** International Harvester Mexico (subsidiary), Mexico City. **Philippines:** International Harvester MacLeod (subsidiary), Manila. **South Africa:** International Harvester S.A. (subsidiary), Johannesburg. **Turkey:** Turk Otomotiv Endustrileri A.S. (joint venture), Istanbul. **United Kingdom:** Sedan Diesel Vehicles Ltd (subsidiary), Oldham. **Venezuela:** Industria Venezolana de Maquinarias C.A. (joint venture), Caracas.

IRAN NATIONAL INDUSTRIAL MANUFACTURING Co. Ltd   Iran

(Make: Paykan)

General Manager: M. Khayyami. Head office, press office and works: Karay Rd., Teheran. 5,700 employees. About 100,000 cars produced in 1977.

ISUZU MOTORS Ltd   Japan

Established in 1937 as result of merger between Ishika-Wajima motor manufacturing factory, which held Wolseley manufacturing licence from 1918 to 1927, and Tokyo Gas & Electric, which began the manufacture of military trucks in 1916. Present title since 1949. In 1971, it became a joint venture company with G.M. Corp. with capital participation of 34.2% by the latter. Chairman: T. Aramaki. President: T. Okamoto. Executive Vice-Presidents: I. Uesugi, Y. Shimizu, H.V. Leonard Jr., T. Tsunoka. Senior Managing Directors: I. Iseki, K. Okumura, S. Beppu, K. Sano. Head office and press office: 22-10 Minami-oi, 6-chome, Shinagawa-ku, Tokyo. Works: Kawasaki, 25-1 Tonomachi 3-chome, Kawasaki City; Fujisawa, 8 Tsuchitana, Fujisawa City. 74,971 employees. 12,230 cars produced in 1977. Most important models: Bellett (1962); Bellett, Bellett Standard (1963); Florian (1967); 117 Coupé (1968); Bellett Gemini (1974).

JAGUAR - see BL Ltd

JEEP - see AMERICAN MOTORS CORPORATION

JOHN BRITTEN GARAGES Ltd   Great Britain

(Make: Arkley)

Founded in 1971. Proprietor: J. Britten. Head office, press office and works: Barnet Rd, Arkley, Barnet, Herts. 15 employees. 60 cars produced in 1977.

JOHNARD VINTAGE CAR REPAIRS Ltd   Great Britain

Specializes in the repair of vintage cars. Car production on limited scale started in January 1976. Directors: J.R. Guppy, D.S. Beck, A.C.A. Head office, press office and works: Blandford Heights, Shaftesbury Lane, Blandford Forum, Dorset. 6 employees. 12 cars produced in 1977.

KELMARK ENGINEERING, Inc.   USA

Established in 1969. President: R. Markham. Vice President and General Manager: R.R. Hendrick. Vice President Marketing: R. Holmes. Head office: 2209 Jolly Rd, Okemos, Mich. 48864. Press office: Kelmark Promotions, P.O. Box K, Okemos, Mich. 48864. Works: Holt, Mich. 50 employees. 500 cars produced in 1977. First GT produced in 1974.

KIA INDUSTRIAL Co. Ltd   Korea

Founded in 1944 as bicycle manufacturer, it became a public company in 1973 and production of passenger cars began in 1974. Chairman: Kim, San Moon. President: Kim, Myung Kee. Executive Managing Director: Kim, Sung Woon Hong, Bok Ryul. Head office: 8, Yang-dong, Choongku, Seoul. Press office: C.P.O.B. 833, Planning and Controlling Division, Seoul. Works: 781-1, Soha-ri, Seo-myun, Shiheung-kun, Kyung Kee-do. 4,500 employees. 10,548 cars produced in 1977. Models: Brisa 1000 (1974); Brisa 1300 (1976).

K.M.B. AUTOSPORTS Ltd   Great Britain

Directors: M.R. Smith, M.A. Fenton, P.W. Jelley. Head office: Finedon Sidings, Finedon, Northants. Press office and works: 228-230 Mill Rd, Wellingborough, Northants.

LAFER S.A. INDUSTRIA E COMERCIO   Brazil

Lafer S.A. Industria e Comercio is a Brazilian corporation controlled by the Lafer brothers, Samuel, Oscar and Percival. In October of 1972 entered the replicar field with the classic 1952 MG TD. A prototype appeared at the

1972 Brazilian Auto Show and the fibreglass car was shown at the 1974 Brazilian Auto Show. Head office and press office: Rua Lavapés 6, São Paulo. Works: Rua Garcia Lorca 301, Vila Paulicéia, São Bernardo do Campo, São Paulo. 350 cars produced in 1975.

LAMBORGHINI - see AUTOMOBILI FERRUCCIO LAMBORGHINI S.p.A.

LANCIA **Italy**

Founded in 1906, noted for production of extremely well-finished prestige cars. In 1969 taken over by the Fiat Group and in 1978 incorporated into Fiat Auto S.p.A. Head office and press office: v. Vincenzo Lancia 27, Turin. Works: as above; v. Caluso 50, Chivasso (Turin); Strada comunale, Verone (Vercelli). 13,000 employees. About 56,000 cars produced in 1978. Most important models: first car 14 hp (1907); Alfa, Dialfa (1908); Beta (1909); Gamma (1910); Delta, Didelta, Epsilon, Eta (1911); Theta (1913); Kappa (1919); Dikappa (1921); Trikappa (1922); Lambda (1923); Dilambda (1928); Artena, Astura (1931); Augusta (1933); Aprilia (1937); Ardea (1939); Aurelia (1950); Aurelia B20 (1951); Appia (1953); Flaminia (1957); Flavia (1960); Flavia Coupé and Convertible (1962); Flavia Sport, Fulvia (1963); Fulvia Coupé, Fulvia Sport (1965); Fulvia Coupé 1.3 HF (1966); Flavia 819 (1967); Fulvia Coupé 1.6 HF (1968); Flavia 2000 (1970); 2000 Berlina, 2000 Coupé (1971); Beta Berlina (1972); Beta Coupé (1973); Stratos (1974); Beta Spider, Beta HPE, Beta Monte Carlo (1975); Gamma, Coupé 1300, Gamma Coupé 1300 (1976).

ASSEMBLY IN OTHER COUNTRIES — **South Africa:** Trans-African Continental Motors Co. Pty Ltd (concessionaire), 174 Anderson St, Johannesburg (assem. Beta Coupé). **Thailand:** Yontrakit Motor Co., 12-14 Rong Huand Soi 5 Rd, Bangkok (assem. Beta Berlina, Beta Coupé).

LAWIL S.p.A. **Italy**

Founded in 1969. President and Managing Director: C. Lavezzarl. Head office, press office and works: v. Maretti 29, Varzi (Pavia). 50 employees. About 1200 cars produced in 1977.

LENHAM MOTOR COMPANY **Great Britain**

Founded in 1962. Incorporating Lenham Sports Car Ltd and The Vintage & Sports Cars Ltd. Directors: J.K. Booty, P.J. Rix, G. Allfrey. Head office, press office and works: 47 West St, Harrietsham 570, Kent. 15 employees. 12 cars produced in 1977. Championship 1600 cc GT cars in 1968.

LEYLAND MOTOR CORPORATION OF AUSTRALIA **Australia**

Founded in 1946 as Nuffield (Australia) Pty Ltd, in 1954 it became British Motor Corporation (BMC). In 1972 it launched fully-manufactured P. 76 but manufacture ended in December 1974. Corporation now assembles Mini-Moke for worldwide markets, also assembling trucks, Land Rover, buses and coaches. Managing Director: R.J. Hancock. Directors: J. Heaven, J. Lamb, J. Wallis, N. Prescott, A. Rae, K. Myler. Head office and press office: 332 Oxford Street, Bondi Junction, NSW. Works: 142 Cosgrove Rd, Enfield, NSW. 1,985 employees. 9,244 cars produced in 1977.

LINCOLN - see FORD MOTOR COMPANY

LOTUS - see GROUP LOTUS CARS COMPANIES Ltd

(THE) LYNX COMPANY **Great Britain**

It is a company formed to produced prototypes and low volume specialist performance cars. It offers a unique service since it has a direct involvment in all aspects of motor car design and development by working alongside its associated company, Lynx Engineering, which specializes in the restoration and development of performance cars concentrating mainly on Jaguars. Head office, press office and works: Station Rd, Northiam, Nr. Rye, Sussex. 10 employees. 20 kits and 18 complete cars produced in 1977.

MASERATI - see OFFICINE ALFIERI MASERATI S.p.A.

MATRA SPORTS **France**

Founded in 1932 as Deutch-Bonnet became René Bonnet in 1961. Present title since 1977. In 1968 a merger was decided with Engins Matra S.A. as "Motoring Division" of latter. President and Managing Director: J.L. Lagardère. Vice-President: S. Floirat. Head office: 4, rue de Presbourg, Paris 75008. Press office: av. Louis Bréguet, B.P.1, 78140 Velizy. Works: 1, av. Saint-Exupéry, 41000 Romorantin; 21 rue Paul Dauthier, 78140 Velizy. About 1,300 employees. 12,094 cars produced in 1977. Models: Deutch-Bonnet (1932-40); René Bonnet (1961-64); Matra-Bonnet (1965); Matra M530 (1966); Matra Simca "Bagheera" (1972); Bagheera Courrèges (1974); Bagheera S (1975); Bagheera S, X, Rancho (1977). Entries and wins in numerous competitions with F2 and F3 cars (Reims, Albi, Magny-Cours in 1965, Monaco, Rouen, GP de Monaco, Palmarès in 1966-67-68, Le Mans in 1972-73). World Champion F1 in 1969. Manufacturers world championship (3-litres Sport prototype) in 1972-73-74.

MAZDA - see TOYO KOGYO COMPANY Ltd

MERCEDES-BENZ - see DAIMLER-BENZ AG

MERCURY - see FORD MOTOR COMPANY and FORD MOTOR COMPANY OF CANADA Ltd

MG - see BL Ltd

MINI - see BL Ltd

MITSUBISHI MOTOR CORPORATION **Japan**

Established in October 1917 as Mitsubishi Shipbuilding & Engineering Co. Ltd, later changed its name to Mitsubishi Heavy Industries Ltd. After the Second World War it split into three companies under Enterprise Reorganization Law, but these again reunited in June 1964 as Mitsubishi Heavy Industries Ltd. Products include ships and other vessels, railway vehicles, aircraft, space equipment, missiles, atomic equipment, heavy machinery. The Automobile Division became an independent company in June 1970 under name of Mitsubishi Motor Corp. In May 1971 it became a joint venture company with Chrysler Corp. (USA), with Mitsubishi holding 65% and Chrysler 35% of shares. President: T. Kubo. Executive Vice Presidents: Y. Sone, K. Sugiura, Y. Mochida. Senior Managing Directors: H. Iwasaki, N. Ichikawa, S. Arai, M. Mizuno, K. Kobayashi, S. Kobayashi, I. Nishina, K. Samema. Head office and press office: No. 33-8 Shiba 5-chome, Minatoku, Tokyo. Works: Mizushima, No. 1, 1-chome, Mizushima, Kaigandori, Kurashiki, Okoyama-Pref.; Nagoya, No. 2, Oyecho, Minato-ku, Nagoya. 22,000 employees. 558,592 cars produced in 1977.

MONOCOQUE ENGINEERING **USA**

Established in 1968 as a design compagny. Present title since 1970. President: D.E. Hanebrink. Head office, press office and works: 1725 B-2 Monrovia St. Costa Mesa, Cal. 92627.

MONTEVERDI - see AUTOMOBILES MONTEVERDI Ltd

MORGAN MOTOR COMPANY Ltd **Great Britain**

Founded in 1910. Managing Director: P.H.G. Morgan. Head office, press office and works: Pickersleigh Rd, Malvern Link, Worcs. WR14 2LL. Production of 4-wheeled vehicles begun in 1936. 110 employees. 447 cars produced in 1978. Most important models: Morgan 4/4, Morgan Plus 8. Entries and wins in numerous competitions since 1911.

MORRIS - see BL Ltd

NISSAN MOTOR Co. Ltd **Japan**

(Makes: Datsun, Nissan)

Founded in 1933 under the name of Jidosha Seizo Co. Ltd. Present title since 1934. In 1966 it took over Price Motors Ltd. Chairman: K. Kawamata. Vice-Chairman: T. Iwakoshi. President: T. Ishihara. Executive Vice-Presidents: S. Sasaki, M. Ohkuma, M. Komaki. Senior Managing Directors: R. Nakagawa, F. Honda, R. Yamazaki, K. Tanaka, H. Takahashi, K. Kanao. Head office and press office: Ginza, Chuo-ku, Tokyo. Works: Mitaka, 8-1, 5-chome, Shimo-Renjaku, Mitaka, Tokyo; Murayama, 6000 Nakafuji, Musashi-Murayama, Kitatama-gun, Tokyo; Agikubo, 5-1, 3-chome, Momoi, Suginami-ku, Tokyo; Oppama, 1, Natsushima-Cho, Yokosuka; Tochigi, 2500, Kaminokawa, Tochigi-ken; Yokohama 2, Takara-cho, Kanagawaku, Yokohama; Yoshiwara, 1-1, Takara-cho, Yoshiwara Fuji, Shizuoka-ken; Zama, 5070, Nagakubo, Zama, Kanagawa-Ken. 52,600 employees. 1,816,376 cars produced in 1977. Most important models: Cedric (1960); Sunny, Gloria (1962); President (1965); Datsun, Nissan Prince Royal (1966); Datsun Bluebird 510 (1967); Laurel (1968); Datsun 240-Z, Nissan Skyline (1969); Cherry (1970); Datsun Bluebird U (1972); Violet Auster, Stanza, Pulsar, Fairlady (1977). First places in Round Australia Rally (1958); East African Safari Rally and Kenya Rally (1966); Shell 4000 Canada Rally (1967-68); South Africa's Moonlight Rally and Beira Rally (1967); Zacateca Race, Malaysian Race, Aussie Race, Southern Cross Rally (1968); South African Castrol 2000 Rally, East African Safari Rally (1969-71).

MANUFACTURE AND ASSEMBLY IN OTHER COUNTRIES — **Australia:** Nissan Motor Manufacturing Co. (Australia) Ltd (subsidiary), Center Rd, Clayton, Victoria 3168. **Costa Rica:** Agencia Datsun S.A. (associated company), Apdo Postal 3219, San José; Motorcentro S.A. (associated company), Apdo 10046, San José. **Ghana:** Japan Motor Trading Co. Ltd (associated company), P.O.B. 5216, Accra. **Indonesia:** P.T. Indokaya Nissan Motors (associated company), 37-38 Jalan Ir. H. Huanda, Djakarta. **Ireland:** Datsun Ltd (associated company), Datsun House, P.O.B. 910, Naas Rd, Dublin 12. **Malaysia:** Tan Chong Motor Assemblies Sdn Bhd (affiliated company), Jalan Segambut, Kuala Lumpur. **Mexico:** Nissan Mexicana S.A. de C.V. (joint venture), Avda. Insurgentes Sur No. 1457, Piso del 1° al 5°, Mexico City 19. **New Zealand:** Nissan Motor Distributors (N.Z.) 1975 Ltd (joint venture), P.O.B. 61133, Otara, Auckland. **Nicaragua:** Distribudora Datsun S.A. (associated company), P.O.B. 3680, Managua. **Peru:** Nissan Motor del Peru S.A. (joint venture), P.O.B. 4265, Lima. **Philippines:** Universal Motor Corp. (associated company) 2232-34, Pason Tamo Ave., Makati, Rizal. **Portugal:** Entreposto Commercial de Automoveis S.a.r.l. (associated company), Av. Eng. Duarte Pacheco, 21-A, Lisbon. **Singapore:** Singapore Nissan Motor (Private) Ltd (affiliated company), 9 Jalan Pesawat, Jurong Town, Singapore-22. **South Africa:** Datsun-Nissan Investment Co. Ltd (associated company), P.O.B. 10, Rosslyn, Pretoria, Transvaal. **Taiwan:** Yue Loong Motor Co. Ltd (associated company), 9th floor, 150 Nanking East Rd, Section 2, Taipei. **Thailand:** Siam Motors & Nissan Co. Ltd (associated company) 865, Rama I Rd, Bangkok. **Trinidad Tobago:** Neal & Massy Ltd (associated company), P.O.B. 1298, Port-of-Spain. **Venezuela:** Ensambladora Carabobo C.A. (associated company), Apdo 754, Valencia, E.do Carabobo. 224,020 vehicles produced outside Japan in 1977.

NOVA CARS Ltd. **Great Britain**

Original company founded in 1971, assumed present title in 1978. Chairman and Managing Director. V. Elam. Director: A. Elam. Head office and press office: Hill Top Garage Brighouse and Denholme Road Mountain, Queensbury, Bradford, W. Yorks. Works: Howden Works, Howden Rd, Silsden, Yorks.

NUOVA INNOCENTI S.p.A. **Italy**

Founded in 1933 as Società Anonima Fratelli Innocenti became Innocenti Anonima per Applicazioni Tubolari Acciaio and Innocenti Società Generale per l'Industria Metallurgica e Meccanica S.p.A. and Innocenti S.p.A. in 1961. Taken over by BLMC in 1972 and in 1976 by GEPI and de Tomaso assuming present title. BL Ltd holds 5% of Nuova Innocenti. Production begun in May 1976. President: R. Spera. Managing Director: A. de Tomaso. General Manager: T. Pirondini. Head office and press office: v. Rubattino 37, Milan. Works: v. Pitteri 84, Milan. 2,322 employees. 38,581 cars produced in 1977. Most important models: Innocenti Austin A40 (1960); Innocenti Morris IM-3S (1963); Innocenti Austin J4 (1964); Innocenti Mini Minor (1965); Innocenti S. Spider (1966); Innocenti Mini Cooper Mk 2 (1968); Innocenti Mini Minor Mk 3, Mini Cooper Mk 3 and J5 (1970); Innocenti Mini 1000, Mini Cooper 1300 Mk 3 Austin J5 (1972); Innocenti Mini 90, Mini 120 and Regent (1974).

OFFICINE ALFIERI MASERATI S.p.A. **Italy**

Founded in 1926, it is famous for its GT and racing cars. Managing Director: A. de Tomaso. Head office, press office and works: v. Ciro Menotti 322, Modena. About 500 employees. About 350 cars produced in 1977. Most important models: A 6/1500 (1948); A6G/2000 (1954); 3500 GT (1956); 5000 GT (1958); 3500 GTI, 5000 GTI (1960); Mistral, Quattroporte (1964); Mexico, Ghibli (1966); Indy (1969); Bora (1971); Merak (1972); Khamsin (1974); Merak SS (1975); Kyalami, Merak 2000, Quattroporte (1976). Victories up to 1957 in all types of motor racing: Targa Florio (1926), Indianapolis 500 Miles (1939-40), European Mountain Championship (1956-57), World Drivers' Championship with J.M. Fangio.

OLDSMOBILE - see GENERAL MOTORS CORPORATION

OPEL - see ADAM OPEL AG

OTOSAN A.S. **Turkey**

Founded in 1959. It is part of Koç Group-Koç Holding and produces cars with fibreglass bodywork and Ford engines. General Manager: E. Gönül. Head office, press office and works: P.K. 102, Kadiköy, Istanbul. 2,630 employees. 5,365 cars produced in 1977.

PANTHER WESTWINDS Ltd **Great Britain**

Founded in 1971. Managing Director: R. Jankel. Deputy Managing Director: L. Jankel. Head office, press office and works: Canada Rd, Byfleet, Surrey. 211 employees. 550 cars produced in 1978. Most important models: J 724.2 litre (1972); Lazer, FF (1973); De Ville Saloon (1974); Rio (1975); Lima, De Ville Convertible (1976); Turbo Lima (1978).

PAYKAN - see IRAN NATIONAL INDUSTRIAL MANUFACTURING Co. Ltd

PEKING **China (People's Republic)**

Works: Dong Fang Hong, Peking. Public Relations office: China National Machinery Import & Export Corp., P.O.B. 49, Peking.

PEUGEOT - see AUTOMOBILES PEUGEOT S.A.

PLYMOUTH - see CHRYSLER CORPORATION

POLSKI-FIAT - see FABRYKA SAMOCHODÓW OSOBOWYCH

PONTIAC - see GENERAL MOTORS CORPORATION and GENERAL MOTORS OF CANADA Ltd

PORSCHE - see Dr. Ing. h.c. F. PORSCHE A.G.

PORTARO (Portugal) - see SEMAL - SOCIEDADE ELECTROMECANICA DE AUTOMOVEIS Lda

(THE) PREMIER AUTOMOBILES Ltd **India**

Founded in 1944. Chairman: L. Hirachand. Managing Director: P.N. Vencatesan. Head office and press office: Construction House, Walchand Hirachand Marg, Ballard Estate, Bombay - 400 038. Works: L.B. Shastri Marg, Kurla, Bombay - 400 070. About 9,000 employees. 17,481 cars produced in 1977.

PRINCESS - see BL Ltd

PUMA INDUSTRIA DE VEICULOS S.A. **Brazil**

Founded in 1964 under name of Sociedade de Automóveis Luminari Ltda. Present title since 1975. Directors: L.R. Alves da Costa, M. Masteguim. J.M. Hellmeister. Head office, press office and works: Av. Presidente Wilson 4385, C.P. 42649, São Paulo. 630 employees. 1,911 cars produced in 1977. Models: Malzoni GT with DKW engine (1964-65); Puma GT with DKW engine (1966-67); Puma 1500 GT with VW engine (1968-69); Puma 1600 GTE with VW engine (1970); Puma 1600 GTE and GTS with VW engine (1971); Puma GTB 4100 with GM engine (1974).

RÉGIE NATIONALE DES USINES RENAULT **France**

Founded in 1898 under the name of Société Anonyme des Usines Renault. Present title since 1945 when it was nationalized. It is today the largest motor manufacturer in France. President and General Manager: B. Vernier-Palliez. Head office and press office: 34 quai du Point du Jour, Boulogne Billancourt 92200. Works: Pierre Lefaucheux, Flins; Usine de Cléon, Cléon: Usine du Mans, Pierre-Piffault; Usine de Choisy, Choisy-le-Roy; Usine d'Orlèans, St. Jean-de-la-Ruelle; Usine du Havre, Sandouville; Usine de Dreux, Dreux; Usine de Douai, Douai. 106,753 employees. 1,745,862 cars produced in 1977. Most important models: 1.75 CV (1898); 2 cylinder (1904); 35 CV (1912); Marne Taxi, Type AG, Type TT (1923); 45 hp (1923-27); Celtaquatre (1934); Viva Grand Sport (1938); 4 CV (1947); Fregate (1951); Dauphine (1957); Floride (1959); Floride S, Caravelle, 8 (1962); Caravelle 1100 (1963); 8 Major (1964); 16 (1965); 4 Parisienne (1966); 16 TE, 6 (1968); 12 (1969); R 5, R 15, R 17 (1971); R 16 TX (1973); R 30, R 20 (1975); R 14 (1976); R 18 (1978). Entries and wins in numerous competitions (Monte Carlo Rally, Alpine Rally, Tour de Corse, Liège-Rome-Liège, Sebring, Reims, Nürburgring, Mobil Economy Run, etc.).

MANUFACTURE AND ASSEMBLY IN OTHER COUNTRIES — **Argentina:** Renault Argentine S.A. (subsidiary), Avda. Santa Maria, C.C. 8, Cordoba (manuf. 4, 6, 12). **Australia:** Renault Australia Pty Ltd (subsidiary), Dougharty Road, P.O. Box 60, West Heidelberg, Victoria (assem. 8, 10, 12, 16, 16 TS). **Belgium:** Rnur (subsidiary), 499 Schaarbeeklei, Vilvoorde 1 (assem. 4, 6, 8, 10). **Chile:** Automotores Franco Chilena (subsidiary), Casilla 10173, Los Andes (assem. 4); Corme Canica (concessionaire), Casilla 10173, Los Andes (assem. 4). **Colombia:** Sofasa (associated company), Apartado Aereo 4529, Medellin (assem. 4, 6); Socofam (associated company), Duitama, Boyaca (assem. 4, 6). **Eire:** Smith Engineering Ltd (subsidiary), Trinity Street, Wexford (assem. 4, 6, 8, 10, 12, 16). **Greece:** Soheca (concessionaire), Athens 126. **Indonesia:** Gaya Motors (concessionaire), Jalan'c Aphd, P.O. Box 2126 DKT, Djakarta Fair, Djakarta. **Iran:** Saipa (concessionaire), 553 av. Eisenhower, Teheran. **Ivory Coast:** Safar (subsidiary), B.P. 2764, Abidjan (assem. 4, 5, 6, 10, 12, 16, 16 TS). **Madagascar:** Somacoa (associated company), Route de Majunga, B.P. 796, Tananarive (assem. 4, 6, 12, 16, 16 TS). **Malaysia:** Champion Motors Sdn Bhd, Jalan Usaha, Shah Alam Selangor, P.O. Box 814, Kuala Lumpur (assem. 10, 16). **Mexico:** Diesel Association (concessionaire), Ciudad Sahagun, Hidalgo (assem. 4, 5, 10). **Morocco:** Somaca, km 12 Autoroute de Rabat, Casablanca (assem. 4, 6, 8, 12, 16, 16 TS). **New Zealand:** Campbell Industries Ltd (concessionaire), Jellicoe Crescent, P.O. Box 84, Thames (assem. 10, 12). **Philippines:** Renault Philippines (subsidiary), P.O. Box 1011, Makati, Rizal (assem. 4, 6, 8, 10, 12, 16, 16 TS). **Portugal:** Industrias Lusitanas Renault (associated company), Fabrica de Guarda, Guarda Gare (assem. 4, 6, 8, 10, 12, 16, 16 TS). **Rumania:** Interprendera de Autoturisme de Pitesti (concessionaire), Casuta Postala I.A.P., Ju de tul Argès, Colibasi (assem. 8, Dacia 1300). **Singapore:** Associated Motors Industries (concessionaire), Taman Jurong, P.O.B. 19, Singapore 22 (assem. 10, 12). **South Africa:** Motors Assemblies Ltd (associated company), P.O. Box 12030, Jacobs, Durban (assem. 4, 6, 10, 12, 16 TS). **Spain:** Fasa-Renault S.A. (subsidiary), Apartado 262, Autopista de Francia, Madrid (assem. 4, 6, 8, 12). **Trinidad:** Amalgamated Industries Ltd, Tumpuna Road, Arima Trinidad, Port of Spain (assem. 10, 12, 16). **Tunisia:** Stia (associated company), Route de Monastir, Sousse (assem. 4). **Turkey:** Oyak Renault (associated company), Zone Industrielle, P.K. 255, Bursa (assem. 12). **Uruguay:** Automotores, Cerro Largo 888, Santa Rosa, Montevideo (assem. 10, 12, 16). **Venezuela:** Cvvca (associated company), Edificio Gran Avenida Piso 4, Apartado del Este 61033, Caracas (assem. 10, 12, 16); Cvvca (associated company), Edo Carabobo, Mariara (assem. 10, 12, 16). **Yugoslavia:** Industrija Motornih Vozil (concessionaire), B.P. 60, Nuovo Mesto (assem. 4, 6, 8, 10, 12, 16).

(THE) RELIANT MOTOR COMPANY Ltd **Great Britain**

Founded in 1934 under the name of Reliant Engineering Co. (Tamworth) Ltd. Present title since 1962. Acquired Bond Cars Ltd in 1969. Chairman: J.F. Nash. Managing Director: R.L. Spencer. Directors: C. Burton, I. J. Jardine, M.E. Smith. Head office and works: Two Gates, Tamworth, Staffs. Public Relations Agents: B.C. Joung & Co., Walton House, Richmond Hill, Bournemouth. 1,000 employees. About 8,000 vehicles produced in 1977. Most important models: first sports car Sabre (1960); Sabre 6 (1961); Regal 3/25 (1962); Scimitar GT, Rebel 700 (1964); Rebel 700 Estate (1967); Scimitar GTE (1968); Scimitar GTE Automatic, Kitten Saloon/Estate (1975); New Scimitar GTE Overdrive/Automatic (1976), Bond Bug (1970); Robin Saloon/Estate and Van (1973), all with glass fibre bodywork. Entries from 1962-64 in numerous competitions (Tulip Rally, RAC Rally of Great Britain, Monte Carlo Rally, Circuit of Ireland, Alpine Rally, Spa-Sofia-Liége Rally; winners of class in Total Economy Run in 1976 and 1977 with 55.5 mpg and 57.5 mpg respectively.

MANUFACTURE IN OTHER COUNTRIES — **Greece:** Mebea SA, 58-60 Aristotelous St, Athens 103 (manuf. TW9, Robin). **Turkey:** Otosan A.S., P.O.B. 102, Kadikoy, Istanbul (manuf. Anadol).

RENAULT (France) - see RÉGIE NATIONALE DES USINES RENAULT

RENAULT ARGENTINA S.A. **Argentina**

Founded in 1955 under the name of Industrias Kaiser Argentina assumed title of Ika-Renault in 1968. Present title since 1977. Head office and press office: Sarmiento 1230, Buenos Aires. Works: Camino a Pajas Blancas, km 4, Cordoba. 7,065 employees. 34,744 cars produced in 1977. Most important models: R4 (1963); Torino (1966); R6 (1970); R12 (1971).

RENAULT ESPAÑA S.A. **Spain**

Founded in 1951. President: J.L. Rodriguez-Pomatta. Vice President: B. Hanon. Managing Director: M.H. Bougler. Head office and press office: Carretera de Alcobendas, km 5.5, Apdo. 262, Madrid 34. Works: Valladolid, Sevilla. About 18,000 employees. 237,502 cars produced in 1977.

REPLICARS Inc. **USA**

Established in 1975. President: J.W. Faircloth. Head office, press office and works: 3175 Belvedere Rd, West Palm Beach, Flo. 33406. 32 employees. 134 cars produced in 1977.

ROLLS-ROYCE MOTORS Ltd **Great Britain**

Rolls-Royce Motors Ltd was formed in April 1971 to take over the assets of the original Rolls-Royce Ltd in the automotive field. The first Rolls-Royce car ran in 1904 and they have always specialised in the production of high class cars of great quality. Chairman: I.J. Fraser, CBE, MC. Group Managing Director: D.A.S. Plastow. Directors: L.W. Harris, G.R. Fenn, T. Neville, C.S. Aston, H. Wuttke, H.P.N. Benson. Head office and works: Crewe, Ches. Press office: 14-15 Conduit St, London W1. 9,500 employees. 2,872 cars produced in 1977. Most important models: first Rolls-Royce in 1904; Silver Ghost (1906-25); Twenty (1911); Phantom I (1925-29); Phantom II (1929-36); Phantom III (1936); Silver Wraith (1946); Phantom IV (1950); Silver Cloud I (1955); Silver Cloud II, Phantom V (1959); Silver Cloud III (1962); Silver Shadow (1965); Phantom VI (1968); Corniche (1971); Camargue (1975); Silver Shadow (1977).

ROM CARMEL INDUSTRIES Ltd **Israel**

Founded in 1958 as private company by L. Schneller and Y. Shubinski. From 1966 to 1971 in partnership with Standard Triumph Motor Co. England. Now Rom Carmel Industries Ltd, member of Clal Group. General Manager: N. Nemirowski. Head office, press office and works: P.O.B. 444, Haifa, Tirat Carmel. 650 employees. 1,800 cars produced in 1977. Most important models: Sussita, Carmel, Bilboa, Rom 1300. All with bodywork in fibreglass reinforced polyester.

ROVER - see BL Ltd

R.V. ALFONSO DMG Inc. **Philippines**

(Make: Toro)

Head office, press office and works: Guevent Bldg., P.O. Box 1263, Manila.

S.A. AUTOMOBILES CITROËN **France**

Founded in 1919 by André Citroën, became S.A. André Citroën in 1927 and Citroën S.A. in 1968. Present title since 1975. December 1974 38.2% of stock acquired by Automobiles Peugeot S.A. Since May 1976 Citroën S.A. is owned by the Peugeot S.A. group (to which Automobiles Peugeot S.A. belongs also). The first car launched since the merger of the two firms is the Citroën LN, presented in the summer of 1976. Directorate: X. Karcher, R. Ravenel, J. Lombard. Head office and press office: 133 quai André Citroën, Paris 15e. Works: as above; Levallois, Aulnay, Clichy, Saint-Ouen, Asnières, Gutenberg, Nanterre, Rennes-La-Barre-Thomas, Rennes-La-Janais, Caen, Froncle, Saint-Etienne, Mulhouse, Reims, Metz. About 57,700 employees. 741,363 cars produced in 1977. Most important models: Torpedo A Type (1919); B2 10 CV (1921); 5 CV (1922); B12 10 CV (1925); B14 (1926); C6 (1928); 7A 7 and 11 CV (1934); 15 Six (1938); 2 CV (1948); 2 CV 425 cc (1954); DS 19 (1955); ID 19 (1957); 2 CV 4 x 4 (1958); Ami 6 3 CV (1961); Ami 6 Break DS Pallas (1964); DS 21 (1965); Dyane (1967); Mehari (1968); Ami 8 (1969); SM and GS (1970); CX (1974); LN (1976); Visa, LNA (1978). Entries and first places in numerous competitions: World distance and speed record at Montlhéry (1932-33), 28th Monte Carlo Rally and Constructors' Cup (1959), Liège-Sofia-Liège Road Marathon (1961), Norwegian Snow and Ice Winter Rally, Lyon-Charbonnière-Solitude, Alpine Trophy, Thousand Lakes Rally, Constructors' Cup, Trophy of Nations (1962), Finnish Snow Rally, Northern Roads, Lyon-Charbonnière-Solitude, Norwegian Winter Rally, International Alpine Criterium, Constructors' Cup in Monte Carlo Rally and Liège-Sofia-Liège Marathon, Tour of Corsica (1963), Spa-Sofia-Liège Marathon (1964), Rallie Neige et Glace, Mobil Economy Run, Coupe des Alpes, Monte Carlo (1966), Constructors' Cup in Morocco Rally 1969-1977); Moroco Rally, TAP Portugal (1969); Chamonix winter run (1970); Morocco Rally (1970-71); World Cup Wembley-Munich 1974); Senegal Car Tour and Constructors' Cup London-Sydney (1977). Morocco Rally (1969, 1970 and 1971).

MANUFACTURE AND ASSEMBLY IN OTHER COUNTRIES — **Argentina:** Citroën Argentina (subsidiary), Zepita 3220, Buenos Aires (2CV, Mehari, Ami 8). **Belgium:** Société Belge des Automobiles Citroën SA (subsidiary), 7 place de l'Yser, Brussels (assem. 2CV, Mehari, LN). **Chile:** Sociedad Importadora e Industrial J. Lhorente y Cia Ltda

(subsidiary), Arica lote 26, Chinthorre (2CV, Ami). **Iran:** Teheran (assem. Dyane). **Madagascar:** Société Industrielle et Commerciale des Automobiles Malgaches (concessionnaire), route de Majunga, Tananarive (assem. 2CV Mehari). **Portugal:** Sociedad Citroën Lusitania SARL (subsidiary), estrada de Nelas, Beira Alto, Mangualde (Dyane, GS, CX). **Spain:** Citroën Hispania (subsidiary), free zone of Vigo (manuf. 2CV, Ami 8, Dyane, Mehari, GS, CX). **Yugoslavia:** Tovarna Motornich Vozil (Tomos) (concessionnaire), Koper (manuf. Dyane, GS, CX).

SAAB-SCANIA AB — **Sweden**

The first Saab car was made in 1950 by the former Svenska Aeroplan Aktiebolaget. Saab cars are currently manufactured by the Saab Car Division of Saab-Scania AB which was formed in 1968 through the merger of Saab Aktiebolag and Scania-Vabis. Other Saab-Scania products include Scania commercial vehicles, aircraft, missiles, avionics, electronic equipment, computers, electromedical equipment, industrial valves, measuring systems, etc. Chairman: M. Wallenberg. President: H.S. Gustafsson. Chief Executive Saab Car Division: S. Wennlo. Group head office: 8-581 88 Linköping. Head office and press office: Saab Car Division: S-611 01 Nyköping. Works: Trollhättan, Nyköping, Kristineham, Arlöv. 14,000 employees. 76,500 cars produced in 1977. Most important models: 92, 93 (1950-60); 95 Estate (1959-78); 96 (1960); 96 V4 (1966); 99 (1968); Sonett III (1969); 99 Combi Coupé (1973). Numerous wins in international rallies including Monte Carlo (twice), RAC (5 times), Tulip Rally, Baja 1000, Swedish KAK, Arctic and 1000 Lakes in Finland, etc.

MANUFACTURE IN OTHER COUNTRIES — **Finland:** Oy Saab-Valmet Ab, Uusikaupunki (manuf. 96, 99, 900). About 30,000 cars produced outside Sweden in 1977.

SBARRO - see SOCIETÉ DE FABRICATION D'AUTOMOBILES SBARRO S.a.r.l.

SCEPTRE MOTOR CAR COMPANY — **USA**

Founded in 1978. Associated with Liberty Manufacturing in Santa Barbara. Chairman: T.W. McBurnie. President: M. Broggie. Director: S. Fields. Head office, press office and works: 7242 Hollister Ave., Goleta Valley, Cal. 93017. 30 employees.

SEAT - SOCIEDAD ESPAÑOLA DE AUTOMOVILES DE TURISMO S.A. — **Spain**

Founded in 1950. President: J.M. Antoñanzas. Managing Directors: P. Vidal, J. Pañella. Head office and press office: Avda. Generalisimo 146, Madrid 16. Works: Zona Franca, Martorell, Barcellona, Landaben, Pamplona. 32,000 employees. 353,413 cars produced in 1977. Most important models: 600 (1957); 1500 (1963); 850 (1966); 124 (1968); 1430 (1969); 127 (1971); 132 (1973); 133 (1974); 131 (1975); 1200 Sport (1976); 124 Berlina, 128 3P (1977); 132 Mercedes Diesel (1978).

SEMAL - SOCIEDADE ELECTROMECANICA DE AUTOMOVEIS Lda. — **Portugal**

(Make: Portaro)

Founded in 1944. Directors: H.M. Pires, J.M. Simões. Head office and press office: Rua Nova de S. Mamede, 3 a 9 Lisboa. Works: En 249/4, km 4,6 Trajouce-Oeiras. 330 employees. 818 cars produced in 1977. Production of Portaro began in 1974.

SEVEN - see CATERHAM CAR Sales Ltd

SHANGHAI — **China (People's Republic)**

Public Relations office: China National Machinery Import & Export Corp., P.O.B. 49, Peking. Works: Shanghai.

SIMCA - see CHRYSLER ESPAÑA and CHRYSLER FRANCE

ŠKODA - AUTOMOBILOVÉ ZÁVODY NÁRODNI PODNIK — **Czechoslovakia**

Founded in 1894 by Laurin and Klement for the construction of velocipedes, assumed title of Laurin & Klement Co. Ltd in 1907, Škoda in 1925, and in 1945 became national corporation (AZNP). Director: M. Zapadlo. Commercial Deputy Director: Z. Rubin. Head office, press office and works: Trída Rudé armady, Mladá Boleslav. 15,000 employees. 150,000 cars produced in 1977. Car production begun in 1905 (2-cylinder cars). Most important models: Laurin & Klement (1905); E 4-cyl. (1907); "S" Type (1911); 100, 105, 110, 120 Type (1923); 4R, 6R (1924); 420, 422 (1934); Popular, Rapid (1935-39); 1101, 1102 (1945-51); 440 (1956); Octavia, Felicia (1958); Octavia Combi, 1202 (1962); 1000 MB (1964); 100 L, 110 L, 1203 (1969); 110R Coupé (1970), 105, 120 (1977).

SOCIETÉ DE FABRICATION D'AUTOMOBILES SBARRO S.a.r.l. — **Switzerland**

Founded in 1973. Proprietor: F. Sbarro. Head office, press office and works: ACA Atelier, 1411 Les Tuileries de Grandson, Yverdon, Lausanne.

SPARTAN CAR COMPANY — **Great Britain**

Specializes in major accident repairs to sports and specialist cars. Designer: J. McIntyre. Head office and press office: Kirby Lane Works Pinxton, Nottinghamshire. 10 employees. 250 cars produced in 1976.

STANDARD MOTOR PRODUCTS OF INDIA Ltd — **India**

Managing Director: C.V. Karthik Narayanan. Head office, press office and works: 134 Mount Rd, Madras - 600 002.

STIMULA - see AUTOMOBILE STIMULA

STUTZ MOTOR CAR OF AMERICA Inc. — **USA**

Established in 1968. President: J.D. O'Donnell. Secretary and Treasurer: R.L. Curotto. Head office: Time-Life Bldg, Rockefeller Center, New York, N.Y. 10020. Press office: Bill Doll, Shannon & Co. Inc., 150 West 52nd St, New York, N.Y. 10019. 50 employees. 50 cars produced in 1977.

SUBARU - see FUJI HEAVY INDUSTRIES Ltd

SUZUKI MOTOR COMPANY Ltd — **Japan**

Founded in 1909 under the name of Suzuki Shokkuki Seisakusho. Present title since 1954. Chairman: J. Suzuki. President: O. Suzuki. Managing Directors: A. Kinoshita, T. Okano. Head office and press office: 300 Kamimura, Hamagun, Shizouka-ken. Works: Kosai, Shirasuka 4520, Kosaishi, Suzuoka-ken; Iwata, Iwai 500, Iwata-shi, Shizouka-ken; Ohsuka, Ombuchi 6333, Omsuka-cho, Ogasagun, Shizouka-ken. 8,764 employees. 91,189 cars produced in 1977. Most important models: Suzulight 360 (1955); Suzuki Fronte 360 LC10 (1967); Fronte 500 (1968); Fronte Coupé (1971).

SYD LAWRENCE SPECIAL CARS Ltd — **Great Britain**

Founded in 1977. Managing Director: S.J. Lawrence. Director: I. Ferguson. Head office and works: 37 High St., Southgate, London N14 6LD.

SYRENA - see FABRYKA SAMOCHODÓW MALOLITRAZOWYCH

TATRA Národní Podnik — **Czechoslovakia**

Tatra is one of oldest European motor manufacturers. In second half of 19th century de luxe coaches were being built in Nesselsdorf. Production of railway carriages was begun in 1882 and first motor-car, called the "President", was produced in 1897. General Director: M. Kopec. Head office and press office: Koprivnice. Works: Tatra Koprivnice okres Novy Jičin, 1,500 cars produced in 1977. Most important models: President (1897); B Type (1902); E Type 12 hp (1905); K Type (1906); T 14/15 (1914); Tatra 4/12, Tatra 11 (1923); 17/31 (1926-30); Tatra 30 (1927-29); Tatra 24/30 (1930-34); Tatra 52 (1930-38); Tatra 57 (1932); Tatra 75 (1933-37); Tatra 77 (1934); Tatra 87 (1936-38); Tatraplan (1949); Tatra 603 (1957); Tatra 2-603 (1964); Tatra 613 (1975). Has been entering competitions since 1900 (Targa Florio, Leningrad-Moscow-Tbilisi-Moscow, Alpine Rally, Polsky Rally, Vltava Rally, Marathon de la Route, etc.).

TECHNICAL EXPONENTS Ltd — **Great Britain**

Founded in 1965. Proprietor and General Manager: T.P. Bennett. Head office and press office: 74 Waterford Rd, London SW6. Works: Denham Green Lane, Denham, Bucks. Most important models: TX Tripper, 1500 and 2000 Dolomite Sprint.

TOFAS - see FIAT S p.A.

TORO - see R.V. ALFONSO DMG Inc.

TOYO KOGYO COMPANY Ltd — **Japa**

(Make: Mazda)

Founded in 1920 under the name of Toyo Cork Kogyo Co Ltd. Present title since 1927. Chairman: K. Matsuda President: Y. Yamasaki. Executive Vice-Presidents: M Kono, T. Murai. Executive Director: T. Wakabayash Managing Directors: H. Mineoka, S. Inomata, T. Hasegawa K. Roppyakuda, K. Yamamoto, M. Watanabe, H. Nakashima Y. Minagawa, A. Fujii. Head office, press office and works 3-1 Shinchi, Fuchucho, Aki-gun, Hiroshima. 28,590 employees. 507,849 vehicles produced in 1977. Car production begun in 1930 with Mazda (3-speed). Most importar models: R360 Coupé (1960); 360 and 600 (1962); 800 Seda (1964); 1000 (1965); 1500 Sedan (1966); 1500 SS, 110 (1967); R110 Coupé, R100 Coupé, 1800 Sedan (1968). RX-2 616 Coupé and Sedan (1970); RX3 (1971); Cosmo RX (1975); 323/GLC (1977); RX7, 626 (1978). Entries numerous competitions: Singapore GP (1966); Macao G (1966-67); 84 hour Marathon (1968); Singapore GP, Franco champs (1969); Francorchamps and Shell Springbok Serie (1970).

TOTAL PERFORMANCE Inc. — **US**

Established in 1971. President: M.V. Lauria. Vice President G.C. Gallicchio. Head office, press office and works 406 S. Orchard St, Rt. 5, Wallingford, CT 06492. 2 employees. 40 cars produced in 1978.

TOYOTA MOTOR COMPANY Ltd — **Japa**

Founded in 1937. Chairman: M. Hanai. President: E Toyoda. Executive Vice-Presidents: S. Toyoda, H. Mori S. Yamamoto. Senior Managing Directors: S. Yamaoto, T Hasegawa, M. Morita, T. Morita. Managing Directors M. Masao, H. Ono, G. Tsuji, K. Matsumoto, K. Kusunoki H. Fuse. Head office and press office: 1, Toyota-cho Toyota City. Works: Housha, 1, Toyota-cho, Toyota City Motomachi, 1 Motomachi, Toyota City; Tokaoka, 1 Honda Toyota City; Tsutsumi, 1 Tsutsumi-cho, Toyota City; Hiyosh 1 Miyoshimachi, Nishikamo-gun. 44,889 employees. 2,162,62 cars produced in 1977. Most important models: Toyo Ac (1954); Toyopet Crown (1955); Toyopet Corona (1957); Toyope Crown Deluxe (1958); Toyopet Crown Diesel (1959) Toyopet New Corona and Publica (1960); Toyopet New Crown (1962); **Crown Eight (1963)**; Toyota Corolla 110 (1966); Toyota Century (1967); Toyota Corona Mk II, Toyot 1000 (1968); Celica, Carina (1970); Sprinter (1971); Corsa Tercel (1978).

MANUFACTURE AND ASSEMBLY IN OTHER COUNTRIES — **Australia:** Australian Motor Industries Ltd, 155 Bertie St Port Melbourne, Victoria 3207. **Costa Rica:** ECASA, Calle 36y Paseo Colon, San José. **Ghana:** Fattal Vehicle Assembly, Ring Rd. W., Industrial Area, Accra. **Indonesia** P.T. Pulti-Astra, Jalan Yos Sudarso (Suntar), Djakarta Utara **Ireland:** Toyota (Ireland) Ltd, J.F. Kennedy Park, Killer Rd Dublin 12. **Kenya:** Associated Vehicle Assemblers Ltd P.O.B. 86334, Mombasa. **Malaysia:** Assembly Services Adn Bhd, P.O.B. 814, Kuala Lumpur, Selangor. **New Zealand** Campbell Industries Ltd, Jellico Crescent, Thames; Stee Motor Assemblies Ltd, 81 Buchanans Rd, Hornbey, Christchurch. **Pakistan:** National Motors Ltd, Hab Chuaki Rd Karachi. **Peru:** Toyota del Peru S.A., Zona Industrial 1- Ventanilla, Puente de Piedra, Lima. **Philippines:** Delta Moto Corp., km 15, South Super Highway, Paranoque Pizol **Portugal:** Salvador Caetano IMVT S.a.r.l., Lugar de Olho Marinko Arada Ovar. **Singapore:** Ford Motor Co. Private Ltd, P.O.B. 4047, Bukit Timah, Timah Rd. Singapore 21 **South Africa:** Motor Assemblies Ltd, P.O.B. 26070 Isipingo Beach, 4115 Natal. **Thailand:** Toyota Motor Thailand Co Ltd, 180 Suriwongse Rd, Bangkok. **Trinidad Tobago:** Amar Auto Supplies Ltd, Las Lamos No. 2. **Venezuela:** Industria Venezolana de Maquinaria C.A., Palo Negro, E.do de Aragua. 110,280 cars produced outside Japan in 1977

TRABANT - see VEB SACHSENRING AUTOMOBILWERKE ZWICKAU

TRIUMPH - see BL Ltd

TVR ENGINEERING Ltd — **Great Britain**

Established in 1954 as Grantura Engineering Ltd. Present title since 1966. Chairman: A. Lilley. Managing Director: M.A. Lilley. Director: S. Halstead. Head office, press office and works: Bristol Ave, Blackpool, Lancs. 84 employees. About 400 cars produced in 1977. Most important models: Mk I (1954-60); Mk II (1960); Mk II A (1962); Mk III (1963-64); Mk III 1800 (1963); Griffith series 200 (1964); Griffith 400 (1965); 200 V8 (1966); Tuscan SE, Vixen 1600 (1967); Vixen S2 (1968); Tuscan V6 (1969); 1600 M (1972-73); 2500 (1970-73); 2500 M, 3000 M (1972); Turbo (1975); Taimar (1976); Convertible (1978). Entries

and wins in numerous competitions. Outright winners of 1970, 1971 and 1972 Modsports Championships. 1976 win in class B production sports cars.

UAZ - ULIANOVSKY AVTOMOBILNY ZAVOD   USSR

Press office: Avtoexport, Ul. Volkhonka 14, Moscow 119902.
Works: Ulianovsk.

VANDEN PLAS - see BL Ltd

VAUXHALL MOTORS Ltd   Great Britain

Founded in 1903. Transferred from Vauxhall district of London to Luton in 1905. Present title since 1907. Taken over by General Motors Corp. in 1925. Chairman and Managing Director: W.R. Price. Directors: R.A. White, G.E. Moore, J.P. McCormack, D. Savage, E.D. Fountain, P.G.H. Newton, N.E. Stasel, S.T. Weber, C.E. Weitz, E.H. Sergo. Head office, press office and works: Kimpton Rd, Luton, Beds. 29,000 employees. 143,612 cars produced in 1977. Most important models: Velox (1949); Cresta (1954); Victor (1957); Viva (1963). Entries in various competitions from 1909 to 1924.

ASSEMBLY IN OTHER COUNTRIES — **Belgium:** General Motors Continental S.A. (associated company), P.B. 549, Antwerp. **Denmark:** General Motors International A.S. (associated company), Aldersrogade 20, Copenhagen. **Eire:** McCairns Motors (concessionaire), Alexandra Rd, East Wall, Dublin. **Malaysia:** Champion Motors (M) Sdn Bhd (concessionaire), P.O.B. 814, Kuala Lumpur. **New Zealand:** General Motors New Zealand Ltd (associated company), Wellington. **Pakistan:** National Motors (concessionaire), Karachi 28. **Philippines:** General Motors Philippines (concessionaire), Manila. **Portugal:** General Motors de Portugal Ltda (associated company), C.P. 2484, Av. Marechal Gomes de Costa, Lisbon 6. **Singapore:** Associated Motors Industries Ltd (concessionaire), P.O.B. 19, Tamar Jurong, Singapore 22. **South Africa:** General Motors South Africa (associated company), P.O.B. 1137, Kempston Rd, Port Elizabeth. **Trinidad:** Neal & Massy Industries Ltd (concessionaire), P.O.B. 1298, Port of Spain.

VAZ - VOLZHSKY AVTOMOBILNY ZAVOD   USSR

Press office: Avtoexport, Ul. Volkhonka 14, Moscow 119902. Works: Togliatti. 75,000 employees. 725,000 cars produced in 1977.

VEB AUTOMOBILWERK EISENACH   Germany (Democratic Republic)

(Make: Wartburg)

Head office and press office: Rennhahn 8, 59 Eisenach.

VEB SACHSENRING AUTOMOBILWERKE ZWICKAU   Germany (Democratic Republic)

(Make: Trabant)

Founded in 1904 under the name of A. Horch Motorwagenwerke AG Zwickau, became Audi-Mobilwagenwerke AG Zwickau in 1909, merged with Auto Union in 1932, nationalized in 1946. Present title since 1958. Head office and press office: W. Rathenau Strasse, Zwickau 95. 9,000 employees. Over 110,000 cars produced in 1978. Most important models: world record 500 hp 16-cyl-rear-engined car (1937-38); DKW 3.5-5 I, F2, F3, F4, F5, F6, F7, F8 (two stroke front drive engine up to 1945); F8 (1949-55); F9 (1949-52); P70, S 240 (1955-59); Trabant P50 (1958-62); 600 (1962-63); 601 (1964). Entries in numerous competitions (Munich-Vienna-Budapest, Semperit, Thousand Lakes, Tulip, Monte Carlo, Vlatava, Pneumat (D.D.R.) Akropolis Rallies, Tour de Belgique).

VOLKSWAGENWERK AG   Germany (Federal Republic)

Founded in 1937 under name of Gesellschaft zur Vorbereitung des Deutschen Volkswagen mbH, became Volkswagenwerk GmbH in 1938. Present title since 1960. For volume of production is foremost German motor manufacturer. President: T. Schmücker. Directors: K.H. Briam, W.R. Habbel, G. Hartwich, H. Münzner, F. Thomée, P. Frerk, E. Fiala, W.P. Schmidt. Head office and press office: 3180 Wolfsburg. Works: as above, Braunschweig, Emden, Hannover, Kassel, Salzgitter. 107,951 employees. 1,274,016 cars produced in 1977. Most important models: Limousine 1200 (1945); 1200 Convertible (1959); 1200 Karmann-Ghia Coupé (1955); 1200 Karmann-Ghia Convertible (1957); 1500 and 1500 Karmann-Ghia Coupé (1961); 1500 N Limousine, 1500 S Limousine, 1500 S Karmann-Ghia Coupé (1963); 1600 TL (1965); 411 (1968); 411 E, 411 LE (1969); 1302, 1302 S, K 70 (1970); 1303 (1972). Passat, Passat Variant (1973); Golf, Scirocco (1974); Polo (1975); Derby (1977).

MANUFACTURE AND ASSEMBLY IN OTHER COUNTRIES — **Belgium:** Volkswagen Bruxelles, S.A., Brussels (Passat).

Indonesia: P.T. Garuda Mataram Motor Co., Djakarta (1200, 181, Golf, Passat). **Mexico:** Volkswagen de México S.A. de C.V. (associated company), Mexico City (1200, 181, Brasilia, Golf). **Nigeria:** Volkswagen of Nigeria (associated company), Lagos-Badagry Highway, km 18, Lagos (manuf. 1200, Brasilia, Passat). **South Africa:** Volkswagen of South Africa Ltd (associated company). Uitenhage (assem. 1200., Passat, Golf). **Yugoslavia:** TAS Tvormica Automobila Sarajevo, Sarajevo (Golf). 648,341 cars produced outside Federal Republic in 1977, including VW do Brasil and VW of America.

VOLKSWAGEN DO BRASIL S.A.   Brazil

Founded in 1953. Chairman: W.F.J. Sauer. Head office, press office and works: v. Anchieta km 23.5, São Bernardo do Campo, São Paulo. CEP 09700. 39,000 employees. 429,048 cars produced in 1977.

VOLKSWAGEN MANUFACTURING CORPORATION OF AMERICA   USA

Founded in September, 1976 as VWMOA. Chairman: T. Schmuecker. President: J. McLernon. Vice Presidents: E.F. Beuler, R.E. Dauch, F. Goes, J.E. Masterson, M.A. Ryan. Head office: 27621 Parkview Blvd, Warren, Mich. 48092. Works: VW Westmoreland, East Huntingdon Township, Pennsylvania. 1,500 employees. Assembly of VW Rabbit begun in 1978.

VOLVO AB   Sweden

Founded in 1926. President and General Manager: P.G. Gyllenhammar. Head office, press office and works: S-405 08, Göteborg. 62,441 employees. 21,371 cars produced in 1977. Most important models: P4 (1927); 53-56 (1939); PV 50 (1944); PV 444 (1947); P 1900 (1954-57); 122S Amazon (1956); P 544 (1958-62); P 1800 (1961); 144 (1966); 164 (1968); 240 (1975); 343 (1976).

ASSEMBLY IN OTHER COUNTRIES — **Australia:** Volvo Australia Pty Ltd, Melbourne (Liverpool). **Belgium:** Volvo Europa N.V. (subsidiary), P.B. 237, Ghent. **Canada:** Volvo (Canada) Ltd, Willowdale. **Holland:** Volvo Car B.V., Steenovenweg, Helmond. **Malaysia:** Swedish Motor Assemblies Sdn Bhd (subsidiary), Batu Tiga, Industrial Estate, Selangor.

VOLVO CAR B.V.   Holland

Founded in 1928 by Hub and Wim van Doorne, assumed title Van Doorne's Automobielfabrieken in 1958. In 1975 A.B. Volvo obtained a controlling interest of 75% in Van Doorne's Automobielfabrieken B.V. which became Volvo Car B.V. a member of the Volvo Group. The Company designes and manufactures the compact medium-sized Volvo cars. Head office and press office: Stenovenweg, Helmond. Works: Born, Oss. Managing Directors: A. van der Padt, A. de Bruin, O. Wibaut. Head office and press office: Steenovenweg, Helmond. About 6,000 employees 74,300 cars produced in 1976.

WARTBURG - see VEB AUTOMOBILWERK EISENACH

YLN - YUE LOONG MOTOR COMPANY Ltd   Taiwan

Founded in 1953 as Yue Loong Engineering Co. Ltd. Present title since 1960. President: T.L. Yen. Executive Vice-President: V. Wu. Special Assistant to Chairman and President: C.C. Yen. Managing Director: V.Z. Faung. Head office and press office: 150 Nanking East Road, Sec II, Taipei. Works: Hsin Tien Taipei. 2,000 employees. 26,646 cars produced in 1977. Under licence of Nissan Motor Co. and American Motors Corp. manufactures various types of sedans and jeeps, including YL-1 and YL-2. Models: 707, 803, 301, 902.

ZAZ - ZAPOROZHSKY AVTOMOBILNY ZAVOD   USSR

Press office: Avtoexport, Ul. Volkhonka 14, Moscow 119902. Works: Zaporozhje. About 190,000 cars produced in 1974.

ZAVODI CRVENA ZASTAVA   Yugoslavia

(Make: ZCZ)

Directors: M. Bojanic, R. Micic. Head office, press office and works: Apanskih boraca 2, 34000 Kragujevac. 30,000 employees. 200,000 cars produced in 1977.

ZIL   USSR

Press office: Avtoexport, Ul. Volkhonka 14, Moscow 119902. Works: Moscow.

COACHBUILDERS

ARCADIPANE DESIGN Ltd   Australia

Founded in 1977. Has produced two major prototypes, six design studies; provides concept studies to manufacturers. General Manager: P. Arcadipane. Head office, press office and works; 148 Northern Rd. West Heidelberg, Melbourne, Victoria 3081.

BERTONE (Carrozzeria) S.p.A.   Italy

Founded in 1912. Produces small and medium series of car bodies; bespoke production for car manufacturing firms and construction of prototypes. President and Managing Director: N. Bertone. Head office: c.so Canonico Allamano 40-46, 10095 Grugliasco, Turin.

BITTER-AUTOMOBILE GmbH & Co. KG   Germany (Federal Republic)

Head office and press office: Stefanstr. 1, Klashammer. 5820 Gevelsberg.

CHRIS HUMBERSTONE DESIGN Ltd   Great Britain

Head office and press office: 4 Monument Rd, Woking. Surrey GU21 5LS.

COGGIOLA Carrozziere   Italy

Proprietor: P. Coggiola. Head office, press office and works: strada S. Luigi 19, 10043 Orbassano, Turin.

COLEMAN-MILNE Ltd   Great Britain

Founded in 1953. Specialist in the manufacture of Grosvenor, Dorchester and Minster limousines. Chairman and Joint Managing Director: R.S.C. Milne. Joint Managing Director: D.H. Hackett. Head office: Colmil Works, Wigan Rd, Hart Common, Westhoughton, Bolton, BL5 2EE.

CRAYFORD AUTO DEVELOPMENT Ltd   Great Britain

Founded in 1960, specialising in convertibles, estate cars and cross country vehicles. Directors: G.D. McMullan, J.J. Smith. Head office: High Street, Westerham, Kent.

DOME Co. Ltd   Japan

Head office and press office: 310-2, Shimozaichi, Iwakura, Sakyo-ku, Kyoto.

PIETRO FRUA (Carrozzerie Speciali)   Italy

Proprietor: P. Frua. Head office, press office and works: v. Papa Giovanni XXIII 13, 10047 Borgo San Pietro - Moncalieri, Turin.

GHIA S.p.A.   Italy

Founded in 1915. Produces car bodies. President and Managing Director: J.D. Head. Members of Board: V. Bonica, S. Cerulli Irelli. Head office: v. A. da Montefeltro 5, 10134 Turin.

GRANDEUR MOTOR CAR CORPORATION   USA

Founded in 1976 by C.R. Northey and C. W. Phillips. Head office, press office and works: 1405 S.W. 8th St., Pompano Beach, Florida 33060.

ITAL DESIGN SIRP S.p.A.   Italy

Founded in 1968. Styling and design of cars in small, medium and large series; construction of models and prototypes. Directors: L. Bosio, G. Giugiaro, A. Mantovani. Head office and press office: v. A. Grandi 11, 10024 Moncalieri, Turin.

KAROSSERIE BAUR GmbH   Germany (Federal Republic)

Directors: K. Baur, H. Baur. Head office, press office and works: Poststr. 40-62, 7 Stuttgart 1 - Berg.

LE VICOMTE CLASSIC COACHBUILDERS, Inc.   Canada

Head office and press office: P.O.B. 430, St. Sauveur des Monts, Quebec, JOR 1RO.

MAGRAW ENGINEERING Ltd Great Britain

Directors: G.J.L. Magraw, M.I. Mech, V.M. Magraw. Head office, press office and works: 135 Widmore Rd, Bromley, Kent BR1 3BA.

MICHELOTTI - Studio Tecnica Design Carrozzeria Italy

Coachbuilding engineering studio for custom-made cars. Proprietor: Giovanni Michelotti. Head office, press office and works: strada dei Boschi 8, 10092 Beinasco, Turin.

MINICARS Inc. USA

Head office and press office: 55 Depot Rd, Goleta, California 93017.

MORETTI S.A.S. FABBRICA AUTOMOBILI & STABILIMENTI CARROZZERIE Italy

Founded in 1926, began motor manufacturing in 1946. Since 1960 no longer produces mechanical parts but is engaged exclusively in production of car bodies. Uses chassis produced by Fiat with whom it has been collaborating for about twenty years. General Partner: G. Moretti. Head office, press office and works: v. Monginevro 278-282, 10142 Turin.

OGLE DESIGN Ltd. Great Britain

Founded in 1954 as design group by late David Ogle. Car production began in 1960. Present head: Tom Karen. Designs include Mini-based Ogle 2-seater, Reliant Scimitar GTE, Bond Bug and Sotheby Special. Head office, press office and works: Birds Hill, Letchworth, Herts SG6 1JA.

PACIFIC COACHWORKS USA

Established as a division of Minicars, Inc., in 1978. General Manager: Meg DiNapoli. Head office and works: 55 Depot Rd, Goleta, California.

PHAETON COACH CORPORATION USA

Founded in 1969 as Eagle Coach Company. Present title since 1974. President and General Manager: R.J. Harris. Products include custom limousines, sport cars and utility vehicles. General offices and showroom: 119 World Trade Center, P.O.B. 58353, Dallas, Texas 75258. Works: 5424 Gregg St., Dallas, Texas 75235.

PININFARINA (Carrozzeria) S.p.A. Italy

Founded in 1930. Produces special and de luxe bodies. President: S. Pininfarina. Managing Director: R. Carli. Member of Board: E. Carbonato. Head office: c. Stati Uniti 61, Turin. Works: v. Lesna 78-80, 10095 Grugliasco, Turin.

THE PHANTOM VEHICLE Co. USA

Founded in 1976 by a small group of designers, engineers and craftsmen. The first prototype is the turbocharged 3-wheel Turbo Phantom. President: R.J. Will. Head office: 630 Center St, Costa Mesa, California 92627. Press office: Box 1704, Newport Beach, California 92663. Works: 779 West 16th St. Costa Mesa, California 92627.

VEHICLE DESIGN FORCE USA

Founded in 1976. President: G. Wiegert. Head office and press office: 1101 West Washington Blvd, Venice, Cal. 90291.

ZAGATO (Carrozzeria) S.p.A. Italy

Founded in 1919. Produces car bodies. President: E. Zagato. Managing Director: G. Zagato. Press office and works: v. Arese, 20017 Terrazzano di Rho, Milan.

ELECTRIC VEHICLE BUILDERS

AM GENERAL CORPORATION USA

Address: 32500 Van Born Road, Wayne, Michigan 48184.

B&Z ELECTRIC CAR USA

Address: 3346 Olive Ave, Signal Hill, California 90807.

BATTRONIC TRUCK CORPORATION USA

Address: Third and Walnut Sts., Boyertown. Pennsylvania 19512.

CEDRE - SEVE France

Address: 09230 Merigon, S.te Croix-Volvestre.

COMMUTER VEHICLES Inc. USA

Address: 50 Sebring Airport, P.O.B. 1479, Sebring, Florida 33870.

COPPER DEVELOPMENT ASSOCIATION Inc. USA

Address: 405 Lexington Avenue, New York, New York 10017.

DAIHATSU KOGYO COMPANY Ltd Japan

Address: 1-1 Daihatsu-cho, Ikeda-shi, Osaka.

DIE MESH CORPORATION USA

Address: 629 Fifth Avenue, Pelham, New York 10803.

EAC - ELECTRIC AUTO CORPORATION USA

Address: 2237 Elliott Avenue, Troy, Michigan 48084.

(US) ELECTRICAR CORPORATION USA

Address: 2342 Main Street, Athol, Massachusetts 01331.

EPC - ELECTRIC PASSENGER CARS Inc. USA

Address: 5127 Galt Way, San Diego, California 92117.

EVA - ELECTRIC VEHICLE ASSOCIATES Inc. USA

Address: 9100 Bank Street, Cleveland, Ohio 44125.

EXXON ENTERPRISES Inc. USA

Address: P.O.B. 192, Florham Park, New Jersey 07932.

FIAT S.p.A. Italy

Address: Corso Marconi 10, 10125 Turin.

FLINDERS UNIVERSITY Australia

Address: Stuart Rd, Bedford Park, Adelaide, SA.

FSM - FABRYKA SAMOCHODÓW MALOLITRAZOWYCH Poland

Address: Ul. R. Luxsemburg 51, Bleisko-Biala.

GARRETT - AIRESEARCH MANUFACTURING Co. of CALIFORNIA USA

A division of The Garrett Corp. Address: 2525 West 190th Street, Torrance, California 90509.

GE - GENERAL ELECTRIC USA

Address: Research and Development Center, P.O. Box 8, Schenectady, New York 12301.

GENERAL MOTORS CORPORATION USA

Address: Chevrolet Motors Division, 3044 W. Grand Blvd, Detroit, Michigan 48202.

GLOBE-UNION Inc. USA

Address: 5757 North Green Bay Ave., Milwaukee, Wisconsin 53201.

GMC TRUCK & COACH DIVISION USA

Address: General Motors, 660 South Boulevard East, Pontiac, Michigan 48053.

GOULD Inc. USA

Address: 30 Gould Center, Rolling Meadows, Illinois 60008.

GURGEL S.A. INDUSTRIA E COMERCIO DE VEHICULOS Brazil

Address: Rodovia Washington Luiz, km 171, Rio Claro 13500, São Paulo.

H-M VEHICLES Inc. USA

Address: 6276 Greenleaf Trail, Apple Valley, Minnesota 55124.

HYBRICON Inc. USA

Address: 11489 Chandler Boulevard, North Holywood, California 91601.

JET INDUSTRIES Inc. USA

Address: 4201 South Congress Avenue, Austin, Texas 78745.

LUCAS BATTERIES Ltd Great Britain

Address: Electric Vehicle Systems, Evelyn Road, Sparkhill, Birmingham B11 3JR.

MARATHON VEHICLES Inc. USA

Address: 900 South Washington Street, Falls Church, Virginia 22046.

McKEE ENGINEERING CORPORATION USA

Address: 411 West Colfax Street, Palatine, Illinois 60067.

MERCEDES-BENZ Germany (FR)

Address: Daimler-Benz AG, Mercedes-Strasse 136, 7 Stuttgart 60.

PGE - PROGETTI GESTIONI ECOLOGICHE Italy

Address: via Rossellini 1, 20124 Milan.

PIAGGIO S.p.A. Italy

Address: v. A. Cecchi 6, 16129 Genoa.

PILCAR Switzerland

Address: rue François-Perréard 22, 1225 Chêne-Bourg, Geneve.

PININFARINA (Carrozzeria) S.p.A. Italy

Address: via Lesna 78-80, 10095 Grugliasco, Turin.

QUINCY-LYNN ENTERPRISES Inc. USA

Address: 2231 W. Shangri-La Road, Phoenix, Arizona 85029.

SAAB-SCANIA Sweden

Address: Saab Car Division, Fack, S-61101 Nyköping.

SEARS ROEBUCK & COMPANY USA

Address: Sears Tower, Chicago, Illinois 60684.

TEILHOL VOITURE ELECTRIQUE France

Address: Zone Industrielle, 63600 Ambert.

TP LABORATORIES Inc. USA

Address: P.O.Box 73, La Porte, Indiana 46350.

VOLKSWAGENWERK AG Germany (Federal Republic)

Address: Abteilung Forschung 6, 3180 Wolfsburg.

VOLVO AB Sweden

Address: Car Division, Advanced Engineering Projects, Department 56500, S-405 08 Göteborg.

(ROBERT STEVEN) WITKOFF USA

Address: 46 Kirkwood Drive, Glen Cove, New York 11542

ZAGATO (Carrozzeria) S.p.A. Italy

Address: v. Arese, 20017 Terrazzano di Rho, Milan.

Indexes

Cars called by names (in alphabetical order)

Model	Make
ACADIAN	PONTIAC (CDN)
ACCORD	HONDA
ALFA ROMEO	FIAT (BR)
ALFASUD	ALFA ROMEO
ALFETTA	ALFA ROMEO
ALLEGRO	AUSTIN
ALPINE	CHRYSLER (GB)
AMBASSADOR	HINDUSTAN
AMIGO	GENERAL MOTORS
ANADOL	OTOSAN
ASCONA	CHEVROLET (ZA), OPEL
ASPEN	DODGE (USA)
AUSTER	NISSAN
AUSTIN-HEALEY	LENHAM
AVENGER	CHRYSLER (GB)
BAGHEERA	MATRA-SIMCA
BEARCAT	BLAKELY, STUTZ
BEL AIR	CHEVROLET (CDN)
BENTLEY DONINGTON	JOHNARD VINTAGE CAR
BETA	LANCIA
BLACKHAWK	STUTZ
BOBCAT	MERCURY (CDN, USA)
BONITO	FIBERFAB
BONNEVILLE	PONTIAC (USA)
BORA	MASERATI
BOX	MONOCOQUE
BRASILIA	VOLKSWAGEN (BR)
BRISA	KIA
BUGATTI	EL-KG, STIMULA
CAMARGUE	ROLLS-ROYCE
CAMARO	CHEVROLET (USA)
CAMPAGNOLA	FIAT (I)
CAPELLA	MAZDA
CAPRI	FORD (D, GB), MERCURY (USA)
CAPRICE	CHEVROLET (USA)
CARINA	TOYOTA
CARLTON	VAUXHALL
CATALINA	PONTIAC (USA)
CAVALIER	VAUXHALL
CEDRIC	NISSAN
CELESTE	MITSUBISHI
CELICA	TOYOTA
CENTURY	BUICK, TOYOTA
CHAIKA	GAZ
CHARADE	DAIHATSU
CHARGER	DODGE (BR)
CHARMANT	DAIHATSU
CHASER	TOYOTA
CHEROKEE	JEEP CORPORATION
CHEVAIR	CHEVROLET (ZA)
CHEVETTE	CHEVROLET (BR, USA) VAUXHALL
CITY	OPEL
CIVIC	HONDA
CLUBMAN	MINI
COMMODORE	CHEVROLET (ZA), HOLDEN, OPEL
COMODORO	CHEVROLET (BR)
CONCORD	AMERICAN MOTORS
CONTINENTAL	LINCOLN
CORCEL	FORD (BR)
CORDOBA	CHRYSLER (USA)
CORNICHE	BENTLEY, ROLLS-ROYCE
COROLLA	TOYOTA
CORONA	TOYOTA
CORONADO	DODGE (RA)
CORSA	TOYOTA
CORTINA	FORD (AUS. GB, ZA)
CORVETTE	CHEVROLET (USA)
COSMO	MAZDA
COUGAR	MERCURY (CDN, USA)

Model	Make
COUNTACH	LAMBORGHINI
CROWN	TOYOTA
CUSTOM	FORD (CDN)
CUSTOM CRUISER	OLDSMOBILE
CUTLASS	OLDSMOBILE
DART	DODGE (BR)
DATSUN	NISSAN
DEAUVILLE	DE TOMASO
DEBONAIR	MITSUBISHI
DELTA	DAIHATSU, OLDSMOBILE
DERBY	VOLKSWAGEN (D)
DE VILLE	CADILLAC, PANTHER
DINO	FERRARI
DIPLOMAT	DODGE (USA)
DOLOMITE	TRIUMPH
DOUBLE-SIX	DAIMLER
DUAL COWL	AUBURN
DYANE	CITROËN
ECLAT	LOTUS
ELECTRA	BUICK
ELEGANTÉ	ELEGANT MOTORS
ELITE	LOTUS
ESCORT	FORD (AUS, D, GB, ZA)
ESPADA	LAMBORGHINI
ESPRIT	LOTUS
ESTATE WAGON	BUICK
EXCELLENCE	FELBER
FAIRLADY	NISSAN
FAIRLANE	FORD (AUS, RA)
FAIRMONT	FORD (AUS, USA)
FALCON	FORD (AUS, RA)
FAMILIA	MAZDA
FIESTA	FORD (D, GB)
FIREBIRD	PONTIAC (USA)
FLEETWOOD	CADILLAC
FLORIAN	ISUZU
FORD « B »	TOTAL REPLICA
FOUR-DOOR	DUESENBERG BROS.
FRAZER NASH	ANTIQUE & CLASSIC AUTOMOTIVE
FRONTE	SUZUKI
GALANT	MITSUBISHI
GALAXIE	FORD (BR)
GAMMA	LANCIA
GAZEL	STANDARD
GEMINI	GENERAL MOTORS, HOLDEN, ISUZU
GIULIETTA	ALFA ROMEO
GLORIA	NISSAN
GOLF	VOLKSWAGEN (D)
GRANADA	FORD (CDN, D, GB, USA, ZA)
GRAND AM	PONTIAC (USA)
GRAND LE MANS	PONTIAC (USA)
GRAND MARQUIS	MERCURY (ÙSA)
GRAND PRIX	PONTIAC (USA)
HARIMAU	GENERAL MOTORS
HORIZON	PLYMOUTH
HURRYCANE	CUSTOCA
IMPALA	CHEVROLET (USA)
JAGUAR	ANTIQUE & CLASSIC AUTOMOTIVE
JEEP	JEEP CORP., MITSUBISHI
JIMNI	SUZUKI
KADETT	OPEL
KHAMSIN	MASERATI
KITTEN	RELIANT
KYALAMI	MASERATI
LADA	VAZ
LAGONDA	ASTON MARTIN
LANCER	MITSUBISHI
LANDCRUISER	TOYOTA
LASER	ELITE
LAUREL	NISSAN
LAURENTIAN	PONTIAC (CDN)

Model	Make
LE BARON	CHRYSLER (USA,, DODGE (BR)
LE MANS	PONTIAC (USA)
LEONE	SUBARU
LE SABRE	BUICK
LIMA	PANTHER
LIMOUSINE	DAIMLER, HONGQI
LONGCHAMP	DE TOMASO
LUCE	MAZDA
MAGNUM	DODGE (BR, USA)
MALAGA	DUTTON
MALIBU	CHEVROLET (USA)
MANTA	OPEL
MARATHON	CHECKER
MARINA	MORRIS
MARK II	TOYOTA
MARQUIS	MERCURY (CDN, USA)
MAVERICK	FORD (BR)
MAX CUORE	DAIHATSU
MAXI	AUSTIN
MEHARI	CITROËN
MERAK	MASERATI
MIDGET	MG
MIGI	DAYTONA
MINI	LEYLAND NUOVA INNOCENTI
MINICA	MITSUBISHI
MONARCH	MERCURY (CDN, USA)
MONTE CARLO	CHEVROLET (USA)
MONZA	CHEVROLET (USA), OPEL
MOSKVICH	AZLK
MURAT	TOFAS
MUSTANG	FORD (USA)
NASR	EL NSR
NEWPORT	CHRYSLER (USA)
NEW YORKER	CHRYSLER (USA)
NINETY-EIGHT	OLDSMOBILE
NOMAD	CHEVROLET (ZA)
NOVA	CHEVROLET (USA)
NUOVA LELE	ENNEZETA
OASIS	FELBER
OMEGA	OLDSMOBILE
OMNI	DODGE (USA)
OPALA	CHEVROLET (BR)
PACER	AMERICAN MOTORS
PADMINI	PREMIER
PANTERA	DE TOMASO
PARISIENNE	PONTIAC (CDN)
PASSAT	VOLKKSWAGEN (D, BR)
PATROL	NISSAN
PHAETON	REPLICARS
PHANTOM	ROLLS-ROYCE
PHOENIX	PONTIAC (USA)
PINTO	FORD (USA)
POLARA	DODGE (BR)
POLO	VOLKSWAGEN (D)
POLONEZ	POLSKI FIAT
PONY	HYUNDAI
PRELUDE	HONDA
PRESIDENT	NISSAN
PULSAR	NISSAN
QUATTROPORTE	MASERATI
RABBIT	VOLKSWAGEN (USA)
RALLYE	OPEL
RANCHO	MATRA-SIMCA
RANGE ROVER	LAND ROVER
REGAL	BUICK
REKORD	CHEVROLET (ZA), OPEL
REPLICA BMW	SBARRO
REX	SUBARU
RITMO	FIAT (I)
RIVIERA	BUICK
ROADPACER	MAZDA
ROADSTER	CLÉNET, REPLICARS
ROBIN	RELIANT
ROM	ROM CARMEL
ROYALE	VAUXHALL

Model	Make
SAFARI	MONTEVERDI
SAHARA	MONTEVERDI
SALOON	PAYKAN
SAVANNA	MAZDA
SCIMITAR	RELIANT
SCIROCCO	VOLKSWAGEN (D)
SCOUT	INTERNATIONAL HARVESTER
SEDAN	SHANGHAI
SENATOR	OPEL
SEVILLE	CADILLAC
SERIES III	EXCALIBUR
SHERPA	FIBERFAB
SIERRA	MONTEVERDI
SIETE	RENAULT (E)
SILHOUETTE	LAMBORGHINI
SILVER SHADOW	ROLLS-ROYCE
SILVER WRAITH	ROLLS-ROYCE
SILVIA	NISSAN
SIMCA	CHRYSLER (E), CHRYSLER FRANCE
SKYHAWK	BUICK
SKYLARK	BUICK
SKYLINE	NISSAN
SOVEREIGN	DAIMLER
SPEEDSTER	AUBURN, INTERMECCANICA
SPIDER JUNIOR	ALFA ROMEO
SPIRIT	AMERICAN MOTORS
SPITFIRE	TRIUMPH
SPORTS	NOVA, SPARTAN CARS
SPRINTER	TOYOTA
STANZA	NISSAN
STARFIRE	OLDSMOBILE
STARLET	TOYOTA
STASH	SBARRO
STRATO	CUSTOCA
ST. REGIS	DODGE (USA)
SUNBEAM	CHRYSLER (GB)
SUNBIRD	HOLDEN, PONTIAC (USA)
SUNNY	NISSAN
SUPER	SEVEN
TAFT	DAIHATSU
TAIMAR	TVR
TAUNUS	FORD (D, RA)
TERCEL	TOYOTA
THUNDERBIRD	FORD (USA)
TORANA	HOLDEN
TORONADO	OLDSMOBILE
TURBO	ARGYLL, GREENWOOD, PORSCHE, TVR
URRACO	LAMBORGHINI
VALIANT	CHRYSLER (AUS)
VANDEN PLAS	DAIMLER
VARIANT	VOLKSWAGEN (BR)
VERANEIO	CHEVROLET (BR)
VERSAILLES	LINCOLN
VIOLET	NISSAN
VISA	CITROËN
VIVA	VAUXHALL
VOLARÉ	PLYMOUTH
VOLGA	GAZ
WAGONEER	JEEP CORPORATION
WINDHOUND	SBARRO
ZASTAVA	ZCZ
ZEPHYR	MERCURY (USA)

Cars called by letters (in alphabetical order)

Model	Make
A4 CITY	LAWIL
A 11	AVALLONE
A 112	AUTOBIANCHI
A 310	ALPINE
AMX	AMERICAN MOTORS
BB	FERRARI
BJ 212	PEKING
B PLUS	DUTTON
CX	CITROËN
D TYPE	LYNX
G	CITROËN
G21	GINETTA
GS	CITROËN
GT	KELMARK
GTB	PUMA
GTE	PUMA
GTM	K.M.B.
GTS	PUMA
HZ	HOLDEN
J 72	PANTHER
LN	CITROËN
LNA	CITROËN
LTD	FORD (AUS, USA)
M 1	BMW (D)
MGB	MG
MK 2	SYD LAWRENCE
PLUS 8	MORGAN
S3 VARZINA	LAWIL
S 110 R	ŠKODA
SS	ARKLEY
SSJ	DUESENBERG
T2	BENTLEY
T 613	TATRA
TR 7	TRIUMPH
TX-S	FAIRTHORPE
TX TRIPPER	TECHNICAL EXPONENTS
V8	ASTON MARTIN
X1/9	FIAT (I)
X-12	GURGEL
X-20	GURGEL
XJ	JAGUAR
XJ-S	JAGUAR

Cars called by numbers (in alphabetical order)

Model	Make
2 CV	CITROËN
4	CLÉNET, RENAULT (E, F)
IV PORTE	STUTZ
4/4 1600	MORGAN
5	RENAULT (E, F)
6	PANTHER, RENAULT (E, F)
6.6 S	SCEPTRE
12	RENAULT (E, F)
14	RENAULT (F)
15	RENAULT (F)
16	RENAULT (F)
17	RENAULT (F)
18	RENAULT (F)
20	RENAULT (F)
30	RENAULT (F)
66	VOLVO (NL)
88	LAND ROVER
96	SAAB
104	PEUGEOT
105	ŠKODA, SYRENA
109	LAND ROVER
114	ZIL
117	ISUZU, ZIL
120	ŠKODA
124	FIAT (I), SEAT
125	FIAT (RA)
125 P	POLSKI-FIAT
126	FIAT (I), GIANNINI
126 P	POLSKI-FIAT
127	FIAT (I), GIANNINI, SEAT
128	FIAT (I, RA), GIANNINI, SEAT

Model	Make
131	FIAT (I), SEAT
132	FIAT (I), SEAT
133	FIAT (RA), SEAT
147	FIAT (BR)
180	CHRYSLER (E)
181	VOLKSWAGEN (D)
200	MERCEDES-BENZ
230	MERCEDES-BENZ
240	ARO, MERCEDES-BENZ
241	ARO
242	VOLVO (S)
243	ARO
244	ARO, VOLVO (S)
245	VOLVO (S)
250	MERCEDES-BENZ, PORTARO
262	VOLVO (S)
264	VOLVO (S)
265	VOLVO (S)
280	MERCEDES-BENZ
300	MERCEDES-BENZ
304	PEUGEOT
305	PEUGEOT
308	FERRARI
316	BMW (D)
318	BMW (D)
320	BMW (D)
323	BMW (D)
343	VOLVO (NL)
350	MERCEDES-BENZ
353	WARTBURG
400	FERRARI
412	BRISTOL
450	MERCEDES-BENZ
469 B	UAZ
504	PEUGEOT
518	BMW (D)
520	BMW (D, ZA)
525	BMW (D)
528	BMW (D, ZA)
530	BMW (ZA)
600	MERCEDES-BENZ
600 S	FIAT (RA, U)
601	TRABANT
603	BRISTOL
604	PEUGEOT
630	BMW (D)
633	BMW (D)
635	BMW (D)
728	BMW (D)
730	BMW (D)
733	BMW (D)
803	YLN
850	MINI
856	ELEGANT MOTORS
898	ELEGANT MOTORS
900	SAAB
902	YLN
911	PORSCHE
924	PORSCHE
928	PORSCHE
968-A	ZAZ
969-A	ZAZ
1000	MINI
1200	VOLKSWAGEN (D, MEX., WAN)
1275	MINI
1300	DACIA, FIAT (RA), TORO, VOLKSWAGEN (BR)
1303	VOLKSWAGEN (D)
1430	SEAT
1500	DODGE (RA), VANDEN PLAS
1600	VOLKSWAGEN (BR)
1700	PRINCESS
2000	ALFA ROMEO, PRINCESS
2200	PRINCESS
2300	ROVER
2600	ROVER
3000	AC, TVR
3500	ROVER

MAXIMUM SPEED

Up to 65 mph

	mph
LAWIL S3 Varzina/A4 City	39
SUZUKI Jimny 55 Series (26 hp)/Jimny 8 Series (26 hp)	55
ZAZ 969-A 4 x 4	56
PEKING BJ 212	61
CITROËN Mehari/Mehari 2 + 2	62
GURGEL X-20	62
TRABANT 601 Limousine/601 Universal	62
CITROËN 2 CV Spécial	63
FIAT (I) 126 Berlina Base/126 Personal	65
POLSKI-FIAT 126 P/650	65
SUBARU Rex 550 SEEC-T Series (31 hp)	65
SUZUKI Fronte 7-S Series (28 hp)	65

From 66 mph to 100 mph

	mph
LAND ROVER 88'' Regular/109'' Estate Car	66
SUZUKI Fronte Hatch 55 Series (25 hp)	67
ARO 240/243	68
CITROËN 2 CV 6	68
DAIHATSU Max Cuore Series (28 hp)	68
FIAT (I) Campagnola Lunga	68
FIAT (RA) 600 S	68
FIAT (U) 600 S	68
MITSUBISHI Minica Ami 55 Series (31 hp)	68
RENAULT (F) 4/4 TL/4 Rodeo	68
ZCZ Zastava 750/Zastava 750 Luxe	68
PORTARO 250	70
ARO 241/244	71
DAIHATSU Taft Series (80 hp)	71
RENAULT (E) 4/4 TL	71
FIAT (I) Campagnola	71
STANDARD Gazel	71
UAZ 469 B	71
VOLKSWAGEN (D) 181/1200 L	71
VOLKSWAGEN (MEX) 1200	71
VOLKSWAGEN (WAN) 1200	71
GURGEL X-12/X-12 TR	73
MINI 850 Saloon	73
RENAULT (F) 6	73
CHEVROLET (ZA) Nomad	74
HINDUSTAN Ambassador Mark 3	74
AZLK Moskvich 2138/Moskvich 2136	75
CITROËN Dyane 6/LN	75
GENERAL MOTORS (MAL) Harimau/Amigo	75
GIANNINI Fiat Giannini 126 Series (30 hp)	75
MITSUBISHI Jeep Series (100 hp)	75
PREMIER Padmini	75
RENAULT (F) 4 GTL	75
RENAULT (RA) 4 S	75
SEAT 133 Lujo	75
SYRENA 105	75
TOYOTA Landcruiser BJ40-KC	75
VOLKSWAGEN (BR) 1300/1300 L Limousine	75
ZCZ Zastava 750 S	75
OPEL (D) City Series (40 hp)/Kadett Series (40 hp)	76
RENAULT (F) 5	76
CITROËN LNA/Visa Spécial/Visa Club	77
FORD (GB) Escort Series (41 hp)	77

	mph
MINI 1000 Saloon	77
JEEP CORPORATION Jeep Series (98 hp)	78
NISSAN Patrol 4WD	78
SEAT 131 Diesel 1760 5 Puertas	78
WARTBURG 353 W Tourist De Luxe	78
YLN 803 DL	78
ZAZ 968-A	78
FORD (D) Escort Series (44 hp)	79
AUSTIN Allegro Series (45 hp)	80
CHRYSLER (GB) Sunbeam Series (42 hp)	80
INTERNATIONAL HARVESTER Scout Series (76.5 hp)	80
PREMIER Padmini De Luxe	80
RELIANT Kitten DL Saloon/Kitten DL Estate Car/Robin 850 Saloon/Robin 850 Super Saloon/Robin 850 Super Estate Car	80
FIAT (RA) 133/133 L	81
FORD (D) Fiesta Series (40 hp)	81
FORD (GB) Fiesta Series (40 hp)	81
LEYLAND Mini-Moke Californian	81
MERCEDES-BENZ 200 D	81
MINI Clubman Saloon/Clubman Estate Car	81
PEUGEOT 304 GLD Berline/304 GLD Break	81
RENAULT (F) 6 Rodeo	81
SEAT 131 Diesel 1760	81
SHANGHAI Sedan	81
ŠKODA 105 S/105 L	81
VOLKSWAGEN (D) 1303 Cabriolet	81
WARTBURG 353 W	81
FORD (GB) Cortina Series (50 hp)	82
VAZ Lada Niva 2121 4 x 4	82
VOLKSWAGEN (D) Polo Series (40 hp)/Derby Series (40 hp)	82
CHEVROLET (BR) Chevette Series (60 hp)	83
RENAULT (E) 6 TL/Siete TL	83
AUTOBIANCHI A 112	84
AZLK Moskvich 2137/Moskvich 2140 Combi IZh	84
DAIHATSU Charade Sedan Series (55 hp)	84
EL NASR Nasr 128	84
RENAULT (E) 5 Series (44 hp)	84
FIAT (BR) 147 Series (57 hp)	84
FIAT (I) 127 Series (45 hp)/132 Diesel 2000	84
GAZ Volga 24 Indenor Diesel	84
MERCEDES-BENZ 220 D	84
PEUGEOT 104 GL Berline/104 ZL Coupé	84
RENAULT (F) 6 TL	84
SEAT 133 Especial Lujo/127 Series (43 hp)/132 Diesel 2200/132 Diesel 2200 Lujo	84
AMERICAN MOTORS (Spirit Series (80 hp)	85
AUSTIN Maxi Series (68 hp)	85
FORD (D) Taunus Series (55 hp)	85
RENAULT (F) 5 TL/5 GTL/12 Berline	85
TRIUMPH Dolomite 1300	85
VOLVO (NL) 66 DL 2-door/66 DL 3-door	85
ZCZ Zastava 101/Zastava 101 Luxe	85
CHEVROLET (ZA) Ascona Series (54 hp)	86
CHRYSLER (E) Simca 1200 Series (52 hp)	86
LAFER MP	86
MAZDA Familia (USA) Series (52 hp)	86
MERCEDES-BENZ 240 D/240 D Long Wheelbase/240 TD	

Model	mph
MORRIS Marina Series (57 hp)	86
OPEL (D) Ascona Series (55 hp)	86
RENAULT (F) 12 Break	86
VAUXHALL Viva Series (57.7 hp)	86
VOLKSWAGEN (BR) 1600 Limousine/Brasilia 2-door/Brasilia 4-door/ Brasilia LS/Variant II/ Variant II Luxe	86
AUTOBIANCHI A 112 Elegant	87
CHRYSLER FRANCE Simca 110 Series (50 hp)	87
DAIHATSU Charade Coupé Series (55 hp)/Delta Wagon Series (92 hp)	87
RENAULT (E) 12 Series (57 hp)	87
FIAT (I) 128 CL 1100/128 Panorama Base 1100	87
FIAT (RA) 128 Berlina/128 Familiar 5 Puertas	87
KIA Brisa 1000	87
MINI 1275 GT	87
NUOVA INNOCENTI Mini 90 N/Mini 90 SL	87
OTOSAN Anadol SL	87
PAYKAN Saloon	87
PONTIAC (USA) Sunbird Series (90 hp)	87
RENAULT (F) 16 TL (55 hp)	87
RENAULT (RA) 12 TL	87
ROM CARMEL Rom 1300	87
ŠKODA 120 L	87
TOYOTA Landcruiser FJ56V-K	87
VAZ Lada Series (60 hp)	87
VOLKSWAGEN (D) Golf Series (50 hp)/Golf Diesel Series (50 hp)	87
ZCZ Zastava 1300/Zastava 1300 Luxe	87
FORD (BR) Corcel II Base/Corcel II L/Corcel II LDO/ Corcel II Belina Base/Corcel II Belina L/Corcel II Belina LDO/Corcel II GT	88
FORD (ZA) Escort 1300 L 4-door Sedan/Cortina 3000 S Sedan	88
RENAULT (F) 12 TL Berline	88
VOLKSWAGEN (D) Passat Diesel Series (50 hp)	88
CHRYSLER (GB) Avenger Series (59 hp)	89
CITROËN Viva Super	89
FORD (D) Granada Series (70 hp)	89
OPEL (D) Manta Series (55 hp)	89
RENAULT (F) 5 Automatic/12 Break TL/12 Break Automatic/14 TL/14 GTL	89
VOLKSWAGEN (D) Scirocco Series (50 hp)	89
AMERICAN MOTORS Concord Series (90 hp)	90
ANTIQUE & CLASSIC AUTOMOTIVE Frazer Nash TT Interceptor/Jaguar SS 100	90
AUDI NSU Audi 80 Series (55 hp)	90
AVALLONE A 11	90
BUICK Century Series (105 hp)/Regal Series (105 hp)	90
CHECKER Marathon Series (110 hp)	90
CHEVROLET (BR) Veraneio Series (151 hp)	90
CHEVROLET (USA) Chevette Series (70 hp)	90
CHRYSLER (USA) Le Baron Series (100 hp)	90
DACIA 1300 Saloon	90
DAYTONA Migi	90
DODGE (RA) 1500	90
DODGE (USA) Aspen Series (100 hp)/Diplomat Series (100 hp)	90
FIAT (I) Ritmo Series (60 hp)	90
FIAT (RA) 128 L Berlina	90
GAZ Volga 24/Volga 24-02	90
JEEP CORPORATION Cherokee Series (114 hp)	90

Model	mph
MATRA-SIMCA Rancho	90
MAZDA Familia AP Series (72 hp)	90
NISSAN Pulsar Series (70 hp)/Sunny Series (70 hp)	90
OTOSAN Anadol SV-1600	90
PEUGEOT 104 GLS Berline/104 SL Berline	90
PLYMOUTH Volaré Series (100 hp)	90
POLSKI-FIAT 125 P 1300/125 P 1300 Estate/Polonez	90
RENAULT (F) 16 TL Automatic	90
ŠKODA S 110 R Coupé	90
VANDEN PLAS 1500	90
VOLKSWAGEN (BR) Passat Series (65 hp)	90
VOLVO (NL) 66 GL 2-door/66 GL 3-door/343 L/343 DL	90
CITROËN G Spécial Break/CX 2500 Diesel Confort/CX 2500 Diesel Break Confort/CX 2500 Diesel Super/CX 2500 Diesel Break Super/CX 2500 Diesel Familiale Super/CX 2500 Diesel Pallas	90
DODGE (USA) Omni Series (70 hp)	90
FORD (GB) Capri II Series (57 hp)	90
OPEL (D) Rekord Series (60 hp)	90
PEUGEOT 305 GL/305 GR/504 Break	90
PLYMOUTH Horizon Series (70 hp)	90
VAUXHALL Chevette Series (57.7 hp)/ Cavalier Series (57.7 hp)	90
ZCZ Zastava 101 Super	90
CHRYSLER FRANCE Simca Horizon Series (59 hp)	91
CITROËN GS Club Berline C Matic/GS Pallas C Matic	91
MERCEDES-BENZ 300 D/300 D Long Wheelbase/300 TD	91
RENAULT (F) 12 Break TS/16 TL (66 hp)	91
TRIUMPH Spitfire 1500 (USA version)	91
VOLVO (S) 240 Diesel Series (82 hp)	91
ALFA ROMEO Alfasud Series (63 hp)	92
AZLK Moskvich 2140/Moskvich 2140 IZh	92
BUICK Le Sabre Series (115 hp)	92
CHEVROLET (USA) Nova Series (90 hp)/Nova Custom Series (90 hp)/Malibu Series (94 hp)/Monte Carlo Series (94 hp)	92
CHRYSLER (USA) Newport Series (110 hp)/New Yorker Series (110 hp)	92
CITROËN G Spécial Berline/GS X/ GS Club Break	92
DAIHATSU Charmant 1300 Series (72 hp)	93
DODGE (RA) 1500 M 1.8/1500 M 1.8 Rural	93
DODGE (USA) St. Regis (110 hp)	93
EL NASR Nasr 125	93
FIAT (I) 131 Series (65 hp)/132 Diesel 2500	93
FORD (CDN) Granada Special Edition Series (97 hp)	93
FORD (USA) Granada Series (97 hp)	93
GIANNINI Fiat Giannini 127 Series (58 hp)	93
HONDA Civic CVCC Series (68 hp)/Civic Wagon Series (70 hp)/Accord 1800 Series (90 hp)	93
KIA Brisa 1300	93
MERCURY (CDN) Monarch Special Editon Series (97 hp)	93
MERCURY (USA) Monarch Series (97 hp)	93
MITSUBISHI Mirage Series (72 hp)/Lancer Series (70 hp)	93

Model	mph
MONTEVERDI Safari	93
NISSAN Violet Series (80 hp)/Auster Series (80 hp)/Stanza Series (80 hp)	93
OLDSMOBILE Starfire Series (85 hp)	93
PEUGEOT 304 GL Berline/304 GL Break/ 304 SL Break	93
PONTIAC (CDN) Acadian Series (70 hp)/Laurentian Series (115 hp)/Parisienne Series (115 hp)	93
PONTIAC (USA) Phoenix Series (115 hp)/Firebird Series (115 hp)/Le Mans Series (115 hp)/ Grand Le Mans Series (115 hp)/Grand Am Series (115 hp)/Catalina Series (115 hp)/Bonneville Series (115 hp)/Bonneville Brougham Series (115 hp)	93
RENAULT (F) 15 TL/15 GTL	93
SAAB 96 GL	93
SEAT 124-D/124-D LS/131 CL 1430 5 Puertas	93
ŠKODA 120 LS	93
SUBARU Leone SEEC-T Series (72 hp)	93
TOFAS Murat 131	93
TOYOTA Corolla Series (72 hp)/Sprinter Series (72 hp)	93
VOLKSWAGEN (D) Passat Series (55 hp)	93
VOLKSWAGEN (USA) Rabbit Series (71 hp)	93
CHRYSLER (E) Chrysler 150 Series (68 hp)	94
CHRYSLER (GB) Alpine GL	94
CHRYSLER FRANCE Simca 1307 GLS	94
CITROËN GS Club Berline/GS Pallas	94
CITROËN GS Club Berline/GS Pallas	94
RENAULT (F) 5 TS	94
TRIUMPH Dolomite 1500/Dolomite 1500 HL	94
DODGE (BR) Polara/Polara Gran Luxo	95
FORD (RA) Taunus L 2000 Sedan/Taunus GXL 2000 Sedan/Falcon Sedan Standard/Falcon Sedan De Luxe/Falcon Station Wagon Standard/Falcon Station Wagon De Luxe	95
MG Midget	95
PEUGEOT 305 SR	95
RENAULT (F) 18 TL/18 GTL	95
AMERICAN MOTORS Pacer Series (110 hp)	96
BUICK Skylark Series (115 hp)	96
CHEVROLET (BR) Opala Sedan/Opala Coupé/Opala Caravan	96
CHEVROLET (USA) Monza Series (90 hp)/Camaro Series (90 hp)	96
CUSTOCA Hurrycane/Strato ES	96
DODGE (RA) Coronado Automatic	96
FORD (AUS) Falcon Series (130 hp)/Falcon 500 Series (130 hp)/Fairmont Series (130 hp)	96
FORD (BR) Maverick Sedan Super/Maverick Sedan Super Luxo/Maverick Sedan LDO/Maverick Coupé Super/Maverick Super Luxo/Maverick Coupé LDO/Maverick Coupé GT-4	96
FORD (CDN) Custom 500 Series (129 hp)	96
FORD (D) Capri II Series (68 hp)	96
FORD (RA) Fairlane LTD 3600 Sedan	96
FORD (USA) Pinto Series (88 hp)/Mustang Series (88 hp)/Fairmont Series (88 hp)/LTD II Series (133 hp)/LTD Series (129 hp)	96
GIANNINI Fiat Giannini 128 Series (66.2 hp)	96
HOLDEN Gemini TD Series (83 hp)/HZ Series (110 hp)	96
LAND ROVER Range Rover	96
MAZDA Luce Series (100 hp)	96

	mph
MERCURY (CDN) Bobcat Series (88 hp)/ Marquis Meteor Series (129 hp)	96
MERCURY (USA) Bobcat Series (88 hp)/Zephyr Series (88 hp)/Capri Series (88 hp)/Marquis Series (129 hp)/Grand Marquis Series (129 hp)	96
MITSUBISHI Celeste Series (80 hp)/Galant Sigma Series (86 hp)/ Galant Lambda Series (86 hp)/Debonair Series (120 hp)	96
NISSAN Skyline Series (95 hp)	96
NUOVA INNOCENTI Mini 120 SL	96
OLDSMOBILE Omega Series (115 hp)/Delta 88 Series (115 hp)/Delta 88 Royale Series (115 hp)/Ninety-Eight Series (115 hp)/Custom Cruiser Series (115 hp)	96
PAYKAN Salon GT	96
PEUGEOT 104 S Berline/104 ZS Coupé/504 Berline	96
POLSKI-FIAT 125 P 1500/125 P 1500 Estate	96
PONTIAC (USA) Grand Prix Series (115 hp)	96
RENAULT (F) 14 TS	96
RENAULT (RA) 12 TS/12 TS Break	96
SEAT 124-D Especial/131 1430/131 1430 Supermirafiori	96
TORO 1300	96
ZCZ Zastava 1500/Zastava 1500 Luxe/Zastava 1500 Familiare	96
HYUNDAI Pony Sedan/Pony Coupé	97
FORD (RA) Falcon Sedan Futura	97
CITROËN GS X3	98
RENAULT (F) 18 TS Automatic/18 GTS Automatic/20 TL Automatic/20 GTL Automatic	98
AMERICAN MOTORS AMX (110 hp)	99
AUDI NSU Audi 100 Series (85 hp)/Audi 100 Avant Series (85 hp)	99
AUTOBIANCHI A 112 Abarth	99
BMW (D) 316/518	99
CHEVROLET (BR) Opala SS-4 Coupé/Opala SS-4 Caravan	99
CHEVROLET (CDN) Bel Air Series (115 hp)	99
CHEVROLET (USA) Impala (90 hp)/Caprice Classic Series (90 hp)	99
DAIHATSU Charmant 1600 Series (88 hp)	99
DODGE (RA) Coronado	99
FIAT (RA) 1300 TV lava	99
FORD (ZA) Cortina 1600 L Sedan/Cortina 1600 L Station Wagon	99
HOLDEN Sunbird Series (81 hp)	99
HONGQI 9-pass. Limousine	99
ISUZU Florian SII Series	99
JEEP CORPORATION Wagoneer Series (129 hp)	99
LANCIA Beta Berlina 1300	99
MAZDA Capella Series (90 hp)	99
MERCEDES-BENZ 200	99
NISSAN Laurel Series (105 hp)/Cedric Series (115 hp)/Gloria Series (115 hp)	99
NUOVA INNOCENTI Mini De Tomaso	99
OLDSMOBILE Cutlass Series (115 hp)	99
OPEL (D) Rallye Series (75 hp)	99
PRINCESS 1700 Series (87 hp)/2000 Series (87 hp)/2200 Series (87 hp)	99
SEAT 128-3P 1200/128-3P 1430/131 CL 1600 5 Puertas	99
TOYOTA Corsa Series (80 hp)/Tercel Series (80 hp)/Corolla (USA) Series (75 hp)/Crown Series (110 hp)	99

	mph
BLAKELY Bearcat 'S'	100
ELITE Laser 917	100
EL-KG Bugatti 35 B	100
FORD (ZA) Escort 1600 GL 4-door Sedan	100
TOTAL REPLICA Ford 'B' Roadster	100
TRIUMPH Spitfire 1500	100

From 101 mph to 120 mph

	mph
FORD (AUS) Escort Series (98 hp)	101
PEUGEOT 504 GL Break/504 Break Familial	101
RENAULT (F) 18 TS	101
CHRYSLER (GB) Alpine S/Alpine GLS	102
CHRYSLER FRANCE Simca 1307 S/ Simca 1308 GT	102
DODGE (BR) Dart De Luxo Sedan/Dart Gran Sedan/Dart De Luxo Coupé	102
FORD (AUS) Fairlane Series (240 hp)	102
FORD (ZA) Granada 2000 GL Sedan	102
HOLDEN Commodore Series (110 hp)	102
PEUGEOT 504 GL Berline	102
SAAB 99 Series (100 hp)/900 Series (100 hp)	102
TRIUMPH Dolomite 1850 HL	102
ALFA ROMEO Giulietta 1.3	103
BMW (D) 318	103
CHEVROLET (ZA) Rekord Series (90 hp)/Commodore Series (120 hp)	103
CHRYSLER (USA) Cordoba (135 hp)	103
DODGE (USA) Magnum XE (135 hp)	103
FIAT (I) 132 1600 Berlina	103
FIAT (RA) 125 Familiar	103
FORD (AUS) Cortina TE Series (112 hp)	103
FORD (BR) Galaxie 500/Galaxie 500 LTD/ Galaxie 500 Landau	103
FORD (GB) Granada Series (99 hp)	103
FORD (USA) Thunderbird Series (133 hp)	103
HOLDEN Torana UC Series (105 hp)	103
ISUZU Gemini Series (100 hp)	103
LANCIA Beta Coupé 1300	103
MAZDA Roadpacer Sedan	103
MERCURY (CDN) Coguar 'S' Series (133 hp)	103
MERCURY (USA) Cougar Series (133 hp)	103
NISSAN Datsun Bluebird Series (95 hp)	103
RENAULT (F) 16 TX Automatic/20 TS Automatic/18 GTS/20 TL/20 GTL	103
SEAT Sport 1430/131 Supermirafiori 1600	103
TOYOTA Starlet Series (72 hp)/Carina Series (88 hp)/Celica Series (88 hp)/ Corona Series (88 hp)/Mark II Series (95 hp)/Chaser Series (95 hp)	103
VOLVO (S) 240 Series (97 hp)	103
YLN 902 SD	103
FORD (ZA) Cortina 2000 GL Sedan/Cortina 2000 GL Station Wagon	104
FAIRTHORPE TX-S 1500	105
FIAT (I) 132 2000 Berlina	105
MORGAN 4-4 1600 2-seater/4-4 1600 4-seater	105
ALFA ROMEO Spider Junior 1300	106
BMW (D) 320 i	106
BUICK Estate Wagon Series (155 hp)/Electra Series (155 hp)	106

	mph
CHEVROLET (BR) Opala SS-6 Coupé/ Opala SS-6 Caravan/Comodoro 4 Sedan/ Comodoro 4 Coupé/ Comodoro 6 Sedan/Comodoro 6 Coupé	106
CHRYSLER (E) Chrysler 180 Series (100 hp)/ Chrysler 2-litros	106
CHRYSLER FRANCE Simca 1309 SX/Simca 2 L Automatic	106
CITROËN CX 2000 Break Confort	106
FELBER Oasis	106
FIAT (BR) Alfa Romeo 2300 B	106
FIAT (I) X1/9 five speed (USA version)	106
FIAT (RA) 125 S/125 SL	106
FORD (RA) Taunus GXL 2300 Sedan/Taunus GT 2300 Coupé	106
GENERAL MOTORS (MAL) Gemini 1.6 Sedan/ Gemini 1.6 Coupé	106
HONDA Prelude Series (90 hp)	106
ISUZU 117 1950 Series	106
LANCIA Beta Berlina 1600	106
MAZDA 626 Series (90 hp)/Cosmo Series (100 hp)	106
MERCEDES-BENZ 230/230 C/230 T	106
MONTEVERDI Sahara	106
NISSAN Silvia Series (105 hp)	106
RENAULT (F) 16 TX/17 TS Cabriolet/ 20 TS	106
REPLICARS Phaeton/Roadster	106
SEAT 132 2000 Lujo	106
VOLVO (S) 260 Series (125 hp)	106
YLN 803 SD	106
MG MGB GT/MGB Sports	107
PEUGEOT 504 TI Berline	107
TRIUMPH TR 7 (USA version)	107
VAUXHALL Carlton 2000 Saloon/Carlton 2000 Estate	107
CITROËN CX 2000 Confort/CX 2000 Super/CX 2000 Pallas/CX 2400 Break Super/CX 2400 Familiale Super	108
GINETTA G 21	108
LANCIA Beta HPE 1600	108
LINCOLN Versailles (130 hp)	108
SPARTAN CARS 2-seater Sports/ 2 + 2-seater Sports	108
TECHNICAL EXPONENTS TX Tripper 1500/TX Tripper 1500 De Luxe	108
ALFA ROMEO Spider Junior 1600/Giulietta 1.6/Alfetta 1.6	109
BMW (ZA) 520	109
BUICK Skyhawk Series (115 hp)	109
CHRYSLER (AUS) Valiant CL Series (138 hp)	109
CHRYSLER FRANCE Simca 1610	109
FIAT (BR) Alfa Romeo 2300 TI	109
FIAT (I) 124 Sport Spider 2000	109
FORD (RA) Fairlane LTD-V8 Sedan	109
LINCOLN Continental Series (159 hp)/ Continental Mark V (159 hp)	109
RENAULT (F) 5 Alpine	109
RENAULT (RA) 12 Alpine	109
TOYOTA Celica (USA) Series (96 hp)	109
ARKLEY SS	110
CHEVROLET (ZA) Chevair Series (105 hp)	110
DUESENBERG SSJ	110
EXCALIBUR Series III (215 hp)	110

	mph
FORD (ZA) Granada 3000 Ghia Sedan	110
INTERMECCANICA Speedster	110
NOVA Sports	110
PANTHER Lima	110
RENAULT (F) 30 TS Automatic	110
TRIUMPH TR 7	110
LANCIA Beta Coupé 1600/Beta Spider 1600	111
PEUGEOT 504 Cabriolet/504 Coupé	111
ALFA ROMEO Alfetta GT 1.6/Alfetta 1.8	112
BMW (D) 320/520	112
CITROËN CX 2400 Super/CX 2400 Pallas/CX 2400 Pallas Injection C Matic	112
BUICK Century Turbo Coupé (175 hp)/Riviera Series (160 hp)	112
CADILLAC De Ville Series (180 hp)/Fleetwood Series (180 hp)	112
DODGE (BR) Le Baron/Charger R-T/Magnum	112
FIAT (I) X1/9 five speed	112
FORD (RA) Falcon Sedan Sprint	112
FORD (ZA) Escort RS 2000 2-door Sedan	112
GAZ Chaika	112
HONKQI 6-pass. Limousine	112
LANCIA Beta Berlina 2000/Beta HPE 2000/Beta ES 2000	112
MAZDA Savanna RX7 Series	112
MERCEDES-BENZ 250/250 Long Wheelbase/250 T	112
NISSAN Fairlady Series (130 hp)/President Series (200 hp)	112
OLDSMOBILE Toronado Brougham Coupé (165 hp)	112
OPEL (D) Commodore Series (115 hp)	112
RELIANT Scimitar GTE	112
ROLLS-ROYCE Phantom VI	112
SBARRO Replica BMW 328 Standard	112
SEVEN Super 7	112
TOYOTA Century Series (180 hp)	112
PEUGEOT 604 SL	113
PUMA GTE 1600 Coupé/GTS 1600 Sport	113
RENAULT (F) 30 TX Automatic	113
FORD (BR) Maverick Coupé GT	114
FORD (ZA) Cortina 3000 Ghia Sedan/Cortina 3000 Ghia Station Wagon/Granada 3000 GL Sedan	114
PANTHER J 72 4.2-Litre	114
RENAULT (F) 30 TS	114
ROVER 2300	114
ALFA ROMEO Alfetta 2000 L	115
CADILLAC Seville (170 hp)/Fleetwood Eldorado (170 hp)	115
DAIMLER Limousine	115
DUESENBERG BROS. Four-door Town Sedan	115
JAGUAR XJ 3.4	115
LANCIA Gamma Berlina 2000/Gamma Coupé 2000	115
MATRA-SIMCA Bagheera	115
PEUGEOT 604 TI	115
RENAULT (RA) Torino Grand Routier	115
VAUXHALL Royale Saloon	115
LANCIA Beta Spider 2000	116
TATRA T 613	116
TRIUMPH Dolomite Sprint	116
CITROËN CX 2400 GTI	117

	mph
LANCIA Beta Coupé 2000	117
PEUGEOT 504 V6 Coupé	117
RENAULT (F) 30 TX	117
ROVER 2600	117
BENTLEY T2 Saloon/Corniche Saloon/Corniche Convertible	118
BMW (D) 323 i	118
CHEVROLET (USA) Corvette (195 hp)	118
CITROËN CX Prestige	118
DAIMLER Sovereign 4.2/Vanden Plas 4.2	118
FAIRTHORPE TX-S 2000	118
FELBER Excellence Coupé/Excellence Roadster	118
JAGUAR XJ 4.2	118
LANCIA Beta Montecarlo	118
MATRA-SIMCA Bagheera S/Bagheera X	118
MERCEDES-BENZ 280/280 C/280 S	118
OPEL (D) Senator Series (140 hp)	118
ROLLS-ROYCE Silver Shadow II/Silver Wraith II/ Silver Wraith II with division/Corniche Saloon/Corniche Convertible/Camargue	118
SBARRO Windhound 4 x 4	118
BMW (D) 728	119
PORSCHE 924 (USA version)	119
AVANTI Avanti II	120
BMW (D) 525	120
K.M.B. GTM Mk 1-3	120
LENHAM Austin-Healey 3000	120
SYD LAWRENCE Mk 2 Sports	120

Over 120 mph

	mph
ALFA ROMEO Alfetta GTV 2000/2000 Spider Veloce	121
CLÉNET Roadster	121
LANCIA Gamma Berlina 2500/Gamma Coupé 2500	121
OPEL (D) Monza Series (140 hp)	121
VAUXHALL Royale Coupé	121
PUMA GTB	123
BMW (D) 730	124
BMW (ZA) 530	124
FORD (AUS) LTD 4-door Sedan	124
MERCEDES-BENZ 280 E/280 CE/280 TE/280 SE/280 SEL/280 SL/280 SLC	124
MONTEVERDI Sierra	124
PORSCHE 924	124
RENAULT (RA) Torino TSX	124
STIMULA Bugatti 55	124
ZIL 114 Limousine/117 Limousine	124
AC 3000 ME	125
FERRARI Dino 208 GT 4	125
KELMARK GT Mark II	125
LOTUS Elite 501/Elite 502/Elite 503/Elite 504	125
MONOCOQUE Box	125
SCEPTRE 6.6 S	125
TECHNICAL EXPONENTS TX Tripper 2000 Sprint	125
ROVER 3500	126
BMW (D) 733 i	127

	mph
LAMBORGHINI Urraco P 200	127
MERCEDES-BENZ 350 SE/350 SEL/350 SL/600/600 Pullman	127
PANTHER De Ville Saloon/De Ville Convertible	128
BMW (D) 528 i	129
ASTON MARTIN V8 Volante	130
BMW (D) 630 CS	130
GREENWOOD Turbo	130
LOTUS Eclat 520	130
MERCEDES-BENZ 350 SLC/450 SE/450 SEL/450 SL/450 SLC	130
MONTEVERDI Sierra Cabriolet	130
BRISTOL 603 S2/412 S2	132
LOTUS Eclat 521/Eclat 522/ Eclat 523/Eclat 524	132
SBARRO Replica BMW 328 America	132
TVR 3000, Turbo and Taimar Series (142 hp)	133
BMW (D) 633 CSi	134
ALPINE A 310 V6	137
LAFER LL	137
MASERATI Merak	137
LOTUS Esprit S2	138
ASTON MARTIN Lagonda	140
BMW (D) 635 CSi	140
DAIMLER Double-Six 5.3/Double-Six Vanden Plas 5.3	140
JAGUAR XJ 5.3	140
JOHNARD VINTAGE CAR Bentley Donington	140
MERCEDES-BENZ 450 SLC 5.0/450 SEL 6.9	140
PORSCHE 924 Turbo/911 SC Coupé/911 SC Coupé (USA version)/911 SC Targa	140
DE TOMASO Deauville	143
MASERATI Quattroporte	143
PORSCHE 928	143
FERRARI Dino 308 GT 4/308 GTS	147
DE TOMASO Longchamp 2 + 2	149
ENNEZETA Nuova Lele Iso Rivolta	149
LAMBORGHINI Urraco P 250	149
MASERATI Kyalami	149
SBARRO Stash HS Cabriolet	149
ARGYLL Turbo GT	150
ELEGANT MOTORS 898 Phaeton/856 Speedster/Eleganté 2 + 2 Sports Phaeton	150
JAGUAR XJ-S	150
LYNX D Type	150
MORGAN Plus 8	150
FERRARI 308 GTB/400 Automatic	152
MASERATI Merak SS	155
LAMBORGHINI Silhouette/Espada 400 GT	155
PORSCHE Turbo Coupé (USA version)	155
DE TOMASO Pantera L	158
ASTON MARTIN V8	160
PORSCHE Turbo Coupé	162
BMW (D) M 1	163
LAMBORGHINI Urraco P 300	165
FERRARI BB 512	169
ASTON MARTIN V8 Vantage	170
MASERATI Khamsin	171
DE TOMASO Pantera GTS	174
MASERATI Bora	174
LAMBORGHINI Countach ''S''	196
PANTHER 6	200

MAKES, MODELS AND PRICES

Page	MAKE AND MODEL	Price in GB £	Price in USA $	Price ex Works	Page	MAKE AND MODEL	Price in GB £	Price in USA $	Price ex Works
	AC (Great Britain),					**ASTON MARTIN** (Great Britain)			
141	3000 ME			11,302*	142	V8		47,425*	23,999*
					142	V8 Vantage		50,550*	25,999*
	ALFA ROMEO (Italy)				142	V8 Volante		71,835*	33,864*
					143	Lagonda			32,620*
188	Alfasud 4-dr Berlina			4,354,000*					
188	Alfasud Super 4-dr Berlina	3,100*		4,921,000*		**AUBURN** (USA)			
188	Alfasud Super 1.3 4-dr Berlina	3,199*		5,109,000*	256	Speedster			24,900
188	Alfasud Giardinetta 1.3 3-dr			5,310,000*	256	Dual Cowl Phaeton			60,000
188	Alfasud ti 1.3 2-dr Berlina	3,400*		5,015,000*					
188	Alfasud ti 1.5 2-dr Berlina	3,600*		5,652,000*		**AUDI NSU** (Germany FR)			
188	Alfasud Sprint 1.3 Coupé			6,579,000*	103	Audi 80 2-dr Limousine			12,295*
188	Alfasud Sprint 1.5 Coupé	4,499*		6,879,000*	103	Audi 80 4-dr Limousine			12,865*
189	Spider Junior 1300			7,281,000*	103	Audi 80 L 2-dr Limousine			13,165*
190	Spider Junior 1600			7,257,000*	103	Audi 80 L 4-dr Limousine			13,735*
190	Giulietta 1.3			7,705,000*	103	Audi 80 S 2-dr Limousine			12,845*
191	Giulietta 1.6	4,499*		8,118,000*	103	Audi 80 S 4-dr Limousine			13,415*
191	Alfetta 1.6			8,118,000*	103	Audi 80 LS 2-dr Limousine		6,295*	13,715*
191	Alfetta GT 1.6	4,999*		8,496,000*	103	Audi 80 LS 4-dr Limousine		6,445*	14,285*
191	Alfetta 1.8			8,531,000*	103	Audi 80 GLS 2-dr Limousine			14,640*
192	Alfetta 2000 L	5,399*	9,695*	9,971,000*	103	Audi 80 GLS 4-dr Limousine			15,210*
192	Alfetta GTV 2000	5,999*	10,495*	9,841,000*	103	Audi 80 GLE 2-dr Limousine			16,340*
192	2000 Spider Veloce		11,195*	9,652,000*	103	Audi 80 GLE 4-dr Limousine			16,910*
					104	Audi 100 2-dr Limousine			15,615*
	ALPINE (France)				104	Audi 100 4-dr Limousine			16,220*
76	A 310 V6			82,000◇	104	Audi 100 L 2-dr Limousine			16,250*
					104	Audi 100 L 4-dr Limousine			17,125*
	AMERICAN MOTORS (USA)				104	Audi 100 GL 4-dr Limousine			18,490*
251	Spirit Sedan			3,899	104	Audi 100 5S 2-dr Limousine			16,440*
251	Spirit Liftback			3,999	104	Audi 100 5S 4-dr Limousine			17,045*
253	AMX			5,899	104	Audi 100 L5S 2-dr Limousine			17,345*
253	Concord 2-dr Sedan			4,049	104	Audi 100 L5S 4-dr Limousine	5,790*		17,950*
253	Concord 4-dr Sedan			4,149	104	Audi 100 GL5S 4-dr Limousine	6,825*		19,315*
253	Concord 2-dr Hatchback			4,149	104	Audi 100 CD5S 4-dr Limousine			22,960*
253	Concord 4+1-dr St. Wagon			4,349	104	Audi 100 5E 2-dr Limousine			17,305*
254	Pacer 2-dr Hatchback			4,699	104	Audi 100 5E 4-dr Liomusine			17,910*
254	Pacer 2+1-dr St. Wagon			4,849	104	Audi 100 L5E 2-dr Limousine			18,210*
					104	Audi 100 L5E 4-dr Limousine			18,815*
	ANTIQUE & CLASSIC AUTOMOTIVE (USA)				104	Audi 100 GL5E 4-dr Limousine	6,940*	8,995*	20,180*
255	Frazer Nash TT Interceptor			9,550	104	Audi 100 CD5E 4-dr Limousine	8,585*		23,265*
255	Jaguar SS 100			12,995	104	Audi 100 5D 2-dr Limousine			18,095*
					104	Audi 100 5D 4-dr Limousine			18,700*
	ARGYLL (Great Britain)				104	Audi 100 L5D 2-dr Limousine			19,000*
141	Turbo GT (turbocharged engine)			10,500	104	Audi 100 L5D 4-dr Limousine			19,605*
141	Turbo GT			9,300	104	Audi 100 GL5D 4-dr Limousine			20,970*
					104	Audi 100 CD5D 4-dr Limousine			24,415*
	ARKLEY (Great Britain)				105	Audi 100 Avant L 5-dr Limousine	5,340*		17,750*
142	SS			2,658	105	Audi 100 Avant GL 5-dr Limousine			19,115*
					105	Audi 100 Avant L5S 5-dr Limousine			18,575*
	ARO (Romania)				105	Audi 100 Avant GL5S 5-dr Limousine	6,545*		19,940*
218	240			—	105	Audi 100 Avant CD5S 5-dr Limousine			—
218	241			—	105	Audi 100 Avant L5E 5-dr Limousine			19,440*
218	243			—	105	Audi 100 Avant GL5E 5-dr Limousine			20,805*
218	244			—	105	Audi 100 Avant CD5S 5-dr Limousine	8,890*		
					105	Audi 100 Avant L5D 5-dr Limousine			20,230*
					105	Audi 100 Avant GL5D 5-dr Limousine			21,595*
					105	Audi 100 Avant CD5D 5-dr Limousine			—
						AUSTIN (Great Britain)			
					143	Allegro 1100 De Luxe 2-dr Saloon			2,601*
					143	Allegro 1100 De Luxe 4-dr Saloon			2,704*

The prices refer to all models listed in the volume. The first column shows the prices of cars imported into the United Kingdom; the second, the prices of cars imported into the United States of America; and the third, the prices of cars in the country of origin. Prices in the USA do not include US transportation fees, state and local taxes.

* Prices including VAT and its equivalent in European countries and also SCT in Great Britain; prices of cars imported into the Unites States (East Coast) including ocean freight, US excise tax and import duty.

◇ Prices ex-showroom in European countries.

Due to the international monetary situation, all the prices shown are subject to confirmation.

Page	MAKE AND MODEL	Price in GB £	Price in USA $	Price ex Works
143	Allegro 1300 Super 2-dr Saloon			2,918*
143	Allegro 1300 Super 4-dr Saloon			3,021*
143	Allegro 1300 Super 2+1-dr Estate Car			3,199*
143	Allegro 1500 Super 4-dr Saloon			3,119*
143	Allegro 1500 Super 2+1-dr Estate Car			3,324*
143	Allegro 1500 Special 4-dr Saloon			3,459*
143	Allegro 1750 HL 4-dr Saloon			3,669*
144	Maxi 1500 Saloon			3,462*
144	Maxi 1750 Saloon			3,621*
144	Maxi 1750 HL Saloon			3,936*
	AUTOBIANCHI (Italy)			
193	A 112			3,800,000◇
193	A 112 Elegant			4,295,000◇
193	A 112 Abarth			4,720,000◇
	AVALLONE (Brazil)			
323	A 11			—
	AVANTI (USA)			
256	Avanti II			17,670
	AZLK (USSR)			
238	Moskvich 2138			—
239	Moskvich 2136			—
239	Moskvich 2140			—
239	Moskvich 2140 IZh			—
239	Moskvich 2137			—
239	Moskvich 2140 Combi IZh			—
	BENTLEY (Great Britain)			
145	T2 Saloon			32,023*
146	Corniche Saloon			46,578*
146	Corniche Convertible			49,479*
	BLAKELY (USA)			
257	Bearcat 'S'			8,500
	BMW (Germany FR)			
106	316	4,599*		15,920*
106	318			16,980*
106	320	5,797*		19,300*
107	320 i		10,165*	—
107	323 i	6,786*		21,850*
107	518	6,099*		19,100*
107	520	7,099*		21,700*
108	525	8,149*		24,380*
108	528 i	9,299*	15,895*	28,450*
108	728	10,276*		31,400*
108	730	12,149*		35,500*
109	733 i	13,249*	24,575*	40,700*
109	630 CS			44,700*
109	633 CSi	15,999*	27,875*	47,300*
109	635 CSi	17,199*		50,400*
110	M 1			—
	BMW (South Africa)			
342	520			—
342	528			—
342	530			—
	BRISTOL (Great Britain)			
146	603 S2			32,382*
146	412 S2			29,264*

Page	MAKE AND MODEL	Price in GB £	Price in USA $	Price ex Works
	BUICK (USA)			
257	Skyhawk S Hatchback Coupé			4,480
257	Skyhawk Hatchback Coupé			4,698
258	Skylark 2-dr Hatchback Coupé			4,357
258	Skylark 2-dr Thin Pillar Coupé			4,208
258	Skylark S 2-dr Thin Pillar Coupé			4,082
258	Skylark 4-dr Thin Pillar Sedan			4,308
258	Skylark S/R 2-dr Thin Pillar Coupé			4,462
258	Skylark S/R 4-dr Thin Pillar Sedan			4,562
259	Century Special 2-dr Coupé			4,716
259	Century Special 4-dr Sedan			4,816
259	Century Special 4+1-dr St. Wagon			5,363
259	Century 2-dr Sport Coupé			5,268
259	Century Custom 3-dr Coupé			4,960
259	Century Custom 4-dr Sedan			5,085
259	Century Custom 4+1-dr St. Wagon			5,677
259	Century Limited 2-dr Coupé			—
259	Century Limited 4-dr Sedan			5,453
260	Century Turbo Coupé			5,738
261	Regal Coupé			5,189
261	Regal Limited Coupé			5,596
261	Regal Sport Coupé			6,355
262	Le Sabre 2-dr Hardtop Coupé			5,788
262	Le Sabre 4-dr Thin Pillar Sedan			5,888
262	Le Sabre 2-dr Limited Hardtop Coupé			6,252
262	Le Sabre 4-dr Limited Thin Pillar Sedan			6,377
262	Le Sabre 2-dr Sport Coupé			6,762
263	Estate Wagon 6-pass. St. Wagon			6,958
263	Estate Wagon 8-pass. St. Wagon			7,152
263	Electra 225 2-dr Coupé			7,827
263	Electra 225 4-dr Sedan			8,002
263	Electra Limited 2-dr Coupé			8,227
263	Electra Limited 4-dr Sedan			8,402
263	Electra Park Avenue 2-dr Coupé			8,669
263	Electra Park Avenue 4-dr Sedan			8,844
264	Riviera Coupé			10,371
264	Riviera Sport Coupé			10,648
	CADILLAC (USA)			
265	Seville	14,894*		15,906
265	De Ville Coupé			11,385
265	De Ville Sedan			11,739
265	Fleetwood Brougham			13,692
265	Fleetwood Limousine			21,233
265	Fleetwood Formal Limousine			21,981
266	Fleetwood Eldorado			14,500
	CHECKER (USA)			
267	Marathon Sedan			6,814
267	Marathon De Luxe Sedan			7,867
	CHEVROLET (Brazil)			
323	Chevette 2-dr Sedan			92,752
323	Chevette L 2-dr Sedan			100,495
323	Chevette SL 2-dr Sedan			104,759
323	Chevette Jeans 2-dr Sedan			—
323	Chevette 4-dr Sedan			—
323	Chevette SL 4-dr Sedan			—
324	Opala Sedan			127,991
324	Opala Coupé			128,897
324	Opala Caravan			141,473
324	Opala SS-4 Coupé			148,409
324	Opala SS-4 Caravan			157,571
325	Opala SS-6 Coupé			186,366
325	Opala SS-6 Caravan			177,775
325	Comodoro 4 Sedan			144,233
325	Comodoro 4 Coupé			143,565
325	Comodoro 6 Sedan			160,827
325	Comodoro 6 Coupé			159,316

Page	MAKE AND MODEL	Price in GB £	Price in USA $	Price ex Works
325	Veraneio Standard			174,621
325	Veraneio De Luxo			182,439
325	Veraneio Super Luxo			215,081
	CHEVROLET (Canada)			
246	Bel Air Coupé			6,424
246	Bel Air Sedan			6,561
246	Bel Air 6-pass. St. Wagon			7,197
246	Bel Air 9-pass. St. Wagon			7,366
	CHEVROLET (South Africa)			
343	Ascona 4-dr Sedan			4,550
343	Ascona « S » 4-dr Sedan			4,845
343	Chevair 2300 De Luxe 4-dr Sedan			5,340
343	Chevair 2300 GL 4-dr Sedan			5,740
343	Chevair 2300 Automatic Berlina 4-dr Sedan			6,420
344	Rekord 4-dr Sedan			6,120
344	Rekord Automatic 4-dr Sedan			6,475
344	Rekord GL 4-dr Sedan			6,420
344	Rekord Automatic GL 4-dr Sedan			6,720
344	Rekord 4+1-dr St. Wagon			6,545
344	Rekord Automatic 4+1-dr St. Wagon			6,930
344	Commodore 3800 4-dr Sedan			6,755
344	Commodore 3800 Automatic 4-dr Sedan			7,185
344	Commodore 3800 GL 4-dr Sedan			8,495
344	Commodore 3800 GL Automatic 4+1-dr St. Wagon			7,995
344	Commodore 4100 GL Automatic 4-dr Sedan			—
345	Nomad			3,845
	CHEVROLET (USA)			
267	Chevette Scooter Hatchback Coupé			3,299
267	Chevette Hatchback Coupé			3,794
267	Chevette Hatchback Sedan			3,914
268	Monza Coupé			3,667
268	Monza St. Wagon			4,090
268	Monza 2+2 Hatchback Coupé			3,960
268	Monza 2+2 Sport Hatchback Coupé			4,407
269	Nova Hatchback Coupé			4,118
269	Nova Coupé			3,955
269	Nova Sedan			4,055
269	Nova Custom Coupé			4,164
269	Nova Custom Sedan			4,264
270	Camaro Sport Coupé			4,777
270	Camaro Rally Sport Coupé			5,173
270	Camaro Berlinetta Coupé			5,498
270	Camaro Z28 Sport Coupé			6,327
272	Malibu Coupé			4,504
272	Malibu Sedan			4,604
272	Malibu St. Wagon			4,851
272	Malibu Classic Coupé			4,784
272	Malibu Classic Landau Coupé			5,026
272	Malibu Classic Sedan			4,909
272	Malibu Classic St. Wagon			5,068
273	Monte Carlo Sport Coupé			5,104
273	Monte Carlo Landau Coupé			6,030
274	Impala Coupé			5,605
274	Impala Landau Coupé			6,082
274	Impala Sedan			5,705
274	Impala 6-pass. St. Wagon			6,308
274	Impala 9-pass. St. Wagon			6,443
274	Caprice Classic Coupé			5,963
274	Caprice Classic Landau Coupé			6,373
274	Caprice Classic Sedan			6,088
274	Caprice Classic 6-pass. St. Wagon			6,598
274	Caprice Classic 9-pass. St. Wagon			6,758
275	Corvette	11,362*		10,515

Page	MAKE AND MODEL	Price in GB £	Price in USA $	Price ex Works
	CHRYSLER (Australia)			
394	Valiant CL Sedan			6,850
394	Valiant CL Station Wagon			7,209
394	Valiant CL Regal Sedan			8,538
394	Valiant CL Regal Station Wagon			8,848
394	Valiant CL Regal SE Sedan			12,202
	CHRYSLER (Great Britain)			
147	Sunbeam 1.0 LS Hatchback Saloon			2,499*
147	Sunbeam 1.0 GL Hatchback Saloon			2,732*
147	Sunbeam 1.3 LS Hatchback Saloon			2,732*
147	Sunbeam 1.3 GL Hatchback Saloon			2,965*
147	Sunbeam 1.6 GL Hatchback Saloon			3,091*
147	Sunbeam 1.6 GLS Hatchback Saloon			3,447*
148	Avenger 1.3 LS Saloon			2,816*
148	Avenger 1.3 LS Estate Car			3,141*
148	Avenger 1.3 GL Saloon			3,239*
148	Avenger 1.3 GL Estate Car			3,585*
148	Avenger 1.6 LS Saloon			2,929*
148	Avenger 1.6 LS Estate Car			3,254*
148	Avenger 1.6 GL Saloon			3,351*
148	Avenger 1.6 GL Estate Car			3,697*
148	Avenger 1.6 GLS Saloon			3,678*
149	Alpine GL			3,637*
149	Alpine S			3,299*
149	Alpine GLS			4,544*
	CHRYSLER (Spain)			
219	Simca 1200 L			292,200
219	Simca 1200 LS			306,800
219	Simca 1200 LS Break			343,600
219	Simca 1200 LX			319,500
219	Simca 1200 GLS			331,400
219	Simca 1200 GLS Confort			345,700
219	Simca 1200 Special TI			375,200
219	Simca 1200 Special TI Break			389,100
220	Chrysler 150 GLS			406,900
220	Chrysler 150 GLS Confort			412,700
220	Chrysler 150 S			445,300
220	Chrysler 150 GT			476,500
221	Chrysler 180	3,949*		537,600
221	Chrysler 180 Automatico			581,700
221	Chrysler 180 Diesel			599,800
221	Chrysler 180 Diesel De Luxe			636,600
222	Chrysler 2-litros			561,200
	CHRYSLER (USA)			
276	Le Baron Coupé			5,133
276	Le Baron Sedan			5,231
276	Le Baron Town and Country St. Wagon			6,083
276	Le Baron Salon Coupé			5,375
276	Le Baron Salon Sedan			5,603
276	Le Baron Medallion Coupé			5,853
276	Le Baron Medallion Sedan			6,081
278	Cordoba			6,173
279	Newport 4-dr Pillared Hardtop			6,215
279	New Yorker 4-dr Pillared Hardtop			8,875
	CHRYSLER FRANCE (France)			
76	Simca 1100 LE 2-dr Berline	2,326*		20,950◇
76	Simca 1100 LE 4-dr Berline	2,396*		22,700◇
76	Simca 1100 LE Break			25,350◇
76	Simca 1100 GLS 4-dr Berline	2,761*		25,850◇
76	Simca 1100 GLS Break	2,803*		27,600◇
77	Simca Horizon LS			27,500◇
77	Simca Horizon GL			29,300◇
77	Simca Horizon GLS			31,700◇

Page	MAKE AND MODEL	Price in GB £	Price in USA $	Price ex Works
77	Simca Horizon SX			35,400◇
78	Simca 1307 GLS			30,500◇
78	Simca 1307 S			34,300◇
78	Simca 1308 GT			36,700◇
78	Simca 1309 SX			41,900◇
79	Simca 1610			35,000◇
79	Simca 2 L Automatic			37,850◇
	CITROËN (France)			
79	2 CV Spécial			15,600◇
80	2 CV 6	1,853*		18,000◇
80	Mehari			21,200◇
80	Mehari 2+2			21,200◇
80	Dyane 6	2,048*		19,100◇
81	LN			21,400◇
81	LNA			21,900◇
81	Visa Spécial			22,660◇
82	Visa Club			23,300◇
82	Visa Super			25,800◇
82	G Spécial Berline	2,933*		27,100◇
82	GS X			28,100◇
82	G Spécial Break	3,193*		27,250◇
82	GS Club Berline	3,249*		29,600◇
83	GS Club Berline C Matic	3,467*		29,750◇
83	GS Club Break	3,477*		31,000◇
83	GS X3			31,000◇
83	GS Pallas	3,621*		31,600◇
83	GS Pallas C Matic			31,850◇
83	CX 2000 Confort	5,097*		40,900◇
84	CX 2000 Break Confort			46,400◇
84	CX 2000 Super	5,336*		43,900◇
84	CX 2000 Pallas			46,800◇
84	CX 2400 Super	5,966*		46,100◇
84	CX 2400 Break Super	6,128*		51,600◇
85	CX 2400 Familiale Super	6,241*		51,100◇
85	CX 2400 Pallas	6,566*		49,000◇
85	CX 2400 GTI	7,160*		58,200◇
85	CX 2400 Pallas Injection C Matic	7,180*		56,100◇
85	CX Prestige	9,590*		74,700◇
85	CX 2500 Diesel Confort	6,199*		47,900◇
85	CX 2500 Diesel Break Confort	6,480*		53,400◇
85	CX 2500 Diesel Super			50,900◇
86	CX 2500 Diesel Break Super			56,400◇
86	CX 2500 Diesel Familiale Super	6,591*		57,900◇
86	CX 2500 Diesel Pallas			53,800◇
	CLÉNET (USA)			
280	Roadster			65,000
281	4-passenger Convertible			—
	CUSTOCA (Austria)			
74	Hurrycane			125,000
74	Strato ES			130,000
	DACIA (Romania)			
219	1300 Saloon			—
219	1300 Break			—
	DAIHATSU (Japan)			
352	Max Cuore Standard 2-dr Sedan			547,000
352	Max Cuore De Luxe 4-dr Sedan			618,000
352	Max Cuore Custom 2-dr Sedan			611,000
352	Max Cuore Custom 4-dr Sedan			645,000
352	Max Cuore Custom EX 2-dr Sedan			637,000
352	Max Cuore Custom EX 4-dr Sedan			671,000
352	Max Cuore Hi-Custom 4-dr Sedan			671,000
352	Max Cuore Hi-Custom EX 4-dr Sedan			697,000
353	Charade Sedan XO			653,000

Page	MAKE AND MODEL	Price in GB £	Price in USA $	Price ex Works
353	Charade Sedan XG			698,000
353	Charade Sedan XT			748,000
353	Charade Sedan XTE			798,000
353	Charade Sedan XGE			768,000
353	Charade Coupé XG			698,000
353	Charade Coupé XT			758,000
353	Charade Coupé XTE			813,000
353	Charmant 1300 De Luxe Sedan			815,000
353	Charmant 1300 Custom Sedan			853,000
353	Charmant 1300 Hi-Custom Sedan			887,000
354	Charmant 1600 Custom Sedan			923,000
354	Charmant 1600 Hi-Custom Sedan			957,000
354	Charmant 1600 SC Sedan			973,000
354	Charmant 1600 GC Sedan			1,007,000
354	Delta Standard Wagon			—
354	Delta De Luxe Wagon			—
354	Delta Custom Wagon			—
354	Delta Custom EX Wagon			—
354	Taft Gran 1600 H-F20S (canvas doors)			—
354	Taft Gran 1600 H-F20SK (steel doors)			—
354	Taft Gran 1600 H-F20J (6-pass., canvas doors)			—
354	Taft Gran 1600 H-F20JK (6-pass., steel doors)			—
354	Taft Gran 1600 H-F20V (4-pass., steel body)			—
354	Taft Diesel F50S (canvas doors)			—
354	Taft Diesel F50SK (steel doors)			—
354	Taft Diesel F50J (6-pass., canvas doors)			—
354	Taft Diesel F50JK (6-pass., steel doors)			—
354	Taft Diesel F50V (4-pass., steel body)			—
	DAIMLER (Great Britain)			
149	Sovereign 4.2			11,646*
150	Vanden Plas 4.2			15,516*
150	Double-Six 5.3			14,906*
150	Double-Six Vanden Plas 5.3			18,219*
150	Limousine			17,640*
	DAYTONA (USA)			
281	Migi			7,000
	DE TOMASO (Italy)			
194	Pantera L	16,146*		22,200,000◇
194	Pantera GTS	16,556*		22,975,000◇
194	Deauville	21,645*		29,840,000◇
195	Longchamp 2+2	19,481*		27,899,000◇
	DODGE (Argentina)			
332	1500			7,584
332	1500 M 1.8			8,660
333	1500 M 1.8 Rural			10,313
333	Coronado			12,062
333	Coronado Automatic			13,784
	DODGE (Brazil)			
325	Polara			90,600
325	Polara Gran Luxo			102,400
326	Dart De Luxo Sedan			140,810
326	Dart De Luxo Gran Sedan			181,680
326	Dart De Luxo Coupé			139,670
326	Le Baron			—
326	Charger R/T			203,610
326	Magnum			—

Page	MAKE AND MODEL	Price in GB £	Price in USA $	Price ex Works
	DODGE (USA)			
282	Omni 024 2-dr Hatchback			4,482
282	Omni 4-dr Hatchback			4,122
282	Aspen Coupé			4,018
282	Aspen Sedan			4,119
282	Aspen St. Wagon			4,495
284	Diplomat Coupé			5,010
284	Diplomat Sedan			5,108
284	Diplomat St. Wagon			5,897
284	Diplomat Salon Coupé			5,252
284	Diplomat Salon Sedan			5,480
284	Diplomat Medallion Coupé			5,730
284	Diplomat Medallion Sedan			5,958
285	Magnum XE			5,886
286	St. Regis			6,342
	DUESENBERG (USA)			
287	SSJ			60,000
	DUESENBERG BROS. (USA)			
288	Four-door Town Sedan			100,000
	DUTTON (Great Britain)			
151	Malaga			—
151	B Plus			—
	ELEGANT MOTORS (USA)			
288	898 Phaeton			50,000
288	856 Speedster			40,000
289	Eleganté 2+2 Sports Phaeton			60,000
	ELITE (USA)			
289	Laser 917			7,500
	EL-KG (Germany FR)			
110	Bugatti 35 B			—
	EL NASR (Egypt)			
341	Nasr 128			—
341	Nasr 125			—
	ENNEZETA (Italy)			
195	Nuova Lele Iso Rivolta			15,000,000*
	EXCALIBUR (USA)			
289	Series III SS Roadster			27,600
289	Series III SS Phaeton			27,600
	FAIRTHORPE (Great Britain)			
152	TX-S 1500			3,087
152	TX-S 2000			3,892
	FELBER (Switzerland)			
234	Excellence Coupé			53,000
234	Excellence Roadster			57,000
234	Oasis			46,500
	FERRARI (Italy)			
195	Dino 208 GT 4			21,240,000*
196	Dino 308 GT 4	15,999*	34,670*	25,650,000*

Page	MAKE AND MODEL	Price in GB £	Price in USA $	Price ex Works
196	308 GTB	17,328*	35,950*	27,675,000*
196	308 GTS	18,169*	37,950*	29,025,000*
196	400 Automatic	28,349*		44,550,000*
197	BB 512	30,193*		48,330,000*
	FIAT (Argentina)			
333	600 S			—
334	133			—
334	133 L			—
334	128 Berlina			—
335	128 L Berlina			—
335	1300 TV lava			—
335	128 Familiar 5 Puertas			—
335	125 S			—
335	125 SL			—
335	125 Familiar			
	FIAT (Brazil)			
327	147			86,385
327	147 L			90,920
327	147 GL			99,145
327	147 GLS			
327	147 Rallye			—
327	Alfa Romeo 2300 B			243,760
327	Alfa Romeo 2300 TI			311,260
	FIAT (Italy)			
197	126 Berlina Base	1,714*		2,608,000◇
198	126 Personal	1,880*		2,814,000◇
198	127 L 2-dr Berlina	2,272*		3,699,000◇
198	127 L 3-dr Berlina	2,389*		3,806,000◇
198	127 C 2-dr Berlina			4,083,000◇
198	127 C 3-dr Berlina	2,498*		4,189,000◇
198	127 CL 2-dr Berlina			4,272,000◇
198	127 CL 3-dr Berlina	2,606*		4,378,000◇
198	127 Sport	2,943*		4,915,000◇
198	128 CL 1100		3,778*	5,092,000◇
199	128 Panorama Base 1100			4,856,000◇
199	Ritmo 60 L 3-dr Berlina			4,620,000◇
199	Ritmo 60 L 5-dr Berlina			4,832,000◇
199	Ritmo 60 CL 3-dr Berlina			4,997,000◇
199	Ritmo 60 CL 5-dr Berlina			5,210,000◇
199	Ritmo 65 L 5-dr Berlina			4,950,000◇
199	Ritmo 65 CL 3-dr Berlina			5,115,000◇
199	Ritmo 65 CL 5-dr Berlina			5,328,000◇
199	Ritmo 75 CL 3-dr Berlina			5,729,000◇
199	Ritmo 75 CL 5-dr Berlina			5,941,000◇
200	X1/9 five speed	4,575*	6,290*	6,531,000◇
201	131 Mirafiori 1300 L 4-dr Berlina	3,016*		5,381,000◇
201	131 Mirafiori 1300 L 5-dr Panorama			5,817,000◇
201	131 Mirafiori 1300 CL 2-dr Berlina			5,835,000◇
201	131 Mirafiori 1300 CL 4-dr Berlina			6,112,000◇
201	131 Mirafiori 1600 CL 4-dr Berlina	3,550*		6,254,000◇
201	131 Mirafiori 1600 CL 5-dr Panorama	3,894*		6,702,000◇
201	131 Supermirafiori 1300 4-dr Berlina	4,102*		6,974,000◇
201	131 Supermirafiori 1600 4-dr Berlina			7,115,000◇
201	131 Supermirafiori 1600 5-dr Panorama			—
201	131 Racing 2000 2-dr Berlina	4,636*		7,629,000◇
201	131 Diesel 2000 L 4-dr Berlina			7,186,000◇
201	131 Diesel 2000 CL 4-dr Berlina			7,611,000◇
201	131 Diesel 2000 CL 5-dr Panorama			8,059,000◇
201	131 Diesel 2500 Super 4-dr Berlina			8,472,000◇
201	131 Diesel 2500 5-dr Panorama Super			8,956,000◇
202	124 Sport Spider 2000		7,090*	—
203	132 1600 Berlina			7,576,000◇
203	132 2000 Berlina	4,850*		8,496,000◇
203	132 Diesel 2000			9,275,000◇
203	132 Diesel 2500			9,747,000◇
204	Campagnola			9,936,000◇
204	Campagnola Lunga			10,242,000◇

424

Page	MAKE AND MODEL	Price in GB £	Price in USA $	Price ex Works
	FIAT (Uruguay)			
323	600 S			47,500
	FIBERFAB (Germany FR)			
111	Bonito			—
111	Sherpa			—
	FORD (Argentina)			
335	Taunus L 2000 Sedan			—
335	Taunus GXL Sedan			—
336	Taunus GXL 2300 Sedan			—
336	Taunus GT Coupé			—
336	Fairlane LTD 3600 Sedan			—
336	Fairlane LTD-V8 Sedan			—
336	Falcon Sedan Standard			—
336	Falcon Sedan De Luxe			—
337	Falcon Station Wagon Standard			—
337	Falcon Station Wagon De Luxe			—
337	Falcon Sedan Futura			—
337	Falcon Sedan Sprint			—
	FORD (Australia)			
395	Escort L 2-dr Sedan			4,438
395	Escort GL 2-dr Sedan			4,859
395	Escort GL 4-dr Sedan			4,938
395	Escort Ghia 4-dr Sedan			5,793
395	Cortina TE L Sedan			5,467
395	Cortina TE L Station Wagon			6,033
395	Cortina TE GL Sedan			5,907
395	Cortina TE GL Station Wagon			6,531
395	Cortina Ghia Sedan			6,496
396	Falcon 4-dr Sedan			5,837
396	Falcon Station Wagon			6,176
396	Falcon 500 4-dr Sedan			6,403
396	Falcon 500 2-dr Hardtop			7,198
396	Fairmont 4-dr Sedan			7,956
396	Fairmont 2-dr Coupé			8,092
396	Fairmont Station Wagon			8,447
396	Fairmont GXL Sedan			9,183
397	Fairlane 500 Sedan			11,340
397	Fairlane Marquis Sedan			13,150
397	LTD 4-dr Sedan			16,602
	FORD (Brazil)			
327	Corcel II Base			115,977
327	Corcel II L			129,229
327	Corcel II LDO			154,229
328	Corcel II Belina Base			134,053
328	Corcel II Belina L			141,982
328	Corcel II Belina LDO			160,368
328	Corcel II GT			97,031
328	Maverick Sedan Super			138,699
328	Maverick Sedan Super Luxo			148,565
328	Maverick Sedan LDO			166,777
329	Maverick Coupé Super			139,624
329	Maverick Coupé Super Luxo			149,427
329	Maverick Coupé LDO			169,214
329	Maverick Coupé GT-4			—
329	Maverick Coupé GT			166,966
329	Galaxie 500			305,494
329	Galaxie LTD			331,737
329	Galaxie Landau			378,617
	FORD (Canada)			
247	Granada Special Edition 2-dr Sedan			4,901
247	Granada Special Edition 4-dr Sedan			5,047
247	Custom 500 2-dr Sedan			6,538
247	Custom 500 4-dr Sedan			6,672

Page	MAKE AND MODEL	Price in GB £	Price in USA $	Price ex Works
	FORD (Germany FR)			
111	Fiesta 3-dr Limousine			9,095*
111	Fiesta L 3-dr Limousine			9,695*
111	Fiesta S 3-dr Limousine			10,995*
111	Fiesta Ghia 3-dr Limousine			11,750*
112	Escort 2-dr Limousine			9,810*
112	Escort 4-dr Limousine			10,355*
112	Escort Turnier			10,540*
112	Escort L 2-dr Limousine			10,380*
112	Escort L 4-dr Limousine			10,925*
112	Escort L Turnier			11,160*
112	Escort GL 2-dr Limousine			11,415*
112	Escort GL 4-dr Limousine			11,960*
112	Escort GL Turnier			12,185*
112	Escort Ghia 2-dr Limousine			13,520*
112	Escort Ghia 4-dr Limousine			14,065*
112	Escort Sport 2-dr Limousine			11,795*
112	Escort Sport 4-dr Limousine			12,340*
112	Escort RS 2000 2-dr Limousine			15,145*
113	Taunus 2-dr Limousine			11,430*
113	Taunus 4-dr Limousine			11,995*
113	Taunus Turnier			12,630*
113	Taunus L 2-dr Limousine			12,065*
113	Taunus L 4-dr Limousine			12,630*
113	Taunus L Turnier			13,265*
113	Taunus GL 2-dr Limousine			13,745*
113	Taunus GL 4-dr Limousine			14,310*
113	Taunus GL Turnier			14,945*
113	Taunus Ghia 2-dr Limousine			16,195*
113	Taunus Ghia 4-dr Limousine			16,760*
113	Taunus S 2-dr Limousine			15,308*
113	Taunus S 4-dr Limousine			15,873*
115	Capri II L Coupé			12,995*
115	Capri II GL Coupé			14,595*
115	Capri II S Coupé			16,950*
115	Capri II Ghia Coupé			19,895
116	Granada 2-dr Limousine			14,535*
116	Granada 4-dr Limousine			15,130*
116	Granada Turnier			15,705*
116	Granada L 2-dr Limousine			15,325*
116	Granada L 4-dr Limousine			15,825*
116	Granada L Turnier			16,755*
116	Granada GL 2-dr Limousine			19,875*
116	Granada GL 4-dr Limousine			20,470*
116	Granada GL Turnier			21,875*
116	Granada Ghia 4-dr Limousine			24,795*
	FORD (Great Britain)			
152	Fiesta 3-dr Saloon			2,362*
152	Fiesta L 3-dr Saloon			2,640*
152	Fiesta S 3-dr Saloon			3,090*
152	Fiesta Ghia 3-dr Saloon			3,471*
153	Escort Popular 1100 2-dr Saloon			2,364*
153	Escort Popular 1100 Plus 2-dr Saloon			2,472*
153	Escort Popular 1100 4-dr Saloon			2,580*
153	Escort 1100 Estate Car			2,640*
153	Escort 1100 L 2-dr Saloon			2,703*
153	Escort 1100 L 4-dr Saloon			2,811*
153	Escort Popular 1300 2-dr Saloon			2,442*
153	Escort Popular 1300 Plus 2-dr Saloon			2,564*
153	Escort Popular 1300 Plus 4-dr Saloon			2,671*
153	Escort 1300 Estate Car			2,776*
153	Escort 1300 L 2-dr Saloon			2,780*
153	Escort 1300 L 4-dr Saloon			2,888*
153	Escort 1300 L Estate Car			3,107*
153	Escort 1300 GL 2-dr Saloon			3,066*
153	Escort 1300 GL 4-dr Saloon			3,174*
153	Escort 1300 GL Estate Car			3,460*
153	Escort 1300 Sport 2-dr Saloon			3,248*
153	Escort 1300 Ghia 2-dr Saloon			3,624*
153	Escort 1300 Ghia 4-dr Saloon			3,732*
153	Escort 1600 Sport 2-dr Saloon			3,345*

Page	MAKE AND MODEL	Price in GB £	Price in USA $	Price ex Works	Page	MAKE AND MODEL	Price in GB £	Price in USA $	Price ex Works
153	Escort 1600 Ghia 4-dr Saloon			3,829*	290	Mustang Ghia 2-dr Sedan			4,757
153	Escort RS 2000 2-dr Saloon			4,077*	290	Mustang Ghia 3-dr Sedan			4,939
153	Escort RS 2000 Custom 2-dr Saloon			4,164*	292	Fairmont 2-dr Sedan			3,770
155	Cortina 1300 2-dr Saloon			2,891*	292	Fairmont 4-dr Sedan			3,870
155	Cortina 1300 4-dr Saloon			3,007*	292	Fairmont St. Wagon			4,217
155	Cortina 1300 L 2-dr Saloon			3,093*	292	Fairmont Futura Coupé			4,131
155	Cortina 1300 L 4-dr Saloon			3,209*	293	Granada 2-dr Sedan			4,457
155	Cortina 1600 4-dr Saloon			3,186*	293	Granada 4-dr Sedan			4,559
155	Cortina 1600 Estate Car			3,551*	293	Granada Ghia 2-dr Sedan			4,831
155	Cortina 1600 L 4-dr Saloon			3,388*	293	Granada Ghia 4-dr Sedan			4,934
155	Cortina 1600 L Estate Car			3,788*	293	Granada ESS 2-dr Sedan			4,991
155	Cortina 1600 GL 4-dr Saloon			3,717*	293	Granada ESS 4-dr Sedan			5,094
155	Cortina 1600 GL Estate Car			4,116*	293	Thunderbird Hardtop			6,200
155	Cortina 1600 Ghia 4-dr Saloon			4,424*	293	Thunderbird Town Landau Hardtop			9,107
155	Cortina 1600 Ghia Estate Car			4,823*	293	Thunderbird Heritage Hardtop			10,928
155	Cortina 2000 GL 4-dr Saloon			3,932*	294	LTD II S 2-dr Hardtop			5,427
155	Cortina 2000 GL Estate Car			4,331*	294	LTD II S 4-dr Pillared Hardtop			5,527
155	Cortina 2000 S 4-dr Saloon			4,189*	294	LTD II 2-dr Hardtop			5,677
155	Cortina 2000 Ghia 4-dr Saloon			4,552*	294	LTD II 4-dr Pillared Hardtop			5,801
155	Cortina 2000 Ghia Estate Car			4,951*	294	LTD II Brougham 2-dr Hardtop			6,013
155	Cortina 2300 GL 4-dr Saloon			4,442*	294	LTD II Brougham 4-dr Pillared Hardtop			6,137
155	Cortina 2300 GL Estate Car			4,841*	295	LTD 2-dr Sedan			6,058
155	Cortina 2300 S 4-dr Saloon			4,700*	295	LTD 4-dr Sedan			6,158
155	Cortina 2300 Ghia 4-dr Saloon			5,062*	295	LTD St. Wagon			6,406
155	Cortina 2300 Ghia Estate Car			5,461*	295	LTD Landau 2-dr Sedan			6,548
157	Capri II 1300 Coupé			2,959*	295	LTD Landau 4-dr Sedan			6,674
157	Capri II 1300 L Coupé			3,336*	295	LTD Country Squire St. Wagon			6,850
157	Capri II 1600 L Coupé			3,524*					
157	Capri II 1600 GL Coupé			3,756*		**GAZ** (USSR)			
157	Capri II 1600 Coupé			4,088*	239	Volga 24			—
157	Capri II 2000 GL Coupé			3,972*	239	Volga 24-02			—
157	Capri II 2000 S Coupé			4,417*	239	Volga 24 Indenor Diesel			—
157	Capri II 2000 Ghia Coupé			5,224*	240	Chaika			—
157	Capri II 3000 S Coupé			4,839*					
157	Capri II 3000 Ghia Coupé			5,921*		**GENERAL MOTORS** (Malaysia)			
158	Granada 2000 L Saloon			4,720*	393	Harimau			—
158	Granada 2000 L Estate Car			5,423*	393	Amigo			—
158	Granada 2100 Diesel Saloon			5,087*	393	Gemini 1.6 Sedan			—
158	Granada 2300 L Saloon			5,001*	393	Gemini 1.6 Coupé			—
158	Granada 2300 L Estate Car			5,705*					
158	Granada 2300 GL Saloon			6,109*		**GIANNINI** (Italy)			
158	Granada 2300 GLS Saloon			6,477*	204	Fiat Giannini 126 GP Base			2,665,000*
158	Granada 2800 GL Saloon (auto)			6,536*	204	Fiat Giannini 126 GP Personal			2,845,000*
158	Granada 2800 GL Estate Car (auto)			7,343*	204	Fiat Giannini 126 GP S Base			2,820,000*
158	Granada 2800 GLS Saloon (auto)			6,905*	204	Fiat Giannini 126 GP S Personal			2,990,000*
158	Granada 2800 GLS Estate Car (auto)			7,466*	204	Fiat Giannini 126 Sport Base DC			3,010,000*
158	Granada 2800i GLS Saloon			7,163*	204	Fiat Giannini 126 Sport Personal DC			3,180,000*
158	Granada 2800i GLS Estate Car			8,107*	205	Fiat Giannini 127 NP 2-dr Berlina Base			3,810,000*
158	Granada 2800 Ghia Saloon (auto)			7,938*	205	Fiat Giannini 127 NP 3-dr Berlina Base			3,930,000*
158	Granada 2800i Ghia Saloon			8,320*	205	Fiat Giannini 127 NP 2-dr Berlina Confort			4,160,000*
					205	Fiat Giannini 127 NP 3-dr Berlina Confort			4,280,000*
	FORD (South Africa)				205	Fiat Giannini 128 NP 2-dr Berlina Confort L			4,385,000*
345	Escort 1300 L 4-dr Sedan			4,260	205	Fiat Giannini 128 NP 4-dr Berlina Confort L			5,350,000*
345	Escort 1600 GL 4-door Sedan			4,810	205	Fiat Giannini 128 NP S 2-dr Berlina Confort L			4,695,000*
345	Escort RS 2000 2-door Sedan			5,965	205	Fiat Giannini 128 NP S 4-dr Berlina Confort L			5,595,000*
345	Cortina 1600 L Sedan			5,450	205	Fiat Giannini 128 5M 2-dr Autostrada Confort L			5,265,000*
346	Cortina 1600 L Station Wagon			5,815	205	Fiat Giannini 128 5M 4-dr Autostrada Confort L			6,085,000*
346	Cortina 2000 GL Sedan			6,330					
346	Cortina 2000 GL Station Wagon			6,330		**GINETTA** (Great Britain)			
346	Cortina 3000 S Sedan			6,780	159	G21			3,959*
346	Cortina 3000 Ghia Sedan			7,660					
347	Cortina 3000 Ghia Station Wagon			8,205					
347	Granada 2000 GL Sedan			6,855					
347	Granada 3000 GL Sedan			8,360					
347	Granada 3000 Ghia Sedan			12,850					
	FORD (USA)								
290	Pinto Sedan			3,664					
290	Pinto Runabout			3,779					
290	Pinto St. Wagon			4,063					
290	Mustang 2-dr Sedan			4,187					
290	Mustang 3-dr Sedan			4,551					

Page	MAKE AND MODEL	Price in GB £	Price in USA $	Price ex Works
	GREENWOOD (USA)			
296	Turbo			28,000
	GURGEL (Brazil)			
329	X-12			105,750
329	X-12 TR			114,809
329	X-20			142,363
	HINDUSTAN (India)			
348	Ambassador Mark 3			—
	HOLDEN (Australia)			
398	Gemini TD 4-dr Sedan			4,481
398	Gemini TD SL 4-dr Sedan			5,121
398	Gemini TD SL Coupé			5,340
398	Gemini TD SL/E 4-dr Sedan			5,930
398	Gemini TD SL/E Coupé			6,025
398	Gemini TD 3 + 1-dr St. Wagon			5,664
398	Sunbird 4-dr Sedan			5,567
398	Sunbird 4-dr Hatchback			5,907
398	Sunbird SL 4-dr Sedan			5,977
398	Sunbird SL Hatchback			6,319
398	Sunbird SL/E 4-dr Sedan			6,589
398	Sunbird SL/E Hatchback			6,929
398	Torana UC S 4-dr Sedan			6,098
398	Torana UC SL 4-dr Sedan			6,706
398	Torana UC SL Hatchback			7,046
399	Commodore S 4-dr Sedan			6,710
399	Commodore SL 4-dr Sedan			8,047
399	Commodore SL/E 4-dr Sedan			10,828
399	HZ Kingswood SL 4-dr Sedan			6,760
399	HZ Kingswood SL St. Wagon			7,065
399	HZ Premier 4-dr Sedan			8,815
399	HZ Premier St. Wagon			9,116
399	HZ GTS 4-dr Sedan			9,584
399	HZ Statesman De Ville 4-dr Sedan			11,586
399	HZ Statesman Caprice 4-dr Sedan			16,640
	HONDA (Japan)			
355	Civic CVCC 1300 Standard 2-dr Sedan			666,000
355	Civic CVCC 1300 De Luxe 3-dr Sedan			721,000
355	Civic CVCC 1300 GL 3-dr Sedan			807,000
355	Civic CVCC 1300 GL-II-5 3-dr Sedan			842,000
355	Civic CVCC 1300 De Luxe 5-dr Sedan			764,000
355	Civic CVCC 1300 Hi-De Luxe 5-dr Sedan			818,000
355	Civic CVCC 1300 GF 5-dr Sedan			845,000
355	Civic CVCC 1300 GF-S 5-dr Sedan			870,000
355	Civic CVCC 1500 RSL 3-dr Sedan			911,000
355	Civic CVCC 1500 GTL-II 3-dr Sedan			897,000
355	Civic CVCC 1500 GF-II 5-dr Sedan			892,000
355	Civic CVCC 1500 GF-II-5 5-dr Sedan			912,000
355	Civic CVCC 1500 Station Wagon		4,759*	—
355	Civic 1500 Van Custom			—
356	Accord 1800 GL 3-dr Hatchback	3,915*		1,033,000
356	Accord 1800 LX 3-dr Hatchback			1,093,000
356	Accord 1800 EX 3-dr Hatchback			1,200,000
356	Accord 1800 EX-L 3-dr Hatchback			1,340,000
356	Accord 1800 SL 4-dr Sedan	4,115*		998,000
356	Accord 1800 GF 4-dr Sedan			1,108,000
356	Accord 1800 EX 4-dr Sedan			1,225,000
356	Accord 1800 EX-L 4-dr Sedan			1,385,000
356	Prelude XT Coupé			1,160,000
356	Prelude E Coupé			1,260,000
356	Prelude XE Coupé			1,400,000
356	Prelude XR Coupé			1,380,000

Page	MAKE AND MODEL	Price in GB £	Price in USA $	Price ex Works
	HONGQI (China People's Republic)			
349	9-pass. Limousine			—
349	6-pass. Limousine			—
	HYUNDAI (Korea)			
350	Pony Sedan			—
350	Pony Coupé			—
	INTERMECCANICA (USA)			
297	Speedster			10,250
	INTERNATIONAL HARVESTER (USA)			
297	Scout II 4 x 2			5,884
297	Scout II 4 x 4			6,604
297	Scout II Diesel 4 x 2			8,465
297	Scout II Diesel 4 x 4			9,241
297	Scout Traveler 4 x 2			6,481
297	Scout Traveler 4 x 4			7,248
297	Scout Traveler Diesel 4 x 2			8,869
297	Scout Traveler Diesel 4 x 4			9,696
297	Scout SS-II 4 x 4			5,825
	ISUZU (Japan)			
357	Gemini 1600 LD 4-dr Sedan			904,000
357	Gemini 1600 LD 2-dr Coupé			934,000
357	Gemini 1600 LT 4-dr Sedan			943,000
357	Gemini 1600 LT 2-dr Coupé			973,000
357	Gemini 1600 LS 4-dr Sedan			1,001,000
357	Gemini 1600 LS 2-dr Coupé			1,073,000
357	Gemini 1600 Minx 4-dr Sedan			983,000
357	Gemini 1600 Minx 2-dr Coupé			1,013,000
357	Gemini 1800 LT 4-dr Sedan			998,000
357	Gemini 1800 LT 2-dr Coupé			1,028,000
357	Gemini 1800 LS 4-dr Sedan			1,056,000
357	Gemini 1800 LS 2-dr Coupé			1,103,000
357	Gemini 1800 Minx 4-dr Sedan			1,093,000
357	Gemini 1800 LS/G 2-dr Coupé			1,178,000
357	Florian SII 1800 De Luxe 4-dr Sedan			1,211,000
357	Florian SII 1800 Super De Luxe 4-dr Sedan			1,383,000
357	Florian SII Diesel 2000 Semi-De Luxe 4-dr Sedan			1,253,000
357	Florian SII Diesel 2000 De Luxe 4-dr Sedan			1,298,000
357	Florian SII Diesel 2000 Super De Luxe 4-dr Sedan			1,470,000
358	117 1950 XT 2-dr Coupé			1,539,000
358	117 1950 XT-L 2-dr Coupé			1,764,000
358	117 1950 XC 2-dr Coupé			1,745,000
358	117 1950 XC-J 2-dr Coupé			1,832,000
358	117 1950 XE 2-dr Coupé			2,533,000
358	117 1950 XG 2-dr Coupé			2,022,000
	JAGUAR (Great Britain)			
160	XJ 3.4			10,338*
160	XJ 4.2		20,000*	10,994*
160	XJ 5.3		22,000*	13,430*
161	XJ-S		25,000*	15,996*
	JEEP CORPORATION (USA)			
298	Jeep CJ-5 Roadster			5,488
298	Jeep CJ-7 Roadster	4,989*		5,582
298	Cherokee 2-dr Station Wagon	7,799*		6,828
298	Cherokee Wide Wheel 2-dr Station Wagon			7,171
298	Cherokee 4-dr Station Wagon	7,899*		6,941

Page	MAKE AND MODEL	Price in GB £	Price in USA $	Price ex Works
299	Wagoneer Standard			8,375
299	Wagoneer Limited			11,688
	JOHNARD VINTAGE CAR (Great Britain)			
162	Bentley Donington			15,500*
	KELMARK (USA)			
299	GT Mark II			—
	KIA (Korea)			
351	Brisa 1000			—
351	Brisa 1300			—
	K.M.B. (Great Britain)			
162	GTM Mk 1-3			—
	LAFER (Brazil)			
329	MP			—
330	LL			—
	LAMBORGHINI (Italy)			
206	Urraco P 200			17,400,000
206	Urraco P 250			17,400,000
207	Urraco P 300			19,000,000
207	Silhouette			23,000,000
207	Espada 400 GT			30,500,000
208	Countach « S »			42,500,000
	LANCIA (Italy)			
208	Beta Berlina 1300	3,564*		7,817,000◊
208	Beta Coupé 1300	4,253*		7,935,000◊
209	Beta Berlina 1600	4,268*	8,217*	8,195,000◊
209	Beta Coupé 1600	4,859*	8,803*	8,691,000◊
209	Beta HPE 1600	5,540*	9,868*	8,691,000◊
209	Beta Spider 1600			8,455,000◊
209	Beta Berlina 2000	4,559*		8,732,000◊
210	Beta Coupé 2000	5,257*		9,410,000◊
210	Beta HPE 2000	5,938*		9,410,000◊
210	Beta Spider 2000	5,720*		8,880,000◊
210	Beta ES 2000	4,955*		—
210	Beta Montecarlo	5,927*		9,635,000◊
210	Gamma Berlina 2000	7,136*		11,888,000◊
211	Gamma Coupé 2000	9,186*		15,122,000◊
211	Gamma Berlina 2500			14,263,000◊
211	Gamma Coupé 2500			17,968,000◊
	LAND ROVER (Great Britain)			
162	88" Regular			4,101*
163	109" Estate Car			4,810*
163	Range Rover			9,815*
	LAWIL (Italy)			
211	S3 Varzina			1,971,000*
212	A4 City			1,947,000*
	LENHAM (Great Britain)			
163	Austin-Healey 3000			6,300
	LEYLAND (Australia)			
400	Mini-Moke Californian			3,775

Page	MAKE AND MODEL	Price in GB £	Price in USA $	Price ex Works
	LINCOLN (USA)			
300	Versailles			13,466
300	Continental Coupé			11,497
300	Continental Sedan			11,713
301	Continental Mark V			13,594
	LOTUS (Great Britain)			
164	Elite 501			12,699*
164	Elite 502			13,633*
164	Elite 503		30,746*	14,141*
164	Elite 504		31,236*	14,318*
165	Eclat 520			11,230*
165	Eclat 521			12,135*
165	Eclat 522			13,093*
165	Eclat 523		29,609*	13,601*
165	Eclat 524		30,138*	13,778*
165	Esprit S2		28,700*	12,611*
	LYNX (Great Britain)			
166	D Type			17,500
	MASERATI (Italy)			
212	Merak	16,883*		20,262,000*
212	Merak SS		29,800*	25,348,000*
213	Quattroporte			—
213	Kyalami	23,342*		31,982,000*
213	Khamsin	25,541*	41,450*	35,438,000*
214	Bora	23,751*	38,790*	35,438,000*
	MATRA-SIMCA (France)			
86	Rancho	5,932*		41,400*
86	Bagheera			42,500*
87	Bagheera S			47,150*
87	Bagheera X			51,350*
	MAZDA (Japan)			
359	Familia AP 1300 Standard 3-dr Sedan			665,000
359	Familia AP 1300 De Luxe 3-dr Sedan			735,000
359	Familia AP 1300 GF 3-dr Sedan			790,000
359	Familia AP 1300 Super Custom 3-dr Sedan			830,000
359	Familia AP 1300 Standard 5-dr Sedan			700,000
359	Familia AP 1300 De Luxe 5-dr Sedan			770,000
359	Familia AP 1300 GL 5-dr Sedan			825,000
359	Familia AP 1300 Super Custom 5-dr Sedan			865,000
359	Familia AP 1400 GF 3-dr Sedan			825,000
359	Familia AP 1400 Super Custom 3-dr Sedan			865,000
359	Familia AP 1400 Touring Custom 3-dr Sedan			890,000
359	Familia AP 1400 GL 5-dr Sedan			860,000
359	Familia AP 1400 Super Custom 5-dr Sedan			900,000
359	Familia AP 1400 Elegant Custom 5-dr Sedan			940,000
359	Familia GLC Regular 3-dr Sedan		3,895*	—
359	Familia GLC De Luxe 3-dr Sedan		4,195*	—
359	Familia GLC De Luxe 5-dr Sedan		4,395*	—
359	Familia GLC De Luxe Station Wagon		4,595*	—
360	Capella 1600 Standard Sedan			850,000
360	Capella 1600 De Luxe Sedan			910,000
360	Capella 1600 GL Sedan			960,000
360	Capella 1600 Super Custom			1,030,000
360	Capella 1600 De Luxe Hardtop			945,000
360	Capella 1600 GL Hardtop			995,000

Page	MAKE AND MODEL	Price in GB £	Price in USA $	Price ex Works
360	Capella 1600 Super Custom Hardtop			1,065,000
360	Capella 1800 GL Sedan			1,040,000
360	Capella 1800 GL Hardtop			1,100,000
360	Capella 1800 Super Custom Sedan			1,110,000
360	Capella 1800 Super Custom Hardtop			1,170,000
360	626			—
360	Luce 1800 Custom Special Sedan			996,000
360	Luce 1800 Custom Sedan			1,100,000
360	Luce 2000 Custom Sedan			1,165,000
360	Luce 2000 Super Custom Sedan			1,230,000
360	Luce 2000 Custom Special 4-dr Hardtop			1,105,000
360	Luce 2000 Custom 4-dr Hardtop			1,230,000
360	Luce 2000 Super Custom 4-dr Hardtop			1,345,000
360	Luce 2000 Super Custom SE 4-dr Hardtop			1,420,000
360	Luce RE Custom Special 4-dr Hardtop			1,250,000
360	Luce RE Super Custom 4-dr Hardtop			1,620,000
361	Luce RE Limited 4-dr Hardtop			2,005,000
361	Cosmo 1800 AP Custom Special Coupé			1,055,000
361	Cosmo 1800 AP Custom Coupé			1,190,000
361	Cosmo 1800 AP Super Custom Coupé			1,355,000
361	Cosmo 2000 AP Custom Coupé			1,280,000
361	Cosmo 2000 AP Super Custom Coupé			1,420,000
361	Cosmo L 2000 AP Custom Special Coupé			1,205,000
361	Cosmo L 2000 AP Custom Coupé			1,340,000
361	Cosmo L 2000 AP Super Custom Coupé			1,480,000
361	Cosmo RE Custom Special Coupé			1,200,000
361	Cosmo RE Custom Coupé			1,330,000
361	Cosmo RE Super Custom Coupé			1,538,000
361	Cosmo L RE Custom Special Coupé			1,285,000
361	Cosmo L RE Custom Coupé			1,415,000
361	Cosmo L RE Super Custom Coupé			1,590,000
361	Cosmo RE Limited Coupé			1,795,000
361	Cosmo L RE Limited Coupé			1,855,000
362	Roadpacer Sedan			3,835,000
362	Savanna RX7 Custom Coupé		6,995*	1,230,000
362	Savanna RX7 Super Custom Coupé		7,695*	1,370,000
362	Savanna RX7 GT Coupé			1,440,000
362	Savanna RX7 Limited Coupé			1,690,000

MERCEDES-BENZ (Germany FR)

Page	MAKE AND MODEL	Price in GB £	Price in USA $	Price ex Works
118	200	7,346*		20,261*
118	230	8,419*		21,336*
118	230 C	10,285*		26,779*
118	230 T			25,704*
118	250	9,705*		24,662*
119	250 Long Wheelbase	13,188*		37,072*
119	250 T			29,030*
119	200 D	7,513*		21,347*
119	240 D	8,435*	14,245*	22,826*
119	240 D Long Wheelbase	13,188*		35,941*
119	240 TD			27,194*
119	300 D	10,468*	19,904*	24,898*
120	300 D Long Wheelbase			37,307*
120	300 TD			29,266*
120	280			27,899*
120	280 C			31,898*
120	280 E	11,599*	20,775*	30,016*
120	280 CE	12,608*	23,337*	34,014*
120	280 TE			34,339*
121	280 S			33,018*
121	280 SE	13,578*	24,556*	35,325*
121	280 SEL			37,621*
121	280 SL			37,912*
121	280 SLC			44,464*
121	350 SE	15,815*		39,357*

Page	MAKE AND MODEL	Price in GB £	Price in USA $	Price ex Works
122	350 SEL			41,653*
122	350 SL	15,655*		41,944*
122	350 SLC			48,496*
122	450 SE	17,035*		44,173*
123	450 SEL	17,995*		49,482*
123	450 SL	16,736*	28,687*	46,760*
123	450 SLC	19,710*	34,760*	53,312*
123	450 SLC 5.0			63,504*
123	450 SEL 6.9	28,621*	47,773*	78,960*
123	600			144,032*
124	600 Pullman			175,392*

MERCURY (Canada)

Page	MAKE AND MODEL	Price in GB £	Price in USA $	Price ex Works
247	Bobcat 2-dr « Special »			3,683
247	Bobcat 2-dr Sedan			4,102
247	Bobcat 3-dr Runabout			4,253
247	Bobcat 2-dr St. Wagon « Special »			4,245
247	Bobcat 2-dr St. Wagon			4,685
248	Monarch Special Edition 2-dr Sedan			4,931
248	Monarch Special Edition 4-dr Sedan			5,078
248	Cougar « S » 2-dr Hardtop			6,149
248	Cougar « S » 4-dr Pillared Hardtop			6,256
249	Marquis Meteor 2-dr Sedan			6,655
249	Marquis Meteor 4-dr Sedan			6,789

MERCURY (USA)

Page	MAKE AND MODEL	Price in GB £	Price in USA $	Price ex Works
301	Bobcat Runabout			3,829
301	Bobcat St. Wagon			4,135
301	Bobcat Villager St. Wagon			4,248
302	Zephyr 2-dr Sedan			3,921
302	Zephyr 4-dr Sedan			4,021
302	Zephyr St. Wagon			4,367
302	Zephyr Z-7 Sports Coupé			4,173
303	Capri Coupé			4,596
303	Capri Ghia Coupé			4,961
304	Monarch 2-dr Sedan			4,516
304	Monarch 4-dr Sedan			4,618
304	Cougar 2-dr Hardtop			5,379
304	Cougar 4-dr Pillared Hardtop			5,524
304	Cougar XR-7 2-dr Hardtop			6,303
305	Marquis 2-dr Sedan			6,165
305	Marquis 4-dr Sedan			6,260
305	Marquis St. Wagon			6,555
305	Marquis Colony Park St. Wagon			7,340
305	Marquis Brougham 2-dr Sedan			6,843
305	Marquis Brougham 4-dr Sedan			7,031
305	Grand Marquis 2-dr Sedan			7,556
305	Grand Marquis 4-dr Sedan			7,744

MG (Great Britain)

Page	MAKE AND MODEL	Price in GB £	Price in USA $	Price ex Works
166	Midget		5,200*	2,971*
167	MGB GT			4,559*
167	MGB Sports		6,550*	3,996*

MINI (Great Britain)

Page	MAKE AND MODEL	Price in GB £	Price in USA $	Price ex Works
167	850 Saloon			2,157*
168	1000 Saloon			2,278*
168	Clubman Saloon			2,537*
168	Clubman Estate Car			2,742*
169	1275 GT			2,854*

MITSUBISHI (Japan)

Page	MAKE AND MODEL	Price in GB £	Price in USA $	Price ex Works
363	Minica Ami 55 Hi De Luxe 2-dr Sedan			563,000
363	Minica Ami 55 Super De Luxe 2-dr Sedan			629,000
363	Minica Ami 55 GL 2-dr Sedan			653,000
363	Minica Ami 55 XL 2-dr Sedan			676,000

Page	MAKE AND MODEL	Price in GB £	Price in USA $	Price ex Works
363	Mirage 1200 EL 2-dr Sedan			728,000
363	Mirage 1200 EL 4-dr Sedan			766,000
363	Mirage 1200 TL 4-dr Sedan			826,000
363	Mirage 1200 GL 2-dr Sedan			828,000
363	Mirage 1200 GL 4-dr Sedan			871,000
363	Mirage 1400 GL 2-dr Sedan			865,000
363	Mirage 1400 GL 4-dr Sedan			913,000
363	Mirage 1400 GLX 2-dr Sedan			922,000
363	Mirage 1400 GLX 4-dr Sedan			965,000
363	Mirage 1400 GLS 2-dr Sedan			1,030,000
364	Lancer 1200 Standard 2-dr Sedan			714,000
364	Lancer 1200 Populaire 2-dr Sedan			778,000
364	Lancer 1200 Populaire 4-dr Sedan			800,000
364	Lancer 1200 GL 2-dr Sedan			817,000
364	Lancer 1200 GL 4-dr Sedan			839,000
364	Lancer 1200 GL-EX 4-dr Sedan			879,000
364	Lancer 1200 SL-5 2-dr Sedan			863,000
364	Lancer 1200 SL-5 4-dr Sedan	3,099*		885,000
364	Lancer 1400 GL 2-dr Sedan	3,399*		875,000
364	Lancer 1400 GL 4-dr Sedan	3,549*		900,000
364	Lancer 1400 GL-EX 4-dr Sedan			940,000
364	Lancer 1400 SL-5 2-dr Sedan			934,000
364	Lancer 1400 SL-5 4-dr Sedan			956,000
364	Lancer 1600 GL-EX 4-dr Sedan			990,000
364	Lancer 1600 GSL 4-dr Sedan			1,014,000
364	Lancer 1600 GSR 2-dr Sedan			1,078,000
364	Celeste 1400 SR Coupé			935,000
364	Celeste 1400 GL Coupé			975,000
364	Celeste 1400 GSL Coupé			1,031,000
364	Celeste 1600 GL Coupé			1,117,000
364	Celeste 1600 XL Coupé			1,115,000
364	Celeste 1600 GT Coupé			1,117,000
364	Celeste 1600 GSR Coupé	4,199*		1,136,000
365	Galant Sigma 1600 L 4-dr Sedan			1,012,000
365	Galant Sigma 1600 GL 4-dr Sedan	4,199*		1,087,000
365	Galant Sigma 1600 SL 4-dr Sedan			1,132,000
365	Galant Sigma 1600 SL Super 4-dr Sedan			1,222,000
365	Galant Sigma Eterna 1600 GL 4-dr Sedan			1,077,000
365	Galant Sigma Eterna 1600 SL Super 4-dr Sedan			1,202,000
365	Galant Sigma 2000 GL 4-dr Sedan			1,210,000
365	Galant Sigma 2000 GSL 4-dr Sedan			1,329,000
365	Galant Sigma 2000 GSL Super 4-dr Sedan			1,415,000
365	Galant Sigma Eterna 2000 GSL 4-dr Sedan			1,309,000
365	Galant Sigma Eterna 2000 GSL Super 4-dr Sedan			1,395,000
365	Galant Sigma 2000 Super Saloon 4-dr Sedan			1,540,000
366	Galant Lambda 1600 SL 2-dr Coupé			1,195,000
366	Galant Lambda 1600 SL Super 2-dr Coupé			1,275,000
366	Galant Lambda Eterna 1600 SR 2-dr Coupé			1,225,000
366	Galant Lambda 2000 GL 2-dr Coupé			1,277,000
366	Galant Lambda 2000 GSL 2-dr Coupé			1,376,000
366	Galant Lambda 2000 GSL Super 2-dr Coupé			1,475,000
366	Galant Lambda 2000 Super Touring 2-dr Coupé			1,641,000
366	Galant Lambda Eterna 2000 XL 2-dr Coupé			1,460,000
366	Debonair De Luxe 4-dr Sedan			2,280,000
366	Debonair Super De Luxe 4-dr Sedan			2,420,000
366	Debonair Super De Luxe 5-seat 4-dr Sedan			2,480,000
367	Jeep H-J 58			1,208,000
367	Jeep H-J 56			1,248,000
367	Jeep J 54			1,343,000
367	Jeep H-J 26			1,332,000
367	Jeep J 24			1,427,000

Page	MAKE AND MODEL	Price in GB £	Price in USA $	Price ex Works
	MONOCOQUE (USA)			
306	Box			18,000
	MONTEVERDI (Switzerland)			
234	Sierra			69,200
235	Sierra Cabriolet			89,000
235	Sahara			37,300
236	Safari			54,900
	MORGAN (Great Britain)			
169	4/4 1600 2-seater			4,347*
169	4/4 1600 4-seater			4,785*
169	Plus 8			6,499*
	MORRIS (Great Britain)			
170	Marina 1300 2-dr Coupé			2,847*
170	Marina 1300 4-dr Saloon			2,967*
170	Marina 1300 4+1-dr Estate Car			3,385*
170	Marina 1300 L 2-dr Coupé			3,078*
170	Marina 1300 L 4-dr Saloon			3,163*
170	Marina 1300 HL 4-dr Saloon			3,501*
170	Marina 1700 4-dr Saloon			3,201*
170	Marina 1700 4+1-dr Estate Car			3,553*
170	Marina 1700 L 4-dr Saloon			3,412*
170	Marina 1700 L 4+1-dr Estate Car			3,801*
170	Marina 1700 HL 4-dr Saloon			3,774*
	NISSAN (Japan)			
367	Pulsar 1200 Custom 4-dr Sedan			774,000
367	Pulsar 1200 Custom D 4-dr Sedan			804,000
367	Pulsar 1200 TS 4-dr Sedan			870,000
367	Pulsar 1200 TS Coupé			918,000
367	Pulsar 1200 Standard Hatchback			740,000
367	Pulsar 1200 Custom Hatchback			766,000
367	Pulsar 1200 Custom D Hatchback			796,000
367	Pulsar 1200 TS Hatchback			860,000
367	Pulsar 1400 TS 4-dr Sedan			945,000
367	Pulsar 1400 TS-G 4-dr Sedan			1,013,000
367	Pulsar 1400 TS Coupé			993,000
367	Pulsar 1400 TS Hatchback			925,000
367	Pulsar 1400 TS-X Hatchback			1,010,000
367	Pulsar 1400 TS-GE 4-dr Sedan			1,108,000
367	Pulsar 1400 TS-XE 4-dr Sedan			1,070,000
367	Pulsar 1400 TS-XE Coupé			1,106,000
367	Pulsar 1400 TS-XE Hatchback			1,080,000
368	Sunny 1200 CT 2-dr Sedan			737,000
368	Sunny 1200 CT 4-dr Sedan			757,000
368	Sunny 1200 City De Luxe 2-dr Sedan			760,000
368	Sunny 1200 City De Luxe 4-dr Sedan			780,000
368	Sunny 1200 De Luxe 2-dr Sedan			788,000
368	Sunny 1200 De Luxe 4-dr Sedan			808,000
368	Sunny 1200 De Luxe Coupé			838,000
368	Sunny 1200 GL 2-dr Sedan			850,000
368	Sunny 1200 GL 4-dr Sedan			870,000
368	Sunny 1200 GL Coupé			910,000
368	Sunny 1400 De Luxe 2-dr Sedan			833,000
368	Sunny 1400 De Luxe 4-dr Sedan			853,000
368	Sunny 1400 De Luxe Coupé			883,000
368	Sunny 1400 GL 2-dr Sedan	3,899*		902,000
368	Sunny 1400 GL 4-dr Sedan			917,000
368	Sunny 1400 GL Coupé			947,000
368	Sunny 1400 SGL 4-dr Sedan			975,000
368	Sunny 1400 SGL Coupé			1,010,000
368	Sunny 1400 GX 4-dr Sedan	4,589*		962,000
368	Sunny 1400 GX Coupé	4,809*		1,001,000
368	Sunny 1400 SGX 4-dr Sedan			1,020,000
368	Sunny 1400 SGX Coupé			1,089,000
368	Sunny 1400 GX-E 4-dr Sedan			1,032,000
368	Sunny 1400 GX-E Coupé			1,071,000

Page	MAKE AND MODEL	Price in GB £	Price in USA $	Price ex Works
368	Sunny 1400 SGX-E 4-dr Sedan			1,090,000
368	Sunny 1400 SGX-E Coupé			1,134,000
369	Violet 1400 Standard Sedan			858,000
369	Violet 1400 De Luxe Sedan			926,000
369	Violet 1400 De Luxe Hatchback Coupé			956,000
369	Auster 1400 De Luxe Sedan			926,000
369	Auster 1400 De Luxe Hatchback Coupé			956,000
369	Violet 1400 GL Sedan			969,000
369	Violet 1400 GL Hatchback Coupé			999,000
369	Violet 1600 De Luxe Sedan			951,000
369	Auster 1600 De Luxe Sedan			951,000
369	Violet 1600 GL Sedan			999,000
369	Violet 1600 GL Hatchback Coupé			1,029,000
369	Violet 1600 GL-L Sedan			1,037,000
369	Auster 1600 CS Sedan			1,042,000
369	Auster 1600 CS Hatchback Coupé			1,072,000
369	Violet 1600 GL-L Hatchback Coupé			1,067,000
369	Violet 1600 GX Sedan			1,035,000
369	Violet 1600 GX Hatchback Coupé			1,065,000
369	Auster 1600 CS-L Sedan			1,094,000
369	Auster 1600 CS-L Hatchback Coupé			1,124,000
369	Stanza 1600 Luxury Sedan			976,000
369	Stanza 1600 Extra Sedan			1,032,000
369	Stanza 1600 Maxima Sedan			1,106,000
369	Violet 1600 GX-EL Sedan			1,181,000
369	Violet 1600 GX-EL Hatchback Coupé			1,211,000
369	Auster 1600 CS-E Sedan			1,112,000
369	Auster 1600 CS-EL Sedan			1,168,000
369	Auster 1600 CS-E Hatchback Coupé			1,142,000
369	Auster 1600 CS-EL Hatchback Coupé			1,198,000
369	Stanza 1600 GT-E Sedan			1,172,000
369	Stanza 1600 Maxima GT-E Sedan			1,222,000
369	Stanza 1800 Extra Sedan			1,057,000
369	Stanza 1800 Maxima Sedan			1,141,000
369	Stanza 1800 Maxima GT-E Sedan			1,262,000
370	Datsun Bluebird 1600 De Luxe Sedan			994,000
370	Datsun Bluebird 1600 GL Sedan			1,071,000
370	Datsun Bluebird 1600 GL-L Sedan			1,114,000
370	Datsun Bluebird 1600 GL-L Hardtop			1,149,000
370	Datsun Bluebird 1800 De Luxe Sedan			1,017,000
370	Datsun Bluebird 1800 GL Sedan			1,127,000
370	Datsun Bluebird 1800 GL Hardtop			1,162,000
370	Datsun Bluebird 1800 GF Sedan			1,284,000
370	Datsun Bluebird 1800 GF Hardtop			1,319,000
370	Datsun Bluebird 1800 SSS Sedan			1,193,000
370	Datsun Bluebird 1800 SSS Hardtop			1,228,000
370	Datsun Bluebird 1800 G4 Sedan			1,156,000
370	Datsun Bluebird 1800 G4 Hardtop			1,192,000
370	Datsun Bluebird 1800 GF-E Sedan			1,364,000
370	Datsun Bluebird 1800 GF-E Hardtop			1,399,000
370	Datsun Bluebird 1800 SSS-E Sedan			1,301,000
370	Datsun Bluebird 1800 SSS-E Hardtop			1,336,000
370	Datsun Bluebird 1800 SSS-ES Sedan			1,451,000
370	Datsun Bluebird 1800 SSS-ES Hardtop			1,451,000
370	Datsun Bluebird 2000 G6-L Sedan			1,366,000
370	Datsun Bluebird 2000 G6-L Hardtop			1,402,000
370	Datsun Bluebird 2000 G6-F Sedan			1,508,000
370	Datsun Bluebird 2000 G6-F Hardtop			1,544,000
370	Datsun Bluebird 2000 G6-E Sedan		8,129*	1,446,000
370	Datsun Bluebird 2000 G6-E Hardtop		8,279*	1,482,000
370	Datsun Bluebird 2000 G6-EL Sedan			1,580,000
370	Datsun Bluebird 2000 G6-EL Hardtop			1,616,000
370	Datsun Bluebird 2000 G6-EF Sedan			1,718,000
370	Datsun Bluebird 2000 G6-EF Hardtop			1,754,000
371	Skyline 1600 TI Sedan			1,021,000
371	Skyline 1600 TI-L Sedan			1,110,000
371	Skyline 1600 TI-L Hardtop			1,145,000
371	Skyline 1800 TI Sedan			1,076,000
371	Skyline 1800 TI-L Sedan			1,199,000
371	Skyline 1800 TI-L Hardtop			1,234,000
371	Skyline 1800 TI-EL Sedan			1,295,000
371	Skyline 1800 TI-EL Hardtop			1,326,000
371	Skyline 1800 TI-EX Sedan			1,387,000
371	Skyline 1800 TI-EX Hardtop			1,419,000
371	Skyline 1800 TI-ES Sedan			1,391,000
371	Skyline 1800 TI-ES Hardtop			1,426,000
371	Skyline 2000 GT Sedan			1,279,000
371	Skyline 2000 GT Hardtop			1,324,000
371	Skyline 2000 GT-L Sedan			1,339,000
371	Skyline 2000 GT-L Hardtop			1,384,000
371	Skyline 2000 GT-E Sedan			1,384,000
371	Skyline 2000 GT-E Hardtop			1,427,000
371	Skyline 2000 GT-EL Sedan			1,444,000
371	Skyline 2000 GT-EL Hardtop			1,487,000
371	Skyline 2000 GT-EX Sedan			1,575,000
371	Skyline 2000 GT-EX Hardtop			1,619,000
371	Skyline 2000 GT-ES Sedan			1,641,000
371	Skyline 2000 GT-ES Hardtop			1,686,000
372	Laurel 1800 Standard 4-dr Sedan			1,098,000
372	Laurel 1800 Custom 4-dr Sedan			1,138,000
372	Laurel 1800 GL 4-dr Sedan			1,212,000
372	Laurel 1800 GL 2-dr Hardtop			1,241,000
372	Laurel 1800 GL 4-dr Hardtop			1,289,000
372	Laurel 1800 SGL 4-dr Sedan			1,344,000
372	Laurel 2000 Diesel Standard 4-dr Sedan			1,190,000
372	Laurel 2000 Diesel De Luxe 4-dr Sedan			1,284,000
372	Laurel 2000 Diesel GL 4-dr Sedan			1,406,000
372	Laurel 2000 Custom 6 4-dr Sedan			1,263,000
372	Laurel 2000 GL6 4-dr Sedan			1,390,000
372	Laurel 2000 GL6 2-dr Hardtop			1,448,000
372	Laurel 2000 GL6 4-dr Hardtop			1,512,000
372	Laurel 2000 SGL 4-dr Sedan			1,498,000
372	Laurel 2000 SGL-E 4-dr Sedan			1,603,000
372	Laurel 2000 SGL-E 2-dr Hardtop			1,659,000
372	Laurel 2000 SGL-E 4-dr Hardtop			1,717,000
372	Laurel 2000 GL6-E 4-dr Hardtop			1,617,000
372	Laurel 2000 Medalist 4-dr Sedan			1,888,000
372	Laurel 2000 Medalist 2-dr Hardtop			1,965,000
372	Laurel 2000 Medalist 4-dr Hardtop			2,032,000
372	Laurel 2800 Medalist 4-dr Sedan			2,011,000
372	Laurel 2800 Medalist 2-dr Hardtop			2,063,000
372	Laurel 2800 Medalist 4-dr Hardtop			2,138,000
373	Silvia LS Coupé			1,075,000
373	Silvia LS Type S Coupé			1,125,000
373	Silvia LS Type L Coupé			1,114,000
373	Silvia LS Type X Coupé	6,229*		1,205,000
373	Silvia LS Type G Coupé			1,305,000
373	Silvia LS-E Type S Coupé			1,209,000
373	Silvia LS-E Type L Coupé			1,225,000
373	Silvia LS-E Type X Coupé			1,283,000
373	Silvia LS-E Type G Coupé			1,383,000
374	Cedric 2000 Standard 4-dr Sedan			1,274,000
374	Cedric 2000 De Luxe 4-dr Sedan			1,381,000
374	Cedric 2000 Custom De Luxe 4-dr Sedan			1,540,000
374	Cedric 2000 Custom De Luxe 4-dr Hardtop			1,649,000
374	Cedric 2000 GL 4-dr Sedan			1,721,000
374	Cedric 2000 GL 4-dr Hardtop			1,859,000
374	Cedric 2000 SGL 4-dr Hardtop			2,229,000
374	Cedric 2000 GL-E 4-dr Sedan			1,826,000
374	Cedric 2000 GL-E 2-dr Hardtop			1,907,000
374	Cedric 2000 GL-E 4-dr Hardtop			1,982,000
374	Cedric 2000 SGL-E 4-dr Sedan			2,188,000
374	Cedric 2000 SGL-E 2-dr Hardtop			2,279,000
374	Cedric 2000 SGL-E 4-dr Hardtop			2,354,000
374	Cedric 2000 SGL-E Extra 4-dr Sedan			2,245,000
374	Cedric 2000 SGL-E Extra 4-dr Hardtop			2,432,000
374	Gloria 2000 Diesel Standard 4-dr Sedan			1,282,000
374	Gloria 2200 Diesel Standard 4-dr Sedan			1,354,000

Page	MAKE AND MODEL	Price in GB £	Price in USA $	Price ex Works
374	Gloria 2200 Diesel De Luxe 4-dr Sedan			1,451,000
374	Gloria 2200 Diesel GL 4-dr Sedan			1,686,000
374	Gloria 2800 SGL-E 4-dr Sedan			2,525,000
374	Gloria 2800 SGL-E 4-dr Hardtop			2,716,000
374	Gloria 2800 Brougham 4-dr Sedan			2,680,000
374	Gloria 2800 Brougham 2-dr Hardtop			2,583,000
374	Gloria 2800 Brougham 4-dr Hardtop			2,826,000
375	Fairlady Z Sports			1,460,000
375	Fairlady ZL Sports			1,625,000
375	Fairlady ZT Sports			1,795,000
375	Fairlady Z 2+2 Sports			1,598,000
375	Fairlady ZL 2+2 Sports			1,793,000
375	Fairlady ZT 2+2 Sports			1,988,000
375	Fairlady 280 ZL Sports			1,800,000
375	Fairlady 280 ZT Sports			2,155,000
375	Fairlady 280 ZL 2+2 Sports			1,965,000
375	Fairlady 280 ZT 2+2 Sports			2,373,000
376	President C Sedan			3,846,000
376	President D Sedan			4,238,000
376	President Sovereign Sedan			4,627,000
376	Patrol 4WD			1,302,000
	NOVA (Great Britain)			
171	Sports			4,800
	NUOVA INNOCENTI (Italy)			
214	Mini 90 N			3,464,000*
214	Mini 90 SL			3,795,000*
215	Mini 120 SL			4,045,000*
215	Mini De Tomaso			4,510,000*
	OLDSMOBILE (USA)			
307	Starfire Sport Coupé			4,195
307	Starfire SX Sport Coupé			4,395
307	Omega Coupé			4,181
307	Omega Hatchback Coupé			4,345
307	Omega Sedan			4,281
307	Omega Brougham Coupé			4,387
307	Omega Brougham Sedan			4,487
308	Cutlass Salon Sedan			4,833
308	Cutlass Salon Coupé			4,733
308	Cutlass Salon Brougham Sedan			5,147
308	Cutlass Salon Brougham Coupé			5,022
308	Cutlass Supreme Coupé			5,172
308	Cutlass Calais Coupé			5,610
308	Cutlass Supreme Brougham Coupé			5,611
308	Cutlass Cruiser St. Wagon			5,094
308	Cutlass Cruiser Brougham St. Wagon			5,646
309	Delta 88 Hardtop Coupé			5,890
309	Delta 88 Sedan			5,990
309	Delta 88 Royale Hardtop Coupé			6,156
309	Delta 88 Royale Sedan			6,281
309	Ninety-Eight Luxury Coupé			7,738
309	Ninety-Eight Luxury Sedan			7,919
309	Ninety-Eight Regency Coupé			8,121
309	Ninety-Eight Regency Sedan			8,309
309	Custom Cruiser St. Wagon			6,990
311	Toronado Brougham Coupé			10,374
	OPEL (Germany FR)			
124	City « J » Hatchback Coupé			9,975*
124	City Hatchback Coupé			9,990*
124	City L Hatchback Coupé	2,751*		10,520*
124	City « Berlina » Hatchback Coupé			11,195*
125	Kadett 2-dr Limousine			9,880*
125	Kadett 4-dr Limousine	2,465*		10,425*
125	Kadett Caravan			10,675*
125	Kadett L 2-dr Limousine	2,686*		10,410*
125	Kadett L 4-dr Limousine			10,955*
125	Kadett L Coupé	3,124*		10,785*
125	Kadett L Caravan			11,205*
125	Kadett «Berlina» 2-dr Limousine			11,085*
125	Kadett « Berlina » 4-dr Limousine			11,535*
125	Kadett « Berlinetta » Coupé			11,460*
125	Kadett «Berlina» Caravan			11,785*
125	Kadett GT/E Coupé			17,470*
126	Rallye 1.6 S Coupé			12,435*
126	Rallye E Coupé	3,873*		14,077*
127	Ascona 1.2 2-dr Limousine			11,460*
127	Ascona 1.2 4-dr Limousine			12,015*
127	Ascona 1.2 L 2-dr Limousine			12,290*
127	Ascona 1.2 L 4-dr Limousine			12,845*
127	Ascona 1.2 « Berlina » 2-dr Limousine			13,110*
127	Ascona 1.2 « Berlina » 4-dr Limuosine			13,515*
127	Ascona 1.6 2-dr Limousine	3,262*		11,900*
127	Ascona 1.6 4-dr Limousine	3,371*		12,455*
127	Ascona 1.6 L 2-dr Limousine	3,654*		12,730*
127	Ascona 1.6 L 4-dr Limousine	3,762*		13,285*
127	Ascona 1.6 « Berlina » 2-dr Limousine			13,550*
127	Ascona 1.6 « Berlina » 4-dr Limousine			13,955*
127	Ascona 2.0 D 2-dr Limousine			—
127	Ascona 2.0 D 4-dr Limousine			—
127	Ascona 2.0 LD 2-dr Limousine			—
127	Ascona 2.0 LD 4-dr Limousine	3,957*		—
127	Ascona 2.0 D « Berlina » 2-dr Limousine			—
127	Ascona 2.0 D « Berlina » 4-dr Limousine	4,293*		—
128	Manta 1.2 2-dr Coupé			12,625*
128	Manta 1.2 L 2-dr Coupé			13,445*
128	Manta 1.2 «Berlinetta» 2-dr Coupé	4,857*		14,265*
128	Manta 1.6 2-dr Coupé			13,065*
128	Manta 1.6 L 2-dr Coupé			13,885*
128	Manta 1.6 « Berlinetta » 2-dr Coupé			14,705*
128	Manta 1.6 CC 2-dr Hatchback Coupé			13,460*
128	Manta 1.6 CC L 2-dr Hatchback Coupé			14,280*
128	Manta 1.6 CC « Berlinetta » 2-dr Hatchback Coupé	4,971*		15,100*
128	Manta 2.0 E Coupé			16,143*
128	Manta 2.0 E « Berlinetta » Coupé			16,930*
128	Manta 2.0 CC E 2-dr Hatchback Coupé			16,538*
128	Manta 2.0 CC E « Berlinetta » 2-dr Hatchback Coupé			17,325*
128	Manta 2.0 GT/E Coupé			16,149*
128	Manta 2.0 CC GT/E 2-dr Hatchback Coupé			16,544*
130	Rekord 2-dr Limousine			14,275*
130	Rekord 4-dr Limousine	4,761*		14,865*
130	Rekord 3-dr Caravan			14,855*
130	Rekord 5-dr Caravan			15,445*
130	Rekord L 2-dr Limousine			15,090*
130	Rekord L 4-dr Limousine			15,525*
130	Rekord L 5-dr Caravan	5,421*		16,260*
130	Rekord « Berlina » 2-dr Limousine			15,849*
130	Rekord « Berlina » 4-dr Limousine	5,029*		16,284*
131	Commodore 2-dr Limousine			16,765*
131	Commodore 4-dr Limousine			17,200*
131	Commodore « Berlina » 2-dr Limousine			17,415*
131	Commodore «Berlina» 4-dr Limousine			17,850*
132	Senator 4-dr Limousine	9,975*		23,380*
132	Senator C 4-dr Limousine			25,340*
132	Senator CD Automatic 4-dr Limousine			37,250*
132	Monza 2-dr Hatchback Coupé	10,250*		25,325*
132	Monza C 2-dr Hatchback Coupé			26,290*
	OTOSAN (Turkey)			
340	Anadol SL			185,000
340	Anadol SV-1600			219,000

Page	MAKE AND MODEL	Price in GB £	Price in USA $	Price ex Works
	PANTHER (Great Britain)			
171	Lima			6,067*
171	J 72 4.2-litre			16,556*
172	De Ville Saloon			44,825*
172	De Ville Convertible			50,895*
172	6			39,950*
	PAYKAN (Iran)			
347	Saloon			—
348	Saloon GT			—
	PEKING (China People's Republic)			
349	BJ 212			—
	PEUGEOT (France)			
87	104 GL Berline	2,464*		23,600◇
87	104 GL6 Berline			24,800◇
87	104 SL Berline	2,985*		26,300◇
88	104 S Berline	3,389*		27,900◇
88	104 ZL Coupé	2,685*		24,000◇
88	104 ZS Coupé	3,134*		27,400◇
88	304 GL Berline			26,300◇
88	304 GL Break	3,210*		27,550◇
89	304 SL Break	3,464*		29,900◇
89	304 GLD Berline			31,100◇
89	304 GLD Break			32,350◇
89	305 GL	3,365*		30,000◇
89	305 GR	3,655*		31,800◇
89	305 SR	3,994*		33,900◇
89	504 Berline	4,130*	7,922*	33,800◇
90	504 Break	4,599*	8,522*	35,300◇
90	504 GL Berline	4,725*	9,432*	36,600◇
90	504 GL Break	5,137*	10,032*	39,000◇
91	504 Break Familial	5,171*		40,600◇
91	504 TI Berline	5,190*		41,700◇
91	504 Cabriolet			57,100◇
91	504 Coupé			57,300◇
91	504 V6 Coupé			69,000◇
92	604 SL	7,314*	11,969*	51,800◇
92	604 TI	8,360*		60,000◇
	PLYMOUTH (USA)			
311	Horizon TC3 2-dr Hatchback			4,482
311	Horizon 4-dr Hatchback			4,122
312	Volaré 2-dr Coupé			4,006
312	Volaré 4-dr Sedan			4,107
312	Volaré St. Wagon			4,483
	POLSKI-FIAT (Poland)			
215	126 P			—
215	126 P 650			—
216	125 P 1300	2,129*		—
216	125 P 1300 Estate	2,449*		—
216	125 P 1500			—
217	125 P 1500 Estate			—
217	Polonez			—
	PONTIAC (Canada)			
250	Acadian S Hatchback Coupé			3,879
250	Acadian Hatchback Coupé			4,360
250	Acadian Hatchback Sedan			4,492
250	Laurentian Coupé			6,618
250	Laurentian Sedan			6,755
250	Laurentian Safari St. Wagon			7,435
250	Parisienne Coupé			7,239

Page	MAKE AND MODEL	Price in GB £	Price in USA $	Price ex Works
250	Parisienne Sedan			7,376
250	Parisienne Safari St. Wagon			8,195
	PONTIAC (USA)			
313	Sunbird Coupé			3,381
313	Sunbird Sport Coupé			4,072
313	Sunbird Sport Hatchback Coupé			4,172
313	Sunbird Sport Safari St. Wagon			4,245
314	Phoenix Hatchback Coupé			4,239
314	Phoenix Coupé			4,089
314	Phoenix Sedan			4,189
314	Phoenix LJ Coupé			4,589
314	Phoenix LJ Sedan			4,689
315	Firebird Hardtop Coupé			4,936
315	Firebird Esprit Hardtop Coupé			5,304
315	Firebird Formula Hardtop Coupé			6,204
315	Firebird Trans Am Hardtop Coupé	9,141*		6,515
317	Le Mans Coupé			4,723
317	Le Mans Sedan			4,823
317	Le Mans Safari St. Wagon			5,330
317	Grand Le Mans Coupé			4,983
317	Grand Le Mans Sedan			5,108
317	Grand Le Mans Safari St. Wagon			5,674
317	Grand Am Coupé			5,199
317	Grand Am Sedan			5,324
318	Grand Prix Hardtop Coupé			5,222
318	Grand Prix LJ Hardtop Coupé			6,394
318	Grand Prix SJ Hardtop Coupé			6,653
319	Catalina Coupé			5,798
319	Catalina Sedan			5,854
319	Catalina Safari St. Wagon			6,491
319	Bonneville Coupé			6,405
319	Bonneville Sedan			6,530
319	Bonneville Safari St. Wagon			6,850
319	Bonneville Brougham Coupé			7,182
319	Bonneville Brougham Sedan			7,371
	PORSCHE (Germany FR)			
133	924	8,549*		26,850*
133	924 (USA)		13,950*	—
133	924 Turbo			37,000*
133	911 SC Coupé	14,549*		42,950*
134	911 SC Coupé (USA)	14,549*	20,775*	—
134	911 SC Targa	14,549*	22,050*	—
134	Turbo Coupé	26,249*		79,900*
134	Turbo Coupé (USA)		38,500*	—
134	928	20,498*	29,775*	—
	PORTARO (Portugal)			
218	250			—
	PREMIER (India)			
348	Padmini			32,975
349	Padmini De Luxe			38,169
	PRINCESS (Great Britain)			
173	1700 L Saloon			3,781*
173	1700 HL Saloon			4,068*
173	2000 HL Saloon			4,254*
173	2200 HL Saloon			4,599*
173	2200 HLS Saloon			5,123*
	PUMA (Brazil)			
330	GTE 1600 Coupé			—
330	GTS 1600 Sport			—
330	GTB			—

Page	MAKE AND MODEL	Price in GB £	Price in USA $	Price ex Works
	RELIANT (Great Britain)			
174	Kitten DL Saloon			2,324*
174	Kitten DL Estate Car			2,494*
174	Robin 850 Saloon			1,883*
174	Robin 850 Super Saloon			2,190*
174	Robin 850 Super Estate Car			2,285*
174	Scimitar GTE			7,704*
	RENAULT (Argentina)			
337	4 S			—
337	6			—
337	12 TL			—
338	12 TS			—
338	12 TS Break			—
338	12 Alpine			—
338	Torino Grand Routier			—
338	Torino TSX			—
	RENAULT (France)			
92	4	2,236*		18,300◊
93	4 TL	2,422*		20,800◊
93	4 GTL			21,900◊
93	4 Rodeo			24,800◊
93	6 Rodeo			27,342◊
93	5	2,345*		21,800◊
94	5 TL	2,640*		24,300◊
94	5 GTL	2,850*	3,895*	26,700◊
94	5 Automatic			29,500◊
94	5 TS	3,187*		28,900◊
94	5 Alpine			39,800◊
95	6			23,400◊
95	6 TL	2,934*		25,000◊
95	12 Berline	2,829*		25,800◊
95	12 Break			28,800◊
96	12 TL Berline	3,145*		27,800◊
96	12 Break TL	3,521*		30,500◊
96	12 Break TS			32,600◊
96	12 Break Automatic			33,900◊
96	14 TL	3,061*		28,900◊
97	14 GTL	3,134*		30,600◊
97	14 TS			33,500◊
97	16 TL (55 hp)	3,791*		33,500◊
97	16 TL (66 hp)			34,200◊
97	16 TL Automatic	4,117*		36,700◊
98	16 TX	4,946*		39,200◊
98	16 TX Automatic			41,600◊
98	18 TL	3,313*		32,500◊
98	18 GTL	3,815*		35,000◊
98	18 TS	3,605*		35,000◊
98	18 TS Automatic	3,956*		38,200◊
99	18 GTS	4,233*		39,500◊
99	18 GTS Automatic	4,503*		41,800◊
99	15 TL			33,300◊
99	15 GTL	3,973*		35,800◊
99	17 TS Cabriolet	4,939*	7,945*	45,300◊
100	20 TL	4,489*		39,800◊
100	20 TL Automatic	4,854*		43,000◊
100	20 GTL			43,200◊
100	20 GTL Automatic			46,400◊
100	20 TS	5,384*		45,000◊
100	20 TS Automatic	5,749*		46,400◊
100	30 TS	6,490*		49,800◊
101	30 TS Automatic	6,855*		53,000◊
101	30 TX			55,000◊
101	30 TX Automatic			57,300◊
	RENAULT (Spain)			
222	4			205,600
222	4 TL			231,700
222	5 TL			275,400

Page	MAKE AND MODEL	Price in GB £	Price in USA $	Price ex Works
222	5 GTL			294,800
222	5 Copa			451,500
223	6 TL			285,900
223	Siete TL			291,600
223	12			331,700
223	12 Familiar			354,100
223	12 TL			349,200
223	12 TL Familiar			368,200
223	12 TS			386,200
223	12 TS Familiar			402,900
	REPLICARS (USA)			
320	Phaeton			14,750
320	Roadster			14,750
	ROLLS ROYCE (Great Britain)			
175	Silver Shadow II		65,400*	32,023*
176	Silver Wraith II		74,500*	37,721*
176	Silver Wraith II with division			39,780*
176	Corniche Saloon		102,900*	46,578*
176	Corniche Convertible		109,800*	49,479*
176	Phantom VI			—
177	Camargue		115,000*	56,757*
	ROM CARMEL (Israel)			
341	Rom 1300			—
	ROVER (Great Britain)			
177	3500			7,996*
178	2600			6,795*
178	2300			5,995*
	SAAB (Sweden)			
228	96 GL			—
229	99 GL 2-dr Sedan	4,495*	6,398*	—
229	99 GL 4-dr Sedan	4,905*		—
229	99 EMS 2-dr Sport Sedan	6,580*		—
229	99 Turbo 2-dr Sport Sedan			—
230	900 GL 3-dr Hatchback Sedan	5,525*	7,798*	—
230	900 GLs 3-dr Hatchback Sedan	5,775*		—
230	900 GLs 5-dr Hatchback Sedan	5,995*		—
230	900 GLE 5-dr Hatchback Sedan	7,675*	8,948*	—
230	900 EMS 3-dr Hatchback Sedan	6,995*	9,073*	—
230	900 Turbo 3-dr Hatchback Sedan	8,675*		—
230	900 Turbo 5-dr Hatchback Sedan	8,995*	11,968*	—
	SBARRO (Switzerland)			
236	Replica BMW 328 Standard			33,000
237	Replica BMW 328 America			42,000
237	Stash HS Cabriolet			100,000
237	Windhound 4 x 4			—
	SCEPTRE (USA)			
320	6.6 S			50,000
	SEAT (Spain)			
224	133 Lujo			225,000*
224	133 Especial Lujo			232,000*
224	127 900 2 Puertas			263,000*
224	127 900 3 Puertas			273,000*
224	127 900 4 Puertas			275,000*
224	127 900 2 Puertas Confort Lujo			294,000*
224	127 900 3 Puertas Confort Lujo			304,000*
224	127 900 4 Puertas Confort Lujo			306,000*
224	127 1000 2 Puertas Especial Confort Lujo			300,000*

Page	MAKE AND MODEL	Price in GB £	Price in USA $	Price ex Works
224	127 1000 3 Puertas Especial Confort Lujo			310,000*
224	127 1000 4 Puertas Especial Confort Lujo			312,000*
225	128/3P 1200			382,000*
225	128/3P 1430			400,000*
225	Sport 1430			425,000*
226	124-D			325,000*
226	124-D LS			362,000*
226	124-D Especial			375,000*
226	131 1430			381,000*
226	131 Supermirafiori 1430			415,000*
227	131 CL 1430 5 Puertas			431,000*
227	131 Supermirafiori 1600			458,000*
227	131 CL 1600 5 Puertas			475,000*
227	131 Diesel 1760			464,000*
227	131 Diesel 1760 5 Puertas			482,000*
228	132 2000 Lujo			588,000*
228	132 Diesel 2200			602,000*
228	132 Diesel 2200 Lujo			659,000*
	SEVEN (Great Britain)			
178	Super 7			4,134*
	SHANGHAI (China People's Republic)			
350	Sedan			—
	ŠKODA (Czechoslovakia)			
74	105 S	1,850*		—
74	105 L	1,949*		—
74	120 L	2,050*		—
75	120 LS	2,299*		—
75	S 110 R Coupé	1,899*		—
	SPARTAN CARS (Great Britain)			
179	2-seater Sports			3,900
179	2 + 2-seater Sports			4,196
	STANDARD (India)			
349	Gazel			—
	STIMULA (France)			
101	Bugatti 55			123,000
	STUTZ (USA)			
321	IV Porte 4-dr Sedan			69,500
321	Blackhawk VI 2-dr Coupé			69,500
321	Bearcat 2-dr Convertible			107,000
	SUBARU (Japan)			
377	Rex 550 SEEC-T Standard 2-dr Sedan			551,000
377	Rex 550 SEEC-T A I 2-dr Sedan			618,000
377	Rex 550 SEEC-T A I 4-dr Sedan			643,000
377	Rex 550 SEEC-T A I 3-dr Swingback			638,000
377	Rex 550 SEEC-T A II 4-dr Sedan			682,000
377	Rex 550 SEEC-T A II 3-dr Swingback			677,000
377	Rex 550 SEEC-T A II G 4-dr Sedan			709,000
377	Rex 550 SEEC-T A II G 3-dr Swingback			704,000
377	Leone SEEC-T 1400 Standard 2-dr Sedan			749,000
377	Leone SEEC-T 1400 De Luxe 2-dr Sedan			836,000

Page	MAKE AND MODEL	Price in GB £	Price in USA $	Price ex Works
377	Leone SEEC-T 1400 De Luxe 4-dr Sedan			861,000
377	Leone SEEC-T 1400 GL 2-dr Sedan			908,000
337	Leone SEEC-T 1400 GL 4-dr Sedan			933,000
377	Leone SEEC-T 1600 De Luxe 4-dr Sedan	2,972*	4,529*	886,000
377	Leone SEEC-T 1600 GL 4-dr Sedan			958,000
377	Leone SEEC-T 1600 Custom 4-dr Sedan			1,008,000
377	Leone SEEC-T 1600 Super Custom 4-dr Sedan			1,130,000
377	Leone SEEC-T 1600 GL Coupé	2,995*		1,016,000
377	Leone SEEC-T 1600 GF Hardtop			1,050,000
377	Leone SEEC-T 1600 Grand Am 4-dr Sedan			1,122,000
377	Leone SEEC-T 1600 Grand Am Hardtop			1,185,000
377	Leone SEEC-T 1600 Super Touring 4-dr Sedan			1,135,000
377	Leone SEEC-T 1600 RX Coupé			1,153,000
377	Leone SEEC-T 1600 GFT Hardtop	3,299*	4,939*	1,149,000
377	Leone SEEC-T 1600 Grand Am T Hardtop			1,307,000
377	Leone SEEC-T 1600 4WD 4-dr Sedan			1,336,000
377	Leone SEEC-T 1600 4WD Station Wagon L	3,990*	5,429*	1,130,000
377	Leone SEEC-T 1600 4WD Station Wagon LG			1,185,000
	SUZUKI (Japan)			
378	Fronte 7-S Standard 2-dr Sedan (2-stroke)			527,000
378	Fronte 7-S Standard 2-dr Sedan (4-stroke)			556,000
378	Fronte 7-S De Luxe 2-dr Sedan (2-stroke)			576,000
378	Fronte 7-S De Luxe 2-dr Sedan (4-stroke)			604,000
378	Fronte 7-S De Luxe 4-dr Sedan (2-stroke)			599,000
378	Fronte 7-S De Luxe 4-dr Sedan (4-stroke)			627,000
378	Fronte 7-S Super De Luxe 4-dr Sedan (2- and 4-stroke)			662,000
378	Fronte 7-S Custom 2-dr Sedan (2- and 4-stroke)			658,000
378	Fronte 7-S Custom 4-dr Sedan (2- and 4-stroke)			698,000
378	Fronte 7-S Cervo Coupé CX (2-stroke)			608,000
378	Fronte 7-S Cervo Coupé CXG (2-stroke)			698,000
378	Fronte 7-SC 100 CXG Coupé			—
379	Fronte Hatch 55 B Station Wagon			507,000
379	Fronte Hatch 55 D Station Wagon			537,000
379	Fronte Hatch 55 T Station Wagon			567,000
379	Jimny 55 Softtop			748,000
379	Jimny 55 Steelbody Wagon			797,000
379	Jimny 8 Softtop			859,000
379	Jimny 8 Steelbody Wagon			908,000
	SYD LAWRENCE (Great Britain)			
179	Mk 2 Sports			16,500
	SYRENA (Poland)			
217	105			—
	TATRA (Czechoslovakia)			
75	T 613			—

Page	MAKE AND MODEL	Price in GB £	Price in USA $	Price ex Works
	TECHNICAL EXPONENTS (Great Britain)			
180	TX Tripper 1500			3,150
180	TX Tripper 1500 De Luxe			3,350
180	TX Tripper 2000 Sprint			3,955
	TOFAS (Turkey)			
340	Murat 131			—
	TORO (Philippines)			
393	1300			—
	TOTAL REPLICA (USA)			
321	Ford « B » Roadster			19,500
	TOYOTA (Japan)			
380	Starlet DX 3-dr Sedan	2,858*		705,000
380	Starlet DX 5-dr Sedan	2,950*		730,000
380	Starlet XL 3-dr Sedan			745,000
380	Starlet XL 5-dr Sedan			770,000
380	Starlet S 3-dr Sedan			798,000
380	Starlet S 5-dr Sedan			823,000
380	Starlet SE 3-dr Sedan			813,000
380	Starlet SE 5-dr Sedan			838,000
380	Corsa Standard 2-dr Sedan			711,000
380	Corsa De Luxe 2-dr Sedan			770,000
380	Corsa De Luxe 4-dr Sedan			795,000
380	Corsa De Luxe 3-dr Coupé			790,000
380	Corsa GL 2-dr Sedan			822,000
380	Corsa GL 4-dr Sedan			847,000
380	Corsa GL 3-dr Coupé			842,000
380	Corsa S 3-dr Coupé			912,000
380	Corsa GSL 4-dr Sedan			931,000
380	Corsa GSL 3-dr Coupé			926,000
380	Tercel Standard 2-dr Sedan			705,000
380	Tercel De Luxe 2-dr Sedan			764,000
380	Tercel De Luxe 4-dr Sedan			789,000
380	Tercel De Luxe 3-dr Coupé			784,000
380	Tercel Hi-De Luxe 2-dr Sedan			810,000
380	Tercel Hi-De Luxe 4-dr Sedan			835,000
380	Tercel Hi-De Luxe 3-dr Coupé			830,000
380	Tercel S 3-dr Coupé			904,000
380	Tercel SE 4-dr Sedan			918,000
380	Tercel SE 3-dr Coupé			918,000
381	Corolla 1300 Standard 2-dr Sedan			698,000
381	Corolla 1300 Standard 4-dr Sedan			723,000
381	Corolla 1300 De Luxe 2-dr Sedan			743,000
381	Corolla 1300 De Luxe 4-dr Sedan			768,000
381	Corolla 1300 De Luxe 2-dr Hardtop			798,000
381	Corolla 1300 De Luxe 2-dr Coupé			811,000
381	Corolla 1300 De Luxe 3-dr Liftback			836,000
381	Corolla 1300 Hi-De Luxe 2-dr Sedan			800,000
381	Corolla 1300 Hi-De Luxe 4-dr Sedan			825,000
381	Corolla 1300 Hi-De Luxe 2-dr Hardtop			851,000
381	Corolla 1300 Hi-De Luxe 2-dr Coupé			863,000
381	Corolla 1300 Hi-De Luxe 3-dr Liftback			892,000
381	Corolla 1300 SL 4-dr Sedan			856,000
381	Corolla 1300 SL 2-dr Hardtop			888,000
381	Corolla 1300 SL 2-dr Coupé			892,000
381	Corolla 1300 SL 3-dr Liftback			935,000
381	Corolla 1300 SR 2-dr Coupé			898,000
381	Corolla 1400 De Luxe 2-dr Sedan			779,000
381	Corolla 1400 De Luxe 4-dr Sedan			804,000
381	Corolla 1400 De Luxe 2-dr Hardtop			834,000
381	Corolla 1400 De Luxe 2-dr Coupé			848,000
381	Corolla 1400 De Luxe 3-dr Liftback			873,000
381	Corolla 1400 Hi-De Luxe 2-dr Sedan			824,000
381	Corolla 1400 Hi-De Luxe 4-dr Sedan			849,000
381	Corolla 1400 Hi-De Luxe 2-dr Hardtop			875,000
381	Corolla 1400 Hi-De Luxe 2-dr Coupé			886,000
381	Corolla 1400 Hi-De Luxe 3-dr Liftback			924,000
381	Corolla 1400 SL 4-dr Sedan			894,000
381	Corolla 1400 SL 2-dr Hardtop			925,000
381	Corolla 1400 SL 2-dr Coupé			929,000
381	Corolla 1400 SL 3-dr Liftback			961,000
381	Corolla 1600 Hi-De Luxe 4-dr Sedan			884,000
381	Corolla 1600 Hi-De Luxe 2-dr Hardtop			910,000
381	Corolla 1600 Hi-De Luxe 2-dr Coupé			919,000
381	Corolla 1600 Hi-De Luxe 3-dr Liftback			978,000
381	Corolla 1600 GSL 4-dr Sedan			970,000
381	Corolla 1600 GSL 2-dr Hardtop			1,003,000
381	Corolla 1600 GSL 2-dr Coupé			1,003,000
381	Corolla 1600 GSL 3-dr Liftback			1,058,000
381	Corolla 1600 SR 2-dr Coupé			1,011,000
381	Corolla 1600 Levin 2-dr Coupé			1,227,000
381	Corolla 1600 Levin GT 2-dr Coupé			1,282,000
381	Corolla 1600 GT 3-dr Liftback			1,332,000
382	Corolla 2-dr Sedan		3,748*	—
382	Corolla Custom 2-dr Sedan		4,133*	—
382	Corolla Custom 4-dr Sedan		4,253*	—
382	Corolla De Luxe 2-dr Sedan		4,338*	—
382	Corolla De Luxe 4-dr Sedan		4,563*	—
382	Corolla De Luxe 4-dr Station Wagon		4,933*	—
382	Corolla De Luxe Sport Coupé		4,758*	—
382	Corolla De Luxe Liftback		4,928*	—
382	Corolla SR-5 Sport Coupé		5,248*	—
382	Corolla SR-5 Liftback		5,388*	—
382	Sprinter 1300 DX 4-dr Sedan			785,000
382	Sprinter 1300 DX Hardtop			819,000
382	Sprinter 1300 DX Coupé			831,000
382	Sprinter 1300 DX Liftback			857,000
382	Sprinter 1300 XL 4-dr Sedan			842,000
382	Sprinter 1300 XL Hardtop			867,000
382	Sprinter 1300 XL Coupé			879,000
382	Sprinter 1300 XL Liftback			916,000
382	Sprinter 1300 ST 4-dr Sedan			873,000
382	Sprinter 1300 ST Hardtop			904,000
382	Sprinter 1300 ST Coupé			908,000
382	Sprinter 1300 ST Liftback			956,000
382	Sprinter 1400 DX 4-dr Sedan			830,000
382	Sprinter 1400 DX Hardtop			859,000
382	Sprinter 1400 DX Coupé			864,000
382	Sprinter 1400 DX Liftback			891,000
382	Sprinter 1400 XL 4-dr Sedan			861,000
382	Sprinter 1400 XL Hardtop			891,000
382	Sprinter 1400 XL Coupé			904,000
382	Sprinter 1400 XL Liftback			943,000
382	Sprinter 1400 ST 4-dr Sedan			909,000
382	Sprinter 1400 ST Hardtop			939,000
382	Sprinter 1400 ST Coupé			943,000
382	Sprinter 1400 ST Liftback			982,000
382	Sprinter 1600 XL 4-dr Sedan			900,000
382	Sprinter 1600 XL Hardtop			930,000
382	Sprinter 1600 XL Coupé			941,000
382	Sprinter 1600 XL Liftback			992,000
382	Sprinter 1600 GS 4-dr Sedan			991,000
382	Sprinter 1600 GS Hardtop			1,023,000
382	Sprinter 1600 GS Coupé			1,023,000
382	Sprinter 1600 GS Liftback			1,078,000
382	Sprinter 1600 SR Coupé			1,033,000
382	Sprinter 1600 Trueno GT			1,302,000
382	Sprinter 1600 Liftback GT			1,352,000
383	Carina 1600 Standard 2-dr Sedan			845,000
383	Carina 1600 Standard 4-dr Sedan			865,000
383	Carina 1600 De Luxe 2-dr Sedan			903,000
383	Carina 1600 De Luxe 4-dr Sedan	3,607*		923,000
383	Carina 1600 De Luxe Hardtop			958,000

Page	MAKE AND MODEL	Price in GB £	Price in USA $	Price ex Works
383	Carina 1600 Super De Luxe 4-dr Sedan			961,000
383	Carina 1600 Super De Luxe Hardtop			996,000
383	Carina 1600 ST 4-dr Sedan			1,026,000
383	Carina 1600 ST Hardtop			1,061,000
383	Carina 1600 SR Hardtop			1,076,000
383	Carina 1600 GT 4-dr Sedan			1,377,000
383	Carina 1600 GT Hardtop			1,412,000
383	Carina 1800 De Luxe 4-dr Sedan			989,000
383	Carina 1800 De Luxe Hardtop			1,024,000
383	Carina 1800 Super De Luxe 4-dr Sedan			1,046,000
383	Carina 1800 Super De Luxe Hardtop			1,087,000
383	Carina 1800 ST 4-dr Sedan			1,117,000
383	Carina 1800 ST Hardtop			1,152,000
383	Carina 1800 SE 4-dr Sedan			1,171,000
383	Carina 1800 SE Hardtop			1,206,000
383	Carina 1800 SR Hardtop			1,167,000
383	Carina 1800 ST 4-dr Sedan			1,177,000
383	Carina 1800 ST Hardtop			1,212,000
383	Carina 1800 SR Hardtop			1,217,000
383	Carina 2000 SE 4-dr Sedan			1,224,000
383	Carina 2000 SE Hardtop			1,259,000
383	Carina 2000 GT 4-dr Sedan			1,487,000
383	Carina 2000 GT Hardtop			1,522,000
384	Celica 1600 ET Coupé			985,000
384	Celica 1600 LT Coupé			1,045,000
384	Celica 1600 LT Liftback			1,125,000
384	Celica 1600 ST Coupé	4,069*		1,080,000
384	Celica 1600 ST Liftback			1,160,000
384	Celica 1600 XT Coupé			1,130,000
384	Celica 1600 XT Liftback			1,226,000
384	Celica 1600 GT Coupé			1,467,000
384	Celica 1600 GT Liftback			1,563,000
384	Celica 1800 ST Coupé			1,110,000
384	Celica 1800 ST Liftback			1,190,000
384	Celica 1800 XT Coupé			1,160,000
384	Celica 1800 XT Liftback			1,256,000
384	Celica 1800 SE Coupé			1,251,000
384	Celica 1800 SE Liftback			1,347,000
384	Celica 1800 ST Coupé			1,193,000
384	Celica 1800 ST Liftback			1,273,000
384	Celica 2000 XT Coupé			1,213,000
384	Celica 2000 XT Liftback	5,130*		1,309,000
384	Celica 2000 SE Coupé			1,304,000
384	Celica 2000 SE Liftback	4,435*		1,400,000
384	Celica 2000 XX-L Liftback			1,466,000
384	Celica 2000 XX-S Liftback			1,576,000
384	Celica 2000 XX-G Liftback			1,696,000
384	Celica 2000 GT Rally Coupé			1,440,000
384	Celica 2000 GT Rally Liftback			1,536,000
384	Celica 2000 GT Coupé			1,577,000
384	Celica 2000 GT Liftback	5,417*		1,673,000
384	Celica 2600 XX-S Liftback			1,713,000
384	Celica 2600 XX-G Liftback			1,839,000
386	Celica ST Hardtop		5,899*	—
386	Celica GT Hardtop		6,329*	—
386	Celica GT Liftback		6,559*	—
386	Corona 1600 Standard 4-dr Sedan			897,000
386	Corona 1600 De Luxe 4-dr Sedan			989,000
386	Corona 1600 De Luxe Hardtop			1,024,000
386	Corona 1600 De Luxe Liftback			1,039,000
386	Corona 1600 GL 4-dr Sedan			1,046,000
386	Corona 1600 GL Hardtop			1,081,000
386	Corona 1600 GL Liftback			1,096,000
386	Corona 1600 SL 4-dr Sedan			1,107,000
386	Corona 1600 SL Hardtop			1,145,000
386	Corona 1600 SL Liftback			1,157,000
386	Corona 1800 De Luxe 4-dr Sedan			1,022,000
386	Corona 1800 De Luxe Hardtop			1,057,000
386	Corona 1800 De Luxe Liftback			1,072,000
386	Corona 1800 GL 4-dr Sedan			1,107,000
387	Corona 1800 GL Hardtop			1,142,000
387	Corona 1800 GL Liftback			1,169,000
387	Corona 1800 SL 4-dr Sedan			1,169,000
387	Corona 1800 SL Hardtop			1,207,000
387	Corona 1800 SL Liftback			1,231,000
387	Corona 1800 SL Touring 4-dr Sedan			1,291,000
387	Corona 1800 SL Touring Hardtop			1,329,000
387	Corona 1800 SL Touring Liftback			1,355,000
387	Corona 2000 GL 4-dr Sedan			1,162,000
387	Corona 2000 GL Hardtop			1,197,000
387	Corona 2000 GL Liftback			1,224,000
387	Corona 2000 SL 4-dr Sedan			1,219,000
387	Corona 2000 SL Hardtop			1,257,000
387	Corona 2000 SL Liftback			1,281,000
387	Corona 2000 CX 4-dr Sedan			1,307,000
387	Corona 2000 CX Hardtop			1,342,000
387	Corona 2000 CX Liftback			1,371,000
387	Corona 2000 GT 4-dr Sedan			1,528,000
387	Corona 2000 GT Hardtop			1,571,000
387	Corona 2000 GT Liftback			1,592,000
388	Mark II 1800 Standard 4-dr Sedan			990,000
388	Mark II 1800 De Luxe 4-dr Sedan			1,066,000
388	Mark II De Luxe 2-dr Hardtop			1,107,000
388	Chaser 1800 De Luxe 4-dr Sedan			1,072,000
388	Chaser 1800 De Luxe 2-dr Hardtop			1,113,000
388	Mark II 1800 GL 4-dr Sedan			1,127,000
388	Mark II 1800 GL 2-dr Hardtop			1,169,000
388	Chaser 1800 XL 4-dr Sedan			1,133,000
388	Chaser 1800 XL 2-dr Hardtop			1,174,000
388	Mark II 2000 De Luxe 4-dr Sedan			1,096,000
388	Mark II 2000 De Luxe 2-dr Hardtop			1,137,000
388	Chaser 2000 De Luxe 4-dr Sedan			1,102,000
388	Chaser 2000 De Luxe 4-dr Hardtop			1,143,000
388	Mark II 2000 GL 4-dr Sedan			1,157,000
389	Mark II 2000 GL 2-dr Hardtop			1,198,000
389	Chaser 2000 XL 4-dr Sedan			1,163,000
389	Chaser 2000 XL 4-dr Hardtop			1,204,000
389	Chaser 2000 GS 4-dr Sedan			1,284,000
389	Chaser 2000 GS 4-dr Hardtop			1,362,000
389	Mark II 2000 GSL 4-dr Sedan			1,278,000
389	Mark II 2000 GSL 2-dr Hardtop			1,354,000
389	Chaser 2000 SXL 4-dr Sedan			1,366,000
389	Chaser 2000 SXL 2-dr Hardtop			1,438,000
389	Mark II 2000 LG 4-dr Sedan			1,459,000
389	Mark II 2000 LG 2-dr Hardtop			1,531,000
389	Chaser 2000 SGS 4-dr Sedan			1,482,000
389	Chaser 2000 SGS 2-dr Hardtop			1,554,000
389	Mark II 2000 LG Touring 4-dr Sedan			1,516,000
389	Mark II 2000 LG Touring 2-dr Hardtop			1,588,000
389	Chaser 2000 SG Touring 4-dr Sedan			1,608,000
389	Chaser 2000 SG Touring 2-dr Hardtop			1,645,000
389	Mark II 2000 Grande 4-dr Sedan			1,835,000
389	Mark II 2000 Grande 2-dr Hardtop			1,872,000
389	Mark II 2600 Grande 4-dr Sedan			—
389	Mark II 2600 Grande 2-dr Hardtop			2,092,000
390	Crown 2000 De Luxe-A 4-dr Sedan			1,370,000
390	Crown 2000 De Luxe 4-dr Sedan			1,508,000
390	Crown 2000 De Luxe 2-dr Hardtop			1,454,000
390	Crown 2000 De Luxe 4-dr Sedan			1,489,000
390	Crown 2000 De Luxe Custom 2-dr Hardtop			—
390	Crown 2000 De Luxe Custom 4-dr Hardtop			—
390	Crown 2000 Super De Luxe 4-dr Sedan			1,690,000
390	Crown 2000 Super De Luxe 4-dr Hardtop			1,800,000
390	Crown 2000 Super Saloon 4-dr Sedan			1,828,000
390	Crown 2000 Super Saloon 4-dr Hardtop			1,976,000
390	Crown 2000 EFI De Luxe-A 4-dr Sedan			1,453,000

Page	MAKE AND MODEL	Price in GB £	Price in USA $	Price ex Works
390	Crown 2000 EFI De Luxe 4-dr Sedan			1,621,000
390	Crown 2000 EFI De Luxe 4-dr Hardtop			1,577,000
390	Crown 2000 EFI De Luxe Custom 2-dr Hardtop			—
390	Crown 2000 EFI De Luxe Custom 4-dr Hardtop			—
390	Crown 2000 EFI Super De Luxe 4-dr Sedan			1,803,000
390	Crown 2000 EFI Super De Luxe 2-dr Hardtop			1,896,000
390	Crown 2000 EFI Super De Luxe 4-dr Hardtop			1,936,000
390	Crown 2000 EFI Super Saloon 4-dr Sedan			1,941,000
390	Crown 2000 EFI Super Saloon 2-dr Hardtop			2,161,000
390	Crown 2000 EFI Super Saloon 4-dr Hardtop			2,131,000
390	Crown 2200 Diesel Standard 4-dr Sedan			1,372,000
390	Crown 2200 Diesel De Luxe-A 4-dr Sedan			1,447,000
390	Crown 2200 Diesel De Luxe 4-dr Sedan			1,585,000
390	Crown 2200 Diesel Super De Luxe 4-dr Sedan			1,765,000
390	Crown 2600 Super Saloon 4-dr Sedan	7,504*		2,243,000
390	Crown 2600 Super Saloon 2-dr Hardtop			2,626,000
390	Crown 2600 Super Saloon 4-dr Hardtop			2,341,000
390	Crown 2600 Royal Saloon 4-dr Sedan			2,597,000
390	Crown 2600 Royal Saloon 4-dr Hardtop			2,626,000
392	Century D Sedan			4,276,000
392	Century C Sedan			3,876,000
392	Landcruiser FJ56V-K		8,998*	—
392	Landcruiser BJ40-KC		7,768*	—
	TRABANT (Germany DDR)			
102	601 Limousine			—
102	601 Universal			—
	TRIUMPH (Great Britain)			
180	Dolomite 1300			3,265*
180	Dolomite 1500			3,492*
180	Dolomite 1500 HL			3,996*
180	Dolomite 1850 HL			4,435*
180	Dolomite Sprint			5,408*
180	Spitfire 1500		5,795*	3,365*
182	TR 7		6,750*	4,764*
	TVR (Great Britain)			
183	3000 M Coupé			7,244*
183	Convertible 3000 S	16,000*		7,591*
183	Turbo Coupé			10,921*
183	Convertible Turbo			11,445*
183	Taimar Hatchback Coupé	16,000*		7,886*
183	Taimar Turbo Hatchback Coupé			11,712*
	UAZ (USSR)			
240	469 B			—
	VANDEN PLAS (Great Britain)			
183	1500			4,180*

Page	MAKE AND MODEL	Price in GB £	Price in USA $	Price ex Works
	VAUXHALL (Great Britain)			
184	Chevette E 2-dr Saloon			2,458*
184	Chevette E 4-dr Saloon			2,566*
184	Chevette E 3-dr Hatchback			2,499*
184	Chevette L 2-dr Saloon			2,705*
184	Chevette L 4-dr Saloon			2,813*
184	Chevette L 3-dr Hatchback			2,746*
184	Chevette L Estate Car			3,031*
184	Chevette GL 3-dr Hatchback			3,064*
184	Chevette GLS 4-dr Saloon			3,131*
184	Chevette 2300 HS Hatchback			5,577*
185	Viva E 2-dr Saloon			2,545*
185	Viva E 4-dr Saloon			2,652*
185	Viva 1300 L 2-dr Saloon			2,792*
185	Viva 1300 L 4-dr Saloon			2,899*
185	Viva 1300 L Estate Car			3,118*
185	Viva 1300 GLS 2-dr Saloon			3,173*
185	Viva 1300 GLS 4-dr Saloon			3,281*
185	Viva 1300 GLS Estate Car			3,499*
185	Viva 1800 GLS 4-dr Saloon			3,459*
185	Cavalier 1300 L 2-dr Saloon			3,134*
185	Cavalier 1300 L 4-dr Saloon			3,242*
185	Cavalier 1600 L 2-dr Saloon			3,312*
185	Cavalier 1600 L 4-dr Saloon			3,420*
185	Cavalier 1600 GL 4-dr Saloon			3,758*
185	Cavalier 1600 GLS Sports Hatchback			4,384*
185	Cavalier 2000 GL 4-dr Saloon			3,966*
185	Cavalier 2000 GLS Coupé			4,551*
185	Cavalier 2000 GLS Sport Hatchback			4,592*
186	Carlton 2000 Saloon			4,831*
187	Carlton 2000 Estate			5,322*
187	Royale Saloon			8,354*
187	Royale Coupé			8,662*
	VAZ (USSR)			
240	Lada 1200 4-dr Sedan	2,056*		—
240	Lada 1200 5-dr Combi	2,340*		—
240	Lada 1300 ES 4-dr Sedan	2,404*		—
240	Lada 1500 4-dr Sedan	2,511*		—
240	Lada 1500 5-dr Combi	2,461*		—
240	Lada 1500 ES 5-dr Combi	2,826*		—
240	Lada 1600 4-dr Sedan	2,666*		—
240	Lada 1600 ES 4-dr Sedan	2,999*		—
242	Lada Niva 2121 4 x 4	4,098*		—
	VOLKSWAGEN (Brazil)			
331	1300			66,164
331	1300 L			69,099
331	1600 Limousine			71,408
331	Passat 2-dr Limousine			105,793
331	Passat LS 2-dr Limousine			112,426
331	Passat LS 3-dr Limousine			115,137
331	Passat LS 4-dr Limousine			115,450
331	Passat TS 2-dr Limousine			124,845
331	Passat LSE 4-dr Limousine			136,757
332	Brasilia 2-dr			86,500
332	Brasilia 4-dr			—
332	Brasilia LS			—
332	Variant II			109,181
332	Variant II Luxe			121,697
	VOLKSWAGEN (Germany FR)			
135	Polo 3-dr Limousine	2,675*		8,970*
135	Polo 3-dr L Limousine	2,965*		9,620*
135	Polo 3-dr GL Limousine			10,400*
135	Polo 3-dr S Limousine			9,290*
135	Polo 3-dr LS Limousine			9,940*
135	Polo 3-dr GLS Limousine	3,333*		10,720*
135	Derby 2-dr Limousine			9,345*
135	Derby 2-dr L Limousine			9,995*

Page	MAKE AND MODEL	Price in GB £	Price in USA $	Price ex Works
135	Derby 2-dr GL Limousine			10,605*
135	Derby 2-dr S Limousine	2,815*		9,665*
135	Derby 2-dr LS Limousine	3,155*		10,315*
135	Derby 2-dr GLS Limousine	3,470*		10,925*
136	Golf 3-dr Limousine	2,965*		9,965*
136	Golf 5-dr Limousine			10,525*
136	Golf 3-dr L Limousine			10,705*
136	Golf 5-dr L Limousine	3,405*		11,265*
136	Golf 3-dr GL Limousine	3,530*		11,515*
136	Golf 5-dr GL Limousine			12,075*
136	Golf 3-dr S Limousine			10,820*
136	Golf 5-dr S Limousine			11,380*
136	Golf 3-dr LS Limousine			11,560*
136	Golf 5-dr LS Limousine			12,120*
136	Golf 3-dr GLS Limousine			12,370*
136	Golf 5-dr GLS Limousine	3,935*		12,930*
136	Golf 3-dr GTI Limousine			15,085*
137	Golf Diesel 3-dr D Limousine			11,470*
137	Golf Diesel 5-dr D Limousine			12,030*
137	Golf Diesel 3-dr LD Limousine		5,199*	12,210*
137	Golf Diesel 5-dr LD Limousine	4,095*	5,339*	12,770*
137	Golf Diesel 3-dr GLD Limousine		5,585*	13,020*
137	Golf Diesel 5-dr GLD Limousine		5,725*	13,580*
138	Scirocco Coupé			12,995*
138	Scirocco L Coupé			14,020*
138	Scirocco S Coupé			13,550*
138	Scirocco LS Coupé			14,575*
138	Scirocco GT Coupé			15,095*
138	Scirocco GL Coupé		6,545*	15,845*
138	Scirocco GTI Coupé			17,595*
138	Scirocco GLI Coupé	4,995*		18,345*
139	Passat 3-dr Limousine			11,695*
139	Passat 5-dr Limousine			12,265*
139	Passat Variant	4,550*		12,645*
139	Passat 3-dr L Limousine			12,480*
139	Passat 5-dr L Limousine			13,050*
139	Passat L Variant			13,430*
139	Passat 3-dr GL Limousine			13,435*
139	Passat 5-dr GL Limousine			14,005*
139	Passat GL Variant			14,385*
139	Passat 3-dr S Limousine			12,195*
139	Passat 5-dr S Limousine			12,765*
139	Passat S Variant			13,145*
139	Passat 3-dr LS Limousine		6,650*	12,980*
139	Passat 5-dr LS Limousine	4,410*	6,810*	13,550*
139	Passat LS Variant		7,080*	13,930*
139	Passat 3-dr GLS Limousine			13,935*
139	Passat 5-dr GLS Limousine	4,725*		14,505*
139	Passat GLS Variant			14,885*
139	Passat Diesel 3-dr D Limousine			13,295*
139	Passat Diesel 5-dr D Limousine			13,865*
139	Passat Diesel D Variant			14,245*
139	Passat Diesel 3-dr LD Limousine		6,950*	14,080*
139	Passat Diesel 5-dr LD Limousine		7,110*	14,650*
139	Passat Diesel LD Variant		7,380*	15,030*
139	Passat Diesel 3-dr GLD Limousine			15,035*
139	Passat Diesel 5-dr GLD Limousine			15,605*
139	Passat Diesel GLD Variant			15,985*
140	1200 L			8,145*
140	1303 Cabriolet		6,245*	13,845*
140	181			14,345*
	VOLKSWAGEN (Mexico)			
322	1200			—
	VOLKSWAGEN (Nigeria)			
342	1200			—
	VOLKSWAGEN (USA)			
322	Rabbit 3-dr Hatchback			4,499

Page	MAKE AND MODEL	Price in GB £	Price in USA $	Price ex Works
322	Rabbit 3-dr Custom			4,899
322	Rabbit 5-dr Custom			5,039
322	Rabbit 3-dr De Luxe			5,349
322	Rabbit 5-dr De Luxe			5,489
	VOLVO (Holland)			
187	66 DL 2-dr			—
187	66 DL 3-dr			—
187	66 GL 2-dr			—
187	66 GL 3-dr			—
187	343 L			—
187	343 DL	3,350*		—
	VOLVO (Sweden)			
231	244 DL 4-dr Sedan	5,285*	7,485*	—
231	244 GL 4-dr Sedan	6,469*		—
231	244 GLE 4-dr Sedan	7,036*		—
231	245 DL 5-dr Station Wagon	5,903*	7,935*	—
231	245 GL 5-dr Station Wagon			—
231	245 GLE 5-dr Station Wagon	7,040*		—
231	242 GT 2-dr Sedan		8,585*	—
232	244 DL D6 4-dr Sedan			—
232	244 GL D6 4-dr Sedan			—
232	245 DL D6 5-dr Station Wagon			—
232	245 GL D6 5-dr Station Wagon			—
232	244 GL D5 4-dr Sedan			—
232	245 GL D5 5-dr Station Wagon			—
233	264 GL 4-dr Sedan	7,649*	11,495*	—
233	264 GLE 4-dr Sedan	8,511*		—
233	264 TE 4-dr Sedan	17,148*		—
233	265 GL 5-dr Station Wagon	7,788*	11,395*	—
233	265 GLE 5-dr Station Wagon	8,288*		—
233	262 C 2-dr Coupé	12,699*	15,995*	—
	WARTBURG (Germany DDR)			
102	353 W			—
103	353 W Tourist			—
103	353 W Tourist De Luxe			—
	YLN (Taiwan)			
351	902 SD			—
352	803 DL			—
352	803 SD			—
	ZAZ (USSR)			
242	968-A			—
242	969-A 4 x 4			—
	ZCZ (Yugoslavia)			
243	Zastava 750			39,337
243	Zastava 750 Luxe			—
243	Zastava 750 S			46,047
244	Zastava 101			65,563
244	Zastava 101 Luxe			68,032
244	Zastava 101 Super			73,723
244	Zastava 1300			62,248
244	Zastava 1300 Luxe			65,768
244	Zastava 1500			64,579
244	Zastava 1500 Luxe			70,190
244	Zastava 1500 Familiare			—
	ZIL (USSR)			
243	114 Limousine			—
243	117 Limousine			—